Published by The Caravan and Motorhome Club Limited

East Grinstead House, East Grinstead

West Sussex RH19 1UA

General Enquiries: 01342 326 944

Travel Service Reservations: 01342 316 101

Red Pennant sales: 01342 336 633

camc.com

Editor: Karla Harris

Publishing service provided by Fyooz Ltd

Printed by MRC

Maps produced by Maproom.

ISBN: 978-1-9993236-9-1

Contents

How to use this guide

The Handbook ... 6
Country Introductions ... 6
Campsite Entries ... 6
Campsite Fees ... 6
Sites Maps ... 6
Satellite Navigation ... 7
Site Report Forms ... 7
Acknowledgements ... 8
Explanation of a Campsite Entry ... 9
Guide to symbols ... 10
Site Description Abbreviations ... 11

Planning your trip

Documents ... 14
Camping Key Europe ... 14
Driving Licence ... 14
EHIC ... 14
Passport ... 15
Regulation for Pets ... 16
Pet Travel Documentation ... 16
Travelling with Children ... 17
Vehicle Documents ... 17
Visas ... 18
Customs ... 20
Caravans and Vehicles ... 20
Currency ... 20
Customs Allowances ... 20
Medicines ... 21
Plants & Food ... 21
Prohibited Goods ... 21
Insurance ... 22
Cover for Your Vehicles ... 22
Holiday Travel Insurance
and Motor Breakdown Cover ... 24
Holiday Insurance for Pets ... 24
Home Insurance ... 24
Money ... 25
Local Currency ... 25
Foreign Currency Bank Accounts ... 25
Prepaid Travel Cards ... 25
Credit & Debit Cards ... 26
Dynamic Currency Conversion ... 26
Emergency Cash ... 26
Crossing the Channel ... 27
Booking Your Ferry ... 27
On the Ferry ... 27
Channel Tunnel ... 28
On the Journey ... 28
Pets ... 28
Gas ... 28
LPG Vehicles ... 29
Club Sites near Ports ... 29
Ferry Routes and Operators ... 30

Motoring advice

Motoring Advice ... 31
Preparing for Your Journey ... 31
Driving in Europe ... 32
Fuel ... 32
Low Emission Zones ... 33
Motorhomes Towing Cars ... 33
Priority & Roundabouts ... 33
Public Transport ... 33
Pedestrian Crossings ... 34
Traffic Lights ... 34
Motoring Equipment ... 35
Essential Equipment ... 35
Child restraint systems ... 35
Fire Extinguisher ... 35
Lights ... 35
Nationality Plate (GB/IRL) ... 36
Reflective Jackets/Waistcoats ... 36
Route Planning ... 36
Seat Belts ... 37
Spares ... 37
Towbar ... 37
Tyres ... 37
Winter Driving ... 38
Warning Triangles ... 39
Essential Equipment Table ... 39
Mountain Roads ... 41
Mountain Passes ... 41
Tunnels ... 42
Table and Map Information ... 42
Major Mountain Passes Table – Alpine ... 43
Major Rail Tunnels Table – Alpine ... 52
Major Road Tunnels Table – Alpine ... 53
Major Mountain Passes Table – Pyrenees ... 55
Major Road Tunnels Table – Pyrenees ... 58

During your stay

Medical Matters ... 59
Before you Travel ... 59
European Health Insurance Card ... 59
Travel Insurance ... 60
First Aid ... 60
Accidents & Emergencies ... 60
Sun Protection ... 60
Tick-Bourne Encephalitis and Lyme Disease ... 61
Water & Food ... 61
Returning Home ... 61
Electricity & Gas ... 62
Electricity – General Advice ... 62
Electrical Connections – CEE17 ... 62
Hooking up to the Mains ... 63
Reversed Polarity ... 64
Shaver Sockets ... 64
Gas – General Advice ... 64

Safety & Security......66
Beaches, Lakes & Rivers 66
Campsite Safety......66
Swimming Pools......68
On The Road......68
Personal Security......69
Money Security......70
Winter sports......70
British Consular Services Abroad......70

Campsites

Booking a Campsite......72
Caravan Storage......73
Facilities & Site Description......73
Finding a Campsite......73
Overnight Stops......74
Municipal Campsites......74
Naturist Campsites......74
Opening Dates......74
Prices and Payment......74
Pets on Campsites......75
Registering on Arrival......76
General Advice......76
Keeping in Touch......77

Site listings

Austria
Country Introduction......78
Site Entries......85
Distance Chart / Sites Location Map......99
Belgium
Country Introduction......101
Site Entries......108
Distance Chart / Sites Location Map......116
Croatia
Country Introduction......118
Site Entries......125
Distance Chart / Sites Location Map......132
Czechia
Country Introduction......134
Site Entries......141
Distance Chart / Sites Location Map......147
Denmark
Country Introduction......149
Site Entries......156
Distance Chart / Sites Location Map......166
Finland
Country Introduction......168
Site Entries......175
Distance Chart / Sites Location Map......178
France
Country Introduction......180
Site Entries......190
Distance Chart / Sites Location Maps......465
Germany
Country Introduction......476
Site Entries......484
Distance Chart / Sites Location Maps......534
Greece
Country Introduction......540
Site Entries......546
Distance Chart / Sites Location Map......550
Hungary
Country Introduction......552
Site Entries......559
Distance Chart / Sites Location Map......562
Italy
Country Introduction......564
Site Entries......573
Distance Chart / Sites Location Map......607
Luxembourg
Country Introduction......612
Site Entries......617
Sites Location Map......621
Netherlands
Country Introduction......622
Site Entries......629
Distance Chart / Sites Location Map......646
Norway
Country Introduction......648
Site Entries......659
Distance Chart / Sites Location Maps......675
Poland
Country Introduction......678
Site Entries......685
Distance Chart / Sites Location Map......691
Portugal
Country Introduction......693
Site Entries......700
Distance Chart / Sites Location Maps......713
Slovakia
Country Introduction......715
Site Entries......721
Distance Chart / Sites Location Map......723
Slovenia
Country Introduction......725
Site Entries......731
Distance Chart / Sites Location Map......735
Spain
Country Introduction......737
Site Entries......748
Distance Chart / Sites Location Maps......805
Sweden
Country Introduction......810
Site Entries......819
Distance Chart / Sites Location Maps......832
Switzerland
Country Introduction......835
Site Entries......843
Distance Chart / Sites Location Map......856

Site Report Forms......859
Subject Index......863

How to use this guide

The Handbook

This section at the front of the book is a comprehensive guide to everything you need to know when touring across Europe. You'll find legal requirements, advice and regulations for before you travel, while you're away and for your return to the UK.

Country Introductions

In the country introductions you'll find more information, regulations and advice specific to that country. You should read the country introduction in conjunction with the handbook chapters before you set off.

Campsite entries

After the country introduction you'll find the campsite entries listed alphabetically under their nearest town or village. Where there are several campsites shown in and around the same town they will be listed in clockwise order from the north.

To find a campsite all you need to do is look for the town or village of where you would like to stay, or use the maps at the back of the book to find a town where sites are listed.

An explanation of the site entries and a guide to symbols is on the following pages.

You'll also find a guide to site entries on the fold out on the rear cover.

Campsite fees

Campsite entries show high season fees per night for an outfit plus two adults. Prices given may not include electricity or showers, unless indicated. Outside of the main holiday season many sites offer discounts on the prices shown and some sites may also offer a reduction for longer stays.

Campsite fees may vary to the prices stated in the site entries, especially if the site has not been reported on for a few years. You're advised to always check fees when booking, or at least before pitching, as those shown in site entries should be used as a guide only.

Site maps

Each town and village listed alphabetically in the site entry pages has a map grid reference number, e.g. 3B4. The map grid reference number is shown on each site entry.

The maps can be found at the end of each country section. The reference number will show you where each town or village is located, and the site entry will tell you how far the site is from that town.

Place names are shown on the maps in two colours:

Red where we list a site which is open all year (or for at least eleven months of the year).

Black where we only list seasonal sites which close in winter.

These maps are intended for general campsite location purposes only; a detailed road map is essential for route planning when touring.

The scale of the map means that it isn't possible to show every town or village where a campsite is listed, so some sites in small villages may be listed under a nearby larger town instead.

Satellite navigation

Most campsite entries now show a GPS (sat nav) reference. There are several different formats of writing co-ordinates, and in this guide we use decimal degrees, for example 48.85661 (latitude north) and 2.35222 (longitude east).

Minus readings, shown as -1.23456, indicate that the longitude is west of the Greenwich meridian. This will only apply to sites in the west of France, most of Spain and all of Portugal as the majority of Europe is east of the Greenwich meridian.

Manufacturers of sat navs all use different formats of co-ordinates so you may need to convert the co-ordinates before using them with your device. There are plenty of online conversion tools which enable you to do this quickly and easily - just type 'co-ordinate converter' into your search engine.

Please be aware if you are using a sat nav device some routes may take you on roads that are narrow and/or are not suitable for caravans or large outfits.

The GPS co-ordinates given in this guide are provided by members and checked wherever possible, however we cannot guarantee their accuracy due to the rural nature of most sites. The Caravan and Motorhome Club cannot accept responsibility for any inaccuracies, errors or omissions or for their effects.

Site report forms

With the exception of campsites in the Club's Overseas Site Booking Service (SBS) network, the Club doesn't inspect sites listed in this guide. Most of the sites listed in Touring Europe are from site reports submitted by users of these guides.

Sites which are not reported on for five years are archived from the guide, so even if you visit a site and find nothing has changed we'd still appreciate an update to make sure that the site isn't archived.

You will find site report forms towards the back of the book, or you can submit them at camc.com/europereport - use the abbreviated site report form if you are reporting no changes, or only minor changes, to a site entry. The full report form should be used for new sites or if sites have changed a lot.

Please submit reports as soon as possible. Information received by mid August will be used wherever possible in the next edition of Touring Europe. Reports received after that date are still very welcome and will appear in the following edition. The editor is unable to respond individually to site reports submitted due to the large quantity that we receive.

Tips for completing site reports

If possible fill in a site report form while a the campsite. Once back at home it can be difficult to remember details of individual sites, especially if you visited several during your trip.

When giving directions to a site, remember to include the direction of travel, e.g. 'from north on D137, turn left onto D794 signposted Combourg' or 'on N83 from Poligny turn right at petrol station in village'. Wherever possible give road numbers, junction numbers and/or kilometre post numbers, where you exit from motorways or main roads. It's also helpful to mention useful landmarks such as bridges, roundabouts, traffic lights or prominent buildings.

We very much appreciate the time and trouble you take submitting reports on campsites that you have visited; without your valuable contributions it would be impossible to update this guide.

Acknowledgements

Thanks go to the AIT/FIA Information Centre (OTA), the Alliance Internationale de Tourisme (AIT), the Fédération International de Camping et de Caravaning (FICC) and to the national clubs and tourist offices of those countries who have assisted with this publication.

Every effort is made to ensure that information provided in this publication is accurate. The Caravan and Motorhome Club has not checked these details by inspection or other investigation and cannot accept responsibility for the accuracy of these reports as provided by members and non-members, or for errors, omissions or their effects. In addition The Caravan and Motorhome Club cannot be held accountable for the quality, safety or operation of the sites concerned, or for the fact that conditions, facilities, management or prices may have changed since the last recorded visit. Any recommendations, additional comments or opinions have been contributed by people staying on the site and are not those of The Caravan and Motorhome Club.

The inclusion of advertisements or other inserted material doesn't imply any form of approval or recognition, nor can The Caravan and Motorhome Club undertake any responsibility for checking the accuracy of advertising material.

Shutterstock/nnattalli

Explanation of a Campsite Entry

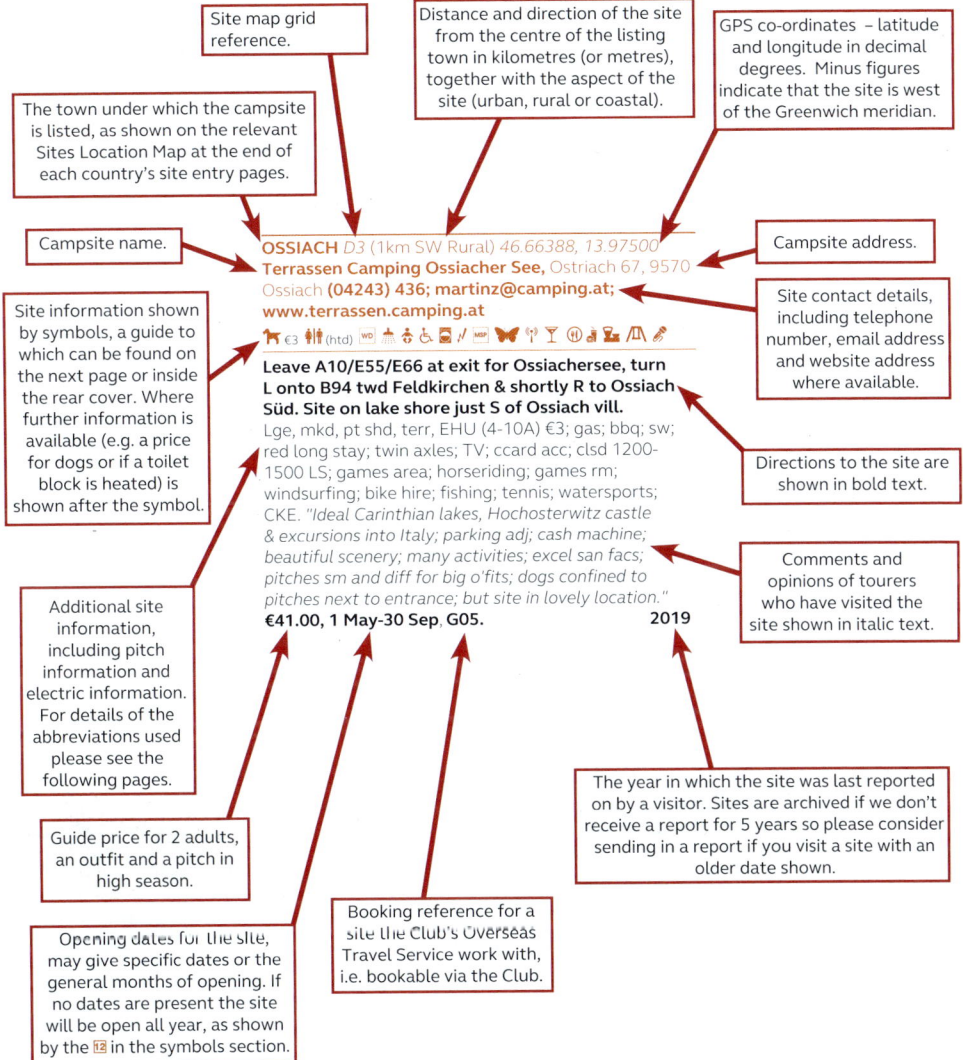

Site map grid reference.

Distance and direction of the site from the centre of the listing town in kilometres (or metres), together with the aspect of the site (urban, rural or coastal).

GPS co-ordinates – latitude and longitude in decimal degrees. Minus figures indicate that the site is west of the Greenwich meridian.

The town under which the campsite is listed, as shown on the relevant Sites Location Map at the end of each country's site entry pages.

Campsite name.

Campsite address.

OSSIACH *D3* (1km SW Rural) *46.66388, 13.97500*
Terrassen Camping Ossiacher See, Ostriach 67, 9570 Ossiach **(04243) 436; martinz@camping.at; www.terrassen.camping.at**
€3 (htd)
Leave A10/E55/E66 at exit for Ossiachersee, turn L onto B94 twd Feldkirchen & shortly R to Ossiach Süd. Site on lake shore just S of Ossiach vill.
Lge, mkd, pt shd, terr, EHU (4-10A) €3; gas; bbq; sw; red long stay; twin axles; TV; ccard acc; clsd 1200-1500 LS; games area; horseriding; games rm; windsurfing; bike hire; fishing; tennis; watersports; CKE. *"Ideal Carinthian lakes, Hochosterwitz castle & excursions into Italy; parking adj; cash machine; beautiful scenery; many activities; excel san facs; pitches sm and diff for big o'fits; dogs confined to pitches next to entrance; but site in lovely location."*
€41.00, 1 May-30 Sep, G05. **2019**

Site contact details, including telephone number, email address and website address where available.

Site information shown by symbols, a guide to which can be found on the next page or inside the rear cover. Where further information is available (e.g. a price for dogs or if a toilet block is heated) is shown after the symbol.

Directions to the site are shown in bold text.

Comments and opinions of tourers who have visited the site shown in italic text.

Additional site information, including pitch information and electric information. For details of the abbreviations used please see the following pages.

The year in which the site was last reported on by a visitor. Sites are archived if we don't receive a report for 5 years so please consider sending in a report if you visit a site with an older date shown.

Guide price for 2 adults, an outfit and a pitch in high season.

Booking reference for a site the Club's Overseas Travel Service work with, i.e. bookable via the Club.

Opening dates for the site, may give specific dates or the general months of opening. If no dates are present the site will be open all year, as shown by the 12 in the symbols section.

Guide to symbols

Symbol	Explanation
12	The site is open all year. Some sites may decide to close if they are not busy so call ahead out of season.
	Dogs are allowed on site, usually at an extra cost (shown if known). Please see the description or member comments for any restrictions.
	Toilets available. If followed by (cont) they will be continental style toilets.
WD	Chemical toilet disposal.
	Showers available.
	Family bathroom or baby and toddler room on site. Facilities may vary.
	Toilet and/or shower facilities available for disabled guests on site. Facilities may vary.
	Laundry facilities available. Facilities and costs may vary.
	Electric hook ups are available. See the description for details of the amperage, costs and any further information.
MSP	Motorhome service point. Low level waste discharge point for motor caravans; fresh water tap and rinse facilities should also be available.

Symbol	Explanation
	Quiet site - set in a peaceful location although at busy times you may still experience noise from other site users.
	Wi-Fi available, usually at an extra cost.
	Bar on site or nearby if followed by nr.
	Restaurant on site or nearby if followed by nr.
	Snack bar, cafe or takeaway on site.
	Shop on site or nearby if followed by nr.
	Playground or play area on site. Age restrictions may apply.
	Entertainment on site - this may either be evening entertainment or organised daytime activities or excursions.
	Pool on site. Where known the listing will specify if heated (htd), covered (covrd).
	Paddling pool for younger children on site.
	Beach nearby, followed by the distance and information about the type of beach where known.

Site Description Abbreviations

Each site entry assumes the following unless stated otherwise:

Level ground, open grass pitches, drinking water on site, clean wc unless otherwise stated (own sanitation required if wc not listed), site is suitable for any length of stay within the dates shown.

aspect
- urban – within a city or town, or on its outskirts
- rural – within or on edge of a village or in open countryside
- coastal – within one kilometre of the coast

size of site
- sm – max 50 pitches
- med – 51 to 150 pitches
- lge – 151 to 500 pitches
- v lge – 501+ pitches

pitches
- hdg pitch – hedged pitches
- mkd pitch – marked or numbered pitches
- hdstg – some hard standing or gravel

levels
- sl – sloping site
- pt sl – sloping in parts
- terr – terraced site

shade
- shd – plenty of shade
- pt shd – part shaded
- unshd – no shade

Site Facilities

adv bkg -
- acc - advance booking accepted
- rec – advance booking recommended
- req - advance booking required

beach - symbol followed by:
- 1km – distance to beach
- sand beach – sandy beach
- shgl beach – shingle beach

bus/metro/tram
- Public transport within 5km

chem disp
- Dedicated chemical toilet disposal facilities;
- chem disp (wc) – no dedicated point; disposal via wc only

CKE
- Camping Key Europe accepted

CL-type
- Very small, privately-owned, informal and usually basic, farm or country site similar to those in the Caravan and Motorhome Club's network of Certificated Locations

el pnts - symbol followed by
- Mains electric hook-ups available for a fee;
- inc – cost included in site fee quoted
- 10A – amperage provided
- conn fee – one-off charge for connection to metered electricity supply
- rev pol – reversed polarity may be present (see Electricity and Gas section

Eng spkn
- English spoken by campsite reception staff

gas
- Supplies of bottled gas available on site or nearby

Mairie
- Town hall (France); will usually make municipal campsite reservations

NH
- Suitable as a night halt

open 1 Apr-15 Oct
- Where no specific dates are given, opening dates are assumed to be inclusive, ie Apr-Oct – beginning April to end October (NB: opening dates may vary from those shown; check before travelling, particularly when travelling out of the main holiday season)

phone
- Public payphone on or adjacent to site

pool - symbol followed by:
- Indoor – indoor pool
- htd – heated pool
- covrd – indoor pool or one with retractable cover

red CCI/CCS
- Reduction in fees on production of a Camping Card International or Camping Card Scandinavia

BBQ
- barbecues allowed (may be restricted to a separate, designated area)

serviced pitch
: Electric hook-ups and mains water inlet and grey water waste outlet to pitch;
all – to all pitches
50% – percentage of pitches

shwrs - symbol followed by:
: inc – cost included in site fee quoted

ssn
: Season;
high ssn – peak holiday season
low ssn – out of peak season

50% statics
: Percentage of static caravans/mobile homes/chalets/fixed tents/cabins or long term seasonal pitches on site, including those run by tour operators

sw
: Swimming nearby;
1km – nearest swimming
lake – in lake
rv – in river

TV
: TV rm – separate TV room (often also a games room)
TV (pitch) – cable or satellite connections to pitches

Other Abbreviations

AIT	Alliance Internationale de Tourisme
a'bahn	Autobahn
a'pista	Autopista
a'route	Autoroute
a'strada	Autostrada
adj	Adjacent, nearby
alt	Alternative
app	Approach, on approaching
arr	Arrival, arriving
avail	Available
Ave	Avenue
bdge	Bridge
bef	Before
bet	Between
Blvd	Boulevard
C	Century, eg 16thC
c'van	Caravan
CC	Caravan and Motorhome Club
ccard acc	Credit and/or debit cards accepted (check with site for specific details)
cent	Centre or central
clsd	Closed
conn	Connection
cont	Continue or continental (wc)
conv	Convenient
covrd	Covered
dep	Departure
diff	Difficult, with difficulty
dir	Direction
dist	Distance
dual c'way	Dual carriageway
E	East
ent	Entrance/entry to
espec	Especially
ess	Essential
excel	Excellent
facs	Facilities
FIA	Fédération Internationale de l'Automobile
FICC	Fédération Internationale de Camping & de Caravaning
FFCC	Fédération Française de Camping et de Caravaning
FKK/FNF	Naturist federation, ie naturist site
foll	Follow
fr	From
g'ge	Garage

gd	Good
grnd(s)	Ground(s)
hr(s)	Hour(s)
immac	Immaculate
immed	Immediate(ly)
inc	Included/inclusive
indus est	Industrial estate
INF	Naturist federation, ie naturist site
int'l	International
irreg	Irregular
junc	Junction
km	Kilometre
L	Left
LH	Left-hand
LS	Low season
ltd	Limited
mkd	Marked
mkt	Market
mob	Mobile (phone)
m'van	Motor caravan
m'way	Motorway
N	North
narr	Narrow
nr, nrby	Near, nearby
opp	Opposite
o'fits	Outfits
o'look(ing)	Overlook(ing)
o'night	Overnight
o'skts	Outskirts
PO	Post office
poss	Possible, possibly
pt	Part
R	Right
rd	Road or street
rec	Recommend/ed
recep	Reception
red	Reduced, reduction (for)
reg	Regular
req	Required
RH	Right-hand
rlwy	Railway line
rm	Room
rndabt	Roundabout
rte	Route
RV	Recreational vehicle, ie large motor caravan
rv/rvside	River/riverside
S	South

Shutterstock/Krivosheev Vitaly

san facs	Sanitary facilities ie wc, showers, etc
snr citizens	Senior citizens
sep	Separate
sh	Short
sp	Sign post, signposted
sq	Square
ssn	Season
stn	Station
strt	Straight, straight ahead
sw	Swimming
thro	Through
TO	Tourist Office
tour ops	Tour operators
traff lts	Traffic lights
twd	Toward(s)
unrel	Unreliable
vg	Very good
vill	Village
W	West
w/end	Weekend
x-ing	Crossing
x-rds	Cross roads

Documents

Shutterstock/ Brian A Jackson

Camping Key Europe

Camping Key Europe (CKE) is a useful touring companion. Not only does it serve as ID at campsites, meaning that you don't have to leave your passport at reception, it also entitles you to discounts at over 2200 sites and offers third party-liability insurance.

You can purchase the CKE from the Club by calling 01342 336 633, or get it free of charge when you purchase a Red Pennant Policy with European Breakdown Cover. Visit campingkeyeurope.com for more information.

Driving licence

Always carry your full driving licence when driving abroad. If stopped by the police and other authorities, you'll need to use your driving licence to prove that you have permission to use your vehicle and that you're insured. Failure to do so may mean you're lliable for a fine and confiscation of your vehicle(s).

If your driving licence is due to expire while you're away, it can be renewed up to three months before expiry - contact the DVLA if you need to renew more than three months ahead.

Rules regarding driving with a provisional licences vary across Europe.

You may not be entitled to drive in some EU countries unless you have a full licence.

All EU countries recognise the photocard driving licence introduced in the UK in 1990, subject to the minimum age requirements (normally 18 years for a vehicle with a maximum weight of 3,500kg carrying no more than 8 people).

Old-style green paper licences or Northern Irish licences issued before 1991 should be updated before travelling as they may not be recognised by local authorities.

If you only have a paper licence or your licence was issued in Gibraltar, Guernsey, Jersey or the Isle of Man you might need an International Driving Permit to drive in some EU countries and Norway, which can be bought at the Post Office for £5.50.

EHIC

The European Health Insurance Card (EHIC) allows any EU citizen access to state medical care when they are travelling in another EU country - although in many circumstances, there are significant limitations to what treatment UK citizens are able to receive.

Existing UK issued European Health Insurance Cards remain valid until their expiry date within the EU but not in Switzerland, Liechtenstein, Norway and Iceland.

New EHICs won't be issued for UK travellers but a replacement Global Health Insurance Card (GHIC) will provide the same access to state healthcare in the EU and Switzerland, but not in Liechtenstein, Norway and Iceland.

Given the limitations of EHIC or GHIC, we always recommend that you have suitable travel insurance before you go on holiday. Make sure you get travel insurance that covers your health needs. Visit gov.uk to check what your travel insurance should cover.

It's now even more important to have personal health and accident cover, and breakdown cover for your vehicle, when travelling overseas. The Club's Red Pennant Emergency Assistance covers all these things and is tailored to your personal situation.

Passport

In many EU countries, everyone is required to carry photographic ID at all times. Enter next-of-kin details in the back of your passport and keep a separate photocopy. It's also a good idea to leave a photocopy with a relative or friend at home.

You can also take a photo of your passport to keep saved on your phone or in a cloud storage service so it's easily accessed.

The following information applies to British passport holders only. For information on passports issued by other countries you should contact the local embassy.

Applying for a passport

Each person travelling out of the UK (including babies) must hold a valid passport - it's no longer possible to include children on a parent's passport. A standard British passport is valid for ten years, or five years for under 16s.

All newly issued UK passports are now biometric, also known as e-passports, which contain a microchip with information which can be used to authenticate the holder's identity.

Full information and application forms are available from main post offices or you can complete an online application for the HM Passport Office (HMPO) via gov.uk.

Allow at least six weeks for first-time passport applications, for which you may need to attend an interview at your nearest HMPO regional office. Allow three weeks for a renewal application or replacement of a lost, stolen or damaged passport.

Passport validity

You must check your passport validity online and renew it if you need to.

If your passport will be older than nine years and six months on the date you plan to travel, the official advice is that you should renew it in advance.

According to the Schengen Border Code, on the day of arrival you'll need your passport to:

- have a 'date of issue' less than 10 years before the date you arrive - if you renewed your passport before 1 October 2018, it may have a date of issue that is more than 10 years ago
- have an 'expiry date' at least three months after the date you plan to leave the Schengen Area

Please note that if you renewed your passport before it expired, extra months may have been added to your current passport expiry date. These extra months on your passport over 10 years may not count towards the six months that should be remaining on your passport.

So, if your passport will be older than nine years and six months on the date of travel to the EU you should renew it in advance.

If you do need to renew your passport, we recommend doing this as soon as possible before you intend to travel as it can take up to three weeks for your new passport to arrive. It may take longer to issue a first adult passport. Note: these rules don't apply if travelling to the Republic of Ireland and you can continue to use your passport as long as it's valid for the length of your stay).

Burgundy passports, whether with 'European Union' on the cover or not, remain valid alongside the new blue passport.

Schengen Agreement

The Schengen Agreement allows people and vehicles to pass freely without border checks from country to country within the Schengen area (29 countries).

Where there are no longer any border checks

Shutterstock/ LightField Studios

you should still not attempt to cross land borders without a full, valid passport.

It's likely that random identity checks will be made for the foreseeable future in areas surrounding borders.

Regulations for pets

Some campsites don't accept dogs at all and some have restrictions on the number and breed of dogs allowed.

Visit camc.com/overseasadvice for more information and country-specific advice.

Pet travel documentation

This information applies to people travelling with their pet cats, ferrets or dogs, including assistance dogs. If you're travelling with any other pets you should check the national rules of the country that you're planning to visit.

Before your pet can travel to the EU or Northern Ireland, you'll need to take these steps to get an Animal Health Certificate (AHC) instead of a pet passport.

- Your pet must be microchipped.
- Your pet must be vaccinated against rabies – your pet must be at least 12 weeks old before it can be vaccinated.
- Wait 21 days after the primary vaccination before travel.
- Visit your vet to get an AHC for your pet, no more than 10 days before travel.
- As long as you keep your pet's rabies vaccinations up to date, you won't need to get repeat vaccinations for repeat trips to the EU.

Getting an animal health certificate (AHC) for travel

Within 10 days of your travel date, take your pet to an official vet who is permitted to sign and issue AHCs. Take proof of your pet's microchipping date and vaccination history.

Your pet's AHC will be valid for:

- 10 days after the issue date for entry into the EU.
- Onward travel within the EU for four months after the date of issue
- Re-entry to GB for four months after the date of issue

Arriving in the EU

Travellers with pets will need to enter through a designated Travellers' Point of Entry (TPE) where you may need to present your pet's original AHC along with proof of:

- Your pet's microchip
- Rabies vaccination
- Tapeworm treatment (if required)

The LeShuttle terminal and all of the ferry ports booked by the Club are designated TPEs.

Repeat trips

Your pet will need a new AHC for each trip. Take your pet to an official vet no more than 10 days before you travel and show proof of your pet's microchipping date and rabies vaccination history. If your pet has an up-to-date vaccination history, they won't need a repeat rabies vaccination before travelling again.

Returning to Great Britain

Your pet must have one of the following documents when returning to GB from the EU:

- An EU pet passport (issued in the EU, or in GB before 1 January 2021)
- The AHC issued in GB used to travel to the EU – which you can use up to four months after it was issued
- A UK pet health certificate (issued outside the UK for travel into GB only)

Dogs should have a tapeworm treatment between 24 and 120 hours before entering Great Britain. This treatment must be approved for use in the country where it's applied and contain praziquantel or an equivalent proven to be effective against tapeworm (Echinococcus Multilocularis).

Your pet won't need this documentation or tapeworm treatment if entering GB directly from Northern Ireland or the Republic of Ireland.

You can travel with up to five pets with an Animal Health Certificate. If there are more than five pets you must either provide proof that they are participating in a competition, exhibition or sporting event or comply with animal health rules which apply to the commercial import of animals into the EU.

For more details please check gov.uk or speak with your vet.

Travelling with children

If you're a lone adult travelling with children some countries require evidence of parental responsibility, especially those who have a different surname to them (including lone parents and grandparents). The authorities may want to see a birth certificate, a letter of consent from the child's parent (or other parent) and some evidence as to your responsibility for the child.

For further information on what will be required at immigration, contact the embassy or consulate of the countries you intend to visit.

Vehicle documents

Caravan Proof of Ownership (CRIS)

In Britain, unlike most other European countries, caravans don't have to be registered in the same way as cars. This may not be fully understood by police and other authorities on the Continent. You're strongly advised to carry a copy of your Caravan Registration Identification Scheme (CRIS) document as it proves you're the registered keeper.

GB sticker

On 28 September 2021, the distinguishing mark (or national identifier) displayed on vehicles registered in the United Kingdom that are driven abroad changed from GB to UK.

This means that vehicles registered in the UK must display the letters 'UK' when driven in the EU. You'lll need to display a UK sticker clearly on the rear of your vehicle if your number plate has any of the following:

- A GB identifier with the Union flag (also known as the Union Jack)
- A Euro symbol
- A national flag of England, Scotland or Wales
- Numbers and letters only - no flag or identifier
- If you're in Spain, you must display a UK sticker no matter what's on your number plate.

If you have a GB sticker, cover or remove it.

Green cards

The European Commission has scrapped the obligation for UK drivers to show a green card when entering the European Union (EU).

This means that you won't need a green card if you're travelling in the following countries/areas:

- The EU (including Ireland)
- Andorra
- Bosnia & Herzegovina
- Iceland
- Liechtenstein
- Montengro
- Norway
- Serbia
- Switzerland

If you plan to drive anywhere else in Europe, you may still need a green card.

Separate green cards are required for cars, motorhomes and anything towed by a motorised vehicle, including caravans, trailers and trailer tents/folding campers. A green card for a car or motorhome needs to have Category A ('Car') ticked; a green card for a caravan, trailer or trailer tent/folding camper needs to have Category F ('Trailer') ticked.

These cards are issued by your vehicle insurer, possibly for a small fee to cover administration costs, and you should contact your insurer in good time prior to departure. The Club cannot provide green cards directly, as we are not an insurance company, however if you have Motorhome Insurance or Car Insurance with The Club, green cards are issued by our partner brokers, Devitt Insurance Ltd.

You can call Devitt on 0345 300 4290.

If you have Caravan Cover with the Club, and Car insurance with the Club, once again, you can call Devitt, who will issue green cards for both the car and the caravan or other towed vehicle. If you have Caravan Cover with the Club, but your car insurance is arranged through another insurance company, you'll need to speak to your car insurance provider and ask them to provide green cards for both vehicles.

Please note that Devitt will charge an administration fee for a green card, but it will be the same whether it's one card or two.

MOT certificate

Carry your vehicle's MOT certificate (if applicable) as you may need to show it to the authorities if your vehicle is involved in an accident, or in the event of random vehicle checks. If your MOT certificate is due to expire while you're away you should have the vehicle tested before you leave home.

Tax

While driving abroad you still need to have current UK vehicle tax. If your vehicle's tax is due to expire while you're abroad you may apply to re-license the vehicle at a post office, by post, or in person at a DVLA local office, up to two months in advance.

Vehicle Registration Certificate (V5C)

You must always carry your Vehicle Registration Certificate (V5C) and MOT Certificate (if applicable) when taking your vehicle abroad. If yours has been lost, stolen or destroyed call DVLA Customer Enquiries on 0300 790 6802 for more information.

Hired or borrowed vehicles

If using a borrowed vehicle you must obtain a letter of authority to use the vehicle from the registered owner. You should also carry the Vehicle Registration Certificate (V5C).

In the case of hired or leased vehicles, including company cars, when you don't possess the V5C, ask the company which owns the vehicle to supply a Vehicle On Hire Certificate, form VE103, which is the only legal substitute for a V5C. The BVRLA, the trade body for the vehicle rental and leasing sector, provide advice on hired or leased vehicles - see bvrla.co.uk or call them on 01494 434 747 for more information.

If you're caught driving a hired vehicle abroad without this certificate you may be fined and/or the vehicle impounded.

Visas

British Citizens don't need a visa for short trips to the EU of up to 90 days in any 180 day period. You may need a visa or permit to stay for longer. we recommend checking GOV.UK for more information on how to get a visa or permit. The Republic of Ireland is not in the Schengen zone so days spent travelling there don't count towards the 90 day limit.

The Entry and Exit System (ESS)

The Entry and Exit System (EES) is an electronic system that the EU is planning to introduce to capture details of all non-EU nationals arriving into and leaving the Schengen area. The information required at the border includes the person's name, travel documents, biometric data such as fingerprints and the place of entry and exit.

The planned launch date has not been confirmed, but when it is in place, this may mean that border checks take a little longer to complete.

The European Travel Information and Authorisation System (ETIAS)

The European Travel Information and Authorisation System (ETIAS) is the electronic system the EU is planning to implement to track individuals entering the area from countries that don't need a visa, much like the ESTA scheme in USA.

The planned launch date is May 2025. UK citizens will need apply for an ETIAS travel authorisation and pay a fee of €7 in advance of travel.

Customs

Shutterstock/mythja

Caravans and vehicles

Vehicles and caravans may be temporarily imported into non-EU countries generally for a maximum of six months in any twelve month period, provided they are not hired, sold or otherwise disposed of in that country.

If you intend to stay longer than six months, dispose of a vehicle in another country or leave your vehicle there in storage, you should seek advice well before your departure from the UK.

Borrowed vehicles

If you're borrowing a vehicle from a friend or relative, or loaning yours to someone, you should be aware of the following:

- The total time the vehicle spends abroad must not exceed the limit for temporary importation (generally six months).
- The owner of the caravan must provide the other person with a letter of authority.
- The owner cannot accept a hire fee or reward.
- The number plate on the caravan must match the number plate on the tow car.
- Both drivers' insurers must be informed if a caravan is being towed and any additional premium must be paid.

Currency

You must declare cash of €10,000 (or equivalent in other currencies) or more when travelling between the UK and a non-EU country. The term 'cash' includes cheques, travellers' cheques, bankers' drafts, notes and coins. You don't need to declare cash when travelling within the EU.

For further information visit the 'Travel abroad' section on the gov.uk website.

Customs allowances

If you're travelling to Great Britain from outside the UK, your personal allowances mean you can bring in a certain amount of goods without paying tax or duty.

If you go over your allowances you must declare all your goods and pay tax and duty on all the goods of the same type in that category.

You cannot combine allowances with other people to bring in more than your individual allowance and there are no personal allowances for tobacco or alcohol if you're under 17.

The allowances are:

- 200 cigarettes, or 100 cigarillos, or 50 cigars, or 250g tobacco, or a combination adding up to the same total (e.g. 100 cigarettes and 25 cigars - both 50% of your allowance)
- 18 litres of wine (not sparkling)
- 42 litres of beer
- 4 litres of spirits or 9 litres of fortified wine (e.g. port or sherry), sparkling wine or alcoholic drinks up to 22% volume, or a combination adding up to the same total (e.g. 2 litres of spirits and 4.5 litres of fortified wine - both 50% of your allowance)
- £390 worth of all other goods including perfume, gifts and souvenirs without having to pay tax and/or duty

For further information visit the 'Travel abroad' section on the gov.uk website.

Medicines

There's no limit to the amount of over the counter medicines you can take abroad. Medicines prescribed by your doctor may contain controlled drugs (e.g. morphine), for which you will need a licence if you're leaving the UK for three months or more.

You don't need a licence for less than three months' supply or if your medication doesn't contain controlled drugs, but you should carry a letter from your doctor stating your name, a list of your prescribed drugs and dosages. You may have to show this letter when going through customs.

Visit gov.uk/travelling-controlled-drugs or call 0300 105 0248 for a list of controlled drugs and to apply for a personal licence.

Plants and food

If you're bringing animal and animal products into the UK, then Andorra, the Canary Islands, Channel Islands, Isle of Man, Liechtenstein, Norway, San Marino and Switzerland also count as EU countries. You can bring:

- meat
- dairy
- other animal products, for example, fish, eggs and honey

You can bring in any plants or plant products as long as they're:

- free from pests and diseases
- for your own use or consumption

When travelling into the EU you cannot take:

- meat and meat products
- milk or dairy products, other than powdered infant milk, infant food, special foods and special pet feed needed for medical reasons

This includes for your immediate personal consumption, for example sandwiches containing meat.

For up to date information contact the Department for Environment, Food and Rural Affairs (Defra) on 0345 33 55 77 or +44 20 7238 6951 from outside the UK. You can also visit defra.gov.uk to find out more.

Prohibited goods

The importation of some goods into the UK is restricted or banned. These include:

- Endangered animals or plants including live animals, birds and plants, ivory, skins, coral, hides, shells and goods made from them such as jewellery, shoes, bags and belts.
- Controlled, unlicensed or dangerous drugs.
- Counterfeit or pirated goods such as watches, CDs and clothes; goods bearing a false indication of their place of manufacture or in breach of UK copyright.
- Offensive weapons such as firearms, flick knives, knuckledusters, push daggers, self-defence sprays and stun guns.
- Indecent and obscene materials, such as books, magazines, films and DVDs.

This list is not exhaustive; if in serious doubt, contact HMRC on 0300 200 3700 (+44 2920 501 261 from outside the UK) or go through the red Customs channel and ask a Customs officer when returning to the UK.

Insurance and Cover

Cover for your vehicles

It's important to make sure your outfit is covered whilst you're travelling abroad. Your car or motorhome insurance may already cover you for driving in the EU, but check what you're covered for before you travel. If you're travelling outside the EU or associated countries you'll need to check with your insurer if they cover you in that country and you may have to pay an additional premium.

Make sure your caravan cover includes travel outside of the UK, speak to your provider to check this. You may need to notify them of your dates of travel and may be charged an extra premium. UK vehicle insurance policies give you a minimum of third party cover to drive your vehicle in EU countries, but you should check with your insurer to see if your policy covers things like theft or damage while overseas. Depending upon where you're travelling, you may need a green card from your insurer as evidence you have the minimum third party cover.

You don't need to carry a green card when you drive in the EU (including Ireland), Andorra, Bosnia and Herzegovina, Iceland, Liechtenstein, Norway, Serbia, and Switzerland. You'll normally need to carry a green card to drive in other countries.

This information is correct at the time of publication, but may change. To see if this advice is still up to date, check the government website on overseas driving:

gov.uk/vehicle-insurance/driving-abroad.

The Caravan and Motorhome Club's Car and Motorhome Insurance and Caravan Cover provide cover for travel within the EU free of charge, provided the total period of foreign travel in any one year doesn't exceed 270 days for Car Insurance, 182 days for Caravan Cover

Shutterstock/Juan Aunion

and 365 days for Motorhome Insurance. It may be possible to extend the Car Insurance and Caravan Cover periods, although a charge may apply. Should you be delayed beyond these limits notify your cover or insurance provider immediately in order to maintain your cover until you can return to the UK.

If your outfit is damaged during ferry travel (including while loading or unloading) it must be reported to the carrier at the time of the incident. Most policies will cover short sea crossings (up to 65 hours) but check with your insurer before travelling.

See camc.com/insurance for full details of the Club's Caravan Cover, Car Insurance and Motorhome Insurance.

European accident statement

Your car or motorhome insurer may provide you with a European Accident Statement form (EAS), or you may be given one if you're involved in an accident abroad. The EAS is a standard form, available in different languages, which gives all parties involved in an accident the opportunity to agree on the facts. Signing the form doesn't mean that you're accepting liability, just that you agree with what has been stated on the form. Only sign an EAS if you're completely sure that you understand what has been written and always make sure that you take a copy of the completed EAS.

Vehicles left behind abroad

If you're involved in an accident or breakdown abroad which prevents you taking your vehicle home, you must ensure that you're covered if you leave your vehicle overseas while you return home. Also check if you're covered for the cost of recovering it to your home address.

In this event, remove all items of baggage and personal belongings from your vehicles before leaving them unattended. If this isn't possible then check if you can extend your cover to protect your belongings.

In all circumstances, you must remove any valuables and items liable for customs duty, including wine, beer, spirits and cigarettes.

Legal costs abroad

If an accident abroad leads to you being taken to court you may find yourself liable for legal costs – even if you're not found to be at fault. Most UK vehicle insurance policies include cover for legal costs or have the option to add cover for a small additional cost – check if you're covered before you travel.

Holiday travel insurance and motor breakdown cover

A standard motor insurance policy won't cover you for all eventualities, for example vehicle breakdown, medical expenses or alternative accommodation, so it's important to also take out adequate travel insurance. Make sure the travel insurance you take out is suitable for a caravan or motorhome holiday.

Remember to check exemptions and exclusions, especially those relating to pre-existing medical conditions and be sure to declare any pre-existing medical conditions to your insurer.

The Club's Red Pennant Emergency Assistance is specifically designed for European touring holidays and can provide cover for both breakdown situations and medical emergencies or cancellations, depending on which option is purchased. Visit camc.com/redpennant for full details or call us on 01342 336 633.

Holiday insurance for pets

If you're taking your pet overseas with you then you'll need to make sure they're covered too. The Club's Red Pennant Overseas Emergency Assistance can be extended to cover the additional costs that you may incur if you and your pet have to be repatriated as a result of an insured incident. Other holiday insurances may cover this.

In order to provide cover for pet injury or illness you'll need a separate pet insurance policy. Make sure you check with your pet insurance provider that you're covered for fees that are incurred overseas.

Home insurance

Your home insurer may require advance notification if you're leaving your home unoccupied for 30 days or more. There may be specific requirements, such as turning off mains services (except electricity), draining water down and having somebody check your home periodically. Read your policy documents or speak to either the Club if your home is insured with us, or your provider.

The Club's Home Insurance policy can provide full cover for up to 90 days when you're away from home (for instance when touring) and usually beyond 90 days on application. Visit camc.com/homeinsurance or call 0345 504 0335 for details.

Personal belongings

The majority of travellers are able to cover their valuables such as jewellery, watches, cameras, laptops, and bikes under a home insurance policy. This includes the Club's Home Insurance.

Specialist gadget insurance is now commonly available and can provide valuable benefits if you're taking smart phones, tablets, laptops or other gadgets on holiday with you.

Money

Shutterstock/ Alohaflaminggo

Being able to safely access your money while you're away is a necessity for you to enjoy your break. It isn't a good idea to rely on one method of payment, so always have a backup plan. A mixture of a small amount of cash plus one or two electronic means of payment are a good idea.

Traveller's cheques have become less popular as fewer banks and hotels are willing or able to cash them. There are alternative options which offer the same level of security but are easier to use, such as prepaid credit cards.

Local currency

It's a good idea to take enough foreign currency for your journey and immediate needs on arrival, don't forget you may need change for tolls or parking on your journey. Currency exchange facilities will be available at ports and on ferries but rates offered may not be as good as you would find elsewhere.

The Post Office, banks, exchange offices and travel agents offer foreign exchange. All should stock euros but during peak holiday times or if you need a large amount it may be sensible to pre-order your currency. You should also pre-order less common currencies.

Shop around and compare commission and exchange rates, together with minimum charges.

Banks and money exchanges in central and eastern Europe won't usually accept Scottish and Northern Irish bank notes and may be reluctant to change any sterling which has been written on or is creased or worn.

Foreign currency bank accounts

Frequent travellers or those who spend long periods abroad may find a Euro bank account useful. Most such accounts impose no currency conversion charges for debit or credit card use and allow fee-free cash withdrawals at ATMs. Some banks may also allow you to spread your account across different currencies, depending on your circumstances. Speak to your bank about the services they offer.

Prepaid travel cards

Prepaid travel money cards are issued by various providers including the Post Office, Travelex, Lloyds Bank and American Express.

They are increasingly popular as the PIN

protected travel money card offers the security of Traveller's Cheques, with the convenience of paying by card. You load the card with the amount you need before leaving home, and then use cash machines to make withdrawals or use the card to pay for goods and services as you would a credit or debit card. You can top the card up over the telephone or online while you are abroad. However, there can be issues with using them with some automated payment systems, such as pay-at-pump petrol stations and toll booths, so you should always have an alternative payment method available.

These cards can be cheaper to use than credit or debit cards for both cash withdrawals and purchases as there are usually no loading or transaction fees to pay. In addition, because they are separate from your bank account, if the card is lost or stolen, your bank account will still be secure.

Credit and debit cards

Credit and debit cards offer a convenient way of spending abroad. For the use of cards abroad, most banks impose a foreign currency conversion charge of up to 3% per transaction. If you use your card to withdraw cash there will be a further commission charge of up to 3% and you'll be charged interest (possibly at a higher rate than normal) as soon as you withdraw the money.

There are credit cards available specifically designed for spending overseas and will give you the best available rates. However, they often have high interest rates so are only economical if you're able to pay them off in full each month.

If you have several cards, take at least two in case you encounter problems. Credit and debit 'Chip and PIN' cards issued by UK banks may not be universally accepted abroad so check that your card will be accepted if using it in restaurants or other situations where you pay after you have received goods or services.

Contact your credit or debit card issuer before you leave home to let them know that you'll be travelling abroad.

Card issuers look out for card fraud and frequently query transactions which they deem unusual or suspicious, causing your card to be declined or temporarily stopped.

You should always carry your card issuer's helpline number with you so that you can contact them if this happens. You'll also need this number should you need to report the loss or theft of your card.

Dynamic currency conversion

When you pay with a credit or debit card, retailers may offer you the choice of currency for payment, e.g. a euro amount will be converted into sterling and then charged to your card account. This is known as a 'Dynamic Currency Conversion' but the exchange rate used is likely to be worse than the rate offered by your card issuer, so will work out more expensive than paying in the local currency.

Emergency cash

If an emergency or theft means that you need cash in a hurry, then friends or relatives at home can send you emergency cash via money transfer services. The Post Office, MoneyGram and Western Union all offer services which, allows the transfer of money to over 233,000 money transfer agents around the world. Transfers take approximately ten minutes and charges are levied on a sliding scale.

Booking your ferry

It`s always wise to make reservations as early as possible to get the best prices but especially so if travelling at peak times, such as Easter or school holidays. Each ferry will have limited room for caravans and large vehicles so spaces can fill up quickly and prices tend to increase as the ship fills up. If you need any special assistance request this at the time of booking.

When booking any ferry crossing, make sure you give the correct measurements for your outfit including bikes, roof boxes or anything which may add to the length or height - if you underestimate your vehicle's size you may be turned away or charged an additional fee.

The Caravan and Motorhom Club is an agent for most major ferry companies operating services. Call the Club's Travel Service on 01342 316 101 or visit camc.com/ferries to book and save the £20 booking fee* that is applied via the Contact Centre.

The table at the end of this section shows ferry routes from the UK to the Continent and Ireland. Some ferry routes may not be operational all year, and during peak periods there may be a limit to the number of caravans or motorhomes accepted.

For the most up-to-date information visit camc.com/ferries or call the Club's Travel Services team.

On the ferry

Arrive at the port with plenty of time before your boarding time. Motorhomes and car/ caravan outfits will usually either be the first or last vehicles boarded onto the ferry. Almost all ferries are now 'drive on – drive off' so you won't be required to do any complicated manoeuvres. You may be required to show ferry staff that your gas is switched off before boarding the ferry.

Be careful using the ferry access ramps, as they are often very steep which can mean there is a risk of grounding the tow bar or caravan hitch. Drive slowly and, if your ground clearance is low, consider whether removing your jockey wheel and any stabilising devices would help.

Vehicles are often parked close together on ferries, meaning that if you have towing extension mirrors they could get knocked or damaged by people trying to get past your

vehicle. If you leave them attached during the ferry crossing then make sure you check their position on returning to your vehicle.

Channel Tunnel

The Channel Tunnel operator, LeShuttle (Eurotunnel), accepts cars, caravans and motorhomes (except those running on LPG) on their service between Folkestone and Calais.

As with ferries, prices increase as it gets closer to the departure time so it's best to book in advance. You must also give accurate outfit dimensions at booking to be sure you aren't charged extra at the terminal.

To book at a discounted price you can call the Club's Travel Service on 01342 316 101 or visit camc.com/ferries to save the £20 booking fee* that is applied via the Contact Centre.

On the journey

Prior to travel you'll be asked to open your roof vents and you'll also need to apply the caravan brake once you have parked your vehicle on the train. You won't be able to use your caravan until arrival.

Pets

It's possible to transport your pet on a number of ferry routes to the Continent and Ireland, as well as on LeShuttle (Eurotunnel) services from Folkestone to Calais. Advance booking is essential as restrictions apply to the number of animals allowed on any one crossing. You'll need to contact an official veterinarian one month prior to travel to check the required vaccinations and documentation needed for your pet to travel. Make sure you understand the carrier's terms and conditions for transporting pets.

Brittany Ferries ask for all dogs to be muzzled when out of the vehicle but this varies for other operators so please check at the time of booking. Once on board pets are normally required to remain in their owner's vehicle or in kennels on the car deck and you won't be able to access your vehicle to check on your pet while the ferry is at sea.

On longer crossings you should make arrangements at the on-board information desk for permission to visit your pet in order to check its well-being. You should always make sure that ferry staff know your vehicle has a pet on board.

On some ships operating longer routes, specific 'pet friendly' cabins are available and as these are very popular we recommend booking well in advance.

Information and advice on the welfare of animals before and during a journey is available via gov.uk/taking-your-pet-abroad.

Gas

UK based ferry companies usually allow up to three gas cylinders per caravan, including the cylinder currently in use, however some may restrict this to a maximum of two cylinders. Some operators may ask you to hand over your gas cylinders to a member of the crew so that they can be safely stored during the crossing. Check that you know the rules of your ferry operator before you travel.

Cylinder valves should be fully closed and covered with a cap, if provided, and should remain closed during the crossing. Cylinders should be fixed securely in or on the caravan in the position specified by the manufacturer.

Gas cylinders must be declared at check-in and the crew may ask to inspect each cylinder for leakage before travel.

The carriage of spare petrol cans, whether full or empty, is not permitted on ferries or through the Channel Tunnel.

LPG vehicles

Vehicles fully or partially powered by LPG can't be carried through the Channel Tunnel. Gas for domestic use (e.g. heating, lighting or cooking) can be carried, but the maximum limit is 47kg for a single bottle or 50kg in multiple bottles. Tanks must be switched off before boarding and must be less than 80% full; you will be asked to demonstrate this before you travel.

Most ferry companies will accept LPG-powered vehicles but you must let them know at the time of booking. During the crossing, the tank must be no more than 75% full and it must be turned off. In the case of vehicles converted to use LPG, some ferry companies also require a certificate showing that the conversion has been carried out by a professional - before you book speak to the ferry company to check their requirements.

Club sites near ports

If you've got a long drive to the ferry port, or want to catch an early ferry then an overnight stop near to the port gives you a relaxing start to your holiday. The following table lists Club Sites which are close to ports.

Club Members can book online at camc.com or call 01342 327 490. Non-members can book by calling the sites directly on the telephone numbers below when the sites are open.

Please note that Commons Wood, Fairlight Wood, Hunter's Moon and Old Hartley are open to Club members only. Non-members are welcome at all other sites listed below.

Port	Nearest Club Campsite	Tel No.
Cairnryan	New England Bay	01776 860275
Dover, Folkestone, Channel Tunnel	Bearsted	01622 730018
	Black Horse Farm*	01303 892665
	Daleacres	01303 267679
	Fairlight Wood	01424 812333
Fishguard, Pembroke	Freshwater East	01646 672341
Harwich	Cambridge Cherry Hinton*	01223 244088
	Commons Wood*	01707 260786
Holyhead	Penrhos	01248 852617
Hull	York Beechwood Grange*	01904 424637
	York Rowntree Park*	01904 658997
Newcastle upon Tyne	Old Hartley	0191 237 0256
Newhaven	Brighton*	01273 626546
Plymouth	Plymouth Sound	01752 862325
Poole	Crossways	01305 852032
	Hunter's Moon*	01929 556605
Portsmouth	Rookesbury Park	01329 834085
Rosslare	River Valley	00353 (0)404 41647
Weymouth	Crossways	01305 852032

** Site open all year*

Sea crossing routes and operators

Route	Operator	Approximate Crossing Time	Maximum Frequency
France			
Dover – Calais	P & O Ferries	1½ hrs	22 daily
Dover – Calais	DFDS Seaways	1½ hrs	10 daily
Dover – Calais	Irish Ferries	1½ hrs	15 daily
Dover – Dunkerque	DFDS Seaways	2 hrs	12 daily
Folkestone – Calais	LeShuttle	35 mins	3 per hour
Newhaven – Dieppe	DFDS Seaways	4 hrs	2 daily
Poole – St Malo (via Channel Islands)*	Condor Ferries	6½ hrs	4 per week
Poole – Cherbourg	Brittany Ferries	5 hrs	1 daily
Plymouth – Roscoff	Brittany Ferries	6 hrs	2 daily
Portsmouth – Caen	Brittany Ferries	6 / 7 hrs	3 daily
Portsmouth – Cherbourg	Brittany Ferries	3 hrs	2 daily
Portsmouth – Le Havre	Brittany Ferries	3¼ / 6 hrs	4 per week
Portsmouth – St Malo	Brittany Ferries	9 hrs	1 daily
Ireland – Northern			
Cairnryan – Larne	P & O Irish Sea	1 / 2 hrs	7 daily
Cairnryan – Belfast	Stena Line	2 / 3 hrs	7 daily
Liverpool (Birkenhead) – Belfast	Stena Line	8 hrs	2 daily
Ireland – Republic			
Cork – Roscoff*	Brittany Ferries	15 hrs	2 per week
Dublin - Cherbourg*	Irish Ferries	19 hrs	5 per week
Fishguard – Rosslare	Stena Line	3½ hrs	2 daily
Holyhead – Dublin	Irish Ferries	2-4 hrs	Max 4 daily
Holyhead – Dublin	Stena Line	2-4 hrs	Max 4 daily
Pembroke – Rosslare	Irish Ferries	4 hrs	2 daily
Rosslare – Cherbourg*	Brittany Ferries	18 hrs	2 per week
Rosslare – Cherbourg	Stena Line	19 hrs	3 per week
Netherlands			
Harwich – Hook of Holland	Stena Line	7 hrs	2 daily
Hull – Rotterdam	P & O Ferries	11-12 hrs	1 daily
Newcastle – Ijmuiden (Amsterdam)	DFDS Seaways	15½ hrs	1 daily
Spain			
Portsmouth – Bilbao	Brittany Ferries	31 / 36 hrs	2 per week
Portsmouth or Plymouth – Santander	Brittany Ferries	20 / 32 hrs	4 per week
Rosslare – Bilbao*	Brittany Ferries	29 - 30 hrs	2 per week
Rosslare – Santander*	Brittany Ferries	29-33 hrs	2 per week (winter only)

** Not bookable through The Club's Travel Service.*

Motoring advice

Shutterstock/ Weston

Preparing for your Journey

The first priority in preparing your outfit for your journey should be to make sure it has a full service. Make sure that you have a fully equipped spares kit, and a spare wheel and tyre for your caravan – it's easier to get hold of them from your local dealer than to have to spend time searching for spares where you don't know the local area.

Caravan and Motorhome Club members should carry their UK Sites Directory & Handbook with them, as it contains a section of technical advice which may be useful when travelling.

The Club also has a free advice service covering a wide range of technical topics – download free information leaflets at camc.com/advice or contact the team by calling 01342 336 611.

Weight limits

For both a legal and safety reasons, it's essential not to exceed vehicle weight limits. Carry documentation confirming your vehicle's maximum permitted laden weight - if this isn't stated on your Vehicle Registration Certificate (V5C) you'll need an alternative certification, e.g. from a weighbridge.

If you are pulled over by the police and don't have certification you will be taken to a weighbridge. If your vehicle(s) are then found to be overweight you will be liable to a fine and may have to discard items to lower the weight before you can continue on your journey.

Some final checks

Before you start any journey make sure you complete the following checks:

- All car and caravan or motorhome lights are working and sets of spare bulbs are packed.
- The coupling is correctly seated on the towball and the breakaway cable is attached.
- Windows, vents, hatches and doors are shut.
- On-board water systems are drained.
- Mirrors are adjusted for maximum visibility.
- Corner steadies are fully wound up and the brace is handy for your arrival on site.
- Any fires or flames are extinguished and the gas cylinder tap is turned off. Fire extinguishers are fully charged and close at hand.
- The over-run brake is working correctly.
- The jockey wheel is raised and secured, the handbrake is released.

Driving in Europe

Driving abroad for the first time can be a daunting prospect, especially when towing a caravan. Here are a few tips to make the transition easier:

- Remember that Sat Navs may take you on unsuitable roads, so have a map or atlas to hand to help you find an alternative route.
- It can be tempting to try and get to your destination as quickly as possible but the Club recommends travelling a maximum of 250 miles a day when towing.
- Share the driving if possible, and on long journeys plan an overnight stop.
- Remember that if you need to overtake or pull out around an obstruction you will not be able to see clearly from the driver's seat. If possible, always have a responsible adult in the passenger seat who can advise you when it's clear to pull out. If that is not possible then stay well back to get a better view and pull out slowly.
- If traffic builds up behind you, pull over safely and let it pass.
- Driving on the right should become second nature after a while, but pay particular attention when turning left, after leaving a rest area, petrol station or site or after a one-way system.
- Stop at least every two hours to stretch your legs and take a break.

Fuel

Grades of petrol sold on the Continent are comparable to those sold in the UK; 95 octane is frequently known as 'Essence' and 98 octane as 'Super'. Diesel may be called 'Gasoil' and is widely available across Europe. E10 petrol (containing 10% Ethanol) can be found in certain countries in Europe.

Most modern cars are E10 compatible, but those which aren't could be damaged by filling up with E10. Check your vehicle handbook or visit www.acea.be and search for 'E10' to find the publication 'Vehicle compatibility with new fuel standards'.

Club members can check current average fuel prices by country at camc.com/overseasadvice.

Away from major roads and towns it's a good idea not to let your fuel tank run too low as you may have difficulty finding a petrol station, especially at night or on Sundays. Petrol stations offering a 24-hour service may involve an automated process, in some cases only accepting credit cards issued in the country you are in.

Automotive Liquefied Petroleum Gas (LPG)

The increasing popularity of dual-fuelled vehicles means that the availability of LPG – also known as 'autogas' or GPL – has become an important issue for more drivers.

There are different tank-filling openings in use in different countries. Currently there is no common European filling system, and you might find a variety of systems.

Most Continental motorway services will have adaptors but these should be used with care.

Low Emission Zones

Many cities in countries around Europe have introduced Low Emission Zones (LEZ) in order to regulate vehicle pollution levels. Some schemes require you to buy a windscreen sticker, pay a fee or register your vehicle before entering the zone. You may also need to provide proof that your vehicle's emissions meet the required standard.

Visit urbanaccessregulations.eu before you travel for maps and details of Low Emission Zones across Europe. Also see the Country Introductions later in this guide for country specific information.

Motorhomes towing cars

If you're towing a car behind a motorhome, our advice would be to use a trailer with all four wheels of the car off the ground. Although most countries don't have specific laws banning A-frames, there may be laws in place which prohibit motor vehicle towing another motor vehicle.

Priority and roundabouts

When driving on the Continent it can be difficult to work out which vehicles have priority in different situations. Watch out for road signs which indicate priority and read the Country Introductions later in this guide for country specific information.

Take care at intersections – you should never rely on being given right of way, even if you have priority; especially in small towns and villages where local traffic may take right of way. Always give way to public service and military vehicles and to buses and trams.

In some countries in Europe priority at roundabouts is given to vehicles entering the roundabout (i.e. on the right) unless the road signs say otherwise.

Public transport

In general in built-up areas be prepared to stop to allow a bus to pull out from a bus stop when the driver is signalling his intention to do so.Take particular care when school buses have stopped and passengers are getting on and off.

Overtaking trams in motion is normally only allowed on the right, unless on a one way street where you can overtake on the left if

Shutterstock/ Monkey Business Images

Shutterstock/ Leonid Andronov

there is not enough space on the right. Don't overtake a tram near a tram stop. These may be in the centre of the road. When a tram or bus stops to allow passengers on and off, you should stop to allow them to cross to the pavement. Give way to trams which are turning across your carriageway. Don't park or stop across tram lines; trams cannot steer round obstructions!

Pedestrian crossings

Stopping to allow pedestrians to cross at zebra crossings is not always common practice on the Continent as it is in the UK. Pedestrians expect to wait until the road is clear before crossing, while motorists behind may be taken by surprise by your stopping. The result may be a rear-end shunt or vehicles overtaking you at the crossing and putting pedestrians at risk.

Traffic lights

Traffic lights may not be as easily visible as they are in the UK, for instance they may be smaller or suspended across the road with a smaller set on a post at the roadside. You may find that lights change directly from red to green, bypassing amber completely. Flashing amber lights generally indicate that you may proceed with caution if it's safe to do so but you must give way to pedestrians and other vehicles.

A green filter light should be treated with caution as you may still have to give way to pedestrians who have a green light to cross the road. If a light turns red as approached, continental drivers will often speed up to get through the light instead of stopping. Be aware that if you brake sharply because a traffic light has turned red as you approached, the driver behind might not be expecting it.

Essential equipment

The equipment that you legally have to carry differs by country. For a full list see the 'Essential Equipment' table at the end of this chapter. Please note equipment requirements and regulations can change frequently. To keep up to date with the latest equipment information visit camc.com/overseasadvice.

Child restraint systems

Children under 10 years of age aren't permitted to travel in front seats of vehicles, unless there are no rear seats in the vehicle, the rear seats are already occupied with other children, or there are no seat belts in the rear. In these situations a child must not be placed in the front seats in a rear-facing child seat, unless any airbag is deactivated. Children up to 10 must travel in an approved child seat or restraint system, adapted to their size. A baby up to 13kg in weight must be carried in a rear facing baby seat. A child between 9kg and 18kg in weight must be seated in a child seat. A child from 15kg in weight up to the age of 10 can use a booster seat with a seat belt.

Children must not travel in the front of a vehicle if there are rear seats available. If they travel in the front, the airbag must be deactivated and again they must use an EU approved restraint system for their size.

Fire extinguisher

As a safety precaution, an approved fire extinguisher should be carried in all vehicles. This is a legal requirement in several countries in Europe.

Lights

When driving on the right, headlights should be adjusted if they're likely to dazzle other road users. You can do this by applying beam deflectors, or some newer vehicles have a built-in adjustment system. Some high-density discharge (HID), xenon or halogen lights, may need to be taken to a dealer to make the necessary adjustment.

Remember to adjust headlights according to the load being carried and to compensate for the weight of the caravan on the back of your car. Even if you don't intend to drive at night, it's important to ensure that your headlights are correctly adjusted as you may need to use them in heavy rain, fog or in tunnels. If using tape or a pre-cut adhesive mask remember to remove it on your return home.

All vehicle lights must be in working condition. If your lights are not in working order you may be liable for a fine of up to €450 and confiscation of your vehicle is a possibility in some European countries.

Headlight flashing

On the Continent headlight flashing is used as a warning of approach or as an overtaking signal at night, and not, as is commonly the case in the UK, an indication that you're giving way. Be more cautious with both flashing your headlights and when another driver flashes you. If a driver flashes his headlights they're generally indicating that they have priority and you should give way, contrary to standard practice in the UK.

Hazard warning lights

Hazard warning lights should not be used in place of a warning triangle, but should be used in addition to it.

Nationality plate

On 28 September 2021, the distinguishing mark (or national identifier) displayed on vehicles registered in the United Kingdom driven abroad changed from GB to UK.

This means that vehicles registered in the UK must display the letters 'UK' when driven in the EU. You'll need to display a UK sticker clearly on the rear of your vehicle if your number plate has any of the following:

- A GB identifier with the Union flag (also known as the Union Jack)
- A Euro symbol
- A national flag of England, Scotland or Wales
- Numbers and letters only - no flag or identifier
- If you're in Spain, you must display a UK sticker no matter what is on your number plate.
- If you have a GB sticker, you need to cover or remove it.

Reflective jackets/waistcoats

If you break down outside of a built-up area it's normally a legal requirement anyone leaving the vehicle must be wearing a reflective jacket or waistcoat. Ensure your jacket is accessible from inside the car. Carry one for each passenger as well as the driver.

Route planning

It's always a good idea to carry a road atlas or map of the countries you plan to visit, even if you have satellite navigation. Websites offering a European route mapping service include google.co.uk/maps, mappy.com or viamichelin.com.

Satellite navigation/GPS

European postcodes don't cover just one street or part of a street in the same way as UK postcodes, they can cover a very large area. GPS coordinates and full addresses are given for site entries in this guide wherever possible, allowing you to programme your device as accurately as possible.

Shutterstock/Pincasso

It's important to remember that sat nav devices don't usually allow for towing or driving a large motorhome and may try to send you down unsuitable roads. Always use your common sense, and if a road looks unsuitable find an alternative route.

Use your sat nav in conjunction with the directions given in the site entries, which have been provided by members who have actually visited. Please note that directions given in site entries have not been checked by the Caravan and Motorhome Club.

In nearly all European countries it's illegal to use car navigation systems which actively search for mobile speed cameras or interfere with police equipment (laser or radar detection).

Car navigation systems which give a warning of fixed speed camera locations are legal in most countries with the exception of France, Germany, and Switzerland where this function must be deactivated.

Seat belts

The wearing of seat belts is compulsory throughout Europe. On-the-spot fines will be incurred for failure to wear them and, in the event of an accident, failure to wear a seat belt may reduce any claim for injury. See the 'Country Introductions' for specific regulations on both seat belts and car seats.

Spares

Caravan spares

Generally, it's much harder to get hold of spare parts for caravans on the Continent, especially for UK manufactured caravans. It's therefore advisable to carry any commonly required spares (such as light bulbs) with you.

Take contact details of your UK dealer or manufacturer with you, as they may be able to assist in getting spares delivered to you in an emergency.

Car spares

Some car manufacturers produce spares kits; contact your dealer for details. The choice of spares will depend on the vehicle and how long you're away, but the following is a list of basic items which should cover the most common causes of breakdown:

- Radiator top hose
- Fan belt
- Fuses and bulbs
- Windscreen wiper blade
- Length of 12V electrical cable
- Tools, torch and WD40 or equivalent water repellent/ dispersant spray

Spare Wheel

Your local caravan dealer should be able to supply an appropriate spare wheel. If you have any difficulty in obtaining one, the Club's Technical Department can provide Club members with a list of suppliers on request.

Tyre legislation across Europe is more or less consistent and, while the Club has no specific knowledge of laws on the Continent regarding the use of space-saver spare wheels, there should be no problems in using such a wheel provided its use is in accordance with the manufacturer's instructions. Space-saver spare wheels are designed for short journeys to get to a place where it can be repaired and there will usually be restrictions on the distance and speed at which the vehicle should be driven.

Towbar

The vast majority of cars registered after 1 August 1998 are legally required to have a European Type approved towbar (complying with European Directive 94/20) carrying a plate giving its approval number and various technical details, including the maximum noseweight.

Your car dealer or specialist towbar fitter will be able to give further advice.

All new motorhomes will need some form of type approval before they can be registered in the UK and as such can only be fitted with a type approved towbar.

Older vehicles can continue to be fitted with non-approved towing brackets.

Tyres

Tyre condition has a major effect on the safe handling of your outfit.

Caravan tyres must be suitable for the highest speed at which you can legally tow, even if you choose to drive slower.

Most countries require a minimum tread depth of 1.6mm but motoring organisations recommend at least 3mm.

If you're planning a long journey, consider if they will still be above the legal minimum by the end of your journey.

Tyre pressure

Tyre pressure should be checked and adjusted when the tyres are cold; checking warm tyres will result in a higher pressure reading. The correct pressures will be found in your car handbook, but unless it states otherwise to add an extra 4-6 pounds per square inch to the rear tyres of a car when towing to improve handling. Make sure you know what pressure your caravan tyres should be. Some require a pressure much higher than that normally used for cars. Check your caravan handbook for details.

Tyre sizes

It's worth noting that some sizes of radial tyre to fit the 13" wheels commonly used on older UK caravans are virtually impossible to find in stock at retailers abroad, e.g. 175R13C.

After a puncture

A lot of cars now have a liquid sealant puncture repair kit instead of a spare wheel. These should not be considered a permanent repair, and in some cases have been known to make repair of the tyre impossible. If you need to use a liquid sealant you should get the tyre repaired or replaced as soon as possible.

Following a caravan tyre puncture, especially on a single-axle caravan, it's advisable to have the non-punctured tyre removed from its wheel and checked inside and out for signs of damage resulting from overloading during the deflation of the punctured tyre.

Winter driving

Snow chains must be fitted to vehicles using snow-covered roads in compliance with the relevant road signs. Fines may be imposed for non-compliance. Vehicles fitted with chains must not exceed 50 km/h (31mph).

They're not difficult to fit but it's a good idea to carry sturdy gloves to protect your hands in freezing conditions. Polar Automotive Ltd sells and hires out snow chains, contact them on 01732 360 638, visit snowchains.com, or email info@snowchains.com.

In Andorra, winter tyres are recommended. Snow chains must be used when road conditions necessitate their use and/or when road signs indicate.

Warning triangles

In almost all European countries, it's compulsory to carry a warning triangle which, in the event of vehicle breakdown or accident, must be placed (providing it's safe to do so) on the carriageway at least 30 metres from the vehicle. In some instances it's not compulsory to use the triangle but only when this action would endanger the driver.

A warning triangle should be placed on the road approximately 30 metres (100 metres on motorways) behind the broken-down vehicle on the same side of the road. Always assemble the triangle before leaving your vehicle and walk with it so that the red, reflective surface is facing oncoming traffic.

If a breakdown occurs round a blind corner, place the triangle in advance of the corner. Hazard warning lights may be used in conjunction with the triangle but they don't replace it.

Essential Equipment Table

The table below shows the essential equipment required for each country.Please note that this information was correct at the time of going to print but is subject to change.

For up-to-date information on equipment requirements for countries in Europe visit camc.com/overseasadvice.

Country	Warning Triangle	Spare Bulbs	First Aid Kit	Reflective Jacket	Additional Equipment to be Carried/Used
Andorra	Yes (2)	Yes	Rec	Yes	Dipped headlights in poor daytime visibility. Winter tyres recommended; snow chains when road conditions or signs dictate.
Austria	Yes	Rec	Yes	Yes	Winter tyres from 1 Nov to 15 April.*
Belgium	Yes	Rec	Rec	Yes	Dipped headlights in poor daytime visibility.
Croatia	Yes (2 for vehicle with trailer)	Yes	Yes	Yes	Dipped headlights at all times from last Sunday in Oct - last Sunday in Mar. Spare bulbs compulsory if lights are xenon, neon or LED. Snow chains compulsory in winter in certain regions.*
Czechia	Yes	Yes	Yes	Yes	Dipped headlights at all times. Replacement fuses. Winter tyres or snow chains from 1 Nov - 31st March.*
Denmark	Yes	Rec	Rec	Rec	Dipped headlights at all times. On motorways use hazard warning lights when queues or danger ahead.
Finland	Yes	Rec	Rec	Yes	Dipped headlights at all times. Winter tyres Dec - Feb.*
France	Yes	Rec	Rec	Yes	Dipped headlights recommended at all times. Legal requirement to carry a breathalyser, but no penalty for non-compliance.

Country	Warning Triangle	Spare Bulbs	First Aid Kit	Reflective Jacket	Additional Equipment to be Carried/Used
Germany	Rec	Rec	Rec	Rec	Dipped headlights recommended at all times. Winter tyres to be used in winter weather conditions.*
Greece	Yes	Rec	Yes	Rec	Fire extinguisher compulsory. Dipped headlights in towns at night and in poor daytime visibility.
Hungary	Yes	Rec	Yes	Yes	Dipped headlights at all times outside built-up areas and in built-up areas at night. Snow chains compulsory on some roads in winter conditions.*
Italy	Yes	Rec	Rec	Yes	Dipped headlights at all times outside built-up areas and in poor visibility. Snow chains from15 Oct - 15 April.*
Luxembourg	Yes	Rec	Rec	Yes	Dipped headlights at night and daytime in bad weather.
Netherlands	Yes	Rec	Rec	Rec	Dipped headlights at night and in bad weather and recommended during the day.
Norway	Yes	Rec	Rec	Rec	Dipped headlights at all times. Winter tyres compulsory when snow or ice on the roads.*
Poland	Yes	Rec	Rec	Rec	Dipped headlights at all times. Fire extinguisher compulsory.
Portugal	Yes	Rec	Rec	Rec	Dipped headlights in poor daytime visibility, in tunnels and in lanes where traffic flow is reversible.
Slovakia	Yes	Rec	Yes	Yes	Dipped headlights at all times. Winter tyres compulsory when compact snow or ice on the road.*
Slovenia	Yes (2 for vehicle with trailer)	Yes	Rec	Yes	Dipped headlights at all times. Hazard warning lights when reversing. Use winter tyres or carry snow chains 15 Nov - 15 Mar.
Spain	Yes (2 Rec)	Rec	Rec	Yes	Dipped headlights at night, in tunnels and on 'special' roads (roadworks).
Sweden	Yes	Rec	Rec	Rec	Dipped headlights at all times. Winter tyres 1 Dec to 31 March.
Switzerland (inc Liechtenstein)	Yes	Rec	Rec	Rec	Dipped headlights recommended at all times, compulsory in tunnels. Snow chains where indicated by signs.

NOTES:
1) All countries: seat belts (if fitted) must be worn by all passengers.
2) Rec: not compulsory for foreign-registered vehicles, but strongly recommended
3) Headlamp converters, spare bulbs, fire extinguisher, first aid kit and reflective waistcoat are strongly recommended for all countries.
4) In some countries drivers who wear prescription glasses must carry a spare pair.
5) Please check information for any country before you travel. This information is to be used as a guide only and it is your responsibility to make sure you have the correct equipment.

* For more information and regulations on winter driving please see the Country Introduction.

Mountain Passes

Mountain passes can create difficult driving conditions, especially when towing or driving a large vehicle. You should only use them if you have a good power to weight ratio and in good driving conditions. If in any doubt as to your outfit's suitability or the weather then stick to motorway routes across mountain ranges if possible.

The tables on the following pages show which passes are not suitable for caravans, and those where caravans are not permitted. Motorhomes aren't usually included in these restrictions, but relatively low powered or very large vehicles should find an alternative route. Road signs at the foot of a pass may restrict access or offer advice, especially for heavy vehicles. Warning notices are usually posted at the foot of a pass if it is closed, or if chains or winter tyres must be used.

Caravanners are particularly sensitive to gradients and traffic/road conditions on passes. The maximum gradient is usually on the inside of bends but exercise caution if it's necessary to pull out. Always engage a lower gear before taking a hairpin bend and give priority to vehicles ascending. On mountain roads it's not the gradient which puts strain on your car but the duration of the climb and the loss of power at high altitudes: approximately 10% at 915 metres (3,000 feet) and even more as you get higher. To minimise the risk of the engine overheating, take high passes in the cool part of the day, don't climb any faster than necessary and keep the engine pulling steadily. To prevent a radiator boiling, pull off the road safely, turn the heater and blower full on and switch off air conditioning. Keep an eye on water and oil levels. Never put cold water into a boiling radiator or it may crack. Check that the radiator is not obstructed by debris sucked up during the journey.

A long descent may result in overheating brakes; select the correct gear for the gradient and avoid excessive use of brakes. Even if you are using engine braking to control speed, caravan brakes may activate due to the overrun mechanism, which may cause them to overheat.

Travelling at altitude can cause a pressure build up in tanks and water pipes. You can prevent this by slightly opening the blade valve of your portable toilet and opening a tap a fraction.

Mountain Pass Information

The dates of opening and closing given in the following tables are approximate. Before attempting late afternoon or early morning journeys across borders, check their opening times as some borders close at night.

Gradients listed are the maximum which may be encountered on the pass and may be steeper at the inside of curves, particularly on older roads.

Gravel surfaces (such as dirt and stone chips) vary considerably; they can be dusty when dry and slippery when wet. Where known to exist, this type of surface has been noted.

In fine weather winter tyres or snow chains will only be required on very high passes, or for short periods in early or late summer. In winter conditions you will probably need to use them at altitudes exceeding 600 metres (approximately 2,000 feet).

Tunnels

Long tunnels are more commonly seen in Europe than in the UK, especially in mountainous regions. Tolls are usually charged for the use of major tunnels.

Dipped headlights are usually required by law even in well-lit tunnels, so switch them on before you enter. Snow chains, if used, must be removed before entering a tunnel in lay-bys provided for this purpose.

'No overtaking' signs must be strictly observed. Never cross central single or double lines. If overtaking is permitted in twin-tube tunnels, bear in mind that it is very easy to underestimate distances and speed once inside. To minimise the effects of exhaust fumes close all car windows and set the ventilator to circulate air, or operate the air conditioning system coupled with the recycled air option.

If you break down, try to reach the next lay-by and call for help from an emergency phone. If you cannot reach a lay-by, place your warning triangle at least 100 metres behind your vehicle. Modern tunnels have video surveillance systems to ensure prompt assistance in an emergency. Some tunnels are miles long and a high number of breakdowns are due to running out of fuel so make sure you have enough before entering the tunnel.

Tables

Much of the information contained in the following tables was originally supplied by The Automobile Association and other motoring and tourist organisations. The Caravan and Motorhome Club haven't checked this information and cannot accept responsibility for the accuracy or for errors or omissions to these tables.

Converting Gradients

20% = 1 in 5	11% = 1 in 9
16% = 1 in 6	10% = 1 in 8
14% = 1 in 7	8% = 1 in 12
12% = 1 in 8	6% = 1 in 16

Abbreviations

MHV	Maximum height of vehicle
MLV	Maximum length of vehicle
MWV	Maximum width of vehicle
MWR	Minimum width of road
OC	Occasionally closed between dates
UC	Usually closed between dates
UO	Usually open between dates, although a fall of snow may obstruct the road for 24-48 hours.

Major Alpine Mountain Passes

Pass Height In Metres (Feet)	From To	Max gradient	Conditions and Comments
Achenpass (Austria – Germany) 941 (3087)	Achenwald *Glashütte*	4%	UO. Well-engineered road, B181/307. Gradient not too severe.
Albula (Switzerland) 2312 (7585)	Tiefencastel *La Punt*	10%	UC Nov-early Jun. MWR 3.5m (11'6") MWV 2.25m (7'6") Inferior alternative to the Julier; fine scenery. **Not recommended for caravans**. Alternative rail tunnel.
Allos (France) 2250 (7382)	Colmars *Barcelonette*	10%	UC early Nov-early Jun. MWR 4m (13'1") Very winding, narrow, mostly unguarded pass on D908 but not difficult otherwise; passing bays on southern slope; poor surface, MWV 1.8m (5'11"). **Not recommended for caravans**.
Aprica (Italy) 1176 (3858)	Tresenda *Edolo*	9%	UO. MWR 4m (13'1") Fine scenery; good surface; well-graded on road S39. Narrow in places; watch for protruding rock. Not recommended for caravanners to attempt this pass E or W. Poor road conditions, repairs reduce width drastically.
Aravis (France) 1498 (4915)	La Clusaz *Flumet*	9%	OC Dec-Mar. MWR 4m (13'1"). Fine scenery; D909, fairly easy road. Poor surface in parts on Chamonix side. Some single-line traffic.
Arlberg (Austria) 1802 (5912)	Bludenz *Landeck*	13%	OC Dec-Apr. MWR 6m (19'8"). Good modern road B197/E60 with several pull-in places. Steeper fr W easing towards summit; heavy traffic. **Caravans prohibited.** Parallel road tunnel (tolls) available on E60 (poss long queues).
Ballon d'Alsace (France) 1178 (3865)	Giromagny *St Maurice-sur-Moselle*	11%	OC Dec-Mar. MWR 4m (13'1") Fairly straightforward ascent/descent; narrow in places; numerous bends. On road D465.
Bayard (France) 1248 (4094)	Chauffayer *Gap*	14%	UO. MWR 6m (19'8") Part of the Route Napoléon N85. Fairly easy, steepest on the S side with several hairpin bends. Negotiable by caravans from N-to-S via D1075 (N75) and Col-de-la-Croix Haute, avoiding Gap.
Bernina (Switzerland) 2330 (7644)	Pontresina *Poschiavo*	12.50%	OC Dec-Mar. MWR 5m (16'5") MWV 2.25m (7'6") Fine scenery. Good with care on open narrow sections towards summit on S-side; on road no. 29.
Bracco (Italy) 613 (2011)	Riva Trigoso *Borghetto di Vara*	14%	UO. MWR 5m (16'5") A two-lane road (P1) more severe than height suggests due to hairpins and volume of traffic; passing difficult. Rec cross early to avoid traffic. Alternative toll m'way A12 available.

Pass Height In Metres (Feet)	From To	Max gradient	Conditions and Comments
Brenner (Europabrücke) (Austria – Italy) 1374 (4508)	Innsbruck *Vipiteno/Sterzing*	14%	UO. MWR 6m (19'8") On road no. 182/12. Parallel toll m'way A13/A22/E45 (6%) suitable for caravans. Heavy traffic may delay at Customs. **Pass road closed to vehicles towing trailers.**
Brouis (France) 1279 (4196)	Nice *Col-de-Tende*	12.50%	UO. MWR 6m (19'8") Good surface but many hairpins on D6204 (N204)/S20. Steep gradients on approaches. Height of tunnel at Col-de-Tende at the Italian border is 3.8m (12'4) **Not recommended for caravans.**
Brünig (Switzerland) 1007 (3340)	Brienzwiler Station *Giswil*	8.50%	UO. MWR 6m (19'8") MWV 2.5m (8'2") An easy but winding road (no. 4); heavy traffic at weekends; frequent lay-bys. On-going road improvement (2009) may cause delays – check before travel.
Bussang (France) 721 (2365)	Thann *St Maurice-sur-Moselle*	7%	UO. MWR 4m (13'1") A very easy road (N66) over the Vosges; beautiful scenery.
Cabre (France) 1180 (3871)	Luc-en-Diois *Aspres-sur-Buëch*	9%	UO. MWR 5.5m (18') An easy pleasant road (D93/D993), winding at Col-de-Cabre.
Campolongo (Italy) 1875 (6152)	Corvara-in-Badia *Arabba*	12.50%	OC Dec-Mar. MWR 5m (16'5") A winding but easy ascent on rd P244; long level stretch on summit followed by easy descent. Good surface, fine scenery.
Cayolle (France) 2326 (7631)	Barcelonnette *Guillaumes*	10%	UC early Nov-early Jun. MWR 4m (13'1") Narrow, winding road (D902) with hairpin bends; poor surface, broken edges with steep drops. Long stretches of single-track road with passing places. **Caravans prohibited.**
Costalunga (Karer) (Italy) 1745 (5725)	Bolzano *Pozza-di-Fassa*	16%	OC Dec-Apr. MWR 5m (16'5") A good well-engineered road (S241) but mostly winding with many blind hairpins. **Caravans prohibited.**
Croix (Switzerland) 1778 (5833)	Villars-sur-Ollon *Les Diablerets*	13%	UC Nov-May. MWR 3.5m (11'6") A narrow, winding route but extremely picturesque. **Not recommended for caravans.**
Croix Haute (France) 1179 (3868)	Monestier-de-Clermont *Aspres-sur-Buëch*	7%	UO on N75. MWR 5.5m (18') Well-engineered road (D1075/N75); several hairpin bends on N side.
Falzárego (Italy) 2117 (6945)	Cortina-d'Ampezzo *Andraz*	8.50%	OC Dec-Apr. MWR 5m (16'5") Well-engineered bitumen surface on road R48; many blind hairpin bends on both sides; used by tour coaches.

Pass Height In Metres (Feet)	From To	Max gradient	Conditions and Comments
Faucille (France) 1323 (4341)	Gex *Morez*	10%	UO. MWR 5m (16'5") Fairly wide, winding road (N5) across the Jura mountains; negotiable by caravans but probably better to follow route via La Cure-St Cergue-Nyon.
Fern (Austria) 1209 (3967)	Nassereith *Lermoos*	8%	UO. MWR 6m (19'8") Obstructed intermittently during winter. An easy pass on road 179 but slippery when wet; heavy traffic at summer weekends. Connects with Holzleiten Sattel Pass at S end for travel to/from Innsbruck – see below.
Flexen (Austria) 1784 (5853)	Lech *Rauzalpe (nr Arlberg Pass)*	10%	UO. MWR 5.5m (18') The magnificent 'Flexenstrasse', a well-engineered mountain road (no. 198) with tunnels and galleries. The road from Lech to Warth, N of the pass, is usually closed Nov-Apr due to danger of avalanche. **Not recommended for caravans.**
Flüela (Switzerland) 2383 (7818)	Davos-Dorf *Susch*	12.50%	OC Nov-May. MWR 5m (16'5") MWV 2.3m (7'6") Easy ascent from Davos on road no. 28; some acute hairpin bends on the E side; bitumen surface.
Forclaz (Switzerland – France) 1527 (5010)	Martigny *Argentière*	8.50%	UO Forclaz; OC Montets Dec-early Apr. MWR 5m (16'5") MWV 2.5m (8'2") Good road over the pass and to the French border; long, hard climb out of Martigny; narrow and rough over Col-des-Montets on D1506 (N506).
Foscagno (Italy) 2291 (7516)	Bormio *Livigno*	12.50%	OC Nov-May. MWR 3.3m (10'10") Narrow and winding road (S301) through lonely mountains, generally poor surface. Long winding ascent with many blind bends; not always well-guarded. Descent includes winding rise and fall over the Passo-d'Eira 2,200m (7,218'). **Not recommended for caravans.**
Fugazze (Italy) 1159 (3802)	Rovereto *Valli-del-Pasubio*	14%	UO. MWR 3.5m (11'6") Very winding road (S46) with some narrow sections, particularly on N side. The many blind bends and several hairpin bends call for extra care. **Not recommended for caravans.**
Furka (Switzerland) 2431 (7976)	Gletsch *Realp*	11%	UC Oct-Jun. MWR 4m (13'1") MWV 2.25m (7'6") Well-graded road (no. 19) with narrow sections (single track in place on E side) and several hairpin bends on both ascent and descent. Fine views of the Rhône Glacier. Beware of coaches and traffic build-up. **Not recommended for caravans.** Alternative rail tunnel available.
Galibier (France) 2645 (8678)	La Grave *St Michel-de-Maurienne*	12.50%	UC Oct-Jun. MWR 3m (9'10") Mainly wide, well-surfaced road (D902) but unprotected and narrow over summit. From Col-du-Lautaret it rises over the Col-du-Telegraphe then 11 more hairpin bends. Ten hairpin bends on descent then 5km (3.1 miles) narrow and rough; easier in N to S direction. Limited parking at summit. **Not recommended for caravans.** (Single-track tunnel under the Galibier summit, controlled by traffic lights; caravans are not permitted).
Gardena (Grödner-Joch) (Italy) 2121 (6959)	Val Gardena *Corvara-in-Badia*	12.50%	OC Dec-Jun. MWR 5m (16'5") A well-engineered road (S243), very winding on descent. Fine views. **Caravans prohibited.**

Pass Height In Metres (Feet)	From To	Max gradient	Conditions and Comments
Gavia (Italy) 2621 (8599)	Bormio *Ponte-di-Legno*	20%	UC Oct-Jul. MWR 3m (9'10") MWV 1.8m (5'11") Steep, narrow, difficult road (P300) with frequent passing bays; many hairpin bends and gravel surface; not for the faint-hearted; extra care necessary. **Not recommended for caravans**. Long winding ascent on Bormio side.
Gerlos (Austria) 1628 (5341)	Zell-am-Ziller *Wald im Pinzgau*	9%	UO. MWR 4m (13'1") Hairpin ascent out of Zell to modern toll road (B165); the old, steep, narrow and winding route with passing bays and 14% gradient is not rec but is negotiable with care. Views of Krimml waterfalls. **Caravans prohibited.**
Gorges-du-Verdon (France) 1032 (3386)	Castellane *Moustiers-Ste Marie*	9%	UO. MWR probably 5m (16'5") On road D952 over Col-d'Ayen and Col-d'Olivier. Moderate gradients but slow, narrow and winding. Poss heavy traffic.
Grand St Bernard (Switzerland – Italy) 2469 (8100)	Martigny *Aosta*	11%	UC Oct-Jun. MWR 4m (13'1") MWV 2.5m (8'2") Modern road to entrance of road tunnel on road no. 21/E27 (UO), then narrow but bitumen surface over summit to border; also good in Italy. Suitable for caravans using tunnel. Pass road feasible but not recommended. See *Road Tunnels* in this section.
Grimsel (Switzerland) 2164 (7100)	Innertkirchen *Gletsch*	10%	UC mid Oct-late Jun. MWR 5m (16'5") MWV 2.25m (7'6") A fairly easy, modern road (no. 6) with heavy traffic at weekends. A long winding ascent, finally hairpin bends; then a terraced descent with six hairpins (some tight) into the Rhône valley. Good surface; fine scenery.
Grossglockner (Austria) 2503 (8212)	Bruck-an-der-Grossglocknerstrasse *Heiligenblut*	12.50%	UC late Oct-early May. MWR 5.5m (18') Well-engineered road (no. 107) but many hairpins; heavy traffic; moderate but very long ascent/descent. Negotiable preferably S to N by caravans. Avoid side road to highest point at Edelweissespitze if towing, as road is very steep and narrow. Magnificent scenery. Tolls charged. Road closed from 2200-0500 hrs (summer). Alternative Felbertauern road tunnel between Lienz and Mittersil (toll).
Hahntennjoch (Austria) 1894 (6250)	Imst *Elmen*	15%	UC Nov-May. A minor pass. **Caravans prohibited.**
Hochtannberg (Austria) 1679 (5509)	Schröcken *Warth (nr Lech)*	14%	OC Jan-Mar. MWR 4m (13'1") A reconstructed modern road (no. 200). W to E long ascent with many hairpins. Easier E to W. **Not recommended for caravans**.
Holzleiten Sattel (Austria) 1126 (3694)	Nassereith *Obsteig*	12.50%	(12.5%), UO. MWR 5m (16'5") Road surface good on W side; poor on E. Light traffic; gradients no problem. **Not recommended for caravans**.
Iseran (France) 2770 (9088)	Bourg-St Maurice *Lanslebourg*	11%	UC mid Oct-late Jun. MWR 4m (13'1") Second highest pass in the Alps on road D902. Well-graded with reasonable bends, average surface. Several unlit tunnels on N approach. **Not recommended for caravans**.

Pass Height In Metres (Feet)	From To	Max gradient	Conditions and Comments
Izoard (France) 2360 (7743)	Guillestre *Briançon*	12.50%	UC late Oct-mid Jun. MWR 5m (16'5") Fine scenery. Winding, sometimes narrow road (D902) with many hairpin bends; care required at several unlit tunnels near Guillestre. **Not recommended for caravans.**
Jaun (Switzerland) 1509 (4951)	Bulle *Reidenbach*	14%	UO. MWR 4m (13'1") MWV 2.25m (7'6") A modern but generally narrow road (no. 11); some poor sections on ascent and several hairpin bends on descent.
Julier (Switzerland) 2284 (7493)	Tiefencastel *Silvaplana*	13%	UO. MWR 4m (13'1") MWV 2.5m (8'2") Well-engineered road (no. 3) approached from Chur via Sils. Fine scenery. Negotiable by caravans, preferably from N to S, but a long haul and many tight hairpins. Alternative rail tunnel from Thusis to Samedan. See *Rail Tunnels* in this section.
Katschberg (Austria) 1641 (5384)	Spittal-an-der-Drau *St Michael*	20%	UO. MWR 6m (19'8") Good wide road (no. 99) with no hairpins but steep gradients particularly from S. Suitable only light caravans. Parallel Tauern/Katschberg toll motorway A10/E55 and road tunnels.
Klausen (Switzerland) 1948 (6391)	Altdorf *Linthal*	10%	UC late Oct-early Jun. MWR 5m (16'5") MWV 2.30m (7'6") Narrow and winding in places, but generally easy in spite of a number of sharp bends. **Caravans prohibited** between Unterschächen and Linthal (no. 17).
Larche (della Maddalena) (France – Italy) 1994 (6542)	La Condamine-Châtelard *Vinadio*	8.50%	OC Dec-Mar. MWR 3.5m (11'6") An easy, well-graded road (D900); long, steady ascent on French side, many hairpins on Italian side (S21). Fine scenery; ample parking at summit.
Lautaret (France) 2058 (6752)	Le Bourg-d'Oisans *Briançon*	12.50%	OC Dec-Mar. MWR 4m (13'1") Modern, evenly graded but winding road (D1091), and unguarded in places; very fine scenery; suitable for caravans but with care through narrow tunnels.
Leques (France) 1146 (3760)	Barrême *Castellane*	8%	UO. MWR 4m (13'1") On Route Napoléon (D4085). Light traffic; excellent surface; narrow in places on N ascent. S ascent has many hairpins.
Loibl (Ljubelj) (Austria – Slovenia) 1067 (3500)	Unterloibl *Kranj*	20%	UO. MWR 6m (19'8") Steep rise and fall over Little Loibl pass (E652) to 1.6km (1 mile) tunnel under summit. **Caravans prohibited.** The old road over the summit is closed to through-traffic.
Lukmanier (Lucomagno) (Switzerland) 1916 (6286)	Olivone *Disentis*	9%	UC early Nov-late May. MWR 5m (16'5") MWV 2.25m (7'6") Rebuilt, modern road.
Maloja (Switzerland) 1815 (5955)	Silvaplana *Chiavenna*	9%	UO. MWR 4m (13'1") MWV 2.5m (8'2") Escarpment facing south; fairly easy, but many hairpin bends on descent; negotiable by caravans but possibly difficult on ascent. On road no. 3/S37.

Pass Height In Metres (Feet)	From To	Max gradient	Conditions and Comments
Mauria (Italy) 1298 (4258)	Lozzo di Cadore *Ampezzo*	7%	UO. MWR 5m (16'5") A well-designed road (S52) with easy, winding ascent and descent.
Mendola (Italy) 1363 (4472)	Appiano/Eppan *Sarnonico*	12.50%	UO. MWR 5m (16'5") A fairly straightforward but winding road (S42), well-guarded, many hairpins. Take care overhanging cliffs if towing. The E side going down to Bolzano is not wide enough for caravans, especially difficult on busy days, not recommended for caravans.
Mont Cenis (France – Italy) 2083 (6834)	Lanslebourg *Susa*	12.50%	UC Nov-May. MWR 5m (16'5") Approach by industrial valley. An easy highway (D1006/S25) with mostly good surface; spectacular scenery; long descent into Italy with few stopping places. Alternative Fréjus road tunnel available.
Monte Croce-di-Comélico (Kreuzberg) (Italy) 1636 (5368)	San Candido *Santo-Stefano- di-Cadore*	8.50%	UO. MWR 5m (16'5") A winding road (S52) with moderate gradients, beautiful scenery.
Montgenèvre (France – Italy) 1850 (6070)	Briançon *Cesana-Torinese*	9%	UO. MWR 5m (16'5") Easy, modern road (N94/S24), some tight hairpin bends, good road surface on French side; road widened & tunnels improved on Italian side, in need of some repair but still easy. Much used by lorries; may need to give way to large vehicles on hairpins.
Monte Giovo (Jaufen) (Italy) 2094 (6870)	Merano *Vipiteno/Sterzing*	12.50%	UC Nov-May. MWR 4m (13'1") Many well-engineered hairpin bends on S44; good scenery. **Caravans prohibited.**
Morgins (France – Switzerland) 1369 (4491)	Abondance *Monthey*	14%	UO. MWR 4m (13'1") A lesser used route (D22) through pleasant, forested countryside crossing French/Swiss border. **Not recommended for caravans**.
Mosses (Switzerland) 1445 (4740)	Aigle *Château-d'Oex*	8.50%	UO. MWR 4m (13'1") MWV 2.25m (7'6") A modern road (no. 11). Aigle side steeper and narrow in places.
Nassfeld (Pramollo) (Austria – Italy) 1530 (5020)	Tröpolach *Pontebba*	20%	OC Late Nov-Mar. MWR 4m (13'1") The winding descent on road no. 90 into Itay has been improved but not rec for caravans.
Nufenen (Novena) (Switzerland) 2478 (8130)	Ulrichen *Airolo*	10%	UC Mid Oct-mid Jun. MWR 4m (13'1") MWV 2.25m (7'6") The approach roads are narrow, with tight bends, but the road over the pass is good; negotiable with care. Long drag from Ulrichen.
Oberalp (Switzerland) 2044 (6706)	Andermatt *Disentis*	10%	UC Nov-late May. MWR 5m (16'5") MWV 2.3m (7'6") Much improved and widened road (no.19) but narrow in places on E side; many tight hairpin bends, but long level stretch on summit. Alternative rail tunnel during the winter. **Not recommended for caravans**.

Pass Height In Metres (Feet)	From To	Max gradient	Conditions and Comments
Ofen (Fuorn) (Switzerland) 2149 (7051)	Zernez *Santa Maria-im-Münstertal*	12.50%	UO. MWR 4m (13'1") MWV 2.25m (7'6") Good road (no. 28) through Swiss National Park.
Petit St Bernard (France – Italy) 2188 (7178)	Bourg-St Maurice *Pré-St Didier*	8.50%	UC mid Oct-Jun. MWR 5m (16'5") Outstanding scenery, but poor surface and unguarded broken edges near summit. Easiest from France (D1090); sharp hairpins on climb from Italy (S26). **Caravans prohibited.**
Pillon (Switzerland) 1546 (5072)	Le Sépey *Gsteig*	9%	OC Jan-Feb. MWR 4m (13'1") MWV 2.25m (7'6") A comparatively easy modern road.
Plöcken (Monte Croce-Carnico) (Austria – Italy) 1362 (4468)	Kötschach *Paluzza*	14%	OC Dec-Apr. MWR 5m (16'5") A modern road (no. 110) with long, reconstructed sections; OC to caravans due to heavy traffic on summer weekends; delay likely at the border. Long, slow, twisty pull from S, easier from N.
Pordoi (Italy) 2239 (7346)	Arabba *Canazei*	10%	OC Dec-Apr. MWR 5m (16'5") An excellent modern road (S48) with numerous blind hairpin bends; fine scenery; used by tour coaches. Long drag when combined with Falzarego pass.
Pötschen (Austria) 982 (3222)	Bad Ischl *Bad Aussee*	9%	UO. MWR 7m (23') A modern road (no. 145). Good scenery.
Radstädter-Tauern (Austria) 1738 (5702)	Radstadt *Mauterndorf*	16%	OC Jan-Mar. MWR 5m (16'5") N ascent steep (road no. 99) but not difficult otherwise; but negotiable by light caravans using parallel toll m'way (A10) through tunnel.
Résia (Reschen) (Italy – Austria) 1504 (4934)	Spondigna *Pfunds*	10%	UO. MWR 6m (19'8") A good, straightforward alternative to the Brenner Pass. Fine views but no stopping places. On road S40/180.
Restefond (La Bonette) (France) 2802 (9193)	Barcelonnette *St Etienne-de-Tinée*	16%	UC Oct-Jun. MWR 3m (9'10") The highest pass in the Alps. Rebuilt, resurfaced road (D64) with rest area at summit – top loop narrow and unguarded. Winding with hairpin bends. **Not recommended for caravans**.
Rolle (Italy) 1970 (6463)	Predazzo *Mezzano*	9%	OC Dec-Mar. MWR 5m (16'5") A well-engineered road (S50) with many hairpin bends on both sides; very beautiful scenery; good surface.
St Gotthard (San Gottardo) (Switzerland) 2108 (6916)	Göschenen *Airolo*	10%	UC mid Oct-early Jun. MWR 6m (19'8") MHV 3.6m (11'9") MWV 2.5m (8'2") Modern, fairly easy two- to three-lane road (A2/E35). Heavy traffic. Alternative road tunnel.

Pass Height In Metres (Feet)	From To	Max gradient	Conditions and Comments
San Bernardino (Switzerland) 2066 (6778)	Mesocco *Hinterrhein*	10%	UC Oct-late Jun. MWR 4m (13'1") MWV 2.25m (7'6") Easy modern road (A13/E43) on N and S approaches to tunnel, narrow and winding over summit via tunnel suitable for caravans.
Schlucht (France) 1139 (3737)	Gérardmer *Munster*	7%	UO. MWR 5m (16'5") An extremely picturesque route (D417) crossing the Vosges mountains, with easy, wide bends on the descent. Good surface.
Seeberg (Jezersko) (Austria – Slovenia) 1218 (3996)	Eisenkappel *Kranj*	12.50%	UO. MWR 5m (16'5") An alternative to the steeper Loibl and Wurzen passes on B82/210; moderate climb with winding, hairpin ascent and descent. **Not recommended for caravans**.
Sella (Italy) 2240 (7349)	Selva *Canazei*	11%	OC Dec-Jan. MWR 5m (16'5") A well-engineered, winding road; exceptional views of Dolomites. **Caravans prohibited.**
Sestriere (Italy) 2033 (6670)	Cesana-Torinese *Pinarolo*	10%	UO MWR 6m (19'8") Mostly bitumen surface on road R23. Fairly easy; fine scenery.
Silvretta (Bielerhöhe) (Austria) 2032 (6666)	Partenen *Galtur*	11%	UC late Oct-early Jun. MWR 5m (16'5") Mostly reconstructed road (188); 32 easy hairpin bends on W ascent; E side more straightforward. Tolls charged. **Caravans prohibited.**
Simplon (Switzerland – Italy) 2005 (6578)	Brig *Domodóssola*	11%	OC Nov-Apr. MWR 7m (23') MWV 2.5m (8'2") An easy, reconstructed, modern road (E62/S33), 21km (13 miles) long, continuous ascent to summit; good views, many stopping places. Surface better on Swiss side. Alternative rail tunnel fr Kandersteg in operation from Easter to September .
Splügen (Switzerland – Italy) 2113 (6932)	Splügen *Chiavenna*	13%	UC Nov-Jun. MWR 3.5m (11'6") MHV 2.8m (9'2") MWV 2.3m (7'6") Mostly narrow, winding road (S36), with extremely tight hairpin bends, not well guarded; care also required at many tunnels/galleries. **Not recommended for caravans**.
Stelvio (Italy) 2757 (9045)	Bormio *Spondigna*	12.50%	UC Oct-late Jun. MWR 4m (13'1") MLV 10m (32') Third highest pass in Alps on S38; 40-50 acute hairpin bends either side, all well-engineered; good surface, traffic often heavy. Hairpin bends too acute for long vehicles. **Not recommended for caravans**.
Susten (Switzerland) 2224 (7297)	Innertkirchen *Wassen*	9%	UC Nov-Jun. MWR 6m (19'8") MWV 2.5m (8'2") Scenic, well-guarded road (no. 11); easy gradients and turns; heavy weekend traffic. East side easier than west. Negotiable by caravans (rec small/medium sized only) with care, not for the faint-hearted. Large summit parking area.
Tenda (Tende) Italy – France 1321 (4334)	Borgo-San Dalmazzo *Tende*	9%	UO. MWR 6m (19'8") Well-guarded, modern road (S20/ND6204) with several hairpin bends; road tunnel (height 3.8m) at summit narrow with poor road surface. Less steep on Italian side. **Caravans prohibited during winter.**

Pass Height In Metres (Feet)	From To	Max gradient	Conditions and Comments
Thurn (Austria) 1274 (4180)	Kitzbühel *Mittersill*	8.50%	UO. MWR 5m (16'5") MWV 2.5m (8' 2") A good road (no. 161) with narrow stretches; N approach rebuilt. Several good parking areas.
Timmelsjoch (Rombo) (Austria – Italy) 2509 (8232)	Obergurgl *Moso*	14%	UC mid Oct-Jun. MWR 3.5m (11'6") Border closed at night 8pm to 7am. On the pass (road no 186/S44b) **caravans are prohibited.** (toll charged), as some tunnels on Italian side too narrow for larger vehicles. Easiest N to S.
Tonale (Italy) 1883 (6178)	Edolo *Dimaro*	10%	UO. MWR 5m (16'5") A relatively easy road (S42); steepest on W; long drag. Fine views.
Tre Croci (Italy) 1809 (5935)	Cortina-d'Ampezzo *Auronzo-di-Cadore*	11%	OC Dec-Mar. MWR 6m (19'8") An easy pass on road R48; fine scenery.
Turracher Höhe (Austria) 1763 (5784)	Predlitz *Ebene-Reichenau*	23%	UO. MWR 4m (13'1") Formerly one of the steepest mountain roads (no. 95) in Austria; now improved. Steep, fairly straightforward ascent followed by a very steep descent; good surface and mainly two-lane; fine scenery. **Not recommended for caravans.**
Umbrail (Switzerland – Italy) 2501 (8205)	Santa Maria-im-Münstertal *Bormio*	9%	UC Nov-early Jun. MWR 4.3m (14'1") MWV 2.3m (7'6") Highest Swiss pass (road S38); mostly tarmac with some gravel surface. Narrow with 34 hairpin bends. **Not recommended for caravans.**
Vars (France) 2109 (6919)	St Paul-sur-Ubaye *Guillestre*	9%	OC Dec-Mar. MWR 5m (16'5") Easy winding ascent and descent on D902 with 14 hairpin bends; good surface.
Wurzen (Koren) (Austria – Slovenia) 1073 (3520)	Riegersdorf *Kranjska Gora*	20%	UO. MWR 4m (13'1") Steep two-lane road (no. 109), otherwise not particularly difficult; better on Austrian side; heavy traffic summer weekends; delays likely at the border. **Caravans prohibited.**
Zirler Berg (Austria) 1009 (3310)	Seefeld *Zirl*	16.50%	UO. MWR 7m (23') South facing escarpment, good, modern road (no. 171). Heavy tourist traffic and long steep descent with one hairpin bend into Inn Valley. Steepest section from hairpin bend down to Zirl. **Caravans not permitted northbound and not recommended southbound.**

Technical information by courtesy of the Automobile Association. Additional update and amendments supplied by caravanners and tourers who have themselves used the passes and tunnels. The Caravan and Motorhome Club has not checked the information contained in these tables and cannot accept responsibility for their accuracy, or for any errors, omissions, or their effects.

Major Alpine Rail Tunnels

Tunnel	Route	Journey Time	General Information and Comments	Contact
Albula (Switzerland) 5.9 km (3.5 miles)	**Chur – St Moritz** Thusis to Samedan	80 mins	MHV 2.85m + MWV 1.40m or MHV 2.50m + MWV 2.20 This tunnel no longer operates a car transport service, but there are regular passenger transport services.	Thusis (081) 2884716 Samedan (081) 2885511 www.rhb.ch
Furka (Switzerland) 15.4 km (9.5 miles)	**Andermatt – Brig** Realp to Oberwald	15 mins	Hourly all year from 6am to 9pm weekdays; half-hourly weekends. MHV 3.5m Saturdays in February and March are exceptionally busy.	(027) 9277777 www.mgbahn.ch
Oberalp (Switzerland) 28 km (17.3 miles)	**Andermatt – Disentis** Andermatt to Sedrun	60 mins	MHV 2.50m 2-6 trains daily when the Oberalp Pass is closed for winter.. Advance booking is compulsory.	(027) 9277777 www.mgbahn.ch
Lötschberg (Switzerland) 14 km (8.7 miles)	**Bern – Brig** Kandersteg to Goppenstein	15 mins	MHV 2.90m Frequent all year half-hourly service. Journey time 15 minutes. Advance booking unnecessary; extension to Hohtenn operates when Goppenstein-Gampel road is closed.	Kandersteg (0)900 553333 www.bls.ch/autoverlad
Simplon (Switzerland – Italy)	**Brig – Domodossola** Brig to Iselle	20 mins	10 trains daily, all year.	(0)900 300300 http://mct.sbb.ch/mct/autoverlad
Lötschberg/ Simplon Switzerland – Italy	**Bern – Domodossola** Kandersteg to Iselle	75 mins	Limited service Easter to mid-October up to 3 days a week (up to 10 times a day) and at Christmas for vehicles max height 2.50m, motor caravans up to 5,000 kg. Advance booking compulsory.	(0)900 553333 www.bls.ch
Tauerbahn (Austria)	**Bad Gastein – Spittal an der Drau** Böckstein to Mallnitz	11 mins	East of and parallel to Grossglockner pass. Half-hourly service all year.	(05) 1717 http://autoschleuse.oebb.at
Vereina (Switzerland) 19.6 km (11.7 miles)	**Klosters – Susch** Selfranga to Sagliains	18 mins	MLV 12m Half-hourly daytime service all year. Journey time 18 minutes. Restricted capacity for vehicles over 3.30m high during winter w/ends and public holidays. Steep approach to Klosters.	(081) 2883737 www.rhb.ch

NOTES: Information believed to be correct at time of publication. Detailed timetables are available from the appropriate tourist offices. Always check for current information before you travel.

Major Alpine Road Tunnels

Tunnel	Route and Height above Sea Level	General Information and Comments
Arlberg (Austria) 14 km (8.75 miles)	**Langen to St Anton** 1220m (4000')	On B197 parallel and to S of Arlberg Pass which is closed to caravans/trailers. **Motorway vignette required; tolls charged.** www.arlberg.com
Bosruck (Austria) 5.5 km (3.4 miles)	**Spital am Pyhrn to Selzthal** 742m (2434')	To E of Phyrn pass; with Gleinalm Tunnel (see below) forms part of A9 a'bahn between Linz & Graz. Max speed 80 km/h (50 mph). Use dipped headlights, no overtaking. Occasional emergency lay-bys with telephones. **Motorway vignette required; tolls charged.**
Felbertauern (Austria) 5.3 km (3.25 miles)	**Mittersill to Matrei** 1525m (5000')	MWR 7m (23'), tunnel height 4.5m (14'9"). On B109 W of and parallel to Grossglockner pass; downwards gradient of 9% S to N with sharp bend before N exit. Wheel chains may be needed on approach Nov-Apr. **Tolls charged.**
Frejus (France – Italy) 12.8 km (8 miles)	**Modane to Bardonecchia** 1220m (4000')	MWR 9m (29'6"), tunnel height 4.3m (14'). Min/max speed 60/70 km/h (37/44 mph). Return tickets valid until midnight on 7th day after day of issue. Season tickets are available. Approach via A43 and D1006; heavy use by freight vehicles. Good surface on approach roads. **Tolls charged.** www.sftrf.fr
Gleinalm (Austria) 8.3 km (5 miles)	**St Michael to Fiesach (nr Graz)** 817m (2680')	Part of A9 Pyhrn a'bahn. **Motorway vignette required; tolls charged.**
Grand St Bernard (Switzerland – Italy) 5.8 km (3.6 miles)	**Bourg-St Pierre to St Rhémy (Italy)** 1925m (7570')	MHV 4m (13'1"), MWV 2.55m (8'2.5"), MLV 18m (60'). Min/max speed 40/80 km/h (24/50 mph). On E27. Passport check, Customs & toll offices at entrance; breakdown bays at each end with telephones; return tickets valid one month. Although approaches are covered, wheel chains may be needed in winter. Season tickets are available. **Motorway vignette required; tolls charged.** For 24-hour information tel: (027) 7884400 (Switzerland) or 0165 780902 (Italy), www.letunnel.com
Karawanken (Austria – Slovenia) 8 km (5 miles)	**Rosenbach to Jesenice** 610m (2000')	On A11. **Motorway vignette required; tolls charged.**
Mont Blanc (France – Italy) 11.6 km (7.2 miles)	**Chamonix to Courmayeur** 1381m (4530')	MHV 4.7m (15'5"), MWV 6m (19'6") On N205 France, S26 (Italy). Max speed in tunnel 70 km/h (44 mph) – lower limits when exiting; min speed 50 km/h. Leave 150m between vehicles; ensure enough fuel for 30km. Return tickets valid until midnight on 7th day after issue. Season tickets are available. **Tolls charged.** www.tunnelmb.net

Tunnel	Route and Height above Sea Level	General Information and Comments
Munt La Schera (Switzerland – Italy) 3.5 km (2 miles)	**Zernez to Livigno** 1706m (5597')	MHV 3.6m (11'9"), MWV 2.5m (8'2"). Open 24 hours; single lane traffic controlled by traffic lights; roads from Livogno S to the Bernina Pass and Bormio closed Dec-Apr. On N28 (Switzerland). **Tolls charged.** Tel: (081) 8561888, www.livigno.eu
St Gotthard (Switzerland) 16.3 km (10 miles)	**Göschenen to Airolo** 1159m (3800')	Tunnel height 4.5m (14'9"), single carriageway 7.5m (25') wide. Max speed 80 km/h (50 mph). No tolls, but tunnel is part of Swiss motorway network (A2). **Motorway vignette required.** Tunnel closed 8pm to 5am Monday to Friday for periods during June and September. Heavy traffic and delays high season. www.gotthard-strassentunnel.ch
Ste Marie-aux-Mines 6.8 km (4.25 miles)	**St Dié to Ste-Marie-aux Mines** 772m (2533')	Re-opened October 2008; the longest road tunnel situated entirely in France. Also known as Maurice Lemaire Tunnel, through the Vosges in north-east France from Lusse on N159 to N59. **Tolls charged.** Alternate route via Col-de-Ste Marie on D459.
San Bernardino (Switzerland) 6.6 km (4 miles)	**Hinterrhein to San Bernadino** 1644m (5396')	Tunnel height 4.8m (15'9"), width 7m (23'). On A13 motorway. No stopping or overtaking; keep 100m between vehicles; breakdown bays with telephones. Max speed 80 km/h (50 mph). **Motorway vignette required.**
Tauern and Katschberg (Austria) 6.4 km (4 miles) & 5.4km (3.5 miles)	**Salzburg to Villach** 1340m (4396') & 1110m (3642')	The two major tunnels on the A10, height 4.5m (14'9"), width 7.5m (25'). **Motorway vignette required; tolls charged.**

NOTES: *Dipped headlights should be used (unless stated otherwise) when travelling through road tunnels, even when the road appears well lit. In some countries police make spot checks and impose on-the-spot fines. During the winter wheel chains may be required on the approaches to some tunnels. These must not be used in tunnels and lay-bys are available for the removal and refitting of wheel chains. Much of the information contained in the table was originally supplied by The Automobile Association and other motoring and tourist organisations. Updates and amendments are supplied by caravanners and tourers who have themselves used the passes and tunnels.*

The Caravan and Motorhome Club has not checked the information contained in these tables and cannot accept responsibility for their accuracy, or for any errors, omissions, or for their effects.

Major Mountain Passes - Pyrenees and Northern Spain

Pass Height In Metres (Feet)	From To	Max Gradient	Conditions and Comments
Aubisque (France) 1710 (5610)	Eaux Bonnes *Argelés-Gazost*	10%	UC mid Oct-Jun. MWR 3.5m (11'6") Very winding; continuous on D918 but easy ascent; descent including Col-d'Aubisque 1709m (5607 feet) and Col-du-Soulor 1450m (4757 feet); 8km (5 miles) of very narrow, rough, unguarded road with steep drop. **Not recommended for caravans**.
Bonaigua (Spain) 2072 (6797)	Viella (Vielha) *Esterri-d'Aneu*	8.5%	UC Nov-Apr. MWR 4.3m (14'1") Twisting, narrow road (C28) with many hairpins and some precipitous drops. **Not recommended for caravans**. Alternative route to Lerida (Lleida) through Viella (Vielha) Tunnel is open all year.
Cabrejas (Spain) 1167 (3829)	Tarancon *Cuenca*	14%	UO. On N400/A40. Sometimes blocked by snow for 24 hours. MWR 5m (16')
Col-d'Haltza and Col-de-Burdincurutcheta (France) 782 (2565) and 1135 (3724)	St Jean-Pied-de-Port *Larrau*	11%	UO. A narrow road (D18/D19) leading to Iraty skiing area. Narrow with some tight hairpin bends; rarely has central white line and stretches are unguarded. Not for the faint-hearted. **Not recommended for caravans**.
Envalira (France – Andorra) 2407 (7897)	Pas-de-la-Casa *Andorra*	12.5%	OC Nov-Apr. MWR 6m (19'8") Good road (N22/CG2) with wide bends on ascent and descent; fine views. MHV 3.5m (11'6") on N approach near l'Hospitalet. Early start rec in summer to avoid border delays. Envalira Tunnel (toll) reduces congestion and avoids highest part of pass.
Escudo (Spain) 1011 (3317)	Santander *Burgos*	17%	UO. MWR probably 5m (16'5") Asphalt surface but many bends and steep gradients. **Not recommended in winter**. On N632; A67/N611 easier route.
Guadarrama (Spain) 1511 (4957)	Guadarrama *San Rafael*	14%	UO. MWR 6m (19'8") On NVI to the NW of Madrid but may be avoided by using AP6 motorway from Villalba to San Rafael or Villacastin (toll).
Ibañeta (Roncevalles) (France – Spain) 1057 (3468)	St Jean-Pied-de-Port *Pamplona*	10%	UO. MWR 4m (13'1") Slow and winding, scenic route on N135.
Manzanal (Spain) 1221 (4005)	Madrid *La Coruña*	7%	UO. Sometimes blocked by snow for 24 hours. On A6.

Pass Height In Metres (Feet)	From To	Max Gradient	Conditions and Comments
Navacerrada (Spain) 1860 (6102)	Madrid *Segovia*	17%	OC Nov-Mar. On M601/CL601. Sharp hairpins. Possible but **not recommended for caravans**.
Orduna (Spain) 900 (2953)	Bilbao *Burgos*	15%	UO. On A625/BU556; sometimes blocked by snow for 24 hours. Avoid by using AP68 motorway.
Pajares (Spain) 1270 (4167)	Oviedo *Léon*	16%	UO. On N630; sometimes blocked by snow for 24 hours. **Not recommended for caravans**. Avoid by using AP66 motorway.
Paramo-de-Masa 1050 (3445)	Santander *Burgos*	8%	UO. On N623; sometimes blocked by snow for 24 hours.
Peyresourde (France) 1563 (5128)	Arreau *Bagnères-de-Luchon*	10%	UO. MWR 4m (13'1") D618 somewhat narrow with several hairpin bends, though not difficult. **Not recommended for caravans**.
Picos-de-Europa: Puerto-de-San Glorio, Puerto-de-Pontón, Puerto-de-Pandetrave (Spain), 1609 (5279)	Unquera *Riaño*	12%	UO. MWR probably 4m (13'1") Desfiladero de la Hermida on N621 good condition. Puerto-de-San-Glorio steep with many hairpin bends. For confident drivers only.
	Riaño *Cangas-de-Onis*		Puerto-de-Ponton on N625, height 1280 metres (4200 feet). Best approach fr S as from N is very long uphill pull with many tight turns.
	Portilla-de-la-Reina *Santa Marina-de-Valdeón*		Puerto-de-Pandetrave, height 1562 metres (5124 feet) on LE245 not rec when towing as main street of Santa Marina steep & narrow.
Piqueras (Spain) 1710 (5610)	Logroño *Soria*	7%	UO. On N111; sometimes blocked by snow for 24 hours.
Port (France) 1249 (4098)	Tarascon-sur-Ariège *Massat*	10%	OC Nov-Mar. MWR 4m (13'1") A fairly easy, scenic road (D618), but narrow on some bends.
Portet-d'Aspet (France) 1069 (3507)	Audressein *Fronsac*	14%	UO. MWR 3.5m (11'6") Approached from W by the easy Col-des-Ares and Col-de-Buret; well-engineered but narrow road (D618); care needed on hairpin bends. **Not recommended for caravans**.
Pourtalet (France–Spain) 1792 (5879)	Laruns *Biescas*	10%	UC late Oct-early Jun. MWR 3.5m (11'6") A fairly easy, unguarded road, but narrow in places. Easier from Spain (A136), steeper in France (D934). **Not recommended for caravans**.

Pass Height In Metres (Feet)	From To	Max Gradient	Conditions and Comments
Puymorens (France) 1915 (6283)	Ax-les-Thermes *Bourg-Madame*	10%	OC Nov-Apr. MWR 5.5m (18') MHV 3.5m (11'6") A generally easy, modern tarmac road (N20). Parallel toll road tunnel available.
Quillane (France) 1714 (5623)	Axat *Mont-Louis*	8.5%	OC Nov-Mar. MWR 5m (16'5") An easy, straightforward ascent and descent on D118.
Somosierra (Spain) 1444 (4738)	Madrid *Burgos*	10%	OC Mar-Dec. MWR 7m (23') On A1/E5; may be blocked following snowfalls. Snow-plough swept during winter months but wheel chains compulsory after snowfalls. Well-surfaced dual carriageway, tunnel at summit.
Somport (France-Spain) 1632 (5354)	Accous *Jaca*	10%	UO. MWR 3.5m (11'6") A favoured, old-established route; not particularly easy and narrow in places with many unguarded bends on French side (N134); excellent road on Spanish side (N330). Use of road tunnel advised - see *Pyrenean Road Tunnels* in this section. NB Visitors advise re-fuelling no later than Sabiñánigo when travelling south to north.
Toses (Tosas) (Spain) 1800 (5906)	Puigcerda *Ribes-de-Freser*	10%	UO MWR 5m (16'5") A fairly straightforward, but continuously winding, two-lane road (N152) with with a good surface but many sharp bends; some unguarded edges. Difficult in winter.
Tourmalet (France) 2114 (6936)	Ste Marie-de-Campan *Luz-St Sauveur*	12.5%	UC Oct-mid Jun. MWR 4m (13'1") The highest French Pyrenean route (D918); approaches good, though winding, narrow in places and exacting over summit; sufficiently guarded. Rough surface & uneven edges on west side. **Not recommended for caravans.**
Urquiola (Spain) 713 (2340)	Durango (Bilbao) *Vitoria/Gasteiz*	16%	UO. Sometimes closed by snow for 24 hours. On BI623/A623. **Not recommended for caravans.**

Major Pyrenean Road Tunnels

Tunnel	Route and Height Above Sea Level	General Information and Comments
Bielsa (France – Spain) 3.2 km (2 miles)	**Aragnouet to Bielsa** 1830m (6000')	Open 24 hours but possibly closed October-Easter. On French side (D173) generally good road surface but narrow with steep hairpin bends and steep gradients near summit. Often no middle white line. Spanish side (A138) has good width and is less steep and winding. Used by heavy vehicles. No tolls.
Cadi (Spain) 5 km (3 miles)	**Bellver de Cerdanya to Berga** 1220m (4000')	W of Toses (Tosas) pass on E9/C16; link from La Seo de Urgel to Andorra; excellent approach roads; heavy weekend traffic. **Tolls charged.**
Envalira (France – Spain via Andorra) 2.8 km (1.75 miles)	**Pas de la Casa to El Grau Roig** 2000m (6562')	Tunnel width 8.25m. On N22/CG2 France to Andorra. **Tolls charged.**
Puymorens (France –Spain) 4.8 km (2.9 miles)	**Ax-les-Thermes to Puigcerda** 1515m (4970')	MHV 3.5m (11'6"). Part of Puymorens pass on N20/E9. **Tolls charged.**
Somport (France – Spain) 8.6 km (5.3 miles)	**Urdos to Canfranc** 1116m (3661')	Tunnel height 4.55m (14'9"), width 10.5m (34'). Max speed 90 km/h (56 mph); leave 100m between vehicles. On N134 (France), N330 (Spain). No tolls.
Vielha (Viella) (Spain) 5.2 km (3.2 miles)	**Vielha (Viella) to Pont de Suert** 1635m (5390')	Tunnel height 5.3m, width 12m. Max speed 80km/h. 3 lane, well lit, modern tunnel on N230. Gentle gradients on both sides. Good road surface. Narrow on approach from Vielha. No tolls.

Shutterstock/ Sunny studio

Before you travel

You can find country specific medical advice, including any vaccinations you may need, from nhs.uk/healthcareabroad, or speak to your GP surgery. For general enquiries about medical care abroad, contact NHS England on 0300 311 22 33, or email england.contactus@nhs.net.

If you have any pre-existing medical conditions, you should check with your GP that you're fit to travel. Ask your doctor for a written summary of any medical problems and a list of medications, which is especially imporant for those who use controlled drugs or hypodermic syringes.

Always make sure that you have enough medication for the duration of your holiday and some extra in case your return is delayed. Take details of the generic name of any drugs you use, as brand names may be different abroad, your blood group and details of any allergies (translations may be useful for restaurants).

An emergency dental kit is available from high street chemists which will allow you temporarily to restore a crown, bridge, or filling or to dress a broken tooth until you can get to a dentist.

Heath insurance cards

The European Health Insurance Card (EHIC) allows any EU citizen access to state medical care when they are travelling in another EU country. Existing European Health Insurance Cards remain valid until their expiry date within the EU, but not in Switzerland, Liechtenstein, Norway and Iceland.

New EHICs will not be issued for UK travellers but a replacement Global Health Insurance Card (GHIC) is available.

In many circumstances, there are significant limitations to what treatment UK citizens are able to receive with their EHIC or GHIC. Therefore, the Caravan and Motorhome Club recommends that you have suitable travel insurance before you go on holiday.

Make sure you get travel insurance that covers your health needs. Visit gov.uk to check what your travel insurance should cover.

Travel insurance

Despite having an EHIC or a GHIC you may incur high medical costs if you fall ill or have an accident. The cost of bringing a person back to the UK in the event of illness or death is never covered by the EHIC or GHIC.

Separate additional travel insurance adequate for your destination is essential, such as the Club's Red Pennant Overseas emergency assistance – see camc.com/redpennant.

First aid

A first aid kit containing at least the basic requirements is an essential item, and in some countries it's compulsory to carry one in your vehicle (see the 'Essential Equipment Table' in the chapter 'Motoring Equipment'). Kits should contain items such as sterile pads, assorted dressings, bandages and plasters, antiseptic wipes or cream, cotton wool, scissors, eye bath and tweezers. Also make sure you carry something for upset stomachs, painkillers and an antihistamine in case of hay fever or mild allergic reactions.

If you're travelling to remote areas, you may find it useful to carry a good first aid manual. The British Red Cross publishes a comprehensive First Aid Manual in conjunction with St John Ambulance and St Andrew's Ambulance Association.

Accidents and emergencies

If you're involved in, or witness a road accident, the police may want to question you about it. If possible, take photographs or make sketches of the scene, and write a few notes about what happened as it may be more difficult to remember the details at a later date.

For sports activities such as skiing and mountaineering, travel insurance must include provision for covering the cost of mountain and helicopter rescue. Visitors to the Savoie and Haute-Savoie areas should be aware that an accident or illness may result in a transfer to Switzerland for hospital treatment. There's a reciprocal healthcare agreement for British citizens visiting Switzerland but you will be required to pay the full costs of treatment and afterwards apply for a refund.

Sun protection

Never underestimate how poorly sun exposure can make you. If you're not used to the heat, it's easy to get heat exhaustion or heat stroke. Avoid sitting in the sun between 11am and 3pm and cover your head if sitting or walking in the sun. Use a high sun protection factor (SPF), reapply frequently, and make sure you drink plenty of fluids.

Shutterstock/Robert Przybysz

Shutterstock/Rido

Tick-borne encephalitis (TBE) and Lyme disease

Hikers and outdoor sports enthusiasts planning trips to forested, rural areas should be aware of tick-borne encephalitis, which is transmitted by the bite of an infected tick. If you think you may be at risk, seek medical advice on prevention and immunisation before you leave the UK.

There's no vaccine against Lyme disease, an equally serious tick-borne infection, which, if left untreated, can attack the nervous system and joints. You can minimise the risk by using an insect repellent containing DEET, wearing long sleeves and long trousers, and checking for ticks after outdoor activity. Avoid unpasteurised dairy products in risk areas.

See tickalert.org for more information.

Water and food

Water from mains supplies throughout Europe is generally safe, but may be treated with chemicals which make it taste different to tap water in the UK.

If in any doubt, always drink bottled water or boil it before drinking.

Food poisoning is potential anywhere, and a complete change of diet may upset your stomach as well. In hot conditions, avoid any food that hasn't been refrigerated or hot food that has been left to cool. Be sensible about the food that you eat – don't eat unpasteurised or undercooked food and if you aren't sure about the freshness of meat or seafood, then it's best avoided.

Returning home

If you become ill on your return home, tell your doctor that you have been abroad and which countries you have visited. Even if you have received medical treatment in another country, always consult your doctor if you have been bitten or scratched by an animal while on holiday. If you were given any medicines in another country, it may be illegal to bring them back into the UK. If in doubt, declare them at Customs when you return.

Electricity and Gas

Shutterstock/ sumroeng chinnapan

Electricity

General advice

The voltage for mains electricity is 230V across the EU, but varying degrees of 'acceptable tolerance' mean you may find variations in the actual voltage. Most appliances sold in the UK are 220-240V so should work correctly. However, some high-powered equipment, such as microwave ovens, may not function well – check your instruction manual for any specific instructions. Appliances marked with 'CE' have been designed to meet the requirements of relevant European directives.

The table below gives an approximate idea of which appliances can be used based on the amperage which is being supplied (although not all appliances should be used at the same time). You can work it out more accurately by making a note of the wattage of each appliance in your caravan. The wattages given are based on appliances designed for use in caravans and motorhomes. Household kettles, for example, have at least a 2000W element. Each caravan circuit will also have a maximum amp rating which should not be exceeded.

Electrical connections – EN60309-2 (CEE17)

EN60309-2 (formerly known as CEE17) is the European Standard for all newly fitted connectors. Most sites should now have these connectors, however there is no requirement to replace connectors which were installed before this was standardised so you may still

Amps	Wattage (Approx)	Fridge	Battery Charger	Air Conditioning	LCD TV	Water Heater	Kettle (750W)	Heater (1kW)
2	400	✓	✓					
4	900	✓	✓		✓	✓		
6	1300	✓	✓	*	✓	✓	✓	
8	1800	✓	✓	✓**	✓	✓	✓	✓**
10	2300	✓	✓	✓**	✓	✓	✓	✓**
16	3600	✓	✓	✓	✓	✓	✓	✓**

* Usage possible, depending on wattage of appliance in question

** Not to be used at the same time as other high-wattage equipment

find some sites where your UK 3 pin connector doesn't fit. For this reason it is a good idea to carry a 2-pin adapter. If you are already on site and find your connector doesn't fit, ask campsite staff to borrow or hire an adaptor. You may still encounter a poor electrical supply on site even with an EN60309-2 connection.

If the campsite does not have a modern EN60309-2 (CEE17) supply, ask to see the electrical protection for the socket outlet. If there is a device marked with IDn = 30mA, then the risk is minimised.

Hooking up to the mains

Connection should always be made in the following order:

- Check your outfit isolating switch is at 'off'
- Uncoil the connecting cable from the drum. A coiled cable with current flowing through it may overheat. Take your cable and insert the connector (female end) into your outfit inlet
- Insert the plug (male end) into the site outlet socket
- Switch outfit isolating switch to 'on'
- Use a polarity tester in one of the 13A sockets in the outfit to check all connections are correctly wired. Never leave it in the socket. Some caravans have these devices built in as standard.

It's recommended that the supply is not used if the polarity is incorrect (see Reversed Polarity).

Warnings:

If you're in any doubt of the safety of the system, if you don't receive electricity once connected or if the supply stops then contact the site staff.

If the fault is found to be with your outfit then call a qualified electrician rather than trying to fix the problem yourself.

To ensure your safety you should never use an electrical system which you can't confirm to be safe. Use a mains tester such as the one shown on the right to test the electrical supply.

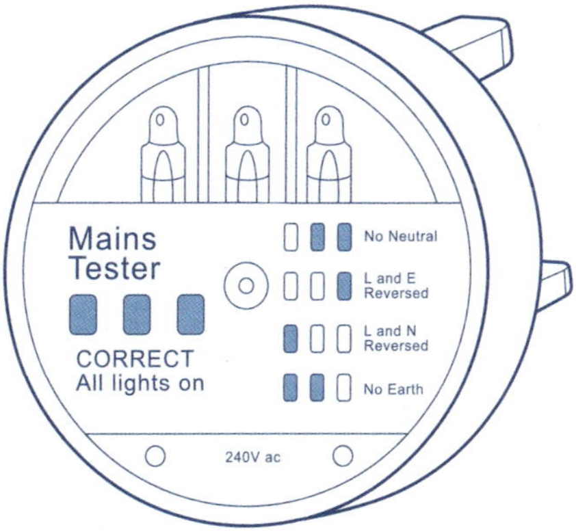

Always check that a proper earth connection exists before using the electrics. Please note that these testers may not pick up all earth faults so if there is any doubt as to the integrity of the earth system do not use the electrical supply.

Disconnection

- Switch your outfit isolating switch to 'off'
- At the site supply socket withdraw the plug
- Disconnect the cable from your outfit

Motorhomes – if leaving your pitch during the day, don't leave your mains cable plugged into the site supply, as this creates a hazard if the exposed live connections in the plug are touched or if the cable is not seen during grass-cutting.

Reversed polarity

Even if the site connector meets European Standard EN60309-2 (CEE17), British caravanners are still likely to encounter the problem known as reversed polarity. This is where the site supply 'live' line connects to the outfit's 'neutral' and vice versa. You should always check the polarity immediately on connection, using a polarity tester available from caravan accessory shops. If polarity is reversed the caravan mains electricity should not be used. Try using another nearby socket instead. Frequent travellers to the Continent can make up an adaptor themselves, or ask an electrician to make one for you, with the live and neutral wires reversed. Using a reversed polarity socket will probably not affect how an electrical appliance works, however your protection is greatly reduced. For example, a lamp socket may still be live as you touch it while replacing a blown bulb, even if the light switch is turned off.

Shaver sockets

Most campsites provide shaver sockets with a voltage of 220V or 110V. Using an incorrect voltage may cause the shaver to become hot or break. The 2-pin adaptor available in the UK may not fit Continental sockets so it's advisable to buy 2-pin adaptors on the Continent. Many modern shavers will work on a range of voltages which make them suitable for travelling abroad. Check your instruction manual to see if this is the case.

Gas

General advice

Gas usage can be difficult to predict as so many factors, such as temperature and how often you eat out, can affect the amount you need. As a rough guide allow 0.45kg of gas a day for normal summer usage.

With the exception of Campingaz, LPG cylinders normally available in the UK cannot be exchanged abroad. If possible, take enough gas with you and bring back the empty cylinders. Always check how many you can take with you as ferry and tunnel operators may restrict the number of cylinders you are permitted to carry for safety reasons.

The full range of Campingaz cylinders is widely available from large supermarkets and hypermarkets, although at the end of

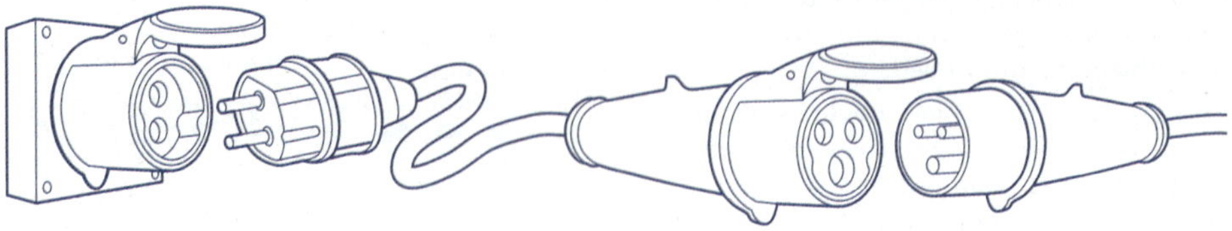

the holiday season stocks may be low. Other popular brands of gas are Primagaz, Butagaz, Totalgaz and Le Cube. A loan deposit is required and if you are buying a cylinder for the first time you may also need to buy the appropriate regulator or adaptor hose.

If you are touring in cold weather conditions use propane gas instead of butane. Many other brands of gas are available in different countries and, as long as you have the correct regulator, adaptor and hose and the cylinders fit in your gas locker these local brands can also be used.

Gas cylinders are now standardised with a pressure of 30mbar for both butane and propane within the EU. On UK-specification caravans and motorhomes (2004 models and later) a 30mbar regulator suited to both propane and butane use is fitted to the bulkhead of the gas locker. This is connected to the cylinder with a connecting hose (and sometimes an adaptor) to suit different brands or types of gas.

Older outfits and some foreign-built ones may use a cylinder-mounted regulator, which may need to be changed to suit different brands or types of gas.

Warnings:

- Refilling gas cylinders intended to be exchanged is against the law in most countries, however you may still find that some sites and dealers will offer to refill cylinders for you.

  Never take them up on this service as it can be dangerous; the cylinders haven't been designed for user-refilling and it's possible to overfill them with catastrophic consequences.
- Regular servicing of gas appliances is important as a faulty appliance can emit carbon monoxide, which could prove fatal. Check your vehicle or appliance handbook for service recommendations.
- Never use a hob or oven as a space heater.

The Caravan and Motorhome Club publishes a range of technical leaflets for its members including detailed advice on the use of electricity and gas – you can request copies or see camc.com/advice-and-training.

Safety and Security

Shutterstock/ hxdbzxy

EU countries have good legislation in place to protect your safety wherever possible. However, accidents and crime will still occur and taking sensible precautions can help to minimise your risk of being involved.

Beaches, lakes and rivers

Check for any warning signs or flags before you swim and ensure that you know what they mean. Check the depth of water before diving and avoid diving or jumping into murky water as submerged objects may not be visible. Familiarise yourself with the location of safety apparatus and/or lifeguards.

Use only the designated areas for swimming, watersports and boating and always use life jackets where appropriate. Watch out for tides, undertows, currents and wind strength and direction before swimming in the sea. This applies in particular when using inflatables, windsurfing equipment, body boards, kayaks or sailing boats. Sudden changes of wave and weather conditions combined with fast tides and currents are particularly dangerous.

Campsite safety

Once you've settled in, take a walk around the campsite to familiarise yourself with its layout and locate the nearest safety equipment. Ensure that children know their way around and where your pitch is.

Natural disasters are rare, but always think about what could happen. A combination of heavy rain and a riverside pitch could lead to flash flooding, for example, so make yourself aware of site evacuation procedures.

Be aware of sources of electricity and cabling on and around your pitch – electrical safety might not be up to the same standards as in the UK.

Poison for rodent control is sometimes used on campsites or surrounding farmland. Warning notices are not always posted and you are strongly advised to check if staying on a rural campsite with dogs or children.

Incidents of theft on campsites are rare but when leaving your caravan unattended, make sure you lock all doors and shut windows. Conceal valuables from sight and lock up any bicycles.

Children

Watch out for children as you drive around the campsite and don't exceed walking pace.

Children's play areas are generally unsupervised, so check which are suitable for your children's ages and abilities. Read and respect the displayed rules. Remember it's your responsibility to supervise your children at all times.

Be aware of any campsite rules concerning ball games or use of play equipment, such as roller blades and skateboards. When your children attend organised activities, arrange when and where to meet afterwards. You should never leave children alone inside a caravan.

Fire

Fire prevention is important on campsites, as fire can spread quickly between outfits. Certain areas of southern Europe experience severe water shortages in summer months leading to an increased fire risk. This may result in some local authorities imposing restrictions at short notice on the use of barbecues and open flames.

Fires can be a regular occurrence in forested areas, especially along the Mediterranean coast during summer months. They're generally extinguished quickly and efficiently, but short-term evacuations are sometimes necessary. If visiting forested areas, familiarise yourself with local emergency procedures in the event of fire. Never use paraffin or gas heaters inside your caravan. Gas heaters should only be fitted when air is taken from outside the caravan. Don't change your gas cylinder inside the caravan. If you smell gas, turn off the cylinder immediately, extinguish all naked flames and seek professional help.

Make sure you know where the fire points and telephones are on site and know the campsite fire drill. Make sure everyone in your party knows how to call the emergency services.

Where site rules permit the use of barbecues, take the following precautions to prevent fire:

- Never locate a barbecue near trees or hedges.
- Have a bucket of water to hand in case of sparks.
- Only use recommended fire-lighting materials.
- Don't leave a barbecue unattended when lit and dispose of hot ash safely.
- Never take a barbecue into an enclosed area or awning – even when cooling they continue to release carbon monoxide which can lead to fatal poisoning.

Shutterstock/ Andrey Armyagov

Swimming pools

Familiarise yourself with the pool area before you venture in for a swim - check the pool layout and identify shallow and deep ends and the location of safety equipment. Check the gradient of the pool bottom as pools which shelve off sharply can catch weak or non-swimmers unawares.

Never dive or jump into a pool without knowing the depth. if there is a 'no diving' rule it usually means the pool isn't deep enough for safe diving.

For pools with a supervisor or lifeguard, note any times or dates when the pool is not supervised. Read safety notices and rules posted around the pool.

On the road

Don't leave valuables on view in cars or caravans, even if they are locked. Make sure items on roof racks or cycle carriers are locked securely.

Near to ports, British owned cars have been targeted by thieves, both while parked and on the move, e.g. by flagging drivers down or indicating that a vehicle has a flat tyre. If you stop in such circumstances, be wary of anyone offering help, ensure that car keys are not left in the ignition and that vehicle doors are locked while you investigate.

Always keep car doors locked and windows closed when driving in populated areas. Beware of thefts through open car windows at traffic lights, filling stations or in traffic jams. When driving through towns and cities keep your doors locked. Keep handbags, valuables and documents out of sight.

If flagged down by another motorist for whatever reason, take care that your own car is locked and windows closed while you check outside, even if someone is left inside.

Be particularly careful on long, empty stretches of motorway and when you stop for fuel. Even if the people flagging you down appear to be officials (e.g. wearing yellow reflective jackets or dark, 'uniform-type' clothing) lock your vehicle doors. They may appear to be friendly and helpful, but could be opportunistic thieves. Have a mobile phone to hand and, if necessary, be seen to use it.

Road accidents are a increased risk in some countries where traffic laws may be inadequately enforced, roads may be poorly maintained, road signs and lighting inadequate, and driving standards poor. It's a good idea to keep a fully charged mobile phone with you in your car with the number of your breakdown organisation saved into it. On your return to the UK, there are increasing issues with migrants attempting to stowaway in vehicles, especially if you're travelling through Calais.

The UK government have issued the following instructions to prevent people entering the UK illegally:

- Where possible, all vehicle doors and storage compartments should be fitted with locks.
- All locks must be engaged when the vehicle is stationary or unattended.
- Immediately before boarding your ferry or train, check that the locks on your vehicle haven't been compromised.
- If you have any reason to suspect someone may have accessed your outfit, speak to border control staff or call the police. Don't board the ferry or train or you may be liable for a fine of up to £2000.

Shutterstock/ Vasik Olga

Overnight stops

Overnight stops should always be at campsites and not at motorway service areas, ferry terminal car parks, petrol station forecourts or isolated 'aires de services' on motorways where robberies are occasionally reported. If you decide to use these areas for a rest then take appropriate precautions, for example, shutting all windows, securing locks and making a thorough external check of your vehicle(s) before departing. Safeguard your property, e.g. handbags, while out of the caravan and beware of approaches by strangers.

For a safer place to take a break, there is a wide network of 'Aires de Services' in cities, towns and villages across Europe, many specifically for motorhomes with good security and overnight facilities. They are often less isolated and therefore safer than the motorway aires. It's rare that you will be the only vehicle staying on such areas, but take sensible precautions and trust your instincts.

Personal security

Petty crime happens all over the world, including in the UK, but as a tourist you are more vulnerable to it. This shouldn't stop you from exploring new horizons, if you take the following precautions to minimise the risk.

- Leave valuables and jewellery at home. If you do take them, fit a small safe in your caravan or lock them in the boot of your car. Don't leave money or valuables in a car glovebox or on view. Don't leave bags in full view when sitting outside at cafés or restaurants, or leave valuables unattended on the beach.

Shutterstock/ DGLimages

- When walking be security conscious. Avoid unlit streets at night, walk away from the kerb edge and carry handbags or shoulder bags on the side away from the kerb. The less of a tourist you appear, the less of a target you are.
- Keep a note of your holiday insurance details and emergency telephone numbers in more than one place, in case the bag or vehicle containing them is stolen.
- Beware of pickpockets in crowded areas, at tourist attractions and in cities. Be especially aware when using public transport in cities.
- Be cautious of bogus plain-clothes policemen who may ask to see your foreign currency or credit cards and passport. If approached, decline to show your money or to hand over your passport but ask for credentials and offer instead to go to the nearest police station.
- Laws and punishment vary from country to country so make yourself aware of anything which may affect you before you travel. Be especially careful on laws involving alcohol consumption (such as drinking in public areas. Never buy or use illegal drugs abroad.
- Respect customs regulations, smuggling is a serious offence and can carry heavy penalties. Don't carry parcels or luggage through customs for other people and never cross borders with people you don't know in your vehicle, such as hitchhikers.

The Foreign and Commonwealth Office produces a range of material to advise and inform British citizens travelling abroad - see gov.uk/foreign-travel-advice for country-specific guides.

Money security

We would rarely walk around at home carrying large amounts of cash, but as you may not have the usual access to bank accounts and credit cards, you are more likely to do so on holiday. You're also less likely to have the same degree of security when online banking as you would in your own home.

Take the following precautions to keep your money safe:

- Carry only the minimum amount of cash and don't rely on one person to carry everything. Never carry a wallet in your back pocket. Concealed money belts are the most secure way to carry cash and passports.
- Keep a separate note of bank account and credit/debit card numbers. Carry your credit card issuer/bank's 24-hour UK contact number with you.
- Be careful when using cash machines (ATMs) – try to use a machine in an area with high footfall and don't allow yourself to be distracted. Put your cash away before moving away from the cash machine.
- Always guard your PIN number, both at cash machines and when using your card to pay in shops and restaurants. Never let your card out of your sight while paying.
- If using internet banking do not leave the PC or mobile device unattended and make sure you log out fully at the end of the session.

Shutterstock/ Rawpixel.com

Winter sports

If you're planning a skiing or snowboarding holiday you should research the safety advice for your destination before you travel. A good starting point may be the relevant embassy for the country you're visiting. All safety instructions should be followed meticulously given the dangers of avalanches in some areas.

The Ski Club of Great Britain offer a lot of advice for anyone taking to the mountains, visit their website skiclub.co.uk to pick up some useful safety tips and advice on which resorts are suitable for different skill levels.

British consular services abroad

British embassy and consular staff offer practical advice, assistance and support to British travellers abroad. They can, for example, issue replacement passports, help Britons who have been the victims of crime, contact relatives and friends in the event of an accident, illness or death, provide information about transferring funds and provide details of local lawyers, doctors and interpreters. There are limits to their powers and a British consul cannot, for example, give legal advice, intervene in court proceedings, put up bail, pay for legal or medical bills, or for funerals or the repatriation of bodies, or undertake work more properly done by banks, motoring organisations and travel insurers.

If you're charged with a serious offence, insist on the British consul being informed. You'll be contacted as soon as possible by a consular officer who can advise on local procedures, provide access to lawyers and insist that you're treated as well as nationals of the country which is holding you. However, they cannot get you released as a matter of course. British and Irish embassy contact details can be found in the 'Country Introduction' chapters.

Campsites

Shutterstock/JGA

The quantity and variety of sites across Europe means you're sure to find one that suits your needs – from full facilities and entertainment to quiet rural retreats. If you haven't previously toured outside of the UK, you may notice some differences, such as pitches being smaller or closer together. In hot climates hard ground may make putting up awnings difficult.

In the high season all campsite facilities are usually open, however bear in mind that toilet and shower facilities may be busy. Out of season, some facilities such as shops and swimming pools may be closed, office opening hours may be reduced, and the sanitary facilities may be reduced to a few unisex toilet and shower cubicles.

Booking a campsite

To save the hassle of arriving to a full site, try to book in advance, especially in high season. If you don't book ahead, arrive no later than 4pm to secure a pitch. After this time, sites fill up quickly. Allow time to find another campsite if your first choice is fully booked.

You can often book directly via a campsite's website. Some sites regard a deposit as a booking or admin fee and will not deduct the amount from your final bill.

Overseas Travel Service

The Caravan and Motorhome Club's Overseas Travel Service offers members a site booking service on over 350 campsites in Europe. Full details of these sites, plus information on ferry special offers and Red Pennant Emergency Assistance can be found in the Club's European Caravan and Motorhome Holidays brochure – call 01342 327 410 to request a copy or visit camc.com/overseas.

Overseas Site Booking Service sites show their booking code (e.g. G04) at the end of their listing. We can't make reservations for any other campsites in this guide.

Overseas Site Night Vouchers

The Club offers Overseas Site Night Vouchers which can be used at over 300 Club inspected campsites in Europe. The vouchers cost £19.95 each (2024 cost) and you'll need one voucher per night to stay on a site in low season and two per night in high season. You'll also be eligible for the Club's special, packaged ferry rates when you're buying vouchers. For more information and to view the voucher terms and conditions visit camc.com/overseasoffers or call 01342 488 102.

Caravan storage

Storing your caravan on a site in Europe can be a great way to avoid a long tow and to save on ferry and fuel costs. Before you leave your caravan in storage always check whether your insurance covers this, as many policies don't.

If you aren't covered then look for a specialist policy - Towergate Insurance (tel: 01242 538 431 or towergateinsurance.co.uk) or Howden Insurance (tel: 01993 894 730 or howdeninsurance.co.uk) both offer insurance policies for caravans stored abroad.

Facilities and site description

All of the site facilities shown in the site listings of this guide have been taken from member reports, as have the comments at the end of each site entry. Please remember that opinions and expectations can differ significantly from one person to the next.

The year of report is shown at the end of each site listing. Sites which haven't been reported on for a few years may have had significant changes to their prices, facilities, and opening dates. It's always best to check any specific details you need to know before travelling by contacting the site or looking at their website.

Sanitary facilities

Facilities normally include toilet and shower blocks with shower cubicles, wash basins and razor sockets. In site listings the abbreviation 'wc' indicates that the site has the kind of toilets we are used to in the UK (pedestal style). Some sites have footplate style toilets and, where this is known, you'll see the abbreviation 'cont', i.e. continental. European sites do not always provide sink plugs, toilet paper or soap so take them with you.

Waste disposal

Site entries show (when known) where a campsite has a chemical disposal and/or a motorhome service point, which is assumed to include a waste (grey) water dump station and toilet cassette-emptying point. You may find fewer waste water disposal facilities as on the continent more people use the site sanitary blocks rather than their own facilities.

Chemical disposal points may be fixed at a high level requiring you to lift cassettes in order to empty them. Disposal may simply be down a toilet. Wastemaster-style emptying points are not very common in Europe. Formaldehyde chemical cleaning products are banned in many countries. In Germany the 'Blue Angel' (Blaue Engel) Standard, and in the Netherlands the 'Milieukeur' Standard, indicates that the product has particularly good environmental credentials.

Finding a campsite

Directions are given for all campsites listed in this guide and most listings also include GPS coordinates. Full street addresses are also given where available. The directions have been supplied by member reports and haven't been checked in detail by the Club.

For information about using satellite navigation to find a site see the 'Motoring Equipment' section.

Shutterstock/Andrey Armyagov

Overnight stops

Many towns and villages across Europe provide dedicated overnight or short stay areas specifically for motorhomes, usually with security, electricity, water and waste facilities. These are known as 'Aires de Services', 'Stellplatz' or 'Aree di Sosta' and are usually well signposted with a motorhome icon. Facilities and charges for these overnight stopping areas will vary significantly.

Many campsites in popular tourist areas will also have separate overnight areas of hardstanding with facilities often just outside the main campsite area. There are guidebooks available which list just these overnight stops, Vicarious Books publish an English guide to Aires including directions and GPS coordinates. Please contact 0131 208 3333 or visit their website vicarious-shop.com.

For security reasons, you shouldn't spend the night on petrol station service areas, ferry terminal car parks or isolated 'Aires de Repos' or 'Aires de Services' along motorways.

Municipal campsites

Municipal campsites are found in towns and villages all over Europe, in particular in France. Once very basic, many have been improved in recent years and now offer a wider range of facilities. They can usually be booked in advance through the local town hall or tourism office. When approaching a town you may find that municipal sites are not always named and signposts may simply state 'Camping' or show a tent or caravan symbol. Most municipal sites are clean, well-run and reasonably priced but security may be basic.

These campsites may be used by seasonal workers, market traders and travellers in low season and as a result there may be restrictions or very high charges for some types of outfits (such as twin axles) in order to discourage this. If you may be affected check for any restrictions when you book.

Naturist campsites

Some naturist sites are included in this guide and are shown with the word 'naturist' after their site name. Those marked 'part naturist' have separate areas for naturists.

Visitors to naturist sites aged 16 and over usually require an INF card or Naturist Licence - covered by membership of British Naturism (tel 01604 620 361, visit bn.org.uk or email headoffice@bn.org.uk) or you can apply for a licence on arrival at any recognised naturist site (a passport-size photograph is required).

Opening dates and times

Opening dates should always be taken with a pinch of salt - including those given in this guide. Campsites may close without notice due to refurbishment work, a lack of visitors or bad weather. Outside the high season, it's best to contact campsites in advance, even if the site advertises itself as open all year.

Most campsites will close their gates or barriers overnight. If you're planning to arrive late or are delayed on your journey, you should call ahead to make sure you'll be able to gain access to the site. There may be a late arrivals area outside of the barriers where you can pitch overnight. Motorhomers should also consider barrier closing times if leaving site in your vehicle for the evening.

Check out time is usually between 10am and 12 noon – speak to the site staff if you need to leave very early to make sure you can check out on departure. Many European campsite receptions close for an extended lunch break, so check-in is not possible until mid-afternoon. If you're planning to arrive or check out around lunchtime, make sure that the office will be open.

Prices and payment

Prices per night (for an outfit and two adults) are shown in the site entries. If you stay on site after midday you may be charged for an extra day. Many campsites have a minimum amount for credit card transactions, meaning they can't be used to pay for overnight or short stays. Check which payment methods are accepted when you check in.

Campsites with automatic barriers may ask for a deposit for a swipe card or fob to operate it.

Extra charges may apply for the use of facilities such as swimming pools, showers or laundry rooms. You may also be charged extra for dogs, Wi-Fi, tents and extra cars.

A tourist tax, eco tax and/or rubbish tax may be imposed by local authorities in some European countries. VAT may also be added to your campsite fees.

Pets on campsites

Dogs are welcome on many sites, although you may have to prove that all of their vaccinations are up to date before they are allowed onto the campsite.

Certain breeds of dogs are banned in some countries and other breeds will need to be muzzled and kept on a lead at all times. A list of breeds with restrictions by country can be found at camc.com/pets.

Campsites usually charge for dogs and may limit the number allowed per pitch. On arrival, make yourself aware of the campsite rules regarding dogs, such as keeping them on a lead, muzzling them, or not leaving them unattended in your outfit.

In popular tourist areas, local regulations may ban dogs from beaches during the summer. Some dogs may find it difficult to cope with changes in climate.

Also, watch out for diseases transmitted by ticks, caterpillars, mosquitoes or sandflies - dogs from the UK will have no natural resistance. Consult your vet about preventative treatment before you travel.

Visitors to southern Spain and Portugal, parts of central France and northern Italy should be aware of the danger of Pine Processionary Caterpillars from mid-winter to late spring. Dogs should be kept away from pine trees if possible, or fitted with a muzzle that prevents the nose and mouth from touching the ground. This will also protect against poisoned bait sometimes used by farmers and hunters.

In the event that your pet is taken ill abroad, a campsite should have information about local vets.

Most European countries require dogs to wear a collar identifying their owners at all times. If your dog goes missing, report the matter to the local police and the local branch of that country's animal welfare organisation.

See the 'Documents' section of this book for more information about the Pet Travel Scheme.

Registering on arrival

Local authority requirements mean you'll usually have to produce an identity document on arrival, which will be held by the site until you check out. If you don't want to leave your passport with reception, most sites accept a document such as the Camping Key Europe (CKE) or Camping Card International (CCI).

CKE are available for Club members to purchase by calling 01342 336 633 or are free to members if you purchase through the Club a Red Pennant Policy with European Breakdown Cover.

General advice

If you've visiting a new campsite, ask to take a look around the site and facilities before booking in. Riverside pitches can be very scenic, but keep an eye on the water level; in periods of heavy rain this may rise rapidly.

Speed limits on campsites are usually restricted to 10 km/h (6 mph). You may be asked to park your car in a separate area away from your caravan, particularly in the high season.

The use of the term 'statics' in the campsite reports in this guide may refer to any long-term accommodation on site, such as seasonal pitches, chalets, cottages, fixed tents and cabins, as well as static caravans.

Complaints

If you want to make a complaint about a campsite issue, take it up with site staff or owners at the time in order to give them the opportunity to rectify the problem during your stay.

The Club has no control or influence over day to day campsite operations or administration of the sites listed in this guide. Therefore, we aren't able to intervene in any dispute you should have with a campsite, unless the booking has been made through our Overseas booking service - see listings that have a booking code in the entry (e.g. G04).

Campsite groups

Across Europe there are many campsite groups or chains with sites in various locations.

You'll generally find that group campsites will be consistent in their format and the quality and variety of facilities they offer. If you liked one site, you can be fairly confident that you'll like other sites within the same group.

If you're looking for a full facility site, with swimming pools, play areas, bars and restaurants on site, you're likely to find these on sites which are part of a group.

You might even find organised excursions and activities such as archery on site.

© Shutterstock/alicja neumiler

Keeping in touch

Internet access

Wi-Fi is available on lots of campsites in Europe, either included in the pitch fee or for an additional charge. Lots of restaurants and cafes offer free Wi-Fi for customers, allowing you to access the internet on your device while you enjoy a coffee or a bite to eat.

Many people now use their smartphones to connect to the internet while overseas. Be aware that you may be charged data roaming charges. If you plan on using your smartphone abroad, speak to your service provider before you leave the UK to make sure you understand the cost, or to add an overseas data roaming package to your phone contract.

Club Together

If you want to chat to other members either at home or while you're away, you can do so on the Club's online community Club Together. You can ask questions and gather opinions on the forums at camc.com/CT.

Radio and television

The BBC World Service broadcasts radio programmes 24 hours a day worldwide and you can listen on a number of platforms: online, via satellite or cable, DRM digital radio, internet radio or mobile phone. You can find detailed information and programme schedules at bbc.co.uk/worldservice.

Satellite television

For English-language TV programmes, the only realistic option is satellite, and satellite dishes are a common sight on campsites all over Europe. A satellite dish mounted on the caravan roof, clamped to a pole, or mounted on a foldable free-standing tripod, will provide good reception and minimal interference. Remember, however, that obstructions to the south east (such as tall trees or even mountains) or heavy rain, can interrupt the signals. A specialist dealer will be able to advise you on the best way of mounting your dish. You will also need a satellite receiver and ideally a satellite-finding meter.

BBC1, ITV1 and Channel 4 can be difficult to pick up in mainland Europe as they are now being transmitted by new narrow-beam satellites. A 60cm dish should pick up these channels in most of France, Belgium and the Netherlands but as you travel further afield, you'll need a progressively larger dish.

Austria

Highlights

From bustling, cosmopolitan cities, packed with culture, to stunning mountain vistas that will take your breath away, Austria is a rich and varied country that caters to every taste.

The Alps offer endless appeal for those looking to enjoy an active, outdoor holiday while the picturesque towns and villages that punctuate the landscape are ideal for relaxing and soaking up the local culture. During the summer months walking and hiking are the order of the day, while winter sports are abundant once the weather turns colder.

Austria is an important centre for European culture; in particular music. As the birthplace of many notable composers – Mozart, Strauss and Haydn to name just a few – Austria is a magnet for classical music fans.

When it comes to food, one of Austria's most famous dishes is strudel, and there are many different varieties of flavours and types available. Also make sure to try Wiener Schnitzel, a meat escalop which is breaded and fried, and Tafelspitz, a beef soup served with apple and horseradish.

Major towns and cities

- Vienna – enjoy a slice of sachertorte in this historic capital.
- Innsbruck – an alpine city famous for winter sports, Imperial architecture and Christmas Markets.
- Graz – the old town is filled with sights and is on the UNESCO World Heritage List.
- Salzburg – this fairytale city was the birthplace of Mozart.

Attractions

- Schönbrunn Palace – a Baroque palace in the heart of Vienna.
- Hallstatt – this alpine village has a fascinating history as well as picturesque views.
- Grossglockner Alpine Road – the highest road in Austria with unparalleled mountain views.
- Innsbruck – a renowned winter sports centre packed with historical sights.

Find out more

Website: austria.info
Email: info@austria.info

Country Information

Capital: Vienna

Bordered by: Czechia, Germany, Hungary, Italy, Liechtenstein, Slovakia, Slovenia, Switzerland

Terrain: Mountainous in south and west; flat or gently sloping in extreme north and east

Climate: Temperate; cold winters with frequent rain in the lowlands and snow in the mountains; moderate summers, sometimes very hot

Highest Point: Grossglockner 3,798m

Language: German

Local Time: GMT or BST + 1, i.e. 1 hour ahead of the UK all year

Currency: Euros divided into 100 cents; £1 = €1.20, €1 = £0.84 (Nov 2024)

Telephoning: From the UK dial 0043 for Austria and leave out the initial zero of the area code of the number you're calling.

Emergency numbers: Police 133; Fire brigade 122; Ambulance 144, or dial 112 for any service (operators speak English).

Public Holidays 2025: Jan 1, 6; Apr 21; May 1, 29; June 9, 19; Aug 15; Oct 26 (National Day); Nov 1; Dec 8, 25, 26.

Schools have Christmas, Easter and half terms breaks; summer holidays are July and August.

Entry Formalities

British and Irish passport holders may stay for up to 90 days in any 180 day period without a visa. You may be asked to show a return or onward ticket at the border to confirm your length of stay, or to prove that you have enough money for your stay.

Your passport will need to have a minimum of 6 months' validity remaining, and be less than 10 years old (even if it has 6 months or more left).

Visitors arriving at a campsite or hotel must complete a registration form.

Medical Services

Minor matters can be dealt with by staff at pharmacies (apotheke). Pharmacies operate a rota system for out of hours access; when closed a notice is often displayed giving the addresses of the nearest open pharmacies.

Free treatment is available from doctors and hospital outpatient departments as long as the doctor is contracted to the local health insurance office (Gebietskrankenkasse). To be covered for hospital treatment you'll need a doctor's referral. In-patient treatment will incur a daily non-refundable charge for the first 28 days.

You'll need to present a Global Health Insurance Card (UK GHIC) to receive treatment. If you have an European Health Insurance Card (EHIC) you may continue to use it until its expiration date. Only a limited amount of dental treatment is covered under the state healthcare system.

Private medical cover and services like mountain rescue are not covered by the EHIC or GHIC.

Opening Hours

Banks: Mon-Fri 8am-12.30pm & 1.30pm-3pm (5.30pm Thu), main branches don't close for lunch; closed Sat/Sun. (Hours may vary).

Museums: Mon-Fri 10am-6pm (summer), 9am-4pm (winter); Sat, Sun & public holidays 9am-6pm

Post Offices: Mon-Fri 8am-12pm & 2pm-6pm; city post offices don't close for lunch; in some towns open Sat 9am-12pm.

Shops: Mon-Fri 8am-6pm; some open until 9.00pm; some close 12pm-2pm for lunch; Sat 8am-6pm; some open Sun and public holidays.

Safety and Security

Take sensible precautions to avoid becoming a victim of crime at crowded tourist sites and around major railway stations and city centre parks after dark. Pickpockets and muggers operate in and around the city centre of Vienna.

Drivers, especially on the autobahns in Lower Austria, should be wary of bogus plain clothes police officers. In all traffic-related matters police officers will be in uniform and unmarked vehicles will have a flashing sign in the rear window which reads 'Stopp –Polizei – Folgen'.

If in any doubt contact the police on the emergency number 133 or 112 and ask for confirmation.

Austria shares with the rest of Europe an underlying threat from terrorism. Please check gov.uk/foreign-travel-advice/austria before you travel.

The winter sports season lasts from December to March, or the end of May in higher regions. There is a danger of avalanches in some areas, particularly in spring. If you plan to ski, check with local tourist offices and ski resort professionals on current snow conditions.

British Embassy

Jauresgasse 12
1030 Vienna
Tel: +43 (1) 716130
gov.uk/world/belgium

Irish Embassy

Rotenturmstraße
16-18, 1010 Vienna
Tel: +43 (0)1 715 4246
ireland.ie/en/austria

Documents

Driving Licence

If you hold a UK driving licence which does not bear your photograph you should carry your passport as further proof of identity, or obtain a photocard licence. You may need an International Driving Permit if you have an old style paper licence or a licence issued in Gibraltar, Guernsey, Jersey or the Isle of Man. These can be obtained from the Post Office before you travel.

Money

Cashpoints (Bankomaten) have instructions in English. Major credit cards are widely accepted in cities although a number of small hotels, shops and restaurants may refuse. Visa and Mastercard are more readily accepted than American Express and Diner's Club.

Passport

You're advised to carry your passport or photocard licence at all times.

Vehicle(s)

You should carry your vehicle registration certificate (V5C), insurance details and MOT certificate.

Driving

Alcohol

The maximum permitted level of alcohol in the bloodstream is 0.049%. Penalties for exceeding this are severe. A limit of virtually zero (0.01%) applies to drivers who have held a full driving licence for less than two years.

Breakdown Service

The motoring organisation, ÖAMTC operates a breakdown service 24 hours a day on all roads.

The emergency number is 120 throughout the country from a land line or mobile phone. Motorists pay a set fee, which is higher at night; towing charges also apply. Payment by credit card is accepted.

Members of AIT and FIA affiliated clubs, such as the Caravan and Motorhome Club, qualify for reduced charges on presentation of a valid Club membership card.

Child Restraint System

Children under 14 years of age and less than 1.5 metres in height must use a suitable child restraint system for their height and weight when travelling in the front and rear of a vehicle. Children under 14 years aren't allowed to travel in two seater sports cars.

Children under 14 years of age but over 1.35 metres are allowed to use a 3-point seat belt without a special child seat, as long as the seat belt does not cut across the child's throat or neck.

Fuel

Most petrol stations are open from 8am to 8pm. Motorway service stations and some petrol stations in larger cities stay open 24 hours. Fuel is normally cheaper at self-service filling stations.

LPG (flüssiggas) is available at a limited number of outlets – a list should be available at oeamtc.at.

Lights

Dipped headlights must be used in poor visibility or bad weather. Headlight flashing is used as a warning of approach, not as an indication that a driver is giving way.

Low Emission Zones

There are Low Emission Zones in force on sections of the A12 motorway, Burgenland, Graz, Niederösterreich, Oberösterreich, Styria and Vienna. See urbanaccessregulations.eu for more information.

Motorways

Orange emergency telephones on motorways are 2 km to 3 km apart. A flashing orange light at the top of telephone posts indicates danger ahead.

Whenever congestion occurs on motorways and dual carriageways drivers are required to create an emergency corridor. Drivers in the left-hand lane must move as far over to the left as possible, and drivers in the central and right-hand lanes must move as far over to the right as possible to provide access for emergency vehicles.

Motorway Tolls (Vehicles under 3,500kg)

Drivers of vehicles up to 3,500kg must display a toll sticker or a digital vignette in order to use motorways and expressways (A and S roads). One vignette covers your caravan as well. Vignettes can be bought at all major border crossings into Austria and from OeAMTC offices, larger petrol stations and post offices in Austria. A two-month vignette for a car (with or without a trailer) or a motorhome costs €29. Also available are a 10-day vignette at €11.50 and a one year vignette at €96.40 (2023 tariffs).

Failure to display a vignette incurs a fine of at least €120, plus the cost of the vignette. Credit cards or foreign currency may be used in payment. If you have visited Austria before, make sure you remove your old sticker.

There are special toll sections in Austria which are excluded from the vignette and where the toll needs to be paid at respective toll points. These include A10 Tauern tunnel, A13 Brenner motorway and S16 Alberg tunnel.

Motorway Tolls (Vehicles over 3,500kg)

Tolls for vehicles over 3,500kg are calculated by the number of axles and EURO emissions category and are collected electronically by means of a small box (called the GO-Box) fixed to your vehicle's windscreen. They're available for a one-off handling fee of €5 from over 175 points of sale – mainly petrol stations – along the primary road network in Austria and neighbouring countries, and at all major border crossing points.

You can pre-load a set amount onto your Go-Box or pay after you have travelled. Tolls are calculated according to the number of axles on a vehicle; those with two axles are charged between €0.211and €0.245 per kilometre + 20% VAT, according to the vehicle's emissions rating. Visit go-maut.at before you travel for more information or to register for the scheme.

This distance-related toll system doesn't apply to a car/caravan combination even if its total laden weight is over 3,500kg, unless the laden weight of the towing vehicle itself exceeds that weight.

Parking

Regulations on the parking of motorhomes and caravans vary according to region, but restrictions apply in areas protected for their natural beauty or landscape and beside lakes. If in doubt, ask the local municipality. You cannot leave a caravan without its towing vehicle in a public place.

A yellow zigzag or dotted line marked on the road indicates that parking is prohibited. Blue lines indicate a blue zone (Kurzparkzone) where parking is restricted to a period for up to two hours and you need to purchase a voucher (Parkschein) from a local shop, bank or petrol station.

Most cities have 'Pay and Display' machines, parking meters or parking discs, and in main tourist areas the instructions are in English. Illegally parked cars may be impounded or clamped. Large areas of Vienna are pedestrianised and parking places are limited. However, there are several underground car parks in Vienna District 1.

Priority

Outside built-up areas, road signs on main roads indicate where traffic has priority or if there are no signs priority is given to traffic from the right.

Buses have priority when leaving a bus stop. Don't overtake school buses with flashing yellow lights which have stopped to let children on and off.

Trams have priority even if coming from the left.

In heavy traffic, drivers must not enter an intersection unless their exit is clear, even if they have priority or if the lights are green.

Prohibited Equipment

Dashboard cameras are prohibited.

Roads

Austria has a well developed and engineered network of roads classified as: federal motorways (A roads), expressways (S' roads), provincial (B roads) and local (L roads). There are over 2180 km of motorways and expressways.

Road Signs and Markings

Most signs conform to international usage. The following are exceptions:

Diversions

Street lights not on all night

Tram turns at yellow or red

You may be stopped and fined in Austria for using roads that prohibit trailers and caravans. This is indicated by the below sign:

If there is an additional sign which shows a weight limit, then this indicates the maximum gross vehicle weight of the trailer. You can also find these signs with a length limit.

Some other signs that are also in use which you may find useful Include:

Austrian	English Translation
Abblendlicht	Dipped headlights
Alle richtungen	All directions
Bauarbeiten	Roadworks
Durchfahrt verboten	No through traffic
Einbahn	One-way street
Fussgänger	Pedestrians
Beschrankung für halten oder parken	Stopping/parking restricted
Lawinen gefahr	Avalanche danger
Links einbiegen	Turn left
Raststätte	Service area
Raststätte Rechts einbiegen	Turn right
Strasse gesperrt	Road closed
Überholen verboten	No passing
Umleitung	Detour

Speed Limits

	Open Road (km/h)	Motorway (km/h)
Car Solo	100	130
Car towing caravan/trailer	80	100
Motorhome under 3500kg	100	130
Motorhome 3500-7500kg	70	80

Exceptions

If the total combined weight of a car and caravan outfit or a motorhome exceeds 3,500 kg, the speed limit on motorways is reduced to 80 km/h (50 mph) and on other roads outside built-up areas to 70 km/h (43 mph).

On motorways where the speed limit for solo vehicles is 130 km/h (81 mph) overhead message signs may restrict speed to 100 km/h (62 mph). Between 10pm and 5am solo cars are restricted to 110 km/h (68 mph) on the A10 (Tauern), A12 (Inntal), A13 (Brenner) and A14 (Rheintal).

A general speed limit of 60 km/h (37 mph) is on most roads in Tyrol, unless indicated otherwise.

The speed limit in built up areas is of 50km/h unless otherwise indicated by road signs. Built-up area begin from the road sign of the place name on entering a town or village.

Some sections of the A12 and A13 are limited to 100 km/h, day and night.

The minimum speed on motorways, as indicated by a rectangular blue sign depicting a white car, is 60 km/h (37 mph). A number of towns have a general speed limit of 30 km/h (18 mph), except where a higher speed limit is indicated.

Traffic Lights

At traffic lights a flashing green light indicates the approach of the end of the green phase. A yellow light combined with the red light indicates that the green phase is imminent.

Traffic Jams

In recent years traffic has increased on the A1 from Vienna to the German border (the West Autobahn). There are usually queues at the border posts with Czech Republic, Slovakia and Hungary. As a result, traffic has also increased on the ring road around Vienna and on the A4 (Ost Autobahn).

Other bottlenecks occur on the A10 (Salzburg to Villach) before the Tauern and Katschberg tunnels, the A12 (Kufstein to Landeck) before the Perjen tunnel and before Landeck, and the A13 (Innsbruck to Brenner) between Steinach and the Italian border. Busy sections on other roads are the S35/S6 between Kirchdorf or Bruck an der Mur and the A9, the B320/E651 in the Schladming and Gröbming areas, and the B179 Fern Pass.

Violation of Traffic Regulations

Police can impose and collect on-the-spot fines of up to €90 from drivers who violate traffic regulations. For higher fines you'll be required to pay a deposit and the remainder within two weeks. An official receipt should be issued. A points system operates which applies to drivers of Austrian and foreign-registered vehicles.

Winter Driving

From 1 November to 15 April vehicles, including those registered abroad, must be fitted with winter tyres marked M&S (mud & snow) on all wheels when there is snow or ice on the road. Snow chains are allowed on roads fully covered by snow or ice, as long as road surfaces will not be damaged by the chains.

The maximum recommended speed with snow chains is generally 50 km/h.

Between 1 November to 15 March vehicles weighing over 3500kg are required to have winter tyres on at least one of the driving axles, regardless of the road conditions. They must also carry snow chains, and use them where road signs indicate that they are compulsory.

It's the driver's legal responsibility to carry the required winter equipment; therefore, it's essential to check that it's included in any hire car.

Essential Equipment

First aid kit

All vehicles must carry a first aid kit kept in a strong, dirt-proof box.

Reflective Jackets/Waistcoats

If your vehicle breaks down or you're in an accident you must wear a reflective jacket or waistcoat when getting out of your vehicle (compliant with EU Standard EN471). This includes when setting up a warning triangle. It's also recommended that a passenger who leaves the vehicle, for example, to assist with a repair, should also wear one. Keep the jackets within easy reach inside your vehicle, not in the boot.

Warning Triangle

An EU approved warning triangle must be used if the vehicle breaks down, has a puncture or is involved in an accident.

Touring

Austria is divided into nine federal regions, namely Burgenland, Carinthia (Kärnten), Lower Austria (Niederösterreich), Salzburg, Styria (Steiermark), Tyrol (Tirol), Upper Austria (Oberösterreich), Vienna (Wien) and Voralberg.

A 10-15% service charge is occasionally included in restaurant bills. Tipping 5-10% is customary if satisfied with the service.

The Vienna Card offers unlimited free public transport and discounts at museums, restaurants, theatres and shops.

AUSTRIA

Depending on your selected pass duration, the pass is valid for three days and is available from hotels, tourist information and public transport offices, see; wienkarte.at.

A Salzburg Card and an Innsbruck Card are also available - see austria.info/uk, or contact the Austrian National Tourist Office for more information.

Camping and Caravanning

There are approximately 500 campsites in Austria, around 150 of which are open all year, mostly in or near to ski resorts.

Casual/wild camping is not encouraged and is prohibited in Vienna, in the Tyrol and in forests and nature reserves. Permission to park a caravan should be obtained in advance from the owners of private land, or from the local town hall or police station in the case of common land or state property.

Cycling

There is an extensive network of cycle routes, following dedicated cycle and footpaths, such as the 360 km cycle lane that follows the Danube. Many cities encourage cyclists with designated cycle lanes. A WienMobil Rad bicycle rental scheme operates in Vienna from more than 185 public cycling stations situated close to underground/metro stations.

See wienmobil.at for more information.

There are eight signposted mountain bike routes between 10 and 42 kilometres long in the Vienna Woods.

Cycle helmets are compulsory for children under 12 years, or 15 years in Lower Austria (Niederösterreich).

Bikes may be carried on the roof or rear of a car. When carried at the rear, the width must not extend beyond the width of the vehicle, and the rear lights and number plate must be visible.

Electricity and Gas

Current on campsites varies from 4-16 amps. Plugs have two round pins and most campsites have CEE connections. Electricity points tend to be in locked boxes, so you'll need to check polarity on arrival before the box is locked. Arrangements also need to be made for the box to be unlocked if making an early departure.

Some sites in Austria make a one-off charge for connection to the electricity supply, which is then metered at a rate per kilowatt hour (kwh) The full range of Campingaz cylinders is widely available.

Public Transport and Local Travel

All major cities have efficient, integrated public transport systems including underground and light rail systems, trams and buses. Two to five people travelling as a group by train can buy an Einfach-Raus-Ticket (ERT), which is good for a day's unlimited travel on all Austrian regional trains - see oebb.at (English option) for more information or ask at any station.

In Vienna there are travel concessions on public transport for senior citizens (show your passport as proof of age). Buy a ticket from a tobacconist or from a ticket machine in an underground station. Otherwise single tickets are available from vending machines in the vehicles themselves - have plenty of coins ready. Tickets are also available for periods of 24 and 72 hours. Children under six travel free and children under 15 travel free on Sundays, public holidays and during school holidays.

Car ferry services operate throughout the year on the River Danube, and hydrofoil and hovercraft services transport passengers from Vienna to Bratislava (Slovakia) and to Budapest (Hungary).

ABERSEE *B3* (3km N Rural) *47.74040, 13.40665* **Seecamping Primus,** Schwand 39, 5342 Abersee **06227 3228; seecamping.primus@aon.at**

nr

B158 fr St Gilgen to Strobl. After 3 km turn L. Camp is last but one. Med, mkd, pt shd, EHU (10A); sw; twin axles; bus 1km; Eng spkn; games area; CCI. *"Very helpful owner; beautiful area nr shipping on lake; ideal for boating; excel; mountain views."* **€25.70, 25 Apr-30 Sep. 2022**

ABERSEE *B3* (3km SE Rural) *47.71336, 13.45138* **Camping Schönblick,** 5350 Abersee **(06137) 7042; info@camping-schoenblick.at; www.camping-schoenblick.at**

€2.90 nr

Fr B158 at km 36 dir Schiffstation & site in 1km on L. Med, mkd, hdstg, pt shd, pt sl, terr, EHU (10A) inc; gas; sw nr; 40% statics; ccard acc; CKE. *"Beautiful, friendly, family-run site nr lakeside opp St Wolfgang town; ferry stn; excel san facs but stretched at busy times; walks & cycle path fr site; vg site."* **€26.90, 1 May-15 Oct. 2024**

ABERSEE *B3* (1.5km NW Rural) *47.73656, 13.43250* **Camping Wolfgangblick,** Seestrasse 115, 5342 Abersee **650-5934297; camping@wolfgangblick.at; www.wolfgangblick.at**

€3.70

Fr B158 fr St Gilgen, on ent Abersee turn L at km 34 twds lake. Site in 1km foll sp to site. Med, hdstg, mkd, pt shd, EHU (12A) metered; 50% statics; Eng spkn; ccard acc. *"Pleasant site; gd, friendly family run site by lake; helpful owners; beautiful scenery; excel for walking & cycling; lake adj; on bus rte to Salzburg and local vills; poss cr, adv bkg advised."* **€42.00, 1 May-30 Sep. 2024**

ABERSEE *B3* (2.5km NW Rural) *47.73910, 13.40065* **Camping Birkenstrand Wolfgangsee,** Schwand 4, 5342 Abersee **(06227) 3029; camp@birkenstrand.at; www.birkenstrand.at**

€3.40 nr nr nr

Fr B158 fr St Gilgen, on ent Abersee turn L at km 32 twds lake. Site on both sides of rd in 1km. 4*, Med, mkd, unshd, pt sl, EHU (10A) metered; bbq; sw nr; TV; 20% statics; Eng spkn; adv bkg acc; boat hire; golf 15km; bike hire. *"Excel area for walking, cycling; lovely situation; immac site; ACSI card acc; new facs (2015)."* **€25.00, 27 Mar-31 Oct. 2022**

ABERSEE *B3* (3km NW Rural) *47.73945, 13.40245* **Romantik Camping Wolfgangsee Lindenstrand,** Schwand 19, 5342 St Gilgen **(06227) 3205; camping@lindenstrand.at; www.lindenstrand.at**

€3.70 (htd) nr

Fr St Gilgen take B158 dir Bad Ischl. In 4km at km 32 foll sp Schwand, site on L on lakeside. Lge, hdstg, mkd, pt shd, serviced pitches; EHU (10A) metered; 10% statics; phone; bus; Eng spkn; adv bkg acc; ccard acc; watersports; CKE. *"Lovely site; rec adv bkg for lakeside pitches; elec conn by staff; lake adj, no dogs in water; poss req long leads; bus & boat to local towns & Salzburg; continental plugs high ssn."* **€34.00, 1 April- 12 Oct. 2024**

ASCHACH AN DER DONAU *B3* (16km N Rural) *48.42026, 13.98400* **Camping Kaiserhof,** Kaiserau 1, 4082 Aschach-an-der-Donau **(07273) 62210; kaiserhof@aschach.at; www.pension-kaiserhof.at**

(htd)

Fr town cent foll site sp. Site adj rv & Gasthof Kaiserhof. Sm, pt shd, EHU; red long stay; 80% statics; Eng spkn; ccard acc; CKE. *"Beautiful location on Danube."* **€19.00, 15 Apr-30 Sep. 2022**

ATTERSEE *B3* (16km S Rural) *47.80100, 13.48266* **Inselcamping,** Unterburgau 37, 4866 Unterach-am-Attersee **(07665) 8311; camping@inselcamp.at; www.inselcamp.at**

€2 shgl

Leave A1 at junc 243 St Georgen/Attersee, foll B151 to Unterach fr Attersee vill. Site sp on app to Unterach. Med, pt shd, EHU (6-16A); gas; sw; 25% statics; Eng spkn; adv bkg acc; CKE. *"Excel site next to lake with sw; helpful owner; 5 min walk to attractive town; conv Salzburg & Salzkammergut; lots to see locally; clsd 1200-1400; gd boat trips; extra for lakeside pitches - some with boat mooring; vg san facs; adv bkg for over 6 days."* **€36.00, 1 May-15 Sep. 2023**

BAD AUSSEE *C3* (11km E Rural) *47.63783, 13.90365* **Campingplatz Gössl,** Gössl 201, 8993 Grundlsee **(03622) 81810; office@campinggoessl.com; www.campinggoessl.com**

€1 nr nr nr

Fr B145 foll sp to Grundlsee, then along lake to Gössl at far end. Ent adj gasthof off mini-rndbt, site on L. Med, EHU (10A) metered + conn fee; sw nr; bus; adv bkg acc; fishing. *"Excel walking cent; scenery v beautiful; boating (no motor boats); local gasthofs vg; daily bus & ferry services; v clean facs."* **€19.50, 1 May-31 Oct. 2024**

AUSTRIA

BAD GLEICHENBERG *C4* (3km E Rural) *46.87470, 15.93360* **Camping im Thermen & Vulkanland Steiermark,** Haus Nr 240, 8344 Bairisch-Kölldorf **(03159) 2342205; camping.bairischkoelldorf@bad-gleichenberg.gv.at; www.bairisch-koelldorf.at**

12 €0.70 (htd) WD MSP (covrd)

Exit A2 at Gleisdorf Süd onto B68 dir Feldbach. Take B66 dir Bad Gleichenberg & at 2nd rndabt turn L, site sp. 4*, Med, unshd, EHU (16A) metered; gas; bbq; sw; 10% statics; adv bkg acc; bike hire; golf 3km; tennis 600m; games area. **€26.40** **2022**

BLUDENZ *C1* (2km N Rural) *47.16990, 9.80788* **Terrassencamping Sonnenberg,** Hinteroferstrasse 12, 6714 Nüziders **(05552) 64035; info@camping-sonnenberg.com; www.camping-sonnenberg.com**

€3-4.50 (htd) WD MSP nr nr

Exit A14/E60 junc 57 onto B190 N, foll sp Nüziders & foll site sp thro Nüziders vill. Med, mkd, hdstg, pt shd, terr, EHU (5-13A) metered over 4kw; red long stay; TV; phone; Eng spkn; adv bkg acc; sep car park. *"Friendly, v helpful owners; superb facs; beautiful scenery - extra for Panorama pitches at top of site; excel mountain views; excel walking; lifts to mountains; ltd opening hrs for recep - use phone at bldg on L at main ent; no arr after 2200 hrs but sep o'night area; rec bk in adv in high ssn; gd for m'vans; highly rec; excel site; gd value."* **€49.00, 17 May-29 Sept.** **2024**

BLUDENZ *C1* (3km S Rural) *47.14651, 9.81630* **Auhof Camping,** Aulandweg 5, 6706 Bürs **(05552) 67044; auhof.buers@aon.at; www.buers.at**

12 (htd) nr

Exit A14/E60 junc 59 dir Bludenz/Bürs, then Brand. Site sp in 300m at Zimba Park shopping cent on edge of sm indus est. Med, unshd, EHU (4A); gas. *"Friendly, tidy, clean site on wkg farm; conv Arlberg Tunnel, m'way, Liechtenstein & mountain resorts; muddy in wet; conv NH for m'way; lovely owners."* **€23.00** **2022**

BREGENZ *C1* (2km W Rural) *47.50583, 9.71221* **Seecamping Bregenz,** Hechtweg, 6900 Bregenz (Vorarlberg) **(05574) 71895; geisselman.guenter@aon.at; www.seecamping.at**

(htd) WD shingle

App Bregenz fr Feldkirch. At bottom of hill on ent town, turn L at camping sp. Fork L at next junc & foll sps, or, fr Bregenz take Bahnhofstrasse (sp St Gallen). In approx 1km site on R sp. Fr Bregenz by-pass foll sps to Bregenz (city tunnel). At end of tunnel turn L at T-junc (sp St Gallen). In 500m turn R at camping sp. Site adj Camping Mexico. 4*, Lge, pt shd, EHU (6A) inc; sw nr; 20% statics; Eng spkn; games area; CKE. *"Footpath to town cent; site in 2 halves; expensive; crowded but excel san facs; friendly reception; in nature reserve; fair."* **€36.00, 15 May-15 Sep.** **2023**

BRUCK AN DER GROSSGLOCKNERSTRASSE *C2* (0.9km SW Urban) *47.28386, 12.81736* **Sportcamp Woferlgut,** Krössenbach 40, 5671 Bruck-an-der-Grossglocknerstrasse **(06545) 73030; info@sportcamp.at; www.sportcamp.at**

12 €5.50 WD MSP (htd, indoor)

Exit A10 junc 47 dir Bischofshofen, B311 dir Zell-am-See. Take 2nd exit to Bruck, site sp fr by-pass, & foll sps thro town to site. 4*, Lge, pt shd, serviced pitches; EHU (10-16A) €2.20 conn fee & €0.80 per kw; sw nr; red long stay; TV; 80% statics; phone; bus to Zell-am-Zee & glacier; Eng spkn; adv bkg acc; ccard acc; tennis; games rm; sauna. *"Extended facs area with R numbered pitches preferable; excel site for sh or long stay; gym & fitness cent; ski cent; farm produce; big pitches; excel mntn walking, local horseriding; helpful recep; tour ops tents & statics; excel for young/teenage families; vg san facs; indoor play area; warm welcome; sm supmkt nrby & plenty of rests & cafes; excel."* **€40.00, G06.** **2022**

See advertisement

DELLACH IM DRAUTAL *D2* (1km S Rural) *46.73085, 13.07846* **Camping Waldbad,** 9772 Dellach-im-Drautal (Kärnten) **(04714) 234-18 or (04714) 288; info@camping-waldbad.at; www.camping-waldbad.at**

€2.50

Clearly sp on B100 & in vill of Dellach on S side or Rv Drau. Med, mkd, hdg, pt shd, EHU (6A) inc; gas; 5% statics; adv bkg acc; ccard acc; games rm; games area. *"Peaceful, wooded site; htd pool complex, paddling pool adj; waterslide adj; vg leisure facs adj."* **€31.00, 15 April-1 Oct.** **2024**

DOBRIACH *D3* (2km S Rural) *46.77020, 13.64788* **Komfort Campingpark Burgstaller,** Seefeldstrasse 16, A-9873 Döbriach (Kärnten) **04246 7774; info@burgstaller.co.at; www.burgstaller.co.at**

12 €4.10 nr nr (htd)

Fr on A10/E55/E66 take exit Millstätter See. Turn L at traff lts on B98 dir Radenthein. Thro Millstatt & Dellach, turn R into Döbriach, sp Camping See site on L by lake after Döbriach. 5*, V lge, hdg, mkd, pt shd, EHU (6-10A) inc; gas; sw; TV; 10% statics; Eng spkn; adv bkg acc; solarium; golf 8km; bike hire; games area; horseriding; boating; sauna; CKE. *"Organised walks & trips to Italy; excel rest; private san facs avail; cinema; some pitches tight; fantastic facs."* **€42.80** **2024**

DOBRIACH *D3* (2km SW Urban) *46.76811, 13.64809* **Camping Brunner am See,** Glanzerstrasse 108, 9873 Döbriach **(04246) 7189 or 7386; info@camping-brunner.at; www.camping-brunner.at**

12 €5

Fr Salzburg on A10 a'bahn take Seeboden-Millstatt exit bef Spittal. Foll rd 98 N of Millstattersee to camping sp. Med, pt shd, EHU (6A) inc; adv bkg acc; ccard acc; tennis; watersports; CKE. *"Great site with excel, clean san facs; pool 300m; gd size pitches; lakeside location; supmkt nrby & rests in vicinity; superb scenery."* **€54.80** **2024**

EBEN IM PONGAU *B2* (1.5km S Rural) *47.39932, 13.39566* **See-Camping Eben,** Familie Schneider, Badeseestraße 54, 5531 Eben I Pg **06458 8231 or 0664 450 2000; info@seecamping-eben.at; www.seecamping-eben.at**

12 €3 (htd)

Head E on A10, take exit 60 - Eben. Turn L onto B99. R onto Badeseestr. Campsite 800m on the L. Med, pt shd, EHU (16A) inc; train 800m; adv bkg acc; games area. *"Helpful owners; saunas; steam rm; lake adj; direct access fr mountains; clean & well organise; gd site."* **€30.00** **2024**

EHRWALD *C1* (3km SW Rural) *47.38249, 10.90222* **Camping Biberhof,** Schmitte 8, 6633 Biberwier (Tirol) **(05673) 2950; info@biberhof.at; www.biberhof.at**

12 €1.90

Fr Reutte, leave B179 sp Lermoos. In Leermoos cent turn R sp Biberwier. At t-junc in Biberwier turn L sp Ehrwald. Site on R in 300mtrs. Med, hdstg, mkd, pt shd, EHU (10A); bbq; twin axles; 80% statics; bus adj; Eng spkn; adv bkg acc; games area. *"Site under power cables; sometimes noisy; trampoline, volleyball, wall climbing, table tennis, walking/cycle rtes adj; mountain views; 3 scenic vill; pool at Lermoos 2km; outstanding san facs; drying rm; beautiful setting; generous pitches; clean san facs; free gd wifi; ideal NH."* **€29.50** **2023**

EHRWALD *C1* (3km W Rural) *47.40250, 10.88893* **Happy Camp Hofherr,** Garmischerstrasse 21, 6631 Lermoos **(05673) 2980; info@camping-lermoos.com; www.camping-lermoos.com**

(htd) nr

On ent Lermoos on B187 fr Ehrwald site located on R. Med, pt shd, pt sl, EHU (16A) metered; gas; TV (pitch); 40% statics; phone; adv bkg acc; ccard acc; site clsd 1 Nov-mid Dec; tennis. *"Ideal for walks/cycling; v picturesque; adj park; ask for guest card for discount on ski lifts etc; ski lift 300m; excel san facs; htd pool 200m; superb rest (clsd Mon & Tue eve); family run site."* **€37.60, 8 May-20 Oct.** **2024**

EISENSTADT *B4* (16km SE Rural) *47.80132, 16.69185* **Storchencamp Rust,** Ruster Bucht, 7071 Rust-am-Neusiedlersee (Burgenland) **2683 5538-0; office@gmeiner.co.at; www.gmeiner.co.at**

€4

Fr Eisenstadt take rd to Rust & Mörbisch. In Rust foll sps to site & Zee; lakeside rd to ent. Lge, pt shd, EHU (16A) €3; sw nr; 60% statics; boating. *"Nr Hungarian border; attractive vill with nesting storks."* **€40.00, 1 Apr-31 Oct.** **2024**

ENGELHARTSZELL *B3* (1km NW Rural) *48.51238, 13.72428* **Camp Municipal an der Donau,** Nibelungenstrasse 113, 4090 Engelhartszell **(0664) 8708787; tourismus@engelhartszell.ooe.gv.at; www.camping-audonau.at**

Fr Passau (Germany) exit SE on B130 along Rv Danube. Site on L in approx 28km just bef Engelhartszell adj municipal pool complex. Sm, unshd, EHU (6A) metered; 50% statics; bus nr. *"Excel, clean, friendly site on rvside; pool adj; Danube cycleway passes site."* **€22.60, 15 Apr-15 Oct.** **2022**

AUSTRIA

AUSTRIA

FURSTENFELD *C4* (2km NW Rural) *47.05631, 16.06255* **Camping Fürstenfeld,** Campingweg 1, 8280 Fürstenfeld **(03382) 54940; camping.fuerstenfeld@chello.at; www.camping-fuerstenfeld.at**

€2 nr nr

Exit A2/E59 sp Fürstenfeld onto B65. Site well sp fr town cent. 4*, Med, pt shd, pt sl, EHU (10A) €2.30 (poss long lead req); 25% statics; phone; golf 5km; waterslide; rv fishing; CKE. *"Pleasant rvside site; ltd facs but clean; conv Hungarian border."*
€21.00, 15 Apr-15 Oct. 2022

GMUND (KARNTEN) *C3* (6km NW Rural) *46.94950, 13.50940* **Terrassencamping Maltatal,** Malta 6, 9854 Malta **(04733) 2340; info@maltacamp.at; www.camping-maltatal.at**

€4 (htd) (htd)

Exit A10/E14 onto B99 to Gmünd. Foll sp Malta & after 6km site sp, on R next to filling stn. 5*, Lge, mkd, pt shd, terr, serviced pitches; EHU (10A) inc; bbq; 5% statics; phone; adv bkg acc; tennis; games area; canoeing; sauna; games rm; trout fishing; CKE. *"Gmund & Spittal gd shopping towns; Millstättersee 15km, Grossglocknerstrasse 1hr's drive; magnificant area with rvs, waterfalls, forests & mountains; guided walks; vg rest; children's mini farm; excel site."*
€39.20, 1 Apr-31 Oct. 2024

GNESAU *D3* (1km W Rural) *46.77966, 13.95062* **Camping Hobitsch,** Sonnleiten 24, 9563 Gnesau (Kärnten) **(0676) 6032848; office@camping-hobitsch.at; www.camping-hobitsch.at**

€1.50 nr nr

Site sp on B95. Sm, pt shd, EHU €3.50; Eng spkn; tennis; games area. *"Beautiful setting in meadow; excel san facs; adj to cycle path."*
€16.60, 1 May-30 Sep. 2022

GRAN *C1* (1km N Rural) *47.51000, 10.55611* **Comfort-Camp Grän,** Engetalstrasse 13, 6673 Grän (Tirol) **(05675) 6570; info@comfortcamp.at; www.comfortcamp.at**

€4 (htd) nr (covrd, htd)

Leave A7 (Germany) at Oy exit, foll 310 via Wertach, Oberjoch to Gran. Rtes fr Sonthofen or Reutte only suitable for MH's. 4*, Med, mkd, unshd, pt sl, terr, EHU (16A) 0.75 per kWh; gas; bbq; TV; 20% statics; phone; bus; Eng spkn; adv bkg acc; games rm; solarium; CKE. *"Ski-rm facs avail; private bthrms avail extra cost; vg facs; luxurious facs, sauna, massage; beautiful area; cable car nrby; walking/cycle rtes fr site; ACSI site."*
€55.00, 10 May-1 Nov & 15 Dec-16 Apr. 2023

GRAN *C1* (6km W Rural) *47.50825, 10.49468* **Panoramacamp Alpenwelt,** Kienzerle 3, 6675 Tannheim **(05675) 43070; alpenwelt@tirol.com; https://alpenwelt-tannheimertal.at**

€3.50 (htd)

Fr N leave A7 junc 137 Oy-Mittelberg onto B310 to Oberjoch, then B199 to Tannheim. Fr S on B198 dir Reutte, turn onto B199 at Weissenbach to Tannheim. 5*, Med, mkd, hdstg, unshd, terr, serviced pitches; EHU (16A) metered; sw nr; TV (pitch); 30% statics; Eng spkn; adv bkg acc; sauna; CKE. *"Excel site & san facs; ski lift 2km; ski bus; gd walking/cycling area; lovely views; pool 4km; wifi at cafe."*
€41.00, 20 Dec-19 Apr & 1 May-30 Oct. 2023

GRAZ *C4* (7km SW Urban) *47.02447, 15.39719* **Stadt-Camping Central,** Martinhofstrasse 3, 8054 Graz-Strassgang **(0316) 697824 or 0676 3785102 (mob); office@reisemobilstellplatz-graz.at; www.reisemobilstellplatz-graz.at**

nr nr

Fr A9/E57 exit Graz-Webling, then dir Strassgang onto B70, site sp on R after Billa supmkt & filling stn. Med, mkd, hdstg, pt shd, EHU (6A) inc; gas; bbq; 20% statics; bus to city; tennis. *"Pleasant, conv site; gd NH; reg bus service fr the nrby main rd (no traff noise); dogs free; pool, paddling pool adj; free ent lido (pt naturist); site manager v helpful; mainly MH."*
€30.00, 1 Apr-31 Oct. 2023

GREIFENBURG *D2* (1.6km W Rural) *46.74805, 13.16416* **Camping Reiter,** Hauzendorf 3, 9761 Greifenburg (Kärnten) **(04712) 389; info@camping-reiter.at; www.camping-reiter.at**

€4 (htd) nr (htd)

Fr Greifenburg on B100, site on L on Drautal Strasse. Sm, pt shd, EHU (10A) metered; bbq (charcoal, elec, gas); sw nr; twin axles; adv bkg acc. *"Beautiful area; excel walking area in Valley of Rv Drau or in Alps; bike hire in Greifenburg; boats on Wiessensee; excel."* **€25.00, 1 May-30 Sep.** 2023

GREIN *B3* (0.7km SW Urban) *48.22476, 14.85428* **Campingplatz Grein,** Donaulände 1, 4360 Grein **676 6679863; info@donaucamping-grein.at; www.donaucamping-grein.at**

€2.50 nr nr

Sp fr A1 & B3 on banks of Danube. Med, pt shd, EHU (6-10A) €3; gas; red long stay; 10% statics; canoeing; fishing; CKE. *"Friendly, helpful owner lives on site; recep in café/bar; vg, modern san facs; htd covrd pool 200m; open air pool 500m; lovely scenery; quaint vill; gd walking; excursions; conv Danube cycle rte & Mauthausen Concentration Camp."*
€33.00, 1 Apr-31 Oct. 2024

HALL IN TIROL *C2* (6km E Rural) *47.28711, 11.57223* **Schlosscamping Aschach,** Hochschwarzweg 2, 6111 Volders **(05224) 52333; info@schlosscamping.com; www.schlosscamping.com**

€2.50 WD MSP (htd)

Fr A12 leave at either Hall Mitte & foll sp to Volders, or leave at Wattens & travel W to Volders (easiest rte). Site well sp on B171. Narr ent bet lge trees. Lge, mkd, pt shd, pt sl, EHU (16A) €2.70 (long cable req some pitches, adaptor lead avail); gas; bbq; red long stay; TV; phone; bus 250m; Eng spkn; adv bkg acc; ccard acc; horseriding; tennis; CKE. *"Well-run, efficient, clean site with vg, modern facs & helpful management; few water & waste points; grassy pitches; beautiful setting & views; gd walking/touring; arr early to ensure pitch; excel."* **€31.00, 1 May-20 Sep.** 2023

HALLEIN *B2* (5km NW Rural) *47.70441, 13.06868* **Camping Auwirt,** Salzburgerstrasse 42, 5400 Hallein **(06245) 80417; info@auwirt.com; www.auwirt.com**

€2 WD MSP

Exit A10/E55 junc 8 onto B150 sp Salzburg Süd, then B159 twd Hallein. Site on L in 4km. Med, pt shd, EHU (10A) €3; bus to Salzburg at site ent; Eng spkn; adv bkg acc; CKE. *"Mountain views; cycle path to Salzburg nr; gd san facs & rest; conv salt mines at Hallein & scenic drive to Eagles' Nest; conv for Berchtesgaden; friendly helpful family owners; flat site; excel; hotel and apartments on site."* **€41.00, 26 Mar-8 Oct, 9 Apr-5 Oct & 1 Dec-31 Dec.** 2023

HALLSTATT *C3* (1km S Rural) *47.55296, 13.64786* **Camping Klausner-Höll,** Lahnstrasse 201, 4830 Hallstatt **+43 6134 8322; camping@hallstatt.net; camping.hallstatt.net**

€3 WD nr

On exit tunnel 500m thro vill, site on R nr lge filling stn. Med, pt shd, EHU (16A) €1 per person; sw; red long stay; Eng spkn; ccard acc; boat trips; CKE. *"Excel, level site; gd, clean san facs; chem disp diff to use; conv Salzkammergut region, Hallstatt salt mines, ice caves; pretty town 10 mins walk; family run site; relaxed & friendly; walks; idyllic quiet setting with mountains all around; cycle path around lake; pool adj; supmkt 300m."* **€48.00, 15 Apr-10 Oct.** 2024

IMST *C1* (1.5km S Rural) *47.22861, 10.74305* **Campingpark FiNK (formerly Imst-West),** Langgasse 62, 6460 Imst **(05412) 66293; info@campingfink.tirol; campingfink.tirol**

12 €1.80-€2 WD MSP nr nr

Fr A12/E60 exit Imst-Pitztal onto B171 N dir Imst. In 1km at rndabt turn L and sweep R round Billa store. Immed turn L & L again to site (sp). Med, mkd, pt shd, pt sl, EHU (6-10A) €4; gas; Eng spkn. *"Gd cent for Tirol, trips to Germany & en rte for Innsbruck; lovely views; pool 1.5km; immac new san facs (2015); ski lift 2km; free ski bus; gd."* **€31.00** 2023

INNSBRUCK *C1* (9.5km SW Rural) *47.23724, 11.33865* **Camping Natterersee,** Natterer See 1, 6161 Natters **(0512) 546732; info@natterersee.com; www.natterersee.com**

12 €5 (htd) WD MSP

App Innsbruck fr E or W on A12 take A13/E45 sp Brenner. Leave at 1st junc sp Innsbruck Süd, Natters. Foll sp Natters - acute R turns & severe gradients (care across unguarded level x-ing), turn sharp R in vill & foll sp to site. Take care on negotiating ent. Narr rds & app. Fr S on A13 Brennerautobahn exit junc 3 & foll dir Mutters & Natters. 5*, Med, pt shd, sl, EHU (10A)€3.75; gas; bbq; sw; TV; bus to Innsbruck; Eng spkn; adv bkg acc; ccard acc; bike hire; waterslide; games rm; tennis; clsd 1 Nov-mid Dec; games area; CKE. *"Well-kept site adj local beauty spot; lakeside pitches gd views (extra charge); gd, scenic cent for walking & driving excursions; gd for children; friendly, helpful staff; excel modern san facs; some sm pitches & narr site rds diff lge o'fits; fantastic setting; sep car park high ssn; no dogs Jul/Aug; guided hiking; special shwr for dogs; excel."* **€40.00, G01.** 2022

"There aren't many sites open at this time of year"

If you're travelling outside peak season remember to call ahead to check site opening dates – even if the entry says 'open all year'.

INNSBRUCK *C1* (7.5km W Urban) *47.25307, 11.32661* **Campingplatz Stigger,** Bahnhofstraße 10, 6176 Völs **(0512) 303533; campingvoels@aon.at; www.camping-stigger.at**

12 WD MSP nr

Exit A12/E60 at Völs exit & foll site sp. 1*, Sm, pt shd, EHU inc; bus adj; Eng spkn; ccard acc; CKE. *"Gd; pool 200m; conv Innsbruck; few lge pitches and quite expensive."* **€34.00** 2023

JENBACH *C2* (6.5km NW Rural) *47.42156, 11.74043* **Camping Karwendel,** 6212 Maurach **(05243) 6116; info@karwendel-camping.at; www.karwendel-camping.at**

12 €3 (htd) WD nr

Exit A12/E45/E50 junc 39 onto B181. Foll sp Pertisau & Maurach. In 8km (climbing fr a'route turn L at Maurach. Foll rd thro vill, turn L at T-junc, then strt across rndabt twd lake. Site sp past recycling cent. Med, unshd, EHU (10A) metered; sw nr; TV; 80% statics; golf 4km; site clsd Nov. *"In open country, glorious views of lake & mountains; diff access lge o'fits; site neglected & rundown."* **€40.00** 2024

AUSTRIA

KITZBUHEL *C2* (3km NW Rural) *47.45906, 12.3619* **Campingplatz Schwarzsee,** Reitherstrasse 24, 6370 Kitzbühel **5356 62806; office@bruggerhof-camping.at; www.bruggerhof-camping.at**
12 €5.50 (htd) WD nr

Site sp fr Kitzbühel dir Kirchberg-Schwarzsee. Lge, pt shd, pt sl, EHU (16A) metered; gas; sw nr; TV (pitch); 80% statics; phone; bus; Eng spkn; adv bkg acc; ccard acc; sauna; CKE. *"Gd walks, cable cars & chair lifts; vg, well-maintained site; poss mosquito & vermin prob; some pitches in statics area; friendly owner; well equipped with lots of activities; excel saunas (site naturist in sauna area only); gd for families."*
€51.00 **2024**

KLAGENFURT *D3* (5km W Rural) *46.61826, 14.25641* **Camping Wörthersee,** Metnitzstrand 5, 9020 Klagenfurt am wörthersee (Kärnten) **463 28 78 10; info@gocamping.at; www.camping-woerthersee.at**
€4.90 WD sand adj

Fr A2/E66 take spur to Klagenfurt-West, exit at Klagenfurt-Wörthersee. Turn R at traff lts & immed L at rd fork (traff lts), then foll sp to site. Lge, shd, EHU (10A) inc; 10% statics; bus; ccard acc; sauna; bike hire. *"V clean facs; local tax €3.50 per visit."*
€44.60, 18 April-22 Sep. **2024**

KLOSTERNEUBURG *B4* (0.7km N Rural) *48.31097, 16.32810* **Donaupark Camping Klosterneuburg,** In der Au, 3402 Klosterneuburg **(02243) 25877; campklosterneuburg@oeamtc.at; www.campingklosterneuburg.at**
(htd) WD nr

Fr A22/E59 exit junc 7 onto B14, site sp in cent of town behind rlwy stn. After passing Klosterneuburg Abbey on L turn 1st R (sharp turn under rlwy). Site immed ahead. 4*, Med, mkd, pt shd, EHU (6-12A) €5; gas; bbq; cooking facs; TV; 5% statics; phone; bus, train to Vienna; ccard acc; bike hire; boat hire; tennis; CKE. *"Well-organised, popular site; leisure cent adj; vg san facs; helpful staff; sm pitches; htd pools adj; conv Danube cycle path & Vienna; church & monastery worth visit."* **€36.00, 13 Mar-5 Nov.** **2023**

KOSSEN *B2* (3km SE Rural) *47.65388, 12.41544* **Eurocamping Wilder Kaiser,** Kranebittau 18, 6345 Kössen **+43 5375 6444; eurocamp@eurocamp-koessen.com; www.eurocamp-koessen.com**
12 €4-6 (htd) WD

Leave A12 at Oberaudorf/Niederndorf junc, head E on 172 thro Niederndorf & Walchsee to Kössen. Strt across at rndabt, in 1km turn R sp Hinterburg Lift. At next junc turn R & site located after 400m. 5*, Lge, mkd, pt shd, serviced pitches; EHU (6A) metered + conn fee; gas; TV (pitch); 50% statics; Eng spkn; adv bkg acc; ccard acc; games area; sauna; tennis; golf 2km; solarium; CKE. *"Lovely site; excel play area & organised activities; htd pool adj; rafting, hang-gliding & canoeing 1km; excel."* **€48.00** **2024**

KOTSCHACH *D2* (1km SW Rural) *46.66946, 12.99153* **Alpencamp Kärnten,** Kötschach 284, 9640 Kötschach-Mauthen **(04715) 429; info@alpencamp.at; www.alpencamp.at**
12 €2 (htd) WD nr
(covrd, htd)

At junc of rds B110 & B111 in Kötschach turn W onto B111, foll camp sps to site in 800m on L. 4*, Med, mkd, pt shd, EHU (16A) inc; TV; phone; Eng spkn; ccard acc; games rm; bike hire; tennis; waterslide; site clsd 1 Nov-14 Dec; boat hire; tennis 400m; sauna; games area. *"Useful for Plöcken Pass; cycle tracks on rv bank nrby; vg san facs; friendly, helpful owner; vg site."* **€37.50** **2022**

LANDECK *C1* (0.5km W Urban) *47.14263, 10.56147* **Camping Riffler,** Bruggfeldstrasse 2, 6500 Landeck **(05442) 64898; info@camping-riffler.at; www.camping-riffler.at**
12 WD nr nr

Exit E60/A12 at Landeck-West, site in 1.5km, 500m fr cent on L. Sm, pt shd, EHU (10A) €2.70 (poss rev pol); gas; ccard acc; bike hire; site clsd May; CKE. *"Well-kept, clean, friendly site; sm pitches; dogs free; narr rds; recep open 1800-2000 LS - site yourself & pay later; pool 500m; excel NH."* **€25.00** **2022**

LIENZ *C2* (2km S Rural) *46.81388, 12.76388* **Dolomiten-Camping Amlacherhof,** Lake rd 20, 9908 Amlach Lienz **4852 62317 / mob 699 17623171; info@amlacherhof.at; www.amlacherhof.at**
€2.90 (htd) WD nr
(htd)

S fr Lienz on B100, foll sp in 1.5km to Amlach. In vill, foll site sp. 4*, Med, hdg, mkd, pt shd, EHU (16A) metered inc; bbq; TV; 5% statics; bus adj; Eng spkn; adv bkg acc; site clsd 1 Nov-15 Dec; games rm; golf 7km; tennis; bike hire. *"Excel touring cent; many mkd walks & cycle rtes; cable cars, ski lifts 3km; attractive, historic town; excel, scenic site; local taxes €5."*
€47.50, 1 Mar-31 Oct. **2024**

LINZ *B3* (14km SE Rural) *48.23527, 14.37888* **Camping-Linz am Pichlingersee,** Wienerstrasse 937, 4030 Linz **(0732) 305314; office@camping-linz.at; www.camping-linz.at**
€1.90 (htd) WD

Exit A1/E60 junc 160; take Enns dir; go L on 1st rndabt; do not go under rndabt thro underpass; site is sp on R. Med, mkd, pt shd, EHU (6A) inc; gas; cooking facs; sw nr; red long stay; 40% statics; bus; Eng spkn; adv bkg acc; tennis. *"Excel modern san facs, well-run, family-run site; friendly staff; site clsd 1300-1500; gd walks around lake; monastery at St Florian worth visit; conv NH; gd."*
€37.90, 15 Mar-15 Oct. **2023**

LOFER *C2* (2km SE Rural) *47.57500, 12.70804* **Camping Park Grubhof,** St Martin 39, 5092 St Martin-bei-Lofer **(06588) 82370; home@grubhof.com; www.grubhof.com**

€3 (htd) nr

Clear sps to camp at ent on rd B311 Lofer to Zell-am-See. Site on L after garden cent. 5*, Lge, pt shd, serviced pitches; EHU (10A) €2; phone; bus to Salzburg; adv bkg acc; CKE. *"Beautiful scenery; roomy, peaceful site; excel san facs; adult only & dog free areas; fitness cent; sh walk to vill; highly rec; mountain views; some meadowside and rvside pitches; delightful rest/bar; excel."* **€50.00, 1 Jan-23 Mar, 11 Apr-2 Nov, 6 Dec-31 Dec, G04. 2022**

See advertisement

LUNZ AM SEE *B4* (0.9km E Urban) *47.86194, 15.03638* **Ötscherland Camping,** Zellerhofstrasse 23, 3293 Lunz-am-See **(07486) 8413; info@oetscherlandcamping.at; www.oetscherlandcamping.at**

12 €1 (htd) nr nr

Fr S on B25 turn R into Lunz-am-See. In 300m turn L, cross rv & take 1st L, site on L on edge of vill. Sm, hdstg, pt shd, EHU (16A) inc; sw nr; 80% statics; Eng spkn. *"Excel walking; immac facs; winter skiing; vg site on Rv Ybbs & Eisenstrasse."* **€19.50 2022**

MARBACH AN DER DONAU *B4* (1km W Rural) *48.21309, 15.13828* **Campingplatz Marbacher,** Campingweg 2, 3671 Marbach a.d. Donau **7413 20733 or 664 735 59 125 (mob); info@marbach-freizeit.at; www.marbach-freizeit.at**

€2 (htd) nr nr

Fr W exit A1 junc 100 at Ybbs onto B25. Cross Rv Danube & turn R onto B3. Site in 7km. Fr E exit A1 junc 90 at Pöchlarn, cross rv & turn L onto B3 to Marbach, site sp. Med, mkd, pt shd, EHU (16A) €1.9; bbq; sw; 5% statics; Eng spkn; adv bkg acc; ccard acc; bike hire; boat hire; tennis 800m; watersports; CKE. *"Beautiful, well-managed site; sm, narr pitches; excel facs & staff; gd rst & bar; gd cycling & watersports; v clean facs; gd NH fr m'way or longer stay for touring."* **€32.00, 1 Apr-31 Oct. 2024**

MARIAZELL *B4* (4km NW Rural) *47.79009, 15.28221* **Campingplatz am Erlaufsee,** Erlaufseestrasse 3, 8630 St Sebastien-bei-Mariazell **(03882) 4937 or (066460) 644400 (mob); gemeinde@st-sebastian.at; www.st-sebastian.at**

€1.90 nr nr

On B20 1km N of Mariazell turn W sp Erlaufsee. Site in 3km on app to lake, turn L thro car park ent to site. Med, pt shd, pt sl, EHU (12A) metered; bus high ssn. *"Cable car in Mariazell; beach nrby; pilgrimage cent; all hot water by token fr owner."* **€16.30, 1 May-15 Sep. 2022**

MATREI IN OSTTIROL *C2* (0.5km S Rural) *46.99583, 12.53906* **Camping Edengarten,** Edenweg 15a, 9971 Matrei-in-Osttirol **(04875) 5111; info@campingedengarten.at; www.campingedengarten.at**

nr nr

App fr Lienz on B108 turn L bef long ascent (by-passing Matrei) sp Matrei-in-Osttirol & Camping. App fr N thro Felbertauern tunnel, by-pass town, turn R at end of long descent, sps as above. Med, pt shd, EHU (10A); gas; 10% statics; bus. *"Gd mountain scenery; helpful owner; beautiful views; pool 300m; pretty town; some rd noise during daytime."* **€31.00, 1 May-15 Oct. 2024**

MATREI IN OSTTIROL *C2* (23km W Rural) *47.01912, 12.63695* **Camping Kals Am Großglockner,** Burg 22, 9981 Kals am Großglockner **4852 67418; info@nationalpark-camping-kals.at; www.nationalpark-camping-kals.at**

€3.70 (htd)

Fr 108 Matrei in Osttirol to Lienz, exit at Huben onto L26 to Kals. 3km after vill foll sp to Dorfertal. National Park campsite on L. Med, unshd, EHU metered; twin axles; Eng spkn; ccard acc; CCI. *"Excel site; ski bus; excel walking & climbing."* **€39.10, 17 May-13 Oct. 2024**

MAYRHOFEN *C2* (1km N Rural) *47.17617, 11.86969* **Camping Mayrhofen,** Laubichl 125, 6290 Mayrhofen **664 8851 8866; camping@alpenparadies.com or info@campingplatz-tirol.at; www.campingplatz-tirol.at**

€4.50 nr

Site at N end of vill off B169. 4*, Lge, hdstg, mkd, pt shd, EHU (10A) metered; gas; 50% statics; adv bkg acc; bike hire; sauna; CKE. *"Modern san facs; diff for lge o'fits, narr rds; some factory noise; gd rest."* **€31.30, 1 Jan-31 Oct & 15 Dec-31 Dec. 2024**

MELK *B4* (3km N Urban) *48.24298, 15.34040* **Donau Camping Emmersdorf,** Bundesstrasse 133, 3644 Emmersdorf-an-der-Donau **(02752) 71707 or (06766) 706652; office@donaucamping-emmersdorf.at; www.donaucamping-emmersdorf.at**

nr nr

Fr A1 take Melk exit. Turn R, foll sp Donaubrücke, cross rv bdge. Turn R, site 200m on L, well sp. Sm, mkd, hdg, pt shd, EHU (6A) inc; bbq; phone; ccard acc; games rm; bike hire; tennis; fishing; CKE. *"Liable to close if rv in flood; clean facs; noise fr rd & disco w/end; attractive vill; vg."* **€34.20, 1 Apr-15 Oct. 2024**

MELK *B4* (3.6km NW Rural) *48.23347, 15.32888* **Camping Fährhaus Melk,** Kolomaniau 3, 3390 Melk **(02752) 53291; info@faehrhaus-melk.at; www.faehrhaus-melk.at**

nr

Skirt Melk on B1, immed after abbey at traff lts, turn N on bdge over rv (sp). Site in 700m. Sm, pt shd, EHU (6A) inc; bbq; fishing. *"Basic site but adequate; abbey adj & boating on Danube; NB all sites on banks of Danube liable to close if rv in flood."* **€12.50, 1 Apr-31 Oct. 2022**

MICHELDORF IN OBERÖSTERREICH *B3* (4km S Rural) *47.851081, 14.146745* **Schön Camping,** Schön 60, 4563 Micheldorf **(07582) 60917; reservierung@schoen-menschen.at; www.schoen-menschen.at**

(indoor)

Fr m'way J28 take rd 138 N dir Micheldorf, foll Schon camping sp (not Schon-Menschen sp) to avoid 3.1m rlwy bdge. Narr country rd. Drive thro complex to camping area at top. Hdstg, pt shd, pt sl, EHU inc; cooking facs; sw nr; phone; bus on rd 138; Eng spkn; adv bkg acc. *"Literally self service, pay in honesty box by facs bldg; part of disabled complex; free minigolf, access to indoor pool; walks witin site and local area; cafe (ltd hrs); vg."* **€25.50, 1 May-30 Sep. 2024**

MILLSTATT *D3* (4km SE Rural) *46.78863, 13.61418* **Camping Neubauer,** Dellach 63, 9872 Millstatt-am-See **+4766 2532; info@camping-neubauer.at; www.camping-neubauer.at**

€2.50 (htd) nr

Exit A10/E55 dir Seeboden & Millstatt. Take lakeside rd B98 fr Millstatt to Dellach, R turn & foll sp camping sp. Med, hdstg, mkd, pt shd, terr, EHU (6A) inc; gas; bbq; sw; 10% statics; ccard acc; tennis; golf 6km; bike hire; watersports. *"Gd touring base; easy access to Italy; superb scenery with lakes & mountains; gd walks; excel facs; boat trips nr; gd rest; steep narr rd's to pitches, tractor avail to help; pt shd on lake pitches."* **€31.70, 1 May-15 Oct. 2024**

MURAU *C3* (3km W Rural) *47.10791, 14.13883* **Camping Olachgut,** Kaindorf 90, 8861 St Georgen-ob-Murau **(03532) 2162 or 3233; office@olachgut.at; www.olachgut.at**

12 €3 nr

Site sp on rd B97 bet Murau & St Georgen. Med, pt shd, EHU (16A) inc; gas; sw; 40% statics; adv bkg acc; sauna; horseriding; bike hire; games area. *"Rural site nr rlwy; ski lift 2.5km."* **€40.00 2024**

NASSEREITH *C1* (2.5km SE Rural) *47.30975, 10.85466* **Camping Rossbach,** Rossbach 325, 6465 Nassereith **(05265) 5154; rainer.ruepp@gmx.at; https://campingrossbach.at**

12 €1.50 (htd) (htd)

On ent vill of Nassereith turn E & foll dir Rossbach/ Dormitz, site in 1.5km. Foll sm green sps. Narr app. 4*, Med, mkd, pt shd, EHU (6A); bbq; TV; 5% statics; phone; adv bkg acc; fishing; games rm; CKE. *"Mountain views; friendly welcome; ACSI prices; ski lift 500m; ski bus; pitch in various sep areas; vg san facs."* **€30.50 2023**

NAUDERS *C1* (4km S Rural) *46.85139, 10.50472* **Alpencamping,** Bundestrasse 279, 6543 Nauders **(05473) 87217; info@camping-nauders.at; www.camping-nauders.com**

€2 (htd)

On W side of B180 just bef Italian border. Sm, hdstg, unshd, EHU €1.90; gas; phone; ccard acc; CKE. *"Conv NH for Reschen pass; gd touring base; excel cycling, walking; excel san facs."* **€35.90, 1 Jan-16 Apr, 2 May-15 Oct, 15 Dec-31 Dec. 2022**

NEUSTIFT IM STUBAITAL *C1* (0.5km NE Rural) *47.10977, 11.30770* **Camping Stubai,** Stubaitalstrasse 94, 6167 Neustift-im-Stubaital **(05226) 2537; info@campingstubai.at; www.campingstubai.at**

12 €2.60 (htd) WD MSP nr nr nr

S fr Innsbruck on B182 or A13, take B183 dir Fulpmes & Neustift. Site sp, in vill opp church & adj Billa supmkt. If app via A13 & Europabrucke, toll payable on exit junc 10 into Stubaital Valley. 4*, Med, mkd, pt shd, pt sl, terr, EHU (6A) €4.40; 50% statics; Eng spkn; adv bkg acc; games rm; sauna; CKE. *"Friendly, family-run site; pitches nr rv poss flood; recep open 0900-1100 & 1700-1900 - barrier down but can use farm ent & find space; htd pool 500m; excel mountain walking & skiing; lovely location."*
€25.40 **2023**

NEUSTIFT IM STUBAITAL *C1* (6km SW Rural) *47.06777, 11.25388* **Camping Edelweiss,** Volderau 29, 6167 Neustift-im-Stubaital **5226 3484; info@camping-edelweiss.at; camping-edelweiss.at**

12 €3 (htd) WD MSP

Fr B182 or A13 exit junc 10 take B183 to Neustift, site on R at Volderau vill. Med, hdstg, unshd, EHU (4A) €3; gas; 30% statics; phone; bus. *"Excel peaceful site in scenic valley; vg, modern san facs; haphazard mix of statics & tourers; winter skiing."* **€22.00** **2024**

OBERNBERG AM INN *B3* (1km SW Rural) *48.31506, 13.32313* **Panorama Camping,** Saltzburgerstrasse 28, 4982 Obernberg-am-Inn **(07758) 30024 or 173 2306 571 (mob); obernberg-panoramacamping@aon.at; http://obernberg-panoramacamping.jimdo.com**

12 WD nr nr

Exit A8/E56 junc 65 to Obernberg. Then take dir Braunau, site well sp. Sm, hdg, pt shd, pt sl, serviced pitches; EHU (10A) metered or €2 (poss rev pol); Eng spkn; adv bkg acc; tennis 800m. *"Friendly, excel sm site; site yourself if office clsd; nr to border; spectacular views; san facs clean; gd walking, birdwatching; o'night m'vans area; network of cycle paths around vills on other side of rv; pool 800m; pleasant walk to town past rv viewpoint."* **€28.00** **2022**

OETZ *C1* (10km S Rural) *47.13533, 10.9316* **Ötztal Arena Camp Krismer,** Mühlweg 32, 6441 Umhausen **(05255) 5390; www.oetztalcamping.com; www.oetztal-camping.at**

12 €5 WD nr

Fr A12 exit junc 123 S onto B186 sp Ötztal. S of Ötztal turn L into Umhausen vill & foll site sp. 4*, Med, mkd, pt shd, pt sl, EHU (16A) metered (poss rev pol); gas; bbq; sw; phone; Eng spkn; adv bkg req. *"Well-run site; immac facs; lots of local info given on arr; friendly owners; poss diff pitching on some sh pitches; pool 200m; excel cent for Stuibenfal waterfall (illuminated Wed night high ssn) & Ötztaler Valley; pool & lake sw 200m; wonderful scenery; gd walking fr site; narr app rd; very cr in high ssn."* **€32.00** **2023**

OSSIACH *D3* (1km SW Rural) *46.66388, 13.97500* **Terrassen Camping Ossiacher See,** Ostriach 67, 9570 Ossiach **(04243) 436; martinz@camping.at; www.terrassen.camping.at**

€3 (htd) WD MSP

Leave A10/E55/E66 at exit for Ossiachersee, turn L onto B94 twd Feldkirchen & shortly R to Ossiach Süd. Site on lake shore just S of Ossiach vill. Lge, mkd, pt shd, terr, EHU (4-10A) €3; gas; bbq; sw; twin axles; red long stay; TV; ccard acc; clsd 1200-1500 LS; games area; horseriding; games rm; windsurfing; bike hire; fishing; tennis; watersports; CKE. *"Ideal Carinthian lakes, Hochosterwitz castle & excursions into Italy; parking adj; cash machine; beautiful scenery; many activities; excel san facs; pitches sm and diff for big o'fits; dogs confined to pitches next to entrance; but site in lovely location."*
€50.00, 15 Apr-15 Oct, G05. **2022**

OSSIACH *D3* (4km SW Rural) *46.65551, 13.93976* **Seecamping Plörz,** Süduferstrasse 289, 9523 Heiligen-Gestade **(04242) 41286 or 0676-3221494 (mob); info@camping-ploerz.at; https://camping-ploerz.at/**

€2 (htd) WD MSP nr nr nr

Fr A10/E55/E65 turn N onto B94 twd Feldkirchen. Almost immed turn R sp Ossiach, site on R just past Camping Mentl. Sm, pt shd, pt sl, EHU (16A) inc; sw nr; TV; phone; Eng spkn. *"Excel sm farm site with gd facs; friendly helpful owners; quiet alt to other busy lakeside sites; play equipment; lge pitches; very clean facs; cycle paths & gd walks; bus stop at gate; ltd facs for children."* **€55.00, Apr-25 Sep.** **2023**

OSSIACH *D3* (5km SW Rural) *46.65321, 13.93344* **Seecamping Berghof,** Ossiachersee Süduferstrasse 241, 9523 Heiligengestade **(04242) 41133; office@seecamping-berghof.at; www.seecamping-berghof.at**

€3 (htd) WD MSP

Exit Villach on rd sp Ossiachersee; take R turn Ossiachersee Süd, site on L bet rd & lake. 5*, Lge, pt shd, pt sl, terr, serviced pitches; EHU (10A) inc; gas; sw; 10% statics; phone; adv bkg acc; sailing; tennis; games area; bike hire; fishing; golf 10km. *"Excel site; gd cent for excursions to castles & lakes; many sports & activities; private bthrms avail; extra for lge/lakeside pitches; sep area for dogs; muddy when wet."*
€51.00, 4 Apr-18 Oct. **2023**

PETTNAU *C1* (0.4km E Rural) *47.29020, 11.16453* **Camping Tiefental "Roppnerhof",** Tiroler Strasse 121, 6408 Pettnau **(0664) 4663003 (mob); tiefental@aon.at; www.camping-tiefental.at**

€3 WD MSP

Leave A12 autoban at junc 101 to join 171 going E twds Zirl and Innsbruck. Site on Tiroler Strabe E end of Unter Pettnau vill. Sm, mkd, pt shd, EHU (13A) €3; bbq; twin axles; Eng spkn; adv bkg acc; CKE. *"Superb views; walking and cycling in the Inn valley; Innsbruck 25km; excel."* **€29.00, 1 May-30 Sep.** **2023**

AUSTRIA

POYSDORF *A4* (1km W Urban) *48.66454, 16.61168* **Veltlinerland Camping,** Laaerstrasse 106, 2170 Poysdorf **(02552) 20371; veltlinerlandcamping.poysdorf@gmx.at; www.poysdorf.at**

nr

Fr rd 7/E461 at traff lts in Poysdorf turn W onto rd 219 dir Laa an der Thaya. Site sp on R in approx 1km on edge of park. Sm, hdstg, mkd, unshd, terr, EHU (6A) €2.20; sw nr; 50% statics; Eng spkn; tennis. *"Gd, under-used site 1hr N of Vienna; htd wc & shwrs at park adj (key issued); no other site in area; conv Czech border."* **€25.00, 1 May-31 Oct.** **2022**

PRUTZ *C1* (0.6km NE Rural) *47.07955, 10.6588* **Aktiv-Camping Prutz,** Pontlatzstrasse 22, 6522 Prutz **(05472) 2648; info@aktiv-camping.at; www.aktiv-camping.at**

€3 (htd)

Fr Landeck to Prutz on rd B180 turn R at Shell stn over rv bdge, site sp. 4*, Med, hdg, mkd, pt shd, EHU (16A) inc; gas; sw nr; red long stay; TV; 20% statics; Eng spkn; adv bkg acc; ccard acc; bike hire; site clsd Nov; CKE. *"Excel, clean facs; gd views; o'night m'vans area; pool complex in vill; office clsd 1000-1630 - find pitch & pay later; walks & cycle rtes; conv NH en rte Italy & for tax-free shopping in Samnaun, Switzerland; gd site; cards given for free bus travel."* **€40.00** **2022**

PURBACH AM NEUSIEDLERSEE *B4* (1km SE Rural) *47.90958, 16.70580* **Storchencamp Purbach,** Türkenhain, 7083 Purbach-am-Neusiedlersee (Burgenland) **(02683) 5170; office@gmeiner.co.at; www.gmeiner.co.at**

€2.90 (htd)

Exit A4/E6 junc 43 onto B50 at Neuseidl-am-See to Purbach. Site sp in town nr pool complex. Sm, pt shd, EHU (6A) €2.30; bbq; 80% statics; bus/train 1km; Eng spkn; games area. *"Open field for tourers; excel sw complex adj free with local visitor card; free public transport & red ent to museums etc; modern facs; conv NH."* **€29.00, 15 Apr-26 Oct.** **2022**

RATTENBERG *C2* (4.5km N Rural) *47.45670, 11.88084* **Seen-Camping Stadlerhof,** Seebühel 15, 6233 Kramsach-am-Reintalersee **(05337) 63371; camping.stadlerhof@chello.at; www.camping-stadlerhof.at**

€4.90 (htd) nr (htd)

Exit A12/E45/E60 junc 32 Rattenberg dir Kramsach. At rndabt turn R, then immed L & foll sp 'Zu den Seen' & site sp. Site on L at Lake Krumsee. 5*, Lge, hdstg, mkd, pt shd, pt sl, EHU (10A) inc; gas; bbq; sw nr; TV (pitch); 50% statics; phone; adv bkg acc; games rm; bike hire; fishing; tennis; sauna. *"Beautiful, well laid-out site in lovely setting; excel san facs."* **€42.40** **2024**

RATTENBERG *C2* (4km NE Rural) *47.46198, 11.90708* **Camping Seehof,** Moosen 42, 6233 Kramsach-am-Reintalersee **(05337) 63541; info@camping-seehof.com; www.camping-seehof.com**

€5 (htd)

Exit A12/E45/E60 junc 32 sp Kramsach, foll sp 'Zu den Seen' for 5km. Site immed bef Camping Seeblick-Toni Brantlhof. 5*, Med, mkd, pt shd, EHU (6-13A) €3; bbq; sw; red long stay; TV (pitch); 30% statics; phone; Eng spkn; adv bkg acc; ccard acc; bike hire; gym; solarium; horseriding nr; CKE. *"Friendly staff; gd views fr some pitches; gd, modern san facs; gd rest; Excel site, local walks, excel museum next door; local taxes €2."* **€42.00** **2024**

REUTTE *C1* (1km S Rural) *47.47763, 10.72258* **Camping Reutte,** Ehrenbergstrasse 53, 6600 Reutte **(05672) 62809 or (06641) 858279 (mob); camping-reutte@aon.at; www.camping-reutte.com**

€2

Foll B179 (Fern pass rd), exit at Reutte Süd. Site sp in 1.5km on L. Med, hdstg, mkd, pt shd, EHU (16A) €2.40; TV (pitch); phone; Eng spkn; adv bkg acc; CKE. *"Conv for Fern Pass; barriers clsd 2100; clean, popular site; excel; ski lift 500m; pool adj; free guest cards for facs & transport."* **€29.70** **2022**

RIED IM OBERINNTAL *C1* (0.6km E Rural) *47.05480, 10.65630* **Camping Dreiländereck,** Gartenland 37, 6531 Ried Im Oberinntal **05472 6025; info@tirolcamping.at; www.tirolcamping.at**

€4 (htd) nr

Fr Landeck take 180 twd Reschenpass. Exit at Ried & foll sp. Sm, unshd, EHU (15A) metered; sw nr; twin axles; TV; bus adj; Eng spkn; adv bkg acc; CCI. *"Wellness cent; conv to vill shops; bike hire; helpful owners; gd clean san facs; adventure sports fac nrby; gd site."* **€40.80** **2024**

ST ANTON AM ARLBERG *C1* (2km E Rural) *47.14505, 10.33890* **Camping Arlberg Life,** Strohsack 235c, 6574 Pettneu-am-Arlberg (Tirol) **0664 1630393; camping@arlberglife.com; en.arlberglifecamping.com**

nr nr nr

Fr W on S16/E60, thro Arlberg tunnel, then take Pettneu exit after St Anton to N; site sp in 200m. 4*, Lge, hdg, mkd, pt shd, EHU (16A) metered; twin axles; 10% statics; phone; bus; Eng spkn; adv bkg acc; sauna; fishing. *"Mountain views; htd private bathrms & sat TV each pitch; o'night m'vans area; beauty treatments avail; excel site;ski & boot rm; ski bus; ski lift 1km; wellness ctr adj with pool; site fees inc free bus, cable car & sw pool for 1 day."* **€41.00, 1 Jun- 31 Sep & 1 Dec - 30 Apr.** **2023**

ST JOHANN IM PONGAU *C2* (1km S Urban) *47.34141, 13.19793* **Camping Kastenhof,** Kastenhofweg 6, 5600 St Johann-im-Pongau **(06412) 5490; info@kastenhof.at; www.camping-kastenhof.at**

12 (htd) WD MSP nr

Take A10 S fr Salzburg onto B311 for Alpendorf. Go over rv & turn L into Liechtensteinklamm twd St Johann, site on L, sp. 1*, Med, unshd, EHU (15A) metered + €3.5 conn fee; TV (pitch); 10% statics; bus; adv bkg acc; sauna; CKE. *"Conv Tauern tunnel, Grossglockner Hochalpenstrasse, Zell-am-See; gd clean site."* **€30.00** **2023**

ST JOHANN IN TIROL *C2* (12km SE Rural) *47.46845, 12.55440* **Tirol Camp,** Lindau 20, 6391 Fieberbrunn (Tirol) **(05354) 56666; office@tirol-camp.at; www.tirol-camp.at**

€8 (htd) WD MSP (covrd, htd)

Fr St Johann thro vill of Fieberbrunn, site sp at end of vill. Turn R up to Streuböden chair lift, site 200m on L. 4*, Lge, pt shd, terr, EHU (6A) metered; sw; TV; 30% statics; phone; train; adv bkg acc; ccard acc; games area; tennis; waterslide; sauna. *"Superb site & facs; gd base for skiing, gd walking; wellness cent; trips to Innsbruck & Salzburg; noise fr adj farm."* **€54.10, 1 Jan-11 Apr, 11 May-7 Nov & 7 Dec-31 Dec.** **2022**

ST MICHAEL IM LUNGAU *C3* (0.2km S Rural) *47.09685, 13.63706* **Camping St Michael,** Waaghausgasse 277, 5582 St Michael-im-Lungau **(06477) 8276; camping-st.michael@sgb.at; www.camping-sanktmichael.at**

12 WD MSP nr nr

Exit junc 104 fr A10/E55, site sp at turn into vill, then on L after 200m bef hill. Sm, pt shd, EHU (16A) €3.50 (poss rev pol); gas; adv bkg acc; ccard acc; CKE. *"Delightful site adj vill; excel san facs (shared with adj sports club); ski lift 1km; pool adj; poss full if arr after 6pm, but o'flow area avail."* **€20.00** **2022**

ST PETER AM KAMMERSBERG *C3* (3km ESE Rural) *47.17905, 14.21671* **Camping Bella Austria,** Peterdorf 100, 8842 St Peter-am-Kammersberg **6641680977; info@camping-bellaustria.com; www.camping-bellaustria.com**

€2 WD MSP (htd)

Fr B96 turn N onto L501 into Katschtal Valley dir Oberdorf, Althofen & St Peter-am-Kammersberg. Site sp. 4*, Lge, hdstg, pt shd, EHU (16A) inc; sw; TV; 70% statics; Eng spkn; adv bkg acc; sauna; games area; bike hire. *"Superb walking area; excel."* **€26.00, 27 Apr-29 Sep.** **2024**

ST PRIMUS *D3* (0.8km N Rural) *46.58569, 14.56598* **Strandcamping Turnersee Breznik,** Unternarrach 21, 9123 St Primus **(04239) 2350; info@breznik.at; www.breznik.at**

€2.40 (htd) WD MSP

Exit A2 at junc 298 Grafenstein onto B70. After 4km turn R & go thro Tainach, St Kanzian twd St Primus. Site is on W side of Turnersee. 5*, Lge, mkd, pt shd, serviced pitches; EHU (6A) inc; bbq; sw; TV; 30% statics; adv bkg acc; fishing; golf 2km; tennis 500m; games area; bike hire; games rm; CKE. *"Lovely situation; cinema rm; excel site."* **€39.60, 10 Apr-2 Oct.** **2022**

ST VEIT AN DER GLAN *D3* (6km NE Rural) *46.80245, 14.41260* **Camping Wieser,** Bernaich 8, 9313 St Georgen-am-Längsee (Kärnten) **(04212) 3535; info@campingwieser.com; www.campingwieser.com**

WD MSP nr

Fr St Veit take B317 NE dir Freisach. After 4km turn R to Bernaich, St Georgen. Site sp on L after 500m. Med, mkd, pt shd, terr, EHU (10A) inc; sw nr; TV; phone; CKE. *"Farm site; pool 5km; friendly owner."* **€27.00, 1 May-10 Oct.** **2022**

ST WOLFGANG IM SALZKAMMERGUT *B3* (1km W Rural) *47.74277, 13.43361* **Seeterrassen Camping Reid,** Ried 18, 5360 St Wolfgang/Salzkammergut **(06138) 3201; camping-ried@aon.at; www.seeterrassencamping-ried.at**

€4 (htd) WD MSP

Fr Salzburg take B158 thro St Gilgen dir Bad Ischl. Exit at sp Strobl & foll sp St Wolfgang. Go thro tunnel to avoid town cent, foll rd along lake to site. Sm, pt shd, pt sl, terr, EHU (16A) metered; gas; sw nr; TV; 10% statics; phone; Eng spkn; watersports adj; tennis nr; fishing adj; CKE. *"Mountain rlwy stn nr; lake views; gd touring base; easy walk into town; friendly site; v clean san facs."* **€37.30, 28 Mar-31 Oct.** **2024**

SALZBURG *B2* (2km N Urban) *47.82683, 13.06296* **Camping Nord-Sam,** Samstrasse 22a, 5023 Salzburg Nord **(0662) 660494; office@camping-nord-sam.com; www.camping-nord-sam.com**

€3 (htd) WD MSP (htd)

Heading E on A1/E55/E69 exit junc 288 Salzburg Nord exit & immed take slip rd on R; then over to L-hand lane for L-hand turn at 2nd traff lts, up narr rd to site, sp. If thro Salzburg foll Wien-Linz sps thro city; turn onto B1 on exit o'skts, camp site posted on L. 4*, Med, hdg, hdstg, pt shd, pt sl, EHU (10A) €3; red long stay; bus adj; Eng spkn; adv bkg req; CKE. *"Sm pitches & high hdgs; san facs clean but old & stretched when site full; friendly staff; many attractions nrby; site sells Salzburg Card; cycle track to city cent; recep open 0800-1200 & 1600-2030 high ssn."* **€49.90, 22 Mar-2 Apr, 19 Apr-13 Oct, 27 Dec-31 Dec.** **2024**

AUSTRIA

SALZBURG *B2* (3km N Rural) *47.82843, 13.05221* **Panorama Camping Stadtblick,** Rauchenbichlerstrasse 21, 5020 Salzburg **(0662) 450652; info@panorama-camping.at; www.panorama-camping.at**

€2 (htd)

Fr A1/E55/E60 exit 288 Salzburg Nord/Zentrum & at end of slip rd turn R & sharp R at traff lts, site sp. If coming fr S, foll ring rd to W then N. Med, mkd, hdstg, pt shd, terr, EHU (4A) inc (long lead req some pitches); gas; red long stay; phone; bus to town nrby (tickets fr recep); Eng spkn; adv bkg acc; CKE. *"Conv a'bahn; views of Salzburg; cycle track by rv to town; Salzburg card avail fr recep; sm pitches - rec phone ahead if lge o'fit; v helpful family owners; vg rest; excel, modern san facs; cash only; rec arr early; also open some dates in Dec & Jan; excel; 'Sound of Music' Tour; v conv for Salzburg, gd views; beautiful city; helpful owner."* **€41.50, 1 Jan-8 Jan, 20 Mar-5 Nov, 6 Dec-17 Dec.** **2023**

SALZBURG *B2* (5km SE Urban) *47.78058, 13.08985* **Camping Schloss Aigen,** Weberbartlweg 20, 5026 Salzburg-Aigen **+43 662 633 089; camping.aigen@elsnet.at; www.campingaigen.com**

€1

Fr S leave A10/E55 at junc 8 Salzburg-Süd & take B150 twds Salzburg on Alpenstrasse. Turn R at rndabt dir Glasenbach, then L into Aignerstrasse. 1km S of Aigen stn turn R into Glasenstrasse & foll sps to site. Lge, pt shd, pt sl, EHU (6-16A) €2.50; gas; red long stay; bus to town 700m; adv bkg acc; CKE. *"Friendly, family-run site; washing machine avail; sl pitches v slippery & boggy when wet; excel rest; conv for city, gd walks."* **€31.00, 1 May-30 Sep.** **2024**

"I like to fill in the reports as I travel from site to site"

You'll find report forms at the back of this guide, or you can fill them in online at camc.com/europereport.

SCHARNSTEIN *B3* (2.5km NE Rural) *47.91580, 13.97372* **Almcamp Schatzlmühle,** Viechtwang 1A, 4644 Scharnstein **07615 20269; office@almcamp.at; www.almcamp.at**

€2

Fr A1 take exit 207 Vorchtdorf to Pettenbach on the L536. Head twd Scharnstein on 120. Turn R 2km bef vill (dir Viechtwang). Foll sp. Alt take A9, exit 5, dir Scharnstein. Sm, hdg, hdstg, mkd, pt shd, EHU (16A); bbq; twin axles; TV; 10% statics; phone; Eng spkn; adv bkg acc; games area; games rm; CCI. *"Child friendly; family run site; site by rv, scenic location; gd cycling & walking rtes; htd, excel site & san facs."* **€39.50, 1 Mar-31 Oct.** **2024**

SEEFELD IN TIROL *C1* (1.6km NW Rural) *47.33716, 11.17859* **Camperpark Seefled (formerly Alpin Camp),** Leutascherstrasse 810, A-6100 Seefeld in Tyrol **(0) 5212 - 20033; info@camperpark-seefeld.at; https://www.camperpark-seefeld.at/**

12 €3 nr

Fr N on B177/E533 turn W into Seefeld. Thro main rd, turn R sp Leutasch, site on L in 2km. Apps fr SE & SW via v steep hills/hairpins, prohibited to trailers. 3*, Med, hdstg, pt shd, pt sl, terr, EHU (16A) €2.80 or metered; gas; 10% statics; bus to town; Eng spkn; adv bkg acc; golf 1.5km; site clsd Nov; bike hire. *"Excel site; htd, covrd pool 1.5km; sauna & steambath inc; excel facs; friendly owners; vg walking; delightful setting; ski tows at gate; lovely vill; free bus to town/funicular; New san facs Aug 23."* **€55.00** **2023**

SOLDEN *C1* (1km S Rural) *46.95786, 11.01193* **Camping Sölden,** Wohlfahrtstrasse 22, 6450 Sölden **(05254) 26270; info@camping-soelden.com; www.camping-soelden.com**

€3 nr nr

Turn L off main rd at cable car terminal. Turn R at rv & foll narr track on rv bank for about 200m, turn R into site. Med, mkd, pt shd, pt sl, terr, serviced pitches; EHU (10A) metered; gas; Eng spkn; adv bkg acc; ccard acc; site clsd mid-Apr to mid-Jun approx; gym; sauna; dog-washing facs. *"Excel for touring or climbing in upper Ötz Valley; pitches tight for lge o'fits; superb site; excel san facs."* **€47.00, 1 Jan-24 Apr, 11 Jun-30 Sep & 29 Oct-31 Dec.** **2022**

SPITTAL AN DER DRAU *D3* (5.6km NE Urban) *46.81510, 13.52001* **Strandcamping Winkler,** Seepromenade 33, 9871 Seeboden **4762 81927; info@camping-winkler.at; www.camping-winkler.at**

€4

Leave A10 Villach-Salzburg at junc 139 twd Seeboden. Cont along main st across 2 rndabts & turn R down narr rd sp Strandcamping Winkler. Sm, mkd, pt shd, pt sl, EHU (16A); sw nr; twin axles; Eng spkn; adv bkg acc; CCI. *"Cycling & walking rtes rnd beautiful Millstätter; gd site."* **€40.60, 13 May-30 Sept.** **2024**

SULZ IM WIENERWALD *B4* (1km N Rural) *48.10510, 16.13348* **Camping Wienerwald,** Leopoldigasse 2, 2392 Sulz-im-Wienerwald **(0)664 4609796; ww-camp@aon.at; www.camping-wienerwald.at**

€1.20 nr nr

Leave A21/E60 at junc 26 dir Sittendorf, Foll sp to site at Sulz (7km fr m'way). Sm, mkd, pt shd, pt sl, EHU (6A) €1.90 (poss long lead req); 10% statics. *"Conv Vienna - 25km; gd walks."* **€17.00, 15 Apr-15 Oct.** **2022**

TELFS *C1* (9km SW Rural) *47.27510, 10.98661* **Camping Eichenwald,** Schiess-Standweg 10, 6422 Stams **(05263) 6159; info@camping-eichenwald.at; www.tirol-camping.at**

12 €2.50 (htd) nr (htd)

Exit A12 at exit Stams-Mötz, foll B171 sp Stams. Turn R into vill, site behind monastery nr dry ski jump; steep app. 4*, Med, pt shd, terr, EHU (6A) €4/4kw then metered; gas; TV; Eng spkn; adv bkg acc; games rm; bike hire; tennis 500m; games area; CKE. *"Beautiful views; friendly owner; private bthrms some pitches; statics (sep area); vg site; gd rest; san facs v clean."* **€31.00** **2023**

VELDEN AM WORTHERSEE *D3* (8km E Rural) *46.61890, 14.10565* **Camping Weisses Rössl,** Auenstrasse 47, Schiefling-am-See, 9220 Velden-Auen **(04274) 2898; office@weisse-roessl-camping.at; www.weisses-roessl-camping.at**

€3 (htd)

Fr A2 exit 335 dir Velden. At rndabt bef town fol sp twd Maria Wörth for 9km on S side of Wörthersee. Site on R up hill. Lge, hdstg, pt shd, pt sl, terr, EHU (16A) inc; gas; bbq; sw nr; TV; phone; Eng spkn; CKE. *"Gd."* **€24.50, 1 May-30 Sep.** **2022**

VILLACH *D3* (7km NE Rural) *46.65641, 13.89196* **Camping Bad Ossiacher See,** Seeuferstrasse 109, 9520 Annenheim **(04248) 2757; office@camping-ossiachersee.at; www.camping-ossiachersee.at**

(htd)

Fr A10/E55/E66 exit sp Villach/Ossiacher See onto B94. Turn R for St Andrä sp Süd Ossiacher See. Site on L in 300m. Lge, pt shd, EHU (10-16A) inc; bbq; sw nr; twin axles; 5% statics; phone; Eng spkn; adv bkg acc; ccard acc; tennis; games area; sailing; waterskiing. *"Well-kept site; barrier clsd 1200-1400; handy NH even when wet; Annenheim cable car; lge level grass pitches; excel."* **€45.00, 7 Apr-26 Oct.** **2023**

VOLKERMARKT *D3* (10km S Rural) *46.58376, 14.62621* **Rutar Lido FKK See-Camping (Naturist),** Lido 1, 9141 Eberndorf **(04236) 22620; fkkurlaub@rutarlido.at; www.rutarlido.at**

12 (covrd, htd)

Take B82 S fr Völkermarkt to Eberndorf. At rndbt on vill by-pass turn R. Site sp on L. Camp ent in 700m down rd. Lge, pt shd, EHU (10A) inc; gas; sw nr; 30% statics; adv bkg acc; ccard acc; tennis adj; sauna; games area; CKE. *"Gd family site; v helpful staff; o'night m'vans area; ltd Eng spkn."* **€20.00** **2024**

WAIDHOFEN AN DER THAYA *A4* (1km SE Rural) *48.81113, 15.28839* **Campingplatz Thayapark,** Badgasse, 3830 Waidhofen-an-der Thaya **(02842) 50356 or 0664 5904433 (mob); stadtamt@waidhofen-thaya.gv.at; www.waidhofen-thaya.at/Campingplatz_Thayapark**

nr nr nr

Site sp fr town cent. Med, pt shd, EHU (10A) €2.30; TV (pitch); 5% statics; CKE. *"Quiet site nr attractive town; pool 300m; recep open 0800-1000 & 1600-1800."* **€26.80, 1 May-30 Sep.** **2022**

> **"I need an on-site restaurant"**
>
> We do our best to make sure site information is correct, but it is always best to check any must-have facilities are still available or will be open during your visit.

WIEN *B4* (9km E Urban) *48.20861, 16.44722* **Aktiv-Camping Neue Donau,** Am Kleehäufel, 1220 Wien-Ost **(1) 2024010; neuedonau@campingwien.at; www.campingwien.at**

€4.50 (htd)

Take A21-A23, exit sp Olhafen/Lobau. After x-ing Rv Danube turn R, sp Neue-Donau Sud. In 150m turn L at traff lts after Shell g'ge; site on R. Fr E on A4 turn R onto A23 & take 1st slip rd sp N-Donau after x-ing rv Danube. Lge, unshd, serviced pitches; EHU (16A) €4 (poss rev pol); bus/metro to city 1km; Eng spkn; adv bkg acc; ccard acc; tennis; games area; CKE. *"Conv Vienna; lovely site; excel facs but poss stretched high ssn; poss v cr due bus tours on site; cycle track to city cent (map fr recep); 3 classes of pitch (extra charge for serviced); recep clsd 1200-1430; standard san facs."* **€44.00, 18 Mar-31 Oct.** **2024**

WIEN *B4* (13km W Urban) *48.21396, 16.2505* **Camping Wien-West,** Hüttelbergstrasse 80, 1140 Wien **(01) 9142314; west@campingwien.at; www.campingwien.at**

€5

Fr Linz, after Auhof enter 3 lane 1-way rd. On app to traff lts get into L hand (fast) lane & turn L at traff lts. At next lts (Linzerstrasse) go strt over into Hüttelburgstrasse & site is uphill. Fr Vienna, foll sp A1 Linz on W a'bahn & site sp to R 100m bef double rlwy bdge. After this turn L on rd with tramlines & foll to v narr section, R at traff lts. Lge, mkd, hdstg, pt shd, EHU (16A) €5; 10% statics; bus; Eng spkn; adv bkg acc; ccard acc; CKE. *"Rec arr early; gd bus service to U-Bahn & city cent - tickets fr recep + Vienna Card; clean facs, but poss stretched high ssn & ltd LS; poss travellers; site poss unkempt LS; sm pitches; sep car park; site clsd Feb; well run; well position for Vienna."* **€34.00, 1 Jan-31 Jan & 16 Feb-31 Dec.** **2023**

AUSTRIA

WORGL *C2* (13km SE Rural) *47.43068, 12.14990* **Camping Reiterhof,** Kelchsauerstrasse 48, 6361 Hopfgarten **(05335) 3512; info@campingreiterhof.at; www.campingreiterhof.at**

12 €2.20 (htd) nr nr nr

Fr Wörgl S on B170, thro Hopfgarten, site sp on R dir Kelchsau. 4*, Med, mkd, pt shd, EHU (10A) €2.80; 45% statics; Eng spkn; adv bkg acc; CKE. *"V friendly, v welcoming, helpful staff; immac san facs; ski lift 2km; excel for families or couples; lge recreation park adj; htd pool 200m; excel walking & cycling area; free ski bus; excel."* **€18.00** **2022**

ZELL AM SEE *C2* (7km N Rural) *47.37740, 12.79583* **Campingplatz Bad Neunbrunnen,** Neunbrunnen 56, 5751 Maishofen **(06542) 68548 or (0664) 3512282 (mob); camping@neunbrunnen.at; www.camping-neunbrunnen.at**

12

Foll B311 N fr Zell-am-See dir Saalfelden; 500m after Maishofen turn L bef tunnel & foll site sp. Med, hdstg, mkd, unshd, EHU (10A) €2.20; sw; ccard acc; fishing; games rm. *"Vg, scenic site; cycle & walking tracks fr site; winter sports area; vg rest."* **€30.90** **2022**

"Satellite navigation makes touring much easier"

Remember most sat navs don't know if you're towing or in a larger vehicle – always use yours alongside maps and site directions.

ZELL AM SEE *C2* (6km SE Rural) *47.30133, 12.8150* **Panorama Camp Zell am See,** Seeuferstrasse 196, 5700 Zell am See **(0) 6542) 56228; info@panoramacamp.at; www.panoramacamp.at**

12 €3.80

S fr Zell on B311 sp Salzburg (using tunnel). At 3rd rndabt turn L dir Thumersbach, site on L in 1.5km, sp. Med, hdg, pt shd, serviced pitches; EHU (16A) metered + conn fee; red long stay; TV; 30% statics; bus; Eng spkn; adv bkg acc; CKE. *"Conv Salzburg & Krimml falls; clsd 1200-1330; cycle & footpaths round lake adj; helpful owners; excel facs; peaceful site; nicely laid out site with adequate pitches; owners take you to pitch and make elec conn; shop nr; rest nr; pizzas & rolls fr recep; lovely view of mountains; easy access."* **€43.90** **2024**

ZELL AM ZILLER *C2* (0.7km SE Rural) *47.22830, 11.88590* **Camping Hofer (Part Naturist),** Gerlosstrasse 33, 6280 Zell-am-Ziller **(05282) 2248; info@campingdorf.at; www.campingdorf.at**

12 €2.50 (htd) nr (htd)

Fr A12/E45/E60 exit junc 39 onto B169 dir Zell-am-Ziller. In vill, site on R, sp. 4*, Med, mkd, pt shd, EHU (10A) €3.50 or metered; gas; bbq; red long stay; phone; Eng spkn; adv bkg acc; games rm; bike hire; CKE. *"Excel site; clean, well-equipped facs; poss fly problem high ssn; friendly, welcoming family; some pitches tight for lge o'fits; gd walking & cycling; owner arranges guided walks; site discount for funicular."* **€43.00** **2024**

ZWETTL *A4* (12km E Rural) *48.58956, 15.31805* **Campingplatz Lichtenfels,** Friedersbach 69, 3533 Friedersbach **(02826) 7492 or 0664 5746866 (mob); camping@thurnforst.at; www.thurnforst.at**

£1

Fr E on B38 fr Zwettl on app Rastenfeld look for rv bdge & ruins of castle. Site sp on L. Med, pt shd, bbq; sw nr; 40% statics; games area. *"Pretty lake setting; open air concerts in ruins of castle high ssn; friendly owner; v clean facs."* **€30.00, 29 Apr-16 Oct.** **2022**

Landeck to Wien (Vienna) = 550km

	Bludenz	Braunau-am-Inn	Bregenz	Bruck an der Mur	Eisenstadt	Fürstenfeld	Gmünd	Gmunden	Graz	Innsbruck	Judenburg	Kitzbühel	Klagenfurt	Landeck	Leibnitz	Lienz	Liezen	Linz	Mariazell	Radstadt	Reutte	Salzburg	Schärding	Sillian	Spittal an der Drau	St. Pölten	Villach	Wien (Vienna)	Wörgl
Braunau-am-Inn	324																												
Bregenz	59	451																											
Bruck an der Mur	562	263	620																										
Eisenstadt	66	345	722	129																									
Fürstenfeld	658	388	715	123	126																								
Gmünd	552	213	611	246	190	369																							
Gmunden	399	80	455	187	280	311	164																						
Graz	590	322	646	56	174	68	299	243																					
Innsbruck	148	245	204	421	513	510	405	251	444																				
Judenburg	503	239	563	63	195	155	261	164	88	354																			
Kitzbühel	243	138	299	291	403	415	296	143	347	95	260																		
Klagenfurt	487	292	544	161	292	215	340	242	140	340	97	243																	
Landeck	70	323	128	498	596	588	482	330	522	79	432	173	415																
Leibnitz	627	359	686	94	200	357	340	282	39	469	126	386	130	547															
Lienz	337	233	395	301	421	227	391	235	290	190	224	94	149	266	280														
Liezen	464	168	521	97	229	308	187	90	126	315	70	190	150	392	198	229													
Linz	454	113	510	185	231	59	99	68	241	304	189	197	268	383	279	293	115												
Mariazell	585	263	643	63	135	186	184	199	118	438	126	329	223	517	155	363	119	149											
Radstadt	367	134	425	167	331	291	291	142	224	220	136	124	182	297	260	158	67	184	187										
Reutte	110	338	133	511	604	601	494	344	535	90	446	187	432	76	558	280	399	397	529	311									
Salzburg	338	64	395	230	331	353	221	68	285	190	198	82	252	269	322	176	126	123	255	75	281								
Schärding	442	47	501	270	309	379	177	74	309	295	237	186	305	372	355	279	151	79	231	183	384	110							
Sillian	368	264	425	331	452	388	422	269	320	222	254	124	181	297	311	32	260	322	394	189	310	208	311						
Spittal an der Drau	413	216	470	210	342	281	393	237	212	263	150	170	75	344	204	76	163	279	276	95	356	155	266	109					
St. Pölten	559	238	617	141	113	196	117	171	198	410	207	304	302	491	236	398	204	125	80	252	503	229	202	430	355				
Villach	449	255	506	189	320	253	368	269	178	303	124	205	38	381	168	113	201	297	253	131	392	191	302	142	36	331			
Wien (Vienna)	619	299	678	150	50	171	141	234	198	470	215	363	312	550	221	440	265	186	140	361	561	300	264	469	386	65	349		
Wörgl	127	180	273	325	437	449	330	177	381	66	394	34	277	144	420	128	224	131	363	158	158	110	220	158	204	338	239	397	
Zell am See	299	141	352	239	408	365	299	145	296	150	209	56	211	230	310	91	142	198	261	74	240	84	188	122	106	305	143	366	90

Motorways
Primary roads
Secondary roads
All year site(s)
Seasonal site(s)
No sites listed
GERMANY
CZECHIA (CZECH REPUBLIC)
SWITZERLAND
ITALY
SLOVENIA
HUNGARY
CROATIA
Regensburg
České Budějovice
Brno
Augsburg
Munchen
Rosenheim
Waidhofen an der Thaya
GMUND
Zwettl
Poysdorf
Engelhartszell
SCHÄRDING
Aschach an der Donau
BRAUNAU AM INN
Obernberg Am inn
LINZ
Grein
Melk
Klosterneuburg
WIEN
Marbach an der Donau
Sulz im Wienerwald
Attersee
Micheldorf in Oberösterreich
Scharnstein
SALZBURG
St Wolfgang im Salzkammergut
Lunz am See
Purbach am Neusiedlersee
Eisenstadt
MARIAZELL
WIENER NEUSTADT
Hallein
Abersee
Bad Aussee
Hallstatt
BREGENZ
GRAN
REUTTE
Kossen
Lofer
Mittenwald
Ehrwald
Rattenberg
Worgl
St Johann in Tirol
KITZBUHEL
St Johann im Pongau
Eben im Pongau
RADSTADT
Nassereith
Telfs
Seefeld
Jenbach
BLUDENZ
St Anton Am Arlberg
Imst
Pettnau
Hall in Tirol
INNSBRUCK
ZELL AM SEE
LANDECK
Prutz
Oetz
Neustift im Stubaital
Mayrhofen
Bruck an der Grossglocknerstrasse
Ried im Oberinntal
Nauders
Solden
Matrei in Osttirol
St Peter am Kammersberg
JUDENBURG
St Michael im Lungau
Murau
GRAZ
FURSTENFELD
Sarvar
LIENZ
SPITTAL AN DER DRAU
Gmund (Karnten)
Millstatt
Gnesau
St Veit an der Glan
Bad Gleichenberg
LEIBNITZ
Zalaegerszeg
Dellach im Drautal
Greifenburg
Dobriach
Ossiach
Kotschach
Villach
Velden am Worthersee
KLAGENFURT
St Primus
Maribor
Mals/ Malles Venosta
Bolzano
Cortina d'Ampezzo
Udine
Ljubljana
A1
A2
A3
A4
A5
A6
A7
A8
A9
A10
A12
A13
A14
A21
S6
S16
S31
S33
S36
N
E
S
W
0
25
50
75
100
125
150 km
20
40
60
80 miles

Belgium

Highlights

Although a country of two halves, with French-speaking Wallonia making up the southern part of the country, and Dutch-speaking Flanders the north, Belgium is very much united when it comes to delicious cuisine, fascinating historic attractions and breathtaking architecture.

With several UNESCO world heritage sites, a diverse landscape and a range of museums and art galleries, you will be spoilt for choice when deciding how best to spend your time in this delightful country.

Most people associate Belgium with chocolate, mussels and beer, but there are other products which share an equal amount of tradition. Lace making has been practiced in Belgium for centuries, Bruges still renowned for the intricate designs and delicacy of its product.

Belgium has also played an important role in the development of comics, and can boast Georges Remi (Hergé), the creator of Tintin, and Pierre Culliford (Peyo) the man behind the smurfs amongst its talented celebrities.

Major towns and cities

- Brussels - this historic city is Belgium's capital.
- Ghent - a city filled with beautiful buildings and important museums.
- Antwerp - Belgium's largest city is filled with stunning landmarks.
- Liège - famous for its folk festivals and for hosting a large annual Christmas Market.

Attractions

- Grand-Place, Brussels - this opulent central square is a UNESCO World Heritage site.
- Gravensteen Castle, Ghent - a magnificent 12th century castle that houses a museum.
- Historic Centre, Bruges - the medieval architecture of the city centre is a must-see.
- Ypres - an ancient town filled with historic monuments, including the Menin Gate.

Find out more

visitbelgium.com

Country Information

Capital: Brussels

Bordered by: France, Germany, Luxembourg, Netherlands

Terrain: Flat coastal plains in north-west; central rolling hills; rugged Ardennes hills and forest in south-east.

Climate: Mild winters with snow likely in the Ardennes. Cool summers, rain any time of the year; coast can be windy

Coastline: 66 km

Highest Point: Signal de Botrange 694m

Languages: Flemish, French, German

Local Time: GMT or BST + 1, i.e. 1 hour ahead of the UK all year

Currency: Euros divided into 100 cents; £1 = €1.20, €1 = £0.84 (Nov 2024)

Emergency numbers: Police 101/112, Fire Brigade 112, Ambulance 112.

Public Holidays 2025: Jan 1; Apr 21; May 1, 29; June 9; Jul 21; Aug 15; Oct 26 (National Day); Nov 1, 11; Dec 25.

Schools have Christmas, Easter and half terms breaks; summer holidays are July and August.

Entry Formalities

British and Irish passport holders may stay in Belgium for up to 90 days in any 180 day period without a visa. You may be asked to show a return or onward ticket at the border to confirm your length of stay, or to prove that you have enough money for your stay.

Your passport will need to have a minimum of 6 months' validity remaining, and be less than 10 years old (even if it has 6 months or more left).

Medical Services

The standard of health care is high. Emergency medical and hospital treatment is available at a reduced cost on production of a European Health Insurance Card (EHIC) or a UK Global Health Insurance Card (UK GHIC).

Check whether a doctor you wish to see is registered with the national health service (conventionné/geconventioneerd) or offers private healthcare.

You'll have to pay for services provided but 75% of the cost of treatment and approved medicines will be refunded if you apply to a local sickness fund office with your EHIC or GHIC.

At night and at weekends at least one local pharmacy will remain open and its address will be displayed in the window of all local pharmacies.

Opening Hours

Banks: Open hours vary from one bank to another, however usual open hours are Mon-Fri 9am-12pm & 2pm-4pm; Sat 9am-12pm (some banks).

Museums: Tue-Sun 10am-5pm; most museums close Monday.

Shops: Mon-Sat 10am-6pm or 8pm (supermarkets); some close 12pm-2pm; most shops closed Sunday.

Safety and Security

Belgium is relatively safe for visitors but you should take the usual precautions to avoid becoming a victim of muggers, bag-snatchers and pickpockets, especially at major railway stations and on the public transport in Antwerp and Brussels.

There have been reports of thefts from luggage racks on high-speed trains, usually just before the train doors close. Never leave luggage unattended.

Belgium shares with the rest of Europe an underlying threat from terrorism. Please check gov.uk/foreign-travel-advice/belgium before you travel.

British Embassy

Avenue d'Auderghem 10
1040 Brussels
Tel: +32 (0)2 2876211
gov.uk/world/belgium

Irish Embassy

Rue Froissart - Froissartstraat 50
1040 Bruselles
Tel: +32 (0)2 2823400
embassyofireland.be
There is also an Honorary Consulate in Antwerp.

Documents

Money

Major credit cards are widely accepted by shops, hotels, restaurants and petrol stations.

Carry your credit card issuer or bank's 24-hour UK contact numbers in case of loss or theft of your cards. If you have difficulty reporting the theft of your card(s) to your UK bank or credit card company, ask the Belgian group 'Card Stop' to send a fax to your UK company to block your card. Card Stop's telephone number is +32 (0)78 170 170.

Passport

Belgian law requires everyone to carry some form of identification, for example passport or photocard driving licence, at all times.

Vehicle(s)

You should carry your vehicle registration certificate (V5C), insurance details and MOT certificate (if applicable).

Driving

Accidents

The police must be called after an accident if an unoccupied stationary vehicle is damaged or if people are injured. If it isn't necessary to call the police to the scene of the accident you must still report it at the local police station within 24 hours.

Alcohol

The maximum permitted level of alcohol in the bloodstream is 0.05%. Penalties for exceeding this limit are severe including heavy fines, suspension of driving licence and a possible jail sentence.

Breakdown Service

The Touring Club Belgium (TCB) operates a breakdown service 24 hours a day throughout the country, tel: +32(2) 233 22 11 or you can dial 112 in an emergency. On motorways, use the roadside telephones called 'telestrade' which are controlled by the police and are situated approximately every 2 km. Ask for 'Touring Secours' or, when in the north of the country, 'Touring Wegenhulp'. It will be necessary to pay a fee which is variable depending on the time of day.

Child Restraint System

Children under 1.35m must be seated in a child seat or child restraint when travelling in the front or rear seat of a vehicle. If a child seat/ restraint is not available, i.e. when two child restraint systems are being used on rear seats and there isn't enough space for a third to be placed, a child must travel in the back of the vehicle using an adult seat belt. If the child is three years or under they must not travel in a vehicle without being seated in a child seat/ restraint.

The child restraint must correspond to the child's weight and be of an approved type. A rear facing child restraint must not be used on a front seat with a front air bag unless it's deactivated.

Fuel

Petrol stations on motorways and main roads are open 24 hours and credit cards are generally accepted. Others may close from 8pm to 8am and often all day Sunday.

LPG, also known as GPL, is widely available at many service stations.

Low Emission Zones

There are Low Emission Zones in force in Antwerp, Brussels, Ghent and the Wallonia Region. See urbanaccessregulations.eu for more information.

Motorways

Belgium has a network of approximately 1,750 km of motorways. Although Belgian motorways are toll free for most vehicles, there is a toll for vehicles over 3,500kg.

Service areas usually have a petrol station, restaurant, shop, showers and toilets. Rest areas have picnic facilities. For detailed information see: autosnelwegen.net.

Some motorways are so heavily used by lorries that the inside lane may become heavily rutted and/or potholed. These parallel ruts are potentially dangerous for caravans travelling at high speed. It's understood that parts of the A2/E314 and A3/E40 are particularly prone to this problem.

Parking

Blue zones indicating limited parking are used to denote where vehicles must display a parking disc on Monday to Saturday, from 9am to 6pm. Discs are available from police stations, petrol stations and some shops. Outside blue zones a parking disc must also be used where the parking sign has a panel showing the disc symbol. Parking areas are also regulated by parking meters and if these exist inside a blue zone parking discs must not be used, except if the parking meter or ticket machine is out of action. Illegally parked vehicles may be towed away or clamped.

Do not park in a street where there is a triangular sign 'Axe Rouge/Ax Rode'.

Priority

Take great care to obey the 'priority to the right' rule which is designed to slow traffic in built-up areas. Drivers must give priority to vehicles joining from the right, even if those vehicles have stopped at a road junction or stopped for pedestrians or cyclists, and even if you're on what appears to be a main road. Exemptions to this rule apply on motorways, roundabouts and roads signposted with an orange diamond on a white background.

Trams have priority over other traffic. If a tram or bus stops in the middle of the road to allow passengers on or off, you must stop.

A zip-merging rule is in place in Belgium. Where a lane is ending or closed, drivers in that lane must continue to where that lane starts to close up before merging into the open lane. Drivers in the lane which remains open must give way in turn to the drivers merging into their lane.

Roads

Roads are generally in good condition and well lit, however, some stretches of motorways have poor surfacing and signs to advise drivers to slow down. Traffic is fast and the accident rate is high, especially at weekends, mainly due to speeding.

Road Signs and Markings

Roads signs and markings conform to international standards. Destination road signs may be signposted either by its French or its Flemish name, according to the predominant language in that particular area.The most important of these towns are:

Flemish	French
Aalst	Alost
Aken (Aachen)	Aix-la-Chapelle (Germany)
Antwerpen	Anvers
Bergen	Mons
Brugge	Bruges
Brussel	Bruxelles
Doornik	Tournai
Gent	Gand
Geraardsbergen	Grammont
Ieper	Ypres
Kortrijk	Courtrai
Leuven	Louvain
Luik	Liège
Mechelen	Maline
Namen	Namur
Rijsel	Lille (France)
Roeselare	Roulers
Tienen	Tirlemont
Veurne	Furnes

Generally signposts leading to and on motorways show foreign destination place names in the language of the country concerned. e.g. German. Exceptions do occur, particularly on the E40 and E314 where city names may be given in Flemish or French.

Roads with the prefix N are regional roads; those with numbers 1 to 9 radiate from Brussels. Motorways have the prefix A and have blue and white signs. When route planning through Belgium follow the green European road numbers with the prefix E which may be the only road numbers displayed.

Road signs you may see include the following:

You may pass right or left

Cyclists have priority over turning traffic

Cyclists have priority at junction

Speed Limits

	Open Road (km/h)	Motorway (km/h)
Car Solo	90*	120
Car towing caravan/trailer	90*	120
Motorhome under 3500kg	90*	120
Motorhome 3500-7500kg	90*	90

**70 in Flanders*

The general speed limit in built-up areas is 50 km/h (31mph). Lower limits of 30 km/h (18 mph) or 20 km/h (12mph) may be imposed and indicated by signs in residential areas, town centres and near schools. Brussels city centre is a 30 km/h (18mph) speed limit zone. The start and finish points of these zones are not always clearly marked. Vehicles over 3,500 kg in weight are restricted to 90 km/h (56mph) outside built-up areas and on motorways.

Traffic Jams

During good weather roads to the coast, the Ardennes and around Brussels and Antwerp are very busy during the weekends.

Other busy routes are the E40 (Brussels to Ostend), the E25 (Liège to Bastogne and Arlon), the E411 (Brussels to Namur and Luxembourg), and the N4 from Bastogne to Arlon around the border town of Martelange caused by motorists queuing for cheap petrol in Luxembourg. Avoid traffic on the E40 by taking the R4 and N49, and on the E411 by taking the N4 Bastogne to Marche-en-Famenne and Namur. These routes are heavily used and consequently the road surface can be poor.

Traffic Lights

A green light (arrow) showing at the same time as a red or amber light means that you can turn in that direction providing you give way to other traffic and pedestrians. An amber light, possibly flashing, in the form of an arrow inclined at an angle of 45 degrees to the left or to the right, shows that the number of traffic lanes will be reduced.

Tunnels

Three road tunnels go under the River Scheldt at Antwerp. In the Liefkenshoektunnel on road R2 to the north of the city a toll of €16-22 (2023) for vehicles over or equal to 3m in height. Vehicles under 3m are charged €4.00-7.00. If you're towing your caravan will be included within this height categorisation. The Kennedy Tunnel on road R1 to the south of the city is toll-free but is heavily congested in both directions for much of the day. The smallest tunnel, the Waasland Tunnel is part of the N59a and is also toll-free.

Violation of Traffic Regulations

The police may impose on-the-spot fines on visitors who infringe traffic regulations such as speeding and parking offences. If you can't pay on the spot your vehicle(s) may be impounded or your driving licence withdrawn. Fines can be paid in cash or with a debit or credit card - make sure you get an official receipt.

In an effort to improve road safety the authorities have increased the number of speed traps throughout the country in the form of cameras and unmarked police vehicles.

Vehicles of 3,500 kg or over are not allowed to use the left lane on roads with more than three lanes except when approaching a fork in a motorway when vehicles have to move to the left or right lane

Essential Equipment

First aid kit

It's not compulsory for foreign registered vehicles to carry a first aid kit, but it's still recommended.

Warning Triangle

An EU approved warning triangle must be used if the vehicle breaks down, has a puncture or is involved in an accident.

Reflective Jacket/Waistcoat

If you have broken down or are in an accident where stopping or parking is prohibited, you must wear a reflective jacket or waistcoat when getting out of your vehicle, or face a €55.00 fine. Anyone leaving the vehicle should also wear one. Keep the jacket(s) to hand in your vehicle, not in the boot.

Touring

Flemish is spoken in the north of Belgium, whilst French is spoken in the south. Brussels is bi-lingual. English is widely spoken.

Prices in restaurants are quoted 'all inclusive' and no additional tipping is necessary. Smoking is severely restricted in public places including restaurants and cafés.

Carrier bags are generally not provided in supermarkets, so take your own.

When visiting Brussels visitors may buy a Brussels Card, valid for 24, 48 or 72 hours, which offers free access to virtually every major museum in the city and unlimited use of public transport, together with discounts at a number of other attractions. The pass is available from the tourist information office in the Hotel de Ville and from many hotels, museums and public transport stations, or visit brusselscard.be to buy online.

Camping and Caravanning

There are more than 900 campsites in Belgium, most of which are near the coast or in the Ardennes. Coastal sites tend to consist largely of mobile homes/statics and can be very crowded in peak season season.
A local tourist tax is usually included in the rates charged.

Twin-axle caravans are not permitted on municipal sites in and around Antwerp. Caravans and vehicles longer than 6 metres are prohibited from Liège city centre.

Casual/wild camping is prohibited in Flanders. Elsewhere permission must first be sought from the landowner or police. Camping is not permitted alongside public highways for more than a 24-hour period, nor is it permitted in lay-bys, in state forests or along the seashore, or within a 100 metre radius of a main water point, or on a site classified for the conservation of monuments.

Cycling

Belgium is well equipped for cyclists, with an extensive network of signposted cycling routes. Cycle lanes are marked on the carriageway by means of a broken double white line or by circular signs depicting a white bicycle on a blue or black background.

Bikes may be carried at the rear of a vehicle as long as its width doesn't extend beyond the width of the vehicle or more than one metre from the rear, and providing the rear lights and number plate remain visible.

Electricity and Gas

The current on most campsites varies from 4-16 amps although on some it's as low as 2 amps. Plugs have two round pins. CEE connections are not yet available at all sites.

Use a mains tester to test a connection before hooking up as problems are more common in Belgium than other EU countries. Issues may include reversed polarity, no earth and/or incorrectly alternating current.

Campingaz cylinders are available.

Public Transport

Anyone under the age of 25 is entitled to free or reduced prices on public transport in Brussels. During periods of severe air pollution public transport in that region is free to all.

Brussels and Antwerp have metro systems and extensive networks of trams and buses. Tram and bus stops are identified by a red and white sign and all stops are request stops; hold out your arm to stop a bus or tram. Tickets, including 10-journeys and one-day travel cards, are available from vending machines at metro stations and some bus stops, newsagents, supermarkets and tourist information centres.

The MOBIB Smartcard, similar to an Oyster card, can be purchased and topped up at metro station kiosks, supermarkets and newsagents, and is valid for all STIB public transport in Brussels (including trams, buses and metros).

Belgium has a good train network and most main routes pass through Antwerp, Brussels or Namur. Trains are modern, comfortable and punctual and fares are reasonable. Buy tickets before boarding the train or you may be charged a supplement.

Grand Place, Brussels

Shutterstock/Zoltan Duray

Sites in Belgium

AISCHE EN REFAIL *B3* (0.4km E Rural) *50.59977, 4.84335* **Camping du Manoir de Là-Bas,** Route de Gembloux 180, 5310 Aische-en-Refail **(081) 655353; europa-camping.sa@skynet.be; www.camping-manoirdelabas.be**

€3 (htd) nr (htd)

Fr E411/A4 exit junc 12 & foll sps to Aische-en-Refail. Site on o'skts of vill. 2*, Lge, pt shd, pt sl, EHU (6A) €3; gas; bbq; 50% statics; phone; Eng spkn; adv bkg acc; fishing; tennis; games rm; CKE. *"Friendly staff; site little run down; ltd hot water; poor san facs, dated & long way fr pitches; some site rds are narr; recep far side of chateau; gd rest & bar (clsd in Sep); site needs updating (2014); poor; NH only; sm pitches; rec NH only."* **€22.00, 1 Apr-31 Oct.** **2023**

ANTWERPEN *A3* (6km NW Urban) *51.23347, 4.39261* **Camping De Molen,** Thonelaan - Jachthavenweg 6, St Annastrand, 2050 Antwerpen **(03) 2198179; info@camping-de-molen.be; www.camping-de-molen.be**

12 nr nr

Clockwise on ring rd, take 1st exit after Kennedy tunnel, exit 6. R at traff lts, 3rd L where cannot go strt on (rv on R), site on R in 1km on bank of Rv Schelde. Or on ent Antwerp foll sp Linkeroever, go strt on at 3 traff lts, then turn L & foll camping sp. Fr A14/E17 exit junc 7 & foll sp for Linkeroever Park & Ride until site sp appear, then foll sp. 2*, Med, pt shd, EHU (10A) €2.50 (poss rev pol) - €30 deposit for adaptor/cable; bus nrby; Eng spkn; adv bkg rec. *"Popular site; max 14 nt stay; pedestrian/cycle tunnel to city cent 1km; metro 1km; gd for rollerblading, cycling; friendly, helpful staff; mosquitoes poss a problem; san facs satisfactory; 30 min walk or bus to city cent; site tired."* **€28.00** **2022**

ARLON *D3* (2km N Urban) *49.70215, 5.80678* **Camping Officiel Arlon,** 373 Rue de Bastogne, Bonnert, 6700 Arlon **(063) 226582; (032) 47176 3144; campingofficiel@skynet.be; www.campingofficielarlon.be**

€2 nr

Fr E411 exit junc 31 onto N82 Arlon for 4km, turn twd Bastogne on N4. Site sp on R. 2*, Med, pt shd, pt sl, EHU (6-10A) €2.50 (check earth); gas; bbq; red long stay; TV; Eng spkn; adv bkg acc; CKE. *"Charming, clean, well laid out, pretty site; c'vans tight-packed when site busy; 5km approx to Luxembourg for cheap petrol; Arlon interesting town; vg NH & longer stay; thoroughly rec for stop over; cash only; 5 sl hdstgs for m'van; levelling blocks/ramps req - supplied by site; pool; san facs updated, v clean; busy but organised; gd vet 0.5m."* **€27.80, 1 Mar-31 Oct.** **2022**

ARLON *D3* (7.6km N Rural) *49.74833, 5.78697* **Camping Sud,** 75 Voie de la Liberté, 6717 Attert **(063) 223715; info@campingsudattert.com; www.campingsudattert.com**

€2 (htd)

Off N4 Arlon rd on E side of dual c'way. Sp to site fr N4 (500m). U-turn into site ent. 4*, Med, hdg, mkd, hdstg, pt shd, EHU (5-10A) €2.50 (check earth); bbq; red long stay; phone; bus; Eng spkn; adv bkg acc; CKE. *"Vg, well-organised site; special NH pitches; fishing & walking; peaceful site; v friendly staff; highly rec."* **€20.50, 1 Apr-15 Oct.** **2024**

AYWAILLE *C3* (1km E Urban) *50.47633, 5.68916* **Domaine Chateau de Dieupart,** Route de Dieupart 37, 4920 Aywaille **(043) 844430; info@dieupart.be; www.dieupart.be**

12

Leave E25 at exit 46 Remouchamps/Aywaille. Turn R at traff lts dir Aywaille, and R by church. Immed L and Rt at Delhaise car park, take ave up to the castle. Site SP. Med, EHU (6A) inc; bbq; 50% statics; bus 500m; Eng spkn; adv bkg acc; CKE. *"Nice site by rv; gd walking and cycling; supmkt 300m."* **€31.50** **2024**

BASTOGNE *C3* (1.6km WNW Urban) *50.00340, 5.69525* **Camping de Renval,** 148 Route de Marche, 6600 Bastogne **(061) 212985; www.campingderenval.be**

€2 (htd) nr

Fr N leave A26 exit 54, foll Bastogne sp. Fr Marche-en-Famenne dir, exit N4 at N84 for Bastogne; site on L in 150m opp petrol stn. Fr E foll Marche, in 1km site on R opp petrol stn. 3*, Med, hdstg, pt shd, pt sl, terr, EHU (10A) inc (poss rev pol); bbq; 95% statics; ccard acc; site clsd Jan; games area; tennis. *"Take care speed bumps; helpful staff; clean san facs but long walk fr tourers' pitches; gd security; facs ltd LS; gd NH."* **€26.00, 1 Mar-1 Dec.** **2024**

BERTRIX *D3* (2km S Rural) *49.83942, 5.25360* **Ardennen Camping Bertrix,** Route de Mortehan, 6880 Bertrix **(061) 412281; info@campingbertrix.be; www.campingbertrix.be**

€5 (htd) (htd)

Exit A4/E411 junc 25 onto N89 for Bertrix & foll yellow sps to site. 4*, Lge, mkd, pt shd, terr, serviced pitches; EHU (10A) €4; gas; TV; 35% statics; Eng spkn; adv bkg acc; ccard acc; bike hire; tennis; sauna; CKE. *"Excel site; scenic location; friendly, helpful owners; gd for families; excel clean facs; gd rest; lg pitches; big pool."* **€40.00, 22 Mar-4 Nov.** **2024**

BRUGGE *A2* (5km E Urban) *51.20722, 3.26305* **Camping Memling,** Veltemweg 109, 8310 Sint Kruis **(050) 355845; info@campingmemling.be; camping-memling.be**

12 €2 (htd) nr nr nr

Exit A10 junc 8 Brugge. In 2km turn R onto N397 dir St Michiels & cont 2km to rlwy stn on R. Turn R under rlwy tunnel & at 1st rndbt take dir Maldegem onto ring rd & in a few kms take N9 sp Maldegem & St Kruis. After 3km at traff lts adj MacDonalds, turn R & immed L sp Camping to site on R in 400m past sw pool. Fr Gent exit E40 sp Oostkamp & foll Brugge sp for 7km to N9 as above. 2*, Med, mkd, hdstg, hdg, pt shd, EHU (6A) inc (poss rev pol); red long stay; 13% statics; bus 200m; Eng spkn; adv bkg acc; ccard acc; bike hire; CKE. *"Busy site; friendly, helpful owners; recep open 0800-2200 (all day to 2200 high ssn); arr early high ssn to ensure pitch; conv Zeebrugge ferry (30mins) & allowed to stay to 1500; conv bus svrs every 20 mins to Bruges; htd pool adj; adv bkgs taken but no pitch reserved; m'van pitches sm, rec pay extra for standard pitch; cycle rte or 35 min walk to Bruges; nice site; rec; facs OAY; pitches nr ent barrier get most sun; vg; automated check-in sys with credit card payment only; immac new san facs (2019)."* **€36.00** **2024**

BRUGGE *A2* (4km S Urban) *51.19634, 3.22573* **Campground Bargeweg,** Off ring rd R30, Buiten Katelijnevest, Brugge **https://www.interparking.be/en/find-parking/Kampeerautoterreinen-1---2/**

12 nr

Exit A10 at junc 7 twd Brugge. After going under rlwy bdge, turn R on ring rd immed after marina to dedicated mv parking adj coach parking, nr marina. Sm, hdstg, pt shd, EHU (10A) inc. *"M'vans only; in great location - gd view of canal, sh walk to town cent thro park; rec arr early high ssn; washrm nr; if full, take ticket & park in coach park opp; NH only; vg for city ctr; narr spaces; traff noise; bef leaving pay at machine & leave thro coach pk; gd."* **€30.00** **2023**

BRUGGE *A2* (13km SW Urban) *51.18448, 3.10445* **Recreatiepark Klein Strand,** Varsenareweg 29, 8490 Jabbeke **(050) 811440; info@kleinstrand.be; www.kleinstrand.be**

12 €2

Fr W leave A10/E40 at Jabbeke exit, junc 6; turn R at rndabt & in 100m turn R into narr rd. Foll site to statics car pk on L & park - walk to check-in at recep bef proceeding to tourer site in 400m. Fr E leave A10/E40 at junc 6 (Jabbeke) turn L at 1st rndabt. Drive over m'way twd vill. Turn L at next rndabt & foll site sp into site car pk as above. Out of ssn carry on along rd to recep by lake. 4*, V lge, hdg, mkd, pt shd, EHU (10A) inc; gas; bbq; sw nr; TV; 75% statics; bus to Brugge; Eng spkn; ccard acc; bike hire; fishing; tennis; watersports; games rm; CKE. *"Busy site; vg touring base; lge pitches; no o'fits over 12m; wide range of entmnt & excursions; direct access to lake adj; bus every 20 mins; v welcoming; ACSI acc; poor hygiene; site dirty; top up card needed for shwrs & sink area."* **€40.00, H15.** **2024**

BRUXELLES *B2* (13km N Rural) *50.93548, 4.38226* **Camping Grimbergen,** Veldkantstraat 64, 1850 Grimbergen **(0479) 760378 or (02) 2709597; camping-grimbergen@webs.com; www.campinggrimbergen.be**

€1 nr nr

Fr Ostend on E40/A10 at ringrd turn E & foll sp Leuven/Luik (Liège)/Aachen. Exit junc 7 N sp Antwerpen/Grimbergen N202. At bus stn traff lts turn R twd Vilvourde N211. Turn L at 2nd traff lts (ignore no L turn - lorries only). Site sp 500m on R. Ent via pool car pk. Med, hdg, pt shd, pt sl, EHU (10A) €4; phone; bus to city (hourly) 200m; Eng spkn; adv bkg acc; bike hire; CKE. *"Well-run, popular site - rec arr early; gd, clean, modern san facs; helpful staff; sh walk to town; train to Brussels fr next vill; red facs LS; gates clsd 1130-1400 and 2000 onwards; gd rest by bus stop; conv Brussels; excel san facs; rec; pool adj; gd NH."* **€26.00, 29 Mar-28 Sep.** **2024**

BRUXELLES *B2* (13km E Urban) *50.85720, 4.48506* **RCCC de Belgique,** Warandeberg 52, 1970 Wezembeek **(02) 78 210 09**

€1 nr nr

Leave ringrd RO at junc 2 sp Kraainem turning E. In 140m 1st intersection on dual c'way (by pedestrian x-ing) turn L into Wezembeek. Foll orange camping sp taking rd to the R around church. Foll rd to crest of hill. Site on L bet houses. Narr ent, easy to miss. 2*, Med, mkd, hdstg, pt shd, pt sl, terr, EHU (6A) inc (poss rev pol & no earth); 65% statics; Eng spkn; adv bkg acc; ccard acc; CKE. *"Poss diff for lge o'fits due narr site ent, v tight corners, metro nr; gates clsd 1200-1400 & 2200-0800; raised kerbs; gd for metro into Brussels fr Kraainem; welcoming wardens; no Eng spkn; unkept; still open 2023 but diff to contact."* **€22.50, 1 Apr-30 Sep.** **2023**

DE HAAN *A1* (2.6km ENE Coastal) *51.28330, 3.05610* **Camping Ter Duinen,** Wenduinesteenweg 143, Vlissegem, 8421 De Haan **(050) 413593; info@campingterduinen.be; www.campingterduinen.be**

€5.75 (htd)

shgl 500m

Exit A10/E40 junc 6 Jabbeke onto N377 dir De Haan. Go thro town dir Wenduine, site on R in 4km. Med, mkd, pt shd, EHU (6A) inc; bbq; sw nr; 85% statics; phone; tram nrby; Eng spkn; adv bkg req; horseriding 1km; fishing 200m; golf 4km; CKE. *"Neat, clean, well-managed site; friendly staff; poss long walk to excel san facs inc novelty wcs!; water complex 1km; htd pool 200m; conv ferries, Bruges; bike hire 200m; excel; hot dish water req tokens, mkt in nrby towns."* **€40.00, 15 Mar-30 Sept.** **2024**

BELGIUM

DE HAAN *A1* (5km SW Urban/Coastal) *51.25698, 2.99150* **Camping 't Rietveld,** Driftweg 210, 8420 De Haan **(0475) 669336; info@camping rietveld.be; www.campingrietveld.be**

€1.85 (htd) sand 1km

Fr Ostend on N34; fork R onto Driftweg bef golf club dir Vosseslag & Klemskerke, site sp. 3*, Sm, mkd, unshd, EHU (16A) €1.95; 80% statics; Eng spkn; CKE. *"Friendly, helpful staff; shop, rest, snacks, bar in town; clean san facs."* **€20.50, 1 Apr-15 Oct.** **2024**

DE PANNE *A1* (3km S Rural) *51.08288, 2.59094* **Camping Ter Hoeve,** Duinhoekstraat 101, 8660 De Panne **(058) 412376; info@campingterhoeve.be; www.camping-terhoeve.be**

12 €1.50 2km

Leave Calais-Ostend m'way at junc 1 (ignore junc 1a) dir De Panne. Foll rd past theme park (Plopsaland), L at filling stn, site 1km on L. 3*, Lge, hdg, pt shd, EHU (4A) inc (poss no earth); 60% statics; tram 1km; Eng spkn; adv bkg rec; ccard acc. *"Nice pitches; lge grassed area for tourers & hdstg area for late arr/early dep; barrier clsd 2200-0800 - go to visitors' car park on R bef booking in; v busy site high ssn, phone to check opening times LS; conv Dunkerque ferries & Plopsaland park; some daytime noise fr nrby theme park; tram tickets avail at filling stn; coin operated dishwash water; san facs basic; Oct-Mar by appointment only; under new management (2018); elec may lack earth; supermkt close."* **€32.50** **2024**

DE PANNE *A1* (4km S Rural) *51.07666, 2.58663* **Familie Camping Kindervreugde,** Langgeleedstraat 1, 8660 Adinkerke **(046) 8040895; info@ kindervreugde.be; www.kindervreugde.be/nl/home**

(htd) nr nr nr

Leave Calais-Ostend m'way at junc 1 (ignore junc 1a) dir De Panne. Foll rd past theme park (Plopsaland), L at filling stn, site 1.3km on L. 2*, Med, hdg, pt shd, EHU (6A) €2.50; bbq; 50% statics; phone; bus 800m; Eng spkn; adv bkg acc; CKE. *"Conv Dunkerque/Calais ferries; final appraoch diff for o'fits over 12ft."* **€35.00, 30 Mar-30 Sep.** **2024**

DINANT *C3* (14km NE Rural) *50.33557, 4.99534* **Camping de Durnal - Le Pommier Rustique,** Rue de Spontin, 5530 Durnal **(083) 699963 or (0475) 407827 (mob); info@camping-durnal.net; www.camping-durnal.net**

Leave E411 at junc 19. Turn S dir Spontin onto D946, then N937, foll site sp. 3*, Sm, mkd, unshd, terr, EHU (10A) inc (check rev pol); TV (pitch); 80% statics; Eng spkn; ccard acc; sauna; games area. *"Friendly, helpful owner; well-run, well-maintained site; ltd touring pitches; sm pitches; conv NH fr m'way; 4 nights for price of 3; v quiet LS; modern san facs."* **€32.00, 1 Mar-30 Dec.** **2024**

DOCHAMPS *C3* (0.7km ESE Rural) *50.23080, 5.63180* **Panorama Campsite Petite Suisse,** Al Bounire 27, 6960 Dochamps **(084) 444030; info@petitesuisse.be; www.petitesuisse.be**

12 €5 (htd) (htd)

Fr E25, take N89 (La Roche) at Samrée turn R onto N841 headed twrds Dochamp. Turn R into rd sp Al Bounire and foll sp to site. 4*, Lge, hdstg, mkd, pt shd, pt sl, terr, EHU (10A) inc; gas; bbq; TV; 50% statics; phone; adv bkg acc; ccard acc; games area; waterslide; games rm; tennis; CKE. *"Outstanding facs; beautiful spot; busy, popular, excel site."* **€66.00** **2023**

EEKLO *A2* (7km E Rural) *51.18093, 3.64180* **Camping Malpertuus,** Tragelstraat 12, 9971 Lembeke **(0) 468 18 41 96; info@campingmalpertuus.be; campingmalpertuus.be**

12 (htd) nr nr

Exit A10/E40 junc 11 onto N44 dir Aalter & Maldegem. Foll sp Eekloo onto N49 & then foll sp Lembeke, site sp. Med, pt shd, EHU (4A) inc; gas; 85% statics; phone; bus 300m; Eng spkn; adv bkg acc; CKE. *"Gd site in lovely area; friendly staff; entmnt/ events at w/end; gd size pitches; gd site; unisex facs."* **€23.00** **2023**

EUPEN *B4* (3km SW Rural) *50.61457, 6.01686* **Camping Hertogenwald,** Oestraat 78, 4700 Eupen **(087) 743222; info@camping-hertogenwald.be; www.camping-hertogenwald.be**

12 €1.60 (htd) nr

Fr German border customs on E40 a'bahn for Liège, take 2nd exit for Eupen. In Eupen L at 3rd traff lts & 1st R in 100m. Drive thro Eupen cent, foll sp to Spa. Camping sp immed at bottom of hill, sharp hairpin R turn onto N629, site on L in 2km. 3*, Med, unshd, EHU (6A) inc (long lead req & poss no earth); 90% statics; phone; Eng spkn; games area. *"Sm tourer area; clean site adj rv & forest; htd covrd pool 3km; muddy after rain; gd walking & cycling beside rv; conv Aachen."* **€19.00** **2022**

FLORENVILLE *D3* (17km E Rural) *49.68499, 5.52058* **Camping Chênefleur,** Norulle 16, 6730 Tintigny **(063) 444078; info@chenefleur.be; www.chenefleur.be**

€4 (htd) (htd)

Fr Liège foll E25 dir Luxembourg. Exit junc 29 sp Habay-la-Neuve to Etalle, then N83 to Florenville. Site sp off N83 at E end of Tintigny vill. 4*, Med, pt shd, EHU (6-8A) inc; gas; Eng spkn; adv bkg acc; ccard acc; games area; bike hire. *"Orval Abbey, Maginot Line worth visit; friendly staff; gd, clean site & modern san facs; well kept site."* **€32.00, 1 Apr-30 Sep.** **2020**

GEDINNE *C3* (1km SW Rural) *49.97503, 4.92719* **Camping La Croix Scaille,** Rue du Petit Rot 10, 5575 Gedinne **(061) 588517; contact@camping croixscaille.be; campingcroixscaille.be**

(htd)

Fr N95 turn W to Gedinne on N935. Site sp S of vill on R after 1km. 2*, Lge, mkd, hdstg, pt shd, terr, EHU (16A) €1.60; gas; TV; 75% statics; ccard acc; bike hire; fishing adj; tennis adj; CKE. **€13.40, 1 Apr-15 Nov.** 2024

"There aren't many sites open at this time of year"

If you're travelling outside peak season remember to call ahead to check site opening dates – even if the entry says 'open all year'.

GEEL *A3* (8km N Rural) *51.22951, 4.97836* **Camping Houtum,** Houtum 51, 2460 Kasterlee **(014) 859216; info@campinghoutum.be; www.campinghoutum.be**

12 (htd) nr

On N19 Geel to Turnhout rd 1km bef Kasterlee site sp on R at windmill opp British WW2 cemetery. Foll sps to site 500m on rd parallel to N19, cross next rd, site in 300m. Lge, mkd, pt shd, EHU (4-6A) €2; red long stay; 60% statics; phone; adv bkg acc, ccard acc; rv fishing adj; bike hire; tennis 300m; boating adj; canoeing adj; CKE. *"Orderly, attractive site; mini golf 300m; nature trails adj; lots for children all ages."* **€33.10** 2024

GHENT *A2* (14km SW Rural) *51.00508, 3.57228* **Camping Groeneveld,** Groenevelddreef 14, Bachte-Maria-Leerne, 9800 Deinze **(09) 3801014; info@ campinggroeneveld.be; www.campinggroeneveld.be**

€2 (htd) nr

E or W E40/E10 on Brussels to Ostend m'way exit junc 13 at sp Gent W/Drongen. Take N466 sp Dienze. Approx 1km beyond junc with N437, turn L just after 2nd 70 km/h sp down narr side rd - house on corner has advert hoarding. Site on L opp flour mill. Sm sp at turning. Med, hdg, pt shd, EHU (10A) inc (poss no earth); red long stay; TV; 40% statics; phone; Eng spkn; adv bkg acc; fishing; CKE. *"Gd welcome; additional san facs at lower end of site; office open 1900-2000 LS but staff in van adj san facs, or site yourself; barrier (€25 deposit for card) clsd until 0800; do not arr bef 1400; 1km fr Ooidonk 16th Castle; OK NH; gd site; bus to vill; some pitches tight; cash only."* **€24.00, 1 Apr-4 Oct.** 2023

GHENT *A2* (4km W Urban) *51.04638, 3.68083* **Camping Blaarmeersen,** Zuiderlaan 12, 9000 Gent **(09) 2668160; blaarmeersen.camping@farys.be; www.blaarmeersen.be / boeken.urban-gardens.be**

€1.25 (htd)

Exit A10/E40 Brussels-Ostend m'way at junc 13 sp Gent W & Drongen. At T-junc turn onto N466 twd Gent. In 4km cross canal then turn R to site, sp (3 rings) Sport & Recreatiecentrum Blaarmeersen. Fr Gent cent foll N34 twd Tielt for 1km past city boundary & turn L to site; adj lake & De Ossemeersen nature reserve. NB Due to rd layout, rec foll camping sp on app to site rather than sat nav. 4*, Lge, hdg, mkd, pt shd, serviced pitches; EHU (10A) metered + conn fee €1.25 (poss rev pol); sw nr; 5% statics; phone; bus to Gent; Eng spkn; ccard acc; tennis; watersports. *"Clean, well-organised, busy site; beautiful lake with path around; helpful staff; rest gd value; full sports facs adj; passport req; gd cycle track fr site; cycle into cent avoiding main rd; gd location for walks & activities; no dep bef 0815 hrs; poss travellers LS; pitches muddy when wet; pool adj; some m'van pitches sm & v shd; excel; best free info pack."* **€35.00, 1 Mar-8 Nov.** 2024

GODARVILLE *B2* (12km E Rural) *50.50501, 4.39928* **Camping Trieu du Bois,** Rue Picolome, 63 6238 Luttre (Pont-a-Celles) (Hainaut) Belgique **(071) 845937 or (0477) 200343; trieudubois@hotmail.com**

12

Fr J21 Luttre, foll sp twrds Luttre. After 1km at T-junc turn L. Site on R after 1km. Sm, hdg, pt shd, EHU (6A) €2; bbq; twin axles; 20% statics; Eng spkn; adv bkg acc. *"Conv for Waterloo & Brussels; adj canal path dir fr site; fair."* **€15.00** 2023

"That's changed – Should I let the Club know?"

If you find something on site that's different from the site entry, fill in a report and let us know. See camc.com/europereport.

HAN SUR LESSE *C3* (0.3km S Rural) *50.12330, 5.18587* **Camping Han-sur-Lesse (formerly de la Lesse),** Rue du Grand Hy, 5580 Han-sur-Lesse **(084) 377596; han. tourisme@skynet.be; www.campingshansurlesse.be**

(htd) nr nr

Site 500m off Han-sur-Lesse main sq adj Office de Tourisme. If app fr Ave-et-Auffe, turn R at Office du Tourisme, take care over rlwy x-ing to site on R in 150m. 3*, Med, mkd, pt shd, EHU (3-6A) inc; gas; 50% statics; phone; adv bkg req; canoeing adj; CKE. *"Gd touring base; undergrnd grotto trip; rv adj; take care on narr rds to site - v high kerbs; excel; san facs immac; pleasant LS."* **€29.00, 1 Apr-15 Nov.** 2024

BELGIUM

BELGIUM

HAN SUR LESSE *C3* (5km SW Rural) *50.11178, 5.13308* **Camping Le Roptai,** Rue Roptai 34, 5580 Ave-et-Auffe **(084) 388319; info@leroptai.be; www.leroptai.be**

12 €1.50 (htd)

Fr A4 exit 23 & take N94 dir Dinant. At bottom of hill turn R onto N86. Turn L in vill of Ave, foll sp, 200m to L. Med, mkd, hdstg, pt shd, pt sl, terr, EHU (6A) €1.80; gas; TV; 80% statics; Eng spkn; adv bkg acc; site clsd Jan; CKE. *"Some pitches awkwardly sl; generally run down & poor facs; ltd facs LS; NH only."* **€23.50** **2024**

HAN SUR LESSE *C3* (0.2km NW Urban) *50.12632, 5.18478* **Camping Le Pirot,** Rue Joseph Lamotte 3, 5580 Han-sur-Lesse **(084) 377596; campingpirot@gmail.com; www.campingshansurlesse.be/FR/pirotfr.html**

nr nr nr

Exit A4/E411 junc 23 sp Ave-et-Auffe & Rochefort. Go over 1st bdge then L immed bef 2nd bdge in Han cent; sh, steep incline. 1*, Sm, unshd, EHU (10A) inc (poss rev pol); bus adj; adv bkg acc; ccard acc; CKE. *"Excel position on raised bank of rv; adj attractions & rests; interesting town; helpful staff; basic, dated san facs; conv NH or sh stay in attractive town."* **€19.20, 1 Apr-30 Oct.** **2022**

HOUTHALEN *B3* (4km E Rural) *51.03222, 5.41613* **Camping De Binnenvaart,** Binnenvaartstraat, 3530 Houthalen-Helchteren **(011) 526720; debinnenvaart@limburgcampings.be; www.limburgcampings.be**

12 (htd)

Exit A2/E314 junc 30 N. In 2km at x-rds turn L, in 2km at rndabt turn R into Binnenvaartstraat, then foll site sp. 2*, Lge, mkd, pt shd, EHU (16A) inc; sw nr; TV; 40% statics; Eng spkn; adv bkg acc. *"Press button at ent for access; friendly welcome; lge serviced pitches; excel NH or longer."* **€40.00** **2023**

KNOKKE HEIST *A2* (1.6km S Urban) *51.33530, 3.28959* **Holiday Village Knokke,** Natiënlaan 70-72, 8300 Knokke-Heist **(050) 601203; info@holidayknokke.be; www.holidayknokke.be/**

1st free, 2nd for 2 euros nr nr 1.5km

On N49/E34 opp Knokke-Heist town boundary sp. Site ent at side of Texaco g'ge. 2*, Med, unshd, EHU (6A) €1.90 (poss rev pol); 60% statics; phone; adv bkg acc; bike hire. *"V clean, tidy site but ltd san facs and waste disp pnts; may need to manhandle c'van onto pitch."* **€27.00, Easter-30 Sep.** **2020**

KOKSIJDE *A1* (2km W Rural) *51.10287, 2.63066* **Camping Noordduinen,** Noordduinen 12, 8670 Koksijde aan Zee **(71)402 5295; noordduinen@molecaten.nl; www.molecaten.nl/noordduinen**

12 €2.50 nr sand 3km

Exit A18/E40 junc 1A onto N8. Foll sp Koksijde to rndabt, strt over into Leopold III Laan, site on L. Do not use SatNav. Sm, hdg, hdstg, pt shd, EHU €2.50; 80% statics; bus 500m; Eng spkn; adv bkg acc; CKE. *"Gd site; adj cycle rte to Veurne - attractive, historic town; san facs now closer to pitches."* **€41.00** **2023**

LONDERZEEL *B2* (3.6km NNE Rural) *51.02041, 4.31936* **Camping Diepvennen,** Molenhoek 35, 1840 Londerzeel **(052) 309492; info@kampeerwoning parkdiepvennen.be; www.camping-diepvennen.be**

12

On A12 exit at Londerzeel, foll sp Industrie Zone & Diepvennen. Foll Diepvennen sp to site. Site on W side of A12. Lge, pt shd, EHU €3; red long stay; 95% statics; games area; tennis. *"Long walk to san facs block; fishing pond; easy access by train to Antwerp & Brussels."* **€18.00** **2024**

NIEUWPOORT *A1* (1.5km NE Rural) *51.13324, 2.76031* **Parking De Zwerver,** Brugsesteenweg 16, 8620 Nieuwpoort **(0474) 669526; de_zwerver@telenet.be; camperparkdezwerver.be/tarieven**

12

Nr Kompass Camping - see dirs under Kompass Camping. Site behind De Zwerver nursery. Sm, mkd, hdstg, unshd, bbq. *"M'vans only; coin & note operated facs; modern & efficient; walking/cycling dist to town cent & port."* **€20.00** **2022**

NIEUWPOORT *A1* (3km E Rural) *51.12960, 2.77220* **Kompascamping Nieuwpoort,** Brugsesteenweg 49, 8620 Nieuwpoort **(058) 236037; nieuwpoort@kompascamping.be; www.kompascamping.be**

€3.20 (htd) (covrd, htd)

Exit E40/A18 at junc 3 sp Nieuwpoort; in 500m turn R at full traff lts; after 1km turn R at traff lts; turn R at rndabt & immed turn L over 2 sm canal bdgs. Turn R to Brugsesteenweg, site on L approx 1km. Fr Ostende on N34 (coast rd) turn L at rndabt after canal bdge as above. 4*, V lge, hdg, mkd, hdstg, pt shd, EHU (10A) inc; gas; red long stay; 50% statics; adv bkg acc; tennis; bike hire; waterslide; golf 10km; CKE. *"Well-equipped site; helpful staff; boat-launching facs; sep area for sh stay tourers; sports/games area adj; very busy w/ends; excel cycle rtes; conv Dunkerque ferry; excel facs; superb san facs; lge site."* **€28.00, 23 Mar-5 Nov, H19.** **2022**

BELGIUM

OOSTENDE *A1* (5km NE Coastal) *51.24882, 2.96710* **Camping 17 Duinzicht,** Rozenlaan 23, 8450 Bredene **(059) 323871; info@campingduinzicht.be; www.campingduinzicht.be**

12 (htd) nr nr sand 500m

Fr Ostend take dual c'way to Blankenberge on N34. Turn R sp Bredene, L into Driftweg which becomes Kappelstraat & turn R into Rozenlaan. Site sp. Lge, mkd, hdstg, unshd, serviced pitches; EHU (10A) inc (poss no earth); gas; bbq; 60% statics; phone; Eng spkn; adv bkg acc; ccard acc; CKE. *"Excel site; poss long walk to san facs; security barrier; take care slippery tiles in shwrs; Bredene lovely, sm seaside town."* **€24.00** **2020**

OOSTENDE *A1* (6km NE Rural) *51.24366, 2.98002* **Camping T Minnepark,** Zandstraat 105, 8450 Bredene-Dorp **(059) 322458; info@minnepark.be; www.minnepark.be**

12 €3 nr sand 2km

Fr Ostend take N34 sp Blankenberge. After tunnel under rlwy turn R sp Brugge. Cross canal & turn L at traff lts in 300m. In 2km after water tower, turn L at X-rds. at Mini rndabt turn R pass Aldi. Site on L in 1km after Zanpolder (sm yellow sp on L). V lge, unshd, EHU (16A) €1 (poss rev pol); TV (pitch); 75% statics; Eng spkn; adv bkg rec. *"Lge pitches; friendly, helpful staff; warm welcome; excel, well-run, well maintained family run site; excel san facs; conv ferries, Bruges & coast; lge pitches; conv for exploring Brugge, Ghent, Ypres & coast."* **€28.00** **2024**

OOSTENDE *A1* (5km E Urban/Coastal) *51.24970, 2.96834* **Camping Astrid,** Koning Astridlaan 1, 8450 Bredene **(059) 321247; info@camping-astrid.be; www.camping-astrid.be**

12 nr sand adj

Foll tourist sp. 2*, Med, unshd, serviced pitches; EHU (10A) inc; TV (pitch); 80% statics; phone; Eng spkn. *"Most sites nrby are statics only; friendly, helpful owners; rec NH; barrier for new arr."* **€30.00** **2024**

OPGLABBEEK *B3* (2km SE Rural) *51.02825, 5.59745* **Wilhelm Tell,** Hoeverweg 87, 3660 Opglabbeek **(089) 854444; wilhelmtell@limburgcampings.be; www.wilhelmtell.com**

12 €5 (covrd, htd)

Leave A2/E314 at junc 32, take rd N75 then N730 N sp As. In As take Opglabbeek turn, site sp in 1km. 4*, Med, mkd, pt shd, EHU (10A) inc; gas; bbq; red long stay; TV; 55% statics; phone; adv bkg acc; golf 10km; tennis; bike hire; waterslide; CKE. *"Nice site; narr ent; superb pools, wave machine; site in nature reserve; helpful staff; san facs dist; bit expensive; not suitable for lge o'fits."* **€32.00** **2020**

OTEPPE *B3* (0.5km N Rural) *50.58239, 5.12455* **Camping L'Hirondelle Château,** Rue de la Burdinale 76A, 4210 Oteppe **(085) 711131; hirondelle@capfun.com; www.lhirondelle.be**

€2.50

App fr E A15/E42 at exit 8; turn W on N643 for 1.5km; turn at sp on R for Oteppe. In vill 3km pass church to x-rds & R by police stn: site 150m on L. Fr W exit A15 at exit 10 onto N80, turn R onto N652 at Burdinne for Oteppe - easier rte. 4*, V lge, shd, pt sl, EHU (6A) inc; gas; bbq; 75% statics; ccard acc; games area; waterslide; tennis; CKE. *"Site in grnds of chateau; excel facs for children; touring pitches at top of site poss diff (steep); gd area for walking, fishing; conv NH; v quiet LS."* **€40.70, 1 Apr-31 Oct.** **2024**

OUDENAARDE *B2* (15km SW Urban) *50.76250, 3.48719* **Panorama Camping,** Boskouter 24, Ruien, 9690 Kluisbergen **(032) 55 38 86 68; info@campingpanorama.be; www.campingpanorama.be**

Fr N8 (Oudenaarde - Berchem) foll sp to Kluisbergen, Ruien. Cont thro Ruien, past church on L turn into Wuipelstraat, then R at rndabt, then L into Boskouter foll sp to site. 1*, Med, mkd, pt shd, pt sl, terr, EHU; 90% statics; Eng spkn; adv bkg acc; CKE. *"Gd site; very sm touring area; helpful owner; excel cycling and walking fr site."* **€25.00, 1 Feb-30 Nov.** **2024**

PHILIPPEVILLE *C2* (11km NW Rural) *50.23920, 4.45927* **Camping Le Chesle,** 1 rue d'Yves, 5650 Vogenee **0475 80 24 63; cheslez.info@gmail.com; www.cheslez.com**

€2.50

N5 Charleroi-Philippeville, exit Yves Gomezee. After rlwy, turn R to Vogenee and foll sp. Med, unshd, pt sl, EHU (16A); bbq; TV; 50% statics; bus 1km; Eng spkn; adv bkg acc; CKE. *"Pleasant walking rtes fr site, ask for map; cycling poss, but v hilly; vg; v friendly, helpful owners."* **€25.00, 1 Feb-15 Dec.** **2023**

ROCHE EN ARDENNE, LA *C3* (0.8km S Rural) *50.17465, 5.57774* **Camping Le Vieux Moulin,** Rue Petite Strument 62, 6980 La Roche-en-Ardenne **(084) 411507; info@strument.com; www.strument.com**

€2 (htd) nr

Off N89 site sp fr La Roche town cent (dir Barrièr-de-Champlon), site in 800m. Med, hdg, shd, pt sl, EHU (6A) €2.50 (poss no earth); bbq; 70% statics; Eng spkn; adv bkg acc; canoeing; fishing; CKE. *"Beautiful site; gd pitches; poss unclean san facs & dishwashing (7/09); poss youth groups; poor security; gd walking (map avail)."* **€14.00, Easter-Nov.** **2020**

BELGIUM

SINT MARGRIETE *A2* (2.6km NW Rural) *51.2860, 3.5164* **Camping De Soetelaer,** Sint Margrietepolder 2, 9981 Sint Margriete **(09) 3798151; camping.desoetelaer@telenet.be; www.campingdesoetelaer.com**

nr

Fr E on N49/E34 to Maldegem or fr W on N9 or N49 turn N onto N251 to Aardenburg (N'lands), then turn R twd St Kruis (N'lands) - site situated 1.5km strt on fr St Margriete (back in Belgium). Med, mkd, pt shd, serviced pitches; EHU (6A) inc; Eng spkn; adv bkg acc; CKE. *"Vg, clean site; excel, modern san facs; peace & quiet, privacy & space; highly rec for relaxation; o'fits pitched v close end to end."* **€36.96, 29 Mar-15 Oct. 2024**

SOUMAGNE *B3* (3.5km S Rural) *50.61099, 5.73840* **Domaine Provincial de Wégimont,** Chaussée de Wégimont 76, 4630 Soumagne **(04) 2372400; wegimont@prov-liege.be; www.prov-liege.be/wegimont**

12 (htd)

Exit A3 at junc 37 onto N3 W twd Fléron & Liège. In 500m at traff lts turn L sp Soumagne. In Soumagne at traff lts form R dir Wégimont, site on top of hill on R directly after bus stop. Med, hdg, pt shd, pt sl, EHU (16A) inc poss rev pol; bbq; 70% statics; bus; site clsd Jan; tennis; games area; CKE. *"Welcoming site in chateau grnds (public access); pool adj high ssn; clean facs; conv sh stay/NH nr m'way."* **€17.00 2022**

SPA *C4* (1.6km SE Rural) *50.48559, 5.88385* **Camping Parc des Sources,** Rue de la Sauvenière 141, 4900 Spa **(087) 772311; info@parcdessources.be; www.parcdessources.be**

€1.50 (htd) nr

Bet Spa & Francorchamps on N62, sp on R. Med, mkd, pt shd, pt sl, EHU (10A) €2.75; gas; 60% statics; phone. *"Excel facs, modern lndry, beautiful location, nr forest; friendly & helpful staff."* **€35.00, 1 Apr-4 Sep. 2022**

STAVELOT *C4* (3km N Rural) *50.41087, 5.95351* **Camping L'Eau Rouge,** Cheneux 25, 4970 Stavelot **(080) 863075; fb220447@skynet.be; www.eaurouge.eu**

€1 (htd) nr

Exit A27/E42 junc 11 onto N68 twd Stavelot. Turn R at T-junc, then 1st R into sm rd over narr bdge. Med, mkd, pt shd, pt sl, EHU (6-10A) €3 rev polarity; bbq; TV; 50% statics; Eng spkn; archery; games area. *"Vg rvside site; friendly, helpful owners; conv Francorchamps circuit."* **€36.50, 29 Mar-30 Oct. 2024**

STEKENE *A2* (4km SW Rural) *51.18366, 4.00730* **Camping Vlasaard,** Heirweg 143, 9190 Stekene **(03) 7798164; info@camping-vlasaard.be; www.camping-vlasaard.be**

(htd) nr

Fr N49 Antwerp-Knokke rd, exit sp Stekene. In Stekene, take dir Moerbeke, site on L in 4km. V lge, mkd, unshd, serviced pitches; EHU (16A); 75% statics; Eng spkn; ccard acc; games area. **€18.00, 7 Jan-20 Dec. 2022**

TELLIN *C3* (5km NE Rural) *50.09665, 5.28579* **Camping Parc La Clusure,** 30 Chemin de la Clusure, 6927 Bure-Tellin **(084) 360050; info@parclaclusure.be; www.parclaclusure.be**

€5 (htd) (covrd, htd)

Fr N on A4 use exit 23A onto N899, fr S exit junc 24. Foll sp for Tellin & then take N846 thro Bure dir Grupont vill. At rndabt at junc N803 & N846 take 2nd exit to site, sp. 4*, Lge, mkd, pt shd, EHU (16A) inc (check rev pol); TV; 35% statics; phone; Eng spkn; adv bkg acc; ccard acc; rv fishing; bike hire; games area; games rm; tennis; CKE. *"V pleasant, lovely, popular rvside site; conv m'way; conv for limestone caves at Han-sur-Lesse & gd touring base Ardennes; friendly owners; clean facs; wild beavers in adj rv; excel site."* **€25.00, 31 Mar - 24 Sept, H09. 2022**

TOURNAI *B2* (2km SE Urban) *50.59967, 3.41349* **Camping de l'Orient,** Jean-Baptiste Moens 8, 7500 Tournai **(069) 222635; campingorient@tournai.be**

12 (htd) nr

Exit E42 junc 32 R onto N7 twd Tournai. L at 1st traff lts, foll sp Aquapark, L at rndabt, site immed on L (no sp). 2*, Med, hdg, hdstg, pt shd, serviced pitches; EHU (10A) inc (poss rev pol/no earth) or metered; gas; Eng spkn; adv bkg req; CKE. *"Well-kept site in interesting area & old town; facs stretched high ssn, but excel site; take care raised kerbs to pitches; max length of c'van 6.5m due narr site rds & high hdgs; helpful wardens; lake adj; E side of site quietest; htd, indoor pool adj; EHU had no earth on a nbr of pitches; rest, bar & playgrnd at leisure complex adj (50% disc to campers); handy for Lille and Dunkerque ferries; renovation work in 2023"* **€20.00 2023**

TURNHOUT *A3* (9.6km SW Rural) *51.28253, 4.83750* **Recreatie de Lilse Bergen,** Strandweg 6, 2275 Lille-Gierle **(014) 557901; info@lilsebergen.be; www.delilsebergen.be**

12 €5 (htd)

Exit A21/E34 junc 22 N dir Beerse; at rndabt foll sp Lilse Bergen. Site in 1.5km. 4*, Lge, mkd, shd, EHU (10A) inc; bbq; sw; 60% statics; phone; Eng spkn; adv bkg acc; ccard acc; bike hire; tennis; games area; sep car park; watersports; CKE. *"Site sep pt of lge leisure complex; pitches amongst pine trees; modern san facs, poss streteched high ssn; excel for children/teenagers; gd."* **€30.00 2022**

VIELSALM *C4* (17km SW Rural) *50.24013, 5.75396* **Camping aux Massotais,** 20 Petites Tailles, Baraque de Fraiture, 6690 Vielsalm **(080) 418560; info@auxmassotais.com; www.auxmassotais.com**

12 (htd) (htd)

Exit A26/E25 junc 50 onto N89 dir Vielsalm. At 1st rndabt turn R onto N30 dir Houffalize. Site on L in 1km behind hotel. Med, hdstg, pt shd, pt sl, EHU (6-16A) inc; TV; 5% statics; Eng spkn; CKE. *"Special pitches for NH (don't need to unhitch); fair."* **€15.00 2024**

VIRTON *D3* (3km NE Rural) *49.57915, 5.54892* **Camping Colline de Rabais,** 1 Rue Clos des Horlès, 6760 Virton **(063) 571195; info@collinederabais.be; www.collinederabais.be**

12 €3.25 (htd) WD MSP

Take junc 29 fr A4/E411 onto N87, 2km fr Virton turn into wood at site sp. At end of rd bef lge building turn R, then 3rd turn R at phone box. 4*, Lge, pt shd, pt sl, terr, EHU (16A) €3.20; sw nr; TV (pitch); 20% statics; phone; Eng spkn; adv bkg acc; ccard acc; bike hire; tennis 1km; fishing 1km; CKE. *"Pleasant site; gd facs."* **€14.00** **2022**

WAASMUNSTER *A2* (2.4km N Rural) *51.12690, 4.08455* **Camping Gerstekot,** Vinkenlaan 30, 9250 Waasmunster **(0323) 7723424; campinggerstekot.be@gmail.com; www.gerstekot.be**

12 (htd) WD MSP

Exit A14/E17 at junc 13 Waasmunster onto N446 S; take 1st L in 100m into Patrijzenlaan & L again into Vinkenlaan, foll camp sp. Med, mkd, pt shd, EHU (16A) inc; bbq; TV; 95% statics; phone; adv bkg acc; ccard acc; games area; games rm; CKE. *"Busy at w/end; water use metered; key req for shwrs; gd."* **€18.00** **2022**

WESTENDE *A1* (0.4km SW Coastal) *51.15728, 2.76561* **Camping Westende,** Westendelaan 341, 8434 Westende **(058) 233254; info@campingwestende.be; www.campingwestende.be**

€2 (htd) WD MSP nr (htd) sand 1km

Fr Middelkerke foll N318; just after Westende vill church take dir Nieuport, site on L in 150m. Lge, mkd, unshd, EHU (10A) inc; gas; 90% statics; phone; bus; Eng spkn; CKE. *"Sm but tidy touring area; friendly owners; beach nrby; tram 1km; excel cycling; gd."* **€34.00, 1 Apr-14 Nov.** **2022**

YPRES *B1* (6km E Rural) *50.85227, 2.93967* **'t hof Bellewaerde,** Bellewaardestraat 2, 8902 Ieper Zillebeke **(468) 584778; info@thofbellewaerde.be; www.thofbellewaerde.be**

€2 WD MSP

N38 onto N308 cont onto N37 (Ypres bypass). At rndabt take 2nd exit. Stay on Zuiderring/N37. After 1.4k at rndabt take 2nd exit onto Meenseweg/N8. After 1.9k turn L onto Bellewaerdestraat. Site on L. Hooge Crater Museum on corner of drive. Sm, hdstg, unshd, pt sl, EHU (6A) €3; bbq (sep area); bus/train; Eng spkn; adv bkg acc; ccard acc; bike hire. *"Located in protected archaeological site (WW1 Battlefield of Bellewaarde Ridge); Bellewaerde amusement pk, Hooge Crater Museum & Hill 62 Sanctuary Wood in walking distance; in Nature Reserve; on cycle routes."* **€21.00, 25 Feb-31 Dec.** **2022**

YPRES/IEPER *B1* (3km E Urban) *50.8467, 2.8994* **Urban Gardens Ieper (formerly Camping Jeugdstadion),** Bolwerkstraat 1, 8900 Leper, Ypres **(057) 217282; ieper@urban-gardens.be; urban-gardens.be/en/ypres**

€1 (htd) WD MSP nr

Fr S ent town cent on N336, after rlwy x-ing turn R at rndabt onto ring rd & L at 2nd rndabt, foll camping sp. Site in 300m on L, sp fr ring rd. If app town cent fr N on N8 fr Veurne take ring rd N37; at rndabt turn L, site in 300m on L, well sp. Fr N38 in Ypres turn off at rndabt sp Industrie/Jeugdstadion, take 2nd L, site at end. NB site open all year for m'vans. Med, hdg, hdstg, mkd, pt shd, pt sl, EHU (10A) inc (poss rev pol); Eng spkn; adv bkg rec; ccard acc; bike hire. *"Automatic registration/check out avail when office clsd; peaceful, well-refurbished site; conv WW1 battle fields & museums; 10 min walk to Menin Gate for daily Last Post Ceremony; helpful staff; gd, modern san facs; sports park adj; soft grass pitches - ask for one with 'rubber tracks' to avoid sinking; hdstg m'van (OAY with own san facs only) pitches in sep area like an Aire; site poss v full local public hols; pool adj; site not fully enclsd; excel, clean, tidy, well run site; rec; noise fr adj processing plant."* **€28.00, 1 Mar-12 Nov.** **2024**

YPRES/IEPER *B1* (10km SW Rural) *50.78643, 2.82035* **Camping Ypra,** Pingelaarstraat 2, 8956 Kemmel-Heuvelland **(057) 444631; info@camping-ypra.be; www.camping-ypra.be**

€1.90 (htd) WD nr

On N38 Poperinge ring rd turn S at rndabt onto N304. Foll sp Kemmel. Site on R in 12km on N edge of Kemmel. 3*, Med, hdstg, mkd, pt shd, pt sl, EHU (16A) inc (poss rev pol); 90% statics; Eng spkn; adv bkg acc; CKE. *"Clean, well-maintained site; gd, modern san facs, but ltd; helpful, friendly staff; access to some pitches poss diff; interesting rest in vill; conv for WW1 battlefields; pitches varied sizes; poss noise fr club hse & bar; gd; some shady pitches."* **€25.00, 1 Mar-30 Nov.** **2022**

BELGIUM

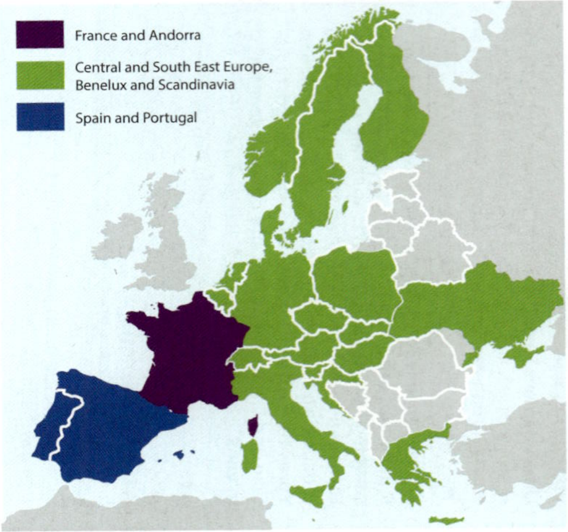

Eupen to Turnhout = 122km

	Aalst	Aalter	Antwerpen	Arlon	Ath	Bastogne	Brugge	Bruxelles (Brussels)	Charleroi	Clervaux (Luxembourg)	Dinant	Eupen	Gent	Hasselt	Huy	Kortrijk	Leuven	Liège	Luxembourg City	Malmedy	Mechelen	Mons	Namur	Oostende	Oudenaarde	Philippeville	Tournai	Turnhout	Ypres
Aalter	48																												
Antwerpen	53	81																											
Arlon	217	262	233																										
Ath	50	83	112	216																									
Bastogne	178	220	196	39	177																								
Brugge	76	26	107	288	113	247																							
Bruxelles (Brussels)	29	73	55	189	54	151	99																						
Charleroi	82	130	115	166	63	129	154	60																					
Clervaux (Luxembourg)	210	253	230	67	207	32	280	181	159																				
Dinant	121	165	135	120	118	82	190	91	55	113																			
Eupen	163	207	154	136	187	97	234	133	129	82	127																		
Gent	33	27	61	245	70	206	55	56	110	231	147	191																	
Hasselt	114	166	81	172	133	131	188	79	93	139	125	67	145																
Huy	109	157	129	123	117	83	183	84	64	100	62	72	141	74															
Kortrijk	70	46	102	274	58	231	59	92	122	263	159	239	48	189	174														
Leuven	59	102	69	188	82	148	129	28	68	180	92	117	88	51	69	129													
Liège	127	171	124	132	149	93	198	96	92	120	91	42	155	43	36	203	80												
Luxembourg City	244	288	262	28	242	67	315	220	195	60	148	130	272	199	150	299	215	180											
Malmedy	182	226	180	123	185	69	253	152	132	56	101	26	210	110	68	242	136	56	116										
Mechelen	51	95	28	207	84	166	123	27	89	199	109	144	82	80	96	115	24	107	234	163									
Mons	89	97	121	196	25	158	136	69	46	190	85	164	121	164	100	76	87	129	225	168	90								
Namur	90	136	110	127	88	89	164	63	36	120	28	99	120	97	34	144	62	62	155	102	81	72							
Oostende	93	42	122	302	121	264	29	115	166	294	205	249	70	202	198	62	144	214	329	268	137	140	179						
Oudenaarde	47	30	81	283	42	224	71	72	111	255	164	207	29	197	165	35	103	172	310	226	96	67	137	86					
Philippeville	108	155	141	149	90	111	182	86	26	142	30	155	136	156	91	146	94	119	177	130	115	72	62	193	138				
Tournai	67	71	127	244	29	203	88	84	93	235	131	211	71	211	148	29	134	175	270	242	116	48	120	91	37	119			
Turnhout	99	128	45	277	155	236	155	94	161	344	177	122	106	55	171	147	112	105	304	166	54	160	146	170	127	185	174		
Ypres	100	77	132	302	90	263	53	122	151	293	189	269	78	217	205	29	161	232	328	272	146	106	175	56	65	175	58	176	
Zeebrugge	90	40	121	302	128	263	15	114	170	263	205	70	201	156	197	74	143	212	331	263	137	151	177	25	86	195	113	167	68

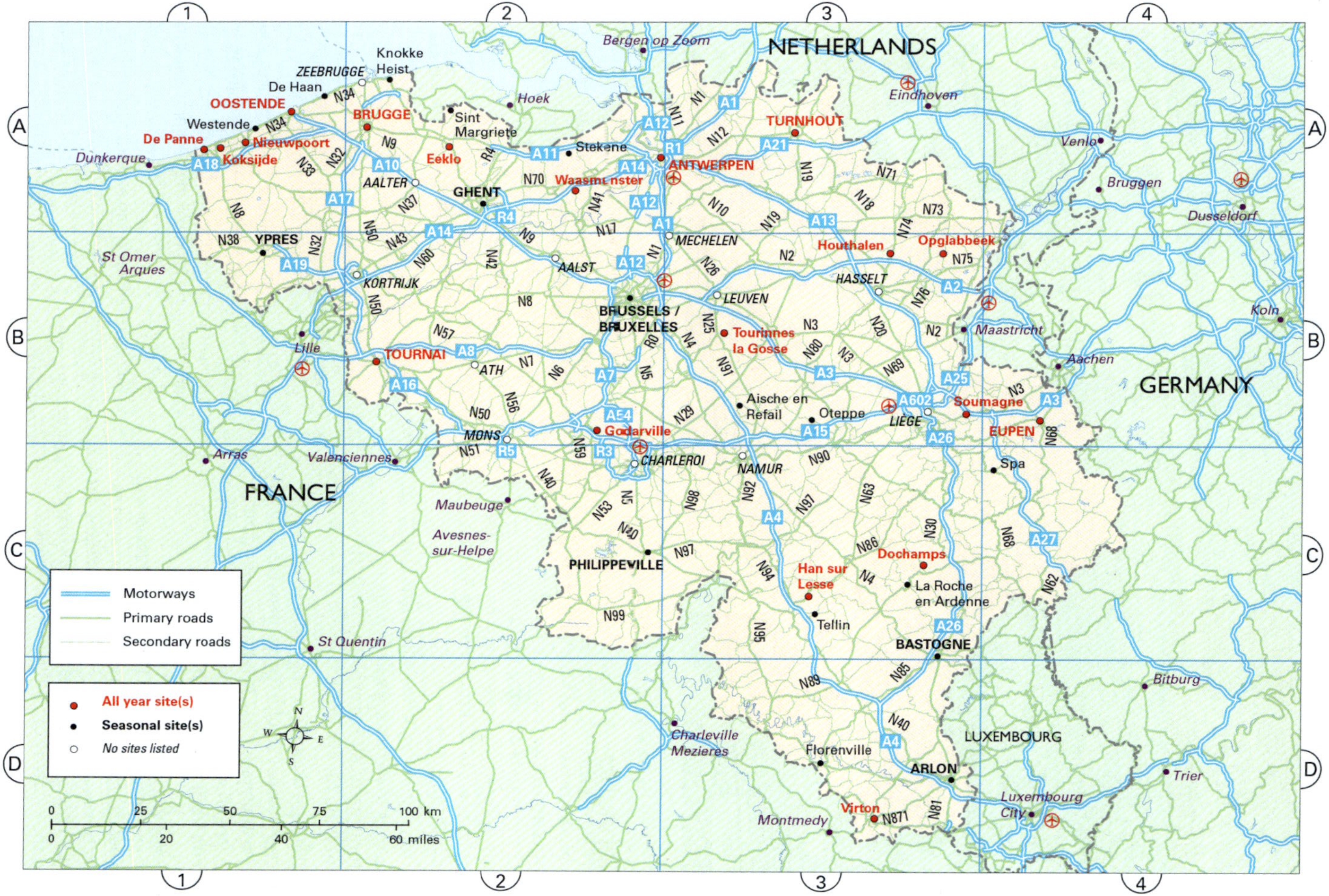
NETHERLANDS
GERMANY
FRANCE
LUXEMBOURG
Bergen op Zoom
Eindhoven
Venlo
Bruggen
Dusseldorf
Koln
Maastricht
Aachen
Hoek
Knokke Heist
ZEEBRUGGE
De Haan
OOSTENDE
Westende
De Panne
Koksijde
Nieuwpoort
Dunkerque
BRUGGE
Sint Margriete
Eeklo
Stekene
ANTWERPEN
TURNHOUT
AALTER
GHENT
Waasmunster
MECHELEN
Houthalen
Opglabbeek
HASSELT
LEUVEN
YPRES
KORTRIJK
AALST
St Omer Arques
BRUSSELS / BRUXELLES
Tourinnes la Gosse
Lille
TOURNAI
ATH
Aische en Refail
Oteppe
LIEGE
Soumagne
EUPEN
MONS
Godarville
CHARLEROI
NAMUR
Spa
Arras
Valenciennes
Maubeuge
Avesnes-sur-Helpe
PHILIPPEVILLE
Dochamps
Han sur Lesse
La Roche en Ardenne
Tellin
BASTOGNE
St Quentin
Bitburg
Charleville Mezieres
Florenville
ARLON
Trier
Virton
Montmedy
Luxembourg City
Motorways
Primary roads
Secondary roads
All year site(s)
Seasonal site(s)
No sites listed
N
E
S
W
0
25
50
75
100 km
0
20
40
60 miles

Croatia

Shutterstock/ trabantos

Highlights

Croatia's Adriatic Coast is a land of sun, beauty and history. Soaked in culture going back thousands of years, there are so many different sights to see, from the 16th century walls of Dubrovnik to the Roman amphitheatre in Pula.

With countless galleries, museums and churches to discover, as well as an exquisite natural landscape to explore, there truly is something for everyone.

Licitars are brightly decorated biscuits made of sweet honey dough. Often given as a gift at celebrations such as Christmas or weddings, they are an integral part of Croatian identity dating from the 16th century.

Croatia is well known for its carnivals, festivals and celebrations, which take place throughout the year. Some of the most important are the Spring Procession of Queens from Gorjani, the Bell Ringer's Pageant from the Kastav Area and the Festivity of St. Blaise, Dubrovnik's patron saint.

Major towns and cities

- Zagreb – the capital of Croatia has a rich history that dates from Roman times.
- Rijeka – Croatia's principal port city overlooking the Adriatic.
- Split – the centre of the city is built around an ancient Roman palace.
- Osijek – a gastronomic centre, and the best place to try a traditional dish.

Attractions

- Dubrovnik – a wonderfully preserved medieval walled city with plenty to see.
- Plitvice Lakes - a stunning series of lakes and waterfalls set in an enchanting woodland.
- Pula Arena – this ancient Roman amphitheatre is one of the best preserved in the world.
- Diocletian's Palace – an ancient monument that makes up the heart of Split.

Find out more

croatia.hr

Country Information

Capital: Zagreb

Bordered by: Bosnia and Herzegovina, Hungary, Serbia, Montenegro and Slovenia

Terrain: Flat plains along border with Hungary; low mountains and highlands near Adriatic coast and islands

Climate: Mediterranean climate along the coast with hot, dry summers and mild, wet winters; continental climate inland with hot summers and cold winters

Coastline: 5,835 km (inc 4,058 km islands)

Highest Point: Dinara 1,830 m

Language: Croatian

Local Time: GMT or BST + 1, i.e. 1 hour ahead of the UK all year

Currency: Euros divided into 100 cents; £1 = €1.20, €1 = £0.84 (Nov 2024)

Emergency Numbers: Police 192; Fire brigade 193; Ambulance 194. Or dial 112 and specify the service you need.

Public Holidays in 2025: Jan 1,6; Apr 20, 21; May 1, 30; June 19, 22; Aug 5, 15; Nov 1, 18; Dec 25, 26.

Some Christian Orthodox and Muslim festivals are also celebrated locally. School summer holidays take place from the last week in June to the end of August.

Entry Formalities

British and Irish passport holders may visit Croatia for up to three months without a visa.

Unless staying at official tourist accommodation (hotel or campsite) all visitors are obliged to register at the nearest police station or tourist agency within 24 hours of arrival. Campsites should carry out this function for their guests but make sure you check with them. If you fail to register you may receive a fine or you may have to leave Croatia.

British citizens intending to stay for an extended period should seek advice from the Croatian Embassy.

Medical Services

For minor ailments, first of all consult staff in a pharmacy (ljekarna). Emergency hospital and medical treatment is available at a reduced cost on production of a valid European Health Insurance Card (EHIC) or a UK Global Health Insurance Card (UK GHIC). You will be expected to pay a proportion of the cost (normally 20%). Only basic health care facilities are available in outlying areas and islands

Opening Hours

Banks: Mon-Fri 8am-7pm; Sat 8am-1pm.

Museums: Tue-Sun 10am-5pm; most close Mon and some close Sun afternoons.

Post Offices: Mon-Fri 7am-7pm (2pm in small villages). In major towns or tourist places, post offices on duty are open until 9pm.

Shops: Mon-Fri 8am-8pm; Sat & Sun 8am-2pm.

Safety and Security

Pickpockets operate in major cities, coastal areas (e.g. pavement cafés). Take sensible precautions when carrying money, credit cards and passports.

Beware of people trying to make you pull over when driving, either by requesting help or indicating that something is wrong with your vehicle. If possible wait until you're in a populated area before pulling over to check.

If you're planning to travel outside the normal tourist resorts you should be aware that there are areas affected by the war, which ended in 1995, where unexploded mines remain. These include Eastern Slavonia, Brodsko-Posavska County, Karlovac County, areas around Zadar County and in more remote areas of the Plitvice Lakes National Park.

Croatia shares with the rest of Europe an underlying threat from terrorism. Please check gov.uk/foreign-travel-advice/croatia before you travel.

British Embassy

Ivana Lučića 4
10000 Zagreb
Tel: +385 (01) 6009100
gov.uk/world/croatia

Irish Honorary Consulate

23 Miramarska Avenue
10000 Zagreb
Tel: +385 (01) 6310025
ireland.ie/zagreb

Customs Regulations

Customs Posts

Main border crossings are open 24 hours.

Foodstuffs

It's not permitted to take meat, milk or products containing them with you into EU countries. There are some exemptions for infant milk, infant food, and special foods or pet food required for medical reasons. Exemptions should be in sealed packages and weigh less than 2km.

Documents

Driving Licence

Full, valid British driving licence are recognised but if you have an old-style green licence then it's advisable to change it for a photocard licence in order to avoid any local difficulties.

Money

Visitors may exchange money in bureaux de change, banks, post offices, hotels and some travel agencies but you're likely to get the best rates in banks. Exchange slips should be kept in order to convert unspent kuna on leaving the country. Many prices are quoted in both kuna and euros, both are widely accepted.

Most shops and restaurants accept credit cards. There are cash machines in all but the smallest resorts.

The police are warning visitors about a recent increase in the number of forged Croatian banknotes in circulation, especially 200 and 500 kuna notes. Take care when purchasing kuna and use only reliable outlets, such as banks and cash points.

Passport

You must be able to show some form of identification if required by the authorities and, therefore, should carry your passport or photocard driving licence at all times.

Vehicle(s)

Carry your vehicle registration certificate (V5C), insurance details and MOT certificate (if applicable).

Driving

Accidents

Any visible damage to a vehicle entering Croatia must be certified by the authorities at the border and a Certificate of Damage issued, which must be produced when leaving the country. In the event of a minor accident resulting in material damage only, call the police and they will assist with the exchange of information between drivers and will issue a Certificate of Damage to the foreign driver. You should not try to leave the country with a damaged vehicle without this Certificate as you may be accused of a 'hit and run' offence.

Confiscation of passport and a court appearance within 24 hours are standard procedures for motoring accidents where a person is injured.

The Croatian Insurance Bureau in Zagreb can assist with Customs and other formalities following road accidents, tel: (01) 4696600, email: huo@huo.hr or see: huo.hr.

Alcohol

The maximum permitted level of alcohol in the bloodstream is 0.05%. Penalties for exceeding this are severe.
For drivers of vehicles over 3,500 kg and for drivers under 24 years of age the alcohol limit is zero. The general legal limit also applies to cyclists.

It's prohibited to drive after having taken any medicine whose side-effects may affect the ability to drive a motor vehicle.

Breakdown Service

The Hrvatski Auto-Klub (HAK) operates a breakdown service throughout the country, telephone 1987 (or +385 1 1987 from a mobile phone) for assistance. On motorways use the roadside emergency phones which are placed at 2 km intervals. Towing and breakdown services are available 24 hours a day in and around most major cities and along the coast in summer (6am to midnight in Zagreb).

Child Restraint Systems

Children under the age of 12 are not allowed to travel in the front seats of vehicles, with the exception of children under 2 years of age who can travel in the front if they are placed in a child restraint system adapted to their size.

It must be rear-facing and the airbag must be de-activated.

Children up to 5 years old must be placed in a seat adapted to their size on the back seat. Children between the ages of 5 and 12 must travel on the back seat using a 3 point seat belt with a booster seat if necessary for their height.

Fuel

Petrol stations are generally open from 7am to 7 or 8pm, later in summer. Some of those on major stretches of road stay open 24 hours a day. Payment by credit card is widely accepted. LPG (Autogas) is fairly widely available.

Lights

Dipped headlights are compulsory at all times, regardless of weather conditions, from the end of October to the end of March and in reduced visibility at other times of the year. It's compulsory to carry spare bulbs, however this rule does not apply if your vehicle is fitted with xenon, neon, LED or similar lights.

Motorways

There are just over 1313 km of motorways. Tolls (cestarina) are levied according to vehicle category. Electronic display panels above motorways indicate speed limits, road conditions and lane closures.
Information on motorways can be found via the website: hac.hr.

Motorway Tolls

Class 1	Vehicle with 2 axles, height up to 1.3m measured from front axle) excluding vans
Class 2	Vehicle with 2 or more axles, height up to 1.3m (measured from front axle), including car + caravan or trailer, motorhomes and vans.
Class 3	Vehicle with 2 or 3 axles, height over 1.3m (measured from front axle), including van with trailer
Class 4	Vehicle with 4 or more axles, height over .3m (measured from front axle)

Tolls can be paid in cash or by credit card. Details of toll prices can be found in English on the website: hac.hr.

Parking

Lines at the roadside indicate parking restrictions. Traffic wardens patrol roads and impose fines for illegal parking. Vehicles, including those registered outside Croatia, may be immobilised by wheel clamps.

Roads

In general road conditions are good in and around the larger towns. The Adriatic Highway or Jadranksa Magistrala (part of European route E65) runs the whole length of the Adriatic coast and is in good condition, despite being mostly single-carriageway. Minor road surfaces may be uneven and, because of the heat-resisting material used to surface them, may be very slippery when wet. Minor roads are usually unlit at night.

Motorists should take care when overtaking and be aware that other drivers may overtake unexpectedly in slow-moving traffic. The standard of driving is generally fair.

Road Signs and Markings

Road signs and markings conform to international standards. Motorway signs have a green background; national road signs have a blue background.

Speed Limits

	Open Road (km/h)	Motorway (km/h)
Car Solo	90-110	130
Car towing caravan/trailer	80	90
Motorhome under 3500kg	90-110	130
Motorhome 3500-7500kg	80	90

In addition to complying with other speed limits, drivers under the age of 25 must not exceed 80 km/h (50 mph) on the open road, 100 km/h (62 mph) on expressways and 120 km/h (74 mph) on motorways.

Traffic Jams

During the summer, tailbacks may occur at the border posts with Slovenia at Buje on the E751 (road 21), at Bregana on the E70 (A3) and at Donji Macelj on the E59 (A1). During July and August there may be heavy congestion, for example at Rupa/Klenovica and at other tourist centres, and on the E65 north-south Adriatic Highway. This is particularly true on Friday evenings, Saturday mornings, Sunday evenings and holidays.

Queues form at ferry crossings to the main islands.Road and traffic conditions can be viewed on the HAK website (in English), hak.hr or tel: (01) 4640800 (English spoken) or (072) 777777 while in Croatia for round the clock recorded information.

Violation of Traffic Regulations

The police may impose on-the-spot fines for parking and driving offences. If you're unable to pay the police may confiscate your passport. Motoring law enforcement, especially for speeding offences, is strictly observed.

Winter Driving

It's compulsory to carry snow chains in your vehicle and they must be used if required by the weather conditions (5cm of snow or black ice). The compulsory winter equipment in Croatia consists of a shovel in your vehicle and a set of snow chains on the driving axel.

Essential Equipment

First aid kit

All vehicles, including those registered abroad, must carry a first aid kit.

Reflective Jacket/Waistcoat

It's obligatory to carry a reflective jacket inside your car (not in the boot) and you must wear it if you need to leave your vehicle to attend to a breakdown, e.g. changing a tyre. Any passenger leaving the vehicle should also wear one.

Warning Triangle(s)

All motor vehicles must carry a warning triangle. If you're towing a caravan or trailer you must have two warning triangles.

Touring

There are a number of national parks and nature reserves throughout the country, including the World Heritage site at the Plitvice lakes, the Paklenica mountain massif, and the Kornati archipelago with 140 uninhabited islands, islets and reefs. Dubrovnik, itself a World Heritage site, is one of the world's best-preserved medieval cities, having been extensively restored since recent hostilities.

While Croatia has a long coastline, there are few sandy beaches; instead there are pebbles, shingle and rocks with man-made bathing platforms.

Croatia originated the concept of commercial naturist resorts in Europe and today attracts an estimated 1 million naturist tourists annually. There are approximately 20 official naturist resorts and beaches and numerous other unofficial or naturist-optional 'free' beaches. Smoking is prohibited in restaurants, bars and public places. A service charge is general included in the bill. English is widely spoken.

Camping and Caravanning

There are more than 150 campsites in Croatia including several well-established naturist sites, mainly along the coast. Sites are licensed according to how many people they can accommodate, rather than by the number of vehicles or tents, and are classed according to a grading system of 1 to 4 stars. There are some very large sites catering for up to 10,000 people at any one time but there are also many small sites, mainly in Dalmatia, situated in gardens, orchards and farms.

Many sites open from April to October; few open all year. They are generally well-equipped.

A tourist tax is around €1.33 per person per day according to region and time of year.

Casual/wild camping is illegal and is particularly monitored at beaches, harbours and rural car parks. Most campsites have overnight areas for late arrivals and there are a number of rest areas established along main roads for overnight stays or brief stopovers.

Electricity and Gas

Current on campsites ranges from 10 to 16 amps. Plugs have 2 round pins. There may not be CEE connections and a long cable might be required.

Campingaz cylinders are not available, so take a good supply of gas with you.

Public Transport

Rail travel is slow and cab be unreliable. By contrast the bus network offers the cheapest and most extensive means of public transport. Buy bus tickets when you board or from kiosks, which you must validate once on board. Trams operate in Zagreb and you can buy tickets from kiosks.

Coastal towns and cities have regular scheduled passenger and car ferry services. Most ferries are drive-on/drive-off – see (jadrolinija.hr) for schedules and maps.

Car ferries operate from Ancona, Bari, Pescara and Venice in Italy to Dubrovnik, Korèula, Mali Lošinj, Poreè, Pula, Rijecka, Rovinj, Sibenik, Split, Starigrad, Vis and Zadar. Full details from:

Viamare Ltd
Suite 108, 582 Honeypot Lane
Stanmore
Middlesex, HA7 1JS
Tel: 020 8206 3420

Email: ferries@viamare.com
Website: viamare.com

VALAMAR CAMPING
Welcome to your 5 000 star residence
CROATIA
• Prime seafront locations on the stunning Croatian coastline
• A variety of accommodation options: spacious pitches, ultra-modern camping homes, villas, suites, and exclusive glamping tents
• Beautiful beaches, outdoor pools, and family water parks
• Endless family activities, fully equipped playrooms, and playgrounds
• Valamar signature restaurants – the finest local cuisine
ISTRIA Valamar Camping Istra 5*/ Valamar Camping Lanterna 4*/ Valamar Camping Marina 4* / Camping Orsera 3* / Camping Solaris 3* - NATURIST / Camping Brioni 2*/ Camping Tunarica 2* KRK ISLAND Valamar Camping Krk 5* / Valamar Camping Ježevac 4* / Valamar Camping Baška 4* / Camping Bunculuka 4* - NATURIST / Camping Škrila 3* RAB ISLAND Valamar Camping Padova 4* / Valamar Camping San Marino 4* DUBROVNIK Camping Solitudo 3*
ADAC Superplatz 2024
ADAC
Erkende camping
TOP 2024
Croatia's Best Campsite
2024
+385 52 465 000 / +385 1 884 865 8
reservations@valamar.com
www.valamar.com

Sites in Croatia

BIOGRAD NA MORU *B3* (12km NW Coastal) *44.00532, 15.36748* **Autokamp Filko,** Aleksandar Colic 23207 Sveti Petar Na Moru **02 33 91 177; info@autokamp-filko.hr; www.autokamp-filko.hr**
12 WD MSP shgl

On D8 bet Zadar & Biograd Na Moru at Sv Petar NM. 1st camp on the R by sea. Sm, pt shd, 30% statics; Eng spkn. *"Some pitches by water on hdstg with views across to islands; dir access fr rd; ideal LS; gd."*
€22.00 **2024**

DUBROVNIK *C4* (10km S Coastal) *42.62444, 18.19301* **Autocamp Matkovica,** Srebreno 8, 20207 Dubrovnik **(098) 725776; u.o.matkovica@hotmail.com**
12 WD nr nr nr shgl adj

Fr Dubrovnik S on coast rd. At Kupari foll sp to site behind Camping Porto. 1*, Sm, mkd, shd, EHU (6A) inc; phone; bus 200m; Eng spkn. *"Well-kept site; friendly, helpful owners; cash only; san facs old but clean; water bus to Dubrovnik 1km."* **HRK 260** **2024**

DUBROVNIK *C4* (7km S Coastal) *42.62471, 18.20801* **Autocamp Kate,** Tupina 1, 20207 Mlini **(020) 487006; info@campingkate.com; www.campingkate.com**
HRK4 WD nr shgl 200m

Fr Dubrovnik on rd 8 foll sp Cavtat or Čilipi or airport into vill of Mlini. Fr S past Cavtat into Mlini. Site well sp fr main rd. Sm, hdstg, pt shd, pt sl, terr, EHU (10-16A) inc; bbq; red long stay; phone; bus to Dubrovnik 150m; Eng spkn; adv bkg acc; CKE. *"Family-run site in lovely setting; v helpful, hard-working, welcoming owners; vg clean facs; boats fr vill to Dubrovnik; long, steep climb (steps) down to beach."*
HRK 200, 4 Apr-27 Oct. **2023**

DUBROVNIK *C4* (5km NW Urban/Coastal) *42.66191, 18.07050* **Camping Solitudo (formerly Autocamp),** Vatroslava Lisinskog 17, 20000 Dubrovnik **(052) 465010; www.valamar.com/en/camping-dubrovnik/solitudo-camping**
€7.30 (htd) WD MSP shgl 500m

S down Adriatic Highway to Tuđjman Bdge over Dubrovnik Harbour. Turn L immed sp Dubrovnik & in 700m take sharp U-turn sp Dubrovnik & carry on under bdge. Site on Babin Kuk across harbour fr bdge. 3*, Lge, hdstg, mkd, pt shd, pt sl, terr, EHU (10A) inc (long lead poss req); bbq; sw; twin axles; phone; bus 150m; Eng spkn; adv bkg acc; ccard acc; tennis; bike hire; fishing; CKE. *"Friendly, clean, well-run, v busy site; sm pitches poss stony &/or boggy; some lge pitches; levelling blocks poss req; pool & paddling pool 200m; san facs poss stretched high ssn & dated; nearest site to city cent; conv Bari ferry; sat nav/map advised as few sp; site in two parts, upper numbered but not mrkd and informal, lower numbered and mkd."*
HRK 400, 26 Apr-6 Oct, X01. **2024**

FAZANA *A3* (1km S Coastal) *44.91717, 13.81105* **Camping Bi-Village,** Dragonja 115, 52212 Fažana **(052) 300300; info@bivillage.com; www.bivillage.com**
HRK53 (htd) WD MSP shgl adj

N fr Pula on rd 21/A9/E751 at Vodnjan turn W sp Fažana. Foll sp for site. 4*, V lge, mkd, pt shd, EHU (10A) inc; gas; bbq; 30% statics; phone; bus; Eng spkn; adv bkg acc; ccard acc; bike hire; waterslide; golf 2km; tennis 1km; boat hire; games area; watersports; CKE. *"Excel, modern, clean san facs; private bthrms avail; site surrounded by pine trees; some beachside pitches; conv Brijuni Island National Park; excel leisure facs for families; vg cycle paths; no emptying point for Wastermaster; vg; prices vary per ssn."*
HRK 420, 20 Apr-14 Oct. **2023**

KARLOVAC *B2* (12km SW Rural) *45.41962, 15.48338* **Autocamp Slapić,** Mrežničke Brig, 47250 Duga Resa **(098) 860601; info@campslapic.hr; www.campslapic.hr**
HRK20 WD nr nr nr

Exit A1/E65 junc 3 for Karlovac; strt over traff lts immed after toll booth sp Split & Rijecka.Take D23 to Duga Resa; turn L by church in Duga Resa; cont over bdge & turn R; foll rd keeping rv on your R; cont thro vill of Mrnžnički Brig in 3km; site sp in another 1km. NB new bdge at Belavici. Site well sp fr Duga Resa. 4*, Sm, mkd, pt shd, EHU (16A) HRK30; bbq; sw nr; phone; train to Zagreb 500m; Eng spkn; adv bkg acc; ccard acc; canoeing; fishing; games area; tennis; bike hire. *"Friendly, pleasant, family-owned site in gd location on rv; lovely area; gd bar/rest; gd clean facs; lge pitches; long hoses req LS; easy drive into Zagreb; excel; new, superb sans block (2014); poss noise fr daytrippers; rds to site narr."*
€33.00, 1 Apr-31 Oct. **2024**

KORENICA *B3* (1.5km NW Urban) *44.76527, 15.68833* **Camping Borje,** Vranovaca bb, 53230 Korenica **(053) 751 015 or 751 014; info@np-plitvicka-jezera.hr; www.np-plitvicka-jezera.hr/camp-borje**
HRK20 (htd) WD MSP nr

Exit A1/A6 at Karlovac & take rd 1/E71 S dir Split. Site on R approx 15km after Plitvička Jezera National Park, well sp. 4*, Med, mkd, pt shd, sl, EHU (10A) inc; bbq; sw nr; twin axles; Eng spkn; adv bkg acc; ccard acc; CKE. *"Vg, clean, well-kept, spacious, sl site - levelling poss tricky; gd, modern, immac facs; helpful staff; well run by Plitvicka National Park; excel for visiting the Lakes & waterfalls; free bus runs to park at 1030 and returns at 1730; excel; mountain views."*
HRK 250, 1 Apr-15 Oct. **2024**

LABIN *A2* (3km SW Rural) *45.08179, 14.10167*
Mini Camping Romantik, HR-52220 Labin, Kapelica 47b
(911) 396423; mario.braticic@pu.t-com.hr; www.kamp-romantik.com

Fr Labin on A21/E751, take 5103 twds Koramomacno for 2km. Site sp on this rd. Turn L into sm lane. Foll sp. 3*, Sm, mkd, hdstg, unshd, EHU (10A); bbq; cooking facs; 10% statics; Eng spkn; adv bkg rec; games area. *"Sm family site; 4 mkd and 4 unmkd pitches; v friendly, helpful, lovely family run site; 2km walk to old Labin."*
HRK 164, 24 Apr-15 Oct. **2022**

NOVIGRAD (DALMATIA) *B3* (0.6km N Coastal) *44.18472, 15.54944* **Camping Adriasol,** 23312 Novigrad **(023) 375618; info@adriasol.com or office@ adriasol.com; www.adriasol.com**
HRK23 nr nr nr adj

Exit A1 at Posedarje & foll sp Novigrad. Site sp at end of vill. 3*, Med, pt shd, EHU (16A) HRK31; cooking facs; TV; 10% statics; adv bkg acc; watersports; bike hire; games area; CKE. *"Well-positioned site - poss windy; gd facs; friendly staff; popular level pitches by beach cost more; freezer avail for camper use; very helpful staff."*
HRK 339, 1 May-30 Sep. **2024**

OMIS *C4* (8km S Coastal) *43.40611, 16.77777*
Autocamp Sirena, Četvrt Vrilo 10, 21317 Lokva Rogoznica **(021) 870266; autocampsirena@gmail.com; www.autocamp-sirena.com**
HRK30 shgl adj

Thro Omiš S'wards on main coastal rd, site up sm lane on R immed bef sm tunnel. Med, hdstg, pt shd, sl, terr, EHU (16A) HRK35; gas; bbq; phone; bus; Eng spkn; adv bkg acc; watersports; CKE. *"Enthusiastic, welcoming staff; improving site; easy access lge o'fits; stunning location above beautiful beach; excel stop bet Split & Dubrovnik; excel rest."* **€35.00** **2024**

OMIS *C4* (1.5km W Coastal) *43.44040, 16.67960*
Autocamp Galeb, Vukovarska bb, 21310 Omiš **(021) 864430; camping@galeb.hr; www.camp.galeb.hr**
HRK33 nr sand

Site sp on rd 2/E65 fr Split to Dubrovnik. 3*, Lge, mkd, pt shd, serviced pitches; EHU (16A) inc; gas; bbq (elec, gas); red long stay; 50% statics; bus; ccard acc; bike hire; games area; tennis; white water rafting; watersports; CKE. *"Excel, well-maintained site in gd position; private bthrms avail; extra for waterside pitch; clean san facs; suitable young children; easy walk or water taxi to town; v friendly staff; excel new rest, with set breakfast."* **HRK 281, X02.** **2022**

OPATIJA *A2* (5km S Coastal) *45.30633, 14.28354*
Camping Opatija (formerly Autocamp Opatija), Liburnijska 46, 51414 Ičići **(051) 704 836; opatijacamping@gmail.com; www.rivijera-opatija.hr**
nr shgl adj

Fr Opatija take Pula rd 66. Site sp on R of rd 5km after Opatija. Sp fr Ičići. Med, pt shd, terr, EHU (10A); Eng spkn; tennis. *"Gd site nr coastal promenade; diff for lge o'fits without motor mover."*
€27.00, 30 Mar-31 Oct. **2024**

OREBIC *C4* (2.6km ENE Coastal) *42.982485, 17.205609*
Camping Lavanda, Dubravica bb, HR 20250 Orebič **(385) 20454484; info@lavanda-camping.com; www.lavanda-camping.com**

On main rd 1km bef Orebic app fr Trpanj. 4*, Med, mkd, hdstg, pt shd, terr, EHU (16A); bbq; TV; 5% statics; phone; bus adj; Eng spkn; adv bkg acc; sauna; CKE. *"Brand new site (2018); excel san facs; dog shwr; ATM; beach for dogs; ferry to island avail; great views fr almost every pitch; supmkt 500m; petrol 200m; excel."* **HRK 248, 15 Apr-31 Oct.** **2023**

OREBIC *C4* (1km E Coastal) *42.9810, 17.1980* **Nevio Camping,** Dubravica bb, 20250 Orebič **(020) 713100; info@nevio-camping.com; www.nevio-camping.com**
HRK15-38 (htd) nr shgl

Fr N take ferry fr Ploče to Trpanj & take rd 415 then 414 dir Orebič, site sp. Fr S on rd 8/E65 turn W at Zaton Doli onto rd 414 to site. Site ent immed after lge sp - not 100m further on. 4*, Sm, pt shd, terr, serviced pitches; EHU (16A) inc; bbq; cooking facs; TV; 40% statics; Eng spkn; adv bkg acc; tennis; bike hire. *"Excel new site in gd location; friendly, helpful, welcoming staff; beach bar; gd views; gd, clean facs; not suitable lge o'fits."* **HRK 339** **2024**

PAKOSTANE *B3* (4km SE Coastal) *43.88611, 15.53305*
Autocamp Oaza Mira, Ul. Dr. Franje Tudmana 2, 23211 Drage **023 635419; info@oaza-mira.hr; www.oaza-mira.hr**
4 - 9 euros (depending on low/high season) adj

A1 Karlovac-Split past Zadar, exit Biograd dir Sibenik on coast rd; sp on coastal side of rd; foll sp site after bay. Med, hdstg, pt shd, terr, EHU inc; bbq; Eng spkn; adv bkg acc; games rm; beach volley court; 2 tennis courts; multi-purpose court for basketball/ soccer. *"Excel new lovely site in beautiful location; generous pitches; rec using ACSI card; 2 beautiful bays adj to site; highly rec."*
HRK 427, 1 Apr-31 Oct. **2020**

POREC *A2* (10km N Coastal) *45.29728, 13.59425*
Valamar Camping Lanterna, Lanterna 1, 52465 Tar
(052) 404 500; lanterna@valamar.com;
www.camping-adriatic.com/camp-lanterna
HRK 55 shgl adj

Site sp 5km S of Novigrad (Istria) & N of Poreč on Umag-Vrsar coast rd. 4*, V lge, hdstg, mkd, hdg, pt shd, pt sl, terr, EHU (10A); gas; bbq; 10% statics; phone; adv bkg req; ccard acc; bike hire; watersports; games area; boat launch; tennis; CKE. *"V busy, well-run site; excel san facs & leisure facs; 2 hydro-massage pools; noise fr ships loading across bay; bkg fee; although many san facs they may be a long walk; variety of shops; gd sightseeing; extra for seaside/hdg pitch; vg."* **€55.00, 12 Apr-10 Oct, X10.** **2024**

POREC *A2* (8km NW Coastal) *45.25680, 13.58350*
Camping Ulika (Naturist), 52440 Poreč (Istra)
(052) 436325; ulika@istracamping.com;
www.istracamping.com/en/camping/ulika
HRK48 shgl

Site sp on rd fr Poreč to Tar & Novigrad. 4*, V lge, shd, pt sl, EHU (6A) HRK23; red long stay; 9% statics; adv bkg acc; ccard acc; watersports; tennis. *"Excel site; picturesque shore; vg facs, poss far fr some pitches; lge site, bike useful for getting around."* **HRK 380, 21 Apr-1 Oct.** **2023**

PRIMOSTEN *B4* (2km N Coastal) *43.60646, 15.92085*
Auto Kamp Adriatic, Huljerat BB, 22202 Primošten
(022) 571223; camp-adriatiq@adriatiq.com;
www.autocamp-adriatiq.com
HRK32 shgl adj

Off Adriatic Highway, rd 8/E65, sp. 3*, V lge, hdstg, unshd, pt sl, terr, EHU (16A) inc; gas; Eng spkn; watersports; games area; tennis; boat hire; CKE. *"Gd sea views; excel san facs; diving cent; some pitches poss diff to get onto; beautiful views fr beach."* **HRK 190, 7 Apr-31 Oct.** **2022**

PULA *A3* (7km S Coastal) *44.82290, 13.85080*
Camping Peškera, Indije 73 52100 Banjole/Pula (Istra)
052 573209; info@camp-peskera.com;
www.camp-peskera.com
HRK22 nr shgl adj

Fr N take A9 to Pula. Cont on m'way twd Premantura. Exit at Banjole, cont twd Indije. Campsite is 100m after Indije. 4*, Sm, pt shd, pt sl, EHU; bus 0.5km; Eng spkn; adv bkg acc; ccard acc; CCI. *"Beautiful situation; helpful & friendly owners; gd clean san facs; vg."* **€28.00, 1 Apr-31 Oct.** **2024**

PULA *A3* (8km S Rural) *44.82472, 13.85885*
Camping Diana, Castagnes b b, 52100 Banjole
(385) 99 293 1963 or (385) 99 738 0313; kristijan.modrusan@gmail.com; www.camp-diana.com
nr

Fr Pula ring rd foll sp Premantura & Camping Indije Site 1km bef Cmp Indije. 3*, Sm, pt shd, pt sl, EHU (16A) inc; adv bkg acc; tennis; games area. *"Pleasant site in garden setting; gd range of facs; immac san facs; welcoming family owners; narr ent poss diff for lge o'fits."* **HRK 254, 15 May-22 Sep.** **2022**

PULA *A3* (9km S Coastal) *44.82012, 13.90252*
Autocamp Pomer, Pomer bb, 52100 Pula **052 573746; acpomer@arenaturist.hr; www.arenacamps.com**
HRK23 shgl adj

Fr N on A9 to Pula, take exit to Pula. At bottom of hill turn L after filling stn & foll dir Medulin/ Premantura. In Premantura turn L by Consum supmkt & foll sp to Pomer & site. Med, mkd, shd, terr, EHU (16A) HRK21 (long lead poss req); bbq; 10% statics; phone; Eng spkn; adv bkg acc; watersports; fishing; games area; CKE. *"Clean san facs poss stretched high ssn; friendly owner; quiet, relaxing site."* **HRK 127, 21 Apr-15 Oct.** **2022**

RABAC *A3* (0.5km W Coastal) *45.08086, 14.14583*
Camping Oliva, Maslinica 1, 52221 Rabac **(0)52 884 170; info@maslinica-rabac.com; www.maslinica-rabac.com**
HRK22 nr shgl

On ent Rabac fr Labin, turn R at sp Autocamp; site ent in 500m. 3*, V lge, mkd, pt shd, EHU (10A) inc (long lead poss req); gas; 30% statics; phone; adv bkg req; ccard acc; boat launch; watersports; CKE. *"Conv historic walled town Labin; sports complex; walk along beach to shops & rest."* **€24.00, 21 Apr-19 Oct.** **2024**

RAKOVICA *B3* (7km SW Rural) *44.95020, 15.64160*
Camp Korana, Plitvička Jezera, 47246 Drežnik Grad
(053) 751888; autokamp.korana@np-plitvicka-jezera.hr; www.np-plitvicka-jezera.hr/camp-korana
HRK23

On A1/E59 2km S of Grabovac, site on L. Site is 5km N of main ent to Plitvička Nat Park, sp. Lge, hdstg, pt shd, pt sl, EHU (16A) inc (poss long lead req); own san req; bbq; 10% statics; Eng spkn; ccard acc; CKE. *"Lovely site, v busy; poss long way fr facs; gd new san facs but inadequate for size of site; efficient, friendly site staff; poss muddy in wet; bus to National Park (6km) high ssn; gd rest."* **HRK 250, 1 Apr-31 Oct.** **2023**

RIJEKA *A2* (9km W Coastal) *45.35638, 14.34222*
Camping Preluk, Preluk 1, 51000 Rijeka
(051) 662185; camp.preluk@gmail.com

On Rijeka to Opatija coast rd. 2*, Sm, shd, EHU (10A) inc; own san req; 80% statics; bus; Eng spkn. *"NH only; many statics; facs recently renovated (2012); bus to town; sm beach on site; gd windsurfing."* **HRK 158, 1 May-30 Sep.** **2020**

CROATIA

RIZVANUSA *B3* (10km W Rural) *44.49580, 15.29165* **Eco Camp Rizvan City,** Rizvanuša 1, 53000 Gospić **385 98 65 65 90; info@adria-velebitica.hr; www.camp-rizvancity.com**

Fr A1 take exit 12 (Gospic). Head 10km E twd Karlobag on highway 25. Turn L off main rd into Vill Rizvanusa. Camp 500m. Sm, pt shd, EHU (16A); bbq; twin axles; Eng spkn; adv bkg acc; games area. *"Walks, high rope course; quad & jeep safari; archery; paintball; zip line; wall climbing; giant swing; bike trails; vg."* **€28.00, 1 Mar-1 Nov. 2024**

ROVINJ *A2* (7km N Coastal) *45.12287, 13.62970* **Campsite Valalta Naturist (Naturist),** Cesta Za Valaltu-Lim 7, 52210 Rovinj (Istra) **052 804800; valalta@valalta.hr; www.valalta.hr**

7km NW fr Rovinj. Foll signs to Valalta. 5*, V lge, hdstg, hdg, mkd, pt shd, EHU (16A); bbq; twin axles; TV; phone; Eng spkn; adv bkg acc; games area; games rm; waterslide; bike hire. *"Excel site."* **€43.50, 1 May-1 Oct. 2024**

ROVINJ *A2* (0.7km NW Coastal) *45.09472, 13.64527* **Autocamp Porton Biondi,** Aleja Porton Biondi 1, 52210 Rovinj **(052) 813557; portonbiondi@web.de; www.porton.hr**

HRK24 nr shgl nrby

Site sp on ent Rovinj. 3*, Lge, shd, pt sl, terr, EHU inc; red long stay; adv bkg acc; ccard acc; watersports; CKE. *"Gd site within walking dist Rovinj old town; beautiful views; new san facs; sm pitches not suitable lge o'fits & care needed when ent site; excel rest; 2nd & subsequent nights at red rate."* **HRK 519, 15 Mar-31 Oct. 2023**

ROVINJ *A2* (5km NW Coastal) *45.10909, 13.61974* **Camping Amarin,** Monsena bb, 52210 Rovinj **(052) 802000; ac-amarin@maistra.hr; www.campingrovinjvrsar.com**

HRK47 (htd) shgl adj

Fr town N in dir Valalta, turn L & foll site sp. 3*, V lge, mkd, pt shd, pt sl, EHU (10A) inc; TV; 30% statics; phone; Eng spkn; adv bkg acc; ccard acc; sports facs; tennis; bike hire; waterslide; CKE. *"Excel site; clean, well-maintained san facs & pool; gd entmnt; views of town & islands; lovely situation in pine & olive trees; water taxi to town; some pitches obstructed by trees & uneven; wifi hotspots but free."* **HRK 1000, 20 Apr-30 Sep. 2023**

SELCE *A2* (1.3km SE Coastal) *45.15361, 14.72488* **Autocamp Selce,** Jasenová 19, 51266 Selce **(051) 764038; autokampselce@jadran-crikvenica.hr; www.jadran-crikvenica.hr**

HRK17 shgl adj

Thro Selce town cent, site is 500m SE of town, sp. 2*, Lge, hdstg, pt shd, pt sl, terr, EHU (10A) HRK27; red long stay; TV; phone; ccard acc; CKE. *"Wooded site; seaside location; helpful staff; long stay; blocks & wedges ess; san facs run down & neglected; long lead rec; door security."* **HRK 247, 1 Apr-15 Oct. 2024**

SIBENIK *B3* (10km NE Rural) *43.80063, 15.94210* **Camp Krka,** Skocici 21, 22221 Lozovac **(022) 778495; goran.skocic@si.t-com.hr; www.camp-krka.hr**

nr

Exit A1 at junc 22 Šibenik, turn E at T-junc, thro tunnel & site in approx 4km. Fr main coast rd at Sibenik turn N onto rte 33 twd Drniš. After 15km turn L dir Skradin, site sp on L. Med, hdstg, pt shd, EHU (16A) HRK23 (poss rev pol, check earth); 10% statics; Eng spkn; CKE. *"Pleasant, basic site in orchard; friendly owner; B&B; gd modern san facs; conv Krka National Park & Krka gorge; gd; clean new shwr/wc facs (2014); rest, cheap basic food."* **€29.50, 1 Mar-31 Oct. 2024**

SIBENIK *B3* (4km S Coastal) *43.69925, 15.87942* **Camping Solaris,** Hotelsko Naselje Solaris, 22000 Šibenik **(052) 465000; www.valamar.com/en/camping-porec/solaris-camping-resort**

(htd) nr

Sp fr E65 Zadar-Split rd, adj hotel complex. 3*, V lge, hdg, mkd, pt shd, serviced pitches; EHU (6A) inc; bbq; red long stay; TV; bus; ccard acc; bike hire; waterslide; tennis; sauna; watersports; CKE. *"Well-situated in olive & pine trees; mv service pnt nr; some pitches adj marina; excel, modern san facs."* **HRK 400, 27 Apr-30 Sep. 2024**

SPLIT *B4* (8km E Coastal) *43.50451, 16.52598* **Camping Stobreč-Split,** Sv Lovre 6, 21311 Stobreč **(021) 325426; camping.split@gmail.com; www.campingsplit.com**

12 HRK56 sand

Fr N foll E65 & m'way thro Split to sp Stobreč. Site sp R off E65 at traff lts in Stobreč. 4*, Lge, hdstg, mkd, shd, pt sl, EHU (16A) inc (long lead poss req); bus to Split; Eng spkn; games area. *"Superb, well-run site in lovely setting with views; helpful, welcoming staff; gd facs; own sandy beach; public footpath thro site; rec arr early to secure pitch; gd value for money; highly rec; Diocletian's Palace worth a visit; excel; wellness ctr - pool, sauna, gym."* **HRK 348 2023**

STARIGRAD PAKLENICA *B3* (0.3km S Coastal) *44.28694, 15.44666* **Autocamp Paklenica,** Dr Franje Tuđjmana 14, 23244 Starigrad-Paklenica **(023) 209066; camping.paklenica@bluesunhotels.com or alan@bluesunhotels.com; www.bluesunhotels.com**

HRK37 WD adj

On rd 8/E65 Adriatic H'way at ent to Paklenica National Park in Zidine vill. Hotel Alan is lge, 10-storey block - ent & cont to site. Lge, shd, pt sl, EHU (16A) inc (long lead poss req); red long stay; TV; 5% statics; phone; Eng spkn; adv bkg acc; ccard acc; games area; bike hire; tennis; CKE. *"Gd clean facs; conv National Park; excel walking & rock climbing; use of facs at adj hotel; pool adj; site muddy when wet; gd res, pleasant helpful staff, san facs being enlarged (2013)."* **HRK 329, 1Apr-15 Nov. 2024**

STARLGRAD PAKLENICA *B3* (1km N Coastal) *44.31340, 15.43579* **Auto-Kamp Plantaža,** Put Plantaza 2, 23244 Starigrad Paklenica **(038) 23 369131; plantaza@hi.t-com.hr; www.pansion-plantaza.com**

12 (htd) WD MSP

Fr Rijeka foll M2/E27 coast rd until 1 km N of Steligrad. V Steep pull out of site. Sm, mkd, hdstg, shd, terr, EHU 10A; bbq; Eng spkn; CKE. *"Vg site; ACSI; excel new facs; handy for NP; shopping for fresh food v ltd locally."* **HRK 114 2020**

TROGIR *B4* (5km W Coastal) *43.51012795, 16.192743494594595* **Amadria Park Camping (formerly Camping Vranjica-Belvedere),** Kralja Zvonimira 62, 21218 Seget Donji **5 21 798 228; trogir@amadriaparkcamping.com; www.amadriaparkcamping.com**

HRK25 WD MSP shgl adj

Site clearly sp on coast rd, W of Trogir, 100m bef start of by-pass. Lge, mkd, pt shd, pt sl, terr, EHU (16A) HRK36; bbq; red long stay; TV; 30% statics; phone; Eng spkn; adv bkg acc; ccard acc; watersports; games area; tennis; CKE. *"Beautiful position with views of bay; bus, water taxi; lovely town; gd facs; vg site; site OK, bit scruffy but clean san facs; private san facs avail; v helpful staff."* **€66.00, 15 Apr-15 Oct. 2024**

TUHELJSKE TOPLICE *B2* (0km S Urban) *46.06583, 15.78513* **Camping Terme Tuhelj,** Ljudevita Gaja 4, 49215 Tuhelj **(049) 203000; info@terme-tuhelj.hr; www.terme-tuhelj.hr**

12 HRK25 WD MSP (htd)

N fr Zagreb on A2 for approx 24km, exit junc 5 Zabok & foll rds 24/301/205 to sp Tuheljske Toplice. Check in at Hotel Toplice. 5*, Sm, pt shd, EHU (6A) HRK25; TV; phone; bus; Eng spkn; adv bkg acc; games area; games rm; waterslide. *"Gd, conv Zagreb & gd alt to Zagreb site; thermal spa adj."* **HRK 433.7 2022**

UMAG *A2* (6km S Coastal) *45.39271, 13.54193* **Autocamp Finida,** Križine br 55A, 52470 Umag **(052) 756296; camp.finida@instraturist.hr; www.istracamping.com**

HRK25 WD MSP shgl adj

Site clearly sp. 4*, Lge, mkd, pt shd, pt sl, EHU (10A) inc; red long stay; TV; 50% statics; phone; bus; Eng spkn; adv bkg acc; ccard acc; bike hire; CKE. *"Gd base for touring Istria; gd, clean, modern facs; lovely site amongst oak trees; friendly staff."* **HRK 125, 23 Apr-30 Sep. 2022**

VRSAR *A2* (0.5km N Urban/Coastal) *45.15555, 13.61055* **Camping Orsera,** 52450 Vrsar **(052) 465000; www.valamar.com/en/camping-porec/orsera-camping-resort**

HRK39 WD MSP shgl adj

S fr Poreč pass Autocamp Funtana, site on R. 3*, V lge, hdg, mkd, pt shd, pt sl, EHU (10A) inc; gas; 15% statics; phone; Eng spkn; adv bkg rec; ccard acc; waterslide; watersports; games area; boat launch; games rm; CKE. *"Gd situation nr Vrsar vill & harbour; money exchange; clean san facs; muddy in rain; conv for town; vg."* **HRK 406, 20 Apr-30 Sep. 2024**

VRSAR *A2* (2km N Coastal) *45.16505, 13.60796* **Camping Valkanela,** Petalon 1, 52450 Vrsar **(052) 225667; info@maistra.hr; www.campingrovinjvrsar.com**

HRK50 WD MSP shgl

Site sp N of town fr coast rd. 4*, V lge, pt shd, pt sl, terr, EHU (6A) inc; TV; 40% statics; phone; Eng spkn; adv bkg acc; ccard acc; watersports; tennis; bike hire; games area; CKE. *"Excel for watersports; vg san facs; vg site for children."* **HRK 275, 19 Apr-6 Oct. 2024**

VRSAR *A2* (1km SE Coastal) *45.14233, 13.60541* **Naturist-Park Koversada (Naturist),** Petalon 1, 52450 Vrsar **(052) 441378; koversada-camp@maistra.hr; www.campingrovinjvrsar.com**

HRK46 WD MSP shgl

Site sp fr Vrsar in dir Koversada. V lge, mkd, hdg, pt shd, pt sl, terr, EHU (10-16A) inc; red long stay; TV; 50% statics; phone; Eng spkn; adv bkg acc; ccard acc; watersports; games area; tennis; bike hire; CKE. *"Vg, modern san facs; diving school; excel leisure facs; peaceful situation; excel; busy noisy hilly site."* **HRK 214, 21 Apr-8 Oct. 2024**

ZADAR *B3* (3.5km N Coastal) *44.13408, 15.21115* **Falkensteiner Camping Zadar,** Majstora Radovana 7, 23000 Zadar **(023) 206 555 602; reservations.camping zadar@falkensteiner.com; www.falkensteiner.com**

12 WD MSP shgl

Exit A2 at Zadar 1/West, cont for approx.19 km. In Zadar, turn R at 2nd x-rds with traff lts and take the bypass (dir Nin, Vir). Cont across 2 x-rds (dir Puntamika). In 70m turn R to Falkensteiner Resort Borik. 5*, V lge, shd, EHU (10A) inc; own san req; phone; bus 450m; Eng spkn; ccard acc; tennis; watersports; CKE. *"Pt of resort complex of 6 hotels; facs poor & some cold water only; poor security; gd sw beach; gd rests nrby; site run down; NH only."* **HRK 630 2022**

CROATIA

ZAGREB *B2* (12km SW Urban) *45.77389, 15.87778*
Camping Motel Plitvice, Lučko, 10090 Zagreb
+385 1 6530 444; motel@motel-plitvice.hr; www.motel-plitvice.hr
(htd) WD

Site at motel attached to Plitvice services on A3/ E70. Access only fr m'way travelling fr N, otherwise long m'way detour fr S. Lge, pt shd, EHU (16A) inc; TV; phone; bus to town fr site; ccard acc; tennis; CKE. *"Ask at motel recep (excel Eng) for best way back fr city &/or details minibus to city; Zagreb well worth a visit; site shabby but facs clean & adequate - stretched when site full & in need of update."*
HRK 168, 1 May-30 Sep. **2022**

ZAGREB *B2* (16km W Rural) *45.80217, 15.82696*
Camp Zagreb, Jezerska 6, 10437 Rakitje
(01) 3324567; info@campzagreb.com; www.campzagreb.com
WD MSP

Exit A3 J2 sp Bestovje. Turn R and cont for approx 3km. At rndabt before x-ing over m'way turn R. Cont for 1km. Site on L. 4*, Med, hdg, mkd, pt shd, EHU (16A); bbq; sw; twin axles; 5% statics; train 1km; Eng spkn; adv bkg acc; games rm; bike hire; CKE. *"Excel site; lake adj; sauna & massage; kayak & bike hire; horse trail; public trans 1.5km; free shuttle to rlw stn into city ctr."* **HRK 280** **2023**

ZAOSTROG *C4* (0.5km SE Coastal) *43.13925, 17.28047*
Camp Viter, Obala A.K. Miosica 1, 21334 Zaostrog (Dalmatija) **021 629190; info@camp-viter.com; www.camp-viter.com**
HRK25 WD MSP nr nr nr

Foll Camp Viter signs 600m on R after Zaostrog sp. Sm, hdstg, pt shd, EHU (16A) HRK25; bbq; twin axles; Eng spkn; adv bkg acc; CCI. *"Very helpful, friendly owners; vg."* **€58.50, 1 Apr-31 Oct.** **2024**

ZATON *B3* (1.5km N Coastal) *44.23434, 15.16605*
Camping Zaton Holiday Resort, Široka ulica bb, 23232 Zaton **023 280215; camping@zaton.hr; www.zaton.hr**
€10 (htd) WD MSP sand adj

Site 16km NW of Zadar on Nin rd. Pt of Zaton holiday vill. Wel sp. 3*, V lge, pt shd, EHU (10A) inc; gas; 15% statics; phone; adv bkg acc; ccard acc; games area; boat hire; watersports; tennis; CKE. *"Excel, well-run, busy site; own beach; excel, modern san facs; cent of site is 'vill' with gd value shops & rests; gd for all ages; nr ancient sm town of Nin, in walking dist; conv National Parks; v expensive outside ACSI discount period but has first class facs and nrby town well worth a visit; Croatia's best campsite; superbly laid out & equipped."* **€75.00, 13 Apr-1 Oct.** **2022**

BRAC ISLAND

BOL *C4* (0.5km W Urban/Coastal) *43.26373, 16.64799*
Kamp Kito, Braćke Ceste bb, 21420 Bol **(021) 635551 or 635091; info@camping-brac.com; www.camping-brac.com**
WD 500m

Take ferry fr Makarska to Brač & take rd 113/115 to Bol (37km). On o'skrts do not turn L into town but cont twd Zlatni Rat. Pass Studenac sup'mkt on R, site on L. Sm, pt shd, EHU (16A) HRK20; gas; bbq; TV; 10% statics; Eng spkn; adv bkg acc. *"Excel for beaches & boating; gd local food in rest; vg, friendly, family-run site; clean, well-equipped; well worth effort to get there."* **HRK 141** **2022**

CRES ISLAND

CRES *A3* (1km N Coastal) *44.96277, 14.39694*
Camping Kovačine (Part Naturist), Melin 1/20, 51557 Cres **(051) 573150 or 573423; campkovacine@kovacine.com; www.camp-kovacine.com**
HRK23 WD

Fr N, foll sp bef Cres on R. Fr S app thro vill of Cres. 4*, V lge, pt shd, EHU (12A) inc; red long stay; Eng spkn; ccard acc; watersports; games area; tennis; CKE. *"Site in olive grove; rocky making driving diff, but amenities gd & well-run; sep area for naturists; welcoming staff; delightful walk/cycle rte to sm vill of Cres; excel site."* **€37.80, 22 Mar-3 Nov.** **2024**

MARTINSCICA *A3* (1km NW Coastal) *44.82108, 14.34298*
Camping Slatina, 51556 Martinšćica **(051) 574127; info@camp-slatina.com; www.camp-slatina.com**
HRK23 WD MSP shgl adj

Fr Cres S on main rd sp Mali Lošinj for 17km. Turn R sp Martinšćica, site in 8km at end of rd. 4*, V lge, hdg, hdstg, shd, terr, EHU (10A) inc (long lead req); 20% statics; phone; Eng spkn; adv bkg acc; ccard acc; boat launch. *"Site on steep slope; newest san facs superb; beautiful island; dog & car washing facs; vg supmkt; ATM on site."* **HRK 338, 23 Apr-1 Oct.** **2022**

KRK ISLAND

BASKA *A3* (1.4km SW Coastal) *44.965613, 14.747772*
Valamar Camping Baška, Put Zablaca 40, 51523 Baska **(052) 465000; www.valamar.com/en/camping-baska/baska-beach-camping-resort**
HKR56 WD MSP (htd)

Drive over bdge to islnd of KRK (no chge on Sun) and take main rd 103 to Krk, then on to the southern tip of islnd and Baska. Site sp on ent town. 4*, Lge, mkd, pt shd, EHU (16A) inc; bbq; twin axles; TV; 20% statics; phone; bus adj; Eng spkn; adv bkg acc; sauna; sports area; bike hire; CKE. *"Excellent, new san facs (2018); kids club; rest adj; perfect experience creator; free use of pool & gym at Baska Wellness Ctr; excel site."* **HRK 604, 19 Apr-6 Oct.** **2024**

BASKA *A3* (1km W Coastal) *44.96911, 14.76671*
Camping Bunculuka (Naturist), 51523 Baška **(052) 465000; bunculuka@hotelibaska.hr; www.valamar.com/en/camping-baska/bunculuka-camping-resort**
HRK25 shgl

Fr Rijeka S on Adriatic highway, in approx 23km turn R over bdge, foll sp Krk & Baška. Site sp. 4*, V lge, mkd, pt shd, terr, EHU (16A) inc (long cable poss req); 10% statics; phone; adv bkg rec; ccard acc; tennis; kayak hire; sailing. *"Pleasant coastal mkd walks; superb site."* **HRK 550, 26 Apr-6 Oct.** **2024**

KRK *A3* (16km SE Coastal) *44.96048, 14.68402*
Camping Škrila (formerly Autocamp), Stara Baška, 51521 Punat **(052) 465000; www.valamar.com/en/camping-krk/skrila-camping**
€2 shgl adj

Fr Krk E on rd 102, turn S dir Punat & Stara Baška. Site on R at bottom of hill approx 8km after Punat. 3*, Lge, mkd, hdstg, unshd, terr, EHU HRK27; Eng spkn. *"Approx 50 touring pitches; friendly, helpful staff; gd security; lovely, isolated position; new excel san facs (2014)."* **HRK 400, 26 Apr-6 Oct.** **2024**

KRK *A3* (4km SE Coastal) *45.01638, 14.62833*
Autocamp Pila, Šetalište Ivana Brusića 2, 51521 Punat **(051) 854020; camp.pila@falkensteiner.com; campingpunat.com**
HRK32 nr adj

Take coast rd, rte 2 twd Split. At Kraljevica, turn R onto rd 103 over Krk toll bdge. Foll sp for Krk, Punat. Site sp at T-junc after Punat Marina & vill. Lge, pt shd, serviced pitches; EHU (10-16A) inc; cooking facs; TV; 80% statics; ccard acc; fishing; watersports; CKE. *"Well-run, big site; clean facs; gd for families with sm children; boat hire; boat trips; sm picturesque vill; lots to do; poss cr."*
€23.00, 12 Apr-18 Oct. **2024**

KRK *A3* (0.3km W Urban/Coastal) *45.01875, 14.56701*
Valamar Camping Ježevac, Planicka bb, 51500 Krk **(052) 465000; jezevac@valamar.com; www.valamar.com**
HRK34 shgl adj

Fr main island rd heading S, app Krk, take 1st rd on R (W) sp Centar. At rndabt take 2nd exit sp Autocamp. App to site thro housing estate. 4*, V lge, hdstg, pt shd, pt sl, serviced pitches; EHU (10-16A) inc; phone; Eng spkn; ccard acc; watersports; tennis; games area; CKE. *"Conv for touring Krk Island; pleasant, gd value rest with view of old town; registration fee payable 1st night; busy site; levelling poss diff for m'vans."* **HRK 652, 1 Mar-3 Nov.** **2024**

NJIVICE *A2* (0.4km N Coastal) *45.16971, 14.54701*
Kamp Njivice, 51512 Njivice **(051) 846168; reservation@kampnjivice.hr; www.kampnjivice.com**
HRK24.50 shgl adj

8km S of Krk Bdge on rd 102 turn R to Njivice. Site not well sp but foll sp to hotel area N of town cent. 2*, V lge, shd, EHU (6-10A) HRK28; 60% statics; phone; bus; Eng spkn; ccard acc; CKE. *"Less cr than other Krk sites; gd facs."*
HRK 173, 1 May-30 Sep. **2022**

LOSINJ ISLAND

MALI LOSINJ *A3* (4km NW Coastal) *44.55555, 14.44166*
Camping Village Poljana, Privlaka 19, 51550 Mali Lošinj **(051) 231726 or (0365) 520682; www.campingpoljana.com**
HRK61 shgl

On main island rd 1km bef vill of Lošinj, sp. Two ferries a day fr Rijeka take car & c'van on 2hr trip to island. 3*, V lge, shd, pt sl, terr, EHU (6-16A) inc; gas; 50% statics; phone; adv bkg acc; ccard acc; bike hire; tennis; games area; boat hire; watersports; CKE. *"Site in pine forest; private washrms avail; sw with dolphins nrby; sep naturist beach."*
HRK 312, 24 Mar-31 Oct. **2022**

RAB ISLAND

LOPAR *A3* (3km E Coastal) *44.82345, 14.73735*
Valamar Camping San Marino, 51281 Lopar **(052) 465000; www.valamar.com/en/camping-rab/san-marino-camping-resort**
HRK29 sand adj

Fr Rab town N to Lopar, sp ferry. At x-rds turn R sp San Marino, site sp. 4*, V lge, mkd, hdstg, shd, terr, EHU (16A) inc; TV; 10% statics; phone; bus; Eng spkn; adv bkg acc; ccard acc; games area; tennis; watersports; CKE. *"Superb, family site on delightful island; pitches on sandy soil in pine woods."*
HRK 625, 19 Apr-1 Oct. **2024**

RAB *A3* (2km SE Coastal) *44.75253, 14.77411*
Valamar Camping Padova, Banjol 496, 51280 Rab **(052) 465000; www.valamar.com/en/camping-rab/padova-camping-resort**
shgl adj

Fr ferry at Mišnjak foll rd 105 N dir Rab town & Banjol, site sp. 4*, Sm, mkd, hdstg, pt shd, terr, EHU (6-16A) inc; bbq; red long stay; phone; Eng spkn; adv bkg acc; ccard acc; tennis; CKE. *"On edge of lovely bay; 2 pools (1 htd, covrd) at Hotel Padova; many sandy beaches on island; coastal path to Rab medieval town."*
HRK 625, 19 Apr-1 Oct. **2024**

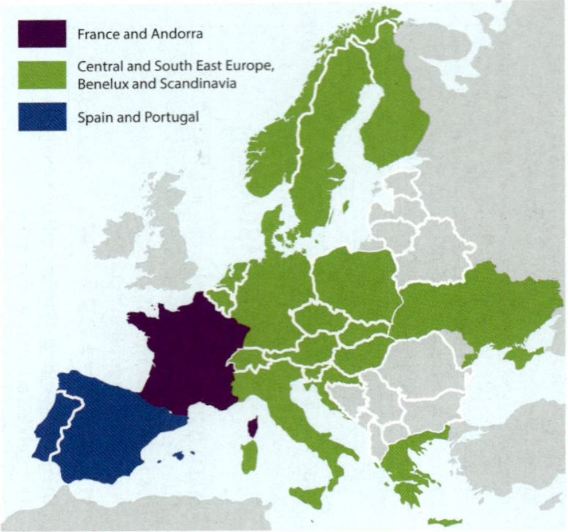

Porec to Virovitica = 410km

	Dubrovnik	Karlovac	Korenica	Krk	Metkovic	Ogulin	Osijek	Pag	Porec	Pula	Rijeka	Šibenik	Senj	Sisak	Split	Trieste (Italy)	Varaždin	Virovitica	Zadar
Karlovac	526																		
Korenica	439	134																	
Krk	659	184	220																
Metkovic	96	481	343	563															
Ogulin	524	49	85	135	432														
Osijek	902	336	463	513	810	378													
Pag	465	288	154	327	369	239	617												
Porec	678	206	242	132	589	157	535	324											
Pula	711	236	275	168	622	190	568	357	56										
Rijeka	601	126	165	58	512	80	462	231	77	110									
Šibenik	305	282	181	333	230	266	644	139	423	416	296								
Senj	251	322	188	408	159	273	651	186	430	463	353	123							
Sisak	667	94	218	278	575	133	235	382	300	333	223	409	406						
Split	225	309	181	430	133	299	677	236	456	503	393	97	26	425					
Trieste (Italy)	684	209	245	135	592	160	538	247	83	190	80	426	433	303	459				
Varaždin	670	154	272	322	619	187	236	426	344	390	280	436	460	149	463	347			
Virovitica	777	204	338	388	685	253	131	492	410	443	333	519	526	110	552	413	102		
Zadar	377	232	131	282	302	216	594	67	301	334	224	72	195	359	169	304	386	469	
Zagreb	572	56	190	261	537	105	280	344	262	292	182	338	378	67	365	265	82	150	288

AUSTRIA
SLOVAKIA
HUNGARY
SLOVENIA
SERBIA
BOSNIA-HERZEGOVINA
MONTENEGRO
ITALY
ADRIATIC SEA
WIEN
BRATISLAVA
Lunz am See
BUDAPEST
Sarvar
Graz
Veszprém
Maribor
Zalakaros
VARAZDIN
LJUBLJANA
Tuheljske Toplice
Pécs
Novo Mesto
ZAGREB
Trieste
VIROVITICA
Umag
Rijeka
KARLOVAC
SISAK
OSIJEK
POREC
Rovinj
Labin
Njivice
Selce
SLAVONSKI BROD
Fazana
Krk
KRK
Baska
Rakovica
Prijedor
Pula
CRES
Lopar
Martinscica
RAB
KORENICA
Banja Luka
LOSINJ
PAG
Rizvanusa
Mali Losinj
PAG
Starigrad Paklenica
Zaton
ZADAR
Zenica
Biograd na Moru
Pakostane
SIBENIK
SARAJEVO
Primosten
SPLIT
Omis
BRAC
Bol
Mostar
Zaostrog
METKOVIC
Orebic
DUBROVNIK
Molunat
PODGORICA
Motorways
Primary roads
Secondary roads
All year site(s)
Seasonal site(s)
No sites listed
0 50 100 150 km
0 20 40 60 80 100 miles
N
S
E
W

Czechia

Castle Loket, Karlovy Vary

Highlights

Lying in the heart of Europe, Czechia is renowned for its ornate castles, fantastically preserved medieval buildings, and numerous other cultural sights.

Considered to be one of the most beautiful cities in the world, the capital, Prague, is a wonderful mix of traditional and modern with treasures old and new waiting to be discovered around every corner.

Traditions are important in Czechia, one of which takes places on April 30 – Walpurgis Night. Known as pálení čarodějnic (the burning of the witches), this is a night of bonfires and celebrations throughout the country.

Czechia is the home of Bohemian glass or crystal, which is international renowned for its beauty, quality and craftsmanship. They are immensely popular as gifts and souvenirs and are one of the best known Czech exports.

Major towns and cities

- Prague – home to an impressive castle and old town.
- Brno – filled with gorgeous architecture and historic sights.
- Plzeň – famous worldwide for Pilsner beer, created here in 1842.
- Olomouc – a quaint city of cobbled streets and historic buildings.

Attractions

- Wenceslas Square, Prague – bursting with monuments, restaurants and shops.
- Český Krumlov – the old town is a UNESCO site and the castle houses a theatre.
- Kutná Hora – Founded in the 12th century, with many spectacular churches.
- Hrad Karlšstejn – this imposing gothic castle is one of the most famous in the country.

Find out more

visitczechia.com

Country Information

Capital: Prague

Bordered by: Austria, Germany, Poland, Slovakia

Terrain: Diverse landscape with rolling hills and plains in the west (Bohemia) surrounded by low mountains; higher hills and heavily forested mountains in the east (Moravia)

Climate: Temperate continental with warm, showery summers and cold, cloudy, snowy winters

Highest Point: Snezka 1,602m

Language: Czech

Local Time: GMT or BST + 1, i.e. 1 hour ahead of the UK all year

Currency: Czech crown (CZK) £1 = CZK 30.27, CZK 100 = £3.30 (Nov 2024)

Emergency numbers: Police 158; Fire brigade 150; Ambulance 155 (operators speak English) or 112.

Public Holidays 2025: Jan 1; Apr 18, 21; May 1, 8; Jul 5, 6; Sep 28, Oct 28; Nov 17; Dec 24, 25, 26.

School summer holidays are from the beginning of July to the end of August.

Entry Formalities

British and Irish passport holders may stay for up to 90 days in any 180 day period without a visa. You may be asked to show a return or onward ticket at the border to confirm your length of stay, or to prove that you have enough money for your stay.

Your passport will need to have a minimum of 6 months' validity remaining, and be less than 10 years old (even if it has more than 6 months validity left).

Visitors arriving at a campsite or hotel must complete a registration form.

Medical Services

For minor ailments first consult staff at a pharmacy (lékárna) who can give advice and are sometimes able to sell drugs normally only available on prescription in the UK. Language may be a problem outside Prague; if you need particular drugs or a repeat prescription, take an empty bottle or remaining pills with you.

For more serious matters requiring a visit to a doctor go to a medical centre (poliklinika) or hospital (nemocnice).

British nationals may obtain emergency medical and hospital treatment and prescriptions on presentation of a European Health Insurance Card (EHIC) or a UK Global Health Insurance Card (UK GHIC). You may have to make a contribution towards costs. Make sure that the doctor or dentist you see is contracted to the public health insurance service, the CMU (most are), otherwise you will have to pay in full for private treatment and for any prescription medicines and the Czech insurance service will not reimburse you.

In parts of the country where few foreign visitors venture, medical staff may not be aware of the rights conferred on you by an EHIC or GHIC. If you have difficulties contact the British Embassy in Prague.

Outbreaks of hepatitis A occur sporadically, particularly in the Prague and Central Bohemia areas, and immunisation is advised for long-stay visitors to rural areas and those who plan to travel outside tourist areas. Take particular care with food and water hygiene.

Opening Hours

Banks: Mon-Fri 9am-5pm. Some foreign exchange bureaux in Prague are open 24 hours.

Museums: Tue-Sun 10am-6pm; closed Monday.

Post Offices: Mon-Fri 8am-6pm, some open on Saturday morning; main post office in Prague (Jindrisska Street 14) is open 2am-12am.

Shops: Mon-Fri 9am-6pm, small shops usually close at lunchtime; Sat 9am-1pm; some food shops open on Sundays.

Safety and Security

There is a high incidence of petty theft, particularly in major tourist areas in Prague, and pickpocketing is common at popular tourist attractions. Care should be taken around the main railway station and on public transport particularly routes to and from Prague Castle where pickpockets may operate.

Beware of fake plain-clothes police officers asking to see your foreign currency and passport. If approached, don't get out your passport. You can call 158 or 112 to check if they are genuine officers, or offer to go to the nearest police station or find a uniformed officer. No police officer has the right to check your money or its authenticity.

If your passport, wallet or other items are lost or stolen you should report the incident immediately to the nearest police station and obtain a police report. A police station that is used to dealing with foreign travellers is at Jungmannovo Nàmìstí 9, Praha 1, 24 hour telephone number 974 851 750; nearest metro: Müstek. Any theft of property must be reported in person to the police within 24 hours in order to obtain a crime number.

Czechia shares with the rest of Europe an underlying threat from terrorism. Please check gov.uk/foreign-travel-advice/czech-republic before you travel.

British Embassy

Thunovska 14
118 00 Prague
Tel: (+420) 257 40 2111
gov.uk/world/czech-republic

Irish Embassy

Tržište 13, 118 00 Prague 1
Tel: (+420) 257 011 280
ireland.ie/prague

Documents

Driving Licence

Czechia authorities require foreign drivers to carry a photocard driving licence. If you still have an old-style driving license you should update it to a photocard before you travel, or obtain an International Driving Permit to accompany your old-style licence. The minimum driving age is 18.

Money

The best place to exchange foreign currency is at banks, where commission rates are generally lower. In Prague some foreign exchange bureaux are open 24 hours. Scottish and Northern Irish bank notes will not be changed. Never exchange money with street vendors as notes are often counterfeit.

Credit cards are often accepted in tourist areas. Cash points are widely available, take care when using them for your own security. Many retail outlets accept Euros.

Passport

You must have a valid passport to enter Czechia. It's recommended that your passport is valid after your planned departure date in case of an unforeseen emergency, which may prevent you from leaving. British nationals with passports in poor condition have been refused entry so you should ensure that your passport is in an acceptable state.

If you hold a British passport where your nationality is shown as anything other than British Citizen contact the Czech Embassy in London to determine whether you require a visa for entry.

Vehicle(s)

Carry your vehicle registration certificate (V5C), insurance details and MOT certificate (if applicable). If you are not the owner of the vehicle you're advised to carry a letter of authority from the owner permitting you to drive it.

Driving

Accidents

If an accident causes injury or damage in excess of CZK 100,000 it must be reported to the police immediately. You should wait at the scene of the accident until the police arrive and then obtain a police report. If your vehicle is only slightly damaged it's still a good idea to report the accident to the police as they will issue a certificate which will facilitate the exportation of the vehicle.

Alcohol

It's prohibited to drink alcohol before or whilst driving. No degree of alcohol is permitted in the blood and driving under the influence of alcohol is considered a criminal offence. This rule also applies to cyclists and horse riders. Frequent random breath-testing takes places and drivers are likely to be breathalysed after an accident, even a minor one.

Breakdown Service

The motoring organisation ÚAMK provides roadside assistance and towing services 24 hours a day, telephone 1230 or 261 104 123. Emergency operators speak English. Breakdown assistance is provided for all motorists at a basic cost. Extra charges apply at night, at weekends and for towing.

The vehicles used for road assistance are yellow Skodas, bearing the ÚAMK and/or ARC Europe logos or the words 'Silnični Služba', together with the telephone number of the emergency centre. ÚMAK also uses the services of contracted companies who provide assistance and towing. These vehicles are also marked with the ÚAMK logo and the telephone number of the emergency centre.

Child Restraint System

Children under 1.5m in height must use a suitable child restraint conforming to ECE standard 44/03 or 44/04. If in the front seat, the restraint must be rear facing with any airbag deactivated. If there are no seatbelts fitted children over the age of 3 may travel in the rear of the vehicle without a child restraint.

Fuel

Some petrol stations on main roads, international routes and in main towns are open 24 hours a day. Most accept credit cards.

Diesel pumps are marked 'Nafta'. LPG is called 'Autoplyn' or 'Plyn' and is widely available at many filling stations. A list of these is available from the ÚAMK and a map is available from filling stations, or see lpg.cz and click on 'Čerpací stanice' / 'Gas station'.

Low Emission Zones

There are Low Emission Zones in force in Prague. See urbanaccessregulations.eu for more information.

Motorways

There are approximately 1240 km of motorways and express roads.

There is a good network of service areas with petrol stations, restaurants and shops, together with rest areas with picnic facilities. Emergency telephones connected to the motorway police are placed at 2 km intervals.

Emergency corridors are compulsory on motorways and dual carriageways. Drivers must create a corridor at least 3m wide for emergency vehicles whenever congestion occurs. Drivers in the left-hand lane must move as far to the left as possible, and drivers in the central and right-hand lanes move to the right.

Motorway Tolls (vehicles under 3,500kg)

To use motorways and express roads you must purchase a vignette (sticker) which must be displayed on the right-hand side of your windscreen. This is available from post offices, ÚAMK branch offices, petrol stations and border posts. Old Vignettes must be removed.

Charges in 2024 are CZK 2,300 for an annual vignette, CZK 430 for one month and CZK 270 for 10 days. For more information please see motorway.cz/stickers.

Motorway Tolls (vehicles over 3,500kg)

Vehicles over 3,500kg are subject to an electronic toll and vehicle owners must register with the toll-collection service to obtain an on-board device which must be fixed on your windscreen inside the vehicle and for which a deposit is required.

Tolls vary according to, emissions category, weight and distance driven. You must be able to show your vehicle documentation when obtaining the device but if your vehicle registration certificate (V5C) does not give an emissions category, then your vehicle will be classified in category Euro 2 for the purposes of this system. For more information please see: mytocz.eu/en.

Parking

Vehicles may only be parked on the right of the road. In a one-way road, parking is also allowed on the left.

Continuous or broken yellow lines indicate parking prohibitions or restrictions. Illegally-parked vehicles may be clamped or towed away.

Prague city centre is divided into parking zones: orange and green zones are limited to two and six hours respectively between 8am and 6pm, and blue zones are for residents only.

Priority

At uncontrolled intersections which are not marked by a priority road sign, priority must be given to vehicles coming from the right. Where there are priority signs, these may easily be missed and care is therefore needed at junctions which, according to recent visitors, may have no road markings.

Trams turning right have priority over traffic moving alongside them on the right. Drivers must slow down and, if necessary, stop to allow buses and trams to merge with normal traffic at the end of a bus lane.

On pedestrian crossings pedestrians have right of way, except if the vehicle approaching is a tram.

Roads

Czech drivers are sometimes described as reckless (particularly when overtaking). Speeding is common and the law on the wearing of seat belts is sometimes ignored.

In general roads are in a good condition and well-signposted. Roads are being upgraded and many have new numbers. It's essential, therefore, to have an up-to-date road map or atlas.

Road Signs and Markings

Road signs and markings conform to international standards. Continuous white lines indicate no overtaking, but are often ignored.

The following road signs may be encountered:

Czech	English Translation
Bez poplatků	Free of charge
Chod'te vlevo	Pedestrians must walk on the left
Dálkový provoz	By-pass
Nebezpečí smyku	Danger of skidding
Nemocnice	Hospital
Objizdka	Diversion
Pozor děti	Attention children
Průjezd zakázán	Closed to all vehicles
Rozsvit' světla	Lights needed
Úsek častých nehod	Accident blackspot
Zákaz zastavení	Stopping prohibited

Speed Limits

	Open Road (km/h)	Motorway (km/h)
Car Solo	90	130
Car towing caravan/trailer	80	80
Motorhome under 3500kg	90	130
Motorhome 3500-7500kg	80	80

Motorhomes over 3,500kg and cars towing a caravan or trailer are restricted to 80 km/h (50 mph) on motorways and main roads and lower limits in urban areas. Speed limits are strictly enforced and drivers exceeding them may be fined on the spot. Police with radar guns are much in evidence.

The use of radar detectors is prohibited and GPS systems which indicate the position of fixed speed cameras must have that function deactivated.

Traffic Lights

A traffic light signal with a green arrow shows that drivers may turn in that direction. If a yellow walking figure accompanies the signal, pedestrians may cross the road and drivers must give them right of way. A green light lit at the same time as a red or yellow light means that drivers may turn in the direction indicated by the arrow, giving way to other traffic and pedestrians.

An illuminated speed signal indicates the speed at which to travel in order to arrive at the next set of traffic lights when they are green.

Traffic Jams

The volume of traffic has increased considerably in recent years, particularly in and around Prague, including its ring road. Traffic jams may also occur on the E50/D1 (Prague-Mirošovice), the E48/R6 (Prague-Kladno), the E50/D5 (Plzeň-Rozvadov) and on the E50/D1 (Prague-Brno).

Traffic may be heavy at border crossings from Germany, Austria and Slovakia, particularly at weekends, resulting in extended waiting times. Petrol is cheaper than in Germany and you may well find queues at petrol stations near the border. Traffic information can be obtained from the ÚAMK Information Centre: tel (+420) 261 104 333, or uamk.cz.

Violation of Traffic Regulations

The police can impose and collect on-the-spot fines up to CZK 5,000 and withdraw a driving licence in the case of a serious offence. An official receipt should be obtained. Efforts are under way to improve enforcement of traffic regulations and a points system has been introduced, together with stricter penalties.

Winter Driving

Winter tyres are compulsory from 1 November to 31 March on all wheels of vehicles up to 3.5 tonnes when there is compacted snow or ice on the road. They are also compulsory whenever the temperature is lower than 4°C and there is a possibility of snow or ice on the road. On roads where there are winter tyres signs (see below), the regulations apply even if the road surface is free of snow and ice, regardless of the weather.

Sign for winter tyres (if shown with a line through indicates the end of restriction)

Vehicles over 3,500kg must be fitted with winter tyres on the driving wheels or carry snow chains.

Essential Equipment

First aid kit

You're required to carry a first aid kit in your vehicle.

Lights

Dipped headlights are compulsory at all times, regardless of weather conditions. Bulbs are more likely to fail with constant use and it's recommended that you carry a complete set of spares.

Drivers are required to signal when leaving a roundabout and when overtaking cyclists.

Reflective Jacket/Waistcoat

If your vehicle has broken down, or in the event of an emergency, you must wear a reflective jacket or waistcoat on all roads, carriageways and motorways when getting out of your vehicle. Passengers who leave the vehicle, for example to assist with a repair, should also wear one. Jackets should, therefore, be kept inside your vehicle, and not in the boot. These must be of an EU standard EN471.

Warning Triangles

You must carry a warning triangle, which must be placed at least 100m behind the vehicle on motorways and highways and 50m behind on other roads.

Drivers may use hazard warning lights in conjunction with the warning triangle.

Touring

Tipping is not mandatory in restaurants but if you have received very good service add 10% to the bill or round it up.

Smoking is not permitted in public places (including public transport) and restaurant owners must provide an area for non-smokers.

A Prague CoolPass offers entrance to over 80 tourist attractions and discounts on excursions and activities. It's available from tourist offices, main metro stations, some travel agents and hotels or order online from www.praguecoolpass.com.

German is the most widely spoken foreign language and a basic understanding is particularly helpful in southern Bohemia. However, many young people speak English.

Camping and Caravanning

Campsites are divided into four categories from 1 to 4 stars. Normally campsites are open from May to mid September, although some campsites stay open all year. They usually close at night between 10pm and 6am.

Campsites are generally good value and in recent years many have upgraded their facilities.

Privacy in the showers may be a problem due to a shortage of, or lack of, shower curtains and only a communal dressing area. Some sites have communal kitchen facilities which enable visitors to make great savings on their own gas supply.

Motorhomes are recommended to carry a very long hose with a variety of tap connectors. Refill the onboard tank whenever possible as few sites have easily accessible mains water.

Casual/wild camping is not permitted and fines are imposed for violation of this law, especially in national parks. It's prohibited to sleep in a caravan or motorhome outside a campsite.

Cycling

There are around 2,500 km of cycle tracks, known as Greenways, in tourist areas. A long-distance cycle track links Vienna and Prague and there are many tracks linking Czechia to Austria and Poland. Helmets are compulsory for cyclists under the age of 18.

Electricity and Gas

Current on campsites varies between 6 and 16 amps. Plugs have two round pins. A few campsites have CEE connections but not many. Reversed polarity may be encountered.

You may find that Campingaz 907 cylinders are available from large DIY warehouses.

Public Transport

Prague city centre is very congested, so park outside and use buses, trams or the metro which are efficient and cheap. There are guarded Park and Ride facilities at a number of metro stations around Prague.

Public transport tickets must be purchased before travelling and are available from newspaper stands ('Trafika'), tobacconists, convenience stores and from vending machines at stations. Special tourist tickets are available for one or three days. Tickets must be validated before the start of your journey at the yellow machines at metro stations or on board trams and buses, including before boarding the funicular tram at Petřín. Failure to do so may result in an on-the-spot fine.

Take extra care when in the vicinity of tram tracks and make sure you look both ways. Trams cannot stop quickly nor can they avoid you if you are on the track.

As a pedestrian you may be fined if you attempt to cross the road or cross tram tracks within 50 metres of a designated crossing point or traffic lights. You may also be fined if you cross at a pedestrian crossing if the green pedestrian light is not illuminated.

For reasons of safety and economy use major taxi companies wherever possible. If you telephone to order a taxi these companies are usually able to tell you in advance the type, number and colour of the car allocated to you. If you do pick up a taxi in the street always check the per kilometre price before getting in. The price list must be clearly displayed and the driver must provide a receipt if requested.

Sites in Czechia

BEROUN *B2* (10km NE Rural) *50.0115, 14.1505* **Camping Valek,** Chrustenice 155, 267 12 Chrustenice **tel 311 672 147; info@campvalek.cz; www.campvalek.cz**

CZK80

SW fr Prague on E50; take exit 10 twd Loděnice then N to Chrustenice. Foll sp. Lge, pt shd, EHU (10A) CZK100; bbq; red long stay; TV; 10% statics; phone; Eng spkn; adv bkg acc; tennis; CKE. *"Vg location; money change on site; entmnt (w/end); excel rest; metro to Prague at Zličín (secure car park adj)."* **CZK 430, 1 May-30 Sep. 2022**

BESINY *C1* (0.5km SW Rural) *49.29533, 13.32086* **Eurocamp Běšiny,** Běšiny 150, 33901 Běšiny **tel 376 375 011; eurocamp@besiny.cz; www.eurocamp.besiny.cz**

12 (htd) nr

Fr E53/rd 27 take rd 171 twd Sušice. Site just outside vill on L. Med, unshd, EHU (6A) inc; bbq; cooking facs; 50% statics; adv bkg acc; ccard acc; games area; tennis; CKE. *"Pleasant setting; nrby vill drab."* **CZK 255 2022**

BOSKOVICE *C3* (12km NE Urban) *49.50980, 16.77308* **Camping de Bongerd,** Benešov U Boskovic C.P. 104. 67953 **tel +31611040721; campingdebongerd@hotmail.com; www.camping-benesov.nl**

Foll sp fr 373 at E end of Benešov on L. Sm, pt shd, sl, terr, Eng spkn; games area; CKE. *"Vg site run by helpful talkative Dutch couple; ent narr, unsuitable for lge o'fits."* **CZK 815, 20 April-20 Sep. 2024**

BOSKOVICE *C3* (15km SE Rural) *49.42296, 16.73585* **Camping Relaxa,** 679 13 Sloup **tel + 420 704 022 518; camp.relaxa@seznam.cz; www.camprelaxa.cz**

(htd) nr nr

Fr Boskovice take dir Valchov; at Ludikov head S & onto rte 373 to Sloup. Site sp up track on R. Sm, unshd, pt sl, EHU (6A) inc (poss rev pol); bus 1km; CKE. *"Conv Moravski Kras karst caves; pool 250m; immed access walking/cycling trails."* **CZK 400, 1 May-30 Sep. 2020**

BRECLAV *D3* (6km NW Rural) *48.78549, 16.82663* **Autocamp Apollo,** Charvátská Nová Ves, 691 44 Břeclav **tel 519 340 414; info@atcapollo.cz; www.atcapollo.cz**

CZK30 nr nr

Fr Breclav take Lednice rd. Site is 3km S of Lednice vill. Lge, pt shd, pt sl, EHU 16A; sw nr; bus; CKE. *"Fair sh stay; site in beautiful area; excel cycling (mkd rtes & walking; Lednice Castle worth a visit; poss school parties; well situated for exploring S Moravia; Chateaux of Lednice & Valtice worth a visit; diff access if app fr Lednice; unmkd pitches; poss crowding when busy; poor san facs."* **CZK 800, 1 May-30 Sep. 2023**

BRNO *C3* (21km W Rural) *49.21182, 16.40745* **Camping Oáza,** Náměstí Viléma Mrštíka 10, 66481 Ostrovačice **tel 606 457 448; info@kempoaza.cz; www.kempoaza.cz**

nr

Leave E65/E50 Prague-Brno at junc 178 for Ostrovačice. At T-junc in vill turn L, site on R 100m. Sm, pt shd, pt sl, EHU (10A) inc; CKE. *"Excel CL-type site, v clean facs; friendly, helpful lady owner; narr, uneven ent poss diff lge o'fits; poss unrel opening dates; super."* **CZK 500, 1 Apr-31 Oct. 2024**

BRNO *C3* (24km NW Rural) *49.27618, 16.4535* **Camping Hana,** Dlouhá ul 135, 664 71 Veverská Bítýška **tel 549 420 331 or 607 905 801 (mob); camping.hana@seznam.cz; www.campinghana.com**

CZK40 nr

On E50 Prague-Brno m'way, exit junc 178 at Ostrovačice & turn N on 386 for 10km to Veverská Bítýška. Site sp bef & in vill. 1*, Med, mkd, pt shd, EHU (10A) CZK60; bbq; cooking facs; twin axles; Eng spkn; CKE. *"Peaceful, well-run site; family owned; clean, dated san facs; hot water runs out by evening if site full; gd security; interesting caves N of town; bus/tram/boat to Brno; excel rest in vill; flexible open-closing dates if reserved in adv; helpful, friendly owners; pleasant walk along rv to vill; gd NH; gd site; lg shwrs but communal chnge rm."* **CZK 612, 27 Apr-30 Sep. 2024**

BUDISOV NAD BUDISOVKOU *B4* (0.8km SE Urban) *49.79089, 17.63668* **Autokemp Budišov,** Nábřeží č. 688, 747 87, Budišov nad Budišovkou **tel 736 767 588; autokemp@budisov.cz; www.autokemp.budisov.cz**

CZK30 nr

Ent town fr E on rd 443; at T junc turn L sp; foll rd which will take you under rlwy; site on R in 100m. Sm, unshd, sl, EHU (6A) CZK80; bbq; 50% statics; CKE. *"Space for 20 vans only, with 4 elec pnts; mini golf onsite & bike hire avail; valid vaccination card req for dogs."* **CZK 240, 1 May-30 Sep. 2022**

CESKY KRUMLOV *C2* (11km NE Rural) *48.83954, 14.37525* **Camping Paradijs,** Rajov 26, 38101 Cesky Krumlov **tel 776 898 022; jakesova.jana@centrum.cz; www.camping-paradijs.eu**

NE of Cesky Krumlov on rte 39 heading twrds Cesky Budejovice. Site sp at bottom of hill. Sm, mkd, pt shd, Eng spkn; adv bkg req; games rm. *"A sm picturesque rural site beside rv; narr app rd, not suitable for lge o'fits; clean but ltd san facs; rafting & canoeing avail."* **CZK 483, 1 Apr-15 Oct. 2023**

CZECHIA

CHEB *B1* (10km W Rural) *50.05258, 12.16572*
Camping Bříza, Bříza 19, 350 02 Briza, Cheb 2
tel (0420) 773 570 196; campingbriza@gmail.com; www.camping bohemen.com

Fr W on 303/E48 thro border take the 2nd exit to Leba, travel back down E48 to Bříza, foll sp to site. Sm, sw; Eng spkn. *"Excel site; lakeside fishing; boat trips; cycling."* **CZK 500** **2020**

CHEB *B1* (8km NW Rural) *50.11715, 12.38808*
Hotel Jadran Autocamping, Jezerní 84/12, 351 01 Františkovy Lázně **tel 00420 603 845 789; info@atcjadran.cz; www.atcjadran.cz**

CZK60 nr

Fr rte 6 turn N dir Libá. After 2km, immed N of new by-pass over bdge, fork L to vill; on o'skirts turn L & foll site/hotel sp, then R in 100m onto narr lane. In 700m turn R. Site in 400m, well sp. Lge, pt shd, EHU (16A) inc (rev pol & long cable req); sw; red long stay; 80% statics; bike hire; CKE. *"Delightful site beside sm lake; many places of interest nr; walk thro woods to beautiful spa town; supmkt on rd to Cheb; run down facs clean, being rebuilt; rec NH only."* **€23.00** **2024**

CHOMUTOV *B1* (1km NE Rural) *50.46899, 13.42278*
Autokemp Kamencové Jezero, Tomáše ze Štítného, 430 01 Chomutov **tel (420) 777 187 843; reception@kamencovejezero.cz; www.kamencovejezero.cz**

(htd) nr nr

Foll site sps in town, look for camp sp on L bet flats. Next sp on R bet more flats. Lge, pt shd, sl, EHU; sw; Eng spkn. *"Site on edge of town with gd bathing facs; gd site based in N Czech Rep in v interesting area."*
CZK 160, 1 May-30 Sept. **2020**

DECIN *A2* (10km ENE Rural) *50.80101, 14.33389*
Rosalka, Stará Oleška 35, Huntiřov, 405 02 Děčín ll **tel 0420 739 674 766; info@rosalka.eu; www.rosalka.eu**

€1 (htd)

On the E442/13 fr Decin turn L at x-rds in vill of Huntirov, in dir of Stara Oleska, site on R within 2km. Sm, unshd, EHU (16A); bbq; twin axles; bus adj; Eng spkn; adv bkg acc; CKE. *"Excel site nr NP attraction; numerous walks & attractions; no smoking on site; welcoming owners; immac facs."*
CZK 567, 1 Mar-31 Oct. **2024**

DOMAZLICE *C1* (11km SE Rural) *49.40314, 13.05763*
Autocamping Hájovna, Na Kobyle 209, 345 06 Kdyně **tel 602 491 855; automotoklub@kdyne.cz; www.camphajovna.cz**

CZK45 nr

In Kdyně going twd Klatovy on rd 22, turn L at end of town sq; then 1st R twd cobbled rd (for 300m); site on L in 2km. 3*, Med, hdstg, pt shd, pt sl, EHU (10A) CZK70 (poss rev pol); TV; 10% statics; phone; CKE. *"Hořovský Týn & Domažlice interesting towns; gd walking; friendly owner; ltd level pitches."*
CZK 307, 1 May-30 Sep. **2022**

FRENSTAT *C4* (750km NW Urban) *49.551722, 18.204618*
Autokemp Frenstat Pod Radhostem, Dolni 1807, 74401 Frenstat pod Radhostem **tel 556 836 624 or 607 265 107; autokemp@mufrenstat.cz; www.autokemp-frenstat.cz**

CZK35 (htd)

Fr S on 58 turn R at Aquapark, site on L in 250m. Med, hdstg, hdg, mkd, pt shd, EHU (10A) CZK100; cooking facs; red long stay; 25% statics; 25m; Eng spkn; adv bkg acc; games area; bike hire. *"Vg site aimed at families/young people; all rds mkd for cycling; school parties visit LS; easy walk to town; gd hill walks & mountain biking area; excel outdoor museum in Roznov."* **CZK 395** **2023**

"There aren't many sites open at this time of year"

If you're travelling outside peak season remember to call ahead to check site opening dates – even if the entry says 'open all year'.

FRYDEK MISTEK *B4* (5km SW Rural) *49.66459, 18.31161*
Autokemp Olešná, Nad Přehradou, 738 02 Frýdek-Místek **tel 558 434 806; olesna@tsfm.cz; www.autokempolesna.cz**

CZK25

Nr Tesco on S side of E462/rte 48 on lakeside. 1*, Sm, unshd, sl, EHU (10A); cooking facs; Eng spkn; fishing. *"Unisex san facs; individual shwr cabins."*
CZK 230, 1 May-30 Sep. **2022**

FRYMBURK *D2* (1km S Rural) *48.65556, 14.17008*
Camping Frymburk, Frymburk 20/55, 382 79 Frymburk **tel 380 735 284 or 733 745 435; info@camping frymburk.cz; www.campingfrymburk.cz**

CZK60 nr

Fr Černa on lake, take rd 163 dir Loucovice to site. Fr Český Krumlov take Rožmberk nad Vltavou rd, turn R at Větřni on rd 162 sp Světlik. At Frymburk turn L to Lipno then site 500m on R on lake shore. 4*, Med, pt shd, sl, terr, EHU (6A) inc; sw; TV; 10% statics; adv bkg acc; bike hire; fishing; boat hire; boating. *"Beautiful lakeside site; modern, clean san facs; some pitches poss tight for lge o'fits; gd rest nrby; v friendly, helpful Dutch owners; private san facs some pitches; gd walking; adv bkg rec bef 1st Apr."*
CZK 764, 29 Apr-25 Sep. **2022**

JICIN *B2* (8km NW Rural) *50.47236, 15.31161*
Chatový tábor Jinolice, Jičín Jinolice, 50601 **tel (0420) 493 591 929; info@kemp-jinolice.cz; www.kempy-ceskyraj.cz**

(htd)

Fr Jicin foll rte 35 twrds Turnov. After 6km turn L to Jinolice and foll sp thro vill. Lge, pt sl, sw; TV; boating. *"In cent of Bohemian Tourist area; sports; cycling."* **CZK 355, 1 May-30 Sep.** **2020**

JIHLAVA *C3* (8km S Rural) *49.44732, 15.59911* **Autocamping Pávov,** Pávov 90, 586 01 Jihlava **tel 776 293 393; camp@pavov.com; www.pavov.com**

Fr D1/E50/E65 exit junc 112 sp Jihlava. Foll sp Pávov & site for 2km. Fr N/S on rte 38, nr a'bahn pick up sp for Pávov. Recep in adj pension/rest. 2*, Med, mkd, unshd, EHU (6A); sw nr; 30% statics; fishing; tennis. *"Grand Hotel in Jihlava gd; m'way noise; friendly rest."* **CZK 400, 1 Apr-30 Oct.** **2022**

KLATOVY *C1* (19km S Rural) *49.28177, 13.24003* **Camping U dvou Orecha,** Splz 13 Strážov na Sumava 34024 **tel (0420) 376 382 421; info@camping-tsjechie.nl; www.camping-tsjechie.nl**

nr

Fr Klatovy twrds Nýrsko on 191, after Janovice turn L twrds Strážov, after 5.5km in Strážov turn R sp Desenice. Site sp on L after 2.4km. Sm, pt shd, terr, EHU 10A; Eng spkn; adv bkg acc; CKE. *"Delightful, vg CL type site; warm welcome fr friendly, helpful Dutch owners."* **CZK 800, 1 May-1 Oct.** **2023**

KUTNA HORA *B2* (3km NE Urban) *49.96416, 15.30250* **Autocamp Transit,** K Malínskému Mostu 35, Kutná Hora **tel 322 320 634 or 792 773 357 (mob); autocamptransit@gmail.com; https://www.autocamp-kutnahora.eu/**

nr nr

Fr N on rd 38 fr Kolín, turn R immed after flyover onto rd No 2 then turn L twrds town, In 1km turn L immed bef rlwy bdge. Sm, pt shd, EHU (16A) CZK130; cooking facs; TV; phone; bus 800m; Eng spkn; CKE. *"Poss noise fr nrby rlwy; sw high ssn; family run; Int UNESCO World Heritage Town; clean, well-kept, with garden area."* **CZK 440, 1 Apr-30 Sep.** **2023**

"That's changed – Should I let the Club know?"

If you find something on site that's different from the site entry, fill in a report and let us know. See camc.com/europereport.

LIPNO NAD VLTAVOU *D2* (3km W Rural) *48.63891, 14.20880* **Autocamp Lipno Modřín,** 382 78 Lipno nad Vltavou **tel 731 410 803; camp@lipnoservis.cz; www.campinglipno.cz**

CZK70 nr

Site sp on rd 163 on lakeside. 1*, Lge, mkd, unshd, EHU (6A) inc; sw; 10% statics; adv bkg acc; games area; bike hire; tennis; boat hire. *"Pleasant, popular site; htd pool complex 500m."* **CZK 601, 1 May-30 Sep.** **2022**

LITOMERICE *A2* (2km SE Urban) *50.53185, 14.13899* **Autocamping Slavoj,** Střelecký Ostrov, 412 01 Litoměřice **tel 416 734 481 or 777 687 667 (mob); kemp.litomerice@post.cz; www.autokemplitomerice.com**

CZK30 WD nr

Fr N on rd 15 N of rv make for bdge over Rv Elbe (Labe) sp Terezín; R down hill immed bef bdge (cobbled rd), L under rlwy bdge, L again, site 300m on R bef tennis courts at sports cent beside rv. Fr S on rd 15 turn L immed after x-ing rv bdge to cobbled rd. Sm, pt shd, EHU (8-16A) CZK75; 10% statics; Eng spkn; tennis; CKE. *"Friendly, family-run site; gd, modern san facs; vg rest; 10 mins walk town cent; Terezín ghetto & preserved concentration camp; v friendly."* **CZK 505, 1 May-30 Sep.** **2024**

MARIANSKE LAZNE *B1* (3km WSW Rural) *49.95234, 12.66656* **Camping La Provence,** Plzenska Street, Velka Hledsebe 35301 **tel 602 165 279; info@camping-laprovence.cz; www.camping-laprovence.cz**

CZK 80 (htd) WD MSP nr

Fr Cheb on Route 21, at Velke Hledesbe turn L twrds Marianske Lazne. Site on R after 1k. Ent obscured by trees. Sm, mkd, pt shd, EHU 10A; bbq (gas, sep area); cooking facs; sw nr; twin axles; TV; 70% statics; phone; Bus; Eng spkn; adv bkg acc; ccard acc; bike hire. *"Famous/historical spa town; 30 min walk to town or bus to Marianske Lazne; other spa towns of historical note nrby; gd."* **CZK 590, 1 May-30 Sep.** **2023**

MARIANSKE LAZNE *B1* (1.5km SE Rural) *49.94419, 12.72797* **Camping Stanowitz-Stanoviště,** Stanoviště 9, 35301 Mariánské Lázně **tel 354 624 673; info@stanowitz.com; www.stanowitz.com**

CZK30 (htd) WD MSP

Fr Cheb on rd 215, then rd 230 dir Karlovy Vary/Bečov. Site sp on R after passing under rlwy bdge. Sm, hdstg, pt shd, pt sl, EHU (16A) CZK90; bbq; TV; phone; Eng spkn; CKE. *"Excel CL-type site with gd rest; conv spa towns & Teplá Monastery; mkd walks in woods; helpful staff."* **CZK 617, 1 Apr-31 Oct.** **2024**

NACHOD *B3* (8km SW Rural) *50.39866, 16.06302* **Autocamping Rozkoš,** Masaryka 836, 552 03 Česká Skalice **tel 491 451 112 or 491 451 108; atc@atcrozkos.com; www.atcrozkos.com**

12 CZK30

On rd 33/E67 fr Náchod dir Hradec Králové, site sp 2km bef Česká Skalice on lakeside. V lge, EHU (16A) CZK70; sw nr; 10% statics; ccard acc; bike hire; windsurfing school; watersports; sauna. *"Lovely countryside."* **CZK 290** **2022**

CZECHIA

PASOHLAVKY *C3* (2km E Rural) *48.89914, 16.56738*
Autocamp Merkur, 691 22 Pasohlávky **tel 519 427 714; kemp@pasohlavky.cz; www.kemp-merkur.cz**
CZK60

S fr Brno on E461/rd 52. After Pohořelice site 5km on R, sp. V lge, hdg, mkd, pt shd, EHU inc; bbq; cooking facs; sw nr; TV; 10% statics; phone; Eng spkn; adv bkg acc; ccard acc; bike hire; games area; tennis; watersports; CKE. *"Vg; secure, pleasant site."*
CZK 519, 1 Apr-31 Oct. **2024**

PLZEN *B1* (6km N Rural) *49.77747, 13.39047*
Autocamping Ostende, 32300 Plzeň-Malý Bolevec **tel 739 604 603; atc-ostende@cbox.cz; www.bolevak.eu**
CZK70 adj

Head N fr Plzeň on rd 27 dir Kaznějov; site sp R on o'skts Plzeň. Foll minor rd over rlwy bdge & sharp R bend to site on L. Beware earlier turning off rd 27 which leads under rlwy bdge with height restriction. Med, shd, pt sl, EHU (10A) poss rev pol CZK140; gas; sw; bus to town; Eng spkn; CKE. *"Pretty, well-run site; bar/rest area untidy - needs upgrade (2009); facs poss gd walk fr c'van area - no shwr curtains; gates not locked at night (2011); cycle rte & walk around lake, site is shabby needs upgrading and thorough cleaning (2011)."* **CZK 660, 1 May-30 Sep.** **2024**

PODEBRADY *B2* (2km SE Rural) *50.13549, 15.13794*
Autocamping Golf, U Nové Vodárny 428, 290 01 Poděbrady **tel 602 330 204; ATCAutokemp@gmail.com; podebrady-ubytovani.cz**
CZK20

Fr D11/E67 (Prague/Poděbrady) take Poděbrady exit N onto rd 32 for 3km; at junc with rte 11/E67 turn W sp Poděbrady (care needed, priority not obvious); site sp on L on E edge of town; site opp town name sp 400m down lane; app fr E if poss. 3*, Med, pt shd, EHU (long cable req) CZK80; own san rec; CKE. *"Conv for touring area; gd supmkt with parking in town; basic site."*
CZK 260, 1 May-31 Sep. **2022**

PRAHA *B2* (12km N Rural) *50.15277, 14.4506*
Camping Triocamp, Ústecká ul, Dolní Chabry, 184 00 Praha 8 **tel 722 242 343; triocamp.praha@telecom.cz; www.triocamp.cz**
12 CZK80

Fr N on D8/E55 take junc sp Zdiby, strt on at x-rds to rd 608 dir Praha. Camp sp in 2km on R just after city boundary. 3*, Med, pt shd, pt sl, EHU (6-10A) CZK90; gas; cooking facs; sw nr; 30% statics; phone; bus/tram to city (tickets fr recep); Eng spkn; ccard acc; CKE. *"Well-organised, clean, family-run site; excel facs; rec arr early; barrier clsd at 2200; rd noise & daytime aircraft noise; free cherries in ssn; helpful staff."*
CZK 1159 **2024**

PRAHA *B2* (6km N Urban) *50.11694, 14.42361*
Camping Sokol Trója, Trojská 171a, 171 00 Praha 7 **tel 797 848 440; info@campsokoltroja.cz; www.campsokoltroja.cz**
12 CZK60

Fr Pilsen (E50/D5) head into cent to rte D8/E55 sp Treplice. Foll N to Trója sp. Immed after rv x-ing take exit under rte 8 & foll camp sp & site on L 100m past Autocamp Trojská. Fr Dresden on E55/D8 foll sp to Centrum to Trója exit on R, foll camping sp. NB: There are 5 sites adj to each other with similar names. Best app fr Treplice. 2*, Med, hdstg, pt shd, EHU (10A) CZK130; ccard acc; CKE. *"Easy tram transport to city; Trója Palace & zoo 1km; v helpful, friendly owner; bar & rest gd value; noise fr bar; facs basic & run down (2017); hostel; 10 min walk to shops."*
CZK 690 **2023**

PRAHA *B2* (22km E Urban) *50.09833, 14.68472*
Camping Praha Klánovice, V Jehličině 1040, 190 14 Praha 9 – Klánovice **tel 00420 774 553 743; info@campingpraha.cz; www.campingpraha.cz**
€2

Fr Prague ring rd exit at Běchovice onto rd 12 dir Kolin. At Újezd nad Lesy turn L at x-rds twd Klánovice & in approx 3km turn R into Šlechtitelská, site on R in approx 1km. 4*, Med, mkd, pt shd, EHU (16A) €4; gas; bbq; TV; 50% statics; phone; bus to Prague; Eng spkn; adv bkg acc; ccard acc; games rm; bike hire; games area; sauna. *"New site 2010; gd public transport to city; excel site, lge woods for walks & cycling."* **CZK 688, 1 May-13 Sep.** **2020**

PRAHA *B2* (18km S Rural) *49.95155, 14.47455*
Camping Oase, Zlatníky 47, 252 41 Dolní Břežany **tel 241 932 044; info@campingoase.cz; www.campingoase.cz**
CZK50 (htd) (covrd, htd, indoor)

Fr Prague on D1 (Prague-Brno). Exit 12 (Jesenice). Head twd Jesenice on rd 101. In vill turn R then immed L at rndabt dir Zlatníky. At Zlatníky rndabt turn L dir Libeň, site in 500m. Beware 'sleeping policemen' on final app. 5*, Med, hdg, pt shd, serviced pitches; EHU (6A) inc (poss rev pol); gas; bbq; cooking facs; TV; phone; bus, tram to city; Eng spkn; adv bkg acc; ccard acc; lake fishing 1km; games area; horseriding; sauna; games rm; bike hire. *"Lovely site; v helpful owners; excel, clean san facs; vg pool; swipe card for barrier & all chargeable amenities; no o'fits over 12m high ssn; well-guarded; bus/train/metro tickets fr recep; rec use metro Park & Ride to city; lge well maintained pitches; excel security."*
CZK 750, 25 Apr-14 Sep, X07. **2022**

PRAHA *B2* (20km S Rural) *49.93277, 14.37294* **Camp Matyáš,** U Elektrárny, 252 46 Vrané nad Vltavou **tel 257 761 228 or 777 016073 (mob); campmatyas@centrum.cz; www.camp-matyas.com**

Fr Plzen take E50/D5 NE twd Prague.Take E48/ E50 heading approx SE twd R4. Exit onto R4 sp Strakonice. Exit R4 twd Zbraslav. Enter vill, turn L in Sq. Foll rd to cross major bdge over Rv Vltava. After bdge turn immed R. Foll this rd keeping rv on your R. Camp is on R in 6km. 3*, Med, pt shd, EHU (10A) CZK120; cooking facs; sw nr; bus, train to city; Eng spkn; adv bkg acc; fishing adj; CKE. *"In lovely location; friendly owners; train & tram service to Prague (1 hr); boat trips on Rv Vltava; superb family site."* **CZK 809, 13 Apr-30 Sep.** **2022**

PRAHA *B2* (10km SW Urban) *50.06233, 14.41331* **Praha Yacht Club Caravan Park,** Cisařská Louka 599, Smíchov, 150 00 Praha 5 **tel 257 318 387; caravanpark.cl@gmail.com; http://kemp-praha.cz**

12 CZK80 nr

Fr E50 access only poss fr S by travelling N on W side of rv. After complex junc (care needed), turn sharp R bef Shell petrol stn to Cisařská Island, foll rd to end. Nr C'van Camping CSK. Diff app fr N due no L turns on Strakonická. Sm, pt shd, EHU (16A) CZK170; adv bkg acc; ccard acc; tennis 100m. *"Boats for hire; launch trips on rv; water taxi fr Prague, book at site recep; helpful staff; friendly, secure site; san facs clean & adequate; unmkd pithces; excel location; views of city; milk etc avail fr Agip petrol stn on Strakonická; busy site, rec arr early; 5 min to ferry & metro to Prague."* **CZK 550** **2023**

PRAHA *B2* (14km SW Rural) *50.04388, 14.28416* **Camp Drusus,** Třebonice 4, 155 00 Praha 5 **tel 235 514 391; drusus@drusus.com; www.drusus.com**

CZK40

Fr Plzeň take E50/D5 to exit 1/23 Třebonice, then E50 dir Brno. Fr Brno exit E50/D5 at junc 19 sp Řeporyje, site in 2km, sp. 1*, Med, pt shd, sl, EHU (10A) CZK150; gas; cooking facs; red long stay; TV; 10% statics; bus; Eng spkn; adv bkg acc; ccard acc; games area; CKE. *"Reg bus service to Prague nrby, tickets fr site; owner v helpful; vg."* **CZK 615, 1 Apr-15 Oct.** **2023**

PROSTEJOV *C3* (8km W Rural) *49.46123, 17.01154* **Autocamping Žralok,** Rudé Armády 302, 798 03 Plumlov **tel 775 568 378 (mob); atczralok@seznam.cz; www.camp-zralok.cz**

CZK35

Fr cent of Prostějov foll sp to Boskovice & thro Čechovice & Plumlov, site clearly sp. Down steep narr lane, cross dam & R to site. Med, unshd, sl, EHU (10A) CZK90(long cable req); 20% statics; CKE. *"O'looking lake; facs basic but clean, needs upgrading; ccards not acc."* **CZK 340, 1 May-30 Sep.** **2024**

ROZNOV POD RADHOSTEM *C4* (2km NE Rural) *49.46654, 18.16376* **Camping Rožnov,** Radhoštská 940, 756 61 Rožnov pod Radhoštěm **tel 731 504 073; camproznov@seznam.cz; www.camproznov.cz**

CZK120 (htd) nr (htd)

On rd 35/E442; on E o'skts of Rožnov on N of rd 200m past ent to Camping Sport, take L fork opp Benzina petrol stn (site sp obscured by lamp post). 4*, Med, pt shd, EHU (16A) CZK150; 60% statics; phone; Eng spkn; ccard acc; tennis; CKE. *"Welcoming; gd cooking & washing facs; pitches v close together; basic, worn san facs; annexe; nr open-air museum; gd walking cent; cycle to town thro park; well run, busy site; lg heated sw pool; gd rest; friendly staff; times shwrs, tokens req in hg ssn; many mkd cycle rte; excel."* **CZK 670, 1 May-31 Oct.** **2023**

STERNBERK *B3* (2km N Rural) *49.74800, 17.30641* **Autocamping Šternberk,** Dolní Žleb, 785 01 Šternberk **tel 585 011 300; info@campsternberk.cz; www.campsternberk.cz**

CZK30 nr

Fr Olomouc take rte 46 to Šternberk. At Šternberk go thro town cent & foll sp Dalov, site just bef vill of Dolní Žleb. Or circumnavigate to W on rds 444 & 445, site sp. Med, pt shd, EHU (10A) CZK75 (poss rev pol); cooking facs; TV; 30% statics; phone; adv bkg acc; CKE. *"Gd, clean facs even when full; helpful staff."* **CZK 215, 15 May-15 Sep.** **2022**

STRIBRO *B1* (16km NE Rural) *49.79073, 13.16869* **Transkemp Hracholusky,** 330 23 Hracholusky **tel 420 337 914 113 or 420 728 470 650; rezervace@hracholusky.com; www.hracholusky.com**

nr shgl adj

Fr Ulice bet Stribro & Plzen on rte 5/E50 turn N, sp Plesnice, & foll vill sp to site in 4km at E end of lake. Med, unshd, pt sl, EHU inc (adaptor for hire); sw; 25% statics; Eng spkn; adv bkg acc; waterskiing; boating. *"Lake steamer trips; gd sh stay/ NH; gd location on lakeside; fair site; facs basic."* **CZK 550, 1 May-31 Dec.** **2024**

STRMILOV *C2* (2km SE Rural) *49.14956, 15.20890* **Autokemp Komorník,** 378 53 Strmilov **tel 384 392 468; recepce@autokempkomornik.cz; www.autokempkomornik.cz**

CZK40 sand adj

Sp fr rd 23 at Strmilov. Lge, pt shd, pt sl, EHU (10A) CZK75 (long lead rec); bbq; 20% statics; CKE. *"V pleasant setting by lake; lake adj; clean, modern san facs; gd rest & bar; conv Telč & Slavonice historic towns."* **CZK 215, 1 Jun-15 Sep.** **2022**

TABOR *C2* (6km E Rural) *49.40985, 14.73157*
Autocamping & Hotel Knížecí Rybník, Měšice 399, 39156 Tábor **tel 381 252 546; knizecak@seznam.cz; www.knizecirybnik.cz**
12 CZK50

On N side of rd 19 fr Tábor to Jihlava, in woods by lake adj hotel. 3*, Lge, hdg, mkd, pt shd, EHU (6-10A) CZK60; sw nr; 10% statics; ccard acc; fishing; tennis; CKE. *"Pleasant, lakeside site; modern san facs."*
CZK 200 **2022**

TANVALD *A2* (3km W Rural) *50.74205, 15.28269*
Camping Tanvaldská Kotlina (Tanvald Hollow), Pod Špičákem 650, 46841 Tanvald **tel 483 311 928; kotlina@tanvald.cz; www.tanvald.cz**
12 CZK20

Fr S on rte 10, in cent Tanvald at rndabt turn foll sp Desnou & Harrachov. In 500m take L fork under rlwy bdge, then immed turn L & foll rd past hospital. Turn R bef tennis courts, site in 600m. Sm, pt shd, EHU CZK30 + metered; bbq; cooking facs; games area. *"Excel; pool in town."* **CZK 230** **2020**

TELC *C2* (10km NW Rural) *49.22785, 15.38442*
Camp Velkopařezitý, Řásná 10, 58856 Mrákotín **tel 567 379 449; campvelkoparezity@tiscali.cz; www.campvelkoparezity.cz**
12 CZK30 1km

Exit Telč on Jihlava rd; turn L in 300m (sp) & foll sp to site beyond Rásná. Well sp fr Telč. Steep site ent. Sm, pt shd, pt sl, EHU CZK100; 10% statics. *"Friendly atmosphere; poor san facs; gd walking & cycling; Telč wonderful World Heritage site."* **CZK 270** **2022**

"I like to fill in the reports as I travel from site to site"

You'll find report forms at the back of this guide, or you can fill them in online at camc.com/europereport.

TREBON *C2* (1km S Rural) *48.99263, 14.76753*
Autocamp Třeboňsky Ráj, Domanin 285, 37901 Třeboň **tel 384 722 586; info@autocamp-trebon.cz; www.autocamp-trebon.cz**
CZK70

Exit town by rd 155 sp Borovany heading SW. Site on L just past lake. Note: site Not accessible fr other end of this rd. 3*, Med, pt shd, pt sl, EHU (6A) CZK120 (long cable req & poss rev pol); bbq; cooking facs; sw; twin axles; TV; 5% statics; phone; bus 2km; Eng spkn; adv bkg acc; bike hire; games area; games rm; boat hire; CKE. *"Attractive unspoilt town; helpful owner; facs stretched when site full; insect repellant rec; gd cycle paths; gd rest on site; indiv shwrs but no curtains, changing area opp shwr; gd cycle paths."*
CZK 460, 27 Apr-30 Sep. **2023**

TURNOV *A2* (6km SSE Rural) *50.5580, 15.1867*
Autocamping Sedmihorky, Sedmihorky 72, 51101 Turnov **tel 481 389 162; camp@campsedmihorky.cz; www.campsedmihorky.cz**
12 CZK90

Fr rte 35/E442 fr Turnov. Turn SW over rlwy x-ing at camping sp S of Sedmihorky. 300m along ave take 1st R. 3*, Lge, pt shd, pt sl, EHU (16A) CZK60; sw; phone; Eng spkn; ccard acc; bike hire; CKE. *"V beautiful site in National Park, sometimes called Bohemian Paradise; v busy site high ssn; dep bef 1000 otherwise charge for extra day; excel site."* **CZK 835** **2023**

UHERSKY BROD *C4* (14km E Urban) *49.04034, 17.79993*
Eurocamping Bojkovice, Stefánikova 1008, 68771 Bojkovice **tel 420 604 236 631; info@eurocamping.cz; www.eurocamping.cz**
CZK50

Off E50 at Uherský Brod turn onto rd 495. Find rlwy stn at Bojkovice on rd 495 at SW end of town. Cross rlwy at NE (town) end of stn & foll sp round L & R turns to site. 4*, Med, pt shd, pt sl, terr, EHU (6A) inc; cooking facs; adv bkg acc; games area. *"Gd walking area."* **CZK 520, 1 May-30 Sep.** **2020**

VRCHLABI *A3* (1km S Rural) *50.61036, 15.60263*
Holiday Park Liščí Farma, Dolní Branná 350, 54362 Vrchlabí **tel 499 421 473; info@liscifarma.cz; www.liscifarma.cz**
12 CZK20 (htd) nr

S fr Vrchlabí on rd 295, site sp. 4*, Lge, mkd, pt shd, EHU (6A) CZK125; cooking facs; TV; adv bkg acc; ccard acc; games area; bike hire; golf 5km; canoeing; horseriding 2km; tennis; sauna. *"Private bthrms avail."*
CZK 220 **2022**

ZAMBERK *B3* (1km E Urban) *50.08638, 16.47527*
Autocamping Jan Kulhanek, U koupaliště, 564 01 Žamberk **tel 465 614 755; kemp@orlicko.cz; www.autocamping.cz**
CZK50 nr nr nr

Fr Zamberk cent on rd 11, foll sp. Sm, pt shd, EHU (16A) CZK70; cooking facs; TV; 50% statics; phone; bus adj, train 1km; Eng spkn; CKE. *"Site is pt of sports cent & aqua park with many diff facs inc mini golf, volleyball & bowling; playgrnd, pool, games area, games rm at sports cent; site leaflet avail at recep showing town plans with supmkt & info office; gd site."* **CZK 241, 1 Apr-31 Oct.** **2022**

ZNOJMO *C3* (8km N Rural) *48.92018, 16.02588*
Camping Country, 67152 Hluboké Mašůvky **tel 515 255 249; camping-country@cbox.cz; www.camp-country.com**
CZK50 nr

N fr Znojmo on E59/38 4km; turn E on 408 to Přímětice; then N on 361 4km to Hluboké Mašůvky. Sharp turn into site fr S. 4*, Med, pt shd, sl, EHU (16A) CZK80 (long lead poss req); sw nr; TV; 20% statics; Eng spkn; tennis; bike hire; horseriding; CKE. *"Gd, clean, well-manicured site; v helpful owner & family; not easy to find level pitch; excel meals."* **CZK 400, 1 May-30 Oct.** **2022**

Klatovy to Tábor = 119km

	Breclav	Brno	Ceské Budejovice	Cheb	Chomutov	Hradec Králové	Jihlava	Karlovy Vary	Klatovy	Liberec	Litomerice	Olomouc	Ostrava	Pardubice	Plzen	Praha (Prague)	Šumperk	Tábor	Zlín
Brno	48																		
Ceské Budejovice	219	184																	
Cheb	430	377	231																
Chomutov	351	298	235	99															
Hradec Králové	203	142	218	288	208														
Jihlava	146	93	126	299	220	111													
Karlovy Vary	388	332	216	43	56	245	257												
Klatovy	340	287	106	132	144	248	194	125											
Liberec	300	239	243	247	150	99	186	205	236										
Litomerice	312	294	198	164	67	166	181	122	154	91									
Olomouc	132	79	259	451	371	150	167	409	360	248	315								
Ostrava	195	165	343	538	457	240	253	495	447	336	411	93							
Pardubice	191	138	198	280	202	21	89	237	241	118	206	147	239						
Plzen	349	296	133	101	103	203	186	84	41	196	112	371	456	199					
Praha (Prague)	255	202	138	175	98	112	123	132	137	103	58	276	362	104	94				
Šumperk	197	133	275	400	319	113	171	356	360	207	315	65	128	119	317	224			
Tábor	221	170	57	214	179	165	75	195	119	185	141	241	329	144	112	84	225		
Zlín	91	100	281	472	394	211	188	425	384	308	389	62	105	208	390	296	127	262	
Znojmo	88	67	144	374	296	185	76	331	253	262	290	140	227	165	290	197	194	148	160

GERMANY
POLAND
SLOVAKIA
AUSTRIA
Dresden
Chemnitz
Hof
Cham
Passau
Linz
Zwettl
WIEN
BRATISLAVA
Trnava
Zvolen
Žilina
Katowice
Opole
Wrocław
Legnica
Jelenia Gora
LIBEREC
Tanvald
Vrchlabi
Turnov
USTI NAD LABEM
Litomerice
Chomutov
Jicin
Nachod
HRADEC KRÁLOVÉ
KARLOVY VARY
Cheb
Marianske Lazne
Podebrady
Zamberk
PRAHA
Beroun
PARDUBICE
Kutna Hora
Stribro
PIZEN
Budisov nad Budisovkou
OSTRAVA
Frydek Mistek
Sternberk
Frenstat
OLOMOUC
Roznov pod Radhostem
Domazlice
KLATOVY
Besiny
TABOR
JIHLAVA
Boskovice
ZLÍN
BRNO
Strmilov
Telc
Uhersky Brod
ČESKÉ BUDĚJOVICE
Trebon
Cesky Krumlov
ZNOJMO
BRECLAV
Frymburk
Lipno nad Vltavou
Motorways
Primary roads
Secondary roads
All year site(s)
Seasonal site(s)
No sites listed
N
E
S
W
0 50 100 150 km
0 20 40 60 80 100 miles

Denmark

Highlights

Regularly found high on the list of the happiest nations on earth, Denmark is a friendly country that welcomes everyone. You can enjoy a charming, fairytale atmosphere working together with modern cities at the forefront of design and sustainability.

The landscape, too, is enchanting, and the beautiful sandy beaches, lakes, rivers and plains are a delight to explore, and ideal for cyclists.

The smørrebrød, a traditional open sandwich made with rye bread, salad and meat or fish, is perhaps one of Denmark's most famous dishes. Equally renowned is the Danish pastry - known locally as Vienna bread or wienerbrød. You'll find these at bakeries throughout the country.

A traditional Scandinavian drink, Akvavit's believed to have originated in Denmark in the 16th century. The spirit takes its distinct flavour from herbs and spices and is often sipped slowly from a small shot glass.

Major towns and cities

- Copenhagen – Denmark's bustling capital city is a perfect mix of old and new.
- Aarhus – this compact city is well known for its musical heritage.
- Odense – one of the country's oldest cities, and home of Hans Christian Anderson.
- Aalborg – a vibrant city with an atmospheric waterfront.

Attractions

- Tivoli Gardens, Copenhagen – one of the oldest amusement parks in the world.
- Kronborg Castle, Helsingør – This renaissance castle is a UNESCO site.
- Frederiksborg Castle, Hillerød – a palatial residence that now houses a museum.
- Skagen Beaches – 60 km of white, sandy beaches and stunning, rugged coastline.

Find out more

visitdenmark.com
contact@visitdenmark.com
T: +45 (0) 32 88 99 00

Country Information

Capital: Copenhagen

Bordered by: Germany

Terrain: Mostly fertile lowland, undulating hills, woodland, lakes and moors

Climate: Generally mild, changeable climate without extremes of heat or cold; cold winters but usually not severe; warm, sunny summers; the best time to visit is between May and September

Coastline: 7,400 km

Highest Point: Ejer Bavnehøj 173m

Languages: Danish

Local Time: GMT or BST + 1, ie 1 hour ahead of the UK all year

Currency: Krone (DKK) divided into 100 øre; £1 = DKK 8.93 DKK 10 = £1.12 (Nov 2024)

Emergency numbers: Police 112 (114 for non-urgent calls); Fire brigade 112; Ambulance 112 (operators speak English).

Public Holidays 2025: Jan 1; Apr 17, 18, 20, 21; May 29; Jun 8, 9; Dec 25, 26.

School summer holidays extend from end June to mid August.

Entry Formalities

British and Irish passport holders may stay for up to 90 days in any 180 day period without a visa. You may be asked to show a return or onward ticket at the border to confirm your length of stay, or to prove that you have enough money for your stay.

Your passport will need to have a minimum of 6 months' validity remaining, and be less than 10 years old (even if it has 6 months or more left).

Visitors arriving at a campsite or hotel must complete a registration form.

Medical Services

The standard of healthcare is high. Citizens of the UK are entitled to the same emergency medical services as the Danish, including free hospital treatment, on production of a European Health Insurance Card (EHIC) or a UK GlobalHealth Insurance Card (GHIC) Tourist offices and health offices (kommunes social og sundhedforvaltning) have lists of doctors and dentists who are registered with the public health service. For a consultation with a doctor you may have to pay the full fee but you will be refunded if you apply to a local health office if they are registered with the Danish Public Health Service. Partial refunds may be made for dental costs and approved medicines. Prescriptions are dispensed at pharmacies (apotek).

Opening Hours

Banks: Mon-Fri 10am-4pm (Thu to 6pm). In the Provinces opening hours vary from town to town.

Museums: Tue-Sun 9am/10am-5pm; most close Mon.

Post Offices: Mon-Fri 9am/10am-5pm/6pm, Sat 9am/10am-12pm/2pm or closed all day.

Shops: Mon-Fri 9am-5.30pm (Fri to 7pm); Sat 9am-1pm/2pm; supermarkets open Mon-Fri 9am-7pm & Sat 9am-4pm/5pm; open on first Sunday of the month 10am-5pm. Most shops close on public holidays but you may find some bakers, sandwich shops, confectioners and kiosks open.

Regulations for Pets

Between April and September all dogs must be kept on a lead. This applies not only on campsites but throughout the country in general.

Safety and Security

Denmark has relatively low levels of crime and most visits to the country are trouble-free. The majority of public places are well lit and secure, most people are helpful and often speak good English. Visitors should, however, be aware of pickpocketing or bag-snatching in Copenhagen, particularly around the central station and in the Christiania and Nørrebro areas, as well as in other large cities and tourist attractions. Car break-ins have increased in recent years; never leave valuables in your car.

Denmark shares with the rest of Europe a general threat from terrorism. Please check gov.uk/foreign-travel-advice/denmark before you travel.

British Embassy

Kastelsvej 36-40
DK-2100 Copenhagen
Tel: +45 35 44 52 00
gov.uk/world/organisations/british-embassy-copenhagen

There are also Honorary Consulates in Aabenraa, Åarhus, Fredericia and Herning

Irish Embassy

Østbanegade 21
2100 Copenhagen Ø
Tel: +45 35 47 32 00
Website: ireland.ie/copenhagen

Documents

Money

Some shops and restaurants, particularly in the larger cities, display prices in both krone and euros and many will accept payment in euros.

Major credit cards are widely, but not always, accepted. Credit cards are not normally accepted in supermarkets. Cash machines are widespread. A 5% surcharge is usually applied to credit card transactions. Some banks and/or cash machines may not accept debit cards issued by non-Danish banks.

It's advisable to carry your passport or photocard driving licence if paying with a credit card as you may well be asked for photographic proof of identity. Carry your credit card issuers'/banks' 24-hour UK contact numbers in case of loss or theft of your cards.

Passport

Your passport must be valid for the proposed duration of your stay, however in case of any unforWeseen delays it's strongly recommended to have a period of extra validity on your passport.

Vehicle(s)

Carry your vehicle documentation, including vehicle registration certificate (V5C), certificate of insurance and MOT certificate (if applicable). You may be asked to produce your V5C if driving a motorhome over the Great Belt Bridge between Funen and Zealand in order to verify the weight of your vehicle. For more information see the 'Motorways' section of this introduction.

The minimum age you can drive, with a valid driver's licence, is 17.

Driving

Alcohol

The maximum permitted level of alcohol is 0.05%. Drivers caught over this limit will be fined and their driving licence withdrawn. Police carry out random breath tests.

Breakdown Service

24 hours assistance is available from SOS Dansk Autohjaelp (Danish Automobile Assistance) call Tel: 70 10 50 52.

The hourly charge between Monday and Friday is 638 DKK + VAT and an administration charge; higher charges apply at night and at weekends and public holidays. On-the-spot repairs and towing must be paid for in cash.

On motorways use the emergency telephones, situated every 2 km, to call the breakdown service. The telephone number to dial in case of an accident is 112.

Child Restraint System

Children under three years of age must be seated in an approved child restraint system adapted to their size. Children over three years old and under 1.35 metres in height must be seated in an approved child restraint suitable for both their height and weight. If the vehicle is fitted with an active airbag children must not use in the front seat in a rear-facing child seat.

Fuel

Some petrol stations in larger towns stay open 24 hours a day and they often have self-service pumps where some will accept cash in DKK (sometimes also in EUR). Few display instructions in English and it's advisable to fill up during normal opening hours when staff are on hand. Unleaded petrol pumps are marked 'Blyfri Benzine'. Major credit cards are normally accepted.

LPG (Autogas or Bilgas) is available from a handful of petrol stations. See mylpg.eu for an overview of filling stations in Denmark.

Lights and Indicators

Dipped headlights are compulsory at all times, regardless of weather conditions. Bulbs are more likely to fail with constant use and you are recommended to carry spares.

On motorways drivers must use their hazard warning lights to warn other motorists of sudden queues ahead or other dangers such as accidents.

By law indicators must be used when overtaking or changing lanes on a motorway and when pulling out from a parked position at the kerb.

Low Emission Zones

Low Emission zones are in force in Aalborg, Aarhus, København (Copenhagen), Frederiksberg and Odense. The rules affect all diesel powered vehicles over 3,500kg, which must meet European Emission Standard 4 (EURO 4) or be fitted with a particulate filter. From 1 October 2023 all Danish LEZ will also affect diesel cars. For more information please see urbanaccessregulations.eu.

Motorways

There are approximately 1,205 km of motorways, mainly two-lane and relatively uncongested. No tolls are levied except on bridges. Lay-bys with picnic areas and occasionally motorhome service points are situated at 25 km intervals. These often also have toilet facilities. Service areas and petrol stations are situated at 50 km intervals and are generally open from 7am to 10pm.

Parking

Parking prohibitions and limitations are indicated by signs. Hours during which parking is not allowed are displayed in black for weekdays, with brackets for Saturdays and in red for Sundays and public holidays. Parking meters and discs are used and discs are available free of charge from post offices, banks, petrol stations and tourist offices. The centre of Copenhagen is divided into red, green and blue zones and variable hourly charges apply round the/ clock Monday to Friday (Saturday to 5pm; Sunday and public holidays free). 'Pay and display' tickets may be bought from machines with cash or a credit card. Cars must be parked on the right-hand side of the road (except in one-way streets). An illegally parked vehicle may be removed by the police.

Priority

At intersections with 'give way' or 'stop' signs and/or a transverse line consisting of triangles (shark's teeth) with one point facing towards the driver, drivers must give way to traffic at an intersection. If approaching an intersection of two roads without any signs you must give way to vehicles coming from the right. Give way to cyclists and to buses signalling to pull out. On the Danish islands take care as many people travel by foot, bicycle or on horseback.

Roads

Roads are generally in good condition, well-signposted and largely uncongested and driving standards are fairly high.

Caravanners should beware of strong crosswinds on exposed stretches of road. Distances are short; it's less than 500 km (310 miles) from Copenhagen on the eastern edge of Zealand, to Skagen at the tip of Jutland, and the coast is never more than an hour away.

Road Signs and Markings

Signs directing you onto or along international E-roads are green with white lettering. E-roads, having been integrated into the Danish network, usually have no other national number.

Signs above the carriageway on motorways have white lettering on a blue background. Signs guiding you onto other roads are white with red text and a hexagonal sign with red numbering indicates the number of a motorway exit.

Primary (main roads) connecting large towns and ferry connections have signs with black numbers on a yellow background. Secondary (local) roads connecting small towns and primary routes are indicated by signs with black numbers on a white background. Signs of any colour with a dotted frame refer you to a road further ahead. Road signs themselves may be placed low down and, as a result, may be easy to miss.'Sharks teeth' markings at junctions indicate stop and give way to traffic on the road you are entering.

General roads signs conform to international standards.

You may see the following:

Place of interest

Recommended speed limits

Dual Carriage-way ends

The following are some other common signs:

Danish	English Translation
Ensrettet kørsel	One-way street
Fare	Danger
Farligt sving	Dangerous bend
Fodgægerovergang	Pedestrian crossing
Gennemkørsel forbudt	No through road
Hold til højre	Keep to the right
Hold til venstre	Keep to the left
Omkørsel	Diversion
Parkering forbudt	No parking
Vejen er spærret	Road closed

Speed Limits

	Open Road (km/h)	Motorway (km/h)
Car Solo	80-90	110-130
Car towing caravan/trailer	70	80
Motorhome under 3500kg	80-90	110-130
Motorhome 3500-7500kg	80	80

Vehicles over 3,500 kg are restricted to 70 km/h (44 mph) on the open road and on motorways. It's prohibited to use radar detectors.

Traffic Jams

There's relatively low density of traffic. At most, traffic builds up during the evening rush hours around the major cities of Copenhagen, Århus, Aalborg and Odense. During the holiday season traffic jams may be encountered at the Flensburg border crossing into Germany, on the roads to coastal areas, on approach roads to ferry crossings and routes along the west coast of Jutland.

Toll Bridges

The areas of Falster and Zealand are linked by two road bridges, 1.6 km and 1.7 km in length respectively.

The areas of Funen and Zealand are linked by an 18 km suspension road bridge and rail tunnel known as the Great Belt Link. (Storebæltsbroen), connecting the towns of Nyborg and Korsør. The toll road is part of the E20 between Odense and Ringsted and tolls for single journeys on the bridge are shown in Table 1 below (2024 prices, subject to change).

Table 1 – Great Belt Bridge

Vehicle(s)	Price
Solo Car up to 6 metres	275 DKK
Car + trailer/caravan	420 DKK
Motorhome (under 3,500 kg) under 6 metres	275 DKK
Motorhome (under 3,500kg) over 6 metres	620 DKK
Motorhome (over 3,500 kg) up to 10 metres	620 DKK
Motorhome (over 3,500 kg) over 10 metres	985 DKK

Day return and weekend return tickets are also available. For more information see storebaelt.dk/en.

The 18 km Øresund Bridge links Copenhagen in Denmark with Malmö in Sweden and means that it's possible to drive all the way from mainland Europe to Sweden by motorway. The crossing is via an 8 km bridge and a 4 km tunnel. Tolls for single journeys (payable in cash, including euros, or by credit card) are levied on the Swedish side, and are shown in Table 2 below (2023 prices, subject to change).

Table 2 – Øresund Bridge

Vehicle(s)	Price
Solo Car or motorhome up to 6 metres	455 DKK
Car + caravan/trailer or motorhome over 6 metres	910 DKK

Speed limits apply, and during periods of high wind the bridge is closed to caravans. Bicycles are not allowed. Information on the Øresund Bridge can be found on oeresundsbron.com.

On both the Øresund and Storebælts bridges vehicle length is measured electronically and even a slight overhang over six metres, e.g. towbars, projecting loads and loose items, will result in payment of the higher tariff.

Violation of Traffic Regulations

The police are authorised to impose and collect on-the-spot fines for traffic offences. Driving offences committed in Denmark are reported to the UK authorities.

Essential Equipment

Reflective Jacket

It's recommended, though not compulsory, to carry a reflective jacket on board the vehicle in the event the driver has to step out of the car in an emergency.

Warning Triangle

An EU approved red warning triangle must be used if the vehicle breaks down, punctures or is involved in an accident.

Touring

The peak holiday season and school holidays are slightly earlier than in the UK and by mid-August some attractions close or operate reduced opening hours.

Service charges are automatically added to restaurant bills although you may round up the bill if service has been good, but it's not expected. Tips for taxi drivers are included in the fare. Smoking is not allowed in enclosed public places, including restaurants and bars. The 3,500 km Marguerite Route, marked by brown signs depicting a flower (see below), takes motorists to the best sights and scenic areas in Denmark.

Tourist Route

A route map and guide (in English) are available from bookshops, tourist offices and Statoil service stations all over Denmark. Stretches of the route are not suitable for cars towing caravans as some of the roads are narrow and twisting.

The capital and major port, Copenhagen, is situated on the island of Zealand. Grundtvig Cathedral, Amalienborg Palace and the Viking Museum are well worth a visit, as are the famous Tivoli Gardens open from mid-April to the third week in September and again for a few weeks in October to early November and from mid November to the end of December (excluding Christmas Eve). The statue of the Little Mermaid, the character created by Hans Christian Andersen, can be found at the end of the promenade called Langelinie. Copenhagen is easy to explore and from there visitors may travel to the north of Zealand along the 'Danish Riviera' to Hamlet's castle at Kronborg, or west to Roskilde with its Viking Ship Museum and 12th century cathedral.

A digital Copenhagen Card is available to buy through the 'Copenhagen Card City Guide' where you can choose to purchase a 'Discover' or a 'Hop' Card. Valid for 24, 48, 72, 96 and 120 hours, a 'Discover' card offers unlimited use of all public transport in the greater Copenhagen Area (in zone 1-99) and free entry to over 80 museums and attractions. Valid for 24, 48 and 72 hours, a 'Hop' card offers access to over 40 attractions in the City and unlimited access to Stromma's Hop On - Hop Off buses. With either a 'Discover' or a 'Hop' card, one adult can bring up to two children for free. Any extra children will require a 'Junior' card.
For more information please see copenhagencard.com.

National Parks in the country include Thy National Park near Thisted along Jutland's north-west coast, Mols Bjerge National Park in eastern Jutland and Wadden Sea National Park in the south-west of the country.

English is widely spoken.

Camping and Caravanning

Denmark has around 570 approved, well-equipped, annually inspected campsites. A green banner flies at each campsite entrance, making it easy to spot. Campsites are graded from 1 to 5 stars, many having excellent facilities including baby-changing areas, private family bathrooms, self-catering cooking facilities and shops. Prices are regulated and there's very little variation.

All except the most basic 1-star sites have water and waste facilities for motorhomes and at least some electric hook-ups. You may find it useful to take your own flat universal sink plug. During the high season it's advisable to book in advance as many Danish holidaymakers take pitches for the whole season for use at weekends and holidays resulting in minimal space for tourers.

A form of ID such as a Camping Key Europe (CKE), Camping or ACSI Club ID is required at all Danish campsites.

Campervans can choose from over 150 DK-Camp campsites offering 'DK-Stellplätze'. These are secure, specially equipped sites with good facilities and flexible check-in/check-out. A list of Stellplätze campsites can be found on dk-camp.dk/en under 'Accomodation types'.

Wild camping is prohibited on common or State land, in stopping bays and parking sites, in the dunes, or on the beaches, unless there's an organised campsite. Farmers or landowners may allow you to pitch on their land, but you must always seek permission from them in advance.

Cycling

Although not as flat as the Netherlands, Denmark is very cyclist-friendly and many major and minor roads, including those in all major towns, have separate cycle lanes or tracks. They have their own traffic lights and signals. Cyclists often have the right of way and, when driving, you should check cycle lanes before turning left or right.

Orange, dockless, city bikes are available to rent in Åarhus and Copenhagen via the Donkey Republic app - please visit the website donkey.bike to see prices and download the app.

There are many separate cycle routes, including eleven national routes, which may be long distance, local or circular, mainly on quiet roads and tracks. Local tourist offices can provide information. When planning a route, take the (often strong) prevailing westerly winds into account.

Bicycles can be carried on the roof of a car if they are attached to an adequate roof-rack and the total height does not exceed 4m, as well as at the rear. When carried at the rear, the lights, indicators and number plate must remain visible.

Electricity and Gas

Current on campsites varies between 6 and 16 amps, a 10 amp supply being the most common. Plugs have 2 round pins. Some sites have CEE17 electric hook-ups or are in the process of converting. If a CEE17 connection is not available site staff will usually provide an adaptor. Visitors report that reversed polarity is common.

Campingaz 904 and 907 butane cylinders are readily available from campsites, or some Statoil service stations and at camping or hardware shops. If travelling on to Norway, Statoil agencies there will exchange Danish propane cylinders.

Public Transport

Public transport is excellent and you can buy a variety of bus, train and metro tickets on the mobile app 'DOT billetter' at station kiosks and at 7-Eleven kiosks. Two children under the age of 12 travel for free on buses and metro trains in the Greater Copenhagen area when accompanied by an adult.
Tickets must be purchased for large dogs and bicycles. Small dogs in pet carriers can travel for free.

Numerous car ferry connections operate daily between different parts of the country. The ferry is a common mode of transport in Denmark and there may be long queues, especially at weekends in summer. The most important routes connect the bigger islands of Zealand and Funen with Jutland using high-speed vessels on day and night services. Vehicle length and height restrictions apply on routes between Odden (Zealand) and Århus and Æbeltoft (Jutland) and not all sailings transport caravans – check in advance. The Danish Tourist Board can provide general information on car ferry services or contact Scandlines for information on inter-island services including timetables and prices - scandlines.dk, email scandlines@scandlines.com or telephone +45 (0) 33 15 15 15.

International ferry services are particularly busy during July and August and it's advisable to book in advance. Popular routes include Frederikshavn to Gothenburg (Sweden), Helsingør to Helsingborg (Sweden), Copenhagen to Oslo (Norway), and Rødby to Puttgarden in Germany (this route involves a road bridge which is occasionally closed to high-sided vehicles because of high winds). The ferry route from Copenhagen to Hamburg is a good alternative to the busy E45 motorway linking Denmark and Germany.

Sites in Denmark

AABENRAA *B3* (2.7km S Coastal) *55.02490, 9.41461* **Fjordlyst Aabenraa City Camping,** Sønderskovvej 100, 6200 Aabenraa **tel 45 74 62 26 99; info@aabenraa-citycamping.dk; aabenraa-citycamping.dk**

DKK10 500m

Fr S take E45 & exit at junc 72 to Aabenraa. Foll Rd 42 then turn L onto Rd 24. Site sp on R. 3*, Med, mkd, pt shd, sl, terr, EHU (16A) DKK35; bbq; twin axles; TV; 10% statics; bus adj; Eng spkn; adv bkg acc; games area; CCI. *"Scenic location with views over the bay; excel facs; friendly, helpful staff; some steep slopes on site rds; vg."* **DKK 240, 9 Apr-13 Sep. 2022**

AALBORG *B1* (3km W Urban) *57.05500, 9.88500* **Strandparken Camping,** Skydebanevej 20, 9000 Aalborg **tel 98 12 76 29; info@strandparken.dk; www.strandparken.dk**

DKK10 nr

Turn L at start of m'way to Svenstrup & Aalborg W, foll A180 (Hobrovej rd) twd town cent. Turn L bef Limfjorden bdge onto Borgergade for 2km, site on R. Fr N turn R after bdge onto Borgergade. 3*, Med, shd, EHU (10A) DKK30 (poss rev pol); cooking facs; TV; 10% statics; phone; bus nr; Eng spkn; adv bkg acc; ccard acc; CKE. *"Gd cent for town & N Jutland; gd security; facs block excel; pool adj; card for elec."* **DKK 248, 24 Marr-11 Sep. 2022**

AALESTRUP *B2* (1km E Rural) *56.69166, 9.49991* **Aalestrup Camping,** Aalestrup Campingplads, Parkvænget 2, 9620 Aalestrup **tel 22 79 92 64; pouledb@ofir.dk; www.rosenparken.dk**

nr

Fr E45 turn W onto rd 561 to Aalestrup; 500m after junc with rd 13 turn L into Borgergade, cross rlwy line. Site sp. 1*, Med, pt shd, EHU DKK30. *"Free ent beautiful rose garden; gd touring base; friendly staff."* **DKK 125, 1 Mar-1 Nov. 2022**

AARHUS *C2* (8km N Rural) *56.22660, 10.16260* **Århus Camping,** Randersvej 400, Lisbjerg, 8200 Århus Nord **tel 86 23 11 33; info@aarhuscamping.dk; www.aarhuscamping.dk**

12 DKK10 (htd)

Exit E45 junc 46 Århus N, then to Ikea rndabt. Then foll sp Lisbjerg & head for smoking factory chimney. Site 400m N of Lisbjerg. 3*, Med, pt shd, pt sl, EHU (16A) metered; gas; bbq; cooking facs; TV; 10% statics; phone; adv bkg acc; golf 10km; games area; CKE. *"Conv Århus; gd, tidy site; modern san facs; conv for bus into Aarhus, helpful owner; elec cards for shwrs."* **DKK 215 2022**

ALBAEK *C1* (9.6km N Coastal) *57.64433, 10.46179* **Bunken Camping,** Ålbækvej 288, Bunken Klitplantage, 9982 Ålbæk **tel 98 48 71 80; info@skagensydstrand.dk; www.skagensydstrandcamping.dk**

DKK15 sand 150m

Site in fir plantation E of A10. 3*, V lge, hdg, pt shd, EHU DKK39 (poss rev pol); gas; cooking facs; TV; phone; adv bkg acc; boating; fishing. *"Beautiful site in trees; spacious pitches."* **DKK 215, 3 Apr-18 Oct. 2022**

ASSENS *B3* (12km N Coastal) *55.33400, 9.89002* **Sandager Naes Camping,** Strandgårdsvej 12, DK 5610 Assens **tel 45 64 79 11 56; info@sandagernaes.dk; www.sandagernaes.dk**

(htd) 0.5km

Fr E20, take exit 57 dir Assens. R at Sandager & foll sp. Med, mkd, hdg, pt shd, pt sl, EHU (13A); bbq; cooking facs; TV; 50% statics; phone; Eng spkn; adv bkg acc; games area; games rm; waterslide; CCI. *"Excel site."* **DKK 330, 23 Mar-15 Sep. 2024**

ASSENS *B3* (1.6km W Urban/Coastal) *55.26569, 9.88390* **Camping Assens Strand,** Næsvej 15, 5610 Assens **tel (45) 63 60 63 62; assens@campone.dk; assensstrand.dk**

DKK25 sand adj

Site on beach at neck of land W of town adj marina. 3*, Med, pt shd, EHU (10A) DKK30; gas; TV; 20% statics; phone; adv bkg acc; watersports; fishing. *"Pleasant site on beach."* **DKK 215, Easter-13 Sep. 2022**

BILLUND *B3* (12km SE Rural) *55.68877, 9.26864* **Randbøldal Camping,** Dalen 9, 7183 Randbøl **tel 75 88 35 75; info@randboldalcamping.dk; www.randboldalcamping.dk**

12 DKK20 (htd)

Fr Vejle take Billund rd. After approx 18km take L turn to Randbol & Bindebolle. Foll sp, site located approx 5km on L. 3*, Med, shd, pt sl, EHU (10A) DKK35; cooking facs; sw; TV; 15% statics; phone; Eng spkn; adv bkg acc; ccard acc; fishing nr; waterslide nr. *"Wooded site nr rv & trout hatchery; facs stretched high ssn; conv Legoland & Lion Park."* **DKK 308 2022**

BLOKHUS *B1* (8km NE Rural) *57.27855, 9.66133* **Jambo Feriepark,** Solvejen 60, 9493, Saltum **tel 98 88 16 66; info@jambo.dk; www.jambo.dk**

sand 1.5km

Take A17/A11 fr Aalborg, L at Saltum Kirke, approx 1.5km, sp on L. 5*, Lge, pt shd, EHU; gas; cooking facs; tennis; sauna. **DKK 530, 22 Mar-19 Oct. 2024**

BOGENSE *C3* (2km SW Urban/Coastal) *55.56144, 10.08530* **Bogense Strand Camping,** Vestre Engvej 11, 5400 Bogense **tel 64 81 35 08; info@bogensecamp.dk; www.bogensecamp.dk**

DKK20 shgl adj

Fr E20 at junc 57 & take 317 NE to Bogense. At 1st traff lts turn L for harbour, site sp at side of harbour. Lge, pt shd, EHU (12A) DKK35; cooking facs; TV; 10% statics; phone; adv bkg acc; CKE. *"Well-run site; excel facs; interesting sm town 5 mins walk."*
DKK 325, 3 Apr-18 Oct. 2022

> **"There aren't many sites open at this time of year"**
>
> If you're travelling outside peak season remember to call ahead to check site opening dates – even if the entry says 'open all year'.

BOGENSE *C3* (1.2km W Urban/Coastal) *55.56770, 10.08336* **Kyst Camping Bogense,** Østre Havnevej 1, 5400 Bogense **tel 64 81 14 43; info@kystcamping.dk; www.kystcamping.dk**

DKK10 200m

Fr E20 at junc 57 take 317 NE to Bogonense, foll sp for harbour, site sp. 3*, Lge, hdg, mkd, unshd, EHU (16A) DKK35; bbq; cooking facs; TV; bus 200m; games rm; games area. *"Vg site; friendly, helpful owners; nice sm town and harbour; ideal cycling."*
DKK 350, 1 Apr-22 Oct. 2024

BORRE *D3* (6km SE Rural) *54.97971, 12.52198* **Camping Møns Klint,** Klintevej 544, 4791 Magleby **tel 55 81 20 25; camping@klintholm.dk; www.campingmoensklint.dk**

shgl 3km

Site nr end of metalled section of rd 287 fr Stege to E of Magleby, site sp. 4*, Lge, pt shd, pt sl, EHU (10A) DKK40; gas; cooking facs; TV; 20% statics; phone; Eng spkn; adv bkg acc; ccard acc; boating; games area; bike hire; tennis; fishing; CKE. *"150m chalk cliffs adj - geological interest; much flora, fauna, fossils; gd walks; friendly staff; excel facs."*
DKK 410, 12 Apr-31 Oct. 2022

BRAEDSTRUP *B2* (6.3km SSE Rural) *55.93552, 9.65314* **Gudenå Camping Brædstrup,** Bolundvej 4, 8740 Brædstrup **tel 75763070; info@gudenaacamping.dk; www.gudenaacamping.dk**

DKK10 (htd)

Fr Silkeborg take rd 52 twds Horsens; site sp R off rd 52 approx 4km fr Braedstrup. 3*, Sm, mkd, unshd, EHU (10A) metered; bbq; TV; 25% statics; adv bkg rec; games rm; CKE. *"Sm, attractive site beside Rv Gudenå; v well run fam site; fishing fr site; excel san facs."*
DKK 223, 29 Apr-27 Sep. 2022

EBELTOFT *C2* (5.2km SE Coastal) *56.16775, 10.73085* **Blushøj Camping,** Elsegårdevej 55, 8400 Ebeltoft **tel 86 34 12 38; info@blushoj.com; www.blushoj-camping.dk**

(htd) shgl

Head Sw on Rte 21 twds Nørrealle. Turn L onto Nørrealle, go thro 1st rndabt, cont ontosteralle, turn L onto Elsegardevej, turn L then R to stay on same rd. Site will be on R. 3*, Lge, mkd, pt shd, EHU (10A) DKK5; gas; bbq; twin axles; TV; bus 0.1km; Eng spkn; adv bkg acc; ccard acc; games rm; fishing; CKE. *"Fantastic location; number of pitches with magnificent sea view; immac facs; friendly owner; highly rec; easy acc to shore."* **DKK 280, 22 Mar-29 Sep. 2024**

ESBJERG *A3* (13km NW Rural/Coastal) *55.54359, 8.33921* **Sjelborg Camping,** Sjelborg Standvej 11, Hjerting, 6710 Esbjerg Vest **tel 75 11 54 32; info@sjelborg.dk; www.sjelborg.dk**

shgl nr

Fr Esbjerg take coast rd N twds Hjerting & Sjelborg. At T-junc, Sjelborg Vej, turn L & in 100m turn R onto Sjelborg Kirkevej (camping sp); in 600m turn L into Sjelborg Strandvej (sp); site on R in 600m. 3*, Lge, hdg, mkd, pt shd, EHU (10A)€4.50; phone; bus to town; adv bkg acc; fishing; golf 5km. *"Excel, well maintained site in a quiet country setting; superb facs & activities all ages; lake adj; spacious on edge of conservation area; mkd walks & bird sanctuary; v welcoming & friendly."*
DKK 190, 11 Apr-20 Sep. 2022

FAABORG *C3* (8.5km W Coastal) *55.10568, 10.10776* **Bøjden Strandcamping,** Bøjden Landevej 12, 5600 Bøjden **tel 63 60 63 60; info@bojden.dk; www.bojden.dk**

DKK25 (htd) nr (htd) sand adj

Rd 8 W fr Fåborg dir Bøjden/Fynshav, site sp nr ferry. 5*, Lge, mkd, hdg, pt shd, pt sl, terr, serviced pitches; EHU (16A) inc; cooking facs; TV; 80% statics; Eng spkn; adv bkg acc; ccard acc; games rm; golf 12km; bike hire; sep car park; boat hire. *"Excel family site with activity cent; blue flag beach; sea views fr pitches; interesting area; excel facs."*
DKK 490, 9 Apr-22 Oct. 2023

FREDERICIA *B3* (12.6km N Coastal) *55.65696, 9.72580* **Morkholt Strand Camping,** Hagenvej 105B, DK-7080 Borkop **tel 75 95 91 22; info@morkholt.dk; morkholt.dk**

12 DKK20 (htd) (htd) adj

Fr Vejle take A28 twrds Fredericia. Exit to Garslev. After Garslev foll sp to Morkholt. Strt on at island. Stay L at junc (camping sp - dead end rd). After 1.5km site on L. 3*, Lge, mkd, hdg, unshd, EHU 6A; bbq (charcoal, elec, gas); cooking facs; twin axles; Eng spkn; adv bkg acc; games area; 2 football pitches; crazy golf; pedal go-karts; 3 bouncy pillows; visitor carpk; sea kayaking courses; CKE. *"Excel."*
DKK 302 2024

DENMARK

FREDERICIA *B3* (6km NE Coastal) *55.62457, 9.83351* **Trelde Næs Camping,** Trelde Næsvej 297, Trelde Næs, 7000 Fredericia **tel 75 95 71 83; info@dancamps.dk; dancamps.dk/trelde-naes**

DKK16 (htd) (htd) sand adj

Route 28 (Vejle-Fredericia). Fr Vejle take Egeskov exit, then Trelde and Trelde-Næs. Fr Fredericia to Trelde, then Trelde Næs. 3*, Lge, unshd, pt sl, EHU (10A) DKK32; bbq; cooking facs; TV; 10% statics; phone; adv bkg acc; ccard acc; waterslide; sauna. *"Vg; friendly; fine views over fjord; conv Legoland & island of Fyn; swipecard for all services - pay on dep."* **DKK 367** **2024**

FREDERIKSHAVN *C1* (2km N Coastal) *57.46415, 10.52778* **Nordstrand Camping A/S,** Apholmenvej 40, 9900 Frederikshavn **tel 98 42 93 50; info@nordstrand-camping.dk; www.nordstrand-camping.dk**

DKK15 (covrd) 1km

Fr E45/Rd40 foll rd N twd Skagen to outside town boundary (over rlwy bdge), turn R at rndabt into Apholmenvej; site sp. 4*, Lge, mkd, unshd, EHU (10-16A) DKK42; gas; red long stay; TV; 10% statics; phone; Eng spkn; adv bkg acc; ccard acc; excursions; CKE. *"Vg NH for ferries; recep open 24hrs peak ssn; well-run, clean site; some pitches sm; cycle track to town."* **DKK 321, 14 Mar-24 Sep.** **2023**

GRASTEN *B3* (2km SW Coastal) *54.9007, 9.57121* **Lærkelunden Camping,** Nederbyvej 17-25, Rinkenæs, 6300 Gråsten **tel 74 65 02 50; info@laerkelunden.dk; www.laerkelunden.dk**

DKK10 (covrd, htd) sand adj

Fr Kruså E on rd 8 twds Gråsten & Sønderborg; on E o'skts of Rinkenæs turn R Nederbyvej (car dealer on corner) & foll sp to site in 400m. 4*, Lge, hdstg, unshd, pt sl, serviced pitches; EHU (10A) DKK50; gas; bbq; cooking facs; TV; 10% statics; phone; Eng spkn; ccard acc; boat launch; sauna; solarium; CKE. *"Gd sailing/surfing; views over Flensburg fjord; coastal footpath; gd cent for S Jutland & N Germany; excel; lovely, well run site."* **DKK 317, 31 Mar-22 Oct.** **2023**

GRENAA *C2* (4km S Coastal) *56.38957, 10.91213* **Grenaa Strand Camping,** Fuglsangsvej 58, 8500 Grenå **tel 86 32 17 18; info@722.dk; www.grenaastrandcamping.dk**

DKK30 sand 250m

Fr Grenå harbour foll coast rd due S foll sp. 3*, V lge, unshd, EHU (10A) DKK35; gas; TV; 10% statics; phone; adv bkg acc; solarium. *"Conv for ferries to Sweden; busy site."* **DKK 264, 1 Apr-16 Sep.** **2022**

GREVE *D3* (9km E Urban/Coastal) *55.59434, 12.34315* **Hundige Strand Familiecamping,** Hundige Strandvej 72, 2670 Greve **tel 20 21 85 84; info@hsfc.dk; www.hundigestrandcamping.com**

nr sand 1km

Leave E20/47/55 at junc 27 & foll sp Hundige, cont strt ahead until T-junc with rd 151. Turn L, ent 200m on L. Or leave at junc 22 & foll rd 151 down coast to site on R in 8km. 2*, Med, mkd, pt shd, terr, EHU inc; gas; bbq; cooking facs; TV; 25% statics; phone; Eng spkn; adv bkg acc; ccard acc; CKE. *"Sh walk to rlwy stn & 15 mins to Copenhagen; bar adj; friendly, helpful staff; hypmkt 1km; lge pool stadium 5km; office open morning & eves only LS; site in two parts; v scenic; site clsd Xmas & New Year; excel, clean facs."* **DKK 267** **2024**

HADERSLEV *B3* (13.6km S Coastal) *55.15313, 9.49424* **Vikaer Strand Camping,** Dundelum 29, Djernaes, 6100 Haderslev **tel 74 57 54 64; info@vikaercamp.dk; www.vikaercamp.dk**

DKK 12

S on Katsund twd Lille Klingbjerg, turn R onto Lille Klingbjerg, L onto Højgade, R onto Møllepladsen, L to stay on Møllepladsen then take rte 170 to Diernæs Strandvej for 10.9km, then take 1st R onto Ny Erlevvej for 450m, turn L onto Omkørselsvejen/Rte 170, cont to foll Rte 170 for 8.1km, go thro 1 rndbt, turn L onto Diernæsvej Strandvej for 2.3km foll Diernæs Strandvej to Dundelum, L onto Diernæs Strandvej, R to stay on same rd, R onto Dundelum, L to stay on Dundelum and site on R. 3*, Lge, mkd, unshd, pt sl, EHU (10-16A); Eng spkn; CCI. *"Super site, many outlets for children; lovely beach; immac san facs."* **€30.00, 22 Mar-29 Sept.** **2024**

HADERSLEV *B3* (1km W Urban) *55.24431, 9.47701* **Haderslev Camping,** Erlevvej 34, 6100 Haderslev **tel 74 52 13 47; haderslev@danhostel.dk; www.danhostel-haderslev.dk/campingplads**

DKK 10 (htd) nr

Turn of E45 at junc 68 sp Haderslev Cent; turn R onto rd 170. On ent town, cross lake & turn R at traff lts. Site on R at rndabt in 500m. 3*, Med, hdstg, mkd, pt shd, pt sl, EHU (16A) DKK35; bbq; cooking facs; sw nr; TV; 10% statics; phone; bus 1km; Eng spkn; adv bkg acc; ccard acc; games rm; CKE. *"Gd, well-kept site conv E45; all facs to high standard; attractive old town; part of youth hostel complex (2018)."* **DKK 180, 23 Mar-21 Oct.** **2023**

HANSTHOLM *B1* (4km E Coastal) *57.10913, 8.66731*
Hanstholm Camping, Hamborgvej 95, 7730 Hanstholm
tel 97 96 51 98; info@hanstholm-camping.de; www.hanstholm-camping.dk

12 DKK10 (htd) WD MSP (htd) sand 1km

Ent town fr S on rte 26. At rndabt turn R onto coast rd sp Vigsø. Site on L in about 4km. 3*, Lge, mkd, hdg, pt shd, pt sl, EHU (10A) DKK40; gas; bbq; TV; 30% statics; phone; Eng spkn; adv bkg acc; ccard acc; horseriding; sauna; fishing; CKE. *"Fine view of North Sea coast; nr wildlife area; gd cycling/walking on coast path; excel, busy, well-maintained site; generous pitches; gd rest; excel childrens facs."* **DKK 230 2022**

HEJLSMINDE *B3* (9km N Coastal) *55.41109, 9.59228*
Gronninghoved Strand Camping, Mosvigvej 21, 6093 Sjolund **tel 75 57 40 45; info@gronninghoved.dk; www.gronninghoved.dk**

WD MSP (htd) shgl 0.2km

Fr E45 at exit 65 take 25 twds Kolding. At lights turn R onto 170. After 3.4km turn L sp Sjolund. On entry Sjolund take 1st L sp Gronninghoved. Take 2nd R in Gronninghoved, then 1st L, foll sp to site. 4*, Lge, hdg, mkd, pt shd, pt sl, EHU (10A) DKK37; cooking facs; twin axles; TV; 75% statics; Eng spkn; adv bkg acc; games area; games rm; CKE. *"Excel site; tennis, mini golf, billards & waterslide."*
DKK 218, 27 Mar-15 Sep. 2022

HELSINGOR *D2* (3km NE Urban/Coastal) *56.04393, 12.60433* **Helsingør Camping Grønnehave,** Strandalleen 2, 3000 Helsingør **tel 49 28 49 50; camping@helsingor.dk; www.helsingorcamping.dk**

12 WD MSP

Site in NE o'skts of town, twd Hornbæk. Site nr beach o'looking channel to Sweden on E side of rd. Foll sps on app or in town (beware: sp are sm & low down). 2*, Med, pt shd, EHU (10A) DKK30; cooking facs; 25% statics; phone. *"10 min walk to Hamlet's castle; 20 min walk to town & stn; gd train service to Copenhagen; max stay 14 days 15 Jun-15 Aug; Baltic ships w/end mid-Aug; v busy/cr high ssn."*
DKK 310 2024

HELSINGOR *D2* (13km SSW Coastal) *55.93949, 12.51643* **Niva Camping,** Sølyst Allé 14, 2290 Nivå
tel 49 14 52 26; info@nivaacamping.dk; www.nivaacamping.dk

(htd) WD MSP nr 800m

Take coast rd bet Copenhagen & Helsingør. Fr N foll sp to Nivå, & site 500m fr main rd, sp. Fr S site 2km after vill. Lge, mkd, hdstg, pt shd, pt sl, EHU (16A); bbq; cooking facs; twin axles; TV; 10% statics; Eng spkn; adv bkg acc; ccard acc; fishing adj; games rm; CKE. *"Conv Helsingborg ferry, Copenhagen, Kronborg Castle (Hamlet); excel san facs; vg location; quiet; best site in Zealand; excel help; upper level pitches quietest & coolest if hot."* **DKK 322, 23 Mar-29 Sep. 2024**

HENNE *A3* (2.7km NNW Rural) *55.73258, 8.22189*
Henneby Camping, Hennebysvej 20, 6854 Henne
tel 75 25 51 63; info@hennebycamping.dk; www.hennebycamping.dk

12 DKK15 (htd) WD MSP 2km

Fr Varde on rd 181 & 465 foll sp Henne Strand. Turn R after Kirkeby. Site sp. 3*, Lge, hdg, pt shd, EHU (10A) DKK32; gas; cooking facs; TV; 10% statics; Eng spkn; ccard acc; bike hire; CKE. *"Superb facs; pool 2.5km; gd, clean site."* **DKK 276 2024**

HILLEROD *D2* (1km SW Urban) *55.9246, 12.2941*
Hillerød Camping, Blytækkervej 18, 3400 Hillerød
tel 48 26 48 54; info@hillerodcamping.dk; www.hillerodcamping.dk

DKK10 WD MSP nr

Fr Roskilde or Copenhagen on A16 twd Hillerød, take 1st L at traff lts sp Hillerød & Frederiksborg Slot Rv233. Site in town cent, not well sp. Med, pt shd, pt sl, EHU (13A) DKK40 (long lead poss req); gas; cooking facs; sw nr; TV; phone; bus, train nr; Eng spkn; adv bkg acc; ccard acc; bike hire; CCI. *"Frederiksborg castle in town cent; gd base for N Sealand; 30 min by train to Copenhagen; v helpful, charming owner; common/dining rm; pleasant, well-run site; excel, new san facs 2010; no mkd pitch, but owner positions o'fits carefully; many personal touches - eg courtyard with herbs, fruit trees, candles & torches; best site; owner takes pride in environment and quality of facs."*
DKK 360, 23 Mar-15 Sept. 2024

HIRTSHALS *C1* (5km SW Coastal) *57.55507, 9.93254*
Tornby Strand Camping, Strandvejen 13, 9850 Tornby **tel 98 97 78 77; mail@tornbystrand.dk; www.tornbystrandcamping.dk**

12 DKK5 WD MSP nr sand 1km

Take rd 55 fr Hjørring twd Hirtshals. In 12km turn L sp Tornby Strand & Camping, site on L in 200m. 3*, Lge, pt shd, EHU (16A) DKK30; gas; TV; 75% statics; phone; Eng spkn; adv bkg acc; CKE. *"Useful for ferries to Kristiansand, Arendal, Faroe & Iceland; helpful owner."* **DKK 275 2022**

HIRTSHALS *C1* (1.5km W Urban) *57.58650, 9.94583*
Hirtshals Camping, Kystvejen 6, 9850 Hirtshals
tel 98 94 25 35; info@hirtshals-camping.dk; www.dk-camp.dk/hirtshals

DKK10 WD MSP nr 200m

Located 16km N of Hjørring. Turn L off rd 14 3km SW of Hirtshals & site on L. Fr ferry foll sp town cent, then site sp. 3*, Med, unshd, terr, EHU (10A) DKK30; sw nr; TV; phone; bike hire; fishing 200m. *"Open site on cliff top; san facs dated; friendly staff; conv ferries; on coastal cycle path; late arr area; busy but efficient; conv for NH."*
DKK 245, 4 Apr-22 Oct. 2022

HJORRING *C1* (14km W Urban) *57.47375, 9.80100* **Lønstrup Camping,** Møllebakkevej 20, Lonstrup, 9800 Hjørring **tel 45 21 44 56 37; loenstrupcamping@mail.dk; www.campingloenstrup.dk**

10DKK (htd) 500m

Fr E39 take Exit 3 dir Hjørring for Rte 35 twd Rte 55. Turn R onto Lonstrupvej. Foll sp to site. 3*, Med, mkd, pt shd, EHU (10A) 35DKK; bbq; cooking facs; twin axles; 30% statics; bus 200m; Eng spkn; adv bkg acc; CCI. *"Vg site; friendly, helpful family owned; lge units may be tight access; close to sm vill & coast."*
DKK 385, 26 Mar-29 Sep. **2024**

HOLBAEK *D3* (4km E Coastal) *55.71799, 11.76020* **FDM Holbæk Fjord Camping,** Sofiesminde Allé 1, 4300 Holbæk **tel 59 43 50 64; c-holbaek@fdm.dk; holbaekfjord.dk**

DKK15 (htd) (htd)

Fr Rv21 exit junc 20 (fr N) or junc 18 (fr S) & foll sp to harbour. Turn R (E) at harbour - Munkholmvej. Approx 1.5km along Munkholmvej, after traff lts, turn L into Sofiesminde Allé dir marina. Site on R, close to marina. 3*, Lge, hdg, mkd, pt shd, EHU (10A) inc; gas; bbq; cooking facs; TV; 80% statics; phone; adv bkg acc; ccard acc; sauna; golf nr; games area; bike hire; games rm; fishing nr; watersports nr. *"Well-run site in attractive position; helpful staff; pitches poss tight lge o'fits; whirlpool; spa; clean san facs; no o'fits over 10m high ssn; gd walks & cycle tracks."*
DKK 235, H17. **2022**

HORSENS *B2* (6km W Rural/Coastal) *55.85928, 9.91747* **Horsens City Camping,** Husoddevej 85, 8700 Horsens **tel 75 65 70 60; camping@horsencity.dk; www.husodde-camping.dk**

DKK10 nr nr sand adj

Site sp to R of Horsens-Odder rd (451), foll rd to fjord, site sp. 3*, Med, mkd, pt shd, pt sl, EHU (10A) DKK35; bbq; cooking facs; TV; 10% statics; phone; Eng spkn; fishing adj; CKE. *"Lovely location; lge pitches; well-maintained, well-managed site; friendly welcome; pool 3km; cycle tracks."* **DKK 287** **2022**

HOVBORG *B3* (0.7km NW Rural) *55.60900, 8.93267* **Holme A Camping,** Torpet 6, 6682 Hovborg **tel 75 39 67 77; info@holmeaacamping.dk; www.holmeaacamping.dk**

DKK10 (htd) nr nr nr

Campsite located besides the 425 Grindsted-Ribe. Well sp after Hovborg. 3*, Med, mkd, pt shd, EHU DKK32; gas; twin axles; TV; bus 0.5km; Eng spkn; ccard acc; CKE. *"Gd cycling; walking; fishing lakes; 20 min fr Legoland; lovely quiet site; immac facs; friendly helpful owner."* **DKK 255** **2024**

HVIDE SANDE *A2* (7.6km S Coastal) *55.94975, 8.15030* **Dancamps Nordsø,** Tingodden 3, Årgab, 6960 Hvide Sande **tel 96 59 17 22; info@dancamps.dk; www.dancamps.dk/nordsoe**

DKK20 (htd) (covrd, htd) sand 200m

Fr E20 take exit 73 onto rd 11 to Varde. Then take rd 181 twd Nymindegab & Hvide Sande. 3*, Lge, hdstg, unshd, serviced pitches; EHU (10A) DKK30; TV; 10% statics; phone; adv bkg acc; fishing; waterslide; tennis; sauna. *"Well-maintained facs; extra charge seaview pitches; private san facs avail; vg."*
DKK 333, 15 Apr-31 Oct. **2022**

JELLING *B3* (13km NW Rural) *55.83138, 9.29944* **Topcamp Riis & Feriecenter,** Østerhovedvej 43, Riis 7323 Give **tel 75 73 14 33; info@riisferiepark.dk; www.riisferiepark.dk**

DKK20 (htd)

Fr S exit E45 at junc 61, turn L & foll rd 28 for approx 8km. Turn R onto rd 441 for 15km, then turn R into Østerhovedvej for 2km & turn L into site. Or fr N on E45 exit junc 57, turn R & foll rd for 25km; turn L & foll 442 for 500m; turn R into Østerhovedvej & cont for 1.5km; turn R into site. 4*, Med, hdstg, mkd, hdg, pt shd, serviced pitches; EHU (13A) inc; gas; bbq; TV; 60% statics; phone; adv bkg acc; ccard acc; sauna; fishing 3.5km; golf 4km; bike hire; games rm; jacuzzi; waterslide; CKE. *"Attractive, well laid-out, well-run site in beautiful countryside; jacuzzi; fitness cent; vg san facs; no o'fits over 15m high ssn; conv for Legoland, Safari Park, Center Mobilium museum in Billund, lakes & E coast; excel; recep 0800-2200; friendly & relaxed; spacious pitches."*
DKK 430, 23 Mar-15 Sep, H11. **2024**

KARISE *D3* (5km S Rural) *55.27086, 12.22281* **Lægårdens Camping,** Vemmetoftevej 2A, Store Spjellerup, 4653 Karise **tel 56 71 00 67; info@laegaardenscamping.dk; www.laegaardenscamping.dk**

DKK10 (htd) nr 3km

Turn S off rd 209 in Karise, site sp. 3*, Med, hdg, mkd, pt shd, EHU DKK30; TV; 60% statics; Eng spkn; adv bkg acc; CKE. **DKK 235** **2022**

KOBENHAVN *D3* (10km N Coastal) *55.74536, 12.58331* **Camping Charlottenlund Fort,** Strandvejen 144B, 2290 Charlottenlund **tel 44 22 00 65; info@campingcopenhagen.dk; www.campingcopenhagen.dk**

nr nr nr sand

Take København-Helsingør coast rd O2/152, site on seaside 2km N of Tuborg factory. Sm, hdstg, mkd, shd, EHU (10A) metered; cooking facs; bus; Eng spkn; adv bkg rec; ccard acc; CKE. *"Experimentarium Science Park at Tuborg brewery; in grnds of old moated fort; conv Copenhagen & Sweden; gd facs but inadequate high ssn; quiet but noisy during mid-summer festivities; friendly staff."* **DKK 330, 30 Apr-6 Sep.** **2024**

KOBENHAVN *D3* (20km N Rural) *55.80896, 12.53062* **Nærum Camping,** Langebjerg 5, Ravnebakken, 2850 Nærum **tel 42 80 19 57; naerum@dcu.dk; www.camping-naerum.dk**

DKK23 WD MSP

Fr Copenhagen take E47/E55/rd 19 N for 16km, turn W to Nærum at junc 14, over bdge x-ing m'way & sharp L. 4*, Lge, pt shd, pt sl, EHU (10A) DKK30; gas; TV; train/bus 500m; Eng spkn; adv bkg acc; ccard acc; CKE. *"Popular nr woods; conv Copenhagen & Helsingor; shopping cent nrby over m'way bdge; gd cycle paths; path fr site for suburban rlwy to Copenhagen; if arr bet 1200 & 1400 select pitch & report to office after 1400; facs stretched in high ssn; excel bus service to Copenhagen."* **DKK 332, 21 Mar-19 Oct. 2024**

KOBENHAVN *D3* (13km S Urban) *55.582578, 12.628996* **Copenhagen Camping,** Bachersmindevej 11, DK-2791 Dragør **tel 32 94 20 07; info@copenhagencamping.dk; copenhagencamping.dk**

12 (htd) WD MSP

Exit E20 at junc 18. 3*, Lge, hdstg, hdg, unshd, 60% statics; Eng spkn; adv bkg acc; ccard acc; CKE. *"Gd; some airport noise; barrier clsd 2300-0700; of for short stay to visit Copenhagen."* **DKK 315 2024**

KOBENHAVN *D3* (9km W Urban) *55.67055, 12.43353* **DCU Absalon Camping,** Korsdalsvej 132, 2610 Rødovre **tel 36 41 06 00; copenhagen@dcu.dk; www.camping-absalon.dk**

12 DKK23 (htd) WD MSP nr

Fr E55/E20/E47 exit junc 24 dir København, site on L in 1km, sp. Or fr København foll A156 W for 9km. Sp Rødovre then Brøndbyøster, shortly after this site sp to R at traff lts; ent on L after 100m down side rd, sp. 2*, V lge, mkd, hdg, unshd, pt sl, EHU (10-16A) DKK30 or metered + conn fee; gas; bbq; cooking facs; twin axles; TV; 10% statics; bus/train nr; Eng spkn; adv bkg acc; ccard acc; games area; golf 10km; games rm; CKE. *"Well located nr Brøndbyøster rlwy stn & bus Copenhagen (rail tickets fr recep); some pitches unrel in wet & dusty when dry; vg, modern san facs; office clsd 1200-1400 LS; htd pool 300m; sep area for c'vans & m'vans; helpful staff; cycle rte to city; excel site; v well run; fitness rm; outdoor chess; attrac & boat trips can be booked; muddy when wet."* **DKK 280 2023**

KOGE *D3* (14km SE Coastal) *55.39793, 12.29022* **Stevns Camping,** Strandvejen 29, 4671 Strøby **tel 60 14 41 54; info@stevnscamping.dk; www.stevnscamping.dk**

12 DKK10 (htd) WD MSP nr nr (htd) shgl 400m

Exit E20/E55 junc 33 twd Køge. In Køge take rd 209 & 260 to Strøby. In Strøby turn L onto Strandvejen. 3*, Lge, mkd, unshd, EHU (10A) inc; bbq; cooking facs; 10% statics; phone; Eng spkn; CKE. *"Gd site nr coast & Koge; access to Copenhagen by public transport."* **DKK 260 2022**

KOLDING *B3* (16km E Coastal) *55.46777, 9.67972* **Gammel Ålbo Camping,** Gammel Aalbovej 30, 6092 Sønder Stenderup **tel 75 57 11 16; camping@gl-aalbo.dk; www.gl-aalbo.dk**

12 (htd) WD MSP shgl adj

Foll rd SE fr Kolding to Agtrup then on to Sønder Bjert & Sønder Stenderup. Foll site sp thro vill twd coast, site at end of rd. 3*, Med, hdg, hdstg, pt shd, terr, EHU (16A) DKK38.50; cooking facs; 10% statics; Eng spkn; fishing; boat hire; CKE. *"Well-kept, relaxing site o'looking Lillebælt; skin-diving; v cr in high ssn."* **DKK 251 2022**

KOLDING *B3* (5km S Urban) *55.53823, 9.45084* **Kolding City Camp,** Dons Landevej 101, 6000 Kolding **tel 75 52 13 88; info@dancamps.dk; dancamps.dk/kolding**

12 DKK20 (htd) WD MSP nr

E45 (Flensbury-Frederikshavn) take exit 65 at Kolding Syd twrds Kolding; at 1st traff lts turn R site 800m on L. Lge, pt shd, pt sl, EHU (10A) DKK40; gas; bbq; cooking facs; TV; phone; bus to town; Eng spkn; adv bkg acc; ccard acc; fishing 5km; tennis; CKE. *"Friendly & v quiet; conv NH Legoland; htd covrd pool 3km; vg san facs; gd site; level pitches; private san facs avail; full kitchen facs."* **DKK 185 2024**

KORSOR *C3* (10km SE Rural) *55.28991, 11.2649* **Boeslunde Camping,** Rennebjergvej 110, 4242 Boeslunde **tel 58 14 02 08; info@campinggaarden.dk; www.campinggaarden.dk**

12 DKK10 WD MSP 1.5km

Take rd 265 S out of Korsør & in 8km, bef Boeslunde at camping sp, turn R. Site on L in 2km. 3*, Med, pt shd, pt sl, EHU DKK30 (long lead poss req); gas; TV (pitch); phone; adv bkg acc; CKE. *"Gd size, grassy pitches; well kept; gate barrier."* **DKK 299 2023**

KRUSA *B3* (0.6km N Rural) *54.85370, 9.40220* **Kruså Camping,** Åbenråvej 7, 6340 Kruså **tel 74 67 12 06; info@krusaacamping.dk; www.krusaacamping.dk**

WD MSP (htd)

S on E45, exit junc 75 twd Kruså. Turn L onto rd 170, site on L. 3*, Lge, pt shd, pt sl, EHU (10A) DKK30; gas; cooking facs; TV; phone; CKE. *"Gd NH; bus to Flensburg (Germany) 1km fr site; new san facs 2010."* **DKK 263, 1 Feb-21 Dec. 2024**

LEMVIG *A2* (4km NW Coastal) *56.56733, 8.29399* **Lemvig Strand Camping,** Vinkelhagevej 6, 7620 Lemvig **tel 23 82 00 45; lemvig@dk-camp.dk; www.lemvigstrandcamping.dk**

DKK10 WD MSP nr (covrd, htd) 300m

Foll camping sps in Lemvig to site. 4*, Med, mkd, unshd, EHU (10A) DKK35; cooking facs; TV; 30% statics; phone; adv bkg acc; ccard acc; games rm; games area; sauna. *"Vg sailing cent; pretty area."* **DKK 298, 22 Mar-20 Oct. 2024**

DENMARK

MIDDELFART *B3* (11km NE Coastal) *55.51948, 9.85025* **Vejlby Fed Camping,** Rigelvej 1, 5500 Vejlby Fed **tel 28 94 02 89; mail@vejlbyfed.dk; www.vejlbyfed.dk**

DKK20 (htd) sand adj

Exit E20 junc 57 or 58. Site sp in Vejlby Fed, NE fr Middelfart dir Bogense, on coast. 4*, Lge, mkd, pt shd, EHU (10A) DKK39; cooking facs; 30% statics; phone; Eng spkn; adv bkg acc; sauna; fishing; tennis; boating; CKE. **DKK 320, 15 Mar-14 Sep. 2024**

MIDDELFART *B3* (5km NW Rural) *55.51694, 9.68225* **Gals Klint Camping,** Galsklintvej 11, 5500 Middelfart **tel 64 41 20 59; mail@galsklint.dk; www.galsklint.dk**

(htd) shgl adj

Fr W on E20 take rd 161. At 2 traff lts turn L & cross Little Belt Bdge. In 300m turn R into Galsklintvej & foll sp. 3*, Lge, hdg, mkd, pt shd, EHU (16A) DKK28; bbq; cooking facs; 10% statics; Eng spkn; adv bkg acc; ccard acc; boat hire; fishing; CKE. *"Site surrounded by forest; gd cycling/walking; vg; well run mod facs shoreside next woodland."* **DKK 208, 18 Mar-3 Oct. 2022**

NYBORG *C3* (4km N Coastal) *55.35853, 10.78660* **Gronnehave Strand,** Regstrupvej 83, 5800 Nyborg **tel 65 36 15 50; info@gronnehave.dk; www.gronnehave.dk**

(htd) nr adj

10 mins N on Skaboeshusevej - sp. Fr E20 junc 46 turn N and foll sp. 3*, Med, mkd, unshd, terr, EHU (10A) DKK36; TV; Eng spkn; games area. *"Friendly owner; gd views; bdge to Zeeland; vg."* **DKK 319, 26 Apr-6 Sep. 2024**

NYBORG *C3* (3km SE Coastal) *55.30457, 10.82453* **Nyborg Strandcamping,** Hjejlevej 99, 5800 Nyborg **tel 65 31 02 56 | 23 20 05 14; mail@strandcamping.dk; www.strandcamping.dk**

nr sand adj

Exit E20 at junc 44. Turn N, site sp in 1km. Lge, mkd, pt shd, EHU (10A) metered; gas; TV; 50% statics; phone; Eng spkn; adv bkg acc; fishing; golf 1km; CKE. *"Conv m'way, rlwy & ferry; excel views of bdge; gd facs; gd site; well difined pitches next to beach."* **DKK 276, 24 Mar-22 Sep. 2024**

NYBORG *C3* (13km S Rural) *55.23693, 10.8080* **Tårup Stand Camping,** Lersey Allé 25, Tårup Strand, 5871 Frørup **tel 65 37 11 99; mail@taarupstrandcamping.dk; www.taarupstrandcamping.dk**

(htd) shgl

S fr Nyborg take 163 twds Svendborg; after 6.5km turn L sp Tårup. In 2.7km turn L sp Tårup Strand. Site 1.5km on R. 3*, Med, mkd, EHU (6-10A) DKK26; TV; 70% statics; phone; adv bkg acc; ccard acc; games rm; CKE. *"Quiet family site; excel views of bdge; fishing; excel site."* **DKK 246, 4 Apr-21 Sep. 2024**

ODENSE *C3* (5km S Rural) *55.36966, 10.39316* **DCU Camping Odense,** Odensevej 102, 5260 Odense **tel 66 11 47 02; odense@dcu.dk; www.camping-odense.dk**

12 DKK23 (htd) nr

Exit E20 junc 51 foll sp 'centrum' (Stenlosevej). After rndabt site on L just after 3rd set traff lts. Ent to R of petrol stn. 3*, Lge, mkd, hdg, pt shd, EHU (16A) DKK30; gas; bbq; cooking facs; twin axles; TV; 10% statics; phone; bus; Eng spkn; adv bkg acc; ccard acc; games area; games rm; CKE. *"Hans Christian Andersen's hse; many attractions; excel, friendly, family-run site; busy high ssn & facs stretched; easy bus access to town cent; lovely, easy cycle rte into town cent; excel san fac; pitches tight for larger units; quick stop area for MH; sep c'van & MH areas; pitches muddy when wet; free WiFi; excel."* **DKK 366 2022**

ODENSE *C3* (11km W Rural) *55.3894, 10.2475* **Campingpladsen Blommenslyst,** Middelfartvej 494, 5491 Blommenslyst **tel 65 96 76 41; info@blommelyst-camping.dk; www.blommenslyst-camping.dk**

DKK10 (htd)

Exit E20 onto 161 (junc 53); sp 'Odense/ Blommenslyst', site on R after 2km; lge pink Camping sp on side of house. Sm, shd, pt sl, EHU (4A) DKK30; 10% statics; bus; Eng spkn; adv bkg req; CKE. *"Picturesque setting round sm lake; gd, clean, rustic facs; welcoming owners; frequent bus to town outside site; excel; lovely site."* **DKK 176, 5 Jan-15 Sept. 2024**

RANDERS *B2* (8km SW Rural) *56.44984, 9.95287* **Randers City Camp,** Hedevej 9, Fladbro, 8920 Randers **tel 45 29 47 36 55; info@randerscitycamp.dk; www.randerscitycamp.dk**

12 DKK10 (htd) (covrd, htd)

Take exit 40 fr E45 & turn twd Randers. Approx 100m fr m'way turn R at traff lts dir Langå. Site clearly sp in 3km & also sp fr rd 16. 3*, Lge, mkd, pt shd, terr, EHU (10A) DKK35; bbq; cooking facs; twin axles; TV; 50% statics; phone; bus 0.5km; Eng spkn; adv bkg acc; ccard acc; games rm; golf adj; fishing; CKE. *"On heather hills with view of Nørreå valley; rec arr early for pitch with view; golf course; Randers tropical zoo; ideal for walkers, cyclist & runners; fishing; gd."* **DKK 259 2023**

RIBE *B3* (2km SE Rural) *55.31725, 8.75952* **Storkesøen Ribe,** Haulundvej 164, 6760 Ribe **tel 75 41 04 11; info@storkesoen.dk; www.storkesoen.dk**

12

Fr S on rte 11, turn R at 1st rndabt onto rte 24 & R at next rndabt. Site 100m on R, sp fishing. Fr S on rte 24, at 1st rndabt after rlwy turn L, site 200m on R. M'vans only - check in at fishing shop on R. Sm, hdstg, unshd, EHU (5A/16A) inc; own san req; lake fishing. *"Picturesque, quiet site o'looking fishing lakes; walking dist Denmark's oldest city; m'vans & c'vans acc, ideal NH; fishing shop; vg facs."* **DKK 140 2022**

RIBE *B3* (2.4km NNW Rural) *55.34115, 8.76506*
Ribe Camping, Farupvej 2, 6760 Ribe **tel 75 41 07 77; info@ribecamping.dk; www.ribecamping.dk**

12 DKK15 (htd) WD MSP (htd)

Fr S foll A11 by-pass W of Ribe to traff lts N of town; turn W off A11 at traff lts; site 500m on R. Fr N (Esbjerg ferry) to Ribe, turn R at traff lts sp Farup. Site on R, sp. 3*, Lge, pt shd, serviced pitches; EHU (10A) DKK35; gas; cooking facs; TV; 10% statics; phone; adv bkg acc; ccard acc; games rm; Quickstop o'night facs; CKE. *"Ribe oldest town in Denmark; much historical interest; helpful, friendly staff; well-run; excel, modern san facs; conv Esbjerg ferry."*
DKK 271 **2022**

RINGKOBING *A2* (5km E Rural) *56.08856, 8.31659*
Ringkøbing Camping, Herningvej 105, 6950 Ringkøbing **tel 97 32 04 20; info@ringkobingcamping.dk; www.ringkøbingcamping.dk**

DKK10 WD MSP sand 3km

Take rd 15 fr Ringkøbing dir Herning, site on L. 3*, Med, hdg, mkd, pt shd, EHU (10A) DKK29; gas; TV; phone; adv bkg acc; Quickstop o'night facs. *"Beautiful site in mixed forest; friendly welcome; excel facs; gd walks; 3km to fjord; 14km to sea."*
DKK 235, 1 Apr-2 Oct. **2022**

ROSKILDE *D3* (4km N Rural) *55.67411, 12.07955*
Roskilde Camping, Baunehøjvej 7-9, 4000 Veddelev **tel 46 75 79 96; mail@roskildecamping.dk; www.roskildecamping.dk**

(htd) WD shgl

Leave rd 21/23 at junc 11 & turn N on rd 6 sp Hillerød. Turn R onto rd 02 (E ring rd); then rejoin 6; (watch for camping sp). At traff lts with camping sp turn L twds city & foll site sp. 3*, Lge, mkd, pt shd, pt sl, EHU (10A) DKK30; own san req; gas; TV; Eng spkn; adv bkg acc; ccard acc; games rm; watersports; CKE. *"Beautiful views over fjord; nr Viking Ship Museum (a must) - easy parking; beautiful Cathedral; excel rest & shop open 0800-2000; bus service to stn, frequent trains to Copenhagen; ltd flat pitches; lovely site; immac, new state of the art san facs block with card for ent (2014); v welcoming & helpful staff."*
DKK 350, 22 Mar-29 Sep. **2024**

RY *B2* (4km NW Rural) *56.10388, 9.74555*
Birkede Camping, Lyngvej 14, 8680 Ry **tel 86 89 13 55; info@birkhede.dk; www.birkhede.dk**

12 WD MSP (htd)

Fr S on rd 52 exit onto rd 445 to Ry, then foll sp N on rd dir Laven. Turn R in 1km to site on lakeside. Clearly sp in cent of Ry. Lge, mkd, pt shd, pt sl, EHU (10A) metered + conn fee; gas; cooking facs; TV; phone; Eng spkn; adv bkg acc; bike hire; golf 10km; fishing; boat hire; games rm; CKE. *"Gd site."*
DKK 336 **2024**

RY *B2* (7km NW Rural) *56.12421, 9.71055*
Terrassen Camping, Himmelbjergvej 9a, 8600 Laven **tel 86 84 13 01; info@terrassen.dk; www.terrassen.dk**

DKK15 WD MSP nr nr (htd)

In Silkeborg take Åarhus rd 15 to Linå. In Linå turn R for Laven. In Laven turn R parallel to lake; site up hill on R in 300m. Sharp turn R into ent. 4*, Lge, pt shd, terr, EHU (10A) DKK32; gas; sw; TV; 15% statics; phone; adv bkg acc; ccard acc; games area; sauna; fishing. *"Excel views of lake & woods; pet zoo; British owner; Jutland's lake district."*
DKK 450, 23 Mar-15 Sep. **2024**

"I like to fill in the reports as I travel from site to site"

You'll find report forms at the back of this guide, or you can fill them in online at camc.com/europereport.

SAEBY *C1* (3.7km N Coastal) *57.36000, 10.50861*
Svalereden Camping And Hytteby, Frederikshavnsvej 112b, 9900 Frederikshavn **tel 98 46 19 37; info@svaleredencamping.dk; svaleredencamping.dk**

12 (htd)

Take coastal rte 180, exit 13 and 12. Site bet Frederikshavn & Saeby. 3*, Med, EHU (16A); bbq; twin axles; TV; bus; Eng spkn; adv bkg acc; ccard acc; games area; CKE. *"Conv for Fredrerikshavn-Gothenburg ferry; outstanding san facs; excel."*
DKK 306 **2023**

SAKSKOBING *C3* (0.8km W Urban) *54.79840, 11.64070* **Sakskøbing Camping,** Saxes Allé 15, 4990 Sakskøbing **tel 45 54 70 45 66 or 45 54 70 47 57; camping@saxsport.dk; www.saxcamping.dk**

MSP nr

N fr Rødby exit E47 at Sakskøbing junc 46, turn L twd town: at x-rds turn R. In 300m turn R into Saxes Allé, site sp. Med, hdg, mkd, pt shd, EHU (6A) DKK30; gas; cooking facs; phone; adv bkg acc; fishing. *"Conv for Rødby-Puttgarden ferry; pool 100m; gd touring base; excel site in pretty area; v welcoming & friendly."*
DKK 316, 22 Mar-3 Oct. **2024**

SILKEBORG *D2* (12km W Rural) *56.14869, 9.39697*
DCU Hesselhus Camping, Moselundsvej 28, Funder, 8600 Silkeborg **tel 86 86 50 66; hesselhus@dcu.dk; www.camping-hesselhus.dk**

12 DKK20 WD MSP (htd)

Take rd 15 W fr Silkeborg twd Herning; after 6km bear R, sp Funder Kirkeby, foll camping sps for several km to site. 3*, Lge, mkd, pt shd, EHU DKK35; gas; TV; 40% statics; phone; adv bkg acc; CKE. *"Great family site; beautiful natural surroundings; 1 hr fr Legoland; busy at w'ends."* **DKK 144** **2022**

SINDAL *C1* (2km W Rural) *57.46785, 10.17851*
Sindal Camping, Hjørringvej 125, 9870 Sindal
tel 98 93 65 30; info@sindal-camping.dk; www.sindal-camping.dk
12 DKK10

On rte 35 due W of Frederikshavn on S side of rd. 4*, Lge, hdg, mkd, pt shd, EHU (16A) metered; gas; bbq; red long stay; twin axles; TV; 50% statics; phone; Eng spkn; adv bkg acc; games area; bike hire; golf 3km; CKE. *"Train & bus v conv; lovely beaches 30 mins; excel modern san facs; helpful owners; hg rec; excel."*
DKK 296 **2023**

SKAELSKOR *C3* (1km NW Rural) *55.25648, 11.28461*
Skælskør Nør Camping, Kildehusvej 1, 4230 Skælskør
tel 58 19 43 84; info@solskinscamping.dk; solskinscamping.dk
12 nr shgl 2km

Exit E20 junc 42 sp Korsør. Take rd 265 S sp Skælskør, site on L just bef town, nr Kildehuset Rest. 4*, Med, mkd, unshd, EHU (10A) DKK35; cooking facs; TV; 80% statics; phone; Eng spkn; adv bkg acc; ccard acc; CKE. *"Lovely location by lake in nature reserve; woodland walks; excel facs; helpful owners."*
DKK 291 **2023**

SKAGEN *C1* (13km SW Rural) *57.65546, 10.45008*
Råbjerg Mile Camping, Kandestedvej 55, 9990 Skagen
tel 98 48 75 00; info@raabjergmilecamping.dk; www.990.dk
12 DKK10 nr (htd) 1.5km

Fr rd 40 Frederikshavn-Skagen, foll sp Hulsig-Råbjerg Mile, site sp. 3*, Lge, hdg, mkd, unshd, EHU (10A) DKK30; cooking facs; TV; 25% statics; phone; Eng spkn; adv bkg acc; ccard acc; bike hire; tennis; golf 1.5km; CKE. *"Gd touring base N tip of Denmark; gd cycling."* **DKK 360** **2024**

SORO *C3* (2km NW Urban) *55.44673, 11.54628*
Sorø Camping, Udbyhøjvej 10, 4180 Sorø **tel 57 83 02 02; info@soroecamping.dk; www.soroecamping.dk**
12 nr

On rd 150 fr Korsør, 300m bef town name board turn L at camping sp, site in 100m on lakeside. 3*, Med, pt shd, pt sl, EHU (10A) DKK30; cooking facs; sw nr; TV; 10% statics; phone; Eng spkn; adv bkg acc; ccard acc; boating; fishing; CKE. *"Conv Copenhagen, friendly owners; busy site; clean facs - up to CC standands."* **DKK 275** **2024**

SVENDBORG *C3* (7km SE Coastal) *55.0537, 10.6304*
Svendborg Sund Camping (formerly Vindebyøre), Vindebyørevej 52, Tåsinge, 5700 Svendborg **tel 21 72 09 13 or 62 22 54 25; maria@svendborgsund-camping.dk; www.svendborgsund-camping.dk**
DKK25 (htd) sand

Cross bdge fr Svendborg (dir Spodsbjerg) to island of Tåsinge on rd 9; at traff lts over bdge turn L, then immed 1st L to Vindeby, thro vill, L at sp to site. 3*, Med, pt shd, pt sl, EHU (16A) DKK35; bbq; cooking facs; TV; 10% statics; phone; adv bkg acc; ccard acc; boat hire; bike hire; CKE. *"V helpful owners; swipe card for facs; excel touring base & conv ferries to islands; beautiful views; o'night area; immac, excel site; narr sandy beach; gd size pitches and san facs."*
DKK 370, 22 Mar-29 Sep. **2024**

THORSMINDE *A2* (0.5km N Coastal) *56.37626, 8.12251*
Thorsminde Camping, Klitrosevej 4, 6990 Thorsminde
tel 20 45 19 76; mail@thorsmindecamping.dk; www.thorsmindecamping.dk
(covrd) 300m

On rd 16/28 to Ulfborg, turn W twd coast & Husby Klitplantage. Turn N onto rd 181 to Thorsminde, 1st turn R past shops, site sp. 3*, Lge, unshd, EHU (10A) DKK30; cooking facs; TV; 10% statics; phone; adv bkg acc; sauna. *"Pleasant site; helpful staff; excel sea fishing."* **DKK 265, 8 Apr-23 Oct.** **2022**

TONDER *B3* (5km W Rural) *54.93746, 8.80008*
Møgeltønder Camping, Sønderstrengvej 2, Møgeltønder, 6270 Tønder **tel 74 73 84 60; info@mogeltonder camping.dk; www.mogeltondercamping.dk**
12 DKK10 (htd) (htd)

N fr Tønder thro Møgeltønder (avoid cobbled main rd by taking 2nd turning sp Møgeltønder) site sp on L in 200m outside vill. 3*, Lge, mkd, pt shd, EHU (10A) DKK25; bbq; cooking facs; TV; 25% statics; phone; Eng spkn; adv bkg acc; CKE. *"Gd cycle paths; beautiful & romantic little vill adj; Ribe worth visit (43km); friendly owner."* **DKK 280** **2024**

VEJERS STRAND *A3* (12km S Coastal) *55.54403, 8.13386* **Hvidbjerg Strand Feriepark,** Hvidbjerg Strandvej 27, 6857 Blåvand **tel 75 27 90 40; info@hvidbjerg.dk; www.hvidbjerg.dk**
12 DKK30 (covrd, htd) sand

Exit rd 11 at Varde on minor rd, sp Blåvand, turn L at sp to Hvidbjerg Strand 2km; site 1km on L. 5*, V lge, hdg, pt shd, serviced pitches; EHU (6A) inc; gas; cooking facs; TV; 10% statics; phone; adv bkg acc; ccard acc; tennis; games area. *"Superb facs; excel family site; young groups not acc."*
DKK 723, 8 Mar-31 Dec. **2024**

VEJLE *B3* (2km ENE Urban) *55.7151, 9.5611*
Vejle City Camping, Helligkildevej 5, 7100 Vejle
tel 75 82 33 35; info@vejlecitycamping.dk; www.vejlecitycamping.dk
DKK5 WD MSP sand 2km

Exit E45 m'way at Vejle N. Turn L twd town. In 250m turn L at camping sp & 'stadion' sp. Med, pt shd, pt sl, EHU (6-10A) DKK30; cooking facs; red long stay; TV; phone; Eng spkn; adv bkg acc; ccard acc. *"Site adj woods & deer enclosure; quickstop o'night facs; walk to town; conv Legoland (26km); lovely well kept site; helpful friendly staff."* **DKK 260, 27 Mar-26 Sep. 2022**

VIBORG *B2* (15km N Rural/Coastal) *56.53452, 9.33117*
Hjarbæk Fjord Camping, Hulager 2, Hjarbæk, 8831 Løgstrup **tel 22 13 15 00; info@hjarbaek.dk; www.hjarbaek.dk**
12 DKK10 (htd) WD sand adj

Take A26 (Viborg to Skive) to Løgstrup, turn R (N) to Hjarbæk, keep R thro vill, site sp. Lge, mkd, pt shd, terr, EHU metered; gas; bbq; cooking facs; TV; 3% statics; phone; Eng spkn; adv bkg acc; ccard acc; lake fishing; CKE. *"Friendly & well-run; gd views; close to attractive vill & harbour."* **DKK 350 2024**

VINDERUP *B2* (6.7km ESE Rural) *56.45901, 8.86918*
Hedelandets Camping (formerly Sevel Camping), Halallé 6, Sevel, 7830 Vinderup **tel 97 44 85 50; info@hedelandetscamping.dk; www.hedelandetscamping.dk**
12 DKK6 (htd) WD MSP nr nr

Fr Struer on rd 513. In Vinderup L nr church then R past Vinderup Camping. Site sp on R on edge of vill. 3*, Sm, hdg, pt shd, pt sl, EHU (16A) DKK30; cooking facs; 10% statics; Eng spkn; adv bkg acc; ccard acc; CKE. *"Family-run site; pleasant, helpful owners; picturesque, historic area."* **DKK 229 2022**

VORDINGBORG *D3* (3.6km W Urban/Coastal) *55.00688, 11.87509* **Ore Strand Camping,** Orevej 145, 4760 Vordingborg **tel 55 77 88 22; mail@orestrandcamping.dk; www.orestrandcamping.dk**
WD MSP shgl adj

Fr E55/47 exit junc 41 onto rd 59 to Vordingborg 7km. Rd conts as 153 sp Sakskøbing alongside rlwy. Turn R at site sp into Ore, site on L. 3*, Med, pt shd, EHU (6A) inc; cooking facs; phone; Eng spkn; adv bkg acc; ccard acc. *"Gd touring cent; fine views if nr water, interesting old town, poss busy san facs."* **DKK 400, 1 May - 1 Oct. 2024**

BORNHOLM ISLAND

GUDHJEM *A1* (2km S Coastal) *55.19566, 14.98602*
Sannes Familiecamping, Melstedvej 39, 3760 Melsted
tel 56 48 52 11; sannes@familiecamping.dk; www.familiecamping.dk
WD MSP nr (htd) sand adj

SW fr Gudhjem on rd 158, in 2km site on L. Pass other sites. NB: Bornholm Is can be reached by ferry fr Sassnitz in Germany or Ystad in Sweden. 5*, Med, mkd, hdstg, pt shd, terr, EHU (6A) DKK30; gas; TV; 10% statics; phone; Eng spkn; adv bkg acc; ccard acc; bike hire; fishing; sauna; fitness rm; CKE. *"Friendly & helpful staff; gd cycle paths in area; bus service fr site."* **DKK 370, 24 Mar-21 Oct. 2022**

"I need an on-site restaurant"

We do our best to make sure site information is correct, but it is always best to check any must-have facilities are still available or will be open during your visit.

LANGELAND ISLAND

LOHALS *C3* (0.4km W Urban) *55.13383, 10.90578*
Lohals Camping, Birkevej 11, 5953 Lohals **tel 62 55 14 60; mail@lohalscamping.dk; www.lohalscamping.dk**
12 WD MSP nr (htd) sand 1km

On island of Langeland. Cross to Rudkøbing, fr island of Tåsinge, then 28km to N of island (only 1 main rd); site in middle of vill nr ferry to Sjælland Island. 3*, Med, shd, EHU (10A) DKK35; TV; 10% statics; phone; adv bkg acc; tennis; bike hire; fishing; boat hire; games area. *"Conv ferry (Lohals-Korsor) 500m."* **DKK 250 2022**

ROMO ISLAND

HAVNEBY *A3* (2km N Coastal) *55.09883, 8.54395*
Kommandørgårdens Camping, Havnebyvej 201, 6792 Rømø **tel 74 75 51 22; info@kommandoergaarden.dk; www.kommandoergaarden.dk**
12 DKK20 (htd) WD MSP (htd) sand 1km

Turn S after exit causeway fr mainland onto rd 175 sp Havneby. Site on L in 8km. 3*, V lge, mkd, pt shd, EHU (10A) DKK35; gas; TV; 30% statics; phone; adv bkg acc; tennis. *"Family-owned site; wellness & beauty cent on site; ferry to German island of Sylt."* **DKK 274 2022**

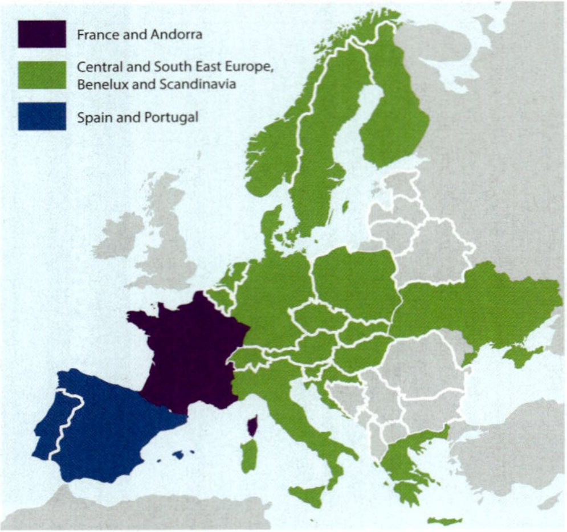

Kolding to Thisted = 195km

	Aalborg	Århus	Billund	Ebeltoft	Esbjerg	Frederikshavn	Grenå	Helsingør	Hjørring	Horsens	Hundested	Kalundborg	København (Copenhagen)	Kolding	Korsør	Kruså	Næstved	Nykøbing (Falster)	Odense	Randers	Ringkøbing	Rødbyhavn	Silkeborg	Skagen	Spodsbjerg	Struer	Svendborg	Thisted	Vejle
Århus	112																												
Billund	193	100																											
Ebeltoft	137	55	100																										
Esbjerg	216	153	56	207																									
Frederikshavn	66	171	261	190	278																								
Grenå	137	62	160	40	216	196																							
Helsingør	422	325	275	381	323	488	394																						
Hjørring	51	156	245	176	267	37	177	473																					
Horsens	162	50	52	102	114	118	109	281	206																				
Hundested	396	303	253	351	298	465	362	56	445	251																			
Kalundborg	325	226	185	280	222	392	291	136	376	182	108																		
København (Copenhagen)	383	285	242	342	278	443	352	46	435	238	66	102																	
Kolding	200	101	41	153	74	259	162	253	246	55	225	156	211																
Korsør	270	172	125	230	170	338	242	152	321	126	123	55	110	102															
Kruså	283	180	120	235	112	342	245	334	328	135	307	236	293	81	183														
Næstved	320	225	180	280	221	389	287	126	372	179	111	72	86	153	51	233													
Nykøbing (Falster)	387	289	241	343	283	450	352	169	435	242	166	135	125	215	113	296	66												
Odense	241	143	100	200	136	304	207	186	290	96	170	100	156	72	36	152	96	150											
Randers	76	35	133	60	171	133	58	363	121	88	339	265	320	135	212	217	262	325	181										
Ringkøbing	170	126	74	175	80	236	190	359	222	118	332	260	317	115	206	196	258	321	175	135									
Rødbyhavn	410	311	268	365	305	475	373	200	456	265	201	156	164	236	135	319	86	46	172	348	343								
Silkeborg	114	40	64	91	120	180	104	322	166	45	295	225	281	97	170	177	220	285	141	52	86	306							
Skagen	103	211	300	233	320	43	233	526	55	260	500	431	485	303	376	383	425	490	345	176	277	513	216						
Spodsbjerg	301	205	162	259	200	367	267	215	351	158	187	115	176	132	66	212	112	175	66	241	237	199	201	405					
Struer	126	125	90	163	120	191	162	370	174	122	343	272	326	144	220	225	269	332	88	106	59	355	86	229	245				
Svendborg	280	180	135	234	175	342	246	186	328	135	161	91	147	107	36	189	86	151	44	216	213	172	176	382	25	225			
Thisted	91	152	142	186	186	140	186	420	116	164	395	325	380	195	270	277	320	384	240	125	123	405	116	172	301	66	277		
Vejle	171	73	25	125	86	234	135	255	219	25	225	156	216	31	106	111	156	218	74	111	102	245	61	273	134	113	112	166	
Viborg	83	65	88	99	136	143	99	346	128	81	320	249	305	120	195	200	245	308	164	42	92	330	37	180	224	62	199	88	93

A
B
C
D
1
2
3
4
NORWAY
SWEDEN
GERMANY
NORTH SEA
SKAGERRAK
KATTEGGAT
SKAGEN
Hirtshals
Albaek
HJORRING
Sindal
Frederikshavn
SAEBY
Hanstholm
AALBORG
Göteborg
Aalestrup
STRUER
Thorsminde
Vinderup
VIBORG
RANDERS
GRENAA
Halmstad
RINGKOBING
Hvide Sande
SILKEBORG
Ry
AARHUS
Braedstrup
HORSENS
HUNDESTED
HELSINGOR
Helsingborg
Hillerod
Vejers Strand
Jelling
BILLUND
VEJLE
KALUNDBORG
Holbaek
KOBENHAVN
ESBJERG
KOLDING
Fredericia
Bogense
Middelfart
ODENSE
SJÆLLAND
Roskilde
Malmö
Hejlsminde
FYN
Ribe
Haderslev
Assens
KORSOR
SORØ
Koge
RØMØ
Havneby
Nyborg
Skaelskor
Karise
Faaborg
Lohals
NÆSTVED
Aabenraa
SVENDBORG
Tonder
Grasten
Vordingborg
Borre
LANGELAND
MØN
Flensburg
Sakskobing
FALSTER
LOLLAND
NYKØBING
RØDBYHAVN
Lindaunis
Kiel
Rostock
Lübeck
Hamburg
Motorways
Primary roads
Secondary roads
All year site(s)
Seasonal site(s)
No sites listed
N
W
E
S
0
25
50
75
100
125 km
0
20
40
60
80 miles

Finland

Highlights

Finland is a country filled with vast forests, crystal clear lakes and a diverse range of flora and fauna. With the Northern Lights visible from Lapland, the outstanding natural world is one of Finland's finest assets, with a vast, pristine wilderness that captures the imagination.

The cities of Finland are not to be missed, with vibrant atmospheres, museums, galleries, delicious restaurants and gorgeous architecture in spades.

Saunas are an important part of life in Finland, and have been for hundreds of years. They are used as a place to relax with friends and family and are generally sociable spaces.

Design and fashion have always been popular in Finland, with one of its most famous companies, Marimekko, a huge contributor to fashion in the 20th century.

Visit Svalbard to witness the unique spectacle of the Midnight Sun. This natural phenomenon occurs each year around the summer solstice.

Major towns and cities

- Helsinki – this capital city is a hub of shopping and architecture.
- Tempere – Finland's cultural home with theatrical, musical and literary traditions.
- Turku – Finland's oldest city and a former European City of Culture.
- Oulu – a quirky city where many technology companies, including Nokia, are based.

Attractions

- Olavinlinna Castle, Savolinna – a medieval stone fortress that houses several exhibitions.
- Lapland – This region is famous for the midnight sun and the Northern Lights.
- Repovesi National Park – a stunning natural area with plenty of walking and hiking trails.
- Temppeliaukio Kirkko, Helsinki – This church is built directly into solid rock.

Find out more

visitfinland.com

Country Information

Capital: Helsinki

Bordered by: Norway, Sweden, Russia

Terrain: Flat, rolling, heavily forested plains interspersed with low hills and over 60,000 lakes; one third lies within the Arctic Circle

Climate: Short, warm summers; long, very cold, dry winters; the best time to visit is between May and September

Coastline: 1,250km (excluding islands)

Highest Point: Haltiatunturi 1,328m

Languages: Finnish, Swedish

Local Time: GMT or BST + 2, ie 2 hours ahead of the UK all year

Currency: Euros divided into 100 cents; £1 = €1.20, €1 = £0.84 (Nov 2024)

Emergency numbers: Police 112; Fire brigade 112; Ambulance 112 (operators speak English)

Public Holidays 2025: Jan 1, 6; Apr 18, 20, 21; May 1, 29; Jun 8, 9, 20, 21; Nov 1; Dec 6, 24, 25, 26.

School summer holidays from early June to mid-August.

Border Posts

The main border posts with Sweden are at Tornio, Ylitornio and Kaaresuvanto. Those with Norway are at Kilpisjärvi, Kivilompolo, Karigasniemi, Utsjoki Ohcejohka and Nuorgam. Border posts are open day and night. The Finnish-Russian border can only be crossed by road at certain official points – contact the Finnish Border Guard website (raja.fi/en) for details.

Border guards patrol the area close to the Russian border and it is important, therefore, to carry identification at all times.

Entry Formalities

British and Irish passport holders may stay for up to 90 days in any 180 day period without a visa. You may be asked to show a return or onward ticket at the border to confirm your length of stay, or to prove that you have enough money for your stay.

Your passport will need to have a minimum of 6 months' validity remaining, and be less than 10 years old (even if it has over 6 months left).

Medical Services

The local health system is good and Finland generally has a high level of healthcare. British citizens are entitled to obtain emergency health care at municipal health centres on presentation of an European Health Insurance Card (EHIC) or an UK Global Health Insurance Card (GHIC). Treatment will either be given free or for a standard fee. Dental care is provided mainly by private practitioners.

There is a non-refundable charge for hospital treatment, whether for inpatient or outpatient visits. Partial refunds for the cost of private medical treatment may be obtained from Sickness Insurance Department, KELA, (kela.fi) up to six months from the date of treatment.

Prescribed drugs can be obtained from pharmacies (apteekki), some of which have late opening hours. Some medicines that are available in stores and supermarkets in other countries, such as aspirin and various ointments, are only available in pharmacies in Finland.

Mosquitoes are abundant and very active during the summer. Ticks are prevalent throughout the country (except for the most northern parts of Finnish Lapland). Wearing long sleeved shirts, clothing that covers your skin and bug repellant is recommended.

Opening Hours

Banks: Mon-Fri 9.15am-4.15pm.

Museums: Check locally as times vary.

Post Offices: Mon-Fri 9am-5pm. During winter some post offices may stay open until 6pm.

Shops: Mon-Fri 7am/8am/9am-9pm; Sat 7am/8am/9am/10am-6pm; Sun noon-6pm (some supermarkets until 11pm). On the eve of a public holiday some shops close early.

Safety and Security

The tourist season attracts pickpockets in crowded areas. You should take the usual precautions to keep yourself and your personal belongings safe.

Finland shares with the rest of Europe an underlying threat from terrorism. Please check (gov.uk/foreign-travel-advice/finland) before you travel.

British Embassy

Itäinen Puistotie 17 00140 Helsinki
Tel: +358 (0)9 2286 5100
gov.uk/world/finland

There are also Honorary Consulates in Åland Islands, Jyväskylä, Kotka, Kuopio, Oulu, Rovaniemi, Tampere, Turku and Vaasa.

Irish Embassy

Erottajankatu 7a00130 Helsinki
Tel: +358 (0)9 682 4240
ireland.ie/helsinki

Documents

Driving Licence/Vehicle(s)

When driving you should carry your driving licence, vehicle registration certificate (V5C), insurance certificate plus MOT certificate (if applicable).

Money

Currency may be exchanged at banks and at bureaux de change.

Major credit cards are widely accepted and cash machines are widespread. Carry your credit card issuers'/banks' 24-hour UK contact numbers in case of loss or theft of your cards.

Passport

You should carry your passport at all times.

Driving

Accidents

Accidents must be reported to the police and if a foreign motorist is involved the Finnish Motor Insurers Centre (lvk.fi./en) should also be informed. Their address is Itämerenkatu 11-13 FI-00180 Helsinki, Finland, tel +358 40 450 4700. At the site of an accident other road users must be warned by the use of a warning triangle.

Alcohol

The maximum permitted level of alcohol in the bloodstream is 0.05%. It's advisable to adopt the 'no drink and drive' rule at all times as anyone exceeding this limit will be arrested immediately and could face a prison sentence. Breath tests and blood tests can be carried out at random.

Breakdown Service

The Automobile & Touring Club of Finland, Autoliitto, has approximately 140 roadside patrols manned by volunteers and these can be called out at weekends and on public holidays. At other times, or if the Autoliitto patrol cannot be reached, contracted partners will provide assistance. For 24-hour assistance telephone 0200 8080. Charges are made for assistance and towing, plus a call-out fee.

Emergency telephone boxes are installed around Helsinki, Kouvola, Jamsa, and Rovaniemi, and on the roads Kouvola-Lappeenranta-Imatra-Simpele and Rovaniemi-Jaatila. Drivers are connected to the national breakdown service.

Child Restraint System

Children under the height of 1.35m must be seated in a suitable child restraint.

If there's not a child restraint/seat available children of 3 years or older must travel in the rear seat using a seat belt or other safety device attached to the seat. Unless in a taxi a child under the age of 3 must not travel in a vehicle without a child restraint. It is the responsibility of the driver to ensure all children under the age of 15 years old are correctly and safely restrained.

Fuel

Petrol stations are usually open from 7am to 9pm on weekdays and for shorter hours at weekends, although a few stay open 24 hours. Their frequency reduces towards the north, so it is advisable not to let your tank run low. Credit cards are accepted at most manned petrol stations. There are many unmanned stations, which have automatic petrol pumps operated with bank notes or credit cards. LPG is not available.

Public charging points for electric vehicles and different types of clean fuel are available in Finland

Low Emission Zones

There is a Low Emission Zone in force in Helsinki. See urbanacessregulations.eu for more information.

Motorways

There are approximately 900 km of motorway (moottoritie) in Finland linking Helsinki, Tampere and Turku. No tolls are levied. There are no emergency phones located on motorways. In the case of breakdown on a motorway drivers of all vehicles must use a warning triangle.

Parking

A vehicle that has been illegally or dangerously parked may be removed by the police and the owner fined. Parking fines may be enforced on the spot and could cost you €60 to €80. Wheel clamps may be used if a vehicle has been parked illegally for more than two days. Parking meters operate for between 15 minutes and four hours; the free use of unexpired time is allowed. In some built-up areas you will need a parking disc obtainable from petrol stations or car accessory shops.

8-17	(8-13)	8-14
Restriction applies 8-17 hrs (Mon-Fri)	Restriction applies 8-13 hrs (Sat)	Restriction applies 8-14 hrs (Sun)

In some towns streets are cleaned on a regular basis. Road signs indicate when the cleaning takes place and the street should be kept clear of parked vehicles. Parked vehicles will be removed and drivers fined.

If you have a low emission car you may be entitled to 50% off parking fees in Helsinki. To qualify for this reduction the parking fees must be made by mobile phone and you'll need to have obtained a green sticker with the letter 'P' from the Helsinki town authorities, which then needs to be attached to the windscreen. For further information see easypark.com.

Priority

At intersections, priority is given to vehicles coming from the right, except when otherwise indicated. The approach to a main road from a minor road is indicated by a 'Give way' sign with a red triangle on a yellow background. When this sign is supplemented by a red octagon with 'Stop' in the centre, vehicles must stop before entering the intersection. Trams and emergency vehicles always have priority, even when coming from the left.

Vehicles entering a roundabout must give way to traffic already on the roundabout.

Roads

Roads are generally in good condition, but there are still some gravelled roads in the countryside which have speed restrictions to avoid windscreens being broken by loose stones. During the spring thaw and during the wet season in September, gravelled roads may be in a poor condition. Roadworks take place during the summer months and sections under repair can extend for many miles.

Drivers should be aware of deer, elks or reindeer wandering across the roads in Finland, especially at dawn and dusk. Slow down or stop your vehicle if you see any animals on the road and use high beams at night where possible. You must notify the police if you collide with an elk, deer or reindeer.
The Finnish Transport Agency operates an online information service on weather and road conditions, recommended driving routes and roadworks, please see the website: liikennetilanne.fintraffic.fi.

Road Signs and Markings

Road markings are generally white and conform to international conventions. Signs for motorway and end of motorway are on a green background, while those for main roads are on a blue background. The following signs may also be found:

Finnish	English Translation
Aja hitaasti	Drive slowly
Aluerajoitus	Local speed limit
Kelirikko	Frost damage
Kokeile jarruja	Test your brakes
Kunnossapitotyö	Roadworks (repairs)
Lossi färja	Ferry
Päällystetyötä	Roadworks (resurfacing)
Tulli	Customs
Tie rakenteilla	Roadworks (road under construction)
Varo irtokiviä	Beware of loose stones

Speed Limits

	Open Road (km/h)	Motorway (km/h)
Car Solo	80-100	120
Car towing caravan/trailer	80	80
Motorhome under 3500kg	100	100
Motorhome 3500-7500kg	80	80

On all roads outside built-up areas, other than motorways, differing speed limits between 70 and 100 km/h (44 and 62 mph) apply – except where vehicles are subject to a lower limit – according to the road quality and traffic. Where there is no sign, the basic speed limit is usually 80 km/h (50 mph) on main roads and 70 km/h (44 mph) on secondary roads, whether solo or towing. The road sign which indicates this basic limit bears the word 'Perusnopeus' in Finnish, and 'Grundhastighet' in Swedish.

Reduced speed limits apply from October to March and these are generally 20 km/h (13 mph) lower than the standard limits.

The maximum speed limit for motorhomes up to 3,500kg is 100 km/h (62 mph).

Recommended maximum speed limits are indicated on some roads by square or rectangular signs bearing white figures on a blue background. The maximum speed limit in residential areas is 20 km/h (13 mph).

Slow moving vehicles must let others pass wherever possible, if necessary by moving onto the roadside verge. Maintain a sufficient distance behind a slow moving vehicle to allow an overtaking vehicle to pull in front.

Radar detectors are prohibited.

Violation of Traffic Regulations

The police can impose, but not collect, fines when road users violate traffic regulations. Fines should be paid at banks.

Winter Driving

Winter tyres are compulsory from 1 December to 28 February and are often needed well into April. Snow chains may be used temporarily when conditions necessitate.

The main arctic road leads from Kemi on the Gulf of Bothnia through Rovaniemi to the Norwegian border. During the winter, all high volume, main roads are kept open including routes to Norway and Sweden. In total between 6,000 and 7,000km of roads are mainly kept free of ice and snow by the use of salt. Other roads will consist of compacted snow. Drivers should expect winter conditions as early as October.

Essential Equipment

Lights

Dipped headlights are compulsory at all times, regardless of weather conditions. Bulbs are more likely to fail with constant use and you are recommended to carry spares.

Reflective Jacket/Waistcoat

Pedestrians must wear reflective devices during the hours of darkness (any type of reflector is acceptable). If you get out of your vehicle you are required to wear one and the standard reflective jacket is probably the best option for driver and passengers.

Warning Triangles

All vehicles must carry a warning triangle and use it when broken down.

Touring

Both Finnish and Swedish are official languages. As a result, many towns and streets have two names, e.g. Helsinki is also known as Helsingfors, and Turku as Åbo. Finnish street names usually end 'katu', while Swedish street names usually end 'gatan' or 'vägen'. Swedish place names are more commonly used in the south and west of the country.

Purchasing a 'Helsinki City Card' includes free and discounted entry to several major museums and other attractions, and unlimited travel for 24, 48 or 72 hours on public transport, plus discounts for sightseeing, restaurants, shopping, concert tickets, sports, etc. For more information and other card options see helsinkicard.com.

The sale of wine and spirits is restricted to Alko shops which are open Monday to Friday until 6pm or 8pm, Saturday until 4pm or 6pm, and closed on Sunday and public holidays. Medium strength beer is also sold in supermarkets and other stores.

A service charge is generally included in most restaurant bills and tips are not expected, but if the service has been good it is customary to round up the bill.

Most lakes are situated in the south east of the country and they form a web of waterways linked by rivers and canals, making this a paradise for those who enjoy fishing, canoeing and hiking. In Lapland the vegetation is sparse, consisting mostly of dwarf birch. Reindeer roam freely so motorists must take special care and observe the warning signs. Rovaniemi is the biggest town in Lapland, just south of the Arctic Circle. It has a special post office and 'Santa Claus Land'.

A number of 'Uniquely Finnish' touring routes have been established including the King's Road along the south coast which takes you through many places of interest including Porvoo, a small town with well-preserved, old, wooden houses, Turku, the former capital, and the famous Imatra waterfall near the southern shore of Lake Saimaa. Swedish influence is evident in this area in local customs, place names and language. These 'Uniquely Finnish' touring routes are marked with brown sign posts; contact the Finnish Tourist Board for more information.

Southern and central Finland are usually snow covered from early December to mid or late April, although in recent years the south coast has had little or no snow. Northern Finland has snow falls from October to May and temperatures can be extremely low. Thanks to the Gulf Stream and low humidity, Finland's winter climate does not feel as cold as temperature readings might indicate but if you plan a visit during the winter you should be prepared for harsh weather conditions.

In the summer many Finnish newspapers have summaries of main news items and weather forecasts in English and radio stations have regular news bulletins in English. English is taught in all schools and is widely spoken.

Camping and Caravanning

There are around 160 campsites in Finland. Campsites are graded from 1 to 5 stars according to facilities available. Most have cabins for hire in addition to tent and caravan pitches, and most have saunas.

At some sites visitors who do not already have one must purchase a Camping Key Europe, which replaced the Camping Card Scandinavia (CCS) in 2012. The Camping Key is valid across Europe and you may purchase it for €16 on arrival at your first campsite or from local tourist offices - for more information see the website: camping.fi.

During the peak camping season from June to mid August it is advisable to make advance reservations. Prices at many campsites may double (or treble) over the midsummer holiday long weekend in June and advance booking is essential for this period. Approximately 70 campsites are open all year.

Casual or wild camping may be allowed for a short period - one or two days. For longer periods, permission must be obtained from the landowner. Camping is be prohibited on public beaches and in public recreation areas campers are often directed to special areas, many of which have facilities provided free of charge.

Cycling

Finland is good for cyclists as it is relatively flat. Most towns have a good network of cycle lanes which are indicated by traffic signs. In built up areas pavements are sometimes divided into two sections, one for cyclists and one for pedestrians. It is compulsory to wear a safety helmet.

Electricity and Gas

Current on campsites is usually between 10 and 16 amps. Plugs are round with two pins. Some sites have CEE connections.

Butane gas is not generally available and campsites and service stations do not have facilities for replacing empty foreign gas cylinders. You will need to travel with sufficient supplies to cover your needs while in Finland or purchase propane cylinders locally, plus an adaptor. The Caravan and Motorhome Club does not recommend the refilling of cylinders.

The Midnight Sun and Northern Lights

Areas within the Arctic Circle have 24 hours of daylight in the height of summer and no sun in winter for up to two months. There are almost 20 hours of daylight in Helsinki in the summer.

The Northern Lights (Aurora Borealis) may be seen in the arctic sky on clear dark nights, the highest incidence occurring in February/March and September/October in the Kilpisjärvi region of Lapland when the lights are seen on three nights out of four.

The Order of Bluenosed Caravanners

Visitors to the Arctic Circle from anywhere in the world may apply for membership of the Order of Bluenosed Caravanners which will be recognised by the issue of a certificate by the International Caravanning Association (ICA).

For more information contact bluenosed@icacaravanning.org and attach a photograph of yourselves and your outfit under any Arctic Circle signpost, together with the date and country of crossing and the names of those who made the crossing.

This service is free to members of the ICA (annual membership £20 plus a £5 joining fee). Coloured plastic decals for your outfit, indicating membership of the Order, are also available at a cost of £4. Please see (icacaravanning.org) for more information.

Public Transport & Local Travel

The public transport infrastructure is of a very high standard and very punctual. You can buy a variety of bus, train, tram and metro tickets at public transport stations, HKL service points, newspaper kiosks and shops all over the country. Single tickets, which are valid for 60 minutes, can be purchased from ticket machines, bus and tram drivers or train conductors. Tourist tickets valid for one, three or five days can also be purchased from kiosks, ticket machines and bus and tram drivers and are valid on all forms of public transport including the Suomenlinna ferry.

Within the Helsinki city area you can hire city bicycles from April to October. For more information see whimapp.com/helsinki.

Vehicle ferries operate all year to Estonia, Germany and Russia and it is now possible to enjoy a visa free ferry trip to St Petersburg for up to 72 hours from Helsinki. Please see visitfinland.com for more information or contact the Finnish Tourist Board.

Internal ferry services (in Finnish 'lossi') transport motor vehicles day and night. Those situated on the principal roads, taking the place of a bridge, are state-run and free of charge. There are regular services on Lake Paijanne, Lake Inari and Lake Pielinen, and during the summer there are daily tours and longer cruises through Finland's lake region. Popular routes are between Hameenlinna and Tampere, Tampere and Virrat, as well as the Saimaa Lake routes. Details are available from the Finnish Tourist Board.

Aurora Borealis over the Arctic Circle

Shutterstock/Jamen Percy

Sites in Finland

HAMINA *C4* (7km SE Coastal) *60.52644, 27.25191* **Hamina Camping,** Vilniementie 375, 49400 Hamina **(40) 1513446; info@hamina-camping.fi; hamina-camping.fi**

(htd) sand

Fr Hamina take rte 7/E18 dir Vaalimaa E. In 3km turn R rd 3513 sp Virolahti, site sp. 3*, Med, hdstg, pt shd, EHU (16A); twin axles; 20% statics; CKE. *"Site in pine forest; secluded pitches; attractive coastline; conv for visiting Russia & Kings Rte; sm museum at Virolahti worth visit; facs poss stretched when site full; interesting town; site under refurb (2016); helpful staff; gd."* **€26.50, 1 May-18 Sep.** **2023**

HANKO/HANGO *B4* (4km NE Coastal) *59.85271, 23.01716* **Camping Silversand,** Hopeahietikko, 10960 Hanko Pohjoinen **(019) 248 5500; cornia@cornia.fi; www.www.cornia.fi**

12 nr

Site sp fr rd 25. 3*, Lge, shd, EHU (16A) inc; cooking facs; TV; 10% statics; Eng spkn; ccard acc; sauna; boat hire; fishing; games rm; bike hire; CKE. *"Beautiful location on edge of sea in pine forest."* **€39.80** **2022**

HELSINKI/HELSINGFORS *C4* (14km ENE Urban/Coastal) *60.20668, 25.12116* **Rastila Municipal Camping,** Karavaanikatu 4, Vuosaari, 00980 Helsinki **(09) 31078517; rastilacamping@hel.fi; www.hel.fi/rastila**

12 nr sand 1.2km

E fr Helsinki on rte 170, over Vuosaari bdge; or get to ring rd 1, turn E dir Vuosaari, site sp. Also sp fr Silja & other ferry terminals & fr rte 170 to Porvoo. Also sp on rte 167. Fr N on E75 exit at Ring I then immed L fork. Foll 101, 170 then sp. 3*, V lge, hdstg, pt shd, EHU (16A) €4.50; cooking facs; red long stay; TV; 10% statics; Eng spkn; ccard acc; games rm; sauna; CKE. *"Conv Helsinki & district; pleasant site; gd san facs; helpful staff; poss ssn workers but site clean & tidy; metro nr; weekly rates avail; best place we stayed at."* **€31.00** **2022**

JUUKA *C3* (35km SE Rural) *63.04004, 29.70994* **Koli Freetime Oy,** Kopravaarantie 27, Juuka **010 322 3040; koli@kolifreetime.fi; www.kolifreetime.fi**

(htd) sand adj

Site is well sp on rte 6 heading N of Juuka. Turn off onto gravel rd as indicated for 2km. Sm, pt shd, sl, EHU (16A) inc; bbq; sw nr; twin axles; TV; 10% statics; Eng spkn; adv bkg acc; ccard acc; games rm; CKE. *"Sauna inc; sm site on edge of lake with sw; in forest; nature walks; 10km fr Koli & nearest supmkt; vg."* **€28.00** **2022**

KOKKOLA *B3* (2.5km N Coastal) *63.85500, 23.11305* **Kokkola Camping,** Vanhansatamanlahti, 67100 Kokkola **(06) 8314006; info@kokkola-camping.fi; www.kokkola-camping.fi**

sand adj

Exit A8 at Kokkola onto rte 749. Site on R, sp fr town. Med, pt shd, EHU inc; cooking facs; games area; sauna; CKE. *"Lovely site, no adv bkg; call ahead in winter for pitching instructions."* **€30.00, 1 Jun-31 Aug.** **2022**

KOTKA *C4* (7.2km SW Coastal) *60.43761, 26.86437* **Santalahti Holiday Resort,** Santalahdentie 150, 48310, Kotka, Kymenlaakso **(358) 52605055; info@santalahti.fi; www.santalahti.fi**

12

Take exit 73 fr E18, turn R onto Mussalontie/Route 352 for 5.6km, turn right onto Merituulentie/Route 355, turn right onto Santalhdentie. Campsite on R. 5*, Med, hdstg, pt shd, EHU (16A); Eng spkn. *"Kotka has lovely parks; site set in nature park with walks; 1.5 hrs fr Helsinki; vg."* **€35.00** **2022**

KUOPIO *C3* (9km SW Rural) *62.86432, 27.64165* **Rauhalahti Holiday Centre,** Kiviniementie, 70700 Kuopio **(017) 473000; sales@visitrauhalahti.fi; www.visitrauhalahti.fi**

(htd)

Well sp fr rte 5 (E63). Site 1.5km fr E63 dir Levänen, on Lake Kallavesi. 5*, Lge, hdstg, pt shd, pt sl, EHU (16A) inc; gas; cooking facs; sw; TV; adv bkg rec; ccard acc; sauna; boat trips; watersports; CKE. *"Hdstg for cars, grass for van & awning; ltd services Sept-May."* **€38.00, 2 May-20 Sep.** **2022**

KUUSAMO *C2* (5km N Rural) *66.00143, 29.16713* **Petäjälammentie,** Kylpyläntie, 93600 Kuusamo/ Petäjälampi **(040) 7379751; pasi.kallunki(at)pp.inet.fi**

12 (htd) sand

Three sites in same sm area on rd 5/E63, sp. Sm, shd, EHU (10A) inc; sw; Eng spkn; ccard acc; sauna; tennis; bike hire; CKE. *"Conv falls area; pool in hotel adj; quiet sm CL-type site nr lake; rented cabins avail; san facs clean; no adv bkg; other sm campsites nrby; gd."* **DKK 27** **2022**

LAHTI *C4* (5km N Rural) *61.01599, 25.64855* **Camping Mukkula,** Ritaniemenkatu 10, 15240 Lahti **(03) 7535380; tiedustelut@mukkulacamping.fi; www.mukkulacamping.fi**

12 (htd) nr nr nr

Fr S on rte 4/E75 foll camping sps fr town cent. 3*, Med, pt shd, EHU (10A) inc; cooking facs; sw; TV; ccard acc; tennis; bike hire; fishing; sauna; CKE. *"Beautiful lakeside views."* **2022**

FINLAND

LAHTI *C4* (8km NW Rural) *61.01872, 25.56387*
Camping Messila, Rantatie 5, 15980 Hollola **3876290; messila@campingmessila.fi; www.campingmessila.fi**
12 (htd) sand

Off A12 onto Messilantie (N), foll rd to lakeshore. Lge, hdg, mkd, hdstg, pt shd, EHU (16A) €6; bbq; sw nr; twin axles; Eng spkn; CKE. *"Gd sized pitches; barrier; v welcoming; well kept; next to marina; golf nr; conv for Lahti; vg."* **€30.00** **2022**

LIEKSA *D3* (3km SW Rural) *63.30666, 30.00532*
Timitranniemi Camping, Timitra, 81720 Lieksa **(04) 51237166; loma@timitra.com; www.timitra.com**
WD nr

Rte 73, well sp fr town on Lake Pielinen. 3*, Med, pt shd, pt sl, EHU (16A) €4; cooking facs; sw; TV; ccard acc; bike hire; sauna; boat hire; fishing; CKE. *"Pt of recreational complex; Pielinen outdoor museum worth visit."* **€28.00, 20 May-10 Sep.** **2022**

"There aren't many sites open at this time of year"

If you're travelling outside peak season remember to call ahead to check site opening dates – even if the entry says 'open all year'.

MERIKARVIA *B4* (3km SW Coastal) *61.84777, 21.47138*
Mericamping, Palosaarentie 67, 29900 Merikarvia **(04) 00 719589; info@mericamping.fi; www.camping.info/en/campsite/mericamping**
WD MSP adj

Fr E8 foll sp to Merikarvia, site sp 2km W beyond main housing area. Med, mkd, unshd, EHU €5; Eng spkn; ccard acc; CKE. *"Vg site on water's edge; some cottages; friendly, helpful staff."* **€22.00, 1 Jun-31 Aug.** **2022**

MUONIO *B1* (3km S Rural) *67.93333, 23.6575*
Harrinivan Lomakeskus, Harrinivantie 35, 99300 Muonio **400 155 110; sales@harriniva.fi; www.harriniva.fi**
(htd) WD nr

On E8 5km S of Muonio, well sp on R going S. Sm, hdstg, pt shd, pt sl, EHU (16A) €4; bbq; twin axles; Eng spkn; adv bkg acc; ccard acc; rv; CCI. *"Canoe hire for white water rafting; huskies; san facs stretch in high ssn; fair."* **€32.00, 1 Jun-30 Sep.** **2024**

PELLO *B2* (1km NW Rural) *66.78413, 23.94540*
Camping Pello, Nivanpääntie 58, 95700 Pello **050 3606611; pello.camping@gmail.com; www.travelpello.fi/palvelu/camping-pello**
(htd) WD MSP nr nr

Foll site sp fr town cent. Med, hdstg, pt shd, EHU (16A) inc; 30% statics; Eng spkn; ccard acc; boat hire; rv fishing adj; sauna. *"Rvside pitches avail - insects!"* **€21.00, 1 Jun-20 Sep.** **2022**

RAUMA *B4* (3km NW Coastal) *61.13501, 21.47085*
Poroholma Camping, Poroholmanti 8, 26100 Rauma **(02)533 5522; info@poroholma.fi; www.poroholma.fi**
12 WD sand

Enter town fr coast rd (8) or Huittinen (42). Foll campsite sp around N pt of town to site on coast. Site well sp. 3*, Lge, shd, pt sl, EHU (16A) €5; ccard acc; sauna; CKE. *"Attractive, peaceful location on sm peninsula in yacht marina & jetty for ferry (foot passengers only) to outlying islands; pool 250m; excel beach; warm welcome fr helpful staff; clean facs."* **€30.00** **2022**

ROVANIEMI *B2* (7km E Rural) *66.51706, 25.84678*
Camping Napapiirin Saarituvat, Kuusamontie 96, 96900 Saarenkylä **50 464 0446 | mob: 40 744 0998; reception@saarituvat.fi; www.saarituvat.fi**
(htd) WD nr

Fr town cent take rd 81, site on R at side of rd on lakeside. NB ignore 1st campsite sp after 2km. Sm, pt shd, terr, EHU (16A) €5.50; bbq; Eng spkn; adv bkg acc; sauna; CKE. *"Excel; friendly staff; vg base for Santa Park & Vill."* **€38.00, 3 June-8 Aug.** **2024**

ROVANIEMI *B2* (1km SE Urban) *66.49743, 25.74340*
Ounaskoski Camping, Jäämerentie 1, 96200 Rovaniemi **(016) 345304 or 504 329965; ounaskoski-camping@windowslive.com; www.ounaskoski-camping-rovaniemi.com**
(htd) WD MSP nr sand

Exit rte 4 onto rte 78 & cross rv. Over bdge turn S on rvside along Jäämerentie. Site on R in approx 500m immed bef old rd & rail bdge, sp. 3*, Med, hdstg, mkd, unshd, EHU (16A) inc; bbq; cooking facs; sw; twin axles; TV; 10% statics; bus 500m; Eng spkn; adv bkg acc; ccard acc; sauna; bike hire; CKE. *"Helpful staff; excel site beside rv in parkland; gd facs; suitable RVs & twin axles; 9km fr Arctic Circle; 6km to Santa Park, 'official' home of Santa; Artikum Museum worth visit; easy walk to town cent; gd flea mkts; excel san facs."* **€45.00, 21 May-26 Sep.** **2023**

SAVONLINNA *C4* (7km W Rural) *61.86216, 28.80513*
Camping Vuohimäki, Vuohimäentie 60, 57600 Savonlinna **(045) 2550073; savonlinna@suncamping.fi; suncampingsavonlinna.sportum.info/stable/Tuotteet**
WD nr

On rte 14, 4km W of Savonlinna turn L immed after bdge twd Pihlajaniemi; site sp for approx 4km on R. 4*, Med, EHU (16A) €5; sw; 10% statics; bus; Eng spkn; adv bkg acc; ccard acc; watersports; sauna; bike hire; CKE. *"Gd area for touring; lake trips; views over lake; gd san facs."* **€31.00, 5 Jun-20 Aug.** **2022**

TORNIO *B2* (3km SE Rural) *65.83211, 24.19953*
Camping Tornio, Matkailijantie, 95420 Tornio
(016) 445945; camping.tornio@co.inet.fi; www.campingtornio.com
12 nr

App Tornio on E4 coast rd fr Kemi sp on L of dual c/way; turn L at traff lts then immed R. Site well sp. 3*, Lge, pt shd, EHU (16A) €4; cooking facs; TV; ccard acc; sauna; tennis; bike hire; CKE. *"Poss boggy in wet."*
€32.00 **2022**

TURKU/ABO *B4* (12km SW Rural) *60.42531, 22.10258*
Ruissalo Camping (Part Naturist), Saaronniemi, 20100 Turku **5590139; ruissalocamping@turku.fi**
12 (htd) WD MSP nr sand adj

Well sp fr m'way & fr Turku docks; recep immed after sharp bend in a layby. 3*, Med, hdstg, pt shd, EHU (16A) inc; TV; 10% statics; bus; Eng spkn; ccard acc; watersports; sauna; games area; CKE. *"Conv for ferry; modern, clean san facs; sep area for naturists; ltd EHU some parts."* **€33.00** **2022**

UUKUNIEMI *D4* (3km NW Coastal) *61.80222, 29.96538*
Papinniemi Camping, Papinniementie 178, Uukuniemi Parikkala 59730, Suomi **(40) 7369852; info@papinniemicamping.net; www.papinniemicamping.net**

Fr Karelia rd foll sp. Fr S take R Niukkalantie. Fr N take L Uukuniementie. Sm, pt shd, EHU (16A) €4; bbq; games area. *"Amazing nature; sauna €15; bicycles; peaceful beautiful place; rowing boats; canoeing; lake water so clean."* **€33.00, 1 May-31 Oct.** **2024**

VIRRAT *B4* (6km SE Rural) *62.20883, 23.83501*
Camping Lakarin Leirintä, Lakarintie 405, 34800 Virrat
(03) 4758639; info@lakaricamping.fi; lakaricamping.fi/wp
(htd) WD

Fr Virrat on rte 66 twd Ruovesi. Fr Virrat pass info/park & take 2nd L, then 1st L. Site 1.7km on R (poor surface), sp. Med, pt shd, pt sl, EHU (16A) €3.40; sw nr; 50% statics; Eng spkn; sauna; boating; fishing; CKE. *"Beautiful lakeside pitches."*
€20.00, 1 May-30 Sep. **2022**

ALAND ISLANDS

VARDO *A4* (4km N Coastal) *60.27073, 20.38819*
Sandösunds Camping, Sandösundsvägen, 22550 Vårdö
(018) 47750; info@sandocamping.aland.fi; sandosund.com
(htd) WD MSP sand adj

Site sp fr ferry at Hummelvik & fr rd 2. 3*, Med, pt shd, pt sl, EHU (10A) €4 (long lead poss req); bbq; cooking facs; 5% statics; phone; Eng spkn; adv bkg acc; bike hire; kayak hire; games area; CKE. *"Well-run site in beautiful location; excel facs."*
€14.00, 15 Apr-31 Oct. **2022**

FINLAND

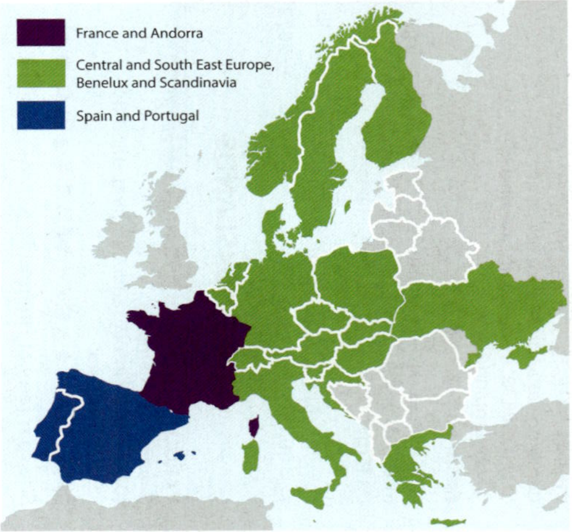

Kuusamo to Turku = 848km

	Forssa	Hanko	Helsinki	Hämeenlinna	Ivalo	Joensuu	Jyväskylä	Kajaani	Kemijärvi	Kokkola	Kouvola	Kuopio	Kurikka	Kuusamo	Kyyjärvi	Lahti	Lappeenranta	Mikkeli	Muonio	Nurmes	Oulu	Pori	Rovaniemi	Savonlinna	Sodankylä	Tampere	Tornio	Turku	Vaasa
Hanko	150																												
Helsinki	114	129																											
Hämeenlinna	56	195	100																										
Ivalo	1091	1238	1122	1041																									
Joensuu	464	546	439	410	839																								
Jyväskylä	238	380	271	187	848	244																							
Kajaani	555	664	556	500	623	229	313																						
Kemijärvi	889	1031	920	835	268	600	646	384																					
Kokkola	417	544	493	391	709	428	241	244	505																				
Kouvola	192	271	143	134	1037	310	192	436	821	432																			
Kuopio	383	493	382	332	800	135	145	170	557	314	264																		
Kurikka	263	390	345	245	882	449	230	385	679	174	356	335																	
Kuusamo	792	910	803	740	406	460	552	245	140	411	680	415	585																
Kyyjärvi	318	474	389	278	802	332	118	293	599	120	310	215	137	503															
Lahti	127	219	107	73	1017	336	170	450	813	409	61	282	294	704	288														
Lappeenranta	275	354	220	221	1062	236	220	437	820	459	82	266	424	682	338	147													
Mikkeli	258	341	231	204	957	208	114	330	718	356	99	162	345	579	233	129	105												
Muonio	975	1121	1004	918	325	782	732	568	275	590	922	670	764	420	686	901	945	840											
Nurmes	514	624	512	459	720	130	272	110	479	342	393	127	434	339	296	414	363	290	660										
Oulu	580	723	612	529	510	392	340	180	308	197	531	286	370	212	290	508	551	447	390	278									
Pori	127	257	242	180	1019	507	273	555	817	310	302	405	177	725	292	236	387	369	900	535	510								
Rovaniemi	807	941	831	747	287	550	561	339	85	420	750	510	593	192	513	730	774	669	230	429	221	730							
Savonlinna	362	449	333	310	958	142	207	332	717	440	207	162	444	578	325	232	155	106	839	272	447	471	671						
Sodankylä	929	1070	960	876	160	680	691	466	108	548	879	640	722	248	643	858	904	798	166	560	352	862	131	798					
Tampere	92	242	173	74	1002	395	152	463	796	324	192	294	171	702	228	128	275	256	882	420	493	115	710	355	841				
Tornio	711	851	742	659	413	523	469	309	210	329	660	416	501	315	423	637	682	578	262	406	129	640	123	576	252	621			
Turku	88	140	165	148	1144	549	304	615	943	434	274	448	283	848	384	217	364	349	1027	577	632	138	855	444	986	153	764		
Vaasa	317	453	418	316	827	494	282	365	626	120	430	379	79	530	164	363	502	398	711	461	317	194	540	489	668	245	448	346	
Varkaus	344	429	320	288	875	118	125	250	634	355	190	75	353	496	242	217	191	87	756	206	362	390	586	88	714	276	494	428	396

A
B
C
D
1
2
3
4
Motorways
Primary roads
Secondary roads
All year site(s)
Seasonal site(s)
No sites listed
N
E
S
W
0
50
100
150
200 km
0
20
40
60
80
100
120 miles
NORWAY
SWEDEN
RUSSIA
GULF OF BOTHNIA
GULF OF FINLAND
Kirkenes
Alta
Karasjok
Tromso
IVALO
Muonio
SODANKYLÄ
Gallivare
Pello
KEMIJÄRVI
Jokkmokk
ROVANIEMI
KUUSAMO
TORNIO
KEMI
Lulea
Kalevala
HAILUOTO
OULU
Skelleftea
KAJAANI
KOKKOLA
Lieksa
Juuka
Umea
KUOPIO
KYYJÄRVI
JOENSUU
VAASA
JYVÄSKYLÄ
Virrat
Savonlinna
MIKKELI
Merikarvia
TAMPERE
PORI
LAPPEENRANTA
Rauma
LAHTI
KOUVOLA
HAMEENLINNA
FORSSA
HAMINA
Kotka
PORVOO
St Petersburg
TURKU/ABO
ÅLAND
Vardo
MARIEHAMN
HELSINKI/HELSINGFORS
HANKO/HANGO

France

Highlights

Home to vibrant cities, exceptional cuisine and beautiful landscapes, each region of France offers a unique holiday. Landscapes range from rolling fields to dramatic mountains and beautiful coastlines.

There's also history around every corner, from the Châteaux of the Loire Valley to the prehistoric sites of the Dordogne. The beaches also rival the best in the world; the Atlantic Coast offers wide sandy expanses perfect for water sports, while the Mediterranean provides glitz and glamour courtesy of Cannes, Nice and St Tropez. The coastline of the North East is dotted with quaint fishing villages and sandy coves.

The cuisine of France is world famous too, from the refined restaurants of Paris to the rich stews and fresh baked bread of the country provinces. Your trip won't be complete without visiting a pâtisserie to sample some traditional French pastries. Visiting a vineyard or winery is another highlight, with over 200 wine varieties grown across France.

Major towns and cities

- Paris - the capital city is brimful with cultural highlights and top-notch cuisine.
- Nice - this coastal gem is known for it's elegance and stunning views.
- Bordeaux - in the heart of the wine growing region, and home to historic architecture.
- Strasbourg - an historic city which offers a mix of French and German cultures.

Attractions

- Eiffel Tower - the symbol of Paris and a must-see if you're in the Capital.
- Palace of Versailles - designed to show off the full glory of the French monarchy.
- Mont Saint-Michel - a dramatic island fortress housing a medieval abbey.
- Rocamadour - this sacred pilgrimage site is carved into a limestone cliff.
- Loire Valley Châteaux - the valley is a UNESCO heritage site.

Find out more

france.fr

Country Information

Capital: Paris

Bordered by: Andorra, Belgium, Germany, Italy, Luxembourg, Monaco, Spain, Switzerland

Terrain: Mostly flat plains or gently rolling hills in north and west; mountain ranges in south and east

Climate: Temperate climate with regional variations; generally warm summers and cool winters; harsh winters in mountainous areas; hot summers in central and Mediterranean areas

Coastline: 3,427km

Highest Point: Mont Blanc 4,807m

Language: French

Local Time: GMT or BST + 1, i.e. 1 hour ahead of the UK all year

Currency: Euros divided into 100 cents; £1 = €1.20, €1 = £0.84 (Nov 2024)

Telephoning: From the UK dial 0033 for France and omit the initial 0 of the 10-digit number you're calling. Mobile phone numbers start 06. For Monaco the code is 00377.

Emergency Numbers: Police 17; Fire brigade 18; Ambulance 15 or 112 for all services.

Public Holidays 2025: Jan 1; April 18, 21; May 1, 8, 29; Jun 8, 9; Jul 14; Aug 15; Nov 1, 11; Dec 25, 26.

Entry Formalities

British and Irish passport holders may stay for up to 90 days in any 180 day period without a visa. You may be asked to show a return or onward ticket at the border to confirm your length of stay, or to prove that you have enough money for your stay.

Your passport will need to have a minimum of 6 months' validity remaining, and be less than 10 years old (even if it has over 6 months left).

Visitors arriving at a campsite or hotel must complete a registration form.

Medical Services

In France a European Health Card (EHIC) or a UK Global Health Card (GHIC) entitles you to state-prrovided medical treatment necesary during your trip.

For the address of a doctor 'conventionné', i.e. working within the French state healthcare system, ask at a pharmacy. After treatment make sure you're given a signed statement of treatment ('feuille de soins') showing the amount paid as you will need this for a refund.

Pharmacies dispense prescriptions and first aid. Your prescription will be returned to you and you should attach this, together with the stickers (vignettes) attached to the packaging of any medication or drugs, to the 'feuille de soins' in order to obtain a refund.

If you're admitted to hospital make sure you present your EHIC or GHIC on admission. This will save you from paying any refundable costs up front and ensure that you only pay the patient contribution. You may have to pay a co-payment towards your treatment and if you're an inpatient you will have to pay a daily hospital charge. These charges are not refundable in France but you may be able to seek reimbursement when back in the UK. Applications for refunds should be sent to a local sickness insurance office (Caisse Primaire d'Assurance-Maladie) and you should receive payment at your home address within about two months.

Andorra is not a member of the EU and there are no reciprocal emergency healthcare arrangements with Britain. You will be required to pay the full cost of medical treatment so make sure that you have comprehensive travel insurance which includes cover for travel to non-EU countries.

Opening Hours

Banks – Mon-Fri 9am-noon & 2pm-4pm/5pm/6pm; in Paris Mon-Fri 10am-5pm; some open Sat & close on Mon. Early closing the day before a public holiday.

Museums – 10am-5pm; closed Mon or Tues. In Paris many open late once a week.

Post Offices – Mon-Fri 8am/9am-6pm/7pm; Sat 8am/9am-noon.

Shops: Food shops - Tues-Sat 7am/9am-6.30pm/7.30pm; some food shops i.e. bakers, grocers, etc, are open sun morning. Other shops - Tues-Sat 9am/10am-7.30pm. Shops generally close all or half day on Mon; in small towns shops close for lunch from noon to 2pm. Major Shops - Mon-Sat 9am/10am-7pm. Supermarkets may stay open until 9pm/10pm. Shops in tourist areas may open on Sunday.

Safety and Security

Take sensible precautions against street and car crime. Mugging, pickpocketing and bag snatching can occur, particularly in areas around railway stations, airports in large cities and at Christmas markets. Don't leave valuables unattended.

France shares with the rest of Europe a general threat from terrorism. Please check gov.uk/foreign-travel-advice/france before you travel.

British Embassy in France

35 Rue du Faubourg St Honore
75363 Paris Cedex 08 Paris
Tel: 01 44 51 31 00
gov.uk/world/france

There are also Consulates in Bordeaux and Marseilles.

Irish Embassy in France

12 Avenue Foch, 75116 Paris
Tel: 01 44 17 67 00
ireland.ie

There are also Irish Consulates-General/ Consulates in Cherbourg, Lyon and Monaco.

Andorra

For Consular help while in Andorra contact the British Consulate-General in Barcelona:
Avda Diagonal 477-13, 08036 Barcelona
Tel: +34 93 366 6200
gov.uk/world/andorra

Documents

Passport

You legally have to carry some form of photographic identification at all times while in France, however this doesn't need to be your passport.

Money

The major debit and credit cards, including American Express, are widely accepted by shops, hotels, restaurants and petrol stations. However, you may find that credit cards are not as widely accepted in smaller establishments as they are in the UK, including campsites, due to the high charges imposed on retailers, and debit cards are preferred. Cash machines are widespread and have instructions in English.

You can be arrested for possession of counterfeit currency and the authorities advise against changing money anywhere other than at banks or bureaux de change.

Carry your credit card issuers'/banks' 24-hour UK contact numbers in case of loss or theft.

Vehicle(s)

Carry your valid driving licence, insurance and vehicle documents with you in your vehicle at all times. It's particularly important to carry your vehicle registration document V5C, as you will need it if entering low emission zones.

Driving

Accidents

Drivers involved in an accident or those who commit a traffic offence may be required to take a saliva or urine drugs test as well as a breathalyser test. In the event of an accident where people are injured or if emergency assistance is required, dial 17 (police) or 112 from any phone.

Alcohol

In both France and Andorra the maximum legal level of alcohol is 0.05%. To ensure you stay under the limit it's best to avoid drinking at all if you plan to drive. For drivers with less than 3 years' experience the limit is 0.02%, which effectively means you cannot drink any alcohol at all. The police carry out random breath tests and penalties are severe.

Blind spot stickers

All vehicles with a total weight exceeding 3.5 tonnes must have a sticker showing other road users the position of blind spots.

The stickers:

- Must be visible from the sides and rear of the vehicle, and at a height between 0.90 and 1.50 meters from the ground.
- Can be glued, painted on the bodywork or affixed by riveting or any other means.
- Must not obstruct the visibility of the vehicle's registration plates and various lights and signalling devices as well as the driver's field of vision.
- Foreign vehicles passing through France are also subject to this signing obligation.

There are no specific blind spot stickers for motorhomes or caravans so you can use either of the stickers listed on the link below. There is no official distribution point for the stickers at present, but these can be purchased online at most big retailers.

To view the stickers and more information, visit securite-routiere.gouv.fr.

Breakdown Service

If you break down on a motorway or in a motorway service area you must call the police from one of the orange emergency telephones placed every 2 km along motorways. If you're in a service area, ask service station staff to contact the police for you, or dial 112 from a public phone and the police will be able to pinpoint your exact whereabouts. The police will arrange breakdown and towing assistance. No breakdown vehicle will enter a motorway without police authority.

Charges for motorway assistance are fixed by the government. If you have taken out breakdown insurance you should contact your insurance provider once the breakdown service has arrived in order to establish a means of payment. Your insurance provider cannot summon the police on your behalf if you breakdown on a motorway.

Headphones

It's illegal to drive a vehicle or cycle while wearing headphones or headsets. This includes listening to music or using headphones or earpieces to make phone calls. It's not illegal to make or receive phone calls using a hands-free system connected via Bluetooth to the car speaker system, or the speaker function on the phone.

Fuel

Unleaded petrol pumps are marked 'Essence Sans Plomb'. Diesel pumps are marked Gas Oil or Gazole.

Petrol stations may close on Sundays. Credit cards are generally accepted. Some automatic pumps are operated by credit cards and may not accept cards issued outside France. Away from major roads and towns don't let your fuel tank run too low as you may have difficulty finding an open petrol station, especially at night or on Sundays.

Fuel containing 10% bioethanol is on sale at many petrol stations in France alongside the regular Euro 95 unleaded fuel. Pumps are labelled SP95-E10. This fuel can be used in most modern vehicles manufactured since 2000 but if you're in any doubt about using it then regular Euro 95 or 98 Super Plus unleaded fuel is still available at most petrol stations. Check your vehicle handbook or visit acea.be for more information.

To find the cheapest fuel in any area log on to zagaz.com and simply click on the map of France to find the locations of petrol stations, together with prices charged.

Automotive Liquefied Petroleum Gas (LPG)

LPG (also called Gepel or GPL) is available in petrol stations across France, especially on motorways. However LPG may not be available in more rural areas so fill up at the first opportunity. Maps showing their company's outlets are issued free by most LPG suppliers, e.g. Shell, Elf, etc. A list of locations is available at the website stationsgpl.fr. LPG is not available in Andorra.

Low Emission Zones

There are Low Emission Zones operating in cities across France. For details of the rules and areas covered by each zone visit urbanaccessregulations.eu before you travel.

Motorhomes Towing Cars

If you're towing a car behind a motorhome, our advice would be to use a trailer with all four wheels of the car off the ground. Although France doesn't have a specific law banning A-frames, they do have a law which prohibits a motor vehicle towing another motor vehicle.

Overtaking and Passing

Crossing a solid single or double centre line is heavily penalised. Outside built-up areas, outfits weighing more than 3,500kg, or more than 7m in length, are required by law to leave at least 50m between themselves and the vehicle in front. They are only permitted to use the two right-hand lanes on roads with three or more lanes and, where overtaking is difficult, should slow down or stop to allow other smaller vehicles to pass.

Parking

As a general rule, all prohibitions are indicated by road signs or by yellow road markings. Stopping or parking on the left-hand side is prohibited except in one-way streets.

In most cities parking is largely by 'pay and display' machines which take coins and credit or debit cards. Where parking signs show 'Horodateur' or 'Stationnement Payant' you must obtain a ticket from a nearby machine.

In Paris two red routes ('axe rouge') have been created on which stopping and parking are prohibited. Car parks are expensive and the best advice is to use public transport, which is cheap and efficient.

Priority

In built up areas, give way to traffic coming from the right, unless otherwise indicated. Outside built-up areas traffic on all main roads of any importance has right of way, indicated by the following signs:

Priority road

Priority road

On entering towns, the same sign will often have a line through it, warning that vehicles may pull out from a side road on the right and will have priority.

End of priority road

On steep gradients, vehicles travelling downhill give way to vehicles travelling uphill.

Public Transport

In built-up areas you must stop to allow a bus to pull out from a bus stop. Take particular care when school buses have stopped and passengers are getting on and off.

Overtaking trams in motion is normally only allowed on the right, unless on a one way street where you can overtake on the left if there is not enough space on the right. Don't overtake a tram near a tram stop, which can be in the centre of the road. When a tram or bus stops to allow passengers on and off, you should stop to allow them to cross to the pavement. Give way to trams which are turning across your carriageway.

Roads

French roads fall into three categories: autoroutes (A) i.e. motorways; national (N) roads; and departmental (D) roads.

Andorra

Conditions on the road from Toulouse to Andorra, the N20/E9, can quickly become difficult in severe winter weather and you should be prepared for delays. Stick to main roads in Andorra when towing and don't attempt the many unsurfaced roads.

Road Signs and Markings

Directional signposting on major roads is generally good. Signs may be placed on walls pointing across the road they indicate and this may be confusing at first. Generally a sign on the right pointing left means that you go straight ahead. The same sign on the right pointing right means 'turn right' at the first opportunity. The words 'tout droit' mean 'go straight ahead' or 'straight on'.

Road signs on approach to roundabouts and at junctions usually don't show road numbers, just destinations, with numbers displayed once you're on the road itself. Once you have seen your destination town signposted continue along the road until directed otherwise.

Lines on the carriageway are generally white. A yellow zigzag line indicates a bus stop, blue markings indicate that parking is restricted and yellow lines on the edge of the roadway indicate that stopping and/or parking is prohibited. A solid single or double white line in the centre of the road indicates that overtaking is not permitted. STOP signs mean stop - you must come to a complete halt otherwise you may be liable to a fine if caught.

While road signs conform to international standards, some other commonly used signs you may see include:

French	English translation
Allumez vos feux	Switch on lights
Attention	Caution
Bouchon	Traffic jam
Chausée deformée	Uneven road
Chemin sans issue	No through road
Col	Mountain pass
Créneau de dépassement	2-lane passing zone, dual carriageway
Déviation	Diversion
Fin d'interdiction de stationner	End of parking restrictions
Gravillons	Loose chippings
Itineraire bis	Alternative route
Péage	Toll
Ralentissez	Slow down
Rappel	Continued restriction
Rétrécissement	Narrow lane
Route barrée	Road closed
Sens interdit	No entry
Sens unique	One-way street
Serrez à gauche/droite	Keep left/right
Stationnement interdit	No parking
Tout droit	Straight on
Toutes directions	All directions
Travaux	Road works
Virages	Bends

Recently-Qualified Drivers

The minimum age to drive in France is 18 years old and this also applies to foreign drivers. Driving without professionally qualified supervision/instruction on a provisional licence is not allowed.

Roundabouts

Drivers must give way to traffic already on the roundabout, i.e. on the left, if indicated by a red-bordered triangular sign showing a roundabout symbol stating 'Vous n'avez pas la priorité' or 'Cédez le passage' underneath.

Traffic on the roundabout has priority

In the absence of these signs traffic entering the roundabout has priority, however It's always very important to be watchful and to take extra care at roundabouts and junctions to avoid accidents.

Traffic Jams

The A6/A7 (the Autoroute du Soleil) from Paris via Lyon to the south are busy motorways prone to traffic jams. Travelling from the north, bottlenecks are often encountered at Auxerre, Chalon-sur-Saône, Lyon, Valence and Orange. An alternative route to the south is the A20, which is largely toll-free, or the toll-free A75 via Clermont-Ferrand.

During periods of congestion on the A6, A7 and A10 Paris-Bordeaux motorways, traffic police close off junctions and divert holiday traffic onto alternative routes or 'Itinéraires Bis' which run parallel to main roads.

Realtime traffic information on traffic conditions on motorways can be found on autoroutes.fr.

In general, Friday afternoons and Saturday mornings are busiest on roads leading south, and on Saturday and Sunday afternoons roads leading north may well be congested. Many French people stop for lunch and, therefore, between noon and 2pm roads are quieter.

At the start of the school holidays in early July, at the end of July and during the first and last few days of August, roads are particularly busy. Avoid the changeover weekend at the end of July/beginning of August when traffic both north and south bound can be virtually at a standstill. Traffic can also be very heavy around the Christmas/New Year period and on the weekend of any public holiday.

Andorra

Main roads are prefixed 'CG' (Carretera General) and side roads are prefixed 'CS' (Carretera Secundaria). CG road signs are white on red and CS signs are white on green.

There is heavy traffic in Andorra-la-Vella on most days of the year. During the summer holiday period you're likely to encounter queues on the Envalira pass from France on the N22. Traffic is at its worst in the morning from France and in the afternoon and evening from Andorra and you're recommended to use the Envalira Tunnel to avoid some of the congestion and reduce travel time.

Traffic Lights

There is no amber light after the red light in the traffic light sequence.

A flashing amber light indicates caution, slow down, proceed but give way to vehicles coming from the right. A flashing red light indicates no entry; it may also be used to mark level crossings, obstacles, etc.

A yellow arrow at the same time as a red light indicates that drivers may proceed in the direction of the arrow, traffic permitting, and providing they give way to pedestrians.

Watch out for traffic lights which may be mounted high above the road and hard to spot.

Violation of Traffic Regulations

Severe fines and penalties are in force for motoring offences and the police are authorised to impose and collect fines on the spot. Violations include minor infringements such as not wearing a seat belt, not carrying a set of spare bulbs or not respecting a STOP sign. More serious infringements such as dangerous overtaking, crossing a continuous central white line and driving at very high speeds, can result in confiscation of your driving licence.

If the offence committed is serious and likely to entail a heavy fine and the suspension of your driving licence or a prison sentence, a motorist who is not resident in France and has no employment there must deposit a guarantee. The police may hold a vehicle until payment is made.

Drivers who are deemed to have deliberately disregarded the safety of others face a maximum fine of €15,000 and a jail sentence. Failure to pay may result in your car being impounded. Your driving licence may also be suspended for up to five years.

By paying fines on the spot (request a receipt) or within three days, motorists can avoid court action and even reduce the fine. Standard fines can now be paid electronically in post offices and newsagents equipped with a dedicated terminal or via amendes.gouv.fr.

Motorways

France has over 11,800 kilometres of excellent motorways. Tolls are payable on most routes according to distance travelled and category of vehicle(s) and, because motorways are privately financed, prices per km vary in different parts of the country. Emergency telephones connected to the police are located every 2 km.

Motorway Service Areas

Stopping is allowed for a few hours at the service areas of motorways, called 'aires', and some have sections specially laid out for caravans. Most have toilet facilities and a water supply but at 'aires' with only basic facilities, water may not be suitable for drinking, indicated by a sign 'eau non potable'. In addition there are 'aires de repos' which have picnic and play areas, whereas 'aires de services' resemble UK motorway service areas with fuel, shop, restaurant and parking facilities for all types of vehicle.

Motorway Tolls

Motorways tolls are common throughout France by a number of different operating companies, although there are numerous stretches, particularly around large cities, where no tolls are levied. Vehicles are classified as follows

Category 1: (Light Vehicles) Vehicle with overall height under 2m and gross vehicle weight not exceeding 3,500kg. Train with overall height under 2m and gross vehicle weight of towing vehicle not exceeding 3,500kg.

Category 2: (Intermediate Vehicles) Vehicle with overall height from 2m to 3m and gross vehicle weight up to 3,500kg. Train with overall height from 2m to 3m and gross vehicle weight up to 3,500kg.

Category 3: (HGV or bus with two axles) Vehicle with overall height of 3m or more. Vehicle with gross vehicle weight of more than 3,500kg. On the A14 all twin-axle buses are in category 4.

Category 4: (HGV or bus with three or more axles) Vehicle with more than two axles and height of 3m or more, or gross vehicle weight of more than 3,500kg. Train with overall height of 3m or more. Train with towing vehicle having gross vehicle weight of more than 3,500kg.

Motorists driving Category 2 vehicles adapted for the transport of disabled persons pay the toll specified for Category 1 vehicles. Holding a disabled person's Blue Badge does not automatically entitle foreign motorists to pay Category 1 charges, and the decision whether to downgrade from Category 2 to 1 will be made by the person at the toll booth.

To calculate the tolls payable on your planned route see viamichelin.com and tick the box marked 'Caravan' (ticking this box will also give the toll for a motorhome) and select the 'Michelin recommended' route. For more detailed information, consult the websites of the individual motorway operating companies, a list of which can be found on autoroutes.fr/index.htm (English option). Alternatively calculate tolls payable on your chosen route on autoroutes.fr.

Toll payments may be made in cash or by credit card, but be aware that when paying with a credit card you may not be asked for a signature or required to key in a PIN. Pre-paid credit cards, Maestro and Electron are not accepted.

On less frequently-used motorways, toll collection is increasingly by automatic machines equipped with height detectors. It's simplest to pay with a credit card but there should be a cash/change machine adjacent. There are lanes at nearly all toll plazas specifically for drivers who have a Liber-t toll tag which allows them to pay for tolls directly from their bank account. Club members can benefit from a free Liber-t tag application (normally €10 + local VAT) - visit camc.com/sanef for details.

Speed Limits

Motorists caught driving more than 40 km/h (25mph) over the speed limit face immediate confiscation of their driving licence. Speed limits on motorways (in dry weather) are higher than in the UK – although they are lower on ordinary roads.

Fixed speed cameras are common on both motorways and major roads. The use of mobile speed cameras and radar traps is frequent, even on remote country roads, and may be operated from parked vans or motorbikes, or they may be hand-held. They may also be in use on exit slip roads from motorways or major roads where there is a posted speed limit. Motorway toll booths will also calculate your speed from the distance you have travelled and the time it has taken.

Radar Detectors

Radar detectors, laser detectors or speed camera jammers are illegal in France. If caught carrying one, even if it's not in use, you're liable to a fine of up to €1,500 and confiscation of the device, and possibly confiscation of your vehicle if you're unable to pay the fine. GPS or sat nav devices which pinpoint the position of fixed speed cameras are also illegal in France. You can still use the device, but you must disable the function which pinpoints speed cameras.

Inside Built-up Areas

The general speed limit is 50 km/h (31 mph) which may be raised to 70 km/h (44 mph) on important through roads, indicated by signs. The beginning of a built-up area is marked by a road sign giving the name of the town or village in blue or black letters on a light background with a red border. The end of the built-up area is indicated by the same sign with a red diagonal line through it. See examples below:

When you enter a town or village, even if there is speed limit warning sign, the place name sign indicates that you're entering a 50 km/h zone. The end of the 50 km/h zone is indicated by the place name sign crossed out. The word 'rappel' on a speed limit sign is a reminder of that limit.

The speed limit on stretches of motorway in built-up areas is 110 km/h (68 mph), except on the Paris ring road which is 80 km/h (50 mph).

Outside Built-up Areas

General speed limits are as follows:

- On single carriageway roads 90 km/h (56 mph)
- On dual-carriageways separated by a central reservation 110 km/h (68 mph)
- On motorways 130 km/h (80 mph)

These general speed limits also apply to private cars towing a trailer tent or caravan, provided the gross train mass (fully laden weight of the car, plus the cars towing limit) of the vehicle does not exceed 3,500kg. If the gross train mass of the towing vehicle is over 3,500kg the speed limits are 90 km/h (56 mph) on motorways, 80-90 km/h (50 mph) on dual carriageways and 80 km/h (50 mph) on single carriageways.

Large motorhomes over 3,500kg have a speed limit of 110 km/h (68 mph) on motorways, 100 km/h (62 mph) on dual carriageways and 80 km/h (50 mph) on single carriageway roads.

Adverse Weather Conditions

In case of rain or adverse weather conditions, general speed limits are lowered as follows:

- On motorways with a toll 110 km/h (68 mph)
- On motorways without a toll and dual carriageways 100 km/h (62 mph)
- Outside built-up areas 80 km/h (50 mph)

A speed limit of 50 km/h (31 mph) applies on all roads (including motorways) in foggy conditions when visibility is less than 50 metres.

Touring

France is divided administratively into 'régions', each of which consists of several 'départements'. There are 101 départements in total including Corsica, and these are approximately equivalent to our counties.

Paris, the capital and hub of the region known as the Ile-de-France, remains the political, economic, artistic, cultural and tourist centre of France. Visit parisjetaime.com for a wealth of information on what to see and do in the city. A Paris Pass, valid for 2 to 6 days, entitles you to free entrance (ahead of the queues) to over 90 attractions in Paris and free unlimited public transport, plus discounts. See parispass.com for more details.

Visitors under the age of 26 are admitted free to permanent collections in national museums; show your passport as proof of age. National museums, including the Louvre, are closed on Tuesday, with the exception of Versailles and the Musée d'Orsay which are closed on Monday. Entrance to national museums is free on the first Sunday of every month.

Restaurants must display priced menus outside and most offer a set menu 'plat du jour' or 'table d'hôte' which usually represents good value. A service charge of 15% is included in restaurant bills but it's also expected to leave a small tip if you have received good service. Smoking is not allowed in bars and restaurants.

France has a large network of well-marked, long-distance footpaths and hiking trails – Les Sentiers de Grande Randonnée – which generally follow ancient tracks. In addition to these 'GR' paths there are also 'PR' paths (Chemins de Petite Randonnée) which are most suited for local hiking. For a list of GR routes see gr-infos.com.

Camping and Caravanning

There are more than 11,000 campsites throughout France classified from 1 to 5 stars, including many small farm sites. Higher rated sites often have a wider range of facilities available. All classified sites must display their classification, current charges, capacity and site regulations at the site entrance.

Following incidents in recent years some authorities in southern France have introduced tighter regulations for sites liable to flooding, including limiting opening dates from April/May until August/September in some areas.

Casual/wild camping is prohibited in many state forests, national parks and nature reserves, and in all public or private forests in the départements of Landes and Gironde, along the Mediterranean coast including the Camargue, parts of the Atlantic and Brittany coasts, Versailles and Paris, and along areas of coast that are covered by spring tides.

Cycling

You may hire bicycles at many local tourist offices and from some railway stations.

Recent initiatives to encourage cycling have included the improvement of cycle tracks along rivers and canals and many former gravel tracks have been replaced with tarmac along the Rivers Rhône, Loire and Yonne/ Canal de Nivernais. Similar improvements have taken place along the Canal de Bourgogne.

In and around Paris there are 620 miles of cycle lanes. Bicycles, known as 'Les Vélibs', are available for hire with 1,400 docking points (one every 300 metres) in Paris.

The French Tourist Board has information on cycle routes and tours throughout France.

Public Transport

Several large cities have metro or tram systems and all have a bus network. The Paris metro network comprises 16 lines and over 300 stations, and has many connections to the RER (regional suburban rail network) and the SNCF national railway system. 'T tickets' can be purchased in the metro stations for single trips on the metro, and are valid on RATP buses.

For tourists Paris Visite travel passes are available allowing unlimited travel for one to five days across some or all of the travel zones and a range of discounts at attractions. For further information see ratp.fr.

People aged 60 and over are entitled to a discount of up to 25% when using French railways. Show your passport as proof of age.

Ferries

Car ferry services operate all year across the Gironde estuary between Royan and Le Verdon eliminating a 155km detour. See bernezac.com for more details.

Ferry services operate from Marseille, Nice and Toulon to Corsica. For information see southernferries.co.uk.

Channel Islands

Ferry services operate for cars and passengers between Poole and Portsmouth and St Malo via Jersey and Guernsey. Caravans and motorhomes are permitted to enter Jersey, subject to certain conditions, including pre-booking direct with a registered campsite and the acquisition of a permit. For further information and details of the campsites on Jersey where caravans are permitted, see jersey.com.

There are four campsites on Guernsey but, for the moment, the authorities in Guernsey don't permit entry to trailer caravans. Motorhomes can only be taken onto the island if they are stored under cover and not used for human habitation. Trailer tents can be taken onto the island without restrictions.

ABBEVILLE *3B3* (14km SE Rural) *50.03416, 1.98383* **Baie de Somme La Peupleraie (formerly Municipal),** Rue de la Chasse À Vaches, 80510 Long **03 22 31 84 27; camping.lapopleraie.long@orange.fr; www.campinglapeupleraie.fr/**

nr nr nr

Exit A16 at junc 21 for D1001 N then turn L at Ailly-le-Haut Clocher onto D32 for Long & foll sp. 2*, Med, mkd, pt shd, EHU (6A) inc (caution - poss rev pol & poss other elec concerns) (long lead req); bbq; red long stay; 90% statics; adv bkg acc; fishing adj; CKE. *"Pretty, busy site beside Rv Somme; gd san facs; gd walking/cycling by rv; site busy 1st week Sep - flea mkt in town; interesting area; old power stn museum; warden lives on site; conv en rte Calais; san facs v clean; quiet peaceful site; highly rec."* **€17.00, 15 Mar-15 Nov. 2023**

ABBEVILLE *3B3* (5km S Urban) *50.07826, 1.82378* **Camp Municipal du Marais-Talsac/Le Marais Communal,** 62 Rue du Marais-Talsac, 80132 Mareuil-Caubert **03 22 31 62 37 or 03 22 24 11 46 (Mairie); mairie.mareuilcaubert@wanadoo.fr; www.spottocamp.com/en/campsites/camping-municipal-le-marais-communal-mareuil-caubert**

nr

Leave A28 at junc 3; at T-junc turn L onto D928; foll camping sp; in 4km turn sharp R onto D3 into Mareuil-Caubert; in 1km turn L thro housing est to site by stadium. Well sp. 2*, Med, hdstg, mkd, pt shd, EHU (6A) €2.90 (poss rev pol); 25% statics; Eng spkn; CKE. *"Well-kept, friendly site; sm pitches; helpful staff; clean dated facs, poss tired LS; no twin axles or o'fits over 8m; hdstgs stony/loose gravel; gates clsd 2000-0800; interesting area; poss travellers LS (2010); vg NH Calais."* **€15.00, 1 Apr-30 Sep. 2024**

ABBEVILLE *3B3* (10km SW Rural) *50.08586, 1.71519* **Camping Le Clos Cacheleux,** Rue des Sources, Route de Bouillancourt, 80132 Miannay **03 22 19 17 47; raphael@camping-lecloscacheleux.fr; www.camping-lecloscacheleux.fr**

€2.10

(covrd, htd, indoor)

Fr A28 exit junc 2 onto D925 sp Cambron. In 5km at Miannay turn S onto D86 sp Bouillancourt. Site thro vill of R opp sister site Camping Le Val de Trie which is sp fr A28. 4*, Med, hdg, mkd, pt shd, pt sl, EHU (10A) inc (poss long lead req); gas; bbq (charcoal, gas); cooking facs; TV; Eng spkn; adv bkg acc; ccard acc; tennis 3km; games area; games rm; sauna; spa; treatment rooms; library; kids' club; bike rental; CKE. *"Pleasant, peaceful, wooded site; lge pitches; charming, helpful owner; farm animals; fishing pond; all services (inc shop, rest & pool) are on sister site 'Le Val de Trie' on opp side of rd, accessed via steep track 500m fr site ent; no o'fits over18m; htd covrd pool, paddling pool adj; jacuzzi; gd walking, cycling; gd for dogs; san facs in a bad state (2019)."* **€28.60, 1 Apr-31 Oct, P12. 2024**

ABBEVILLE *3B3* (10km SW Rural) *50.08570, 1.71480* **Camping Le Val de Trie,** 1 Rue des Sources, Bouillancourt-sous-Miannay, 80870 Moyenneville **03 22 31 48 88; raphael@camping-levaldetrie.fr; www.camping-levaldetrie.fr**

€2.10 (htd)

(covrd, htd)

Fr A28 exit junc 2 onto D925 sp Cambron. In 5km at Miannay turn S onto D86 sp Bouillancourt. Site thro vill on L. Site sp fr A28. NB Last pt of app narr with bends. 4*, Med, hdstg, mkd, hdg, shd, pt sl, EHU (6-10A) inc; gas; bbq; red long stay; TV; 1% statics; phone; Eng spkn; adv bkg acc; ccard acc; lake fishing; games rm; CKE. *"Beautiful, well-run site; well- shd; welcoming, helpful, conscientious owner; excel, clean, modern, san facs, ltd LS; gd family site; woodland walks; interesting area; conv Calais; great location for visiting the Somme area."* **€28.00, 1 Apr-31 Oct. 2024**

ABBEVILLE *3B3* (7km NW Rural) *50.14166, 1.76237* **Camping Le Château des Tilleuls,** Rue de la Baie, 80132 Port-le-Grand **03 22 24 07 75; contact@chateaudestilleuls.com; www.chateaudestilleuls.com**

(htd) (htd)

Fr N on A16 join A28 dir Rouen. At junc 1 take D40 dir St Valery-sur-Somme, site on R in approx 3km. 3*, Med, hdstg, mkd, hdg, pt shd, sl, terr, EHU (10-16A) €4; bbq; red long stay; TV; Eng spkn; adv bkg acc; ccard acc; games rm; bike hire; tennis; CKE. *"Pleasant site; lge, v sl pitches; find suitable pitch bef booking in; long uphill walk fr recep; gd unisex san facs; new pitches far fr ent; site updated; well run; v clean but maybe in adequate in HHS; excel; mostly static, separate area for tourers; gd sized hdg pitches with ehu & fresh water tap; lots of onsite activies; suitable for family holiday."* **€29.80, 1 Mar-30 Oct. 2023**

ABRETS, LES *9B3* (2km E Rural) *45.54065, 5.60834* **Kawan Village Le Coin Tranquille,** 6 Chemin des Vignes, 38490 Les Abrets **04 76 32 13 48; contact@coin-tranquille.com; www.coin-tranquille.com**

€2 (covrd, htd)

Fr N exit A43 at junc 10 Les Abrets & foll D592 to town cent. At rndbt at monument take D1006 twd Chambéry/Campings; cont for 500m then turn L sp Le Coin Tranquille; cross level x-ing & cont for 500m to site. Fr S on A48 exit junc 10 at Voiron onto D1075 to Les Abrets; turn R at rndabt onto D1006 twd Le Pont-de-Beauvoisin, then as above. 4*, Lge, mkd, hdg, pt shd, EHU (10A) €5; gas; bbq; TV; Eng spkn; adv bkg req; ccard acc; bike hire; archery; games area; games rm; CKE. *"Well-kept, well-run site in gd location; no o'fits over 8m unless bkd in adv; lge narr pitches; busy/noisy site, but some quiet pitches avail; helpful & friendly staff; horseriding 7km; fishing 7km; golf 15km; well-kept, clean san facs, ltd LS; lovely pool; vg activities for children; poss flooding in wet weather; excel."* **€20.00, 1 Apr - 1 Nov, M05. 2022**

ABRETS, LES *9B3* (3km S Rural) *45.47079, 5.54688* **Camping Le Calatrin,** 799 Rue de la Morgerie, 38850 Paladru **04 76 32 37 48; camping.le.calatrin@gmail.com; www.camping-paladru.fr**

€3.50 WD MSP

S fr Les Abrets on D1075; turn R onto D50 to Paladru; site 1km beyond vill on L, on brow of hill. Or exit A48 junc 9 & foll sp 'Lac de Paladru'; 3km after rndabt junc of D50 & D17, site on R (by another rndabt). 3*, Med, mkd, hdg, shd, terr, EHU (10A) €4 (long lead poss req); gas; bbq; sw nr; red long stay; TV; 30% statics; bus 200m; Eng spkn; adv bkg acc; fishing; games area; watersports; games rm; tennis 500m; bike hire; CKE. *"Attractive site; direct access to lake; lge pitches; welcoming & helpful owners; gd recreational facs; nice walks; excel."* **€17.00, 1 Apr-30 Sep. 2023**

ABRETS, LES *9B3* (11km SW Rural) *45.44621, 5.53183* **Camp Municipal le Bord du Lac,** 687 route du Bord du Lac, 38850 Bilieu **04 75 39 03 80 or 04 76 06 62 41 (Mairie); camping@ville-bilieu.fr; www.camping-leborddulac-bilieu.fr**

(htd) WD

S on D1075 fr Les Abrets. Turn R onto D50. Just bef Paladru, turn L to Charavines. site on R on ent Bilieu, by lakeside. Med, mkd, pt shd, pt sl, terr, EHU (10A) €3; 10% statics; ccard acc; CKE. *"Nice site by lake; san facs vg; staff helpful; no sw in lake fr site, only boat launch; pitch access poss diff; gd."* **€27.60, 13 Apr-6 Oct. 2024**

ACCOUS *8G2* (0.5km NW Rural) *42.97717, -0.60592* **Camping Despourrins,** Route du Somport, D'Arrechau, 64490 Accous **www.campingdespourrins.com**

WD nr nr nr

On N134 rte to & fr Spain via Somport Pass. Site sp on main rd. 2*, Sm, pt shd, EHU (6A) €2.70; bbq; 10% statics; fishing. *"Clean, tidy NH; conv Col de Somport."* **€10.50, 1 Mar-31 Oct. 2024**

AGAY *10F4* (0.7km E Coastal) *43.4328, 6.86868* **Camping Agay Soleil,** 1152, Boulevard de la plage RD559, 83530 Agay **04 94 82 00 79; camping-agay-soleil@wanadoo.fr; www.agay-soleil.com**

€2 (htd) WD MSP sand adj

E fr St Raphaël on D559 site on R after passing Agay dir Cannes. Or (to avoid busy St Raphaël) fr A8 exit junc 38 on D37 & foll sp St Raphaël, then Agay/ Valescure on D100 for approx 8 km; L at rndabt by beach in Agay; site far side of bay immed after watersports club. 3*, Med, mkd, hdstg, pt shd, pt sl, terr, EHU (10A) €5; gas; bbq (elec); train & bus 500m; Eng spkn; adv bkg rec; games area; watersports; CKE. *"Superb location on sea front; excel modern facs; many pitches too sm for awning; extra for beach pitches; dogs not acc high ssn;excel; sm pleasant site; direct access to beach; lge o'fits phone ahead; vg."* **€39.00, 16 Mar-10 Nov. 2024**

> **"There aren't many sites open at this time of year"**
>
> If you're travelling outside peak season remember to call ahead to check site opening dates – even if the entry says 'open all year'.

AGAY *10F4* (1.5km S Coastal) *43.41995, 6.85696* **Royal Camping,** Plage de Camp-Long, 83530 Agay **04 94 82 00 20; contact@royalcamping.net; www.royalcamping.net**

WD nr nr sand adj

On D559 twd St Raphaël. Turn at sp Tiki Plage & site. Stop in ent rd at recep bef ent site. 3*, Sm, mkd, hdstg, pt shd, EHU (6A) €3.50; gas; 10% statics; phone; bus 200m; Eng spkn; adv bkg acc; CKE. *"Gd walks; lovely site; some pitches adj to beach in sep area; vg."* **€30.00, 10 Feb-4 Nov. 2023**

FRANCE

AGAY *10F4* (4km NW Rural/Coastal) *43.45408, 6.83254* **Esterel Caravaning,** 4 481 avenue des golfs, 83530 Agay Saint-Raphaël **04 94 82 03 28; contact@esterel-caravaning.fr; www.esterel-caravaning.fr**

€4 (htd) (covrd, htd) sand 3km

Fr A8 foll sps for St Raphaël & immed foll sp 'Agay (par l'interieur)/Valescure' into D100/Ave des Golfs, approx 6km long. Pass golf courses & at end of rd turn L at rndabt twds Agay. Site ent immed after a L hand bend. 5*, Lge, hdstg, mkd, hdg, pt shd, pt sl, terr, serviced pitches; EHU (16A) inc; gas; bbq (charcoal, elec, gas); red long stay; twin axles; TV; 50% statics; Eng spkn; adv bkg acc; ccard acc; squash; waterslide; tennis; golf nr; archery; bike hire; games rm; games area; CKE. *"Superbly situated, busy site adj Esterel forest; undergrnd disco; 8 local golf clubs; friendly, helpful staff; gd san facs; gd for families - excel leisure activities; excel rest & shop; now classified as a 5 star site; conv Gorges du Verdon, Massif de l'Estérel, Monaco, Cannes & St Tropez; individual san facs to some pitches (extra charge); min stay 1 week high ssn (Sun to Sun); various pitch prices; ltd lge pitches avail; some pitches v sl & poss diff; ltd facs LS; mkt Wed; excel."* **NP 33, 9 Apr - 1 Oct, C21. 2022**

AGDE *10F1* (3km SE Coastal) *43.27949, 3.48114* **Camping Le Rochelongue,** Chemin des Ronciers, Route de Rochelongue, 34300 Le Cap d'Agde **04 67 21 25 51; le.rochelongue@wanadoo.fr; www.camping-le-rochelongue.fr**

€4 (cont) (htd) sand 500m

Exit A9 junc 34 sp Agde. Foll D612 to Le Cap d'Agde then thro Rochelongue. Site on L just bef rndabt. 4*, Med, mkd, hdstg, pt shd, EHU (6A) inc; gas; bbq; 50% statics; phone; Eng spkn; adv bkg acc; bike hire; table tennis; golf 1.5km; CKE. *"Friendly, well-kept site; takeaway; sh walk to vill & beach."* **€67.00, 13 May-15 Sep. 2024**

AGDE *10F1* (7km SE Coastal) *43.29645, 3.52255* **Centre Hélio-Marin René Oltra (Naturist),** 1 Rue des Néréïdes, 34307 Le Cap-d'Agde **04 67 01 06 36 or 04 67 01 06 37; contact@centrenaturiste-oltra.fr; www.centrenaturiste-oltra.fr**

€3.80 sand adj

S fr m'way A9 Agde-Pézenas junc on N312/D612 for 14km to Cap d'Agde turn-off; foll Camping Naturist sp to site on E side of Le Cap-d'Agde. 4*, V lge, hdg, mkd, pt shd, serviced pitches; EHU (6A) inc; 50% statics; bus adj; Eng spkn; adv bkg rec; ccard acc; INF card. *"Naturist area in Cap-d'Agde has all facs; lovely beach; gd size pitches; friendly atmosphere; modern san facs; gd family facs; excel; great location; gd public transport & walking; facs upgraded (2015); v busy but mostly quiet."* **€50.50, 15 Mar-14 Oct. 2023**

AGDE *10F1* (2km SW Rural) *43.29806, 3.45639* **Camping Le Neptune,** 46 Boulevard du St Christ, 34300 Agde **04 67 94 23 94; info@campingleneptune.com; www.campingleneptune.com**

€3 nr (htd) sand 2km

Fr A9 exit junc 34 onto N312, then E on D612. Foll sp Grau d'Agde after x-ing bdge. Site on D32E on E bank of Rv Hérault on 1-way system. 4*, Lge, mkd, hdg, pt shd, EHU (6-10A) inc; gas; bbq; TV; 40% statics; phone; Eng spkn; adv bkg rec; ccard acc; games area; tennis; CKE. *"Peaceful, pleasant, clean site; helpful owners; dog breed restrictions - check bef travel; modern facs, ltd LS; liable to flood after heavy rain; easy rvside walk/cycle to vill; gd cycleways; rv cruises; boat launch/slipway 500m; v popular site; gd facs; excel."* **€55.00, 1 Apr-30 Sep. 2023**

AGEN *8E3* (8km NW Rural) *44.24368, 0.54290* **Camping Le Moulin de Mellet,** Route de Prayssas, 47450 St Hilaire-de-Lusignan **05 53 87 50 89 or 06 79 93 48 54; moulin.mellet@orange.fr; www.camping-moulin-mellet.com**

€3.80 nr

NW fr Agen on N113 twd Bordeaux for 5km. At traff lts just bef Colayrac-St Cirq take D107 N twd Prayssas for 3km. Site on R. 3*, Sm, mkd, shd, EHU (10A) €3.80 (poss rev pol); gas; bbq; phone; Eng spkn; adv bkg acc; games rm; CKE. *"Delightful, well-run site; helpful, friendly new owners; sm children's farm; RVs & twin axles phone ahead; excel; spotless facs; rest & bar open in LS; pretty location; gd for long stay."* **€30.00, 1 Apr-10 Oct. 2024**

AGON COUTAINVILLE *1D4* (0.3km NE Urban/Coastal) *49.05105, -1.59112* **Camp Municipal Le Martinet,** Blvd Lebel-Jéhenne, 50230 Agon-Coutainville **02 33 47 05 20; campingsmunicipaux@agoncoutainville.fr; lemartinetlemarais.wixsite.com**

€3.20 nr sand 600m

Fr Coutances take D44 to Agon-Coutainville; site sp nr Hippodrome. 2*, Med, hdg, mkd, pt shd, EHU (6A) €3.50; bbq; 55% statics; bus; Eng spkn; adv bkg acc; ccard acc; CKE. *"V pleasant site; ltd facs LS; horse racecourse adj; vg."* **€14.60, 1 Apr-30 Oct. 2023**

AIGNAN *8E2* (0.6km S Rural) *43.69290, 0.07528* **Camping Le Domaine du Castex,** 32290 Aignan **05 62 09 25 13; info@domaine-castex.com; www.gers-vacances.com**

€4 nr

Fr N on D924/N124 turn S on D20 thro Aignan onto D48; in 500m g'ge on R, immed after turn L; site sp. Fr S on D935 turn E at Monplaisir onto D3/D48 to Aignan; site on R bef vill. 3*, Sm, hdg, mkd, hdstg, pt shd, EHU (10A) €3; bbq; sw nr; TV; 4% statics; phone; Eng spkn; adv bkg acc; ccard acc; tennis adj; games area; CKE. *"Lovely site in grnds of medieval farmhouse; helpful Dutch owners; modern san facs; excel pool & rest; squash adj; gd touring cent for Bastide vills; mkt Mon; phone ahead LS; vg."* **€27.20, 20 Mar-20 Oct.** **2022**

AIGREFEUILLE D'AUNIS *7A1* (2km N Rural) *46.14621, -0.94571* **Camp Municipal de la Garenne,** 47 Avenue de l'île Madame 17730 PORT DES BARQUES **05 46 84 80 66; camping@ville-portdesbarques.fr; www.camping-municipal-portdesbarques.com/**

€3 nr

Fr Aigrefeuille-d'Aunis take D112 2.5km N to vill of St Christophe, site sp. 3*, Sm, mkd, hdg, pt shd, EHU (4A) €2.50; adv bkg acc; lake fishing 3km; horseriding; tennis; CKE. *"V clean site in sm vill; unrel opening dates, phone ahead LS."* **€23.00, 1 Apr -31 Oct.** **2020**

AIGUES MORTES *10F2* (3km NE Rural) *43.57314, 4.21836* **Camping à la Ferme (Loup),** Le Mas de Plaisance, 30220 Aigues-Mortes **04 66 53 92 84 or 06 22 20 92 37 (mob); info@ot-aiguesmortes.fr; www.ot-aiguesmortes.fr**

Site sp in Aigues-Mortes or foll D58 E dir Stes Maries-de-la-Mer, then sharp R along farm rd (v narr & potholed) at end of rv bdge. NB Fr town narr rd with much traff calming & sharp bends. Either way for v sm o'fits only. 4*, Sm, pt shd, EHU inc; bbq; CKE. *"Excel sm site; superb san facs; helpful owners; rec not to use water at m'van service point as off irrigation system - other water points avail; video security at gate."* **€22.00, 1 Apr-30 Sep.** **2024**

AIGUES MORTES *10F2* (3.5km W Rural) *43.56300, 4.15910* **Yelloh! Village La Petite Camargue,** 30220 Aigues-Mortes **04 66 53 98 98; info@yellohvillage-petite-camargue.fr; www.yellohvillage-petite-camargue.com**

€6

sand 3km

Heading S on N979 turn L onto D62 bef Aigues-Mortes & go over canal bdge twd Montpellier; site on R in 3km; sp. 5*, V lge, mkd, pt shd, EHU (10A) inc; bbq (charcoal, gas); red long stay; TV; 50% statics; Eng spkn; adv bkg acc; ccard acc; games rm; serviced; horseriding; bike hire; tennis; games area; jacuzzi; CKE. *"Lively, busy, well-run, youth-oriented commercial site with many sports facs; no o'fits over 7m; clean san facs, poss stretched high ssn; excel pool complex; bus to beach high ssn; some sm pitches; take care o'head branches; gd cycling; mkt Wed & Sun; some pitches diff to access."* **€57.00, 10 Apr-14 Sep, C04.** **2022**

AIGUILLES *9D4* (1km NE Rural) *44.78783, 6.88849* **Camp Municipal Le Gouret,** Camp Municipal Le Gouret, Aiguilles-en-Queyras, **06 46 42 50 64; www.camping-gouret.fr; https://lequeyras.com/offres/camping-municipal-le-gouret-aiguilles-fr-3259709/**

€1 nr nr nr

Fr Aiguilles on D947 dir Abriès, sp to site on R across rv bdge. 2*, Lge, shd, EHU (3-10A) €2.20-3.20; bbq; 10% statics; phone; bus 100m; games area. *"Site on bank of Rv Guil; random pitching in lge area of larch forest; excel cent for Queyras National Park; vg."* **€21.60, 17 May-15 Sept.** **2024**

AIRE SUR LA LYS *3A3* (2km NE Urban) *50.64390, 2.40630* **Camp Municipal de la Lys,** 56 rue du Fort Gassion, Bassin des Quatre Faces, 62120 Aire-sur-la-Lys **03 91 93 42 28; camping@www.ville-airesurlalys.fr; www.ville-airesurlalys.fr**

12 (htd)

Fr town cent, find main sq & exit to R of town hall. Thro traff lts turn R into narr lane just bef rv bdge dir of Hazebrouck. Site poorly sp. High vehicles beware low bdge at site ent. 2*, Sm, mkd, hdg, hdstg, pt shd, EHU (6A) €2.10; 95% statics. *"Ltd touring pitches; ltd but clean san facs; not suitable lge o'fits; rec for NH only; v welcoming; waterside pitches; vg NH; easy walk to town."* **€12.00** **2023**

AIRE SUR L'ADOUR *8E2* (0.7km NE Urban) *43.70259, -0.25792* **Camping Les Ombrages de l'Adour,** Rue des Graviers, 40800 Aire-sur-l'Adour **05 58 71 75 10; hetapsarl@yahoo.fr; www.camping-adour.com/FR**

€1.80

Turn E on S side of bdge over Rv Adour in town. Site close to bdge & sp, past La Arena off rd to Bourdeaux. 2*, Med, pt shd, EHU (10A) inc; bbq; adv bkg acc; ccard acc; fishing 500m; tennis 500m; games area. *"Vg; htd pool 500m; canoeing 500m; v clean facs but dated."* **€21.00, 13 Mar-1 Nov.** **2022**

FRANCE

AIRE SUR L'ADOUR *8 E2* (14.6km SW Rural) *43.63582, -0.38150* **Camping Municipal de Geaune,** 11 Route de Cledes, Geaune **05 58 44 50 27; https://geaune.fr**

nr nr

Foll D2 fr Aire sur l'Adour to Geaune. Thro town ctr and L on D111 twrds Cledes. Site on L in 300m. Sm, mkd, pt shd, terr, EHU 6A; bbq (sep area); sw nr; CKE. *"Vg."* **€17.00, 1 Apr-31 Oct.** **2024**

AIRVAULT *4H1* (1km N Rural) *46.83200, -0.14690* **Camping de Courte Vallée,** 8 Rue de Courte Vallée, 79600 Airvault **05 49 64 70 65; info@caravanning france.com; www.caravanningfrance.com**

€1.50 (htd)

Fr N, S or W leave D938 sp Parthenay to Thouars rd at La Maucarrière twd Airvault & foll lge sp to site. Site on D121 twd Availles-Thouarsais. NB If app fr NE or E c'vans not permitted thro Airvault - watch carefully for sp R at Gendarmerie. Well sp fr all dirs. 3*, Sm, hdstg, mkd, hdg, pt shd, pt sl, EHU (13A) inc (poss long lead req); gas; bbq; red long stay; twin axles; TV; 8% statics; adv bkg acc; ccard acc; games rm; bike hire; fishing; CKE. *"Peaceful, popular; pleasant, helpful British owners; excel, clean & vg facs, poss stretched high ssn; conv Futuroscope & Puy du Fou theme park; mkt Sat; not as well kept & expensive compared to similar sites; c'van storage; town dissapointing, empty shops; new rest & bar(2018)."* **€31.00, 1 Mar-31 Oct, L14.** **2022**

AIX EN PROVENCE *10F3* (9km E Rural) *43.51771, 5.54128* **FFCC Camping Ste Victoire,** Quartier La Paradou, 613 avenue Jullien Gautier, 13100 Beaurecueil **04 42 66 91 31; campingvictoire@orange.fr; www.campingsaintevictoire.com**

€1.10 (htd) nr

Exit A8/E80 junc 32 onto D7n dir Aix, then R onto D58 & foll sp for 3km. 2*, Sm, hdstg, hdg, mkd, shd, EHU (10A) inc; red long stay; TV; phone; bus; adv bkg acc; archery; bike hire; CKE. *"Well-run site in attractive hilly, wooded area; friendly, helpful owners; clean, basic, dated & small san facs, ltd LS, but clean; various pitch sizes; lge o'fits poss diff manoeuvring; pool 9km; some pitches too soft for lge o'fits when wet; no twin axles; no lighting at night; gd walking & climbing; lovely location; shady; frequent cheap bus to Aix; narr rds; site can be diff to find."* **€31.00, 5 Mar-30 Nov.** **2023**

AIX EN PROVENCE *10F3* (3km SE Urban) *43.51556, 5.47431* **Airotel Camping Chantecler,** 41 Avenue du Val Saint André, 13100 Aix-en-Provence **04 42 26 12 98; info@campingchantecler.com; www.campingchantecler.com**

€3.60 (htd)

Fr town inner ring rd foll sps Nice-Toulon, after 1km look for sp Chantecler to L of dual c'way. Foll camp sp past blocks of flats. Well sp in Val-St André. If on A8 exit at junc 31 sp Val-St André; R at rndabt; R at Rndabt; L at 2nd traff lts onto Ave Andre Magnan; R ar rndabt; site sp. If app fr SE on D7n turn R immed after passing under A8. 4*, Lge, hdstg, hdg, pt shd, sl, terr, EHU (5A) €4.10 (long lead poss req); gas; bbq (elec, gas); red long stay; TV; bus; adv bkg acc; ccard acc; site clsd 1 & 2 Jan; CKE. *"Lovely, well-kept, wooded site; facs ltd LS; some site rds steep - gd power/weight ratio rec; access poss diff some pitches; rec request low level pitch & walk to pitch bef driving to it; ent narr; recep clsd 12.30-13.30; gd pool; conv city; vg touring base; access diff to some pitches, refurb san facs now htd & excel (2014)."* **€28.70, 1 May - 20 Oct.** **2024**

AIX EN PROVENCE *10F3* (8.6km SE Urban) *43.51250, 5.47196* **Camping L'Arc-en-Ciel,** Ave Henri Malacrida, Pont des 3 Sautets, 13100 Aix-en-Provence **04 42 26 14 28; camping-arcenciel@neuf.fr; www.campingarcenciel.com**

Free (htd) nr nr nr

Fr E or W exit A8 at junc 31 for D7n dir SE; (turn N for 300m to 1st rndabt where turn R; in 200m at 2nd rndabt turn R again onto D7n dir SE); pass under m'way; site ent immed on R; sp. Take care at ent. NB Access easier if go past site for 1km to rndabt, turn round & app fr S. 4*, Sm, mkd, hdg, shd, terr, EHU (6A) inc; gas; bbq; TV; phone; bus adj; Eng spkn; adv bkg acc; fishing; canoeing; golf 1km; games area; CKE. *"Delightful, well-kept, well-run, great site; friendly, helpful owner; some pitches sm; some steep site rds, tow avail; vg immac facs; superb pool; if recep clsd use intercom in door; gd dog walk adj; bus to Marseille; conv NH nr a'route; highly rec; v secure; easy access to Aix town; bank cards not acc."* **€29.50, 15 May-30 Sept.** **2024**

AIX LES BAINS *9B3* (7km SW Rural) *45.65511, 5.86142* **Camp Municipal L'Ile aux Cygnes,** La Croix Verte, 501 Blvd Ernest Coudurier, 73370 Le Bourget-du-Lac **04 79 25 01 76; camping@lebourgetdulac.fr; www.lebourgetdulac.fr / www.ileauxcygnes.fr/**

€1.50

Fr N foll Bourget-du-Lac & Lac sp soon after Tunnel Le Chat. Fr Chambéry take D1504 dir Aix-les-Bains; foll sp to Le Bourget-du-Lac & Le Lac, bear R at Camping/Plage sp to site at end of rd. 3*, Lge, shd, EHU (6A) inc; gas; sw; TV; 10% statics; phone; bus; adv bkg acc; watersports; boating; waterslide; CKE. *"On beautiful lake; mountain scenery; grnd stoney; tight pitches; poss cr; reasonable facs; site badly sp."* **€32.00, 6 Apr-30 Sept.** **2024**

AIX LES BAINS *9B3* (3km W Rural) *45.70005, 5.88666* **Camp Municipal International du Sierroz,** Blvd Robert Barrier, Route du Lac, 73100 Aix-les-Bains **04 79 61 89 89; info@camping-sierroz.com; www.camping-sierroz.com**

€1.60 (htd) WD MSP

Fr Annecy S on D1201, thro Aix-les-Bains, turn R at site sp. Keep to lakeside rd, site on R. Nr Grand Port. 3*, Med, mkd, hdg, unshd, EHU (6A) inc; gas; twin axles; TV; 5% statics; bus (ask at recep for free pass); adv bkg acc; ccard acc; golf 4km; games area; CKE. *"Pleasant location; lake adj for watersports; lge pitches; site crowded; pitches close together; san facs dirty."* **€27.90, 25 Mar-2 Nov.** 2023

AIXE SUR VIENNE *7B3* (0.8km NE Rural) *45.79887, 1.13928* **Camp Municipal Les Grèves,** Ave des Grèves, 87700 Aixe-sur-Vienne **06 73 67 23 48; camping@mairie-aixesurvienne.fr; www.mairie-aixesurvienne.fr**

WD MSP nr nr nr

SW fr Limoges for approx 13km, on N21 twds Périgueux, cross bdge over Rv Vienne & in about 600m turn to R (site sp) by rv. Steep down hill app & U-turn into site - take care gate posts! 2*, Med, shd, EHU (10A) €2.50 (poss rev pol); red long stay; adv bkg acc; fishing. *"Pleasant, clean site by rv; spacious pitches; helpful, friendly warden; gd san facs, but ltd LS; conv Limoges area & Vienne valley; several chateaux in easy reach; pool adj; no twin axles; vg."* **€20.40, 1 May-30 Sep.** 2024

AIZELLES *3C4* (0.4km NW Rural) *49.49076, 3.80817* **Camping du Moulin (Merlo),** 16 Rue du Moulin, 02820 Aizelles **03 23 22 41 18 or 06 14 20 47 43 (mob); magali.merlo@orange.fr; www.camping-du-moulin.fr**

WD nr

Fr Laon take D1044 dir Reims; in 13km turn L on D88 to Aizelles; site sp in vill 'Camping à la Ferme'. Fr Reims on A26 exit junc 14 onto D925 then D1044 N. Turn R to Aizelles on D889 past Corbeny. Turn onto Rue du Moulin & site on R in 250m. Camping sp at church says 100m but allow 300m to see ent. NB Lge o'fits take care sharp R turn at ent to site. Sm, pt shd, pt sl, EHU (6A) inc €3.80; Eng spkn; ccard acc; fishing 800m; CKE. *"Attractive, well-kept CL-type farm site; v friendly, helpful owners; basic san facs need update; gates clsd 2200-0700; wonderful well maintained site in a sm pretty vil; conv Calais 3 hrs; vg site; conv for Zeebrugge; few statics."* **€14.90, 1 Apr-15 Oct.** 2023

AIZENAY *2H4* (8km NW Rural) *46.75282, -1.68645* **Camping Val de Vie,** Rue du Stade, 85190 Maché **02 51 60 21 02; campingvaldevie@bbox.fr; www.campingvaldevie.fr**

€3 WD nr (htd)

Fr Aizenay on D948 dir Challans. After 5km turn L onto D40 to Maché. Fr vill cent cont twd Apremont. Sm, blue site sp 100m on L. 3*, Med, hdg, mkd, pt shd, pt sl, serviced pitches; EHU (6-10A) €3.50-4; gas; bbq; twin axles; red long stay; 20% statics; Eng spkn; adv bkg acc; fishing; bike hire; tennis adj; boat hire. *"Lovely, peaceful, well-run site in pretty vill; new young owners upgrading facs & rds (2011); warm welcome; clean san facs; steel pegs useful; gd touring base; gd cycling; excel."* **€25.90, 4 Apr-30 Sep.** 2022

"I need an on-site restaurant"

We do our best to make sure site information is correct, but it is always best to check any must-have facilities are still available or will be open during your visit.

ALBAN *8E4* (1km NW Rural) *43.89386, 2.45416* **Camp Municipal La Franquèze,** 81250 Alban **05 63 55 82 09 01 83 64 69 21; mairie.alban@wanadoo.fr; www.campingtarn.com/fr/camping-municipal-la-franqueze**

12

W of Albi on D999 turn L at ent to Alban. Site 300m on R, sp. 5*, Sm, hdg, pt shd, pt sl, terr, EHU (6A) €2.10; adv bkg acc; rv fishing; CKE. *"Beautiful area, conv Tarn Valley; vg; water taps scarce; gd hilltop site with views."* **€14.00** 2024

ALBERT *3B3* (1.5km N Urban) *50.01136, 2.65556* **Camp Municipal du Vélodrome,** Ave Henri Dunant, 80300 Albert **07 85 13 32 36; contact@campingalbert.fr; www.camping-albert.com**

WD MSP nr

Fr town cent take Rue Godin E adj to Basilica & foll sp for site. Easiest access fr Bapaume (N) twds Albert; turn R at camping sp on edge of town. 3*, Med, mkd, pt shd, EHU (4-10A) €2.20-4.40 (rev pol); red long stay; 40% statics; Eng spkn; adv bkg acc; fishing adj; CKE. *"Pleasant, well-run, well maintained, clean site; nr lake; friendly, helpful warden; poss security prob; conv for Lille, Arras & Amien by train & for WW1 battlefields etc; poss rlwy noise; facs basic but rates reasonable; if office close find pitch and inform warden later; gates clsd fairly early, will need ent code if late; easy walk into Albert; semi sep aire; unisex shwrs & wc."* **€19.50, 1 Apr-11 Oct.** 2024

FRANCE

ALBERT *3B3* (14km SW Rural) *49.91930, 2.57985* **FFCC Camping Les Puits Tournants,** 6 Rue du Marais, 80800 Sailly-le-Sec **03 22 76 65 56; camping.puits tournants@wanadoo.fr; http://www.camping-puits tournants.com**

(htd) (htd)

Fr N exit A1 junc 14 onto D929 dir Amiens, at Albert take D42 S to Sailly-Laurette then turn R onto D233 to Sailly-le-Sec & foll sp. Or fr S exit junc 13 twd Albert onto D1029. At Lamotte-Warfusée R onto D42 to Sailly-Laurette, turn L to Sailley-le-Sec. 3*, Med, mkd, hdstg, pt shd, EHU (6A) €4; gas; bbq; sw; TV; 60% statics; Eng spkn; adv bkg acc; ccard acc; games area; bike hire; canoe hire; fishing; horseriding 5km; tennis 2km. *"Lovely, pleasant family-run site; amiable staff; gd clean san facs, need updating; grass pitches muddy when wet; tight ent, lge o'fits poss diff; gd pool; walks by rv; excel; picturesque site nr rv Somme; nice dog walks by rv; facs poss stretched in HS; new pools & rest under construction (2017)."* **€21.20, 1 Apr-31 Oct.** **2023**

ALBI *8E4* (2km NE Urban) *43.93485, 2.16213* **Albirondack Park, Camping Lodge & Spa,** 31 Allée de la Piscine, 81000 Albi **05 63 60 37 06 or 06 84 04 23 13 (mob); albirondack@orange.fr; www.albirondack.fr**

€5 (htd) nr (htd)

Fr Albi ring rd/bypass exit sp Lacause/St Juéry (do not turn twd Millau). Strt over & foll sp Géant-Casino hypmkt & 'Centre Ville', then foll camping/ piscine sp. 3*, Med, mkd, pt shd, pt sl, EHU (10A) €5.70; bbq; 10% statics; bus; adv bkg acc; CKE. *"Vg, popular site in conv position; pitches unlevelled - soft in wet & some poss diff lge o'fits due trees; gd walk (40 min) by rv to town cent; Albi Cathedral; spa; Toulouse Lautrec exhibitions; spa & pool inc; excel rest; excel clean modern san facs; beware of low lying wooden & concrete posts; v cramped site; rec arr early."* **€36.50, 20 Jan-10 Nov & 2 Dec-31 Dec.** **2023**

ALBINE *8F4* (1km SW Rural) *43.45406, 2.52706* **Camping Le Stap,** Le Suc, 81240 Albine **05 63 98 34 74; campinglestap@orange.fr; www.campinglestap.com**

€2 nr

Fr Mazamet on D612 dir Béziers for approx 12km; turn R onto D88 sp Albine. On app to vill turn R at sp 'Camping du Lac'. Site in 1km. 3*, Sm, hdg, mkd, hdstg, pt shd, terr, EHU (6A) €4; gas; bbq (gas); Eng spkn; adv bkg acc; ccard acc; fishing; games area; CKE. *"Well-kept, clean site; superb views; facs adequate; excel touring base; poss diff lge o'fits due sm pitches & steep access; vg; new friendly French owners."* **€25.00, 27 Apr-5 Oct.** **2024**

ALENCON *4E1* (3km SW Rural) *48.42566, 0.07321* **Camp Municipal de Guéramé,** 65 Rue de Guéramé, 61000 Alençon **02 33 26 34 95; camping.gueramé@orange.fr; www.ville-alencon.fr**

€1.90 (htd) nr nr

Located nr town cent. Fr N on D38 take N12 W (Carrefour sp). In 5km take D1 L sp Condé-sur-Sarthe. At rndabt turn L sp Alençon then R immed after Carrefour supmkt, foll site sp. Site is sp fr D112 inner ring rd. 2*, Med, hdstg, hdg, pt shd, EHU (5A) €3.10 (check EHU carefully) (poss long lead req); bbq; TV; Eng spkn; adv bkg acc; bike hire; horseriding; rv fishing; tennis; canoeing; CKE. *"Helpful warden; clean san facs; o'night m'vans area; pool complex 700m; barrier/recep clsd 1800 LS; LS phone ahead to check site open; some pitches poss flood in heavy rain; rvside walk to town thro arboretum; peaceful site; great site; v interesting town; excel."* **€16.00, 1 Apr-30 Sep.** **2022**

ALERIA *10H2* (7km N Coastal) *42.16155, 9.55265* **Camping-Village Riva-Bella (Part Naturist),** 20270 Aléria **04 95 38 81 10; riva-bella@orange.fr; www.naturisme-rivabella.com**

12 €3.50 sand adj

Fr Bastia S on N198 for 60km, site sp to L. Poor rd access (2011). 3*, Med, pt shd, EHU €4.30; red long stay; TV; 10% statics; adv bkg acc; fishing; games area; watersports; bike hire; tennis; INF card. *"Site untidy early ssn (2011); fitness rm; steam rm; sauna; spa treatments; poss insect problem; naturist site 15 May-20 Sep, non-naturist rest of year - but always sm end beach avail for naturists."* **€36.00** **2023**

"Satellite navigation makes touring much easier"

Remember most sat navs don't know if you're towing or in a larger vehicle – always use yours alongside maps and site directions.

ALET LES BAINS *8G4* (0.3km W Rural) *42.99490, 2.25525* **Camping Val d'Aleth,** Ave Nicolas Pavillon, 11580 Alet-les-Bains **04 68 69 90 40; info@valdaleth.com; www.valdaleth.com**

12 €2.50 (htd) nr

Fr Limoux S on D118 twd Quillan; in approx 8km ignore 1st L turn over Aude bdge into vill but take alt rte for heavy vehicles. Immed after x-ing rv, turn L in front of casino & ent town fr S; site sp on L. 2*, Sm, hdg, mkd, hdstg, shd, pt sl, EHU (4-10A) €2.60-4.10; gas; bbq (gas); red long stay; 25% statics; phone; Eng spkn; adv bkg acc; ccard acc; bike hire; CKE. *"Rvside (no sw) site in attractive, medieval vill; sm pitches (lge o'fits need to book); friendly, helpful British owner; gd clean san facs; v few facs in vill; poss unkempt early ssn; conv Carcassonne & Cathar country - scenic; ACSI acc."* **€19.80** **2023**

ALLEGRE LES FUMADES *10E2* (2km NE Rural) *44.2089, 4.25665* **Camping Le Château de Boisson,** 30500 Allègre-les-Fumades **04 66 24 85 61 or 04 66 24 82 21; reception@chateaudeboisson.com; www.chateaudeboisson.com or www.les-castels.com**

€5 WD MSP (covrd, htd)

Fr Alès NE on D904, turn R after Les Mages onto D132, then L onto D16 for Boisson. Fr A7 take exit 19 Pont l'Esprit, turn S on N86 to Bagnols-sur-Cèze & then D6 W. Bef Vallérargues turn R onto D979 Lussan, then D37 & D16 to Boisson. 4*, Lge, mkd, hdg, shd, pt sl, EHU (6A) inc; gas; bbq (elec, gas); red long stay; 80% statics; phone; Eng spkn; adv bkg acc; ccard acc; games rm; tennis; bike hire. *"Vg, well-run, peaceful site; no o'fits over 7m high ssn; no dogs 9 Jul-20 Aug; gd sized pitches, poss some v sm; helpful staff; excel san facs; excel rest & facs; superb pool complex."* **€39.00, 12 Apr-27 Sep, C34.** **2023**

ALTKIRCH *6F3* (1km SE Rural) *47.61275, 7.23336* **Camp Municipal Les Acacias,** Rue de Hirtzbach, 68130 Altkirch **03 89 40 69 40 or 03 89 40 00 04 (Mairie); les-acacias@orange.fr; camping-acacias-altkirch.com/**

12 (htd) WD

Sp on D419 on app to town fr W. Sp in town. 3*, Sm, mkd, shd, EHU (10A) €3; 20% statics; Eng spkn; adv bkg rec; CKE. *"Lovely quiet site; gd, clean facs; office clsd until 1700 - site yourself & pay later; gd NH."* **€13.50** **2024**

AMBAZAC *7B3* (3km NE Rural) *45.97158, 1.41315* **Camping L'Ecrin Nature,** 87240 Ambazac **06 52 92 71 65 or 05 55 56 60 25; contact@campinglecrinnature.com; www.campinglecrinnature.com**

WD MSP (htd)

Fr A20 foll sp to Ambazac; site on D914. 3*, Med, mkd, hdg, pt shd, pt sl, terr, EHU (6A) €3.50; bbq; 15% statics; Eng spkn; adv bkg acc; ccard acc; lake fishing. *"Excel waterside site with lovely lake views, o'looking lake; v friendly new owners, who cont to improve this eco site; san facs clean; ctr for mountain biking & walking; much improved site; gd pool; hg rec; use barrier intercom to contact bureau on arr (bureau clsd midday-3pm); shgl beach adj (sw not allowed); excel site; peaceful; use intercom to gain access."* **€16.00, 5 Apr-29 Sept.** **2024**

AMBERT *9B1* (1km S Urban) *45.53951, 3.72867* **Camping Les Trois Chênes,** Rue de la Chaise-Dieu, 63600 Ambert **04 73 82 34 68; tourisme@ville-ambert.fr; www.camping-ambert.com**

€1 WD nr nr

On main rd D906 S twd Le Puy on L bet Leisure Park & Aquacentre. 3*, Med, mkd, hdg, pt shd, serviced pitches; EHU (10A) €3.25; 80% statics; adv bkg acc; waterslide; CKE. *"Excel, well-kept site; gd, clean san facs; rvside walk to town; htd pool adj; rec arrive bef noon peak ssn; recep & barrier clsd 1900 LS; steam museum & working paper mill nr; steam train 1.5km; vg."* **€19.00, 5 Apr-3 Nov.** **2024**

AMBIALET *8E4* (0.8km ESE Rural) *43.94181, 2.38686* **Camping La Mise à l'Eau,** Fédusse, 81430 Ambialet **05 63 79 58 29; rikkimayze@gmail.com; www.campinglamisealeau.com**

€1.50 nr nr nr

Fr Albi E on D999; in 15km, after Villefranche-d'Albigeois, turn L onto D74 to Ambialet; turn R at junc; in 100m bear L; site on L. Sharp turn, turning pnt avail down rd. NB App via D74 as v narr tunnels on D172/D700 to E & W of Ambialet. 2*, Sm, mkd, pt shd, EHU (6-10A) €2.15; adv bkg acc; kayaking; CKE. *"Easy walk to pretty vil; bar 500ml; clean facs; excel; pretty rvside site; no chem disp facs on site, use public toilet in vill."* **€21.90, 1 May-31 Oct.** **2022**

AMBOISE *4G2* (1km N Rural) *47.41763, 0.98717* **Camp Municipal L'Ile d'Or,** 37400 Amboise **02 47 57 23 37 or 02 47 23 47 38 (Mairie); camping@ville-amboise.fr; www.camping-amboise.com**

€1.60 (htd) WD MSP nr

Fr N exit A10 exit junc 18 onto D31/D431 to Amboise; at turn R onto D751 dir Blois & get in L lane to cross bdge on D431; site a turning L off bdge, on lge wooded island in Rv Loire. Fr S exit A85 junc 11 onto D31 dir Amboise; foll Centre Ville sp to rv on D431; get in L/H lane to cross bdge (dir Nazelles); turn R off bdge to site on island. 2*, Lge, mkd, pt shd, EHU (10A) inc (poss rev pol) €5.50; red long stay; TV; phone; Eng spkn; adv bkg acc; ccard acc; fishing; games area; tennis; CKE. *"Lovely, spacious, secure site in gd location adj Rv Loire & park; well-kept; lge pitches; htd pool & waterslide 500m (high ssn); nice rest & bar; easy walk to interesting old town; vg dog walking; conv Parc Léonardo Da Vinci (last place he lived) & Château d'Amboise; midsummer week music festival in adj park - check date; no twin axles; m'van o'night area open all year, excel stop out of ssn; gd value; vg; excel san facs, stretched in high ssn; v busy; excel facs."* **€17.00, 31 Mar-9 Oct.** **2024**

AMBOISE *4G2* (7km NE Rural) *47.44580, 1.04669* **Camping Le Jardin Botanique,** 9 bis, Rue de la Rivière, 37530 Limeray **02 47 30 13 50; campingjardin botanique@wanadoo.fr; www.camping-jardinbotanique.com**

€1.50 (htd) WD MSP nr

NE fr Amboise on D952 on N side of Rv Loire dir Blois; in approx 6km turn L for Limeray & then immed turn L onto Rue de la Rivière; site on L in 500m. NB Rec not to app fr Limeray, narr rds & diff for lge o'fits. 3*, Med, hdg, mkd, hdstg, pt shd, EHU (10A) €5 (poss rev pol); gas; bbq; red long stay; TV; 20% statics; Eng spkn; adv bkg acc; bike hire; tennis; games area; CKE. *"Gd for Loire chateaux; 500m fr rv; friendly & helpful owner; gd for children; gd gourmet rest adj; poss muddy when wet; gd cycle rtes; poorly maintained facs (2014)."* **€22.80, 3 Apr-1 Nov.** **2022**

FRANCE

AMBRIERES LES VALLEES *4E1* (2km SW Rural) *48.39121, -0.61680* **Camping Le Parc de Vaux,** 35 Rue des Colverts, 53300 Ambrières-les-Vallées **02 43 04 90 25; contact@parcdevaux.com; www.parcdevaux.com**

€1.80 nr (htd)

Fr S on D23 turn R at sp 'Parc de Loisirs de Vaux'. Site in approx 100m on bank Rv Varenne. Check in at Office de Tourisme bef site recep. 3*, Med, hdg, mkd, hdstg, pt shd, terr, EHU (10A) €3.20 (poss long lead req) (poss rev pol); bbq; red long stay; TV; 40% statics; Eng spkn; adv bkg acc; tennis; canoe hire; fishing; games area; bike hire; waterslide; CKE. *"Excel site in beautiful surroundings; lake adj; helpful recep; nice rvside site adj to leisure pool; vill 20 mins along rv."*
€19.00, 1 Apr-31 Oct. **2024**

AMIENS *3C3* (10km N Rural) *49.97240, 2.30150* **FFCC Camping du Château,** Rue du Château, 80260 Bertangles **09 51 66 32 60; camping@chateaubertangles.com; www.chateaubertangles.com**

nr

Foll N25 N of Amiens; after 8km turn W on D97 to Bertangles. Well sp in vill. 2*, Sm, hdg, pt shd, EHU (5A) €3.70 (poss rev pol); red long stay; bus; CKE. *"Pleasant, peaceful, well-kept site by chateau wall; pitches gd size; busy high ssn, early arr rec (bef 1600); pleasant welcome; clean, old san facs; ltd recep hrs, pitch yourself; grnd soft when wet; Amiens attractive city; gd walks; conv a'routes & NH; excel; gd value; basic site, needs updating; lovely location; gd dogs walk adj; bread avail fr recep in morning."*
€21.00, 21 Apr-11 Sep. **2023**

"There aren't many sites open at this time of year"

If you're travelling outside peak season remember to call ahead to check site opening dates – even if the entry says 'open all year'.

AMIENS *3B3* (32km N Rural) *50.13813, 2.36842* **Camping Familial Au Bord De l'Authie,** Route d'Albert 80600 Authieule **03 22 32 56 13 or 06 74 59 92 65 (mob); contact@campingauborddelauthie.com; www.campingauborddelauthie.com**

Fr Amiens N25 twd Rue de Longpré, turn R at Doullens onto D938. After 2.6 km site on R. Sm, mkd, shd, pt sl, terr, EHU (6A); bbq; 80% statics; Eng spkn; adv bkg acc; CCI. **€13.00, 1 Feb-1 Dec.** **2024**

AMIENS *3C3* (5km NW Urban) *49.92091, 2.25883* **Camping Parc des Cygnes,** 111 Ave des Cygnes, 80080 Amiens-Longpré **03 22 43 29 28; contact@amiens-campingdescygnes.com; www.parcdescygnes.com**

€2 (htd)

Exit A16 junc 20 twds Amiens onto ring rd Rocade Nord exit junc 40. At 1st rndabt foll sp Amiens, Longpré D412; foll sp Parc de Loisirs & site. 4*, Med, mkd, pt shd, EHU (10A) inc on most pitches (poss long lead req); gas; bbq; twin axles; TV; phone; bus to city adj; adv bkg rec; ccard acc; fishing nr; bike hire; games rm; kayaking; CKE. *"Peaceful, well-kept, secure site in parkland; leisure park adj; lge pitches; helpful, welcoming staff; gd, clean san facs, ltd LS; ring bell by recep if office clsd; no o'fits over 11m high ssn; access to grass pitches off hard areas - m'vans can keep driving wheels on in wet weather; gd canal-side cycling/walk to city; Amiens cathedral worth visit; longer leads req for some pitches; conv Somme battlefields; gd; rec; 50% of pitches have EHU; new san facs (2019); Veloroute Vallee de la Somme adj."*
€23.00, 1 Apr-16 Oct, P11. **2023**

ANCENIS *2G4* (12km E Rural) *47.36702, -1.01275* **Camping de l'Ile Batailleuse,** St Florent-le-Vieil, 44370 Varades **02 40 96 70 20; camping.ecoloire@mauges-sur-loire; naxiresa.inaxel.com/etape1-criteres.php?compte=ecoloire44**

€1.20 nr nr

On Ancenis-Angers rd D723 turn S in Varades onto D752 to St Florent-le-Vieil. After x-ing 1st bdge over Rv Loire site on L on island immed bef 2nd bdge. 2*, Med, pt shd, EHU (10A) €2; Eng spkn; bike hire; games area; tennis 1km; CKE. *"Basic, clean site; main shwr facs up stone staircase; panoramic views of Rv Loire in town; gd cycle rtes along rv; new san facs (2014); v pleasant sites."* **€18.00, 30 May-14 Sep.** **2024**

ANCENIS *2G4* (5km SW Rural) *47.34400, -1.20693* **Camp Municipal Beauregret,** 49530 Drain **02 40 98 20 16 (Mairie); mairie-sg.drain@wanadoo.fr**

nr

Fr Ancenis take D763 S for 2km, turn R onto D751 & cont for 3km. Site on R bef vill of Drain on L. 2*, Sm, hdg, pt shd, EHU (10A) inc (poss rev pol); bbq; TV; adv bkg acc; games area. *"Secluded, tranquil site; immac san facs up steps - ltd number; poss not suitable lge o'fits; warden calls am & pm; gd fishing; lake nrby; nice quiet site."* **€13.00, 1 May-30 Sep.** **2024**

ANCENIS *2G4* (1.5km W Rural) *47.36201, -1.18721* **FFCC Camping de l'Ile Mouchet,** 44156 Ancenis Cedex **02 40 83 08 43 or 06 62 54 24 73 (mob); camping-ile-mouchet@orange.fr; www.camping-estivance.com**

(htd) nr

Fr S, exit N249 at Vallet onto D763 to Ancenis; turn L immed after x-ing Rv Loire & foll sp; site on banks of rv. Or fr N, exit A11 junc 20 onto D923 to Ancenis; cont on D923 over rndabt; foll D923 along rv; in 400m, at next rndabt, do not cross rv but cont strt on onto D23; site sp to L in 700m. 3*, Med, mkd, pt shd, EHU (6-10A) €4 (rev pol); gas; TV; 12% statics; Eng spkn; adv bkg acc; ccard acc; waterslide; tennis 50m; games rm; CKE. *"Excel touring base; ltd facs LS; some steps; rvside walks; gd site with modern facs; worth a couple of nights; recep clsd 1200-1430."*
€23.30, 2 Apr-23 Oct. **2022**

ANDELYS, LES *3D2* (2.5km SW Rural) *49.23582, 1.40016* **Camping de L'Ile des Trois Rois,** 1 rue Gilles Nicolle, 27700 Les Andelys **02 32 54 23 79; contact@camping-troisrois.com; www.camping-troisrois.com**

€4 (htd) (htd)

Fr Rouen S on A13, exit junc 18 onto D135 & foll sp Les Andelys. Cross bdge over Rv Seine & turn immed R at rndabt, site on R on rvside. Site sp fr town cent. Med, hdstg, mkd, hdg, pt shd, EHU (10A) inc; gas; bbq; red long stay; TV; 20% statics; phone; Eng spkn; adv bkg acc; ccard acc; fishing; bike hire; games rm; CKE. *"Well-kept site on Rv Seine; extra lge pitches avail; friendly, helpful staff; gd security; conv Rouen, Evreux, Giverny; bowling alley; view ruins of Château Gaillard; nice place, nice people; excel; refurbished, clean, modern san facs, sw pool, vg bar & rest; easy walk to old town; hugh site; gd dog walk adj."* **€29.00, 15 Mar-15 Nov.** **2024**

See advertisement

ANDERNOS LES BAINS *7D1* (5km NW Coastal) *44.77792, -1.14280* **FLOWER Camping La Canadienne,** 82 Rue du Général de Gaulle, 33740 Arès **44.778539, -1.143136; info@lacanadienne.com; www.lacanadienne.com or www.flowercampings.com**

€2.50 sand 2km

N fr town sq at Arès on D3 (Rue du Général de Gaulle) dir Cap Ferret. Site on R after 1km. 4*, Med, shd, EHU (15A) inc; gas; TV; adv bkg rec; bike hire; archery; tennis; windsurfing 1km; fishing 1km; canoe hire; games rm; sailing 1km.
€31.00, 1 Feb-30 Nov. **2020**

ANDUZE *10E1* (1.5km SE Rural) *44.03824, 3.99454* **Camping Le Bel Eté,** 1870 Route de Nîmes, 30140 Anduze **04 66 61 76 04; contact@camping-bel-ete.com; www.camping-bel-ete.com**

€1.50 nr

S fr Alès on D6110; W on D910A to Anduze. In Anduze take D907 SE twds Nîmes. Site on L, 200m after rlwy bdge. 4*, Med, mkd, pt shd, serviced pitches; EHU (6A) €4.50; gas; 10% statics; phone; adv bkg req; ccard acc; CKE. *"Delightful, well-kept site in superb location; vg facs but ltd LS; helpful owner; rv adj; gd base for Cévennes area; Thurs mkt."*
€33.50, 8 May-17 Sep. **2020**

ANDUZE *10E1* (1.4km NW Rural) *44.06430, 3.97694* **Camping Castel Rose,** 610 Chemin de Recoulin, 30140 Anduze **04 66 61 80 15; castelrose@wanadoo.fr; www.castelrose.com**

€2

Fr Alès S on D6110 & W on N910A to Anduze. Foll sp Camping L'Arche. 3*, Lge, shd, EHU (6-10A) €3.20-4; gas; TV; Eng spkn; adv bkg rec; fishing; boating. *"Excel site by rv; friendly, helpful owners; attractive countryside; gd cent touring Cévennes."*
€50.00, 12 Apr-22 Sep. **2024**

FRANCE

ANDUZE *10E1* (2km NW Rural) *44.06785, 3.97336*
Camping L'Arche, Route de Saint Jean du Gard, 30140 Anduze **04 66 61 74 08; contact@camping-arche.fr; www.camping-arche.fr**
€3.80 (htd) (covrd, htd)

Fr Alès S on D6110/D910A to Anduze. On D907, sp on R. Access poss dff lge o'fits/m'vans. 5*, Lge, mkd, shd, EHU (10A) €2; gas; bbq; red long stay; TV; 10% statics; Eng spkn; adv bkg acc; waterslide; CKE. *"Well-run site; gd san facs; beautiful area; bamboo gardens worth visit; 24hr security patrols; excel rest; outstanding site; vg value."*
€48.00, 7 Apr-27 Sep. 2024

ANET *3D2* (0.5km N Urban) *48.86183, 1.44166*
Camp Municipal Les Eaux Vives, 1 Route des Cordeliers, 28260 Anet **02 37 41 42 67 or 06 09 74 16 90 (mob); martine.desrues@cegetel.net; www.camping-anet.fr**
€1.10 (htd) nr

Take D928 NE fr Dreux; in Anet thro town & take 1st L after chateau; turn L on rd to Ezy & Ivry (camp sp on corner), site in 150m N of rv.
2*, Lge, pt shd, serviced pitches; EHU (10A) €3; sw nr; 95% statics; Eng spkn; tennis; fishing 2km; CKE. *"Rvside pitches; helpful warden; clean, v basic san facs, poss stretched high ssn; rv adj; grnd soft in wet - site poss clsd early; gd walks in forest; chateau in vill; easy drive to Paris; untidy statics (2010); conv NH."*
€14.00, 1 Mar-31 Oct. 2024

ANET *3D2* (1km N Urban) *48.86278, 1.41552*
Camp Municipal Les Trillots, Chemin des Trillots, 27530 Ezy-sur-Eure **02 37 64 73 21 or 02 37 64 73 48 (Mairie)**
(htd) nr nr nr

N fr Dreux on D928/D143. Site on N side of Rv Eure. Med, pt shd, EHU (4A) inc; bbq; 95% statics. *"Quiet site adj rvside walks; gd san facs; helpful warden; poss not suited to tourers; not rec."*
€13.00, 1 Mar-15 Nov. 2020

ANGERS *4G1* (15km SE Rural) *47.44332, -0.40881*
Camping du Port Caroline, Rue du Pont Caroline, 49800 Brain-sur-l'Authion **02 41 80 42 18; info@campingduportcaroline.fr; www.campingduportcaroline.fr**
€3 (htd) nr (htd)

E fr Angers on D347 turn onto D113, site sp at ent to vill. 3*, Med, hdstg, hdg, mkd, pt shd, EHU (10A) inc; bbq; TV; 5% statics; adv bkg acc; ccard acc; games rm; tennis nr; fishing nr. *"Gd touring base; games area adj; skateboarding; site clsd Feb; lge pitches."*
€41.00, 1 Apr-31 Oct. 2023

ANGERS *4G1* (7km SE Urban) *47.42442, -0.52701*
Slow Camp Loire Vallée (formerly Camping L'Ile du Château), Ave de la Boire Salée, 49130 Les Ponts-de-Cé **02 85 35 97 47; contact@slow-camp.fr; www.slow-village.fr/loire-vallee**
€2 sand 500m

Fr Angers take D160 (sp Cholet) to Les Ponts-de-Cé. Foll sp 'Centre Ville' & turn R at rndabt in town opp Hôtel de Ville, & site on R in 200m on banks of Rv Loire. 3*, Med, hdg, shd, EHU (10A) inc (poss rev pol); bbq; TV; 4% statics; phone; Eng spkn; tennis; games rm; golf 5km; waterslide adj; games area; CKE. *"Well-kept, scenic site; excel pool adj; gd touring base for chateaux, vineyards; htd pool adj; gd dog walking; highly rec; v shd, few sunny pitches; v busy area; organised entmnt."* **€31.00, 6 Apr-3 Nov. 2024**

ANGERS *4G1* (6km SW Urban) *47.41878, -0.61160*
Camping Aire d'Accueil de Camping Cars, 25 Rue Chevrière, 49080 Bouchemaine **02 41 77 11 04 or 02 41 22 20 00 (Mairie); www.ville-bouchemaine.fr**
12 nr nr

Fr Angers take D160 S, at intersection with D112 W sp Bouchemaine. Cross Rv Maine via suspension bdge. At rndabt on W bank turn L, site on L in 100m dir La Pointe adj rv. Fr Château-Gontier take N162, then D106, then D102E. Bouchemaine well sp.
2*, Sm, hdstg, pt shd, EHU (16A) €2.55 (poss rev pol); phone; bus; adv bkg acc; games area; CKE. *"M'vans & tents only; warden calls am & pm; free Oct-Apr but no EHU; san facs upstairs; poss flooding nr rv; vg NH; automated access; pool 500m; excel cycling, track into Angers."* **€11.00 2024**

ANGERS *4G1* (6km SW Urban) *47.45387, -0.59463*
Camping d'Angers - Lac de Maine, Ave du Lac de Maine, 49000 Angers **02 41 81 97 37; www.campingangers.com**
€2.30 (htd) nr (htd)

W fr Angers on D723, exit at 'Quartier du Lac de Maine' then foll sp to site & Bouchemaine. After 4 rndabts site on L; sp W of Rv Maine. Fr S on D160 or A87, turn onto D4 at Les Ponts-de-Cé. In 6km, cross Rv Maine to Bouchemaine & turn R to Pruniers dir Angers. Site on R at Pruniers town exit sp. 4*, Med, hdstg, mkd, hdg, pt shd, serviced pitches; EHU (10A) inc (rev pol); gas; bbq; sw nr; red long stay; twin axles; TV; 10% statics; phone; bus adj; Eng spkn; adv bkg rec; ccard acc; boating; fishing; tennis 800m; games area; windsurfing 500m; jacuzzi; bike hire; CKE. *"Excel, lge, well-run site in leisure park; pitches narr, some suitable v l'ge o'fits; height barrier at ent 3.2m; conv Loire chateaux; pay 6 nights, stay 7; hypmkt 2km; facs ltd in LS; solar shwrs; few lights on site; gd cycling & walking rte; canoeing; gd bus svrs; excel san facs; v helpful recep; bread avail; easy cycle route to Angers Chateau and along La Loire Rv."* **€30.90, 3 Apr-3 Nov. 2024**

ANGOULEME *7B2* (6.7km N Rural) *45.68573, 0.14994* **Camping du Plan d'Eau,** 1 rue du Camping, 16710 St Yrieix-sur-Charante **05 45 92 14 64; camping@grandangouleme.fr; www.camping-angouleme.fr**

(htd)

Fr N or S on N10/E606 turn NW & foll sp St Yrieix-sur-Charante, 'Plan d'Eau' & 'Nautilis - Centre Nautique'. Site sp. 4*, Med, mkd, hdg, pt shd, EHU (10A) €3.50; gas; bbq; sw nr; TV; 10% statics; Eng spkn; adv bkg acc; ccard acc; games area; watersports. *"Superb location; gd; rather bare site; notices warn of poss flooding."* **€21.10, 1 Apr-16 Oct. 2022**

ANGOULEME *7B2* (23km NW Rural) *45.79769, 000.63639* **Camping Du Lac de Bignac (formerly Camping Marco de Bignac),** Chemin de la Résistance, 16170 Bignac **05 45 21 78 41; www.campingdulacdebignac.fr**

(htd)

Fr N10 approx 14km N Angoulême take exit La Touche & foll D11 W thro Vars; at Basse turn R onto D117 & foll sp in Bignac. (Foll sp not Sat Nav due to new rd layout at Basse). 3*, Med, mkd, pt shd, EHU (3-6A) €3-4; bbq (charcoal, elec, gas); twin axles; red long stay; 3% statics; bus adj; Eng spkn; adv bkg acc; ccard acc; games area; tennis; fishing; watersports; bike hire; pets corner; CKE. *"Attractive, peaceful, tidy, lakeside site; worth long drive; scenic area; lge pitches; welcoming, helpful British owners; clean refurb san facs; gd rest; pleasant walk round lake; lake adj; ideal for Angoulême Circuit des Remparts; excel; pets corner; excel."* **€29.00, 14 Mar-14 Oct. 2024**

ANNECY *9B3* (10km SE Rural) *45.84070, 6.16450* **Camping Le Solitaire du Lac,** 615 Route de Sales, 74410 St Jorioz **04 50 68 59 30 or 06 88 58 94 24 (mob); contact@campinglesolitaire.com or campinglesolitaire@wanadoo.fr; www.campinglesolitaire.com**

€4 nr

Exit Annecy on D1508 twd Albertville. Site sp on N o'skts of St Jorioz. 3*, Med, mkd, pt shd, EHU €6; gas; bbq; sw; red long stay; TV; 10% statics; Eng spkn; adv bkg acc; ccard acc; boat launch; games area; bike hire; CKE. *"Nice, well-run site in excel location; water to MH's charge €0.20 per 60l; popular but quiet; cycle track; sm pitches; clean, modern san facs; direct access to Lake Annecy; sh walk to public beach & water bus; cycle path nr; gd touring base; excel; perfect for boating & cycling; v helpful staff."* **€30.00, 8 Apr-23 Sep. 2023**

ANNECY *9B3* (11km SE Rural) *45.82423, 6.18523* **Camping Le Familial,** 400 Route de Magnonnet, 74410 Duingt **04 50 68 69 91; contact@annecy-camping-familial.com**

€1.70

Fr Annecy on D1508 twd Albertville. 5km after St Jorioz turn R at site sp Entrevernes onto D8, foll sp past Camping Champs Fleuris. 2*, Sm, mkd, hdstg, pt shd, pt sl, EHU (6A) €4.30; bbq; twin axles; TV; Eng spkn; adv bkg rec; ccard acc; games area; CKE. *"Gd site in scenic area; gd atmosphere; generous pitches; friendly, helpful owner; communal meals & fondu evenings; conv lakeside cycle track; mobile homes for rent, sleeps 6; excel."* **€32.50, 1 Apr-30 Sep. 2023**

ANNECY *9B3* (8km SE Rural) *45.86305, 6.19690* **Camping Le Clos Don Jean,** Route du Clos Don Jean, 74290 Menthon-St-Bernard **04 50 60 18 66; donjean74@orange.fr; www.campingclosdonjean.com**

€1

Fr N site clearly sp fr vill of Menthon. L uphill for 400m. 2*, Med, mkd, pt shd, pt sl, EHU (3-6A) €2.60-3; gas; sw nr; Eng spkn; Bakery; CKE. *"Excel site in orchard; clean san facs, ltd LS; fine views chateau & lake; walk to lake."* **€21.00, 1 Jun-31 Aug. 2020**

ANNECY *9B3* (10km S Rural) *45.82995, 6.18215* **Village Camping Europa,** 1444 Route d'Albertville, 74410 St Jorioz **04 50 68 51 01; info@camping-europa.com; www.campingeuropa.com**

€3 nr (htd)

Fr Annecy take D1508 sp Albertville. Site on R 800m S of St Jorioz dir Albertville. Look for lge yellow sp on o'skirts of St Jorioz. 4*, Med, hdg, pt shd, serviced pitches; EHU (6A) inc; bbq (elec, gas); red long stay; twin axles; TV; 20% statics; Eng spkn; adv bkg acc; ccard acc; bike hire; jacuzzi; boat hire; fishing; waterslide; games rm; tennis 700m; windsurfing; CKE. *"Peaceful site; friendly staff; facs stretched high ssn; vg rest; excel for m'vans; conv Chamonix & Mont Blanc; variable pitch prices; cycle track adj; some pitches tight lge o'fits; gd tourist base; excel; no water points around site, collect fr toilet block; brilliant pool complex; no hot water in sinks; gd cycling area."* **€58.00, 30 Apr-17 Sep. 2023**

ANNECY *9B3* (6km S Urban) *45.85482, 6.14395* **Camping au Coeur du Lac,** Les Choseaux, 74320 Sévrier **04 50 52 46 45; info@aucoeurdulac.com; www.campingaucoeurdulac.com**

S fr Annecy on D1508 sp Albertville. Pass thro Sévrier cent. Site on L at lakeside 1km S of Sévrier. 300m after McDonald's. 3*, Med, mkd, hdstg, pt shd, pt sl, terr, EHU (4A) €3.60, long cable rec; sw; bus nrby; Eng spkn; adv bkg req; ccard acc; boat hire; bike hire; CKE. *"Busy, nice site in lovely location; gd views of lake fr upper terr; tight for lge o'fits - sm, sl pitches; dogs not acc high ssn; ok san facs; gd access to lake beach & cycle path; excel, espec LS; v popular site."* **€32.20, 1 Apr-24 Sep. 2022**

FRANCE

FRANCE

ANNECY *9B3* (6km S Rural) *45.84333, 6.14175*
Camping Le Panoramic, 22 Chemin des Bernets, Route de Cessenaz, 74320 Sévrier **04 50 52 43 09; info@camping-le-panoramic.com; www.camping-le-panoramic.com**
€1.60 (htd) 2km

Exit A41 junc 16 Annecy Sud onto D1508 sp Albertville. Thro Sévrier to rndabt at Cessenaz (ignore all prior sp to site) & take 1st R onto D10. In 200m turn R up hill to site in 2km. 3*, Lge, mkd, pt shd, pt sl, terr, EHU (4-6A) €3.20-4.20 (some rev pol); sw; TV; Eng spkn; ccard acc; games rm; CKE. *"Fantastic views fr many pitches; blocks/wedges ess for sl pitches; excel pool/bar area; rec for families; new san facs (2012); excel views of lake; v friendly staff; high rec."* **€31.00, 19 Apr-29 Sep. 2024**

"I like to fill in the reports as I travel from site to site"

You'll find report forms at the back of this guide, or you can fill them in online at camc.com/europereport.

ANNECY *9B3* (6.5km S Urban) *45.84412, 6.15354*
Camping de l'Aloua, 492 Route de Piron, 74320 Sévrier **04 50 52 60 06; camping.aloua@wanadoo.fr; www.camping-aloua-lac-annecy.com**
€4 shgl 300m

Foll sp for Albertville D1508 S fr Annecy. Site on E side, approx 1.4km S of Sevrier vill. Turn L at Champion supmkt rndabt & foll sp twd lake. 2*, Lge, hdg, mkd, shd, EHU (10A) €6; sw nr; TV; phone; Eng spkn; adv bkg acc; fishing adj; watersports adj; archery; boating adj; CKE. *"Gd base for lake (no dir access fr site); cycle track around lake; night security; poss noisy at night with youths & some rd noise; basic san facs; pleasant owners; well run & maintained site; nr lac Annecy, Carrefour & g'ge; bike track or bus to Annecy; vg."* **€32.00, 18 Apr-19 Sep. 2023**

ANNECY *9B3* (6.5km S Rural) *45.84806, 6.15129*
FFCC Camping Les Rives du Lac, 331 Chemin du Communaux, 74320 Sévrier **04 50 52 40 14; lesrivesdulac-annecy@ffcc.fr; www.lesrivesdulac-annecy.com**
€1.20 nr shgl

Take D1508 S fr Annecy sp Albertville, thro Sévrier sp FFCC. Turn L 100m past (S) Lidl supmkt, cross cycle path & turn R & foll sp FFCC keeping parallel with cycle path. Site on L in 400m. 3*, Med, mkd, pt shd, EHU (10A) €4; bbq; sw; bus nr; Eng spkn; adv bkg acc; sailing; fishing; CKE. *"Beautiful situation; generous pitches; helpful staff; excel new toilet block; water bus to Annecy nr; gd touring base; walking; red CC members (check first); walking, sailing & cycling; cycle rte adj."* **€32.00, 30 Mar-30 Sep. 2024**

ANNECY *9B3* (9km S Rural) *45.49484, 6.1055*
Camping International du Lac d'Annecy, 1184 Route d'Albertville, 74410 St Jorioz **04 50 68 67 93; contact@camping-lac-annecy.com; www.camping-lac-annecy.com**
€2.50 (htd)

Fr Annecy take D1508 sp Albertville. Site on R just after St Jorioz. 4*, Med, hdstg, mkd, hdg, pt shd, EHU (6-10A) €4-5.60; gas; bbq (elec, gas); sw nr; TV; 30% statics; phone; bus 500m; Eng spkn; adv bkg acc; ccard acc; bike hire; games area; Mini Club - children's entertainment (July and August); CKE. *"Lovely site; gd san facs; excel for touring lake area; site ent tight for med/lge o'fits (2009); vg cycling; gd rest nrby."* **€36.00, 30 April -21 Sep. 2020**

ANNECY *9B3* (7km SW Rural) *45.86131, 6.05214*
Aire Naturelle La Vidome (Lyonnaz), 18 route de la vidome, 74600 Montagny-les-Lanches **04 50 46 61 31; j.lyonnaz@wanadoo.fr**
12 €0.80 nr

Exit Annecy on D1201 sp Aix-les-Bains/Chambéry; after 6km at Le Treige turn R sp Montagny-les-Lanches. In 1km turn R in Avulliens; site on R in 100m. 2*, Sm, pt shd, pt sl, EHU (3-10A) €2.10-4; adv bkg acc; horseriding 1km; fishing 1km; CKE. *"Excel site; gd views; meals avail; friendly owners; vg san facs; access poss tight for lge o'fits; beach & mini golf 10km; pool 3km; gd touring base."* **€15.00 2024**

APREMONT *2H4* (2km N Rural) *46.77848, -1.73394*
Camping Les Charmes, Route de la Roussière, 85220 Apremont **02 28 17 67 77; accueil@campingles charmes.com; www.campinglescharmes.com**
€2.80

Fr D948 Challans to Aizenay turn W onto D94 sp Commequiers; after 2km L, sp Les Charmes. 4*, Med, mkd, pt shd, EHU (6-10A) €3.30-4 (poss rev pol); gas; sw nr; red long stay; TV; 60% statics; Eng spkn; adv bkg acc; ccard acc; CKE. *"Beautiful, well-kept site; generous pitches but soft when wet; welcoming, friendly, helpful owners; excel, clean san facs; a great find."* **€28.80, 1 Jun-30 Sep. 2024**

APT *10E3* (8km N Rural) *43.92050, 5.34120*
Domaine des Chenes Blancs, Route de Gargas, 84490 St Saturnin-lès-Apt **04 88 70 00 07; contact@ leschenesblancs.com; www.luberon-camping.fr/en**
€4 (htd)

Fr W on D900 twd Apt, at NW o'skts of Apt turn N on D101, cont approx 2km turn R on D83 into Gargas; thro Gargas & in 4km turn L at camp sp; site on R in 300m. Narr rd. 3*, Lge, hdg, shd, EHU (6A) inc; bbq; TV; Eng spkn; adv bkg rec; ccard acc; lake fishing 5km; games area. *"Well-run, popular site in gd location; pitches amongst oaks poss diff lge o'fits; steel pegs req due stony grnd; friendly staff; vg, modern san facs; nice pool; excel touring base; lots of facs; dated san facs (2015); dusty."* **€29.50, 1 Apr-6 Nov. 2022**

APT *10E3* (0.5km NE Urban) *43.87753, 5.40302* **Camping des Cèdres (formerly Camp Municipal Les Cèdres),** 63 Impasse de la Fantaisie, 84400 Apt **04 90 74 14 61 or 04 90 36 52 20; www.escapade-vacances.com**

€1 (htd) WD MSP

In town turn N off D900 onto D22 twd Rustrel, site sp. Site on R in 200m immed after going under old rlwy bdge. 2*, Med, mkd, pt shd, EHU (6-10A) €3.50; gas; cooking facs; adv bkg acc; ccard acc; CKE. *"Excel site in lovely location; sm pitches; pitching poss haphazard LS; friendly staff; clean san facs; some pitches muddy when wet; cycle tracks; conv Luberon vills & ochre mines; phone ahead to check open LS; v lge mkt Sat; gd NH; site in 2 parts; popular; gd touring cent."* **€23.50, 1 Mar-31 Oct.** 2024

ARAMITS *8F1* (0.3km W Rural) *43.12135, -0.73215* **Camping Barétous-Pyrénées,** Quartier Ripaude, 64570 Aramits **05 59 34 12 21; contact@camping-pyrenees.com; www.camping-pyrenees.com**

€2.80 WD MSP nr nr (htd)

SW fr Oloron-Ste Marie take D919 sp Aramits, Arette. Fr Aramits cont on D919 sp Lanne; site on R; well sp. 4*, Sm, mkd, pt shd, serviced pitches; EHU (10A) €4.90; twin axles; TV; 50% statics; Eng spkn; adv bkg acc; games rm; bike hire; CKE. *"Friendly, helpful owner; well-kept, clean, lovely site but muddy when wet; ltd facs LS; dated but v clean; gd base for Pyrenees; poss unrel opening dates - phone ahead LS; excel bistro 400m; vg."* **€33.80, 4 Apr-1 Oct.** 2022

ARBOIS *6H2* (1.5km E Urban) *46.90331, 5.78691* **Camping Les Vignes (formerly Camp Municipal Les Vignes),** 5 Rue de la Piscine, 39600 Arbois **06 46 51 91 54; camping@au-coeur-des-vignes.com; https://au-coeur-des-vignes.com**

€2.50 WD MSP

Fr N or S, ent town & at rndabt in cent foll camp sp on D107 dir Mesnay. Site adj stadium & pool. NB Steep slopes to terr & narr ent unsuitable lge o'fits. 3*, Med, hdg, mkd, hdstg, pt shd, pt sl, terr, EHU (10A) inc; gas; twin axles; TV; Eng spkn; adv bkg acc; ccard acc; tennis; fishing 1km; CKE. *"Beautiful setting; clean san facs but poss stretched high ssn; site clsd 2200-0800 LS; ltd facs LS; pitches on lower tier mostly sl; pleasant sm town, home of Louis Pasteur a must see; htd pool adj; Roman salt works, grottoes nr, lge fair 1st w/end in Sep; excel; linear site; shd pitches at W end furthest fr main facs; poss rallies."* **€24.50, 1 Apr-30 Sep.** 2024

ARC EN BARROIS *6F1* (0.5km W Urban) *47.95052, 5.00523* **Camp Municipal Le Vieux Moulin,** 2 Aubepierre Road, 52210 Arc-en-Barrois **03 25 02 51 33 (Mairie); contact@arc-en-barrois.fr; www.arc-en-barrois.com**

€2.18 (htd) WD MSP nr

Exit A5 junc 24 onto D10 S to Arc-en-Barrois; turn R onto D3 thro vill; site on L on o'skirts. Or fr D65 turn L onto D6 about 4km S of Châteauvillain; site on R on D3 at ent to vill, adj rv. 4*, Med, pt shd, EHU (6A) inc; bbq; TV; tennis adj; CKE. *"Attractive, peaceful, lovely, well-kept site by sm rv; adj vill sports field; basic, clean san facs but need update - excel hot shwrs; warden calls early eve, poss not on Sundays; gd wildlife; gd facs; beautiful vill; conv NH fr A5 or longer."* **€12.00, 1 Apr-1 Oct.** 2024

ARCACHON *7D1* (0.5km E Coastal) *44.65089, -1.17381* **Camping Club d'Arcachon,** 5 Allée de la Galaxie, 33312 Arcachon **05 56 83 24 15; info@camping-arcachon.com; www.camping-arcachon.com**

€4 (htd) WD MSP sand 1.5km

Exit A63 ont A660 dir Arcachon. Foll sp 'Hôpital Jean Hameau' & site sp. 4*, Lge, hdstg, mkd, hdg, pt shd, terr, EHU (10A) €4; gas; bbq; TV; 40% statics; Eng spkn; adv bkg acc; ccard acc; bike hire; site clsd mid-Nov to mid-Dec; CKE. *"Vg site in pine trees; excel touring base; gd facs; access rds narr - poss diff manoeuvring into pitches; gd network cycle tracks; private san facs avail; easy walk to town."* **€44.00, 1 Jan-14 Nov, 15 Dec-31 Dec.** 2023

> **"We must tell the Club about that great site we found"**
>
> Get your site reports in by mid-August and we'll do our best to get your updates into the next edition.

ARCACHON *7D1* (9km E Coastal) *44.64400, -1.11167* **Camping de Verdalle,** 2 Allée de l'Infante, La Hume, 33470 Gujan-Mestras **05 56 66 12 62; camping.verdalle@wanadoo.fr; www.campingdeverdalle.com**

€1.50 WD MSP nr sand adj

Fr A63 take A660 twd Arcachon. Turn R at rndabt junc with D652 sp La Hume. In vill at junc with D650 turn L, then R at rndabt; then 3rd turning on R after rlwy line. 2*, Med, hdg, pt shd, EHU (10A) inc; bbq (sep area); phone; bus adj; Eng spkn; adv bkg acc; ccard acc; CKE. *"Lovely, well-kept site in excel position in Arcachon bay; friendly, helpful owner; cycling/walking; conv local attractions; vg."* **€32.50, 1 Apr-27 Oct.** 2024

FRANCE

ARCIS SUR AUBE *4E4* (0.5km N Urban) *48.53907, 4.14270* **Camping de l'Ile Cherlieu,** Rue de Châlons, 10700 Arcis-sur-Aube **03 25 37 98 79; camping-arcis@hermans.cx**

€1.60 nr nr nr

Fr A26 junc 21 foll sp to Arcis. Fr town cent take D677/N77 dir Châlons-en-Champagne. Turn R after rv bdge, site sp. 3*, Med, mkd, shd, EHU (10-16A) inc (poss rev pol); bbq; Eng spkn; rv fishing adj; CKE. *"Pleasant, well-kept site on island surrounded by rv; friendly, helpful Dutch owners; gd, clean san facs; popular NH, rec arr early; bar 500m; vg site; quiet by 10pm; muddy in wet weather; gd site, improves each year; excel facs."* **€25.00, 15 Apr-1 Oct. 2023**

ARDRES *3A3* (0.5km N Urban) *50.85726, 1.97551* **Camping Ardresien,** 64 Rue Basse, 62610 Ardres **03 21 82 82 32; www.campingardresien.com**

Fr St Omer on D943 to Ardres, strt on at lights in town onto D231; site 500m on R - easy to o'shoot; v narr ent, not suitable twin-axles. 2*, Sm, hdg, pt shd, EHU (16A) €3.10; 95% statics; CKE. *"Basic site; friendly staff; walk to lakes at rear of site; ltd touring pitches; conv Calais & local vet; NH only."* **€15.00, 1 May-30 Sep. 2023**

ARDRES *3A3* (9km NE Rural) *50.88147, 2.08618* **Camp Municipal Les Pyramides,** Rue Nord Boutillier, 62370 Audruicq **03 21 85 56 98 or 06 62 33 91 29**

Fr Calais take A16 dir Dunkerque, after 8km exit S at junc 21 onto D219 to Audruicq; foll camp sp. Fr Ardres NE on D224 to Audruicq. Site on NE side of Audruicq nr canal. 2*, Med, hdg, unshd, EHU (6A); gas; 80% statics; CKE. *"Conv Calais; few sm pitches for tourers; rec phone ahead."* **1 Apr-30 Sep. 2024**

ARDRES *3A3* (10km SE Rural) *50.83865, 1.97612* **Camping St Louis,** 223 Rue Leulène, 62610 Autingues **03 21 35 46 83; camping-saint-louis@sfr.fr; www.campingstlouis.com**

Fr Calais S on D943 to Ardres; fr Ardres take D224 S twd Licques, after 2km turn L on D227; site well sp in 100m. Or fr junc 2 off A26 onto D943 dir Ardres. Turn L just after Total g'ge on R on app to Ardres. Well sp. If app fr S via Boulogne avoid Nabringhen & Licques as narr, steep hill with bends. NB Mkt Thurs am - avoid R turn when leaving site. 3*, Med, hdg, mkd, pt shd, EHU (10A) inc (long lead poss req, poss rev pol); gas; bbq; 70% statics; phone; Eng spkn; adv bkg req; ccard acc; games rm; CKE. *"Peaceful, well-kept, well-run, busy site; conv Dunkerque, Calais ferries; some gd sized pitches; gd welcome & friendly; clean san facs poss stretched high ssn; ltd touring pitches, phone ahead to check avail high ssn; early dep/late arr area; automatic exit barrier; barrier opens 0600 high ssn; gd rest; vg vet in Ardres; vg, conv NH; lovely clean, improved site; newly refurb san facs, excel (2015); well maintained; can be booked thro Pitchup.com."* **€25.00, 1 Apr-18 Oct. 2023**

ARDRES *3A3* (10km SE Rural) *50.80867, 2.05569* **Hôtel Bal Caravaning,** 500 Rue du Vieux Château, 62890 Tournehem-sur-la-Hem **03 21 35 65 90; contact@hotel-camping-bal.fr; www.hotel-camping-bal.fr**

nr nr

Fr S on A26 leave at exit 2; turn R onto D217 then R onto D943 dir St Omer. Turn R in Nordausques onto D218 (approx 1km), pass under A26, site is 1km on L - ent thro Bal Parc Hotel gates. Fr N or S on D943, turn R or L in Nordausques, then as above. 3*, Med, hdg, mkd, hdstg, pt shd, pt sl, EHU (10A) inc (poss rev pol); gas; 80% statics; Eng spkn; adv bkg acc; ccard acc; tennis; CKE. *"Tidy area for tourers, but few touring pitches; sports grnd & leisure cent adj; htd wc (in hotel in winter); gd rest & bar; 25km Cité Europe mall; gd NH; ltd facs in LS."* **€20.00, 1 Apr-31 Oct. 2022**

ARDRES *3A3* (9km SE Rural) *50.82193, 2.07577* **Camping Le Relax,** 318 Route de Gravelines, 62890 Nordausques **03 21 35 63 77; camping.le.relax@cegetel.net**

nr

Fr N on D943 in vill 25km S of Calais at beginning of vill, turn L at sp. Site 200m on R. Or fr S on A26, leave at junc 2 & take D943 S for 1km into Nordausques, then as above. NB Ent diff, beware low o'hanging roof on recep. 2*, Med, hdg, pt shd, EHU (6A) €2.20 (poss rev pol); 90% statics; adv bkg req; CKE. *"Obliging owner; sm pitches & sharp access, not suitable lge o'fits; basic san facs, poss tired high ssn; conv A26, Calais & war sites; NH only."* **€13.00, 1 Apr-30 Sep. 2023**

ARGELES GAZOST *8G2* (1km N Rural) *43.01218, -0.09709* **Camping Sunêlia Les Trois Vallées,** Ave des Pyrénées, 65400 Argelès-Gazost **05 62 90 35 47; www.camping3vallees.com**

€2 (htd) nr (htd)

S fr Lourdes on D821, turn R at rndabt sp Argelès-Gazost on D821A. Site off next rndabt on R. 4*, Lge, mkd, pt shd, EHU (6A) inc (poss rev pol); TV; 30% statics; adv bkg req; ccard acc; sauna; games area; bike hire; waterslide; games rm; golf 11km. *"Excel touring base; views of Pyrenees; conv Lourdes; interesting area; red facs LS; excel san facs; v helpful staff."* **€46.00, 7 Apr-1 Oct. 2022**

ARGELES GAZOST *8G2* (4km NE Rural) *43.01124, -0.07748* **Camping Deth Potz,** 40 route de Silhen, 65400 Boô-Silhen **05 62 90 37 23 or 06 80 92 11 99; contact@deth-potz.fr; www.deth-potz.fr**

€1

Fr Lourdes on D821 to Argeles Gazost. At 2nd rndabt foll Luz-St-Sauveur sp for 100m over rv and turn L sp Boo-Silhen. Site on L in 1km. 2*, Med, mkd, pt shd, pt sl, terr, EHU (3-10A) inc; bbq; twin axles; TV; 20% statics; Eng spkn; adv bkg acc; games rm; games area; CKE. *"Family run site, o'looking woodland; site has upper (terr) and lower (flat) area; gd for walking, climbing, stunning scenery; vg site; ltd wifi."* **€17.00, 11 Jan-15 Dec. 2024**

ARGELES GAZOST *8G2* (7km SE Rural) *42.98120, -0.06535* **Camping Le Viscos,** 16 Route de Préchac, 65400 Beaucens **05 62 97 05 45; domaineviscos@orange.fr**

€1 nr

Fr Lourdes S twd Argelès-Gasost on D821. Cont twd Luz & Gavarnie to L of Argelès town, & turn L within 500m, sp Beaucens. Turn R to D13, site 2.5km on L. 2*, Med, shd, pt sl, EHU (2-10A) €2-4.50 (rev pol); gas; bbq; red long stay; adv bkg req; lake fishing 500m; CKE. *"Delightful site; landscaped grnds; excel, clean san facs; pool 4km; gd rests in area."*
€17.50, 1 May-15 Oct. **2022**

ARGELES GAZOST *8G2* (1km S Rural) *42.98670, -0.08854* **Camping Les Frênes,** 46 Route des Vallées, 65400 Lau-Balagnas **05 62 97 25 12; campinglesfrenes.fr**

(htd) nr

Site on R of D821 twd S. 3*, Med, hdg, shd, EHU (10A)€4.40; gas; bbq; red long stay; TV; 10% statics; adv bkg rec; games rm; rv fishing 1km. *"Gd site."*
€20.60, 15 Dec-15 Oct. **2023**

ARGELES GAZOST *8G2* (2km S Rural) *42.98826, -0.08923* **Yelloh! Village Le Lavedan,** 44 Route des Vallées, 65400 Lau-Balagnas **05 62 97 18 84; contact@lavedan.com; www.lavedan.com**

€2.50 (htd) nr (covrd, htd)

Fr Lourdes S on D821 dir Argelès-Gazost/Cauterets; 2km after Argelès on D921 site on R after vill of Lau-Balagnas. 4*, Med, mkd, shd, EHU (6-10A) €3; gas; bbq; TV; 80% statics; phone; Eng spkn; adv bkg acc; ccard acc; games rm; CKE. *"In beautiful valley; friendly, relaxed staff; clean modern san facs; rd noise if pitched adj to rd & poss noise fr entmnt in café; excel cycle rte to Lourdes; vg; quiet pleasant site."*
€43.00, 26 Apr-15 Sep. **2023**

ARGELES GAZOST *8G2* (3km S Rural) *42.9871, -0.1061* **Camping du Lac,** 29 Chemin d'Azun, 65400 Arcizans-Avant **05 62 97 01 88; campinglac@campinglac65.fr; www.campinglac65.fr**

€2.50 nr (htd)

Fr Lourdes S thro Argelès-Gazost on D821 & D921. At 3rd rndabt take exit for St Savin/Arcizans-Avant. Cont thro St Savin vill & foll camp sp, site on L just thro Arcizans-Avant vill. NB: Dir rte to Arcizans-Avant prohibited to c'vans. 4*, Med, hdg, mkd, pt shd, pt sl, EHU (5-10A) €4.30-5; gas; TV; Eng spkn; adv bkg acc; bike hire; games rm; CKE. *"Excel, beautiful, peaceful, scenic & attractive site; mountain views; gd size pitches; clean san facs; gd for touring; excel rest."*
€34.00, 1 Jun-15 Sep. **2022**

ARGELES GAZOST *8G2* (11km SW Rural) *42.94139, -0.17714* **Camping Pyrénées Natura,** Route du Lac, 65400 Estaing **05 62 97 45 44; info@camping-pyrenees-natura.com; www.camping-pyrenees-natura.com**

€3 (htd)

Fr Lourdes take D821 to Argelès Gazost; fr Argelès foll sp Col d'Aubisque & Val d'Azun onto D918; after approx 7.5km turn L onto D13 to Bun; after Bun cross rv & turn R onto D103 twd Estaing; site in 3km - rd narr. NB Rd fr Col d'Aubisque steep, narr & not suitable c'vans or lge m'vans. 4*, Med, hdg, mkd, pt shd, terr, EHU (3-10A) €2-5 (poss rev pol); gas; bbq; TV; 20% statics; Eng spkn; adv bkg acc; ccard acc; sauna; games area; solarium; games rm; CKE. *"Superb, peaceful, well-kept, scenic site; friendly, helpful owners; clean unisex san facs; vg takeaway; gd for young families; no plastic grnd-sheets allowed; adj National Park; birdwatching area; excel; home cooked food at bar; no o'fits over 7.5m high ssn; pool 4km; vg site, one of the best ever visited."*
€30.00, 14 May - 30 Sept, D22. **2022**

ARGELES SUR MER *10G1* (1km N Coastal) *42.56320, 3.03498* **Camping Les Marsouins,** Ave de la Retirada, 66702 Argelès-sur-Mer **04 68 81 14 81; lesmarsouins@cielavillage.com; www.campsud.com**

€6 (htd) sand 800m

Fr Perpignan take exit 10 fr D914 & foll sp for Argelès until Shell petrol stn on R. Take next L just bef rv into Allée Ferdinand Buisson to T-junc, turn L at next rndabt dir Plage-Nord. Take 2nd R at next rndabt, site on L opp Spanish war memorial. 4*, V lge, hdg, mkd, shd, EHU (5A) inc; gas; bbq (elec, gas); 20% statics; Eng spkn; adv bkg acc; ccard acc; games area; windsurfing 1km; games rm; bike hire; sailing 1km. *"Lovely, well-kept, well-run site; clean san facs; busy rd to beach, but worth it; many sm coves; gd area for cycling; TO on site; excel; gd pool/slides; v conv for town/beach."* **€68.00, 14 Apr-8 Oct.** **2023**

ARGELES SUR MER *10G1* (3km NE Coastal) *42.55583, 3.04222* **Camping Les Pins,** Ave du Tech, Zone des Pins, 66700 Argelès-sur-Mer **04 68 81 10 46; camping@les-pins.com; www.les-pins.com**

€4 sand 200m

Exit D914 junc 10, foll sp Pujols & Plage-Nord, site sp. 3*, Lge, hdg, mkd, pt shd, EHU (6A) inc; gas; Eng spkn; adv bkg rec; ccard acc; games area; CCI. *"Cent for beach & town; pleasant, helpful staff; clean, modern san facs; quiet peaceful site; supmkt nrby."*
€48.00, 11 Apr-1 Oct. **2024**

ARGELES SUR MER *10G1* (4km NE Coastal) *42.57245, 3.04115* **Camping La Marende,** Avenue du Littoral, 66702 Argelès-sur-Mer **04 68 81 03 88; info@marende.com; www.marende.com**

€2.50 WD MSP sand adj

Fr Perpignan S on D914 exit junc 10 Argelès-sur-Mer; foll sp Plage Nord; after 2km at rndabt turn L sp St Cyprian; at next rndabt turn R sp Plages Nord & Sud; site on L in 800m. L onto unmade rd. 4*, V lge, mkd, hdg, shd, serviced pitches; EHU (6-10A) inc; gas; bbq (elec, gas); TV; 12% statics; phone; Eng spkn; adv bkg acc; ccard acc; jacuzzi; games area; CKE. *"Beautiful site; lge pitches; friendly, helpful family owners; 1st class facs; excel pool; many static tents high ssn; gd area for cycling & walking; aquarobics, scuba diving lessons Jul & Aug; v quiet Sept; shared facs."* **€38.00, 29 Apr-24 Sep. 2022**

"I need an on-site restaurant"

We do our best to make sure site information is correct, but it is always best to check any must-have facilities are still available or will be open during your visit.

ARGELES SUR MER *10G1* (2km E Urban/Coastal) *42.55317, 3.04375* **Camping La Chapelle,** Ave du Tech, 66702 Argelès-sur-Mer **04 68 81 28 14; campingla chapelle@marvilla-parks.com; www.camping-la-chapelle.com**

€4 nr nr 200m

Fr A9 exit junc 42 onto D900/D914 to Argelès-sur-Mer. At junc 10 cont thro Argelès vill & foll sp Argelès-Plage. In 2.5km turn L at rndabt, bear L at Office de Tourisme, site immed L. 3*, Lge, hdg, mkd, shd, EHU (6A) €6.50; 30% statics; Eng spkn; adv bkg acc; tennis 200m; CKE. *"Narr site rds poss diff lge o'fits; ltd facs LS; gd."* **€30.00, 4 Apr- 28 Sep, C25. 2024**

ARGELES SUR MER *10G1* (4.5km SE Coastal) *42.53147, 3.07167* **Camping Les Amandiers,** Route des Campings, 66190 Collioure **04 68 81 14 69; info@camping-les-amandiers.com; www.camping-les-amandiers.com**

€3 (htd) WD MSP shgl 200m

On D914 SE fr Perpignan, leave at junc 13 sp Collioure. After rndabt foll rd to Collioure. Climb coastal rd; site on L, steep descent, not rec lge o'fits. 2*, Med, mkd, shd, pt sl, terr, EHU (10A) inc; gas; 10% statics; Eng spkn; adv bkg rec; CKE. *"Site access v diff, espec for lge/med o'fits, manhandling prob req - rec investigation bef ent; sm pitches; facs stretched high ssn; many trees - dusty site; steep site rds; friendly, helpful owners; Collioure historic port; gd."* **€43.10, 30 Mar-30 Sep. 2024**

ARGELES SUR MER *10G1* (5km SE Coastal) *42.53413, 3.06826* **Camping Les Criques de Porteils,** RD114, road to Collioure, 66700 Argeles sur Mer **04 68 81 12 73; contactcdp@lescriques.com; https://www.lescriques.fr/**

€5 (htd) WD MSP (htd) shgl adj

Fr N on A9/E15 take exit junc 42 onto D914 Argelès-sur-Mer. Fr S exit junc 43 onto D618. In abt 16km R onto D914. At exit 13 leave D914 sp Collioure & foll site sp. Site by Hôtel du Golfe 1.5km fr Collioure. 5*, Lge, mkd, hdg, pt shd, pt sl, terr, EHU (5A) €6; gas; TV; 15% statics; phone; Eng spkn; adv bkg acc; fishing; tennis; games area; games rm; watersports; CKE. *"Excel, well-run site; variable size pitches, some uneven - not all suitable for lge o'fits; splendid views fr many terr pitches; steps to beach; scuba diving; clean, modern, well kept san facs; exposed, poss v windy; gd walks; v challenging (30 min) walk to Collioure but stunning; some narr site rds; gd rest; site shop fully stocked."* **€58.00, 8 Apr - 29 Oct, C16. 2022**

ARGELES SUR MER *10G1* (8km W Urban) *42.52667, 2.93515* **Camp Municipal Le Vivier,** 31 Rue du Stade, 66740 Laroque-des-Albères **04 68 89 00 93 or 04 68 95 49 97; tourisme@laroque-des-alberes.fr; www.laroque-des-alberes.fr**

€4 WD nr

D2 fr Argelès-sur-Mer to Laroque-des-Albères; foll sp in cent of vill. Site on rvside. 2*, Lge, mkd, pt shd, pt sl, EHU (6A) €3; bbq; 5% statics; bus 300m; adv bkg acc; CKE. *"Peaceful, simple site on edge Pyrenees, pleasant vill; vg."* **€24.00, 15 Jun-15 Sep. 2022**

"Satellite navigation makes touring much easier"

Remember most sat navs don't know if you're towing or in a larger vehicle – always use yours alongside maps and site directions.

ARGELES SUR MER *10G1* (8km W Rural) *42.52366, 2.94446* **Camping Les Albères,** Route Moulin Cassagnes, 66740 Laroque-des-Albères **04 68 89 23 64; contact@camping-des-alberes.com; www.camping-des-alberes.com**

WD MSP nr (covrd, htd)

Fr A9 exit junc 43 onto D618 dir Argelès-sur-Mer/ Port Vendres. Turn R onto D50 to Laroque-des-Albères. In vill at T-junc turn L, then turn R at rndabt & foll sp to site on D11. 4*, Med, mkd, pt shd, terr, EHU (6A) €5; bbq (gas); TV; 5% statics; phone; Eng spkn; tennis; games area; CKE. *"Attractive, peaceful site under slopes of Pyrenees; friendly owners; gd san facs; gd walking area; excel."* **€36.00, 12 May - 19 Sep. 2024**

ARGENTAN *4E1* (0.5km SE Urban) *48.73991, -0.01668* **Camp Municipal du Parc de la Noé,** 34 Rue de la Noé, 61200 Argentan **02 33 36 05 69; camping@argentan.info; tourisme.terresdargentan.fr/camping-municipal-de-la-noe**

(htd) nr

S fr Caen on D958 foll camping sp fr by-pass. At rndabt in town cent foll sp to Alencon (Blvd Carnot). In 300m turn L and foll camping signs. NB. Site ent immed on R on entering Rue de la Noe. 2*, Sm, shd, EHU (10A) €4; TV; 10% statics; adv bkg req; games area; rv. *"Superb, clean, tidy site adj town park; excel, clean san facs; gd touring base; lovely town; park adj; lake adj; immac site run by efficient, helpful warden; busy even mid Sept, rec arr early; gates close at 8pm, use adj aire."* **€11.50, 2 Apr-1 Oct.** **2023**

ARGENTAN *4E1* (3.6km S Rural) *48.71841, -0.01077* **FFCC Aire Naturelle du Val de Baize (Huet des Aunay),** 18 Rue de Mauvaisville, 61200 Argentan **02 33 67 27 11; mhuetdesaunay@orange.fr; www.normandiealaferme.com**

nr

Take D958 fr Argentan twd Sées & Alençon; site clearly sp on D958 - turn R just bef leaving Argentan boundary. Site adj T-junc N of farm buildings. Sm, hdstg, pt shd, EHU (6A); 10% statics; Eng spkn; adv bkg acc; CKE. *"Charming, well-kept site; pool 2.5km; B&B; lge pitches in orchard; clean but dated facs, ltd LS; friendly welcome; NH only; ring in advance to check opening dates."* **€13.00, Unknown-30 Sep.** **2022**

ARGENTAT *7C4* (1km NE Urban) *45.10205, 1.94390* **Camp Municipal Le Longour,** Route d'Egletons, 19400 Argentat **05 55 28 13 84; camping.municipal@argentat-sur-dordogne.fr; www.argentat.fr**

€1.30 nr

Fr cent of Argentat head N dir Egletons on D18. 3*, Med, pt shd, EHU (10A) €3.20; phone; ccard acc; tennis; fishing. *"Efficiently run, clean site; pleasant rvside walk to old quay & cafés; htd pool adj; sports complex adj; gd touring base; excel; beautiful town."* **€21.40, 10 May -30 Sept.** **2024**

ARGENTAT *7C4* (4km NE Rural) *45.11151, 1.95908* **Camping Château de Gibanel,** Sea Green Camping le Gibanel, 19400 ARGENTAT **+33 (0)5 64 10 20 20; reservation@seagreen.fr; www.camping-gibanel.com**

€2 (free LS)

Exit Argentat on D18 twd Egletons & fork R on lakeside past hydro-elec dam. Sp fr all dir. Site in grnds of sm castle on N bank of Rv Dordogne. App rd narr but satisfactory. 4*, Lge, mkd, pt shd, pt sl, EHU (10A) €3.70; gas; bbq; sw; TV; 15% statics; Eng spkn; adv bkg acc; ccard acc; boating; fishing; games area; games rm; CKE. *"Excel, well-managed site in idyllic location; helpful owner; gd san facs; various pitch sizes; lovely sm town; excel."* **€29.50, 8 Jul-26 Aug.** **2024**

ARGENTAT *7C4* (4km SW Rural) *45.07531, 1.91689* **Camping Sunêlia au Soleil d'Oc,** 19400 Monceaux-sur-Dordogne **05 55 28 84 84; info@campingsoleildoc.com; www.campingsoleildoc.com**

€3

Fr N exit A20 junc 46a dir Tulle, then D1120 to Argentat. Fr Argentat take D12 sp Beaulieu. In 4km in Laygues turn L over bdge x-ing Rv Dordogne, site in 300m. 4*, Med, mkd, hdg, pt shd, terr, EHU (6A) €4.10; gas; bbq; red long stay; TV; 10% statics; phone; Eng spkn; adv bkg acc; ccard acc; canoeing; games area; games rm; bike hire; rv; archery; CKE. *"Ideal family site high ssn & peaceful LS; some pitches on rv bank; ltd water points; gd walking & other activities; many beautiful vills in area; tours arranged."* **€20.70, 16 Apr-30 Oct.** **2022**

ARGENTIERE LA BESSEE, L' *9C3* (2.5km S Rural) *44.77775, 6.55798* **Camp Municipal Les Ecrins,** Avenue Pierre Sainte, 05120 L'Argentière-la-Bessée **06 20 97 09 73; contact@camping-les-ecrins.com; www.campinglesecrins.com/**

€2.10 (htd)

Fr L'Argentière on N94, turn R onto D104, site sp. 3*, Med, mkd, pt shd, EHU (10A) €2.40; phone; adv bkg acc; tennis 300m; games area. *"Mountain scenery; pool 300m."* **€22.20, 22 Apr-15 Sep.** **2024**

ARGENTIERE LA BESSEE, L' *9C3* (5km S Rural) *44.75765, 6.57995* **FFCC Camping Le Verger,** 05310 La Roche-de-Rame **04 92 20 92 23; info@campingleverger.com; www.campingleverger.com**

12 nr nr nr

S fr Briançon on N94; site 500m L of rd bef vill; sp. 3*, Sm, hdg, shd, terr, EHU (3-10A) €5.50; sw nr; TV; 25% statics; phone; Eng spkn; adv bkg acc. *"Grass pitches in orchard; excel, well-maintained facs; beautiful; ideal loc for visiting Ecrins area; fantastic value; hg rec."* **€17.00** **2023**

ARGENTIERE LA BESSEE, L' *9C3* (4km NW Rural) *44.82455, 6.52575* **Campéole Camping Le Courounba,** Le Village, 05120 Les Vigneaux **04 11 11 03 03; courounba@vacances-andretrigano.com; vacances-andretrigano.co.uk/camping/hautes-alpes/le-courounba-les-vigneaux**

(htd) nr (htd)

Take N94 S fr Briançon to L'Argentiere-la-Bessée, turn R onto D994E dir Vallouise. Site on L over rv bdge. 3*, Lge, hdstg, pt shd, EHU (6A) €4.10 (poss long lead req); bbq; TV; 20% statics; phone; Eng spkn; adv bkg acc; ccard acc; tennis; horseriding nr; bike hire; fishing; waterslide; CKE. *"Gd site, beautifully situated in woods by rv in mountains; gd clean san facs; no site lighting."* **€34.50, 15 May-15 Sep.** **2024**

FRANCE

ARGENTIERE LA BESSEE, L' *9C3* (8km NW Rural) *44.84354, 6.48989* **Camping Indigo Vallouise (formerly Les Chambonnettes),** Chemin des Chambonnettes, 05290 Vallouise **04 92 23 30 26; vallouise@camping-indigo.com; https://europe.huttopia.com/site/camping-vallouise**

€5 (htd) nr nr nr (htd)

Take N94 Briançon-Gap, on N o'skts of L'Argentière-la-Bessée take D994 W dir Vallouise. In cent of Vallouise turn L over bdge & immed L, site in 200m on rvside. 3*, Med, mkd, pt shd, pt sl, EHU (10A) €5.30; bbq; twin axles; TV; 25% statics; phone; Eng spkn; adv bkg acc; ccard acc; games area; games rm; tennis; CKE. *"Mountain scenery; gd facs; bar 500m; gd cent for walking, skiing, canoeing; pool 3km; white-water rafting at nrby rv; interesting vill; gd."* **€27.00, 22 May - 28 Sep and 13 Dec-23 Mar, M17.** **2024**

ARGENTON LES VALLEES *4H1* (0.9km N Rural) *46.9877, -0.4504* **Camp Municipal du Lac d'Hautibus,** Rue de la Sablière, 79150 Argenton-les-Vallées **05 49 65 54 25; contact@camping-lacdhautibus.com; camping-lacdhautibus.com/en/home**

nr

Fr E or W on D759, site well sp in town, on lakeside. 2*, Med, hdg, pt sl, EHU (6A) €2.50; sw nr; 10% statics; Eng spkn; games rm; tennis 100m; CKE. *"Beautifully-situated, well-kept site; pool 100m; interesting, quiet town; excel."* **€14.00, 1 Apr-30 Sep.** **2022**

"There aren't many sites open at this time of year"

If you're travelling outside peak season remember to call ahead to check site opening dates – even if the entry says 'open all year'.

ARGENTON SUR CREUSE *7A3* (13km SW Rural) *46.54192, 1.40328* **Camping La Petite Brenne (Naturist),** La Grande Metairie, 36800 Luzeret **02 54 25 05 78; info@lapetitebrenne.com; www.lapetitebrenne.com**

(covrd, htd)

Fr A20 exit junc 18 sp Luzeret/Prissac; foll D55 to Luzeret vill. After bdge in vill turn L, then next L to site. Med, pt shd, pt sl, EHU (10A) €7 (long leads poss req); bbq; red long stay; twin axles; 10% statics; phone; Eng spkn; adv bkg rec; ccard acc; games rm; sauna; horseriding; games area; CKE. *"Excel family site; friendly Dutch owners; lge pitches; excel san facs; ideal for children; pools excel; gd rest; gd walking in National Park; great facs."* **€37.00, 22 Apr-1 Oct.** **2023**

ARGENTON SUR CREUSE *7A3* (2km NW Rural) *46.59636, 1.50619* **Camp Municipal Les Chambons,** 37 Rue des Chambons, 36200 Argenton-sur-Creuse **06 47 81 59 35 & 09 66 84 06 01; campingleschambons@gmail.com; www.campingleschambons.fr**

12 nr nr

Fr A20 exit junc 17 onto D937 dir Argenton; turn R at rndabt, then L at mini rndabt nr supmkt sp St Marcel; foll rd downhill over rlwy bdge; then 1st R in 100m. But best app fr N on D927 to avoid traff calming rd humps; at town sp cross rlwy bdge & turn R immed past LH turn for Roman archaeological museum; foll camping sp on narr, busy app rd. 3*, Med, mkd, hdstg, shd, pt sl, EHU (5A) €3.60 (poss long lead req); gas. *"Beautiful, peaceful, well-kept site by rv; helpful warden; v muddy after heavy rain & poss uneven pitches by rv; rvside walk into interesting old town; no need to unhitch so useful for early start; quiet in day, busy in evening as popular NH high ssn; excel."* **€22.00** **2024**

ARLES *10E2* (8km NE Rural) *43.72336, 4.71861* **Huttopia Fontvieille,** Rue Michelet, 13990 Fontvieille **04 90 54 78 69; fontvieille@huttopia.com; europe.huttopia.com/camping-fontvieille-provence/**

€1.50 nr

Take D570 fr Arles to Avignon, in 2km turn R on D17 to Fontvieille, at far end of vill turn R at rndabt, foll sp. 3*, Med, hdg, mkd, pt shd, pt sl, EHU (6A) €3; red long stay; TV; bus; Eng spkn; adv bkg acc; games area; games rm; CKE. *"Delightful, pleasant quiet site in pines; friendly staff; vg san facs; 15-20 mins walk to lively vill with rests & 2 supmkts; quiet forest walks; tennis in vill; nr Arles; lots of attractions locally; vg."* **€38.00, 30 Mar-14 Oct.** **2023**

ARLES *10E2* (7km E Rural) *43.64799, 4.70625* **Camping La Bienheureuse,** 13280 Raphèle-les-Arles **04 90 98 48 06; contact@labienheureuse.com**

€2.50

Fr Arles E on D453, site on L 5km after Pont-de-Crau. W fr Salon-de-Provence on A54/N113; exit N113 junc 12 onto N1435 to St Martin-de-Crau; cont past St Martin-de-Crau on N1435; in 2km rd becomes D435 to Raphèle-les-Arles; site on R 900m after Raphèle-les-Arles. 3*, Med, hdg, pt shd, EHU (16A); twin axles; 50% statics; phone; bus adj; Eng spkn; adv bkg acc; horseriding nr; CKE. *"Pleasant site; obliging British owners; 700m to shops/bar in vill; gd facs; gd dog walk along nrby lanes and canal."* **€21.00, 1 Mar-30 Sept.** **2024**

ARLES *10E2* (5km SE Urban) *43.65942, 4.65416* **Camping L'arlesienne,** 149 Draille Marseillaise, Pont de Crau, 13631, Arles **04 90 96 02 12; info@camping-larlesienne.com; www.camping-larlesienne.com**

€1.50 (htd) nr (htd)

Exit Arles E by D453 sp Pont-de-Crau or junc 7 fr N113 dir Raphèle-les-Arles; 200m after exit vill take 1st exit at rndabt then R at Flor Hotel sp on D83E. Site in 50m on R adj hotel. 3*, Med, pt shd, EHU (6A) €4; TV; 80% statics; bus fr rndabt; Eng spkn; games area. *"Many mosquitoes; red facs LS; v muddy after rain; visit Les Baux citadel early morning bef coach parties arr; no o'fits over 5.5m allowed (but poss not enforced); gd birdwatching; poss no site lighting LS; conv Arles."* **€27.00, 1 Apr-1 Nov. 2022**

ARMENTIERES *3A3* (3km E Rural) *50.68774, 2.93279* **Camping Les Alouettes et L'Image,** 140 Rue Brune, 59116 Houplines **06 81 61 56 82; www.natureetvacances.fr**

12 (htd)

Exit A25 junc 8 sp Armentières, onto D945 N twd Houplines; pass on R Chemin du Pilori in 1.8km; then pass on R Hameau de L'Hépinette in 2.2km; turn R into Rue Brune in 3km; site in 1km on R. Ent not v clearly sp. 3*, Med, hdg, shd, serviced pitches; EHU (6-10A) inc; 90% statics; Eng spkn; adv bkg acc; tennis; games area; CKE. *"Mainly statics, adv bkg rec; friendly, helpful staff; dated san facs, poss unclean & unkempt (2011); pitches exposed & poss v windy; gd NH prior to ferry."* **€28.00 2023**

ARNAY LE DUC *6H1* (1km E Rural) *47.13388, 4.49835* **Camping L'Etang de Fouché,** Rue du 8 Mai 1945, 21230 Arnay-le-Duc **03 80 90 02 23; info@campingfouche.com; www.campingfouche.com**

€2 (htd) (htd)

App by D906 to Arnay (site sp); turn E onto D17, site on R in 2km. 4*, Lge, hdstg, mkd, hdg, pt shd, EHU (6A) €4; bbq; sw nr; TV (pitch); TV; Eng spkn; adv bkg acc; ccard acc; bike hire; waterslide; fishing; tennis; games rm; CKE. *"Excel lakeside site with pleasant views; lge pitches; friendly staff; gd san facs; attractive sm town; gd touring base S Burgundy; gd for young families."* **€32.00, 3 Apr-28 Sep. 2024**

ARQUES *8G4* (0.8km S Rural) *42.94924, 2.37670* **Camping Innature,** 7 Chemin du Lac, 11190 Arques **04 68 47 74 64; contact@camping-innature.com; www.camping-innature.com**

12 (htd) lake

Fr A61 J23 Carcassonne Ouest take D118 to Couiza for 63km then D613 to Arques 13km. Site sp on R on leaving vill. 4*, Med, hdg, mkd, hdstg, pt shd, terr, serviced pitches; EHU (10A); twin axles; 40% statics; Eng spkn; adv bkg acc; ccard acc; CKE. *"Walks fr site; site still being developed (2022); vg."* **€42.00 2022**

ARRAS *3B3* (14km E Rural) *50.27347, 2.94852* **Camping La Paille Haute,** 145 Rue de Sailly, 62156 Boiry-Notre-Dame **03 21 48 15 40; lapaillehaute@wanadoo.fr; www.la-paille-haute.com**

(htd)

Fr Calais take A26/A1 twd Paris, exit junc 15 onto D939 twd Cambrai; in 3km take D34 NE to Boiry-Notre-Dame & foll camp sp. Fr D950 Douai-Arras rd, at Fresnes turn S onto D43, foll sp to Boiry in 7km, site well sp in vill. 3*, Med, hdg, hdstg, pt shd, terr, EHU (6A) €4 (poss rev pol); bbq; red long stay; 60% statics; Eng spkn; ccard acc; tennis; games rm; site open w/ends in winter; lake fishing; CKE. *"Popular NH; useful & reliable; pretty site with views; rec arr early; lge pitches; friendly, helpful owner; gd for children; Calais over 1hr; conv WW1 sites & A26; gd reg used site; gd for long stay; peaceful vill; pitches muddy in wet weather; san facs updated and excel; gd dogs walk adj; cycle route, 15km canal side to Arras."* **€27.50, 27 Mar-23 Oct. 2024**

ARRENS MARSOUS *8G2* (0.8km E Rural) *42.9613, -0.2034* **Camping La Hèche,** 54 Route d'Azun, 65400 Arrens-Marsous **05 62 97 02 64; laheche@free.fr; www.campinglaheche.com**

€0.50 (htd)

Fr Argelès-Gazost foll D918. Site on L immed bef Arrens. If towing c'van do not app fr Col d'Aubisque. Lge, mkd, pt shd, EHU (3A) €2.70; gas; TV; 10% statics; phone; games area; waterslide; tennis; CKE. *"Beautiful location; pool in vill high ssn; gd san facs."* **€16.50, 1 Apr-31 Nov. 2024**

ARRENS-MARSOUS *8G2* (0.9km NE Rural) *42.95991, -0.20645* **Camping Mialanne,** 63 route du Val d'Azun, 65400 Arrens-Marous **05 62 92 67 14; mialanne@orange.fr; www.campingmialanne.fr**

(€0.50) nr nr nr

Sp on D918 bet Arrens-Marsous, 10km WSW of Argeles-Gazost. (Opp ent of Camping La Heche). 3*, Med, mkd, pt shd, terr, EHU (10A) €3.10; bbq (charcoal, gas); twin axles; phone; bus 300m; Eng spkn; adv bkg acc; ccard acc; games rm; CKE. *"Friendly fam site; htd pool 300m; 300m to vill, conv Arrens & Estaing; san facs extended (2015); vg."* **€19.60, 1 Jun-30 Sep. 2022**

ARROMANCHES LES BAINS *3D1* (3km E Coastal) *49.33963, -0.58188* **Camp Municipal Quintefeuille,** Ave Maurice Schumann, 14960 Asnelles **02 31 22 35 50; contact@camping-asnelles.com; www.camping-asnelles.com**

nr nr nr sand 300m

Site sp on D514, but visible fr vill sq in Asnelles. 4*, Med, mkd, unshd, EHU; fishing; tennis; games area. **€22.00, 15 Mar-15 Jan. 2024**

FRANCE

ARROMANCHES LES BAINS *3D1* (0.5km W Urban/ Coastal) *49.33793, -0.62647* **Camp Municipal,** Ave de Verdun, 14117 Arromanches-les-Bains **02 31 22 36 78; camping.arromanches@wanadoo.fr**
€1 sand 500m.

App fr Bayeux on D516. Turn R on onto D65 on app to Arromanches to site on L. 2*, Med, pt shd, pt sl, terr, EHU (10A) inc; gas. *"Conv Mulberry Harbour exhibition & invasion beaches; friendly warden; gd san facs; levelling blocks req most pitches; grnd soft when wet; sh stay pitches stony; water access diff for m'vans (2010); town centre nrby; v gd."* **€22.00, 1 Apr-30 Sep. 2024**

ARROU *4F2* (0.9km NW Rural) *48.10189, 1.11556* **Camp Municipal du Pont de Pierre,** 28290 Arrou **02 37 97 02 13 (Mairie); mairie.arrou@wanadoo.fr**
WD MSP nr nr nr sand adj

Take D15 fr Cloyes. Site sp in vill of Arrou. 2*, Med, hdg, mkd, unshd, pt sl, EHU (6-10A) €2-3; bbq; 10% statics; phone; adv bkg acc; horseriding; lake fishing; bike hire; tennis; CKE. *"Lovely, peaceful, well-kept site in park-like setting; lge pitches; excel, clean san facs; gd security; htd pool, paddling pool adj; gd rvside walks/cycle rides; excel value; rec; gd site but diff to contact; no arrivals after 6pm."* **€8.00, 1 May-30 Sep. 2023**

ARTIGAT *8F3* (0.7km NE Urban) *43.13776, 1.44407* **Camping Les Eychecadous,** 09130 Artigat **(033) 05 67 44 51 65; campingartigat@hotmail.fr; www.campingartigat.com/**
12 WD MSP

Fr Toulouse take A64 S, take exit 28 twrds Capens. Marquefave, St. Sulpice. Turn L onto D10, at rndabt take 2nd exit onto D622, turn L sp Av. Antonin Triqué, cont twrds Lombardi on D622, go thro 1 rndabt, turn R sp Rue de la République/ D622 cont on D622, to Av. Des Pyrénées/D4 cont onto D919 cont thro 3 rndabts then L onto Chemin du Comté then L twrds Les Eychecadous, then R, then L to site. 3*, Sm, mkd, pt shd, EHU (10A); bbq; twin axles; TV; 10% statics; adv bkg acc; CKE. *"Vg site on edge of Lèze; warm welcome; fishing, boating, & horseriding."* **€12.00 2020**

ARZON *2G3* (2km NE Coastal) *47.56031, -2.87854* **Camping de Bilouris,** Route de Kerners, 56640 Arzon **02 97 53 70 55; campingbilouris@gmail.com; www.campingdebilouris.com**
€3.50 WD

Fr Vannes foll D780 for abt 23km. On app Arzon foll sp for site. Sm, hdg, pt shd, pt sl, EHU (10A) €5.30; bbq; 60% statics; Eng spkn; adv bkg rec. *"Coastal walks, boating & kayaking; miles of off-rd cycling; vg."* **€27.00, 1 Apr-1 Nov. 2023**

ARZON *2G3* (2km W Coastal) *47.54403, -2.90945* **Camp Municipal de Port-Sable,** Port Navalo, 56640 Arzon **02 97 53 71 98; portsable@arzon.fr; www.camping-arzon.fr**
€1.40 WD MSP nr sand adj

Fr N165/E60 take D780 to Sarzeau, cont to Arzon. Site sp fr last rndabt bef fort. 3*, Med, pt shd, pt sl, EHU (6A) €2.30; gas; Eng spkn; ccard acc; fishing; sailing school. *"Vg, spacious site; beautiful position nr beach with views; gd beach for children; walk into marina; boat excursions; gd facs; gd for m'vans - rests nrby."* **€18.50, 1 Apr-15 Oct. 2022**

ASPRES SUR BUECH *9D3* (6.5km W Rural) *44.53048, 5.68371* **Camping La Source,** 05140 St Pierre-d'Argençon **04 92 58 67 81 or 06 78 32 30 40 (mob); info@lasource-hautesalpes.com; www.lasource-hautesalpes.com**
12 €2.50 WD MSP

Fr S on D1075 at Aspres-sur-Buëch turn onto D993 dir Valence to St Pierre-d'Argençon; after 6km site sp. Fr N on D93, cont onto D993 over Col de Cabre; site sp on L bef St Pierre-d'Argençon. Sm, mkd, pt shd, pt sl, EHU (6/10A) €6.50; bbq; red long stay; twin axles; phone; Eng spkn; adv bkg acc; ccard acc; CKE. *"Peaceful, well-kept CL-type site in woodland/open field; friendly, helpful British owners; clean san facs; takeaway; chambre d'hôte on site; htd pool (4km); highly rec; ideally located for all mountain sports, walking, climbing, watersports, gliding, flying & cycling; 3 luxury Teepees for hire; excel; own facs req Nov - Mar as site facs clsd."* **€21.00 2023**

ASSERAC *2G3* (5km NW Coastal) *47.44533, -2.44766* **Camping Le Moulin de l'Eclis,** Pont Mahé, 5 bis rue de la Plage, 44410 Assérac **02 40 01 76 69 or 04 11 32 90 00; info@camping-leclis.com; https://www.sandaya.fr/nos-campings/moulin-de-l-eclis**
€3 WD MSP nr
(covrd, htd) sand adj

Fr D774 turn N onto D83 to Assérac. Take D82 two coast to Pont Mahé, site sp. 4*, Lge, hdg, mkd, pt shd, EHU (6-10A) €3.60-4; bbq (elec, gas); TV; 60% statics; phone; Eng spkn; adv bkg acc; ccard acc; games area; bike hire; waterslide; sailing school; watersports. *"Excel family site; conv Guérande; vg touring base; superb new (2013) san facs."* **€53.00, 4 Apr-28 Sep. 2024**

AUBENAS *9D2* (2km E Rural) *44.61885, 4.43220* **Camping Le Plan d'Eau,** Route de Lussas, 07200 St Privat **04 75 35 44 98; info@campingleplandeau.com; www.campingleplandeau.fr**

€2.70 nr (htd)

Exit A7 at Montélimar dir Aubenas. Bef Aubenas turn R at rndabt onto D104 dir St Privat. In approx 1km turn R twd Lussas & foll site sp. Site on R on rvside. 3*, Med, mkd, pt shd, EHU (8A) €4.20; bbq (gas); cooking facs; red long stay; TV; 25% statics; phone; Eng spkn; adv bkg acc; games rm Animation from July 6 to August 24; CKE. *"Vg, peaceful site; gd san & sports facs."* **€43.00, 27 Apr-16 Sep. 2020**

AUBENAS *9D2* (7km NW Rural) *44.65157, 4.32384* **Camp Municipal le Pont des Issoux,** 150 Allée de Vals, 07380 Lalevade-d'Ardèche **06 20 03 09 41 or 04 27 52 96 64; familyscampinglesissoux@gmail.com; www.sud-ardeche-camping.fr**

€1.20 nr nr nr

Fr Aubenas, N102 sp Mende & Le Puy-en-Velay; Lalevade in 10km; R in vill; well sp. 4*, Med, mkd, pt shd, EHU (10A) €3.10 (poss rev pol); gas; sw nr; bus 250m; Eng spkn; adv bkg acc; tennis nr; CKE. *"Pleasant, shady site beside Rv Ardèche; friendly, helpful warden; san facs dated but clean, poss scruffy LS; children's park nrby; no twin axles; close to vill; conv touring base; vg."* **€11.50, 19 Apr-16 Sept. 2024**

"I like to fill in the reports as I travel from site to site"

You'll find report forms at the back of this guide, or you can fill them in online at camc.com/europereport.

AUBERIVES SUR VAREZE *9B2* (8km E Rural) *45.42830, 4.92823* **Kawan Village Camping Le Bontemps,** 5 Impasse du Bontemps, 38150 Vernioz **04 66 60 07 00; contact@camping-lebontemps.fr; www.camping-lebontemps.com**

€3 (covrd, htd, indoor)

Take N7 S fr Vienne. At Le Clos turn L onto D37 thro Cheyssieu & Vernioz, site approx 9km E of Vernioz. Fr S, on N7 N of vill of Auberives R onto D37, site on R in 8km. Tight ent - rec swing wide. NB Also sp Hotel de Plein Air. 4*, Lge, mkd, pt shd, terr, EHU (6A) inc (poss long lead req); bbq; TV; 30% statics; adv bkg acc; ccard acc; games rm; tennis; lake fishing; games area; CKE. *"Attractive, well-kept site; popular NH high ssn; wildlife sanctuary; helpful staff; no o'fits over 10m high ssn; excel sports facs; vg NH/long stay; new san facs (2014)."* **€30.00, 13 Apr - 29 Sep, M10. 2022**

AUBERIVES SUR VAREZE *9B2* (1.6km S Rural) *45.41284, 4.81358* **Camping des Nations,** 38550 Clonas-sur-Varèze **04 74 84 95 13 or 04 14 42 42 84; contact@campingdesnations.com; www.campingdesnations.com**

€1 (htd) nr

Fr Vienne S on N7; site sp on R in 12km. Or fr S exit A7 junc 12 onto N7 dir Vienne; do not go into Clonas vill; site on L adj Hotel des Nations. 3*, Med, hdg, mkd, shd, EHU (9A) inc; bbq; adv bkg req; CKE. *"Pleasant, well-kept, well-laid out site; gd sized pitches; gd, v clean san facs; site muddy when wet; poss under-used; ltd facs LS; poss irreg cleaning end of ssn; useful NH/touring base for Spain & the Med; vg site; friendly, helpful staff."* **€26.00, 15 Mar-15 Oct. 2022**

AUBETERRE SUR DRONNE *7C2* (1km SE Rural) *45.26786, 0.17474* **Camping Base de Loisirs d'Aubeterre Sur Dronne (formerly Municipal),** Route de Ribérac, 16390 Aubeterre-sur-Dronne **05 45 98 75 43 or 06 23 01 03 47; accueil@campingaubeterre.fr; www.camping-aubeterre-sur-dronne.fr**

€1 (cont) nr nr

On D2 fr Chalais, take D17 around S end of town. Turn R over rv & site on R adj sports grnd. 3*, Med, pt shd, EHU (10A) €2.50; 10% statics; Eng spkn; rv fishing adj; bike hire; tennis adj; boating adj. *"Excel site; gd for children; friendly staff; picturesque town; conv touring Périgord."* **€20.00, 1 May-30 Sep. 2024**

AUBIGNY SUR NERE *4G3* (1.5km E Rural) *47.48435, 2.45703* **FLOWER Camping des Etangs,** Route de Sancerre, 18700 Aubigny-sur-Nère **02 48 58 02 37; camping.aubigny@orange.fr; www.camping-aubigny.com or www.flowercampings.com**

€2 (htd) nr (covrd, htd)

D940 fr Gien, turn E in vill of Aubigny onto D923, foll sp fr vill; site 1km on R by lake, after Camp des Sports & just bef end of vill sp. Avoid town cent due congestion. 4*, Med, mkd, hdstg, pt shd, EHU (6-10A) inc; bbq; TV; 10% statics; phone; Eng spkn; adv bkg acc; bike hire; fishing; games rm; CKE. *"Vg site with lake views; pretty medieval vill with historical links to Scotland; mkt Sat; 2nd w/e July Scottish Son & Lumière event adj site!"* **€26.00, 29 Mar-30 Sep. 2024**

AUBUSSON *7B4* (10km N Rural) *46.02133, 2.17052* **Camping La Perle,** Fourneaux, 23200 St Médard-la-Rochette **05 55 83 01 25 or 06 18 99 05 48; info@camping-laperle.fr; camping laperle.fr/en**

12 (htd)

On D942 N fr Aubusson dir Guéret; site on R bef Fourneaux. 3*, Sm, hdg, mkd, hdstg, pt shd, terr, EHU (10A) poss rev pol €3.50; bbq; TV; 10% statics; Eng spkn; adv bkg acc; bike hire; CKE. *"Site ever improving (2011); various sized pitches; Dutch owners; tapestry museum in Aubusson & other historical attractions; vg site."* **€24.00, 6 Apr-4 Nov. 2024**

AUBUSSON *7B4* (5km S Rural) *45.91939, 2.17044* **Camping des Combes,** 73 Les Combes, 23500 Felletin **(0)5 87043581 / (0)6 46746617; info@campingdescombes.com; www.campingdescombes.com**

Fr Aubusson on D982 to Felletin, when in Felletin & immed bef rlwy line, turn R at cemetery. Foll camping sp approx 4km. Sm, hdg, mkd, pt shd, EHU (10A) €2 (long lead poss req); phone; adv bkg acc; fishing; boating. *"Peaceful, British-owned site on edge Lake Combes; ideal touring base; vg; spotless."* **€37.50, 1 Mar-30 Sep.** **2024**

AUCH *8F3* (8km N Rural) *43.7128, 0.5646* **Kawan Village Le Talouch,** Au Cassou, 32810 Roquelaure **05 62 65 52 43; info@yellohvillage-letalouch.com; www.camping-talouch.com**

€2.40 (covrd, htd)

Head W on N124 fr Auch, then N on D148 for 7km to site. 4*, Med, mkd, pt shd, EHU (6A) inc; gas; bbq; TV; 15% statics; Eng spkn; adv bkg acc; golf driving range; tennis; games area; CKE. *"Well-kept site; set in lovely countryside with lge grassed pitches, maintained to high standard; friendly Dutch owners who spk excel Eng; steam rm; sauna; recreational facs superb for all age groups; gd walking & nature trails; poss liable to flooding."* **€41.80, 13 Apr-16 Sep.** **2024**

AUCUN *8F2* (0.7km E Rural) *42.97338, -0.18496* **Camping Azun Nature,** 1 Route des Poueyes, 65400 **05 62 97 45 05; azun.nature@orange.fr; www.camping-azun-nature.com**

Fr Toulouse- A64 exit Tarbes W. Fr Bordeaux or Bayonne- A64 Exit Soumoulou. Fr Lourdes- drive twd Argeles-Gazost, take exit Aubisque col-Val d'Azun; Fr town cent of Argeles-Gazost go twd Aubisque col, Soulor col; Cross Arras-en-Lavedan, go on twd Aucun vill, turn L sp Las Poueyes, site ent 100m on R bet barns. 4*, Sm, mkd, pt shd, EHU (3-6A) €2.50-3.50; bbq; TV; 50% statics; adv bkg acc; games area; games rm; CKE. *"Stunning setting; ideal walking & cycling area; gd for exploring the Pyrenees, visits to Lourdes; well maintained; pool 3km; friendly, helpful owner."* **€27.60, 1 May-30 Sep.** **2024**

AUDIERNE *2F1* (3km SE Coastal) *48.00723, -4.50799* **Camping de Kersiny-Plage,** 1 Rue Nominoé, 29780 Plouhinec **02 98 70 82 44; info@kersinyplage.com; www.kersinyplage.com**

€2 sand

Fr Audierne on D784 turn R at 2nd traff lts in Plouhinec, cont for 1km; turn L into Rue Nominoé (sp diff to see) for 100m. Or fr Quimper on D784 to Plouhinec, turn L at 1st traff lts & as bef. 2*, Med, hdg, pt shd, terr, EHU (8A) €3; bbq (gas); Eng spkn; CKE. *"Quiet, peaceful site; beautiful location & beach; most pitches superb sea views; welcoming, friendly owner; clean san facs; barrier clsd 2300-0730; not much in area for children except beach; gd coastal walks; vg, rec."* **€19.90, 25 May-7 Sep.** **2022**

AULUS LES BAINS *8G3* (0.5km NW Rural) *42.79402, 1.33197* **Camp Municipal Le Coulédous,** 09140 Aulus-les-Bains **05 61 66 43 56; campinglecouledous@orange.fr; www.camping-aulus-couledous.com**

€1 (htd) nr

Take D618 fr St Girons. After 13km cross rv; turn R onto D3 sp Aulus-les-Bains. On app to Oust turn L onto D32, site approx 17km on R at ent to vill on rvside. 2*, Med, mkd, hdstg, pt shd, sl, EHU (3-10A) €3-6.50; 10% statics; Eng spkn; adv bkg acc; site clsd mid-Nov to mid-Dec; CKE. *"Gd walking & skiing (16km); sm spa in vill; bar 300m; excel; san facs clean but tired; church clock chimes thro night."* **€16.50** **2023**

AUMALE *3C3* (0.5km W Rural) *49.76618, 1.74618* **Camp Municipal Le Grand Mail,** Chemin du Grand Mail, 76390 Aumale **02 35 93 40 50 (Mairie); communeaumale@wanadoo.fr**

€2 nr

Clearly sp in town; long steep climb to ent. 2*, Med, pt shd, EHU (6A) €2.40; bike hire; fishing 1km. *"Gd site; clean, modern san facs; conv Channel ports; steep slope fr town to site; gd NH."* **€18.00, 20 Mar-30 Sep.** **2024**

AURAY *2F3* (7km SE Rural) *47.64320, -2.89890* **Aire Naturelle La Fontaine du Hallate (Le Gloanic),** 8 Chemin du Poul Fétan, La Hallate, 56400 Plougoumelen **09 64 04 90 16 or 06 16 30 08 33 (mob); clegloanic@orange.fr; www.camping-morbihan.bzh/fr/**

€2.88 nr

Fr N165 Vannes-Lorient, turn S onto D101E to Plougoumelen; watch for sp after Plougoumelen, site in La Hallate. Narr, bumpy app rd. 2*, Sm, hdg, mkd, pt shd, pt sl, EHU (6A) €3.40 (poss rev pol); 2% statics; phone; adv bkg req; tennis adj; golf adj; CKE. *"Gd alt to lge/noisier sites; gd coast paths; conv local boat trips & Ste Anne-d'Auray; vg."* **€18.60, 1 Apr-30 Oct.** **2024**

AURAY *2F3* (8km SW Rural) *47.64256, -3.05406* **FFCC Camping de Kergo,** Route de Carnac, 56400 Ploemel **02 97 56 80 66; contact@campingkergo.com; www.campingkergo.com**

€0.70 nr sand 5km

Fr Auray take D768 SW sp Carnac. After 4km turn NW on D186 twd Ploemel & foll sp. 3*, Med, mkd, pt shd, EHU (6-10A) inc; 10% statics; adv bkg rec; CKE. *"Lovely, peaceful site, lots of trees; gd, clean san facs but dated (2015), ltd LS; welcoming, friendly, helpful owners; gd size pitches; ideal for cycling into Carnac."* **€33.00, 1 May-30 Sep. 2023**

AURAY *2F3* (8km W Rural) *47.66406, -3.09985* **FFCC Camp Municipal Le St Laurent,** Kergonvo, 56400 Ploemel **02 97 56 85 90; contact@camping-saint-laurent.fr; www.camping-saint-laurent.fr**

12 €1.40 (htd) (htd)

Fr Auray on D22 twd Belz/Etel; after 8km turn L on D186 to Ploemel & site on L in 200m. 3*, Med, hdstg, shd, EHU (10A) €4; bbq; 10% statics; adv bkg acc; games area. *"Peaceful site; friendly staff; red facs LS."* **€23.50 2024**

AURILLAC *7C4* (1.4km NE Urban) *44.93551, 2.45596* **Camping De l'Ombrade,** Chemin du Gué Bouliaga, 15000 Aurillac **04 71 48 28 87 or 07 88 85 28 50; www.campingombrade.fr**

nr

Take D17 N fr Aurillac twd Puy-Mary; site on banks of Rv Jordanne. Well sp fr town. 3*, Lge, mkd, shd, pt sl, EHU 10A (inc); bbq; TV; games rm. *"Well-managed, spacious site; lge pitches; interesting, lge mkt town; vg; excel new san fac (2014)."* **€17.40, 15 Jun-15 Sep. 2024**

AUTRANS *9C3* (0.5km E Rural) *45.17520, 5.54770* **Camping Les 4 Montagnes (formerly Kawan Village au Joyeux Réveil),** Le Château, 38880 Autrans **04 76 95 33 44; camping-au-joyeux-reveil@wanadoo.fr; www.camping-au-joyeux-reveil.fr**

(htd) nr nr (htd)

Fr Villard-de-Lans take D531 to Lans-en-Vercors & turn L onto D106 to Autrans. On E side of vill site sp at 1st rndabt. NB App on D531 fr W fr Pont-en-Royans not rec - v narr rd & low tunnels. 4*, Med, mkd, pt shd, pt sl, EHU (2-10A) €2-8; gas; bbq; TV (pitch); TV; 60% statics; phone; bus 300m, Eng spkn; adv bkg acc; ccard acc; golf 20km; games area; tennis 300m; bike hire; rv fishing; waterslide; CKE. *"Site in Vercors National Park with excel views; winter sport facs, 1050m altitude; modern san facs; excel; well run site; friendly staff."* **€44.00, 11 May-10 Sep. 2024**

AUTUN *6H1* (2km N Rural) *46.96478, 4.29381* **Camping D'Auton (formerly Camp de la Porte d'Arroux),** Les Chaumottes, Rue du Traite d'Anvers, 71400 Autun **03 85 52 10 82; camping.autun@aquadis-loisirs.com; www.aquadis-loisirs.com**

Fr Autun foll dir for Saulieu on D980; site on L 500m after passing thro Roman Arch; only site in Autun. 3*, Sm, hdg, hdstg, pt shd, EHU (10A) €3.30 (poss rev pol); bbq; sw; twin axles; TV; phone; Eng spkn; adv bkg acc; ccard acc; bike hire; fishing; canoeing; games area; CKE. *"Lovely, quiet, clean site; busy NH high ssn; sm pitches, views fr some pitches; friendly, helpful staff; gd san facs, poss stretched high ssn; no twin axles; v muddy when wet (tow avail); vg, lively rest & bar; medieval architecture & Roman walls around town; m'van Aire de Service nr lake in town; mkt Wed/Fri; poss overpriced for nature of site."* **€21.90, 1 May-22 Oct. 2023**

AUTUN *6H1* (12km NW Rural) *47.01227, 4.19150* **Camping Les Deux Rivières,** Le Pré Bouché, 71400 La Celle-en-Morvan **03 85 52 81 23; les2rivieres@camping-morvan.fr; www.camping-morvan.fr**

(htd)

Fr Autun take D978 sp to Chateau-Chinon for approx 12km. Site on R as entering vill. 300m fr main rd. 3*, Med, hdg, mkd, pt shd, bbq; twin axles; Eng spkn; adv bkg acc; games area; CKE. *"V friendly Dutch owners; well kept clean site; supmkt in Autun; excel."* **€29.80, 13 May-13 Oct. 2022**

AUXERRE *4F4* (10km S Rural) *47.70704, 3.63563* **FFCC Camping Les Ceriselles,** Route de Vincelottes, 89290 Vincelles **03 86 42 50 47; campingvincelles@night-day.fr; www.campingceriselles.com**

2.50 € (htd) nr (covrd, htd)

Leave A6 at Auxerre Sud. Fr Auxerre, take D606 S twd Avallon. 10km fr Auxerre turn L into Vincelles. In 400m immed after 'Atac Marche', turn L into site access rd, sp as Camping Les Ceriselles. Site is approx 16km fr a'route exit. 4*, Med, hdstg, mkd, pt shd, EHU (10A) inc (poss rev pol); bbq; red long stay; TV; 10% statics; phone; Eng spkn; adv bkg acc; ccard acc; bike hire; CKE. *"Excel, busy site by canal, poss full late Jun; friendly, helpful owner; 1st dog free, max 2; gd san facs, poss insufficient high ssn & ltd LS; lovely walks to vill & along canal; cycle track to Auxerre & Clamecy; highly rec; high ssn over flow area; secure o'night area; gas adj; v popular."* **€21.00, 29 Mar-30 Oct. 2024**

FRANCE

FRANCE

AUXI LE CHATEAU *3B3* (0.5km NW Rural) *50.2341, 2.1058* **Camping Au vert de l'Authie (formerly Municipal),** 22 Rue du Cheval, 62390 Auxi-le-Château **03 21 04 00 67 or 07 87 07 72 31; contact@campingpasdecalais.fr; www.auvertdelauthie.com**

nr nr nr

Fr S on D925, turn N onto D933 at Bernaville to Auxi-le-Château; turn W onto D941; then turn R in 300m into Rue du Cheval; site sp on R in 500m by football stadium. Or take D928 S fr Hesdin; in 11km take D119 to Auxi-le-Château. 4*, Med, hdg, unshd, EHU (3-6A) inc; 5% statics; adv bkg acc; fishing; sailing. *"Easy walk into town; dir access to rv; gd supmkt 300m; excel NH or short stay; helpful staff; town 1m; gd."* **€23.50, 15 Mar-15 Oct.** **2023**

AUXONNE *6G1* (1km NW Rural) *47.19838, 5.38120* **Camping L'Arquebuse,** Route d'Athée, 21130 Auxonne **03 80 31 06 89; camping.arquebuse@wanadoo.fr; www.campingarquebuse.com**

€2.20 (htd) nr

On D905 Dijon-Geneva, site sp on L bef bdge at ent to Auxonne. 3*, Med, pt shd, EHU (10A) €3.70 (poss rev pol); gas; bbq; twin axles; TV; 40% statics; Eng spkn; adv bkg acc; ccard acc; waterskiing; fishing; clsd 2200-0700; windsurfing; sailing; CKE. *"Pleasant rvside site; friendly staff; san facs tatty & dated; htd pool adj; poss busy w/ends as NH; interesting town; child friendly site."* **€22.00, 4 Mar-16 Dec.** **2023**

AVAILLES LIMOUZINE *7A3* (7km E Rural) *46.12342, 0.65975* **FFCC Camp Municipal Le Parc,** 86460 Availles-Limouzine **05 49 48 51 22; camping.leparc@wanadoo.fr; http://www.camping-le-parc-availles.fr/**

€3.50 nr

Fr Confolens N on D948 & turn R on D34 to Availles-Limouzine. Site on Rv Vienne by town bdge. 2*, Med, pt shd, EHU (10A) inc; gas; Eng spkn; adv bkg acc; CKE. *"Attractive, well-run site in beautiful position; rv views; vg playgrnd; barrier clsd 2200-0800; poss scruffy LS; vg value; permanent warden."* **€19.00, 1 Apr-30 Sep.** **2023**

AVALLON *4G4* (2km SE Rural) *47.48030, 3.91246* **Camp Municipal Sous Roche,** Rue Sous Roche; 89200 Avallon **03 86 34 10 39; campingsousroche@ville-avallon.fr; www.campingsousroche.com**

nr

App town fr a'route or fr SE on N6. Turn sharp L at 2nd traff lts in town cent, L in 2km at sp Vallée du Cousin (bef bdge), site 250m on L. If app fr S care needed when turning R after bdge. 3*, Med, hdstg, pt shd, terr, EHU (10A) inc; bbq; rv fishing adj; CKE. *"Popular, well-kept site in lovely location nr rv; friendly, helpful staff; excel immac san facs; conv Morvan National Park; poss flood warning after heavy rain; no twin axles or o'fits over 2,500kg; attractive town; steep walk to town; excel; M'vans max 3,500kg."* **€19.50, 30 Mar -15 Oct.** **2024**

AVESNES-SUR-HELPE *3D4* (9km ENE Rural) *50.143096, 4.028659* **Camping Municipal de La Boissellerie,** rue de la Place 59740, Felleries **01 83 64 69 21; campingdaboissellerifelleries@orange.fr; www.felleries.fr/le-camping**

nr nr

Fr N2 19km S of Maubeuge. Turn E on D962. At Sars-Poteries turn S on D80 or D104. Site sp in vill. Med, pt shd, EHU (6A) €4; bbq (charcoal, elec, gas); Eng spkn; adv bkg acc. *"Conv N2 N/S or D1043 W/E; lovely area of wooded hills; Rock Fest 1 w/e per year; excel."* **€12.00, 1Apr-30 Sep.** **2024**

AVIGNON *10E2* (9km NE Rural) *43.99057, 4.91340* **Camping Avignon Parc,** 385 Route d'Entraigues, 84270 Vedène **04 90 31 00 51; avignonparc@cielavillage.com; www.campingavignonparc.com**

€2.50

(covrd, htd)

Fr A7 exit 23 dir Carpentras for 3km then Vedene. 3*, Lge, mkd, pt shd, pt sl, EHU (10A) €4 (poss rev pol); gas; bbq; twin axles; 15% statics; phone; bus; Eng spkn; adv bkg acc; games area; games rm; CKE. *"Conv touring base Vaucluse; uneven pitches & paths; facs poss stretched high ssn & ltd LS; lovely pool; vg."* **€29.00, 24 May-24 Sep.** **2023**

AVIGNON *10E2* (8km S Urban) *43.88361, 4.87010* **Camping de la Roquette,** 746 Ave Jean Mermoz, 13160 Châteaurenard **04 90 94 46 81; contact@camping-la-roquette.com; www.camping-la-roquette.com**

€2 nr

Exit A7/D907 Avignon S to Noves; take D28 to Châteaurenard 4km; foll sp to site & Piscine Olympic/Complex Sportiv. 3*, Med, hdg, mkd, pt shd, serviced pitches; EHU (10A) €4; TV; phone; Eng spkn; adv bkg rec; ccard acc; tennis; CKE. *"Gd touring cent; sm pitches; owners friendly, helpful; clean facs; gd walks."* **€24.00, 30 Mar-19 Oct.** **2024**

AVIGNON *10E2* (12km W Rural) *43.95155, 4.66451* **Camping Le Bois des Ecureuils,** 947 Chemin De La Beaume, 30390 Domazan **04 66 57 10 03; contact@camping-boisdesecureuils.fr; camping-boisdesecureuils.fr**

12 €4 nr (htd)

Exit A9/E15 at Remoulins junc 23 twd Avignon on N100. Site on R in 6km. Fr S on N7 foll sp for Nîmes onto N100. Go over 2 lge rndabts, site about 6km on L at rndabt. 2*, Sm, hdstg, mkd, shd, EHU (6A) inc; gas; bbq; TV; 5% statics; phone; Eng spkn; adv bkg rec; CKE. *"Ideal for touring Avignon & Pont du Gard; friendly owners; clean facs; steel awning pegs ess; many long-stay residents LS; v shd; tired site; mostly residential in LS."* **€27.00** **2023**

AVIGNON *10E2* (1km NW Urban) *43.95670, 4.80222* **Camping du Pont d'Avignon,** 10 Chemin de la Barthelasse, 84000 Avignon **03 86 37 95 83 or 04 90 80 63 50; camping.avignon@aquadis-loisirs.com; www.aquadis-loisirs.com**

€2.70

Exit A7 junc 23 Avignon Nord dir Avignon Centre (D225) then Villeneuve-les-Avignon. Go round wall & under Pont d'Avignon; then cross rv dir Villeneuve, Ile de la Barthelasse. Turn R onto Ile de la Barthelasse. 4*, Lge, mkd, hdg, shd, EHU (10A) inc; gas; bbq; cooking facs; red long stay; TV; phone; Eng spkn; adv bkg req; ccard acc; games rm; car wash; games area; tennis; CKE. *"Superb, well-run, busy site; welcoming, helpful staff; lovely pool; gd sized pitches but most with high kerbs; poss flooded LS; extra for c'vans over 5.5m; Avignon festival Jul/Aug; best site for Avignon - 20 mins walk or free ferry; rec arr early even LS; san facs ltd but recently refurbished (2014)."*
€39.00, 1 Mar-3 Nov. 2024

AVIGNON *10E2* (5km NW Rural) *43.99573, 4.81843* **Campéole Camping L'Ile des Papes,** 1497 departmental road 780, Quartier l'Islon, 30400 Villeneuve-lès-Avignon **04 90 15 15 90 or 04 11 32 90 00; https://www.sandaya.fr/nos-campings/l-ile-des-papes**

€3.50

Fr A9 exit sp Roquemaure; head S on D980. Site adj to rv 2km NW of city. Fr D907 (A7) exit Avignon Nord, twds Avignon cent & cross bdge twds Villeneuve. Turn off after x-ing rv bef x-ing canal. Site bet rv & canal. 4*, Lge, pt shd, EHU (10A) inc; bbq; cooking facs; red long stay; TV; 35% statics; Eng spkn; adv bkg acc; ccard acc; archery; lake fishing adj; CKE. *"Lovely area; hiking; well-run site; pleasant staff; lge pitches; gd site rest."*
€25.00, 11 Apr-28 Sept. 2024

AVRILLE *7A1* (0.5km N Rural) *46.47641, -1.49373* **Camping Le Domaine des Forges,** Rue des Forges, 85440 Avrillé **02 51 22 38 85; forges@capfun.com; www.campingdomainedesforges.com or www.les-castels.com**

€4 (covrd, htd)

Fr N on D747 turn R at Moutiers-les-Mauxfaits onto D19 to Avrillé. In town cent cont strt & after sm rndabt foll yellow/white site sp. Turn R into Rue des Forges, site on R in 600m. 5*, Med, mkd, pt shd, EHU (16A) inc; gas; bbq; TV; Eng spkn; adv bkg acc; ccard acc; lake fishing; games area; bike hire; games rm; tennis. *"Attractive site in lovely location; no o'fits over 10m Apr-Oct; spacious, well-kept pitches; fitness rm; helpful, friendly owner; gd, clean, modern san facs; lots of fish in lake; highly rec."*
€43.00, 18 Apr-27 Sep. 2024

AX LES THERMES *8G4* (1km NW Rural) *42.72870, 1.82541* **Camping Sunêlia Le Malazéou,** 09110 Ax-les-Thermes **05 61 64 69 14; camping.malazeou@wanadoo.fr; www.campingmalazeou.com**

12 €3 (htd)

Sp on N20 to Foix. 4*, Lge, hdg, shd, pt sl, EHU (6A) inc; gas; 70% statics; train 500m; Eng spkn; adv bkg acc; CKE. *"Pleasant site by rv; lovely scenery; gd fishing; gd htd san facs; site poss clsd Nov; rvside walk to town; gd."* **€33.00 2024**

AXAT *8G4* (2km E Rural) *42.80775, 2.25408* **Camping de la Crémade,** 11140 Axat **04 68 20 80 64; lecampinglacremade@orange.fr; www.camping-la-cremade.com**

€1

S fr Quillan on D117, cont 1km beyond junc with D118 twd Perpignan. Turn R into site, sp, narr access. 2*, Med, hdg, pt shd, pt sl, EHU (6A) €2.50; bbq; 5% statics; Eng spkn; adv bkg acc; games rm; CKE. *"Pleasant, well-maintained site in beautiful location; few level pitches; gd san facs; conv for gorges in Aude Valley."* **€26.00, 3 Mar-27 Oct. 2024**

AYDAT *9B1* (2km NE Rural) *45.66777, 2.98943* **Camping du Lac d'Aydat,** Forêt du Lot, 63970 Aydat **04 73 79 38 09; info@camping-lac-aydat.com; www.camping-lac-aydat.com**

€1.50 nr

Exit A75 S fr Clermont-Ferrand at junc 5 onto D13 W. Foll sp Lake Aydat. At x-rds at end of Rouillas-Bas, turn L at rndabt & foll site sp.
3*, Med, mkd, hdstg, shd, terr, serviced pitches; EHU (10A) €4; sw nr; 30% statics; phone; adv bkg acc; fishing; CKE. *"On shore of Lake Aydat; gd for m'vans; bar 500m; charming woodland pitches, facs tired."*
€24.00, 1 Apr-30 Sep. 2020

AYDAT *9B1* (3km W Rural) *45.66195, 2.94857* **Camping Les Volcans,** La Garandie, 63970 Aydat **04 73 79 33 90; contact@campinglesvolcans.com; www.campinglesvolcans.com**

€2 nr (htd)

sand 3km

Fr N exit A75 junc 2 onto D2089 dir Bourboule; in 18km turn S onto D213 to Verneuge; in 1km fork R onto D5 dir Murol; in 1.5km turn R onto D788 sp La Grandie; turn R into vill; turn R again & site on L in 100m. Fr S exit A75 junc 5 onto D213 W; in 16km turn S in Verneuge onto D5; after 1.5km turn W onto D788 sp La Garandie; in vill turn R just after phone box, site on L in 100m. 3*, Sm, mkd, pt shd, pt sl, EHU (6A) €5; sw nr; 2% statics; Eng spkn; adv bkg acc; games area; horseriding 3km; watersports 3km. *"Relaxing site; friendly, helpful new owners improving (2011); lge pitches; no twin axles; excel walking & cycle rtes nr; beautiful area; gd touring base; excel clean & well stocked facs; loads of hot water always on supply."*
€24.50, 26 Apr-22 Sep. 2024

FRANCE

FRANCE

AZAY LE FERRON *4H2* (8km N Rural) *46.91949, 1.03679* **Camping Le Cormier,** Route de St Flovier, 36290 Obterre **02 54 39 27 95 or 06 66 53 07 90; mike@loireholidays.biz; www.loireholidays.biz**

12 (htd) nr

Fr Azay-le-Ferron N on D14, site on R just N of Obterre. Or fr Loches S on D943 for 3.5km, turn onto D41 to St Flovier then turn L onto D21 sp Obterre. In 1km turn R onto D14, site on L in 4km. Sm, hdg, hdstg, mkd, pt shd, EHU (10A) €4; bbq; twin axles; TV; Eng spkn; adv bkg acc; ice; games area; games rm. *"Friendly, helpful British owners (CC members); dogs free; spacious pitches; gd san facs; excel touring/walking base; nr Brenne National Park; excel birdwatching; vg."* **€20.00** **2024**

"I need an on-site restaurant"

We do our best to make sure site information is correct, but it is always best to check any must-have facilities are still available or will be open during your visit.

BADEN *2F3* (0.9km SW Rural) *47.61410, -2.92540* **Camping Mané Guernehué,** 52 Rue Mané er Groëz, 56870 Baden, Morbihan Bretagne **02 97 57 02 06; info@camping-baden.com; www.camping-baden.com or www.yellohvillage.co.uk**

€6 (htd) (covrd, htd) sand 3km

Exit N165 sp Arradon/L'Ile aux Moines onto D101 to Baden (10km); in Baden vill turn R at camp sp immed after sharp L-hand bend; in 200m bear R at junc; site on R. Sp at both ends of vill. 5*, Lge, mkd, hdg, pt shd, terr, serviced pitches; EHU (10A) €4.70; bbq; sw nr; red long stay; TV; 35% statics; phone; Eng spkn; ccard acc; sauna; jacuzzi; games rm; golf 1.5km; waterslide; lazy river; spa treatments; fishing; bike hire; games area; tennis 600m; horse riding school; kids' clubs; gym; mini golf; watersports 3km. *"Mature, pleasant site; fitness rm; gd views; excel san facs; some narr site rds; excel."* **€35.00, 8 Apr - 25 Sep, B26. 2022**

BAERENTHAL *5D3* (2km N Rural) *48.98170, 7.51230* **Camp Municipal Ramstein-Plage,** Rue de Ramstein, 57230 Baerenthal **04 66 60 07 00; ramstein@koawa.com; www.camping-ramstein-plage.fr**

€1.90 (htd) nr (htd)

Fr N62 turn onto D36 sp Baerenthal, site sp on lakeside. 3*, Lge, hdg, mkd, pt shd, pt sl, EHU (12A) €3.50; sw nr; 80% statics; Eng spkn; adv bkg acc; tennis; games area. *"Attractive location in important ecological area; generous pitches; modern san facs; m'van o'night area; gd walks; birdwatching; conv Maginot Line; excel."*
€23.50, 1 Apr-30 Sep. **2022**

BAGNERES DE BIGORRE *8F2* (3km E Rural) *43.08180, 0.15139* **Camping Le Monlôo,** 6 Route de la Plaine, 65200 Bagnères-de-Bigorre **05 62 95 19 65; campingmonloo@yahoo.com; www.lemonloo.com**

€1.50 nr

Fr A64 exit junc 14 onto D20/D938 to Bagnères-de-Bigorre. At traff lts on ent turn R onto D8, site on R in 1km, sp at ent. Fr Tarbes (N) on D935 turn L at 1st rndabt, L again over old rlwy line, site on R. 4*, Med, pt shd, sl, EHU (10A) €5.20; TV; 30% statics; phone; Eng spkn; adv bkg acc; ccard acc; waterslide; tennis; CKE. *"Pleasant, peaceful, scenic site; spacious & well-kept site; friendly, welcoming, helpful owners; ltd water points; gd facs, poss stretched high ssn; pleasant town; conv Pyrenean mountain passes; nice views of Pyrenees."* **€44.10, 1 Apr-5 Nov.** **2024**

BAGNERES DE BIGORRE *8F2* (2km SE Rural) *43.05566, 0.16510* **Camping La Pommeraie,** 2 Ave Philadelphe, 65200 Gerde **05 62 91 32 24; campinglapommeraie@gmail.com; www.campinglapommeraie.com**

12 €1.30 (htd) nr nr

App fr E, exit A64 junc 14 (Tournay) onto D20/D938 to Bagnères-de-Bigorre; on ent town turn L at traff lts & foll sp to site. App fr W, exit A64 junc 12 (Tarbes); leave ring rd at junc with D935 & cont to Bagnères-de-Bigorre; foll site sps fr town. 2*, Sm, hdstg, mkd, shd, pt sl, EHU (3-10A) €2.50-6; bbq; 10% statics; phone; Eng spkn; adv bkg acc; games rm; CKE. *"Mountain views; htd covrd pool 2km; friendly owners; bike hire in Bagnères; excel walking, mountain biking & touring base; gd, clean, well mainteined site; ideal tourist area."* **€12.50** **2023**

BAGNERES DE BIGORRE *8F2* (2km SE Urban) *43.07485, 0.16869* **Camping Les Palomieres,** 20 Route Palomieres, 65200 Bagnères-de-Bigorre **05 62 95 59 79; camping-les-palomieres@wanadoo.fr; www.camping-les-palomieres.com**

12

Take D938 fr Bagnères dir Toulouse, after 2km turn R at Haut de la Côte. Site sp. Sm, pt shd, pt sl, EHU (A-6A) €1.50-4.25; sw nr; 50% statics; adv bkg rec. *"Gd views of Pyrenees; simple site; local specialities."*
€12.50 **2023**

BAGNERES DE BIGORRE *8F2* (13km NW Rural) *43.11196, 0.04931* **Aire Naturelle Le Cerf Volant (Dhom),** 7 Cami de la Géline, 65380 Orincles **05 62 42 99 32; lecerfvolant1@yahoo.fr**

Fr Bagnères-de-Bigorre on D935; turn L onto D937 dir Lourdes; site on L opp D407. Single track app rd for 150m. Sm, pt shd, EHU (15A) €2.30; CKE. *"Farm site - produce sold Jul-Aug; conv Lourdes & touring Pyrenees; gd, clean site; lovely site; quiet."*
€12.00, 15 May-15 Oct. **2022**

BAGNOLES DE L'ORNE *4E1* (1.6km SW Urban) *48.54783, -0.41995* **Camp Municipal de la Vée,** Avenue du President Coty, 61140 Bagnoles-de-l'Orne **02 33 37 87 45; info@campingbagnolesdelorne.com; www.campingbagnolesdelorne.com**

€1.70 (htd) nr

Access fr D335 in vill of Bagnoles-Château. Or fr La Ferté-Macé on D916 for 6km sp Couterne. Well sp fr all dirs. 3*, Lge, hdg, mkd, pt shd, pt sl, EHU (10A) €3.50 (poss rev pol); gas; bbq; TV; phone; bus adj; Eng spkn; ccard acc; golf nr; tennis nr; CKE. *"Excel, well-kept, well-run site in vg location; vg, spotless facs; htd pool 1.5km; mini golf nr; easy walk to beautiful thermal spa town & lake; free bus to town cent at site ent; forest walks; archery nrby; gd for dogs; gd value; town bus €1 per day."* **€18.00, 3 Mar-11 Nov.** 2022

BAGNOLS SUR CEZE *10E2* (1.5km N Rural) *44.17585, 4.63540* **Camping La Coquille,** 1534 Route de Carmignan, 30200 Bagnols-sur-Cèze **06 80 01 26 09; contact@campinglacoquille.com; www.campinglacoquille.com**

(cont) nr

Head N fr Bagnols-sur-Cèze over rv bdge turn R at Total stn, site 2km on RH side. 3*, Sm, pt shd, EHU (4-6A) €4-4.50; adv bkg rec; ccard acc; canoe hire; fishing; CKE. *"Site under military aircraft flightpath, otherwise gd, friendly, family-run site."* **€29.00, 1 Apr-31 Aug.** 2024

BAGNOLS SUR CEZE *10E2* (3km NE Rural) *44.17358, 4.63694* **Camping Les Genêts d'Or,** Chemin de Carmigan, 30200 Bagnols-sur-Cèze **04 66 89 58 67; info@camping.genets-dor.com; www.camping-genets-dor.com**

(htd) (htd)

N fr Bagnols on N86 over rv bdge, turn R into D360 immed after Total stn. Foll sp to site on rv. 4*, Med, mkd, hdstg, pt shd, pt sl, EHU (6A) €5.50 (poss rev pol); gas; 10% statics; Eng spkn; adv bkg req; ccard acc; games rm; fishing 2km; games area. *"Excel, clean site; welcoming Dutch owners; gd pool; canoeing 2km; no dogs Jul/Aug; wildlife in rv; gd rest; highly rec."* **€38.50, 15 Apr-25 Sep.** 2022

BAGNOLS SUR CEZE *10E2* (8km NW Rural) *44.18865, 4.52448* **Camping Les Cascades,** Route de Donnat, 30200 La Roque-sur-Cèze **04 66 82 72 97; infos@campinglescascades.com; www.campinglescascades.com**

€1.85 (htd) (htd)

Fr Bagnols take D6 W twd Alès. After 4km turn N on D143 & foll sp to La Roque-sur-Cèze. Site on R in 7km. App fr N not rec. Long narr bdge (2.3m). 4*, Med, pt shd, pt sl, EHU (6-10A) €4.10-4.30; gas; bbq; TV; adv bkg acc; boating; rv fishing adj; tennis. *"Tranquil site; modern san facs."* **€75.00, 24 Apr-15 Sep.** 2024

BAILLEUL *3A3* (3.5km N Rural) *50.76160, 2.74956* **Camping De La Ferme Des Saules,** 453 Route du Mont Noir, 59270 Bailleul **03 28 49 13 75; www.ferme-des-saules.com**

Free

N fr Lille on A25 exit junc 10 & head N into Bailleul cent; in town cent at traff lts turn R onto D23/N375; after 400m turn L on D23; in 2km just bef Belgian border turn L onto D223. Site on L in 300m. Sm, hdstg, pt shd, EHU (6A) €3.50; bbq; 90% statics; Eng spkn; CKE. *"Farm site; friendly owner; conv Calais, Dunkerque & WW1 sites; lovely, excel site, highly rec well kept and comfortable site; 1st class farm shop; unkempt in LS; 2 pin adapter ess; new san facs (2017)."* **€17.00, 1 Apr-31 Oct.** 2023

BAIN DE BRETAGNE *2F4* (0.5km SE Rural) *47.83000, -1.67083* **Camping du Lac,** Route de Launay, 35470 Bain-de-Bretagne **02 99 43 85 67; info@campinglac.fr; www.campinglac.fr**

€2 nr (covrd, htd)

Fr Bain-de-Bretagne take N772 SE dir Châteaubriant, foll sp. Up hill & turn R into narr lane & foll site sp; narr ent. Not rec to tow thro Bain-de-Bretagne. 2*, Med, hdg, mkd, pt shd, EHU (10A) €2.50; sw nr; 10% statics; phone; Eng spkn; sauna; CKE. *"Pretty site with lake views; friendly, helpful new owners (2010) - much improved site; attractive sm town; many leisure facs in walking dist; conv NH; sailing school nr; lovely location, conv for a'route, Vitre & Fougeres; modern & clean facs, but stretched in high ssn."* **€24.00, 15 Mar-15 Oct.** 2024

BAIN DE BRETAGNE *2F4* (13km W Rural) *47.8200, -1.8299* **Camp Municipal Le Port,** Rue de Camping, 35480 Guipry **02 99 34 72 90 (Mairie) or 02 99 34 28 26**

nr nr

W fr Bain-de-Bretagne on D772, cross rv at Messac; cont on D772 sharp L at Leader supmkt into Ave du Port; site sp bef ent Guipry. NB Do not app after dark as rv is at end of app rd. V sharp turn at Leader supmkt into Ave du Camping. 2*, Med, hdg, mkd, pt shd, EHU (10A) €3 (poss long lead req); rv fishing; CKE. *"Excel, pretty site; friendly; warden on duty am & late pm; barrier 1.9m locked at times but phone for help or go to pitch 30; delightful rv walks & cycle paths; cruising & hire boats avail; nr classic cars museum; phone Mairie for warden's number, who calls early PM; vg value; lovely rvside loc; vg walk to town; Creperie nrby."* **€13.00, Easter-15 Oct.** 2022

FRANCE

BALARUC LES BAINS *10F1* (0.3km NE Coastal) *43.44084, 3.68320* **Camp Municipal du Pech d'Ay,** Ave de la Gare, 34540 Balaruc-les-Bains **04 67 48 50 34; pechday@mairie-balaruc-les-bains.fr; www.pechday-balaruc.com/**

(htd) nr nr nr shgl nr

Exit N113 to Balaruc-les-Bains; foll sp Centre Commercial & then head for prom. Site on prom. 2*, Lge, mkd, pt shd, pt sl, EHU (10A) €3.40; bus; Eng spkn; adv bkg rec; CKE. *"Delightful holiday resort; busy site all ssn, rec arr early; vg, clean san facs poss stretched peak timesshops adj; many gd rests adj; thermal baths in vill; bus to Sète."* **€28.00, 16 Mar-19 Oct. 2024**

BALAZUC *9D2* (1km NE Rural) *44.51199, 4.38667* **FFCC Camping La Falaise,** Hameau Les Salles, 07120 Balazuc **04 75 37 74 27; contact@campingdelafalaise.com; www.camping-balazuc.com**

€1.50

Sp on D579 on rvside. 3*, Sm, hdg, shd, pt sl, EHU (6A) €3.80; gas; phone; Eng spkn; adv bkg acc; rv; canoe hire; CKE. *"Site beside Rv Ardèche; helpful and friendly owners; vg."* **€32.00, 1 Apr-20 Sep. 2024**

BALAZUC *9D2* (2km E Rural) *44.50778, 4.40333* **Camping Le Chamadou,** Mas de Chaussy, 07120 Balazuc **06 83 76 92 04 or 04 75 37 00 56; infos@camping-le-chamadou.com; www.camping-le-chamadou.com**

€4 (htd)

Fr Ruoms foll D579 dir Aubenas. After approx 9km turn R under viaduct, site sp. Keep R up narr rd to site. App recep on foot fr car pk. 3*, Med, hdstg, hdg, pt shd, pt sl, EHU (10A) €6 (some rev pol); bbq (elec); TV; 10% statics; phone; Eng spkn; adv bkg rec; ccard acc; canoe hire; kayak hire; waterslide; CKE. *"Excel, well-run, family site; panoramic views; most pitches spacious."* **€28.00, 1 Apr-31 Oct. 2023**

BALBIGNY *9B1* (2.7km NW Rural) *45.82558, 4.16196* **Camping La Route Bleue,** Route D56 du Lac de Villerest, Pralery, 42510 Balbigny **04 77 27 24 97; camping.balbigny@wanadoo.fr; https://www.campingdelaroutebleue.com/**

Free nr

Fr N on D1082, take 1st R after a'route (A89/72) junc N of Balbigny onto D56. Fr S on D1082, turn L at RH bend on N o'skirts of Balbigny, D56, sp Lac de Villerest & St Georges-de-Baroille. Well sp. 3*, Med, hdg, mkd, pt shd, pt sl, EHU (16A) €4.50 (poss long lead req); bbq; red long stay; adv bkg acc; ccard acc; fishing; games rm; CKE. *"Nice site on rv bank; views over rv some pitches; helpful, friendly & welcoming staff; sports complex adj; ltd EHU; extra for twin axles; conv A72; excel; lovely area; lge pitches; gd NH; ok long stay; fishing."* **€21.00, 15 Mar-31 Oct. 2023**

BANDOL *10F3* (3km NW Rural) *43.15980, 5.72905* **Camping Le Clos Ste Thérèse,** Route de Bandol, 83270 St Cyr-sur-Mer **04 94 32 12 21; camping@clos-therese.com; www.clos-therese.com**

€2.30 (htd) nr (htd) sand 4km

Fr Bandol take D559 twd St Cyr & Marseilles. Site on R after 3km. Caution - site ent sharp U turn fr rd. Site service rds steep & narr; not suitable lge vans. 4*, Med, shd, terr, EHU (6-10A) €4-5.20; gas; TV; 30% statics; adv bkg rec; golf nr; tennis nr; horseriding nr. *"Many beaches & beauty spots in area; tractor will site c'vans."* **€51.00, 5 Apr-30 Sep. 2024**

BANON *10E3* (2km S Rural) *44.02607, 5.63088* **Camping L'Epi Bleu,** Les Gravières, 04150 Banon **04 92 73 30 30 or 06 15 61 68 63 (mob); campingepibleu@aol.com; www.campingepibleu.com**

€4 (htd)

Fr D4100 8km S of Forcalquier turn R onto D5 N thro St Michel-L'Observatoire & Revest twd Banon (approx 25km). Turn L on D51 twds Simiane-la-Rotunde. Site on R in 500m immed bef town, sp at junc. 4*, Med, shd, EHU (10A) €5; bbq; TV; 70% statics; Eng spkn; adv bkg acc; games area; CKE. *"Vg, wooded site; pleasant owners; gd walking & cycling tours; access to some pitches diff for lge o'fits; san fac tired but clean (2015); uphill 30m walk to vill with sm supmkt."* **€28.30, 15 May-25 Sep. 2022**

BANYULS SUR MER *10H1* (1.5km SW Rural) *42.47665, 3.11904* **Camp Municipal La Pinède,** 2 route du Mas Reig, 66650 Banyuls-sur-Mer **04 68 88 32 13; camp.banyuls@banyuls-sur-mer.com; www.campinglapinede-banyuls.com**

€3 nr shgl 1km

On D914 foll sp to Banyuls-sur-Mer; turn R at camping sp at cent of sea-front by town hall; foll sp to site. 2*, Lge, hdg, mkd, pt shd, pt sl, terr, EHU (10A) €6.50; Eng spkn; ccard acc; CKE. *"Busy, friendly site; spacious pitches, some with sea view; narr site rds; vg, clean facs."* **€29.00, 23 Feb-12 Nov. 2023**

BAR LE DUC *6E1* (2km E Urban) *48.77433, 5.17415* **Camping du Château,** Rue Jean Bernard, 55000 Bar-le-Duc **03 29 79 17 33 (TO) or 03 29 79 11 13 (LS); barleduc.tourisme@wanadoo.fr; www.tourisme-barleduc.com**

nr

Fr town cent foll Camping sps. Rue de St Mihiel is pt of D1916 dir Verdun. Fr NW on D994/D694 or fr SE on N1135, at rndabt turn E onto D1916 sp Metz, Verdun & St Mihiel. In 200m turn L into Rue du Stade sp Camping. Site on L in 100m. 1*, Sm, pt shd, EHU (16A) €3 (poss long lead req). *"Barrier clsd 1100-1500; delightful site in grnds of chateau; friendly & helpful warden; clean, modern san facs; no twin axles; check gate opening times; lovely walk into historic town; gd NH; vg site; nice open plan site."* **€10.00, 1 May-15 Oct. 2023**

BARBIERES *9C2* (1km SE Rural) *44.94470, 5.15100* **Camping Le Gallo-Romain,** 1090 Route de Col de Tourniol, 26300 Barbières **04 75 05 90 12; info@legalloromain.net; www.legalloromain.net**

€5.50

Exit A49 junc 7 onto D149 dir Marches & Barbières. Go thro vill & ascend Rte du Col de Tourniol for 2km, site on R, well sp. 4*, Med, mkd, pt shd, pt sl, terr, EHU (6A) €3.75; bbq; TV; 15% statics; phone; Eng spkn; adv bkg acc; CKE. *"Mountain setting; welcoming, friendly, helpful Dutch owners; ltd facs LS; gd; nice location."* **€35.50, 22 Apr-17 Sep. 2024**

BARCARES, LE *10G1* (1km SW Coastal) *42.78094, 3.02267* **Yelloh! Village Le Pré Catalan,** Route de St Laurent, 66420 Le Barcarès **04 68 86 12 60; info@precatalan.com; www.precatalan.com or www.yellohvillage.co.uk**

€3 (htd) sand 1km

Exit A9 junc 41 onto D83; app Le Barcarès turn R onto D81, then L onto D90 to Le Barcarès, site sp. 4*, Lge, shd, EHU (6A) €4; gas; TV; phone; adv bkg rec; tennis; games area; games rm. **€32.00, 04 May-15 Sep. 2024**

BARCELONNETTE *9D4* (9km W Rural) *44.39686, 6.54605* **Domaine Loisirs de l'Ubaye,** Vallée de l'Ubaye, 04340 Barcelonnette **04 92 81 01 96; info@loisirsubaye.com; domaineubaye.com**

€3.50 (htd)

Site on S side of D900. 4*, Lge, mkd, shd, terr, EHU (6A) €3.50; gas; red long stay; TV; phone; watersports; bike hire; CKE. *"Magnificent scenery; gd site; friendly."* **€33.00, 15 May-15 Sep. 2022**

BARFLEUR *1C4* (0.7km NW Urban/Coastal) *49.67564, -1.26645* **Camp Municipal La Blanche Nef,** 12 Chemin de la Masse, 50760 Gatteville-le-Phare **02 33 23 15 40; camping.barfleur.fr/en/**

€2.50 (htd) nr sand adj

Foll main rd to harbour; half-way on L side of harbour & turn L at mkd gap in car pk; cross sm side-rd & foll site sp on sea wall; site visible on L in 300m. Site accessible only fr S (Barfleur). 3*, Med, unshd, pt sl, EHU (10A) €5; 45% statics; Eng spkn; adv bkg acc; ccard acc; CKE. *"Gd sized pitches; vg facs; lovely site; sea views; gd beach; gd birdwatching, walking, cycling; m'vans all year; walking dist to fishing vill; clean washing facs; bread van at 9am."* **€18.00, 15 Feb-15 Nov. 2023**

BARFLEUR *1C4* (1km NW Coastal) *49.67971, -1.27364* **Camping La Ferme du Bord de Mer,** 43 Route du Val de Saire, 50760 Gatteville-Phare **060 895 2434; camping.gatteville@gmail.com; www.camping-gatteville.fr**

12 €1.45 nr sand adj

On D901 fr Cherbourg; on o'skts of Barfleur turn L onto D116 for Gatteville-Phare. Site on R in 1km. 2*, Sm, mkd, hdg, pt shd, pt sl, serviced pitches; EHU (3-10A) €3.40-5.30; gas; 25% statics; phone; games rm. *"CL-type site; sheltered beach; coastal path to vill & lighthouse; conv ferries (30 mins); Sep 2002 member reported high-strength poison against rodents in field adj site - no warning notices displayed, beware children or dogs; great seaside loc; friendly; helpful; v gd."* **€20.40 2022**

BARROU *4H2* (0km S Rural) *46.86500, 0.77100* **FFCC Camping Les Rioms,** Les Rioms, 37350 Barrou **02 47 94 53 07; contact@camping-lesrioms.com; www.camping-lesrioms.com/en**

nr nr (htd)

Fr D750 Descartes to La Roche-Posay rd turn R at sp Camping at ent to Barrou vill. Site sp. NB Site has barriers, phone if clsd. 2*, Sm, hdg, mkd, pt shd, EHU (16A) €4; bbq; 35% statics; Eng spkn; adv bkg acc; CKE. *"Pleasant, peaceful site on bank of Rv Creuse; clean san facs; friendly owners; gd pool; excel."* **€18.40, 6 Apr-9 Oct. 2024**

BASTIA *10G2* (5km N Coastal) *42.74039, 9.45982* **Camping Les Orangers,** 4 Chemin de Fiumicellu, 20200 San-Martino-di-Lota, Corsica **06 12 53 73 33; camping.lesorangers@gmail.com; www.camping-lesorangers.com**

shgl adj

Foll main coast rd D80 N 4km fr ferry. Site well sp on L of rd. 1*, Sm, shd, EHU; TV; Eng spkn; CKE. *"Poss run down LS; friendly owners; vg rest; site ent tight for lge o'fits; no m'vans (2011); poss unrel opening dates."* **€19.00, 1 Apr-30 Sep. 2020**

BASTIA *10G2* (11km S Coastal) *42.62922, 9.46835* **Camping San Damiano,** Lido de la Marana, 20620 Biguglia **04 95 33 68 02; san.damiano@wanadoo.fr; www.campingsandamiano.com**

€0.90 sandy adj

S fr Bastia on N193 for 4km. Turn SE onto Lagoon Rd (sp Lido de Marana). Site on L in 7km. 4*, Lge, pt shd, EHU (6A) €3.40; red long stay; 60% statics; Eng spkn; ccard acc; games area; games rm; CKE. *"San facs basic but clean; cycle path; big site, spread out; no water points; rd and aircraft noise."* **€34.00, 30 Mar-3 Nov. 2024**

FRANCE

BASTIDE DE SEROU, LA *8G3* (1km S Rural) *43.00150, 1.44472* **Camping L'Arize,** Route de Nescus, 09240 La Bastide-de-Sérou **05 61 65 81 51; mail@camping-arize.com; www.camping-arize.com**

€2 (htd) nr

Fr Foix on D117 on ent La Bastide-de-Sérou turn L at TO/Gendarmerie on D15 sp Nescus, site 1km on R. 4*, Med, hdg, mkd, pt shd, serviced pitches; EHU (6A) inc (poss rev pol); gas; sw nr; 10% statics; Eng spkn; adv bkg acc; ccard acc; golf nr; fishing; horseriding adj; golf 5km; bike hire; CKE. *"Pleasant, scenic site on bank Rv Arize; modern facs; gd mkd walking/cycle rtes."*
€31.00, 30 Apr-30 Sep. **2024**

BAUD *2F3* (7km W Rural) *47.88239, 3.10818* **Camp Municipal de Pont Augan,** Pont Augan, 56150 Baud **02 97 51 04 74 or 06 84 82 44 13; camping.p.augan@live.fr; camping-pontaugan.com**

(htd) nr nr

Fr Baud, W on D6. Site on R on ent vill. 2*, Sm, hdg, mkd, pt shd, EHU (10A) €4; bbq; Eng spkn; adv bkg acc; canoeing adj; fishing adj; games area; bike hire; CKE. *"Peaceful site; barrier & office ltd opening hrs but parking area avail; warden calls morning & teatime; ltd groceries; 4 gites on site; vg."*
€15.50, 1 Apr-30 Sep. **2023**

BAULE, LA *2G3* (2km NE Rural) *47.29833, -2.35722* **Airotel Camping La Roseraie,** 20 Ave Jean Sohier, Route du Golf, 44500 La Baule-Escoublac **02 40 60 46 66; camping@laroseraie.com; www.laroseraie.com**

€5 nr (covrd, htd) sand 2km

Take N171 fr St Nazaire to La Baule. In La Baule-Escoublac turn R at x-rds by church, site in 300m on R; sp fr La Baule cent. 4*, Lge, hdstg, mkd, hdg, pt shd, EHU (6-10A) €5.50-€7.50; gas; bbq; red long stay; TV; 80% statics; phone; Eng spkn; adv bkg acc; ccard acc; games rm; waterslide; watersports; tennis; fishing; games area; CKE. *"Gd site & facs; sm pitches; fitness rm; clean unisex san facs; ltd facs LS; easy walk into La Baule-Escoublac; excel beach nrby; vg."*
€40.00, 1 Apr-25 Sep. **2020**

BAUME LES DAMES *6G2* (0.5km S Rural) *47.34050, 6.35752* **Camping Du Domaine D'Aucroix,** 33 Quai du Canal, 25110 Baume-les-Dames **03 81 84 38 89 or 04 77 56 66 09; camping-baume-les-dames@orange.fr; www.vacances-ulvf.com**

12 €3.50 nr nr nr (htd)

Fr D683 in Baume-les-Dames turn S onto D50, cross canal & turn W. Site sp. Sm, hdstg, mkd, pt shd, EHU (16A) inc; TV; 20% statics; Eng spkn; adv bkg acc; ccard acc; CKE. *"Peaceful site; gd NH/long stay, v conv fr m'way; on Euro Velo 5 cycle rte along Le Doub rv; easy access to town by bike; off open 5:30pm; site self and register later; v quiet; new san facs (2023); gd."*
€11.50 **2023**

BAYEUX *3D1* (0.5km N Urban) *49.28392, -0.69760* **Camp Municipal des Bords de L'Aure,** Blvd d'Eindhoven, 14400 Bayeux **02 31 92 08 43; camping-bayeux.fr; http://www.camping-bayeux.fr**

Site sp off Périphérique d'Eindhoven (Bayeux by-pass, D613). Fr W (Cherbourg) exit N13 junc 38, turn L over N13, then R onto D613 thro Vaucelles. At rndabt cont on D613 (3rd exit) Blvd d'Eindhoven. Site on R immed after traff lts, almost opp Briconaute DIY store. Fr E (Caen) on N13 exit junc 36 onto D613 N; foll ring rd across 2 rndabts, 4 traff lts, site on L opp Bayeux town sp. 3*, Lge, hdstg, hdg, pt shd, EHU (6A) inc (poss rev pol); gas; sw nr; red long stay; phone; Eng spkn; adv bkg req; CKE. *"Excel, well-kept site; indoor pool adj; avoid perimeter pitches (narr hdstgs & rd noise); no twin axles; office open LS; gd footpath to town along stream; Bayeux festival 1st w/end July; conv ferries; lge mkt Sat; new, clean san facs & lndry facs (2018)."* **€26.50, 30 Mar-3 Nov.** **2024**

BAYEUX *3D1* (18km SE Rural) *49.15722, -0.76018* **Camping Caravaning Escapade,** Rue de l'église, 14490 CAHAGNOLLES **02 31 21 63 59; info@campinglescapade.net; www.campinglescapade.net**

€2.70 (htd)

Fr Saint Paul du Varnay take D99 Cahagnolles on the L; foll rd for aprrox 2.5km; turn L & aft church campsite on R. 4*, Med, mkd, pt shd, EHU (10A) €3.90; bbq; adv bkg acc; ccard acc. *"Lovely site; well looked after & cared for; clean san facs; friendly owners & staff; recep rm for events; pt of Flower Campings chain."* **€28.00, 1 Apr-30 Sep.** **2024**

BAYEUX *3D1* (7km SE Rural) *49.24840, -0.60245* **Camping Le Château de Martragny,** 52 Hameau Saint-Léger, 14740 Martragny **02 31 80 21 40; chateau.martragny@wanadoo.fr; www.chateau-martragny.com or www.chateau-martragny.fr**

€1 (htd)

Fr Caen going NW on N13 dir Bayeux/Cherbourg, leave at Martragny/Carcagny exit. Strt on & take 2nd R (past turn for Martragny/Creully) into site & chateau grnds. Fr Bayeux after leaving N13 (Martragny/Carcagny), go L over bdge to end of rd, turn L then take 2nd R into Chateau grnds. 4*, Lge, mkd, pt shd, pt sl, EHU (15A) €5.50 (long lead poss req, poss rev pol); gas; bbq; TV; Eng spkn; adv bkg acc; ccard acc; games rm; tennis; fishing; horseriding 500m; CKE. *"Popular, attractive, 1st class site on lawns of chateau; attractive area; relaxed atmosphere; friendly, helpful staff; new superb, modern san facs (2013); gd rest; no o'fits over 8m; poss muddy when wet; conv cemetaries; D-Day beaches 15km; Sat mkt in Bayeux; conv Caen ferry; excel."*
€35.00, 23 May - 25 Aug, N06. **2022**

BAYEUX *3D1* (9km NW Rural) *49.33120, -0.80240* **Camping Reine Mathilde,** 14400 Etréham **02 31 21 76 55; campingreinemathilde@gmail.com; www.camping-normandie-reinemathilde.com**

€2.50 (htd) (htd) sand 5km

NW fr Bayeux on D6 turn L to Etréham (D100); site 3km (sp). Or W fr Bayeux on N13 for 8km, exist junc 38. At x-rds 1.5km after vill of Tour-en-Bessin turn R on D206 to Etréham & bear L at church. 3*, Med, mkd, hdg, pt shd, EHU (6A) €4.70; TV; 15% statics; phone; Eng spkn; adv bkg acc; fishing 1km; bike hire; CKE. *"Well-kept, attractive site; lge, well spaced hdg pitches; mv service pnt nr; app rds quite narr; friendly, helpful warden; gd, clean san facs; conv D-Day beaches etc; excel."* **€26.70, 1 Apr-30 Sep.** **2024**

BAYONNE *8F1* (11km NE Rural) *43.52820, -1.39157* **Camping Lou P'tit Poun,** 110 Ave du Quartier Neuf, 40390 St Martin-de-Seignanx **05 59 56 55 79; contact@louptitpoun.com; www.louptitpoun.com**

€5 nr

Fr Bordeaux exit A63 junc 6 dir Bayonne Nord; then take D817 dir Pau & St Martin-de-Seignanx; site sp on R in 7km. 4*, Lge, mkd, hdg, pt shd, terr, serviced pitches; EHU (10A) inc; gas; bbq (elec, gas); sw nr; red long stay; TV; 17% statics; phone; Eng spkn; adv bkg acc; ccard acc; games area; games rm; tennis; CKE. *"Charming, spacious, family-run site; gd sized pitches; friendly staff; gd clean san facs; ltd facs LS; conv Biarritz, St Jean-de-Luz & a'route; excel."* **€75.00, 9 Jun - 15 Sep, A39.** **2022**

BAYONNE *8F1* (8km NE Rural) *43.54858, -1.40381* **Aire Naturelle L'Arrayade (Barret),** 280 Chemin Pradillan, 40390 St Martin-de-Seignanx **05 59 56 10 60; guide-des-landes.com/en/tourism/accommodation/camping/campervan-sites/saint-martin-de-seignanx-270/aire-naturelle-l-arrayade-1033.html**

On D26 midway bet D810 & D817, 3km W of St Martin. (Opp tall crenellated building). Sm, pt shd, pt sl, EHU €2.50 (long lead rec); bbq. *"Delightful little site; warm welcome; helpful owner; simple facs poss stretched high ssn; gd base for exploring Basque country."* **€12.00, 1 Jun-30 Sep.** **2024**

BAZAS *7D2* (2km SE Rural) *44.43139, -0.20167* **Campsite Le Paradis de Bazas,** Route de Casteljaloux, 33430 Bazas **05 56 65 13 17; paradis@capfun.com; www.camping-paradis-bazas.fr**

€3 nr (htd)

Exit A62 junc 3 onto N524 twd Bazas, then D655. Cont thro town cent & foll sp Casteljaloux/Grignols. Site sp on R. 4*, Sm, hdg, mkd, pt shd, pt sl, EHU (6-16A) €3.25-4.90; gas; red long stay; TV; 6% statics; Eng spkn; adv bkg acc; CKE. *"Pleasant, relaxed, well-kept site in picturesque location; views of chateau & town; friendly, helpful staff; san facs v smart but poss stretched high ssn; pleasant walk/cycle track to interesting, walled town; vineyards nr."* **€25.00, 1 Apr-29 Sep.** **2023**

BEAUGENCY *4F2* (0.8km E Rural) *47.77628, 1.64294* **Camp Municipal du Val de Flux,** Route de Lailly-en-Val, 45190 Beaugency **02 38 14 72 66; camping.beaugency@gmail.com; www.camping-beaugency.fr**

€2 (htd) nr sand

Exit A10 junc 15 onto D2152. In Beaugency turn L at traff lts nr water tower onto D925 & again over rd bdge. Site sp on S bank of Rv Loire. 3*, Lge, mkd, pt shd, EHU (10A) inc (rev pol); red long stay; 10% statics; Eng spkn; ccard acc; fishing; watersports; CKE. *"Beautiful, welcoming, well-kept site; views over Loire; helpful, friendly staff; free 1 night site for m'vans over rv on other side of town; poss unrel opening dates LS, rec phone ahead; vg location close to town; coded ent barrier; next to rv and bdge to town; some rd noise at busy times; facs gd but far away fr pitches; scruffy & unkempt; town dilapidated; free WiFi around shop; gd cycling."* **€23.00, 1 Apr-20 Sep.** **2024**

BEAUGENCY *4F2* (8km S Rural) *47.68679, 1.55802* **Camp Municipal L'Amitié,** 17 Rue du Camping, Nouan-sur-Loire, 41220 St Laurent-Nouan **02 54 87 01 52; campingdelamitie@stlaurentnouan.fr; www.campingdelamitie.fr**

12 €1 (htd) nr nr

On D951 SW fr Orléans cont past power stn into Nouan-sur-Loire. Site on R sp. 2*, Med, hdg, mkd, pt shd, EHU (6A) €4.60; 50% statics; adv bkg acc; CKE. *"Interesting area; view of Rv Loire; workers poss resident on site; friendly, helpful staff; well-maintained site; poor condition portacabins, better san facs nr ent; phone ahead LS to check open; dir access to rv; being redeveloped; excel facs; sports activities nrby; site clsd Xmas & New Year; conv for Chateau Chambord; supmkt 100m fr ent."* **€8.00** **2024**

"Satellite navigation makes touring much easier"

Remember most sat navs don't know if you're towing or in a larger vehicle – always use yours alongside maps and site directions.

BEAULIEU SUR DORDOGNE *7C4* (3km N Rural) *45.00911, 1.85059* **Aire Naturelle La Berge Ombragée (Lissajoux),** Valeyran, 19120 Brivezac **+33 670786563; contact@berge-ombragee.com; www.berge-ombragee.com**

€0.30

N fr Beauliew-sur-Dordogne on D940; in 500m turn R onto D12; site on R in 2km. Office down on rv bank. NB Front wheel drive tow cars may find diff on gravel hill leading up fr office. Sm, pt shd, pt sl, EHU (6A) €3; bbq; sw nr; Canoeing; Volleyball; Badminton; CKE. *"CL-type site; friendly; canoeing fr site; gd."* **€22.40, 1 May-15 Sep.** **2020**

FRANCE

BEAULIEU SUR DORDOGNE *7C4* (5km N Rural) *45.02167, 1.83960* **Camping la Champagne,** La Champagne, 19120 Brivezac **06 48 47 23 51; info@campinglachampagne.com; www.campinglachampagne.com**

€2.50

Fr Beaulieu-sur-Dordogne take D940, sp Tulle. R onto D12, sp Argentat. R onto D136. R again after bdge. Site 600m on R. 2*, Sm, mkd, pt shd, terr, EHU (6A) €3; bbq; sw nr; twin axles; phone; Eng spkn; adv bkg acc; CCI. *"Aire Naturella (max 25 vans); fishing; canoeing; horseriding nr; peaceful, spacious rvside location; Dutch owners."*
€28.00, 1 May-15 Sep. **2024**

BEAULIEU SUR DORDOGNE *7C4* (0.3km E Urban) *44.97950, 1.84040* **Huttopia Beaulieu Sur Dordogne (formerly Camping des Iles),** Blvd Rodolphe-de-Turenne, 19120 Beaulieu-sur-Dordogne **05 55 91 02 65; https://europe.huttopia.com/site/camping-beaulieu-sur-dordogne/**

€5 (htd)

Exit A20 junc 52 ont D158/D38 dir Collonges-la-Rouge; cont on D38 & turn R onto D940 to Beaulieu-sur-Dordogne; site sp fr o'skts of town. Or on D940 N fr Bretenoux, turn R in Beaulieu town sq, site about 200m on island in Rv Dordogne. NB 3m height limit at ent. 4*, Med, mkd, shd, EHU (10A) inc (poss long lead req); bbq (gas); red long stay; 15% statics; Eng spkn; adv bkg rec; games rm; rv; fishing; bike hire; games area; canoeing. *"Delightful, wooded site; pitches by rv excel (extra charge); plenty shd; friendly staff; gd clean san facs, ltd LS; attractive medieval town; gd value; highly rec."*
€40.00, 14 Apr - 25 Sep, A21. **2022**

BEAULIEU SUR LOIRE *4G3* (0.3km E Rural) *47.54407, 2.82167* **FFCC Camp Municipal du Canal,** Route de Bonny, 45630 Beaulieu-sur-Loire **01 83 64 69 21; renault.campingbeaulieu@orange.fr; www.beaulieu-sur-loire.fr**

12 nr nr nr

Exit A77 junc 21 Bonny-sur-Loire, cross rv to Beaulieu-sur-Loire on D296. On E o'skirts of vill on D926, nr canal. 2*, Sm, hdg, mkd, hdstg, pt shd, EHU (10A) €4; Eng spkn; adv bkg acc; CKE. *"Well-kept site in pleasant area; direct access to canal; some sm pitches diff lge o'fits; site yourself, warden calls 0800-0900 & 1830-1930; no security; clean modern san facs; gd walking along canal & Rv Loire; boat trips; poss workers' statics LS; mkt Wed; lovely hdg pitches; conv Aqueduct at Briare; on san facs req Oct - Apr as site facs clsd."* **€12.00** **2023**

BEAUMONT DU PERIGORD *7D3* (7km SW Rural) *44.75603, 0.70216* **Centre Naturiste de Vacances Le Couderc (Naturist),** 24440 Naussannes **05 53 22 40 40; info@lecouderc.com; www.lecouderc.com**

€5 (htd)

Fr D660 at D25 W thro Naussannes & hamlet of Leydou. Just beyond Leydou turn R into site, well sp. 1*, Lge, mkd, pt shd, pt sl, EHU (5A) €5.50; red long stay; 10% statics; adv bkg req; ccard acc; jacuzzi; sauna; bike hire. *"Beautiful site with relaxed atmosphere; friendly, helpful Dutch owners; gd san facs; superb pool; naturist walks on site; gd walking/cycling area; Bastide towns nrby; new sauna,steam rm/spa (2015); new camping field; pond cleaned & enlarged; vg entmnt & activity prog for kids & adults."* **€41.60, 1 Apr-15 Oct.** **2023**

BEAUMONT SUR SARTHE *4F1* (1km E Rural) *48.22563, 0.13440* **FFCC Camp Municipal du Val de Sarthe,** Rue de l'Abreuvoir, 72170 Beaumont-sur-Sarthe **02 43 97 01 93; camping-beaumontssarthe@orange.fr; www.camping-val-de-sarthe.fr**

€2 nr nr

Fr D338 Alençon-Le Mans, turn sharp L at 2nd set of traff lts in cent of Beaumont & foll site sp twd E of town. Fr Le Mans on A28 exit 21 onto D6, R onto D338 & R at traff lts & foll sp. NB Narr, sloping app thro town rds with blind corners. Narr site access. 3*, Med, hdg, mkd, pt shd, EHU (10A) €3.50; TV; Eng spkn; adv bkg rec; ccard acc; fishing adj; rv boating adj; CKE. *"Beautiful, peaceful, well-run rvside site; lge pitches, some by rv; no twin axles & poss no c'vans over 2,000 kg; barrier clsd 2200; easy walk to interesting, pretty town; mkt Tues; rec; nice clean site; pleasant & friendly; well maintained site; recep open 1000-1200, 1600-1900 (May, Jun & Sep), 900-1200, 1500-2000 (Jul & Aug); barrier unattended bet 1200-1400; pool 500m; admission only aft 4pm; popular NH; excel value; well equipped indoor rm for campers."*
€16.40, 1 May-30 Sep. **2024**

BEAUNE *6H1* (1km N Urban) *47.03304, 4.83911* **Camp Municipal Les Cent Vignes,** 10 Rue Auguste Dubois, 21200 Beaune **03 80 22 03 91; campinglescentvignes@mairie-beaune.fr; www.campinglescentvignes.fr**

(htd)

Fr N on A31 & fr S on A6 at junc with m'ways A6/A31 take A6 sp Auxerre-Paris; after 1km leave at junc 24 to join D974 twd Beaune; after approx 1.5km, turn R at 2nd traff lts fr a'route to site (sp) in 200m. If app fr S on D974 site well sp fr inner ring rd & foll sp to Dijon (not a'route sps). Also sp fr Mersault/L'Hôpital x-rds. 4*, Med, hdg, mkd, hdstg, pt shd, EHU (16A) inc (some rev pol); gas; bbq; TV; phone; Eng spkn; ccard acc; bike hire; games area; tennis; CKE. *"Popular, well-run site; rec arr early even LS; gd modern san facs; vg rest; most pitches gd size but narr site rds makes access some pitches diff, a mover useful; tight turns & low trees poss diff lge o'fits; twin axles; in walking dist of Beaune; v conv site; hypmkt 2km; superb new san facs 2013; excel site; adv bkg in writing only bef 30 May; pool 800m; many pitches with own service pnts; v busy site."* **€22.30, 15 Mar-20 Nov.** **2023**

BEAUNE *6H1* (3.5km NE Rural) *47.02668, 4.88294* **Camping Les Bouleaux,** 11 Rue Jaune, 21200 Vignoles **03 80 22 26 88; campinglesbouleaux.wixsite.com/lesbouleaux**

12 (htd)

Exit A6 at junc 24.1; 500m after toll turn R at rndabt, in 1.5km turn R sp Dole rndabt. Immed after x-ing m'way turn L sp Vignoles. L again at next junc then R & foll camping sp. Site in approx 1.5km in cent Chevignerot; fr town cent take D973 (E) sp Dole. In 2km cross a'route & 1st L (N) sp Vignoles. Well sp. 3*, Sm, hdg, mkd, pt shd, EHU (6A) inc (rev pol altered on request); adv bkg rec; CKE. *"Attractive, well-kept, busy site, even in LS; rec arr early high ssn; some gd sized pitches, most sm; superb clean new san facs, poss stretched high ssn & ltd LS; poss muddy after rain - park on rdways; conv NH fr a'route; basic site; long lead may be req'd; excel site; excel walking in area; helpful owner; cash only."* **€23.10** **2023**

"There aren't many sites open at this time of year"

If you're travelling outside peak season remember to call ahead to check site opening dates – even if the entry says 'open all year'.

BEAUNE *6H1* (8km SW Rural) *46.98573, 4.76855* **La Grappe d'Or (formally Kawan Village),** 2 Route de Volnay, 21190 Meursault **03 80 21 22 48; info@camping-meursault.com; www.camping-meursault.com**

€1.40 (htd)

Fr N-S, Exit A6 Junc 24.1 SP Beaune Centre Hospices, at rndabt foll sp to Chalon sur Saône RN 74, after 7km foll sp to Meursault, turn r, foll sp for site. 4*, Med, mkd, pt shd, terr, EHU (10A) inc; gas; sw; phone; Eng spkn; adv bkg req; waterslide; bike hire; tennis; games area; CKE. *"Lovely family site; busy high ssn - arr early; all pitches views over vineyards; friendly, helpful owners; basic facs stretched; ltd water pnts & poss steep climb fr lower pitches; some pitches uneven, sm or obstructed by trees - poss diff access lge o'fits; poss muddy when wet; barrier clsd 2200-0730; rambling; sh walk to lovely vill; gd cycle paths; vg; popular site; well run; if full use site at Santenay."* **€35.00, 3 Apr-2 Nov.** **2024**

BEAUREPAIRE *9C2* (10km S Rural) *45.25332, 5.02803* **Camping du Château,** Route de Romans, 26390 Hauterives **04 75 68 80 19; contact@camping-hauterives.com; www.camping-hauterives.com**

€2.20 nr (htd)

Take D538 S to Hauterives, site sp in vill adj Rv Galaure. 4*, Med, mkd, pt shd, EHU (6-10A) €2.50-3; 10% statics; adv bkg acc; rv fishing adj; games area; tennis. *"Gd NH; friendly; gd pool; Do not use sat nav, inaccurate."* **€19.50, 5 Apr-22Sep.** **2024**

BEAUVAIS *3C3* (16km E Rural) *49.40506, 2.25803* **Camping de la Trye,** Rue de Trye, 60510 Bresles **03 44 07 80 95 or 06 10 40 30 29 (mob); www.camping-de-la-trye.com**

12

Exit N31 (Beauvais to Clermont) at Bresles; foll site sp. Med, hdg, mkd, pt shd, sl, EHU (6A) inc; bbq; 75% statics; adv bkg acc; ccard acc; bike hire; CKE. *"Helpful Dutch owners; cycle & walking rtes; theme parks nrby; trampoline; largely a holiday chalet/static site with ltd no of touring pitches; pony rides; fair NH/sh stay."* **€21.40** **2022**

BEAUVILLE *7D3* (0.5km SE Rural) *44.27210, 0.88850* **Camping Les Deux Lacs,** 47470 Beauville **05 53 95 45 41; camping-les-2-lacs@wanadoo.fr; les2lacs.com**

€3.30 nr

Fr D656 S to Beauville, site sp on D122. NB Steep descent to site - owners help when leaving if necessary. 3*, Med, hdg, mkd, shd, terr, EHU (10A) €6.70; sw nr; red long stay; 10% statics; Eng spkn; adv bkg acc; ccard acc; fishing; games area; watersports; CKE. *"Peaceful; gd fishing; pleasant walk to vill; vg; Dutch owners; facs inadequate when site full."* **€31.70, 1 Apr-31 Oct.** **2023**

BEDOIN *10E2* (1.5km NE Rural) *44.13363, 5.18738* **Camping Domaine de Bélézy (Naturist),** 132 Maraval Road 84410 Bédoin **04 90 65 60 18; info@belezy.com; www.belezy.com**

(htd) (htd)

Fr Carpentras D974 to Bédoin. Go thro vill & turn R at rndabt sp Mont Ventoux. In 300m turn L & foll sp to site. 4*, Lge, shd, pt sl, EHU (12A) €5.60; gas; cooking facs; red long stay; TV; 20% statics; phone; Eng spkn; adv bkg acc; ccard acc; tennis; golf 20km; INF card; horseriding 2km; games area. *"Delightful, peaceful, well-kept site in lovely location; warm welcome, helpful staff; sep car park high ssn; extensive facs; sauna; steam rm; many acitivies; some sm & awkward pitches; gd base for Mt Ventoux, Côtes du Rhône; excel; no pets; pitches v close together."* **€57.00, 2 Apr-2 Oct.** **2024**

BEDOIN *10E2* (0.5km W Rural) *44.12468, 5.17249* **Camp Municipal de la Pinède,** 502 Chemin des Sablières, 84410 Bédoin **04 90 65 61 03; campingmunicipal@bedoin.fr; www.camping-lapinede-ventoux.fr/**

€1.50 (htd) nr (htd)

Take D938 S fr Malaucène for 3km, L onto D19 for 9km to Bédoin. Site adj to vill & sp. 2*, Med, mkd, hdstg, shd, sl, terr, EHU (16A) €4; bus; Eng spkn; adv bkg acc; ccard acc; CKE. *"Pool clsd Mon; 5 min walk to vill; mkt Mon; steep terr site; vans towed to pitch if req; steep climb to some san facs; v clean; v friendly; excel pool; v popular; MH site adj; easy walk to town."* **€19.00, 15 Mar-31 Oct.** **2023**

FRANCE

FRANCE

BELCAIRE *8G4* (4km SW Rural) *42.79207, 1.92477*
Camping Les Sapins, Ternairols, 11340 Camurac **04 68 20 38 11; info@lessapins-camurac.com; www.lessapins-camurac.com**
€2 (htd) nr

Easiest app fr N - at Bélesta on D117 turn S onto D16/D29/D613 to Belcaire then cont to Camurac, site 1km SE of vill. Or take D613 fr Ax-les-Thermes (1st 10km over Col de Chioula diff climb - gd power/weight ratio). Site sp in vill of Camurac & visible fr rd. App rd fairly steep for sh dist. 2*, Med, mkd, pt shd, pt sl, EHU (10A) €4; bbq (elec, gas); TV; 33% statics; Eng spkn; adv bkg acc; ccard acc; horseriding; games area; site clsd 1 Nov-15 Dec; CKE. *"Lovely, peaceful site in beautiful surroundings; welcoming, friendly, helpful Dutch owners; excel walking; in Cathar region; vg; highly rec; winter sports; mountain biking; ltd facs LS."*
€24.00, 1 Jan-1 Nov, 15 Dec-31 Dec. **2023**

BELCAIRE *8G4* (0.3km W Rural) *42.81598, 1.95098*
Les Chalets Du Lac (formerly Municipal), 4 Chemin Lac, 11340 Belcaire **04 68 20 39 47; contact@leschaletsdulacbelcaire.fr; www.camping-pyrenees-cathare.fr**
12

Site on D613 bet Ax-les-Thermes & Quillan. 4*, Sm, mkd, shd, pt sl, EHU (10A) €2; sw nr; phone; tennis nr; horseriding nr; CKE. *"Site by lake; site yourself, warden calls; gd cent for walking; historic vill of Montaillou nr; excel; conv for Georges de la Frau."* **€20.30** **2024**

BELFORT *6G3* (1.8km N Urban) *47.65335, 6.86445*
FFCC Camping de l'Etang des Forges, 11 Rue du Général Béthouart, 90000 Belfort **03 84 22 54 92; contact@camping-belfort.com; www.camping-belfort.com**
€2 (htd) nr nr

Exit A36 junc 13; go thro cent of Belfort; then foll sp Offemont on D13, then site sp. Or fr W on N19 site well sp. 3*, Med, mkd, hdg, pt shd, EHU (6A) €3.50; bbq; red long stay; twin axles; TV; 5% statics; bus; Eng spkn; adv bkg acc; ccard acc; fishing adj; watersports adj; archery; CKE. *"Pleasant, well-kept, basic site; some lovely pitches; friendly; modern, unisex san facs with third cont wc, but needs updating (2014); lovely walk around lake fr site ent; cycle paths; conv for Corbusier's chapel at Ronchamp."* **€30.00, 1 Apr-30 Oct.** **2022**

BELLAC *7A3* (11km SW Rural) *46.05718, 0.97766*
Fonclaire Holidays, 87300 Blond **06 14 65 58 35; fonclaireholidays@gmail.com; www.fonclaireholidays.com**
12 nr nr (htd)

Fr Bellac take D675 S dir St Junien. Site on L in approx 7km, 2km bef Mortemart. Sm, hdstg, pt shd, EHU (6A) €4 (poss long lead req); sw; Eng spkn; adv bkg acc; Badminton; CKE. *"Lovely & peaceful, spacious CL-type site in lovely location; welcoming, helpful British owners; Glamping units on site; gd facs; gd hdstg in wet; nr Oradour-sur-Glane martyr vill; conv Futuroscope; gd cycling; gd; v quiet rural location; no night lighting; gd NH/longer; excel."* **€23.50** **2024**

BELLEME *4E2* (1km SW Urban) *48.37420, 0.55370*
Camp Municipal Le Val, Route de Mamers, 61130 Bellême **02 33 25 30 77 or 06 24 70 55 17; campingduperchebellemois@gmail.com; www.campingduperchebellemois.com**
€0.50 nr

Fr Mortagne, take D938 S to Bellême; turn R ent town on D955 Alençon rd; site sp on L half-way down hill. 2*, Sm, hdg, pt shd, pt sl, EHU (8A) €2.65 (poss long lead req); adv bkg rec; tennis adj; fishing. *"Pretty, well-kept site; some pitches v sl; warden visits twice daily; gd san facs; poss long water hoses req; pitches poss soft when wet; steep walk to town."*
€14.50, 15 Apr-15 Oct. **2024**

BELLEY *9B3* (8km E Rural) *45.76860, 5.76985*
Camping Du Lac du Lit du Roi, La Tuilière, 01300 Massignieu-de-Rives **04 79 42 12 03; info@camping-savoie.com; www.camping-savoie.com**
€4 (htd)

Fr D1504 turn E onto D992 to Massignieu-de-Rives, site sp. Site on NE of lake nr Les Mures. 4*, Med, mkd, hdg, pt shd, terr, EHU (10A) inc (long lead req); gas; bbq; sw; red long stay; TV; 20% statics; phone; Eng spkn; adv bkg req; ccard acc; boating; tennis; bike hire; CKE. *"Superb location; many pitches on lake with lovely views; some lge pitches, others v sm; lack of site maintenance (2010); few water pnts (2009); bkg fee; v friendly site, idyllic location; recep clsd 1200-1330."*
€33.00, 26 Mar-2 Oct. **2022**

BELVES *7D3* (12km SW Rural) *44.75813, 0.90222*
Camping Terme d'Astor (Naturist), 24540, St Avit-Rivière **05 53 63 24 52; camping@termedastor.com; www.termedastor.com**

Leave D710 at Belvès onto D53; in 4km turn R onto D26 to Bouillac; pass thro vill; then turn 2nd L. Well sp. 3*, Med, mkd, shd, pt sl, EHU (6A) €5.20; gas; bbq; TV; 10% statics; phone; Eng spkn; adv bkg acc; ccard acc; INF; rafting; games rm; jacuzzi; archery; canoeing nr; tennis nr; excursions. *"Gd cent for Dordogne rv & chateaux; vg; horserding nrby; poss low ampage & rev pol on some pitches."* **€37.00, 1 May-30 Sep.** **2022**

BELVES *7D3* (5km SW Rural) *44.75258, 0.98330*
FLOWER Camping Les Nauves, Le Bos-Rouge, 24170 Belvès **05 53 29 12 64; campinglesnauves@hotmail.com; www.lesnauves.com or www.flowercampings.com**
€4 nr

On D53 fr Belvès. Site on L just after junc to Larzac. Avoid Belves cent - use lorry rte dir Monpazier. 3*, Med, hdg, pt shd, pt sl, EHU (6A) inc; bbq; twin axles; TV; 10% statics; Eng spkn; adv bkg acc; ccard acc; bike hire; games area; games rm; horseriding; CCI. *"Excel site; gd views fr some pitches; sl site; interesting towns nrby; sm pool."* **€28.00, 11 Apr-26 Sep.** **2022**

BELZ *2F3* (2.6km NW Coastal) *47.68268, -3.18796*
Camping St Cado, 3 rue pen perleieu, 56550 Belz
06 49 66 67 01; info@camping-saintcado.com; www.camping-saintcado.com

€1.60 nr nr

W fr Auray on D22 then D16. Well sp fr Belz. 2*, Med, hdg, pt shd, EHU (3-6A) €2.60-3.60; 10% statics; Eng spkn; adv bkg acc; games rm; fishing 300m; tennis; games area. *"Popular site in beautiful location; boat hire 300m; seas views fr some pitches; helpful owner; volleyball; boules; rec phone ahead high ssn; vg; rec."* **€15.00, 1 April-30 Sep. 2024**

BENODET *2F2* (1.5km E Coastal) *47.86670, -4.09080*
Camping Du Letty, Rue du Canvez, 29950 Bénodet
02 98 57 04 69; reception@campingduletty.com; www.campingduletty.com

€5 WD MSP (covrd, htd) sand adj

Fr N ent town on D34, foll sp Fouesnant D44. Le Letty sp R at rndabt. Fr E on N165 take D44 sp Fouesnant & foll rd to o'skirts Bénodet. After town sp, site is sp. 4*, Lge, hdstg, mkd, hdg, pt shd, pt sl, EHU (10A) inc; gas; bbq (gas); TV; phone; Eng spkn; adv bkg acc; ccard acc; golf nr; tennis; games area; kayak hire; sauna; games rm; gym; squash; horseriding nr; waterslide; CKE. *"Excel, well-run, beautifully laid-out site; clean & well-equipped; lovely beach adj; excel playgrnd; many activities; aqua park; library; friendly, helpful staff; highly rec."* **€53.00, 11 Jun-5 Sep. 2023**

BENODET *2F2* (0.5km SE Coastal) *47.86780, -4.09750*
Camping du Poulquer, 23 rue du Poulquer, 29950 Bénodet **02 98 57 04 19; contact@campingdupoulquer.com; www.campingdupoulquer.com**

€3.50 WD nr (covrd, htd, indoor) sand adj

Fr N ent town on D34. At rndabt after junc with D44 strt onto Rue Penfoul. At next rndabt (tourist info office on R after rndabt) go strt dir La Plage until reach seafront; turn L at seafront then L at end of prom at camping sp; site in 100m on R. Fr E on N165 take D44 sp Fouesnant & foll rd to o'skirts Bénodet. After town sp, site is sp. 4*, Lge, mkd, hdg, pt shd, pt sl, EHU (6-10A) €5.50 (long lead poss req, poss rev pol); bbq; TV; 5% statics; Eng spkn; adv bkg acc; jacuzzi; games rm; waterslide; golf nr; tennis; CKE. *"Lovely, well-kept, family-run site; bike hire 1km; boat trips nrby; friendly, helpful owner; aqua park; no c'fits over 7.5m high ssn; quiet site LS; mkt Mon; rec; vg; gd cafe/bar & shop; indoor pool open LS; 1st class san facs."* **€30.00, 1 May-30 Sep, B16. 2022**

BERCK *3B2* (4km E Rural) *50.41861, 1.60556*
Camping L'Orée du Bois, 251 Chemin Blanc, 62180 Rang-du-Fliers **03 21 84 28 51; contact@oreedubois.fr; www.oreedubois.fr**

€4 WD MSP nr (covrd, htd) sand 4km

Exit A6 junc 25 onto D140 & D917. Thro Rang-du-Fliers, turn R bef pharmacy into Chemin Blanc, site sp. 4*, V lge, mkd, hdg, pt shd, serviced pitches; EHU (6A) inc; gas; red long stay; 80% statics; phone; Eng spkn; adv bkg acc; ccard acc; games area; bike hire; tennis; lake fishing; CKE. *"Conv Le Touquet, Boulogne, Montreuil & Calais; peaceful site in woodland; ltd space for tourers; tropical waterpark; vg pools; pleasant, helpful owners; m'van pitches cramped."* **€47.00, 1 Apr - 31 Oct. 2024**

BERGERAC *7C3* (2km S Urban) *44.84902, 0.47635*
Camping La Pelouse, 8 bis Rue Jean-Jacques Rousseau, 24100 Bergerac **05 53 57 06 67; campinglapelouse@orange.fr; www.night-and-day.fr**

€1.60 (htd) WD MSP nr

On S bank of Rv Dordogne 300m W of old bdge opp town cent. Do not ent town, foll camping sp fr bdge, ent on R after L turn opp block of flats. Well sp, on Rv Dordogne. 3*, Med, mkd, pt shd, pt sl, EHU (6A) €4.65; gas; Eng spkn; adv bkg acc; rv fishing adj; CKE. *"Peaceful, spacious site on rv bank; friendly warden; san facs ltd LS; easy walk by rv into attractive old town; no twin axles & c'vans over 6m; site poss clsd earlier if weather bad; pitches poss muddy when wet; rec arr bef 1400 high ssn site has lots of trees so not all pitches in sun; facs updated 2012."* **€15.40, 1 Apr-31 Oct. 2023**

"That's changed – Should I let the Club know?"

If you find something on site that's different from the site entry, fill in a report and let us know. See camc.com/europereport.

BERGERAC *7C3* (14km W Rural) *44.83849, 0.33052*
FFCC Camping Parc Servois, 11 Rue du Bac, 24680 Gardonne **06 89 31 50 47; www.parcservois.com**

€0.70 WD MSP nr nr

Fr D936 Bergerac to Bordeaux, in vill of Gardonne turn R into sm rd 100m after traff lts; site at end of rd by rv. Well sp in vill. 1*, Sm, pt shd, EHU (10A) poss rev pol; Eng spkn; CKE. *"Pretty, CL-type site on bank of Rv Dordogne; lge pitches; helpful warden; facs immac but dated & poss stretched when site full; gates clsd 2200-0800 with pedestrian access; sm mkt Wed & Sun; excel, well run site."* **€16.44, 15 Apr-13 Oct. 2024**

FRANCE

BERGUES *3A3* (0.6km N Urban) *50.97248, 2.43420* **Camping Le Vauban,** Blvd Vauban, 59380 Bergues **03 28 68 65 25; contact@campingvauban.fr; www.campingvauban.fr**

€1.05 (cont) nr nr nr

Exit A16 junc 60 twd Bergues on D916. In 2km turn L onto D2 dir Coudekerque vill. In 2km turn R at rndabt onto D72 to Bergues thro Couderkerque vill, then turn R immed after canal. Site on R as rd bends to L. 3*, Med, hdg, mkd, pt shd, terr, EHU (6A) inc (poss rev pol); 60% statics; adv bkg acc; CKE. *"Pleasant site; sm pitches poss diff lge o'fits; ltd manoeuvring in site rds; friendly & helpful; gates clsd 2130-0700 & poss clsd 1230-1730; lovely fortified town; conv Dunkerque & Calais; NH only; san facs updated (2015)."* **€16.00, 1 Apr-31 Oct.** **2022**

BERNY RIVIERE *3C4* (1.5km S Rural) *49.40603, 3.12860* **Camping La Croix du Vieux Pont,** Rue de la Fabrique, 02290 Berny-Rivière **03 23 55 50 02; info@la-croix-du-vieux-pont.com; www.la-croix-du-vieux-pont.com**

(htd) (covrd, htd)

On N31 bet Soissons & Compiègne. At site sp turn onto D13, then at Vic-sur-Aisne take next R, R again then L onto D91. Foll sp to site on o'skts of Berny. 5*, V lge, hdstg, hdg, pt shd, serviced pitches; EHU (6A) €2.50 (poss rev pol, no earth & ltd supply); gas; sw; TV; Eng spkn; adv bkg rec; ccard acc; games rm; waterslide; gym; tennis; bike hire; horseriding; boating; archery; fishing; golf; CKE. *"Pleasant, v lge, well-run, clean site; busy LS; lge pitches, some rvside; excel for families or older couples; friendly, helpful staff; vg san facs, ltd LS; some sh stay pitches up steep bank; beauty cent; some pitches worn/uneven end of ssn (2010); some pitches liable to flood; many tour op statics high ssn; site open all yr but no services Nov-Mar; excel; tourers pitch on open area."* **€41.00, 9 Apr-30 Oct, P15.** **2022**

BERNY RIVIERE *3C4* (6km S Rural) *49.39280, 3.15161* **Camping La Halte de Mainville,** 18 Chemin du Routy, 02290 Ressons-le-Long **03 23 74 26 69; lahaltedemainville@wanadoo.fr; www.lahaltedemainville.fr**

(htd) nr (htd)

Fr Soissons W on N31 dir Compiègne, in approx 8km look for site sp on L. Clearly sp. 3*, Lge, hdg, mkd, pt shd, EHU (10A) €3 (poss rev pol); bbq; 60% statics; phone; Eng spkn; adv bkg rec; games area; tennis; fishing; CKE. *"Pleasant, clean, conv NH; friendly, helpful staff; 1 hr fr Disneyland; vg; lovely area."* **€22.00, 8 Jan-8 Dec.** **2022**

BESANCON *6G2* (6km NE Rural) *47.26472, 6.07255* **Camping Besancon Chalezeule,** 12 Route de Belfort, 25220 Chalezeule **03 81 88 04 26; contact@campingdebesancon.com; www.campingdebesancon.com**

€1.35 (htd) nr nr

Exit A36 junc 4 S; foll sp Montbéliard & Roulons onto D683; site in 1.5km on R, 200m after rlwy bdge; well sp fr D683. Fr Belfort 2.65m height restriction; foll sp to Chalezeule & 300m after supmkt turn L to rejoin D683, site in 200m on rvside. 3*, Med, mkd, pt shd, terr, EHU (16A) (poss rev pol); bbq; twin axles; 50% statics; bus to city; Eng spkn; ccard acc; kayaking; CKE. *"Helpful staff; htd pool adj; excel modern san facs; access to opp side of dual c'way under sm tunnel, suggest going to rndabt to make the turn; tram to city 1.5km uphill."* **€25.00, 15 Mar-31 Oct.** **2023**

BESSINES SUR GARTEMPE *7A3* (1.5km SW Urban) *46.10013, 1.35423* **Camp Municipal Lac de Sagnat,** Route de St Pardoux, 87250 Bessines-sur-Gartempe **05 55 76 01 66; ot.bessines@wanadoo.fr; http://www.tourisme-hautevienne.co.uk/objet_touristique/2570**

nr nr

Exit A20 junc 24 sp Bessines-sur-Gartempe onto D220; then D27 sp lake. Foll sp to Bellevue Restaurant. At rest, turn R foll site sp. Well sp fr junc 24. 2*, Med, hdg, mkd, pt shd, pt sl, terr, EHU (6A) inc; sw nr; TV; Eng spkn. *"Pretty site with lake views; peaceful location; friendly staff; gd, clean san facs; poss unkempt LS (Jun 2009); hotel for meals nrby; conv NH A20."* **€18.70, 15 Jun-15 Sep.** **2020**

BEZIERS *10F1* (10km NE Rural) *43.39849, 3.37338* **Camping Le Rebau,** 34290 Montblanc **04 67 98 50 78; gilbert@camping-lerebau.fr; www.camping-lerebau.fr**

€2.80 nr nr

NE on N9 fr Béziers-Montpellier, turn R onto D18. Site sp, narr ent 2.50m. 3*, Lge, hdstg, hdg, mkd, pt shd, EHU (5A) €4.50; TV; 10% statics; phone; bus 1km; Eng spkn; adv bkg acc; CKE. *"Gd site; tight ent & manoeuvring onto pitches; some facs old, but modern shwrs; ltd facs LS, but clean; helpful owner; gd pool; gd touring base; LS phone ahead to check open."* **€19.50, 1 May-31 Aug.** **2020**

BEZIERS *10F1* (7km SE Urban) *43.3169, 3.2842* **Camping Les Berges du Canal,** Promenade des Vernets, 34420 Villeneuve-les-Béziers **04 67 39 36 09; contact@campinglbdc.com; www.campinglesbergesducanal.com**

€3 (htd)

Fr A9 exit junc 35 & foll sp for Agde. Exit 1st rndabt for D612 dir Béziers then 1st L onto D37 sp Villneuve-les-Béziers. Foll site sp to site adj canal. 4*, Med, hdg, mkd, shd, EHU (16a) inc; 45% statics; Eng spkn; adv bkg acc; bike hire; CKE. *"Pleasant site; facs clean & modern but poss stretched in ssn; noisy, fr rlwy yard; some pitches tight lge o'fits; pleasant stroll along canal."* **€28.00, 14 Mar-17 Oct.** **2024**

BEZIERS *10F1* (12km SW Rural) *43.31864, 3.14276* **Camping Les Peupliers,** 7 Promenade de l'Ancien Stade, 34440 Colombiers **04 67 37 05 26; contact@camping-colombiers.com; www.camping-colombiers.com**

12 €3 nr nr

SW fr Béziers on D609 (N9) turn R on D162E & foll sp to site using heavy vehicle rte. Cross canal bdge & fork R; turn R & site on L. Easier ent fr D11 (Béziers-Capestang) avoiding narr vill rds, turn L at rndabt at end of dual c'way sp Colombiers; in 1km at rlwy bdge, go strt on; in 100m turn L (bef canal bdge) where rd turns sharp R. 3*, Med, mkd, pt shd, EHU (10A) €3.50 (inc in high ssn) (poss rev pol); gas; bbq; red long stay; 25% statics; adv bkg acc; CKE. *"Nr Canal du Midi away fr busy beach sites; modern san facs; no twin axles; excel walking & cycling; pleasant sm vill, conv NH; gd rest in vill; diff for lge o'fits; touring pitches among statics; 45km to stn for Carcassonne."*

€28.50 **2024**

BIARRITZ *8F1* (4.6km S Coastal) *43.45305, -1.57277* **Yelloh! Village Ilbarritz,** Ave de Biarritz, 64210 Bidart **05 59 23 00 29; contact@camping-ilbarritz.com; www.camping-ilbarritz.com**

€6 (htd) sand 900m

S fr Bayonne on D810, by-pass Biarritz. 1km after A63 junc turn R at rndabt immed after Intermarché on R; sp to Pavillon Royal. Site 1km on R sp. 4*, Lge, mkd, pt shd, pt sl, terr, EHU (25A) inc; gas; TV; 80% statics; phone; Eng spkn; adv bkg req; ccard acc; games area; horseriding; bike hire; golf nr; CKE. *"Attractive, mature site, lge pitches, need blocks as v sl; narr access rds poss diff long o'fits; excel pool; gd beaches nrby; gd."*

€100.00, 5 Apr-28 Sep. **2022**

See advertisement

BIARRITZ *8F1* (5km S Coastal) *43.43371, -1.59040* **Camping Ur-Onéa,** Rue de la Chapelle, 64210 Bidart **05 59 26 53 61; contact@uronea.com; www.uronea.com**

€2.50 (htd) sand 600m

Exit A63 junc 4 dir Bidart, fr Bidart on D810 sp St Jean de Luz, L at traff lts in town where site sp, then 2nd R, L at motel, site is 300m on L. Access fr main rd a bit tricky, 2nd access further S is easier for lge o'fits. 3*, Lge, hdstg, mkd, pt shd, terr, serviced pitches; EHU (10A) inc; gas; bbq; TV; 20% statics; phone; Eng spkn; adv bkg acc; ccard acc; CKE. *"Well-kept site 600m fr Bidart; various pitch sizes, most not terr; suitable for o'fits up to 8m; staff friendly & helpful; excel, clean san facs; conv Pays Basque vills; new covrd/open pool (2014)."*

€46.70, 6 Apr-22 Sep. **2024**

BIARRITZ *8F1* (2km SW Coastal) *43.4625, -1.5672* **Camping Biarritz,** 28 Rue Harcet, 64200 Biarritz **05 59 23 00 12; info@biarritz-camping.fr; www.biarritz-camping.fr**

(htd) sand 1km

S fr Bayonne on D810, by-pass Biarritz & cont to junc of D810 coast rd sp Bidart & Biarritz; double back on this rd, take 1st exit at next rndabt, 1st L dir Biarritz Cent, foll sp to site in 2km. Lge, mkd, pt shd, pt sl, terr, EHU (10A) €4; gas; 10% statics; bus at gate; adv bkg acc; ccard acc; tennis 4km; CKE. *"One of better sites in area, espec LS."*

€55.50, 8 Apr-30 Oct. **2022**

BIARRITZ *8F1* (3.5km SW Coastal) *43.45525, -1.58119* **Camping Pavillon Royal,** Ave du Prince de Galles, 64210 Bidart **05 59 23 00 54; info@pavillon-royal.com; www.pavillon-royal.com**

(htd) sand adj

Exit A63/E4 junc 4; then take D810 S dir Bidart. At rndabt after Intermarché supmkt turn R (sp Biarritz). After 600m turn L at site sp. 5*, Lge, hdg, mkd, pt shd, pt sl, serviced pitches; EHU (10A) inc (long lead poss req); gas; bbq; TV; Eng spkn; adv bkg rec; ccard acc; tennis nr; golf 500m; games rm; horseriding 2km; bike rental; spa treatments; massages; gym. *"Lovely, well-kept, busy site in beautiful location beside beach; various pitch sizes, some with sea views, some sm & diff lge o'fits; direct access via steps to excel beach; fitness rm; san facs poss irreg cleaning LS; mkt Sat; excel; adv bkg rec as ess; no o'fits over 8m; avoid pitches on perimeter fence as damage to vehicles fr stray golf balls; vg, helpful, friendly staff; excel shwrs, wc, shop, bar & rest."* **€65.00, 13 May - 30 Sep, A06. 2022**

See advertisement

BINIC *2E3* (2.5km S Coastal) *48.58269, -2.80477* **Camping Les Madières,** Rue du Vau Madec, 22590 Pordic **02 96 79 02 48; campinglesmadieres@wanadoo.fr; www.campinglesmadieres.com**

€2.50 (htd) (htd) shgl 800m

Site at E end of Pordic vill, sp. 3*, Med, pt shd, pt sl, EHU (10A) €4; gas; 10% statics; adv bkg acc; watersports 3km; CKE. *"Pleasant, clean, child-friendly site; helpful, friendly owners; immac facs; poss diff access to shgl beach, Binic beach OK; highly rec; beach sand 3km; quiet site."* **€26.70, 1 Apr-15 Oct. 2024**

BINIC *2E3* (4km S Coastal) *48.57875, -2.78498* **Camping Le Roc de l'Hervieu,** 19 Rue d'Estienne d'Orves, 22590 Pordic **02 96 79 30 12; herviroc@gmail.com; www.campingrocdelhervieu.fr**

sand 600m

Site on E side of vill off N786, Binic-St Brieuc rd. Turn E in cent of vill, sp to Les Madières then sp Le Roc de l'Hervieu. 3*, Med, hdg, pt shd, EHU (10A) €3.50; bbq; 10% statics; fishing. *"Gd walking; pleasant, gd site."* **€19.50, 1 May-30 Sep. 2023**

BISCARROSSE *7D1* (3km N Coastal) *44.42955, -1.16792* **Campéole Camping Navarrosse,** 712 Chemin de Navarrosse, 40600 Biscarrosse **05 5809 84 32; navarrosse@campeole.com; www.campeole.co.uk/camping/landes/navarrosse-biscarrosse**

(htd) nr nr

Fr Biscarrosse N on D652 dir Sanguinet; 1km beyond turning to L to Biscarrosse-Plage, turn L onto D305 & foll sp to Navarrosse. 4*, V lge, mkd, pt shd, EHU (10A) inc (poss rev pol); bbq; sw nr; red long stay; TV; 40% statics; Eng spkn; ccard acc; games area; sailing; games rm; fishing; bike hire; tennis; Entertainment tent; Library; Inflatable structure; CKE. *"Pleasant site; vg for children; helpful staff; late arr area; gd walking; sailing lessons; cycle rtes; gd value."* **€33.00, 3 Apr-27 Sep. 2020**

BISCARROSSE *7D1* (4.5km N Rural) *44.42715, -1.16078* **Camping Bimbo,** 176 Chemin de Bimbo, 40600 Biscarrosse **05 58 09 82 33; info@campingbimbo.fr; www.campingbimbo.fr**

(htd)

Fr Biscarrosse take D652 N. At rndabt take 2nd exit (D305) sp Biscarrosse Lac. After 1.5km turn R twds Chemin de Bimbo, site on R in 500m. 4*, Med, shd, EHU (3-10A) inc (poss rev pol); 80% statics; adv bkg acc; games area; watersports 1km. *"Excel full facs site; beach 10km excel for surfing; bakery, pizzeria & creperie on site."* **€54.00, 3 May-15 Sep. 2024**

BISCARROSSE *7D1* (5km N Rural) *44.43996, -1.14068* **Aire Naturelle Le Frézat (Dubourg),** 2583 Chemin de Mayotte, 40600 Biscarrosse **06 22 65 57 37; www.lefrezat.fr**

nr

Fr Biscarrosse on D652 dir Sanguinet; after 5km turn L at water tower onto D333; site 2nd on R in 1km. Med, shd, EHU (6A) inc; bbq; Eng spkn; adv bkg acc; CKE. *"Lovely site; friendly owners; clean facs; cycle paths."* **€25.00, 15 Jun-15 Sept. 2024**

BISCARROSSE *7D1* (8km NE Rural) *44.46230, -1.12900* **Camping de la Rive,** Route de Bordeaux, 40600 Biscarrosse **05 58 78 12 33; info@larive.fr; www.larive.fr**

€13 (htd) (covrd, htd)

Fr Bordeaux on A63 dir Bayonne/San Sebastian; at junc 22 turn off onto A660; cont until 1st junc where turn L onto D216; cont for 17km to Sanguinet; cont on A652 for 3km; site sp on R nr Lake Cazaux. 4*, V lge, mkd, hdg, pt shd, EHU (6A) inc; gas; bbq (gas); sw nr; TV; 30% statics; phone; Eng spkn; adv bkg acc; ccard acc; games rm; jacuzzi; tennis; waterslide; bike hire; watersports; games area; CKE. *"On banks of Lake Cazaux-Sanguinet in delightful area; bustling site high ssn; many acitivies for all ages; no c'van/m'van over 9m; some pitches diff lge o'fits due trees; gd beaches; gd cycling; lovely rest, pleasant staff."* **€76.00, 12 Apr-30 Aug. 2024**

BISCARROSSE *7D1* (8km NW Coastal) *44.45804, -1.23968* **Campéole Camping Le Vivier,** 681 Rue du Tit, 40600 Biscarrosse-Plage **05 58 78 25 76; contact@andretriganogroupe.com; www.ms-vacances.com/**

€2.50 (htd) sand 800m

Fr Arcachon & Pyla-sur-Mer, take D218, D83 to Biscarrosse Plage. Town o'skts site sp to R. Foll sps. 3*, Lge, pt shd, EHU (10A) inc (poss rev pol); 25% statics; ccard acc; fishing; bike hire; games rm; boating; tennis; horseriding nr. *"Sandy site in pine forest; access to beach via path thro dunes."* **€52.00, 28 Apr-17 Sep. 2023**

BISCARROSSE *7D1* (9km NW Coastal) *44.44133, -1.24558* **Campéole Camping Plage Sud,** 230 Rue des Bécasses, 40600 Biscarrosse-Plage **02 53 81 70 00; www.ms-vacances.com**

€3.50 nr (htd) sand 800m

Clearly sp on D146 on ent to Biscarrosse-Plage in pine forest. 4*, V lge, mkd, pt shd, pt sl, EHU (6A) inc; bbq; 50% statics; Eng spkn; adv bkg rec; ccard acc; bike hire; CKE. *"Gd site, lively high ssn; helpful staff; facs stretched high ssn; gd beach, inc surfing; some pitches on soft sand; sm, modern town, lots of rests; new entmnt, pool and san facs (2013); excel for sh or long stay."* **€47.50, 4 May-22 Sep. 2024**

BLANC, LE *4H2* (2km E Rural) *46.63202, 1.09389* **Camping L'Ile d'Avant,** Route de Châteauroux, 36300 Le Blanc **02 54 37 88 22; info@tourisme-leblanc.fr; www.tourisme-leblanc.fr**

nr nr nr

Fr town cent take D951 twd St Gaultier/Argenton; site on R 1km after supmkt. 3*, Med, hdg, mkd, pt shd, EHU (6A) inc; bbq; adv bkg acc; fishing; tennis adj Canoeing; Service area. *"Gd pitches; htd pool adj inc; adj sports field & club house; open Apr with adv bkg only, otherwise May."* **€14.00, 1 May-17 Sep. 2020**

BLANGY LE CHATEAU *3D1* (0.5km N Rural) *49.24670, 0.27370* **Camping Le Domaine du Lac,** 14130 Blangy-le-Château **02 31 64 62 00 or 06 85 43 43 14; info@domaine-du-lac.fr; www.domaine-du-lac.fr**

Fr Pont-l'Evêque & A13 S on D579 twd Lisieux. In 5km turn L onto D51 to Blangy where at fountain (rndabt) turn L, taking care. In 200m at end of vill turn L onto D140 Rte de Mesnil & site 200m on R. Site is 5km SE of Pont-l'Evêque. 2*, Med, mkd, pt shd, pt sl, EHU (6A) inc (long lead poss req); gas; bbq; 70% statics; adv bkg acc; ccard acc; games rm; tennis; lake fishing; CKE. *"Peaceful NH in lovely area; friendly British owner; poss uneven pitches; tired, access to pitches diff when wet; pretty vill; gd walks; conv Honfleur; 1hr to Le Havre ferry; NH only; mainly statics; facs poorly maintained."* **€24.00, 1 Apr-31 Oct. 2024**

BLANGY LE CHATEAU *3D1* (3km SE Rural) *49.22525, 0.30438* **Camping Le Brévedent,** 14130 Le Brévedent **02 31 64 72 88; contact@campinglebrevedent.com; www.campinglebrevedent.com**

(htd) (htd)

Fr Pont l'Evêque & A13 go S on D579 twd Lisieux; after 5km turn L onto D51 twd Blangy-le-Château. In Blangy bear R at rndabt to stay on D51 & foll sp to Le Brévedent & Moyaux; site on L in just after le Breveden vill. 4*, Med, mkd, pt shd, pt sl, EHU (10A) (poss long leads req, poss rev pol); bbq; TV; 10% statics; phone; Eng spkn; adv bkg acc; ccard acc; horseriding 2km; games area; bike hire; tennis; games rm; golf 11km; lake fishing; kids' club; playground; CKE. *"Pleasant, busy site with all amenities, around lake in grnds of chateau; welcoming, helpful staff; no o'fits over 8m; some modern san facs, ltd LS; gd pool; rallies welcome; excel."* **€45.00, 4 May-14 Sep, N01. 2024**

FRANCE

FRANCE

BLANGY SUR BRESLE *3C2* (2km SE Rural) *49.92378, 1.65693* **Camping Aux Cygnes d'Opale (formerly Municipal),** Zone de Loisirs, 76340 Blangy-sur-Bresle **02 35 94 55 65 or 09 72 32 88 40; contact@auxcygnesdopale.fr; www.auxcygnesdopale.fr**

€2 WD MSP nr nr nr

Leave A28 at junc 5, R at T-junc onto D49, site on L in 800m. 3*, Med, mkd, unshd, EHU (5-16A) €3 (poss rev pol); bbq; 20% statics; phone; adv bkg rec; tennis nr; CKE. *"Attractive, well-kept site adj lakes; conv Calais, A28 & D928; gd san facs; adv bkg rec lge o'fits high ssn; no twin axles; pleasant & helpful warden; rec wait for warden for pitching; mini golf nr; poss waterlogged in wet (& ent refused); avoid during Int'l Petanque Competition 3rd w/end June on adj leisure cent; excel NH; new owners (2013), many improvements; new pool."* **€23.50, 1 Apr-31 Oct.** **2022**

"I need an on-site restaurant"

We do our best to make sure site information is correct, but it is always best to check any must-have facilities are still available or will be open during your visit.

BLANGY SUR BRESLE *3C2* (8km W Rural) *49.95430, 1.55098* **Camp Municipal La Forêt,** 4 rue de la Forêt, 76340 Bazinval **02 32 97 04 01; bazinval2@wanadoo.fr; www.tourisme-aumale-blangy.fr**

WD nr

NW fr Blangy on D49 for 6km, then D149 to Bazinval. Site sp. 1*, Sm, hdg, pt shd, pt sl, EHU (10A) €4.50 (poss rev pol); twin axles; Eng spkn; games area; games rm; CKE. *"Gd san facs, poss inadequate; site yourself, warden calls early eve; poss travellers on site; NH only; lovely, peaceful site; conv Dieppe; vg."* **€10.80, 1 Apr-30 Oct.** **2023**

BLAYE *7C2* (5km NE Rural) *45.16708, -0.61666* **Aire Naturelle Les Tilleuls (Paille),** Domaine Les Alberts, 33390 Mazion **05 57 42 18 13; chateau-alberts@hotmail.com; guide-bordeaux-gironde.com/en/tourism/accommodation/campings/campsites-mobile-homes/mazion-276/aire-naturelle-de-camping-les-tilleuls-4379.html**

Fr Blaye on D937 N, sp to site on L. Sm, pt shd, pt sl, EHU (3-10A) €2.50; own san req; bbq; Eng spkn; CKE. *"Lovely, family-run site in vineyards; charming owners; clean basic san facs; wine-tasting; easy cycling nrby, cycle track to Blaye."* **€12.50, 1 May-15 Oct.** **2024**

BLERE *4G2* (0.6km E Urban) *47.32791, 0.99685* **Camping La Gâtine Onlycamp,** Rue de Cdt Le Maître, 37150 Bléré **02 47 57 92 60; campinglagatin@onlycamp.fr; https://camping-blere.fr/en/**

€2 (htd) WD MSP nr nr nr (htd)

Exit A10 S of Tours onto A85 E. Exit A85 junc 11 dir Bléré. Site in 5km adj sports cent on S side of Rv Cher. 3*, Lge, mkd, pt shd, pt sl, EHU (10A) €4 (poss rev pol & long lead poss req); bbq (elec, sep area); cooking facs; twin axles; red long stay; TV; bus (100mtrs), train (2km),; Eng spkn; adv bkg acc; ccard acc; rv fishing adj; games area; games rm; CKE. *"Excel, well-kept, peaceful, pleasant site; clean san facs, some dated & stretched when site full, some modernised; some dated EHU poss unrel in wet; gd cent for wine rtes & chateaux; htd pool adj high ssn; unrel opening dates LS; excel cycle routes adj; boating nrby; off clsd 12-4pm, find own pitch; excel."* **€25.40, 5 Apr-29 Sep.** **2024**

BLOIS *4G2* (12km NE Rural) *47.68666, 1.48583* **Camping Le Château de la Grenouillère,** 41500 Suèvres **02 54 90 13 66; www.les-castels.com**

WD MSP (covrd)

Exit A10 junc 16 sp Chambord, Mer; take rd to Mer; go thro Mer on D2152 dir Blois; site in 5km, 2km NE of Suèvres. 5*, Lge, mkd, pt shd, EHU (10A) inc; gas; bbq (charcoal, gas); TV; Eng spkn; adv bkg req; ccard acc; bike hire; sauna; waterslide; gym; fishing; tennis; boating; games rm; CKE. *"Ideal for Loire area; clean modern san facs, poss ltd LS; no o'fits over 15m; statics (tour ops); some superb leisure facs; mkt Wed & Sat Blois."* **€34.00, 18 Apr-12 Sep, L04.** **2024**

BLOIS *4G2* (5km NE Rural) *47.605289, 1.374560* **Camping Le Val de Blois,** RD951 Lac de Loire 41350, Blois/Vineuil **02 54 79 93 57; contact@camping-loisir-blois.com; www.camping-loisir-blois.com**

€1.20 (htd) WD MSP

Fr N exit 17 from A10 onto D200 thro Blois. Over bdge, turn off to D951. Site sp 3km to E. Fr S on d174, turn off D951 before bdge. Site sp 3km to E. 3*, Med, hdg, pt shd, pt sl, EHU 6A; gas; bbq (charcoal, elec, gas); sw nr; 10% statics; Eng spkn; ccard acc; bike hire; CKE. *"Situated on Loire rv; vast cycling area; facs stretched in high ssn; vg."* **€23.60, 30 Mar-5 Oct.** **2024**

BLOIS *4G2* (10km E Rural) *47.59149, 1.45894* **Camping de Chatillon (formerly Aire Naturelle),** 6 Rue de Châtillon, 41350 Huisseau-sur-Cosson **02 54 20 35 26**

€1.50 WD MSP nr

Fr Blois cross Rv Loire on D765 dir Vineuil. 1km S turn L onto D33. Site at E end of vill of Huisseau on R. Sm, mkd, hdg, pt shd, pt sl, EHU (10A) €4.20 (poss rev pol); gas; adv bkg acc; CKE. *"Pretty, peaceful, garden site; lovely, even LS; beautiful area; friendly owner; gd clean san facs, but ltd; conv Loire Valley chateaux; cycle rte thro Chambord forest; Son et Lumière show in town; rec; delightful, spacious and spotless site."* **€18.00, 1 May-8 Sep.** **2024**

BLOIS *4G2* (18km W Rural) *47.54427, 1.15712* **Ferme de Prunay,** 41150 SEILLAC **09 53 86 02 01 or 06 98 99 09 86; contact@prunay.com; www.prunay.fr**

Take exit Blois on the A10; foll dir for Angers Chateau Renault until Molineuf, then Chambon sur Cisse and Seillac, rd D131. 4*, Med, mkd, pt shd, EHU (10A) inc; bbq; TV; Eng spkn; ccard acc; bike hire; games area; fishing. *"In the heart of the Loire Valley; spacious pitches; v nice site; san facs tired."* **€37.00, 6 Apr-2 Nov. 2024**

BOIS DE CENE *2H4* (0.9km S Rural) *46.93395, -1.88728* **Camping Le Bois Joli,** 2 Rue de Châteauneuf, 85710 Bois-de-Céné **02 51 68 20 05; contact@camping-leboisjoli.com; www.camping-leboisjoli.com**

€4 (max 1) nr (covrd, htd)

Fr D21 turn R at church in cent of vill, site on R in 500m on rd D28. 3*, Med, hdg, pt shd, EHU (6A) €4; gas; bbq; 10% statics; phone; bus in vill; Eng spkn; adv bkg acc; fishing; bike hire; games area; tennis; CKE. *"Friendly, helpful owner; clean san facs; gd walks; lovely pool; great site; ltd facs LS; rec; excel."* **€25.00, 1 Apr-4 Oct, A35. 2022**

BOLLENE *9D2* (5.5km E Rural) *44.29811, 4.78645* **FFCC Camping et Centre Equestre La Simioune,** Quartier Guffiage, 84500 Bollène **06 70 73 50 54 or 04 90 63 17 91; camping@la-simioune.fr; www.la-simioune.fr**

€4 nr

Exit A7 junc 19 onto D994/D8 dir Carpentras (Ave Salvatore Allende D8). At 3rd x-rd turn L into Ave Alphonse Daudet dir Lambique & foll rd 3km to sp for camping on L, then site 1km. 3*, Sm, shd, pt sl, EHU (6A) inc; bbq; 10% statics; adv bkg rec; horseriding; CKE. *"In pine forest; facs ltd in winter; pony club for children & adults; NH only; lovely site."* **€31.00, 1 Mar-31 Oct. 2023**

BOLLENE *9D2* (6km SW Rural) *44.24335, 4.72931* **FFCC Camping La Pinède en Provence,** Quartier des Massanes, 84430 Mondragon **04 90 40 82 98; contact@camping-pinede-provence.com; www.camping-pinede-provence.com**

€2 (htd)

Exit A7 junc 19 dir Bollène & take D26 S, site 1.5km N of Mondragon. Steep access. 3*, Med, mkd, pt shd, pt sl, terr, EHU (8-13A) €4.40-4.85; bbq; 10% statics; adv bkg acc; CKE. *"Gd, clean site; gd touring base; conv Ardèche Gorge."* **€33.00, 1 Feb-31 Oct. 2024**

BONIFACIO *10H2* (15km N Coastal) *41.47326, 9.26318* **Camping Rondinara,** Suartone, 20169 Bonifacio **04 95 70 43 15; reception@rondinara.fr; www.rondinara.fr**

€2.60 sand 400m

Fr Bonifacio take N198 dir Porte-Vecchio for 10km, then turn R onto D158 dir Suartone (lge camp sp at turning). Site in 5km. NB D158 single track, many bends & hills. 4*, Med, pt shd, pt sl, EHU (6A) €3.60; bbq; 10% statics; Eng spkn; ccard acc; games area; watersports; games rm; CKE. *"Excel rest; idyllic location by bay; excel new san facs 2013; rd to campsite steep and narr in places; adv bkg for mkd pitches fr May."* **€35.70, 15 May-30 Sep. 2024**

BONIFACIO *10H2* (4km NE Rural) *41.39986, 9.20141* **Camping Pian del Fosse,** Route de Sant' Amanza, 20169 Bonifacio **04 95 73 16 34 or 06 70 92 73 43; pian.del.fosse@wanadoo.fr; www.camping-piandelfosse.com**

€2.50 shgl 3km

Leave Bonifacio on D58 dir Sant' Amanza, site on L in 4km. 3*, Sm, hdg, mkd, shd, terr, EHU (4A) €3.80; bbq; red long stay; 20% statics; Eng spkn. *"Pitches poss diff lge m'vans due o'hanging trees, vg; ccard acc."* **€39.50, 1 May-15 Oct. 2024**

> **"Satellite navigation makes touring much easier"**
>
> Remember most sat navs don't know if you're towing or in a larger vehicle – always use yours alongside maps and site directions.

BONNAC LA COTE *7B3* (1.4km S Rural) *45.93238, 1.28977* **Camping Le Château de Leychoisier,** 1 Route de Leychoisier, 87270 Bonnac-la-Côte **05 55 39 93 43; contact@leychoisier.com; chateau-de-leychoisier.pagesperso-orange.fr**

€3

Fr S on A20 exit junc 27 & L at T-junc onto D220. At rndabt take 3rd exit then 1st L onto D97. At mini-rndabt in Bonnac take 2nd exit, site on L in 1km. Fr N exit A20 junc 27, turn R at T-junc onto D97, then as above. 5*, Med, mkd, hdg, pt shd, sl, EHU (10A) inc; bbq (charcoal, gas); twin axles; TV; phone; Eng spkn; adv bkg acc; ccard acc; games rm; fishing; tennis; CKE. *"Peaceful site in grnds of chateau; lge pitches; welcoming, friendly & helpful staff; no o'fits over 20m; clean san facs but dated, unisex; excel rest; extra for m'vans; blocks req some pitches; rallies welcome; conv NH nr m'way; excel; ccard not acc for 1 night stay; access for lge o'fits diff; gd rest/pool area; less commercial then other Les Castels sites."* **€35.00, 15 Apr - 20 Sep, L11. 2022**

FRANCE

BONNAL *6G2* (3.5km N Rural) *47.50777, 6.35583* **Camping Le Val de Bonnal,** 1 Chemin du Moulin, 25680 Bonnal **03 81 86 90 87; www.camping-valdebonnal.com or www.les-castels.com**

€4 WD MSP

Fr N on D9 fr Vesoul or Villersexel to Esprels, turn S onto D49 sp 'Val de Bonnal'. Fr S exit A36 junc 5 & turn N onto D50 sp Rougemont, site sp to N of Rougemont. 5*, Lge, mkd, pt shd, EHU (5-10A) inc (poss rev pol); gas; bbq; sw nr; twin axles; TV; 40% statics; Eng spkn; adv bkg acc; ccard acc; fishing; golf 6km; games rm; gym; bike hire; waterslide; canoe hire; watersports; CKE. *"Attractive, busy site; lge accessible pitches; excel welcome; modern, clean san facs; gd child activities; ltd facs LS; tour ops."* **€57.00, 6 May - 11 Sep, J01. 2022**

BONNEVILLE *9A3* (0.5km NE Rural) *46.08206, 6.41288* **Camp Municipal Le Bois des Tours,** 314 Rue des Bairiers, 74130 Bonneville **04 50 97 04 31**

WD nr

Fr A40 junc 16 take D1203, or fr Cluses take D1205 to Bonneville. Cross rv bdge into town cent; site sp. 2*, Med, pt shd, EHU (5A) €2.50; bbq; adv bkg acc; Ironing room. *"Well-maintained, immac site; gd san facs."* **€8.00, 1 Jul-6 Sep. 2020**

BORDEAUX *7C2* (7km N Rural) *44.89701, -0.58317* **Camping Le Village du Lac Bordeaux,** Blvd Jacques Chaban Delmas, 33520 Bordeaux-Bruges **05 57 87 70 60; contact@village-du-lac.com; www.camping-bordeaux.com**

12 €5 (htd) WD MSP

On ring rd A630 take exit 5 twd lake; site sp on N side of lake, 500m N of Parc des Expositions. 4*, Lge, hdstg, mkd, pt shd, EHU (10A) inc; bbq; sw; TV; 50% statics; bus/tram to city; Eng spkn; adv bkg acc; ccard acc; fishing adj; games rm; bike hire; CKE. *"Busy, poorly laid out, modern site; friendly staff; san facs poss streched high ssn; plenty elec & water pnts; excel rest; conv Bordeaux; easy access fr ring rd; pitches poss soft and muddy after rain; bus/tram conn to city; vg rest; gd unisex facs."* **€34.00 2023**

BORDEAUX *7C2* (4km S Urban) *44.75529, -0.62772* **Camping Beausoleil,** 371 Cours du Général de Gaulle, 33170 Gradignan **05 56 89 17 66; campingbeausoleil@orange.fr; www.camping-beausoleil-gradignan.fr**

12 €1 (htd) WD nr nr nr

Fr N take exit 16 fr Bordeaux ring rd onto D1010 sp Gradignan. Fr S exit A63 junc 24 onto D211 to Jauge then D1010 to Gradignan. Site S of Gradignan on R after Beau Soleil complex, sp. 2*, Sm, hdg, mkd, hdstg, pt shd, pt sl, EHU (6-10A) €1.50 -3 (poss rev pol); bbq (elec, gas); sw nr; 70% statics; bus/tram 250m; Eng spkn; adv bkg rec; CKE. *"Pleasant, family-run site; helpful owners; vg, modern, clean san facs; ltd touring pitches; sm pitches not suitable lge o'fits; adv bkg rec; excel; gd sm site; booking necessary; htd pool & waterslides 5km; highly rec; excel & cheap park & ride tram sys 6km away; lovely quiet gdn site; easy bus rte to city."* **€23.50 2023**

BOULOGNE SUR MER *3A2* (17km E Rural) *50.73337, 1.82440* **Camping à la Ferme Le Bois Groult (Leclercq),** 120 impasse du Bois Groult, 62142 Henneveux Le Plouy **03 21 33 32 16; leclercq.gilbert0643@orange.fr; www.leboisgroult.fr**

12 €1 nr

Take N42 fr Boulogne twd St Omer, take exit S dir Desvres (D127). Immed at rndabt foll sp Colembert. On ent Le Plouy turn R at the calvary & foll sp to site in 1km. Sm, hdstg, pt shd, pt sl, EHU (6-10A) €5; adv bkg acc. *"Charming, well-kept, peaceful CL-type site; pleasant & helpful owner; no barrier; WWI places of interest; easy access fr N42; ideal NH to/fr ferry/tunnel; excel; v clean & tidy site; vg; shwrs €2."* **€10.00 2023**

BOULOGNE SUR MER *3A2* (8km E Rural) *50.73111, 1.71582* **Camp Municipal Les Sapins,** Route de Crémarest, 62360 La Capelle-lès-Boulogne **06 75 16 63 61**

nr nr nr sand 4km

Exit A16 junc 31 E onto N42 to La Capelle vill; cont to next rndabt & take sp Crémarest; site on L opp horse riding school. 2*, Sm, pt shd, EHU (4-6A) €2.35-4.60 (poss rev pol); bbq; bus 1km; adv bkg acc; CKE. *"Helpful warden; gd modern san facs but insufficient amount; office 0800-0900 & 1600-1700; gd NH for Calais; poss travellers."* **€17.00, 29 Jun-2 Oct. 2024**

BOULOGNE SUR MER *3A2* (7km S Urban) *50.67752, 1.64335* **Camping Les Cytises,** Chemin Georges Ducrocq, 62360 Isques **06 84 94 34 50; campinglescytises@orange.fr; www.campinglescytises.com**

€1 (htd) WD MSP nr sand 4km

S fr Boulogne on D901 to Isques; site 150m fr D901. Or on A16 exit junc 28 & foll sp Isques & camp sp. 2*, Med, hdg, hdstg, pt shd, terr, EHU (6A) inc (poss rev pol); gas; 50% statics; Eng spkn; adv bkg acc; ccard acc; games area; games rm; CKE. *"Pleasant site; poss sm pitches; friendly staff; clean, modern san facs, ltd LS; barrier clsd 2300-0700; conv Channel Tunnel & 5 mins fr Nausicaá; poss unkempt LS; conv NH nr m'way; gd."* **€25.00, 29 Mar-19 Oct. 2024**

BOULOGNE SUR MER *3A2* (8km SSW Coastal) *50.67128, 1.57079* **FFCC Camp Municipal La Falaise,** Rue Charles Cazin, 62224 Equihen-Plage **03 21 31 22 61; camping.equihen.plage@orange.fr; www.camping-equihen-plage.fr**

€2.60 WD MSP (htd) sand 200m

Exit A16 junc 28 onto D901 dir Boulogne, then D940 S. Turn R to Condette then foll sp Equihen-Plage, site sp in vill. Access fr D901 via narr rds. 3*, Med, hdg, pt shd, sl, terr, EHU (10-16A) inc (poss rev pol); 85% statics; phone; adv bkg acc; ccard acc; games rm; watersports; CKE. *"Pleasant, well-run site in excel location, but poss windy; excel clean facs; sl pitches poss diff long o'fits; steep rd to beach; gd site approx 1hr fr Calais."* **€27.00, 1 Apr-31 Oct. 2024**

BOULOU, LE *8G4* (3.5km N Rural) *42.54157, 2.83431* **Camping Le Mas Llinas,** 66160 Le Boulou **04 68 83 25 46; info@camping-mas-llinas.com; www.camping-mas-llinas.com**

€2.20 (htd)

Fr Perpignan, take D900 S; 1km N of Le Boulou turn R at Intermarché supmkt 100m to mini rndabt, turn L & foll sp to Mas-Llinas to site in 2km. Or fr A9 exit 43 & foll sp Perpignan thro Le Boulou. L at rndabt adj Leclerc supmkt, site well sp. 3*, Med, mkd, pt shd, terr, EHU (5-10A) €4.10-5.20; gas; bbq; TV; 10% statics; phone; Eng spkn; adv bkg acc; bike hire; games area; games rm; CKE. *"Peaceful, scenic site, mountain views; beware poss high winds on high pitches; ltd water points at top levels; ltd facs LS; facs clean; gd sized pitches; golden orioles on site; no longer family owned now company owned; pitches smaller, diff to manouver average sized MH onto sm pitch; WiFi €2 an hour; busy; poor."*
€27.00, 10 Mar-30 Nov. **2022**

BOULOU, LE *8G4* (5km S Rural) *42.49083, 2.79777* **Camping Les Pins/Le Congo,** Route de Céret, 66480 Maureillas-las-Illas, Pyrénées Orientales Occitanie **09 65 01 13 50; lespinslecongo@hotmail.fr; https://www.campinglespinslecongo.com/en/**

3,00 € (htd) nr

Fr Le Boulou take D900 S, fork R after 2km onto D618 dir Céret. Site on L 500m after Maureillas. 4*, Med, hdg, shd, EHU (10A) €3.50; gas; bbq; 10% statics; phone; Eng spkn; adv bkg acc; ccard acc; Gym; Bowling green; Game room. *"Shabby and expensive, shwrs OK (2010)."*
€23.00, 1 Apr-30 Oct. **2020**

BOULOU, LE *8G4* (4km SW Rural) *42.50664, 2.79502* **Camping de la Vallée,** Route de Maureillas, 66490 St Jean-Pla-de-Corts **04 68 83 23 20; campingdelavallee@yahoo.fr; www.campingdelavallee.com**

€2.50 (htd) nr

Exit A9 at Le Boulou. Turn W on D115. Turn L after 3km at rndabt, into St Jean-Pla-de-Corts, thro vill, over bdge, site on L. 3*, Med, mkd, pt shd, EHU (10A) €4.40; sw nr; red long stay; TV; 50% statics; phone; bus adj; Eng spkn; adv bkg acc; ccard acc; fishing 1km; archery; CKE. *"Lovely well-kept site; easy access lge, well mkd pitches; friendly, helpful owners with gd local info; excel san facs; conv NH fr A9 or longer; gd rest; quiet site; nice pool with sun loungers, best site in area; gd value; free WiFi all over site; highly rec; excel."*
€24.20, 1 Apr-31 Oct. **2022**

BOULOU, LE *8G4* (4km W Rural) *42.50908, 2.78429* **Camping Les Casteillets,** 66490 St Jean Pla-de-Corts **04 68 83 26 83; jc@campinglescasteillets.com; www.campinglescasteillets.com**

12

Exit A9 at Le Boulou; turn W on D115; after 3km turn L immed after St Jean-Pla-de-Corts; site sp on R in 400m. NB Narr app last 200m. 3*, Med, mkd, pt shd, serviced pitches; EHU (6A) €3.30 (poss rev pol); gas; red long stay; TV; 10% statics; Eng spkn; adv bkg rec; tennis; games area. *"Lovely, friendly, scenic, well run site; lge pitches; conv for touring & en rte NE Spain; low lying; gd food in rest; gd."* **€27.20** **2023**

BOURBON LANCY *9A1* (1km S Rural) *46.61949, 3.75506* **Camping de Bourbon-Lancy (formerly Le Plan d'Eau du Breuil),** 11 rue des Eurimants, 71140 Bourbon Lancy **03 85 89 20 98; camping.bourbonlancy@aquadis-loisirs.com; www.aquadis-loisirs.com**

Site sp fr town, on lakeside. 3*, Sm, pt shd, pt sl, EHU (6A); bbq; TV; Eng spkn; adv bkg acc; CKE. *"Excel; 2km to town; lake adj; bike rec."*
€22.10, 9 Mar-13 Nov. **2023**

BOURBON LANCY *4H4* (0.3km WNW Urban) *46.62098, 3.76557* **Camping St Prix,** Rue de St Prix, 71140 Bourbon-Lancy **03 85 89 20 98 or 03 86 37 95 83; aquadis1@wanadoo.fr; www.aquadis-loisirs.com**

€3.10 (htd) (htd)

Fr N turn L fr D979 on D973 & foll into Bourbon-Lancy. Turn R at traff lts after Attac Sup'mkt, keep L, site on R after mini-rndabt. 3*, Med, hdg, hdstg, shd, pt sl, terr, EHU (10A) €2; sw; 25% statics; Eng spkn; fishing; CKE. *"Tidy, well-run site; helpful staff; new san facs; lovely old town 10 min uphill walk; rec."*
€20.35, 9 Mar-3 Nov. **2024**

BOURBON L'ARCHAMBAULT *9A1* (1km W Rural) *46.58058, 3.04804* **Camp Municipal de Bourbon l'Archambault,** 03160 Bourbon-l'Archambault **Camp Municipal Parc Capitaine 04 70 67 08 83 or 06 82 82 62 50; camping@mairie-bourbon.com; www.allier-auvergne-tourisme.com and bourbonlarchambault.com/camping-municipal**

nr

Exit D953 at Bourbon-l'Archambault onto D1 northwards; in 400m turn L into Blvd Jean Bignon. Site sp. 3*, Lge, pt shd, sl, EHU (6-10A) €2-2.20; 75% statics; tennis nr. *"Beautifully laid-out in park surroundings; htd pool 300m; waterslide 300m; gd pitches; excel updated san facs (2013); charming town; excel."* **€13.00, 1 Mar-12 Nov.** **2024**

FRANCE

FRANCE

BOURBOULE, LA *7B4* (1km E Rural) *45.58980, 2.7525210* **Camping Les Vernières,** 170 Avenue Maréchal de Lattre de Tassigny 63150 La Bourboule **047 38 110 20; contact@camping-la-bourboule.fr; www.camping-la-bourboule.fr**

€1 (htd) nr nr (covrd, htd)

Fr N on N89 or S on D922 turn E onto D130 dir Le Mont-Dore, site sp. 4*, Lge, hdg, pt shd, terr, EHU (10A) €3.50; Eng spkn; adv bkg acc; fishing nr. *"Lovely setting in mountains; gd clean facs; sh walk to fine spa town; gd family site; rec."* **€10.00, 9 Feb-30 Sep.** **2020**

BOURBOULE, LA *7B4* (4km E Rural) *45.59456, 2.76347* **Camping Les Clarines,** 1424 Ave Maréchal Leclerc, 63150 La Bourboule **04 73 81 02 30; clarines.les@wanadoo.fr; www.camping-les-clarines.com**

€2 (htd) nr nr (htd)

Fr La Bourboule take D996/D88 on N bank of rv (old rd sp Piscine & Gare); fork L at exit fr town. Site sp on R, nr junc with D219. 3*, Lge, pt shd, terr, EHU (6-10A) €3.50-€5.80; gas; bbq; TV; adv bkg rec; games area; outdoor fitness space. *"Gd winter sports cent; excel htd facs."* **€16.00, 21 Dec-11 Oct.** **2020**

BOURDEAUX *9D2* (1km SE Rural) *44.57854, 5.12791* **Camping Les Bois du Châtelas,** Route de Dieulefit, 26460 Bourdeaux **04 75 00 60 80; contact@chatelas.com; www.chatelas.com**

€5 (htd) (covrd, htd)

Fr N exit A7 m'way junc 16 onto D104, head twd Crest. Shortly bef Crest turn R onto D538 S thro Bourdeaux & cont dir Dienlefit (still on D538), site in 1km on L, well sp. 5*, Med, mkd, pt shd, terr, EHU (10A) inc; gas; bbq (elec, gas); cooking facs; TV; 30% statics; phone; Eng spkn; adv bkg req; ccard acc; games area; horseriding 5km; bike hire; games rm; waterslide; sauna; fitness rm; CKE. *"In lovely, scenic area; site on steep slope; no o'fits over 8m high ssn; gd walking."* **€56.00, 10 Apr-6 Sep, M11.** **2022**

BOURG ACHARD *3D2* (1km W Rural) *49.35330, 0.80814* **Camping Le Clos Normand,** 235 Route de Pont Audemer, 27310 Bourg-Achard **02 32 56 34 84 or 06 40 25 53 14 (mob); contact@leclosnormand-camping.com; leclosnormand-camping.fr**

1km W of vill of Bourg-Achard, D675 Rouen-Pont Audemer or exit A13 at Bourg-Achard junc. 3*, Med, hdg, mkd, pt shd, pt sl, EHU (6A) €3.40 (poss rev pol & poss long lead req); gas; 10% statics; adv bkg acc; ccard acc; CKE. *"Vg, clean san facs; plenty hot water; many pitches uneven; gd; muddy when wet."* **€28.00, 15 Mar-15 Oct.** **2022**

BOURG ARGENTAL *9C2* (2km E Rural) *45.29910, 4.58183* **Camping L'Astrée,** L'Allier, 42220 Bourg-Argental **04 77 39 72 97; contact@campinglastree.fr; www.campinglastree.fr**

12 €1.60 nr

S fr St Etienne on D1082 to Bourg-Argental, thro town, site well sp on R soon after rndabt & opp filling stn. Fr Annonay or Andance site on L of D1082 at start of Bourg-Argental, adj rv. 3*, Sm, mkd, hdstg, pt shd, EHU (4-6A) inc (long cable poss req); gas; bbq; 60% statics; phone; ccard acc; waterslide; games rm; tennis; fishing; bike hire; CKE. *"Pleasant site with modern facs; htd pool 600m; vg."* **€21.00** **2023**

BOURG D'OISANS, LE *9C3* (1.5km NE Rural) *45.06557, 6.03980* **Camping à la Rencontre du Soleil,** Route de l'Alpe-d'Huez, La Sarenne, 38520 Le Bourg-d'Oisans **04 76 79 12 22; contact@rencontresoleil.fr; www.rencontre-du-soleil.com**

€1.20 (htd) nr (covrd, htd)

Fr D1091 approx 800m E of town turn N onto D211, sp 'Alpe d'Huez'. In approx 500m cross sm bdge over Rv Sarennes, then turn immed L to site. (Take care not to overshoot ent, as poss diff to turn back). 5*, Med, hdg, mkd, pt shd, EHU (10A) inc; bbq; TV; 45% statics; adv bkg req; ccard acc; games rm; tennis; fishing; horseriding 1.5km; games area; CKE. *"Busy site with lovely views; various pitch sizes/shapes; excel, spotless san facs, some unisex; helpful owner; excel rest; La Marmotte cycle race (early Jul) & Tour de France usually pass thro area & access poss restricted; no o'fits over 7m high ssn; pitches poss flooded after heavy rain, but staff excel at responding; mkt Sat; highly rec."* **€60.00, 1 May - 30 Sep.** **2022**

BOURG D'OISANS, LE *9C3* (13km SE Rural) *44.98611, 6.12027* **Camping Le Champ du Moulin,** Bourg d'Arud, 38520 Vénosc **04 76 80 07 38; info@champ-du-moulin.com; www.champ-du-moulin.com**

€2.10

On D1091 SE fr Le Bourg-d'Oisans sp Briançon for about 6km; turn R onto D530 twd La Bérarde & after 8km site sp. Turn R to site 350m after cable car stn beside Rv Vénéon. NB Site sp bef vill; do not cross rv on D530. 3*, Med, mkd, hdg, pt shd, EHU (6-10A) €7.20-9.80 (extra charge in winter, poss rev pol); gas; bbq; red long stay; TV; 20% statics; Eng spkn; adv bkg req; ccard acc; fishing nr; rafting nr; horseriding nr; sauna; games rm; tennis nr; CKE. *"Lovely, well-run site by alpine torrent (unguarded); friendly, helpful owners; ltd facs LS; htd pool adj; access to pitches poss diff lge o'fits; ideal for walking, climbing & relaxing; no o'fits over 10m; lots of outdoor activities to enjoy; cable car to Les Deux Alpes adj (closes end Aug); mkt Tue Vénosc (high ssn); highly rec."* **€33.00, 15 Dec - 23 Apr, 25 May -15 Sep, M03.** **2022**

BOURG D'OISANS, LE *9C3* (4km NW Rural) *45.09000, 6.00750* **Camping Ferme Noémie,** Chemin Pierre Polycarpe, Les Sables, 38520 Le Bourg-d'Oisans **04 76 11 06 14; ferme.noemie@orange.fr; www.fermenoemie.com**

On D1091 Grenoble to Briançon; Les Sables is 4km bef Le Bourg-d'Oisans; turn L next to church, site in 400m. 2*, Sm, mkd, unshd, EHU (16A) €3.50; bbq (gas); red long stay; 25% statics; phone; bus 500m; adv bkg acc; ccard acc; cycling; fishing; games area; CKE. *"Simple site in superb location with excel facs; helpful British owners; lots of sports; skiing; walking; gd touring base lakes & Ecrins National Park; pool 3km; excel site."* **€34.50, 29 Apr-14 Oct.** **2023**

"There aren't many sites open at this time of year"

If you're travelling outside peak season remember to call ahead to check site opening dates – even if the entry says 'open all year'.

BOURG D'OISANS, LE *9C3* (7km NW Rural) *45.11388, 6.00785* **RCN Camping Belledonne,** Rochetaillée, 38520 Le Bourg-d'Oisans **04 76 80 07 18; belledonne@rcn.fr; https://www.rcn.nl/nl/campings/frankrijk/alpe-d-huez/rcn-belledonne**

Fr S of Grenoble take N85 to Vizille then D1091 twd Le Bourg-d'Oisans; in approx 25km in Rochetaillée turn L onto D526 sp Allemont. Site 100m on R. 4*, Med, hdg, shd, EHU (10A) inc; bbq; TV; Eng spkn; ccard acc; sauna; games area; tennis; games rm; fishing 500m; horseriding; windsurfing; CKE. *"Beautiful, well-run site in lovely location; no o'fits over 7.5m high ssn; friendly Dutch owners; access to many pitches tight; no twin axles; gd for teenagers; excel pool with views; many walks; gd touring base; La Marmotte cycle race (early Jun) & Tour de France usually pass thro area & access poss restricted; mkt Sat; excel new san facs (2018), gd rest; v helpful staff."* **€40.00, 6 May - 25 Sept, M02.** **2022**

BOURG EN BRESSE *9A2* (11km NE Rural) *46.29078, 5.29078* **Camp Municipal du Sevron,** Chemin du Moulin, 01370 St Etienne-du-Bois **04 74 24 05 47; campingdusevron@gmail.com; www.campingdusevron.fr**

On D1083 at S end of vill of St Etienne-du-Bois on E side of rd. 2*, Sm, hdg, pt shd, EHU (10A) €2.05; 50% statics; Eng spkn; ccard acc; rv fishing; tennis. *"Gd NH; dated but clean facs; friendly; sm pitches; late arr get v sm pitches; poss rd & rlwy noise; gd shwrs & plenty hot water; gd facs."* **€17.40** **2023**

BOURG ET COMIN *3D4* (0.5km NE Rural) *49.39871, 3.66072* **Camping de la Pointe,** 5 Rue de Moulins, 02160 Bourg-et-Comin **03 23 25 87 52; sejouraucamping@gmail.com; campingdelapointe.fr**

Leave A26/E17 at junc 14 & turn W along D925 dir Soissons for 15km. Site on R on ent vill. 2*, Sm, hdg, pt shd, EHU (6A) €3.20; bbq; phone; bus 500m; Eng spkn; adv bkg acc; CKE. *"CL-type site in orchard; narr ent & access to pitches poss diff lge o'fits; most pitches sm & not suitable lge o'fits; EHU is only 2 pin; gd rest; gd walking area; 10 mins fr Parc Nautique de l'Ailette with watersports; conv Aisne Valley; bar 500m; v accommodating owner; htd pool OAY; wifi not reliable."* **€29.00** **2023**

BOURG ST MAURICE *9B4* (1km E Rural) *45.62241, 6.78503* **Camping Le Versoyen,** Route des Arcs, 73700 Bourg-St Maurice **04 79 07 03 45; versoyen@camping-indigo.com; www.camping-bourgsaintmaurice.com**

Fr SW on N90 thro town turn R to Les Arcs. Site on R in 1km. Do not app fr any other dir. 3*, Lge, hdstg, pt shd, EHU (4-10A) €4.60-5.20; Eng spkn; fishing; sauna; games area; tennis adj; canoeing; CKE. *"Excel for winter sports; mountain views; mkd walks fr site; 2 pools adj; rvside walk to town; well-organised site; dated but clean facs."* **€12.80, 15 Dec-28 Apr, 25 May-2 Nov, 14 Dec-31 Dec.** **2024**

"That's changed – Should I let the Club know?"

If you find something on site that's different from the site entry, fill in a report and let us know. See camc.com/europereport.

BOURG SUR GIRONDE *7C2* (0.5km S Urban) *45.03880, -0.56065* **Camp Municipal La Citadelle,** 2 Quai des Chantiers, 33710 Bourg, France **05 56 68 40 06; commune-de-bourg@wanadoo.fr; www.campingfrance.com/recherchez-votre-camping/nouvelle-aquitaine/gironde/bourg/camping-la-citadelle**

Take D669 fr St André-de-Cubzac (off A10) to Bourg. Foll sp Halte Nautique & Le Port into Rue Franklin on L twd town cent & foll sp to site. Or fr Blaye, foll Camping sp on app Bourg, cont round by-pass to other end of town to Rue Franklin. NB Do not attempt to take c'van thro town. 2*, Sm, mkd, pt shd, EHU (3-10A) €3-6 (poss long lead req); bbq; adv bkg acc; CKE. *"Scenic, CL-type rvside site; well-maintained but basic facs; poss variable opening dates; pool adj; excel."* **€18.50, 1 April-15 Oct.** **2024**

FRANCE

FRANCE

BOURGES *4H3 (2km S Urban) 47.07228, 2.39497*
Camping de Bourges (formerly Municipal Robinson), 26 Blvd de l'Industrie, 18000 Bourges **02 48 20 16 85; camping.bourges@aquadis-loisirs.com; www.aquadis-loisirs.com/camping-nature/camping-de-bourges**

€1.35 (htd) nr nr

Exit A71/E11 at junc 7, foll sp Bourges Centre & bear R at 'Autres Directions' sp; foll site sp; site at traff lts on N side of S section of inner ring rd half-way bet junc with D2144 & D2076. NB: site access is via a loop - no L turn at traff lts, but rndabt just past site if turning missed. If on outer ring rd D400, app city on D2144 & then as above. Sp on app rds to site gd. 3*, Med, hdg, mkd, hdstg, pt shd, serviced pitches; EHU (10-16A) €3.40-8 (poss rev pol); bbq (elec, gas); twin axles; red long stay; bus adj; Eng spkn; ccard acc; CKE. *"Attractive, well-kept, well-organised, busy, rvside site in gd location; helpful, friendly staff; pool 300m inc; excel, immac san facs; some v lge pitches, some sm & poss diff ent; most pitches hdstg; excel NH or longer; 20 min walk to historic town; easy acc to Canal de Berry cycle rte."* **€24.20, 1 Mar-3 Nov. 2024**

BOURGUEIL *4G1 (0.8km S Rural) 47.26991, 0.16873*
Camp Municipal Parc Capitaine, 37140 Bourgueil **02 47 97 85 62 or 02 47 97 25 00 LS; camping@bourgueil.fr; www.bourgueil.fr**

€1.50 nr

N on D749 fr junc 5 of A85, site 1km on R. Fr W (Longue) via D10 & by-pass, S at rndabt on D749 to site on L in 200m. Do not app fr N via D749 thro town cent. 3*, Med, hdg, mkd, pt shd, EHU (10A) €2.65 (poss long lead req); gas; bbq; sw; ccard acc; CKE. *"Ideal cent Loire châteaux; 2 sites - one on R for tourers; excel; barrier ent & exit by code; office clsd 1230-1500 but warden lives upstairs; conv fr A85 & Loire valley; vg; san facs need refurb."* **€15.65, 1 May-15 Oct. 2024**

BOUSSAC *7A4 (2km NE Rural) 46.37192, 2.20036*
Camping du Château de Poinsouze, Route de la Châtre, 23600 Boussac-Bourg **05 55 65 02 21; camping-de-poinsouze@gmail.com; www.camping-de-poinsouze.com**

€3

Fr junc 10 on A71/E11 by-pass Montluçon via N145 dir Guéret; in 22km turn L onto D917 to Boussac; cont on D917 dir La Châtre; site 3km on L. Or fr Guéret on N145, exit Gouzon, at rndabt take D997 to Boussac, then as above. 4*, Med, mkd, unshd, pt sl, serviced pitches; EHU (6-20A) inc (poss rev pol); bbq; TV; 10% statics; Eng spkn; adv bkg req; ccard acc; horseriding 5km; games area; games rm; waterslide; lake fishing; golf 20km; bike hire; CKE. *"Peaceful, relaxed site by lake in chateau grnds; well-kept & well-run; lge pitches, some sl; no o'fits over 15m; dogs not acc Jul/Aug welcoming, helpful owners; superb san facs; excel rest & snacks; gd for young children; gd walking."* **€35.00, 9 Jun - 10 Sep, L16. 2022**

BOUSSAC *7A4 (2km W Rural) 46.34938, 2.18662*
Camping Creuse-Nature (Naturist), Route de Bétête, 23600 Boussac **05 55 65 18 01; creuse-nature@wanadoo.fr; www.creuse-nature.com**

€5.50 (covrd, htd)

Fr Boussac take D917 N twd La Châtre. In 500m turn L (W) on D15 sp Bétête. Site on R in 2.5km, clearly sp. 2*, Med, hdg, mkd, pt shd, pt sl, EHU (10A) €4.50 (poss long lead req); 10% statics; Eng spkn; adv bkg acc; ccard acc; fishing; games area. *"Excel site in lovely area; great pitches; charming & helpful owners; clean facs; easy walk to town & interesting château; great location."* **€37.00, 12 Apr-30 Sept. 2024**

BRACIEUX *4G2 (0.5km N Urban) 47.55060, 1.53743*
Camping Indigo les Châteaux, 11 Rue Roger Brun, 41250 Bracieux **02 54 46 41 84; chateaux@camping-indigo.com; https://europe.huttopia.com/site/camping-les-chateaux/**

€5 nr nr (covrd)

Fr S take D102 to Bracieux fr Cour-Cheverny. Fr N exit Blois on D765 dir Romorantin; after 5km take D923 to Bracieux & site on R on N o'skts of town opp church, sp. 3*, Lge, hdg, mkd, hdstg, pt shd, EHU (10A) €2.75 (poss long lead req); red long stay; TV; 10% statics; Eng spkn; adv bkg acc; ccard acc; tennis; games rm; bike hire; CKE. *"Peaceful spot; attractive forest area; busy high ssn; gd security; gd touring base; gas 300m; bike tracks; well run site; all san blocks replaced (2013); superb; excel, well run site."* **€30.00, 31 Mar - 6 Nov. 2022**

BRANTOME *7C3 (1km E Rural) 45.36074, 0.66035*
Camping Brantôme Peyrelevade, 46 Ave André Maurois, 24310 Brantôme **05 53 05 75 24; info@camping-dordogne.net; www.camping-dordogne.net**

€2 (htd) nr sand adj

Fr N on D675 foll sp Centre Ville; ent vill & turn L onto D78 Thiviers rd, site sp at turn; in 1km on R past stadium opp g'ge. Fr S D939 foll sp 'Centre Ville' fr rndabt N of town. Then L onto D78 Thiviers rd & foll sp. Do not foll 'Centre Ville' sp fr rndabt S of town, use by-pass. Football stadium best ref point for ent. 4*, Lge, mkd, hdg, pt shd, EHU (10A) inc; bbq; sw nr; 7% statics; Eng spkn; adv bkg acc; ccard acc; tennis nr; CKE. *"Spacious, well-kept rvside site; attractive courtyard layout; friendly, helpful owners; excel, modern, gd san facs; facs stretched in high ssn; grnd poss soft after heavy rain; 10 min walk to lovely town (the Venice of Périgord); mkt Wed; games area adj; beautiful countryside; gd walking & cycling; excel; some pitches heavily shd; excel family camping."* **€34.00, 29 Apr-22 Sep. 2023**

BRANTOME *7C3* (4km SW Rural) *45.32931, 0.63690* **Camping du Bas Meygnaud,** 24310 Valeuil **05 53 05 58 44; camping-du-bas-meygnaud@wanadoo.fr; www.basmeygnaud.fr**

€2.50 nr

Fr Brantôme, take D939 S twd Périgueux; in 4.5km turn R at sp La Serre. In 1km turn L to in 500m, well sp. Winding, narr app thro lanes; poss diff lge o'fits. 2*, Sm, pt shd, pt sl, EHU (6A) €3.50; bbq; phone; Eng spkn; CKE. *"Most pitches shd by pine trees; helpful & friendly owner; dated san facs; unspoilt countryside."* **€27.50, 1 Apr-30 Sep. 2024**

BRASSAC *8F4* (11km SE Rural) *43.59700, 2.60732* **Camping Le Rouquié,** Lac de la Raviège, 81260 Lamontélarie **05 63 70 98 06; contact@campingrouquie.fr; www.campingrouquie.fr**

Fr Brassac take D62 to N side of Lac de la Raviège; site on lakeside. 2*, Med, mkd, pt shd, terr, EHU (3-6A) €4; bbq; sw; TV; 50% statics; adv bkg acc; ccard acc; bike hire; watersports adj; games area; fishing; sailing; CKE. *"Ltd facs LS; gd lake views; site needs TLC."* **€28.00, 1 May-31 Oct. 2024**

BRASSAC *8F4* (5km S Rural) *43.60835, 2.47148* **FFCC Camping Le Plô,** 23 Rue du Plô du Catussou, Le Bourg, 81260 Le Bez **05 63 74 00 82; info@leplo.com; www.leplo.com**

€1.50 nr

Fr Castres on D622 to Brassac; then D53 S to Le Bez, site sp W of Le Bez. 3*, Med, mkd, pt shd, terr, EHU (6A) €3; bbq; Eng spkn; adv bkg acc; games area; games rm; bike hire; CKE. *"Lovely location; well-equipped site; excel, clean san facs; friendly, helpful Dutch owners; beautiful, historical area with National Park; much wildlife; cafés & gd rest nrby; vg."* **€31.50, 1 May-30 Sep. 2024**

BRAUCOURT *6E1* (9km W Rural) *48.55754, 4.70629* **Camping Le Clos du Vieux Moulin,** 33 Rue du Lac, 51290 Châtillon-sur-Broué **03 26 41 30 43; leclosduvieuxmoulin@orange.fr; www.leclosduvieuxmoulin.fr**

12 (htd) nr

Fr N take D13 fr Vitry-le-François. Turn R at sp for Châtillon-sur-Broué; site 100m on R. Fr S 2nd L fr Giffaumont (1km); site 100m on R. 3*, Med, hdg, mkd, hdstg, pt shd, pt sl, EHU (5A) €3.70; gas; 80% statics; phone; ccard acc; watersports; CKE. *"Busy high ssn; birdwatching, san facs need refurb (2010) & ltd LS; site poss unkempt (2010); grnd soft after rain."* **€20.00 2024**

BRENGUES *7D4* (0.5km S Rural) *44.57509, 1.83261* **Camp Municipal de Brengues,** 46320 Brengues **06 11 17 57 10 or 05 81 48 06 99; labrenguette.camp46@gmail.com; www.brengues.org**

nr

W fr Figeac on D13. After 6km turn L onto D41. After 17km, turn L at x-rds with D38, site ent 100m on R bef bdge over Rv Célé. 3*, Sm, mkd, pt shd, EHU (10A) inc (rev pol); sw; tennis; CKE. *"Warden now onsite."* **€15.00, 1 Jun-30 Sep. 2023**

BRESSE, LA *6F3* (3.2km E Rural) *47.99893, 6.91801* **FFCC Camp Municipal Le Haut des Bluches,** 5 Route des Planches, 88250 La Bresse **03 29 25 64 80; www.hautdesbluches.com**

12 (htd)

Leave La Bresse on D34 Rte de la Schlucht. Site on R in 3km. 3*, Med, mkd, pt shd, terr, EHU (4-13A) €2-4.80; bbq; TV; 10% statics; Eng spkn; adv bkg acc; ccard acc; games rm; site clsd early Nov-mid Dec; games area; CKE. *"Excel site in attractive setting; NH area for m'vans; excel san facs; pool in vill; gd walks fr site; conv winter sports."* **€21.70 2023**

BRESSUIRE *4H1* (2.6km S Rural) *46.82923, -0.50223* **Camping Le Puy Rond,** Allee du Puy Rond, Cornet, 79300 Bressuire **05 16 72 93 14 or 06 85 60 37 26 (mob); puyrondcamping@gmail.com; www.puyrondcamping.com**

€2 (htd) nr nr

Fr N149 foll site sp on rte 'Poids Lourds' to site on D38. Fr 'Centre Ville' foll sp for Fontenay-Le-Comte; turn R 100m after overhead bdge & go across junc to site. Well sp. 3*, Med, mkd, pt shd, pt sl, terr, EHU (6-10A) €5; bbq; red long stay; twin axles; 95% statics; Eng spkn; adv bkg acc; ccard acc; fishing 1km; CKE. *"Gd touring base; friendly British owners; adv bkg ess for twin axles; winter storage avail; vg; poss rev pol."* **€21.00, 02 Mar-5 Nov. 2020**

BRETENOUX *7C4* (0.2km N Urban) *44.91650, 1.83816* **Camping La Bourgnatelle,** 46 Al Port, 46130 Bretenoux **05 81 48 02 94 or 06 23 05 34 52; la.bourgnatelle@gmail.com; www.camping-lot-bretenoux.com**

€1.50 nr

In town 100m fr D940. 3*, Lge, pt shd, EHU (5-10A) €3; adv bkg acc; canoe hire; rv; fishing. *"Lovely site along banks of Rv Cère; clean site; gd fishing; lovely town MD Tues."* **€25.00, 1 Apr-31 Oct. 2024**

BRETEUIL SUR L'ITON *4E2* (0.3km SSE Urban) *48.83175, 0.91258* **Camping Les Berges de l'Iton,** 53 rue du Fourneau, 27160 Breteuil-sur-Iton **02 32 62 70 35 or 06 84 75 70 32 (mob); campinglesberges-de-liton@orange.fr; www.campinglesbergesdeliton.com**

(htd)

Fr Evreux take D830 twd Conches-en-Ouche. L onto D840 to Breteuil, then foll sp for site. 3*, Med, hdstg, hdg, mkd, pt shd, pt sl, EHU (6A) inc; gas; bbq; 66% statics; adv bkg acc; INF; CCI. *"Well kept, landscaped site; gd NH; mkt on Wednesdays; helpful staff; vg."* **€23.70, 29 Mar-27 Sep. 2024**

FRANCE

FRANCE

BRETIGNOLLES SUR MER *2H3* (1km E Urban) *46.63583, -1.85861* **Camping La Trévillière,** Route de Bellevue, 85470 Bretignolles-sur-Mer **02 51 90 09 65 or 02 51 33 05 05; info@chadotel.com; La Trévillière**

€4 (max 1) (covrd, htd) sand 1.5km

S along D38 fr St Gilles Croix-de-Vie twd Olonne-sur-Mer, site is sp to L in Bretignolles-sur-Mer. Site 1km fr town cent nr football stadium. Sp fr town cent. 4*, Lge, mkd, hdg, pt shd, serviced pitches; EHU (6A) inc; gas; bbq (gas); red long stay; TV; 70% statics; phone; Eng spkn; adv bkg acc; ccard acc; bike hire; waterslide; fishing; horseriding 5km; watersports 3km; games rm; CKE. *"Friendly, family site; lge pitches; no c'van/m'van over 8m high ssn; quiet; gd cycling area; salt marshes worth a visit; mkt Thu & Sun; busy in July, pool overcrowded, loud music; wc no seat or toilet paper; vill 15min walk; lge Sunday mkt; new management, poor welcome ltd help/assistance."* **€40.00, 7 Apr-24 Sep, A26.** 2023

"I like to fill in the reports as I travel from site to site"

You'll find report forms at the back of this guide, or you can fill them in online at camc.com/europereport.

BRETIGNOLLES SUR MER *2H3* (5km E Rural) *46.64021, -1.80708* **Camping L'Oree de l'Océan,** Rue Capitaine de Mazenod, 85220 Landevieille **02 51 22 96 36; contact@oreeocean.fr; www.camping-oreedelocean.com**

€3 nr (htd) sand 5km

Take D12 fr La Mothe-Achard to St Julien-des-Landes & cont to x-rds bef La Chaize-Giraud. Turn L onto D32, take 1st R in Landevieille to site on L in 50m. Adj Mairie. 4*, Med, hdg, mkd, pt shd, pt sl, EHU (10A) €4; red long stay; TV; 95% statics; phone; Eng spkn; adv bkg acc; ccard acc; tennis; CKE. *"Gd, friendly, family site; many gd beaches & mkd cycle tracks nr; gd for NH."* **€23.00, 1 Apr-30 Sep.** 2024

BRETIGNOLLES SUR MER *2H3* (3.4km S Coastal) *46.603957, -1.840665* **Camping L'Ocean,** 17 rue du Brandais, 85470 Brem-sur-Mer **+332 51 90 59 16; contact@cybelevacances.com; www.campingdelocean.fr**

€6 (covrd, htd) sand

Fr La Roche-sur-Yon and Les Sables d'Olonne foll A87. Then D160. Take dir of Bretignolles-sur-Mer. 5*, Med, pt shd, bbq (gas); bus/train; adv bkg acc. *"Biggest indoor waterpark in Vendée; cycling rte fr site."* **NP 30, 9 Apr-6 Nov.** 2022

BRETIGNOLLES SUR MER *2H3* (4km S Coastal) *46.60413, -1.83231* **Camping Le Chaponnet,** 16 Rue du Chaponnet, 85470 Brem-sur-Mer **02 51 90 55 56; contact@le-chaponnet.com; www.le-chaponnet.com**

€6 (covrd, htd) sand 1km

Fr La Roche-sur-Yon on N160 dir Les Sables-d'Olonne. Turn R onto D87 thro St Mathurin vill & take 1st R (just after church) D38 dir L'Ile d'Olonne. Foll sp Brem-sur-Mer, go thro vill & foll sp 'Océan' (nr bakery & bar); turn L opp hairdresser, site in 50m along 1-way rd. 4*, Lge, hdg, pt shd, EHU (10A) inc; gas; bbq; TV; 75% statics; phone; adv bkg acc; ccard acc; gym; games area; sauna; bike hire; waterslide; games rm; jacuzzi; tennis; CKE. *"Gd beaches adj; vg."* **€34.00, 14 Apr-15 Sep, A05.** 2024

BRIANCON *9C4* (6km NE Rural) *44.93034, 6.68169* **Camp Municipal du Bois des Alberts,** 1245 Route des Alberts, Les Alberts, 05100 Montgenèvre **04 92 21 16 11 or 04 92 21 52 52; camping@montgenevre.com; camping.montgenevre.com/**

12 (htd)

Take N94 fr Briançon sp Italie. In 4km turn L onto D994, site 200m past Les Alberts vill on L. 2*, Lge, hdstg, shd, EHU (6-10A) €4.25 (rev pol); 30% statics; adv bkg acc; ccard acc; fishing; tennis; games area; CKE. *"Pleasant, friendly site in pine trees; cycle & walking paths; x-country skiing; random pitching; facs dated but clean, ltd LS; lge pine cones can fall fr trees - park away fr tall ones; kayak tuition; gd touring base; nice site."* **€11.50** 2024

BRIARE *4G3* (6km S Rural) *47.60018, 2.76101* **Camping Municipal L'ecluse des Combles,** Chemin de Loire, 45360 Châtillon-sur-Loire **02 38 36 34 39 or 06 32 07 83 45; camping.chatillonsurloire@orange.fr; www.camping.chatillon-sur-loire.com**

€1.20 (htd) nr nr nr

SE fr Briare on N7, in 4km turn SW onto D50. Site immed bef rv bdge on R. Care needed over bdge after ent. 2*, Med, pt shd, terr, EHU (6A) inc; gas; bbq; Eng spkn; fishing; games rm; CKE. *"Basic site with some nice pitches by Rv Loire & historic canal; pleasant staff; right of way along rv bank passes thro site; mkt 2nd Thurs of month; vg; canal viaduct at Briare worth visit; site neglected; pitch yourself; warden in off late afternoon."* **€16.90, 1 Mar-30 Oct.** 2023

BRIARE *4G3* (0.5km W Rural) *47.64137, 2.72560* **Camping Le Martinet,** Quai Tchékof, 45250 Briare **02 38 31 24 50 or 02 38 31 24 51; campingbriarelecanal@night-day.fr; www.night-and-day.fr/camping/13-camping-le-martinet**

€1 nr nr nr

Exit N7 into Briare. Fr N immed R after canal bdge; fr S L bef 2nd canal bdge; sp. 3*, Lge, mkd, unshd, EHU (10A) €3.60; Eng spkn; adv bkg acc; fishing adj. *"Gd views some pitches; pretty bars & rests along canal; gd walking & cycling; interesting town; gates close 2200; slightly neglected (2009); OK sh stay; san facs old style but clean."* **€22.20, 1 Apr-31 Oct. 2023**

BRIGNOLES *10F3* (9km SE Rural) *43.33919, 6.12579* **Camping La Vidaresse,** 83136 Ste Anastasie-sur-Issole **04 94 72 21 75; info@campinglavidaresse.com; www.campinglavidaresse.com**

€3 WD MSP nr (covrd, htd)

On DN7 2km W of Brignoles at rndabt take D43 dir Toulon. In about 10km turn L at rndabt to D15. Do not ent vill, go strt & site is approx 250m on R. 3*, Med, mkd, hdg, pt shd, terr, EHU (10A) €5 (poss rev pol); gas; bbq (elec, gas); 40% statics; adv bkg acc; ccard acc; tennis; fishing 200m; games area; CKE. *"Well-managed, family site in lovely area; peaceful; friendly & helpful; facs adequate; excel pool; gd touring base Haute Provence, Gorges du Verdon & Riviera; vineyard adj; gd."* **€26.00, 20 Mar-30 Sep. 2024**

BRILLANE, LA *10E3* (5km E Rural) *43.92282, 5.92369* **Camping Les Oliviers,** Chemin St Sauveur, 04700 Oraison **04 92 78 20 00; camping-oraison@wanadoo.fr; www.camping-oraison.com**

12 €2.50 WD MSP

Exit A51 junc 19; take rd E to Oraison in 2km; site sp in vill. 4*, Med, mkd, pt shd, pt sl, terr, EHU (16A) €4.50; gas; TV; 10% statics; Eng spkn; adv bkg acc; ccard acc; games area; bike hire; games rm; CKE. *"Pleasant, family-run site among olive trees; friendly, helpful owners; walks fr site; conv Verdon gorge; adj elec sub-stn, elec cables run over small pt of site, not obtrusive; gd."* **€29.20 2023**

BRIONNE *3D2* (0.5km N Urban) *49.20256, 0.71554* **Camp Municipal La Vallée,** Rue Marcel Nogrette, 27800 Brionne **02 32 44 80 35 or 07 69 72 34 37; evasioncampinglocation@orange.fr; www.ville-brionne.fr**

WD MSP nr nr

Fr D438 N or S on by-pass, turn N at D46 junc, pass Carrefour supmkt on L & take 1st R, site on L. 2*, Sm, hdg, pt shd, EHU (8A) €3.45; gas; bbq; CKE. *"Excel, well maintained site in lovely vill; gd san facs, poss ltd LS; sh walk to supmkt; clean facs but ltd."* **€15.00, 30 Apr-30 Sep. 2024**

BRIONNE *3D2* (6km N Rural) *49.24174, 0.70339* **Camp Municipal Les Marronniers,** Rue Louise Givon, 27290 Pont-Authou **02 32 42 75 06 or 06 27 25 21 45 (mob); lesmarroniers27@orange.fr or campingmunicipaldesmarronniers@orange.fr; www.normandie-accueil.fr**

12 €1.35 (htd) WD MSP nr nr

Heading S on D438 take D130 just bef Brionne sp Pont-Audemer (care req at bdge & rndabts). Site on L in approx 5km, well sp on o'skts of Pont-Authou; foll sp in vill. 2*, Med, hdstg, mkd, pt shd, EHU (10A) €3.40 (poss rev pol); bbq; 50% statics; adv bkg acc; fishing; bike hire; CKE. *"Useful, clean stop nr Rouen & m'way; friendly recep; clean san facs; best pitches far side of lake; few hdstg; adv bkg rec; some statics unsightly; stream runs thro site; beautiful valley with many historic towns & vills; excel walking; gd NH; pretty but basic site; recep & security gate cls 1800 in LS."* **€15.00 2023**

BRIONNE *3D2* (9km N Rural) *49.23648, 0.72265* **Camping Saint Nicolas,** 15 Rue St Nicolas, 27800 Le Bec-Hellouin **02 32 44 83 55 or 06 84 75 70 32 (Mob); campingstnicolas@orange.fr; www.campingsaintnicolas.fr**

€1.50 (htd) WD MSP nr nr (htd, indoor)

Exit A28 junc 13 onto D438 then take D581 to Malleville-sur-le-Bec; site on R 1km after Malleville. Well sp. 4*, Med, pt shd, EHU (10A) €3.50; bbq; 10% statics; tennis nr; horseriding nr; CKE. *"Attractive, peaceful, well-kept site in pleasant location; spacious pitches; friendly, helpful warden; vg, clean san facs; gate clsd 2200-0700; gd dog walks; vg cycling; attractive countryside; conv NH nr Calais; rec; delightful vill; rec dir in book; vist to Abbey at Bec Hellouin a must."* **€26.20, 27 Mar-11 Oct. 2022**

BRIOUDE *9C1* (2km S Rural) *45.2813, 3.4045* **Camping La Bageasse,** Ave de la Bageasse, 43100 Brioude **03 86 37 95 83; camping.brioude@aquadis-loisirs.com; www.aquadis-loisirs.com**

€1.50 WD (htd)

Turn off N102 & foll sp for Brioude town cent; then foll site sp. Narr app rd. Site on Rv Allier. 3*, Med, mkd, pt shd, terr, EHU (6A) €2 (some rev pol); bbq; red long stay; 8% statics; phone; Eng spkn; adv bkg acc; ccard acc; canoe hire; boating adj; fishing adj; CKE. *"Well-kept site; lge pitches; helpful warden; gd, clean san facs; phone ahead to check open LS; interesting basilica; easy cycle to Brioude."* **€20.00, 1 Mar-3 Nov. 2024**

BRISSAC QUINCE *4G1* (2km NE Rural) *47.35944, -0.43388* **Le Domaine de L'Etang,** 603 impasse de l'Étang, 49320 Brissac Quincé **02 41 91 70 61; www.campingetang.com**

€2 (htd) (covrd, htd)

Fr N on A11, exit junc 14 onto N260 passing E of Angers, following sp for Cholet/Poitiers. After x-ing Rv Loire, foll sp to Brissac-Quincé on D748. Foll sp for St Mathurin/Domaine de l'Etang on D55 to site. 4*, Med, hdstg, mkd, hdg, pt shd, serviced pitches; EHU (16A) inc; gas; bbq (charcoal, gas); red long stay; twin axles; TV; Eng spkn; adv bkg acc; ccard acc; bike hire; waterslide; games rm; lake fishing; golf 8km; CKE. *"Excel, well-cared for site amongst vineyards; lge pitches; staff pleasant & helpful; clean, modern facs; leisure facs gd for children; pleasant 15 min rvside walk to Brissac-Quincé; wine tasting; gd touring base Loire valley; mkt Thu; rec Apocalypse Tapestry at Chateau d'Angers; gd for walks & sightseeing; extensive site; bar/rest might be clsd from September; excel."*
€35.00, 7 Apr-17 Sep, L15. 2023

BRIVE LA GAILLARDE *7C3* (8km S Rural) *45.10049, 1.52423* **FFCC Camping à la Ferme (Delmas),** Malfarges, 19600 Noailles **05 55 85 81 33**

12 €2.60 nr

Fr A20/E9 take exit 52 sp Noailles; in vill take 1st R across yellow paving at vill café/shop (to avoid steep dangerous hill); turn R at T-junc, site on L. Sp fr m'way. NB All vill rds have 3,500kg limit. Sm, mkd, pt shd, terr, EHU (5A) €2.70-5.30 (poss rev pol); 10% statics; adv bkg acc; fishing 200m; CKE. *"Conv NH/sh stay adj A20; friendly, helpful farmer; if owner not around choose a pitch; farm meals & produce; basic san facs; parking on terr poss awkward; fly problem in hot weather; strict silence after 2200; excel."* **€16.00** 2024

BRIVE LA GAILLARDE *7C3* (6km SW Rural) *45.09975, 1.45115* **Camping Intercommunal La Prairie,** 207 La Prairie, 19600 Lissac-sur-Couze **05 55 85 37 97; www.campingdulacducausse.com**

€3

A20 exit 51; D1089 to Larche; L onto D19 sp Lissac; take 1st L after St Cernin-de-Larche onto D59 round N side of Lac de Causse, sharp R down hill then bear L over dam; R to site in 2km. Site sp as 'Camping Nautica'. 3*, Med, mkd, hdstg, pt shd, terr, serviced pitches; EHU (16A) €2; sw; 5% statics; Eng spkn; adv bkg acc; boating; windsurfing; CKE. *"Beautiful site in idyllic setting o'looking lake; friendly recep; clean san facs; recep poss clsd Tues & Sun - site inaccessible when recep clsd, phone ahead rec; many outdoor activities."* **€34.00, 1 Apr-30 Oct.** 2024

BROGLIE *3D2* (0.4km S Rural) *49.00684, 0.53067* **Aire de Camping-Car Broglie,** Route de la Barre-en-Ouche, 27270 Broglie **02 32 44 60 58; mairie-broglie@wanadoo.fr**

12 nr nr

Exit A28 junc 15 onto D49 E dir Broglie. Turn R in vill onto D6138 Rue des Canadiens, then L into Rue de la Victoire over rv, site on R in former rlwy yard, nr municipal library. Sm, mkd, hdstg, pt shd,. *"M'vans only; gate secured at night; lndry 200m; ideal NH."*
€11.50 2024

BROMMAT *7D4* (0.3km E Rural) *44.83083, 2.68638* **Camping Municipale,** Le Bourg, 12600 Brommat **05 65 66 00 96 or 06 72 08 83 72; mairie-de.brommat @wanadoo.fr; www.brommat.fr or www.camping-brommat.fr**

Fr D98, cross rv bdge, cont uphill to Mairie. Turn R in front of Mairie and cont strt on. Campsite on R. 2*, Sm, hdg, pt shd, EHU (6A); sw nr; TV; bus 50m; adv bkg acc; tennis 2km; fishing; CCI. *"Beautiful adj walk; vg."* **€17.00, 15 May-15 Sep.** 2024

BROUSSES ET VILLARET *8F4* (0.5km S Rural) *43.33932, 2.25201* **Camping Le Martinet Rouge,** 11390 Brousses-et-Villaret **04 68 26 51 98 or 06 91 34 41 60 (mob); info@camping-martinet.com; www.camping-martinet.fr**

€2

Fr D118 Mazamet-Carcassonne, turn R 3km after Cuxac-Carbades onto D103; turn L in Brousses & foll sp. 3*, Med, hdg, pt shd, pt sl, EHU (6-10A); TV; 20% statics; phone; bus; Eng spkn; adv bkg acc; horseriding; waterslide; trout fishing; games area; canoeing; CKE. *"Helpful owners, great for walking or mountain biking; cather castles, abbeys & churchs, Canal du Midi; forest, lakes, rv & caverns; excel site."*
€25.00, 1 Apr-30Oct. 2024

BRULON *4F1* (0.5km SE Rural) *47.96275, -0.22773* **Camping Le Septentrion,** Le Bord du Lac, 72350 Brûlon **02 43 95 68 96; le.septentrion@ orange.fr; www.campingleseptentrion.com**

€1.20 (htd) nr (htd)

Exit A81 junc 1; foll D4 S to Brûlon; site sp on ent to town to L; turn on L down narr rd (Rue de Buet); then turn R in 300m. Site well sp. 3*, Sm, shd, pt sl, EHU (6A) €3; bbq; sw; red long stay; TV; 50% statics; phone; adv bkg acc; fishing; bike hire; games rm; boating. *"Attractive, well-kept site; spacious pitches; welcoming staff; gd, clean san facs - unisex LS; poss a bit unkempt early ssn; gd cycling & walking area; excel."*
€13.50, 1Apr-30 Oct. 2024

BUGUE, LE *7C3* (1km SE Urban) *44.90980, 0.93160* **Camping du Bournat (formerly Les Trois Caupain),** Le Port, 24260 Le Bugue Dordogne **05 53 07 24 60; www.campingdubournat.fr**

€2 nr (covrd, htd)

Exit Le Bugue town cent on D703 twd Campagne. Turn R at sp after 400m to site in 600m on rvside. 3*, Med, mkd, pt shd, EHU (6-16A) €4-4.30 (rev pol); gas; 25% statics; adv bkg acc. *"Beautiful, lovely, well run site; pleasant, helpful owners; cycle along rv to pretty town; excel; new pool; mkt in Le Bugue well worth a visit; rv adj; games area adj; ideal cent for touring the Dordogne region; lots of attractions; gd rest."* **€25.90, 8 Apr-30 Sep. 2023**

BUGUE, LE *7C3* (3km SE Rural) *44.90663, 0.97412* **Camping Le Val de la Marquise,** Le Petit Moulin, 24260 Campagne **05 53 54 74 10; contact@levaldelamarquise.com; www.camping-dordogne-marquise.com**

€2 nr

Fr D703 bet Le Bugue & Les Eyzies take D35 at Campagne dir St Cyprien, site sp. 4*, Med, mkd, pt shd, terr, EHU (10-15A); bbq; 5% statics; phone; Eng spkn; adv bkg acc; lake fishing; games area; CKE. *"Peaceful, attractive site; poss diff access to pitches for lge c'vans due narr site rds & low terrs; clean san facs; beautiful pool; Michelin starred rest nrby; brilliant site; great loc; excel fam facs; warm welcome fr new owner; pleasant town, great mkt; high rec."* **€30.00, 28 Apr-30 Sep. 2023**

BUGUE, LE *7C3* (5km SW Rural) *44.89323, 0.87955* **Camping La Ferme des Poutiroux,** 24 510 Limeuil en Périgord **05 53 63 31 62; campinglespoutiroux@orange.fr; www.poutiroux.com**

€1 (htd)

W fr Le Bugue on D703 twd Bergerac; in 2km take D31 S for 4km; bef bdge take R fork twd Trémolat/Lalinde; in 300m fork R (sp), site well sp. 4*, Sm, mkd, pt shd, pt sl, terr, EHU (6A) €4; sw nr; 50% statics; phone; Eng spkn; adv bkg acc; CKE. *"Peaceful, well-kept, well-positioned, family-run site; friendly, canoeing nr; helpful farmer; facs clean; vg value LS; highly rec."* **€17.40, 1 Apr-2 Oct. 2024**

BUGUE, LE *7C3* (6km SW Rural) *44.87990, 0.88576* **Camping du Port de Limeuil,** 24480 Alles-sur-Dordogne **05 53 63 29 76; contact@leportdelimeuil.com; www.leportdelimeuil.com**

€3 (htd)

Exit Le Bugue on D31 sp Le Buisson; in 4km turn R on D51 sp Limeuil; at 2km turn L over rv bdge; site on R after bdge. 4*, Med, hdg, mkd, pt shd, pt sl, serviced pitches; EHU (5A) €3.50; gas; bbq; 40% statics; Eng spkn; adv bkg acc; bike hire; canoe hire; games rm; CKE. *"Superb location & site for all ages; rv adj; lge pitches; clean san facs, ltd LS; tour ops."* **€50.00, 29 Apr - 23 Sep, A16. 2022**

BUIS LES BARONNIES *9D2* (0.6km N Urban) *44.27558, 5.27830* **Camp Municipal,** Quartier du Jalinier, 26170 Buis-les-Baronnies **04 75 28 07 34; mairie@buislesbaronnies.fr; www.buislesbaronnies.fr/camping-municipal**

€1.20

Fr Vaison-la-Romaine S on D938; turn L onto D54/D13/D5 to Buis-les-Baronnies; cont N onto D546; at bend turn R over rv bdge; turn L along rv, then 1st R. Site split into 2 either side of sw pool; recep in upper site. Med, hdg, mkd, pt shd, pt sl, EHU (6A) €3; 5% statics; phone; bus 300m; CKE. *"Lovely views; san facs dated but clean; not suitable lge o'fits but lger, more accessible pitches on lower level; attractive town; gd mkt Wed & Sat; fair; warden in off 1900-2000 only."* **€11.50, 1 Mar-11 Nov. 2022**

BURTONCOURT *5D2* (1km W Rural) *49.22485, 6.39929* **FFCC Camping La Croix du Bois Sacker,** 57220 Burtoncourt **03 87 35 74 08; camping.croixsacker@wanadoo.fr; www.campingcroixsacker.com**

€1.70 nr

Exit A4 junc 37 sp Argancy; at rndabt foll sp Malroy; at 2nd rndabt foll sp Chieuilles & cont to Vany; then take D3 for 12km dir Bouzonville; turn R onto D53A to Burtoncourt. 2*, Lge, hdg, mkd, hdstg, pt shd, terr, EHU (6A) inc; gas; TV; 10% statics; phone; bus 300m; Eng spkn; adv bkg acc; fishing; tennis; games area; CKE. *"Lovely, wooded site in beautiful location; lge pitches; pleasant, friendly owners; clean san facs; forest walks; gd security; gd NH or sh stay en rte Alsace/Germany; conv Maginot Line; excel; Hachenberg Ouvrage tour highly rec (30km)."* **€20.30, 1 Apr-15 Oct. 2022**

BUXIERES-SOUS-MONTAIGUT *7A4* (3.8km SW Rural) *46.19271, 2.81994* **Camping Les Suchères,** Les Sucheres, 63700 Buxierères-sous-Montaigut **04 73 85 92 66 or 06 64 15 40 76; campinglessucheres@outlook.com; www.campinglessucheres.com**

€1.50

Head SE on D92, cont on Buxières. Take Les Gouttes to Les Sucheres; 1st R onto Buxières; cont onto Les Gouttes after 7m turn R twd Les Sucheres, L twd Les Sucheres, 1st R onto Les Sucheres, turn L to stay on Les Sucheres, take the 1st L to stay on Les Sucheres; site on R. Sm, pt sl, EHU (6A) €3; bbq; TV; Eng spkn; CCI. *"Helpful Dutch owners; lovely peaceful site; gd walking area; Montaiqut within walking dist; shop; access to the site could be diff for lge o'fits as rd narr for last km; quiet."* **€27.50, 1 Apr-30 Sep. 2024**

FRANCE

FRANCE

BUZANCAIS *4H2* (0.5km N Urban) *46.89309, 1.41801* **Camp Municipal La Tête Noire,** Allée des Sports, 36500 Buzançais **06 59 88 78 32 or 02 54 84 17 27; campinglatetenoire@gmail.com; www.campinglatetenoire.fr**

€1.50 nr nr nr

D943 fr Châteauroux thro town cent, cross rv, immed turn R into sports complex. 3*, Lge, hdstg, pt shd, EHU (16A) inc; red long stay; 10% statics; adv bkg acc; CKE. *"Pleasant, peaceful, well-kept site on rv; clean facs; no access when office clsd but ample parking; no twin axles; pool 500m; gd fishing."* **€21.50, 8 Apr-31 Oct.** **2024**

BUZANCY *5C1* (1.5km SW Rural) *49.42647, 4.93891* **Camping La Samaritaine,** 3 allée des étangs, 08240 Buzancy **03 24 30 08 88; contact@camping-lasamaritaine.fr; www.camping-lasamaritaine.fr**

€2 nr

Fr Sedan take D977 dir Vouziers for 23km. Turn L onto D12, cont to end & turn L onto D947 for Buzancy. On ent Buzancy in 100m turn 2nd R immed after g'ge on R sp Camping Stade. Foll sp to site on L past football pitches. 3*, Med, hdstg, mkd, hdg, pt shd, serviced pitches; EHU (10A) inc; bbq (charcoal, gas); sw nr; TV; 10% statics; phone; Eng spkn; adv bkg acc; tennis; games rm; horseriding nr; fishing; CKE. *"Beautiful area for walking/cycling; library; helpful, pleasant staff; excel facs, ltd LS."* **€19.00, 8 Apr - 24 Sep, L30.** **2022**

CABANNES, LES *8G3* (2km SE Rural) *42.77444, 1.70328* **Camp Municipal La Coume,** 09310 Albiès **05 61 64 98 99; camping.albies09@orange.fr; campingalbies09.wixsite.com/camping-la-coume09**

Free (htd) nr nr

Site sp fr N20 in vill. 2*, Med, hdg, pt shd, pt sl, terr, EHU (5-10A) inc; bbq; 10% statics; fishing; games area. *"Gd san facs; Rv Ariège 100m; not suitable for lge o'fits."* **€17.60, 9 Mar - 31 Oct.** **2024**

CABANNES, LES *8G3* (2km SW Rural) *42.77269, 1.67172* **FFCC Camping Le Pas de l'Ours,** Les Gesquis, 09310 Aston **05 61 64 90 33; campinglepasdelours@orange.fr; www.lepasdelours.fr/**

€2 (htd) nr nr

S on N20, after Tarascon-sur-Ariège turn R sp Plateau de Beille/Les Cabannes. Pass thro Aulos, site well sp. 3*, Sm, hdg, mkd, pt shd, pt sl, EHU (6A) €4; bbq; TV; 50% statics; phone; Eng spkn; adv bkg acc; ccard acc; games area; bike hire; tennis; CKE. *"Attractive site surrounded by mountains; v clean san facs; not suitable lge o'fits; helpful owners; pool adj; gd touring base; access poss diff for lge o'fits."* **€32.00, 26 May-15 Sep.** **2024**

CABOURG *3D1* (6km W Coastal) *49.28319, -0.19098* **Camping Le Point du Jour,** 75 Route de Cabourg, 14810 Merville-Franceville-Plage **02 31 24 23 34; camping.lepointdujour@gmail.com; www.camping-lepointdujour.com**

€3 (htd)

(covrd, htd) sand adj

Fr Ouistreham on D514 turn E at Bénouville onto D224, cross bdge onto D514, site on L dir Cabourg, 8km beyond Pegasus Bdge at far end of Merville. Or fr A13/D675 exit Dozulé dir Cabourg, then D514 to site. 4*, Med, hdg, pt shd, EHU (10A) inc; gas; bbq; red long stay; TV; 40% statics; bus; adv bkg acc; ccard acc; games rm; CKE. *"Site with sea views; direct access to Sword Beach (D-Day) & sand dunes; conv Pegasus Bdge; some pitches might be diff for lge o'fits; open till 2300 for late ferry arr, v obliging; ent & exit diff; sm-med pitches, many sl; facs tired."* **€50.20, 29 Mar-27 Oct, N03.** **2024**

CABOURG *3D1* (6km W Coastal) *49.28296, -0.19072* **Camping Village Ariane,** 100 Route de Cabourg, 14810 Merville-Franceville-Plage **02 31 24 52 52; info@loisirs-ariane.com; www.camping-ariane.com**

€3 (htd) nr sand 300m

Fr Ouistreham on D514 turn E at Bénouville onto D224, cross bdge onto D514 to site dir Cabourg. Or fr A13/D675 exit Dozulé dir Cabourg, then D514 to site. 3*, Lge, mkd, pt shd, EHU (6-10A) €4; gas; red long stay; TV; 10% statics; Eng spkn; adv bkg acc; games area; tennis nr; games rm; watersports nr; CKE. **€12.00, 1 Apr-5 Nov.** **2023**

CABRERETS *7D3* (1km NE Rural) *44.50771, 1.66234* **Camping Cantal,** 46330 Cabrerets **05 65 31 26 61; mairie@cabrerets.fr; www.cabrerets.fr**

Fr Cahors take D653 E for approx 15km bef turning R onto D662 E thro Vers & St Géry. Turn L onto D41 to Cabrerets. Site 1km after vill on R. 2*, Sm, pt shd, pt sl, serviced pitches; EHU €2.50; rv canoeing nr; CKE. *"Superb situation; v interesting vill; peaceful site; warden calls; grnd slightly bumpy; excel san facs; not suitable lge o'fits; conv Pech Merle; gd cycling rte; quiet; friendly; overhanging trees, care when pitching; unisex san facs; vg."* **€13.00, 1 Apr-15 Oct.** **2023**

CADENET *10E3* (5km N Rural) *43.767986, 5.372672* **Les Hautes Prairies,** 28 route de Vaugines 84160, Lourmarin **04 90 68 02 89; leshautesprairies@campasun.eu; www.campasun-lourmarin.eu**

€5 nr

Fr D973 take exit to Cadenet. Fork L (eastbnd) at rd junc twrds Lourmarin. In Lourmarin turn R at 2nd rndabt. Site on R in 0.5km. 4*, Med, hdg, mkd, hdstg, pt shd, pt sl, EHU (10A) inc; bbq (sep area); twin axles; bus adj; Eng spkn; adv bkg acc; ccard acc; jacuzzi; sm shop in recep; games area; CKE. *"Gd gateway for Luberon area; lovely spacious site; v clean, well maintained facs (new 2016); v helpful staff; gd security (barrier); excel & enjoyable experience; excel."* **€45.00, 5 Apr-13 Oct.** **2024**

CADENET *10E3* (10km NE Rural) *43.76871, 5.44970* **Camping Lou Badareu,** La Rasparine, 84160 Cucuron **04 90 77 21 46; contact@loubadareu.com; www.loubadareu.com**

€1.80

In Cadenet foll sp for church (église) onto D45 dir Cucuron; S of Cucuron turn onto D27 (do not go into town); site is E 1km. Well sp fr D27. 2*, Sm, mkd, pt shd, pt sl, EHU (10A) €4.50 (long lead poss req); own san rec; 10% statics; phone; CKE. *"Pretty farm site in cherry orchard, vineyard and olive grove adj; basic but adequate san facs; natural spring-fed pool; friendly, helpful owner; sep access for high vans; lge shd camping field."* **€17.80, 1 Apr-15 Oct. 2023**

CAEN *3D1* (20km N Coastal) *49.32551, -0.39010* **Sandaya La Côte de Nacre,** 17 Rue du Général Moulton, 14750 St Aubin-sur-Mer **02 31 97 14 45; cdn@sandaya.fr; www.sandaya.fr/cdn**

€5 (htd) (covrd, htd) sand 500m

Fr Caen on D7 dir Douvres-la-Délivrande, Langrune-sur-Mer & St Aubin. Site in St Aubin-sur-Mer on S side of D514; clearly sp on o'skts. 5*, Lge, hdstg, mkd, hdg, pt shd, EHU (10A); bbq (charcoal); sw nr; TV; 70% statics; phone; Eng spkn; adv bkg rec; ccard acc; sauna; waterslide; bike hire; games rm; tennis 200m; CKE. *"Ideal for families; lge pitches; conv Caen ferry, Normandy beaches, WW2 sites; helpful staff; excel modern san facs; poss waterlogging; gd cycle tracks along sea front LS; easy walk into quiet vill; vg; payment on arr, no refund for early dep; vg site."* **€54.00, 8 Apr - 25 Sep, N11. 2022**

CAGNES SUR MER *10E4* (4km N Rural) *43.68717, 7.15589* **Camping Le Val Fleuri,** 139 Vallon-des-Vaux, 06800 Cagnes-sur-Mer **04 93 31 21 74; valfleur2@wanadoo.fr; www.campingvalfleuri.fr**

€1.50 nr (htd) shgl 4km

Fr Nice take D6007 W twd Cannes. On app Cagnes turn R & foll sp Camping; site on R after 3km, well sp. NB 3.3m height restriction on this rte. 3*, Sm, pt shd, terr, EHU (3-10A); Eng spkn; adv bkg acc. *"Gd, clean, improving site, efficient NH; divided by rd (not busy); some sm pitches; helpful, friendly owners; bus to Nice; dated facs (2014); diff access lge o'fits; no offsite parking."* **€36.00, 25 May-2 Nov. 2024**

CAGNES SUR MER *10E4* (5km S Coastal) *43.63128, 7.12993* **Camping Parc des Maurettes,** 730 Ave du Docteur Lefebvre, 06270 Villeneuve-Loubet **04 93 20 91 91; info@parcdesmaurettes.com; www.parcdesmaurettes.com**

€4 (htd) nr nr nr (htd, indoor) shgl 1km

Fr Nice exit A8 junc 47, turn L onto D6007 dir Antibes; foll sp Intermarché, then R into Rue des Maurettes; site in 250m. N fr Cannes on A8 exit Villeneuve-Loubet-Plage junc 46; foll D241 over D6007 & rwly line, U-turn back over rwly line, then R onto D6007 dir Antibes as above. NB Site on steep cliff with narr winding rds packed with trees; diff ent. 3*, Med, mkd, pt shd, terr, serviced pitches; EHU (3-10A) €5.30; gas; bbq (charcoal, sep area); red long stay; twin axles; TV (pitch); train Nice 400m; Eng spkn; adv bkg rec; ccard acc; jacuzzi; CKE. *"Well-kept site; variable pitch size/price; excel base for Nice, Cannes, Antibes & Monaco; trains & bus fare gd value."* **€43.40, 10 Jan-15 Nov. 2024**

CAGNES SUR MER *10E4* (1km NW Urban) *43.67159, 7.13845* **Camping Le Colombier,** 35 Chemin de Ste Colombe, 06800 Cagnes-sur-Mer **04 93 73 12 77; campinglecolombier06@gmail.com; www.campinglecolombier.com**

€2.50 (htd) nr nr 2.5km

N fr Cagnes cent foll 1-way system dir Vence. Half way up hill turn R at rndabt dir Cagnes-sur-Mer & R at next island. Site on L 300m, sp fr town cent. 3*, Sm, mkd, hdg, pt shd, EHU (2-16A) (poss rev pol) €2-8; red long stay; TV; 10% statics; phone; Eng spkn; bike hire; CKE. *"Friendly, family-run site; dogs not acc Jul/Aug; sm pool adj."* **€33.50, 1 Apr-1 Oct. 2024**

CAGNES SUR MER *10E4* (4km NW Rural) *43.68272, 7.08391* **Camping Les Pinèdes,** 1402 Route du Pont de Pierre, 06480 La Colle-sur-Loup **04 93 32 98 94; info@lespinedes.com; www.lespinedes.com**

€4 (htd)

Exit A8 junc 47; take D6007 dir Nice, then D2 sp Villeneuve-Loubet; turn R at rndabt sp Villeneuve-Loubet & cross rv bdge; go thro sh tunnel, other side is Cagnes-sur-Mer & rndabt; turn L onto D6 to Colle-sur-Loup; site on R sh dist after Colle-sur-Loup. NB Take 2nd turning into site (1st leads to rest). 4*, Lge, hdstg, mkd, hdg, pt shd, pt sl, terr, serviced pitches; EHU (6-10A) €4.60-5.90 (poss rev pol); bbq (elec, gas); sw nr; red long stay; TV; 20% statics; Eng spkn; adv bkg acc; ccard acc; rv fishing adj; games rm; archery; tennis adj; horseriding adj; games area; solarium; CKE. *"Excel, family-run site set in pine & oak trees; no c'vans over 6m (excluding towbar) & m'vans over 8m high ssn; helpful & friendly; spacious pitches; steep access to pitches - poss diff lge o'fits, help avail; adequate san facs; gd rest at site ent; highly rec; vg site has everything you need; spacious pitches; excel pool."* **€58.00, 1 Apr - 30 Sep, C30. 2022**

FRANCE

FRANCE

CAHORS *7D3* (2km N Urban) *44.46318, 1.44226*
Camping Rivière de Cabessut, 1180 Rue de la Rivière, 46000 Cahors **05 65 30 06 30; contact@cabessut.com; www.cabessut.com**
€2

Fr N or S on D820, at S end Cahors by-pass take L onto D620 sp Rodez. At traff lts by bdge do not cross rv but bear R on D911. In 1km at site sp turn L. Site on E bank of Rv Lot, well sp fr town. Site at end of long lane. 1.8km to site fr bdge (Pont Cabessut). (NB: Fr N if leaving A20 at J57 - Do not foll Sat Nav.) 3*, Med, mkd, hdg, pt shd, serviced pitches; EHU (10A) inc (poss rev pol); gas; bbq (gas); 5% statics; phone; bus to Cahors 600m; adv bkg req; CKE. *"Lovely, well-run site by rv; beautiful area; pleasant, mostly lge pitches, sm pitches diff access when site full; gd for children; walk to town by rv 1.8km; food mkt Wed, full mkt Sat; hypmkt 1.5km; excel san facs; well maintained site, helpful, commited owners; rv adj; great site with lge sunny or shd pitches; pre-ordered bread delivered daily; lge o'fits turned away if grnd is damp; adv bkg req Jul/Aug; free shuttle bus to Cahors 600m at park & ride."* **€24.50, 1 Apr-30 Sep. 2024**

CAHORS *7D3* (8km N Rural) *44.52585, 1.46048*
Camping Les Graves, 1459, avenue Saint Pierre 46090, St Pierre-Lafeuille **05 65 36 83 12; infos@camping-lesgraves.com; www.camping-lesgraves.com**
€1.50

Leave A20 at junc 57 Cahors Nord onto D820. Foll sp St Pierre-Lafeuille; at N end of vill, site is opp L'Atrium wine cave. 3*, Med, hdg, pt shd, sl, EHU (6-10A) €2.50-3.50 (poss rev pol); 5% statics; Eng spkn; adv bkg rec; ccard acc; bike hire; CKE. *"Scenic site; lge pitches; poss clsd during/after wet weather due boggy grnd; disabled facs over stony rd & grass; ltd facs LS; conv A20; nice, quiet, clean site."* **€23.90, 1 Apr-31 Oct. 2023**

CAHORS *7D3* (8km N Rural) *44.53136, 1.45926*
Camping Quercy-Vacances, Mas de la Combe, 46090 St Pierre-Lafeuille **05 65 36 87 15; www.quercy-vacances.com**
€1.50

Heading N on D820, turn L at N end of St Pierre-Lafeuille turn W at site sp N of vill, site in 700m down lane. Site sp fr main rd. Fr A20 exit junc 57 & foll sp N20. 4*, Med, mkd, pt shd, pt sl, EHU (10A) €3.30-5.30; gas; twin axles; TV; 50% statics; phone; Eng spkn; adv bkg acc; ccard acc; games area; CKE. *"Pretty site; most pitches slightly sl; clean, modern san facs; poss unkempt LS; helpful owner; vg; tennis & horse riding nrby; gd for Cahors & Lot Valley."* **€27.00, 1 Mar-11 Nov. 2023**

CAHORS *7D3* (13km W Rural) *44.47968, 1.35906*
Camping de L'écluse, Lieu dit Le Payras, 46140 Douelle **09 84 45 33 78; antinea.loisirs@orange.fr; www.tourisme-lot.com/en**
12

Fr N foll D820 past D811 junc, over rv lot bdge, immed take D8 on R, sp Pradines Douelle. In Douelle cont thro vill, take R sp Antinea Campings. Take R sp Camping, park outside barrier, walk to Antinea (by rv). Sm, mkd, pt shd, EHU (6A) €1.50; bbq; sw nr; twin axles. *"Quiet rvside site by disused lock; basic but clean facs; level pitches but uneven & long grass; check in at Antinea Bar; barrier open on req; gd rvside walk into Douelle; attractive vill; fair."* **€13.50 2024**

CAJARC *7D4* (6.4km NE Rural) *44.50612, 1.89667*
Camping Les Cournoulises, 46160 Montbrun **06 03 23 13 56; accueil@lescournoulises.fr; lescournoulises.com**
€0.50

Fr Cahors foll D662 or fr Figeac D19. Foll D622 along N bank of R Lot for 6km. Site well sp on app. 2*, Sm, mkd, pt shd, EHU (6A) €3; bbq (charcoal, sep area); red long stay; twin axles; bus adj; Eng spkn; adv bkg acc; games area; canoe hire; tennis nr; fishing; CKE. *"Lge pitches; teepee & trapper tents on site (for hire); many attractions within 30km radius; dir access to rv; fishing rods avail; friendly, helpful owner; excel; paragliding; trekking; htd pool 6km; beautiful site; spotless facs; wonderful; highly rec."* **€14.00, 1 Apr-10 Oct. 2023**

CAJARC *7D4* (0.3km SW Urban) *44.48374, 1.83928*
Camp Le Terriol (formerly Municipal), Rue Le Terriol, 46160 Cajarc **05 65 40 72 74; info@campingleterriol.com; www.campingleterriol.com**
(cont) nr nr nr

Fr Cahors dir Cajarc on D662 on L foll sp to site. 2*, Sm, hdg, mkd, hdstg, pt shd, EHU (10A) inc (poss rev pol); bbq; phone; Eng spkn; adv bkg acc; tennis 500m; CKE. *"Gd sized pitches; clean, basic facs; lovely sm town on Rv Lot; pool 500m; vg."* **€15.50, 1 May-30 Sep. 2023**

CAJARC *7D4* (6km SW Rural) *44.4667, 1.7500*
Camp Municipal Le Grand Pré, 46330 Cénevières **06 32 58 56 29 or 06 20 95 06 66; mairie.cenevieres@wanadoo.fr; www.cenevieres.fr**
nr nr nr

Fr Villefranche on D911 twd Cahors turn R onto D24 at Limogne for Cénevières. Foll sp. Fr St Cirq-Lapopie on D24 thro vill & over rlwy. 2*, Sm, mkd, hdg, pt shd, EHU (10A) inc; bbq; sw; phone; bus. *"Peaceful site by rv; wonderful views of cliffs; vg san facs; site self & warden calls am & pm; excel highly rec."* **€12.50, 1 Jun-30 Sep. 2024**

CAJARC *7D4* (6km W Rural) *44.4735, 1.7835*
Camping Ruisseau du Treil, Le Ruisseau, 46160 Larnagol **05 65 31 23 39; contact@lotcamping.com; www.lotcamping.com**
€3.90 WD

Exit A20 junc 57 onto D49 sp St Michel; in 4km turn R onto D653; after 5.5km in Vers at mini-rndabt turn L onto D662; site on L immed after leaving Larnagol. Or fr Figeac foll D19 thro Cajarc. At top of hill leaving Cajarc turn R onto D662 sp Cahors & Larnagol. Site sp on R 300m bef Larnagol on blind bend. 3*, Sm, mkd, pt shd, pt sl, EHU (6A) €4; bbq; sw nr; TV; 4% statics; adv bkg acc; canoeing adj; fishing adj; games rm; bike hire; horseriding; CKE. *"Beautiful, spacious, peaceful site in lovely area; well-run; friendly, helpful British owners; clean san facs but ltd when site full; lge pitches poss uneven; many long-stay/returning campers; library; guided walks; vg touring base; excel."* **€29.90, 1 May-30 Sep. 2024**

CALAIS *3A3* (12km E Coastal) *50.99657, 2.05062*
Camping Clairette, 525 Route des Dunes, 62215 Oye-Plage **03 21 35 83 51 or 06 14 22 92 71 (mob); www.campingclairette62.com**
€1.40 (htd) WD MSP nr 500m

Exit A16 junc 50 & foll sp Oye-Plage. At traff lts at D940 cont strt. At junc with D119 turn R then L, site on L in 2km. Foll sp 'Réserve Naturelle'. 2*, Med, hdg, mkd, unshd, pt sl, EHU (10A) €4; bbq; 95% statics; Eng spkn; adv bkg acc; ccard acc; clsd 16 Dec-14 Jan; CKE. *"Ltd touring pitches, rec phone/email in adv; warm welcome; helpful owners; security barrier; nature reserve nrby; conv ferries; fair; san facs OK (2013)."* **€14.00, 15 Jan - 15 Dec. 2024**

"I need an on-site restaurant"

We do our best to make sure site information is correct, but it is always best to check any must-have facilities are still available or will be open during your visit.

CALAIS *3A3* (12km E Rural) *50.96613, 2.05270*
Camping Le Pont d'Oye, 308 Rue de la Rivière, 62215 Oye-Plage **06 21 85 65 25; campingdupontdoye@gmail.com; www.campingdupontdoye.fr**
12 WD nr sandy 5km

Exit A16 at junc 50 onto D219 to Oye-Plage; cross rv & immed turn R sp camping; foll rv; site on L. 2*, Sm, hdg, unshd, EHU (6A) €2.50; gas; bbq; 85% statics; Eng spkn; adv bkg acc; CKE. *"Basic CL-type site; few touring pitches; grassed field for c'vans; friendly, helpful owners; san facs adj statics park - v dated but clean; conv ferries; NH only; new owner (2012); site improved."* **€13.50 2024**

CALAIS *3A3* (13km SW Rural) *50.91160, 1.75127*
Camping Les Epinettes, Impasse de Mont Pinet, 62231 Peuplingues **03 21 85 21 39; lesepinettes@aol.com; www.lesepinettes.fr**
€1.50 WD MSP nr sand 3km

A16 fr Calais to Boulogne, exit junc 40 W on D243 sp Peuplingues, go thro vill & foll sp; site on L in 3km. 2*, Lge, hdg, pt shd, pt sl, EHU (4-6A) €2.90-3.90; bbq; 80% statics; phone; adv bkg acc; ccard acc; CKE. *"Pleasant, easy-going, quiet site; conv NH for m'way, ferries & tunnel; some pitches sm; san facs clean; when bureau clsd, site yourself - warden calls eve or call at cottage to pay; library; if arr late, park on grass verge outside main gate - use facs excel elec, pay half price; few touring pitches."* **€15.50, 1 Apr-31 Oct. 2024**

CALAIS *3A3* (4km SW Coastal) *50.95677, 1.81101*
Camp du Fort Lapin, Route Provincial 940, 62231 Sangatte-Blériot Plage **03 21 97 67 77; campingdufortlapin@sfr.fr; camping-du-fort-lapin.fr**
WD nr sand adj

Fr E exit junc 43 fr A16 Calais cent, dir beach (Blériot-Plage). Turn L along coast onto D940 dir Sangatte; site on R in dunes shortly after water tower, opp sports cent; site sp fr D940. Fr S exit A16 junc 41 to Sangatte; at T-junc turn R onto D940; site on L just bef water tower. 3*, Med, mkd, unshd, pt sl, EHU (10A) inc (poss rev pol); bbq; 50% statics; phone; bus; adv bkg acc; CKE. *"Conv ferry; warden lives on site; rec arr bef 1700 high ssn; gates clsd 2300-0700; recep 0900-1200 & 1600-2000, barrier clsd when recep clsd; ltd parking outside espec w/end - phone ahead for access code; gd bus service; basic, clean, adequate san facs (shwrs and lndry clsd after 2100); conv Auchan & Cité Europe shops; poss youth groups high ssn; conv NH; close to beach; clean tidy site; adequate facs; grnd v well drained; easy cycle into Calais or walk along the promenade to the harbour ent."* **€18.60, 1 Apr-31 Oct. 2023**

CALAIS *3A3* (5km W Coastal) *50.94610, 1.75798*
Camping des Noires Mottes, Rue Pierre Dupuy, 62231 Sangatte **03 21 82 04 75; www.campingdesnoiresmottes.fr**
€1.30 WD MSP nr sand 500m

Fr A16 exit junc 41 sp Sangatte onto D243, at T-junc in vill turn R then R again bef monument. 3*, Lge, mkd, hdg, pt shd, pt sl, EHU (10A) €4.10; 90% statics; bus 500m; Eng spkn; adv bkg rec; CKE. *"Conv ferries & Eurotunnel; lge pitches; san facs clean; barrier - no arr bef office opens 1500 (1600 LS); san facs clsd o'night & poss 1200-1600; some pitches boggy when wet; windy spot; OK NH; well maintained site."* **€24.60, 1 Apr-31 Oct. 2023**

FRANCE

CALAIS 3A3 (3km NW Coastal) 50.959323, 1.831833 **Camping Municipal Le Grande Gravelot,** 62100 Calais **03 91 91 52 34; camping@mairie-calais.fr**

250m

Head for Calais beach. Site at end of Port de Plaisance dock on rd behind hses & flats o'look beach. Med, mkd, hdg, unshd, EHU (16A) inc; twin axles; TV; phone; bus; Eng spkn; adv bkg acc; sauna; games rm; bike hire; CCI. *"Excel; aire de svr adj to site all year round; site patrolled at night; local cafes nrby; short walk to town; vg site for Blerlot Plage/Valais; excel facs."* **€21.90, 1 Apr-31 Oct. 2022**

"Satellite navigation makes touring much easier"

Remember most sat navs don't know if you're towing or in a larger vehicle – always use yours alongside maps and site directions.

CALVI 10G2 (1.8km SE Coastal) 42.55228, 8.76423 **Camping Paduella,** Route de Bastia, 20260 Calvi, Corsica **04 95 65 06 16 or 04 95 65 13 20; info@campingpaduella.com; www.campingpaduella.com**

sand 300m

On N197 fr Calvi; on R 200m after rndabt by Casino supmkt. 3*, Med, mkd, pt shd, pt sl, terr, EHU (6A) €3.65; 25% statics; Eng spkn; CKE. *"Poss best site in Calvi; immac san facs but slippery when wet, espec ramp; vg."* **€35.50, 8 May-8 Oct. 2024**

CALVI 10G2 (22.5km SW Urban) 42.46451, 8.68012 **La Morsetta Camping,** Route Calvi-Porta, 20260 Calvi **04 95 65 25 28; info@lamorsetta.net; www.lamorsetta.net**

€1.70

Drive via the D81 fr Calvi to Galeria. Then about 12 km via the D81b coastal rd dir Calvi. Take the direct rte D81b fr Calvi, 20 km. Med, pt shd, EHU €3.20. **€46.60, 1 May-15 Oct. 2024**

CAMARET SUR MER 2E1 (3km NE Coastal) 48.28070, -4.56490 **Camping Le Grand Large,** Lambézen, 29570 Camaret-sur-Mer **02 98 27 91 41; contact@campinglegrandlarge.com; www.campinglegrandlarge.com**

€3 (htd) shgl 500m

On D8 bet Crozen & Camaret, turn R at ent to Camaret onto D355, sp Roscanvel. Foll sps to site in 3km. 4*, Med, mkd, hdg, pt shd, pt sl, EHU (10A) inc; gas; bbq; TV; adv bkg acc; ccard acc; tennis; boating. *"Coastal views fr some pitches, lovely beach; pleasant, helpful owners; 45 min cliff top walk to town; excel; excel location; do not arr bef 2pm if not prebooked."* **€21.00, 29 Apr-28 Oct. 2023**

CAMARET SUR MER 2E1 (4km NE Coastal) 48.28788, -4.56540 **Camping Plage de Trez-Rouz,** Route de Camaret à Roscanvel, 29160 Crozon **02 98 27 93 96; contact@trezrouz.com; www.trezrouz.com**

€2.50 (htd) sand

Foll D8 to Camaret-sur-Mer & at rndabt turn N sp Roscanvel/D355. Site on R in 3km. 3*, Med, hdg, mkd, pt shd, pt sl, EHU (16A) €3.50; 10% statics; adv bkg acc; horseriding 2km; tennis 500m; CKE. *"Great position opp beach; conv for Presqu'île de Crozon; gd facs but stretched high ssn; site scruffy LS; friendly helpful owner; gd hot shwrs; gd 3km coastal path to Camaret-sur-Mer."* **€27.10, 15 Mar-15 Oct. 2020**

CAMBO LES BAINS 8F1 (3km SW Rural) 43.33863, -1.40129 **Camping L'Hiriberria,** 64250 Itxassou **05 59 29 98 09; Campinghiriberria64@gmail.com; www.hiriberria.com**

€1 (htd) nr nr nr (covrd, htd)

Fr Cambo-les-Bains on D932 to Itxassou. Site on L 200m fr D918. 3*, Lge, hdstg, mkd, hdg, pt shd, pt sl, EHU (5A) €3.25; gas; bbq; red long stay; TV; 20% statics; phone; Eng spkn; games area; CKE. *"Popular site, phone ahead rec; gd views Pyrenees; pretty vill in 1km; vg walks; friendly owners."* **€30.00, 26 Feb - 25 Nov. 2024**

CAMBO LES BAINS 8F1 (5km W Rural) 43.33969, -1.47000 **Camping Alegera,** 209 Route d'Espelette, 64250 Souraïde **05 59 93 91 80 or 06 13 76 66 87 (mob); campingalegera@gmail.com; www.camping-alegera.com**

€1.30 (cont)

Fr St Jean-de-Luz take D918 to Souraïde, site sp on L on rvside. 3*, Lge, hdg, mkd, pt shd, EHU (4-10A) €3.40-4 (poss rev pol); gas; bbq (elec, gas); 10% statics; adv bkg acc; fishing 4km; golf; games rm; tennis. *"Excel for coast & Pyrenees; spacious pitches; red facs LS; pretty vill; v quiet, clean, lovely site."* **€32.00, 1 Apr-31 Oct. 2024**

CAMBRAI 3B4 (2.5km W Urban) 50.17533, 3.21534 **FFCC Camp Municipal Les Trois Clochers,** 77 Rue Jean Goudé, 59400 Cambrai **03 27 70 91 64**

(htd) nr nr

Exit A2 junc 14; at rndabt after slip rd (with 6 exits) take D630 dir Cambrai; in 1km (by Buffalo Grill) turn L onto D630; in 200m turn L onto D939; in 100m turn L into Rue Jean Goudé. Or fr Cambrai W on D939; after x-ing rv bdge cont on D939 until traff lts in 300m; go strt over traff lts, then in 100m turn L into Rue Jean Goudé. Site sp fr all dirs on ent town. 3*, Sm, hdg, unshd, EHU (5-8A) €2.50; Eng spkn. *"Beautiful, well-kept site; gd, spacious pitches; v conv Calais; early arr rec high ssn; v helpful, friendly manager; gd san facs, ltd & stretched when site full; interesting town; excel; 5 min walk to Aldi supmkt; hg rec."* **€14.50, 15 Apr-15 Oct. 2023**

CANCALE *2E4* (3km N Coastal) *48.70369, -1.84829* **Camp Municipal La Pointe du Grouin,** 35260 Cancale **02 99 89 63 79 or 02 99 89 60 15; campingcancale@ville-cancale.fr; www.ville-cancale.fr**

€1.75 nr shgl adj

Take D76 twd Cancale & cont on D201 sp Pointe de Grouin; site on R in 3km on cliffs above sea, on N side of Cancale (diff to see, on RH bend mkd with chevrons); sp 'Camp Municipal'. Care req at ent. 2*, Med, pt sl, EHU (8-13A) €3.40-445 (poss long lead req); bbq; Eng spkn; ccard acc; fishing; watersports. *"Lovely, well-kept site in gd location; sea views; some pitches uneven; excel san facs; gates clsd 2300-0700; conv Dinan, Mont-St Michel, St Malo; gd walking."*
€17.00, 18 Mar-18 Oct. 2024

CANCALE *2E4* (10km S Coastal) *48.61592, -1.85151* **Camping de l'Ile Verte,** 42 Rue de l'Ile Verte, 35114 St Benoît-des-Ondes **02 99 58 62 55; welcome@campingdelileverte.com; www.campingdelileverte.com**

€2.50 (htd) nr nr sand adj

Site on S side of vill. Fr Cancale, take D76 SW for approx 4km, then turn L onto D155 into St Benoît. Foll site sp. 3*, Sm, hdg, pt shd, EHU (6A) €4 (poss rev pol); gas; 3% statics; phone; adv bkg acc; CKE. *"Well-kept, tidy site on edge of vill; facs poss stretched high ssn; big pitches but narr access rds."*
€32.00, 1 Apr-1 Oct. 2023

CANCALE *2E4* (2.3km NW Coastal) *48.68995, -1.86130* **Camping Les Close Fleuris,** La Ville es Poulains et Les, Clos Fleuris, La Ville es Polains, 35260 Cancale **02 99 89 97 68; campingdosfleuris@free.fr; www.canale-camping.fr**

€2

Foll D76 to D355, foll D355 to Blvd d'Armor, cont on Boulrvard D'Armor. Drive on to La Ville Es Poulains, exit the rndbt onto Blvd d'Armor, go over rdbt, bear L twrds Rue du Saussaye, cont onto Rue du Saussaye, turn L onto La Ville Es Poulains, take 1st R to stay on La Ville Es Poulains and the site will be on your L. Med, mkd, pt shd, EHU (16A) €4.40; Eng spkn; games rm. *"Lots of walking trails and coastal walks."*
€20.00, 15 Mar-15 Nov. 2024

CANCALE *2E4* (7km NW Coastal) *48.68861, -1.86833* **Camping Le Bois Pastel,** 13 Rue de la Corgnais, 35260 Cancale **02 99 89 66 10; contact@campingboispastel.fr; www.campingboispastel.fr**

4€/day. (covrd, htd, indoor) sand 800m

Fr Cancale take D201 dir Pointe du Grouin & St Malo by Rte Touristique. Site sp on L 2.5km after Pointe du Grouin. 3*, Med, mkd, pt shd, EHU (6A) €4; bbq; red long stay; 25% statics; adv bkg acc; ccard acc; games area; games rm; fishing. *"Conv Mont-St Michel, St Malo; gd touring base."*
€22.00, 3 Apr-4 Oct. 2020

CANDE SUR BEUVRON *4G2* (0.9km S Rural) *47.48952, 1.25834* **La Grande Tortue,** 3 Route de Pontlevoy, 41120 Candé-sur-Beuvron **02 54 44 15 20; camping@grandetortue.com; www.grandetortue.com**

€4.50 (htd) (covrd, htd)

Exit A10 junc 17 (Blois) & foll 'Autres/Toutes Directions' or 'Vierzon' to cross Rv Loire; immed after bdge R onto D951/D971 dir Chaumont; ignore D173 R fork & foll D751 thro Chailles & Villelouet; R at rndabt to go thro Cande; fork L after Cande; site on L in abt 100m. 5*, Lge, hdstg, mkd, hdg, pt shd, pt sl, EHU (10A) €3.50; gas; bbq; TV; 50% statics; Eng spkn; adv bkg acc; ccard acc; bike hire; games area; CKE. *"Excel, rustic site amongst trees; poss diff access due trees; helpful staff; vg, clean san facs; gd pool; gd for children; gd cycling; gourmet rest by rv bdge in vill; conv Loire chateaux; gd rest."*
€50.80, 6 Apr-14 Sep. 2024

CANET PLAGE *10G1* (3km N Coastal) *42.70808, 3.03332* **Camping Le Brasilia,** 2 Ave des Anneux du Roussillon, 66140 Canet-en-Roussillon **04 68 80 23 82; info@lebrasilia.fr; www.brasilia.fr**

€4 (htd) sand 150m

Exit A9 junc 41 sp Perpignan Nord & Rivesaltes onto D83 dir Le Barcarès & Canet for 10km; then take D81 dir Canet for 10km until lge rndabt which goes under D617 (do not foll sp to Canet to R) - cont round rndabt & foll sp Ste Marie-le-Mer (to go back the way you came). Then take 1st R sp Le Brasilia. 5*, V lge, mkd, hdg, pt shd, serviced pitches; EHU (10A) inc; gas; bbq (elec, gas); twin axles; TV; 35% statics; bus to Canet; Eng spkn; ccard acc; bike hire; tennis; fishing; archery; games rm; CKE. *"Excel, well-run, well laid-out site; gd sized pitches; friendly staff; immac san facs; excel facs, espec for families/children/teenagers; rvside walk adj; conv day trips to Barcelona,Carcassonne etc; daily mkt in Canet except Mon."*
€54.00, 16 Apr - 8 Oct, C01. 2022

CANET PLAGE *10G1* (3.5km N Coastal) *42.70905, 3.03285* **Camping Marina Canet (formerly Camping Le Bosquet),** Ave des Anneaux du Roussillon, 66140 Canet-Plage **01 59 00 05 95; www.marina-de-canet.com**

€3 sand 400m

Exit A9 junc 41 onto D83 dir Le Barcarès; then turn R onto D81 dir Canet; in Canet at lge rndabt go R round until exit dir Torreilles & Ste Marie; then immed after rndabt take sm rd on R; site sp. Or E on D617 fr Perpignan, turn L on D11 in Canet & foll sp. 4*, Med, hdg, mkd, pt shd, EHU (5A) €3.50; gas; bbq; TV; phone; bus adj; Eng spkn; adv bkg acc; ccard acc; games rm; games area; CKE. *"Family-run site nr excel sand beach; shops 2km - plenty of choice; gd touring base; vg."* **€49.00, 6 Apr-5 Oct. 2024**

FRANCE

CANET PLAGE *10G1* (0.5km S Coastal) *42.67540, 3.03120* **Camping Club Mar Estang,** Route de St Cyprien, 66140 Canet-Plage **04 68 80 35 53; contact@marestang.com; www.marestang.com**

€4 (htd) sand adj

Exit A9 junc 41 Perpignan Nord dir Canet, then foll sp St Cyprien, site sp. Site on D81A bet Canet-Plage & St Cyprien-Plage. 3*, V lge, hdstg, mkd, pt shd, EHU (6A) €7; gas; red long stay; TV; 50% statics; Eng spkn; adv bkg acc; ccard acc; tennis; waterslide; bike hire; CKE. *"Conv Spanish border & Pyrenees; fitness rm; gd birdwatching."* **€51.40, 26 Apr-14 Sep. 2024**

CANET PLAGE *10G1* (4km W Rural) *42.68914, 2.99877* **FFCC Camping Les Fontaines,** 23 Avenue de Saint Nazaire, 66140 Canet-en-Roussillon **04 68 80 22 57 or 06 77 90 14 91 (mob); info@campinglesfontaines.fr; www.campinglesfontaines.fr**

€3.50 sand 2.5km

Take D11 fr Canet dir St Nazaire; site sp on L in 1.5km. Easy access. 3*, Lge, mkd, hdg, unshd, EHU (10A) €3.50; bbq (elec, gas); 30% statics; phone; bus; Eng spkn; adv bkg acc; games area. *"Pitches lge; conv Etang de Canet et St Nazaire nature reserve with flamingos; excel; relaxed atmosphere; friendly staff."* **€49.00, 7 Apr-30 Sep. 2024**

"There aren't many sites open at this time of year"

If you're travelling outside peak season remember to call ahead to check site opening dates – even if the entry says 'open all year'.

CANET PLAGE *10G1* (4km W Urban) *42.70114, 2.99850* **Kawan Village Ma Prairie,** 1 Ave des Coteaux, 66140 Canet-en-Roussillon **+33 (0)4 68 73 26 17; ma.prairie@wanadoo.fr; www.maprairie.com**

€5 nr sand 3km

Leave A9/E15 at junc 41, sp Perpignan Centre/ Canet-en-Roussillon. Take D83, then D81 until Canet-en-Roussillon. At rndabt, take D617 dir Perpignan & in about 500m leave at exit 5. Take D11 dir St Nazaire, pass under bdge & at rndabt turn R. Site on L. 4*, Lge, hdg, shd, serviced pitches; EHU (10A) inc; gas; bbq (elec, gas); TV; 20% statics; bus to town nr; Eng spkn; adv bkg req; ccard acc; waterslide; games rm; sailing; waterskiing; canoeing; CKE. *"Peaceful, popular site; friendly, helpful owners; o'fits 7.5m & over by request; reg bus to beach (Jul/Aug); daily mkt Perpignan; gd."*
€70.00, 5 May - 19 Sep, C05. 2022

CANNES *10F4* (3km NE Urban) *43.55610, 6.96060* **Camping Parc Bellevue,** 67 Ave Maurice Chevalier, 06150 Cannes **04 93 47 28 97; info@parcbellevue.com; www.parcbellevue.com**

(htd) sand 1.5km

A8 exit junc 41 twd Cannes. Foll N7 & at junc controlled by traff lts, get in L lane. Turn L & in 100m turn L across dual c'way, foll sp for site. Site in 400m on L after sports complex - steep ramp at ent. 3*, Lge, mkd, pt shd, EHU (6A) €4; gas; TV (pitch); 80% statics; phone; bus/train nr; Eng spkn; adv bkg acc; CKE. *"Site on 2 levels; gd security; gd san facs; some pitches long way fr facs; many steps to gd pool; helpful; conv beaches & A8; green oasis in busy area; gd bus to prom; no m'van facs; rec use sat nav; not rec in wet weather; no hdstg; o'fits have to be towed off pitches in bad weather."* **€46.00, 30 Mar-31 Dec. 2024**

CANNET DES MAURES, LE *10F3* (4km N Rural) *43.42140, 6.33655* **FFCC Camping Domaine de la Cigalière,** Route du Thoronet, 83340 Le Cannet-des-Maures **04 94 73 81 06; www.domaine-lacigaliere.com**

€2 (htd)

Exit A8 at Le Cannet-des-Maures onto D17 N dir Le Thoronet; site in 4km on R, sp. 4*, Med, hdg, mkd, hdstg, pt shd, pt sl, EHU (6A) €4; bbq (elec, gas); 20% statics; CKE. *"Peaceful site; lge pitches; St Tropez 44km; vg site."* **€38.40, 15 Apr-15 Oct. 2024**

CANOURGUE, LA *9D1* (2km E Rural) *44.40789, 3.24178* **Camping Le Val d'Urugne,** Route des Gorges-du-Tarn, 48500 La Canourgue **04 66 32 84 00; lozereleisure@wanadoo.fr; www.lozereleisure.com**

€2 nr nr

Exit A75 junc 40 dir La Canourgue; thro vill dir Gorges-du-Tarn. In 2km site on R 600m after golf clubhouse. 3*, Sm, hdg, pt shd, pt sl, EHU (6A) €3.50; TV; Eng spkn; adv bkg acc; ccard acc; CKE. *"Vg site; golf adj; conv A75 & Gorges-du-Tarn; some statics adj; LS stop at golf club for key to site; site poss tired end of ssn."* **€16.40, 1 May-30 Sep. 2024**

CANOURGUE, LA *9D1* (7.4km W Rural) *44.43638, 3.1475* **Municipal la Vallèe,** Miége Rivière 48500 Canilhac **04 66 32 91 14; www.camping-vallee-du-lot.com**

€1 (htd)

Leave A75 at junc 40. Take D988 W, sp St Laurent d'Olt. Site on L at level x-ing after 10 mins. 2*, Sm, hdg, pt shd, EHU (16A) €3; bbq; TV; 10% statics; phone; adv bkg acc; games rm; fishing; CCI. *"Sm shop; supmkt 5km; next to rv (sw not allowed); horseriding nr; golf nr; canoeing nr; paint-balling & quad biking nrby; conv for Gorges du Tarn & Aubrac; St laurent d'Olt worth a visit."* **€23.30, 1 May-30 Sep. 2024**

CANY BARVILLE *3C2* (0.5km S Urban) *49.78335, 0.64214* **Camp Municipal,** Route de Barville, 76450 Cany-Barville **02 35 97 70 37; camping@cany-barville.fr; www.cany-barville.fr**

€1.35 (htd) nr

Sp fr town cent, off D268 to S of town, adj stadium. 3*, Med, hdg, mkd, hdstg, pt shd, EHU (10A) €3.25 (poss rev pol); red long stay; 25% statics; adv bkg acc; ccard acc; CKE. *"Vg facs but poss stretched at high ssn; poss no check-in on Sun; within reach of Dieppe & Fécamp chateau; gd cycling; poss mkt traders on site."*
€14.00, 1 Apr-30 Sep. **2024**

CAPESTANG *10F1* (0.5km W Urban) *43.32759, 3.03865* **Camp Municipal de Tounel,** 1 Rue Georges Brassens, Ave de la République, 34310 Capestang **06 07 97 52 09 or 04 67 32 31 87; camping@ville-capestang.fr; www.capestang.fr**

(cont) nr nr

Fr Béziers on D11, turn R twd vill of Capestang, approx 1km after passing supmkt. Site on L in leisure park opp Gendamarie. 1*, Med, hdg, pt shd, EHU (6A) €3; tennis; bike hire; fishing. *"300m fr Canal de Midi; excel walks or bike rides; lovely rest in vill; LS site yourself, fees collected; facs poss tired LS; poss diff access to pitches for long o'fits; ltd EHU; poss resident workers; NH only."* **€15.00, 1 Jun-30 Sep.** **2024**

CARCASSONNE *8F4* (10km NE Rural) *43.28305, 2.44166* **Camping Le Moulin de Ste Anne,** Chemin de Ste Anne, 11600 Villegly-en-Minervois **04 68 72 20 80; contact@moulindesainteanne.com; www.moulindesainteanne.com**

€5 (cont, htd) nr (htd)

Leave A61 junc 23 Carcassone Ouest dir Mazamet; after approx 14km onto D620 to Villegly, site sp at ent to vill. NB Turning R off D620 hidden by trees, then over narr bdge; long o'fits need wide swing in. 4*, Med, mkd, hdg, pt shd, pt sl, terr, EHU (10A) inc; bbq (gas); red long stay; 25% statics; Eng spkn; adv bkg acc; ccard acc; games area; CKE. *"Pretty, clean site; lge pitches; friendly, helpful owner; ltd san facs; pitches poss diff/muddy in wet; gd touring base; poss local youths congregate on motorbikes nrby in eve; min 3 nights high ssn; vg."*
€35.00, 29 Mar - 15 Oct, C28. **2022**

CARCASSONNE *8F4* (10km E Rural) *43.21498, 2.47031* **Camping La Commanderie,** 6 Chemin Eglise, 11800 Rustiques **04 68 78 67 63; contact@campinglacommanderie.com; www.campinglacommanderie.com**

€2 (htd) nr

Fr Carcassonne take D6113/D610 E to Trèbes (approx 8km); at Trèbes take D610 & after 2km L onto D906, then L onto D206; site on R; foll sp 'Rustiques'. Or fr A61 ext junc 24 onto D6113 to Trèbes & then as bef. 3*, Sm, mkd, pt shd, pt sl, EHU (6A) inc; 10% statics; phone; Eng spkn; adv bkg acc; ccard acc; CKE. *"Pleasant, helpful owner & staff; modern san facs; patron sells own wines; gd cycling along canal fr Trèbes; conv A61; gd NH en rte Spain; superb refurbished pool; excel; quiet relaxing site; excel site improving year on year, running track and 12 fitness machines added this year."*
€30.10, 8 Apr-24 Sep. **2023**

CARCASSONNE *8F4* (15km NW Rural) *43.29861, 2.22277* **Camping de Montolieu,** L'Olivier, 11170 Montolieu **04 68 76 95 01 or 06 31 90 31 92 (mob); campingdemontolieu@gmail.com; www.camping-de-montolieu.com**

€2.50 nr nr nr

Fr D6113 4km W Carcassonne, take D629 twd Montolieu; site on R in 2.5km after Moussoulens. Sp fr D6113, approx 5km dist. App thro Montolieu not rec. 3*, Sm, mkd, hdg, pt shd, EHU (5A) inc; gas; bbq; 10% statics; phone; adv bkg acc; games area; games rm; CKE. *"Well-run site in lovely countryside; pool 100m; manoeuvring tight; excel facs; conv Carcassonne; highly rec."*
€27.00, 22 Apr-20 Oct. **2024**

CARCES *10F3* (0.5km SE Urban) *43.47350, 6.18826* **Camping Les Fouguières,** 165 chemin des Fouguières, 83570 Carcès **34 94 59 96 28 or 06 74 29 69 02 (mob); info@camping-les-fouguieres.com; www.camping-les-fouguieres.com**

€2 (htd)

Exit A8 junc 35 at Brignoles onto D554 to Le Val; then take D562 to Carcès. Site sp off D13. Narr app rd, diff entry & exit for long o'fits. Med, pt shd, EHU (14A) €3; gas; sw nr; TV; 80% statics; phone; bus; Eng spkn; canoeing nr; fishing nr. *"Pleasant, clean, well-shd site; friendly, helpful owner; Rv Caramy runs thro site; interesting, medieval town; Lake Carcès 2km; don't miss Entrecasteaux chateau; mkt Sat; excel."*
€32.00, 10 Mar-30 Nov. **2024**

FRANCE

CARENTAN *1D4* (0.6km NE Urban) *49.30864, -1.239117*
Camping Le Haut Dick, 30 Chemin du Grand-Bas Pays, 50500 Carentan Les Marais **02 33 42 16 89; contact@camping-lehautdick.com; www.camping-lehautdick.com**
€2 (covrd, htd, indoor)

Exit N13 at Carentan; clearly sp in town cent, nr pool, on L bank of canal, close to marina.Foll sp to Port de Plaisance. 3*, Med, mkd, hdg, pt shd, EHU (6A) €4 (rev pol); gas; bbq; 5% statics; phone; adv bkg acc; games rm; bike hire; ping pong; go-kart rental; CKE. *"Some pitches poss tight for lge o'fits; gd security; eve meals avail; gates locked 2200-0700; conv Cherbourg ferry & D-Day beaches; crazy golf; gd birdwatching & cycling; htd pool adj; mkt Mon."*
€25.50, 3 Apr-26 Sep. 2020

CARGESE *10H2* (4km N Coastal) *42.1625, 8.59791*
Camping Le Torraccia, Bagghiuccia, 20130 Cargèse **04 95 26 42 39; contact@camping-torraccia.com; www.camping-torraccia.com**
nr sand 1km

N fr Cargèse twd Porto on D81 for 3km. Site on L. 3*, Med, pt shd, terr, EHU ltd (6A) €3.10; games area. *"Nearest site to Porto without diff traff conditions."*
€19.00, 15 May-30 Sep. 2024

CARNAC *2G3* (1km N Rural) *47.59683, -3.06035*
Camping La Grande Métairie, Route des Alignements de Kermario, 56342 Carnac **02 30 26 02 29; info@lagrandemetairie.com; www.lagrandemetairie.com**
€4 (htd) (covrd, htd) sand 2.5km

Fr Auray take N768 twd Quiberon. In 8km turn L onto D119 twd Carnac. La Métairie site sp 1km bef Carnac (at traff lts) turn L onto D196 to site on R in 1km. 4*, V lge, mkd, hdg, pt shd, EHU (6A) €3; gas; bbq; TV; 80% statics; Eng spkn; adv bkg acc; ccard acc; games rm; watersports 2.5km; sailing 2.5km; tennis; waterslide. *"Excel facs; vg pool complex; friendly, helpful staff; rec."* **€42.00, 2 Apr-10 Sep. 2023**

CARNAC *2G3* (3km N Rural) *47.60801, -3.09049*
Camping Les Bruyères, Kerogile, 56340 Plouharnel **02 97 52 30 57; contact@camping-lesbruyeres.com; www.camping-lesbruyeres.com**
€2 (htd) sand 3km

Fr Vannes W on E60/N165, at Auray take D768 dir Quiberon. At rndabt approx 2km fr Plouharnel turn L into Rte du Hahon, site in 500m, sp.
3*, Med, hdstg, mkd, hdg, pt shd, EHU (6A) €3.70; bbq; TV; 30% statics; Eng spkn; adv bkg acc; ccard acc; tennis; games area; CKE. *"V pleasant, well-run, peaceful site; library; bicycles; pony rides; vg."*
€30.00, 6 Apr-29 Sep. 2024

CARNAC *2G3* (2km NE Rural) *47.60820, -3.06605*
Camping Le Moustoir, 71 Route du Moustoir, 56340 Carnac **02 97 52 16 18; lemoustoir@vagues-oceanes.com; www.lemoustoir.com**
€1 (covrd, htd) sand 4km

Fr N165 take D768 at Auray dir Carnac & Quiberon. In 5km take D119 dir Carnac, site on L at ent to Carnac. 4*, Lge, mkd, hdg, pt shd, pt sl, EHU (10A) inc; bbq; TV; 60% statics; phone; Eng spkn; adv bkg acc; ccard acc; games area; waterslide; bike hire; tennis; CKE. *"Attractive, friendly, well-run site; facs clean but stretched; megaliths nrby; Sun mkt."*
€43.00, 8 Apr-23 Sep, B19. 2023

CARNAC *2G3* (3.5km NE Rural) *47.60198, -3.03672*
Camping de Kervilor, Route du Latz, 56470 La Trinité-sur-Mer **02 97 89 95 10; www.camping-kervilor.com**
€2.90 (covrd, htd) sand 4km

Sp fr island in cent of Trinité-sur-Mer. 4*, Lge, hdstg, mkd, hdg, pt shd, EHU (6-10A) €3.85-4.35; gas; bbq; 5% statics; Eng spkn; adv bkg acc; ccard acc; waterslide; solarium; bike hire; games area; tennis; CKE. *"Busy, well-kept family site; lge pitches; clean dated unisex san facs; 20 min walk into La Trinité-sur-Mer (1.5km); gd cycling to Carnac & megaliths; great site; excel loc; easy walk to lovely town."*
€41.10, 7 Apr-29 Sep. 2023

CARNAC *2G3* (2km E Rural/Coastal) *47.5810, -3.0576*
Camping Les Druides, 55 Chemin de Beaumer, 56340 Carnac **02 97 52 08 18; contact@camping-les-druides.com; www.camping-les-druides.com**
€2.50 nr nr (htd) sand 500m

Go E on seafront Carnac Plage to end; turn N onto Ave d'Orient; at junc with Rte de la Trinité-sur-Mer, turn L, then 1st R; site 1st on L in 300m. 3*, Med, hdg, pt shd, pt sl, EHU (6A) €3.70; TV; 5% statics; Eng spkn; adv bkg acc; ccard acc; games rm; CKE. *"Friendly welcome; Super-u in easy walking distance."*
€42.50, 22 Apr-2 Sep. 2023

CARNAC *2G3* (3km E Rural) *47.61122, -3.02908*
Camping du Lac, Passage du Lac, 56340 Carnac **02 97 55 78 78; info@lelac-carnac.com; www.lelac-carnac.com**
€2 nr (htd) sand 3km

Fr Auray (by-pass) take D768 sp Carnac; in 4km turn L on D186; after 4km look for C105 on L & foll sp to site. Fr E end of quay-side in La Trinité-sur-Mer take main Carnac rd & in 100m turn R onto D186; in 2km R on C105, R on C131; sp. 3*, Med, hdg, pt shd, pt sl, serviced pitches; EHU (6A) €3.60; gas; bbq; TV; 50% statics; phone; Eng spkn; adv bkg acc; ccard acc; bike hire; CKE. *"Excel, beautiful, woodland site o'looking tidal lake; helpful owner; clean, well-cared for; multi-sport court; fitness rm; superb pool; gd cycling & walking; vg; lovely sunsets & sunrises."*
€36.20, 11 Apr-26 Sep. 2023

CARNAC *2G3* (2km SE Coastal) *47.58116, -3.05804*
Camping Le Dolmen, Chemin de Beaumer, 56340 Carnac **02 97 52 12 35; contact@campingledolmen.com; www.campingledolmen.com**
€3 (htd) nr (htd) sand 500m

Fr N on D768 twd Quiberon; turn L onto D781 twd La Trinité-sur-Mer. At Montauban turn R at rndabt dir Kerfraval & Beaumer, site in 700m, sp. 4*, Med, hdstg, mkd, hdg, pt shd, pt sl, EHU (10A) €4.70; bbq; 2% statics; adv bkg acc; ccard acc; games area; games rm; CKE. *"Excel, v friendly, clean, pleasant site; v well maintained; generous size pitches; modern, clean san facs; highly rec."* **€41.50, 1 Apr-30 Sep.** **2023**

CARNAC *2G3* (1km S Coastal) *47.57667, -3.06817*
Camping Les Menhirs, Allé saint michel, 56343 Carnac **02 97 52 94 67; contact@lesmenhirs.com; www.lesmenhirs.com**
(htd) sand 350m

Fr Auray foll sps to Carnac, Carnac Plage. Site past shopping cent rd on L, sp by camping sps. 4*, Lge, pt shd, pt sl, EHU (6A) €4.80; gas; 50% statics; adv bkg acc; sauna; jacuzzi; games rm. *"Extra charge for larger pitches; excel san facs; excel location, nr rest, shops & beach."* **€56.00, 1 Apr-30 Sep.** **2023**

CARNAC *2G3* (3.5km NW Rural) *47.59468, -3.09659*
Camping Les Goélands, Kerbachic, 56340 Plouharnel **02 97 52 31 92; contact@camping-lesgoelands.com; www.camping-lesgoelands.com**
€1 nr sand 3km

Take D768 fr Auray twd Quiberon. In Plouharnel turn L at rndabt by supmkt onto D781 to Carnac. Site sp to L in 500m. 2*, Med, pt shd, EHU (3-6A) €3.50; gas; adv bkg rec. *"Good facs; gd-sized pitches; gate clsd at 2200; nr beaches with bathing & gd yachting; bells fr adj abbey not too intrusive; conv for megalithic sites; high standard, pleasant, quiet site; facs basic; clean and tidy; new owners (2015)."*
€20.00, 1 Apr-31 Oct. **2022**

CARPENTRAS *10E2* (7km N Rural) *44.12246, 5.03437*
Camp Municipal de Roquefiguier, 84190 Beaumes-de-Venise **04 90 62 95 07 or 04 90 62 94 34 (Mairie); camping.roquefiguier@orange.fr; www.beaumes-de-venise.fr**
€1.45

Leave A7 exit 22, take N7 S then L onto D950 sp Carpentras. At rndabt after Sarrians sp turn L onto D21 to Beaumes-de-Venise. Cross Beaumes & foll site sp. Turn L bef Crédit Agricole to site on R. 2*, Med, hdg, mkd, pt shd, pt sl, terr, EHU (6A) €3; bbq; phone; ccard acc; CKE. *"Gd site; gd views; facs clean; steel pegs req for pitches; poss diff access lge o'fits; steep access some pitches; gate clsd 1900-0830; 5 mins walk to Beaumes-de-Venise; pool in vill; wine caves adj; mini golf; mkd walks & cycle ways; conv for Mt Ventoux, Orange & Avignon MD Tues, excel hot shwrs."* **€13.60, 1 Mar-31 Oct.** **2024**

CARPENTRAS *10E2* (7km N Rural) *44.09723, 5.03682*
Camping Le Brégoux, 410 Chemin du Vas, 84810 Aubignan **04 90 62 62 50; www.camping-lebregoux.fr**
€1.90 nr nr nr

Exit Carpentras on D7 sp Bollène. In Aubignan turn R immed after x-ing bdge, 1st R again in approx 250m at Club de Badminton & foll site sp at fork. 3*, Lge, hdstg, hdg, mkd, pt shd, EHU (10A) €3.80 (poss long lead req); bbq; TV; 2% statics; phone; Eng spkn; adv bkg acc; ccard acc; games rm; golf nr; tennis; CKE. *"Popular site in beautiful area; lge pitches & gd access; helpful, friendly staff; gates clsd 2200-0700; go-karting nrby; poss flooding in heavy rain; excel walking & cycling nrby; gd value; gd; san facs upgraded, modern & clean (2015)."* **€26.40, 1 Mar-31 Oct.** **2023**

CARPENTRAS *10E2* (6km S Urban) *43.99917, 5.06591*
Camp Municipal Coucourelle, Ave René Char, 84210 Pernes-les-Fontaines **04 90 66 45 55 or 04 90 61 31 67 (Mairie); camping@perneslesfontaines.fr; www.tourisme-pernes.fr**
€0.50 nr nr

Take D938 fr Carpentras to Pernes-les-Fontaines; then take D28 dir St Didier (Ave René Char pt of D28). Site sp (some sps easily missed). Foll sp sports complex, site at rear of sw pool. 2*, Sm, hdg, mkd, shd, EHU (10A) €3.50; bbq; adv bkg acc; ccard acc; tennis adj; fishing 2.5km; CKE. *"Pleasant, well-run site; views of Mont Ventoux; most pitches lge but some sm & narr; excel clean facs; m'vans can park adj to mv point free when site clsd; pool 2.5km; gates close 1930; no twin axles; free use of adj pool; attractive old town, easy parking; adv bkg rec LS; vg."*
€15.50, 1 Apr-30 Sep. **2022**

CARPENTRAS *10E2* (4km SW Rural) *44.0398, 5.0009*
Camp Municipal de Bellerive, 54 Chemin de la Ribière, 84170 Monteux **04 90 66 81 88 or 04 90 66 97 52 (TO); camping.bellerive@orange.fr; www.provenceguide.com**
€1 nr nr nr

Site on N edge of Monteux cent, sp off ring rd Monteux N, immed after rlwy x-ing. 2*, Sm, hdg, mkd, hdstg, pt shd, serviced pitches; EHU (6-10A) €2.50; red long stay; 10% statics; phone; bus; CKE. *"Gd, busy, lovely site; rec arr early high ssn; helpful, friendly, v helpful warden lives adj; gd security; vg, clean, modern san facs; trees a problem for sat TV - choose pitch carefully; park adj gd for children; 5 min walk to vill; poss muddy when wet; poss some workers' statics LS; Mistral blows early & late ssn; pool 4km; gd touring base; free WiFi; no grey water drainage."*
€14.40, 1 Apr-15 Oct. **2023**

FRANCE

FRANCE

CASSIS *10F3* (1.5km N Coastal) *43.22417, 5.54126* **Camping Les Cigales,** 43 Ave de la Marne, 13260 Cassis **04 42 01 07 34; www.campingcassis.com**

€1.30 shgl 1.5km

App Cassis on D41E, then at 2nd rndabt exit D559 sp Cassis, then turn 1st R sp Les Calanques into Ave de la Marne, site immed on R. Avoid town cent as rds narr. 4*, Lge, hdg, mkd, hdstg, pt shd, pt sl, EHU (3A) €2.60 (poss rev pol & poss long lead req); gas; 30% statics; phone; Eng spkn; ccard acc; CKE. *"Gd base for Calanques; v busy w/ends; popular attractive resort, but steep walk to camp site; poss tired san facs end ssn; poss diff lge o'fits due trees; v strong pegs req to penetrate hardcore; bus to Marseille cent fr campsite."*
€32.00, 25 Mar-5 Nov. 2024

CASTELJALOUX *7D2* (10km SE Rural) *44.27262, 0.18969* **Camping Moulin de Campech,** 47160 Villefranche-du-Queyran **05 53 88 72 43; camping@moulindecampech.co.uk; www.moulindecampech.co.uk**

€2.40 (htd)

Fr A62 exit junc 6 (sp Damazan & Aiguillon). Fr toll booth take D8 SW sp Mont-de-Marsan. In 3km turn R in Cap-du-Bosc onto D11 twd Casteljaloux. Site on R in 4km. Or fr Casteljaloux S on D655 then SW on D11 after 1.5km. Site on L after 9.5km. 3*, Sm, hdg, mkd, pt shd, EHU (6A) €4; bbq; sw nr; phone; adv bkg acc; ccard acc; lake fishing; games rm; golf nr; CKE. *"Superb, peaceful rvside site in wooded valley; well-run; lge pitches; friendly, helpful & welcoming British owners; clean, dated san facs, needs refurb (2014); gd pool; excel, gd value rest; BBQ suppers; gd cycling; no o'fits over 8.2m; interesting area ideal for nature lovers; excel site; many social events."*
€33.00, 5 May - 22 Sept, D16. 2022

CASTELLANE *10E3* (2.7km SE Rural) *43.83833, 6.54194* **Camping La Ferme de Castellane,** Quartier La Lagne, 04120 Castellane **04 92 83 67 77; accueil@camping-la-ferme.com; www.camping-la-ferme.com**

€1 nr nr nr

Fr Castellane take D6085 dir Grasse. In 1km turn R (at Rest L'Escapade) then site in 1km, sp. Narr app rd with passing places. 3*, Sm, mkd, pt shd, terr, EHU €3.50; TV; 25% statics; Eng spkn; adv bkg acc; ccard acc; games rm; CKE. *"Vg, clean, friendly site; gd touring base; breakfast and BBQ evenings at rest."*
€29.20, 15 Mar-15 Nov. 2022

CASTELLANE *10E3* (0.3km SW Urban) *43.84623, 6.50995* **Camping Frédéric Mistral,** 12 Ave Frédéric Mistral, 04120 Castellane **04 92 83 62 27; camping-fredericmistral.fr**

(htd) nr

In town turn onto D952 sp Gorges-du-Verdon, site on L in 100m. 2*, Med, mkd, pt shd, serviced pitches; EHU (6A) €3 (poss rev pol); 2% statics; adv bkg acc; CKE. *"Friendly owners; pool 200m; gd san facs but poss stretched in ssn; gd base for gorges etc; gd."*
€18.50, 1 Mar-11 Nov. 2023

CASTELLANE *10E3* (0.5km SW Rural) *43.84570, 6.50447* **Camping Notre Dame,** Route des Gorges du Verdon, 04120 Castellane **04 92 83 63 02 or 06 86 71 26 53; camping-notredame@wanadoo.fr; www.camping-notredame.com**

nr

N fr Grasse on D6085, turn L in Castellane at sq onto D952 to site on R in 500m. 3*, Sm, pt shd, EHU (6A) €3.50; gas; 20% statics; phone; Eng spkn; adv bkg acc; CKE. *"Ideal touring base; helpful owners; poss a bit unkempt early ssn; excel."*
€26.50, 12 Apr-6 Oct. 2024

CASTELLANE *10E3* (1.5km SW Rural) *43.83921, 6.49370* **Sandaya Domaine du Verdon,** D952, 04120 Castellane **04 92 83 61 29; ver@sandaya.fr; https://www.sandaya.fr/nos-campings/domaine-du-verdon**

€5 (htd)

Fr Castellane take D952 SW twd Grand Canyon du Verdon & Moustiers-Ste Marie. After 1.5km turn L into site. NB To avoid Col de Lèques with hairpins use N202 & D955 fr Barrême instead of D6085. 5*, V lge, mkd, hdg, pt shd, serviced pitches; EHU (6A) inc; gas; bbq (elec, gas); sw; TV; 60% statics; Eng spkn; ccard acc; games rm; rv fishing adj; waterslide; canoeing; archery; games area; horseriding nr; CKE. *"Excel site by rv; no o'fits over 8m; gd sized pitches; gd, clean san facs, modern & dated blocks; quiet, rural walk to town; mkt Wed & Sat."*
€37.00, 20 May - 18 Sep. 2022

CASTELLANE *10E3* (12km SW Rural) *43.79596, 6.43733* **Camp Municipal de Carajuan,** 04120 Rougon **09 71 21 70 94; campingverdon.carajuan@gmail.com; camping-gorgesduverdon-carajuan-rougon.com/**

€1.20

Fr N on D4085 turn R on D952 & foll sps for 16km to rv bank of Gorges du Verdon nr Carajuan bdge; site on L. Fr E on D952 ignore turning to Rougon; site sp in 5km. 2*, Med, mkd, pt shd, EHU (6A) €2.70; red long stay; 10% statics; phone; bus Jul/Aug; Eng spkn; adv bkg acc; CKE. *"Natural, unspoilt site nr rvside with shingle beach (no sw); friendly staff; basic, dated facs, poss unclean LS; gd walking; fair; gd morning sun despite valley."* **€20.50, 11 Apr-6 Oct. 2024**

CASTELLANE *10E3* (9km W Rural) *43.82276, 6.43143* **Camping Indigo Gorges du Verdon,** Clos d'Aremus, 04120 Castellane **04 92 83 63 64; gorgesduverdon@camping-indigo.com; www.camping-indigo.com**

(htd)

On D6085 fr Grasse turn L on D952 in Castellane. Camp in 9km on L. Look for sp Chasteuil on R of rd; site in 500m. 4*, Lge, mkd, shd, EHU (6A) inc; gas; TV; 10% statics; Eng spkn; adv bkg req; games rm; fishing; boating; games area; canoeing; CKE. *"Some sm pitches; rd along Gorges du Verdon poss diff for lge o'fits; pool & san facs renovated 2015."*
€40.90, 11 May-29 Sep. 2024

CASTELLANE *10E3* (2km NW Rural) *43.85861, 6.49795* **CAMPING TERRA VERDON (formerly Kawan Village Camping International),** 384 Route du Hameau de la Palud, 04120 Castellane **04 92 83 66 67; terraverdon@cielavillage.com; https://camping-terra-verdon.com**

€2 (htd) WD MSP

Site sp fr D4085 & D602. 5*, Lge, hdg, pt shd, pt sl, serviced pitches; EHU (6A) €4.50; gas; sw nr; TV; 50% statics; Eng spkn; adv bkg acc; ccard acc; golf; horseriding; games area; CKE. *"Busy site; friendly, helpful owners; main san facs vg, some dated, but clean; most pitches on gentle slope; conv Gorges de Verdon; gd walking; gd."*
€45.00, 31 Mar-1 Oct. **2024**

CASTELNAUDARY *8F4* (7km E Rural) *43.31723, 2.01582* **FFCC Camping à la Ferme Domaine de la Capelle (Sabatte),** St Papoul, 11400 St Martin-Lalande **04 68 94 91 90; www.domaine-la-capelle.fr/en**

€1 (htd) WD nr

Fr D6113 Castelnaudary/Carcasonne, take D103 E & foll sp to St Papoul & site in 2km. Well sp. NB Ent poss awkward lge o'fits. Sm, hdg, mkd, pt shd, pt sl, EHU (4A) €2.50; bbq; phone; Eng spkn; CKE. *"Delightful, peaceful, spacious CL-type site; friendly, helpful owner; vg san facs, poss stretched when site full; ltd EHU; gd walking; nr St Papoul Cathar vill with abbey; ideal NH for Spain; excel; close to ind site, gd cycling."* **€14.50, 1 Apr-30 Sep.** **2022**

CASTIES LABRANDE *8F3* (1.5km W Rural) *43.32502, 0.99046* **Camping Le Casties,** Le Bas de Lebrande, 31430 Casties-Labrande **05 61 90 81 11 / mobile 06 44 01 54 15; contact@camping-lecasties.fr / online form; www.camping-lecasties.fr**

€1 WD

S fr Toulouse, exit A64 junc 26 onto D626; after Pouy-de-Touges turn L onto & foll camping sp. 1*, Med, hdg, pt shd, EHU (5A) €1; bbq; 10% statics; phone; Eng spkn; adv bkg acc; ccard acc; tennis; fishing; CKE. *"Remote; lge hdg pitches; staff friendly & helpful; value for money; lovely pool; excel; new vg san facs (2013); v peaceful; sm farm for children."*
€12.50, 1 May-30 Sep. **2024**

CASTILLON LA BATAILLE *7C2* (0.6km E Urban) *44.85350, -0.03550* **Camping Les Batailleurs (formerly Municipal La Pelouse),** 2 promenade du Bourdieu, 33350 Castillon-la-Bataille **05 57 40 42 83**

Site in town on N bank of Rv Dordogne. After x-ing rv on D17 fr S to N, take 1st avail rd on R to rv. 2*, Sm, shd, EHU (15A) inc; adv bkg acc; CKE. *"Peaceful, lovely site by rv; busy high ssn; pitches poss rough & muddy when wet; helpful warden; facs dated but clean; conv town; trans, St Emillion & wine area; gd NH."* **€17.40, 1 May-15 Oct.** **2022**

CASTRES *8F4* (2km NE Urban) *43.62054, 2.25401* **Camping de Gourjade,** Ave de Roquecourbe, 81100 Castres **05 63 59 33 51; contact@campingdegourjade.net; www.campingdegourjade.net**

€2 WD MSP nr

Leave Castres NE on D89 sp Rocquecourbe; site on R in 2km. Well sp. Ave de Roquecourbe is pt of D89. 3*, Med, hdg, pt shd, terr, EHU (6-16A) inc (poss rev pol); gas; bbq; 5% statics; bus; ccard acc; cycling; golf adj; CKE. *"Lovely site in beautiful park on Rv Agout; lge pitches; helpful staff; gd, tired clean san facs; 9 hole golf course adj; some lower pitches sl & poss soft; boat fr site to town; extra charge twin axles; gd security; poss groups workers LS; leisure cent & golf adj; vg cycling; highly rec; rest open evenings only; well run; excel for long or sh stay."*
€20.80, 8 Apr-23 Sep. **2023**

CASTRIES *10E1* (2.6km NE Rural) *43.69406, 3.99585* **Camping Domaine de Fondespierre,** 277 Route de Fontmarie, 34160 Castries **04 67 91 20 03; accueil@campingfondespierre.com; www.campingfondespierre.com**

€3 (htd) WD MSP nr

Fr A9 exit junc 28 sp Vendargues, foll sp for Castries on D610. Cont thro Castries in dir of Sommieres. Aprox 1.5km past Castries turn L and foll camp sp. 3*, Med, hdstg, mkd, hdg, pt shd, terr, EHU (10A) inc (poss long lead req); bbq (sep area); sw nr; 40% statics; phone; Eng spkn; adv bkg acc; ccard acc; games area; tennis adj; bike hire; golf 2.5km; CKE. *"Gd walking area; poss travellers & site poss unkempt LS; site rds narr with sharp, tree-lined bends - poss diff access to pitches for lge o'fits; NH; superb vill."*
€34.00, 4 Jan-19 Dec. **2022**

"I like to fill in the reports as I travel from site to site"

You'll find report forms at the back of this guide, or you can fill them in online at camc.com/europereport.

CAUNES MINERVOIS *8F4* (1km S Rural) *43.32380, 2.52592* **Camp Municipal Les Courtals,** Ave du Stade, 11160 Caunes-Minervois **09 52 17 09 45; mairie.de.caunes@wanadoo.fr**

MSP nr

Sp fr D620 at stadium & adj rv. 1*, Sm, pt shd, EHU (4A) inc; phone; games area. *"Pleasantly situated site; office opens 1800; gate locked 2100; site self, warden calls; pool 6km; rv adj; interesting town."*
€11.00, 15 Feb-15 Dec. **2024**

FRANCE

FRANCE

CAUSSADE *8E3* (9km NE Rural) *44.18273, 1.60305* **Lodges & Camp du Bois Dodo (formerly Camping de Bois Redon),** 10 Chemin de Bonnet, 82240 Septfonds **05 63 64 92 49 or 06 78 35 79 97 (Mob); lodgesboisdodo@gmail.com; lodges-bois-dodo.com**

€3

Exit A20 junc 59 to Caussade, then onto D926 to Septfonds (narr rds); after rndabt turn 3rd L; site sp. Site in 2km. One-way system when leaving site. 3*, Sm, mkd, pt shd, pt sl, EHU (10A) inc; bbq; 10% statics; Eng spkn; adv bkg req; bike hire; CKE. *"Well-shd, spacious site in ancient oak forest with walks; charming Dutch owners; Septfonds nr with all facs; new shwrs (2013/14); enthusiastic owners continually making improvements; excel site; immac new san fac block."* **€25.00** **2024**

CAUSSADE *8E3* (10km NW Rural) *44.24323, 1.47735* **Camping Le Faillal,** 46 Blvd Pasteur, 82270 Montpezat-de-Quercy **05 63 02 07 08 or 07 68 59 25 32; contact@parcdufaillal.com; www.parcdufaillal.com**

€1.50 nr

N on D820, turn L onto D20, site clearly sp on R in 2km. (Do not take D38 bef D20 fr S). 3*, Med, hdg, pt shd, pt sl, terr, EHU (10A) €3.70; bbq; TV; phone; Eng spkn; adv bkg acc; games rm; tennis adj; games area; CKE. *"Pretty, well-kept site; friendly, helpful staff; gd, clean san facs, poss ltd; super pool; many pitches unavail after heavy rain; access to some pitches diff; old town a 'must'; rec pay night bef dep; excel; horse drawn carriage rides, pony rides, kayaking, rafting, paintball."* **€22.50** **2023**

CAUTERETS *8G2* (2.5km NE Rural) *42.91092, -0.09934* **Camping GR10,** Route de Pierrefitte, 65110 Cauterets **06 20 30 25 85; contact@gr10camping.com; www.gr10camping.com**

€1.30 (htd) nr (htd)

N fr Cauterets on D920; site in 2.5km on R. 3*, Med, mkd, shd, terr, EHU €4; TV; 25% statics; Eng spkn; games rm; tennis; games area. *"Pretty site; canyoning (guide on site); excel."* **€29.50, 6 Jul-31 Aug.** **2024**

CAVAILLON *10E2* (8km E Rural) *43.84220, 5.13284* **Camp Municipal Les Royères du Prieuré,** La Combe-St Pierre, 84660 Maubec **04 90 76 50 34; camping.maubec@c-lmv.fr; www.campingmaubec-luberon.com**

€2 nr

Heading E fr Cavaillon on D2, thro vill of Robion, in 400m at end vill sp turn R to Maubec. Site on R in 1km bef old vill. (Avoid any other rte with c'van). Diff access at ent, steep slope. Sm, pt shd, terr, EHU (6-10A) €5; 10% statics; CKE. *"Awkward site for lge o'fits, otherwise vg; san facs stretched high ssn; conv A7; san facs refurbed; restful site; wine tasting on Tue eve."* **€13.00, 1 Apr-15 Oct.** **2023**

CAVAILLON *10E2* (1km S Rural) *43.82107, 5.03723* **Camp Municipal de la Durance,** 495 Ave Boscodomini, 84300 Cavaillon **04 90 71 11 78; contact@camping-durance.com; www.camping-durance.com**

€1.50 (htd) nr

S of Cavaillon, nr Rv Durance. Fr A7 junc 25 foll sp to town cent. In 200m R immed after x-ing rv. Site sp (Municipal Camping) on L. 3*, Lge, pt shd, EHU (4A-10A) €2.50- 6.50; TV; 30% statics; adv bkg acc; tennis; fishing; games area. *"Site OK; gd NH only; close to town; decent facs; reasonably priced."* **€23.20, 1 Apr-30 Sep.** **2024**

CAVAILLON *10E2* (9km S Rural) *43.78182, 5.04040* **Camping de la Vallée Heureuse,** Quartier Lavau, 3660 Orgon **04 84 80 01 71; camping.valleeheureuse@gmail.com; www.valleeheureuse.com**

€1.70 nr

Sp in Organ town cent. 3*, Lge, mkd, shd, terr, EHU (16A); bbq; sw nr; TV; Eng spkn; adv bkg acc; CKE. *"Site adj to old quarry in beautiful position; friendly, helpful staff; superb san facs; gd pool; gd walking; café; interesting area; conv m'way; isolated site; vill 1.5km."* **€25.50, 1 Apr-6 Nov.** **2022**

CAVAILLON *10E2* (12km SW Rural) *43.76058, 4.95154* **FFCC Camping Les Oliviers,** Ave Jean Jaurès, 13810 Eygalières **04 90 95 91 86; campinglesoliviers13@gmail.com**

€1 (htd) nr nr nr

Exit A7 junc 25; D99 dir St Rémy-de-Provence; in 8km camping sp on L; in vill well sp. Sm, hdg, pt shd, EHU (6A) inc; bbq (elec, gas); adv bkg acc. *"Lovely, friendly site in olive grove nr scenic vill; quiet site; facs rustic but v clean; pitches cramped for lge o'fits; simple site; diff acc for lge o'fits; free WiFi."* **€19.00, 30 Mar-30 Sep.** **2023**

CAVALAIRE SUR MER *10F4* (2km NE Rural) *43.18220, 6.51610* **Kawan Village Cros de Mouton,** Chemin de Cros de Mouton, 83240 Cavalaire-sur-Mer **04 94 64 10 87; campingcrosdemouton@wanadoo.fr; www.crosdemouton.com**

€2 (htd) sand 1.8km

Exit A8 junc 36 dir Ste Maxime on D125/D25, foll sp on D559 to Cavalaire-sur-Mer. Site sp on coast app fr Grimaud/St Tropez & Le Lavandou; diff access. 4*, Lge, mkd, shd, terr, serviced pitches; EHU (10A); gas; TV; 10% statics; phone; Eng spkn; adv bkg rec; ccard acc; bike hire; CKE. *"Attractive, well-run, popular site in hills behind town - rec adv bkg even LS; lge pitches avail; poss diff access to pitches due steep site rds - help avail; pleasant, welcoming & efficient staff; gd san facs; gd pool; vg rest & bar; buses to St Tropez; excel; lovely views; steep walk fr town."* **€43.30, 1 Apr-31 Oct.** **2023**

CAVALAIRE SUR MER *10F4* (3km NE Coastal) *43.19450, 6.55495* **Sélection Camping,** 12 Blvd de la Mer, 83420 La Croix-Valmer **04 94 55 10 30; camping.selection@gmail.com; www.selectioncamping.com**
€4 (htd) (htd) sand 400m

Off N559 bet Cavalaire & La Croix-Valmer, 2km past La Croix at rndabt turn R sp Barbigoua, site in 200m. 4*, Lge, hdg, mkd, shd, terr, EHU (10A) €5; gas; TV; 20% statics; phone; bus; Eng spkn; adv bkg req; games area. *"Excel location; sm pitches; private bthrms avail; dogs not acc Jul/Aug; vg san facs; excel pool; excel site."* **€60.30, 15 Mar-31 Oct.** **2023**

CAVALAIRE SUR MER *10F4* (0.9km S Urban) *43.16956, 6.53005* **Camping de La Baie,** Blvd Pasteur, 83240 Cavalaire-sur-Mer **04 94 64 08 15 or 04 94 64 08 10; contact@camping-baie.com; www.camping-baie.com**
€4 (htd) (htd) sand 400m

Exit A8 sp Ste Maxime/St Tropez & foll D25 & D559 to Cavalaire. Site sp fr seafront. 4*, Lge, mkd, pt shd, pt sl, EHU (10A) €6; bbq; 10% statics; Eng spkn; adv bkg acc; ccard acc; sailing; games area; jacuzzi; watersports; games rm. *"Well-run, busy site; pleasant staff; excel pool & facs; nr shops, beach, marina & cafes; cycle paths; gd location; diving 500m; sm pitches; narr rd."* **€55.00, 15 Mar-126 Nov.** **2024**

CAVALAIRE SUR MER *10F4* (0.5km SW Coastal) *43.17203, 6.52461* **Camping La Pinède,** Chemin des Mannes, 83240 Cavalaire-sur-Mer **04 94 64 11 14; camping.lapinede83@orange.fr; www.la-pinede.com**
sand 500m

Sp on R (N) of N559 on S o'skts of Cavalaire. 4*, Lge, mkd, shd, pt sl, EHU (5A) €3; gas; adv bkg req. *"Cavalaire pleasant, lively resort."* **€27.00, 15 Mar-15 Oct.** **2024**

CAYEUX SUR MER *3B2* (2km NE Coastal) *50.19765, 1.51675* **Camping Le Bois de Pins,** Rue Guillaume-le-Conquérant, Brighton, 80410 Cayeux-sur-Mer **03 22 26 71 04; info@campingleboisdepins.com; www.campingleboisdepins.com**
€2 (htd) nr 500m

Take D940 out of St Valery to Cayeux, then D102 NE for 2km & foll sp. 3*, Lge, mkd, hdg, shd, terr, EHU (6-10A) inc; bbq; red long stay; 80% statics; Eng spkn; adv bkg acc; ccard acc; fishing adj; bike hire; sailing adj; horseriding; CKE. *"Friendly, clean, busy site; gd food vans visit site; attractive sm town; gd cycling & birdwatching area; hg quality food vans serve the site; quiet & attractive; conv for Saint Valery-sur-Somme; excel."* **€32.00, 1 Apr-1 Nov.** **2022**

CAYLAR, LE *10E1* (4km SW Rural) *43.83629, 3.29045* **Camping Mas de Messier,** St Félix-de-l'Héras, 34520 Le Caylar **06 85 81 54 91; info@masdemessier.com; www.masdemessier.com**
nr

Fr N exit A75 junc 49 onto D9 thro Le Caylar. Turn R sp St Félix & foll sp St Félix-de-l'Héras; at x-rds in St Félix turn R, site in 1km on L. Fr S exit A75 junc 50; foll sp to St Félix-de-l'Héras; at x-rds turn R & as bef. 2*, Sm, hdg, pt shd, pt sl, EHU (10A) €3; Eng spkn; adv bkg req; CKE. *"Excel views fr some pitches; friendly, helpful Dutch owner; facs excel; access unsuitable lge o'fits; meals avail some eves; gd walking; excel long or sh stay; dogs free; low rates in LS."* **€33.00, 13 May-23 Sep.** **2023**

CAYLUS *8E4* (0.5km E Rural) *44.23368, 1.77636* **FFCC Camping de la Bonnette,** 672 route de la Bonnette, 82160 Caylus **05 63 65 70 20 or 06 07 34 61 99; info@campingbonnette.com; www.campingbonnette.com**
€1.50 nr

Fr A20 exit junc 59 dir Caylus; thro Caylus to g'ge on L. Turn R in 1km over next crossrds & foll site sps to site on R in 1km. 3*, Med, hdg, mkd, pt shd, EHU (10A) €3.50; bbq; red long stay; 10% statics; Eng spkn; adv bkg rec; games area. *"Nice, tidy, scenic site on edge of medieval vill - worth a visit; friendly owner; pitches in groups of 4, not v private."* **€19.00, 29 Mar-4 Oct.** **2024**

CEAUCE *4E1* (1km N Rural) *48.49812, -0.62481* **Camp Municipal de la Veillotière,** Chemin de la Veillotière, 61330 Ceaucé **02 33 38 31 19 or 06 19 10 86 11 (mob); mairie.ceauce@wanadoo.fr; www.mairie-ceauce.fr**

S fr Domfront on D962 dir Mayenne, at rndabt in Ceaucé turn L. Site in 200m on R adj sm lake. Sm, hdg, pt shd, pt sl, EHU (6A); fishing adj. *"Well-kept site on edge vill; gd; nice as always; bar 200m; quiet cycle rte to Ambrieves Les Vallees; warden calls eves, otherwise visit mairie."* **€11.00, 1 May-30 Sep.** **2024**

CERCY LA TOUR *4H4* (0.9km S Urban) *46.86680, 3.64328* **Camp Municipal Le Port,** 58360 Cercy-la-Tour **03 86 25 09 38; camping.cercylatour@gmail.com; campingleport.e-monsite.com**

At Decize take D981 E; in 12 km L onto D37, then L onto D10 to Cercy-la-Tour; site sp in vill. Adj municipal pool, Rv Aron & canal. Med, hdstg, pt shd, EHU inc; phone; Eng spkn; CKE. *"Clean & tidy site; immac san facs; gd cycling/walking along canal; excel value; excel."* **€16.00, 1 Apr-15 Oct.** **2023**

FRANCE

CERESTE *10E3* (2.5km SW Rural) *43.84564, 5.56394* **Camping Bois de Sibourg (Vial-Ménard),** 04280 Céreste **04 92 79 02 22 or (mobs) 06 30 88 63 29 or 06 70 64 62 01; campingsibourg@orange.fr; www.sibourg.com**

(cont)

W fr Céreste on D900/D4100; turn L in 2km (site sp); site on L in 1km. Sm, pt shd, EHU (6A) €2.80; phone; Eng spkn; CKE. *"Delightful 'green' farm site; St Michel l'Observatoire 15km; gd NH or longer; excel."* **€14.50, 15 Apr-15 Oct.** **2024**

CERET *8H4* (1km E Rural) *42.48981, 2.76305* **Camping Les Cerisiers,** Mas de la Toure, 66400 Céret **09 70 35 85 82; www.campingcerisiers.fr**

12 nr nr nr

Exit A9 junc 43 onto D115, turn off for cent of Céret. Site is on D618 approx 800m E of Céret twd Maureillas, sp. Tight ascent for lge o'fits. 2*, Med, mkd, shd, EHU (4A); gas; sw nr; TV; 60% statics; phone; site clsd Jan; CKE. *"Site in cherry orchard; gd size pitches; facs dated & ltd LS; footpath to attractive vill with modern art gallery; pool 600m; conv Andorra, Perpignan, Collioure."* **€18.00** **2024**

CERILLY *4H3* (10km N Rural) *46.68210, 2.78630* **Camping des Ecossais,** La Salle, 03360 Isle-et-Bardais **04 70 66 62 57 or 04 70 67 50 96; ecossais@campingstroncais.com; www.campingstroncais.com**

€1.50 nr

Fr Lurcy-Lévis take D978A SW, turn R onto D111 N twd Isle-et-Bardais & foll camp sp. Ent tight. 2*, Med, hdg, pt shd, pt sl, EHU (10A) inc; bbq; sw; twin axles; 10% statics; adv bkg acc; games area; games rm; fishing; CKE. *"Excel; v busy high ssn; ltd facs LS; gd cycling; site in oak forest; rec; mountain bike nec on forest tracks."* **€16.90, 1 Apr-31 Oct.** **2022**

CERNAY *6F3* (6km S Rural) *47.74684, 7.12423* **Camping Les Castors,** 4 Route de Guewenheim, 68520 Burnhaupt-le-Haut **03 89 48 78 58; info@camping-les-castors.fr; www.camping-les-castors.fr**

€15 (htd) nr

Exit A36 junc 15 sp Burnhaupt-le-Haut onto D83, then D466 sp Masevaux. Site on R. 4*, Med, mkd, pt shd, EHU (5-10A) €4-5; gas; bbq; 40% statics; phone; Eng spkn; adv bkg acc; games rm; CKE. *"Conv German & Swiss borders, Black Forest; wine rte; Mulhouse motor museum; gd san facs; vg; excel site, nice area; friendly owner; gd cycle path."* **€20.30, 15 Mar-15 Oct.** **2024**

CERNAY *6F3* (0.9km SW Urban) *47.80448, 7.16999* **Camping Les Cigognes,** 16 Rue René Guibert, 68700 Cernay **03 89 75 56 97; campinglescigognes@orange.fr; www.camping-les-cigognes.com**

€1.20

Fr N on D83 by-pass, exit Cernay Est. Turn R into town at traff lts, immed L bef rv bdge, site sp on L; well sp. 3*, Lge, mkd, pt shd, EHU (5A) €3.50 (poss rev pol); red long stay; 25% statics; CKE. *"Friendly staff; clean, tidy site; storks nesting over some pitches; sh walk to town."* **€18.00, 1 Apr-30 Sep.** **2022**

CERNAY LA VILLE *4E3* (0.8km NW Rural) *48.67630, 1.97208* **Cernay Vacances,** 37 Rue de la Ferme, 78720 Cernay-la-Ville **33 13 48 52 123; albert.koning@free.fr; www.cernayvacances.com**

12

Fr Rouen take A13 twrds Paris, then A12 twrds Rambouillet. Aft Leon de Bruxelles rest & metro take exit Mesnil - St. Denis. At rndabt pass by D58 twrds le-Mesnil, dir Dampierre. In Dampierre turn R onto D91 then L onto D149 twrds Senlisse. At top of this rd turn onto D906, aft 500mtrs at Peugeot g'ge turn R on Rue des Moulins strt to fm. Sm, pt shd, EHU €4; cooking facs; Eng spkn; adv bkg acc; games area. *"Vg."* **€21.00** **2023**

CERVIONE *10G2* (6km SE Coastal) *42.32155, 9.54546* **Camping Calamar,** Prunete, 20221 Cervione **04 95 38 03 54 or 04 95 34 08 44 (LS); contact@campingcalamar.eu**

nr sand adj

On N198 S fr Prunete for 6km. Turn L at x-rds, site in 500m beside beach, sp. Sm, pt shd, EHU €2.50; bbq; Eng spkn; adv bkg acc; watersports; games area; sailing. *"Friendly owner; pleasant site with trees & shrubs; excel."* **€25.00, 13 Apr-31 Oct.** **2024**

CHABLIS *4F4* (0.6km SE Rural) *47.81376, 3.80563* **Camp Municipal Le Serein,** Quai Paul Louis Courier, 89800 Chablis **03 86 42 44 39 or 03 86 42 80 80 (Mairie); mairie-chablis@chablis.net; www.chablis.net**

€1.50 nr nr

W fr Tonnere on D965; in approx 16km exit D965 for Chabilis; in 300m, just bef x-ing Rv Serein, turn L at camping sp onto Quai Paul Louis Courier; site in 300m on R. 2*, Med, hdg, mkd, shd, EHU (5A) €2; Eng spkn; adv bkg acc; CKE. *"Attractive, tidy site; facs poss stretched high ssn; friendly & helpful warden, calls 0800-1200 & 1600-2000; easy walk to attractive town; vineyards & wine cellars nrby; excel Sun mkt; warden attaches elec supply to locked post."* **€12.00, 2 Jun-15 Sep.** **2022**

CHAGNY *6H1* (0.7km W Urban) *46.91187, 4.74567* **Camping du Pâquier Fané,** 20 Rue du Pâquier Fané, 71150 Chagny **03 85 87 21 42; camping-chagny@orange.fr; www.campingchagny.com**

€3 WD MSP nr nr nr

Clearly sp in town. 3*, Med, hdg, mkd, pt shd, EHU (16A) inc; gas; Eng spkn; fishing; tennis adj; CKE. *"Well laid-out, well-lit vg site; friendly, helpful resident wardens; clean san facs; htd pool adj; many pitches sm & diff med/lge o'fits; on wine rte; gd cycling nrby (voie verte); new sm sw pool on site; rlwy noise at night; v popular site, full off ssn."* **€24.20, 7 Apr-22 Oct. 2023**

CHAILLAC *7A3* (0.6km SW Rural) *46.43260, 1.29602* **Camp Municipal Les Vieux Chênes,** 36310 Chaillac **02 54 25 61 39 or 02 54 25 74 26 (Mairie); chaillac-mairie@wanadoo.fr; www.chaillac36.fr/tourisme-economie/tourisme/hebergements/camping**

12 (htd) WD nr nr nr

Exit N20 S of Argenton-sur-Creuse at junc 20 onto D36 to Chaillac. Thro vill, site 1st L after sq by 'Mairie', adj Lac du Rochegaudon. Fr S exit J21, take D10 sp St Benoit du Sault. Fr there turn L onto D36 and foll instructions above. 3*, Sm, hdg, mkd, pt shd, pt sl, EHU (16A) inc (poss rev pol); bbq; sw nr; Eng spkn; adv bkg acc; waterslide; fishing adj; tennis adj; CKE. *"Excel site, beautiful location, friendly wardens, well kept san facs, gd local supmkt 2 mins walk (clsd Mon); lake nrby."* **€11.40 2023**

CHALAIS *7C2* (10km NW Rural) *45.32758, -0.02385* **Chez Sarrazin,** 16480 Brossac **05 45 78 21 57 or 07 78 21 08 36; chezsarrazin@orange.fr; www.chezsarrazin.net**

€2 WD

N10 S fr Angouleme, leave exit for Barbezieux to Brossac & Chalais on D731, 700m after rndabt at Brossac Gare, L twd Brie Sous Chalais. After 1.4km R at 4 wheelie bins sp Chez Sarrazin Camping. Sm, shd, pt sl, EHU (10A); bbq; Eng spkn; adv bkg acc; games area. *"Natural site in beautiful setting; many historical vills; walks; san facs & pool excel; charming & peaceful; excel; steep path to shwrs; helpful owners; well equipped."* **€25.00, Easter-31 Oct. 2023**

CHALANDRAY *4H1* (0.8km N Rural) *46.66728, -0.00214* **Camping du Bois de St Hilaire,** Rue de la Gare, 86190 Chalandray **05 49 60 20 84 or 01246 852823 (UK); acceuil@camping-st-hilaire.com; www.camping-st-hilaire.com**

€1 (htd) WD MSP nr (htd)

Foll N149 bet Parthenay & Vouille; at xrds in vill, turn N into Rue de la Gare (D24); site 750m on R over rlwy line. 3*, Sm, mkd, hdg, shd, EHU (10A) €3.95; bbq (charcoal, elec, gas); twin axles; TV; phone; bus 750m; Eng spkn; adv bkg acc; ccard acc; tennis; games rm; games area; mini golf; boules pitch; fire pit; CCI. *"Friendly, helpful British owners; situated in mature forest area, sh walk fr vill; 20 mins fr Futuroscope; lge pitches; excel, clean site & pool; c'van storage; poss muddy in wet weather; woodland walks; excel bakery in vill."* **€25.00, 1 May-30 Sep. 2024**

CHALLANS *2H4* (10km SE Rural) *46.81522, -1.77472* **Camping Domaine de Bellevue,** Bellevue Du Ligneron, 85670 Saint Christophe du Ligneron **02 51 93 30 66 or 06 21 55 54 29 (mob); contact@vendee-camping-bellevue.com; www.vendee-camping-bellevue.com**

12 €3 (htd)

Fr S: On Route National D948 exit Saint Christophe du Lingeron; turn W in dir Saint Gilles Croix de Vie/ Commequirers; at rndbt cont strt on; take 2nd R at Bellevue du Ligneron. 3*, Med, hdg, EHU (16) €4; bbq; 50% statics; Eng spkn; adv bkg acc; ccard acc; fishing; games rm; bike hire; CKE. *"Gd value for money; in lovely Vendee region; gd fishing on site; new site with friendly owners; takeaway; v lge pitches."* **€26.40 2022**

CHALLANS *2H4* (4km S Rural) *46.81869, -1.88874* **FFCC Camping Le Ragis,** Chemin de la Fradinière, 85300 Challans **02 51 68 08 49; info@camping-leragis.com; www.camping-leragis.com**

€4 (htd) WD MSP nr (htd)

Fr Challans go S on D32 Rte Les Sables, turn R onto Chemin de la Fradinière & foll sp. 3*, Lge, mkd, hdg, pt shd, EHU (10A) €4; gas; bbq; twin axles; TV; 50% statics; bus 1km; Eng spkn; adv bkg acc; ccard acc; waterslide; games area. *"Vg; homegrown veg; tickets for Puy Du Fou; night car park; conv Vendee coast; lake fishing; petanque; traditional French site; kids club 4-10; v friendly staff."* **€25.00, 1 Apr-31 Oct. 2022**

CHALON SUR SAONE *6H1* (3km E Rural) *46.78411, 4.87136* **Camping du Pont de Bourgogne,** 12 Rue Julien Leneveu, 71380 St Marcel **03 85 48 26 86; campingchalon71@wanadoo.fr; www.camping-chalon.com**

€2.60 (htd) WD MSP

Fr A6 exit junc 26 (sp Chalon Sud) onto N80 E; foll sp Chalon-sur-Saône; at 1st rndabt go strt over (sp Louhans & St Marcel) & over flyover; take 4th exit on 2nd rndbt; immed after this rndabt fork R thro Les Chavannes (still on N80). Turn R at traff lts bef bdge. (DO NOT CROSS BDGE). Site in 500m. 3*, Med, hdstg, hdg, mkd, pt shd, terr, EHU (6-10A) inc (rev pol); gas; bbq; TV; 2% statics; Eng spkn; adv bkg acc; ccard acc; games rm; bike hire; canoeing nr; rv fishing; CKE. *"Peaceful, well-run rvside site in gd location; lge pitches, some by rv; helpful, friendly staff; excel clean san facs, poss stretched high ssn; vg rest/bar; pool 500m; no o'fits over 12m; rvside walks; lovely town, 20 min walk; conv NH fr A6; vg; gd cycling; shopping ctr nrby."* **€29.50, 1 Apr - 30 Sep, L17. 2023**

FRANCE

CHALONNES SUR LOIRE *2G4* (1.5km E Rural) *47.35164, -0.74679* **Camping Les Portes de la Loire,** Le Candais, 49290 Chalonnes-sur-Loire **41 78 02 27; contact@lesportesdelaloire.fr; www.onlycamp.fr/portes-de-loire-chalonnes-loire**

Fr D723 cross bdge to Challones. In town turn L sp Rochefort-Sur-Loire. Site on L of this rd in abt 1km. 3*, Lge, mkd, pt shd, EHU (10A) €3; bbq; twin axles; adv bkg acc. *"Close to rv & town; peaceful setting; lge pitches; gd touring base; vg; excel san facs."* **€20.00, 20 May-20 Sep.** 2022

CHALONNES SUR LOIRE *2G4* (8km SE Rural) *47.32285, -0.71428* **Camp Municipal Les Patisseaux,** Route de Chalonnes, 49290 Chaudefonds-sur-Layon **02 41 78 04 10 (Mairie); mairie@chaudefonds-sur-layon.fr**

nr nr

Fr Chalonnes on D961 S dir Cholet; Turn L onto D125 after 3km at narr rlwy bdge. Foll sp to site vill by Rv Layon. 2*, Sm, hdg, mkd, pt shd, EHU. *"V basic, clean, delightful site nr rv; lots of interest in area; reverse polarity; ltd san facs; lovely peaceful site; warden calls."* **€14.00, 1 May-31 Aug.** 2024

CHALONNES SUR LOIRE *2G4* (10km NW Urban) *47.39211, -0.87082* **Camping La Promenade,** Quai des Mariniers, 49570 Montjean-sur-Loire **02 41 39 02 68 or 06 26 32 60 28 (mob); contact@campinglapromenade.com; www.campinglapromenade.com**

€2 nr (htd) sand 600m

Exit Angers on N23 twd Nantes. Exit 1km beyond St Germain-des-Prés dir Montjean-sur-Loire. Cross rv then R on D210 to site in 500m. 3*, Lge, mkd, hdg, pt shd, EHU (10A) €4; gas; bbq; twin axles; TV; 30% statics; Eng spkn; adv bkg acc; ccard acc; games area; CKE. *"Friendly, young owners; interesting sculptures in vill & at Ecomusée; gd for Loire cycling; diff exit to R for lge vehicles; fishing nr; on 'Loire á Vélo' route; vg value LS."* **€22.50, 1 Apr-30 Sep.** 2020

CHALONS EN CHAMPAGNE *5D1* (3km S Urban) *48.93579, 4.38299* **Camping de Châlons en Champagne,** Plaisance street, 51000 Châlons-en-Champagne **03 26 68 38 00; camping.chalons@aquadis-loisirs.com; www.aquadis-loisirs.com/camping-nature/camping-de-chalons-en-champagne**

Free (htd) nr

Fr N on A26 exit junc 17, on D3 foll sp to Chalons en Champagne, then to Fagnières. Strt on at traff lts, then L at 1s rndabt. Turn R, sp Vitry le François, site sp. Fr S exit junc 18 onto D977, then D5 over rv & canal nr town cent; then foll site sp to R. Fr N44 S of Châlons sp St Memmie; foll site sp. D977 fr N into Châlons, cont on main rd to traff lts at 6 x-rds & turn R, site well sp. Or exit A4 junc 27 onto N44; turn R at St Memmie; site sp. NB some sps in area still show old town name 'Châlons-sur-Marne'. Do not use SatNav. 4*, Med, hdg, hdstg, mkd, pt shd, EHU (6-10A) (poss long lead req & rev pol, 2 pin adapter req); bbq; red long stay; twin axles; TV; bus; Eng spkn; adv bkg acc; ccard acc; tennis; games area; CKE. *"Popular site adj park; generous pitches, inc hdstg; rec arr early or phone ahead; check barrier arrangements if need early dep; gates shut 2130 LS & 2300 high ssn; ltd bus service; poss noisy high ssn - pop concerts in adj area; hypmkt 1km; flat walk to lovely, interesting town; conv touring base & NH; friendly helpful recep; seasonal workers in Sep; san facs neglected but clean; bkg thro pitchup.com; busy site; v quiet area; beautiful loc & site; strongly rec; elec pnts sparse; gd."* **€23.00, 1 Mar-3 Nov.** 2024

CHALUS *7B3* (10km NW Rural) *45.71540, 0.91956* **Camping Parc Verger,** Le Halte, 87150 Champagnac-la-Rivière, Limousin **0844 232 8500 (Fr UK) or 05 55 01 22 83 or 06 04 09 05 20 (mob); pvbureau@parcverger.com; www.parcverger.com**

(htd) nr nr

N fr Châlus on D901; in 9km turn L onto D75 sp Champagnac-la-Rivière; site on L in 150m. Sm, mkd, hdstg, unshd, EHU (16A) inc; bbq; sw; twin axles; red long stay; bus 150m; Eng spkn; adv bkg acc; ccard acc; CKE. *"Lovely site; welcoming, friendly, helpful British owners; lge pitches suitable for RVs; gd clean san facs, poss stretched high ssn; gd mkd walks nrby; 15km-long walk/cycle path adj (old rwly track); red grass pitch; excel local vet; excel area for walking; bike hire."* **€18.00** 2022

CHAMBERY *9B3* (5km E Rural) *45.55151, 5.98416* **Family Camping Le Savoy (formerly Municipal),** Parc des Loisirs, Chemin des Fleurs, 73190 Challes-les-Eaux **09 88 66 77 80; contact@family-camping-le-savoy.com; www.family-camping-le-savoy.com**

12 €1.40 nr nr

On o'skts of town app fr Chambéry on D1006. Pass airfield, lake & tennis courts on L, L at traff lts just bef cent of Challes-les Eaux sp Parc de Loisirs, at Hôtel Les Neiges de France foll camp sp to site in 100m. Fr A41 exit junc 20, foll sp Challes-les-Eaux, then 'Centre Ville', then D1006 N. 3*, Med, mkd, hdstg, shd, serviced pitches; EHU (6-10A) €2.90; gas; sw nr; red long stay; bus; adv bkg acc; ccard acc; fishing adj; tennis adj. *"Well-designed, well-run, clean site in beautiful setting; diff sized pitches; level (suitable wheelchairs); friendly, helpful staff; excel modern san facs; excel walking; well run site, rec hotel school rest in term time."* **€28.60** **2023**

> **"Satellite navigation makes touring much easier"**
>
> Remember most sat navs don't know if you're towing or in a larger vehicle – always use yours alongside maps and site directions.

CHAMBON LA FORET *4F3* (0.8km N Rural) *48.06381, 2.28192* **Camping Domaine La Rive du Bois,** Route de la Forêt, 45340 Chambon-la-Forêt **02 38 32 29 73 or 06 79 95 26 53 (mob); rive.bois@wanadoo.fr; www.larivedubois.com**

12 (htd)

Fr Pithiviers take D921 S. Immed after x-ing over A19 turn L onto D30 sp Chambon-la-Forêt, Sully-sur-Loire. At La Rive-du-Bois traff lts foll sp to site on R. 3*, Sm, pt shd, EHU (10A) inc; bbq; 70% statics; Eng spkn; adv bkg acc; bike hire; fishing; tennis; games area; CKE. *"Helpful, friendly manager; gd walking & cycling fr site; deer & red squirrels in woods around; gd; lovely woodland setting."* **€15.00** **2024**

CHAMBON SUR LAC *7B4* (2km W Rural) *45.57127, 2.89067* **Camping de Serrette,** Serrette, 63790 Chambon-sur-La **04 73 88 67 67; camping.de.serrette @wanadoo.fr; campingdeserrette.com**

€2.50

Fr A75, exit 6, foll D996 dir Mont Dore. Foll site sp after Lac Chambo. After 1.5km turn L onto D636. Site on R. Sharp turn at ent. 3*, Sm, mkd, hdg, pt shd, pt sl, terr, EHU (10A) €4.80; bbq; sw nr; twin axles; TV; 50% statics; phone; Eng spkn; adv bkg acc; table tennis; games rm; CKE. *"Excel walking area; watersports on Lac Chambon; gd site."* **€26.70, 28 Apr-17 Sep.** **2022**

CHAMONIX MONT BLANC *9B4* (3km NE Rural) *45.9378, 6.8925* **Camping La Mer de Glace,** 200 Chemin de la Bagna, Praz de Chamonix, 74400 Chamonix **04 50 53 44 03; info@chamonix-camp.com; www.chamonix-camping.com**

(htd) nr nr nr

Foll sp on D1506 thro Chamonix dir Argentière & Swiss Frontier; site well sp on R in 3km but ent under bdge 2.4m. Rec, to avoid low bdge cont to 1st rndabt in Praz-de-Chamonix & foll sp to site (R at rndabt). 3*, Med, hdg, mkd, hdstg, pt shd, pt sl, EHU (10A) €3; bbq; bus & train 500m; Eng spkn; CKE. *"Well-run, wooded site with superb views; sm pitches; helpful staff; vg facs; bar 500m; v conv trains/buses; close to Flégère lift; sports cent nr; htd pool 2km; path to town via woods & rv; excel."* **€25.00, 4 May-9 Oct.** **2022**

CHAMONIX MONT BLANC *9B4* (7km NE Rural) *45.97552, 6.92224* **Camping Le Glacier d'Argentière,** 161 Chemin des Chosalets, 74400 Argentière **04 50 54 17 36; info@campingchamonix.com; www.campingchamonix.com**

€0.50 nr

On Chamonix-Argentière D1506 rd bef Argentière take R fork twd Argentière cable car stn. Site immed on R. 2*, Med, pt shd, pt sl, EHU (2-10A); bbq; Eng spkn; adv bkg acc; games area; CKE. *"Alpine excursions; cable cars adj; mountain views; friendly, helpful owners; gd friendly site; Alpine views; quiet relaxed site; bus stop 1 min; 10 min walk to Argentiere Vill', train stn & cable car; mkd paths fr site; free travel on local buses & trains inc."* **€24.00, 15 May-30 Sep.** **2024**

CHAMONIX MONT BLANC *9B4* (3.5km SW Rural) *45.90203, 6.83716* **Camping Les Deux Glaciers,** 80 Route des Tissières, Les Bossons, 74400 Chamonix **04 50 53 15 84; info@les2glaciers.com; www.les2glaciers.com**

(htd)

Exit Mont Blanc tunnel foll sps Geneva turn L on D1506 (Chamonix-Geneva rd), in 2km turn R for Les Bossons & L under bdge. Fr W foll sps Chamonix & Mont Blanc tunnel. On dual c/way turn R at sp `Les Bossons' & site after Mercure Hotel; adj Les Cimes site; site clearly sp fr D1205. 3*, Med, pt shd, sl, EHU (2-10A) €2.80-4.50; bus; Eng spkn; games rm; table tennis; CKE. *"Pleasant, well-kept site in wonderful location just under Mont Blanc; roomy pitches; clean facs; poss diff site for lge o'fits over 6m; if recep clsd pitch & wait until 1730; ideal for walking; skating rink 4km; funicular adj to Glacier des Bossons; rec arr early high ssn; pool 4km; highly rec; rest vg; vg."* **€23.00, 1 Jan-15 Nov & 15 Dec-31 Dec.** **2022**

FRANCE

FRANCE

CHANAC *9D1* (0.5km S Urban) *44.46519, 3.34670* **Camp Municipal La Vignogue,** Rue de Plaisance, 48230 Chanac **04 66 48 24 09; gites-camping-chanac@orange.fr; www.camping-chanac.fr**

€1 (htd) nr nr nr

Exit A75 junc 39.1 onto N88 to Chanac; site well sp in vill. Sm, mkd, pt shd, pt sl, EHU (6A) inc; bbq; 10% statics; Eng spkn; adv bkg acc. *"Excel; bar 500m; pool adj; rec arr early (bef 1800)."*
€17.50, 15 Apr-30 Sep. **2023**

CHANTILLY *3D3* (5km NW Rural) *49.22571, 2.42862* **Camping Campix,** 60340 St Leu d'Esserent **03 44 56 08 48; campix@orange.fr; campingcampix.com/index.php/fr**

€2 (htd)

Exit A1 junc 8 to Senlis; cont W fr Senlis on D924 thro Chantilly, x-ing Rv Oise to St Leu-d'Esserent; leave town on D12 NW twd Cramoisy thro housing est; foll site sp for 1km, winding app. 3*, Med, hdstg, mkd, shd, terr, EHU (6-10A) €3.50 (min 25m cable poss req); gas; bbq; sw nr; red long stay; phone; Eng spkn; adv bkg acc; ccard acc; fishing; games rm; CKE. *"Beautiful, peaceful site in former quarry - poss unguarded, vertical drops; helpful owner & friendly staff; wide variety of pitches - narr, steep access & o'hanging trees on some; conv Paris Parc Astérix & Disneyland (Astérix tickets fr recep); sh walk to vill; rec; gd facs; long elec leads maybe needed."*
€27.00, 7 Mar-30 Nov. **2023**

> **"There aren't many sites open at this time of year"**
>
> If you're travelling outside peak season remember to call ahead to check site opening dates – even if the entry says 'open all year'.

CHANTILLY *3D3* (7km NW Rural) *49.21225, 2.40270* **Camping L'Abbatiale,** 39 Rue Salvador Allendé, 60340 St Leu-d'Esserent **03 44 56 38 76; contact@camping-abbatiale.fr; www.camping-abbatiale.com**

(htd) nr nr sandy 1km

S twds Paris on A1 exit Senlis; cont W fr Senlis on D924/D44 thro Chantilly x-ing Rv Oise to St Leu-d'Esserent; cont on D44, x-ing D603 which becomes Rue Salvador Allendé in 700m; foll site sps; avoid rv x-ing on D17 fr SW; v narr bdge. 3*, Sm, hdg, mkd, hdstg, pt shd, EHU (3A) €2.50 (some rev pol); bbq (sep area); twin axles; red long stay; phone; bus adj; Eng spkn; adv bkg acc; ccard acc; games rm; games area. *"Chantilly & chateau interesting; conv for Chantilly, Paris & L'oise Valley; gd walks nrby (woodland & rvside); v friendly family owned & managed; lge nbr of statics on site but does not detract fr touring pitches nor impact on facs; best site in area."* **€16.00** **2024**

CHANTONNAY *2H4* (12km NE Rural) *46.75168, -0.94568* **Camping La Baudonnière,** Route des Salinières, 85110 Monsireigne **02 51 66 43 79; tombann1962@gmail.com; www.labaudonniere.com**

Fr Chantonnay take D960B NE dir St Prouant & Pouzauges. In St Prouant take D23 to Monsireigne. Foll rd downhill, cross sm rv & as rd starts to climb take 2nd L sp Reaumur; in 400m L onto Rue des Salinières. Site on L in 800m. Sm, pt shd, pt sl, EHU (10A) €4; bbq; Eng spkn; adv bkg acc; games rm; tennis 2km. *"V relaxing, peaceful, pretty CL-type site; welcoming, friendly, helpful Irish owners; excel san facs; conv Puy de Fou theme park; vg; v well kept site."*
€22.00 **2024**

CHAPELLE EN VERCORS, LA *9C3* (0.2km S Urban) *44.9695, 5.4156* **Camp Municipal Les Bruyères,** Ave des Bruyères, 26420 La Chapelle-en-Vercors **04 75 48 21 46**

€1 (htd) nr nr nr

Take D518 N fr Die over Col de Rousset. Fr N on A49 exit 8 to N532 St Nazaire-en-Royans, then D76 thro St Thomas-en-Royans, then D216 to St Laurent-en-Royans. Take D2 round E flank of Combe Laval (2 sh 2-lane tunnels). Fr Col de la Machine foll D76 S 1km, then D199 E over Col de Carri to La Chapelle. (D531 fr Villard de Lons, D76 over Combe Laval & D518 Grandes Goulet not suitable for c'vans & diff lge m'vans due narr rds & tunnels & 5km of o'hanging ledges.) 2*, Med, hdstg, pt shd, pt sl, EHU (6A); TV; 10% statics; adv bkg acc; cycling; fishing; horseriding; CKE. *"Excel base for beautiful Vercors plateau; friendly welcome; climbing; pool 300m; excel value; choose own pitch; clean & immac san facs; excel cycling; vg."*
€13.50, 1 May-1 Oct. **2022**

CHAPELLE HERMIER, LA *2H4* (4km SW Rural) *46.66652, -1.75543* **Camping Le Pin Parasol,** Châteaulong, 85220 La Chapelle-Hermier **02 51 34 64 72; contact@campingpinparasol.fr; www.campingpinparasol.fr**

€6 nr (htd)

Exit A83 junc 4 onto D763/D937 dir La Roche-sur-Yon; turn R onto D948; at Aizenay turn R onto D6 twd St Gilles Croix-de-Vie; after 10km at x-rds turn L onto D21; in La Chapelle-Hermier foll D42 twds L'Aiguillon-sur-Vie; site sp in 4km. 5*, Lge, mkd, hdg, unshd, pt sl, terr, EHU (16A) inc; gas; bbq; sw nr; TV; 45% statics; Eng spkn; adv bkg acc; ccard acc; games rm; fishing 200m; excursions; fitness rm; archery; bike hire; games area; waterslide; tennis; CKE. *"On banks of Lake Jaunay; access to lake down sm path; lge pitches; friendly staff; no o'fits over 11m; boating 200m; canoeing 200m; excel facs; adventure zone; lovely pools; away fr crowds but close to beaches; pleasant walks & cycle tracks around lake; beautiful site; v well kept."* **€42.00, 20 May - 11 Sept, A36.** **2022**

CHARITE SUR LOIRE, LA *4G4* (0.5km W Urban) *47.17683, 3.01058* **FFCC Camp Municipal La Saulaie,** Quai de la Saulaie, 58400 La Charité-sur-Loire **03 86 70 00 83 or 03 86 70 15 06 (LS); campinglasaulaie@outlook.fr; entreprisefrery.fr/lacharitesurloire**

€1.50 nr

Exit A77 junc 30 & foll sp 'Centre Ville'. Turn L over Rv Loire sp Bourges; take 2nd R bef next bdge. Fr Bourges on N151, turn L immed after x-ing 1st bdge over Rv Loire. Foll sp. NB Take care when turn R over narr rv bdge when leaving site - v high kerb. 3*, Med, mkd, pt shd, EHU (10A); sw nr; red long stay; CKE. *"Lovely, well-kept site on rv island; warm welcome, helpful staff; gd security; poss school groups high ssn; LS phone to check open; beautiful town; playgrnd & htd pool, paddling pool adj inc (pool opens 1 Jul); welcoming staff; new san facs (2016); site v well maintained."* **€18.90, 1 Apr-30 Sep. 2023**

CHARLEVILLE MEZIERES *5C1* (12km N Urban) *49.87757, 4.74187* **Camp Municipal au Port à Diseur,** Rue André Compain, 08800 Monthermé **03 24 29 36 81; camping-port-disseur@orange.fr; www.camping-port-diseur.com**

nr nr nr

Fr D988 at Revin turn E onto D1 TO Monthermé. Site is on D1 S of town. Site on R, 100m past supmkt on L. 2*, Med, hdg, mkd, pt shd, pt sl, EHU (4-10A) inc; 10% statics; phone; CKE. *"Pleasant, rvside site in conv location; lge pitches; excel, clean san facs, poss stretched if site full; gd rvside walks; 20 min easy walk to Monthermé; gd cycling & walking; popular with fishermen & canoeists; excel site; some pitches adj rv; gas 100m; picturesque hilly wooded countryside."* **€14.50, 1 Apr-30 Sep. 2024**

CHARLEVILLE MEZIERES *5C1* (3.5km N Urban) *49.77813, 4.72245* **Camp Municipal Mont Olympe,** 139 Rue des Pâquis, 08000 Charleville-Mézières **03 24 33 23 60; contact@camping-mont-olympe.fr; www.camping-mont-olympe.fr**

€1.60 (htd) nr nr

Fr N43/E44 head for Hôtel de Ville, with Hôtel de Ville on R, cont N along Ave des Arches, turn R at 'Gare' sp & cross rv bdge. At 'Gare' turn sharp L immed along Rue des Pâquis, site on L in 500m, visible fr rd. Well sp fr town cent. 4*, Med, hdg, mkd, hdstg, pt shd, serviced pitches; EHU (10A) €3.95; gas; bbq; TV; 10% statics; Eng spkn; ccard acc; fishing; boating; games rm; CKE. *"Lovely, spacious, well-kept site on Rv Meuse; v lge pitches extra; helpful staff; htd covrd pool adj; san facs clean, new (2018); useful snack bar; easy walk to charming town; excel; NH for m'van's."* **€22.40, 1 Apr-30 Oct. 2023**

CHARLIEU *9A1* (1km E Urban) *46.15851, 4.18088* **Camping de Charlieu (formerly Municipal de la Douze),** rue du Camping, 42190 Charlieu **04 77 69 89 72; contact@campingcharlieu.com; campingcharlieu.com/en**

(htd) nr

N fr Roanne on D482 to Pouilly-sous-Charlieu, then E on D487 to Charlieu town cent, site sp in town, by sw pool. NB Do not confuse with Camp Municipal Pouilly-sous-Charlieu which is sp fr main rd. 3*, Med, hdg, pt shd, EHU (6A) inc; sw nr; twin axles; 5% statics; Eng spkn; adv bkg acc; boating adj; fishing adj; games area; CKE. *"Gd clean new san facs (2018); vg value; quiet; new cycle rte to Loire; canal cycle paths; sw & tennis adj; historical town."* **€22.00, 1 Apr-30 Oct. 2023**

CHARMES *6E2* (1km N Rural) *48.37706, 6.28974* **Camp Municipal Les Iles,** 20 Rue de l'Ecluse, 88130 Charmes **03 29 38 85 85 or 03 29 38 15 34; andre.michel63@wanadoo.fr; www.ville-charmes.fr**

nr

Exit N57 for Charmes, site well sp on Rv Moselle. Do not confuse with sp for 'Camping Cars'. 3*, Med, mkd, pt shd, EHU (10A) inc; gas; bbq; red long stay; phone; Eng spkn; adv bkg acc; kayak hire; fishing; CKE. *"Lovely site bet rv & canal; lge pitches; friendly staff; footpath to town; m'van o'night area in town; vg value; gd; v lge pitches."* **€22.00, 1 Apr-15 Oct. 2024**

CHARNY *4F3* (0.9km N Rural) *47.89078, 3.09419* **FFCC Camping des Platanes,** 41 Route de la Mothe, 89120 Charny **03 86 91 83 60; info@campinglesplatanes.fr; www.campinglesplatanes.fr**

€3 (htd) nr

Exit A6 junc 18 onto D943 to Montargis. Turn S onto D950 to Charny, site on R as ent vill; sp. 3*, Med, hdg, mkd, pt shd, serviced pitches; EHU (10A) inc; gas; bbq; red long stay; TV; 60% statics; Eng spkn; adv bkg acc; bike hire; tennis 500m; rv fishing 150m; CKE. *"Pleasant, peaceful site; gd sized pitches; friendly, helpful owners; excel, clean san facs; sh walk to vill; gd walking; gd touring base."* **€29.00, 1 Apr-30 Oct. 2024**

CHAROLLES *9A2* (0.5km E Rural) *46.43972, 4.28208* **FFCC Camp Municipal,** 3 Route de Viry, 71120 Charolles **03 85 24 04 90; camping@ville-charolles.fr; www.campingcharolles.fr**

€1.50 (htd) nr (htd)

Exit N79 at E end of by-pass sp Vendenesse-lès-Charolles; at rndabt foll camping sp; then sharp R bottom hill bef town; site on L, next to Municipal pool. 3*, Med, hdg, mkd, hdstg, pt shd, pt sl, EHU (6A) €2; bbq; twin axles; 2% statics; adv bkg rec; ccard acc; games rm; CKE. *"Well-kept site; sm pitches; friendly, helpful warden; gd, modern san facs; pool adj high ssn (proper sw trunks req); m'van area outside site; negligible security; canoe's avail, launching stn to rv on site; excel."* **€13.50, 1 Apr-30 Sep. 2023**

CHARTRE SUR LE LOIR, LA *4F2* (0.5km W Rural) *47.73220, 0.57451* **Camping Le Vieux Moulin,** Chemin des Bergivaux, 72340 La Chartre-sur-le Loir **06 47 50 10 52; directeurcamping@lachartresurleloir.fr; campingduvieuxmoulin-lachartresurloir.fr**

€1.50 (htd) WD MSP nr (htd)

Sp fr D305 in town. Fr S exit A28 junc 27 onto D766 dir Beaumont-la-Ronce; then take D29 to La Chartre-sur-le Loir; go over rv, turn L immed after bdge. Fr N leave A20 at junc 24 & foll D304 to Chartre, site well sp on R bef bdge. 3*, Med, mkd, hdg, pt shd, EHU (5-10A) €4-5 (poss rev pol); bbq; TV; 20% statics; Eng spkn; adv bkg rec; 15% red CC members; rv fishing; bike hire; CKE. *"Beautiful, well-kept rvside site; helpful, friendly staff; excel pool; gd for dogs; v lge MH's acc; gd base for chateaux, forest & Loir Valley; excel; pleasant walk to town."* **€24.00, 1 Mar-30 Nov.** **2023**

CHARTRES *4E2* (3km SE Urban) *48.43433, 1.49914* **Camping de Chartres (formerly Les Bords de l'Eure),** 9 Rue de Launay, 28000 Chartres **02 34 40 30 40; camping-de-chartres.com**

(htd) WD MSP

Exit N123 ring rd at D935, R at T-junc dir Chartres; then R at 2nd traff lts dir Chartres immed after rlwy bdge; site on L in 400m; inside of ring rd. Also sp fr town cent on N154 fr N, foll sp town cent under 2 rlwy bdges, L at traff lts sp Orléans, after 1km site sp. Fr SE on N154 cross ring rd, foll site sp & turn L at 2nd traff lts; site on R. 3*, Med, mkd, hdg, shd, EHU (6A) inc (poss rev pol); bbq; 10% statics; Eng spkn; adv bkg acc; ccard acc; fishing; CKE. *"Popular, spacious, pleasant, well laid-out, dir access to rv; unisex san facs refurbished (2022), stretched when busy; some pitches diff lge o'fits; gates clsd 2200-0700; poss ssn workers; poss unkempt early ssn; when wet grnd soft & muddy in places; easy walk or cycle along rv to Chartres, well lit at night; rec Son et Lumière; ideal NH & longer; vg; attractive site, bottom of hill, some awkward pitches; friendly helpful staff; excel situation; ltd water points; ACSI discount."* **€26.00, 1 Mar-31 Oct.** **2023**

CHASSENEUIL SUR BONNIEURE *7B3* (10km E Rural) *45.83283, 0.55811* **Camping Le Paradis,** Mareuil, 16270 Mazières **05 45 31 53 47 or 06 46 51 69 37 or 07769 970829 (UK); contact@campingleparadis.eu; campingleparadis.eu/en**

12 WD MSP nr nr

Fr Limoges W on N141 twd Angoulême, turn L at 1st traff lts in Roumazières-Loubert D161. Site sp in 2km at t-junc. 4*, Sm, hdg, mkd, hdstg, pt shd, EHU (10-16A) €5.50-8.50; bbq; sw nr; 20% statics; phone; bus 1km; adv bkg rec; fishing nr; tennis nr; games area; watersports 5km; CKE. *"Clean, tranquil site; gd sized pitches; vg, immac san facs; welcoming, helpful British owners, helpful & friendly; gd touring base; adv bkg rec lge o'fits; excel; min €30 for 1 night stays; storage avail; highly rec; dog exercise field adj."* **€28.50** **2024**

CHATAIGNERAIE, LA *2H4* (8km N Rural) *46.7325, -0.7425* **Camping Le Grand Fraigneau,** Le Grand Fraigneau, 85700 Menomblet Vendée **02 51 51 68 21 or 06 42 68 48 12 (mob); info@legrandfraigneau.com**

NE fr La Châtaigneraie on D938T to St Pierre-du-Chemin; turn L onto D49 to Menomblet; in 500m turn L to Le Grand Fraigneau. Site sp. Sm, pt shd, EHU (10A) €3; bbq; sw; twin axles; Eng spkn; adv bkg acc. *"CL-type site; friendly, helpful British owners; fenced pond; walks in lovely countryside; dogs free; boating 9km; excel."* **€9.00, 15 Apr-30 Oct.** **2024**

CHATEAU ARNOUX *10E3* (3km NE Rural) *44.10476, 6.01680* **Camping Sunêlia L'Hippocampe,** Route Napoléon, 04290 Volonne **04 92 33 50 00; camping@l-hippocampe.com; www.l-hippocampe.com**

€2 WD MSP (htd)

Exit A51 junc 21 onto D4085 12km S of Sisteron twd Volonne vill over rv. Turn R on D4 on ent vill & foll camp sp 1km. 5*, Lge, hdstg, mkd, hdg, pt shd, serviced pitches; EHU (10A) inc (poss rev pol); bbq (elec, gas); red long stay; TV; 10% statics; Eng spkn; adv bkg acc; ccard acc; canoeing; fishing; games area; waterslide; bike hire; rafting; tennis; games rm; CKE. *"Pleasant, busy, well-run site; spacious, well-screened pitches; various pitch sizes/prices, some by lake; some pitches poss diff due trees; scruffy."* **€31.00, 30 Apr - 9 Sep, C09.** **2022**

CHATEAU CHINON *4H4* (6km S Rural) *47.00587, 3.90548* **Camping La Fougeraie,** Hameau de Champs, 58120 St Léger-de-Fougeret **03 86 85 11 85; www.camping-fougeraie-bourgogne-morvan.com/en/**

€1.70 WD

Fr Château-Chinon S on D27; in approx 3km turn R onto D157 to St Léger-de-Fougeret; in vill foll sps S dir Onlay to site in 2.5km. 3*, Med, hdg, mkd, pt shd, terr, EHU (6A) €3.20; bbq; sw; TV; Eng spkn; games area; bike hire; games rm; fishing; CKE. *"Beautiful, tranquil situation; most pitches lge & face lake; donkey rides; welcoming, efficient owners; facs at top of terr - poss stretched high ssn & ltd LS; gd rest; poss diff lge o'fits; pitches muddy when wet; excel."* **€29.00, 1 Apr-30 Sep, L24.** **2024**

CHATEAU DU LOIR *4G1* (8km E Rural) *47.71250, 0.49930* **Camping du Lac des Varennes,** Route de Port Gauthier, 72340 Marçon **02 43 44 13 72; contact@lacdesvarennes; www.lacdesvarennes.com**

€1.80 (htd) WD MSP

Fr N on D338 fr Château-du-Loir dir Vendôme for 3km. Turn L onto D305 sp Marçon. In vill turn L onto D61 over bdge. Site on R by lake. 3*, Lge, hdstg, mkd, hdg, pt shd, EHU (10A) €3.40 (poss rev pol, poss long lead req); bbq; sw nr; red long stay; 11% statics; Eng spkn; adv bkg rec; ccard acc; boat hire; watersports; horseriding; tennis; bike hire; CKE. *"Pretty site in lovely situation bet lake & rv; friendly, helpful staff; gd security; gd walks & cycling; san facs basic & unisex; LS off clsd 1200-1600; new owners (2016)."* **€20.00, 1 Apr-30 Oct.** **2022**

CHATEAU GONTIER *4F1* (11km N Rural) *47.92109, -0.68334* **Camping Village Vacances et Pêche,** Rue des Haies, 53170 Villiers-Charlemagne **02 43 07 71 68; vvp@villiers.charlemagne.fr; www.vacancesetpeche.fr**

12 WD

N fr Château-Gontier on N162; turn R onto D20 to Villiers-Charlemagne; site on R. 3*, Sm, pt shd, EHU (6A) inc; bbq; cooking facs; twin axles; 10% statics; Eng spkn; fishing; tennis; bike hire; games rm; CKE. *"Sm wooded site in rural surroundings; each pitch has own san facs & kitchenette; site is amazing; helpful, friendly staff; v peaceful; well maintained."* **€27.00** **2024**

CHATEAU GONTIER *4F1* (2km N Urban) *47.83851, -0.69965* **Camping Le Parc,** 15 Route de Laval, 53200 Château-Gontier **02 43 07 35 60; camping.parc[@]chateaugontier.fr; camping-chateau-gontier.fr**

12 (htd) WD MSP nr

App Château-Gontier fr N on N162, at 1st rndabt on bypass take 1st exit. Site on R in 250m. 3*, Sm, mkd, pt shd, sl, EHU (6-10A) inc (rev pol); TV; 20% statics; ccard acc; tennis; fishing; games rm; CKE. *"V pleasant, beautiful site; most pitches sl, some o'look rv; superb clean unisex san facs; rvside path to attractive town; mkt Thurs; excel site, gd pitches; superb clean san facs; helpful staff; pool 800m; lots of activity on rv to watch."* **€15.00** **2023**

CHATEAU GONTIER *4F1* (12km SE Rural) *47.74985, -0.64258* **Camping des Rivières,** Rue du Port, 53200 Daon **02 43 06 94 78; www.campingdaon.fr**

WD nr

On town side of rv bdge, turn down lane & site ent on R at bottom of hill. 3*, Med, pt shd, EHU (10A) €3; sw nr; adv bkg acc; tennis nr; CKE. *"Vg clean & well-cared for site; some pitches diff to access; mini golf nr; boating on adj Rv Mayenne; great san facs."* **€14.00, 1 Apr-30 Sep.** **2022**

CHATEAU RENAULT *4G2* (7km S Urban) *47.54471, 0.88786* **Camp Municipal du Moulin,** Rue du Lavoir, 37110 Villedômer **02 47 55 05 50 or 02 47 55 00 04 (Mairie); mairie.villedomer@wanadoo.fr**

€1 WD nr nr nr

Fr A10 exit junc 18 onto D31 dir Château-Renault. Turn W onto D73 sp to Auzouer & Villedômer. Fr Château-Renault S on D910, site sp dir Villedômer. 1*, Sm, hdg, shd, EHU (10A) €3; adv bkg rec; rv fishing; fishing 2km. *"Gd, clean facs but old-fashioned; pitch yourself if warden not present; does not accept twin axles."* **€14.00, 15 Jun-15 Sep.** **2022**

CHATEAU RENAULT *4G2* (0.5km W Urban) *47.59283, 0.90687* **Camp Municipal du Parc de Vauchevrier,** Rue Paul-Louis-Courier, 37110 Château-Renault **02 47 29 54 43 or 02 47 29 85 50 (LS); camping.vauchevrier@orange.fr; ww.ville-chateau-renault.fr**

WD MSP nr nr nr (htd)

At Château-Renault foll sp to site 800m fr D910. If app fr a'route turn L on ent town & site on R of main rd adj Rv Brenne. 2*, Med, hdg, mkd, pt shd, EHU (6A) €2.20 (long lead poss req); tennis; fishing; CKE. *"Pleasant site by rv in park; lge pitches; friendly, helpful warden; clean, modern san facs, ltd LS; bar 300m; gd NH nr D910; no twin axles."* **€14.00, 1 May-15 Sep.** **2022**

CHATEAUBRIANT *2F4* (1.5km S Urban) *47.70305, -1.37789* **Camp Municipal Les Briotais,** Rue de Tugny, 44110 Châteaubriant **02 40 81 14 38 or 02 40 81 02 32; h.menet@ville-chateaubriant.fr; www.tourisme-chateaubriant.fr/camping-municipal-des-briotais**

€0.35 MSP nr nr nr

App fr Nantes (D178) site sp on S end of town. Or fr Angers on D963/D163 foll sp at 1st rndabt; fr town cent, foll sps thro town. 2*, Sm, hdg, pt shd, EHU €2.70; games area. *"11thC chateau in town; site locked o'night; site on municipal playing field; gd NH; pool in town."* **€6.00, 1 May-30 Sep.** **2022**

CHATEAUDUN *4F2* (2km N Urban) *48.08008, 1.33141* **Camp Municipal Le Moulin à Tan,** Rue de Chollet, 28200 Châteaudun **01 83 64 69 21; tourisme-chateaudun@wanadoo.fr**

WD MSP nr nr

App Châteaudun fr N on N10; turn R onto D3955 at 2nd rndabt (supmkt & Buffalo Grill on L); L at next rndabt onto D955; in 800m turn L into Rue de Chollet. App Châateaudun fr S on N10, turn L onto D3955 & then as bef. Site adj Rv Loir & well sp fr D955. 2*, Med, mkd, pt shd, EHU (6A) inc; TV; 5% statics; fishing; games area; canoeing; CKE. *"Gd touring base; quiet/under-used LS; helpful warden; some night flying fr nrby military airfield; htd covrd pool 2km; security gate 2.1m height; no twin axles; gd; rec open fr 0700 - 2200; walks fr site; automated credit card sys, req an account; OK NH."* **€14.00, 1 Apr-30 Sep.** **2024**

FRANCE

FRANCE

CHATEAULIN *2E2* (2km S Rural) *48.18754, -4.08515* **Camping La Pointe,** Route de St Coulitz, 29150 Châteaulin **02 98 86 51 53; lapointecamping@gmail.com; www.lapointesuperbecamping.com**

€1 (htd) WD MSP nr nr

Exit N165 onto D887 to Châteaulin; in town cent, cross bdge & turn L along rv on D770; after approx 750m, turn L at sp for St Coulitz; in 100m turn R into site. NB if app fr S to Châteaulin on D770, do not attempt to turn R at sp for St Coulitz (tight turn); go into town & turn round. 3*, Med, hdstg, hdg, mkd, pt shd, pt sl, EHU (10A) €4 (poss rev pol); bbq; phone; Eng spkn; adv bkg acc; rv fishing nrby; games rm; bike hire; CKE. *"Charming, peaceful, spacious site in wooded setting; well-run; helpful & friendly British owners; immac san facs; rvside path to town; gd cycling, walking & fishing; gd touring base; excel well-kept & equipped site."* **€18.00, 15 Apr-15 Oct.** **2024**

CHATEAULIN *2E2* (0.5km SW Urban) *48.19099, -4.08597* **Camping de Rodaven,** Rocade de Prat Bihan 29150 Châteaulin **02 56 70 98 91; campingchateaulin@night-day.fr; www.night-and-day.fr/camping/2-camping-de-rodaven**

€1.20 WD MSP nr nr sand 20km

Fr N165 dir Brest, exit junc 60 dir Chateaulin onto D887. In town ctr turn L onto D770 along rvbank, at rndabt take 2nd exit. Site on R in 800m. 3*, Med, mkd, hdg, shd, pt sl, EHU (10A) €2.90; bbq (charcoal, elec, gas); twin axles; 6% statics; Eng spkn; adv bkg acc; fishing; rv; CKE. *"Well-kept site; pleasant, helpful owner; htd covrd pool 300m; vg clean facs; walk along rv bank to town; gd touring base; Locronan vill well worth the visit; central to many attractions; walking/cycling adj site on banks of Aulne; excel."* **€20.60, 1 Apr-30 Sep.** **2023**

CHATEAUMEILLANT *7A4* (0.5km NW Rural) *46.56807, 2.18823* **Camp Municipal L'Etang Merlin,** Route de Vicq-Exemplet 18370 Chateaumeillant **02 48 61 31 38; www.camping-etangmerlin.e-monsite.com**

€1 WD MSP nr (htd)

Rec app fr W to avoid narr town rds. Site sp fr rndabt at W end of town on D80 N of Châteaumeillant on lakeside. Fr Culan by pass town on D943, then as above. 3*, Sm, hdg, mkd, pt shd, serviced pitches; EHU (5A) inc; bbq; TV; Eng spkn; adv bkg acc; ccard acc; fishing; tennis adj; CKE. *"Superb, well-kept site; lge pitches; friendly & helpful staff; basketball at sports complex adj; lake adj (no sw); rec arr early high ssn to secure pitch; easy walk to town."* **€11.50, 1 May-30 Sep.** **2020**

CHATEAUNEUF DU FAOU *2E2* (1km S Urban) *48.18306, -3.80986* **Gites & Camping de Penn ar Pont,** Rue de la Liberation, 29520 Chateauneuf du Faou **02 98 81 81 25; gites.pennarpont@orange.fr; www.pennarpont.com**

€2 WD MSP nr nr

Take D36 S, go over bdge, site at 1st R turn. Sm, mkd, hdg, pt shd, terr, EHU (16A) €3.50; bbq; Eng spkn; adv bkg acc. *"Steep rd on site, diff for lge o'fits; jazz fest last w/end of July; gd; san facs clean but needs upgrade; typical sm municipal site in beautiful setting."* **€12.70, 1 Apr-31 Oct.** **2023**

CHATEAUNEUF SUR ISERE *9C2* (5km W Rural) *44.99710, 4.89333* **Le Soleil Fruité,** 480 chemin des Communaux, 26300 Châteauneuf-sur Isère **04 75 84 19 70; contact@lesoleifruite.com; www.lesoleilfruite.com**

(covrd, htd)

Fr Valence, take A7 dir Lyon. Take exit 14 Valence Nord twd Bourg les Valence. At rndabt take 1st exit onto N7. Turn R onto D877 and foll sp. 4*, Med, hdg, mkd, pt shd, EHU (6A); bbq; TV; Eng spkn; adv bkg acc; bike hire; games area; waterslide; CCI. *"Immac site; lovely pool; gd rest; sh drive to vill."* **€44.00, 19 Apr-15 Sep.** **2024**

CHATEAUNEUF SUR LOIRE *4F3* (1km S Rural) *47.85643, 2.22426* **FFCC Camping de la Maltournée,** Route de Châteauneuf, 45110 Châteauneuf-sur-Loire **02 38 58 42 46 or 06 32 11 41 13 (mob); contact@lamaltournee.fr; www.lamaltournee.fr**

€1.50 (htd) WD MSP

S fr Chateauneuf cent, cross rv on D11; take 1st L, site in 300m on S bank of Rv Loire. 2*, Lge, pt shd, EHU (10A) inc; 75% statics; adv bkg acc; canoeing; CKE. *"Well-kept, busy site; helpful, pleasant staff; clean, modern san facs; chem disp v basic via narr pipe; some m'van pitches beside rv; conv Orléans; security barrier; poss ssn workers; gd cycling base for Evro Velo."* **€18.00, 1 Apr-31 Oct.** **2024**

CHATEAUPONSAC *7A3* (0.2km SW Rural) *46.13163, 1.27083* **Camping De La Gartempe,** Ave de Ventenat, 87290 Chateauponsac **05 55 76 55 33 or 07 49 40 39 34; campingdelagartempe@gmail.com; www.campingdelagartempe.fr**

12 €1 (htd) WD nr

Fr N exit A20 junc 23.1 sp Châteauponsac; go thro vill, well sp on L on rvside. Fr S exit A20 junc 24 sp Châteauponsac & then as above. 3*, Sm, hdg, mkd, pt shd, terr, EHU (6A) €3 (poss rev pol); Eng spkn; adv bkg acc; kayaking; archery; CKE. *"Pleasant site; gd san facs; pitches muddy in wet; not suitable lge m'vans; activities down steep hill by rv; poss noise fr parties in rest; children's activites; adj to holiday bungalows/gites; helpful owners; nice vill."* **€20.00** **2023**

CHATEAUROUX *4H2* (2km N Rural) *46.82368, 1.69496* **Camp Municipal Le Rochat-Belle Isle,** Rue du Rochat, 36000 Châteauroux **06 02 71 14 55 or 02 54 08 96 29; campinglerochat@gmail.com; www.camping-lerochat.fr**

12 €1.50 WD MSP nr nr nr

Exit A20 junc 13 onto D943/N143 S; foll sp Châteauroux; site sp bef town. Site on banks of Rv Indre, just S of Lac de Belle-Isle. Sp in town. 3*, Med, pt shd, EHU (5-10A) inc; gas; Eng spkn. *"Leisure park adj with pool & windsurfing on lake; friendly welcome & helpful; gd, modern, clean san facs; poss music till late w/end high ssn; poss travellers; pleasant walk into town along rv; lge brocante mkt 1st Sun of month Oct-Jul; vg; nice site; excel family site."* **€21.20** **2023**

CHATEL DE NEUVRE *9A1* (1.3km NE Rural) *46.4131, 3.31884* **Camping Deneuvre,** Route De Moulins, 03500 Châtel-de-Neuvre **04 70 42 04 51; campingdeneuvre@wanadoo.fr; www.camping-deneuvre.fr**

€1 WD MSP

S fr Moulins on D2009; sp N of vill on E side of D2009. 3*, Med, mkd, hdstg, pt shd, EHU (4A) inc; gas; Eng spkn; adv bkg acc; canoe hire; CKE. *"Site by Rv Allier in nature reserve; clean but not smart; useful NH without unhitching; friendly welcome; excel clean san facs; ltd facs LS; meals avail; splendid place for walking, fishing, cycling & birdwatching; diff ent/exit for lge o'fits; no twin axles."* **€20.00, 1 Apr-30 Sep.** **2022**

CHATEL DE NEUVRE *9A1* (0.4km W Rural) *46.40320, 3.31350* **Canoe Camping la Courtine,** 7 Rue de St Laurant, 03500 Châtel-de-Neuvre **04 70 42 06 21 or 06 24 93 01 35; mail@camping-lacourtine.com; www.camping-lacourtine.com**

12 (htd) WD MSP nr nr

Fr N on D2009 to cent of vill, turn L at x-rds onto D32; site in 500m. 2*, Sm, hdstg, mkd, pt shd, EHU (6-10A) €3-5 (poss rev pol); TV; Eng spkn; adv bkg acc; CKE. *"Friendly welcome; untidy ent masks v nice site; German family-owned site; access to Rv Allier for canoeing, fishing; walking in nature reserve; liable to flood & poss clsd LS, phone ahead to check; conv LS NH; lovely woodland setting."* **€18.00** **2023**

CHATELAILLON PLAGE *7A1* (2km N Urban) *46.08632, -1.09489* **Camping L'Océan,** Ave d'Angoulins, 17340 Châtelaillon-Plage **05 46 56 87 97; reception@oceancamping.fr; www.oceancamping.fr**

€2 WD nr nr nr sand 500m

Fr La Rochelle take D602 to Châtelaillon-Plage, site sp on L in 300m (after passing g'ge & L'Abbaye camp site). 3*, Med, hdg, mkd, EHU (10A) €5; bbq; phone; bus; Eng spkn; ccard acc; waterslide; ice. *"Very nice, excel site; gd cycle rtes; top class facs; occasional noise fr rlwy & clay pigeon range; park & ride 400m; beautiful man made lake/beach; new owner (2017)."* **€41.30, 15 May-17 Sep.** **2023**

CHATELAILLON PLAGE *7A1* (2.5km SE Coastal) *46.05491, -1.08331* **Camping Au Port Punay,** Les Boucholeurs, Allée Bernard Moreau, 17340 Châtelaillon-Plage **05 17 81 00 00; contact@camping-port-punay.com; www.camping-port-punay.com**

€2.50 nr sand 500m

Fr N exit D137 La Rochell-Rochefort rd onto D109; strt on at 1st rndabt, L at 2nd rndabt; then cont for 2.8km to end (harbour); turn L, keep R along narr one-way st; at next junc to L, site sp. Fr S exit D137 onto D203 sp Les Boucholeurs; at rndabt in 1km foll site sp to edge of Châtelaillon & turn R, foll sp. Site in 500m. 4*, Lge, pt shd, EHU (10A) €5; gas; TV; 25% statics; Eng spkn; adv bkg acc; bike hire; games area. *"Busy but quiet site; immac san facs; friendly, energetic, helpful owners; steel pegs req; sm pitches; excel; lovely area & location."* **€44.80, 5 May-17 Sep.** **2023**

See advertisement

FRANCE

CHÂTEL-GUYON *9B1* (5km NW Rural) *45.91597, 3.07682* **Camping Le Ranch des Volcans,** Route de la Piscine, 63140 Châtel-Guyon **04 73 86 02 47; contact@ranchdesvolcans.com; www.ranchdesvolcans.com**

€1.50

Fr Riom take D227 to Châtelguyon, site on R on o'skts of town. Tight turn into ent. 4*, Lge, pt shd, pt sl, EHU (6A) inc; gas; red long stay; Eng spkn; adv bkg acc; tennis; poss open until 31 Dec. *"Pleasant, well-run site; san facs dated; some pitches steep & poss uneven; sh walk to town; m'vans/campers not allowed up to Puy-de-Dôme - must use bus provided; conv for A71, gd NH; gd quiet site; conv for Clermont-Ferrand and Puy de Dôme."* **€25.70, 1 Apr-29 Oct.** **2023**

CHATILLON COLIGNY *4F3* (0.5km S Rural) *47.81717, 2.84447* **Camp Municipal La Lancière,** Rue de la Lancière, 45230 Châtillon-Coligny **01 83 64 69 21; contact@campingcarpark.com; www.chatillon-coligny.fr/decouvrir-se-divertir/se-loger-a-chatillon-coligny/camping-municipal-de-la-lanciere/**

nr nr nr

N fr Briare twd Montargis on N7; E fr Les Bézards on D56 twd Châtillon-Coligny; site sp on ent town on R immed bef canal bdge. Fr town cross Canal de Briare on D93 twd Bléneau; immed turn S along canal rd sp Camping & Marina. 2*, Med, mkd, pt shd, EHU (3-6A) €2-3.10 (poss long lead req & rev pol); 25% statics; games area; rv fishing; CKE. *"Attractive, peaceful, tidy site; many lge pitches; clean, dated facs; site yourself, warden calls; gd walking/cycling along canal & historic vill; superb site for simple caravaning, excel value."* **€11.00, 1 July-30 Sep.** **2024**

CHATILLON EN DIOIS *9D3* (0.6km E Urban) *44.69450, 5.48817* **Camp Municipal Les Chaussières,** 26410 Châtillon-en-Diois **04 75 21 10 30; contact@leschaussieres.fr; www.camping-chatillonendiois.com**

€2.10 nr nr

Fr Die take D93 S for 6km then L on D539 to Châtillon (8km) site sp on R on ent to town. 2*, Med, mkd, pt shd, EHU (10A) €3.60; bbq; 30% statics; phone; Eng spkn; adv bkg acc; ccard acc; ice; canoeing; fishing; cycling; horseriding; tennis; CKE. *"Wardens off site 1130- 1630; pool adj; pleasant sweet site, wardens friendly and helpful."* **€26.00, 1 Apr-5 Nov.** **2024**

CHATILLON SUR CHALARONNE *9A2* (0.5km SE Urban) *46.11622, 4.96172* **FFCC Camp Municipal du Vieux Moulin,** Ave Jean Jaurès, 01400 Châtillon-sur-Chalaronne **04 74 55 04 79; camping@chatillon-sur-chalaronne.org; www.camping-vieuxmoulin.com**

€2 nr nr nr

Exit A6 junc 30 to Châtillon-sur-Chalaronne; pick up D7 on S site of vill; site on R in 400m. Ave Jean Jaurès is pt of D7. Site sp in town. 4*, Med, hdstg, hdg, shd, EHU (10A) €4 (long lead req on some pitches); 50% statics; phone; adv bkg acc; ccard acc; fishing; CKE. *"Lovely site in picturesque area; helpful warden; immac facs, ltd LS; check office opening hrs for early dep; leisure cent adj; if office clsd ring bell, warden will open barrier; lovely medieval town cent; pool adj inc; excel model rlwy; bar adj; mkt Sat; site remains excel, new municipal pool under construction next door."* **€25.80, 15 Apr-30 Sep.** **2024**

CHATILLON SUR INDRE *4H2* (0.8km N Rural) *46.99116, 1.17382* **Camping De Mon Village (formerly Les Rives de L'Indre),** Rue de Moulin de la Grange, 36700 Châtillon-sur-Indre **07 61 39 81 62 or 02 54 38 17 86; camping-chatillon-sur-indre@orange.fr; www.chatillon-sur-indre.fr**

nr nr

Site well sp in vill. N twd Loches then foll sp. 3*, Med, hdg, mkd, pt shd, EHU (6A) €3; bbq; CKE. *"Lovely, relaxed, well-kept site; friendly, helpful warden; 4 chalets; gd, clean san facs; conv Loire chateaux; gd birdwatching area; interesting old town; htd pool 400m (proper sw trunks only); lge mkt Fri; excel value; call warden if barrier clsd; warden onsite 0800-1100/1630-2000."* **€13.30, 1 Apr-31 Oct.** **2023**

CHATILLON SUR SEINE *6F1* (1km E Urban) *47.85955, 4.57975* **Camp Municipal Louis Rigoly,** Esplanade Saint Vorles, 21400 Châtillon-sur-Seine **03 80 91 03 05 or 03 80 91 13 19 (LS); contact@camping-chatillonsurseine.com; camping-chatillonsurseine.com**

nr

Fr N, cross rv bdge (Seine); cont approx 400m twd town cent; at lge metal fountain forming rndabt turn L, foll sp to site. Fr S turn R & foll camping sp. Rec lge o'fits proceed thro town to metal fountain. Turn R & foll sp to site. 2*, Med, hdg, mkd, pt shd, pt sl, EHU (6A) €2.30-4.65; gas; Eng spkn; adv bkg acc; jacuzzi; tennis; fishing; CKE. *"Pretty site adj park; clean, tidy, well-spaced pitches; helpful, welcoming warden; htd pool adj; excel, clean new san facs; easy walk to old town & famous museum housing Celtic Vix treasures; vg; excel disabled san facs."* **€17.30, 1 Apr-30 Sep.** **2023**

CHATRE, LA *7A4* (3km N Rural) *46.60131, 1.97808* **Camp Municipal Solange-Sand,** 2 Rue du Pont, 36400 Montgivray **02 54 06 10 36 or 02 54 06 10 34; mairie.montgivray@wanadoo.fr; www.montgivray.fr/camping/**

Fr La Châtre take rd to Montgivray, foll camping sp. Fr Châteauroux on D943 SE twd La Châtre turn R 2km S of Nohant on D72. Site behind church. 2*, Med, mkd, pt shd, EHU (10A) inc (poss rev pol); bbq; CKE. *"Pleasant site in chateau grnds; gd san facs; gd access; warden calls am & pm; gd walks; quiet but occ noise fr nrby hall; excel; v gd for stop over or sh stay; welcoming staff; town 2km."* **€13.60, 15 Mar-30 Sep. 2022**

CHAUMONT SUR LOIRE *4G2* (1km NE Rural) *47.48444, 1.19417* **Camp Municipal Grosse Grève,** Ave des Trouillas, 41150 Chaumont-sur-Loire **02 54 20 95 22 or 02 54 20 98 41 (Mairie); mairie.chaumontsloire@wanadoo.fr; www.camping-chaumont-sur-loire.com**

(htd) nr nr

Fr N side of rv on D952 cross bdge to Chaumont on D1, turn R immed & R under bdge. Site sp in vill on D751. 2*, Med, pt shd, EHU (6-16A) €2-3.50 (poss long lead req); bbq; canoeing; tennis; fishing; bike hire; horseriding; CKE. *"Pleasant site by rv; gd, clean san facs; no twin axles; interesting chateau; cycle track along Loire; gd value; excel."* **€12.00, 29 Apr-30 Sep. 2022**

"I need an on-site restaurant"

We do our best to make sure site information is correct, but it is always best to check any must-have facilities are still available or will be open during your visit.

CHAUVIGNY *7A3* (1km E Urban) *46.57072, 0.65326* **Camp Municipal de la Fontaine,** Rue de la Fontaine, 86300 Chauvigny **05 49 46 31 94; camping-chauvigny@cg86.fr; www.chauvigny.fr**

€1.80 (htd) nr

N151 fr Poitiers to Chauvigny. Turn L in cent Chauvigny just bef gate. Site well sp fr Chauvigny. 3*, Med, pt shd, EHU (15A) inc; bbq; adv bkg acc; tennis 1km; bike hire; CKE. *"Popular; well-kept; well-run site adj park & lake; views of castle; lge pitches; helpful, friendly staff; excel immac san facs; o'night m'vans area; delightful walk to cent; mkts Tue, Thur & Sat; a real find; gd value; rec; vg; interesting town; gd touring base; €20 for barrier key; v interesting beautiful town & location."* **€19.50, 2 Apr-30 Sep. 2023**

CHEF BOUTONNE *7A2* (2km W Rural) *46.10767, -0.09342* **Camping Le Moulin,** 1 Route de Niort, 79110 Chef-Boutonne **05 49 29 73 46 or 06 89 60 00 49 (mob); info@campingchef.com; www.campingchef.com**

12 €1.50 (htd) nr (htd)

Fr D950 to or fr Poitiers, turn E onto D740 to Chef-Boutonne, site on R. Fr N10 turn onto D948 to Sauzé-Vaussais then L onto D1 to Chef-Boutonne; then take D740 dir Brioux-sur-Boutonne; site on L. 3*, Sm, hdstg, mkd, hdg, pt shd, EHU (10A); bbq (charcoal, elec, gas); twin axles; red long stay; 10% statics; Eng spkn; adv bkg acc; ccard acc; ice; CKE. *"Well-kept site; lge pitches; friendly, helpful British owners; v gd rest; much bird life; conv Futuroscope & La Rochelle; vg; clean san facs refurbed with disabled facs (2018); peaceful; mv service pnt 1km; rest & bar refurb (2018); site acc rallies; excel; chge for wifi."* **€21.60 2024**

"Satellite navigation makes touring much easier"

Remember most sat navs don't know if you're towing or in a larger vehicle – always use yours alongside maps and site directions.

CHEMILLE *2G4* (1.5km SW Rural) *47.20182, -0.73486* **FFCC Camping Coulvée,** Route de Cholet, 49120 Chemillé **02 41 30 42 42 or 02 41 30 39 97 (Mairie); camping-chemille-49@wanadoo.fr; www.camping-coulvee-chemille.com**

€1.70 sand

Fr Chemillé dir Cholet on D160, turn R in 1km. 3*, Sm, hdg, pt shd, terr, EHU (10A) €3.60; bbq; sw; red long stay; Eng spkn; adv bkg acc; CKE. *"Clean facs; helpful staff; gd pitches, soft when wet; poss unrel opening dates; pedalos; mkt Thurs; mkd cycling and walking rtes fr site."* **€23.60, 1 May-15 Sep. 2022**

CHENONCEAUX *4G2* (1.5km E Rural) *47.32905, 1.08816* **Camping de l'Ecluse,** Route de la Plage, 37150 Chisseaux **02 47 23 87 10 or 06 15 83 21 20 (mob); sandrine@campingdelecluse-37.fr; www.campingdelecluse-37.fr**

€1.50 nr

E fr Chenonceaux on D176; cross bdge; immed hard R & foll rv bank; site in 300m. 2*, Med, mkd, pt shd, EHU (16A) €3.90 (rev pol); phone; Eng spkn; adv bkg acc; ccard acc; canoeing; watersports; fishing; CKE. *"Rv trips; fishing; gd walking; some rd/rlwy noise; gd."* **€12.50, 1 Mar-31 Oct. 2024**

FRANCE

CHENONCEAUX *4G2* (1.5km S Rural) *47.32765, 1.08936* **Camping Le Moulin Fort,** Port Oliver, 37150 Francueil **02 47 23 86 22; lemoulinfort@wanadoo.fr; www.lemoulinfort.com**

€3

Exit A85 junc 11 N, then take D976 E dir Montrichard; site on S bank of Rv Cher just off D976. Fr Tours take D976 sp Vierzon; keep on D976 by-passing Bléré until sm rndabt (5km) where site sp to L twd rv. Take sm rd on R to site, bef actually x-ing bdge. Site well sp. 3*, Med, hdg, mkd, pt shd, EHU (6A) inc (long lead poss req); gas; bbq (charcoal, gas); TV; Eng spkn; adv bkg rec; ccard acc; games rm; bike hire; fishing; CKE. *"Lovely, well-kept site on rv bank; beautiful area; gd san facs; easy access most pitches; many sm & v shady pitches; no o'fits over 8m high ssn; lge o'fits check in adv; some pitches suitable for lge o'fits; footpath by rv with view of chateau; gd cycle rtes; poss security probs due access to site fr rv bank; Fri mkt Montrichard & Sun mkt Amboise; excel; well laid site to rv view for many pitches; use of pool diff for those with red mobility due to poor design of ladder; new owners (2023); rest redeveloped, food is simple, inexpensive and excel."*
€32.20, 7 May - 27 Sep, L08. **2023**

CHERBOURG *1C4* (18km NE Coastal) *49.6928, -1.4387* **Camping De La Plage,** 2 Village de Fréval, 50840 Fermanville **02 33 54 38 84; campingdelaplage.fermanville@gmail.com; www.campingdelaplage-fermanville.com**

€2.50 300m, sand

Fr Cherbourg on D116 dir Barfleur, site in 12km on L. 3*, Med, hdg, unshd, EHU (10A); 70% statics; Eng spkn; adv bkg req. *"Friendly owner; conv for ferry & D-Day landing beaches; poss unrel opening dates; vg."*
€24.00, 1 Apr-15 Oct. **2023**

CHERBOURG *1C4* (10km E Coastal) *49.66720, -1.48772* **Camping L'Anse du Brick,** 18 L'Anse du Brick, 50330 Maupertus-sur-Mer **02 33 54 33 57; contact@adbcamping.com; www.anse-du-brick.com or www.les-castels.com**

€5 (htd, indoor) sand adj

At rndabt at port take 2nd exit sp Caen, Rennes & Mont St Michel; at 2nd rndabt take 3rd exit sp Caen & Mont St Michel (N13); at 3rd rndabt take 2nd exit onto dual c'way sp St Lô, Caen (N13), Bretteville-sur-Mer; exit on D116 & foll sp thro Bretteville-en-Saire (take care lge speed hump in Le Becquet); turn R for site just after R-hand blind bend & turning for Maupertus; up v steep incline. 5*, Med, mkd, hdg, shd, sl, terr, serviced pitches; EHU (10A) inc (poss rev pol); gas; bbq; sw nr; TV; adv bkg acc; ccard acc; archery; waterslide; bike hire; tennis; games rm; kayak rental; CKE. *"Attractive, well-kept site in beautiful setting; conv ferry; gd clean san facs; max 2 dogs per pitch; some pitches for lge o'fits; no o'fits over 8m; conv Landing Beaches, Barfleur, coastal nature reserve."*
€60.00, 8 Apr - 25 Sep, N14. **2022**

CHERBOURG *1C4* (3.6km NW Urban/Coastal) *49.65576, -1.65257* **Camp Municipal de la Saline,** Rue Jean Bart, 50120 Equeurdreville-Hainneville **02 33 93 88 33 or 02 33 53 96 00 (Mairie); mairie-equeurdreville@dialoleane.com; www.equeurdreville.com**

12 €0.50 (htd) nr nr nr sand adj

Fr ferry terminal foll D901 & sp Beaumont-Hague. On dual c'way beside sea look out for site sp to L at traff lts. 2*, Med, hdg, mkd, hdstg, pt shd, pt sl, terr, EHU (10A) €4.56; 50% statics; phone; adv bkg acc; fishing; CKE. *"Sea views; boules & skateboard park adj; aquatic cent 500m; mv service pnt nr; cycle path to town; secured at night; excel NH for ferry."*
€17.50 **2022**

CHEVERNY *4G2* (3km S Rural) *47.47798, 1.45070* **Camping Les Saules,** 102 Route de Contres, 41700 Cheverny **02 54 79 90 01; contact@camping-cheverny.com; www.camping-cheverny.com**

€2 (htd) (htd)

Exit A10 junc 17 dir Blois Sud onto D765 to Romorantin. At Cour-Cheverny foll sp Cheverny & chateau. Fr S on D956 turn R onto D102 just N of Contres, site on L just bef Cheverny. Well sp fr all dirs. 4*, Lge, mkd, shd, EHU (10A) €3.50 (poss long lead req); gas; bbq; red long stay; TV; 2% statics; phone; Eng spkn; adv bkg rec; ccard acc; fishing; golf nr; games rm; tennis nr; excursions; bike hire; CKE. *"Beautiful, well-run site; friendly, welcoming, helpful owners; excel san facs; castle 2 mil; excel pool; all pitches under trees; muddy after heavy rain; many excel cycle & walking rtes nr; Cheverny chateau worth visit; little train & boat rides; excel; gd rest."*
€36.00, 1 Apr-17 Sep, L01. **2022**

CHINON *4G1* (0.5km SW Rural) *47.16397, 0.23377* **Camping de L'Ile Auger,** Quai Danton, 37500 Chinon **02 47 93 08 35; campingchinon@night-day.fr; www.night-and-day.fr/camping/14-camping-de-lile-auger**

€1.20 nr

On S side of rv at bdge. Fr S foll sp Chinon St Jacques; when app 2nd bdge on 1-way 'loop', avoid R lane indicated for x-ing bdge & cont strt past S end of main bdge to site on R. Fr N foll sp 'Centre Ville' round castle, cross bdge, site on R. Well sp in town & opp castle. 2*, Lge, mkd, hdg, pt shd, EHU (12A) inc (poss rev pol); red long stay; TV (pitch); phone; ccard acc; canoe hire; CKE. *"Excel, well-kept site in gd location; twin axles discretionary; poss midge prob; poss travellers; gd cycle rtes; gd views of chateau; rec; automatic ent barrier; htd pool 300m; well laid out; new san facs (2017); 5min walk to town; exc value; hg rec boat trip on Rv Vienne; gd value; gd touring base."* **€16.00, 1 Apr-3 Oct.** **2024**

CIOTAT, LA *10F3* (4km NE Coastal) *43.18733, 5.65810* **Campsite La Baie des Anges,** Chemin des Plaines Baronnes, 13600 La Ciotat **04 88 80 89 58; www.camping-la-ciotat.com**

nr nr nr shgl 800m

Fr La Ciotat, foll D559 coast rd sp Bandol & Toulon. Site in 4km, look for lge sp on L. Caution x-ing dual c'way. 4*, V lge, shd, pt sl, terr, EHU (6A) (poss rev pol); gas; 80% statics; bus 300m; Eng spkn; adv bkg acc; ccard acc; tennis; CKE. *"Sea views many pitches; friendly staff; gd touring base; v nice."*
€35.00, 12 Apr-1 Oct. **2024**

CIVRAY *7A2* (1km NE Urban) *46.15835, 0.30169* **Camping Le Rivage Civraisien (formerly Camping de Civray),** Route de Roche, 86400 Civray **05 17 34 50 02; www.camping-lerivagecivraisien.fr**

nr (htd)

Civray 9km E of N10 halfway bet Poitiers & Angoulême. Site outside town SE of junc of D1 & D148. Sp on D148 & on S by-pass. Avoid town cent narr rds. 2*, Med, pt shd, pt sl, EHU (6-10A) €3 (poss long lead req); bbq; sw nr; 50% statics; Eng spkn; ccard acc; golf; bike hire; fishing adj; CKE. *"Pleasant rvside site, walk to town; pitches soft when wet; vg rest; conv town cent; mkt Wed; vg; new owners; ltd san facs."*
€20.00, 7 Apr-15 Oct. **2023**

CLAIRVAUX LES LACS *6H2* (1.2km SE Rural) *46.56431, 5.7562* **Yelloh! Village Le Fayolan,** Chemin de Langard, 39130 Clairvaux-les-Lacs **03 84 25 88 52; fayolan@odesia.eu; www.campinglefayolan.fr**

€6 (covrd, htd)

Fr town foll campsite sp, last site along lane adj to lake. 4*, V lge, mkd, hdg, pt shd, terr, serviced pitches; EHU (6A) inc (poss rev pol); gas; sw nr; twin axles; TV; 16% statics; Eng spkn; adv bkg rec; ccard acc; waterslide; games rm; tennis 1km; bike hire; sauna; CKE. *"Excel, clean site; extra for lakeside pitches high ssn; pleasant sm town in easy walking dist; lovely area."*
€43.00, 3 May - 8 Sep, J11. **2022**

CLAIRVAUX LES LACS *6H2* (1km S Rural) *46.56761, 5.75480* **Camping La Grisière et Europe Vacances,** 7 Chemin Langard, 39130 Clairvaux-les-Lacs **03 84 25 80 48; grisiere@clicochic.com; www.clicochic.com/camping-france -franche_comte-grisiere-FR.html**

€1.40 (htd)

Turn S off D678 in Clairvaux opp church onto D118; fork R in 500m & foll site sps to lake. Sp in vill. Camping La Grisière ent after Camping Les Lacs. 3*, V lge, mkd, pt shd, pt sl, EHU (6-10A) inc; bbq; sw nr; TV; 5% statics; phone; bus 700m; Eng spkn; ccard acc; bike hire; watersports; tennis 1km; fishing; canoe hire; CKE. *"Lovely views of lake in beautiful area; lge pitches; excel site; quiet; few facs."*
€22.70, 1 May-15 Sep. **2023**

CLAIRVAUX LES LACS *6H2* (10km SW Rural) *46.52311, 5.67350* **Camping de Surchauffant,** Pont de la Pyle, 39270 La Tour-du-Meix **03 84 25 41 08; info@camping-surchauffant.fr; www.camping-surchauffant.fr**

€1.60 nr

Fr Clairvaux S on D27 or D49 to D470. Foll sp Lac de Vouglans, site sp. 3*, Med, mkd, pt shd, pt sl, EHU (6A) €3; bbq; TV; 10% statics; Eng spkn; adv bkg acc; ccard acc; watersports; sailing. *"Vg facs; lovely location; dir access to lake; hiking trails."*
€19.00, 22 Apr-19 Sep. **2022**

CLAIRVAUX LES LACS *6H2* (7km W Rural) *46.59976, 5.68824* **Sites & Paysages Camping - Camping Beauregard,** 2 Grande Rue, 39130 Mesnois **03 84 48 32 51; reception@juracampingbeauregard.com; www.juracampingbeauregard.com**

€2.20 (htd) nr nr nr (htd) sand 800m

S fr Lons-le-Saunier on D52/D678, about 1km bef Pont-de-Poitte turn L on D151. Site 1km on L opp rd junc to Pont-de-Poitte. 3*, Lge, hdstg, hdg, mkd, pt shd, pt sl, terr, EHU (6A) €4 (poss long lead req); gas; 10% statics; Eng spkn; adv bkg acc; tennis; bike hire; games rm. *"Super site, clean & well-run; different sized pitches; excel san facs, ltd LS; excel rest; kayaking nr; poss muddy when wet; new indoor pool with jacuzzi and sauna (2012), extremely gd quality."*
€31.00, 28 Mar-30 Sep, J13. **2024**

CLAMECY *4G4* (5km NE Rural) *47.51665, 3.48001* **Camping Le Bois Joli,** 2 Route de Villeprenoy, 89480 Andryes **03 86 81 70 48; info@campingauboisjoli.com; www.campingauboisjoli.com**

€3 (htd)

S on N151 fr Auxerre to Coulanges-sur-Yonne; W on D39 to Andryes. Foll sps `Camping Andryes'; site in 500m after vill. 4*, Med, mkd, shd, terr, EHU (10A) €4.80 (poss rev pol); gas; bbq; sw nr; TV; 10% statics; phone; Eng spkn; ccard acc; fishing 2km; bike hire; tennis; CKE. *"Dutch owners; beautiful countryside; boat hire 2km; gd pitches; muddy in rain; excel facs & site; quiet; nice site in wooded area."*
€44.00, 1 Apr - 31 Oct. **2022**

CLAMECY *4G4* (1.3km SE Urban) *47.45133, 3.52770* **Camp Municipal du Pont-Picot,** Rue de Chevroches, 58500 Clamecy **07 86 86 14 31; clamecycamping@orange.fr; www.clamecy.fr**

nr

On N151 fr S, exit N151 at rndabt 3km SW of town cent, cross level x-ing then R at rndabt on D23, take 1st L, site sp in 2.4km. Narr app rd. App fr N or E thro town not rec. Do not use sat nav thro town. 2*, Med, pt shd, pt sl, EHU (6A) inc; sw; CKE. *"Pleasant, peaceful site bet rv & canal in beautiful location; friendly, helpful staff; facs poss inadequate when busy; town 10 min walk on towpath; gd cycling; gd NH; narr bdge just bef ent."* **€17.00, 1 Apr-30 Sep.** **2024**

FRANCE

CLAMECY 4G4 (8km SE Rural) 47.41390, 3.60828 **Camp Municipal Les Fontaines,** 58530 Brèves **03 86 24 25 26; mairie-breves@wanadoo.fr**

On D985 (Clamecy-Corbigny) at Brèves. Both app clearly sp. 2*, Med, unshd, pt sl, EHU (6A) €2; bbq; 4% statics; phone; adv bkg rec; CKE. *"Quiet site in pretty area nr Rv Yonne & canal; friendly staff; grnd soft after heavy rain; ltd level sites for m'van vg."* **€15.00, 7 May-28 Sep.** **2024**

CLAYETTE, LA 9A2 (0.5km E Urban) 46.29159, 4.32020 **Camping des Bruyères,** 9 Route de Gibles, 71800 La Clayette **09 72 77 61 85 or 03 85 28 09 15; contact@campingbruyeres.com; campingbruyeres.com**

€1.60 (htd) nr nr

Site on D79, 100m fr D987 & lake. 3*, Med, hdstg, hdg, mkd, shd, sl, EHU (6A) inc; gas; bbq; 10% statics; phone; adv bkg acc; boating; games area; tennis; CKE. *"Pleasant, well-kept site o'looking lake & chateau; friendly, helpful staff; gd-sized pitches; htd pool adj Jun-Aug inc; excel; 20 min walk to town; supmkt 10 min walk."* **€25.00, 18 Apr-30 Sep.** **2024**

CLAYETTE, LA 9A2 (13km S Rural) 46.2011, 4.3391 **FFCC Camping Les Feuilles,** 18 Rue de Châtillon, 71170 Chauffailles **03 85 26 48 12; campingchauffailles@gmail.com or chalets@chalets-decouverte.com; www.chauffailles.fr**

(htd) nr

S fr La Clayette on D985 (dir Les Echarmeaux), turn R at camp sp down hill & cross Rv Botoret to site. 3*, Med, mkd, hdstg, pt shd, EHU (5A) inc; TV; Eng spkn; adv bkg req; games rm; tennis; fishing; CKE. *"Attractive site; poss rallies May/June & Sep (poss noisy); gd san facs but hot water to shwrs & dishwashing only; easy walk to interesting town; pool adj; sep m'van Aire de Service adj rear ent."* **€19.60, 1 Apr-30 Sep.** **2024**

CLECY 3D1 (1.4km E Rural) 48.91491, -0.47374 **FFCC Camping Les Rochers des Parcs,** La Cour, 14570 Clécy **02 31 69 70 36; camping.normandie@gmail.com; www.camping-normandie-clecy.fr**

€1.60 (htd) nr nr

Fr Condé take D562 dir Caen; turn R onto D133a sp Clécy & Le Vey; do not take turning to Clécy cent but cont downhill, past museum on L & then over bdge; turn R in 150m at campsite sp; site on R. 3*, Med, mkd, hdstg, pt shd, pt sl, EHU (6A) €3.50; bbq; red long stay; 10% statics; phone; Eng spkn; games area; bike hire; rv fishing. *"Lovely rvside situation; friendly, helpful owner; facs poss stretched high ssn & ltd LS; excel cent for walking."* **€26.50, 1 Apr-30 Sep.** **2023**

CLERMONT FERRAND 9B1 (16km SE Rural) 45.70027, 3.16953 **Camping Le Clos Auroy,** Rue de la Narse, 63670 Orcet **04 73 84 26 97; www.camping-le-clos-auroy.com**

12 €17.5 p/w (htd) (htd)

S on A75 take exit 5 sp Orcet; foll D213 to Orcet for 2km, at rndabt onto D52, take 1st L, site on R. Do not foll SatNav to site. 4*, Med, hdstg, mkd, hdg, pt shd, terr, EHU (10A) inc; gas; red long stay; 10% statics; phone; Eng spkn; adv bkg acc; ccard acc; tennis; rv fishing 500m; CKE. *"Excel, well-kept; site poss open all year; easy access; lge pitches, poss v high hedges; superb htd san facs; pitches by rv poss liable to flood; extra charge for sh stay m'vans; ltd fresh water points & diff to use for refill; vg winter site; interesting town; gd dog walks adj; snack & bar only open high ssn; vg value; helpful staff; gd site."* **€33.80** **2024**

CLERMONT FERRAND 9B1 (9km SE Urban) 45.74015, 3.22247 **Camp Municipal Le Pré des Laveuses,** Rue des Laveuses, 63800 Cournon-d'Auvergne **04 73 84 81 30; camping@cournon-auvergne.fr; www.cournon-auvergne.fr/camping**

€2.70 (htd)

Fr S o'skts Clermont-Ferrand take D212 E to Cournon & foll sp in town; by Rv Allier, 1km E of Cournon. 3*, Lge, mkd, pt shd, EHU (5-10A) €3.30; sw nr; 40% statics; Eng spkn; ccard acc; fishing; boating; CKE. *"Well-kept site - even LS; lge pitches; helpful manager; sports grnd adj; excel; clean new facs."* **€33.00, 1 Apr-25 Oct.** **2024**

"There aren't many sites open at this time of year"

If you're travelling outside peak season remember to call ahead to check site opening dates – even if the entry says 'open all year'.

CLERMONT FERRAND 9B1 (6km SW Urban) 45.73866, 3.06168 **Camp Municipal Le Chanset,** Rue de camping, 63122 Ceyrat **04 73 61 30 73; contact@camping-ceyrat.fr; www.camping-ceyrat.fr**

€1.80 (htd) (htd)

Exit A75 junc 2 onto D2089 dir Aubière/Beaumont. Foll sp Beaumont then in approx 7km at rndabt junc foll sp Ceyrat. Uphill into Ceyrat; curve R to traff lts; cross main rd & take L fork up hill. Site at top on R - turn poss diff so cont 50m for U-turn back to site. 3*, Lge, mkd, hdg, pt shd, pt sl, terr, EHU (10A) €4.50 (poss rev pol); gas; bbq; red long stay; TV; 25% statics; phone; bus; Eng spkn; adv bkg acc; ccard acc; games rm; CKE. *"Gd base for Clermont Ferrand - gd bus service; friendly, helpful staff; security barrier; shops & supmkt in Vill; late arr can park nr recep."* **€17.00, 26 Mar-2 Nov.** **2024**

CLERMONT FERRAND *9B1* (5km W Rural) *45.75845, 3.05453* **Huttopia Royat (was Camping Indigo Royat),** Route de Gravenoire, 63130 Royat **04 73 35 97 05; royat@camping-indigo.com; www.europe.huttopia.com**

€5 (htd) (htd)

Site diff to find fr Clermont-Ferrand cent. Fr N, leave A71 at Clermont-Ferrand. Foll sp Chamalières/Royat, then sp Royat. Go under rlwy bdge & pass thermal park on L. At mini-rndabt go L & up hill. At statue, turn L & go up long hill. Look for site sp & turn R. Site on R. NB Do not go down steep rd with traff calming. NB sat nav directs up v narr rds & steep hills. 4*, Lge, hdstg, mkd, pt shd, terr, serviced pitches; EHU (10A) €5.20; gas; bbq; TV; 10% statics; phone; Eng spkn; adv bkg acc; ccard acc; bike hire; tennis; CKE. *"Excel, clean, spacious, lovely site; set on hillside in trees; gd size earth pitches; views at top levels over Clermont; clean san facs; facs ltd in LS; conv touring base; new recep; vg."*
€35.00, 31 Mar - 6 Nov, L18. **2022**

CLERMONT L'HERAULT *10F1* (5km NW Rural) *43.64491, 3.38982* **Camp Municipal du Lac du Salagou,** 34800 Clermont-l'Hérault **04 67 96 13 13; www.campinglacdusalagou.fr**

€1.70 (htd) nr

Fr N9 S take D909 to Clermont-l'Hérault, foll sp to Lac du Salagou 1.5km after town sp. Fr by-pass foll sp Bédarieux. Well sp. 4*, Lge, mkd, pt shd, pt sl, EHU (5-10A) €2.90-3.40; bbq; TV; 80% statics; phone; Eng spkn; adv bkg acc; fishing; watersports; CKE. *"Unique location; poss muddy LS & poss windy; facs dated; gd undeveloped beaches around lake; beautiful scenery."*
€22.00, 5 Apr-30 Sep. **2024**

CLISSON *2H4* (1.3km N Urban) *47.09582, -1.28216* **Camp Municipal du Vieux Moulin,** Rue de la Fontaine Câlin, Route de Nantes, 44190 Clisson **02 40 54 44 48 or 06 20 29 08 42 (mob); campingdumoulin@onlycamp.fr; camping.clissonsevremaine.fr**

€1.12 nr nr

1km NW of Clisson cent on main rd to Nantes, at rndabt. Look for old windmill nr ent on L of rd. Leclerc hypmkt on opp side of rd; site sp fr town cent. Narr ent. 3*, Sm, hdg, pt shd, pt sl, EHU 10A inc; TV; Eng spkn; adv bkg acc; fishing adj; boating; horseriding adj; tennis adj; game rm. *"Gd municipal site; lge pitches; gd clean san facs; if office clsd pitch self, book in later; picturesque town 15 min walk; bar 500m; hypmkt 500m; mkd walks; interesting old town with castle ruins; next to retail park; excel rest in town."*
€24.50, 1 Mar-30 Nov. **2023**

CLOYES SUR LE LOIR *4F2* (1km N Rural) *48.00240, 1.23304* **Parc Le Val Fleuri,** 13A Route de Montigny, 28220 Cloyes-sur-le-Loir **02 37 98 50 53; info@val-fleuri.fr; www.val-fleuri.fr**

€2 (htd) (htd)

Located on L bank of Rv Loir off N10; site sp. 4*, Lge, hdg, pt shd, EHU (5A) inc; bbq; twin axles; 50% statics; phone; Eng spkn; adv bkg acc; ccard acc; waterslide; bike hire; €3; CKE. *"Facs gd for children but ltd LS; well-run, pleasant site in wooded valley; site fees inc use of sm leisure park, pedalos & rowing boats on Rv Loir; vg san facs."* **€40.50, 15 Mar-15 Nov.** **2024**

CLUNY *9A2* (0.5km E Urban) *46.43086, 4.66756* **Camp Municipal St Vital,** 30 Rue de Griottons, 71250 Cluny **03 85 59 08 34; www.campingsaintvital.fr**

(htd)

E fr Cluny on D15 (sp Azé & Camping) across narr rv bdge; in 200m turn R into Rue de Griottonste; site on L in 100m. Site adj sw pool. To avoid bdge app fr S on D15. 3*, Lge, mkd, hdstg, pt shd, sl, EHU (6A) €4.50 (poss rev pol); gas; bbq; twin axles; adv bkg rec; ccard acc; fishing; horseriding nr; bike hire; games rm; tennis. *"Well-run, tidy site; helpful staff; gd clean san facs; cycle & walking rte adj (Voie Verte); frequent rlwy noise daytime; interesting town; htd pool adj inc; excel, reliable site; well organised and pleasant; busy site."*
€26.60, 1 Apr-1 Oct. **2023**

"That's changed – Should I let the Club know?"

If you find something on site that's different from the site entry, fill in a report and let us know. See camc.com/europereport.

CLUNY *9A2* (12km S Rural) *46.33744, 4.61123* **Flower Camping Lac De Saint Point (formerly du Lac),** Lac de Saint Point Lamartine, 71520 St Point **06 62 02 17 53; contact@campingsaintpoint.com; www.campingsaintpoint.com**

€2 (htd) nr

Turn S off N79, Mâcon/Paray-le-Monial rd, turn L bef Ste Cécile on D22; site sp at junc; site 100m on R after St Point vill. 3*, Med, hdg, mkd, pt shd, pt sl, terr, EHU (16A) inc; bbq; sw nr; TV; 30% statics; phone; adv bkg acc; fishing; boat hire; tennis 4km; CKE. *"Cluny attractive town & abbey; lge pitches; clean & basic san facs & ltd LS; lovely scenery & pleasant lake; on edge of Beaujolais; sp walks fr site; peaceful area with wooded hills & valleys."*
€17.60, 15 Apr-15 Oct. **2023**

FRANCE

CLUSAZ, LA *9B3* (6km N Rural) *45.93972, 6.42777*
Camping L'Escale, Route de la Patinoire, 74450 Le Grand-Bornand **04 50 02 20 69; contact@campinglescale.com; www.campinglescale.com**
€2.70 (htd) nr (covrd, htd)

Exit A41 junc 17 onto D16/D909 E dir La Clusaz. At St Jean-de-Sixt turn L at rndabt sp Le Grand Bornand. After 1.5km foll camping sp on main rd & at junc turn R sp for site & 'Vallée du Bouchet'. Site is 1st exit R at rndabt at end of this rd. D4 S fr Cluses not rec while towing as v steep & winding. 3*, Med, mkd, pt shd, pt sl, terr, EHU (10A) inc poss rev pol); gas; bbq; TV; 20% statics; adv bkg req; ccard acc; archery; tennis; fishing; games rm; CKE. *"Family-run site in scenic area; bike hire 250m; gd san facs; no c'vans over 8.5m or m'vans over 8m high ssn, Feb & wk of New Year; serviced pitch in summer; vg rest; sh walk to attractive vill; lovely alpine mountain views; winter sports; free use htd ski/boot rm in winter; boggy in wet weather; loads of flies May and June; vg mkt Wed; excel site; ski bus; gd sports facs."*
€40.00, 18 May -18 Sept, 10 Dec - 2 Apr, M07. 2022

COEX *2H4* (2.5km W Rural) *46.67679, -1.76899*
RCN Camping La Ferme du Latois, 85220 Coëx **03 43 74 50 90; contact@rcn.nl; www.rcn.nl/en/camping/france/vendee/rcn-la-ferme-du-latois**
€5 (htd)

Exit D948 at Aizenay onto D6 dir St Gilles-Croix-de-Vie; at Coëx take D40 SW sp Brétignolles; site in 1.5km on L. 4*, Lge, pt shd, EHU inc (poss rev pol); bbq (gas); 20% statics; phone; Eng spkn; adv bkg acc; games rm; games area; lake fishing; bike hire. *"Spacious pitches; cycle rtes adj; conv Lac du Jaunay & Lac du Gué-Gorand; excel."*
€41.00, 19 Apr-27 Sep. 2024

COGNAC *7B2* (2.5km NE Rural) *45.70920, -0.31284*
Camping de Cognac, Blvd de Châtenay, 16100 Cognac **05 45 32 13 32; campingcognac@night-day.fr; www.night-and-day.fr/camping/10-camping-de-cognac**
€1.50

Fr N141 foll 'Camping' sp to town cent. Turn R at 'Speedy' g'ge, site immed on R in 2km after x-ing rv; foll sp 'Base de Plein Air'. Take care ent barrier. 3*, Med, hdg, mkd, hdstg, pt shd, EHU (6A) inc (poss long leads req & poss rev pol); bbq; red long stay; 5% statics; phone; bus; Eng spkn; adv bkg acc; ccard acc; games area; rv boating; rv fishing; CKE. *"Excel lge park with many facs; helpful staff; clean modern san facs but dated; gates clsd 2200-0700 (1800 LS); night watchman high ssn; no twin axles; footpath to town; conv Cognac distilleries (vouchers fr site recep); cycle rte to town cent."* **€22.80, 1 May-30 Sep. 2023**

COGNAC *7B2* (10km E Rural) *45.67160, -0.22718*
Camping De Bourg Charente, 16200 Bourg-Charente **06 15 16 67 82 or 06 03 06 85 07; campingbourgcharente@gmail.com; campingbourgcharente.wixsite.com/lecamping**
nr nr

Exit N141 onto D158 dir Bourg-Charente; turn L in 800m & site on R. Site sp fr D158. Chicane-type ent gates. 1*, Sm, pt shd, pt sl, EHU (6A) €3; red long stay; fishing; tennis. *"Delightful site on banks of Rv Charante; friendly staff; facs v basic & ltd but clean, poss stretched high ssn; site on 2 levels, lower one sl; gd walks & cycle path to Jarnac & Cognac; gd; find placement, owner will call; vg value; v quiet site."*
€15.50, Easter-1 Nov. 2023

COGNAC *7B2* (16km E Urban) *45.67606, -0.17349*
Camping l'Ile Madame, 16200 Gondeville **06 26 91 40 92; campingjarnac@nigh-day.fr; www.night-and-day.fr/camping/9-camping-de-lile-madame**
€2.50 nr nr

Turn E at S end of rv bdge at S end of town. Fr Angoulême on N141, exit junc sp 'Jarnac Est'; foll sp Jarnac thro 1 rndabt into Jarnac; at traff lts (LH lane) turn L sp Tourist Info/Camping; cross rv bdge & immed turn L to site. 3*, Lge, pt shd, EHU (6-10A) €3.20 (rev pol); red long stay; TV; adv bkg acc; golf nr; games area; CKE. *"Pleasant, well-run site; gd sized pitches; easy walk into Jarnac with shops & rests; gd walks along rv; nr Courvoisier bottling plant; excel; boat trips along rv; canoe hire nr; poss noise fr adj sports grnd & disco; site redesigned & new san facs (2015)."*
€22.90, 1 May-30 Sep. 2023

COGNAC *7B2* (8km S Rural) *45.60148, -0.36067*
Camping Le Chiron (Chainier), 8, Chemin du Chiron, 16130 Salles-d'Angles **05 45 83 72 79; jacky.chainier@orange.fr**
12 (htd) nr

Fr Cognac D731 Barbezieux to Salles-d'Angles, R at bottom hill onto D48; then in 3km turn L onto D151; site on L in 500m (foll Chambres d'Hôtes sps). Sm, pt shd, pt sl, EHU (10A) inc (rev pol); Eng spkn. *"Vg; meals avail at farm; v basic; own san facs rec."*
€12.00 2024

COGNAC LA FORET *7B3* (1.5km SW Rural) *45.82494, 0.99674* **Camping des Alouettes,** Les Alouettes, 87310 Cognac-la-Forêt **05 55 03 26 93; info@camping-des-alouttes.com; www.camping-des-alouettes.com**
€1 nr

Fr Aixe-sur-Vienne on D10, site W of Cognac-la-Forêt on D10, sp to L. 3*, Med, hdg, pt shd, pt sl, EHU (10A) €3; bbq; sw nr; 10% statics; Eng spkn; adv bkg acc; tennis 700m; CKE. *"Beautiful location; friendly Dutch owners; conv war vill Oradour-sur-Glane & Richard Lion Heart sites; excel facs, peaceful, relaxing, vg site; lge pitches; well run site."*
€24.50, 1 Apr-30 Sep. 2023

COLMAR *6F3* (2km E Urban) *48.07942, 7.38665*
Camping de l'Ill, 1 Allée du Camping, 68180 Horbourg-Wihr **03 89 41 15 94; colmar@camping-indigo.com; www.campingdelill.com**
€4.50 (htd) (htd)

Exit A35 junc 25 onto D415, foll Freibourg sp. At 2nd rndabt turn L to Colmar cent, site on rvside on L bef bdge. 3*, Lge, hdstg, mkd, hdg, shd, pt sl, terr, EHU (10A) inc (poss rev pol); TV; 10% statics; bus/train to city cent; Eng spkn; adv bkg acc; ccard acc; bike hire; CKE. *"Lovely, clean, rvside site; gd san facs; gd rest; some pitches req steel pegs; much noise fr a'route on some pitches; gd for town; sep area for NH, ltd bus svr only to town, supmkt 900m; helpful recep."* **€24.00, 30 Mar - 2 Jan, J12. 2023**

"I like to fill in the reports as I travel from site to site"

You'll find report forms at the back of this guide, or you can fill them in online at camc.com/europereport.

COLMAR *6F3* (7km SW Rural) *48.04272, 7.29970*
Camping des Trois Châteaux, 10 Rue du Bassin, 68420 Eguisheim **03 89 23 19 39; reception@camping-eguisheim.fr; www.camping-eguisheim.fr**
€3 nr nr nr

Foll D83 S (Colmar by-pass) R at sp Eguisheim. R into vill to site at top of vill, foll camp sp. 3*, Med, mkd, pt shd, pt sl, terr, EHU (8-10A) €3-5 (poss rev pol); gas; adv bkg req; ccard acc; CKE. *"Popular, well-run, clean, busy site; no c'vans over 7m (inc draw bar); mv pitches flat but some c'van pitches sl & poss diff; gd touring base; weekly wine-tasting events; stork park adj; rec arr early; excel; cycle rte to cent of Colmar; gd."* **€23.80, 26 Mar-2 Nov & 25 Nov-24 Dec. 2024**

COLMAR *6F3* (7km W Urban) *48.08517, 7.27253*
Camping Le Medieval, Quai de la Fecht, 68230 Turckheim **03 89 27 02 00; reception@camping-turckheim.fr; www.camping-turckheim.fr**
€2.50 (htd) nr

Fr D83 twd Turchkeim turn W onto D11 to Turckheim. On ent vill, turn immed L down 1-way rd after x-ing rlwy lines. Do not cross rv bdge. Site on L bef bdge, adj stadium. 3*, Med, hdg, pt shd, EHU (16A) €4; bbq; twin axles; TV; bus adj, train 250m; Eng spkn; ccard acc; games rm; CKE. *"Lovely site with med pitches; cycle rtes nr; resident storks; sh walk to interesting, beautiful old vill with rests; gd touring base; gd, excel san facs; poss cr in June, high ssn & w/ends; new management (2016); friendly helpful staff; open 26 Dec-28 Dec for Christmas mkt; vg; close to historic sites and medieval castles; wine tasting & sales; great site; new shwr block (2017); cycle rte to Colmar & vineyards."* **€19.00, 7 Apr-23 Oct & 30 Nov-24 Dec. 2024**

COLMARS *9D4* (0.4km S Rural) *44.17731, 6.62151*
Aire Naturelle Les Pommiers, Chemin des Mélèzes, 04370 Colmars-les-Alpes **07 86 40 21 76; contact@camping-pommier.com; www.tourisme-alpes-haute-provence.com/**
€2 nr nr nr

Fr N on D908 on ent Colmars take 1st R over rd bdge & foll site sp. Col d'allos on D908 v narr, best to avoid. Sm, pt shd, terr, EHU (10A) €2; bbq; phone; adv bkg acc; CKE. *"Beautifully-situated, well-maintained CL-type site nr medieval town; friendly owner; htd pool 800m; gd walking."* **€21.00, 1 Jun-15 Sep. 2024**

COLMARS *9D4* (1km S Rural) *44.17472, 6.61629*
Camping Le Bois Joly, Chemin des Buissières, 04370 Colmars-les-Alpes **04 92 83 40 40; camping-le-bois-joly@sfr.fr**

Fr S on D955 & D908 twds Colmars, go thro Beauvezer & Villars-Colmars. Ignore two other sites en rte. Site sp. Sm, hdstg, mkd, shd, EHU (6A) €2.43; gas; bbq; phone; adv bkg acc; rv fishing adj; CKE. *"Well-kept, wooded site with gd atmosphere; gd facs; ideal base for walking in Haute Provence; bar & shop 1km; friendly owners."* **€11.00, 1 May-1 Oct. 2024**

COLMARS *9D4* (2km SW Rural) *44.19148, 6.59690*
Camping Le Haut Verdon, 04370 Villars-Colmars **04 92 83 40 09; info@lehautverdon.com; www.lehautverdon.com**
€4 (htd) (htd)

Only app fr S on D955 & D908 fr St André-les-Alps thro Beauvezer. Clearly sp on ent Villars-Colmars on R. Do not take D908 via Annot/Le Fugeret with a caravan(Do not confuse with Municipal site approx 5km bef this site). 4*, Sm, hdstg, mkd, pt shd, EHU (6-10A) €3-4; gas; bbq; sw nr; twin axles; TV; 50% statics; 50m; adv bkg acc; rv fishing; games area; games rm; bike hire; CKE. *"Superb setting on Rv Verdon; gd, clean san facs; helpful staff; conv Colmars, flower meadows, Allos Lake; site nr Mercantour National Pk; scenic rte to Barcelonnette via Col d'Allos, not suitable for c'vans; ski area at Allos; gd."* **€28.00, 28 Apr-14 Oct. 2023**

COMBOURG *2E4* (8km NE Rural) *48.45304, -1.65031*
Camping Le Bois Coudrais (Ybert), 35270 Cuguen **02 99 73 27 45; info@vacancebretagne.com; www.vacancebretagne.com**
(htd)

Fr Combourg take D796 twd Pleine-Fougères, 5km out of Combourg turn L on D83 to Cuguen; 500m past Cuguen, turn L, site sp. Or fr Dol-de-Bretagne, take D795 then turn L onto D9 to Cuguen. Sm, hdg, pt shd, EHU (10A) €3; bbq (gas); twin axles; Eng spkn; adv bkg acc; ccard acc; golf nr; watersports nr; fishing nr; animal petting area; CCI. *"CL-type site, friendly British owners, gd clean facs, great for young children, sm animal-petting area, gd touring base; zoo nrby; adventure park nr; excel."* **€20.00, 8 May-8 Sep. 2024**

COMBOURG *2E4* (6km SW Rural) *48.38090, -1.83290* **Camping Domaine du Logis,** 35190 La Chapelle-aux-Filtzméens,Ille-et-Vilaine **02 99 45 25 45; domainedulogis@wanadoo.fr; www.domainedulogis.com**

€1.60 WO MSP nr (htd)

Fr N176 at junc for Dol-de-Bretagne branch R onto D155 sp Dol & take D795 S to Combourg. Then take D13 twd St Domineuc, go thro La Chapelle-aux-Filtzméens & site on R in 1km. 5*, Lge, mkd, hdg, pt shd, serviced pitches; EHU 16A (€4.50); gas; bbq (elec, gas); red long stay; twin axles; TV; 10% statics; phone; Eng spkn; adv bkg rec; ccard acc; gym; games area; games rm; fishing nr; bike hire; fitness rm; CKE. *"Set in chateau grnds; lge flat grassy pitches; helpful, pleasant staff; gd, clean san facs; gd touring base, conv St Malo, Mont St Michel, Dinan & Channel Islands; mkt Mon; excel; no o'fits over 12m; beautiful; v child oriented; canoe 800m; superb pool; excel."* **€40.00, 1 Apr-30 Sept, B02.** **2022**

COMPS SUR ARTUBY *10E3* (1km NW Rural) *43.71543, 6.49862* **Camp Municipal du Pontet,** 83840 Comps-sur-Artuby **04 94 76 91 40 or 06 03 96 91 86; mairie.compsurartuby@wanadoo.fr; comps-sur-artuby.fr/campings**

WO

Fr Comps-sur-Artuby take D71 sp Grand Canyon du Verdon. Site sp on R in 1km. 2*, Med, mkd, pt shd, terr, EHU (6A) €3; phone; CKE. *"Vg, well-laid out, wooded site; conv Gorges du Verdon; easy access; ltd san facs at top of site."* **€8.00, 1 May-31 Oct.** **2024**

CONCARNEAU *2F2* (6km S Coastal) *47.85628, -3.89999* **Camping Le Cabellou Plage,** Ave de Cabellou, Kersaux, 29185 Concarneau **02 98 97 37 41; info@le-cabellou-plage.com; www.le-cabellou-plage.com**

€4 (cont) WO (htd) sand adj

Fr N165 turn onto D70 dir Concarneau. At 5th rndabt (Leclerc supmkt) foll dir Tregunc. After Moros bdge take 2nd exit at next rndabt dir Le Cabellou-Plage. Site sp on L. 4*, Lge, hdg, mkd, hdstg, pt shd, EHU (10A) inc; TV; 20% statics; bus at site ent; Eng spkn; adv bkg acc; ccard acc; games area; bike hire; games rm; watersports. *"Pleasant seaside site; vg san facs; gd walking fr site; gd for town via ferry."* **€36.00, 28 Apr - 15 Sep, B34.** **2022**

See advertisement opposite

CONCARNEAU *2F2* (1.5km NW Urban/Coastal) *47.8807, -3.9311* **Camping Les Sables Blancs,** Ave du Dorlett, 29900 Concarneau **02 98 97 16 44; contact@camping-lessablesblancs.com; www.camping-lessablesblancs.com**

Free (htd) WO MSP nr (htd) sand 400m

Exit N165 to Concarneau dir 'Centre Ville'. Then foll sp 'La Côte' 300m after traff lts. Site on R, sp. 4*, Med, hdstg, mkd, hdg, pt shd, pt sl, terr, EHU (10A); bbq; red long stay; TV; 3% statics; phone; bus 300m; Eng spkn; adv bkg acc; ccard acc; jacuzzi; games rm; games area; CKE. *"Nice, clean, family site in woodland; many sm pitches; friendly staff; excel san facs; superb pool; gd rest; pleasant walk to town, 1.5km; mkt Mon & Thurs; vg; well run; some pitches uneven; steep walk to san facs."* **€32.00, 1 Apr-31 Oct.** **2024**

CONCARNEAU *2F2* (3km NW Coastal) *47.89054, 3.93847* **Camping Les Prés Verts aux 4 Sardines,** Kernous-Plage, 29900 Concarneau **02 98 97 09 74 or 07 87 90 90 01 (mob); info@presverts.com; www.presverts.com**

€2 WO MSP nr (htd)

Exit N165 onto D70 dir Concarneau. At rndabt by Leclerc supmkt foll sp 'Centre Ville' (Town Centre) with Leclerc on L. Strt over at 2nd rndabt then bear R at the next rndabt onto Rue de Kerneach & down slope. Bear L at 1st rndabt & R at next. Keep R to join Rue des Sables Blancs, pass Hôtel l'Océan; site 3rd rd on L in 1.5km. 3*, Med, hdg, mkd, pt shd, pt sl, serviced pitches; EHU (6A-10A) inc (poss rev pol & long lead req); bbq (charcoal, gas); TV; 10% statics; adv bkg acc; ccard acc; games rm; horseriding 1km; sailing 1km. *"Peaceful, scenic, busy site; path to sandy cove below; gd sized pitches, lge pitches extra; family-run, friendly helpful staff; basic san facs, run down, ltd LS; poss unkempt LS; dir access to beach; no o'fits over 8m; gd touring base; walk along coastal path to Concarneau; mkt Mon & Fri; cycle track to old town (old rlwy track) 300m fr site; gd location."* **€28.00, 1 May-30 Sep, B24.** **2020**

CONDE SUR NOIREAU *3D1* (0.5km W Urban) *48.85146, -0.55703* **Camp Municipal du Stade,** Rue de Vire, 14110 Condé-sur-Noireau **02 31 69 02 93; contact@paysdevire-tourisme.fr; www.paysdevire-normandie-tourisme.fr/**

WO nr nr nr

On D562 (Flers to Caen rd). In town, turn W on D512 twd Vire. After Zone Industrielle, sports complex on L, no L turn. Go 1 block further & foll lge white sp 'Espace Aquatique' to site. Site 500m on R in grnds of sports cent. 2*, Sm, pt shd, EHU (6-10A) inc; tennis; CKE. *"Well-kept clean site in grnds of leisure cent; gd size pitches; gd clean san facs; htd pool adj; staff friendly & helpful; pleasant town; gd NH."* **€8.00, 2 May-30 Sep.** **2024**

FRANCE

CONDOM *8E2* (4km NE Rural) *43.97491, 0.42038* **Camping à la Ferme (Rogalle),** Guinland, 32100 Condom **05 62 28 17 85; rogalle.guinland@wanadoo.fr; http://campingdeguinland.monsite-orange.fr**

NE fr Condom on D931, turn R onto D41. Pass water tower on R, site ent on L at bottom of hill just bef sm lake on R. Sm, shd, EHU (6-10A) €3; bbq; 10% statics; tennis nr. *"Vg CL-type site in pine grove; canoe hire nr; gd views; friendly owner; clean facs."*
€9.00, 1 Apr-30 Oct. **2023**

CONDOM *8E2* (7.4km SE Rural) *43.92929, 0.42698* **Ferme d'accueil de Bordeneuve,** Bordeneuve Grazimis, 32100 CONDOM **+33 (0)5 62 28 07 09 or 06 35 23 90 83; fermedebordeneuve@gmail.com; www.campingdebordeneuve.fr**

E fr Condom on D7 to Caussens; far end of vill turn R on D204, sp St Orens; in 1.2km turn R sp Béraut, bear R at fork, site on L in 400m. Also sp fr D654. Sm, pt shd, pt sl, EHU (12A) €2.50 (long lead poss req); adv bkg acc. *"Peaceful & secluded CL-type site; friendly owners; basic san facs; waymkd trails nr; phone ahead to check open LS - poss not open until Apr."*
€12.00 **2020**

CONDOM *8E2* (1.5km SW Rural) *43.94813, 0.36435* **Camping de l'Argenté (formerly Camp Municipal de l'Argenté),** Chemin de l'Argenté, Gauge, 32100 Condom **05 62 28 17 32; campingdelargente@onlycamp.fr; camping-condom.fr**

Fr Condom, take D931 twd Eauze; site ent on L opp municipal sports grnd. 3*, Med, mkd, pt shd, EHU (6A) €3.60; phone; fishing; tennis adj. *"Pleasant, spacious, well-kept site adj rv; lge pitches; well shd; friendly staff; excel san facs but ltd LS; levelling blocks useful; pool 200m; no twin axles; lots for older children to do; interesting, unspoilt town nr pilgrim rte; rec visit Armagnac distilleries; excel."*
€12.00, 5 Apr-29 Sep. **2024**

CONDRIEU *9B2* (4km N Rural) *45.50949, 4.77330* **Camping Domaine du Grand Bois (Naturist),** Tupin et Semons, 69420 Condrieu **04 74 87 89 00 or 07 62 77 19 60; domainedugrandbois@free.fr; www.domainedugrandbois.fr**

Fr Vienne take D502 dir Rive-de-Gier; site well sp after x-ing Rv Rhône. NB Do not app fr Condrieu - v steep with hairpins. Lge, pt shd, sl, EHU (6A) €4.50; TV; 75% statics; phone; adv bkg acc; INF card. *"Spectacular views; v basic san facs."*
€23.10, 15 Apr-15 Oct. **2024**

FRANCE

CONDRIEU *9B2* (5.7km SE Rural) *45.42413, 4.78251* **Camping Le Daxia,** Route du Péage, 38370 St Clair-du-Rhône **04 74 56 39 20; ledaxia.camping@gmail.com; www.campingledaxia.com**

€1.85

S fr Vienne on D386; turn L in Condieu sp D28 Les Roches-de-Condrieu & Le Péage-de-Roussillon; foll sp A7 Valance & 'Camping' onto D4. Site on L well sp fr Condrieu. 3*, Med, hdg, mkd, pt shd, EHU (5-10A) €2.40-2.85; bbq; adv bkg acc; games rm; CKE. *"Vg site; on edge of sm rv with beach."*
€29.50, 1 Apr-30 Sep. **2024**

CONFOLENS *7A3* (0.5km N Rural) *46.01905, 0.67531* **Camping des Ribières,** Ave de St Germain, 16500 Confolens **05 45 85 35 27; www.campingdesribieres.fr**

nr

Fr N foll D951 dir Confolens turn L sp St Germain-de-Confolens, site on R in 7km at edge of town bet rd & rv. NB Diff app fr S thro vill. 3*, Med, mkd, pt shd, EHU (16A); gas; bbq; sw nr; 3% statics; phone; Eng spkn; adv bkg req; bike hire; boating; fishing; games area. *"Interesting, pretty town; facs neglected & ltd LS; m'van o'night area outside site; pool 200m; warden calls am & pm; great site; lovely location; excel."* **€24.50, 1 Apr-1 Oct.** **2023**

CONQUES *7D4* (8km E Rural) *44.55948, 2.46184* **Camping L'Etang du Camp,** 12320 Sénergues **05 65 46 01 95; info@etangducamp.fr; www.etangducamp.fr**

€1.60

Fr S on D901 dir Conques; at St Cyprien turn R onto D46 sp Sénergues; foll sp Sénergues up hill for 6km; 2nd L at the top; foll Camping sp. 3*, Med, mkd, hdg, pt shd, EHU Inc; bbq (charcoal); 10% statics; Eng spkn; adv bkg acc; fishing in private lake; ice; bike hire; games area; canoeing nr; games rm; CKE. *"Well-situated, well-kept site; quiet & relaxing; warm welcome, British owners; modern, clean san facs; gd base for touring, walking & cycling; htd pool 6km; conv Conques; highly rec; excel"*
€23.00, 1 Apr-30 Sep. **2024**

CONQUET, LE *2E1* (2km N Coastal) *48.36748, -4.75990* **Camping Les Blancs Sablons,** 29217 Le Conquet **02 98 36 07 91; www.camping-blancs-sablons.com**

nr nr (htd) sand 100m

Exit Brest on D789 to Le Conquet. Turn R after 22km (1.8km bef Le Conquet) on D67 twd St Renan, turn L after 700m on D28 twd Ploumoguer. After 2km, turn L at x-rds twd Plage des Blancs Sablons, site on L in 1km. 2*, Lge, mkd, unshd, pt sl, EHU (16A) €3 (long lead poss req); adv bkg acc; ccard acc; CKE. *"Gd views fr some pitches; some soft pitches; ltd facs LS & dated but clean with gd hot water; bar 500m; lovely old fishing town."*
€21.00, 1 Apr-31 Oct. **2023**

CORCIEUX *6F3* (1km ESE Rural) *48.16826, 6.89006* **Camping Le Clos de la Chaume,** 671 Rue d'Alsace, 88430 Corcieux **03 29 50 76 76 or 06 85 19 62 55; info@camping-closdelachaume.com; www.camping-closdelachaume.com**

€2.20 nr nr nr (covrd, htd)

Take D145 fr St Dié, then D8 thro Anould & bear R onto D60. Site in 3km on R at ent to vill. 3*, Med, hdstg, mkd, hdg, pt shd, serviced pitches; EHU (8-10A) €5; gas; bbq; twin axles; red long stay; TV; 15% statics; phone; Eng spkn; adv bkg acc; ccard acc; fishing; games area; games rm; CKE. *"Lovely, peaceful site in beautiful area; stream runs thro; friendly & helpful owners; bike hire 800m; san facs poss stetched & busy high ssn; conv Gérardmer & Alsace wine rte; excel; acess rd vg; highly rec; family owned; v well run; excel covrd pool."* **€36.00, 11 Apr - 30 Sep, J08.** **2022**

CORDES SUR CIEL *8E4* (5km SE Rural) *44.04158, 2.01722* **Camping Redon,** Livers-Cazelles, 81170 Cordes-sur-Ciel **06 47 46 13 62 (mob); info@campredon.com; www.campredon.com**

€2.25 nr

Off D600 Albi to Cordes rd. Exit on D107 to E. Site sp. 3*, Sm, hdg, pt shd, pt sl, EHU (6-16A) €4.25; gas; red long stay; TV; phone; bus 1km; Eng spkn; adv bkg acc; CKE. *"Well-kept, well-run site; views fr some pitches; friendly, helpful Dutch owner; excel facs, poss stretched high ssn; ecological septic tank - environmentally friendly liquid sold on site; conv Bastides in area; highly rec; lovely."*
€30.60, 1 Apr-15 Oct. **2023**

CORMATIN *9A2* (0.5km N Rural) *46.54841, 4.68351* **Camping Le Hameau des Champs,** Route de Chalon, 71460 Cormatin **03 85 50 76 71; contact@le-hameau-des-champs.com; www.le-hameau-des-champs.com**

€1 (htd) nr

Fr Cluny N on D981 dir Cormatin for approx 14km, site N of town sp on L, 300m after chateau. Look for line of European flags. Ent 100mtrs down hdg lane. 3*, Sm, mkd, hdg, pt shd, pt sl, EHU (13A) €3.70 (long lead poss req); bbq (elec, gas); cooking facs; sw nr; TV; 10% statics; phone; Eng spkn; adv bkg acc; ccard acc; bike hire; CKE. *"Well-kept, secure site in lovely countryside; welcoming, friendly owner; lge pitches; ltd EHU, adv bkg rec; gd facs, poss stretched high ssn; rest open LS; Voie Verte cycling rte adj; excel municipal site; sm town but gd local store; Chateau closeby."*
€29.90, 1 Apr-30 Sep. **2024**

CORMATIN *9A2* (6km NW Rural) *46.57139, 4.66245* **Camping du Gué,** Messeugne, 71460 Savigny-sur-Grosne **06 74 96 81 81; camping@camping-messeugne.com; camping-messeugne.com/en/home-page**

€1.20 (htd)

Fr Cluny N on D981, 2km N of Cormatin fork L sp Malay. Site 3km on R bef rv bdge. 3*, Med, mkd, shd, EHU €3; bbq; 90% statics; rv; fishing; games area; CKE. *"Pleasant, friendly site; nr St Genoux-le-National (national monument), Cluny & Taizé; on Burgundy wine rte; fairly boggy when wet; c'vans parked on concrete bases."* **€26.00, 1 Apr-3 Nov. 2024**

CORNY SUR MOSELLE *5D2* (0.7km N Rural) *49.03768, 6.05736* **Camping Le Pâquis,** rue de la Moselle, 57680 Corny-sur-Moselle **07 67 59 05 55 or 03 24 37 60 37 or 06 32 56 79 29; campinglepaquis@orange.fr; http://campinglepaquis.free.fr**

€1.30 (htd) nr

SW fr Metz on D657; site sp on ent to vill. Or S on A31 take junc 29 Féy & turn R onto D66 into Corny-sur-Moselle; at rndabt in vill turn R & foll sp. Site 300m on L. 3*, Lge, pt shd, EHU (6A) inc (long cable poss req); sw nr; TV; adv bkg acc; ccard acc; games rm; CKE. *"Gd, well-run site on Rv Moselle; friendly, helpful owners; opening dates vary according to public holidays; rec arr early for quieter pitch at far end site; many pitches long, drive-thro so no need unhitch; pleasant."* **€23.00, 1 May-10 Sep. 2024**

CORPS *9C3* (0.3km W Urban) *44.81909, 5.94323* **Camping Municipal Les Aires,** Route du Sautet, 38970 Corps **07 50 44 39 22; amandine300784@hotmail.fr; www.isere-tourisme.com**

Fr N85, Route de Napoleon, Grenoble to Gap. Vill of Corps turn R on D537, site on L in 400m. Sm, mkd, pt shd, EHU (6A) inc; 30% statics; games rm. *"Quiet site; san facs old but clean; in pretty vill on the Route de Napoleon."* **€16.00, 1 June-30 Sep. 2024**

COSNE COURS SUR LOIRE *4G3* (5km SW Rural) *47.40923, 2.91792* **Camping de l'Ile,** Ile de Cosne, 18300 Bannay **03 86 24 48 43; camping.cosne@aquadis-loisirs.com; www.aquadis-loisirs.com/camping-nature/camping-de-l-ile**

€0.90 (htd)

Fr Cosne take Bourges rd, D955, over 1st half of bdge, ent immed on L, 500m strt. On rv island. 3*, Lge, shd, EHU (10A) €4; bbq; TV; 10% statics; Eng spkn; ccard acc; bike hire; CKE. *"Helpful staff; views of Rv Loire; gd san facs; gd NH; supmkt Carrefour closeby; gd rest opp; town within walking dist."* **€24.00, 1 Apr-24 Oct. 2024**

COUHE *7A2* (8.5km SW Rural) *46.25652, 0.08892* **Camping La Grande Vigne,** 11 Rue du Paradis, 79120 Messé **05 49 29 39 93 or 0800 073 8385; bonjour@naturaserena.fr**

€0.75 (htd) (htd)

Fr N10 exit at Chaunay onto D35/D55 sp Lezay, thro Vanzay & in approx 1.5km turn R onto C11. Site sp. Sm, pt shd, EHU (10A) €3.50; bbq; twin axles; adv bkg acc; games area; bike hire; CKE. *"Gd walking, cycling; gd birdwatching; 2 gîtes to rent; British owners; dogs by prior agreement; friendly welcome; excel."* **€26.00, 1 Apr-15 Oct. 2024**

COULANGES SUR YONNE *4G4* (9km E Rural) *47.53610, 3.63326* **Camping Municipal Le Petit Port,** 516 Le Petit Port, 89660 Châtel-Censoir **06 27 46 01 06; contact@campinglepetitport.com; www.campinglepetitport.com**

€0.50 nr

Fr Auxerre or Clamecy on N151 at Coulanges turn E onto D21, S side of rv & canal to Châtel-Censoir; site sp. 1*, Med, pt shd, EHU (6A) inc; bbq; sw nr; twin axles; 10% statics; phone; Eng spkn; fishing adj; CKE. *"Attractive, peaceful site bet rv & canal; friendly, busy resident warden; OK san facs; some pitches muddy when wet; beautiful area with gd cycling; concerts at w/ends; excel."* **€15.50, 27 Apr-30 Sep. 2023**

COULANGES SUR YONNE *4G4* (0.6km S Rural) *47.52269, 3.53817* **Camping des Berges de l'Yonne,** 89480 Coulanges-sur-Yonne **03 86 81 76 87; lesbergesdelyonne@orange.fr**

nr

On N151 dir Nevers. 2*, Med, pt shd, EHU (10A) €2.80; bbq; tennis; fishing. *"V pleasant site in beautiful area; dated facs but adequate & clean; superb pool."* **€14.40, 1 May-30 Sep. 2020**

COULON *7A2* (5km SE Rural) *46.31307, -0.53495* **Camping le Martin-Pêcheur,** 155 av. Du Marais Poitevin, 79460 Magné **05 49 35 71 81; info@camping-le-martin-pecheur.com; www.camping-le-martin-pecheur.com**

(htd) nr

Fr S take A10, exit 33 dir Marais Poitevin. Then Sansais, La Garette, Magne. Fr Nantes A83, exit 9 twds Marais Poitevin, Coulon & Magne. 4*, Med, hdg, mkd, pt shd, EHU (10A) inc; bbq; red long stay; bus; Eng spkn; adv bkg acc; CKE. *"Excel; beautiful area; interlaced with canals; gd walking & cycling; boats & gondolas for hire, with or without boatman; new facs (2014)."* **€27.50, 6 Apr-29 Sep. 2024**

FRANCE

COULON *7A2* (2km W Rural) *46.31444, -0.60888* **Camping La Venise Verte,** 178 Route des Bords de Sèvre, 79510 Coulon **05 49 35 90 36; accueil@camping-laveniseverte.fr; www.camping-laveniseverte.fr**

€3 (htd)

Exit A83 junc 9 onto D148 to Benet. Turn R at rndabt onto D25E sp Benet cent & foll sp for Coulon thro Benet. In Coulon turn R at traff lts onto D123 sp Le Vanneau-Irleau & Arcais. Cont for approx 3km with canal on L to site R bef canal bdge. Site sp. 4*, Med, mkd, pt shd, EHU (10A) inc (poss rev pol); bbq (charcoal, gas); twin axles; 20% statics; phone; Eng spkn; adv bkg acc; ccard acc; canoe hire; fishing; bike hire; games rm; boating; CKE. *"Superb, peaceful eco site in park-like setting; v friendly helpful owner; excel facs; gd rest; gd sized pitches (some with reinforced plastic grid), but some sm & diff due trees & posts; ACSI; excel touring base for nature lovers; gd walking & cycle paths beside waterways; pretty town; lovely area; much revisited site; well placed pitches; gd facs; beautiful, tranquil location; highly rec; excel family run site; charming vill walkable."*
€32.10, 1 Apr-1 Oct, A37. **2023**

COULON *7A2* (6km W Rural) *46.33020, -0.67524* **Camping Le Relais du Pêcheur,** 85420 Le Mazeau **02 51 52 93 23; campinglerelaisdupecheur@orange.fr; www.lerelaisdupecheur.fr**

nr

Fr Fontenay-le-Comte take N148 SE. At Benet turn R onto D25 thro vill to Le Mazeau. Turn L in vill then R over canal bdge. Site on L in 500m. 3*, Med, hdg, pt shd, EHU (16A) €3.50; Eng spkn; adv bkg acc; CKE. *"Pleasant, clean site in delightful location; gd cyling & walks; new owners, resident warden; facs being updated (2016)."* **€15.00, 4 Apr-10 Oct.** **2023**

COURBIAC *7D3* (1.7km W Rural) *44.37818, 1.01807* **FFCC Le Pouchou,** 47370 Courbiac **06 80 25 15 13; lepouchou@gmail.com; www.camping-le-pouchou.com**

€1.80

S fr Fumel on D102 thro Tournon-d'Agenais; Courbiac sp to L on S side of town; site on R in 2.5km (1.5km bef Courbiac). 3*, Sm, pt shd, pt sl, EHU (10A) €4 (poss rev pol); TV (pitch); 10% statics; Eng spkn; adv bkg req; fishing; horseriding; bike hire; site clsd 21 Dec-9 Jan; archery; CKE. *"Vg site in lovely setting; lge pitches each with picnic table; many sl pitches poss diff; gd, clean facs; gd views; friendly, hospitable owners; gd cycling; peaceful location."*
**€16.00, 1 Mar-30 Jun,
1 Jul-31 Aug, 1 Sep-30 Nov.** **2024**

COURPIERE *9B1* (5km NE Rural) *45.79199, 3.60583* **Camping Le Grün du Chignore,** Les Plaines, 63120 Vollore-Ville **04 73 53 73 37; lesplaines.grundechignore@gmail.com; www.campingauvergne.fr**

€1.50 nr

D906 S fr Thiers; at Courpière turn L onto D7 to Vollore-Ville; cont on D7 past vill; site on R in 500m. 3*, Sm, hdg, mkd, pt shd, EHU (10A) €4; bbq (sep area); 10% statics; Eng spkn; adv bkg acc; ccard acc; games area. *"Situated above fishing lake; rolling hills; helpful & welcoming owners; facs poss stretched high ssn; poss clsd on Weds in April; gd walks; chateau in Vollore-Ville; bar pt of vill life; highly rec; excel; vg, new deep pool; gd size level pitches; gd value pizza rest; hiking guide maps at recep; excel value; some rd noise on upper terrace."* **€22.50, 1 Apr-15 Oct.** **2023**

COURPIERE *9B1* (10km E Rural) *45.79966, 3.61633* **Campsite Le Montbartoux,** Montbartoux, 63120 Vollore-Ville, Auvergne **04 73 53 7005; camping.montbartoux63@gmail.com; campingmontbartoux.com**

12 €1

D906 S fr Thiers to Courpiere. Then E on D7 to Vollore-Ville. Cont twd Vollore-Montagne. Sp to camp. 3*, Sm, mkd, pt shd, sl, terr, EHU (10A); bbq; twin axles; TV; Eng spkn; adv bkg acc; games rm; games area; CCI. *"Attractive site, beautiful views of Auvergne Valley and Vocanoes of Puy-de-Dome; helpful owner; gd; lge o'fits should phone for dir to avoid hairpin on app rd; new san fac's being built(2013)."* **€22.00** **2024**

COURSEULLES SUR MER *3D1* (8km SW Rural) *49.28949, -0.52970* **Camp Municipal des Trois Rivières,** Route de Tierceville, 14480 Creully **02 31 80 90 17; contact@camping-les-3-rivieres.com; www.camping-les-3-rivieres.com**

€1.20 (htd) nr nr nr

sand 5km

Fr Caen ring rd, exit junc 8 onto N13 dir Bayeux; in 15km turn R onto D82 to Creully; site on R 500m past cent of Creully. 3*, Med, hdg, mkd, pt shd, pt sl, EHU (10A) €4.10 (long leads req, poss rev pol); bbq (charcoal, gas); twin axles; 9% statics; Eng spkn; adv bkg acc; ccard acc; games area; games rm; table tennis; tennis; CKE. *"Friendly, helpful warden; facs not v clean, stretched high ssn; pool 5km; conv D-Day beaches, Bayeux; barrier clsd 1500-1700; gd cycling; standard of maintenance is poor; run down site and unkept (2019); many ssn vans."*
€20.40, 6 Apr-13 Oct. **2024**

FRANCE

COURVILLE SUR EURE *4E2* (0.5km S Urban) *48.44629, 1.24157* **Camp Municipal Les Bords de l'Eure,** Ave Thiers, 28190 Courville-sur-Eure **02 37 23 76 38 or 02 37 18 07 90 (Mairie); camping@courville-sur-eure.fr; www.courville-sur-eure.fr**

(htd) nr nr

Turn N off D923 19km W of Chartres. Site on bank of rv. Foll sp. 2*, Med, hdg, pt shd, EHU (16A) inc; Eng spkn; ccard acc. *"Lovely, peaceful rvside site; spacious pitches; friendly warden; no twin axles; conv Chartres; mkt Thurs; easy walk into town; gd security, oniste warden; mv service pnt adj; pool 200m; site basic but lge pitches and v well kept; ltd facs gd and spotless; excel cycling; key for gates (dep req)."*
€15.00, 30 Apr-18 Sep. **2023**

COUTRAS *7C2* (7.5km NW Rural) *45.07929, -0.20839* **Camping Le Chene du Lac,** 3 Lieu-dit Chateauneuf, 33230 Bayas **05 57 69 13 78 or 06 07 98 92 65 (mob); lechenedulac@orange.fr; www.camping-lechenedulac.com**

€2

Fr Coutras W on D10 to Guitres; N fr Guitres on D247 to Bayas; site 2km N of Bayas, sp. 3*, Sm, mkd, shd, EHU 6A; gas; bbq (elec); sw; 2% statics; Eng spkn; adv bkg acc; CCI. *"Helpful owner; pedalos & canoes adj; vg; red facs in winter; great site; friendly, helpful new owners; v relaxed atmosphere; lake adj; excel."*
€29.30, 1 Apr-31 Oct. **2024**

COZES *7B1* (0.7km NW Urban) *45.58650, -0.83568* **Camping Le Sorlut,** Rue de Stade, 17120 Cozes **05 46 90 75 99 or 06 45 46 07 90; contact@camping-charente-maritime-cozes.com; www.camping-charente-maritime-cozes.com/**

nr

Fr bypass D730 turn into Cozes at Royan end. Foll sp for camping. Turn L at supmkt, site 400m on L. 2*, Med, mkd, pt shd, EHU (6A) €2.50; tennis; CKE. *"Pleasant site close to Royan; friendly, helpful warden; no twin axles; popular with long stay British; excel new san facs (2016); number plate recognition barrier."*
€22.20, 21 Apr-6 Nov. **2023**

CRAON *2F4* (1.7km E Urban) *47.84819, -0.94409* **Camp Municipal du Mûrier,** 5 Rue Alain Gerbault, 53400 Craon **02 43 06 96 33 or 02 43 06 13 09 (Mairie); www.campingdecraon53.fr**

Fr Laval take D771 S to Craon. Site sp fr town cent. 3*, Sm, hdg, pt shd, EHU (6-10A) €2.90; red long stay; adv bkg acc; tennis. *"Lge pitches; easy walk to town; pool 200m; office clsd Tues & Sun LS, when barrier key req (2010); local chateau gardens; vg; modern san block; excel rest nrby; close to town."*
€16.60, 1 May-21 Sep. **2022**

CREMIEU *9B2* (4km NW Rural) *45.74829, 5.22486* **Camping à la Ferme des Epinettes,** 11 Rue de l'Eglise, 38460 St Romain-de-Jalionas **04 74 90 94 90 or 06 19 31 03 50; info@camping-cremieu.com; www.camping-cremieu.com**

12 €1 (htd) nr

N fr Crémieu on D517; in 3km site sp on R, immed bef rndabt on edge of St Romain-de-Jalionas. 200m after turning R off D517 (into Rue de l'Eglise), turn L into Rue des Epinettes & site ent. Site on R in 100m. 1*, Sm, mkd, pt shd, EHU (16A); 20% statics; jacuzzi. *"Gd NH for interesting & historic town of Lyon and Crémieu; helpful owners; ltd facs LS; gd touring base; Pérouges worth visit; trams/metro fr Meyzieu to Lyon; rec; lovely, peaceful site; run down (2014); narr rds; statics mainly for workers; movers needed for lge o'fits; no resident warden."* **€17.00** **2024**

CREON *7D2* (3km NW Rural) *44.78372, -0.37108* **FFCC Camping Caravaning Bel Air,** 150 Route Departementale 671, 33670 Créon **05 56 23 01 90; contact@camping-bel-air.com; www.camping-bel-air.com**

€2.50 (htd) nr

Fr A10/E70 at junc 24 take D936 E fr Bordeaux sp Bergerac. Approx 15km E turn SE onto D671 sp Créon & cont for 5km. Site on L, 1.5km after Lorient. 3*, Med, hdstg, mkd, hdg, pt shd, pt sl, EHU 5A-10A; bbq (elec, gas); TV; 60% statics; bus 300m; adv bkg acc; ccard acc; games area; games rm; CKE. *"Helpful owners; immac, modern san facs; rest sm & ltd; facs v ltd LS; no twin axles; some pitches v restricted and tight; phone ahead to check open LS; gd NH; poss music festival in next field; clsd to vehicles 2200-0800; poss rd noise; nr cycle path to Bordeaux and Sauverne; gd."* **€30.20, 29 Mar-3 Nov.** **2024**

CRESPIAN *10E1* (0.5km S Rural) *43.87850, 4.09590* **Kawan Village Le Mas de Reilhe,** 169 chemin du Mas de Reilhe, 30260 Crespian **04 66 77 82 12; info@camping-mas-de-reilhe.fr; www.camping-mas-de-reilhe.fr**

€3.50 (htd) (htd)

Exit A9 at Nîmes Ouest N onto N106 dir Alès for 5km. Fork R, then L over bdge onto D999 dir Le Vigan. Foll rd for 24km, R at x-rds onto D6110 to site on R just on ent Crespian. Take care - ent on a bend on busy rd. 4*, Med, mkd, pt shd, pt sl, terr, EHU (10A) inc; bbq (elec, gas); red long stay; TV; Eng spkn; ccard acc; games area; table tennis; games rm; CKE. *"Quiet, relaxing & lovely site; friendly staff; no o'fits over 7.5m; clean, modern excel san facs; wine-tasting adj; conv Nîmes, Uzès & Cévennes National Park; excel."* **€25.00, 1 Apr - 30 Sep, C10.** **2022**

FRANCE

CREST *9D2* (8km W Rural) *44.72717, 4.92664* **Camping Les Quatre Saisons,** Route de Roche-sur-Grâne, 26400 Grane **04 75 62 64 17; contact@camping-4-saisons.com; www.camping-4-saisons.com**

nr (htd)

Exit A7 at junc for Loriol or Crest, take D104 E for 18km. Turn R thro vill twd Roche-sur-Grane, site well sp. If a lge unit, access thro 4th junc to Grane. Site well sp fr Crest. 4*, Med, pt shd, pt sl, terr, EHU (6A) €4; bbq; red long stay; TV; 10% statics; phone; Eng spkn; adv bkg acc; ccard acc; games area; bike hire; tennis; CKE. *"Beautiful views; well-run site; pleasant, helpful owner; sm & lge pitches; excel san facs; gd pool; Grane (supmkt, rest etc) in walking dist; some pitches far fr EHU and san facs up steep hill; paths a bit uneven - need attention; pleasant stay."* **€35.00 2024**

CREVECOEUR LE GRAND *3C3* (7km SE Rural) *49.59161, 2.16018* **Fontana Sébastien (formerly Camping à la Ferme),** 8 Hameau de la Neuve Rue, 60480 Ourcel-Maison **03 44 46 81 55; sebastien-fontana@orange.fr; www.gite-camping-beauvais.com**

NE fr Beauvais on D1001 to Froissy; turn W at traff lts onto D151. Avoid 1st sp to Francastel but cont to x-rds & turn into vill on D11. Francastel adjoins Ourcel-Maison & site at far end. Or fr A16 exit junc 16 W onto D930 & foll sp. Sm, pt shd, EHU (5A) inc (rev pol); bbq. *"Farm produce avail; no hdstg & poss muddy/diff in wet; gd NH; site yourself, owner calls."* **€10.00 2024**

CREVECOEUR LE GRAND *3C3* (13km SW Rural) *49.57569, 1.93899* **Camping du Vieux Moulin,** 2 Rue des Larris, 60690 Roy-Boissy **06 32 10 66 96; accueil@pausevieuxmoulin.com; pausevieuxmoulin.com**

Fr Marseille-en-Beauvasis SW onto D930 dir Gournay-en-Bray; in 1.5km site sp to R at Roy-Boissy. 3*, Sm, pt shd, EHU inc (poss rev pol); 10% statics; phone. *"Farm site in area with few sites; beautiful countryside; pitch yourself, owner calls eves; excel."* **€20.00, 1 Apr-31 Oct. 2023**

CRIEL SUR MER *3B2* (1.5km NW Coastal) *50.03048, 1.30815* **Camping Les Mouettes,** Rue de la Plage, 76910 Criel-sur-Mer **02 35 86 70 73; contact@camping-lesmouettes.fr; www.camping-lesmouettes.fr**

€2

Fr D925 take D222 thro Criel to coast, site sp. Care needed with narr, steep access. 2*, Sm, mkd, unshd, terr, EHU (6A) €3.70; bbq; TV; 10% statics; Eng spkn; adv bkg acc; games area; games rm. *"Pleasant, well-kept site; friendly, helpful owner; gd san facs; sea views; 3 min walk to Stoney Beach."* **€16.00, 1 Apr-1 Nov. 2024**

CROTOY, LE *3B2* (1.3km N Urban/Coastal) *50.22396, 1.61908* **Camping La Prairie,** 2 Rue de Mayocq, 80550 Le Crotoy **03 22 27 02 65; info@camping-laprairie.fr; www.camping-laprairie.fr**

€1 sand 400m

Fr S exit A16 at Abbeville onto D86/D940 to Le Crotoy to rndabt at ent to town. Cont strt for 1.5km then 2nd L, site on L in 500m. Fr N exit A16 for Rue onto D32, then D940, then as above. 2*, Lge, hdg, pt shd, EHU (3A) inc; 90% statics; phone. *"Busy site; ltd pitches for tourers; conv beach & town; gd san facs; gd cycle paths; gd tourist train & bird walks; everything in walking dist."* **€25.00, 1 Apr-30 Sep. 2024**

CROTOY, LE *3B2* (1.5km N Rural) *50.22968, 1.64140* **Camping La Tarteron,** Route de Rue, 80550 Le Crotoy **03 22 27 06 75; contact@letarteron.fr; www.letarteron.fr**

(htd) sand 1.5km

Fr A16 exit junc 24 onto D32, then D940 around Rue twd Le Crotoy. Pass D4 dir St Firmin site on L. 3*, Med, hdg, mkd, pt shd, EHU (4-10A) €3.50-8; gas; 80% statics. *"Conv Marquenterre bird park & steam train fr Le Crotoy; v clean, basic san facs; 2km walk to town, off rd; barrier ent."* **€32.00, 1 Apr-31 Oct. 2023**

CROTOY, LE *3B2* (3km N Rural/Coastal) *50.23905, 1.63182* **Camping Le Ridin,** Mayocq, 80550 Le Crotoy **03 22 27 03 22; info@yellohvillage-le-ridin.com; www.campingleridin.com**

€2 (htd) (htd) sand 1km

Fr N exit A16 junc 24 dir Rue & Le Crotoy; at rndabt on D940 on app to Le Crotoy take D4 (due W) sp St Firmin; take 2nd rd to L, site sp. Or fr S exit A16 junc 23 onto D40/D940 to Le Crotoy; at rndabt cont strt over onto D4; in 800m turn R; site on R in 1km. NB Do not ent Le Crotoy town with c'van. 4*, Lge, hdstg, mkd, hdg, unshd, EHU (4-10A) €3-5.50; gas; bbq; red long stay; TV; 60% statics; Eng spkn; adv bkg acc; ccard acc; golf 10km; bike hire; games rm; tennis 4km; gym; CKE. *"Some sm, tight pitches bet statics; narr site rds not suitable lge o'fits; helpful staff; fitness rm; clean san facs, unisex LS; bird sanctuary at Marquenterre; quiet except noise fr adj gravel pit/lorries; Le Crotoy interesting town; vg site."* **€30.00, 3 Apr-30 Sep. 2020**

CROZON *2E2* (6.5km E Coastal) *48.24204, -4.42932* **Camping L'Aber,** Tal-ar-Groas,50 Route de la Plage de l'Aber, 29160 Crozon **09 52 78 63 33 or 06 75 62 39 07 (mob); contact@camping-aber.com; www.camping-aber.com**

€1.50 (htd) sand 1km

On D887 turn S in Tal-ar-Groas foll camp sp to site in 1km on R. 3*, Med, mkd, pt shd, pt sl, terr, EHU (5A) €3.40; gas; 50% statics; adv bkg acc; fishing; sailing; windsurfing. *"Great views."* **€21.00, 1 Apr-28 Oct. 2023**

CUISEAUX *9A2* (5km W Rural) *46.49570, 5.32662*
Camping Le Domaine de Louvarel, 71480 Champagnat **03 85 76 62 71; info@louvarel.com; www.louvarel.com**
€2 (htd) (htd) sand

Exit A39 junc 9 dir Cuiseaux; foll sp 'Base de Loisirs de Louvarel'. Or fr D1083 exit Champagnat & foll sp to site on lakeside. 4*, Med, mkd, hdg, pt shd, terr, EHU (10A) incl; bbq; sw nr; 7% statics; phone; Eng spkn; adv bkg acc; bike hire; games area; boating; fishing; CKE. *"Excel, clean site; helpful manager; o'night m'vans area; excel, immac san facs; nice rest & bar; gd walking; free use of canoes; busy."*
€46.00, 28 Apr-23 Sep. **2024**

CUVILLY *3C3* (1.5km N Rural) *49.56750, 2.70790*
Camping de Sorel, 24 Rue St Claude, 60490 Orvillers-Sorel **03 44 85 02 74; contact@aestiva.fr; www.camping-sorel.com**
12 (htd)

Exit A1/E15 at junc 12 (Roye) S'bound or 11 (Ressons) N'bound. Site on E of D1017. 3*, Med, mkd, pt shd, EHU (10A) €3; bbq; TV; 50% statics; games area. *"Pleasant situation; conv NH A1 & Calais; friendly staff; facs need updating (2014); rec early arr in ssn; rv fishing 10km; busy at w/end; 30 mins Parc Astérix; plenty to visit."* **€23.20** **2024**

DARBRES *9D2* (10km NE Rural) *44.63370, 4.50740*
Camping Les Charmilles, Le Clapas, 07170 Darbres, Ardèche **04 75 88 56 27; info@campinglescharmilles.eu; www.campinglescharmilles.fr**
€2

E fr Aubenas on D259; turn L on D224 at Lussas; fork R after Darbres & site in 2km on L sp. Steep app. 4*, Med, pt shd, terr, EHU (5-10A) inc; 10% statics; Eng spkn; adv bkg acc. *"Free tow if in trouble on app."*
€47.80, 18 May-28 Sep. **2024**

DAX *8E1* (1.5km W Rural) *43.71189, -1.07304*
Camping Les Chênes, Allée du Bois de Boulogne, 40100 Dax **05 58 90 05 53; campingleschenes@bala-dax.fr; www.camping-leschenes-dax.com**
€1.50 (htd) nr

Fr D824 to Dax, foll sp Bois de Boulogne, cross rlwy bdge & rv bdge & foll camp sp on rv bank. Well sp. 4*, Lge, mkd, shd, serviced pitches; EHU (10A) inc; gas; bbq; TV; 80% statics; Eng spkn; adv bkg acc; ccard acc; games rm; bike hire; CKE. *"Excel position; easy walk along rv into town; poss noise fr school adj; conv thermal baths at Dax; modernised site with uptodate htd, clean san facs; lovely pool and child area; interesting spa town."* **€23.00, 15 Mar-31 Oct.** **2023**

DAX *8E1* (11km W Rural) *43.68706, -1.14687*
FFCC Camping à la Ferme Bertranborde (Lafitte), 975 Route des Clarions, 40180 Rivière-Saas-et-Gourby **05 58 97 58 39; bertranborde@orange.fr; camping-chambres-bertranborde.fr**
12 €0.50 nr

Turn S off D824 5km W of Dax onto D113, sp Angoumé; at x-rd in 2km turn R (by water tower); then immed L; site on R in 100m, well sp. Or fr N10/A63, exit junc 9 onto D824 dir Dax; in 5km turn R onto D113, then as bef. Sm, pt shd, pt sl, EHU (4-10A) €2.50-4.50; own san rec; bbq; Eng spkn; adv bkg acc; ice; CKE. *"Peaceful CL-type site; beautiful garden; friendly, helpful owners; meals on request; min 2 nights high ssn; poss travellers festival time; excel; lovely site."*
€16.40 **2022**

DAX *8E1* (3km NW Rural) *43.72020, -1.09365*
FFCC Camping Les Pins du Soleil, Route des Minières, La Pince, 40990 St Paul-les-Dax **05 58 91 37 91; info@pinsoleil.com; www.pinsoleil.com**
€2 (htd) nr

Exit N10 junc 11 sp Dax onto D16. Cross D824 & turn R onto D459 S. Cross rndabt & cont on D459, Route des Minières. Site sp in pine forest. 4*, Med, mkd, hdg, pt shd, pt sl, serviced pitches; EHU (5A) €2; gas; bbq; red long stay; TV; 25% statics; phone; Eng spkn; ccard acc; tennis 2km; games area; bike hire. *"Nice, quiet site (LS); various pitch sizes, some spacious; soft, sandy soil poss problem when wet; helpful, friendly staff; excel pool; spa 2km; conv Pyrenees & Biarritz; vg; not well maintained (2018); NH only."*
€27.60, 1 Apr-31 Oct. **2023**

DEAUVILLE *3D1* (3km S Urban) *49.32903, 0.08593*
Camping La Vallée de Deauville, Ave de la Vallée, 14800 St Arnoult **02 31 88 58 17; contact@campingdeauville.com; www.camping-deauville.com**
€4.20 (htd) (covrd, htd) sand 4km

Fr Deauville take D27 dir Caen, turn R onto D278 to St Arnoult, foll site sp. 5*, Lge, hdg, mkd, hdstg, pt shd, EHU (10A) inc; gas; 80% statics; phone; Eng spkn; ccard acc; waterslide; games rm; lake fishing; CKE. *"Easy access to beaches & resorts; conv Le Havre using Pont de Normandie; lake walks & activities on site; excel san facs."* **€50.20, 29 Mar-31 Oct.** **2024**

DECAZEVILLE *7D4* (9km NE Rural) *44.62920, 2.32030*
Camping Pittoresque (formerly Camp La Plaine), Le Bourg, 12300 St Parthem **06 15 32 28 33 or 06 81 42 37 64; info@campingpittoresque.nl; www.campingpittoresque.nl**
€1.50

N fr Decazeville on D963; in 6km over narr bdge take 1st turn R onto D42 to St Parthem. Site 1km past vill on R. 2*, Med, hdg, mkd, pt shd, EHU (6A) inc; bbq; 5% statics; phone; Eng spkn; adv bkg acc; tennis; CKE. *"Idyllic setting on banks of Rv Lot; friendly Dutch owners; excel walking; vg."*
€24.50, 1 Jun-31 Aug. **2023**

FRANCE

DECAZEVILLE *7D4* (3km NW Rural) *44.58819, 2.22145* **FFCC Camping Le Roquelongue,** 12300 Boisse-Penchot **05 65 63 39 67; info@camping-roquelongue.com; www.camping-roquelongue.com**

12 (htd)

Fr D963 N fr Decazeville turn W onto D140 & D42 to Boisse-Penchot. Rte via D21 not rec (steep hill & acute turn). Site mid-way bet Boisse-Penchot & Livinhac-le-Haut on D42. 2*, Med, hdg, mkd, pt shd, EHU (6-10A) €4.20-4.80; gas; 10% statics; phone; adv bkg acc; canoeing; tennis; fishing; bike hire; CKE. *"Direct access Rv Lot; pitches gd size; san facs clean; no twin axles; excel base for Lot Valley."* **€18.30 2022**

DECIZE *4H4* (0.5km NE Urban) *46.83487, 3.45552* **Camping des Halles,** Allée Marcel Merle, 58300 Decize **07 49 67 89 20; campingdeshalles@onlycamp.fr; camping-des-halles-decize.fr**

€1.60

Fr Nevers take D981 to Decize, look for sp for 'Stade Nautique Camping'. 3*, Lge, mkd, pt shd, EHU (6A) €2.30 (poss rev pol); gas; TV (pitch); Eng spkn; ccard acc; CKE. *"Site on banks of Rv Loire; lge pitches, some by rv; helpful staff; san facs clean but need update; no twin axles; poss diff access pitches due trees; shady, flat walk into town; mkt Fri; town v interesting,15 min walk."* **€19.30, 5 Apr-3 Nov. 2024**

DEYME *8F3* (0.4km NE Rural) *43.48672, 1.5322* **Camping Les Violettes,** Porte de Toulouse, 31450 Deyme **05 61 81 72 07; campinglesviolettes@wanadoo.fr; www.campinglesviolettes.com**

12 €0.70 (htd)

SE fr Toulouse to Carcassonne on N113, sp on L, 12km fr Toulouse (after passing Deyme sp). 3*, Med, mkd, hdstg, pt shd, EHU (6A) €4; bbq; TV; 60% statics; CKE. *"Helpful, friendly staff; facs run down (Jun 2009); poss muddy when wet; 800m fr Canal du Midi & 10km fr Space City; Park & Ride 2.5km & metro to Toulouse; san facs updated (2018); sw pool nrby."* **€27.70 2023**

DIE *9D2* (1km NE Rural) *44.75444, 5.37778* **FFCC Camping Le Riou-Merle,** Route de Romeyer, 26150 Die **04 75 22 21 31; lerioumerle@gmail.com; www.camping-lerioumerle-drome.com**

€2 nr

Fr Gap on D93 heading twd Valence. Cont on D93 twd town cent; R on D742 to Romeyer. Site on L in 200m. On D93 fr Crest foll sp round town cent onto D742. 3*, Med, pt shd, pt sl, EHU (10A) inc; 30% statics; Eng spkn; fishing. *"Clean, well laid out site; friendly, helpful staff; gd san facs; 15 min walk to attractive town with gd shops; gd base for touring; rec."* **€30.80, 1 Apr-10 Oct. 2023**

DIE *9D2* (2km NW Rural) *44.76250, 5.34674* **Camping de Chamarges,** Route de Crest, 26150 Die **04 75 22 14 13; campingchamarges@orange.fr; www.camping-chamarges-die.fr**

€1.60 nr

Foll D93 twd Valence, site on L by Rv Drôme. 2*, Med, mkd, pt shd, EHU (3-6A) €2.90-3.60; gas; bbq (gas); sw nr; TV; phone; Eng spkn; adv bkg rec; ccard acc; fishing; canoeing; table tennis; CKE. *"Beautiful mountainous area; vg; friendly owners."* **€12.00, 1 Apr-13 Sep. 2020**

DIEPPE *3C2* (3km S Urban) *49.90040, 1.07472* **Flower Camping Dieppe Vitamin,** 865 Chemin des Vertus, 76550 St Aubin-sur-Scie **02 35 82 11 11; camping-vitamin@wanadoo.fr; www.camping-vitamin.com**

€3 nr (covrd) shgl 2km

Fr E or W leave Peripherique (D925) S at D927 (sp Rouen). At rndabt take exit onto Canadiens Ave/ N27. About 850m take exit twrds Belvedere. Then R onto Rue de la Briqueterie. Site on the R. 4*, Med, hdg, mkd, unshd, EHU (10A) inc; 80% statics; adv bkg acc; ccard acc; games area; CKE. *"Lovely, well-kept site; san facs immac; poss boggy in wet; conv ferries; excel; auto barrier for early dep; v useful & gd value; on bus rte to Dieppe; off clsd 1200-1430; lots of statics & ssn workers; lge retail pk nrby; Aldi at ent; fully equipped site; fair."* **€31.00, 15 Mar-1 Oct. 2023**

DIEPPE *3C2* (5km S Rural) *49.87063, 1.14426* **Camping des 2 Rivières,** 76880 Martigny **02 35 85 60 82; martigny.76@orange.fr; www.camping-2-rivieres.com**

€1.70

Martigny vill on D154 S fr Dieppe. If appr fr Dieppe, ent is on L bef vill sp. 3*, Med, pt shd, EHU (6A) €3.05; adv bkg rec; horseriding nr; watersports nr. *"Attractive, pleasant, spacious site by lge lake; access poss diff long o'fits due parked vehicles; mountain biking nrby; Arques forest nrby; cycle paths; highly rec."* **€20.60, 31 Mar-08 Oct. 2023**

DIEPPE *3C2* (4km SW Rural) *49.89820, 1.05705* **Camping La Source,** 63 Rue des Tisserands, Petit-Appeville, 76550 Hautot-sur-Mer **02 35 84 27 04; info@camping-la-source.fr; www.camping-la-source.fr**

€2.20 nr (htd) sand 3km

Fr Dieppe ferry terminal foll sp Paris, take D925 W dir Fécamp. In 2km at Petit Appeville turn L, site in 800m on rvside. NB 4m bdge bef ent & narr rd to site - not suitable v lge o'fits. 3*, Med, mkd, pt shd, EHU (10A) €4.20; sw nr; TV; 10% statics; adv bkg acc; ccard acc; golf 4km; bike hire; games area; boating adj; games rm; fishing adj; CKE. *"Lovely, well-kept site in attractive setting; pleasant, vg, clean san facs; footpath to Le Plessis vill; gd cycling; excel NH for ferry; MH pitches sm, but backs onto delightful stream and fmland."* **€30.00, 1 Apr-30 Sep. 2024**

DIEPPE 3C2 (6km SW Rural) *49.90886, 1.04069* **Camping Marqueval,** 1210 Rue de la Mer, 76550 Pourville-sur-Mer **02 35 82 66 46; contact@camping lemarqueval.com; www.campinglemarqueval.com**

€2 (htd) WD MSP (htd) sand 1.2km

Site well sp fr D75. 4*, Lge, mkd, hdg, pt shd, EHU (6A) €2.50; bbq; TV; 70% statics; Eng spkn; adv bkg acc; ccard acc; games rm; lake fishing; CKE. *"Attractive, well-kept site; san facs clean but tired; delightful coastal area close by; Bois Du Moutiers gdns highly rec; spa; dog walk on site."*
€31.10, 3 Apr-15 Oct. **2023**

"I need an on-site restaurant"

We do our best to make sure site information is correct, but it is always best to check any must-have facilities are still available or will be open during your visit.

DIEPPE 3C2 (9km SW Urban) *49.87297, 1.04497* **Camp Municipal du Colombier,** 453 Rue Loucheur, 76550 Offranville **02 35 85 21 14; camping@ offranville.fr; www.offranville.fr/2019-05-28-11-57-57/le-camping-municipal**

WD shgl 5km

W fr Dieppe on D925, take L turn on D55 to Offranville, site clearly sp in vill to Parc du Colombier. NB Pt of site cul-de-sac, explore on foot bef towing in. 3*, Med, hdg, mkd, pt shd, EHU (10A) €2.20 (poss rev pol); gas; 80% statics; Eng spkn; CKE. *"Pleasant setting in ornamental gardens; vg clean site & facs; helpful staff; gates clsd 2200-0700; ask warden how to operate in his absence; conv ferries; easy walk to town; rec; gd site; michelin star rest adj."*
€21.00, 1 Apr-30 Sep. **2023**

DIEULEFIT 9D2 (1km SW Urban) *44.52129, 5.06126* **Le Domaine des Grands Prés,** Chemin de la Bicoque, 26220 Dieulefit **04 75 49 94 36 or 06 30 57 08 43 (mob); info@lesgrandspres-dromeprovencale.com; www.lesgrandspres-dromeprovencale.com**

€2 WD

Fr N of A7 take exit 17 twd Dieulefit/Montelimar. At rndabt, take 2nd exit onto N7. Turn L onto D74. Drive thro the vill of Souzet, La Batie-Rolland & la Begude de Mazenc. Campsite located bef town on S side of the rd on the R. 3*, Med, mkd, hdstg, pt shd, EHU (10A) €3.90; bbq; TV; bus 0.2km; Eng spkn; adv bkg acc; ccard acc; CCI. *"Site on o'skirts of vill (10 min walk) with all facs with unusual accomodations; attractive, well run site."*
€24.00, 20 Mar-1 Nov. **2022**

DIGNE LES BAINS 10E3 (1.5km SE Rural) *44.08646, 6.25028* **Camping Les Eaux Chaudes,** 32 Ave des Thermes, 04000 Digne-les-Bains **04 92 32 31 04 or 06 80 47 17 31; info@campingleseauxchaudes.com; www.campingleseauxchaudes.com**

€1.50 (htd) WD nr

Fr S foll N85 sp 'Centre Ville' over bdge keeping L to rndabt, turn 1st R sp Les Thermes (D20). Past Intermarché, site on R 1.6km after leaving town. 3*, Med, mkd, pt shd, EHU (4-10A) €2-3.50 (poss rev pol); gas; sw nr; 50% statics; adv bkg acc; games area; CKE. *"Pleasant site with plenty shd; vg san facs; gd pool; gd touring base; 500m fr thermal baths; National Geological Reserve in town cent; phone ahead LS to check open."* **€28.00, 1 Apr-31 Oct.** **2024**

DIGOIN 9A1 (1km W Urban) *46.47985, 3.96780* **Camping de la Chevrette,** 41 Rue de la Chevrette, 71160 Digoin **03 85 53 11 49; info@lachevrette.com; www.lachevrette.com**

€1 (htd) WD MSP nr

Fr S exit N79/E62 at junc 24 sp Digoin-la-Grève D994, then on D979 cross bdge over Rv Loire. Take 1st L, sp campng/piscine. 3*, Med, hdg, hdstg, pt shd, pt sl, terr, EHU inc (10A) rev pol; 5% statics; Eng spkn; adv bkg acc; fishing; CKE. *"Pleasant, well-run site by rv; diff sized pitches, some lge; friendly, helpful owner; ltd facs LS; barrier clsd 2200-0700; htd pool adj; pleasant walk & dog walking by rv to town; lovely cycle rides along canals; gd NH; canoe hire avail."*
€22.00, 1 Apr-30 Sep. **2023**

"Satellite navigation makes touring much easier"

Remember most sat navs don't know if you're towing or in a larger vehicle – always use yours alongside maps and site directions.

DIJON 6G1 (3km W Urban) *47.32127, 5.01108* **Camping du Lac Kir,** 3 Blvd du Chanoine Kir, 21000 Dijon **06 66 96 56 26; reservation@camping-du-lac-dijon.com; www.camping-du-lac-dijon.com**

€2 WD nr

Site situated nr N5, Lac Kir. Fr Dijon ring rd take N5 exit (W) sp A38 twd Paris. At traff lts L sp A31, site immed on R under 3m high bdge. Do not tow thro town cent. 2*, Med, mkd, hdstg, pt shd, EHU (10-16A) inc (poss rev pol & long lead req); gas; sw; bus adj; Eng spkn; ccard acc; fishing; boating; CKE. *"Rvside path to town; wonderful surrounding area; proof of dog vaccination req, dogs must be on leads; easy bus to town; gd security; poss flooding; Aire for MH at ent (€10 per night); one point for chem disp."*
€21.00, 1 Apr-31 Oct. **2023**

FRANCE

DINAN *2E3* (3km N Rural) *48.48903, -2.00855* **Camping Beauséjour,** La Hisse, 22100 St Samson-sur-Rance **02 96 39 53 27; beausejour-stsamson@orange.fr; www.beausejour-camping.com**

€2.05 (htd)

Fr Dinan take N176/D766 N twd Dinard. In 3km turn R onto D12 dir Taden then foll sp thro Plouer-sur-Rance to La Hisse; site sp. Fr N exit N176/E401 dir Plouer-sur-Rance, then foll sp La Hisse. 3*, Med, hdg, mkd, pt shd, pt sl, EHU (10A) €3.45 (poss rev pol); red long stay; 40% statics; phone; Eng spkn; adv bkg acc; ccard acc; tennis; games area; sailing; CKE. *"Pleasant, well-kept site; gd pool; quiet & spacious Jun & Sep; no twin axles; excel rv walks; excel well maintained site; footpath down to Rance and rvside walks; gd facs; off open 1000-1230 & 1600-1930; new plots may be diff for lge o'fits."* **€16.00, 1 May-30 Sep. 2024**

DINAN *2E3* (4km NE Rural) *48.47138, -2.02277* **Camping la Hallerais,** 4 rue de la Robardais, 22100 Taden **02 96 39 15 93; contact@camping-lahallerais.com; www.camping-lahallerais.com**

(htd) nr nr nr (htd) shgl 10km

Fr Dinan take N176/D766 N twd Dinard. In 3km turn R onto D12 to Taden. Foll La Hallerais & Taden sp to site. Fr N176 take exit onto D166 dir Taden; turn onto D766 dir Taden, then L onto D12A sp Taden & Camping. At rndabt on ent Taden take 1st exit onto D12 sp Dinan; site rd is 500m on L. Do not ent Dinan. Site adj Rv Rance. 4*, Lge, mkd, pt shd, terr, serviced pitches; EHU (10A) inc (rev pol); gas; bbq; TV; 80% statics; Eng spkn; adv bkg acc; ccard acc; tennis; fishing; horseriding 500m; games rm. *"Lovely site, well maintained; some shady pitches; clean san facs; vg pool; phone ahead if arr late at night LS; ltd office hrs LS - report to bar; sh walk to Taden; gd rvside walk to Dinan medieval town; rv trips; no o'fits over 9m (check in adv rec); storage facs; convenient for St Malo port; gd walking, cycling; mkt Thur am & Fri eve; rec; excel; san facs refurb (2017); busy site; v helpful owner."* **€22.00, 13 Mar-7 Nov, B01. 2022**

DINAN *2E3* (0.9km S Urban) *48.44743, -2.04631* **Camp Municipal Châteaubriand,** 103 Rue Châteaubriand, 22100 Dinan **02 96 39 11 96 or 02 96 39 22 43 (LS); campingmunicipaldinan@wanadoo.fr; www.brittanytourism.com**

€1.50 nr nr nr

Fr N176 (E or W) take slip rd for Dinan cent; at lge rndbt in cent take 2nd R; down hill to site on L (500m) after 2nd set of traff lts. 2*, Sm, mkd, pt shd, pt sl, EHU (6A) €2.70; bbq; phone; Eng spkn; adv bkg acc; ccard acc; games area; CKE. *"Pleasant, helpful staff; high kerb onto pitches; poss mkt traders; opening dates vary each year; check time when barrier locked, espec LS; gd cent for Rance valley, St Malo & coast; gd location; bar adj; san facs old but clean; 20 min walk to chateau & town; excel position nr park; more level pitches in lower area of site beyond san block."* **€15.00, 1 Jun-30 Sep. 2023**

DINARD *2E3* (0km W Coastal) *48.6309, -2.08413* **Camping La Touesse,** 171 Rue de la Ville Gehan, La Fourberie, 35800 St Lunaire **02 99 46 61 13; camping.la.touesse@wanadoo.fr; www.campinglatouesse.com**

€1.50 sand 300m

Exit Dinard on St Lunaire coast rd D786, site sp. 4*, Med, mkd, pt shd, EHU (5-10A) €3.30-3.70; TV; adv bkg req; golf 2km; tennis 1.5km; CKE. *"Vg well-kept site; gd beach & rocks nr; friendly recep."* **€32.20, 1 Apr-30 Sep. 2023**

DINARD *2E3* (1km W Coastal) *48.63486, -2.07928* **Camping Le Port Blanc,** Rue de Sergent Boulanger, 35800 Dinard **02 99 46 10 74; info@camping-port-blanc.com; www.camping-port-blanc.com**

€1.90 nr sand adj

Fr Dinard foll sp to St Lunaire on D786 for 1.5km. Turn R at traff lts by football grnd to site. 3*, Lge, mkd, pt shd, pt sl, terr, EHU (10A) €3.95; 40% statics; phone; bus; adv bkg acc; ccard acc; CKE. *"O'looks sand beach; gd san facs; excel site; walk along coast to town; well run site; gd pitches; gd access to beach."* **€26.20, 25 Feb-16 Nov. 2024**

DINARD *2E3* (5km W Coastal) *48.63406, -2.12039* **Camping Longchamp,** Blvd de St Cast, 35800 St Lunaire **02 99 46 33 98; longchamp@clicochic.com; www.camping-longchamp.com**

€2 sand 300m

Fr St Malo on D168 turn R sp St Lunaire, In 1km turn R at g'ge into St Lunaire, site sp to W of vill on D786 dir St Briac. 4*, Lge, hdg, mkd, pt shd, EHU (4-10A) €3.40-4.20; gas; bbq; 30% statics; bus 500m; Eng spkn; adv bkg rec. *"Excel, well-run site; clean facs; friendly, helpful staff; clean beach 300m; conv Brittany Ferries at St Malo; site under new ownership, much improved (2013); pool htd; quiet site nr beautiful seaside town."* **€35.00, 8 Apr-6 Nov. 2024**

DIVONNE LES BAINS *9A3* (3km N Rural) *46.37487, 6.12143* **Camping Huttopia Divonne-les-Bains,** Quartier Villard, 01220 Divonne-les-Bains **04 50 20 01 95; www.huttopia.com**

€5 (htd) (htd)

Exit E62 dir Divonne-les-Bains approx 12km N of Geneva. Fr town on D984, foll sp to site. 3*, Lge, hdg, mkd, shd, sl, terr, EHU (4A) €5; gas; sw nr; TV; 50% statics; Eng spkn; adv bkg acc; ccard acc; tennis; games area; CKE. *"Helpful owner; levellers req; Lake Geneva 8km; new recep & san facs renovated (2015)."* **€34.30, 25 Apr-29 Sep. 2024**

DOL DE BRETAGNE *2E4* (7km NE Coastal) *48.60052, -1.71182* **Camping de l'Aumône,** 35120 Cherrueix **02 99 48 84 82**

WD MSP nr 1km

Exit D797 Pontorson-Cancale rd S onto D82, opp rd leading into vill of Cherrueix. Site in 100m. 3*, Med, unshd, EHU (10A) €3.50; gas; bbq; 20% statics; Eng spkn; adv bkg rec; bike hire; CKE. *"Sm chateau; gd sized pitches; modern san facs; noise fr adj rd daytime; sand yachting nrby; beach not suitable for sw; vg; pleasant, friendly owners."* **€26.50, 1 Apr-30 Oct. 2023**

DOL DE BRETAGNE *2E4* (7km SE Rural) *48.49150, -1.72990* **Les Ormes, Domaine & Resort,** Domaine des Ormes, 35120, Dol-de-Bretagne, France **02 99 73 53 00; www.lesormes.com**

€3 WD (htd)

Exit N176/E401 at W end of Dol-de-Bretagne; then S fr Dol on D795 twd Combourg & Rennes, in 7km site on L of rd, clearly sp. 5*, V lge, mkd, hdg, pt shd, pt sl, serviced pitches; EHU (6-16A) inc (poss long lead req); gas; bbq (charcoal, gas); TV; 80% statics; Eng spkn; adv bkg acc; ccard acc; lake fishing; bike hire; tennis; archery; golf; waterslide; canoeing; games rm; horseriding; CKE. *"Busy site set in well-kept chateau grnds; cricket; o'fits 8m & over by request only; helpful staff; clean san facs; covrd aquacentre; conv Mont St Michel, St Malo & Dinan; pedalos; disco at night; mkt Sat; golfing discount for campers; poss noisy (disco); excel all round."* **€65.00, 14 Apr-16 Sep**, B08. **2022**

DOLE *6H2* (1.6km E Rural) *47.08937, 5.50339* **Camping Du Pasquier,** 18 Chemin Victor et Georges Thévenot, 39100 Dole **03 84 72 02 61; lola@camping-le-pasquier.com; www.camping-le-pasquier.com**

€3 (htd) WD MSP

Fr A39 foll sp dir Dole & Le Pasquier. Fr all dir foll sp 'Centre ville' then foll site name sp & 'Stade Camping' in town; well sp. Site on rvside private rd. Narr app. 3*, Lge, hdg, mkd, pt shd, EHU (10A) inc (rev pol); twin axles; red long stay; 10% statics; Eng spkn; ccard acc; fishing; rv; CKE. *"Generous pitches; aqua park 2km; friendly recep; gd clean san facs; pleasant pool; walk along rv (otters!) into Dole; dir access rv 500m; mkt Tues, Thur, Sat; poss cr; lovely site; on Euro Velo 6 cycle rte; v popular site; mini sw pool."* **€22.80, 15 Mar-15 Oct. 2024**

DOLE *6H2* (8km SE Rural) *47.01660, 5.48160* **FFCC Camping Les Bords de Loue,** 39100 Parcey **03 84 71 03 82; contact@jura-camping.fr; www.jura-camping.fr**

€2 must keep on lead WD adj

Leave A39 at junc 6 onto D905 dir Chalon-sur-Saône. Turn L (SE) at rndabt after going under A39 & in 6km turn R into vill of Parcey at 'Camping' sp. 3*, Lge, pt shd, serviced pitches; EHU (6A) inc; bbq; 20% statics; phone; Eng spkn; adv bkg acc; ccard acc; fishing; boating; CKE. *"Pleasant site."* **€28.50, 6 Apr-29 Sep. 2024**

DOMFRONT *4E1* (0.5km S Urban) *48.58808, -0.65045* **Camp Municipal Champ Passais,** 4 Rue du Champ Passais, 61700 Domfront **02 33 37 37 66 or 02 33 38 92 24 (LS); mairie-de-domfront@wanadoo.fr; http://camping-municipal-domfront.jimdo.com**

€0.80 WD nr nr nr

Fr N on D962 foll Laval sps into Domfront; then take D976 W dir Mont-St Michel; site turning in 400m on L; well sp bet old quarter & town cent. Fr S on D962 well sp fr edge of town. 2*, Sm, hdstg, hdg, mkd, pt shd, terr, EHU (10A) €3; TV; phone; Eng spkn; rv fishing nrby; CKE. *"Pleasant, well-kept terr site; helpful, charming staff; gd security; sh, steep walk to medieval town; no twin axles; vg; site still excel value; shade improving with growing trees."* **€12.50, 1 Apr-30 Sep. 2022**

DOMPIERRE LES ORMES *9A2* (0.5km NW Rural) *46.36369, 4.47460* **Camp Municipal Le Village des Meuniers,** 71520 Dompierre-les-Ormes **03 85 50 36 60; villagedesmeuniers@yahoo.fr; www.villagedesmeuniers.com**

€3 WD MSP nr (covrd, htd, indoor)

Fr A6 exit Mâcon Sud onto N79 dir Charolles. After approx 35km take slip rd onto D41 for Dompierre-les-Ormes. Well sp nr stadium. 4*, Med, hdg, mkd, pt shd, terr, serviced pitches; EHU (16A) €4.50; gas; adv bkg req; ccard acc; tennis; bike hire; waterslide; CKE. *"Excel, clean site with views; v lge pitches; o'flow field with full facs high ssn; facs stretched high ssn; excel for children; gd sp walks in area; pools, rest, bar etc used by public; free m'van hdstg outside site ent."* **€26.00, 15 Apr - 2 Oct**, L25. **2022**

"There aren't many sites open at this time of year"

If you're travelling outside peak season remember to call ahead to check site opening dates – even if the entry says 'open all year'.

DOMPIERRE SUR BESBRE *9A1* (1.5km S Urban) *46.51378, 3.68276* **Camp Municipal,** La Madeleine, Parc des Sports, 03290 Dompierre-sur-Besbre **04 70 34 55 57 or 04 70 48 11 39 (Mairie); camping@mairie-dsb.fr; www.dompierre-sur-besbre.fr**

€1 (htd) WD MSP nr

At E end of town nr rv behind stadium; sp. 2*, Med, hdg, pt shd, pt sl, EHU (10A) inc; bbq; phone; Eng spkn; adv bkg acc; CKE. *"Well-run, busy site; v well kept dated san facs, but poss stretched high ssn; excel sports complex; gd for Loire Valley, vineyards & chateaux; highly rec LS; lge easy acc pitches; gd adj park for dog walking; rv walks; cycling & running tracks; town v close; full sports facs adj; v friendly recep; snacks, takeaway & rest in town; gd; rec."* **€15.00, 15 May-15 Sep. 2022**

FRANCE

DONZENAC *7C3* (1.5km S Rural) *45.21978, 1.51784* **FFCC Camping La Rivière,** Route d'Ussac, 19270 Donzenac **05 55 85 63 95; info@campingdonzenac.com; www.campinglariviere.jimdo.com**

€1.10 (htd)

Fr N exit A20 at junc 47 (do not use junc 48); take exit at rndabt dir Donzenac D920. In 3km on ent Donzenac keep on D920 & go down hill to rndabt. Take 2nd exit D170 sp Uzzac, site on R in 500m. NB Avoid app thro Donzenac as narr & diff for lge o'fits. Fr S exit junc 49 to Ussac. 3*, Med, mkd, pt shd, EHU (10A) €3.10; gas; TV; adv bkg rec; bike hire; games rm; fishing 5km; tennis; games area. *"Excel facs."* **€22.50, 2 May-30 Sep.** **2024**

DORAT, LE *7A3* (0.6km S Urban) *46.21161, 1.08237* **Camp Municipal,** Route de la Planche des Dames, 87210 Le Dorat **06 40 06 70 58; ledorat.fr/camping-municipal/**

nr nr nr

Site sp fr D675 & in town cent. 1*, Sm, mkd, hdg, pt shd, EHU (16A) €3.10; Eng spkn; CKE. *"Excel, basic site; permanent barrier, code fr TO; clean facs, but ltd & own san rec high ssn; warden calls evenings; public uses footpath as sh-cut; v clean, quiet site, must book in TO in town sq; friendly & helpful."* **€6.00, 3 Apr - 30 Sep.** **2024**

DORCEAU *4E2* (2km N Rural) *48.43717, 0.82742* **Camping Forest View,** L'Esperance, Dorceau, 61110 Remalard en Perche, Orne **02 33 83 78 55; graham@forestviewfrance.com; www.forestviewfrance.com**

€1.40

Fr D920 (ring rd) in Rémalard take D38 sp Bretoncelles; site in 4km on corner on L. Sm, pt shd, pt sl, EHU (10A) inc; 10% statics; adv bkg acc; lake fishing; CKE. *"Simple, well-kept site in beautiful countryside; helpful, friendly British owners; painting workshops; gd touring base or NH; excel; evening meal avail with hosts, reasonable price."* **€10.00, 1 May-28 Sept.** **2024**

DORMANS *3D4* (9km NE Rural) *49.10638, 3.73380* **Camping Rural (Nowack),** 10 Rue de Bailly, 51700 Vandières **03 26 58 02 69 or 03 26 58 08 79; champagne@nowack.fr; www.champagne-nowack.com**

Fr N3, turn N at Port Binson, over Rv Marne, then turn W onto D1 for 3km, then N into Vandières. Site on R about 50m fr start of Rue Bailly, sp 'Champagne Nowack' or 'Camping Nowack.' Sm, pt shd, pt sl, EHU (6-10A) inc; bbq; TV; adv bkg acc; ccard acc; tennis 2km; fishing 1km; CKE. *"Charming, peaceful, CL-type site in orchard; friendly owners; lovely, well-kept, clean, modern san facs; fresh water tap beside chem disp; boating 6km; site poss muddy when wet; site pt of vineyard, poss grape pickers in Sep, champagne can be bought; pool 8km; excel value; busy in July, book ahead; excel."* **€24.00, 1 Apr-1 Nov.** **2022**

DOUARNENEZ *2E2* (14km W Coastal) *48.08416, -4.48194* **Camping Pors Péron,** 29790 Beuzec-Cap-Sizun **02 98 70 40 24; info@campingporsperon.com; www.campingporsperon.com**

€1.60 sand 200m

W fr Douarnenez take D7 sp Poullan-sur-Mer. Thro Poullan & in approx 4km turn R sp Pors-Piron, foll site & beach sp. Site bef Beuzec-Cap-Sizun vill. 2*, Med, hdg, mkd, pt shd, pt sl, EHU (10A) inc (long lead req); gas; bbq; 5% statics; adv bkg acc; bike hire; games area; CKE. *"Pleasant, quiet site nr beautiful sandy cove; friendly, helpful British owners; immac san facs, poss insufficient high ssn & long way fr some pitches; poss ltd privacy in ladies' facs; gd; excel site leaflet; gd pitches; excel well maintained site; highly rec; best pitches now taken up by cabins."* **€25.40, 5 Apr-29 Sep.** **2024**

DOUARNENEZ *2E2* (2km W Rural) *48.09270, -4.35220* **Camping de Trézulien,** 14 Route de Trézulien, 29100 Douarnenez **02 98 74 12 30 or 06 80 01 17 98 (mob); contact@camping-trezulien.com; www.camping-trezulien.com**

€3.50 nr sand 1.5km

Ent Douarnenez fr E on D7; foll sp 'Centre Ville'; turn L at traff lts sp to Tréboul. Cross rv bdge into Ave de la Gare, at PO turn L, then 1st L. Turn R at island, foll site sp. 2*, Lge, pt shd, terr, EHU (10A) inc (poss rev pol, long lead req); gas. *"Pleasant site; steep hill fr ent to recep; 1km by foot to Les Sables Blancs; conv Pointe du Raz."* **€25.50, 1 Apr-30 Sep.** **2020**

DOUARNENEZ *2E2* (6km W Rural) *48.08166, -4.40722* **Camping de la Baie de Douarnenez,** 69 Avenue du Bois d'Isis, 29100 Douarnenez Tréboul **+33 2 98 74 05 67; info@camping-douarnenez.com; https://europe.huttopia.com/en/site/douarnenez**

€2.50 (htd) (covrd, htd, indoor) sand 5km

Fr E take circular rd around Douarnenez on D7/D765 dir Audierne & Poullan-sur-Mer, Tréboul & Pointe-du-Van. Site on L off D7 1km fr Poullan-sur-Mer vill, shortly after church spire becomes visible. 4*, Med, mkd, hdg, pt shd, EHU (10A) inc; gas; bbq (charcoal, gas); sw nr; TV; Eng spkn; adv bkg acc; ccard acc; bike hire; watersports 4km; games area; tennis; games rm; lake fishing; pools; mini golf; CKE. *"Tranquil site in woodland; gd sized pitches; staff friendly; ltd facs LS; entmnt well away fr most pitches; gd for families; mkd walks, guided high ssn; no o'fits over 10m high ssn; statics (tour ops); mkt Mon & Fri; pools & water slides great fun."* **€40.00, 29 Apr- 30 Sep, B37.** **2022**

DOUCIER *6H2* (6km N Rural) *46.71221, 5.79709* **Camping du Gît,** Monnet-le-Bourg, 39300 Montigny-sur-l'Ain **03 84 51 21 17 or 07 85 57 53 28 (off-season); olivierraph@orange.fr; www.campingdugit.com**

€2 nr

W fr Champagnole on D471 foll sp Monnet-la-Ville, foll camp sp thro vill, turn L at x-rds to church; site immed afterwards on R behind church in Monnet-la-Ville (also known as Monnet-le-Bourg). 3*, Med, mkd, pt shd, pt sl, EHU (5A) €2.50; bbq; sw nr; TV; adv bkg acc; fishing 1.5km; games area; CKE. *"Peaceful site; beautiful views; kayaking 1.5km; lge pitches; gd san facs."* **€12.00, 1 May-27 Sep.** **2020**

DOUE LA FONTAINE *4G1* (1km N Rural) *47.20338, -0.28165* **Camp Municipal Le Douet,** Rue des Blanchisseries, 49700 Doué-la-Fontaine **02 41 59 14 47 or 06 22 71 25 53 (mob); contact@camping-lesrives dudouet.fr; www.camping-lesrivesdudouet.fr**

nr nr

Fr Doué N on D761 twd Angers; site in sports grnd on o'skts of town; sp. 2*, Med, mkd, pt shd, EHU (6A) inc; 10% statics; tennis; CKE. *"Clean, well-run site; gd, flat pitches; helpful warden; gd san facs; lovely park & museum; htd pool adj high ssn; conv zoo, rose gardens & Cadre Noir Equestrian Cent; poss ssn workers LS; gd shd; shop will order bread; vg."* **€21.50, 1 Apr-15 Oct.** **2024**

DOUE LA FONTAINE *4G1* (2km SW Rural) *47.17390, -0.34750* **Camping La Vallée des Vignes,** 49700 Concourson-sur-Layon **02 41 59 86 35; info@camping-vdv.com; camping-vdv.com**

€3 (htd) (htd)

D960 fr Doué-la-Fontaine (dir Cholet) to Concourson-sur-Layon; site 1st R 250m after bdge on leaving Concourson-sur-Layon. Or fr Angers foll sp dir Cholet & Poitiers; then foll sp Doué-la-Fontaine. 4*, Med, mkd, pt shd, serviced pitches; EHU (10A) €4; gas; bbq; red long stay; TV; 5% statics; bus; Eng spkn; adv bkg acc; ccard acc; bike hire; CKE. *"Peaceful site poss open all yr weather permitting - phone to check; vg, clean, well-maintained facs; pool open & htd early ssn; some pitches diff lge o'fits due o'hanging trees; conv for Loire chateaux & Futuroscope; new French owners (2016), v helpful."* **€26.20, 29 May-15 Sep.** **2023**

DOUE LA FONTAINE *4G1* (18km W Rural) *47.18032, -0.43574* **Camping Kathy Dave,** Les Beauliers, 49540 La Fosse de Tigné **02 41 67 92 10 or 06 14 60 81 63 (mob); kathy.irvin@wanadoo.fr; www.camping-kathydave.co.uk**

nr nr

Fr Doue la Fontaine on D84 sp. St Georges sur Layon. 12km West to Tigne, turn S thro La Fosse de Tigne (2km). Turn sharp R at 30kph, site sp. After 70mtrs turn L on Chemin des Plantes. Site mkd 100mtrs on R. Sm, mkd, pt shd, pt sl, EHU (8A) €5; bbq (sep area); TV (pitch); Eng spkn; adv bkg rec. *"Tranquil, rural orchard site in middle of vineyards; welcoming, helpful, v. friendly British owners, many regular repeat visitors, gd san facs, some pitches restricted by trees, gd centre for touring; adults only; phone ahead rec (6 pitches only); excel for relaxing holiday; excel."* **€16.00, 1 Mar-30 Oct.** **2024**

DOUE LA FONTAINE *4G1* (8km W Rural) *47.19355, -0.37075* **Camping Les Grésillons,** Chemin des Grésillons, 49700 St Georges-sur-Layon **02 41 50 02 32 or 07 82 83 86 18; contact@camping-lesgresillons.fr; www.camping-gresillons.com**

(htd) nr (htd)

Fr Doué-la-Fontaine on D84, site sp. In St Georges-sur-Layon turn L opp church. 3*, Sm, hdg, hdstg, pt shd, terr, EHU (6-10A) €2.90-3.50; red long stay; 28% statics; Eng spkn; adv bkg acc; ccard acc; rv fishing 200m; games area; CKE. *"Delightful site in area of vineyards; friendly, helpful owner; gem of a site."* **€20.80, 1 Apr-30 Sep.** **2023**

DOUHET, LE *7B2* (2km S Rural) *45.81080, -0.55288* **Camping La Roulerie,** 17100 Le Douhet **05 46 96 40 07 or 06 49 48 25 67 (mob); campinglaroulerie.com**

€1

Fr Niort to Saintes, site on W side of D150 in vill of La Roulerie. Sm, mkd, hdstg, hdg, pt shd, EHU (16A) €3.50; 10% statics; Eng spkn; adv bkg acc; games area; CKE. *"Sm pitches; full by early eve; friendly, helpful owner; gd san facs; vg value; gd NH."* **€9.00, 1 May-15 Oct.** **2024**

DOURDAN *4E3* (0.7km NE Urban) *48.52572, 2.02878* **Camping Les Petits Prés,** 11 Rue Pierre Mendès France, 91410 Dourdan **01 64 59 64 83 or 01 60 81 14 17; camping@mairie-dourdan.fr; www.camping-dourdan.com**

(htd) nr nr nr

Exit A10 junc 10 dir Dourdan; foll by-pass sp Arpajon; after 5th rndabt site 200m on L. 3*, Med, mkd, unshd, pt sl, EHU (4A) €3.40; TV; 75% statics; Eng spkn; adv bkg acc; bread delivery Jul/Aug; meeting rm. *"Gd NH; friendly welcome; gas & supmkt 500m; clean dated san facs, ltd LS; pool 500m; town worth visit."* **€14.00, 1 Apr-30 Sep.** **2020**

FRANCE

DOUSSARD *9B3* (3km N Rural) *45.80256, 6.20960* **Camping La Ravoire,** Route de la Ravoire, Bout-du-Lac, 74210 Doussard **04 50 44 37 80; www.campingsannecy.com/fr/la-ravoire**

(htd) (htd)

Fr Annecy, turn R at traff lts in Bredanaz, then immed L & foll rd across cycle track & uphill for 1km, at vill take L fork, site immed on L. Fr Albertville on B1508, turn L opp Complex Sportif, Bout de Lac sp Lathule; cont, x-ing cycle track to rndabt; turn R & cont 2km past other sites; at junc turn sharp R, site immed on L. 4*, Med, hdstg, mkd, hdg, pt shd, pt sl, serviced pitches; EHU (5A) inc (poss rev pol); gas; sw nr; TV; 10% statics; phone; Eng spkn; adv bkg rec; ccard acc; bike hire; sailing adj; horseriding adj; games area; waterslide; fishing adj; windsurfing adj; golf adj; CKE. *"Excel, well-kept, busy site with mountain views; friendly staff & atmosphere; immac facs; lake ferry fr Doussard; cycle paths adj."* **€40.60, 19 Apr-22 Sep.** **2024**

DOUSSARD *9B3* (3km N Rural) *45.80302, 6.20608* **Camping Le Taillefer,** 1530 Route de Chaparon, 74210 Doussard **04 50 44 30 30; info@campingletaillefer.com; www.campingletaillefer.com**

€2.50 shgl 3km

Fr Annecy take D1508 twd Faverges & Albertville. At traff lts in Bredannaz turn R, then immed L for 1.5km; site immed on L by vill sp 'Chaparon'. Do NOT turn into ent by Bureau but stop on rd & ask for instructions as no access to pitches fr Bureau ent. Or, to avoid Annecy, fr Faverges, along D1508, turn L (sp Lathuile) after Complex Sportif at Bout-du-Lac. Turn R at rndabt (sp Chaparon), site is on R after 2.5km. 2*, Sm, mkd, pt shd, pt sl, terr, EHU (6A) €4.50 (check rev pol); bbq (charcoal, gas); sw nr; red long stay; TV; Eng spkn; adv bkg acc; games rm; bike hire; watersports 2km; sailing; tennis 100m; rafting. *"Peaceful, simple, family-run site nr Lake Annecy; fantastic mountain views; access some pitches poss diff due steep terraces; friendly, helpful owners; dated, clean san facs; no o'fits over 8m high ssn; canyoning; climbing; vg rest in easy walking dist; mkt Mon; worth another visit."* **€25.00, 1 Apr - 04 Nov, M06.** **2022**

DOUVILLE *7C3* (2km S Rural) *44.99271, 0.59853* **Camping Lestaubière,** Pont-St Mamet, 24140 Douville **05 53 82 98 15 or 06 82 28 23 97; lestaubiere@gmail.com; camping-lestaubiere.fr**

€3.50 (htd)

Well sp fr N & S on N21. Approx 21km N of Bergerac. Exit fr N21 sp Pont St. Mamet. 3*, Med, mkd, pt shd, EHU (6-10A) €4-5; gas; bbq; sw; twin axles; TV; 10% statics; phone; Eng spkn; adv bkg acc; ccard acc; tennis 5km; games area; lake fishing; games rm; CKE. *"Spacious, park-like site with beautiful views; v lge pitches; owned by friendly, helpful Dutch couple; twin axles (high ssn only); vg modern san facs; superb out of ssn; site in 2 sep sections; a few v lge drive thro pitches; excel."* **€35.00, 8 Apr-30 Sep.** **2023**

DRAGUIGNAN *10F3* (4km S Rural) *43.51796, 6.47836* **Camping La Foux,** Quartier La Foux, 83300 Draguignan **04 94 68 18 27; www.camping-lafoux.com**

€3.90

Fr A8, take Le Muy intersection onto N555 N to Draguignan. Site ent on R at ent to town sp Sport Centre Foux. Fr Draguignan, take N555 S; just after 'End of Draguignan' sp, double back at rndabt & turn R. 2*, Lge, unshd, pt sl, EHU (4-10A) €3.50-5; TV; fishing. *"Friendly staff; v poor san facs; care needed long vehicles on ent site; unshd, but many trees planted (2011); poss flooding when wet; easy access to Riviera coast."* **€16.00, 20 Jun-30 Sep.** **2022**

"I like to fill in the reports as I travel from site to site"

You'll find report forms at the back of this guide, or you can fill them in online at camc.com/europereport.

DREUX *4E2* (9.5km NW Rural) *48.76149, 1.29041* **Camping Etangs de Marsalin,** 3 Place du Général de Gaulle, 28500 Vert-en-Drouais **02 37 82 92 23; contact@campingdemarsalin.fr; www.campingdemarsalin.fr**

12 (htd) nr nr

Fr W on N12 dir Dreux, cross dual c'way bef petrol stn onto D152 to Vert-en-Drouais; on ent turn R to church, site on L. Well sp. 2*, Med, hdg, mkd, hdstg, pt shd, pt sl, EHU (6-10A), €4.60 (poss rev pol, long leads poss req, avail at recep); 80% statics; Eng spkn; lake fishing 2km; CKE. *"Peaceful location; working families on site; friendly, helpful staff; basic, clean san facs; touring pitches at far end far fr facs; muddy when wet; lovely vill; conv Versailles; NH only; site tidy and clean; bar 100m; facs refurb (2016)."* **€14.00** **2023**

DUNKERQUE *3A3* (12km NE Coastal) *51.07600, 2.55524* **Camping Perroquet Plage,** 59123 Bray-Dunes **03 28 58 37 37; contact@campingleperroquet.com; www.campingleperroquet.com**

€0.50 (htd) sand adj

On Dunkerque-Ostend D601, about 100m fr Belgian frontier, thro vill on D947; cont 1km to traff lts, R on D60 thro vill, past rlwy stn to site on L. NB Take care some speed humps. 4*, V lge, hdstg, hdg, pt shd, EHU (4A) €4.50; TV; 85% statics; Eng spkn; adv bkg req; sauna; watersports; gym; tennis; mini-golf; CKE. *"Busy, well-kept site; lge pitches; if parked nr site ent, v long walk to beach; lge bar & rest nr beach (long walk fr ent); gd san facs, poss far; many local attractions; conv NH for ferries; gd."* **€15.00, 1 Apr-20 Sept.** **2020**

DUNKERQUE *3A3* (4.6km NE Coastal) *51.05171, 2.42025* **Camp Municipal La Licorne,** 1005 Blvd de l'Europe, 59240 Dunkerque **03 28 69 26 68; lalicorne@vagues-oceanes.com; www.campingdelalicorne.com**

€0.90 (htd) nr sand adj

Exit A16 junc 62 sp 'Malo'; at end of slip rd traff lts turn L sp Malo-les-Bains; in 2km (at 5th traff lts) turn R at camping sp; at 2nd traff lts past BP g'ge turn L. Site on L (cont strt to rndabt & return on opp side of dual c'way to ent). 3*, Lge, mkd, unshd, pt sl, EHU (10A) (poss long lead); gas; 50% statics; bus fr site ent; Eng spkn; adv bkg acc; ccard acc; clsd 2200-0700; CKE. *"V gd, secure NH for ferries - obtain gate code for early depart; pitches uneven; many site rd humps; promenade along sea front to town cent; site backs onto sand dunes & beach (used for Dunkirk evacuation of Allied Forces in 1940); poss windy; m'van o'night area; gd san facs; bus stop nr site ent; very attractive site; site tired, clean san facs."*
€31.00, 27 Apr-3 Nov. **2024**

DURAS *7D2* (0.5km N Rural) *44.68293, 0.18602* **Camping Le Cabri,** Malherbe, Route de Savignac, 47120 Duras **05 53 20 16 67; info@lecabriresort.com; www.lecabriresort.com**

12 €3 (htd) nr

Fr N on D708, turn R on ent Duras onto D203 at mini-rndabt by tourist info shop; site in 800m. Sm, hdg, hdstg, unshd, terr, EHU (4-10A) €3-5; bbq; 30% statics; bus 500m; Eng spkn; adv bkg acc; ccard acc; games area; tennis 1km; games rm, mini-golf; CKE. *"Spacious site with wide views; lge pitches; British owners (CC members); san facs poss tired high ssn (2011); vg rest; Duras an attractive town; excel."*
€17.00 **2020**

DURBAN CORBIERES *8G4* (0.5km N Rural) *43.00017, 2.81977* **Municipal Camping L'Espazo (formerly Municipal De Durban-Corbieres),** Lespazo, 11360 Durban-Corbieres **04 68 45 06 81 or 06 42 48 69 05; camping@mairiededurban.fr; www.audetourisme.com**

Fr A61 take exit 25, foll D611 S across to Durban Corbieres. Site sp on R on entering Vill. Sm, hdg, pt shd, pt sl, EHU (10A); bbq; twin axles; 10% statics; bus 0.5km; adv bkg acc; CCI. *"Tranquil site surrounded by rugged hills; pool 0.5km; Cathar castle in vill; vg."*
€11.00, 15 Jun-15 Sep. **2024**

DURTAL *4G1* (0.2km W Urban) *47.67115, -0.23798* **Camping Les Portes de l'Anjou,** 9 Rue du Camping, 49430 Durtal **02 41 76 31 80; contact-camping@lesportesdelanjou.com; en.lesportesdelanjou.com**

€2.50 nr (htd)

On A11 take exit 11 for Durtal, cont on RD859, turn R on last rndabt to Durtal, Foll sp. 3*, Med, hdg, pt shd, EHU (10A); own san rec; bbq (elec, gas); sw; red long stay; 12% statics; Eng spkn; adv bkg acc; ccard acc; canoeing; fishing; games area; games rm; CKE. *"Site in need of TLC, in pleasant position on Rv Loir; office clsd 12.30-3.30; helpful staff; interesting vill; v gd."* **€25.00, 7 Apr-31 Oct.** **2023**

EAUX PUISEAUX *4F4* (1km SW Rural) *48.11696, 3.88317* **Camping à la Ferme des Haut Frênes,** 6 Voie de Puiseaux, 10130 Eaux-Puiseaux **03 25 42 15 04; les.hauts.frenes@wanadoo.fr; www.les-hauts-frenes.com**

12 €2 (htd) nr nr

N fr St Florentin or S fr Troyes on N77. Ignore D374 but take next turning D111 in NW dir. Site in 2km; well sp. Long o'fits take care at ent gate. 3*, Med, hdg, mkd, hdstg, pt shd, EHU (6-15A) €2-3 (poss some rev pol); gas; bbq; red long stay; TV; Eng spkn; adv bkg acc; games rm; tennis 3km; CKE. *"Well-kept, tidy farm site in beautiful setting; lge, level pitches; helpful, friendly owners; gd san facs; meals on request; own facs adv high ssn; loyalty card; cider museum in vill; conv m'way; excel NH en rte S; super; v quiet site; gd."*
€17.00 **2023**

ECHELLES, LES *9B3* (0.2km SE Urban) *45.43462, 5.75615* **Camping L'Arc-en-Ciel,** Chemin des Berges, 38380 Entre-Deux-Guiers **04 76 66 06 97; info@camping-arc-en-ciel.com; www.camping-arc-en-ciel.com**

€1.10 nr nr nr

Fr D520 turn W sp Entre-Deux-Guiers. On ent vill turn R into Ave de Montcelet dir Les Echelles & R again in 100m. Site sp fr D520. 3*, Med, hdg, mkd, pt shd, pt sl, EHU (2-4A) €2.50-4.30; gas; 40% statics; CKE. *"Conv La Chartreuse area with spectacular limestone gorges; gd."* **€24.00, 1 Apr-3 Nov.** **2024**

ECHELLES, LES *9B3* (6km S Rural) *45.39107, 5.73656* **Camp Municipal Les Berges du Guiers,** Le Revol, 38380 St Laurent-du-Pont **04 76 55 20 63 or 04 76 06 22 55 (LS); camping.st-laurent-du-pont@wanadoo.fr; www.camping-chartreuse.com**

€1 nr nr nr

On D520 Chambéry-Voiron S fr Les Echelles. On ent St Laurent-du-Pont turn R just bef petrol stn on L. 2*, Sm, mkd, pt shd, EHU (5A) €3.50; bbq; Eng spkn; tennis 100m; CKE. *"Clean & well-kept; pool 300m; pleasant area; gates clsd 1100-1530; vg."*
€19.40, 3 Jun-17 Sep. **2023**

FRANCE

ECOMMOY *4F1* (0.4km NE Urban) *47.83367, 0.27985* **Camp Municipal Les Vaugeons,** 19 Rue de la Charité, 72220 Ecommoy **06 49 55 03 70; lau66san@aol.fr; www.camping-ecommoy.com**

nr

Heading S on D338 foll sp. Turn E at 2nd traff lts in vill; sp Stade & Camping. Also just off A28. 2*, Med, pt shd, pt sl, EHU (6A) €2.35; Eng spkn; adv bkg acc; tennis; CKE. *"Site full during Le Mans week (nr circuit); gd san facs; new arr no access when recep clsd, hrs 0900-1130 & 1500-2030; coarse sand/grass surface."* **€10.00, 1 Apr-18 Oct.** **2024**

"I need an on-site restaurant"

We do our best to make sure site information is correct, but it is always best to check any must-have facilities are still available or will be open during your visit.

ECOMMOY *4F1* (4km SE Rural) *47.81564, 0.33358* **Camp Municipal Le Chesnaie,** 72220 Marigné-Laillé **02 43 42 12 12 (Mairie); mairie.marigne-laille@wanadoo.fr or mairie.marigne-laille.catherine@wanadoo.fr; www.tourisme-en-sarthe.com**

nr

S on D338 Le Mans-Tours, turn E 3km after Ecommoy twds Marigné-Laillé. Site in 1.5km. 2*, Sm, hdstg, mkd, pt shd, EHU (10A) inc; fishing adj; tennis; CKE. *"Lovely site; clean, adequate san facs; pleasant warden; if height barrier down, use phone at ent; lake adj; easy access A28; v warm welcome; basic site, but clean; pool 5km; pretty site, great NH."* **€8.00, 1 May-30 Sep.** **2024**

ECRILLE *4H2* (2.7km WNW Rural) *46.50973, 5.62042* **Camping La Faz,** 4 Pont de Vaux 39270 Ecrille **03 08 25 40 27; campinglafaz@gmail.com; www.jura-camping-lafaz.com**

€1.40

Fr Stye at the rndabt (the only rndabt onmain rd thro Stye) take dir Geneva, then 50m down on R is Ecrille. Site is 1.5km fr Stye. 3*, EHU €3.10. *"Excel."* **€27.50, 28 Apr-15 Oct.** **2024**

EGLETONS *7C4* (2km NE Rural) *45.41852, 2.06431* **Camping du Lac,** 10 Le Pont, 19300 Egletons **05 55 93 14 75; campingegletons@orange.fr; www.camping-egletons.com**

12 €1.30 nr

Fr Egletons on D1089 for approx 2km, site 300m past Hôtel Ibis on opp site of rd. 3*, Med, mkd, pt shd, terr, EHU (10A) inc; gas; sw nr; TV; 30% statics; phone; Eng spkn; fishing 300m; watersports 300m; CKE. *"Lovely, wooded site in attractive area; on busy rd; lge pitches; friendly owners; vg; san facs being updated (2022)."* **€14.00** **2022**

EGUZON CHANTOME *7A3* (1.5km NE Urban) *46.44556, 1.58314* **Camping Vallée de la Creuse (formerly Camp Eguzon La Garenne),** 1 Rue Yves Choplin, 36270 Éguzon-Chantôme **02 54 47 44 85; info@campingvalleedelacreuse.fr; campingvalleedelacreuse.fr**

€1.50 nr (htd)

Exit A20 junc 20 onto D36 to Eguzon; on ent vill sq cont strt on, foll sp; site on L in 300m. 4*, Med, hdg, pt shd, pt sl, EHU (6-10A) inc; bbq; sw nr; TV; 3% statics; phone; Eng spkn; adv bkg acc; watersports 4km; cycling; CKE. *"All you need on site or in vill; excel; well run, attractive site; poss OAY, phone ahead; only 2 hdstg; gas 300m; site is improving; gd; clean, tidy; v friendly Dutch owners; ACSI acc."* **€30.00, 1 May-1 Oct.** **2023**

EGUZON CHANTOME *7A3* (3km SE Rural) *46.43372, 1.60399* **Camp Municipal du Lac Les Nugiras,** Route de Messant, 36270 Eguzon-Chantôme **02 54 47 45 22; contact@camping-municipal-eguzon.com; www.camping-municipal-eguzon.com**

12 (htd) sand 300m

Fr A20 exit junc 20, E on D36 to Eguzon; in vill turn R & foll site sp. 3*, Lge, hdg, mkd, pt shd, pt sl, terr, EHU (10A) €3 (rev pol); 10% statics; games rm; watersports; CKE. *"Scenic site & region; security barrier; ample, clean facs but v ltd LS; site yourself on arr; waterski school; warden avail early eves; gd winter site; muddy after heavy rain."* **€9.40** **2024**

"Satellite navigation makes touring much easier"

Remember most sat navs don't know if you're towing or in a larger vehicle – always use yours alongside maps and site directions.

ELNE *10G1* (3km E Coastal) *42.60695, 2.99098* **Camping Le Florida,** Route Latour-Bas-Elne, 66200 Elne **04 68 37 80 88; info@campingleflorida.com; www.campingleflorida.com**

12 nr nr sand 4km

Exit A9 junc 42 Perpignan-Sud onto D914 dir Argelès-sur-Mer. Exit D914 junc 7 onto D11 dir Elne Centre, then D40 sp St Cyprien to Latour-Bas-Elne, site sp. 4*, Lge, mkd, pt shd, EHU (6A) €4; bbq; TV; 70% statics; phone; Eng spkn; adv bkg acc; ccard acc; games area; games rm; tennis; CKE. *"Excel site; bus to beach high ssn."* **€43.00** **2022**

ELNE *10G1* (4km S Rural) *42.57570, 2.96514* **Kawan Village Le Haras,** Sant Galdric Estate, 1 Ter Avenue Joliot Curie, 66690 Palau del Vidre **04 68 22 14 50; contact@camping-le-haras.com; www.camping-le-haras.com**

€5

Exit A9 junc 42 sp Perpignan S dir Argelès-sur-Mer on D900 (N9) & then D914; then exit D914 junc 9 onto D11 to Palau-del-Vidre. Site on L at ent to vill immed after low & narr rlwy bdge. 4*, Med, shd, EHU (10A) €5; bbq (elec, gas); TV; 10% statics; Eng spkn; adv bkg acc; ccard acc; tennis 1km; fishing 50m; archery; games rm; CKE. *"Peaceful, well-kept, family-owned site in wooded parkland; helpful, friendly warden; san facs poss red LS; gd rest & pool; 5 mins walk to delightful vill; no o'fits over 7m high ssn; rds around site poss liable to flood in winter; many walks in area; Collioure worth visit; conv Spanish border; excel."* **€63.00, 1 Apr - 30 Sep, C26. 2022**

EMBRUN *9D3* (6km N Rural) *44.60290, 6.52150* **FFCC Camping Les Cariamas,** Fontmolines, 05380 Châteauroux-les-Alpes **04 92 43 22 63 or 06 30 11 30 57 (mob); contact@cariamas.fr; www.cariamas.fr**

12 €4.50 nr nr (htd)

Fr Embrun on N94; in 6km slip rd R to Châteauroux & foll sp to site. Site in 1km down narr but easy lane. 3*, Med, mkd, pt shd, pt sl, terr, EHU (6A) €3.15; bbq; sw nr; 20% statics; phone; Eng spkn; adv bkg acc; ccard acc; watersports; bike hire; fishing; tennis 500m; CKE. *"Excel for watersports & walking; mountain views; National Park 3km."* **€21.50 2020**

EMBRUN *9D3* (3.5km S Urban) *44.54725, 6.48852* **Camping le Petit Liou,** Ancienne route de Baratier, 05200 Baratier **04 92 43 19 10; info@camping-lepetitliou.fr; www.camping-lepetitliou.com**

€1.50 (htd)

On N94 fr Gap to Briancon turn R at rndabt just bef Embrun. First L after 150m then 1st R. Site on L in 250m, sp. 3*, Lge, hdg, mkd, pt shd, pt sl, EHU (3-10A) €3.60-€4.20; bbq; 5% statics; Eng spkn; adv bkg acc; games rm; bike hire; CKE. *"Lovely mountain views; vg."* **€24.90, 1 May-22 Sep. 2022**

EMBRUN *9D3* (2.4km SW Urban) *44.55440, 6.48610* **Camping La Vieille Ferme,** Chemin sous le Roc, 05200 Embrun **04 92 43 04 08; info@campingembrun.com; www.campingembrun.com**

€3 nr

On N94 fr Gap, at rndabt 3rd exit sp Embrun cross Rv Durance then take 1st R, sp La Vielle Ferme, keep L down narr lane, site ent on R. Access poss diff for lge o'fits. 4*, Med, mkd, pt shd, EHU (6-10A) €5-6 (pos rev pol); red long stay; Eng spkn; adv bkg acc; rafting; watersports. *"Friendly, Dutch family-run site; canyoning; gd facs; pretty town."* **€37.70, 1 May-1 Oct. 2023**

ENTRAYGUES SUR TRUYERE *7D4* (4km NE Rural) *44.67777, 2.58279* **Camping Le Lauradiol (Formaly Municipal),** Banhars, 12460 Campouriez **05 65 44 53 95; Campinglelauradiol@orange.fr; www.camping-lelauradiol.com**

€2 nr (htd)

On D34, sp on rvside. 3*, Sm, hdg, mkd, pt shd, EHU (6A) inc; 10% statics; tennis; CKE. *"Beautiful setting & walks; excel; power mover needed for lge o'fits to access pitches; beautiful site; rv adj; v friendly helpful staff; a real gem."* **€17.50, 29 Jun-31 Aug. 2024**

ENTRAYGUES SUR TRUYERE *7D4* (1.6km S Rural) *44.64218, 2.56406* **Camping Le Val de Saures,** 12140 Entraygues-sur-Truyère **05 65 44 56 92; info@camping-valdesaures.com; www.camping-valdesaures.com**

€1.50 nr

Fr town cent take D920 (twds Espalion) & in 200m turn R over narr rv bdge and then R onto D904. In 200m fork R onto new rd and thro sports complex to site. 3*, Med, mkd, pt shd, EHU (6A) €3.50; 10% statics; Eng spkn; ccard acc. *"Pleasant, friendly, gd site; in great situation; footbdge to town over rv; vg, well-kept san facs; recep clsd Sun & pm Mon LS; pool adj; gd touring base."* **€25.60, 20 May-29 Sep. 2024**

ENTREVAUX *10E4* (1.5km NW Rural) *43.96163, 6.79830* **Camping Le Brec,** 04320 Entrevaux **04 93 05 42 45; info@camping-dubrec.com; www.camping-dubrec.com**

€1 (htd)

Site sp on R just after bdge 2km W of Entrevaux on N202. Rd (2km) to site narr with poor surface, passing places & occasional lge lorries. 3*, Med, mkd, pt shd, pt sl, EHU (10A) €3 (poss long lead req); bbq; sw nr; TV; 10% statics; phone; Eng spkn; adv bkg acc; ccard acc; watersports cent; fishing adj; boating adj; CKE. *"In beautiful area lake on site; friendly family owners; popular with canoeists; easy rv walk to town; beautiful area; gd."* **€22.50, 15 Mar-15 Oct. 2024**

EPERNAY *3D4* (1km NW Urban) *49.05734, 3.95042* **Camp Municipal d'Epernay,** Allées de Cumières, 51200 Epernay **03 26 55 32 14; camping.epernay@free.fr; www.epernay.fr**

€1.80 (htd)

Fr Reims take D951 twd Epernay, cross rv & turn R at rndabt onto D301 sp Cumières (look for sp 'Stade Paul Chandon'), site sp. Site adj Stadium. Avoid town at early eve rush hr. 3*, Med, hdg, mkd, pt shd, EHU (10A) inc (poss long lead req); bbq; red long stay; phone; Eng spkn; adv bkg acc; ccard acc; fishing; tennis; bike hire; games area; canoeing; CKE. *"Attractive, well-run site on Rv Marne in lovely location; generous pitches; friendly, helpful staff; gd spacious san facs; barrier open 0800-2100 & 0700-2200 high ssn; parking outsite; rec arr early; footpaths along rv into town; htd covrd pool 2km; waterslide 2km; Mercier train tour with wine-tasting; site used by grape pickers; no twin axles or c'vans over 6m acc; gd value; boulangerie and cafe nrby."* **€24.20, 30 Apr-1 Oct. 2023**

FRANCE

FRANCE

EPESSES, LES *2H4* (0.5km N Rural) *46.88920, -0.89950* **FFCC Camping La Bretèche,** Base De Loisirs, 85590 LES EPESSES **02 51 20 41 94; contact@olela.fr; www.camping-la-breteche.com**

€ 5.00 / night (htd)

Fr Les Herbiers foll D11 to Les Epesses. Turn N on D752, site sp on R by lake - sp fr cent Les Epesses. 4*, Med, hdg, mkd, pt shd, EHU (10A) €3 (poss rev pol); bbq; TV; 30% statics; Eng spkn; adv bkg acc; ccard acc; fishing; horseriding; tennis; games room; CKE. *"Well-kept, well-run site; htd pool adj inc; busy high ssn; helpful staff; plenty of attractions nr; events staged in park by lake high ssn; conv Puy du Fou; vg; no waste or water on site, long leads req."*
€22.00, 4 Apr-1 Nov. **2020**

EPINAL *6F2* (2km E Urban) *48.17930, 6.46780* **Camping Parc du Château,** 37 Rue du Petit Chaperon Rouge, 88000 Epinal **03 29 34 43 65 or 03 29 82 49 41 (LS); parcduchateau@orange.fr**

€3 (htd)

Sp fr town cent. Or fr N57 by-pass take exit sp Razimont, site sp in 1km. 2*, Med, hdg, mkd, hdstg, pt shd, terr, EHU (6-10A) €5-6; gas; bbq; red long stay; TV; 20% statics; Eng spkn; adv bkg acc; ccard acc; tennis; CKE. *"Lge pitches; ltd facs LS; walk thro park to town; helpful new owners who have improved site; sep m'van park adj, fr €12; exceptionally clean; ACSI acc."*
€12.70, 1 Apr-30 Sep. **2024**

EPINAL *6F2* (8km W Rural) *48.16701, 6.35975* **Kawan Village Club Lac de Bouzey,** 19 Rue du Lac, 88390 Sanchey **03 29 82 49 41; lacdebouzey@orange.fr; www.lacdebouzey.com**

12 €4 (htd) (htd)

Fr Epinal take D460 sp Darney. In vill of Bouzey turn L at camp sp. Site in few metres, by reservoir. 4*, Lge, hdstg, mkd, hdg, pt shd, pt sl, terr, EHU (10A) €7; gas; bbq; red long stay; TV; 15% statics; phone; Eng spkn; adv bkg acc; ccard acc; bike hire; fishing; horseriding; games area; CKE. *"Excel site; lake adj; sl slightly but pitches fairly level; ACSI discount in LS; gd cycling area; nice cycle ride to Epinal; pleasant position opp lake."* **€40.20** **2022**

ERQUY *2E3* (5km SSW Coastal) *48.604565, -2.489502* **Camping La Vallée,** St Pabu, 22430 Erquy **02 96 72 06 22; contact@campinglavallee.fr; www.campinglavallee.fr**

€2 500m

Foll d786 fr Val Andre twrds Erquy. As dual c'way ends, becoming 2 way, turn L immed. Foll sp for 750m. 3*, Sm, hdg, mkd, pt shd, terr, EHU (10A) €4.50; bbq; 20% statics; Eng spkn; adv bkg acc; sauna; games area; bike hire; CKE. *"Vg site."*
€26.90, 1 Apr-1 Oct. **2023**

ERVY LE CHATEL *4F4* (1km E Rural) *48.04018, 3.91900* **Camp Municipal Les Mottes,** 10130 Ervy-le-Châtel **03 25 70 07 96 or 03 25 70 50 36 (Mairie); mairie-ervy-le-chatel@wanadoo.fr; www.ervy-le-chatel.fr**

€1.50 nr

Exit N77 sp Auxon (int'l camping sp Ervy-le-Châtel) onto D374, then D92; site clearly sp. 2*, Med, pt shd, EHU (5A) €2.50; adv bkg acc; tennis; rv fishing 300m; CKE. *"Pleasant, well-kept, grassy site; lge pitches; vg facs; v friendly, helpful staff; no twin axles; rests in vill; rec; excel sm site; v clean."*
€16.00, 15 May-4 Oct. **2023**

ESPALION *7D4* (0.3km E Urban) *44.52176, 2.77098* **Camping Roc de l'Arche,** 12500 Espalion **05 65 44 06 79; info@rocdelarche.com; www.rocdelarche.com**

€0.50 nr

Sp in town off D920 & D921. Site on S banks of Rv Lot 300m fr bdge in town. 3*, Med, hdg, mkd, pt shd, EHU (6-10A); bbq; adv bkg acc; canoeing; fishing; tennis. *"Well-kept site; gd sized pitches, water pnts to each; service rds narr; pool adj inc; friendly, helpful warden; clean, modern san facs; excel."*
€22.40, 6 May-15 Sep. **2024**

ESSARTS, LES *2H4* (0.8km W Urban) *46.77285, -1.23558* **Camping Le Petit Bocage (formerly Camp Municipal Le Pâtis),** Rue de la Piscine, 85140 Les Essarts **06 18 86 86 64; campinglepetitbocage@onlycamp.fr; camping-essarts-en-bocage.fr**

€1.60 (htd) nr nr

Exit A83 junc 5 onto D160. On ent Les Essarts, foll sp to site. Site on L just off rd fr Les Essarts to Chauché. 2*, Med, mkd, pt shd, EHU (6A) €2.80; bbq (charcoal, gas); 40% statics; tennis adj; CKE. *"Excel NH off A83; gd, clean san facs; sports cent adj with 2 pools (1 Olympic size) adj; warden resident."*
€19.00, 15 Apr-15 Sep. **2024**

ESSAY *4E1* (0.6km S Rural) *48.53799, 0.24649* **FFCC Camp Municipal Les Charmilles,** Route de Neuilly, 61500 Essay **02 33 29 15 46; lescharmillescamping@gmail.com; www.camping-lescharmilles.com**

Exit A28 junc 18 (Alençon Nord) onto D31 to Essay (sp L'Aigle); turn R in vill dir Neuilly-le-Bisson; site on R in 400m. 2*, Sm, hdg, pt shd, EHU (6A) €3 (reverse pol); 50% statics; adv bkg acc. *"Lge pitches, some diff to access; site yourself, warden calls in eve to pay; historical vill; fair NH; no hot water; old style European EHU."* **€10.00, 1 Apr-30 Sep.** **2024**

ESTAGEL *8G4* (3km W Rural) *42.76566, 2.66583* **Camping La Tour de France,** Route d'Estagel, 66720 Latour-de-France **04 68 29 16 10; www.camping-latourdefrance.fr**

€3 WD MSP nr nr nr

Fr D117 at Estagel turn S onto D612 then R onto D17 to Latour. Site on R on ent to vill. 2*, Med, mkd, shd, EHU (10A) €3.50; sw nr; red long stay; 13% statics; phone; Eng spkn; adv bkg acc; ccard acc. *"Pretty vill & wine 'cave' in walking dist; rec visit Rv Agly barrage nrby; htd pool 3km; helpful staff; excel; peaceful; welcoming, helpful, young owners; many ptiches with trees, diff for lge o'fits."* **€28.00, 8 Apr-23 Sep.** **2023**

ESTANG *8E2* (0.5km E Rural) *43.86493, -0.10321* **Camping Les Lacs de Courtès,** 23 route de Panjas, 32240 Estang **05 62 09 61 98 or 06 68 00 09 03; www.camping-lacsdecourtes.com**

12 €3 WD MSP nr nr (htd)

W fr Eauze site sp fr D30. Fr Mont-de-Marsan D932 take D1 to Villeneuve-de-Marsan, then D1/D30 to Estang. 3*, Sm, hdg, mkd, pt shd, terr, EHU (6A) €3; TV; 50% statics; Eng spkn; adv bkg acc; lake fishing; tennis; games area. *"Gd family site; no bar/rest end of Aug; excel walking area; area for m'vans open all yr; gd rest in vill; vg."* **€34.20** **2023**

ETABLES SUR MER *2E3* (1km S Coastal) *48.63555, -2.83526* **Camping L'Abri Côtier,** Rue de la Ville-ès-Rouxel, 22680 Etables-sur-Mer **02 96 70 61 57 or 06 07 36 01 91 (mob LS); camping.abricotier@wanadoo.fr; www.camping-abricotier.fr**

€2 (htd) WD MSP (htd) sand 500m

Fr N12 round St Brieuc take D786 N thro Binic & 500m after Super U supmkt turn L to Etables. Go thro vill for approx 3 km & turn L into Rue de la Ville-es-Rouxel just after R turn for Plage-du-Moulin. Site ent just after sm x-rds. NB Long c'vans & big m'vans (to avoid going thro vill): cont on D786, past Chapel, down hill & turn L at boatyard dir Etables; take 2nd turn on R. To avoid manoeuvring, park on rd & go to recep on foot. 3*, Med, mkd, pt shd, pt sl, serviced pitches; EHU (10A) inc; gas; bbq; TV; 10% statics; adv bkg acc; ccard acc; watersports 2km; games rm; jacuzzi; golf 4km; CKE. *"Popular, immac site; tennis in vill; excel beach (poss strong currents); entry narr & steep, narr corners on site rds poss diff lge o'fits; mkt Tues & Sun; vg."* **€31.00, 1 Apr-15 Oct, B09.** **2024**

ETANG SUR ARROUX *4H4* (0.9km SE Rural) *46.86190, 4.19177* **FFCC Camping des 2 Rives,** 26-28 Route de Toulon, 71190 Etang-sur-Arroux **03 85 82 39 73; camping@des2rives.com; www.des2rives.com**

12 €2.40 WD MSP nr

Fr Autun on N81 SW for 11km; turn L onto D994 to Etang-sur-Arroux; site on R after passing thro main pt of town. 3*, Med, shd, EHU (6-10A) €3.60; sw nr; 20% statics; phone; Eng spkn; adv bkg acc; canoeing; kayaking; CKE. *"Well-kept site bet two rvs; Dutch owners; dated but adequate san facs; gd rv sports; ltd opening Jan & Feb; nice site; pool 500m; helpful owners."* **€24.60** **2024**

ETRETAT *3C1* (5km E Rural) *49.69880, 0.27580* **Camping de l'Aiguille Creuse,** 24 Rue de l'Aiguille, 76790 Les Loges **02 35 29 52 10; camping@aiguillecreuse.com; www.campingaiguillecreuse.com**

€3 WD MSP nr nr (covrd, htd) 3km

On S side of D940 in Les Loges; sp. 4*, Med, mkd, unshd, EHU (10A) inc; bbq; TV; adv bkg acc; tennis; games rm. *"Facs ltd LS; conv Etretat; gd; gd ctr for cliff top walks and inland villages."* **€30.00, 1 Apr - 16 Sep, N08.** **2022**

ETRETAT *3C1* (1km SE Urban/Coastal) *49.70053, 0.21428* **Camp Municipal,** 69 Rue Guy de Maupassant, 76790 Éetretat **02 35 27 07 67**

(htd) WD MSP nr shgl 1km

Fr Fécamp SW on D940 thro town cent of Etretat & site on L. Or fr Le Havre R at 2nd traff lts; site on L in 1km on D39. 2*, Med, mkd, hdstg, pt shd, pt sl, EHU (6A) €6 (poss rev pol); gas; bbq; phone; ccard acc; CKE. *"Busy, well-kept site; lge pitches; conv Le Havre ferry; friendly & helpful staff; clean san facs but dated; level walk to pleasant seaside resort, attractive beach nr; gd cliff top walks nr; m'van o'night area adj (no EHU) open all yr €8; early arr high ssn rec; excel; lovely site; clsd 1200-1500."* **€23.40, 1 Apr-15 Oct.** **2023**

EU *3B2* (0.3km W Rural) *50.05065, 1.40996* **Camp Municipal du Parc du Chateau,** Le Parc du Château, 76260 Eu **02 35 86 20 04 or 03 86 33 93 50; camping-du-chateau@ville-eu.fr; www.ville-eu.fr**

WD nr shgl 3km

App fr Blangy on D1015 turn L at junc with D925 & foll camp sp to site in grnds of Hôtel de Ville (chateau). Fr Abbeville on D925 fork R at 1st rndabt in town S of rlwy then immed strt on over cobbled rd to chateau walls. Turn R at chateau walls into long, narr app rd thro trees. 2*, Med, hdstg, hdg, pt shd, terr, EHU (16A) (poss rev pol); gas; 10% statics; Eng spkn. *"Louis-Philippe museum in chateau; poor san facs; easy uphill walk to town thro forest behind chateau; Eu worth visit, an alt to seaside towns nrby; vg Fri mkt; gd local dog walks; recep 0900-1200/1400-2100; rec."* **€12.70, 1 Apr-30 Sep.** **2024**

FRANCE

EVIAN LES BAINS *9A3* (6km W Rural) *46.39388, 6.52805* **FFCC Camping Les Huttins,** 350 Rue de la Plaine, Amphion-les-Bains, 74500 Publier **04 50 70 03 09; campingleshuttins@gmail.com; www.camping-leshuttins.com**

€1 nr nr

Fr Thonon on D1005 twds Evian, at start of Amphion turn L onto Rte du Plaine sp; ent 200m on R after rndabt. Fr Evian on D1005 twds Thonon, at end of Amphion turn R & foll sp. 2*, Med, mkd, shd, EHU €3; gas; bbq; sw nr; TV; 5% statics; Eng spkn; adv bkg acc; tennis adj. *"Spacious, simple, relaxed site in beautiful area; hypmkt 300m; enthusiastic, helpful owners; pool 200m; sports complex 200m; basic, clean san facs; gd base for Lake Léman; poss unrel opening dates - phone ahead; excel; site run by siblings."*
€24.80, 1 May-30 Sep. 2024

"There aren't many sites open at this time of year"

If you're travelling outside peak season remember to call ahead to check site opening dates – even if the entry says 'open all year'.

EVRON *4F1* (9km SE Rural) *48.09423, -0.35642* **Glamping Sainte-Suzanne,** 10 Rue de la Croix Couverte, 53270 Ste Suzanne **02 43 10 49 60; contact@glamping-saintesuzanne.fr; www.glamping-saintesuzanne.fr**

nr nr nr

Take D7 SW fr Evron sp Ste Suzanne. Site 800m S (downhill) after this sm fortified town.
2*, Sm, hdg, mkd, pt shd, pt sl, EHU (10A) inc; bbq; 25% statics; Eng spkn; adv bkg acc; horseriding adj; CKE. *"Remodelled site with new facs (2017); llovely area; unspoilt town & castle with historic Eng conns; walking adj; 8 EHU pnts; excel; rec."*
€27.00, 16 May-10 Sep. 2023

EYMET *7D2* (0.2km W Urban) *44.66923, 0.39615* **Camping du Château (formerly Municipal),** Rue de la Sole, 24500 Eymet **05 53 23 80 28 or 06 98 16 97 93 (mob); eymetcamping@aol.com; www.camping-eymet.fr**

nr nr nr

Thro Miramont onto D933 to Eymet. Turn opp Casino supmkt & foll sp to site. Sp on ent to Eymet fr all dirs. 2*, Sm, hdg, mkd, pt shd, EHU (10A) €3 (poss rev pol); sw nr; red long stay; Eng spkn; adv bkg acc; bike hire; boat hire; CKE. *"Lovely site by rv behind medieval chateau; friendly, helpful owner; clean but tired san facs; pool 1.5km; gas 300m; wine tasting on site; lake nrby; Thur mkt; excel; peaceful site nr lovely Bastide town; no arr bet 1200-1500."*
€11.50, 1 Apr-30 Sep. 2022

EYMOUTIERS *7B4* (8km N Rural) *45.80560, 1.84342* **Camping Les 2 Iles (formerly Municipal Les Peyrades),** Auphelle, Lac de Vassivière, 87470 Peyrat-le-Château **05 55 35 60 81; les2iles.camping@orange.fr; www.campings-vassiviere.com/camping-les-2-iles**

nr nr nr sand adj

Fr Peyrat E on D13, at 5km sharp R onto D222 & foll sp for Lac de Vassivière. At wide junc turn L, site on R. Med, pt shd, pt sl, EHU (5A) €2.50; bbq; sw nr; twin axles; 25% statics; Eng spkn; adv bkg acc; games area; games rm. *"Helpful warden; some pitches o'look lake; new fac block (2015); v gd."*
€20.70, 2 Apr-31 Oct. 2022

EYZIES DE TAYAC, LES *7C3* (5km NE Rural) *44.96935, 1.04623* **Camping Le Pigeonnier,** Le Bourg, 24620 Tursac **05 53 06 96 90; campinglepigeonnier@orange.fr; www.campinglepigeonnier.fr**

€1 nr shgl

NE fr Les Eyzies for 5km on D706 to Tursac; site is 200m fr Mairie in vill cent; ent tight. 2*, Sm, hdg, mkd, shd, pt sl, terr, EHU (10A) €3; gas; sw nr; adv bkg acc; horseriding; fishing 1km; bike hire; CKE. *"Freshwater pool (v cold); spacious, grass pitches; facs poss stretched high ssn; canoeing 1km; v quiet hideaway site in busy area; chem disp in vill; close to prehistoric sites; friendly Brit owners."*
€20.50, 1 Jun-15 Sep. 2020

FANJEAUX *8F4* (2.5km S Rural) *43.16558, 2.02702* **Camping Les Brugues,** 11270 Fanjeaux **04 68 24 77 37 or 06 72 74 85 21 (mob); lesbrugues.fanjeaux@gmail.com; www.lesbrugues-camping.com**

nr nr nr

Exit A61 junc 22 onto D4/D119 (dir Mirepoix) to Fanjeaux; cont on D119 dir Mirepoix; at top of hill turn L onto D102 sp La Courtète (past rest La Table Cathare & fuel stn) & in 100m turn R to site in 2.5km. Site well sp fr Fanjeaux. Sm, hdg, mkd, shd, pt sl, terr, EHU (10-16A) inc (rev pol); 10% statics; Eng spkn; adv bkg acc; games rm; CKE. *"Delightful, peaceful, 'off the beaten track' site adj sm lake; care req sm children; well-kept; v lge pitches, some o'looking lake; friendly, helpful owners; gd clean san facs; many walks; beautful countryside; excel touring base; rec."*
€21.60, 1 Jun-30 Sep. 2023

FAVERGES *9B3* (7.3km NW Urban) *45.77510, 6.22585* **Camping La Serraz,** Rue de la Poste, 74210 Doussard **05 79 87 02 59; www.grouperomanee.com**

€2.50 (htd)

Exit Annecy on D1508 twd Albertville. At foot of lake ignore sp on R for Doussard Vill & take next turn R. Site on L in 1km, bef PO, sp. 5*, Med, pt shd, EHU (16A) inc; bbq; sw nr; twin axles; 50% statics; Eng spkn; adv bkg acc; games area; bike hire; games rm; sauna; CCI. *"Excel site; diving course for 8-14 year olds in Jul & Aug; spa opening 2014."* **€47.00, 5 Apr-29 Sep. 2024**

FAYENCE *10E4* (6km W Rural) *43.3500, 6.39590* **Camping La Tuquette (Naturist),** The High Suanes 83440 Fayence **04 94 76 19 40; robert@tuquette.com; www.tuquette.com**

€2 (htd)

Fr Fayence take N562. At km 64.2 sp turn R, site ent 100m. 2*, Sm, mkd, pt shd, terr, EHU (6A) €4.60; bbq; 10% statics; Eng spkn; adv bkg acc; INF card. *"Vg, lovely, clean site; friendly owners, family run."* **€36.40, 10 Apr-26 Sep. 2023**

FECAMP *3C1* (6km SE Rural) *49.74041, 0.41660* **Camping Les Falaises de Toussaint,** D926 76400 Toussaint **02 35 29 78 34; info-lesfalaises@ka-vacances.com**

(htd) nr nr nr 4km

On D926 N of Toussaint. Sp fr main rd. 2*, Med, hdg, mkd, pt shd, pt sl, EHU (4-10A) inc; bbq (gas); twin axles; 70% statics; Eng spkn; adv bkg acc; games area; CKE. *"Lovely quiet site; helpful warden; clean san facs; gd; excel."* **€18.00, 15 Mar-15 Nov. 2021**

FERRIERES EN GATINAIS *4F3* (0.3km N Rural) *48.09198, 2.78482* **Camp Municipal Le Perray/Les Ferrières,** Rue du Perray, 45210 Ferrières-en-Gâtinais **06 71 43 25 95 (mob) or 02 38 87 15 44 (Mairie); camping@ferrieresengatinais.fr; www.ferrieresengatinais.fr/camping-municipal-du-perray**

nr nr

N fr Mantargis on N7; R onto D96/D32 sp Ferrières & foll camp sp. 2*, Med, mkd, pt shd, EHU (10A) inc; 50% statics; tennis; rv fishing adj. *"Vg site; direct access to sm rv; sports facs adj; gd facs & security; old pretty town with lovely church; supmkt clsd Sun-Mon; pool adj; call to check if open; free WiFi; off clsd 1200-1500, no access to site at this time."* **€12.00, 1 Apr-30 Oct. 2023**

FERRIERES SUR SICHON *9B1* (0.3km SE Rural) *46.02246, 3.65326* **Camp Municipal,** 03250 Ferrières-sur-Sichon **04 70 41 10 10; mairie.ferrieres@wanadoo.fr; www.ferrieres-sur-sichon.fr/**

(htd) nr

Well sp in Ferrières-sur-Sichon. At x-rds of D995 & D122. Sm, pt shd, pt sl, EHU €2.20. *"CL-type site; friendly warden visits 1930; gd san facs; excel NH; lake adj; pleasant vill."* **€7.00, 1 Jun-30 Sep. 2024**

FERTE VIDAME, LA *4E2* (1.2km SW Rural) *48.60760, 0.89005* **Camping Les Abrias du Perche,** Route de la Lande, 28340 La Ferte Vidame **02 37 37 64 00; info@campingperchenormandie.fr; www.campingperchenormandie.fr**

€2.50 (covrd, htd)

Fr N12 take D45 (D24) twds Moussenvilliers and la Ferte Vidame. Site on R (D15.1). Sm, hdstg, mkd, pt shd, EHU (6A) €2.50; bbq; twin axles; 50% statics; bus 1km; adv bkg acc; games rm; bike hire; CKE. *"Close to sports ctr, forest walks and fishing; vg; max 2 dogs; fishing nr; long cable poss req; poss rev pol."* **€22.00, 1 Mar-30 Nov. 2023**

FEUILLERES *3C3* (0.4km W Rural) *49.94851, 2.84364* **Camping du Château et de l'Oseraie,** 12 Rue du Château, 80200 Feuillères **03 22 83 17 59 or 06 16 97 93 42 (mob-LS); info@camping-chateau-oseraie.fr; www.camping-chateau-oseraie.com**

€1.20 (htd)

Fr A1/E15 exit 13.1 Maurepas onto D938 dir Albert & then L onto D146; R at staggered x-rds in Feuillères (by church) & site on R in 500m. 3*, Med, hdg, mkd, hdstg, pt shd, EHU (10A) inc (poss rev pol); gas; bbq; red long stay; 10% statics; Eng spkn; adv bkg rec; ccard acc; games rm; fishing; tennis; games area; CKE. *"Excel, well-kept, well-run site; gd sized pitches; friendly staff; clean san facs; conv A1 a'route, WW1 battlefields & Disneyland Paris."* **€25.50, 15 Mar-31 Oct. 2023**

FEURS *9B2* (1km N Urban) *45.75457, 4.22595* **Camp Municipal Le Palais,** Route de Civens, 42110 Feurs **06 63 37 24 57; www.camping-rhonealpes.com**

€0.61 (htd)

Site sp fr D107 on N o'skts of town. Site in corner of sports campus next to Boulodrome. 3*, Lge, pt shd, EHU (6A) €3.05; gas; 80% statics; phone; CKE. *"Pleasant, spacious, beautifully-kept site; busy, espec w/ends; pool adj; clean san facs."* **€18.50, 1 Apr-31 Oct. 2023**

FIGEAC *7D4* (2km E Rural) *44.60989, 2.05015* **Camping Caravanning Domaine Du Surgie,** Base de Loisirs Surgié, 46100 Figeac **05 61 64 88 54; contact@marc-montmija.com; www.domainedusurgie.com**

€2.50

Fr Figeac foll sp Rodez (on D840 S) to site by Rv Célé adj leisure complex. Foll sps 'Base Loisirs de Surgie'. Narr ent, light controlled. Or appr fr E on D840, immed after passing under rlwy arch a v sharp R turn into narr rd (keep R thro traff lts); site on L in 700m. NB Recep at beginning of rd to leisure cent & camping. 3*, Med, mkd, hdg, pt shd, EHU (10A) inc; red long stay; 30% statics; Eng spkn; adv bkg acc; boating; bike hire; tennis. *"Excel pool complex adj (free to campers, clsd Sundays); peaceful LS; pleasant 2km walk or car park just outside town; ent clsd 1200-1600 LS; adj rv unfenced; htd pool & waterslide adj; mkt Sat; rd noise nrby; lge plots; gd cycling routes adj; vg."* **€22.90, 1 May-31 Oct. 2024**

FIGEAC *7D4* (7km SW Rural) *44.57833, 1.93750* **FFCC Camping de Pech-Ibert,** Route de Cajarc, 46100 Béduer **05 65 40 05 85; camping.pech.ibert@orange.fr; www.camping-pech-ibert.com**

€2 (htd)

SW fr Figeac on D662/D19 twds Cajarc. Site well sp on R after Béduer. 2*, Sm, pt shd, EHU (16A) €3.50 (poss rev pol); bbq; sw nr; 10% statics; Eng spkn; adv bkg req; fishing 1km; tennis; bike hire; CKE. *"Peaceful, relaxing site on pilgrimage rte; pleasant, helpful owners; gd clean san facs; gd walking fr site (mkd trails); Sat mkt Figeac; excel; rock pegs req."* **€16.00, 15 Mar-15 Nov. 2024**

FRANCE

FLECHE, LA *4G1* (10km E Rural) *47.70230, 0.07330* **Camping La Chabotière (formerly municipal),** Place des Tilleuls, 72800 Luché-Pringé **02 43 45 10 00; contact@lachabotiere.com; www.lachabotiere.com or www.loir-valley.com**

€1.50 nr

SW fr Le Mans on D323 twd La Flèche. At Clermont-Créans turn L on D13 to Luché-Pringé. Site sp. 3*, Med, hdg, mkd, pt shd, pt sl, EHU (10A) inc (poss rev pol); TV; 10% statics; phone; Eng spkn; adv bkg acc; bike hire; CKE. *"Lovely, well-kept site by Rv Loir; helpful, friendly warden; pool adj high ssn; clean, modern facs; gd site for children; many cycle rtes; conv chateaux; nice vill nrby; avoid Le Mans motor bike week - poss many bikers on site; excel."* **€17.10, 1 Apr-30 Sep.** **2023**

FLECHE, LA *4G1* (0.9km W Urban) *47.69514, -0.07936* **Camping Municipal de la Route d'Or,** Allée du Camping, 72200 La Flèche **02 43 94 55 90; info@camping-laroutedor.com; camping-lafleche.com**

€1 (htd) nr (htd)

Fr NW dir Laval D306, keep to W of town, leave S on D306 twd Bauge; site on L after x-ing rv; sp. Fr S take dir for A11 & Laval, site clearly sp on R on rvside. 4*, Lge, hdg, hdstg, mkd, pt shd, EHU (10A) €3.80 (poss long lead req); gas; bbq; TV; phone; Eng spkn; adv bkg acc; ccard acc; fishing nr; canoeing nr; games area; tennis; CKE. *"Lovely, busy site in beautiful location by rv; well kept, run & maintained site; lge pitches; v friendly, welcoming, helpful staff; facs ltd LS; ring for ent code if office clsd; no twin axles; attractive, easy, sh walk across rv to attractive town; mkt Wed; rec; mkt Sun & Wed; defibrillator on site; new excel san facs (2016); recep clsd 1200-1400; gd value; hg rec."* **€18.00, 15 Mar-4 Nov.** **2024**

FLEURIE *9A2* (0.7km S Rural) *46.18758, 4.69895* **Vivacamp La Grappe Fleurie,** 161 rue de la Grappe, 69820 Fleurie **04 74 69 80 07; info@beaujolais-camping.com; www.beaujolais-camping.com**

€3.10 nr nr nr

S dir Lyon on D906 turn R (W) at S end of Romanèche onto D32; 4km to vill of Fleurie (beware sharp turn in vill & narr rds) & foll site sp. 5*, Med, hdg, mkd, pt shd, terr, serviced pitches; EHU (10A) inc; gas; 10% statics; Eng spkn; adv bkg rec; ccard acc; tennis; CKE. *"Clean, well-run, busy site; friendly staff; excel san facs; lovely pool; gates & wash rms clsd 2200-0700; clean, spacious san facs; path to town thro vineyards (uphill); wine tasting; sm mkt Sat; excel."* **€36.00, 7 Apr-1 Oct.** **2023**

FLORAC *9D1* (1km N Rural) *44.33569, 3.59002* **FFCC Camping Le Pont du Tarn,** Route de Pont de Montvert, 48400 Florac **04 66 45 18 26; contact@camping-florac.com; www.camping-florac.com**

€2 (htd) nr nr nr

Exit Florac N on N106 & turn R in 500m by by-pass on D998; site on L in 300m. 3*, Lge, hdg, mkd, pt shd, EHU (10A) €4.20; bbq (charcoal, elec); sw nr; 60% statics; phone; Eng spkn; adv bkg rec; rv fishing adj; CKE. *"Nice, well-kept, well-run site in beautiful area; clean san facs, needs updating (2016); no twin axles; 20 min walk to town; gd touring base; lge pitches; lge mkt Thurs; vg value; excel site on rv; well situated."* **€37.50, 15 Apr-1 Oct.** **2023**

FLORAC *9D1* (2.5km NE Rural) *44.34528, 3.61008* **FFCC Camping Chantemerle,** La Pontèze, 48400 Bédouès **04 66 45 19 66; chante-merle@wanadoo.fr; www.camping-chantemerle.com**

€1.50

Exit Florac N on N106; in 500m turn R onto D998; in 2.5km site on L, past Bédouès vill cent. 2*, Med, mkd, pt shd, pt sl, EHU (6A) €2.80; sw nr; 10% statics; Eng spkn; games rm; CKE. *"Lovely location; helpful owner; gd walking; conv Gorges du Tarn, Cévennes National Park; vg; water and EHU now avail on lower pitches; sm rest, home cooked food; excel site."* **€26.90, 7 Apr-1 Nov.** **2023**

FLORAC *9D1* (4km NE Rural) *44.34433, 3.60533* **Camping Chon du Tarn,** 48400 Bédouès **04 66 45 09 14; info@camping-chondutarn.com; www.camping-chondutarn.com**

€1 nr

Exit Florac N on N106, turn R in 500m onto D998 (sp Pont de Monvert), site on L in 3km in vill. 2*, Med, mkd, pt shd, pt sl, terr, EHU (6A) €2 (poss rev pol); gas; sw; adv bkg acc; games area; CKE. *"Beautiful rvside site with views; helpful staff; clean dated san facs, ltd LS; conv Tarn Gorges, Causses & Cévennes National Park; lovely rural setting; excel."* **€19.90, 27 Apr-6 Oct.** **2024**

FOIX *8G3* (2km N Rural) *42.98911, 1.61565* **Camping du Lac,** Quartier Labarre, 09000 Foix **05 61 65 11 58; camping-du-lac@wanadoo.fr; www.vap-camping.fr/camping-foix**

€1.50 nr

Fr N on N20 foll sp for 'Centre Ville', site on R in 2km. Fr S onto on N20 thro tunnel & take 1st exit N of Foix & foll sp 'Centre Ville', then as above. Site opp Chausson building materials store. 3*, Lge, mkd, pt shd, EHU (6A) inc; bbq; TV; 75% statics; bus to Foix adj (not Sun); Eng spkn; adv bkg rec; ccard acc; windsurfing; boating; tennis; CKE. *"Busy site w/end; quiet, spacious pitches on L of camp; modern san facs, poss stretched high ssn; site & facs poss uncared for early ssn (2011); gates clsd 2300-0700; pleasant town; NH only LS."* **€32.10, 1 Mar-1 Nov.** **2023**

FOIX *8G3* (4km S Urban) *42.93081, 1.63883* **FFCC Camping Roucateille,** 15 Rue du Pradal, 09330 Montgaillard **05 61 64 05 92; info@roucateille.com; www.camping-roucateille.com**

nr nr

Fr N exit N20 junc 11, fr S exit N20 junc 12; foll sp Montgaillard; site sp fr main rd thro vill. NB Swing wide at ent - sharp turn. 3*, Med, hdg, mkd, shd, EHU (4-10A) €2.50-4.90; bbq; red long stay; 25% statics; Eng spkn; adv bkg acc; ccard acc; CKE. *"Lovely, picturesque, informal site; clean & well cared for; charming, helpful young owners; excel facs; care needed to avoid trees; garden produce in ssn; gd touring base; gd cycling; Forges de Pyène eco-museum worth visit; excel; historical area; pool 3km; nr stream with cherry orchard behind."* **€24.00, 1 May-30 Sep. 2024**

FONTAINE SIMON *4E2* (0.8km N Rural) *48.51314, 1.01941* **Camping du Perche,** 3 Rue de la Ferrière, 28240 Fontaine-Simon **02 37 81 88 11 or 06 23 82 90 28 (mob); campingduperche@orange.fr; www.campingduperche.com**

12 €2 (htd)

Fr La Loupe on D929 take D25 N to Fontaine-Simon, site sp. 3*, Med, hdg, pt shd, pt sl, EHU €3.60; bbq; sw nr; 10% statics; adv bkg acc; fishing; CKE. *"Undulating, lakeside site; htd covrd pool adj; gd."* **€15.00 2020**

FONTAINEBLEAU *4E3* (5km NE Rural) *48.42215, 2.74872* **Camping Municipal de Samoreau,** Rue de l'Abreuvoir/Rue de l'Eglise, 77210 Samoreau **06 89 16 25 68; camping@samoreau.fr; www.samoreau.fr**

(htd) nr nr nr

Fr cent of Fontainebleau take D210 (dir Provins); in approx 4km at rndabt cross bdge over Rv Seine; take R at rndabt; site sp at end of rd thro Samoreau vill; site twd rv. 1*, Med, mkd, hdg, pt shd, pt sl, EHU (10A) inc (poss rev pol); phone; bus; adv bkg acc; CKE. *"Peaceful site in attractive location by Rv Seine; gd sized pitches; helpful staff; gd, immac san facs; adj vill hall poss noisy w/end; jazz festival late Jun; conv palace, Paris (by train) & Disneyland; clsd 2200-0700; excel; waterpoints around site could do with upgrade; bus stop adj; dedicated cycle route to Chateau."* **€23.10, 1 Mar-31 Oct. 2024**

FONTAINEBLEAU *4E3* (10km S Rural) *48.31740, 2.69650* **Camping Les Prés,** Chemin des Prés, 77880 Grez-sur-Loing **01 64 45 72 75; camping-grez@wanadoo.fr; www.camping-grez-fontainebleau.info**

nr nr

Fr Fontainebleau on D607 twd Nemours (S) for 8km; look for camping sps. At traff island turn L onto D40D, in 1km immed after x-ing bdge turn R; site on L. Do not tow into Grez-sur-Loing. 2*, Med, hdg, mkd, pt shd, EHU (5A) €3; gas; red long stay; 80% statics; phone; Eng spkn; adv bkg acc; ccard acc; fishing; canoe hire; bike hire; CKE. *"In attractive area; helpful British owner; 80% statics; site poss unkempt/scruffy end of ssn; vg; busy; rest in vill."* **€20.30, 14 Mar-6 Nov. 2022**

FONTAINEBLEAU *4E3* (14km S Rural) *48.33362, 2.75386* **Camping Le Parc du Gué,** Route de Montigny, La Genevraye, 77690 Montigny-sur-Loing **01 64 45 87 79; contact@camping-parcdugue.com; www.camping-parcdugue.com**

€3.70 (htd) (htd)

Do not tow thro Montigny-sur-Loing, v narr tight turns. Site is E of Montigny, N of La Genevraye off D104. App fr S Nemours on D40, slow rd but safe, or fr NE, Moret-sur-Loing D606/D104. 2*, Lge, hdg, mkd, pt shd, EHU (10A) €3.60; bbq; sw nr; 70% statics; Eng spkn; adv bkg acc; ccard acc; fishing; games area; watersports; CKE. *"Beautiful, wooded country; kayaks; mkt Sat 2km; excel walking & cycling; new pool (2015); vg."* **€21.00, 15 Mar-30 Nov. 2022**

FONTENAY TRESIGNY *4E3* (7km NE Rural) *48.75050, 2.89728* **Camping des Quatre Vents,** 22 Rue de Beauregard, 77610 Crèvecoeur-en-Brie, Île de France **01 64 07 41 11; contact@caravaning-4vents.fr; www.caravaning-4vents.fr**

€3 (htd) nr

At Calais take A26/E15 dir Arras; at Arras take A1/E15 dir Paris; next take A104 dir A4 Metz/Nancy/Marne-la-Vallée, then A4 dir Metz/Nancy, exit junc 13 onto D231 dir Provins; after rndabt with lge monument turn R dir Crèvecoeur-en-Brie & foll site sp. Site in 13km. 3*, Lge, hdg, mkd, pt shd, serviced pitches; EHU (6A) inc; bbq; TV; 50% statics; phone; Eng spkn; adv bkg req; ccard acc; games rm; horseriding; games area; CKE. *"Friendly, well-run, beautiful site; lge, well-kept pitches; welcoming, helpful staff; san facs spacious & v clean; pleasant pool; conv Disneyland & Paris; poss muddy when wet; vg; beautiful countryside ideal for cycling; no o'fits over 10m high ssn; restfull even in high ssn."* **€30.00, 20 Mar - 1 Nov, P09. 2022**

FONTES *10F1* (0.9km N Rural) *43.54734, 3.37999* **FFCC Camping L'Evasion,** Route de Cabrières, 34320 Fontès **04 67 25 32 00; www.campingevasion.com**

€2.80

Fr A75 exit junc 59 (Pézenas). At rndabt take D124 to Lézignan-la-Cèbe then fork L, cont on D124 to Fontès. In vill foll sp to site. 3*, Sm, hdg, mkd, pt shd, pt sl, EHU (10A) €3.50; gas; bbq; 75% statics; phone; adv bkg acc; CKE. *"Excel san facs; touring pitches amongst statics (long-term residents); helpful owners."* **€22.50, 14 Mar-2 Nov. 2022**

FONTES *10F1* (3km E Rural) *43.54491, 3.41743* **Camping Les Clairettes,** Route de Péret, 34320 Fontès **04 67 25 01 31; campinglesclairettes.fr**

12 nr

Sp on D609. Turn onto D128 sp Adissan, Fontès. Fr A75 exit junc 58. Foll sp for Adissan & site. 3*, Med, hdg, mkd, pt shd, serviced pitches; EHU (6A); gas; bbq; TV; 50% statics; adv bkg acc. *"V quiet; friendly owners; ltd facs LS; nice site; no m'van drive-over drain; convly nr m'way but away fr coastal crowds."* **€23.00 2024**

FRANCE

FRANCE

FORCALQUIER *10E3* (0.7km E Urban) *43.96206, 5.78718* **Camping Les Routes de Provence (formerly Forcalquier),** Avenue Claude Delorme, 04300 Forcalquier **04 66 60 07 00; lesroutesdeprovence@outlook.com; www.camping-routes-de-provence.fr**

€4.50 nr (htd)

Fr A51 exit junc 19 La Brillane onto D4100 to Forcalquier. Site sp. 3*, Med, mkd, pt shd, pt sl, serviced pitches; EHU (10A) inc; bbq; TV; 10% statics; phone; Eng spkn; adv bkg acc; games area; CKE. *"Pleasant site in lovely location; excel m'van facs; access for lge o'fits & m'vans poss diff due v narr site rds & awkward corners; walking dist fr town cent; v friendly & helpful staff; famous lge mkt on Mon."* **€31.80, 4 Apr-22 Sep.** **2024**

FORCALQUIER *10E3* (8km SE Rural) *43.89752, 5.80609* **FLOWER Camping La Rivière,** Lieu-Dit 'Les Côtes', 04300 St Maime **04 92 79 54 66; contact@camping-lariviere.com; https://camping-lariviere.com/fr/**

12 €2.50

S fr Sisteron on D4085, then D4096. Turn R at Voix onto D13, site on R in about 5km. 2*, Med, hdg, mkd, pt shd, EHU (10A) inc; bbq; TV; 50% statics; adv bkg acc; ccard acc; games area; games rm; lake fishing adj; CKE. *"Vg, relaxing, friendly site; gd touring base for hilltop towns."* **€35.50** **2024**

FORCALQUIER *10E3* (6.5km S Urban) *43.91096, 5.78210* **Au Tylo Soleil Camping (formerly Camp l'Eau Vive),** 04300 Dauphin **04 92 79 51 91; info@leauvive.fr; autylosoleil.fr**

€3.50 (htd)

S fr Forcalquier on D4100 dir Apt; in 2.5km turn L onto D13 (at Mane); site on R in 3km. Or fr D4096, turn onto D13 at Volx; site on L in 6km (800m past Dauphin). 3*, Med, mkd, shd, EHU (3-6A) €3.50-4.50; bbq (gas, sep area); TV; bus 800m; Eng spkn; adv bkg acc; games area; tennis; games rm; bike hire. *"Well-run, super site; helpful owners; vg pools; vg for children; excel."* **€34.00, 1 Apr-13 Nov.** **2023**

FORCALQUIER *10E3* (4km NW Rural) *43.97235, 5.73800* **Camping Le Domaine des Lauzons (Naturist),** 04300 Limans **04 92 73 00 60; leslauzons@wanadoo.fr; www.camping-lauzons.com**

€4 (htd)

Exit A51 junc 19 onto N100 dir Avignon; in Forcalquier at rndabt turn L onto D950/D313 sp Banon; site on R in approx 6km. Lge site sp. Diff app. 4*, Med, mkd, pt shd, pt sl, terr, EHU (6A) €4.50; gas; bbq (charcoal, gas); TV; 25% statics; phone; Eng spkn; adv bkg acc; ccard acc; waterslide; games area; ice; sauna; games rm; INF card req; archery. *"Pleasant site in wooded valley; wonderful scenery; excel family site; helpful, friendly staff; most san facs modern, ltd LS; excel pool area; walks fr site; Forcalquier lovely town; excel touring base; pony rides; many activities; access diff lge o'fits, tractor help avail; INF not compulsory."* **€41.20, 22 Apr-30 Sep.** **2023**

FORGES LES EAUX *3C2* (0.5km S Urban) *49.60597, 1.54262* **Camping De La Miniere (formerly Aire de Service),** Blvd Nicolas Thiessé, 76440 Forges-les-Eaux **02 359 053 91; campingforges@gmail.com; www.campingforges.com/fr/bienvenue-a-la-miniere**

12

Fr Forges-les-Eaux cent, take D921 S sp Lyons-la-Forêt. In 500m turn R foll sp, camp on L in 250m opp municipal site. Med, mkd, hdstg, unshd, EHU (poss rev pol). *"No power, water etc Nov to Mar; water points; max 2 nights; warden visits or pay at Municipal site opp; town cent easy walk; views of open countryside; excel."* **€7.00** **2024**

FORGES LES EAUX *3C2* (1km S Urban) *49.60603, 1.54302* **Camp Municipal La Minière,** 3 Blvd Nicolas Thiese, 76440 Forges-les-Eaux **02 35 90 53 91; campingforges@gmail.com; www.campingforges.com/en**

nr

Fr Forges-les-Eaux cent, take D921 S sp Lyons-la-Forêt. In 750m turn R foll sp, camp on R in 150m. NB 3,500kg limit in town all dirs. 2*, Med, mkd, hdg, pt shd, pt sl, EHU (6A) inc (rev pol); CKE. *"Well-presented site; mv service pnt adj; lge pitches; friendly warden, warm welcome; v basic, clean san facs; poss diff access some pitches; m'van o'night area opp; htd pool in town; pleasant town with excel WWII Resistance Museum; gd local vet; useful NH; gd access to town; dog walk on site."* **€19.50, 26 Mar-29 Oct.** **2023**

FOUGERES *2E4* (2.5km E Urban) *48.3544, -1.1795* **Camp Municipal de Fougeres (formerly de Paron),** Route de la Chapelle-Janson, 35300 Fougères **02 99 99 40 81; camping.fougeres.fr**

nr nr

Fr A84/E3 take junc 30 then ring rd E twd N12. Turn L at N12 & foll sp. Site on D17 sp R after Carrefour. Well sp on ring rd. 3*, Med, hdg, hdstg, pt shd, pt sl, serviced pitches; EHU (5-10A) €3.60-4.10 (poss rev pol); adv bkg acc; ccard acc; tennis; horseriding adj; CKE. *"Well-kept site in pleasant parkland setting; lge pitches, poss soggy when wet; popular NH; helpful warden; gd clean facs; gates clsd 2200-0900 & 1230-1730 card pass avail, parking avail in adj car park; tours of 12thC castle; old town worth visit; Sat mkt; excel; excel san facs."* **€22.00, 1 Apr-31 Oct.** **2023**

FOURAS *7A1* (0.5km NE Coastal) *45.99264, -1.08680*
Camp Municipal du Cadoret, Blvd de Chaterny, 17450 Fouras **05 46 82 19 19; campinglecadoret@fouras-les-bains.fr; www.campings-fouras.com**
12 €2.15 nr (htd)
sand adj

Fr Rochefort take N137, L onto D937 at Fouras, fork R at sp to site in 1km. At next rndabt take 3rd exit into Ave du Cadoret, then 1st R at next rndabt. 3*, Lge, hdg, mkd, pt shd, pt sl, EHU (6-10A) €3.50-5.40 (poss long lead req); gas; 50% statics; bus to La Rochelle, Rochefort, ferry to Ile d'Aix; Eng spkn; adv bkg acc; golf 5km; fishing; games area; tennis 1km; boating; CKE. *"Popular, well-kept site; vg location; well shd; lge pitches; clean san facs, unisex LS; coastal footpath; pleasant town; a favourite; highly rec; gd conv site."* **€24.00** **2024**

FOURAS *7A1* (1km E Rural) *45.99023, -1.05184*
Camping Domaine Les Charmilles, 1541 Route de l'OcÃcan, 17450 Fouras **05 46 84 00 05; lescharmilles@vagues-oceanes.com; www.domainedescharmilles.com**
12 (htd) (covrd, htd)
sand 3km

N fr Rochefort on N137, after 2km L onto D937. Site on L in 2km bef ent Fouras. 4*, Lge, hdg, mkd, pt shd, EHU (6A) €4; gas; bbq; red long stay; 20% statics; adv bkg acc; ccard acc; waterslide; bike hire; games rm; CKE. *"Gd site; friendly staff; bus to beach high ssn; unisex facs."* **€37.50** **2024**

FREJUS *10F4* (5km SW Rural) *43.39890, 6.67531*
Camping Domaine de la Bergerie, Vallée-du-Fournel, Route du Col-du-Bougnon, 83520 Roquebrune-sur-Argens **04 98 11 45 45; info@domainelabergerie.com; www.domainelabergerie.com**
€6 (covrd, htd)

On DN7 twd Fréjus, turn R onto D7 sp St Aygulf & Roquebrune-sur-Argens; after passing Roquebrune, site sp in approx 6km on R. 5*, V lge, mkd, hdg, pt shd, terr, serviced pitches; EHU (6A) inc (extra for 10A); gas; red long stay; 70% statics; Eng spkn; adv bkg acc; ccard acc; tennis; jacuzzi; sauna; archery; games area; lake fishing; waterslide. *"Well-organised site; entmnt/activities for all ages; mini farm; early bkg ess for summer; excel."*
€57.30, 20 Apr-2 Nov. **2024**

FREJUS *10F4* (10km W Rural) *43.45070, 6.63320*
Village camping Les Pêcheurs, Quartier Verseil, 83520 Roquebrune-sur-Argens **04 94 45 71 25; info@camping-les-pecheurs.com; www.camping-les-pecheurs.com**
€3.50 (htd) (htd)

Exit A8 junc 36 dir Le Muy, onto DN7 then D7 sp Roquebrune; camp 800m on L (bef bdge over Rv Argens) at ent to vill. Alt rte, leave A8 at junc 37, turn R at rndabt twrds Le Muy and cont as above. 4*, Lge, hdstg, mkd, hdg, pt shd, EHU (10A) €5.50; gas; bbq (elec, gas); sw nr; TV; 25% statics; phone; Eng spkn; adv bkg acc; ccard acc; horseriding; canoeing adj; tennis 2km; fishing adj; CKE. *"Lovely site; popular with families; helpful staff; sauna; spa; jacuzzi; some pitches v shady; bike hire 1km; some site rds/pitch access tight for lge o'fits, OK with mover; gd walking, cycling."*
€71.00, 5 Apr - 12 Oct, C08. **2022**

FREJUS *10F4* (3km NW Rural) *43.46335, 6.7247*
Camping Le Fréjus, 3401, rue des Combattants, d'Afrique du Nord, 83600 FREJUS **04 94 19 94 60; frejus@capfun.com; www.lefrejus.com**
(leashed) €4 (htd) (htd)

Exit A8 junc 38, at 1st rndabt turn L, then L at 2nd rndabt & L again at 3rd rndabt, Site on R in 200m. 3*, Lge, mkd, pt shd, pt sl, terr, EHU (10A) inc; 80% statics; Eng spkn; adv bkg acc; ccard acc; waterslide; games rm; tennis; CKE. *"Ideal position for coast bet Cannes & St Tropez; lge pitches; pleasant, friendly staff; gd san facs; muddy after rain; quiet; vg site; basin cold water at each pitch."*
€46.20, 1 Apr-15 Dec. **2024**

FREJUS *10F4* (4km NW Urban) *43.46616, 6.72203*
Camping La Baume - La Palmeraie, Route de Bagnoles, Rue des Combattants d'Afrique du Nord, 83600 Fréjus **04 94 19 00 00; reception@labaume-lapalmeraie.com; www.labaume-lapalmeraie.com**
€6 (htd) (covrd, htd, indoor) sand 5km

Fr A8 exit junc 38 sp Fréjus cent. Fr E'bound dir foll Bagnols sp at 2 rndabts & Fréjus cent/Cais at 3rd. Fr W'bound dir foll Bagnols at 3 rndabts & Fréjus cent/Cais at 4th. Site on L in 300m. 4*, V lge, pt shd, pt sl, EHU (6A) inc; gas; 80% statics; adv bkg req; horseriding; tennis; waterslide; spa.
€51.00, 28 Mar-26 Sep. **2020**

FREJUS *10F4* (6km NW Rural) *43.46944, 6.67805* **Camping La Bastiane,** 1056 Chemin des Suvières, 83480 Puget-sur-Argens **04 94 55 55 94; info@labastiane.com; www.labastiane.com**

€4 WD (htd)

Exit A8 at junc 37 Puget/Fréjus. At DN7 turn R dir Le Muy & in 1km turn R immed after 2nd bdge. Foll sp to site. Fr DN7 turn L at traff lts in Puget, site is 2km N of Puget. 4*, Lge, mkd, hdg, shd, pt sl, EHU (10A) inc; bbq (elec); red long stay; TV; 40% statics; phone; Eng spkn; adv bkg acc; ccard acc; bike hire; tennis; games area; games rm; watersports; CKE. *"Excel, family-run, friendly site; cinema; car wash area; conv m'way (no m'way noise); clean san facs; gd rest."* **€50.20, 21 Apr-9 Oct. 2023**

"I need an on-site restaurant"

We do our best to make sure site information is correct, but it is always best to check any must-have facilities are still available or will be open during your visit.

FRESNAY SUR SARTHE *4E1* (0.2km NW Rural) *48.28297, 0.0158* **Camp Municipal Le Sans Souci,** Rue du Haut Ary, Ave Victor Hugo, 72130 Fresnay-sur-Sarthe **02 43 97 32 87; fresnaycamping@gmail.com; camping.fresnaysursarthe.fr**

€3 WD MSP nr nr nr

Fr Alençon S on D338; in 14km at La Hutte turn R on D310 to Fresnay; sp in town on traff lts bef bdge; bear R imm after x-ing bdge, then sharp R, sp diff to see, if missed V diff for c'vans to turn fr opp dir. Fr Beaumont-sur-Sarthe NW on D39 to Fresnay. 3*, Med, mkd, hdg, pt shd, pt sl, terr, EHU (10A) €4 (poss rev pol); gas; twin axles; Eng spkn; adv bkg acc; ccard acc; rv fishing adj; bike hire; canoe hire; games area; tennis courts; CKE. *"Pleasant, clean site adj Rv Sarthe; gd rvside pitches; 3 pitches for lge o'fits, mover rec; htd pool adj inc; facs poss stretched high ssn; gd cycling; vg."* **€15.60, 1 Apr-31 Oct. 2023**

FRONTIGNAN *10F1* (1km S Coastal) *43.42998, 3.75968* **Camping Méditerranée,** 11 Ave des Vacances, Quartier L'Entrée, 34110 Frontignan-Plage **04 99 04 92 32 or 06 73 65 48 74; camping-mediterranee@orange.fr; www.camping-mediterranee34.com**

€1.50 nr sand 100m

3km fr Sète on D612 to Montpellier, turn R at rlwy bdge, in approx 1km L at x-rds to site. Or on D129 fr Frontignan to Frontignan-Plage site on R 100m past reclamation area. 2*, Med, pt shd, EHU (6A) €3.50; bus adj; adv bkg rec; games area; tennis. " **€26.00, 24 Mar-29 Sep. 2024**

FRONTIGNAN *10F1* (6km S Coastal) *43.44970, 3.80540* **Sandaya Les Tamaris,** 140 Ave d'Ingril, 34110 Frontignan-Plage **04 67 43 44 77; tam@sandaya.fr; www.sandaya.co.uk**

€3 (htd) WD MSP (htd) sand adj

Fr A9/E15 exit junc 32 St Jean-de-Védas & foll sp Sète. At next rndbt foll sp Sète N112. After approx 8km turn L sp Vic-la-Gardiole onto D114. Cross rlwy & Canal du Rhône. Pass Les Aresquiers-Plages & turn L in 500m, site sp on L in 500m. Fr N on D613, take N300 to Sète; then N112 to Frontignan-Plage. 5*, Lge, hdstg, mkd, hdg, pt shd, serviced pitches; EHU (10A) inc; bbq; red long stay; TV; 50% statics; phone; adv bkg rec; ccard acc; lake fishing; bike hire; watersports; horseriding nr; games rm. *"Popular, family-run site; direct access to beach; sm pitches; archery; weights rm; friendly, helpful staff; gd clean san facs; vg for families; excel pool; late arr area; gd rest; lovely town; mkt Thu & Sat am; excel."* **€73.30, 27 Mar-5 Oct. 2024**

FUMEL *7D3* (2km E Rural) *44.48929, 0.99704* **Camping de Condat/Les Catalpas,** Path of the Plaine de Condat, 47500 Fumel **05 53 71 11 99 or 06 30 24 20 04; contact@les-catalpas.com; www.les-catalpas.com**

(htd) WD MSP nr nr

Take D811 fr Fumel E twd Cahors. Clearly sp after Condat. 3*, Med, mkd, hdstg, pt shd, pt sl, EHU (10A) €3; bbq; TV; 15% statics; Eng spkn; adv bkg acc; fishing adj; CKE. *"New owners, friendly helpful, improvements to site, sec barrier, by rv."* **€21.00, 1 Apr-31 Oct. 2020**

"Satellite navigation makes touring much easier"

Remember most sat navs don't know if you're towing or in a larger vehicle – always use yours alongside maps and site directions.

FUMEL *7D3* (4km E Rural) *44.48925, 1.02048* **Aire Naturelle Le Valenty (Baillargues),** Rue de Chantegrue 46700 Soturac, Lot **06 50 74 21 59 09 83 34 77 78; campingdevalenty@gmail.com; www.campinglevalenty.fr**

€1 nr nr nr

Fr Fumel take D911/811 dir Cahors. Thro Soturac, site immed on L outside vill. 2*, Sm, pt shd, terr, EHU (4-10A) €2.50; 20% statics; bus 200m; Eng spkn; adv bkg acc; games rm; CKE. *"Delightful CL-type site; helpful owners; tranquil but secure; pony rides; organic produce for sale; mini golf; poss not open LS - phone ahead."* **€17.00, 1 Mar-12 Nov. 2024**

FUMEL *7D3* (8km E Rural) *44.49810, 1.06670*
Camping Le Ch'Timi, La Roque, 46700 Touzac
05 65 36 52 36; receptie@campinglechtimi.com; www.campinglechtimi.com
€1.90

Exit N20-E9 junc 57 onto D820 dir Cahors; turn R at rndabt onto D811 sp Villeneuve-sur-Lot; in Duravel take 3rd exit at rndabt onto D58, sp Vire-sur-Lot; in 2.5km cross bdge & turn R at rndabt onto D8, sp Touzac; site on R on rvside, on hill, in about 1.5km. Well sp. NB D8 not suitable lge c'vans or m'vans. 3*, Med, mkd, hdg, pt shd, pt sl, EHU (6A) €4.20; gas; bbq; twin axles; TV; 13% statics; phone; Eng spkn; adv bkg acc; ccard acc; tennis; games area; games rm; archery; bike hire; fishing 100m; CKE. *"Site in gd position; friendly, helpful Dutch owners; immac facs, ltd LS; rv nr site, down steep steps; access some pitches poss diff lge o'fits; gd local rests; no o'fits over 7m high ssn; canoeing 100m; wine-tasting tours; mkt Puy l'Evêque Tue; wonderful stay, rec; v well kept; rv view fr some pitches; ACSI acc."* **€32.00, 15 Apr - 30 Sep, D05. 2022**

GACE *4E1* (0.2km E Urban) *48.79475, 0.29926*
Camp Municipal Le Pressoir, Ave de Tahiti, 61230 Gacé **02 33 35 50 24; ville.gace@wanadoo.fr; www.camping-lepressoir-gace.fr**
12 nr nr

Exit A28 junc 16 onto D932/D438; in 2km turn R off D438 opp Intermarché onto D724; site immed on L. Foll sp. NB Take care corners on app if o'fit v long. 2*, Sm, mkd, hdg, pt shd, sl, EHU (6A) €2.50 (poss long lead req); twin axles. *"Clean, well-run site; rec early arr; san facs dated but clean; mv service pnt in vill; most pitches gd size, sm pitches poss diff for lge o'fits; pitches rather sl for m'van; warden calls am & pm; conv NH fr A28; nice site, well kept."* **€13.00 2024**

GAILLAC *8E4* (5km E Urban) *43.90929, 1.98311*
Camping Les Pommiers d'Aigueleze, Espace de Loisirs d'Aigueleze, 81600 Rivières **05 63 33 02 49; info@camping-lespommiers.com; www.camping-lespommiers.com**
€2 (htd)

Fr A68, Albi - Toulouse take exit 10, foll sp Espace Loisirs d'Aigueleze. 4*, Med, hdstg, mkd, hdg, pt shd, EHU (10-13A) €4.50; bbq; sw; twin axles; red long stay; TV; 25% statics; phone; Eng spkn; adv bkg acc; games area; bike hire; CCI. *"Visit Albi by sightseeing boat on Rv Tarn or by train; canoe hire 150m; bike hire 150m; vg; conv Albi, Cordes, P&R Toulose; excel; well kept clean site; friendly, welcoming owners; conv for bastide vill; sm eve mkt Mon in hg ssn nr."*
€30.00, 1 May-30 Sep. 2023

GAILLAC *8E4* (2km W Urban) *43.89674, 1.88522*
Camping Municipal des Sources, 9 Ave Guynemer, 81600 Gaillac **05 63 57 18 30; camping-gaillac@orange.fr; www.camping-gaillac.fr**
€2 (htd) nr

Exit A68 junc 9 onto D999 then in 3.5km at rndabt turn onto D968 dir Gaillac. In 100m turn R immed past Leclerc petrol stn, then L by Aldi. Site 200m on R, well sp fr town cent. Sharp turn into ent. 3*, Med, hdg, mkd, hdstg, pt shd, terr, EHU (10A) €3; TV; 10% statics; ccard acc; CKE. *"Peaceful, clean & tidy site; friendly, helpful staff; gd, modern san facs; steep walk to recep & bar but san facs at pitch level; purpose-made dog-walk area; gd touring base Tarn & Albi region & circular tour Bastides; cent of wine area; not suitable lge o'fits; gd; call recep fr Aldi carpk to operate barrier."*
€14.50, 1 Apr-31 Oct. 2023

GANGES *10E1* (7km E Rural) *43.92630, 3.78951*
Camp Municipal Le Grillon, Place de l'Eglise, 34190 Montoulieu **04 67 73 79 31 or 06 61 75 35 11; camping.montoulieu@sfr.fr; http://camping.montoulieu.fr**
12

Fr Ganges take D999 E. At La Cadière-et-Cambo turn R onto D195 (site sp). Site on R in 3km. 3*, Sm, hdg, hdstg, pt shd, pt sl, EHU (6A) inc; 40% statics. *"Gd cent for outdoor activities; gd, modern facs; useful winter NH; fairly isolated."* **€18.90 2024**

GANNAT *9A1* (10km W Rural) *46.11077, 3.08082*
Camp Municipal Les Nières, Rue des Nières, 03450 Ebreuil **04 70 90 70 60 or 04 70 90 71 33 (Mairie); contact@campingdesnieres.fr; www.camping-sioule.fr**
€ 3 (cont) (htd)

Site 1km SW of Ebreuil, sp fr D915. 3*, Sm, shd, EHU (4-8A) €1.95-2.80; bbq; Eng spkn; fishing; rv; tennis. *"Nice setting on Rv Sioule; san facs dated but clean, poss stretched high ssn; warden present 1700-2000 only LS; sh walk into vill."* **€8.00, 24 Apr-27 Sep. 2020**

GAP *9D3* (1.5km N Rural) *44.58030, 6.08270*
Camping Alpes-Dauphiné, Route Napoléon, 05000 Gap **04 92 51 29 95; info@alpesdauphine.com; www.alpesdauphine.com**
€2.10 (htd) (htd)

On N85, sp. 4*, Med, hdstg, mkd, pt shd, pt sl, terr, EHU (6A) €3; gas; TV; 20% statics; phone; Eng spkn; adv bkg rec; ccard acc; games area; CKE. *"Pleasant site with views; modern, well maintained san facs; m'vans need levellers; gd touring base; lack of maintenance early ssn (2011); conv NH; gd site; excel rest."*
€30.10, 15 Apr-15 Oct. 2023

FRANCE

GAP *9D3* (10km S Rural) *44.45708, 6.04785*
Camping Le Chêne, Route de Marseille, 05130 Tallard **04 92 54 13 31 or 06 15 99 50 89 (mob); contact@camping-lechene.com; www.camping-lechene.com**
nr (htd)

Fr S take N85 twds Gap; turn R at traff lts onto D942; site on R after 3km. Fr Gap take N85 S; turn L at traff lts, D942; site on R 3km. 3*, Sm, mkd, hdstg, pt shd, sl, terr, EHU (6A) €3.5; bbq (sep area); phone; adv bkg acc; tennis; CKE. *"Poss unsuitable for lgs o'fits, sm pitches; lovely setting; new san facs (2018), but ltd for site size; site needs tlc."*
€20.00, 15 Apr-9 Oct. **2023**

GAVARNIE *8G2* (4km N Rural) *42.75896, 0.00069*
Camping Le Pain de Sucre, quartier Couret, 65120 Gavarnie **05 62 92 47 55 or 06 75 30 64 22 (mob); camping-gavarnie@wanadoo.fr or info@camping-gavarnie.com; www.camping-gavarnie.com**
€2.15 nr nr

N of Gavarnie, across rv by sm bdge; clearly visible & sp fr rd. 2*, Med, pt shd, EHU (2-10A) €2.30-6.50 (long lead poss req); bbq; ccard acc. *"Gd base for walking; gd facs; access to national park; vg; gd clean san facs; fantastic view of Cirque."* **€21.20, 1 Jan-15 Apr, 29 May-30 Sep & 15 Dec-31 Dec.** 2022

GENNES *4G1* (0.7km NE Rural) *47.34205, -0.22985*
Camping Au Bord de Loire, Ave des Cadets-de-Saumur, 49350 Gennes **02 41 38 04 67; contact@camping-auborddeloire.com; www.camping-auborddeloire.com**
€1.60 nr

At Rv Loire bdge cross S to Gennes on D751B. Site 200m on L. Ent to site thro bus terminus/car park on ent to Gennes. 3*, Med, pt shd, pt sl, EHU (10A) €3.40; bbq; red long stay; 2% statics; CKE. *"Delightful, relaxing, well-kept site by Rv Loire, spacious pitches, main san facs block up 18 steps, vg; htd pool in vill; Loire cycle rte passes gate; new san facs block (2015); v easy walk to vill."* **€19.90, 8 Apr-30 Sep.** **2023**

GERARDMER *6F3* (2km SW Urban) *48.06472, 6.85388*
Camping de Ramberchamp, 21 Chemin du Tour du Lac, 88400 Gérardmer **03 29 63 03 82; info@camping-de-ramberchamp.com; www.camping-de-ramberchamp.com**
€1 (htd) nr

S bank of Lake Gérardmer. Fr W turn R off D417, 1km bef Gérardmer. Fr E thro cent of town foll sps to La Bresse, fork R onto D69, sp Vagney. Foll lakeside rd & camping sps. 3*, Lge, hdg, mkd, pt shd, EHU (4A) €3.50; bbq; sw; TV; Eng spkn; ccard acc; fishing; CKE. *"Comfortable site in excel location; friendly staff; some sm pitches; easy-going walks; walk along lake to town; games for children, giant chessboard, mini golf; excel, stunning area; rec open fr 0830 to 2030, san facs stretched when busy, access rds thro site very narr for lge o'fits, superb location at edge of lake."* **€20.40, 4 Apr-30 Sep.** **2024**

GERAUDOT *6E1* (1km E Rural) *48.30268, 4.33752*
Camping Les Rives du Lac/L'Epine aux Moines, 10220 Géraudot **03 25 41 24 36; camping.lepineauxmoines@orange.fr; www.campinglesrivesdulac.com**
12 €2 (htd) nr

Exit A26 at junc 23 onto D619 to Lusigny-sur-Barse; foll sp Parc de la Forêt d'Orient. Turn N along lake to site. Or fr Troyes D960 E. At Rouilly head S on D43 sp Géraudot. Site 1km E of vill. 2*, Lge, hdg, mkd, pt shd, pt sl, EHU (6A) inc (poss rev pol & long lead req); sw nr; adv bkg acc; boat hire; CKE. *"Nice, well-kept site in attractive area; clean san facs; poss mosquitoes; gd walking & cycle paths; nr bird observatory; lovely vill; conv NH."* **€31.80** **2024**

GEX *9A3* (1.4km E Urban) *46.33430, 6.06744*
Camping Les Genêts, 400 Ave des Alpes, 01170 Gex **04 56 82 14 04 or 06 43 11 23 70 (mob); campinglesgenets01@gmail.com; www.camping-les-genets-gex.com**
€1 nr

Fr all dir head for 'Centre Ville'; at rndabt take D984 twd Divonne/Lausanne. Site sp to R (tight turn) after rlwy sheds (poor sp in town) & Musée Sapeurs Pompiers. 3*, Med, hdg, hdstg, pt shd, pt sl, EHU (16A) €2.90; TV; phone; Eng spkn; adv bkg acc; games area; CKE. *"Excel, attractive, well-kept site; excel games facs/playgrnd; friendly, helpful staff; clean san facs; quiet with lots of privacy; conv Geneva; wifi in recep; gates clsd 2200-0800; 20 mins fr Geneva airport."* **€19.50, 9 Apr-8 Oct.** **2023**

GIEN *4G3* (8km S Rural) *47.64152, 2.61528*
Les Bois du Bardelet, Route de Bourges, Poilly 45500 Gien **02 38 67 47 39; contact@bardelet.com; www.bardelet.com**
€4 (htd)
(covrd, htd, indoor)

Fr Gien take D940 dir Bourges; turn R onto D53, then R again onto unclassified rd to go back across D940; foll sp to site on L side of this rd. Site well sp fr D940. 5*, Lge, hdstg, mkd, hdg, pt shd, pt sl, EHU (10-16A) inc (some rev pol); gas; bbq; red long stay; twin axles; TV; 17% statics; phone; adv bkg acc; ccard acc; archery; bike hire; fitness rm; jacuzzi; canoeing; games area; tennis; lake fishing; horseriding 5km; games rm; CKE. *"Pleasant, well-kept, well-run site; friendly welcome; modern, immac san facs, poss stretched high ssn; some pitches poss diff access; beautiful o'door pool; gd for young children; guided walks; remote site in countryside."*
€40.00, 7 May - 11 Sep, L05. **2022**

GISORS *3D3* (7km SW Rural) *49.25639, 1.70174* **Camp Municipal de l'Aulnaie,** Rue du Fond-de-l'Aulnaie, 27720 Dangu **02 32 55 43 42; contact@campingdelaulnaie.com; www.campingdelaulnaie.com**

€2.60 (htd) nr nr

On ent Gisors fr all dirs, take ring rd & exit dir Vernon D10, then L onto D181 dir Dangu. Site on L bef Dangu. Site sp fr D10. NB speed humps. 3*, Lge, mkd, pt shd, EHU (10A); gas; sw; 90% statics; Eng spkn; adv bkg acc; fishing; CKE. *"Lakeside site; Gisors attractive town; conv Giverny & Gisors local attractions; beautiful site; rest in town; gd."* **€18.10, 1 Apr-31 Oct.** **2022**

GIVET *5B1* (0.5km N Urban) *50.14345, 4.82614* **Caravaning Municipal La Ballastière,** 16 Rue Berthelot, 08600 Givet **03 24 42 30 20; sa.mairiegivet@wanadoo.fr; www.tourisme-champagne-ardenne.com**

12 €0.85 (htd) nr nr nr

Site at N end of town on lake. Foll 'Caravaning' sp fr W end of rv bdge or Dinant rd. 2*, Med, mkd, hdstg, hdg, pt shd, EHU (10A) inc; bbq; 60% statics; CKE. *"Nr Rv Meuse; adj sports & watersports complex; picturesque town; walking dist to shops & rest; vg; pool adj; conv for Rv Meuse cycleway; fair NH; scruffy & unkept san facs, rundown but clean (2018)."* **€10.00** **2023**

GIVORS *9B2* (10km NW Urban) *45.61498, 4.67068* **Camping La Trillonnière,** Boulevard du General de Gaulle, 69440 Mornant **04 78 44 16 47; contact@la-trillonniere.fr; www.la-trillonniere.fr**

€1 nr nr

Exit A7 at Givors & foll sp for St Etienne via D488, thro Givors onto D2 till sp seen for Mornant via D34, cont on D34 up hill for 7km, cross D342 & cont 1km to o'skts of Mornant, L at junc island & site on L. 2*, Med, pt shd, pt sl, EHU (10A) inc; twin axles; 20% statics; Eng spkn; adv bkg acc; CKE. *"Well managed, quiet site on edge of lovely vill in Monts du Lyonnais; walks in hills; Lyon accessible by bus (outsite gate) & metro; excell new san facs; 6 chalets."* **€25.00, 15 May-30 Sep.** **2023**

GIVRE, LE *7A1* (1.5km S Rural) *46.44472, -1.39832* **Camping La Grisse,** 85540 Le Givre **02 51 30 83 03; lagrisse@wanadoo.fr; www.campinglagrisse.com**

12 €2

Fr Luçon take D949 & turn L at junc with D747 (La Tranche rd). Turn L in 3km & foll sps. 3*, Sm, pt shd, EHU (16A) €4; 50% statics; Eng spkn; adv bkg acc; ccard acc; games area; CKE. *"Peaceful, friendly, farm site; lge pitches; clean, modern facs; beautiful area/beach; gd for dogs; knowledgeable owner of local area."* **€30.30** **2023**

GIVRY EN ARGONNE *5D1* (0.2km S Rural) *48.94835, 4.88545* **Camp Municipal du Val d'Ante,** Rue du Pont, 51330 Givry-en-Argonne **03 26 60 04 15 or 03 26 60 01 59 (Mairie)**

€1.20 nr

Exit A4 junc 29 at Ste Menéhould; S on D382 to Givry-en-Argonne; site sp on R on lakeside. 2*, Sm, pt shd, pt sl, EHU (6A) €2.10; sw. *"Attractive, basic site; boat hire adj; clean san facs; warden calls am & pm; gd birdwatching."* **€12.40, 1 May-31 Aug.** **2024**

GORDES *10E2* (2km N Rural) *43.92689, 5.20207* **Camping Les Sources,** Route de Murs, 84220 Gordes **04 90 71 12 48; sources-de-gordes@clicochic.com; www.campingdessources.com**

€5

Fr A7 junc 24, E on D973; then D22; then D900 twds Apt. After 18km at Coustellet turn N onto D2 then L on D15 twds Murs; site on L in 2km beyond Gordes. 2*, Med, mkd, hdstg, pt shd, terr, EHU (6A) €4.40 (long lead poss req); red long stay; 25% statics; Eng spkn; adv bkg acc; ccard acc; games rm; bike hire; games area; CKE. *"Lovely location & views; friendly staff; modern, clean san facs; gd pool; access rds narr; sm pitches v diff lge o'fits; ask for easy pitch & inspect on foot; some steep rds to pitches as site on hillside; 24 hr security barriers; gd walking; mkt Tues."* **€37.70, 6 Apr-28 Sep.** **2024**

GOUAREC *2E3* (0.6km SW Rural) *48.22555, -3.18307* **Camping de Gouarec (formerly Camping Tost Aven),** Au Bout du Pont, 22570 Gouarec **07 68 58 19 22; info@campingdegouarec.com; www.campingdegouarec.com**

nr nr nr

Sp fr town cent bet rv & canal. 2*, Med, pt shd, EHU (10A) €2.40; bbq; sw nr; bus 200m; Eng spkn; adv bkg acc; bike hire; canoe hire. *"Clean, relaxed, tidy site bet Nantes-Brest canal & rv on edge of vill; gas adj; towpath for cycling; great!"* **€15.00, 5 May-21 Sep.** **2023**

GOUDARGUES *10E2* (1km NE Rural) *44.22056, 4.47884* **Camping Les Amarines,** La Vérune Cornillon, 30630 Goudargues **04 66 82 24 92; les.amarines@orange.fr; www.campinglesamarines.com**

€3 (htd) (htd)

Fr D980 foll sp onto D23 & site bet Cornillon & Goudargues. 4*, Med, hdg, mkd, shd, EHU (6A) €3.50, adv bkg acc; rv fishing. *"Lge pitches; site liable to flood after heavy rain; excel."* **€32.00, 1 Apr-1 Oct.** **2024**

GOURDON *7D3* (21km S Rural) *44.64953, 1.43482* **Camping Le Moulin du Bel-Air,** Claux de Bouyssole, 46310 St. Germain-du-Bel-Air **05 65 31 00 71; contact@lot-camping.com**

€2 (htd)

Fr A20 autoroute junc 56 head for Saint Germain du Bel-Air via D2 and D23 about 14km. 3*, Med, mkd, pt shd, EHU (16A); bbq; Eng spkn; adv bkg acc; ccard acc; games rm. *"Excel."* **€22.00, 15 Apr-25 Sep.** **2022**

FRANCE

GOURDON *7D3* (2km SW Rural) *44.72214, 1.37381* **Aire Naturelle Le Paradis (Jardin),** La Peyrugue, 46300 Gourdon **05 65 41 65 01 or 06 40 93 33 81 (mob); www.campingleparadis.fr**

€2 nr

S on D673 Gourdon/Fumel rd, after Intermarché supmkt on L, turn L onto track sp site. If full, overflow area avail - 2 hookups. Sm, pt shd, pt sl, terr, EHU (6A) €2; 10% statics; adv bkg acc. *"Gd welcome; facs poss stretched if full; farm produce; delightful site; no entmnt; excel san facs."* **€14.00, 1 May-31 Aug. 2024**

GOURDON *7D3* (10km W Rural) *44.75491, 1.23999* **Camping Le Convivial,** La Gréze, 24250 St Martial de Nabirat **05 53 28 43 15; contact@campingle convivial.com; www.campingleconvivial.com**

€1.60 (htd) nr

SW fr Gourdon, take D673 twd Salviac. Bef Pont Carral turn R onto D6 which becomes D46. Site 1.5km N St Martial on L. Sm, hdg, pt shd, pt sl, EHU (8A); bbq; twin axles; 25% statics; Eng spkn; ccard acc; games area; fishing 1km; CCI. *"Beautiful, spacious site off tourist track; friendly & welcoming owners; cycle trail in pretty valley of Céon nrby; vg."* **€19.70, 1 Apr-31 Oct. 2024**

GOURDON *7D3* (1.5km NW Rural) *44.74637, 1.37700* **Camping Domaine La Quercy,** Ecoute S'il Pleut, 46300 Gourdon **05 65 41 06 19; contact@ domainequercy.com; www.domainequercy.com**

€2.50

Fr N site on R of D704 1.5km bef Gourdon. Sp fr Gourdon. 4*, Med, hdstg, mkd, pt shd, pt sl, terr, EHU (6A) €3.50; bbq; cooking facs; TV; 30% statics; phone; Eng spkn; adv bkg rec; ccard acc; waterslide; games area; watersports 200m; tennis; games rm; fishing; sailing 200m. *"Gd leisure facs - gd for families; badminton, bowling; volleyball; football; lake adj; ACSI; gd san facs; Gourdon attractive town; vg."* **€24.40, 1 Jun-14 Sep. 2024**

GRANDCAMP MAISY *1C4* (0.5km W Coastal) *49.38814, -1.05204* **Camping Le Joncal,** Le Petit Nice, 14450 Grandcamp-Maisy **04 92 28 38 48 or 02 31 22 61 44; campingdujoncal@hotmail.fr; www.capfun.com/ camping-france-basse_normandie-joncal-FR.html**

€1.10 nr nr sand adj

Ent on Grandcamp port dock area; visible fr vill. Fr N13 take D199 sp Grandcamp-Maisy & foll Le Port & Camping sps. 3*, Lge, hdg, mkd, pt shd, EHU (6-10A) €5.40-7.50; gas; bbq; 80% statics; bus. *"Conv for D Day beaches; some pitches at water's edge; excel morning fish mkt close by; gd NH."* **€23.50, 1 Apr-30 Sep. 2024**

GRANVILLE *1D4* (6km NE Coastal) *48.86976, -1.56380* **Kawan Village La Route Blanche,** 6 La Route Blanche, 50290 Bréville-sur-Mer **02 33 50 23 31; route-blanche@ capfun.com; www.campinglarouteblanche.com**

€3 (htd) (htd) sand 500m

Exit A84 junc 37 onto D924 dir Granville. Bef Granville turn L onto D971, then L onto D114 which joins D971e. Site on R bef golf club. Nr Bréville sm airfield. 5*, Lge, hdstg, mkd, hdg, pt shd, serviced pitches; EHU (6-10A) €4-5; gas; bbq; red long stay; TV; 40% statics; phone; Eng spkn; adv bkg acc; ccard acc; tennis nr; waterslide; sailing school; golf nr; games area; CKE. *"Pleasant, busy site with vg clean facs; staff friendly & helpful; disabled seatlift in pool; gd walking, cycling & beach; pleasant old walled town & harbour; vg."* **€48.80, 8 Apr-18 Sep. 2023**

GRANVILLE *1D4* (8km SE Rural) *48.79790, -1.5244* **Camping Le Château de Lez-Eaux,** 240 Avenue de Lez-Eaux, 50380 St Aubin des Préaux **02 33 51 66 09; bonjour@lez-eaux.com; www.lez-eaux.com**

(htd) (covrd, htd) sand 4km

App site on D973 Granville to Avranches rd (not via St Pair). Cont strt thro 1st rndabt at Geant and next rndabt for 2km, site sp on R. 5*, Lge, mkd, pt shd, pt sl, serviced pitches; EHU (10-16A) inc; bbq; twin axles; TV; 80% statics; ccard acc; games rm; lake fishing; bike hire; tennis; horseriding 4km; waterslide; games area; CKE. *"Superb, beautiful site in grnds of chateau; children's indoor aqua park; easy access; spacious pitches, various prices; helpful & friendly staff; clean, modern san facs; excel pool complex; gd for children; boat hire 7km; great for dogs; gd cycling & gd cycle rte to beach; gd touring base; conv Mont St Michel, Dol & landing beaches; mkt Thu St Pair; highly rec."* **€46.00, 15 Apr - 11 Sep, N02. 2022**

See advertisement opposite

GRASSE *10E4* (8km NE Rural) *43.70230, 6.99515* **FFCC Camping des Gorges du Loup,** Chemin des Vergers, 06620 Le Bar-sur-Loup **04 93 42 45 06; info@ lesgorgesduloup.com; www.lesgorgesduloup.com**

€3 shgl

E fr Gasse on D2085 sp Chateauneuf-Grasse; in 4km turn L onto D2210 to Le Bar-sur-Loup. Site well sp. 4*, Med, mkd, hdstg, pt shd, terr, EHU (6-10A) €3.50-5.50 (poss rev pol); gas; TV; 20% statics; phone; bus 1km; Eng spkn; adv bkg acc; ice; CKE. *"Peaceful, well-kept site with superb views; table tennis; basketball; helpful, pleasant owners; bowls; clean san facs; steep access rds; owner will site c'van; gd hilly cycling; highly rec."* **€35.80, 6 Apr-21 Sep. 2024**

GRASSE *10E4* (5.5km SE Urban) *43.63507, 6.94859* **Camping Caravaning La Paoute,** 160 Route de Cannes, 06130 Grasse **04 93 09 11 42; camppaoute@hotmail.com; www.campinglapaoute.com**

12 WD MSP nr (htd)

Sp fr Grasse town cent on Route de Cannes (secondary rd to Cannes, NOT D6185), a 10 min drive. 3*, Med, hdg, mkd, pt shd, sl, terr, EHU (10A) €4; 15% statics; bus 500m; games rm; CKE. *"Gd, quiet site; m'vans acc out of ssn but adv bkg req."* **€39.50 2024**

GRASSE *10E4* (8km S Rural) *43.60650, 6.90216* **Camping Le Parc des Monges,** 635 Chemin du Gabre, 06810 Auribeau-sur-Siagne **04 93 60 91 71; parcdesmonges@dsonevacances.com; www.parcdesmonges.com**

€2.50 (htd) WD MSP nr nr (htd)

Exit A8 junc 40 or 41 onto D6007 dir Grasse; then onto D109 becoming D9; foll sp to Auribeau-sur-Siagne; site on rd to Le Gabre. 3*, Med, hdg, shd, EHU (4-10A) €3.50-5.50; sw nr; 7% statics; phone; bus adj; Eng spkn; adv bkg acc; ccard acc; ice; fishing nr Jacuzzi onsite; Bowling alley; CKE. *"Vg site by Rv Siagne; rv not accessible fr site; activities; watch out for branches when manoeurvering."* **€23.00, 4 Apr-27 Sep. 2020**

GRAVELINES *3A3* (3km N Coastal) *51.00777, 2.11777* **Camping des Dunes,** Rue Victor-Hugo, Plage de Petit-Fort-Philippe, 59820 Gravelines **03 28 23 09 80; www.camping-des-dunes.com**

€2.10 (htd) WD nr nr sand adj

E fr Calais on D940 foll sp to Gravelines. Heading W fr Dunkerque exit D601 E of Gravelines; turn R into Blvd de L'Europe & foll sp for Petit-Fort-Philippe & site. Site on both sides of rd. 4*, Lge, hdg, mkd, hdstg, pt shd, EHU (10A) €4.05; TV; 10% statics; phone; bus; Eng spkn; adv bkg req; ccard acc; games rm; CKE. *"Site in 2 parts, various prices; gd site rds; helpful, friendly staff; poss uneven pitches & raised manhole covers; conv Dunkerque ferries (15km); vg; excel NH or sh stay; v clean & welcoming."* **€20.00, 1 Apr-31 Oct. 2024**

GREOUX LES BAINS *10E3* (1.2km S Rural) *43.75158, 5.88185* **Camping Le Verseau,** Route de St Pierre, 04800 Gréoux-les-Bains **04 92 77 67 10 or 06 22 72 93 25 (mob); info@camping-le-verseau.com; www.camping-le-verseau.com**

€2.50 WD MSP nr

Fr W on D952 to Gréoux. Go under bdge then bear L just bef petrol stn. Cross rv (narr bdge), site on R in 500m. 3*, Med, hdg, pt shd, pt sl, EHU (10A) €3.90; bbq (elec, gas); phone; adv bkg acc; tennis 1km; CKE. *"Friendly owners; interesting spa town; great views."* **€23.00, 1 Mar-31 Oct. 2022**

GRIGNAN *9D2* (0.5km S Urban) *44.41731, 4.90950* **Camping de Grignan,** 2 Avenue de Grillon, 26230 Grignan **04 75 01 92 23; contact@camping-grignan.com; www.camping-grignan.com**

WD (htd)

N7 S fr Montelimar on N7 N fr Orange, then D133 onto D541, dir Nyons for 17km. Grignan sp Camping Municipal in vill. Sm, lge, hdg, mkd, pt shd, EHU (6A); bbq; twin axles; bus; Eng spkn; adv bkg rec; CKE. *"10 min walk to town & Chateau and Saint Sauveur Church; excel."* **€21.50, 29 Apr-1 Oct. 2023**

GRILLON *9D2* (1.5km S Rural) *44.38307, 4.93046* **Camping Le Garrigon,** Chemin de Visan, 84600 Grillon **04 90 28 72 94; contact@camping-garrigon.com; www.camping-garrigon.com**

WD nr (htd)

A7, exit Montelmar-Sud, twds Gap. Take D541 then Grillon cent & foll sp to site. 4*, Med, mkd, pt shd, EHU (10A), bbq (elec, gas); 10% statics; Eng spkn; adv bkg acc; ccard acc; games rm; CKE. *"Pleasant site in attractive area; nice pool; updated san facs (2015); level but some rough or uneven grnd; vg."* **€28.50, 14 Mar-13 Nov. 2022**

FRANCE

GRIMAUD *10F4* (5km E Urban) *43.27512, 6.56032* **Camping La Pinède,** 1968 route de Ste Maxime, 83310 Grimaud **04 94 56 04 36; la-pinede@capfun.com; www.capfun.co.uk/camping-france-provence_alpes_cote_d_azur-la_pinede-EN.html**

sand 2.5km

Fr Ste Maxine to St Tropez turn R at St Pons-Les-Mûres on D14 twd Grimaud. Site in 1.6km on L. 4*, Lge, mkd, hdg, pt shd, pt sl, EHU (2A); gas. *"Vg; excel beaches in easy driving dist; open location with plenty of rm for o'fit."* **€32.50, Easter-1 Nov. 2024**

GRIMAUD *10F4* (6.8km E Coastal) *43.28205, 6.58614* **Camping de la Plage,** 98 Route National, St Pons-les-Mûres, 83310 Grimaud **04 94 56 31 15; contact@campingplage.fr; www.camping-de-la-plage.fr**

€2.20 sand

Fr St Maxime turn onto D559 sp to St Tropez; site 3km on L on both sides of rd (subway links both parts). 3*, Lge, pt shd, EHU (4-16A) €4.70-14; gas; adv bkg req; ccard acc; tennis; CKE. *"Pitches in shd woodland - some sm; site tired but lovely situation & views compensate; clean facs, refurb 2015; cycle tracks; site poss flooded after heavy rain; used every yr for 44 yrs by one CC member (2011); conv for ferry to St Tropez, rec as beautiful, helpful friendly efficient staff; acc ACSI."* **€48.50, 31 Mar-16 Oct. 2023**

GRIMAUD *10F4* (7.3km E Coastal) *43.283754, 6.591659* **Camping Les Mures,** 2721 route du Littoral 83310, Grimaud **04 94 56 16 97 or 04 94 56 16 17 (mob); info@camping-des-mures.com; www.camping-des-mures.com**

€3 (htd) adj

Fr St Maxine take coast rd D559 twrds St Tropez. Site on R after 5km. 4*, Lge, mkd, pt shd, pt sl, terr, EHU 6-10A; bbq; twin axles; TV; 10% statics; phone; bus adj; Eng spkn; adv bkg acc; games area; CCI. *"Excel; gd access rds; site split both sides of rd; beach pitches avail for extra cost; v friendly staff; gd rest; ACSI acc."* **€53.90, 22 Mar-13 Oct. 2024**

GRUISSAN *10F1* (5km NE Coastal) *43.1358, 3.1424* **Camping Les Ayguades,** Ave de la Jonque, 11430 Gruissan **04 68 49 81 59; infos@loisirs-vacances-languedoc.com; www.camping-soleil-mer.com**

€2.50 (htd) sand adj

Exit A9 junc 37 onto D168/D32 sp Gruissan. In 10km turn L at island sp Les Ayguades, foll site sp. 4*, Lge, mkd, hdg, unshd, EHU (6A) inc; TV; 75% statics; Eng spkn; adv bkg acc; ccard acc; fitness rm; bike hire; sports grnd; CKE. *"Pleasant site; extensive cycle network, 6 night min stay high ssn."* **€31.00, 20 Mar-8 Nov. 2020**

GUDAS *8G3* (2km S Rural) *42.99269, 1.67830* **Camping Naturiste Millefleurs (Naturist),** Le Tuillier, 09120 Gudas **05 61 60 77 56; info@camping-millefleurs.com; www.camping-millefleurs.com**

€2.25

Do not use SatNav thro Dalou. App Foix on the N20 fr Toulouse foll sp Foix-Tarbes. Pass Camping du lac on R, cont approx 2.2km, at traff lghts turn L sp D1 Laroque d'Olmes, Lieurac, l'Herm). Foll D1 for 6.5km until junc D13 (Care req, sharp bend). Turn L sp Col de Py, Mirepoix, cont past quarry, L fork (sp Gudas, Varhilles). After 2km sp Millefleurs, le Tuilier, turn L over bdge. Site in approx 2km bef Gudas. 1*, Sm, hdg, mkd, pt shd, pt sl, terr, EHU (6-10A) €3.75; bbq; twin axles; phone; Eng spkn; adv bkg rec; sauna; INF card req. *"Excel, scenic, beautiful, peaceful site; lovely owners; gd pitches; 2 c'vans for hire; clean facs; gd base Andorra, Toulouse & Carcassonne; great touring base."* **€34.40, 1 Apr-31 Oct. 2023**

GUEMENE PENFAO *2G4* (1km SE Rural) *47.62575, -1.81857* **Camping De L'Hermitage,** 46 Ave du Paradis, 44290 Guémené-Penfao **02 40 79 23 48; camping.hermitage@orange.fr; www.campinglhermitage.com**

€2 nr

On D775 fr cent of Guémené-Penfao, dir Châteaubriant for 500m, turn R, site sp. 3*, Med, mkd, hdstg, pt shd, EHU (6A) €3.50; gas; bbq; sw nr; TV; 20% statics; phone; Eng spkn; adv bkg acc; jacuzzi; games rm; waterslide; bike hire; fishing 300m; tennis; canoeing; games area; CKE. *"Gd walking in area; htd covrd pool adj; site not ready early ssn."* **€26.00, 1 Apr-31 Oct. 2023**

GUERANDE *2G3* (3km N Rural) *47.34954, -2.43170* **Camping La Fontaine,** Kersavary, Route de St-Molf, 44350 Guérande **02 40 24 96 19 or 06 08 12 80 96 (mob); lafontaine.guerande@orange.fr; www.camping-lafontaine.com**

€2 nr nr (htd)

Fr Guérande take N774 N sp La Roche-Bernard; in 1 km, opp windmill, fork L onto D233 sp St-Molf; site on L in 500m. 3*, Med, hdg, mkd, hdstg, pt shd, EHU (6A) €4; bbq; twin axles; 10% statics; Eng spkn; adv bkg rec; games area; CKE. *"Pleasant, peaceful site; lge pitches; helpful staff; san facs clean & new (2015); gd."* **€24.00, 3 Apr-18 Oct. 2022**

GUERANDE *2G3* (2km NE Rural) *47.34340, -2.41935* **Domaine de Bréhadour,** Route de Bréhadour, 44350 Guérande **02 43 53 04 33; www.domainedebrehadour.com**

€3.70 (htd)

Exit N165 onto D774 to Guérande. After 20km at rndabt take 3rd exit onto D99E. Turn L twd Route de Bréhadour, take first R and site is on L. 4*, Lge, hdg, pt shd, EHU (4A) €3-4.70; gas; bbq; 40% statics; Eng spkn; adv bkg acc; ccard acc; golf; tennis; CKE. *"Beautiful, quiet site; redeveloped for 2014."* **€43.20, 5 Apr-22 Sep. 2024**

GUERANDE 2G3 (7km W Coastal) *47.32856, -2.49907* **Camping Les Chardons Bleus,** Blvd de la Grande Falaise, 44420 La Turballe **02 40 62 80 60; campingleschardonsbleus@mairielaturballe.fr; www.camping-laturballe.fr**

€5 (htd) sand adj

Foll D99 to La Turballe. Site well sp fr town cent along D92. 3*, Lge, mkd, hdg, unshd, EHU (10A) inc (poss rev pol, long lead poss req); gas; phone; Eng spkn; ccard acc; CKE. *"Well-run, well-kept site in great location; mv service pnt adj; warm welcome; gd, clean san facs, poss stretched high ssn; ltd EHU when full; variable opening dates, phone ahead early ssn; nature reserve adj with bird life; superb beach adj, pt naturist; walk along beach to pretty La Turballe with rests; vg modern facs & pool area; pinewoods; gd kids club for younger children; gd base for cycling, excel."* **€27.00, 1 Mar-29 Sep, A46. 2020**

GUERANDE 2G3 (7km NW Rural) *47.34252, -2.47159* **Camping Le Parc Ste Brigitte,** Manoir de Bréhet, 44420 La Turballe **02 40 24 88 91; reservation.saintebrigitte@gmail.com; www.campingsaintebrigitte.com**

€1.50 (covrd, htd) sand 2km

Take D99 NW fr Guérande twd La Turballe thro vill of Clis. Sp on R in 900m. 4*, Lge, mkd, shd, serviced pitches; EHU (6-10A) inc; gas; TV; 10% statics; phone; adv bkg acc; ccard acc; fishing; bike hire; CKE. *"V peaceful; excel rest & bar; some sm pitches; poss unkempt LS; gd."* **€32.00, 1 Apr-1 Oct. 2024**

GUERET 7A4 (10km S Rural) *46.10257, 1.83528* **Camp Municipal Le Gué Levard,** 5 Rue Gué Levard, 23000 La Chapelle-Taillefert **05 55 51 09 20 or 05 55 52 36 17 (Mairie); www.ot-gueret.fr**

Take junc 48 fr N145 sp Tulle/Bourganeuf (D33 thro Guéret); S on D940 fr Guéret, turn off at site sp. Foll sp thro vill, well sp. 1*, Sm, hdstg, pt shd, sl, terr, EHU (16A) €2.50; bbq (sep area); 20% statics; adv bkg acc; fishing in Rv Gartempe; CKE. *"Attractive, peaceful, well-kept site hidden away; vg san facs; site yourself, warden calls 1900; all pitches sl so m'van levelling diff; gd auberge in vill (clsd most of Jul & Aug); gd walking; sports facs nr; phone ahead to check open LS; excel little site."* **€11.00, 1 Apr-1 Nov. 2022**

GUERET 7A4 (1.4km W Rural) *46.16387, 1.85882* **Camping de Courtille,** Rue Georges Aullon, 23000 Guéret **05 55 81 92 24**

nr nr nr

Fr W on N145 take D942 to town cent; then take D914 W; take L turn bef lake sp; site in 1.5km along lakeside rd with speed humps. Site sp. 3*, Med, hdg, mkd, pt shd, pt sl, EHU (10A) inc; bbq; sw; phone; watersports; CKE. *"Pleasant scenery; well-managed site; beach sand; narr ent to pitches; mkd walks nrby; pool 1.5km; ramps needed for m'vans; bread delivered; busy NH."* **€18.70, 1 Apr-30 Sep. 2023**

GUIGNICOURT 3C4 (0.5km SE Urban) *49.43209, 3.97035* **Camping au Bord de l'Aisne (Formaly Municipal),** 14b Rue des Godins, 02190 Guignicourt **03 23 79 74 58; campingguignicourt@orange.fr; www.camping-aisne-picardie.fr**

€2 (htd) nr nr (covrd, htd)

Exit A26 junc 14 onto D925 to Guignicourt; after passing under rlway bdge cont on D925 for 800m; then turn R at Peugeot g'ge down narr rd to site (12% descent at ent & ramp). Site sp in vill on rv bank. 4*, Med, mkd, hdg, pt shd, EHU (6-10A) inc (poss rev pol, poss long cable req); bbq; red long stay; 20% statics; phone; train 500m; Eng spkn; adv bkg acc; ccard acc; fishing; CKE. *"Pretty, well-kept/run, excel site in beautiful setting on banks of rv; v pretty & quiet; popular gd NH, conv A26; well-guarded; friendly, v helpful staff; poss muddy when wet; pleasant town; excel touring base Reims, Epernay; easy access despite gradient; excel; v clean, refurbished & modern facs; facs stretched in high ssn; fair."* **€30.00, 1 Apr - 31 Oct, P02. 2022**

GUILVINEC 2F2 (2.5km W Coastal) *47.80388, -4.31222* **Camping la Plage,** Chemin des Allemands, Penmarc'h, 29760 Guilvinec **02 98 58 61 90; www.villagelaplage.com**

€6 (covrd, htd) sand adj

Fr Quimper, Pont l'Abbé on D785 SW to Plomeur; turn S onto D57 sp Guilvinec. Bear R on app to town & v soon after turn R sp Chapelle de Tremor. Foll site to site in 1.5km. 4*, Lge, pt shd, EHU (5A) inc; gas; bbq; 60% statics; adv bkg acc; ccard acc; sauna; fitness rm; archery; tennis; games rm; waterslide; bike hire. *"Ideal for families; spacious pitches; no o'fits over 8m high ssn; site rds poss diff lge o'fits; excel touring base; mkt Tue & Sun."* **€50.00, 12 Apr-14 Sep, B15. 2022**

GUILVINEC 2F2 (3.5km NW Coastal) *47.81819, -4.30942* **Camping Cap Finistère (formerly Camping Les Genêts),** 20 Rue Gouesnac'h Nevez, 29760 Penmarc'h **02 98 58 66 93 or 06 83 15 85 92 (mob); capfinistere@flowercampings.com; www.camping-finistere-bretagne.fr**

€2 (htd) (covrd, htd) sand 1.5km

S fr Pont-l'Abbé on D785 to Plomeur; cont on D785 for another 4km, then turn L onto D53 sp Guilvinec; in 300m turn L into Rue Gouesnac'h Nevez to site. 4*, Med, mkd, hdg, pt shd, EHU (10A) €3.40; gas; bbq; red long stay; TV; 25% statics; phone; bus; Eng spkn; adv bkg acc; games area; horseriding 800m; games rm; waterslide; ice; CKE. *"Peaceful, well-kept site in beautiful, unspoilt area; family-run; friendly atmosphere; welcoming, helpful owners; easy access to spacious pitches; excel, clean, modern san facs; bike hire nrby; gd value; excel."* **€19.00, 1 Apr-30 Sep. 2024**

FRANCE

FRANCE

GUINES *3A3* (1km SW Rural) *50.86611, 1.85694* **Camping De La Bien Assise,** Route D231 62340 Guînes **03 21 35 20 77; castels@bien-assise.com; www.camping-la-bien-assise.com**

€3 (htd) (covrd, htd, indoor)

Fr Calais or Boulogne, leave A16 at junc 43; foll D305 then D127 to Guines; cont to junc with D231; turn R (across S of vill and cont to rndabt) site ent on L. Fr S (A26 or D943), take D231 to Guines. 5*, Lge, mkd, hdg, pt shd, pt sl, EHU (10A) inc (poss rev pol); gas; bbq (charcoal, gas); red long stay; twin axles; TV; 20% statics; Eng spkn; adv bkg req; ccard acc; bike hire; games rm; horseriding 3km; waterslide; golf nr; tennis; CKE. *"Pleasant, busy, excel site in grnds of chateau; well-kept & well-run; gd sized pitches with easy access; conv ferries - late arr area; pleasant, cheerful, helpful staff; clean san facs, stretched when site full; excel rest, clsd in Jan; vg pool complex; grass pitches, some soft LS & boggy when wet; vet in Ardres (9km), site will book for you; even if notice says 'Complete' check for sh stay; mkt Fri; ACSI acc; v popular NH stop; one san fac block newly refurb (2016)."*
€36.20, 7 Apr-24 Sep, P05. **2023**

See advertisement

GUISE *3C4* (0.5km SE Urban) *49.89488, 3.63372* **FFCC Camping de la Vallée de l'Oise,** 33 Rue du Camping, 02120 Guise **06 74 08 50 54; camping.guise@outlook.fr**

nr

Foll Vervin sp in town & camp clearly sp fr all dirs in town. 3*, Lge, pt shd, EHU (6-10A) €5.50 (rev pol); TV; 50% statics; Eng spkn; adv bkg acc; rv fishing adj; bike hire; games rm; CKE. *"Spacious, beautifully kept, friendly site; busy w/ends; gd san facs; barrier always open, warden not always on site; canoe hire adj; if arr late, pitch & pay next morning; interesting old town; gd value."* **€15.00, 15 Mar-30 Nov.** **2023**

HAGUENAU *5D3* (2.6km SW Urban) *48.80233, 7.76439* **Camp Municipal Les Pins,** 20 Rue de la Piscine, 67500 Haguenau **03 88 73 91 43 or 03 88 93 70 00; tourisme@ville-haguenau.fr; www.camping-haguenau.alsace**

€1 (htd) nr nr nr

Fr S on D263, after passing Haguenau town sp turn L at 2nd set of traff lts (opp Peugeot g'ge). Site sp fr D263. 1*, Med, mkd, pt shd, terr, EHU (6A) inc; gas; bbq; phone; bus 500m; Eng spkn; adv bkg acc; CKE. *"Lge pitches; helpful staff; clean, modern san facs; meals avail fr warden; grnd firm even after heavy rain; excel; pleasant town."* **€13.00, 1 May-30 Sep.** **2022**

"There aren't many sites open at this time of year"

If you're travelling outside peak season remember to call ahead to check site opening dates – even if the entry says 'open all year'.

HARDELOT PLAGE *3A2* (3km NE Urban) *50.64661, 1.62539* **Caravaning du Château d'Hardelot,** 21 Rue Nouvelle, 62360 Condette **03 21 87 59 59; contact@camping-caravaning-du-chateau.com; www.camping-caravaning-du-chateau.com**

nr sand 3km

Take D901 S fr Boulogne, R turn onto D940 dir Le Touquet; then R at rndabt on D113 to Condette; take 2nd turning to Château Camping, R at next rndabt & site 400m on R. Fr S leave A16 at exit 27 to Neufchâtel-Hardelot, take D940 twd Condette & turn L at 1st rndabt onto D113, then as above. Not well sp last 3km. Tight turn into site ent. 3*, Med, hdg, mkd, pt shd, pt sl, EHU (10A) €4.70 (poss rev pol); 30% statics; Eng spkn; adv bkg rec; horseriding; games rm; tennis 500m; golf; CKE. *"Lovely, well-run, wooded site; busy high ssn; vg LS; sm pitches; helpful, friendly owners; sm multi-gym; clean, modern san facs; tight access some pitches; conv Calais (site barrier opens 0800)."* **€30.60, 1 Apr-31 Oct.** **2022**

HARDINGHEN *3A3* (0.5km SE Rural) *50.79462, 1.81369* **Camping à la Ferme Les Piloteries,** Rue de l'Eglise, 62132 Hardinghen **03 21 85 01 85; lespiloteries@free.fr; http://lespiloteries.free.fr**

WD

Fr N exit A16 junc 36 at Marquise onto D191 to Hardinghen; turn R onto D127 (where D191 turns sharp L); site in 1km (concealed ent). Sm, pt shd, pt sl, EHU (6A) €2; bbq. *"Vg CL-type site; friendly owner; lovely site; well looked after; rec; narr ent; gd NH."*
€11.00, 16 Apr-2 Oct. 2023

HAUTEFORT *7C3* (3km NE Rural) *45.27248, 1.16861* **Camping Belle Vue,** La Contie 24390 Boisseuilh **05 53 51 62 71; cbv@dordogne-camping.org; www.dordogne-camping.org**

€2 WD MSP

Fr Limoges take D704 and cont until St Agnan. Take turning for Hautefort and pass supmkt on Land the Chateau on R. At next x-rds turn L onto D72 and cont over 3 bdges until La Contie. Site is last hse on R. Sm, shd, EHU (6A); bbq; twin axles; 25% statics; Eng spkn; adv bkg acc; CKE. *"Beautiful views of chateau Hautefort, illuminated at night; excel customer svrs; breakfast delivered to pitch each morning; excel."*
€28.00, 1 May-30 Sep. 2023

HAUTEFORT *7C3* (4km NE Rural) *45.28081, 1.15917* **Camping La Grenouille,** Brégérac, 24390 Hautefort **05 53 50 11 71; info@lagrenouillevacances.com; www.lagrenouillevacances.com**

WD

Fr N on D704 at Cherveil-Cubas take D77 dir Boisseuilh/Teillots. In 4km turn R & in 800m turn L to site. Fr S on D704 at St Agnan take D62 sp Hautefort/Badefols d'Ans. Pass 'Vival' (sm shop on L) in Hautefort & turn L dir Boisseuilh. After 1st bdge turn L to La Besse & site in 2km. Sm, pt shd, pt sl, EHU (8A) €3.50; bbq; Eng spkn; adv bkg acc; ice; CKE. *"Tranquil, scenic, well-kept CL type site; friendly, helpful, Dutch owners; vg san facs; meals avail; goats, guinea pigs, chickens in pens on site; gd walking; dogs free; highly rec."* **€21.50, 22 Apr-15 Oct. 2022**

HAUTEFORT *7C3* (8km W Rural) *45.28032, 1.04845* **Camping Les Tourterelles,** Clos Faure, 24390 Tourtoirac **05 53 51 11 17; camping24390@gmail.com; les-tourterelles.fr**

€5 WD MSP nr

Fr N or S on D704 turn W at Hautefort on D62/D5 to Tourtoirac. In Tourtoirac turn R over rv then L. Site in 1km. 4*, Med, hdg, mkd, pt shd, terr, EHU (6A) €4.50; gas; TV; 20% statics; phone; bus 1km; Eng spkn; adv bkg acc; ccard acc; horseriding; tennis; CKE. *"Beautiful Auvézère valley; rallies welcome; owners helpful; equestrian cent; gd walks."*
€37.00, 25 Apr-27 Sep. 2024

HAYE DU PUITS, LA *1D4* (6km N Urban) *49.38725, -1.52755* **FFCC Camp Municipal du Vieux Château,** Ave de la Division-Leclerc, 50390 St Sauveur-le-Vicomte **02 33 41 79 06; basedeloisirs@sslv.fr; www.ville-saint-sauveur-le-vicomte.fr**

€1.50 nr nr

Fr Cherbourg on N13/D2 site on R after x-ing bdge at St Sauveur-le-Vicomte, sp. 1*, Med, mkd, pt shd, pt sl, EHU (10A) €2.50 (poss rev pol); bbq; TV; phone; adv bkg acc; ccard acc; games area; games rm; tennis 1km; CKE. *"Excel site in chateau grnds; friendly warden; gd clean facs but unreliable; ideal 1st stop fr Cherbourg; office open until 2200 for late arr; barrier clsd 2200-0800; vg auberge opp; helpful warden; Eng not spkn; sh walk to friendly, nice town."*
€12.22, 15 May-17 Sep. 2022

HAYE DU PUITS, LA *1D4* (3km SW Rural) *49.27292, -1.55896* **Camping La Bucaille,** 50250 Montgardon **02 33 07 46 38; info@labucaille.com; www.labucaille.com**

WD nr nr nr sand 4km

Fr Cherbourg S on N13 & D2 twd St Sauveur-le-Vicomte, then D900 to La Haye-du-Puits. Fr cent of La Haye turn onto D136 Rte de Bretteville-sur-Ay for approx 2km, site sp at L turn, site on L. Sm, pt shd, pt sl, EHU (10A) €5; bbq; adv bkg acc. *"Pleasant quiet, 'hide-way' CL-type site; lge grassy pitches; width restriction 3m; friendly British owners; ideal for walking; dogs free; excel; peaceful, well kept with super hosts."* **€17.00, 1 Apr-30 Sep. 2022**

HEMING *6E3* (5km SW Rural) *48.69130, 6.92769* **Camping Les Mouettes,** 4 Rue de Diane Capelle, 57142 Gondrexange **06 45 29 83 21; otsi-gondrexange.pagesperso-orange.fr**

€1.55 (htd) WD MSP nr nr

Exit Héming on N4 Strasbourg-Nancy. Foll sp Gondrexange & site sp. App fr W on D955 turn to site sp on L about 1km bef Héming. 2*, Lge, mkd, unshd, pt sl, EHU (16A) inc; sw nr; 60% statics; phone; Eng spkn; fishing adj; sailing adj; bike hire; tennis; CKE. *"Pleasant site by lake; clean; good facs."*
€18.00, 1 Apr-30 Sep. 2024

HERBIGNAC *2G3* (0.3km E Rural) *47.44802, -2.31073* **Camp Le Ranrouet,** 7 Allee des Pres Blancs, 44410 Herbignac **02 40 15 57 56 or 06 20 89 44 69; campingleranrouet@orange.fr; www.camping-parc-de-la-briere.com**

WD MSP nr nr nr (htd)

Site at intersection D774 & D33 on E edge of vill. 3*, Med, mkd, pt shd, EHU (6A); TV; CKE. *"Immac san facs; gd cent for Guérande."*
€18.00, Easter-30 Oct. 2024

FRANCE

HERIC *2G4* (2km W Rural) *47.41329, -1.67050* **Camping La Pindière,** La Denais, Route de la Fay-de-Bretagne, 44810 Héric **02 40 57 65 41; contact@camping-la-pindiere.com; www.camping-la-pindiere.com**

12 €1.40 (htd)

Exit N137 twd Héric at traff lts in town, leave town & turn W onto D16 (sp Camping). Site on L after rndabt supmkt, turn at sp Notre Dames-des-Landes. 3*, Med, hdstg, mkd, hdg, pt shd, EHU (6-10A) €3.20-4.80; gas; bbq (charcoal); twin axles; TV; 80% statics; phone; Eng spkn; adv bkg rec; ccard acc; sports facs; horseriding 200m; tennis; CKE. *"Pleasant site; lge, grass pitches, soft in wet weather; warm welcome; helpful owners; gd clean san facs; gd NH before St Malo; gd walks."* **€22.50** 2024

"That's changed – Should I let the Club know?"

If you find something on site that's different from the site entry, fill in a report and let us know. See camc.com/europereport.

HERISSON *7A4* (0.8km WNW Rural) *46.51055, 2.70576* **Camp Municipal de l'Aumance,** Rue de Crochepot, 03190 Hérisson **04 70 06 88 22, 04 70 06 80 45 or 06 63 46 21 49 (mob); www.allier-tourisme.com**

Exit A71 junc 9 onto D2144 N; turn R onto D11 dir Hérisson; immed bef T-junc with D3 turn L at blue sp (high on L) into Rue de Crochepot; site on R down hill. NB-Avoid towing thro town. 2*, Med, mkd, pt shd, EHU (6A) €2.80; phone; games area. *"Delightful rvside site; idyllic setting; old san facs but gd & clean; warden calls eves; rec; peaceful and picturesque; easy walk to vil; lovely site; sm gd supmkt & fuel at Vallons; rv fishing reserved for campers - permit necessary; remarkable value; site on 2 levels, higher level better in wet weather."* **€8.00, 1 Apr-31 Oct.** 2022

HIRSON *3C4* (10km N Rural) *50.00585, 4.06195* **FFCC Camping Les Etangs des Moines,** 100 rue des Etangs, 59610 Fourmies **03 27 63 05 26; contact@etangs-des-moines.fr; www.etangsdesmoines.fr**

€1 nr (htd)

Fr D1043 Hirson by-pass head N on D963 to Anor. Turn L onto D156 dir Fourmies, site sp on R on ent town. Site also well sp off D42 & thro Fourmies. 3*, Med, hdstg, hdg, pt shd, EHU (10A) €3.30; bbq; 80% statics; Eng spkn; CKE. *"Textile & eco museum in town; shwrs run down, other facs gd; vg."* **€15.80, 1 Apr-31 Oct.** 2024

HONFLEUR *3C1* (6km S Rural) *49.40083, 0.30638*
Camping Domaine Catinière, 910 Route de la Morelle, 27210 Fiquefleur-Equainville **02 32 57 63 51; info@camping-catiniere.com; www.camping-catiniere.com**

€2 (covrd, htd)

Fr A29/Pont de Normandie (toll) bdge exit junc 3 sp Le Mans, pass under m'way onto D580/D180. In 3km go strt on at rndabt & in 100m bear R onto D22 dir Beuzeville; site sp on R in 500m. Do not app fr Beuzeville, c'vans not allowed in vill. 4*, Sm, mkd, hdg, pt shd, EHU (4A) inc or (8-13A) €1-1.50 (long lead poss req, poss rev pol); bbq; TV; 15% statics; Eng spkn; adv bkg rec; ccard acc; rv fishing; waterslide; games rm; CKE. *"Attractive, well-kept, busy site; pleasant, helpful, friendly owners; clean but dated unisex san facs, stretched high ssn & ltd LS; some pitches quite sm; unfenced stream on far boundary; gd touring base & NH; gd walks; easy parking for m'vans nr town; 20 mins to Le Havre ferry via Normandy bdge; no o'fits over 8.50m; conv A13; highly rec; lovely pool; ACSI acc."* **€32.00, 1 Apr - 1 Nov, N16. 2022**

HONFLEUR *3C1* (3.5km SW Rural) *49.39777, 0.20861*
Camping La Briquerie, 14600 Equemauville
02 31 89 28 32; info@campinglabriquerie.com; www.campinglabriquerie.com

€3 nr (htd)
sand 2.5km

Fr Honfleur head S on D579A. At rndabt cont strt onto D62, site on R. Fr S take D579 dir Honfleur Cent. Pass water tower n turn L at Intermarché rndabt, site on R in 300m. 5*, Lge, hdg, pt shd, EHU (5-10A) €4-5 (poss rev pol); gas; bbq; TV; 50% statics; bus nr; Eng spkn; adv bkg req; games rm; tennis 500m; horseriding 500m; fitness rm; waterslide; CKE. *"Lge pitches; staff helpful; gd clean san facs; late/early ferry arr; local vets geared up for dog inspections, etc; gd; cash only."* **€34.70, 1 Apr-30 Sep. 2022**

HONFLEUR *3C1* (1km NW Coastal) *49.42445, 0.22753*
Camping du Phare, Blvd Charles V, 14600 Honfleur
02 98 83 45 06; camping.du.phare@orange.fr; www.camping-du-phare.com

€3 nr nr sand 100m

Fr N fr Pont de Normandie on D929 take D144; at ent to Honfleur keep harbour in R; turn R onto D513 sp Trouville-sur-Mer & Deauville (avoid town cent); fork L past old lighthouse to site entry thro parking area. Or fr E on D180; foll sp 'Cent Ville' then Vieux Bassin dir Trouville; at rectangular rndabt with fountain turn R sp Deauville & Trouville, then as above. 2*, Med, hdg, pt shd, EHU (16A) inc; gas; bbq; 10% statics; phone; Eng spkn; fishing; CKE. *"Gd clean site in excel location; conv NH Le Havre ferry; busy high ssn, rec arr early; friendly owners; san facs basic & tired but clean, ltd LS; barrier clsd 2200-0700; m'van pitches narr & adj busy rd; some soft, sandy pitches; easy walk to town/harbour; sep m'van Aire de Service nr harbour; new disabled san facs (2015); conv Honfleur by foot; nice site; own san facs rec."* **€25.00, 1 Apr-30 Sep. 2022**

HOULGATE *3D1* (1km E Coastal) *49.29390, -0.06820*
Camping La Vallée, 88 Rue de la Vallée, 14510 Houlgate **02 31 24 40 69 or 04 88 81 15 62; camping.lavallee@wanadoo.fr; www.campinglavallee.com**

€5 (htd) (covrd, htd)
sand 900m

Exit junc 29 or 29a fr A13 onto D45 to Houlgate. Or fr Deauville take D513 W. Bef Houlgate sp, turn L & foll sp to site. 5*, Lge, mkd, hdg, pt shd, pt sl, terr, serviced pitches; EHU (6A) inc; gas; TV; 85% statics; Eng spkn; adv bkg req; ccard acc; games rm; bike hire; waterslide; lake fishing 2km; tennis; golf 1km; CKE. *"Superb, busy site; friendly recep; clean san facs; some pitches poss sm for lge o'fits; sep area m'vans; 1,5km walk to sandy beach and town; bkg fee; ACSI acc; fam/child orientated site."* **€58.00, 1 May-28 Sep. 2024**

HOURTIN *7C1* (7.5km SSW Rural) *45.13915, -1.07096*
Aire Naturelle de Camping l'Acacia, Route de Carcans, 33990 (Gironde) **05 56 73 80 80 or 06 72 94 12 67 (mob); camping.lacacia@orange.fr; www.campinglacacia.com**

Fr Carcans on main rd to Hourtin, sp for site about 5km. Turn off rd on L and travel for 1.5km. Sm, pt shd, EHU inc; cooking facs; twin axles; adv bkg acc; games area; games rm. *"Site well maintained; immac san facs; owner v helpful, ltd Eng; v lge pitches; volleyball; bicycles; table tennis; v lge field; quiet peaceful site; great for families and couples; excel."* **€23.00, 7 Jun-30 Sep. 2024**

HOURTIN *7C1* (1.5km W Rural) *45.17919, -1.07502*
Camping Les Ourmes, 90 Ave du Lac, 33990 Hourtin Port **05 56 09 12 76; info@lesourmes.com; www.lesourmes.com**

€2 nr nr nr

Fr vill of Hourtin (35km NW Bordeaux), foll sp Houtin Port. In 1.5km, L at sp to site. 4*, Lge, mkd, pt shd, EHU (6A) inc; gas; bbq; sw nr; TV; 50% statics; phone; bus; Eng spkn; adv bkg acc; horseriding; fishing; games rm; watersports; CKE. *"Excel for family holiday; Lake Hourtin shallow & vg for bathing, sailing etc; vg beaches nrby; nr Les Landes & Médoc vineyards."* **€32.00, 16 Apr-25 Sep. 2022**

HOURTIN *7C1* (10km W Coastal) *45.22296, -1.16472*
Camping La Côte d'Argent, Rue de la Côte d'Argent, 33990 Hourtin-Plage **05 56 09 10 25; info@cca33.com; www.cca33.com**

€5.50
(covrd, htd) sand 300m

On D1215 at Lesparre-Médoc take D3 Hourtin, D101 to Hourtin-Plage, site sp. 4*, V lge, mkd, shd, pt sl, terr, EHU (10A) inc; bbq; sw nr; red long stay; 30% statics; phone; Eng spkn; adv bkg acc; ccard acc; bike hire; watersports; horseriding; fishing 4km; games area; ice; waterslide; games rm; jacuzzi; CKE. *"Pleasant, peaceful site in pine trees & dunes; poss steel pegs req; conv Médoc region chateaux & vineyards; ideal for surfers & beach lovers."* **€53.00, 14 May-18 Sep. 2022**

See advertisement opposite

HUELGOAT *2E2* (3km E Rural) *48.36275, -3.71532* **FFCC Camping La Rivière d'Argent,** La Coudraie, 29690 Huelgoat **02 98 99 72 50; contact@larivieredargent.com; www.larivieredargent.com**

€2.30 WD MSP nr (covrd, htd, indoor)

Sp fr town cent on D769A sp Poullaouen & Carhaix. 2*, Med, mkd, hdg, shd, EHU (6-10A) €3.70; red long stay; adv bkg acc; tennis. *"Lovely wooded site on rv bank; some rvside pitches; gd walks with maps provided; san facs updated (2017) well maintained, v clean; gd unisex facs; site self; poss rev pol; excel dog walks fr site; v friendly & helpful new owners (2018); excel."* **€22.10, 1 Apr-30 Sep. 2024**

HYERES *10F3* (8km E Coastal) *43.1186, 6.24693* **Miramar Camping,** 1026 Blvd Louis Bernard, 83250 La Londes-les-Maures **04 94 66 80 58; camping.miramar.lalonde@wanadoo.fr; www.campingmiramar.com**

WD sand 200m

On D98 in cent of La Londes-les-Maures, turn S at traff lts; in 1km turn R over white bdge & foll rd for 1.5km dir Port Miramar; site on R 150m bef port. 3*, Lge, hdg, mkd, shd, EHU (4-10A) €4.50-6.50; 25% statics; phone; Eng spkn; ccard acc; games rm; CKE. *"Vg shd; beach, port, rests & shops 200m, but food shops 2km; vg marina; excel site out of ssn; vg."* **€22.00, 15 Mar - 15 Nov. 2024**

HYERES *10F3* (9km S Coastal) *43.02980, 6.15490* **Camping La Tour Fondue,** Ave des Arbanais, 83400 Giens **04 94 58 23 59; info@camping-latourfondue.com; www.camping-latourfondue.com**

€3 WD MSP adj

D97 fr Hyères, site sp. Med, hdg, pt shd, pt sl, terr, EHU (6A) €4.70; 10% statics; Eng spkn; adv bkg acc; ccard acc; games area. *"Pleasant, sister site of Camping Presqu'île de Giens with easier access; sm pitches; no dogs on beach; only water point at 'Sanitaires' (by recep); superb new san facs (2014)."* **€41.60, 23 Mar-6 Oct. 2024**

ILE BOUCHARD, L' *4H1* (0.5km N Urban) *47.12166, 0.42857* **Camping Les Bords de Vienne,** 4 Allée du Camping, 37220 L'Ile-Bouchard **07 81 07 23 44; campinglesbordsdevienne@onlycamp.fr; camping-ile-bouchard.fr**

€1.50 WD nr

On N bank of Rv Vienne 100m E of rd bdge nr junc of D757 & D760. Fr E, turn L bet supmkt & pharmacy. 3*, Med, mkd, pt shd, pt sl, EHU (6-16A) €3.50; gas; sw nr; red long stay; 10% statics; Eng spkn; adv bkg acc; ccard acc; tennis 500m; CKE. *"Lovely, clean rvside site; attractive location; poss travellers; conv Loire chateaux."* **€14.60, 3 Mar-22 Sep. 2024**

ILLIERS COMBRAY *4E2* (2km SW Rural) *48.28667, 1.22697* **Camping Le Bois Fleuri,** Route de Brou, 28120 Illiers-Combray **02 37 24 03 04; contact@camping-chartres.com; www.camping-chartres.com/fr**

€2 (htd) WD nr nr

S on D921 fr Illiers for 2km twd Brou. Site on L. 3*, Med, hdg, hdstg, pt shd, serviced pitches; EHU (6A) €3.50; gas; 30% statics; adv bkg acc; fishing adj; games area; CKE. *"Many pitches wooded & with flowers; popular NH; excel san facs; ltd water/EHU; htd pool 200m; uneven grnd makes access diff; gd security; excel cycle path to vill."* **€31.10, 1 May-30 Sep. 2024**

INGRANDES *4H2* (1km N Rural) *46.88700, 0.58800* **Camping Le Petit Trianon de St Ustre,** 1 Rue du Moulin de St Ustre, 86220 Ingrandes-sur-Vienne **05 49 02 61 47; contact@domaine-petit-trianon.com; www.domaine-petit-trianon.com**

€4 WD MSP (htd)

Leave A10/E5 at Châtellerault Nord exit 26 & foll sp Tours. Cross rv heading N on D910 twd Tours & Dangé-St Romain. At 2nd traff lts in Ingrandes (by church), turn R. Cross rlwy line & turn L at site sp in 300m. After 1.5km turn R at site sp, site at top of hill. NB Site ent narr, poss diff lge o'fits. 4*, Med, mkd, pt shd, pt sl, EHU (10A) inc; gas; bbq; TV; Eng spkn; adv bkg acc; ccard acc; horseriding 1km; rv fishing 3km; games rm; tennis 1.5km; bike hire; games area; CKE. *"Lovely site in chateau grnds; charming old buildings; gd sized pitches; friendly, helpful staff; excel facs."* **€40.00, 6 Apr-24 Sep, L07. 2022**

ISIGNY SUR MER *1D4* (0.5km NW Rural) *49.31872, -1.10825* **Camping Le Fanal,** Rue du Fanal, 14230 Isigny-sur-Mer **02 31 21 33 20; info@camping-lefanal.com; http://www.camping-normandie-fanal.fr**

€5 WD MSP (htd, indoor)

Fr N13 exit into Isigny, site immed N of town. Foll sp to 'Stade' in town, (just after sq & church on narr rd just bef R turn). 4*, Med, hdg, mkd, pt shd, EHU (16A) inc (long cable poss req); TV; 50% statics; phone; adv bkg acc; ccard acc; games rm; horseriding; tennis; games area; lake fishing adj; CKE. *"Friendly staff; aqua park; poss boggy in wet weather; vg site."* **€30.50, 1 Apr-30 Sep. 2020**

ISLE SUR LA SORGUE, L' *10E2* (2km E Rural) *43.91451, 5.07181* **Camping Airotel La Sorguette,** 871 Route d'Apt, 84800 L'Isle-sur-la-Sorgue **04 90 38 05 71; info@camping-sorguette.com; www.camping-sorguette.com**

€3.50 WD MSP nr adj

Fr L'Isle-sur-la-Sorgue take D901 twd Apt, on L site in 1.5km, sp. 3*, Med, hdg, mkd, pt shd, EHU (10A) €4.70; gas; bbq; 10% statics; Eng spkn; adv bkg acc; ccard acc; tennis; fishing adj; games area; canoeing; CKE. *"Lovely, well-run site; useful & busy; friendly, helpful staff; beware low trees; dated but clean san facs; rvside walk to attractive town; Sun mkt (shuttle fr site); highly rec."* **€23.00, 15 Mar-15 Oct. 2024**

ISPAGNAC *9D1* (1km W Rural) *44.37232, 3.53035*
Camping Le Pré Morjal, 48320 Ispagnac **04 66 45 43 57 or 06 81 32 46 23; contact@camping-premorjal.com; camping-premorjal.com**
€1.20 (htd) nr

On D907B 500m W of town, turn L off D907B & then 200m on R, sp. 3*, Med, hdg, pt shd, EHU (10-16A) €3; bbq; sw nr; TV; games area; games rm. *"Lovely family site; gd sized pitches on rocky base, poss muddy when wet; pool 50m inc; friendly staff; gd rvside walks; vg base for Tarn & Joute Gorges; early ssn poss unkempt & irreg cleaning of san facs (2010)."*
€27.40, 30 Mar-1 Nov. **2024**

ISSOIRE *9B1* (3km E Rural) *45.55113, 3.27423*
FFCC Camp Municipal du Mas, Ave du Dr Bienfait, 63500 Issoire **06 09 80 52 63; www.camping-issoire.fr/fr**
€0.70 (htd) nr nr nr

Fr Clermont-Ferrand S on A75/E11 take exit 12 sp Issoire; turn L over a'route sp Orbeil; at rndabt, take 1st exit & foll site sp. 3*, Med, mkd, hdg, pt shd, pt sl, serviced pitches; EHU (10-13A) inc; bbq (elec, gas); red long stay; TV; 5% statics; phone; Eng spkn; adv bkg rec; ccard acc; fishing adj; tennis 500m; boule; ten pin bowling; CKE. *"Lovely, well-kept, basic site in park-like location; lge pitches; helpful warden; new, modern san facs; site poss boggy after rain; conv A75; excel touring base or NH; easy cycle rte to Issoire; vg."*
€22.00, 1 Apr-1 Nov. **2024**

ISSOIRE *9B1* (6km SE Rural) *45.50908, 3.2848*
FFCC Camping Château La Grange Fort, 63500 Les Pradeaux **04 73 71 05 93 or 04 73 71 02 43; chateau@lagrangefort.com; www.lagrangefort.com**
€3 (htd) nr
(covrd, htd)

S fr Clermont Ferrand on A75, exit junc 13 onto D996 sp Parentignat. At 1st rndabt take D999 sp St Rémy-Chargnat (new rd); at next rndabt take 1st exit onto D34 & foll sp to site on hill-top. Narr app rd & narr uphill ent. 3*, Med, mkd, hdg, shd, EHU (6A) €3.50; gas; TV; 10% statics; phone; Eng spkn; adv bkg req; ccard acc; bike hire; rv fishing; sauna; canoe hire; tennis; CKE. *"Pleasant, peaceful Dutch-run site in chateau grnds with views; excel san facs but long walk fr some pitches & ltd LS; some sm pitches; most pitches damp & gloomy under lge trees & muddy after rain; bkg fee; mosquito problem on shadiest pitches; ltd parking at recep; conv A75; gd."* **€27.00, 1 Apr-31 Oct.** **2024**

ISSOIRE *9B1* (11km S Rural) *45.47373, 3.27161*
Camping Les Loges, 63340 Nonette **04 73 71 65 82; campingnonette@lesloges.com; www.lesloges.com**
€3 (htd)

Exit 17 fr A75 onto D214 sp Le Breuil, dir Nonette. Turn L in 2km, cross rv & turn L to site. Site perched on conical hill. Steep app. 3*, Med, hdg, mkd, pt shd, EHU (10A) €3.50; gas; bbq; sw nr; TV; 30% statics; adv bkg acc; sports facs; volleyball; pétanque; table tennis; games area; bouncy castle; games rm; fishing adj; CKE. *"Friendly site; conv Massif Cent & A75; gd NH."*
€21.00, 30 Mar-30 Sep. **2020**

ISSOUDUN *4H3* (3km N Rural) *46.96361, 1.99011*
Camp Municipal Les Taupeaux, 37 Route de Reuilly, 36100 Issoudun **02 54 03 13 46 or 02 54 21 74 02; tourisme@issoudun.fr; www.tourisme.issoudun.fr/o-dormir**

Fr Bourges SW on N151, site sp fr Issoudun on D16 nr Carrefour supmkt. Sm, hdg, mkd, pt shd, EHU €3.70. *"Pleasant site off RR; mv service pnt adj; conv A71 & N151."* **€11.00, 15 May-15 Sep.** **2022**

JARD SUR MER *7A1* (2km NE Rural) *46.42624, -1.56564* **Camping La Mouette Cendrée,** Les Malécots, 85520 St Vincent-sur-Jard **02 51 33 59 04; camping.mc@orange.fr; www.mouettecendree.com**
€3 (max 2) nr sand 2km

Fr Les Sables-d'Olonne take D949 SE to Talmont-St-Hilaire; then take D21 to Jard-sur-Mer; at rndabt stay on D21 (taking 2nd exit dir La Tranche-sur-Mer & Maison-de- Clemanceau); in 500m turn L onto D19 sp St Hilaire-la-Forêt & foll site sps. Site on L in 700m. 3*, Med, hdg, mkd, pt shd, EHU (10A) inc; bbq (elec, gas); sw nr; 30% statics; Eng spkn; adv bkg acc; ccard acc; golf 10km; waterslide; windsurfing 2km; fishing; horseriding 500m; bike hire; games rm; CKE. *"Busy site high ssn; gd pitches; welcoming, helpful owners; san facs poss stretched when site full; no o'fits over 7.5m high ssn; vg pool; gd woodland walks & cycle rtes nr; mkt Mon."*
€29.50, Early April - Mid October, A20. **2022**

JARD SUR MER *7A1* (2km SE Coastal) *46.41980, -1.52580* **Camping La Bolée d'Air,** Route du Bouil, Route de Longeville, 85520 St Vincent-sur-Jard **02 51 90 36 05 or 02 51 33 05 05; info@chadotel.com; www.chadotel.com**
€4 (htd)
(covrd, htd) sand 900m

Fr A11 junc 14 dir Angers. Take N160 to La Roche-sur-Yon & then D747 dir La Tranche-sur-Mer to Moutier-les-Mauxfaits. At Moutiers take D19 to St Hilaire-la-Forêt & then L to St Vincent-sur-Jard. In St Vincent turn L by church sp Longeville-sur-Mer, site on R in 1km. 4*, Lge, mkd, hdg, pt shd, serviced pitches; EHU (10A) inc; gas; bbq (charcoal, gas); red long stay; TV; 25% statics; Eng spkn; adv bkg acc; ccard acc; sauna; bike hire; games rm; waterslide; jacuzzi; tennis; CKE. *"Popular, v busy site high ssn; mkt Sun; no o'fits over 8m; whirlpool; access some pitches poss diff lge o'fits; excel."*
€34.00, 1 Apr-24 Sep, A31. **2022**

JAULNY *5D2* (0.5km S Rural) *48.96578, 5.88524*
Camping La Pelouse, Chemin de Fey, 54470 Jaulny
03 83 81 91 67; info@campingdelapelouse.com; www.campingdelapelouse.com
€2 (htd)

SW fr Metz on D657, cross rv at Corny-sur-Moselle onto D6/D1; in 1.5km turn R onto D952 dir Waville & Thiaucourt-Regniéville; in 6km turn L onto D28 dir Thiaucourt-Regniéville; cont on D28 to Jaulny; site sp to L in Jaulny. 3*, Med, pt shd, sl, EHU (6A) €4; bbq; sw nr; 80% statics; adv bkg acc; fishing; volleyball; table tennis; CKE. *"Vg site; friendly owner and staff; basic san facs, poss stretched high ssn; no fresh or waste water facs for m'vans; conv NH."*
€20.60, 1 Apr-30 Sep. 2020

JAUNAY CLAN *4H1* (7km NE Rural) *46.72015, 0.45982*
Camping du Lac de Saint-Cyr, 86130 St Cyr
05 49 62 57 22; contact@campinglacdesaintcyr.com; www.campinglacdesaintcyr.com
€3

Fr A10 take Châtellerault Sud exit & take D910 dir Poitiers; at Beaumont turn L at traff lts for St Cyr; foll camp sp in leisure complex (Parc Loisirs) by lakeside - R turn for camping. Or fr S take Futuroscope exit to D910. 4*, Lge, mkd, hdg, pt shd, pt sl, serviced pitches; EHU (10A) inc (poss rev pol); gas; bbq; sw; red long stay; TV; 15% statics; Eng spkn; adv bkg acc; ccard acc; games area; boat hire; golf adj; watersports; games rm; fishing; sailing; canoeing; tennis; fitness rm; bike hire; CKE. *"Excel, well-kept site in leisure complex; lovely setting by lake; gd sized pitches; helpful recep; no o'fits over 8m; gd, clean san facs, poss stretched high ssn; gd rest; some pitches poss diff lge o'fits; rec long o'fits unhitch at barrier due R-angle turn at barrier - poss diff long o'fits; Futuroscope approx 13km; highly rec; excel site; gd size pitches; friendly helpful staff."*
€34.10, 1 Apr-30 Sep, L09. 2023

JAUNAY CLAN *4H1* (2km SE Urban) *46.66401, 0.39466* **Kawan Village Le Futuriste,** Rue du Château, 86130 St Georges-les-Baillargeaux **05 49 52 47 52; camping-le-futuriste@wanadoo.fr; www.camping-le-futuriste.fr**
12 €2.50 (htd) (covrd, htd)

On A10 fr N or S, take Futuroscope exit 28; fr toll booth at 1st rndabt take 2nd exit. Thro tech park twd St Georges. At rndabt under D910 take slip rd N onto D910. After 150m exit D910 onto D20, foll sp. At 1st rndabt bear R, over rlwy, cross sm rv & up hill, site on R. 4*, Med, mkd, hdg, pt shd, serviced pitches; EHU (6A) inc (check earth & poss rev pol); gas; bbq; TV; 10% statics; Eng spkn; adv bkg acc; ccard acc; games area; games rm; lake fishing; waterslide; CKE. *"Lovely, busy, secure site; well-kept; friendly, helpful family owners; vg clean facs, ltd LS - facs block clsd 2200-0700; vg pool; vg for families; hypmkt 2km; ideal touring base for Poitiers & Futuroscope (tickets fr recep); vg value, espec in winter; conv a'route; excel."*
€35.30 2023

JOIGNY *4F4* (8km E Urban) *47.955286, 3.507431*
Camping Les Confluents, Allée Léo Lagrange, 89400 Migennes **03 86 80 94 55; contact@les-confluents.com; www.les-confluents.com**
€1 (htd)

A6 exit at junc 19 Auxerre Nord onto N6 & foll sp to Migennes & site, well sp. 3*, Med, hdstg, mkd, hdg, pt shd, EHU (6-10A) €3.50-4.90; gas; bbq; red long stay; TV; 8% statics; phone; bus 10 mins; adv bkg acc; ccard acc; bike hire; watersports 300m; games area; canoe hire; volleyball; ping pong; bowling green; library; CKE. *"Friendly, family-run, clean site nr canal & indust area; no twin axles; medieval castle, wine cellars, potteries nrby; walking dist to Migennes; mkt Thurs; excel."*
€24.00, 28 Mar-1 Nov. 2020

JOIGNY *4F4* (2km W Rural) *47.98143, 3.37439*
FFCC Camp Municipal, 68 Quai d'Epizy, 89300 Joigny
03 86 62 07 55; contact.camping@ville-joigny.f; https://camping.ville-joigny.fr
nr nr

Fr A6 exit junc 18 or 19 to Joigny cent. Fr cent, over brdg, turn L onto D959; turn L in filter lane at traff lts. Foll sp to site. 2*, Sm, hdg, hdstg, pt shd, EHU (10A) inc; sw nr; fishing adj; tennis; horseriding; CKE. *"V busy site; liable to flood in wet weather; v helpful warden; pool 4km; interesting town; v modern clean san facs; quiet in May; some sm pitches; v helpful warden; local wine avail to buy."*
€16.50, 17 May-30 Sep. 2023

JOSSELIN *2F3* (1.5km W Rural) *47.95230, -2.57338*
Domaine de Kerelly, Le bas de la lande, 56120 Guégon **02 97 22 22 20 or 06 27 57 22 79 (mob); domainedekerelly@orange.fr; www.camping-josselin.com**
nr

Exit N24 by-pass W of town sp Guégon; foll sp 1km; do not attempt to cross Josselin cent fr E to W. Site on D724 just S of Rv Oust (canal).
3*, Med, hdg, pt shd, terr, EHU (6-10A) €3.80-4.50; bbq; TV; phone; Eng spkn; adv bkg acc; ccard acc; bike hire; CKE. *"Vg, clean san facs; site rds steep; pleasant walks; poss diff if wet; walk to Josselin, chateau & old houses; gd cycling; family run; gd food; mini golf."*
€20.00, 1 Apr-31 Oct. 2023

JUGON LES LACS *2E3* (1km S Rural) *48.40166, -2.31678* **Camping au Bocage du Lac,** Rue Du Bocage, 22270 Jugon-les-Lacs **02 96 31 60 16; contact@campinglacbretagne.com; www.camping-location-bretagne.com**
€3.20 nr (htd)

Bet Dinan & Lamballe by N176. Foll `Camping Jeux' sp on D52 fr Jugon-les-Lacs. Situated by lakes, sp fr cent of Jugon. 4*, Lge, pt shd, pt sl, EHU (10A) €3-4.60; TV; 10% statics; adv bkg acc; fishing adj; waterslide; games area; watersports adj; games rm. *"Well-situated nr pretty vill; many sports & activities; vg, modern san facs; vg, attractive site."*
€31.50, 5 Apr-29 Sep. 2024

JUMIEGES *3C2* (1km E Rural) *49.43490, 0.82970* **Camping de la Forêt,** Rue Mainberte, 76480 Jumièges **02 35 37 93 43; info@campinglaforet.com; www.campinglaforet.com**

(htd) nr (htd)

Exit A13 junc 25 onto D313/D490 N to Pont de Brotonne. Cross Pont de Brotonne & immed turn R onto D982 sp Le Trait. Cont thro town & in 1km turn R onto D143 sp Yainville & Jumièges. In Jumièges turn L at x-rds after cemetary & church, site on R in 1km. NB M'vans under 3.5t & 3m height can take ferry fr Port Jumièges - if towing do not use sat nav dirs. 4*, Med, hdg, mkd, pt shd, EHU (10A) €5 (poss rev pol); gas; bbq; TV; 30% statics; phone; bus to Rouen; Eng spkn; adv bkg acc; ccard acc; watersports; bike hire; games rm; fishing; tennis; games area. *"Nice site, well-situated in National Park; busy; some sm pitches; gd, clean san facs but poss stretched high ssn; interesting vill; conv Paris & Giverny; no o'fits over 7m high ssn; gd walking, cycling; ferries across Rv Seine; gd for dogs; children loved it; v friendly helpful owners."* **€29.60, 1 Apr - 31 Oct, N15.** **2022**

KAYSERSBERG *6F3* (1km NW Rural) *48.14899, 7.25405* **Camping Municipal de Kayserberg,** Rue des Acacias, 68240 Kaysersberg **03 89 47 14 47 or 03 89 78 11 11 (Mairie); camping@villekaysersberg.fr; www.camping-kaysersberg.com**

12 €2 nr

Fr A35/N83 exit junc 23 onto D4 sp Sigolsheim & Kaysersberg; bear L onto N415 bypass dir St Dié; site sp 100m past junc with D28. Or SE fr St Dié on N415 over Col du Bonhomme; turn L into Rue des Acacias just bef junc with D28. 4*, Med, hdg, mkd, pt shd, EHU (8-13A) inc (may need cable); gas; TV; fishing adj; tennis adj. *"Excel, well-kept, busy site; rec arr early high ssn; no dogs Jul/Aug; many gd sized pitches; friendly staff; clean san facs; rv walk to lovely town, birth place Albert Schweitzer; bread delivery; many mkd walks/cycle rts; Le Linge WWI battle grnd nr Orbey; excel site; if arr when clsd, choose pitch nbr bef registering; recep clsd 12-14pm, no access to site at this time."* **€18.90** **2024**

KAYSERSBERG *6F3* (7km NW Rural) *48.18148, 7.18449* **Camping Les Verts Bois,** 3 Rue de la Fonderie, 68240 Fréland **07 86 02 60 93; gildas.douault@sfr.fr; www.camping-lesvertsbois.com**

€0.70 (htd) nr

Sp off N415 Colmar/St Dié rd bet Lapoutroie & Kaysersberg. Site approx 5km after turn fr main rd on D11 at far end of vill. Turn L into rd to site when D11 doubles back on itself. 2*, Sm, pt shd, pt sl, terr, EHU (6-10A) €2.70-3.20; gas; bbq; Eng spkn; adv bkg acc; ccard acc; CKE. *"Lovely site in beautiful, peaceful setting adj rv; friendly welcome; excel; fishing & bird watching; cheese farms 2 miles away; a must for cheese lovers; v helpful owners; excel rest."* **€19.00, 1 Apr-31 Oct.** **2024**

"We must tell the Club about that great site we found"

Get your site reports in by mid-August and we'll do our best to get your updates into the next edition.

KEMBS *6F3* (0.5km E Rural) *47.686816, 7.508359* **Camping du Canal,** 12 rue Paul Bader, 68680 Kembs **07 83 89 72 50; campingkembs@gmail.com; www.camping-du-canal.fr**

€5 (htd) nr (htd)

Exit Junc 35 on A35 onto the Rue De La Liberation (E). Then N on the D468 to Kembs. Site is sp down Rue Paul Bader. 3*, Sm, hdstg, mkd, pt shd, EHU inc; bbq (charcoal, elec, gas); 15% statics; bus; train; Eng spkn; adv bkg acc; ccard acc; games area. *"Lovely site; clean face; between 2 canals; walking distance fr the Rhine; friendly owners; gd for walkers/cyclists; gd nh; no shops except Lidl; 15 mins from Swiss border and German border; vg."* **€22.20, 1 Apr-30 Sep.** **2024**

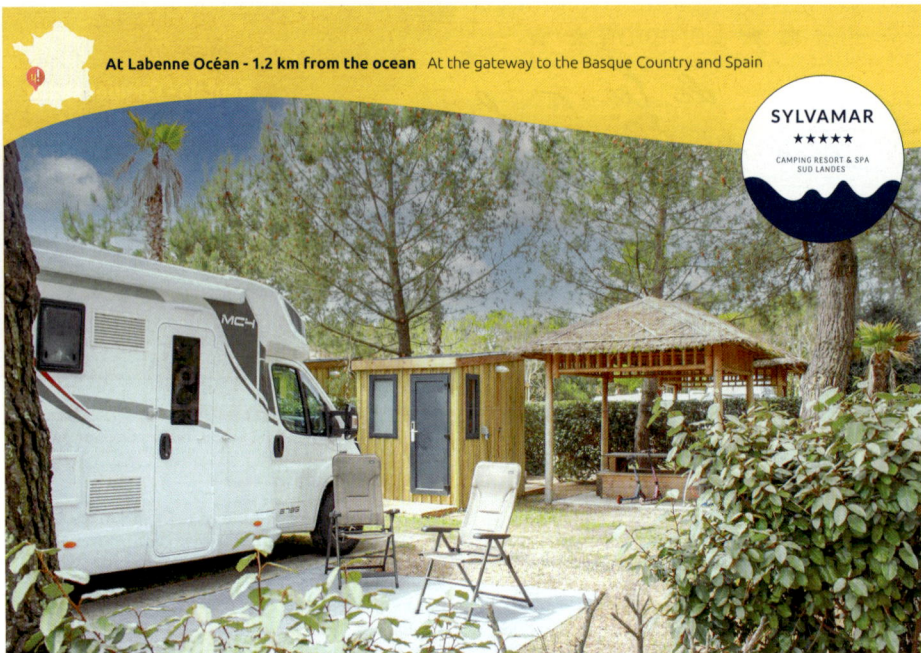

LABENNE *8E1* (3km SW Coastal) *43.59533, -1.45651* **Camping Le Sylvamar,** Ave de l'Océan, 40530 Labenne **05 59 45 75 16; camping@sylvamar.fr; www.sylvamar.fr or www.yellohvillage.co.uk**

nr (htd) sand 800m

Exit A63 junc 7 onto D85; then take N10 N to Labenne; turn L onto D126; site sp. Lge, hdg, mkd, pt shd, serviced pitches; EHU (10A) inc; bbq; 50% statics; Eng spkn; adv bkg acc; ccard acc; waterslide; CKE. *"Site amongst pine trees; sauna; spa; creche; sandy pitches; fitness rm; beauty cent; gd location; vg facs."* **€70.00, 8 Apr-29 Oct.** **2022**

See advertisement

LABENNE *8E1* (3km W Coastal) *43.59628, -1.46104* **Camping Le Boudigau (formerly Camp Atlantique Le Boudigau),** 45 Avenue de la Plage, 40530 Labenne-Océan **05 59 45 42 07; leboudigau@vagues-oceanes.com; www.camping-vagues-oceanes.com/camping-landes/le-boudigau.html**

(covrd, htd) sand 500m

Turn W off N10 in Labenne at traff lts in town cent onto D126 to Labenne-Plage. Site 2km on R. 4*, Lge, shd, EHU (6A) inc; gas; bbq; 90% statics; adv bkg rec; games area. *"Sm touring area - only 25 pitches; excel san facs; gd site; 1 dog per pitch; lively high ssn - gd kids activities."* **€28.00, 22 Mar-22 Sep.** **2024**

LACANAU *7C1* (3.3km NNW Rural) *45.00178, -1.09241* **Camping Les Fougères,** Ave de l'Océan, 33680 Talaris **05 56 03 56 76; lacanau@campingsliberte.com; www.libertelacanau.com**

€2.10

A630 bypass exit at junc 8 sp Lacanau - Le Verdon. 3*, Med, pt shd, EHU (4A) inc; bbq; sw nr; twin axles; 10% statics; Eng spkn; adv bkg acc; games area; CKE. *"Excel site; watersports 1.5km; tennis 9km."* **€39.20, 17 Jun-9 Sep.** **2024**

LACANAU OCEAN *7C1* (1km N Coastal) *45.00823, -1.19322* **Airotel L'Océan Camping & Spa,** 24 Rue du Repos, 33680 Lacanau-Océan **05 56 03 24 45; contact@airotel-ocean.com; www.airotel-ocean.com**

€5 (htd, indoor) sand 800m

On ent town at end of sq in front of bus stn turn R, fork R & foll sp to site (next to Camping Grand Pins). 4*, Lge, pt shd, pt sl, EHU (16A) inc; gas; TV; Eng spkn; adv bkg acc; watersports; bike hire; tennis; CKE. *"Attractive site/holiday vill in pine woods behind sand dunes; surfing school nrby; care in choosing pitch due soft sand; gd, modern san facs; some pitches tight access."* **€33.00, Easter-27 Sep.** **2024**

See advertisement opposite

LACANAU OCEAN *7C1* (5km SE Rural) *44.98620, -1.13410* **Camping Le Tedey,** Par Le Moutchic, Route de Longarisse, 33680 Lacanau-Océan **05 56 03 00 15; contact@letedey.com; www.campingletedey.com**

Fr Bordeaux take D6 to Lacanau & on twd Lacanau-Océan. On exit Moutchic take L fork twd Longarisse. Ent in 2km well sp on L. 4*, V lge, mkd, shd, EHU (10A) €4.30; gas; sw nr; TV; 10% statics; Eng spkn; adv bkg rec; ccard acc; bike hire; boating; golf 5km; CKE. *"Peaceful, friendly, family-run site in pine woods - avoid tree sap; golf nr; gd cycle tracks; no EHU for pitches adj beach; access diff some pitches; excel site."* **€43.20, 5 Apr-23 Sep. 2024**

LACAPELLE VIESCAMP *7C4* (1.6km SW Rural) *44.91272, 2.24853* **Camping La Presqu'île du Puech des Ouilhes,** 15150 Lacapelle-Viescamp **04 71 46 42 38 or 06 80 37 15 61 (mob); contact@cantal-camping.fr; www.camping-lac-auvergne.com**

€2 nr sand adj

W fr Aurillac on D120; at St Paul-des-Landes turn S onto D53 then D18 to Lacapelle-Viescamp. Foll sp Base de Loisirs, Plage-du-Puech des Ouilhes & Camping. Site beside Lake St Etienne-Cantalès. 3*, Med, mkd, hdstg, hdg, pt shd, EHU (16A) €3; sw nr; 10% statics; Eng spkn; fishing; canoeing; tennis; games rm; watersports. *"Friendly, helpful young owners; excel."* **€30.00, 15 Jun-15 Sep. 2024**

FRANCE

LAGRASSE 8F4 (0.7km N Rural) 43.09516, 2.61893 **Camp Municipal de Boucocers,** Route de Ribaute, 11220 Lagrasse **04 68 43 10 05 or 04 68 43 15 18; mairielagrasse@wanadoo.fr; www.audetourisme.com**

€2.10 nr nr

1km on D212 fr Lagrasse to Fabrezan (N). 1*, Sm, hdstg, pt shd, pt sl, EHU (15A) €2.80; sw nr; phone; adv bkg acc; CKE. *"At cent of 'off-the-beaten-track' beautiful touring area; helpful warden; simple but gd san facs; gd walking; path down to lagrasse cent; o'looks superb medieval town; rec arr early; hillside walk into vill needs care; site run down at then of ssn; no entry barrier, site self, pay when warden calls; excel, well kept site; Lagrasse Abbey & town worth a visit."*
€15.00, 15 Mar-15 Oct. **2023**

LAGUEPIE 8E4 (1km E Rural) 44.14780, 1.97892 **Camping Les Tilleuls,** 82250 Laguépie **07 86 23 12 61; campinglestilleulslaguepie82@gmail.com; campinglestilleuls-laguepie82.fr**

nr nr

Exit Cordes on D922 N to Laguépie; turn R at bdge, still on D922 sp Villefranche; site sp to R in 500m; tight turn into narr lane. NB App thro Laguépie poss diff lge o'fits. Med, pt shd, terr, EHU (10A) €2.70; sw; TV; 44% statics; phone; adv bkg acc; canoe hire; fishing; tennis; games area. *"Attractive setting on Rv Viaur; friendly welcome; excel playgrnd; gd touring base; conv Aveyron gorges."*
€17.90, 1 Apr-28 Oct. **2023**

LAGUIOLE 7D4 (0.5km NE Rural) 44.68158, 2.85440 **Camp Municipal Les Monts D'Aubrac,** 12210 Laguiole **05 65 44 39 72 or 05 65 51 26 30 (LS); campinglesmontsdaubraclaguiole.jimdofree.com**

nr nr nr

E of Laguiole on D15 at top of hill. Fr S on D921 turn R at rndabt bef ent to town. Site sp. Med, mkd, hdg, pt shd, pt sl, EHU (16A) inc; phone; CKE. *"Clean & well cared for site; pleasant vill."*
€19.00, 15 May-15 Sep. **2024**

LAISSAC 7D4 (3km SE Rural) 44.36525, 2.85090 **Village La Grange de Monteillac,** Chemin de Monteillac, 12310 Sévérac-l'Eglise **05 65 70 21 00; info@le-grange-de-monteillac.com; www.aveyron-location.com/fr**

€1.50

Fr A75, at junc 42, go W on N88 twds Rodez; after approx 22km; bef Laissac; turn L twds Sévérac-l'Eglise; site sp. 4*, Med, hdg, mkd, unshd, pt sl, terr, EHU (6A) inc (long lead poss req); TV; 10% statics; phone; Eng spkn; adv bkg rec; bike hire; tennis; horseriding; CKE. *"Beautiful, excel site; bar & shops high ssn."* **€40.10, 17 May-29 Sep.** **2024**

LALINDE 7C3 (2km E Urban) 44.83956, 0.76298 **Camping Moulin de la Guillou,** 24150 LALINDE, Dordogne **05 53 58 31 84 or 05 53 73 44 60 (Mairie); moulindelaguillou@ville-lalinde.fr; www.moulindelaguillou.fr**

€2 nr

Take D703 E fr Lalinde (Rv Dordogne on R) & keep strt where rd turns L over canal bdge. Site in 300m; sp. 2*, Med, shd, EHU (5A) €2.60; sw nr; adv bkg rec; tennis adj; fishing adj. *"Charming, peaceful site on bank of Rv Dordogne; lovely views; clean san facs, in need of upgrade; poss travellers; vg."*
€15.00, 1 May-30 Sep. **2020**

LALLEY 9D3 (0.3km S Rural) 44.75490, 5.67940 **Camping Belle Roche,** Chemin de Combe Morée, 38930 Lalley **04 76 34 75 33; contact@campingbelleroche.com; www.campingbelleroche.com**

€1.50 nr (htd)

Off D1075 at D66 for Mens; down long hill into Lalley. Site on R thro vill. 3*, Med, hdstg, hdg, pt shd, pt sl, EHU (10A) €4 (poss rev pol, poss long lead req); gas; bbq; TV; 10% statics; adv bkg acc; ccard acc; games area; tennis 500m; CKE. *"Well-kept, scenic site; spacious pitches but little shd; friendly, welcoming owners; clean, vg modern san facs, poss stretched high ssn; pleasant pool area; nr Vercors National Park; vg walking/cycling; don't miss The Little Train of La Mure; conv NH; v nice site; highly rec superb in every way."* **€29.50, 31 Mar-14 Oct.** **2024**

LAMALOU LES BAINS 10F1 (2km SE Rural) 43.57631, 3.06842 **Camping Domaine de Gatinié,** Route de Gatinié, 34600 Les Aires **04 67 95 71 95 or 04 67 28 41 69 (LS); contact@domainegatinie.com; www.domainegatinie.com**

€2

Fr D908 fr Lamalou-les-Bains or Hérépian dir Poujol-sur-Orb, site sp. Fr D160 cross rv to D908 then as above. 3*, Med, hdg, mkd, pt shd, pt sl, EHU (6A) inc; bbq; sw nr; red long stay; 10% statics; Eng spkn; adv bkg acc; fishing; horseriding 2km; tennis 2km; canoeing; games area; golf 2km; CKE. *"Beautiful, peaceful situation; many leisure activities; vg; helpful staff, leafy pleasant site in a lovely area."*
€19.00, 1 Apr-31 Oct. **2024**

LAMASTRE 9C2 (5km NE Rural) 45.01173, 4.62410 **Camping Les Roches,** 07270 Le Crestet **06 46 23 27 43; campinglesroches07@gmail.com; www.campinglesroches.com**

€4.50 (htd)

Take D534 fr Tournon-sur-Rhône dir Lamastre. 3km fr vill. Do not use Sat Nav. 4*, Sm, hdstg, mkd, pt shd, terr, EHU (6A) €4.50; bbq; sw nr; TV; 30% statics; bus 1km; Eng spkn; adv bkg acc; ccard acc; games area; tennis 3km; fishing 500m; CKE. *"Friendly family-run site; clean facs; lovely views; gd base for touring medieval vills; gd walking; site rd steep; on hillside abv rv valley; diff for lge o'fits; excel rest."*
€31.70, 1 Apr-15 Sep. **2024**

LANDEDA 2E1 (2km NW Coastal) 48.59333, -4.60333 **Camping des Abers,** 51 Toull Tréaz, 29870 Landéda, Finistère North, Brittany **02 98 04 93 35; info@camping-des-abers.com; www.camping-des-abers.com**

€2.50 nr nr sand adj

Exit N12/E50 at junc with D788 & take D13 to Lannilis. Then take D128A to Landéda & foll green site sp. 4*, Lge, mkd, hdg, pt shd, terr, EHU (10A) €3 (long lead poss req); gas; bbq; red long stay; TV; 10% statics; Eng spkn; adv bkg rec; ccard acc; bike hire; fishing; games rm; classes; CKE. *"Attractive, landscaped site on wild coast; views fr high pitches; friendly, helpful manager; san facs clean, some new, others old; some pitches muddy when wet; no o'fits over 8m high ssn; access to many pitches by grass tracks, some sl; gd walks, cycling; excel; some problems with voltage."* **€22.00, 1 May-30 Sep**, **B30.** **2022**

LANDEDA 2E1 (3km NW Coastal) 48.60310, -4.59882 **Camp Municipal de Penn-Enez,** 551 place called Penn-Enez, 29870 Landéda **02 98 04 99 82 or 02 98 89 55 78; info@camping-penn-enez.com; www.camping-penn-enez.com**

€1.65 sand 500m

Proceed NW thro Landéda, turn R in 1km sp Penn-Enez then L in 600m. Site sp. 1*, Med, hdg, unshd, pt sl, EHU (16A) €2.80; 2% statics; Eng spkn. *"Site on grassy headland; beach views fr some pitches; site self if warden absent; friendly, helpful staff; vg clean san facs; gd walks; excel."* **€19.30, 1 Apr-30 Sep.** **2024**

LANDIVISIAU 2E2 (9.3km NE Urban) 48.57724, -4.03006 **Camp Municipal Lanorgant,** Rue du Plan D'eau, 29420 Plouvorn **02 98 61 32 40 (Mairie); www.plouvorn.com/aire-de-camping-cars**

nr nr nr sand

Fr Landivisiau, take D69 N twd Roscoff. In 8km turn R onto D19 twd Morlaix. Site sp, in 700m turn R. NB Care req entry/exit, poss diff lge o'fits. 2*, Sm, mkd, hdg, pt shd, terr, EHU (10A) inc; bbq; sw; adv bkg acc; tennis; fishing; canoe hire. *"Ideal NH for ferries; lge pitches; sailboards hire; nr lake."* **€10.00, 1 May-30 Sep.** **2023**

LANGEAIS 4G1 (1km E Urban) 47.32968, 0.41848 **Camp Municipal du Lac,** rue Carnot, 37130 Langeais **06 26 65 03 40; patrimoine@langeais.fr; langeais-camping-loisirs.fr**

nr nr (htd)

Exit A85 junc 7 onto D952 dir Langeais & foll 'Camping Municipal' sp. 2*, Med, mkd, pt shd, EHU (6A) €3.50; 5% statics; ccard acc; fishing nr; CKE. *"Busy site high ssn; easy walk to town; dated san facs, inadequate when busy; nr Rv Loire cycle path; lovely chateau; gd; poss rd/rlwy noise."* **€19.00, 1 Jun-15 Sep.** **2024**

LANGOGNE 9D1 (2km W Rural) 44.73180, 3.83995 **Camping Les Terrasses du Lac,** 48300 Naussac **04 66 69 29 62; hello@naussac.com; www.naussac.com**

€3.30 nr

S fr Le Puy-en-Velay on N88. At Langogne take D26 to lakeside, site sp. 3*, Lge, pt shd, terr, EHU (6A) €2.50; bbq; sw nr; TV; 10% statics; phone; Eng spkn; adv bkg acc; horseriding 3km; games area; sailing school; bike hire; golf 1km; watersports adj; CKE. *"Vg views; steep hill bet recep & pitches; vg cycling & walking."* **€23.70, 15 Apr-30 Sep.** **2023**

LANGRES 6F1 (6km NE Rural) 47.89505, 5.39510 **Camping Hautoreille,** 6 Rue du Boutonnier, 52360 Bannes **03 25 84 83 40; contact@camping hautoreille.com; www.campinghautoreille.com**

€1 (htd)

N fr Dijon on D974/D674 to Langres; foll rd around Langres to E; onto D74 NE to Bannes; site on R on ent vill. Or exit A31 junc 7 Langres Nord onto D619, then D74 NE to Bannes. 3*, Med, mkd, hdstg, pt shd, pt sl, EHU (10A) €4; sw nr; 10% statics; phone; Eng spkn; adv bkg acc; horseriding 5km; tennis 5km; bike hire; CKE. *"Peaceful, clean, tidy site; basic facs, ltd LS & poss inadequate high ssn; pleasant owner; gd rest; site muddy when wet - parking on hdstg or owner will use tractor; on Sundays site yourself - recep opens 1700; gd NH."* **€23.30, 1 Mar-24 Nov.** **2024**

LANGRES 6F1 (6km E Rural) 47.87190, 5.38120 **Kawan Village Le Lac de la Liez,** Rue des Voiliers, 52200 Peigney **03 25 90 27 79; contact@camping-liez.fr; www.campingliez.com**

€4 (htd) (covrd, htd, indoor)

Exit A31 at junc 7 (Langres Nord) onto DN19; at Langres turn L at traff lts onto D74 sp Vesoul, Mulhouse, Le Lac de la Liez; at rndabt go strt on sp Epinal, Nancy; after Champigny-lès-Langres cross over rlwy bdge & canal turning R onto D52 sp Peigney, Lac de la Liez; in 3km bear R onto D284 sp Langres Sud & Lac de la Liez; site on R in 800m. Well sp fr N & S. 5*, Lge, hdstg, mkd, hdg, pt shd, terr, EHU (10A) €5.50; bbq; sw nr; TV; 15% statics; phone; Eng spkn; ccard acc; bike hire; sauna; golf 10km; boat hire; watersports; fishing; horseriding 10km; tennis; games rm; CKE. *"Popular, well-run, secure site; lake views fr some pitches; various sized pitches; helpful, friendly staff; san facs ltd LS; blocks poss req some pitches; some sm pitches & narr access rds diff manoeuvre lge o'fits; no o'fits over 10m; spa; vg rest; rec arr bef 1600 high ssn; gd walks & cycle rte by picturesque lake; interesting & historic town; poor."* **€39.00, 1 Apr - 25 Sep**, **J05.** **2022**

FRANCE

LANGRES *6F1* (15km S Rural) *47.74036, 5.30727* **Camping du Lac,** 14 rue Cototte, 52190 Villegusien le Lac **25 88 45 24; richard-emmanuel@hotmail.fr; www.tourisme-langres.com**

Take N19, foll N19 to Ave du Capitaine Baudoin, then foll Ave du Général de Gaulle, foll D974 to D26 in Villegusien-le-Lac, cont on D26, turn L onto D26, turn L, turn R,site on L. 1*, Med, mkd, shd, pt sl, EHU; bbq (gas); sw; twin axles; adv bkg acc; windsurfing; trekking; games rm; tennis; fishing; sailing. *"V pleasant site in lovely setting, some slight rd noise; beach lifeguard."* **€22.00, 15 Mar-30 Oct. 2024**

LANGRES *6F1* (7.5km S Rural) *47.81210, 5.32080* **Camping de la Croix d'Arles,** 52200 Bourg **03 25 88 24 02; contact@campinglacroixdarles.fr; www.campinglacroixdarles.fr**

Site is 4km S of Langres on W side of D974 (1km S of junc of D974 with D428). Site opp junc of D51 with D974. Fr Dijon poss no L turn off D974 - can pull into indust est N of site & return to site, but memb reported that L turn now poss (2011). 3*, Med, hdg, mkd, hdstg, pt shd, pt sl, EHU (10A) €4 (poss rev pol) (long cable req); phone; Eng spkn; ccard acc; CKE. *"Popular site, fills up quickly after 1600; friendly staff; some lovely secluded pitches in woodland; gd san facs; access poss diff lge o'fits; muddy after rain; unkempt LS; poss haphazard pitching when full; conv NH Langres historic town; nice, sm rest on site; easy to reach."* **€25.10, 15 Mar-31 Oct. 2023**

LANGRES *6F1* (1km SW Urban) *47.86038, 5.32894* **Camp Municipal Navarre,** 9 Blvd Maréchal de Lattre de Tassigny, 52200 Langres **03 25 87 37 92 or 06 10 74 10 16; camping.navarre@gmail.com; www.tourisme-langres.com/nl/CAMPING-LANGRES-01_camping-navarre**

App fr N or S on D619/D674, cont on main rd until lge rndabt at top of hill & go thro town arched gateway; site well sp fr there. NB Diff access for lge o'fits thro walled town but easy access fr D619. Med, pt shd, pt sl, EHU (10A) (long lead req & poss rev pol); bbq; phone; Eng spkn; CKE. *"Well-situated, busy NH, gd views fr some pitches; on arr site self & see warden; rec arr bef 1630; helpful staff; excel, modern unisex san facs; lovely walk round citadel ramparts; delightful town; vg site, views and location; warden mulit-lingual and helpful; conv for shops, rest, Friday mkt, cathedral; cash only; facs locked till recep open, closes at 5pm."* **€19.80, 11 Mar-5 Nov. 2023**

LANGRES *6F1* (13km SW Rural) *47.79528, 5.23278* **Camping de la Croisée,** 3 Route De Auberive, 52250 Flagey **03 25 88 01 26; yannick.durenne52@orange.fr; www.campingdelacroisee.com**

Exit A31 at J6 direction Langres D428. Campsite 1km on L (opp junc to Flagey). Med, mkd, hdstg, hdg, pt shd, bbq (charcoal, gas); ccard acc; red low ssn.. *"Conv NH stop as 2km fr A31 m'way; farm animals; gd."* **€17.00 2023**

LANILDUT *2E1* (1km N Coastal) *48.48012, -4.75184* **Camping du Tromeur,** 11 Route du Camping, 29840 Lanildut **07 89 00 00 24; swtromeur@gmail.com; www.tromeur.fr**

Site well sp on app rds to vill. 2*, Med, EHU €3 (poss long lead req & poss rev pol); bbq; phone. *"Clean, sheltered site; san facs gd; harbour & sm beach; LS warden am & pm only - site yourself; wooded walk into vil."* **€16.00, 30 Mar-22 Sep. 2024**

"I need an on-site restaurant"

We do our best to make sure site information is correct, but it is always best to check any must-have facilities are still available or will be open during your visit.

LANLOUP *2E3* (0.4km W Rural) *48.71369, -2.96711* **FFCC Camping Le Neptune,** 22580 Lanloup **02 96 22 33 35; contact@leneptune.com; www.leneptune.com**

Take D786 fr St Brieuc or Paimpol to Lanloup, site sp. NB Take care sat nav dirs (2011). 3*, Med, mkd, hdg, pt shd, EHU inc; gas; bbq; TV; 15% statics; phone; Eng spkn; adv bkg acc; horseriding 4km; bike hire; tennis 300m; CKE. *"Excel, well-maintained site nr beautiful coast; various pitch sizes; clean san facs; friendly, helpful owner; highly rec."* **€30.00, 2 Apr-1 Oct. 2023**

LANNE *8F2* (1km NW Rural) *43.17067, 0.00186* **Camping La Bergerie,** 79 Rue des Chênes, 65380 Lanne **05 62 45 40 05; contact@camping-la-bergerie.com; www.camping-la-bergerie.com**

Fr Lourdes take N21 N dir Tarbes; turn R onto D16 (Rue des Chênes) dir Lanne; site on R in 200m. 3*, Med, mkd, shd, EHU (10A) €3.8 (poss rev pol); gas; bus 200m; Eng spkn; adv bkg acc; tennis; CKE. *"Well-run site; friendly owners; some rd noise & aircraft noise at night; gd san facs; poss unkempt LS; poss flooding wet weather."* **€21.50, 15 Apr-15 Oct. 2023**

LANNION *1D2* (2.6km SE Urban) *48.72300, -3.44600* **Camp Municipal Les Deux Rives,** Rue du Moulin du Duc, 22300 Lannion **02 56 74 82 79 or 02 96 46 64 22; campinglesdeuxrives@onlycamp.fr; camping-lannion.fr**

12 €1.10

SW fr Perros-Guirec on D788 to Lannion; fr Lannion town cent foll dir Guincamp on D767; site well sp, approx 1.5km, turn R at Leclerc supmkt (do not confuse with hypmkt). Fr S on D767 sp at rndabts; turn L at Leclerc supmkt. 3*, Med, mkd, unshd, EHU (6A) €2.50; adv bkg acc; CKE. *"Rvside walk to old town; vg, clean san facs; phone ahead LS to check open; security barrier; warden lives on site but poss no arr acc Sun."* **€20.00** **2024**

LANNION *1D2* (9km NNW Coastal) *48.73833, -3.54500* **FFCC Camping Les Plages de Beg-Léguer,** Route de la Côte, 22300 Lannion **02 96 47 25 00; info@campingdesplages.com; www.campingdesplages.com**

€1 (covrd, htd) sand 500m

Fr Lannion take rd out of town twd Trébeurden then twd Servel on D65, then head SW off that rd twd Beg Léguer (sp). 3*, Lge, mkd, hdg, pt shd, EHU (6A) €3.50 (poss long lead req); gas; red long stay; TV; 20% statics; phone; bus 400m; Eng spkn; adv bkg acc; ccard acc; windsurfing; fishing; sailing; tennis; CKE. *"Pleasant, peaceful, well-run family site; charming French owner who speaks excel Eng; superb pool complex & vg children's play area; lge grass pitches; immac, modern san facs; one of the best sites in France; many superb rest in nrby seaside resorts; stunning beaches; cliftop location; adj to GR34 coastal path; phone LS; excel, fam oriented facs; conv for beach."* **€31.70, 29 May-22 Sep.** **2024**

"Satellite navigation makes touring much easier"

Remember most sat navs don't know if you're towing or in a larger vehicle – always use yours alongside maps and site directions.

LANSLEBOURG MONT CENIS *9C4* (0.3km SW Rural) *45.28417, 6.87380* **Camp Municipal Les Balmasses,** Chemin du Pavon, 73480 Lanslebourg-Mont-Cenis **06 38 28 92 84; cotesoleil@yahoo.fr; www.camping-les-balmasses.com**

nr

Fr Modane, site on R on rv on ent to town. 2*, Med, mkd, pt shd, EHU (6-10A) €4.50-5.40; bbq; phone; Eng spkn; CKE. *"Pleasant, quiet site by rv; mountain views; clean facs; conv NH bef/after Col du Mont-Cenis."* **€14.00, 1 Jun-20 Sep.** **2024**

LAON *3C4* (3km W Rural) *49.56190, 3.59583* **Camp La Chênaie (formerly Municipal),** Allée de la Chênaie, 02000 Laon **03 23 23 38 63 or 03 23 20 25 56; contact.camping.laon@gmail.com; www.camping-aisne.fr**

€1.80 (htd) (htd)

Exit A26 junc 13 onto N2 sp Laon; in 10km at junc with D1044 (4th rndabt) turn sp Semilly/Laon, then L at next rndabt into site rd. Site well sp. 3*, Sm, hdstg, mkd, hdg, pt shd, sl, terr, EHU (10A) €5.10 (poss rev pol); bbq; twin axles; red long stay; 10% statics; phone; Eng spkn; adv bkg acc; fishing 50m; CKE. *"Peaceful, pleasant site in gd location; popular NH; well-mkd pitches - lgest at end of site rd; pool (2.5km); extremely helpful staff; if travelling Sept phone to check site open; m'van parking nr cathedral; vg; woodland glades; gd NH; site now privately owned; 20min walk up steep path to historic town."* **€30.70, 1 Apr-30 Sep.** **2022**

"There aren't many sites open at this time of year"

If you're travelling outside peak season remember to call ahead to check site opening dates – even if the entry says 'open all year'.

LAPALISSE *9A1* (0.3km S Urban) *46.24322, 3.63950* **Camping de la Route Bleue,** Rue des Vignes, 03120 Lapalisse **04 70 99 26 31, 04 70 99 76 29 or 04 70 99 08 39 (LS); contact@lapalissetourisme.com; www.lapalisse-tourisme.com**

€1 (htd) nr

S fr Moulins on N7; at rndabt junc with D907 just bef Lapalisse, take 3rd exit onto Ave due Huit Mai 1945 (to town cent), foll rd for 1.5km, over rv bdg, round RH bend onto Rue des Vignes, site on R in 500m. 3*, Med, mkd, pt shd, EHU (6-9A) €2.40; Eng spkn; CKE. *"Popular, excel NH off N7 in pleasant parkland setting; gd clean san facs; pleasant 10 min walk thro adj park to town; no twin axles; poss flooding after heavy rain; adequate sans but need upgrade."* **€16.00, 15 Apr-13 Oct.** **2024**

LARGENTIERE *9D2* (5km SE Rural) *44.50347, 4.29430* **Camping Les Châtaigniers,** Le Mas-de-Peyrot, 07110 Laurac-en-Vivarais **06 30 81 66 38; chataigniers07@orange.fr; www.chataigniers-laurac.com**

€2

Fr Aubenas S on D104 dir Alès; site sp fr D104. Site on one of minor rds leading to Laurac-en-Vivarais. 3*, Med, mkd, pt shd, pt sl, EHU (10A) €3; bbq (gas); 15% statics; adv bkg acc. *"Attractive, great, clean site; some pitches deep shd; sun area; gd pool; sh uphill walk to vill shops & auberge; vg."* **€25.00, 1 Apr-30 Sep.** **2022**

LARGENTIERE *9D2* (1.6km NW Rural) *44.56120, 4.28615* **Domaine Les Ranchisses,** Route de Rocher, Chassiers, 07110 Largentière **04 75 88 31 97; reception@lesranchisses.fr; www.lesranchisses.fr**

€6 (covrd, htd)

Exit A7/E15 junct 17/18 (Montelimar N or S) on to N7 dir Montelimar to take N102. Fr Aubenas S on D104 sp Alès. 1km after vill of Uzer turn R onto D5 to Largentière. Go thro Largentière on D5 in dir Rocher/Valgorge; site on L in 1.5km. DO NOT use D103 bet Lachapelle-Aubenas & Largentière - too steep & narr for lge vehicles & c'vans. NB Not rec to use sat nav dirs to this site. 5*, Lge, mkd, pt shd, EHU (10A) inc; gas; bbq (elec, gas); sw; TV; 30% statics; adv bkg req; ccard acc; games rm; fishing; tennis; bike hire; games area; canoeing. *"Lovely, well-run, busy site adj vineyard; gd sized pitches; friendly, helpful staff; gd, immac san facs; o'fits over 7m by request; excel rest & takeaway; lovely pools; gd choice of sporting activities; wellness cent; poss muddy when wet; noisy rd adj to S end of site; mkt Tues am; first class; 5 star site in lovely location."* **€65.00, 16 Apr - 25 Sep, C32.** **2022**

LARUNS *8G2* (6km N Rural) *43.02085, -0.42043* **FFCC Camp Municipal de Monplaisir,** 1 rue de la Fontaine, Quartier Monplaisir, 64260 Gère-Bélesten **05 59 82 61 18; camping-gere-belesten@orange.fr; campingmonplaisir.odoo.com**

12 (htd) nr nr

Site sp on E side of D934 S of Gère-Bélesten. 2*, Med, mkd, pt shd, EHU (6A) €3.90; TV; 75% statics; Eng spkn; adv bkg acc; fishing. *"Helpful warden calls am & pm; htd pool 4km."* **€17.00** **2024**

LARUNS *8G2* (6km SE Rural) *42.96972, -0.38220* **Camping d'Iscoo,** 64440 Eaux-Bonnes **06 79 95 92 76 or 06 98 23 54 93 (mob); camping.iscoo@live.fr; campingiscoo-valleedossau.fr**

nr

Site is on R 1.4km fr Eaux-Bonnes on climb to Col d'Aubisque. Site ent in middle of S-bend so advise cont 500m & turn on open grnd on L. 2*, Sm, mkd, pt shd, pt sl, EHU (2-5A) €2.50; CKE. *"V pleasant location; friendly owner; beautiful sunny site in hills; pool 3km; excel shwrs."* **€17.50, 26 Jun-9 Sep.** **2024**

LAURENS *10F1* (1km S Rural) *43.53620, 3.18583* **Camping L'Oliveraie,** Chemin de Bédarieux, 34480 Laurens **04 67 90 24 36 or 06 03 93 75 89; oliveraie.laurens@gmail.com; www.oliveraie.com**

12 €2 (htd)

Clearly sp on D909 Béziers to Bédarieux rd. Sp reads Loisirs de L'Oliveraie. 3*, Med, hdstg, mkd, pt shd, terr, EHU (10A) €3.20-4.60 (poss rev pol); TV; 30% statics; phone; adv bkg acc; ccard acc; site clsd 15 Dec-15 Jan; games rm; CKE. *"Helpful staff; gd, clean san facs; sauna high ssn; site becoming tatty (2011); in wine-producing area; gd winter NH."* **€35.00** **2024**

LAVANDOU, LE *10F3* (2km E Coastal) *43.14471, 6.38084* **Caravaning St Clair,** Ave André Gide, 83980 Le Lavandou **04 94 01 30 20; caravaningstclair@orange.fr; www.caravaningstclair.com**

€2 (htd) nr nr nr sand adj

N559 thro Le Lavandou twd St Raphaël; after 2km at sp St Clair turn R immed after bend 50m after blue 'caravaning' sp (easy to overshoot). 3*, Med, mkd, shd, EHU (16A) €4.10 (rev pol); TV; adv bkg req; boat hire; fishing. *"Popular with British; pitch & ent screened by trees; conv beach & rests; no tents; quiet site."* **€34.00, 23 Mar-15 Oct.** **2024**

LAVANDOU, LE *10F3* (8.6km E Coastal) *43.15645, 6.44821* **Parc-Camping de Prasmousquier,** Faverolle Road, 83980 Le Lavandou **04 94 05 83 95; camping-lavandou@wanadoo.fr; www.campingpramousquier.com**

€2.10 sand 400m

Take D559 E fr Le Lavandou. At Pramousquier site sp on main rd; awkward bend. 3*, Lge, pt shd, terr, EHU (3-6A) €3.304; gas; Eng spkn. *"Pleasant, relaxing, clean site; site lighting poor; gd cycle track to Le Lavandou; excel."* **€35.20, 13 Apr-3 Nov.** **2024**

LAVANDOU, LE *10F3* (2km S Coastal) *43.11800, 6.35210* **Camping du Domaine,** La Favière, 2581 Route de Bénat, 83230 Bormes-les-Mimosas **04 94 71 03 12; mail@campdudomaine.com; www.campdudomaine.com**

(not acc Jul/Aug) sand adj

App Le Lavandou fr Hyères on D98 & turn R on o'skts of town clearly sp La Favière. Site on L in 2.3km about 200m after ent to Domaine La Favière (wine sales) - ignore 1st lge winery. If app fr E do not go thro Le Levandou, but stay on D559 until sp to La Favière. 4*, V lge, mkd, pt shd, terr, EHU (10A) inc (long lead poss req); gas; bbq (gas); TV; 10% statics; phone; Eng spkn; adv bkg req; ccard acc; tennis; games rm; CKE. *"Lge pitches, some with many trees & some adj beach (direct access); well-organised site with excel facs; gd walking & attractions in area."* **€55.00, 4 Apr-31 Oct.** **2024**

LAVANDOU, LE *10F3* (1.5km SW Coastal) *43.13386, 6.35224* **Camping Beau Séjour,** 379 Route de Bénat, Quartier St Pons, 83980 Le Lavandou **04 94 71 25 30; caravaning.beau.sejour@gmail.com; www.caravaning-beausejour.com**

nr nr nr 900m

Take Cap Bénat rd on W o'skts of Le Lavandou. Site on L in approx 500m. 2*, Med, mkd, pt shd, EHU (3A) €4. *"Well-kept, clean site; rd noise on W side; gd sized pitches."* **€23.00, 15 Apr-31 Oct.** **2024**

LAVANDOU, LE *10F3* (2.7km W Urban) *43.13630, 6.35439* **Camping St Pons,** Ave Maréchal Juin, 83960 Le Lavandou **04 94 71 03 93; info@campingstpons.com; www.campingstpons.com**

€3.90 nr sand 800m

App fr W on D98 via La Londe. At Bormes keep R onto D559. At 1st rndabt turn R sp La Favière, at 2nd rndabt turn R, then 1st L. Site on L in 200m. 2*, Med, mkd, shd, EHU (6A) inc; 10% statics; phone; Eng spkn; CKE. *"Much improved site; helpful owner."* **€26.00, 6 May-8 Oct. 2023**

LAVELANET *8G4* (1km SW Urban) *42.92340, 1.84477* **Village des Bons Hommes Le Pré Cathare,** Rue Jacquard, 09300 Lavelanet **05 61 01 55 54 or 06 83 36 94 30; leprecathare@orange.fr; www.villagedesbonshommes.com**

€1 (htd) nr

Fr Lavelanet, take D117 twd Foix & foll sp (foll sp for sports complex). Adj 'piscine'. 3*, Med, mkd, pt shd, EHU (15A) €3; bbq; sw nr; TV; 95% statics; adv bkg acc; games area; tennis 800m; CKE. *"Gd sized pitches, some with mountain views; san facs ok; poss open in winter with adv bkg; pool adj; gates locked 2200; quiet town; scruffy; few pitches; €25 booking fee; vg."* **€32.20, 1 Apr-30 Sep. 2023**

LE BUISSON *9D1* (10km NNE Rural) *44.705795, 3.282804* **Camping Municipal Aumont Aubrac,** D809 48130 Peyre en Aubrac **04 66 42 88 70; www.ot-aumont-aubrac.fr**

Travelling on A75 between Millau and St Flour South. Leave at J35. Med, pt shd, EHU 6A; twin axles; CKE. *"V pleasant quiet campsite; perfect for NH; gd walk in area; vg."* **€12.00, 1 Jun-30 Sep. 2024**

LEGE *2H4* (7km S Rural) *46.82899, -1.59368* **Camp Municipal de la Petite Boulogne,** 12 Rue du Stade, 85670 St Etienne-du-Bois **02 51 34 52 11 or 02 51 34 54 51; la.petite.boulogne@wanadoo.fr; www.stetiennedubois-vendee.fr**

12 €2.10 nr

S fr Legé on D978 dir Aizenay. Turn E onto D94 twd St Etienne-du-Bois. Foll sp to site. 2*, Sm, mkd, pt shd, pt sl, terr, EHU (10A) €2.70; TV; Eng spkn; adv bkg acc; CKE. *"Pleasant, clean site; helpful warden; san facs would be stretched if site full."* **€15.00, 1 May-1 Oct. 2024**

LEGE *2H4* (10km SW Rural) *46.82121, -1.64844* **Camp Municipal Les Blés d'Or,** 10 rue de la Piscine, 85670 Grand'Landes **02 51 98 51 86; mairie@grandlandes.fr; www.vendee-tourisme.com**

nr nr

Take D753 fr Legé twd St Jean-de-Monts. In 4km turn S on D81 & foll sp. Fr S on D978, turn W sp Grand-Landes. 3km N of Palluau. 2*, Sm, pt shd, pt sl, EHU (16A) €2.30; gas; 30% statics; Eng spkn; adv bkg acc. *"V pleasant site; height barrier only, cars 24hr access; immac but dated facs; pay at Mairie adj; v useful."* **€10.50, 1 May-30 Sep. 2023**

LEGE-CAP-FERRET *7D1* (6km W Coastal) *44.73443, -1.1960* **Camping Les Viviers,** Ave Léon Lesca, Claouey, 33950 Lège-Cap-Ferret **05 56 60 70 04; reception@lesviviers.com; www.lesviviers.com**

€5 (htd) (covrd, htd) sand adj

Fr N exit A10/A630 W of Bordeaux onto D106 sp Cap-Ferret. Foll D106 thro Arès & vill of Claouey on W side of Bassin d'Arcachon, site on L after LH bend (approx 1.5km after Claouey). 4*, V lge, mkd, hdg, pt shd, EHU (10A) inc; gas; bbq (elec, gas); red long stay; TV; 27% statics; bus; Eng spkn; adv bkg req; ccard acc; games rm; sauna; windsurfing; fishing; tennis; waterslide; games area; bike hire; sailing; CKE. *"Sand pitches, various positions & prices; clean san facs; sea water lagoon with private sand beach adj; cinema; vg leisure facs and waterpark on site; free night bus along peninsular; vg site."* **€50.00, 28 Mar-13 Sep. 2022**

LEMPDES SUR ALLAGNON *9C1* (1.2km N Rural) *45.38699, 3.26598* **Camping Le Pont d'Allagnon,** Rue René Filiol, off Route de Chambezon, 43410 Lempdes-sur-Allagnon **04 71 76 53 69; centre.auvergne.camping@orange.fr; www.campingenauvergne.com**

nr

Going S on A75 exit junc 19 (ltd access) onto D909; turn R on D654 bef vill, site sp at junc. Or fr junc 20 going N; foll sp. Site just outside vill. 3*, Med, hdg, pt shd, EHU (16A) €3.40; phone; adv bkg acc; ccard acc; games rm; tennis; rv fishing; games area. *"Pleasant site in beautiful area; pool 100m; conv NH A75; gd."* **€23.10, 18 Mar-31 Oct. 2024**

LEON *8E1* (4km N Rural) *43.90260, -1.31030* **Camping Sandaya Le Col Vert,** Lac de Léon, 40560 Vielle-St Girons **05 58 42 94 06; www.sandaya.co.uk/our-campsites/le-col-vert**

€5 (covrd, htd)

Exit N10 junc 12; at Castets-des-Landes turn R onto D42 to Vielle-St Girons. In vill turn L onto D652 twd Léon sp Soustons. In 4km, bef Vielle, take 2nd of 2 RH turns twd Lac de Léon. Site on R at end of rd in 1.5km. 4*, V lge, shd, serviced pitches; EHU (3A) inc; gas; bbq (elec, gas); sw nr; red long stay; TV; 60% statics; adv bkg acc; ccard acc; canoeing nr; games rm; windsurfing nr; archery; tennis; sailing nr; bike hire; fishing nr; horseriding; CKE. *"Lakeside site in pine forest; fitness rm; some pitches 800m fr facs; ideal for children & teenagers; wellness cent; no c'van/m'van over 6.5m; daily mkt in Léon in ssn; excel location."* **€35.00, 8 Apr - 25 Sep, A08. 2022**

FRANCE

FRANCE

LEON *8E1* (9km NW Coastal) *43.90830, -1.36380* **Domaine Naturiste Arnaoutchot (Naturist),** Arnaoutchot, 5006 Route de Pichelèbe, 40560 Vielle-St Girons **05 58 49 11 11; contact@arna.com; www.arna.com**

€3.50 (covrd, htd) sand adj

Fr St Girons turn R onto D328 at Vielle sp Pichelèbe. Site in 5km on R. 3*, Lge, hdstg, shd, pt sl, EHU (3-10A) €4.50-6.10 inc; gas; bbq (elec, gas); red long stay; TV; 80% statics; Eng spkn; adv bkg acc; ccard acc; games area; golf nr; bike hire; waterslide; games rm; tennis; watersports 5km; archery. *"Excel site in pine forest; Arna Forme Spa; some pitches soft sand; clean san facs, ltd LS; no o'fits over 6.5m; lake adj; spa cent; excel LS site; access lge o'fits poss diff due trees; superb beach; daily mkt in Léon in ssn; new hdstg pitches with elec/water for MH's; great facs."* **€78.30, 1 Apr-24 Sep.** **2023**

LERAN *8G4* (2km E Rural) *42.98368, 1.93516* **Camping La Régate,** Route du Lac, 09600 Léran **05 61 03 09 17 or 06 08 48 08 63 (mob); contact@campinglaregate.com; www.campinglaregate.com**

€1 nr nr

Fr Lavelanet go N on D625, turn R onto D28 & cont to Léran. Site sp fr vill. Ent easily missed - rd past it is dead end. 3*, Med, mkd, hdg, shd, terr, EHU (8A) €3.70; bbq; 10% statics; phone; adv bkg acc; ccard acc; watersports. *"Conv Montségur chateau; leisure cent nr; pony trekking; clean san facs; lake adj; gd location; pool adj; mkd walking & cycle rtes around adj lake."* **€33.60, 30 Mar-26 Oct.** **2024**

LES MOUTIERS EN RETZ *2H3* (4km SSE Coastal) *47.036544, -1.984846* **Domaine du Collet,** Route Verte, 44760 Les Moutiers-en-Retz **00 33 2 40 21 40 92; contact@domaine-du-collet.com; www.domaine-du-collet.com**

€5 (covrd, htd) 100m

SW fr Nantes on D723, after 9km turn L D751 sp Noirmoutier; in abt 8km at Port-Saint-Père turn L sp D758/Noirmoutier; in abt 18km foll D758 thro Bourgneuf-en-Retz (beware narr sharp turn); at mini-rndabt go L onto D758; at rndabt take 2nd exit sp Port du Collet; in abt 2km turn R over bdge; aft 1km fork R and site on R aft 1km. 4*, Lge, pt shd, TV; 70% statics; games rm. *"Very quiet; gd for families."* **€40.00, 1 Apr - 31 Oct, B36.** **2024**

LESCHERAINES *9B3* (2.5km SE Rural) *45.70279, 6.11158* **L'lle du Cheran (formerly Municipal de l'Ile),** Base de Loisirs, Les Iles du Chéran, 73340 Lescheraines **04 79 63 80 00; contact@savoie-camping.com; www.savoie-camping.com**

€1.50 nr

Fr Lescheraines foll sp for Base de Loisirs. 3*, Lge, mkd, pt shd, EHU (6-10A) €2.40-3.50; bbq; sw; 5% statics; phone; Eng spkn; boat hire; fishing; canoe hire; CKE. *"Beautiful, scenic, lakeside setting; v helpful staff; gd walks."* **€16.50, 19 Apr-28 Sep.** **2024**

LESPERON *8E1* (4km SW Rural) *43.96657, -1.12940* **Le Laha Camping,** 3000 Route de Linxe, 40260 Lesperon **05 58 89 60 15 or 06 18 96 36 49; www.lelaha.com**

€1 nr

Exit N10 junc 13 to D41 sp Lesperon; in 1km turn L, thro vill of Lesperon; L at junc onto D331; bottom of hill turn R & immed L; site on R in 3km dir Linxe. 3*, Sm, mkd, pt shd, EHU (6A); gas; bbq (elec, gas); sw nr; red long stay; twin axles; 10% statics; phone; Eng spkn; adv bkg acc; ccard acc; CKE. *"Lovely but isolated site on edge of wine country; gd facs on lakes for sailing, windsurfing; British owners; clean san facs; vg; new owners."* **€27.50, Apr-Oct.** **2024**

LEUCATE PLAGE *10G1* (0.2km S Coastal) *42.90316, 3.05178* **Camp Municipal du Cap Leucate,** Chemin de Mouret, 11370 Leucate-Plage **04 68 40 01 37; camping.capleucate@mairie-leucate.fr; campingmunicipalcapleucate.ellohaweb.com**

€2 nr nr nr sand 100m

Exit A9 junc 40 onto D627 thro Leucate vill to Leucate-Plage approx 9km. Site sp. 2*, Lge, hdg, shd, EHU (6A) €2.10 long lead req; bbq; TV; 60% statics; phone; adv bkg acc; games area; CKE. *"Nice, spacious, sandy site in gd position; popular with surfers; htd pool 100m; m'van area outside; gd NH; immac new san facs (2012)."* **€18.50, 1 Feb-30 Nov.** **2024**

LEZIGNAN CORBIERES *8F4* (10km S Rural) *43.11727, 2.73609* **Camping Le Pinada,** Villerouge la Crémade, 11200 Fabrezan **04 68 43 32 29; contact@lepinada.com; www.lepinada.com**

€3

Fr Lézignan-Corbières on D611 S, pass airfield & fork L thro Ferrals-les-Corbières (steep, narr) on D106. Site sp & on L after 4km. Alt rte to avoid narr rd thro Ferrals: exit A61 junc 25 & foll D611 thro Fabrezan. At T-junc turn L onto D613 & after 2km turn L onto D106. Site on R after Villerouge-la-Crémade. 3*, Med, hdg, mkd, shd, pt sl, terr, EHU (6A) €5; bbq; sw nr; TV; 25% statics; Eng spkn; adv bkg req; fishing 3km; games area; tennis; CKE. *"Friendly owners; gd base for Carcassonne & Med coast; bkg fee; well-run site; dated san facs; excel."* **€18.50, 1 Mar-30 Oct.** **2020**

LEZINNES *4F4* (0.4km S Urban) *47.79955, 4.08957* **La Graviere du Moulin,** 7 route de Frangey, 89160 Lezinnes **03 86 75 68 67 or 02 29 59 27 (mob); lagravieredumoulin@lezinnes.fr; gravieredumoulin.lezinnes.fr**

Fr N on Route Nationale D905 turn L onto D200, foll rd round to the R onto Route de Frangey to site. 3*, Sm, EHU €2.70; tennis; canoeing. *"Gated site; football; basketball; handball; strictly run; great café in vill."* **€17.80, 1 Apr-3 Oct.** **2024**

LICQUES 3A3 (2.5km E Rural) 50.77905, 1.95567 **Camping-Caravaning Le Canchy,** Rue de Canchy, 62850 Licques **03 21 82 63 41 or 06 88 70 66 79; campinglecanchylicques@orange.fr; www.camping-lecanchy.com**

nr

Fr Calais D127 to Guînes, then D215 sp Licques; site sp in vill on D191; site on L in 1km with narr app rd. Or fr Ardres take D224 to Liques then as above. Or A26 fr Calais exit junc 2 onto D217 dir Zouafques/ Tournehem/Licques. Foll site sp in vill. 2*, Med, mkd, hdg, pt shd, EHU (6A) €3.70; bbq; 50% statics; Eng spkn; adv bkg acc; ccard acc; fishing nr; CKE. *"Busy site; friendly, helpful owners; dated san facs, ltd LS; gd walking/cycling; conv Calais & ferries; vg."* **€18.00, 30 Mar-3 Nov.** **2020**

LICQUES 3A3 (1.8km SE Rural) 50.77974, 1.94766 **Camping Les Pommiers des Trois Pays,** 273 Rue du Breuil, 62850 Licques **03 21 35 02 02; contact@pommiers-3pays.com; www.pommiers-3pays.com**

€1 nr (covrd, htd)

Fr Calais to Guînes on D127 then on D215 to Licques; take D191 fr vill & foll sp; site on L in 1km. Or exit A26 junc 2 onto D217 to Licques; turn L onto D215; cont strt on & site on L on far side of vill. NB sloping ent, long o'fits beware grounding. 4*, Med, mkd, hdg, pt shd, sl, EHU (16A) €4.80; bbq; red long stay; TV; 65% statics; Eng spkn; adv bkg acc; ccard acc; games rm; golf 25km; fishing 2km; sailing 25km; games area. *"Site v full early Jun, adv bkg rec; lge pitches; friendly, helpful owners; gd quality facs, ltd LS, rest clsd; gd beaches nr; gd walking; conv Calais/ Dunkerque ferries; gd; excel san facs; busy, well-run site; sm pool for children; clean facs; only 0.75h fr Calais ferry."* **€29.00, 15 Mar-31 Oct.** **2024**

LIGNY EN BARROIS 6E1 (0.5km W Rural) 48.68615, 5.31666 **Camp Municipal Chartel,** Rue des Etats-Unis, 55500 Ligny-en-Barrois **03 29 77 09 36 or 03 29 78 02 22 (Mairie); mairie@lignyenbarrois.fr; http://www.lignyenbarrois.com/wp/tourisme/camping-municipal/**

(cont) nr

If app fr E, leave N4 at Ligny-en-Barrois N exit, turn S twd town; in approx 500m turn R at junc (bef rd narr); foll sm sp, site 500m on L. If app fr W, leave N4 at exit W of town onto N135 (Rue des Etats-Unis); site sp on R. 2*, Sm, hdstg, pt shd, terr, EHU inc; own san rec; sw nr; Eng spkn; fishing 500m; CKE. *"Poss diff lge o'fits; modern san facs; further modernisation planned (2010); gd NH; great site and location."* **€11.00, 1 May-30 Sep.** **2020**

LIGNY LE CHATEL 4F4 (0.5km SW Rural) 47.89542, 3.75288 **Camp Municipal La Noue Marrou,** 89144 Ligny-le-Châtel **03 86 47 56 99 or 03 86 47 41 20 (Mairie); camping.lignylechatel@orange.fr; www.mairie-ligny-le-chatel-89.fr**

Exit A6 at junc 20 Auxerre S onto D965 to Chablis. In Chablis cross rv & turn L onto D91 dir Ligny. On ent Ligny turn L onto D8 at junc after Maximart. Cross sm rv, foll sp to site on L in 200m. 2*, Sm, mkd, pt shd, EHU (16A) inc; bbq (charcoal, elec, gas); sw nr; phone; bus 200m; Eng spkn; ccard acc; tennis; games area; CKE. *"Well-run site; lge pitches; no twin axles; v welcoming, friendly warden lives on site; san facs dated but clean; pleasant vill with gd rests; popular NH; excel."* **€12.00, 15 Apr-1 Oct.** **2024**

LILLEBONNE 3C2 (4km W Rural) 49.53024, 0.49763 **Camping Hameau des Forges,** 76170 St Antoine-la-Forêt **02 35 39 80 28 or 06 07 44 03 08; mondeamical@hotmail.fr; www.normandie-tourisme.fr/camping/camping-les-forges**

12

Fr Le Havre take rd twds Tancarville bdge, D982 into Lillebonne, D81 W to site on R in 4km (pt winding rd). Fr S over Tancarville bdge onto D910 sp Bolbec. At 2nd rndabt turn R onto D81, site 5km on L. NB Concealed ent by notice board and post-box. 1*, Med, pt shd, EHU (5A) inc; 90% statics; adv bkg acc; CKE. *"Basic, clean, open site; staff welcoming & helpful; poss statics only LS & facs ltd; site muddy when wet; conv NH for Le Havre ferries late arr & early dep; Roman amphitheatre in town worth visit; site & facs tired (2019); fair."* **€16.40** **2024**

LIMOGNE EN QUERCY 7D4 (0.6km W Rural) 44.39571, 1.76396 **Camp Municipal Bel-Air,** 46260 Limogne-en-Quercy **06 79 23 30 99; camping.lebelair@hotmail.com; www.campinglebelair-limogne.com**

nr nr

E fr Cahors on D911 just bef Limogne vill. W fr Villefranche on D911 just past vill; 3 ents about 50m apart. 3*, Sm, mkd, shd, sl, EHU (6A) inc; adv bkg rec. *"Friendly welcome; if warden absent, site yourself; pleasant vill."* **€18.00, 1 Apr-1 Oct.** **2024**

LISIEUX 3D1 (2km N Rural) 49.16515, 0.22054 **Camp Municipal de La Vallée,** 9 Rue de la Vallée, 14100 Lisieux **02 31 62 36 37; contact@camping-lisieux.fr; www.lisieux-tourisme.com**

nr nr nr

N on D579 fr Lisieux twd Pont l'Evêque. Approx 500m N of Lisieux take L to Coquainvilliers onto D48 & foll sp for Camping (turn L back in Lisieux dir). Site on D48 parallel to main rd. On app to site look for Volvo dealer & Super U supmkt. 3*, Med, hdstg, pt shd, EHU (6A) €2.50-4.50; gas; 20% statics; bus fr ent; CKE. *"Interesting town, childhood home of St Thérèse; helpful warden; v clean san facs; gd."* **€15.00, 15 Apr-8 Oct.** **2023**

FRANCE

LISLE *7C3* (6km SW Rural) *45.25731, 0.49573* **Camp Municipal Le Pré Sec,** 24350 Tocane-St Apre **05 53 90 40 60 or 05 53 90 70 29; campinglepresec@tocanesaintapre.fr; www.campingdupresec.com**

nr

Fr Ribérac E on D710 sp Brantôme. Fr E or W at Tocane St Apre, take bypass rd at rndabt. Site sp at both rndabts - dist 500m. Site is on N side of D710 (fr Riberac dir, there is a gab bet cent reservation to turn L.) Ent thro lge car park for Tocan Sports, barrier to site 100m back. 3*, Med, hdg, shd, EHU (6-10A) €1.80; bbq; twin axles; 10% statics; phone; bus 200m; Eng spkn; adv bkg acc; CKE. *"Gd; canoeing nrby on Rv Dronne."* **€10.00, 2 May-30 Sep.** **2024**

LOCHES *4H2* (1km S Urban) *47.12255, 1.00175* **Camping La Citadelle,** Ave Aristide Briand, 37600 Loches **02 47 59 05 91 or 06 21 37 93 06 (mob); camping@lacitadelle.com; www.lacitadelle.com**

€3 (htd) (htd)

Fr any dir take by-pass to S end of town & leave at Leclerc rndabt for city cent; site well sp on R in 800m. 4*, Lge, mkd, hdg, pt shd, EHU (10A) €5 (poss rev pol) (poss long lead req); gas; bbq; red long stay; TV; 30% statics; Eng spkn; adv bkg rec; ccard acc; golf 9km; tennis nr; boating; games area; bike hire; fishing; CKE. *"Attractive, well-kept, busy site nr beautiful old town; views of citadel; gd sized pitches, poss uneven; helpful staff; facs poss stretched; barrier clsd 2200-0800; poss no night security (2010); rvside walk into town; poss mosquitoes; site muddy after heavy rain; mkt Wed & Sat am; excel site; lge serviced pitches; sh walk to a beautiful medieval town; new san facs; 3 pool complex."* **€32.50, 29 Mar-30 Sep.** **2024**

LOCMARIAQUER *2G3* (2km S Coastal) *47.55598, -2.93939* **Camp Municipal de la Falaise,** Route de Kerpenhir, 56740 Locmariaquer **02 97 57 31 59 or 02 97 57 32 32 (LS); campinglafalaise@locmariaquer.bzh; www.campingmunicipallafalaise.com**

€2.10 nr sand adj

Site sp fr Locmariaquer. On ent vill, site sp R avoiding narr cent (also sp fr vill cent). 2*, Lge, mkd, pt sl, EHU (6A) inc; gas; ccard acc. *"Gd, quiet, well run site in pleasant countryside; clean san facs, some modern & some dated; archaeological remains; gd fishing, boating, cycling & coastal walking; rest simple but superb food."* **€16.50, 15 Mar-15 Oct.** **2024**

LOCMARIAQUER *2G3* (2km NW Coastal) *47.57982, -2.97394* **Camping Lann Brick,** Lieu Dit Lann-Brick, 56740 Locmariaquer **02 97 57 32 79 or 06 42 22 29 69 (mob); camping.lanbrick@wanadoo.fr; www.camping-lannbrick.com**

€2.60 (cont) nr (htd) 0.5km

N165/E60, exit Crach via D28 dir Locmariaquer. L Onto D781. Sp on R 2km bef Locmariaquer. 3*, Med, mkd, hdg, shd, EHU (6/10A); bbq; twin axles; TV; 40% statics; phone; bus adj; Eng spkn; adv bkg acc; ccard acc; bike hire; CKE. *"Gd; quiet well managed site; helpful & friendly owners; facs well maintained & spotless; easy walk to beach; delightful site; gd location for Gulf of Morbihan; easy cycle rte; hg hdg."* **€27.60, 16 Mar-31 Oct.** **2024**

LOCQUIREC *2E2* (2km SW Coastal) *48.67940, -3.65320* **Camping Municipal Du fond de la Baie,** Route de Plestin, 29241 Locquirec **02 98 67 40 85; campingdufonddelabaie@gmail.com; www.campinglocquirec.com**

12 €1 sand adj

Fr D786 Morlaix-Lannion, turn L (traff lts) at Plestin-Les-Graves onto D42. At T junc on reaching Bay turn L onto D64. Site on R on app Locquirec. 2*, Lge, mkd, pt shd, gas; bbq; twin axles; 6% statics; phone; bus adj; Eng spkn; adv bkg acc; ccard acc. *"Beautifully situated beachside site; vill 1.5km; flat site; fishing, boating & shellfishing; gd."* **€19.00** **2022**

LOCRONAN *2E2* (1km ESE Urban) *48.09657, -4.19774* **Camping de Locronan,** Rue de la Troménie, 29180 Locronan **02 98 91 87 76 or 06 28 80 44 74**

€2.20 nr nr nr (covrd, htd)

Fr Quimper/Douarnenez foll sp D7 Châteaulin; ignore town sp, take 1st R after 3rd rndabt. Fr Châteaulin, turn L at 1st town sp & foll site sp at sharp L turn. NB Foll sp around town, do not ent Locronan. Med, hdg, pt shd, terr, EHU (10A) €4.30; phone; Eng spkn; adv bkg rec; ccard acc; games area; CKE. *"Gd touring cent with gd views; gd walks; historic town; excel; ltd san facs LS."* **€32.00, 13 Apr-10 Nov.** **2024**

LODEVE *10E1* (9km S Rural) *43.67182, 3.35429* **Camp Municipal Les Vailhés,** Baie des Vailhes, Lac du Salagou, 34700 Lodève **04 84 31 00 99; camping@lodevoisetlarzac.fr; www.campinglesvailhes.com**

Fr N exit A75 junc 54 onto D148 dir Octon & Lac du Salagou. Foll site sp. Fr S exit A75 junc 55. 3*, Lge, hdg, mkd, pt shd, terr, EHU (16A) inc; bbq; sw; 20% statics; Eng spkn; fishing; watersports; CKE. *"Peaceful, remote site by lake; pleasant staff; no facs nrby; excel walks; gd."* **€25.20, 31 Mar-1 Oct.** **2023**

LODEVE *10E1* (5.6km W Rural) *43.73631, 3.26443* **Camping Domaine de Lambeyran (Naturist),** Lambeyran, 34700 Lodève **04 67 44 13 99; lambeyran@wanadoo.fr; www.lambeyran.com**

nr

Fr N or S on N9 take sliprd to Lodève. Leave town on D35 W twd Bédarieux. In 2km take 2nd R, sp L'Ambeyran & St Martin. Foll sp 3.7km up winding hill to site. 3*, Lge, hdg, mkd, pt shd, pt sl, terr, EHU (6A) €4.20; gas; bbq; red long stay; 5% statics; phone; Eng spkn; adv bkg acc; ccard acc; windsurfing 10km; CKE. *"Superb location with views; lge pitches; sailing 10km; gd walking, inc on site; gates clsd 2000; Lac du Salagou with sports facs 12km."* **€34.20, 7 May-30 Sep. 2024**

LONGEVILLE SUR MER *7A1* (2km S Coastal) *46.40402, -1.50673* **Camp Le Petit Rocher,** 1250 Ave du Dr Mathevet, 85560 Longeville-sur-Mer **02 51 20 41 94; www.olela.fr/campings/camping-petit-rocher**

€3 nr nr sand 150m

Fr La Tranche-sur-Mer take D105 N. In 8km site clearly sp 'Le Rocher' at 3rd exit fr rndabt (Ave du Dr Mathevet). Site on R in 1km at beginning of beach rd. 4*, Lge, hdg, mkd, shd, pt sl, EHU (6A) inc; gas; 10% statics; adv bkg acc; bike hire; games area; games rm; CKE. *"Gd beach holiday; gd facs."* **€33.00, 5 Apr - 21 Sep. 2024**

LONGEVILLE SUR MER *7A1* (2km S Coastal) *46.39499, -1.48736* **Camping Le Sous-Bois,** La Haute Saligotière, 85560 Longeville-sur-Mer **02 51 33 36 90; lesousbois85@gmail.com; lesousbois85.com**

€1.60 sand 1km

Sp fr D105 fr La Tranche-sur-Mer. 3*, Med, hdg, shd, EHU (10A) €4 (poss rev pol); TV; 15% statics; phone; tennis; CKE. *"Nice, well-managed, family site; pleasant 1km woodland walk to beach; gd walks; cycle tracks; excel; great for cycling; lovely sandy beach."* **€19.00, 1 Jun-30 Sep. 2024**

LONGEVILLE SUR MER *7A1* (3km SW Coastal) *46.41310, -1.52280* **Camping Les Brunelles,** Rue de la Parée, Le Bouil, 85560 Longeville-sur-Mer **02 53 81 70 00; reservation@ms-vacances.com; www.ms-vacances.com**

€5.50 nr (covrd, htd) sand 000m

Site bet Longeville-sur-Mer & Jard-sur-Mer; foll D21. 5*, Lge, mkd, pt shd, pt sl, serviced pitches; EHU (10A) inc; TV; 75% statics; Eng spkn; adv bkg acc; ccard acc; gym; sauna; bike hire; horseriding 2km; games area; waterslide; watersports; tennis; golf 15km. *"Gd san facs."* **€25.00, 7 Apr-17 Sep, A02. 2023**

LONS LE SAUNIER *6H2* (2.7km NE Rural) *46.68437, 5.56843* **Camping La Marjorie,** 640 Blvd de l'Europe, 39000 Lons-le-Saunier **03 84 24 26 94; info@camping-marjorie.com; www.camping-marjorie.com**

€2.60 (covrd, htd)

Site clearly sp in town on D1083 twd Besançon. Fr N bear R dir 'Piscine', cross under D1083 to site. 4*, Lge, hdg, hdstg, pt shd, terr, EHU (10A) inc (poss rev pol); gas; twin axles; phone; Eng spkn; ccard acc; golf 8km; games area; CKE. *"Lovely site in beautiful area; conv location; lge pitches; welcoming, friendly, helpful owners; excel, spotless san facs; 20 mins walk to interesting old town & Laughing Cow Museum; ideal touring base; rec; excel; by busy main rd; well run; aquatic cent adj; red facs in LS; upper terr nr to superior facs; long lead poss needed."* **€28.00, 1 Apr-15 Oct. 2022**

LORIENT *2F2* (6km N Rural) *47.82041, -3.40689* **Camping Ty Nénez,** Route de Lorient, 56620 Pont-Scorff **02 97 32 51 16; contact@camping-tynenez.com; www.lorient-camping.com**

12 €1 (htd) nr (htd)

N fr N165 on D6, look for sp Quéven in approx 5km on R. If missed, cont for 1km & turn around at rndabt. Site sp fr Pont-Scorff. 3*, Med, hdg, pt shd, EHU (16A) €3; bbq; 10% statics; Eng spkn; adv bkg acc; games area. *"Site barrier locked 2200-0800; excel LS; peaceful NH; tidy, organised site; excel htd facs; gd base for S Brittany."* **€28.20 2023**

LORIENT *2F2* (10km NE Rural) *47.80582, -3.28347* **Camping d'Hennebont,** Quai St Caradec, 56700 Hennebont **02 97 35 49 15 or 06 70 79 12 24; contact@campinghennebont.com; campinghennebont.wixsite.com/bretagne**

nr

Fr S on D781 to Hennebont. In town cent turn L & cross bdge, then sharp R along Rv Blavet for 1km. On R on rv bank. 2*, Med, mkd, pt shd, EHU inc; 10% statics; Eng spkn; adv bkg acc; bike hire; CKE. *"Pretty site; excel fishing; peaceful; pleasant sh walk into sm town; site barrier locked 2200-0700; tel on arri; excel customer care."* **€13.00, 1 Apr-15 Sep. 2024**

LOUDEAC *2E3* (2km E Urban) *48.17764, -2.72834* **Campsite Seasonova Aquarev,** Les Ponts es Bigots, 22600 Loudéac **02 96 26 21 92; contact@camping-aquarev.com; www.vacances-seasonova.com**

Fr Loudeac take N164 twrds Rennes. Site on L by lake. 3*, Med, mkd, pt shd, EHU (10A) inc; 10% statics; adv bkg acc; games area; CKE. *"Walks; tennis; fishing; archery; vg."* **€22.00, 1 Apr-30 Sep. 2023**

FRANCE

LOUDUN *4H1* (1km W Rural) *47.00379, 0.06337* **Camp Municipal de Beausoleil,** Chemin de l'Etang, 86200 Loudun **05 49 98 14 22 or 05 49 98 15 38; mairie@ville-loudun.fr; www.ville-loudun.fr**

nr

On main rte fr Poitiers to Saumur/Le Mans; N on D347 around Loudun, foll sp; turn L just N of level x-ing, then on R approx 250m. 3*, Sm, hdg, mkd, pt shd, terr, EHU (10A) inc; bus adj; Eng spkn; lake fishing adj; CKE. *"Beautiful, well-kept site; lge pitches; site yourself, warden calls am & pm; friendly & helpful; excel; long way fr the town."* **€22.00, 15 May-31 Aug.** **2024**

LOUHANS *6H1* (2km W Urban) *46.62286, 5.21733* **Camping Les 3 Rivieres Louhans,** 10, Chemin de la Chapellerie, 71500 Louhans **03 85 75 19 02 or 03 85 76 75 10 (Mairie); campinglhs@gmail.com; www.camping-louhans.com/**

Free WD (covrd)

In Louhans foll sp for Romenay on D971. Go under rlwy & over rv. Site on L just after stadium. 3*, Med, hdg, mkd, hdstg, shd, EHU €3.60; bbq; sw nr; adv bkg acc; Tennis, volleyball, table tennis; CKE. *"Rv location; clean & well-appointed; sports complex adj; lovely cycling area; tennis courts adj; mv service pnt nr; lge town mkt Mon am; poss travellers; vg."* **€7.40, 28 Mar-30 Sep.** **2020**

LOURDES *8F2* (1km NE Urban) *43.10247, -0.02789* **Camping de Sarsan,** 4 Ave Jean Moulin, 65100 Lourdes **05 62 94 43 09 or 06 07 94 36 74 (mob); camping.sarsan@wanadoo.fr; www.camping-sarsan.fr**

WD MSP

Fr N on N21 past airport, on app to Lourdes turn L sp 'Zone Indust du Monge'. Pass Cmp Le Moulin du Monge & foll site sp for approx 2km. Site on L immed after x-rds. 3*, Med, pt shd, pt sl, EHU (4-10A) pos rev pol €2.50-4.60; TV; 10% statics; adv bkg acc; games rm; games area. *"Easy 25min walk to town cent; ACSI acc."* **€26.80, 1 Apr-15 Oct.** **2023**

LOURDES *8F2* (3km W Rural) *43.09561, -0.07463* **Camping La Forêt,** Route de la Forêt, 65100 Lourdes **05 62 94 04 38; hello@camping-hautes-pyrenees.com; www.camping-hautes-pyrenees.com**

€1.90 MSP

Fr N on N21 exit onto D914 to Lourdes; on ent Lourdes turn L off D914 under rlwy bdge dir Cent Ville & hospital; in 100m turn R onto Rue de Pau sp St Pé & Bétharram; in 1km turn L over rv bdge; site in 1km. 3*, Med, mkd, pt shd, EHU (3-10A) €2.60-7.60; gas; bbq; 10% statics; phone; Eng spkn; adv bkg acc; ccard acc; CKE. *"Lovely site; helpful owners; conv town cent & grotto (1km); poss open outside stated dates - adv bkg req; ideal site to visit Lourdes."* **€28.00, 1 Apr - 31 Oct.** **2022**

LOUROUX, LE *4G2* (0.4km N Rural) *47.16270, 0.78697* **Camping à la Ferme La Chaumine (Baudoin),** 37240 Le Louroux **02 47 92 82 09 or 06 85 45 68 10 (mob); bruno.baudoin@free.fr; www.lelouroux.com**

WD

Fr Tours, take D50 S for 30km. Site immed on R bef Le Louroux. Sm, hdg, shd, EHU (10A) inc; bbq; bus 200m; Eng spkn; adv bkg acc. *"Superb CL-type site nr quaint vill; helpful owners; gd, clean san facs; gd walks fr site."* **€11.50, 1 May-15 Oct.** **2024**

LOUVIE JUZON *8F2* (0.5km S Rural) *43.08277, -0.42050* **Camp Municipal de la Vallée d'Ossau,** Route d'Ossau, 64260 Izeste **05 59 05 68 67; mairie.izeste@9business.fr**

nr nr

Site 300m fr rv bdge in Louvie-Juzon, on L heading S on D934. Sm, mkd, shd, EHU (6A) inc; adv bkg acc; CKE. *"Vg, attractive site adj fast-flowing rv & weir; ideal for access to Vallée d'Ossau; some rd & water noise; incredibly helpful & friendly site manager."* **€14.60, 1 Jun-15 Sep.** **2024**

LOUVIERS *3D2* (3.5km W Rural) *49.21490, 1.13279* **Camping Le Bel Air,** Route de la Haye-Malherbe, Hameau de St-Lubin, 27400 Louviers **02 32 40 10 77; www.camping-lebelair.fr**

€2.50 WD MSP nr (htd)

Site well sp in Louviers. Fr cent foll D81 W for 2.5km dir La Haye-Malherbe; twisting rd uphill; site on R. Or if travelling S leave A13 at junc 19 to Louviers & as bef. NB In town cent look for sm green sp after Ecole Communale (on L) & bef Jardin Public - a narr rd (1-way) & easy to miss. 3*, Med, hdg, mkd, hdstg, shd, EHU (6A) €4.90; gas; 30% statics; Eng spkn; adv bkg acc; ccard acc; CKE. *"Access to pitches diff long o'fits, poss mover req; check barrier opening times; bowling; poss NH only (2013); gd site and dog walks on site; handy for Newhaven Dieppe rte."* **€24.00, 15 Mar-15 Oct.** **2022**

LUCON *7A1* (17km SE Rural) *46.39174, -01.01952* **Camping l'île Cariot,** Rue Du 8 Mai, 85450 Chaillé-les-Marais **02 51 56 75 27; camping.ilecariot@gmail.com; camping-chaille-les-marais.com**

€1.65 (htd) WD MSP nr (htd)

In Chaille take D25, sp in town. 3*, Sm, mkd, pt shd, EHU (10A) €3.90; bbq; TV; bus adj; Eng spkn; adv bkg acc; games area; games rm; CKE. *"Cycle & walking rtes fr site; nr 'Green Venice'; free canoeing on canal; excel."* **€19.00, 1 Apr-30 Sep.** **2022**

LUDE, LE *4G1* (1km NE Rural) *47.65094, 0.16221* **Camp Municipal au Bord du Loir,** Route du Mans, 72800 Le Lude **02 43 94 67 70; camping@ville-lelude.fr; www.camping-lelude.com**

nr nr

Fr town cent take D305 (E); in 1km take D307 (N) sp 'Le Mans'; site immed on L. Well sp. Fr E on D305, avoid cent of Vaas, use HGV route. 3*, Med, hdg, mkd, pt shd, EHU (10A) inc; bbq (gas); TV; 10% statics; phone; Eng spkn; adv bkg acc; ccard acc; fishing; cycling; tennis; canoeing; CKE. *"Well-kept, well-run site; warm welcome, helpful staff; modern san facs; vg walk to town; Château du Lude & excel rest nrby; highly rec; gd."* **€13.00, 1 Apr-4 Oct. 2022**

LUSIGNAN *7A2* (0.5km N Rural) *46.43712, 0.12369* **Camp Municipal de Vauchiron,** Chemin de la Plage, 86600 Lusignan **05 49 43 30 08 or 05 49 43 31 48 (Mairie); lusignan@cg86.fr; www.lusignan.fr**

nr nr

Site sp fr D611, 22km SW of Poitiers; foll camp sp in Lusignan to rvside. 2*, Med, pt shd, EHU (15A) €2.40 (poss rev pol); bbq; sw nr; phone; Eng spkn; adv bkg acc; ccard acc; fishing; boat hire; CKE. *"Beautiful, peaceful site in spacious park; lge pitches; forest & rv walks adj; friendly, helpful resident warden; excel clean san facs; steep walk to historic town; highly rec; rv fishing; vg."* **€14.30, 1 May-17 Sep. 2022**

LUSSAC LES CHATEAUX *7A3* (13km SW Rural) *46.32231, 0.67384* **Camp Municipal du Renard,** 8 route de la Mairie, 86150 Queaux **06 70 04 30 87; contact@queaux.fr; www.queaux.fr**

nr

Fr Lussac cross rv bdge sp Poitiers & immed turn L. Foll sp to Gouex & Queaux. Site on D25 S of vill. 2*, Med, mkd, pt shd, pt sl, EHU (6A) €2.50; 10% statics; Eng spkn. *"Lovely rvside site nr pleasant vill; manned high ssn or apply to Mairie."* **€10.00, 1 Apr-30 Sep. 2023**

LUSSAC LES CHATEAUX *7A3* (6km SW Rural) *46.36912, 0.69330* **Camp Municipal du Moulin Beau,** 86320 Gouex **05 49 48 46 14; www.tourisme-vienne.com**

Fr Lussac on N147/E62 dir Poitiers, cross rv bdge sp Poitiers & immed turn L on D25; foll sp to Gouex; site on L in 4km at sw pool/camping sp. Sm, pt shd, EHU (15A) €1.60 (check pol); Tennis; CKE. *"Excel site on bank Rv Vienne; bakery in vill; facs clean but ltd; bollards at site ent, care needed if van over 7m or twin axles; pool 300m; highly rec."* **€4.00, 15 Jun-15 Sep. 2020**

LUXEUIL LES BAINS *6F2* (0.5km N Rural) *47.82315, 6.38200* **Domaine Du Chatigny Camping,** 14 Rue Grammont, 70300 Luxeuil-les-Bains **03 84 93 97 97; camping.lechatigny@chainethermale.fr; www.domaine-du-chatigny.com**

€1.70 (htd)

N fr Vesoul on N57; turn L at rndabt into Luxeuil-les-Bains; foll Camping sp. Vehicular access fr Rue Ste Anne. 3*, Med, hdstg, mkd, hdg, pt shd, terr, EHU (16A) €3.50-4.50; gas; bbq; TV; 20% statics; bus 300m; Eng spkn; adv bkg acc; ccard acc; CKE. *"New (2009), high standard site; indoor tennis court; gd."* **€8.00, 1 Mar-31 Oct. 2024**

LUZ ST SAUVEUR *8G2* (1km N Rural) *42.88140, -0.01258* **Airotel Camping Pyrénées,** 46 Ave du Barège, La Ferme Theil, 65120 Esquièze-Sère **05 62 92 89 18; contact@airotel-pyrenees.com; www.airotel-pyrenees.com**

€1.50 (htd) (covrd)

On main rd fr Lourdes to Luz on L past Int'l Campsite. L U-turn into ent archway needs care - use full width of rd & forecourt. 5*, Med, mkd, shd, pt sl, EHU (3-10A) €3.50-6.50 (rev pol); gas; TV; 30% statics; Eng spkn; adv bkg acc; ccard acc; horseriding; sauna; site clsd Oct & Nov; fishing; CKE. *"Beautiful area; facs poss stretched high ssn; ski in winter; walking; excel walking & wildlife; lovely vill; well organised; ACSI discount."* **€40.60, 15 May-18 Sep. 2023**

LUZ ST SAUVEUR *8G2* (1.5km N Rural) *42.88285, -0.01354* **Camping International,** 50 Ave de Barège, 65120 Esquièze-Sère **05 62 92 82 02; camping.international.luz@wanadoo.fr; www.international-camping.fr**

(htd) nr (htd)

On E side of D921, clearly sp. Ave de Barège is pt of D921. 4*, Lge, mkd, hdg, pt shd, pt sl, EHU (2-6A) €2-5; TV; 10% statics; phone; Eng spkn; adv bkg acc; tennis; horseriding; games area; games rm; waterslide; CKE. *"Beautiful views fr site; friendly, helpful owners; vg clean san facs, ltd LS; gd walking; gd base for cycling inc Col du Tourmalet; skiing; mkt Mon; vg; Excel modern san facs."* **€41.00, 25 May-20 Sep. 2024**

FRANCE

LUZ ST SAUVEUR *8G2* (0.5km E Rural) *42.87362, 0.00293* **Camping Le Bergons,** 12 Route de Barèges, 65120 Esterre **05 62 92 90 77 or 06 76 95 17 34; info@camping-bergons.com; www.camping-bergons.com**

€0.80 (htd) nr

On D918 to Col du Tourmalet, site on R. 2*, Med, mkd, pt shd, pt sl, terr, EHU (2-6A) €2.10-5; gas; bbq; red long stay; 10% statics; phone; CKE. *"Well-kept site; friendly, helpful owner; gd san facs; levelling blocks poss req; v tight ent for lge o'fits; excel walking; Donjon des Aigles at Beaucens worth visit; pool 500m; mkt Mon; vg."* **€20.00, 9 Feb-20 Oct and 22 Dec-7 Jan. 2024**

LUZ ST SAUVEUR *8G2* (8km E Rural) *42.89451, 0.05741* **Camping La Ribère,** Route de Labatsus, 65120 Barèges **05 62 92 69 01; contact@laribere.fr; www.laribere.fr**

€0.95 (htd) nr

On N side of rd D918 on edge of Barèges, site sp as `Camping Caraveneige'. Phone kiosk at ent. 2*, Sm, pt shd, pt sl, EHU (2-6A) €2-6; 10% statics; site clsd end Oct-mid Dec. *"Conv, attractive site; gd facs; magnificent views; site refurb (2015)."* **€25.10, 15 May-15 Oct. 2024**

LUZ ST SAUVEUR *8G2* (2km NW Rural) *42.88218, -0.02270* **Camping Le Pyrénévasion,** Route de Luz-Andiden 65120 Sazos **05 62 92 91 54; info@camping pyrenevasion.com; www.campingpyrenevasion.com**

€2.50 (htd) nr

Fr Lourdes S on D921 twd Gavarnie. Shortly bef Luz-St Sauveur after petrol stn & campsites sp, take R fork onto D12 sp Sazos. Cont thro vill & turn R sp Luz-Andiden, then immed R again sp Sazos (D12) & Luz-Andiden. Cont uphill, site on R just after Sazon sp. 4*, Med, mkd, hdg, pt shd, EHU (3A/6A/10A) €3.5/€7/€8; gas; bbq (charcoal, elec, gas); 60% statics; Eng spkn; fishing; games rm; site clsd 20 Oct-19 Nov. *"Fair site in mountains; no o'fits over 7.5m high ssn; long, steep trek to/fr shops."* **€45.10, 1 May-10 Oct. 2023**

LUZY *4H4* (1km NE Rural) *46.79622, 3.97685* **Camping La Bédure,** Route d'Autun, 58170 Luzy **06 13 30 76 60 or 06 42 66 90 77; info@campingla bedure.com; www.campinglabedure.com**

12 €1.50 nr

Foll sps on D981 to site. 2*, Med, mkd, pt shd, pt sl, EHU (6A) €3 (poss rev pol); Eng spkn. *"Pleasant site; pool adj; gd walking & touring base; adjoins Lidl."* **€21.60 2023**

LUZY *4H4* (7km NE Rural) *46.81680, 4.05650* **Camping Domaine de la Gagère (Naturist),** 58170 Luzy **03 86 30 48 11; info@la-gagere.com; www.la-gagere.com**

€4 (htd)

Fr Luzy take D981 dir Autun; in 6.5km over rlwy, turn R onto unclassified rd sp 'La Gagère'. Site at end of rd in 3.5km on L; this rd narr in places. 4*, Med, hdstg, mkd, pt shd, pt sl, terr, EHU (6A) €4.50; bbq; TV; 20% statics; phone; bus 10km; Eng spkn; adv bkg acc; ccard acc; INF card req; sauna; ACSI acc. *"Excel, wooded, scenic site in beautiful area; gd views; friendly, helpful owners; superb san facs; gd touring base."* **€40.10, 15 Apr-1 Oct. 2024**

LYON *9B2* (12km E Rural) *45.79082, 4.99223* **Camping Le Grand Large,** 81 Rue Victor Hugo, 69330 Meyzieu **04 72 45 30 29**

€1 (htd) nr

Exit N346 junc 6, E onto D6 dir Jonage. In approx 2 km turn L twd Le Grand Large (lake), site in 1km. 2*, Lge, pt shd, EHU (5A) inc; gas; sw nr; TV; 90% statics; bus 1km; adv bkg acc; ccard acc; fishing; boating; games area; CKE. *"Pleasant location; san facs scruffy & unclean (2011); stn 2km for trains to Lyon; mainly statics and chalets; NH only high ssn."* **€28.00, 1 Apr-31 Oct. 2024**

LYON *9B2* (8km NW Urban) *45.81948, 4.76168* **Camping de Lyon,** Ave de la Porte de Lyon, 69570 Dardilly **04 78 35 64 55; contact@camping-lyon.com; www.camping-lyon.com**

12 €4.90 (htd) nr (htd)

Fr D306 Paris rd, take Limonest-Dardilly-Porte de Lyon exit at Auchan supmkt. Fr A6 exit junc 33 Porte de Lyon. Site on W side of A6 adj m'way & close to junc, foll sp (poss obscured by trees) for 'Complexe Touristique'. Fr E take N ring rd dir Roanne, Paris, then as above. 4*, Lge, hdstg, mkd, hdg, pt shd, serviced pitches; EHU (10A) inc; twin axles; TV; 10% statics; phone; bus/train to city nr; Eng spkn; adv bkg acc; ccard acc; games rm; CKE. *"Well-run, secure site; Lyon easy by bus & metro, tickets can be bought fr recep; bar 100m; gd touring base for interesting area; helpful recep; gd, clean san facs; gas 100m; cafes nrby."* **€30.00 2022**

MACHECOUL *2H4* (0.5km SE Urban) *46.98987, -1.81562* **Camping La Rabine,** Allée de la Rabine, 44270 Machecoul **02 40 02 30 48 or 06 08 49 22 88; camprabine@wanadoo.fr; camping-la-rabine.com**

€0.90 nr

Sp fr most dirs. Look out for prominent twin-spired church in cent; take sm one-way rd that leads away fr spire end; site on R in 400m. 2*, Med, pt shd, EHU (4-13A) €2-3.20; bbq (gas); adv bkg acc. *"Pleasant site with lge generous size pitches & gd facs; excel base for birdwatching & cycling over marshes; pleasant town; mkt Wed & Sat; pool adj; lovely friendly well managed site; excel facs; lovely site rv fishing."* **€14.30, 1 Apr-30 Sep. 2023**

MACON *9A2* (4km N Urban) *46.33023, 4.84491*
Camp Municipal Les Varennes, 1 Route des Grandes Varennes, Sancé, 71000 Mâcon **03 85 38 16 22; camping@ville-macon.fr; www.campingmacon.com**
€1.40 (htd) WD MSP

Fr both N & S exit A6 junc 28 & cont S on N6 twd Mâcon; site on L in approx 3km, sp. (Fr S, leaving A6 at junc 28 avoids long trip thro town). 4*, Lge, mkd, pt shd, pt sl, EHU (5-10A) inc (poss rev pol); gas; twin axles; red long stay; TV; phone; bus; Eng spkn; adv bkg acc; ccard acc; golf 6km; tennis 1km; CKE. *"Well-kept, busy NH nr A6; rec arr early as poss full after 1800; friendly staff; vg, immac san facs; hypmkt 1km; excel rest; gates clsd 2200-0630; poss flooding bottom end of site; long level walk to town; excel; perfect new facs (2014)."* **€27.00, 15 Mar-31 Oct. 2024**

MACON *9A2* (8km S Rural) *46.25167, 4.82610*
Base de loisirs du lac de Cormoranche, Les Luizant, 01290 Cormoranche-sur-Saône **03 85 23 97 10; contact@lac-cormoranche.com; www.lac-cormoranche.com**
€2.20 (htd) WD MSP

Exit A26 junc 29 sp Mâcon Sud onto N6 S to Crêches-sur-Saône. Turn L in town at traff lts onto D31 sp Cormoranche, then D51A. Cross rv, site sp on L. Alt rte: exit N6 in Mâcon & turn E onto D1079 dir St Laurent-sur-Saône then take D933 S to Pont-de-Veyle. Cont on D933 & foll sp to Cormoranche. 4*, Med, hdg, mkd, pt shd, EHU (10A) inc; bbq; sw nr; TV; 25% statics; Eng spkn; adv bkg acc; ccard acc; fishing; bike hire; CKE. *"Spacious pitches, some with narr access; vg; tight access to some pitches; gd for families."* **€31.40, 1 May-30 Sep. 2024**

MAICHE *6G3* (1km S Rural) *47.24705, 6.79952*
Camp Municipal St Michel, 23 Rue St Michel, 25120 Maîche **03 81 64 12 56 or 03 81 64 03 01 (Mairie); contact@mairie-maiche.fr; www.mairie-maiche.fr**
12 (htd) WD nr

Fr S turn R off D437 onto D442. App on D464 L on o'skts of town. Sp fr both dir. 3*, Med, pt shd, sl, terr, EHU (6A) inc; 10% statics; phone; adv bkg acc; games area; site clsd 3rd week Nov & Dec; games rm. *"Beautiful, neat, well-run site with lovely views; many trees & wild flowers; lower pitches are quieter; pool adj; clean facs; phone ahead LS to check open; gd walks in woods."* **€18.00 2023**

MAILLEZAIS *7A2* (0.4km S Rural) *46.36921, -0.74054*
Camp Municipal de l'Autize, Rue du Champ de Foire, 85420 Maillezais **02 51 00 70 79 or 06 43 19 14 90 (mob); camping.lautize@orange.fr; www.maillezais.fr**
WD nr

Fr Fontenay take D148 twd Niort; after 9km, turn R onto D15 to Maillezais; pass church in vill on L, site on R after 200m. Or fr A83, exit junc 9 onto D148, then D15 (do not use v minor rds, as poss directed by sat nav). 2*, Sm, hdg, mkd, pt shd, EHU (4-13A) €3-5; twin axles; TV; adv bkg acc; ccard acc; games rm; games area; CKE. *"Lovely, clean site; spacious pitches, gd views fr some; friendly, helpful warden; excel, immac san facs; warden calls am & pm; some low branches (2010); excel mkd cycle paths; conv Marais Poitevin area & Venise Verte; nrby abbey worth a visit; vg NH fr A83; excel; boat rides fr Vieux Port."* **€17.00, 1 Jun-30 Sep. 2023**

MAILLEZAIS *7A2* (6km S Rural) *46.31308, -0.73342*
FFCC Camping Les Conches, Route du Grand Port, 85420 Damvix **02 51 87 17 06; campingdesconches@orange.fr; http://campingdesconches.free.fr**
€1 WD MSP nr nr

Fr Fontenay-le-Comte exit D148 at Benet then W on D25 thro Le Mazeau to sp on L for Damvix. Or exit A83 junc 8 then S on D938 & E on D25 dir Benet. Site 1km thro vill on R over bdge (sp). 2*, Med, mkd, shd, EHU (6-10A) €3; adv bkg rec; golf; rv fishing adj; boating adj; tennis; horseriding; CKE. *"Gd rest; friendly staff; gd cycling."* **€17.50, 1 Apr-15 Oct. 2024**

MAILLY LE CHATEAU *4G4* (5km S Rural) *47.56267, 3.64671* **Camping Merry Sur Yonne (formerly Municipal Escale),** 5 Impasse de Sables, 89660 Merry-sur-Yonne **+33 (0)3 86 34 59 55; campingmerrysuryonne@yahoo.com; www.campingmerrysuryonne.com**
12 WD MSP

Fr N on D100, turn R over bdge, sp Merry Sur Yonne. At t-junc in vill turn L. At end of vill bear L at war memorial into site. 4*, Med, hdstg, mkd, pt shd, EHU (16A); bbq; cooking facs; sw nr; twin axles; Eng spkn; adv bkg acc; games rm; games area; CCI. *"Charming English owners; takeaway; beautiful location nr rv and canal; canal walks adj; excel rest; hdstdg on concrete surrounded by grass, shaded by trees; close to Rv Yonne, Nivernais canal, Roches du saussois; excel."* **€21.40 2024**

MAINTENON *4E2* (6km NW Rural) *48.60890, 1.54760* **Camping Les Ilots de St Val,** Le Haut Bourray, 28130 Villiers-le-Morhier **02 37 82 71 30; campinglesilotsdestval@orange.fr; www.campinglesilotsdestval.com**

€2 (htd) nr

Take D983 N fr Maintenon twd Nogent-le-Roi, in 5km 2nd L onto D101 sp Néron/Vacheresses-les-Basses/Camping to site in 1km on L at top of hill. NB New by-pass around Nogent le Roi fr N. 3*, Lge, hdstg, hdg, mkd, pt shd, EHU (6-10A) €4-7; gas; bbq; red long stay; 50% statics; Eng spkn; adv bkg acc; games rm; rv fishing 1km; tennis; CKE. *"Pleasant, peaceful site in open countryside; lge private pitches; some vg, modern san facs; helpful staff; gd value site; conv Chartres, Versailles, Maintenon Château, train to Paris; dog walking fr the site is gd; improved access for lge o'fits; pool 4km; phone ahead late Dec to mid Feb as site may be clsd to tourers; friendly owners."* **€32.00, 1 Feb-22 Dec. 2022**

MALAUCENE *10E2* (4km N Rural) *44.20101, 5.12535* **Camping La Saousse,** La Madelaine, 84340 Malaucène **04 90 65 14 02; lcamping.lasaousse@orange.fr; www.lasaousse.com**

nr nr

Fr Malaucène take D938 N dir Vaison-la-Romaine & after 3km turn R onto D13 dir Entrechaux where site sp. After 1km turn R, site 1st on R. Sm, hdg, shd, terr, EHU (5A) €2.50; bbq; adv bkg rec; CKE. *"CL-type site o'looking vineyards with views to Mt Ventoux; some pitches in woods with steep incline - rec pitch on lower level for easy access; friendly, helpful owners; pool 4km; basic, clean facs; v peaceful, excel."* **€14.00, 1 Apr-30 Sep. 2020**

MALAUCENE *10E2* (0.4km NW Rural) *44.17789, 5.12533* **Camping Le Bosquet,** Route de Suzette, 84340 Malaucène **04 90 65 29 09; lebosquet84@gmail.com; www.provence.guideweb.com/camping/bosquet**

€1 (htd) nr

Fr S on D938 dir Vaison-la-Romaine turn L onto D90 at Malaucène dir Suzette. Site on R in 300m. Do not tow thro Malaucène. 2*, Sm, hdg, hdstg, pt shd, terr, EHU (10A) €3.20 (poss rev pol); gas; 2% statics; phone; adv bkg acc; CKE. *"Clean san facs; friendly owner; gd touring base Mt Ventoux; mkt Wed; easy 15 min walk to the town."* **€21.10, 6 Apr-16 Oct. 2024**

MALBUISSON *6H2* (2km S Rural) *46.77449, 6.27370* **Camping du Lac,** 10 Rue du Lac, 25160 Labergement-Ste Marie **03 81 69 31 24; camping.lac.remoray@wanadoo.fr; www.camping-lac-remoray.com**

€1.50 adj

Exit N57/E23 junc 2 onto D437 thro Malbuisson to Labergement. Site sp to R of D437 after x-ing Rv Doubs. 3*, Med, mkd, pt shd, EHU (6A) €3.50; gas; TV; 5% statics; phone; Eng spkn; adv bkg acc; ccard acc; fishing; tennis nr; cycling; games area; CKE. *"Roomy site by Lake Remoray with forest views; kind & helpful owner; clean san facs; walking; statics sep area; vill 500m with gd shops; excel."* **€21.00, 17 May-15 Sep. 2024**

MALBUISSON *6H2* (1.4km SW Urban) *46.79176, 6.29257* **Camping Les Fuvettes,** 24 Route de la Plage et des Perrières, 25160 Malbuisson **03 81 69 31 50; les-fuvettes@wanadoo.fr; www.camping-fuvettes.com**

€1.50 (htd)

Site 19km S of Pontarlier on N57 & D437 to Malbuisson, thro town, R down rd to Plage. 3*, Lge, pt shd, pt sl, EHU (4-6A) €3.60-4; gas; sw; 30% statics; fishing; games rm; boating; CKE. *"Popular, lakeside, family site; mkd walks/cycle paths in adj woods; petting zoo (llamas etc) nrby."* **€28.00, 5 Apr-30 Sep. 2024**

MALENE, LA *9D1* (0.2km W Rural) *44.30120, 3.31923* **FFCC Camp Municipal Le Pradet,** 48210 La Malène **04 66 48 58 55 or 04 66 48 51 16 (LS); camping.lamalene@gmail.com; www.gorgesdutarn-camping.com**

€0.30 nr nr nr

W fr La Malène on D907B dir Les Vignes. Site on L in 200m. Well sp. 2*, Sm, mkd, hdstg, pt shd, pt sl, EHU (10A) €2.50; bbq; sw; phone; adv bkg acc; ccard acc; fishing; CKE. *"Kayak hire; boat trips fr vill; helpful warden; excel; v narr pitches; rvside site; steep slope down to recep; spectacular scenery."* **€27.00, 1 Apr-30 Sep. 2023**

MALESHERBES *4E3* (5km S Rural) *48.25659, 2.43574* **FFCC Camping Ile de Boulancourt,** 6 Allée des Marronniers, 77760 Boulancourt **01 64 24 13 38; hello@iledeboulancourt.com; www.campingiledeboulancourt.com**

12 €1 (htd) nr

Exit A6 at junc 14 Ury & Fontainebleau. SW on D152 to Malesherbes; S on D410 for 5km into Boulancourt. Site sp fr D410 & in vill. 3*, Med, pt shd, EHU (3-6A) €2.70; bbq; 90% statics; Eng spkn; waterslide 5km; fishing 3km; tennis; CKE. *"Attractive rv thro site; well-maintained facs, ltd LS; sep field for tourers; friendly, helpful staff; golf course in vill; chateau nr; excel."* **€15.70 2022**

MALESTROIT *2F3* (0.5km E Urban) *47.80865, -2.37922* **Domaine Les Rives de l'Oust (formerly Municipal de la Daufresne),** Chemin des Tanneurs, 56140 Malestroit **02 97 75 13 33 or 06 83 69 88 17; contact@campingmalestroit.com; www.campingmalestroit.com**

nr nr nr

S fr Ploërmel on N166 dir Vannes for 9km. Turn L onto D764 to Malestroit; site sp just off Blvd du Pont Neuf on E bank of Rv Oust, not well sp. 2*, Sm, hdg, pt shd, EHU (10A) €2.70 (poss long lead req); adv bkg acc; ccard acc; rv fishing adj; tennis; canoeing nr; CKE. *"Pleasant site in excel location; narr site rds, some pitches poss diff to manoeuvre; no twin axles; clean san facs, basic but ok, poss stretched high ssn; canal towpath adj; gd cycle rtes; Museum of Breton Resistance in St Marcel; v nice, pretty site, highly rec."* **€10.00, 1 May-15 Sep. 2023**

MAMERS *4E1* (0.5km N Rural) *48.35778, 0.37181*
Portes du Perche, Route de Contilly, 72600 Mamers
02 43 97 68 30; camping@mairie-mamers.fr; www.campingdesportesduperche.com
€0.50 (htd)

Fr W on D311, at rndabt at top of hill on circular rd, turn R (sp); then easy L (sp). Fr E on D311, strt thro rndabt (at Super U), ignore 1st camping sp, turn R at traff its & 2nd camping sp; at mini-rndabt turn L, sp Contilly; see lake & site. 3*, Sm, hdg, hdstg, pt shd, pt sl, terr, EHU (10A) inc (long lead poss req); TV; 30% statics; adv bkg acc; games area; CKE. *"Well-kept, secure site; admittance LS 1700-1900 only; Mamers pretty; pool 200m; lakeside; easy walk to town."*
€15.00, 15 Apr-30 Sep. **2022**

MANOSQUE *10E3* (4km E Rural) *43.82352, 5.85424*
Camping Tikayan Oxygene, 2949 Route du Val de Durance, 04210 Valensole **04 92 72 41 77; info@camping-oxygene.com; www.tikayan.com/fr/camping-oxygene-accueil**
€2.50

Exit A51 junc 18 onto D907 E dir Vinon-sur-Verdon; in 1km turn L at rndabt onto D4 N dir Oraison; site in 2.5km on L, at Les Chabrands, just bef Villedieu. 3*, Med, hdg, mkd, pt shd, EHU (6-10A) €3.50-4.50; bbq (elec, gas); gym; horseriding nr; games area. *"Peaceful, well-kept site with hill views; excel well-run site; vg pool; many places of interest nrby, inc Gorges du Verdon; canyoning, angling & rafting nr; paragliding nr; vg farm shop nr."* **€31.20, 6 Apr-31 Oct.** **2024**

MANOSQUE *10E3* (1.5km W Rural) *43.82986, 5.76384*
FFCC Camping Les Ubacs, 1138 Ave de la Repasse, 04100 Manosque **04 92 72 28 08; lesubacs.manosque@ffcc.fr**
€1 (cont)

Exit A51 junc 18 onto D907 dir Manosque; then D907 dir Apt; site sp at last rndabt on W side of Manosque. NB easy to overshoot. 1*, Med, hdg, mkd, pt shd, pt sl, EHU (3-9A) €3.34-4.20; sw nr; red long stay; ccard acc; tennis; CKE. *"Conv Gorges du Verdon; helpful."* **€15.40, 1 Apr-30 Sep.** **2024**

MANS, LE *4F1* (7.6km NE Rural) *48.01904, 0.27996*
Camping Le Pont Romain, Allée des Ormeaux, Lieu-dit La Châtaigneraie, 72530 Yvré-l'Evêque **02 43 82 25 39; campinglepontromain@onlycamp.fr; camping-le-mans.fr**
€1 (htd) (htd)

Fr Le Mans take D314 to Yvré-l'Evêque - but do not ent town; just after rv bdge take 1st L into Allée des Ormeaux; site on L in 800m. Or exit A28 junc 23 onto D314 dir 'Le Mans Cent'; site on R just bef Yvré-l'Evêque. Avoid direct rte into vill over bridge. 4*, Med, mkd, hdstg, hdg, pt shd, EHU (16A) inc; gas; bbq; 15% statics; phone; bus; Eng spkn; adv bkg acc; games rm; CKE. *"Excel modern san facs; sep car park; conv Le Mans & m'way; vg; uneven pitches, need TLC; pleasant rural site; easy access to city; recep open 0830-1200 & 1430-2000; gd; bus to Le Mans 1.5km; beautiful site; easy access to bus; excel pitches; gd MV service pnt."* **€28.60, 13 Mar-8 Nov.** **2024**

MANS, LE *4F1* (20km SW Urban) *47.88985, 0.03038*
Aire De Camping Car, Rue de La Port, Suze Sur Sarthe **02 43 77 30 49; contact@lasuze.fr; www.lasuze.fr/tourisme/laire-de-camping-cars/**
(cont) nr nr nr

Fr A11 Lemans-Angers take exit 9 twds Tours/Allonnes on A11.1, 1st exit on rndabt onto D309. Then take D233 to La Suze-sur-Sarthe. Turn L immed bef Rv brdg onto site. Sm, hdstg, pt shd, EHU (6A) inc; own san rec; bus/train. *"Excel site; no c'vans allowed; on edge of rv bank with views; conv for Le Mans."*
€8.00, 3 May - 30 Sept. **2024**

MANS, LE *4F1* (20km SW Urban) *47.889024, 0.033594*
Camp Municipal Le Port, Ave de la Piscine, 72210 La Suze-sur-Sarthe **02 43 77 30 49; contact@lasuze.fr; www.lasuze.fr**
12 €0.45 (htd)

Fr A11 take exit 9 twrds Tours/Allonnes on A11.1, 1st exit on rndabt onto D309. Foll sp to La Suze Sur Sarthe on D233. Cross rlwy and turn L as you come into town, foll sp for MH. Turn R into Ave de la Piscine, then right into parking area. Pay at barrier to be let thro to site. 2*, Med, mkd, pt shd, EHU (10A) €2.30; bbq; red long stay; TV; boating; rv adj; own san; tennis; adv bkg; fishing. *"Narr gate to site; ample hdstg for m'vans in adj car park."* **€11.00** **2023**

MANSLE *7B2* (0.4km NE Urban) *45.87841, 0.18175*
Camp Municipal Le Champion, Rue de Watlington, 16230 Mansle **05 45 20 31 41 or 05 45 22 20 43; mairie.mansle@wanadoo.fr; www.mansle.fr**
nr nr

N on N10 fr Angoulême, foll sp Mansle Ville. Leave N10 at exit to N of town, site rd on L, well sp. Rec ent/leave fr N as rte thro town diff due to parked cars. Site beside Rv Charente. 3*, Med, hdg, pt shd, EHU (16A) €2.80 (poss long lead req); bbq; sw nr; 5% statics; phone; Eng spkn; adv bkg acc; fishing; boating adj; CKE. *"Popular, peaceful, well-kept NH nr N10; lge pitches, choose own; helpful warden; immac san facs; grnd poss boggy after heavy rain; mkt Tues, Fri am; great site in excel location, well run; vg; gd rest; easy walk to town."* **€16.40, 12 May-17 Sep.** **2023**

MANSLE *7B2* (10km SE Rural) *45.84137, 0.27319*
Camping Devezeau, 4 Rue du Camping,16230 St Angeau **05 45 93 92 68 or 01622 370 662; ask@campingdevezeau.com; www.campingdevezeau.com**
12 (htd) nr

N or S on N10 exit Mansle; in cent vill at traff lts foll sp twd La Rochefoucauld (D6); past Super U supmkt; over bdge; 1st R onto D6. In approx 9km at T-junc turn R, site sp. App down narr rd. 2*, Sm, hdg, hdstg, pt shd, sl, EHU (6A-10A) €2; gas; bbq; twin axles; 25% statics; Eng spkn; adv bkg acc; cycling; canoeing; horseriding; fishing; CKE. *"Nice CL-type site; v friendly British owners; excel san facs modernised (2015); traction diff in wet (4x4 avail); blocks & steel pegs needed; gd cycling country; phone ahead in winter; lovely tranquil site; walking; vg; friendly atmosphere; bar snacks & English breakfast."* **€22.00** **2023**

FRANCE

MARANS *7A1* (1km N Rural) *46.31682, -0.99158* **Camp Municipal Le Bois Dinot,** Route de Nantes, 17230 Marans **05 46 01 10 29; campingmarans@orange.fr; www.ville-marans.fr**

€1.10 nr nr nr

Heading S, site on L of D137 bef ent Marans. Heading N, site is well sp on R 300m after supmkt on L. 3*, Lge, shd, EHU (6-10A) €3; red long stay; Eng spkn; adv bkg rec; fishing; boat hire; CKE. *"Well-kept, wooded site; v helpful, efficient staff; quieter pitches at back of site; vg pool adj; poss mosquitoes; gd cycling; mkt Tues & Sat; excel; v clean san facs; grass pitch avail subj to rainfall; woodland pitches quietest; poss diff lger o'fits."* **€16.50, 1 Apr-30 Sep. 2024**

MARCENAY *6F1* (1km N Rural) *47.87070, 4.40560* **Camping Les Grèbes du Lac de Marcenay,** 5 Route du Lac, 21330 Marcenay **03 80 81 61 72 or 06 98 07 28 43; info@campingmarcenaylac.com; www.campingmarcenaylac.com**

€1 (htd) nr nr

On D965 bet Laignes & Châtillon-sur-Seine. Fr Châtillon sp on R 8km after vill of Cérilly. Foll sp to lake & camp. 2*, Med, hdstg, mkd, hdg, shd, EHU (10A) €3; gas; bbq; sw nr; TV; 5% statics; phone; Eng spkn; adv bkg rec; ccard acc; horseriding; games rm; boat hire; watersports; fishing; canoe hire; games area; golf; bike hire; CKE. *"Lovely, peaceful, well-run site by lake; beautiful area; friendly, helpful Dutch owners; excel san facs; pitches poss soft after rain; bar adj; gd touring base; gd walking & cycling; Châtillon museum & Abbey de Fontenay worth visit."* **€23.50, 1 Apr-31 Oct. 2024**

MARCIAC *8F2* (1.5km NW Rural) *43.53228, 0.16633* **FFCC Camping du Lac,** Bezines, 32230 Marciac **06 88 84 87 33; info@camping-marciac.com; www.camping-marciac.com**

€1.50 nr

E fr Maubourguet take D943 to Marciac. Take D3 to lake dir Plaisance. At lake turn R & R again at sp. Site on L in 200m. Fr N exit A62 at junc 3 & foll D932 sp Pau to Aire-sur-Adour then E on D935 & D3 & foll sp. 3*, Med, mkd, hdstg, pt shd, pt sl, EHU (6A) inc; gas; bbq; red long stay; 8% statics; phone; adv bkg acc; ccard acc; CKE. *"Friendly British owners; peaceful site; lge pitches with easy access; interesting old town; lake adj; jazz festival 1st 2 weeks Aug (extra charge); Wed mkt."* **€31.00, 20 Mar-12 Oct. 2024**

MARCIGNY *9A1* (7km W Rural) *46.26489, 3.95756* **Camping La Motte aux Merles,** 71110 Artaix **03 85 25 37 67; campingpicard@yahoo.fr**

€1

Leave D982 (Digoin-Roanne) at Marcigny by-pass. Take D989 twd Lapalisse. In 2km at Chambilly cont on D990, site sp in 5km on L, 200m down side rd. Sm, pt shd, pt sl, EHU (8A) €2.40; bbq; fishing nr; tennis nr; golf nr. *"Friendly owners; gd sightseeing in peaceful area; site diff in wet; excel."* **€10.00, 1 Apr-31 Oct. 2020**

MARCILLAC LA CROISSILLE *7C4* (2km SW Rural) *45.26896, 2.00838* **Camp Municipal Le Lac,** 28 Route du Viaduc, 19320 Marcillac-la-Croisille **05 55 27 81 38 or 05 55 27 82 05 (Mairie); camping.marcillac@aquadis-loisirs.com; aquadis-loisirs.com/en/nature-campsite/camping-du-lac**

€0.90 nr

S fr Egletons on D16 & D18. Site sp at S end of vill at intersection with D978. 3*, Lge, shd, pt sl, EHU (6A) €2.80; TV; 10% statics; adv bkg acc; tennis adj. *"Spacious park like setting; lake adj."* **€18.00, 1 Mar-3 Nov. 2024**

MARENNES *7B1* (10.5km SE Rural) *45.77324, -0.96301* **Camping Le Valerick,** La Petite Mauvinière, 17600 St Sornin **05 46 85 15 95; www.camping-le-valerick.fr**

€1.40 (htd)

Fr Marennes take D728 sp Saintes for 10km; L to St Sornin; site sp in vill. Fr Saintes D728 W for 26km; take 2nd R turn R in vill D118, site on L sp La Gripperie. 2*, Sm, mkd, pt shd, pt sl, EHU (4-6A) €3-€3.70 (poss rev pol); bbq (charcoal, gas); adv bkg acc; ccard acc; CKE. *"Nice, friendly site; gd san facs; plenty of bird life - herons, storks etc; poss mosquito problem; excel; spotless san facs; lge pitches; v warm welcome; highly rec."* **€19.00, 1 Apr-30 Sep. 2024**

MARENNES *7B1* (5km SE Rural) *45.81083, -1.06027* **Camping Séquoia Parc,** La Josephtrie, 17320 St Just-Luzac **05 46 85 55 55; info@sequoiaparc.com; www.sandaya.fr/nos-campings/sequoia-parc**

€7 (covrd, htd)

Fr A10/E05 m'way exit at Saintes, foll sp Royan (N150) turning off onto D728 twd Marennes & Ile d'Oléron; site sp to R off D728, just after leaving St Just-Luzac. Or fr Rochefort take D733 & D123 S; just bef Marennes turn L on D241 sp St Just-Luzac. Best ent to site fr D728, well sp fr each dir. 5*, Lge, mkd, hdg, unshd, sl, serviced pitches; EHU (6A) inc (poss rev pol); gas; bbq; red long stay; TV; 60% statics; adv bkg acc; ccard acc; fishing 1.5km; bike hire; watersports 3km; games area; horseriding; tennis; games rm; CKE. *"High standard site; aqua park: o'fits over 8m on request; max 1 dog; waterslides, waterjets & whirlpool; barrier clsd 2230-0700; 3 pools (2 htd); lge pitches; cash machine; clean san facs; superb pools; excel free club for children."* **€55.00, 15 Apr-18 Sep, A28. 2022**

MARENNES *7B1* (2km NW Coastal) *45.83139, -1.15092* **Camp Municipal La Giroflée,** 17560 Bourcefranc-le-Chapus **05 46 85 06 43 or 05 46 85 02 02 (Mairie); campinglagiroflee@orange.fr; www.bourcefranc-le-chapus.fr**

nr adj

Fr Saintes on D728/D26 to Boucefranc, turn L at traff lts. Site on L after 1km (after sailing school) opp beach. 2*, Med, pt shd, EHU (6A) €3. *"Gd NH stop; busy hg ssn; gd cafe Pirate next door."* **€17.00, 1 May-30 Sep. 2022**

MAREUIL *7B2* (5km N Rural) *45.49504, 0.44860* **FFCC Camping Les Graulges,** Le Bourg, 24340 Les Graulges **05 53 60 74 73; info@lesgraulges.com; www.lesgraulges.com**

€2

Fr D939 at Mareuil turn L onto D708 & foll sp to Les Graulges in 5km. 1*, Sm, mkd, pt shd, pt sl, terr, EHU (6A) €3.50; bbq; red long stay; TV; 10% statics; Eng spkn; adv bkg acc; lake fishing. *"Tranquil site in forested area; ideal touring base; friendly Dutch owners; excel rest; not suitable for elderly; pool dirty; lge dog lives on site (2012)."* **€20.50, 1 Apr-30 Sep.** **2020**

MAREUIL *7B2* (4km SE Rural) *45.44481, 0.50474* **Camping L'Etang Bleu,** 24340 Vieux-Mareuil **03 35 53 60 92 70; letangbleu@ornage.fr; www.letangbleu.com**

€3

On D939 Angoulême-Périgueux rd, after 5km turn L cent of Vieux-Mareuil onto D93, foll camping sp to site in 2km. Narr app thro vill, care needed. 2*, Lge, hdg, mkd, pt shd, EHU 6-10A (poss rev pol); gas; bbq; TV; 10% statics; adv bkg acc; ccard acc; lake fishing 500m; CKE. *"Pleasant site in unspoilt countryside; lge pitches, but narr site rds; access diff lge o'fits without mover; friendly British owners; gd san facs, ltd LS; gd walking/ cycling area; excel."* **€26.00, 1 Apr-20 Oct.** **2023**

MARNAY (HAUTE SAONE) *6G2* (0.5km SE Urban) *47.28975, 5.77628* **Camping Vert Lagon,** Route de Besançon, 70150 Marnay **03 84 31 73 16 or 06 40 78 58 13; camping.marnay@woka.fr; www.camping-vertlagon.com**

€1 nr nr (htd)

Fr N stay on D67 Marnay by-pass; ignore old camping sp into town. Proceed to S of town on by-pass then turn L at junc. Bef bdge in 1km take gravel rd on S side, round under bdge to site (app thro town fr N v narr). 4*, Med, hdg, mkd, pt shd, EHU (10A) €4; bbq; 40% statics; adv bkg acc; ccard acc; games area; canoeing; fishing; CKE. *"Pleasant, popular, family site by Rv Ognon; gd san facs; lake adj; tree-top walks; vg."* **€28.00, 2 May-30 Sep.** **2023**

MARQUION *3B4* (2.7km NE Rural) *50.22280, 3.10863* **FFCC Camping de l'Epinette,** 7 Rue du Calvaire, 62860 Sauchy-Lestrée **03 21 59 50 13; lepinette62@wanadoo.fr; www.lepinette62.com**

nr

Fr A26 exit junc 8 onto D939 to Marquion. On ent Marquion turn R at x-rds to Sauchy-Lestrée; on ent vill turn R at 1st T-junc & site on L in 100m. Fr Cambrai take D939 twd Arras, then as above. 2*, Sm, pt shd, pt sl, EHU (10A) €3 (poss rev pol); own san rec; gas; 80% statics; adv bkg acc; games area; CKE. *"Charming, well-kept site in tranquil spot; sm CL-type area for tourers; clean, simple, dated but adequate facs, no facs LS, NH only; levelling blocks ess for m'vans; conv Calais/Dunkerque; quiet but some military aircraft noise; WW1 cemetary nr; gd value; popular excel NH."* **€15.00, 1 Apr-31 Oct.** **2024**

MARQUISE *3A3* (5km SW Rural) *50.78389, 1.66917* **Camping L'Escale,** 15 Route Nationale, 62250 Wacquinghen **03 21 32 00 69; camp-escale@wanadoo.fr; www.escale-camping.fr**

(cont)

Fr A16 S fr Calais exit junc 34. Fr A16 N fr Boulogne exit junc 33. Foll sp. 3*, Lge, pt shd, EHU (4A) €3.50 (poss rev pol); gas; 90% statics; ccard acc. *"Pleasant, busy site; open 24 hrs; conv NH nr ferries, A16, Channel tunnel & WW2 coastal defences; o'fits staying 1 night pitch on meadow at front of site for ease of exit (but some noise fr m'way); m'van 'aire' open all yr; vg; site relandscaped (2017), vg; comfort pitches."* **€30.50, 1 Apr-15 Oct.** **2023**

MARSANNE *9D2* (2.5km NE Rural) *44.65769, 4.89098* **Camping Les Bastets,** Quartier Les Bastets, 26740 Marsanne **04 75 90 35 03; contact@campingles bastets.com; www.campinglesbastets.com**

€4 (htd)

Exit A7 junc 17 onto N7; pass thro Les Tourettes & La Coucourde to Marsanne. In La Coucourde turn L onto D74 & in 6km L onto D105 thro Marsanne. Site sp fr D105. App fr N on D57 not rec. 4*, Med, hdg, mkd, pt shd, sl, terr, EHU (10A); bbq; TV; 10% statics; Eng spkn; adv bkg acc; games rm; archery; bike hire; games area. *"Pleasant site; gd views; beautiful area; vg; infinity pool with views over Valdaine Plaine; 30 new easy access level hdg pitches, some in woods; welcoming site; mini golf, golf 10km; highly rec."* **€24.50, 1 Apr-1 Oct.** **2022**

MARSEILLAN PLAGE *10F1* (7km SE Coastal) *43.31904, 3.55655* **Flower Camping Robinson,** Quai de Plaisance, 34340 Marseillan Plage **04 67 21 90 07; reception@camping-robinson.com; www.camping-robinson.com**

opp

Fr Agde take D612 twds Sete. In Marseillan Plage cont on D612 & cross canal bdge. In abt 300m turn R and foll sp to site. 3*, Med, mkd, pt shd, EHU (10A); twin axles; 33% statics; Eng spkn; adv bkg acc; games area; CKE. *"Gd."* **€38.00, 23 Apr-23 Sep.** **2022**

MARSEILLAN PLAGE *10F1* (0.7km SW Urban/Coastal) *43.31365, 3.54779* **Camping Beauregard Plage,** 250 Chemin de l'Airette, 34340 Marseillan-Plage **04 67 77 15 45; reception@beauregardplage.com; www.camping-beauregard-plage.com**

€2 (allowed LS only) nr nr nr sand adj

On N112 Agde-Sète rd, turn S at rndabt to Marseillan-Plage onto D51 & foll camping sp thro town. Site immed on leaving town cent. 3*, Lge, hdg, pt shd, EHU (6A) inc; bbq; TV; 5% statics; Eng spkn; adv bkg acc; fishing. *"Superb sand beach sheltered by dunes; some pitches soft & sandy; excel for beach holiday; delightful staff; onsite bistro gd value; town is tourist resort & v new; plenty of bars, rest, supermrkt & shops nr."* **€63.80, 15 Mar-13 Oct.** **2024**

FRANCE

MARSEILLAN PLAGE *10F1* (1km SW Coastal) *43.31275, 3.54638* **Camping La Créole,** 74 Ave des Campings, 34340 Marseillan-Plage **04 67 21 92 69; contact@campinglacreole.com; www.campinglacreole.com**

€4 nr nr sand adj

Fr Agde-Sète rd N112, turn S at rndabt onto D51 & foll sp thro town. Narr ent easily missed among lger sites. 3*, Med, mkd, hdstg, hdg, pt shd, EHU (6A) €3.50; 10% statics; phone; adv bkg acc; ccard acc; tennis 1km; games area; CKE. *"Vg, well-kept site; min stay 7 nights Jul-Aug; dir access to excel beach; naturist beach 600m."* **€34.50, 28 Mar-11 Oct. 2020**

MARTRES TOLOSANE *8F3* (1.5km S Rural) *43.19060, 1.01840* **Camping Le Moulin,** 31220 Martres-Tolosane **05 61 98 86 40; info@domainelemoulin.com; www.domainelemoulin.com or www.campinglemoulin.com/en/toulouse-campsite-france/**

€3 nr (htd)

Exit A64 junc 22 (fr N or S) & foll camping sps. Site sp adj Rv Garonne. 4*, Med, hdg, pt shd, pt sl, EHU (6-10A) €4-6; gas; bbq; red long stay; TV; 20% statics; Eng spkn; adv bkg rec; ccard acc; games area; tennis; games rm; bike hire; rv fishing adj; outdoor fitness; canoeing; massages; canoeing; CKE. *"Excel, well-maintained site; friendly welcome; gd, modern san facs; water on all pitches; gd touring base for Spain, Lourdes, etc."* **€30.00, 1 Apr-27 Sep, D28. 2022**

MARVEJOLS *9D1* (1km NE Rural) *44.55077, 3.30440* **Camping Village Le Coulagnet,** Quartier de l'Empery, 48100 Marvejols **06 81 26 71 52 or 04 66 49 28 31; contact@camping-marvejols.com; camping-marvejols.com**

Exit A75 junc 38 onto D900 & N9. Foll E ring rd onto D999, cont over rv & foll sp to site; no R turn into site, cont 500m to Aire de Retournement, & turn L into site. Foll sp 'VVF', camping pt of same complex. NB U-turn bef ent impossible long o'fits; nasty speed humps on app rd. 2*, Sm, hdg, pt shd, EHU (5A) inc (poss rev pol); bbq (sep area); TV; 50% statics; phone; Eng spkn; adv bkg acc; ccard acc; games rm; tennis; games area. *"Well equiped site; san facs immac; sep area for tourers; interesting walled town; rv adj; excel; ent too tight to make u-turn."* **€21.00, 5 May-15 Sep. 2024**

MARVILLE *5C1* (1km N Rural) *49.46294, 5.45859* **Camp Syndicat Mixte de la Vallée de l'Othain,** 55600 Marville **03 29 88 19 06 or 03 29 88 15 15; marville.accueil@wanadoo.fr**

Sp on D643 on app Marville fr both dirs. 1*, Med, hdg, pt shd, EHU (3A); 20% statics; CKE. *"Easy access adj lake; htd covrd pool adj; gd NH."* **1 Feb-30 Nov. 2024**

MASEVAUX *6F3* (1km N Urban) *47.77820, 6.99090* **Camping Les Rives de la Doller (formerly de Masevaux),** 3 Rue du Stade, 68290 Masevaux **03 89 39 83 94 or 06 33 49 44 88 (mob); www.masevaux-camping.fr**

€0.50 (htd) nr

Fr N83 Colmar-Belfort rd take N466 W to Masevaux; site sp. NB D14 fr Thann to Masevaux narr & steep - not suitable c'vans. 3*, Med, mkd, pt shd, EHU (3-6A) €3.20-3.80; red long stay; TV; 40% statics; Eng spkn; adv bkg acc; ccard acc; CKE. *"Pleasant walks; htd pool adj; interesting town - annual staging of Passion Play; helpful, friendly owners; excel facs; sports complex adj; gd cycle rtes; excel; gd site in nice little town; supmkt nrby; close to Ballon d'Alsace."* **€20.00, 1 Apr-19 Oct. 2024**

MASSERET *7B3* (11km N Rural) *45.61142, 1.50110* **Camping de Montréal,** Rue du Petit Moulin, 87380 St Germain-les-Belles **05 55 71 86 20; contact@campingdemontreal.com; www.campingdemontreal.com**

€2.60 (htd) nr (htd)

S fr Limoges on A20; exit junc 42 onto D7B to St Germain-les-Belles; turn R onto D216; site on L in 500m. Site sp in vill. NB Care needed due narr rds. 3*, Med, mkd, hdg, pt shd, terr, EHU (10A) €3; bbq; sw nr; 12% statics; phone; Eng spkn; adv bkg acc; ccard acc; tennis; fishing; watersports; CKE. *"Peaceful, lovely, well-run site in attractive setting o'looking lake; excel, modern, spotless san facs; bike hire 1km; conv A20; a gem of a site; gd rest; vg NH; shops 10 min walk."* **€19.60 2023**

MASSERET *7B3* (5km E Rural) *45.53880, 1.57790* **Camping Domaine des Forges,** Complexe Touristique Bourg, 19510 Lamongerie **05 55 73 44 57; www.domaine-des-forges.fr**

Exit A20 at junc 43 sp Masseret & foll sp Lamongerie. At rndabt turn R, site sp. Site ent bet 2 lge stone pillars. 3*, Med, shd, sl, EHU (5A) €2.30 (poss long lead req some pitches); sw; TV; ccard acc; fishing; golf nr; tennis. *"Pleasant situation; fitness course thro woods & round lake; clean facs; gd NH & longer; crazy golf, tennis on site; gd area for walks."* **€19.00, 1 Apr-30 Sep. 2022**

MASSEUBE *8F3* (0.4km E Rural) *43.42914, 0.58516* **Camping Berges du Gers,** Ave Henri Trilha, 32140 Masseube **06 30 47 26 47 or 05 62 66 01 75; camping.masseube@orange.fr; www.berges-du-gers.fr**

nr nr nr

S fr Auch on D929 to Masseube; turn L onto D27 dir Simorre; site on L in 500m. 3*, Med, shd, EHU (6A) €3; bbq; TV; 10% statics; Eng spkn; adv bkg acc; ccard acc; games area; tennis; bike hire; games rm;.CKE. *"Well-run site in pleasant setting; security barrier; htd pool adj; access to rv; vg."* **€18.00, 1 May-31 Oct. 2023**

MASSEUBE *8F3* (2km E Rural) *43.42748, 0.61142* **Camping Aux Mêmes,** 32140 Bellegarde **05 62 66 91 45 or 06 83 62 02 22; info@gascogne-camping.fr; www.gascogne-camping.fr**

Fr Masseube take D27 E dir Simorre & Bellegarde; in 2.5km turn L (having past sports stadium & driven up hill thro trees); site is 1st farm on R in 300m. Site sp. 3*, Sm, unshd, pt sl, EHU (6A) €3; bbq; TV; Eng spkn; adv bkg acc; tennis nr; canoeing; games rm; sailing nr; golf nr; watersports; bike hire; windsurfing nr; fishing. *"Excel; v friendly & helpful Eng owners."* **€28.00, 1 Apr-15 Sep.** **2023**

MATHES, LES *7B1* (1km WSW Urban) *45.71517, -1.15520* **Camping Monplaisir,** 26 avenue de la Palmyre, 17250 Les Mathes **05 46 22 50 31; camping-monplaisir@orange.fr; www.campingmonplaisirlesmathes.fr**

nr nr nr beach 3.5km

Fr Saujon take D14 to the o'skirts of Tremblade, avoid vill of Arvert & Etaule if towing c'van, rd surface poor & narr. At rndabt take D25 for a sh dist & take L onto D268 twrds La Palmyre. Cont along D141 to o'skirts of Les Mathes, then L at rndabt. Site on L within approx 450m opp cycle hire. 3*, Med, pt shd, pt sl, EHU €4.50; bbq; TV; Eng spkn; ccard acc; games area; games rm. *"Bike hire nrby; crazy golf & childrens car track on site; friendly family owned site, clean & tidy; gd cycle tracks in area; bar 300m; zoo 4km; vg; v clean san facs; open mkt in vill most days."* **€20.00, Apr-Sep.** **2022**

"Satellite navigation makes touring much easier"

Remember most sat navs don't know if you're towing or in a larger vehicle – always use yours alongside maps and site directions.

MATHES, LES *7B1* (2.5km N Rural) *45.72333, -1.17451* **Camping La Palombière,** 1551 Route de la Fouasse, 17570 Les Mathes **05 46 22 69 25 or 06 80 34 31 91; contact@camping-lapalombiere.com; www.camping-lapalombiere.com**

€3 (htd) (htd) sand 5km

Fr La Tremblade bypass foll sp Dirée on D268; site on R in 5km just past Luna Park. 3*, Med, pt shd, EHU (6-10A) €4.50-5; gas; bbq; 10% statics; phone; bus; Eng spkn; ice; games area; CKE. *"Spacious, tranquil site under oaks & pines; lge pitches; palatial san facs; superb beaches 5km (some naturist); excel, spacious site, helpful staff; immac maintained."* **€38.50, 1 Apr-15 Oct.** **2024**

MATHES, LES *7B1* (3.5km N Rural) *45.72980, -1.17929* **Camping Sandaya L'Orée du Bois,** 225 Route de la Bouverie, La Fouasse, 17570 Les Mathes **05 46 22 42 43; www.sandaya.fr/nos-campings/l-oree-du-bois**

€3.60 (htd) sand 4km

Fr A10 to Saintes, then dir Royan. Fr Royan take D25 thro St Palais & La Palmyre twd Phare de la Coubre. Cont 4km past Phare & turn R on D268 to La Fouasse. Site on R in 4km. 4*, Lge, hdstg, mkd, hdg, pt shd, EHU (6A) inc; gas; bbq; red long stay; TV; 50% statics; Eng spkn; adv bkg rec; ccard acc; games rm; bike hire; waterslide; games area; golf 20km; tennis; CKE. *"Well-kept site in pine wood; local beaches ideal for sw & surfing; helpful staff; excel pool area; private san facs some pitches; zoo in La Palmyre worth visit; excel."* **€40.00, 24 May-14 Sep.** **2024**

MATHES, LES *7B1* (3km SW Urban) *45.70133, -1.16613* **Camping Atlantique Parc,** 26 Ave des Mathes, 17570 La Palmyre **05 46 02 17 17; atlantiqueparc@capfun.com; www.camping-atlantique-parc.com**

(€5, 1 per pitch) (htd) sand 2km

Fr N150, in Saujon turn R onto D14 sp Les Mathes for 22km. At 3rd rndabt take 3rd exit sp D14 Ètaules. In Arvert turn L on D141 sp Les Mathes, La Palmyre Zoo. Foll D141 thro Les Mathes, at rndabt take 3rd exit onto Ave des Mathes sp La Palmyre, site ent on L after 1.5km, sp fr rd. 5*, Lge, pt shd, EHU (10A) €7 (poss rev pol); gas; TV; 80% statics; waterslide; fishing 3km; watersports 3km; games rm. *"€30 refundable deposit for card for barriers and san fac access; gd site, espec for families; gd san fac."* **€49.00, Apr-Sep.** **2024**

MATHES, LES *7B1* (2.5km NW Rural) *45.72098, -1.17165* **Camping La Clé des Champs,** 1188 Route de la Fouasse, 17570 Les Mathes **05 56 07 90 17**

€3.80 (htd) (covrd, htd) sand 3.5km

S of La Tremblade, take D141 twd La Palmyre, site sp. 4*, Lge, mkd, pt shd, EHU (6-10A) inc; gas; bbq; TV; 30% statics; Eng spkn; adv bkg acc; ccard acc; fishing 3km; jacuzzi; games area; gym; watersports 3km; games rm; bike hire; sauna; CKE. *"Well-equipped, busy site; many excel beaches in area; modern san facs; local oysters avail; Cognac region; Luna Park nrby."* **€40.00, 2 Apr-5 Nov.** **2021**

MATOUR *9A2* (1km W Rural) *46.305161, 4.482047* **Camp Municipal Le Paluet,** 2 Rue de la Piscine, 71520 Matour **03 86 37 95 83; contact@aquadis-loisirs.com; http://www.matour.fr/en/welcome-to-matour/**

nr (htd)

On W o'skts of Matour off Rte de la Clayette D987. 3*, Med, hdg, mkd, pt shd, EHU (10A) inc; bbq; TV; Eng spkn; adv bkg acc; ccard acc; lake fishing adj; tennis; games area; waterslide; badminton; volleyball; ping pong; CKE. *"Conv touring vineyards; highly rec; facs poss inadequate high ssn."* **€18.50, 1 Apr-25 Oct.** **2020**

MAURS *7D4* (0.8km S Rural) *44.70522, 2.20586* **Camp Municipal Le Vert,** Route de Decazeville, 15600 Maurs **04 71 49 00 32; camping@ville-maurs.fr; www.ville-maurs.fr/tourisme/camping**

Fr Maurs take D663 dir Decazeville. Site on L 400m after level x-ing thro sports complex. Narr ent. 3*, Med, mkd, shd, EHU (15A) inc; adv bkg acc; rv fishing; tennis. *"V pleasant on side of rv; sports complex adj; friendly helpful warden."* **€11.00, 2 May-30 Sep. 2024**

MEAUX *3D3* (4km NE Rural) *49.00301, 2.94139* **Camping Village Parisien,** 13 Route des Otages, 77910 Varreddes **01 64 33 68 74; village-parisien@capfun.com; www.capfun.com/camping-france-ile_de_france-le_village_parisien-FR.html**

Fr Meaux foll sp on D405 dir Soissons then Varreddes, site sp on D121 dir Congis. 4*, Med, hdg, mkd, pt shd, EHU (6A) €2; gas; bbq; red long stay; TV; 85% statics; Eng spkn; adv bkg acc; waterslide; games area; golf 5km; tennis; games rm; fishing; bike hire; CKE. *"Conv Paris cent (drive to metro), Parc Astérix & Disneyland - tickets avail fr site; friendly, helpful staff; cash only; sm pitches; narr site rds; v busy, well-used site."* **€41.00, 1 Apr-5 Nov. 2023**

MEAUX *3D3* (10km SW Rural) *48.91333, 2.73416* **Camping L'International de Jablines,** 77450 Jablines **01 60 26 09 37; welcome@camping-jablines.com; www.camping-jablines.com**

Fr N on A1 then A104 exit Claye-Souilly. Fr E on A4 then A104 exit Meaux. Fr S on A6, A86, A4, A104 exit Meaux. Site well sp 'Base de Loisirs de Jablines'. 3*, Lge, mkd, pt shd, pt sl, EHU (10A) inc; bbq; sw nr; bus to Eurodisney; Eng spkn; adv bkg req; ccard acc; horseriding; windsurfing; bike hire; tennis 500m; fishing; sailing; CKE. *"Clean, well-run, well-guarded site; vg pitches; pelasant staff; san facs poss tired high ssn; ideal for Disneyland (tickets for sale), Paris & Versaille."* **€33.80, 31 Mar-29 Sep. 2023**

MEES, LES *10E3* (11km S Rural) *43.95377, 5.93304* **Little Carpe Diem,** Hameau-Les-Pourcelles, 04190 Les Mées **04 92 34 18 97; contact@littlecarpediem.com; www.littlecarpediem.com/**

Exit A51 junc 20 (fr N) or 19 (fr S) & cross Rv Durance onto D4. Site bet Oraison & Les Mées. Turn onto D754 to Les Pourcelles & foll site sp. 3*, Sm, hdg, mkd, pt shd, pt sl, terr, EHU (6-10A) €4.90; 5% statics; Eng spkn; adv bkg acc. *"Views over beautiful area; friendly owners; occasional out of ssn pitches avail; unrel opening; vg."* **€33.50, 29 Apr-30 Sep. 2022**

MEGEVE *9B3* (2km SW Rural) *45.84120, 6.58887* **FFCC Camping Gai Séjour,** 332 Route de Cassioz, 74120 Megève **04 50 21 22 58**

On D1212 Flumet-Megève rd, site on R 1km after Praz-sur-Arly, well sp. 2*, Med, mkd, pt shd, sl, EHU (4A); Eng spkn; adv bkg acc; CKE. *"Pleasant site with gd views, lge pitches; gd walks; 40km fr Mont Blanc; helpful owners; no free parking in Megeve."* **€15.00, 6 Jan-15 Sep. 2024**

MEHUN SUR YEVRE *4H3* (0.5km N Urban) *47.14797, 2.21725* **Camp Municipal,** Ave du Champ de Foire, 18500 Mehun-sur-Yèvre **02 48 57 44 51; www.ville-mehun-sur-yevre.fr/tourisme/accueil/hebergement-de-plein-air**

Leave A71 junc 6 onto D2076 (N76) dir Bourges. App Mehun & turn L into site at 2nd traff lts. Ave Jean Châtelet is pt of D2076. 2*, Sm, mkd, pt shd, EHU (6A) €2.80 (poss rev pol & long lead req some pitches); twin axles; tennis adj. *"Excel NH conv for m'way; clean, modern san facs; water pnts poss long walk; gates locked 2200-0700 (high ssn); facs open to elements; pool adj; town rather run down, nice park."* **€12.00, 8 May-30 Sep. 2023**

MELE SUR SARTHE, LE *4E1* (0.5km SE Rural) *48.50831, 0.36298* **Camp Intercommunal La Prairie,** La Bretèche, St Julien-Sarthe, 61170 Le Mêle-sur-Sarthe **02 33 27 18 74; camping-la-prairie.com**

Turn off N12 onto D4; site sp in vill. 2*, Med, mkd, pt shd, EHU (6A) inc; adv bkg acc; sailing; tennis; CKE. *"Pt of excel sports complex; vg."* **€11.00, 1 April-31 Oct. 2024**

MELLE *7A2* (11km SW Rural) *46.14421, -0.21983* **Camp Municipal,** Rue des Merlonges, 79170 Brioux-sur-Boutonne **05 49 07 50 46**

On ent Brioux fr Melle on D150 turn R immed over bdge; site on R in 100m. 1*, Sm, pt shd, EHU (6A) €1.80. *"Pleasant rural setting; tidy, well-cared for site; ltd facs but clean; choose own pitch & pay at Mairie on dep if no warden; conv for town; great value; vg sh stay/NH."* **€8.00, 1 Apr-31 Oct. 2023**

MENAT *7A4* (2km E Rural) *46.09579, 2.92899* **Camp Municipal des Tarteaux,** 23 Pont de Menat, 63560 Menat **04 73 85 52 47; campingdemenat@orange.fr; www.camping-lestarteaux.fr/**

Heading SE fr St Eloy-les-Mines on D2144 foll sp Camping Pont de Menat. Exit D2144 at Menat opp Hôtel Pinal. Site alongside Rv Sioule. 2*, Med, shd, pt sl, terr, EHU (16A) €2.70; adv bkg acc; rv fishing 2km; CKE. *"Beautiful site beside rv; Chateau Rocher ruins nrby; boating 2km; OK NH; delightful site; modern san facs in new block (2014)"* **€8.00, 26 Apr-15 Sep. 2024**

MERDRIGNAC *2E3* (2km N Rural) *48.19786, -2.41622* **Camping Le Val de Landrouët,** 14 rue du Gouède, 22230 Merdrignac **02 96 28 47 98; contact@valdelandrouet.com; www.valdelandrouet.com**

nr (htd)

Sp fr town cent, 500m fr town on D793 twd Broons, site on L. Med, hdg, mkd, pt shd, pt sl, EHU (4A) €3; bbq; sw nr; twin axles; 5% statics; bus adj; adv bkg acc; ccard acc; fishing; tennis; CKE. *"Superb, spacious site; mv service pnt (emptying only); gd touring ctr; activities adj; excel."* **€19.00, 30 Apr-30 Sep. 2024**

> **"There aren't many sites open at this time of year"**
>
> If you're travelling outside peak season remember to call ahead to check site opening dates – even if the entry says 'open all year'.

MERENS LES VALS *8G4* (1km W Rural) *42.64633, 1.83083* **Camping de Mérens (formerly Camp Municipal Ville de Bau),** Ville de Bau, 09110 Mérens-les-Vals **05 61 02 85 40 or 05 61 64 33 77; camping.merens@wanadoo.fr; www.camping.merenslesvals.fr**

12 €0.70 (htd)

Fr Ax-les-Thermes on N20 sp Andorra past Mérens-les-Vals turn R nr start of dual c'way sp Camp Municipal. Site on R in 800m. 3*, Med, hdg, EHU (6-10A) inc (poss rev pol); bbq; 20% statics; ccard acc; CKE. *"Excel site; gd clean san facs; gd walks fr site; conv Andorra, Tunnel de Puymorens; all pitches have water taps; pool 8km; lovely walk fr site past Eglise Romane in vill to hot spring with natural bathing pools."* **€20.40 2023**

MERS LES BAINS *3B2* (1.5km NE Rural) *50.07730, 1.41540* **Flower Camping Le Rompval,** Lieudit Blengues, 154 Rue André Dumont, 80350 Mers-les-Bains **02 35 84 43 21; campinglerompval@gmail.com; www.camping-lerompval.com**

€3 (htd) (covrd, htd) sand 2.5km

Fr Calais on A16, exit junc 23 at Abbeville onto A28. In 5km exit junc 2 onto D925 dir Friville-Escarbotin, Le Tréport. In approx 20km at rndabt junc with D19 foll sp Ault & at next rndabt take D940 twd Mers-les-Bains. In St Quentin-la-Motte turn R, site on R, sp. Fr S on A28 exit junc 5 onto D1015 to Mers-les-Bains & foll sp Blengues & site. 3*, Med, hdstg, mkd, hdg, unshd, EHU (6-13A) €4-6.50; gas; bbq; red long stay; TV; 25% statics; Eng spkn; adv bkg acc; ccard acc; tennis 3km; games rm; bike hire; games area; CKE. *"Vg site; library; gd facs."* **€32.00, 4 Apr-2 Nov. 2024**

MESNIL ST PERE *6F1* (2km NE Rural) *48.26329, 4.34633* **Kawan Village Camping Lac d'Orient,** Rue du Lac, 10140 Mesnil-St Père **03 25 40 61 85; info@camping-lacdorient.com; www.camping-lacdorient.com**

€3 (htd) nr (covrd, htd)

On D619 foll sps Lac de la Forêt d'Orient. Approx 10km fr Vendeuvre or 20km fr Troyes turn N on D43A, to Mesnil-St Père; site sp. Sp at ent to site: 'Camping Lac d'Orient' (with 'Kawan Village' in v sm lettering). 4*, Lge, hdstg, mkd, hdg, pt shd, pt sl, EHU (10A) inc; bbq; sw nr; 10% statics; phone; Eng spkn; adv bkg acc; ccard acc; watersports 500m; games rm; fishing; games area; tennis; jacuzzi; CKE. *"Peaceful site with mature trees next to lake & forest; lge pitches; 1st class san facs; no o'fits over 10m high ssn; poss muddy when wet; conv Nigloland theme park & Champagne area; conv A26; excel spacious site; excel cycle rte; private san facs some pitches; fantastic rest over looking lake; vg."* **€47.00, 8 Apr - 25 Sep, J07. 2022**

MESSANGES *8E1* (2km SW Coastal) *43.79790, -1.40135* **Airotel Camping Le Vieux Port,** 850 Route de la Plage Sud, 40660 Messanges, Landes **01 76 76 70 00; contact@levieuxport.com; contact@resasol.com**

€3.90 (covrd, htd, indoor) sand 400m

Fr S take D652 past Vieux-Boucau; site sp. Turn W at Super U rndabt. 5*, V lge, hdstg, mkd, shd, EHU (6A) inc; gas; bbq; red long stay; TV; 10% statics; Eng spkn; adv bkg acc; ccard acc; horseriding; waterslide; tennis; bike hire; games area; CKE. *"V pleasant, clean site; dir access to sand beach; quad bikes; superb, v lge pool complex; excel touring base."* **€26.00, 24 Mar - 4 Nov, A14. 2022**

METZ *5D2* (1.5km NW Urban) *49.12402, 6.16917* **Camp Municipal Metz-Plage,** Allée de Metz-Plage, 57000 Metz **03 87 68 26 48; campingmetz@mairie-metz.fr; www.metz.fr**

€0.60

Fr W exit A31 junc 33 Metz-Nord/Pontiffroy exit; cross rv bdges Pont Canal & Pont des Morts; then immed turn L into Allée de Metz-Plage; site in 200m (or after leaving A31 at junc 33, at rndabt turn R & foll sps). Fr E foll 'Autres Directions' over A31 & Rv Moselle, then as above. 3*, Lge, mkd, hdstg, pt shd, pt sl, EHU (10A) inc (poss rev pol); twin axles; Eng spkn; adv bkg acc; ccard acc; rv fishing adj; CKE. *"Spacious, well-situated on rv with views; some gd sized pitches; helpful staff; poss long walk to san facs; rv unfenced; facs stretched if site full; early arr ess high ssn; vg; fac's need updating; wifi in designated areas; pool adj; excel."* **€24.00, 15 Apr-30 Sep. 2024**

FRANCE

MEYRAS *9 D2* (4.7km SE Rural) *44.66480, 4.29409* **Camping La Charderie,** 410 route de Bayzan, 07380 Pont-de-Labeaume **04 75 38 00 52; la.charderie@wanadoo.fr; www.camping-lacharderie.com**

river sand beach

Fr Aubenas twrds Le Puy-en-Velay on the N102. At Pont de Labeaume, R over narr stone bdge. Site on R in 200m. 3*, Sm, mkd, pt shd, pt sl, EHU 10A (€4.50); gas; bbq (elec); sw; Eng spkn; adv bkg acc; ccard acc; games area; games rm; CCI. *"Excel; gd walks."* **€27.70, 18 Apr-3 Oct. 2024**

MEYRUEIS *10E1* (0.5km E Rural) *44.18075, 3.43540* **Camping Le Jardin des Cevennes,** Route de la Brèze, 48150 Meyrueis **04 66 45 60 51; infocamping@jardindescevennes.com; www.campinglejardindescevennes.com/**

€1 nr (htd)

Fr W on D907 dir Gorges de la Jonte into Meyrueis. Foll sp Château d'Ayres & site. 3*, Med, hdg, mkd, pt shd, pt sl, EHU (6A) €3; bbq; 15% statics; phone; Eng spkn; adv bkg acc; ccard acc; games rm; games area; bike hire; CKE. *"Helpful owners; rec."* **€26.50, 27 Apr-25 Sep. 2020**

MEZE *10F1* (1km N Coastal) *43.43019, 3.61070* **Kawan Village Beau Rivage,** 113 Route Nationale, 34140 Mèze **0466 600 700; beau-rivage@koawa.com; www.camping-beaurivage.fr**

€6 (htd) sand 700m

Fr Mèze cent foll D613 dir Montpellier, site on R 100m past rndabt on leaving town; well sp. 4*, Lge, mkd, pt shd, EHU (3-6A) inc; bbq; TV; 50% statics; phone; Eng spkn; adv bkg acc; ccard acc; sailing; tennis 900m; fishing; CKE. *"Well equipped site; trees & narr access rds poss diff lge o'fits; vg modern san facs; lovely pool; pitches poss worn end of ssn; fitness rm; poor security - rear of site open to public car park; diff exit onto busy coast rd; conv Sète & Noilly Prat distillery; vg; excel site; close to town with gd mkt, marina and rest."* **€40.00, 10 Apr-17 Sep. 2024**

MEZE *10F1* (3km N Rural) *43.44541, 3.61595* **Camp Municipal Loupian,** Route de Mèze, 34140 Loupian **04 67 43 57 67 or 04 67 43 82 07 (LS); camping@loupian.fr; www.loupian.fr**

€1 sand 3km

Fr Mèze tak D613 & turn L at 1st Loupian sp, then foll sp for site. 3*, Med, mkd, hdg, pt shd, EHU (6A); bbq; phone; Eng spkn; adv bkg acc; tennis; CKE. *"Pleasant site in popular area; plenty shd; friendly, helpful staff; vg san facs; takeaway; gd beaches; excel fisherman's rest; gd rests at Mèze & Bouzigues; superb cycling on old rlwy rte fr site to Mèze (Voie Verte); rec; cent to main attractions; gd value site; excel."* **€19.00, 6 Apr-14 Oct. 2024**

MEZIERES EN BRENNE *4H2* (6km E Rural) *46.79817, 1.30595* **Camping Bellebouche,** 36290 Mézières-en-Brenne **02 54 38 28 28; contact@bellebouche.fr; www.village-vacances-bellebouche.com**

(cont)

Sp on D925. 3*, Med, mkd, pt shd, pt sl, EHU €3.50; bbq (elec); sw nr; 10% statics; phone; ccard acc; fishing; watersports; CKE. *"In country park; gd walking, cycling, birdwatching; vg; san facs dated."* **€11.00, 30 Apr-30 Sep. 2024**

MEZOS *8E1* (1km SE Rural) *44.07980, -1.16090* **Le Village Tropical Sen Yan,** 40170 Mézos, Landes **05 58 42 60 05; reception@sen-yan.com; www.sen-yan.com**

€6 (covrd, htd, indoor)

Fr Bordeaux on N10 in 100km at Laharie turn W onto D38 dir Mimizan; in 12km turn L onto D63 to Mézos; turn L at mini-rndabt; site on L in approx 2km. Site 1.5km fr D63/D38 junc NE of Mézos. 5*, Lge, mkd, hdg, shd, EHU (6A) inc; gas; bbq (gas); TV; 80% statics; phone; Eng spkn; adv bkg acc; ccard acc; waterslide; tennis; watersports 15km; jacuzzi; bike hire; rv fishing adj; games rm; sauna; CKE. *"Attractive, restful site; many plants, inc banana trees; fitness cent; no o'fits over 8m; canoe hire 1km; modern, many sports & games; clean san facs; excel facs for families; mkt Mimizan Fri & Morcenx Wed."* **€47.00, 1 Jun-9 Sep. 2020**

MILLAS *8G4* (7km SW Urban) *42.67165, 2.62907* **Camp Municipal Le Colomer,** Rue Colonel Fabien, 66130 Ile-sur-Tet **04 68 56 79 67; contact@camping-le-colomer.fr; www.camping-le-colomer.fr**

€1.50

Exit N116 on NE of town, R twds Ille sur Tet on D916, L at next rndabt foll sp to site. Med, hdg, pt shd, EHU (10A) €4; 30% statics; bus adj, train 0.5km; Eng spkn; adv bkg req; games area; CKE. *"Conv for Les Orgues cliffs & Prieure de Serrabone; gd rests in attractive town; pool 200m; adj rlwy not busy but conv for Perpignan; vg."* **€11.30, 1 Nov-30 Sep. 2022**

MILLAU *10E1* (7km N Rural) *44.15188, 3.09899* **Camping La Belle Etoile,** Chemin des Prades, 12520 Aguessac **05 65 72 91 07 ou 06 72 23 10 56 (mob); contact@camping-labelleetoile.fr; www.camping-labelleetoile.fr**

€2 nr

Site on N907 in vill; ent on R v soon after level x-ing when app fr Millau. 2*, Med, mkd, pt shd, EHU (6A) inc; gas; canoeing; games area; rv fishing adj; CKE. *"Nice, spacious, clean rvside site; gd position with mountain views; gd sized pitches; helpful & friendly staff; public footpath thro site along rv to picturesque vill; poss youth groups high ssn; sports grnd adj; excel touring base; vg location; vg quiet site."* **€23.00, 27 Apr-30 Sep. 2024**

MILLAU *10E1* (1km NE Urban) *44.10500, 3.08833* **Camping du Viaduc,** Millau-Cureplat, 121 Ave du Millau-Plage, 12100 Millau **05 65 60 15 75; info@camping-du-viaduc.com; www.camping-du-viaduc.com**

€3 (htd) (htd)

Exit Millau on N991 (sp Nant) over Rv Tarn via Cureplat bdge. At rndabt take D187 dir Paulhe, 1st campsite on L. 4*, Lge, mkd, hdg, shd, serviced pitches; EHU (6A) €4 (poss long lead req); gas; bbq; sw; red long stay; 20% statics; Eng spkn; ccard acc; CKE. *"Peaceful, well-run site; helpful, welcoming staff; excel, clean san facs; barrier clsd 2200-0700; many sports & activities in area; conv for gorges & viaduct tours; quiet; super site."* **€36.00, 13 Apr-30 Sep. 2024**

MILLAU *10E1* (1.6km NE Rural) *44.10640, 3.08800* **Camping Les Erables,** Ave de Millau-Plage, 12100 Millau **05 65 59 15 13; camping-les-erables@orange.fr; www.campingleserables.fr**

€1.20 (htd)

Exit Millau on D991 (sp Nant) over Rv Tarn bdge; take L at island sp to Millau-Plage & site on L immed after Camping du Viaduc & bef Camping Larribal. On ent Millau fr N or S foll sps 'Campings'. 3*, Med, hdg, mkd, shd, EHU (10A) €3 (rev pol); bbq; sw nr; TV; phone; Eng spkn; adv bkg acc; ccard acc; canoeing adj; CKE. *"Peaceful, well-kept, clean site on banks of Rv Tarn; lge shd pitches; friendly, helpful owners; excel modern san facs; some pitches poss diff lge o'fits; excel walking; beavers nrby; Millau Viaduct Vistor Cent a must; excel."* **€20.00, 1 Apr-30 Sep. 2023**

MILLAU *10E1* (2km NE Urban) *44.10240, 3.09100* **Camping Indigo Millau,** Ave de l'Aigoual, 12100 Millau **05 65 61 18 83; millau@camping-indigo.com; www.camping-indigo.com or www.europe.huttopia.com/site/camping-millau**

€4.60 (htd)

Fr N exit A75 junc 45 to Millau. Turn L at 2nd traff island sp 'Camping'. Site on R over bdge in 200m. Fr S exit A75 junc 47 onto D809 & cross rv on by-pass, turn R at 1st traff island sp Nant on D991, cross bdge, site on R in 200m, sp. Site a S confluence of Rv Dourbie & Rv Tarn. 3*, Med, mkd, shd, pt sl, EHU (5A) €3.50; gas; sw nr; 10% statics; Eng spkn; adv bkg acc; fishing nr; games; CKE. *"Excel site; gd san facs, renovated 2015; hang-gliding nrby; pleasant, helpful owner; canoe hire nr; conv Tarn Gorges; lge mkt Fri."* **€28.90, 19 Apr-29 Sep, D17. 2024**

MILLAU *10E1* (1km E Urban) *44.10287, 3.08732* **Camping des Deux Rivières,** 61 Ave de l'Aigoual, 12100 Millau **01 40 44 78 70 or 06 44 78 61 60; camping-chaumont-montmarte@gmail.com; www.camping-des-deux-rivieres.fr**

12 €1.50 (htd) nr

Fr N on D911 foll sp for Montpellier down to rv. At rndabt by bdge turn L over bdge, site immed on L well sp. Fr S on D992 3rd bdge, sp camping. 3*, Sm, mkd, shd, EHU (8-10A) €3 (poss long lead req); gas; phone; fishing; CKE. *"Basic site in gd situation by rv; friendly, helpful owners; gd san facs; gd base for touring gorges."* **€28.00 2024**

MILLAU *10E1* (1km E Rural) *44.10166, 3.09611* **Camping Les Rivages,** Ave de l'Aigoual, 12100 Millau **05 65 61 01 07; info@campinglesrivages.com; www.campinglesrivages.com**

€4 (htd) (htd)

Fr Millau take D991 dir Nant (sp Gorges de la Dourbie & Campings). Cross Rv Tarn & cont on this rd, site is 500m after bdge on R. 4*, Lge, pt shd, serviced pitches; EHU (10A) inc (poss rev pol); bbq; sw nr; red long stay; twin axles; TV; 10% statics; phone; Eng spkn; adv bkg acc; ccard acc; canoeing nr; squash; fishing; games area; tennis; games rm; CKE. *"Pleasant, busy, scenic site - esp rv/side pitches; helpful & friendly staff; immac, clean san facs; vg rest/snack bar - home cooked & inexpensive; gd security; views of Millau viaduct; hang-gliding; spa; easy access to town; mkt Wed & Fri; pleasant cycle ride along rvbank; v nice site."* **€45.00, 15 Apr - 30 Sep, D20. 2022**

MILLAU *10E1* (2.5km E Rural) *44.10029, 3.11099* **FFCC Camping St Lambert,** Ave de l'Aigoual, 12100 Millau **05 65 60 00 48; contact@campingsaintlambert.fr; www.campingsaintlambert.fr**

€1

Fr N on either D809 or D11 foll dir D992 St Affrique/Albi. Turn L at rndabt over bdge onto D991 dir Nant. Site on R, sp. Fr S on D992 turn R at rndabt & dir as above. 3*, Med, mkd, shd, EHU (6A); gas; sw nr; 10% statics; adv bkg acc; ccard acc; CKE. *"Spacious, gd site; sm pitches, all under trees; stretched high ssn; site needed gd tidy up, but nice atmosphere; 30min walk into Millau; gd LS; owners pleasant & helpful; lovely area."* **€20.50, 27 Apr-20 Oct. 2024**

MIMIZAN *7D1* (2km N Rural) *44.21997, -1.22968* **Camping du Lac,** Ave de Woolsack, 40200 Mimizan **05 58 09 01 21; lac@mimizan-camping.com; https://siblu.co.uk/camping/france/south-west-coast/nouvelle-aquitaine/mimizan-lac**

€1.70

Fr Mimizan N on D87, site on R. 2*, Lge, mkd, pt shd, EHU (3A) inc; gas; bbq; 10% statics; adv bkg acc; boating; fishing. *"Nice site in lovely location; lake adj - no sw; o'night m'vans area; rec."* **€20.00, 27 Apr-20 Sep. 2024**

FRANCE

MIMIZAN *7D1* (3km E Rural) *44.22296, -1.19445* **Camping Aurilandes,** 1001 Promenade de l'Etang, 40200 Aureilhan **05 58 09 10 88; www.campingaurilandes.com**

€3 (htd)

Fr N10 S of Bordeaux take D626 W fr Labouheyre twds Mimizan. Site 1km fr D626 by Lake Aureilhan. V lge, mkd, pt shd, EHU (6-10A) inc; Eng spkn; adv bkg acc; ccard acc; watersports; sauna; tennis; games rm. *"Dir access to lake; spa."* **€44.00, 27 Apr-9 Sep.** 2024

MIMIZAN PLAGE *7D1* (0.7km E Coastal) *44.21629, -1.28584* **Camping de la Plage,** Blvd d'Atlantique, 40200 Mimizan-Plage **05 58 09 00 32; contact@mimizan-camping.com; www.campingsgrandsud.fr/camping/camping-mimizan-plage**

€1.80 sand 850m

Turn off N10 at Labouheyre on D626 to Mimizan (28km). Approx 5km after Mimizan turn R. Site in approx 500m. 3*, V lge, shd, pt sl, EHU (10A) inc; bbq; 20% statics; games area. *"Gd facs; town nrby; big busy coastal site; many cycle paths; excel."* **€24.00, 7 Apr-30 Sep.** 2023

MIMIZAN PLAGE *7D1* (3km E Coastal) *44.20420, -1.2908* **Club Marina-Landes,** Rue Marina, 40200 Mimizan-Plage-Sud **05 58 09 12 66; marina-landes@vagues-oceanes.com; www.camping-club-marina.com**

€5 (covrd, htd) sand 500m

Turn R off N10 at Labouheyre onto D626 to Mimizan (28km). Approx 5km fr Mimizan-Plage turn L at Camping Marina sp on dual c'way. Site sp on S bank of rv. 4*, V lge, hdstg, hdg, pt shd, EHU (10A) €7; gas; bbq; TV; 10% statics; Eng spkn; adv bkg acc; ccard acc; ice; golf 7km; games area; horseriding; games rm; bike hire; waterslide; fitness rm; tennis; CKE. *"Excursions to Dax, Biarritz & Bordeaux areas; excel leisure facs; excel; great location."* **€66.00, 13 May-25 Sep.** 2023

MIRAMBEAU *7C2* (0.5km N Urban) *45.37822, -0.56874* **Aire Park Mirambeau (formerly Municipal Le Carrelet),** 92 Ave de la République, 17150 Mirambeau **05 46 49 60 73; accueil.mairie@mirambeau17.fr; https://www.aireparkreservation.com/aires-camping-cars/nouvelle-aquitaine/charente-maritime/mirambeau**

(cont) nr

Exit 37 fr A10 onto D730/D137 dir Mirambeau. Site opp Super U supmkt, behind TO. 2*, Sm, pt shd, pt sl, EHU (10A) inc; gas; 80% statics; phone; ccard acc. *"Basic site; clean but tired facs; obliging warden; site yourself & warden calls evening; v muddy when wet; poss neglected LS; conv NH for A10; no longer a campsite; now a camperstop (2019); toilet block clsd; Ccd payment at machine allws access."* **€8.00, 1 Apr-31 Oct.** 2024

MIRAMBEAU *7C2* (8km S Rural) *45.31430, -0.60290* **Camping Chez Gendron,** 2 Chez Jandron, 33820 Saint Palais **05 57 32 96 47; info@chezgendron.com; www.chezgendron.com**

(htd) nr

N fr Blaye on N137; turn to St Palais, past church 1km; turn L twd St Ciers. Site sp R down narr lane. Or N fr Bordeaux on A10 exit juncs 37 or 38 onto N137 to St Palais & as above. 3*, Sm, mkd, pt shd, pt sl, terr, EHU (6A) inc; bbq; TV; phone; Eng spkn; adv bkg rec; games rm; tennis 3km; games area; CKE. *"Peaceful & relaxed site in vineyards; lovely ambience; friendly, helpful Dutch owners; sep car park high ssn; superb san facs; ltd facs LS; pitches nr bar/recep poss noisy till late peak ssn; poss waterlogged after heavy rain; chem disp poor; excel Sun mkt."* **€23.20, 15 Mar-15Oct.** 2024

MIRAMBEAU *7C2* (15km W Coastal) *45.38333, -0.72250* **Camping L'Estuaire,** 3 Route de l'Estuaire, 17150 St Thomas-de-Cônac **05 46 86 08 20; info@lestuaire.com; www.lestuaire.com**

12 €4 (htd)

Exit A10 junc 37 Mirambeau onto D730 dir Royan. At St Ciers-du-Taillon foll sp St Thomas-de-Cônac, site sp. 4*, Lge, mkd, hdg, unshd, EHU (16A) inc; bbq; TV; 60% statics; adv bkg acc; games area; gym; bike hire; watersports nr; fishing; tennis. *"Interesting area nr Gironde estuary; gd walking & cycling."* **€20.00** 2022

MIRAMONT DE GUYENNE *7D2* (7km NW Rural) *44.62877, 0.29135* **Camp Municipal d'Allemans du Dropt,** Rue du Pont, 47800 Allemans-du-Dropt **05 53 20 25 59 or 05 53 20 23 37 (Mairie)**

nr nr nr

Fr D668 site well sp in vill. Sm, shd, EHU (20A); canoeing; kayaking; CKE. *"Attractive site on opp side of Rv Dropt to vill; friendly warden lives on site; ltd pitches for c'vans & lge o'fits due trees & o'hanging branches; basic but clean facs; easy walk to vill; excel."* **€13.40, 1 Apr-15 Oct.** 2022

MIRANDE *8F2* (1km NE Rural) *43.55235, 0.31371* **Camping Pouylebon (Devroome),** Pouylebon, 32320 Montesquiou **662 73 83 62 or 662 73 83 62; domainedecalabel@gmail.com; www.domainedecalabel.com**

Exit N21 NW at Mirande onto D159; in 10km, at Pouylebon, turn R onto D216; in 900m site on R, 600m down track. Sm, pt shd, pt sl, EHU (6A) €2.85; bbq; TV; Eng spkn; adv bkg acc; games area; games rm; tennis nr; horseriding nr; fishing nr. *"Rural retreat; charming, Dutch owners; meals on request; dogs free; excel."* **€26.00, 15 Apr-15 Oct.** 2024

MIRANDE *8F2* (0.5km E Rural) *43.51432, 0.40990* **Camping Paradis Île du Pont,** Au Batardeau, 32300 Mirande **05 62 66 64 11; www.camping-iledupont.com**

€1 (htd)

On N21 Auch-Tarbes, foll sp to site on island in Rv Grande Baise. 3*, Med, pt shd, EHU (6A) inc; bbq; 20% statics; adv bkg rec; bike hire; games rm; sailing; canoeing; windsurfing; tennis; waterslide; fishing; CKE. *"Excel site; helpful staff; quiet location; 5min walk to town; gd stopover if heading to pyrenees."* **€20.00, 15 Apr-30 Sep.** **2022**

MIREPOIX (ARIEGE) *8F4* (1km E Rural) *43.08871, 1.88585* **Camping Les Nysades,** Route de Limoux, 09500 Mirepoix **05 61 60 28 63; campinglesnysades@orange.fr; www.camping-mirepoix-ariege.com**

€2 nr

E fr Pamiers on D119 to Mirepoix. Site well sp on D626. 2*, Med, hdg, mkd, shd, EHU (6A) €3.50; 10% statics; fishing 1km; tennis. *"Lge pitches; san facs ok; site a bit tired; interesting medieval town; mkt Mon rec; gd little site, walks along rv; barrier open 0700-2300, if warden not on site he will collect fees later."* **€15.00, 16 Apri-31 Oct.** **2023**

MODANE *9C4* (1km W Rural) *45.19437, 6.66413* **Camping Les Combes,** Refuge de La Sapinière, Route de Bardonnèche, 73500 Modane **04 79 05 00 23 or 06 10 16 54 61 (mob); camping-modane@wanadoo.fr; http://camping-modane.chez-alice.fr**

12 €1.50 (htd) nr

Exit A43 junc 30 onto D1006 thro Fourmeaux to o'skirts Modane; at Casino supmkt turn R onto D215; site in 500m on bend on hill (at junc with D216). Fr Fréjus tunnel site on L 1km bef Modane. 2*, Med, pt shd, pt sl, EHU (6A) €3; 10% statics; tennis. *"Excel & conv NH for Fréjus tunnel; warm welcome; winter sports; superb scenery; ltd san facs; LS recep opens 1700 - site yourself."* **€13.00** **2024**

MOISSAC *8E3* (2km S Rural) *44.09664, 1.08878* **Camping Le Moulin du Bidounet,** St Benoît, 82200 Moissac **05 63 32 52 52; info@camping-moissac.com; www.camping-moissac.com**

€1.50 nr nr

Exit A62/E72 at junc 9 at Castelsarrasin onto D813 dir Moissac. Or fr N on D813 cross Rv Tarn, turn L at 1st rndabt & foll camp sp, site on L by rv. NB Height restriction 3.05m for tunnel at ent & tight turn lge o'fits. 3*, Med, hdg, mkd, hdstg, shd, EHU (6A) €3.10, bbq; red long stay; 10% statics; phone; Eng spkn; adv bkg acc; ccard acc; canoe hire; fishing; bike hire; watersports; boat hire; CKE. *"Excel, pleasant, rvside site in lovely area; extra for twin axles; helpful staff; basic, clean san facs; conv lovely town & abbey; gd fishing; walking/cycling; vg cycle track by canal; gd NH; entry tight for lge o'fits; passport identity needed."* **€24.20, 1 Apr-30 Sep.** **2024**

MOLIETS ET MAA *8E1* (2km W Coastal) *43.85166, -1.38375* **Camping Les Cigales,** Ave de l'Océan, 40660 Moliets-Plage **05 58 48 51 18; reception@camping-les-cigales.fr; www.camping-les-cigales.fr**

€2 sand 300m

In Moliets-et-Maa, turn W for Moliets-Plage, site on R in vill. 3*, Lge, shd, pt sl, EHU (5A) €3.50; bbq; TV; 80% statics; adv bkg acc; ccard acc; games area; CKE. *"Site in pine wood - sandy soil; narr access tracks; excel beach & surfing; many shops, rests 100m; gd forest walk to N."* **€30.70, 1 Apr-30 Sep.** **2024**

MOLIETS ET MAA *8E1* (2km W Coastal) *43.85210, -1.38730* **Camping St Martin,** Ave de l'Océan 40660 Moliets-Plage **05 58 48 52 30; contact@camping-saint-martin.fr; www.camping-saint-martin.fr**

€5 (htd) (covrd, htd) sand 300m

On N10 exit for Léon, Moliets-et-Maa. At Moliets foll sp to Moliets-Plage. Camp site after Les Cigales, by beach. 4*, V lge, mkd, hdg, pt shd, pt sl, terr, serviced pitches; EHU (10A) €5.30; gas; TV; Eng spkn; adv bkg rec; ccard acc; games area; jacuzzi; tennis nr; watersports; golf nr; sauna; CKE. *"Excel family site; cycle paths; vg san facs; gd for teenagers; gd cycling, walking."* **€63.20, 8 Apr-31 Oct.** **2023**

MOLSHEIM *6E3* (0.9km SE Urban) *48.54124, 7.50003* **Camp Municipal de Molsheim,** 6 Rue des Sports, 67120 Molsheim **03 88 49 82 45 or 03 88 49 58 58 (LS); camping-molsheim@orange.fr; www.mairie-molsheim.fr**

€1.30

On ent town fr Obernai on D1422 site sp on R immed after x-ing sm rv bdge. 2*, Med, mkd, pt shd, EHU (10A) €3.40; bbq; train to Strasbourg 700m; Eng spkn; adv bkg acc; bike hire; CKE. *"Pleasant site; excel san facs; pool adj; easy walk to town cent & shops; Bugatti museum in town; vg."* **€22.80, 25 Mar-31 Oct.** **2023**

MONASTIER SUR GAZEILLE, LE *9C1* (1km SW Rural) *44.93662, 3.98453* **Camping Estela,** Route du Moulin de Savin, 43150 Le Monastier-sur-Gazeille **06 87 48 60 28 (mob) or 04 71 03 82 24; estelacamping@gmail.com; campingestela.fr/camping-lestela-chemin-de-stevenson**

€2.50

Fr Le Puy-en-Velay E on D535; in 4km fork R continuing on D535 to Le Monastier-sur-Gazeille; site sp fr ent to vill. App only fr N end of vill. Site in bottom of valley; gd power-weight ratio needed on dep. 2*, Sm, pt shd, EHU (3-10A) €3.20; bbq; sw. *"Lovely rvside site in beautiful area; friendly staff; Le Monastier was start of RL Stevenson's 'Travels with a Donkey'."* **€18.00, 1 Jun-30 Sep.** **2024**

MONETIER LES BAINS, LE *9C3* (1km NW Rural) *44.98059, 6.49537* **Camp Municipal Les Deux Glaciers,** 05220 Le Monêtier-les-Bains **07 89 56 58 77; camping.monetier@orange.fr; www.monetier.com**

€1 (htd) nr nr nr

On D1091 12km NW of Briançon; pass thro Le Monêtier-les-Bains, in 1km site sp on L. 2*, Med, mkd, hdstg, shd, terr, EHU (16A) €3.50; bus 1km; adv bkg acc; CKE. *"Excel, scenic site bef x-ing Montgenèvre pass; gd base for Ecrins National Park; easy access fr D1091; footpath to vill; v friendly helpful staff; immac gd facs; excel for hiking, cycling, wildlife & flowers; fantastic loc; clean."* **€15.50, 1 Jun-30 Sep.** **2023**

MONFORT *8E3* (0.1km N Urban) *43.79628, 0.82315* **Pays de Montfort (Formerly Camp Municipal de Monfort),** 32120 Monfort **05 62 06 83 26 (Mairie); www.paysdemontfort.com**

€0.50 nr nr nr

SE fr Fleurance on D654 to Monfort, then foll sp to 'Cent Ville' & camping sp. Town has narr rds so foll sp & v narr app rd. 1*, Sm, hdg, pt shd, pt sl, EHU (5A) €1.50; bbq; CKE. *"Well-kept, scenic, CL-type site on ramparts of attractive Bastide vill; pitch yourself, warden calls am & pm; ltd pitches big enough for c'van; long walk to waste disposal; excel; pitches well prepared and solid."* **€9.50, 1 May-15 Oct.** **2024**

MONISTROL D'ALLIER *9C1* (4km N Rural) *44.99148, 3.67781* **Camp Municipal Le Marchat,** 43580 St Privat-d'Allier **04 71 57 22 13; info@mairie-saint privatdallier.fr; www.mairie-saintprivatdallier.fr**

nr nr

Fr Le Puy-en-Velay W on D589. Turn R in cent of vill at petrol stn, site on R in 200m. 2*, Sm, hdg, shd, terr, EHU (10A) €1.10. *"Beautifully-kept, superb sm site; friendly warden; not suitable lge o'fits; bars & shop within 200mtrs."* **€6.00, 1 May-1 Nov.** **2023**

MONISTROL SUR LOIRE *9C1* (7km SE Rural) *45.21630, 4.21240* **Kawan Village Camping de Vaubarlet,** 43600 Ste Sigolène **04 71 66 64 95; camping@vaubarlet.com; www.vaubarlet.com**

€4 (htd)

Fr Monistrol take D44 SE twd Ste Sigolène & turn R into vill. In vill take D43 dir Grazac for 6km. Site by Rv Dunière, ent L bef bdge. Site well sp fr vill. 4*, Med, mkd, pt shd, EHU (6A) €3 (poss rev pol); bbq; sw nr; TV; 15% statics; phone; Eng spkn; adv bkg acc; ccard acc; trout fishing; games area; bike hire; CKE. *"Friendly, helpful staff; well-run site; excel, spotless san facs; interesting museums nrby; ideal for families."* **€45.00, 8 Apr - 31 Oct, L23.** **2022**

MONPAZIER *7D3* (3km SW Rural) *44.65875, 0.87925* **Camping Moulin de David,** Route de Villeréal, 24540 Gaugeac-Monpazier **05 53 22 65 25; contact@ moulindedavid.com; www.moulindedavid.com**

€3 (htd)

Fr Monpazier, take D2 SW twd Villeréal, site sp on L after 3km. Narr app rds. 4*, Lge, mkd, hdg, pt shd, serviced pitches; EHU (10A) inc gas; bbq; sw; TV; 80% statics; Eng spkn; adv bkg acc; ccard acc; games rm; waterslide; archery; bike hire; tennis; fishing adj; games area; CKE. *"Charming site nr lovely town; welcoming, helpful owners; excel facs, ltd LS; poss mosquitoes nr rv thro site; mkt Thur Monpazier; highly rec; v rural; superb rest."* **€31.00, 1 May-15 Sep.** **2024**

MONS LA TRIVALLE *10F1* (2.5km SE Rural) *43.56247, 2.97306* **Camping le Claps(formerly Camp Municipal de Tarassac),** 34390 Mons-la-Trivalle **04 67 97 72 64; camping@monslatrivalle.fr; camping-leclaps.fr/en/**

Fr D908 turn S onto D14, sp Béziers; site off D14 on Rv Orb. Lge, hdstg, mkd, shd, pt sl, EHU; sw nr; 10% statics; phone; fishing adj. *"Fair sh stay; watersports cent adj; pitches bounded by boulders; beautiful area; site a bit unkept; v natural enviroment; vg."* **€16.00, 6 April-21 Sept.** **2024**

MONT DORE, LE *7B4* (4km SE Rural) *45.571474, 2.817692* **Domaine de la Grande Cascade,** Route de Besse, 63240 Le Mont-Dore **04 73 65 06 23; contact@ camping-grandecascade.com; www.camping-grande cascade.com**

€1

Fr Le Mont-Dore take D36 (12% incline) via col rte twd Besse-en-Chandesse. Site on R visible fr rd after 4km. App fairly steep & winding with poor surface. 2*, Med, hdg, mkd, pt shd, pt sl, EHU (6A); cooking facs; 5% statics; Eng spkn; adv bkg acc; games area; CKE. *"Excel; simple with magnificent, stunning mountain views; walk to waterfall; modern clean san facs; helpful staff."* **€15.00, 13 May-15 Oct.** **2023**

MONT LOUIS *8G4* (5km W Rural) *42.50636, 2.04671* **Camping Huttopia Font-Romeu,** Route de Mont-Louis, 66120 Font-Romeu **04 68 30 09 32; font-romeu@ huttopia.com; www.huttopia.com**

€3.50 (htd) (htd)

W fr Mont-Louis on D618. Site on L bef Font-Romeu, opp stadium. Fr Aix-les-Thermes or Puigcerdà turn E at Ur up longish hill, thro town to site on R at o'skts. Lge, pt shd, sl, EHU (6-10A) €4.20-6.20; 10% statics; phone; adv bkg acc; tennis 500m; horseriding 1km. *"Gd cent for mountain walks; site at 1800m altitude."* **€30.50, 29 May-15 Sep, D29.** **2024**

MONT ST MICHEL, LE *2E4* (10km E Rural) *48.62822, -1.41508* **Camping St Michel,** Route du Mont-St Michel, 50220 Courtils **02 33 70 96 90; infos@campingsaintmichel.com; www.campingsaintmichel.com**

€2-3 (htd) WD MSP (htd)

Fr A84 exit J33. Foll sp for Courtils on Mont St Michel rd. Site on L at far end of vill. 3*, Med, mkd, hdg, pt shd, pt sl, EHU (6A) €3.50; gas; bbq; TV; 40% statics; phone; bus adj; Eng spkn; adv bkg acc; ccard acc; bike hire; games area; games rm; CKE. *"Excel, flat site; helpful, friendly owner; excel modern san facs (unisex); cycle paths adj; gd NH for St Malo; attractive; rest 1km; conv drive to Mont St Michel, parking area for free shuttle to monument; sm animal fm onsite; vg."* **€29.00, 31 Mar-1 Nov.** **2022**

MONT ST MICHEL, LE *2E4* (4km S Rural) *48.59622, -1.51244* **Camping aux Pommiers,** 28 Route du Mont-St Michel, 50170 Beauvoir **01 59 00 84 99; www.camping-auxpommiers.com**

€1.20 (htd) WD MSP (htd) shgl 2km

N fr Pontorson foll D976 sp Le Mont St Michel. Site 5km on R on ent vill of Beauvoir. 4*, Med, hdstg, mkd, hdg, pt shd, EHU (6A) €4; gas; bbq; TV; 30% statics; Eng spkn; adv bkg acc; ccard acc; games area; waterslide; bike hire; games rm; tennis 900m; CKE. *"Busy site, rec arr early; friendly, helpful staff & owner; tired clean facs; gd touring base; easy cycle ride to Mont St Michel or pleasant walk; excel site; modern; v highly rec."* **€33.75, 4 May-3 Nov.** **2024**

MONTAIGU *2H4* (10km SE Rural) *46.93769, -1.21975* **Camping Heart of Vendée (formerly Camping L'Eden),** La Raillière, 85600 La Boissière-de-Montaigu **04 30 05 15 19; contact@camping-domaine-eden.fr; www.tohapi.fr**

12 €2 (htd)

Fr Montaigu S on D137, in 8km turn E on D62, thro Le Pont-Legé. Site sp on L off D62. 3*, Med, mkd, shd, EHU (10A) inc; gas; TV; 40% statics; adv bkg acc; tennis; CKE. *"Pleasant, quiet site in woodlands; site poss open all year; clean facs; motor mover useful; site looking a bit tired."* **€23.00** **2023**

MONTBARD *6G1* (1km N Urban) *47.6314, 4.33303* **Camp Municipal Les Treilles,** Rue Michel Servet, 21500 Montbard **03 80 92 69 50; camping.montbard@wanadoo.fr; www.montbard.com**

€2 WD nr

Lies off N side D980. Camping sp clearly indicated on all app including by-pass. Turn onto by-pass at traff lts at rndabt at junc of D905 & D980. Site nr pool. 3*, Med, hdg, pt shd, EHU (16A) €4; bbq; sw nr; phone; bike hire; CKE. *"Pleasant & well-kept site; gd pitches; lge, smart san facs; poss contract worker campers; pool complex adj inc; quiet but rd/rlwy noise at far end; interesting area; excel NH."* **€20.00, 26 Mar-30 Oct.** **2022**

MONTBARREY *6H2* (1km SW Rural) *47.01230, 5.63161* **FLOWER Camping Les Trois Ours,** 28 Rue du Pont, 39380 Montbarrey **03 84 81 50 45; h.rabbe@orange.fr; www.camping-les3ours-jura.com or www.flowercampings.com**

(htd) WD MSP nr

Exit A39 junc onto D905 E; 1km after Mont-sur-Vaudrey on D472 turn L dir Montbarrey. Cross rv, site on L at rvside on edge of vill. 3*, Med, hdg, mkd, shd, EHU (10A) inc; bbq; TV; 10% statics; phone; bus; Eng spkn; adv bkg acc; ccard acc; games rm. *"Improvements planned; vg walking/cycling fr site; excel menu in rest."* **€25.00, 13 Apr-28 Sep.** **2024**

MONTBAZON *4G2* (0.8km N Rural) *47.29044, 0.71595* **Camping La Vallée de l'Indre,** parc la Grange Rouge, 37250 Montbazon **02 47 26 06 43; contact@camping-montbazon.com; www.camping-montbazon.com**

€2 WD nr nr nr (htd)

On D910 thro Montbazon fr S to N, after x-ing bdge (pt of D910) immed turn L to site. Clearly visible & clearly sp on W side of rd at N end of town. 3*, Med, mkd, pt shd, EHU (10A) €4; TV; 10% statics; Eng spkn; adv bkg acc; ccard acc; fishing; tennis; CKE. *"Lovely, spacious rvside site in pretty town (walkable); helpful, friendly owner; bar adj; conv Tours & a'routes; facs being renewed (2019)."* **€22.80, 1 Apr-11 Oct.** **2024**

MONTBERT *2H4* (0.5km SE Rural) *47.05133, -1.47930* **Camping Le Relais des Garennes,** La Bauche Coiffée, 44140 Montbert **02 40 04 78 73; lerelaisdesgarennes@gmail.com; www.camping-lerelaisdesgarennes.com**

(htd) WD

Fr Nantes on N937 dir La Roche, at Geneston turn L dir Montbert & foll site sp. Or fr Nantes on N137 dir La Rochelle turn R at Aigrefeuille-sur-Maine for Montbert. Sm, mkd, pt shd, pt sl, EHU (10A) inc; Eng spkn; adv bkg acc; lake fishing adj; tennis nr; CKE. *"Peaceful, picturesque site; lge pitches; friendly owners; immac facs, but no individual wash rms; rabbits & hens on site; toys for children; many attractions nrby; pleasant walk to town; gd value; sports facs nrby; excel; highly rec; bus avail to Nantes fr vill; excel."* **€16.00, 1 Jun-30 Sep.** **2023**

MONTBRISON *9B1* (1.5km S Urban) *45.59133, 4.07806* **Camp Municipal Le Surizet,** 31 Rue du Surizet, Moingt, 42600 Montbrison **04 77 58 08 30**

€0.85 WD MSP nr

Fr St Etienne on D8, at rndabt junc with D204 turn L sp St Anthème & Ambert. Cross rlwy & turn R in 400m, site sp. 3*, Med, pt shd, EHU (5-10A) inc; bbq; 10% statics; bus (every hr); adv bkg acc; fishing; tennis 2km; CKE. *"Pleasant, well-kept site; no twin axles; vg value; highly rec NH or sh stay; bird reserve (20km)."* **€17.70, 15 Apr-15 Oct.** **2023**

FRANCE

FRANCE

MONTBRON *7B3* (11km NE Rural) *45.74042, 0.58678* **Camping de l'Etang,** Les Geloux, 16310 Le Lindois **05 45 65 02 67; lelindoiscampingdeletang@gmail.com; www.campingdeletang.com**

€1.50 (htd) WD adj

Fr S take D16 N fr Montbron, in 9km turn R onto D13, in 3km turn R onto D27. Site sp in vill opp lake. 2*, Sm, hdg, mkd, pt shd, pt sl, EHU (16A) €4.50; gas; sw; phone; Eng spkn; adv bkg rec; ccard acc; fishing; CKE. *"Loads of wildlife in attractive surroundings; sm library; v pleasant & restful; gd quality rest; gd value; rec."* **€17.50, 1 Apr-1 Nov.** **2024**

MONTBRON *7B3* (6km SE Rural) *45.65972, 0.55805* **Camping Les Gorges du Chambon,** 861 rue de la tardoire 16220 EYMOUTHIERS **0466 600 700; gorges-chambon@koawa.com; www.camping-gorges-chambon.fr**

€3 (htd) WD MSP (htd)

Fr N141 turn SE onto D6 at La Rochefoucauld; cont on D6 out of Montbron; after 5km turn L at La Tricherie onto D163; foll camp sp to site in approx 1.9km. NB Fr La Tricherie narr in places & some sharp bends. 4*, Med, hdstg, mkd, pt shd, pt sl, EHU (10A) inc; gas; bbq (charcoal, gas); red long stay; twin axles; TV; 25% statics; Eng spkn; adv bkg acc; ccard acc; horseriding nr; games rm; tennis; bike hire; games area; golf nr; canoe hire; rv fishing; CKE. *"Beautiful, 'away fr it all', scenic site in grnds of old farm; welcoming, helpful & friendly staff; lge pitches but some sl; excel san facs; superb rest; gd mkd walks; birdwatching & wildlife; poss motorbike rally on site end June; excel."* **€25.00, 1 Apr-30 Sep, D11.** **2022**

MONTECH *8E3* (1km E Rural) *43.96608, 1.24003* **Camping de Montech,** Chemin de la Pierre, 82700 Montech **05 63 31 14 29; contact@camping-montech.fr; www.camping-montech.fr**

€2.80 WD MSP

Exit A20 junc 65 Montauban Sud onto D928 dir Auch. In Montech turn R just bef canal, site well sp. 3*, Lge, mkd, hdg, unshd, EHU (16A) €4; bbq; twin axles; 60% statics; Eng spkn; adv bkg acc; games area; lake fishing nrby; CKE. *"Gd cycle paths."* **€24.00, 1 Mar-31 Oct.** **2024**

MONTENDRE *7C2* (4km NW Rural) *45.30037, -0.43495* **Camping Twin Lakes,** La Faiencérie, 17130 Souméras **06 61 05 17 20; bookings@twinlakesfrance.com; www.twinlakesfrance.com**

12 €1.50 WD nr (htd)

Exit N10/E606 at Montlieu-la-Garde onto D730 thro Montendre dir Mirambeau; go past Souméras vill on R, site sp on L. Or exit A10 junc 37; turn R onto D730; at rndabt turn R onto N137; in Mirambeau turn L onto D730; site on R in approx 14 km. Sm, hdg, pt shd, pt sl, EHU (10-16A) €3; gas; bbq; red long stay; TV; 15% statics; Eng spkn; adv bkg acc; clsd 15 Dec-5 Jan; lake fishing; games rm. *"Vg British-owned site; meals arranged; gd touring base; vg; best to pitch on field beside lake."* **€30.00** **2023**

MONTFERRAND *8F4* (4.8km N Rural) *43.39007, 1.82788* **FFCC Domaine St Laurent,** Les Touzets, 11320 Montferrand **04 68 60 15 80; info@camping-carcassonne-toulouse.com; www.camping-carcassonne-toulouse.com**

€2 WD

S fr Toulouse on N113/D1113 past Villefranche-de-Lauragais. Turn L onto D43 for 4.2km; then R to St Laurent. Or turn L onto D218 bypassing Montferrand & cont directly to St Laurent; turn L at church. Site well sp. 3*, Sm, hdg, pt shd, EHU (6A) inc; TV; 10% statics; Eng spkn; adv bkg acc; tennis; bike hire; games rm; sauna; archery. *"Attractive, peaceful, well-kept site; clean san facs; friendly owners; gd views; woodland walks; vg site but narr access rds."* **€26.00, 2 Apr-30 Oct.** **2023**

MONTFERRAND *8F4* (6km SE Rural) *43.31451, 1.80246* **Camping Le Cathare,** Château de la Barthe, 11410 Belflou **04 68 60 32 49; contact@camping-lecathare.com; www.auberge-lecathare.com**

€3.25 WD nr shgl

Fr Villefranche-de-Lauragais on N113/D6113, foll D622 sp Toulouse/Carcassonne over rlwy, canal, then immed L on D625 for 7km. Thro St Michel-de-Lanes then take D33 to Belflou; foll sp to Le Cathare. 3*, Sm, mkd, pt shd, EHU (3-10A) €3-7.50; bbq; sw nr; 10% statics; boules pitch; mini golf; common rm; CKE. *"Poss long walk to basic san facs - sh timer for lts & might prefer to use your own facs; Cent Nautique on lake; dramatic position o'looking lake."* **€18.00, 15 Apr-15 Nov.** **2020**

"I like to fill in the reports as I travel from site to site"

You'll find report forms at the back of this guide, or you can fill them in online at camc.com/europereport.

MONTIGNAC *7C3* (7km E Rural) *45.05375, 1.23980* **Yelloh! Village Lascaux Vacances,** Route des Malénies, 24290 St Amand-de-Coly **05 53 50 81 57; mail@campinglascauxvacances.com; www.campinglascauxvacances.com or www.yellohvillage.co.uk**

€4 WD MSP

Exit A89 junc 17 (Peyrignac) SE onto D6089 to Le Lardin-St Lazare. Join D62 S to Coly & then foll sp to Saint Amand-de-Coly. Site well sp. 3*, Med, hdg, mkd, pt shd, EHU (10A) inc; bbq; red long stay; TV; 60% statics; phone; adv bkg acc; ccard acc; fishing nr; waterslide; games area; sauna; games rm. *"Excel, peaceful, renovated site in superb location; warm welcome; lge pitches; excel touring base."* **€33.00, 15 Apr-11 Sep.** **2023**

MONTIGNAC *7C3* (8km SE Rural) *45.07211, 1.23431* **Camping La Tournerie Ferme,** La Tournerie, 24290 Aubas **05 53 51 04 16; la-tournerie@orange.fr; www.la-tourneriecamping.com/**

(htd) nr nr

Fr Montignac on D704 dir Sarlat-la-Canéda; in 5.5km turn L onto C1 sp St Amand-de-Coly; in 1.6km at x-rds turn L sp Malardel & Drouille; in 400m at Y-junc foll rd to R sp Manardel & La Genèbre; cont on this rd ignoring minor rds; in 1.6km at elongated junc take rd to R of post box; immed after passing Le Treuil farm on R turn R at x-rds La Tournerie. Site opp farm. Sm, hdstg, unshd, sl, terr, EHU (6A) inc; bbq; twin axles; Eng spkn; adv bkg req. *"Lovely, tranquil site; adults only; lge pitches with beautiful views; friendly, helpful British owners (CC members); excel san facs; request detailed dirs or see website - sat nav not rec; excel touring base; excel site; fenced dog pitches."* **€23.00, 1 Mar-30 Nov. 2022**

MONTIGNAC *7C3* (0.5km S Urban) *45.05980, 1.15860* **Camping Le Moulin du Bleufond,** Ave Aristide Briand, 24290 Montignac **05 53 51 83 95; info@bleufond.com; www.bleufond.com**

€3 (htd) (htd)

S on D704, cross bdge in town & turn R immed of rv on D65; site sp in 500m nr stadium, adj Rv Vezere. 3*, Med, hdg, pt shd, EHU (10A) €3.50; bbq; red long stay; TV; adv bkg acc; ccard acc; fishing; tennis adj; wellness area with jacuzzi and sauna (additional charge and reservation required); table football; table tennis; pinball machine; bowling. *"Pleasant site; pleasant, helpful owners; facs excel; poss diff lge o'fits due trees; conv Lascaux caves & town; gd walking area; lovely site."* **€31.40, 31 Mar-14 Oct. 2020**

MONTIGNAC *7C3* (14km SW Rural) *45.00178, 1.07155* **Camping Le Paradis,** 5667 Route De La Vallée, 24290 St Léon-sur-Vézère **55 30 72 64; contact@le-paradis.com; www.le-paradis.fr**

€3 (htd) (covrd, htd, indoor) adj

On W bank of Rv Vézère on D706 Montignac-Les Eyzies rd, 1km fr Le Moustier. D706 poss rough rd. 5*, Med, hdg, pt shd, EHU (10A); bbq; sw; red long stay; TV; 25% statics; phone; Eng spkn; adv bkg acc; ccard acc; boat hire; tennis; fishing; sauna; games area; bike hire; CKE. *"Excel, high standard site in gd location; friendly, conscientious Dutch owners; immac san facs; gd pool, rest & takeaway; vg for families; tropical vegetation around pitches, grnds like a garden; excel, espec LS; ACSI acc."* **€54.00, 1 Apr - 20 Oct, D30. 2023**

See advertisement

MONTIGNAC *7C3* (8km SW Rural) *45.04107, 1.11915* **Camping La Castillonderie,** 24290 Thonac **07 86 09 86 18; lacastillonderie@gmail.com; www.dordogne-castillonderie.fr/en**

€0.50 (htd)

Take D706 dir Les Eyzies. At rndabt in Thonac turn R onto D65 sp Fanlac in 1km after x-rd take R, site is sp 1.5km. Narr app rd. 4*, Med, hdstg, mkd, hdg, pt shd, pt sl, EHU (10A) €4; bbq; TV; 10% statics; phone; Eng spkn; adv bkg acc; ccard acc; CKE. *"Peaceful, well-kept site; friendly, helpful Dutch owners; on site lake fishing; canoeing 3km; gd cent for historic visits & walks."* **€30.80, 1 May-30 Sep. 2024**

MONTIGNY LE ROI *6F2* (1km N Rural) *48.00084, 5.49637* **Camping du Château,** Rue Hubert Collot, 52140 Montigny-le-Roi **01 83 64 69 21; contact@campingcarpark.com; www.campingduchateau.com**

(htd)

Fr A31 junc 8 for Montigny-le-Roi. Site well sp in cent vill on D74. 3*, Med, pt shd, terr, EHU (5A) €3; bbq; tennis; bike hire. *"Modern facs; steep ent; rests & shops in vill."* **€22.00, 30 Apr-1 Oct. 2024**

MONTLUCON *7A4* (4.6km SW Rural) *46.327547, 2.556069* **Camping De L'Etang De Sault,** 8 Rue Du Plan D'Eau, 03410 Premilhat **07 89 51 07 50; campingdeletangdesault@gmail.com; campingetangdesault.fr**

Fr W on E62/N145 twrds Montlucon. Turn R at rndabt before Auchan S'mkt onto D745. Past Lake on L, turn L across bdge to site. Sm, mkd, pt shd, EHU €6; bbq; Eng spkn; adv bkg acc; ccard acc; CKE. *"Family run; new Belgian owners; v welcoming, wkg hard to renovate site; bike hire; excel rest; fishing on lake but no sw; family orientated; pk nrby; san facs dated, clean, stretched; gd short stay/NH; fair."* **€16.00** **2023**

MONTMAUR *9D3* (0.5km E Rural) *44.56866, 5.88326* **Camping Mon Repos,** Le Cadillon, 05400 Montmaur **04 92 58 03 14 or 06 76 84 40 13 (mob); info@campingmonrepos.fr; www.campingmonrepos.fr**

Fr D994 Veynes-Gap, foll D937 N, turning R at bdge to keep on D937. Site sp. 2*, Med, mkd, pt shd, EHU (2-5A) €3-4; gas; bbq (sep area); cooking facs; sw nr; TV; 30% statics; bus, 400mtrs; Eng spkn; adv bkg acc; games rm. *"Friendly, family-run site; excel walking; beautiful, v quiet site; excel loc; v clean but rustic san facs; excel priced; lovely staff; highly rec; excel."* **€20.00** **2024**

MONTMAUR *9D3* (7km SE Rural) *44.55003, 5.95114* **Camping au Blanc Manteau,** Route de Céüse, 05400 Manteyer **92 57 82 56 or 92 57 85 89; pierre.wampach@wanadoo.fr; www.campingaublancmanteau.fr**

Take D994 fr Veynes twd Gap, past Montmaur; site sp fr vill of La Roche-des-Arnauds on D18 in 1km. 3*, Sm, mkd, pt shd, EHU (10A) €5.35; adv bkg rec; tennis. *"Gd sized pitches; pleasant owner; pretty, in wooded area with beautiful views of mountains."* **€24.00** **2024**

MONTMEDY *5C1* (0.7km NW Urban) *49.52126, 5.36090* **Camp Municipal La Citadelle,** Rue Vauban, 55600 Montmédy **03 29 80 10 40 (Mairie); mairie.montmedy@wanadoo.fr; www.montmedy.fr**

Fr D643 foll sp to Montmédy cent & foll site sp. Steep app. 2*, Sm, hdg, pt shd, pt sl, EHU (4-10A) €2.80-3.97; red long stay; CKE. *"Warden calls am & pm; facs clean, ltd LS; nr Montmedy Haut fortified town; 10A hook-up not avail high ssn; vg; lovely, delightful little site; gd views."* **€9.60, 1 May-30 Sep.** **2024**

MONTMORILLON *7A3* (0.8km S Urban) *46.42035, 0.87554* **Camp Municipal de l'Allochon,** 31 Ave Fernand Tribot, 86500 Montmorillon **05 49 91 02 33 or 05 49 91 13 99 (Mairie); www.montmorillon.fr**

On D54 to Le Dorat, approx 400m SE fr main rd bdge over rv at S of town. Site on L. Fr S v sharp RH turn into site. 3*, Med, mkd, pt shd, terr, EHU (10A); bbq; TV; Eng spkn; adv bkg acc; ccard acc; games area; fishing; CKE. *"Delightful, peaceful, well-kept site; lge pitches; friendly, hard-working warden; gd touring base; vg value; v clean facs, old but working shwrs; htd covrd pool adj; relaxing; rec; security barrier; gd walking area, maps fr TO; ltd facs LS."* **€12.00, 1 Mar-31 Oct.** **2023**

MONTOIRE SUR LE LOIR *4F2* (0.5km S Rural) *47.74750, 0.86351* **Camp Municipal Les Reclusages,** Ave des Reclusages, 41800 Montoire-sur-le Loir **02 54 85 02 53; camping.reclusages@orange.fr; www.mairie-montoire.fr**

Foll site sp, out of town sq, over rv bdge & 1st L on blind corner at foot of old castle. 3*, Med, mkd, pt shd, EHU (6-10A) €3.10-3.93; 5% statics; Eng spkn; adv bkg acc; ccard acc; canoeing; fishing; CKE. *"Lovely location nr Rv Loir; peaceful, well-kept, secure site; some rvside pitches; friendly, helpful warden; excel clean san facs, ltd LS; gd cycling; conv troglodyte vills; excel; pleasant sh walk into town across rv; htd pool adj; attractive town; Int'l Folk Festival mid Aug."* **€18.40, 1 May-30 Sep.** **2023**

MONTPELLIER *10F1* (8km N Rural) *43.65135, 3.89630* **Sandaya Le Plein Air des Chênes,** 531 Avenue Georges France, 34830 Clapiers **04 67 02 02 53; pac@sandaya.fr; www.sandaya.co.uk**

Exit A9 junc 28 onto N113/D65 twd Montpellier. Leave at junc with D21 sp Jacou & Teyran, site sp on L. NB Site ent/exit v narr & no place to stop when leaving. 4*, Med, mkd, pt shd, pt sl, terr, serviced pitches; EHU (10A) inc; gas; red long stay; 75% statics; horseriding; tennis; games area; waterslide. *"Vg site; site rds tight for lge o'fits; private san facs some pitches (extra charge); pitches muddy in wet."* **€25.00, 3 Apr-13 Sep.** **2024**

MONTPELLIER *10F1* (9.7km SE Rural) *43.57611, 3.92583* **FFCC Camping Le Parc,** Route de Mauguio, 34970 Lattes **04 67 65 85 67; camping-le-parc@wanadoo.fr; www.leparccamping.com**

Exit A9 junc 29 for airport onto D66. In about 4km turn R onto D172 sp Lattes & campings, cross over D21. Site ent in 200m on R. 3*, Med, hdg, shd, EHU (10A) inc; gas; 15% statics; Eng spkn; adv bkg req; CKE. *"Friendly, helpful owners; lge pitches but dusty; gd facs, excel pool & snack bar; conv Cévennes mountains & Mediterranean beaches; hiking & mountain biking; barrier locked 2200."* **€28.00** **2024**

MONTPON MENESTEROL *7C2* (1km N Rural) *45.01280, 0.15828* **Camping La Cigaline,** 1 Rue de la Paix, Route de Ribérac, 24700 Montpon-Ménestérol **05 53 80 22 16; contact@lacigaline.fr; www.camping-dordogne-lacigaline.com**

€1.50 WD nr

Fr Montpon town cent traff lts take D730 N to Ménestérol. Site on L bef bdge beside Rv Isle. 3*, Med, hdg, mkd, shd, EHU (10A) inc; bbq; sw nr; 1% statics; train 1km; Eng spkn; adv bkg acc; ccard acc; fishing; tennis 200m; boat hire; CKE. *"Gd touring base for St Emilion region; gd walking, cycling; vg; new young owners (2014); leisure park nrby; bike hire 500m; gd food in bar/rest; terr o'looks rv; site improving."* **€23.40, 19 Apr-4 Oct.** **2024**

MONTREJEAU *8F3* (7km S Rural) *43.02864, 0.57852* **Camping Es Pibous,** Chemin de St Just, 31510 St Bertrand-de-Comminges **05 61 88 31 42 or 09 74 56 74 63; contact@es-pibous.fr; www.espibous.fr**

(htd) WD MSP nr nr

Turn S fr D817 onto D825 sp Bagnères-de-Luchon & Espagne. Foll past 'Super U' to lge rndabt & turn R sp St Bertrand-de-Comminges/Valcabrère then at 1st traff lts turn R & foll sp for St Bertrand. Turn R off N125 onto D825 to roman excavation site. Site on L. Or exit A64 junc 17 onto A645 sp Bagnères-de-Luchon to lge rndabt, then as above. 3*, Med, mkd, hdg, pt shd, EHU (10A) inc; gas; TV; 20% statics; adv bkg acc; ccard acc; fishing 3km; tennis 3km. *"Peaceful, friendly site; pitches among trees; clean dated san facs, ltd LS; lndry is owner's washing machine, not always avail (2010); gd touring area nr mountains; picturesque town in walking dist."* **€21.20, 1 Mar-31 Oct.** **2023**

MONTRESOR *4H2* (3km W Rural) *47.15782, 1.16026* **Camping Les Coteaux du Lac,** 37460 Chemillé-sur-Indrois **02 47 92 77 83; lescoteauxdulac@wanadoo.fr; www.lescoteauxdulac.com**

€1.70 WD MSP (htd)

Fr Loches on D764; then D10 dir Montrésor; cont to Chemillé-sur-Indrois. 4*, Med, pt sl, EHU (6A) €3.90; bbq; TV; phone; Eng spkn; fishing; games rm; boating. *"Excel setting by lake; immac, modern san facs; beautiful vill 600m; trekking in Val d'Indrois; 3km along cycle track (old rlwy)."* **€34.00, 3 Mar-15 Oct.** **2024**

MONTREUIL *3B3* (0.5km W Rural) *50.46853, 1.76280* **FFCC Camping La Fontaine des Clercs,** 1 Rue de l'Eglise, 62170 Montreuil **03 21 06 07 28; desmarest.mi@wanadoo.fr; www.campinglafontainedesclercs.fr**

12 €2 (htd) WD MSP nr

Fr N or S turn SW off D901 at rndabt onto D349 to Montreuil; turn R immed after rlwy x-ing (onto Rue des Préaux); in 120m turn R; site in 100m on R; sp on Rv Canche. Or take 2nd R ALMOST immed after (20m) rlwy-xing (onto Grande Ville Basse); in 50m fork R (Rue de l'Eglise); site in 200m on R. NB Poss difff access lge o'fits. 2*, Med, mkd, hdstg, pt shd, pt sl, terr, EHU (6-10A) €3.70-€4.80; bbq; 60% statics; adv bkg rec; rv fishing adj; site clsd over New Year; games rm; CKE. *"Busy, basic site in beautiful spot; helpful, friendly owner; gd san facs; steep & narr site rd with tight turns to terr pitches, some sm; pool 1.5km; not suitable lge o'fits; some generous pitches beside rv; vet in Montreuil; attractive, historic town with amazing restaurants- uphill walk; conv NH Le Touquet, beaches & ferry; wine society outlet; excel site; some Eng spkn."* **€21.90** **2022**

MONTREUIL BELLAY *4H1* (4km E Rural) *47.15263, -0.13599* **FFCC Camping Le Thouet,** Les Côteaux-du-Chalet, route Bron 49260 Montreuil-Bellay **02 41 38 74 17 or 06 19 56 32 75 (mob); campinglethouet@alicepro.fr; www.campinglethouet.com**

12 €2 WD nr

Fr D347 N of Montreuil-Bellay take dir 'Cent Ville'; turn L immed bef rv bdge & foll sp to Les Côteaux-du-Chalet. Access via narr, rough rd for 1km. Med, pt shd, EHU (10A) €3; gas; bbq; 5% statics; phone; adv bkg acc; ccard acc; boating; fishing; CKE. *"Peaceful, spacious, British-owned site; lge area grass & woods surrounded by vineyards; pitches in open grass field; poss unkempt LS; gd walks; vill not easily accessed by foot; unguarded rv bank poss not suitable children; v lge pitches."* **€26.00** **2024**

MONTREUIL BELLAY *4H1* (1km W Urban) *47.13191, -0.15897* **Camping Paradis Les Nobis D'Anjou,** Rue Georges Girouy, 49260 Montreuil-Bellay **02 41 52 33 66; contact@campinglesnobis.com; www.campinglesnobis.com**

WD MSP (htd)

Fr S on D938 turn L immed on ent town boundary & foll rd for 1km to site; sp fr all dir. Fr N on D347 ignore 1st camping sp & cont on D347 to 2nd rndabt & foll sp. Fr NW on D761 turn R onto D347 sp Thouars to next rndabt, foll site sp. 4*, Lge, hdg, mkd, pt shd, EHU (10A) €3 (poss long cable req, rev pol); gas; red long stay; TV; 50% statics; phone; Eng spkn; adv bkg acc; ccard acc; bike hire; CKE. *"Spacious site bet castle & rv; gd, modern san facs; local chateaux & town worth exploring; 'aire de service' for m'vans adj; gd patissiere in town; some pitches o'look rv Thouet; extremely well managed, friendly site; nr Saumur vineyards; excel."* **€29.00, 8 Apr-24 Sep.** **2023**

FRANCE

FRANCE

MONTREVEL EN BRESSE *9A2* (0.5km E Rural) *46.201520, 5.136681* **Camping La Plaine Tonique,** Base de loisirs - 599, route d'Etrez - 01340 Malafretaz **04 74 30 80 52; contact@laplainetonique.com; www.laplainetonique.com**

€4 (covrd, htd)

Exit A40 junc 5 Bourg-en-Bresse N onto D975; at Montrevel-en-Bresse turn E onto D28 dir Etrez & Marboz; site sp on L in 400m. Or exit A6 junc 27 Tournus S onto D975. 4*, V lge, hdg, mkd, shd, EHU (10A) inc; bbq; sw nr; Eng spkn; adv bkg acc; ccard acc; waterslide; fishing; watersports; bike hire; games area; tennis. *"Excel, busy, family site; superb leisure facs; mountain biking; archery; vg clean san facs; some pitches boggy after rain."* **€30.00, 22 Apr-6 Sep. 2020**

MONTRICHARD *4G2* (1km S Rural) *47.33384, 1.18766* **Camping Couleurs du Monde,** 1 Rond Point de Montparnasse, 41400 Faverolles-sur-Cher **02 54 32 06 08 or 06 74 79 56 29 (mob); contact@camping-couleurs-du-monde.com; www.camping-couleurs-du-monde.com**

€2 nr (covrd, htd)

E fr Tours on D796 thro Bléré; at Montrichard turn S on D764 twd Faverolles-sur-Cher, site 200m fr junc, adj to Carrefour supmkt - on L by 2nd rndabt. 4*, Med, hdstg, mkd, pt shd, EHU (10A) €4; bbq; sw nr; TV; Eng spkn; adv bkg acc; ccard acc; tennis 500m; games rm; sauna; bike hire; games area; waterslide 500m; CKE. *"Level site in gd location nr vineyards; beauty cent; gd sports activities; vg; excel facs; gd sw pool with canopy; ideal for exploring Cher & Loire Valley; access to Cher Rv."* **€34.00, 6 Apr-21 Sep. 2024**

MONTRICOUX *8E3* (0.5km W Rural) *44.07660, 1.61103* **FFCC Camping Le Clos Lalande,** Route de Bioule, 82800 Montricoux **05 63 24 18 89; contact@camping-lecloslalande.com; www.camping-lecloslalande.com**

€2.50 nr

Fr A20 exit junc 59 to Caussade; fr Caussade take D964 to Montricoux, where site well sp. 3*, Med, hdg, mkd, pt shd, EHU (6A) €3.60; bbq; TV; 10% statics; phone; bus 400m; Eng spkn; adv bkg rec; games area; rv fishing 400m; canoe hire; watersports; tennis; bike hire; CKE. *"Peaceful, quiet, well-kept site by rv at mouth of Aveyron gorges; beautiful area, inc Bastide vills; great family site; friendly, helpful owners; mkt Weds; easy walk to town; highly rec."* **€25.40, 30 Mar-6 Oct. 2024**

MONTROLLET *7B3* (0.1km N Rural) *45.98316, 0.89702* **Camping Auberge La Marchadaine,** Beaulieu, 16420 Montrollet **05 45 71 09 88 or 06 63 07 82 48 (mob); aubergedelamarchadaine@gmail.com**

nr

N fr St Junien on D675, turn W onto D82 to Montrollet. Auberge sp in vill. Sm, pt shd, EHU (6A) inc; gas; bbq; twin axles; phone; adv bkg acc; games area; fishing; CKE. *"Delightful CL-type site nr beautiful lake; vg rest; many mkd walks; Oradour sur Glane nrby (wartime museum); Vienne rv; gd; rund down (2017)."* **€12.00 2023**

MONTSOREAU *4G1* (1.3km NW Rural) *47.21805, 0.05270* **Camping L'Isle Verte,** Ave de la Loire, 49730 Montsoreau **+33 241 517 660; isleverte49@orange.fr; www.campingisleverte.com**

€4 nr (htd)

At Saumur on S side of rv turn R immed bef bdge over Rv Loire; foll sp to Chinon & site. Fr N foll sp for Fontevraud & Chinon fr Rv Loire bdge; site on D947 in vill on banks of Loire opp 'Charcuterie' shop. 4*, Med, mkd, pt shd, EHU (16A) poss long lead req; gas; TV; 20% statics; bus to Saumur; Eng spkn; adv bkg rec; ccard acc; games area; rv fishing; bike hire; watersports; golf 13km; tennis; CKE. *"Pleasant rvside site in beautiful situation; v busy high ssn, still busy out of high ssn; various sized/shaped pitches; car hire; gd san facs, poss irreg cleaning LS; vg rest; barrier clsd 2200-0700; gd security; pleasant vill; gd; excel; helpful staff."* **€50.00, 4 Apr-9 Oct, L34. 2022**

MORESTEL *9B3* (8km S Urban) *45.63521, 5.57231* **Camping del Padel (formerly Camping Couleur Nature,** 6 Rue du Stade, 38630 Les Avenières **04 74 33 92 92; camping@lesavenieres.fr; www.campingdelpadel.fr**

(htd)

S fr Morestel on D1075, turn onto D40 to Les Avenières, site well sp. 3*, Med, hdg, mkd, hdstg, pt shd, EHU (10A); bbq; sw nr; TV; 35% statics; phone; adv bkg acc; ccard acc; CKE. *"Phone ahead LS to check open; pool adj; noise fr adj stadium."* **€27.00, 1 May-30 Sep. 2024**

MORLAIX *2E2* (13km N Coastal) *48.65950, -3.84847* **Camping De La Baie de Terenez,** 29252 Plouezoch **02 98 67 26 80; contact@campingbaiedeterenez.com; www.campingbaiedeterenez.com**

(htd) sand 2km

Take D46 on exit Morlaix, turn L on D76 to site. 3*, Lge, pt shd, pt sl, EHU (10A) inc; gas; TV; adv bkg acc; fishing; windsurfing; games rm. *Quiet, rural site; variety of plants & trees; coastal path adj;* **€26.50, 4 Apr-27 Sep. 2024**

MORLAIX *2E2* (11km E Rural) *48.60283, -3.73833* **La Ferme de Croas Men,** Garlan, 29610 Plouigneau **02 98 79 11 50 or 06 52 97 65 91; info@ferme-de-croasmen.com; www.ferme-de-croasmen.com**

€1 WD MSP

Fr D712 rndabt W of Plouigneau twd Morlaix (exit fr N12) 2km R sp Garlan; thro Garlan site 1km on L, well sp. Sm, hdg, pt shd, serviced pitches; EHU (6A) €3.50; 10% statics; Eng spkn; horseriding 200m; CKE. *"Lovely, well-kept CL-type farm site; excel facs; farm museum; donkey/tractor rides; ideal for children; produce avail inc cider & crêpes; vg."* **€20.90, 1 Apr-31 Oct. 2023**

MORMOIRON *10E2* (4km E Rural) *44.05713, 5.22798* **Camping Les Verguettes,** Route de Carpentras, 84570 Villes-sur-Auzon **04 90 61 88 18; info@provence-camping.com; www.provence-camping.com**

€2.60- 3.60 (htd) WD nr

E on D942 fr Carpentras dir Sault. Site at ent to Villes-sur-Auzon beyond wine cave. Or at Veulle-les-Roses turn E onto D68. Cont thro Sottenville-sur-Mer. Site on L in 2km. 4*, Lge, hdg, mkd, pt shd, pt sl, EHU (6A) inc; TV; adv bkg rec; tennis; fishing 300m; games rm. *"Scenic location; gd walking & cycling; friendly, helpful owner; families with children sited nr pool, others at end of camp away fr noise; poss muddy when it rains; sm pitches not suitable lge o'fits; red facs LS; new san facs block."* **€35.80, 26 Apr-6 Oct. 2024**

MORTAGNE SUR GIRONDE *7B2* (1km SW Coastal) *45.47600, -0.79400* **camping Municipal Bel Air (formerly Aire Communale Le Port),** 17120 Mortagne-sur-Gironde **06 419 160 19; mairie-mortagne@smic17.fr; www.campingfrance.com**

12 WD MSP nr nr nr

Fr Royan take D730 dir Mirambeau for approx 28km. Turn R in Boutenac-Touvent onto D6 to Mortagne, then foll sp Le Port & Aire de Camping-Car. M'vans only. Sm, unshd, EHU (10A) inc. *"Car/c'vans poss acc; shwrs & mv service pnt 800m fr site; fees collected 0900; all pitches have views; excel."* **€6.00 2024**

MORTAIN *2E4* (12km S Rural) *48.57039, -0.94883* **Camping Les Taupinières,** La Raisnais, 50140 Notre-Dame-du-Touchet **02 33 69 49 36 or 06 33 26 78 82 (mob); belinfrance@fsmail.net; www.lestaupinieres.com**

WD nr nr

Fr Mortain S on D977 sp St Hilaire-du-Harcouët; shortly after rndabt take 2nd L at auberge to Notre-Dame-deTouchet. In vill turn L at PO, sp Le Teilleul D184, then 2nd R sp La Raisnais. Site at end of lane on R (haycart on front lawn). Sm, hdstg, pt shd, pt sl, EHU (10A) inc (poss long lead req); adv bkg acc. *"Pleasant, tranquil, spacious CL-type site adj farm; lovely outlook; washing machine on request; adults only; NB no wc or shwrs Dec-Feb but water & EHU all year; DVD library; friendly, helpful British owners; htd pool 8km; well-kept, clean san facs; adv bkg rec; highly rec."* **€18.50, 1 Mar-31 Oct. 2023**

MOSNAC *7B2* (0km E Rural) *45.50557, -0.52304* **Camp Municipal Les Bords de la Seugne,** 34 Rue de la Seugne, 17240 Mosnac **05 46 70 48 45; camping@commune-mosnac.fr; www.commune-mosnac.fr**

(htd)

Fr Pons S on N137 for 4.5km; L on D134 to Mosnac; foll sp to site behind church. 2*, Sm, mkd, pt shd, EHU (10A) €4; gas; red long stay; Eng spkn; adv bkg acc; CKE. *"Charming, clean, neat site in sm hamlet; site yourself, warden calls; helpful staff; excel, spotless san facs; conv Saintes, Cognac & Royan."* **€10.50, 1 May-30 Sep. 2023**

"I need an on-site restaurant"

We do our best to make sure site information is correct, but it is always best to check any must-have facilities are still available or will be open during your visit.

MOTHE ACHARD, LA *2H4* (5km NW Rural) *46.65285, -1.74759* **Camping La Guyonnière,** 85150 St Julien-des-Landes **02 51 46 62 59; info@laguyonniere.com; www.laguyonniere.com**

€4 WD (covrd, htd)

Leave A83 junc 5 onto D160 W twd La Roche-sur-Yon. Foll ring rd N & cont on D160 twd Les Sables-d'Olonne. Leave dual c'way foll sp La Mothe-Achard, then take D12 thro St Julien-des-Landes twd La Chaize-Giraud. Site sp on R. 5*, Lge, hdg, pt shd, pt sl, EHU (6A) inc (long lead rec); gas; bbq; sw nr; TV; 10% statics; phone; Eng spkn; adv bkg acc; ccard acc; waterpark; lake fishing 400m; waterslide; windsurfing 400m; bike hire. *"V lge pitches; canoe hire 400m; gd views; friendly owners; gd walking area."* **€47.00, 26 Apr-28 Sep, A12. 2022**

MOTHE ACHARD, LA *2H4* (6km NW Rural) *46.64469, -1.73346* **FLOWER Camping La Bretonnière,** 85150 St Julien-des-Landes **02 51 46 62 44; info@la-bretonniere.com; www.la-bretonniere.com or www.flowercampings.com**

€2-5 WD MSP nr (covrd, htd)

Fr La Roche-sur-Yon take D160 to La Mothe-Achard, then D12 dir St Gilles-Croix-de-Vie. Site on R 2km after St Julien. 4*, Med, mkd, pt shd, pt sl, EHU (6-12A) €2-4.50; bbq; sw nr; TV; 20% statics; Eng spkn; adv bkg acc; ccard acc; bike hire; fishing; ice; games area; sailing 2km; tennis; games rm; CKE. *"Excel, friendly site adj dairy farm; v lge pitches; san facs stretched in high ssn; 10 mins fr Bretignolles-sur-Mer sand dunes."* **€33.00, 9 Apr-30 Sep. 2023**

FRANCE

MOTHE ACHARD, LA *2H4* (7km NW Rural) *46.66280, -1.71380* **Camping La Garangeoire,** 85150 St Julien-des-Landes **02 51 46 65 39; info@garangeoire.com; www.camping-la-garangeoire.com or www.les-castels.com**

€5 (covrd, htd)

Site sp fr La Mothe-Achard. At La Mothe-Achard take D12 for 5km to St Julien, D21 for 2km to site. Or fr Aizenay W on D6 turn L dir La Chapelle-Hermier. Site on L, well sp. 5*, Lge, mkd, hdg, shd, pt sl, serviced pitches; EHU (16A) inc (poss rev pol); gas; bbq (gas); red long stay; twin axles; TV; 50% statics; phone; Eng spkn; adv bkg rec; ccard acc; lake fishing; games rm; waterslide; bike hire; games area; tennis; horseriding; webcam computer; CKE. *"Busy, well-run site set in chateau parkland; some v lge pitches; pleasant helpful owners; excel, clean facs; gd for families & all ages; pitches quiet - entmnt well away fr pitches; super site; gd site in every way."* **€37.00, 7 May -20 Sep.** **2020**

MOULINS *9A1* (21km N Rural) *46.709544, 3.323283* **Camping Municipal des Baillys,** Les Bailly, 58390 Dornes **06 74 82 04 02 or 33 86 50 60 86**

nr nr nr

On the D22 bet Dornes and Chantenay Saint Imbert. 2nd turning on the left after Dornes. Sm, pt shd, EHU; adv bkg acc. *"O'looking fishing lake (no sw); v welcoming warden; no fixed pitches but warden allocates; vg."* **€11.00** **2024**

MOURIES *10E2* (2km E Rural) *43.68207, 4.91769* **Camping à la Ferme Les Amandaies,** Mas de Bou Malek, 13890 Mouriès **04 90 47 50 59; bou.malek@orange.fr; http://campinglesamandaies.fr/**

Fr Mouriès take D17 E sp Salon-de-Provence. Site sp on R 200m past D5 junc. Foll site sp to farm in 2km. Sm, pt shd, EHU €2 (rec long lead) (poss rev pol); bbq. *"Simple CL-type site; a few lge pitches; friendly owners; dated, dimly-lit san facs; conv coast & Avignon; book in using intercom on LH wall at ent to shwr block."* **€13.00** **2023**

MOURIES *10E2* (7km NW Urban) *43.72138, 4.80950* **Camp Municipal Les Romarins,** Avenue des Alpilles, 13520 Maussane-les-Alpilles **04 90 54 33 60; camping-municipal-maussane@wanadoo.fr; www.campinglesromarins.fr**

€3.50 nr

Fr Mouriès N on D17, turn onto D5 on o'skts of vill dir St Rémy-de-Provence, turn immed L site on R adj municipal pool. 4*, Med, hdg, mkd, pt shd, EHU (10A) €4.80; twin axles; red long stay; TV; phone; bus in ssn; Eng spkn; adv bkg rec; ccard acc; bike hire; games area; games rm; tennis; CKE. *"Well-kept, well-run site in lovely area; on edge of vill; excel san facs; pool adj inc; some pitches diff m'vans due low trees; gd security; in Natural Park; hiking; mountain biking; excel."* **€30.00, 15 Mar-3 Nov.** **2023**

MOUSTIERS STE MARIE *10E3* (0.5km W Rural) *43.84497, 6.21555* **Camping Manaysse,** 04360 Moustiers-Ste Marie **04 92 74 66 71; manaysse@orange.fr; www.camping-manaysse.com**

€1.40 nr

Fr Riez take D952 E, pass g'ge on L & turn L at 1st rndabt for Moustiers; site on L off RH bend; strongly advised not to app Moustiers fr E (fr Castellane, D952 or fr Comps, D71) as these rds are diff for lge vehicles/c'vans - not for the faint-hearted. 2*, Med, mkd, pt shd, pt sl, EHU (6-10A) €2.50-3.50; bbq; adv bkg acc; ccard acc; volleyball court; field balls; ping pong tables; CKE. *"Welcoming, family-run site; super views; gd unisex san facs; cherry trees on site - avoid parking under during early Jun; steep walk into vill; lge o'fits do not attempt 1-way system thro vill, park & walk; gd."* **€14.00, 28 Mar-1 Nov.** **2020**

MOYAUX *3D1* (3.4km NE Rural) *49.20860, 0.39230* **Camping Château Le Colombier,** Chemin du Val Séry, 14590 Moyaux **02 31 63 63 08; mail@camping-le colombier.com; www.camping-normandie-le colombier.com**

(htd)

Fr Pont de Normandie on A29, at junc with A13 branch R sp Caen. At junc with A132 branch R & foll sp Lisieux, D579. Turn L onto D51 sp Blangy-le-Château. Immed on leaving Moyaux turn L onto D143 & foll sp to site on R in 3km. 4*, Lge, mkd, pt shd, EHU (10A) inc (poss lead req); gas; bbq; red long stay; TV; 30% statics; phone; Eng spkn; adv bkg acc; ccard acc; excursions; games rm; bike hire; tennis; horseriding nr; games area; CKE. *"Beautiful, peaceful, spacious site in chateau grnds; ltd san facs LS; lge pool, but no shd, seats or sunshades around; vg for children; gd shop & crêperie; some static tents/tour ops; shgl paths poss diff some wheelchairs/pushchairs; if dep bef 0800 must move to car park o'night; mkt Sun; gd site; some pitches boggy when wet; no o'fits over 7m high ssn; gd facs; excel site to explore Normandy landing beaches; easy walk to vill with shops and rest and sh drive to larger town, lovely site, v helpful owners; poss travellers on site."* **€33.70, 19 Apr-29 Sep, N04.** **2024**

MUIDES SUR LOIRE *4G2* (1km N Rural) *47.67191, 1.52596* **Camp Municipal BelleVue,** Ave de la Loire, 41500 Muides-sur-Loire **02 54 87 01 56 or 07 57 76 41 47; campingmunicipalbellevue@orange.fr; www.muides.fr**

€3 nr nr

Fr A10/E5/E60 exit junc 16 S onto D205. Turn R onto D2152 then D112 over rv. Site on S bank of rv on D112 W of bdge. Tight U-turn into site fr N. 2*, Med, mkd, pt shd, EHU (6A) inc (poss long lead req),(poss rev pol); sw nr; rv fishing adj; cycling; CKE. *"Neat, clean, basic, spacious site; ladies shwrs need upgade (2011); vehicle barrier; gd views over rv; some pitches by fast-flowing (unfenced) rv; little shd; excel cycling; site self when off clsd (open 0800-1000 & 1700-1900)."* **€18.00, 1 May-15 Sep.** **2023**

MUIDES SUR LOIRE 4G2 (6km E Rural) 47.64803, 1.61165 **Camp Municipal du Cosson,** Route de la Cordellerie, 41220 Crouy-sur-Cosson **06 31 46 38 80 or 02 54 87 08 81; mairie-de-crouy-sur-cosson@orange.fr; www.crouysurcosson.fr**

Fr Muides-sur-Loire, take D103 E dir Crouy-sur-Cosson. In vill, turn R onto D33 dir Chambord. Site 200m fr vill, well sp. 2*, Med, mkd, pt shd, EHU (6A) inc (poss rev pol); bbq; 10% statics; phone; adv bkg acc; rv fishing nrby; CKE. *"V pleasant site; woodland setting; nr Rv Loire; poss long-stay workers; attractive site in nice vill; bar 300m; excel."*
€16.00, 1 Apr-15 Oct. **2024**

MUIDES SUR LOIRE 4G2 (0.5km S Rural) 47.66611, 1.52916 **Sandaya Château des Marais,** 27 Rue de Chambord, 41500 Muides-sur-Loire **02 54 87 05 42; mar@sandaya.fr; https://www.sandaya.fr/nos-campings/chateau-des-marais**

€5 (htd) (covrd, htd)

Exit A10 at junc 16 sp Chambord & take D2152 sp Mer, Chambord, Blois. At Mer take D112 & cross Rv Loire; at Muides-sur-Loire x-rds cont strt on for 800m; then turn R at Camping sp; site on R in 800m. 5*, Lge, mkd, shd, pt sl, serviced pitches; EHU (6A) inc (poss rev pol); gas; bbq (charcoal); twin axles; TV; 65% statics; Eng spkn; adv bkg acc; ccard acc; watersports nr; lake fishing; games area; bike hire; waterslide; tennis; jacuzzi; games rm; sauna; CKE. *"Busy lively site in wooded area in chateau grnds; gd sized pitches; excel, clean san facs; friendly staff; plenty of gd quality children's play equipment; sh walk to rv; conv Loire chateaux; plenty to do in area; mkt Sat Blois; pitches grass, can be a problem when wet."*
€25.00, 14 Apr - 24 Sep, L10. **2022**

MULHOUSE 6F3 (2km SW Rural) 47.73405, 7.3235 **Camping de l'Ill,** 1 Rue de Pierre Coubertin, 68100 Mulhouse **03 89 42 64 76; reception@camping-mulhouse.com; www.camping-mulhouse.com**

€2.50

Fr A36 take Mulhouse/Dornach exit & foll sp Brunstatt at 1st traff lts. At 2nd traff lts turn R, foll University/Brunstatt/Camping sps, site approx 2.5km on rvside. 3*, Lge, mkd, pt shd, pt sl, EHU (10A) €6.60; gas; tram 500m; CKE. *"Welcoming recep; cycle/walk along rv to town cent; OK NH."*
€21.70, 1 Apr-30 Sep. **2023**

MULHOUSE 6F3 (30km W Rural) 47.73554, 7.01497 **Flower Camping du Lac de la Seigneurie,** 3 Rue de la Seigneurie, 90110 Leval **03 84 23 00 13; contact@camping-lac-seigneurie.com; www.camping-lac-seigneurie.com**

(htd)

Off N83 dir Belfort-Mulhouse. D11 NW Petitefontaine twds Roughmont sp to Leval. 3*, Med, hdg, mkd, pt shd, pt sl, EHU (6-10A); bbq; 6% statics; adv bkg acc; ccard acc; games area.
€21.00, 1 Apr-31 Oct. **2022**

MUNSTER 6F3 (4km E Rural) 48.05160, 7.20527 **Camping La Route Verte,** 13 Rue de la Gare, 68230 Wihr-au-Val **03 89 71 10 10 or 06 47 42 49 62; info@camping-routeverte.com; www.camping-routeverte.com**

€1.50

Take D417 out of Colmar twd Munster & turn R int Wihr-au-Val. Site on L 800m. Well sp. 2*, Med, mkd, shd, pt sl, EHU (4-6A) €2.80-3.95; red long stay; phone; adv bkg acc; games rm; CKE. *"Delightful, popular, clean site amid vineyards; owner helpful & friendly; not suitable lge c'vans (6m max); pool 4km; excel san facs; highly rec; excel."*
€17.00, 5 May-15 Sep. **2024**

MUNSTER 6F3 (2km SW Rural) 48.03105, 7.11350 **Camping Les Amis de la Nature,** 4 Rue du Château, 68140 Luttenbach-près-Munster **03 89 77 38 60; an-munster@wanadoo.fr; https://an-camping.fr**

€2 (htd) (htd)

Fr Munster take D10 sp Luttenbach; site sp. 3*, Lge, mkd, pt shd, EHU (6A) €3.90; bbq; TV; 50% statics; Eng spkn; ccard acc; games rm; sauna; fishing; tennis 1km; games area. *"Lovely setting by stream; dir access to rv; gd value; new san facs (2017); pleasant walk to town; excel rest; gd touring area."*
€14.80, 21 Mar-11 Nov. **2023**

MUR DE BRETAGNE 2E3 (6km N Rural) 48.25568, -2.98801 **Le Boterff Gites and Camping (Formerly Camping Le Boterff d'en Haut),** 22320 St Mayeux **www.brittanyforholidays.com and 02 96 24 00 65 +33 (0) 2 96 57 97 70; info@leboterff.com; https://www.leboterff.com/**

12 €1

N fr Mur-de-Bretagne on D767 to St Mayeux. Turn R into vill & R after vill hall (Salle Municipal); to T-junc, turn R & site on L. App via 750m single-track lane. Car parking in rd outside. Sm, unshd, EHU (6A) inc; bbq; red long stay; adv bkg acc; watersports 8km. *"Peaceful, remote CL-type site; gd san facs; gd touring cent; gd walks & cycling; when wet, cars parked off site; excel; (2013) new owner, 2 dogs max; still British, very welcoming; superb CL type site; beautiful area."*
€20.00 **2024**

MUR DE BRETAGNE 2E3 (2km SW Rural) 48.19872, -3.01282 **Camping Le Point de Vue,** 104 Rue du Lac, 22530 Mur-de-Bretagne **02 96 26 01 90 and 06 80 25 87 21; camping-lepointdevue@orange.fr; www.camping-lepointdevue.fr**

€1

Fr Mur-de-Bretagne take D18 & foll site sp; ent opp view point of Lake Guerlédan. 2*, Med, pt shd, pt sl, terr, EHU (10A) inc; CKE. *"Gd watersports; hot water may be ltd to a few hrs a day in LS; gd walking & cycling around lake."* **€15.00, 15 Feb-15 Nov.** **2024**

FRANCE

FRANCE

MUR DE BRETAGNE *2E3* (4km NW Rural) *48.20950, -3.05150* **Camping Nautic International,** Route de Beau Rivage, 22530 Caurel **02 96 28 57 94; location@villagenautic.fr; www.campingnautic.fr**

€2.50 (htd)

Fr Loudéac on N164 into Caurel. Fork L 100m past church, site is 1st on L, beside Lac de Guerlédan. NB App fr Pontivy on D767 via Mur-de-Bretagne v steep in places & not rec when towing. 4*, Med, mkd, pt shd, terr, EHU (10A)€4.90; bbq; TV; adv bkg acc; ccard acc; lake fishing; games rm; horseriding nr; bike hire; watersports nr; jacuzzi; sauna; tennis; CKE. *"Peaceful site in attractive countryside by lake; gd pitches, some poss diff lge o'fits; dated facs, poss stretched when site full; fitness rm; no o'fits over 8m; wonderful pool & lake."* **€24.00, 15 May-25 Sep. 2024**

MURAT *7C4* (1km SW Urban) *45.10303, 2.86599* **Camp Municipal de Stalapos,** 8 Rue de Stade, 15300 Murat **01 83 64 69 21 or 04 71 20 03 80; agyl@camping-murat.com; www.murat.fr**

(cont) nr

Fr N122 site sp fr cent of Murat dir Aurillac (thro indus est), adj Rv Alagnon. 2*, Lge, hdstg, pt shd, pt sl, EHU (6-16A) €2.50-6.30; rv fishing adj; CKE. *"Peaceful location; winter ssn, phone ahead; basic but clean san facs; warden lives on site; excel touring base; gd views medieval town."* **€16.00, 12 June-30 Sep. 2024**

MURAT *7C4* (5km SW Rural) *45.07781, 2.83047* **Aire Naturelle Municipal,** 15300 Albepierre-Bredons **04 71 20 20 49**

nr nr nr

SW fr Murat on D39 dir Prat-de-Bouc; site sp fr cent of Albepierre. Sm, pt shd, EHU (10A) €2; CKE. *"Excel, peaceful location; basic, clean facs; warden visits am & pm; bar 300m; vg walking amidst extinct volcanoes; gd; beautiful sm friendly site."* **€9.00, 15 Jun-15 Sep. 2022**

MURAT *7C4* (5.4km W Rural) *45.11697, 2.81275* **Camp Municipal Le Vallognon,** 15300 Laveissière **04 71 20 11 34; www.camping-le-vallagnon.fr**

nr

Site sp fr N122 W fr Murat Sp Aurilla, after 4km turn R onto D439 site on L after 300m. 2*, Med, pt shd, EHU inc; CKE. *"Conv for Cantal Mountains; htd pool adj; gd hill walking; gd site."* **€14.60, 1 Jan-3 Apr, 1 Jun-4 Sep, 20 Dec-31 Dec. 2024**

MUROL *7B4* (1km S Rural) *45.57400, 2.95735* **Camp Le Repos du Baladin,** Groire, 63790 Murol **09 77 95 74 49; reposbaladin@free.fr; www.camping-auvergne-france.com**

€3 (htd) nr (htd)

Fr D996 at Murol foll sp 'Groire' to E, site on R in 1.5km just after vill. 3*, Med, hdg, mkd, shd, pt sl, terr, EHU (10A); sw nr; Eng spkn; sauna; CKE. *"Lovely site with immac san facs; friendly, helpful owners; easy walk into town thro fields."* **€28.00, 29 Apr-16 Sep. 2023**

MUROL *7B4* (2km W Rural) *45.57516, 2.91428* **Camping Le Pré Bas,** 63790 Chambon-sur-Lac **04 73 88 63 04; prebas@campingauvergne.com; www.campingauvergne.com**

€2.10 (covrd, htd)

Take D996 W fr Murol twd Mont-Dore. Site 1.5km on L, twd lake. 5*, Lge, mkd, hdg, pt shd, pt sl, serviced pitches; EHU (6A) €4.70; bbq; sw; TV; 40% statics; phone; Eng spkn; adv bkg acc; games area; waterslide; ice; fitness room; CKE. *"Excel family-run site by Lac Chambon; library; superb views; friendly, helpful staff; immac san facs; excel pool complex; rock pegs ess; access to sm pitches poss diff lge o'fits; excel walking area."* **€24.00, 25 Apr-13 Sep. 2020**

MUROL *7B4* (5km W Rural) *45.56979, 2.90185* **Camping Les Bombes (formerly Municipal),** Chemin de Pétary, 63790 Chambon-sur-Lac **04 73 88 64 03 or 06 88 33 25 94 (mob); lesbombes@orange.fr; www.camping-les-bombes.com**

€5 (htd)

Site is on D996. Nr exit fr vill Chambon. Well sp. 3*, Med, mkd, pt shd, EHU (6A) €4.50; bbq; sw nr; TV; 5% statics; phone; Eng spkn; adv bkg acc; homeball; mini golf; playhse for kids; soccer field; volleyball; terrain balls; table tennis; chess; bowling; CKE. *"Beautiful area; gd, clean, well-maintained facs stretched in high ssn; lge pitches; friendly, helpful owners; excel."* **€24.00, 30 Apr-13 Sep. 2020**

MUZILLAC *2G3* (8km SW Coastal) *47.51780, -2.55539* **Camping Ty Breiz,** 15 Grande Rue, Kervoyal, 56750 Damgan **02 97 41 13 47; campingtybreiz@orange.fr; www.campingtybreiz.com**

€1.50 sand 300m

Fr Muzillac on D153 dir Damgan, turn S for Kervoyal; site on L opp sm church. 2*, Med, hdg, mkd, pt shd, EHU (6-10A) €3-3.50; bbq; TV; Eng spkn; adv bkg rec; ccard acc; table tennis; CKE. *"Pleasant, welcoming, family-run site; excel san facs; quiet; cycle path to Damgan; mkt Wed; vg."* **€21.00, 1 Apr-31 Oct. 2020**

NAJAC *8E4* (1.7km W Rural) *44.22011, 1.96985* **Camping Le Païsserou,** 12270 Najac **05 65 29 73 96; campingnajac@gmail.com; www.campingnajac.com**

€2 nr (htd)

Take D922 fr Villefranche-de-Rouergue. Turn R on D39 at La Fouillade to Najac. Site by rv, sp in vill. Or fr A20 exit junc 59 onto D926. At Caylus take D84 to Najac. All appr v steep. 3*, Med, hdg, shd, EHU €3; bbq; 10% statics; phone; Eng spkn; adv bkg acc; tennis adj; CKE. *"Conv for Aveyron gorges; friendly owners; ltd facs LS; lovely vill; unrel opening LS, phone ahead; htd covrd pool adj (free); site yourself if recep clsd, avail pitches listed."* **€23.00, 1 May-30 Sep. 2020**

NAMPONT ST MARTIN *3B3* (3km W Rural) *50.33595, 1.71230* **La Ferme des Aulnes,** Camping Ferme des Aulnes, Fresne, 80120 NAMPONT SAINT MARTIN **03 22 29 22 69; lesaulnes@vagues-oceanes.com; www.fermedesaulnes.com**

€4 (htd) nr (covrd, htd)

D901 S fr Montreuil 13km thro Nampont-St Firmin to Nampont-St Martin; turn R in vill onto D485; site in 3km; sp fr D901. 4*, Med, hdg, pt shd, pt sl, EHU (6-10A) €6-12; bbq (charcoal, gas); TV; 80% statics; Eng spkn; adv bkg acc; games area; golf 1km; archery; CKE. *"Attractive site nr Calais; some pitches sm, some very sl; friendly welcoming staff; clsd 2200-0800; cinema rm; old fm bldgs retain character of an old fmstead; clean san facs."* **€32.50, 1 Apr-31 Oct, P13.** **2022**

NANCAY *4G3* (0.9km NW Rural) *47.35215, 2.18522* **Camping Les Pins (Formerly Municipal),** Route de Salbris, La Chaux, 18330 Nançay **02 48 51 81 80; campinglespins@onlycamp.fr; camping-nancay.fr**

(htd) nr

Site on D944 fr Salbris twd Bourges on L immed bef ent Nançay. 2*, Med, mkd, hdstg, shd, EHU (6A) inc; gas; adv bkg acc; golf 2km; fishing; tennis; CKE. *"Lovely spot in pine woods; friendly recep; clean san facs; poor site lighting; beautiful vill; gd walking; rec open am and pm."* **€8.50, 1 May-30 Sep.** **2023**

NANCY *6E2* (6.5km SW Rural) *48.65730, 6.14028* **Camping Bel Air Village Le Brabois,** 2301 Ave Paul Muller, 54600 Villers-lès-Nancy **03 83 27 18 28; campingbrabois@belairvillage.com; campingbrabois.fr**

€4 (htd)

Fr A33 exit junc 2b sp Brabois onto D974 dir Nancy; after 400m turn L at 2nd traff lts; at slip rd after 2nd further traff lts turn R on slip rd & site on R; site well sp. 3*, Lge, mkd, pt shd, EHU (4-15A) €5.90; gas; bbq; TV; 10% statics; bus adj; Eng spkn; adv bkg acc; ccard acc; games area; CKE. *"Popular, well-run site; mostly lge pitches, but some sm, all grass; supmkt & petrol 2km; friendly, helpful staff; gd, clean, all new san facs; no twin axles over 5.5m (m'vans OK); interesting town; rec arr early; vg NH; excel."*
€26.00, 30 Mar-14 Oct, J03. **2023**

NANCY *6E2* (10km NW Rural) *48.74733, 6.05700* **Camping Les Boucles de la Moselle,** 7 Ave Eugène Lerebourg, 54460 Liverdun **03 83 24 43 78; francis.iung@orange.fr; www.lesbouclesdelamoselle.com**

€1.50 (htd)

Fr A31 exit junc 22 to Frouard. In Frouard bear L onto D90 to Liverdun; cross rv bdge (sp Liverdun); turn L immed after rv bdge; foll rv and sp to camp. 2*, Lge, pt shd, EHU (6-10A) €5-7; 10% statics; CKE. *"Lovely site & area; helpful staff; Nancy worth visit; pleasant rvside site."* **€21.00, 1 May-30 Sep.** **2024**

NANT *10E1* (2km N Rural) *44.03578, 3.29008* **Camping Le Roc Qui Parle,** Les Cuns, 12230 Nant **05 65 62 22 05; contact@camping-roc-qui-parle-aveyron.fr; www.camping-roc-qui-parle-aveyron.fr**

Fr Millau take D991E to site passing Val de Cantobre. Fr La Cavalerie take D999E to Nant & at T-junc on o'skts of Nant turn N; Millau & Les Cuns approx 2km; site on R. NB Steep decent into site. 3*, Med, hdg, mkd, pt shd, pt sl, serviced pitches; EHU (10A) €3.50; bbq; sw; adv bkg acc; fishing; CKE. *"Excel, well-run site in magnificent surroundings; lge pitches with views; warm welcome, friendly & helpful; excel facs; rv walk; rec; same price year round."* **€15.00, 13 Mar-21 Oct.** **2022**

NANT *10E1* (4km N Rural) *44.04550, 3.30170* **RCN Camping Le Val de Cantobre,** Domaine de Vellas, 12230 Nant **08 50 40 07 00 or 09 70 73 10 38; contact@rcn.fr; www.rcn-valdecantobre.fr**

€5.50 (htd)

Exit A75 junc 47 (La Cavalerie/Nant); foll sp D999 E dir La Cavalerie/Nant for 12 km. At Nant at T-junc turn L onto D991 sp Val de Cantobre. Site on R in 4km. NB Steep access rd, care req. Rec park in parking area at ent to site & walk down drive to recep. 4*, Lge, hdstg, mkd, pt shd, terr, EHU (10A) inc; gas; bbq; TV; Eng spkn; adv bkg acc; ccard acc; tennis; games area; bike hire; games rm; waterslide; CKE. *"Busy, popular, Dutch-owned site; in gd position - views fr most pitches; helpful, welcoming staff; clean, modern san facs but long walk fr some pitches; some tour op statics & tents; steep site rds & many steps; no o'fits over 7m high ssn; mkt Tue (July/Aug only); excel; gd cent for exploring the causse & gorges; gd walks fr site"* **€51.50, 16 Apr-10 Oct.** **2022**

"Satellite navigation makes touring much easier"

Remember most sat navs don't know if you're towing or in a larger vehicle – always use yours alongside maps and site directions.

NANT *10E1* (11km E Rural) *44.01117, 3.20457* **Camping La Dourbie,** Route de Nant, 12230 Saint-Jean-du-Bruel, Aveyron **05 65 46 06 40; campingladourbie@orange.fr; www.camping-dourbie-aveyron.com**

(htd)

Fr A75 take exit 47, twrds La cavalerie, Nat, St-Eulalie-de-Cernon. At rndabt take 3rd exit onto D999, go thro next rndabt, turn R cont D999 to site. 4*, Med, hdg, pt shd, EHU (10A); bbq; 20% statics; canoeing. *"Excel site, such a lot to do & see; very friendly; bungee jumping; paragliding; clean san facs; spa; 1 dog per pitch; rest open Fri & Sat nights in LS."*
€25.50, 14 Apr-30 Sep. **2023**

FRANCE

NANT *10E1* (1km S Rural) *44.01698, 3.30125* **Camping Les Deux Vallées,** 12230 Nant **05 65 62 26 89 or 05 65 62 10 40; contact@lesdeuxvallees.com; www.lesdeuxvallees.com**

€1 nr

Exit A75 junc 47 onto D999 for 14km to Nant; site sp. 3*, Med, mkd, pt shd, serviced pitches; EHU (6A) €2 (poss rev pol); own san req; TV; phone; adv bkg acc; rv fishing; CKE. *"Peaceful, well-kept, scenic site; friendly; clean, modern san facs; pool 500m; 15 mins walk fr vill cent; gd walking; rec."* **€21.50, 15 Apr-17 Oct. 2022**

NANTES *2G4* (3km N Urban) *47.24261, -1.55703* **Nantes Camping,** 21 Blvd de Petit Port, 44300 Nantes **02 40 74 47 94; nantes-camping@nge-nantes.fr; www.nantes-camping.fr**

12 €4 (htd)

Fr ring rd exit junc 39 sp Porte de la Chapelle & foll sp Cent Ville, Camping Petit Port or University when ent o'skts of Nantes. Site ent opp Hippodrome & nr racecourse & university; well sp. Take care tram lines. 5*, Lge, hdstg, mkd, hdg, pt shd, serviced pitches; EHU (16A) €5; gas; bbq (charcoal); red long stay; twin axles; TV; 30% statics; bus & tram to city cent adj; Eng spkn; adv bkg req; ccard acc; bike hire; CKE. *"Well kept and maintained; htd covrd pool adj; waterslide adj inc; excel san facs; tram stop next to site, easy access to Nantes cent; excel site, great location; o'night m'van area; ACSI red LS; popular; recep clsd 1230-1500."* **€56.00 2023**

NANTES *2G4* (20km E Urban) *47.24930, -1.37118* **Camping Le Chêne,** 44450 St Julien-de-Concelles **02 40 54 12 00; camping-duchene@vacances-seasonova.com; vacances-seasonova.com/fr**

€1 nr (covrd)

Fr Nantes, cross Rv Loire dir Poitiers; immed turn E sp St Sébastien; thro town onto D751 to Le Bout-des-Pont; turn S onto D57 sp Camping. Site on L immed after lake. 3*, Med, shd, EHU (10A) €2.60; bbq; adv bkg rec; fishing; sailing; golf; windsurfing; tennis; bike hire. *"Under new ownership (2013); lake adj; very helpful staff."* **€16.00, 29 Mar-27 Oct. 2024**

NANTES *2G4* (6km E Rural) *47.25416, -1.45361* **Camping Belle Rivière,** Route des Perrières, 44980 Ste Luce-sur-Loire **02 40 25 85 81; belleriviere@wanadoo.fr; www.camping-belleriviere.com**

12 €1.50 (htd) nr nr

Fr 'Nantes Périphérique Est' take exit 43 (at Porte d'Anjou) onto A811; exit A811 junc 24 dir Thouaré-sur-Loire on D68; at double rndabt by car showroom turn S & foll sp over rlwy bdge; site sp. Fr E via D68, thro Thouaré dir Ste Luce; at double rndabt by car showroom, S over rlwy bdge twd rv; site sp. 3*, Med, hdg, mkd, hdstg, pt shd, EHU (10A) €4.50; gas; bbq; 50% statics; Eng spkn; adv bkg acc; CKE. *"Beautifully-kept site; helpful owners; gd clean san facs; rvside walks; conv Nantes Périphérique & city cent; gd touring base; excel."* **€21.00 2023**

NANTUA *9A3* (1km W Urban) *46.14999, 5.60017* **Camping Le Signal,** 17 Ave du Camping, 01130 Nantua **04 74 75 02 09 or 04 48 20 03 19; direction.signal@olydea.com; www.olydea.com**

€10 nr

E on D1084 fr Pont d'Ain, rd passes alongside Nantua lake on R. At end of lake bef ent town turn R & foll sps. 2*, Sm, hdg, mkd, unshd, EHU (16A) inc; sw nr; 10% statics. *"Attractive, spacious, well-kept site in lovely setting; nice lrg pitches; friendly staff; town & shops mins away; conv for m'way; sports cent nr; Lidl store 3 mins away; gd shwrs."* **€20.00, 1 Apr-31 Oct. 2023**

NAPOULE, LA *10F4* (3km N Urban/Coastal) *43.5234, 6.9308* **Camping Coté Mer,** Blvd du Bon Puits, 06210 Mandelieu-la-Napoule **+33 (0)4 42 16 89 90; www.campingcotemer.com**

€4 sand 700m

Fr A8 exit junc 40 & turn L in Mandelieu cent sp Fréjus; 200m after rndabt with palm tree cent, fork R into Ave Maréchal Juin & strt into Blvd du Bon Puits. Avoid La Napoule vill when towing. 2*, Med, shd, EHU (10A) inc; gas; 10% statics; adv bkg acc. *"Nice atmosphere; some pitches very sm; friendly, helpful staff; dated but clean facs; pleasant sm bar & rest."* **€36.00, 25 Mar-1 Oct. 2024**

NARBONNE *10F1* (10km N Rural) *43.26009, 2.95552* **Camp Municipal,** Rue de la Cave Coopérative, 11590 Sallèles-d'Aude **04 68 46 68 46 (Mairie) or 06 47 97 75 78; ot.sallelesdaude@wanadoo.fr; www.camping-sallelesdaude.fr**

nr

Fr A9/E15 exit junc 36 onto D64 N & in approx 4km turn L to join D11 W. Cont on this rd for approx 18km, then turn L onto D13 S to Ouveillan. In vill, turn R onto D418 SW to Sallèles-d'Aude. Site in vill. NB Nr Canal du Midi some narr app rds. 1*, Sm, hdg, mkd, pt shd, EHU €2.50; bbq; adv bkg acc. *"Clean site nr canal; 16 pitches; warden calls am; phone warden bef pitching; site not maintained but nice."* **€16.00, 1 May-30 Sep. 2024**

NARBONNE *10F1* (12km SW Rural) *43.16296, 2.89186* **Camping La Figurotta,** Route de Narbonne, 11200 Bizanet **04 68 45 16 26 or 06 88 16 12 30 (mob); camping.figurotta@gmail.com; www.camping-figurotta.com**

12 €3 (htd)

Exit A9 at Narbonne Sud onto slip rd N9/D6113 twd Lézignan-Corbières; in 3km at new rndabt head L twd D613 & then D224 sp Bizanet & site. App fr W not rec due narr D rds. 1*, Sm, hdstg, mkd, shd, pt sl, terr, EHU (10A) €5 (poss long lead req); gas; red long stay; 5% statics; phone; Eng spkn; adv bkg acc; games area; CKE. *"Pleasant, simple, well-run, scenic site; friendly & helpful owners; sm dogs only; gd pool with new snack bar o'looking; gusty & stony site - steel pegs req; excel drainage; gd NH en rte Spain; vg; new san facs (2018)."* **€22.00 2023**

NASBINALS *9D1* (1km N Rural) *44.67016, 3.04036* **Camp Municipal,** Route de St Urcize, 48260 Nasbinals **06 07 13 49 29; camping.nasbinals@orange.fr; www.nasbinals.fr/camping-municipal/**

(htd) nr nr

Fr A75 exit 36 to Aumont-Aubrac, then W on D987 to Nasbinals. Turn R onto D12, site sp. Med, pt shd, pt sl, EHU (16A) €3; bbq; CKE. *"Lovely location; gd views; no shd; facs inadequate peak ssn; excel communal rm."* **€12.00, 15 May-30 Sep. 2022**

NAVARRENX *8F1* (0.2km S Urban) *43.31988, -0.76143* **Camping Beau Rivage,** Allée des Marronniers, 64190 Navarrenx **05 59 66 10 00; beaucamping@free.fr; www.beaucamping.com**

€4 (htd) nr nr nr

Fr E exit A64 junc 9 at Artix onto D281 dir Mourenx, then Navarrenx. Fr N on D947 thro Orthez to Navarrenx (D947 fr Orthez much improved). Site well sp bet walled (Bastide) town & rv. 3*, Med, hdstg, mkd, hdg, pt shd, pt sl, terr, serviced pitches; EHU (6-10A) inc; bbq; sw nr; 15% statics; phone; Eng spkn; adv bkg acc; ccard acc; rv fishing; games rm; rafting; tennis; CKE. *"Lovely, peaceful, well-run site; no o'fits over 9m high ssn; nr interesting walled town; helpful, friendly, British owners; bike hire in town; clean san facs; gd pool; bar 300m; gd area for walking, cycling; conv local shops & rests; mkt Wed; rec; outstanding."* **€30.00, 8 Apr - 15 Oct, D26. 2022**

NAY *8F2* (2km N Rural) *43.20027, -0.25722* **Camping Les Ô Kiri,** Ave du Lac, 64800 Baudreix **05 59 92 97 73; contact@lesokiri.com; www.lesokiri.com**

€2 (htd)

Exit A64 junc 10 onto Pau ring rd D317 S, then D938 dir Nay & Lourdes. Exit sp Baudreix & in 2km turn R at rndabt & foll sp to lake & site. 4*, Med, mkd, hdg, pt shd, EHU (6-10A) €4-5.50; bbq; sw; 50% statics; adv bkg acc; ccard acc; tennis; waterslide; bike hire. *"Conv Biarritz, N Spain & Pyrenees; lake sw complex booking ess; on arr use carpark for recep; excel rest; superb lake facs; picturesque; basic but OK san facs, poss stretched if site full."* **€19.50, 1 Apr-30 Sep. 2024**

NEBOUZAT *9B1* (2km NW Rural) *45.72569, 2.89008* **Camping Les Domes,** Les Quatre Routes de Nébouzat, 63210 Nébouzat **04 73 87 14 06 or 06 80 23 92 73 (LS); camping-les-domes@wanadoo.fr; www.les-domes.com**

(covrd, htd)

Exit 5 fr A75 onto D213 twd Col de la Ventouse; turn L on D2089 sp Tulle. Do not ent vill of Nébouzat but cont for 1km. Take L onto D216 sp Orcival then immed L. Site on L in 100m. 3*, Med, mkd, hdstg, pt shd, EHU (10-15A) €6 (poss long lead req); gas; TV; phone; Eng spkn; adv bkg acc; sailing; windsurfing; CKE. *"Immac site; walking; boules area; warm welcome; friendly, helpful staff; sm pitches; gd san facs; conv Vulcania; excel rest nrby; gd base for Auvergne."* **€26.50, 23 Apr-3 Oct. 2022**

NERET *4H3* (3km N Rural) *46.58885, 2.13425* **Campsite Le Bonhomme,** Mulles 36400 Neret **02 54 31 46 11; info@camping-lebonhomme.com; www.camping-lebonhomme.com**

Fr Vierzon on the A20 take exit 12 to Chateauroux, then the D943 twds Montlucon.Turn L at Neret exit and foll Aire Naturelle signs. Site is 2km beyond Neret on L. 2*, Sm, hdstg, mkd, pt shd, sl, EHU (16A); bbq; Eng spkn; adv bkg acc; games area. *"Excel; lovely rural, quiet site; food avail fr owners."* **€20.50, 1 Apr-1 Oct. 2022**

NERIS LES BAINS *7A4* (1km NW Urban) *46.28695, 2.65215* **Le Camping du Lac,** Ave Marx Dormoy, 03310 Néris-les-Bains **04 70 03 17 59 or 04 70 03 24 70 (recep); campingdulac@nerislesbains.fr; www.campingdulac-neris.com**

€1 nr

Site on N side of Néris off D2144. Turn W at rndabt by blue TO, opp park, & foll sp round 1 way system to site in 500m. 3*, Med, hdstg, hdg, mkd, pt shd, pt sl, terr, EHU (10A); gas; red long stay; 10% statics. *"6 pitches for m'vans at ent to site; covrd pool 500m; space to wait on car park if barrier clsd; pleasant town; vg; gd facs, quiet lower pitches, gd NH."* **€15.00, 1 Apr-22 Oct. 2024**

NEUF BRISACH *6F3* (1km E Urban) *48.01638, 7.53565* **Camp Municipal Vauban,** Entrée Porte de Bâle, 68600 Neuf-Brisach **03 89 72 54 25 or 03 89 72 51 68 (Mairie); contact@camping-vauban.fr; www.camping-vauban.fr**

€1 nr

Fr D415 (Colmar-Freiburg) at E of Neuf-Brisach turn NE on D1 bis (sp Neuf-Brisach & Camping Vauban). At next junc turn L & immed R into site rd. 2*, Med, pt shd, EHU (10A) €4; 5% statics; adv bkg acc; CKE. *"Gd, well-run site; fascinating ramparts around town; lge pitches; friendly, helpful staff; excel cycle rtes fr site along Rhine & thro historic vill; pool 3km; site won many awards; long elec leads req; ideal long stay; supmkt 2km."* **€26.00, 1 Apr-31 Oct. 2022**

NEUF BRISACH *6F3* (6km SE Rural) *47.97988, 7.59639* **Camping L'Orée du Bois,** 5 Rue du Bouleau, 68600 Geiswasser **03 89 72 80 13; valerie.schappler@orange.fr; https://campingaloreedubois.fr/**

€0.50 (htd)

Site in vill cent; rd name on bungalow; ent bet bungalow & vegetable garden - tight turn, watch out bungalow gutters. 1*, Sm, hdg, pt shd, EHU (10A) €3.85; bbq; 60% statics; bus adj; Eng spkn; adv bkg acc; CKE. *"Gd touring base; friendly owner; gd."* **€16.80, 1 Apr-30 Sep. 2023**

FRANCE

NEUFCHATEL EN BRAY *3C2* (1.4km NW Urban) *49.73781, 1.42803* **Camping Sainte Claire,** 19 rue Grande Flandre, 76270 Neufchâtel-en-Bray
02 35 93 03 93; www.camping-sainte-claire.com

Fr N & S exit A28 junc 9 onto D928 sp Neufchâtel; in 1km at mini rndabt at bottom hill, turn L into Rue de la Grande Flandre, foll Leclerk supmkt sp; cont past supmkt for 400m to Rue Ste Claire. (NB Motorvan aire immed bef site ent, do not turn in by mistake as there are charges). 3*, Med, hdstg, mkd, hdg, pt shd, pt sl, terr, serviced pitches; EHU (6-10A) inc; bbq; twin axles; red long stay; 20% statics; phone; bus 400m; Eng spkn; adv bkg acc; ccard acc; bike hire; fishing; CKE. *"Beautiful, spacious, well-run, well-kept, busy site by rv; lge, med & sm pitches; not all pitches have 10A, poss 6A pitches better; friendly, helpful owner; excel clean san facs - poss long walk LS; wet rm for disabled; wheelchair access/easy walking; pleasant walk along cycle rte (old rlwy line) to town & vet; Sat mkt; conv Le Havre/Dieppe ferries & A28; sep o'night area; some drive-thro pitches; gd value sh or long stay; popular NH; excel; nice site as always; Aire for m'vans now open adj (OAY, €12, all hdstg, full facs, 10A elec & acc ccards only); busy, efficient site; gd easy access fr a'route; ent tight for lge o'fits; best book for twin axles; excel rest; adj 40km greenway cycle ride; ACSI acc; lge Leclerc nrby."* **€20.40, 1 Apr-15 Oct. 2022**

NEUNG SUR BEUVRON *4G3* (0.5km NE Rural) *47.53893, 1.81488* **FFCC Camp Municipal de la Varenne,** 34 Rue de Veilleas, 41210 Neung-sur-Beuvron
02 54 83 68 52 or 06 27 92 39 14 (mob); camping.lavarenne@wanadoo.fr; www.neung-sur-beuvron.fr/camping

nr nr nr

On A10 heading S take Orléans Sud exit & join N20 S. At end of La Ferté-St Aubin take D922 SW twd Romorantin-Lanthenay. In 20km R onto D925 to Neung. Turn R at church pedestrian x-ing in cent of vill ('stade' sp), R at fork (white, iron cross) & site on R in 1km. Site by rvside. Fr A71 exit junc 3 onto D923; turn R onto D925 & as above.
2*, Sm, hdg, mkd, pt shd, pt sl, EHU (6A) €3.10; gas; 10% statics; Eng spkn; adv bkg acc; ccard acc; tennis. *"Friendly, helpful warden; gd, immac facs; lge pitches; barrier clsd 2200-0800; vg cent for hiking, cycling, birdwatching; mkt Sat; excel well maintained site."*
€12.00, Easter-20 Oct. 2023

NEUVE LYRE, LA *3D2* (0.4km W Urban) *48.90750, 0.74486* **Camp Municipal De La Risle (Formerly Le Salle),** Rue de l'Union, 27330 La Neuve-Lyre
02 32 30 50 01 (Mairie); mairie.la-neuve-lyre@wanadoo.fr; http://laneuvelyre.e-monsite.com

nr

Fr NE on D830 into vill turn R at church (sp not visible), fr S (Rugles) foll sp. Well sp fr vill.
1*, Med, pt shd, EHU (5A) inc (poss long lead req); 2% statics; fishing; CKE. *"Delightful, peaceful, clean site; site yourself, warden calls; excel sh stay/NH."*
€12.00, 15 Mar-15 Oct. 2023

NEUVEGLISE *9C1* (5km S Rural) *44.89500, 3.00157* **Flower Camping Le Belvédère,** Le Pont-de-Lanau, 15260 Neuvéglise **04 71 23 50 50; contact@campinglebelvedere.com; www.campinglebelvedere.com**

(htd)

S on A75/E11 exit junc 28 at St Flour; take D921 S twd Chaudes-Aigues. Turn R sp 'Villages de Vacances de Lanau' & site - do not app site thro Neuvéglise. Steep access poss diff lge o'fits. 4*, Med, pt shd, terr, EHU (6A) inc; gas; bbq (charcoal, gas); red long stay; twin axles; TV; 25% statics; adv bkg acc; ccard acc; sauna; fishing; windsurfing nr; horseriding 20km; canoeing nr; games rm; tennis nr; sailing 15km; CKE. *"Views over Rv Truyère; fitness rm; friendly, peaceful, family-run site; steep terrs & tight pitches poss diff; gd, clean san facs; mkt Neuvéglise Fri; excel site, beautiful views."* **€35.80, 26 Apr-6 Oct. 2024**

NEUVIC (CORREZE) *7C4* (4km N Rural) *45.38245, 2.22901* **Camping Domaine de Mialaret,** Route d'Egletons, 19160 Neuvic **05 55 46 02 50; info@lemialaret.com; www.lemialaret.com**

(htd)

Fr N on A89 exit 23 twds St Angel then D171 to Neuvic or foll sp fr Neuvic on D991. 4*, Med, hdg, pt shd, pt sl, EHU (10A) €3-4; red long stay; TV; 30% statics; phone; bus 4km; Eng spkn; adv bkg acc; games rm; watersports nr; CKE. *"Excel site in grnds of chateau; 2 carp fishing pools; charming owner, friendly staff; facs ltd LS; blocks req most pitches; mini farm; walking tours; mountain bike trails; children's mini zoo & rare sheep breeds nrby."* **€42.60, 26 Apr-5 Oct. 2024**

NEVERS *4H4* (1km S Rural) *46.98210, 3.16110* **Camping de Nevers,** Rue de la Jonction, 58000 Nevers
03 86 36 40 75; camping.nevers@aquadis-loisirs.com; www.aquadis-loisirs.com/camping-de-nevers

€2 (cont) nr nr
sand 200m

Fr E exit A77 junc 37 & foll dir 'Cent Ville'. Site on R immed bef bdge over Rv Loire. Fr W (Bourges) on D976 foll sp 'Nevers Centre' onto D907. In approx 3km bef bdge turn R, site on L. 3*, Sm, hdstg, mkd, hdg, shd, pt sl, terr, EHU (10A); bbq; TV; 3% statics; phone; bus 20m; Eng spkn; adv bkg rec; ccard acc; rv fishing; bike hire; CKE. *"Pleasant, scenic site on bank of Rv Loire; on 3 levels - ltd EHU on lower; gd clean san facs, poss stretched high ssn; cycle paths along Loire; no twin axles; poss noisy when events at Nevers Magny-Cours racing circuit; gd site; easy walk over bdge to interesting town; nr town; excel recep staff; ltd no of elec pitches, arr early; off open 3pm; v popular site."* **€22.50, 1 Mar-30 Oct. 2023**

NEXON *7B3* (6km SSW Rural) *45.63471, 1.16176* **Camping L'Air Du Lac,** Impasse du Lac Plaisance, 87800 St Hilaire-les-Places **05 55 58 79 18; campinglairdulac@flowercampings.com; www.campinglairdulac.com**

€2 adj

S fr Nexon on D11. Soon after ent St Hilaire-les-Places take a L sp Lac Plaisance & Camping. Site adj to lake. 3*, Med, hdg, shd, pt sl, EHU (10A) €6; bbq; sw; TV; 20% statics; Eng spkn; adv bkg acc; ccard acc; games rm; games area; CKE. *"Pleasant site adj to lake sw beach; dep req; very helpful staff; gd sized pitches; clean facs; vg for families; interesting touring area; excel."* **€16.00, 15 Apr-30 Sep. 2023**

NIEDERBRONN LES BAINS *5D3* (1.5km SW Rural) *48.92958, 7.60428* **Camping Seasonova Les Vosges du Nord,** 3 Rue de Frohret, 67110 Oberbronn **09 83 32 65 10; www.vacances-seasonova.com/fr/camping/oberbronn/; www.opale-dmcc.fr**

€2.65 (covrd, htd)

Fr D1062 turn S on D28 away fr Niederbronn; thro Oberbronn, site sp. 3*, Lge, mkd, pt shd, pt sl, EHU (6A) €4.30; bbq; red long stay; 20% statics; adv bkg rec; ccard acc; golf; cycling; fishing 2km; sauna; games rm; clsd 1200-1300; tennis; CKE. *"Vg site with views; pt of leisure complex; sl area for tourers; horseriding rtes; some san facs tired; walking; wellness cent; fitness rm; site gravel paths not suitable wheelchair users."* **€15.00, 1 Apr-30 Sep. 2022**

"There aren't many sites open at this time of year"

If you're travelling outside peak season remember to call ahead to check site opening dates – even if the entry says 'open all year'.

NIMES *10E2* (8km S Rural) *43.78776, 4.35196* **Camp La Bastide,** route de Générac, 30900 Nîmes **04 66 62 05 82; bastide@capfun.com; www.camping-nimes.com**

12 €2.70 (htd) nr

Fr A9 exit junc 25 onto A54 dir Arles; in 2km exit A54 junc 1 onto D42 sp St Gilles; in 1.5km (at 2nd rndabt) turn R onto D135; in 2.5km at rndabt turn R onto D13; site on L. Or N fr Montpellier on N113/D6113 to Nimes; at Périphique Sud turn S onto D13 sp Générac; site on R 500m after rndabt junc with D613. Site well sp fr town cent. 4*, Lge, mkd, hdstg, hdg, shd, EHU (10A) inc; gas; TV; 50% statics; phone; bus; Eng spkn; adv bkg acc; games area; CKE. *"Excel, well-run site; lge pitches; friendly, helpful recep; Nîmes 20 mins by bus fr site; gd site; exciting water complex; vg bistro on site; child's entmnt; old san facs; busy, used by workers; gd NH."* **€27.50 2024**

NOIRETABLE *9B1* (1km S Rural) *45.80817, 3.76844* **Camp Municipal de la Roche,** Route de la Roche, 42440 Noirétable **04 77 24 72 68; www.noiretable.fr/plan_eau_camping_Roche.aspx**

€1.70 (htd) nr nr

Leave A72/E70 junc 4 sp Noirétable; thro toll & turn SW onto D53. Ignore narr tourist rte sp to W; cont downhill to T-junc & turn R onto D1089. Take next L & site on R in 750m. 2*, Sm, hdstg, mkd, pt shd, pt sl, terr, EHU (10A) €3.80; own san rec; 40% statics; Eng spkn. *"Warden lives on site, but barrier poss locked LS; recep open 0900-1230, 1800-1930; camperstop 100m; lake adj; €3 for water & chem disp, token fr site."* **€10.00, 1 Apr-1 Nov. 2023**

NOIRMOUTIER EN L'ILE *2H3* (2km E Coastal) *46.99697, -2.22057* **Huttopia Noirmoutier,** Bois de la Chaize, 23 Rue des Sableaux, 85330 Noirmoutier-en-l'Ile **02 51 39 06 24; www.europe.huttopia.com**

€4.50 sand adj

Ent Noirmoutier on D948, strt on over bdge & foll sp for Bois-de-la-Chaize, then 'campings'. 3*, Lge, pt shd, EHU (10A); sw nr; 10% statics; phone; adv bkg acc; bike hire; fishing; boat launch; CKE. *"Peaceful site in pine forest nr salt water marshes; gd for children; excel new san facs (2022)."* **€34.30, 7 Apr- 25 Sept, A45. 2022**

NOIRMOUTIER EN L'ILE *2H3* (10km SE Coastal) *46.94503, -2.18542* **Sandaya Domaine le Midi,** 17 Rue du Camping, 85630 Barbâtre **02 51 39 63 74; mid@sandaya.fr; www.sandaya.co.uk**

€5 (htd) sand adj

Cross to island by Passage du Gois D948 (low tide - 2.5 hrs per day) or bdge D38. Turn L after 2.5km off dual c'way to Barbâtre. Site sp N thro vill. 5*, Lge, pt shd, pt sl, EHU (10A) inc; gas; bbq (gas); 45% statics; ccard acc; games area; tennis. *"Gd site; sandy but firm pitches; excel base for cycling island."* **€53.20, 8 Apr-25 Sep. 2022**

NOIRMOUTIER EN L'ILE *2H3* (6.3km SE Coastal) *46.96659, -2.22027* **Domaine Les Moulins,** 54 Rue des Moulins, 85680 La Guérinière **0251 39 51 38; moulins@originalcamping.com; www.domaine-les-moulins.com**

(htd) nr

Cross to island on D38, sp to La Guérinière, Imm turn L, site dir ahead. 5*, Lge, hdg, mkd, pt shd, pt sl, EHU (10A); 40% statics; adv bkg acc; ccard acc; games area; games rm; CKE. *"Excel site; bike hire 100m."* **€67.00, 1 Apr-30 Sep. 2024**

FRANCE

NONTRON 7B3 (11km NE Rural) 45.55138, 0.79472 **Kawan Village Le Château Le Verdoyer,** Château le Verdoyer, 24470 Champs Romain **05 53 56 94 64; chateau@verdoyer.fr; www.verdoyer.fr**

€3 (covrd, htd, indoor)

Fr Limoges on N21 twd Périgueux. At Châlus turn R sp Nontron (D6 bis-D85). After approx 18km turn L twd Champs Romain on D96 to site on L in 2km. 4*, Lge, hdg, pt shd, terr, EHU (5-10A) inc (poss rev pol); gas; bbq (charcoal, gas); sw nr; TV; 20% statics; phone; Eng spkn; adv bkg acc; ccard acc; lake fishing; games rm; waterslide; bike hire; tennis; golf 25km; boating; CKE. *"Peaceful, Dutch-run site in grnds of chateau; B&B in chateau; lovely location; no o'fits over 10m; gd sized pitches, but terr; friendly staff, superb facs; poss steep access some pitches; grnd hard, but awnings poss; excel; highly rec."* **€40.00, 20 Apr - 30 Sep, D21.** 2022

NONTRON 7B3 (8km NE Rural) 45.56185, 0.71979 **Camping Manzac Ferme,** Manzac, 24300 Augignac **07 49 55 45 30; info@manzac-ferme.com; www.manzac-ferme.com**

(htd) nr nr

Fr Nontron take D675 N dir Rochechouart & after 7km on ent Augignac turn R sp Abjat-sur-Bandiat then immed R sp Manzac. Site on R 3.5km. Sm, mkd, hdstg, pt shd, pt sl, EHU (6A) inc; bbq; sw nr; Eng spkn; adv bkg acc; rv fishing; CKE. *"Superb, peaceful, well-kept CL-type, adults only site; helpful British owners; dogs by prior arrangement; excel san facs; phone ahead in winter; ideal for birdwatching & wildlife; highly rec; most pitches in dense shd; excel."* **€24.00, 15 May-15 Sep.** 2022

NONTRON 7B3 (1km S Urban) 45.51992, 0.65876 **Camping L'Agrion Blue (Formerly Camping de Nontron),** St Martiel-de-Valette, 24300 Nontron **05 53 56 02 04 or 06 30 66 25 74 (mob); camping@lagrionbleu.fr; https://campinglagrionbleu.com/**

€1 (htd) nr nr nr

Thro Nontron S twd Brantôme on D675. Site on o'skts of town on L nr stadium. Sp. Med, hdg, mkd, pt shd, EHU (10A) €3.50; gas; TV; Eng spkn; games area; games rm; CKE. *"Pleasant owners; site clsd mid-Dec to early Jan; excel, modern san facs; gd touring base; town 1km walk along footpath."* **€32.00** 2023

NORT SUR ERDRE 2G4 (1km S Rural) 47.42770, -1.49877 **Camping Seasonova du Port Mulon,** Rue des Mares Noires, 44390 Nort-sur-Erdre **02 36 81 00 01 or 02 40 72 23 57; contact@camping-portmulon.com; www.camping-portmulon.com**

€0.90 nr

Sp fr all ents to town; foll 'Camping' & 'Hippodrome' sp. NB: C'vans banned fr town cent, look for diversion sp. 3*, Med, shd, EHU (6A) €2.40; adv bkg acc; fishing; boating; tennis; CKE. *"Delightful, spacious, under-used site; gd walking & cycling area, espec along Nantes canal & Rv Erdre; Barrier perm locked, access when warden on site only; friendly staff; beautiful site; pool v busy; lovely location vg san facs; helpful owner."* **€22.00, 1 Apr-31 Oct.** 2022

NOUAN LE FUZELIER 4G3 (0.7km S Urban) 47.53328, 2.03508 **Camping La Grande Sologne,** Rue des Peupliers, 41600 Nouan-le-Fuzelier **02 54 88 70 22; info@campingrandesologne.com; www.campingrandesologne.com**

€1 nr

On E side of D2020, at S end of Nouan opp rlwy stn. Sp fr town cent & opp rlwy stn. NB sat nav not rec. 3*, Med, mkd, pt shd, EHU (10A) €3; red long stay; 2% statics; Eng spkn; adv bkg acc; golf 15km; tennis; fishing; games area; CKE. *"Pretty site adj lake (no sw); some pitches boggy when wet; facs poss stretched high ssn; ltd facs end of ssn & poss unclean; htd pool adj; public park at ent to site, but quiet; rec arr early; excel NH; phone for entry LS; excel site; office open 0700-1500; voucher for nrby sw pool; san facs dated; friendly owners."* **€24.50, 1 Apr-15 Oct.** 2024

NOUVION EN THIERACHE, LE 3B4 (2km S Rural) 50.00538, 3.78292 **Camp du Lac de Condé,** Promenade Henri d'Orléans, Rue de Guise (Le Lac), 02170 Le Nouvion-en-Thiérache **03 23 98 98 58; campinglacdeconde@gmail.com; www.camping-thierache.com**

€1 nr nr nr

Sp fr cent of Le Nouvion fr D1043 on D26, dir Guise opp chateau. 2*, Sm, hdg, mkd, hdstg, pt shd, pt sl, EHU (4-8A) €4-5.20; bbq; red long stay; 70% statics; phone; Eng spkn; adv bkg acc; ccard acc; tennis nr; horseriding nr; CKE. *"Beautiful, spacious, lakeside site; busy even LS - rec phone ahead; gd sized pitches; warm welcome, staff helpful; htd pool adj; gd san facs; gd for families; canoe hire nr; some pitches not suitable m'vans due slope; muddy when wet; walk around lake; conv NH; excel; coarse fishing in adj lake."* **€12.00, 1 Apr-30 Sep.** 2023

NOYERS *4G4* (0.2km S Rural) *47.69423, 3.99421* **Camp Municipal,** Promenade du Pré de l'Echelle, 89310 Noyers-sur-Serein **03 86 82 83 72 (Mairie); mairie-de-noyers@wanadoo.fr**

Exit A6 at Nitry & turn R onto D944. In 2km at N edge of Nitry, turn R onto D49 sp Noyers. In 10km in Noyers, turn L onto D86 sp Cent Ville/Camping. Immed after x-ing rv & bef gate, turn L bet 2 obelisks. Site at end of track. Sm, mkd, shd, terr, EHU €1.05; own san req; bbq. *"Attractive, secluded site nr Rv Serein (6 pitches); ent key fr Mairie on R after going thro town gate; pretty old vill; ltd san facs."*
€4.00, 1 April - 30 Oct. **2024**

NOYON *3C3* (4.5km E Rural) *49.58882, 3.04370* **FFCC Camping L'Etang du Moulin,** 54 Rue du Moulin, 60400 Salency **03 44 09 99 81**

Take D1032 fr Noyon dir Chauny. On ent Salency turn L & foll site sp. Site in 1km. 2*, Sm, shd, pt sl, EHU (10A) €1.60; gas; bbq; 75% statics; fishing; tennis; CKE. *"Site adj to fishing lake; gd facs; very clean & tidy; elec french 2 pin; security barrier card; pool 3km; v quiet location."* **€13.00** **2022**

NOYON *3C3* (10km S Rural) *49.50667, 3.01765* **FFCC Camping Les Araucarias,** 870 Rue du Général Leclerc, 60170 Carlepont **03 44 75 27 39; camping-les-araucarias@wanadoo.fr; www.camping-les-araucarias.com**

Fr S, fr A1 exit junc 9 or 10 for Compiègne. There take D130 sp Tracy-le-Val & Carlepont. Site on L 100m fr Carlepont vill sp. Or fr N on D934 Noyon-Soissons rd take D130 dir Carlepont & Tracy-le-Val. Site on R after vill on SW twd Compiegne - not well sp. 2*, Sm, mkd, pt shd, pt sl, EHU (6-10A) €3 (poss rev pol); gas; bbq; 80% statics; Eng spkn; adv bkg acc; CKE. *"Secluded site, previously an arboretum; close Parc Astérix & La Mer-de-Sable (theme park); 85km Disneyland; san facs poss scruffy LS; vg."* **€12.50, 1 Apr-31 Oct.** **2022**

NUITS ST GEORGES *6G1* (5km S Urban) *47.10323, 4.94148* **Camping Le Moulin de Prissey,** 14 rue du Moulin de Prissey, 21700 Premeaux-Prissey **03 80 62 31 15 or 07 50 55 05 80; cpg.moulin.prissey@free.fr; www.cpg-moulin-prissey.fr**

Fr A31 take D8 to Nuits St Georges then D974 twrds Beaune. After Premeaux turn L onto D115E. Thro Prissey and site on R. 3*, Sm, mkd, pt shd, pt sl, EHU (6A) inc; gas; bbq; adv bkg acc; ccard acc; CKE. *"Popular NH - arr early; sm pitches; access poss diff lge o'fits; basic facs; gd cycling; noisy rlwy adj; site well laid out & tidy (2015)."* **€20.00, 4 Apr-15 Oct.** **2024**

NYONS *9D2* (1km NE Rural) *44.36523, 5.15365* **Camping Les Clos,** Route de Gap, 26110 Nyons **04 75 26 29 90; info@campinglesclos.com; www.campinglesclos.com**

Fr rndabt in town cent take D94 sp Gap & site on R in 1km. 4*, Med, hdg, mkd, hdstg, pt shd, EHU (10A) inc; gas; bbq (elec, gas); 20% statics; phone; Eng spkn; adv bkg acc; ccard acc; rv; fishing; CKE. *"Quiet, well-kept site in lovely area; friendly, helpful staff; excel touring base; 20 min walk to town along quiet side rd; mkt Thu & Sat; popular site."*
€22.00, 1 Apr-30 Sep. **2024**

NYONS *9D2* (12km NE Rural) *44.42569, 5.21904* **Camping de Trente Pas,** 26110 St Ferréol-Trente-Pas **04 75 27 70 69; contact@campingtrentepas.com; www.campingtrentepas.com**

Exit A7 junc 19 Bollène onto D994 & D94. L on D70 to St Ferréol-Trente-Pas. Site 100m fr vill on banks of stream. 2*, Med, shd, EHU (6A) €4.80; TV; 5% statics; bike hire; tennis; games rm; horseriding 4km. *"Peaceful site nr rv; scenic area, views fr site; gd, clean san facs; gd pool; on flood plain; excel value; rec."*
€22.60, 1 May-31 Aug. **2023**

NYONS *9D2* (12km NE Rural) *44.43507, 5.21248* **FFCC Camping Le Pilat,** 26110 St Ferréol-Trente-Pas **04 75 27 72 09; info@campinglepilat.com; www.campinglepilat.com**

Fr D94 N or Nyons turn N at La Bonté onto D70 to St Ferréol, site sp 1km N of vill. 3*, Med, hdg, shd, EHU (6A) €4; bbq; red long stay; TV; 25% statics; phone; Eng spkn; games area, ping pong table.; CKE. *"Site among lavender fields; pleasant, helpful owners; gd clean san facs; outdoor gym; gd walking & off-rd cycling; Thurs mkt Nyons; excel."*
€23.60, 1 Apr-30 Sep. **2020**

NYONS *9D2* (18km E Rural) *44.34319, 5.28357* **Camp Municipal Les Cigales,** Allée des Platanes, 26110 Ste Jalle **04 75 27 34 88 or 04 75 27 32 78 (mairie); mairie.saintejalle@orange.fr**

Fr Nyons take D94 dir Serres; In 10 km at Curnier turn R onto D64 to Ste-Jalle. In vill turn R onto D108 dir Buis-les-Baronnies. Site on R in 300m. NB Dist by rd fr Nyons is 20km. 2*, Sm, hdg, pt shd, EHU (10A) €2.20; 15% statics; adv bkg acc. *"Vg site in attractive old vill; friendly warden; facs dated but clean."*
€13.00, 1 May-30 Sep. **2022**

FRANCE

OBERNAI *6E3* (16.5km ESE Urban) *48.41413, 7.66983* **Camping Municipal Le Wagelrott,** 1 rue de la Sugarrie, 67150 Erstein **33 88 98 09 88 or 33 88 98 14 33 (Municipal); campingerstein@gmail.com; https://www.camping-erstein-wagelrott.fr/**

€2.30 (htd) nr nr

Fr Strasbourg on A35 then D1083. R onto D426. At rndabt turn L then 1st R to site. Med, hdg, mkd, unshd, EHU (16A) €3.50; 50% statics; phone; Eng spkn; adv bkg acc; ccard acc. *"Gd municipal site; cls to Strasbourg; gd cycle rts; clean facs."* **€16.00, 1 Apr-30 Sep. 2023**

OBERNAI *6E3* (1.5km W Urban) *48.46460, 7.46750* **Camp Municipal Le Vallon de l'Ehn,** 1 Rue de Berlin, 67210 Obernai **03 88 95 38 48; camping@obernai.fr; www.obernai.fr**

€1.10 (htd)

Fr N exit A35 junc 11 onto D426 sp Obernai. Foll D426 W around Obernai & foll sp Mont St Odile & Camping VVF; at final rndabt turn R & immed L to site. Fr S on A35 exit junc 12 sp Obernai. At 3rd rndabt turn L onto D426 Ottrott-Mont Ste Odile (look for sp Camping VVF). Do not tow into Obernai. 3*, Lge, mkd, hdstg, pt shd, pt sl, serviced pitches; EHU (10-16A) €4.50; bbq; twin axles; red long stay; phone; bus to Strasbourg & Obernai adj, train; Eng spkn; adv bkg acc; ccard acc; horseriding adj; tennis adj; CKE. *"Attractive, well-kept, busy site on edge of picturesque town; sm pitches; welcoming, helpful staff; superb, excel, modern clean san facs; no entry after 1930; rec arr early high ssn; lge pool 200m;10% red CC members LS; c'vans, m'vans & tents all sep areas; excel bus/train links; ideal NH; highly rec; very well run, gd site; office clsd 1230-1400; popular."* **€23.40, 1 Jan-7 Jan & 15 Mar-31 Dec. 2024**

OCTON *10F1* (2km NE Rural) *43.65948, 3.32052* **Camping Le Village du Bosc (Naturist),** Chemin de Ricazouls, 34800 Octon **04 67 96 07 37; r.villagedubosc@free.net; www.villagedubosc.net**

€3 (htd)

Exit 54 or 55 fr N9/A75 dir Octon onto D148, foll sp to Ricazouls/site. 2*, Med, hdg, mkd, pt shd, pt sl, terr, EHU (6-10A); sw; red long stay; TV; 5% statics; Eng spkn; adv bkg acc; watersports; INF card; games area; games rm. *"Lovely, quiet site with wooded walks; friendly owners; clean facs; tight turns on terr access for lge o'fits; Octon vill pretty; wheelchair facs in san facs."* **€30.00, 21 Apr-30 Sep. 2023**

OCTON *10F1* (0.6km SE Rural) *43.65100, 3.30877* **Camping Le Mas des Carles,** 34800 Octon **04 67 96 32 33; toocamp.co.uk/france/camping-le-mas-des-carles-c27865.html**

nr nr

Leave A75 at junc 54, foll sp for Octon, 100m after vill sp turn L & foll white site sp keeping L. Ent on L opp tel kiosk (sharp turn). 2*, Sm, hdg, mkd, pt shd, pt sl, terr, EHU (6-10A) inc; 30% statics; phone; adv bkg acc; watersports 800m; CKE. *"Pleasant site with views; helpful owner; facs a little tired (2006); boating 800m; take care low branches on pitches; Lac de Salagou with abandoned vill of Celles 1km."* **€21.40, 1 Apr-10 Oct. 2024**

OLARGUES *8F4* (0.4km N Rural) *43.55798, 2.91440* **Camp Municipal Le Baoüs,** 34390 Olargues **04 67 97 71 50; otsi.olargues@wanadoo.fr; www.olargues.org**

(cont) nr

Take D908 W fr Bédarieux, site immed bef ent Olargues. Site sp over sm bdge on L. At end of bdge turn R to site. Last 50m rough track & narr turn into site. 2*, Sm, pt shd, EHU (6A); adv bkg req; canoeing; bike hire. *"Helpful warden; hill climb to services block; site poss flooded by Rv Jaur in spring; sh walk to amazing hilltop vill."* **1 Jul-15 Sep. 2024**

OLONZAC *8F4* (9km E Rural) *43.28372, 2.82688* **FFCC Camping Les Auberges,** 11120 Pouzols-Minervois **04 68 46 26 50; vero.pradal@neuf.fr; www.campinglesauberges.hubside.fr**

nr

Fr D5 site 500m S of vill of Pouzols-Minervois. 2*, Sm, mkd, pt shd, EHU (5A) €3.50; bbq; 30% statics; Eng spkn; adv bkg rec; tennis; CKE. *"V popular site; friendly owners; gas adj; sm Sat mkt at 'cave' opp."* **€16.00, 1 Apr-1 Nov. 2020**

OLORON STE MARIE *8F2* (3km SW Urban) *43.17886, -0.62328* **Camping Pyrenees Nature,** Chemin de Lagravette, 64400 Oloron-Ste Marie **05 59 39 11 26; camping.pyrenees.nature@gmail.com; www.campingpyreneesnature.fr**

12 €1.20 nr

Fr N on ring rd foll sp to Saragosse (Spain); at rndabt take 2nd exit onto D6 still sp Saragosse, site sp on R just after sports field. Fr S on D55 join ring rd & turn W at rndabt by McDonalds; sp. 3*, Med, hdg, mkd, pt shd, EHU (6-10A) €4-6 (some rev pol); bbq; sw nr; twin axles; TV; adv bkg acc; tennis; rv fishing 1km; bike hire; CKE. *"Well-kept site; lge pitches; helpful staff; clean facs but ltd LS & stretched high ssn; take care low tree; grnd poss soft & damp after rain; barrier clsd 1200-1500; excel base for Pyrenees; pool adj; gd walking."* **€23.60 2024**

FRANCE

ONESSE ET LAHARIE *8E1* (0.5km N Rural) *44.06344, -1.07257* **L'Orée des Landes Camping (formerly Le Bienvenu),** 259 Route de Mimizan, 40110 Onesse-et-Laharie **05 54 54 10 05; contact@loreedeslandes.com; www.loreedeslandes.com**

€1 nr nr nr

On N10 Bordeaux-Bayonne rd, turn W onto D38 at Laharie. Site in 5km. 2*, Med, mkd, pt shd, EHU (10A) €4; red long stay; TV; 10% statics; adv bkg acc; CKE. *"Well-run, nice, family site; gd facs; very helpful staff."* **€18.00, 1 Mar-30 Sep.** 2024

ONZAIN *4G2* (6km W Rural) *47.51030, 1.10400* **Yelloh! Village Le Parc du Val de Loire,** 155 Route de Fleuray, 41150 Mesland **02 54 70 27 18; parcduvaldeloire@orange.fr; www.parcduvaldeloire.com**

€4 (covrd, htd, indoor)

Fr Blois take D952 SW twd Amboise. Approx 16km outside Blois turn R to Onzain & foll sp to Mesland; go thro Mesland vill & turn L dir Fleuray; site on R after 1.5km. 5*, Lge, mkd, hdg, pt shd, pt sl, serviced pitches; EHU (10A) inc; gas; bbq (charcoal, gas); TV; 30% statics; Eng spkn; adv bkg acc; ccard acc; waterslide; bike hire; tennis; games area; games rm; CKE. *"Secluded site; wine-tasting; excursions to vineyards; mkt Thur Onzain; excel."* **€35.00, 8 Apr - 11 Sep, L02.** 2022

ORANGE *10E2* (12km NE Rural) *44.16222, 4.93531* **Camping des Favards,** 1335 Route d'Orange, 84150 Violès **04 90 70 90 93; campingfavards@gmail.com; www.favards.com**

€3 (htd)

Fr N exit A7 junc 19 Bollène. Foll D8 dir Carpentras & Violès. In Violès foll dir Orange & look for camp sp. Fr S exit A7 junc 22 sp Carpentras, take dir Avignon, then dir Vaison-la-Romaine to Violès. Avoid cent of Orange when towing. 3*, Sm, hdg, mkd, unshd, EHU (6-10A) inc (poss rev pol); Eng spkn; adv bkg acc; ccard acc; CKE. *"Well-kept site; excel pitches - some very lge (extra charge); superb san facs, poss stretched; wine-tasting on site high ssn; gd touring base; poss dust clouds fr Mistral wind; pitches muddy when wet; gd."* **€33.70, 13 Apr-30 Sep.** 2023

ORLEANS *4F3* (11km E Rural) *47.88830, 2.02744* **Camp Municipal Les Pâtures,** 55 Chemin du Port, 45430 Chécy **02 38 91 13 27; camping@checy.fr; https://www.checy.fr/camping/**

€2 nr

Take D960 E twd Châteauneuf. In Chécy, foll site sp. Access thro town via narr rds. 2*, Sm, hdg, pt shd, EHU (16A) €3.50; bbq; twin axles; red long stay; Eng spkn; adv bkg acc; fishing; golf 5km; tennis; CKE. *"Excel, well-run site on Rv Loire; vg location; friendly, helpful warden; gd san facs; conv Orléans, park & ride tram; poss open bef & after dates given; popular NH."* **€20.00, 12 May-25 Sep.** 2023

ORLEANS *4F3* (5km S Rural) *47.85603, 1.92555* **Camp Municipal d'Olivet,** Rue du Pont-Bouchet, 45160 Olivet **02 38 63 53 94; infos@camping-olivet.org; https://www.night-and-day.fr/camping/22-camping-dolivet**

€2 (htd)

To avoid height restriction, best app fr A71 exit junc 2 onto N271 dir Orléans-La Source. Cont on N271 until rd crosses N20 into Rue de Bourges. Pass commercial estate & hotel on L & turn L at traff lts into Rue de Châteauroux. Pass university (Parc Technologique), cross tramway & turn L at traff lts onto D14, Rue de la Source, then in 500m turn R (watch for pharmacy on L & green site sp) into Rue du Pont-Bouchet (narr rd). Site well sp on D14. NB Beware height restrictions on junc underpasses in Orléans cent. 2*, Sm, hdg, pt shd, pt sl, EHU (16A) €3.10 (rev pol); bus 400m; Eng spkn; adv bkg rec; CKE. *"Well-run, busy site by Rv Loiret; friendly; excel clean san facs; guided tours of Orléans by site staff; gd walking; vineyards nr; vg."* **€21.70, 1 Apr-30 Sep.** 2023

ORLEANS *4F3* (3km W Urban) *47.89492, 1.86196* **Camp Municipal Gaston Marchand,** Rue de la Roche, 45140 St Jean-de-la-Ruelle **06 58 48 73 48; camping@ville-saintjeandelaruelle.fr; www.ville-saintjeandelaruelle.fr**

€2 nr

App Orléans fr Blois on D2152/D152; 500m after passing under A71, turn R into Rue de la Roche. Or app Orléans fr E on D2151/D215; 1km after passing Pont de l'Europe (still on D2151/D215) turn L into Rue de la Roche. Site sp. 2*, Sm, mkd, shd, EHU (6A) inc; bbq; cooking facs; twin axles; bus; Eng spkn; adv bkg rec; ccard acc; bike hire. *"Well-kept site on bank of Rv Loire; pool 1.5km; ltd san facs; gd value; conv Orléans; NH only; fair."* **€21.00, 7 Jun-25 Sep.** 2023

ORNANS *6G2* (1km E Rural) *47.10064, 6.16036* **Camping La Roche d'Ully,** Allée de la Tour de Peiltz, 25290 Ornans **03 81 57 17 79; contact@larochedully.com; www.camping-larochedully.com**

€3 (htd) (covrd, htd)

Fr Ornans foll blue sps to site nr rvside. 4*, Med, mkd, unshd, EHU (10A) €4; bbq; 20% statics; adv bkg acc; ccard acc; rv fishing; bike hire; sauna; canoeing; games area. *"Pleasant, family-run site in gd location in rv valley; popular with students; some noise in ssn."* **€36.00, 2 Apr-9 Oct.** 2022

FRANCE

ORPIERRE *9D3* (0.5km E Rural) *44.31110, 5.69650* **Camping Les Princes d'Orange,** Flonsaine, 05700 Orpierre **04 66 60 07 00; princes-orange@koawa.com; www.campingorpierre.com**

€1.60 (htd)

N75 S fr Serres for 11km to Eyguians. Turn R in Eyguians onto D30, 8km to Orpierre, turn L in vill to site (sp). 4*, Med, mkd, hdstg, pt shd, pt sl, terr, EHU (10A) €4.50; gas; TV; 10% statics; adv bkg acc; fishing; games area; waterslide; tennis. *"Rock-climbing area; gd walking; beautiful, interesting vill."* **€46.40, 1 Apr-3 Nov.** **2024**

OUISTREHAM *3D1* (1km S Urban) *49.26909, -0.25498* **Camping Le Riva Bella,** Rue de la Haie Breton, 14150 Ouistreham **02 31 97 12 66; camping-rivabella@vacances-seasonova.com; www.vacances-seasonova.com/camping-riva-bella**

€1.50 (htd) (covrd, htd, indoor) sand 1.8km

Fr ferry terminal foll sp Caen on D84 (Rue de l'Yser/ Ave du Grand Large); in approx 1.5km site sp at rndabt; take 3rd exit. 4*, Lge, hdg, pt shd, EHU (10A) inc; gas; twin axles; 40% statics; bus; Eng spkn; adv bkg acc; ccard acc; games area; tennis; bike hire; CKE. *"V conv for late or early ferry (5 mins to terminal), site stays open for late Brittany ferry, essential to ring or email ahead; busy high ssn; gd sized pitches; sandy soil; gates open 0630-2300 (dep out of hrs, by request); opens for late arr; no twin axles; nice walk/cycle along canal to town; wonderful beaches; interesting area; mkt Thur; conv & sep area for NH without unhitching; British twin axle c'vans acc; gd for long stay; takeaway food and bread shop on site; new management has improved site (2017); new san facs & pool."* **€34.00, 5 Apr - 30 Sep, N10.** **2024**

OUISTREHAM *3D1* (12km NW Coastal) *49.31799, -0.35824* **Camp Municipal La Capricieuse,** 2 Rue Brummel, 14530 Luc-sur-Mer **02 31 97 34 43; info@campinglacapricieuse.com; www.campinglacapricieuse.com**

€2.50 nr sand adj

Fr ferry terminal turn R at 3rd traff lts (D514) into Ave du G. Leclerc. Cont to Luc-sur-Mer; 1st turn L after casino; site on R in 300m. Ave Lecuyer is sp & Rue Brummel is off that rd. 4*, Lge, hdg, mkd, pt shd, terr, EHU (6-10A) €4.65-6.25; gas; TV; Eng spkn; adv bkg rec; ccard acc; games rm; tennis; excursions; CKE. *"Excel location; some lge pitches with easy access; clean, ltd facs LS; conv beach & Luc-sur-Mer; conv WW2 beaches; excel site; conv for ferries."* **€26.40, 1 Apr-30 Sep.** **2024**

OUNANS *6H2* (1km N Rural) *47.00290, 5.66550* **Huttopia La Plage Blanche,** 3 Rue de la Plage, 39380 Ounans **03 84 37 69 63; plageblanche@camping-indigo.com; europe.huttopia.com/en/site/la-plage-blanche**

€5 nr (covrd, htd, indoor)

Exit A39 junc 6 sp Dole Cent. Foll N5 SE for 18km dir Pontarlier. After passing Souvans, turn L on D472 sp Mont-sous-Vaudrey. Foll sp to Ounans. Site well sp in vill. 3*, Lge, hdstg, mkd, pt shd, EHU (6A) €4 (poss rev pol); sw nr; TV; 1% statics; Eng spkn; adv bkg rec; ccard acc; lake fishing; bike hire; horseriding; canoeing; CKE. *"Superb rvside pitches; trout & carp fishing; friendly recep; excel san facs, recently updated (2013); gd rest; excel."* **€35.00, 19 May - 18 Sep, J02.** **2022**

OUST *8G3* (2km N Rural) *42.89343, 1.21381* **Camp Municipal La Claire,** Rue La Palere, 09140 Soueix-Rogalle **05 61 66 85 85; laclaire.camping@gmail.com; www.soueix-rogalle.fr**

€2 (htd) nr nr

S fr St Girons on D618; in 13km, just bef rndabt, turn R onto D32 (thro rock arch) to Soueix-Rogalle; turn L at vill sq; site in 100m, just after x-ing rv bdge. NB Narr ent, rec park in sq & walk down first. 2*, Sm, pt shd, EHU (10A) inc (poss long lead req); 10% statics; phone; fishing; CKE. *"Pleasant, well-maintained, rvside site; lge pitches; basic san facs."* **€14.00, 1 Apr-31 Oct.** **2024**

OUST *8G3* (0.6km S Rural) *42.87042, 1.21947* **Camping Les Quatre Saisons,** Route d'Aulus-les-Bains, 09140 Oust **06 72 44 62 68; camping.ariege@gmail.com; www.camping4saisons.com**

12 €1.50 (htd) nr

Take D618 S fr St Girons; then D3 to Oust; on N o'skts of town turn L (sp Aulus) onto D32; in 1km site on R nr Rv Garbet. 3*, Med, hdg, pt shd, EHU (10A) inc; TV; 25% statics; phone; Eng spkn; adv bkg rec; ccard acc; games area; CKE. *"In beautiful, unspoilt area; friendly site; excel boulangerie 5mins walk on footpath to vill; excel."* **€20.00** **2022**

PACAUDIERE, LA *9A1* (0.2km E Rural) *46.17512, 3.87639* **Camp Municipal Beausoleil,** Route de Vivans, 42310 La Pacaudière **04 77 64 11 50 or 04 77 64 30 18 (Mairie); lapacaudiere@wanadoo.fr; www.roannais-tourisme.com/camping-municipal-beausoleil**

NW on N7 Roanne to Lapalisse; turn R in La Pacaudière, D35; site well sp; fork R in 50m; site ent in 400m. 2*, Sm, hdstg, hdg, unshd, sl, EHU (10A) inc; gas; TV. *"Pleasant NH in beautiful countryside; public pool high ssn; ltd facs LS; interesting area; Sat mkt."* **€16.00, 1 May-30 Sep.** **2023**

PAIMPOL *1D3* (2.5km SE Coastal) *48.76966, -3.02209* **Camp Municipal Crukin,** Rue de Crukin, Kérity, 22500 Paimpol **02 96 20 78 47 or 02 96 55 31 70 (Mairie); contact@camping-paimpol.com; www.camping-paimpol.com**

€2 (htd) nr shgl 250m

On D786 fr St Brieuc/Paimpol, site sp in vill of Kérity 80m off main rd shortly bef abbey. 2*, Med, hdg, pt shd, EHU (6A) €4.50 (poss rev pol); TV; 10% statics; bus 100m; watersports; fishing; CKE. *"Sep m'van area; Beaufort Abbey nrby; excel sh stay/NH; plenty of space; facs ltd LS; walk to town along coast rd gd views; site unkept; boggy when wet; gd; tourist train runs past site ent to/fr Paimpol, hourly svrs."* **€17.30, 1 Apr-30 Sep. 2023**

PALAVAS LES FLOTS *10F1* (0.5km N Coastal) *43.53000, 3.92400* **Aire Communale/Camping-Car Halte,** Base Paul Riquet Rue Frédéric Mistral, 34250 Palavas-les-Flots **04 67 07 73 45 or 04 67 07 73 48; tourisme@ot-palavaslesflots.com; ot-palavaslesflots.com/en/touristic_sheet/aire-de-camping-car-palavas-les-flots-en-3095230/**

12 nr nr nr sand 500m

Fr Montpellier on D986 to Palavas. On ent town at 1st rndabt 'Europe' foll sp Base Fluviale & site sp. Med, hdstg, mkd, pt shd, EHU (16A) €2; phone; bus 200m; ccard acc; CKE. *"M'vans only; special elec cable req - obtain fr recep (dep); some pitches on marina quay; conv Montpellier, Camargue; 3 night max stay."* **€10.00 2024**

PALAVAS LES FLOTS *10F1* (1km NE Coastal) *43.53346, 3.94820* **Camping Montpellier Plage,** 95 Ave St Maurice, 34250 Palavas-les-Flots **04 67 68 00 91; camping.montpellier.plage@wanadoo.fr; www.camping-montpellier-plage.com**

sand adj

Site on D21ES on o'skts of vill twd Carnon. 3*, V lge, mkd, pt shd, EHU (10A) inc; gas; bbq; 50% statics; bus high ssn; Eng spkn; adv bkg rec; games area; CKE. *"Gd location;spa facs; basic san facs, but lge pitches & friendliness of site outweigh this; gd security; poss somewhat unkempt; easy walk into Palavas - interesting sm port; flamingoes on adjoining lake; gd."* **€38.00, 16 Apr-18 Sep. 2023**

PALAVAS LES FLOTS *10F1* (2km E Urban/Coastal) *43.53867, 3.96076* **Camping Les Roquilles,** 267b Ave St Maurice, 34250 Palavas-les-Flots **04 67 68 03 47; roquilles@wanadoo.fr; www.camping-les-roquilles.fr**

(htd) sand 100m

Exit A9 junc 30 onto D986 dir Palavas. In Palavas foll sp Carnon-Plage on D62, site sp. 4*, V lge, mkd, hdstg, pt shd, serviced pitches; EHU (6A) €3.90; red long stay; TV; 30% statics; phone; bus; Eng spkn; adv bkg acc; ccard acc; waterslide; CKE. *"Excel pizza bar on site; gas 100m; vg sw pools."* **€37.50, 20 Apr-15 Sep. 2024**

PARAY LE MONIAL *9A1* (1km NW Urban) *46.45750, 4.10472* **Camping Au Bon Endroit (formerly Camp de Mambré),** 19 Route du Gué-Léger, 71600 Paray-le-Monial **03 85 88 89 20; contact@campingaubonplace.fr; www.campingaubonendroit.fr**

€3 (covrd)

Fr N79 Moulin to Mâcon; site at W end of town; just after level x-ing turn NE into Rte du Gué-Léger. Turn R into site after x-ing rv; well sp. 4*, Lge, mkd, pt shd, EHU (10A) inc; CKE. *"Paray-le-Monial is pilgrimage cent; lovely site & facs; well maintained; new covered sw pool (2023); 15min walk to town along rv; excel cycling cent; clean, well run site; hg rec."* **€26.00, 15 Apr-30 Sep. 2024**

PARENTIS EN BORN *7D1* (6km SW Rural) *44.34562, -1.09241* **Camping L'Arbre d'Or,** 75 Route du Lac, 40160 Landes **05 58 78 41 56; contact@arbre-dor.com; www.arbre-dor.com**

nr

Leave the Bordeaux m'way A63/N10 in Liposthey and drive twds Parentis (D43). The campsite is sp in Parentis. 4*, Med, mkd, pt shd, EHU (10A) inc; bbq; sw nr; twin axles; 25% statics; phone; Eng spkn; adv bkg acc; ccard acc; games area; CKE. *"Vg; lake 500m fr site, watersports in lake; v friendly mgmt; bike hire."* **€36.00, 1 Apr-30 Oct. 2023**

PARENTIS EN BORN *7D1* (3km NW Rural) *44.35153, -1.10959* **Camping Calède,** Quartier Lahitte, 40160 Parentis-en-Born **05 58 78 44 63; contact@camping-calede.com; www.camping-calede.com**

€0.50 nr

Exit N10 junc 17 onto D43 to Parentis-en-Born; then take D652 dir Biscarrosse; site in 3km on L. Sp adj lake. 2*, Med, hdg, pt shd, EHU (10A) €3.30; gas; bbq; sw nr; phone; Eng spkn; adv bkg acc; sailing; fishing; CKE. *"Peaceful site in remote location; well-kept pitches & san facs; friendly, helpful staff; site yourself if office clsd; rec."* **€22.00, 6 Apr-26 Oct. 2024**

PARIS *3D3* (12km E Urban) *48.85385, 2.53794* **Camp Municipal La Haute Ile,** Chemin de l'Ecluse, 93330 Neuilly-sur-Marne **01 43 08 21 21; camping.rivesdeparis@neuillysurmarne.fr; camping.lesrivesdeparis.fr**

€2.85 nr

Fr Périphérique (Porte de Vincennes) foll N34 sp Vincennes. Shortly after passing Château de Vincennes on R, L at fork, sp Lagny. At next major x-rds sharp L (still N34) sp Chelles. Thro Neuilly-Plaisance to Neuilly-sur-Marne. In cent lge x-rds turn R sp N370 Marne-la-Vallée & A4 Paris. In 200m, bef rv bdge, foll Camp Municipal sp (no tent or c'van symbols on sp) turn L. Site at junc of rv & canal. 2*, Lge, mkd, pt shd, EHU (10A) inc (check rev pol); gas; bbq; 25% statics; bus/train 900m; Eng spkn; adv bkg rec; rv fishing. *"Lovely location bet rv & canal (almost on an island); additional; wooden posts on pitches poss diff manoeuvring lge o'fits; some sm pitches; lndry adj; poss unkempt (2011); soft after rain; gd base & transport for Paris & Disney; gd dog walks adj; gd NH; san facs are run down."* **€25.00, 1 Mar-30 Sep. 2024**

FRANCE

PARIS *3D3* (11km W Urban) *48.86843, 2.23471*
Camping Indigo Paris Bois de Boulogne, 2 Allée du Bord de l'Eau, 75016 Paris **01 45 24 30 00; paris@camping-indigo.com; www.campingparis.fr**
€4.70 (htd) nr nr

Site bet bdge of Puteaux & bdge of Suresnes. App fr A1: take Blvd Périphérique W to Bois de Boulogne exit at Porte Maillot; foll camp sp. App fr A6: Blvd Périphérique W to Porte Dauphine exit at Porte Maillot; foll camp sp. App fr Pont de Sèvres (A10, A11): on bdge take R lane & take 2nd rd R mkd Neuilly-sur-Seine; rd runs parallel to Seine; cont to site ent. App fr A13: after St Cloud Tunnel foll sp twd Paris; immed after x-ing Rv Seine, 1st R sp Bois de Boulogne; foll camp sps; traff lts at site ent. NB Sharp turn to site, poorly sp fr N - watch for lge 'Parking Borne de l'Eau 200m'. 4*, V lge, mkd, hdstg, hdg, pt shd, pt sl, EHU (10A) €6.20; gas; twin axles; TV; 10% statics; phone; bus to metro; Eng spkn; adv bkg rec; ccard acc; CKE. *"Busy site in excel location; easy access A13; conv cent Paris - Metro Porte Maillot 4km; some v sm pitches; walk over Suresne bdge for shops, food mkt, supmkt etc; some tour ops on site; gd security; refurbished san facs (2014); vg; food truck; new rest (2015)."* **€40.20, P18.** **2024**

"I need an on-site restaurant"

We do our best to make sure site information is correct, but it is always best to check any must-have facilities are still available or will be open during your visit.

PARIS *3D3* (22km NW Urban) *48.94001, 2.14563*
Sandaya Paris Maisons Laffitte, 1 Rue Johnson, 78600 Maisons-Laffitte **01 39 12 21 91; pml@sandaya.fr; https://www.sandaya.co.uk/our-campsites/paris-maisons-laffitte**
€5 (htd) (htd)

Easy access fr A13 sp Poissy; take D308 to Maisons-Laffitte; foll site sp bef town cent. Fr A15 take N184 S fr Poissy, foll sp St Germain; approx 6km after x-ing Rv Seine & approx 300m after x-ing lge steel bdge, take L lane ready for L turn onto D308 to Maison-Laffitte; foll camp sp. Or D301 to St Denis, then A86 exit Bezons, then dir Poissy, Noailles, Sartrouville & Maisons-Laffitte. NB Narr app rd diff due parked cars & high kerbs. 4*, Lge, mkd, hdg, pt shd, serviced pitches; EHU (10-16A); gas; TV; 40% statics; Eng spkn; adv bkg acc; ccard acc; games area; CKE. *"V busy, popular site on island in Rv Seine; ideal for visiting Paris (20 min by RER), Disneyland & Versailles; RER stn 1km; mobilis ticket covers rlwy, metro & bus for day in Paris; friendly, helpful staff; poss ltd facs LS."* **€25.00, 8 Apr - 6 Nov, P03.** **2022**

PARTHENAY *4H1* (1km SW Urban) *46.64160, -0.26740*
Camping Flower du Bois Vert, 14 Rue Boisseau, Le Tallud, 79200 Parthenay **05 49 64 78 43; campingboisvert@outlook.fr; www.camping-boisvert.com**
€3 (htd) nr (htd)

Site on D743 to Niort. Sp fr N & S. Fr S 1km bef town turn L at sp La Roche-sur-Yon immed after rv bdge turn R; site on R in 500m. 4*, Med, hdstg, mkd, hdg, pt shd, pt sl, EHU (6 or 10A) inc; bbq; TV; 10% statics; phone; adv bkg acc; fishing; games rm; bike hire; tennis; boating; CKE. *"1 hr rvside walk to town; m'van o'night area adj; noisy nr main rd & bar; Wed mkt; gd NH to Spain; conv Futuroscope; new facs, plenty hot water; well spaced hdg grass pitches; 20 min cycle ride to Medieval town; excel facs."* **€25.50, 1 Apr-15 Oct.** **2022**

PARTHENAY *4H1* (9km W Urban) *46.62214, -0.35139*
Camp Municipal Les Peupliers, 79130 Azay-sur-Thouet **05 49 95 37 13 (Mairie); mairie-azaysurthouet@cc-parthenay.fr; www.tourisme-gatine.com**
nr

Fr Parthenay take D949 dir Secondigny to Azay-sur-Thouet; turn L onto D139 dir St Pardoux; site on L in 200m. Site adj stadium on rvside. 2*, Sm, mkd, pt shd, EHU (10A) €3.50; bbq. *"Pleasant, peaceful site; barrier open ltd hrs; clean dated san facs, poss inadequate number high ssn; MH area outside of campsite; gd."* **€9.00, 15 Jun-30 Sep.** **2023**

PARTHENAY *4H1* (9km W Rural) *46.65738, -0.34816*
Camping La Chagnée, 79450 St Aubin le Cloud **05 49 95 31 44 or 06 71 10 09 66 (mob); gerard.baudoin3@wanadoo.fr; www.lachagneevacances.fr**
nr

Fr Parthenay on D949BIS dir Secondigny. Turn R in Azay-sur-Thouet onto D139 dir St Aubin, site on R in 2km, look for 'Gîte' sp. 3*, Sm, hdg, pt shd, terr, EHU (10A) €5; Eng spkn; fishing. *"Charming, CL-type organic fm site o'looking lake; friendly, extremely helpful & welcoming owners; v clean, modern facs; OAY providing use own san in winter; maps loaned for walks; excel; m'van only during period Nov-Mar; fmhse meal avail weekly; vg lake fishing; rec."* **€15.00** **2023**

PAU *8F2* (5km E Rural) *43.28909, -0.26985*
FFCC Camping Les Sapins, Route de Tarbes, 64320 Ousse **05 59 81 79 03 or 05 59 81 74 21 (LS); lessapins64@orange.fr; camping-les-sapins-64.com**
nr nr

Site adj Hôtel des Sapins on S side of D817 (Pau-Tarbes rd). 3*, Sm, pt shd, EHU (4-10A) inc; fishing. *"Popular, pleasant NH; red facs LS; helpful owners; NH only; bus svrs infrequent."* **€17.00** **2024**

PAU 8F2 (6km W Rural) 43.32081, -0.45096
Camping Le Terrier, Ave du Vert-Galant, 64230 Lescar **07 45 22 87 39; sasfihlt@gmail.com; www.camping-terrier64.com**
12 (htd) nr (covrd)

Exit A64 junc 9.1 onto D817; in 3km, at rndabt junc with D509, turn L onto Blvd de L'Europe; in 1.5km at rndabt turn R onto Av du Vert Galant; site on R in 1km, 200m bef rv bdge. NB. If app on Av du Galant fr S, rec cont to next rndabt & app fr opp dir due tight, concealed ent. 3*, Med, mkd, hdg, shd, EHU 6A; gas; bbq (elec); TV; 50% statics; bus; adv bkg acc; ccard acc; car wash; rv fishing adj; tennis; games rm; CCI. *"Gd base for Pau & district; helpful new owners (2010); improved access (2011); vg clean san facs; excel food; no twin axles; 2 golf courses nr; excel."*
€21.00 **2024**

PAUILLAC 7C2 (1km S Rural) 45.18515, -0.74218
Camp Municipal Les Gabarreys, Route de la Rivière, 33250 Pauillac **05 56 59 10 03; camping@mairie-pauillac.fr; www.campinglesgabarreys.com/**
€3 nr

On ent Pauillac on D206, turn R at rndabt, sp site. On app Quays, turn R bef 'Maison du Vin'. Site on L in 1km. 4*, Med, hdg, mkd, hdstg, pt shd, EHU (10A) €6; bbq; TV; 6% statics; Eng spkn; adv bkg acc; ccard acc; games rm; CKE. *"Peaceful, well-kept, well-equipped site on estuary; nice clean san facs; conv wine chateaux; cycle rtes; mkt Sat; excel."*
€23.00, 3 Apr-8 Oct. **2023**

PAYRAC 7D3 (1km N Rural) 44.80574, 1.47479
Camping Le Picouty (formerly Camping Panoramic), Route de Loupiac, 46350 Payrac-en-Quercy **05 65 37 78 97; camping.lepicouty[at]wanadoo.fr; www.camping-picouty.com**
12 (htd) nr

N fr Payrac on D820, turn L onto D147 sp Loupiac (200m after 'end of vill' sp), site 300m on R. 2*, Sm, hdstg, pt shd, pt sl, EHU (5A) €3 (poss rev pol); gas; bbq; sw nr; TV; 10% statics; phone; Eng spkn; adv bkg acc; bike hire; canoe hire; CKE. *"Well-run, clean site; OK san facs - poss inadequate if site full; poss muddy in bad weather but hdstg avail; pool 400m; friendly, helpful Dutch owner; gd walking; excel winter NH"* **€15.00** **2024**

PAYRAC 7D3 (6km N Rural) 44.83527, 1.46008
Camping Les Hirondelles, Lieu Dit "Le Pech", 46350 Loupiac **05 65 37 66 25; camp.les-hirondelles@orange.fr; camping-leshirondelles.com/en/**
€2.50 (htd) (htd)

Fr Souillac foll D820 for about 12km. Site on R bef dual c'way. 3*, Sm, mkd, hdg, shd, pt sl, EHU (6A) inc (poss rev pol); gas; TV; 40% statics; phone; Eng spkn; adv bkg acc; bike hire; games area; CKE. *"Vg friendly, helpful owners; clean site; gd views fr some pitches; excel."* **€34.00, 6 Apr-22 Sep.** **2024**

PEILLAC 2F3 (2km N Rural) 47.72635, -2.21430
Camping du Pont d'Oust, 56220 Peillac **02 99 91 39 33 or 06 65 20 65 21; campingdupontdoust@gmail.com; www.campingdupontdoust.com**
Free (htd) nr nr nr

SW fr La Gacilly on D777; in 6km turn L onto D14 sp Les Fougerêts; cont thro Les Fougerêts, site on R in 1km opp canal. Or N fr Peillac on D14, folls sp Pont d'Oust; site on L. 2*, Med, pt shd, EHU (10A) inc (poss rev pol); bbq. *"Nice, peaceful site by Rv Oust & canal; spacious pitches, soft when wet; helpful warden calls, site yourself; v flat, ideal for cycling; pretty vill; vg; mkd cycling and walking rtes fr site; pool adj; pay at Mairie during May."* **€25.00, 1 May-30 Sep.** **2023**

PELUSSIN 9B2 (1km SE Rural) 45.41375, 4.69143
Camping Bel'Epoque du Pilat, La Vialle, Route de Malleval, 42410 Pélussin **04 74 87 66 60; contact@camping-belepoque.fr; www.camping-belepoque.fr**
€3 (htd) nr (htd)

Exit A7 junc 10 just S of Lyon foll N86 dir Serrières; in Chavanay turn R onto D7 to Pélussin, then at rndabt turn L and foll D79 S & foll site sp. Rec do not use sat nav! 3*, Sm, hdg, pt shd, pt sl, EHU (6A) €3.50; gas; bbq; phone; train 10km; Eng spkn; adv bkg acc; ccard acc; games area; tennis; CKE. *"In nature reserve; excel touring base; vg walking; vg, peaceful site; supmkt in Pelussin; friendly, helpful owners."*
€28.00, 1 Apr - 30 Sep. **2022**

PENESTIN 2G3 (3km S Coastal) 47.44527, -2.48416
Camping Les Iles, La Pointe du Bile, 56760 Pénestin **02 99 90 30 24; https://www.chadotel.com/camping-les-iles-penestin**
€4 (htd, indoor) sand direct access

Fr La Roche Bernard take D34 to Pénestin; cont on D201 for 2.5km & foll site sp. 5*, Lge, mkd, hdg, pt shd, serviced pitches; EHU (10A) inc (poss rev pol); gas; bbq (charcoal, elec); TV; 10% statics; Eng spkn; adv bkg acc; ccard acc; bike hire; waterslide; fishing adj; horseriding; tennis; games rm; CKE. *"Lovely site o'looking sea; no o'fits over 7m high ssn; direct access to shoreline; some pitches sm; max 1 dog; helpful staff; clean modern unisex san facs; mkt Sun (also Wed in Jul/Aug); gd cycling, walking; vg."*
€50.00, 12 Apr-30 Sep, B06. **2022**

PERIERS 1D4 (6km NE Rural) 49.21581, -1.35093
Camping Le Clos Castel, 50500 Raids **09 77 24 23 80 or 07 71 9 39 31 34 (mob); lecloscastel@live.com; www.lecloscastel.co.uk**
12 nr

S fr Carentan on D791 to Raids; cont past vill on D791 for 300m; turn R to site, ent on R in 100m. Or N fr Periers on D791; turn L 300m bef Raids & then as bef. Site well sp. Sm, hdstg, unshd, EHU (6A) inc; bbq; Eng spkn; adv bkg acc. *"Site has B&B; helpful British owners; dogs free; conv D-day beaches; excel."*
€17.50 **2022**

FRANCE

PERIERS *1D4* (5km SE Rural) *49.16638, -1.34916* **Aire Naturelle Le Clos Vert,** 50190 St Martin-d'Aubigny **02 33 07 73 92 (Mairie); mairie-st-martin-daubigny@wanadoo.fr; https://mairie-saintmartindaubigny.fr/**
nr nr nr

E fr Périers on D900 dir St Lô; in 4km turn R sp St Martin-d'Aubigny; site on L in 500m adj church. Sm, pt shd, EHU (6A) €2.50; bbq; golf 2km; fishing 2km; tennis 2km; CKE. *"Charming, sm, well-kept, useful site; facs basic but OK; easy 70km run to Cherbourg; no twin axles; basic quiet site in vill, bar & rest within walking dist; conv for ports; pay at Marie if no one calls for payment."* **€13.00, 15 Apr-15 Oct. 2023**

"Satellite navigation makes touring much easier"

Remember most sat navs don't know if you're towing or in a larger vehicle – always use yours alongside maps and site directions.

PERIGUEUX *7C3* (13km NE Rural) *45.21975, 0.86383* **Camping Le Bois du Coderc,** Route des Gaunies, 24420 Antonne-et-Trigonant **05 53 05 99 83; coderc-camping@wanadoo.fr; www.campinglecoderc.com**
12 €2.20 nr nr (htd) shgl adj

NE fr Périgueux on N21 twd Limoges, thro Antonne approx 1km turn R at x-rds bet car park & rest. Site in 500m. 3*, Med, hdg, pt shd, EHU (10A) €4.70; bbq; sw nr; TV; 10% statics; phone; Eng spkn; adv bkg acc; ccard acc; games rm; ice; games area; CKE. *"Secluded, pleasant, peaceful site; most pitches spacious; rallies welcome; gd value, inc rest; highly rec; quiet; well maintained; excel site; view of website a must; gd birdwatching; v helpful owners, v eager to please; excel htd pool; excel wifi fr some pitches; new san block (2018); excel."* **€18.30 2023**

PERIGUEUX *7C3* (8km SE Rural) *45.14900, 0.77880* **Camping Le Grand Dague,** Route du Grand Dague, 24750 Atur **05 53 04 21 01; www.sandaya.fr/nos-campings/le-grand-dague**
€2 (htd) (htd)

Fr cent Périgueux, take N21 & A89 twd Brive. Fork L onto D2 to Atur (main rd bears R). In Atur turn L after bar/tabac; foll site sp for 2.5km. 4*, Lge, shd, pt sl, EHU (6A) inc; bbq; TV; 70% statics; phone; Eng spkn; adv bkg acc; ccard acc; games rm; bike hire; games area; CKE. *"Gd family site; friendly owners; site immac, even end of ssn; poss unkempt early ssn; lots to do; ltd touring pitches; excel."* **€39.00, 22 Apr-25 Sep. 2022**

PERONNE *3C3* (2.6km S Rural) *49.91805, 2.93227* **Camping du Port de Plaisance,** Route de Paris, 80200 Péronne **03 22 84 19 31; contact@camping-plaisance.com; www.camping-plaisance.com**
€1.30 (htd) nr (htd)

Exit A1/E15 junc 13 dir Peronne on D1029 to D1017. Site on L o'looking canal. Well sp fr all dirs. 3*, Med, mkd, pt shd, EHU (6-10A) €4.30-7.95 (some rev pol & long lead poss req); red long stay; Eng spkn; ccard acc; jacuzzi; fishing. *"Popular NH; helpful, pleasant staff & owners; gd play park & pool; gates locked 2200-0800 - when clsd, park outside; vg rest adj; rec visit to war museum in Péronne castle; popular with ralliers; facs need upgrading; vg site, pleasant situation nr a canal; gd size pitches; gd dog walk along canal; hypmkt 3km; san facs clean but tired; site self if recep clsd; may need long EHU lead."* **€29.30, 1 Mar-31 Oct. 2022**

PERPIGNAN *8G4* (6km S Rural) *42.63754, 2.89819* **Camping Les Rives du Lac,** Chemin de la Serre, 66180 Villeneuve-de-la-Raho **04 68 55 83 51; camping.villeneuveraho@wanadoo.fr; www.villeneuvedelaraho.fr**
€1.60 (htd) (htd) 1.5km

Fr A9 exit Perpignan Sud, dir Porte d'Espagne. In 3km turn R onto N9 dir Le Boulou. In 1km after Auchan supmkt take slip rd to N91 dir Villeneuve-de-la-Raho. In 2km rd becomes D39, turn R to site, site on L in 1km. Beware ford on D39 in v wet weather (usually dry). 2*, Med, hdstg, mkd, pt shd, pt sl, EHU (6A) inc; bbq (elec, gas); sw nr; 10% statics; phone; Eng spkn; adv bkg acc; ccard acc; tennis 2km; watersports 1.5km; fishing 1.5km; CKE. *"Lakeside site with views; poor san facs & insufficient for site size; busy cycling/jogging path adj; conv trips to Spain; busy public beach nr."* **€20.00, 15 Mar-15 Nov. 2024**

PERROS GUIREC *1D2* (1km SE Coastal) *48.79657, -3.42689* **Camp Municipal Ernest Renan,** 22700 Louannec **02 96 23 11 78; www.camping-louannec.fr**
€3 (htd) sand adj

1km W of Louannec on D6. 3*, Lge, unshd, EHU (6A) €4.50; gas; TV; Eng spkn; adv bkg acc; watersports adj; fishing adj; games rm. *"Well-kept site; pitches on seashore; clean san facs; clsd 1200-1530, little parking space outside; highly rec."* **€17.50, 1 Jun-30 Sep. 2023**

PERROS GUIREC *1D2* (3km NW Coastal) *48.82798, -3.47623* **Sandaya Le Ranolien,** Boulevard du Semaphore, Ploumanac'h, 22700 Perros-Guirec **020 76 60 85 83; ranolien@sandaya.fr; www.sandaya.fr**
€5 (htd) (covrd, htd) sand

At Perros-Guirec harbour turn R at Marina foll sp Trégastel. Up hill above coast into Perros Guirec town. Cont strt thro traff lts & into La Clarté vill; strt at traff lts & sharp R at Camping & Le Ranolien sp. Ent shortly on L. Foll Trégastel sp all way. 5*, V lge, mkd, pt shd, pt sl, serviced pitches; EHU (16A) inc; 75% statics; Eng spkn; adv bkg acc; ccard acc; waterslide; horseriding; fishing; tennis; golf. *"Excel beaches; spa; many tour op statics; vg coastal walks nrby."* **€71.00, 5 Apr-5 Oct. 2024**

PERS *7C4* (4.8km NE Rural) *44.90619, 2.25568* **Camping Du Viaduc,** 12, Rue du Viaduc Le Ribeyrès, 15290 Pers **04 71 64 70 08; campingduviaduc@wanadoo.fr; www.camping-cantal.com**

€2-3.10

Fr Aurillac take N122 S twrds Figeac. After Sansac turn R onto D61 sp Pers. Site well sp fr here. Final 2km narr rd with passing places. 3*, Med, hdg, mkd, pt shd, terr, EHU (10A) €3.60; bbq; twin axles; 20% statics; adv bkg acc; CKE. *"Adj to lge lake with watersports avail; takeaway; nearest town for shops is Aurillac 25km; local shops in Le Rouget 7km; beautiful location; many pitches with lake view; excel."*
€26.50, 13 Apr-2 Nov. **2024**

PERTUIS *10E3* (8km N Rural) *43.75860, 5.50407* **Camping de La Bonde,** Etang de la Bonde, 84240 Sannes **04 90 77 63 64; campingdelabonde@campasun.eu; www.campasun.eu/**

12 €6

NE fr Pertuis on D956, fork L onto D9 (sp Cabrières & Etang de la Bonde). At x-rds in 8km turn R onto D27. Site on L in 200m. 2*, Med, pt shd, EHU (10A) (poss rev pol) inc; gas; sw; 80% statics; adv bkg acc; ccard acc; tennis; fishing; watersports; games area; CKE. *"Lovely lakeside & beach; ltd facs LS; phone ahead to check site open; pool 8km; gd cycling area."*
€29.50 **2023**

PESMES *6G2* (0.5km S Rural) *47.27612, 5.56451* **Camp Municipal La Colombière,** 3 La Colombiere, 70140 Pesmes **03 84 31 20 15; campcolombiere@aol.com;https://campinglacolombiere.business.site/**

€1.20 nr nr

On D475 halfway bet Gray & Dole. S fr Pesmes immed on L after x-ing rv bdge. N fr Dole, site sp on R immed bef rest at rv bdge. 2*, Med, hdg, pt shd, EHU (6-10A) €2.30-3.60; phone; Eng spkn; adv bkg rec; ccard acc; bike hire. *"Picturesque vill; helpful, friendly staff; gd san facs; vg; no twin axles."*
€12.60, 1 May-31 Oct. **2023**

PEYRELEAU *10E1* (1km N Rural) *44.19126, 3.20470* **Camp Municipal de Brouillet,** 48150 Le Rozier **05 65 62 63 98; contact@campinglerozier.com; www.camping-lerozier.com**

nr (htd)

Fr Millau take D809 N to Aguessac, onto D907; in Le Rozier, cross bdge over Rv Tarn onto D996 & in 200m (opp church); take rd on R to site; sp. 3*, Lge, mkd, pt shd, EHU (6A) €3.50; adv bkg rec; CKE. *"V pleasant, busy, spacious site adj rv; friendly recep; vg for m'vans; poss facs stretched & unclean; gd base for Tarn Gorges; gd area walking & birdwatching."*
€28.50, 1 Apr-30 Sep. **2024**

PEYRELEAU *10E1* (1km W Rural) *44.19470, 3.20210* **Camping Saint Pal,** Route des Gorges du Tarn, 12720 Mostuéjouls **05 65 62 64 46 or 05 65 58 79 82 (LS); saintpal@orange.fr; www.campingsaintpal.com**

€2

Exit A75 exit junc 44.1 onto D29 to Aguessac then L onto D907 to Mostuéjouls. Or fr Millau take D809 N to Aguessac, turn R onto D907 to Mostuéjouls. Site in 10km 500m fr Rozier bdge. 3*, Med, hdg, mkd, shd, EHU (6A) €3.20; gas; bbq; sw nr; red long stay; TV; 20% statics; phone; Eng spkn; adv bkg acc; ccard acc; games rm; CKE. *"Excel site & facs; organised walks; gd walks, canoeing, fishing & birdwatching, beavers on rv bank opp; poss diff for lge o'fits."*
€40.90, 15 Jun-2 Sep. **2024**

PEYRELEAU *10E1* (1.2km NW Rural) *44.19810, 3.19442* **FFCC Camping Les Bords du Tarn,** 12720 Mostuéjouls **05 65 62 62 94; contact@campinglesbordsdutarn.com; www.campinglesbordsdutarn.com**

€2 (htd)

Exit A75 junc 44.1 onto D29 to Aguessac; turn L onto D907 dir Le Rozier & Peyreleau; site on R 1km bef Le Rozier. NB Do not use exit 44 fr A75 (as sat nav might instruct). 3*, Med, mkd, pt shd, pt sl, EHU (10A) €3.50; bbq (charcoal, gas); sw nr; 10% statics; phone; Eng spkn; adv bkg acc; ccard acc; cycling; fishing; games rm; canoe hire; tennis; CKE. *"Site in beautiful area by rv; some v lge pitches; climbing; gd for rv sports; paragliding; modern san facs; gd walking; conv Gorges du Tarn & Gorges de la Jonte; excel."*
€36.00, 16 Jun-2 Sep. **2024**

> **"There aren't many sites open at this time of year"**
>
> If you're travelling outside peak season remember to call ahead to check site opening dates – even if the entry says 'open all year'.

PEZENAS *10F1* (2.8km S Rural) *43.4419049, 3.41767072* **Camping les Cigales,** 2 bis impasse des Cigalous, Hameau de Conas, 34120 Pezenas **04 67 98 97 99; informations@campinglescigales.com; www.campinglescigales.com**

€4 (htd)

Fr N on A75, 3km. Exit 60 dir D13, Nézignan-l'Évêque, Vias, Agde. 1st exit on D13, Conas. Foll site sp. Fr S on A75, 4km. Exit 61, Pézenas, Roujan, Bédarieux. Foll sp to Pézenas and A9. When on D13 1st exit Conas. Foll site sp. Fr A9, 9km. Exit 34, Pézenas, Agde. Take de D13 N dir Pézenas. Take Conas exit foll site sp. Sm, mkd, hdg, pt shd, EHU; bbq (charcoal, elec, gas); 32% statics; Eng spkn; adv bkg rec; ccard acc; bike hire. *"Close to Pézenas; excel."*
€24.00, 30 Mar-30 Sep. **2024**

FRANCE

PEZENAS *10F1* (0.5km SW Urban) *43.45419, 3.41573* **Campotel Municipal de Castelsec,** Chemin de Castelsec, 34120 Pézenas **04 67 98 04 02; contact@camping-pezenas.com; www.camping-gites-herault.com**

€1.40 nr

Fr Béziers take N9 to Pézenas; foll Cent Ville sps fr rndabt at edge of town onto Route de Béziers; in 600m at next rndabt (at junc with D13) go strt over into Ave de Verdun; in 400m take 1st L after McDonalds & pharmacy at ent to Carrefour supmkt; foll Campotel sps; site on L in 300m. 2*, Sm, mkd, pt shd, pt sl, terr, EHU (10A) €2.90; TV; 30% statics; adv bkg acc; tennis adj; CKE. *"Great little site; friendly staff; some pitches unsuitable lge o'fits; easy walk/cycle to interesting town; toy museum worth visit; vg; updated san facs (2019)."* **€16.00, 1 Apr-30 Oct. 2024**

PICQUIGNY *3C3* (0.3km E Urban) *49.9445, 2.1458* **Camping De L'Abime,** 66 Rue du Marais, 80310 Picquigny **03 22 51 25 83 or 06 51 64 40 25; contact@campingdelabime-picquigny.fr; www.campingdelabime-picquigny.fr**

€3 nr

Site sp fr town cent. 2*, Med, pt shd, EHU (10A) €6; 80% statics; adv bkg rec; rv; fishing. *"Pleasant, well laid out site; gd, clean, modern san facs; some shd pitches bet statics; occasional noise fr rlwy line; WW1 war cemetery nr town; nice, small, simple site; easy walking dist fr town; many places to visit."* **€24.00, 1 Apr-31 Oct. 2023**

PIERRE BUFFIERE *7B3* (2km SE Rural) *45.68937, 1.37101* **Camping de Pierre Buffière (Formerly Camp Intercommunal Chabanas),** 87260 Pierre-Buffière **05 55 00 96 43; ccbshv@orange.fr; www.tourisme-briancesudhautevienne.fr/**

€2 nr

Approx 20km S of Limoges on A20, take exit 40 onto D420 S bound; site on L in 500m. Foll sps for 'Stade-Chabanas'. 3*, Med, hdg, mkd, pt shd, pt sl, EHU (10A) inc (poss rev pol); phone; adv bkg acc; fishing; CKE. *"Clean, quiet site; helpful staff; excel clean san facs; some pitches diff for lge o'fits; no twin axles; warden on site 1600-2200, but gate poss locked all day LS (code issued, phone ahead); conv Limoges; excel NH fr A20; conv for Oradour Sur Glane; gd size plots."* **€13.50, 15 May-30 Sep. 2023**

PIERREFITTE SUR SAULDRE *4G3* (6km NE Rural) *47.54444, 2.19138* **Sandaya Les Alicourts,** Domaine des Alicourts, 41300 Pierrefitte-sur-Sauldre **02 54 88 63 34; www.sandaya.fr/nos-campings/les-alicourts**

€7 (covrd, htd, indoor)

Fr S of Lamotte-Beuvron, turn L on D923. After 14km turn R on D24E sp Pierrefitte. After 750m turn L, foll sp to site approx 750m on R. 5*, Med, pt shd, EHU (6A) inc; bbq; sw; 10% statics; Eng spkn; adv bkg acc; ccard acc; waterslide; bike hire; games rm; tennis; CKE. *"Excel, peaceful site; skating rink; kayak/pedalo hire; extra for lakeside pitches; fitness cent; gd, clean facs; v lge pitches."* **€56.00, 20 May- 18 Sep, L22. 2022**

PIERREFONDS *3D3* (0.5km N Urban) *49.35427, 2.97564* **Camping Le Coeur de la Foret,** 34 Rue de l'Armistice, 60350 Pierrefonds **03 44 42 80 83 or 06 45 31 64 21 (mob); contact@lecoeurdelaforet.fr; www.lecoeurdelaforet.fr**

€1 (htd) nr nr

Take D973 fr Compiegne; after 14km site on L adj sp for Pierrefonds at ent to vill. 3*, Med, hdg, pt shd, serviced pitches; EHU (10A) €2.80 (poss rev pol); red long stay; adv bkg acc; CKE. *"Attractive, well-run, busy site; tight pitches for lge o'fits; clean san facs; poss unkempt LS; site yourself if recep clsd; cycle rte to Compiegne; nr Armistice train & museum; gd site; walking dist to vill, Chateau Pierrefonds; bike rental avail."* **€20.40, 6 Apr-30 Sep. 2024**

PIEUX, LES *1C4* (3km SW Coastal) *49.49444, -1.84194* **Le Grand Large,** 11 Route de Grand Large, 50340 Les Pieux **02 33 52 40 75; info@legrandlarge.com; www.legrandlarge.com**

Free (htd) nr (htd, indoor) sand adj

Fr ferry at 1st rndabt take 1st exit sp Cent Ville. Closer to town cent foll old N13 sp Caen. In about 1.5km branch R onto D900 then L onto D650 sp Carteret. Foll this rd past Les Pieux, cont on D650 to sp Super U. Turn R & foll site sp onto D517, then D117 for 3km until reaching beach rd to site, site on L in 2km. 4*, Lge, hdg, mkd, pt shd, EHU (10A) €6.50; gas; bbq; red long stay; TV; 40% statics; phone; Eng spkn; adv bkg acc; ccard acc; tennis; horseriding 4km; games rm; outdoor games. *"Well-run site; rec for families; 1 dog per pitch; dir access to superb lge beach; friendly staff; clean modern san facs; o'fits over 8m by request; barrier clsd 22.00-08.00; conv Cherbourg ferries but arr not rec after dark due sm country lanes; outside pitches avail for early dep for ferries; mkt Fri."* **€37.00, 9 Apr - 18 Sep, N07. 2022**

PIEUX, LES *1C4* (4km SW Coastal) *49.48022, -1.84216* **Camping Le Ranch,** 50340 Le Rozel **02 33 10 07 10 and 02 50 79 51 92; contact@camping-leranch.com; www.camping-leranch.com**

€3.20 (htd) sand adj

S fr Cherbourg on D650 & turn R to Les Pieux, then take D117 to Le Rozel. Turn L thro Rozel, foll sps to site. Site is on R at end rd. 5*, Med, unshd, pt sl, EHU (10A) €4.50; red long stay; 80% statics; fishing; waterslide; games area; watersports; CKE. **€46.60, 1 Apr-30 Sep. 2024**

PISSOS *7D1* (0.5km E Rural) *44.30469, -0.76817* **Camp Municipal l'Arriu,** 40410 Pissos **05 58 04 41 40; tourisme@pissos.fr; sejour-pissos.fr/le-camping-municipal**

Fr N exit N10 junc 18 onto D834 to Pissos; at x-rds turn L onto D43 sp Sore; site on R in 500m, sp. 3*, Med, shd, EHU (6A) inc; red long stay; ice; rv fishing 300m. *"Lge pitches; pool 500m; excel."*
€15.00, 1 Jul-15 Sep. **2024**

PITHIVIERS *4F3* (8km S Rural) *48.10365, 2.24142* **Camping Le Clos des Tourterelles,** Rue des Rendillons, 45300 Bouzonville-aux-Bois **02 38 33 01 00 or 06 79 48 36 18 (mob); leclosdestourterelles@sfr.fr; www.camping-clos-tourterelles.fr**

12 (htd)

S fr Pithiviers on D921 twds Jargeau; enter Bouzonville; turn R immed bef cafe; site 500m on R; sp in vill. 2*, Med, pt shd, EHU (16A) inc; 90% statics; adv bkg acc; CKE. *"Ltd space for tourers - phone ahead rec; friendly, helpful owners; gd NH; cash only."*
€15.00 **2024**

PLAISANCE *8F2* (0.5km S Urban) *43.92511, 2.54616* **Camping Municipal Le Moulin De L'Horte,** 12550 Plaisance **05 65 99 72 07 or 05 65 99 75 07; mairie.plaisance12@laposte.net; plaisance12.com/tourisme-et-loisirs/camping-sud-aveyron**

Fr D999 Albi-Millau, exit at D127 to Plaisance. R onto D77. Site on R after bdge. 1*, Sm, mkd, pt shd, EHU (6A); gas; bbq; sw nr; twin axles; TV; 10% statics; phone; Eng spkn; adv bkg acc; games rm. *" Vg, great quiet site with rv adj to swim in; excel rest & café nrby 0.2km; sm town but v pleasant."*
€12.00, 15 Jun-15 Sep. **2024**

PLELAN LE GRAND *2F3* (7km SW Rural) *47.95950, -2.15260* **Camping du Château d'Aleth,** Rue de l'Ecole, 56380 St Malo-de-Beignon **06 78 96 10 62 (mob); contact@camping-aleth.com; www.camping-aleth.com**

12

Fr N24 twds Rennes exit N onto D773 to St Malo-de-Beignon in 5km, site L by church. 3*, Sm, pt shd, pt sl, EHU (10A) inc; bbq. *"Pleasant, tranquil, well-kept site by lake; clean san facs; themed cowboy & indian site."*
€19.50 **2024**

PLESTIN LES GREVES *2E2* (4km NE Coastal) *48.66805, -3.60060* **Camp Municipal St Efflam,** Rue Lan-Carré, 22310 Plestin-les-Grèves **02 96 35 62 15; camping municipalplestin@wanadoo.fr; www.camping-municipal-bretagne.com**

€1.30 nr sand 150m

Fr Morlaix on D786 thro Plestin-les-Grèves; foll D786 sp St Efflam down hill to bay; site on R 850m along bay; sp. 3*, Lge, mkd, pt shd, pt sl, terr, EHU (10A) €2.50; gas; bbq; sw nr; Eng spkn; adv bkg req; ccard acc; boating adj; fishing adj; CKE. *"Excel; helpful recep; v well kept; modern san facs; municipal pool on site; superb beach nrby; grass pitches liable to waterlogging in wet weather."*
€14.00, 26 Mar-3 Oct. **2022**

PLOEMEUR *2F2* (5.2km S Coastal) *47.70583, -3.42419* **Camping Bella Plage,** Rue de l'Anse du Stole, 56270 Ploemeur **97 56 77 17; info@yellohvillage-belle-plage.com; www.yellohvillage.co.uk/camping/belle_plage#content**

(htd) (htd)

On N165/E60 take exit 43 via D29 direction Larmor Plage, via D152 sp to Kerpape. 4*, Med, mkd, pt shd, EHU (10A); bbq (charcoal, gas); TV; 15% statics; Eng spkn; adv bkg rec; ccard acc; games rm.
€40.10, 2 Apr-30 Sep. **2022**

PLOERMEL *2F3* (2km N Rural) *47.94866, -2.42077* **Camping du Lac,** Les Belles Rives, 56800 Taupont **02 97 74 01 22; campingdulactaupont@gmail.com; camping-lac-au-duc.fr**

€2.40 (htd)

Fr N24 foll D766e around Ploërmel or foll sp for Taupont (D8). Cent, take D8 twds Taupont & Lac-au-Duc 3km. Site clearly sp on R on edge of lake. 2*, Med, hdg, mkd, pt shd, EHU (5A) €3.50; gas; bbq; sw nr; 10% statics; Eng spkn; adv bkg acc; ccard acc; tennis; waterslide nr; watersports adj; CKE. *"Pleasant site in lovely location; golf 1km; horseriding 1km; friendly staff; vg; excel shopping in Ploermel; excel cent to explore Brittany."* **€15.00, 1 Apr-30 Sep.** **2024**

PLOERMEL *2F3* (7.6km N Rural) *47.98425, -2.38191* **Camping Parc Merlin l'Enchanteur,** 8 Rue du Pont, Vallée de l'Yvel, 56800 Loyat **02 97 93 05 52 or 02 97 73 89 45; camelotpark@wanadoo.fr; www.campingmerlin.com**

12 €3 (htd) nr nr (covrd, htd)

Fr Ploërmel take D766 N sp St Malo. In 5km turn L to Loyat. Site on L on ent vill opp g'ge, adj sm lake. 2*, Med, hdg, mkd, pt shd, EHU (10-16A) €5 (poss rev pol); gas; bbq; sw nr; red long stay; 10% statics; adv bkg acc; ccard acc; games area; tennis; bike hire; fishing; watersports 4km; CKE. *"Peaceful site; spacious pitches; welcoming British owners; vg clean facs; gd indoor pool; poss soggy in winter; new 60km tarmac cycle trail adj; conv Château Josselin, Lizio & Brocéliande forest with legend of King Arthur; pleasant site; excel walking and cycling; site rather unkept."*
€20.40 **2023**

FRANCE

FRANCE

PLOMBIERES LES BAINS *6F2* (10km S Rural) *47.92460, 6.47545* **Camping l'Orée des Vosges (Formerly Val d'Ajol),** Rue des Oeuvres, 88340 Le Val-d'Ajol **03 29 66 55 17; campingoreedesvosges@onlycamp.fr; camping-val-dajol.fr/**

nr

Fr N on N57 after Plombières-les-Bains turn onto D20 sp Le Val-d'Ajol. Site sps in vill. 2*, Sm, hdg, pt shd, EHU (6A) €2.50; TV; phone; adv bkg acc; CKE. *"Excel site; excel, clean san facs; vg touring base; lovely; htd covrd pool adj; attractive area."*
€13.00, 15 Apr-30 Sep. **2023**

PLONEVEZ PORZAY *2E2* (3km W Coastal) *48.14458, -4.26915* **Camping La Plage de Tréguer,** Plage de Ste Anne-la-Palud, 29550 Plonévez-Porzay **02 98 92 53 52; camping-treguer-plage@wanadoo.fr; www.camping-treguer-plage.com**

€2.20 (htd) nr (indoor) sand adj

On D107 S fr Châteaulin. After 8km turn R to Ste Anne-la-Palud & foll sp. 2*, Lge, mkd, hdg, unshd, EHU (10A) €5; gas; bbq; TV; 10% statics; Eng spkn; adv bkg acc; ccard acc; games area; games rm; CKE. *"Well-situated touring base; vg, friendly site; excel beach with direct access; new san facs (2019)."* **€31.90, 27 Apr-21 Sep.** **2024**

PLOUGASNOU *1D2* (1.5km SE Rural) *48.68548, -3.78530* **Camping Le Trégor,** 130 route du Cosquerou, 29630 Plougasnou **02 98 67 37 64; bookings@campingdutregor.com; www.campingdutregor.com**

€1 nr sand 1.2km

At junc of D46 to Plougasnou. Site is on L just bef town sp. Sm, mkd, hdg, pt shd, EHU (6-10A) inc; gas; bbq; sw nr; 40% statics; adv bkg acc; watersports 3km; CKE. *"Well-run site in beautiful area; dated but clean facs; ideal for walking, cycling & fishing; conv Roscoff ferries & Morlaix; phone if req NH after end Oct."*
€15.00, Easter-11 Nov. **2024**

PLOUGASNOU *1D2* (3km NW Coastal) *48.71421, -3.81563* **Camp Municipal de la Mer,** 29630 Primel-Trégastel **02 98 72 37 06 or 02 98 67 30 06; primel-tregastel.camping-de-la-mer@wanadoo.fr**

€1 nr nr nr sand 500m

Fr Morlaix take D46 to Plougastel on to Primel-Trégastel. Bear R in vill & 1st L opp cafe to site on R in 100 m. 2*, Med, unshd, EHU (10A) inc; phone; CKE. *"Fine coastal views; gd walking & cycling; ltd facs LS."*
€17.00, 1 Jun-30 Sep. **2024**

PLOUGRESCANT *1D3* (2km ENE Coastal) *48.8472138, -3.2073686* **Camping Beg Ar Vilin,** lieu dit Beg-Ar-Vilin, 22820 Plougrescant **02 96 92 56 15; camping@plougrescant.fr; www.plougrescant.fr/camp**

nr nr sand/shingle adj

Fr centre of Plougrescant turn R at church with wonky spire. Foll sp to Camping Beg At Villin or Camping Municipal for 2 km. Site on spit of land by oyster sheds. ///bravest.milkmaid.invest Med, mkd, unshd, EHU (16A); bbq (sep area); 5% statics; Eng spkn; adv bkg rec; ccard acc. *"Very good."*
€20.00, Apr-Nov. **2024**

PLOUGUENAST *2E3* (2km NW Rural) *48.28653, -2.72145* **Pinábre Camping & Caravaning,** 15 Lingouet 22150 **06 11 35 85 72; pinabrecampsite.com**

Site is 50 miles fr St. Malo ferry port, bet Loudeac and Moncontour off the D768. Sm, pt shd, pt sl, EHU (16A) €3; bbq; Eng spkn; adv bkg acc; CKE. *"Gd for walks & cycling; sm friendly site; excel facs; close to N & S coast; open plan, grassy site; quiet; excel."*
€20.00, Apr-Sep. **2023**

PLOUGUERNEAU *2E2* (3km N Coastal) *48.63048, -4.52402* **Camping La Grève Blanche,** St Michel, 29880 Plouguerneau **02 98 04 70 35 or 06 83 26 51 91; lroudaut@free.fr; www.campinggreveblanche.com**

(htd) nr sand

Fr Lannilis D13 to Plouguerneau, D32 sp La Grève, St Michel (look out for lorry rte sp). Avoid Plouguerneau vill when towing - tight RH bend. 2*, Med, mkd, hdg, unshd, pt sl, terr, EHU (9A) €2.80 (long cable poss req, rev pol); bbq (charcoal, elec, gas); twin axles; 20% statics; bus adj; Eng spkn; adv bkg acc; games area; games rm; CCI. *"Excel location; sea views; helpful staff; facs clean & well-kept; LS recep open eves only; in fog lighthse sounds all night otherwise quiet; walking coastal rte; san facs clean but dated."*
€11.10, 23 Mar-8 Oct. **2023**

PLOUHARNEL *2F3* (7km S Coastal) *47.55458, -3.13198* **Camping Municipal De Penthievre,** Avenue Duquesne, Penthievre 56510 St Pierre, Quiberon **02 07 52 33 86; www.saintpierrequiberon.fr**

€1.04 adj

Take D768 fr N165 at Auray dir Quiberon. Foll sp at Penthievre. V lge, pt shd, pt sl, EHU (10A) €1.83; gas; bbq; twin axles; phone; bus, train; Eng spkn; ccard acc; games area. *"Traditional French municipal; v friendly; ideal watersports & cycling; coastal scenery; Quiberon magnificent; rests, mkt; park & ride; ideal base for visiting southern Brittany; pool 6km; excel."*
€15.00, 1 Apr-30 Sep. **2022**

POET LAVAL, LE *9D2* (2km SE Rural) *44.52889, 5.02300* **Camp Municipal Lorette,** 26160 Le Poët-Laval **04 75 91 00 62 or 04 75 46 44 12 (Mairie); camping. lorette@wanadoo.fr; www.campinglorette.fr**

€1.80 (htd) nr nr nr

Site 4km W of Dieulefit on D540. 2*, Sm, mkd, pt shd, pt sl, EHU (1A) €3; bus; Eng spkn; adv bkg acc; ccard acc; tennis; CKE. *"Well-kept site with views; lge pitches; clean, modern facs; nr lavender fields (Jun/Jul); mkt in Dieulefit Fri; excel; gd welcome."* **€12.50, 1 May-30 Sep.** 2022

POILLY-LEZ-GIEN *4G3* (3km S Rural) *47.68233, 2.62289* **Camping Touristique de Gien,** Rue des Iris, 45500 Poilly-lez-Gien **02 38 67 12 50; info@camping-gien.com; www.camping-gien.com**

€2 (htd) nr (covrd)

Off D952 Orléans-Nevers rd; turn R over old rv bdge in Gien & then R again onto D951; site on R on Rv Loire. Alt dir fr D940 (Argent-sur-Sauldre - Gien) at rndbt take rd sp Gien. Take L at traff lts bef old bdge; site on R, 1km S of rv. 3*, Lge, hdstg, mkd, hdg, pt shd, pt sl, EHU (10A) €5; bbq; sw nr; red long stay; TV; 20% statics; phone; Eng spkn; adv bkg acc; ccard acc; tennis; canoeing; games rm; bike hire; CKE. *"Lovely rvside site; views of old bdge & town some pitches; excel staff; gd san facs; vg facs; no sw allowed in rv; easy walk to town across bdge; porcelain factory 'seconds'; vg value; gd rest; san facs unisex; excel site, highly rec; nice situation; bar adj; gas adj; flock of sheep/goats traverse the site daily."* **€27.00, 9 Mar-31 Oct.** 2024

POITIERS *7A2* (12km N Rural) *46.65611, 0.30194* **Camping du Futur,** 9 Rue des Bois, 86170 Avanton **05 49 54 09 67; contact@camping-du-futur.com; www.camping-du-futur.com**

€1.50 nr nr

Exit A10 junc 28. After toll take 1st exit at rndabt sp Avanton. Site well sp fr Avanton, but care needed thro Martigny & hotel complex. 3*, Med, mkd, hdg, pt shd, EHU (6-10A) €3.50-3.8; TV; adv bkg acc; games area; games rm; CKE. *"Attractive, spacious site; well-kept & well-run; helpful owners; vg clean san facs, ltd early ssn; c'van storage; 5 mins Futuroscope & A10; ideal NH or longer; bread, pastries and breakfast can be ordered; mv service pnt; nr Futurscope attraction; ltd shd; lovely & peaceful; quiet parkland setting; conv for Poitiers; excel."* **€30.90, 1 Apr-1 Nov.** 2022

POIX DE PICARDIE *3C3* (0.3km SW Rural) *49.77621, 1.97467* **Camp Municipal Le Bois des Pêcheurs,** Route de Forges-les-Eaux, 80290 Poix-de-Picardie **03 22 90 11 71; camping@ville-poix-de-picardie.fr; www.ville-poix-de-picardie.fr**

€1.50 nr nr nr

Fr town cent on D901 dir Beauvais, in 100m turn R onto D919 opp Citroën agent sp Camping; site on R in 500m. Fr Beauvais, turn L at bottom of steep hill opp Citroën agent; site in 500m on R. 3*, Med, hdg, mkd, hdstg, pt shd, EHU (6A) €4 (poss long lead req); bbq; red long stay; TV; Eng spkn; adv bkg acc; rv fishing adj; tennis 800m; bike hire; games rm; CKE. *"Pleasant, peaceful, tidy site in delightful area; v clean modern san facs; htd covrd pool 800m; gd touring base; vg walking & cycling; bar 500m; train to Amiens; lovely mkt Sun; rec; every 3rd night free; gas 300m; sh walk to town and supmkt; vg."* **€18.00, 1 Apr-30 Sep.** 2023

POLIGNY *6H2* (1km SW Rural) *46.83455, 5.69840* **Camping La Tulip De Vigne (formerly Camp Communautaire de la Croix du Dan),** Road to Lons-le-Saunier, 39800 Poligny **07 86 62 43 19; latulipedevigne@gmail.com; www.camping-poligny.com**

nr

Fr SW on N83 turn R at rndabt sp 'Centre'; site on R immed bef town sp Poligny. Fr N & NW take D905 into & thro town cent (no L turn on N83 S of Poligny), then foll sp Lons-Le Saunier. Site on L bef sportsgrnd - look for m'van sp. Do not overshoot ent, as diff to see. N5 fr E not rec as steep & hairpins. 2*, Med, mkd, pt shd, EHU (10A) €6.40; twin axles; phone; Eng spkn; CKE. *"Excel, clean, tidy site; helpful warden; pretty town; if recep clsd ring number on board to open barrier."* **€15.00, 15 Jun-20 Sep.** 2023

PONS (CHARENTE MARITIME) *7B2* (0.5km W Urban) *45.57791, -0.55552* **Camp Municipal Le Paradis,** 1 Ave de Poitou, 17800 Pons **05 46 91 36 72; campingmunicipalpons@voila.fr; www.pons-ville.org**

12 €1.76 nr

Well sp fr town o'skts. 3*, Med, mkd, pt shd, EHU (6-10A) inc (poss rev pol); TV; Eng spkn; rv fishing 200m. *"Excel site in attractive grnds; helpful, friendly, super wardens; interesting town; conv for Saintes, Cognac, Royan; free wifi in snack bar; gd sized pitches; pool 100m; waterslide 100m; easy but uphill walk to old city; excel; some rd noise."* **€23.00** 2024

FRANCE

FRANCE

PONT AUDEMER *3D2* (8km W Rural) *49.31433, 0.40344* **Camping La Lorie (Lehaye),** 5 La Lorie, 27210 Fort-Moville **02 32 57 15 49**

nr nr

Fr Pont-Audemer take D675 twrds Beauzeville. Then L onto D27. Take 3rd exit at rndabt to stay on D27. Then 3rd exit at next rndabt onto Haut Rue de Fort Moville; slight L then strt on; site on L. Sm, pt shd, EHU (10A) inc; bbq; 10% statics; CKE. *"CL-type site in attractive area; basic facs but clean; conv Le Havre, Honfleur; gd base."* **€13.50, Easter-1 Nov.** **2024**

PONT AUDEMER *3D2* (2km NW Rural) *49.36660, 0.48739* **Camp Municipal Risle-Seine Les Etangs,** 19 Route des Etangs, 27500 Toutainville **02 32 42 46 65; infos@camping-risle-seine.com; https://www.camping-risle-seine.com/**

€2.50 nr (covrd, htd)

Fr Le Havre on A131/E05 cross rv at Pont de Normandie (toll). Take D580 & at junc 3 branch R & take 2nd exit onto D22 sp Beuzeville. At edge of Fiquefleur take D180, then D675 dir Pont-Audemer. In Toutainville, turn L just aft A13 underpass, site signposted, site approx 2km on R. 3*, Med, hdg, mkd, pt shd, serviced pitches; EHU (5-10A) €3.95; bbq; sw nr; red long stay; TV; bus; Eng spkn; adv bkg acc; ccard acc; fishing; bike hire; watersports; games area; tennis 1.5km; games rm; canoeing. *"Lovely, well-run site; helpful warden; barrier clsd 2200-0830 but flexible for ferry; many leisure activities; htd pool 1.5km; poss school groups at w/end; vg for dogs; 1hr Le Havre ferry; Fri mkt Pont-Audemer; conv NH; excel; facs not stretched LS; boggy when wet; pitches are narr which means car has to go at the front of your pitch."* **€35.00, 1 Apr - 31 Oct, N13.** **2022**

"I need an on-site restaurant"

We do our best to make sure site information is correct, but it is always best to check any must-have facilities are still available or will be open during your visit.

PONT AVEN *2F2* (8km SE Coastal) *47.78799, -3.70064* **Camping de l'Ile Percée,** Plage de Trénez, 29350 Moëlan-sur-Mer **02 98 71 16 25; contact@camping-ile-percee.fr; www.camping-ile-percee.fr**

€1 shgl adj

App thro Moëlan-sur-Mer, 6km SE of Pont-Aven or 6km SW of Quimperlé - watch for R turn after Moëlan. Take D116 sp to Kerfany. Keep strt at Kergroës, turn L after 500m sp L'Ile Percée. 3*, Med, unshd, pt sl, EHU (4-6A) €2.60-3.70; bbq; sw nr; TV; 10% statics; phone; adv bkg acc; watersports adj; fishing adj; games area. *"Well-run site; sea views; ent narr & winding; sm pitches; manhandling ess; not suitable lge o'fits; san facs poss stretched high ssn."* **€17.50, 1 Apr-19 Sep.** **2024**

PONT AVEN *2F2* (11km SSW Coastal) *47.79640, -3.77489* **Camping Les Chaumières,** 5 Hameau de Kerascoët, 29920 Névez **02 98 06 73 06; info@camping-des-chaumieres.com; www.camping-des-chaumieres.com**

€1.50 nr nr nr sand 800m

S fr Pont-Aven thro Névez to Kerascoët. 2*, Med, mkd, hdg, pt shd, serviced pitches; EHU (4-10A) €3.40-4.30; bbq; Eng spkn; adv bkg req; CKE. *"Excel, well-organised, peaceful, beautiful site; immac facs poss stretched high ssn; gd play & games areas; sandy bay/beaches, cliff walks; san facs refurbished and upgraded; highly rec; friendly owner; recep clsd LS, but owner avail via mob."* **€31.30, 15 May-19 Sep.** **2023**

PONT AVEN *2F2* (5km SW Rural) *47.81749, -3.79959* **Camping Les Genêts,** Route St Philibert, 29920 Névez **02 98 06 86 13 or 02 98 06 72 31; campingfrance.com/uk/find-your-campsite/brittany/finistere/nevez/les-genets3**

€1 nr sand

Turn S off D783 onto D77 to Névez. At church in town, bear R & turn immed R to exit Névez with PO on R. Site on L, clearly sp. 2*, Med, hdg, mkd, pt shd, EHU (3-6A) €2.40-5; 10% statics; Eng spkn; adv bkg acc; CKE. *"Excel beaches adj; vg."* **€15.00, 15 May-15 Sep.** **2024**

PONT AVEN *2F2* (6km SW Coastal) *47.79906, -3.79033* **Sandaya Deux Fontaines,** Raguenès, 29920 Névez **02 98 06 81 91; fon@sandaya.fr; www.sandaya.co.uk**

€5 (htd) sand 4km

Leave N165/E60 at Kérampaou foll sp D24 twds Pont Aven. In approx 4.5km turn R (S) foll sp Névez then Raguenès. Site 3km fr Névez. 4*, Lge, mkd, pt shd, EHU (10A) inc; bbq (charcoal); 80% statics; adv bkg acc; tennis. *"Busy high ssn; popular with British families; o'night facs for m'vans; 25 meter conn lead req'd; price inc waterpark acc & kids club."* **€33.00, 10 Apr-13 Sep.** **2024**

PONT AVEN *2F2* (8km SW Coastal) *47.79597, -3.79877* **Camping du Vieux Verger,** Raguenès-Plage, 29920 Névez **02 98 06 86 08; contact@campingduvieuxverger.com; www.campingduvieuxverger.com**

sand 500m

Fr Pont-Aven take D783 dir Concarneau; in 2.5km L onto D77 to Névez; foll sp Raguenès-Plage; 1st site on R. Foll 'Vieux Verger' sps. 2*, Med, mkd, hdg, pt shd, EHU (4-10A) €3.20-4.20 (poss rev pol); phone; CKE. *"Well-run, well-kept site with pool & waterslides; statics (sep area); highly rec LS; excel; gd for young children; excel site; gd value; many attractive beaches nrby."* **€21.50, 14 Apr-15 Sep.** **2023**

PONT AVEN *2F2* (8km SW Coastal) *47.79330, -3.80110* **Camping Raguénès-Plage,** 15 - 19 Rue des Îles à Raguénès, 29920 Névez **02 98 06 80 69; contact@camping-le-raguenes-plage.com; www.camping-le-raguenes-plage.com**

€1.50 (htd) WD MSP (covrd, htd) sand adj

Fr Pont-Aven take D783 dir Trégunc; in 2.5km turn L for Névez, foll sps to Raguénès fr Névez. Or fr N165 take D24 at Kérampaou exit; in 3km turn R to Nizon; at church in vill turn R onto D77 to Névez; site on L 3km after Névez. 4*, Lge, hdstg, mkd, pt shd, EHU (6-15A) €4-6.90; gas; bbq; sw nr; 20% statics; Eng spkn; adv bkg rec; ccard acc; games rm; watersports school adj; sauna; tennis nr; bike hire; games area; waterslide; horseriding; CKE. *"Pretty, wooded, family-run site; trampoline; statics sep area; private path to beach; clean facs; 1st class site."*
€33.00, 8 Apr-2 Nov, B12. **2022**

See advertisement

PONT D'AIN *9A2* (1.4km SE Urban) *46.04680, 5.34446* **Camping de l'Oiselon,** Rue E'mile Lebreüs, 01160 Pont-d'Ain **04 74 39 05 23; campingoiselon@free.fr; www.campingpontdain.e-monsite.com**

WD

Fr A42 exit Pont-d'Ain foll D90 to vill. In vill cent turn R on D1075. Turn L immed after x-ing Rv L'Ain. Foll rd passing tennis club on L. Site on L, clearly sp. 3*, Lge, pt shd, EHU (6-10A) €2.40-3.10 (poss rev pol); bbq; sw; 30% statics; Eng spkn; adv bkg acc; fishing; canoeing; tennis adj; games area; horseriding 5km; bike hire; CKE. *"Gd, well-run site with easy access, v lge; helpful, friendly staff; gd clean san facs; cash only; site needs TLC (early ssn 2010); gd NH; excel site."*
€18.60, 17 Mar-14 Oct. **2023**

PONT DE L'ARCHE *3D2* (0.8km N Urban) *49.3060, 1.1546* **Camp Municipal Eure et Seine,** Quai Maréchal Foch, 27340 Pont-de-l'Arche **02 35 23 06 71 or 02 32 98 90 70 (Mairie); campeure@pontdelarche.fr; www.pontdelarche.fr**

€1.50 WD nr

Fr Rouen S on D6015 turn 1st L after x-ing rv bdge, drive downhill then L under bdge & strt on for 300m (foll Camping Car sp at traff lts, do not go into town), site on R. Restricted width on app. Or exit A13 junc 20 onto D321 to Pont-de-l'Arche; turn L at War Memorial onto Place du Souvenir; in 300m to R at rv; site on L in 200m. 2*, Med, mkd, pt shd, EHU (6-10A) inc; red long stay; TV; 4% statics; phone; adv bkg rec; ccard acc; rv fishing adj; CKE. *"Pleasant, peaceful, clean rvside site in attractive medieval town; sm pitches; helpful warden; gd, modern san facs; recep 1000-1200 & 1600-2000; access only after 1600, Aire outside site accessible 24/7; many shops clsd Wed pm; bus fr town to Rouen; popular NH & longer; beautiful site nr Gothic church; excel; superb setting; v busy so arrive early or ring ahead; sh walk to town; o'night parking for M'van outside site €5 pn "*
€12.00, 1 Apr-30 Oct. **2024**

PONT DE SALARS *7D4* (1.5km N Rural) *44.29150, 2.72571* **Parc Camping du Lac,** Le Lac, 12290 Pont-de-Salars **05 65 46 84 86; camping.du.lac@wanadoo.fr; www.campingdulacaveyron.com**

WD

Fr Rodez on D911 La Primaube-Millau rd, turn L bef ent Pont-de-Salars. Site sp. 3*, Lge, mkd, pt shd, pt sl, terr, EHU (3-6A) €2.50-3.50; gas; bbq; sw; TV; 90% statics; phone; adv bkg acc; ccard acc; fishing; sailing. *"Beautiful situation; poor for c'vans, OK m'vans; diff lge o'fits; blocks req; site poss unclean end of ssn; ltd facs."* **€25.50, 1 Jun-30 Sep.** **2023**

FRANCE

PONT DE SALARS *7D4* (8km S Rural) *44.21500, 2.77777* **Camping Soleil Levant,** Lac de Pareloup, 12290 Canet-de-Salars **05 65 46 03 65; contact@camping-soleil-levant.com; www.camping-soleil-levant.com**

€2 (htd) nr

Exit A75 junc 44.1 onto D911 to Pont-de-Salars, then S on D993 dir Salles-Curan. Site in 8km bef bdge on L. 3*, Lge, mkd, pt shd, pt sl, terr, EHU (6A) inc; gas; bbq; sw nr; TV; 50% statics; Eng spkn; adv bkg acc; ccard acc; watersports; games area; tennis; games rm; fishing; CKE. *"Lovely lakeside site; excel san facs; vg; well run by friendly couple."* **€32.90, 1 May-30 Sep. 2023**

PONT DE VAUX *9A2* (4km NE Rural) *46.44394, 4.98313* **Camping Les Ripettes,** St Bénigne, 01190 Chavannes-sur-Reyssouze **03 85 30 66 58; info@camping-les-ripettes.com; www.les-ripettes.fr**

€1.50 (htd)

Take D2 fr Pont-de-Vaux sp St Trivier-des-Courtes for 3km. Immed after water tower on R turn L onto D58 sp Romenay, then immed L. Site well sp on L in 100m. 3*, Med, hdg, mkd, pt shd, pt sl, EHU (10A) €4; 1% statics; phone; Eng spkn; adv bkg rec; ccard acc; games area; CKE. *"Lovely, popular site in beautiful location; spacious pitches; friendly, helpful owner; immac facs; gd pool area; gd touring base; hard to beat; ACSI card acc; one of the best; cycle rte maps at TO in Pont de Vaux; memb of La Via Natura; promoting many eco ideas; excel."* **€21.00, 1 Apr-30 Sep. 2023**

PONT DE VAUX *9A2* (0.5km W Urban) *46.42979, 004.93296* **Camping Champ d'Été,** Lieu-dit Champ D'Eté, 01190 Reyssouze **03 85 23 96 10; campinglechampdete@onlycamp.fr; www.camping-champ-dete.com**

€3 (htd) nr nr nr

Fr A6 N J27, take D906 dir Pont-de-Vaux. In town, foll Base-de-Loisirs & camping sp. 4*, Med, mkd, hdstg, pt shd, EHU (10A) inc; bbq; TV; 20% statics; bus adj; Eng spkn; adv bkg acc; ccard acc; games rm; CKE. *"Walking dist to town; adj to pk & free sw pool; v clean san facs; friendly owners; htd pool adj; gd for touring Burgundy area; gd for long or sh stays; some pitches tight for lge o'fits; vg."* **€23.00, 25 Mar-15 Oct. 2022**

PONT FARCY *1D4* (0.5km N Rural) *47.46810, 4.35709* **Camp Municipal Pont-Farcy,** Quai de la Vire, 14380 Pont-Farcy **02 31 68 32 06 or 02 31 68 86 48; pontfarcy@free.fr; www.pont-farcy.fr**

€1 nr nr nr

Leave A84 junc 39 onto D21 to Pont-Farcy; site on L at ent to vill. 3*, Med, hdg, mkd, pt shd, terr, EHU (10A) €2.50; 30% statics; phone; adv bkg acc; boating adj; rv fishing adj; tennis; bike hire; CKE. *"Barrier poss locked periods during day but parking avail; bar 500m; helpful, friendly warden; clean facs; mosquitoes at dusk."* **€12.50, 3 April-30 Sep. 2024**

PONT L'ABBE *2F2* (7km S Rural) *47.81241, -4.22147* **Camping L'Océan Breton,** Route Kerlut, 29740 Lesconil **02 98 82 23 89; info@yellohvillage-loceanbreton.com; www.camping-bretagne-oceanbreton.fr or www.yellohvillage.co.uk**

€6 (htd)

(covrd, htd, indoor) sand 2km

Fr Pont l'Abbé S on D102 to Plobannalec & head for Lesconil; site on L after supmkt. 5*, Lge, hdstg, mkd, hdg, pt shd, serviced pitches; EHU (5A) inc; gas; sw nr; red long stay; 80% statics; phone; Eng spkn; adv bkg acc; ccard acc; tennis; games area; sauna; waterslide; bike hire; kids clubs; bowling; adventure trail; CKE. *"Excel site for families; fitness rm; spacious pitches."* **€35.00, 25 May - 11 Sep, B39. 2022**

PONT L'ABBE *2F2* (8.6km S Rural/Coastal) *47.79715, -4.22868* **Camping des Dunes,** 67 Rue Paul Langevin, 29740 Plobannalec-Lesconil **02 98 87 81 78; contact@camping-desdunes.com; www.camping-desdunes.com**

€2.10 nr nr sand 100m

Fr Pont l'Abbé, S on D102 for 5km to Plobannelec; over x-rds; in 1km turn R, 100m after sports field; green sp to site in 1km. 3*, Med, mkd, hdg, pt shd, EHU (8A) €3.70; bbq; adv bkg acc; ccard acc; games area; games rm; CKE. *"Helpful owner; nr fishing port; gd walking, cycling & birdwatching; site gd for children; access to beach with amazing granite rock formations; red early ssn; well cared for."* **€25.70, 30 Mar-29 Sep. 2024**

PONT L'ABBE *2F2* (3km W Rural) *47.86113, -4.26766* **Aire Naturelle Keraluic,** 8 Keraluig, 29120 Plomeur **02 98 82 10 22; info@keraluic.fr; www.keraluic.fr**

€1.50

Leave Quimper S on D785 to o'skts Pont L'Abbe; turn R at 1st rndabt (junc with D44); strt on at 2nd rndabt (junc with D2); in 1km turn R at 3rd rndabt up narr rd sp St Jean-Trolimon; site on R in 1.5km. Site 2km NE of Plomeur & well sp. Sm, pt shd, EHU (6A) €2.90; gas; bbq; Eng spkn; adv bkg rec; ccard acc; games area; games rm; CKE. *"Excel, well-kept, family-run site; friendly, helpful Dutch owners; spacious pitches; no dogs high ssn; gd leisure facs; ideal for children; gd walking; gd surfing nrby; surfing 5km; facs poss stretched high ssn, highly rec LS; no motorhomes."* **€19.00, 1 May-31 Oct. 2024**

PONT L'ABBE *2F2* (10km NW Rural) *47.89462, -4.32863* **Camping Kerlaz,** Route de la Mer, 29720 Tréguennec **02 98 87 76 79; contact@kerlaz.com; www.kerlaz.com**

€1.30 nr (covrd, htd)

sand 2km

Fr Plonéour-Lanvern take D156 SW to Tréguennec. 3*, Med, hdg, pt shd, EHU (10A); bbq; 30% statics; Eng spkn; adv bkg acc; ccard acc; bike hire. *"Nice, friendly site; pleasant owners; attractive site; gd for cycling."* **€25.00, 1 Apr-30 Sep. 2023**

PONT ST ESPRIT *9D2* (6km NW Rural) *44.30388, 4.58443* **Camping Le Pontet,** 07700 St Martin-d'Ardèche **04 75 04 63 07 or 04 75 98 76 24; contact@campinglepontet.com; www.campinglepontet.com**

€2

N86 N of Pont-St Esprit; turn L onto D290 at sp Gorges de l'Ardèche & St Martin-d'Ardèche, site on R after 3km, sp. 3*, Med, mkd, pt shd, EHU (6A) €5; gas; sw nr; 5% statics; phone; Eng spkn; adv bkg acc; CKE. *"Vg; helpful owners; peaceful out of ssn; facs stretched when busy; online bkg fee €10."* **€25.00, 8 Apr-25 Sep. 2023**

PONT ST ESPRIT *9D2* (8km NW Rural) *44.28950, 4.58923* **Camping Le Peyrolais,** Route de Barjac, 30760 St Julien-de-Peyrolas **04 66 82 14 94; contact@camping-lepeyrolais.com; www.camping-lepeyrolais.com**

€2

N fr Pont-St. Esprit on D6086 turn L onto D901 sp Barjac. In 2.5km turn R at site sp, site in 500m up narr track on bank of Rv Ardèche. 3*, Med, mkd, pt shd, EHU (3-10A) €2.30-3.80; sw nr; TV; phone; adv bkg acc; ccard acc; horseriding; kayaking; fishing; bike hire; games area; canoe hire; CKE. *"Attractive, well-maintained site in beautiful location; clean facs; hiking; friendly owners; vg; great site."* **€32.00, 3 May-30 Sep. 2024**

PONT ST ESPRIT *9D2* (8km NW Rural) *44.34423, 4.60434* **Camping Les Truffières,** 252 Impasse Les Truffières, 07700 St Marcel-d'Ardèche **04 75 04 68 35; soulier.valerie@wanadoo.fr; www.camping-les-truffieres.com**

12 €1.60 (htd) nr

S fr Bourg-St Andéol, turn W on D201; in vill foll sp to site located approx 3km W of vill. 2*, Med, mkd, pt shd, terr, EHU (6A) €6.60 (poss rev pol); gas; 70% statics; adv bkg acc; CKE. *"Friendly owners; glorious views; gd san facs; conv NH nr A7; v pleasant; tricky without motor mover (trees)."* **€28.00 2023**

PONT ST ESPRIT *9D2* (9km NW Rural) *44.30043, 4.57069* **Camping Indigo Le Moulin,** 07700 St Martin-d'Ardèche **04 75 04 66 20; moulin@camping-indigo.com; europe.huttopia.com/site/camping-le-moulin-ardeche**

€4 (htd) nr (htd)

Exit A7 junc 19 to Bollène, then D994 to Pont-St Esprit & D6068/D86 to St Just. Turn L onto D290 to St Martin in 4km. Site on L on rvside. 3*, Med, pt shd, pt sl, EHU (10A) €4.90; sw nr; TV; 5% statics; phone; Eng spkn; ccard acc; canoe hire; games area; tennis 500m; bike hire; fishing. *"Friendly site; gd modern san facs; footpath to vill; quiet low ssn; gd local walks; rec."* **€38.50, 30 Apr-28 Sep. 2024**

PONTAILLER SUR SAONE *6G1* (0.8km E Rural) *47.30817, 5.42518* **Camping La Chanoie,** 46 Rue de la Chanoie, 21270 Pontailler-sur-Saône **03 80 67 21 98; camping.municipal1@orange.fr; www.camping-lachanoie.com**

€1.55 (htd) nr

E fr Pontailler-sur-Saône on D959; pass town hall & TO on R; after bdg take 1st L sp Camping; site in 500m. Fr W on D959 turn R bef bdg & bef ent town. 3*, Med, hdg, mkd, pt shd, EHU (6-10A) €2.85-4.10; bbq; sw nr; red long stay; 80% statics; bus; adv bkg acc; games area; tennis; watersports adj; games rm; fishing adj; CKE. *"Attractive sm town; polite & helpful owner; clean san facs, poss stretched high ssn; vg; OK NH."* **€17.30, 15 Mar-15 Oct. 2024**

PONTARLIER *6H2* (1km SE Rural) *46.90024, 6.37425* **FFCC Camping Le Larmont,** Rue du Toulombief, 25300 Pontarlier **03 81 46 23 33; contact@camping-pontarlier.fr; www.camping-pontarlier.fr**

€1 (htd)

Leave N57 at Pontarlier Gare & foll site sp. Site uphill, turning nr Nestlé factory. 3*, Med, hdstg, unshd, terr, EHU (10A) €4; gas; 20% statics; Eng spkn; adv bkg acc; horseriding adj; CKE. *"Friendly; easy access; clean san facs; ltd pitches for awnings; site self out of office hrs; skiing winter; well-behaved zebra on site; excel; horseriding next to site; rec."* **€22.50, 1 Jan-11 Nov. 2024**

PONTARLIER *6H2* (12km S Rural) *46.81176, 6.30326* **Camping Saint-Point-Lac,** 8 Rue du Port, 25160 St Point-Lac **03 81 69 61 64; contact@camping-saintpointlac.fr; www.camping-saintpointlac.fr**

€1.50 (htd) nr adj

Exit Pontarlier S on N57 dir Lausanne, turn R on D437 dir Malbuisson; in 6km turn R onto D129 thro Les Grangettes to St Point-Lac. Site sp on L. 3*, Med, mkd, hdstg, pt shd, EHU (16A) €4.50; bbq; 5% statics; Eng spkn; adv bkg rec; ccard acc; games area; CKE. *"Delightful, well-kept lakeside site in beautiful position; sm pitches, some may be diff for large units to get in to; friendly staff; vg, clean san facs; m'van o'night area with facs opp; gd fishing, walking, birdwatching; sw; gd touring; rec adv bkg wkends/high ssn; excel."* **€17.10, 1 May-30 Sep. 2023**

PONTAUBAULT *2E4* (4km E Rural) *48.61690, -1.29475* **Camp Municipal La Sélune,** Rue de Boishue, 50220 Ducey-les-Chéris **02 33 48 46 49; camping@ducey.fr; ducey.fr/camping**

€1.30 nr nr

Exit A84 junc 33 onto N176 E fr Pontaubault. In Ducey turn R onto D178 twd St Aubin-de-Terregatte. Ent at sports grnd in 200m. 2*, Sm, hdg, shd, pt sl, EHU (5A) €1.85 (poss rev pol, poss long lead req); gas; 10% statics; phone; bus; Eng spkn; adv bkg acc; tennis adj; CKE. *"Well-maintained site; warden calls am & pm; poss travellers; excel; v clean facs; friendly, helpful owners."* **€15.00, 1 Jul-31 Aug. 2024**

FRANCE

PONTAUBAULT *2E4* (6km SW Coastal) *48.56583, -1.47111* **Campéole Camping St Grégoire,** Le Haut Bourg, 50170 Servon **02 33 60 26 03; saint-gregoire@campeole.com; www.campeole.com**

€2.60

Foll N175 fr Pontaubault twd Pontorson. After 6km site sp on R twd Servon vill. 3*, Med, hdg, mkd, hdstg, pt shd, EHU (6A) inc; bbq; TV; 30% statics; adv bkg acc; ccard acc; games rm; CKE. *"Conv ferries; quiet but some rd noise on S side of site; useful stop en rte to Cherbourg."* **€35.00, 4 Apr-21 Sep. 2024**

PONTAUBAULT *2E4* (0km W Urban) *48.62983, -1.35205* **Camping La Vallée de la Sélune,** 7 Rue Maréchal Leclerc, 50220 Pontaubault **02 33 60 39 00; campselune@wanadoo.fr; www.camping-manche.com**

€1.30

Foll sp to Pontaubault (well sp fr all dirs). In vill head twd Avranches. Turn L immed bef bdge over Rv Sélune. In 100m turn L, site strt in 100m, well sp. 2*, Med, mkd, pt shd, pt sl, EHU (10A) inc; red long stay; 10% statics; adv bkg rec; ccard acc; horseriding nr; fishing adj; golf nr; tennis adj; CKE. *"Relaxing, clean, tidy, pleasant site in sm vill; vg, clean san facs; conv Mont St Michel & Cherbourg ferries; gd NH; cycling nr; friendly, v helpful Yorkshire owner; on cycle rte; gd site; gd loc; busy HS."* **€21.50, 1 Apr-15 Oct. 2022**

PONTCHATEAU *2G3* (7km W Rural) *47.44106, -2.15981* **Le Château du Deffay,** Ste Reine-de-Bretagne, 44160 Pontchâteau **02 40 88 00 57; info@camping-le-deffay.com; www.camping-le-deffay.com**

€2 (covrd, htd)

Leave N165 at junc 13 onto D33 twd Herbignac. Site on R approx 1.5km after Le Calvaire de la Madeleine x-rds, 270m past Chateau ent. Site sp fr by-pass. 4*, Lge, mkd, hdg, pt shd, pt sl, terr, EHU (10A); bbq (charcoal, gas); TV; 40% statics; Eng spkn; adv bkg acc; ccard acc; lake fishing; bike hire; tennis; games rm; golf 10km; CKE. *"Excel, beautiful site with trees in grnds of chateau by lake; free pedalos; friendly, helpful, welcoming staff; bar & restaurant only open Tues & Friday out of HS; excel clean san facs; some pitches lakeside & not fenced; mkt Mon; gd value rest."* **€38.00, 1 May-30 Sep, B25. 2022**

PONTGIBAUD *7B4* (3km NE Rural) *45.84436, 2.87672* **Camping Bel-Air,** 63230 St Ours **04 73 88 72 14; campingbelair63@orange.fr; www.campingbelair.fr**

€1 nr

Exit A89 junc 26 onto D941 dir Pontgibaud; cont past Pontigibaud; in 1.5km turn L onto D943; site in 1.3km on L. Site sp. 2*, Med, mkd, shd, pt sl, EHU (6A) €3.30; gas; bbq; 5% statics; Eng spkn; adv bkg acc; golf; games area; CKE. *"Peaceful, basic site in beautiful area; helpful owner; clean facs, ltd LS; conv Vulcania; excel."* **€18.00, 1 May-27 Sep. 2024**

PONTGIBAUD *7B4* (0.2km S Rural) *45.82978, 2.84517* **Camp Municipal La Palle,** 3 Avenue du General de Gaulle, 63230 Pontgibaud **04 73 88 96 99; camping.pontgibaud@orange.fr; www.ville-pontgibaud.fr/camping-municipal**

(htd) nr

At W end of Pontgibaud turn S over bdge on D986 & site in 500m on L, past site for La Palle Chalets. 3*, Med, hdg, mkd, hdstg, pt shd, EHU (10-16A) inc; bbq; sw nr; red long stay; Eng spkn; adv bkg acc; games area; tennis 400m; CKE. *"Pleasant, clean, tidy site nr sm rv; helpful staff; gd touring base; pop concerts once a week high ssn; conv Vulcania exhibition cent; bike hire 400m; v lge hdg plots; minimal rd & rlwy noise; well maintained; friendly; easy flat walk to town; gd base for Puy de Dome."* **€17.80, 15 Apr-30 Sep. 2023**

"Satellite navigation makes touring much easier"

Remember most sat navs don't know if you're towing or in a larger vehicle – always use yours alongside maps and site directions.

PONTORSON *2E4* (0.9km NW Rural) *48.55805, -1.51444* **Camping Haliotis,** Chemin des Soupirs, 50170 Pontorson **02 33 68 11 59; camping.haliotis@wanadoo.fr; www.camping-haliotis-mont-saint-michel.com**

€3 (htd) nr (htd)

Exit A84 junc 33 onto N175 dir Pontorson; foll sp Cent Ville/Mont-St-Michel. Site well sp. 3*, Lge, mkd, hdg, pt shd, pt sl, EHU (10-16A) inc (poss rev pol); gas; bbq; 25% statics; phone; bus 400m; Eng spkn; adv bkg rec; ccard acc; boating; games area; tennis; rv fishing; games rm; bike hire; sauna; CKE. *"Popular, well-kept, busy, superb site; lge pitches; friendly, helpful owners; immac, unisex san facs; lovely pool & bar; rvside walk to town; cycle rte/bus to Mont St Michel; highly rec; serviced pitches; pitches with private bthrms avail; spa; library; avoid pitches 77-89 due to noise fr bins; excel."* **€40.00, 8 Apr - 31 Oct, N17. 2022**

PONTORSON *2E4* (8km NW Rural) *48.59415, -1.59855* **Camping Les Couesnons,** 8 L'Hôpital, 35610 Roz-sur-Couesnon **02 99 80 26 86; courrier@lescouesnons.com; www.lescouesnons.com**

€2 (htd)

Exit N175/N176 NW onto D797 dir St Malo on coastal rd; site sp 700m past Roz-sur-Couesnon on R. Turn R at Les Couesnons Rest. Site behind. 3*, Sm, hdg, mkd, pt shd, EHU (6A) €3; bbq (charcoal, gas); red long stay; TV; 10% statics; Eng spkn; adv bkg acc; ccard acc; games rm; games area; CKE. *"Excel site; Mont St Michel 8km; ACSI acc; vg, spotless, htd facs; gd rest & bar; highly rec."* **€23.00, 1 Apr-31 Oct. 2023**

PONTRIEUX *2E3* (0.5km W Rural) *48.69493, -3.16365* **Camping Traou-Mélédern,** Traou-Mélédern, 22260 Pontrieux **02 96 95 69 27; campingpontrieux@free.fr; www.camping-pontrieux.com**

12 €1 nr

N on D787 fr Guingamp; on ent town sq turn sharp L sp Traou Mélédern, cross rv bdge & turn R alongside church. Site in 400m. Access poss diff for lge o'fits; steep exit on 1-way system. 2*, Med, hdg, mkd, pt shd, pt sl, EHU (8A) €3.50; bbq; phone; Eng spkn; adv bkg acc; CKE. *"In orchard; excel touring base; friendly owner; quiet but some daytime factory noise; steep junc nr site poss problem for lge o'fits; gd."*
€20.20 **2023**

PORGE, LE *7C1* (9km W Coastal) *44.89430, -1.20181* **Camping La Grigne,** Ave de l'Océan, 33680 Le Porge **05 56 26 54 88; info@lagrigne.com; www.camping-leporge.fr**

€1.90 600m

Fr Bordeaux ring rd take N215 twd Lacaneau. In 22km at Ste Hélène D5 to Saumos & onto Le Porge. Site on L of rd to Porge-Océan in approx 9km. 3*, V lge, mkd, shd, pt sl, terr, EHU (10A) €5; gas; red long stay; TV; adv bkg acc; tennis; games area. *"Vg facs; great beach; excel cycle path network."*
€22.00, 1 Apr-30 Sep. **2022**

PORNIC *2G3* (10km N Urban) *47.20315, -2.03716* **Camping du Grand Fay,** Rue du Grand Fay, 44320 St Père-en-Retz **02 40 21 72 89 or 06 85 87 47 39; contact@grandfay.fr; www.grandfay.fr**

€2 nr (htd)

Fr Mairie in cent St Père-en-Retz take D78 E twds Frossay. After 500m turn R into Rue des Sports, after 200m turn L into Rue du Grand Fay. Site on L in 200m adj sports cent. 3*, Med, mkd, pt shd, pt sl, EHU (6A) €3.80; 10% statics; lake fishing adj; games area; CKE. *"Pleasant site nr sandy beaches."*
€20.00, 1 Apr-15 Oct. **2024**

PORNIC *2G3* (4km E Rural) *47.11885, -2.07296* **Camping La Chênaie (formerly Patisseau),** 36 Rue du Patisseau, 44210 Pornic **02 40 82 07 31; chenaie@capfun.com; www.lepatisseau.com**

€6 (htd) (covrd, htd) sand 2.5km

Fr N or S on D213, take slip rd D751 Nantes. At rndabt take exit sp to Le Patisseau, foll sp. 4*, Med, hdstg, mkd, hdg, pt shd, pt sl, EHU (6A) inc; bbq; TV; 35% statics; Eng spkn; adv bkg rec; ccard acc; sauna; fitness rm; waterslide; golf 2km; tennis 1km; bike hire; games area; games rm; jacuzzi. *"Excel, modern, family site; modern san facs block - lovely shwrs; 1hr walk on path fr back of site to Pornic."*
€42.00, 7 Apr-12 Sep. **2023**

PORNIC *2G3* (5km E Coastal) *47.09748, -2.0525* **Airotel Camping Village La Boutinardière,** 23 Rue de la Plage de la Boutinard, 44210 Pornic **02 40 82 05 68; info@laboutinardiere.com; www.camping-boutinardiere.com**

€5 (covrd, htd) sand 200m

SW fr Nantes on D723; after abt 6km turn L on D751 sp Pornic; after abt 30km L at 2nd rndabt onto D13 sp la Bernerie en Retz; site rd on R after abt 3km in la Rogere abt 50m bef rndabt; recep on R; park on gravel next to low walls on R. 4*, Lge, hdg, pt shd, pt sl, serviced pitches; EHU (6-10A) €5-6 (poss rev pol); gas; bbq; sw nr; red long stay; TV; 15% statics; bus nrby; Eng spkn; adv bkg acc; ccard acc; waterslide; bike hire; tennis; sauna; golf 5km; games rm; jacuzzi; CKE. *"Excel family site; vg pool complex; activities; v busy high ssn; Pornic interesting town."* **€62.00, 1 Apr-30 Sep.** **2024**

PORNIC *2G3* (6km SE Rural/Coastal) *47.08450, -2.03650* **Camping Les Ecureuils,** 24 Ave Gilbert Burlot, 44760 La Bernerie-en-Retz **02 40 82 76 95; info@chadotel.com; www.chadotel.com/camping-les-ecureuils-la-bernerie-en-retz**

€4 nr (covrd, htd) sand 350m

Fr Pornic take D13 S for 5km, then D66 for 1km; site sp. 4*, Lge, hdg, pt shd, pt sl, EHU (10A) inc; bbq; 30% statics; Eng spkn; adv bkg acc; ccard acc; waterslide; golf 5km; tennis; CKE. *"Excel; children's club; v clean modern san facs; hg rec."*
€50.00, 1 Apr-30 Sep, L29. **2022**

"There aren't many sites open at this time of year"

If you're travelling outside peak season remember to call ahead to check site opening dates – even if the entry says 'open all year'.

PORNIC *2G3* (10km S Coastal) *47.07500, -2.00741* **Camping Les Brillas,** Le Bois des Treans, 44760 Les Moutiers-en-Retz **02 40 82 79 78; info@campinglesbrillas.com; www.campinglesbrillas.com**

Fr Nantes ring rd, take D723 SW. Take exit D751 twd Pornic. Turn L on D66. Foll sp. 3*, Med, hdg, mkd, EHU (6A); Eng spkn; CCI. *"Sm coastal vill; easy walk to beach; excel; lovely location & beach; basic facs."* **€31.20, 14 Apr-1 Oct.** **2023**

FRANCE

PORNIC *2G3* (5km W Rural) *47.14079, -2.15306* **Les Vallons de L'Océan,** 2 route de la Tabardière 44770 La Plaine sur Mer **02 40 21 58 83; https://www.camping-lesvallonsdelocean.com**

€5 (htd) (covrd, htd) sand 3km

Take D13 NW out of Pornic sp Préfailles & La Plaine-sur-Mer. In about 5.5km turn R (nr water tower). Foll sps to site, about 1km fr main rd. NB C'vans not allowed in Pornic town cent, use by-pass. 4*, Lge, hdstg, mkd, hdg, pt shd, terr, serviced pitches; EHU (10A); gas; bbq (charcoal, gas); TV; 40% statics; Eng spkn; adv bkg acc; ccard acc; tennis; games rm; fishing 3km; waterslide; horseriding 5km; CKE. *"Excel, peaceful site; multi-sport area; no o'fits over 7.5m high ssn; vg facs for families; v clean unisex san facs; gates clsd 2230-0800; recep clsd lunchtime; conv for Pornic; site in fairly steep sided valley."*
€50.20, 12 Apr-20 Sep, B31. **2024**

PORNIC *2G3* (9km NW Coastal) *47.15995, -2.16813* **Camping Thar-Cor,** 43 Ave du Cormier, 44730 St Michel-Chef-Chef **02 40 27 82 81; camping@letharcor.com; www.camping-le-thar-cor.com**

€3 (htd) nr sand 200m

Fr Pornic take D213 twds Saint Michel Chef Chef. Turn L onto Rue de la Dalonnerie. L at rndabt onto D96. Foll sp to site. Lge, mkd, hdg, pt shd, EHU (10A) €5; bbq; twin axles; TV; 50% statics; phone; Eng spkn; adv bkg rec; ccard acc; games area. *"Vg town site, mkt at Tharon-Plage high ssn; 200m to promenade & sandy beach; friendly staff; mainly French; beach excel."*
€26.50, 10 Apr-25 Sep. **2022**

PORT EN BESSIN HUPPAIN *3D1* (1km N Coastal) *49.34693, -0.77095* **Camping Port'land,** Chemin du Sémaphore, 14520 Port-en-Bessin **02 31 51 07 06; campingportland@wanadoo.fr; https://www.camping-portland.fr/**

€3 (htd) (covrd, htd, indoor) sand 4km

Site sp fr D514 W of Port-en-Bessin. 4*, Lge, hdstg, mkd, hdg, pt shd, EHU (16A) €5; bbq; red long stay; TV; 30% statics; Eng spkn; adv bkg acc; ccard acc; waterslide; tennis 800m; games area; games rm; CKE. *"Pleasant site; friendly, helpful staff; vg san facs; extra charge lger pitches; excel touring base for landing beaches etc; well kept clean, well spaced lge hdged pitches; well positioned for Bayeaux, Arromanche and D Day museums and cemetaries."*
€37.50, 1 Jul - 31 Oct, N09. **2022**

PORT LESNEY *6H2* (0.2km N Rural) *47.00358, 5.82366* **Camping Les Radeliers,** 1 Rue Edgar Faure, 39600 Port-Lesney **09 53 21 44 22; contact@camping-les-radeliers.com; www.camping-les-radeliers.com**

€2 nr nr nr

N fr Arbois on N83, cross junc with D472 & turn L in 1.5km sp Port-Lesney. Site sp. 3*, Med, mkd, pt shd, EHU (13A) €4; sw nr; twin axles; 2% statics; bus adj; Eng spkn; adv bkg acc; canoeing; kayak hire; CKE. *"Tranquil site in delightful rvside setting; helpful staff; poss youth groups high ssn; gd walking & cycling; Salt Mine Museum in Salins-les-Bains worth visit; canyoning; bar 200m; plenty rvside pitches."*
€23.00, 1 May-30 Sep. **2022**

PORT SUR SAONE *6F2* (0.8km S Rural) *47.68056, 6.03937* **Camping de la Maladière (formerly Municipal Parc),** 70170 Port-sur-Saône **03 84 78 18 00; secretariat@port-sur-saone.fr; www.ville-port-sur-saone.fr**

(cont) nr nr nr

Take N19 SE fr Langres or NW fr Vesoul. Site sp in vill bet rv & canal off D6 at municipal bathing area. 2*, Med, hdg, pt shd, EHU (6A) €3 (poss rev pol); own san rec; adv bkg acc; ccard acc; fishing; tennis; CKE. *"Peaceful site on island; rvside cycle path; gd walks; gd sh stay/NH; san facs basic & tired; pool adj; 25m cable needed; vg value."* **€15.40, 15 May-15 Sep.** **2023**

PORTIRAGNES PLAGE *10F1* (1km N Coastal) *43.28003, 3.36396* **Camping Les Sablons,** Plage-Est, 34420 Portiragnes-Plage **04 67 90 90 55; les.sablons@wanadoo.fr; www.les-sablons.com**

€4 (htd) sand adj

Fr A9 exit Béziers Est junc 35 onto N112. Then take D37 S to Portiragnes-Plage & foll sp. 5*, V lge, mkd, shd, EHU (6A) inc; gas; bbq; 50% statics; phone; Eng spkn; adv bkg acc; ccard acc; waterslide; boating; games area; tennis; bike hire; fishing. *"Gd site on beach; modern san facs; diving; nightly disco but quiet after midnight."* **€71.80, 29 Mar-29 Sep.** **2024**

PORTIRAGNES PLAGE *10F1* (2km NE Coastal) *43.29138, 3.37333* **Camping Les Mimosas,** Port Cassafières, 34420 Portiragnes-Plage **04 67 90 92 92; www.mimosas.com**

€5.50 sand 1km

Exit A9 junc 35 Béziers Est & take N112 sp Vias, Agde. After 3km at rndabt foll sp Portiragnes & cont along side of Canal du Midi. Cross canal, site sp. 4*, Lge, hdstg, mkd, pt shd, EHU (6-10A) €4; gas; bbq (gas); 50% statics; Eng spkn; adv bkg acc; ccard acc; games area; jacuzzi; sauna; games rm; waterslide; bike hire; CKE. *"Excel touring base in interesting area; friendly welcome; superb waterpark; fitness rm; private san facs avail; 4 star site; gd for families."*
€51.90, 1 Jun-7 Sep, C35. **2024**

POSES *3D2* (1.6km SE Urban) *49.29552, 1.24914* **Lery-Poses en Normandie (formerly Base de Loisirs),** Rue du Souvenir French, 27740 Poses **02 32 59 13 13; lery.poses@wanadoo.fr; www.lery-poses.fr**

Fr Poses head NE on Rue du Bac twrd Rue das Masures, take 1st R onto Rue des Masures, turn R onto Rue du Roussillon, after 350m turn L onto Rue du Souvenir Francais, site after 220m on L. Lge, pt shd, EHU (16A); table tennis; canoeing. *"Gd san facs; gravel rdway throughout site; water ski; hiking; pedalo hire; mini golf; site adj to & overlooking the Rv Seine with direct access to the rvside; plenty of pitches for tourers; beach volleyball; supmkt 5km; older san block needs updating (2018)."* **€15.00, 1 Apr-31 Oct. 2023**

POUANCE *2F4* (1.5km N Rural) *47.74850, -1.17841* **Camp Muncipal La Roche Martin,** 23 Rue des Etangs, 49420 Pouancé **02 41 92 43 97 or 02 41 92 41 08 (Mairie); contact@anjousportnature.com; anjousportnature.com**

nr nr nr

Take D6 (sp St Aignan) N fr town. After level x-ing turn L onto D72 (sp La Guerche-de-Bretagne). In 300m, site on L. 3*, Sm, mkd, pt sl, terr, EHU (10A); gas; adv bkg rec; watersports; tennis; games area. *"Well-kept, friendly site o'looking lge lake; dir access to lake; noise fr rd & sailing school."* **1 Apr-30 Sep. 2024**

POUILLY EN AUXOIS *6G1* (0.8km NW Urban) *47.26534, 4.54804* **Camping Vert Auxois,** 15 Voûte du Canal du Bourgogne, 21320 Pouilly-en-Auxois **03 80 90 71 89; contact@camping-vert-auxois.com; www.camping-vert-auxois.fr**

Exit A6 at Dijon/Pouilly-en-Auxois onto A38. Exit A38 at junc 24. Thro vill & turn L after church on R, site sp adj Burgandy canal. 3*, Sm, hdg, pt shd, EHU (6-10A) long cable req; 10% statics; bus 300m; Eng spkn; adv bkg acc; ccard acc; rv fishing adj; CKE. *"Beautiful position, relaxed & peaceful; lge pitches, unusual layout; run by delightful, friendly couple; gd cycling; interesting area; sh walk to sm town; vg; san facs poss stretched."* **€23.00, 1 Apr-7 Oct. 2023**

POUILLY SUR LOIRE *4G3* (1km N Rural) *47.28742, 2.94427* **Camp Municipal Le Malaga,** Rue des Champs-sur-Loire, Les Loges, 58150 Pouilly-sur-Loire **03 33 86 39 12 55; www.ot-pouillysurloire.fr**

€1

Fr S exit A77 junc 26 onto D28a, turn L onto D59/ D4289 W, bef rv bdge turn R, site in 1km on rv. Fr N on ent vill turn R at site sp into narr rd. Turn R along rv as above. 3*, Med, pt shd, EHU (10A) inc (poss long lead req & poss rev pol); bbq; phone; Eng spkn. *"Beautifully kept site on banks of Loire; busy NH; spacious but uneven pitches; mixed reports san facs; poss youth groups; beautiful area; wine tasting nrby; no twin axles or o'fits over 5m; poss mosquitoes; excel; delightful site adj to the Loire, spacious and leafy areas, wonderful wines in Pouilly and Sancerre, excel museum closeby."* **€16.00, 1 May-15 Sep. 2022**

POULDU, LE *2F2* (0.3km N Coastal) *47.76850, -3.54540* **Camping Les Embruns,** 2 Rue du Philosophe Alain, Clohars-Carnoët, 29360 Le Pouldu **02 98 39 91 07; camping-les-embruns@wanadoo.fr; www.camping-les-embruns.com**

€2.70 (htd)
(covrd, htd) sand 250m

Exit N165 dir Quimperlé Cent, onto D16 to Clohars-Carnoët. Cont on D16/D24/D1214 to Le Pouldu. Site on R on ent 1-way traff system. Site sp. 4*, Lge, hdstg, mkd, hdg, pt shd, terr, serviced pitches; EHU (10A) inc; gas; bbq; TV; 40% statics; bus nrby; Eng spkn; adv bkg acc; ccard acc; watersports; games area; tennis; horseriding nr; tennis 200m; games rm; bike hire; fishing; CKE. *"Excel family-run site in great location; children's farm; luxury pitches extra charge; friendly, helpful owners; vg clean san facs; superb facs; gd walking along coastal paths; cycle rtes; great for dogs; town was home of Paul Gauguin; highly rec."* **€31.50, 10 Apr-19 Sep. 2022**

See advertisement

FRANCE

POULDU, LE *2F2* (2km N Coastal) *47.78401, -3.54463* **FFCC Camping de Croas An Ter,** Quelvez, Le Pouldu, 29360 Clohars-Carnoët **02 98 39 94 19 or 06 64 25 48 58 (mob); campingcroasanter@orange.fr; www.campingcroasanter.com**
nr nr nr 1.5km

On D49 fr Quimperlé to Le Pouldu. Site on L 3km after junc with D224. 2*, Med, pt shd, pt sl, EHU (6A) €3.20; Eng spkn; CKE. *"Lge pitches; friendly owners; cash only; gd bathing & sailing; walks in wood & rv fr site; Tues mkt; vg."* **€13.60, 1 May-15 Sep.** **2022**

POULDU, LE *2F2* (2km E Rural/Coastal) *47.77466, -3.50616* **Jardins De Kergal,** Route des Plages, 56520 Guidel **02 97 05 98 18; jardins.kergal@wanadoo.fr; www.camping-lorient.com**
€3 nr (covrd) sand 1.5km

Fr N165 Brest-Nantes take Guidel exit; thro Guidel & onto Guidel-Plages; camp sp in 1km. 4*, Lge, hdstg, mkd, hdg, pt shd, pt sl, EHU (10A) inc; gas; bbq; TV; 75% statics; adv bkg acc; waterslide; games area; tennis; games rm; bike hire; CKE. *"Friendly, helpful, welcoming staff; well-run, peaceful site; conv beaches & touring."* **€41.00, 29 Mar-30 Sep.** **2024**

POULE LES ECHARMEAUX *9A2* (1.5km W Rural) *46.15028, 4.45419* **Camp Municipal Les Echarmeaux,** 69870 Poule-les-Echarmeaux **06 74 05 91 38; campingpoulelesecharmeaux69@gmail.com; www.poulelesecharmeaux.eu**
nr

Turn E off D385 to Poule-les-Echarmeaux, site sp. Sm, hdg, pt shd, terr, EHU inc; adv bkg rec. *"Beautifully situated site adj lake; nr Beaujolais wine area; excel sh stay; mkd walks."* **€11.00, 1 May-30 Sep.** **2024**

PRADES *8G4* (10km NE Urban) *42.64269, 2.53367* **Camping Lac De Vinca,** Rue des Escoumes, 66320 Vinça **04 68 05 84 78 or 06 72 32 27 07 (mob); campinglesescoumes@orange.fr; www.camping-lac-de-vinca.com**
€3.50 nr nr nr

Fr Prades take N116 E twd Perpignan. Vinca on R about 5m from Prades outskirts. Ignore 1st R into Vinca - narr rds. Take 2nd R then foll sp. 2*, Med, mkd, pt shd, pt sl, EHU (6-10A) €3; gas; sw; 20% statics; Eng spkn; fishing; bike hire. *"Beautiful, quiet, excel site; helpful staff; gd sized pitches; gd touring base; lake not suitable for toddlers (no sand, entry via steps); rec."* **€17.00, 1 Apr-31 Oct.** **2024**

PRALOGNAN LA VANOISE *9B4* (0.5km S Rural) *45.37667, 6.72236* **Camping Le Parc Isertan,** Route de l'Isertan, 73710 Pralognan-la-Vanoise **04 79 08 75 24; camping@camping-isertan.com; www.camping-isertan.com**
€1.50 (htd) nr

Fr Moûtiers, take D915 E to Pralognan. Pass under concrete bdge & foll camping sp. Site behind pool adj municipal site. 3*, Lge, hdstg, pt shd, terr, EHU (2-10A) €4-6.50; bbq; red long stay; 10% statics; phone; Eng spkn; adv bkg acc; ccard acc; horseriding 500m; CKE. *"Peaceful site with superb scenery; recep in hotel on site; vg walking; sports cent adj; htd covrd pool adj; cable car in vill; drying rm & ski boot rm; cross country skiing at side of site; free naveltte to ski lift; new spa facs (2012); excel site."* **€24.00, 18 Dec-18 Apr & 21 May-24 Sep.** **2024**

PRALOGNAN LA VANOISE *9B4* (13.7km NW Rural) *45.44274, 6.64874* **Camping Huttopia Bozel en Vanoise (formerly Municipal),** Route de Chevelu, 73350 Bozel **04 79 41 70 83; camping.lechevelu.bozel@gmail.com; www.camping-bozel.com**
€5 nr

Foll D915 thro Bozel dir Pralognan. Site on R immed beyond vill. 2*, Med, mkd, hdstg, shd, pt sl, terr, EHU (6-10A) €3.50-4.50; sw nr; phone; Eng spkn; adv bkg acc; lake fishing 1km; CKE. *"In wood by rv; excel walking & climbing; vg; pleasant vill; lunchtime rest v popular with locals."* **€25.00, 19 May - 25 Sep.** **2022**

PRECY SOUS THIL *6G1* (0.4km NW Rural) *47.38721, 4.30645* **Camping du Parc de L'Hotel de Ville (formerly Municipal),** 17 Rue de l'Hôtel de Ville, 21390 Précy-sous-Thil **03 80 64 57 18 (Mairie); www.burgundy-tourism.com/campsites/camping-du-parc-de-lhotel-de-ville**
€1.30 nr nr nr

Exit A6 at junc 23 Bierre-lès-Semur exit onto D980 to Précy. Site sp in vill. 3*, Sm, pt shd, pt sl, EHU (6A) inc; TV; 10% statics; tennis nr; horseriding. *"In grnds of Town Hall; warden calls 1900-2100; bar 300m; rv adj; mostly sl pitches, conv NH on way S."* **€12.00, Easter-1 Nov.** **2024**

PRESSAC *7A3* (8km SW Rural) *46.09696, 0.48081* **Camping Rural des Marronniers,** La Bussière, 16490 Pleuville **05 45 71 42 19; campingruraldesmarronniers@gmail.com; www.campingruraldesmarronniers.com**
12 Free (htd) nr nr

S fr Poitiers on D741 to Pressac; turn R onto D34 to Pleuville then turn onto D30 dir Charroux, site on L in 1.5km - look for sp La Bussière. Sm, unshd, pt sl, EHU (10A) inc; bbq; twin axles; adv bkg acc; games rm; CKE. *"Friendly, British-owned, peaceful, lovely sm CL-type farm site; open field - chickens & ducks roaming; gd touring base; ideal for exploring SW France; fam/couples welcome; excel."* **€15.00** **2024**

PRIVAS *9D2* (1.5km S Urban) *44.72668, 4.59730* **Kawan Village Ardèche Camping,** Blvd de Paste, Quartier Ouvèze, 07000 Privas **04 75 64 05 80; jcray@wanadoo.fr; www.ardechecamping.fr**
€4 nr (htd)

Exit A7 junc 16 dir Privas. App Privas cross rv bdge & at rndabt take 2nd exit. Site ent opp supmkt, sp. 4*, Lge, mkd, pt shd, pt sl, EHU (10A) inc; bbq; red long stay; TV; 80% statics; Eng spkn; adv bkg acc; ccard acc; rv fishing; tennis adj; CKE. *"Very gd, friendly owners; gd rest and shady pitches; interesting area to visit; pleasant site; walk to town up extremely steep rd."* **€60.00, 29 Apr - 25 Sep.** **2022**

PUGET THENIERS *10E4* (2km NW Rural) *43.95801, 6.85980* **Origan Village Naturiste (formerly Camping L'Origan) (Naturist),** 2160 Route de Savé, 06260 Puget-Théniers **04 93 05 06 00; origan@orange.fr; www.origan-village.com**
€2.50 (htd) (htd)

On N202 fr Entrevaux (dir Nice) at Puget-Théniers, immed turn L at rlwy x-ing (sp), site approx 1km up track. 3*, Med, hdg, mkd, hdstg, pt shd, pt sl, terr, EHU (6A) €4; bbq; TV; 50% statics; phone; train to Nice; Eng spkn; adv bkg acc; ccard acc; INF card; tennis; fishing; waterslide; sauna; archery. *"Sm pitches not suitable o'fits over 6m; hilly site but pitches level; san facs dated (2018); interesting area; great views; ent noise poss high ssn; attractive bar/rest; tourist steam train bet Puget-Theniers & Annot on certain days."* **€26.00, Easter-3 Oct.** **2023**

PUIMOISSON *10E3* (6.5km NE Rural) *43.89836, 6.18011* **Camping à la Ferme Vauvenières (Sauvaire),** 04410 St Jurs **06 50 74 37 11; ferme.de.vauvenieres@gmail.com; www.ferme-de-vauvenieres.fr**
€0.75 nr

Fr Riez take D953 N to 1km beyond Puimoisson then fork R onto D108 sp St Jurs & site sp. Sm, pt shd, EHU (6A) €2.90; bbq; sw nr; Eng spkn; adv bkg acc; games area; CKE. *"Peaceful, basic site off beaten track; wonderful views; lavendar fields; friendly Dutch owner; clean san facs, poss stretched if site full; gd for mountain walking; D17 to Majastres v narr; vg mkt on Wed & Sat in Riez; sm supmkt at filling stn at ent Puimoisson; v lge mkd pitches."* **€18.00, 1 Apr-15 Oct.** **2024**

PUIVERT *8G4* (0.5km S Rural) *42.91596, 2.0441* **Camping FontClaire (formerly Camping de Puivert),** Fontclaire, 11230 Puivert **04 68 20 00 58; campingdulacfontclaire@gmail.com; www.campings11.fr**
nr

Take D117 W fr Quillan dir Lavelanet for 16km; at Puivert turn L onto D16; site in 500m by lake; well sp. Or E fr Foix on D117 for 45km; at Puivert turn R onto D16 & as bef. 2*, Med, hdstg, hdg, pt shd, terr, EHU (16A) €3; bbq (sep area); sw nr; fishing adj. *"Attractive area; lge pitches, some lakeside, some hill views; dated san facs but adequate & clean; museum in vill; chateau nrby; vg."* **€19.00, 20 Apr-20 Sep.** **2024**

PUY EN VELAY, LE *9C1* (0.5km N Urban) *45.05014, 3.88044* **Camping du Puy-en-Velay (formerly Camping de Bouthezard),** Chemin de Bouthezard, Ave d'Aiguilhe, 43000 Le Puy-en-Velay **04 71 09 55 09; camping.puyenvelay@aquadis-loisirs.com; www.aquadis-loisirs.com/camping-de-bouthezard**
€2

Fr Le Puy heading NW on N102 to city cent; look for sp Clermont & Vichy; turn R at traff lts in Place Carnot at sp for Valence; site on L on bank of rv. Site ent immed opp Chapel St Michel & 200m fr volcanic core. 3*, Med, hdg, pt shd, EHU (10A) inc (rev pol); sw nr; bus stn 1.5km; Eng spkn; adv bkg acc; tennis adj; games rm; CKE. *"Popular, well-kept site in gd location; busy - rec arr early; efficient staff; gates clsd 2100-0700 LS; no twin axles; may flood & grnd soft in v heavy rain; unrel opening dates - phone ahead LS; vg touring base on pilgrim rte to Spain; immac; very helpful owners; spectacular town; highly rec; pool adj; excel."* **€18.60, 1 Apr-20 Oct.** **2024**

PUY EN VELAY, LE *9C1* (1.4km N Urban) *45.05047, 3.88088* **Campsite du Puy en Valey,** Avenue de Bonneville, 43000 Aiguilhe **04 71 09 55 09; camping.puyenvelay@aquadis-loisirs.com; www.aquadis-loisirs.com/camping-nature/camping-du-puy-en-velay**
€1 nr nr

Sp in Le Puy en Velay. Campsite at foot of High Rock Church on N88 (Avenue de Bonneville). 3*, Med, mkd, pt shd, EHU (10-16A); red long stay; phone; bus/train; Eng spkn; adv bkg acc; ccard acc; games rm; CKE. *"UNESCO World Heritage town; many mkd walks and cycle routes in and around city and along rivers; vg."* **€18.90, 11 Apr-23 Oct.** **2022**

PUY EN VELAY, LE *9C1* (9km N Rural) *45.12473, 3.92177* **Camping Les Ombrelles (formerly Camp Municipal Les Longes),** 16 Avenue Jules Vallès, 43800 Lavoûte-sur-Loire **04 71 08 18 79; contact@campinglesombrelles.fr; www.campinglesombrelles.fr**
€1.50

Fr Le Puy take N on D103 sp Lavoûte & Retournac. In Lavoûte turn R onto D7 bef rv bdge, site on L in 1km on rvside. 3*, Med, mkd, shd, EHU (6A) €2.50; sw nr; tennis; fishing 50m. *"Gd, friendly site; gd walking; lovely quiet site by Haute Loire; san facs clean; rec; mostly statics."* **€15.50, 1 May-14 Sep.** **2023**

FRANCE

FRANCE

PUY EN VELAY, LE *9C1* (3km E Urban) *45.04431, 3.93030* **Camping d'Audinet,** Ave des Sports, 43700 Brives-Charensac **04 71 09 10 18; camping.audinet@wanadoo.fr; www.camping-audinet.fr**

Fr Le Puy foll green sp E twd Valence. Fr S on N88 foll sp twd Valence & on E side of town foll white sp. 3*, Lge, pt shd, EHU (6A) €3.30; bbq; sw; red long stay; bus to town; fishing. *"Spacious site on rvside; friendly, helpful staff; poss travellers - but not a prob; no twin axles; vg; 12 min bus to town every 1/2 hr; san facs dated but satisfactory; gd onsite takeaway/restaurant; barrier clsd 2200-0700."* **€19.00, 14 Apr-18 Sep. 2023**

PUY L'EVEQUE *7D3* (2.5km S Rural) *44.47780, 1.14214* **FFCC Village-Camping Les Vignes,** Le Méoure, Le Cayrou, 46700 Puy-l'Evêque **05 65 30 81 72; contact@camping-lesvignes.fr; www.camping-lesvignes.fr**

€1.50 nr

App fr E on D911 dir Villeneuve-sur-Lot, just bef ent Puy-l'Evêque turn L, foll sp for 3km. Site adj Rv Lot. Avoid town cent while towing. 3*, Med, shd, EHU (10A) €2.90; gas; TV; games area; tennis; fishing; bike hire. *"Lovely, peaceful site in beautiful countryside; well-kept; warm welcome, friendly owners; gd san facs."* **€25.10, 1 Apr-31 Oct. 2024**

PUYSSEGUR *8E3* (0.2km N Rural) *43.75064, 1.06065* **FFCC Camping Namasté,** 31480 Puysségur **05 61 85 77 84; contact@camping-namaste.com; www.camping-namaste.com**

€1.50

Fr Toulouse NW on N224/D1 sp Cadours; at Puysségur in 30km foll Camping Namasté sp. (Puysségur is 1km NE of Cadours). 4*, Sm, pt shd, EHU (4-10A) €3-5; bbq; 10% statics; sauna; bike hire; games area; games rm; fishing. **€30.00, 1 May-15 Oct. 2024**

PYLA SUR MER *7D1* (7km S Coastal) *44.58517, -1.20868* **Plya Camping (formerly Camping Village Centre La Forêt),** Route de Biscarosse, 33115 Pyla-sur-Mer **05 56 22 73 28; reception@pylacamping.fr; www.pyla-camping.com**

€2 sand 600m

Fr Bordeaux app Arcachon on A660 by-pass rd; at La Teste-de-Buch at rndabt foll sp for Dune du Pilat & 'campings'. At T-junc in 4km turn L; foll 'plage' & camping sp on D218. Site on R. 3*, Lge, hdg, mkd, shd, sl, EHU (6A) inc; bbq; 80% statics; adv bkg acc; ccard acc; solarium; tennis; bike hire; CKE. *"Forest setting at foot of sand dune (own steps); well-organised; many facs; hang-gliding, surfing, sailing, cycle rtes nrby."* **€20.00, 4 Apr-20 Sep. 2023**

PYLA SUR MER *7D1* (8km S Rural/Coastal) *44.57474, -1.22217* **Yelloh! Village Panorama du Pyla,** Route de Biscarosse, 33115 Pyla-sur-Mer **05 56 22 10 44; mail@camping-panorama.com; www.camping-panorama.com or www.yellohvillage.co.uk**

€5 (htd)
sand adj

App Arcachon fr Bordeaux on A63/A660, at rndabt foll sp for Dune-du-Pilat & 'campings'. Foll sp for 'plage' & 'campings' on D218. Site on R next to Camping Le Petit Nice. 4*, Lge, hdstg, mkd, shd, sl, terr, EHU (3-10A) inc; gas; bbq; TV; 20% statics; Eng spkn; games area; tennis; games rm; sauna; waterslide; CKE. *"Pleasant site on wooded dune; pitches clsd together; adv bkg not acc; some pitches poor; direct steep access to excel beach; site rds v narr; ltd pitches for v lge o'fits; some pitches sandy; gd facs; paragliding adj."* **€46.00, 9 Apr-3 Oct. 2022**

QUETTEHOU *1C4* (2.5km E Urban/Coastal) *49.58520, -1.26858* **Camping La Gallouette,** Rue de la Gallouette, 50550 St Vaast-la-Hougue **02 33 54 20 57; contact@camping-lagallouette.fr; www.camping-lagallouette.fr**

€1.80 (htd)
sand 300m

E fr Quettehou on D1, site sp in St Vaast-la-Houge to S of town. 4*, Lge, hdg, mkd, pt shd, EHU (6-10A) €3.80-4.60; gas; bbq; 10% statics; phone; adv bkg acc; games area; games rm; CKE. *"Lovely friendly site; some lge pitches; gd range of facs; sh walk to interesting town; excel site."* **€34.40, 1 Apr-30 Sep. 2023**

QUIBERON *2G3* (3.6km N Coastal) *47.49978, -3.12021* **Sauvage Quiberon (formerly Camping Do Mi Si La Mi),** 8 Rue de la Vierge, 56170 Quiberon **02 97 50 22 52; contact@sauvage-quiberon.com; www.sauvage-quiberon.com**

€2.40 nr nr shgl 100m

Take D768 down Quiberon Peninsular, 3km after St Pierre-Quiberon & shortly after sp for rlwy level x-ing turn L into Rue de la Vierge, site on R in 400m. 3*, Lge, hdg, mkd, pt shd, pt sl, serviced pitches; EHU (3-10A) €2.80-4.30; gas; bbq; 40% statics; Eng spkn; ccard acc; bike hire; tennis nr; horseriding nr; sailing nr; games area; CKE. *"Gd touring base; vg; excel site; great location; excel rest."* **€33.00, 31 Mar-30 Sep. 2023**

QUIBERON *2G3* (1.5km SE Rural/Coastal) *47.47641, -3.10441* **Camping Le Bois d'Amour,** Rue St Clément, 56170 Quiberon **02 97 50 13 52; camping.boisdamour@flowercampings.com; www.quiberon-camping.com**

€5 (htd)
200m

Exit N165 at Auray onto D768. In Quiberon foll sp 'Thalassothérapie', site sp. 3*, Lge, hdg, mkd, pt shd, EHU (16A) €5; gas; bbq; Eng spkn; adv bkg acc; ccard acc; tennis; horseriding; bike hire; games area; CKE. *"Shwrs clean but hot water can be temperamental; lovely friendly clubhse with reasonable food prices."* **€20.00, 2 Apr-24 Sep. 2022**

QUIBERON *2G3* (2km SE Coastal) *47.47424, -3.10563*
Camp Municipal Le Goviro, Blvd du Goviro, 56170 Quiberon **02 97 50 13 54; campingdugoviro@ville-quiberon.fr; www.campingdugoviro.fr**

€1.65 nr sand adj

Fr D768 at Quiberon foll sp Port Maria & 'Cent Thalassothérapie'. Site 1km on L nr Sofitel hotel. 2*, Lge, mkd, hdg, pt shd, terr, EHU (13A) €3; gas; fishing adj; watersports adj. *"Popular, well-run site in excel location; lovely bay, gd sea views & coastal path into town; smallish pitches; clean, adequate san facs, ltd LS."* **€32.00, 1 Apr-12 Oct.** **2022**

QUILLAN *8G4* (1.2km W Urban) *42.87358, 2.17565*
FFCC Camp Municipal La Sapinette, 21 Ave René Delpech, 11500 Quillan **04 68 20 13 52; campingsapinette@wanadoo.fr**

€1.60 (htd) nr

Foll D118 fr Carcassonne to Quillan; turn R at 2nd traff lts in town cent; site sp in town. 3*, Med, hdg, mkd, hdstg, pt shd, sl, terr, EHU (6A) €3.10; TV; 25% statics; adv bkg acc; ccard acc; CKE. *"Gd touring base; sm pitches, some level, mostly sl; early arr rec; helpful staff; san facs a little tired; excel pool; site poss tired end ssn; mkt Wed & Sat; leisure cent 500m; vet adj; highly rec; 15min walk to nice town."* **€25.00, 1 Apr-30 Oct.** **2022**

QUIMPER *2F2* (10km SE Rural) *47.94133, -4.02453*
Camping de Keromen, 38 Rue de Cornouaille, 29170 Saint-Evarzec **02 98 64 09 59 or 06 23 05 58 25; keromenlff@yahoo.fr; www.campingdekeromen.fr**

Heading S fr Quimper on D783 at end of dual c'way fork R sp Evarzec. Cont over mini rndabt, site on R in 1.5km, well sp. Med, hdg, mkd, pt shd, EHU (10A); twin axles; TV; 40% statics; bus; adv bkg acc; games area; games rm. *"Adj lake area; donkeys & goats in enclosure; free fishing on sm lake; gd."* **€16.80, 1 Apr-30 Oct.** **2023**

QUIMPER *2F2* (9km SE Rural) *47.93811, -3.99959*
Camping Vert, 202 Route de Concarneau, 29170 St Evarzec **02 98 56 29 88 or 06 68 46 97 25 (mob); campingvert@orange.fr; www.campingvertdecreachlann.com**

nr nr (htd)

S fr Quimper on D783, 1.5km fr St Evarzec rndabt at brow of hill (easily missed). Sm, hdg, pt shd, pt sl, EHU (4-13A) €3-3.50; bbq; 60% statics; Eng spkn; adv bkg acc; games rm. *"Lovely spacious site; lge pitches; friendly, helpful owner; gd playgrnd; poss to stay after end Sep by arrangement; lovely old town; gd touring base; daily mkt; excel."* **€17.80, 1 Jun-30 Sep.** **2023**

"I like to fill in the reports as I travel from site to site"

You'll find report forms at the back of this guide, or you can fill them in online at camc.com/europereport.

QUIMPER *2F2* (3.5km S Rural) *47.97685, -4.11060*
Camping L'Orangerie de Lanniron, 90 Allée de Lanniron, 29000 Quimper **02 98 90 62 02; camping@lanniron.com; https://www.tohapi.co.uk/brittany/campsite-orangerie-de-lanniron.php**

€5.70 (htd)

Fr Rennes/Lorient: on N165 Rennes-Quimper, Quimper-Centre, Quimper-Sud exit, foll dir Pont l'Abbé on S bypass until exit sp Camping de Lanninon on R. At top of slip rd turn L & foll site sp, under bypass then 2nd R to site. Recep at Old Farm 500m bef site. 5*, Lge, mkd, pt shd, serviced pitches; EHU (10A) inc; gas; bbq; TV; 40% statics; phone; bus; Eng spkn; adv bkg acc; ccard acc; bike hire; tennis; golf; canoeing; rv fishing; games rm; CKE. *"Excel, busy, family-run site in grnds of chateau by Rv Odet; 9-hole golf on site; aqua park; well-spaced pitches; vg san facs; vg leisure facs; easy walk to town."* **€37.00, 9 Apr - 11 Sept, B21.** **2022**

See advertisement

*Last year of report

FRANCE

QUIMPERLE *2F2* (7km NE Rural) *47.90468, -3.47477* **Camping Le Ty-Nadan,** Route d'Arzano, 29310 Locunolé **04 30 05 15 19; www.tohapi.fr/bretagne/camping-ty-nadan.php**

€5.50 (htd) (covrd, htd)

To avoid Quimperlé cent exit N165 dir Quimperlé. As ent town turn R onto D22 dir Arzano. In 9km turn L at W end of Arzano (un-numbered rd) sp Locunolé & Camping Ty Nadan; site on L just after x-ing Rv Elle. Or fr Roscoff on D69 S join N165/E60 but take care at uneven level x-ing at Pen-ar-Hoat 11km after Sizun. 5*, Lge, mkd, hdg, pt shd, serviced pitches; EHU (10A) inc (long lead poss req); gas; bbq (charcoal, gas); TV; 40% statics; Eng spkn; adv bkg acc; ccard acc; waterslide; games area; horseriding; rv fishing adj; tennis; archery; games rm; sauna; bike hire; canoeing adj; CKE. *"Excel, peaceful site by rv; pitches poss narr for lge o'fits; friendly staff; spa; no o'fits over 8.5m high ssn; barrier clsd 2300-0800; many activities; gd touring base."* **€45.00, 9 Apr- 2 Sept, B20.** **2022**

"We must tell the Club about that great site we found"

Get your site reports in by mid-August and we'll do our best to get your updates into the next edition.

QUINTIN *2E3* (0.6km SE Urban) *48.40128, -2.90672* **Camp Municipal du Lac,** Chemin des Côtes, 22800 Quintin **02 96 74 92 54 or 02 96 74 84 01 (Mairie); mairie@quintin.fr; www.quintin.fr**

nr nr nr

Fr N exit D790 at rndabt & foll sp 'Cent Ville'; at 2nd rndabt site sp; site on L 200m after 5th ped x-ing (narr rd, easy to miss). Fr S on D790 do not take slip rd (D7) but cont to rndabt - narr rds in town; then as above. Site N (100m) of town gardens & boating lake. 2*, Sm, pt shd, pt sl, EHU (6A) €2.80; bbq; fishing. *"Fair site; helpful warden; poss insufficient of security (2011); interesting town."* **€8.50, 15 Apr-30 Sep.** **2022**

RABASTENS *8E3* (2km NW Rural) *43.83090, 1.69805* **Les Auzerals Camping du Lac (formerly Camp Municipal des Auzerals),** Route de Grazac, 81800 Rabastens **07 72 13 64 84; mairie.rabastens@libertysurf.fr**

nr nr

Exit A68 junc 7 onto D12. In Rabastens town cent foll sp dir Grazac, site sp. 1*, Sm, hdg, mkd, pt shd, pt sl, terr, EHU (10A) inc; adv bkg req; CKE. *"Attractive lakeside site; facs old but clean; office 0900-1200 & 1500-1900, otherwise height barrier in place; conv m'way NH; pool adj high ssn; highly rec; gd hedges around plots; call to check if site open."* **€11.00, 1 Apr-30 Sep.** **2023**

RAMBOUILLET *4E3* (3km SE Rural) *48.6252, 1.84495* **Camping Huttopia Rambouillet,** Route du Château d'Eau, 78120 Rambouillet **01 30 41 07 34; rambouillet@huttopia.com; https://europe.huttopia.com/site/camping-rambouillet/**

€4.20 (htd) (htd)

Fr N exit D910 at 'Rambouillet Eveuses' & foll sp to site in 2.5km. Fr S exit at 'Rambouillet Cent' & foll sp to site back onto D910 (in opp dir), exit 'Rambouillet Eveuses' as above. Avoid Rambouillet town cent. 3*, Lge, hdg, pt shd, EHU (10A) inc; bbq (elec, gas); 10% statics; phone; Eng spkn; adv bkg rec; ccard acc; fishing adj; sep car park; CKE. *"Excel, busy, wooded site; conv Paris by train - parking at stn 3km; gd cycling rtes; interesting town."* **€42.00, 7 Apr - 6 Sept, P17.** **2022**

RAON L'ETAPE *6E3* (2km SE Rural) *48.39474, 6.86232* **Camping Vosgina,** 1 Rue la Cheville, 88420 Moyenmoutier **03 29 41 47 63; info@camping-vosgina.com; www.camping-vosgina.com**

€1.50

On N59 St Dié-Lunéville rd, take exit mkd Senones, Moyenmoutier. At rndabt take rd twd St Blaise & foll camping sp. Site is on minor rd parallel with N59 bet Moyenmoutier & Raon. 2*, Med, hdg, pt shd, terr, EHU (4-10A) €3-6; gas; TV; 20% statics; Eng spkn; adv bkg acc; ccard acc; CKE. *"Gd site for quiet holiday in a non-touristy area of Alsace; friendly recep; lovely countryside; many cycle/walking rtes in area; barrier clsd 2200-0700; park like setting; beautifully maintained; friendly Swiss owners; excel for sh stay or NH."* **€20.00, 25 Mar-31 Oct.** **2022**

RAUZAN *7D2* (0.2km N Rural) *44.78237, -0.12712* **Camping du Vieux Château,** 6 Blabot-Bas, 33420 Rauzan **05 57 84 15 38; contact@vieuxchateau.fr; www.camping-levieuxchateau.com**

€2 nr

Fr Libourne S on D670, site is on D123 about 1.5km fr D670, sp. 3*, Sm, mkd, shd, EHU (6A) €5 (poss rev pol); gas; TV; 10% statics; Eng spkn; adv bkg acc; ccard acc; tennis; bike hire; horseriding; CKE. *"Lovely site but take care tree roots on pitches; quiet wooded area; pleasant family run site; helpful owners; basic san facs - ltd LS & poss not well-maintained, & poss stretched high ssn; access to some pitches diff when wet; conv vineyards; walking dist to vill; nice sw pool; wine-tasting; TV rm & bar open to 9pm; events avail."* **€22.00, 30 Mar-18 Oct.** **2023**

REALMONT *8E4* (2.5km SW Rural) *43.77092, 2.16336* **Camp Municipal La Batisse,** Route Graulhet, 81120 Réalmont **05 63 55 50 41; camping@realmont.fr; www.camping-realmont.fr**

nr nr nr

On D612 fr Albi heading S thro Réalmont. On exit Réalmont turn R on D631 where site sp. Site 1.5km on L on Rv Dadou. 2*, Sm, pt shd, EHU (3A) inc; gas; 10% statics; rv fishing adj. *"Pleasant, peaceful, well-kept site in rv valley; friendly, pleasant warden; dated but clean san facs; nr Albi-Castres cycle rte; excel value; mkt Wed; gd; hg rec."* **€15.00, 1 Apr-30 Sep.** **2023**

REGUINY *2F3* (1km S Urban) *47.96928, -2.74083* **Camping de l'Étang à Réguiny (formerly Municipal),** Rue de la Piscine, 56500 Réguiny **06 72 64 08 71; www.camping-etang-reguiny.fr**

€2 nr nr nr

On D764 fr Pontivy to Ploërmel, turn R into D11 to Réguiny then foll sp. 2*, Med, pt shd, EHU (10A) €2.50; phone; Eng spkn; ccard acc. *"Gd facs; htd pool 500m; gd touring base; deposit for gate remote control (€100); v pleasant site; rec rest in vill; gd acc to S Brittany."* **€14.00, 15 Jun-15 Sep.** **2023**

REIMS *3D4* (19km SE Rural) *49.16687, 4.21416* **Camping Intercommunalité Val de Vesle (formerly Municipal),** 8 Rue de Routoir, Courmelois, 51360 Val-de-Vesle **03 26 03 91 79; valdevesle.camping@orange.fr; www.reims-tourism.com**

€1.30 nr

Fr Reims twd Châlons-en-Champagne on D944, turn L by camp sp on D326 to Val-de-Vesle, foll camp sp; look for tall grain silos by canal. NB do not turn L bef D326 due narr lane. 2*, Med, mkd, shd, EHU (6-10A) €3.70 (long lead poss req); bbq; adv bkg acc; ccard acc; rv fishing; CKE. *"Charming, well-kept, busy site amongst trees; popular NH, rec arrive early; informal pitching; friendly, helpful staff; new security gate, booking in req for code (2011); in sm vill (no shops); poss mosquito prob; cycle rte to Reims along canal; gd touring base; lge pitches; lovely, clean facs; well sp fr D944; conv for Champagne caves."* **€17.20, 1 Apr-15 Oct.** **2022**

"I need an on-site restaurant"

We do our best to make sure site information is correct, but it is always best to check any must-have facilities are still available or will be open during your visit.

REMOULINS *10E2* (2km NW Rural) *43.94805, 4.54583* **Camping La Sousta,** Ave du Pont de Gard, 30210 Remoulins **04 66 37 12 80; info@lasousta.fr; www.lasousta.fr**

€2 nr

Fr A9 exit Remoulins, foll sp for Nîmes, then sp 'Pont du Gard par Rive Droite' thro town. Immed over rv bdge turn R sp 'Pont du Gard etc'; site on R 800m fr Pont du Gard. 4*, Lge, hdstg, mkd, shd, pt sl, EHU (6A); gas; bbq (sep area); sw nr; TV; 20% statics; Eng spkn; adv bkg acc; ccard acc; bike hire; fishing; watersports; tennis; CKE. *"Friendly, helpful staff; poss diff lge o'fits due trees; excel touring base; in walking dist Pont-du-Gard; set in lovely woodland with plenty of shd; vg; can be dry & dusty in Jul & Aug; bar & rest open in LS; sw pool clsd until 5th May."* **€36.20, 12 Mar-1 Nov.** **2023**

REMOULINS *10E2* (4km NW Rural) *43.95594, 4.51588* **Camping Clicochic Gorges du Gardon (formerly Camping International),** Chemin de la Barque Vieille, Route d'Uzès, 30210 Vers-Pont-du-Gard **04 66 22 81 81 or 04 92 28 38 48; gorges-gardon@clicochic.com; www.clicochic.com**

€2 (htd)

Exit A9 junc 23 Remoulins & head NW twd Uzès on D981. Pass turn for Pont-du-Gard & site on L in 1.5km. Or fr E on N100 turn N onto D6086 then D19A to Pont-du-Gard (avoiding Remoulins cent). 4*, Lge, mkd, hdg, pt shd, EHU (6A) inc; gas; sw nr; red long stay; TV; 10% statics; Eng spkn; adv bkg acc; ccard acc; tennis; games rm; boating; fishing; games area; CKE. *"Beautiful location; many sm pitches - some lge pitches to back of site; friendly, cheerful owners; excel san facs, ltd LS; no twin axles or o'fits over 5m; beavers in rv; site poss subject to flooding & evacuation; superb; conv for the Pont du Gard, thoroughly rec staying several nights, unique site."* **€29.00, 15 Mar-30 Sep, C18.** **2023**

RENNES *2F4* (4km NE Urban) *48.13529, -1.64597* **Camp Municipal des Gayeulles,** Rue du Maurice Audin, 35700 Rennes **02 99 36 91 22; camping-rennes@citedia.com; www.camping-rennes.com**

12 €1 nr

Exit Rennes ring rd N136 junc 14 dir Maurepas & Maison Blanche, foll sp 'Les Gayeules' & site. Narr app to site. 3*, Med, mkd, hdstg, pt shd, pt sl, serviced pitches; EHU (10A) inc; bbq; red long stay; phone; bus; Eng spkn; adv bkg acc; ccard acc; tennis nr; CKE. *"Lovely, well-kept, well-run site adj activity park; friendly, helpful staff; lge pitches; slight sl for m'vans; 1st class facs; office clsd 1200-1400; reg bus to Rennes, a lovely city; sm m'van Aire de Service adj; excel; mini golf nr; archery nrby; no dogs allowed in park adj; m'van o'night area; pool adj; noise fr disco & football; great location; new san facs close to ent."* **€17.10** **2023**

REVEL *8F4* (0.5km E Urban) *43.45454, 2.01515* **Camping Le Moulin du Roy,** Chemin de la Pergue, 31250 Revel **05 61 83 32 47 or 06 29 78 22 43; campinglemoulinduroy@gmail.com; www.camping-lemoulinduroy.com**

€0.90 nr

Fr Revel ring rd take D1/D85 dir Sorèze, site sp. 2*, Med, hdg, pt shd, EHU €320; sw nr; phone; bus; Eng spkn; tennis adj; CKE. *"Pleasant, immac site; htd pool adj; helpful staff; Sat mkt; vg."* **€23.50, 2 Jun-7 Sep.** **2023**

FRANCE

REVEL *8F4* (6km E Urban) *43.45446, 2.06953*
Camping St Martin, Les Vigariés, 81540 Sorèze
05 63 50 20 19; campingsaintmartin@gmail.com; www.campingsaintmartin.com
€1.50

Fr Revel take D85 sp Sorèze; site sp on N side of vill; turn L at traff lts; site on R in 100m. 3*, Sm, hdg, mkd, hdstg, pt shd, EHU (10A) €3.60; bbq; sw nr; TV; 20% statics; tennis; games rm; CKE. *"Vg, well-kept site; friendly staff; excel san facs; fascinating medieval town; nr Bassin de St Ferréol; excel mkt in Revel; rec; noise fr adj sports facs & pitches nr san fac beware of being hit by footballs."* **€24.00, 1 Apr-30 Sep. 2023**

REVIGNY SUR ORNAIN *5D1* (0.4km S Urban) *48.82663, 4.98412* **Camping Revigny-sur-Ornain (formerly Camp Municipal du Moulin des Gravières),** Rue du Stade, 55800 Revigny-sur-Ornain **03 29 78 73 34; camping-ry@orange.fr; www.revigny-sur-ornain.fr/camping-aire-camping-car.php**
nr

N fr Bar-le-Duc on D994 to Revigny-sur-Ornain; fr town cent take D995 twd Vitry-le-François. Site on R, sp. 2*, Sm, hdg, mkd, pt shd, EHU (6A) €2.70; TV; 3% statics; Eng spkn; adv bkg acc; CKE. *"Pleasant, well-kept site; lge pitches; vg, modern facs; trout stream runs thro site; bike hire in town; tennis in town; gd cycling along canal; mkt Wed adj; highly rec; excel site, beautifully kept; park like setting; far better than any other municipal site we have stayed on."* **€20.00, 1 May-30 Sep. 2023**

RHINAU *6E3* (0.5km NW Rural) *48.32123, 7.69788*
Camping Ferme des Tuileries, 1 Rue des Tuileries, 67860 Rhinau **03 88 74 60 45 or 06 85 74 98 97; camping.fermetuileries@neuf.fr; www.fermedestuileries.com**
nr (htd)

Take D1083 (between Strasbourg and Selestat). Exit at Benfield or Sand and take D5 through Boofzheim to Rhinau. Site sp. 3*, Med, mkd, hdstg, pt shd, EHU (6A) €3.20; gas; bbq; sw; 20% statics; Eng spkn; games area; games rm; bike hire; tennis. *"Spacious site with excel facs; regimented; free ferry across Rv Rhine adj; vg; excel for cycling; hdstdg for MH's."* **€18.00, 1 Apr-30 Sep. 2023**

RIBEAUVILLE *6E3* (2km E Urban) *48.19490, 7.33648*
Camp Municipal Pierre-de-Coubertin, Rue de Landau, 68150 Ribeauville **03 89 73 66 71; camping@ribeauville.fr; www.camping-alsace.com**
€1 (htd)

Exit N83 junc 20 at Ribeauville onto D106 & foll rd to o'skts; at traff lts turn R & then immed R again. Site on R in 500m. Camp at sports grnd nr Lycée. 4*, Lge, mkd, pt shd, pt sl, EHU (16A) €3.50; gas; CKE. *"Well-run site; friendly, helpful staff; park outside site bef checking in; clean, excel san facs; resident storks; gd size pitches; gd touring base; mkt Sat; pool adj; highly rec; excel."* **€19.00, 15 Mar-15 Nov. 2024**

RIBERAC *7C2* (0.5km N Rural) *45.25755, 0.34128*
Camp Municipal La Dronne, Route d'Angoulême, 24600 Ribérac **05 53 92 41 61; ot.riberac@perigord.tm.fr**
€0.50 nr

Site on W of main rd D708 immed N of bdge over Rv Dronne on o'skts of Ribérac. 2*, Med, hdg, pt shd, EHU (10A) €2.50. *"Vg, well-run site; pitches in cent hdgd & shady; facs gd & clean but inadequate high ssn; Fri mkt; v friendly, helpful owner; excel value; rvside loc; lively, nice town."* **€16.00, 1 Jun-15 Sep. 2022**

"Satellite navigation makes touring much easier"

Remember most sat navs don't know if you're towing or in a larger vehicle – always use yours alongside maps and site directions.

RIBES *9D2* (0.7km S Rural) *44.29545, 4.12436*
Camping Les Cruses, Ribes 07260 Joyeuse
33 04 75 39 54 69; les-cruses@wanadoo.fr; www.campinglescruses.com
€3 (htd) 1km

Head NW on rue du Mas de Laffont twd Le Chateâu after 120m turn L onto Le Chateâu. Turn R onto D550, sharp R twds Laffont, L onto Laffont, sharp R twd D450 after 40m turn L onto D450. Sm, mkd, shd, EHU (10A) €4.30; bbq; TV; Eng spkn; adv bkg acc; ccard acc; games area; CCI. *"Excel on site pool and jacuzz; v helpful and friendly owners; nr lively town and places to see."* **€31.70, 1 Apr-30 Sep. 2024**

RICHELIEU *4H1* (0.5km S Rural) *47.00774, 0.32078*
Camp Municipal, 6 Ave de Schaafheim, 37120 Richelieu **09 67 75 32 80 or 06 81 14 03 31; campinglecardinal37@orange.fr; campinglecardinal.fr**
nr

Fr Loudun, take D61 to Richelieu, D749 twd Châtellerault; site sp. 2*, Sm, hdg, mkd, pt shd, EHU (5-15A); fishing; tennis; CKE. *"Phone ahead to check site open LS; clean site and facs; pool 500m; gd value."* **€16.00, 5 Apr-30 Sep. 2024**

RILLE *4G1* (4km W Rural) *47.45750, 0.21840*
Camping Huttopia Rillé, Base de Loisirs de Pincemaille, Lac de Rillé, 37340 Rillé **02 47 24 62 97; rille@huttopia.com; europe.huttopia.com/site/village-lac-de-rille**
€3.50 (htd) (htd)

Fr N or S D749 to Rillé, foll sp to Lac de Pincemaille, site sp on S side of lake. 3*, Med, shd, EHU (6-10A) €4.20-6.20; sw nr; 10% statics; adv bkg rec; sep car park; watersports; fishing; games rm; tennis. *"Peaceful site; vg walking; excel."* **€38.00, 13 Apr-29 Sep. 2024**

RIOM *9B1* (6km NW Rural) *45.90614, 3.06041* **Camping de la Croze,** St Hippolyte, 63140 Châtel-Guyon **04 73 86 08 27 or 06 87 14 43 62 (mob); campinglacroze@wanadoo.fr; www.campingdelacroze.com**
€1.80 (htd) WD nr (htd)

Fr A71 exit junc 13; ring rd around Riom sp Châtel-Guyon to Mozac, then D455. Site L bef ent St Hippolyte. Fr Volvic on D986 turn L at rndabt after Leclerc supmkt & L again to D455. NB Not rec to tow thro Riom. 3*, Lge, mkd, pt shd, pt sl, EHU (6-10A) €3.80; 10% statics; CKE. *"Gd sightseeing area; mini-bus to Châtel-Guyon (2km) high ssn; vg; supmkt nrby; gd rest."* **€18.50, 26 Mar-30 Oct.** **2023**

RIOZ *6G2* (0.9km E Rural) *47.42525, 6.07524* **Camp Municipal du Lac,** Rue de la Faïencerie, 70190 Rioz **03 84 91 91 59, 03 84 91 84 84 (Mairie) or 06 33 78 63 75 (mob); camping@rioz.fr; camping.rioz.fr**
€1.50 (htd) nr nr

Site sp off D15. 3*, Med, hdg, hdstg, pt shd, EHU (16A) €2.50; gas. *"Site yourself, warden calls; some lge pitches; gd facs; pool adj; footpath to vill shops."* **€16.00, 1 Apr-30 Sep.** **2023**

RIVIERE SUR TARN *10E1* (2km E Rural) *44.19100, 3.15675* **FLOWER Camping Le Peyrelade,** Route des Gorges du Tarn, 12640 Rivière-sur-Tarn **05 65 62 62 54; campingpeyrelade@orange.fr; www.campingpeyrelade.com**
€2 WD MSP (htd)

Exit A75 junc 44.1 to Aguessac, then take D907 N thro Rivière-sur-Tarn to site in 2km. Fr Millau drive N on N9 to Aguessac, then onto D907 thro Rivière-sur-Tarn, & site sp on R. 4*, Lge, mkd, hdg, shd, terr, EHU (6A) €4; gas; bbq; cooking facs; sw nr; TV; phone; bus; adv bkg acc; ccard acc; canoeing; games rm; CKE. *"Excel touring base in interesting area; bike hire 100m; lovely quiet site with pitches next to Rv Tarn; gd pool; excel facs; rvside pitches extra charge."* **€46.90, 15 May-15 Sep.** **2024**

RIVIERE SUR TARN *10E1* (2.5km E Rural) *44.20319, 3.15806* **FFCC Camping Le Pont,** Boyne, 12640 Rivière-sur-Tarn **5 65 59 96 33; campinglepont.fr/**
€1 WD MSP nr nr

Fr Millau head N on N9, R after 7km onto D907 sp Gorges du Tarn, site in 9km on R on ent to vill. 3*, Sm, pt shd, EHU (8A) €2.50; sw nr; fishing adj; CKE. *"Gd base for Tarn gorges; canoeing & climbing nrby; facs dated but clean; helpful owner; excel."* **€14.00, 1 Apr-30 Sep.** **2024**

ROANNE *9A1* (5km SW Rural) *45.98830, 4.04531* **Camping L'Orée du Lac,** 68 Route du Barrage, 42300 Villerest **04 77 69 60 88; camping@loreedulac.net; www.loreedulac.net**
€1 WD nr

Take D53 SW fr Roanne to Villerest; site sp in vill. 3*, Sm, mkd, pt shd, pt sl, EHU (6A) €3.50; sw; TV; phone; Eng spkn; adv bkg rec; watersports; fishing; CKE. *"Attractive, lovely site nr medieval vill; much of site diff lge/med o'fits; lower pt of site diff when wet; sandy sw beach 800m on lake; gd facs; helpful owners."* **€24.00, 14 Apr-28 Oct.** **2024**

ROCAMADOUR *7D3* (7km E Rural) *44.81805, 1.68638* **Campsite Padimadour,** 1775 La Châtaigneraie-Varagne, 46500 Rocamadour **05 65 33 72 11; camping@padimadour.fr; www.padimadour.fr**
(htd) WD MSP

Fr N of A20, take exit 54 dir Gramat D840. Turn L onto Pounou. Sharp L onto La Chataigneraie after Pounou. 4*, Sm, mkd, pt shd, pt sl, EHU (10A) inc; bbq; 30% statics; phone; Eng spkn; adv bkg acc; ccard acc; games rm; games area; CCI. *"Excel & clean san facs & pool; helpful, friendly owners; homemade pizza's in high ssn; highly rec; new level pitches (2016)."* **€40.00, 4 Apr-29 Sept.** **2024**

ROCHE BERNARD, LA *2G3* (0.3km NW Urban) *47.51946, -2.30517* **Camp Municipal Le Patis,** Chemin du Patis, 56130 La Roche-Bernard **02 99 90 60 13 or 02 99 90 60 51 (Mairie); mairie-lrb@wanadoo.fr; www.laroche-bernard.com/camping-le-patis**
€2.30 (cont) WD MSP nr nr

Leave N165 junc 17 (fr N) junc 15 (fr S) & foll marina sp. NB Arr/exit OK on mkt day (Thurs) if avoid town cent. 3*, Med, mkd, hdstg, hdg, pt shd, EHU (6A); red long stay; Eng spkn; adv bkg acc; ccard acc; boating adj; games area; sailing adj. *"Excel clean site in lovely spot on rv bank; helpful staff; facs poss stretched high ssn; grass pitches poss soft - heavy o'fits phone ahead in wet weather; Thurs mkt; m'van o'night area; organic mkt Sat; ancient, pretty town up steep hill; gd walks; yacht harbour adj; highly rec."* **€20.00, 15 Mar-14 Oct.** **2024**

ROCHE CHALAIS, LA *7C2* (0.5km S Rural) *45.14892, -0.00245* **Camping Du Meridien (formerly Municipal Les Gerbes),** Rue de la Dronne, 24490 La Roche-Chalais **05 53 91 40 65; campingdumeridien@larochechalais.fr; campingdumeridien.wixsite.com/campinglarochechalai**
nr

Fr S on D674 turn sharp L in vill at site sp. Site on R in 500m. Fr N take Coutras-Libourne rd thro vill; site sp on L beyond sm indus est. 3*, Med, mkd, pt shd, terr, EHU (5-10A) €2.60-3.60 (poss rev pol); sw nr; red long stay; adv bkg acc; canoeing adj; fishing adj; boating adj; CKE. *"Pleasant, well-kept, well-run site nr rv; gd sized pitches, some rvside; leisure pk 5km; gd clean san facs; rec pitch N side of site to avoid factory noise; mkt Sat am; rec."* **€14.00, 1 Apr-31 Oct.** **2024**

FRANCE

FRANCE

ROCHE POSAY, LA 4H2 (1.5km N Rural) 46.7989, 0.80961 **Camping La Roche-Posay,** Route de Lésigny, 86270 La Roche-Posay **05 49 86 21 23; info@larocheposay-vacances.com; www.larocheposay-vacances.com**

€6 (htd) nr (covrd, htd)

On A10 take exit 26 Châtellerault-Nord, La Roche-Posay; foll sp La Roche-Posay; foll the D725 to La Roche-Possay; at rndabt foll sp for 'Camping-Hippodrome'. 4*, Lge, mkd, hdg, shd, serviced pitches; EHU (10A) inc; gas; bbq (elec, gas); sw nr; red long stay; 40% statics; Eng spkn; adv bkg acc; bike hire; fishing 1.5km; tennis; waterslide; CKE. *"Excel, popular, well-maintained site; aquatic park; 1st class facs; barrier locks automatically 2300; parking avail outside; walk to town on busy rd with no pavement; spa town."* **€50.00, 9 Apr-16 Sep, L21.** **2022**

ROCHE POSAY, LA 4H2 (3km E Rural) 46.78274, 0.86942 **Camp Municipal Les Bords de Creuse,** Rue de Pont, 37290 Yzeures-sur-Creuse **07 83 08 79 97; campinglesbordsdecreuse@onlycamp.fr; www.yzeuressurcreuse.com**

nr

Fr Châtellerault take D725 E twds La Roche-Posay; after x-ing Rv Creuse, turn L onto D750 twds Yzeures-sur-Creuse; at traff lts in vill turn S onto D104; site on R in 200m at T-junc. 1*, Med, mkd, pt shd, pt sl, EHU (6A) inc; bbq; sw nr; games rm; tennis adj. *"Pool adj."* **€15.40, 15 Jun-31 Aug.** **2024**

"There aren't many sites open at this time of year"

If you're travelling outside peak season remember to call ahead to check site opening dates – even if the entry says 'open all year'.

ROCHE SUR YON, LA 2H4 (8.2km SW Rural) 46.62281, 1.44983 **Campilo,** L'Auroire, 85430 Aubigny **02 51 31 68 45; accueil@campilo.com; www.campilo.com**

12 €3

Take Rue du Maréchal Joffre, D248 Rue du Maréchal Lyautey and D747 to Les Gâts in Aubign, take Rue des Mésanges and Le Champt des Landes to La Guyonnière, turn R onto Les Gâts, turn L onto Route de l'Auroire, cont onto Rue des Mésanges, turn L onto Le Champt des Landes, take the 2nd R onto La Guyonnière. Med, mkd, pt shd, sl, EHU (10A); bbq; Eng spkn. *"Tow cars not allowed besides c'vans sep car park; fishing lake on site; walks and cycling rtes; lge sports area; bicycles; sm gym; friendly staff; new san facs and pool."* **€26.00** **2024**

ROCHEFORT 7B1 (1.5km N Coastal) 45.94986, -0.99499 **Camping Le Bateau,** Rue des Pêcheurs d'Islande, 17300 Rochefort **05 46 99 41 00; lebateau@orange.fr; www.campinglebateau.net**

€1.70

Exit A837/E602 at junc 31 & take D733 dir Rochefort. At 1st rndabt by McDonalds, take D733 dir Royan. At next rndabt 1st R onto Rue des Pêcheurs d'Islande. Site at end of rd on L. Med, hdg, pt shd, EHU (8A) €4; 25% statics; watersports; tennis; fishing; waterslide; games rm; CKE. *"Sm pitches, a few o'look estuary; helpful staff; basic, clean san facs; poss scruffy LS - ducks & geese on site; no twin axles; gd cycling, walking; mkt Tues & Sat; lake fishing; Lidl 10 mins walk; intersting town; friendly non-english speaking owners; site adj to rv."* **€26.50, 22 Mar-3 Nov.** **2024**

ROCHEFORT 7B1 (1km S Urban) 45.93013, -0.95826 **Camping Municipal Le Rayonnement,** 3, Avenue de la Fosse Aux Mâts, 17300 Rochefort **05 46 82 67 70; camping.municipal@ville-rochefort.fr; www.ville-rochefort.fr/decouvrir/camping**

€1.05 nr

Exit E602 at junc 31 & take D733 dir Rochefort. At rndabt by McDonalds, take D733 dir Royan. Cont on D733. At rndabt with plane take 3rd exit onto Bd Edouard Pouzet. At rndabt take 3rd exit onto Bd de la Résistance, at next rndabt take 1st exit & then turn L onto ave de la Fosse aux Mâts. Site on L. Med, hdg, hdstg, shd, EHU (15A) inc; bbq; TV; 15% statics; phone; bus 100m; Eng spkn; adv bkg rec; games rm; bike hire. *"Bikes hire free; rv Charente & cycle path to cent 800m away; v helpful staff; no c'vans over 6m & twin axles; san facs v clean; Ecolabel campsite; vg; excel transporter bdge & access to town; excel."* **€18.00, 27 Feb-3 Dec.** **2022**

ROCHEFORT 7B1 (8km W Coastal) 45.94828, -1.09592 **Camping la Garenne,** Ave de l'Ile-Madame, 17730 Port-des-Barques **05 46 84 80 66; campingportdesbarques@night-day.fr; www.night-and-day.fr/camping/6-camping-la-garenne**

€1.26 nr nr nr (htd) shgl adj

Fr Rochefort S on D773, cross Rv Charente bdge & take 1st exit sp Soubise & Ile Madame. Cont strt thro Port-des-Barques, site on L opp causeway to Ile-Madame. 3*, Lge, mkd, unshd, EHU (10A) inc; red long stay; 25% statics; phone; bus adj; adv bkg acc; ccard acc; CKE. *"Pleasant site; lge pitches; pitches a little scruffy, but level; facs dated but clean; refurb (2016) nice location to sea."* **€17.00, 1 Apr-31 Oct.** **2023**

ROCHEFORT EN TERRE *2F3* (9.8km NE Urban) *47.74455, -2.25997* **Camp Municipal de La Digue,** Route 77 Le Guélin, 56200 St Martin sur Oust **02 99 91 49 45; st-martin-oust@wanadoo.fr**

€0.50 nr

On D873 14km N of Redon at Gacilly, turn W onto D777 twd Rochefort-en-Terre; site sp in 10km in St Martin. 2*, Med, pt shd, EHU (3-5A) €3.20; bbq; adv bkg acc; rv fishing 50m. *"Towpath walks to vill & shops; clean facs but ltd LS; well-maintained site; site yourself, warden calls am & eve; excel, refurbished facs (2013)."* **€10.00, 1 May-30 Sep. 2023**

ROCHEFORT EN TERRE *2F3* (0.6km S Rural) *47.695193, -2.349117* **Camping Au Gré des Vents,** Chemin de Bogeais, Route de Limerzel, 56220 Rochefort-en-Terre **02 97 43 37 52; gredesvents@orange.fr; www.campingaugredesvents.com**

€3 nr nr (htd)

Fr Redon W on D775 twd Vannes, approx 23km turn R onto D774 sp Rochefort-en-Terre; immed after vill limit sp, turn sharp L up slope to ent. NB Do not drive thro vill. 3*, Med, hdg, mkd, pt shd, pt sl, terr, EHU ltd (10A) €4.50; bbq; sw nr; 10% statics; adv bkg acc; ccard acc; games area; CKE. *"Peaceful base for touring area; helpful, lovely owners; no vehicle movement or shwrs 2200-0700 (0800 LS), but wcs open; no twin axles; excel; bit scruffy; v nr vill."* **€26.00, 31 Mar-30 Sep. 2024**

ROCHELLE, LA *7A1* (12km N Rural/Coastal) *46.25239, -1.11972* **Camping Animal King (formerly Municipal Les Misottes),** 46 Rue de l'Océan, 17137 Esnandes **06 59 33 80 49 or 05 16 59 01 86; cak@camping-animal-king.com; camping-animal-king.com**

€2.50 (cont) nr

shgl 2km

Fr N on D938 or N1327 turn W at Marans onto D105. In 7.5km turn S onto D9 then D202 to Esnandes. Enter vill, at x-rds strt, site on R in 200m. Fr La Rochelle D105 N to cent Esnandes, site sp. 2*, Med, mkd, pt shd, EHU (10A) €3; 5% statics; Eng spkn; adv bkg acc; fishing; CKE. *"Site on the edge of marshlands; v nice & quiet; excel bus svrs; canal fishing; liable to flood; vg; new manager (2018) enthusiastic and determined to update site; v clean basic san facs; vg for La Rochelle and area; rec for sh stay; san facs tired."* **€15.50, 1 Apr-15 Oct. 2024**

ROCHELLE, LA *7A1* (5km S Rural/Coastal) *46.11659, -1.11939* **Camping Les Sables,** Chemin du Pontreau, 17440 Aytré **05 46 45 40 30; contact@camping-les-sables.com; www.camping-les-sables.com**

€1.50

(covrd, htd)

Fr S (Rochefort) on D137, exit sp Aytré. At 2nd traff lts turn L & foll site sp. Lge, hdg, pt shd, EHU (6A) €3; bbq; 50% statics; phone; Eng spkn; adv bkg acc; ccard acc; bike hire; games area; games rm; waterslide; CKE. *"Vg."* **€42.00, 1 May-15 Oct. 2023**

ROCHELLE, LA *7A1* (5km NW Rural/Coastal) *46.19583, -1.1875* **Camping au Petit Port de l'Houmeau,** Rue des Sartières, 17137 L'Houmeau **05 46 50 90 82; info@aupetitport.com; www.aupetitport.com**

€2 nr nr

shgl 1.5km

Exit N237 onto D104/D105 sp Lagord; at rndabt in 1km turn L onto D104; in 2.5km fork L onto D106 to L'Houmeau; at ent to town turn R into Rue des Sarthières sp Camping; site on R in 100m. 4*, Med, hdg, mkd, hdstg, shd, terr, EHU (10A) €4.60 (poss rev pol); bbq (gas); bus 400m; Eng spkn; adv bkg rec; ccard acc; bike hire; games rm; CKE. *"Pleasant, friendly site; helpful owners; clean facs; no vehicle access 2230-0730; gd walking & cycling; under new management (2013); conv Ile de Ré bdge; excel."* **€30.00, 1 Apr-30 Sep. 2024**

ROCROI *5C1* (12km SE Rural) *49.87200, 4.60446* **Camp Départemental du Lac des Vieilles Forges,** 08500 Les Mazures **03 24 40 17 31; cmpingvieillesforges@cg08.fr**

€1 (htd)

Fr Rocroi take D1 & D988 for Les Mazures/Renwez. Turn R D40 at sp Les Vieilles Forges. Site on R nr lakeside. 3*, Lge, mkd, hdstg, shd, pt sl, EHU (6-10A) €2.50-4.30 (long leads req); sw; TV; 20% statics; adv bkg acc; bike hire; boating; tennis; fishing. *"Attractive walks; lake views fr some pitches; vg site; recep clsd 1200-1500."* **€20.00, 11 Apr-15 Sep. 2022**

ROHAN *2F3* (0.2km NW Rural) *48.07078, -2.75525* **Camp du Val d'Oust,** Rue de St Gouvry, 56580 Rohan **02 97 51 57 58; mairie@rohan@.fr; www.campingvaldoust-rohan56.jimdosite.com**

€0.90 nr nr nr

Rue de St Gouvry runs NW fr Rohan parallel to D11, but other side of canal. 2*, Sm, mkd, pt shd, EHU €3.10; bbq; phone; adv bkg acc; CKE. *"Pleasant site beside Nantes/Brest canal; gd cycling; market in vill; some rd noise."* **€14.10, 1 Jun-15 Sep. 2023**

ROMAGNE *7A2* (1.3km NE Rural) *46.277709, 0.313029* **Camping Le Jardin de Rose,** 24 Lieu dit Feuillebert, Romagne 86700 **06 37 08 61 91 or 07779 418735 (UK mob); campinglejardin.grance@gmail.com; campinglejardin.fr**

12 (htd) nr

Take Couhe turning fr N10. Foll sp for Romagne for approx 13km. NB: Google maps takes you to site with no problems. Sm, mkd, pt shd, EHU (16A); bbq (charcoal, elec, gas); twin axles; TV; Eng spkn; adv bkg rec; ccard acc; bike hire. *"V helpful English owners; around 10 pitches so adv bkg rec; great area for cycling, walking etc; fabulous peaceful site for those wishing to get off beaten track; B&B avail; excel."* **€20.00 2022**

FRANCE

ROMIEU, LA *8E2* (0.3km NE Rural) *43.98299, 0.50183* **Kawan Village Le Camp de Florence,** 32480 La Romieu **05 62 28 15 58; info@lecampdeflorence.com; www.lecampdeflorence.com**

€3 nr nr

Take D931 N fr Condom & turn R onto D41, where La Romieu sp next to radio mast. Go thro La Romieu & turn L at sp just bef leaving vill. 4*, Lge, hdstg, hdg, pt shd, EHU (10A) inc (poss rev pol); bbq; twin axles; TV; 80% statics; Eng spkn; adv bkg req; ccard acc; bike hire; games area; games rm; tennis; CKE. *"Peaceful, Dutch-run site in pleasant location; gd sized pitches, most with views; welcoming, helpful staff; waterslide; jacuzzi; leisure complex 500m; gd clean san facs; gd rest; poss muddy when wet; archery; some noise fr disco, ask for pitch away fr bar; rest in 16thC farmhouse; gd pool but take care sl ent; gd cycling; historic 11thC vill; mkt Wed Condom."* **€25.00, 23 Apr - 25 Sep, D19.** 2022

ROMILLY SUR SEINE *4E4* (4km W Rural) *48.5259, 3.6646* **Camping du Domaine de la Noue des Rois,** Chemin des Brayes, 10100 St Hilaire-sous-Romilly **03 25 24 41 60; contact@lanouedesrois.com; www.lanouedesrois.com**

(on lead) €3.50 (htd) (covrd, htd)

Site sp fr D619, on rvside. 4*, Lge, mkd, pt shd, EHU (16A) €3.50-5; gas; red long stay; 90% statics; Eng spkn; adv bkg acc; ccard acc; waterslide; fishing; games area; watersports; sailing; tennis; CKE. *"Gd situation in wooded area; conv Paris & Disneyland; ltd pitches/facs for tourers."* **€37.00, 1 Feb-30 Nov.** 2024

ROMORANTIN LANTHENAY *4G2* (1km E Urban) *47.35486, 1.75568* **Camping de Tournefeuille,** Rue de Long Eaton, 41200 Romorantin-Lanthenay **02 54 76 16 60; campingromorantin@night-day.fr; www.campingromorantin.com**

€1.80 (htd) nr

Fr town cent on D724 to Salbis, foll sp thro several traff lts over bdge turn R into Rue de Long-Eaton, site sp. 3*, Med, pt shd, EHU (6A) inc; gas; bbq; TV; ccard acc; fishing; bike hire. *"Rv walk to town rec; pool adj; excel modern san facs; helpful staff."* **€30.00, 1 Apr-31 Oct.** 2024

ROQUEBRUN *10F1* (0.3km SE Rural) *43.49775, 3.02834* **Camping Campotel Le Nice de Roquebrun,** Rue du Temps Libre, 34460 Roquebrun **04 67 89 61 99 or 04 67 89 79 97; campoteldelorb@orange.fr; www.camping-lenice.com**

€1.30 nr nr nr

N112 to St Chinian & take D20 dir Cessenon-sur-Orb, turn L onto D14 twd Roquebrun; site on L bef bdge over rv. Narr app rd. 2*, Sm, mkd, hdstg, pt shd, pt sl, terr, EHU (6A) €2.50; sw nr; 15% statics; phone; adv bkg acc; ccard acc; fishing adj; tennis; sailing adj; CKE. *"Excel cent for walking & cycling; beautiful scenery; ltd touring pitches; some gd, modern san facs; canoe hire adj; not suitable for lge o'fits; need key for WC block; off clsd Sundays LS."* **€23.20, 11 Mar-14 oct.** 2024

ROSANS *9D3* (2.5km SW Rural) *44.38273, 5.46172* **Camping des Rosieres,** Quartiers des Quinces, 05150 Rosans **04 92 65 35 17; contact@camping-rosieres.com; www.camping-rosieres.com/fr**

(htd)

On D94 Nyons to Gap on RH side just prior to ent Rosans. 3*, Sm, hdg, shd, EHU (6A); twin axles; Eng spkn; adv bkg acc; games area; CKE. *"Horseriding; canyoning; tennis; boules; steep narr rd fr recep & sw pool to pitches; gd."* **€24.00, 1 May-30 Sep.** 2023

ROSCOFF *1D2* (7km SW Rural/Coastal) *48.67246, -4.05326* **Camp Municipal du Bois de la Palud,** 29250 Plougoulm **02 98 29 81 82 or 02 98 29 90 76 (Mairie); contact@plougoulm.bzh; www.plougoulm.bzh**

nr sand 500m

Fr D58 turn W on D10 sp Cléder/Plouescat; after 3km on ent Plougoulm foll sp to site. 2*, Sm, hdg, mkd, pt shd, terr, EHU (8A) €3.50; phone; Eng spkn; adv bkg acc; ccard acc; CKE. *"Clean, tidy site in delightful area; lovely views to sandy inlet; conv ferry; if arr late, site yourself; warden calls am & pm; access all hrs with c'van; walk in first, turning diff inside; also lower field with EHU; sh walk to vill; excel; late arr & late dep; beautiful beaches to the west."* **€14.00, 15 Jun-4 Sep.** 2022

ROSIERS SUR LOIRE, LES *4G1* (1km N Rural) *47.35908, -0.22500* **Camping Les Voiles d'Anjou (formerly FLOWER Camping Val de Loire),** 6 Rue Ste Baudruche, 49350 Les Rosiers-sur-Loire **02 41 51 94 33; contact@camping-valdeloire.com; www.camping-voilesdanjou.com/fr**

€3 (htd)

Take D952 fr Saumur in dir Angers. Site on D59 1km N of vill cent on L dir Beaufort-en-Vallée. 4*, Med, hdstg, mkd, hdg, pt shd, serviced pitches; EHU (10A) €4.50; gas; bbq; red long stay; TV; 15% statics; Eng spkn; adv bkg acc; waterslide; tennis; games rm; CKE. *"Close to Rv Loire; lge pitches; friendly, helpful staff; excel san facs; gd touring base for chateaux region; excel."* **€38.00, 4 Apr-27 Sep.** 2024

ROSNAY *4H2* (0.8km N Rural) *46.70647, 1.21161* **Camp Municipal Les Millots,** Route de St Michel-en-Brenne, 36300 Rosnay **02 54 37 80 17; rosnay-mairie@wanadoo.fr**

(htd) nr nr

NE on D27 fr Le Blanc to Rosnay; site sp 500m N of Rosnay on D44. 2*, Sm, mkd, pt shd, EHU (6-10A) inc (poss rev pol); bbq; phone; adv bkg acc; lake fishing; tennis; cycling; CKE. *"Lovely, tranquil, popular site; well-kept; excel modern san facs; warden collects fees twice daily; lakeside walks; excel walking, cycling, birdwatching & fishing; gd base for exploring Brenne National Park; vg value; excel; friendly."* **€11.40, 16 Feb-15 Nov.** 2023

ROUEN *3C2* (5km E Urban) *49.43154, 1.15387* **Camping L'Aubette,** 23 Rue du Vert- Buisson, 76160 St Léger-du-Bourg-Denis **02 32 08 47 69; camping aubette@gmail.com; www.rouentourisme.com**

12 Free nr

Fr Rouen E on N31 dir Darnétal & Beauvais; in 1km cont strt on onto D42/D138 dir St Léger-du-Bourg-Denis; in 400m turn L onto Rue du Vert Buisson; site on r in 800m just past stop sp. Site well sp as 'Camping' fr Rouen cent. 2*, Med, pt shd, pt sl, terr, EHU 4A; bbq; 40% statics; bus 150m; CKE. *"In attractive rv valley; conv city cent; conv bus to town; v ltd touring pitches; cash only; v basic site, gd NH only; v poor."* **€15.00** **2024**

"That's changed – Should I let the Club know?"

If you find something on site that's different from the site entry, fill in a report and let us know. See camc.com/europereport.

ROUSSILLON *10E2* (2.5km SW Rural) *43.88973, 5.27596* **Camping L'Arc-en-Ciel,** Route de Goult, 84220 Roussillon **04 90 05 73 96 or 06 35 23 58 90; campingarcenciel@wanadoo.fr; www.camping-arc-en-ciel.fr**

€3.50

Take D900 W out of Apt, then R on D201 sp Roussillon, then R on D4 for 1.5km, then L on D104 twd Roussillon. Take L fork twd Goult, site well sp 2.5km on L. No access for c'vans & m'vans in Roussillon vill. 3*, Med, mkd, hdstg, pt shd, pt sl, terr, EHU (4A) €3.80; gas; phone; adv bkg acc; games area; CKE. *"Tranquil woodland site; tight access some pitches; poss diff lge o'fits due trees; helpful staff; old san facs; beware rd humps & drainage channels on site access rds; some pitches poss diff lge o'fits; worth a detour; vg."* **€30.00, 15 Mar-31 Oct.** **2024**

ROYAN *7B1* (5km SE Coastal) *45.58345, -0.98720* **Camping Bois Soleil,** 2 Ave de Suzac, 17110 St Georges-de-Didonne **05 46 05 05 94; info@bois-soleil.com; www.bois-soleil.com**

€3 (not acc end Jun-Aug inc) (htd) (htd) sand adj

Fr A10 exit junc 35 dir Saintes & Royan; on app Royan foll St Georges-de-Didonne sp onto bypass D25/D730/D25/D25E; go over 2 rndabts (with underpass bet); at 3rd rndabt turn L sp Meschers-sur-Gironde; site on R in 500m. Site well sp. 5*, Lge, hdstg, mkd, hdg, pt shd, terr, EHU (6A) inc (poss rev pol); gas; bbq (gas); TV; 30% statics; phone; Eng spkn; adv bkg rec; ccard acc; bike hire; tennis; games area; CKE. *"Superb wooded site in vg location nr beach; popular & busy; generous pitches, some sandy; excel, clean san facs; vg shop & rest; many sandy beaches nrby."* **€61.30, 6 Apr-6 Oct.** **2024**

See advertisement

"I like to fill in the reports as I travel from site to site"

You'll find report forms at the back of this guide, or you can fill them in online at camc.com/europereport.

ROYAN *7B1* (6km SE Coastal) *45.59253, -0.98713* **Camping Idéal,** 16 Ave de Suzac, 17110 St Georges-de-Didonne **05 46 05 29 04; info@ideal-camping.com; www.ideal-camping.com**

(htd) sand 200m

Fr Royan foll coast rd sp St Georges-de-Didonne. Site sp on D25 2km S of St Georges, opp Cmp Bois-Soleil. 4*, Lge, mkd, shd, EHU (6-10A) €4.50-5.50; gas; 10% statics; phone; ccard acc; bike hire; games area; horseriding 300m; tennis 500m; games rm; jacuzzi; waterslide; CKE. *"Helpful staff; site popular with families."* **€37.00, 2 May-8 Sep.** **2024**

FRANCE

ROYAN *7B1* (4km NW Urban/Coastal) *45.6309, -1.0498* **Campéole Camping Clairefontaine,** 16 Rue du Colonel Lachaud, Pontaillac, 17200 Royan **05 46 39 08 11; clairefontaine@campeole.com; www.campeole.com**

€3 (htd) WD MSP sand 300m

Foll Pontaillac sp fr Royan. Site sp in Clairefontaine (& Pontaillac). 4*, Lge, mkd, pt shd, serviced pitches; EHU (10A); gas; bbq; TV; 80% statics; phone; Eng spkn; adv bkg req; ccard acc; tennis; CKE. *"Lovely coastline; gd for family holiday; helpful owner; clean, unisex san facs; ltd touring pitches, some sm; gd security; site poss dusty; vg walking & cycling; casino 300m; coastal path Pontaillac to Royan; gd site; easy walk/bike/bus into town; nice sw; bar & shop onsite; conv for city; vg."* **€49.20, 31 Mar-1 Oct.** **2023**

ROYBON *9C2* (1.6km S Rural) *45.24639, 5.24806* **Camping de Roybon,** Route de St Antoine, 38940 Roybon **04 76 36 23 67 or 06 86 64 55 47; campingroybon38@gmail.com; www.campingroybon.com**

€2.65 WD nr

Fr Roybon go S on D71 & foll sp. 2*, Med, mkd, pt shd, pt sl, EHU (10A) €3.50; sw nr; adv bkg acc; watersports adj. *"V peaceful; gd, modern facs new; vg; can be boggy when wet."* **€18.40, 1 May-30 Sep.** **2022**

ROYERE DE VASSIVIERE *7B4* (6km SW Rural) *45.78869, 1.89855* **Camping Les Terrasses du Lac,** Vauveix, 23460 Royère-de-Vassivière **05 55 64 76 77; lesterrassesdulac.camping@gmail.com; www.camping-vassiviere.fr**

€1 (htd) WD nr nr adj

Fr Eymoutiers take D43 for approx 10km then take D36 to Vauveix & foll sp. 1*, Med, hdg, mkd, pt shd, terr, EHU (10A) €3.10 (poss rev pol); TV; 50% statics; cycling; horseriding; watersports adj; CKE. *"Helpful staff; walking; lovely setting."* **€19.00, 2 Apr-31 Oct.** **2023**

RUE *3B2* (6km N Rural) *50.31367, 1.69472* **Caravan Le Val d'Authie (formerly Kawan Village),** 20 Route de Vercourt, 80120 Villers-sur-Authie **03 22 29 92 47; valdauthie@capfun.com; www.capfun.com/camping-france-picardie-val_authie-FR.html**

€1.50 (htd) WD MSP (covrd, htd)

Exit 24 on A16 twrds Vron, foll sp Camping Vercourt thro town. 5*, Lge, mkd, hdg, pt shd, pt sl, EHU (6-10A) (rev pol); gas; TV; 60% statics; phone; Eng spkn; adv bkg acc; ccard acc; games area; games rm; fitness rm; tennis; CKE. *"Set in pleasant countryside; sauna; steam rm; helpful, friendly owners; clean, unisex facs & spacious shwrs; sm sep area for tourers, but many touring pitches bet statics (2009); poss diff for lge o'fits; gd pool; v cr & noisy high ssn; excel."* **€31.00, 1 Apr-30 Sep.** **2023**

RUE *3B2* (4km SE Rural) *50.25278, 1.71224* **Camping de la Mottelette,** Ferme de la Mottelette, 80120 Forest-Montiers **06 72 85 73 77; contact@la-mottelette.com; www.la-mottelette.com**

€1 WD nr

Exit A16 junc 24 onto D32 dir Rue & L Crotoy; at rndabt junc with D235 cont on D32; site on L in 1.5km. Site sp on leaving A16. 2*, Sm, hdg, mkd, unshd, EHU (6A) €4; bbq; 50% statics; Eng spkn; adv bkg acc; games area; games rm; CKE. *"Basic, CL type, clean site on wkg fm; welcoming, friendly owners; mkt Sat; conv A16; gd touring base or NH; vg; pleasant atmosphere; new facs (2015)."* **€18.00, 1 Apr-31 Oct.** **2023**

RUFFEC *7A2* (3km SE Rural) *46.01500, 0.21304* **Camping Le Réjallant,** Les Grands Champs, 16700 Condac **05 45 31 29 06 or 06 58 12 88 18; contact@camping-du-rejallant.com; www.camping-du-rejallant.com**

12 WD nr

Site sp fr N10 & fr town. App 1km fr turn-off. 3*, Med, hdg, mkd, shd, pt sl, EHU (10A) inc; sw nr; Eng spkn; fishing 100m; CKE. *"Gd NH; friendly, sm nbr of touring sites; lovely vill 2km, gd Leclerc and Lidl supmkt; gd pool; clean facs; nearby restaurant may be closed LS, esp Mondays; bar 100m; great for families."* **€21.00** **2021**

RUOMS *9D2* (4km SW Urban) *44.43101, 4.32945* **Camping La Chapoulière,** 07120 Ruoms **04 75 39 64 98 or 04 75 93 90 72; camping@lachapouliere.com; www.lachapouliere.com**

€3.50 MSP

Exit Ruoms S on D579. At junc 2km S, foll D111 sp St Ambroix. Site 1.5km fr junc. 4*, Med, mkd, shd, pt sl, EHU (6A) €4.60; gas; sw nr; TV; Eng spkn; adv bkg rec; games area; tennis 2km; canoeing; fishing adj. *"Beautiful pitches on rv bank; friendly; ltd facs LS; vg; excel modern san facs; lge pitches demarcated by trees."* **€46.00, 23 Mar-28 Sep.** **2024**

SABLE SUR SARTHE *4F1* (0.5km S Rural) *47.83101, -0.33177* **Camp Municipal de l'Hippodrome,** Allée du Québec, 72300 Sable-sur-Sarthe **02 43 95 42 61; camping@sablesursarthe.fr; camping.sablesursarthe.fr**

Sp in town (foll sm, white sp with c'van symbols or Hippodrome). Fr N on D306; at traff lts at junc with D309, go strt over & under rlwy brdg sp Centre Ville; foll camping sps. 3*, Med, hdg, pt shd, EHU (15A) €2.40; gas; bbq; red long stay; TV; Eng spkn; ccard acc; boat hire; canoeing; rv fishing; bike hire. *"Excel site next to racecourse; gd, clean facs; helpful staff; conv for town; some pitches diff for lge fits."* **€16.40, 3 Apr-15 Oct.** **2023**

SABLES D'OLONNE, LES *7A1* (2km E Rural) *46.48098, -1.73146* **Camping Le Puits Rochais,** 25 Rue de Bourdigal, 85180 Château-d'Olonne **02 51 21 09 69; info@puitsrochais.com; www.puitsrochais.com**

€3.30 (htd) sand 2km

Fr Les Sables-d'Olonne take D949 twd La Rochelle. Pass rndabt with lge hypermrkt 'Magasin Géant' & turn R at 1st traff lts at Mercedes g'ge, then 1st L to site. 4*, Med, mkd, hdg, pt shd, EHU (6-10A) inc; bbq (gas); TV; 60% statics; phone; adv bkg acc; ccard acc; games area; waterslide; bike hire; games rm; tennis; CKE. *"Friendly, welcoming site; gd for families; san facs gd but ltd."* **€46.00, 19 Apr-30 Sep. 2024**

SABLES D'OLONNE, LES *7A1* (10km ESE Coastal) *46.471521, -1.725812* **Camping Bel Air,** 6 allee de la Chevreuse, Chateau d'Olonne 85180 **02 51 22 09 67; dubelair@cybelevacances.com; www.campingdubelair.com**

€6 (covrd, htd) sand

Fr La Roche-sur-Yon take D160 twrds Les Sables d'Olonne. Take D949 twrds Niort then the D2949 on Avenue de Talmont. At rndabt take D32A, 3rd exit on Rue du Brandais. Turn R onto Chemin de Bel air. Med, pt shd, bbq (gas); adv bkg acc. **€46.00, 1 Apr-1 Nov. 2024**

SABLES D'OR LES PINS *2E3* (1km NW Rural/Coastal) *48.63230, -2.41229* **Camping Les Salines,** 11 rue de l'Islet, 22240 Plurien **02 96 72 17 40; ccontact@campinglessalines.fr; www.campinglessalines.fr**

€0.50 nr sand 400m

Fr D786 turn N at Plurien onto D34 to Sables-d'Or. In 1km turn L & site on L after 200m. 2*, Med, pt shd, pt sl, terr, EHU (6A) €2.35; phone; Eng spkn; adv bkg acc; CKE. *"Lovely, quiet, tranquile hillside site; some sea views; vg san facs; gates clsd 2200-0700; no pitching when office clsd, but lge car park opp; excel access to nature reserve & beautiful beaches; enthusiastic, helpful new owners (2017); lge pitches; lovely estuary walks; conv St Malo; wonderful coast; highly rec."* **€16.00, 1 Apr-12 Nov. 2023**

SACQUENAY *6G1* (0.5km S Rural) *47.58924, 5.32178* **Aire Naturelle La Chênaie (Méot),** 16 Rue du 19 Mars, 21260 Sacquenay **03 80 75 89 43 or 03 80 75 97 07; eric.meot@wanadoo.fr; www.cotedor-tourisme.com**

nr

S on D974 turn L onto D171A sp Occey & Sacquenay, site sp. Sm, pt shd, pt sl, EHU (6A); red long stay; Eng spkn; adv bkg acc; CKE. *"Peaceful site in orchard."* **€12.00, 1 Apr-1 Oct. 2024**

ST AFFRIQUE *8E4* (1km E Urban) *43.95025, 2.89248* **Camp Municipal,** Parc des Sports, La Capelle Basse, 12400 St Affrique **05 65 99 08 57; mairie-de-vabres-labbaye@wanadoo.fr**

nr nr nr

Site on D99 Albi-Millau rd to St Affrique sp fr all dir in E end of town. Nr stn & sports complex. 2*, Med, pt shd, EHU €2.75; sw; adv bkg acc; rv fishing; tennis. *"Gd clean facs; NH."* **€12.00, 14 Jun-13 Sep. 2024**

ST AIGNAN SUR CHER *4G2* (9km N Rural) *47.32361, 1.36983* **FFCC Camping Domaine du Bien Vivre,** 13-15 Route du Petit Village, 41140 St Romain-sur-Cher **02 54 71 73 74; domainedubienvivre@free.fr; www.domainedubienvivre.fr**

12 nr nr

Fr St Aignan-sur-Cher N on D675; in 6km in St Romain-sur-Cher site sp to L; foll sps for 3km. Sm, mkd, pt shd, pt sl, EHU (6A) inc; bbq; Eng spkn; ccard acc; CKE. *"A vineyard site; helpful owner; ltd facs in winter; sale of wines; conv Blois; gd."* **€16.50 2022**

ST AIGNAN SUR CHER *4G2* (4km NW Rural) *47.29411, 1.33041* **Camp Municipal Le Port,** 3 rue du Passeur, 41110 Mareuil-sur-Cher **02 54 75 10 01; camping-leport@orange.fr; www.camping-leport.fr**

€2 (htd) nr

Fr St Aignan take D17 twd Tours (on S bank of Cher); site in 4km in vill of Mareuil-sur-Cher behind church, thro new archway, on Rv Cher. By Mareuil chateau. Or fr A85 sp. 3*, Sm, mkd, pt shd, EHU (16A) €5.50; sw; Eng spkn; canoe hire; fishing; CKE. *"Beautiful, simple, rvside site; friendly staff; clean san facs but ltd; opening/closing dates variable, phone ahead to check; if office clsd enquire at supmkt adj (same owners); gas 50m; no access 1300-1500; diff lge o'fits; no twin axles; m'vans extra; gd touring area."* **€28.60, 15 Apr-30 Sep. 2024**

ST AMAND LES EAUX *3B4* (4km SE Rural) *50.43535, 3.46290* **FFCC Camping du Mont des Bruyères,** 806 Rue Basly, 59230 St Amand-les-Eaux **03 27 48 56 87; lemontdesbruyeres@orange.fr; www.campingmontdesbruyeres.com**

€1 (htd)

Exit A23 m'way at junc 5 or 6 onto ring rd D169, site sp. Fr N exit E42 junc 31 onto N52/N507 then D169. Avoid St Amand cent. 4*, Med, hdg, mkd, shd, pt sl, terr, EHU (6A-10A) inc; bbq; 60% statics; adv bkg acc; CKE. *"Attractive site on forest edge; most touring pitches under trees; access to some pitches diff due slopes; gd cycling; excel birdlife on site; fac gd & clean; some pitches untidy; own toilet paper & soap req'd in toilet block."* **€28.00, 15 Mar-30 Oct. 2022**

FRANCE

ST ANDRE DE CUBZAC *7C2* (4km NW Rural) *45.00703, -0.47724* **FFCC Camping Le Port Neuf,** 1125 Route du Port Neuf, 33240 St André-de-Cubzac **05 57 43 16 44; contact@camping-port-neuf.com; www.camping-port-neuf.com**

€1 (htd) WD MSP

Fr A10 or N10 take exit sp St André. Well sp fr St André (narr rds) on D669. 2*, Sm, hdg, mkd, hdstg, pt shd, EHU (6A) €3.50 (poss long lead req); train to Bordeaux fr vill; Eng spkn; adv bkg acc; bike hire; lake fishing 100m; boating 100m; horseriding nr; CKE. *"Lovely spot; friendly, helpful staff; san facs clean; pedalo hire; scruffy site (2015)."*
€15.00, 1 May-30 Sep. **2022**

ST ANTONIN NOBLE VAL *8E4* (1.5km N Rural) *44.1595, 1.7564* **Camping Ponget,** Route de Caylus, 82140 St Antonin-Noble-Val **05 63 68 21 13 or 05 63 30 60 23 (Mairie); camping-leponget@wanadoo.fr**

€1.20 (htd) MSP nr nr nr

Fr Caylus take D19 S to St Antonin; site on R, well sp. 2*, Sm, hdg, pt shd, EHU (3-6A) €2.50-3.70; gas; sw nr; phone; CKE. *"Well-kept site adj sports field; modern san facs; poss diff lge o'fits; gd walking; vg friendly site; excel mkt Sun; discount for 7 days; lovely medival town; gd for Aveyron Gorges & Bastide towns."*
€11.40, 2 May-30 Sep. **2023**

ST ASTIER *7C3* (0.6km E Rural) *45.14735, 0.53308* **Flower Camping Le Pontet,** 2 Impasse du Pontet, 24110 Saint-Astier **05 53 54 14 22; contact@camping-le-perigord.com; camping-le-perigord.com/**

WD nr sand adj

Take D6089 SW fr Périgueux; in 14km turn R sp St Astier; site on R on D41 on banks of Rv Isle. 3*, Med, mkd, shd, EHU (6A) €2.55; gas; bbq; adv bkg acc; canoeing; fishing; CKE. *"Some areas soft in wet weather."* **€19.00, 1 Apr-30 Sep.** **2024**

ST AYGULF *10F4* (0.5km N Coastal) *43.39151, 6.72648* **Camping de St Aygulf Plage,** 270 Ave Salvarelli, 83370 St Aygulf Plage **04 94 17 62 49; info@campingdesaintaygulf.fr; www.campingdesaintaygulf.fr**

€3 WD sand adj

Fr Roquebrunne on D7 at rndabt 100m after vill sp St Aygulf take 3rd exit leading to Rue Roger Martin du Gard. Keep turning L. Fr Fréjus on D559, rd bends R after bdge over beach access, turn R bef rd climbs to L. 2*, V lge, hdg, mkd, shd, EHU (5A) €3.50; gas; twin axles; red long stay; adv bkg acc; ccard acc; fishing; watersports nr; games area; CKE. *"Gd; shop clsd LS; sports facs nrby; pool (2017)."*
€40.00, 1 Apr-28 Oct. **2023**

ST AYGULF *10F4* (4km S Coastal) *43.40963, 6.72491* **Camping Le Plage d'Argens,** 541 route Départementale 559 (RN 98), 83370 St Aygulf **+33 (0)4 94 17 62 49; info@campingdesaintaygulf.fr; www.laplagedargens.fr/?utm_source=google&utm_medium=organic&utm_campaign=gmb_search**

€2.50 (htd) WD MSP (htd) sand adj

Well sp fr D559 bet Fréjus & St Aygulf, by Rv Argens. If app fr W pass site on R & return via next rndbt. 2*, Lge, mkd, pt shd, EHU (6A) €2; gas; TV; 5% statics; Eng spkn; adv bkg acc; ccard acc; bike hire; CKE. *"Excel, well-run site by rv; sh walk to uncrowded beach (pt naturist); excel facs & pool; hypmkt 1km; cycle track to St Aygulf & pt way to Fréjus."*
€30.00, 1 Apr-20 Oct. **2024**

ST AYGULF *10F4* (2.5km W Coastal) *43.36566, 6.71264* **Camping Au Paradis des Campeurs,** La Gaillarde-Plage, 83380 Les Issambres **04 94 96 93 55; info@campingpdc.fr; auparadisdescampeurs.com**

€3 (htd) WD MSP sand adj

Exit A8/E80 junc 37 at Puget-sur-Argens onto DN7 to by-pass Fréjus, then onto D559 twd Ste Maxime. Site on R 2km after passing thro St Aygulf, on LH bend bef hill. Or exit junc 36 onto D125 to Ste Maxime, then D559 dir Fréjus. Site on L after ent Les Issambres. 4*, Med, mkd, hdstg, pt shd, pt sl, terr, serviced pitches; EHU (6A) €4 (poss rev pol); bbq; TV; Eng spkn; ccard acc; golf 4km; games rm; bike hire; CKE. *"V popular LS; direct access via underpass to beach; excel san facs; superb views fr top level pitches - worth extra; gates shut at night & guarded; helpful owners; old rd to St Aygulf suitable for cycling; excel; adj beach small."* **€45.00, 1 Apr-5 Oct.** **2024**

ST BENOIT SUR LOIRE *4F3* (0.5km SE Rural) *47.80711, 2.29528* **FFCC Camping Le Port,** Rue du Port, 45730 St Benoît-sur-Loire **02 38 35 12 34; campingleport@onlycamp.fr**

(htd) WD MSP nr nr sand adj

Fr Orléans take N60 & bypass Châteauneuf-sur-Loire. Take D60 twd Sully-sur-Loire to St Benoît-sur-Loire. Foll sp fr vill, site on L side of 1-way rd. 2*, Sm, pt shd, pt sl, EHU (13A) €2.50; bbq; sw nr; fishing adj; canoeing adj; CKE. *"Gd cycling, walking; pleasant town; splendid views over Loire fr some pitches, others in wooded area; excel."* **€20.00, 1 May-15 Sep.** **2024**

ST BREVIN LES PINS *2G3* (2km N Coastal) *47.26553, -2.16918* **Camping de Mindin,** 32 Ave du Bois, 44250 St Brévin-les-Pins **02 40 27 46 41; contact@campingmindin.com; www.camping-de-mindin.com**

12 €2.35 (htd) WD MSP (htd) sand adj

On beach rd at N end of St Brevin. 3*, Med, shd, EHU (16A) €5.05; 80% statics; adv bkg acc; ccard acc; CKE. *"Sm, sandy pitches; 6 touring pitches, area unkept; san facs being updated."* **€37.00** **2023**

ST BREVIN LES PINS *2G3* (2km S Coastal) *47.21375, -2.15409* **Camping Les Rochelets,** Chemin des Grandes Rivières, 44250 St Brévin-les-Pins **02 40 27 40 25; info@rochelets.com; www.rochelets.com**

12 €4 (htd) 100m

Fr N or S on D213 exit sp Les Rochelets, site sp. 4*, Lge, mkd, hdg, pt shd, EHU (6-10A) €5-6.50; 30% statics; adv bkg acc; ccard acc; games rm; games area; bike hire. *"Gd site for families; lots of entmnt & activities in high ssn; great location."* **€29.60** **2024**

ST BREVIN LES PINS *2G3* (2.4km S Coastal) *47.23514, -2.16739* **Camping Le Fief,** 57 Chemin du Fief, 44250 St Brévin-les-Pins **02 40 27 23 86; camping@lefief.com; www.lefief.com**

€7 (covrd, htd) sand 800m

Fr Nantes dir St Nazaire. After St Nazaire bdge S on D213. Pass Leclerc & exit sp St Brévin-l'Océan/La Courance. At rndabt foll sp Le Fief. 4*, Lge, hdstg, mkd, pt shd, EHU (8A) €6; gas; bbq (charcoal, gas); red long stay; TV; 30% statics; Eng spkn; adv bkg acc; ccard acc; sauna; gym; games area; waterslide; games rm; jacuzzi; CKE. *"Excel for families; wellness cent; fitness rm; waterpark & waterslide etc adj; vg leisure facs."* **€34.00, 4 Apr-20 Sep.** **2024**

See advertisement

ST BRIAC SUR MER *2E3* (0.5km S Coastal) *48.61493, -2.12779* **Camping Le Pont Laurin,** Route de la Vallée Gatorge, 35800 St Briac-sur-Mer **02 99 88 34 64; contact@ouest-camping.com; www.ouest-camping.com**

€1.50 sand 1km

Fr St Briac, 500m S on D3. 2*, Lge, hdg, mkd, hdstg, pt shd, EHU (10A) €3 (poss rev pol); 40% statics; Eng spkn; adv bkg acc; ccard acc; games area; sailing; tennis nr; CKE. *"Peaceful site; welcoming, helpful staff; clean, modern san facs; excel beaches; canoe hire nr; sports cent adj; gd walking; walking dist to shops, rest etc; interesting town; highly rec."* **€26.00, 1 Apr-30 Sep.** **2023**

ST CAST LE GUILDO *2E3* (0.5km N Coastal) *48.63690, -2.26900* **Camping Le Châtelet,** Rue des Nouettes, 22380 St Cast-le-Guildo **02 96 41 96 33; info@lechatelet.com; www.lechatelet.com**

€7 (covrd, htd) sand 300m

Site sp fr all dir & in St Cast-le-Guildo but best rte: fr D786 at Matignon take D13 into St Cast-le-Guildo, turn L after Intermarché supmkt on R; foll sm site sp. Or app on D19 fr St Jaguel. Care needed down ramp to main site. (NB Avoid Matignon cent Wed due to mkt). 5*, Lge, mkd, hdg, pt shd, pt sl, terr, EHU (10A) inc; gas; bbq (charcoal, elec); TV; 50% statics; adv bkg acc; ccard acc; games rm; golf 2km; fishing. *"Site o'looks coast; o'fits over 7m by req; extra for sea view pitches; gd for families; helpful staff; modern unisex san facs; bike hire 500m; gates clsd 2230-0700; access to some pitches diff lge o'fits; mkt Mon; excel site."* **€50.00, 8 Apr-17 Sep, B11.** **2022**

ST CAST LE GUILDO *2E3* (3.5km S Rural) *48.58441, -2.25691* **Camping Le Château de Galinée,** Camping Château de Galinée, Rue de Galinée, 22380 Saint Cast Le Guildo **02 96 41 10 56; galinee@capfun.com; www.chateaudegalinee.com**

€4.50 (htd) (covrd, htd, indoor) sand 4km

W fr St Malo on D168 thro Ploubalay. At La Ville-es-Comte branch onto D786 & go thro Notre Dame-du-Guildo. Approx 2km after Notre Dame-du-Guildo turn 3rd L into Rue de Galinée & foll sp to site. Do not go into St Cast. 4*, Lge, mkd, hdg, pt shd, EHU (10A) inc; bbq; cooking facs; red long stay; TV; 30% statics; Eng spkn; adv bkg acc; ccard acc; sauna; games area; waterslide; horseriding 6km; games rm; tennis; golf 3km; fishing; mini golf; CKE. *"Peaceful, family site in lovely area; spacious, well laid-out pitches; helpful staff; modern, clean, excel san facs; pitches poss muddy after rain; fishing pond; excel rest; mkt Fri & Mon; identity bracelet to be worn at all times."* **€55.00, 10 May-5 Sep, B27.** **2022**

ST CHELY D'APCHER *9D1* (3km N Rural) *44.81644, 3.27074* **Cosy Camping,** 48200 St Chély-d'Apcher **06 42 10 49 04; cosycamping48@gmail.com; cosy-camping.com**

€1 nr nr nr

Fr N on A75 J33 onto D809, 2nd exit of rndabt, site 100m on L. Fr S J34 onto D809 thro vill dir Clermont Ferand. Site 1km on R after vill. 2*, Med, hdg, pt shd, EHU (10A) inc; twin axles; TV; 5% statics; Eng spkn; adv bkg acc; games area; games rm; CKE. *"Friendly, helpful staff; gd walks; gd NH/long stay; horse riding adj; gd."* **€18.30, 1 Apr-6 Oct.** 2023

ST CHINIAN *10F1* (2km W Rural) *43.42082, 2.93395* **Camp Municipal Les Terrasses,** Route de St Pons, 34360 St Chinian **06 12 90 14 55; campinglesterrasses@outlook.fr; www.campinglesterrasses.net**

nr

On main Béziers-St Pons rd, D612, heading W on o'skts of St Chinian. Site on L. Med, unshd, terr, EHU (10A) €4. *"Attractive site with gd views; sm pitches; diff access some pitches; terraced site; quiet until school hols; pool; friendly hosts."* **€12.00, 1 Apr-6 Nov.** 2022

ST CHRISTOPHE *7A3* (2.5km NE Rural) *46.01467, 0.87679* **Camping & Gites En Campagne,** Essubras, 16420 St Christophe **05 45 31 67 57; info@encampagne.com; www.encampagne.com**

€2 (htd) (covrd, htd)

Fr Bellac take D675 direction Saint-Junien. In Chene Pignier turn R on D9/D82 to Confolens. In Saint-Christophe turn R on D330 to Nouic. Site on L in 2.6km. 3*, Sm, mkd, hdg, pt shd, EHU (6-10A) inc; bbq; Eng spkn; adv bkg acc; games area; games rm; bike hire; pingpong table; petanque court; CCI. *"Excel; tourist attractions info avail; hiking/biking rtes; gd site but busy due to festival; gd value for money."* **€28.00, 1 Apr-1 Oct.** 2022

ST CIRQ LAPOPIE *7D3* (2km N Rural) *44.46926, 1.68135* **Camping La Plage,** Porte Roques, 46330 St Cirq-Lapopie **05 65 30 29 51; camping-laplage@wanadoo.fr; www.campingplage.com**

€2

Exit Cahors on D653, in Vers take D662 sp Cajarc. In 20km turn R at Tour-de-Faure over narr bdge, sp St Cirq-Lapopie, site 100m on R beside Rv Lot. 4*, Med, mkd, shd, EHU (6-16A) €4-5; bbq; 5% statics; Eng spkn; adv bkg acc; watersports; canoeing; CKE. *"Pleasant, clean & tidy rvside site; v shady; LS site yourself, pay later; friendly, helpful owner; gd walking; excel."* **€29.10, 6 Apr-28 Sep.** 2024

ST CIRQ LAPOPIE *7D3* (2.5km S Rural) *44.44871, 1.67468* **FFCC Camping La Truffière,** Route de Concots, 46330 St Cirq-Lapopie **05 65 30 20 22; contact@camping-truffiere.com; www.camping-truffiere.com**

€1.50 (htd) (htd)

Take D911, Cahors to Villefranche rd; in 20km turn N onto D42 at Concots dir St Cirq for 8km - site clearly sp. NB Do not app fr St Cirq-Lapopie. 3*, Med, shd, pt sl, terr, EHU (10A) €4; TV; phone; Eng spkn; adv bkg acc; ccard acc; fishing 3km; bike hire; CKE. *"Well-kept site in gd location; friendly owners; excel but dated san facs (2014), ltd LS; most pitches in forest clearings; muddy when wet; lovely pool; gd; 2m fr fairytale vill of St Cirq Lapopie, a must see; site 11m fr nearest supmkt."* **€27.10, 6 Apr-29 Sep.** 2024

ST CLAUDE *9A3* (2km S Rural) *46.37153, 5.87171* **Campsite Flower Camping Le Martinet,** 12 le Martinet, 39200 St Claude **03 84 45 00 40 or 03 84 41 42 62 (LS); campinglemartinet@mairie-saint-claude.fr; www.camping-saint-claude.fr**

nr

On ent town foll 1-way, under bdge mkd 4.1m high, then take R turn 'Centre Ville' lane to next traff lts. Turn R then immed L sp Genève, turn R 300m after Fiat g'ge onto D290, site on R. 3*, Med, pt shd, EHU (5A) €2.30; gas; Eng spkn; adv bkg acc; ccard acc; tennis; fishing; CKE. *"Site now pt of Flower camping group (2014), completely renovated; htd pool adj; has 3 modern san blocks; excel walking; v attractive town; gd."* **€23.00, 1 Apr-30 Sep.** 2024

ST CYPRIEN PLAGE *10G1* (3km S Coastal) *42.59939, 3.03761* **Camping Cala Gogo,** Ave Armand Lanoux, Les Capellans, 66750 St Cyprien-Plage **04 68 21 07 12; camping@calagogo66.fr; www.camping-le-calagogo.fr**

€3-4 (htd) sand adj

Exit A9 at Perpignan Nord onto D617 to Canet-Plage, then D81; site sp bet St Cyprien-Plage & Argelès-Plage dir Les Capellans. 5*, V lge, hdg, mkd, pt shd, EHU (6A) €2-4; TV; 30% statics; Eng spkn; adv bkg acc; ccard acc; tennis; games area; CKE. *"Excel site; gd pitches; lovely beach; v helpful staff."* **€57.90, 8 Apr-30 Sep.** 2023

ST DENIS D'OLERON *7A1* (3.7km S Coastal) *46.00480, -1.38480* **Camping Les Seulières,** 1371 Rue des Seulières, 17650 Saint-Denis-d'Oléron **05 46 47 90 51; contact@lesseulieres.com; www.lesseulieres.com**

€2 nr sand 0.3km

Fr D734 Cheray-Saint-Denis-d'Oleron. L twd La Jausiere, cont onto Grande Rue a Chaucre and foll sp to campsite. 4*, Med, mkd, pt shd, EHU (10A); gas; 45% statics; Eng spkn; adv bkg acc; ccard acc; CCI. *"Very nice beach; sep cycling rtes (plan provided)."* **€24.00, 5 Apr-29 Sep.** 2024

ST DONAT SUR L'HERBASSE *9C2* (0.5km S Rural) *45.11916, 4.99290* **Camping Domaine Les Ulèzes,** Route de Romans, 26260 St Donat-sur-l'Herbasse **04 75 47 83 20; www.camping-des-ulezes.fr**

€2 (htd)

Exit A7 junc 13 onto D532 dir Romans-sur-Isère. In 5km turn N onto D67 thro St Donat. Site on edge of vill off D53 dir Peyrins, well sp. 4*, Med, mkd, hdg, pt shd, EHU (6-10A) €3.50-4.50; bbq (elec, gas); TV; 10% statics; Eng spkn; adv bkg acc; ccard acc; games rm; ice; games area; CKE. *"Lovely rvside site; gd size pitches; immac; excel facs; welcoming, friendly owners; canal-side walk to town; gd touring base; vg; rec; serviced pitches."* **€30.00, 30 Mar-25 Oct.** 2024

"We must tell the Club about that great site we found"

Get your site reports in by mid-August and we'll do our best to get your updates into the next edition.

ST EMILION *7C2* (3km N Rural) *44.91695, -0.14160* **Camping Yelloh Saint Emilion,** 1000 route de Trimoulet, 33330 St Emilion **05 57 24 75 80; info@camping-saint-emilion.com; www.camping-saint-emilion.com**

€6 (covrd, htd)

NB Trailer c'vans not permitted in cent of St Emilion. Fr A10 exit junc 39a sp Libourne onto D670. In Libourne turn E on D243 twd St Emilion. On o'skts of St Emilion turn L onto D122 dir Lussac & Montagne; site on R by lake in 3km. Or fr S, foll site sp off D670 to Libourne, nr Les Bigaroux. NB D122 S of St Emilion unsuitable for c'vans. 4*, Lge, hdstg, mkd, hdg, shd, EHU (10A) inc; gas; bbq (gas); sw nr; TV; 40% statics; phone; Eng spkn; adv bkg acc; ccard acc; waterslide, bike hire; watersports nr; tennis; canoeing; fishing; CKE. *"Lovely, peaceful, well-run lakeside site; owners friendly & helpful; gd sized & shd pitches; pedalos avail; suitable lge o'fits; no o'fits over 10m; mountain bike circuit; clean, modern san facs but inadequate; free shuttle bus service to St Emilion; gd cycle rtes; poss boggy when wet; excel."* **€48.00, 23 May - 13 Sep, D08.** 2024

See advertisement

FRANCE

ST EMILION *7C2* (9km SE Rural) *44.85138, -0.10683* **Aire St Emilion Domaine du Château Gerbaud,** 33000 St Pey-d'Armens **06 03 27 00 32 (mob) or 05 57 41 34 92; contact@chateau-gerbaud.com; www.chateau-gerbaud.com**

12 MSP

Fr Libourne SE on D670/D936 dir Castillon-la-Bataille. In St Pey-d'Armens at bar/tabac foll sp Château Gerbaud vineyard. Eng spkn. *"Parking for max 48 hrs; friendly, lovely site among the vines."* **€5.00** **2024**

STE ENGRACE *8F1* (5km NW Rural) *43.01600, -0.85786* **FFCC Camping Ibarra,** Quartier Les Casernes, 64560 Ste Engrâce **05 59 28 73 59; www.ibarra-chantina.com**

D918 S fr Tardets-Sorholus; in 2km turn R onto D26; in 6km to L onto D113 sp Ste Engrâce; site on R in 5km. Site clearly sp just bef La Caserne. NB not suitable car+c'van. Sm, mkd, pt shd, EHU (5A) €1.80; bbq (sep area); 8% statics; CKE. *"Pleasant site on rv bank; scenic views; spectacular Kakuetta gorges nrby; vg; narr rd thro gorge for several kms bef site."* **€11.50, 1 Apr-30 Sep.** **2024**

ST ETIENNE DE BAIGORRY *8F1* (0.5km N Rural) *43.18370, -1.33569* **Camp Municipal L'Irouleguy,** Borciriette, 64430 St Etienne-de-Baïgorry **05 59 37 43 96 or 05 59 37 40 80 (Mairie); camping.baigorri@orange.fr; animazioa5.wixsite.com/camping-de-baigorri**

nr

W on D15 fr St Jean-Pied-de-Port to St Etienne-de-Baigorry; site on R 300m bef junc with D948; ent next to wine co-operative. Fr N on D948, on ent St Etienne-de-Baïgorry turn L onto D15; site in 300m on L. NB Don't be put off by entry down track L of winery - can't see site fr rd. 3*, Med, shd, EHU (6A) €2.70; adv bkg acc; trout fishing; tennis adj. *"Scenic site by rv; lge pitches; plenty hot water; gas 100m; gd hill walking cent; birdwatching; htd pool adj; out of ssn call at Mairie to open site for NH; gd modern san facs."* **€9.00, 1 May-30 Nov.** **2024**

ST ETIENNE DE MONTLUC *2G4* (0.2km N Rural) *47.28002, -1.77967* **Camp Municipal de la Coletterie,** Rue de Tivoli, 44360 St Etienne-de-Montluc **02 40 86 97 44 or 02 40 86 80 26 (Mairie); campinglacoletterie@st-etienne-montluc.net / on line form; www.st-etienne-montluc.net**

12 €1.20 (htd) nr nr nr

Well sp fr N165 (E60) in both dirs. 3*, Sm, hdg, mkd, pt shd, pt sl, EHU (15A) €3.80; phone; adv bkg acc; fishing; games area; CKE. *"Vg; check open bef travelling."* **€10.00** **2024**

ST FLOUR *9C1* (4km N Rural) *45.05120, 3.10778* **Camping International La Roche Murat,** N9 15100 St Flour **04 71 60 43 63; www.camping-saint-flour.com**

(htd) nr

Fr N or S on A75 exit junc 28; sp off rndabt on St Flour side of m'way. Site ent visible 150m fr rndabt. 3*, Med, hdg, mkd, pt shd, terr, EHU (16A) inc (poss rev pol); gas; Eng spkn; adv bkg acc; CKE. *"Busy site with gd views; sunny & secluded pitches; gd, clean facs; some pitches sm; when pitches waterlogged use site rds; old town high on hill worth visit; excel touring cent & conv NH fr A75; vg; v clean facs."* **€18.00, 1 Apr-1 Nov.** **2023**

ST FORT SUR GIRONDE *7B2* (4km SW Rural) *45.43278, -0.75185* **Camping Port Maubert,** 8 Rue de Chassillac, 17240 St Fort-sur-Gironde **05 46 04 78 86; bourdieu.jean-luc@wanadoo.fr; www.campingport maubert.com**

€2 nr

Exit A10 junc 37 onto D730 dir Royan. Foll sp Port Maubert & site. 2*, Sm, hdg, mkd, shd, EHU (10A) €3.50; gas; bbq; red long stay; TV; 10% statics; Eng spkn; adv bkg acc; ccard acc; bike hire; games rm; CKE. *"Pleasant, well-run site; LS ltd facs, OK NH; great loc; slightly scruffy san facs."* **€16.00, 1 Apr-30 Oct.** **2022**

STE FOY LA GRANDE *7C2* (1km NE Rural) *44.84426, 0.22468* **Camping de la Bastide,** Allée du Camping, 2 Les Tuileries, Pineuilh, 33220 Ste Foy-la-Grande **05 57 46 13 84; contact@camping-bastide.com; www.camping-bastide.com**

€2 nr nr

Fr W go thro town & turn off at D130 to site, well sp on Rv Dordogne. 3*, Med, mkd, pt shd, EHU (10A) €3 (poss rev pol); 10% statics; phone; Eng spkn; adv bkg acc; ccard acc; canoeing; games rm; jacuzzi; fishing; CKE. *"Pretty, well-cared for site; sm pitches; helpful, lovely British owners; immac, modern san facs; high kerb stones onto pitches - poss diff lge o'fits; mkt Sat; excel; ACSI acc; walking dist to supmkt & town; v clean site; v peaceful."* **€27.00, 14 Apr-16 Oct.** **2024**

ST GAUDENS *8F3* (1km W Rural) *43.11000, 0.70839* **Camp Municipal Belvédère des Pyrénées,** Rue des Chanteurs du Comminges, 31800 St Gaudens **05 61 94 78 00; mairie@stgo.fr; www.stgo.fr**

€1.50 (htd) nr

Foll camping sp fr St Gaudens town cent on D817 dir Tarbes. Site ent at top of hill on N side. Last rd sp is 'Belvédère'. 3*, Med, pt shd, EHU (4-13A) €3.50-6; gas. *"Pleasant site; facs clean; gates clsd 1200-1500 & 2300-0700."* **€15.00, 1 Jun-30 Sep.** **2024**

ST GAULTIER *4H2* (1km W Rural) *46.63406, 1.40863* **Camping L'Oasis du Berry,** Rue de la Pierre Plate, 36800 St Gaultier **02 54 47 17 04 or 06 79 90 77 97; contact@camping-oasisduberry.fr; camping-oasisduberry.fr**

€1.40 (htd)

Appr fr W (fr Le Blanc) on D951; turn R at sp St Gaultier, then foll sp L'Oasis du Berry. Look out for sp in vill. 4*, Med, hdg, mkd, pt shd, terr, EHU (4-10A) €2.50-3.50; bbq; 60% statics; Eng spkn; adv bkg acc; games area; CKE. *"Pleasant site in wooded surroundings; nice clean san facs; takeaway; gd pool; gd walks nrby; nr Voie Verte track; nr Brenne Regional Park; most pitches sl; gd."* **€19.00, 1 Apr-6 Nov. 2024**

ST GENIX SUR GUIERS *9B3* (0.3km SE Urban) *45.58878, 5.64252* **Les Bords du Guiers,** Route de Pont Beauvoisin, 73240 Saint Genix sur Guiers **04 76 31 71 40; info@lesbordsduguiers.com; www.lesbordsduguiers.com**

On reaching vill on D1516 foll sp Le-Pont-de-Beauvoisin, site 300m on R. 3*, Med, mkd, hdg, pt shd, EHU (8-10A); bbq; twin axles; Eng spkn; games area; games rm. *"Excel, quiet site; bike hire; v helpful owners; gd base for site seeing or star watching; town cent 5 mins walk; mkt day Wed."* **€25.70, 29 Mar-28 Sep. 2024**

"I need an on-site restaurant"

We do our best to make sure site information is correct, but it is always best to check any must-have facilities are still available or will be open during your visit.

ST GEORGES DU VIEVRE *3D2* (0.2km W Rural) *49.24248, 0.58040* **Camp Municipal du Vièvre,** Route de Noards, 27450 St Georges-du-Vièvre **02 32 42 76 79; www.camping-eure-normandie.fr**

(htd) nr

Fr traff lts on D130 in Pont Authou turn W onto D137 to St Georges-du-Vièvre; turn L after town square uphill sp camping; site 200m on L. If app fr S on N138 at Bernay take D834 sp Le Havre to Lieurey. Turn R onto D137 to St Georges, then turn R at camping sp by sw pool. 2*, Sm, hdg, pt shd, serviced pitches; EHU (5A) inc; bbq; sw nr; Eng spkn; adv bkg rec; bike hire; tennis 50m; CKE. *"Peaceful; gd facs & pitches; pool 150m; well-run site; interesting area; gd cycling; vg; basic but attractive site on edge of v picturesque vill; gd sized pitches."* **€12.00, 1 Apr-30 Sep. 2023**

ST GEORGES LES BAILLARGEAUX *4H1* (1km S Rural) *46.66452, 0.39477* **Camping Le Futuriste,** Rue du Château, 86130 St Georges-les-Baillargeaux **05 49 52 47 52; camping-le-futuriste.@wanadoo.fr; www.camping-le-futuriste.fr**

12 €2.80 (htd) (covrd, htd)

On A10 fr N or S, take Futuroscope exit 28; fr toll booth at 1st rndabt take 2nd exit. Thro tech park twd St Georges. At rndabt under D910 take slip rd N onto D910. After 150m exit D910 onto D20, foll sp. At 1st rndabt bear R, over rlwy, cross sm rv & up hill, site on R. 4*, Med, mkd, hdg, pt shd, serviced pitches; EHU (6A) inc (check earth & poss rev pol); gas; bbq; twin axles; TV; 10% statics; Eng spkn; adv bkg acc; ccard acc; games area; waterslide; games rm; lake fishing; CKE. *"Lovely, busy, secure site; well-kept; friendly, helpful family owners; vg clean facs, ltd LS - facs block clsd 2200-0700; vg poolwith waterslide for kids & adults; hypmkt 2km; vg for families; ideal touring base for Poitiers & Futuroscope (tickets fr recep); vg value, espec in winter; conv a'route; excel."* **€33.00 2023**

ST GERVAIS D'AUVERGNE *7A4* (8km E Rural) *46.02741, 2.89894* **Camp Municipal Les Prés Dimanches,** 22, Rue de la Sioule, 63390 Châteauneuf-les-Bains **04 73 86 41 50 or 06 50 02 05 97; campingdelasioule@gmail.com; campingdelasioule.com**

(htd) nr nr

Fr Montaigut take N144 S twd Riom & Clermont-Ferrand. In 9km at La Boule S onto D987 to St Gervais. Take D227 E to Chateuneuf-les-Bains. In 7km L onto D109. Site thro vill on R. 3*, Sm, hdg, mkd, pt shd, EHU (6A) inc; adv bkg acc; fishing nr; canoeing nr; tennis nr; CKE. *"Lovely, well-kept site; helpful warden; spa baths 500m; excel; gd walks."* **€18.00, 30 Apr-15 Oct. 2024**

ST GERVAIS LES BAINS *9B4* (10km SE Rural) *45.80275, 6.72207* **Camping Le Pontet,** 2485 Route de Notre-Dame-de-la-Gorge, 74170 Les Contamines-Montjoie **04 50 47 04 04; welcome@campinglepontet.fr; www.campinglepontet.fr**

12 (htd) nr

Fr St Gervais take D902 to Les Contamines-Montjoie (sp); go thro vill & foll sp to Notre Dame-de-la-Gorge; site in 2km on L, clearly sp. 3*, Lge, hdstg, mkd, pt shd, EHU (2-10A) €3-9.90; phone; Eng spkn; adv bkg acc; ccard acc; tennis; horseriding; fishing. *"Mkd alpine walks; ski lift 200m; leisure/sports park adj; lake adj; excel new owners; owner is a ski instructor & mountain guide."* **€26.00 2024**

FRANCE

FRANCE

ST GERVAIS LES BAINS *9B4* (2.6km S Rural) *45.87333, 6.72000* **Camping Les Dômes de Miage,** 197 Route des Contamines, 74170 St Gervais-les-Bains **04 50 93 45 96; info@camping-mont-blanc.com; www.natureandlodge.fr**

€2 (htd) nr nr

Exit A40 junc 21; fr N thro St Gervais, at sm rndabt in cent foll sp Les Contamines onto D902, site 2km on L. 4*, Med, mkd, pt shd, EHU (6A) €3.50 (poss rev pol); gas; bbq; TV; bus adj; Eng spkn; adv bkg req; ccard acc; tennis 800m; fishing 1km; games area; CKE. *"Superb, well-kept, perfect, family-owned site in beautiful location at base of Mt Blanc; welcoming, helpful & friendly; lux chalet to rent; bike hire 800m; immac san facs; conv Tramway du Mont Blanc excursions; mkt Thurs; bkg fee; htd pool 800m; excel; free bus service to delightful sm town."* **€31.00, 15 May-16 Sep.** **2023**

"Satellite navigation makes touring much easier"

Remember most sat navs don't know if you're towing or in a larger vehicle – always use yours alongside maps and site directions.

ST GILLES CROIX DE VIE *2H3* (4km SE Coastal) *46.67095, -1.90874* **Camping Les Cyprès,** 41 Rue du Pont du Jaunay, 85800 St Gilles-Croix-de-Vie **02 51 55 38 98; contact@camping-lescypres85.com; www.camping-lescypres85.com/en**

€3.30 (covrd, htd) sand 600m

Site on S end of St Gilles-Croix-de-Vie off D38, after rndabt sp Le Jaunay turn sharp L - hard to spot. 4*, Lge, hdg, shd, EHU (10A) €3; gas; red long stay; 12% statics; Eng spkn; adv bkg req; ccard acc; jacuzzi; CKE. *"Excel for family hols; family-run site; red facs LS; footpath along rv to town cent; busy & noisy in high ssn."* **€38.70, 8 Apr-18 Sep.** **2024**

See advertisement

ST GILLES CROIX DE VIE *2H3* (4km SE Urban/Coastal) *46.67113, -1.90356* **Chadotel Le Domaine de Beaulieu,** Rue du Parc, Route des Sables-d'Olonne, 85800 Givrand **02 51 33 05 05; info@chadotel.com; www.chadotel.com**

€3.20 sand 1km

S on D38 fr St Gilles Croix-de-Vie, site sp on L. 4*, Lge, hdg, mkd, pt shd, serviced pitches; EHU (6A) inc (poss long lead req); gas; bbq (gas); red long stay; TV; adv bkg acc; ccard acc; waterslide; tennis; golf 5km; CKE. *"Gd site for families; red facs LS; low trees poss diff; gd; excel value for money; lovely site; friendly, helpful Eng spkn staff."* **€55.00, 5 Apr-20 Sep.** **2024**

ST GIRONS PLAGE *8E1* (0.8km NE Coastal) *43.95436, -1.35689* **Campéole Camping Les Tourterelles,** 40560 Vielle St Girons **02 53 81 70 00; tourterelles@campeole.com; www.ms-vacances.com**

€1 nr sand 200m

Exit N10 at Castets & take D42 W to St Girons, then to St Girons-Plage. 4*, Lge, shd, pt sl, EHU (6A) €3.90; bbq; games rm; games area. *"Site in pine trees; footpath to dunes & beach."* **€42.72, 4 May-22 Sep.** **2024**

ST GIRONS PLAGE *8E1* (1km E Coastal) *43.95105, -1.35276* **Camping Eurosol,** Route de la Plage, 40560 St Girons-Plage **05 58 47 90 14; contact@camping-eurosol.com; www.camping-eurosol.com**

€5 (covrd, htd) sand 700m

Turn W off D652 at St Girons on D42. Site on L in 4km. 4*, Lge, pt shd, pt sl, serviced pitches; EHU (10A) inc; gas; sw nr; TV; 10% statics; tennis; games rm; bike hire; games area; horseriding adj. *"Pitches poss tight for long vans; excel for beach."* **€30.00, 21 May - 18 Sep, A27.** **2022**

STE HERMINE *2H4* (11km NE Rural) *46.59764, -0.96947* **Camping Le Colombier (Naturist),** 85210 St Martin-Lars **02 51 27 83 84; contact@lecolombier.fr; www.lecolombier-naturisme.com**

€4.50 nr

Fr junc 7 of A83 take D137 N; 3km past Ste Hermine turn R onto D52 to Le Poteau; turn L onto D10 to St Martin-Lars; 150m past St Martin-Lars turn R sp Le Colombier. Site ent on L in 200m.
4*, Lge, hdstg, hdg, mkd, pt shd, pt sl, EHU (16A) €4.50; gas; 50% statics; Eng spkn; adv bkg acc; ccard acc; jacuzzi; sauna. *"Well-run site; diff areas diff character; lge pitches; friendly Dutch owners; san facs clean but tired; gd walking in site grnds & local area; conv Mervent National Park; excel; superb facs; gd loc."*
€29.00, 1 Apr-1 Oct. **2023**

"There aren't many sites open at this time of year"

If you're travelling outside peak season remember to call ahead to check site opening dates – even if the entry says 'open all year'.

ST HILAIRE DE RIEZ *2H3* (6km N Rural) *46.76332, -1.95839* **Camping La Puerta del Sol,** 7 Chemin des Hommeaux, 85270 St Hilaire-de-Riez **02 51 49 10 10; info@campinglapuertadelsol.com; www.campinglapuertadelsol.com**

€4 (htd) sand 4.5km

N on D38 fr Les Sables-d'Olonne; exit onto D69 sp Soullans, Challans, Le Pissot. At next rndabt take 3rd exit & foll lge sp to site. Site on R in 1.5km.
4*, Lge, mkd, hdg, pt shd, pt sl, serviced pitches; EHU (10A) inc (poss rev pol); bbq (elec, gas); TV; 50% statics; Eng spkn; adv bkg acc; ccard acc; tennis; games area; watersports 5km; horseriding; sauna; games rm; jacuzzi; bike hire; waterslide; fishing 2km; golf; CKE. *"Vg site; med sized pitches, some diff lge o'fits due odd shape; clean san facs; gd for families; no o'fits over 10m high ssn; gd touring base; lovely pools and playgrnd."* **€33.00, 1 Apr-30 Sep.** **2022**

ST HILAIRE DE RIEZ *2H3* (3.5km W Coastal) *46.72289, -1.97931* **Camp Municipal de La Plage de Riez,** Allée de la Plage de Riez, Ave des Mimosas, 85270 St Hilaire-de-Riez **02 51 54 36 59; www.campingplagederiez.com**

€3.90 sand adj

Fr St Hilaire take D6A sp Sion-sur-l'Océan. Turn R at traff lts into Ave des Mimosas, site 1st L.
3*, V lge, mkd, shd, pt sl, serviced pitches; EHU (10A) €3.40; gas; TV; 30% statics; Eng spkn; bike hire. *"Vg for dogs; pool 5km; exceptionally helpful manager."*
€22.00, 30 Mar-31 Oct. **2022**

ST HILAIRE DU HARCOUET *2E4* (1km W Urban) *48.58105, -1.09771* **FFCC Camp Municipal de la Sélune,** 50600 St Hilaire-du-Harcouët **02 33 49 43 74 or 02 33 49 70 06; info@st-hilaire.fr; www.st-hilaire.fr**

€0.70 nr

Sp on N side of N176 twd Mont St Michel/St Malo/ Dinan, on W side of town; well sp.
3*, Med, hdg, pt shd, pt sl, EHU (16A) €1.95; red long stay; CKE. *"Peaceful, beautifully maintained site; pool 300m; easy access; helpful, pleasant warden; superb san facs; gate locked 2200-0730; excel."*
€22.50, 23 Apr-16 Sep. **2024**

ST HONORE LES BAINS *4H4* (0.5km W Urban) *46.90413, 3.83919* **Camp Municipal Plateau du Guet,** 13 Rue Eugène Collin, 58360 St Honoré-les-Bains **03 86 30 74 87 (Mairie); mairie@sainthonorelesbains.fr; www.st-honore-les-bains.com**

(htd) nr nr nr

On D985 fr Luzy to St Honoré-les-Bains. In cent vill turn L on D106 twd Vandenesse. Site on L in 150m. Or N fr Château-Chinon 27km. Then D985 to St Honoré. 2*, Med, mkd, hdstg, pt shd, terr, EHU (10A) €2.90; adv bkg acc; CKE. *"Gd, modern san facs (part unisex); htd pool 300m; pleasant, conv site town, gd walking; get barrier key for early dep."*
€8.60, 1 Apr-26 Oct. **2024**

ST JEAN D'ANGELY *7B2* (3km WNW Rural) *45.94868, -0.53645* **Camping Val de Boutonne,** 56 Quai de Bernouet, 17400 St Jean-d'Angély **05 46 32 26 16; contact@campingcharentemaritime17.com; www.camping-charente-maritime-17.com/**

€2 nr nr

Exit A10 at junc 34; head SE on D939; turn R at 1st rndabt into town. Site sp. 3*, Med, mkd, shd, EHU (10A) €4; red long stay; TV; 10% statics; Eng spkn; adv bkg acc; ccard acc; CKE. *"Pleasant, friendly, well-kept site by Rv Boutonne; helpful owners; aquatic cent 500m; lovely pool, strict rules, men must wear speedos; gd, clean san facs, outdated; poss open in Oct - phone ahead; vg; lake with sm boating facs; rec; gd NH just off the A10; 10min walk to historic town; lge Sat mkt; no admittance until 14:30; gd rests."*
€25.20, 1 Apr-30 Sep. **2023**

ST JEAN DE LOSNE *6H1* (0.8km E Rural) *47.10232, 5.27521* **Camp Municipal Les Herlequins,** 17 chemin de la plage, 21170 St Jean-de Losne **03 80 39 22 26; 06 23 96 19 33; camping.les.herlequins@gmail.com; www.campinglesherlequins.fr/en**

12 (htd) nr sand

Fr A36 take Exit 1, Seurre, then D976 to St Jean-de-Losne. Fr rndabt with water tower foll site sp. Don't use Sat Nav which may take you around the town.
3*, Med, hdstg, mkd, hdg, pt shd, EHU (10A); bbq; TV; phone; Eng spkn; adv bkg acc; ccard acc. *'Boat hire adj R Saone; vg site.'* **€20.00** **2022**

ST JEAN DE LUZ *8F1* (2km NE Coastal) *43.40563, -1.64216* **Camping de la Ferme Erromardie,** 40 Chemin d'Erromardie, 64500 St Jean-de-Luz **05 59 26 34 26; contact@camping-erromardie.com; www.camping-erromardie.com**

€3 nr nr (htd, indoor) sand adj

Exit A63 junc 3 onto D810 sp St Jean-de-Luz. After 1km cross rlwy and turn immed sharp R sp Erromardie. Site ent on R in 3km just bef rest/bar. 4*, Lge, mkd, hdg, shd, EHU (6-16A) inc; gas; 80% statics; Eng spkn; adv bkg acc; CKE. *"Well-run, popular site; cheerful, helpful staff; ltd water pnts in 2nd field; lovely, sandy beaches; coastal walk into St Jean-de-Luz; Basque museum nrby; site in 3 sections, lge o'fits should ask for pitch on touring field; excel modern san facs."* **€45.00, 15 Mar-30 Sep.** **2024**

ST JEAN DE LUZ *8F1* (3km NE Coastal) *43.41339, -1.61710* **Camping Itsas-Mendi,** Acotz, 64500 St Jean-de-Luz **05 59 26 56 50; contact@itsas-mendi.com; www.itsas-mendi.com**

€2.20 (htd) (htd) 500m

Exit A63 junc 3 sp St Jean-de-Luz; take D810 dir Biarritz; in 3km turn L sp Acotz Plage & Camping; site well sp. 4*, Lge, hdg, shd, pt sl, terr, EHU (10A) inc; bbq; TV; phone; Eng spkn; games area; tennis; sauna; CKE. *"Friendly staff; excel; waterslides & aquatic area."* **€50.00, 22 Mar-3 Nov.** **2024**

ST JEAN DE LUZ *8F1* (10km SE Rural) *43.35748, -1.57465* **Camping d'Ibarron,** 64310 St Pée-sur-Nivelle **05 59 54 10 43; ibarron@natureetresidenceloisirs.com; www.camping-ibarron.com**

€1.60

Fr St Jean take D918 twd St Pée, site 2km bef St Pée on R of rd. 3*, Lge, shd, EHU (6A) €3.95; TV; 5% statics; phone; Eng spkn; adv bkg acc; games rm; CKE. *"Well-kept site in scenic location; spacious pitches; welcoming, helpful owner; gd san facs; on main rd & no footpath to vill; walk along rv into vill; mkt Sat; excel."* **€22.00, 23 Apr-30 Sep.** **2023**

ST JEAN DE LUZ *8F1* (8km SE Rural) *43.34591, -1.61724* **Camping Chourio,** 64310 Ascain **05 59 85 30 93; www.camping-chourio.fr**

nr nr

Fr St Jean-de-Luz take D918 sp Ascain. In 6km turn R at traff lts, in 250m over rv bdge & turn L at mini-rndabt. Site sp in town. 1*, Med, pt shd, EHU (6A) €2.80; phone; CKE. *"Friendly, family-owned, relaxed site in lovely countryside; conv Spanish border; Tues & Sat mkt St Jean-de-Luz; vg; v helpful owners; bar only 300mtrs."* **€12.00, 20 Mar-15 Nov.** **2023**

"That's changed – Should I let the Club know?"

If you find something on site that's different from the site entry, fill in a report and let us know. See camc.com/europereport.

ST JEAN DE LUZ *8F1* (3km SW Rural) *43.37064, -1.68629* **Camping Larrouleta,** 210 Route de Socoa, 64122 Urrugne **05 59 47 37 84; info@larrouleta.com; www.larrouleta.com**

12 €3 (htd) (covrd, htd) sand 3km

Exit A63 junc 2 St Jean-de-Luz Sud. Pass under D810 & take 1st L sp Urrugne. Loop back up to N10 & turn R, site sp in 500m. Or fr S on D810, 2km beyond Urrugne vill (by-pass vill), turn L into minor rd, site 50m on R. 3*, Lge, hdstg, mkd, hdg, pt shd, EHU (10A) inc (poss rev pol); gas; sw; phone; bus 200m; Eng spkn; adv bkg req; ccard acc; games area; boating; tennis; fishing; CKE. *"Pleasant, well-run family site nr lake; satisfactory san facs (unisex LS) & pool; friendly & helpful (ask for dir on dep to avoid dangerous bend); some pitches unrel in wet but can park on site rds/hdstg; poss ltd facs LS; conv A63, Biarritz & en rte Spain; excel; conv m'way & hypmkt/fuel 1.5km; nice walk to Urrugne & St Jean to Luz; lots of hot water shwrs."* **€24.00** **2022**

See advertisement

ST JEAN DE LUZ *8F1* (9km SW Rural) *43.33277, -1.68527* **Le Camping du Col d'Ibardin,** Route d'Ascain, 64122 Urrugne **05 59 54 31 21; info@col-ibardin.com; www.col-ibardin.com**

€3 (htd)

Exit A63 junc 2, ignore slip rd to R 50m, turn L & in 100m turn R onto D810 S. In 2km at rndabt foll sp Col d'Ibardin, Ascain; after 4km site on R immed past minor rd to Col d'Ibardin. 4*, Med, hdstg, mkd, hdg, pt shd, pt sl, terr, serviced pitches; EHU (10A) inc; gas; bbq; sw nr; red long stay; TV; 50% statics; phone; Eng spkn; adv bkg acc; ccard acc; games rm; tennis; games area; CKE. *"Lovely, well-run site in woodland; fair sized pitches; helpful, friendly owner; gd san facs; pleasant bar/rest; mountain rlwy nr; gd touring base for Pyrenees & N Spain; excel."*
€63.00, 26 Mar - 11 Nov, A15. **2022**

ST JEAN DE MAURIENNE *9C3* (1km SE Urban) *45.27034, 6.35023* **Camp Municipal des Grands Cols,** 422 Ave du Mont-Cenis, 73300 St Jean-de-Maurienne **09 52 17 46 55; info@campingdesgrandscols.com; www.campingdesgrandscols.com**

€1 nr

Site sp fr D1006 in St Jean-de-Maurienne; site behind shops 100m fr town cent behind trees/ parking. 3*, Med, hdg, mkd, hdstg, pt shd, pt sl, serviced pitches; EHU (16A) €3; TV; Eng spkn; games rm; CKE. *"Warm welcome; helpful staff; clean san facs; pool 1.5km; interesting town; excel for serious cycling; gd NH for Fréjus tunnel; excel."*
€26.80, 10 May-21 Sep. **2024**

ST JEAN DE MONTS *2H3* (8km SE Coastal) *46.75638, -2.00749* **Camping La Yole,** Chemin des Bosses, Orouët, 85160 St Jean-de-Monts **02 51 58 67 17; contact@la-yole.com; www.vendee-camping.eu**

€8 (covrd, htd) sand 2km

Take D38 S fr St Jean-de-Monts dir Les Sable d'Olonne & Orouet. At Orouet turn R at L'Oasis rest dir Mouette; in 1.5km turn L at campsite sp; site on L. Situated bet D38 & coast, 1km fr Plage des Mouettes. On arr, park in carpark on R bef registering. 4*, Lge, mkd, hdg, pt shd, serviced pitches; EHU (10A) inc; bbq (gas); sw nr; TV; 80% statics; Eng spkn; adv bkg req; ccard acc; tennis; watersports 6km; fishing; jacuzzi; games rm; waterslide; horseriding 3km; CKE. *"Busy, gd, well-run site; no o'fits over 8m; sm dogs only; san facs clean, not spacious; excel cycle paths, mkt Wed & Sat; vg; friendly & helpful staff."*
€66.35, 11 Apr-24 Sep, A23. **2022**

ST JEAN DE MONTS *2H3* (1km W Coastal) *46.79931, -2.07378* **Camping Le Bois Joly,** 46 Route de Notre Dame-de-Monts, 85165 St Jean-de-Monts **02 51 59 11 63; bois-joly@vagues-oceanes.com; www.camping-leboisjoly.com**

€3 nr (covrd, htd) sand 1km

N on D38 circular around St Jean-de-Monts; at rndabt past junc with D51 turn R dir Notre Dame-de-Monts, site on R in 300m. 4*, Lge, hdg, mkd, pt shd, EHU (6A) inc rev pol; TV; 25% statics; phone; Eng spkn; adv bkg acc; ccard acc; games area; waterslide; sauna; CKE. *"Ideal for families; ACSI; gd san facs; lge pitches; coastal & inland cycleways nrby; excel."*
€48.00, 12 Apr-15 Sep. **2024**

ST JEAN DE MONTS *2H3* (1km NW Rural) *46.80083, -2.08013* **Camping La Buzelière,** 79 Rue de Notre Dame, 85169 St Jean-de-Monts **02 51 58 64 80; info@buzeliere.com; www.buzeliere.com**

€2.50 nr (htd) sand 1km

Take D38 fr St Jean-de-Monts to Notre Dame-de-Monts. Site on L. 4*, Med, hdg, mkd, pt shd, pt sl, serviced pitches; EHU (10A) inc; gas; bbq; TV; 20% statics; Eng spkn; adv bkg acc; ccard acc; games area; games rm; CKE. *"Many sports inc golf nrby; clean san facs; red facs LS; excel."*
€37.00, 1 May-22 Sep. **2024**

ST JEAN DE MONTS *2H3* (2.5km NW Coastal) *46.80311, -2.09300* **La Prairie,** 146 Rue du Moulin Casse, 85160 Saint-Jean-de-Monts **02 51 58 16 04; contact@campingprairie.com; campingprairie.com**

sand

Fr St Jean de Monts take D38 twds Notre Dame de Monts. Site abt 1.5km N of St Jean de Monts. Foll sp. Sm, mkd, pt shd, EHU (6A); bbq; twin axles; 40% statics; bus adj; Eng spkn; adv bkg acc; bike hire; games rm; sauna; games area. *"Gd site."*
€34.00, 1 Apr-9 Oct. **2022**

ST JEAN DE MONTS *2H3* (4km NW Coastal) *46.80978, -2.10971* **Camping Les Places Dorées,** Route de Notre Dame de Monts, 85160 St Jean-de-Monts **02 51 59 02 93 or 02 40 73 03 70 (LS); abridespins@aol.com; www.placesdorees.com**

€2.80 nr (htd) sand 800m

Fr Nantes dir Challons & St Jean-de-Monts. Then dir Notre Dame-de-Monts. 4*, Med, shd, pt sl, EHU (10A) inc; gas; Eng spkn; adv bkg acc; games area; games rm; waterslide; CKE. *"Vg; free entmnt children/adults; organised excursions; friendly family-run site; mountain views."* **€32.00, 1 Jun-10 Sep.** **2022**

FRANCE

ST JEAN DU GARD *10E1* (3.6km W Rural) *44.11250, 3.85320* **Camping Mas de La Cam,** Route de St André-de-Valborgne, 30270 St Jean-du-Gard **04 66 85 12 02; camping@masdelacam.fr; www.camping-cevennes.info**

nr

On S side of D 907, 1.1km W of W end of town by-pass, W of sp Camping les Baigneurs on non-Corniche rd to Florac. NB: Due to acute angle of slip rd off D907, if app fr W on D907 must go 500m past slip rd & make U-turn at layby opp D907-D9 junc. Slip rd sh but v narr; turn L after x-ing rv, L twd tennis court. Med, mkd, hdg, shd, pt sl, EHU (6A) €4.5; TV; bike hire; tennis. *"Excel site; friendly owners."* **€16.00, Easter-30 Sep.** 2024

ST JEAN PIED DE PORT *8F1* (3km W Rural) *43.17745, -1.25970* **Camping Narbaïtz Vacances Pyrénées Basques,** Route de Bayonne, 64220 Ascarat **05 59 37 10 13 or 06 09 39 30 42 (mob); camping-narbaitz@wanadoo.fr; www.camping-narbaitz.com**

(htd) WD MSP (htd)

Site on L of D918 St Jean to Bayonne 3km fr St Jean, sp. 4*, Med, hdg, mkd, pt shd, pt sl, EHU (6-10A) €4.50-5.50 (poss rev pol); 5% statics; phone; Eng spkn; adv bkg acc; ccard acc; trout fishing; kayaking; canoeing; cycling; CKE. *"Attractive, clean, pleasant, family-run site; lovely views; helpful owners; vg facs; rec m'vans use top of site when wet; nr Spanish border (cheaper petrol); excel; gd san facs."* **€43.00, 29 Apr-24 Sep.** 2023

ST JEAN PIED DE PORT *8F1* (2.4km NW Rural) *43.17304, -1.25416* **Europ Camping,** 64220 Ascarat **05 59 37 12 78; europcamping64@orange.fr; www.europ-camping.com**

€2.50 WD MSP nr

Site on D918 bet Uhart-Cize & Ascarat. Well sp. 4*, Med, hdg, mkd, pt shd, EHU (6A) €4 (poss rev pol); 30% statics; adv bkg acc; ccard acc; sauna; games area; games rm; CKE. *"Beautiful location; helpful staff; ltd facs LS; only basic food in bar/rest; grnd v soft when wet; vg."* **€33.00, 4 Apr-30 Sep.** 2022

ST JULIEN EN GENEVOIS *9A3* (5km SE Rural) *46.12015, 6.10565* **Kawan Village La Colombière,** 166 Chemin Neuf-Chef-Lieu, 74160 Neydens **04 50 35 13 14; contact@domaine-la-colombiere.com; www.camping-la-colombiere.com**

€2.50 (htd) WD MSP (covrd, htd)

Exit A40 junc 13 onto D1201 dir Cruseilles; in 1.75km turn L to Neydens; turn R at church; site on R in 200m. Site sp. NB: Do not go into St Julien-en-Genevois when towing. 4*, Med, hdstg, mkd, hdg, pt shd, pt sl, EHU (6-10A) inc, extra for 15A; gas; bbq; TV; 10% statics; Eng spkn; adv bkg acc; ccard acc; bike hire; lake fishing 1km; games rm; CKE. *"Family-owned site; friendly, helpful staff; boggy after heavy rain; farm produce; conv Geneva - guided tours high ssn; no o'fits over 10m high ssn; park & ride bus; open for m'vans all year; gd NH; excel; highly rec."* **€40.00, 1 Apr - 31 Oct, M08.** 2022

ST JUNIEN *7B3* (4km E Rural) *45.88078, 0.96539* **FFCC Camp Municipal de Chambery,** 87200 St Brice-sur-Vienne **05 55 02 42 92; mairiest-brice@wanadoo.fr; www.tourismelimousin.com**

(htd) nr

Fr St Junien take D32 E sp St Brice & St Victurnien; on leaving St Brice on D32 turn L & foll sp; site on L in 500m, on E edge of vill. Or app on D32 fr E, turn R onto C2 bef St Brice-sur-Vienne town sp, sp 'Campings & Gite Rural'. 2*, Sm, hdg, mkd, hdstg, pt shd, pt sl, serviced pitches; EHU (10A) €3.40; adv bkg acc; CKE. *"Peaceful, clean site in park; spacious pitches o'look lake & countryside; site yourself, office open 1hr am & pm; barrier clsd 2200-0700; conv Oradour-sur-Glane; excel; beautiful location; excel san facs; each pitch has own tap & drain; call to check if open."* **€10.00, 1 May-1 Sep.** 2024

ST JUST (CANTAL) *9C1* (0.5km W Urban) *44.89035, 3.21079* **FFCC Camp Municipal,** 15320 St Just **04 71 73 72 57, 04 71 73 70 48 or 06 31 47 05 15 (mob); info@saintjust.com; www.saintjust.com**

(htd) WD MSP

Exit junc 31 fr A75, foll sp St Chély-d'Apcher D909; turn W onto D448 twds St Just (approx 6km); sp with gd access. 3*, Med, mkd, pt shd, pt sl, terr, EHU (10A) €2.30; red long stay; phone; Eng spkn; ccard acc; tennis; bike hire; fishing. *"Vg site; friendly, helpful warden; ltd facs LS; excel tennis & pool; gd touring base; area for m'vans."* **€10.20, 1 May-30 Sep.** 2023

ST JUST EN CHEVALET *9B1* (1km NW Rural) *45.91459, 3.84026* **Camp Municipal Le Verdillé,** 42430 St Just-en-Chevalet **06 80 12 63 33; campingleverdille@sfr.fr; www.leverdille.com**

€1.70 WD MSP nr nr nr

Exit A72 at junc 4, join D53 NE twd St Just-en-Chevalet. Foll sp in town to camping/piscine. Due to steep gradients avoid D1 when towing. 2*, Med, hdg, pt shd, pt sl, EHU (16A) €3; 10% statics; phone; Eng spkn; adv bkg acc; tennis adj; CKE. *"Friendly owners; htd pool adj."* **€19.00, 1 May-30 Sep.** 2024

ST JUSTIN *8E2* (2.5km NW Rural) *44.00166, -0.23502* **Camping Le Pin,** Route de Roquefort, 40240 St Justin **05 58 44 88 91; campingdeslandes.40240@orange.fr; www.campingdeslandes40.com**

€2.50 WD MSP

Fr D933 in St Justin take D626 sp Requefort, site on L in 2km (sp says 3). 3*, Sm, mkd, hdg, pt shd, EHU (6-10A) inc; bbq; TV; 10% statics; Eng spkn; adv bkg acc; rv fishing 2km; games area; bike hire; horseriding; CKE. *"Pleasant, spacious site; new facs (2016); beautiful vill; rustic wooded setting; gd welcome; helpful owner; bread avail daily; sm pond, free fishing for campers; highly rec; excel modern clean san facs; Bastide town nrby; conv to & fr Spain; excel."* **€23.60, 3 Mar-1 Dec.** 2024

ST LARY SOULAN *8G2* (4km NE Rural) *42.84482, 0.33836* **Camping Le Lustou,** 89 Chemin d'Agos, 65170 Vielle-Aure **05 62 39 40 64; contact@lustou.com; www.lustou.com**

12 €1.80 (htd) WD nr

Exit A64 junc 16 & head S on D929. Thro Arreau & Guchen turn R onto D19 dir Vielle-Aure. Site on R just bef Agos. 3*, Med, hdg, pt shd, pt sl, EHU (6-10A) €6.80; gas; bbq; TV; 5% statics; phone; adv bkg acc; canoeing nr; fishing nr; tennis nr; games area; CKE. *"Organised walks in mountains by owner; excel skiing; immac facs; communal meals organised weekly (high ssn); excel site."* **€19.00** **2022**

ST LAURENT EN GRANDVAUX *6H2* (0.5km SE Rural) *46.57645, 5.96214* **Camp Municipal Le Champs de Mars,** 8 Rue du Camping, 39150 St Laurent-en-Grandvaux **03 84 60 19 30 or 06 03 61 06 61; champmars.camping@orange.fr; camping-saint-laurent-jura.fr**

(htd) WD MSP nr

E thro St Laurent on N5 twd Morez, site on R, sp `Caravaneige' at ent. 3*, Med, mkd, hdstg, pt shd, pt sl, serviced pitches; EHU (4-10A) €5-6.4; TV; 20% statics; phone; adv bkg acc; CKE. *"Gd site; peaceful LS; gd NH; friendly staff."* **€17.60, 1 Jan-30 Sep, 15 Dec-31 Dec.** **2024**

ST LAURENT SUR SEVRE *2H4* (1km W Rural) *46.95790, -0.90290* **Camping Le Rouge Gorge,** Route de la Verrie, 85290 St Laurent-sur-Sèvre **02 51 67 86 39; campinglerougegorge@wanadoo.fr; www.camping-lerougegorge-vendee.com**

€2.10 (htd) WD MSP

Fr Cholet on N160 dir La Roche-sur-Yon; at Mortagne-sur-Sèvre take N149 to St Laurent-sur-Sèvre. In St Laurent foll sp La Verrie on D111. Site on R at top of hill. Or take 762 S fr Cholet to St Laurent. Site sp in town. 3*, Med, hdg, mkd, pt shd, pt sl, EHU (4-13A) €2.95-4.10; 30% statics; adv bkg acc; lake fishing 800m; golf 15km; games area; CKE. *"Peaceful family site; woodland walks & mountain biking; attractive sm town; close to Puy du Fou Theme Park."* **€35.00, 1 Apr-30 Sep.** **2023**

ST LEGER SOUS BEUVRAY *4H4* (1km N Rural) *46.93157, 4.10088* **Camping De La Boutière,** 71990 St Léger-sous-Beuvray **06 80 40 81 28 or 03 85 82 48 86 (LS); camping@la-boutiere.com; www.la-boutiere.com**

€2.70 WD nr

Take N81 SW fr Autun dir Bourbon-Lancy & in approx 10km, turn R onto D61 to St Léger. Site sp in vill. Sm, mkd, pt shd, pt sl, EHU (6-10A) €3.70; twin axles; 5% statics; phone; CKE. *"Pleasant, well-kept, Dutch-owned site; gd, modern san facs; vg."* **€16.00, 1 Apr-31 Aug.** **2024**

ST LEONARD DE NOBLAT *7B3* (15km N Rural) *45.94311, 1.51459* **Camping Pont du Dognon,** 87240 St Laurent-les-Eglises **06 75 73 25 30; www.aupontdudognon.fr**

€2 (htd) WD shgl

Take D941 fr St Léonard-de-Noblat; after 1.5km turn L (N) on D19 thro Le Châtenet-en-Dognon. Site in approx 4km, bef St Laurent-les-Eglises. 3*, Med, hdg, mkd, pt shd, terr, EHU (6-16A) €3.50; gas; bbq; twin axles; adv bkg acc; tennis; bike hire; canoeing. *"Vg site."* **€13.00, 2 Apr-1 Oct.** **2022**

ST LEONARD DE NOBLAT *7B3* (2km S Rural) *45.82300, 1.49200* **Camping de Beaufort,** 87400 St Léonard-de-Noblat **06 17 12 86 18; camping@ville-saint-leonard.fr; www.campingdebeaufort.fr**

€1.50 (htd) WD

Leave A20 S-bound at junc 34 dir St Léonard, onto D941. In 18km on ent St Léonard, 300m after x-ing Rv Vienne, fork R (sp). Site on R in 2km. 3*, Med, hdg, pt shd, pt sl, EHU (15A) €3-4; phone; adv bkg acc; ccard acc; fishing; CKE. **€19.00, 2 Apr-7 Nov.** **2024**

ST MAIXENT L'ECOLE *7A2* (1.5km SW Urban) *46.40836, -0.21856* **Camp Municipal du Panier Fleuri,** Rue Paul Drévin, 79400 St Maixent-l'Ecole **05 49 05 53 21**

MSP nr nr

Take D611 twd Niort, at 2nd set of traff lts nr top of hill out of town turn L. Foll camping sps into ent. 3*, Med, mkd, pt shd, pt sl, EHU (10A); tennis. *"Warden on site am & eve, if office locked go to hse nr wc block; ltd/basic facs LS; htd pool adj; interesting town; NH en rte Spain; immac new htd san facs (2014)."* **€10.50, 1 Apr-15 Oct.** **2024**

ST MALO *2E4* (10km NE Rural) *48.67368, -1.92732* **Camping a la ferme La Vignette,** 35350 St Coulomb **02 99 89 08 42; francoise.morin600@orange.fr; www.facebook.com/campinglavignette**

12 WD 1km

Fr St Malo foll D355 E twds St Coulomb. Just bef vill turn L, sp 'Camping a la ferme'. Site in 400m on R. Sm, pt shd, pt sl, EHU (10A). *"Vg site; excellent for St Malo Ferry to Portsmouth, 20 mins drive to Port."* **€14.00** **2022**

ST MALO *2E4* (11km NE Coastal) *48.69000, -1.94200* **Camping des Chevrets,** La Guimorais, 35350 St Coulomb **02 99 89 01 90; contact@campingdeschevrets.fr; www.campingdeschevrets.fr**

WD MSP sand adj

St Malo to Cancale coast rd D201; La Guimorais on L 3km E of Rothéneuf, strt thro vill; fairly narr app. 3*, V lge, mkd, hdg, pt shd, pt sl, EHU (6A) €3.35 (poss rev pol); gas; bbq; red long stay; 50% statics; Eng spkn; adv bkg acc; ccard acc; games area; bike hire; CKE. *"Vg, beautiful location with 2 bays; vg, busy, well run site; bus fr St Malo to Cancale in the summer; statics in sep area; vg value LS; vg facs; conv for ferry."* **€35.50, 30 Mar-16 Oct.** **2023**

ST MALO *2E4* (5km SE Rural) *48.60916, -1.98663* **Camping Le P'tit Bois,** La Chalandouze, 35430 St Jouan des-Guérets **02 99 21 14 30; camping.ptitbois @wanadoo.fr; www.ptitbois.com**

€4-6 (covrd, htd) sand 2km

Fr St Malo take D137 dir Rennes; after o'skts of St Malo turn R twd St Jouan-des-Guérets, site sp. 4*, Lge, mkd, hdg, pt shd, serviced pitches; EHU (10A) inc; gas; bbq (elec, gas); TV; 75% statics; adv bkg acc; ccard acc; waterslide; games rm; tennis; bike hire; watersports 2km; CKE. *"Well-kept, well-run site; lge o'fits by request; busy even LS; min 3 persons high ssn; tidal rv fishing 2km; jacuzzi; turkish bath; friendly, helpful staff; gd clean san facs, one block unisex; some narr site rds poss diff lge o'fits; conv Le Mont-St Michel & ferries; excel."*
€52.00, 8 Apr-12 Sep, B03. **2022**

ST MALO *2E4* (2.7km S Coastal) *48.63558, -2.02731* **Camp Municipal Cité d'Alet,** Allée Gaston Buy, Saint-Servan 35400 St Malo **02 99 81 60 91; campsaintmalo@gmail.com; www.ville-saint-malo.fr/campings**

€2.95 nr nr nr sand 500m

Fr ferry terminal go twd St Malo, site sp at rndabt immed past docks. Fr all other dir foll sp for port/ ferry, then site sp. Site off Place St Pierre, St Servan-sur-Mer. App thro old pt of city poss diff for lge o'fits. 2*, Lge, hdstg, pt shd, pt sl, EHU (10A) inc (poss rev pol & long elec cable poss req); bbq (charcoal, elec, gas); twin axles; phone; bus 1km; Eng spkn; adv bkg acc; ccard acc; CKE. *"Well-run, scenic site; staff helpful & friendly; sm pitches, access to some diff lge o'fits; san facs basic but OK (poss v slippery); WW2 museum adj; noise fr harbour when foggy; mkt Fri; parts of site steep, lovely walks, cliff top views of Dinard & St Malo, walk to St Malo worth while; site feels cosy."*
€22.50, 26 Apr-21 May & 1 Jul-25 Sep. **2023**

ST MALO *2E4* (6km S Rural) *48.61469, -1.98663* **Camping Domaine de la Ville Huchet,** Rue de la Passagère, Quelmer, 35400 St Malo **02 99 81 11 83; info@lavillehuchet.com; www.lavillehuchet.com**

€3.50 (covrd, htd, indoor) sand 4km

Fr ferry port, foll sps for D137 dir Rennes; site sp fr 'Madeleine' rndabt on leaving St Malo. Or fr S on D137 take D301 sp St Malo cent. Take 1st exit at next 2 rndabts (thro indus est) & cont on this rd (sharp R-hand bend), then under bdge, site on R. Fr S head N on D137, merge onto D301, at rndabt take 1st exit onto Rue de la Grassinais, thro next rndabt. At next rndabt take 1st exit. Site on the L. 4*, Lge, hdg, mkd, pt shd, pt sl, EHU (6A) inc; bbq (charcoal, gas, sep area); TV; 40% statics; Eng spkn; adv bkg acc; waterpark; games area; games rm. *"Spacious site in grnds of sm chateau; helpful team; modern san facs; no o'fits over 7.4m except by request; lge pitches avail; some pitches v shady; conv ferries & Mont St Michel; excel; bus to St Malo adj."*
€40.00, 8 Apr- 18 Sep, B32. **2022**

See advertisement

STE MARIE DU MONT *1D4* (3km SE Coastal) *49.36564, -1.17721* **Camping La Baie des Veys,** Le Grand Vey, 50480 Ste Marie-du-Mont **02 33 71 56 90; contact@campinglabaiedesveys.com; www.campinglabaiedesveys.com**

€1.50 (htd)

N of Carentan exit N13 onto D913 thro Ste Marie-du-Mont. At lge calvary 2km after vill, turn R onto D115 sp Le Grand Vey. Turn R at sea edge, site on R in 100m. 3*, Med, hdg, mkd, pt shd, EHU (10A) €4; bbq; 10% statics; Eng spkn; adv bkg acc; bike hire. *"Site beside salt flats; helpful, friendly owners; gd birdwatching, fishing; conv Utah Beach, D-Day museums etc; nature reserve adj; nice site"*
€34.20, 6 Apr-20 Sep. **2024**

STES MARIES DE LA MER *10F2* (0.8km E Coastal) *43.45633, 4.43576* **Camping La Brise,** Rue Marcel Carrière, 13460 Les Stes Maries-de-la-Mer **04 90 97 84 67; info@camping-labrise.fr; www.camping-labrise.fr**

€5.20 (htd) MSP nr (htd) adj

Sp on o'skts on all rds. Take N570 fr Arles or D58 fr Aigues-Mortes. 3*, V lge, unshd, EHU (16A) €4.90; bbq; TV; 10% statics; fishing; site clsd mid-Nov to mid-Dec. *"Gd facs; v cr Aug; poss mosquitoes; gd security; beach improved with breakwaters; m'vans can use free municipal car park with facs; fitness area; recep open fr 0900-1700 but clsd 1200-1400; vg winter NH; pitches poorly mrkd, dirty & dusty."* **€17.00, 1 Jan-12 Nov & 15 Dec-31 Dec. 2022**

STES MARIES DE LA MER *10F2* (2.6km W Coastal) *43.45014, 4.40163* **Camping Le Clos du Rhône,** Route d'Aigues-Mortes, 13460 Stes Maries-de-la-Mer **04 90 97 85 99; info@camping-leclos.fr; www.camping-leclos.fr**

€6 WD MSP (htd) sand

Fr Arles take D570 to Stes Maries; fr Aigues Mortes, D58/D570. 4*, Lge, mkd, pt shd, serviced pitches; EHU (16A) inc; gas; bbq; cooking facs; twin axles; TV; 30% statics; phone; Eng spkn; adv bkg acc; ccard acc; horseriding adj; games area; games rm; bike hire; waterslide; CKE. *"Excel pool & facs; san facs clean, poss ltd & stretched LS; popular with families; private gate to beach; mosquitoes; rv boat trips adj; off rd bike & foot paths to town; vg."* **€42.20, 29 Mar-3 Nov. 2024**

ST MARTIN DES BESACES *1D4* (1.2km W Rural) *49.00889, -0.85955* **Camping Sous Les Etoiles,** La Groudière, 14350 St Martin-des-Besaces Calvados **06 37 87 99 53; info@sous-les-etoiles.camp; www.sous-les-etoiles.camp**

(htd) WD MSP

Fr Caen SW on A84 dir Rennes, Villers-Bocage & exit junc 41 to St Martin-des-Besaces. At traff lts in vill turn R. Site on L at end of Vill after gge after 500m. Fr Cherbourg foll sp St Lô onto m'way. After Torini-sur-Vire at junc with A84 foll sp Caen & exit J41, then as above. 2*, Sm, hdg, pt shd, pt sl, serviced pitches; EHU (6A) (poss rev pol); bbq; red long stay; twin axles; TV; Eng spkn; adv bkg acc; ccard acc; fishing; cycling; games rm; CKE. *"Pleasant CL-type orchard site; no arr bef 1400; lge pitches with garden; 'super' pitches extra cost; B&B in farmhouse; equestrian trails; lake adj; suitable for rallies up to 30 vans; c'van storage; war museum in vill; conv Caen ferries; new excel san facs (2019);excep helpful, new English owners (2018); easy reach of D Day beaches, Bayeaux, Falaises and Villers Bocage; excel."* **€26.00, 1 Mar-15 Nov. 2024**

ST MARTIN EN CAMPAGNE *3B2* (2km N Coastal) *49.96631, 1.20469* **Camping Domaine Les Goélands,** Rue des Grèbes, 76370 St Martin-en-Campagne **02 35 83 82 90; camping@mairie-petit-caux.fr; www.camping-les-goelands.fr**

€2 (htd) WD nr nr shgl 500m

Fr Dieppe foll D925 twd Le Tréport & Abbeville. Turn L at rndabt on D113 twd St Martin-en-Campagne. Cont thro vill to St Martin-Plage (approx 3km) & foll 'Camping' sp to site on L. 4*, Lge, hdg, mkd, hdstg, pt shd, pt sl, terr, serviced pitches; EHU (16A) inc (poss rev pol); gas; bbq; TV; 40% statics; Eng spkn; adv bkg acc; ccard acc; bike hire; waterslide 1km; tennis; fishing; CKE. *"Gd touring area; ltd recep hrs LS; no late arr area; poss resident workers LS; mkt Dieppe Sat; golf 20km; horseriding 15km; vg site; immac modern san facs(2017); v helpful recep."* **€23.00, 1 Apr-31 Oct. 2023**

ST MARTIN SUR LA CHAMBRE *9B3* (0.5km N Rural) *45.36883, 6.31458* **Camping Le Petit Nice,** Notre Dame-de-Cruet, 73130 St Martin-sur-la-Chambre **04 79 56 37 72 or 06 76 29 19 39 (mob); campinglepetitnice@yahoo.fr; www.campinglepetitnice.com**

12 €1 (htd) WD

Fr N on A43 exit junc 26 & foll sp to cent of La Chambre, thro town to rndabt & turn R into Rue Notre Dame-du-Cruet. Foll site sp & in 2km turn R thro housing, site on L in 200m. 3*, Sm, pt shd, terr, EHU (3-10A); 80% statics; Eng spkn; adv bkg acc; CKE. *"By stream with mountain views; clean, dated facs; gd location for hilly cycling; fair."* **€16.00 2022**

ST MARTIN SUR LA CHAMBRE *9B3* (1km SW Rural) *45.36146, 6.31300* **Camping Le Bois Joli,** 73130 St Martin-sur-la-Chambre **09 66 97 21 28 or 06 48 21 64 27; camping.le.bois.joli@wanadoo.fr; www.campingleboisjoli.com**

€4 WD

Leave A43 at junc 26 onto D213 sp La Chambre & Col de la Madeleine; foll camping sp (rd narr & winding in places); site on L. 2*, Med, mkd, pt shd, pt sl, terr, EHU (6A) inc; gas; bbq; red long stay; 20% statics; phone; Eng spkn; adv bkg acc; fishing; CKE. *"Helpful staff; mountain scenery; gd walking, skiing; guided walks; ltd facs LS; conv Fréjus Tunnel."* **€16.50, 5 Apr-6 Oct, A35. 2023**

ST MATHIEU 7B3 (3km E Rural) 45.71413, 0.78835 **Camp Municipal du Lac,** Les Champs, 87440 St Mathieu **05 55 00 34 30 (Mairie) or 05 55 00 30 26; mairie.saint.mathieu@orange.fr; www.saint-mathieu.fr/camping.html**

€3.50 nr nr

On D699 heading E in dir of Limoges 1.8km fr vill turn on L (N). Sp fr vill cent. 3*, Med, hdg, mkd, pt shd, terr, EHU €3; sw; windsurfing. *"Attractive, well-kept site; pleasant situation on lakeside; lge pitches; pedalos; site yourself, warden calls; beautiful lake with lots of activities."* **€14.00, 1 May-30 Sep. 2024**

STE MAURE DE TOURAINE 4H2 (6km NE Rural) 47.14831, 0.65453 **Camping Le Parc de Fierbois,** 37800 Ste Catherine-de-Fierbois **02 47 65 43 35; contact@fierbois.com; www.fierbois.com or www.les-castels.com**

€5 (covrd, htd, indoor)

S on D910 fr Tours, thro Montbazon & cont twd Ste Maure & Châtellerault. About 16km outside Montbazon nr vill of Ste Catherine look for site sp. Turn L off main rd & foll sp to site. Or exit A10 junc 25 onto D760E, then D910 N sp Tours; in 6.5 km turn R to Ste Catherine-de-Fierbois; site on L 1.5km past vill. 5*, Lge, mkd, hdg, pt shd, EHU (10A) €5; bbq; twin axles; TV; Eng spkn; adv bkg acc; ccard acc; games area; waterslide; tennis; bike hire; games rm; boating; fishing; CKE. *"Excel, well-kept family site; helpful staff; gd touring base; peaceful LS; rec."* **€64.00, 16 May - 28 Aug, L20. 2022**

See advertisement

STE MAURE DE TOURAINE *4H2* (1.5km SE Rural) *47.10483, 0.62574* **Camp Municipal Marans,** Rue de Toizelet, 37800 Ste Maure-de-Touraine **02 47 65 44 93; camping@sainte-maure-de-touraine.fr; http://www.sainte-maure-de-touraine.fr/**

€1.42 WD MSP nr nr nr

Fr A10 take Ste Maure exit junc 25 & foll D760 twd Loches. At 4th rndabt turn L & then immed R. Site on R in 500m. Site sp fr m'way. 2*, Med, mkd, pt shd, EHU (10A) €3.20 (poss long cables req); bbq; phone; Eng spkn; adv bkg acc; fishing; tennis. *"Well-kept, basic site; cheerful staff; gd, clean facs - poss stretched when busy; pool 1.5km; if office clsd site yourself; barrier down 2200-0700; roller blade court; late arr area outside barrier; no twin axles; poss travellers in sep area; vg; wifi around office area; lovely peaceful site."* **€9.00, 10 Apr-30 Sep.** **2023**

STE MAURE DE TOURAINE *4H2* (1.5km S Rural) *47.10861, 0.61440* **Aire de Service Camping-Cars Bois de Chaudron,** 37800 Ste Maure-de-Touraine **06 84 97 84 22**

12 MSP

Fr S on D910 dir Tours, as ent town, site on R adj junc at traff lts; sm sp on dual-c'way. Sm, EHU €2 (on only some pitches); Eng spkn. *"M'vans only; New Aire de Service (2009); warden calls; conv N/S journeys; easy to park; level, grass; friendly."* **€5.00** **2023**

STE MAURE DE TOURAINE *4H2* (10km W Rural) *47.10705, 0.51016* **Camping du Château de la Rolandière,** 37220 Trogues **02 47 58 53 71; contact@larolandiere.com; www.larolandiere.com**

€3 WD nr (htd)

Exit A10 junc 25 onto D760 dir Chinon & L'Ile-Bouchard. Site sp on S side of rd in 5.5km. 4*, Sm, hdg, mkd, pt shd, pt sl, EHU (10A) €4.40 (poss long lead req); bbq; TV; Eng spkn; adv bkg acc; games area; games rm; CKE. *"Beautiful, well-maintained, family-run site in chateau grnds; friendly, helpful owners; gd clean san facs; excel for young families, sh or long stay; gd dog walking; conv Loire chateaux; excel pool & sports field; highly rec; Villandry gdns to N; Richlieu worth a visit; secluded and peaceful; gd size pool; football pitch & games for children; great location for Loire chateaux; gd for o'night stay."* **€42.00, 14 May - 17 Sep.** **2022**

ST MAURICE LES CHARENCEY *4E2* (0km N Rural) *48.64747, 0.75575* **Camp Municipal de la Poste,** Rue de Brest, 61190 St Maurice-lès-Charencey **02 33 25 63 26; mairiedecharencey@orange.fr**

12 nr nr nr

Vill on N12 halfway bet Verneuil-sur-Avre & Mortagne-au-Perche. Site in vill cent, opp Mairie & church. 2*, Sm, hdg, mkd, pt shd, EHU; bbq; 50% statics; phone; fishing. *"Phone ahead LS to check open; helpful warden; facs basic but adequate; gd NH; lake adj; site self; gd site."* **€7.60** **2022**

SAINT MAURICE SOUS LES COTES *5D2* (0.4km N Rural) *49.01796, 5.67539* **Camping Du Bois Joli,** 12 rue haute Gaston Parant, 55210 St Maurice-sous-les-Côtes **06 43 00 43 47; campingduboisjoli@gmail.com; www.forest-campingbj.com**

nr nr

Well sp in vill. If app on D23, turn R at t-junc & foll sp. 2*, Sm, pt shd, sl, EHU (7A) €2.20 (ltd points, long cable useful); bbq; Eng spkn. *"Conv Verdun & WW1 sites; gd view during World Air Balloon Festival."* **€19.80, 1 May-15 Sep.** **2024**

ST MAURICE SUR MOSELLE *6F3* (4.5km NE Urban) *47.88888, 6.85758* **Sunêlia Domaine de Champé,** 14 Rue des Champs Navés, 88540 Bussang **03 29 61 61 51; reception@domaine-de-champe.com; domaine-de-champe.fr**

€3 (htd) WD MSP nr (covrd, htd)

Fr N66/E512 in Bussang, site sp fr town sq. Opp Avia filling stn. 5*, Med, mkd, pt shd, pt sl, terr, EHU (6-10A) €5-6; bbq; TV; 50% statics; phone; bus 1km; Eng spkn; adv bkg acc; ccard acc; sauna; waterslide; games rm; bike hire; tennis; games area; CKE. *"Excel site behind hospital grnds; lovely views; welcoming, helpful owners; fitness rm; immac, state of art facs; vg rest; excel walks, cycle path; hg rec."* **€45.00, 1 Jan-6 Mar, 24 Mar-6 Nov, 23 Nov-31 Dec.** **2024**

ST MAURICE SUR MOSELLE *6F3* (14km E Rural) *47.88170, 6.94435* **Camp Municipal Bénélux-Bâle,** Rue de la Scierie, 68121 Urbès **03 89 82 78 76; mairie.urbes@wanadoo.fr; camping-urbes.fr**

(htd) WD MSP

Site off N66 on N side of rd at foot of hill rising W out of Urbès. At foot of Col de Bessang. Fr Bussang on N66, immed on ent Urbes turn L doubling back & foll rd, site on L. 2*, Lge, mkd, pt shd, EHU (6-10A) €6.80; bbq; sw nr; 10% statics; phone; adv bkg rec; fishing adj; games area; CKE. *"Gd sh stay/ NH; beautiful area; friendly, welcoming staff; meals avil on site; facs bit cramped & ltd with poor shwrs; horse riding; hang gliding; cycle paths fr site; walks."* **€8.50, 1 May-30 Sep.** **2023**

ST MAXIMIN LA STE BAUME *10F3* (3km S Rural) *43.42848, 5.86498* **Camping Caravaning Le Provençal,** Route de Mazaugues, 83470 St Maximin-la-Ste Baume **04 94 78 16 97; campingprovencal@orange.fr; www.camping-le-provencal.com**

MSP

Exit St Maximin on N560 S twd Marseilles. After 1km turn L onto D64. Site on R after 2km. 3*, Lge, mkd, shd, pt sl, EHU (6-10A) €3.40-4.40; gas; TV; 40% statics; adv bkg acc; CKE. *"Gd NH; easy access fr A8."* **€29.00, 1 Apr-30 Sep.** **2024**

FRANCE

FRANCE

SAINT MEEN LE GRAND *2E3* (1km S Urban) *48.183972, -2.188716* **Camping Municipal La Porte Juhel,** 35290 Saint-Meen-le-Grand **02 99 09 58 or 06 45 72 70**

nr nr nr

On N164 E or W leave at junc to E of town D125. Turn L at rndabt and foll rd for 1km. Site on L after gge by level x-ing. Sm, mkd, hdg, pt shd, pt sl, EHU 4A; own san rec; bbq; twin axles; bus; Eng spkn. *"Gd site for NH; facs basic, not v clean; if barrier down phone for warden, only 2 mins away."*
€10.45, 1 Jun-30Sep. **2024**

STE MENEHOULD *5D1* (1km E Rural) *49.08937, 4.90969* **Camp Municipal de la Grelette,** Chemin de l'Alleval, 51800 Ste Menéhould **03 26 60 24 76; mairie@ste-menehould.fr; www.ste-menehould.fr**

€3 nr nr nr

Exit A4 junc 29 to Ste Menéhould; foll sp 'Centre Ville' thro town to Mairie & cent sq on D3; then foll sp 'Piscine' & 'Camping' on D3; cont uphill with rlwy on R; turn R over narr rlwy bdge, then L to site in 200m. 2*, Sm, pt shd, pt sl, EHU (10A) €4; Eng spkn; adv bkg acc; CKE. *"Delightful site; helpful warden 0830-1000 & 1700-1930, gate open at other times, access to o'fits over 2m poss restricted; confirm dep with warden; vg, clean but dated san facs(2017); interesting old town; well maintained site; new indoor pool opened nrby; conv for Reims & Verdun; ok for NH; park away fr bungalows."*
€19.40, 1 May-30 Sep. **2024**

STE MERE EGLISE *1C4* (9.5km NE Coastal) *49.46650, -1.23540* **Camping Le Cormoran,** 2 Rue du Cormoran, 50480 Ravenoville-Plage **02 33 41 33 94; lecormoran@wanadoo.fr; www.lecormoran.com**

€3 (covrd, htd) sand adj

NE on D15 fr Ste Mère-Eglise to Ravenoville, turn L onto D14 then R back onto D15 to Ravenoville Plage. Turn R on D421, Rte d'Utah Beach, site on R in 1km. Or fr N13 sp C2 Fresville & ent Ste Mère-Eglise, then take D15. 5*, Lge, hdstg, mkd, hdg, unshd, EHU (6A) inc; gas; bbq (charcoal, gas); sw nr; twin axles; TV; 60% statics; Eng spkn; adv bkg acc; ccard acc; jacuzzi; games rm; archery; tennis; bike hire; games area; horseriding; sauna; CKE. *"Popular, family-run site; lge pitches; warm welcome, helpful recep; well-kept san facs, poss tired end of ssn; poss v windy; vg children's facs; special pitches for early dep for ferry; m'van o'night area; excel."*
€33.00, 31 Mar - 30 Sep, N12. **2022**

ST MICHEL DE MAURIENNE *9C3* (0.5km SE Rural) *45.21276, 6.47858* **FFCC Camping Le Marintan,** 1 Rue de la Provalière, 73140 St Michel-de-Maurienne **04 79 59 16 91; info@le-marintan.com; camping-maurienne.com**

12 €1 (htd) nr

Fr D1006 foll sp in town to 'Centre Touristique' & 'Maison Retraite'. Rue de la Provalière is a L turn fr D1006 immed bef rlwy bdge. 3*, Sm, hdg, unshd, EHU inc; 10% statics. *"Gd touring base, but no character; conv for skiing at Val Thorens via gondola lift at Orelle."* **€12.00** **2024**

ST MICHEL EN GREVE *2E2* (1km NE Coastal) *48.69277, -3.55694* **Camping Les Capucines,** Voie Romaine, Kervourdon, 22300 Trédez-Locquémeau **02 96 35 72 28; les.capucines@wanadoo.fr; www.lescapucines.fr**

€2.10 (covrd, htd) sand 1km

Fr Lannion on D786 SW twd St Michel-en-Grève, sp Morlaix; in approx 700m, after steep descent & 'Landebouch' sp, turn R & R again in 100m at x-rds. Fr Roscoff take D58 to join N12 at junc 17; NE of Morlaix at next junc turn onto D786 twd Lannion; site down narr app rd on L on leaving St Michel-en-Grève (slow down at town exit sp), then R at x-rds. 4*, Med, mkd, hdg, pt shd, pt sl, serviced pitches; EHU (10A) inc; gas; bbq (charcoal, gas); red long stay; TV; 15% statics; phone; Eng spkn; adv bkg acc; ccard acc; games area; watersports 1km; bike hire; games rm; CKE. *"Excel, peaceful, well-kept site; no o'fits over 9.5m high ssn; gd sized pitches; helpful owners; clean san facs; gd pool; gd touring base; mkt Lannion Thu."*
€40.00, 1 Apr-30 Sep, B13. **2023**

ST MIHIEL *5D2* (1km NW Rural) *48.90209, 5.53978* **Camping Des Dames De Meuse (formerly Camping Base de Plein Air),** 1Chemin du Gué Rappeau, 55300 St Mihiel **06 07 43 38 99 and 03 29 45 28 79; campingbpa55300@orange.fr; https://campingbasepleinair.wixsite.com/**

(htd) nr nr nr

Site on W bank of rv. Sp app St Mihiel. Fr town cent take rd sp Bar-le-Duc (D901) 1st R after rv bdge. 2*, Med, mkd, pt shd, EHU (10A) €2.60; TV; 10% statics; bus 1km; adv bkg acc; sailing; games area; canoeing; CKE. *"Site developed as youth cent; facs clean but tired; pleasant scenery; htd pool 1km; lge pitches; v friendly."*
€9.00, 1 Apr-1 Nov. **2024**

ST NECTAIRE *9B1* (1km SE Rural) *45.57971, 3.00173* **Camping Le Viginet,** chemin du Manoir, 63710 St Nectaire **04 73 88 53 80 or 08 25 80 14 40; campingviginet@gmail.com; www.camping-viginet.com**

€2 nr nr nr

Exit A75/E11 junc 14 onto D996 dir Mont-Doré. In E side of St Nectaire (opp Ford g'ge) turn sharp L up v steep hill; rd widens after 100m; site on R after bends. Car park at site ent. 3*, Med, hdg, mkd, pt shd, pt sl, EHU (10A) €4; gas; Eng spkn; adv bkg acc; CKE. *"Nice pitches; gd views; gd sm pool; gd walking in hills around site."*
€30.00, 1 Apr-30 Sep. **2024**

ST NECTAIRE *9B1* (0.5km S Rural) *45.57556, 3.00169* **Camping La Clé des Champs,** 2 Rue du Pont Romain, 63710 St Nectaire **04 73 88 52 33; campingcledechamps@free.fr; www.campingcledeschamps.com**

S bound exit A75 at junc 6 to join D978 sp Champeix; N bound exit junc 14 to join D996 sp Champeix/St Nectaire. In St Nectaire turn L at g'ge on L (site sp); site 300m on L. 4*, Med, hdg, mkd, pt shd, pt sl, EHU (2-6A) €2.10-3.50 (poss rev pol); gas; 10% statics; adv bkg acc; CKE. *"Well-kept, clean site; spectacular scenery; helpful owner; vg san facs."* **€13.00, 1 Apr-30 Sep. 2024**

ST NECTAIRE *9B1* (1km S Rural) *45.57541, 2.99942* **Camping La Vallée Verte,** Route des Granges, 63710 St Nectaire **04 73 88 52 68; contact@valleeverte.com; www.valleeverte.com**

Fr A75 exit junc 6 onto D978 & D996 to St Nectaire. On ent o'skts St Nectaire turn L immed at site sp, site in 300m. 3*, Med, pt shd, EHU (5-8A) €3-3.50; sw nr; 20% statics; phone; Eng spkn; adv bkg acc; CKE. *"Vg, friendly, well-maintained, family-run site."* **€21.00, 15 Apr-18 Sep. 2023**

ST NICOLAS DU PELEM *2E3* (1.5km SW Rural) *48.30983, -3.17923* **Camp Municipal de la Piscine,** Croas-Cussuliou, Rue de Rostrenen, 22480 St Nicolas-du-Pélem **02 96 29 56 12 or 02.96.29.51.27 (outside opening hours); www.stnicolasdupelem.fr/le-camping-municipal/**

Fr Rostrenen, take D790 NE twd Corlay. In 11km, turn L sp St Nicolas-du-Pélem. Site in 500m on R, opp pool. Med, pt shd, EHU (10A) inc; CKE. *"Clean, well-kept site; choose own pitch, warden will call; htd pool opp; excel touring base."* **€12.00, 15 Jun-31 Aug. 2024**

ST OMER *3A3* (11km E Rural) *50.73490, 2.37463* **FFCC Camping Le Bloem Straete,** 1 Rue Bloemstraete, 59173 Renescure **03 28 49 85 65 or 06 50 01 08 16 (mob); lebloemstraete@gmail.com; www.lebloemstraete.fr**

E fr St Omer on D642 thro Renescure dir Hazebrouck; turn L (site sp) onto D406 Rue Andre Coo on bend on leaving Renescure; over level x-ing; site on L thro gates. 3*, Sm, hdg, mkd, hdstg, pt shd, EHU (2-6A) €2.50 (poss rev pol); bbq (charcoal, gas); 20% statics; Eng spkn; adv bkg acc; tennis; games area; CKE. *"Conv Calais ferry & tourist sites; manoeuvring poss diff due high kerbs; m'van area; site clean and tidy; worth finding!; excel facs; easy access to ports; new owners, v helpful & planning on improving site (2015)."* **€27.00, 15 Apr-15 Oct. 2022**

ST OMER *3A3* (6.5km E Urban) *50.74612, 2.30566* **Camp Municipal Beauséjour,** Rue Michelet, 62510 Arques **03 21 88 53 66; beausejour@natureetvacances.fr; www.camping-arques.fr**

Fr junc 4 of A26 foll sp Arques to town cent. Foll sp Hazebrouck. After x-ing canal site sp 'Camping *' on L. NB Drive 25m bef correct turning to site. Site signs sm and easily missed.** 4*, Med, hdg, mkd, EHU (6-10A) €3 (poss rev pol); bbq; 80% statics; phone; Eng spkn; adv bkg acc; ccard acc; lake fishing; CKE. *"Neat, tidy site; well-run; lge pitches but tight access; friendly, helpful warden; excel, clean facs; m'van o'night area adj (no EHU); gd cycling along canal; lakes & nature park nrby; conv Cristal d'Arques; canal lift & preserved rlwy in town; Calais & Dunkerque 50 mins drive; useful NH; vg."* **€17.50, 1 Apr-5 Nov. 2024**

ST OMER *3A3* (12.8km SW Rural) *50.66938, 2.16490* **Camping du Moulin,** 14 bis rue Bernard Chochoy, 62380 Remilly- Wirquin **03 21 93 05 99 or 0614528532; campinglemoulin62380@orange.fr; www.campingdumoulin.com/**

Fr A26 N or S take exit 3 sp St Omer; at rndabt take D342 sp Lumbres; in 2m at Setques turn L onto D211 sp Esquerdes; in 2m at Esquerdes turn R onto D192E to Crehem; at Crehem turn R on D192; site on L in 1m; sharp turn into site. 2*, Med, hdg, pt shd, EHU (3A) €2.50; bbq; twin axles; 75% statics; phone; bus 45m; adv bkg acc; games rm; CKE. *"Rando rail 6km; horseriding 5km; gd walking country; rv fishing on site; golf 10mins away."* **€16.50, 1 Jan-31 Nov. 2024**

ST OMER *3A3* (10km NW Rural) *50.81890, 2.17870* **Kawan Village Château du Gandspette,** 133 Rue du Gandspette, 62910 Eperlecques **03 21 93 43 93; contact@chateau-gandspette.com; www.chateau-gandspette.com**

Fr Calais SE on A26/E15 exit junc 2 onto D943 foll sp Nordausques-St Omer. 1.5km after Nordausques turn L onto D221 twd Eperlecques; site 5km on L. Do not ent Eperlecques. (Larger o'fts should cont on D943 fr Nordausques to Tilques; at rndabt foll sp for Dunkerque (D300) then D221 dir Eperlecques, site on R. 4*, Med, hdg, mkd, hdstg, pt shd, pt sl, EHU (6A) €5.20 (some rev pol); gas; bbq (charcoal, gas); TV; 15% statics; phone; Eng spkn; adv bkg acc; ccard acc; tennis; bike hire; fishing 3km; golf 5km; games rm; horseriding 5km; playground; CKE. *"Beautiful, well-kept, busy site; spacious, mainly sl pitches; charming, helpful friendly owners; superb, clean san facs; excel rest; site poss muddy in wet; gd for dogs; no o'fits over 8m; rec visit WW2 'Le Blockhaus' nr site; conv A26; highly rec; conv for Calais & for ferry to Dover; spectacular location; excel ctr for visits & activities; vg; security guard with dog; ACSI card; excel site."* **€39.00, 1 Apr-30 Sep, P08. 2024**

FRANCE

ST PABU *2E1* (2km NW Coastal) *48.57643, -4.62854* **Camping FFCC de L'Aber Benoît,** 89 Rue de Corn ar Gazel, 29830 St Pabu **02 98 89 76 25; info@camping-aber-benoit.com; www.camping-aber-benoit.com**

€1 100m

E fr Ploudalmézeau on D28; in 5km L to St Pabu. Site sp in vill. 2*, Med, hdg, pt shd, EHU (6A) €3; bbq; TV; 10% statics; CKE. *"Facs stretched high ssn; vg."* **€12.00, Easter-30 Sep. 2024**

ST PALAIS SUR MER *7B1* (7km N Rural) *45.67550, -1.09670* **Camping Le Logis du Breuil,** 17570 St Augustin **05 46 23 23 45; info@logis-du-breuil.com; www.logis-du-breuil.com**

€4.25 (htd) sand 5km

N150 to Royan, then D25 dir St Palais-sur-Mer. Strt on at 1st rndabt & 2nd rndabt; at next rndabt take 2nd exit dir St Palais-sur-Mer. At next traff lts turn R dir St Augustin onto D145; site on L. NB sat nav can direct thro diff & narr alt rte. 4*, Lge, mkd, pt shd, pt sl, serviced pitches; EHU (6-10A) €6-8 (50m cable poss req); gas; bbq (elec, gas); TV; 10% statics; phone; Eng spkn; adv bkg acc; ccard acc; tennis; fishing 1km; golf 3km; excursions; games area; bike hire; games rm; horseriding 400m; CKE. *"Nice peaceful site; lge pitches in wooded area; gd alt to cr beach sites; friendly owner; san facs clean; no c'vans over 12m; gd for young families; excel."* **€50.00, 23 Apr-30 Sep, A04. 2022**

ST PALAIS SUR MER *7B1* (0.5km NE Coastal) *45.64245, -1.07677* **Camping de Bernezac,** 2 Ave de Bernezac, 17420 St Palais-sur-Mer **05 46 39 00 71; acccf-bernezac@acccf.com; bernezac.acccf.com**

€1 nr adj

Leave A10 at junc 35 fr N. N150 then D25, at 2nd rndabt take 3rd exit (Rue de la Roche), cross 2 rndabt then L onto Ave de Bernezac. Site on R in under 1km. 3*, Med, hdg, mkd, pt shd, pt sl, serviced pitches; EHU (6A) €4.60 (poss rev pol); bbq; twin axles; TV; 60% statics; Eng spkn; adv bkg acc; lake fishing 1km; games area. *"Helpful, friendly staff; clean, spacious pitches; new shwrs (2016); free wifi; cycle rtes nr; sm quiet site; direct access to beach; pleasant coastal walks; off rd bike rides fr beach gate; lots of activities in area; vg."* **€34.50, 15 Mar-15 Oct. 2023**

ST PALAIS SUR MER *7B1* (1.5km E Rural/Coastal) *45.64656, -1.07300* **Camping Les Ormeaux,** 22 Ave des Peupliers, 17420 St Palais-sur-Mer **05 46 39 02 07; campingormeaux@aliceadsl.fr; www.campinglesormeaux.com**

€4 (htd) sand 800m

Foll sp fr D25 Royan-St Palais rd. Rec app ent fr R. Ent & camp rds narr. 3*, Lge, pt shd, EHU (6-10A) €7.50; gas; TV; 98% statics. *"Ltd touring area & access diff for lge o'fits or m'vans - tents or sm m'vans only; one of the best campsites we have stayed in; clean spacious pitches, amazing staff, new san facs; dir access to 41km cycle rtes, mostly off-rd; no TV on pitches."* **€25.00, 1 Apr-31 Oct. 2022**

ST PALAIS SUR MER *7B1* (2km E Coastal) *45.64396, -1.06325* **Camping Le Val Vert,** 108 Ave Frédéric Garnier, 17640 Vaux-sur-Mer **05 46 38 25 51; www.val-vert.com**

€6.50 (htd) sand 900m

Fr Saintes on N150 dir Royan; join D25 dir St Palais-sur-Mer; turn L at rndabt sp Vaux-sur-Mer & Centre Hospitaliers; at traff lts ahead; at 2nd rndabt take 3rd exit & then turn immed R. Site on R in 500m. 3*, Med, hdg, EHU (10A) inc; gas; bbq (elec, gas); adv bkg acc; ccard acc; tennis 400m; bike hire; horseriding 5km; games rm; fishing; watersports; games area; golf 5km. *"Well-kept, family-run site; no o'fits over 6.5m high ssn; gd sized pitches; unisex san facs; a stream runs alongside site; sh walk to pleasant vill; daily mkt in Royan."* **€50.00, 27 Apr-24 Sep, A25. 2022**

"I need an on-site restaurant"

We do our best to make sure site information is correct, but it is always best to check any must-have facilities are still available or will be open during your visit.

ST PALAIS SUR MER *7B1* (2km SE Urban/Coastal) *45.64272, -1.07183* **Camping Nauzan-Plage,** 39 Ave de Nauzan-Plage, 17640 Vaux-sur-Mer **05 46 38 29 13; contact@campinglenauzanplage.com; www.campinglenauzanplage.com**

€5 sand 450m

Take either coast rd or inland rd fr Royan to Vaux-sur-Mer; site not well sp. 4*, Lge, mkd, pt shd, EHU (10A) €5.50; gas; red long stay; TV; 10% statics; adv bkg rec; tennis 200m; games rm; CKE. *"Gd site, busy high ssn; helpful staff; gd cycling rte; pt of Flower Camping group."* **€45.00, 1 Apr-15 Oct. 2023**

ST PALAIS SUR MER *7B1* (3km NW Coastal) *45.6500, -1.1193* **Camping La Côte de Beauté,** 157 Ave de la Grande Côte, 17420 St Palais-sur-Mer **05 46 23 20 59; campingcotedebeaute@wanadoo.fr; www.camping-cote-de-beaute.com**

€3 (htd) sand 200m

Fr St Palais-sur-Mer foll sp to La Tremblade & Ronce-les-Bains. Site on D25, 50m fr beach, look for twin flagpoles of Camping Le Puits de l'Auture & lge neon sp on R; site in 50m. 3*, Med, hdg, shd, EHU (6A) €4.20; 10% statics; adv bkg acc; tennis adj; golf 2km. *"Clean, tidy site; friendly staff; steep descent to beach opp - better beach 600m twd La Tremblade; bike hire adj; cycle track to St Palais & Pontaillac; town 3km; clean san facs; gd pitches."* **€31.00, 1 May-30 Sep. 2023**

ST PALAIS SUR MER *7B1* (6.5km NW Coastal) *45.64930, -1.11785* **Camping Le Puits de l'Auture,** La Grande Côte, 17420 St Palais-sur-Mer **05 46 23 20 31; contact@camping-puitsdelauture.com; www.camping-puitsdelauture.com**

(htd) (htd) sand adj

Fr Royan take D25 onto new rd past St Palais foll sp for La Palmyre. At 1-way section turn back L sp La Grande Côte & site is 800m; rd runs close to sea, flags at ent. 4*, Lge, pt shd, serviced pitches; EHU (10A) inc; gas; 25% statics; Eng spkn; adv bkg rec; ccard acc; fishing; games area; CKE. *"Well-maintained, well laid-out, excel site; san facs stretched high ssn & 'tired'; poss cr but carefully controlled; friendly, helpful staff; gd cycle paths."* **€38.00, 28 Apr-3 Oct. 2022**

ST PANTALEON *7D3* (4km NE Rural) *44.36760, 1.30634* **Camping des Arcades,** Moulin de St Martiel, 46800 St Pantaléon **+33(0)6 60 98 80 39; info@des-arcades.com; www.des-arcades.com**

€1.50 WD (htd)

Fr N20 3km S of Cahors take D653 sp Montcuq, after 17km site in hamlet of St Martial on L. 3*, Med, mkd, pt shd, pt sl, EHU (6A) €4; bbq; sw nr; 5% statics; Eng spkn; adv bkg acc; ccard acc; fishing adj; CKE. *"Vg Dutch-owned site with restored 13thC windmill; sm lake; clean facs."* **€20.00, 29 Jun-31 Aug. 2024**

ST PANTALEON LES VIGNES *9D2* (2km E Rural) *44.39752, 5.06099* **Camping Les Cyprès,** Hameau Font de Barral, 26770 Saint Pantaleon les Vignes **06 81 53 78 03 or 06 82 27 19 14; contact@lescypres-camping.com; www.lescypres-camping.com**

€1.80 WD nr nr

D541 fir Nyons. Fr highway A7 exit Montèlimar-Sud Bollène or Orange Cent. 1*, Sm, pt shd, pt sl, EHU (4,6,10A) €2.50-3.60; bbq; twin axles; games rm. *"Beautiful surroundings; friendly owners."* **€11.00, 1 Apr-31 Oct. 2024**

ST PARDOUX *7A3* (1.6km S Rural) *46.04955, 1.27893* **Campsite de Fréaudour,** Site de Freaudour 87250 St Pardoux **05 55 76 57 22; camping.freaudour@orange.fr; www.aquadis-loisirs.com**

WD

Fr A20 dir Limonges, take exit 25, onto D219. Cont onto D44 thro Razes & foll sp to Lac De Saint-Pardoux. Turn R onto D103A to Freaudour. 4*, Med, mkd, pt shd, EHU (6A); bbq; TV; 20% statics; Eng spkn; adv bkg rec; games area. *"Fair site."* **€20.40, 1 Apr-27 Oct. 2024**

ST PARDOUX *9A1* (7.5km SW Rural) *46.03202, 2.95704* **Camping La Coccinelle (formerly Camping Elan),** Route de Villemorie, 63440 Blot-l'Eglise **04 73 64 93 15; info@campingcoccinelle.com; www.campingcoccinelle.com**

€1 WD nr

Fr N on N144 take D16 to Blot, fr S take D50, foll site sp. 2*, Sm, hdg, mkd, pt shd, EHU (5-10A) €2.50-4.50; red long stay; TV; Eng spkn; adv bkg acc; tennis; games area; CKE. *"In beautiful area; lge pitches; friendly Dutch owners; clean but basic san facs; site open LS by arrangement; gd touring base; conv Vulcania; gd."* **€23.00, 26 Apr-13 Sept. 2024**

ST PAUL DE FENOUILLET *8G4* (7km E Rural) *42.80811, 2.6058* **Camping Le Maurynate,** La Caunette Basse, 66460 Maury **27 17 71 85; campinglemaurynate@gmail.com; lemaurynate-campingdesoliviers.com**

€2 (htd) WD MSP

W fr St-Paul-de-Fenouillet on D117 to Maury in 6km; cont past Maury on D117; site on L in 1km, just bef level x-ing. 2*, Sm, mkd, hdg, pt shd, EHU (10A) €3.50; bbq; Eng spkn; adv bkg acc; CKE. *"Vg site; prehistoric history region."* **€25.00, 1 Apr-31 Aug. 2024**

ST PAUL DE FENOUILLET *8G4* (7km E Rural) *42.80782, 2.60579* **Camping Le Maurynate (formerly Municipal Les Oliviers),** Departmental 117, 66460 Maury **336 27 17 71 85; campinglemaurynate@gmail.com; https://lemaurynate-campingdesoliviers.com/**

(cont) nr nr nr

Heading W on D117. Site immed after level x-ing on R 500m bef Maury. 2*, Sm, mkd, shd, EHU; CKE. *"Some rd noise fr level x-ing; immac san facs."* **€28.50, 1 May-30 Sep. 2024**

"Satellite navigation makes touring much easier"

Remember most sat navs don't know if you're towing or in a larger vehicle – always use yours alongside maps and site directions.

ST PAUL DE FENOUILLET *8G4* (0.4km S Rural) *42.80762, 2.50235* **Camping de l'Agly,** Ave 16 Août 1944, 66220 St Paul-de-Fenouillet **04 68 59 09 09; contact@camping-agly.com; www.camping-agly.com**

12 WD nr

Heading W on D117; turn L at traff lts in St Paul; site on R in 200m, well sp. 2*, Sm, hdg, mkd, pt shd, pt sl, EHU (16A) €4.50; sw nr; site clsd Jan; CKE. *"Vg site; friendly warden; mountain scenery; gd climbing & cycling; conv for Château's Payrepertuse & Quéribus; sm pitches, diff access for lge o'fits; conv NH."* **€16.00 2023**

FRANCE

ST PAUL EN FORET *10E4* (3.5km N Rural) *43.58449, 6.69016* **Camping Le Parc,** Quartier Trestaure, 83440 St Paul-en-Forêt **04 94 76 15 35; contact@campingleparc.com; www.campingleparc.com**

€4.50 (htd)

(htd)

Exit A8 at junc 39, foll D37 (dir Fayence) for 8.4km to lge rndabt on D562. Take 3rd exit at rndabt (sp draguignan/Fayence). Foll D562 for 4.8km thro 4 more rndabts. At 5th rndabt (Intermarche Supmkt on L) take 3rd exit D562 sp Draguignan. After 4.2km take 3rd exit at rndabt onto D4, after 2km turn L at bus stop. Foll rd to site. 4*, Sm, mkd, shd, sl, EHU (10A) €5 high ssn only; twin axles; TV; 65% statics; phone; Eng spkn; adv bkg acc; games rm; fishing; games area; tennis; CKE. *"Conv hill vills of Provence; gd rests in St Paul; many medieval vill; excel."*
€29.00, 2 Apr-30 Sep. **2022**

"There aren't many sites open at this time of year"

If you're travelling outside peak season remember to call ahead to check site opening dates – even if the entry says 'open all year'.

ST PIERRE EN PORT *3C2* (0.5km N Coastal) *49.80943, 0.49354* **Les Falaises,** 130 Rue du Camping, 76540 St Pierre-en-Port **02 35 29 51 58; lesfalaises@cegetel.net; www.campinglesfalaises.com**

nr 2km

Fr D925 turn onto D79 bet St Valery & Fecamp. Site sp in St Pierre. 2*, Med, hdg, unshd, EHU (10A); bbq; 60% statics; bus 0.5km; Eng spkn; games area; games rm; CKE. *"Cliff top site; path to beach steep with steps; narr app rd; facs dated but clean; well kept site; takeaway snacks avail high ssn only; v quiet, pleasant site; gd."* **€36.10, 1 Apr-5 Oct.** **2023**

ST PIERRE LE MOUTIER *4H4* (8km SW Rural) *46.75722, 3.03328* **Camp Municipal de St Mayeul,** Rue de Saint-Mayeul, 03320 Le Veurdre **04 70 66 40 67; mairie.le.veurdre@wanadoo.fr; www.allier-auvergne-tourisme.com**

nr

Fr N7 at St Pierre-le-Moûtier SW onto D978A to Le Veurdre. Site sp on far side of Le Veurdre. 2*, Sm, hdg, mkd, pt shd, pt sl, EHU €4; bbq; adv bkg acc. *"Pleasant spot; site yourself, warden calls; friendly staff; clean, basic facs; shops in pleasant vill; rec NH; vg."* **€12.10, 1 May-15 Sep.** **2023**

ST POL DE LEON *1D2* (2km E Coastal) *48.69355, -3.96930* **Camping de Trologot,** Grève du Man, 29250 St Pol-de-Léon **02 98 69 06 26; camping-trologot@wanadoo.fr; www.camping-trologot.com**

€2.40 nr

(htd) sand adj

Fr the port of Roscoff take D58 go briefly on the D769 then back on to the D58 foll the sp to Morlaix over six rndabts (approx 4miles/6.5km). Just after passing under a rlwy bdge, take the exit for the D769 (sp St Pol de Léon, Kerlaudy, Penzé) then turn L. Stay on the D769 for 1.8 km, just past the graveyard turn R at the rndabt and go strt over the next rndabt (sp Campings/Plage) at the end of the rd turn L and the turning for the site will be on L after 1km and is sp. Do not use sat nav. Fr the E on the N12 take the exit for the D19 (sp Morlaix St pol de Leon) at the rndabt take the 2nd exit cont twds St-Pol-de Leon on the D58. Take the exit to the D769 (SP St-Pol-de Leon) then foll above dirs fr the graveyard. 3*, Med, mkd, hdg, pt shd, EHU (10A) €4.50; bbq (charcoal, gas); red long stay; TV; 20% statics; adv bkg acc; ccard acc; games rm; bouncy castle; CKE. *"Lovely, well-kept site; ideal NH for Roscoff ferry; gd sized pitches; helpful owners; clean, modern san facs; no o'fits over 7m high ssn; gd for family beach holiday; peaceful area, many walks nrby; beautiful town; gd cycling area; hg rec; excel."*
€35.00, 31 March-27 Oct, B29. **2022**

"That's changed – Should I let the Club know?"

If you find something on site that's different from the site entry, fill in a report and let us know. See camc.com/europereport.

ST POL DE LEON *1D2* (5km SE Coastal) *48.65805, -3.92805* **Les Mouettes,** La Grande Grève, 29660 Carantec **02 98 67 02 46; camping@les-mouettes.com; www.les-mouettes.com**

€6 (covrd, htd)

shgl 1km

Fr Morlaix take D58 N sp Roscoff; at lge rndabt turn R sp Carantec on D173; turn L at 1st rndabt; strt on at 2nd & 3rd rndabt past Casino supmkt; turn L next rndabt; site on L. Or fr Roscoff take D58 sp Mortaix, then D173 to Carantec; foll sp town cent, then site. 5*, Lge, mkd, pt shd, EHU (10A) inc (poss rev pol); gas; bbq (charcoal); TV; 50% statics; Eng spkn; adv bkg acc; ccard acc; tennis; bike hire; fishing; games area; golf 1.5km; waterslide; games rm; CKE. *"Attractive site with sea views; no o'fits over 8m; clean, modern san facs; sauna; jaccuzi; impressive pool complex; plenty to do on site; mkt Thu; noise fr boatyard; conv Carnac."*
€38.00, 8 Apr-11 Sep, B14. **2022**

ST PONS DE THOMIERES *8F4* (2km E Rural) *43.49055, 2.78527* **Camping Les Cerisiers du Jaur,** Les Marbrières-du-Jaur, Route de Bédarieux, 34220 St Pons-de-Thomières **04 67 95 30 33; info@cerisierdujaur.com; www.cerisierdujaur.com**

€1.50 WD MSP nr

Fr Castres on D612 to St Pons; go thro town cent under rlwy bdge; turn L onto D908 sp Olargues. Site on R in 500m. 3*, Med, hdg, mkd, pt shd, terr, EHU (10A) €4; bbq; phone; Eng spkn; ccard acc; games area; bike hire; CKE. *"Excel site nr Rv Jaur; welcoming, friendly, helpful owner; cycle rte fr site; an oasis!; hot water not v hot; expensive in LS; san facs unkept."*
€22.00, 29 Mar-26 Oct. **2023**

ST POURCAIN SUR SIOULE *9A1* (0.7km SE Urban) *46.30643, 3.29207* **Camp Municipal de l'île de la Ronde,** Quai de la Ronde, 03500 St Pourçain-sur-Sioule **04 70 35 13 69; les.perches.pah@gmail.com; ile-de-la-ronde.fr**

0,50 € WD MSP nr

On D2009, 31km S of Moulins; in St Pourçain-sur-Sioule town cent turn R immed bef rv bdge; site ent on L in 100m. NB Sp in town easily missed. 3*, Med, hdg, pt shd, EHU (10A) inc; adv bkg acc; CKE. *"Well-run, magnificent, busy, pleasant site in pretty town; extra charge for lger pitches; barrier clsd 2000-0800; gd rest nr; mkt Sat; great value; excel; recep and barrier clsd 1200-1400; 2 supmkt in town; 2 pin adapter ess; set amongst trees; walks/rvside path adj; san facs stretched at times; gd value."*
€14.00, 1 Apr-1 Oct. **2024**

ST QUENTIN *3C4* (12km SW Urban) *49.78222, 3.21333* **Camping du Vivier aux Carpes,** 10 Rue Charles Voyeux, 02790 Seraucourt-le-Grand **03 23 60 50 10; contact@camping-picardie.com; www.camping-picardie.com**

€1.50 (htd) WD MSP (covrd, htd)

Fr A26 take exit 11 St Quentin/Soissons; S 4km on D1 dir Tergnier/Soissons. Fork R onto D8 to Essigny-le-Grand & in vill foll camping sp W to Seraucourt. Fr St Quentin, S 10km on D930 to Roupy, E on D32 5km to Seraucourt-le-Grand. Site N of Seraucourt on D321. Narr ent fr rd unsuitable lge o'fits. 3*, Med, hdstg, mkd, hdg, pt shd, EHU (10A) inc (poss rev pol); gas; bbq; 30% statics; Eng spkn; adv bkg acc; tennis adj; golf adj; horseriding adj; games rm; CKE. *"Delightful, lovely, well-run site; busy, even LS - rec arr early; ltd hdstg; peaceful LS; gd, lge pitches; narr site rds; friendly, helpful staff; pitches by lake poss boggy when wet; poss flooding; mkd footpaths round lakes; vg angling; mosquito probs; Disneyland 90 mins; conv Channel ports; c'van storage; warn staff night bef if v early dep; excel; facs stretched but clean & gd; lovely cycle rte along canal to St Quentin; nice bistro in vill; coded security barrier; heard laughing duck; nice walks; clean facs; vg onsite rest/bar."*
€30.50, 1 Apr-30 Sep, P14. **2023**

ST QUENTIN EN TOURMONT *3B2* (0.5km S Rural) *50.26895, 1.60263* **Camping Le Champ Neuf,** 8 Rue du Champ Neuf, 80120 St Quentin-en-Tourmont **03 22 25 07 94; campinglechampneuf@orange.fr; www.camping-lechampneuf.com**

€1.50 (htd) WD MSP (covrd, htd) 2km

Exit D1001 or A16 onto D32 to Rue, take D940 around Rue & foll sp St Quentin-en-Tourmont, Parc Ornithologique & Domaine du Marquenterre to site. Site sp fr D204. 3*, Lge, hdg, mkd, pt shd, EHU (5-10A) inc; bbq; 80% statics; phone; adv bkg acc; ccard acc; horseriding 500m; bike hire; games area. *"Excel Ornithological Park nrby; well-kept, pleasant site; friendly, helpful owner; gd cycle paths."*
€30.00, 1 Apr-1 Nov. **2022**

See advertisement

FRANCE

ST RAPHAEL *10F4* (8.6km WSW Coastal) *43.408915, 6.708677* **Camping Sandaya Rivièra d'Azur,** 189 Les Grands Chat.de Villepey, RD7 83370, Saint Aygulf **04 11 32 90 00; www.sandaya.fr/nos-campings/riviera-d-azur**

€5 (htd) (htd) sandy 2.5km

Leave A8 exit 36 Le Muy on N555 twrds Draguignan then N7 twrds Frejus. R on d7 sp St Aygulf. Site on R in 2.5km before town. 5*, Lge, hdg, mkd, hdstg, pt shd, serviced pitches; EHU 10A inc; bbq (elec, gas); cooking facs; sw nr; 60% statics; Eng spkn; adv bkg rec; ccard acc; bike hire; beauty ctr; fishing; tennis; security. *"10m extension lead req for EHU; Gd walking and cycling. Serviced pitch inc private shower, toilet, and dishwash. In April/May booking through Club site fees were 16 euros/ night only."* **€74.00, 7 Apr - 5 Nov.** 2022

"We must tell the Club about that great site we found"

Get your site reports in by mid-August and we'll do our best to get your updates into the next edition.

ST RAPHAEL *10F4* (4.5km N Rural) *43.44611, 6.80610* **Sandaya Douce Quiétude,** 3435 Blvd Jacques Baudino, 83700 St Raphaël **04 94 44 30 00; www.sandaya.fr/nos-campings/douce-quietude**

€5 (htd) (htd) sand 2km

Exit A8 at junc 38 onto D37 then D100 sp Agay. Foll sp Valescure-Boulouris, site sp. NB c'vans not permitted on St Raphaël seafront. 5*, Lge, hdstg, mkd, hdg, pt shd, pt sl, serviced pitches; EHU (10A) inc; gas; bbq (gas); TV; phone; bus; Eng spkn; adv bkg acc; ccard acc; games area; gym; waterslide; games rm; bike hire; mini golf; CKE. *"Lge pitches; excel facs; takeway; disco nightly high ssn; many tour ops statics; sm touring pitches mostly amongst statics; vg."* **€71.30, 5 Apr-2 Nov.** 2024

ST REMY DE PROVENCE *10E2* (0.5km NE Rural) *43.79622, 4.83878* **Camping Le Mas de Nicolas,** Ave Plaisance-du-Touch, 13210 St Rémy-de-Provence **04 90 92 27 05; contact@camping-masdenicolas.com; www.camping-masdenicolas.com**

€2.15-€2.80 (htd) (htd)

Take D99 E twrds Saint Remy de Provence. Turn L at 2nd rndabt after town ctr & foll sp to campsite. 4*, Lge, hdstg, mkd, hdg, pt shd, EHU (6A) €3.80; bbq; TV (pitch); TV; 20% statics; bus 1km; Eng spkn; adv bkg req; ccard acc; games area; games rm; CKE. *"Family-owned site; gd clean modern san facs; some pitches diff access long o'fits; v helpful staff; interesting town; excel pool with gym/jacuzzi; easy walk to St Remy; excel."* **€33.00, 1 Apr-14 Oct.** 2023

ST REMY DE PROVENCE *10E2* (2km NW Rural) *43.7967, 4.82378* **Camping Monplaisir,** 435 Chemin Monplaisir, 13210 St Rémy-de-Provence **04 90 92 22 70; reception@camping-monplaisir.fr; www.camping-monplaisir.fr**

€2.50 (htd)

Exit D99 at St Rémy onto D5 going NW dir Maillane, in 110m turn L & foll sp in 500m. Avoid going thro town. 4*, Med, hdstg, hdg, shd, EHU (10A) inc; gas; bbq (elec, gas); red long stay; phone; bus 1km; Eng spkn; adv bkg acc; ccard acc; bike hire; CKE. *"Immac, well-run site; mostly gd sized pitches; clean, modern san facs; gd touring base; highly rec; site clsd last Sat in Oct; excel site; lovely pool; walk to nice town; fills up quickly."* **€62.00, 10 Mar-19 Oct.** 2023

ST ROME DE TARN *8E4* (0.3km N Rural) *44.05302, 2.89978* **Camping de la Cascade des Naisses,** Route du Pont, 12490 St Rome-de-Tarn **05 65 62 56 59; contact@camping-cascade-aveyron.com; www.camping-cascade-aveyron.com**

12 €6 (htd)

Fr Millau take D992 to St Georges-de-Luzençon, turn R onto D73 & foll sp to St Rome. In St Rome turn R along Ave du Pont-du-Tarn, site sp. Diff, steep app for sm/underpowered car+c'van o'fits. 4*, Med, hdg, mkd, hdstg, pt shd, terr, EHU (6A) inc; own san req; 40% statics; Eng spkn; adv bkg acc; boating; rv fishing; tennis; bike hire; CKE. *"Lovely rvside pitches; pleasant vill; friendly, helpful staff; each level has a wc but steep walk to shwr block; owners will site vans; conv Millau viaduct; excel tranquil, scenic site."* **€35.00** 2022

"I need an on-site restaurant"

We do our best to make sure site information is correct, but it is always best to check any must-have facilities are still available or will be open during your visit.

ST SAVIN *7A3* (0.5km N Rural) *46.56892, 0.86772* **Camping du Moulin de la Gassotte,** 10 Rue de la Gassotte, 86310 St Savin-sur-Gartempe **05 49 48 18 02; camping@moulindelagassotte.fr; www.moulindelagassotte.fr**

Free nr nr nr

E fr Chauvigny on D951 to St Savin; fr St Savin N on D11; well sp. Fr S on D5 cross rv; meet D951, turn R & site on R. Fr S on D11 use 'poids lourds' (heavy vehicles) rec rte to meet D951. 2*, Sm, pt shd, EHU (12A) inc; bbq; TV; rv fishing adj; CKE. *"Beautiful, peaceful, park like site by rv; views of Abbey; helpful warden; san facs old but clean; sh walk to vill; murals in Abbey restored by UNESCO; defined pitches."* **€13.00, Apr-Oct.** 2024

FRANCE

ST TROPEZ *10F4* (11km SW Rural) *43.21804, 6.57830* **Domaine de Verdagne (formerly Camping Moulin),** Chemin du Moulin de Verdagne, 83580 Gassin **04 94 79 78 21; contact@domaine-verdagne.com; www.domaine-verdagne.com**

€3 WD nr sand 5km

Foll N559 N fr Cavalaire for 6km. Take 1st R after town traff lts in La Croix-Valmer, site sp. Site in 2km, surrounded by vineyards. Rough app rd/track. 3*, Med, mkd, pt shd, terr, EHU (6A) €4; red long stay; 60% statics; phone; Eng spkn; ccard acc. *"Vg, lovely site; tight bends & narr pitches poss diff long o'fits; pool 2m deep; c'van best app fr La Croix vill; new owners (2016); helpful; new pool (2017)."* **€37.50, 1 Apr-31 Oct. 2023**

"Satellite navigation makes touring much easier"

Remember most sat navs don't know if you're towing or in a larger vehicle – always use yours alongside maps and site directions.

ST VALERY EN CAUX *3C2* (1.6km N Coastal) *49.86839, 0.71154* **Aire Communale,** Quai d'Aval, Plage Ouest, 76460 St Valery-en-Caux **02 35 97 00 22 or 02 35 97 00 63 (TO); servicetourisme@ville-saint-valeryen-caux.fr**

12 WD MSP nr nr

Sp fr cent of St Valery-en-Caux along rv/seafront to harbour. Sm, phone. *"M'vans only; rec arr early; LS free except Fri, Sat & Sun; water fill €4; free parking for 48 hrs."* **€4.00 2024**

ST VALERY SUR SOMME *3B2* (4.6km S Rural) *50.15333, 1.63583* **Le Domaine du Château de Drancourt,** 80230 Estréboeuf **03 22 26 93 45; chateau.drancourt@wanadoo.fr; www.chateau-drancourt.fr**

€6 WD MSP (covrd, htd)

Exit A28/E402 junc 1 at Abbeville onto D40 twd Noyelles-sur-Mer. At rndabt with D940 turn L sp St Valery-sur-Somme. At next rndabt go strt over dir Le Tréport, then at next rndabt at junc with D48 take last exit (sp Estréboeuf), turn immed L & foll sps to site. NB.1-way system at recep area. 5*, Lge, mkd, hdg, pt shd, pt sl, EHU (10A) inc (poss rev pol); gas; bbq; 80% statics; Eng spkn; adv bkg acc; ccard acc; bike hire; fishing adj; golf driving range; tennis; horseriding 12km; games rm; watersports 2km; CKE. *"Conv, busy, popular NH in grnds of chateau; friendly staff; facs poss stretched when site full; red facs LS; bird sanctuary in estuary nrby; gd."* **€40.00, 15 Apr - 11 Sep, P06. 2022**

ST VALERY SUR SOMME *3B2* (1km SW Urban/Coastal) *50.18331, 1.61786* **Camping Le Walric,** Route d'Eu, 80230 St Valery-sur-Somme **03 22 26 81 97; info@campinglewalric.com; www.campinglewalric.com**

€3 WD MSP (htd, indoor)

Ringrd round St Valery D940 dir Le Tréport. Cont to 3rd rndabt (1st rndabt Carrefour supmkt on L) 3km & take 1st exit (R) sp St Valery & Cap Hornu D3. Site on R in 2km at ent to town sp. 4*, Lge, hdstg, mkd, hdg, pt shd, EHU (6A) inc; gas; bbq; red long stay; 70% statics; phone; Eng spkn; adv bkg acc; ccard acc; tennis; games area; bike hire; games rm; boat hire; fishing; CKE. *"Well-kept, well-run, busy site in excel location; clean san facs; cycle rtes, canal track; steam train; beach nrby; delightful medieval town; mkt Sun; excel; easy to find; sh walk to town."* **€37.00, 1 Apr-30 Oct. 2024**

ST VALERY SUR SOMME *3B2* (3km SW Rural) *50.17632, 1.58969* **Camping de la Baie,** Routhiaville, 80230 Pendé **03 22 60 72 72; contact@campingdelabaie.eu; campingdelabaie.eu**

WD nr

Just off D940 twd Tréport, well sp. 2*, Sm, hdg, EHU (6A) €4; 95% statics; adv bkg acc; CKE. *"Well-run, clean, tidy site & san facs; friendly, helpful owners; low trees in places need care; cycle rte to St Valery; adequate NH."* **€15.50, 27 Mar-16 Oct. 2024**

ST VALERY SUR SOMME *3B2* (1km W Urban) *50.18447, 1.62263* **Camping de la Croix l'Abbé,** Place de la Croix l'Abbé, 80230 St Valery-sur-Somme **03 22 60 81 97; info@campingdelacroixlabbe.fr; www.campingdelacroixlabbe.fr**

WD nr (covrd, htd) shgl 1km

Ringrd round St Valery D940 dir Le Tréport. Cont to 2nd rndabt (1st rndabt Champion supmkt on L) 3km & take exit sp St Valery & Cap Hornu D3. Site 250m beyond Camping Le Walric. Lge, hdg, mkd, unshd, pt sl, EHU (10A) inc; TV; 90% statics; bus adj; Eng spkn. *"San facs needs updating (2017); gd location for walk to town; sh stay/NH only; super town; rec steam rlwy to Le Crotoy."* **€20.00, 1 Apr-30 Nov. 2023**

ST VALLIER *9C2* (2km N Rural) *45.18767, 4.81225* **Camp Municipal Les Iles de Silon,** 26240 St Vallier **04 75 23 22 17 or 07 44 56 84 05; camping@saintvallier.fr; www.camping-saintvallier.fr**

€2.30 WD

On N7 just N of town, clearly sp in both dirs on rvside. 3*, Med, hdg, pt shd, EHU (10A) €2.30 (poss long cable req); bbq; 10% statics; Eng spkn; adv bkg acc; ccard acc; watersports; tennis adj; CKE. *"Attractive, gd quality site; views over rv; lge pitches; friendly warden; gd immac san facs; rec arr bef 1600 high ssn; gd value; cycle/walking track adj, along Rhône; excel well managed site; vg facs and staff; free WiFi; no twin-axles/o'fits over 3.5 tonnes; gd value; excel."* **€14.50, 15 Mar-15 Nov. 2024**

FRANCE

SAINTES 7B2 (0.5km N Urban) 45.75511, -0.62871 **Camp Municipal au Fil de l'Eau,** 6 Rue de Courbiac, 17100 Saintes **05 46 93 08 00 or 06 75 24 91 96 (mob); contact@camping-saintes-17.com; www.camping-saintes-17.com**

€1.60

Well sp as 'Camping Municipal' fr rndbts on by-pass N & S on D150 & D137 (thro indus area), adj rv. If app fr W on D128 (N side of Saintes), turn R at rndabt onto Rue de l'Abbatoir; in 800m turn L into Rue de Courbiac; site on R in 200m. NB 1st Mon in month st mkt & many rds clsd. 3*, Lge, pt shd, EHU (10A) €3.60; bbq; sw nr; red long stay; Eng spkn; adv bkg acc; ccard acc; boating adj; fishing adj; CKE. *"Excel site; vg, clean, upgraded (2019) san facs; excel rest; grnd poss boggy when wet; gd touring base; mkt Wed & Sat; easy walk to attractive Roman town; huge open site, efficent recep; friendly staff; gd NH just off A10; rest clsd on Sundays;spacious, well positioned for town; fab town with Roman Amphitheatre & museums."* **€21.00, 1 May-30 Sep.** 2022

SALBRIS 4G3 (1km N Urban) 47.43006, 2.05427 **Camping de Sologne,** 8 Allée de la Sauldre, Route de Pierrefitte, 41300 Salbris **02 54 97 06 38 or 06 80 13 60 59 (mob); campingsolognesalbris@orange.fr; www.campingdesologne.fr**

€1 nr

Fr N exit A71 J4. Take D724 bypass (2nd exit on rndabt). At next rndabt take D2020 N sp Salbris. Cont thro town. After x-ing bdge at next traff lts turn R onto D55 (Rte de Perrelefitte). Impass de la Sauldre leading to Allee de la Sauldre is 2nd turning on R in 200m (narr and easy to miss). Fr S to avoid Peage leave A71 at J5. Take D2020 N to Salbris then as abv. 3*, Med, hdg, mkd, pt shd, EHU (10A) inc (some rev pol); gas; TV; 25% statics; phone; Eng spkn; adv bkg acc; ccard acc; fishing; boat hire; CKE. *"Excel, well-kept site in pleasant lakeside location; friendly, helpful owners; karting 6km; lake adj; gd san facs poss stretched if site busy & ltd LS; gd rest; gd dog walks adj; conv NH for m'way; hypmkt 1km; beautiful site; easy access to town; new shwr block (2015); ACSI accepted."* **€26.50, 1 Apr-30 Sep.** 2024

SALERS 7C4 (0.8km NE Rural) 45.14756, 2.49857 **Camp Municipal Le Mouriol,** Route de Puy-Mary, 15140 Salers **04 71 40 73 09 or 06 47 37 10 73 (mob); www.salers.fr**

nr nr nr

Take D922 SE fr Mauriac dir Aurillac; turn onto D680 E dir Salers; site 1km NE of Salers on D680 dir Puy Mary, opp Hôtel Le Gerfaut; sp fr all dir. 2*, Med, hdg, mkd, pt shd, sl, EHU (16A) €4.60 (long lead poss req); bbq; red long stay; phone; bus 1km; tennis; CKE. *"Generous pitches; san facs gd but stretched if site full; peaceful LS; hill walking; excel cycling & walking; beautiful medieval vill; vg; well kept; footpath fr site to Salers."* **€14.00, 1 Apr-30 Oct.** 2023

SALERS 7C4 (0.8km W Rural) 45.13304, 2.48762 **Camping à la Ferme d'Apcher,** Apcher, 15140 Salers **04 71 40 72 26; www.salers-tourisme.fr**

nr

D922 S fr Mauriac for 17km; L on D680 sp Salers; in lane on R sp Apcher - immed after passing Salers town sp. Sm, pt shd, EHU (10A) €2.30; CKE. *"Sm farm, CL type site; welcoming, friendly owner; excel clean san facs, plenty hot water; beautiful countryside; gd; run down end of ssn."* **€9.30, 1 May-30 Sep.** 2023

SALIES DE BEARN 8F1 (3km S Rural) 43.45277, -0.92055 **Domaine d'Esperbasque,** Chemin de Lagisquet, 64270 Salies de Béarn **06 78 12 44 33; info@esperbasque.com; www.esperbasque.com**

€1.50-€3.50 nr

Site well sp on D933. E of rd bet Salies de Bearn and Sauveterre. Fr N pass the site, turn at next exit & app fr southern side. 2*, Med, mkd, hdstg, pt shd, sl, terr, EHU (6A) €3.50; bbq; twin axles; TV; Eng spkn; adv bkg acc; ccard acc; games area; games rm; CKE. *"Gd touring; horse riding at site highly rec; excel; go-karts; petanque; scenic, rural, visits to wine growers & Salies de Bearn; gd."* **€30.00, 1 Mar-31 Oct.** 2023

SALIES DU SALAT 8F3 (2km S Rural) 43.07621, 0.94683 **Complex Touristique de la Justale,** Chemin de St Jean, 31260 Mane **05 61 90 68 18; contact@village-vacances-mane.fr; www.village-vacances-mane.fr**

€1.20 (htd) nr

Fr A64 exit 20 onto D117, turn R in vill at sp 'Village de Vacances'. Site on R in approx 500m. 2*, Sm, hdg, mkd, pt shd, EHU (16A) €3.60 (poss rev pol); TV; phone; Eng spkn; adv bkg rec; horseriding; tennis; fishing. *"Lovely, peaceful site; lge pitches; helpful staff; excel facs; sinage poss diff to foll; well maint hdg emplacements; v quiet at night; modern, immaculate san facs."* **€19.50, 1 Apr-31 Oct.** 2022

SALINS LES BAINS 6H2 (0.5km N Rural) 46.94650, 5.87896 **Camping Le Salins les Bains (formerly Municipal),** 39110 Salins-les-Bains **07 61 14 69 01; sandrine@campinglesalinslesbains.fr; www.salinscamping.com**

nr

SE fr Besançon on N83. At Mouchard take D472 E to Salins. Turn L at rndabt at N of Salins, well sp nr old stn. If app fr E take 2nd exit fr rndabt (blind app). 2*, Sm, pt shd, EHU (10A) €3.10; 10% statics; adv bkg acc. *"Well-run site; clean, modern san facs; excel touring base N Jura; not often visited by British; far end of site quieter; htd pool adj; gd NH; barrier locked 1000-0700; chalets being built (2016)."* **€18.50, 31 Mar-1 Oct.** 2023

SALLANCHES *9A3* (4km SE Rural) *45.92388, 6.65042* **Camping Village Center Les Iles,** Lac de Passy 245 Chemin de la Cavettaz, 74190 Passy **04 30 05 15 04; www.campinglesiles.fr**

€3 (htd)

E fr Geneva on A40, exit junc 21 onto D339 dir Passy; in 400m turn L onto D39 dir Sallanches; at rndabt in 1.5km turn L onto D199 dir Domancy; immed after rlwy x-ing in 500m turn R into Chemin de Mont Blanc Plage; site at end of rd in 1km. Or E fr Sallanches on D1205 dir Chamonix; in 3km turn L (1st into filter to turn L) onto D199; in 1km turn L immed bef level x-ing; site at end of rd. 3*, Lge, hdg, mkd, pt shd, EHU (8A) inc; sw nr; phone; Eng spkn; adv bkg acc; ccard acc; fishing; CKE. *"Mountain views; conv Chamonix; vg site; v overgrown; nr rlwy and m'way; pitches bare of grass, some v muddy after rain, v shady; not rec."* **€16.00, 1 Apr-1 Oct.** **2022**

SALLE EN BEAUMONT, LA *9C3* (4km SE Rural) *44.87593, 5.83710* **Camping Belvédère de l'Obiou,** Les Egats, 38350 St Laurent-en-Beaumont **04 76 30 40 80; info@camping-obiou.com; www.camping-obiou.com**

€2 (htd) (covrd, htd)

Clearly sp on D1085. 3*, Sm, pt shd, pt sl, terr, EHU (4-10A) €3-6 (poss rev pol); red long stay; TV; 5% statics; Eng spkn; games rm; CKE. *"Superb, immac, family-run site; excel facs; helpful owners; excel rest & pool; picturesque & interesting area; gd local walks."* **€30.00, 15 Apr-15 Oct.** **2024**

> **"There aren't many sites open at this time of year"**
>
> If you're travelling outside peak season remember to call ahead to check site opening dates – even if the entry says 'open all year'.

SALLES (GIRONDE) *7D1* (0.5km SW Rural) *44.54475, -0.87506* **FFCC Camping Parc du Val de l'Eyre,** 8 Route du Minoy, 33770 Salles **05 56 88 47 03; levaldeleyre33@gmail.com; www.girondecamping.fr**

€4 nr (htd)

Exit junc 21 fr A63, foll dir to Salles on D3. On edge of Salles turn L on D108 at x-rds. Ent to site on L after rv opp Super U supmkt building. 4*, Lge, pt shd, EHU (6A) €4 (poss rev pol); gas; bbq; sw; 80% statics; ccard acc; tennis 500km; games area; canoeing; fishing; horseriding 8km. *"Attractive site; gd san facs but poss stretched when site busy; ltd facs LS; gd NH only; peaceful site by rv; gd size mkd pitches with access to water & drainage; refurbished unizex san facs (2013) v clean; conv for m'way; Carrefour opp; gd for long/sh stay."* **€50.00, 1 Apr-15 Oct.** **2024**

SALLES (GIRONDE) *7D1* (4km SW Rural) *44.52039, -0.89631* **Camping Le Bilos,** 37 Route de Bilos, 33770 Salles **05 56 88 36 53 or 06 25 70 17 46 (mob); lebilos@aol.com; www.lebilos.wixsite.com/camping-lebilos**

12 (htd)

Exit A63 junc 21; foll sp Salles on D3; turn L onto D108/D108E3 sp Lugos; pass Carrefour supmkt on R; in 2km bear R & site on R in 2km. 2*, Med, pt shd, EHU (6A) inc; gas; bbq (sep area); 80% statics; adv bkg acc. *"Pleasant, peaceful site in pine forest; sm, well-drained pitches, ltd space for tourers, friendly owners, old but clean san facs, ltd LS, cycle lane thro forest, vg NH en rte Spain; friendly welcome; site cr."* **€22.40** **2024**

SALLES CURAN *8E4* (3km N Rural) *44.20167, 2.77705* **Camping Beau Rivage,** Route des Vernhes, 12410 Salles-Curan **05 65 46 33 32; camping-aveyron-beau-rivage.fr**

€3.90

Fr Rodez D911 turn S onto the D993 sp Salles Curan.Foll rd for approx 7km; turn R after lake bdge to site on R in approx 1.5km. 4*, Med, pt shd, EHU (6A) inc; TV; adv bkg rec; fishing; watersports nr; games rm; horseriding nr. *"Excel site on lake location; lovely area, gd walks & lots of activities nrby."* **€35.00, Jun-Sep.** **2024**

SALLES CURAN *8E4* (2km NW Rural) *44.18933, 2.76693* **Camping Les Genêts,** Lac de Pareloup, 12410 Salles-Curan **05 65 46 35 34; contact@camping-les-genets.fr; www.camping-les-genets.fr**

€8.50 (htd)

and lake adj. to site

Fr D911 Rodez-Millau rd take D993 S for approx 9km, then R onto D577, site sp on R by lake. 4*, Lge, shd, pt sl, EHU (10A) inc; sw; red long stay; 40% statics; adv bkg acc; fishing; sailing; bike hire; games area. *"Beautiful area; ltd facs LS; excel site."* **€69.00, 14 May - 18 Sep, D07.** **2022**

SALLES SUR VERDON, LES *10E3* (2km N Rural) *43.78129, 6.21298* **Camp Municipal Les Ruisses,** 83630 Les Salles-sur-Verdon **04 98 10 28 15; info@campinglesruisses.fr; www.campinglesruisses.fr/en/municipal-campsite-les-ruisses-les-salles-sur-verdon-home**

€1.70

Fr Moustiers foll D957, site on L just bef Les Salles. 2*, Lge, mkd, pt shd, EHU (6A) €3.20; ccard acc; fishing; CKE. *"Pleasant site; lake nrby; ltd facs LS but gd hot shwrs & clean facs."* **€19.00, 15 Feb-15 Nov.** **2024**

FRANCE

SALLES SUR VERDON, LES *10E3* (0.5km W Rural) *43.77552, 6.20719* **Camping La Source,** Lac de Sainte Croix, Quartier Margaridon, 83630 Les Salles-sur-Verdon **04 94 70 20 40; contact@camping-la-source.eu; www.camping-la-source.eu**

€2.20 nr nr nr

Fr Moustiers on D957, foll sp Camping Les Pins (adj) via rd round vill. 4*, Med, hdg, mkd, hdstg, pt shd, terr, serviced pitches; EHU (10A) €3.80 (poss rev pol); gas; bbq; sw nr; TV; phone; Eng spkn; adv bkg acc; ccard acc; watersports; canoe hire; CKE. *"Excel facs; superb situation; well-run site conv Gorges du Verdon; dir access to lake; friendly, helpful owners; gates clsd 2200-0700; some sm pitches - manhandling poss req; highly rec."* **€32.00, 15 Mar-15 Sept.** **2024**

SALON DE PROVENCE *10E2* (12km NE Rural) *43.72125, 5.20495* **FFCC Camping Durance Luberon,** Domaine du Vergon, 13370 Mallemort **04 90 59 13 36 or 06 63 53 13 36 or 07 60 62 49 09; duranceluberon @orange.fr; campingduranceluberon.fr**

€2 (htd) nr (htd)

Exit A7 junc 26 onto D7n dir Aix-en-Provence. In 11km turn L at rndabt onto D561 dir Charleval (passing Pont-Royal golf course). In 1km turn L dir Mallemort, site on R in 1km, sp. 4*, Med, hdg, mkd, pt shd, EHU inc (6-10A) €3.80-4.50; gas; bbq; 5% statics; phone; Eng spkn; adv bkg acc; rv fishing 1km; horseriding adj; tennis; bike hire; CKE. *"Gd site with lge pitches; friendly owners; clean, modern san facs; gd touring base; excel."* **€22.00, 1 Apr-30 Sept.** **2024**

SALON DE PROVENCE *10E2* (5km NW Rural) *43.67820, 5.06480* **Camping Nostradamus,** Route d'Eyguières, 13300 Salon-de-Provence **04 90 56 08 36; camping.nostradamus@gmail.com; www.camping-nostradamus.com**

€3 nr

Exit A54/E80 junc 13 onto D569 N sp Eyguières. After approx 1.5km turn R opp airfield onto D72d, site on R in approx 4km just bef T-junc. Or fr N exit A7 junc 26 dir Salon-de-Provence. Turn R onto D17 for 5km dir Eyguières, then L onto D72, site on L. 3*, Med, mkd, hdg, pt shd, EHU (4-6A) €2.95-5.15; gas; bbq; TV; 15% statics; phone; Eng spkn; adv bkg req; ccard acc; games area; CKE. *"Pleasant site; busy high ssn; welcoming owner with vg sense of humour!; bkg fee; poss diff access lge o'fits; dusty when dry; gd walking."* **€24.00, 1 Mar-30 Oct.** **2024**

SAMOENS *9A3* (0.8km S Rural) *46.07731, 6.71851* **Camping Caravaneige Le Giffre,** 1064 Route du Lac aux Dames, La Glière, 74340 Samoëns **04 50 34 41 92; camping.samoens@wanadoo.fr; www.camping-samoens.com**

12 €2 (htd) nr nr nr

Leave A40 at junc 15 sp Fillinges/St Jeoire. Foll D907 thro Taninges E for 11km, sp Samoëns. At W town boundary turn R immed after wooden arch over rd, foll sp to Parc des Loisirs. Site on R after sw pool & park. 3*, Lge, mkd, pt shd, EHU (6-10A) €3.20-4.75; bbq; TV; 5% statics; phone; adv bkg req; ccard acc; bike hire; tennis; lake fishing adj; CKE. *"Friendly staff; some facs ltd LS; on arr, park on rdside bef checking in; htd pool adj; htd ski storage/drying rm; private san facs avail; Samoëns ski gondola 150m; excel winter site."* **€31.00** **2024**

SAMOENS *9A3* (6km W Rural) *46.08944, 6.67874* **Camp Municipal Lac et Montagne,** 74440 Verchaix **06 79 57 69 59; www.verchaix.com**

12 €1.40 nr nr nr

Fr Taninges take D907 sp Samoëns for 6km, site to R of main rd in Verchaix. 2*, Med, shd, EHU (10A) €4.10; 10% statics; phone; adv bkg acc; tennis. *"Gd touring base; clean facs; rv & lake adj; barrier locked 2200-0700; off clsd on Mondays, call."* **€22.40** **2024**

SANARY SUR MER *10F3* (4km NE Urban) *43.13147, 5.81483* **Campasun Mas de Pierredon,** 652 Chemin Raoul Coletta, 83110 Sanary-sur-Mer **04 94 74 25 02; pierredon@campasun.eu; www.campasun.eu/mas-pierredon/le-camping**

€4 (htd) (htd) 3km

Take D11 fr Sanary, cross m'way & 1st L. Site on R in approx 1km. 4*, Med, shd, EHU (10A) inc; TV; adv bkg rec; tennis; waterslide; CKE. *"Gd family site."* **€47.00, 19 Apr-30 Sep.** **2024**

SANCERRE *4G3* (4km N Rural) *47.34215, 2.86571* **Camping Les Portes de Sancerre,** Quai de Loire, 18300 St Satur **02 48 72 10 88; camping.sancerre@flower campings.com; www.camping-cher-sancerre.com**

€2 nr nr

Fr Sancerre on D955 thro cent St Satur & St Thibault. Turn L immed bef Loire bdge. Site on R in 100m. 3*, Med, hdg, shd, EHU (16A) inc (long lead poss req); sw; TV; 50% statics; Eng spkn; adv bkg acc; bike hire; games area; tennis; CKE. *"Nice site; some pitches sm, some with rv view; friendly & helpful staff; pool adj; canoe hire adj; gd clean excel san facs, rec own in peak ssn; rvside walks; gd touring cent; vg; highly rec; gd rest nrby."* **€25.00, 1 Apr-1 Oct.** **2023**

FRANCE

SANCERRE *4G3* (9.4km SW Rural) *47.30353, 2.74555* **Camping Paulin Roulin (formerly Crezancy en Sancerre),** 9 Route de Veagues, 18300 Crezancy en Sancerre **06 12 55 69 98; campingcrezancy@orange.fr**

Fr Sancerre take D955 dir Bourges. In 5km turn R onto D22 sp Crezancy, Henrichement. After 5km at vill turn L onto D86 sp Veagues. Site 100m on L. Sm, hdg, mkd, shd, EHU (6A); bbq; cooking facs; twin axles; phone; bus 100m; Eng spkn; adv bkg acc; CKE. *"Site in Sancerre vineyards with wine tasting & to buy; gd walks & cycling, but a bit hilly; easy acc to Sancerre and The Loire; hospitable site manager; excel; lovely sm friendly site; indiv hdg bays; rural, quiet & clean; new shwrs (2016)."* **€25.00, 1 Apr-31 Oct.** **2023**

SANGUINET *7D1* (3km N Rural) *44.49915, -1.07911* **Camping Lou Broustaricq,** 2315 Route de Langeot, 40460 Sanguinet **05 58 82 74 82; reception@lou-broustaricq.com; www.lou-broustaricq.com**

(htd)

Take Arcachon exit off Bordeax-Bayonne m'way. After 5km twd S on D3 & D216 to Sanguinet. Site sp in town off Bordeaux rd. 4*, V lge, mkd, pt shd, EHU (10A) inc; bbq; sw nr; TV; 60% statics; Eng spkn; adv bkg acc; ccard acc; watersports; games area; golf nr; bike hire; waterslide; tennis; sailing school; CKE. *"In lovely wooded area; gd cycle tracks; gd for children; vg; touring pitches sep fr statics; nice pool; nr army base, some aircraft noise."* **€51.00, 1 Apr-30 Sep.** **2024**

SANGUINET *7D1* (1.5km W Rural) *44.483045, -1.088951* **Sandaya Sanguinet Plage,** 1039 Avenue de Losa, 40460 Sanguinet **05 58 76 61 74; sap@sandaya.fr; www.sandaya.co.uk**

€5 (htd)

sand 100mtrs

Foll Le Lac sp at rndabt in Sanguinet, turn L on lakeside, site on L in 600m. 5*, Lge, mkd, pt shd, EHU (10A); sw nr; twin axles; 80% statics; Eng spkn; games rm; games area; sailing nr; bike hire; watersports; CKE. *"Spacious site; cycle path around lake; watersports on lake; friendly, helpful staff."* **€62.00, 27 Mar-21 Sep.** **2024**

SARLAT LA CANEDA *7C3* (12km N Rural) *44.97450, 1.18832* **Camping Les Tailladis,** 24200 Marcillac-St Quentin **05 53 59 10 95; contact@tailladis.com; www.tailladis.com**

€2.20

N fr Sarlat on D704 dir Montignac. After 7km turn L & foll sp to site. NB Access along fairly narr lane. 3*, Med, hdg, pt shd, pt sl, terr, EHU (10A) €4.20; gas; sw; 6% statics; phone; Eng spkn; adv bkg acc; ccard acc; canoeing; fishing. *"Excel site; friendly & helpful Dutch owners; immac san facs, ltd early ssn; vg food in rest; c'van storage."* **€36.00, 15 Apr-31 Oct.** **2024**

SARLAT LA CANEDA *7C3* (10km NE Rural) *44.95778, 1.27280* **Sandaya Les Péneyrals,** Le Poujol, 24590 St Crépin-et-Carlucet **05 53 28 85 71; pen@sandaya.fr; https://www.sandaya.fr/nos-campings/peneyrals**

€5 (htd)

(covrd, htd)

Fr Sarlat N on D704; D60 E dir Salignac-Eyvignes to Le Poujol; S to St Crépin. Site sp. 5*, Lge, hdg, pt shd, pt sl, terr, serviced pitches; EHU (5-10A); bbq (gas); 50% statics; Eng spkn; adv bkg acc; ccard acc; games area; waterslide; fishing; tennis. *"Friendly owners; superb family & touring site; excel aquatic ctr; some pitches require mover."* **€54.00, 14 Apr - 24 Sep, A18.** **2022**

SARLAT LA CANEDA *7C3* (9.7km NE Rural) *44.91905, 1.27789* **Camping Domaine des Mathévies,** Les Mathévies, 24200 Ste Nathalène **05 53 59 20 86 or 06 14 10 95 86 (mob); info@mathevies.com; www.mathevies.com**

€5

Exit A20 junc 55 Souillac & foll sp Roufillac. At Roufillac, foll sp to Carlux & cont to Ste Nathalène, site sp N of Ste Nathèlene. 2*, Sm, mkd, hdg, pt shd, EHU (10A) €4; sw nr; TV (pitch); 10% statics; adv bkg acc; tennis; games area; playground; games rm. *"Gd, British-owned site; lge pitches, most with views; max. 2 dogs per pitch; excel site; gd for kids."* **€40.00, 21 May - 21 Sep, D04.** **2022**

SARLAT LA CANEDA *7C3* (12km E Rural) *44.86345, 1.37350* **Camping Le Mondou,** Le Colombier, 24370 St Julien-de-Lampon **05 53 29 70 37; contact@camping-lemondou.com; camping-lemondou.com**

€1 nr

Fr Sarlat-la-Canéda take D704/D703 E; cross rv at Rouffillac, ent St Julien-de-Lampon & turn L at x-rds; site sp on R in 2km. 3*, Med, mkd, hdg, pt shd, EHU (6A) €3.50; bbq; sw nr; 10% statics; phone; Eng spkn; adv bkg acc; games rm; bike hire; fishing 300m; games area; watersports 300m. *"Beautiful views; friendly, helpful owners; gas 700m; sm, uneven pitches; gd cycle paths."* **€23.60, 30 Apr-8 Oct.** **2024**

SARLAT LA CANEDA *7C3* (10km SE Rural) *44.81536, 1.29245* **Camping Les Granges,** 175 Rte de la Borie Grande, 24250 Groléjac **05 53 28 11 15; contact@lesgranges-fr.com; www.camping-vagues-oceanes.com**

€3 (htd)

Fr Sarlat take D704 SE, sp Gourdon. Site sp nr cent of Groléjac on R. Care on acute corner after rlwy bdge. 4*, Med, hdg, pt shd, terr, serviced pitches; EHU (6A) €3.80; gas; TV; 40% statics; Eng spkn; adv bkg acc; ccard acc; lake fishing 1km; bike hire; waterslide; games rm; CKE. *"Historical & beautiful area; vg site & facs."* **€26.50, 23 Apr-11 Sep.** **2024**

FRANCE

SARLAT LA CANEDA *7C3* (11km SE Rural) *44.83274, 1.26626* **Camping Le Plein Air des Bories,** 24200 Carsac-Aillac **05 53 28 15 67; contact@camping-desbories.com; www.camping-desbories.com**

€3 (htd)

Take D704 SE fr Sarlat sp Gourdon; diff RH turn to site after Carsac vill. Easier access on D703 fr Vitrac. 3*, Med, shd, pt sl, EHU (16A) €4.50; gas; sw; Eng spkn; canoe hire; fishing; boating; tennis 700m; CKE. *"Clean, shady rvside site; friendly owners."* **€25.00, 1 Jun-15 Sep. 2023**

SARLAT LA CANEDA *7C3* (10km S Rural) *44.81521, 1.22362* **Camping La Rivière de Domme,** 24250 Domme **05 53 28 33 46 or 06 07 96 77 38; contact@camping-riviere-domme.com; www.camping-riviere-domme.com**

WD nr

Fr Sarlat take D46 to Vitrac. Cross rv bdge on D46E. In 1km at T-junc turn R on D50 & in 1km turn R at sp into site. 2*, Sm, pt shd, EHU (10A) €2.50 (poss rev pol); 10% statics; Eng spkn; adv bkg acc; games area. *"Generous pitches; pleasant owner; modern san facs; many walks fr site."* **€16.00, 11 Apr-31 Oct. 2024**

SARLAT LA CANEDA *7C3* (10km S Rural) *44.82181, 1.22587* **Camping Le Bosquet,** La Rivière, 24250 Domme **05 53 28 37 39; info@lebousquet.com; www.lebosquet.com**

€2 WD

Fr Sarlat take D46 S to Vitrac cross rv on D46E. Sp at junc, site 500m on R. 3*, Sm, hdg, mkd, pt shd, EHU (6A) €2.50 (long lead poss req); gas; sw nr; 50% statics; Eng spkn; adv bkg acc; fishing 500m; CKE. *"Lovely peaceful site with friendly, helpful owners; excel updated san facs but poss stretched high ssn; gd shd but sm pitches; gd views of Domme."* **€27.70, 11 Apr-27 Sep. 2024**

SARLAT LA CANEDA *7C3* (10km S Rural) *44.81725, 1.21944* **Camping Le Perpetuum,** 24250 Domme **05 53 28 35 18; leperpetuum.domme@orange.fr; www.campingleperpetuum.com**

€2 WD MSP

Fr Sarlat take D46 to Vitrac; cross rv bdge to D46E; in 1km turn R onto D50, R again in 1km at site sp. 4*, Med, hdg, mkd, hdstg, pt shd, EHU (10A); bbq; sw nr; TV; Eng spkn; adv bkg acc; ccard acc; games area; canoeing; CKE. *"Site fronts rv; busy high ssn; relaxed, friendly atmosphere; gd sized pitches; cheerful, helpful owners; v clean san facs; gd pool; Rv Dordogne adj; gd local dog walks; late arr area at ent; excel campsite; generous, well hdg pitches."* **€36.00, 27 May-5 Oct. 2024**

SARLAT LA CANEDA *7C3* (10km S Rural) *44.82525, 1.25360* **Domaine de Soleil-Plage,** Caudon-par-Montfort, 24200 Vitrac **05 35 37 14 13; info@soleilplage.fr; www.soleilplage.fr**

€3.50 (htd) WD MSP (htd)

On D46, 6km S of Sarlat twd Vitrac, turn L onto D703 to Château Montfort, R to site dir Caudon, sp. Site beyond Camping La Bouysse on rvside, 2km E of Vitrac. If coming fr Souillac on D703, when app Montfort rd v narr with overhanging rock faces. Narr access rds on site. 5*, Lge, hdg, pt shd, serviced pitches; EHU (16A) inc (poss rev pol); gas; bbq; TV; 45% statics; phone; Eng spkn; adv bkg req; ccard acc; waterslide; bike hire; tennis; golf 1km; canoeing; rv fishing adj; horseriding 5km; games rm; CKE. *"Lovely site in beautiful location; friendly, welcoming owner; variety of pitches - extra for serviced/rvside (shady); no o'fits over 7m Jun-Aug; san facs clean; superb aquatic complex; poss muddy when wet; red groups; highly rec; first class comprehensive site; poss best site we've ever stayed at; lge private pitches; lovely cycling, but some on fairly steep rds."* **€44.00, 8 Apr - 29 Sep, D15. 2022**

SARLAT LA CANEDA *7C3* (12km S Rural) *44.79175, 1.16266* **Camping Bel Ombrage,** 24250 St Cybranet **05 53 28 34 14; belombrage@wanadoo.fr; www.belombrage.com**

WD nr nr

Fr Sarlat take D46 sp Bergerac, rd then conts as D57; after 8km turn L at Vézac sp Castelnaund. After 1.6km at T-junc turn L onto D703 & in 180m turn R onto D57. Cont thro Castelnaund on D57; site on L in 3km. 3*, Lge, hdg, shd, EHU (10A) inc; bbq; sw; red long stay; TV; adv bkg acc; ccard acc; tennis 800m; horseriding 2km; fishing; games area; bike hire; games rm; CKE. *"Attractive, well-run site by rv; popular with British; lge pitches; no o'fits over 8m high ssn; modern san facs; peaceful early ssn; library; ideal base for Dordogne; mkt Thur; excel."* **€25.00, 1 Jun - 5 Sep, D01. 2022**

SARLAT LA CANEDA *7C3* (6km S Rural) *44.82375, 1.25080* **Camping La Bouysse,** 1583 Route de la Plage de Caudon, 24200 Vitrac **05 53 28 33 05; info@labouysse.com; www.labouysse.com**

€3.80 WD (htd)

S fr Sarlat on D46 dir Vitrac. At Vitrac 'port' bef bdge turn L onto D703 sp Carsac. In 2km turn R & foll site sp, site on L. Well sp. 3*, Med, mkd, hdg, pt shd, EHU (10A) €6.80; gas; bbq; sw; 10% statics; phone; Eng spkn; adv bkg req; ccard acc; canoe hire; tennis; fishing; games area; CKE. *"Beautiful family-run site on Rv Dordogne; helpful owner; plenty gd clean san facs; gd access rv beach; muddy when wet; many Bastides in area; excel."* **€28.90, 12 Apr-17 Sep. 2023**

SARLAT LA CANEDA *7C3* (9km S Rural) *44.81628, 1.21508* **Camping Beau Rivage,** Gaillardou, 24250 La Roque-Gageac **05 53 28 32 05; beaurivage@vagues-oceanes.com; www.beaurivagedordogne.com**

€3 (htd) nr (htd)

On S side of D703, 1km W of Vitrac adj Rv Dordogne. 3*, Lge, mkd, pt shd, EHU (6A) €3.50; gas; TV; 10% statics; phone; Eng spkn; adv bkg rec; games area; horseriding; bike hire; rv; archery; canoeing; tennis; golf 2km. *"Gd touring base."* **€23.60, 4 Apr-20 Sep. 2024**

SARLAT LA CANEDA *7C3* (9km S Rural) *44.82442, 1.16939* **Camping La Plage,** 83 Près La Roque-Gageac, 24220 Vézac **05 53 29 50 83 or 06 83 36 41 68; contact@campinglaplagevezac.fr; www.camping-laplage.fr**

nr

On banks of Rv Dordogne, 500m W of La Roque-Gageac on D703. 3*, Med, mkd, shd, EHU (3A) €2.40; gas; bbq; sw; 10% statics; adv bkg acc; canoeing; fishing; CKE. *"Attractive site; excel pitches; kind, helpful owers; ltd facs LS; highly rec; upgraded (2014) immac, well kept san facs."* **€23.80, 1 Mar-30 Oct. 2024**

SARLAT LA CANEDA *7C3* (9km S Rural) *44.78648, 1.20930* **Camping Le Pech de Caumont,** 24250 Cénac-et-St-Julien **05 53 28 21 63; www.pech-de-caumont.com**

nr

D46 fr Sarlat to Cénac, cross rv & cont on D46 thro Cénac; site ent on L 500m past End of Vill sp. Do not go thro Domme. 3*, Med, hdg, mkd, pt shd, pt sl, terr, EHU (6A) €3.10; bbq; sw nr; TV; 20% statics; phone; Eng spkn; adv bkg acc; ccard acc; CKE. *"Views fr most pitches; modern, clean san facs; helpful owners; popular, tidy, family-run site; excel."* **€24.90, 27 Apr-21 Sep. 2024**

SARLAT LA CANEDA *7D3* (18km SSW Rural) *44.76762, 1.17590* **Camping Le Moulin de Paulhiac,** 24250 Daglan **05 53 28 20 88; info@moulin-de-paulhiac.com; www.moulin-de-paulhiac.com**

€3 (htd) shgl

D57 SW fr Sarlat, across rv into St Cybranet & site in 2km. Fr Souillac W on D703 alongside Rv Dordogne; x-ing rv onto D46 (nr Domme) & D50, to site. Med, mkd, hdg, shd, EHU (10A) €6; gas; TV; 20% statics; Eng spkn; adv bkg acc; ccard acc; canoeing; waterslide; rv fishing adj; CKE. *"Pretty site; friendly, helpful staff; vg fruit/veg mkt Sun in vill; highly rec."* **€25.00, 3 May-6 Sep. 2024**

See advertisement

SARLAT LA CANEDA *7C3* (10km SW Rural) *44.80519, 1.15852* **Camping Maisonneuve,** Vallée de Céou, 24250 Castelnaud-la-Chapelle **05 53 29 51 29; contact@campingmaisonneuve.com; www.campingmaisonneuve.com**

(htd) (htd)

Take D57 SW fr Sarlat sp Beynac. Cross Rv Dordogne at Castelnaud; site sp 500m on L out of Castelnaud on D57 twd Daglan. Foll narr rd across bdge (or alt ent - cont on D57 for 2km, sp on L for c'vans). 4*, Med, hdstg, mkd, hdg, pt shd, EHU (6-10A) €3.10-6.40; gas; bbq; sw; TV; 10% statics; Eng spkn; adv bkg req; ccard acc; rv; games rm; tennis 2km; bike hire; fishing; CKE. *"Vg, spacious site; helpful owners; excel, modern, clean facs (hot water unreliable); gd walks, cycling; outstanding."* **€32.40, 1 Apr-31 Oct. 2022**

FRANCE

SARLAT LA CANEDA *7C3* (8km SW Rural) *44.83560, 1.15873* **Camping Les Deux Vallées,** La Gare, 24220 Vézac **+33(0)608406158; contact@campingles2vallees.com; www.campingles2vallees.com**

€2 (htd)

Exit A20 junc 55 onto D804 dir Sarlat-la-Caneda; cont onto D703/D704A/D704 to Sarlat; then take D57 SW to Vézac; immed after sp for vill take 1st R to site. Or fr E leave D703 onto D57; 250m after junc with D49 turn L & foll sp to site. 3*, Med, hdg, mkd, hdstg, pt shd, EHU (6-10A) €4.10; gas; bbq; red long stay; TV; 6% statics; Eng spkn; adv bkg req; ccard acc; games area; bike hire; games rm; ice; CKE. *"Excel site; helpful, friendly Dutch owners; ltd san facs LS; poss muddy when wet; entmnt July/Aug (in Dutch); gd local walks; poss long leads req; some reverse polarity; ltd water points; pitch 71,72 &73 too restricted for c'van access."* **€41.00, 17 Feb-12 Nov.** **2024**

SARLAT LA CANEDA *7C3* (9km W Rural) *44.90805, 1.11527* **Camping Le Moulin du Roch,** Le Roch, Route des Eyzies, 24200 Sarlat-la-Canéda **06 73 63 88 96; moulin@capfun.com; www.moulin-du-roch.com**

(htd) (htd)

Fr A20 take exit 55 at Souillac dir Sarlat. Head for D704 twds Sarlat La Caneda. At rndabt in Sarlat (just under rlwy viaduct) take 2nd exit onto bypass. Take 2nd exit at next rndabt staying on D704. At next rndabt take 2nd exit onto D6 dir Les Eyzies (becomes D47). Site on L in approx 9 km on D47. Fr N on D704 to Sarlat, turn R at hypmkt, then as above. 4*, Lge, mkd, hdg, pt shd, terr, serviced pitches; EHU (6A) inc; gas; bbq (charcoal, gas); sw nr; red long stay; twin axles; TV; 45% statics; Eng spkn; adv bkg rec; ccard acc; horseriding nr; games rm; canoeing nr; lake fishing; outdoor sports; playground; CKE. *"Well-run, family owned site; lge pitches; clean facs but poss long, steep walk; some noise fr adj rd; gd rest & pool; m'vans poss not acc after prolonged heavy rain due soft grnd; mkt Sat."*
€52.00, 25 May-22 Sep, D02. **2022**

SARZEAU *2G3* (8km SE Coastal) *47.50551, -2.68308* **Camping Manoir de Ker An Poul,** 1 Route de la Grée, Penvins, 56370 Sarzeau **02 49 88 07 45; keranpoul@edenvillages.fr; www.manoirdekeranpoul.com**

€4 nr (htd, indoor) sand 1km

Fr E exit N165 1km E of Muzillac, sp Sarzeau D20 & cont approx 20km to junc of D20 & D199, S on D199 sp Penvins. Fr W, 6km E of Vannes, exit N165 onto N780 sp Sarzeau, in 9.5km S onto D199 sp Penvins. 4*, Lge, hdg, pt shd, pt sl, EHU (6-10A) €4; bbq; TV; 30% statics; Eng spkn; adv bkg acc; tennis; games area; bike hire; CKE. *"Spacious pitches; warm welcome; excel staff; no dog walk on site; san facs recently renovated (2015); noisy weekend nr pool, quieter mid week."* **€60.10, 7 Apr-23 Sep.** **2023**

SARZEAU *2G3* (2.5km S Coastal) *47.50720, -2.76083* **Camping La Ferme de Lann Hoëdic,** Rue Jean de la Fontaine, Route de Roaliguen, 56370 Sarzeau **02 97 48 01 73; contact@camping-lannhoedic.fr; www.camping-lannhoedic.fr**

€2.60 (htd) nr nr nr sand 800m

Fr Vannes on N165 turn onto D780 dir Sarzeau. Do not ent Sarzeau, but at Super U rndabt foll sp Le Roaliguen. After 1.5km turn L to Lann Hoëdic. 3*, Med, mkd, pt shd, EHU (16A) €4.10; gas; 10% statics; phone; Eng spkn; adv bkg acc; ccard acc; bike hire; CKE. *"Peaceful, well-managed, popular, family-run site; warm welcome; excel, clean facs; beautiful coastline - beaches & dunes; highly rec; gd cycling routes."* **€24.50, 28 Mar-01 Nov.** **2020**

SARZEAU *2G3* (2km SW Rural) *47.52255, -2.79713* **Lodge Club Presqu'île de Rhuys (formerly Le Bohat),** Lieu Dit Le Bas Bohat, 56370 SARZEAU **02 97 41 29 93; lodge@capfun.com; www.lodgeclub.fr**

€3.70 (covrd, htd) sand 4km

Fr Vannes on N165, exit onto D780 to Sarzeau. Do not turn off this main rd to Sarzeau (town not suitable for m'vans or c'vans) but cont twd Arzon; 1km after 2nd rndabt turn L for Le Bohat & Spernec, then take 1st R. Fr S on N165 take D20 at Muzillac, thro Surzur & cont to join D780 to Sarzeau. Then as above. 4*, Lge, mkd, hdg, pt shd, EHU (10A) inc; gas; bbq (charcoal, gas); TV; 4% statics; phone; Eng spkn; adv bkg acc; ccard acc; bike hire; fishing; golf 6km; waterslide; horseriding 2km; games rm; watersports 4km; CKE. *"Busy, well-kept, Dutch-owned site; pony rides; lge pitches; excel, helpful staff; clean san facs; excel pools; gd for families; cycle tracks; gd touring base; mkt Thu; vg."* **€34.00, 5 Apr-22 Sep.** **2024**

SAULIEU *6G1* (1km N Rural) *47.28936, 4.22401* **Camping de Saulieu,** Route de Paris, 21210 Saulieu **03 80 64 16 19; camping.salieu@wanadoo.fr; www.aquadis-loisirs.com**

€1.50 (htd)

On D906 on L of rd on ent fr N. Sp. 3*, Lge, hdg, mkd, pt shd, pt sl, EHU (10A) €3.90; gas; adv bkg acc; tennis; lake fishing; CKE. *"Nr town but rural feel; quiet at far end of site, away fr pool & playgrnd; no twin axles; many rests in town; gd walking area; gd."*
€22.00, 18 Mar-3 Nov. **2024**

SAUMUR *4G1* (2km N Urban) *47.25990, -0.06440*
Flower Camping de L'Ile d'Offard, Rue de Verden, 49400 Saumur **02 41 40 30 00 or 02 52 56 03 11; iledoffard@flowercampings.com; www.saumur-camping.com or www.flowercampings.com**
€3 (htd) (htd)

Exit A85 junc 3 onto D347 and then D347E; ent town past rlwy stn & cross Rv Loire bdge; turn L immed over bdge & alongside rv. At rndabt turn L & take 1st L to site; foll sp. Site on island facing Saumur castle. 4*, Lge, hdstg, mkd, hdg, pt shd, pt sl, EHU (10A) (poss rev pol); gas; sw nr; TV; 20% statics; Eng spkn; adv bkg req; ccard acc; tennis; boating adj; fishing adj; games area; jacuzzi; bike hire; CKE. *"Pleasant, busy, well-run site; ideal for children; hdstg pitches in winter; helpful staff; clean, most pitches lge but some v sm pitches bet statics - lge o'fits check in advance; gd bar & rest; can be muddy when wet; gd cycle rtes; nice rvside and bdge walk to town; excel, but busy; great facs; easy acc to city; san facs refurb, modern & clean (2015); recep clsd 1300-1400; lovely loc; gd base for visiting Loire Valley or Saumur town; 35 placement municiple area adj, acc by card; v welcoming."*
€36.00, 15 Mar-13 Oct. **2024**

SAUMUR *4G1* (7km NE Rural) *47.29937, -0.01218*
Camping Le Pô Doré, 49650 Allonnes **02 41 38 78 80; camping.du.po.dore@wanadoo.fr; www.camping-lepodore.com**
€1.50 (htd)

NE fr Saumur on N347 & turn R onto D10. Site 3km W of Allonnes on R. 4*, Med, hdg, mkd, hdstg, pt shd, EHU (6-10A) €3-4 (poss rev pol); 25% statics; phone; Eng spkn; ccard acc; bike hire; CKE. *"Gd, clean & tidy site; helpful staff; dirty, sandy soil; conv wine rtes, caves, museums & a'route; conv NH/sh stay; excel san facs; spectacular laggon."*
€28.60, 15 Mar-15 Nov. **2023**

SAUMUR *4G1* (6km E Rural) *47.24755, -0.00033*
Camping Domaine de la Brèche, 5 Impasse de la Brèche, 49730 Varennes-sur-Loire **+33(0) 241 512 292; mail@etang-breche.com; www.domainedelabreche.com**
(covrd, htd)

Exit 3 of A85, then D767 & D347 twrds Saumur, then D952 twd Tours & site sp fr either dir. Site on N side of rd (6km W of Varennes) app fr lge lay-by giving easy ent. 5*, Lge, hdg, pt shd, serviced pitches; EHU (16A); gas; TV; 50% statics; phone; Eng spkn; adv bkg rec; ccard acc; waterslide; tennis; bike hire; games rm; CKE. *"Spacious site & pitches; well-organised; excel facs; auto barrier clsd 2300-0700; helpful staff; excel."*
€45.00, 21 Apr-10 Sep, A32. **2022**

SAUMUR *4G1* (7.5km NW Rural) *47.29440, -0.14120*
Huttopia Saumur, 1 Chemin Chantepie, Saint-Hilaire-Saint-Florent, 49400 Saumur **02 41 67 95 34; https://europe.huttopia.com/site/camping-saumur**
€5 (htd) (covrd, htd)

Fr Saumer take D751 on S bank of Rv Loire sp Gennes. Turn L 3km N of St Hilaire-St-Florent just bef lge sp for a supmkt & bef mushroom museum. Site sp. Or fr N after x-ing rv on N347, take turn sp St Hilaire-St-Florent & join D751 for Gennes; site is 3km N of St Hilaire-St Florent, well sp fr D751. NB Easy to miss turning. 5*, Lge, mkd, hdg, pt shd, EHU (10A) inc (poss rev pol); gas; bbq; TV; 10% statics; Eng spkn; adv bkg acc; ccard acc; golf 2km; games rm; horseriding 5km; tennis 2km; bike hire; fishing; CKE. *"Excel well-run site nr rv; well-spaced, lge pitches, some with excel rv views (supplement); access to some pitches diff lge o'fits; friendly, helpful staff; no o'fits over 10m; boating 5km; excel san facs, conv Loire cycle rte; mkt Sat Saumur; excel views, bar & rest; excel cycle track; TV recep may be diff due to many trees."*
€40.00, 14 Apr-25 Sep, L06. **2022**

SAUMUR *4G1* (9km NW Rural) *47.30982, -0.14492*
Camping Terre d'Entente, Lieu dit de la Croix Rouge, 49160 St Martin-de-la-Place **09 72 30 31 72 or 07 70 07 69 37; contact@terre-dentente.fr; terre-dentente.fr**
€1.50 nr nr nr

Exit A85 junc 3 sp Saumur. Take slip rd immed bef bdge then L sp 'Angers Touristique'. Site on L at vill sp. Fr Saumur take D347 N across rv then turn L onto D952 dir Angers. At St Martin-de-la-Place foll sp for site. 2*, Med, mkd, pt shd, EHU (6-10A) €3-4; sw nr; bus 150m; Eng spkn; adv bkg acc; sailing adj; CKE. *"Beautiful, tranquil site on Rv Loire; friendly, helpful owners; 26 steps to spacious san facs; disabled facs at grnd level; 2m high security fence by rv; barrier clsd 2200-0700; no twin axles; conv Saumur; bar 200m; v pleasant site; poor."* **€19.00, 8 Apr-30 Sep.** **2023**

SAVENAY *2G3* (2.5km E Rural) *47.35651, -1.92136*
Camp Municipal du Lac de Savenay, Route du Lac, 44260 Savenay **02 40 58 31 76; www.camping-lac-savenay.fr**
€1.20 (htd)

Site well sp in Savenay. Can avoid Savenay Town by turning off N165 SW of town on new rd, dir LAC. 2*, Med, mkd, pt shd, terr, EHU (10A) €2.07; Eng spkn; fishing. *"Vg, clean site in attractive lakeside park; lge pitches; gas adj; pool adj; excel modern san block; terr pitches req long elec leads."*
€26.00, 1 Mar-31 Oct. **2022**

FRANCE

SAVERNE *6E3* (2km SW Urban) *48.73329, 7.35371* **Camping Les Portes d'Alsace (formerly Camping de Saverne),** Rue du Père Libermann, 67700 Saverne **03 88 91 35 65; contact@camping-lesportes dalsace.com; www.vacances-seasonova.com**
€1.60 (htd) nr (covrd)

Take Saverne exit fr A4, junc 45. Site well sp nr town cent. 3*, Med, mkd, hdstg, hdg, pt shd, pt sl, terr, EHU (6-10A) €3.10-5.70 (poss rev pol); 20% statics; adv bkg acc; ccard acc; CKE. *"Pleasant, busy, well-run site; pitches mostly terr; warm welcome, friendly staff; long steep walk back fr town; m'van aire de service nr ent; trains to Strasbourg fr town; poss travellers; v gd."*
€27.00, 26 Mar - 1 Nov, J06. **2022**

SAVIGNY EN VERON *4G1* (0.5km W Rural) *47.20059, 0.13932* **FFCC Camping La Fritillaire,** Rue Basse, 37420 Savigny-en-Véron **02 47 58 03 79 or 06 81 27 96 72; lafritillaire@orange.fr; www.campinglafritillaire.com**
€1 (htd) nr nr

Fr Montsoreau on D751 or D7 on S bank of Rv Loire, foll sp to Savigny-en-Véron & site. 3*, Med, mkd, pt shd, EHU (10A) inc (poss rev pol); bbq; 10% statics; adv bkg acc; bike hire; horseriding; tennis; CKE. *"Excel, peaceful site; htd covrd pool 4km; friendly owners; gd clean facs, ltd LS; gd touring base Loire chateaux; vg cycle rtes; games area (under-7s); poss workers staying on site (2009)."* **€13.00, 29 Mar-20 Oct.** **2024**

SEES *4E1* (1km S Urban) *48.59875, 0.17103* **Camp Municipal Le Clos Normand,** Ave du 8 mai 1945, 61500 Sées **02 33 28 87 37 or 02 33 28 74 79 (LS); contact@camping-sees.fr; www.ville-sees.fr**
€1.25 nr nr nr

C'vans & lge m'vans best app fr S - twd rndabt at S end of by-pass (rec use this rndabt as other rtes diff & narr). Well sp. Narr ent. 3*, Sm, hdg, pt shd, EHU (10A) €2.50; gas; 10% statics; Eng spkn; adv bkg acc; fishing; CKE. *"Spacious, well-cared for pitches; helpful, friendly warden; gd san facs, poss stretched if site full; excel mv service pnt; gates clsd 2100 (2000 LS); easy walk to town; shop nr; vg."*
€13.00, 16 Apr-30 Sep. **2023**

SEILHAC *7C4* (4km SW Rural) *45.35018, 1.64642* **Camp Municipal du Pilard,** La Barthe, 19700 Lagraulière **05 55 73 71 04; mairie@lagrauliere.fr; www.lagrauliere.correze.net**
€1 nr nr nr

Exit A20 junc 46 onto D34 to Lagraulière, site sp. NB Lge o'fits rec take D44 & D167E fr Seilhac. 2*, Sm, mkd, pt shd, EHU (3-6A) €3 (poss rev pol); bbq; Eng spkn; tennis; CKE. *"Quiet, clean site nr pleasant interesting vill; htd pool adj; warden calls; mkts on Thurs."* **€10.00, 15 Jun-15 Sep.** **2024**

SELESTAT *6E3* (7km N Rural) *48.30647, 7.50057* **Camping Rural (Weiss),** 10 Rue du Buhl, 67600 Ebersheim **06 85 10 95 54; theo.sonntag@wanadoo.fr; www.selestat-haut-koenigsbourg.com/lei/detail/114/222000308/1884/camping-rural-foyer-saint-martin-ebersheim.htm**
nr

Fr S or N on N83 in vill of Ebersheim foll green Camping Rural sps. Sm, pt shd, EHU (16A) inc; bbq; cooking facs; bus 0.5km; Eng spkn; adv bkg acc; CKE. *"Gd touring base; friendly, helpful staff; excel Boulangerie in vill; dogs free; site self, staff visit pm; excel for sh or lg stay."* **€15.00, 15 Jun-15 Sep.** **2024**

SELESTAT *6E3* (1km SW Urban) *48.25470, 7.44781* **Camping Les Cigognes,** Rue de la 1ère D.F.L, 67600 Sélestat **03 88 92 03 98; camping@ville-selestat.fr; http://camping.selestat.fr**
€1 nr nr

Site sp D1083 & D424. Fr S town cent turn E off D1083 & foll sps to site adj schools & playing fields. 2*, Med, mkd, pt shd, EHU (6-16A) inc; gas; train to Strasbourg nrby; Eng spkn; adv bkg rec; CKE. *"Great, well-run site; helpful staff; pool 300m; some noise fr local football area; excel new san blocks; easy walk to old town; mkt Sat; rec."*
€15.50, 1 Apr-15 Oct & 15 Nov-24 Dec. **2022**

SELESTAT *6E3* (12km W Rural) *48.27287, 7.29052* **Camping du Haut-Koenigsbourg,** Rue de la Vancelle, 68660 Lièpvre **03 68 61 14 60; contact@camping-haut koenigsbourg.com; www.camping-hautkoenigs bourg.com**
€2 (htd) nr

Fr Sélestat W on N59 twd Lièpvre vill then R at factory car park & foll site sps. Fr Ste Marie-aux-Mines on N59 turn L at rndabt after tunnel. 3*, Med, mkd, pt shd, pt sl, EHU (4-8A) €3-4.20; bbq; TV; 10% statics; CKE. *"V well maintained site; gd location; rec; gd walks & cycling; lovely site."*
€23.90, 15 Mar-4 Nov, 1 Dec-24 Dec. **2024**

SEMUR EN AUXOIS *6G1* (3.5km S Rural) *47.46812, 4.35589* **Camping Pont du Lac (formerly Lac de Pont),** 16 Rue du Lac, 21140 Pont-et-Massène **03 80 97 01 26; contact@camping-lacdepont.fr or camping-lacdepont @orange.fr; www.camping-du-lac-de-pont.business.site**
12 €2 nr

Exit A6 junc 23 twd Semur-en-Auxois on D980; after sh dist turn R sp 'Lac de Pont' D103. 3*, Med, hdg, pt shd, pt sl, EHU (6A) €3.50; gas; bbq; sw nr; phone; Eng spkn; ccard acc; tennis; watersports; games rm; bike hire; CKE. *"Warm welcome, helpful owners; generous pitches, some shady; san facs dated; vg for teenagers - games/meeting rm; 'Petit Train' goes round site & into Semur; cycle rte/walks adj; gd touring base; nr A6 m'way; diving platform; walled, medieval town; muddy pitches; site neglected (2017), NH only."* **€15.00** **2023**

SENNECEY LE GRAND *6H1* (7km E Rural) *46.65480, 4.94461* **Château de L'Epervière,** Rue du Château, 71240 Gigny-sur-Saône **03 85 94 16 90; info@domaine-eperviere.com; www.domaine-eperviere.com**

€3 (htd) (covrd, htd, indoor)

Fr N exit A6 junc 26 (Chalon Sud) onto N6 dir Mâcon & Tournus; at Sennecey-le-Grand turn E onto D18 sp Gigny-sur-Saône; site sp 1km S of Gigny-sur-Saône. Or fr S exit A6 junc 27 (Tournus) onto N6 N to Sennecey-le-Grand, then as above. NB Diff to find signs fr main rd. 5*, Lge, hdstg, mkd, hdg, pt shd, EHU (6A) inc; gas; bbq; TV; Eng spkn; adv bkg acc; ccard acc; sauna; bike hire; tennis 400m; fishing; games rm; jacuzzi; CKE. *"Superb, spacious, well-run site in grnds of chateau nr sm lake; lovely, lge pitches; warm welcome, pleasant staff; excel san facs; gd pools & rest; vg for families; wine tasting; tour op statics; lake nrby; interesting wild life; no o'fits over 18m high ssn; boggy when wet; conv NH fr a'route; fantastic site; level pitches; great facs."* **€45.00, 1 Apr - 30 Sep, L12. 2022**

"I need an on-site restaurant"

We do our best to make sure site information is correct, but it is always best to check any must-have facilities are still available or will be open during your visit.

SENNECEY LE GRAND *6H1* (5km NW Rural) *46.67160, 4.83301* **Camping La Héronnière,** Les Lacs de Laives, 71240 Laives **03 85 44 98 85; camping.laives@wanadoo.fr; www.camping-laheronniere.com**

€1.60 nr (htd)

Exit A6 junc 26 (fr N) or junc 27 (fr S) onto N6. Turn W at Sennecey-le-Grand to Laives. Foll sp 'Lacs de Laives'. Sp on D18. 3*, Med, hdg, mkd, hdstg, pt shd, EHU (6A) €4.80; sw nr; Eng spkn; adv bkg acc; fishing; windsurfing; bike hire; watersports; CKE. *"Lovely, level, lakeside site; busy NH; may fill up after 1500; popular with bikers; vg; pretty site; laid back helpful staff; gd NH; romantic rest by lakeside 3 mins walk (high ssn); excel facs; san facs ok but dirty."* **€27.00, 3 Mar-4 Nov. 2023**

SENS *4F4* (1km S Urban) *48.18312, 3.28803* **Camp Municipal Entre Deux Vannes,** Ave de Senigallia, 89100 Sens **03 86 65 64 71 or 03 86 65 37 42 (LS); http://ville-sens.fr**

nr nr

D606/D1060 S of town. Take D606a sp sens. Site on R in 600m. 2*, Med, mkd, pt shd, EHU (16A) inc; adv bkg rec; ccard acc; CKE. *"Excel site; opp rv & superb park area; friendly, helpful warden; san facs old but clean; gate locked 2200; easy walk to town; ensure height barrier moved bef ent."* **€13.50, 15 May-15 Sep. 2024**

SERIGNAC *7D3* (5km W Rural) *44.43103, 1.06902* **Camping Le Clos Barrat Naturiste (Naturist),** 46700 Sérignac **06 47 50 09 78 or 04 74 24 60 82; info@leclosbarrat.fr; www.leclosbarrat.fr**

€2.50 (htd)

Fr Fumel by-pass turn S on D139 to Montayral, rd cont but becomes D4. Site sp bet Mauroux & St Matré. 3*, Med, mkd, pt shd, pt sl, EHU (6A) inc; own san rec; gas; bbq (gas); twin axles; TV; 2% statics; phone; Eng spkn; adv bkg acc; ccard acc; games rm; CKE. *"Nr Rv Lot; INF card req - can be bought on site; new owners (2015); helpful staff; excel & friendly site; beautiful area."* **€29.00, 1 May-25 Sep. 2023**

SERIGNAN PLAGE *10F1* (1km W Coastal) *43.26398, 3.3210* **Sérignan Plage,** Les Orpelières, 34410 Sérignan-Plage **04 67 32 35 33; info@leserignanplage.com; www.leserignanplage.com**

€4 (covrd, htd)

Exit A9 junc 35. After toll turn L at traff lts onto N112 & at 1st rndabt strt on to D64. In 5km turn L onto D37E Sérignan-Plage, turn R on narr 1-way rd to site. Adj to Camping Sérignan-Plage Nature (Naturist site). 3*, V lge, mkd, hdg, pt shd, EHU (5A) inc; gas; bbq; sw; TV; 80% statics; Eng spkn; adv bkg acc; tennis; horseriding; CKE. *"Busy, even LS; excel pool; Club Nautique - sw, sailing & water-ski tuition on private beach; use of naturist private beach & facs adj; some tourers amongst statics & sm sep touring area."* **€78.00, 24 Apr-28 Sept. 2022**

SERIGNAN PLAGE *10F1* (1.6km W Coastal) *43.26308, 3.31976* **Camping Le Sérignan-Plage Nature (Naturist),** Les Orpelière, 34410 Sérignan-Plage **04 67 32 09 61; info@leserignannature.com; www.leserignannature.com**

€6 sand

Exit A9 junc 36 Beziers Est onto D64. At Sérignan town turn L on D37E to Sérignan-Plage. After 4km turn R on dual c'way. At T-junc turn L & immed L again in 50m to site. 5*, Lge, mkd, pt shd, EHU (5A) inc (poss rev pol); gas; bbq; red long stay; TV; 75% statics; Eng spkn; adv bkg rec; golf 15km; bike hire; CKE. *"Lovely, clean site & facs; max 2 dogs; helpful staff; Cmp Le Sérignan Plage (non-naturist) adj with use of same private beach & facs; pool also shared - for naturists' use 1000-1200 only; beauty cent; cycle rtes adj; excel."* **€63.30, 28 Apr-2 Oct. 2024**

SERIGNAN PLAGE *10F1* (5km W Rural) *43.26965, 3.28631* **FFCC Camping Le Paradis,** Route de Valras-Plage, 34410 Sérignan **04 67 32 24 03; paradis camping34@aol.com; www.camping-leparadis.com**

sand 2km

Exit A9 junc 35 Béziers Est onto D64 dir Valras-Plage. Site on L on rndabt at S end of Sérignan by-pass, 1.5km S of Sérignan. 4*, Med, mkd, pt shd, EHU (6A) inc; gas; red long stay; Eng spkn; adv bkg rec; CKE. *"Excel, well-kept, family-run site; immac san facs; nr gd beaches; vg value LS; EHU poss no earth."* **€41.00, 1 Apr-30 Sep. 2024**

FRANCE

SERRES *9D3* (1.4km S Rural) *44.41941, 5.71840* **Camping des Barillons,** Route de Nice, 05700 Serres **04 92 67 17 35 or 06 30 50 31 58; campingdes barillons@free.fr; campingdesbarillons.free.fr**

€1.60 (covrd, htd)

D4075 dir Sistoron fr town ctr. Sm, pt shd, EHU (6A); bbq; adv bkg acc.; CKE. *"Gd."* **€18.50, 1 Apr-30 Sep. 2023**

"Satellite navigation makes touring much easier"

Remember most sat navs don't know if you're towing or in a larger vehicle – always use yours alongside maps and site directions.

SERRIERES *9C2* (3km W Rural) *45.30872, 4.74622* **Camping Le Bas Larin,** 88 Route de Larin Le Bas, 07340 Félines **04 75 34 87 93; info@campingbas larin.com; www.campingbaslarin.com**

nr nr

Exit A7 junc 12 Chanas or fr N7, exit at Serrières onto D1082; cross canal & rv; cont over rndabt up winding hill, camp on L nr hill top. Sp fr N7 & D1082, but easily missed - foll sp Safari de Peaugres. 3*, Med, shd, terr, EHU (4-10A) €2.50-3.80; 10% statics; Eng spkn; games area; games rm; CKE. *"Friendly, family-run site; beautiful views; helpful staff; easy access pitches; popular with Dutch; excel; v nice site but ent to pitches may be diff."* **€23.00, 1 Apr-30 Sep. 2023**

SETE *10F1* (11km SW Coastal) *43.34194, 3.58440* **Camping Le Castellas,** Cours Gambetta, 34200 Sète **04 30 63 38 80; www.campinglecastellas.com**

€3 (htd) sand 150m

On D612/N112 bet Agde and Sète. Foll sp for 'Plages-Agde'. 4*, Lge, hdg, pt shd, EHU (6A) inc; gas; red long stay; Eng spkn; adv bkg acc; bike hire; tennis; games area; CKE. *"Bull-fighting in ssn; superb beach; twin axles welcome."* **€59.00, 6 Apr-29 Sep. 2024**

SEVERAC LE CHATEAU *9D1* (1km SW Urban) *44.31841, 3.06412* **Camping Les Calquières,** Ave Jean Moulin, 12150 Sévérac-le-Château **05 65 47 64 82; contact@ camping-calquieres.com; www.camping-aveyron.fr**

€1.50 (htd) nr (covrd, htd)

Exit A75 junc 42 sp Sévérac & Rodez; foll 'Camping' sps to avoid narr town rds. 4*, Med, hdg, pt shd, serviced pitches; EHU (6-16A) €4.20 (poss long lead & rev pol); bbq; red long stay; 10% statics; adv bkg acc; tennis; fishing; games area; CKE. *"Lovely, spacious site with gd views; lge pitches; friendly, v helpful owners; v gd touring base & NH; conv A75; busy NH, espec w/end; gd for main holiday stay; new excel san facs (2015); vg rest; chge for wifi."* **€29.10, 1 Apr-30 Sep. 2023**

SEYNE *9D3* (0.8km S Rural) *44.34270, 6.35896* **Camping Les Prairies,** Haute Gréyère, 04140 Seyne-les-Alpes **04 92 35 10 21; info@campinglesprairies. com; www.campinglesprairies.com**

€2 (htd) nr nr (htd)

Fr Digne-les-Bains, take D900 N to Seyne. Turn L on ent Seyne onto D7, site sp beside Rv La Blanche. 3*, Med, mkd, pt shd, EHU (10A) €3.50; gas; bbq; phone; Eng spkn; adv bkg acc; ccard acc; tennis 300m; horseriding 500m; CKE. *"Immac, tidy, peaceful site; excel; beautifully sited and maintained; rest fr mid June; highly rec."* **€27.70, 7 May-7 Sep. 2024**

SEZANNE *4E4* (2km NW Rural) *48.72115, 3.70247* **Camp Municipal,** Route de Launat, 51120 Sézanne **03 26 80 57 00; campingdesezanne@wanadoo.fr; www.tourisme-en-champagne.com**

€1.05 nr nr

W'bound on N4 Sézanne by-pass onto D373 & foll site sp. Fr E turn R at 1st junc on Sézanne bypass & foll sps 'Camping & Piscine'. Avoid town cent. 2*, Med, pt shd, sl, serviced pitches; EHU (10A) inc; waterslide; CKE. *"Nice, well-kept site, v busy high ssn; generous pitches, some v sl; helpful manager; excel, immac san facs; levelling blocks req some pitches; request gate opening/closing at back bungalow of 2 opp site; nice vill; vg; well run site; pool adj; excel value; barrier clsd until 1500 unless adj pool open."* **€6.40, 1 Apr-30 Sep. 2023**

SIERCK LES BAINS *5C2* (6km SW Rural) *49.426188, 6.300037* **Camp Municipal de Malling,** 2 rue du plan d'eau 57480 Malling **03 82 50 12 97; camping.malling@ orange.fr; www.malling.fr/camping**

€2 nr nr

W of D654, well sp. Lge, mkd, pt shd, EHU 4A; bbq; sw; adv bkg acc. *"Beautifully situated between Plan d'eau and Rv Moselle; v helpful staff; v clearly sp fr D654; lovely site with wildlife on lake."* **€20.00, 1 Apr-30 Sep. 2024**

SIERCK LES BAINS *5C2* (1.7km W Rural) *49.44544, 6.34899* **Camp Municipal les Tilleuls,** Allée des Tilleuls, 57480 Sierck-les-Bains **03 82 83 72 39; camping@ siercklesbains.fr; www.siercklesbains.fr/index.php/ le-camping**

Fr S on D654 turn L onto D64 sp Contz. Fr Schengen (Lux) turn L immed bef Moselle Bdge sp Contz. Well sp on banks of Moselle. 2*, Sm, mkd, hdg, pt shd, EHU (16A); bbq; Eng spkn; adv bkg acc; bike hire; CKE. *"Excel site."* **€19.70, 12 Apr-13 Oct. 2024**

SIGEAN *10G1* (5km N Rural) *43.06633, 2.94100* **Camping La Grange Neuve,** 17 La Grange Neuve Nord, 11130 Sigean **04 68 48 58 70; info@camping-sigean.com; www.campingsigean.com**

12 €3 sand 5km

Exit junc 39 fr A9; pass over A9 (fr N) then 1st R sp La Réserve Africaine, then turn R just bef entering Sigean sp La Grange Neuve. 3*, Med, hdg, mkd, hdstg, pt shd, pt sl, terr, EHU (6A) inc; TV; 5% statics; adv bkg acc; waterslide; CKE. *"Easy access; gd san facs; excel pool; ltd facs LS; phone ahead to check open LS; gd NH."* **€33.20** **2023**

SIGEAN *10G1* (10km S Rural) *42.95800, 2.99586* **Camping Le Clapotis (Naturist),** 11480 La Palme **04 68 48 15 40 or 05 33 09 20 92; info@leclapotis.com; www.leclapotis.com**

€2 (cont)

On D6009 S fr Narbonne turn L 8km S of Sigean. After 350m turn R at camping sp. Site in 150m. Final app rd narr but negotiable for lge vans. 2*, Lge, mkd, pt shd, EHU (4A) €4; gas; 80% statics; Eng spkn; adv bkg acc; ccard acc; games area; tennis. *"Pleasant, basic, friendly site; sm pitches; Naturists INF card req; helpful owners; san facs dated but clean; gd pool; poss strong winds - gd windsurfing; La Palme vill 15 mins walk; great location."* **€33.40, 11 Apr-10 Oct.** **2023**

SIGOULES *7D2* (1.5km N Rural) *44.77135, 0.41076* **Camping Pomport Beach,** Route de la Gardonnette, 24240 Pomport-Sigoulès **05 24 10 61 13; info@pomport-beach.com; www.pomport-beach.com**

€6 nr (htd)

S fr Bergerac take D933 S. After 6km at top of hill turn R by La Grappe d'Or Rest onto D17 sp Pomport/Sigoulès. Thro Pomport, site at bottom of hill on R by lake. 4*, Med, mkd, shd, pt sl, EHU (6A); bbq (charcoal, gas); sw nr; TV; 25% statics; phone; Eng spkn; adv bkg rec; ccard acc; lake; fishing; tennis; canoeing; games area; bike hire; games rm; CKE. *"Barrier ent; gd security; gd site; 2 san facs blocks, clean and up to date (2019); kids loved the site; rec."* **€74.00, 14 May - 3 Sep.** **2022**

SILLE LE GUILLAUME *4F1* (3km N Rural) *48.20352, -0.12774* **Lac de Sillé,** Sillé-Plage, 72140 Sillé-le-Guillaume **02 43 20 16 12; https://europe.huttopia.com/site/camping-lac-de-sille**

€5 (htd) (htd)

Fr Sillé-le-Guillaume take D5 N, D203 to site. 3*, Med, shd, EHU (13A) inc; sw; 10% statics; ccard acc; watersports; fishing; bike hire; games area. *"Site in pine forest; gd dog walk around lake."* **€30.00, 14 Apr-25 Sep.** **2022**

SILLE LE GUILLAUME *4F1* (2km NW Rural) *48.18943, -0.14130* **Camping Les Tournesols,** Route de Mayenne, Le Grez, 72140 Sillé-le-Guillaume **02 43 20 12 69; campinglestournesols@orange.fr; www.campinglestournesols.com**

€2

Exit Sillé on D304/D35 sp Mayenne; in 2km at x-rds turn R; site in 150m on L, easily visible & sp. 3*, Med, hdg, mkd, pt shd, pt sl, EHU (6A) inc (poss long lead req); bbq (gas); sw nr; red long stay; TV; 20% statics; Eng spkn; adv bkg acc; ccard acc; bike hire; fishing 1km; CKE. *"Beautiful site; friendly owners; facs dated but spotless; rabies cert req for dogs; badminton; bouncy castle; pleasant town; canoeing 2km; mini golf; football; volleyball; jeux de boules; conv Le Mans; gd; welcoming, helpful owner; excel value; pretty, 'natural' site; onsite family owners."* **€18.00, 1 May-30 Sep.** **2022**

SILLE LE PHILIPPE *4F1* (1.4km W Rural) *48.10880, 0.33730* **Camping Le Château de Chanteloup,** Parc de l'Epau Sarl, 72460 Sillé-le-Philippe **02 43 27 51 07; www.chateau-de-chanteloup.com**

€0 (htd) (htd)

Leave A11/E50 at junc 7 Sp Le Mans Z1 Nord. After toll turn L onto N338. Foll this & turn L onto D313 sp Coulaines, Mamers & Ballon. Take D301 (at lge supmkt) & in approx 13km site is sp just after ent to Sillé-le-Philippe. Avoid cent Sillé-le-Philippe. 5*, Med, mkd, pt shd, pt sl, EHU (10A) €4 (poss rev pol); gas; bbq; twin axles; TV; Eng spkn; adv bkg acc; ccard acc; golf 10km; games area; lake fishing; games rm; horseriding 10km; CKE. *"Lovely, tranquil, spacious site in chateau grnds; pleasant, helpful staff; some pitches in wooded areas poss tight lge o'fits; gd rest; twin axles & lge o'fits by request; gd for Le Mans; sep o'night area with elec & water; rec; no facs to drain waste water fr m'van; higher charge during Le Mans events; excel san facs; clean & well maintained park."* **€54.90, 29 May-31 Aug, L13.** **2022**

SISTERON *10E3* (2.5km N Rural) *44.21467, 5.93643* **Camp Municipal Les Prés Hauts,** 44 Chemin des Prés Hauts, 04200 Sisteron **04 92 61 19 69; info@camping-sisteron.com; www.camping-sisteron.com**

€2

On W of D951. 4*, Lge, hdg, pt shd, pt sl, serviced pitches; EHU (10A) inc; Eng spkn; ccard acc; fishing; tennis; CKE. *"Lovely, well-kept, busy, excel site; excel location, gd views; lge pitches & gd for m'vans; site yourself LS; vg facs, ltd LS; interesting old town, gd mkt; conv a'route; vg; ent Barrier clsd at 2000; stunning pool; huge pitches; gd facs; friendly helpful staff; handy for m'way; 30min walk to Sisteron."* **€26.60, 1 Apr-30 Sep.** **2024**

FRANCE

SIZUN *2E2* (1km S Rural) *48.40038, -4.07635* **Camp Municipal du Gollen,** 29450 Sizun **02 98 24 11 43 or 02 98 68 80 13; camping-de-sizun@orange.fr; www.mairie-sizun.fr**

nr

Fr Roscoff take D788 SW onto D69 to Landivisiau, D30 & D764 to Sizun. In Sizun take D18 at rndabt. At end of by-pass, at next rndabt, take 3rd exit. Site adj pool. 2*, Sm, pt shd, EHU (10A) €3 (poss rev pol); phone; CKE. *"Lovely little site; simple & restful by rv in nature park; friendly recep; htd pool adj high ssn; site yourself if warden not avail; vg."* **€17.50, 16 Apr-30 Sep.** 2023

SOISSONS *3D4* (2km N Urban) *49.39295, 3.32701* **Camp Municipal du Mail,** 14 Ave du Mail, 02200 Soissons **03 23 74 52 69; camping@ville-soissons.fr; www.soissons.fr/camping-municipal-de-soissons**

€1 (htd) nr

Fr N on D1; foll town cent sp to 1st rndabt; turn R, cross rv & immed R into Ave du Mail. Foll sp 'Camping Piscine'. Site well sp beside sw pool. Rd humps & tight ent on last 500m of access rd. (Poss to avoid tight ent by going 150m to rndabt & returning). Or fr S on D1, turn R sp Centre Ville along Ave de Château-Thiery; at 3rd rndabt turn R into Rue du Général Leclerc to Place de la Republique; cont strt over into Blvd Gambette for 500m, then turn L into Ave de l'Aisne, leading into Ave du Petit Mail; then as above. 2*, Med, hdg, mkd, hdstg, pt shd, EHU (6A) €3.15 (poss rev pol); bbq; 5% statics; phone; ccard acc; bike hire; clsd 1 Jan & 25 Dec; CKE. *"Pleasant, excel, clean & well-run site in interesting area; gd sized pitches, some nr rv; poss muddy, park on site rds in winter; m'van pitches all hdstg; helpful, friendly staff; gd clean, modern san facs, updated (2015); rvside walks/cycling; gate clsd 2200-0700; pool adj; lge mkt Wed & Sat; vg winter NH; conv for town (15mins)."* **€22.50, 1 Apr-31 Oct.** 2024

SOMMIERES *10E1* (2km SE Rural) *43.77550, 4.09280* **Camping Domaine de Massereau,** The heights of Sommières,1803 route d'Aubais – 30250 Sommières **04 66 53 11 20; camping@massereau.com; www.massereau.com**

€4

(covrd, htd)

Exit A9 junc 26 at Gallargues, foll sp Sommières; site sp on D12. NB Danger of grounding at ent fr D12. Use this rte 24/7 - 03/08 (due to festival in Sommières). Otherwise exit A9 junc 27 onto D34 to Sommières, foll sps to "Centre Historique" dir Aubias; cross bdge (sharp turn) & turn R onto D12; site on L in 3km. 5*, Med, mkd, hdg, pt shd, pt sl, serviced pitches; EHU (16A) inc; gas; bbq (gas); sw nr; TV; 50% statics; phone; Eng spkn; adv bkg acc; ccard acc; games rm; jacuzzi; bike hire; waterslide; canoeing nr; sauna; games area; tennis; horseriding nr; CKE. *"Lovely, tranquil, well-run site adj vineyard; lge pitches, some uneven; pleasant, cheerful staff; running track; no o'fits over 7m high ssn; trampoline; modern san facs; narr site rds, sl/uneven pitches & trees diff lge o'fits; tight ents, diff without mover; excel; pool not htd."* **€55.00, 9 Apr - 31 Oct, C33.** 2022

SOMMIERES *10E1* (3km SE Rural) *43.76120, 4.11961* **Camping Les Chênes,** 95 Chemin des Teullières Basses, 30250 Junas **04 66 80 99 07; camping-les-chenes@orange.fr; www.camping-les-chenes.com**

€4

Fr Sommières take D12 S (sp Gallargues) 3km to junc with D140 L (N) for 1km. Site on R 300m up side rd. Sp. 2*, Med, mkd, pt shd, pt sl, EHU (10A) €5.40 (long lead poss req); gas; bbq (charcoal, gas); sw nr; 10% statics; adv bkg acc; games area; sep car park; CKE. *"Gd shd; gd san facs; friendly, helpful staff; vg; 2km fr disused rlwy cycle track; vg site."* **€20.70, 7 Apr-14 Oct.** 2023

SOMMIERES *10E1* (6km SE Urban) *43.77052, 4.12592* **Camping L'Olivier,** 112 Route de Conqénies Junas, 30250 Sommieres **04 66 80 39 52; contact@campinglolivier.fr; www.campinglolivier.fr**

(€3) nr

Fr Nîmes, take D40 twd Sommieres. At Congenies take D140 L to Junas, site sp in vill. 3*, Sm, mkd, pt shd, pt sl, EHU (6-10A) €5, poss inc on certain pitches; cooking facs; 40% statics; phone; Eng spkn; adv bkg acc; fishing; tennis; games area; CKE. *"Excel home made pizzas; jazz festival in summer; elec BBQ for hire; excel; lovely site; ping pong; entmnt (Thur eves); trampoline; homemade jams & olive oil for sale; less than 1km fr Nimes-Sommiere Voie Verte; mini golf; new owners (2017)."* **€19.00, 30 Mar-20 Oct.** 2023

SOMMIERES *10E1* (0.5km NW Urban) *43.78672, 4.08702* **Camping Le Garanel,** 99 Chemin de la Princesse, 30250 Sommières **04 66 80 33 49 or 06 59 65 79 00; contact@camping-garanel.fr; https://camping-garanel.fr**

€2 (htd) nr nr nr

Fr S on A9 exit junc 27 N & foll D34 then take D610 twd Sommières. By-pass town on D610, over rv bdge; turn R for D40, Rue Condamine. After L turn for Nîmes pull out to make sharp R turn sp 'Camping Arena' (easy to miss this R turn). At T-junc turn R, site thro car park. Fr N on D610 turn L at 4th junc sp 'Ville Vieille' & site adj rv. Site sp fr D610 fr N. NB Narr rds nr site. 2*, Sm, hdg, mkd, pt shd, EHU (10A) inc; bbq; bus 500m; Eng spkn; adv bkg acc; tennis adj; CKE. *"Well-kept site in great location nr medieval town cent & rv; some open views; friendly, helpful warden; nice sm pool; poss some workers' statics LS; rv walks; bar 200m; Voie Verte cycle rte; interesting town & area; site subject to flooding at any time; mkt Sat; twin axle restrictions; diff in/out for lge o'fits; email for avail in Jul/Aug; san facs updated (2018)."* **€21.90, 1 Apr-30 Sep.** 2023

SONZAY *4G1* (0.5km W Rural) *47.52620, 0.45070* **Kawan Village L'Arada Parc,** 88 Rue de la Baratière, 37360 Sonzay **02 47 24 72 69; info@laradaparc.com; www.laradaparc.com**

€3 (covrd, htd)

Fr N exit A28 junc 27 to Neuillé-Pont-Pierre; then D766 & D6 to Sonzay; turn R in town cent. Site on R on o'skirts immed past new houses; sp. Fr S & E use Sat Nav. 4*, Med, mkd, hdg, pt shd, pt sl, serviced pitches; EHU (10A) inc (poss rev pol); gas; bbq; red long stay; TV; 15% statics; phone; bus to Tours; Eng spkn; adv bkg acc; ccard acc; bike hire; rv fishing 500m; gym; games area; CKE. *"Peaceful, well-kept site; spa; friendly, helpful owners & staff; clean, modern facs; gd views; vg rest; poss diff for lge o'fits when site full/cr; barrier clsd 2300-0800; many walks, inc in attractive orchards; 60km fr Le Mans circuit; rec; gd size pitches; bread to order; gd NH en route Spain."* **€36.00, 6 Apr-22 Sept.** 2024

SOSPEL *10E4* (4km NW Rural) *43.89702, 7.41685* **Camping Domaine Ste Madeleine,** Route de Moulinet, 06380 Sospel **04 93 04 10 48; camp@camping-sainte-madeleine.com; www.camping-sainte-madeleine.com**

€1.50

Take D2566 fr Sospel NW to Turini & site 4km on L; sp fr town. Rd to site fr Menton steep with many hairpins. 3*, Med, mkd, shd, pt sl, terr, EHU (10A) €2.90; gas; Eng spkn; adv bkg rec; CKE. *"Friendly, busy site; gd pool but has no shallow end; stunning scenery; beautifully kept site; gd, immac facs; v well run."* **€27.50, 28 Mar-3 Oct.** 2023

SOUILLAC *7C3* (7km SE Rural) *44.87716, 1.57361* **Camping Les Borgnes,** 46200 St Sozy **02 35 21 69 63; www.campinglesborgnes.fr**

€1 nr nr

Exit A20 junc 55; foll sp Martel on D803; in 5km turn R onto D15 to St Sozy; site just bef rv bdge. 2*, Med, pt shd, EHU €3; gas; bbq; sw nr; 60% statics; phone; Eng spkn; adv bkg acc; ccard acc; canoe hire; CKE. *"Helpful British owners; gd."* **€12.00, 1 May-30 Sep.** 2024

SOUILLAC *7C3* (1km S Rural) *44.88197, 1.48253* **Camp Municipal du Pont de Lanzac,** 46200 Lanzac **05 65 37 02 58; mairie.lanzac@wanadoo.fr; www.lanzac.fr**

nr

S on D820 thro Souillac; immed after x-ing Rv Dordogne site visible on R of D820. 2*, Sm, shd, EHU (6A) €3; gas; sw; TV; 10% statics; adv bkg acc; canoe hire; fishing; CKE. *"Gd site in lovely location; free-style pitching; helpful warden; clean, basic san facs; easy stroll into Souillac along rv; unrel opening dates - phone ahead; gd NH."* **€12.00, June-Sept.** 2024

SOUILLAC *7C3* (5km S Rural) *44.86602, 1.49715* **Camping Verte Rive,** 46200 Pinsac **05 65 37 85 96 or 06 50 41 58 73; www.camping-laverterive.com**

€2

Fr Souillac S on D820. Turn L immed bef Dordogne rv bdge on D43 to Pinsac. Site on R in 2km on rvside. 4*, Med, hdg, mkd, shd, EHU (10A) €4; gas; 20% statics; Eng spkn; adv bkg req; ccard acc; games rm; canoeing; CKE. *"Pleasant, peaceful, wooded site on Rv Dordogne; gd san facs; poss mosquitoes by rv; gd pool; excel."* **€31.00, 1 Apr-15 Sep.** 2024

SOUILLAC *7C3* (5km SW Rural) *44.87340, 1.43389* **Camping Les Belles Rives (formerly Municipal La Borgne),** 24370 Cazoulès **05 53 28 27 13; ushuaiavillageslesbellesrives@alphacamping.fr; camping-cazoules.com**

€1

Fr Souillac, take D804/D703 twd Sarlat. In 4km in vill of Cazoulès turn L & foll site sps. Site on R just bef rv bdge & adj Rv Dordogne. 2*, Lge, pt shd, EHU (10A) €3; bbq; 15% statics; fishing; tennis adj; boat hire. *"Poss mosquito problem; canoe trips; helpful staff."* **€15.00, 15 Jun-15 Sep.** 2024

SOUILLAC *7C3* (1km W Urban) *44.88895, 1.47418* **FLOWER Camping Les Ondines,** Ave de Sarlat, 46200 Souillac **05 65 37 86 44; camping.les.ondines@flowercampings.com; www.camping-lesondines.com or www.flowercampings.com**

€2 nr (htd)

Leave A20 junc 55. D804 then D820 to Souillac. In cent of town turn W onto D804 to Sarlat. In 225m turn R into Rue des Ondines. Site on R after 200m (opp Quercyland). 4*, Lge, mkd, pt shd, EHU (6A) inc; bbq; 10% statics; phone; Eng spkn; horseriding; tennis; canoeing; fishing; CKE. *"Gd touring base nr rv; helpful staff; clean facs; conv NH Rocamadour & caves; easy access fr A20/D820; aquatic park nrby; vg; ACSI accepted."* **€29.20, 1 May-29 Sep.** 2024

SOUILLAC *7C3* (7km NW Rural) *44.93599, 1.43743* **Camping La Draille,** La Draille, 46200 Souillac **05 65 32 65 01; info@ladraille.com; www.beteruitvakantieparken.nl**

€3

Leave Souillac on D15 sp Salignac-Evvigues; at Bourzoles in 6km take D165; site sp in 500m on L. Med, hdg, pt shd, pt sl, EHU (4A) €4; bbq; 25% statics; phone; Eng spkn; adv bkg acc; ccard acc; CKE. *"Lovely location; friendly; gd walks; highly rec."* **€26.00, 27 Apr-5 Oct.** 2024

FRANCE

SOUILLAC *7C3* (8km NW Rural) *44.94510, 1.44140* **Domaine de la Paille Basse,** 46200 Souillac **05 65 37 85 48; info@lapaillebasse.com; www.lapaillebasse.com**

€6

Exit Souillac by D15 sp Salignac, turn onto D165 at Bourzolles foll sp to site in 3km. NB Narr app, few passing places. 4*, Lge, hdg, pt shd, terr, EHU (3-10A) €4-6; gas; bbq; TV; adv bkg acc; ccard acc; golf 5km; tennis; bike hire; games area; waterslide. *"Excel site in remote location; friendly, helpful staff; clean facs; organised outdoor activities; cinema rm; some shwrs unisex; restored medieval vill."*
€57.00, 9 Apr - 17 Sep, D06. **2022**

SOULAC SUR MER *7B1* (1km S Coastal) *45.50136, -1.13185* **Camping Le Palace,** 65 Blvd Marsan-de-Montbrun, Forêt Sud, 33780 Soulac-sur-Mer **05 56 09 80 22; info@camping-palace.com; www.camping-palace.com**

€3-6 (covrd, htd) sand 400m

Fr ferry at Le Verdon-sur-Mer S on D1215, site sp. Or fr S on D101. 4*, V lge, mkd, hdg, shd, EHU; bbq; 65% statics; adv bkg acc; waterslide; bike hire. *"Ideal for family beach holiday."*
€36.00, 1 May-27 Sep. **2024**

SOULAC SUR MER *7B1* (13km S Coastal) *45.41600, -0.12930* **Centre Naturiste Euronat (Naturist),** 33590 Grayan-l'Hôpital **05 56 09 33 33; info@euronat.fr; www.euronat.fr**

€3 (htd) (covrd, htd) sand adj

Fr Soulac, take D101 twd Montalivet, turn W at camp sp onto rd leading direct to site. Fr Bordeaux, take D1215 sp Le Verdon-sur-Mer. Approx 8km after Lesparre-Médoc turn L onto D102. In Venday-Montalivet bear R onto D101. In 7.5km turn L sp Euronat. 4*, V lge, hdstg, mkd, shd, serviced pitches; EHU (10A) inc; gas; bbq; TV; 30% statics; phone; Eng spkn; adv bkg acc; bike hire; horseriding; tennis; archery; INF card req; golf driving range. *"Expensive, but well worth it; cinema; thalassotherapy & beauty treatment cent; gd lge pitches, many with elec/water; shwrs basic/dated; excel."*
€58.00, 1 Apr-29 Oct. **2023**

SOULAC SUR MER *7B1* (5km SSW Coastal) *45.480917, -1.145109* **Sandaya Soulac Plage,** Lieu-dit l'Amelie, 33780 Soulac-sur-Mer **05 56 09 87 27; www.sandaya.co.uk**

€5 (htd) (covrd, htd) sand adj

Fr S on D1215 dir Le Verdon, turn R onto D1E4 dir Soulac-sur-Mer, in 1.8km turn R onto Av de L'Europe sp Centre Ville & Plages. At rndabt go R sp plages, site sp. 4*, V lge, hdg, mkd, pt shd, EHU (10A) inc; bbq (gas); 60% statics; adv bkg acc; sauna; tennis. *"Excel site; direct access to beach."*
€65.00, 5 Apr-21 Sep. **2024**

SOULAC SUR MER *7B1* (1.5km SW Coastal) *45.49958, -1.13899* **Camping Les Sables d'Argent,** Blvd de l'Amélie, 33780 Soulac-sur-Mer **05 56 09 82 87; sables@lelilhan.com; www.sables-d-argent.com**

€2.95 sand adj

Drive S fr Soulac twd L'Amélie-sur-Mer. Clearly sp on R. 3*, Med, mkd, pt shd, pt sl, EHU (10A) inc (poss long lead req); TV; 60% statics; tennis; fishing. *"Nice area, but major erosion of coast so no access to beach; poss diff lge o'fits; Soulac sm, lively mkt town."*
€18.00, 1 Apr-30 Sep. **2023**

SOULAINES DHUYS *6E1* (0.5km N Rural) *48.37661, 4.73829* **Camping La Croix Badeau,** 6 Rue Croix Badeau, 10200 Soulaines-Dhuys **03 25 27 25 63; lacroixbadeau@orange.fr; www.croix-badeau.com**

€1 nr

500m N of junc D960 & D384, behind lge church of Soulaines-Dhuys, well sp. 3*, Sm, hdg, mkd, hdstg, pt shd, EHU (10A) €2.50; phone; Eng spkn; tennis; CKE. *"Excel, clean site in interesting vill."*
€25.50, 15 Apr-15 Oct. **2024**

SOUSTONS *8E1* (6.5km NE Rural) *43.78430, -1.30473* **Camping Azu'Rivage,** 720 Route des Campings, 40140 Azur **05 58 48 30 72; info@campingazurivage.com; www.campingazurivage.com**

€2

Exit m'way A10 at exit Magescq & take D150 W for 8km to Azur, site sp fr church adj La Paillotte. 3*, Med, pt shd, EHU (10A) €7.40; sw; red long stay; TV; 80% statics; adv bkg acc; ccard acc; boating; tennis; watersports. *"Delightful forest setting adj lake; v busy high ssn; san facs poss stretched high ssn; rec; lovely pool; no easy access to lake; v few touring pitches; heavily commercialised."*
€29.00, 15 May-30 Sep. **2024**

"There aren't many sites open at this time of year"

If you're travelling outside peak season remember to call ahead to check site opening dates – even if the entry says 'open all year'.

SOUSTONS *8E1* (9km W Coastal) *43.75579, -1.35384* **Camping Sandaya Souston Village,** 63 Avenue de Port d'Albret, 40140 Soustons **05 58 77 77 98 or 04 11 32 90 00; www.sandaya.fr/nos-campings/soustons-village**

(htd, indoor)

Head S on N10. Leave at Magesq exit and head for Soustons on D116. Then follow sp. 5*, TV; adv bkg rec; Ccard acc; bike hire; fishing; watersports; spa; games area; gym; cinema. **14 Apr-1 Oct.** **2024**

SOUTERRAINE, LA *7A3* (2km NE Rural) *46.24368, 1.50606* **Camping Suisse Océan,** 26 chemin du Cheix, 23300 La Souterraine **05 55 63 59 71; laquarelledulimousin@gmail.com; camping-creuse-limousin.com/**

12 €1.20 (htd)

Fr N145/E62 take D72 sp La Souterraine. Strt over 1st rndabt, at 2nd rndabt turn R, then L to L'Etang de Cheix. Fr N exit A20 junc 22 onto D912 sp La Souterraine; at T-junc turn L & foll outer rd D912b; at rndabt turn L to Etang-du-Cheix; in 50m turn L to site. Sp fr D912b. 3*, Sm, hdg, mkd, hdstg, pt shd, pt sl, terr, EHU (10A) €3.50; 10% statics; Eng spkn; adv bkg acc; tennis; fishing adj; sailing adj; CKE. *"Superb location by lake; lge pitches; sl rds on site could grnd lge o'fits - walk site bef pitching; san facs in portacabin; diving (summer); ltd facs LS inc EHU & inadequate when site full; quiet but night noise fr factory nrby; lake adj; pleasant sm town; mkt Thur & Sat; site fair."*
€15.00 **2024**

SOUTERRAINE, LA *7A3* (6km E Rural) *46.24534, 1.59083* **Camp Municipal Etang de la Cazine,** 23300 Noth **01 83 64 69 21; mairiedenoth@wanadoo.fr; www.tourisme-creuse.com/en/offers/camping-de-la-cazine-noth-en-4240914**

€1.50

Exit A20 junc 23 onto N145 dir Guéret; turn L on D49 sp Noth. Site opp lake. 1*, Sm, mkd, pt shd, pt sl, EHU (16A) €3; sw nr; lake fishing adj; CKE. *"Gd touring base; gd; san facs portacabins; excel NH and sh stay; rural location."* **€16.00, 31 Mar-7 Nov.** **2024**

STRASBOURG *6E3* (3km W Urban) *48.57537, 7.71724* **Camping Indigo Strasbourg,** 9 rue de l'Auberge de Jeunesse, 67200 Strasbourg **03 88 30 19 96; info@camping-strasbourg.com; www.camping-strasbourg.com**

12 €4.50

(htd)

Fr A35 exit junc 4, then foll (white) sp to Montagne Verte. Then foll D392 to site. 4*, Lge, hdg, pt shd, pt sl, EHU (10A); bbq; twin axles; red long stay; TV; 50% statics; bus; Eng spkn; adv bkg req; bike hire; games area; games rm; CKE. *"Excel site; site renovated (2015); bus/tram/cycle path to city; v busy."*
€31.00, J10. **2022**

SULLY SUR LOIRE *4F3* (2km NW Rural) *47.77180, 2.36200* **Camping Le Jardin de Sully,** 1 RUE D'ORLÉANS, 45600 SAINT-PÈRE-SUR-LOIRE **02 38 67 10 84; lejardindesully@gmail.com; www.camping-bord-de-loire.com**

12 €2 (htd)

(htd) sand adj

Fr N on D948 to Sully then turn R at rndabt immed bef x-ing bdge over Rv Loire onto D60 in St Père-sur-Loire, dir Châteauneuf-sur-Loire. Sp to site in 200m. Fr S thro Sully on D948, cross Rv Loire & turn L at rndabt onto D60. Well sp fr town. 3*, Med, hdg, mkd, hdstg, pt shd, serviced pitches; EHU (10-16A) inc (poss rev pol); gas; bbq; red long stay; TV (pitch); 18% statics; phone; bus; Eng spkn; adv bkg rec; ccard acc; tennis; bike hire; games rm; CKE. *"Pleasant, well-kept, well laid-out site on rvside adj nature reserve; pleasant walk along rv to town; long dist footpath (grande randonnée) along Loire passes site; gd dog walks; htd covrd pool 500m; gd cycling; gd winter site & NH en rte S; recep might be clsd LS, need to phone for barrier code ent; fairy-tale chateau in Sully; gd loc; helpful, friendly new owner keen to bring the standards up; excel new san fac (2018); excel; poss cr."*
€35.70 **2022**

SURIS *7B3* (1km N Rural) *45.85925, 0.63739* **Camping La Blanchie,** 16270 Suris **05 45 89 33 19; contact@lablanchie.co.uk**

Fr N141 halfway bet Angoulême & Limoges take D52 S at La Péruse to Suris; in 3km turn E up a narr lane to site. 2*, Sm, hdstg, pt shd, pt sl, EHU (10A) €4; bbq; sw nr; red long stay; twin axles; 10% statics; Eng spkn; adv bkg acc; golf nr; tennis nr; CKE. *"Welcoming, friendly British owners; clean site in lovely area; Futuroscope nrby; ltd facs; c'van storage; gd touring base; poor."* **€20.40, 1 Mar-31 Sep.** **2024**

TAIN L'HERMITAGE *9C2* (5km NE Rural) *45.10715, 4.89105* **Camping Chante-Merle,** 26600 Chantemerle-les-Blés **04 75 07 49 73; campingchantemerle@wanadoo.fr; www.campingchantemerle.fr**

12 €2 (htd) nr

Exit A7 at Tain-l'Hermitage. After exit toll turn L twd town, next turn R (D109) to Chantemerle; site sp. Cont for 5km, site on L. 3*, Sm, hdg, mkd, pt shd, serviced pitches; EHU (10A) €4.50; 10% statics; adv bkg req; tennis 500m; site clsd Jan; CKE. *"Helpful manager; popular site; excel facs."* **€21.00** **2023**

FRANCE

TAIN L'HERMITAGE *9C2* (1.4km S Urban) *45.06727, 4.84880* **Camp Municipal Les Lucs,** N7, 56 Ave du Président Roosevelt, 26600 Tain-l'Hermitage **04 75 08 32 82; camping.tainlhermitage@orange.fr; www.camping-tain.fr**

€1.40 nr nr

Fr N or S exit A7 junc 13 dir Tain-l'Hermitage onto N7. Cont N twd town cent; at fuel stn on R & Netto supmkt sp prepare to turn L in 80m; ent to site in 35m. Fr N on N7 prepare to turn R after fuel stn on R. Site alongside Rv Rhône via gates (locked o/night). Well sp adj sw pool/petrol stn. 3*, Med, hdg, hdstg, mkd, pt shd, EHU (6A) inc (poss rev pol); phone; Eng spkn; CKE. *"Pretty, well-kept, well-run site by Rhône; lovely views; secure site; friendly staff; excel, clean san facs; no twin axles, no c'vans over 5.5m & no m'vans over 6m (poss high ssn only); rvside walk to town; Valrhona chocolate factory shop nrby; mkt Sat; gd touring base; popular NH; highly rec; access gate with PIN; v sm pitches."* **€25.30, 15 Feb-15 Nov.** **2024**

TALMONT SAINT HILAIRE *7A1* (8km WSW Coastal) *46.451713, -1.702118* **Camping Sandaya Le Littoral,** Le Porteau 85440, Talmont-St-Hilaire **02 51 22 04 64; www.sandaya.fr/nos-campings/le-littoral**

(htd) (htd) shgl

Fr Talmont-St-Hilaire to Les Sables d'Olonne on D949. Turn L after racecourse. Site sp. 5*, Mkd, pt shd, EHU 10A; gas; bbq (elec, gas); twin axles; Eng spkn; adv bkg rec; ccard acc; bike hire; fishing; scuba diving; games rm; security. **€56.20, 29 Mar-5 Oct.** **2024**

TANINGES *9A3* (1km S Rural) *46.09899, 6.58806* **Camp Municipal des Thézières,** 166 Rte du Stade, 74440 Taninges **04 50 34 25 59; camping.taninges@wanadoo.fr; www.camping-taninges.fr**

€1.30 (htd) nr nr

Take D902 N fr Cluses; site 1km S of Taninges on L - just after 'Taninges' sp on ent town boundary; sp Camping-Caravaneige. 2*, Lge, pt shd, EHU (6-10A) €2.50-4; bbq; TV; phone; Eng spkn; ccard acc; tennis; CKE. *"Splendid site with magnificent views; pool at Samoens 11km; peaceful & well-kept; lge pitches; friendly, helpful staff; excel facs; conv for N Haute Savoie & Switzerland to Lake Geneva; excel; wooded site; bit of rd noise."* **€20.90, 1 Jan-3 Nov & 7 Dec-31 Dec.** **2023**

TARASCON *10E2* (5km SE Urban) *43.78638, 4.71789* **Camping Porte Des Alpilles (formerly Camp Municipal du Grès),** 2 Avenue of Doctor Barberin, 13103 Saint-Étienne-du-Grès **09 52 42 71 39; www.camping-porte-des-alpilles.com**

12 €1 nr

Fr Arles take N570 dir Avignon D99 E dir St Rémy. Site sp on o'skts of St Etienne. 2*, Sm, hdg, pt shd, EHU (16A) €4; CKE. *"Gd, peaceful site; lge pitches; friendly staff; gd san facs, recently updated."* **€14.00** **2024**

TARASCON *10E2* (5km SE Rural) *43.76744, 4.69331* **Camping St Gabriel,** Route de Fontvieille, 13150 Tarascon **04 90 91 19 83; contact@campingsaintgabriel.com; www.campingsaintgabriel.com**

€2 (htd) nr (htd)

Take D970 fr Tarascon, at rndabt take D33 sp Fontvieille, site sp 100m on R. 3*, Med, hdg, shd, EHU (6A) €3.3; gas; TV; 30% statics; adv bkg acc; games rm; site clsd mid-Feb & Xmas/New Year; rv fishing; CKE. *"Well-kept, charming site; excel base for Camargue & Arles; modern san facs; sm pitches poss not suitable lge o'fits; gd; 10 min walk into cent."* **€27.00, 14 Mar-14 Nov.** **2022**

TARASCON SUR ARIEGE *8G3* (4km N Rural) *42.87910, 1.62829* **Camping du Lac,** 1 Promenade du Camping, 09400 Mercus-Garrabet **05 61 05 90 61 or 06 86 07 24 18 (mob); info@campingdulacmercus.com; www.campingdulacmercus.com**

€2 nr nr (htd)

N20 S fr Foix, after 10km exit Mercus over N20 sp, cross rlwy line. At T-junc turn R thro Mercus, site of R over level x-ing. Tight bend into site off long, narr ent drive. 4*, Med, hdg, mkd, shd, terr, EHU (6-10A) €3.40-4.90; bbq; sw nr; red long stay; 20% statics; phone; Eng spkn; adv bkg req; fishing adj; games rm; watersports adj; CKE. *"Clean facs; friendly owners; sm pitches; bkg fee; steep entry rd with tight turn to get thro barrier; 60km Andorra; a real find!"* **€26.00, 5 Apr-4 Oct.** **2024**

TARASCON SUR ARIEGE *8G3* (3km SW Rural) *42.81311, 1.58908* **Camping Des Grottes,** Dumaines de la Hille, 09400 Alliat **05 61 05 88 21; info@campingdesgrottes.com; www.campingdesgrottes.com**

€2 nr (htd)

S fr Foix on N20 dir Andorra, turn R onto D8 just past Tarascon-sur-Ariège sp Niaux/Vicdessos. Site on R in 2km. 3*, Med, hdstg, hdg, mkd, pt shd, EHU (6-10A) €2; TV; 20% statics; phone; adv bkg acc; waterslide; games area. *"Lovely, peaceful site in valley; ideal NH for Andorra or long stay; Miglos Castle & Niaux cave nr; excel modern san facs; excel."* **€28.00, 1 Mar-15 Oct.** **2023**

TARDETS SORHOLUS *8F1* (1km S Rural) *43.11143, -0.86362* **Camping du Pont d'Abense,** 64470 Tardets-Sorholus **06 78 73 53 59; camping.abense@wanadoo.fr; www.campingdupontdabense.fr**

12 €2 nr nr nr

Take D918 S to Tardets, turn R to cross bdge onto D57. Site sp on R. Tardets cent narr. 2*, Med, shd, EHU (3A) €3.20; 10% statics; adv bkg acc; rv fishing nr; CKE. *"Informal pitching; facs old; gd birdwatching; lovely, quaint site, a gem; nr gorges; heavenly!"* **€24.00** **2023**

TELGRUC SUR MER *2E2* (1km S Coastal) *48.22386, -4.37223* **Camping Le Panoramic,** 130 Route de la Plage, 29560 Telgruc-sur-Mer **02 98 27 78 41; info@camping-panoramic.com; www.camping-panoramic.com**

€4 (htd) sand 700m

Fr D887 Crozon-Châteaulin rd, turn W on D208 twd Trez-Bellec Plage, site sp on R in approx 1.5km. 4*, Med, mkd, hdg, pt shd, terr, EHU (6-10A) inc; bbq; TV; 10% statics; adv bkg acc; ccard acc; jacuzzi; bike hire; tennis; games rm; CKE. *"Vg, well-run, welcoming site; access to pitches poss diff due trees & narr site rds; rec; some facs tired need updating; sea views; excel rest, pool & all facs; helpful owner."* **€26.50, 4 Jan-9 Sep.** **2024**

THENON *7C3* (3km SE Rural) *45.11883, 1.09119* **Camping Le Verdoyant,** 211 Chemin du Jarry Carrey, 24210 Thenon **05 53 05 20 78; contact@campingleverdoyant.fr; www.campingleverdoyant.fr**

€1.75 nr

Sp fr A89, take D67 fr Thenon to Montignac. Site on R in 4km. 3*, Med, mkd, pt shd, sl, terr, EHU (10A) inc; gas; 20% statics; Eng spkn; adv bkg acc; lake fishing; CKE. *"Beautiful setting away fr tourist bustle; friendly owners; excel base for area."* **€21.00, 4 Apr-30 Sep.** **2024**

THIERS *9B1* (7km NE Rural) *45.89874, 3.59888* **Camping Les Chanterelles,** Chapon 63550 St Rémy-sur-Durolle **04 73 93 60 00; contact@revea-vacances.com; www.revea-vacances.fr**

€1.50 (htd) (htd)

On A72/E70 W dir Clermont-Ferrand, exit at junc 3 sp Thiers. Foll sp twd Thiers on N89 into L Monnerie. Fr vill, take D20 & foll sp St Rémy. In St Rémy, foll 'Camping' sp. Do not app thro Thiers as narr rds v diff for lge o'fits. 3*, Med, pt shd, terr, EHU (10A) €3.50; gas; bbq; sw nr; TV; 10% statics; adv bkg acc; ccard acc; waterslide; tennis 600m; windsurfing; CKE. *"Vg site in beautiful situation with views; modern, clean facs; some noise at w/end fr statics; excel."* **€26.00, 30 Apr-15 Sep.** **2024**

THIEZAC *7C4* (0.5km E Rural) *45.01360, 2.67027* **Camping La Bédisse,** 3 Rue de la Bédisse, 15800 Thiézac **0471 47 00 41; campinglabedisse@gmail.com; www.campinglabedisse.com**

12

Fr Murat, take N122 twds Vic sur Cere & Aurillac. In approx 24km foll sp to Thiezac. Site posted fr vill cent. EHU €4; bbq; sw; twin axles; 10% statics; Eng spkn; adv bkg acc; games area; CKE. *"Tennis court; lovely rvside site; sh uphill walk to vill & shops; view of mountains; gd walks; rec; excel."* **€13.00** **2022**

THILLOT, LE *6F3* (1km NW Rural) *47.88893, 6.75683* **Camp Municipal du Clos de Chaume,** 36 Rue de la Chaume, 88160 Le Thillot **06 30 23 50 05 or 07 88 44 62 43; campingmunicipal@ville-lethillot88.fr; www.ville-lethillot88.fr**

(htd) nr

Site sp on N o'skts of town N on N66, on R behind sports cent. 2*, Med, pt shd, pt sl, EHU (6A) €1.80; gas; 10% statics; adv bkg acc; tennis adj. *"Attractive, well-maintained site; friendly staff; vg san facs; excel touring base."* **€6.00, 1 Mar - 30 Nov.** **2024**

THIONVILLE *5C2* (0.5km NE Urban) *49.36127, 6.17534* **Camping Municipal Thionville (formerly Camp Municipal Touristique),** 6 Rue du Parc, 57100 Thionville **03 82 53 83 75; camping.municipal@mairie-thionville.fr; www.thionville.fr**

€1.20 nr nr nr

Exit A31 at sp Thionville Cent; foll sp 'Centre Ville'; foll site sp dir Manom. 2*, Sm, mkd, hdstg, pt shd, EHU (3-10A) €2.40-4.65; red long stay; Eng spkn; adv bkg acc; fishing; boating; CKE. *"Well-kept site; some rvside pitches which can be noisy in eve; friendly warden; gd san facs; rec arr early high ssn; 5 min walk thro lovely adj park to town; vg; walk alongside rv as adj."* **€16.50, 1 May-30 Sep.** **2023**

THIVIERS *7C3* (10km N Rural) *45.50255, 0.91447* **Camping Moulin du Touroulet,** Moulin du Tourelet, 24800 Chaleix **05 53 55 23 59; touroulet3@gmail.com; www.camping-touroulet.com**

€0.50 (htd) nr

Fr Limoges on N21 S twd Périgueux, thro vill of La Coquille, in about 4.5km turn R onto D98 twd St Jory-de-Chalais & Chaleix. In 4km turn L to vill & site 1km further on. Take care narr bdge & site ent. Sm, hdstg, pt shd, pt sl, EHU (8A) €3; bbq; adv bkg acc; fishing; games rm; CKE. *"Beautiful site in tranquil rvside setting; spacious & well-kept; welcoming, helpful British owners; fishing avail on site; basic, ltd san facs, stretched high ssn; excel bar/rest; hdstg pitches sl & uneven; Xmas package; excel."* **€18.00, 1 Mar-31 Dec.** **2024**

THIVIERS *7C3* (2km E Rural) *45.41299, 0.93209* **Camping Le Repaire,** Ave de Verdun, 24800 Thiviers **05 53 52 69 75; contact@camping-le-repaire.fr; www.camping-le-repaire.fr**

€2 (htd) nr (covrd)

N21 to Thiviers; at rndabt take D707 E dir Lanouaille; site in 1.5km on R. 3*, Med, hdg, mkd, pt shd, pt sl, terr, EHU (12A) €3; bbq; TV; 5% statics; phone; Eng spkn; adv bkg acc; games rm; lake fishing; CKE. *"Lovely site, one of best in area; friendly owners; clean san facs; some pitches unrel in wet weather; excel; v nice tree shd plots."* **€25.00, 1 Apr-4 Nov.** **2023**

THONNANCE LES MOULINS *6E1* (2km W Rural) *48.40630, 5.27110* **Camping La Forge de Ste Marie,** 52230 Thonnance-les-Moulins **+33 (0)5 79 87 02 59; info@laforgedesaintemarie.com; www.laforgedesaintemarie.com**

€5 (covrd, htd)

Fr N67 exit sp Joinville-Est, foll D60 NE sp Vaucouleurs. In 500m turn R onto D427 sp Poissons & Neufchâteau. Site on R in 11km. NB Swing wide at turn into site fr main c'way, not fr what appears to be a run in. Site ent narr. 5*, Lge, mkd, hdg, pt shd, pt sl, terr, serviced pitches; EHU (6A) inc; gas; bbq; TV; 25% statics; phone; Eng spkn; adv bkg acc; ccard acc; games rm; bike hire; boating; lake fishing; games area; CKE. *"Vg, well-kept, busy site; friendly, helpful owners; freshwater fishing; access poss diff to some terr pitches/sharp bends on site rds; muddy after rain; vg rest; no o'fits over 8m; mkt Fri; lovely spacious, well run site, beautiful area; swing wide at ent; poss no mob phone recep; san facs fair."*
€34.00, 18 Apr - 4 Sep, J04. 2022

THONON LES BAINS *9A3* (3km NE Rural) *46.39944, 6.50416* **Camping Le Saint Disdille,** 117 Ave de St Disdille, 74200 Thonon-Les-Bains **04 50 71 14 11; camping@disdille.com; www.disdille.com**

€3

Exit A41/A40 junc 14 Annemasse onto D1005 & foll sp Thonon twd Evian. At Vongy rndabt foll sp St Disdille & site. Site 200m fr Lake Geneva. 3*, V lge, mkd, shd, EHU (6-10A) €4; gas; bbq; sw nr; 30% statics; adv bkg req; ccard acc; fishing; watersports; tennis; games area; bike hire; games rm; CKE. *"Well-situated; well-equipped site; gd touring base for v nice area; excel campsite; generous pitches; v clean san facs; Wi-Fi throughout campsite; lge well stocked superette; staff friendly, helpful, welcoming."* **€25.00, 15 Apr-25 Sep.** 2024

See advertisement

THURY HARCOURT *3D1* (0.9km NE Rural) *48.98930, -0.46966* **FFCC Camping Vallée du Traspy,** Rue du Pont Benoit, 14220 Thury-Harcourt **02 31 29 90 86 or 07 86 18 60 13; contact@campingdutraspy.com; www.campingdutraspy.com**

€2.90 nr

App fr N on D562 fr Caen, take L fork into town after pool complex. In 100m turn L at Hôtel de la Poste, 1st L to site, clearly sp adj Rv Orne. 3*, Med, mkd, pt shd, terr, EHU (4A) inc; gas; bbq; 20% statics; phone; Eng spkn; adv bkg rec; fishing; canoeing; CKE. *"Friendly owners; well-maintained pitches; o'night m'vans area; gd walking; site under new management with some refurbishment (2014); rec."*
€27.20, 1 Apr-30 Sep. 2024

TINTENIAC *2E4* (0.5km N Rural) *48.33111, -1.83315* **Camp Municipal du Pont L'Abbesse,** Rue du 8 Mai 1945, 35190 Tinténiac **02 99 68 09 91 or 02 99 68 02 15 (Mairie)**

(htd) nr nr nr

Fr D137 turn E onto D20 to Tinténiac; go strt thro vill to canal; sp just bef canal bdge; turn L. Site behind Brit Hôtel La Guinguette, on Canal d'Ille et Rance. 2*, Sm, hdg, mkd, pt shd, pt sl, EHU inc; 10% statics; fishing; CKE. *"Delightful, busy site; gd san facs; lovely walks/cycling along canal; vg; unreliable end of ssn closing; clsd at night by barrier; NH; site shut on bank holidays & Sundays."*
€10.00, 1 Mar-30 Sep. 2022

TINTENIAC *2E4* (2km S Rural) *48.31058, -1.82027* **Camping Les Peupliers,** Manoir de la Besnelais, 35190 Tinténiac **02 99 45 49 75; contact@domainelespeupliers.fr; www.domainelespeupliers.fr**

€1.60 nr (htd)

On D137 Rennes to St Malo rd; after Hédé foll rd to Tinténiac about 2km; site on main rd on R, sp. 3*, Med, hdg, mkd, pt shd, pt sl, EHU (6A) €2.90 (poss rev pol); TV; 30% statics; phone; adv bkg acc; games area; tennis; lake fishing; CKE. *"Pleasant, quiet, well-kept site; gd pool & park; on pilgrim rte to Spain; conv for acc to canal."* **€24.50, 1 Apr-1 Oct.** 2023

TONNERRE *4F4* (1.5km NE Urban) *47.86003, 3.98429* **Camp Municipal de la Cascade,** Ave Aristide Briand, 89700 Tonnerre **03 86 55 22 55 (Mairie) or 03 36 11 23 24 52; camping@mairie-tonnerre.fr; camping.ville-tonnerre.com**

(htd)

Best app via D905 (E by-pass); turn at rndabt twd town cent L after x-ing 1st rv bdge. Foll site sp to avoid low bdge (height 2.9m, width 2.4m). On banks of Rv Armançon & nr Canal de l'Yonne, 100m fr junc D905 & D944. 2*, Med, pt shd, EHU 3 euros; bbq; sw nr; TV; 10% statics; Eng spkn; adv bkg acc; ccard acc; fishing; CKE. *"Pleasant, spacious, shady site in arboretum; friendly warden; lge pitches; excel clean san facs; often damp underfoot; no twin axles; interesting town; gd cycling/walking along canal; conv site; excel."* **€18.00, 6 Apr-13 Oct. 2024**

TORIGNI SUR VIRE *1D4* (1km S Rural) *49.02833, -0.97194* **Camping Le Lac des Charmilles,** Route de Vire, 50160 Torigni-sur-Vire **02 33 75 85 05 or 06 09 35 29 94; contact@camping-lacdescharmilles.com; www.camping-lacdescharmilles.com**

€3 (htd) (htd)

Exit A84 junc 40 onto D974 dir Torigni-sur-Vire/ St Lô; site on R in 4km. Opp municipal stadium. 3*, Med, hdstg, mkd, hdg, pt shd, pt sl, EHU (10A) inc (long lead poss req); gas; bbq; sw nr; twin axles; TV; 30% statics; phone; Eng spkn; adv bkg acc; ccard acc; games area; bike hire; games rm; CKE. *"Lovely, well-kept, well-laid out site; clean, modern san facs, new shwr (2016); attractive, interesting town; excel; excel shopping in the town within walking dist; v helpful,friendly new owner (2016); picturesque lakes; tree-lined walks."* **€29.60, 30 Mar-1 Nov. 2024**

TORREILLES PLAGE *10G1* (0.9km N Coastal) *42.76750, 3.02972* **Les Tropiques,** Blvd de la Méditerranée, 66440 Torreilles-Plage **04 68 28 05 09; contact@campinglestropiques.com; www.campinglestropiques.com**

€4 sand 400m

Exit A9 junc 41 onto D83 E dir Le Barcarès, then D81 dir Canet-Plage. At 1st rndabt turn L onto D11 sp Torreilles-Plage, site sp. 4*, Lge, hdg, mkd, shd, EHU (6A) inc; gas; red long stay; TV; 80% statics; Eng spkn; ccard acc; waterslide; gym; bike hire; tennis; games area; CKE. *"Vg family site; excel leisure & san facs."* **€48.50, 9 Apr-1 Oct. 2023**

TOULON SUR ARROUX *4H4* (0.5km W Urban) *46.69419, 4.13233* **Camp Municipal Le Val d'Arroux,** Route d'Uxeau, 71320 Toulon-sur-Arroux **03 85 79 51 22 or 03 85 79 42 55 (Mairie); www.campingcarpark.com**

nr

Fr Toulon-sur-Arroux NW on D985 over rv bdge; rturn L in 100m, site sp. 2*, Med, pt shd, EHU (6A) €3.25; sw nr; 30% statics. *"Rvside site; boules park adj; beautiful Buddhist temple 6km; gd."* **€9.50, 16 Apr-15 Oct. 2024**

TOULOUSE *8F3* (5km N Urban) *43.65569, 1.41585* **Camping Toulouse Le Rupé,** 21 Chemin du Pont de Rupé, 31200 Toulouse **05 61 70 07 35; campinglerupe31@wanadoo.fr; www.vap-camping.fr/camping-de-toulouse**

12 €1.50 (htd)

N fr Toulouse on D820, sp. Poss tricky app fr N for long vans, suggest cont past Pont de Rupé traff lts to next rndabt & double back to turn. Fr S on ring rd exit junc 33A (after junc 12), turn immed R & foll sp. 3*, Lge, hdstg, hdg, mkd, pt shd, EHU (10A) inc; TV; 50% statics; phone; bus; Eng spkn; ccard acc; games rm; lake fishing; CKE. *"If site clsd 1200-1500, park in layby just bef site & use speakerphone; gd clean san facs; rock pegs poss req; ssn workers camp opp but no probs, site security excel; conv Airbus factory tours; space theme park 10km; well maintained; v helpful staff; ideal for dogs, children or walkers."* **€36.40 2024**

TOUQUET PARIS PLAGE, LE *3B2* (5km N Rural) *50.55270, 1.61887* **Camping La Dune Blanche,** Route d'Etaples, 62176 Camiers **04 30 05 15 18; www.campingladuneblanche.com**

12 €2.50 (htd) nr sand 3km

Leave A16 junc 26 dir Etaples or junc 27 dir Neufchâtel onto D940 dir Etables, Le Touquet. Site well sp. 3*, Lge, mkd, shd, pt sl, EHU (6A) €6; gas; bbq; red long stay; TV; 90% statics; phone; adv bkg acc; ccard acc; CKE. *"Amongst trees; remote, quiet by rlwy line; bus to beach at Ste Cécile; staff friendly & helpful."* **€17.50, 29 Apr-13 Sept. 2024**

TOUQUET PARIS PLAGE, LE *3B2* (6km S Coastal) *50.47343, 1.59178* **Camping La Forêt,** 149 Blvd de Berck, 62780 Stella-Plage **03 21 94 75 01; contact@laforetstella.fr; camping-touquet-parisplage.fr**

€2.50 sand 2km

Exit A16 junc 26 onto D393 to Etaples; turn L onto D940 dir Berck; foll sp Stella-Plage. Blvd de Berck is turning S off D144 W to Stella-Plage. 3*, Med, hdg, mkd, unshd, EHU €5; gas; 90% statics; phone; bus adj; Eng spkn; adv bkg acc; games rm; fishing nr; sailing; tennis 900m; windsurfing; games area. *"Gd site; tourist attractions nrby; narr aves to pitches with tight corners; not suitable for lge o'fits; unisex facs; not a touring site."* **€27.00, 1 Apr-31 Oct. 2024**

FRANCE

TOUQUIN *4E4* (2.5km W Rural) *48.73305, 3.04697* **Camping Les Etangs Fleuris,** Route de la Couture, 77131 Touquin **01 64 04 16 36; contact@etangs-fleuris.com; www.etangsfleuris.com**

€1.50 (htd) (htd)

On D231 fr Provins, turn R to Touquin. Turn sharp R in vill & foll sp to site on R in approx 2km. Or fr Coulommiers, take D402 SW twd Mauperthuis, after Mauperthuis L twd Touquin. Foll sp in vill. NB Beware two unmkd speed bumps on entering vill. 3*, Med, hdstg, mkd, hdg, pt shd, EHU (10A) inc; gas; bbq; TV; 20% statics; phone; adv bkg acc; ccard acc; games rm; fishing; games area; CKE. *"Peaceful site; no twin axles high ssn; conv Paris & Disneyland; helpful, supportive staff; no noise after 11pm."*
€30.00, 13 Apr-14 Sep. **2024**

TOURNIERES *1D4* (0.5km S Rural) *49.23017, -0.93256* **Camping Le Picard,** 14330 Tournières **02 31 22 82 44; lepicard14@orange.fr; camping-lepicardnormandy.com**

12 (htd) nr (htd)

Fr Bayeux foll D5/D15 W to Tournières, 5km past Le Molay-Littry. Fr N13 Cherbourg-Bayeux, E of Carentan turn S onto N174 then E on D15 to Tournières. Site sp opp Tournières church. 3*, Sm, hdg, pt shd, serviced pitches; EHU (10A) €4.30; 10% statics; phone; adv bkg acc; ccard acc; fishing; boating; CKE. *"Delightful, British-owned site; conv Normandy beaches, Bayeux, Cherbourg ferry; friendly, helpful owners bake croissants & will do laundry; san facs need refurb/update; c'van storage; clean well maintained site; nice fishing pool with carp; home cooked food avail; themed evenings inc food."*
€21.00 **2024**

TOURNON SUR RHONE *9C2* (0.4km N Rural) *45.07000, 4.83000* **Camping Le Rhône,** 1 Promenade Roche-de-France, 07300 Tournon-sur-Rhône **04 75 08 05 28; camping@camping-tournon.com; www.camping-tournon.fr**

12 €2 (htd) nr nr nr

Fr Tain l'Hermitage cross Rhône, turn R onto D86; in approx 1km R at end of car park; turn L after 50m, site on R on Rv Rhône. Or fr N on D86, sp on L by car park. 3*, Med, shd, EHU (6-10A) €4-6.50; gas; red long stay; 10% statics; phone; Eng spkn; adv bkg rec; canoeing; CKE. *"Pleasant, well-kept site in wooded location; rvside pitches; friendly owners; clean, dated san facs (unisex LS); m'van o'night area; c'van storage avail; some sm pitches & narr site rds poss diff lge o'fits; gd security; footbdge to Tain-l'Hermitage; fr mid-Jun rock concerts poss held nrby at w/end; gd; conv NH; interesting old town."* **€24.00** **2022**

TOURNON SUR RHONE *9C2* (6km N Rural) *45.12116, 4.80023* **Camping Iserand,** Rue Royal, 07610 Vion **04 75 08 01 73; camping@iserand.com; www.iserandcampingardeche.com**

€3 (htd) nr

Take D86 N fr Tournon, site 1km N of Vion on L. 3*, Med, mkd, hdg, pt shd, sl, terr, EHU (10A) €3; gas; bbq; TV; 20% statics; phone; bus 1km; Eng spkn; adv bkg acc; bike hire; CKE. *"Excel site; friendly owner lives on site - will take LS visitors."*
€24.00, 7 Apr-15 Sep. **2023**

TOURNON SUR RHONE *9C2* (4km W Rural) *45.06786, 4.78516* **Camping Le Castelet,** 113 Route du Grand Pont, 07300 St Jean-de-Muzols **04 75 08 09 48; courrier@camping-lecastelet.com; www.camping-lecastelet.com**

€2

Exit Tournon on D86 N; in 500m turn L on D532 twd Lamastre; in 4km turn R on D532 over bdge & turn immed R into site. 2*, Med, mkd, hdstg, pt shd, terr, EHU (10A) €4.50; gas; bbq; TV; adv bkg acc; fishing; games rm. *"Lovely, family-run site in beautiful setting; excel facs."* **€37.00, 5 Apr-13 Sep.** **2024**

TOURNUS *9A2* (1km N Urban) *46.57244, 4.90854* **Camping de Tournus,** 14 Rue des Canes, 71700 Tournus **03 85 51 16 58; camping-tournus@orange.fr; www.camping-tournus.com**

€2.60

Fr N6 at N of town turn E opp rlwy stn & rest 'Le Terminus;' foll site sp. 3*, Med, mkd, hdstg, pt shd, pt sl, EHU (10A) €4.70 (long lead poss req)(poss rev pol); gas; bbq; TV; Eng spkn; rv fishing 100m; CKE. *"Peaceful, rvside site in nice position; popular NH, conv A6 - rec arr early; helpful staff; clean facs poss stretched high ssn & ltd LS; htd pools adj; poss extra charge twin axles; rv walk into town; gd cycling nrby; quiet but rd & rlwy noise some pitches; abbey worth visit; vg; well kept site; helpful staff."*
€29.90, 1 Apr-30 Sep. **2023**

TOURNUS *9A2* (9km S Rural) *46.48768, 4.91286* **Camping Le National 6,** 71700 Uchizy **03 85 40 53 90; camping.uchizylen6@wanadoo.fr; www.camping-lenational6.com**

€1

Exit A6 junc 27 & foll N6 S; sp on L, turn L over rwly bdge on lane to site on L. Adj Rv Saône. 2*, Med, shd, EHU (6A) €3.90; gas; adv bkg acc; fishing; boat hire. *"Attractive, well-maintained site; gd, modern san facs; pitches soft & muddy in rain; cash only; arr early for rvside pitch; lovely position."*
€22.70, 1 Apr-30 Sep. **2023**

TOURS 4G2 (8km E Rural) *47.39273, 0.81085*
Camping de Montlouis-sur-Loire (formerly Les Peupliers), 37270 Montlouis-sur-Loire **02 47 50 81 90; aquadis1@wanadoo.fr; www.aquadis-loisirs.com**
€1.90 (htd) nr

On D751, 2km W of vill of Montlouis. Fr N foll sp to Vouvray (keep on N side of Rv Loire to avoid Tours) & cross rv by bdge to Montlouis. Sp at last min. NB App fr E a 'Q-turn' to get into site. 3*, Lge, hdg, pt shd, EHU (6A) €2; 12% statics; Eng spkn; adv bkg acc; ccard acc; tennis; CKE. *"Clean, tidy site; poss clsd mid-Oct; lge pitches; mkt Sun in Amboise; vg."*
€23.00, 1 Apr-20 Oct. **2024**

"I need an on-site restaurant"

We do our best to make sure site information is correct, but it is always best to check any must-have facilities are still available or will be open during your visit.

TOURS 4G2 (8km E Rural) *47.40226, 0.77845*
Camping Les Acacias, Rue Berthe Morisot, 37700 La Ville-aux-Dames **02 47 44 08 16; contact@camping-tours.fr; www.camping-tours.fr**
12 €2 (htd) nr

Fr Tours take D751 E sp Amboise; after 6km at rndabt where La Ville-aux-Dames sp to R, go strt on for 200m, then turn R, site sp. 3*, Med, hdg, mkd, hdstg, pt shd, EHU (10A) inc; bbq; red long stay; 10% statics; bus nr; Eng spkn; adv bkg acc; ccard acc; tennis 600m; fishing 100m; games area; bike hire; CKE. *"Well-kept, well-run, level site; excel san facs, ltd LS; conv town cent; fitness trail; many long-term residents; gd site; conv NH; lovely friendly helpful owners; mountain bike circuit; lge supmkt nr; bus to city nr; pool 500m; gd for long or sh stays; country park adj for dog walks; gd for Chateaux."* **€32.00, L03.** **2024**

TOURS 4G2 (5km SE Urban) *47.37070, 0.72305*
Camping Tours Loire Valley (formerly Camping Les Rives du Cher), 61 Rue de Rochepinard, 37550 St Avertin **02 47 27 87 47; campingtoursvaldeloire@onlycamp.fr; campingtours.fr**
€1.20 nr nr nr

Fr Tours, take D976 S of rv sp Bléré/Vierzon into St Avertin vill. Take next L at traff lts over 1st of 2 bdges. Site on R in 450m, not well sp. 3*, Med, hdg, mkd, hdstg, pt shd, EHU (10A) €4.20 (poss rev pol); red long stay; phone; bus nrby; Eng spkn; adv bkg acc; ccard acc; tennis; fishing; CKE. *"Clean & tidy site but needs updating; some lge pitches; friendly owner; htd pool adj; some resident workers; frequent bus to Tours."* **€19.00, 1 Apr-15 Oct.** **2024**

TOURS 4G2 (8km SW Urban) *47.35530, 0.63401*
Camping La Mignardière, 22 Ave des Aubépines, 37510 Ballan-Miré **02 47 73 31 00; info@mignardiere.com; www.mignardiere.com**
(htd) nr (covrd, htd)

Fr A10 exit junc 24 onto N585 & D37 by-pass. At exit for Joué-lès-Tours foll sp Ballan-Miré onto D751. Turn R at 1st set traff lts & foll site sp to W of lake. 4*, Lge, hdstg, mkd, hdg, pt shd, serviced pitches; EHU (6-10A) €3.50; bbq; TV; phone; Eng spkn; adv bkg acc; squash; bike hire; tennis; windsurfing 1km; fishing 1km; CKE. *"Conv Loire valley & chateaux; friendly, helpful staff; unisex facs LS; gd cycle paths; vg site; rec; bar 200m; gd san facs; v conv for bus/tram to Tours."*
€29.00, 1 Apr-25 Sep. **2023**

TOURS 4G2 (10km W Rural) *47.35054, 0.54964*
Camp La Confluence, Route du Bray, 37510 Savonnières **02 47 50 00 25; contact@campinglaconfluence.fr; www.onlycamp.fr**
€1.20 nr nr nr

Fr Tours take D7 on S of Rv Cher. Site on R on ent Savonnières on rvside. 3*, Med, mkd, hdstg, hdg, pt shd, EHU (10A) €4.20; bbq; phone; bus 200m; Eng spkn; adv bkg acc; tennis adj; canoe hire; CKE. *"Well-kept, clean, pleasant site; friendly, efficient staff; modern unisex san facs (a bit dated, 2018); some pitches narr & awnings diff; lovely vill with basic facs; gd touring base; gd birdwatching, cycling; bar adj; highly rec; gd touring base; on cycle rte; Vallendry Chateau 3.5km."* **€28.00, 19 Apr-22 Sep.** **2024**

TOURS 4G2 (8km W Rural) *47.38950, 0.59616*
Camping L'Islette, 23 Rue de Vallières, 37230 Fondettes **02 47 42 26 42; www.camping-de-lislette.ruedesloisirs.com**
nr

Foll D952 W fr Tours twd Saumur. In approx 6km turn R at traff lts onto D276 at Port-de-Vallières. Site on L in approx 2km. 2*, Sm, hdg, pt shd, EHU (10A) €2.50; bus; adv bkg acc; CKE. *"Pleasant site; helpful owners; facs poss stretched if site full; poss boggy when wet; pool 4km; conv for Langeais & Luynes chateaux."* **€9.40, 1 Apr-31 Oct.** **2024**

TRANCHE SUR MER, LA 7A1 (0.5km E Coastal) *46.34945, -1.43280* **Camping Bel,** Rue de Bottereau, 85360 La Tranche-sur-Mer **02 51 30 47 39; belcampsite@gmail.com; www.campingbel.com**
nr nr

Ent La Tranche on D747, take 2nd R at rndabt, R at traff lts, ent on L. 4*, Med, hdg, mkd, pt shd, EHU (10A) inc; TV; phone; Eng spkn; adv bkg acc; table tennis; CKE. *"Ideal for families with young children; bike hire nrby; adv bkg is only for current year."*
€28.00, 25May-1 Sep, A34. **2024**

FRANCE

TRANCHE SUR MER, LA *7A1* (0.5km E Coastal) *46.34611, -1.43225* **Camping La Baie d'Aunis,** 10 Rue de Pertuis-Breton, 85360 La Tranche-sur-Mer **02 51 27 47 36; info@camping-baiedaunis.com; www.camping-baiedaunis.com**

(not Jul/Aug) €2.30 (htd) nr (htd) sand adj

Fr La Roche-sur-Yon on D747 to La Tranche-sur-Mer; at 1st rndabt turn R, at 2nd rndabt (by Super U) turn L, at 3rd rndabt turn R - (all sp Centre Ville); ahead at min-rndabt & site on L in 100m. 4*, Med, hdstg, mkd, hdg, pt shd, EHU (10A) inc; gas; bbq; TV; 10% statics; Eng spkn; adv bkg rec; ccard acc; sea fishing; watersports; games rm; tennis 500m; sailing; CKE. *"Vg, friendly site; bike hire adj; helpful staff; excel san facs; excel rest; poss diff ent for lge o'fits; gd beaches, lovely area."* **€35.00, 26 Apr-15 Sep. 2024**

TRANCHE SUR MER, LA *7A1* (3km E Coastal) *46.34810, -1.38730* **Camping du Jard,** 123 Blvd du Lattre de Tassigny, 85360 La Tranche-sur-Mer **02 51 27 43 79; info@campingdujard.fr; www.campingdujard.fr**

(covrd, htd) sand 700m

Foll D747 S fr La Roche-sur-Yon twd La Tranche; at rndabt on o'skirts of La Tranche turn L onto D46 sp La Faute-sur-Mer; cont for approx 5km. At rndabt turn R sp La Faute-sur-Mer 'par la côte'; then R at next rndabt onto D46 sp La Tranche-sur-Mer 'par la côte' & La Grière-Plage (ignore all previous La Grière sps); site on R in 1km. Rough app rd. 4*, Lge, mkd, hdg, pt shd, serviced pitches; EHU (10A) inc; bbq (charcoal, gas); red long stay; TV; 75% statics; Eng spkn; adv bkg acc; ccard acc; horseriding 10km; games area; bike hire; games rm; waterslide; tennis; golf 20km; sauna; CKE. *"Lovely, well-run, clean & tidy site; busy high ssn; gd sized pitches, some sm; gd, well-kept san facs; fitness cent; no c'vans over 8m high ssn; gd pool; superb beach across busy coastal rd; easy parking at other beaches; poss flooding in wet weather; mkt Tue & Sat."* **€36.00, 17 May-12 Sep, A03. 2023**

TRANCHE SUR MER, LA *7A1* (4km E Coastal) *46.34781, -1.38303* **Camping La Grande Vallée,** 145 blvd de Lattre de Tassigny, 85360 La Tranche-sur-Mer **02 51 30 12 82; c.lagrandevallee@orange.fr; www.campinglagrandevallee.com**

700m

Fr La Roche Sur Yon on D747 to Latranche. At rndabt turn L onto D46, in 5km at rndabt turn R sp Le Gote L'Aiguillon. R at next rndabt. Site sp on R past Spar. 2*, Med, mkd, pt shd, EHU (4-10A); bbq; red long stay; 10% statics; bus; Eng spkn; adv bkg acc; ccard acc. *"Vg; rec long stay; bike hire; coastal bus Jul-Aug; friendly young owners; bkg fee for mid/high ssn."* **€30.00, 1 Apr-30 Sep. 2024**

TREBEURDEN *1D2* (3.5km NW Coastal) *48.79905, -3.58386* **Camp Municipal Le Dourlin,** L'Île Grande, 22560 Pleumeur-Bodou **02 96 91 92 41 or 02 96 23 91 17 (Mairie); camping.ig@pleumeur-bodou.fr; www.pleumeur-bodou.com**

€0.60 nr shgl adj

Off D788 N fr Trébeurden. Foll minor rd thro vill to site on coast. Well sp. 2*, Med, mkd, unshd, EHU (6A) €2.35; bbq; phone; bus; Eng spkn; sailing; games area; fishing; CKE. *"Popular site in excel location - fine sea views; excel facs; gd walking, cycling; ornithological cent nr; 8km circular coast rd round peninsula; gd; lovely coastal walk; well stocked shop in vill."* **€19.00, 30 Apr-27 Sep. 2023**

TREGASTEL *1D2* (3km NE Coastal) *48.82549, -3.49135* **Tourony Camping,** 105 Rue de Poul-Palud, 22730 Trégastel **02 96 23 86 61; contact@camping-tourony.com; www.camping-tourony.com**

€1.50 nr sand adj

On D788 fr Trébeurden dir Perros Guirec, site on R immed after exit Trégastel town sp & immed bef bdge over Traouieros inlet, opp Port de Ploumanac'h. 3*, Med, hdg, mkd, pt shd, EHU (6A) €3; gas; bbq; red long stay; TV; 15% statics; Eng spkn; adv bkg acc; ccard acc; tennis; bike hire; games area; horseriding nr; lake fishing; golf nr; CKE. *"Pleasant, lovely sm site in gd location; friendly, helpful staff; gd touring base Granit Rose coast; sm pitches dif for lge o'fits; clean but dated san facs (2015)."* **€26.10, 31 Mar-22 Sep. 2023**

TREGUIER *1D3* (10km N Coastal) *48.85810, -3.22013* **FFCC Camping Le Varlen,** 4 Pors-Hir, 22820 Plougrescant **02 96 92 52 15; info@levarlen.com; www.levarlen.com**

€1.50 shgl 300m

Take D8 N out of Tréguier to Plougrescant. Go past old chapel then immed bef church turn R sp Pors-Hir to site in 1km on R. 3*, Sm, mkd, pt shd, pt sl, EHU (6-10A) €3.50-3.90 (poss rev pol); 90% statics; adv bkg acc; ccard acc; games area. *"Friendly, helpful owners; some pitches sm & poss diff lge o'fits/m'vans; coastal walks."* **€15.00, 1 Mar-15 Nov. 2024**

TREGUNC *2F2* (3.5km SW Coastal) *47.83384, -3.89173* **Camping La Plage Loc'h Ven,** Plage de Pendruc, 29910 Trégunc **02 98 50 26 20; contact@lochven.com; www.lochven.com**

€1.60 (htd) nr nr shgl adj

Fr N165 exit at Kérampaou sp Trégunc. At rndbt W of Trégunc foll Loc'h Ven sp thro Lambell, site on coast. 2*, Med, mkd, hdg, pt shd, pt sl, EHU (4-10A) €3.50-4.70; gas; TV; 40% statics; Eng spkn; adv bkg acc; games area. *"Easy walk to beach, rock pools & coastal footpath; helpful owners."* **€18.50, 28 Apr-20 Sep. 2024**

FRANCE

TREIGNAC *7B4* (4.5km N Rural) *45.56023, 1.81369*
Camping La Plage, Lac des Barriousses, 19260 Treignac **05 55 98 08 54; camping.laplage@flowercampings.com; www.camping-correze.com**
€1.20 (htd) nr

On D940 opp Lac des Barriousses. 3*, Med, mkd, shd, pt sl, terr, EHU (6A) €2.80; sw nr; 5% statics; adv bkg acc; fishing adj; boating adj; CKE. *"Beautiful area & outlook; friendly; facs unclean LS."*
€22.70, 30 Mar-29 Sep. 2024

TREIGNAC *7B4* (10km SE Rural) *45.50262, 1.86911*
Camping Le Fayard (Naturist), Cors, 19260 Veix **05 55 94 00 20 or 0031 113301245 (N'lands); veen514@zonnet.nl; www.le-fayard.com**
€2 (htd)

Fr Treignac take D16 dir Lestards. 1km after Lestards take D32 S & in 2km turn R dir Cors, site sp. 2*, Sm, mkd, pt shd, pt sl, EHU (6A) €3.50; adv bkg acc; games area; CKE. *"Friendly Dutch owners; relaxing site in National Park of Limousin."*
€16.00, 18 May-1 Sep. 2024

TREPORT, LE *3B2* (1km N Urban) *50.05805, 1.38860*
Camping Paradise Les Boucaniers (formerly Municiple), Rue Pierre Mendès-France, 76470 Le Tréport **02 35 86 35 47; campingboucaniers@gmail.com; www.camping-lesboucaniers.com**
€1.60 (htd) sand 2km

Fr Eu take minor rd sp to Le Tréport under low bdge. On ent o'skts of Le Tréport, turn R at traff lts, camp ent 100m on R. Site nr stadium. 3*, Lge, hdstg, pt shd, EHU (6A) inc; TV; 10% statics; games rm. *"Busy, well-kept, well-run site; some lge pitches; gd, clean san facs; gd sep m'van area; lots to see in Le Tréport; m'van Aire de Service adj; gd value; excel; check elec lead is long enough bef unhitching."*
€40.00, 28 Mar-30 Sep. 2024

TREPT *9B2* (3km E Rural) *45.68701, 5.35190*
Camping les 3 Lacs du Soleil, La Plaine de Serrières, 38460 Trept **04 74 92 92 06; info@les3lacsdusoleil.com; www.camping-les3lacsdusoleil.com**
€2.50

Exit A432 at junc 3 or 3 & head twd Crémieu then Morestel. Trept bet these 2 towns on D517, site sp by lakes. 4*, Lge, pt shd, EHU (6A) inc; bbq (gas); sw nr; TV; 5% statics; phone; Eng spkn; adv bkg acc; ccard acc; waterslide; fishing; tennis; games area; archery; horseriding 2km. *"Gd family site; gd, modern san facs; fitness rm; lge & busy site with lots of activities."*
€38.00, 27 Apr-8 Sep. 2024

TRETS *10F3* (4km SW Rural) *43.44178, 5.62847*
Camping Le Devançon, Chemin de Pourachon, 13790 Peynier **04 42 53 10 06; reservation@ledevancon.fr; www.ledevancon.fr**
€2 (htd)

Leave A8 at Canet or Pas-de-Trets or leave D6 at Trets & take D908 to Peynier. In vill cont on D908 sp Marseille. Site on R at end vill after g'ge. 3*, Med, hdstg, mkd, shd, pt sl, EHU (10A) €6.5; gas; bbq; red long stay; TV; 50% statics; Eng spkn; adv bkg acc; ccard acc; tennis; CKE. *"Excel facs & site; helpful owner; poss diff manoeuvring onto pitches for lge o'fits; few water points; gd touring area."*
€29.20, 1 Mar-5 Nov. 2023

TREVIERES *1D4* (1.4km NE Rural) *49.31308, -0.90578*
Camp Municipal Sous Les Pommiers, Rue du Pont de la Barre, 14710 Trévières **02 31 92 89 24 or 07 45 28 79 34; campingsouslespommiers@onlycamp.fr; www.onlycamp.fr/sous-les-pommiers**
(cont) nr

Turn S off N13 onto D30 sp Trévières. Site on R on ent to vill. 2*, Med, hdg, mkd, pt shd, EHU (10A) €3; adv bkg rec; rv fishing adj; CKE. *"Delightful site in apple orchard; lge pitches; vg san facs; conv D-Day beaches; excel site; sm town in walking dist."*
€18.90, 30 Mar-15 Oct. 2024

TRIE-SUR-BAISE *8F2* (22km WNW Urban) *43.388595, 0.155504* **Camping Municipal La Galotte,** 44 Rue de Mirande, 65140 Rabastens de Bigorre **05 62 36 57 64 or 06 10 35 34 95; camping.lagalotte@gmail.com**
nr

Turn R (fr Tarbes, S) in ctr of Rabastens-de-Bigorre and foll N21. Site on R on outskirts of town abt 1km. Sm, shd, EHU (10A); gas; bbq (charcoal, elec, gas, sep area); twin axles; Eng spkn; adv bkg acc; CKE. *"Gd, basic site on edge of vill; suitable for short stays."*
NP 20, 1 Apr-30 Sep. 2023

TROYES *4E4* (16km E Rural) *48.28998, 4.28279*
Camping La Fromentelle, Ferme Fromentelle, 10220 Dosches **03 25 41 52 67; www.tourisme-champagne-ardenne.com**
€2 nr sand 5km

Exit A26 junc 23 onto D619 dir Bar-sur-Aube. In 8.5km turn L onto D1 sp Géraudot (take care bends) Site on L in 5km. 2*, Sm, mkd, pt shd, pt sl, EHU (6-10A) €3 (long lead poss req)(poss rev pol); bbq; sw nr; adv bkg acc; games area; CKE. *"Beautiful, lovely farm/CL-type site in old orchard; well-kept & well-run; warm welcome, charming owner; v clean san facs; gd for birdwatching, sailing, watersports on lakes; excel cycle tracks; nr nature reserve, lakes & forest; conv A26; excel spacious pitches; gd facs; some rd noise; hg rec old town in Troyes; owner sells own champagne."*
€18.00, 1 Apr-1 Oct. 2023

TROYES *4E4* (14km SE Rural) *48.20106, 4.16620* **Les Terres Rouges,** 10390 Clérey **06 70 00 76 75; lesterresrouges10@gmail.com; www.les-terres-rouges.com**

Exit A5 junc 21 onto D671 S dir Bar-sur-Seine & Dijon; site on R in 3.5km. Or SE fr Troyes on D671 dir Bar-sur-Seine, foll sp Clérey; then as bef. Site well sp. App over gravel track thro gravel quarry area. 2*, Sm, hdstg, pt shd, EHU (5-10A) €3.20 (poss rev pol); sw; 10% statics; phone; adv bkg acc; tennis; waterskiing; fishing; boating; CKE. *"Gd, basic NH; clean, v basic san facs; friendly, helpful new owners(2017); gate opens 0600, recep clsd 1900; conv fr a'route to Calais; commuter traff noise."* **€22.60, 2 April-30 Sep.** **2023**

TUCHAN *8G4* (1km S Rural) *42.88302, 2.71861* **Camping La Peiriere,** route de Paziols, 11350 Tuchan **04 68 45 46 50; lapeiriere@lapeiriere.com; www.camping-la-peiriere.com**

Fr Tuchan dir Paziols on L, 200m fr edge of town. Med, mkd, hdg, shd, EHU (9A); bbq; 10% statics; bus adj; Eng spkn; adv bkg acc; CKE. *"Mini farm & free lake fishing on site; excel base; access rds are v tight; vg."* **€26.00, 1 Apr-30 Sep.** **2022**

TUFFE *4F1* (1km N Urban) *48.11866, 0.51148* **FFCC Camping du Lac,** Route de Prévelles, 72160 Tuffé **02 43 93 88 34; campingdulac.tuffe@orange.fr; www.camping.tuffe.fr**

Site on D33, sp. 4*, Med, hdg, mkd, pt shd, EHU (6A) €2.50; bbq; sw nr; TV; 10% statics; Eng spkn; adv bkg acc; fishing; CKE. *"Well-kept, pretty lakeside site; adj tourist train; clean san facs; friendly staff."* **€24.70, 30 Mar-30 Sep.** **2024**

TULETTE *9D2* (2km S Rural) *44.26485, 4.93180* **Camping Les Rives de L'Aygues,** 142 chemin des rives de l'Eygues, 26790 Tulette **04 75 98 37 50; camping.aygues@wanadoo.fr; www.lesrivesdelaygues.com**

Exit D94 at Tulette onto D193 S; site in 2.2km on L. Site sp. Med, hdstg, hdg, mkd, shd, EHU (6A) €4.20; gas; 5% statics; phone; Eng spkn; adv bkg acc; ccard acc; games area; CKE. *"Lovely, peaceful, family-run site in woodland by Rv Aygue; gd san facs; gd pool; vineyards & lavendar fields nr; dir access to rv; excel."* **€35.00, 1 May-25 Sep.** **2024**

UGINE *9B3* (7km NW Rural) *45.76141, 6.33702* **Camping Champ Tillet,** 28 Rue Chenevier, 74210 Marlens **04 50 44 33 74; duchamptillet@wanadoo.fr; www.champtillet.com**

D1508 S fr Annecy after leaving Lake. Take by-pass past Faverges dir Ugine. After rndabt, site on R at junc bef Marlens, sp. 3*, Med, hdg, pt shd, EHU (10A) €4 (poss rev pol); 10% statics; ccard acc; bike hire; rv fishing 500m; CKE. *"Gd walks; lovely views; barrier clsd 2300-0700; some rd noise - adj extensive cycle track; helpful staff; shops 4km."* **€39.00, 1 Apr-30 Sep.** **2024**

URCAY *4H3* (6km NE Rural) *46.6430, 2.6620* **Camping Champ de la Chapelle,** St Bonnet-Tronçais, 03360 Braize **00 33 470 07 82 46; campingbraize@gmail.com; www.champdelachapelle.com**

Fr D2144 take D978A for Tronçais. 1.5km on L fr rndabt(Montaloyer) x-ing D28. Site sp. 3*, Med, mkd, pt shd, pt sl, EHU (10A) inc; sw nr; 10% statics; Eng spkn; adv bkg acc; ccard acc; games area; CKE. *"Excel walking & flora/fauna in ancient oak forest; some lge pitches; peaceful site; new British owner (2016)."* **€24.50, 1 May-30 Sep.** **2024**

URDOS *8G2* (0.5km N Rural) *42.87705, -0.55670* **Camping Le Gave d'Aspe,** 64490 Urdos **05 59 34 88 26; campingaspe@gmail.com; www.campingaspe.com**

Turn W off N134 onto site access rd by disused Urdos stn approx 1km bef vill, clear sp. Other access rds in vill v diff lge o'fits. 2*, Sm, mkd, pt shd, pt sl, EHU (10A) €2.40; bbq; phone; Eng spkn; adv bkg acc; ccard acc; rv; CKE. *"Adj Rv Aspe; 14km fr Col du Somport/Tunnel; surrounded by mountains; conv x-ing into Spain; vg; lovely sm site; beautiful mountain scenery; gd facs; gd walking."* **€14.00, 1 May-15 Sep.** **2023**

URT *8F1* (0.9km E Rural) *43.49353, -1.27960* **Camping Ferme Mimizan,** 64240 Urt **05 59 56 21 51; contact@lafermedemimizan.fr; www.lafermedemimizan.fr**

E fr Bayonne on A64/E80, exit junc 4 sp Urt; in vill turn sharp R at PO & foll sps; site on R in 1km. Fr N on D12 cross Rv Adour by metal bdge & turn L immed past church, site on R in 1.5km. 2*, Med, pt shd, EHU (10A) €3.50; 10% statics; adv bkg acc; CKE. *"V peaceful out of ssn; friendly owners; gd walking & cycling; conv coast & Pyrenees; gd NH."* **€19.50** **2023**

UZERCHE 7B3 (8km NE Rural) 45.45200, 1.65056 **Camping Aimée Porcher (Naturist),** 19140 Pingrieux Eyburie **05 55 73 20 97 or 06 01 11 51 90; aimeeporcher@hotmail.com; www.aimee-porcher.com**

Fr Uzerche take D3 NE to Eyburie & in Eyburie turn R at site sp (Cheyron/Pingrieux). In 1km turn L at site sp; site at end of narr lane. 2*, Sm, mkd, pt shd, terr, EHU (6A) (poss long lead req); bbq; sw nr; red long stay; adv bkg acc; games area; INF card. *"Beautiful views; wonderful location; INF not req; excel san facs; spacious pitches; basic; site rd steep in places; superb; v friendly Dutch owners."* **€19.00, 20 May-11 Sep.** **2023**

UZERCHE 7B3 (0.2km SE Rural) 45.42148, 1.56592 **Camp Municipal La Minoterie,** Route de la Minoterie, 19140 Uzerche **05 55 73 12 75 or 05 55 73 02 84; nicolas@uzerche.fr; http://camping.uzerche.fr**

nr

Fr N exit A20 at junc 44 for Uzerche on D920; proceed thro tunnel & cross town bdge. Site clearly sp on ent to town on rvside. Steep app rd & sharp bend. NB Narr app rd used by lorries fr nrby quarry. Site well sp. NB Steep exit. 3*, Sm, mkd, shd, pt sl, EHU (10A) €2.90; bbq; TV; Eng spkn; watersports; fishing; tennis; games rm; kayak hire; CKE. *"Lovely pitches on rv's edge; helpful warden; rock climbing; clean san facs; not suitable lge o'fits or lge m'vans; sh walk along rv to beautiful old vill; gd local walks; poss risk of flooding; v quiet end of ssn with ltd pitches; conv NH; excel."* **€15.40, 1 May-30 Oct.** **2024**

UZERCHE 7B3 (9km SW Rural) 45.36861, 1.53849 **Camp Municipal du Lac du Pontcharal,** Pontcharal Lake, 19410 Vigeois **05 55 98 91 93 (Mairie) or mob +33 6 32 95 44 53; campingpontcharal@orange.fr; www.vigeois.com**

€0.90

Fr A20 exit 45 onto D3 to Vegeois then D7. Site is 2.5km SE of Vigeois. 3*, Med, shd, pt sl, EHU (15A) €3.50 (poss rev pol); gas; sw; TV; adv bkg acc; watersports; fishing; tennis 2km; games area. *"Delightful, well-kept site in picturesque setting; excel san facs."* **€19.50, 18 Mar - 31 Oct.** **2024**

UZES 10E2 (2km E Rural) 44.03202, 4.45557 **Camping Le Moulin Neuf,** 30700 St Quentin-la-Poterie **04 66 22 17 21; lemoulinneuf@yahoo.fr; www.le-moulin-neuf.fr**

€1.50 (htd)

N fr Uzès on D982; after 3km turn L onto D5; in 1.5km fork R, keeping on D5; in 200m turn R onto D405 (Chemin du Moulin Neuf); site on L in 500m. 3*, Med, mkd, pt shd, EHU (5A) €3.50; 10% statics; fishing; horseriding; bike hire; tennis. *"Site off beaten track; busy high ssn, rec phone in adv; conv touring base; o'night m'van area; barrier clsd 2230-0700; poss mosquito problem; Uzès a lovely town; wonderful helpful staff; excel facs."* **€23.00, 1 Apr-22 Sep.** **2023**

UZES 10E2 (3km SW Rural) 43.99843, 4.38424 **Camping Le Mas de Rey,** Route d'Anduze, 30700 Arpaillargues **04 66 22 18 27; info@campingmasderey.com; www.campingmasderey.com**

€2

Sp fr Uzès. Exit by D982 sp Anduze. After 2.5km cross narr bdge, turn L in 100m on site app rd. 4*, Med, hdg, mkd, hdstg, pt shd, pt sl, EHU (10A) €4 (rev pol); bbq; TV; phone; Eng spkn; adv bkg acc; CKE. *"Clean, comfortable, busy site; helpful Dutch owners; some v lge pitches; gd for sm children; excel cycling; Uzès interesting; LS red for snr citizens."* **€41.00, 23 Mar-15 Oct.** **2024**

VAISON LA ROMAINE 9D2 (1.5km NE Urban) 44.24472, 5.07861 **Camping du Théâtre Romain,** Chemin du Brusquet, 84110 Vaison-la-Romaine **04 90 28 78 66; info@camping-theatre.com; www.camping-theatre.com**

€2 (htd) nr

Fr D975, cont onto Ave de Martigny to Chemin du Brusquet. Foll sp for Théâtre Romain & site. Ent to Chemin du Busquet on rndabt at Théâtre Romain. Or site sp off Orange-Nyons rd thro town (do not ent town cent). 4*, Med, hdg, mkd, pt shd, serviced pitches; EHU (5-10A); bbq; 10% statics; Eng spkn; adv bkg req; ccard acc; games rm; CKE. *"Excel, well-kept, friendly site; busy LS due long stay residents, rec book in adv; mainly gd sized pitches but some sm; most pitches suitable m'vans; clean, unisex san facs; attractive town; mkt Tues; highly rec; excel as usual; old Roman town cent, 10 mins walk fr campsite; conv for town; refurbed sw & new paddling pool (2016); long stay red."* **€33.00, 15 Mar-31 Oct.** **2024**

"Satellite navigation makes touring much easier"

Remember most sat navs don't know if you're towing or in a larger vehicle – always use yours alongside maps and site directions.

VAISON LA ROMAINE 9D2 (4km NE Rural) 44.26240, 5.12950 **Camping L'Ayguette,** D86 Quartier l'Ayguette, 84110 Faucon **04 90 46 40 35 or 07 77 26 38 65; info@ayguette.com; www.ayguette.com**

€1.80 (htd) nr (htd)

Exit Vaison NE on D938, R on D71, thro St Romain-en-Viennois. Then R onto D86 sp Faucon. Site on R, well sp. 3*, Med, mkd, shd, terr, EHU (10A) €2.50 (poss long lead req); bbq; red long stay; adv bkg acc; ccard acc; CKE. *"Excel, well-run site; lge pitches in forest setting; friendly, helpful owners; excel mod facs inc hairdryers & children's shwrs; tractor tow avail."* **€38.00, 19 Apr-27 Sep.** **2024**

VAISON LA ROMAINE *9D2* (4.5km NE Rural) *44.26806, 5.10651* **Camping Le Soleil de Provence,** Route de Nyons, Quartier Trameiller, 84110 St Romain-en-Viennois **04 90 46 46 00 or 02 51 28 10 20; info@camping-soleil-de-provence.fr; www.camping-soleil-de-provence.fr**

Leave A7 at junc 19 Bollène onto D94 dir Nyons. After Tullette turn R onto D20 & then D975 to Vaison-la-Romaine; fr Vaison take D938 sp Nyons; in 4km R & in 150m L to site; well sp. 4*, Lge, hdg, mkd, pt shd, terr, serviced pitches; EHU (10A) €4.50; gas; adv bkg acc; CKE. *"Popular, scenic, attractive, well-kept, family-run site; gd pools; lovely town; poss strong Mistral winds Sep; mkt Tues; excel; newly extended section & new san block (2014)."*
€30.00, 15 Mar-31 Oct. **2024**

VAISON LA ROMAINE *9D2* (0.8km SE Rural) *44.23440, 5.08955* **FFCC Camping Club International Carpe Diem,** Route de St Marcellin, 84110 Vaison-la-Romaine **04 90 36 02 02; carpe-diem@capfun.com; www.camping-carpe-diem.com**

S on A7 exit Orange; foll sp to Vaison; at Vaison on Nyons rd (D938) turn S at rndabt by supmkt dir Carpentras. In 1km turn L at junc to St Marcellin, site immed on L. 4*, Lge, hdg, mkd, pt shd, terr, EHU (6-10A) €4.70-5.70; gas; TV; 10% statics; Eng spkn; adv bkg acc; ccard acc; waterslide; site clsd 21 Dec-16 Jan; CKE. *"Lively site; helpful staff; poss dust fr nrby quarry; poss muddy pitches; gd san facs; gd cent for Provence."* **€31.00** **2024**

VAISON LA ROMAINE *9D2* (3.7km SE Rural) *44.22357, 5.10428* **Camping Le Voconce,** route de St Marcellin, 84110 St Marcellin **04 90 36 28 10; contact@camping-voconce.com; www.camping-voconce.com**

Fr Vaison S on D977. Turn L onto D938 after 1km. Turn R onto D151 after 0.5km to St Marcellin-les-Vaison. Turn R at rndabt by a chapel & foll sp to site. 3*, Med, hdg, mkd, pt shd, EHU (10A) €5; gas; 15% statics; Eng spkn; adv bkg acc; ccard acc; games area; CKE. *"Tranquil site bet 2 vineyards; friendly, fam run site; vg base for cycling, walking & exploring; boules; great views; acc to rv; vg."*
€24.00, 1 Apr-15 Oct. **2022**

VAISON LA ROMAINE *9D2* (5km NW Rural) *44.26446, 5.05242* **Camping Domaine de La Cambuse,** Route de Villedieu, 84110 Vaison-la-Romaine **04 90 36 14 53 or 07.78.12.62.20 or 06.31.61.89.81; dom.lacambuse@wanadoo.fr; campingdomainedelacambuse.wordpress.com/**

Fr Vaison-la-Romaine N on D51 sp Villedieu. After 4km fork R onto D94 sp Villedieu. Site on R after 300m. Sm, pt shd, terr, EHU (6A) €3; 5% statics; phone; CKE. *"Site in vineyard on hillside; friendly, helpful owners."* **€22.00, 1 May-31 Oct.** **2024**

VAL D'ISERE *9B4* (1km E Rural) *45.44622, 6.99218* **Camping Les Richardes,** Le Laisinant, 73150 Val-d'Isère **04 79 06 26 60; campinglesrichardes@free.fr; www.campinglesrichardes.free.fr**

Leave Val d'Isère going E twds Col de l'Iseran on D902, site on R 1.5km bef Le Fornet vill. 1*, Med, unshd, pt sl, EHU (3-6A) €1.90-3.80; CKE. *"Peaceful site; pool 1.5km; delightful owner."*
€13.00, 15 Jun-15 Sep. **2022**

VALENCE *9C2* (8.5km N Rural) *44.99723, 4.89383* **Camping Le Soleil Fruité,** Les Pêches, 26300 Chateauneuf-sur-Isère **04 75 84 19 70; contact@lesoleilfruite.com; www.lesoleilfruite.com**

Exit A7 junc 14 Valence Nord onto D67 sp Chateauneuf-sur-Isère, site sp to W of vill. Alt rte foll N7 turn onto D877 twrds Chateauneuf and foll sp to campsite. 4*, Med, hdg, mkd, pt shd, EHU (10A) €4; bbq; TV; 15% statics; phone; Eng spkn; adv bkg acc; ccard acc; CKE. *"Vg, family-run site; lge pitches; friendly owner; no dogs high ssn; excel, clean, modern san facs; rest/takeaway open early Jun (2011); ltd water pnts; cycle friendly; gd bar/rest; smart site; v busy HS; gd for families with young children."*
€33.00, 26 Apr-15 Sep. **2022**

VALENSOLE *10E3* (5.4km E Rural) *43.83862, 6.02029* **Domaine du Petit Arlane (Naturist),** Route de Riez, 04210 Valensole **04 92 74 82 70; contact@domainepetitarlane.fr; www.domainepetitarlane.fr**

Leave A51 junc 18 to Valensole 15km, fr Valensole take D6 signed Riez, site on L 5km (v bendy rds). Med, hdstg, mkd, pt sl, EHU (6- 15A) €3.90-8; bbq; twin axles; TV; 10% statics; Eng spkn; adv bkg acc; ccard acc; games area. *"Beautiful site, many pitches face lakes; dogs leashed; INF card advised;gd local walks fr local villages; bkg ess."*
€25.00, 26 Apr-30 Sep. **2024**

VALLON EN SULLY *7A4* (1.2km SE Rural) *46.53019, 2.61447* **Camp Municipal Les Soupirs,** Allée des Soupirs, 03190 Vallon-en-Sully **04 70 06 50 10 or 06 30 65 92 58; mairie.vallonensully@wanadoo.fr**

N fr Montluçon on D2144; in 23km at traff lts where D11 crosses D2144 turn L & foll camping sp for Vallon-en-Sully. After bdge over Rv Cher turn L in 50m. Site in 500m. If N or S on A71 exit at junc 9 Vallon-en-Sully; turn N on D2144; in 3km at traff lts turn L. 2*, Med, pt shd, EHU (6-20A) €2-4; TV; bus 500m; adv bkg acc. *"Peaceful, spacious site on banks of rv & canal; immac san facs; lge pitches; risk of flooding in wet; gd cycling along canal; gd NH; vg."*
€10.40, 1 Jul-12 Sep. **2023**

VALLON PONT D'ARC *9D2* (6km N Rural) *44.46611, 4.4125* **Domaine de Chadeyron,** 07150 Lagorce Vallon-Pont-d'Arc **04 75 88 04 81 or 06 70 67 88 78 (mob); infos@campingchadeyron.com; www.campingchadeyron.com**

(htd)

Fr S Vallon Pont d'Arc take D390 sp St Remeze/ Lagorce. R onto D1, foll sp to site. (NB Rd thro vill narr). Fr N (rec large o'fits) Vogue foll D579 sp Ruoms/Vallon Pont d'Arc, after 1.5km turn L D1 Rochecolmbe/Lagorce, 8km to site. 4*, Sm, mkd, pt shd, EHU (10A); twin axles; TV; 50% statics; Eng spkn; adv bkg acc; CCI. *"Gd walks; canoeing; vg site."* **€39.00, 26 Apr-6 Oct. 2024**

VALLON PONT D'ARC *9D2* (1km SE Rural) *44.39777, 4.39861* **Camping Nature Park L'Ardéchois,** Route des Gorges de l'Ardèche, 07150 Vallon-Pont-d'Arc **04 75 88 06 63; info@ardechois-camping.com; www.ardechois-camping.com**

€9 (htd) (htd)

Fr Vallon take D290 Rte des Gorges & site on R bet rd & rv. 5*, Lge, hdstg, mkd, hdg, shd, pt sl, serviced pitches; EHU (6-10A) inc; gas; bbq; sw nr; TV; Eng spkn; adv bkg acc; ccard acc; tennis; bike hire; canoeing; games area; CKE. *"Spectacular scenery; private bthrm avail (by reservation); excel rvside site; helpful staff; price depends on size of pitch; gd san facs; short drive to Pont D'Arc or Chauvet 2 cave paintings; 5 star site."* **€104.00, 2 Apr - 1 Oct, M14. 2022**

See advertisement

VALLON PONT D'ARC *9D2* (1km SE Rural) *44.39783, 4.40005* **Rives D'Arc (formerly Camping Le Provençal),** Route des Gorges, 07150 Vallon-Pont-d'Arc **04 75 88 00 48; contact@rivesdarc.com; www.rivesdarc.com**

€4 (htd) (htd)

Fr Aubenas take D579 thro Vallon-Pont-d'Arc to S. Turn L on D290 N of rv; site on R in 500m (middle of 3 sites). Fr Alès, N on D904/D104. At St Ambroix turn R onto D51 then D579 to Vallon-Pont-d'Arc. 3*, Lge, pt shd, EHU (8A) €3.90; gas; 10% statics; Eng spkn; adv bkg acc; ccard acc; tennis; fishing; sailing; canoeing. *"Friendly, helpful staff; site at NW end of spectacular Gorges de l'Ardèche."* **€59.00, 13 Apr-20 Sep. 2024**

"There aren't many sites open at this time of year"

If you're travelling outside peak season remember to call ahead to check site opening dates – even if the entry says 'open all year'.

VALLON PONT D'ARC *9D2* (1.5km SE Rural) *44.39467, 4.39909* **Mondial Camping,** Route des Gorges, 07150 Vallon-Pont-d'Arc **04 75 88 00 48; contact@rivesdarc.com; www.mondial-camping.com**

€4.50 (htd) (htd)

Fr N exit A7 Montélimar Nord junc 17 onto N7 then N102 dir Le Teil, Villeneuve-de-Berg. Turn S onto D103/D579 dir Vogűé, Ruoms then Vallon-Pont-d'Arc. Take D290, Rte des Gorges de l'Ardèche to site in 1.5km. Fr S exit A7 junc 19 at Bollène, dir Bourg-St Andéol, then D4 to St Remèze & Vallon-Pont-d'Arc. App to Vallon fr E thro Gorges de l'Ardeche not rec. 4*, Lge, mkd, hdg, shd, serviced pitches; EHU (6-10A) inc; gas; TV; 10% statics; phone; Eng spkn; adv bkg acc; ccard acc; tennis adj; canoeing; games rm; CKE. *"Dir access to rv, Ardèche gorges & canoe facs; gd touring base; waterslides & aqua park; excel site."* **€42.00, 1 Apr-30 Sep. 2023**

VALLON PONT D'ARC *9D2* (2km W Rural) *44.41517, 4.37796* **Domaine de L'Esquiras,** chemin du Fez, 07150 Vallon-Pont-d'Arc **04 75 88 04 16; esquiras@orange.fr; www.camping-esquiras.com**

€3.50

Fr Ruoms L at rndabt bef the Lidl nr the vill. Foll sp. Fr Vallon foll dir Ruoms. R after Lidl. 4*, Med, mkd, pt shd, pt sl, gas; twin axles; TV; phone; Eng spkn; adv bkg acc; ccard acc; games area; games rm; CKE. *"Lovely vill (10 min walk) with lots of bars & rest; caving, climbing or kayaking; excel; ACSI acc."* **€40.00, 25 Mar-30 Sep.** **2022**

VALLON PONT D'ARC *9D2* (4km W Rural) *44.41251, 4.35018* **Camping Arc en Ciel,** Route de Ruoms, Les Mazes, 07150 Vallon-Pont-d'Arc **04 75 88 04 65; camping.arcenciel@wanadoo.fr; www.campingarcencielardeche.com**

€3.50

Fr Ruoms take D579 dir Vallon. After 4km bear R for Les Mazes. Pass thro vill & in about 1.7km bear L at camp sp. 3*, Lge, pt shd, pt sl, EHU (10A) €4; bbq (elec, gas); 10% statics; bus; adv bkg acc; ccard acc; games rm; rv; canoeing; horseriding nr; tennis nr; fishing. *"Pleasant site on rv bank; excel; some pitches diff to access."* **€41.00, 29 Apr-18 Sep.** **2022**

VALLORCINE *9A4* (1km SE Rural) *46.0242, 6.92370* **Camping des Montets,** Le Buet, 74660 Vallorcine **06 79 02 18 81; b.stam@orange.fr; http://camping-montets.com**

nr

N fr Chamonix on D1506 via Col de Montets; Le Buet 2km S of Vallorcine; site sp nr Le Buet stn. Fr Martigny (Switzerland) cross border via Col de la Forclaz; then D1506 to Vallorcine; cont to Le Buet in 1km. 2*, Med, hdg, mkd, pt shd, EHU (3-6A) €2-3; red long stay; train 500m; Eng spkn; tennis adj; CKE. *"Site with spectacular views; friendly owners; ltd flat pitches for o'fits (others for tents in field), rec phone ahead; clean san facs; excel walking direct fr site; free train pass to Chamonix; vg."* **€16.00, 1 Jun-15 Sep.** **2022**

VALOGNES *1C4* (1km N Urban) *49.51154, -1.47534* **Camp Municipal Le Bocage,** 2 ter Rue Neuve, 50700 Valognes **06 33 67 62 30 - 02 33 95 82 01; Camping@valognes.fr; www.mairie-valognes.fr**

€0.66 nr nr nr

Off N13 Cherbourg to Carentan take 1st exit to Valonges, turn L just past Champion at Lidl sp; site sp bef & in town. Fr Carentan dir, take 3rd R after 4th set traff lts. 2*, Sm, hdg, mkd, hdstg, pt shd, EHU (10A) €3.55 (poss rev pol); gas; CKE. *"Super little site; clean san facs; friendly staff; conv Cherbourg ferries (17km) & town; poss travellers; warden calls 1900-2000, site self if office clsd; gates clsd 2200-0600; ideal NH; excel as always."* **€15.30, 1 Apr-15 Oct.** **2024**

VALRAS PLAGE *7E3* (2.5km SW Coastal) *43.227408, 3.243536* **Camping Sandaya Blue Bayou,** Vendres Plage Ouest 34350, Valras-Plage **04 67 37 41 97 or 04 11 32 90 00; www.sandaya.fr/nos-campings/blue-bayou**

(htd) (htd) sandy 0.5

Take exit 36 off the A9. Then onto the D64 twrds Vendres-Plage. 5*, Mkd, unshd, EHU 10A; bbq (elec, gas); TV; Eng spkn; ccard acc; bike hire; beauty ctr; fishing; watersports. **€69.00, 27 Mar-28 Sep.** **2024**

VALRAS PLAGE *10F1* (3km SW Coastal) *43.23750, 3.26166* **Camping Domaine de la Yole,** Avenue de la Méditerranée, 34350 VALRAS-PLAGE **+33 (0)4 88 80 89 59; infocamping@layolewineresort.com; www.campinglayole.com**

€4.50 (covrd, htd, indoor) sand 400m

Leave A9/E15 at Béziers-Ouest junc 36; foll D64 twd coast dir Valras-Plage, then Valras-Plage-Ouest & site sp. 5*, V lge, mkd, hdstg, hdg, shd, EHU (4A) inc; gas; bbq (charcoal, gas); TV; Eng spkn; adv bkg acc; ccard acc; games rm; bike hire; tennis; horseriding 3km; waterslide; games area; CKE. *"Lovely, excel site; v busy high ssn; some gd sized pitches with plenty of shd - book ahead high ssn; gd for all age groups; mkt Mon & Fri; lge clean sw pool complex; site extremely lge; tour ops statics; gd beach in 15 mins walk."* **€63.00, 23 Apr - 25 Sep, C03.** **2022**

VALRAS PLAGE *10F1* (3km SW Coastal) *43.23101, 3.25330* **Sandaya Les Vagues,** Chemin des Montilles, 34350 Vendres-Plage **04 67 37 03 62; vag@sandaya.fr; www.sandaya.co.uk**

€5 (htd) sand 400m

Exit A9 junc 36 onto D64 to Valras-Plage then Vendres-Plage. Site sp. 4*, Lge, pt shd, EHU (10A) inc; bbq (sep area); TV; 75% statics; Eng spkn; adv bkg acc; games area; horseriding 5km; waterslide; jacuzzi. *"Recep helpful; clean san facs; wave machine excel."* **€25.00, 24 May-29 Sep.** **2024**

VALRAS PLAGE *10F1* (3km W Coastal) *43.23502, 3.26845* **Camping La Plage et du Bord de Mer,** Route de Vendres, 34350 Valras Plage **04 67 37 34 38; reservation@camping-plageetmer.com; www.camping-plageetmer.com**

€4.50 (htd) adj

Leave A9 at Junc 9 onto D64. Foll signs for Valras Plage Ouest. Site on R, past La Yole. Lge, mkd, pt shd, EHU (6A) inc; bbq; cooking facs; twin axles; 20% statics; phone; Eng spkn; adv bkg acc; bike hire; games area; waterslide; games rm; tennis; CCI. *"Excel site; watersports mkt Mon & Fri (am)."* **€54.00, 20 Apr-23 Sep.** **2024**

VALRAS PLAGE *10F1* (6km NW Rural) *43.29273, 3.26710* **Camping La Gabinelle,** 7 Rue de la Grille, 34410 Sauvian **04 67 39 50 87; info@lagabinelle.com; www.lagabinelle.com**

€3.50 nr nr sand 5km

Exit A9 at Béziers Ouest, turn R twd beaches sp S to Sauvian on D19. Site 500m on L thro town. 3*, Med, pt shd, EHU (6A) €3; red long stay; TV; adv bkg acc; fishing 1km; tennis; games area; games rm. *"Friendly, helpful staff; suitable lge m'vans; canoeing 2km; LS ltd san facs & poss unkempt; sh walk to delightful old vill; popular; bar/pool shut LS."*
€13.80, 12 Apr-12 Sep. **2022**

VALREAS *9D2* (1km N Rural) *44.39264, 4.99245* **Camping La Coronne,** Route de Pègue, 84600 Valréas **07 62 71 05 21; contact@lacoronne.com; https://lacoronne.fr/en/la-coronne-english**

€4

Fr Nyons take D538 W to Valréas. Exit town on D10 rd to Taulignan, immed after x-ing bdge over Rv Coronne turn R into D196 sp Le Pègue. Site on R in 100m on rvside. Sp app fr E but easy to miss; app fr W; well sp in Valréas. 3*, Med, hdg, mkd, pt shd, EHU (6A) inc; gas; bbq; TV; phone; Eng spkn; adv bkg acc; ccard acc; fishing; CKE. *"Sm pitches; excel pool; facs need refurb & poss unclean; site clsd 2200-0700."*
€21.00, 31 Mar-15 Oct. **2023**

VALREAS *9D2* (8km W Rural) *44.41131, 4.89112* **Camping Les Truffières,** 1100 Chemin de Bellevue-d'Air, Nachony, 26230 Grignan **04 75 46 93 62; info@lestruffieres.com; www.lestruffieres.com**

nr

Fr A7 take D133 E twds Grignan. On W o'skts of vill turn S on D71. In 1km turn L at sp. Site is 200m on R. Fr Nyons take D538 W to Grignan. 3*, Sm, mkd, shd, EHU (10A) €4.20; gas; bbq; 5% statics; Eng spkn; adv bkg acc; fishing; CKE. *"Excel, well-wooded site by lavender fields; pleasant owners; immac san facs; gd pool; some pitches diff access; site poss dusty; 20 min stroll to town."* **€32.00, 12 Apr-13 Oct.** **2024**

VANDENESSE EN AUXOIS *6G1* (2.5km NE Rural) *47.23661, 4.62880* **Camping Le Lac de Panthier,** 1 Chemin du Lac, 21320 Vandenesse-en-Auxois **03 80 49 21 94; info@lac-de-panthier.com; www.lac-de-panthier.com**

€3.50 (covrd, htd, indoor)

Exit A6 junc 24 (A38) at Pouilly-en-Auxois; foll D16/ D18 to Vandenesse; turn L on D977bis, cross canal bdge & cont strt for 3km to site on L. Fr SW (Autun) on D981 approx 12km after Arnay-le-Duc turn R onto D994 sp Châteauneuf. At x-rds cont onto D977bis then as above. 4*, Lge, hdg, mkd, pt shd, pt sl, terr, EHU (6A) inc (some rev pol); bbq; TV (pitch); adv bkg req; fishing; waterslide; bike hire; sauna; CKE. *"Lovely area; Oct open Fri, Sat & Sun; views fr higher pitches; well-run site operating with Les Voiliers adj; lge pitches, most sl & blocks req; facs poss stretched high ssn, adequate; gd cycling & walks round lake; popular NH; vg."* **€44.00, 1 Apr - 28 Sep, L31.** **2022**

VANNES *2F3* (5km N Rural) *47.73035, -2.72795* **Camping du Haras,** 5 Kersimon-Vannes/Meucon, 56250 Monterblanc **02 97 44 66 06 or 06 71 00 05 59 (mob); lesjardinsdumorbihan@natureetresidence loisirs.com; www.campingvannes.com**

12 €4 (htd) (covrd, htd)

App fr N165 turn L onto D767 sp Airport. Go N for 7km & turn R onto D778 for 1km & turn R again. After 1km approx, turn L onto Airport Perimeter Rd, site sp on W side. App fr N on D767, join D778 & as above. 5*, Med, hdstg, mkd, hdg, pt shd, EHU (4-16A) €3-8; gas; bbq; sw nr; red long stay; 30% statics; Eng spkn; adv bkg acc; ccard acc; horseriding 300m; fishing; tennis; waterslide; bike hire; games rm; CKE. *"Lovely site; outdoor fitness; ltd facs LS; NH; sauna; wellness cent; trampoline; ltd space for tourers; rec."*
€36.00 **2024**

VANNES *2F3* (3km S Rural) *47.62754, -2.74117* **FFCC Camping Moulin de Cantizac,** 2 Rue des Orchidées, 56860 Séné **02 98 92 53 52; info@camping-vannes.com; www.camping-vannes.com**

12 €2.30 (htd) sand 4km

S fr Vannes on D199 twds Séné. Site on L at rndabt beside rv. 3*, Med, hdg, pt shd, pt sl, EHU (10A) €3.90; gas; 50% statics; ccard acc; games rm; boating; games area. *"Superb cent for birdwatching; excel new facs; buses to Vannes."* **€29.00** **2024**

FRANCE

FRANCE

VANNES *2F3* (4km SW Coastal) *47.63365, -2.78008* **Flower Camping Le Conleau,** 188 Ave Maréchal Juin, 56000 Vannes **02 97 63 13 88; camping.conleau@flowercampings.com; en.vannes-camping.com**
€3 (covrd, htd) sand 300m

Exit N165 at Vannes Ouest junc; Conleau sp on R. Site twd end of rd on R. If on N165 fr Auray take 1st exit sp Vannes & at 2nd rndabt R (sp) to avoid town cent. C'vans not allowed thro town cent. 4*, Lge, mkd, hdg, pt shd, pt sl, EHU (6A) €3.50 (some rev pol); bbq; twin axles; TV; 20% statics; phone; bus adj; Eng spkn; adv bkg acc; ccard acc; games area; bike hire; CKE. *"Most pitches sl; sep area for m'vans by rd - little shd & poss long walk to san facs; v busy/noisy in high ssn; sea water pool nr; lovely easy walk to Port Conleau; site full of atmosphere - rec; excel; great location & facs."* **€35.10, 1 Apr-1 Oct.** 2023

VANNES *2F3* (5km SW Coastal) *47.62190, -2.80056* **Camping de Penboch,** 9 Chemin de Penboch, 56610 Arradon **02 97 44 71 29; camping.penboch@orange.fr; www.camping-penboch.fr**
€3.50 (covrd, htd, indoor) sand 200m

Exit Brest-Nantes N165 Vannes by-pass at junc with D127 sp Ploeren & Arradon. Foll sp Arradon. Site well sp. 4*, Lge, mkd, hdg, pt shd, EHU (10A) inc (poss rev pol); gas; bbq; TV; 10% statics; Eng spkn; adv bkg rec; ccard acc; games rm; waterslide; games area; playground; CKE. *"Excel site; gd clean san facs; bike hire 2km; some pitches sm; steel pegs req; o'flow area with facs; no o'fits over 7m high ssn; plenty for youngsters; 20 mins walk to Arradon; gd coast walks."* **€40.00, 9 Apr- 24 Sep, B33.** 2022

VANNES *2F3* (6km SW Coastal) *47.62108, -2.84025* **Camping de l'Allée,** 56610 Arradon **02 97 44 01 98; contact@camping-allee.com; www.camping-allee.com**
€2 (htd) shgl 600m

Fr Vannes take D101 & D101A to Arradon. Take by-pass & take 1st exit at rndabt & foll sp. Site to SW of Arradon. Fr Auray on D101 turn R on C203 immed after Moustoir. App rd to site is narr. 3*, Med, hdg, mkd, pt shd, pt sl, EHU (10A) €4.60 (poss long leads req); gas; TV; 5% statics; Eng spkn; adv bkg acc; games rm; CKE. *"Delightful, helpful, family-run site partly in orchard; site yourself if office clsd; immac modern san facs; gd walks; gd touring base; highly rec; roomy site with gd atmosphere; rec."* **€25.60, 13 Apr-2 Sep.** 2024

VANS, LES *9D1* (2.5km E Rural) *44.40953, 4.16768* **Camping Domaine des Chênes,** 07140 Chassagnes-Haut **04 75 37 34 35; reception@domaine-des-chenes.fr; www.domaine-des-chenes.fr**
€2.50

Fr town cent take D104A dir Aubenas. After Peugeot g'ge turn R onto D295 at garden cent twd Chassagnes. Site on L after 2km; sp adj Rv Chassezac. 3*, Med, pt shd, pt sl, terr, EHU (10A) inc; bbq; 80% statics; adv bkg acc; ccard acc; rv fishing 500m; CKE. *"Lovely shady site; ideal for birdwatchers; gd rest; rec."* **€18.00, 4 Apr-27 Sep.** 2022

VARENNES EN ARGONNE *5D1* (0.4km N Rural) *49.22935, 5.03424* **Camp Municipal Le Pâquis,** Rue St Jean, 55270 Varennes-en-Argonne **03 29 87 86 55 or 03 29 80 71 01 (Mairie); mairievarennesenargonne@orange.fr; www.varennesenargonne.fr/pages/camping-municipal.html**
€0.40 nr

On D946 Vouziers/Clermont-en-Argonne rd; sp by bdge in vill, on banks of Rv Aire, 200m N of bdge. NB Ignore sp by bdge to Camping Lac Vert (not nr). 2*, Med, pt shd, EHU (6-16A) €3.65; bbq; Eng spkn; rv fishing. *"Pleasant site with gd facs; gd (hilly) cycle ride taking in US WWI cemetary."* **€18.90, 12 Apr-12 Oct.** 2024

VARILHES *8G3* (0.4km NE Urban) *43.04714, 1.63096* **FFCC Camp Municipal du Parc du Château,** Ave de 8 Mai 1945, 09120 Varilhes **05 61 67 42 84; campingdevarilhes@orange.fr**
12 (htd) nr nr nr

Exit N20/E9 at sp Varilhes. Turn N in town on D624. Site 250m on L (sp) just bef leisure cent adj Rv Ariège. 2*, Med, mkd, pt shd, terr, EHU (5-10A) €5.90-6.40; 20% statics; adv bkg acc; rv fishing adj; games area. *"Shwr & sinks locked 2100-0700; hot water unreliable."* **€13.00** 2023

VARILHES *8G3* (3km NW Rural) *43.06258, 1.62101* **Camping Les Mijeannes,** Route de Ferriès, 09120 Rieux-de-Pelleport **05 61 60 82 23; accueil-lesmijeannes@orange.fr; www.camping-les-mijeannes.fr**
12 €1.10 (htd)

Exit N20 sp Varilhes; on app Varilhes cent join 1-way system; 1st R at Hôtel de Ville; over rv bdge; foll camp sps; site 2km on R. 3*, Med, hdg, pt shd, EHU (10A) €4.60; bbq; TV; Eng spkn; adv bkg acc; fishing; games area; CKE. *"Peaceful site by rv, on island formed by rv; ACSI; helpful owner; kids club; badminton; gd size pitches; excel san facs; weekly theme nights high ssn; volley; excel; ltd facs LS."* **€31.60** 2023

VATAN *4H3* (0.5km W Urban) *47.07131, 1.80573* **Camp Municipal de la Ruelle au Loup,** 31 Rue du Collège, 36150 Vatan **02 54 49 91 37 or 02 54 49 76 31 (Mairie); vatan-mairie1@wanadoo.fr; www.vatan-en-berry.com**

nr nr

Exit A20 junc 10 onto D922 to town cent. Take D2 dir Guilly & foll site sp - 2nd on L (easily missed). 2*, Med, mkd, hdg, pt shd, EHU (10A) inc (rev pol); adv bkg acc; CKE. *"Pleasant, well-kept, beautiful site in park o'looking lake; spacious pitches; v clean, gd san facs (2019); twin axles; warden onsite daytime into early eve; easy access fr a'route; pool adj; conv Loire chateaux."* **€17.00, 15 Apr-15 Sep.** **2024**

VAYRAC *7C4* (3.5km S Rural) *44.93462, 1.67981* **FFCC Camping Les Granges,** Les Granges-de-Mezel, 46110 Vayrac **05 65 32 46 58; www.les-granges.com**

€1.60

App Vayrac on D803; turn S at sq in town sp "Campings"; site in 3.5km on banks of Rv Dordogne. Sp in Vayrac. Alt rte fr D803 in St Denis-les-Martel on D80 S - shorter on narr rds; site sp. 3*, Lge, pt shd, EHU (10A) €4; gas; TV; adv bkg acc; cycling; fishing; canoeing; games area. *"Vg children's amenities; facs fair; poss mosquitoes."* **€25.40, 4 May-28 Sep.** **2024**

VENACO *10G2* (3km E Rural) *42.22388, 9.19364* **Camping La Ferme de Peridundellu,** 20231 Venaco **06 95 73 20 66; campingvenaco@orange.fr; campingvenaco.e-monsite.com**

(htd) WD nr nr nr

S on N200 fr Corte for 15km; R on D143; at bdge keep R twds Venaco; site on L in 1.5km on bend. Sm, pt shd, pt sl, EHU (6-10A) €5; CKE. *"CL-type site; beautifully situated; gd walking country; friendly owner; highly rec."* **€17.00, Apr-Sep.** **2024**

VENCE *10E4* (3km W Rural) *43.7117, 7.0905* **Camping Domaine La Bergerie,** 1330 Chemin de la Sine, 06140 Vence **04 93 58 09 36; info@camping-domainedelabergerie.com; www.camping-domainedelabergerie.com**

WD MSP

Fr A8 exit junc 47 & foll sp Vence thro Cagnes-sur-Mer. Take detour to W around Vence foll sp Grasse/Tourrettes-sur-Loup. At rndabt beyond viaduct take last exit, foll site sp S thro La Sine town; long, narr rd to site, up driveway on R. 3*, Lge, mkd, hdstg, shd, pt sl, EHU (5A); gas; bbq (gas); red long stay; Eng spkn; adv bkg acc; ccard acc; lake fishing; games area; tennis; CKE. *"Shady site; helpful staff; clean san facs; no twin axles or c'vans over 5m; gd dog walks; Vence lovely & excel touring base."* **€33.40, 25 Mar-16 Oct.** **2024**

VENCE *10E4* (6km W Rural) *43.69958, 7.00785* **Camping Les Rives du Loup,** Route de la Colle, 06140 Tourrettes-sur-Loup **04 93 24 15 65; info@rivesduloup.com; www.rivesduloup.com**

€3.50

Exit A8 junc 47 at Cagnes-sur-Mer. Foll sp La Colle-sur-Loup, then Bar-sur-Loup (D6). Site in Gorges-du-Loup valley, 3km bef Pont-du-Loup. 3*, Sm, pt shd, EHU (5A) €3.50 (poss rev pol); 60% statics; adv bkg acc; horseriding 5km; tennis; fishing. *"Many activities avail; guided walks; beautiful location; cramped pitches."* **€29.50, 1 Apr-30 Sep.** **2024**

VENDAYS MONTALIVET *7C1* (8.6km W Coastal) *45.36325, -1.14496* **Camping CHM Montalivet (Naturist),** 46 Ave de l'Europe, 33930 Vendays-Montalivet **05 33 09 20 92; infos@socnat.fr; www.chm-montalivet.com**

12 €6.90 WD MSP (htd) sand adj

D101 fr Soulac to Vendays-Montalivet; D102 to Montalivet-les-Bains; site bef ent to vill; turn L at petrol stn; site 1km on R. 3*, V lge, hdstg, mkd, pt shd, pt sl, EHU (6A) inc; gas; red long stay; TV; 50% statics; phone; Eng spkn; adv bkg acc; ccard acc; games rm; bike hire; INF card; games area. *"Vast, peaceful site in pine forest; superb lge naturist beach adj; excel facs for children of all ages; vg; excel; hdstg with elec for MH's."* **€56.60** **2023**

VENDOIRE *7B2* (3km W Rural) *45.40860, 0.28079* **Camping du Petit Lion,** 24320 Vendoire **05 53 91 00 74; contact@camping-petit-lion.com; www.camping-petit-lion.com**

12 €3 (htd)

S fr Angoulême on D939 or D674, take D5 to Villebois-Lavalette, then D17 to Gurat. Then take D102 to Vendoire, site sp. 1*, Sm, hdg, hdstg, pt shd, EHU (10A) €4; 10% statics; adv bkg acc; lake fishing; tennis; CKE. *"British owners; rally fields."* **€17.00** **2022**

VENDOME *4F2* (0.5km E Urban) *47.79122, 1.07586* **Camping Au Coeur de Vendôme,** Rue Geoffroy-Martel, 41100 Vendôme **02 54 77 00 27; camping@aucoeurdevendome.net; www.aucoeurdevendome.com**

€2.50 WD nr nr nr

Fr N10 by-pass foll sp for town cent; in town foll sp Camping; site adj to pool 500m. 3*, Lge, mkd, pt shd, EHU (10A) inc, long leads req, some rev polarity; bbq; red long stay; 5% statics; phone; Eng spkn; rv fishing adj; tennis; CKE. *"Pleasant rvside setting; clean san facs - a trek fr outer pitches; sports cent, pool & theatre adj; statics sep area; recep 0900-2100; htd pool adj; games area adj; barrier clsd 2200-0630; vg; friendly; bar 500m; level site; narr ent/exit over bdge, poss diff for lge o'fits; 400m fr beautiful historic centre."* **€25.60, 1 Apr-31 Oct.** **2024**

FRANCE

VERDUN *5D1* (2km SW Urban) *49.15428, 5.36598* **Camping Les Breuils,** 8 Allée des Breuils, 55100 Verdun **03 29 86 15 31; contact@camping-lesbreuils.com; www.camping-lesbreuils.com**

€2.10

Fr W (Paris) on A4/E50, exit junc 28 onto D1916/ D603/D330; cont over rndabt junc with D34 onto D330; at next rndabt in 100m turn R into Allée des Breuils. Or fr E (Metz) exit junc 31 onto D964/D330; cont on D330 past junc with D34A; at rndabt in 150m turn L into Allée des Breuils. Site sp nr Citadel. Avoid Verdun town cent due to 1-way rds. Allée des Breuils runs parallel to D34 on E side of rwly. Site well sp fr D603 & all other dirs. Steepish ent. 3*, Lge, hdg, mkd, hdstg, pt shd, pt sl, EHU (16A) (poss some rev pol); gas; red long stay; phone; Eng spkn; adv bkg rec; ccard acc; fishing; bike hire; waterslide; CKE. *"Pleasant, clean, well-kept, lovely, busy site; grass pitches beside lge pond, some lge; poss long walk to water taps; some site rds tight for lge o'fits; gd pool; poss lge youth groups Sept; interesting historial town; cycle rtes around WWI battlefields; easy walk to Citadel with WWI museum; excel; gd rest; friendly staff; sports cent; san facs block refurbished (2018); facs expanding."* **€27.60, 1 Apr-30 Sep.** **2024**

VERDUN SUR LE DOUBS *6H1* (0.5km W Rural) *46.90259, 5.01777* **Camping La Plage,** Quai du Doubs Prolongé, 71350 Verdun-sur-le-Doubs **mairie.verdunsurledoubs@wanadoo.fr; www.tourisme-verdun-en-bourgogne.com**

€1 nr nr nr

SE on D970 fr Beaune to Verdun-sur-le-Doubs & foll sp in town. Or on D973 or N73 twd Chalon fr Seurre, turn R onto D115 to Verdun; site on bank of Rv Saône. 2*, Lge, mkd, shd, pt sl, EHU (10A) €2.10; bbq; phone; waterslide; tennis; fishing. *"Lovely rvside location; lge pitches; helpful warden; interesting sm town; confluence of 3 rvs: La Saône, Le Doubs & La Dheune; htd pool adj; fishermen's paradise; excel."* **€12.00, 1 May-15 Sep.** **2023**

VERMENTON *4G4* (0.9km S Rural) *47.65897, 3.73087* **Camp Municipal Les Coullemières,** route de Coullemières, 89270 Vermenton **03 86 81 53 02; contact@camping-vermenton.com; www.camping-vermenton.com**

€1 (htd) nr nr

Lies W of D606 - turn off D606 into Rue Pasteur (tight turn & narr rd), strt on at x-rds into Ave de la Gare. Turn R at stn, L over level x-ing. Well sp in vill adj to rv but sps low down & easy to miss. 3*, Med, hdg, mkd, pt shd, EHU (6A) inc; TV; 5% statics; bus; adv bkg rec; ccard acc; fishing; boating; tennis; bike hire. *"Peaceful, well-run rvside site; excel san facs; absolutely immac; weight limit on access rds & pitches; no twin axles; gd walks & cycling; conv Chablis vineyards; town with 12thC church; excel site; staff helpful; delightful site in interesting area."* **€17.00, 1 Apr-30 Sep.** **2024**

VERNANTES *4G1* (7km NW Rural) *47.43717, 0.00641* **Camping La Fortinerie,** La Fortinerie, 49390 Mouliherne **02 41 67 59 76; north.john.a@gmail.com; www.lafortinerie.com**

nr nr

Fr Vernantes take D58 dir Mouliherne; opp Château Loroux (Plaissance) turn L; at x-rds turn R, site over 1.5km on L. Sm, pt shd, EHU (16A) €5 (poss rev pol); bbq; adv bkg acc. *"Peaceful CL-type site; only sound is crickets!;dogs by prior arrangement; lge pitches; helpful, friendly British owners; B&B avail; beautiful chateau town; conv Loire valley & vineyards; excel."* **€12.00, 1 May-30 Sep.** **2022**

VERNET LES BAINS *8G4* (4km S Rural) *42.53330, 2.39847* **Camping Domaine St Martin,** 6 Boulevard de la Cascade 66820 Casteil **04 68 30 34 87 or 06 27 49 14 70 (mob); domainesaintmartin.com**

nr

Fr Prade to Villefranche on N116. Twd Vernet-les-Bains/Casteil at rndabt. Sp to campsite. 4*, Med, hdstg, mkd, shd, terr, EHU (10A); bbq; cooking facs; TV; 20% statics; phone; bus adj; Eng spkn; adv bkg acc; games rm; CCI. *"Mountain hiking/biking; Grottoes 6km; Abbey in vill; friendly, helpful staff; excel rest; vg."* **€24.00, 28 Mar-15 Sep.** **2024**

VERNET, LE *9D3* (0.8km N Rural) *44.28170, 6.39080* **Camping Lou Passavous,** Route de Roussimat, 04140 Le Vernet **04 92 35 14 67; loupassavous@orange.fr; www.loupassavous.com**

€1.50 (htd)

Fr N on A51 exit junc 21 Volonne onto N85 sp Digne. Fr Digne N on D900 to Le Vernet; site on R. Fr S exit A51 junc 20 Les Mées onto D4, then N85 E to Digne, then as above. 3*, Sm, pt shd, pt sl, EHU (6A) €4; TV; 10% statics; Eng spkn; adv bkg acc; fishing; games area; CKE. *"Scenic location; gd, clean facs; Dutch owners; gd walking, mkd walks fr site, escorted walks by owner; excel; highly rec."* **€24.00, 1 May-15 Sep.** **2022**

VERNEUIL SUR SEINE *3D3* (1.5km N Rural) *48.99567, 1.95681* **Camping-Caravaning 3* du Val de Seine,** Chemin du Rouillard, 78480 Verneuil-sur-Seine **01 39 71 88 34 or 01 39 28 16 20; contact@valdeseine.iledeloisirs.fr; www.terres-de-seine.fr/hotellerie_plein_air/camping-caravaning-du-val-de-seine-4/**

€2 (htd)

Exit A13 junc 8 & foll sp to Verneuil; site sp twd rvside. 3*, Med, mkd, hdstg, pt shd, EHU (6A) €4.25; bbq; sw nr; 10% statics; Eng spkn; ccard acc; horseriding; watersports; fishing; games area. *"V pleasant site adj Rv Seine; friendly, helpful staff; gd facs & activities; Paris 20 mins by train; site and area run down."* **€26.00, 19 Apr-30 Sep.** **2024**

VERSAILLES *4E3* (3km E Urban) *48.79455, 2.16038* **Camping Huttopia Versailles,** 31 Rue Berthelot, Porchefontaine, 78000 Versailles **01 39 51 23 61; versailles@huttopia.com; https://europe.huttopia.com/site/camping-versailles/**

€5 (htd) nr (htd)

Foll sp to Château de Versailles; fr main ent take Ave de Paris dir Porchefontaine & turn R immed after twin gate lodges; sp. Narr access rd due parked cars & sharp bends. No sp rec use sat nav. 3*, Lge, mkd, pt shd, pt sl, terr, EHU inc (6-10A) €4.60-6.80; gas; bbq; red long stay; TV; 20% statics; bus 500m; Eng spkn; adv bkg acc; ccard acc; bike hire; games area; CKE. *"Wooded site; sm, sl, uneven pitches poss diff lge o'fits; friendly, helpful staff; excel, clean san facs, stretched high ssn; conv Paris trains & Versailles Château; bus 171 to town."* **€55.00, 31 Mar - 6 Nov, P19.** **2022**

VERTEILLAC *3 B3* (3km W Rural) *45.340833, 0.340833* **La Grande Evasion (formerly HighThorn At Haute Epine),** 24320 St Martial Viveyrols **05 57 25 46 11 or 06 80 96 40 61 (mob); info@lagrande-evasion.com; www.lagrande-evasion.com**

(htd) nr nr (htd)

Fr Vertaillac foll D97 W for 2km. Then turn L at x-rds, S for 200m to site. Sm, hdg, unshd, serviced pitches; EHU 10A; bbq (charcoal, elec, gas); cooking facs; sw nr; twin axles; bus; Eng spkn; adv bkg rec; ccard acc. *"Adults only; tranquil site; only 4 pitches, each with own enclosed secure bathroom; separate utility and freezer rm; pick of fruit and veg in gdn; plenty of rest in area; lge shopping area and mkts in Riberac (12km); many beautiful vill, historic towns and vineyards to visit; owners live on site, friendly and welcoming, runs rest onsite only avail to site guest; dog sitting avail; hg rec; excel."* **€39.00, 1 May-30 Sep.** **2024**

"I need an on-site restaurant"

We do our best to make sure site information is correct, but it is always best to check any must-have facilities are still available or will be open during your visit.

VERVINS *3C4* (8.5km N Rural) *49.90676, 3.91977* **Camping du Val d'Oise,** 3 Rue du Mont d'Origny, 02580 Etréaupont **03 23 97 48 04**

€0.30 nr

Site to E of Etréaupont off N2, Mons-Reims rd. Site adj football pitch on banks of Rv Oise. Well sp fr main rd. 2*, Sm, hdg, mkd, pt shd, EHU (10A) €4 (poss rev pol); Eng spkn; adv bkg acc; rv fishing adj; tennis; CKE. *"Pretty, tidy site; sports field adj; warm welcome; v clean san facs; site self if recep clsd; conv rte to Zeebrugge ferry (approx 200km); gd walking & cycling; gd; delightful site; canoe hire adj; vg."* **€18.60, 1 Apr-31 Oct.** **2023**

VESOUL *6G2* (3km W Rural) *47.63026, 6.12858* **Camping Vesoul,** Ave des Rives du Lac, 70000 Vesoul **03 84 76 22 86; https://vacances-seasonova.com/fr/camping/vesoul/**

12 €2 (htd) nr

2km fr D619, sp fr W end of by-pass, pass indus est to lge lake on W o'skts. Ent opp Peugeot/Citroën factory on lakeside. 3*, Lge, mkd, pt shd, EHU (6A) €3; gas; 10% statics; adv bkg acc; ccard acc; tennis; fishing; waterslide 300m; games area; CKE. *"Super site screened fr indus est by trees; pool & paddling pool 300m; site clsd mid-Dec to early Jan; gd size pitches but poss soft after rain; excel aqua park nr; gd cycle rtes; vg."* **€19.00** **2022**

VEULES LES ROSES *3C2* (3.5km E Rural) *49.88351, 0.85188* **Camp Municipal Le Mesnil,** Route de Sotteville, 76740 St Aubin-sur-Mer **02 35 83 02 83; contact@campinglemesnil.com; www.campinglemesnil.com**

(htd) sand 1.5km

On D68 2km W of St Aubin-sur-Mer. 4*, Med, hdg, unshd, terr, EHU (10A) €3.70 (pos rev pol); 30% statics; ccard acc; CKE. **€24.40, 1 Apr-29 Oct.** **2024**

VEULES LES ROSES *3C2* (6km E Rural) *49.86083, 0.89079* **Camping Les Garennes de la Mer,** 12 Route de Luneray, 76740 Le Bourg-Dun **02 35 83 10 44; camping_lesgarennesdelamer@hotmail.fr; www.lesgarennes.fr**

€1 nr shgl 3km

Fr Veules-les-Roses, take D925 twd Dieppe. Site sp in Le Bourg-Dun - 1km SE. 2*, Sm, mkd, pt shd, pt sl, EHU (16A) €4; gas; 60% statics; Eng spkn; adv bkg acc; ccard acc; CKE. *"Well-kept site; vg san facs."* **€26.00, 1 Apr-15 Oct.** **2024**

VEULES LES ROSES *3C2* (0.3km S Rural/Coastal) *49.87586, 0.80314* **Camping Les Mouettes,** 7 Ave Jean Moulin, 76980 Veules-les-Roses **02 35 97 61 98; camping.lesmouettes.normandie@gmail.com; www.camping-lesmouettes-normandie.com**

€2 (htd) (covrd, htd) shgl 800m

On ent vill fr Dieppe on D925, turn R onto D68, site in 500m up hill (14%). 3*, Lge, mkd, hdg, pt shd, EHU (6A) €4.70; gas; bbq; red long stay; TV; 10% statics; Eng spkn; adv bkg acc; ccard acc; games area; games rm; fitness rm; CKE. *"Pleasant area; peaceful, well-kept site; vg; site a bit scruffy start of ssn (2017)."* **€31.80, 1 Apr-15 Oct.** **2023**

FRANCE

FRANCE

VEYNES *9D3* (2km SW Rural) *44.51889, 5.79880*
FFCC Camping Les Rives du Lac, Les Iscles, 05400 Veynes **04 92 57 20 90; contact@camping-lac.com; www.camping-lac.com**
€2.50 (covrd)

Off D994. Sp on lakeside. 3*, Med, mkd, hdstg, pt shd, pt sl, EHU (10A) €3.50; bbq; sw nr; phone; bus 500m; adv bkg acc; ccard acc; watersports; CKE. *"Attractive, well-run site on shore of sm lake; welcoming staff; beach games in high ssn; climbing; mountain biking; open air cinema twice weekly; san facs excel; something for all ages."* **€23.00, 1 May-30 Sep.** 2024

VEZELAY *4G4* (2km SE Rural) *47.45879, 3.77150*
Camp Municipal, 89450 St Père **03 86 33 36 58 or 03 86 33 26 62 (Mairie); camping-saint-pere89@orange.fr; www.saint-pere.fr**
(cont) nr

Fr Vézelay take D957, turn onto D36 to St Père. Site sp. Med, pt shd, EHU (10A) €2.20 (poss rev pol); 10% statics; tennis; rv fishing adj; canoeing. *"Pleasant site; conv Morvan National Park; warden comes am & pm; basic san facs need update; gd walking area."*
€11.00, 1 Apr-30 Oct. 2024

VIAS *10F1* (3km S Coastal) *43.29055, 3.39863*
Camping Californie Plage, 34450 Vias-Plage **04 67 21 64 69; info@californie-plage.fr; www.californie-plage.fr**
€4.60 (covrd, htd)
sand adj

W fr Agde on D612 to Vias; turn S in town & foll sps 'Mer' over canal bdge & sp to site. 4*, Lge, mkd, shd, EHU (5-10A) €1.50-3.50; gas; TV; 10% statics; Eng spkn; adv bkg acc; ccard acc; bike hire; waterslide; CKE.
€33.00, 1 Apr-30 Oct. 2022

VIAS *10F1* (3km S Coastal) *43.29800, 3.41750*
Camping Les Salisses, Avenue of the Mediterranean, 34450 Vias-Plage **04 67 21 64 07; info@salisses.com; www.salisses.com**
€3.50
(covrd, htd) sand 1km

Turn S off D612 (Agde-Béziers rd) in Vias & foll sp to Vias-Plage. Cross Canal du Midi bdge & site on R. 4*, Lge, mkd, pt shd, EHU (6A) inc; gas; bbq; TV; 80% statics; ccard acc; bike hire; waterslide; tennis; games area. *"Vg family hols; sauna; steam rm; interesting town & mkt in Agde; sm pitches."*
€42.00, 13 Apr-15 Sep. 2024

VIAS *10F1* (3km S Coastal) *43.29083, 3.41783*
Yelloh! Village Le Club Farret, Farinette-Plage, 34450 Vias-Plage **04 67 21 64 45; info@farret.com; www.camping-farret.com**
€6 (htd)
sand adj

Fr A9, exit Agde junc 34. Foll sp Vias-Plage on D137. Sp fr cent of Vias-Plage on L, immed after Gendarmerie. 4*, V lge, mkd, pt shd, EHU (6A) inc; gas; TV; 10% statics; Eng spkn; adv bkg acc; ccard acc; games rm; bike hire; fitness rm; games area; tennis; watersports; CKE. *"Excel facs, entmnt; excursions; gd security."* **€70.20, 12 Apr-29 Sep.** 2023

VIAS *10F1* (3km W Rural) *43.31222, 3.36320*
Camping Sunêlia Le Domaine de la Dragonnière, 34450 Vias **04 67 01 03 10; contact@dragonniere.com; www.dragonniere.com**
€5 (htd)
sand 3km

Exit A9 junc 35 onto D64 twd Valras-Plage, then D612 dir Agde & Vias. Site on R bef Vias. Or exit junc 34 onto D612A. At Vias turn R onto D612 sp Béziers, site on L. NB Take care high speed humps at sh intervals. 5*, V lge, mkd, hdg, pt shd, EHU (16A) inc; gas; bbq; TV; 80% statics; phone; Eng spkn; adv bkg acc; ccard acc; games area; spa; bike hire; tennis; CKE. *"Vg site; excel for children & teenagers high ssn; Canal du Midi nrby; opp Béziers airport; free bus to beach; site poss flooded after heavy rain; touring pitches have individual shwr block on pitch; v busy at w/ends."*
€109.00, 8 Apr - 2 Oct, C06. 2022

"Satellite navigation makes touring much easier"

Remember most sat navs don't know if you're towing or in a larger vehicle – always use yours alongside maps and site directions.

VICHY *9A1* (4km S Rural) *46.11555, 3.43006*
Camping Beau Rivage, Rue Claude Decloître, 03700 Bellerive-sur-Allier **04 70 32 26 85; contact@camping-beaurivage.com; www.camping-beaurivage.com**
€1 (covrd, htd)

Fr Vichy cross rv bdge over Rv Allier onto D1093, turn L at rndabt foll sp Campings, sp to Beau Rivage. Site on L on rv bank, past Cmp Les Acacias. 4*, Med, shd, EHU (10A) €3.10; gas; bbq; TV; 50% statics; tennis 2km; games area; bike hire; archery; waterslide; canoeing; fishing. *"Lovely rvside site, but no rv sw allowed; lge o'fits have diff pitching; easy cycle ride to lovely city."*
€28.00, 1 Apr-8 Oct. 2023

VIERZON 4G3 (2.5km SW Urban) 47.20937, 2.08079 **Camp O'village Vierzon,** 115 Route de Bellon, 18100 Vierzon **02 48 53 99 89; vierzon@campovillage.com; www.campovillage.com**

Fr N on A71 take A20 dir Châteauroux, leave at junc 7 onto D2020 & then D27 dir Bourges; pass Intermarché supmkt on L, after next traff lts turn L into Route de Bellon; site in 1km on R, sp. NB Do not go into town cent. 2*, Med, mkd, hdg, pt shd, pt sl, EHU (6A) €3 (some rev pol); gas; bbq (elec, gas); phone; Eng spkn; adv bkg acc; boat hire; fishing; CKE. *"Attractive, well-kept site by rv; gd sized pitches but some poss diff to negotiate; nice little rest o'looking rv; gates clsd 2300-0700; helpful staff; off clsd 12-4, no site access; poss travellers; ideal NH; gd site; friendly recep; facs v clean; acc to Berry canal & town ctr by bike, use acc rd not rv footpath."* **€24.38, 15 Jun-14 Sep. 2024**

VIEURE 7A4 (2km NE Rural) 46.50305, 2.90754 **Plan d'eau de Vieure,** La Borde, 03430 Vieure **07 64 76 12 93; www.plandeaudevieure.fr**

Exit A71-E11 at junc 10. Take D94 NE to Cosne d'Allier, then R onto D11. L onto D459, 1st R onto La Bordé. Foll sp to campsite. Med, hdg, pt shd, pt sl, EHU (10A) €3.10; sw; twin axles; 35% statics; phone; ccard acc; CCI. *"Large, open & shd pitches; dated san facs; v pleasant remote site by lake; fishing & canoeing; family friendly; gd."* **€11.50, 11 Apr-30 Sep. 2024**

VILLARD DE LANS 9C3 (1.5km N Rural) 45.07750, 5.55620 **Camping Caravaneige L'Oursière,** 38250 Villard-de-Lans **04 76 95 14 77; oursiere@franceloc.fr; www.camping-oursiere.fr**

Site clearly visible on app to town fr D531 Gorges d'Engins rd (13km SW Grenoble). App fr W on D531 not rec for c'vans & m'vans due o'hangs. 3*, Lge, unshd, terr, EHU (10A) €4-6; gas; bbq; 20% statics; Eng spkn; adv bkg acc; ccard acc; CKE. *"Excel all winter sports; friendly owners; drying rm; san facs need upgrade (2010); pool 800m; waterpark 800m; new htd indoor sw pool (2015)."* **€26.00 2022**

VILLARD DE LANS 9C3 (12km N Rural) 45.12951, 5.53215 **Camping Caravaneige Les Buissonnets,** 38112 Méaudre **04 76 95 21 04; camping-les-buissonnets@wanadoo.fr; www.camping-les-buissonnets.com**

Fr Grenoble take D1532 to Sassenage then D531 to Lans-en-Vercors. Turn R at rndabt onto D106 twrds Meaudre. Turn L just bef rndabt in vill off D106. Approx 30km SW of Grenoble by rd & 18km as crow flies. 3*, Med, unshd, sl, EHU (6-10A) €4-6; bus to ski slopes; games area; clsd 1 Dec-10 Nov. *"Gd skiing cent; conv touring Vercours; levellers ess; highly rec; friendly, v well managed site; higher price in winter; pool 300m; lovely area; slightly sl, levelling necessary; v pleasant."* **€22.00, 1 Jan-31 Oct & 12 Dec-31 Dec. 2023**

VILLARS LES DOMBES 9A2 (0.2km S Urban) 45.99763, 5.03163 **Camping Le Nid du Parc,** 164 Ave des Nations, 01330 Villars-les-Dombes **04 74 98 00 21; camping@parcdesoiseaux.com; www.lenidduparc.com**

N fr Lyon on N83, site in town cent on R by sw pool. 4*, Lge, hdstg, pt shd, EHU (10A) €4.50; bbq (gas); 60% statics; games area; rv fishing adj; bike hire; tennis. *"Excel site; lge pitches; modern, gd san facs; htd pool adj inc; gd security; bird park 10 mins walk; popular NH."* **€31.70, 1 Apr-1 Nov. 2024**

VILLEDIEU LES POELES 1D4 (0.6km S Urban) 48.83638, -1.21694 **Camping Les Chevaliers de Malte,** 2 Impasse Pré de la Rose, 50800 Villedieu-les-Poêles **02 33 59 49 04; contact@camping-deschevaliers.com; www.camping-deschevaliers.com**

Exit A84 junc 38 onto D999 twd Villedieu, then R onto D975 & R onto D924 to avoid town cent. Foll sp fr car park on R after x-ing rv. Site behind PO & cinema. 3*, Med, hdstg, mkd, hdg, pt shd, EHU (6A) inc (poss rev pol); bbq; TV; 40% statics; phone; Eng spkn; adv bkg acc; games area; boating; games rm; rv fishing; tennis; CKE. *"Peaceful, lovely site; lge pitches but kerbs poss diff lger o'fits; interesting historic town; avoid arr Tue am due mkt; conv A84 & Cherbourg ferry; vg; gd modern facs, all new; well worth a visit to town; excel site; rest extended 2011; staff v helpful; bell foundry worth a visit; new owners (2016); vg."* **€25.00, 1 Apr-15 Oct. 2023**

VILLEFORT (LOZERE) 9D1 (0.6km S Rural) 44.43536, 3.93323 **Le Mas Les Sédariès,** Ave des Cévennes, 48800 Villefort **04 66 46 25 20 or 06 52 36 91 49 (mob); vacances48@gmail.com; www.sedaries.com**

On D906 heading S fr Villefort twd Alès. 2*, Sm, pt shd, terr, EHU (6A) €2; bbq; sw nr; phone; fishing 2km; CKE. *"Attractive, scenic site; bureau clsd 1000-1830; privately owned now (2014); not many touring places."* **€15.00, 1 Jun-30 Sep. 2024**

VILLEFRANCHE DE LAURAGAIS 8F3 (8km SW Rural) 43.35498, 1.64862 **Camping Le Lac de la Thésauque,** Nailloux, 31560 Montgeard **05 61 81 34 67; camping@thesauque.com; www.camping-thesauque.com**

Fr S exit A61 at Villefrance-de-Lauragais junc 20 onto D622, foll sp Auterive then Lac after Gardouch vill, site sp. Fr N turn off A61 at 1st junc after tolls S of Toulouse onto A66 (sp Foix). Leave A66 at junc 1 & foll sp Nailloux. Turn L on ent vill onto D662 & in 2km turn R onto D25 & immed R to site, sp. 3*, Med, mkd, hdstg, pt shd, terr, EHU (10A) inc; bbq; 70% statics; ccard acc; boating; fishing; tennis; CKE. *"Scenic, peaceful location; conv NH for A61; helpful owners; ltd facs LS; gd security; steep app to sm terr pitches poss diff lge o'fits; facs basic but adequate."* **€24.00 2024**

VILLEFRANCHE DE ROUERGUE *7D4* (9km SE Rural) *44.26695, 2.11575* **Camping Le Muret,** 12200 St Salvadou **05 65 81 80 69 or 06 72 48 11 02; contact@campinglemuret.com; www.campinglemuret.com**

€2

Fr Villefranche on D911 twd Millau, R on D905A sp camping & foll camping sp 7km. 3*, Sm, hdg, mkd, shd, EHU (16A) €4.50; red long stay; phone; adv bkg acc; fishing; CKE. *"Lovely setting; gas & ice at farm; lake adj; gd sized pitches."* **€23.00, 5 Apr-22 Oct. 2023**

VILLEFRANCHE DE ROUERGUE *7D4* (1km SW Urban) *44.34207, 2.02731* **FFCC Camping du Rouergue,** Avenue de la Libération 12200 Villefranche-de-Rouergue **05 65 45 16 24; campingdurouergue@onlycamp.fr; www.campingdurouergue.com**

€1

Best app fr N on D922, then D47 dir Monteils & Najac; avoid 1-way system in town; ent thro sports stadium. Site well sp. 3*, Med, hdstg, mkd, hdg, shd, serviced pitches; EHU (16A) €3.50; red long stay; twin axles; TV; 15% statics; bus high ssn; Eng spkn; adv bkg req; ccard acc; tennis 1km; CKE. *"Well-kept, peaceful site; easy access; lge pitches; pleasant, friendly owner; excel clean san facs; pool v sm; gd security; sports stadium adj; easy walk/cycle to town; m'van services outside site; rec; v hot water, gd supply; excel."* **€23.70, 3 May-22 Sep. 2024**

VILLEFRANCHE DU PERIGORD *7D3* (1km E Urban) *44.62757, 1.08159* **FFCC Camping La Bastide,** Route de Cahors, 24550 Villefranche-du-Périgord **05 53 28 94 57 or 06 89 65 32 95; contact@camping-la-bastide.com; www.camping-la-bastide.com**

€1 nr

On N660 fr Villefranche-du-Périgord dir Cahors; site past PO on R nr top of hill on town o'skts. 3*, Med, hdg, mkd, pt shd, terr, EHU (6-10A) €3-4; 25% statics; adv bkg acc; tennis 300m; fishing; CKE. *"Steep, terr site but easy access, can be soft in wet weather; charming owners; ACSI; excel touring base; vg; v nice town within walking dist."* **€25.60, 1 Apr-30 Oct. 2024**

VILLEFRANCHE SUR CHER *4G3* (8km SE Rural) *47.26917, 1.86265* **FFCC Camp Municipal Val Rose,** Rue du Val Rose, 41320 Mennetou-sur-Cher **02 54 98 11 02 or 02 54 98 01 19 (Mairie); mairie.mennetou@wanadoo.fr**

€0.20 (htd) nr nr

Site sp fr D976/D2076 fr Villefranche (sm white sp); site on R in SW side of vill of Mennetou. To avoid narr bdge in town fr N76 onto A20, just outside town, turn imm R, site sp after L turn. 2*, Sm, mkd, pt shd, EHU 4A (rev polarity); Eng spkn; adv bkg acc; ccard acc. *"Pleasant, well-kept site; friendly, helpful warden; excel, spotless san facs but dated; excel lndry; pretty, walled town 5 mins walk along canal; mkt Thurs; htd pool adj; vg value; access for lge o'fits diff; 2 excel rest in town; excel NH; barrier clsd 21:00-07:30; site self; ltd facs; bread to order."* **€14.50, 13 May-18 Sep. 2023**

VILLEFRANCHE SUR SAONE *9B2* (10km E Rural) *45.99104, 4.81802* **FFCC Camp Municipal le Bois de la Dame,** 590 Chemin du Bois de la Dame, 01480 Ars-sur-Formans **04 74 00 77 23 or 04 74 00 71 84 (Mairie); camping.boisdeladame@orange.fr; www.ars-village.fr**

€3 (cont)

Exit A6 junc 31.1 or 31.2 onto D131/D44 E dir Villars-les-Dombes. Site 500m W of Ars-sur-Formans on lake, sp. 3*, Med, mkd, pt shd, pt sl, terr, EHU (10-16A) €3-5; 60% statics; adv bkg rec; lake fishing; tennis court; CKE. *"Average site, but pretty & interesting vill; ltd facs LS; no twin axles; higher pitches have unguarded precipices; gd."* **€21.60, 8 Apr-14 Oct. 2024**

VILLEFRANCHE SUR SAONE *9B2* (10km SE Rural) *45.93978, 4.76811* **Camping Kanopee,** Rue Robert Baltie, 01600 Trévoux **04 74 08 44 83; contact@kanopee-village.com; www.kanopee-village.com**

nr

Fr Villefranche take D306 S to Anse. Turn L onto D39/D6 for Trévoux, site sp in town, on bank of Rv Saône. 3*, Lge, pt shd, EHU (6A) inc; sw nr; 75% statics; adv bkg req; rv fishing adj; CKE. *"Spacious rvside site nr vill; helpful staff; well maintained; access poss diff lge o'fits due statics; gd cycling rtes nrby; Trévoux interesting history; m'van o'night area at ent; excel shwr blocks; Aire at ent to camp; vg."* **€23.00, 1 Apr-30 Sep. 2023**

"There aren't many sites open at this time of year"

If you're travelling outside peak season remember to call ahead to check site opening dates – even if the entry says 'open all year'.

VILLEFRANCHE SUR SAONE *9B2* (5km S Rural) *45.94050, 4.72680* **Camping Les Portes du Beaujolais,** 495 Ave Jean Vacher, 69480 Anse **04 74 67 12 87; beaujolais@capfun.com**

€2 (htd)

Exit A6 junc 31.2 at Villefranche & foll D306 S to Anse (foll sp Champion supmkt). Site well sp off D39, on banks of Rvs Saône & L'Azergues. 4*, Lge, hdg, mkd, hdstg, pt shd, EHU (10A) €5.50; sw; TV; 20% statics; phone; Eng spkn; adv bkg acc; bike hire; CKE. *"Pleasant, friendly site; pitches poss tired end of ssn; some pitches sm, uneven & diff lge o'fits; ltd facs LS & poss stretched high ssn; shwrs sometimes cold (2011); pool poss overcrowded; poss muddy when wet; lge field avail at rear but no shd; rvside walk; rd noise fr A6 nrby & some rwly noise; Anse 10 min walk - bus to Lyons; narr gauge rlwy adj; lge o'night area; conv NH."* **€37.50, 1 Mar-31 Oct. 2024**

VILLENEUVE SUR LOT *7D3* (8km E Urban) *44.39576, 0.80491* **Camping Les Berges du Lot,** 1, Lot Banks Alley, 47140 St Sylvestre-sur-Lot **05 53 41 22 23 or 05 53 41 24 58 (Mairie); e.cassagne@orange.fr; www.saintsylvestresurlot.com**

nr nr nr

Exit Villeneuve-sur-Lot on D911 sp Cahors. Site in cent of St Sylvestre-sur-Lot. Foll Camping sp to rear of La Mairie (Town Hall) & supmkt; site accessed via car park to R of main rd. 2*, Sm, mkd, pt shd, EHU (6A) €3.30 (poss long lead req); Eng spkn; boating; fishing. *"Popular, comfortable, scenic site; clean facs; helpful staff; adv bkg rec; 2 pin cont el conn; many long term residents, inc British; mkt Wed & Sun am, when access diff; rec; cramped; untidy; birdwatching; not suitable for large o'fits."* **€11.50** **2024**

VILLENEUVE SUR LOT *7D3* (3km S Urban) *44.39483, 0.68680* **Camping Lot et Bastides,** Allée de Malbentre, 47300 Pujols **05 53 36 86 79; contact@camping-lot-et-bastides.fr; www.camping-lot-et-bastides.fr**

€2

Fr Villeneuve Sur Lot on D911 take L onto D118. At rndabt take 1st exit onto D911. Turn L onto Rue du General. Site on the R. 3*, Med, hdg, pt shd, EHU (16A); bbq; twin axles; 25% statics; bus adj; adv bkg acc; ccard acc; games area; CCI. *"New site 2012; neat and clean; views of Pujols, most beautiful vill in France; lots to see & do in area; v scenic; friendly staff; bike hire."* **€24.00, 30 Mar-2 Nov.** **2024**

VILLENEUVE-LOUBET *10E4* (6km S Rural) *43.62027, 7.12583* **Camping La Vieille Ferme,** 296 Blvd des Groules, 06270 Villeneuve-Loubet-Plage **04 93 33 41 44; info@vieilleferme.com; www.vieilleferme.com**

12 €2.50 (htd) nr (covrd, htd) shgl 1km

Fr W (Cannes) take Antibes exit 44 fr A8, foll D35 dir Antibes 'Centre Ville'. At lge junc turn onto D6007, Ave de Nice, twd Biot & Villeneuve-Loubet sp Nice (rlwy line on R). Just after Marineland turn L onto Blvd des Groules. Fr E (Nice) leave A8 at junc 47 to join D6007 twd Antibes, take 3rd turning after Intermarché supmkt; site well sp fr D6007. 4*, Med, mkd, hdg, pt shd, pt sl, terr, serviced pitches; EHU (2A-10A) €3 - €7; gas; bbq (elec, gas); red long stay; TV; 40% statics; bus, train nr; Eng spkn; adv bkg acc; ccard acc; games rm. *"Peaceful, well-kept family-run site; well-drained pitches, some lge; beach not suitable children & non-swimmers; no o'fits over 8m; excel pool; gd walking, cycling & dog walking as lge park adj; some aircraft & rd noise; vg value LS; excel; be wary of bike thieves; nice bar/rest; friendly staff; v quiet at night; bus & train nrby; ehu use restricted."*
€45.00, C22. **2023**

VILLEREAL *7D3* (2km N Rural) *44.65723, 0.72820* **Camping Château de Fonrives,** 47210 Rives, Villeréal **05 53 36 63 38; www.campingchateaufonrives.com**

€6 (covrd, htd)

Fr Bergerac take N21 S for 8km, turn L onto D14 thro Issigeac; site is just outside vill of Rives in grnds of chateau. 4*, Med, pt shd, pt sl, EHU (6A) inc; gas; sw; 10% statics; Eng spkn; adv bkg acc; ccard acc; fishing; golf; bike hire; games rm; waterslide; CKE. *"Spacious site; gd, 3 pools; van poss manhandled on some shady pitches; easier access pitches without shd; some noise fr weekly disco; friendly owners; B&B avail; interesting town; mkt Sat; huge pitches nr pool/bar; poss noisy."* **€47.00, 7 Jun-7 Sep.** **2024**

VILLEREAL *7D3* (7km NE Rural) *44.65331, 0.80953* **Camping Le Moulin de Mandassagne,** Mandassagne, 47210 Parranquet **05 53 36 04 02; isabelle.pimouguet@orange.fr; www.tourisme-lotetgaronne.com**

Fr D104/D2 bet Villeréal & Monpazier turn N sp Parranquet, site sp. 3*, Sm, mkd, pt shd, EHU (6A) inc; gas; TV; Eng spkn; adv bkg acc; fishing; tennis. *"Lovely countryside; v relaxing; slightly bohemian site; friendly owners."* **€15.00, 1 Apr-1 Oct.** **2024**

VILLEREAL *7D3* (9km SE Rural) *44.61426, 0.81889* **Camping Fontaine du Roc,** Les Moulaties, 47210 Dévillac **05 53 36 08 16; reception@fontainedu roc.com; www.fontaineduroc.com**

€3.50

Fr Villeréal take D255 sp Dévillac, just beyond Dévillac at x-rds turn L & L again sp Estrade; site on L in 500m. 3*, Med, hdg, mkd, hdstg, pt shd, EHU (5-10A) €3.50-4.50 gas; bbq; red long stay; TV; 2% statics; phone; Eng spkn; adv bkg acc; fishing 500m; bike hire; games rm; CKE. *"Peaceful, well-cared for site; helpful owner; lge pitches; ACSI acc (LS); excel."* **€15.00, 1 Apr-15 Oct.** **2022**

VILLEREAL *7D3* (3km NW Rural) *44.65253, 0.72375* **Camping de Bergougne,** 47210 Rives **05 53 36 01 30; info@camping-de-bergougne.com; www.camping-de-bergougne.fr/**

nr (htd)

Fr Villeréal, take D207 NW sp Issigeac/Bergerac. In 1km turn L onto D250 W sp Doudrac. Foll sm green sp to site. 3*, Med, mkd, hdg, pt shd, pt sl, terr, EHU (6A) inc; gas; bbq (sep area); TV; 15% statics; Eng spkn; adv bkg acc; ccard acc; games rm; fishing; games area; CKE. *"Vg site; small café; bread del in Jul & Aug; friendly welcoming new owners; occasional events in bar/rest; v peaceful rustic ambience; vg."*
€31.00, 1 May-30 Sep. **2023**

*Last year of report

FRANCE

VILLERSEXEL *6G2* (1km N Rural) *47.55763, 6.43628* **Camping Le Chapeau Chinois,** 92 Rue du Chapeau Chinois, 70110 Villersexel **03 84 63 40 60; contact@camping-villersexel.eu; https://campingvillersexel.com/**

nr nr

Leave vill on D468 N, site on R immed after rv bdge. 3*, Med, hdg, mkd, pt shd, EHU (10A) €3.30; bbq; sw; 5% statics; Eng spkn; adv bkg acc; games area; CKE. *"Vg."* **€19.00, 1 Apr-6 Oct. 2022**

VILLEVAUDE *3D3* (2km E Rural) *48.91258, 2.67025* **Camping Le Parc de Paris,** Rue Adèle Claret, Montjay-la-Tour, 77410 Villevaudé **01 60 26 20 79; info@campingleparc.fr; www.campingleparc.fr**

12 €6 (htd) nr

Fr N, A1 twds Paris, then A104 to Marne-la-Vallée, exit at junc 6B (Paris Bobigny), then D105 to Villevaudé, then to Montjay & site sp. Fr S exit A104 at junc 8 to Meaux & Villevaudé. 3*, Lge, mkd, hdg, pt shd, pt sl, serviced pitches; EHU (10A) €5; sw nr; TV; 50% statics; phone; Eng spkn; adv bkg acc; ccard acc; games rm; tennis 200m; games area; CKE. *"Conv Disneyland, Paris, Parc Astérix (Disney tickets fr recep); gd san facs; twin axles acc if adv bkg; drive to local stn (10mins) & park free; shuttle service to Disneyland; gd sh stay; san facs tired, pitches sm and uneven."* **€33.00 2022**

VILLIERS SUR ORGE *4E3* (0.6km SE Urban) *48.65527, 2.30409* **Camping Le Beau Village,** 1 Voie des Prés, 91700 Villiers-sur-Orge **01 60 16 17 86; contact@campingaparis.com; www.campingaparis.com**

12 €2 (htd) nr

Fr S on N20 turn off onto D35 heading E twrds Villiers sur Orge. Cont strt on to traff lts & sm Renault g'ge, turn R alongside rv. Turn just bef St Genieve des Bois. 3*, Med, hdg, pt shd, EHU (10A) (poss rev pol); gas; bbq; phone; train 700m; games rm; kayaking; fishing. *"Pleasant, well-run site; conv Paris; some statics/chalets; ltd space for lge o'fits; helpful staff."* **€28.90 2023**

VIMOUTIERS *3D1* (0.6km N Urban) *48.93236, 0.19646* **Camping La Campière - Vimoutiers,** Ave Dr Dentu, 61120 Vimoutiers **02 33 39 18 86; https://www.camping-campiere-vimoutiers.fr**

€1.50 (htd) nr nr

App Vimoutiers fr N on on D579/D979/D916, site on R 300m after passing junc with D16; turn R at flag poles (200m after Avia petrol stn). Or appr fr Gacé on D979 turn L at flag poles (on D916 just bef junc with D16). Site nr stadium & not well sp. 2*, Sm, hdg, pt shd, EHU (6A) €2.85; sw nr; 10% statics; adv bkg acc; tennis; bike hire; rv fishing 2km; CKE. *"Excel, well-maintained, pretty site at cent of Camembert cheese industry; helpful, friendly warden; sports facs 2km; vg, clean san facs; noise fr nrby factory; boating 2km; unrel opening dates - phone ahead LS; attractive town; gd value."* **€16.10, 1 Apr-31 Oct. 2023**

VIRIEU LE GRAND *9B3* (5km NE Rural) *45.87483, 5.68428* **Camping Le Vaugrais,** Chemin de Vaugrais, 01510 Artemare **04 79 87 37 34; contact@camping-le-vaugrais.fr; www.camping-savoie-levaugrais.com**

€3 nr nr (htd)

N fr Belley on D1504 then D904 to Artemare; sp in vill. Well sp fr D904 on rvside. 3*, Sm, hdg, pt shd, EHU (10A); bbq; 10% statics; Eng spkn; adv bkg acc; fishing; CKE. *"Charming site in gd location; some lge pitches with views; friendly owners; clean san facs, poss inadequate high ssn; nice pool; Artemare within walking dist; gd food at hotel in town; vg local walks; excel; app over narr bdge; gd views; highly rec."* **€43.00, 1 Apr - 1 Oct, M12. 2022**

VITRE *2F4* (14km N Rural) *48.23090, -1.18087* **Camp Municipal du Lac,** Rue Rouxière, 35210 Châtillon-en-Vendelais **02 99 76 48 84 or 06 84 74 58 24; info@campinglesrivesdulac.fr; www.campinglesrivesdulac.fr**

Take D178 fr Vitré to Fougères. In 11km branch L onto D108, sp Châtillon-en-Vendelais. Foll sp thro vill & turn R immed after level x-ing & bef bdge; site in 1km. 3*, Med, pt shd, pt sl, EHU (6A) €3.10 (poss rev pol); 10% statics; fishing; tennis; CKE. *"Pleasant site; clean san facs; warden on site 0900-1000 only; levelling blocks req most pitches; lake adj; quiet; gd walks; nature reserve (birds) nr."* **€11.50, 15 May-30 Sep. 2024**

VITRE *2 F4* (2.7km SSE Urban) *48.11000, -1.19891* **Camping Municipal de Vitré,** 109 Boulevard des Rochers, 35500 Vitre **02 99 75 25 28; camping@marie-vitre**

Fr Vitre ring rd D173 take D88 heading SE sp Argentre du P. Site on L in 450m. Well sp. Sm, hdg, pt shd, EHU 10A (€2.60); bbq (charcoal, elec, gas); sw nr; bus fr site ent; public pool 1km; CKE. *"Interesting, attractive medieval town; quiet cycling rds nrby; excel."* **€12.20, 1 Mar-15 Dec. 2023**

VITRY LE FRANCOIS *6E1* (6km SE Rural) *48.69673, 4.63039* **Aire Naturelle Camping Nature (Scherschell),** 13 Rue de l'Evangile, 51300 Luxémont-et-Villotte **03 26 72 61 14 or 06 83 42 83 53 (mob); eric.scherschell@wanadoo.fr; www.camping-nature.net**

€1

Fr N44 at rndabt take N4 sp St Dizier. Take exit sp Luxemont. At rndabt take 1st exit D396, at next rndabt take 4th exit sp Luxemont (D316). After 2.1km turn R, site on L in 100km. Sm, hdstg, shd, pt sl, EHU (6A) inc (poss rev pol & long lead req); bbq; sw nr; Eng spkn; adv bkg acc; fishing; CKE. *"Delightful, CL-type site; well-kept & immac; helpful, friendly owners; gd, clean unisex san facs; nr canal & cycle paths; interesting area to visit; excel; poss mosquitoes."* **€16.00, 1 May-15 Oct. 2024**

VIVONNE *7A2* (0.5km E Rural) *46.42511, 0.26409* **Camp Municipal,** Chemin de Prairie, 86370 Vivonne **05 49 43 25 95 or 05 49 43 41 05 (Mairie); camping@vivonne.fr; www.vivonne.fr**

Exit N10 where it by-passes Vivonne & ent town. Site in municipal park to E of town. 2*, Med, pt shd, EHU (10A) €2.35. *"Welcoming, helpful resident warden; clean facs; sh walk to town cent; noise fr rlwy, quieter w/end; worth a visit; as gd as ever; ideal NH."* **€18.00, 13 Apr-13 Oct. 2024**

VIZILLE *9C3* (0.5km N Urban) *45.08660, 5.76814* **FFCC Camping Le Bois de Cornage,** Chemin du Camping, 38220 Vizille **04 76 68 12 39; campingvizille@orange.fr; www.campingvizille.com**

€0.80 nr (htd)

Site sp at x-rds of Rte Napoléon, N85 & Rte de Briançon D1091. Site on N o'skirts of town. Well sp. 3*, Med, hdg, mkd, shd, pt sl, terr, EHU (10-16A) €4.50-5.50 (long lead poss req); red long stay; 10% statics; bus; Eng spkn; adv bkg rec; CKE. *"Helpful owner; excel clean facs; gd cycling & climbing nrby; mkd walks nrby; no vans over 5m acc; poss mosquitoes; frequent buses to Grenoble & Bourg-d'Oisans; vg."* **€16.00, 24 Apr-10 Oct. 2024**

VOLLORE-VILLE *9B1* (1km NE Rural) *45.79199, 3.60583* **Camping Le Grün de Chignore (formerly Camping Des Plaines),** Le Grun de Chignore, Les Plaines, 63120 Vollore-Ville **04 73 53 73 37; jenny-loisel@orange.fr; www.campingauvergne.fr**

12 nr

Leave A89/E70 at junc 29 onto D906 S to Courpiere. Fr Courpiere take D7 to Vollore-Ville. Site on the R at turning to Chabrier. 2*, Sm, hdg, mkd, pt shd, gas; bbq; twin axles; 20% statics; adv bkg acc; ccard acc; CKE. *"Excel, well-kept little site; friendly owners; pleasant vill; conv for A89/E70."* **€15.00 2024**

VOLVIC *9B1* (0.7km E Urban) *45.87208, 3.04591* **Camping Onlycamp Pierre et Sources (formerly Camp Municipal Pierre et Sources),** Rue de Chancelas, 63530 Volvic **04 73 33 50 16; campingvolvic@onlycamp.fr; www.camping-volvic.com**

€1.50 (htd)

Exit Riom on D986: foll sp for Pontgibaud & Volvic. Site sp to R on app to town. 3*, Sm, shd, EHU (12A) €3.50, 10% statics; Eng spkn; adv bkg acc. *"Pleasant, tidy site with lovely views; welcoming & helpful; excel, clean san facs; access some pitches poss diff, particularly for lge o'fits; conv Volvic factory tour; no access for new arrivals when off is clsd."* **€20.00, 1 May-30 Sep. 2023**

VONNAS *9A2* (0.3km NW Rural) *46.22152, 4.98805* **Camp Municipal Le Renom,** 240 Ave des Sports, 01540 Vonnas **04 74 50 02 75 or 07 56 19 41 89; www.camping-renom.com/fr/accueil-p1**

€1 nr

Fr Bourg-en-Bresse take D1079 W sp Mâcon. In 15km take D26 or D47 S to Vonnas; turn R in town cent (ignore sp on o'skts of town) & site on R in 300m by leisure cent. 3*, Med, hdg, mkd, pt shd, EHU (10A) €4.50; bbq; 30% statics; tennis adj; rv fishing. *"Warm welcome; interesting town- 10min walk; mkt Thurs; htd pool adj; gd site, but expensive; extremely well kept."* **€23.00, 2 Apr-2 Oct. 2024**

VOUECOURT *6E1* (0.1km E Rural) *48.26774, 5.13671* **Camp Municipal Rives de Marne,** Rue de Verdun 52320 Vouécourt

nr nr

N fr Chaumont on N67; sp to site in 17km; thro vill by Rv Marne; site on L bef main rv bdge, almost opp Mairie; well sp. 2*, Sm, mkd, pt shd, EHU (10A) €2.50 (poss rev pol); gas; adv bkg acc; ccard acc; fishing; CKE. *"Lovely, peaceful, rvside site; gd sized pitches; friendly warden calls pm; clean; rv poss floods in winter; forest walks & cycling; popular NH; new excel san facs (2015); crowded; excel."* **€13.00, 29 Apr-30 Sep. 2023**

VRAIGNES EN VERMANDOIS *3C4* (0.2km N Rural) *49.88538, 3.06623* **Camping des Hortensias,** 22 Rue Basse, 80240 Vraignes-en-Vermandois **03 22 85 64 68; campingdeshortensias@gmail.com; www.campinghortensias.com**

12 €2 (htd) nr nr

Fr N on A1/E15 take exit 13 onto D1029 sp St Quentin; strt rd 16km until rndabt, take D15 (Vraignes) exit; site sp 1st on R in vill. Or fr S & A26, take junc 10 onto D1029 sp Péronne; after 15km at rndabt take D15 as bef. 2*, Sm, hdg, hdstg, pt shd, EHU (4-8A) (poss long lead req); bbq; red long stay; 10% statics; CKE. *"Lovely farm site; v helpful, friendly owners; little English spkn; lovely site; vg, clean san facs; conv for Somme battlefields & m'way; excel; rec torch."* **€20.00 2023**

WASSELONNE *6E3* (1km W Urban) *48.63739, 7.43209* **Camping Wasselonne (formerly FFCC Camp Municipal),** Rue des Sapins, 67310 Wasselonne **03 88 87 00 08; campingdewasselonne@onlycamp.fr; www.campingwasselonne.fr**

€0.60 (covrd, htd)

Fr D1004 take D244 to site. 2*, Med, mkd, pt shd, terr, EHU (5-10A) €2.30-3.70; gas; 30% statics; CKE. *"Pleasant, pretty town; facs excel; cycle rte & bus (adj) to Strasbourg; gd NH."* **€23.50, 15 Apr-15 Oct. 2023**

FRANCE

WATTEN *3A3* (0.6km N Urban) *50.83521, 2.21047*
Camping Le Val Joly, Rue de Aa, 59143 Watten
03 21 88 23 26 or 03 21 88 24 75
€1.55 nr

NW fr St Omer on D943; N of Tilques turn N onto D300; in 5km at rndabt turn R onto D207 sp Watten; at T-junc turn L onto D213; cross rv brdg & turn L in 500m at camping sp. 2*, Med, mkd, pt shd, EHU (6A) €4; 90% statics; adv bkg acc; fishing. *"Spacious, attractive, well-kept site; conv NH for ferries; welcoming, friendly, helpful owner; basic, clean san facs; secure gates, locked 2200-0700, but off rd parking; cycling along rv/canal; no site lighting (2010); few touring pitches - arr early or phone ahead high ssn; access to rv walk; glass works at Arques; vet nr; new management, some facs updated (2023); conv for Calais; gd sm town 5m walk; gd NH/sh stay."*
€16.00, 1 Apr-31 Oct. **2023**

WIMEREUX *3A2* (1km S Coastal) *50.76131, 1.60769*
Camp Municipal L'Olympic, 49 Rue de la Libération, 62930 Wimereux **03 21 32 45 63; camping.wimereux@orange.fr; www.ville-wimereux.fr**
€2 nr 800m

A16 exit 32 & foll sp Wimereux Sud to vill; turn R at rndabt to site. Or N fr Boulogne on D940, at vill sp Wimereux & rndabt, turn R. 3*, Med, hdg, mkd, unshd, pt sl, EHU (6A) €4; bbq; 80% statics; Eng spkn; ccard acc; sailing; fishing; CKE. *"Conv Boulogne; basic facs, stretched high ssn & poss irreg cleaning LS (2010); hot water runs out early; poss waterlogging after rain; gd vet in attractive seaside town; poor security, take care thieves at night (2009); useful NH only; pool 4km; off clsd 1300-1500."* **€18.00, 16 Mar-18 Oct.** **2024**

WIMEREUX *3A2* (1.5km S Coastal) *50.75277, 1.60722*
Caravaning L'Eté Indien, Hameau de Honvault, 62930 Wimereux **03 21 30 23 50; contact@campingeteindien.eu; www.eteindien.eu**
€3 (htd)
sand 1.5km

Fr Calais on A16 exit junc 32 sp Wimereux Sud. Thro Terlincthun R after x-ing rlwy, site in 700m on R (do not enter 1st site, correct site is the 2nd one clearly sp above gate with site name) - narr, v rough rd. 4*, Med, unshd, pt sl, terr, serviced pitches; EHU (10A) inc; gas; bbq (gas); red long stay; 90% statics; phone; Eng spkn; adv bkg acc; games area; games rm. *"Conv A16, Calais ferries; rec LS phone to check site open; ltd touring pitches & poss steep; muddy & unpleasant in winter; rlwy runs along one side of site; NH only if desperate!; new sw pool and MV area; gd clean facs (2012); poor facs for waste water."* **€25.00** **2024**

WISSANT *3A2* (7.6km NE Coastal) *50.91226, 1.72054*
Camping Les Erables, 23 Rue du Château d'Eau, 62179 Escalles **03 21 85 25 36 or 06 29 68 66 20; sabine@camping-les-erables.fr; www.camping-les-erables.fr**
(htd) nr nr sand 2km

Fr A16 take exit 40 onto D243 thro Peuplingues. Site sp to L on ent Escalles (on sharp R bend). Steep ent. Don't be put off by No Entry sp - 1-way system for c'vans on app rd. 1*, Sm, hdstg, mkd, pt shd, terr, EHU (6-10A) €3.50-€4.50; bbq; phone; Eng spkn; adv bkg rec; CKE. *"Lovely, well-kept open site with great views; family owned; spacious pitches but poss haphazard pitching; immac, modern facs; gates open 0800-2200; 2 pitches for disabled visitors with san facs; coast walks; sh walk to vill; private san facs extra; conv tunnel & ferries; gd site with view of Channel; excel grass pitch site; friendly, welcoming, helpful owners; popular site; ideal NH."*
€18.00, 24 Mar-11 Nov. **2022**

WISSANT *3A2* (4km E Rural) *50.88290, 1.70938*
Camping Les Voiles Des 2 Caps (formerly Camping La Vallée), 901 Rue Principale, 62179 Hervelinghen **06 19 45 34 30 or 03 21 36 73 96; contact@lesvoilesdes2caps.fr; www.lesvoilesdes2caps.fr**
€1 (htd) shgl 3km

Fr Calais exit A16 onto D244 & foll sp St Inglevert. Site on L at end Hervelinghen vill. 3*, Med, hdg, pt shd, pt sl, EHU (6A) (poss rev pol); gas; bbq; 60% statics; Eng spkn; adv bkg acc; ccard acc; games area; games rm; CKE. *"Family-run site; clean san facs; conv Calais, Cité Europe; gd walking in area; 24hr hot pizza machine; gd."* **€22.00, 1 Apr-14 Oct.** **2023**

YCHOUX *7D1* (10km E Rural) *44.33060, -0.97975*
Camp Municipal du Lac des Forges, 40160 Ychoux
05 58 78 20 07 or 06 25 23 59 96; campingdesforges@hotmail.fr; www.campingdesforgeslandes.fr
€1.50 nr

Fr Bordeaux take N10 S & turn onto D43 at Liposthey W twd Parentis-en-Born. Site in 8km on R, past vill of Ychoux. 2*, Sm, pt shd, pt sl, EHU (5-10A) €3.50 (rev pol); TV; fishing; sailing. *"Levelling blocks poss req; lake adj; pitches nr rd poss noisy."*
€14.00, 15 Jun-10 Sep. **2024**

YPORT *3C1* (0.9km SE Rural) *49.73221, 0.32098*
Flower Camping La Chênaie (formerly Camp Municipal La Chênaie), Rue Henri-Simon, 76111 Yport
02 35 27 33 56; www.camping-normandie-yport.com
nr shgl 1km

Take D940 fr Fécamp SW, D211 to Yport to site. 3*, Med, pt shd, EHU (10A); 80% statics. *"Conv Le Havre."* **€33.00, 31 Mar-30 Sep.** **2023**

CORSICA

GHISONACCIA *10H2* (4km E Coastal) *41.99850, 9.44220* **Camping Arinella Bianca,** Route de la Mer, Bruschetto, 20240 Ghisonaccia **04 95 56 04 78; arinella@arinellabianca.com; www.arinellabianca.com**

€6 (htd) sand adj

S fr Bastia on N193/N198 approx 70km to Ghisonaccia. At Ghisonaccia foll sp opp pharmacy to beach (plage) & Rte de la Mer. In 3km turn R at rndabt & site well sp. NB When towing keep to main, coastal rds. 4*, Lge, mkd, hdg, shd, EHU (6A) €5.50 (poss rev pol); gas; bbq; TV; 45% statics; Eng spkn; adv bkg acc; ccard acc; games area; horseriding adj; games rm; bike hire; fishing; watersports; tennis; CKE. *"Clean, well-run site; attractive lake in cent; trees make access to pitches diff; helpful owner & staff."* **€38.00, 16 Apr-30 Sep. 2022**

PIANOTTOLI CALDARELLO *10H2* (3.5km SE Coastal) *41.47272, 9.04327* **Camping Kevano Plage,** Route du bord de mer 20131 Pianottoli-Caldarello **603 36 57 36; www.campingkevano.com**

€1 sand 400m

Turn off N196 in Pianottoli at x-rds onto D122 for 1km. Turn R in Caldarello, site on L in 2km. 3*, Med, mkd, pt shd, pt sl, terr, EHU (4-6A) €2.50; TV; 10% statics; phone; Eng spkn; adv bkg rec; ccard acc; CKE. *"Beautiful, family-run site in macchia amongst huge boulders; san facs tired but clean; no dogs on beach Jul/Aug."* **€42.00, 27 Apr-30 Sep. 2024**

PIETRACORBARA *10G2* (4km SE Coastal) *42.83908, 9.4736* **Camping La Pietra,** Marine de Pietracorbara, 20233 Pietracorbara **04 95 35 27 49; lapietra@wanadoo.fr; www.la-pietra.com**

€3.50 (htd) sand 600m

Fr Bastia on D80 N. In 20km ent vill & turn L onto D232. Site on R in 1km at marina beach. Well sp. 3*, Med, hdg, mkd, shd, EHU (20A) €3.60; bbq; TV; bus nr; Eng spkn; ccard acc; lake fishing; tennis; CKE. *"Generous pitches; helpful owners; excel facs; beautiful pool; gd beach rest."* **€28.90, 20 Mar-4 Nov. 2023**

PORTO VECCHIO *10H2* (7.3km N Rural) *41.646168, 9.296385* **Camping Cupulatta,** 20137 Porto Vecchio **06 12 81 50 89; www.campingcorse-cupulatta.com**

€2 (cont) nr 10km shgl

Fr Lecci on N198 (T10). Site on R after dbl bdge direction Porto Vecchio in 4km. 3*, Sm, mkd, pt shd, EHU (6A) €4; bbq (elec, gas); twin axles; 90% statics; phone; adv bkg acc; CKE. *"Driving distance fr coast with all facs; close to scenic mountains; rest on access rd; gd."* **€25.00, 1 Apr-31 Sep. 2024**

PORTO VECCHIO *10H2* (5km NE Coastal) *41.62273, 9.2997* **Camping Les Ilots d'Or,** Ste Trinité, Route de Marina di Fiori, 20137 Porto-Vecchio **04 95 70 01 30; info@campinglesilotsdor.com; www.campinglesilotsdor.com**

(cont) sand adj

Turn E off N198 5km N of Porto-Vecchio at Ste Trinité twd San Ciprianu. In 1km fork R, site in 300m on L. 3*, Med, shd, pt sl, terr, EHU (6A) €3.5; gas. *"Well-organised site; helpful family owners; many vg beaches in easy reach."* **€29.08, 2 May-15 Oct. 2024**

PORTO VECCHIO *10H2* (14km W Rural) *41.61788, 9.21236* **Campsite U Furu (Naturist),** Route de Muratello, 20137 Porto-Vecchio, Corsica **04 95 70 10 83; contact@u-furu.com; www.u-furu.com**

Fr N on N198 turn R at rndabt sp Muratello. Foll sp to U-Furu. 2*, Sm, mkd, pt shd, terr, EHU (6A); gas; sw nr; twin axles; 10% statics; Eng spkn; adv bkg acc; games area; CCI. *"Site on beautiful sm rv with rock pools and waterfalls; fabulous beaches within 40 mins; easy access to Ospedale area & Bavella Pass."* **€32.50, 15 May-15 Oct. 2024**

ST FLORENT *10G2* (1km SW Coastal) *42.67394, 9.29205* **Camping U Pezzo,** Route de la Roya, 20217 St Florent **04 95 37 01 65; contact@upezzo.com; www.upezzo.com**

€3.50 sand adj

Exit St Florent for L'Ile-Rousse on D81 then N199 Route de la Plage. After 2km sharp R immed after x-ing bdge. 2*, Med, pt shd, terr, EHU (10A) €4; adv bkg acc; horseriding; sailing; windsurfing; waterslide; fishing; CKE. *"Pleasant site; mini farm for children."* **€19.00, 1 Apr-15 Oct. 2024**

SOLENZARA *10H2* (12km W Rural) *41.83495, 9.32144* **Camping U Ponte Grossu,** Route de Bavella, 20145 Sari-Solenzara **04 95 48 26 61 or 06 64 79 80 46 (mob); lucchinitoussaint@gmail.com; www.upontegrossu.com**

Fr N198, take D268 to U Ponte Grossu. Sm, mkd, pt shd, terr, EHU (6A); adv bkg acc; CCI. *"Site alongside rv; rv adj; canyoning; rafting; access to fab mountain areas; vg."* **€31.00, 1 May-20 Sep. 2024**

FRANCE

ILE DE RE

ARS EN RE *7A1* (0.3km NW Coastal) *46.21130, -1.53017* **Camping Le Cormoran,** Route de Radia, 17590 Ars-en-Ré **05 46 29 46 04; info@cormoran.com; www.cormoran.com**

€5.00 nr (htd) 500m

Fr La Rochelle take D735 onto Ile-de-Ré, site sp fr Ars-en-Ré. 5*, Med, mkd, hdstg, hdg, pt shd, EHU (10A) €6; 10% statics; Eng spkn; adv bkg acc; ccard acc; games rm; sauna; golf 10km; bike hire; tennis; games area; CKE. *"Delightful vill; vg site."* **€58.00, 1 Apr-30 Sep.** 2024

COUARDE SUR MER, LA *7A1* (5km SE Coastal) *46.17405, -1.37865* **Sunêlia Parc Club Interlude,** 8 Route de Gros Jonc, 17580 Le Bois-Plage-en-Ré **05 46 09 18 22; infos@interlude.fr; www.interlude.fr**

€8 (htd) (covrd, htd) sand

Fr toll bdge at La Rochelle foll D201 to Gros-Jonc. Turn L at rndabt at site sp. Site 400m on L. 4*, Lge, hdstg, mkd, hdg, pt shd, serviced pitches; EHU (10A) inc; gas; bbq; TV; 45% statics; Eng spkn; adv bkg req; bike hire; watersports; fitness rm; boat hire; solarium; sauna; tennis nr; games area; jacuzzi. *"Excel, well-run, clean, relaxing site; busy but not noisy; vg facs; some sm, sandy pitches - extra for lger; gd rest; nrby beaches excel; o'night m'vans area; walk to great beach; gd atmosphere, entmnt and shop."* **€50.00, 11 Apr-20 Sep.** 2022

COUARDE SUR MER, LA *7A1* (1km W Urban/Coastal) *46.19348, -1.43427* **Le Remondeau,** 12 Route Petite Noue, 17670 La Couarde-sur-Mer **05 46 29 84 27; leremondeau@lacouardesurmer.fr; www.leremondeau.fr**

€3 (htd) sand adj

Fr toll bdge foll D735 to rndabt on W side of La Couarde-sur-Mer & take D201. Foll sp to site. 3*, Lge, pt shd, pt sl, EHU (10A) €4.70; bbq; red long stay; 10% statics; Eng spkn; CKE. *"Vg site; great cycling base."* **€28.50, 15 Mar-7 Nov.** 2023

COUARDE SUR MER, LA *7A1* (2km NW Coastal) *46.20473, -1.44470* **Camping La Tour des Prises,** Route d'Ars D735, 17670 La Couarde-sur-Mer **05 46 29 84 82; camping@lesprises.com; www.lesprises.com**

€4 (htd) (covrd, htd) 600m

Fr toll bdge foll D735 or D201 to La Couarde, then Rte d'Ars for 1.8km to R turn; site sp & 200m on R. 4*, Med, hdg, mkd, pt shd, EHU (16A) €5.50; 30% statics; Eng spkn; adv bkg acc; ccard acc; bike hire; sailing school; games rm; CKE. *"Excel, well-managed, clean site; lge individual pitches, mixed sizes; helpful owner & staff; excel pool; many cycle/walking tracks; beach 10 mins walk; ideal for families; lge o'fits drive cautiously, no one way; v busy; v friendly staff; cent located on Isle de Re; acc to cycle paths fr site gate."* **€47.00, 4 Apr-27 Sep.** 2024

ST CLEMENT DES BALEINES *7A1* (0.5km E Rural/Coastal) *46.24041, -1.56070* **Camping Les Baleines,** Chemin Devaude, 17590 St. Clement-des-Baleines **05 46 29 40 76; camping.lesbaleines@wanadoo.fr; www.camping-lesbaleines.com**

€2-€3 nr nr nr sand adj

Fr bdge foll sp for Phare De Baleines. Sp 500m bef lighthouse. Do not foll sat nav. Narr vill rds. 4*, Lge, hdg, mkd, pt shd, EHU (10A) €5-6; bbq; twin axles; TV; 10% statics; phone; bus 200m; Eng spkn; ccard acc; games area; games rm; CKE. *"Vg, quiet site in natural surroundings; helpful staff; clean modern shwrs; direct access to beach; bar 500m; 5mins walk to lighthouse."* **€49.30, 4 May-21 Sep.** 2024

ST CLEMENT DES BALEINES *7A1* (0.9km S Coastal) *46.22567, -1.54424* **Camping La Côte Sauvage - Marvilla Parks,** 336 Rue de la Forêt, 17590 St Clément-Des-Baleines **04 30 05 15 13; www.campinglacotesauvage.com**

€3 nr shgl adj

Fr cent of vill, foll sp to site at edge of forest. 3*, Lge, mkd, pt shd, pt sl, EHU (10A) €4 (poss long lead req); sw; phone; Eng spkn; CKE. *"Gd location; some pitches uneven; gd modern san facs; poss unrel opening dates; cycle rtes adj; gd."* **€42.40, 3 May-22 Sep.** 2024

STE MARIE DE RE *7A1* (1km S Coastal) *46.14504, -1.31509* **Camp Municipal La Côte Sauvage,** La Basse Benée 17740 Ste Marie-de-Ré **05 46 30 21 74 or 05 46 30 21 24 (LS); europe.huttopia.com/site/camping-cote-sauvage-ile-de-re**

sand adj

Site sp fr main rd. V narr rds thro town. 2*, Med, mkd, pt shd, EHU (16A) €3.50; ccard acc; fishing; CKE. *"Excel location but poss windy; helpful owners; gd value snack bar; free parking for m'vans adj; highly rec."* **€15.00, 1 Apr-19 Oct.** 2024

STE MARIE DE RE *7A1* (4km NW Coastal) *46.16112, -1.35428* **Camping Les Grenettes,** Route De L'Ermitage, 17740 Ste Marie De Re **05 46 30 22 47; contact@hotel-les-grenettes.com; www.campinglesgrenettes.com**

12 €4 200m

Foll sp for D201 'Itinéraire Sud' after toll bdge in the dir of Le Bois-de-Plage; after approx 2km turn L. 2*, Med, mkd, pt shd, EHU (6A) €4.50; gas; bbq; TV; Eng spkn; adv bkg acc; ccard acc; tennis; fishing; waterslide; bike hire. *"Nice site close to sea; vg rest; many facs, but stretched in high ssn."* **€44.00** 2022

ST MARTIN DE RE *7A1* (5km SE Rural) *46.18740, -1.34390* **Camping La Grainetière,** Route St Martin, 17630 La Flotte-en-Ré **05 46 09 68 86; la-grainetiere@orange.fr; www.la-grainetiere.com**

€4.50 (htd) sand 3km

10km W fr toll bdge, site sp on La Flotte ring rd. Med, pt shd, EHU (10A) €4.50; gas; TV; 70% statics; Eng spkn; adv bkg acc; bike hire; CKE. *"Beautiful, clean, wooded site; haphazard pitching; helpful owners; gd san facs; gd pool; daily mkt; vg."*
€23.00, 2 Apr-30 Sep. **2024**

ST MARTIN DE RE *7A1* (0.5km S Urban) *46.19913, -1.36682* **Camp Municipal Les Remparts,** Rue Les Remparts, 17410 St Martin-de-Ré **05 46 09 21 96; camping.stmartindere@wanadoo.fr; www.saint-martin-de-re.fr**

€2 sand 1.3km

Foll D735 fr toll bdge to St Martin; sp in town fr both ends. 2*, Med, hdg, mkd, pt shd, pt sl, EHU (10A) €3.70; bbq; Eng spkn; adv bkg acc; ccard acc; CKE. *"Busy site in brilliant location; san facs dated but clean; gd basic rest; poss children's groups mid-ssn; some pitches boggy when wet; gd cycling; site poss unkempt end ssn; vg mkt; beautiful situation on o'skirts of a lovely town, gd size pitches; pool 3km; superb position."* **€25.00, 12 Mar-18 Nov.** **2022**

ILE D'OLERON

BREE LES BAINS, LA *7A1* (0.8km NW Coastal) *46.01861, -1.35446* **Camp Municipal Le Planginot,** Allée du Gai Séjour, 17840 La Brée-les-Bains **05 46 47 82 18; camping.planginot@orange.fr; www.labreelesbains.com**

€2 (htd) adj

N fr St Pierre d'Oléron on D734, turn R for La Brée on D273, site sp (if sp diff to see - foll 'plage' sp). 2*, Lge, mkd, pt shd, EHU (10A) €3.60; 15% statics; Eng spkn; adv bkg acc. *"Well-kept site in quiet location; friendly, helpful staff; gd cycling; daily mkt nrby; cont to be excel value; wonderful location; gd."*
€20.00, 15 Mar-15 Oct. **2022**

CHATEAU D'OLERON, LE *7B1* (2.5km NW Coastal) *45.90415, -1.21525* **Camping La Brande,** Route des Huîtres, 17480 Le Château-d'Oléron **05 46 47 62 37; info@camping-labrande.com; www.camping-labrande.com or www.campings-oleron.com**

€3 (covrd, htd) sand 300m

Cross bdge on D26, turn R & go thro Le Château-d'Oléron. Foll Rte des Huîtres to La Gaconnière to site. 5*, Lge, shd, EHU (6-10A) €4-6; gas; bbq; TV; 60% statics; Eng spkn; adv bkg acc; ccard acc; tennis; golf 6km; games area; sep car park; bike hire; waterslide; CKE. *"Pleasant owners; pitches at far end adj oyster farm - some noise fr pumps & poss mosquitoes; sauna; steam rm; 10 min cycle ride into town; vg."* **€44.00, 1 Apr-5 Nov.** **2023**

ST GEORGES D'OLERON *7A1* (7km E Coastal) *45.96820, -1.24483* **Camping Signol (formerly Camp Atlantique Signol),** Ave des Albatros, Boyardville, 17190 St Georges-d'Oléron **02 51 20 41 94; www.olela.fr/campings/camping-signol**

€4 (htd, indoor) sand 800m

Cross bdge onto Ile d'Oléron & cont on main rd twd St Pierre-d'Oléron. Turn R at Dolus-d'Oléron for Boyardville & foll sp in vill. 4*, Lge, mkd, hdg, pt shd, pt sl, EHU (6A); gas; 70% statics; Eng spkn; adv bkg acc. *"Size of pitches variable; san facs stretched in high ssn; impressive pool complex; narr site rds; 1 dog per pitch; gd site & facs; vg activities for kids; low overhanging branches."*
€56.00, 3 Apr-20 Sep. **2023**

ST GEORGES D'OLERON *7A1* (2km SE Rural) *45.96796, -1.31874* **Camping Le Domaine d'Oléron,** La Jousselinière, 17190 St Georges-d'Oléron **02 51 33 05 05; info@chadotel.com; www.chadotel.com/camping-le-domaine-doleron-saint-georges-doleron**

€4 (htd) sand 3km

After x-ing Viaduct (bdge) onto island foll sp dir St Pierre d'Oléron & St Georges-d'Oléron on D734; turn R on rndabt immed see Leclerc supmkt on R; at next rndabt turn L sp 'Le Bois Fleury'; pass airfield 'Bois 'Fleury' on R; take next R & then immed L. Site on L in 500m. 4*, Lge, mkd, hdg, pt shd, terr, EHU (6A) inc; gas, bbq (gas, sep area); red long stay; TV; 40% statics; Eng spkn; adv bkg rec; ccard acc; bike hire; games area; games rm; waterslide; CKE. *"Popular, well-organised, clean site; friendly, helpful staff; lovely pool; no o'fits over 8m high ssn; max 1 dog; cycle paths; fair."* **€50.00, 1 Apr-30 Sep, A41.** **2022**

FRANCE

Les Gros Joncs
★★★★★
1962
www.camping-les-gros-joncs.com
On the west coast of the island of Oléron, 200 metres from the ocean, our campsite offers you a haven of peace, between dunes and nature,for a refreshing holiday.

ST GEORGES D'OLERON *7A1* (6km SW Coastal) *45.95386, -1.37932* **Camping Les Gros Joncs,** Les Sables Vigniers, 17190 St Georges-d'Oléron **05 46 76 52 29; info@camping-les-gros-joncs.com; www.camping-les-gros-joncs.com**

€3 (htd) shgl 200m

Fr bdge D734 to St Pierre, at 2nd traff lts (police stn) turn L to La Cotinière 4km, at x-rds turn R dir Domino (Ave De Pins) for 5km. Site on L past Le Suroit. 5*, V lge, pt shd, EHU (10A) €3; TV; 10% statics; adv bkg acc; games area; jacuzzi. *"Excel pool; beach sand 1km; hydrotherapy sprays; great location; clean facs; rec."* **€50.00** **2022**

See advertisement

ST GEORGES D'OLERON *7A1* (7km SW Coastal) *45.94756, -1.37386* **Camping Le Suroit,** L'Ileau de la Grande Côte, 17190 St Georges-d'Oléron **05 46 47 07 25 or 06 80 10 93 18 (mob); camping@lesuroit.fr; www.camping-lesuroit.com**

€5 (htd) (covrd, htd) sand adj

Fr Domino cent foll sp for beach, turn L for L'Ileau. Strt at x-rds. Fork L for La Cotinière, site on R in 150m. 4*, Lge, mkd, shd, EHU (10A) €4.50; gas; bbq; TV; 10% statics; adv bkg acc; ccard acc; bike hire; games area; tennis; CKE. *"Excel, well-organised site."* **€45.20, 1 Apr-1 Oct.** **2022**

ST PIERRE D'OLERON *7B1* (4km SW Coastal) *45.92315, -1.34130* **Camping Le Sous Bois,** avenue des Pins, 17310 Saint Pierre d'Oleron **05 46 47 22 46; resa.lesousbois@orange.fr; www.camping-lesousbois-oleron.com**

€4 nr nr

Fr St Pierre take D274 to La Cotiniere. In La Cotiniere foll dir L'lleau, turn R onto Ave des Pins. Campsite 500m out of town on R. 3*, Med, hdg, mkd, pt shd, EHU (3A, 6A-10A) €5-7; Eng spkn; adv bkg acc; sauna; games area; beac 200m. *"Gd cycle tracks; sailing school; jet ski; equestrian ctr in Cotiniere; conv location; bar 20m; vg."* **€33.50, 1 Apr-31 Oct.** **2022**

ST PIERRE D'OLERON *7B1* (3.5km W Coastal) *45.92394, -1.34273* **FFCC Camp Municipal La Fauche Prère,** Ave des Pins, La Cotinière, 17310 St Pierre d'Oléron **05 46 47 10 53; camping@saintpierreoleron.com; www.saintpierreoleron.com**

€2 sand adj

Fr bdge foll D734 N to St Pierre-d'Oléron. Turn L onto D274 for La Cotinière, site bef vill on L, sp. Med, mkd, shd, pt sl, EHU (12A) €4.10; CKE. *"Direct access to beach; most pitches sandy; gd; lovely site amongst pine trees; new san facs (2017); quiet."* **€16.00, 1 Apr-30 Sep.** **2023**

ST TROJAN LES BAINS *7B1* (1.5km SW Rural) *45.82947, -1.21632* **Camping St-Tro'Park (formerly Camping La Combinette),** 36 Ave des Bris, 17370 St Trojan-les-Bains **05 46 76 00 47; info@st-tro-park.com; www.st-tro-park.com**

2km

Fr toll bdge stay on D26 for 1km, L onto D275 & L onto D126 to St Trojan-les-Bains. Strt ahead at rndabt with figure sculpture, then R at next rndabt sp Campings. In 1km turn L at rd fork, site on R in 1km. 4*, Lge, shd, EHU (5-10A) (poss rev pol); gas; games area; bike hire. *"Gd touring base; some super pitches; poss flooding in heavy rain; lovely site amongst pine trees; sauna; spa; gym; new san facs (2017); vg."* **€39.00, 15 Apr-15 Oct.** **2023**

ANDORRA

ANDORRA LA VELLA (ANDORRA) *8G3* (0.6km S Urban) *42.50166, 1.51527* **Camping Valira,** Ave de Salou, AD500 Andorra-la-Vella **722 384; campvalira@andorra.ad; https://campingvalira.com/en**

€2.10 (htd) (covrd, htd)

Site on E site of main rd S fr Andorra-la-Vella; behind sports stadium; clearly sp. 2*, Lge, mkd, hdstg, pt shd, terr, EHU (3-10A) €3.50-6 (no earth); gas; Eng spkn; adv bkg acc; CKE. *"Conv NH for shopping; 25mins walk to main shops; excel immac facs; vg rest; beware of sudden storms blowing up."* **€37.20** **2024**

La Rochelle to Toulouse = 424km

	Andorra-la-Vella	Annecy	Bayonne	Besançon	Bordeaux	Bourges	Brest	Caen	Calais	Cherbourg	Clermont-Ferrand	Dieppe	Dijon	Grenoble	Le Havre	Lille	Limoges	Le Mans	La Rochelle	Lyon	Marseille	Metz	Montpellier	Mulhouse	Nancy	Nantes	Nice	Orléans	Paris	Perpignan	Poitiers	Reims	Rennes	Rouen	Strasbourg	Toulon	Troyes	Toulouse	Tours
Annecy	701																																						
Bayonne	415	912																																					
Besançon	861	230	1042																																				
Bordeaux	432	691	190	855																																			
Bourges	678	505	630	544	446																																		
Brest	1051	1092	822	965	632	672																																	
Caen	1026	790	775	659	581	425	380																																
Calais	1141	832	1067	653	884	553	722	340																															
Cherbourg	1085	910	843	773	657	549	403	117	460																														
Clermont-Ferrand	591	332	545	416	356	189	842	612	726	725																													
Dieppe	1052	751	863	613	679	388	555	182	177	301	568																												
Dijon	783	263	955	95	764	246	868	558	575	679	352	521																											
Grenoble	601	106	821	352	776	476	1133	822	879	941	295	781	305																										
Le Havre	1051	754	823	621	632	393	468	91	270	[illegible]	579	109	526	781																									
Lille	1105	756	1003	585	812	477	743	369	113	485	652	197	502	807	301																								
Limoges	516	580	409	501	225	189	612	465	701	569	180	540	438	549	550	630																							
Le Mans	873	709	624	569	434	275	403	158	420	273	453	262	477	738	215	433	309																						
La Rochelle	627	782	375	749	183	330	440	451	766	470	464	565	652	744	535	701	232	281																					
Lyon	615	143	828	258	538	353	1029	715	766	831	181	673	199	106	676	703	431	628	630																				
Marseille	477	401	695	572	650	663	1265	1049	1104	1162	482	1008	530	312	1005	1039	732	920	830	320																			
Metz	1084	528	1099	268	902	506	913	571	465	684	616	466	272	571	530	366	721	522	791	465	780																		
Montpellier	320	383	533	559	490	529	1116	952	1088	1071	347	909	515	293	916	1017	445	795	668	302	172	782																	
Mulhouse	989	358	1183	139	990	473	1101	793	676	905	544	750	224	484	755	649	627	701	882	391	708	259	688																
Nancy	1013	472	1081	206	898	480	972	590	486	702	560	492	216	514	556	420	652	578	789	410	744	62	727	195															
Nantes	762	886	522	750	329	369	303	299	602	313	482	471	658	768	382	613	306	185	144	645	975	711	815	886	729														
Nice	641	529	850	732	810	816	1441	1204	1260	1321	633	1168	685	465	1157	1192	883	1081	991	474	203	951	329	690	901	1139													
Orléans	748	532	651	399	462	125	552	321	433	432	301	279	298	582	285	364	272	155	345	453	767	456	641	525	433	302	926												
Paris	875	542	769	405	580	251	599	242	299	357	428	201	313	572	206	227	402	202	469	463	799	328	776	542	353	386	954	131											
Perpignan	158	533	491	702	451	631	1081	1032	1235	1093	447	1011	662	443	1015	1165	520	882	627	451	318	927	155	838	875	776	476	741	865										
Poitiers	663	629	436	613	248	192	516	348	634	452	317	429	517	601	403	563	124	186	141	483	784	662	733	742	652	217	942	213	336	697									
Reims	989	557	911	382	717	386	729	385	279	501	563	286	301	603	344	210	531	340	604	496	829	191	810	401	210	522	985	267	142	956	473								
Rennes	871	846	634	716	445	422	246	189	527	207	602	365	622	882	279	578	426	155	259	774	1070	670	929	846	692	108	1217	298	349	888	332	486							
Rouen	995	690	812	559	622	326	503	125	213	241	511	60	459	723	95	250	488	206	507	611	945	478	851	689	489	386	1095	217	142	952	375	286	311						
Strasbourg	1093	452	1256	261	1066	580	1082	730	623	843	665	625	338	553	693	520	751	684	950	511	825	162	808	125	145	865	793	611	492	957	816	349	829	629					
Toulon	551	480	760	623	718	725	713	1120	1131	[illegible]	525	1085	560	371	1033	1075	640	1005	890	383	79	855	245	763	785	1055	140	838	841	380	890	871	1141	981	904				
Troyes	967	411	911	245	745	235	735	408	397	[illegible]	381	366	186	462	365	341	404	351	611	371	663	250	663	282	233	516	833	207	168	806	611	127	133	316	378	761			
Toulouse	203	626	295	802	240	504	869	825	998	[illegible]	405	850	752	535	854	932	315	675	424	538	406	1025	246	931	965	572	566	579	710	210	492	838	684	793	1058	485	739		
Tours	771	623	538	510	345	159	492	249	536	359	310	336	421	593	301	468	222	90	231	475	772	561	642	646	551	216	932	116	235	796	105	375	243	278	709	851	323	583	
Valence	519	178	729	360	683	443	1092	830	889	943	266	785	315	94	796	819	518	708	715	103	215	584	196	492	526	735	371	555	582	345	568	608	848	727	612	294	474	445	566

A
B
C
D
1
2
3
4
UNITED KINGDOM
ENGLISH CHANNEL
Southampton
Portsmouth
Bournemouth
Poole
Exeter
Plymouth
BILBAO
SANTANDER
DUBLIN
ROSSLARE
CORK
ROSSLARE
GUERNSEY
JERSEY
Barfleur
Quettehou
Cherbourg
Les Pieux
Ste Mere Eglise
Grandcamp Maisy
Isigny sur Mer
Trevieres
Ste Marie du Mont
Carentan
La Haye du Puits
Periers
Agon Coutainville
Granville
Torigni sur Vire
St Martin des Besaces
Pont Farcy
Hambye
Villedieu les Poeles
N13
N174
D2
D972
D971
D999
A84
D524
Roscoff
St Pol de Leon
Plougasnou
Trebeurden
Locquirec
Tregastel
Perros Guirec
Lannion
St Michel en Greve
D786
Paimpol
Lanloup
Motorways
Primary roads
Secondary roads
All year site(s)
Seasonal site(s)
No sites listed

 Map 1

E
F
G
H
1
2
3
4
Mortain
Pontaubault
St Hilaire du Harcouet
Fougeres
Romagne
Pontorson
Mont St Michel
Dol de Bretagne
Combourg
Tinteniac
Cancale
St Malo
Dinard
Dinan
St Cast le Guildo
St Briac sur Mer
Sables d'Or les Pins
Erquy
Binic
ST-BRIEUC
Quintin
Plouguenast
Merdrignac
Saint Meen le Grand
Loudeac
Gouarec
Pontrieux
Rennes
Vitre
Craon
Segre
Chateaubriant
Bain de Bretagne
Guemene Penfao
Ploermel
Malestroit
Rochefort en Terre
Peillac
Josselin
Rohan
Reguiny
Baud
Vannes
Auray
Baden
Locmariaquer
Arzon
Sarzeau
Carnac
Plouharnel
Quiberon
Lorient
Ploemeur
Le Pouldu
Quimperle
Pont Aven
Concarneau
Tregunc
Benodet
Pont l'Abbe
Guilvinec
Quimper
Douarnenez
Plonevez Porzay
Audierne
Chateaulin
Chateauneuf du Faou
Huelgoat
Plestin les Greves
Morlaix
Landivisiau
Sizun
Plouguerneau
Landeda
Lanildut
Le Conquet
BREST
Telgruc sur Mer
Crozon
Camaret sur Mer
Muzillac
Penestin
La Roche Bernard
Herbignac
Asserac
Pontchateau
Savenay
Guerande
La Baule
Heric
Nort sur Erdre
Ancenis
Nantes
Chalonnes sur Loire
Chemille
Clisson
St Brevin Les Pins
Pornic
Les Moutiers en Retz
Noirmoutier en l'Ile
Bois de Cene
Machecoul
Montbert
Lege
Challans
St Jean de Monts
St Hilaire de Riez
St Gilles Croix de Vie
Coex
Aizenay
La Chapelle Hermier
Bretignolles sur Mer
La Mothe Achard
La Roche sur Yon
St Laurent sur Sevre
Les Epesses
Chantonnay
La Chataigneraie
Ste Hermine
BAY OF BISCAY
A84
A81
A11
A83
A87
N12
N24
N137
N157
N136
N165
N164
N166
N171
N176
N249
D976
D177
D155
D771
D775
D178
D163
D963
D723
D137
D766
D768
D700
D790
D767
D887
D789
D213
D751
D948
D763
D746
D949B
0 25 50 75 100 km
0 20 40 60 miles
N E S W

Map 2

Motorways
Primary roads
Secondary roads
All year site(s)
Seasonal site(s)
No sites listed
0 25 50 75 100 km
0 20 40 60 miles
UNITED KINGDOM
BELGIUM
Newhaven
Dover
Channel Tunnel
Portsmouth
Brussels
Ghent
Mons
Tournai
Ypres
LILLE
Dunkerque
Bergues
Calais
Guines
Ardres
Hardinghen
Licques
Watten
St Omer
Arques
Aire sur la Lys
Bailleul
Armentières
Wissant
Marquise
Wimereux
Boulogne sur Mer
Hardelot Plage
St Amand les Eaux
Avesnes-sur-Helpe
Le Nouvion en Thiérache
Cambrai
Marquion
Arras
Auxi le Chateau
Nampont St Martin
Rue
St Quentin en Tourmont
Le Crotoy
St Valery sur Somme
Cayeux sur Mer
Abbeville
Mers les Bains
Le Treport
Eu
St Martin en Campagne
Dieppe
Albert
Feuilleres
Peronne
Amiens
Picquigny
Blangy sur Bresle
Aumale
Poix de Picardie
Hirson
Guise
Vervins
St Quentin
Vraignes en Vermandois
Montaigu
Guignicourt
Reims
Laon
Aizelles
Bourg et Comin
Soissons
Noyon
Cuvilly
Berny Riviere
Pierrefonds
Crevecoeur le Grand
Beauvais
Forges les Eaux
Neufchatel en Bray
Gisors
Chantilly
Charny
Meaux
Villevaude
Montreuil
PARIS
Epernay
Dormans
Rouen
Pont de l'Arche
Poses
Les Andelys
Louviers
Anet
Breteuil sur l'Iton
La Neuve Lyre
Brionne
St Georges du Vievre
Bourg Achard
Jumieges
Lillebonne
Pont Audemer
Veules les Roses
St Pierre en Port
Fecamp
Yport
Etretat
LE HAVRE
Honfleur
Deauville
Blangy le Chateau
Moyaux
Lisieux
Vimoutiers
Houlgate
Cabourg
Ouistreham
Courseulles sur Mer
Arromanches les Bains
Port en Bessin Huppain
Bayeux
Caen
Thury Harcourt
Clecy
A
B
C
D
1
2
3
4
5

E
F
G
H
1
2
3
4
6
7
Troyes
Arcis sur Aube
Sezanne
Eaux Puiseaux
Ervy le Chatel
Tonnerre
Chablis
Ligny le Chatel
Mailly le Chateau
Avallon
Vermenton
Auxerre
Joigny
Sens
Clamecy
Coulanges sur Yonne
Chateau Chinon
St Honore les Bains
Luzy
Bourbon Lancy
Cercy la Tour
St Pierre Le Moutier
Nevers
La Charite sur Loire
Cosne Cours sur Loire
Bourbon l'Archambault
Touquin
Fontenay Tresigny
Fontainebleau
MELUN
Ferrieres en Gatinais
Briare
Beaulieu sur Loire
Sancerre
Pouilly sur Loire
Cerilly
Villiers sur Orge
Malesherbes
Pithiviers
St Benoit sur Loire
Sully sur Loire
Gien
Poilly-lez-Gien
Aubigny sur Nere
Bourges
Mehun sur Yevre
Urcay
Versailles
Cernay La Ville
Rambouillet
Dourdan
Chateauneuf sur Loire
Orleans
La Ferte St Aubin
Nouan le Fuzelier
Pierrefitte sur Sauldre
Nancay
Vierzon
Salbris
Issoudun
La Chatre
Dreux
Maintenon
Chartres
Chateaudun
Beaugency
Neung sur Beuvron
Romorantin Lanthenay
Villefranche sur Cher
Vatan
Chateauroux
Argenton sur Creuse
St Maurice les Charencey
La Ferte Vidame
Fontaine Simon
Courville sur Eure
Illiers Combray
Cloyes sur le Loir
Arrou
Muides sur Loire
Blois
Bracieux
Cheverny
Cande sur Beuvron
Montrichard
St Aignan sur Cher
Montresor
Chatillon sur Indre
Buzancais
Azay le Ferron
Rosnay
Le Blanc
Vendome
Montoire sur le Loir
Chateau Renault
Onzain
Chaumont sur Loire
Amboise
Chenonceaux
Blere
Loches
La Roche Posay
Belleme
St Calais
Chateau du Loir
Tours
Montbazon
Ste Maure de Touraine
Ingrandes
Chauvigny
Argentan
Sees
Essay
Le Mele sur Sarthe
Mamers
Sille le Philippe
Beaumont sur Sarthe
Le Mans
Alencon
Fresnay sur Sarthe
Ecommoy
Chateau du Loir
Le Lude
Sonzay
Rille
Vernantes
Bourgueil
Azay le Rideau
L'Ile Bouchard
Chinon
Montsoreau
Saumur
Montreuil Bellay
Loudun
St Georges les Baillargeaux
Jaunay Clan
Poitiers
Chalandray
Airvault
Flers
Domfront
Bagnoles de l'Orne
Ceauce
Ambrieres les Vallees
Sille le Guillaume
Evron
Sable sur Sarthe
Chateau Gontier
Durtal
Angers
Brissac Quince
Gennes
Doue la Fontaine
Argenton les Vallees
Bressuire
Parthenay

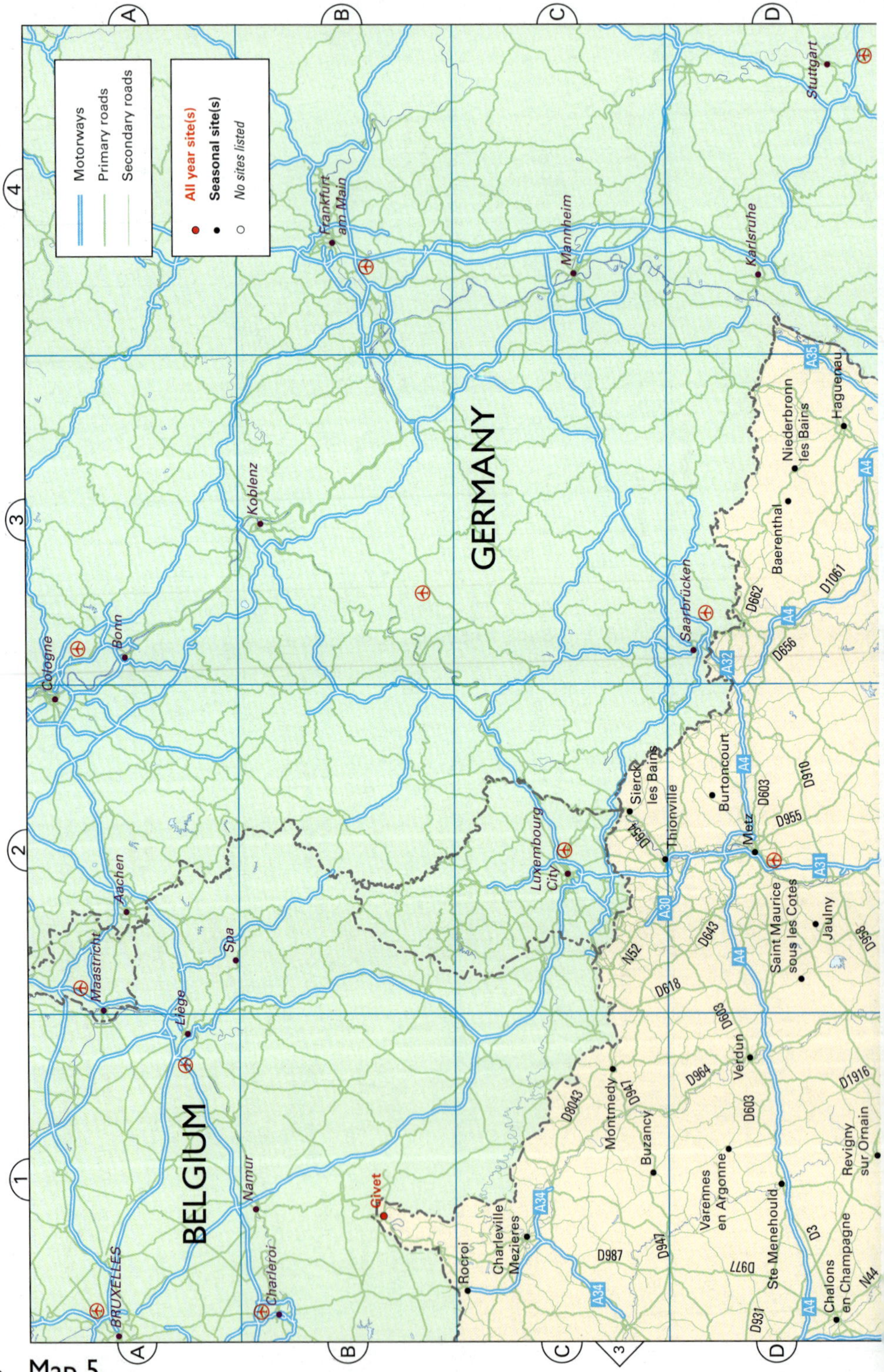
Motorways
Primary roads
Secondary roads
All year site(s)
Seasonal site(s)
No sites listed
GERMANY
BELGIUM
BRUXELLES
Charleroi
Namur
Givet
Liege
Maastricht
Spa
Aachen
Cologne
Bonn
Koblenz
Frankfurt am Main
Mannheim
Karlsruhe
Stuttgart
Luxembourg City
Saarbrücken
Sierck les Bains
Thionville
Burtoncourt
Metz
Saint Maurice sous les Cotes
Jaulny
Verdun
Montmedy
Buzancy
Varennes en Argonne
Ste Menehould
Revigny sur Ornain
Chalons en Champagne
Rocroi
Charleville Mezieres
Baerenthal
Niederbronn les Bains
Haguenau
A4
A31
A30
A32
A34
A35
D603
D955
D910
D643
D618
N52
D654
D964
D947
D8043
D987
D977
D931
D3
N44
D1916
D958
D656
D662
D1061
A
B
C
D
1
2
3
4

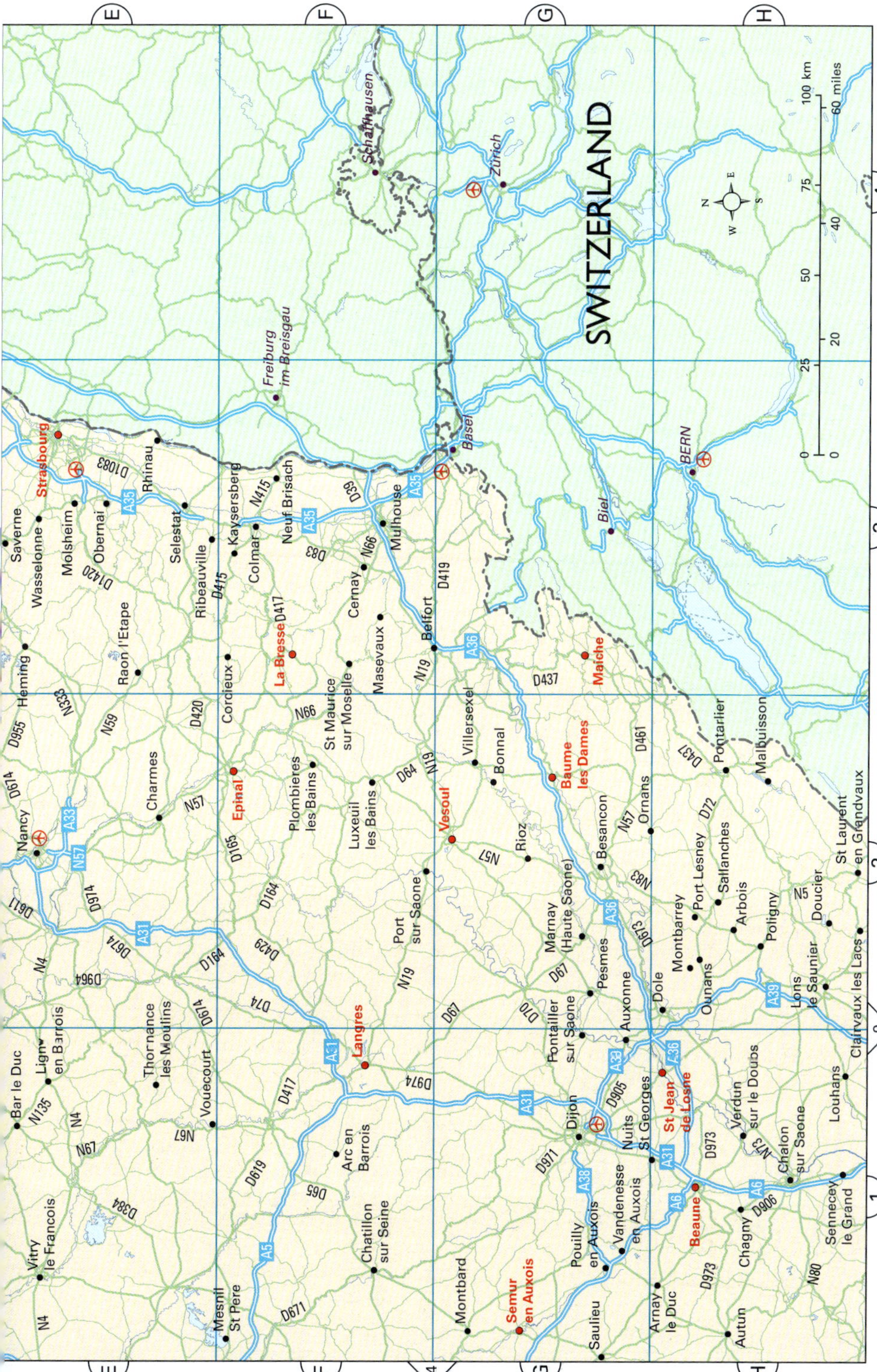
SWITZERLAND
Strasbourg
Saverne
Wasselonne
Molsheim
Obernai
Rhinau
Selestat
Ribeauville
Kaysersberg
Colmar
Neuf Brisach
Freiburg im Breisgau
Schaffhausen
Zürich
Basel
Mulhouse
Cernay
Masevaux
Belfort
La Bresse
Corcieux
St Maurice sur Moselle
Heming
Raon l'Etape
Charmes
Nancy
Epinal
Plombieres les Bains
Luxeuil les Bains
Vesoul
Villersexel
Bonnal
Rioz
Maiche
Baume les Dames
Besancon
Ornans
Pontarlier
Malbuisson
Biel
BERN
Port sur Saone
Marnay (Haute Saone)
Pesmes
Auxonne
Dole
Montbarrey
Port Lesney
Sallanches
Arbois
Ounans
Poligny
Doucier
Lons le Saunier
St Laurent en Grandvaux
Clairvaux les Lacs
Fontailler sur Saone
Langres
Thornance les Moulins
Vouecourt
Ligny en Barrois
Bar le Duc
Vitry le Francois
Mesnil St Pere
Arc en Barrois
Chatillon sur Seine
Montbard
Semur en Auxois
Pouilly en Auxois
Vandenesse en Auxois
Saulieu
Dijon
Nuits St Georges
St Jean de Losne
Verdun sur le Doubs
Chalon sur Saone
Louhans
Beaune
Chagny
Arnay le Duc
Autun
Sennecey le Grand
A35
A36
A31
A33
A39
A38
A6
A5
N57
N19
N66
N415
N4
N67
N135
N59
N333
N73
N80
N83
N5
D1083
D1420
D415
D417
D420
D955
D614
D611
D674
D964
D164
D429
D165
D74
D417
D619
D65
D671
D384
D971
D905
D973
D906
D67
D70
D974
D64
D437
D461
D72
D673
D39
D83
D419
E
F
G
H
1
2
3
4
9
0
25
50
75
100 km
20
40
60 miles
N
E
S
W

A
B
C
D
1
2
3
4
9
Les Sables d'Olonne
Talmont St Hilaire
Le Givre
Jard sur Mer
Longeville sur Mer
Lucon
La Tranche sur Mer
St Clement des Baleines
ÎLE DE RÉ
Ars en Re
St Martin de Re
La Couarde sur Mer
Ste Marie de Re
La Rochelle
St Denis d'Oleron
St Pierre d'Oleron
St Georges d'Oleron
Fouras
Chatelaillon Plage
Rochefort
St Pierre d'Oleron
StTrojan les Bains
ÎLE D'OLÉRON
StTrojan les Bains
Les Mathes
St Palais sur Mer
Royan
Soulac sur Mer
Vendays Montalivet
BAY OF BISCAY
Hourtin
Lacanau Ocean
Le Porge
Lege-Cap-Ferret
Andernos les Bains
Arcachon
Pyla sur Mer
Sanguinet
Biscarrosse
Parentis en Born
Mimizan Plage
Pissos
Salles (Gironde)
D148
A83
Marans
Maillezais
Coulcn
N11
St Christophe
Aigrefeuille d'Aunis
A837
Saintes
N150
Cozes
N141
D730
St Fort sur Gironde
Pons (Charente Maritime)
Mosnac
Cognac
Mirambeau
Montendre
Pauillac
D1215
D137
A10
St Andre de Cubzac
A630
Bordeaux
A63
A660
D1010
Creon
St Emilion
St Maixent l'Ecole
A10
Lusignan
D611
D150
Melle
D948
D910
D950
Chef Boutonne
Ruffec
St Jean d'Angely
Mansle
D939
Chasseneuil sur Bonnieure
N141
Angouleme
N10
Vendoire
Verteillac
Chalais
Aubeterre sur Dronne
La Roche Chalais
N10
Coutras
Montpon Menesterol
A89
Castillon la Bataille
D936
Ste Foy la Grande
Rauzan
Duras
Bazas
A62
Casteljaloux
A65
Aiguillon
Chauvigny
D347
St Savin
Montmorillon
Lussac les Chateaux
D347
Civray
Availles Limouzine
Pressa:
Confc lens
Montrollet
D948
St Junien
Suris
Montbron
D939
Nont on
Ma euil
Brantome
-isle
Riberac
Perigueux
N21
Douville
Bergerac
Sigoules
Eymet
N21
Miramont de Guyenne
Villeneuve sur Lot
D666
D911
Fumel
Serignac
Courbiac
Beauville
Lalinde
Le Bugue
Les Eyzies de Tayac
Beaumont du Perigord
Belves
Villereal
Monpazier
Argenton sur Creuse
Chaillac
Bellac
Chateauponsac
Bessines sur Gartempe
St Pardoux
Bonnac la Cote
Cognac La Foret
N21
LIMOGES
Chalus
Nexon
Thiviers
Hautefort
Thenon
Montignac
Ambazac
Pierre Buffiere
Masseret
A20
Uzerche
Donzenac
BRIVE
Souillac
Payrac
Cabrerets
Cahors
St Cirq Lapopie
A20
La Chatre
Neret
Chateaumeillant
Ste Severe sur Indre
Eguzon Chantome
A20
Boussac
N145
Gueret
D942
St Leonard De Noblat
Royere de Vassiviere
D941
Eymoutiers
Seilhac
Eglotons
A89
Neuvic (Correze)
Argentat
Beaulieu sur Dordogne
Bretenoux
D1120
Lacapelle Viescamp
N122
B engues
D840
Figeac
Cajarc
Limogne en Quercy
D926
Villefranche de Rouergue
Maurs
Conques
Decazeville
D840
Vallon en Sully
Herisson
Vieure
A71
Montlucon
N145
Buxieres-sous-Montaigut
Pontgibaud
Nebouzat
La Bourboule
Le Mont Dore
Chambon sur Lac
D922
Salers
N122
Murat
D922
Thiezac
Aurillac
Brommat
Laguiole
Entraygues sur Truyere
Espalion
Laissac
Pont de Salars

Motorways
Primary roads
Secondary roads
All year site(s)
Seasonal site(s)
No sites listed
0 25 50 75 100 km
0 20 40 60 miles
SPAIN
ANDORRA
Mezos
Onesse et Laharie
St Girons Plage
Lesperon
Moliets et Maa
Messanges
Soustons
Dax
Labenne
Bayonne
Biarritz
Urt
St Jean de Luz
Salies de Bearn
Navarrenx
St Jean Pied de Port
Tardets Sorholus
Oloron Ste Marie
Aramits
Pau
Nay
Lanne
TARBES
Lourdes
Accous
Argeles Gazost
Arrens-Marsous
Urdos
Cauterets
Luz St Sauveur
Gavarnie
Bagneres de Bigorre
St Lary Soulan
St Justin
Condom
Nerac
La Romieu
Aignan
Plaisance
Mirande
Masseube
Trie-sur-Baise
Agen
Moissac
Montech
Puyssegur
Caussade
Montricoux
Caylus
St Antonin Noble Val
Najac
Laguepie
Cordes sur Ciel
Gaillac
Albi
Ambialet
Alban
Rabastens
Realmont
Belmont sur Rance
Salles Curan
St Rome de Tarn
Toulouse
Deyme
Villefranche de Lauragais
Castres
Brassac
Olargues
Mazamet
St Pons de Thomieres
Revel
Montferrand
Brousses et Villaret
Caunes Minervois
Castelnaudary
Carcassonne
Olonzac
Lezignan Corbieres
Fanjeaux
Le Vernet
Casties Labrande
Martres Tolosane
Montrejeau
Salies du Salat
Artigat
Varilhes
Gudas
Mirepoix (Ariege)
Leran
Lagrasse
Alet les Bains
Durban Corbieres
Tuchan
Foix
Lavelanet
Puivert
Quillan
St Paul de Fenouillet
Tarascon Sur Ariege
Oust
Aulus les Bains
Belcaire
Axat
Estagel
Estang
Les Cabannes
Merens les Vals
Millas
Prades
Perpignan
Vernet les Bains
Mont Louis
Le Boulou
Ceret
Andorra
Pamplona
Lumbier
Jaca
Vielha
Ainsa
Banyoles
A63
A64
A65
A62
A20
A68
A620
A66
A61
A9
D817
D932
D918
D933
D834
D824
D9335
D932
D8
D933
D931
N21
D934
D928
N124
D935
D929
D2
N134
D825
D125
N126
D612
D820
D6113
N88
N20
N116
D117
E
F
G
H
1
2
3
4
10

SWITZERLAND
ITALY
Sion
Aosta
Turin
Geneve
Evian les Bains
Thonon les Bains
Divonne les Bains
Gex
St Julien en Genevois
Taninges
Bonneville
Vallorcine
Chamonix Mont Blanc
St Gervais les Bains
Megeve
La Clusaz
Annecy
Faverges
Doussard
Lescheraines
Rumilly
Aix les Bains
Chambery
St Genix sur Guiers
Les Echelles
Les Abrets
Belley
Virieu le Grand
Morestel
Trept
Cremieu
St Claude
Nantua
Pont d'Ain
Cuiseaux
Montrevel en Bresse
Bourg en Bresse
Villars les Dombes
Tournus
Pont de Vaux
Macon
Cluny
Cormatin
Matour
Fleurie
Chatillon sur Chalaronne
Villefranche sur Saone
Lyon
Marennes
Givors
Condrieu
Pelussin
Serrieres
Auberives sur Vareze
Roybon
St Donat sur l'Herbasse
Tain l'Hermitage
Tournon sur Rhone
St Vallier
Lamastre
Valence
Bourg Argental
Autrans
Villard de Lans
La Chapelle en Vercors
GRENOBLE
Le Bourg d'Oisans
St Martin sur la Chambre
St Jean de Maurienne
Pralognan la Vancise
Val d'Isere
Lanslebourg Mont Cenis
Le Monetier les Bains
L'Argentiere la Bessee
Embrun
Gap
Barcelonnette
Colmars
Montmaur
Aspres sur Buech
Serres
Orpierre
Lalley
Chatillon en Diois
Die
Rosans
Buis Les Baronnies
Vaison La Romaine
Nyons
Valreas
Grillon
Grignan
Bollene
Pont St Esprit
St Pantaleon les Vignes
Dieulefit
Le Poet Laval
Bourdeaux
Marsanne
St Vincent de Barres
Privas
Aubenas
Balazuc
Ruoms
Vallon Pont d'Arc
Largentiere
Ribes
Les Vans
Meyras
Langogne
Villefort (Lozere)
Ispagnac
Chanac
Marvejols
La Canourgue
La Malene
Severac le Chateau
Le Buisson
Nasbinals
St Chely d'Apcher
St Just (Cantal)
St Flour
Monistrol d'Allier
Le Puy en Velay
St Paulien
Monistrol sur Loire
SAINT-ETIENNE
Montbrison
Feurs
Balbigny
Boen sur Lignon
Noiretable
Ambert
Vollore-Ville
Courpiere
Clermont Ferrand
Issoire
St Nectaire
Murol
Aydat
Volvic
Riom
Châtel-Guyon
Gannat
Vichy
St Pourcain sur Sioule
Lapalisse
La Pacaudiere
Roanne
Charlieu
La Clayette
Charolles
Paray le Monial
Digoin
Marcigny
Dompierre les Ormes
Dompierre sur Besbre
Moulins
Chatel de Neuvre
Bourbon l'Archambault
Lempdes sur Allagnon
A
B
C
D
1
2
3
4
6
7
A6
A39
A40
A404
A41
A410
A42
A43
A430
A432
A46
A47
A48
A49
A51
A7
A72
A75
A71
A719
A89
D1005
D902
D1212
D1508
D884
D910
D1006
D1075
D1083
D975
D936
D1084
D389
D1085
D519
D538
D1091
D1091
D1075
D900
N94
N90
N85
D994
N86
D104
D93
D533
D1082
D105
N88
D15
D985
D982
D482
N7
N79
D1089
D906
N102
D806
D46
D2009
A89

Riviere sur Tarn
Peyreleau
Millau
Meyrueis
Nant
D999
Le Caylar
Ganges
D986
Lodeve
Lamalou les Bains
Octon
Fontes
Laurens
Pezenas
St Chinian
Beziers
Capestang
Vias
Agde
Serignan Plage
Portiragnes Plage
Narbonne
Gruissan
Sigean
Meze
Marseillan Plage
Frontignan
Montpellier
Castries
Sommieres
Crespian
D6110
Anduze
Allegre les Fumades
Seyne
D981
N106
Goudargues
Bagnols sur Ceze
Uzes
D6086
Remoulins
Nimes
A9
Avignon
Orange
Tarascon
D6113
Arles
A54
D6572
Aigues Mortes
Palavas les Flots
D613
A75
Stes Maries de la Mer
St Remy de Provence
D7N
Mouries
N568
Malaucene
Bedoin
Carpentras
Gordes
Cavaillon
Salon de Provence
A7
A55
MARSEILLE
Cassis
La Ciotat
Aix en Provence
A51
A52
Trets
Cadenet
Pertuis
Apt
D900
Manosque
Banon
Forcalquier
Sisteron
Chateau Arnoux
Les Mees
La Brillane
Puimoisson
Greoux les Bains
Moustiers Ste Marie
N85
D4085
St Maximin la Ste Baume
D560
DN8
A50
TOULON
Hyeres
A57
D5
Brignoles
A8
Carces
Draguignan
Le Cannet des Maures
Grimaud
D98
Le Lavandou
St Tropez
Cavalaire sur Mer
Frejus
DN7
Agay
St Raphael
St Aygulf
St Paul en Foret
Fayence
Comps sur Artuby
D6085
Grasse
Gourdon
Castellane
N202
Puget Theniers
D6202
Vence
Sospel
D6204
Cagnes sur Mer
Antibes
NICE
MONACO
Torreilles Plage
Canet Plage
St Cyprien Plage
Elne
D914
Argeles sur Mer
Banyuls sur Mer
Figueres
SPAIN
0 25 50 km
0 10 20 30 miles
Pietracorbara
Bastia
T30
Aleria
T20
Ghisonaccia
T10
Solenzara
T40
Porto Vecchio
Bonifacio
CORSICA
MEDITERRANEAN SEA
N
W
E
S
0 25 50 75 100 km
0 20 40 60 miles
Motorways
Primary roads
Secondary roads
All year site(s)
Seasonal site(s)
No sites listed
E
F
G
H
1
2
3
4
8

Germany

Highlights

Home to beautiful landscapes, architectural delights and diverse cities, Germany has a rich culture and history for you to discover. Berlin is undoubtedly one of the culture and arts capitals of the world, while the picturesque timbered villages and castles have inspired countless works of literature, film and art.

Often thought of as the home of beer and bratwurst, Germany has much more to offer on a gastronomic level, with Riesling wine, Black Forest Gateaux and Stollen just some of the treats that are waiting to be discovered and enjoyed.

Germany is the home of the modern car, and its automobile industry is one of the most innovative in the world. BMW, Audi, Porsche and Mercedes all have museums to visit.

Oktoberfest, the largest beer festival in the world, is held annually in Munich and attracts people from around the globe. This 17-day festival only serves traditional beers that are brewed within Munich city limits.

Major towns and cities

- Berlin – this capital is an exciting city of culture and science.
- Hamburg – enjoy stunning and varied architecture in this gorgeous city.
- Munich – a magnificent city of culture and technology.
- Cologne – this city is brimming with bars, restaurants and pubs.

Attractions

- Neuschwanstein, Füssen – this fairytale castle inspired Sleeping Beauty's palace.
- Holstentor, Lübeck – a UNESCO relic of the medieval city fortifications.
- Cologne Cathedral – This gothic cathedral is Germany's most visited landmark.
- Lindau – an enchanting island town boasting beautiful architecture and wonderful gardens.

Find out more

germany.travel

Country Information

Capital: Berlin (population approx 3.4 million)

Bordered by: Austria, Belgium, Czechia, Denmark, France, Luxembourg, Netherlands, Poland, Switzerland

Terrain: Lowlands in north; uplands/ industrialised belt in the centre; highlands, forests and Bavarian alps in the south

Climate: Temperate throughout the year; warm summers and cold winters; rain throughout the year

Coastline: 2,389km

Highest Point: Zugspitze 2,962m

Language: German

Local Time: GMT or BST + 1, i.e. 1 hour ahead of the UK all year

Currency: Euros divided into 100 cents; £1 = €1.20, €1 = £0.84 (Nov 2024)

Emergency numbers: Police 112; Fire brigade 112; Ambulance 112. Operators speak English

Public Holidays 2025: Jan 1; Apr 18, 21; May 1, 29; Jun 9; Oct 3; Dec 25, 26.

Public holidays vary according to region. The dates shown here may not be celebrated throughout the country. School summer holidays also vary by region but are roughly July to mid/end Aug or Aug to mid-Sept.

Entry Formalities

British and Irish passport holders may stay for up to 90 days in any 180 day period without a visa. You may be asked to show a return or onward ticket at the border to confirm your length of stay, or to prove that you have enough money for your stay.

Your passport will need to have a minimum of 6 months' validity remaining, and be less than 10 years old (even if it has over 6 months left).

Visitors arriving at a campsite or hotel must complete a registration form.

Regulations for Pets

Certain breeds of dogs, such as pit bull terriers and American Staffordshire terriers, are prohibited from entering Germany unless you have a Certificate of Personality Test, which must be given by a vet on entering Germany. Other breeds such as Dobermann, Mastiff and Rottweiler may need to be kept on a lead and muzzled in public, including in your car. You're advised to contact the German embassy in London before making travel arrangements for your dog and check the latest available information from your vet or from the Pet Travel helpline on 0370 241 1710.

Medical Services

Local state health insurance fund offices offer assistance round-the-clock and telephone numbers can be found in the local telephone directory. EU citizens are entitled to free or subsidised emergency care from doctors contracted to the state health care system on presentation of a European Health Insurance Card (EHIC). Private treatment by doctors or dentists is not refundable under the German health service. You will be liable for a percentage of prescribed medication charges at pharmacies and this is also non-refundable. Pharmacies offer an all-night and Sunday service and the address of the nearest out-of-hours branch will be displayed on the door of every pharmacy.

There's a fixed daily charge for a stay in hospital (treatment is free for anyone under 18 years of age) which is not refundable. If you're required to pay an additional patient contribution for treatment then reduced charges apply to holders of an EHIC. For refunds of these additional charges you should apply with original receipts to a local state health insurance fund office.

Opening Hours

Banks: Mon-Fri 8.30am-12.30pm & 1.30pm-3.30pm (to 5pm or 6pm on Thurs).

Museums: Check locally as times vary.

Post Offices: Mon-Fri 7/8am-6/8pm; Sat 8am-12pm.

Shops: Mon-Fri 8/9am-6pm/8pm. Sat 8/9am-12/4pm; bakers may be open Sun mornings.

Safety and Security

Most visits to Germany are trouble free but visitors should take the usual commonsense precautions against mugging, pickpocketing and bag snatching, particularly in areas around railway stations, airports in large cities and at Christmas markets. Do not leave valuables unattended.

Germany shares with the rest of Europe an underlying threat from terrorism. Please check gov.uk/foreign-travel-advice/germany before you travel.

British Embassy

Wilhelmstrasse 70, D-10117 Berlin
Tel: +49 (0) 30 204570,
gov.uk/world/germany

British Consulates-General

Willi-Becker-Allee 10
40227 Düsseldorf
Tel: +49 (0) 211 94480

Möhlstrasse 5, 81675 München
Tel: +49 (0) 89 211090

Irish Embassy

Jägerstrasse 51, 10117 Berlin
Tel: +49 (0) 30 220720
ireland.ie/en/berlin

There are also Irish Honorary Consulates in Frankfurt, Hamburg, Köln (Cologne), München (Munich) and Stuttgart.

Documents

Passport

It's a legal requirement to carry your passport at all times. German police have the right to ask to see identification and for British citizens the only acceptable form of ID is a valid passport.

Money

The major debit and credit cards, including American Express, are widely accepted by shops, hotels, restaurants and petrol stations. However, you may find that credit cards are not as widely accepted in smaller establishments as they are in the UK, including many shops and campsites, due to the high charges imposed on retailers, and debit cards are preferred. Cash machines are widespread and have instructions in English.

British visitors have been arrested for possession of counterfeit currency and the authorities advise against changing money anywhere other than at banks or legitimate bureaux de change.

Carry your credit card issuers'/banks' 24-hour UK contact numbers in case of loss or theft of your cards.

Vehicle(s)

Carry your valid driving licence, insurance and vehicle documents with you in your vehicle at all times. It's particularly important to carry your vehicle registration document V5C, as you will need it if entering a low emission zone (see later in this chapter for more information).

If you're driving a hired or borrowed vehicle, you must be in possession of a letter of authorisation from the owner or a hire agreement.

Driving

Roads in Germany are of an excellent standard but speed limits are higher than in the UK and the accident rate is greater. Drivers undertaking long journeys in or through Germany should plan their journeys carefully and take frequent breaks.

Accidents

In the event of a road accident the police must always be called even if there are no injuries.

Alcohol

The maximum permitted level of alcohol is 0.05%. For novice drivers who have held a driving licence for less than two years, and for drivers under the age of 21, no alcohol is permitted in the bloodstream. Penalties for driving under the influence of alcohol or drugs are severe.

Breakdown Service

The motoring organisation Allgemeiner Deutscher Automobil-Club (ADAC - adac.de) operates road patrols on motorways and in the event of a breakdown, assistance can be obtained by calling from emergency phones placed every 2 km. Members of clubs affiliated to the AIT or FIA, such as The Caravan and Motorhome Club, must ask specifically for roadside assistance to be provided by ADAC as they should be able to receive assistance free of charge. You must pay for replacement parts and towing. ADAC breakdown vehicles are yellow and marked 'ADAC Strassenwacht'.

If ADAC Strassenwacht vehicles are not available, firms under contract to ADAC provide towing and roadside assistance, against payment.

Vehicles used by firms under contract to ADAC are marked 'Strassendienst im Auftrag des ADAC'.

On other roads the ADAC breakdown service can be reached 24 hours a day by telephoning 01802 22 22 22 or 22 22 22 from a mobile phone.

Child Restraint Systems

Children under three years of age must be placed in an approved child restraint and cannot be transported in a vehicle otherwise. Children of three years and over must travel in the rear of vehicles. Children under 12 years old and 1.5 metres in height must be seated in an approved child restraint. If a child restraint won't fit into the vehicle because other children are using a child restraint, then children of three years and over must use a seat belt or other safety device attached to the seat.

Fuel

Most petrol stations are open from 8am to 8pm. In large cities many are open 24 hours. In the east there are fewer petrol stations than in the south and west. Some have automatic pumps operated using credit cards.

LPG (autogas or flussiggas) is widely available. You can view a list of outlets throughout the country, including those near motorways, on the website autogastanken.de (follow the links under 'Driving with LPG' and 'Autogas filling stations). On some stretches of motorway petrol stations may be few and far between, e.g. the A45, A42 and A3 to the Dutch border, and it's advisable not to let your fuel tank run low.

Low Emission Zones

There are Low Emission Zones in force in many towns and cities across Germany. See urbanaccessregulations.eu for more information.

Motorways

With around 13,000 toll free kilometres, Germany's motorways (autobahns) constitute one of the world's most advanced and efficient systems. For a complete list of autobahns, including the location of all junctions and roadworks in progress, see autobahn-online.de.

Some motorways are so heavily used by lorries that the inside lane has become heavily rutted. These parallel ruts are potentially dangerous for caravans travelling at high speed and vigilance is necessary. It's understood that the A44 and A7 are particularly prone to this problem. Caution also needs to be exercised when driving on the concrete surfaces of major roads.

On motorways emergency telephones are placed at 2 km intervals; some have one button to request breakdown assistance and another to summon an ambulance. Other telephones connect the caller to a rescue control centre. A vehicle that has broken down on a motorway must be towed away to the nearest exit.

There are hundreds of motorway service areas offering, at the very least, a petrol station and a restaurant or cafeteria. Tourist information boards are posted in all the modern motorway service areas. Recent visitors have reported an increase in service facilities just off Autobahn exit ramps, in particular with 'Autohof' (truck stops). The facilities at Autohofs are reported to be comparable to service areas, but usually with considerably lower prices.

Parking

Zigzag lines on the carriageway indicate a stopping (waiting) and parking prohibition, e.g. at bus stops, narrow roads and places with poor visibility, but double or single yellow lines are not used. Instead look out for 'no stopping', 'parking prohibited' or 'no parking' signs.

Except for one-way streets, parking is only permitted on the right-hand side. Don't park in the opposite direction to traffic flow. Parking meters and parking disc schemes are in operation and discs may be bought in local shops or service stations.

Priority

At crossroads and junctions, where no priority is indicated, traffic coming from the right has priority. Trams don't have priority over other vehicles but priority must be given to passengers getting on or off stationary trams. Trams in two-way streets must be overtaken on the right. Drivers must give way to a bus whose driver has indicated his intention to pull away from the kerb.

Don't overtake a stationary school bus which has stopped to let passengers on or off. This may be indicated by a red flashing light on the bus.

Traffic already on a roundabout has right of way, except when signs show otherwise. Drivers must use their indicators when leaving a roundabout, not when entering.

Always stop to allow pedestrians to cross at marked pedestrian crossings. In residential areas where traffic-calming zones exist, pedestrians are allowed to use the whole street, so drive with great care.

Road Signs and Markings

Most German road signs and markings conform to the international pattern. Other road signs that may be encountered are:

Keep distance shown

Street lights not on all night

Lower speed limit applies in the wet

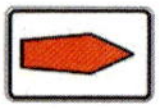
Recommended route on motorways

One way street

Tram or bus stop

German	English Translation
Einsatzfahrzeuge Fre	Emergency vehicles only
Fahrbahnwechsel	Change traffic lane
Freie Fahrt	Road clear
Frostchaden	Frost damage
Gefährlich	Danger
Glatteisgefahr	Ice on the road
Notruf	Emergency roadside telephone
Radweg Kreuzt	Cycle-track crossing
Rollsplitt	Loose grit
Stau	Traffic jam
Strassenschaden	Road damage
Umleitung	Diversion
Vorsicht	Caution

Road signs on motorways are blue and white, whereas on B roads (Bundesstrasse) they are orange and black. If you're planning a route through Germany using E road numbers, be aware that E roads may be poorly signposted and you may have to navigate using national A or B road numbers.

Speed Limits

	Open Road (kmph)	Motorway (kmph)
Solo Car	100	130
Car towing caravan/trailer	80*	80
Motorhome under 3500kg	100	130
Motorhome 3500-7500kg	80	80

* 100 km/h with some restrictions: The permissible maximum weight ratio between the caravan/trailer and the car is:

0.3 for caravan/trailers without brakes or without hydraulic suspension.

0.8 for trailers with fixed platform and hydraulic suspension.

1.1 for other trailers with hydraulic suspension.

1.2 for trailers with stabilisation mechanism who have a certificate.

The tyres on the caravan/trailer must not be more than 6 years old.

A "100 km/h" sticker has to be affixed on the back of the caravan/trailer.

There's a speed limit of 50 km/h (31 mph) in built-up areas for all types of motor vehicles, unless otherwise indicated by road signs. A built-up area starts from the town name sign at the beginning of a town or village.

The number of sections of autobahn with de-restricted zones, i.e. no upper speed limit, is diminishing and the volume of traffic makes high speed motoring virtually impossible.

Regulations on many stretches of two-lane motorway restrict lorries, together with cars towing caravans, from overtaking.

Speed cameras are frequently in use but they may be deliberately hidden behind crash barriers or in mobile units. A GPS navigation system which indicates the location of fixed speed cameras must have the function deactivated. The use of radar detectors is prohibited.

A car towing a caravan or trailer is prohibited to 80km/h (50 mph) on motorways and other main roads. You may occasionally see car/caravan combinations displaying a sign indicating that their maximum permitted speed is 100 km/h (62 mph). This is only permitted for vehicles that have passed a TUV test in Germany, who will then need to apply for a sticker at a Zulassungsstelle. The application process can be complicated as some Zulassungsstelles will insist they see a registration certificate for your caravan. Obtaining a 100 km/h sticker without a registration certificate is best done in Aachen as they are the only Zulassungsstelle familiar with this process. If you're having difficulty at a different Zulassungsstelle ask them to call the Zulassungsstelle in Aachen to confirm that a registration document is not required.

In bad weather when visibility is below 50 metres, the maximum speed limit is 50 km/h (31 mph) on all roads.

Towing

Drivers of cars towing caravans and other slow-moving vehicles must leave enough space in front of them for an overtaking vehicle to get into that space, or they must pull over from time to time to let other vehicles pass.

If you're towing a car behind a motorhome, our advice would be to use a trailer with all four wheels of the car off the ground. Although Germany doesn't have a specific law banning A-frames, they do have a law which prohibits a motor vehicle towing another motor vehicle. Outside built-up areas the speed limit for such vehicle combinations is 80 km/h (50 mph) or 60 km/h (37 mph) for vehicles over 3,500 kg.

Traffic Jams

Roads leading to popular destinations in Denmark, the Alps and Adriatic Coast become very congested during the busy holiday period of July and August and on public holidays. In those periods traffic jams of up to 60 km are not unheard of.

Congestion is likely on the A3 and A5 north-south routes. Traffic jams are also likely to occur on the A7 Kassel-Denmark, the A8 Stuttgart-Munich-Salzburg and on the A2 and A9 to Berlin. Other cities where congestion may occur are Würzburg, Nürnberg (Nuremberg), Munich and Hamburg. Alternative routes, known as U routes, have been devised; those leading to the south or west have even numbers and those leading to the north or east have odd numbers. These U routes often detour over secondary roads to the following motorway junction and the acquisition of a good road map or atlas is recommended.

ADAC employs 'Stauberater' (traffic jam advisors) who are recognisable by their bright yellow motorbikes. They assist motorists stuck in traffic and will advise on alternative routes.

Upgrading of motorways to Berlin from the west and improvements to many roads in the old east German suburbs may result in diversions and delays, and worsened traffic congestion.

Violation of Traffic Regulations

Police are empowered to impose and collect small on-the-spot fines for contravention of traffic regulations. Fines vary according to the gravity of the offence and have in recent years been increased dramatically for motorists caught speeding in a built-up area (over 50 km/h – 31 mph). A deposit may be required against higher fines and failure to pay may cause the vehicle to be confiscated.

It's an offence to use abusive language, or make rude gestures in Germany, including to other drivers while driving. It's also an offence to stop on the hard shoulder of a motorway except in the case of mechanical failure - please note that running out of fuel is not classed as a mechanical failure so you may be liable for a fine of up to €70 if you do run out of fuel and stop on the hard shoulder.

It's illegal for pedestrians to cross a road when the red pedestrian light is displayed, even if there's no traffic approaching the crossing. Offenders could be fined and will find themselves liable to all costs in the event of an accident.

Winter Driving

All vehicles, including those registered outside Germany, must be fitted with winter tyres (or all season tyres) during winter conditions, bearing the mark 'M+S' (Mud + Snow) or the snowflake symbol. Failure to use them can result in a fine and penalty points. There must also be anti-freeze in the windscreen cleaning fluid.

The use of snow chains is permitted and for vehicles fitted with them there's a maximum speed limit of 50 km/h (31 mph).
In mountainous areas the requirement for chains is indicated by signs. The use of spiked tyres is not authorised.

Essential Equipment

Lights

Dipped headlights are recommended at all times and must always be used in tunnels, as well as when visibility is poor and during periods of bad weather. Bulbs are more likely to fail with constant use and you're recommended to carry spares.

Reflective jacket

If you have broken down or are in an accident, it's advisable you and other occupants of your vehicle wear a reflective jacket if you're required to leave your vehicle.

Warning triangle

It's compulsory for vehicles with four wheels or more to carry a warning triangle at all times for use in the event of an accident or breakdown.

Touring

German food is generally of high quality and offers great regional range and diversity. In the country there's at least one inn – 'gasthof' or 'gasthaus' – in virtually every village.

A service charge is usually included in restaurant bills but it's usual to leave some small change or round up the bill by 5-10% if satisfied with the service.

Smoking is generally banned on public transport and in restaurants and bars, but regulations vary from state to state.

The German National Tourist Board (GNTB) produces guides to walking and cycle paths throughout the country, as well an extensive range of other brochures and guides. The individual tourist offices for the 16 federal states can also supply a wealth of information about events, attractions and tourist opportunities within their local regions.

Christmas markets are an essential part of the run-up to the festive season and they range in size from a few booths in small towns and villages, to hundreds of stalls and booths in large cities. The markets generally run from mid-November to 22 or 23 December.

There are 54 UNESCO World Heritage sites in Germany, including the cities of Lübeck, Potsdam and Weimar, the cathedrals of Aachen, Cologne and Speyer, together with numerous other venues of great architectural and archaeological interest.

The Berlin Welcome Card is valid for 2 to 6 days and includes free bus and train travel (including free travel for three accompanying children up to the age of 14), as well as discounted or free entrance to museums, and discounts on tours, boat trips, restaurants and theatres. It can be extended to include Potsdam and the Museuminsel and is available from tourist information centres, hotels and public transport centres or from visitberlin.de. The 3-day Berlin Museum Pass is also available, valid in over 30 museums in the city.

Other cities, groups of cities or regions also offer Welcome Cards, including Bonn, Cologne, Dresden, Düsseldorf, Frankfurt, Hamburg, Heidelberg and Munich. These give discounts on public transport, museums, shopping, dining and attractions. Enquire at a local tourist office or at the German National Tourist Office in London.

Camping and Caravanning

There are approximately 3,500 campsites in Germany, which are generally open from April to October. Many (mostly in winter sports areas) stay open in winter and have all the necessary facilities for winter sports enthusiasts. Sites may have a very high proportion of statics, usually in a separate area. In the high summer season visitors should either start looking for a pitch early in the afternoon or book in advance.

Campsites are usually well equipped with modern sanitary facilities, shops and leisure amenities, etc. Some sites impose a charge for handling rubbish, commonly €1 to €2 a day. Separate containers for recycling glass, plastic, etc, are now the norm.

A daily tourist tax may also be payable of up to €2 or €3 per person per night.

Naturism is popular, particularly in eastern Germany, and sites which accept naturists will generally display a sign 'FKK'.

Many sites close for a two hour period between noon and 3pm (known as Mittagsruhe) and you may find barriers down so that vehicles cannot be moved on or off the site during this period. Some sites provide a waiting area but where a site entrance is off a busy road parking or turning may be difficult.

Casual/wild camping is discouraged and is not allowed in forests and nature reserves. In the case of private property permission to pitch a tent or park a caravan should be obtained in advance from the owners, or on common land or state property, from the local town hall or police station.

Cycling

There's an extensive network of over 70,000 km of cycle routes across all regions. Children under eight years are not allowed to cycle on the road. Under 10 year olds may ride on the pavement but must give way to pedestrians and dismount to cross the road. Bicycles must have front and rear lights and a bell.

Cyclists can be fined €55 for using a mobile phone without a hands-free kit while cycling

Electricity and Gas

Current on campsites varies between 2 and 16 amps, 6 to 10 amps being the most common. Plugs have two round pins. Most campsites have CEE connections.

Many sites make a one-off charge – usually €1 or €2 however long your stay – for connection to the electricity supply, which is then metered at a rate per kilowatt hour (kwh) of approximately €0.50-€0.70, with or without an additional daily charge. This connection charge can make one night stays expensive. During the summer you may find only a flat, daily charge for electricity of €2-€5, the supply being metered during the rest of the year.

Campingaz is available and the blue cylinders in general used throughout Europe may be exchanged for German cylinders which are green-grey. At some campsites in winter sports areas a direct connection with the gas mains ring is available and the supply is metered.

Public Transport

Most major German cities have underground (U-bahn), urban railway (S-bahn), bus and tram systems whose convenience and punctuality are renowned. Pay your fare prior to boarding public transport using the automated ticketing machines. Your ticket must then be date stamped separately using the machines on board the vehicle or at the entry gates at major stops. Daily tickets permit the use of trains, buses and trams.

A number of car ferries operate across the Weser and Elbe rivers which allow easy touring north of Bremen and Hamburg. Routes across the Weser include Blexen to Bremerhavn, Brake to Sandstedt and Berne to Farge. The Weser Tunnel (B437) connects the villages of Rodenkirchen and Dedesdorf, offering an easy connection between the cities of Bremerhaven and Nordenham. Across the Elbe there's a car ferry route between Wischhafen and Glückstadt. An international ferry route operates all year across Lake Constance (Bodensee) between Konstanz and Meersburg. There's also a route between Friedrichshafen and Romanshorn in Switzerland.

Sites in Germany

AACHEN *1A4* (18km SE Rural) *50.69944, 6.22194* **Camping Vichtbachtal,** Vichtbachstrasse 10, 52159 Roetgen-Mulartshütte **(02408) 5131; camping@vichtbachtal.de; www.vichtbachtal.de**

12 WD MSP nr

On E40/A44 exit junc 3 Aachen/Brand onto B258 dir Kornelimünster. In 5km at R-hand bend turn L sp Mulartshütte. Thro Venwegen. Site ent on L 50m bef T-junc app Mulartshütte, site sp. 3*, Med, shd, pt sl, EHU (16A) €1.50 or metered (rev pol); 80% statics; site clsd Nov; CKE. *"Sm area for tourers; v friendly Eng spkn owners; gd site for visiting Aachen; gd walks adj; gd bus service to Aachen; v pretty wooded area."* **€21.50** **2022**

ALPIRSBACH *3C3* (2km N Rural) *48.35576, 8.41224* **Camping Alpirsbach,** Grezenbühler Weg 18-20, 72275 Alpirsbach **(07444) 6313; info@camping-alpirsbach.de; www.camping-alpirsbach.de**

12 €1 WD MSP

On B294 leave Alpirsbach twds Freudenstadt. 1st site sp on L. 4*, Med, pt shd, serviced pitches; EHU (16A) metered; gas; red long stay; 10% statics; Eng spkn; tennis; golf 5km; CKE. *"Excel site; helpful, informative & friendly owner; vg welcome, free bottle of local beer per person; immac san facs; gd rest; gd walking; o'night area for m'vans €10; guest card for free transport on some local transport; some rvside pitches (v shd)."* **€30.00** **2024**

ALTENBURG *2F4* (12km NNE Rural) *51.045799, 12.500404* **See Camping Altenburgh-Pahna,** 04617 Pahna **(03434) 351914; info@camping-pahna.de; www.camping-pahna.de**

12 €2.50 (htd) WD MSP

A4 exit 60 (Ronneburg) then B7 to Altenburg. B93 direction Leipzig, right B7 direction Frohburg, foll sp at Eschefeld. 4*, V lge, pt shd, serviced pitches; EHU €2; bbq; cooking facs; sw; red long stay; 25% statics; Eng spkn; adv bkg acc; lake adj; games area; CKE. *"Vg; nature walks; conv Dresden, Leipzig & Colditz; quiet LS but busy on w/ends and hg ssn."* **€24.00** **2024**

ALTENKIRCHEN *2F1* (9km W Coastal) *54.62905, 13.22281* **Caravancamp Ostseeblick,** Seestr. 39a, 18556 Dranske **(03839) 18196; www.caravancamp-ostseeblick.de**

WD MSP

Clearly sp fr main rd bet Kuhle & Dranske. Sm, mkd, hdstg, hdg, pt shd, EHU €2.50; twin axles; 20% statics; Eng spkn; adv bkg rec. *"Excel; sea adj."* **€14.60, 1 Apr-31 Oct.** **2023**

ALTENSTEIG *3C3* (3km W Rural) *48.58456, 8.57866* **Schwarzwald Camping Altensteig,** Im Oberen Tal 3-5, 72213 Altensteig **(07453) 8415; info@schwarzwaldcamping.de; www.schwarzwaldcamping.de**

12 €2 WD

Take Obere Talstrasse (L362) due W fr town ctr. Aft 2km site on L. Easy access. Sm, pt shd, EHU; bbq; twin axles; 75% statics; Eng spkn; games area. *"Gd; table tennis, beach volleyball, boating, walking fr site; Black Forest; cross country skiing."* **€25.00** **2023**

AUGSBURG *4E3* (7km N Rural) *48.41168, 10.92371* **Camping Bella Augusta,** Mühlhauserstrasse 54B, 86169 Augsburg-Ost **(0821) 707575; info@bella-augusta.de; www.bella-augusta.de**

12 €2.55 WD MSP nr

Exit A8/E52 junc 73 dir Neuburg to N, site sp. 2*, Lge, pt shd, EHU (10A) inc; sw nr; 80% statics; ccard acc; boating. *"V busy NH; excel rest; camping equipment shop on site; vg san facs but site looking a little run down; noise fr a'bahn; cycle track to town (map fr recep); vg; nice lake."* **€31.00** **2024**

AUGSBURG *4E3* (8km N Rural) *48.43194, 10.92388* **Camping Ludwigshof am See,** Augsburgerstrasse 36, 86444 Mühlhausen-Affing **(08207) 9621500; info@campingludwigshof.de; www.campingludwigshof.de**

€2 WD MSP nr

Exit A8/E52 junc 73at Augsburg Ost/Pöttmes exit; foll sp Pöttmes; site sp on L on lakeside. 3*, Lge, unshd, EHU (16A) €3.50 (long cable req); bbq; sw; twin axles; red long stay; 70% statics; bus; Eng spkn; ccard acc; tennis; CKE. *"Pleasant site; unmkd field for tourers, close to san facs; both 6A panel & 16A panels for EHU -16A only accepts German type of plug; beautiful clean, modern facs; nr A8 m'way; conv NH on way to E Italy; clsd 1300-1500; gd for long stay, special rates can be negotiated; poss need long cable as EHU in corner of field."* **€31.50, 1 Apr-31 Oct.** **2023**

AUGSBURG *4E3* (9km NE Rural) *48.4375, 10.92916* **Lech Camping,** Seeweg 6, 86444 Affing-Mühlhausen **(08207) 2200; info@lech-camping.de; www.lech-camping.de**

€5 (htd) WD MSP nr

Exit A8/E52 at junc 73 Augsburg-Ost; take rd N sp Pöttmes; site 3km on R. 5*, Sm, hdstg, mkd, pt shd, EHU (16A); bbq; sw nr; bus to Augsburg, train Munich; Eng spkn; adv bkg rec; ccard acc; boating. *"Lovely, well-ordered site; friendly, helpful owners; excel san facs; gd play area; deposit for san facs key; camping accessory shop on site; cycle rte to Augsburg; excel NH for A8; excel site espec lakeside pitch; statics (sep area); c'vans close together; constant rd noise; recep shut 12-2pm."* **€40.00, 1 May - 14 Sep, G19.** **2022**

BAD ABBACH *4F3* (6km W Rural) *48.93686, 12.01992* **Campingplatz Freizeitinsel,** Inselstraße 1a, D93077 Bad Abbach **(09405) 9570401 or (0176) 96631729; info@campingplatz-freizeitinsel.de; www.campingplatz-freizeitinsel.de**

A93 Regensburg, exit Pentling B16 dir twrds Kelheim. Cont on B16 past Bad Abbach and take next exit R to Poikam/Inselbad. Over rv and foll rd round to R past Poikam sp. At junc turn R sp Inselbad. Site on R. Med, mkd, EHU; bbq; cooking facs; sw nr; twin axles; 20% statics; Eng spkn; adv bkg acc; bike hire; CKE. *"New (2014) family run developing site; vg, modern, clean facs; some deluxe serviced pitches avail with supp; gd area for touring, cycling & walking; nrby lake, sw & thermal baths; gd rest in vill 1km; train to Regensburg 1km; excel site."* **€33.00, 19 Mar-7 Nov.** **2023**

BAD BEDERKESA *1C2* (1km S Rural) *53.62059, 8.84879* **Regenbogen-Camp Bad Bederkesa,** Ankeloherstrasse 14, 27624 Bad Bederkesa **(04745) 6487 or (04312) 372370 or (04745) 7820192; urlaub@regenbogen.ag; www.regenbogen.ag**

Exit A27 junc 5 Debstedt, dir Bederkesa, site sp. 2*, V lge, pt shd, EHU (16A) metered + conn fee; red long stay; TV; 60% statics; adv bkg acc; ccard acc; games area; golf 4km; CKE. *"O'night m'vans area; clsd 1300-1500."* **€27.00** **2024**

BAD BENTHEIM *1B3* (3km E Rural) *52.29945, 7.19361* **Campingplatz am Berg,** Suddendorferstrasse 37, 48455 Bad Bentheim **(05922) 990461; info@campingplatzamberg.de; www.campingplatzamberg.de**

Exit A30 ad junc 3 onto B403, foll sp to Bad Bentheim. After sh incline, passing g'ge on R at traff lts, at next junc turn R round town to hospital (sp Orthopäde). Turn L & cont past hospital to rndabt, strt over then 1.5km on L. Sm, mkd, pt shd, EHU (16A) €2.50; gas; cooking facs; 50% statics; phone; Eng spkn; adv bkg acc; site clsd 24 Dec-26 Jan; CKE. *"Friendly, helpful owners; easy drive to Europort & ferries; rlwy museum on Dutch side of border."* **€24.50, 4 Mar-24 Dec.** **2024**

BAD BIRNBACH *4G3* (800km N Rural) *48.450201, 13.094024* **Camping Theresienhof,** Breindoblweg 6, 84364 Bad Birnbach **08563-96320; www.camping-bad-birnbach.com**

Off B388 W fr A3 fr Schaarding. Mkd, hdstg, pt shd, terr, EHU (16A); bbq (charcoal, elec, gas); cooking facs; twin axles; adv bkg rec; bike hire. *"Ideal stopover."* **NP 26.9** **2024**

BAD BRAMSTEDT *1D2* (1km N Rural) *53.9283, 9.8901* **Kur-Camping Roland,** Kielerstrasse 52, 24576 Bad Bramstedt **(04192) 6723**

Exit A7 junc 17 dir Bad Bremstedt; site sp, ent immed at Nissan g'ge at top of hill at start of dual c'way. Fr N exit A7 junc 16 dir Bad Bremstedt; site on L in 4km. 3*, Sm, shd, EHU (6-16A) €2 & metered; Eng spkn; CKE. *"Excel CL-type site; friendly owner; EHU not rec if site v full; gd sh stay/NH."* **€28.00, 1 Apr-31 Oct.** **2023**

BAD DOBERAN *2F1* (10km N Coastal) *54.15250, 11.89972* **Ferien-Camp Borgerende (Part Naturist),** Deichstrasse 16, 18211 Börgerende **(038203) 81126; info@ostseeferiencamp.de; www.ostseeferiencamp.de**

In Bad Doberan, turn L off B105 sp Warnemunde. In 4km in Rethwisch, turn L sp Börgerende. In 3km turn R at site sp. 5*, V lge, hdg, unshd, EHU (10-16A) €3; cooking facs; 10% statics; phone; bus 500m; Eng spkn; games area; bike hire; sauna; CKE. *"Excel beaches; o'night m'vans area; cycle paths; sep naturist beach; excel site."* **€43.00, 21 Mar-30 Oct.** **2022**

BAD DURKHEIM *3C2* (3km S Rural) *49.43741, 8.17036* **Campingplatz im Burgtal,** Waldstrasse 105, 67157 Wachenheim **(06322) 2689; campingburgtal@vg-wachenheim.de; https://www.campingimburgtal.de/home.html**

Fr Bad Dürkheim, take B271 S dir Neustadt for approx 2km. After passing Villa Rustica rest area, turn L for Wachenheim, then R. Go strt at traff lts, up hill thro vill (narr). Site on L. Med, mkd, hdstg, hdg, pt shd, serviced pitches; EHU (16A) inc; 50% statics; tennis; golf 12km; CKE. *"Forest walks in Pfalz National Park; in heart of wine-tasting country; v busy during wine festival - adv bkg rec; helpful owners; gd facs; site bit shabby (2017); upper area unshd."* **€27.50, 1 Mar-30 Nov.** **2024**

BAD FALLINGBOSTEL *1D2* (3km NE Rural) *52.87686, 9.73147* **Camping Bohmeschlucht,** Vierde 22, D 29683 Fallingbostel-Vierde **(05162) 5604; info@boehmeschlucht.de; www.boehmeschlucht.de**

A7 junc 47 Bad Fallingbostel. Foll sp Dorfmark/Soltau. On leaving Fallingbostel, go strt at rndabt and cont for approx 1 km. Site sp on R. 4*, Med, mkd, pt shd, EHU (16A) - €2; bbq; sw; 60% statics; Eng spkn; adv bkg acc; games rm. *"Excel walking, cycling & boat/canoe tours fr site; vg rest; library; helpful staff; excel for exploring Luneburger Heide, Hamburg or Walsrode Bird Park; excel site."* **€21.00** **2024**

GERMANY

BAD FUSSING *4G3* (3km S Rural) *48.33255, 13.31440* **Kur-Camping Max,** Falkenstrasse 12, 94072 Egglfing-Bad Füssing **(08537) 96170; info@campingmax.de; www.campingmax.de**

€2 (htd) nr

Across frontier & bdge fr Obernberg in Austria. Site sp in Egglfing. On B12 Schärding to Simbach turn L immed bef vill of Tutting sp Obernberg. Site on R after 7km, sp. 5*, Med, pt shd, EHU (16A) metered + conn fee; cooking facs; sw; TV; 20% statics; fishing; golf 2km; tennis 2km; bike hire; CKE. *"Gd rest for snacks & meals on site; well managed site; excel clean facs; wellness cent; thermal facs in Bad Füssing; pool 3km; private san facs avail; new indoor thermal bath & outdoor sw pool (2014)."* **€22.60** **2024**

BAD GANDERSHEIM *1D3* (2km E Rural) *51.86694, 10.04972* **Kur-Campingpark,** 37581 Bad Gandersheim **0431 237 237 0; www.regenbogen.ag/ferienanlagen/bad-gandersheim.html**

€1

Exit A7/E45 at junc 67 onto B64 dir Holzminden & Bad Gandersheim. Site on R shortly after Seboldshausen. 4*, Lge, pt shd, EHU (10A) metered + conn fee; 40% statics; bike hire. *"Excel; pool 1.5km; always plenty of space; sep o'night area."* **€25.00** **2024**

BAD HONNEF *1B4* (9km E Rural) *50.65027, 7.30166* **Camping Jillieshof,** Ginsterbergweg 6, 53604 Bad Honnef-Aegidienberg **(02224) 972066; information@camping-jillieshof.de; www.camping-jillieshof.de**

€2

Exit E35/A3 junc 34 & foll sp Bad Honnef. In Himburg bef pedestrian traff lts turn L, then R. Site in 300m. 3*, Lge, mkd, pt shd, sl, EHU (16A) €2 or metered; 85% statics; Eng spkn; fishing. *"Excel facs; pool 9km; gated."* **€17.50** **2020**

BAD KOSEN *2E4* (1.5km S Rural) *51.12285, 11.71743* **Camping an der Rudelsburg,** 06628 Bad Kösen **(034463) 28705; campkoesen@aol.com; www.campingbadkoesen.de**

€3.50 nr nr

Site sp fr town. 4*, Med, pt shd, EHU (16A) metered + conn fee; gas; 10% statics; CKE. *"O'night m'vans area."* **€33.00, 23 Mar-1 Nov.** **2022**

BAD KREUZNACH *3C2* (8km N Rural) *49.88383, 7.85712* **Campingplatz Lindelgrund,** Im Lindelgrund 1, 55452 Guldental **(06707) 633; info@lindelgrund.de; www.lindelgrund.de**

€3.50

Fr A61 exit junc 47 for Windesheim. In cent immed after level x-ing, turn L & pass thro Guldental. Site sp on R in 500m. Sm, hdstg, pt shd, terr, EHU (10-16A) €2 or metered; red long stay; 60% statics; tennis; golf 12km. *"Lovely, peaceful site; friendly, helpful staff; wine sold on site; narr gauge rlwy & museum adj; gd NH; htd covrd pool 2km; san facs nr touring pitches; conv base for Rhine & Mosel Valleys."* **€28.00, 1 Mar-15 Dec.** **2022**

BAD MERGENTHEIM *3D2* (3km SE Rural) *49.46481, 9.77673* **Campingplatz Bad Mergentheim,** Willinger Tal 1, 97980 Bad Mergentheim **(01784) 727670; campingplatz@silvago24.de; campingplatz-bad-mergentheim.de**

€2.50 (covrd, htd)

Fr Bad Mergentheim foll B19 S, sp Ulm. After 1km take rd to L (sps). Ent 2.7m. Med, pt shd, sl, EHU (10A) metered + conn fee or €1.90; gas; 20% statics; bus nr; tennis; CKE. *"Nice site; sep o'night area; friendly, helpful owner."* **€17.00** **2024**

BAD NEUENAHR AHRWEILER *3B1* (8km W Rural) *50.53400, 7.04800* **Camping Dernau,** Ahrweg 2, 53507 Dernau **(02643) 8517; www.camping-dernau.de**

€1 (htd) nr

Exit A61 junc 30 for Ahrweiler. Fr Ahrweiler on B267 W to Dernau, cross rv bef Dernau & turn L into Ahrweg, site sp. 3*, Sm, hdstg, shd, EHU (16A) €2; bus, train. *"In beautiful Ahr valley - gd wine area; train to Ahrweiler Markt rec; immac, modern san facs; v nice."* **€17.00, 1 Apr-31 Oct.** **2024**

BAD PYRMONT *1D3* (13km W Rural) *51.98671, 9.10833* **Ferienpark Teutoburgerwald,** Badeanstaltsweg 4, 32683 Barntrup **(05263) 2221; info@ferienparkteutoburgerwald.de; www.ferienparkteutoburgerwald.de**

€2.25 nr nr

On B1 bet Blomberg & Bad Pyrmont turn W for 1km to Barntrup & foll sp fr vill cent. 4*, Med, hdstg, pt shd, terr, EHU (16A) inc; gas; red long stay; 10% statics; Eng spkn; adv bkg acc; tennis adj. *"Excel site; quiet; rural; delightful; gd WiFi; sep m'van area; outstanding san facs but poss stretched in high ssn; conv Hameln (Hamelin)."* **€28.50, 1 Apr-6 Oct.** **2022**

BAD RIPPOLDSAU *3C3* (7km S Rural) *48.38396, 8.30168* **Schwarzwaldcamping Alisehof,** Rippoldsauerstrasse 8, 77776 Bad Rippoldsau-Schapbach **(07839) 203; camping@alisehof.de; www.alisehof.de**

€2 (htd)

Exit A5/E35 junc 55 Offenburg onto B33 dir Gengenbach & Hausach to Wolfach. At end of Wolfach vill turn N dir Bad Rippoldsau. Site on R over wooden bdge after vill of Schapbach. 2 steep passes fr other dir. 5*, Med, mkd, pt shd, pt sl, serviced pitches; EHU (16A) metered + conn fee; gas; red long stay; 20% statics; phone; Eng spkn; adv bkg acc; CKE. *"Highly rec; clean, friendly site; site clsd 1230-1430; many gd walks in area; not a NH."* **€28.20** **2024**

BAD SCHANDAU *2G4* (3km E Rural) *50.92996, 14.19301* **Campingplatz Ostrauer Mühle,** Kirnitzschtal, 01814 Bad Schandau, Sachsen **+49 35022 - 42742; campmuehle@hotmail.com; www.ostrauer-muehle.de**

12 €2 WD MSP

SE fr Dresden on B172 for 40km (Pirna-Schmilka). In Bad Schandau turn E twds Hinterhermsdorf; site in approx 3km. Med, pt shd, terr, EHU (10A) €1.75 + conn fee; sep car park; CKE. *"In National Park; superb walking area; rec arr early high ssn; site yourself if office clsd on arr."* **€18.50** **2020**

BAD SEGEBERG *1D2* (5km NE Rural) *53.96131, 10.33685* **Klüthseecamp Seeblick,** Stripdorfer Weg, Klüthseehof 2, 23795 Klein Rönnau **(04551) 82368; info@kluethseecamp.de; www.kluethseecamp.de**

12 €3 WD MSP (htd)

Exit A21 junc 13 at Bad Sedgeberg Süd onto B432; turn L sp Bad Sedgeberg; cont on B432 dir Scharbeutz & Puttgarden thro Klein Rönnau, look out for sp, site on R. 5*, V lge, pt shd, serviced pitches; EHU (16A) inc; gas; bbq; sw nr; twin axles; TV; 75% statics; bus adj, train to Hamburg, Lübeck; Eng spkn; adv bkg acc; ccard acc; fishing; golf 6km; games rm; horseriding; tennis; bike hire; CKE. *"Spacious, well-kept nr lakeside site; relaxing atmophere; lge pitches; sauna; steam rm; helpful staff; gd facs & pool; site clsd Feb; wide range of activities; spa; gd cycling, walking; conv Hamburg, Lübeck; excel; peaceful 50 min lakeside walk to town; excel."* **€30.00, G12.** **2022**

BAD TOLZ *4E4* (7km S Rural) *47.70721, 11.55023* **Alpen-Camping Arzbach,** Alpenbadstrasse 20, 83646 Arzbach **(08042) 8408; info@alpen-campingplatz.de; www.alpen-campingplatz.de**

12 WD nr (covrd)

S fr Bad Tölz on B13. Exit Lenggries, turn R to cross rv & R on Wackersburgerstrasse twds Arzbach; in 5km on ent Arzbach turn L. Site ent past sw pool. 3*, Med, hdstg, pt shd, EHU (10-16A) €2; gas; bbq; sw nr; twin axles; 50% statics; bus 300m; Eng spkn; adv bkg acc; tennis 100m; CKE. *"Gd walking, touring Bavarian lakes, excel facs & rest; care needed with lge c'vans due trees & hedges; vg site with superb rest; easy excess to Munich; excel."* **€24.00** **2023**

BAD WILDBAD IM SCHWARZWALD *3C3* (9km E Rural) *48.73715, 8.57623* **Camping Kleinenzhof,** Kleinenzhof 1, 75323 Bad Wildbad **(07081) 3435; info@kleinenzhof.de; www.kleinenzhof.de**

12 €3.80 WD MSP

(covrd, htd, indoor)

Fr Calmbach foll B294 5km S. Site sp on R, in rv valley. Fr Bad Wildbad site is on L. 5*, Lge, pt shd, pt sl, serviced pitches; EHU (16A) metered + conn fee; gas; red long stay; 80% statics; adv bkg acc; sauna; bike hire. *"Nature trails fr site; o'night m'vans area; clsd 1300-1500; mountain views; distillery on site; modern san facs; ski lift 8km; sm pitches."* **€40.00** **2022**

BENSERSIEL *1B2* (0km W Coastal) *53.67531, 7.57001* **Familien & Kurcampingplatz Bensersiel,** 26427 Esens-Bensersiel **(04971) 917121; nordseeurlaub@bensersiel.de; www.bensersiel.de**

WD MSP (htd) adj

Fr B210 turn N at Ogenbargen; thro Esens to Bensersiel. Site adj to harbour in cent of vill - clearly sp. 5*, V lge, unshd, EHU (16A) €2.50; gas; TV; 70% statics; adv bkg acc; tennis; bike hire; games area. *"Cycling country; spa cent nrby; gd boat trips; gd san facs; open site adj sea; gd access vill, rests & island ferries; elec metered after 3 days - if staying longer, check meter on arr."* **€34.50, Easter-23 Oct.** **2023**

> **"There aren't many sites open at this time of year"**
>
> If you're travelling outside peak season remember to call ahead to check site opening dates – even if the entry says 'open all year'.

BERCHTESGADEN *4G4* (5km NE Rural) *47.64742, 13.03993* **Camping Allweglehen,** Allweggasse 4, 83471 Berchtesgaden-Untersalzberg **(08652) 2396; camping@allweglehen.de; www.allweglehen.de**

12 €2.95 (htd) WD MSP

(htd)

On R of rd B305 Berchtesgaden dir Salzburg, immed after ent Unterau; sp. App v steep in places with hairpin bend; gd power/weight ratio needed. 4*, Lge, hdstg, pt shd, pt sl, terr, serviced pitches; EHU (16A) metered + conn fee; 20% statics; phone; bus 500m; adv bkg rec; ccard acc; CKE. *"Gd touring/walking cent; wonderful views some pitches; cycles; beautiful scenery; Hitler's Eagles' Nest worth visit (rd opens mid-May) - bus fr Obersalzburg; ski lift; site rds poss o'grown & uneven; steep app some pitches - risk of grounding for long o'fits; friendly, family-run site; excel rest."* **€45.50** **2024**

BERCHTESGADEN *4G4* (9km NW Rural) *47.67666, 12.93611* **Camping Winkl-Landthal,** Klaushäuslweg 7, 83483 Bischofswiesen **(08652) 8164; info@camping-winkl.de; www.camping-winkl.de**

€3.50 WD nr

Fr Munich-Salzburg m'way take rd 20 sp Bad Reichenhall. Where rd turns L, foll rd 20 twd Berchtesgaden. Site on R in 9km. 4*, Med, hdg, pt shd, terr, serviced pitches; EHU (10A) €4.50; gas; red long stay; 50% statics; Eng spkn; adv bkg acc; ccard acc; CKE. *"Some pleasant, shd pitches adj sm rv; htd pool 3.5km; clean san facs; vg."* **€40.00, 1 Apr-30 Oct.** **2023**

GERMANY

BERLIN *2G3* (23km SW Rural) *52.4650, 13.16638* **DCC Campingplatz Gatow,** Kladower Damm 207-213, 14089 Berlin-Gatow **(030) 3654340; gatow@dccberlin.de; www.dccberlin.de**

12 €2 (htd) nr sand 1km

Fr A10 to W of Berlin turn E on rd 5 sp Spandau/ Centrum. Go twd city cent & after 14km turn R onto Gatowerstrasse (Esso g'ge) sp Kladow/Gatow. Site 6.5km on L almost opp Kaserne (barracks). 3*, Med, pt shd, EHU (10-16A) metered + conn fee; gas; 60% statics; bus at gate; Eng spkn; CKE. *"Excel site; bus tickets fr friendly recep; frequent bus to Berlin cent at gate; highly rec; excel, clean san facs; bicycles can be taken on nrby Kladow ferry to Wannsee S Bahn; gates close bet 1300 & 1500 and at 2200; rec."* **€26.50** **2022**

BERLIN *2G3* (26km SW Rural) *52.55111, 13.24900* **City Campingplatz Hettler & Lange,** Bäkehang 9a, 14532 Kleinmachnow-Dreilinden **(033203) 79684; kleinmachnow@city-camping-berlin.de; www.city-camping-berlin.de**

12 €2 (htd)

Fr S exit A115/E51 junc 5 sp Kleinmachnow, turn L at T-junc & cont to rndabt. Turn L & foll site sp in 800m. 3*, Lge, pt shd, pt sl, EHU (6A) €2.50; gas; sw nr; phone; bus nr; Eng spkn; adv bkg acc; boat hire; CKE. *"Excel location on canal side; immac, modern san facs; twin axles by arrangement; gd walking in woods; gd public transport conv Berlin 45 mins - parking at Wannsee S-bahn (family ticket avail for bus & train); v busy sandy site under trees; 20 min walk to bus stop; vg."* **€24.00** **2023**

BERLIN *2G3* (13km NW Urban) *52.54861, 13.25694* **City-Camping Hettler & Lange,** Gartenfelderstrasse 1, 13599 Berlin-Spandau **(030) 33503633; spandau@city-camping-berlin.de; www.city-camping-berlin.de**

12 €2 nr

Fr N on A111/A115/E26 exit junc 10 sp Tegel Airport & head W on Saatwinkler Damm. Fr S on A100 exit junc 11 onto Saatwinkler Damm. Cont 3.2km to traff lts, turn R, then R again immed bef 2nd bdge. Site on island in rv. Med, shd, pt sl, EHU (16A) €2; Eng spkn; ccard acc; CKE. *"Conv Berlin; 15 min walk to bus stn; gd location beside a canal but aircraft noise; gd san facs; NH/sh stay only; poss to cycle along canal to Potsdam."* **€22.50** **2024**

BERNKASTEL KUES *3B2* (20km NE Rural) *49.96556, 7.10475* **Camping Rissbach,** Rissbacherstrasse 155, 56841 Traben-Trarbach **(06541) 3111; info@moselcampingplatz.de; www.mosel-camping-platz.de**

€3.50 (htd) nr

Fr Bernkastel on B53, after Kröv do not cross Mosel bdge but cont strt on twd Traben, site on R in 1km. NB 20km by rd fr Bernkastel to site. Med, mkd, shd, pt sl, EHU (16A) €2.50; bbq; 30% statics; phone; boat launch. *"In lovely position nr rv; extra for pitches nr rv; well-run site; excel san facs; vg sw pools in town; htd pool adj; poss flooding at high water; Sept wine fest."* **€16.00, 1 Apr-31 Oct.** **2024**

BERNKASTEL KUES *3B2* (2km SW Rural) *49.90883, 7.05600* **Knaus Campingpark (formerly Kueser Werth Camping),** Am Hafen 2, 54470 Bernkastel-Kues **(06531) 8200; www.knauscamp.de**

(htd) nr nr

A'bahn A1/48 (E44) exit Salmtal; join rd sp Bernkastel. Bef rv bdge turn L sp Lieser, thro Lieser cont by rv to ent on R for boat harbour, foll camping sp to marina. Diff access via narr single-track rd. 3*, Lge, mkd, pt shd, EHU (16A); bbq; 10% statics; bus 1km; Eng spkn; adv bkg acc; CKE. *"Excel cent for touring Mosel Valley; covrd pool 2km; Bernkastel delightful sm town with gd parking, sailing, boat excursions, wine cent; cycle lanes; site low on rv bank - poss flooding in bad weather; efficient staff; gd site; not rec for NH/sh stay high ssn as pitches & position poor; san facs old but gd condition; newly taken over by Knaus."* **€45.50, 1 Mar-17 May, 11 Jun-28 Jun, 1 Sep-5 Nov.** **2023**

BERNKASTEL KUES *3B2* (10km NW Rural) *49.97972, 7.0200* **Camping Erden,** Moselufer 1, 54492 Erden **(06532) 4060; info@camping-erden.de; camping-erden.de**

€2 (htd) nr

Exit A1/48 junc 125 onto B50 to Zeltingen. Cross bdge over Mosel, turn L to Erden, site sp. 3*, Med, shd, pt sl, EHU (16A) metered + conn fee; gas; red long stay; TV; 90% statics; phone; bus; adv bkg acc; ccard acc. *"Pleasant, less cr site on opp side of rv to main rd; wonderful setting in scenic area; water point & san facs long way fr tourer pitches; pool 5km; barrier locked 1300-1500 & o'night."* **€18.00, 1 Apr-31 Oct.** **2024**

BERNKASTEL KUES *3B2* (3km NW Rural) *49.93736, 7.04853* **Mosel Camping (Formerly Camping Schenk),** Hauptstrasse 165, 54470 Bernkastel-Wehlen **(06531) 8176; info@mosel-camping-bernkastel.de; www.mosel-camping-bernkastel.de**

€3 (htd) nr nr

On Trier/Koblenz rd B53, exit Kues heading N on L bank of rv & site on R in 4km at Wehlen, sp. Steep exit. Med, mkd, hdstg, pt shd, pt sl, terr, serviced pitches; EHU (16A) metered + conn fee; gas; 40% statics; phone; bus; Eng spkn; adv bkg acc; CKE. *"In apple orchard on Rv Mosel; price according to pitch size; friendly helpful owners; debit cards acc; pool deep - not suitable non-swimmers; poorly ventilated san facs; rv walks & cycle path to town."* **€28.00, 19 Mar-31 Oct.** **2022**

BERNKASTEL KUES *3B2* (4km NW Rural) *49.94122, 7.04653* **Weingut Studert-Prum,** Uferallee 22, 54470 Bernkastel Kues **(06531) 2487; info@studert-pruem.de; www.studert-pruem.com**

nr nr nr

Fr Bernkastel-Kues, co N on W Bank of Rv Mosel, site on R in 4km at ent to Wehlen. Adj to Camp Schenk. Sm, hdstg, mkd, unshd, terr, own san rec; adv bkg acc. *"M'homes only; no san facs; terr site with lovely views of Rv Mosel; covrd pool 2km; vineyards; sh walk to pretty vill; walk/cycle path by rv; boat trips; wineries; excel."* **€10.00, 1 Apr-31 Oct.** **2022**

BIELEFELD *1C3* (8km SW Rural) *52.00624, 8.45681* **Campingpark Meyer Zu Bentrup,** Vogelweide 9, 33649 Bielefeld **(0521) 4592233; bielefeld@meyer-zu-bentrup.de; www.camping-bielefeld.de**

Fr N or S on A2 - At interchange 21 take A33 Osnabruck. Cont till m'way ends, cont onto A61 dir Bielefeld. After 2km take A68 exit, dir Osnabruck/Halle West. Site on L after 3km. 3*, Lge, unshd, pt sl, EHU (10-16A) €1.50; cooking facs; 70% statics; games area; games rm; CKE. *"Vg; immac but dated san facs (2015); conv for Bielefeld; well maintained; warm welcome; excel shop at adj fruit farm."* **€25.00, 1 Mar-30 Nov. 2023**

BINGEN *3C2* (3km E Urban) *49.97029, 7.93916* **Camping Hindenburgbrucke,** Bornstrasse 22, 55411 Kempton-Bingen **(06721) 17160; bauer@bauer-schorsch.de; www.bauer-schorsch.de**

Foll rd on Rhine twd Mainz, site on L bef traff lts. Turn into tarmac rd, bear R, L under rlwy bdge, strt to site ent by Rhine. Lge, hdg, unshd, EHU (watch rev pol); bbq; twin axles; 40% statics; bus/train adj. *"Open site on W bank of Rhein; staff conn elec pnts; lovely position for sh stay; mosquitoes abound; close to Rüdesheim-Bingen ferry, vineyards, castles, cruising."* **€19.00, 1 May-31 Oct. 2024**

BINZ *2G1* (6km NW Coastal) *54.44817, 13.56152* **Wohnmobil-Oase Rügen,** Proraer Chaussee 60, 18609 Ostseebad Binz OT Prora **+49 (0) 38393. 699 777; info@wohnmobilstellplatz-ruegen.de; www.wohnmobilstellplatz-ruegen.de**

Fr Binz foll coast rd to Prora, site on L past traff lts. Med, hdstg, pt shd, EHU (16A); gas; bus/tram adj; Eng spkn. *"Vg site, m'vans only, track to beach."* **€15.00 2020**

BITBURG *3B2* (10km W Rural) *49.95895, 6.42454* **Prümtal Camping,** In der Klaus 5, 54636 Oberweis **(06527) 92920; info@pruemtal.de; www.pruemtal.de**

On B50 Bitburg-Vianden rd. On ent Oberweis sharp RH bend immed L bef rv bdge - sp recreational facs or sp Köhler Stuben Restaurant-Bierstube. V lge, pt shd, EHU (16A) €2.75 or metered; 60% statics; Eng spkn; adv bkg acc; ccard acc; bike hire; CKE. *"Excel facs; san facs stretched high ssn; vg rest."* **€26.00 2020**

BONN *1B4* (13km SE Rural) *50.65388, 7.20111* **Camping Genienau,** Im Frankenkeller 49, 53179 Bonn-Mehlem **(0228) 344949; genienau@freenet.de; campingplatz-genienau.de**

Fr B9 dir Mehlem, site sp on Rv Rhine, S of Mehlem. Med, pt shd, EHU (6A) €3 or metered; 60% statics; bus; Eng spkn; CKE. *"Excel site on rv bank; liable to flood when rv v high; nr ferry to cross Rhine; late arr no problem; san facs up steps but disabled facs at grnd level; lots to see & do."* **€20.00 2022**

BRANDENBURG AN DER HAVEL *2F3* (9km E Rural) *52.39833, 12.43665* **Camping und Ferienpark am Plauer See,** Plauer Landstrasse 200, 14774 Brandenburg **33 81 80 45 44; info@camping-plauersee.de; www.camping-plauersee.de**

Fr A2 take 102 to Brandenburg. L onto 1, cont 4km. Just after sp for Plauerhof is a campsite sp. Turn L & foll rd for 1.5km to site on the side of lake. Med, mkd, pt shd, pt sl, EHU (10A) €1.90; bbq; 75% statics; Eng spkn; adv bkg acc; games area; bike hire; CCI. *"Next to sm lake; boat, cycles & BBQ hire; nr historic town of Brandenburg; vg site, mainly statics but tourers and MH given gd pitches next to lake; gd rest and bar; rec Potsdam."* **€33.00 2024**

BRAUNEBERG *3B2* (0.9km W Rural) *49.90564, 6.97603* **Wohnmobilstellplatz Brauneberger Juffer,** Moselweinstraße 101, 54472 Brauneberg **6534 933 333; mfrollison@yahoo.co.uk or info@brauneberg.de; www.brauneberg.de**

Fr NE of A1 take exit 127-Klausen onto L47 twds Mulheim. Cont onto L158, then turn L onto B53. Supermkt 20m fr site ent which is down side rd twds rv. Sm, hdg, mkd, hdstg, pt shd, EHU (16A); bbq; sw nr; bus 100m; Eng spkn. *"Aire-type site; no adv bkg; Gd cycle paths along rv; vg site."* **€10.00 2024**

BRAUNLAGE *2E4* (8.6km NE Rural) *51.75713, 10.68345* **Campingplatz am Schierker Stern,** Hagenstrasse, 38879 Schierke **(039455) 58817; info@harz-camping.com; www.harz-camping.com**

Fr W on B27 fr Braunlage for 4km to Elend. Turn L & cross rlwy line. Site on L in 2km at x-rds. Med, hdstg, pt shd, pt sl, EHU (6A) €2.60; bbq; cooking facs; TV; bus at site ent, train 1km; adv bkg acc. *"Conv & pleasant site in Harz mountains; excel san facs; friendly, helpful owners live on site; sm pitches; vg."* **€24.00 2024**

GERMANY

BRAUNLAGE *2E4* (12km SE Rural) *51.65697, 10.66786* **Campingplatz am Bärenbache,** Bärenbachweg 10, 38700 Hohegeiss **(05583) 1306; campingplatz-hohegeiss @t-online.de; www.campingplatz-hohegeiss.de**

12 €1.50 (htd) WO MSP nr (htd)

Fr Braunlage S on B4 thro Hohegeiss; site sp on L downhill (15%) on edge of town. 4*, Med, mkd, hdg, pt shd, terr, EHU (10A); bbq; cooking facs; 10% statics; Eng spkn; adv bkg acc; bike hire. *"Gd walking; friendly; walking dist to vill; vg."* **€22.50** **2024**

BREISACH AM RHEIN *3B4* (7km E Rural) *48.03104, 7.65781* **Kaiserstuhl Camping,** Nachwaid 5, 79241 Ihringen **(07668) 950065; info@kaiserstuhl camping.de; www.kaiserstuhlcamping.de**

€2.50 WO MSP nr nr

Fr S exit A5/E35 junc 64a, foll sp twds Breisach, then camping sp to Ihringen. At Ihringen site sp dir Merdingen. Fr N exit junc 60 & foll sp. Med, unshd, EHU (16A) metered + conn fee; red long stay; 10% statics; tennis adj; golf 8km; CKE. *"Can get cr in high ssn; htd pool adj."* **€32.00, 15 Mar-31 Oct.** **2024**

BREMEN *1C2* (16km SW Rural) *53.01055, 8.68972* **Marchencamping (formerly Camp Wienberg),** Zum Steller See 83, 28816 Stuhr-Gross Mackenstedt **(04206) 9191; info@maerchen-camping.com; maerchen-camping.com**

12 €2 (htd) WO MSP

Exit A1/E37 junc 58a onto B322 sp Stuhr/ Delmenhorst. Foll Camping Steller See sp. Sp also call site Marchen Camping. Lge, mkd, hdstg, pt shd, pt sl, EHU (16A) metered or €3; TV; 50% statics; Eng spkn; adv bkg acc; ccard acc; bike hire; CKE. *"Helpful staff; basic facs; gd."* **€23.00** **2023**

BREMEN *1C2* (17km SW Rural) *53.00694, 8.69277* **Campingplatz Steller See,** Zum Stellersee 15, 28816 Stuhr-Gross Mackenstedt **(04206) 6490; steller.see@t-online.de; www.steller-see.de**

(htd) WO MSP nr

Exit A1/E37 junc 58a onto B322 sp Stuhr/ Delmenhorst. Foll site sp. 3*, Lge, unshd, EHU (10-16A) inc; gas; bbq; sw nr; red long stay; 80% statics; phone; adv bkg acc; ccard acc; games area; CKE. *"Site officially clsd but owner may accommodate you; well-appointed, lakeside site; adequate, clean san facs; friendly owners; conv NH fr m'way & for trams to Bremen; gd space, easy to position; pretty site; vg."* **€30.00, 1 Apr-30 Sep.** **2022**

BREMEN *1C2* (5km NW Rural) *53.11483, 8.83263* **Camping Hanse (formerly Camping am Stadtwaldsee),** Hochschulring 1, 28359 Bremen **(0421)30746825; info@hansecamping.de; www.HanseCamping.de**

12 €4 (htd) WO MSP

Fr A27 take exit 19 for Universitat, foll sp for Universitat and camping. Site on L in 1km after leaving University area. 3*, Lge, hdstg, mkd, pt shd, EHU (16A) metered; gas; bbq; cooking facs; sw nr; red long stay; 10% statics; phone; bus 100m; Eng spkn; adv bkg acc; ccard acc; CKE. *"Excel, spacious lakeside site; superb san facs; cycle path to beautiful city; gd bus service; v gd rest adj; spacious pitches but unkept & poorly maintained."* **€35.50** **2023**

BRIESELANG *2F3* (5km W Rural) *52.57138, 12.96583* **Campingplatz Zeestow im Havelland,** 11 Brieselangerstrasse, 14665 Brieselang **(033234) 88634; info@campingplatz-zeestow.de; www.campingplatz-zeestow.de**

12 €2 WO

Exit A10/E55 junc 27; turn W dir Wustermark; site on L after canal bdge in 500m. 3*, Lge, unshd, pt sl, EHU (16A) metered; gas; 75% statics; bus; CKE. *"Gd NH nr a'bahn; facs dated but clean; 13km fr Berlin & 25km fr Potsdam; fair."* **€20.00** **2022**

BRUGGEN *1A4* (2km SE Rural) *51.23416, 6.19815* **Camping-Forst Laarer See,** Bruggenerstrasse 27, 41372 Niederkrüchten **(02163) 8461 or 0172 7630591 (mob); info@campingforst-laarersee.com; www.campingforst-laarersee.com**

12 €1 (htd) WO MSP nr nr

Fr A52 junc 3 or A61 junc 3 - take B221 to Brüggen, turn R at 1st traff lts into site. Lge, pt shd, pt sl, EHU (16A) inc; bbq; 80% statics; Eng spkn; adv bkg acc; games area; CKE. *"Unspoilt area nr pretty town; many leisure amenities nr site - gd for children; vg site; ltd touring pitches; pleasant site with lake; walking/bike paths."* **€21.00** **2022**

BUHL *3C3* (7km NW Rural) *48.72719, 8.08074* **Campingplatz Adam,** Campingstrasse 1, 77815 Bühl-Oberbruch **(07223) 23194; info@campingplatz-adam.de; www.campingplatz-adam.de**

€4.50 WO MSP nr

Exit A5 at Bühl take sp Lichtenau & foll sp thro Oberbruch, then L twd Moos to site in 500m. If app on rd 3 take rd sp W to Rheinmünster N of Bühl. Site sp to S at W end of Oberbruch. 4*, Lge, mkd, hdstg, pt shd, serviced pitches; EHU (10A) €3; bbq (charcoal, elec, gas); sw; twin axles; red long stay; 25% statics; Eng spkn; adv bkg acc; sailing; tennis; fishing; boating; games area; CKE. *"Excel, clean san facs; conv for Strasbourg, Baden-Baden & Black Forest visits; o'night area tarmac car park; extra for lakeside pitches; if recep clsd use area outside gate; vg; excel camp with own lake; gd rest; friendly staff; handy for m'way but still quiet; o'night tarmac area excel for NH but worth a longer stay; highly rec; 45 mins to Europe Pk; nice san facs; lndry facs old; some rd noise; excel."* **€28.00, 1 Mar-30 Nov.** **2021**

GERMANY

BURGEN *3B2* (0.6km N Rural) *50.21457, 7.38976*
Happy Life Camping Burgen (Formerly Camping Burgen), 56332 Burgen **(02605) 2396; burgen@haeppy-life.de; www.haeppy-life.de**
€2 nr

Leave A61 at J39; foll B411 twds Dieblich to reach S bank of Mosel; turn L and foll B49 for approx 12km; site on L bet rd and rv bef vill. Sat nav uses rte thro vill, not suitable. 4*, Med, mkd, unshd, EHU (10A) metered + conn fee (poss rev pol); gas; 30% statics; Eng spkn; boat launch; CKE. *"Scenic area; ideal for touring Mosel, Rhine & Koblenz areas; gd shop; poss liable to flood; lovely, clean site; gd san facs; rec."*
€23.00, 11 Apr-19 Oct. **2024**

CALW *3C3* (12km SW Rural) *48.67766, 8.68990*
Camping Erbenwald, 75387 Neubulach-Liebelsberg **(07053) 7382; info@camping-erbenwald.de; www.camping-erbenwald.de**
12 €2 (htd)

On B463 S fr Calw, take R slip rd sp Neubulach to go over main rd. Foll Neubulach sp until camping sp at R junc. Site well sp. 4*, Lge, hdg, mkd, pt shd, EHU (10A) metered; 60% statics; phone; Eng spkn; adv bkg acc; games area. *"Gd size pitches; child-friendly site; no vehicles in or out fr 1300-1500; excel; cash only."*
€22.00 **2024**

CANOW *2F2* (2km E Rural) *53.19636, 12.93116*
Camping Pälitzsee, Am Canower See 165, 17255 Canow **(039828) 20220; info@mecklenburg-tourist.de; www.mecklenburg-tourist.de**
12 €2 nr

Fr N on B198 turn S dir Rheinsberg to Canow vill, site sp. Lge, pt shd, EHU (16A) metered or €3; sw; 50% statics; adv bkg acc; boating. *"Canow charming vill; vg touring base for lakes; cash only - no cards accepted."* **€20.00** **2022**

CHEMNITZ *2F4* (10km SW Rural) *50.76583, 13.01444*
Waldcampingplatz Erzgebirgsblick, An der Dittersdorfer Höhe 1, 09439 Amtsberg **(0371) 7750833; info@waldcamping-erzgebirge.de; www.waldcamping-erzgebirge.de**
12 (htd)

Fr A4 take A72 S & exit junc 15. Foll sp 'Centrum' & join 'Südring' ring rd. Turn onto B174 & foll sp Marienberg twd junc with B180. Site sp 500m fr junc. Med, mkd, pt shd, EHU (16A) metered; gas; red long stay; TV; bus 800m; Eng spkn; games area; site clsd 6-27 Nov; CKE. *"Gd san facs; relaxing site; gd walking; dogs free; vg standard of site; cash only - no cards accepted."* **€35.00** **2022**

CHIEMING *4F4* (2km NW Rural) *47.902103, 12.519891*
Camping Seehäusl, Beim Seehäusl 1, 83339 Chieming **(8664) 303; info@camping-seehaeusl.de; www.camping-seehaeusl.de**
(htd) lake, shgl

J109 N off A8 twrds Chieming. Foll sp. Diff access for v lge o'fits (narr lane) 4*, Med, mkd, hdstg, pt shd, EHU (16A); bbq (elec, gas); sw nr; twin axles; Eng spkn; adv bkg rec; ccard acc; fishing; watersports. *"Gd san facs."* **€32.50, 1 Apr-1 Oct.** **2024**

COBURG *4E2* (15km SW Rural) *50.19433, 10.83809*
Campingplatz Sonnland, Bahnhofstrasse 154, 96145 Sesslach **(09569) 220; info@camping-sonnland.de; www.camping-sonnland.de**
12 €3.50 (htd) nr nr

Exit A73 junc 10 Ebersdorf onto B303 W. Then at Niederfüllbach turn S onto B4, then turn W dir Sesslach. Site sp N of Sesslach dir Hattersdorf; turn R at sp opp filling stn, site in 150m. Med, mkd, hdstg, pt shd, terr, serviced pitches; EHU (16A) metered; bbq; sw; 70% statics; adv bkg acc; CKE. *"Sesslach unspoilt, medieval, walled town; site well laid-out."*
€26.00 **2022**

COCHEM *3B2* (1.5km N Rural) *50.15731, 7.17360*
Mosel Camping Cochem (formerly Campingplatz am Freizeitzentrum), Moritzburgerstrasse 1, 56812 Cochem **(02671) 4409; info@mosel-camping-cochem.de; www.mosel-camping-cochem.de**
€3 nr nr

On rd B49 fr Koblenz, on ent town go under 1st rv bdge then turn R over same bdge. Foll site sp. 3*, Lge, mkd, pt shd, pt sl, EHU (10-16A) €2.50 + conn fee (some rev pol); gas; 10% statics; bike hire; CKE. *"Gd, clean site adj Rv Mosel; pitches tight & poss diff access fr site rds; gd for children; easy walk along rv to town; train to Koblenz, Trier, Mainz."*
€23.00, 1 Apr-31 Oct. **2022**

COCHEM *3B2* (10km E Rural) *50.17056, 7.29285*
Camping & Watersports Mosel-Islands, Yachthafen, 56253 Treis-Karden/Mosel **(02672) 2613; campingplatz@mosel-islands.de; www.mosel-islands.de**
€4 nr

Fr Cochem take B49 to Treis-Karden (11km), cross Mosel bdge bear L then 1st sharp L back under Mosel bdge & parallel with rv. After 300m at bdge over stream turn R then thro allotments. Site over bdge by boating cent. Fr A61 Koblenz/Bingen a'bahn descend to rv level by Winningen Valley Bdge, turn L onto B49 (Moselweinstrasse). Do not descend thro Dieblich as c'vans are prohibited. After 25km; turn R immed bef Mosel bdge & then as above. Avoid Treis vill (narr with thro traff priorities). 5*, Med, mkd, pt shd, serviced pitches; EHU (6A) metered & conn fee; gas; bbq; 50% statics; adv bkg acc; tennis 300m. *"Ideal for touring Mosel valley; rv cruising & historical sites; vg san facs 1st floor; poss midges; gd site."* **€42.00, 27 Mar-27 Oct.** **2024**

COCHEM *3B2* (6km SE Rural) *50.10999, 7.23542*
Campingplatz Happy-Holiday, Moselweinstrasse,
56821 Ellenz-Poltersdorf **(02673) 1272;**
www.camping-happy-holiday.de

🐕 €1.50 ⛺ (htd) ᵂᴰ ▲ 🛒 💧 ⫫ ⛾ 🅣 🕘 🚲 🛥

Fr Cochem, take B49 S to Ellenz; site sp on bank
of Rv Mosel. Med, shd, pt sl, EHU (6A) metered; gas;
70% statics; Eng spkn; fishing; watersports. *"Pleasant
situation; gd value rest; pool 300m; clean facs; conv
touring base."* €19.50, 1 Apr-31 Oct.   2024

COCHEM *3B2* (7km SE Rural) *50.08231, 7.20796*
Camping Holländischer Hof, Am Campingplatz 1,
56820 Senheim **(02673) 4660; info@moselcamping.
com; https://www.moselcamping.com**

⫫ ᵂᴰ ▲ 🛒 ♿ 🛒 💧 ⫫ ᴹˢᴾ 🦋 ⛾ 🅣 🚲 🛥

Fr Cochem take B49 twd Traben-Trarbach; after
approx 15km turn L over rv bdge sp Senheim; site on rv
island. 4*, Med, mkd, pt shd, EHU (6-10A) metered; gas;
sw nr; red long stay; 20% statics; phone; Eng spkn; adv
bkg acc; tennis; CKE. *"Pleasant, well-run site; beautiful
location; helpful staff; sm pitches on loose pebbles; excel
cycle paths; poss flooding when wet weather/high water;
poss overcr."* €16.00, 9 Apr-31 Oct.   2020

"I like to fill in the reports as I travel from site to site"

You'll find report forms at the back of this
guide, or you can fill them in online at
camc.com/europereport.

COCHEM *3B2* (7km SE Rural) *50.13253, 7.23029*
Campingplatz Bruttig, Am Moselufer, 56814 Bruttig-
Fankel **(02671) 915429; www.campingplatz-bruttig.de**

⫫ (htd) ᵂᴰ ▲ 🛒 💧 🦋 ⛾ 🚲 🛥

Leave Cochem on B49 twd Trier. In 8km turn L over
bdge to Bruttig-Fankel. Thro vill, site on R on banks
Rv Mosel. Sm, mkd, pt shd, EHU (16A) metered; sw nr;
50% statics; phone; Eng spkn. *"Pleasant site in pretty
vill; gd walking, cycling; Mosel boat trips fr Bruttig."*
€16.00, Easter-31 Oct.   2022

COCHEM *3B2* (15km S Rural) *50.09162, 7.16319*
Campingplatz zum Feuerberg, 56814 Ediger-Eller
(02675) 701; info@zum-feuerberg.de;
www.zum-feuerberg.de

🐕 €2 ⫫ ᵂᴰ ▲ 🛒 💧 🦋 ⛾ 🅣 🚲 🛥 nr ⛺ ⛵

On A49 fr Cochem to Bernkastel Kues, just bef vill
of Ediger on L - 17km by rd. Lge, hdg, mkd, EHU
(16A) metered + conn fee; gas; 40% statics; phone;
bus, train to Cochem; Eng spkn; adv bkg acc; bike
hire; CKE. *"Well-kept site in lovely area; charming vill;
boat mooring; helpful staff; facs at 1st floor level, via
key (deposit); gd selection of rests & pubs; rv bus high
ssn; gd touring base; gd; pitches next to rv cost more."*
€23.00, 18 Mar-31 Oct.   2022

COLBITZ *2E3* (3km NE Rural) *52.33158, 11.63123*
Campingplatz Heide-Camp, Angerschestrasse,
39326 Colbitz **(039207) 80291; info@heide-
camp-colbitz.de; www.heide-camp-colbitz.de**

12 🐕 €2.80 ᵂᴰ ▲ 🛒 ♿ 🛒 💧 ᴹˢᴾ 🅣 🕘 nr 🚲 🛥 nr ⛺

Exit A2/E30 junc 70 onto B189 N dir Stendal. In
Colbitz foll sp Angern. Site in 2km. 4*, Lge, mkd, pt
shd, EHU (6-16A) metered + conn fee; gas; 20% statics;
Eng spkn; adv bkg acc; ccard acc; games area; CKE.
"Site on woodland, lge pitches." €19.00   2024

COLDITZ *2F4* (4km E Rural) *51.13083, 12.83305*
Campingplatz am Waldbad, Im Tiergarten 5, 04680
Colditz **(034381) 43122; info@campingplatz-colditz.de;**
www.campingplatz-colditz.de

🐕 €1 ⫫ ᵂᴰ ▲ 💧 🕘 🛥 nr

Fr Leipzig A14 to Grimma, foll B107 to Colditz.
Cross rv, foll B176 sp Dobeln. Turn L immed bef
town exit sp. After 1km turn R at camping sp. Foll
track thro woods for 500m, site on R immed
after sw pool. 4*, Med, pt shd, pt sl, EHU (10A) inc;
30% statics; phone; Eng spkn; sauna; CKE. *"V nice
peaceful site; gd clean facs, overrun when busy; gd value;
tight turn into site fr narr rd; helpful, friendly manager &
staff; 30 mins walk to Colditz Castle; leisure cent adj; sm
rest 200m; chem point."* €22.00, 1 Apr-30 Sep.   2022

CREGLINGEN *3D2* (3.5km S Rural) *49.43945,
10.04210* **Campingpark Romantische Strasse,**
Münster 67, 97993 Creglingen-Münster **(07933)
20289; camping.hausotter@web.de;**
www.camping-romantische-strasse.de

🐕 €1 ⫫ (htd) ᵂᴰ ▲ 🛒 ♿ 🛒 💧 ᴹˢᴾ 🦋 ⫫ ⛾ 🅣 🕘 🚲 🛥 ⛺
⛵ (covrd, htd) 🎣

Fr E43 exit A7/junc 105 at Uffenheim. At edge of
Uffenheim turn R in dir of Bad Mergentheim; in
approx 17km at T-junc turn L for Creglingen, thro
vill & then R sp Münster with camping sp - approx
8km further. Site on R after Münster. (Avoid rte bet
Rothenburg & Creglingen as includes some v narr
vills & coaches). 4*, Med, pt shd, serviced pitches;
EHU (6A) €2.20; bbq; 20% statics; phone; sauna; bike
hire; lake fishing; CKE. *"Site ent needs care; helpful
owner; lovely welcome; excel rest & facs; Romantische
Strasse with interesting medieval churches locally;
gd cent for historic towns; clsd 1300-1500; gd value;
facs stretched high ssn; poss long walk fr facs."*
€27.50, 15 Mar-15 Nov.   2023

DAHME *2E1* (1.5km N Coastal) *54.24254, 11.08030*
Camping Stieglitz, Im Feriengebiet Zedano, 23747
Dahme **(04364) 1435; info@camping-stieglitz.de;**
www.camping-stieglitz.de

🐕 (not Jul-Aug) €5 ⫫ (htd) ᵂᴰ ▲ 🛒 ♿ 🛒 💧 ᴹˢᴾ 🦋 ⛾ 🕘 🛥 ⛺
🐎 ⛱ sand 200m

Exit A1/E47 junc 12 at Lensahn E twd coast.
Fr B501 foll sp Dahme-Nord to sea wall, site
sp. 4*, Lge, mkd, hdg, pt shd, EHU (16A) €2.60
or metered; TV; 50% statics; adv bkg acc; ccard
acc; fishing; bike hire; watersports. *"Excel site."*
€32.50, 26 Mar-24 Oct & 5-31 Dec.   2024

DAHN *3B3* (0.5km W Rural) *49.14416, 7.76805* **Campingplatz Büttelwoog,** Am Campingplatz 1, 66994 Dahn **(06391) 5622; buettelwoog@t-online.de; www.camping-buettelwoog.de**

€3

Fr rte 10 Pirmasens-Karlsruhe turn S at traff lts at Hinterweidenthal onto B427 to Dahn. In Dahn cent turn R, foll Youth Hostel sp; over single track rlwy & up hill; site on R in 500m, clearly sp opp Youth Hostel (Jugendherberge). 4*, Med, pt shd, terr, EHU (4A) inc (rev pol); gas; 10% statics; Eng spkn; adv bkg acc; bike hire; Quickstop o'night facs; CKE. *"Welcoming, informal site; covrd pool adj; clsd to arr 1200-1400 & 2200-0800; facs dated & stretched high ssn; picturesque area; gd walks fr site."* **€31.00, 15 Mar-4 Nov.** **2024**

DAUN *3B2* (19km SE Rural) *50.13111, 6.93331* **Feriendorf Pulvermaar,** Auf der Maarhöhe, Vulkanstrasse, 54558 Gillenfeld **(06573) 287; info@feriendorf-pulvermaar.de; www.feriendorf-pulvermaar.de**

12 €1

Fr A1/A48/E44 exit junc 121 onto B421 dir Zell/ Mosel. After approx 5km turn R to Pulvemaar, site sp nr lakeside. 3*, Med, pt shd, sl, EHU (16A) metered + conn fee; bbq; 60% statics; Eng spkn; adv bkg acc; fishing adj; games area; CKE. *"Conv Mosel valley & Weinstrasse; attractive site; helpful owner."* **€21.00** **2022**

DETTELBACH *3D2* (6km S Rural) *49.82603, 10.20083* **Camping Katzenkopf,** Am See, 97334 Sommerach **(09381) 9215; info@camping-katzenkopf.de; www.camping-katzenkopf.de**

€2

Fr A7/E45 junc 101 dir Volkach. Cross rv & foll sp S to Sommerach, site sp. Fr S exit A3/E43 junc 74 dir Volkach & foll sp. NB Town unsuitable c'vans; foll site sps bef town ent (beware - sat nav rte poss thro town). Lge, pt shd, EHU (16A) €2.50 or metered; gas; sw; red long stay; ccard acc; boating; golf 10km; fishing; CKE. *"Beautiful surroundings; sm pitches; clean, modern facs; m'van o'night area outside site; barrier clsd 1300-1500; easy walk to wine-growing vill; gd rest; gd NH nr A3."* **€21.60, 1 Apr-25 Oct.** **2020**

DIESSEN *4E4* (1.5km N Rural) *47.96528, 11.10308* **Camping St Alban am Ammersee,** Seeweg Süd 85, 86911 St Alban **(08807) 7305; ivian.pavic@t-online.de; www.camping-ammersee.de**

€1 shgl

Exit A96 junc 29 & foll rd S to Diessen; site on L 150m after Diessen town sp. Med, unshd, EHU (16A) inc; sw; 60% statics; train nr; Eng spkn; adv bkg acc; ccard acc; boating; windsurfing; games rm. *"Friendly helpful staff; excel rest; clsd 1200-1400; gd, immac san facs."* **€34.00, 15 Mar-15 Oct.** **2024**

DINKELSBUHL *3D3* (2km NNE Rural) *49.08194, 10.33416* **DCC Campingpark Romantische Strasse,** Kobeltsmühle6, 91550 Dinkelsbühl **(09851) 7817; campdinkelsbuehl@aol.com; www.campingplatz-dinkelsbuehl.de**

12 €1

On Rothenburg-Dinkelsbühl rd 25. Turn sharp L at camp sp immed bef rlwy x-ing (at Jet petrol stn) at N end of town. Site on R in 1km on lakeside. Or exit A7/E43 junc 112; turn R at T-junc. Site well sp. 4*, Lge, mkd, pt shd, terr, EHU (10-16A) metered; gas; sw; 40% statics; phone; adv bkg acc; ccard acc; site clsd 1300-1500 & 2200-0800; boating; dog wash; CKE. *"Pitches poss long way fr san facs; gd, modern san facs; NH area with easy access; close to beautiful medieval town (25min walk); m'van o'night area with EHU; quiet, peaceful, well-equipped & well-managed site; excel rest; gd cycle paths in area; gd; recep open 9-1230 & 1500-1700."* **€23.00** **2024**

DONAUESCHINGEN *3C4* (7km SE Rural) *47.93754, 8.53422* **Riedsee-Camping,** Am Riedsee 11, 78166 Donaueschingen **(0771) 5511; info@riedsee-camping.de; www.riedsee-camping.de**

12 €3.50

Fr Donaueschingen on B31 to Pfohren vill, site sp. Lge, mkd, pt shd, EHU (16A) metered, €0.50 (check for rev pol); sw; 90% statics; Eng spkn; ccard acc; bike hire; golf 9km; boating; tennis; CKE. *"Vg facs; clean, well-run site; sm pitches; site busy at w/end; office clsd Mon (poss LS only); gd value rest; conv Danube cycle way."* **€24.00** **2022**

DONAUWORTH *4E3* (5km SE Rural) *48.67660, 10.84100* **Donau-Lech Camping,** Campingweg 1, 86698 Eggelstetten **(09090) 4046; info@donau-lech-camping.de; www.donau-lech-camping.de**

12 €2.20 (htd) nr nr

Fr B2 take Eggelstetten exit & foll sp to vill. Site immed bef vill on R, foll 'Int'l Camping' sp. 4*, Med, hdg, mkd, hdstg, pt shd, EHU (16A) inc (some rev pol); gas; sw; 80% statics; phone; Eng spkn; adv bkg acc; archery; golf nr; boat hire; site clsd Nov; fishing nr; horseriding nr; CKE. *"Superb, well-maintained, site but poss unkempt & boggy LS; ltd area for tourers; friendly, helpful staff & owner; facs clean but update req; owner sites vans; conv base for touring Danube & Romantic Rd; nr Danube cycle way."* **€25.00** **2024**

GERMANY

DORTMUND *1B4* (10km SE Rural) *51.42078, 7.49514* **Camping Hohensyburg,** Syburger Dorfstrasse 69, 44265 Dortmund-Hohensyburg **(0231) 774374; info@camping-hohensyburg.de; www.camping-hohensyburg.de**

€3

Exit Dortmund a'bahn ring at Dortmund Sud onto B54 sp Hohensyburg. Foll dual c'way S & strt at next traff lts. Turn L twd Hohensyburg, up hill to Y junc. Turn L (camping sp) & cont over hill to Gasthof. Turn R immed bef Gasthof down narr, steep rd (sharp bends) to site in 100m. Lge, pt shd, pt sl, EHU (16A) €2.50 or metered; bbq; twin axles; 80% statics; Eng spkn; adv bkg acc; golf 3km; boat launch. *"Lovely, friendly site; narr lane at ent not suitable lge o'fits; excel, clean san facs; gd; lge site; immac san facs."*
€26.50 **2022**

DORUM *1C2* (6km NE Coastal) *53.73938, 8.51680* **Knaus Campingpark Dorum,** Am Kuterhafen, 27632 Dorum/Neufeld **(04741) 5020; dorum@knauscamp.de; www.knauscamp.de/dorum-nordsee**

adj

Fr A27 Bremerhaven-Cuxhaven, take exit 4 to Dorum. Then foll signs to Dorum-Neufeld. Cont over dyke to harbour, campsite on R. Lge, unshd, EHU (6A); twin axles; 40% statics; bus 0.5km; Eng spkn; adv bkg acc; bike hire; CCI. *"Vg; temporary ssnal site; scenic fishing port."*
€41.00, 1 Apr-30 Sep. **2024**

DRESDEN *2G4* (17km NE Rural) *51.12027, 13.98000* **Camping- und Freizeitpark Lux Oase,** Arnsdorferstrasse 1, 01900 Kleinröhrsdorf **(035952) 56666; info@luxoase.de; www.luxoase.de**

€6.50 (covrd) adj

Leave A4/E40 at junc 85 dir Radeberg. S to Leppersdorf, Kleinröhrsdorf. Sp on L end vill, well sp fr a'bahn. 5*, Lge, mkd, pt shd, serviced pitches; EHU (10A) inc; gas; bbq; sw nr; red long stay; twin axles; TV; 30% statics; bus to city; Eng spkn; ccard acc; fishing; games area; horseriding; bike hire; sauna; games rm; CKE. *"Excel site by lake; vg san facs; new luxury san facs 2011; v helpful staff; gd rest; site bus to Dresden Tues - 15 mins walk to reg bus; fitness cent; weekly bus to Prague fr site & other attractions in easy reach; new spa 2013."* **€35.00, 13 Apr-5 Nov, G14.** **2022**

DRESDEN *2G4* (16km SE Rural) *50.99839, 13.86919* **Campingplatz Wostra,** At 7 Wostra, 01259 Dresden **(351) 20278678; cp-wostra@dresden.de; https://www.dresden.de/de/leben/sport-und-freizeit/sport/campingplatz.php**

(htd) nr nr (htd)

Take exit 6 fr E55 Prague-Dresden in dir of Pirna, then take B172 Dresden-Pirna to Heidenau, foll sp to site. Med, pt shd, EHU (16A); bbq (sep area); cooking facs; twin axles; bus/tram adj; Eng spkn; ccard acc; games rm; table tennis; CKE. *"Excel quiet site."*
€20.00, 6 Apr-1 Nov. **2020**

DRESDEN *2G4* (7km S Urban) *51.01416, 13.7500* **Campsite Dresden-Mockritz,** Boderitzerstrasse 30, 01217 Dresden-Mockritz **(0351) 4715250; camping-dresden@t-online.de; www.camping-dresden.de**

€1 (htd)

Exit E65/A17 junc 3 onto B170 N sp Dresden. In approx 1.5km turn E at traff lts sp Zschernitz, site sp. 2*, Med, mkd, pt shd, pt sl, EHU (6A) €2.70; 5% statics; bus; Eng spkn; adv bkg rec; site clsd Christmas to end Jan; CKE. *"V conv city cent & buses; poss muddy after rain; helpful staff; excel; office clsd 1300-1500 find a pitch and inform recep; WiFi variable; gd rest; conv for Dresden; highly rec."*
€27.20, 1 Jan-31 Jan, 1 Mar-31 Dec. **2022**

DUSSELDORF *1B4* (19.5km NNW Urban) *51.30180, 6.72560* **Rheincamping Meerbusch,** Zur Rheinfähre 21, 40668 Meerbusch **(02150) 911817; info@rheincamping.com; www.rheincamping.com**

€2.80 (htd) nr

Exit A44 junc 28, turn R twd Strümp. Thro vill, turn L at sp for Kaiserswerth ferry, site on rv. Lge, pt shd, EHU (10A) €3.50; gas; bbq; 40% statics; Eng spkn; adv bkg acc; boat launch; CKE. *"Pleasant, busy, well-organised, open site with gd views of Rv Rhine; all facs up steps; ferry x-ring rv, then tram/train to Dusseldorf; ferry/tram; site may flood when rv at v high level; long lead req'd; gd NH."* **€28.00, 4 Apr-12 Oct.** **2024**

ECHTERNACHERBRUCK *3A2* (1km SW Rural) *49.81240, 6.43160* **Camping Freibad Echternacherbrück,** Mindenerstrasse 18, 54668 Echternacherbrück **(06525) 340; info@echternacherbrueck.de; www.echternacherbrueck.de**

€3.30-€4.70 (htd) nr nr (covrd, htd)

Fr Bitburg on B257/E29 site is at Lux'burg border, sp. Fr Trier take A64 dir Luxembourg; exit junc 15 onto N10 to Echternacherbrück; cross bdg dir Bitburg, then 1st L sp camping & foll sp. 4*, Lge, pt shd, EHU (10A) €2.70 + conn fee; sw nr; TV; 30% statics; Eng spkn; games area; boat hire; tennis 400m; horseriding 4km; bike hire; waterslide; CKE. *"Poss flooding in v wet weather; private bthrms avail; excel facs; o'night m'van area; gd, well-organised site; gd bus service to Luxembourg and Trier; ACSI card acc; rvside pitches lger."* **€29.00, 18 Mar-15 Oct.** **2022**

ECKERNFORDE *1D1* (12km NE Coastal) *54.50280, 9.95802* **Ostsee-Camping Gut Ludwigsburg,** Ludwigsburg 4, 24369 Waabs **(49043) 58370; info@ostseecamping-ludwigsburg.de; www.ostseecamping-ludwigsburg.de**

€2-6 adj

Fr Eckernforde take coastal rd NE, sp Ludwigsburg & Waabs. Site sp in approx 12km on R; turn R down single track rd. Site in 2km. Lge, hdstg, mkd, pt shd, EHU (16A) €3; bbq; twin axles; TV; 60% statics; Eng spkn; games area; games rm; CKE. *"Fishing in lake adj; excel san facs; horseriding & watersports adj; gd walking and cycling rtes nrby; gd site."* **€26.00, 28 Mar-1 Oct.** **2024**

EISENACH *1D4* (10km S Rural) *50.90888, 10.29916* **Campingplatz Eisenach am Altenberger See,** Am Altenberger See, 99819 Wilhelmsthal **(03692) 9798007; campingpark-eisenach@t-online.de; www.campingpark-eisenach.de**

€2

Leave E40/A4 at junc 39 Eisenach Ost onto B19 sp Meiningen; site 2km S of Wilhelmsthal, sp. Med, hdstg, pt shd, pt sl, serviced pitches; EHU (16A) inc; 80% statics; bus to Eisenach nr; ccard acc; sauna; boating; site clsd Nov; CKE. *"Helpful staff; clsd 1300-1500; conv Wartburg & Thuringer Wald, Bach & Luther houses in Eisenach; lake adj; lge carpk in town suitable for MH's."* **€25.50, 1 Jan-31 Oct & 1 Dec-31 Dec. 2023**

ERFURT *4E1* (10km NW Urban) *51.03895, 10.97870* **Campingplatz "Erfurt am See",** Steinfeld 4, 99189 Erfurt-Kühnhausen **(0176) 517 52386; mail@erfurtamsee.de; www.erfurtamsee.de**

12 (htd) adj

Fr A71 take exit 9 twds Kühnhausen. Turn L onto August-Röbling-Straße. Turn L onto Kühnhäuser Str, turn R onto Steinfeld, site on L. Med, unshd, pt sl, EHU; train 1km; CKE. *"Basic clean site bet angling & sw lakes; conv for visiting Erfurt; no laundry rm; gd site."* **€19.50 2023**

ERLANGEN *4E2* (7km NW Rural) *49.63194, 10.9425* **Camping Rangau,** Campingstrasse 44, 91056 Erlangen-Dechsendorf **(09135) 8866; infos@camping-rangau.de; www.camping-rangau.de**

€2.50 (htd) nr

Fr A3/E45 exit junc 81 & foll camp sp. At 1st traff lts turn L, strt on at next traff lts, then L at next traff lts, site sp. 4*, Med, pt shd, EHU (6A) €4.50 (long lead poss req); sw; red long stay; Eng spkn; adv bkg acc; ccard acc; boat hire; CKE. *"Gd site, espec for families; clean facs; welcoming & well-run; some sm pitches; popular NH - overflow onto adj sports field; vg, busy NH; arrive early; gates clsd 1300-1500 & 2200 hrs; dog wash facs; recep clsd 1200-1400; ltd parking on app rd."* **€30.00, 26 Mar-3 Oct. 2023**

ESSEN *1B4* (8km S Urban) *51.38444, 6.99388* **DCC Campingpark Stadtcamping,** Im Löwental 67, 45239 Essen-Werden **(0201) 492978; essen@knauscamp.de; www.knauscamp.de/essen-werden**

12

Exit A52 junc 28 onto B224 S dir Solingen. Turn R bef bdge over Rv Ruhr at traff lts & immed sharp R into Löwental, site sp. 3*, Med, mkd, hdstg, pt shd, EHU (16A) metered; gas; 95% statics; phone; Eng spkn; adv bkg acc; games area; games rm. *"Rv trips; poss ssn workers; site clsd 1300-1500 & 2130-0700; car park adj; gd."* **€27.30 2022**

FASSBERG *1D2* (6km E Rural) *52.87593, 10.22718* **Ferienpark Heidesee (Part Naturist),** Lüneburger-Heidesee, 29328 Fassberg-Oberohe **(05827) 970546; heidesee@ferienpark.de; www.campingheidesee.com**

12 €2 (htd)

Leave A7/E45 at exit 44 onto B71. Turn S to Müden, then dir Unterlüss. Foll site sp. V lge, pt shd, terr, EHU (10A) €3; gas; sw; 65% statics; Eng spkn; ccard acc; sauna; bike hire; fishing; horseriding; tennis; games rm; CKE. *"Naturist camping in sep area; long leads maybe req; pool 250m; friendly helpful staff; places of interest nrby; private bthrms avail; gd mkd cycling and walking rtes fr site."* **€21.00 2024**

"I need an on-site restaurant"

We do our best to make sure site information is correct, but it is always best to check any must-have facilities are still available or will be open during your visit.

FELDBERG *2G2* (2km NE Rural) *53.34548, 13.45626* **Camping am Bauernhof,** Hof Eichholz 1-8, 17258 Feldberg **(039831) 21084; info@campingplatz-feldberg.de; www.campingplatz-am-bauernhof.de**

12 €3 nr

Fr B198 at Möllenbeck turn dir Feldburg, thro Feldburg dir Prenzlau, site sp. 4*, Med, mkd, unshd, pt sl, EHU (16A) metered + conn fee; sw; 30% statics; fishing; CKE. *"Well-situated, vg site among lakes; many cycle paths in area."* **€18.00 2022**

FICHTELBERG *4F2* (2.5km N Rural) *50.01673, 11.85525* **Kur-Camping Fichtelsee,** Fichtelseestrasse 30, 95686 Fichtelberg **(09272) 801; info@camping-fichtelsee.de; www.camping-fichtelsee.de**

€2.50 nr nr

Exit junc 39 fr A9/E51. Foll B303 twd Marktredwitz. After Bischofsgrün take R turn sp Fichtelberg, site on L in 1km. 5*, Lge, mkd, hdstg, pt shd, pt sl, terr, EHU (16A) metered + conn fee (poss rev pol); TV; 20% statics; phone; Eng spkn; ccard acc; site clsd 7 Nov-15 Dec; dog wash; CKE. *"Gd cent for walking in pine forests round lake & winter sports; peaceful site; pool 800m; barrier clsd 1230-1430; excel san facs."* **€25.00, 1 Jan-31 Oct, 18 Dec-31 Dec. 2023**

FINSTERAU *4G3* (1km N Rural) *48.94091, 13.57180* **Camping Nationalpark-Ost,** Buchwaldstrasse 52, 94151 Finsterau **(08557) 768; berghof-frank@berghof-frank.de; www.camping-nationalpark-ost.de**

12 €2 nr

Fr B12 turn N dir Mauth. Cont to Finsterau & site 1km adj parking for National Park. Sm, pt shd, EHU (6-16A) metered + conn fee or €2.50; gas; TV; CKE. *"Gd walking & mountain biking; site in beautiful Bavarian forest."* **€17.60 2022**

GERMANY

FLENSBURG *1 D1* (7.4km S Rural) *54.74445, 9.43812* **Jarplund Campsite,** Europastrasse 80, 24976 Handewitt **(04619) 79024; campingplatz.jarplund@web.de; www.campingplatz-jarplund.de**

€1 nr nr

Due S on Flensburg on old main road to Jarplund, Oeversee. Med, mkd, hdg, pt shd, EHU 10A (€2.50); bbq; cooking facs; Eng spkn; adv bkg acc; ccard acc. *"Conv for historic Flensburg port; sm supmkt next door; pool not always filled; gd NH/short stay; gd".*
€26.00, 15 Mar-15 Nov. **2023**

FRANKFURT AM MAIN *3C2* (8km NE Rural) *50.81700, 8.46550* **Campingplatz Mainkur,** Frankfurter Landstraße 107, 63477 Maintal **(069)-412193; info@campingplatz-mainkur.de; www.campingplatz-mainkur.de**

Fr Frankfurt head NE B4 and Hanua cross over A661 and cont over 8 sets of traff lts pass car showrooms and Bauhaus on L. 100m aft flyover bear R into single track tarmac rd to site. Sp on B8/B4. Med, mkd, pt shd, bbq; 35% statics; Eng spkn; adv bkg acc; boating; lounge with sm library. *"Family run site o'looking rv; conv for Frankfurt; vg, rec."*
€28.00, 1 Apr-30 Sept. **2020**

"Satellite navigation makes touring much easier"

Remember most sat navs don't know if you're towing or in a larger vehicle – always use yours alongside maps and site directions.

FREIBURG IM BREISGAU *3B4* (21km NE Rural) *48.02318, 8.03253* **Camping Steingrubenhof,** Haldenweg 3, 79271 St Peter **(07660) 210; info@camping-steingrubenhof.de; www.camping-steingrubenhof.de**

€2.50 nr nr

Exit A5 junc 61 onto B294. Turn R sp St Peter. Steep hill to site on L at top of hill. Or fr B31 dir Donaueschingen, after 4km outside Freiburg turn N sp St Peter; by-pass vill on main rd, turn L under bdge 1st R. Fr other dir by-pass St Peter heading for Glottertal; site on R 200m after rd bdge on by-pass. Med, hdg, mkd, hdstg, unshd, terr, serviced pitches; EHU (16A) €2.50; bbq; red long stay; 70% statics; phone; Eng spkn; adv bkg acc; ccard acc; CKE. *"Peaceful site in heart of Black Forest; wonderful location; pleasant staff; immac facs; gate clsd 1200-1400 & 2200-0800; v diff to manoeuvre twin axle vans onto pitches as narr access paths; pitches are sm & few for tourers; great site."*
€25.00, 1 Jan-10 Nov & 15 Dec-31 Dec. **2024**

FREIBURG IM BREISGAU *3B4* (4km E Rural) *47.99250, 7.87330* **Camping Hirzberg,** Kartäuserstrasse 99, 79104 Freiburg-im-Breisgau **(0761) 35054; hirzburg@freiburg-camping.de; www.freiburg-camping.de**

12 €1 (htd)

Exit A5 at Freiburg-Mitte & foll B31 past town cent sp Freiburg, Titisee. Foll camping sp twd Freiburg-Ebnet, nr rocky slopes on R. Then approx 2.5km on narr, winding rd. Site on R just after start of blocks of flats on L. Med, pt shd, pt sl, terr, EHU (10A) €2.50; gas; bbq; 40% statics; bus 300m; Eng spkn; adv bkg acc; bike hire; CKE. *"Pleasant, v helpful owner; site clsd 2000 - ltd outside parking; gd cycle path & easy walk to town; busy in high ssn; clsd 1300-1500; pool 500m; excel, v clean & modern san facs; gd value rest."*
€34.50 **2023**

FREIBURG IM BREISGAU *3B4* (11km SE Rural) *47.96015, 7.95001* **Camping Kirchzarten,** Dietenbacherstrasse 17, 79199 Kirchzarten **(07661) 9040910; info@camping-kirchzarten.de; www.camping-kirchzarten.de**

12 €2.50 (htd) nr nr

Sp fr Freiburg-Titisee rd 31; into Kirchzarten; site sp fr town cent. 5*, Lge, mkd, pt shd, serviced pitches; EHU (16A) €2.50 or metered; bbq; red long stay; 20% statics; train 500m; Eng spkn; adv bkg rec; ccard acc; tennis adj; CKE. *"Gd size pitches; choose pitch then register at office (clse fr 1200-1400); spacious, well-kept site; office clsd 1300-1430; Quickstop o'night area; excel san facs; gd rest; 3 htd pools adj; winter sports area; site fees inc free bus & train travel in Black Forest region; helpful staff; dogs not acc Jul/Aug."*
€35.00 **2022**

FREIBURG IM BREISGAU *3B4* (5km SE Urban) *47.98126, 7.88127* **Busses Camping am Möslepark,** Waldseestrasse 77, 79117 Freiburg-im-Breisgau **(0761) 7679333; info@camping-freiburg.com; camping-freiburg.com**

€1.90 nr nr

Fr A5 exit junc 62 onto B31 & foll sp Freiburg strt thro city sp Donauschingen. Bef ent to tunnel take L lane & foll site sp (do not go thro tunnel). Site nr Möselpark Sports Stadium. When sps run out, cross level x-ing and turn L. 3*, Med, shd, pt sl, EHU (16A) €2.50; tram to city nr; Eng spkn; ccard acc; tennis 1km; sauna; bike hire; CKE. *"Conv Freiburg & Black Forest (footpath adj); wooded site easily reached fr a'bahn; clsd 1200-1430 & 2200-0800 - waiting area in front of site; o'night m'van area; excel, modern san facs; noise fr stadium adj; public transport tickets fr recep; parking nr tram stop; v helpful staff; red CC Members."*
€34.50, 1 Mar-18 Dec. **2024**

FREUDENSTADT *3C3* (8km ENE Rural) *48.48011, 8.5005* **Höhencamping Königskanzel,** Freizeitweg 1, 72280 Dornstetten-Hallwangen **(07443) 6730; info@camping-koenigskanzel.de; www.camping-koenigskanzel.de**

12 €2.50 (htd)

Fr Freudenstadt head E on rte 28 foll sp Stuttgart for 7km. Camping sp on R, sharp R turn foll sp, sharp L on narr, winding track to site in 200m. Fr Nagold on R28, 7km fr Freudenstadt fork L; sp as bef. NB: 1st sharp R turn is v sharp - take care. Med, hdg, pt shd, pt sl, terr, serviced pitches; EHU (10A) metered; gas; bbq; red long stay; 60% statics; phone; Eng spkn; adv bkg req; site clsd 3 Nov-15 Dec; golf 7km; sauna; bike hire; CKE. *"Pleasant owners; friendly welcome; excel shwr facs, inc for dogs; well run family site; hill top location with gd views of Black Forest; bkg fee; ski lift 7km; recep clsd 1300-1400; excel value rest."* **€30.40** **2024**

FREUDENSTADT *3C3* (5km W Rural) *48.45840, 8.37255* **Camping Langenwald,** Strassburgerstrasse 167, 72250 Freudenstadt-Langenwald **(07441) 2862; info@camping-langenwald.de; www.camping-langenwald.de**

€3 (htd) (htd)

Foll sp fr town on B28 dir Strassburg. 5*, Med, pt shd, terr, serviced pitches; EHU (16A) metered; gas; red long stay; 10% statics; Eng spkn; ccard acc; bike hire; golf 4km; CKE. *"Gd, clean san facs & site; woodland walks fr site; gd rest; friendly owners."* **€39.50, 26 Mar-1 Nov.** **2022**

> **"There aren't many sites open at this time of year"**
>
> If you're travelling outside peak season remember to call ahead to check site opening dates – even if the entry says 'open all year'.

FRICKENHAUSEN AM MAIN *3D2* (1km W Rural) *49.66916, 10.07444* **Knaus Campingpark Frickenhausen,** Ochsenfurterstrasse 49, 97252 Frickenhausen/Ochsenfurt **(09331) 3171; info@knauscamp.de; www.knauscamp.de**

12 €3 (htd)

Turn off B13 at N end of bdge over Rv Main in Ochsenfurt & foll camping sp. 4*, Lge, hdg, mkd, pt shd, serviced pitches; EHU (16A) €2.40 or metered; gas; red long stay; TV; 40% statics; Eng spkn; adv bkg acc; bike hire. *"Vg, well-managed site on rv island; excel, clean facs; located on Romantischestrasse with many medieval vills; site clsd 1300-1500; v clean, cared for site; gd rest; friendly staff; gd sized pitches; site clsed bet 1-3pm."* **€48.20** **2023**

FRIEDRICHSHAFEN *3D4* (8km W Rural) *47.66896, 9.40253* **Camping Fischbach,** Grenzösch 3, 88048 Friedrichshafen-Fischbach **(07541) 42059; info@camping-fischbach.de; www.camping-fischbach.de**

sand adj

Take B31 fr Friedrichshafen to Meersburg. Site sp on L at end of vill. Turning lane avail for easy access off busy rd. 3*, Med, mkd, hdstg, pt shd, EHU (10-16A) €2 (poss rev pol); sw nr; 40% statics; phone; Eng spkn; CKE. *"Tranquil, relaxing site; some lake view pitches, worth the extra; excel, clean, modern san facs; ferries to Konstanz nrby; Zeppelin/Dornier museums nrby; cr; on Lake Constance cycle rte."* **€30.50, 6 Apr-8 Oct.** **2023**

FRIESOYTHE *1C2* (13km SE Rural) *52.93703, 7.92923* **Campingplatz Wilken,** Thülsfelder Str. 3, 26169 Friesoythe **(04495) 9219150; info@camping-wilken.de; www.camping-wilken.de**

12 (htd)

Fr B72 Cloppenburg-Friesoythe. After 13km turn L onto Thülsfelder Straße. Site next to Thülsfeld Reservoir on L. Lge, mkd, hdstg, unshd, EHU (16A) metered. *"Excel site for long stay; spacious pitches; v clean san facs; would rec."* **€13.50** **2024**

FUSSEN *4E4* (6km N Rural) *47.61553, 10.7230* **Camping Magdalena am Forggensee,** Bachtalstrasse 10, 87669 Osterreinen **(08362) 4931; info@sonnen-lage.de; www.sonnen-lage.de**

€3

Fr Füssen take rd 16 sp Kaufbeuren & Forggensee for 5km; R sp Osterreinen for 500m; L at T-junc foll site sp; site on R in 50m; app rd steep with sharp bends. Site well sp. 3*, Med, mkd, hdg, pt shd, terr, EHU (10A) metered + conn fee; gas; 40% statics; Eng spkn; adv bkg rec; sailing; watersports; CKE. *"Ltd touring pitches; superb views over lake; peaceful; gd site; sm pitches; conv for Zugspitze, Royal Castles, Oberammergau; lakeside cycle track to Füssen & to Neuschwanstein Castle."* **€23.90, 1 Apr-31 Oct.** **2024**

FUSSEN *4E4* (6km NE Rural) *47.59638, 10.73861* **Camping Brunnen,** Seestrasse 81, 87645 Brunnen **(08362) 8273; info@camping-brunnen.de; www.camping-brunnen.de**

12 €4.50 nr nr adj

S on rte 17 twd Füssen turn R in vill of Schwangau N to Brunnen; turn R at ent to vill at Spar shop, site clearly sp. Fr Füssen N on B17; turn L in Schwangau; well sp on lakeside. 5*, Lge, mkd, hdstg, pt shd, pt sl, serviced pitches; EHU (10-16A) metered + conn fee; gas; sw nr; bus; Eng spkn; adv bkg acc; ccard acc; bike hire; golf 3km; site clsd 5 Nov-20 Dec; CKE. *"Lovely location, next to lake; o'fits poss tightly packed; steel pegs ess; excel san facs; some pitches cramped; gd for Royal castles; gd cycle rtes; 10% red visits to Neuschwanstein Castle nrby; gates clsd 2200-0700; excel, busy, vg site; yachting in Lake Forggensee adj; handy rest, supmkt & g'ge."* **€38.00** **2024**

FUSSEN *4E4* (5km NW Rural) *47.60198, 10.68333* **Camping Hopfensee,** Fischerbichl 17/Uferstrasse, 87629 Hopfen-am-See **(08362) 917710; info@camping-hopfensee.de; www.camping-hopfensee.com**

€4.15 (covrd, htd)

Fr Füssen N on B16 twd Kaufbeuren in 2km L on rd sp Hopfen-am-See, site at ent to vill on L thro c'van car park. 5*, Lge, hdstg, mkd, pt shd, serviced pitches; EHU (16A) metered; gas; sw nr; free bus to Fussen; Eng spkn; adv bkg rec; sauna; boating; fishing; CKE. *"Gd location; excel facs; helpful staff; gd rest on site; no tents allowed except for awnings; tight squeeze in high ssn; vans need manhandling; fitness cent; solarium; winter sports area; gd walking & cycling; lakeside pitches rec; excel; highly rec; 5 star facs; WiFi €2 per day, recep clsd 12-2pm."* **€46.70, 1 Jan-6 Nov & 15 Dec-31 Dec. 2023**

FUSSEN *4E4* (6km NW Rural) *47.60883, 10.66918* **Haus Guggemos,** Uferstrasse 42, 87629 Hopfen-am-See **(08362) 3334; haus.guggemos@t-online.de; www.haus-guggemos.de**

€2 nr nr nr

Fr Füssen take B16 N dir Kaufbeuren; in 2km turn L sp Hopfen-am-See. Drive thro vill; site on R opp lake. Sm, hdstg, pt shd, EHU (10A) metered; sw nr; bus adj; Eng spkn; adv bkg acc; CKE. *"Excel, family-run, farm site in beautiful area; views across lake to Alps."* **€16.00, 1 Apr-31 Oct. 2024**

GANDERKESEE *1C2* (7km W Rural) *53.04666, 8.46388* **Ferienpark Falkensteinsee,** Am Falkensteinsee 1, 27777 Ganderkesee-Steinkimmen **(04222) 9470077; camping@falkensteinsee.de; www.falkensteinsee.de**

€1.50 nr

Exit A28/E22 junc 18 dir Habbrügge. Site on R in 2km. 4*, Lge, pt shd, EHU (16A) €3.50 or metered; sw nr; 70% statics; Eng spkn; golf 8km; sauna; CKE. *"Conv Oldenburg & Bremen; new owners; completely refurb (2015); lake sw with 2 sandy beaches; pleasant holiday park; well organised; o'night m'van area; friendly staff; sep naturist beach; new facs & v high quality; excel; sep sw area for dogs."* **€21.50 2022**

GARMISCH PARTENKIRCHEN *4E4* (4km W Rural) *47.4798, 11.05331* **Campingplatz Zugspitze,** Griesenerstrasse 9, 82491 Garmisch-Grainau **(08821) 9439115; office@perfect-camping.de; www.perfect-camping.de/5-sterne-camping-resort-zugspitze-garmisch-partenkirchen-bayern**

€7 (htd) nr nr nr

Fr Garmisch-Partenkirchen on rd 23 dir Griesen, site sp. 1*, Sm, hdg, pt shd, serviced pitches; EHU (16A) metered; adv bkg acc; ccard acc; CKE. *"Conv Oberammergau, Zugspitze & castles; cycle track to Garmisch; facs clean but need refurb; ski lift 2.5km; htd pool 2km; pitching haphazard & site becoming run down; sh stays sited adj noisy rd; vg."* **€60.00 2023**

GARTOW *2E2* (4km NW Rural) *53.03972, 11.41583* **Camping Laascher See,** Ortsteil Laasche 13, 29471 Gartow **(05846) 342; pewsdorf@campingplatz-laascher-see.de; www.elbtalaue-camping.de**

€1.50 nr nr

Fr S on B493 to Gartow, turn N on L256 (Rondelerstrasse) dir Gartower See & Laasche See, site sp on R. Or E fr Dennenberg on L256 dir Gorleben & Gartow, site sp approx 5km after Gorleben. Med, hdg, pt shd, pt sl, EHU (6A) inc; sw nr; 60% statics; adv bkg acc; CKE. *"Pleasant owners; clean, modern san facs; vg."* **€19.50, 1 Apr-31 Oct. 2022**

GEESTHACHT *1D2* (9km SW Rural) *53.42465, 10.29470* **Campingplatz Stover Strand International,** Stover Strand 10, 21423 Drage **(04177) 430; info@camping-stover-strand.de; www.camping-stover-strand.de**

€2 (htd)

Fr N on A25 to Geesthacht, then B404 dir Winsen to Stove. Site at end Stover Strand on banks of Rv Elbe. Fr S on A7 to Maschen, then A250 to Winsen then B404, as above. 5*, V lge, mkd, pt shd, EHU (6-16A) €2 or metered; bbq; cooking facs; sw; 80% statics; adv bkg acc; ccard acc; bike hire; fishing; games area; watersports; CKE. *"Excel rvside site; marina; site clsd 1300-1500; Hamburg Card avail."* **€20.00 2020**

GEMUNDEN AM MAIN *3D2* (5km W Rural) *50.05260, 9.65656* **Spessart-Camping Schönrain,** Schönrainstrasse 4-18, 97737 Gemünden-Hofstetten **(09351) 8645; info @spessart-camping.de; www.spessart-camping.de**

€2.80 (htd)

Rd B26 to Gemünden, cross Rv Main & turn R dir Hofstetten, site sp. 5*, Lge, hdg, mkd, hdstg, pt shd, terr, EHU (10A) metered + conn fee €2.15; TV; 50% statics; phone; Eng spkn; bike hire; sauna; fitness rm; solarium; games area; CKE. *"Clean, well-kept, wooded site; interesting towns nrby; variable pitch sizes/prices; excel; v well kept new facs block; welcoming."* **€25.00, 1 Apr-30 Sep. 2024**

GERSFELD (RHON) *3D2* (2.5km N Rural) *50.46223, 9.91953* **Camping Hochrhön,** Schachen 13, 36129 Gersfeld-Schachen **(06654) 7836; info@camping-hochrhoen.de; www.rhoenline.de/camping-hochrhoen**

nr nr

Exit A7 exit Fulda-Süd S onto B27/B279 to Gersfeld, then B284 sp Ehrenberg, Turn L dir Schachen, foll sp to site. 3*, Med, hdg, mkd, hdstg, pt shd, EHU (16A) metered; 10% statics; CKE. *"Conv for gliding & air sports at Wasswerkuppe; ski lift 3km; friendly."* **€18.00 2020**

GLUCKSBURG (OSTSEE) *1D1* (6km NE Coastal) *54.85901, 9.59109* **Ostseecamp,** An der Promenade 1, 24960 Glücksburg-Holnis **(04631) 622071; info@ostseecamp-holnis.de; www.ostseecamp-holnis.de**

€2.50 (htd) nr sand adj

Fr Flensburg on rd 199 turn off thro Glücksburg & further 6km to Holnis. 4*, Med, mkd, hdstg, pt shd, EHU (16A) €3; bbq; cooking facs; 30% statics; adv bkg acc; windsurfing 1km; fishing; bike hire; CKE. *"Lovely coastal loc; v friendly staff; clean facs."* **€29.00, 28 Mar-16 Oct.** **2022**

GOPPINGEN *3D3* (13.5km SW Rural) *48.63946, 9.55508* **Campingplatz Aichelberg,** Bunzenberg 1, 73101 Aichelberg **(07164) 2700; mail@camping-aichelberg.de; camping-aichelberg.de**

€2 nr

Exit E52/A8 junc 58 sp Aichelberg-Goppingen & foll sp to camp site in 1km. 3*, Med, pt shd, EHU (10A) €2; 80% statics; adv bkg acc. *"Fills up after 1600 hrs but gd overflow field with EHU for NH; family-run site; new excel facs; owner helpful; nr A8; gd conv NH."* **€26.00, 7 Apr-8 Oct.** **2023**

GOSLAR *1D3* (4km SW Rural) *51.88958, 10.39889* **Harz Camp Goslar (formerly Sennhütte),** Clausthalerstrasse 28, 38644 Goslar **(05321) 22502; info@harz-camp-goslar.de; www.campingplatz-goslar.de**

12

Fr Goslar on B241 twd Clausthal, Zellerfeld site on R in 2km. Ent thro car pk of Hotel Sennhütte. 2*, Med, pt shd, EHU (16A) metered + €2 conn fee (poss long lead req); 30% statics; bus at ent to town; ccard acc. *"Gd NH/sh stay nr beautiful town; neat, modern, well organised site; gd rest, san facs, WiFi; redeveloped in 2020; in Harz Mountains; attractive villages in area; rec; vg."* **€29.40** **2023**

GRAFENDORF *3D2* (11km SE Rural) *50.10678, 9.78241* **Camping Rossmühle,** Rossmühle 7, 97782 Gräfendorf-Weickersgrüben **(09357) 1210; www.campingplatz-rossmuehle.de**

12 €2

Exit A7 junc 96 onto B27 sp Karlstadt. At Hammelburg foll sps to Gräfendorf & site in 8km on rvside, beyond Weickersgrüben. 3*, Lge, mkd, pt shd, terr, EHU (6-10A) €2; TV; 50% statics; adv bkg acc; bike hire; canoe hire; watersports; solarium. *"Poss liable to flooding after heavy rain; o'night m'vans area; clean san facs; fitness rm; excel; cycle rte tourers sep fr statics."* **€18.00** **2020**

GREFRATH *1A4* (4km N Rural) *51.36492, 6.32328* **Campingplatz Waldfrieden,** An der Paas 13, 47929 Grefrath-Vinkrath **(02158) 3855; info@ferienpark-waldfrieden.de; www.ferienpark-waldfrieden.de**

12 €2 (htd) nr

Fr A40-E34 S to Duisburg; turn S at exit 3 sp Grefrath; site sp on L in 3km; 1km down side rd beside Am Blumenfeld. 4*, Lge, hdg, hdstg, pt shd, EHU (10A) €3.50; gas; sw nr; 80% statics; Eng spkn; CKE. *"Conv NH North Sea ports; WWII cemetaries at Reichswald; sw pools 1.5km; site over-used & weary; site clsd 1300-1500."* **€25.00** **2023**

"That's changed – Should I let the Club know?"

If you find something on site that's different from the site entry, fill in a report and let us know. See camc.com/europereport.

GREIFSWALD *2G1* (16km NE Coastal) *54.12666, 13.52196* **Campingplatz Loissin (Part Naturist),** 17509 Loissin **(038352) 243; kontakt@campingplatz-loissin.de; www.campingplatz-loissin.de**

€2 sand adj

Fr Greifswald E to Kemnitz, then head N twds Loissin; site on coast N, well sp fr the vill. 3*, Lge, mkd, pt shd, EHU (16A) inc; 40% statics; adv bkg acc; games area; windsurfing; clsd 1300-1430 & 2200-0800; bike hire; CKE. *"Vg site; approx 40km to foot x-ing fr car park to Poland for shopping; excel san facs; sep naturist beach; main attraction is immed proximity to sea."* **€32.00, 1 Apr-31 Oct.** **2023**

GREVEN *1B3* (6km SW Rural) *52.08328, 7.55806* **Campingplatz Westheide,** Altenbergerstrasse 23, 48268 Greven **(02571) 560701; kontakt@campingplatz-westheide.de; www.campingplatz-westheide.de**

12 €1 (htd) sand adj

Exit A1 junc 76 onto B481 around E side of Greven, then turn L onto B219 for 2km. Turn R onto L555 Nordwalderstrasse & in 2km at Westerode turn L into Altenbergerstrasse, site on L in 1km. Med, hdg, pt shd, EHU (16A) metered; 80% statics; ccard acc; games rm; fishing; CKE. *"Gd for sh stay; lake adj; walks around lake."* **€18.00** **2022**

GYHUM *1D2* (4km SE Rural) *53.19308, 9.33638* **Waldcamping Hesedorf,** Zum Waldbad 3, 27404 Gyhum-Hesedorf **(04286) 2252; info@waldcamping-hesedorf.de; www.waldcamping-hesedorf.de**

12 €0.50 (htd) nr

Exit A1/E22 junc 49 in dir Zeven. In 1km turn R sp Gyhum & foll site sp to Hesedorf. Med, unshd, EHU (16A) inc; 70% statics; Eng spkn; CKE. *"Clean, well-kept site; attractive area; htd pool 150m inc; gd rest; lge sep area for tourers; barrier clsd 1300-1500; dated san facs but clean; gd NH."* **€20.00** **2024**

GERMANY

HALBERSTADT *2E3* (3km NE Rural) *51.90981, 11.0827* **Camping am See (Part Naturist),** Warmholzberg 70, 38820 Halberstadt **(03941) 609308 or (01768) 4042782; info@camping-am-see.de; www.camping-am-see.de**

12 €2

Sp on B81 (Halberstadt-Magdeburg). Med, unshd, terr, EHU (10A) metered + conn fee €2.50 (poss rev pol); sw nr; 75% statics; sep car park; CKE. *"Conv Harz mountains & Quedlinburg (770 houses classified as historic monuments by UNESCO); quiet, green site; sep naturist beach; some individual shwrs; pool adj; clsd 1300-1500."* **€34.00** **2024**

HAMBURG *1D2* (7km NW Urban) *53.5900, 9.93083* **Campingplatz Buchholz,** Keilerstrasse 374, 22525 Hamburg-Stellingen **(040) 5404532; info@camping-buchholz.de; www.camping-buchholz.de**

12 €4 nr nr

Exit A7/E45 junc 26 & foll dir 'Innenstadt' - city cent. Site sp in 600m on L. Sm, mkd, hdg, hdstg, pt shd, EHU (16A) €4; 10% statics; bus, train nr; adv bkg acc. *"Fair NH nr a'bahn & Hamburg cent; conv transport to city - tickets fr recep; friendly management; sm pitches; busy site, rec arr early; diff access for lge o'fits."* **€35.00** **2024**

HAMBURG *1D2* (9km NW Urban) *53.64916, 9.92970* **Knaus Campingpark Hamburg,** Wunderbrunnen 2, 22457 Hamburg **(040) 5594225; hamburg@knauscamp.de; www.knauscamp.de/hamburg**

12 €3.50 nr

Heading N on A7 exit junc 23 to Schnelsen Nord; L at traff lts, foll sp Ikea & site behind Ikea. 4*, Med, mkd, pt shd, EHU (6A) inc; TV; phone; bus to city; Eng spkn; ccard acc; CKE. *"Useful NH; helpful staff; stn adj; gates clsd 2200 hrs & 1300-1600 LS; elec pylons & cables cross site; deposit for key to san facs & el box; 3-day Hamburg card excel value."* **€43.50** **2024**

HAMELN *1D3* (2km W Urban) *52.10916, 9.3475* **Campingplatz Hameln An Der Weser (formerly zum Fährhaus),** Uferstrasse 80, 31787 Hameln **(05151) 67489; info@campingplatz-hameln.de; www.campingplatz-hameln.de**

€1 (htd) nr

Fr A2/E30 at Bad Eilsen junc 35 onto B83 to Hameln on NE side of Rv Weser; in town foll sp Detmold/ Paderborn; cross bdge to SW side (use Thiewall Brücke); turn R on minor rd twd Rinteln; foll site sp. 3*, Med, unshd, EHU (10-16A); 20% statics; phone; clsd 1300-1430; CKE. *"Picturesque & historic district; open-air performance of Pied Piper in town on Sun to mid-Sep; sm pitches & poss uneven; helpful, lovely owner; san facs refurb, best in Europe!(2017); gd cycle paths by rv to town; site beautifully kept."* **€34.50, 1 Mar-4 Nov.** **2023**

HAMELN *1D3* (8km W Rural) *52.10725, 9.29588* **Camping am Waldbad,** Pferdeweg 2, 31787 Halvestorf **(05158) 2774; hello@campingamwaldbad.de; www.campingamwaldbad.de**

nr (htd)

Fr Hameln on B83 dir Rinteln. In approx 10km turn L, cross rv & foll sp Halvestorf & site. 4*, Med, unshd, pt sl, EHU (16A) €2; 80% statics; adv bkg acc. *"Pleasant site - better than site in Hameln; gd facs."* **€26.50, 1 Apr-31 Oct.** **2023**

HAMM *1B3* (13km E Rural) *51.6939, 7.9710* **Camping Uentrop,** Dolbergerstrasse 80, 59510 Lippetal-Lippborg **(02388) 437 or (0172) 2300747; info@camping-helbach.de; www.camping-helbach.de**

12 €2 (htd) nr nr

Exit A2/E34 junc 19, site sp; behind Hotel Helbach 1km fr a'bahn. 3*, Lge, pt shd, pt sl, EHU (16A) €2; gas; 90% statics; Eng spkn; ccard acc. *"Friendly; gd security; barrier clsd 1300-1500 & 2200-0500; fair NH."* **€18.00** **2022**

HAMMELBACH *3C2* (0.6km S Rural) *49.63277, 8.83000* **Camping Park Hammelbach,** Gasse 17, 64689 Grasellenbach/Hammelbach **(06253) 3831; info@camping-hammelbach.de; www.camping-hammelbach.de**

€2.50 (htd) nr nr nr

Exit A5/E35 exit junc 31 onto B460 E. Turn S in Weschnitz to Hammelbach & foll site sp. 5*, Med, hdg, pt shd, EHU (16A) metered; gas; bbq; 70% statics; bus 300m; Eng spkn; adv bkg acc, ccard acc; CKE. *"Excel family run site with views; sauna adj; v pleasant, helpful staff; red for snrs; conv Heidelberg; immac hotel like san facs; htd pool 300m; well up to CC standards."* **€24.50, 1 Apr-31 Oct.** **2024**

HANNOVER *1D3* (14km NE Urban) *52.45383, 9.85611* **Campingplatz Parksee Lohne,** Alter Postweg 12, 30916 Isernhagen **05139 88260; parksee-lohne@t-online.de; www.parksee-lohne.de**

(htd)

Fr A2 take exit 46 to Altwarmbüchen. Cont onto K114, turn R onto Alter Postweg & foll sp to campsite. V lge, pt shd, cooking facs; 95% statics; Eng spkn. *"Vg site; next to golf course; excel san facs; narr cobbled rd 1/2 m; under flight path, but quiet at night."* **€29.60, 1 Apr-15 Oct.** **2024**

HANNOVER *1D3* (16km SE Rural) *52.30447, 9.86216* **Camping Birkensee,** 30880 Laatzen **(0511) 529962; info@camping-birkensee.de; www.camping-laatzen.de**

12 €2.50 (covrd)

Fr N leave A7 junc 59 dir Laatzen, turn R, then turn L & site well sp on L after traff lts. Fr S exit junc 60 twd Laatzen, site sp on L on lakeside. 3*, Lge, pt shd, EHU (10A) €2.50 (poss rev pol); sw; 60% statics; Eng spkn; fishing; games area; sauna; CKE. *"Gd, clean facs; sm touring area; site needs TLC; v helpful staff."* **€27.00** **2024**

HANNOVER *1D3* (10km S Rural) *52.30133, 9.74716* **Campingplatz Arnumer See,** Osterbruchweg 5, 30966 Hemmingen-Arnum **(05101) 3534; info@camping-hannover.de; www.camping-hannover.de**

12 €1.50 (htd) WD MSP nr

Leave A7 junc 59 onto B443 dir Pattensen, then B3 dir Hannover. Site sp in Hemmingen dir Wilkenburg. 4*, Lge, hdg, mkd, pt shd, EHU (16A) €3; gas; cooking facs; sw; 95% statics; bus to Hannover 1.5km; tennis; fishing; bike hire; CKE. *"Friendly staff; excel, modern, clean san facs; sm area for tourers - gd size open pitches; gd lake sw & boating; insect repellent ess!"* **€31.00** **2024**

HANNOVER *1D3* (16km NW Rural) *52.42083, 9.54638* **Camping Blauer See,** Am Blauen See 119, 30823 Garbsen **(05137) 89960; info@camping-blauer-see.de; www.camping-blauer-see.de**

12 €2.50 (htd) WD MSP

Fr W exit A2 at junc 41 onto Garbsen rest area. Thro service area, at exit turn R, at T-junc turn R (Alt Garbson). All sp with int'l camp sp. Fr E exit junc 40, cross a'bahn & go back to junc 41, then as above. Lge, hdstg, pt shd, serviced pitches; EHU (16A) €2.70; gas; bbq; sw nr; 90% statics; phone; bus to Hannover 1.5km; Eng spkn; ccard acc; watersports adj; CKE. *"Excel san facs; well-organised site; helpful staff; conv bus/train to Hannover; barrier clsd 2300-0500 & 1300-1500; rec pitch by lake."* **€29.00** **2024**

HANNOVERSCH MUNDEN *1D4* (0.9km W Rural) *51.41666, 9.64750* **Campingplatz Hann-Münden (formerly Grüne Insel Tanzwerder),** Tanzwerder 1, 34346 Hannoversch-Münden **(05541) 12257; www.camping-und-kanu.de**

€2 WD MSP nr nr nr

A7/E45 exit junc 76 onto B496 to Hann-Münden. Cross bdge & site sp on an island on Rv Fulda next to town cent. App over narr swing bdge. Fr junc 75 foll sp to Hann-Münden. At Aral g'ge in town take next L & foll sp to site (sp Weserstein). 3*, Med, mkd, pt shd, EHU (16A) metered + conn fee; red long stay; Eng spkn; adv bkg acc; CKE. *"Pleasant, well looked after site on island bordered by rv both sides; noisy bdge traff; easy stroll to historic old town."* **€32.00, 1 Apr-16 Oct.** **2022**

HATTINGEN *1B4* (3km NW Urban) *51.40611, 7.17027* **Camping Ruhrbrücke,** Ruhrstrasse 6, 45529 Hattingen **(02324) 80038; info@camping-hattingen.de; www.camping-hattingen.de**

€2 (htd) WD nr nr nr

Fr A40 bet Essen & Bochum exit junc 29 dir Höntrop & Hattingen. Foll sp Hattingen on L651 & B1, site sp bef rv bdge. 3*, Med, unshd, pt sl, EHU (16A) €3; bbq; sw nr; phone; bus, train adj; Eng spkn; adv bkg acc; windsurfing adj; canoeing adj; CKE. *"Beautiful rvside setting; plentiful, clean facs; friendly owner; excel cycle tracks."* **€18.00, 1 Apr-20 Oct.** **2022**

HAUSEN IM TAL *3C4* (0.1km E Rural) *48.08365, 9.04290* **Camping Wagenburg,** Kirchstr. 24, 88631 Beuron / i Tal Hausen **(07579) 559; info@camping-wagenburg.de; www.camping-wagenburg.de**

€1.50 WD MSP nr nr

Fr E on B32 stay on Sigmaringen bypass and take minor rd L227 sp Gutenstein/Beuron to Hausen, site in vill beside Rv Donau. 3*, Med, hdstg, pt shd, EHU (16A) metered + conn fee; sw nr; red long stay; TV; Eng spkn; adv bkg acc; tennis 300m. *"Beautiful location in Danube Gorge; friendly, helpful owner; clsd 1230-1430; poss flooding in wet weather/high rv level; gd walking/cycling; vg; excel site gd for walking cycling; rv canoeing."* **€26.00, 30 Apr-22 Sep.** **2020**

HEIDELBERG *3C2* (10km E Rural) *49.40175, 8.77916* **Campingplatz Haide,** Ziegelhäuser Landstrasse 91, 69151 Neckargemünd **(06223) 2111; info@camping-haide.de; www.camping-haide.de**

€2 WD MSP nr

Take B37 fr Heidelberg, cross Rv Neckar by Ziegelhausen bdge by slip rd on R (avoid vill narr rd); foll site sp. Site on R bet rv & rd 1km W of Neckergemünd on rvside. Lge, hdstg, unshd, EHU (6A) €2.50 (long lead req); bbq; 5% statics; Eng spkn; bike hire; CKE. *"Conv Neckar Valley & Heidelberg; some rd, rlwy (daytime) & rv noise; NH/sh stay only; long attractive site along rv."* **€20.30, 1 Apr-31 Oct.** **2022**

HEIDELBERG *3C2* (12km E Urban) *49.39638, 8.79472* **Campingplatz an der Friedensbrücke,** Falltorstrasse 4, 69151 Neckargemünd **(06223) 2178; info@camping-bei-heidelberg.de; www.campingplatz-am-neckar.de**

€1.50 (htd) WD MSP nr

Exit Heidelberg on S side of rv on B37; on ent Neckargemünd site sp to L (grey sp) mkd Poststrasse; site adj rv bdge. Fr S on B45 turn L sp Heidelberg, then R at camping sp. Fr A6 exit junc 33 onto B45 sp Neckargemünd, then as above. Foll sp - do not foll sat nav. 4*, Lge, unshd, EHU (6-16A) €5 or metered (poss rev pol); gas; TV; phone; Eng spkn; adv bkg acc; tennis. *"Gd location by busy rv, poss liable to flood; immac, well-run, relaxing site; ask for rvside pitch (sm) - extra charge; transport to Heidelberg by boat, bus & train 10 mins walk fr site; owner will site o'fits; warm welcome; helpful staff; kayaking 500m; no plastic grndsheets; 26 steps up to main san facs; pool adj; gd rvside walks & cycling; TO 500m; gd NH facs, nr ent; recep clsd 1-3pm; Wifi €2 per day."* **€28.00, 1 Apr-15 Oct.** **2023**

HEIDENAU *1D2* (2.6km W Rural) *53.30851, 9.62038* **Ferienzentrum Heidenau,** Minkens Fuhren, 21258 Heidenau **(04182) 4272 or 4861; info@ferienzentrum-heidenau.de; www.ferienzentrum-heidenau.de**

12 (htd) WD MSP (htd)

Exit A1 Hamburg-Bremen m'way junc 46 to Heidenau; foll sp. 4*, Lge, pt shd, EHU (16A) €2.50 (poss long lead req); bbq (sep area); 75% statics; phone; Eng spkn; sauna; cycling; games area; tennis; lake fishing; CKE. *"Pleasant, wooded site; tourers on grass areas by lakes; clean, modern facs; ltd shop; gd; visa ccards not acc; pitches maybe unusable in v wet weather."* **€26.00** **2022**

HERBOLZHEIM *3B3* (2km E Rural) *48.21625, 7.78796* **Terrassen-Campingplatz Herbolzheim,** Laue-Dietweg 1, 79336 Herbolzheim **(07643) 1460; s.hugoschmidt@t-online.de; www.laue-camp.de**

€2 (not acc mid-Jul to mid-Aug) WD MSP

Fr E35/A5 exit 58 to Herbolzheim. Turn R in vill. Turn L on o'skts of vill. Site in 1km next to sw pool, sp. 4*, Med, pt shd, terr, EHU (10A) €2; red long stay; 30% statics; adv bkg acc; ccard acc; tennis nr; CKE. *"Excel friendly, well-maintained site; o'nights facs for m'vans; conv Vosges, Black Forest & Europapark; clsd 1300-1500; ACSI; gd simple rest, spotless and supmkt nrby, excel staff; immac grass on firm base."* **€30.00, 23 Mar-3 Oct.** **2024**

HIRSCHAU *4F2* (6km E Rural) *49.55608, 12.00634* **Campingplatz am Naturbad,** Badstrasse 13, 92253 Schnaittenbach **(09622) 1722 or (09622) 70250; info@campingplatz.schnaittenbach.de; www.schnaittenbach.de**

WD nr nr

On B14 bet Rosenberg & Wernberg, clearly sp in vill. 3*, Med, unshd, sl, EHU (16A) €1.50 or metered + conn fee; 80% statics; games area; CKE. *"Gd NH; scenic area; v pleasant site."* **€17.50, 1 Apr-30 Sep.** **2024**

HOCHDONN *1D1* (1.5km E Rural) *54.02395, 9.29381* **Campingplatz Klein Westerland,** Zur Holstenau 1, 25712 Hochdonn **04948 252345; info@campingplatz-klein-westerland.de; www.campingplatz-klein-westerland.de**

€1.50

Fr A23, take exit 5 to Süderhastedt. Turn L on 431 to Hochdonn. Site sp. Canal ferry maybe diff for trailer c'vans, steep ramps. Med, pt shd, EHU; 70% statics; gd. *"Interesting canal traff & lge locks at Brunsbüttel, 20km S; noisy, passing ships; only site on the Northsea-Baltic sea canal."* **€18.00, 1 Apr-31 Oct.** **2022**

HOF *4F2* (10km NW Rural) *50.37494, 11.83804* **Camping Auensee,** 95189 Joditz-Köditz **(09295) 381; rathaus@gemeinde-koeditz.de; www.auensee-camping.de**

12 €1.50 MSP nr

Exit A9 at junc 31 Berg/Bad Steben. Turn R fr m'way & in 200m L to Joditz, foll site sp in vill (1-way ent/exit to site). 3*, Med, unshd, terr, EHU (16A) €1.80 or metered; sw; 75% statics; tennis; fishing; clsd 1230-1500; CKE. **€20.30** **2022**

HOHENSTADT *3D3* (0.5km NE Rural) *48.54693, 9.66794* **Camping Waldpark Hohenstadt,** Waldpark 1, 73345 Hohenstadt **(07335) 6754; camping@waldpark-hohenstadt.de; www.waldpark-hohenstadt.de**

€1 (htd) WD MSP (htd)

Exit A8/E52 junc 60 Behelfs & foll sp to Hohenstadt & site in approx 5km. Med, hdstg, pt shd, pt sl, EHU (16a) €2.50; bbq; 75% statics; Eng spkn; CKE. *"Gd, peaceful NH to/fr Austria; handy off A8 - conv for mway; helpful & friendly staff; gd facs; long walk to shwrs fr tourer parking; lovely site; area ideal for walking, cycling, climbing, skiing and cross country skiing; excel."* **€27.50, 1 Mar-31 Oct.** **2024**

HOOKSIEL *1C2* (2km N Coastal) *53.64100, 8.03400* **Nordsee Camping Hooksiel (Part Naturist),** Bäderstrasse, 26434 Wangerland **(04425) 958080; info@wangerland.de; www.wangerland.de**

€3.10 WD MSP

Exit A29 at junc 4 sp Fedderwarden to N. Thro Hooksiel, site sp 1.5km. 4*, V lge, hdstg, unshd, EHU (6-10A) inc; gas; 50% statics; bike hire; fishing; games area; watersports; sailing. *"Main san facs excel but up 2 flights steps - otherwise facs in Portakabin; naturist site adj with same facs."* **€24.00, 25 Mar-17 Oct.** **2022**

HORB AM NECKAR *3C3* (4km W Rural) *48.44513, 8.67300* **Camping Schüttehof,** Schütteberg 7-9, 72160 Horb-am-Neckar **(07451) 3951; info@camping-schuettehof.de; www.camping-schuettehof.de**

12 €2 WD (htd)

Fr A81/E41 exit junc 30; take Freudenstadt rd out of Horb site sp. Med, mkd, pt shd, pt sl, EHU (16A) metered + conn fee; gas; 75% statics; adv bkg acc. *"Horb delightful Black Forest town; site close to saw mill & could be noisy; steep path to town; site clsd 1230-1430; superb, new, state of the art facs; peaceful; v pleasant helpful staff."* **€31.50** **2023**

HORSTEL *1B3* (5km N Rural) *52.32751, 7.60061* **Campingplatz Herthasee,** Herthaseestrasse 70, 48477 Hörstel **(05459) 1008; contact@hertha-see.de; www.hertha-see.de**

WD MSP nr

Exit A30/E30 junc 10 to Hörstel, then foll sp Hopsten. Site well sp fr a'bahn. 4*, V lge, shd, pt sl, EHU (16A) €2.40 or metered + conn fee (poss long lead req); gas; bbq; sw nr; TV; 70% statics; Eng spkn; tennis; bike hire; CKE. *"Excel site."* **€31.00, 22 Mar-29 Sep.** **2024**

HOXTER *1D3* (2km S Rural) *51.76658, 9.38308* **Wesercamping Höxter,** Sportzentrum 4, 37671 Höxter **(05271) 2589; info@wesercamping-hoexter.de; www.wesercamping-hoexter.de**

€1.50

Fr B83/64 turn E over rv sp Boffzen, turn R & site sp almost on rv bank. Turn R in 300m at green sp, turn L in car park. Med, pt shd, EHU (10-16A) €2; 60% statics; CKE. *"Lge open area for tourers; clsd 1300-1500; spaces beside rv; easy walk along rv to town."* **€19.50, 15 Mar-15 Oct. 2024**

HUCKESWAGEN *1B4* (4km NE Rural) *51.15269, 7.36557* **Campingplatz Beverblick,** Grossberghausen 29, Mickenhagen, 42499 Hückeswagen **(02192) 83389; info@beverblick.de; www.beverblick.de**

12 (htd)

Fr B237 in Hückeswagen at traff lts take B483 sp Radevormwald. Over rv & in 500m turn R sp Mickenhagen. In 3km strt on (no thro rd), turn R after 1km, site on R. Steep app. Med, hdstg, unshd, pt sl, EHU (10A) metered; 90% statics. *"Few touring pitches; helpful owners; gd rest & bar; gd touring base; vg."* **€15.00 2020**

HUNFELD *1D4* (5km SW Rural) *50.65333, 9.72388* **Knaus Campingpark Praforst,** Dr Detlev-Rudelsdorff Allee 6, 36088 Hünfeld **(06652) 749090; huenfeld@knauscamp.de; www.knauscamp.de/huenfeld-praforst**

12 €2

Exit A7 junc 90 dir Hünfeld, foll sp thro golf complex. 5*, Med, mkd, pt shd, pt sl, EHU (16A) metered or €3.50; 40% statics; fishing; golf adj; games area; games rm. *"Excel san facs; gd walking/cycling."* **€44.00 2023**

IDAR OBERSTEIN *3B2* (15km N Rural) *49.80455, 7.26986* **Camping Harfenmühle,** 55758 Asbacherhütte **(06786) 1304; mail@harfenmuehle.de; www.camping-harfenmuehle.de**

12 €3

Fr rte 41 fr Idar twd Kirn, turn L at traff lts at Fischbach by-pass sp Herrstein/Morbach, site 3km past Herrstein vill. Sharp turn to site. 4*, Med, pt shd, EHU (16A) metered; gas; sw nr; TV; 50% statics; phone; Eng spkn; adv bkg acc; tennis; games rm; sauna; fishing; games area; golf 10km; CKE. *"Vg rest; o'night m'vans area; gd san facs but poss inadequate in high ssn; sep area late arr; barrier clsd 2200; gd site."* **€31.00 2024**

ILLERTISSEN *3D4* (11km S Rural) *48.14138, 10.10665* **Camping Christophorus,** Werte 6, 88486 Kirchberg-Sinningen **(07354) 663; info@camping-christophorus.de; www.camping-christophorus.de**

12 €3.50 (htd) (covrd)

Exit A7/E43 junc 125 at Altenstadt. In cent of town turn L, then R immed after level x-ing. Foll site sp. 4*, Lge, pt shd, EHU (16A) €2.50 or metered; sw nr; 80% statics; Eng spkn; adv bkg acc; bike hire; fishing; sauna; CKE. *"Gd site; sm sep area for tourers; excel san facs."* **€34.70 2023**

ILLERTISSEN *3D4* (2km SW Rural) *48.21221, 10.08773* **Camping Illertissen,** Dietenheimerstrasse 91, 89257 Illertissen **(07303) 7888; info@camping-illertissen.de; www.camping-illertissen.de**

€2 nr

Leave A7 at junc 124, twd Illertissen/Dietenheim; after rlwy x-ing turn R then L foll site sp. Off main rd B19 fr Neu Ulm-Memmingen fr N, turn R in Illertissen, foll sp. 4*, Sm, mkd, pt shd, terr, EHU (16A) €2 or metered; gas; 65% statics; ccard acc; CKE. *"Trains to Ulm & Kempten; 20 mins walk to town or cycle track; some pitches poss unrel in wet; site clsd bet 1300-1500 & 2200-0700; obliging owner; conv a'bahn; vg."* **€34.00, 1 Apr-5 Nov. 2023**

IMMENSTADT IM ALLGAU *3D4* (3km NW Rural) *47.57255, 10.19358* **Buchers Alpsee Camping,** Seestrasse 25, 87509 Bühl-am-Alpsee **(08323) 7726; mail@alpsee-camping.de; www.alpsee-camping.de**

12 €3

Fr Immenstadt, W on B308; turn R dir Isny & Missen. In 1.3km turn L sp Bühl & site sp. 2*, Lge, unshd, EHU (16A) €2.50 (poss rev pol); gas; sw nr; Eng spkn; adv bkg acc. *"Lake sm but pleasant; gd mountain walks; friendly welcome; ski lift 3km; excel site, first class facs."* **€45.00 2024**

INGOLSTADT *4E3* (4.5km E Rural) *48.75416, 11.46277* **Campingpark Am Auwaldsee,** 85053 Ingolstadt **(0841) 9611616; ingolstadt@azur-camping.de; https://www.azur-camping.com/en/ingolstadt/**

12 €6 nr

Exit A9/E45 junc 62 Ingolstadt Süd, foll sp for camp site & Auwaldsee. Lge, pt shd, EHU (10A) inc; gas; sw; 50% statics; bus; adv bkg rec; fishing; boating. *"Wooded site by lake; useful NH nr m'way; modern & clean san facs; gd location; excel facs; gd rest; excel."* **€43.00, G07. 2022**

INZELL *4F4* (0.8km SW Rural) *47.76722, 12.75341* **Camping Lindlbauer,** Kreuzfeldstraße 44, 83334 Inzell **08665 928 99 88; info@camping-inzell.de; www.camping-inzell.de**

12 €4 (htd) (covrd, htd)

Fr A8 exit 112 Traunstein-Siegsdorf. Take B306 twds Inzell. Foll sp in vill to campsite. Med, mkd, hdstg, unshd, terr, EHU (16A); twin axles; bus adj; Eng spkn; adv bkg acc; games area; CCI. *"Excel site; beautiful views; friendly, family run site; excel location for walking & cycling."* **€44.70 2024**

JENA *2E4* (2km NE Rural) *50.93583, 11.60833*
Campingplatz Unter dem Jenzig, Am Erlkönig 3, 07749 Jena **(03641) 666688; post@jenacamping.de; www.jenacamping.de**
12 €1 WD MSP nr nr

Exit A4/E40 junc 54 to Jena, then B88 for 4m N dir Naumberg. Turn R just outside Jena at campsite sp, R over blue bdge; site nr sports stadium/sw pool on L, sp. Med, unshd, EHU (10A) €2.50; phone; bus 1km; Eng spkn; adv bkg acc. *"Gd san facs in Portakabin; pool adj; sh walk to interesting town; gd cycle paths."*
€17.00 **2024**

JESTETTEN *3C4* (0.8km SW Urban) *47.64802, 8.56648*
Campingplatz & Schwimmbad, Waldshuterstrasse 13, 79798 Jestetten **(07745) 1220; info@jestetten.de; www.jestetten.de**
(htd) WD nr nr (htd)

Site in town on B27 main rd, sp. Sm, pt shd, pt sl, EHU (10A) metered; bus at gate, train 1.1km; Eng spkn; adv bkg acc. *"Gd for walk or train Rhine Falls & Switzerland; shwr token inc; friendly owner; sw pool free; site in Schwimmbad grnds."*
€22.00, Mid May-Mid Sep. **2024**

"I need an on-site restaurant"

We do our best to make sure site information is correct, but it is always best to check any must-have facilities are still available or will be open during your visit.

KALKAR *1A3* (5km N Rural) *51.76100, 6.28483*
Freitzeitpark Wisseler See, Zum Wisseler-See 15, 47546 Kalkar-Wissel **(02824) 96310; info@wisseler-see.de; www.wisseler-see.de**
12 €3 WD MSP

Fr A3 take junc 4 onto B67 dir Kalkar & Wissel. Fr Kleve take B57 SE for 8km twd Kalkar, E to Wissel & foll camp sp. V lge, hdg, mkd, pt shd, serviced pitches; EHU (16A) inc; 75% statics; Eng spkn; adv bkg rec; bike hire; games area; watersports; tennis. *"Commercialised & regimented but conv NH Rotterdam ferry; gd facs; gd for children & teenagers."*
€32.00 **2022**

KAMENZ *2G4* (7km NE Rural) *51.30465, 14.15272*
Campingplatz Deutschbaselitz, Grossteichstrasse 30, 01917 Kamenz **(03578) 301489; info@campingplatz-deutschbaselitz.com; www.campingplatz-deutschbaselitz.com**
(htd) WD MSP

Fr Kamenz N on rd S95 dir Wittichenau; at Schiedel turn R twd lake, site sp. 3*, Med, pt shd, EHU (16A) €3; bbq; cooking facs; sw; 10% statics; adv bkg acc; bike hire; games area; watersports; games rm; CKE.
€23.00, 1 Mar-31 Oct. **2022**

KARLSHAGEN *2G1* (2km E Coastal) *54.11769, 13.84477*
Dünencamp, Zeltplatzstraße; 17449 Ostseebad; Karlshagen **038371 20291; camping@karlshagen.de; www.duenencamp.de**
12 €4 (htd) WD MSP adj

Site sp fr Karlshagen along Zeltplatzstrasse. 5*, Lge, mkd, shd, pt sl, EHU (16A) €2 (or metered); phone; Eng spkn. *"Site has direct access to long clean sandy beach; long mains lead may be needed for some pitches; conv for visiting Peenemünde; gd site."*
€47.60 **2022**

KARLSRUHE *3C3* (7km E Rural) *49.00788, 8.48303*
Azur Campingpark Turmbergblick, Tiengenerstrasse 40, 76227 Karlsruhe-Durlach **(0721) 497236; karlsruhe@azur-camping.de; www.azur-camping.de**
€3.50 (htd) WD MSP

Exit A5/E35 junc 44 dir Durlach/Grötzingen onto B10 & foll sp to site 3km. Lge, mkd, pt shd, EHU (10A) €3 (long lead poss req); gas; 20% statics; Eng spkn; adv bkg acc; ccard acc; tennis; CKE. *"NH conv to a'bahn; adequate, clean san facs; clsd 1230-1400; expensive for average site; Karlsruhe worth a visit."*
€32.00, 1 Apr-31 Oct. **2022**

KASSEL *1D4* (22km S Rural) *51.17757, 9.47781*
Camping Fuldaschleife, zum Bruch 6, 34302 Guxhagen-Büchenwerra **(0566) 5961044; info@fuldaschleife.de; www.fuldaschleife.de**
€1.50 (htd) WD MSP nr

Exit A7 at J81 twrds Guxhagen. Foll sp. Site in 4km. 4*, Sm, mkd, pt shd, bbq; twin axles; 60% statics; bus adj; Eng spkn; adv bkg acc; ccard acc; games area; CKE. *"Pleasant site adj rv; helpful staff; boating, canoeing & cycling rtes fr site; Hann Munden & Gottingen worth visiting; conv for N, S, E & W Germany; excel."* **€22.00, 1 Mar-31 Oct.** **2022**

KEHL *3B3* (12km ESE Rural) *48.54375, 7.93518*
Europa-Camping, Waldstrasse 32, 77731 Willstätt-Sand **(07852) 2311 or (0170) 9361255; europacamping.sand@gmail.com; www.europa-camping-sand.de**
€2 (htd)

Exit A5/E35/E52 at junc 54 almost immed turn R at Int'l Camping sp; foll site sp. 3*, Med, hdstg, pt shd, EHU (16A) €2.50 (long lead poss req); cooking facs; red long stay; 30% statics; Eng spkn; ccard acc; CKE. *"Easy reach Black Forest & Strasbourg; 1km fr a'bahn exit; well-managed, clean, tidy site; gd san facs; friendly helpful owner; cycle tracks fr site."*
€26.00, 1 Feb-30 Nov. **2024**

KEHL *3B3* (3km S Urban) *48.5615, 7.80861* **DCC Campingpark Kehl-Strassburg,** Rheindammstrasse 1, 77694 Kehl-Kronenhof **(07851) 2603; info@campingpark-kehl.de; campingpark-kehl.de**

€2 (htd)

Fr A5/E35, take exit 54 onto B28 at Appenweier twd Kehl & foll site sp. 4*, Lge, pt shd, EHU (16A) metered + conn fee (long lead poss req); gas; 15% statics; bus 1km; Eng spkn; adv bkg acc; ccard acc; CKE. *"Peaceful site adj Rv Rhine; excel rest & modern san facs; sm pitches; pleasant rv walk & cycle paths to town; sw pool adj; barrier clsd 1300-1500."* **€25.00, 15 Mar-31 Oct. 2024**

KEMPTEN (ALLGAU) *3D4* (25km E Rural) *47.80283, 10.55377* **Camping Platz Elbsee,** Am Elbsee 3, 87648 Aitrang **08 34 32 48; info@elbsee.de; www.elbsee.de**

12 €4.50 (htd)

S on A7. Take J134 dir Marktobedorf on B12. Take exit twd Unterthingau on OAL10. Turn L on OAL3, cont onto OAL 5. Turn R on Am Elbsee. Foll sp. 5*, Lge, hdg, mkd, hdstg, pt shd, EHU (16A); bbq; cooking facs; twin axles; bus 0.75km; Eng spkn; adv bkg acc; ccard acc; games rm; CCI. *"Excel site; gd base; lake adj; many local historical places & amazing architecture; camp has much to offer - peace & quiet, spa art, yoga."* **€29.70 2024**

KINDING *4E3* (5km E Rural) *49.00328, 11.45200* **Camping Kratzmühle,** Mühlweg 2, 85125 Kinding-Pfraundorf **(08461) 64170; info@kratzmuehle.de; www.kratzmuehle.de**

12 €2

Exit A9/E45 junc 58, dir Beilngries. Site sp. 4*, Lge, pt shd, serviced pitches; EHU (16A) €2.50; gas; cooking facs; sw nr; red long stay; 40% statics; adv bkg acc; ccard acc; games area; sauna; CKE. *"Beautiful situation; conv NH for a'bahn; ideal boating & bathing, public access to lake; clsd 1300-1500; poss mosquito prob; helpful staff."* **€36.00 2023**

KIRCHHEIM *1D4* (5km SW Rural) *50.81435, 9.51805* **Camping Seepark,** Reimboldshäuserstraße, 36275 Kirchheim **(06628) 1525; info@campseepark.de; www.campseepark.de**

12 €2 (htd) (covrd)

Exit A7 at Kirchheim junc 87, site clearly sp. 5*, Lge, mkd, pt shd, pt sl, terr, EHU (16A) €3 metered; gas; sw; red long stay; 50% statics; phone; bus 500m; adv bkg acc; ccard acc; sauna; golf 3km; games area; tennis; CKE. *"Gd walking; helpful owner; o'night m'vans area; excel site - leisure facs pt of lge hotel complex; NH only."* **€30.00 2023**

KIRKEL *3B3* (1km S Urban) *49.28175, 7.22860* **Caravanplatz Mühlenweiher,** Unnerweg 5c, 66459 Kirkel-Neuhäusel **(06849) 1810555; info@camping-kirkel.de; www.caravanplatz-kirkel.de**

12 €1.15 (htd) nr

Fr A6 junc 7 & fr A8 junc 28, take dir into town & foll sp for 'schwimmbad'. Site on L past pool, well sp. 3*, Med, mkd, hdstg, pt shd, EHU (10A) €3 or metered + conn fee (poss rev pol); gas; TV (pitch); 60% statics; phone; CKE. *"Gd welcome; excel area for cycling; noise fr pool & church bells all night; pool adj; site/office clsd 1230-1500."* **€20.00 2022**

KITZINGEN *3D2* (3km E Urban) *49.73233, 10.16833* **Camping Schiefer Turm,** Marktbreiter Straße 20, 97318 Kitzingen-Hohenfeld **(09321) 33125; info@camping-kitzingen.de; www.camping-kitzingen.de**

€1.50

Fr A3 take exit junc 74 sp Kitzingen/Schwarzach or exit 72 Würzburg-Ost, or fr A7 exit junc 103 Kitzingen. Site sp in town 'Schwimmbad'. 3*, Med, mkd, pt shd, EHU (16A) €2 or metered; gas; bus; ccard acc. *"Bird reserve; pleasant town in evening; gd cycling; busy NH high ssn; san facs up steps; excel Lido adj."* **€18.00, 1 Apr-11 Oct. 2020**

"Satellite navigation makes touring much easier"

Remember most sat navs don't know if you're towing or in a larger vehicle – always use yours alongside maps and site directions.

KOBLENZ *3B2* (4km NE Urban) *50.36611, 7.60361* **Knaus Campingpark Rhein-Mosel,** Schartwiesenweg 6, 56070 Koblenz-Lützel **(0261) 82719; koblenz@knauscamp.de; www.camping-rhein-mosel.de**

12 nr nr nr

Fr Koblenz heading N on B9 turn off dual c'way at sp for Neuendorf just bef Mosel rv bdge; foll sp to Neuendorf vill. Or heading S on B9 exit dual c'way at camping sp (2nd sp) bef Koblenz; fr Koblenz cent foll sp for 'Altstadt' until Baldwinbrücke (bdge); N over bdge instead of foll sp along S bank of Rv Mosel; R after bdge, then foll sp; site on N side of junc Rhine/Mosel rvs. 2*, Med, hdstg, pt shd, pt sl, EHU (6-16A) €2.05 or metered (long lead poss req); cooking facs; sw; Eng spkn; adv bkg rec; ccard acc; CKE. *"Pleasant, informal site in beautiful location; muddy in wet; staff helpful; no veh acc after 2200; adj ferry to city & easy cycle rte; mkt Sat; sep dog shwrs; flea mkt Sun; 'Rhine in Flames' fireworks 2nd Sat in Aug - watch fr site; MH stopover called Knaus Campingpark just outside main gates, basic price €12.50, both sites under same owner; vg."* **€46.00 2023**

 *Last year of report

GERMANY

KOBLENZ *3B2* (12km SW Urban) *50.30972, 7.50166* **Camping Winninger Ferieninsel Ziehfurt,** Inselweg 10, 56333 Winningen **(02606) 357 or 1800; camping@ferieninsel-winningen.de; www.ferieninsel-winningen.de**

€3

Exit A61/E31 junc 38 to Winningen. In Winningen turn R twds Cochem B416, then L at sw pool. In approx 100m turn R and then in 700m turn L over bdge to site recep. Lge, pt shd, EHU (16A) €2.50; 50% statics; Eng spkn. *"Cent of wine-growing country; boat trips avail fr Koblenz; cycle rtes; scenic area; poss flooding if v high water; pool 300m; lively site when busy; gd, modern san facs up steep steps but poss stretched when busy; excel rest; excel site."*
€30.50, 6 Apr-3 Oct. 2023

KOBLENZ *3B2* (8km SW Rural) *50.33194, 7.55277* **Camping Gülser Moselbogen,** Am Gülser Moselbogen 20, 56072 Koblenz-Güls **(0261) 44474; info@moselbogen.de; www.moselbogen.de**

€4 (htd) nr nr

Fr A61/E31 exit 38 dir Koblenz/Metternich. After 400m turn R at rndabt dir Winningen. Stay on this rd to T-junc in Winningen, turn L dir Koblenz-Güls, site sp on R in 3km. 4*, Med, hdg, mkd, pt shd, EHU (16A) €1.50 + conn fee; gas; TV (pitch); 50% statics; phone; Eng spkn; adv bkg acc; ccard acc; bike hire; CKE. *"High quality, high-tech san facs; no vehicles 1200-1400; poss subject to flooding; excel."*
€28.00 2024

KOCHEL AM SEE *4E4* (3km SW Rural) *47.63642, 11.34827* **Camping Kesselberg,** Altjoch 2 ½, 82431 Kochel-am-See **(08851) 464; mailto@campingplatz-kesselberg.de; www.campingplatz-kesselberg.de**

€3

S fr Kochel on Bundestrasse 11. After 3km fork R for Walchensee Kraftwerk, many hairpins, site 150m on R. Med, mkd, pt shd, pt sl, EHU (10A) metered; gas; bbq; sw nr; red long stay; 40% statics; Eng spkn; adv bkg acc; sailing; CKE. *"Friendly site; beautifully situated by Kochelsee; attractive peaceful lakeside site; clean san facs; friendly & helpful staff; vg."*
€29.50, 22 Mar-15 Oct. 2024

KOLN *1B4* (4km NE Urban) *50.96305, 6.98361* **Reisemobilhafen Köln,** An der Schanz, 50735 Köln **017 84674591 (mob); info@reisemobilhafen-koeln.de; www.reisemobilhafen-koeln.de**

nr nr nr

Fr A1 Köln ring rd exit junc 100 dir Köln 'Zentrum' until reach rv. Turn L & foll sp to site. M'vans only. Sm, mkd, hdstg, EHU (10A) €1 for 12 hrs; own san req; bus, train nr. *"Adj Rv Rhine; must have change for elec & water (metered) - €0.50, parking (€10 note) etc; easy access to city cent; site is unmanned; cycle rte to city, zoo & botanic gdns."* **€16.00** 2023

KOLN *1B4* (8km SE Rural) *50.8909, 7.02306* **Camping Berger,** Uferstrasse 71, 50996 Köln-Rodenkirchen **(0221) 9355240; inquiry@camping-berger.koeln; www.camping-berger-koeln.de**

€1 (htd)

Fr A4 turn S onto A555 at Köln-Sud exit 12. Leave A555 at Rodenkirchen exit 3. At 1st junc foll site sp to R. Fr A3 Frankfurt/Köln a'bahn, take A4 twd Aachen (Köln ring rd); exit at Köln Sud; foll sp Bayenthal; at lge rndabt turn R sp Rheinufer & R again at camp sp, under a'bahn. App rd narr & lined with parked cars. Lge, pt shd, EHU (4-10A) €1.50; gas; cooking facs; red long stay; 80% statics; phone; bus 500m; Eng spkn; ccard acc; bike hire; CKE. *"Pleasant, popular, wooded site on banks of Rhine; rvside pitches best; excel rest; helpful staff; gd dog walking; cycle path to city cent; conv cathedral, zoo & museums; some noise fr Rhine barges; don't arr early eve at w/end as narr app rd v busy; pitches poss muddy after rain; san facs up steps - poss clsd 2300-0600; gd site; vg facs; need car/bike to get around."* **€34.50** 2023

KOLN *1B4* (6km S Urban) *50.90263, 6.99070* **Campingplatz der Stadt Köln,** Weidenweg 35, 51105 Köln-Poll **(0221) 831966; info@camping-koeln.de; www.camping-koeln.de**

€2.50 nr

Exit fr A4 (E40) at junc 13 for Köln-Poll-Porz at E end of bdge over Rv Rhine, 3km S of city. At end of slip rd, turn L twd Poll & Köln. Cont about 1000m turn L at sp just bef level x-ing, then foll site sp. Narr lane to ent. Lge, pt shd, EHU (10A) €3.50 (some rev pol & long lead poss req); gas; cooking facs; phone; Eng spkn; CKE. *"Tram to city over rv bdge; rural site in urban setting on bank of Rv Rhine & subject to flooding; clsd 1230-1430; gd undercover cooking facs; gd refurbished san facs on 1st floor; friendly site; v busy at w/end; rvside cycle track to city; cycle theft a problem (store in caged kitchen o'night); friendly owner; site in green zone."* **€30.00, 15 Mar-23 Oct.** 2022

KONIGSSEE *4G4* (1km N Rural) *47.5992, 12.98933* **Camping Mühlleiten,** Königsseerstrasse 70, 83471 Königssee **(08652) 4584; info@camping-muehlleiten.de; www.camping-muehlleiten.de**

€5 nr 1km

On on R of B20 Berchtesgaden-Königssee. 3*, Med, pt shd, EHU (16A) €3 or metered; gas; bbq (elec, gas); twin axles; 10% statics; bus; Eng spkn; adv bkg acc; ccard acc; golf 6km; CKE. *"Beautiful area; friendly staff; excel san facs; excel site with mixed MH's, c'van and camping; walking trails; free/red bus fares with visitor card; ski lift 500m; off clsd 1200-1500 daily."*
€43.70, 1 Dec-5 Nov. 2023

KONIGSTEIN *2G4* (1km E Rural) *50.92222, 14.08833* **Camping Königstein,** Schandauerstrasse 25e, 01824 Königstein **(035021) 68224; info@camping-koenigstein.de; www.camping-koenigstein.de**

12 €3 nr

Foll B172 SE fr Dresden/Pirna. Site 500m past Königstein rlwy stn. Turn L over rlwy x-ing & R into site ent on Rv Elbe. 3*, Med, unshd, pt sl, EHU (10-16A) €2.60; gas; red long stay; 15% statics; adv bkg acc; sep car park. *"Gd san facs; lovely location nr national parks & Czech border; on Elbe cycle path; frequent trains to Dresden; boat trips; gates clsd 1300-1500; dogs not acc Jul/Aug; site updated to hg std (2018)."* **€26.50** **2023**

KONIGSTEIN *2G4* (3km E Rural) *50.91500, 14.10730* **Caravan Camping Sächsische Schweiz,** Dorfplatz 181d, 01824 Kurort-Gohrisch **350 21 59107; Info@caravan-camping-saechsischeschweiz.de; www.caravan-camping-saechsischeschweiz.de**

12 €2 nr

Fr Königstein foll B172 E dir Bad Schandau. Fork R dir Gohrisch for 2.5km, turn L into Dorfplatz & foll site sp. Med, hdstg, hdg, mkd, pt shd, pt sl, EHU (16A) metered; bbq; cooking facs; red long stay; TV (pitch); 5% statics; bus 500m; Eng spkn; adv bkg acc; bike hire; games area; sauna. *"Excel site; gd touring base; htd covrd pool 4km; interesting area; guided walks."* **€22.00** **2020**

KONSTANZ *3D4* (13km N Rural) *47.74596, 9.14701* **Camping Klausenhorn,** Hornwiesenstrasse, 78465 Dingelsdorf **(07533) 6372; info@camping-klausenhorn.de; www.camping-klausenhorn.de**

(htd) nr

Site sp N of Dingelsdorf on lakeside. 4*, Lge, mkd, hdstg, pt shd, EHU (10A) inc; bbq; 50% statics; bus 500m; Eng spkn; adv bkg acc; ccard acc; boating; games area; sep car park; CKE. *"Excel site; lake adj; 1st class san facs; v helpful recep; free bus svrs fr site."* **€35.00, 1 Apr-3 Oct.** **2022**

KONSTANZ *3D4* (12km W Rural) *47.69871, 9.04603* **Camping Sandseele,** Bradlengasse 24, 78479 Niederzell **(07534) 7384; info@sandseele.de; www.sandseele.de**

Clearly sp off B33 Konstanz-Radolfzell rd. Foll sp on island & sm multiple sp. Lge, pt shd, EHU (16A) €3.50; gas; sw; 30% statics; watersports. *"Insect repellent rec, excel san facs; sep car park high ssn; excel walking & cycling all over island; poor layout."* **€33.00, 18 Mar-9 Oct.** **2022**

KRANICHFELD *2E4* (4km NW Rural) *50.87216, 11.17843* **Campingplatz Stausee Hohenfelden,** 99448 Hohenfelden **(036450) 42081; info@stausse-hohenfelden.de; www.stausee-hohenfelden.de**

12 €2.50

Fr A4/E40 take exit 47a S twd Kranichfeld. Site clearly sp by lake along rough rd. 4*, V lge, mkd, pt shd, pt sl, terr, EHU (16A); bbq; cooking facs; sw; red long stay; 50% statics; adv bkg acc; ccard acc; bike hire; boating; lake adj; CKE. *"Woodland, lakeside walks; gd; well run; excel WiFi; excel san facs."* **€24.00** **2022**

"There aren't many sites open at this time of year"

If you're travelling outside peak season remember to call ahead to check site opening dates – even if the entry says 'open all year'.

KRESSBRONN AM BODENSEE *3D4* (9km NE Rural) *47.63395, 9.6477* **Gutshof-Camping,** Badhütten 1, 88069 Laimnau **(07543) 96330; gutshof.camping@t-online.de; www.gutshof-camping.de**

€2

Fr Kressbronn take B467 to Tettnang & Ravensburg. In 3km immed after x-ing Rv Argen turn R & site sp for approx 3km. Take care on final app rd. Dark, steep and twisty, great care needed. 4*, V lge, hdg, mkd, pt shd, serviced pitches; EHU (16A) metered; gas; sw nr; red long stay; 40% statics; adv bkg acc; CKE. *"Sep area for naturists; gd facs; v rural site; clean, quiet & pleasant; excel."* **€30.00, 1 Apr - 31 Oct, G15.** **2022**

KRESSBRONN AM BODENSEE *3D4* (2km SW Rural) *47.58718, 9.58281* **Campingplatz Irisweise,** Tunau 16, 88079 Kressbronn **(07543) 8010; info@campingplatz-irisweise.de; www.campingplatz-iriswiese.de**

€2.50 (htd)

Fr E or W take exit off B31 bypass for Kressbronn, site well sp. 4*, Lge, hdg, mkd, pt shd, EHU (10A) metered + conn fee; gas; bbq; sw nr; 10% statics; phone; Eng spkn; watersports; sailing; CKE. *"Steamer trips on lake; no car access 2100-0700, park outside site; sep naturist beach; excel san facs but some dist fr touring pitches; gd."* **€28.00, 22 Mar-21 Oct.** **2024**

KRUMBACH *4E4* (7km SW Rural) *48.22720, 10.29280* **See Camping Günztal,** Oberrieder Weiherstrasse 5, 86488 Breitenthal **(08282) 881870; info@see-camping-guenztal.de; www.see-camping-guenztal.de**

€2 (htd) nr nr

W fr Krumbach on rd 2018, in Breitenthal turn S twd Oberried & Oberrieder Weiher, site sp on lakeside. Med, mkd, hdstg, pt shd, EHU (10A) inc; bbq; sw; TV; 30% statics; adv bkg acc; games area; watersports; fishing. **€30.00, 15 Apr-30 Oct.** **2022**

GERMANY

KULMBACH *4E2* (11km NE Rural) *50.16050, 11.51605* **Campingplatz Stadtsteinach,** Badstrasse 5, 95346 Stadtsteinach **(09225) 800394 or (0151) 20837917; info@campingplatz-stadtsteinach.de; www.campingplatz-stadtsteinach.de**

€2 (htd) WD MSP nr (htd)

Fr Kulmbach take B289 to Untersteinach (8km); turn L to Stadtsteinach; turn R at camping sp & foll rd for 1km. Site also sp fr N side of town on B303. Or fr A9/E51 exit junc 39 onto B303 NW to Stadtsteinach. 4*, Med, mkd, pt shd, pt sl, EHU (6-16A) €2.50; bbq (charcoal, gas); sw; 60% statics; Eng spkn; adv bkg acc; ccard acc; rv fishing; bike hire; tennis; CKE. *"Excel site in beautiful countryside; htd pool adj; excel, modern facs; highly rec."* **€24.00, 1 Mar-1 Nov.** **2024**

LAHNSTEIN *3B2* (3km E Urban) *50.30565, 7.61313* **Kur-Campingplatz Burg Lahneck,** Am Burgweg, 56112 Lahnstein-Oberlahnstein **(02621) 2765; http://www.camping-burg-lahneck.de**

€1 WD MSP nr

Take B42 fr Koblenz over Lahn Rv, if fr low bdge turn L immed after church & sp fr there; if fr high level bdge thro sh tunnel turn L at 1st rd on L sp to Burg-Lahneck - site sp on L. 4*, Med, pt shd, pt sl, EHU (16A) metered + conn fee; 10% statics; Eng spkn. *"Gd views over Rhine; scenic area; delightful, helpful owner v particular about pitching; gd size pitches; immac, well-run site."* **€21.50, 29 Mar-3 Nov.** **2020**

LAICHINGEN *3D3* (6km SE Rural) *48.47560, 9.7458* **Camping & Freizeitzentrum Heidehof,** Heidehofstrasse 50, 89150 Laichingen-Machtolsheim **(07333) 6408; info@heidenhof.info; www.camping-heidehof.de**

12 WD MSP (htd)

Exit A8 junc 61 dir Merklingen. At T-junc turn R sp Laichingen. In 3km site sp to L. 4*, V lge, hdg, mkd, hdstg, pt shd, pt sl, EHU (10-16A) €2 or metered; gas; red long stay; 95% statics; adv bkg acc; bike hire; sauna; CKE. *"Blaubeuren Abbey & Blautopf (blue pool of glacial origin) worth visit; sep area for o'nighters immed bef main camp ent - poss unrel when wet; hdstg pitches sm & sl; vg rest; gd NH; clean modern facs; lack of elec boxes; no water taps excep at facs; whole site on uneven sl; arr early to get nr elec."* **€27.50** **2024**

LANDAU IN DER PFALZ *3C3* (13km W Rural) *49.20138, 7.97222* **Camping der Naturfreunde,** Victor von Scheffelstrasse 18, 76855 Annweiler-am-Trifels **(06346) 3870; campingplatz@naturfreunde-annweiler.de; www.naturfreunde-annweiler.de**

€2 (htd) WD MSP nr nr

Fr Landau take B10 dir Pirmasens, take 1st exit to Annweiler then turn L into vill along Landauerstrasse. Turn L immed after VW/Audi g'ge, site sp. Tight access at ent. 3*, Sm, hdstg, pt shd, EHU (10A) €2; 80% statics; CKE. *"Friendly, helpful owner poss on site evenings only; immac, modern san facs; ltd space for tourers but adequate facs; vg views across valley & forest; Ent is up steep hill with acute L turn; advise use campingplatz on R."* **€16.00, 1 Apr-31 Oct.** **2024**

LANDSHUT *4F3* (3km NE Urban) *48.55455, 12.1795* **Camping Landshut Mitterwöhr,** Breslauerstrasse 122, 84028 Landshut **(0871) 53366; info@isarcamping.de; isarcamping.de**

€1.50 WD MSP nr nr

Fr A92/E53 exit junc 14 onto B299 dir Landshut N. After approx 5km turn L at int'l camping sp & foll site sp. 2*, Med, pt shd, EHU (16A) €2.50; bbq; 10% statics; CKE. *"Well-run, friendly site; gd san facs; htd pool 3km; beautiful medieval town & castle - easy cycle rte."* **€17.00, 1 Apr-30 Sep.** **2022**

LANGWEDEL *1D1* (1km W Rural) *54.21465, 9.91825* **Caravanpark am Brahmsee,** Mühlenstrasse 30a, 24631 Langwedel **(04329) 1567; info@caravanpark-am-brahmsee.de; www.caravanpark-am-brahmsee.de**

12 (htd) WD MSP nr nr

Exit A7 at junc 10 dir Tierpark Warder (animal park) & foll site sp to lakeside. Or exit A215 at Blumenthal onto L298 thro Langwedel dir Tierpark Warder, site sp. 3*, Med, mkd, hdstg, hdg, pt shd, EHU (16A) €2.50; bbq; cooking facs; sw nr; 80% statics; adv bkg acc; fishing. *"Peaceful site in nature park; gd; diff access to some pitches for lge o'fits; excel san facs; dedicated hdstg area for campers; v cramped."* **€15.00** **2024**

LECHBRUCK *4E4* (3km NE Rural) *47.71169, 10.81872* **Via Claudia Camping,** Via Claudia 6, 86983 Lechbruck **(08862) 8426; info@camping-lechbruck.de; www.via-claudia-camping.de**

12 €3.50 WD MSP

A7 exit 138 Nesselwang. Sp Seeg, foll Oa1 round Seeg to Roßhaupten. Then B16 sp Markt-Oberdorf. 1st exit to Lechbruck. Thro Lechbruch to site on R by lake. 4*, Lge, hdstg, mkd, pt shd, terr, EHU (10-16A) €2.65; gas; bbq; sw; red long stay; twin axles; TV; 50% statics; Eng spkn; adv bkg acc; ccard acc; watersports; games rm; CKE. *"Pleasant, peaceful, lakeside site; o'night m'van area; fac to a high standard; pool 500m; mini golf; gd welcome; v helpful; volleyball; archery; cont investment in site fr new owners; bus 1.5km; watersports; mountain tours; hiking; cycle trails; model aircraft; spa; rafting; traditional craft demos; skiing; local historic buildings; excel."* **€34.00** **2023**

LEER (OSTFRIESLAND) *1B2* (7km W Rural) *53.22416, 7.41891* **Camping Ems-Marina Bingum,** Marinastrasse 14-16, 26789 Leer-Bingum **(0491) 64447; into-camping-bingum@t-online.de; www.ems-marina-bingum.de**

12 €3.50 nr

Leave A32/E12 junc 12; site 500m S of Bingum; well sp. Lge, pt shd, EHU (16A) €2.50 or metered; gas; red long stay; 65% statics; adv bkg acc; bike hire; CKE. *"Gate clsd 1230-1500."* **€23.00** **2022**

LEIPHEIM *3D3* (3.5km NNW Rural) *48.46566, 10.2035* **Camping Schwarzfelder Hof,** Schwarzfelderweg 3, Riedheim, 89340 Leipheim **(08221) 72628; info@schwarzfelder-hof.de; www.schwarzfelder-hof.de**

12 €3.90 (htd) nr nr

Fr A8 exit junc 66 Leipheim onto B10. In Leipheim foll sp Langenau & Riedheim, site sp. Do not confuse with Laupheim 25km S of Ulm on B30. Sm, hdstg, pt shd, serviced pitches; EHU (16A) €2.50; bbq; 50% statics; train 1km; Eng spkn. *"Peaceful, delightful, farm-based site on site of old quarry; ideal for children & adults; welcoming, helpful owner; lge pitches; vg san facs but ltd; farm animals & riding for children; conv Ulm; recep open 0800-1000 & 1730-2000; poss noisy youth groups; conv NH for m'way."* **€25.50** **2024**

LEIPZIG *2F4* (7km NW Urban) *51.37030, 12.31375* **Campingplatz Auensee,** Gustav-Esche Strasse 5, 04159 Leipzig **(0341) 4651600; leipzig@knauscamp.de; www.knauscamp.de**

12 €2 (htd) nr

Fr A9/E51 exit junc 16 onto B6 two Leipzig. In Leipzig-Wahren turn R at 'Rathaus' sp Leutzsch (camping symbol), site on R in 1.5km, sp. 4*, Lge, mkd, hdstg, pt shd, EHU (16A) €3; bbq; cooking facs; TV; phone; bus; Eng spkn; adv bkg acc; ccard acc; CKE. *"Roomy, well-run, clean site; plentiful, excel, modern san facs; gd size pitches; friendly, helpful staff; Lake Auensee 500m; tram 1.5km; 10 mins walk to tram for city cent or bus stop at site ent; excel."* **€41.60** **2023**

LIMBURG AN DER LAHN *3C2* (2km SSW Urban) *50.38916, 8.07333* **Camping Resort Limburg (Formerly Lahn Camping),** Schleusenweg 16, 65549 Limburg-an-der-Lahn **(01609) 1996659; info@camping-resort-limburg.de; camping-resort-limburg.de**

€1.50

Exit A3/E35 junc 42 Limburg Nord, site sp. By Rv Lahn in town, easy access. 3*, Lge, pt shd, EHU (6A) €2.60 (long lead poss req); gas; sw; 20% statics; bus; Eng spkn; fishing; CKE. *"Busy, well-organised site; delightful location by rv; sm pitches - some poss diff to manoeuvre; gd views; friendly staff; poss flooding in wet weather; htd pool 100m; sh walk to interesting town; gates clsd 1300-1500; useful NH."* **€19.90, 28 Mar-27 Oct.** **2024**

LINDAU (BODENSEE) *3D4* (5km NE Rural) *47.58509, 9.70667* **Campingpark Gitzenweiler Hof,** Gitzenweiler 88, 88131 Lindau-Gitzenweiler **(08382) 94940; www.gitzenweiler-hof.de**

12 €3.50

Exit A96/E43/E54 junc 4 onto B12 sp Lindau. Turn off immed after vill of Oberreitnau twd Rehlings. Site well sp fr all dirs. Lge, mkd, pt shd, pt sl, serviced pitches; EHU (6-16A) inc; gas; red long stay; TV; 50% statics; bus 1km; Eng spkn; adv bkg acc; boating; fishing; CKE. *"Well-run, busy site in scenic area; gd facs; friendly staff; excel site for children; max 2 dogs; o'night facs for m'vans; gd cycling; poss prone to flooding after v heavy rain; pitches poorly maintained; poss cr."* **€36.00, G18.** **2024**

LINDAU (BODENSEE) *3D4* (9km SE Coastal) *47.53758, 9.73143* **Park-Camping Lindau am See,** Fraunhoferstrasse 20, 88131 Lindau-Zech **(08382) 8899999; info@park-camping.de; www.park-camping.de**

€3 shgl

On B31 fr Bregenz to Lindau, 200m after customs turn L to site in 150m; ent could be missed; mini-mkt on corner; ent rd crosses main rlwy line with auto barriers. B31 fr Friedrichshafen, site well sp fr o'skts of Lindau. 4*, Lge, mkd, hdstg, pt shd, EHU (10A) €1 (long lead poss req); sw; 20% statics; Eng spkn; bike hire; golf 3km. *"Busy site; immac san facs; sh stay pitches poss diff to manoeuvre as v cramped; office/gate clsd 1300-1400; helpful staff; m'van o'night area €10; shwr rm for dogs; excel walking in Pfänder area; excel; Korridor scheme round Bregenz abolished; Pfander tunnels complete; Austria m'way vignette req; cyc rtes fr site."* **€46.10, 22 Mar-10 Nov.** **2023**

LINDAUNIS *1D1* (1km SSW Rural) *54.58626, 9.8173* **Camping Lindaunis,** Schleistrasse 1, 24392 Lindaunis **(04641) 7317; info@camping-lindaunis.de; www.camping-lindaunis.de**

€2 (htd)

Exit A7/E45 junc 5 onto B201 sp Brebel & Süderbrarup. At Brebel turn R & foll dir Lindaunis, site approx 12km on R beside Schlei Fjord. 3*, Lge, hdg, mkd, pt shd, terr, EHU (16A); bbq; twin axles; TV; 80% statics; Eng spkn; adv bkg rec; games area; boat hire; games rm; boating; fishing; bike hire; canoeing; CKE. *"Vg, family-run site ideally placed for exploring Schlei fjord & conv Danish border; lakeside setting; boat & canoe rentals; gd walks & cycle rtes; attractive area; vg."* **€27.00, 27 Mar-15 Oct.** **2022**

GERMANY

LINGERHAHN *3B2* (1km NE Rural) *50.09980, 7.57330* **Campingpark am Mühlenteich,** Am Mühlenteich 1, 56291 Lingerhahn **(06746) 533; info@muehlenteich.de; www.muehlenteich.de**

€3.50

Exit A61/E31 exit junc 44 to Laudert & Lingerhahn. In Lingerhahn foll sp Pfalzfeld, site sp. 4*, Lge, unshd, serviced pitches; EHU (6A) €2; 75% statics; adv bkg acc; golf 12km; tennis; CKE. *"Delightful rest & beer garden; ent clsd 1300-1500 & 2200; excel site."* **€22.50** 2024

LIPPSTADT *1C4* (8km NE Rural) *51.70095, 8.40808* **Campingparadies Lippstadter Seenplatte,** Seeufer Straße 16, 59558 Lippstadt **02 948 22 53; info@camping-lippstadt.de; www.camping-lippstadt.de**

€2.50

Turn R off B55 to Lipperode. In town turn R onto Niederdedinghauser. After 2.5km turn L onto Seeuferstraße. Site 200m on R. Sm, mkd, pt shd, EHU (16A); twin axles; 25% statics; bus 200m; adv bkg acc; bike hire; CCI. *" Vg site; fishing in adj lake; excel modern facs; lge pitches; friendly owners; Paderborn lovely city; off clsd 1230-1430."* **€23.00, 1 Mar-31 Oct.** 2023

"We must tell the Club about that great site we found"

Get your site reports in by mid-August and we'll do our best to get your updates into the next edition.

LUBECK *2E2* (6km W Rural) *53.86943, 10.63086* **Campingplatz Lübeck-Schönböcken,** Steinrader Damm 12, 23556 Lübeck-Schönböcken **(0451) 893090; info@camping-luebeck.de; www.camping-luebeck.de**

€1

Fr A1 exit junc 23 on sh slip rd, stay in L lane, foll sp to Schönböcken & then camp sp (not v obvious); turn R at traff lts bef Dornbreite, site in 1km on L. 3*, Med, unshd, pt sl, EHU (6A) inc; gas; bbq; bus to town; Eng spkn; ccard acc; games rm; CKE. *"Helpful owners; busy site; gd san facs but poss stretched if site full; conv Travemünde ferries; Lübeck interesting town; cycle path to town; vg; nice place; gd hypmkt nr; gd site; gd bus service to fascinating town."* **€24.00** 2024

LUNEBURG *1D2* (6km S Rural) *53.20925, 10.41000* **Camping Rote Schleuse,** Rote Schleuse 4, 21335 Lüneburg **(04131) 791500; kontakt@camp-rote-schleuse.de; www.camproteschleuse.de**

€1 nr

Exit A250 junc 4 onto Neu Häcklingen twd Lüneburg. Site sp to R in 300m. 3*, Med, pt shd, EHU (16A) €2.50 or metered; bbq; 60% statics; bus fr site ent; Eng spkn; adv bkg acc; ccard acc; games rm; bike hire. *"Pleasant, friendly owners; clsd 1300-1500; interesting town; gd rest."* **€30.50** 2023

LUTHERSTADT WITTENBERG *2F3* (14km S Rural) *51.79135, 12.56995* **Camping Bergwitzsee,** Strandweg 1, 06901 Bergwitz **(034921) 28228; reception@bergwitzsee.de; www.bergwitzsee.de**

€3

S fr Berlin on B2 thro Wittenberg, then thro Eutzsch, bear R onto B100 into Bergwitz; at cent site is sp, foll to lake, turn R & site ahead. Fr main rd to site thro vill 1.5km, cobbled. Site on lakeside. Lge, shd, EHU (10-16A) €2; sw; TV; 90% statics; adv bkg rec; watersports; bike hire; games area; fishing; CKE. *"Interesting town - Martin Luther Haus; gd cycling/walking area; quiet, restful site; Lakeside site nr Ferropolis, popular with families."* **€34.00** 2024

LUTHERSTADT WITTENBERG *2F3* (5km S Rural) *51.85465, 12.64563* **Marina Camp Elbe,** Brückenkopf 1, 06888 Lutherstadt-Wittenberg **(03491) 4540; info@marina-camp-elbe.de; www.marina-camp-elbe.de**

€1.50 nr

Site on S side of Elbe bdge on B2 dir Leipzig; well sp. 5*, Med, pt shd, serviced pitches; EHU (16A)€2.50; gas; bbq; cooking facs; TV; bus at gate; ccard acc; bike hire; sauna; CKE. *"Delightful rvside site; marina adj; excel, modern san facs."* **€37.00** 2023

MAGDEBURG *2E3* (15km N Rural) *52.21888, 11.65944* **Campingplatz Barleber See,** Wiedersdorferstrasse, 39126 Magdeburg **(0391) 503244; checkin@cbs-md.de; www.cvbs.de**

€2 sand adj

Exit A2/E30 junc 71 sp Rothensee-Barleber See; site 1km N of a'bahn. 4*, Lge, mkd, pt shd, EHU (10A) €2; gas; sw; red long stay; 80% statics; Eng spkn; bike hire; CKE. *"Gd beach & watersports; pleasant site; gd sports facs; gd touring base; v noisy due to adj gravel quarry; unhelpful staff; v busy at w/end; crowded beach."* **€26.50, 15 Apr-1 Oct.** 2023

MALLISS *2E2* (2km SE Rural) *53.19596, 11.34046* **Camping am Wiesengrund,** Am Kanal 4, 19294 Malliss **(038750) 21060; sielaff-camping@t-online.de; www.camping-malliss.m-vp.de**

€2.50 nr

Sp in Malliss on rd 191 fr Ludwigslust to Uelzen. 4*, Sm, pt shd, EHU (16A) €2; gas; sw nr; 30% statics; phone; watersports; bike hire; CKE. *"Well-run, pleasant, family site; beautiful surroundings; barrier clsd 1200-1400; m'van o'night facs; visit Ludwigslust Palace & Dömitz Fortress; vg; lovely site and v friendly staff."* **€16.50** 2020

MALSCH *3C3* (4km S Rural) *48.86165, 8.33789* **Campingpark Bergwiesen,** Waldenfelsstrasse 1, 76316 Malsch **(07246) 1467; email@campingpark-bergwiesen.eu; www.campingpark-bergwiesen.eu**

12 €2 nr

Fr Karlsruhe on B3 thro Malsch vill over level x-ing to Waldprechtsweier. Foll site sp, take care tight L turn & steep app thro residential area. 4*, Lge, hdg, mkd, hdstg, pt shd, terr, serviced pitches; EHU (16A); gas; sw nr; 80% statics; Eng spkn; adv bkg req; CKE. *"1st class facs; well-run site in beautiful forest setting; v friendly site & owner; not rec for long o'fits or lge m'vans; gd walks fr site; no wifi."* **€19.00** **2022**

MANNHEIM *3C2* (8km S Urban) *49.44841, 8.44806* **Camping am Strandbad,** Strandbadweg 1, 68199 Mannheim-Neckarau **(0176) 55422268; Online form; www.campingplatz-mannheim-strandbad.de**

€1.50 nr nr

Exit A6 Karlsruhe-Frankfurt at AB Kreuz Mannheim (junc 27) L onto A656 Mannheim-Neckarau. Exit junc 2 onto B36 dir Neckarau, site sp. 2*, Med, pt shd, EHU (16A) metered; gas; sw; 60% statics; CKE. *"Some noise fr barges on Rhine & factories opp; poss flooding at high water; interesting area; barrier down & recep clsd 1200-1500."* **€20.00, 1 Apr-15 Oct.** **2024**

MARBURG AN DER LAHN *1C4* (2km S Urban) *50.80000, 8.76861* **Camping Lahnaue,** Trojedamm 47, 35037 Marburg-an-der-Lahn **(06421) 21331; info@lahnaue.de; www.lahnaue.de**

€2.50 nr nr

Site by Rv Lahn, app fr sports cent. Exit a'bahn at Marburg Mitte & sp fr a'bahn. 3*, Med, mkd, pt shd, EHU (10A) €2; sw nr; 10% statics; Eng spkn; ccard acc; tennis nr; rv canoeing; CKE. *"Busy site; some pitches v narr; boating nrby; quiet but m'way & rlwy noise; clsd 1300-1500; cycle & footpath to interesting town; pool adj; excel pool adj; gd."* **€27.00, 1 Apr-30 Oct.** **2024**

MARKTHEIDENFELD *3D2* (5km S Rural) *49.81885, 9.58851* **Camping Main-Spessart-Park,** Spessartstrasse 30, 97855 Triefenstein-Lengfurt **(09395) 1079; info@camping-main-spessart.de; www.camping-main-spessart.de**

12 €2.50

Exit A3/E41 junc 65 or 66 sp Lengfurt. In Lengfurt foll sp Marktheidenfeld; site in 1km. 5*, Lge, pt shd, pt sl, terr, serviced pitches; EHU (6-10A) €3; 50% statics; Eng spkn; adv bkg acc; ccard acc; watersports; CKE. *"Excel, high quality site; vg rest; vg san facs; easy access A4; sep NH area; helpful owners; access diff parts of site due steep terrs; busy site; pool adj; gd facs."* **€27.50** **2022**

MEDELBY *1D1* (0.7km W Rural) *54.81490, 9.16361* **Camping Kawan Mitte,** Sonnenhügel 1, 24994 Medelby **(04605) 189391; info@camping-mitte.de; www.camping-mitte.de**

12 (htd) nr (htd)

Exit A7 junc 2 onto B199 dir Niebüll to Wallsbüll, turn N dir Medelby, site sp. 5*, Lge, mkd, pt shd, EHU (16A) metered; bbq; cooking facs; TV; 20% statics; adv bkg acc; fitness rm; horseriding 600m; sauna; games area; bike hire; golf 12km; CKE. *"Conv m'way & Danish border; vg."* **€32.00** **2022**

MEISSEN *2G4* (5km S Rural) *51.13942, 13.49883* **Camping Rehbocktal,** Rehbocktal 4, 01665 Scharfenberg-bei-Meissen **(01514) 2497758; info@camping-rehbocktal.de; www.camping-rehbocktal.de**

€2 nr

Exit E40/A4 at Dresden Altstadt; foll sp Meissen on B6 to Scharfenberg; site on L opp Rv Elbe. 3*, Med, pt shd, pt sl, EHU (16A) €3; 10% statics; bus; CKE. *"In wooded valley opp vineyard; friendly staff; conv Colditz; Meissen factory & museum worth visit; cycle path to Meissen nr."* **€26.00, 15 Mar-31 Oct.** **2024**

MELLE *1C3* (8km NW Rural) *52.22428, 8.2661* **Campingplatz Grönegau-Park Ludwigsee,** Nemdenerstrasse 12, 49326 Melle **(05402) 2132; info@ludwigsee.de; www.ludwigsee.de**

12 €3 nr

Exit A30/E30 junc 22 twd Bad Essen, site sp on lakeside. 4*, Lge, hdg, mkd, pt shd, EHU (10A) inc; sw; 80% statics; adv bkg acc; ccard acc; games area; bike hire; CKE. *"Beautiful & pleasant site; sep car park; barrier clsd 1300-1500; helpful owners; sep area for tourers."* **€37.00** **2023**

MENDIG *3B2* (7km N Rural) *50.42151, 7.26448* **Camping Laacher See,** Am Laacher See, 56653 Wassenach **(02821) 3939997; info@camping-laacher-see.de; www.rcn.nl/laachersee**

€4 (htd)

Fr A61, exit junc 34 Mendig. Foll tents sp to Maria Laach. Site on Laacher See. 4*, Lge, hdstg, mkd, hdg, pt shd, pt sl, terr, EHU (16A) metered + conn fee; gas; sw; 50% statics; bus 500m; Eng spkn; adv bkg acc; ccard acc; fishing; sailing; CKE. *"Beautiful, neat, clean, relaxing site; all pitches lake views; busy at w/end; modern, outstanding san facs; gd woodland walks, cycling & sw; excel sailing facs & sw; excel site & rest; close to m'way; rec; helpful staff; avoid arr bet 11am-2pm when recep clsd."* **€48.00, 1 Apr-30 Sep.** **2023**

GERMANY

MENDIG *3B2* (2km NNW Rural) *50.38646, 7.27237* **Camping Siesta,** Laacherseestrasse 6, 56743 Mendig **(02652) 1432; service@campingsiesta.de; www.campingsiesta.de**

€2

Fr A61 exit junc 34 for Mendig dir Maria Laach; foll camp sps; site on R in 300m by ent to car park. 3*, Med, hdg, pt shd, sl, EHU (16A) €2.5; gas; 60% statics; Eng spkn; CKE. *"Useful NH; easy access fr A61; owner helpful in siting NH o'fits; longest waterslide in Europe; gd base for region's castles & wines; friendly owners; spotless site; gd rest; site has so much more to offer than only a NH; v welcoming; vg refurbished; new san facs (2014)."* **€24.00** **2024**

"I need an on-site restaurant"

We do our best to make sure site information is correct, but it is always best to check any must-have facilities are still available or will be open during your visit.

MESCHEDE *1C4* (10km S Rural) *51.29835, 8.26425* **Knaus Campingpark Hennesee,** Mielinghausen 7, 59872 Meschede **(0291) 952720; hennesee@knauscamp.de; www.knauscamp.de**

€3.80

S fr Meschede on B55 for 7km; at sp for Erholungszentrum & Remblinghausen turn L over Lake Hennesee, site on L in 500m, sp. 5*, Lge, mkd, pt shd, terr, serviced pitches; EHU (6A) conn fee; gas; sw nr; 60% statics; Eng spkn; adv bkg acc; bike hire; sauna; CKE. *"Conv Sauerland mountains & lakes; 50m elec cable advisable; vg."* **€28.70** **2020**

MITTENWALD *4E4* (4km N Rural) *47.47290, 11.27729* **Naturcamping Isarhorn,** Am Horn 4, 82481 Mittenwald **(08823) 5216; info@camping-isarhorn.de and anfrage@camping-isarhorn.de; www.camping-isarhorn.de**

€4.50

E fr Garmisch-Partenkirchen on rd 2; at Krün turn S on D2/E533 dir Mittenwald. Site on R in approx 2km at int'l camping sp. Ent on R fr main rd. NB: Rd thro to Innsbruck via Zirlerberg improved & no longer clsd to c'vans descending S; long & steep; low gear; not to be attempted N. 4*, Lge, hdstg, pt shd, EHU (16A) inc; bbq; bus adj; Eng spkn; ccard acc; tennis; site clsd 1 Nov-mid Dec; site clsd 1300-1500 & 2200-0700; canoeing. *"Relaxed, secluded site in pines; mountain views; excel base for walking; htd covrd pool 4km; cycle track to attractive town; poss some noise fr nrby military base; ski lift; owner v keen on recycling waste; facs gd, warm and modern; highly rec; v conv NH en route to Italy; helpful staff."* **€36.00, 1 Jan - 4 Nov.** **2024**

MITTENWALD *4E4* (8km N Rural) *47.49040, 11.25438* **Alpen-Caravanpark Tennsee,** Am Tennsee 1, 82493 Klais-Krün **(08825) 170; info@camping-tennsee.de; www.camping-tennsee.de**

€3.30 (htd)

N fr Mittenwald on main Innsbruck-Garmisch rd turn off for Krun, foll Tennsee & site sp. 2km SE of Klais, not well sp. 5*, Lge, mkd, hdstg, pt shd, terr, serviced pitches; EHU (16A) metered; gas; phone; Eng spkn; adv bkg acc; ccard acc; bike hire; CKE. *"Excel area for Bavarian Alps, Tirol; barrier clsd 1200-1500; gd size pitches; ski lift 2.5km; red snr citizens; vg, clean, friendly, family-run site; price inc use of tourist buses."* **€35.00, 1 Jan-2 Nov, 18 Dec-31 Dec.** **2022**

MITTERTEICH *4F2* (3km NW Rural) *49.97311, 12.22497* **Campingplatz Großbüchlberg,** Großbüchlberg 32, 95666 Mitterteich **09633 40 06 73; camping@freizeithugl.de; www.freizeithugl.de**

€1.50 (htd)

Fr A93 Marktredwitz-Mitterteich take exit 16 Mitterteich. At xrds in town cent foll Freizeithugl signs. Turn L after 200m twds Grossbuchberg. Foll sp. 5*, Med, hdg, mkd, hdstg, pt shd, pt sl, terr, EHU (16A); twin axles; TV; bus adj; Eng spkn; adv bkg acc; ccard acc; CCI. *"Excel site; superb htd san facs; washing machine €3; close to mini golf, toboggan run, etc; extensive views; v friendly."* **€32.00** **2023**

MONSCHAU *3A1* (3km SW Rural) *50.54305, 6.23694* **Camping Perlenau,** 52156 Monschau **(02472) 4136; familie.rasch@monschau-perlenau.de; www.monschau-perlenau.de**

€2.60 (htd)

Fr N (Aachen) foll B258 past Monschau dir Schleiden. Site on L just bef junc with B399 to Kalterherberg. Steep & narr app. Fr Belgium, exit A3 junc 38 for Eupen & foll rd thro Eupen to Monschau. Site on rvside. 3*, Med, hdstg, mkd, hdg, pt shd, pt sl, terr, EHU (10-16A) €2.60 or metered; gas; bbq; cooking facs; red long stay; 20% statics; phone; bus 500m; Eng spkn; adv bkg acc; CKE. *"Gd touring base for Eifel region; attractive site beside stream; historic town in walking dist."* **€27.60, 20 Mar-31 Oct.** **2024**

MONTABAUR *3C2* (8km E Rural) *50.43761, 7.90498* **Camping Eisenbachtal,** 56412 Girod **(06485) 766; www.facebook.com/campingeisenbachtal**

€2 (htd) nr

S on A3/E35 exit junc 41 dir Montabaur; at Girod turn L to site, well sp. Med, hdg, mkd, hdstg, pt shd, pt sl, serviced pitches; EHU (10A) inc (poss rev pol); gas; sw nr; red long stay; 75% statics; Eng spkn; adv bkg acc; CKE. *"Beautiful, well-equipped site in Naturpark Nassau; conv NH fr a'bahn & worth longer stay; friendly, welcoming staff; gd for nature lovers & children; gd walking & cycling; adj rest excel; site clsd 1300-1500 but car park opp; conv Rhine & Mosel valleys."* **€18.00** **2024**

GERMANY

MORFELDEN *3C2* (3km E Rural) *49.97986, 8.59461* **Campingplatz Mörfelden,** Am Zeltzplatz 5-15, 64546 Mörfelden-Walldorf **(06105) 22289; info@campingplatz-moerfelden.de; www.campingplatz-moerfelden.de**

12 €1.50 (WD) (MSP)

Fr A5 exit 24, turn W on 486 twds Morfelden. In 200m turn L, opp Holiday Inn. Site on R in 100m. 3*, Med, pt shd, EHU (16A) metered or €2.50; gas; phone; Eng spkn. *"Conv NH/sh stay for Frankfurt; excel, modern san facs; helpful owner; vg."*
€34.00 **2022**

"Satellite navigation makes touring much easier"

Remember most sat navs don't know if you're towing or in a larger vehicle – always use yours alongside maps and site directions.

MUNCHEN *4E4* (7km S Urban) *48.09165, 11.54516* **Camping München-Thalkirchen,** Zentralländstrasse 49, 81379 München **(089) 7231707 or 72430450; info@campingmuenchen.de; campingplatz-thalkirchen.de**

(htd) (WD) (MSP)

Fr S on A95/E533 at end of a'bahn keep strt on (ignore zoo sp). After tunnel exit R at sp Thalkirchen. Turn L at traff lts & foll sp to camp. If app fr S on A8/E45 turn L at traff lts at end twd Garmish & strt on to tunnel, site sp. Fr NW at end of A8 in 200m turn R & foll sp to zoo (Tierpark). Cont to foll zoo sp until in approx 10km pick up sp to site. (Zoo on E side of Rv Isar, site on W side.) App fr N not rec due v heavy traff. 3*, V lge, mkd, pt shd, serviced pitches; EHU (10A) €2 (long lead req); sw nr; phone; bus 100m; Eng spkn; ccard acc; games rm; CKE. *"Busy site; some m'van/o'night pitches v sm; bus/U-bahn tickets avail fr recep; cycle track/walk along rv to town cent, avoiding traff; helpful staff; san facs clean, stretched when site full; gd site when visiting Munich; gd canoeing; rec; gd."*
€35.00, 15 Mar-15 Oct. **2023**

MUNCHEN *4E4* (12km NW Urban) *48.19888, 11.49694* **Campingplatz Nord-West,** Auf den Schrederwiesen 3, 80995 München-Moosach **(089) 1506936; info@campingplatz-nord-west.de; www.campingplatz-nord-west.de**

12 €2 (htd) (WD) (MSP) nr

Fr N exit A99 junc 10 Lugwigsfeld onto B304 S - Dachauerstrasse, sp München. Turn L in approx 800m at traff lts. Turn R at T-junc to site on R. Med, hdstg, shd, EHU (10-16A) €5 or metered; 50% statics; phone; bus to city; Eng spkn; adv bkg acc; ccard acc; CKE. *"Friendly, helpful welcome; enquire about public transport tickets; ltd facs LS; Dachau - pretty town 10km; gd; Dachau Concentration Camp Memorial worth a visit."* **€28.00** **2023**

MUNCHEN *4E4* (17km NW Rural) *48.19821, 11.41161* **Campingplatz am Langwieder See,** Eschenriederstrasse 119, 81249 München-Langwied **(089) 8641566; info@camping-langwieder-see.de; www.camping-langwieder-see.de**

12 €1.70 (htd) (WD)

Exit A8 junc 80 at Langwieder See & foll sp Dachau; site within 200m. Fr ring rd A99 junc 8 join A8 to N, then as above. Med, hdstg, pt shd, EHU (10A) metered + conn fee €1; gas; sw nr; 95% statics; Eng spkn; CKE. *"Pleasant owners; tourers in a row outside recep area parked v close together; v sm pitches, mostly on gravel; gd san facs; site used by workers; easy access to Munich by train fr Dachau; lge free car park at stn; NH/sh stay only."* **€21.50** **2022**

MUNSTER *1B3* (9km SE Rural) *51.94638, 7.69027* **Camping Münster,** Laerer Wersuefer 7, 48157 Münster **(0251) 311982; mail@campingplatz-muenster.de; www.campingplatz-muenster.de**

12 €3 (htd) (WD) (MSP)

Fr A43 exit junc 2 or A1/E37 exit junc 78 onto B51 dir Münster then Bielefeld. On leaving built-up area, turn R after TV mast on R. Cross Rv Werse & turn L at 1st traff lts, site sp. (Site is also sp fr Münster S by-pass). 5*, Lge, mkd, hdstg, pt shd, serviced pitches; EHU (16A) inc; bbq; twin axles; 50% statics; bus 150m; Eng spkn; adv bkg acc; ccard acc; tennis; bike hire; fishing; CKE. *"Excel; quiet mid wk; Münster very interesting; radio/TV mast useful landmark fr S; gd cycle rtes; o'night m'van area; barrier clsd 1300-1500; htd pool adj; vg site, tokens for shwrs; sep motor parking outside camp; excel for bus to Munster; helpful staff; clean facs & plentiful; well organised; pitches cramped; gd rest."* **€24.00** **2022**

MUNSTERTAL *3B4* (2km WNW Rural) *47.85995, 7.76370* **Feriencamping Münstertal,** Dietzelbachstrasse 6, 79244 Münstertal **(07636) 7080; info@camping-muenstertal.de; www.camping-muenstertal.de**

12 €3.50 (WD) (MSP) (covrd, htd)

Exit A5 junc 64a at Bad Krozingen-Staufen-Münstertal. By-pass Stauffen & foll Münstertal sps. Site on L 1.5km past Camping Belchenblick off rd L123. 5*, Lge, mkd, shd, serviced pitches; EHU (16A) metered; gas; red long stay; TV (pitch); 10% statics; phone; adv bkg rec; fishing; tennis; horseriding; games area; games rm; CKE. *"Superb, well-managed site; luxurious, clean facs; beauty treatments avail; winter sports nrby; ski lift 10km; sauna; steam rm; solarium; private bthrms avail; many organised activities for all family; gd walking; vg rest; conv Freiburg & Black Forest; new premium pitches (2016); rlwy stn 200m; gates clsd 1300-1430 & 2200-0730; m'van o'night area; friendly staff."* **€46.60** **2023**

GERMANY

MURNAU AM STAFFELSEE *4E4* (3.5km NW Rural) *47.68493, 11.17918* **Camping Halbinsel Burg,** Burgweg 41, 82418 Murnau-Seehausen **(08841) 9870 and (08841) 9434; info@camping-staffelsee.de; www.camping-staffelsee.de**

Exit A95 junc 9 Sindelsdorf/Peissenberg to Murnau. Site sp at traff lts in cent of Murnau, dir Seehausen. 3*, Med, pt shd, EHU (16A) €2.50; sw; 20% statics; watersports; CKE. *"Wonderful sw & boating; pleasant, lovely, well-equipped site in superb location for alps, lakes & local amenities."*
€26.00, 6 Jan-25 Oct. **2024**

NEEF *3B2* (0.5km N Rural) *50.09500, 7.13694* **Wohnmobilplatz Am Frauenberg,** Am Moselufer, 56858 Neef **(06542) 1512; info@verkehrsverein-neef.de**

nr nr

Exit A1/E44 junc 125 onto B49 to Neef. In Neef cross rv bdge, site sp on L beside rv. M'vans only. Med, pt shd, EHU (10A) inc. *"Gd; owner calls am & pm for payment; beautiful location."*
€5.00, 1 Mar-30 Oct. **2024**

NEEF *3B2* (4km S Urban) *50.05294, 7.13115* **Bären Camp Bullay,** Am Moselufer 1+3, D-56859 Bullay (Mosel) **06542 900097; info@baeren-camp.de; www.baeren-camp.de**

(htd)

Foll B49 to Alf, cross Moselle bdge to Bullay. Turn L and drive under the rlwy bdge, foll the rd. At the vill sq turn into Fährstrasse, drive across Moselle car park past the football grnd foll sp to site. 4*, Sm, mkd, pt shd, bbq; Eng spkn; CKE. *"Fair site; handy for Mosel Cycle Rte; diff ent, barrier down rest time."* **€35.60, 28 Mar-3 Nov.** **2024**

NENNIG *3A2* (1.6km N Rural) *49.54195, 6.37126* **Mosel-Camping Dreiländereck,** Am Moselufer, 66706 Perl-Nennig **(06866) 322; info@mosel-camping.de; www.mosel-camping.de**

€1 (htd) nr

Site on bank of Mosel opp Remich (Luxembourg), access on R just bef bdge (fr German side). Fr Luxembourg cross rv bdge, turn L after former border post cont to rv & turn L under bldg; site is ahead. Med, unshd, EHU (16A) inc; bbq; red long stay; 65% statics; phone; Eng spkn; adv bkg acc; golf 15km; cycling; fishing; CKE. *"Nice, lovely site; dishwashing & chem disp adj; ltd, tired facs; conv vineyards, Roman mosaic floor in Nennig; cycle track along rv; sh walk to Remich; shwr €2 for 5 mins; lndry €5; cash only; friendly welcome; 4km walk/cycle into Wesel via cycle path."* **€25.00, 1 Apr-15 Oct.** **2024**

NENNIG *3A2* (1.8km N Rural) *49.54331, 6.37207* **Camping Mosella am Rothaus (formerly Moselplatz),** Zur Moselbrücke 15, 66706 Perl-Nennig **(06866) 510 or 1522 8601461; info@camping-mosella.de; camping-mosella.de**

(htd) nr

Site on bank of Mosel opp Remich (Luxembourg), access on R just bef bdge. Fr Luxembourg cross rv bdge, turn L after former border post, site is ahead, opp Mosel-Camping Dreiländereck. Med, hdg, pt shd, EHU (10A) inc; bbq; 50% statics; bus 100m; Eng spkn; CKE. *"Lovely, well placed site by rv for sh or long stay; helpful, friendly owner; ltd facs, a bit tired; rest nr; rvside pitch sm extra charge; gd touring base; frequent bus to Luxembourg City."*
€12.00, 1 Apr-15 Oct. **2023**

NESSLBACH *4G3* (0.7km W Rural) *48.69400, 13.11638* **Donautal Camping,** Schillerstrasse 14, 94577 Nesslbach-Winzer **(01512) 6245360; info@camping-donautal.de; www.camping-donautal.de**

12 (htd) nr nr

Exit A3/E56 junc 112 to Nesslbach. Site adj sports stadium, sp. Sm, mkd, unshd, EHU (6A) inc; 20% statics; games area. *"Adj Danube cycleway; lovely, open site; dogs free; friendly staff; lge pitches - easy access lge o'fits; ltd san facs but clean; site yourself instructions if site not manned; vg."* **€15.00** **2024**

NEUMARKT IN DER OBERPFALZ *4E3* (10km N Rural) *49.32944, 11.42876* **Campingplatz Berg,** Hausheimerstrasse 31, 92348 Berg **(09189) 1581; campingplatz-herteis@t-online.de; www.camping-in-berg.de**

12 €2 nr nr

Exit A3 junc 91 & foll sp Berg bei Neumarkt. In cent of Berg, turn R, site on R in 800m, sp. On ent turn R to tourers area & walk to recep. 3*, Med, unshd, pt sl, EHU (20A) €2.50; 60% statics; Eng spkn; golf 8km. *"Well-run, friendly, family-owned site; excel san facs; sh walk to Berg cent; excel touring base; gd NH fr m'way; pleasant views of countryside; canal walk."*
€24.00 **2022**

NEUMUNSTER *1D1* (6km SW Rural) *54.04636, 9.92306* **Familien-Camping Forellensee,** Humboldredder 5, 24634 Padenstedt **(04321) 82697; info@familien-campingplatz.de; www.familien-campingplatz.de**

12 €1.50 nr

Exit A7 junc 14 for Padenstedt, join dual c'way for 1km & turn L sp Centrum. In 1km turn L at traff lts sp Padenstedt for 3km, under m'way. Site on L in vill. 4*, Lge, mkd, pt shd, EHU (16A) €3.50 or metered; sw; 75% statics; phone; Eng spkn; tennis; trout fishing; games area; CKE. *"Gd NH; conv for trains to Hamburg/Lübeck; swimming lake with section for dogs."*
€26.00 **2024**

NEUREICHENAU *4G3* (8km E Urban) *48.74861, 13.81694* **Knaus Campingpark Lackenhäuser,** Lackenhäuser 127, 94089 Neureichenau **(08583) 311; lackenhaeuser@knauscamp.de; www.knauscamp.de**

12 €2.50 (htd)

Leave A3/E56 at junc 14 (Aicha-vorm Wald) & go E for 50km via Waldkirchen, Jandelsbrunn, Gsenget & Klafferstrasse to Lackenhäuser. 4*, Lge, mkd, hdg, pt shd, pt sl, terr, serviced pitches; EHU (16A) €2.60 or metered; gas; bbq; red long stay; TV; 40% statics; adv bkg acc; ccard acc; horseriding adj; fishing; tennis 500m; games rm; sauna; bike hire. *"Lge site with little waterfalls & walkways; ski lift on site - equipment for hire; mv service pnt diff to access; excel shop; 2km to 3 point border with Austria & Czech Republic; excursions booked; solarium; hairdresser; recep clsd 1200-1500 & after 1800."* **€43.50** **2022**

NEUSTADT AN DER AISCH *4E2* (9km N Rural) *49.64058, 10.59975* **Campingplatz Münchsteinach,** Badstrasse 10, 91481 Münchsteinach **(09166) 750; gemeinde@muenchsteinach.de; www.muenchsteinach.de**

12 €2 nr

Turn NW fr rd 470 Neustadt-Höchstadt at camp sp 8km fr Neustadt & thro Gutenstetten. Int'l camping sp in 5km turn R, foll camp sp. Lge, unshd, EHU (16A) metered; red long stay; 60% statics; CKE. *"Sm touring area; clean facs; pool adj; site muddy when wet."* **€11.00** **2022**

NEUSTADT AN DER WALDNAAB *4F2* (1km NW Urban) *49.73750, 12.17222* **Waldnaab Camping,** Gramaustrasse 64, 92660 Neustadt-an-der-Waldnaab **(09602) 94340; poststelle@neustadt-waldnaab.de; www.neustadt-waldnaab.de**

12 €1.50 (htd) nr nr

Exit A93 junc 21a onto B15 for 4km S into Neustadt. Site sp fr N side of vill. 3*, Sm, hdg, pt shd, EHU (16A) inc; games area. *"Helpful owners; clean facs; excel value for money."* **€17.00** **2024**

NEUSTADT/HARZ *2E4* (2km NW Rural) *51.56897, 10.82836* **Campingplatz am Waldbad,** An der Burg 3, 99762 Neustadt/Harz **(036331) 479891; info@neustadt-harz-camping.de; www.neustadt-harz-camping.de**

12 €2 (htd)

Fr A38, exit J10 for B243 to Nordhausen. Turn L onto B4 dir Niedersachswerfen. Turn R onto L1037, L onto Osteroder Straße and R onto Klostergasse. Foll sp to campsite. 4*, Med, hdg, pt shd, pt sl, EHU (10A) metered + con fee; twin axles; 50% statics; adv bkg acc; games area; CCI. *"Gd site; conv for Harz; helpful owners; vg san facs."* **€18.90** **2024**

NEUSTRELITZ *2F2* (10km SW Rural) *53.30895, 13.00305* **Camping- und Ferienpark Havelberge,** An der Havelbergen 1, 17237 Gross Quassow **(03981) 24790; info@haveltourist.de; www.haveltourist.de**

nr

Fr Neustrelitz foll sp to Userin on L25 & bef Userin turn L sp Gross Quassow. Turn S in vill at camping sp, cross rlwy line & rv, sm ent in 1.5km. Site 1.7km S of Gross Quassow twd lake, sp. 5*, Lge, pt shd, pt sl, EHU (16A) €2.90; sw; 30% statics; watersports; sauna; bike hire. *"Lovely wooded area; poss diff lge o'fits; not rec as NH."* **€40.00, 01 Apr-03 Nov, G11.** **2022**

NIESKY *2H4* (3km W Rural) *51.30156, 14.80302* **Campingplatz Tonschächte (Part Naturist),** Raschkestrasse, 02906 Niesky **(03588) 205771; info@campingplatz-tonschacht.de; campingplatz-tonschacht.de**

nr

Leave A4/E40 at junc 93 onto B115 sp Niesky; cont on B115 site sp on L; do not go into Niesky but stay on B115. 2*, Lge, shd, EHU (10A); 50% statics; games area. *"Conv Polish border x-ing & a'bahn; sep naturist area."* **€12.50, 15 Apr-15 Oct.** **2022**

> **"There aren't many sites open at this time of year"**
>
> If you're travelling outside peak season remember to call ahead to check site opening dates – even if the entry says 'open all year'.

NOHFELDEN *3B2* (10km SW Rural) *49.56072, 7.06105* **Campingplatz Bostalsee,** 66625 Nohfelden-Bosen **6851 801 8050; campingplatz@bostalsee.de; www.bostalsee.de/campingplatz**

12 €2 (htd) nr

Fr A62 exit junc 3 sp Nohfelden/Türkismühle & Bostalsee. Turn R & foll camp sp. Site on R in 1.6km after passing thro vill of Bosen. 5*, V lge, mkd, unshd, pt sl, EHU (16A) €2; sw nr; 75% statics; adv bkg acc; sauna; golf 7km; watersports. *"Vg san facs; pleasant lakeside site but poss unrel in wet; clsd to vehicles 1300-1500 & 2200-0700; spacious, hdstg pitches; conv NH."* **€20.00** **2024**

NORDEN *1B2* (5km W Coastal) *53.60471, 7.13863* **Nordsee-Camp Norddeich,** Deichstrasse 21, 26506 Norden-Norddeich **(04931) 8073; info@nordsee-camp.de; www.Nordsee-Camp.de**

€3.80 200m

Off B70 N of Norden. Well sp. V lge, mkd, pt shd, EHU (6A) €2.20; 25% statics; ccard acc; fishing; bike hire; CKE. *"Immac san facs; friendly atmosphere; day trips to Frisian Islands; excel rest; vg site."* **€37.00, 20 Mar-22 Oct.** **2022**

NURNBERG *4E2* (8km SE Urban) *49.42305, 11.12138* **Knaus Campingpark Nürnberg,** Hans-Kalb-Strasse 56, 90471 Nürnberg **(0911) 9812717; nuernberg@knauscamp.de; www.knauscamp.de**

12 €5 (on request) (htd) WD MSP nr

Exit E45/A9 junc 52 or E50/A6 junc 59 dir Nürnberg-Langwasser heading N, or Nürnberg-Fischbach exit travelling S; foll sp to 'Stadion', turn L. Site ent off wide rd opp Nürnberg Conference Cent. 4*, Lge, mkd, pt shd, EHU (6-16A) €3 (long cable rec); gas; red long stay; TV; 25% statics; tram/metro 1.2km; Eng spkn; adv bkg acc; ccard acc; tennis; CKE. *"Friendly, helpful staff; peaceful, surrounded by trees; san facs poss stretched high ssn; quiet; htd pool adj; gd security; office & access clsd 1300-1500 & 2200-0700; gd cycle rte to town; national rlwy museum in town worth visit; 1.2km to metro to town cent; red squirrels on site."* **€40.00** **2024**

NURNBERG *4E2* (12km W Rural) *49.43174, 10.92541* **Camping Zur Mühle,** Seewaldstraße 75, 90513 Zirndorf/Leichendorf **(0911) 693801; camping.walther@t-online.de; www.camping-zur-muehle.de**

€2 (htd) WD

Head W on Adlerstraße twd Stangengäßchen, cont onto Josephspl, then Vordere Lederg. Cont onto Schlotfegerg then onto Further Tor; Cont onto Dennerstraße then slight R onto Am Plärrer. Cont onto Rothenburger Str, turn L to stay on Rothenburger. Turn R twd Seewaldstraße, keep R. Site on L. Med, mkd, pt shd, EHU metered; bbq; ccard acc; CKE. *"Mastercard acc not Visa; local style rest in traditional building on site; conv for visiting Nurnberg; vg site."* **€24.00, 1 Apr-31 Dec.** **2024**

"That's changed – Should I let the Club know?"

If you find something on site that's different from the site entry, fill in a report and let us know. See camc.com/europereport.

OBERAMMERGAU *4E4* (1km S Rural) *47.58988, 11.0696* **Campingpark Oberammergau,** Ettalerstrasse 56B, 82487 Oberammergau **(08822) 94105; info@camping-oberammergau.de; www.campingpark-oberammergau.de**

12 €2 WD MSP nr nr

Fr S turn R off B23, site on L in 1km. Fr N turn L at 2nd Oberammergau sp. Do not ent vill fr N - keep to bypass. 4*, Med, hdg, mkd, hdstg, pt shd, EHU (16A) metered + conn fee; gas; red long stay; 25% statics; bus; Eng spkn; adv bkg rec; sep car park; bike hire; CKE. *"Plenty of space; helpful recep; excel san facs; excel rest adj; easy walk to vill; well run site, visitor tax does not apply to one night stays."* **€29.60** **2023**

OBERSTDORF *3D4* (2km N Rural) *47.42370, 10.27843* **Rubi-Camp,** Rubingerstrasse 34, 87561 Oberstdorf **(08322) 959202; info@rubi-camp.de; www.rubi-camp.de**

12 €4 (htd) WD MSP nr

Fr Sonthofen on B19, just bef Oberstdorf at rndabt take exit sp Reichenbach, Rubi. Site in 1km over level x-ing, 2nd site on R. 5*, Med, hdstg, unshd, serviced pitches; EHU (8A) metered; bbq; TV; 10% statics; phone; bus; Eng spkn; adv bkg acc; site clsd Nov; CKE. *"Well-run, well-maintained site; immac facs; block paved paths to pitches; block hdstg with grass growing thro; ski lift 1km; excel scenery; excel facs; easy 20 min level walk to town."* **€38.80** **2024**

OBERSTDORF *3D4* (3km N Rural) *47.42300, 10.27720* **Campingplatz Oberstdorf,** Rubingerstrasse 16, 87561 Oberstdorf **(08322) 6525; info@camping-oberstdorf.de; www.camping-oberstdorf.de**

12 €0.50 WD MSP nr nr

Turn off B19 at rndabt dir Oberstdorf, L at next rndabt, R after rly level x-ing. 3*, Med, hdstg, hdg, pt shd, serviced pitches; EHU (10A) €4.50; 45% statics; Eng spkn; adv bkg acc; golf 5km. *"Cable cars to Nebelhorn & Fellhorn in town; ski lift 3km; ski bus; Oberstdorf pedestrianised with elec buses fr o'skirts; vg."* **€29.00** **2023**

OBERWESEL *3B2* (8km N Urban) *50.15995, 7.70875* **Camping Loreleystadt,** Wellmicher Str 55, 56346 St Goarshausen **(06771) 2592; info@camping-loreleystadt.de; www.camping-loreleystadt.de**

WD MSP nr

Site on B42, E side of Rhine on N o'skts of St Goarshausen, sp, but take care not to overshoot. Med, unshd, EHU (10A) metered + conn fee €1.28; gas; sw; 10% statics; adv bkg acc. *"Poss flooding in heavy rain."* **€24.00, 20 Mar-31 Oct.** **2024**

OBERWESEL *3B2* (7.6km SE Rural) *50.05111, 7.7750* **Camping Sonnenstrand,** Strandbadweg 9, 55422 Bacharach **(06743) 1752; info@camping-sonnenstrand.de; www.camping-rhein.de**

€1 WD MSP adj

S on A61. Exit 44 Laudert via Oberwesel to Bacharach (B9). Turn Sat Nav off after Laudert. Foll sp to Oberwesel-Bacharach. Med, mkd, hdstg, pt shd, EHU (6A); bbq; twin axles; red long stay; 25% statics; Eng spkn; boating; golf 6km; games area; bike hire; games rm; CKE. *"Helpful, knowledgeable owner; poss lge groups m'cyclists; scenic area; busy, noisy rvside site; sm pitches; wine cellar visits; shwrs/san facs ltd & poss stretched high ssn; plenty of rv activities; excel rest; sh walk to sm medieval town; sh stay/NH; gd."* **€19.50, 25 Mar-31 Oct.** **2022**

OBERWESEL *3B2* (0.9km S Urban) *50.10251, 7.73664* **Camping Schönburgblick,** Am Hafendamm 1, 55430 Oberwesel **(06744) 714501; info@camping-oberwesel.de; www.camping-oberwesel.de**

nr nr

Fr A61/E31 exit sp Oberwesel, site sp on L at ent to sports stadium, on rvside. Sm, pt shd, EHU (6A) €4.20; red long stay; adv bkg acc; tennis adj; CKE. *"Clean, modern san facs in Portacabins - stretched when site full; o'night m'vans area; rv trips, cycling, walking."* **€24.50, 11 Mar-1 Nov. 2023**

OHRDRUF *2E4* (10km W Rural) *50.82452, 10.61060* **Campingplatz Paulfeld,** Catterfeld, 99894 Leinatal **(036253) 25171 or (036253) 40993; info@paulfeld-camping.de; www.paulfeld-camping.de**

12 €2

Fr E exit A4 junc 42 onto B88 sp Friedrichroda & foll sp Catterfeld & site on R. Or fr W exit junc 41a at Gotha. Take B247 S twd Ohrdruf. After 6km bear R sp Georgenthal. In Georgenthal vill, bear R onto B88. After 2km site sp L on app Catterfeld vill. Foll rd 2km thro forest to site, sp. Site approx 12km fr A4. 5*, Lge, hdg, pt shd, EHU (16A) inc; gas; bbq; sw; red long stay; twin axles; 40% statics; games rm; sauna; fishing; bike hire; games area; CKE. *"Excel, well-kept site; sm pets corner; gd access to pitches; clean san facs; gd for families with young children; solarium; woodland walks; conv stop en rte eastern Europe; happy family site; helpful friendly owners."* **€26.50 2024**

OLPE *1B4* (8km N Rural) *51.0736, 7.8564* **Feriencamp Biggesee - Vier Jahreszeiten,** Am Sonderner Kopf 3, 57462 Olpe-Sondern **(02761) 944111; biggesee@freizeit-oasen.de; biggesee.freizeit-oasen.de/**

12 €5

Exit A45/E41 junc 18 & foll sp to Biggesee. Pass both turnings to Sondern. Take next R in 200m. Ent on R in 100m. NB: Other sites on lake. 4*, Lge, mkd, pt shd, terr, EHU (16A) inc; gas; cooking facs; sw nr; 20% statics; Eng spkn; adv bkg acc; sauna; tennis; watersports inc diving; solarium; bike hire; CKE. *"Gd facs; well-organised site; barrier clsd 1300-1500 & 2200-0700; rollerskating rink; conv Panorama Theme Park & Cologne; vg cycling area; footpaths."* **€25.00 2022**

OSNABRUCK *1C3* (14km SW Rural) *52.22944, 7.89027* **Regenbogen-Camp Tecklenburg,** Grafenstrasse 31, 49545 Leeden **(05405) 1007; www.regenbogen.ag**

€4 (covrd, htd)

Exit A1/E37 junc 73 or fr A30/E30 junc 13; foll sp to Tecklenburg, then Leeden & foll site sp. V lge, pt shd, pt sl, serviced pitches; EHU (16A) €2.90; 45% statics; adv bkg acc; ccard acc; bike hire; games area; CKE. *"Gd views; o'night area for m'vans open all yr; site clsd 1 Nov-15 Dec; clsd 1300-1500; excel san facs; gd rest."* **€42.00, 1 Apr-31 Oct. 2023**

PAPENBURG *1B2* (1km S Rural) *53.06481, 7.42691* **Camping Poggenpoel,** Am Poggenpoel, 26871 Papenburg **(04961) 974026; campingpcp@aol.com; www.papenburg-camping.de**

12 €2.50 (htd)

Fr B70, site sp fr town. 4*, Med, pt shd, EHU (10A) inc; sw nr; red long stay; TV (pitch); 40% statics; phone; games area; golf 1km; CKE. *"O'night facs for m'vans."* **€27.50 2022**

PAPPENHEIM *4E3* (1.8km N Rural) *48.93471, 10.96993* **Natur Camping Pappenheim,** Badweg 1, 91788 Pappenheim **(09143) 1275; info@camping-pappenheim.de; www.camping-pappenheim.de**

€1 nr

B2 heading S, site sp after passing thro Weissenburg, on edge of Pappenheim. Med, pt shd, EHU (16A) €2; sw; 25% statics; Eng spkn. *"Mountain views; excel site in historical town; castle worth visiting; grass pitches; san facs dated."* **€18.50, 1 Apr-25 Oct. 2023**

PASSAU *4G3* (10km NW Rural) *48.60605, 13.34583* **Drei-Flüsse Campingplatz,** Am Sonnenhang 8, 94113 Irring **(08546) 633; info@dreifluesse-camping.de; dreifluesse-camping.de**

€1.50 (covrd)

On A3/E56, junc 115 (Passau Nord); foll sps to site. 3*, Med, pt shd, pt sl, terr, serviced pitches; EHU (16A) €4; gas; bbq; red long stay; phone; bus 200m; adv bkg acc; ccard acc; CKE. *"Interesting grotto on site; gd rest; rec arr early; facs need updating; poor surface drainage after heavy rain; interesting town at confluence of 3 rvs; on Danube cycle way; conv NH fr A3/E56."* **€28.00, 1 Apr-31 Oct. 2024**

PEISSENBERG *4E4* (1.7km E Rural) *47.78746, 11.08386* **Campingplatz Ammertal,** Badstrasse 51, 82380 Peissenberg **(08803) 2797; info@camping-ammertal.de; www.camping-ammertal.de**

12 €3.50 (htd)

Fr B472, 15km E Schongau turn L over bdge dir Worth. Site sp. Foll sp thro Worth onto Badstrasse. After 1k take bdge over B472, then keep R to site ent. 4*, Med, hdg, mkd, hdstg, pt shd, EHU 10A (metered); gas; bbq (sep area); twin axles; red long stay; TV; 60% statics; phone; bus, train; Eng spkn; adv bkg acc; ccard acc; games area. *"Gd sh stay; helpful owner; gd."* **€31.00 2023**

GERMANY

PFALZFELD *3B2* (1km SW Rural) *50.10612, 7.56804* **Country-Camping Schinderhannes,** Hausbayerstrasse, 56291 Hausbay **(06746) 3889797; info@countrycamping.de; www.countrycamping.de**

€2 (htd) nr

Fr A61/E31 exit J43, foll sps for 3km to Pfalzfeld & onto Hausbay, site sp. 4*, Med, mkd, hdstg, pt shd, terr, EHU (6-16A) inc; sw; twin axles; 10% statics; adv bkg acc; ccard acc; fishing; games rm; tennis; CKE. *"Pleasant, peaceful, clean site; spacious pitches, some far fr san facs; helpful, friendly staff; sep NH area; excel, immac san facs; htd pool 8km; scenic area close Rv Rhine; vg cycle track; nice area for walking; conv m'way; excel NH with sep area to stay hitched-on; wonderful touring area; excel."* **€26.00** **2024**

PFORZHEIM *3C3* (13km S Rural) *48.81800, 8.73400* **International Camping Schwarzwald,** Freibadweg 4, 75242 Neuhausen-Schellbronn **(07234) 6517; famfrech@t-online.de; www.camping-schwarzwald.de**

Fr W on A8 exit junc 43 for Pforzheim; fr E exit junc 45. In town cent take rd 463 sp Calw, but immed after end of town sp take minor rd L thro Huchenfeld up hill to Schellbronn; go R in vill. Site in vill of Schellbronn on N side of rd to Bad Liebenzell - sp at church on R. 4*, Lge, pt shd, pt sl, EHU (17A) €2 or metered; gas; red long stay; 80% statics; bus; adv bkg acc; bike hire; CKE. *"Scenic area; dance & fitness cent; no vehicle access after 2200; htd pool adj; v clean, well-maintained site; vg san facs; excel rest/takeaway; v rural."* **€25.50** **2022**

PIRMASENS *3B3* (20km NE Rural) *49.27546, 7.72121* **Camping Clausensee,** 67714 Waldfischbach-Burgalben **(06333) 5744; info@campingclausensee.de; www.campingclausensee.de**

€4.20 (htd)

Leave a'bahn A6 at junc 15 Kaiserslautern West; S onto B270 for 22km. E 9km on minor rd sp Leimen, site sp. 4*, Lge, mkd, pt shd, serviced pitches; EHU (6-16A) inc; gas; bbq; sw nr; red long stay; TV; 50% statics; Eng spkn; adv bkg acc; ccard acc; fishing; games rm; boating; CKE. *"Peaceful situation in Pfalzerwald Park; helpful staff; clean san facs; busy at w/ends; gd walking & cycling; gd; lovely setting on shore of Lake Clausensee; noisy at wkends when permanent o'fits inhabited."* **€31.50** **2022**

PIRNA *4G1* (3km N Urban) *50.98169, 13.92508* **Camping Pirna (formerly Waldcampingplatz Pirna-Copitz),** Außere Pillnitzerstrasse 19, 01796 Pirna **(03501) 523773; info@camping-pirna.de; camping-pirna.de**

€2.50 (htd) nr nr

Fr B172 fr Dresden to Pirna-Copitz or fr A17/E55. Site well sp. 3*, Med, mkd, pt shd, EHU (10A) €3; 20% statics; bus 200m; adv bkg acc. *"Clean, well-run site; modern facs."* **€33.00, 27 Mar-1 Nov.** **2024**

PLAUEN *4F1* (7km NE Rural) *50.53860, 12.18495* **Camping Gunzenberg Pöhl,** 08543 Möschwitz **+49 (0)37439 - 45050; tourist-info@talsperre-poehl.de; www.camping-poehl.de**

€3

Exit A72/E441 junc 7 & foll sp for Möschwitz & white sp for Talsperre Pöhl. 4*, V lge, hdg, mkd, pt shd, terr, EHU (10A) €2 or metered + conn fee; sw nr; 60% statics; clsd 1230-1400; golf 2km; CKE. *"Excel, v formal, clean site; helpful, friendly staff."* **€30.50, 27 Mar-3 Nov.** **2024**

PORTA WESTFALICA *1C3* (8km SW Rural) *52.22146, 8.83995* **Camping Grosser Weserbogen,** Zum Südlichen See 1, 32457 Porta Westfalica **(05731) 6188 or 6189; info@grosserweserbogen.de; www.grosserweserbogen.de**

€1.50

Fr E30/A2 exit junc 33, foll sp to Vennebeck & Costedt. Site 12km by rd fr Bad Oeynhausen. Site sp fr m'way. 4*, Lge, mkd, hdstg, pt shd, EHU (16A) €2.90; bbq; sw nr; twin axles; Eng spkn; adv bkg acc; ccard acc; fishing; watersports; games rm; CKE. *"Site in cent of wildlife reserve; v tranquil, lovely lakeside location; gd base Teutoburger Wald & Weser valley; barrier clsd 1300-1500 & o'night; 80% statics; lge area for tourers; gd for families; excel san facs & rest; shwrs charged to electronic card; level access; highly rec."* **€27.00** **2022**

"We must tell the Club about that great site we found"

Get your site reports in by mid-August and we'll do our best to get your updates into the next edition.

POTSDAM *2F3* (10km SW Rural) *52.36088, 12.94663* **Camping Riegelspitze,** Fercherstrasse, 14542 Werder-Petzow **(03327) 42397; info@campingplatz-riegelspitze.de; www.campingplatz-riegelspitze.de**

€3

Fr A10/E55 Berlin ring a'bahn take exit 22 dir Glindow or Werder exits & foll sp to Werder; then foll B1 for 1.5km twd Potsdam, R after Strengbrücke bdge twd Petzow. 4*, Lge, pt shd, terr, EHU (16A) €0.50 (poss rev pol & long lead req); sw; 50% statics; bus; Eng spkn; adv bkg acc; watersports; bike hire; CKE. *"Friendly recep; haphazard pitching; no dogs high ssn; transport tickets fr recep; recep clsd 1300-1500 and 2200-0700; bus outside site; Sanssouci visit a must; train to Berlin £6; vg."* **€26.50, 1 Apr-25 Oct.** **2022**

POTSDAM *2F3* (7km SW Rural) *52.36055, 13.00722* **Camping Sanssouci,** An der Pirschheide 41, 14471 Potsdam **(0331) 9510988; info@camping-potsdam.de; www.camping-potsdam.de**

€0

Fr A10 Berlin ring rd take exit 22 at Gross Kreutz onto B1 twd Potsdam cent for approx 17km, past Werder (Havel) & Geltow. Site sp approx 2km after Geltow immed bef rlwy bdge. 5*, Lge, shd, serviced pitches; EHU (6A) inc (poss rev pol); gas; bbq; sw nr; 25% statics; Eng spkn; adv bkg acc; horseriding 8km; games rm; bike hire; watersports; fishing; CKE. *"V helpful, friendly owners; lovely area; sandy pitches; poss diff lge o'fits manoeuvring round trees; excel clean facs inc music & underfloor heating; camp bus to/fr stn; gate clsd 1300-1500; fitness cent; gd security; covrd pool 200m; conv Schlosses & Berlin by rail - minibus to stn; excel site and rest (lge portions); 5 star facs; sm pitches; site & rest cash only; gate opens 7.30am; kitchen, washup and dog shwr; rec."*
€33.00, 1 Apr - 2 Nov, G16. **2022**

"I need an on-site restaurant"

We do our best to make sure site information is correct, but it is always best to check any must-have facilities are still available or will be open during your visit.

POTTENSTEIN *4E2* (3km NW Rural) *49.77942, 11.38411* **Feriencampingplatz Bärenschlucht,** 12 Weidmannsgesees, 91278 Pottenstein **(09243) 206; info@baerenschlucht-camping.de; www.baerenschlucht-camping.de**

12 €1.90 nr

Note - narrow roads and sp difficult to see. Exit A9 junc 44 onto B470 dir Forchheim; cont past Pottenstein; site in 2km on R. Sm, pt shd, pt sl, EHU (8-16A) metered; own san req; gas; cooking facs; 40% statics. *"Surrounded by trees & rocky cliffs, run by friendly farmer; vg; scenic area; local caves & climbing; No san facs; water & EHU metered; excel local rest; adv bkg via email."* **€20.00** **2022**

PREETZ *1D1* (6km SE Rural) *54.21073, 10.31720* **Camp Lanker See,** Gläserkoppel 3, 24211 Preetz Gläserkoppel **(04342) 81513; camp@lankersee.de; www.camp-lankersee.de**

€1

Sp off B76 bet Preetz & Plön. 4*, Lge, mkd, pt shd, terr, EHU (6A) metered; sw; 10% statics; phone; adv bkg acc; ccard acc; horseriding; boating; CKE. *"Barrier clsd 1300-1500 & o'night; gd."*
€22.00, 1 Apr-31 Oct. **2022**

PRIEN AM CHIEMSEE *4F4* (4km SE Rural) *47.83995, 12.37170* **Panorama-Camping Harras,** Harrasserstrasse 135, 83209 Prien-Harras **(08051) 904613; info@camping-harras.de; www.camping-harras.de**

€3.20 (htd)

Exit A8/E52/E60 junc 106 dir Prien. After 2.5km turn R at rndabt sp Krankenhaus & site. 4*, Lge, pt shd, EHU (6A) €2 (poss no earth); gas; sw; 20% statics; Eng spkn; ccard acc; canoeing; golf 3km; bike hire; boat hire; CKE. *"Beautiful, scenic area; on Chiemsee lakeside (extra for lakeside pitches); 15% extra if staying fewer than 4 nights; htd covrd pool 3km; sm pitches; popular, busy site - rec arr early; modern, clean facs; poor drainage after rain; site rather run down end of ssn."*
€33.00, 1 Apr-31 Oct. **2024**

PRUCHTEN *2F1* (1km W Rural/Coastal) *54.37960, 12.66181* **Naturcamping Pruchten,** Zeltplatzstrasse 30, 18356 Pruchten **(038231) 2045; info@naturcamp.de; www.naturcamp.eu**

€2 (htd) sand 500m

Fr Rostock on B105, at Löbnitz take L23 N sp Barth & Zingst to Pruchten & foll site sp. 4*, Lge, mkd, pt shd, EHU (16A) €2; 20% statics; adv bkg acc; games area; horseriding 500m. *"Gd birdwatching, surfing, fishing; m'van o'night area; vg."*
€43.50, 1 Apr-31 Oct. **2024**

PRUM *3A2* (2km NE Rural) *50.21906, 6.43811* **Waldcamping Prüm,** 54591 Prüm **(06551) 2481; info@waldcamping-pruem.de; www.waldcamping-pruem.de**

12 €2.50 nr

Site sp fr town cent dir Dausfeld. 4*, Med, pt shd, EHU (10-16A) inc; gas; 60% statics; Eng spkn; adv bkg acc; ccard acc; tennis adj; bike hire; CKE. *"Pleasant site in lovely surroundings; pool complex adj; friendly staff; clean facs; m'van o'night facs; ski lift 2km; o'night facs for m'vans; do not arr bef 1900 on Sundays due local rd closures for family cycling event."* **€28.20** **2024**

QUEDLINBURG *2E3* (10km SW Urban) *51.75614, 11.04956* **Kloster Camping Thale,** Burghardt Wilsdorf, Wendhusenstraße 3, 06502 Thale **(03947) 63185; info@klostercamping-thale.de; www.klostercamping-thale.de**

12 (htd) nr nr

Head S twds Steinholzstraße. 1st R onto Steinholzstraße. Bear L onto Stauffenberg-Platz. Turn L onto Weststraße cont onto Wipertistraße for 1.4km then onto Unter der Altenburg. Cont onto K2356, turn L onto Thalenser Str. Cont onto L240 then turn L onto L92. After 1.4km turn L onto Schmiedestraße. Then R onto Breiteweg & bear R onto Wendhusenstraße. Site on LH side. Med, hdstg, mkd, pt shd, EHU (10A) €2.50; 10% statics; bus 0.3km; CKE. *"San facs excel; lovely site with gdn & lake."*
€25.00 **2023**

GERMANY

RADEVORMWALD *1B4* (5km SW Rural) *51.18498, 7.31362* **Camping-Ferienpark Kräwinkel,** Kräwinkel 1, 42477 Radevormwald **(01722) 908445; kraewinkel@ferienpark.de; www.camping-radevormwald.de**

12 €2 (htd) WD

Exit A1 at junc 95B, take B229 sp Radevormwald, foll B229 for 6km over lake bdge to 1st rndabt, R sp Heide & Krawinkel, site on L in 3km. Sm, hdg, pt shd, terr, EHU (20A) inc; sw nr; 80% statics; Eng spkn; adv bkg acc; CKE. *"Lge pitches; pleasant area; key needed for all facs €10 deposit; friendly owner; call nbr on noticeboard for access."* **€17.00** **2023**

RADOLFZELL AM BODENSEE *3C4* (16km S Rural) *47.65972, 8.93388* **Campingplatz Wangen,** Seeweg 32, 78337 Öhningen-Wangen **(07735) 919675; camping-wangen@oehningen.de; www.camping-wangen.de**

€2 WD MSP nr

Site in Wangen vill, 5km E of Stein am Rhien. 4*, Med, hdstg, pt shd, EHU (10A) metered + conn fee; bbq; sw nr; twin axles; 40% statics; phone; Eng spkn; adv bkg acc; games area; fishing; CKE. *"Lovely scenery; site in vill but quiet; dogs by prior arrangement only; helpful recep; gd cycling & sw; lake steamer trips; Stein-am-Rhein 5km; watersports in adj lake."* **€22.00, 3 Apr-3 Oct.** **2024**

RADOLFZELL AM BODENSEE *3C4* (6km SW Urban) *47.72942, 9.02432* **Campingplatz Willam,** 78315 Markelfingen **(049) 7533 6211; info@campingplatz-willam.de; www.campingplatz-willam.de**

WD adj

Fr S on A81 at junc 40 take A98 for 9m, at end of m'way turn L, site ent on L in 0.75m. Lge, mkd, pt shd, EHU (€0.7/kWh); gas; bbq; Eng spkn; boat hire; CKE. *"Gd site; cycle track; modern san facs; some noise fr rlwy; 2.6m low bdge nr site ent (can be avoided)."* **€20.50, 23 Mar-3 Oct.** **2022**

REINSBERG *2G4* (1km W Rural) *51.00381, 13.36012* **Campingplatz Reinsberg,** Badstrasse 17, 19629 Reinsberg **(037324) 82268; campingplatz-reinsberg@web.de; www.campingplatz-reinsberg.de**

€2 (htd) WD nr nr

Exit A4/E40 junc 75 Nossen. Take 1st R to Siebenlehn & foll sp Reinsberg. In Reinsberg take 1st R sp camping & 'freibad' to site. 3*, Med, pt shd, EHU (16A) €2; 40% statics; phone; Eng spkn; adv bkg acc. *"Friendly, helpful owner; sports facs adj; excel san facs; gd walking; conv Meissen, Dresden & Freiberg; v clean; peaceful; pool adj; gd for dogs, walks and cycling."* **€16.00, 25 Mar-31 Oct.** **2022**

REIT IM WINKL *4F4* (16km NW Rural) *47.73556, 12.41565* **Camping Zellersee,** Zellerseeweg 3, 83259 Schleching-Mettenham **(08649) 986719; info@camping-zellersee.de; www.camping-zellersee.de**

(htd) WD nr nr nr

Fr A8 exit junc 109 S sp Reit im Winkel. Just after Marquartstein turn R onto B307 sp Schleching, site sp just N of Schleching. 4*, Med, mkd, pt shd, pt sl, terr, EHU (16A) metered; gas; sw; red long stay; 50% statics; phone; Eng spkn; adv bkg acc; ccard acc; tennis; CKE. *"Excel, high quality facs; many footpaths fr site; mountain views; nr Alpenstrasse."* **€35.00, 3 May-8 Sep.** **2024**

REMAGEN *3B1* (1km ENE Urban) *50.57666, 7.25083* **Campingplatz Goldene Meile,** Simrockweg 9-13, 53424 Remagen **(02642) 22222; info@camping-goldene-meile.de; www.camping-goldene-meile.de**

12 €1.70 WD MSP

Fr A61 exit dir Remagen onto B266; foll sp 'Rheinfähre Linz'; in Kripp turn L, site sp. Or fr B266 1km beyond Bad Bodendorf at rndabt take B9 (dir Bonn & Remagen); in 1km take exit Remagen Süd; foll sp to sports cent/camping. Site adj Luddendorf Bdge. Fr S on A48 exit junc 10 onto B9 twd Bonn. Site sp in 22km after junc with B266. 4*, Lge, hdg, mkd, hdstg, pt shd, serviced pitches; EHU (16A) €2.60 (50m cable rec some pitches); gas; 50% statics; train into Bonn; Eng spkn; adv bkg acc; bike hire; CKE. *"Tourers on flat field away fr rvbank; sm pitches tightly packed in high ssn; gd rest; helpful staff; EHU up ladder; access to facs not gd; cycle path along Rhine; m'van o'night area adj; site clsd 1300-1500; vg, well-organised site; pool adj; interesting old town."* **€30.50** **2023**

RERIK *2E1* (1km NE Urban) *54.11133, 11.63234* **Campingpark Ostseebad Rerik,** Straße am Zeltplatz 18230 Ostseebad Rerik **038296 75720; info@campingpark-rerik.de; www.campingpark-rerik.de**

12 €3 (htd) WD MSP

Fr A20 junc 12 to Kröpelin on L12 thro Kröelin twrds Rerik then foll sp to site. 5*, Med, mkd, hdg, pt shd, EHU (16A); Eng spkn; ccard acc. *"Gd site; new modern facs."* **€34.00** **2022**

RETGENDORF *2E2* (0.4km N Rural) *53.72947, 11.50279* **Natur Camping Retgendorf,** Seestrasse 7A, 19067 Retgendorf **(03866) 400040; anfrage@naturcamping-retgendorf.de; naturcamping-retgendorf.de**

€1.50 WD nr

Exit A241 at junc 4 onto B104 dir Schwerin, in 2km turn N onto lakeside rd dir Retgendorf & Flessenow. On ent Retgendorf, site on L by bus stop. 1*, Med, mkd, pt shd, EHU (10A) €2; sw nr; 70% statics; phone; fishing. *"Views of lake; conv beautiful towns of Schwerin & Wismar; gd cycling area; san facs clean & functional but dated; shwrs lack privacy; staff/ static owners friendly & helpful; lovely peaceful site if prepared to rough it a bit."* **€15.00, 1 Apr-15 Oct.** **2024**

RETGENDORF *2E2* (4.6km N Rural) *53.75194, 11.49638* **Seecamping Flessenow,** Am Schweriner See 1A, 19067 Flessenow **(03866) 81491; info@seecamping.de; www.seecamping.de**

(htd) WD MSP

Exit A14 at junc 4 Schwerin-Nord onto B104 dir Schwerin. In 2km turn R along lakeside sp Retgendorf & Flessenow, site in approx 10km. 4*, Med, mkd, pt shd, EHU (10A) €2.50; gas; bbq (charcoal); sw nr; twin axles; TV; 50% statics; phone; bus adj; adv bkg acc; ccard acc; watersports; games area; CKE. *"Fair site in gd location; gd long stay for touring."* **€30.00, 30 Mar-14 Oct. 2023**

RIBNITZ DAMGARTEN *2F1* (13km NE Coastal) *54.28194, 12.31250* **Camping in Neuhaus,** Birkenallee 10, 18347 Dierhagen-Neuhaus **(038226) 539930; ostsee@camping-neuhaus.de; www.camping-neuhaus.de**

12 €3 (htd) WD nr 100m

Exit E55/A19 junc 6 onto B105 N. At Altheide turn N thro Klockenhagen dir Dierhagen, then turn L at camping sp & foll site sp to sea. Med, hdg, pt shd, EHU (16A); 40% statics; adv bkg acc. *"Friendly site; vg."* **€28.00 2022**

RIBNITZ DAMGARTEN *2F1* (13km NW Coastal) *54.29188, 12.34375* **Ostseecamp Dierhagen,** Ernst Moritz Arndt Strasse, 18347 Dierhagen-Strand **(038226) 80778; info@ostseecamp-dierhagen.de; www.ostseecamp-dierhagen.de**

€2.80 WD MSP nr sand 800m

Take B105 fr Rostock dir Stralsund. Bef Ribnitz, turn L sp Dierhagen & Wustrow & cont for 5km to traff lts & camp sp. Turn L to site on R in 300m. Lge, pt shd, EHU (6A) €3; gas; 20% statics; phone; adv bkg req; bike hire. *"Site low-lying, poss v wet after heavy rain; bkg fee; charge for chem disp."* **€39.50, 15 Mar-31 Oct. 2022**

RIEGEL AM KAISERSTUHL *3B4* (1.5km N Rural) *48.16463, 7.74008* **Camping Müller-See,** Zum Müller-See 1, 79359 Riegel-am-Kaiserstuhl **(07642) 3694; info@muellersee.de; www.muellersee.de**

(htd) WD MSP nr nr

Exit A5/E35 at junc 59 dir Riegel, foll site sp. 4*, Med, pt shd, EHU (16A) €2; sw nr; phone; CKE. *"Excel cycle paths in area; excel san facs; gd NH; train to Freiburg; sep excel MH area (unshd, €15 inc acc to all facs); elec fr pay boxes."* **€25.00, 1 Apr-31 Oct. 2022**

RIESTE *1C3* (0.2km W Rural) *52.48555, 7.99003* **Alfsee Ferien - und Erholungspark,** Am Campingpark 10, 49597 Rieste **(05464) 92120; info@alfsee.de; www.alfsee.de**

12 €5 (htd) WD MSP

Exit A1/E37 junc 67; site in 10km, sp. 5*, V lge, mkd, pt shd, EHU (16A) metered; sw nr; 50% statics; phone; Eng spkn; ccard acc; tennis; watersports; bike hire; CKE. *"Site pt of lge watersports complex; modern san facs; gd for famiies, conv for Osnotbruk old town; excel pitch; vg facs; may be noisy."* **€37.30 2024**

RINTELN *1C3* (2km W Rural) *52.1865, 9.05988* **Camping Doktorsee,** Am Doktorsee 8, 31722 Rinteln **(05751) 964860; info@doktorsee.de; www.doktorsee.de**

12 €1.60 WD MSP

Exit A2/E30 a'bahn, junc 35; foll sp 'Rinteln' then 'Rinteln Nord'. Turn L at traff lts, foll 'Stadtmitte' sp over rv bdge. immed turn R, bear L at fork, site in 1km on R. 3*, V lge, pt shd, EHU (16A) €1.90; sw nr; 60% statics; phone; Eng spkn; adv bkg acc; ccard acc; bike hire; tennis; CKE. *"NH on hdstg by ent; picturesque town with gd shops; 1 excel san facs block, other run down; pleasant staff."* **€20.00 2024**

ROCKENHAUSEN *3C2* (7km NE Rural) *49.67000, 7.88666* **Camping Donnersberg (formerly Azur Campingpark Pfalz),** Kahlenbergweiher 1, 67813 Gerbach **(06361) 8287; info@campingdonnersberg.com; www.campingdonnersberg.com**

€2.80 WD MSP

Fr Rockenhausen take local rd to Gerbach then foll site sp on rd L385. 4*, Med, pt shd, EHU (16A) metered or €2.80; gas; cooking facs; 60% statics; adv bkg acc; tennis; CKE. *"Conv Rhein & Mosel wine regions; gd walking."* **€27.00, 14 Apr-31 Oct. 2024**

ROSENHEIM *4F4* (9km N Rural) *47.92518, 12.13571* **Camping Erlensee,** Rosenheimerstrasse 63, 83135 Schechen **(08039) 1695; info@camping-erlensee.de; www.camping-erlensee.de**

12 €2 WD nr

Exit A8 junc 102, avoid Rosenheim town cent by foll B15 sp Landshut. Site on E side of B15 at S end Schechen. 3*, Med, pt shd, serviced pitches; EHU (16A) €2; sw; 60% statics; Eng spkn; adv bkg acc; CKE. *"Pleasant, gd & simple site; helpful owners; excel facs; mosquito prob."* **€25.00 2024**

ROSENHEIM *4F4* (14km SW Rural) *47.78978, 12.00575* **Kaiser Camping (formerly known as Tenda-Park),** Reithof 2, 83075 Bad Feilnbach **(08066) 884400; info@kaiser-camping.com; www.kaiser-camping.com**

12 €3 (htd)

Take exit 100 fr A8/E45/E52 & foll sp to Brannenburg. Site in 5km on R, 1km N of Bad Feilnbach. 4*, V lge, pt shd, EHU (16A) €2 or metered + conn fee (poss rev pol); gas; 80% statics; Eng spkn; adv bkg acc; bike hire. *"V busy, clean, well-run site; pleasant, wooded pitches; useful NH; pleasant helpful staff; some of the best san facs; ski lift 12km; discount vouchers for local shops/rest."* **€34.00 2023**

GERMANY

GERMANY

ROSTOCK *2F1* (23.5km NNE Rural/Coastal) *54.194259, 12.155333* **Camp & Ferienpark Markgrafenheide,** Budentannenweg 2, 18146 Markgrafenheide **(938166) 11510 or (45448) 00313; info@baltic-freizeit.de; www.baltic-freizeit.de**
(covrd, htd) 100m

Take B105/E22 fr Rostock twrds Stralsund. Aft 9km exit twrds Markgrafenheide & Niederhagen. Aft 3.5km turn L. Aft approx 4km sharp R, site immed on L. V lge, mkd, shd, EHU (16A); bbq; TV; Eng spkn; adv bkg acc; sauna; games area; bike hire; CKE. *"Vg site; 20mins fr ferry terminal; max 2 dog; wellness ctr; gd for children; WiFi hotspot on site; spotless san facs; ACSI discounted area."* **€36.00** **2022**

ROTENBURG (WUMME) *1D2* (10km SE Rural) *53.06977, 9.49413* **Camping Ferienpark Hanseat,** Am Campingplatz 4, 27386 Bothel **(04266) 335; info@campingpark-hanseat.de**
€2 (htd)

Exit A1 junc 50 Sottrum twd Rotenburg, then take B71 E dir Soltau. Site sp in Bothel. 3*, Med, unshd, EHU; bbq; sw nr; TV; 60% statics; adv bkg acc; games area; tennis; fishing 1km. *"Gd for NH, a bit run down; htd pool 100m."* **€22.00** **2024**

ROTHENBURG OB DER TAUBER *3D2* (3km NW Rural) *49.38805, 10.16638* **Camping Tauber-Idyll,** Detwang 28, 91541 Rothenburg-ob-der-Tauber **(09861) 3177 or 6463; www.campingplatz-rothenburg.de**
€1 (htd) nr

NW on Rothenburg-Bad Mergentheim rd in vill of Detwang. Sp. Site behind inn nr church. Care on tight R turn into ent. Sm, pt shd, EHU (6-16A) €2 or metered + conn fee; gas; bus; Eng spkn; adv bkg rec; bike hire. *"Church clock chimes each hr; clsd to vehicles 2200-0800; old walled town, gd cent for Romantische Strasse & Hohenlohe Plain; owners helpful, friendly; pleasant, peaceful, excel site; gd, clean san facs; sm c'van pitches at busy times; gd walking & cycle rte along valley; playgrnd at church; rec."* **€28.60, 1 Apr-1 Oct.** **2023**

ROTHENBURG OB DER TAUBER *3D2* (3km NW Rural) *49.38888, 10.16722* **Campingplatz Tauber-Romantik,** Detwang 39, 91541 Rothenburg-ob-der-Tauber **(09861) 6191; info@camping-tauberromantik.de; www.camping-tauberromantik.de**
€2 (htd) nr

NW on Rothenburg-Bad Mergentheim rd in vill of Detwang; turn L at camp sp & immed R; site sp fr Rothenburg. Sharp turn into site ent. Med, mkd, hdstg, pt shd, pt sl, terr, EHU (16A) €2.40; gas; 10% statics; phone; bus adj; Eng spkn; adv bkg acc; ccard acc; CKE. *"Pleasant, gd value site; excel, clean, vg facs; gd sized pitches; picturesque town; gd cycle rte; pleasant atmosphere; gd facs for children; conv NH for Rothenburg, Austria, Italy; busy over festival w/ends; vg; well managed."* **€26.00, 15 Mar-6 Nov & 25 Nov-6 Jan.** **2023**

ROTTENBUCH *4E4* (0.5km S Rural) *47.72763, 10.96691* **Terrasencamping am Richterbichl,** Solder 1, 82401 Rottenbuch **(08867) 1500 or (01713) 4471; info@camping-rottenbuch.de; www.camping-rottenbuch.de**
€2 nr

S fr Schongau for 10km on B23 dir Oberammergau, site just S of Rottenbuch. 4*, Med, mkd, pt shd, terr, EHU (10A) metered + conn fee; gas; sw nr; red long stay; 40% statics; Eng spkn; adv bkg acc; ccard acc; CKE. *"Walks & cycle paths fr site; local castles, churches & interesting towns; excel facs; friendly, helpful owners."* **€29.80** **2024**

"Satellite navigation makes touring much easier"

Remember most sat navs don't know if you're towing or in a larger vehicle – always use yours alongside maps and site directions.

RUDESHEIM *3C2* (3km E Urban) *49.97944, 7.95777* **Camping Geisenheim Rheingau,** Am Campingplatz 1, 65366 Geisenheim **(06722) 75600; info@rheingaucamping.de; www.rheingaucamping.de**
€1.50 (htd) nr

Well sp fr B42, on rvside. 3*, Lge, mkd, pt shd, EHU (16A) metered €1 + 0.76 per kWh; bbq; 50% statics; bus adj; Eng spkn; adv bkg acc; games area; CKE. *"Vg site bet Rv Rhine & vineyards; walks and cycling by rv; lots to do."* **€42.00, 24 Apr-15 Oct.** **2023**

RUDESHEIM *3C2* (2km SE Urban) *49.97777, 7.94083* **Camping am Rhein,** Auf der Lach, 65385 Rüdesheim-am-Rhein **(06722) 2528 or 49299 (LS); info@campingplatz-ruedesheim.de; www.campingplatz-ruedesheim.de**
€3 (htd) nr

Fr Koblenz (N) on B42 pass car ferry to Bingen on app to Rüdesheim; turn L & over rlwy x-ing, foll Rheinstrasse & rlwy E for 1km; cont under rlwy bdge, turn R sp to Car Park 6; turn R at T-junc, pass coach park; turn L at x-rds & foll rd to site on R. When arr via Bingen ferry turn R onto B42 & foll above dir fr level x-ing. Fr S on B42 ent Rüdesheim, turn L immed after o'head rlwy bdge (3.1m); foll camping sp. Lge, pt shd, EHU (10A) inc (poss rev pol & poss long lead req); gas; bbq (charcoal, gas); bus 500m; Eng spkn; adv bkg acc; horseriding 4km; tennis adj; bike hire; CKE. *"Pleasant, busy, family-run, well-kept site; gd, clean modern facs; poss long walk to water supply; pleasant 1km walk/cycleway by rv to town; warden sites you & connects elec - no mkd pitches; perforated grnd sheets only allowed; recep 0800-2200; rallies welcome; htd pool, paddling pool adj; Harley Davidson w/end bike festival in June; no o'fits over 11m; pool adj; shwrs far; pleasant loc by rv; shops conv."* **€33.00, 30 Apr - 3 Oct, G08.** **2024**

GERMANY

SAARBURG *3B2* (5km S Urban) *49.59937, 6.54143* **Camping Leukbachtal,** 54439 Saarburg **(06581) 2228; service@campingleukbachtal.de; www.camping-leukbachtal.de**
€2 nr

Fr B51 Trier-Sarbrucken rd on S end Saarburg ring rd, take exit sp Nennig, Wincheringen, site sp. Site on o'skirts of Saarburg on L of B407. 3*, Med, hdg, pt shd, EHU (6A); bbq; sw nr; Eng spkn; adv bkg acc; CKE. *"Gd walking area; m'van o'night rate; interesting scenic town; vg."* **€27.50, 1 Mar-2 Nov.** **2022**

SAARBURG *3B2* (3km W Rural) *49.60083, 6.52833* **Campingplatz Waldfrieden,** Im Fichtenhain 4, 54439 Saarburg **(06581) 2255; info@campingwaldfrieden.de; www.campingwaldfrieden.de**
12 €2 nr

Fr B51/B407 bypass foll sp 'krankenhaus' (hospital). Site sp off L132. 4*, Med, hdg, hdstg, pt shd, pt sl, serviced pitches; EHU (16A) metered; gas; bbq; cooking facs; red long stay; TV; 60% statics; Eng spkn; adv bkg acc; bike hire; CKE. *"Highly rec; helpful owners; warm welcome; clean facs; pitches poss tight lge o'fits; Aldi & Rewe supmkt 1km."* **€23.00** **2022**

SAARBURG *3B2* (4km NW Rural) *49.62010, 6.54274* **Camping Landal Warsberg,** In den Urlaub, 54439 Saarburg **31-(0)70 300 35 06; warsberg@landal.de; www.landal.de**
€3 (covrd, htd)

Fr Trier foll B51 S and turn at rd sp Saarbrücken at Konz, after 25km on leaving Ayl vill turn R sp Saarburg. Cont over bdge turn R sp Centre. At rndabt turn L thro cent, at rndabt L into rd sp Warsburg, after 300m turn L uphill sp Landal. 5*, V lge, mkd, pt shd, pt sl, EHU (6A) inc; gas; bbq; ccard acc; games rm; tennis; bike hire. *"Excel; gd san facs; chem disp diff to use; excel pool; site clsd 1300-1500; chairlift to attractive town cent; gd views; many activities all ages."* **€32.00, 3 Apr-9 Nov.** **2020**

SAARLOUIS *3B2* (2km NW Urban) *49.31833, 6.73972* **Campingpark Saarlouis Dr Ernst Dadder,** Marschall-Ney-Weg 2, 66740 Saarlouis **(06831) 3691; info@campingplatz-saarlouis.de; www.campingplatz-saarlouis.de**
€0.60 nr

Exit A620/E29 junc 2. Foll sp to city cent. At 500m approx turn L at traff lts sp 'Schiffanlegestelle'. At 500m approx site on R. 3*, Med, pt shd, EHU (16A) €2.30 or metered; gas; red long stay; 50% statics; Eng spkn; adv bkg acc; ccard acc; CKE. *"Castles, Roman remains, ruins & forest rds at Saarland & Saarbrücken; htd pool 150m; beautifully situated & clean; conv for A8; 15min walk to town; friendly, helpful owner; gd rest; cycle rte along R Saar; recep clsd 1200-1400."* **€40.00, 15 Mar-31 Oct.** **2023**

SALEM *3D4* (2.6km NE Rural) *47.76926, 9.30693* **Gern-Campinghof Salem,** Weildorferstrasse 46, 88682 Salem-Neufrach **(07553) 829695; info@campinghof-salem.de; www.campinghof-salem.de**
€2 (htd) nr

Site well sp on all app to Neufrach on rvside. 4*, Med, mkd, unshd, pt sl, EHU (16A) €2; gas; bbq; cooking facs; sw nr; TV (pitch); 5% statics; phone; bus; Eng spkn; adv bkg acc; ccard acc; tennis; games rm; CKE. *"Excel touring base for Lake Constance away fr busy lakeside sites; htd covrd pool 4km; barrier clsd 1230-1500 & 2200-0700; avoid pitches by recep - noise & dust; gd, clean san facs; friendly, helpful owners; no dogs Jul/Aug; gd for families; vg."* **€29.00, 1 Apr-31 Oct.** **2023**

SCHILLINGSFURST *3D3* (2km S Rural) *49.27353, 10.26587* **Campingplatz Frankenhöhe,** Fischhaus 2, 91583 Schillingsfürst **(09868) 5111; info@campingplatz-frankenhoehe.de; www.campingplatz-frankenhoehe.de**
12 €1.50 (htd)

Fr A7/E43 exit junc 109; fr A6/E50 exit junc 49. Site situated bet Dombühl & Schillingsfürst. 3*, Med, pt shd, pt sl, EHU (16A) €2.50 or metered + conn fee; gas; sw nr; red long stay; 40% statics; phone; adv bkg acc; CKE. *"Very clean facs; barrier clsd 1300-1500 & 2100-0700; poss unkempt early ssn (2009); gd cycle paths; ACSI prices; gd NH."* **€23.00** **2023**

SCHOMBERG *3C3* (2km N Rural) *48.79820, 8.63623* **Höhen-Camping,** Schömbergstrasse 32, 75328 Langenbrand **(07084) 6131; info@hoehencamping.de; www.hoehencamping.de**
12 €2 (htd) nr

Fr N exit A8 junc 43 Pforzheim, take B463 dir Calw. Turn R sp Schömberg & foll sp Langenbrand. 5*, Med, hdg, mkd, pt shd, pt sl, EHU (10-16A) €3; TV; 70% statics; phone; adv bkg acc; CKE. *"Clean, well-maintained site in N of Black Forest; no recep, ring bell on house adj site ent; blocks req for sl pitches; vg site with excel san facs."* **€21.00** **2023**

SCHONAU IM SCHWARZWALD *3B4* (1km N Rural) *47.79127, 7.90076* **Camping Schönenbuchen,** Friedrichstrasse 58, 79677 Schönau **(07673) 7610; info@camping-schoenau.de; www.camping-schoenau.de**
12 €1 nr (htd)

Fr Lörrach on B317 dir Todtnau for approx 23km. Site thro Schönau main rd on R on rvside, ent thro car park. Narr access diff for l'ge o'fits. 3*, Med, hdg, pt shd, EHU inc (16A) (poss rev pol); sw nr; red long stay; 70% statics; adv bkg acc; watersports adj; bike hire; horseriding; sauna; tennis; CKE. *"Friendly staff; site poss not well-kept; gd walking & cycling; lovely old town."* **€25.00** **2024**

GERMANY

SCHUTTORF *1B3* (2km N Rural) *52.33960, 7.22617* **Camping Quendorfer See,** Weiße Riete 3, 48465 Schüttorf **05923 90 29 39; info@camping-schuettorf.de; www.camping-schuettorf.de**

€2 (htd) nr

A1/A30, exit J4 Schüttorf-Nord. Or A31 exit J28 Schüttorf-Ost twds town cent. Foll sp to site. Sm, hdg, mkd, unshd, EHU (16A); sw nr; twin axles; adv bkg acc; ccard acc; games area; CCI. *"Excel site; immac san facs; mostly fully serviced pitches; conv NH for ferries fr Holland; flat cycling & walking."* **€26.50, 1 Apr-31 Oct.** **2024**

SCHWAAN *2F2* (3.6km S Rural) *53.92346, 12.10688* **Camping Schwaan,** Güstrowerstrasse 54/Sandgarten 17, 18258 Schwaan **(03844) 813716; info@campingplatz-schwaan.de; www.campingplatz-schwaan.de**

€2 (htd)

Fr A20 exit junc 13 to Schwaan, site sp. Fr A19 exit junc 11 dir Bad Doberan & Schwaan. Site adj Rv Warnow. 4*, Lge, mkd, pt shd, EHU (16A) €2.20 or metered; cooking facs; TV; 30% statics; adv bkg acc; sauna; site clsd 21 Dec-4 Jan; canoeing; games area; bike hire; tennis 700m; boat hire. *"Pleasant rvside site; gd touring base; tight app thro Schwaan town (esp fr N)."* **€21.00, 1 Mar-31 Oct.** **2024**

SCHWEICH *3B2* (1.6km S Urban) *49.81459, 6.75019* **Campingplatz zum Fährturm,** Am Yachthafen, 54338 Schweich **(06502) 91300; camping@kreusch.de; www.kreusch.de**

nr

Fr exit 129 or 130 fr A1/E44. Site by rv bank by bdge into town, sp. 4*, Lge, mkd, pt shd, EHU (16A) €1.60; gas; bbq; twin axles; bus to Trier nr; Eng spkn; adv bkg acc; bike hire; watersports; CKE. *"Poss long wait for conn to EHU; poss long walk to san facs - dated; m'van o'night area outside site - no EHU; sports cent adj; on banks of Mosel with cycle rte; yacht/boating harbour adj; gd rest/bar; pool adj; vg."* **€27.00, 11 Apr-17 Oct.** **2023**

SCHWEPPENHAUSEN *3B2* (1km N Rural) *49.93392, 7.79194* **Campingplatz Aumühle,** Naheweinstraße 65, 55444 Schweppenhausen **06724 602392; info@camping-aumuehle.de**

(htd)

Fr A61 take exit 47 - Waldlaubersheim. Foll signs to Schweppenhausen. Sp to camp site. Med, mkd, pt shd, EHU (10A); twin axles; 50% statics; Eng spkn; adv bkg acc; CKE. *"V gd site; cycle rtes fr site; v helpful Dutch owners; gd san facs; touring vans in sep area nr m'way; excel NH; gd base for Rhine."* **€24.00, 1 Apr-31 Oct.** **2023**

SEEFELD *4E4* (1.3km W Rural) *48.030463, 11.199018* **Camping Am Pilsensee,** Am Pilseesee 2, 82229 Seefeld am Pilsensee **(08152) 999741; info@camping-pilsensee.de; www.camping-pilsensee.de**

12

W on 96 fr Munchi, exit 31, turn R onto 2349. Aft abt 6km turn R onto 2068. Cont for 4.5km, site 500m S of junc with 2070 to Seefeld to the R. V lge, hdg, mkd, pt shd, EHU (10A); bbq; sw; twin axles; TV; 80% statics; phone; Eng spkn; adv bkg acc; games area; CKE. *"Gd site; boat hire on lake; Andechs monastery nrby."* **€33.50** **2023**

SEESHAUPT *4E4* (4km E Rural) *47.82651, 11.33906* **Camping beim Fischer,** Buchscharnstrasse 10, 82541 St Heinrich **(08801) 802; info@camping-beim-fischer.de; www.camping-beim-fischer.de**

12 (htd) nr nr

Exit A95 junc 7 & foll sp Seeshaupt for 1.6km to T-junc. Turn R, site in 200m on R. 4*, Med, mkd, unshd, EHU (16A) metered; gas; sw nr; TV; 45% statics; bus adj; Eng spkn; adv bkg acc; games area; CKE. *"Well-maintained, friendly, lovely, honest family-run site; immac facs; conv Munich & Bavarian castles."* **€26.40** **2024**

SIMMERATH *1A4* (8km E Rural) *50.61777, 6.37690* **Camping Rursee,** Seerandweg 26, D 52152 Simmerath/Rurberg **(02473) 2365; info@camping-rursee.de; camping-rursee.de**

Fr Simmerath L166 to Kesternich; R on 266 for 1 km; then L on L166 twds Rurberg. L on L128 twds Woffelsbach then sp R to site. Sm, mkd, unshd, EHU €3; games area. **€18.50, 1 Apr-Nov.** **2024**

"There aren't many sites open at this time of year"

If you're travelling outside peak season remember to call ahead to check site opening dates – even if the entry says 'open all year'.

SOEST *1C4* (12km S Rural) *51.47722, 8.10055* **Camping Delecke-Südufer,** Arnsbergerstrasse 8, 59519 Möhnesee-Delecke **(02924) 8784210; info@campingplatz-moehnesee.de; www.campingplatz-moehnesee.de**

12 nr

Exit A44/E331 at junc 56 onto B229 sp Arnsberg/Mohnesee. Cont to lake, cross bdge. At next junc turn L & site immed on L, sp. 4*, Med, hdg, unshd, pt sl, EHU (16A); sw nr; 50% statics; phone; Eng spkn; adv bkg acc; clsd 1300-1500 & 2000-0800; boating; CKE. *"Excel site on boating lake; san facs locked o'night; gd walking & sailing; v busy at w/ends; gd disable facs."* **€28.50** **2022**

SOLINGEN *1B4* (6km S Rural) *51.13388, 7.11861* **Waldcamping Glüder,** Balkhauserweg 240, 42659 Solingen-Glüder **(0212) 242120; info@camping-solingen.de; www.camping-solingen.de**

12 €2.30 (htd) WD nr nr

Exit A1 junc 97 Burscheid onto B91 N dir Hilgen. In Hilgen turn L onto L294 to Witzhelden then R on L359 dir Solingen. Site sp in Glüder by Rv Wupper. 3*, Med, hdg, mkd, hdstg, unshd, EHU (6-10A) €3; gas; TV; 80% statics; bus; Eng spkn; CKE. *"Beautiful location in wooded valley; clsd 1300-1500; resident owner; excel san facs; easy walk to Burg-an-der-Wupper Schloss - worth visit."* **€27.40** **2024**

SOTTRUM *1D2* (5km SW Rural) *53.08335, 9.17697* **Camping-Paradies Grüner Jäger,** Everinghauser Dorfstrsse 17, 27367 Sottrum/Everinghausen **(04205) 319113 or (01703) 868672; info@camping-paradies.de; www.camping-paradies.de**

12 € 2 (htd) WD MSP

Exit A1 junc 50 at Stuckenborstel onto B75 dir Rotenburg. In approx 500m turn R & foll sp Everinghausen. Site in 4km. Med, mkd, unshd, EHU (16A) inc; bbq; 30% statics; Eng spkn; CKE. *"Excel NH; new superb facs block (2016)."* **€31.00** **2024**

SPEYER *3C3* (3km N Rural) *49.33600, 8.44300* **Camping Speyer,** Am Rübsamenwühl 31, 67346 Speyer **(06232) 42228; info@camping-speyer.de; www.camping-speyer.de**

€2 nr

Fr Mannheim or Karlsruhe take rd 9 to exit Speyer Nord dir Speyer. At 3rd traff lts turn L into Auestrasse, then at 2nd rndabt L into Am Rübsamenwühl. Site in 500m. Sm, mkd, EHU €3; sw; red long stay; 90% statics. *"Speyer pleasant town, cathedral & Technik Museum worth visit; v basic site; scruffy & not well-kept; fair NH/sh stay."* **€29.00, 15 Mar-25 Sep.** **2024**

SPEYER *3C3* (1km SE Urban) *49.31250, 8.44916* **Camping Technik Museum,** Am Technik Museum 1, Geibstrasse, 67346 Speyer **(06232) 67100; info@hotel-speyer.de; www.hotel-speyer.de**

12 (htd) WD MSP nr nr nr

Exit A61/E34 at junc 64, foll sp to museum. Med, unshd, EHU inc (10A); bus; Eng spkn; adv bkg acc; ccard acc. *"Book in at hotel adj; 3 nights max stay; excel museum & IMAX cinema on site; conv Speyer cent and cathedral; dogs free; site unkept; excel san facs; 24hr CCTV controlled ent gate."* **€22.00** **2022**

STAUFEN IM BREISGAU *3B4* (1.4km SE Rural) *47.87194, 7.73583* **Ferien-Campingplatz Belchenblick,** Münstertälerstrasse 43, 79219 Staufen-im-Breisgau **(07633) 7045; info@camping-belchenblick.de; www.camping-belchenblick.de**

12 €3.50 WD MSP nr (htd, indoor)

Exit A5/E35 junc 64a dir Bad Krozingen-Staufen-Münstertal. Avoid Staufen cent, foll Münstertal sp. Camp on L 500m past Staufen. Visibility restricted fr Münstertal dir. 4*, Lge, pt shd, EHU (16A) metered; gas; bbq; TV; 60% statics; phone; Eng spkn; adv bkg rec; horseriding 500m; games rm; bike hire; sauna; tennis nr; CKE. *"Well-run, family-owned site; some pitches sm; no o'fits over 8m high ssn; no veh access 1230-1500 & night time - parking area avail; strict pitching rules; beautiful area & Staufen pleasant town; beware train app round blind corner at x-ing; gd walking, cycling, horseriding; san facs tired, need refurbishing (2013); better cheaper sites close by."* **€30.00, G02.** **2022**

STOCKACH *3C4* (7.5km SSW Rural) *47.80860, 8.97000* **Campinggarten Wahlwies,** Stahringerstrasse 50, 78333 Stockach-Wahlwies **(07771) 3511; info@camping-wahlwies.de; www.camping-wahlwies.de**

WD MSP nr nr

Exit A98 junc 12 Stockach West onto B313 to Wahlwies. In vill turn L immed after level x-ing, site on R bef next level x-ing, sp. 3*, Med, pt shd, EHU (16A) €2; sw nr; 50% statics; phone; Eng spkn; adv bkg rec; CKE. *"Pleasantly situated, orchard site 6km fr Bodensee; friendly, helpful staff; female san facs inadequate; gd touring cent; gd local train service; excel cycle tracks."* **€31.80, 1 Jan-9 Jan & 24 Feb-15 Nov.** **2022**

STOCKACH *3C4* (2.5km SW Urban) *47.84194, 8.99500* **Camping Papiermühle,** Johann Glatt Strasse 3, 78333 Stockach **(07771) 9190490; campingpark-stockach@web.de; www.campingpark-stockach-de.webnode.com**

€2.20 (htd) WD MSP nr

Fr Stockach at junc rndabt of B31 & B313, turn L (E) to Caramobil C'van Sales Depot. Site adj under same management. Med, mkd, hdstg, pt shd, pt sl, terr, EHU (6A) €2; bbq; 50% statics; phone; bus 200m; Eng spkn; adv bkg acc; ccard acc; CKE. *"Sep m'van area adj; v clean facs; helpful staff; conv location for town; gd walking & cycling; vg site."* **€21.50, 1 Mar-30 Nov.** **2022**

STORKOW *2G3* (6km NE Rural) *52.29194, 13.98638* **Campingplatz Waldsee,** 15526 Reichenwalde-Kolpin **(033631) 5037; mail@campingplatz-waldsee.de; www.campingplatz-waldsee.de**

12 €1 WD nr

Fr A12/E30, exit junc 3 Storkow. Just bef ent Storkow, turn N twd Fürstenwalde. In 6km turn R leaving Kolpin, site sp. 3*, Med, pt shd, pt sl, EHU (16A) €2; sw nr; 60% statics; Eng spkn; adv bkg acc; ccard acc; sauna; bike hire; CKE. *"Gd san facs; haphazard pitching; conv NH en rte to/fr Poland; gd cycling area; Bad Saarow lakeside worth visit; facs dated (2012); staff friendly."* **€16.00** **2024**

STRAUBING *4F3* (1km N Urban) *48.89346, 12.5766* **Camping Straubing,** Wundermühlweg 9, 94315 Straubing **(09421) 89794; info@campingplatzstraubing.de; www.campingplatzstraubing.de**

(htd) WD MSP nr

Fr A3/E56 exit junc 105 or 106 to Straubing. Foll sp over Danube bdge, site sp on R in approx 1km. Also foll sp to stadium. 4*, Med, shd, EHU (16A) inc; bbq; cooking facs; sw nr; twin axles; phone; bus; adv bkg acc; golf 2km; CKE. *"Gd, clean, well-kept site In grnds of sports stadium; quaint town with attractive shops; gd san facs; pool 5km; conv Danube cycle way; easy walk to town; dogs not acc Aug; excel stop over fr A3, gd for longer breaks; excel."* **€34.50, 1 May-15 Oct.** **2023**

STUTTGART *3D3* (5km E Urban) *48.79395, 9.21911* **Campingplatz Cannstatter Wasen,** Mercedesstrasse 40, 70372 Stuttgart **(0711) 556696; info@campingplatz-stuttgart.de; www.campingplatz-stuttgart.de**

12 €3 (htd) WD MSP nr

Fr B10 foll sp for stadium & Mercedes museum & then foll camping sp. Access poss diff when major events in park adj. Lge, hdstg, pt shd, serviced pitches; EHU (16A) metered + conn fee; bbq; bus nr; Eng spkn; adv bkg acc; ccard acc; CKE. *"Helpful staff; clean san facs (2015); town cent best by train, tickets fr recep; cycle ride to town thro park; Mercedes museum 15 mins walk; fr Sep site/office open 0800-1000 & 1700-1900 only; site within low emission zone; camping field for tents."* **€22.00** **2022**

SULZBURG *3B4* (1km NW Rural) *47.84778, 7.69848* **Camping Sulzbachtal,** Sonnmatt 4, 79295 Sulzburg **(07634) 592568; a-z@camping-sulzbachtal.de; www.camping-sulzbachtal.de**

12 €2.60 (htd) WD MSP nr nr

Fr A5/E35 exit junc 64a Bad Krozingen onto L120/ L123 dir Staufen-in-Breisgau. Cont on L125, site sp on L. 5*, Med, mkd, hdstg, pt shd, terr, serviced pitches; EHU (16A) metered; red long stay; 10% statics; phone; Eng spkn; adv bkg acc; ccard acc; tennis; CKE. *"Gd base for S Black Forest & Vosges; well laid-out site; clean facs; conv m'way; 45 mins to Basel; helpful, pleasant owners; ask about bus/train pass; m'van o'night facs; high standards; well maintained; excel san facs; lge pitches; in wine growing area; excel walks."* **€35.40** **2024**

TENGEN *3C4* (1km NW Rural) *47.82365, 8.65296* **Hegau Familien-Camping,** An der Sonnenhalde 1, 78250 Tengen **(07736) 92470; info@hegau-camping.de; www.hegau-camping.de**

12 €4 (htd) WD MSP (covrd, htd)

Exit A81 junc 39 thro Engen dir Tengen, site sp. 5*, Lge, hdstg, mkd, pt shd, pt sl, serviced pitches; EHU (16A) metered or €2; gas; sw; red long stay; 40% statics; bus 500m; Eng spkn; adv bkg acc; ccard acc; tennis adj; sauna; games area; horseriding 2km; bike hire; games rm; canoeing; dog shwr; CKE. *"Site of high standard; fairly isolated; gd family facs; clsd 1230-1430; o'night m'vans area; excel; same price in high ssn; beautifully maintained; well run; 1st rate pool complex; wonderful children's play facs; rec."* **€42.00** **2022**

TIEFENSEE *2G3* (1km E Rural) *52.68019, 13.85063* **Country-Camping Tiefensee,** Schmiedeweg 1, 16259 Tiefensee **(033398) 90514; info@country-camping.de; www.country-camping.de**

12 €1.50 (htd) WD MSP

Site sp fr B158 on lakeside. 4*, Lge, hdg, mkd, pt shd, EHU (16A) metered or €2.50; bbq; sw nr; red long stay; TV; 75% statics; Eng spkn; adv bkg acc; ccard acc; fishing; games area; sauna. *"Family-owned site; sep m'van pitches; sep naturist area at lake; sep car park; o'night m'vans area; clsd 1300-1500; gd cycling & walking; train to Berlin fr Arensfeldt; working ship lift at Niederfinow; vg."* **€20.00** **2024**

TITISEE NEUSTADT *3C4* (7km SW Rural) *47.88693, 8.13776* **Terrassencamping Sandbank,** Seerundweg 9, 79822 Titisee-Neustadt **(07651) 8243 or 8166; info@camping-sandbank.de; www.camping-sandbank.de**

€1.50 (htd) WD MSP

Fr rte 31 Freiberg-Donauschingen turn S into Titisee. Fork R after car park on R, foll sp for Bruderhalde thro town. After youth hostel fork L & foll sp at T junc. 4*, Lge, mkd, hdstg, terr, EHU (16A) €1.40; sw; red long stay; 50% statics; Eng spkn; ccard acc; boating; bike hire; CKE. *"Ltd touring pitches; steel pegs ess; clean, well-run, well laid-out site in gd position; terr gives gd lake views; helpful owner; gd welcome; larger pitches avail at extra cost; gd touring base for Black Forest; gd walks round lake; lakeside walk into town thru woods (approx 30 mins); ask for Konus card for free travel on local buses; clsd 1200-1400; excel; rd to site tarmaced."* **€40.70, 25 Mar-31 Dec.** **2022**

TITISEE NEUSTADT *3C4* (7.6km SW Rural) *47.89516, 8.13789* **Camping Bühlhof,** Bühlhofweg 13, 79822 Titisee-Neustadt **(07652) 1606; kontakt@camping-buehlhof.de; www.camping-buehlhof.de**

12 €2.30 WD MSP nr

Take rd 31 out of Freiburg to Titisee; R fork on ent Titisee; bear R to side of lake, site on R after end of Titisee, up steep but surfaced hill, sharp bends. 2*, Lge, mkd, pt shd, pt sl, terr, serviced pitches; EHU (16A); gas; bbq; 30% statics; Eng spkn; horseriding; boat hire; site clsd Nov to mid-Dec; tennis; watersports; CKE. *"Beautiful situation on hillside above Lake Titisee; 300m fr Lake Titisee (but no access; recep 0700-2200; lower terr gravel & 50% statics; top terr for tents & vans without elec; winter sports area, ski lift 6km; pitches sm; woodland walks; pleasant walk to town; gd san facs."* **€36.00** **2023**

TITISEE NEUSTADT *3C4* (8km SW Rural) *47.88996, 8.13273* **Natur-Campingplatz Weiherhof,** Bruderhalde 26, 79822 Titisee-Neustadt **(01772) 190959; info@camping-titisee.de; www.camping-titisee.de**

€2 (htd) WD

Fr B31 Frieberg-Donaueschingen, turn S into Titisee & fork R after car park on R, foll sp Bruderhalde thro town. Site on L on lakeside. Lge, shd, EHU (10A) €2.50; sw nr; 20% statics; phone; golf 2km; bike hire playground; CKE. *"Site in woodland next to the lake; no mkd pitches but ample rm; vg; trip to town along lakeside well worth a visit."* **€23.00, 1 May-15 Oct.** **2024**

TRAUNSTEIN *4F4* (8km SW Rural) *47.81116, 12.5890* **Camping Wagnerhof,** Campingstrasse 11, 83346 Bergen **(08662) 8557; info@camping-bergen.de; www.camping-bergen.de**

12 €2 WD MSP nr shgl 10km

Exit A8/E52/E60 junc 110. On ent Bergen take 2nd R turn (sp). 4*, Med, mkd, pt shd, EHU (10A); red long stay; 30% statics; Eng spkn; adv bkg acc; tennis; site clsd 1230-1500; CKE. *"Excel, v clean, pleasant site in beautiful location; htd pool adj; debit & euro card acc; helpful owner; when not full owner tries to offer pitches with empty pitches adjoining; conv a'bahn; cable car to Hockfelln; well mkd walking & cycling rtes."* **€31.50** **2024**

TRAVEMUNDE *2E2* (4km SW Rural) *53.94196, 10.84417* **Camping Ivendorf,** Frankenkrogweg 2, 23570 Ivendorf **(04502) 4865; mail@camping-travemuende.de; www.camping-travemuende.de**

12 €2 WD nr

Fr A1 exit junc 19 take B226 to Ivendorf, then B75 dir Travemünde, site well sp. 3*, Med, mkd, pt shd, EHU €3.50 or metered; 10% statics; Eng spkn; CKE. *"Sep disabled pitches; conv ferries to/fr Sweden; pool 4km; easy access to Lübeck, a beautiful city; spacious, well maintained site; hedged; WiFi nr recep; excell san facs; gd for Lubeck."* **€32.00** **2022**

TRIER *3B2* (2km SW Urban) *49.74385, 6.62523* **Camping Treviris,** Luxemburgerstrasse 81, 54294 Trier **(0651) 86921; info@camping-treviris.de; www.camping-treviris.de**

€1.70 WD MSP nr

On E side of Rv Mosel on A1/A603/B49/B51 cross to W side of rv on Konrad Adenauerbrücke. Cont in R lane & foll sp Koln/Aachen - Luxemburgerstrasse. In 500m turn R to site, site on R. Well sp fr W bank of rv. Med, mkd, pt shd, EHU (10A) metered; bbq; bus 200m; ccard acc; site clsd 1-10 Jan; CKE. *"Cycle/walk to town cent; m'van park adj open all yr - ltd facs; clean, modern, clean san facs; swipe card for all facs; elec pylon in cent of site; gd touring base; gd sh stay/NH; well placed; sm pitches; 20min walk to city."* **€24.00, 18 Mar-30 Oct.** **2023**

TRIER *3B2* (8.4km SW Rural) *49.70460, 6.57398* **Camping Konz,** Saarmünding, 54329 Konz **(06501) 2577; camping@campingplatz-konz.de; www.campingplatz-konz.de**

€0.70 MSP nr

On B51 S of rv at rndabt just bef rv x-ing, go L & foll sp Camping Konz (not Konz-Könen). Do not go into Konz. Med, mkd, pt shd, EHU metered + conn fee; Eng spkn; watersports. *"Conv NH/sh stay for Trier - cycle rte or public transport; facs clean; poss flooding; sm pitches."* **€15.00, 15 Mar-15 Oct.** **2024**

TRIER *3B2* (9km SW Rural) *49.70555, 6.55333* **Campingplatz Igel,** Moselstrasse, 54298 Igel **(06501) 12944; info@camping-igel.com; www.camping-igel.com**

€2 (htd) WD MSP nr

SW on A49 Luxembourg rd fr Trier; in cent of Ige vill, turn L by Sparkasse Bank, thro narr tunnel (3.6m max height); in 200m turn L along rv bank; site 300m on L; café serves as recep. Med, pt shd, EHU (6A) €2 (poss rev pol); 90% statics; lake fishing adj; CKE. *"Excel, friendly, well-run site; immac san facs; gd rest; ltd touring pitches; rv bank foot & cycle path to Trier; conv Roman amphitheatre in Trier (bus/train); close to Luxembourg border for cheap petrol; conv for bus into Trier."* **€19.00, 1 Apr-31 Oct.** **2024**

TRITTENHEIM *3B2* (4km N Urban) *49.84933, 6.89283* **Camping Neumagen-Dhron,** Moselstrasse 100, 54347 Neumagen-Dhron **(01749) 678296; info@marina-mittelmosel.de; www.marina-mittelmosel.de**

WD

On B53 fr Trittenheim twd Piesport. Immed after x-ing rv turn R, then R again sp Neumagen. Site sp in vill on rvside. 5*, Med, mkd, pt shd, EHU (6A) metered + conn fee; bbq; 40% statics; adv bkg acc; boating; fishing; CKE. *"Gd; site clsd if rv in flood; marina adj; rvside park; excel site; interesting Roman town; poss noise fr adj rest; main san facs up 25 steps; Hot water 7am-9pm."* **€19.00, 1 Apr-31 Oct.** **2023**

GERMANY

TRITTENHEIM *3B2* (0.4km E Urban) *49.82472, 6.90305* **Reisemobil/Wohnmobilstellplatz (Motorhome Camping),** Am Moselufer, 54349 Trittenheim **(06507) 2227; info@trittenheim.de; www.trittenheim.de**

WD MSP nr nr

Fr Trier foll B53 dir Bernkastel Kues. Site sp in Trittenheim dir Neumagen-Dhron, on rvside. Sm, hdstg, unshd, pt sl, EHU (16A) €2.50; own san req. *"M'vans only; pleasant site poss clsd if rv floods; warden calls for payment."*
€5.00, 1 Apr-31 Oct. 2024

TRITTENHEIM *3B2* (0.4km SE Rural) *49.82131, 6.90201* **Campingplatz im Grünen,** Olkstrasse 12, 54349 Trittenheim **(06507) 2148; cp-trittenheim@t-online.de; www.camping-trittenheim.de**

€1.50 WD nr nr

Foll B53 along Rv Mosel fr Trier dir Bernkastel Kues; turn R in Trittenheim at camping symbol sp Leiwen as if to go over rv & site on R immed bef x-ring rv. 3*, Sm, mkd, pt shd, EHU €2.60 or metered + conn fee; 20% statics; Eng spkn; CKE. *"Lovely, quiet site by Rv Mosel o'looking vineyards; boat trips; beautiful area; excel, clean san facs; mv service pnt point in adj vills; friendly owner; gd cycle paths; close to vill; infrequent bus to Trier; recep clsd 1200-1500; interesting area; adv bkg fr March; no plastic materials on lawns; close to local rests and seasonal boat cruises."*
€36.00, 15 Apr-15 Oct. 2024

TRITTENHEIM *3B2* (5km S Rural) *49.80305, 6.89111* **Ferienpark Landal Sonnenberg,** 54340 Leiwen **(06507) 4913900; sonnenberg@landal.org; www.landal.de**

€3 WD MSP (covrd, htd)

Fr Bernkastel Kues or Trier on B53 take bdge over Rv Mosel to S bank at Thörnich & foll sp Leiwen. Turn R to top of hill, site sp. Long, winding ascent. 5*, Med, mkd, pt shd, terr, EHU (6A) inc; gas; adv bkg acc; tennis; games rm; sauna; CKE. *"Vg family site with rv views; fitness rm; excel san facs."*
€46.00, 15 Mar-15 Nov. 2024

TUBINGEN *3C3* (5km SW Rural) *48.51008, 9.03525* **Neckarcamping Tübingen,** Rappenberghalde 61, 72070 Tübingen **(07071) 43145; mail@neckarcamping.de; www.neckarcamping.de**

€1.50 WD MSP

B28 to Tübingen, site well sp fr main rds. Site on N bank of Rv Neckar. 3*, Med, pt shd, EHU (6A) metered + conn fee (rev pol); 70% statics; bike hire; clsd 1230-1430 & 2200-0800; CKE. *"Easy walk to attractive old town & lge pool complex; Neckar cycle path rn; cramped pitches; NH only; bus stop nr camp ent."* **€36.50, 1 Apr-30 Oct.** 2023

UBERLINGEN *3D4* (3km SE Coastal) *47.75186, 9.19315* **Campingplatz Nell,** Zur Barbe 7, 88662 Überlingen-Nussdorf **(07551) 4254; info@campingplatz-nell.de; www.campingplatz-nell.de**

WD nr nr nr

Exit B31 to Nussdorf. In vill cent turn L under rlwy bdge at 2nd campsite sp, site on R on lakeside. Sm, pt shd, EHU (10A) metered; bbq; sw nr; adv bkg acc. *"Beautifully-kept site; friendly owner; all amenities nr; gd cycling; excel; lge plots; cash only; ltd places for tourers so arrive early."*
€21.00, 21 Mar-20 Oct. 2022

UBERLINGEN *3D4* (13km NW Rural) *47.81720, 9.03802* **Campingplatz Schachenhorn,** Radolfzeller Str. 23, 78351 Bodman-Ludwigshafen **07773 9376851; info@camping-schachenhorn.de; www.camping-schachenhorn.de**

WD

Exit A98/E54 junc 12 onto B34. Site sp 1.5km on Bodensee fr Ludwigshafen. Med, pt shd, EHU (16A); bbq; sw nr; twin axles; TV; 20% statics; Eng spkn; games rm. *"Taken over in 2013, formerly Camping See-Ende; lovely location at W end of Bodensee; excel san facs; many cycle paths; bit disorganised; poss muddy after rain; rec visit Mainau Gdns."*
€32.00, 15 Mar-15 Oct. 2022

ÜBERSEE *4F4* (16km W Rural) *47.816891, 12.363742* **Camping Mariengrund,** Prienerstr. 42, D-83233 Bernau am Chiemsee **(08051) 7894; mariengrund@aol.com; campingplatz-mariengrund.de**

12 WD MSP nr

Exit m'waysp Bernau. Turn twrds Prien. Ent to site v sharp R immed after Munich slip rd. Lge o'fits can cont twrds Prien and u turn at next rndabt. Hdstg, pt shd, EHU (16A) inc; bbq (charcoal, elec, gas); sw nr; Eng spkn; adv bkg acc; ccard acc. *"Hdstng area sometimes crowded with NH'ers; facs basic but ok; vast numbers of flies & mosquitoes in summer; fair."*
€31.00 2024

UFFENHEIM *3D2* (10km W Rural) *49.52277, 10.12583* **Camping Paradies Franken,** Walkershofen 40, 97215 Simmershofen **(09848) 969633; camping-paradies-franken@web.de; www.camping-paradies-franken.de**

12 €1.50 (htd) MSP

Fr N exit A7 junc 105 Gollhofen or fr on B13 to Uffenheim. In Uffenheim turn W thro Adelhofen to Simmershofen, then turn L twd Walkershofen, site sp. 4*, Med, mkd, pt shd, EHU inc; bbq; 10% statics; adv bkg acc; bike hire; games area. *"Interesting area; gd touring base; gd rest, cycling gd."* **€37.80** 2024

GERMANY

VLOTHO *1C3* (5km NE Rural) *52.17388, 8.90666* **Camping Sonnenwiese,** Borlefzen 1, 32602 Vlotho **(05733) 8217; info@sonnenwiese.com; www.sonnenwiese.com**

12 €2.20 (htd)

Fr S exit A2 junc 31 to Vlotho; cross rv bdge (Mindenerstrasse) & in 500m turn R into Rintelnerstrasse to site - 2 sites share same access. Fr N exit A2 junc 32 to Vlotho; turn L bef bdge into Rintelner Strasse. 4*, Lge, hdstg, unshd, serviced pitches; EHU (10A) inc; bbq; sw; TV (pitch); 75% statics; phone; Eng spkn; adv bkg acc; games rm; CKE. *"Excel site; v helpful staff, abundant wildlife; rv adj for boats/canoes; recep clsd 1300-1500."*
€25.50 **2022**

VOLKACH *3D2* (2km NW Rural) *49.869215, 10.214989* **Campingplatz Ankergrund,** Fahrerstraße 7, 97332 Volkach am Main **(09381) 6713 or (09381) 4114; info@campingplatz-ankergrund.de; www.campingplatz-ankergrund.de**

€3.50

Exit A3 J74 sp Kitzingen/Schwarzach/Volkach. Site sp in town approx 10km fr A3. Med, hdg, mkd, pt shd, EHU (10A) €0.60kwh; bbq; sw nr; red long stay; twin axles; 25% statics; 800m; adv bkg acc; games area; CKE. *"Excel; super pitches avail with rv view; adj to Rv Main; sports ctr nrby with pool; san facs raised with disabled access via lift; in wine area; excel cycling & walking; gd rests; gd supmkt."*
€34.00, 1 Apr-22 Oct. **2023**

WAGING AM SEE *4F4* (2km NE Rural) *47.94333, 12.74741* **Strandcamping Waging-am-See,** Am See 1, 83329 Waging-am-See **(08681) 552; info@strandcamp.de; www.strandcamp.de**

€2.90 (not acc Jul & Aug)

Exit A8 junc 112 to Traunstein, then foll sp to Waging-am-See; in vill site sp on rd to Tittmoning. 5*, V lge, hdg, mkd, pt shd, serviced pitches; EHU (10A) metered + conn fee; gas; sw nr; red long stay; 30% statics; adv bkg acc; fishing; sailing; tennis; games area; bike hire; windsurfing; CKE. *"Excel, clean, family site; gd cycling country; site clsd 1200-1400; well-equipped shop."* **€23.60, 1 Apr-31 Oct.** **2024**

WALDMUNCHEN *4F2* (3km N Rural) *49.39598, 12.69913* **Campsite Ferienpark Perlsee,** Alte Ziegelhütte 6, 93449 Waldmünchen **(09972) 1469; info@ferienpark-perlsee.de; www.ferienpark-perlsee.de**

12 €2 (htd)

N fr Cham on B22 to Schontal, NE to Waldmünchen for 10km. Foll site sp 2km. 4*, Med, hdg, mkd, pt shd, terr, EHU (16A) metered; bbq; sw nr; 50% statics; games area; watersports; CKE. *"Vg san facs; superb site; long leads poss req."* **€25.30** **2024**

WALDSHUT *3C4* (5.6km SW Urban) *47.61083, 8.22526* **Rhein Camping,** Jahnweg 22, 79761 Waldshut-Tiengen **(07751) 3152; info@rheincamping.de; www.rheincamping.de**

12 €3 (htd) nr

Site on rvside on E o'skts of vill. Fr N foll rd 500 in dir Tiengen fr Switzerland, take 1st L after Koblenz border x-ing & foll site sp. 4*, Med, hdstg, mkd, unshd, EHU (16A) metered + conn fee €1; bbq (elec, gas); cooking facs; sw nr; red long stay; 40% statics; Bus; Eng spkn; adv bkg acc; ccard acc; CCI. *"Nr Rhine falls at Schaffhausen; boat for Rhine trips fr site; excel rest; bread to order;; gd walk path to town; pleasant walk along Rhine; excel; conv NH mobil park adj."*
€36.00 **2024**

WALKENRIED *2E4* (1km NE Rural) *51.58944, 10.62472* **Knaus Campingpark Walkenried,** Ellricherstrasse 7, 37445 Walkenried **(05525) 778; walkenried@knauscamp.de; www.knauscamp.de**

12 €2.80 (covrd, htd)

A7, exit Seesen, then B243 to Herzberg-Bad Sachsa-Walkenried, sp. 4*, Lge, mkd, pt shd, pt sl, terr, EHU (6-10A) €2.40; gas; red long stay; TV; 20% statics; Eng spkn; adv bkg acc; games area; solarium; site clsd Nov; sauna. *"Vg rest; winter sports; lovely old vill; excel site."*
€45.80 **2023**

WARNITZ *2G2* (0.7km S Rural) *53.17754, 13.87400* **Camping Oberuckersee,** Lindenallee 2, 17291 Warnitz **(039863) 459; info@camping-oberuckersee.de; www.camping-oberuckersee.de**

€2 nr nr

Fr A11/E28 exit 7. Site sp fr Warnitz on lakeside. 3*, Lge, shd, pt sl, EHU (10A) €2; sw; TV; 50% statics; fishing; bike hire; boating. *"Lovely site in pine trees on edge lge lake; conv NH en rte to Poland; deposit for san facs key; clsd 1300-1500; gd cycle rte nrby."*
€29.00, 1 May-15 Sep. **2022**

WAXWEILER *3A2* (0.7km W Rural) *50.09270, 6.35866* **Camping Park Eifel (formerly Eifel Ferienpark Prümtal),** Schwimmbadstrasse 7, 54649 Waxweiler **(06554) 92000; info@ferienpark-waxweiler.de; www.campingparkeifel.de**

€2.50 (htd) nr

Exit A60/E42/E29 junc 5 to B410 to Waxweiler. Site sp dir Prüm on rvside. 3*, Med, mkd, hdg, pt shd, EHU (10A) inc; bbq; 50% statics; Eng spkn; adv bkg acc; waterslide; games area; sauna; tennis; bike hire; fishing. *"V nice site in the valley; htd pool adj; v warm welcome fr staff; lovely pool adj."*
€29.00, 1 Apr-31 Oct. **2024**

GERMANY

WEIKERSHEIM *3D2* (4km S Rural) *49.45640, 9.92565* **Camping Schwabenmühle,** Weikersheimer Straße 21, 97990 Weikersheim **07934 99 22 23; info@camping-schwabenmuehle.de; www.camping-schwabenmuehle.de**

€1

Fr Weikersheim twd Laudenbach, site on R in 3km. 4*, Med, hdstg, hdg, mkd, pt shd, EHU (16A); twin axles; Eng spkn; bike hire; CCI. *"Excel; bread can be ordered."* **€26.00, 17 Apr-12 Oct.** **2024**

WEILBURG *3C1* (4km SW Rural) *50.4757, 8.23966* **Campingplatz Odersbach,** Runkelerstrasse 5A, 35781 Weilburg-Odersbach **(06471) 7620; info@camping-odersbach.de; www.camping-odersbach.de**

€1 nr

Fr Limburg exit B49 sp Weilburg & Bad Homburg, turn S (R) opp Shell stn at top of hill at Weilburg o'skts. Site on L at foot of hill in Odersbach. 4*, Lge, unshd, EHU (16A) metered + conn fee; 75% statics; ccard acc; boating; bike hire; golf 8km; CKE. **€25.00, 1 Apr-31 Oct.** **2024**

WEINHEIM *3C2* (9km N Rural) *49.59776, 8.64013* **Camping Wiesensee,** Ulmenweg 7, 69502 Hemsbach **(06201) 72619; info@camping-wiesensee.de; www.camping-wiesensee.de**

12 €2

Exit A5/E35 junc 32; foll sp Hemsbach. On ent vill strt at 1st rndbt & traff lts, at 2nd rndabt turn L & foll camping sp about 1km. 4*, Lge, hdg, pt shd, serviced pitches; EHU (16A) €1.90 or metered + conn fee; gas; sw; 75% statics; Eng spkn; adv bkg rec; boating; tennis 100m; golf 12km; bike hire. *"Superb facs to CC standard; htd pool 100m; friendly welcome; helpful staff; supmkt in walking dist; gd NH for A5."* **€21.50** **2024**

WERTHEIM *3D2* (3.6km N Urban) *49.77805, 9.50916* **Azur Campingpark Wertheim,** An den Christwiesen 35, 97877 Wertheim-Bestenheid **(09342) 83111; wertheim@azur-camping.de; www.azur-camping.com/wertheim**

€3 (htd)

Exit A3/E41 junc 65 twrds Wertheim. After x'ing rv turn R twrds Bestenheid. Site sp on R. Crozz r'way, turn immed R down single track rd. Site in 300mtrs. 4*, V lge, hdstg, mkd, pt shd, pt sl, serviced pitches; EHU (10A); gas; bbq (sep area); cooking facs; red long stay; TV; 10% statics; phone; bus 100m, train 1km; Eng spkn; adv bkg acc; ccard acc; games area; games rm; tennis 500m; boat hire; waterslide; fishing; bike hire; CKE. *"Interesting town in walking dist; helpful staff; gd rvside cycle paths; historic towns of Wurzburg & Rothernburg worth a visit; on Romanthische Strasse; gd."* **€44.00, 1 Apr-31 Oct.** **2023**

WERTHEIM *3D2* (11km NE Rural) *49.78097, 9.56553* **Campingpark Wertheim-Bettingen,** Geiselbrunnweg 31, 97877 Wertheim-Bettingen **(09342) 7077; info@campingpark-wertheim-bettingen.de; www.campingpark-wertheim-bettingen.de**

€3

Fr A3/E41 exit junc 66 - 2nd Wertheim exit; then turn off to vill of Bettingen; site sp. 4*, Med, pt shd, pt sl, EHU (10A) inc (long lead req for rvside pitches); gas; red long stay; 80% statics; Eng spkn; adv bkg acc; ccard acc; bike hire; boating; fishing; CKE. *"On bank of Rv Main; conv, popular NH for A3 - rec arr early; NH tourers on sep, lge, level meadow outside main site (but within barrier); gd rest; htd pool, paddling pool adj; waterslide adj; fuel stn nrby; effcnt check-in."* **€25.00, 1 Apr - 31 Oct.** **2022**

"I need an on-site restaurant"

We do our best to make sure site information is correct, but it is always best to check any must-have facilities are still available or will be open during your visit.

WESEL *1B3* (3km W Rural) *51.66795, 6.55620* **Erholungszentrum Grav-Insel,** 46487 Wesel-Flüren **(0281) 972830; info@grav-insel.com; www.grav-insel.com**

12 €1

Exit A3/E35 junc 6 dir Wesel. Then foll sp Rees & Flüren, site sp. 4*, V lge, unshd, EHU (10A) inc; 65% statics; Eng spkn; tennis 3km; boat hire; fishing; games area; bike hire; watersports; golf 7km. *"Rv Rhine adj; many activities; gd touring base; htd pool 3km; modern san facs but pss far fr pitches; v lge site with comprehensive facs & v well kept; poss cr during high ssn; excel shwrs in main building."* **€23.50** **2024**

WESTERSTEDE *1C2* (1km S Rural) *53.2508, 7.93506* **Camping Westerstede,** Süderstrasse 2, 26655 Westerstede **(04488) 78234; camping@westerstede.de; www.westerstede.de/camping**

12 €2 (htd) nr

Exit E35/A28 junc 6 to Westerstede; cont thro town dir Bad Zwischenahn on L815 for 1km; then foll L815 to L onto Oldenburgerstrasse (rd conts strt on as L821); in 200m turn L to site. Med, mkd, hdstg, pt shd, EHU (9A) €2.50; bus, train 400m; Eng spkn; CKE. *"Pleasant, friendly, relaxing, well-managed site; recep open 08:30-11:00; if arr after 11 barrier open/closes automatically; pay at bkg machine for toilet block card; sm pitches; outer field (nr mv svc pnt and rest) cheaper but rd noise and abt 100mtrs fr facs; o'night m'van facs; gd touring base; many cycle paths; gd town for shopping; gd midway stop to/fr Denmark."* **€30.00** **2022**

WETTRINGEN *1B3* (10km N Rural) *52.27408, 7.3204* **Campingplatz Haddorfer Seen,** Haddorf 59, 48493 Wettringen **(05973) 2742; info@campingplatz-haddorf.de; campingpark-haddorf.de**

12 €3 (htd) WD MSP

Exit A30 junc 7 at Rheine Nord dir Neuenkirchen. At end city limits turn R dir Salzbergen then L in 4km & foll site sp. 4*, V lge, mkd, pt shd, EHU (16A) metered + conn fee; sw; 90% statics; adv bkg acc; fishing; boat hire; games area; watersports; CKE. *"Family-friendly site; modern san facs; gd bistro; gd walking, cycling."*
€26.00 **2022**

WILDBERG *3C3* (2km SSW Rural) *48.61248, 8.73507* **Camping Carpe Diem,** Martinshölzle 6-8, 72218 Wildberg **(07054) 931851; campingcarpedeum@live.de; www.campingcarpediem.de**

€2.50 high ssn only WD

Take the A8, exit 43 Pforzheim-West dir Calw. In Calw foll the B463 dir Nagold. Foll the rd in Wildberg. Foll the camping signs. Med, hdg, pt shd, EHU (16A) inc; twin axles; 70% statics; Eng spkn; adv bkg rec; bike hire. *"Cycling and walks by rv Nagold; takeaway; gd site."* **€26.00, 29 Mar-20 Oct.** **2024**

WINSEN (ALLER) *1D3* (1.5km W Rural) *52.67506, 9.89968* **Campingplatz Winsen,** Auf der Hude 1, 29308 Winsen **(05143) 6698399 or (0151) 56620333; Allerklause@online.de; www.lueneburger-heide.de/service/unterkunft/13578/campingplatz-winsen.html**

12 €2 (htd) WD MSP

Fr A7/E45 exit junc 50 Wietze onto B214Thro Wietze & in 6km turn L to Oldau & Winsen. Foll site sp. Med, mkd, pt shd, EHU (10-16A) inc; gas; 50% statics; phone; bus 1km; CKE. *"Attractive site; rv adj; helpful staff; some rvside pitches - poss liable to flood; htd covrd pool 200m; m'van o'night area; easy walk to picturesque town cent; lovely cycle paths."*
€31.00 **2024**

WINTRICH *3B2* (30km NE Rural) *49.96541, 7.10537* **Mosel Stellplatz Wintrich,** Rissbacherstraße 155, 56841 Traben-Trarbach **(06541) 3111; info@moselcampingplatz.de; www.mosel-camping-platz.de**

12 WD MSP

Fr S of A1 take exit 125 Wittlich-Mitte for B50 twds Wittlich. Merge onto B49, cont onto L55 to Urzig, then turn R onto B53 & foll sp to camp. 4*, Med, shd, EHU (6A). *"Vg site."* **€8.00** **2024**

WISMAR *2E2* (0.4km S Urban) *53.89388, 11.45166* **Wohnmobilpark Westhafen,** Schiffbauerdamm 12, 23966 Wismar **(01723) 905368 or 884003; info@wohnmobilpark-wismar.de; www.wohnmobilpark-wismar.de**

12 nr nr

Exit A20/E22 junc 8 to cent of Wismar; foll sp to 'hafen', site sp. 4*, Sm, hdstg, unshd, EHU (10A) €1 for 8 hrs; adv bkg acc. *"Superb NH in stunning town; quayside noise; m'vans only - no c'vans allowed."*
€9.00 **2022**

WISMAR *2E2* (9km NW Coastal) *53.93441, 11.37160* **Ostsee Camping,** Sandstrasse 19c, 23968 Zierow **(038428) 63820; info@ostsee-camping.de; www.ostsee-camping.de**

12 €2.70 (htd) WD MSP adj

Fr Wismar-Lübeck rd B105/22 to Gägelow, turn N to Zierow; thro vill to site at end of rd. 4*, V lge, unshd, EHU (16A) €2.80; TV; 75% statics; games area; sauna; horseriding adj; bike hire; CKE. *"Busy site in superb location; gd san facs; a first class campsite."*
€32.00 **2022**

WISSEN *1B4* (3km SW Rural) *50.76108, 7.72086* **Zum Hahnhof,** Paffrather Str. 192, 57537 Wissen **49 27 42 56 10; info@zumhahnhof.de; www.zum-hahnhof.de**

12 WD MSP

Take B62 twds Roth. After 1km turn R onto Koblenzer Str (rd doubles back onto overpass) then 1st R onto Nistertais Str. Site approx 3km on R. Sm, hdstg, pt shd, terr, EHU (6A) €1.50; bbq; sw nr; twin axles; TV; 25% statics; Eng spkn; adv bkg acc; CKE. *"Modern san facs, very clean; some hdstg pitches, rest in meadow - long elec leads req; app rd (K133) fairly narr in places; gd site."* **€10.00** **2022**

WOLFSBURG *2E3* (3km NE Urban) *52.4316, 10.8158* **Camping am Allersee,** In den Allerwiesen 5, 38446 Wolfsburg **(05361) 63395; allerseecamping@gmx.de; www.camping-allersee.de**

12 €1 (htd) WD nr adj

Exit A39 junc 5 twd Zentrum, foll sp VW Autostadt until start of flyover, keep R and foll sp. 3*, Med, hdstg, mkd, pt shd, EHU (10A) €2.50 or metered; cooking facs; sw nr; 80% statics; Eng spkn; adv bkg acc; sailing; clsd 1300-1500 & 2200-0700; canoeing. *"Vg, clean site beside lake; conv VW factory visits (not w/end or bank hols) - check time of tour in Eng; o'night m'vans area; gd lake perimeter path adj; friendly, helpful owners; ice rink & indoor water cent other side of lake."* **€19.00** **2022**

WURZBURG *3D2* (6km NE Urban) *49.83286, 9.99783* **Camping Estenfeld,** Maidbronnerstrasse 38, 97230 Estenfeld **(09305) 228; cplestenfeld@freenet.de; www.camping-estenfeld.de**

€1.50 WD nr

Exit A7/E45 junc 101. Foll sp to Estenfeld & site sp. Sm, hdstg, pt shd, EHU (16A) €2.50 or metered & conn fee; red long stay; 10% statics; Eng spkn; CKE. *"Helpful owner; clsd 1300-1500; clean, tidy site; rec NH."*
€21.50, 29 May-14 Oct. **2024**

WURZBURG *3D2* (8km S Rural) *49.74471, 9.98433* **Camping Kalte Quelle,** Winterhäuserstrasse 160, 97084 Würzburg-Heidingsfeld **(0931) 65598; info@kalte-quelle.de; www.kalte-quelle.de**

12 WD MSP

Exit A3/E43 at Heidingsfeld junc 70 onto A19 dir Würzburg. Take 1st exit & foll sp Ochsenfurt + camping sp. Site on L in approx 5km. 3*, Med, mkd, pt shd, EHU (16A) conn fee + €2; 50% statics; Eng spkn; adv bkg acc; ccard acc; clsd 1330-1430; bike hire; CKE. *"No doors on shwrs & run down facs, but clean; pleasant situation on rv; NH only; conv Würzburg & Nürnberg; bus to centrum 2km; no mkd pitches for NH."* **€16.00 2024**

WUSTENWELSBERG *4E2* (0.5km SE Rural) *50.13750, 10.82777* **Camping Rückert-Klause,** Haus Nr 16, 96190 Wüstenwelsberg **(09533) 288**

WD nr

Fr Coburg on B4, turn W at Kaltenbrunn; site sp thro Untermerzbach & Obermerzbach. Or fr B279 fr Bamberg to Bad Königshofen, turn R just S of Pfarrweisch, sp. Sm, pt shd, pt sl, EHU (16A) metered + conn fee; 50% statics; Eng spkn; adv bkg acc; games rm; CKE. *"Many castles nrby; beautiful countryside; super situation."* **€18.20, 1 Apr-31 Oct. 2022**

"Satellite navigation makes touring much easier"

Remember most sat navs don't know if you're towing or in a larger vehicle – always use yours alongside maps and site directions.

ZELL *3B2* (4km N Rural) *50.03375, 7.17365* **Campingplatz Mosella,** 56856 Zell-Kaimt **(06542) 961216; info@capingpark-zell.de; www.campingpark-zell.de**

€1 WD MSP

Fr Cochem S on B49, in Alf take B53 dir Bernkastel-Kues. In Zell site sp to Kaimt. Med, mkd, hdstg, unshd, EHU (16A) inc; gas; watersports. *"Scenic area; v quiet at night; site soggy after rain; excel well kept site, rest and bar being built (2012); cycles and boats for hire."* **€26.50, 27 Mar-31 Oct. 2024**

ZELL *3B2* (6km NW Rural) *50.05391, 7.13041* **Bären Camp,** Am Moselufer 1-3, 56859 Bullay **(06542) 900097; info@baeren-camp.de; www.baeren-camp.de**

€2 WD MSP

Exit A1 junc 125 at Wittlich onto B49 to Alf. At Alf cross rv to Bullay & foll sp to site. 4*, Med, pt shd, EHU (16A) metered; bbq; Eng spkn. *"Conv Cochem, Bernkastel-Kues; gd cycling along tow-path; extra for rvside pitch; recep clsd 1230-1400; narr rd to recep; friendly staff; gd location on the Mosel."* **€35.60, 28 Mar-3 Nov. 2024**

ZEVEN *1D2* (2km NE Urban) *53.30401, 9.29793* **Campingplatz Sonnenkamp Zeven,** Sonnenkamp 10, 27404 Zeven **(04281) 951345; info@campingplatz-sonnenkamp.de; www.campingplatz-zeven.de**

12 €0.50 (htd) WD MSP

Fr A1 exit 47 or 49 to Zeven. Fr Zeven dir Heeslingen/Buxtehude rd, site sp fr all dir twd stadium. 5*, Lge, mkd, hdstg, unshd, EHU (16A) metered; gas; 75% statics; phone; Eng spkn; adv bkg acc; ccard acc; bike hire; games area; tennis; games rm; sauna; CKE. *"Sports facs adj."* **€23.50 2022**

FEHMARN ISLAND

WULFEN *2E1* (0.6km E Coastal) *54.40611, 11.1772* **Camping-und Ferienpark Wulfener Hals (Part Naturist),** Wulfener Hals Weg, 23769 Wulfen **(04371) 86280; camping@wulfenerhals.de; www.wulfenerhals.de**

12 €10 (htd) WD MSP sand adj

Turn off B207/E47 to Avendorf, site sp. 5*, V lge, mkd, shd, serviced pitches; EHU (160A) inc; gas; 20% statics; phone; adv bkg acc; ccard acc; golf adj; sauna; watersports; sailing; CKE. *"Excel."* **€39.00, G10. 2023**

ZIERENBERG *1D4* (1km E Rural) *51.36809, 9.31494* **Campingplatz Zur Warme,** Im Nordbruch 2, 34289 Zierenberg **(05606) 3966; campingplatz-zierenberg@t-online.de; www.campingplatz-zierenberg.de**

12 €2 (htd) WD nr (covrd)

Exit A44 at junc 67 to Zierenberg. In vill cent foll sp for Freizeit Centrum. Site on R on leaving vill, well sp. 4*, Med, mkd, hdstg, unshd, EHU (16A) €1.70 or metered; TV; 75% statics; Eng spkn; adv bkg acc; fishing. *"Scenic, well-kept site with stream & sm lake adj; clean, modern facs but poss stretched if site full."* **€17.50 2022**

ZINGST AM DARSS *2F1* (3km W Coastal) *54.44055, 12.66031* **Camping am Freesenbruch,** Am Bahndamm 1, 18374 Zingst-am-Darss **(038232) 15786; info@camping-zingst.de; www.camping-zingst.de**

12 €5 WD MSP adj

On rd 105/E22 at Löbnitz take rd thro Barth to Zingst; site on coast rd. 4*, Lge, mkd, pt shd, EHU (16A) €4; 20% statics; adv bkg acc; ccard acc; games area; bike hire; CKE. *"Well-maintained site in National Park; sep car park; o'night facs for m'vans; sep fr beach by sea wall & rd; well-maintained; card operated barrier."* **€42.00 2022**

ZISLOW *2F2* (2km N Rural) *53.44555, 12.31083* **Naturcamping Zwei Seen,** Waldchaussee 2, 17209 Zislow **(039924) 2550; info@zwei-seen-naturcamping.de; www.zwei-seen-naturcamping.de**

12 €2.50 nr

A19/E55 exit 17 dir Adamshoffnung. Turn R at x-rds in 4km. Site sp. Also sp fr W of Stuer on B198. 3*, Lge, pt shd, EHU (6A) €2; sw; 40% statics; phone; Eng spkn; adv bkg acc; ccard acc; games area; bike hire; watersports; CKE. *"Ideal for country lovers; remote spot; vg lakeside pitches."* **€22.70** **2022**

ZITTAU *2H4* (3km W Rural) *50.8943, 14.77005* **See-Camping Zittauer Gebirge,** Zur Landesgartenschau 2, 02785 Olbersdorf **(03583) 69629-2; info@seecamping-zittau.com; www.seecamping-zittau.com**

€2 nr nr

Fr Zittau foll Olbersdorfer See sp, site on lakeside. 3*, Lge, unshd, sl, EHU (10A) €2; sw nr; 10% statics; Eng spkn; ccard acc; CKE. *"Excel san facs; excel base for hill walking; close Polish & Czech borders."* **€26.50, 1 Apr-31 Oct.** **2022**

RUGEN ISLAND

ALTEFAHR *2F1* (1km NW Coastal) *54.33200, 13.12206* **Sund Camp,** Am Kurpark 1, 18573 Altefähr **(038306) 75483; info@sund-camp.de; www.sund-camp.de**

€2 (htd) nr nr shgl 500m

Fr Stralsund, cross bdge on B96 to Rügen Island. Foll sp to Altefähr. Site well sp fr vill. Med, mkd, pt shd, pt sl, EHU (16A) inc (poss rev pol); red long stay; TV; 25% statics; phone; Eng spkn; sep car park; bike hire:WiFi hotspot. *"Conv Rugen Is (walks, cycle tracks, beaches, steam rlwy); easy walk to vill & harbour; splendid, but busy island; well worth visit; ferry to Stralsund Altstadt nrby; excel, friendly site; muddy when wet; excel, clean san facs; ltd nbr of touring pitches; busy in ssn; delightful site; vg."* **€29.40, 1 Apr-15 Oct.** **2022**

BINZ *2G1* (3km NW Coastal) *54.42315, 13.57808* **Camping Prora (formerly Camping Meier),** Proraer Chaussee 30, 18609 Prora **(038393) 2085; info@camping-prora-ruegen.de; www.camping-prora-ruegen.de**

€3.50 nr sand 500m

On B96 Stralsund to Bergen cont on 196 to Karow. Turn L on 196a to Prora, at traff lts turn R onto L29 to Binz. After 1.5km at camp sp turn R thro wood to site. Med, mkd, pt shd, EHU (6A) €2.50; red long stay; phone; adv bkg req; ccard acc; bike hire; tennis. *"Gd location for touring Rügen area; gd sandy beach 5-10 min walk thro woods; bkg fee; vg rest; vg san facs."* **€36.10, 1 Mar-6 Nov.** **2022**

SYLT ISLAND

WESTERLAND *1C1* (5km N Coastal) *54.94251, 8.32685* **Camping Wenningstedt,** Am Dorfteich, 25996 Wenningstedt **(04651) 944004; camp@wenningstedt.de; www.campingplatz.wenningstedt.de**

€3.50 (covrd, htd)

Fr Westerland foll sp to Wenningstedt or List. Site app rd on sharp bend bef Wenningstedt. 4*, Lge, unshd, pt sl, EHU (16A) metered; adv bkg acc; fishing 300m. **€28.00, Easter-31 Oct.** **2022**

ZWEIBRUCKEN *3B3* (17km SW Rural) *49.15888, 7.24388* **Camping Walsheim,** Am Campingplatz 1, 66453 Gersheim-Walsheim **(06843) 800180; info@campingwalsheim.de; www.campingwalsheim.de**

€0.50 nr nr nr

Fr A8/E50 exit junc 9 onto B423 dor Blieskastel. In Webenheim turn L twd Gersheim, after 11km turn L for Walsheim. Site on L beyond vill. 3*, Med, pt shd, pt sl, EHU €2 or metered (10A); bbq; 85% statics; phone; adv bkg acc; CKE. *"Helpful warden; htd pool adj; sep area for tourers; pleasant countryside; walking & cycle paths nr; site barrier clsd 1300-1500 & 2200."* **€19.00, 15 Mar-31 Oct.** **2024**

"There aren't many sites open at this time of year"

If you're travelling outside peak season remember to call ahead to check site opening dates – even if the entry says 'open all year'.

ZWEIBRUCKEN *3B3* (5km SW Rural) *49.20638, 7.33111* **Camping Hengstbacher-Mühle,** Hengstbacher Mühle 1, 66482 Zweibrücken-Mittelbach **(06332) 18128; www.camping-hengstbachermuehle.de**

nr

Fr A8 exit junc 33 onto B424 sp Zweibrücken-Ixheim & Mittelbach. At T-junc turn R dir Bitsch & in 50m turn R at camping sp. Site on L in 4km after end of Mittelbach vill. 2*, Sm, pt shd, EHU (15A) €2.50 or metered (poss rev pol); 70% statics; Eng spkn. *"Friendly owner; lovely setting; basic site but clean san facs; gd NH, liable to flooding; CL type size."* **€13.50, 15 Apr-31 Oct.** **2024**

GERMANY

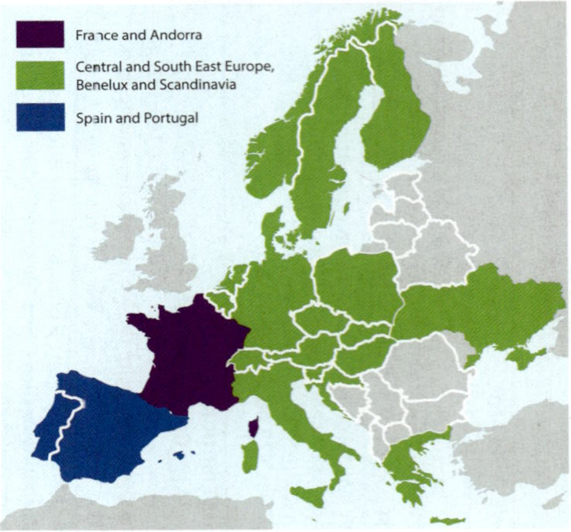

Karlsruhe to Trier = 233km

	Aachen	Augsburg	Bayreuth	Berlin	Bonn	Bremen	Dresden	Düsseldorf	Erfurt	Essen	Frankfurt-am-Main	Frankfurt-an-der-Oder	Freiburg-im-Breisgau	Fulda	Garmisch-Partenkirchen	Hamburg	Hannover	Heidelberg	Karlsruhe	Kassel	Kiel	Koblenz	Köln (Cologne)	Leipzig	Lübben	Magdeburg	München (Munich)	Münster	Neubrandenburg	Nürnberg (Nuremberg)	Osnabrück	Passau	Regensburg	Rostock	Saarbrücken	Schwerin	Stuttgart	Trier	Wilhelmshaven
Augsburg	565																																						
Bayreuth	538	243																																					
Berlin	642	600	356																																				
Bonn	90	482	406	585																																			
Bremen	369	723	580	380	340																																		
Dresden	651	473	237	216	611	479																																	
Düsseldorf	85	567	472	555	75	297	619																																
Erfurt	447	426	187	290	391	355	225	410																															
Essen	125	605	500	481	98	251	586	35	368																														
Frankfurt-am-Main	241	362	268	570	179	448	490	223	270	260																													
Frankfurt-an-der-Oder	728	655	416	95	705	465	178	651	368	605	664																												
Freiburg-im-Breisgau	460	338	460	811	405	725	702	477	535	529	263	882																											
Fulda	330	335	190	476	259	386	395	355	182	302	96	552	362																										
Garmisch-Partenkirchen	745	120	340	689	641	845	586	745	515	730	506	763	495	482																									
Hamburg	471	723	600	281	445	110	495	410	370	346	511	390	765	413	873																								
Hannover	354	603	465	263	311	120	385	275	295	255	365	336	630	278	745	156																							
Heidelberg	302	279	311	639	230	559	542	300	329	345	124	720	175	156	426	570	423																						
Karlsruhe	351	225	340	654	271	600	570	349	404	397	137	750	132	241	365	643	500	40																					
Kassel	309	432	280	370	279	290	403	231	132	192	192	442	455	107	578	310	166	255	335																				
Kiel	552	830	700	345	557	206	578	510	462	450	603	448	863	506	972	88	241	661	732	406																			
Koblenz	146	432	350	608	85	415	535	151	320	163	128	690	340	228	583	526	411	127	209	245	603																		
Köln (Cologne)	62	540	434	550	30	320	585	36	375	76	190	630	436	282	679	386	296	246	311	245	490	113																	
Leipzig	578	432	201	187	551	370	145	556	172	480	412	212	645	315	516	390	259	487	516	280	486	456	490																
Lübben	697	574	342	85	642	454	110	132	315	595	580	69	795	462	692	481	336	655	665	470	469	613	663	132															
Magdeburg	503	533	296	131	463	255	229	419	207	388	445	205	703	348	616	275	139	495	578	247	381	500	419	110	196														
München (Munich)	653	61	244	596	560	770	499	643	425	650	415	676	403	384	92	776	645	329	271	485	882	516	582	439	610	526													
Münster	201	624	523	450	169	175	600	155	384	89	283	530	553	306	763	263	185	332	425	203	349	244	146	450	537	343	670												
Neubrandenburg	725	733	500	130	437	353	360	707	440	603	708	280	953	610	816	240	396	751	818	509	232	762	650	325	215	272	731	531											
Nürnberg (Nuremberg)	472	185	76	428	429	592	326	481	267	460	237	503	381	205	272	618	478	230	256	308	707	353	419	268	406	360	163	493	567										
Osnabrück	260	583	641	411	221	121	585	192	376	135	341	488	550	294	759	203	132	400	429	191	301	306	203	410	486	296	650	61	435	486									
Passau	691	236	275	629	645	800	372	697	462	676	438	563	486	415	300	823	678	426	459	510	905	583	612	463	498	569	182	700	762	207	748								
Regensburg	571	165	160	515	529	695	342	581	346	563	329	588	482	306	196	713	569	325	355	404	803	449	511	352	460	443	109	585	645	108	586	131							
Rostock	645	790	550	232	630	274	444	591	439	525	692	320	926	582	872	145	320	730	798	480	200	690	563	376	340	320	775	472	100	615	368	825	705						
Saarbrücken	321	360	450	749	260	585	670	330	456	361	192	823	312	293	511	693	558	135	192	386	776	206	285	589	750	611	415	427	881	360	479	563	456	850					
Schwerin	590	748	568	201	581	230	422	542	482	476	631	308	871	528	862	120	269	685	756	429	142	639	525	365	317	311	776	395	189	608	320	795	703	91	831				
Stuttgart	410	152	270	622	351	640	535	416	435	472	200	706	210	263	302	672	526	120	80	365	763	275	368	472	612	575	211	506	765	215	558	401	290	818	211	792			
Trier	259	480	490	719	188	526	648	261	430	295	240	806	363	350	613	620	490	128	233	362	716	128	219	569	735	605	526	362	862	311	415	620	506	832	104	759	311		
Wilhelmshaven	421	819	690	485	385	110	662	375	453	294	500	563	720	451	925	220	225	578	592	348	309	461	362	485	556	336	832	220	475	646	162	871	741	425	639	339	711	515	
Würzburg	362	243	150	492	322	490	385	372	292	363	132	641	321	100	389	511	372	131	196	211	506	248	301	410	567	462	298	383	753	106	392	323	209	706	315	618	160	356	559

Federal States of Germany

SCHLESWIG-
HOLSTEIN
MECKLENBURG-VORPOMMERN
(Mecklenburg-
Western Pomerania)
Hamburg
HAMBURG
BREMEN
Bremen
NIEDERSACHSEN
(Lower Saxony)
Hannover
BERLIN
Berlin
BRANDENBURG
SACHSEN-ANHALT
(Saxony-Anhalt)
NORDRHEIN-WESTFALEN
(North Rhine-Westphalia)
Düsseldorf
Köln
Bonn
Leipzig
SACHSEN
(Saxony)
Dresden
THÜRINGEN
(Thuringia)
HESSEN
(Hesse)
Frankfurt-am-Main
RHEINLAND-PFALZ
(Rhineland-Palatinate)
SAARLAND
Nürnberg
BAYERN
(Bavaria)
Stuttgart
BADEN-
WÜRTTEMBERG
München

Motorways
Primary roads
Secondary roads
All year site(s)
Seasonal site(s)
No sites listed
A
B
C
D
1
2
3
4
NORTH SEA
DENMARK
NETHERLANDS
BELGIUM
SYLT
Westerland
Aabenraa
Medelby
Glucksburg
Flensburg
Lindaunis
Eckernforde
KIEL
Preetz
Neumunster
Hochdonn
Bad Bramstedt
Bad Segeberg
Hamburg
Geesthacht
Norden
Bensersiel
Hooksiel
Dorum
BREMERHAVEN
EMDEN
Leer (Ostfriesland)
Westerstede
OLDENBURG
Zeven
Gyhum
Sottrum
Bremen
Ganderkesee
Papenburg
Friesoythe
Fassberg
Bad Fallingbostel
Leeuwarden
Groningen
Assen
Emmen
Hoorn
Utrecht
Arnhem
Rieste
Schuttorf
Osnabruck
Wettringen
Greven
Munster
Hannover
Porta Westfalica
Vlotho
Hameln
Bielefeld
Lemgo
Bad Pyrmont
Bad Gandersheim
Hoxter
Kalkar
Wesel
Hamm
Lippstadt
Soest
Dortmund
Essen
DUISBURG
Eindhoven
Hattingen
Meschede
Zierenberg
Hannoversch Munden
Kassel
Dusseldorf
WUPPERTAL
Bruggen
Radevormwald
Hueckeswagen
Hasselt
Maastricht
Olpe
Koln
Aachen
Liège
Bonn
Bad Honnef
Wissen
Altenkirchen
Simmerath
Remagen
Hunfeld
3

E
F
G
H
1
2
3
4
0 25 50 75 100 km
0 20 40 60 miles
N
S
E
W
BALTIC SEA
Svendborg
Sakskobing
FEHMARN
Wulfen
Zingst am Darss
RÜGEN
Binz
Altefahr
STRALSUND
Ribnitz Damgarten
Bad Doberan
Rerik
Rostock
Karlshagen
Greifswald
Travemunde
Wismar
Lubeck
Schwaan
Retgendorf
SCHWERIN
Zislow
Neustrelitz
Szczecin/Stettin
Malliss
Canow
Warnitz
Gartow
POLAND
Brieselang
BERLIN
Brandenburg an der Havel
Wolfsburg
Colbitz
Potsdam
BRAUNSCHWEIG
Magdeburg
Zielona Góra
Lutherstadt Wittenberg
Quedlinburg
Braunlage
Walkenried
Neustadt/Harz
Ortrand
Leipzig
Niesky
Kamenz
Bad Kosen
Colditz
Dresden
Heidenau
Erfurt
Altenburg
Reinsberg
Jena
Konigstein
Bad Schandau
Zittau
GERA
Liberec
Kranichfeld
Chemnitz
Usti nad Labem
CZECHIA (CZECH REPUBLIC)
4

A
B
1
C
D
Eindhoven
NETHERLANDS
Dortmund
Essen
Hattingen
Soest
Hannoversch Munden
Bruggen
Dusseldorf
WUPPERTAL
Meschede
Zierenberg
Kassel
Radevormwald
Hueckeswagen
Olpe
Maastricht
Koln
Eisenach
Aachen
Bonn
Wissen
Liege
Simmerath
Altenkirchen
Bad Honnef
Remagen
Hunfeld
Spa
Bad Neuenahr Ahrweiler
Montabaur
Weilburg
Gersfeld (Rhon)
BELGIUM
Mendig
Koblenz
Limburg An Der Lahn
Lahnstein
Prum
Daun
Cochem
Pfalzfeld
Frankfurt Am Main
Lingerhahn
Oberwesel
Grafendorf
Bitburg
Zell
Rudesheim
Gemunden Am Main
Brauneberg
Bernkastel Kues
Bingen
MAINZ
Morfelden
Echternacherbruck
Wintrich
Burgen
Schweppenhausen
Marktheidenfeld
Volkach
Schweich
Trittenheim
Bad Kreuznach
Dettelbach
LUXEMBOURG
Trier
Idar Oberstein
Wurzburg
Wertheim
Kitzingen
LUXEMBOURG
Saarburg
Hammelbach
Frickenhausen am Main
Nennig
Weinheim
Bad Durkheim
Mannheim
Weikersheim
Creglingen
Heidelberg
Saarlouis
Kirkel
Speyer
Rothenburg Ob Der Tauber
Zweibrucken
Metz
Pirmasens
Schillingsfurst
Karlsruhe
Dinkelsbuhl
Pforzheim
Malsch
Bad Wildbad im Schwarzwald
Schomberg
Stuttgart
Nancy
Calw
Goppingen
Buhl
Strasbourg
Kehl
Kirchheim
Altensteig
Tubingen
Freudenstadt
Bad Rippoldsau
Horb am Neckar
Laichingen
Leipheim
FRANCE
Alpirsbach
Riegel Am Kaiserstuhl
Krumbach
Breisach Am Rhein
Illertissen
Freiburg im Breisgau
Hausen Im Tal
Titisee Neustadt
Donaueschingen
Staufen im Breisgau
Munstertal
Stockach
Sulzburg
Feldberg
Tengen
Uberlingen
Schonau im Schwarzwald
Radolfzell Am Bodensee
Friedrichshafen
Kempten (Allgau)
Konstanz
Immenstadt Im Allgau
Basel
Kressbronn Am Bodensee
Lindau (Bodensee)
Zurich
Oberstdorf
SWITZERLAND
Motorways
Primary roads
Secondary roads
All year site(s)
Seasonal site(s)
No sites listed
2
3
4

Walkenried
Neustadt/harz
Leipzig
Ortrand
Kamenz
Niesky
POLAND
Bad Kosen
Colditz
Dresden
Erfurt
Jena
Altenburg
Reinsberg
Heidenau
Zittau
Konigstein
Bad Schandau
Kranichfeld
GERA
Chemnitz
Liberec
Usti Nad Labem
Hof
Coburg
Wustenwelsberg
Kulmbach
PRAHA
CZECHIA
(CZECH REPUBLIC)
Fichtelberg
Mitterteich
Pottenstein
Erlangen
Neustadt an der Aisch
Hersbruck
Nurnberg
Klatovy
Waldmunchen
Neumarkt in der Oberpfalz
Kinding
Pappenheim
Bad Abbach
Straubing
Finsterau
České Budějovice
Neureichenau
Ingolstadt
Donauworth
Passau
Landshut
Bad Birnbach
Augsburg
Bad Fussing
Linz
Munchen
AUSTRIA
Chieming
Rosenheim
Traunstein
Seeshaupt
Salzburg
Peissenberg
Bad Tolz
Ubersee
Inzell
Lechbruck
Murnau Am Staffelsee
Oberammergau
Berchtesgaden
Konigssee
Fussen
Garmisch Partenkirchen
Mittenwald
Innsbruck
N
W
E
S
0
25
50
75
100 km
0
20
40
60 miles

Highlights

Whether you want to marvel at ancient ruins, lay on an idyllic sandy beach or sample local dishes, Greece is undoubtedly the place to be.

From rugged hillsides to the sparkling blue waters of the Mediterranean, this is a country steeped in myths of gods and heroes. The country is also famed for the friendly and hospitable nature of its people, so you're sure to receive a warm welcome.

Music is an integral part of Greek society and laïkó is a modern folk music genre that boomed in the 1960s and 70s. There are now many different forms of this music, but it still retains a sense of being a song of the people.

Greece can be considered the birthplace of wine, and the origins of wine-making in Greece go back well over 6000 years. Although not as well-known as other European nations for its wine, Greece has a thriving industry and the local varieties pair up well with food dishes from the same area.

Major towns and cities

- Athens – the cradle of Western civilization and one of the world's oldest cities.
- Thessalonika – a charming city filled with museums to explore.
- Patras – this amazing city is home to fascinating sites from ancient times.
- Larissa – surrounded by mountains and home to several ancient sites.

Attractions

- The Acropolis, Athens – an ancient citadel containing the Parthenon and other ruins.
- Meteora – stunning monasteries built on natural sandstone pillars.
- Delphi – this site boasts some of Greece's most important ancient ruins.
- Cape Sounion – fantastic views over the Aegean and the ruins of an ancient temple.

Find out more

visitgreece.gr

Country Information

Capital: Athens

Bordered by: Albania, Bulgaria, Macedonia, Turkey

Coastline: 13,676km

Terrain: Mainly mountain ranges extending into the sea as peninsulas and chains of islands

Climate: Warm Mediterranean climate; hot, dry summers; mild, wet winters in the south, colder in the north; rainy season November to March; winter temperatures can be severe in the mountains

Highest Point: Mount Olympus 2,919m

Language: Greek

Local Time: GMT or BST + 2, i.e. 2 hours ahead of the UK all year

Currency: Euros divided into 100 cents; £1 = €1.15, €1 = £0.87 (Nov 2023)

Emergency numbers: Police 100/112; Fire brigade 199/112; Ambulance 166/112. Operators speak English. Dial 171 for emergency tourist police.

Public Holidays 2025: Jan 1, 6; Mar 25; Apr 18, 20, 21; May 1; Jun 8, 9; Aug 15; Oct 28; Dec 25, 26.

School summer holidays run from the beginning of July to the first week in September.

Border Posts

Borders may be crossed only on official routes with a Customs office. These are usually open day and night. Customs offices at ports are open from 7.30am to 3pm Monday to Friday.

Entry Formalities

British and Irish passport holders may stay for up to 90 days in any 180 day period without a visa. You may be asked to show a return or onward ticket at the border to confirm your length of stay, or to prove that you have enough money for your stay.

Your passport will need to have a minimum of 6 months' validity remaining, and be less than 10 years old (even if it has over 6 months left).

Visitors arriving at a campsite or hotel must complete a registration form.

Medical Services

For minor complaints seek help at a pharmacy (farmakio). In major cities there's usually one member of staff in a pharmacy who speaks English. You should have no difficulty finding an English speaking doctor in large towns and resorts.

Medications containing codeine are restricted. If you're taking any medication containing it, you should carry a letter from your doctor and take no more than one month's supply into the country.

There are numerous public and private hospitals and medical centres of varying standards. Wards may be crowded and the standards of nursing and after care, particularly in the public health sector, are generally below what is normally acceptable in Britain. Doctors and facilities are generally good on the mainland, but may be limited on the islands. The public ambulance service will normally respond to any accident but there are severe shortages of ambulances on some islands.

Emergency treatment at public medical clinics (yiatria) and in state hospitals registered by the Greek Social Security Institute, IKA-ETAM, is free on presentation of a European Health Insurance Card (EHIC) or Global Health Insurance Card (GHIC).

You may consult a doctor or dentist privately but you'll have to present your EHIC or GHIC and pay all charges up front. You can then claim back the charges later from the IKA-ETAM.

If staying near a beach, ensure that you have plenty of insect repellent as sand flies are prevalent. Don't be tempted to befriend stray dogs as they often harbour diseases which may be passed to humans.

Opening Hours

Banks: Mon-Fri 8am-2pm (1.30pm on Friday); 8am-6pm in tourist areas.

Museums: Check locally for opening hours. Normally closed on Mon or Tues and some bank holidays.

Post Offices: Mon-Fri 8am-2pm; 8am-7pm in tourist areas; many in Athens open Sat mornings in summer.

Shops: 9am-9pm (large cities).

Working hours for suburban stores are split shifts and can vary. Shops are generally closed on Sundays with exception to tourist areas.

Safety and Security

Normally visits to Greece are trouble free, but the tourist season results in an increase in incidents of theft of passports, wallets, handbags, etc, particularly in areas or at events where crowds gather.

Take care when visiting well-known historical sites; they're the favoured haunts of pickpockets, bag-snatchers and muggers. Women should not walk alone at night and lone visitors are strongly advised never to accept lifts from strangers or passing acquaintances at any time.

Multilingual tourist police are available in most resorts offering information and help; they can be recognised by a 'Tourist Police' badge, together with a white cap band. There's also a 24-hour emergency helpline for tourists; dial 171 from anywhere in Greece.

Certain areas near the Greek borders are militarily sensitive and you should not take photographs or take notes near military or official installations. Seek permission before photographing individuals.

Greece shares with the rest of Europe an underlying threat from terrorism. Please check gov.uk/foreign-travel-advice/greece before you travel.

During especially hot and dry periods there's a danger of forest fires. Take care when visiting or driving through woodland areas. Ensure that cigarette ends are properly extinguished, don't light barbecues and don't leave rubbish or empty bottles behind.

Some motorists have encountered stowaway attempts while waiting to board ferries to Italy from Patras. Keep a watch on your vehicle(s).

In order to comply with the law, always ensure that you obtain a receipt for goods purchased.

British Embassy

1 Ploutarchou Street
106 75 Athens
Tel: +30 (210) 727 2600
gov.uk/world/greece

There are also British Consulates/Vice-Consulates/Honorary Consulates in Corfu, Heraklion (Crete), Rhodes and Zakynthos.

Irish Embassy

7 Leof.vas
Konstantinou, 106 74 Athens
Tel: +30 (210) 723 2771
ireland.ie/en/greece/athens

There are also Honorary Consulates in Corfu, Crete, Rhodes and Thessaloniki.

Documents

Money

Major credit cards are accepted in hotels, restaurants and shops and at some petrol stations. They may not be accepted at shops in small towns or villages. There's an extensive network of cash machines in major cities.

Carry your credit card issuers'/banks' 24-hour UK contact numbers in case of loss or theft.

Passport

Carry your passport at all times as a means of identification.

Vehicle(s)

Carry your vehicle registration certificate (V5C), insurance certificate and MOT certificate (if applicable) at all times.

Driving

Accidents

It's not essential to call the police in the case of an accident causing material damage only, however motorists are advised to call at the nearest police station to give a description of the incident to the authorities.

Whenever an accident causes physical injury, drivers are required to stop immediately to give assistance to the injured and call the police. Drivers who fail to do this are liable to imprisonment for up to three years.

If a visiting motorist has an accident, especially one causing injuries, they should inform the motoring organisation, ELPA, at its head office in Athens, on +30 (210) 6068800, email: info@elpa.gr, as they should be able to offer you assistance.

Alcohol

The maximum permitted level of alcohol is 0.05%. This is reduced to 0.02% for motorcyclists and newly-qualified drivers who have held a driving licence for less than three years. Police carry out random breath tests and refusal to take a test when asked by the police, and/or driving while over the legal limit, can incur high fines, withdrawal of your driving licence and even imprisonment.

Breakdown Service

The Automobile & Touring Club of Greece (ELPA) operates a roadside assistance service (OVELPA) 24 hours a day on all mainland Greek roads as well as on most islands. The number to dial from most towns in Greece is 10400.

Members of AIT/FIA affiliated clubs, such as The Caravan and Motorhome Club, should present their valid membership card in order to qualify for reduced charges for on-the-spot assistance and towing. Payment by credit card is accepted.

Child Restraint System

Children under three years of age must be seated in a suitable and approved child restraint. Children between the ages of 3 and 11 years old that are less than 1.35 metres in height must be seated in an appropriate child restraint for their size. From 12 years old children that are over 1.35 metres in height can wear an adult seat belt.

A rear facing child restraint can be placed in the front seat only if the airbag is deactivated.

Fuel

Petrol stations are usually open from 7am to 7pm; a few are open 24 hours. Some will accept credit cards but those offering cut-price fuel are unlikely to do so. In rural areas petrol stations may close in the evening and at weekends, so keep your tank topped up.

There are no automatic petrol pumps operated with either credit cards or bank notes.

LPG (autogas) is available from a limited number of outlets.

Low Emission Zones

There are Low Emission Zones in force in Athens and Thessaloniki. See urbanaccessregulations.eu for more information.

Motorways

There are over 2,300 km of motorways in Greece. Service areas provide petrol, a cafeteria and shops. The main motorways are A1 Agean, A2 Egnatia,A6 Attiki, A7 Peloponissos, A8 Pathe, A29 Kastorias.

Motorway Tolls

Tolls are charged according to vehicle classification and distance travelled. By European standards the tolls are generally quite low. Cash is the preferred means of payment.

The Egnatia Highway

The 804 km Egnatia Motorway (the A2), connects Alexandroupolis on the border of Turkey and Igoumenitsa which is close to Albania. The route includes many bridges and tunnels with frequent emergency telephones for which the number to call from a landline or mobile phone is 1077. The road provides a continuous high-speed link from west to east. There are 11 toll sections on the route, which cost from €1.00 to €2.40.

Patras – Antirrio Bridge

A 2.8 km long toll suspension bridge between Rio (near Patras) and Antirrio links the Peloponnese with western central Greece and is part of the A8/E55 motorway. It has cut the journey time across the Gulf of Corinth – formerly only possible by ferry – to just five minutes. Tolls are charged.

Preveza – Aktio Tunnel

This undersea toll tunnel links Preveza with Aktio near Agios Nikolaos on the E55 along the west coast of mainland Greece and is part of a relatively fast, scenic route south from Igoumenitsa to central and southern regions.

Parking

Parking is only permitted in the Athens 'Green Zone' where there are parking meters. Special parking sites in other areas are reserved for short-term parking for tourists.

There may be signs on the side of the road indicating where vehicles should be parked.

Parking restrictions are indicated by yellow lines at the side of the road. The police are entitled to remove vehicles.

Police can also confiscate the number plates of vehicles parked illegally and, while this usually applies only to Greek-registered vehicles, drivers of foreign registered vehicles should nevertheless avoid illegal parking.

You cannot park within three metres of a fire hydrant, five metres of an intersection, stop sign or traffic light, and fifteen metres of a bus stop, tram stop and level crossings.

Roads

The surfaces of all major roads and of the majority of other roads are in good condition. Some mountain roads, however, may be in poor condition and drivers must beware of unexpected potholes (especially on corners), precipitous, unguarded drops and single-carriageway bridges. Even on narrow mountain roads you may well encounter buses and coaches.

British motorists visiting Greece should be extra vigilant in view of the high incidence of road accidents. Driving standards are generally poorer than in the UK and you may well have to contend with dangerous overtaking, tailgating, weaving motorcycles and scooters, constant use of the horn, roaming pedestrians and generally erratic driving. Greece has one of the highest rate of road fatalities in Europe and overtaking and speeding are common causes of accidents, particularly on single lane carriageways. Drive carefully and be aware of other drivers at all times.

August is the busiest month of the year for traffic and the A1/E75 between Athens and Thessalonika is recognised as one of the most dangerous routes, together with the road running through the Erimanthos mountains south of Kalavrita. Mountain roads in general can be dangerous owing to narrow carriageways, blind bends and unprotected embankments, so keep your speed down.

You must have a valid motorcycle licence if you're planning to hire a motorcycle, moped or scooter. The wearing of crash helmets is a legal requirement and not wearing one will incur a fine of €350. Never hand over your passport when hiring a vehicle.

Where there's a shortage of parking spaces drivers park on pavements so pedestrians are forced to walk in the road.

Road Signs and Markings

Road signs conform to international conventions. Motorway signs have white lettering on a green background, signs on other roads are on a blue background. All motorways, major and secondary roads are signposted in Greek and English.

Some open roads have a white line on the nearside, and slower-moving vehicles are expected to pull across it to allow vehicles to overtake.

Speed Limits

	Open Road (km/h)	Motorway (km/h)
Car Solo	90-110	130
Car towing caravan/trailer	80	80
Motorhome under 3500kg	80	90
Motorhome 3500-7500kg	80	80

Traffic Jams

There's heavy rush hour traffic in and around the major cities and traffic jams are the norm in central Athens any time of day. During the summer months traffic to the coast may be heavy, particularly at weekends. Traffic jams may be encountered on the A1/E75 Athens to Thessalonika road and on the A8/E65 Athens to Patras road. Traffic may also be heavy near the ferry terminals to Italy and you should allow plenty of time when travelling to catch a ferry. Delays can be expected at border crossings to Turkey and Bulgaria.

Violation of Traffic Regulations

The Greek police are authorised to impose fines in cases of violation of traffic regulations, but fines may not be collected on the spot. Motorists must pay fines within ten days, otherwise legal proceedings will be started.

Essential Equipment

First Aid Kit

All vehicles must carry a first aid kit.

Fire Extinguisher

All vehicles must carry a fire extinguisher.

Warning Triangles

The placing of a warning triangle is compulsory in the event of an accident or a breakdown. It must be placed 100 metres behind the vehicle.

Touring

Mainland Greece and most of the Greek islands that are popular with British tourists are in seismically active zones, and small earth tremors are common. Serious earthquakes are less frequent but can, and do, occur.

Smoking is prohibited in bars and restaurants. In restaurants, if the bill doesn't include a service charge, it's usual to leave a 10 to 20% tip. Taxi drivers don't normally expect a tip but it's customary to round up the fare.

The best known local wine is retsina but there's also a wide range of non-resinated wines. Beer is brewed under licence from German and Danish breweries; Ouzo is a popular and strong aniseed-flavoured aperitif.

The major Greek ports are Corfu, Igoumenitsa, Patras, Piraeus and Rhodes. Ferry services link these ports with Cyprus, Israel, Italy and Turkey. The routes from Ancona and Venice in Italy to Patras and Igoumenitsa are very popular and advance booking is recommended.

For further information contact:

Viamare Ltd
Suite 108
582 Honeypot Lane
Stanmore
Middlesex
HA7 1JY
Tel: 020 8206 3420,
viamare.com
ferries@viamare.com

Some ferries on routes from Italy to Greece have 'camping on board' facilities whereby passengers can sleep in their outfits. Mains hook-ups, showers and toilets are available.

There are several World Heritage sites in Greece, including such famous sites as the Acropolis in Athens, the archaeological sites at Olympia and Mistras, and the old towns of Corfu and Rhodes. See whc.unesco.org for more information. When visiting churches and monasteries dress conservatively, i.e. long trousers for men and no shorts, sleeveless T-shirts or short skirts for women.

Camping and Caravanning

There are over 300 campsites licensed by the Greek National Tourist Office. These can be recognised by a sign displaying the organisation's blue emblem. Most are open from April until the end of October, but those near popular tourist areas stay open all year. There are other unlicensed sites but visitors to them cannot be assured of safe water treatment, fire prevention measures or swimming pool inspection.

Casual/wild camping is not allowed outside official sites in Greece.

Electricity and Gas

Usually current on campsites varies between 4 and 16 amps. Plugs have two round pins. There are few CEE connections.

The full range of Campingaz cylinders are available from hypermarkets and other shops, but when purchasing a cylinder you may not be given a refundable deposit receipt.

Public Transport

Greece has a modern, integrated public transport system, including an extensive metro, bus, tram and suburban railway network in and around Athens. There are many ferry and hydrofoil services from Piraeus to the Greek islands and between islands.

Buy bus/tram tickets from special booths at bus stops, newspaper kiosks or from metro stations. A ticket is valid for a travel time of 90 minutes.

All licensed taxis are yellow and are equipped with meters (the fare is charged per kilometre) and display a card detailing tariffs and surcharges. In certain tourist areas, you may be asked to pay a predetermined (standard) amount for a ride to a specific destination. Taxis run on a share basis, so they often pick up other passengers on the journey.

Sites in Greece

ALEXANDROUPOLI *C1* (2km W Coastal) *40.84679, 25.85614* **Camping Municipal Alexandroupolis,** Makris Ave, 68100 Alexandroupolis **(25510) 28735 or 26055; camping@tieda.gr; www.tieda.gr**
12 sand adj

Site on coast - after drainage channel, at 2nd set traff lts close together. Lge, hdstg, mkd, hdg, shd, EHU (8A) €3.60; gas; 20% statics; phone; Eng spkn; watersports; games area; tennis; CKE. *"Spacious, secure, well-run site; clean, hot shwrs; easy walk to pleasant town cent; site a little tired (2019); ACSI acc."* **€29.50** **2024**

ATHINA *B3* (7km NW Urban) *38.00916, 23.67236* **Camping Athens,** 198-200 Athinon Ave, 12136 Athens **(210) 5814114 or 5814101 winter; info@camping athens.com.gr; www.campingathens.com.gr**
12

Fr Corinth on E94 m'way/highway, stay on this rd to Athens o'skts; site is approx 4km past Dafni Monastery, set back on L of multi-lane rd, sh dist beyond end of underpass. Go past site to next traff lts where U-turn permitted. Fr N use old national rd (junc 8 if on toll m'way). Med, pt shd, EHU (16A) €4; TV; bus to Athens; ccard acc. *"V dusty but well-managed site; gd san facs but poss insufficient high ssn; helpful staff; bus tickets to Athens sold; visitors rec not to use sat nav to find site, as it misdirects!"* **€33.00** **2024**

"There aren't many sites open at this time of year"

If you're travelling outside peak season remember to call ahead to check site opening dates – even if the entry says 'open all year'.

DELFI *B2* (5km W Rural) *38.47868, 22.47461* **Camping Delphi,** Itea Road, 33054 Delfi **(22650) 82745; info@delphicamping.com; www.delphicamping.com**

App fr Itea-Amfissa rd or Levadia; well sp. Med, shd, terr, EHU (16A) €3.90; gas; TV; phone; bus to Delfi; adv bkg acc; ccard acc; tennis; CKE. *"Visit grotto, refuge of Parnassus; Delfi archaeological sites 3km; friendly, helpful staff; Sunshine Group site; magnificent views; gd pool; dogs free; tired facs; 20% discount for Minoan Line ticketholders; delightful site; san facs bit tired but clean & tidy; excel site."* **€29.00, 1 Apr-31 Oct.** **2024**

DELFI *B2* (8.5km W Rural) *38.47305, 22.45926* **Chrissa Camping,** 33055 Chrissa **(22650) 82050; info@chrissacamping.gr; www.chrissacamping.gr**
12 shgl 10km

1st site on Itea to Delfi rd, sp. 4*, Med, shd, pt sl, terr, EHU (10A) €4 first 4KWh/day then metered; gas; TV; adv bkg acc; ccard acc; games area; tennis 300m; CKE. *"Excel, scenic site."* **€28.50** **2023**

"That's changed – Should I let the Club know?"

If you find something on site that's different from the site entry, fill in a report and let us know. See camc.com/europereport.

DREPANO *B3* (12km E Coastal) *37.49710, 22.99028* **Iria Beach Camping,** Iria Beach 21060, Nafplio **02 75 20 94 253; info@iriabeachcamp.gr; iriabeachcamp.gr**
12 adj

Fr Drepano head E on Epar. Od. Drepanou-Kantias. Cont onto Kantias-Irion. 800m after Iria Beach Hotel turn R. Site on L after 1.5km. Med, hdstg, shd, EHU (16A); bbq; cooking facs; twin axles; TV; 5% statics; Eng spkn; adv bkg acc; CCI. *"Opp beach; gd sw; site quiet & relaxing; helpful staff; vg site."* **€25.00** **2024**

GERAKINI *B2* (3km SE Coastal) *40.26464, 23.46338* **Camping Kouyoni,** 63100 Gerakini **(23710) 52226; info@kouyoni.gr; www.kouyoni.gr**
sand adj

Take main rd S fr Thessaloniki to Nea Moudania, then turn E twd Sithonia. Site is 18km on that rd past Gerakini on R, past filling stn. Well sp. Med, hdg, mkd, shd, pt sl, EHU (16A) €3.30; bbq; red long stay; TV; 30% statics; phone; adv bkg acc; games area; boat launch; CKE. *"Gd touring base set in olive grove; friendly owner; gd facs; gd beach; influx of w/enders high ssn."* **€29.00, 1 May-30 Sep.** **2022**

IGOUMENITSA *A2* (10km S Coastal) *39.46346, 20.26037* **Camping Elena's Beach,** 46100 Plataria **(26650) 71414; bteo@altecnet.gr or info@ campingelena.gr; www.campingelena.gr/en**
shgl adj

Sp on Igoumenitsa-Preveza rd, 2km NW of Plataria. Med, hdstg, pt shd, terr, EHU (5A) inc; gas; bbq; red long stay; 10% statics; phone; bus; adv bkg acc; CKE. *"Well-maintained, family-run, friendly site; clean, modern san facs; beautiful location with pitches next to sea; excel rest; conv ferries Corfu, Paxos."* **€26.50, 1 Apr-31 Oct.** **2024**

IGOUMENITSA *A2* (5km W Coastal) *39.51014, 20.22133* **Camping Drepanos,** Beach Drepanos, 46100 Igoumenitsa **(26650) 26980; camping@drepano.gr; www.drepano.gr**

12 WD MSP nr sand

Fr Igoumenitsa take coast rd N. Foll sp for Drepanos Beach. Fr either port turn L and head N up coast. Med, hdstg, pt shd, sl, bbq; twin axles; 10% statics; bus adj; Eng spkn; adv bkg acc; CKE. *"Beside nature reserve; amazing sunsets; friendly; dated san facs; attractive walks/cycle; vg."* **€33.00** **2024**

KALAMBAKA *A2* (4km SE Rural) *39.68250, 21.65510* **Camping Philoxenia,** 42200 Kalambaka **(24320) 24466; philoxeniacamp@ath.forthnet.gr**

(htd) WD MSP nr

Site on N side of E92 Trikala rd, behind barrier. 3*, Med, hdstg, shd, EHU (6A) inc; gas; bbq; cooking facs; TV; 30% statics; Eng spkn; adv bkg acc; ccard acc; waterslide; bike hire; CKE. *"Interesting area esp during Easter religious festivals; Still open 2016 but call bef travelling."* **€20.00, 1 Mar-30 Nov.** **2023**

KALAMBAKA *A2* (2km NW Rural) *39.71315, 21.61588* **Camping Vrachos,** Meteoron Street, 42200 Kastraki **(24320) 22293; tsourvaka@yahoo.gr; www.campingkastraki.com**

12 WD MSP (htd)

Fr cent of Kalambaka take rd at app to vill of Kastraki. Site is 2km N of E92. Med, hdstg, mkd, hdg, pt shd, pt sl, terr, EHU (16A) inc; gas; bbq; cooking facs; twin axles; TV; phone; bus adj, train 1km; Eng spkn; adv bkg acc; CKE. *"V friendly management; clean san facs; vg views fr some pitches; ltd facs open in winter; dogs free; Harmonie Group site; conv for monasteries, tour bus fr camp."* **€33.00** **2023**

KAVALA *C1* (4km SW Urban/Coastal) *40.91573, 24.37851* **Camping Multiplex Batis,** 65000 Kavala **(2510) 245918; nfo@batis-sa.gr; www.batis-sa.gr**

12 (htd) WD sand adj

On W app to town on old coast rd, ent on a curving hill. Med, hdg, mkd, shd, pt sl, EHU (6A) €4; phone; bus; Eng spkn; adv bkg acc; ccard acc; CKE. *"Beautiful location but v developed; conv ferry to Thassos & archaeological sites; clean facs but site poss unkempt LS; vg."* **€26.00** **2022**

KYLLINI *A3* (10km S Coastal) *37.88539, 21.11175* **Campsite Melissa,** 27050 Kastro Kyllinis Ilia **02 62 30 95 213; camping_melissa@yahoo.gr; www.campingmelissa.gr/en**

WD MSP

S fr Patras twd Pygros on E55. Turn R twds Lehena after 58km marker. Foll signs to Kastro Kyllinis. Med, hdg, shd, EHU (10A); bbq; cooking facs; twin axles; TV; 2% statics; Eng spkn; adv bkg acc; CCI. *"Great campsite to chill; excel rest, bar & shop; lovely sandy beach; excel sw; fabulous views across the bay."* **€25.00, 1 Apr-31 Oct.** **2024**

KYLLINI *A3* (17km S Coastal) *37.83828, 21.12972* **Camping Aginara Beach,** Lygia, 27050 Loutra Kyllinis **(26230) 96211; info@camping-aginara.gr; www.camping-aginara.gr**

12 WD MSP shgl adj

S fr Patras on E55 twds Pyrgos; exit Gastouni & turn W thro Vartholomio twd Loutra Kyllinis; turn L about 3km bef Kyllinis then foll sps. 3*, Lge, hdg, hdstg, shd, pt sl, EHU (10A); gas; bbq; TV; 25% statics; phone; Eng spkn; adv bkg acc; ccard acc; watersports; CKE. *"Friendly proprietor; excel, modern facs; site on lovely beach; beautiful views."* **€28.00** **2024**

METHONI *A3* (1km ESE Coastal) *36.81736, 21.71515* **Camp Methoni,** 24006 Methoni **(27230) 31188; info@camping-methoni.gr or hello@camping-methoni.gr; camping-methoni.gr**

sand

Fr Pylos on rd 9, strt thro Methoni to beach, turn E along beach, site sp. 2*, Med, hdstg, pt shd, EHU (10A) inc; bbq; phone; Eng spkn; adv bkg acc; CKE. *"Superb Venetian castle; close to pleasant vill; park away fr taverna & rd to avoid noise; excel sw; v dusty site; clean san facs; new owner & undergoing renovations (2013); quiet & gd site."* **€21.40, 1 May-31 Oct.** **2024**

MIKINES *B3* (0.1km E Urban) *37.71922, 22.74676* **Camping Mikines/Mykenae,** 21200 Mikines **(27510) 76247; dars@arg.forthnet.gr; www.ecogriek.nl**

12 WD nr

In town of Mikines (Mycenae) nr bus stop. On R as heading to archeological site, sp. 2*, Sm, mkd, hdstg, pt shd, EHU (10A) €4.50; Eng spkn; CKE. *"Quaint family-run site; v warm welcome; conv ancient Mycenae; meals served; friendly staff; vg."* **€21.00 2024**

NAFPLIO *B3* (12km SE Coastal) *37.5287, 22.87553* **Kastraki Camping,** Kastraki Assinis, 21100 Assini **(27520) 59386 or 59387; sgkarmaniola@kastrakicamping.gr; www.kastrakicamping.gr**

WD MSP sand

Fr Nafplio take rd to Tolon. Immed after Assini, take L fork sp Ancient Assini. Site 3km on L. Lge, shd, EHU (16A) shared €4; TV; ccard acc; tennis; games area. *"Vg location with own private beach & excel facs; day trips to several islands fr Tolón harbour; many pitches too sm for lge m'vans."* **€35.00, 1 Apr-30 Sep.** **2024**

OLIMBIA *A3* (1km W Rural) *37.64337, 21.61943* **Camping Alphios,** 27065 Olimbia **(26240) 22951; alphios@otenet.gr; www.campingalphios.gr**

WD MSP

Fr E55 Pyrgos to Tripoli rd take exit sp 'Ancient Olympia' & foll site sp. 4*, Med, hdg, mkd, hdstg, pt shd, pt sl, terr, EHU (16A) inc; gas; bbq; cooking facs; TV; ccard acc. *"Superb views fr some pitches; excel pool; very friendly; walking dist to ancient Olympic site."* **€29.00, 1 Apr-25 Oct.** **2024**

GREECE

GREECE

PARGA *A2* (2km W Coastal) *39.28550, 20.38997* **Camping Valtos,** Valtos Beach, 48060 Parga **(26840) 31287; info@campingvaltos.gr; www.campingvaltos.gr**
sand adj

Foll sp fr Parga twd Valtos Beach, site sp. Site at far end of beach behind bar/club. Med, mkd, shd, pt sl, EHU (10A); Eng spkn; CKE. *"Helpful owners; gd walking area; steep walk to town; poor san facs."* **€31.00, 1 May-30 Sep.** **2022**

PATRA *A2* (21km SW Coastal) *38.14986, 21.57740* **Camping Kato Alissos,** 25002 Kato Alissos **(26930) 71249 or 71914; demiris-cmp@otenet.gr; www.camping-kato-alissos.gr**
shgl adj

W of Patra on old national rd turn R at Kato Alissos & foll site sp for 600m. 3*, Med, shd, EHU (10A) €4; cooking facs; 10% statics; phone; bus 1km; Eng spkn; adv bkg acc; ccard acc; watersports; CKE. *"Clean ltd facs; Sunshine Camping Group site; steps to beach; gd NH."* **€19.00, 1 Apr-25 Oct.** **2024**

PLAKA LITOHOROU *B2* (10km N Coastal) *40.18230, 22.55885* **Camping Stani,** 60200 Kalivia Varikou **(23520) 61277; campingstani@gmail.com**

Leave E75 (Athens-Thessaloniki) at N Efesos/Variko, foll sp Varikou & site. Lge, mkd, shd, EHU; TV; phone; CKE. *"Ltd facs LS; conv Dion; fair site."* **€22.00** **2024**

PYLOS *A3* (7km N Coastal) *36.94784, 21.70635* **Camping Navarino Beach,** 24001 Gialova **(27230) 22973; info@navarino-beach.gr; www.navarino-beach.gr**
nr

Fr Pylos N twds Kiparissia for 5km around Navarino Bay, site at S end of Gialova vill; sp. Med, hdstg, pt shd, EHU (16A) €4; gas; bbq; cooking facs; red long stay; bus; Eng spkn; adv bkg acc; ccard acc; windsurfing; boat launch; CKE. *"Management v helpful; gd, clean, modern facs; several rest & shops in easy walking dist; some pitches on beach; vg."* **€32.50** **2024**

STYLIDA *B2* (4km SE Coastal) *38.89638, 22.65555* **Camping Interstation,** Rd Athens-Thessalonika, Km 230, 35300 Stylida **(22380) 23828 or (69720) 11585; info@campinginterstation.gr; campinginterstation.gr**
adj

Fr Lamia take rd E to Stylis; cont for further 3km & site situated to side of dual-c'way opp petrol stn. Med, shd, EHU (16A); gas; TV; 10% statics; Eng spkn; adv bkg acc; tennis; watersports; CKE. *"Day visitors have access to beach via site; do not confuse with Cmp Paras adj - not rec; Sunshine Camping Group site; poss poor san facs LS; NH only."* **€27.40** **2023**

VARTHOLOMIO *A3* (10km SW Coastal) *37.83555, 21.13333* **Camping Ionion Beach,** 27050 Glifa **(26230) 96828; ioniongr@otenet.gr; www.ionion-beach.gr**
(htd) nr adj

Fr E55 Patras-Pirgos rd turn W to Gastouni, Ligia & Glifa, then Glifa Beach. Site is 1km SW of Glifa. Med, hdg, hdstg, pt shd, serviced pitches; EHU (16A); gas; bbq; TV; Eng spkn; adv bkg acc; ccard acc; watersports; games area; CKE. *"Excel, well-run site; superb facs."* **€32.50** **2022**

VOLOS *B2* (18km SE Coastal) *39.31027, 23.10972* **Camping Sikia,** 37300 Kato Gatzea **(24230) 22279 or 22081; info@camping-sikia.gr; www.camping-sikia.gr**
shgl

Fr Volos take coast rd S to Kato Gatzea site on R, sp immed next to Camping Hellas. Med, shd, terr, EHU (16A) €3; gas; red long stay; 20% statics; phone; Eng spkn; adv bkg acc; ccard acc; CKE. *"Highly rec; some beautiful, but sm, pitches with sea views; Sunshine Group site; excel, friendly family-run site; v clean; v helpful staff; take care o'hanging trees."* **€33.00** **2022**

GREEK ISLANDS

AGIA GALINI (CRETE) *C4* (2km E Rural/Coastal) *35.10004, 24.69514* **Camping No Problem!,** 74056 Agia Galini **(28320) 91239; gogalini.com/camping**
shgl 500m

Site sp on Tympaki rd. Sm, mkd, pt shd, EHU (6A) €4; bbq; 10% statics; bus 500m; Eng spkn; adv bkg acc. *"Vg, family-run site; dogs free; gd walks."* **€22.00** **2022**

LEFKADA (LEFKAS) *A2* (26km SE Coastal) *38.67511, 20.71475* **Camping Santa Maura,** Dessimi, 31100 Vlycho **(26450) 95007, (00306) 976085621, (00306) 932902309; campingsantamavra@yahoo.gr; www.campingsantamaura.com**
shgl adj

Take coast rd S fr Lefkada to Vlycho, turn L for Dessimi, site in 2.5km (after Camping Dessimi). Access via v steep hill - severe gradients both sides. 3*, Med, mkd, pt shd, terr, EHU (6A) inc; gas; bbq; TV; phone; CKE. *"Excel site & beach; gd, clean san facs; friendly owners; pls call for prices."* **1 Apr-31 Oct.** **2022**

PEFKARI (THASSOS) *C2* (0.3km W Coastal) *40.61630, 24.60021* **Camping Pefkari Beach,** 64002 Pefkari **(25930) 51190; reservation@camping-pefkari.gr; www.camping-pefkari.gr**
sand adj

SW fr Thassos port approx 43km to Limenaria, Pefkari is next sm vill. Site well sp in vill. Med, hdstg, pt shd, EHU (6A) €2.90; own san req; bbq; 5% statics; bus 1km; Eng spkn; CKE. *"Lovely spot; worth putting up with poor, dated san facs; gd local rest; vg; improving site; beautiful; easy walk to Pefkari and Potos; excel on site rest; lovely spot."*
€31.00, 1 May-30 Sep. **2024**

RETHYMNO (CRETE) *C4* (3km E Coastal) *35.36795, 24.51487* **Campsite Camping Elizabeth Rethymno (Crete)(Formerly Camping Elizabeth),** Ionias 84 Terma, 74100 Missiria **30-28310 28694; info@camping-elizabeth.net; www.camping-elizabeth.net**
adj

W fr Iraklio/Heraklion exit Platanes/Arkadi. Site 1km bef Platanes, on R on sh unsurfaced rd. Lge, hdg, shd, EHU (12A) inc; bbq; cooking facs; 3% statics; phone; bus 500m; Eng spkn; adv bkg acc; CKE. *"Gd walking on mkd rtes; gd cycling; excursion programme; vg; san facs tired."*
€28.50, 1 Mar-22 Dec. **2024**

TINOS (TINOS) *C3* (0.5km E Coastal) *37.53994, 25.16377* **Tinos Camping Bungalows,** Louizas Sohou 5, 84200 Tinos **(22830) 22344 or 23548; tinoscamping@gmail.com; www.wiw.gr/english/agios_fokas_tinos_camping_bungalows**
shgl 500m

Clearly sp fr port. Sm, hdg, mkd, hdstg, shd, EHU €4.50; bbq; cooking facs; red long stay; phone; Eng spkn; adv bkg acc; ccard acc; CKE. *"1,600 Venetian dovecots & 600 churches on island; monastery with healing icon."* **€21.50, 1 May-31 Oct.** **2022**

GREECE

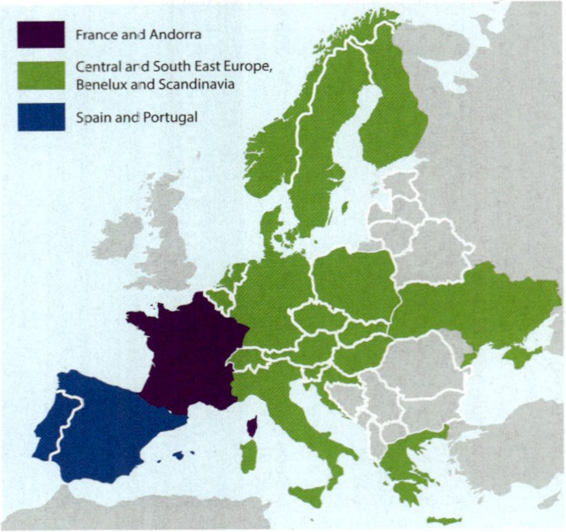

Kavala to Trikala = 377km

	Alexandroupoli	Athina (Athens)	Korinthos (Corinth)	Florina	Igoumenista	Ioanina	Kalamata	Kastoria	Kavala	Lamia	Larisa	Nafplio	Neos Marmaras	Patra	Pirgos	Sparti (Sparta)	Thessaloniki	Trikala	Tripoli
Athina (Athens)	468																		
Korinthos (Corinth)	884	88																	
Florina	497	592	251																
Igoumenista	816	473	393	353															
Ioanina	716	447	364	320	96														
Kalamata	1060	284	175	759	505	467													
Kastoria	535	485	519	67	286	204	694												
Kavala	177	682	659	320	611	525	882	358											
Lamia	643	214	244	360	353	263	415	274	470										
Larisa	503	361	389	231	309	209	561	239	323	151									
Nafplio	947	165	63	668	482	427	163	586	770	307	455								
Neos Marmaras	427	636	667	282	575	481	838	343	250	426	277	733							
Patra	844	224	138	513	281	247	220	483	660	193	341	201	615						
Pirgos	944	320	230	643	367	347	119	542	743	284	432	208	830	96					
Sparti (Sparta)	1056	225	145	763	521	487	60	664	852	385	533	119	838	236	180				
Thessaloniki	349	513	544	459	452	362	715	220	169	303	154	614	123	492	580	711			
Trikala	346	330	356	233	247	148	516	159	377	115	62	419	339	310	400	497	216		
Tripoli	964	191	110	685	457	426	90	635	824	324	472	81	751	176	155	60	620	466	
Volos	552	326	355	293	371	271	518	301	383	119	62	417	337	308	412	524	214	124	439

A
B
C
D
1
2
3
4
SERBIA
PRISTINA
KOSOVO
SOFIA
BULGARIA
Burgas
Plovdiv
SKOPJE
NORTH MACEDONIA
TIRANA
Bitola
ALBANIA
Edirne
SERES
XANTHI
KOMATINI
Kavala
Alexandroupoli
Tekirdağ
THESSALONIKI
THASSOS
Pefkari
POLYGYROS
Gerakini
KATERINI
Plaka Litohorou
Çanakkale
KERKIRA
IOANINA
Kalambaka
CORFU
Igoumenitsa
Parga
Volos
AEGEAN SEA
LESBOS
MITILINI
TURKEY
Lefkada
LEVKAS
AGRINIO
LAMIA
Stylida
CHIOS
İzmir
HIOS
CHALKIDA
Delfi
PATRA
Drepano
Kyllini
Vartholomio
ATHINA
TINOS
Tinos
ERMOUPOLI
PIRGOS
Mikines
TRIPOLI
KALAMATA
SPARTI
Pylos
Methoni
KOS
RODOS
RHODES
HANIA
Rethymno
Agia Galini
SITIA
CRETE
MEDITERRANEAN SEA
A1
A2
A3
A5
A7
A8
A25
A29
A52
A71
Motorways
Primary roads
Secondary roads
All year site(s)
Seasonal site(s)
No sites listed
N
W
E
S
0
50
100
150
200
250 km
150 miles

Hungary

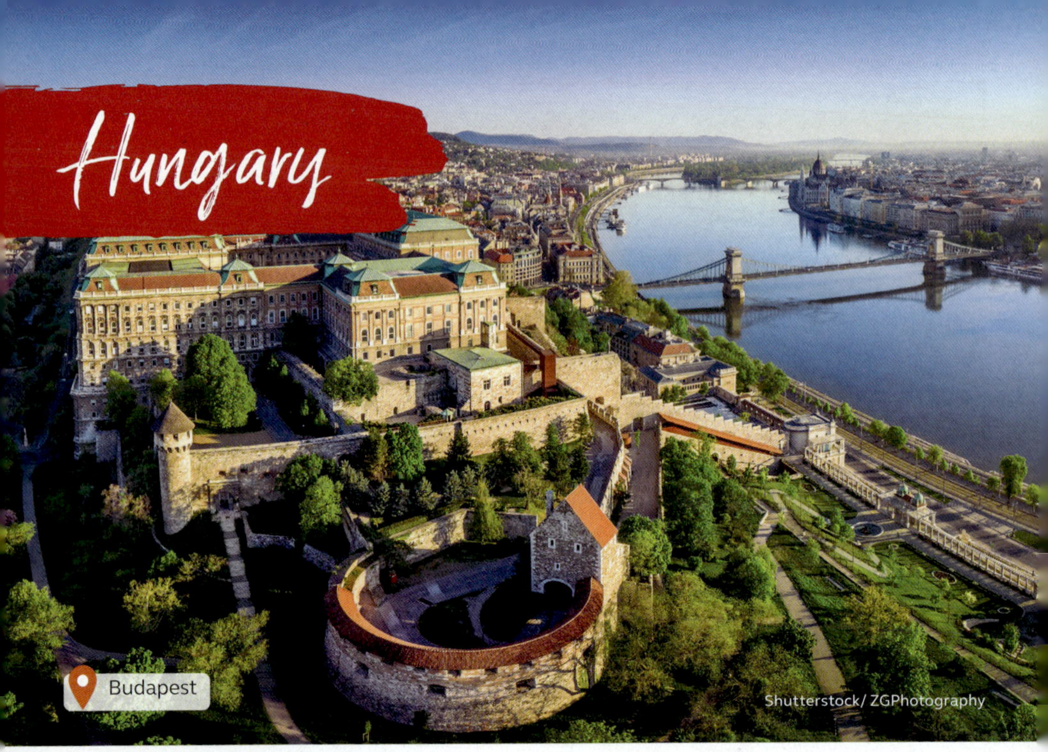

Shutterstock/ ZGPhotography

Highlights

Hungary is home to some of the most dramatic and exotic architecture found in Europe, with buildings spanning from the Art Nouveau era to Ancient Rome. Turkish, Slavic, Magyar and Roman influences entwine with its own unique culture to make Hungary a fascinating place.

There are more medicinal spas in Hungary than anywhere else in Europe and spa culture is an important part both of tourism and everyday life. You can enjoy spas that range from traditional bathhouses to modern wellness centres that cater for the whole family.

Many folk festivals are celebrated in Hungary throughout the year, the biggest of which is the Festival of Folk Arts/Crafts held every August in Buda Castle. Thousands of visitors attend to view the fantastic traditional crafts on offer.

One of the most renowned crafts is pottery making, with Hungary having a long tradition of creating both fine porcelain, such as Herend, and tiling and stoneware.

Major towns and cities

- Budapest – an enchanting city full of galleries, theatres and museums.
- Debrecen – this former capital is one of Hungary's most important cultural centres.
- Pécs – an ancient city with countless things to see and do.
- Eger – a city famous for its fine red wines.

Attractions

- Fisherman's Bastion, Budapest – enjoy unmatched views over the city.
- Hungarian Parliament Building, Budapest – a magnificent building on the banks of the Danube.
- Lake Hévíz – one of the largest thermal lakes in the world with its own unique ecosystem.
- Esztergom Basilica – a spectacularly enormous cathedral with Renaissance art.

Find out more

hungary.com

Country Information

Capital: Budapest

Bordered by: Austria, Croatia, Romania, Serbia, Slovakia, Slovenia, Ukraine

Terrain: Mostly flat and rolling plains; hills and low mountains to the north

Climate: Temperate, continental climate; cold, cloudy winters; warm, sunny summers; changeable in spring and early summer with heavy rain and storms. The best times to visit are spring and autumn

Highest Point: Kekes 1,014m

Language: Hungarian

Local Time: GMT or BST + 1, i.e. 1 hour ahead of the UK all year

Currency: Forint (HUF); £1 = HUF 491.51, HUF 1000 = £2.03 (Nov 2024)

Emergency numbers: Police 107; Fire brigade 105; Ambulance 104. Operators speak English.

Public Holidays 2025: Jan 1; Mar 15; Apr 18, 21; May 1; Jun 9; Aug 20; Oct 23; Nov 1; Dec 25, 26.

School summer holidays are from mid-June to the end of August

Entry Formalities

British and Irish passport holders may stay for up to 90 days in any 180 day period without a visa. You may be asked to show a return or onward ticket at the border to confirm your length of stay, or to prove that you have enough money for your stay.

Your passport will need to have a minimum of 6 months' validity remaining, and be less than 10 years old (even if it has over 6 months left).

Visitors arriving at a campsite or hotel must complete a registration form.

Medical Services

British nationals may obtain emergency medical and dental treatment from practitioners contracted to the national health insurance scheme, Országos Egészségbiztosítási (OEP), together with emergency hospital treatment, on presentation of a European Health Insurance Card (EHIC) or a Global Health Insurance Card (GHIC) and a British passport.

Fees are payable for treatment and prescribed medicines, and aren't refundable in Hungary. You may be able to apply for reimbursement when back in the UK.

Pharmacies (gyógyszertár) are well stocked. The location of the nearest all-night pharmacy is displayed on the door of every pharmacy.

Opening Hours

Banks: Mon-Thurs 8am-3pm. Fri 8am - 1pm. Hours may vary slightly.

Museums: Tue-Sun 10am-6pm; closed Mon.

Post Offices: Mon-Fri 8am-6pm; post office at Budapest open Mon-Sat 7am-9pm.

Shops: Mon-Fri 10am-6pm (supermarkets from 7am-7pm with some grocery stores open 24 hours); open half day Saturdays.

Safety and Security

Petty theft in Budapest is common in areas frequented by tourists, particularly on busy public transport, at markets and at popular tourist sites. Beware of pickpockets and bag snatchers, don't carrying large amounts of cash.

Theft of and from vehicles is common. Don't leave your belongings, car registration documents or mobile phones in your car and ensure that it's properly locked with the alarm on, even if leaving it for just a moment. Beware of contrived 'incidents', particularly on the Vienna-Budapest motorway, designed to stop motorists and expose them to robbery.

Visitors have reported in the past that motorists may be pestered at service areas on the Vienna to Budapest motorway by people insisting on washing windscreens and demanding money.

During the summer season in Budapest, uniformed tourist police patrol the most frequently visited areas of the city. Criminals sometimes pose as tourist police and ask for visitors' money, credit cards or travel documents in order to check them.

Always ensure that a uniformed police officer is wearing a badge displaying the word 'Rendörség' and a five-digit identification number, together with a name badge. Plain clothes police carry a badge and an ID card with picture, hologram and rank. If in doubt, insist on going to the nearest police station.

There are still occasional incidents of excessive overcharging in certain restaurants, bars and clubs in Budapest, accompanied by threats of violence. Individuals who have been unable to settle their bill have frequently been accompanied by the establishment's security guards to a cash machine and made to withdraw funds. Visitors are advised to ask for a menu and only order items which are priced realistically. A five digit price for one dish is too high. Never accept menus which don't display prices and check your bill carefully.

Taxi drivers are sometimes accomplices to these frauds, receiving 'commission' for recommending restaurants and bars which charge extortionate prices to visitors. Never ask a taxi driver to recommend a bar, club or restaurant. If a driver takes you to one or you're approached on the street with an invitation to an unfamiliar bar or restaurant, you should treat such advice with extreme caution.

Don't change money or get involved in gambling in the street; both are illegal.

If you need help, go to the nearest police station or the Tourist Information Point open 8am - 8pm, Deák Ferenc Square, 1052 Budapest, Sütő Street 2 +36 (1) 438 8080

Hungary shares with the rest of Europe an underlying threat from terrorism. Please check gov.uk/foreign-travel-advice/hungary before you travel.

British Embassy

Fuge Utca 5-7 Budapest 1022
Tel: +36 (1) 429 6200
gov.uk/world/hungary

Irish Embassy

Bank Centre, Granit Tower, Floor VII,
Szabadság Tér 7, Budapest 1054
Tel: +36 (1) 301 4960
ireland.ie/en/hungary/budapest

Documents

Money

Hungarian currency is available from banks in Austria before crossing the border. For emergency cash reserves, it's advisable to have euros, rather than sterling. Foreign currency is best exchanged at banks as they aren't allowed to charge commission. Private bureaux de change do charge commission, but the rate of exchange may be better.

Credit cards are accepted at many outlets in large towns and cities and cash dispensers, 'bankomats', are widespread even in small towns. There's a high incidence of credit card fraud and payment in cash wherever possible is advisable. Carry your credit card issuers'/banks' 24 hour UK contact numbers separately in case of loss or theft of your cards.

Don't use street money changers. Take care not to accept bank notes that are no longer valid but which are still in circulation. There have been a small number of reports of taxi drivers deliberately passing these notes to tourists - as well as notes from neighbouring countries that aren't valid in Hungary.

Euros are widely accepted in shops and restaurants frequented by tourists, but check the exchange rate.

When leaving Hungary on the MI motorway (Budapest-Vienna), it's important to change back your forints on the Hungarian side of the border by crossing the carriageway to the left at the designated crossing-point, as visitors report that there are no facilities on the right hand side and none on the other side in Austria.

Passport

Carry your passport at all times. A photocopy is not acceptable.

Vehicle(s)

Carry your vehicle registration certificate (V5C), vehicle insurance certificate and MOT certificate (if applicable) with you when driving.

Driving

Accidents

Accidents causing damage to vehicles or injury to persons must be reported to the nearest police station and to the Hungarian State Insurance Company (Hungária Biztositó) within 24 hours. The police will issue a statement which you may be asked to show when leaving the country.

If entering Hungary with a conspicuously damaged vehicle, it's recommended that you obtain a report confirming the damage from the police in the country where the damage occurred, otherwise difficulties may arise when leaving Hungary.

Alcohol

There's a zero tolerance policy on drink-driving. It's illegal to drive after consuming any alcohol whatsoever.

Breakdown Service

The motoring organisation, Magyar Autóklub (MAK), operates a breakdown service 24 hours a day on all roads. Drivers in need of assistance should telephone 188 or +36 (1) 345 1601. The number (1) is the area code for Budapest. On motorways emergency phones are placed at 2 km intervals.

MAK road patrol cars are yellow and marked 'Segélyszolgálat'. Their registration numbers begin with the letters MAK.

The roadside breakdown service is chargeable, higher charges applying at night. There's a scale of charges by vehicle weight and distance for towing vehicles to a garage. Payment is required in cash.

Child Restraint System

Children under the height of 1.5m must be seated in a suitable child restraint system appropriate for their size in the rear of the vehicle.

If no child restraint is available a child over 3 who is over 1.35m in height may travel in the rear seat with a seatbelt. Children younger or shorter than this may not ever travel without a suitable restraint system in the vehicle.

Fuel

Leaded petrol is no longer available. The sign 'Ólommentes üzemanyag' or 'Bleifrei 95' indicates unleaded petrol. LPG is widely available.

Most petrol stations are open from 6am to 8pm. Along motorways and in large towns they're often open 24 hours. Some petrol stations accept credit and debit cards but cash is the most usual means of payment.

Lights

Outside built-up areas dipped headlights are compulsory at all times, regardless of weather conditions. Bulbs are more likely to fail with constant use and you're recommended to carry spares. At night in built-up areas dipped headlights must be used as full beam is prohibited.

Headlight flashing often means that a driver is giving way, but don't carry out a manoeuvre unless you're sure that this is the case.

Motorways

All motorways (autópálya) and main connecting roads run to or from Budapest. In recent years the road network has been extended and improved and there are now approximately 1,715 kilometres of motorway and dual carriageways or semi-motorways. However, most roads are still single carriageway, single lane and care is recommended. The M0 motorway is a 75 km ringroad around Budapest which links the M1, M7, M6, M5 and Highway 11. The Megyeri Bridge on the Danube is part of the M0 and considerably reduces traffic congestion to the north of Budapest.

Emergency corridors are compulsory on motorways and dual carriageways. Drivers are required to create a precautionary emergency corridor to provide access for emergency vehicles whenever congestion occurs. Drivers in the left-hand lane must move as far over to the left as possible, and drivers in the central and right-hand lanes must move as far over to the right as possible.

Motorway Vignettes

An e-vignette (sticker) must be purchased before entering any toll motorway. They're from motorway customer service offices, at large petrol stations near the motorways and online via the e-Matrica website or smartphone app.
You can pay in forints or by credit card.

Leaflets are distributed to motorists at the border and a telephone information centre is available in Hungary – tel 36 587 500. Vignettes should only be purchased from outlets where the prices are clearly displayed at the set rates. For full details (in English), including how to buy online and toll-free sections, see nemzetiutdij.hu/en.

When purchasing an e-vignette a confirmation message will be sent or a coupon issued and this must be kept for a year after its expiry date. There's no need to display the vignette in your windscreen as the motorway authorities check all vehicles electronically (without the need for you to stop your vehicle) and verify registration number, category of toll paid and validity of an e-vignette. Charges in forints (2024 charges, subject to change) are shown below:

Category of Vehicle	Period of Validity	
	10 Days	1 month
Vehicle up to 3,500kg with or without caravan or trailer	6,400	10,360
Motorhome	9,310	14,670

Hungary's State Motorway Management company (AAK) impose on-the-spot fines for motorists who don't have a vignette. Fines amount to HUF 14,875 for vehicles under 3,500kg or HUF 66,925 for vehicles between 3,500kg and 7,500kg if paid within 30 days. 78% of the motorists fined so far have been foreign nationals, so ensure you have a vignette before travelling on motorways.

Parking

Zigzag lines on the carriageway and road signs indicate a stopping/parking prohibition. Illegally-parked vehicles will be towed away or clamped. On two-way roads, vehicles must park in the direction of traffic; they may park on either side in one-way streets.

In certain circumstances, parking on the pavement is allowed.

Budapest is divided into various time restricted parking zones (maximum three hours) where tickets must be purchased from Monday to Friday from a machine. For longer periods 'Park and Ride' car parks are located near major metro stations and bus terminals.

Priority

Pedestrians have priority over traffic at pedestrian crossings and at intersections. They don't have priority on the roadway between central tram loading islands and pavements, and drivers must exercise care on these sections. Major roads are indicated by a priority road ahead sign. At the intersection of two roads of equal importance, where there's no sign, vehicles coming from the right have priority. Trams and buses have priority at any intersection on any road and buses have right of way when leaving bus stops after the driver has signalled his intention to pull out.

Roads

Hungary has a good system of well surfaced main roads and driving standards are higher than in many other parts of Europe. There are few dual carriageways and care is required, therefore, when overtaking with a right-hand drive vehicle. Extra care is required on provincial roads which may be badly lit, poorly maintained and narrow. In the countryside at night be on the alert for unlit cycles and horse drawn vehicles

Road Signs and Markings

Road signs and markings conform to international conventions. Square green road signs indicate the number of km to the next town. At traffic lights a flashing amber light indicates a dangerous intersection. Destination signs feature road numbers rather than the names of towns, so it's essential to equip yourself with an up-to-date road map or atlas. Signs for motorways have white lettering on a blue background; on other roads signs are white and green.

Speed Limits

	Open Road (km/h)	Motorway (km/h)
Car Solo	90-110	130
Car towing caravan/trailer	70	80
Motorhome under 3500kg	90-110	130
Motorhome 3500-7500kg	70	80

A speed limit of 30 km/h (18 mph) is in force in many residential, city centre and tourist resort areas.

Traffic Jams

Roads around Budapest are busy on Friday and Sunday afternoons. In the holiday season roads to Lake Balaton (M7) and around the lake (N7 and N71) may be congested. There are regular traffic hold ups at weekends at the border crossings to Austria, the Czechia and Serbia. Motorway traffic information (in English) is available on utinform.hu.

Violation of Traffic Regulations

The police make spot vehicle document checks and are keen to enforce speed limits. They're permitted to impose on-the-spot fines of up to HUF 300,000. Credit cards are accepted for the payment of fines in some circumstances.

Winter Driving

The use of snow chains can be made compulsory on some roads when there's severe winter weather.

Essential Equipment

First Aid Kit

It's a legal requirement that all vehicles should carry a first aid kit.

Reflective Jackets/Waistcoats

If your vehicle is immobilised on the carriageway outside a built-up area, or if visibility is poor, you must wear a reflective jacket or waistcoat when getting out of your vehicle.

Passengers who leave the vehicle, for example, to assist with a repair, should also wear one. Keep the jackets inside your vehicle, not in the boot.

In addition, pedestrians and cyclists walking or cycling at night or in poor visibility along unlit roads outside a built-up area must also wear a reflective jacket.

Warning Triangles

In the event of accident, it's compulsory to place a warning triangle 100 metres behind the vehicle on motorways and 50 metres on other roads.

Touring

Hungary boasts eight World Heritage sites including the national park at Aggtelek which contains Europe's largest cave network, the Christian cemetery at Pécs and the monastery at Pannonhalma. Lake Balaton, the largest lake in Central Europe, offers swimming, sailing, fishing and windsurfing. With 200 km of sandy shoreline and shallow warm waters, it's very popular with families.

The best way to make the most of the city is with a Budapest Card. This allows unlimited travel on public transport from one to five consecutive days, free city walking tours, discounted entry to museums and other attractions, plus discounts on many guided tours, events, shops and restaurants. Cards are available to buy from metro stations, tourist information offices, many travel agencies, hotels, museums and main Budapest transport ticket offices, as well as from the Hungarian National Tourist Office in London. You can also order online from budapest-card.com.

A tip of 10-15% of the bill is expected in restaurants. Check your bill first to ensure that a service charge has not already been added.

Hungarian is a notoriously difficult language for native English speakers to decipher and pronounce. English is not widely spoken in rural areas, but it's becoming increasingly widespread elsewhere as it's now taught in schools. German is widely spoken and a dictionary may be helpful.

Camping and Caravanning

There are approximately 100 organised campsites in Hungary rated from 1 to 4 stars. These are generally well signposted off main routes, with the site name shown below a blue camping sign.

Most campsites open from May to September and the most popular sites are situated by Lake Balaton and the Danube. A Camping Key Europe (CKE) or Camping Card International (CCI) is essential.

Facilities vary from site to site, but visitors will find it useful to carry their own flat universal sink plug. There has been improvement in recent years in the general standard of campsites, but communal changing areas for showers aren't uncommon. Many sites have communal kitchen facilities which enable visitors to make great savings on their own gas supply.

Many campsites require payment in cash. Prices have risen in recent years.

Therefore, prices in this guide for sites not reported on for some time might not reflect the current prices.

Casual/wild camping is prohibited.

Cycling

There are approximately 2,000 km of cycle tracks, around 200 km of which are in Budapest and over 200 km around Lake Balaton. Tourinform offices in Hungary provide maps of cycling routes.

Children under 14 years aren't allowed to ride on the road and all cyclists must wear a reflective jacket at night and in poor daytime visibility.

Electricity and Gas

Current on campsites varies between 6 and 16 amps. Plugs have two round pins. There are some sites that don't have CEE connections.

Only non-returnable and/or non-exchangeable Campingaz cylinders are available.

Public Transport & Local Travel

Cars aren't permitted within the Castle District and on Margaret Island in Budapest. It's advisable to use public transport when travelling into the city and there's an excellent network of bus, tram and metro routes (BKV). All public transport in Hungary is free for over 65s, and this also applies to foreign visitors with proof of age (passport).

There are a number of ticket options, including family tickets, 1, 3 and 7 day tickets, and they can be bought at metro stations, ticket machines, tobacconists and newsagents.

Validate your bus and metro tickets before use at each stage of your journey and every time you change metro lines at the red machines provided. Tickets are often checked on vehicles or at metro station exits by controllers wearing arm bands and carrying photo ID. For further information on public transport in Budapest see bkk.hu.

As a general rule, it's better to phone for taxis operated by reputable local companies, rather than flag them down in the street, and always ensure that fares are metered. A tip of approximately 10% of the fare is customary.

Mahart, the Hungarian Shipping Company, operates a regular hydrofoil service from April to October along the Danube between Budapest and Vienna. The journey lasts six hours and covers 288 km.

Local companies Legenda (legenda.hu/en) and Mahart also offer city cruises between May and October, as well as regular trips to tourist attractions outside Budapest, such as Szentendre, Visegrád and Esztergom.

A ferry service takes cars across Lake Balaton from Szántód to Tihany. There are crossings every 10 minutes from June to September and every hour during the low season. Regular bus and train services link the towns and villages along the lakeside.

Sites in Hungary

AGGTELEK *A3* (1km NW Rural) *48.47094, 20.49446* **Baradla Camping,** Baradla Oldal 1, 3759 Aggtelek **(06) 308619427; szallas@anp.hu**

nr nr

Fr Slovakia turn off E571/A50 at Plesivec onto rd 587 S via Dlha Ves to border x-ing. Cont S for approx 800m & hotel/campsite complex is on L. Fr Miskolc 45km N on rte 26, turn onto rte 27 sp Perkupa then foll sp Nemzeti National Park & Aggtelek. Site sp in vill. 1*, Med, pt shd, pt sl, EHU (16A) inc; bbq; cooking facs; 10% statics. *"Gd NH to/fr Slovakia; ent to lge Barlang Caves system adj; facs poss stretched high ssn."* **HUF 5070, 15 Apr-15 Oct. 2022**

BALATONALMADI *C2* (2km SW Rural) *47.0205, 18.00828* **Balatontourist Camping Yacht,** Véghely Dezsö út 18, 8220 Balatonalmádi **(88) 584101; yacht@balatontourist.hu; www.balatontourist.hu**

HUF990 WD MSP adj

Fr rd 71, km post 25.5, site sp at lakeside. 2*, Lge, hdg, mkd, pt shd, EHU (4A) inc (rev pol); TV; 10% statics; Eng spkn; adv bkg acc; ccard acc; watersports; bike hire; CKE. *"Excel san facs; excel rest; several sites in close proximity; great site with friendly owners."* **HUF 9980, 1 May-15 Sep. 2024**

BALATONBERENY *C1* (1km NW Rural) *46.71340, 17.31080* **FKK Naturista Camping (Naturist),** Hetvezer u.2, 8649 Balatonberény **(85) 377299; bereny@balatontourist.hu; www.balatontourist.hu**

€2.60 WD

Fr Keszthely foll rte 71 & rte 76 round SW end of lake. Lge sp indicates Balatonberény & site. Sps change fr Naturista Camping to FKK at turn off main rd. Med, mkd, hdg, pt shd, EHU (12-16A) inc; bbq; sw nr; TV; 10% statics; phone; adv bkg acc; games area; red INF; windsurfing; watersports. *"Vg site; gd sized pitches; direct access to lake adj; excel san facs."* **HUF 8695, 15 May-15 Sep. 2024**

BALATONSZEPEZD *C1* (4km SW Rural) *48.82950, 17.64000* **Balatontourist Camping Napfény,** H-8200 Veszprém, Levendula u. 1. **+36/88/544-444; info@balatontourist.hu; www.balatontourist.hu**

HUF900 WD MSP

Take m'way E71/M7 & exit junc 90 along N shore of lake, passing Balatonalmádi & Balatonfüred to Révfülöp. Site sp. 3*, Lge, mkd, pt shd, EHU (6A) inc; bbq; sw nr; twin axles; TV; 2% statics; phone; adv bkg acc; ccard acc; tennis 300m; boat hire; watersports; games rm; fishing; horseriding 5km; bike hire; games area. *"Warm welcome; excel, well-organised lakeside site; spa; gd pitches; gd for families; private san facs avail; fees according to pitch size & location."* **HUF 9449, 25 Apr-27 Sep, X06. 2024**

BOLDOGASSZONYFA *D2* (1km S Rural) *46.17807, 17.83812* **Camping Horgásztanya,** Petőfi út 53, 7937 Boldogasszonyfa **+3673471603; csukabeno@ciromail.hu; www.horgasztanya.hu**

WD

Take rte 67 S fr Kaposvár. Immed after vill of Boldogasszonyfa turn L, site sp on rvside. Sm, hdg, shd, pt sl, EHU (10A); fishing; CKE. *"Simple, rural site; conv Pécs & border area; rec use own facs."* **1 May-30 Sep. 2024**

BUDAPEST *B2* (10km N Urban) *47.57434, 19.05179* **Római Camping,** Szentendrei útca 189, 1031 Budapest **(1) 3887167; info@romaicamping.hu; www.romaicamping.hu**

12 HUG590 WD nr (htd)

Fr Gyor/Budapest m'way M1/E50 foll rte 11 twd Szentendre/Esztergom for approx 9km. Turn R at site sp. Site adj Római Fürdő rlwy stn. 3*, Med, mkd, shd, EHU (16A) HUF600; bbq; TV; phone; train 300m; Eng spkn; waterslide; CKE. *"V conv for city."* **HUF 10613 2024**

BUDAPEST *B2* (10km E Urban) *47.50421, 19.15834* **Camping Arena,** Pilisi Str 7, 1106 Budapest **06 30 29 691 29; info@budapestcamping.hu; arenacamping.eu**

12 WD MSP

Do not use Sat Nav. Leave M0 at exit 60 Kistarcsa & foll Rd 3 twd city cent for 7.5km. Turn L just bef rlwy bdge. Site 200m on R. Sm, hdg, pt shd, EHU (16A) inc; cooking facs; 10% statics; bus 400m; Eng spkn; adv bkg acc; CCI. *"Some rlwy & aircraft noise; supmkt 400m; shopping arcade 1km; metro 1km; rec all day travel card for metro, trams & busses; vg; v helpful staff."* **HUF 7650 2024**

BUDAPEST *B2* (5km SE Urban) *47.47583, 19.08305* **Haller Camping,** 27 Haller útca, 1096 Budapest **(20) 3674274; info@hallercamping.hu; www.hallercamping.hu**

WD MSP nr nr

Fr S on M5 twd Budapest cent. At ring rd foll dir Lagnymanyosi Hid (bdge). Bef bdge by lge shopping cent (Lurdy-Ház) turn R. Site sp. Or fr SE on rd 4 sp airport/Cegléd, turn R 100m bef new church steeple on L, foll sp Haller Piac. Med, hdstg, pt shd, EHU (16A) inc; bbq; red long stay; phone; tram & bus 100m; Eng spkn; adv bkg acc; CKE. *"V friendly; vg security; gd, clean san facs; dogs free; tram stop opp site; lge shoping cent 500m; conv for city cent; v helpful staff."* **HUF 8985, 10 May-30 Sep. 2024**

HUNGARY

BUDAPEST *B2* (7km WNW Rural) *47.514437, 18.972951* **Ave Natura Camping,** Csermely u. 3, 1121 Budapest **(36) 12003470 or (36) 705507069; campingavenatura@gmail.com; www.campingavenatura.hu**

Fr Austria via M1/M7 fr Balaton exit 14 Budakeszi. Fr M0, foll rd to end then Route 1 direction Budakeszi. Fr Budakeszi foll camping sp. Fr city to Moskva Ter then foll sp. Sm, hdg, hdstg, pt shd, terr, EHU (16A) HUF1200; bbq; cooking facs; phone; bus 300m; Eng spkn; adv bkg acc; CKE. *"Guaranteed warm and informative welcome by family run peaceful, wooded site; 10min downhill walk to bus into Budapest; vg."* **HUF 10560, 1 May-31 Oct.** 2023

CSERKESZOLO *C3* (0.8km S Urban) *46.86386, 20.2019* **Thermal Camping Cserkeszölö,** Beton út 5, 5465 Cserkeszölö **(6) 56568450; hotelcamping@cserkeszolo.hu; www.touring-hotel.hu/en**

12 HUF (htd) nr (covrd, htd)

On rte 44 bet Kecksemet & Kunszentmárton. Site sp in Cserkeszölö. 4*, Lge, pt shd, EHU (10A) inc; bbq; cooking facs; 10% statics; phone; bus 200m; waterslide; sauna; tennis; games area; CKE. *"Use of sw pools & thermal pools inc in site fee; gd."* **HUF 8326** 2022

DOMOS *B2* (0.5km E Rural) *47.7661, 18.91495* **Dömös Camping,** Dömös Dunapart, 2027 Dömös **(30) 3106580; info@domoscamping.hu; www.danukanyar.hu/kemping-domos**

HUF500

On rd 11 fr Budapest, site on R on ent Dömös, adj Rv Danube. 3*, Med, hdg, pt shd, EHU (10A) HUF950; cooking facs; red long stay; TV; phone; bus to Budapest; Eng spkn; adv bkg acc; CKE. *"Delightful site with views Danube bend; spacious pitches - lower ones poss subject to flooding; excel, clean facs & rest."* **HUF 10465, 1 May-24 Sep.** 2023

DUNAFOLDVAR *C2* (2km NE Rural) *46.81227, 18.92664* **Kék-Duna Camping,** Hösök Tere 23, 7020 Dunafoldvár **(75) 541107; kemping@tolna.net; dunafoldvarfurdo.hu/kemping**

12 (covrd)

Fr rndabt S of Dunafoldvár turn twd town cent. At traff lts turn R down to rv, then turn L, under green bdge & foll towpath 300m to site. 2*, Sm, shd, EHU (16A) inc; bbq; adv bkg acc; fishing; bike hire; tennis; watersports; CKE. *"Pleasant position o'looking Danube; adequate, clean san facs but dated; gd touring base Transdanubia."* **HUF 4280** 2022

GYOR *B1* (7km NE Rural) *47.72547, 17.71446* **Piheno Camping,** Weg 10, 9011 Gyor **(96) 523008 or (36) 704536330; piheno@piheno.hu; www.piheno.hu**

HUF1000 (htd)

E fr Gyor on rte 1 twds Budapest, stay on rte 1 for Komarom. Site on L 3km past m'way (M1) junc. Sm, hdg, mkd, pt shd, pt sl, EHU (16A); gas; bbq; cooking facs; TV; 10% statics; phone; bus; Eng spkn; adv bkg acc; ccard acc; CKE. *"Gd facs; fair."* **HUF 4593, 1 May-30 Sep.** 2023

HAJDUSZOBOSZLO *B4* (2km N Urban) *47.45756, 21.39396* **Thermál Camping,** Böszörményi út 35A, 4200 Hajdúszoboszló **(52) 558552; thermalcamping@hungarospa.hu; www.hungarospa.hu**

12 HUF440

Fr W on rte 4/E573 thro town, site sp on L. Fr Debrecen, turn R 500m past Camping Hadjdútourist on lakeside. 3*, Lge, hdg, pt shd, EHU (12A) inc; bbq; cooking facs; TV; phone; Eng spkn; ccard acc; waterslide; CKE. *"Pleasant site; htd covrd pool adj; sm naturist island in lake; thermal baths adj."* **HUF 9136** 2022

JASZAPATI *B3* (1.5km S Urban) *47.50537, 20.14012* **Tölgyes Strand Camping,** Gyöngyvirág u 11, 5130 Jászapáti **(57) 441187; info@tolgyesstrand.hu; www.tolgyesstrand.hu**

(covrd, htd)

Fr Budapest E on M3, exit at Hatvan & take rd 32 to Jászberény then foll rd 31 to Jászapáti. Site sp fr town cent. 3*, Med, mkd, pt shd, EHU (10A); TV; 10% statics; adv bkg acc; games area; site clsd 1 Nov to mid-Dec; bike hire; tennis 200m. *"Gd, modern facs."* **1 Apr-30 Nov.** 2022

KESZTHELY *C1* (8km NW Rural) *46.78393, 17.19575* **Kurcamping Castrum,** Tópart, 8380 Héviz **(83) 343198; heviz@castrum.eu; www.castrum-group.hu**

€4 (htd)

Fr Keszthely foll sp to Héviz & site 700m to E, opp Héviz thermal lake. 4*, Lge, mkd, pt shd, serviced pitches; EHU (6-16A) €3; sw nr; TV (pitch); Eng spkn; adv bkg acc; CKE. *"Lake fed by hot springs so gd for sw; casino adj; easy cycle ride/walk into lovely spa town & cycle path to Keszthely; excel san facs; excursions Budapest fr gate; htd pool adj; v nice site; gd location to explore by foot or bike."* **HUF 3113, 1 Mar-31 Dec.** 2024

MATRAFURED *B3* (4km N Rural) *47.84416, 19.95725* **Mátra Camping Sástó,** Farkas út 4, 3232 Mátrafüred **(37) 374025; recepcio@matrakemping.hu; www.matrakemping.hu**

nr nr nr

Take rte 24 N fr Gyöngyös. Site on L 2km after Mátrafüred. 4*, Med, hdstg, pt shd, pt sl, EHU (10A) inc; cooking facs; TV; 10% statics; ccard acc. *"Site pt of controlled sports complex; vg secure site."* **HUF 5543, 1 Apr-31 Oct.** 2022

MOSONMAGYAROVAR *B1* (1km E Urban) *47.87718, 17.27874* **Termál Aqua Camping,** Kigyó út 1, 9200 Mosonmagyaróvár **(96) 579168; aquahotel@t-online.hu; aquahoteltermal.hu**

€2 (htd) nr

Foll sp fr town cent to Termál Hotel Aqua; site in grnds, just behind lge thermal baths. Sm, hdg, mkd, shd, EHU €3; bbq; cooking facs; phone; bus, train 1km; Eng spkn. *"Vg site; htd covrd thermal adj; pool adj; price inc ent to thermals & sauna."*
HUF 9028, 1 Apr-30 Oct. 2022

MOSONMAGYAROVAR *B1* (3km SE Urban) *47.84224, 17.28591* **Camping Kis-Duna,** Gabonarakpart 6, 9200 Mosonmagyaróvár **(96) 216433; kisdunamotel@gmail.com; www.halaszkertvendeglo.hu**

12 HUF500 nr

Site on L of M1 Mosonmagyaróvár-Gyõr in grnds of motel & rest, 15km fr border. 2*, Sm, hdstg, unshd, EHU (16A) HUF500; TV. *"Gd, clean, facs; thermal pool 2.5km; rest gd but busy; gd alt to Bratislava site (Slovakia); ideal NH."* **HUF 10050** 2023

PAPA *B1* (2km N Urban) *47.33797, 17.47367* **Termál Camping Pápa,** Várkert út 7, 8500 Pápa **36 89 320 735; info@thermalkemping.hu; www.thermalkemping.hu**

12 €2 (htd) nr

Fr 83 exit at Gyori Way. Foll sp. Lge, hdstg, mkd, hdg, pt shd, EHU (16A); gas; bbq; cooking facs; sw nr; twin axles; 20% statics; phone; bus 500m; Eng spkn; adv bkg acc; games rm; games area; CCI. *"Onsite kids club; boccia; basketball; archery; disco adj; thermal baths with indoor & outdoor pools, slides; excel; htd pool adj; well managed site; gd area for long stay & touring; very helpful staff."* **HUF 11570** 2024

SAROSPATAK *A4* (2km NE Rural) *48.33274, 21.58245* **Tengerszem Camping,** Herceg Ferenc ut 2, 3950 Sárospatak **(47) 312744; info@tengerszem-camping.hu; www.tengerszem-camping.hu**

NW fr Tokaj on R38; then NE on R37 to Sárospatak; foll camp sp. 3*, Med, hdg, pt shd, EHU (10A) inc; TV; games area; tennis; CKE. *"Refurbished thermal sw baths next door; gd site for mountains."*
HUF 6441, 30 Apr-15 Oct. 2022

SARVAR *B1* (2km SE Urban) *47.24671, 16.9473* **Sárvár Thermal Camping,** Vadkert út 1, 9600 Sárvár **(95) 523610; info@thermalcamping.com; www.thermalcamping.com**

12 €2 (htd) nr

E fr Szombathely via rtes 86 & 88. Site on Sopron-Lake Balaton rte 84. 4*, Med, hdstg, pt shd, EHU (16A) €3; bbq; cooking facs; red long stay; 10% statics; ccard acc; waterslide; lake fishing; tennis 500m; sauna; CKE. *"Barrier clsd 1330-1500; htd thermal pools adj; private san facs avail; free ent to spa & fitness cent adj."*
HUF 21762 2022

SOPRON *B1* (8km SE Rural) *47.6525, 16.6575* **Kurcamping Castrum Balf-Sopron,** Fürdö Sor 59-61, 9494 Balf **(83) 314422; info@castrum.eu; www.castrum.eu**

€2.50 (htd) nr nr

On rte 84 S of Sopron turn E sp Balf. In 2km turn N sp Sopron & foll sps. Site at W end Balf vill. 3*, Med, hdg, mkd, pt shd, EHU (6A) HUF800; TV; phone; Eng spkn; ccard acc; bike hire; sauna; CKE. *"Thermal baths avail; Tesco hypmkt on app to Sopron 6km, with ATM; pitches uneven; ltd facs LS & poss unkempt; poss cold shwrs; site in need of maintenance; overpriced NH."*
HUF 4770, 1 Apr-31 Oct. 2022

TAMASI *C2* (1km S Urban) *46.62577, 18.28734* **Thermál Camping,** Hársfa út 1, 7090 Tamási **(74) 471738; camping@tamasistrand.hu; www.tamasikemping.hu**

HUF67 nr nr (htd)

Site & thermal baths sp on rd 65 adj motel. 2*, Med, pt shd, EHU (10A) HUF575 (long lead req); 10% statics; phone; CKE. *"Security gate; free access to lge thermal pool complex; vg; perfect location for spa next door; nice town and surrounding area."*
HUF 5099, 1 May-15 Oct. 2024

TURISTVANDI *A4* (1km SW Rural) *48.04710, 22.64300* **Vizimalom Camping,** Malom út 3, 4944 Túristvándi **(30) 289 9808; vizimalompanzio@gmail.com; www.turvizimalom.hu**

nr

Fr Fehérgyarmat foll rd 491 NE for 4km to Penyige, turn L to Túristvándi. After approx 12km site on R adj 18thC water mill on Rv Túr. Sm, hdstg, pt shd, EHU (10A); bbq; TV; games rm; canoeing; games area. *"Excel location; no hdstg."*
HUF 5853, 1 Mar-1 Nov. 2022

"There aren't many sites open at this time of year"

If you're travelling outside peak season remember to call ahead to check site opening dates – even if the entry says 'open all year'.

ZALAKAROS *C1* (3km S Rural) *46.53165, 17.12443* **Kurcamping Castrum,** Ady Endre út, 8754 Galambok **(93) 358610; zalakaros@castrum.eu; www.castrum-group.hu**

(htd) nr nr (covrd, htd)

Fr rte 7 N dir Zalakaros, site sp. 4*, Med, hdg, mkd, pt shd, EHU (6A) inc; bbq; 10% statics; bus; ccard acc; sauna; CKE. *"Thermal complex 2km."*
HUF 9375, 1 May-30 Sep. 2023

HUNGARY

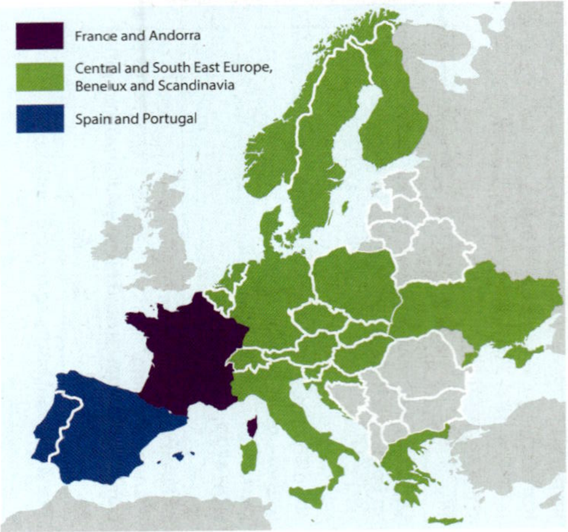

Salgótarján to Tatabánya = 168km

	Békéscsaba	Budapest	Debrecen	Győr	Kecskemét	Keszthely	Miskolc	Mosonmagyaróvár	Nyíregyháza	Pécs	Salgótarján	Sopron	Szeged	Székesfehérvár	Szekszárd	Szolnok	Szombathely	Tatabánya	Veszprém
Budapest	202																		
Debrecen	129	224																	
Győr	329	122	348																
Kecskemét	122	86	193	206															
Keszthely	354	155	381	158	230														
Miskolc	231	181	98	306	203	334													
Mosonmagyaróvár	364	159	388	41	244	176	338												
Nyíregyháza	181	245	51	368	239	400	96	410											
Pécs	282	199	366	238	176	150	375	277	419										
Salgótarján	241	112	206	219	172	269	127	257	215	310									
Sopron	415	215	432	88	296	133	390	90	453	284	322								
Szeged	95	169	221	292	87	308	288	334	272	189	255	379							
Székesfehérvár	258	67	290	85	137	123	247	125	307	153	178	172	207						
Szekszárd	230	144	315	188	121	169	322	226	362	64	259	273	141	99					
Szolnok	109	97	131	221	60	252	160	261	182	235	132	309	132	161	186				
Szombathely	406	221	445	103	278	99	405	112	469	247	334	71	354	155	241	320			
Tatabánya	257	55	284	70	139	188	237	104	302	210	168	155	227	59	159	155	174		
Veszprém	292	113	337	75	171	74	287	114	357	165	226	144	240	45	129	210	113	103	
Zalaegerszeg	389	224	450	155	272	49	401	166	464	192	338	126	345	164	210	322	54	221	121

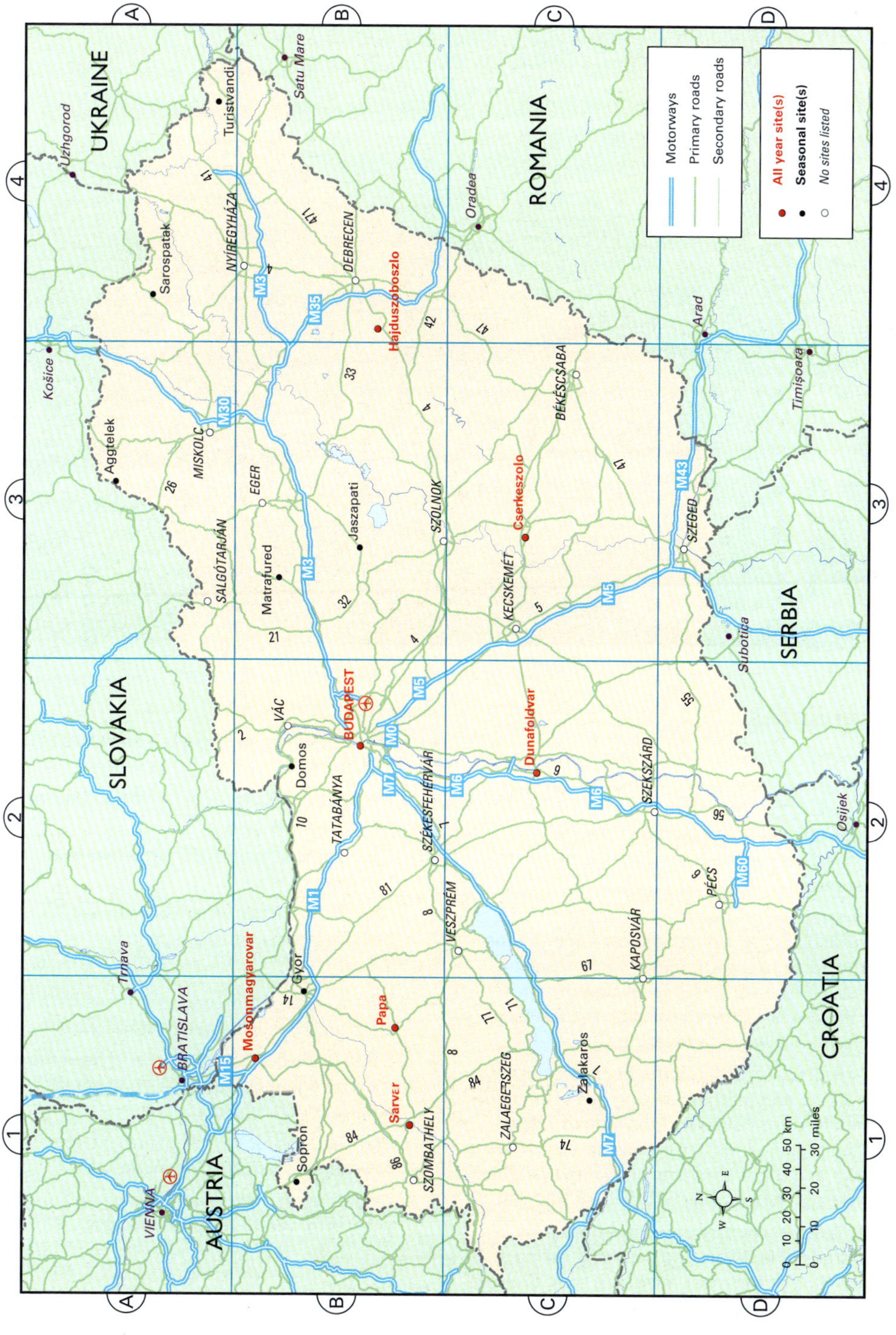
Motorways
Primary roads
Secondary roads
All year site(s)
Seasonal site(s)
No sites listed
UKRAINE
SLOVAKIA
AUSTRIA
ROMANIA
SERBIA
CROATIA
Uzhgorod
Satu Mare
Košice
Trnava
BRATISLAVA
VIENNA
Oradea
Arad
Timişoara
Subotica
Osijek
Turistvandi
Sarospatak
NYÍREGYHÁZA
DEBRECEN
Hajduszoboszlo
Aggtelek
MISKOLC
EGER
SALGÓTARJÁN
Matrafured
Jaszapati
SZOLNOK
Cserkeszolo
BÉKÉSCSABA
KECSKEMÉT
SZEGED
VÁC
Domos
BUDAPEST
TATABÁNYA
SZÉKESFEHÉRVÁR
Dunafoldvar
SZEKSZÁRD
PÉCS
KAPOSVÁR
VESZPRÉM
Gyor
Mosonmagyarovar
Papa
Sarver
SZOMBATHELY
Sopron
ZALAEGERSZEG
Zalakaros
M1
M3
M5
M6
M7
M15
M30
M35
M43
M60
M0
0 10 20 30 40 50 km
0 10 20 30 miles
A
B
C
D
1
2
3
4

Italy

Highlights

One of the greatest cultural jewels in Europe's crown has to be Italy. It's a country alive with art and fashion that is envied across the world, and boasts some of the most extraordinary architectural masterpieces in existence.

Alongside the grandeur is a country with great natural diversity, from the snow-capped Alps in the north to the stunning Mediterranean coastline. The variety of local customs and traditions encountered through the different regions are always captivating.

Italy is often considered the fashion capital of the world, and leather working has often been at the forefront of its fashion industry. The Italian tanning industry is considered a world leader and there are many products available from bags to belts which showcase this skill.

Italy is also a country of celebration, with hundreds of festivals and carnivals taking place. One of the most famous is the Carnival of Venice, where traditional masks and costumes are worn by attendees.

Major towns and cities

- Rome - this remarkable city is known as the 'Capital of the World'.
- Milan - a global centre of fashion and known for its exquisite galleries.
- Turin - famous for its baroque architecture and monuments.
- Naples - boasting a wealth of historical buildings from a variety of periods.

Attractions

- Venice – one of the world's most beautiful cities and boasting a wealth of historic sites.
- Santa Maria del Fiore, Florence – one of the most recognisable cathedrals that houses several important works of art.
- Pompeii – the remains of an ancient Roman town in the shadow of Mount Vesuvius.
- Cinque Terree – five beautiful and traditional villages that lie on the Italian Riviera.

Find out more

italia.it
italia.it@ministeroturismo.gov.it

Country Information

Capital: Rome

Bordered by: France, Switzerland, Austria, Slovenia

Terrain: Mountainous in the north descending to rolling hills in the centre; some plains and coastal lowlands

Climate: Predominantly Mediterranean climate, alpine in the far north, hot and dry in the south

Coastline: 7,600km

Highest Point: Monte Bianco (Mont Blanc) 4,810m

Language: Italian, German (in the northern Alps)

Local Time: GMT or BST + 1, i.e. 1 hour ahead of the UK all year

Currency: Euros divided into 100 cents; £1 = €1.20 €1 = £0.84 (Nov 2024)

Emergency numbers: Police 112; Fire brigade 115; Ambulance 118

Public Holidays 2025: Jan 1, 6; Apr 20, 21, 25; May 1; Jun 2; Aug 15; Nov 1; Dec 8, 25, 26.

Each locality also celebrates its patron saint's day. School summer holidays run from mid June to mid September.

Entry Formalities

British and Irish passport holders may stay for up to 90 days in any 180 day period without a visa. You may be asked to show a return or onward ticket at the border to confirm your length of stay, or to prove that you have enough money for your stay.

Your passport will need to have a minimum of 6 months' validity remaining, and be less than 10 years old (even if it has over 6 months left).

Visitors arriving at a campsite or hotel must complete a registration form.

Medical Services

Ask at a pharmacy (farmacia) for the nearest doctor registered with the state health care scheme (SSN) or look in the telephone directory under 'Unita Sanitaria Locale'. The services of a national health service doctor are normally free of charge.

A European Health Insurance Card (EHIC) or a UK Global Health Insurance Card (GHIC) entitles you to emergency treatment and medication at local rates and to hospital treatment under the state healthcare scheme. Any charges you do incur are non-refundable in Italy but you may be able to make a claim on your return to the UK. Dental treatment is expensive and you will be charged the full fee.

Emergency services (Guardia Medica) are available at weekends and at night and there are first aid posts at major train stations and airports. Staff at pharmacies can advise on minor ailments and at least one pharmacy remains open 24 hours in major towns.

Opening Hours

Banks: Mon-Fri 8.30am-1.30pm & 3pm-4pm.

Museums: Check locally as may vary. The Vatican museums and Sistine Chapel are not open to visitors Sun. Visitors under 18 or over 60 are admitted free to State museums on production of a passport.

Post Offices: Mon-Fri 8.30am-2pm/5.30pm, Sat 8.30am-12 noon.

Shops: Mon-Sat 8.30am/9am-1pm & 3.30pm/4pm-7.30pm/8pm. In southern Italy and tourist areas shops may stay open later. There's no lunch time closing in large cities. Shops are closed half a day each week (variable by region).

Regulations for Pets

All dogs, including those temporarily imported, must be on a leash at all times. It's advisable to carry a muzzle as the police/authorities can insist on your dog wearing one if they consider your dog to be dangerous. Some sites and some public transport operators insist that all dogs are muzzled at all times - check local requirements on arrival.

A domestic animal may be transported in a car provided it does not distract the driver. More than one animal may be transported provided they're kept in the rear of the car, separated from the driver by bars, or kept in special cages.

Safety and Security

Visitors should take care on public transport and in crowded areas where pickpockets and bag snatchers may operate. In Rome take particular care around the main railway station, Roma Termini, and on the bus to and from St Peter's Square.

Also take care in and around railway stations in large cities. Be particularly wary of groups of children who may try to distract your attention while attempting to steal from you. Don't carry your passport, credit cards and cash all together in one bag or pocket and only carry what you need for the day. Don't wear expensive jewellery, particularly in the south of Italy.

Take care in bars and don't leave drinks unattended. Recently there have been cases of drinks being spiked. Check prices before ordering food and insist on seeing a priced menu. Be particularly careful when ordering items, such as lobster, which are charged by weight.

When driving in towns keep your car windows shut and doors locked and never leave valuables on display. Around Rome and Naples moped riders may attempt to snatch bags from stationary cars at traffic lights. Always lock your vehicle and never leave valuables in it, even if you will only be away for a short time or are nearby. Avoid leaving luggage in cars for any length of time or overnight.

Increasingly robberies are taking place from cars at rest stops and service stations on motorways. Treat offers of help with caution, for example with a flat tyre, particularly on the motorway, as sometimes the tyre will have been punctured deliberately.

Don't be tempted to enter or bathe in Italy's many fountains – there are heavy fines if you do. Dress conservatively when visiting places of worship, i.e. cover shoulders and upper arms and don't wear shorts. Avoid queues in the peak season by visiting early.

The authorities are making strenuous efforts to stamp out the illegal production and sale of counterfeit goods. Illegal traders operate on the streets of all major cities, particularly tourist cities such as Florence and Rome. You're advised not to buy from them at the risk of incurring a fine.

Italy shares with the rest of Europe an underlying threat from terrorism. Please check (gov.uk/foreign-travel-advice/italy) before you travel.

British Embassy

Via XX Settembre 80a,
00187 Rome
Tel: +39 06 4220 0001 (24-hour emergency number)
gov.uk/world/italy

British Consulate-General

Via San Paolo 7,
20121 Milan
Tel: +44 20 7008 5000 (24-hour)
There's also a British Consulates in Naples.

Irish Embassy

Villa Spada, Via Giacomo Medici 1,
00153 Rome
Tel: +39 06 5852 381
ireland.ie/en/italy/rome
There's also an Irish Honorary Consulate in Milan.

Documents

Driving Licence

The standard pink UK paper driving licence is recognised in Italy but holders of the old-style green UK licence are recommended to change it for a photocard licence. Alternatively an International Driving Permit may be purchased from the AA, the RAC or selected post offices.

Money

There are few bureaux de change, so change cash at a bank.

Major credit cards are widely accepted including at petrol stations, but not as widely as in some other European countries. Automatic cash machines (Bancomat) are widespread. Carry your credit card issuers'/banks' 24-hour UK contact numbers in case of loss or theft of your cards.

Vehicle(s)

Carry your valid driving licence, insurance and vehicle documents with you in your vehicle at all times. It's particularly important to carry your vehicle registration document V5C, as you will need it if entering low emission zones.

Driving

Alcohol

The maximum permitted level of alcohol is 0.05%. Penalties for driving under the influence of alcohol can be severe. A lower level of 0.02% applies to drivers who have held a driving licence for less than three years i.e virtually nil. It's advisable to adopt the 'no drink and drive' rule as penalties are severe.

Breakdown Service

The motoring organisation, Automobile Club d'Italia (ACI) operates a breakdown service 24 hours a day throughout Italy, including San Marino and Vatican City. Telephone 803116 from a landline or mobile phone from within Italy, or or 800 116 800 from a foreign mobile phone. ACI staff speak English. These numbers also give access to the ACI emergency information service, operated by multilingual staff, for urgent medical or legal advice. There are emergency phones placed every 2 km on motorways.

On all roads, including motorways, standard charges are made for assistance and/or recovering a vehicle weighing up to 2,500kg to the nearest ACI garage. Higher charges apply for vehicles over 2,500kg, at night, over weekends and public holidays and for towing to anywhere other than the nearest ACI garage. Payment is required in cash.

Road police, 'Polizia Stradale', constantly patrol all roads and motorways and can assist when vehicles break down.

Congestion Charge

To access the historical centre of Milan (Area C) from 7.30am–7.30pm on Monday, Tuesday, Wednesday and Friday and from 7.30am-6pm on Thursday you must pay a fee of €5 a day.

For more information, or to register your details and buy a ticket, visit areac.atm-mi.it. Petrol vehicles classed as Euro 0 and diesel vehicles in classes Euro 0 - 3 are not allowed to enter Area C at all during the above times.

Child Restraint System

Children travelling in UK registered vehicles must be secured according to UK legislation.

Fuel

Unleaded petrol is sold from pumps marked 'Super Unleaded' or 'Super Sensa Piombo'. Diesel is called 'gasolio' and LPG is known as 'gas auto' or 'GPL'.

Fuel is sold 24 hours a day on motorways but elsewhere petrol stations may close for an extended lunch break and overnight from approximately 7pm. Opening hours are clearly displayed, as are the addresses of the nearest garages which are open.

Major credit cards are accepted, but possibly not in rural areas, so always carry some cash. Look for the 'Carta Si' sign. Recent visitors report that many petrol stations in rural areas and on major routes between towns are now unmanned and automated. Payment may be made with bank notes but the machines will usually only accept credit cards issued by Italian banks.

Lights

It's compulsory for all vehicles to have dipped headlights at all times when driving outside built-up areas, on motorways and major roads, when driving in tunnels and when visibility is poor, e.g. in rain or snow. Bulbs are more likely to fail with constant use so you're advised to carry spares.

Low Emission Zones

Many Italian cities and towns operate low emission zones. They often affect all vehicles, but rules vary from city to city. For more information visit urbanaccessregulations.eu

Motorways

There are approximately 6,700 km of motorway (autostrade) in Italy. Tolls (pedaggio) are levied on most of them. On some motorways, tolls are payable at intermediate toll booths for each section of the motorway used. On a few others the toll must be paid on entering the motorway.

Motorway Tolls

Category A	Cars with height from front axle less than 1.30m.
Category B	Motor vehicles with 2axles with height from front axle over 1.30m including motorhomes.
Category C	Motor vehicles with 3 axles, e.g. car plus caravan.
Category D	Motor vehicles with 4 axles, e.g. car plus twin-axle caravan.

To calculate the tolls payable and find traffic and motorway services information see (autostrade.it) which allows you to enter your route and class of vehicle.

Tolls can prove to be expensive especially over long distances.

Cash (euro only), debit and credit cards are accepted. Credit cards are also accepted for payment in the Fréjus, Mont-Blanc and Grand St Bernard tunnels. However, visitors advise that on some stretches of motorway automated pay desks which accept credit cards will only do so for solo vehicles. If you're towing a caravan it's advisable to have cash available as you may need to pass through the manned white channel for cash payments.

Overtaking

On roads with three traffic lanes, the middle lane is reserved for overtaking, but overtaking is only allowed if a vehicle travelling in the opposite direction isn't already overtaking.

When pulling out to overtake on motorways check for cars travelling at well over the maximum speed limit of 130 km/h (81 mph).

Parking

In major towns parking zones where payment is required are indicated by blue road signs. Pay either at a machine with coins or buy a card from local tobacconists or newspaper shops and display it inside your vehicle. Some cities also have green zones where parking is prohibited on working days during the morning and afternoon rush hours.

Parking against the traffic flow and parking on the pavement are not allowed. Illegally parked vehicles may be clamped or towed away.

Priority

In general, priority must be given to traffic coming from the right except if indicated by road signs. At traffic lights a flashing amber light indicates that traffic must slow down and proceed with caution, respecting the priority rules.

Roads

The road network is of a high standard and main and secondary roads are generally good. Many main roads are winding and hilly but provide a more interesting route than the motorways. Stopping places for refreshments may be few and far between in some areas.

Standards of driving may be erratic, especially overtaking, and lane discipline poor; some roads have a particularly bad reputation for accidents. Those where special vigilance is called for include the Via Aurelia between Rome and Pisa, which is mostly two lane and is extremely busy at weekends, the A12 to the north with its series of tunnels and curves, the A1 between Florence and Bologna, the Rome ring road, roads around Naples and Palermo, and mountain roads in the south and in Sicily.

Road Signs and Markings

Road signs conform to international standards. White lettering on a green background indicates motorways (autostrada), whereas state and provincial roads outside built-up areas have white lettering on a blue background.

Snow chains required

Horizontal traffic light

Carabinieri (police)

Ecopass zone (Milan)

Other frequently encountered signs include the following:

Italian	English Translation
Attenzione	Caution
Autocarro	Lorries
Coda	Traffic jam
Curva pericolosa	Dangerous bend
Destra	Right
Deviazione	Diversion
Divieto di accesso	No entry
Divieto di sorpasso	No overtaking
Divieto di sosta	No parking
Ghiaia	Gravel
Incidente	Accident
Incrocio	Crossroads
Lavori in corso	Roadworks ahead
Pericoloso	Danger
Rallentare	Slow down
Restringimento	Narrow lane
Senso unico	One-way street
Senso vietato	No entry
Sinistra	Left
Sosta autorizzata	Parking permitted (times shown)
Sosta aietata	No parking
Svolta	Bend
Uscita	Exit
Vietato ingresso veicili	No entry for vehicles

A single or double unbroken line in the centre of the carriageway must not be crossed.

Speed Limits

	Open Road (km/h)	Motorway (km/h)
Car Solo	90-110	130
Car towing caravan/trailer	70	80
Motorhome under 3500kg	90-110	130
Motorhome 3500-7500kg	80	100

Motorhomes over 3,500 kg are restricted to 80 km/h (50 mph) outside built-up areas and 100 km/h (62 mph) on motorways.

Speed on some sections of Italian motorways is electronically controlled. When you leave a motorway the toll booth calculates the distance a vehicle has travelled and the journey time. The police are automatically informed if speeding has taken place, and fines are imposed.

In bad weather the maximum speed is 90 km/h (56 mph) on roads outside built-up areas and 110 km/h (68 mph) on motorways.

The transportation or use of radar detectors is prohibited.

Traffic Jams

During the summer months, particularly at weekends, the roads to the Ligurian and Adriatic coasts and to the Italian lakes are particularly busy, as are the narrow roads around the lakes. Travelling mid week may help a little. Bottlenecks are likely to occur on the A1 north-south motorway at stretches between Milan and Bologna, Rioveggio and Incisa and on the ring road around Rome. Other traffic jams occur on the A14 to the Adriatic coast; on the A4 between Milan and Brescia caused by heavy traffic to Lakes Iseo and Garda; the A11 Florence to Pisa (before the A12 junction); the A12 Rome to Civitavecchia; the A23 Udine to Tarvisio and before the tunnels on the A26 between Alessandria and Voltri.

Italians traditionally go on holiday during the first weekend of August when traffic density is at its worst. Traffic jams regularly occur on the ring roads for Milan, Rome and Naples.

Violation of Traffic Regulations

The police may impose on the spot fines, which are particularly heavy for speeding and drink and/or drug related driving offences. Payment is required in cash and a receipt must be given. It can take up to a year for notice of a traffic violation and resulting fine to reach the owner of a foreign registered vehicle.

Winter Driving

In the area of Val d'Aosta vehicles must be equipped with winter tyres or snow chains must be carried between 15 October and 15 April. This rule may apply in other areas and over other periods as conditions dictate.

Essential Equipment

Reflective Jackets/Waistcoats

It's compulsory to wear a reflective jacket when getting out of your vehicle on a motorway or main road. Pedestrians walking at night or in bad visibility outside built-up areas must also wear one.

Warning Triangle

A warning triangle must be used to give advance warning of any vehicle parked outside a built-up area near a bend, or on a hill if rear side lights have failed, or in fog. Place the triangle at least 50 metres behind the vehicle (100 metres on motorways). Failure to use a triangle may result in a fine.

Touring

Italy's great cities, with their religious, artistic and historic treasures, are high on the short break list and are worthy destinations in their own right. Visitors over 65 often qualify for reduced or free entrance to museums and other attractions, so carry your passport as proof of age.

In Rome an Archaeology Card is available for purchase. The card is valid for seven days, offering entry (ahead of any queues) to many of Rome's most famous sites, together with discounts on guided tours. The cards are available from participating sites and museums.

Smoking isn't permitted in public places including restaurants and bars.

In bars prices shown are for drinks taken standing at the bar. Prices are higher if you're seated at a table. In restaurants a service or cover charge is usually added to the bill but it's customary to add 50 cents or €1 per person if you're happy with the service provided. Not all restaurants accept credit cards; check before ordering.

The east coast of Italy has many holiday resorts with fine, sandy beaches, from Ravenna, to Pescara and beyond. However, most beaches in Italy are commercially managed and unless a campsite or hotel has its own private beach, be prepared to pay to enjoy a day by the sea. By law a part of every beach must have free access, but usually it's the least attractive part.

Many parts of Italy lie on a major seismic fault line and tremors and minor earthquakes are common. Visitors climbing Mount Etna should follow the marked routes and heed the advice of guides. There's also ongoing low-intensity volcanic activity on the island of Stromboli.

Parts of Venice are liable to flood in late autumn and early spring.

There are more than 50 World Heritage sites in Italy (more than any other country) including the historic centres of Florence, Siena, Naples, Pienza, Urbino and the Vatican City.

The Vatican museums and Sistine Chapel are closed on Sundays, except on the last Sunday of the month. When visiting art galleries in Florence, in particular the Uffizi and Accademia, you're advised to buy timed tickets in advance, either online or in person. Otherwise you will encounter long queues.

There are numerous ferry services transporting passengers and vehicles between Italy and neighbouring countries. Major ports of departure for Croatia, Greece and Turkey are Ancona, Bari, Brindisi, Trieste and Venice. Services also operate to Corsica from Citavecchia, Genoa, Livorno, Porto Torres (Sardinia), Santa Teresa di Gallura (Sardinia) and Savona.

For further information contact:

Viamare Ltd
Suite 108, 582 Honeypot Lane
Stanmore
Middlesex HA7 1JS
Tel: 020 8206 3420
Website: viamare.com
Email: ferries@viamare.com

If you're planning a skiing holiday contact the Italian State Tourist Board for advice on safety and weather conditions before travelling, or visit avalanches.org.

Italy has a law requiring skiers and snowboarders to carry tracking equipment, a snow probe and a shovel if going off-piste. The law also obliges children under 18 years of age to wear a helmet.

Camping and Caravanning

There are over 2,000 organised and supervised campsites in Italy. They're usually well signposted and are open from April to September. Advance booking is recommended in high season, especially by the lakes and along the Adriatic coast. About 20% of campsites are open all year including some in the mountains and around large towns. Campsites organised by the Touring Club Italiano (TCI) and the Federcampeggio are particularly well equipped.

In general pitch sizes are small at about 80 square metres and it may be difficult to fit a large outfit plus an awning onto a pitch. You will frequently find that hot water is supplied to showers only, for which you will be charged. Published opening and closing dates may be unreliable - phone ahead if travelling during the low season.

It's not compulsory to have a Camping Key Europe (CKE) or Camping Card International (CCI), but it's recommended as a means of identification. If for any reason details are missing from the CKE or CCI a site will insist on holding a visitor's passport instead.

Casual camping isn't recommended and isn't permitted in national parks or in state forests.

Motorhomes

Many local authorities permit motorhomes to park overnight in specially designated places known as 'Camper Stops' or 'Aree di Sosta' and a list of their locations and the services provided are contained in a number of publications and on a number of websites including the French 'Guide Officiel Aires de Service Camping-Car' published by the Fédération Française de Camping et de Caravaning, ffcc.fr.

Transportation of bicycles

You can carry your bikes on the roof of your car provided they are attached to an adequate roof-rack and the total height does not exceed 4m.

You can also carry your bikes on the back of your vehicle, provided they don't obscure lights, indicators or number plates. Bike racks can only rest on the towbar if the maximum weight on the towbar is not exceeded.

Any overhanging load must be indicated by an aluminium square panel (panello) measuring 50 cm x 50 cm with reflective red and white diagonal stripes. Panels can be purchased from Fiamma stockists are available in aluminium and plastic. In Spain you can use either, however, in Italy the panel must be aluminium. At night, outside built-up areas, cyclists must wear a reflective jacket and must ride in single file.

Electricity and Gas

Current at campsites varies between 2 and 16 amps and often it's very low, offering a maximum of only 4 amps across the whole site. Many sites have CEE connections. Plugs have three round pins in line.

Campingaz cylinders are generally available, except in the south of Italy, Sardinia and Sicily where exchange may be difficult outside of marinas and holiday resorts.

Public Transport & Local Travel

Traffic is restricted in the historical centre of most Italian cities in order to reduce congestion and pollution levels, and you're advised to use out of centre car parks and public transport. The boundaries of historic centres are usually marked with signs displaying the letters ZTL (zona traffico limitato). A crossed hammer on the sign means the restriction does not apply on Sundays and public holidays. Don't pass the ZTL sign as your registration number is likely to be caught on camera and fined.

Many northern Italian regions have banned traffic, except buses and taxis, in town and city centres on Sundays.

Public transport is usually cheap and efficient. All the major cities have extensive bus networks and Messina, Milan, Padova, Rome and Turin also have trams. At present only Rome, Naples, Milan and Turin have an underground network and Perugia has a 'minimetro'. Bus and metro tickets cannot be purchased on board and must be obtained prior to boarding from newsagents, tobacconists, ticket kiosks or bars. Books of tickets and daily, weekly and monthly passes are also available. Validate your ticket at the yellow machines positioned at the entrance to platforms in railway stations, in the entrance hall of metro stations and on board buses and trams. Officials patrol all means of public transport and will issue an on the spot fine if you don't hold a validated ticket. Tickets for buses and the metro tend to be time limited (75 minutes) and it's therefore necessary to complete your journey within the allotted time and purchase a new ticket for any additional travel.

Only use taxis which are officially licensed. They will have a neon taxi sign on the roof and are generally white or yellow. Also ensure that the meter in the taxi has been reset before starting your journey. Fares are quite high and there are additional charges for luggage and pets, at night and on public holidays. A tip is expected (up to 10%) and this is sometimes already added to the fares for foreigners.

Car ferry services operate between Venice and the Lido, the Italian mainland and the Aeolian Islands, Sardinia, Sicily, Elba and Capri, Corsica (France) and on Lakes Maggiore, Como and Garda.

Parking in Venice is very difficult; instead park at a mainland car park and use a bus or ferry to the city. Be aware that thieves may operate in car parks in Mestre. Driving and parking in Naples are not recommended in any circumstances.

Cars towing caravans are prohibited from using the S163 south of Naples because it's narrow and has many bends. Motorhomes are prohibited in summer between Positano and Vietri-a-Mare. at the entrance to platforms in railway stations, in the entrance hall of metro stations and on board buses and trams.

Colosseum, Rome

Shutterstock/prochasson frederic

AGEROLA *3A3* (3.5km SE Urban) *40.62537, 14.56761* **Camping Beata Solitudo,** Piazza Generale Avitabile 4, San Lazzaro, 80051 Agerola (NA) **081 8025048; beatasol@gmail.com; www.beatasolitudo.it**

12 (cont) nr nr nr

Exit A3/S145 at Castellammare-di-Stabia & foll dirs S on S366 to Agerola. Turn L sp San Lazzaro, site in vill sq - narr access rds. Do not app via Amalfi coast rd. Sm, shd, terr, EHU (3A) inc; 70% statics; bus adj; Eng spkn; adv bkg acc; CKE. *"Vg access to Amalfi coast via bus; site at 650m - sea views; v helpful owner; bungalows & hostel accomm avail in restored castle building on site; vg but suitable m'vans only; facs tired."* **€20.00** **2022**

ALBA *1B2* (1km SW Urban) *44.68507, 8.01019* **Camping Village Alba,** Corso Piave 219, San Cassiano, 12051 Alba (CN) **0173 280972; info@albavillagehotel.it; www.albavillagehotel.it**

12 (htd) nr

Fr A21 exit Asti Est onto S231 to Alba ring rd. Take Corso Piave dir Roddi & Castiglione Falletto, site sp (Campo Sportivo) on L - red block. Or fr A6 exit at SP662 & foll sp Cherasco & Marene, then at rndabt foll sp Pollenza, then Roddi. Fr Roddi site sp dir Alba. 3*, Med, hdg, mkd, pt shd, EHU (16A) €2.50; bbq; red long stay; bus; Eng spkn; adv bkg acc; ccard acc; games area; bike hire; CKE. *"Excel, friendly, clean site; mv service pnt adj; open country to rear; htd pool adj; vg facs; some statics or apartmnts; sports cent adj; conv Barolo vineyards; attractive town & area; camper van stop adj €5."* **€30.00** **2023**

ALBENGA *1B2* (2km E Rural/Coastal) *44.08277, 8.21611* **Camping Baciccia,** Via Torino 19, 17023 Ceriale (SV) **0182 990743; info@campingbaciccia.it; www.campingbaciccia.it**

€4 (htd) shgl 600m

Exit A10 for Albenga, turn L onto SS1 Via Aurelia dir Savona for 3km. Turn L inland at traff lts bef Famiglia Supmkt in Ceriale, site in 200m on L, sp. 1*, Med, mkd, pt shd, pt sl, serviced pitches; EHU (6A) inc; gas; bbq; red long stay; TV; 5% statics; Eng spkn; adv bkg acc; ccard acc; golf 10km; tennis 500m; sep car park; horseriding 2km; bike hire; CKE. *"Family-run site; ltd touring pitches; narr site rds & ent & sm pitches; friendly owners; bus to beach; gd san facs & pool; busy w/ends; lovely pool & café; private beach nrby; conv many historical attractions."* **€50.00, 1 Apr-3 Nov & 1 Dec-10 Jan.** **2024**

ALBEROBELLO *3A4* (1.5km N Rural) *40.80194, 17.25055* **Camping Dei Trulli,** Via Castellana Grotte, Km 1.5, 70011 Alberobello (BA) **0804 323699; info@campingdeitrulli.it; campingdeitrulli.it**

Fr Alberobello, site sp on R. Lift barrier to ent if clsd. 3*, Med, mkd, hdstg, pt shd, EHU (6A) €2.50; red long stay; phone; Eng spkn; ccard acc; bike hire; CKE. *"Gd touring base; some pitches sm due to trees; mv service pnt nr; ltd, basic facs LS; hot water to shwrs only; site run-down."* **€30.00, 1 Apr-2 Nov.** **2024**

ALBEROBELLO *3A4* (1km S Rural) *40.77507, 17.24040* **Camping Bosco Selva,** 27 Via Bosco Selva, 70011 Alberobello (BA) **080 4323726; info@campingboscoselva.it; www.campingboscoselva.it**

12 nr

Sp fr S172/S239 Alberobello ring rd. 3*, Med, hdstg, shd, pt sl, EHU (2A) inc; Eng spkn; CKE. *"In heart of 'Trulli' region of sm beehive-shaped houses; wooded site; friendly owner; vg facs; v nice site; tennis courts; walks in forest adj."* **€35.00** **2024**

> **"There aren't many sites open at this time of year"**
>
> If you're travelling outside peak season remember to call ahead to check site opening dates – even if the entry says 'open all year'.

ANGHIARI *1D3* (0.6km S Urban) *43.53666, 12.05204* **Agrturism Vel della Pieve,** Via della Fossa, 8 - 52031(AR) **0575 788593; info@agriturismovaldellapieve.it; www.agriturismovaldellapieve.it**

12 (htd) nr nr (htd)

Fr N on the SP47 turn L on to Via della Fossa rd to the site. Sm, hdstg, pt shd, EHU (6A) inc; twin axles; Eng spkn; adv bkg acc; CKE. **€25.00** **2024**

AOSTA *1B1* (4km E Rural) *45.74088, 7.39355* **Lazy Bee Camping Village (formerly Camping Aosta),** Villaggio Clou 29, 11020 Quart (AO) **0165 765862; info@campingaosta.com; www.lazybee.it**

12

Site 1km fr Villefranche at Quart on SS26. 2*, Med, shd, pt sl, terr, EHU (6A) inc; 80% statics; phone; bike hire. *"Ltd touring pitches; poorly-maintained site; pool 5km; NH only."* **€36.00** **2024**

ITALY

AOSTA *1B1* (5km SW Rural) *45.71706, 7.26161*
Camping Monte Bianco, St Maurice 15, 11010 Sarre (AO) **0165 258514; info@campingmontebianco.it; www.campingmontebianco.it**
WD MSP nr nr nr

Fr A5/E25 exit Aosta W twd Aosta, site on R, well sp. Fr Mont Blanc tunnel on S26 site on R at Sarre 500m past St Maurice sp. W fr Aosta, site on L 100m past boundary sp St Maurice/Sarre, yellow sp. Turn into site poss tight for lge o'fits. 2*, Sm, pt shd, terr, EHU (6-10A) €2.80; gas; red long stay; phone; bus fr site to Aosta; Eng spkn; adv bkg acc; CKE. *"Sm, gd, family-run site set in orchard on rv; friendly, helpful; excel tourist info; beautiful alpine scenery & walks; last tunnel is close to exit when coming fr Mont Blanc do not rely on sat nav to restart in time; bar 100m; pool 4km; pleasant site; supmkt 2km; fascinating walled Roman town; many archaeological sites to visit."*
€28.00, 1 May-30 Sep. **2023**

AQUILEIA *2E1* (0.3km NE Rural) *45.77786, 13.36943*
Camping Aquileia, Via Gemina 10, 33051 Aquileia (UD) **0431 91042; info@campingaquileia.it; www.campingaquileia.it**
€3 WD MSP nr

Fr A4/E70 take Grado/Palmanova exit & foll sp Grado on SS352. Turn L at traff lts at ent to Aquileia. Site in 400m on R. Fr SS14 turn onto SS352, site sp. 2*, Med, shd, EHU (6A) inc; red long stay; 10% statics; bus 300m; ccard acc; CKE. *"Excel site; lge pitches; 10 mins walk thro Roman ruins to magnificent, unique basilica & mosaics; poss noisy concerts July festival week; gd, friendly site; great site."*
€30.50, 1 May-30 Sep. **2024**

AQUILEIA *2E1* (3km S Coastal) *45.72640, 13.39860*
Camping Village Belvedere Pineta, Via Martin Luther King, 33051 Belvedere-di-Grado (UD) **0431 91007; info@belvederepineta.it; www.belvederepineta.it**
€7.50 WD MSP sand adj

Fr Venezia/Trieste a'strada, exit for Palmanova & foll Grado sp on S352 to Aquileia. Drive thro Belvedere, & site is nr lagoon. Slow app to site due to uneven surface. 4*, V lge, mkd, shd, EHU (3-6A) inc; gas; bbq; red long stay; 50% statics; train 10km at Cervignano; adv bkg acc; bike hire; tennis; excursions; waterslide; games rm; watersports; golf 5km; games area; CKE. *"Wooded site - poss mosquitoes; steamer trips fr Grado; gd touring base, inc Venice; red for Seniors; excel site with v clean san facs."*
€59.00, 1 May-30 Sep. **2024**

ARCO *2D1* (6km SSW Coastal) *45.87614, 10.86779*
Camping Bellavista, Via Gardesana, 31, 38062 Arco **0464 505644; info@camping-bellavista.it; www.camping-bellavista.it**
€3.50 WD MSP

Fr A22 take exit for Roveretto Sud-Lago di Garda; at rndabt take 4th exit twrds Riva Del Garda; in 3km turn L onto SS240. After town cent in 8km take L into site bef lakeside tunnel, just after Lidl supmkt on L. Med, mkd, shd, EHU (3A) inc; bbq; twin axles; phone; bus 100m; Eng spkn; bike hire. *"Lakeside; v busy but v pleasant site; direct access to beach; takeaway; excel, immac san facs; vg & reasonable rest; next to supmkt; town cent 5 min walk along lakeside path; vg touring area for northern towns of lake Garda; excel site."* **€38.00, 1 Apr-30 Oct.** **2024**

AREZZO *1D3* (10km SW Rural) *43.44982, 11.78990*
Camping Villaggio Le Ginestre, Loc Ruscello 100, 52100 Arezzo **0575 363566; info@campingleginestre.it; www.campingleginestre.it**
(htd) WD MSP nr

Onto A1 sp Arezzo. Foll sp to Battifolle & Ruscello, proceed for 2km to rndabt, turn L to Ruscello and foll sp to site which is on the L. 3*, Med, hdstg, pt shd, pt sl, terr, EHU (5-10A) inc; 5% statics; bus; adv bkg acc; ccard acc; tennis; site clsd Jan; games area; games rm; CKE. *"Pleasant tiered grassy site with views; friendly owner; gd rest (clsd Mon); trains fr Arezzo to Florence, Rome etc; gd touring base/NH."*
€29.00, 10 Mar-31 Oct. **2023**

ARONA *1B1* (8km N Rural) *45.81583, 8.54992*
Camping Solcio, Via al Campeggio, 28040 Solcio-de-Lesa (NO) **0322 7497; info@campingsolcio.com; www.campingsolcio.com**
€3.80 (htd) WD MSP

Foll S33 N fr Arona, thro Meina campsite on R of rd app Solcio; well sp, adj boatyard.
2*, Med, mkd, pt shd, EHU (6A) inc; gas; bbq; sw nr; red long stay; 40% statics; phone; Eng spkn; adv bkg acc; fishing; boat hire; watersports; CKE. *"Gd site adj lake; some sm pitches; premium for lakeside pitches; gd rest; gd cent for area; conv Stresa and Borromeo Islands; friendly; highly rec; beach has permanent wooden parasols; immac san facs; lovely site."*
€43.90, 12 Mar-17 Oct. **2023**

ASSISI *2E3* (3km W Rural) *43.07611, 12.57361* **Green Village Assisi,** Via San Giovanni Campiglione 110, 06081 Assisi (PG) **075 813710 or 075 816813; prenotazioni@greenvillageassisi.it; www.greenvillageassisi.it**

€2

Fr Perugia SS75 to Ospedalicchio, then SS147 twd Assisi. Site well sp on R bef Assisi. Fr Assisi take SS147 to Perugia. Site on L in 3km adj Hotel Green. 3*, Lge, mkd, shd, EHU 6A inc; gas; 40% statics; phone; bus; Eng spkn; adv bkg rec; ccard acc; tennis; car wash; CKE. *"Helpful staff; minibus to Assisi; lovely, tidy, clean site; busy even in LS; immac san facs; gd rest; sm pitches; caves at Genga worth visit; excel; 10% red on next site if pt of same chain; v conv for visiting local area."* **€34.00, 23 Mar-2 Nov. 2024**

ASTI *1B2* (15km S Rural) *44.79688, 8.24183* **International Camping Le Fonti,** Via Alle Fontane 54, 14041 Agliano Terme **0141 954820; info@campinglefonti.eu; www.campinglefonti.eu**

(htd)

Fr A21 Torino to Alessandria exit Asti Est, dir Alba. Then Isola d'Asti exit, rd 456. Camp sp at the end of Montegrosso d'Asti vill, R twds Agliano Terme. 3*, Med, mkd, shd, terr, EHU (6A); bbq; twin axles; TV; 10% statics; Eng spkn; games area. *"Beautiful (if challenging) area for cycling; v friendly & helpful staff; some pitches small & diff to access; v gd."* **€28.50, 25 Mar-30 Oct. 2022**

ASTI *1B2* (2km NW Rural) *44.94087, 8.18726* **Camping Umberto Cagni,** Loc Valmanera 152, 14100 Asti **0141 271238; info@campingcagniasti.it; www.campingcagniasti.it**

€2

Leave A21 at Asti E. Foll sp to Asti. At beg of town cntre with Asti Service Stn on L; turn R foll sp to camping site. 2*, Med, shd, pt sl, EHU €3; 50% statics; games area; CKE. *"Fair NH/sh stay; friendly staff; not suitable lge o'fits; poss travellers; gates clsd 1300-1500."* **€23.50, 1 Apr-30 Sep. 2020**

BARDOLINO *1D2* (1.2km N Rural) *45.56388, 10.71416* **Camping La Rocca,** Loc San Pietro, Via Gardensana 37, 37011 Bardolino (VR) **045 7211111; info@campinglarocca.com; www.campinglarocca.com**

€5.90 shgl adj

Exit A22/E45 Affi/Lago di Garda Sud & foll SR249 sp Bardolino. Camp 1st site on both sides of rd exit town at km 53/IV. 3*, V lge, shd, EHU (10A) inc; bbq; sw; TV; 15% statics; phone; Eng spkn; ccard acc; bike hire; fishing; CKE. *"Pleasant, popular site; gd views; avoid field nr lake; lakeside walk to Garda or Bardolino 20mins; mkt Thurs Bardolino, Fri Garda; red snr citizens."* **€52.00, Easter-6 Oct. 2024**

BARDOLINO *1D2* (2km S Rural) *45.52525, 10.72977* **Camping Cisano/San Vito,** Via Peschiera 48, 37011 Cisano (VR) **045 6229098; cisano@camping-cisano.it; www.camping-cisano.it**

Sites on S boundary of Cisano, on SE shore of Lake Garda. 4*, V lge, mkd, shd, sl, terr, EHU (16A) inc; gas; sw nr; TV; Eng spkn; windsurfing; canoeing; waterskiing; waterslide; bike hire; games area; tennis. *"Two lovely, clean, lakeside sites run as one - San Vito smaller/quieter; helpful staff; san facs in need of refurb; some pitches diff access & chocks req; passport req at site check-in; Verona Opera excursions arranged high ssn; gd; v popular; helpful staff; gd walking/cycling; gd rest."* **€54.00, 23 Mar-15 Oct. 2023**

BAROLO *1B2* (1km W Rural) *44.61246, 7.92106* **Camping Sole Langhe,** Piazza della Vite e Del Vino, Frazione Vergne, 12060 Barolo (CN) **0173 560510; info@solelanghe.com; www.solelanghe.com**

nr

Fr S exit A6 E sp Carru. At Carru turn N onto SP12 & foll sp Barolo. Site sp on ent Barolo. Sm, hdg, pt shd, EHU (6A) inc; bbq; Eng spkn; games area. *"Lovely orchard site in cent Barolo wine region; v helpful owner; highly rec."* **€30.00, 20 Mar-30 Nov. 2023**

BARREA *2F4* (2km S Rural) *41.74978, 13.99128* **Camping La Genziana,** Loc Tre Croci 1, 67030 Barrea (AQ) **0864 88101; info@campinglagenziana.it; www.campinglagenzianapasetta.it**

€3 nr

Fr S83 to S end Lago di Barrea, thro Barrea S, site immed on L on uphill L-hand bend. 2*, Med, mkd, pt shd, terr, EHU (3A) €2.60; bbq; sw nr; bus; Eng spkn; adv bkg acc. *"Knowledgeable owner; delightful site; excel area cycling; trekking, skiing; ltd shops Barrea 10 mins walk; conv Abruzzi National Park; updated facs (2015)."* **€33.50, 5 Apr-20 Oct. 2022**

BASCHI *2E3* (13km NE Rural) *42.70722, 12.2920* **Camping Il Falcone,** Loc Vallonganino 2A, Loc Civitella-del-Lago, 05023 Baschi (TR) **0744 950249 & 075 843690 & 328 3272851; info@campingilfalcone.com; www.campingilfalcone.com**

Fr Orvieto take SS205 dir Baschi then S448 alongside Lago di Corbaro. Turn R sp Civitella. Uphill for 4km to site. 2*, Sm, mkd, hdstg, pt shd, terr, EHU (3A) inc; gas; bbq; red long stay; TV; Eng spkn; adv bkg acc; ccard acc; games rm; sep car park; CKE. *"Lovely site in olive grove & woods; quiet; excel clean san facs; some pitches poss diff lge o'fits."* **€34.10, 1 Apr-30 Sep. 2023**

ITALY

BASTIA MONDOVI *1B2* (1km N Rural) *44.44871, 7.89417* **Camping La Cascina,** Loc Pieve 3, 12060 Bastia-Mondovi (CN) **0174 60181; info@campinglacascina.it; www.campinglacascina.it**

Fr Cuneo on S564 turn R at rndabt adj to Rv Tanaro sp to Bastìa Mondovi, site on R in 500m. 2*, Lge, pt shd, EHU (6A) €2.50; 90% statics; phone; Eng spkn; ccard acc; site clsd Sep; games area; CKE. *"Touring vans on edge of sports field; conv wine vills; hot water poss erratic; v busy w/end high ssn."* **€35.50, 2 Jan-24 Dec. 2024**

BELLAGIO *1C1* (1.8km S Rural) *45.97093, 9.25381* **Clarke Camping,** Via Valassina 170/C, 22021 Bellagio, Como **031 951325; elizabethclarke54@icloud.com; www.bellagio-camping.com**

Fr Como, on arr in Bellagio foll sp Lecco to R, foll site sps uphill. Narr rds & site ent. Med, pt shd, terr, EHU (16A) €2; sw nr. *"Friendly British owner; views over lake; uphill walk fr town to campsite; town is on lakeside; site & ent not suitable for o'fits over 7m; ferries, water taxis 1.5km; no twin axles; beautiful, peaceful site; basic san facs but clean; use vehicle ferry fr Cadenabbis or Varenne €20 for m'van & 2 people, then foll dirs."* **€34.00, 1 May-20 Sep. 2022**

BELLARIA *2E2* (2km NE Coastal) *44.16076, 12.44836* **Happy Camping Village,** Via Panzini 228, San Mauro a Mare, 47814 Bellaria (RN) **0541 346102; info@happycamping.it; www.happycamping.it**

Fr A14 exit Rimini Nord onto S16 N. Turn off dir San Mauro Mare & Bellaria Cagnona, foll sp Aquabell Waterpark. Over rlwy x-ing, turn R, site on L. 4*, Lge, mkd, hdstg, pt shd, pt sl, EHU (8-10A) €3.50; gas; TV; 40% statics; phone; Eng spkn; adv bkg acc; tennis; games area; games rm; CKE. *"Conv Rimini, San Marino; variable size pitches; clean, private beach; pool clsd 1300-1530 & after 1900; lge shopping cent & cinema complex 2km; Bellaria pleasant resort with port & marina."* **€39.00 2020**

BERGAMO *2C1* (25km N Rural) *45.78866, 9.94705* **Camping La Tartufaia,** Via Nazionale 2519, 24060 Ranzanico al Lago di Endine **39 035 819 259; info@latartufaia.com; www.latartufaia.com**

Fr A4 Milan-Venice, exit at Seriate. Take SS42 dir Lovere. Campsite on L past Ranzanico exit. 3*, Med, mkd, hdstg, pt shd, terr, EHU (6A) inc; gas; bbq; sw nr; twin axles; bus adj; Eng spkn; ccard acc; games rm; CCI. *"Excel site; beautiful views over lake & mountains; gd bus conns; foothpath around lake; v friendly & helpful owners."* **€41.50, 23 Apr-30 Sep. 2024**

BIBIONE *2E1* (6km W Coastal) *45.63055, 12.99444* **Camping Village Capalonga,** Viale della Laguna 16, 30020 Bibione-Pineda (VE) **0431 438351 or 0431 216100 LS; capalonga@bibionemare.com; www.capalonga.com**

Well sp approx 6km fr Bibione dir Bibione Pineda. 4*, V lge, shd, EHU (10A) inc; gas; bbq; TV; 25% statics; phone; adv bkg acc; ccard acc; excursions; watersports; games rm; archery; horseriding 6km; fishing; golf 10km; tennis. *"Well-organised site; gd for families; various activities; extra for pitches on beach; spacious, clean san facs; no o'fits over 10m high ssn; rest o'looking lagoon; blue flag sand beach; voracious mosquitoes!"* **€52.00, 24 Apr-21 Sep, Y15. 2022**

BIELLA *1B1* (88km NNW Rural) *45.84781, 7.93980* **Campeggio Alagna,** Localita Miniere, 3, 13020 Riva Valdobbia VC **0163 922947; info@campeggioalagna.it; www.campeggioalagna.it**

Site on R hand side up valley on the S299 at Riva Valdobbia, just bef Alagna Valsesia. 2*, Sm, shd, EHU; twin axles; phone; bus adj; Eng spkn; adv bkg acc; ccard acc; games area. *"Excel site."* **€20.00 2022**

BOBBIO *1C2* (1.5km S Rural) *44.75340, 9.38456* **Camping PonteGobbo Terme,** Via San Martino 4, 29022 Bobbio (PC) **0523 936927 or 0523 936068; camping.pontegobbe@iol.it; www.campingpontegobbo.com**

Heading twd Genova on S45 turn L on long bdge & immed R. Site sp. 3*, Lge, shd, pt sl, EHU (4A) €2; gas; TV; 40% statics; phone; Eng spkn; ccard acc; games area; sep car park; CKE. *"Trout-fishing in rv; gd scenery; lovely town; hot water to shwrs only; no dogs; rvside walks and cycling."* **€21.50 2024**

BOLOGNA *1D2* (2km NE Rural) *44.52333, 11.37388* **Centro Turistico Campeggio Città di Bologna,** Via Romita 12/4a, 40127 Bologna **051 325016; info@hotelcamping.com; www.hotelcamping.com**

Access is fr A14 Bologna to Ancona. Leave at junc 7 sp Fiera & Via Stalingrado. Can be accessed fr the parallel 'Tangenziale' at same junc. Sp at 1st junc after toll. 3*, Med, mkd, pt shd, EHU (6A) inc; bbq (charcoal, gas); red long stay; TV; bus to city; Eng spkn; adv bkg acc; ccard acc; site clsd 20 Dec-9 Jan; games rm; CKE. *"Conv Bologna Trade Fair & Exhibition cent; friendly, helpful staff; excel, clean san facs; fitness cent; excel pool; tourist pitches at rear nr san facs block; no o'fits over 15m on hdstg & over 9m on grass; gd bus service fr ent into city; access to pitches poss diff lge o'fits; sat nav dir may take you down narr rds; poss lots mosquitoes; excel site."* **€35.00, 20 Jan-18 Dec, Y14. 2022**

ITALY

BOLSENA *1D3* (2km S Rural) *42.62722, 11.99444* **Camping Village Lido di Bolsena,** Via Cassia, Km 111, 01023 Bolsena (VT) **0761 799258 or 0761 797048; info@bolsenacamping.it; www.bolsenacamping.it**
sand adj

Fr S on a'strada A1 foll sp Viterbo & Lago di Bolsena, then take SR2 N to site; sp. Fr N exit A1 at Orvieto onto SS71 to Bolsena. At traff lts in cent of town turn L, site on R in approx 2km. 4*, V lge, pt shd, EHU (3A) inc (poss rev pol); gas; sw; 10% statics; phone; Eng spkn; adv bkg acc; tennis; games area; sep car park; bike hire; watersports. *"Beautiful lakeside location; gd size pitches; all facs excel; cycle path around lake to town; private bthrms avail; sm dogs acc; charge for pool."* **€38.00, 22 Apr-30 Sep.** **2024**

BOLZANO/BOZEN *1D1* (10km S Rural) *46.42982, 11.34357* **Camping-Park Steiner,** Kennedystrasse 32, 39055 Laives/Leifers (BZ) **0471 950105; info@campingsteiner.com; www.campingsteiner.com**
€5 (htd) (covrd)

Fr N take Bolzano/Bozen-Sud exit fr A22/E45 & pick up rd S12 twd Trento to site; site on R on ent Laives at N edge of vill. Fr S leave A22 at junc for Egna onto rd S12 dir Bolzano. Poorly sp. 3*, Lge, hdg, mkd, shd, pt sl, EHU (6A) inc; gas; TV; 10% statics; phone; Eng spkn; adv bkg rec; bike hire; CKE. *"Pleasant, well-run, excel site on edge of Dolomites; attractive pitches; helpful staff; gd, clean, modern san facs; gates clsd 1300-1500 & 2200-0700; no dogs high ssn; beautiful area; vg walking; well stocked shop; highly rec; easy 5 min walk into town; excel rest; busy in high ssn; excel value transport passes fr TO."* **€40.00, 12 Mar-31 Oct.** **2022**

BOLZANO/BOZEN *1D1* (2km NW Rural) *46.50333, 11.3000* **Camping Moosbauer,** Via San Maurizio 83, 39100 Bolzano **0471 918492; info@moosbauer.com; www.moosbauer.com**
12 €4 (htd) (htd)

Exit A22/E45 at Bolzano Sud exit & take S38 N dir Merano (keep L after toll booths). After tunnel take 1st exit sp Eppan & hospital, & turn L at top of feeder rd sp Bolzano. After approx 2km at island past 08 G'ge turn L & foll site sp. Site on R in 1km by bus stop on S38, sp. 4*, Med, hdstg, mkd, hdg, pt shd, pt sl, serviced pitches; EHU (5A) inc; TV (pitch); bus; Eng spkn; adv bkg acc; games rm; CKE. *"Popular, well-maintained, attractive site; gd welcome fr friendly owners; pitches narr; excel, modern san facs; gate shut 1300-1500; bus service adj for archaeological museum (unique ice man); gd cent for walks in Dolomites."* **€34.00** **2020**

BORGO SAN LORENZO *1D3* (5km W Rural) *43.96144, 11.30918* **Camping Mugello Verde,** Via Massorondinaio 39, 50038 San Piero-a-Sieve (FI) **055 848511 or 0331 6991844; mugelloverde@florencecamping.com; campingmugelloverde.com**
(htd)

Exit A1 at Barberino exit & foll Barberino sp twd San Piero-a-Sieve & Borgo San Lorenzo. Turn S on S65 twd Florence. Site sp immed after Cafaggiolo. 3*, Lge, pt shd, sl, terr, EHU (6A) inc; gas; 50% statics; bus/train; ccard acc; tennis; bike hire; CKE. *"Hillside site; bus to Florence high ssn (fr vill LS) or 20 mins drive; hard grnd diff for awnings; poss long walk to recep & shop; helpful, friendly staff; refurbed, gd, clean san facs; avoid early Jun - Italian Grand Prix!."* **€40.00, 21 Mar-3 Nov.** **2024**

BORGO SAN LORENZO *1D3* (28km NW Rural) *44.09810, 011.26836* **Camping La Futa,** Via Bruscoli Futa, 889/h, Firenzuola **3289248746; info@campinglafuta.it; www.campinglafuta.it**
€2 (htd)

A1 Bologna to Firenze - exit Roncobiaccio SS65 to Passo Della Futa. Site close to pass. 2*, Med, mkd, pt shd, terr, EHU (10A); bbq; twin axles; TV; 25% statics; phone; Eng spkn; adv bkg acc; games rm; games area; CKE. *"Excel site."* **€28.00, 15 Apr-30 Sep.** **2022**

BRACCIANO *2E4* (3km N Rural) *42.1300, 12.17333* **Kwan Village Roma Flash Sporting,** Via Settevene Palo 42, 00062 Bracciano **0699 805458 or 3389 951738 LS; info@romaflash.it; https://www.camping.it/en/lazio/romaflash/**
€5.50

Fr A1 exit at Magliano Sabina dir Civita Castellana. Then foll sp Nepi, Sutri, Trevignano & Bracciano. Sp on lakeside rd N of Bracciano. 3*, Lge, mkd, pt shd, EHU (6A) inc; bbq (charcoal, gas); sw; TV; 5% statics; bus to Bracciano, bus/train to Rome; Eng spkn; ccard acc; games rm; sauna; horseriding 4km; bike hire; fishing; watersports; tennis. *"Attractive, well-kept lakeside site; clean, modern san facs; fitness cent; no o'fits over 12m; sep car park; conv Rome."* **€42.00, 1 Apr-29 Sep, Y16.** **2022**

BRUNICO/BRUNECK *1D1* (10km E Rural) *46.77600, 12.03688* **Camping Residence Corones,** Niederrasen 124, 39030 Rasun di-Sotto/Niederrasen (BZ) **0474 496490; info@corones.com; www.corones.com**
€4.20 (htd)

On SS49 dir Rasun, turn N to site to Antholz, bear L in front of Gasthof, over bdge turn L, site in 400m. 4*, Med, pt shd, serviced pitches; EHU (3A) metered; gas; 10% statics; phone; Eng spkn; adv bkg acc; ccard acc; solarium; tennis; bike hire; sauna; games area. *"Gd cent for walking & skiing - outings arranged; superb facs, inc in winter; private bthrms avail; conv day visit to Dolomites; helpful owner & staff; excel."* **€33.00, 1 Dec-19 Apr & 20 May-25 Oct.** **2024**

ITALY

CANNOBIO *1C1* (0.2km N Rural) *46.06515, 8.6905* **Camping Riviera,** Via Casali Darbedo 2, 28822 Cannobio (VB) **0323 71360; riviera@riviera-valleromantica.com; www.riviera-valleromantica.com**

€4.50

N of Cannobio twd Switzerland on main rd. Over rv at o'skts of town, site ent on R in 30m; sp. 2*, Lge, mkd, hdg, shd, EHU (4A) €4; gas; sw nr; 10% statics; adv bkg rec; boat hire; windsurfing. *"Popular, peaceful, well-maintained site bet rv & lake; extra for lakeside pitch; gd sailing; private san facs some pitches; v helpful staff."* **€47.00, 1 Apr-18 Oct.** **2024**

CANNOBIO *1C1* (0.5km N Urban) *46.06678, 8.69507* **Camping Del Sole,** Via Sotto i Chiosi 81/A, 28822 Cannobio (VB) **0323 70732; info@campingsole.it; www.campingsole.it**

€3 nr

Fr S fr A26 foll Verbania sp then sp Cannobio or Locarno. Ent vill, over cobbles, 2nd R in 750m. Bef rv bdge immed sharp R under main rd, site on L after quick R turn. Fr N ent Cannobio, 1st L after x-ing rv, then as above. 2*, Lge, hdg, mkd, hdstg, pt shd, EHU (4A) €3; gas; sw nr; red long stay; 60% statics; Eng spkn; CKE. *"Attractive vill & lake frontage; friendly, family-run site; poss tight access some pitches; lovely pool area; cramped pitches; diff to park m'van; dated clean san facs; close to town; fair."* **€50.00, 1 Jan-7 Jan, 9 Feb-31 Dec.** **2024**

CANNOBIO *1C1* (1km N Rural) *46.07791, 8.69345* **Villaggio Camping Bosco,** Punta Bragone, 28822 Cannobio (VB) **0323 739647**

€4 shgl

On W side of lakeshore rd bet Cannobio & Swiss frontier. Sh steep app to site & hairpin bend fr narr rd, unsuitable for car/c'van o'fits & diff for m'vans. 2*, Med, pt shd, terr, EHU (3A) €3.90; gas; bbq; sw; Eng spkn; adv bkg rec; CKE. *"All pitches with magnificent lake view; beautiful town; hot water to shwrs only."* **€37.30, 31 Mar-8 Oct.** **2023**

CANNOBIO *1C1* (1.5km N Urban) *46.07136, 8.69366* **Camping Campagna,** Via Casali Darbedo, 20-22 - 28822 Cannobio (VB) **0323 70100; info@campingcampagna.it; www.campingcampagna.it**

€5 shgl

Brissago-Cannobio rd, site on L on ent town. 2*, Med, shd, EHU (6-10A) €4; gas; 10% statics; Eng spkn; adv bkg acc. *"Steamer trips on Lake Maggiore; vg Sunday mkt in Cannobio; vg, modern facs; friendly staff; clean; friendly staff; fabulous views of lake."* **€47.00, 15 Mar-15 Nov.** **2024**

CANNOBIO *1C1* (1.5km SW Rural) *46.05756, 8.67831* **Camping Valle Romantica,** Via Valle Cannobina, 28822 Cannobio (VB) **0323 71249; valleromantica@riviera-valleromantica.com; www.riviera-valleromantica.com**

€4

Turn W on S o'skirts of Cannobio, sp Valle Cannobina. In 1.5km at fork keep L. Site immed on R. On ent site cont to bottom of hill to park & walk back to recep. 2*, Lge, hdg, mkd, pt shd, pt sl, terr, EHU (4-6A) €4.50; 25% statics; adv bkg acc; golf 12km. *"Vg; some sm pitches; particularly helpful& friendly staff; narr site rds poss diff m'vans; masses of flowers; beautiful situation; footpath to town, poss cr high ssn; v well kept; req to show passport."* **€49.00, 1 Apr-13 Sep.** **2023**

CAORLE *2E2* (5km SW Coastal) *45.56694, 12.79416* **Camping Villaggio San Francesco,** Via Selva Rosata 1, Duna Verde, 30020 Porto-Santa-Margherita (VE) **0421 2982; info@villaggiosfrancesco.com; www.villaggiosfrancesco.com**

€3 adj

Fr A4/E70 exit Santo Stino di Livenza, then dir Caorle. By-pass town & cont on coast rd, site sp on L. 4*, V lge, shd, EHU (6A) inc; gas; TV; 60% statics; phone; waterslide; windsurfing; games area; solarium; bike hire; games rm; tennis; boat hire; waterskiing; CKE. *"Excel family facs; min 2 nights' stay."* **€44.60, 24 Apr-25 Sep.** **2022**

CAPRAROLA *2E4* (6km NW Rural) *42.33504, 12.20488* **Camping Natura,** Loc Sciente Le Coste, 01032 Caprarola (VT) **333 2505792; campingnatura@gmail.com; www.camping-natura.com**

€3

Fr Viterbo take Via Cimina sp Ronciglione. After approx 19km bef Ronciglione turn R sp Nature Reserve Lago di Vico, in 200m turn R, site sp on R in 3km. 3*, Med, mkd, pt shd, EHU (4A) €3; sw nr; ccard acc. *"Friendly site; guided walks in nature reserve; run down LS & ltd facs."* **€18.00, Easter-30 Sep.** **2020**

CASALBORDINO *2F4* (7km NE Coastal) *42.20018, 14.60897* **Camping Village Santo Stefano,** S16, Km 498, 66020 Marina-di-Casalbordino (CH) **0873 918118; booking@campingsantostefano.com; www.campingsantostefano.com**

adj

Exit A14 Vasto N onto S16 dir Pescara, site at km 498 on R. 3*, Med, mkd, shd, EHU (6A) inc; 10% statics; Eng spkn; adv bkg acc; CKE. *"Pleasant, well-maintained, family-run site; sm pitches; beautiful private beach & pool area; gd rest."* **€48.00, 21 Apr-23 Sep.** **2024**

CASTIGLIONE DEL LAGO *2E3* (1km N Rural) *43.13460, 12.04383* **Camping Listro,** Via Lungolago, Lido Arezzo, 06061 Castiglione-del-Lago (PG) **075 951193; listro@listro.it; www.listro.it**

nr

Fr N A1 Val di Chiana exit 75 bis Perugia, site clearly sp on N edge of town on lakeside. 2*, Med, mkd, pt shd, EHU (3A) inc (poss rev pol); gas; sw nr; red long stay; Eng spkn; adv bkg acc; ccard acc; tennis nr; bike hire; CKE. *"On W shore of Lake Trasimeno; facs stretched when site full; v helpful staff; sand beach & lake sw adj; bus to Perugia; rlwy stn 1km for train to Rome; 'tree fluff' a problem in spring; new san facs (2016); poor elecs."* **€22.30, 1 Apr-30 Sep.** **2022**

CAVALLINO *2E2* (2.5km S Coastal) *45.46726, 12.53006* **Union Lido Park & Resort,** Via Fausta 258, 30013 Cavallino (VE) **041 2575111; info@unionlido.com; www.unionlido.com**

(htd)

Exit a'strada A4 (Mestre-Trieste) at exit for airport or Quarto d'Altino & foll sp for Jesolo & then Punta Sabbiono; site on L 2.5km after Cavallino. 5*, V lge, mkd, shd, serviced pitches; EHU (6A) inc; gas; 50% statics; Eng spkn; adv bkg acc; ccard acc; gym; bike hire; watersports; horseriding; tennis; boating; golf; sauna; fishing. *"Variable pitch size; sat TV; late arr (after 2100) area with EHU; min stay 7 days high ssn; children's lagoon with slides; some pitches soft sand (a spade useful!); church; banking facs; Italian lessons; wellness cent; many long-stay campers; skating rink; hairdresser; babysitting; no admissions 1230-1500 (poss busy w/end); excursions; varied entmnt programme high ssn; well-organised, well-run; clean facs; worth every penny! excel."* **€75.20, 21 Apr-2 Oct.** **2023**

CAVALLINO *2E2* (5km SW Coastal) *45.45638, 12.4960* **Camping Enzo Stella Maris,** Via delle Batterie 100, 30013 Cavallino-Treporti (VE) **041 966030; info@enzostellamaris.com; www.enzostellamaris.com**

(htd) sand adj

Exit A4 at sp for airport. Foll sp Jesolo, Cavallino, Punta Sabbioni rd SW. Site sp after Ca'Ballarin. 5*, Lge, mkd, pt shd, serviced pitches; EHU (10A) inc; gas; red long stay; TV; 25% statics; phone; Eng spkn; ccard acc; fitness rm; clsd 1230-1600 & 2300-0700; games area; CKE. *"Well-run, friendly, family-owned site; excel facs; beware mosquitoes; indoor htd pool; wellness cent; €30 in LS."*
€71.30, 8 Apr-21 Oct. **2023**

CAVALLINO *2E2* (6km SW Coastal) *45.44872, 12.47116* **Camping Dei Fiori,** Via Vettor Pisani 52, 30010 Cavallino-Treporti (VE) **041 966448; fiori@vacanze-natura.it; www.deifiori.it**

sand adj

Fr Lido di Jesolo foll sp to Cavallino; site on L approx 6km past Cavallino & bef Ca'Vio. 4*, Lge, mkd, shd, serviced pitches; EHU (5A) inc (poss rev pol); gas; red long stay; Eng spkn; adv bkg req; ccard acc; games area. *"V clean & quiet even in Aug; excel facs & amenities; conv water bus stop at Port Sabbioni; hydro massage therapy; 3/5 day min stay med/high ssn; highly rec; excel."* **€22.50, 19 Apr-30 Sep.** **2022**

CECINA *1D3* (3km NW Coastal) *43.31850, 10.47440* **Camping Mareblu,** Via dei Campilunghi, Mazzanta, 57023 Cecina Mare (Li) **0586 629191; info@campingmareblu.com; www.campingmareblu.com**

sand adj

Fr S on SS1 exit sp Cecina Nord & foll dir Mazzanta, site sp. Fr N exit sp Vada then Mazzanta. 3*, Lge, hdg, mkd, pt shd, EHU (3A) inc; gas; bbq (gas); 10% statics; phone; Eng spkn; adv bkg acc; ccard acc; CKE. *"Lge pitches; gd facs & pool area; car must be parked in sep car park; no dogs Jul/Aug; ATM; well-organised, friendly site."*
€46.50, 25 Mar-21 Oct. **2023**

CERVIA *2E2* (3.6km S Coastal) *44.24760, 12.35901* **Camping Adriatico,** Via Pinarella 90, 48015 Cervia (RA) **0544 71537; info@campingadriatico.net; www.campingadriatico.net**

€6 (htd)

sand 600m

On SS16 S fr Cervia twd Pinarella, turn L at km post 175, over rlwy line & take 1st R, site sp. 3*, Lge, shd, EHU (6A) inc; TV; 40% statics; Eng spkn; adv bkg acc; ccard acc; fishing; tennis 900m; golf 5km; CKE. *"V pleasant site; friendly staff; gd san facs; excel pizza at rest; ACSI acc."* **€33.70, 14 Apr-19 Sep.** **2022**

CESENATICO *2E2* (1.5km N Coastal) *44.21545, 12.37983* **Camping Cesenatico,** Via Mazzini 182, 47042 Cesenatico (FC) **0547 81344; info@campingcesenatico.it; www.campingcesenatico.com**

12 €8.70 (htd)

(htd) sand adj

Travelling S on S16 look for Esso g'ge on R on app Cesenatico. Take 2nd L after Erg g'ge, over rlwy x-ing, site on L, sp. 3*, V lge, hdstg, mkd, pt shd, EHU (4A) €3.60; gas; red long stay; TV; 80% statics; phone; Eng spkn; adv bkg acc; ccard acc; games area; tennis; CKE. *"Many long stay winter visitors; gd touring base; unspoilt seaside resort with canal (designed by Da Vinci), port & marina; hairdresser; medical cent; excel; in easy walking/cycling dist fr Cesenatico."*
€55.00 **2024**

ITALY

CESENATICO *2E2* (2km N Coastal) *44.21584, 12.37798* **Camping Zadina,** Via Mazzini 184, 47042 Cesenatico (FC) **0547 82310; info@campingzadina.it; www.campingzadina.it**

€7 (WD) (MSP) sand

Leave A14 at Cesena Sud; foll sp Cesenático; after 10.5km turn R at T-junc onto SS16; after 2km fork L over level x-ing; site on L. Lge, mkd, pt shd, terr, EHU (6A) inc; gas; bbq; 80% statics; Eng spkn; adv bkg acc; sep car park; fishing. *"Sea water canal runs thro site; pitches poss tight lge o'fits; gd."*
€43.00, 15 Apr-20 Sep. **2024**

CHIOGGIA *2E2* (2km E Urban/Coastal) *45.19027, 12.30361* **Camping Miramare,** Via A. Barbarigo 103, 30015 Sottomarina (VE) **041 490610; info@miramarecamping.com; www.miramarecamping.com**

€3.50 (WD) (MSP) sand

Fr SS309 foll sp Sottomarina. In town foll brown sp to site. 4*, Lge, mkd, pt shd, EHU (6A) inc; gas; 75% statics; adv bkg acc; ccard acc; games area; CKE. *"Busy site; friendly staff; gd entmnt facs for children; cycle tracks to picturesque Chioggia; site 10 min walk fr ferry point and beach or free shuttle bus service until mid Sept; free sun umbrella for the beach front; rec; visit Venice by bus/ferry; pitches generous; private beach beautifully kept; site rest vg."*
€43.60, 20 Apr-25 Sep. **2023**

CHIUSA/KLAUSEN *1D1* (0.7km E Rural) *46.64119, 11.57332* **Camping Gamp,** Via Griesbruck 10, 39043 Chiusa/Klausen (BZ) **0472 847425; info@camping-gamp.com; www.camping-gamp.com**

€3.50 (htd) (WD) (MSP)

Exit A22 Chiusa/Klausen & bear L at end of slip rd (sp Val Gardena). Site on L at rd fork 800m, sp. 3*, Sm, mkd, pt shd, EHU (6A) €2.60; TV (pitch); phone; Eng spkn; CKE. *"Excel cent for mountain walks; Chiusa attractive town; immac facs, sep m'van o'night area; busy site; table tennis; htd ski & boot rm; some pitches sm for lge o'fits; sep m'van o'night facs; discount with Camping Euro card."*
€53.40, 1 Apr-1 Nov, 28 Nov-31 Dec. **2024**

COMO *1C1* (5km S Urban) *45.78385, 9.06034* **Camping No Stress,** Breccia, Via Cecilio, 22100 Como **031 521435; campingint@hotmail.com; camping-internazionale.business.site**

€2

Fr E to Como, on SS35 Milano rd foll sp a'strada Milano; site on Como side of rndabt at junc S35 & S432; ent/exit diff unless turn R. Or take 2nd exit off m'way after border (Como S), site sp. 2*, Med, pt shd, pt sl, EHU (4-6A) €2.50 (rev pol); gas; ccard acc; golf 5km; bike hire. *"Conv NH for m'way."*
€24.00, 1 Apr-31 Oct. **2024**

CORIGLIANO CALABRO *3A4* (10km N Coastal) *39.69130, 16.52233* **Camping Thurium,** Contrada Ricota Grande, 87064 Ricota Grande (CS) **0983 851101 or 03280 728061; info@campingthurium.com; www.campingthurium.com**

€4.80 (WD) (MSP) sand adj

Exit SS106 at km stone 21. Site sp on gd app rd for 2km. Rd narr and bumpy in places. Do not foll sat nav. 4*, Lge, mkd, pt shd, EHU inc (3-6A); gas; twin axles; 20% statics; Eng spkn; games area; tennis; bike hire; CKE. *"Vg well-run site; windsurfing lessons; site rdways narr on corner, tight for lge o'fits; fair."*
€61.00, 1 Mar-30 Nov. **2024**

CORIGLIANO CALABRO *3A4* (7km N Coastal) *39.70333, 16.52583* **Camping Onda Azzurra,** Contrada Foggia, 87064 Corigliano-Calabro (CS) **0983 851157 or 0983 851253; info@ondaazzurracamping.com; ondaazzurracamping.com**

12 €3 (htd) (WD) (MSP) sand adj

On SS106-bis Taranto to Crotone rd, after turn off for Sibari, cont S for 6km. Turn L at 4 lge sp on 1 notice board by lge sep building, 2km to site on beach. 3*, Lge, mkd, shd, EHU (6-10A) €3-4; red long stay; 10% statics; adv bkg acc; ccard acc; tennis; bike hire; CKE. *"Excel, well-run site all ssns - facs open all yr; popular long stay; clean facs; lge pitches; water not drinkable; v friendly helpful owner; popular in winter; special meals Xmas/New Year; site conv Sybaris & Rossano; high standard site; excel friendly welcome; free acitivities LS."* **€33.00** **2024**

CORIGLIANO CALABRO *3A4* (8km N Coastal) *39.68141, 16.52160* **Camping Il Salice,** Contrada da Ricota Grande, 87064 Corigliano-Calabro (CS) **0983 851169; info@salicevacanze.it; www.salicevacanze.it**

12 €4 (htd) (WD) (MSP) sand adj

Exit A3 dir Sibari onto SS106 bis coast rd dir Crotone. At 19km marker after water tower on L, turn L sp Il Salice - 1.5km to new access rd to site on L. Site sp easily missed. 4*, Lge, mkd, hdstg, pt shd, pt sl, serviced pitches; EHU (3-6A) inc; gas; bbq; TV; 70% statics; phone; Eng spkn; watersports; games area; tennis; games rm; bike hire; CKE. *"Narr rds thro vill to site - care needed when busy; v popular, well-run winter destination; haphazard siting in pine trees; clean, private beach; modern san facs; ltd facs LS; big price red LS; scenic area."* **€48.00** **2020**

ITALY

CORTINA D'AMPEZZO *2E1* (3.5km S Rural) *46.51858, 12.1370* **Camping Dolomiti,** Via Campo di Sotto, 32043 Cortina-d'Ampezzo (BL) **0436 2485; campeggio dolomiti@tin.it; www.campeggiodolomiti.it**

(htd) (htd)

2km S of Cortina turn R off S51. Site beyond Camping Cortina & Rocchetta. 4*, Lge, mkd, pt shd, EHU (4A) inc (check earth); gas; 10% statics; phone; bus; Eng spkn; ccard acc; games area; games rm. *"Superb scenery in mountains, gd walks; cycle rte into Cortina; helpful owner; beautiful setting; choice of open meadow or shd woodland pitches; gd facs; excel shwrs."* **€24.00, 1 Jun-20 Sep.** **2024**

CORVARA IN BADIA *1D1* (2km W Rural) *46.55111, 11.8575* **Camping Colfosco,** Via Sorega 15, 39030 Corvara-in-Badia (BZ) **0471 836515; info@camping colfosco.org; www.campingcolfosco.org**

€4 nr

Leave A22 (m'way fr Brenner) at Bressanone exit foll E66/S49 E. At San Lorenzo turn S on S244 for 28km to Corvara. In town turn R dir Colfosco, foll sp. 1*, Lge, hdstg, unshd, pt sl, EHU (16A) €0.70 per kWh; bbq; twin axles; Eng spkn; adv bkg acc; ccard acc; sep car park; golf 4km; site clsd 1200-1500; games rm. *"Fine scenery & walks; well-managed site; sh walk to vill; gd base for skiing (ski in & out of site) & mountain biking; ski lift 300m; ski bus; lift/ bus passes avail; vg san facs; somewhat bleak hdstg area; site lies at 5000ft - cool nights; cycle track, walking routes nr; gd base for Passo Pordoi; vg."* **€35.50, 2 Dec-11 Apr & 3 Jun-25 Sep.** **2023**

COURMAYEUR *1A1* (6.2km NE Rural) *45.83293, 6.99095* **Campsite Grandes Jorasses,** Via per la Val Ferret 53, 11013 Courmayeur (Valle d'Aosta) **0165 869708; info@grandesjorasses.com; www.grandesjorasses.com**

Foll the brown 'Val Ferret' signs bet Courmayeur and the Mont Blanc tunnel, and the campsite is located a few km on the L of the rd. Med, hdstg, pt shd,; games rm; CKE. *"Beautiful site at the foot of Mt Blanc; nature trails thro forest; trekking expeditions arranged; gd rest."* **€26.00, 20 Jun-15 Sep.** **2024**

COURMAYEUR *1A1* (6km SE Rural) *45.76333, 7.01055* **Camping Arc en Ciel,** Loc Feysoulles, 11017 Morgex (AO) **0165 809257; info@campingarcenciel.it; www.campingarcenciel.it**

12 €1 (htd) nr

Fr A5/E25 take Morgex exit, turn L to vill & foll sp dir Dailley. Site in 1km on L, sp. Fr tunnel take SS25 to Morgex, then as above. 1*, Med, pt shd, terr, EHU (3-6A) €1-€2; bbq; 30% statics; adv bkg acc; ccard acc; sep car park; site clsd 6 Nov-8 Dec; rafting; CKE. *"Gd, clean san facs; views Mont Blanc fr some pitches; vg; ski lift 8km; mountain climbing; ski bus; views of the mountains marvellous; helpful manager."*
€27.00 **2024**

DEIVA MARINA *1C2* (3km E Coastal) *44.22476, 9.55146* **Villaggio Camping Valdeiva,** Loc Ronco, 19013 Deiva-Marina (SP) **0187 824174; camping@ valdeiva.it; www.valdeiva.it**

shgl 3km

Fr A12 exit Deiva Marina, site sp on L in approx 4km by town sp. 3*, Med, mkd, hdstg, pt shd, pt sl, EHU (3-6A) inc; bbq; TV (pitch); 90% statics; phone; bus to stn; Eng spkn; adv bkg rec; ccard acc; CKE. *"Free minibus to stn - conv Cinque Terre or Portofino; helpful, friendly staff; gd rest; sep car park high ssn; excel walking; v quiet LS & shwrs ltd; gd facs; can be long waits at rest; late night disco."* **€36.00, 1 Jan-8 Jan, 5 Feb-15 Nov & 3 Dec-31 Dec.** **2024**

DEMONTE *1B2* (1.5km N Rural) *44.32260, 7.29222* **Camping's Sun Melchio (formerly Campeggio IL Sole),** Frazione Perosa 3/B, 12014 Demonte (CN) **0334 1132724; erikamelchio@virgilio.it**

12

Fr lge town sq on S21 go E for 100m, fork L & in 100m turn L. Pass 2 churches on L, turn L, then R over rv into Via Colle dell'Urtica to N. Foll this rd uphill for 1.2km, turn L at T-junc & in 300m L at T-junc again. Site on R. Town cent side rds v narr with arches & app rd narr & steep in places. 2*, Sm, mkd, unshd, EHU €2; bbq. *"Lovely, peaceful site in mountains; vg value rest."* **€17.00** **2024**

DEMONTE *1B2* (1.5km W Rural) *44.31357, 7.27275* **Camping Piscina Demonte,** Loc Bagnolin, 12014 Demonte (CN) **338 2464353; info@campingde monte.com; www.campingdemonte.com**

€1.60 nr nr

App only fr Borgo on S21, 500m after Demonte turn L, foll sp. 1*, Med, pt shd, EHU (6A) €1.50; gas; 90% statics; adv bkg acc; ccard acc; CKE. *"Gd NH bef Col d'Larche; helpful, friendly owner; gd mountain scenery."* **€16.50, 15 Jun-15 Sep.** **2024**

DESENZANO DEL GARDA *1D2* (5km SE Rural) *45.46565, 10.59443* **Camping San Francesco,** Strada V San Francesco, 25015 Desenzano-del-Garda (BS) **030 9110245; booking@campingsanfrancesco.com; www.campingsanfrancesco.com**

E fr Milan on A4 a'strada take exit Sirmione & foll sp twd Sirmione town; join S11 twd Desenzano & after Garden Center Flowers site 1st campsite on R after rndabt; site sp twd lake bet Sirmione & Desanzano. Or fr Desenzano, site just after Rivoltella. 5*, Lge, mkd, shd, pt sl, EHU (6A) inc; gas; bbq (charcoal, gas); sw; TV; 50% statics; phone; Eng spkn; adv bkg acc; ccard acc; games area; sailing; boat hire; windsurfing; canoe hire; golf 10km; fishing; bike hire; tennis; CKE. *"Lovely lakeside pitches for tourers (extra); no o'fits over 6m high ssn; muddy if wet; poss diff lge o'fits due trees; helpful staff; well managed site; gd position on edge of lake; recep clsd 1300-1500 & no vehicle movement; handy for local bus; excel site; v clean facs; gd rest."* **€53.70, 1 Apr-30 Sep.** **2024**

ITALY

DIANO MARINA *1B3* (4km NE Coastal) *43.92177, 8.10831* **Camping del Mare,** Via alla Foce 29, 18010 Cervo (IM) **0183 400130 or 0183 405556; info@campingdelmare-cervo.com; www.campingdelmare-cervo.com**

shgl adj

Exit A10/E80 at San Bartolomeo/Cervo onto Via Aurelia. Turn L at traff lts twd Cervo. Sp adj rv bdge. R turn acute - long o'fits app fr NE.
2*, Med, mkd, hdstg, hdg, shd, EHU (6A) €2; gas; TV; 40% statics; phone; Eng spkn; adv bkg rec; ccard acc. *"Immac site; spacious pitches; friendly, helpful staff; picturesque beach & perched vill (Cervo); easy walk San Bartolomeo; gd mkts; highly rec site; pitches close together; office closes 1200-1500."*
€45.00, 1 Apr-15 Oct. 2024

"I need an on-site restaurant"

We do our best to make sure site information is correct, but it is always best to check any must-have facilities are still available or will be open during your visit.

EDOLO *1D1* (1.5km W Rural) *46.17648, 10.31333* **Camping Adamello,** Via Campeggio 10, Loc Nembra, 25048 Edolo (BS) **0364 71694 or 0333 8275354; info@campingadamello.it; www.campingadamello.it**

€3 nr

On rd 39 fr Edolo to Aprica; after 1.5km turn sharp L down narr lane by rest; camping sp on rd; diff app.
3*, Med, pt shd, pt sl, terr, EHU (6A) €1.50; 50% statics. *"Useful NH; beautiful mountain site; steep rds all round; v diff app fr W; quiet for couples; nothing for children."* **€27.00 2022**

FIANO ROMANO *2E4* (2km W Rural) *42.15167, 12.57670* **Camping I Pini,** Via delle Sassete 1/A, 00065 Fiano-Romano **0765 453349; ipini@huopenair.com; https://ipini.huopenair.com/**

€2 (htd)

Fr A1/E35 exit sp Roma Nord/Fiano Romano (use R-hand lane for cash toll), foll sp Fiano at rndabt. Take 1st exit at next rndabt sp I Pini & stay on this rd for approx 2km. Take 2nd exit at next rndabt, L at T-junc under bdge, site sp on R. 4*, Med, mkd, hdg, pt shd, pt sl, terr, EHU (6A) inc (poss rev pol); bbq; TV; 60% statics; phone; bus; Eng spkn; adv bkg rec; ccard acc; fishing; games rm; tennis; horseriding nr; bike hire; CKE. *"Well-run, clean, excel san facs; helpful, friendly staff; excel rest; access poss diff lge o'fits; kerbs to all pitches; most pitches slope badly side to side req double height ramps; no o'fits over 10m high ssn; excursions by coach inc daily to Rome or gd train service; super site."* **€38.00, 28 May-4 Sep, Y13. 2022**

FIE/VOLS *1D1* (3km N Rural) *46.53334, 11.53335* **Camping Alpe di Siusi/Seiser Alm,** Loc San Constantino 16, 39050 Fiè-allo-Sciliar/Völs-am-Schlern (BZ) **0471 706459; info@camping-seiseralm.com; www.camping-seiseralm.com**

€4.50 (htd)

Leave Bolzano on SS12 (not A22) sp Brixen & Brenner. After approx 7km take L fork in tunnel mouth sp Tiers, Fiè. Foll rd thro Fiè, site in 3km dir Castelrotto, sp on L.
4*, Lge, mkd, hdstg, unshd, terr, EHU (16A) metered; TV (pitch); 20% statics; phone; bus; Eng spkn; adv bkg acc; golf 1km; sauna; site clsd 5 Nov to 20 Dec; CKE. *"Well-organised site with gd views; impressive, luxury undergrnd san facs block; private san facs avail; vg walking/skiing; an amazing experience; v popular site; efficiently run!"*
€47.00, 1 Jan-2 Nov & 20 Dec-31 Dec. 2024

FIESOLE *1D3* (1km NE Rural) *43.80666, 11.30638* **Camping Panoramico,** Via Peramonda 1, 50014 Fiesole (FI) **055 599069; panoramico@florencevillage.com; https://www.campingpanoramicofiesole.com/en/**

Foll sp for Fiesole & Camping Panoramico fr Florence; site on R. Rd to Fiesole v hilly & narr thro busy tourist area. 3*, Lge, pt shd, terr, EHU (3A) inc; gas; 20% statics; Bus; Eng spkn; ccard acc. *"Access v diff - more suitable tenters; site soggy in wet; ltd water points; Florence 20 mins bus but 1.5km steep walk to stop; excel views; excel site."* **€39.00 2020**

FIGLINE VALDARNO *1D3* (20km SW Rural) *43.53847, 11.41380* **Camping Orlando in Chianti,** Localita Caffggiolo, 52022 Cavriglia **055 967 422; info@campingorlandoinchianti.it; www.campingorlandoinchianti.it**

Fr A1 Firenze-Roma, exit Incisa. Foll Figline Val d'Arno. Dir Greve in Chianti, exit at Lucolena, then foll signs to 'Piano Orlando Parco Cavriglia'.
Med, hdstg, mkd, shd, pt sl, EHU (16A); bbq; 10% statics; Eng spkn; adv bkg acc; CCI. *"Vg site; excel priced rest; rural; v friendly staff."* **€62.00, 18 Apr-13 Oct. 2024**

FIGLINE VALDARNO *1D3* (2.5km W Rural) *43.61111, 11.44940* **Camping Norcenni Girasole Club,** Via Norcenni 7, 50063 Figline-Valdarno (FI) **055 915141; girasole@ecvacanze.it; https://norcenni.huopenair.com/**

(covrd, htd)

Fr a'strada A1, dir Rome, take exit 24 (sp Incisa SS69) to Figline-Valdarno; turn R in vill & foll sp to Greve; site sp Girasole; steep app rd to site with some twists for 3km. 4*, V lge, hdg, pt shd, terr, EHU (6A) inc; gas; bbq; twin axles; TV; bus to Florence; Eng spkn; adv bkg acc; ccard acc; sauna; horseriding; games area; tennis; excursions; jacuzzi; games rm; bike hire. *"Excel, well-run site; some pitches sm; fitness cent; steep site rds poss diff lge o'fits; private bthrm extra; steel pegs rec; upper level pool area excel for children; site clsd 1330-1530; site hilly; gd touring base."* **€35.00, 23 Apr-25 Sept, Y07. 2022**

FINALE LIGURE *1B2* (1.5km N Rural) *44.18395, 8.35349* **Eurocamping Calvisio,** Via Calvisio 37, 17024 Finale-Ligure (SV) **019 601240; info@eurocampingcalvisio.it; www.eurocampingcalvisio.it**

sand 2km

On SS1 Savona-Imperia, turn R at ent to Finale-Ligure; sp to site in Calvisio vill. 3*, Med, hdg, mkd, shd, EHU (6A) inc; 80% statics; adv bkg acc; ccard acc; solarium. *"Security guard at night; sep car park high ssn; clean, well-maintained san facs."*
€54.50, Easter-5 Nov. **2022**

FIRENZE *1D3* (24km SE Rural) *43.70138, 11.40527* **Camping Village Il Poggetto,** Via Fiorentina, 212 - 50067 Troghi **055 8307323; info@campingilpoggetto.com; www.campingilpoggetto.com**

€2.20

Fr S on E35/A1 a'strada take Incisa exit & turn L dir Incisa. After 400m turn R dir Firenze, site in 5km on L. Fr N on A1 exit Firenze-Sud dir Bagno a Ripoli/S. Donato; go thro S. Donato to Troghi, site on R, well sp. Narr, hilly app rd & sharp turn - app fr S easier. Lge, mkd, hdg, pt shd, pt sl, terr, EHU (7A) inc (poss rev pol); gas; red long stay; 5% statics; phone; bus adj; Eng spkn; adv bkg req; ccard acc; table tennis; bike hire; CKE. *"Superb, picturesque, family-run site in attractive location inc vineyard; clean, modern facs; lovely pool; bus to Florence 45mins - tickets fr recep; trains fr Incisa Valdarno (free parking at stn); excursions; gd rest; LS offers for long stay (7+ days); money exchange; vg site; helpful staff; private san facs avail; lge o'fits come fr S; highly rec."*
€47.00, 1 Apr-31 Oct. **2023**

FORNI DI SOPRA *2E1* (2km E Rural) *46.42564, 12.56928* **Camping Tornerai,** Stinsans. Via Nazionale, 33024 Forni-di-Sopra (UD) **0433 88035; www.campingtornerai.it**

12 €2 (cont)

Site sp on SS52 Tolmezzo-Pieve di Cadore rd, 2km E of Forni-di-Sopra (approx 35km by rd fr Pieve-di-Cadore). Sm, pt shd, pt sl, EHU (2A) €1 (extra for 6A) (long lead poss req); 50% statics; Eng spkn; ccard acc. *"Conv CL-type site for Forni-di-Sopra chairlift & Passo-della-Mauria; gd san facs."* **€20.00** **2022**

GALLIPOLI *3A4* (4km SE Coastal) *39.99870, 18.02590* **Camping Baia di Gallipoli,** Litoranea per Santa Maria di Leuca, 73014 Gallipoli (LE) **0833 273210 or 338 8322910 LS; info@baiadigallipoli.com; www.baiadigallipoli.com**

€3 (htd) sand 800m

Fr Brindisi/Lecce take S101 to Gallipoli. Exit at sp Matino-Lido Pizzo & foll sp to site, on coast rd bet Gallipoli & Sta Maria di Leuca. 4*, V lge, pt shd, EHU (6A) inc; bbq; TV; ccard acc; tennis; excursions; games area; sep car park. *"Gd site; small dogs only."*
€65.00, 25 May-30 Sep. **2024**

GENOVA *1C2* (15km W Coastal) *44.41437, 8.70475* **Caravan Park La Vesima,** Via Aurelia, Km 547, 16100 Arenzano (GE) **010 6199673 or 6199672; info@caravanparklavesima.it; www.caravanparklavesima.it**

12 (htd) shgl adj

E of Arenzano on coast rd, clearly sp. Or leave A10 at Arenzano & go E on coast rd. 2*, Med, hdstg, mkd, unshd, EHU (3A) inc (poss rev pol); gas; 90% statics; Eng spkn; adv bkg acc; CKE. *"Useful LS NH/sh stay; gd security; gd, clean san facs; v cr, noisy high ssn; some pitches sm; vg site."* **€42.00** **2023**

GRAVEDONA *1C1* (3km SW Rural) *46.13268, 9.28954* **Camping Magic Lake,** Via Vigna del Lago 60, 22014 Dongo (CO) **034 480282; camping@magiclake.it; www.magiclake.it**

€3 (htd) nr

Site sp on S340d adj Lake Como. 2*, Sm, pt shd, pt sl, EHU (6A) inc; bbq; sw nr; red long stay; TV; 40% statics; bus 100m; Eng spkn; adv bkg acc; CKE. *"Excel, friendly, family-run site; walk, cycle to adj vills along lake; excel facs; v clean mod facs; bike/kayak hire on site; bike repairs on site; helpful staff."*
€30.00, 1 Apr-10 Oct. **2022**

GUBBIO *2E3* (1.2km W Urban) *43.35213, 12.56704* **Camper Club Gubbio,** Via Bottagnone 06024 Area Communale P4 **07 59 27 20 37 / 07592 77316; sede@camperclubgubbio.it; camperclubgubbio.it**

12

Head NW on SR298 twd Via Bruno Buozzi, at rndbt take 2nd exit onto Viale Parruccini cont for 500m, take 1st exit at rndabt onto Viale Leonardo da Vinci, after 250m turn L onto Via Botagore. Sm, pt shd,. *"Only campervan parking allowed; no san facs; gd NH; historical town worth a visit."* **€5.00** **2024**

IDRO *1D1* (2km NE Rural) *45.7540, 10.4981* **Rio Vantone,** Via Vantone 45, 25074 Idro (BS) **0365 83125; idro@azur-camping.de; www.idrosee.eu**

€6

Fr Brescia, take S237 N. At S tip of Lago d'Idro, turn E to Idro. thro Crone, on E shore of lake, thro sh tunnel, site 1km on L, last of 3 sites.
4*, Lge, shd, serviced pitches; EHU (6A) inc; gas; TV; phone; adv bkg acc; ccard acc; games area; boat hire; windsurfing; bike hire; tennis; CKE. *"Idyllic on lakeside with beautiful scenery; lake adj; superb san facs; excel."*
€40.00, 1 Apr-16 Oct, Y08. **2022**

*Last year of report

ITALY

IMPERIA *1B3* (1km SW Coastal) *43.86952, 7.99810*
Camping de Wijnstok, Via Poggi 2, 18100 Porto-Maurizio (IM) **0183 64986; info@campingdewijnstok.com; www.campingdewijnstok.com**
nr shgl 500m

Exit A10/E80 Imperia W twds sea, take coast rd SS1 Via Aurelia dir San Remo. At km 651/1 turn dir Poggi, site sp. Med, shd, EHU (3A) €2; gas; TV; 80% statics; phone; ccard acc; sep car park; site clsd mid-Dec to mid-Jan. *"Shabby facs ltd LS; sm pitches diff for lge o'fits; sh walk to town; NH only."*
€31.00 **2022**

ISEO *1C1* (0.5km NE Rural) *45.66416, 10.05722*
Camping Iseo, Via Antonioli 57, 25049 Iseo (BS) **030 980213; info@campingiseo.it; www.campingiseo.it**
€3.50 nr adj

Fr A4 exit sp Rovato & immed foll brown sp Lago d'Iseo. Site well sp in vill. 3*, Med, hdg, pt shd, serviced pitches; EHU (6-10A) €2; gas; 10% statics; phone; Eng spkn; adv bkg acc; windsurfing; golf 3km (red for campers); games area; bike hire; CKE. *"V scenic; friendly, welcoming owner; well-organised, smart site; sm pitches; extra for lakeside pitches; well-maintained, clean facs but ltd; cruises on lake; many rests nr; excel; site next to a rlwy line, poss sm noise; sm pitches."* **€42.00, 20 Mar-1 Nov.** **2023**

ISEO *1C1* (0.5km NE Rural) *45.66388, 10.05638*
Camping Punta d'Oro, Via Antonioli 51-53, 25049 Iseo (BS) **030 980084; info@camping-puntadoro.com; www.puntadoro.com**
€5 nr nr shgl

Fr Brescia-Boario Terme into Iseo, look for `Camping d'Iseo' sp on corner; after 200m cross rlwy, 1st R to site in 400m on lakeside. Med, pt shd, pt sl, EHU (4A) inc; sw; Eng spkn; boating; golf 6km; CKE. *"Gd security; beautiful area; friendly family run site, eager to help."*
€36.00, 1 Apr-17 Oct. **2023**

ISEO *1C1* (1km NE Rural) *45.66527, 10.06277*
Camping Quai, Via Antonioli 73, 25049 Iseo (BS) **030 9821610; info@campingquai.it; www.campingquai.it**
nr nr

Fr Brescia-Boario Terme rd by-passing Iseo, take NE exit; look for 'Camping d'Iseo' sp on corner. After 200m cross rlwy, site sp (sps obscured - go slow). Site adj Punta d'Oro on lakeside. 3*, Med, mkd, shd, EHU (4A) inc (poss rev pol); bbq; sw nr; red long stay; 25% statics; phone; bus, train 1km; Eng spkn; adv bkg acc; ccard acc; watersports; boat launch; sep car park; games area. *"Well-kept; lake views fr some pitches; helpful manager; some noise fr nrby rlwy."*
€43.00, 15 Apr-25 Sep. **2024**

ISEO *2F2* (1km E Urban) *45.66700, 10.06766*
Camping Covelo, Via Covelo 18, 25049 Iseo **030 982 13 05; info@campingcovelo.it; www.campingcovelo.it**
€3.50

Fr A4 Bergamo-Brescia, take exit Palazzolo/SP469. Cont Onto SP12. At rndabt take 2nd exit SPxi. Take 3rd exit at next rndabt and foll sp to camp. 3*, Med, pt shd, EHU (6A); sw nr; Eng spkn; adv bkg acc; ccard acc; games area. *"Excel site; v well run; adj to lake; beautiful views; range of watersports; v helpful staff."*
€44.00, 24 Apr-28 Oct. **2024**

ISEO *1C1* (1.5km W Rural) *45.65689, 10.03739*
Camping Del Sole Village, Via per Rovato 26, 25049 Iseo (BS) **030 980288; info@campingdelsole.it; www.campingdelsole.it**
€3.50 (htd)

Exit Brescia-Milan a'strada at Rivato-Lago d'Iseo exit & foll sp to Iseo. At complex rd junc with rndabts on Iseo o'skirts, site ent on L (lge sp). Site bet lakeside & rd, bef API petrol stn on R. 5*, Lge, mkd, shd, EHU (6A) inc; sw; TV; 75% statics; Eng spkn; adv bkg acc; ccard acc; sep car park; bike hire; waterskiing; tennis; games area. *"Glorious views; excel facs; htd private bthrms avail; well-run, pleasant, popular lakeside site; pitches poss closely packed; ltd waste/water disposal; no dogs high ssn; narr site rds."*
€50.00, 6 Apr-15 Oct. **2023**

ISEO *1C1* (1.5km W Rural) *45.65690, 10.03429*
Camping Sassabanek, Via Colombera 2, 25049 Iseo (BS) **030 980300; camping@sassabanek.it; www.sassabanek.it**

On periphery of Iseo by lakeside. 4*, Lge, pt shd, EHU (6A) inc; gas; bbq; TV; 50% statics; phone; adv bkg acc; ccard acc; boating; sep car park; bike hire; tennis; windsurfing; sauna. *"Clean facs; sh walk to pretty lakeside & vill; helpful staff; gd NH/sh stay; nice location; cramped pitches; vg."*
€41.40, 1 Apr-4 Oct. **2023**

LAVENA *1C1* (9km SW Rural) *45.95960, 8.86340*
International Camping di Rimoldi Claudio, Via Marconi 18, 21037 Lavena-Ponte-Tresa (VA) **0332 550117; info@internationalcamping.com; www.internationalcamping.com**
nr

On rte S233 going SW into Italy fr Switzerland, turn SE after border twd Lavena-Ponte-Tresa. Going twd Switzerland fr Italy on same rte turn R twd vill. Site sp in vill. 3*, Med, hdg, pt shd, pt sl, EHU (2-6A) €1.50; 80% statics; adv bkg acc; CKE. *"On smallest, most W bay of Lake Lugano; sand beach on lake; excel facs; ACSI card acc; friendly, helpful staff; wall around site so no lake views."* **€40.50** **2024**

LAZISE *1D2* (1.5km N Urban) *45.50807, 10.73166*
Camping Lazise Campeggio Comunale (former Municipale), Via Roma 1,37017 Lazise (VR) **045 7580020; camping.municipale@comune.lazise.vr.it; www.comune.lazise.vr.it**

€3 nr nr nr

N on S249 fr Peschiera, thro Pacengo & Lazise, at rndabt cont on S249 then turn L into Via Roma. Site sp at end of rd. Care req in 100m, sharp R turn; site ent pt hidden. 2*, Med, hdg, mkd, pt shd, EHU (10A) inc; sw nr; 5% statics; Eng spkn; ccard acc. *"Gd touring cent; some pitches v muddy; gd, clean facs; friendly staff; avoid arr bef 1500 Wed (mkt on app rd); easy walk along lake to interesting sm town."*
€33.00, 22 Mar-2 Nov. 2023

LAZISE *1D2* (0.9km S Rural) *45.49861, 10.7375*
Camping Du Parc, Via Gardesana, 110 I, 37017 Lazise (VR) **045 7580127; duparc@campingduparc.com; www.campingduparc.com**

€5.70

Site on W side of lakeside rd SR249. 3*, Lge, hdg, pt shd, pt sl, EHU (5A) inc (rev pol); sw; 15% statics; Eng spkn; adv bkg acc; ccard acc; boat hire; waterslide; gym; bike hire; watersports. *"Sh walk to old town & ferry terminal; lovely lakeside position; excel, well-maintained site; vg san facs; gd size pitches, some on lake - long walk to water point; vg pizzeria & pool; quiet; ideal for families; gd security; Magic of Europe discount; vg; site improved every year; most pitches have water & drain."* **€61.00, 10 Mar-5 Nov. 2023**

LAZISE *1D2* (1.5km S Rural) *45.49277, 10.73305*
Camping La Quercia, Loc Bottona, 37017 Lazise (VR) **045 6470577; laquercia@laquercia.it; www.laquercia.it**

€6.90 (htd) sand

Exit A22/E45 at Affi/Lago di Garda Sud or exit A4/E70 at Peschiera-del-Garda. Site on SR249, on SE shore of lake. 4*, V lge, hdg, mkd, shd, pt sl, EHU (6A) inc; gas; 15% statics; phone; adv bkg rec; watersports; jacuzzi; gym; waterslide; games area; tennis. *"Superb site for family holidays; many excel sports & leisure facs; vehicle safety checks for cars/m'vans; some pitches on lakeside; easy walk to town along beach; highly rec."* **€61.00, 26 Mar-11 Oct. 2020**

LAZISE *1D2* (3.5km S Urban) *45.47912, 10.72635*
Camping Amici di Lazise, Loc Fossalta Nuova, Strada del Roccolo 8, 37017 Lazise (VR) **045 6490146; info@campingamicidilazise.it; www.campingamicidilazise.it**

12 €4.50 shgl 300m

S fr Lazise, immed bef high rest with Greek columns (bef Gardaland) take side rd on R, site on R.
3*, Med, pt shd, serviced pitches; EHU (6A) inc; 40% statics; Eng spkn; adv bkg acc. *"Gd; nice friendly site; gd pool; noise fr theme pk next door."*
€34.00 2022

LECCO *1C1* (6km S Coastal) *45.81555, 9.39969*
Camping Village Riviera, Via Foppaola 113, 23852, Garlate **0341 680346; info@campingvillageriviera.com; www.campingvillageriviera.com**

(htd) nr

Head S on SS36, take exit Pescate/Lecco, cont strt, at rndbt take 3rd exit onto Via Roma, over rndbt, cont onto Via Statale, turn L onto Via Foppaola, site on L. Sm, hdg, pt shd, pt sl, EHU (10A); bbq (sep area); sw; bus; adv bkg acc; CKE. *"Lake location with free kayak, pedalo, gym, site poor; facs dirty and unkept (2019); very noisy day and night."* **€25.00 2024**

LECCO *1C1* (4km W Rural) *45.81730, 9.34307*
Camping Due Laghi, Via Isella 34, 23862 Civate (LC) **0341 550101; erealin@tin.it; www.duelaghicamping.com**

€3 (cont)

S side of Lecco-Como rd on lake. Use slip rd mkd Isella/Civate. Turn L at T-junc, then L over bdge; foll v narr app rd to site, sp. 2*, Med, shd, pt sl, EHU (10A) inc; gas; 80% statics; Eng spkn; games area. *"Lovely lakeside pitches; gd facs; quiet except weekends; app to site is v narr."* **€29.00, 28 Mar-15 Sep. 2024**

LECCO *1C1* (9km NW Rural) *45.92138, 9.28777*
Camping La Fornace, Via Giuseppe Garibaldi, 52 23865 Oliveto-Lario (LC) **031 969553; lafornace@libero.it; www.lafornace.it**

Fr Lecco SP583 twd Bellagio. Site on R at '37km' sp. Fr Bellagio on SP583 site on L 100m after Onno boundary sp. V sharp L turn at yellow sp. App diff for lge o'fits, narr app rd. 1*, Sm, mkd, hdstg, pt shd, pt sl, EHU (5A) inc; sw nr; adv bkg acc; games rm; CKE. *"Peaceful, lakeside site but poss loud music fr bar until sm hrs; delightful setting; simple, clean facs."*
€22.00, 1 Apr-30 Sep. 2024

LEVANTO *1C2* (1km NE Coastal) *44.17364, 9.62550*
Camping Cinque Terre, Sella Mereti, 19015 Levanto (SP) **0187 801252; info@campingcinqueterre.it; www.campingcinqueterre.it**

(except high ssn) (htd) nr nr shgl 1km

Clearly sp fr cent of Lèvanto. Fr E turn L off SS1 to Lèvanto, sp Carradano, site on R bef town.
1*, Sm, hdg, mkd, shd, terr, EHU (3A) inc; gas; TV; adv bkg acc; sep car park; games rm; CKE. *"Excel, friendly, family-run site; gd, modern san facs; steep ent, but site level; bus to beach high ssn; quiet and secluded; helpful staff; sm pitches."* **€35.00, Easter-30 Sep. 2024**

ITALY

ITALY

LEVANTO *1C2* (4km NE Rural) *44.17561, 9.63665* **Camping San Michele,** Localita' Busco, 19015 Levanto (SP) **3281 689 750 or 0187 800 449; info@campinglevanto.eu; campinglevanto.eu/en/home-en**

(cont)

Head S on SS566 dir Carrodano Inferiore-Levanto. At 2nd rndabt take 3rd exit, then turn L onto Localita Albero D'Oro. Campsite on the R after 2.3km. Lge, hdstg, pt shd, terr, Eng spkn. *"Helpful staff; fair site; scooter hire; clean but tired facs."*
€29.00 **2024**

LEVICO TERME *1D1* (1km S Rural) *46.00638, 11.28944* **Camping Lago Levico,** Via Pleina 5, 38056 Levico-Terme (TN) **0461 706491; info@campinglevico.com; www.campinglevico.com**

€2-6 shgl 200m

Foll sp to Levico fr A22 or SS12 onto SS27; site sp. 4*, Lge, mkd, shd, serviced pitches; EHU (6A) inc; gas; bbq; 30% statics; adv bkg acc; golf 7km. *"Health spa nr; vg; supp for lakeside pitch (no dogs on these pitches)."* **€50.00, 21 Apr-15 Oct.** **2023**

LIDO DI JESOLO *2E2* (5.8km NE Coastal) *45.52862, 12.69693* **Campsite Parco Capraro,** Via Corer 2 ramo, 4 30016 Lido di Jesolo **0421 961073; info@parcocapraro.it; www.parcocapraro.it**

(htd)

Fr Jesolo head NE on Via Roma Destra twrds Via Giotto da Bondone. Cont onto Via Loghetto, then onto Via Cà Gamba, L onto Via Corer. Site on L. 3*, Lge, pt shd, EHU (16A); bbq; twin axles; TV; Eng spkn; games rm; bike hire. *"Vg; v well kept family site; public transport 1km; takeaway; path thro sm pine forest leads to beach & bus stop to cent of town; vg rest/bar; superb sw pool."*
€55.50, 24 Apr-16 Sep. **2024**

"There aren't many sites open at this time of year"

If you're travelling outside peak season remember to call ahead to check site opening dates – even if the entry says 'open all year'.

LUCCA *1D3* (0.8km NW Urban) *43.85000, 10.48583* **Camper Il Serchio,** Via del Tiro a Segno 704, Santa Anna, 55100 Lucca (LU) **0583 317385; info@camperilserchio.it; www.camperilserchio.it**

nr

Sp fr main rds to Lucca & fr town. Gd access rds. Med, hdg, mkd, hdstg, pt shd, EHU (5A) inc; bbq; Shuttle service to the city centre; adv bkg acc; bike hire; tennis opp. *"Attractive pitches; mainly for m'vans - not suitable lge car/c'van o'fits or lge tents; games area opp; vg site."* **€25.00** **2020**

LUINO *1C1* (6km N Rural) *46.04189, 8.73279* **Camping Lido Boschetto Holiday,** Via Pietraperzia 13, 21010 Maccagno (VA) **0332 560250; lido@boschettoholiday.it; www.boschettoholiday.it/lido**

€3

On E shore of Lake Maggiore on SS394 bet Bellinzona & Laveno. Fr Luino pass under 2 rlwy bdges & foll sp L twd lake, site clearly sp. Med, pt shd, EHU (3-4A) €3.50 (poss rev pol); sw nr; 4% statics; adv bkg acc; ccard acc; watersports; CKE. *"Hydrofoil/ferries fr vill to all parts of lake; trains to Locarno; barrier clsd 1300-1500, no place to pk outside; well kept."* **€31.00, 31 Mar-22 Oct.** **2023**

MAGIONE *2E3* (10km S Rural) *43.08140, 12.14340* **Camping Polvese,** Via della Sapienza - Sant'Arcangelo di Magione - 06063 **075 848078; polvese@polvese.com; www.polvese.com**

€2 (cont) sand adj

Fr A1 exit dir Lake Trasimeno to Castiglione-del-Lago, then S599 to San Arcangelo. 3*, Med, mkd, pt shd, EHU (10A) inc; gas; red long stay; 40% statics; phone; adv bkg acc; lake fishing; bike hire; games area; watersports; CKE. *"Gd touring base for Umbria; lakeside pitches avail; helpful staff."*
€22.00, 1 Apr-30 Sep. **2020**

MALCESINE *1D1* (0km N Urban) *45.76583, 10.81096* **Camping Villaggio Turistico Priori,** Via Navene 31, 37018 Malcesine (VR) **045 7400503; info@appartement-prioriantonio.it; www.appartement-prioriantonio.it**

nr nr nr

Well sp in town cent. Take care if app fr N. 1*, Sm, mkd, hdstg, pt shd, pt sl, terr, EHU (3A) inc; sw nr; phone; Eng spkn; adv bkg acc; CKE. *"Vg; conv all amenities & Monte Baldo funicular."*
€24.00, 15 Apr-16 Oct. **2022**

MALCESINE *1D1* (3km N Rural) *45.78971, 10.82609* **Camping Martora,** Campagnola, Martora 2, 37018 Malcesine (VR) **338 1453795; martora@martora.it; www.martora.it**

nr

On E side of lake on rd SS249 at km 86/11. Ent up concrete rd bet iron gates at 'Prinz Blau' sp. 2*, Med, mkd, pt shd, pt sl, EHU (4A) inc; sw nr; 10% statics; adv bkg acc; windsurfing adj. *"Lakeside cycle path to town."* **€27.00, 1 Apr-3 Oct.** **2023**

MALS/MALLES VENOSTA *1D1* (3km S Rural) *46.67305, 10.5700* **Campingpark Gloria Vallis,** Wiesenweg 5, 39020 Glurns/Glorenza (BZ) **0473 835160; info@gloriavallis.it; www.gloriavallis.it**

€4 (htd)

Sp on rd S41 E of Glorenza. 4*, Med, mkd, unshd, terr, EHU (10A) inc; gas; 5% statics; phone; Eng spkn; adv bkg acc; ccard acc; tennis; games area; CKE. *"Excel mountain views; dog shwr rm; higher prices in winter; excel well run site; serviced pitches; 7 day travel pass in 'all inc' package."* **€37.00, 23 Mar-31 Oct.** **2022**

MANERBA DEL GARDA *1D2* (2km N Rural) *45.56138, 10.55944* **Camping Rio Feriengl ück,** Via del Rio 37 Pianarolli, 25080 Manerba-del-Garda (BS) **0365 551450 summer 0365 551075 winter; info@campingrioferiengluck.com; www.gardalake.it/rioferiengluck**

€2 WD MSP nr (htd)

Fr S572 rd turn E at traff lts sp Manerba Centro. At TO turn L down hill & at petrol stn turn R into Viale Degli Alpini. At next rndabt turn L & foll site sp. Site 1.5km N of Manerba opp Hotel Zodiaco. 2*, Lge, mkd, pt shd, EHU (6A) €3; gas; bbq; sw nr; 10% statics; Eng spkn; watersports; CKE. *"Excel, family-run lakeside site with lge, level, grass pitches; welcoming vill nr; cent for Garda sightseeing; conv for train to Venice & Milan; beautiful area; cr but delightful situation."* **€40.50, 23 Mar-20 Oct. 2024**

MANERBA DEL GARDA *1D2* (2.5km N Rural) *45.56333, 10.56611* **Camping San Biagio,** Via Cavalle 19, 25080 Manerba-del-Garda (BS) **0365 551549; info@campingsanbiagio.net; www.campingsanbiagio.net**

€5 (htd)

Fr S572 rd turn E at sp Manerba, site sp 1.5km N fr Manerba. 3*, Lge, mkd, hdstg, shd, terr, EHU (16A) metered; bbq; sw; Eng spkn; adv bkg acc; ccard acc. *"Terr pitches with views over Lake Garda; v clean, modern san facs; easily got twin axle into lge pitch (reserved); beautiful site; extra for lakeside pitches; gd cent for touring area - Verona, Mantua, Sigurta, Torri."* **€31.00, 23 Mar-30 Sep. 2022**

MANERBA DEL GARDA *1D2* (3km S Rural) *45.52555, 10.54333* **Camping Fontanelle,** Via del Magone 13, 25080 Moniga-del-Garda (BS) **0365 502079; info@campingfontanelle.it; www.campingfontanelle.it**

€4 WD MSP

Exit A4 m'way dir Desenzano del Garda & foll sp Salo. In 10km arr at Moniga del Garda take 2nd exit off 1st rndabt twd Salo, then 1st R into Via Roma sp Moniga Centro. Immed after 'Api' g'ge on L turn R into into Via Caccinelli; at end of this narr rd turn R into Via del Magone; site on L by lake. Access poss diff lge o'fits due narr vill rds. 4*, Lge, mkd, pt shd, sl, terr, EHU (6A) inc; gas; bbq (charcoal, gas); sw; TV; 20% statics; phone; Eng spkn; adv bkg acc; ccard acc; tennis; fishing; golf 5km; games rm; horseriding 8km; watersports; boat trips; CKE. *"Vg site; excursions to Venice, Florence, Verona; bike hire 2km; friendly, helpful staff; excel san facs; no o'fits over 6.5m high ssn; levellers needed all pitches; extra for lakeside pitches; pitches poss tight lge o'fits due trees; mkt Mon; lovely site."* **€32.00, 18 Apr-26 Sep, Y01. 2022**

MANFREDONIA *2G4* (10.5km SSW Coastal) *41.55477, 15.88794* **Camping Lido Salpi,** SS159 delle Saline Km 6,200, 71043 Manfredonia **0884 571160; lidosalpi@alice.it; www.lidosalpi.it**

12 WD MSP

Head S on A14, exit at Foggia dir Manfredonia/ SS89. Take ramp to Manfredonia Sud and cont strt. Turn R onto SS159, site on the R. Sm, mkd, pt shd, EHU (6A) €2; bbq; twin axles; 10% statics; bus 0.5km; Eng spkn. *"V well located for San Giovanni Rotondo & Gargano; gd o'night stop fr A14; some pitches awkward for lge o'fits due to trees & site furniture; gd site."* **€24.00 2024**

MARINA DI CAULONIA *3B4* (1km NE Coastal) *38.35480, 16.48375* **Camping Calypso,** Contrada Precariti, 89040 Marina-di-Caulonia (RC) **0964 82028; info@villaggiocalypso.com; www.villaggiocalypso.com**

€2.50 WD MSP sand adj

On o'skts of Marina-di-Caulonia on S106. 3*, Med, mkd, shd, EHU (2A) €3.50; TV; 5% statics; phone; Eng spkn; ccard acc; tennis 500m; games area; CKE. *"Superb sandy beach; gd (if dated) facs; sep car park high ssn; close to early Byzantine church at Stilo & medieval hill vill of Gerace."* **€28.50, 1 Apr-30 Sep. 2024**

MARINA DI MINTURNO *2F4* (6km SE Coastal) *41.20731, 13.79138* **Camping Villlagio Baia Domizia,** Via Pietre Bianche, 81030 Baia-Domizia (CE) **0823 930164; info@baiadomizia.it; www.baiadomizia.it**

WD MSP sand adj

Exit A1 at Cassino onto S630, twd Minturno on S7 & S7quater, turn off at km 2, then foll sp Baia Domizia, site in 1.5km N of Baia-Domizia. 4*, V lge, hdg, shd, EHU (10A) inc (poss rev pol); gas; TV; ccard acc; boat hire; windsurfing; games area; tennis; bike hire. *"Excel facs; 30/7-16/8 min 7 night stay; site clsd 1400-1600 but adequate parking area; top class site with all facs; gd security."* **€55.00, 19 May-18 Sep, Y10. 2022**

MARTINSICURO *2F3* (1km S Urban/Coastal) *42.88027, 13.92055* **Camping Riva Nuova,** Via dei Pioppi 6, 64014 Martinsicuro (TE) **0861 797515; info@rivanuova.it; www.rivanuova.it**

WD MSP sand adj

Fr N exit A14/E55 sp San Benedetto-del-Tronto onto S16 dir Pescara to Martinsicuro, site sp. 3*, Lge, shd, EHU inc; TV; adv bkg acc; ccard acc; games area; excursions; gym; watersports; bike hire. *"San facs were exceptionally gd & spotless; quiet."* **€43.00, 14 May-18 Sep. 2022**

ITALY

MATERA *3A4* (2km S Rural) *40.65305, 16.60694* **Azienda Agrituristica Masseria del Pantaleone,** Contrada Chiancalata 27, 75100 Matera (MT) **0835 335239; info@agriturismopantaleonematera.it; www.agriturismopantaleonematera.it**

12 (cont) WD MSP

Do not use sat nav. Fr S on SS7 take Matera Sud exit, site 2km on L, not well sp. Opp Ospedale Madonna delle Grazie. Sm, hdstg, pt shd, terr, EHU (16A) inc; bbq; Eng spkn; CKE. *"Conv Matera - World Heritage site; helpful owners provide transport to/fr Matera cent."* **€12.00** **2024**

MENAGGIO *1C1* (0.5km N Rural) *46.02516, 9.23996* **Camping Europa,** Loc Leray, Via dei Cipressi 12, 22017 Menaggio (CO) **344 31187; info@campingeuropa menaggio.it**

nr

On ent Menaggio fr S (Como) on S240 turn R & foll 'Campeggio' sp along lakeside prom. On ent fr N turn L at 'Campeggio' sp, pass site ent & turn in boatyard. 1*, Sm, mkd, pt shd, terr, EHU; sw; 80% statics; Eng spkn; adv bkg acc; bike hire; boat hire; CKE. *"V sm pitches cramped high ssn; narr site rds diff for lge o'fits; old-fashioned facs but clean; poor security; helpful owner; m'vans rec to arr full of water & empty of waste; hardly any rd noise, Menaggio delightful place; v friendly."* **€26.50, 25 Mar-30 Sep.** **2022**

MENAGGIO *1C1* (6km S Urban) *45.96937, 9.19298* **Camping La'vedo,** Via degli Artigiani 1, 22016 Lenno (CO) **0344 56288; info@campinglavedo.com; www.campinglavedo.it**

(cont) WD MSP nr nr

Fr Como foll S340 along W shore of lake, site SE of Lenno 200m fr lake, adj to supmkt. 2*, Sm, pt shd, pt sl, EHU (3A) inc; bbq; 25% statics; games area; CKE. *"Picturesque, friendly site in sm town; basic facs; 15 mins to boat stn for other towns on lake; great care needed on S340 - v narr & busy rd."* **€20.00, 1 Apr-30 Sep.** **2024**

MERANO/MERAN *1D1* (5km E Rural) *46.67144, 11.20091* **Camping Hermitage,** Via Val di Nova 29, 39012 Meran **0473 232191; info@einsiedler.com; www.einsiedler.com**

€3 WD MSP

Exit SS38 at Meran Süd & foll sp twds Merano to Meran 2000 past Trautmannsdorf. Site sp. 4*, Med, hdstg, mkd, pt shd, terr, EHU (10-16A); bbq; twin axles; phone; bus 100m; adv bkg acc; bike hire; sauna. *"Tennis; serviced pitches; mountain views; hotel facs avail to campers; forest walk; ACSI site; excel."* **€45.50, 1 Jan-8 Jan & 1 Apr-31 Dec.** **2023**

MERANO/MERAN *1D1* (1km S Urban) *46.66361, 11.15638* **Live Merano,** Via Piave/Piavestrasse 44, 39012 Merano/Meran (BZ) **0473 426388; info@live meranocamping.com; www.livemeranocamping.com**

12 €3.30 WD MSP nr nr (htd)

Exit S38 at Merano Sud & foll rd into town. Brown site sps to Camping & Tennis (no name at main juncs in town cent). Site ent mkd 'Camping Tennis'. Site also sp fr N. 3*, Med, hdstg, pt shd, EHU (6A) €3; red long stay; phone; tennis adj; CKE. *"Sh walk to town cent; fine site surrounded by spectacular mountain scenery; helpful staff; pitches soft after rain; gd clean san facs; helpful staff; 10% surcharge for 1 night; excel thermal baths; take car pk ticket to acc site recep at barrier, ticket to exit car park provided free at recep."* **€29.00** **2022**

MERANO/MERAN *1D1* (15km S Rural) *46.59861, 11.14527* **Camping Völlan,** Zehentweg 6, 39011 Völlan/Foiana **0473 568056; info@camping-voellan.com; www.camping-voellan.com**

€3 WD MSP nr

Leave S38 dual c'way (Merano-Bolzano) S of Merano sp Lana. Drive thro Lana, turn uphill sp Gampenpass. Turn R sp Foliana/Völlan & foll sp to site. 3*, Sm, mkd, pt shd, terr, serviced pitches; EHU (4A) €2.50; 10% statics; phone; Eng spkn; golf 6km; CKE. *"Long drag up to site fr Lana, but worth it; beautiful situation o'looking Adige Valley; excel facs & pool; barriers clsd 1300-1500 & 2200-0700; v helpful owners; some pitches with steep acc & tight for lge units."* **€42.80, 23 Mar-4 Nov.** **2024**

MESTRE *2E2* (3km E Urban) *45.48098, 12.27516* **Venezia Camping Village,** Via Orlanda 8/C, 30170 Mestre/Venezia (VE) **041 5312828; info@venezia village.it; www.veneziavillage.it**

€2 (htd) WD MSP (htd, indoor)

On A4 fr Milan/Padova take exit SS11 dir Venice. Exit SS11 for SS14 dir Trieste & airport. 200m after Agip g'ge on R watch for sp and take 1st exit R fr rdbt bet two major dealerships. Keep in R lane all way to site. 2*, Med, hdstg, hdg, pt shd, EHU (6A) inc (poss rev pol); gas; bbq (charcoal, elec, gas); sw nr; red long stay; twin axles; 10% statics; bus to Venice; Eng spkn; adv bkg acc; ccard acc; CKE. *"V conv Venice - tickets/maps fr recep; clean, well-run site; popular with m'vans; friendly, helpful owners; pitches poss cramped when site full; mosquitoes; pool 3km; bus to Pizzale Roma fr campsite; excel."* **€44.70, 22 Feb-31 Dec.** **2024**

MESTRE *2E2* (4km E Urban) *45.48425, 12.28227* **Camping Rialto,** 16 Via Orlanda, Loc Campalto, 30175 Mestre (VE) **041 5420295; info@campingrialto.com; https://www.campingrialto.it/en/home-page-english/**

€3

Fr A4 take Marco Polo Airport exit, then fork R onto SS14 dir Venice. Site on L 1km past Campalto opp lge car sales area, well sp. Do not enter Mestre. Med, pt shd, EHU (15A) €1.50; phone; bus to Venice; Eng spkn; adv bkg acc; CKE. *"Site in need of refurb but v conv Venice; bus tickets fr recep; friendly, helpful staff; vg san facs, vg rest; rec."*
€33.00, 7 Apr-31 Oct. **2024**

MILANO *1C2* (8km W Urban) *45.47390, 9.08233* **Camping Citta di Milano,** Via Gaetano Airaghi 61, 20153 Milano **0248 207017; info@campingmilano.it; www.campingmilano.it**

12 €3.50 nr

Fr E35/E62/A50 Tangentiale Ovest ring rd take Settimo-Milanese exit & foll sp San Siro along Via Novara (SS11). Turn R in 2km at Shell petrol stn, then R at traff lts in 500m & L to site in 600m. Site ent at Gardaland Waterpark, poorly sp. 4*, Lge, hdstg, mkd, pt shd, EHU (6A) inc; phone; bus 500m; Eng spkn; ccard acc; CKE. *"Gd san facs; noise fr adj concerts high ssn; conv bus/metro Milan; penned animals for kid to enjoy; rd, aircraft noise, disco at w/end & waterpark adj; gd security; peacocks roaming site; excel well organised site; gd for NH; wet, muddy in winter."* **€34.00** **2024**

MONOPOLI *2H4* (5km S Coastal) *40.91333, 17.34387* **Camping Atlantide,** Contrada Lamandia 13E, 70043 Capitolo Monopoli (BA) **080 801212; dematti a@residenceatlantide.it; www.residenceatlantide.it**

12 €4 on leash (not acc Aug) nr

On SS379 (Bari Brindisi coast rd), 3km S of Monopoli, fr SS16 (Adriatica) take exit Capitolo. Lge, mkd, hdstg, pt shd, pt sl, terr, serviced pitches; EHU (6A) inc (poss rev pol); 40% statics; bus adj; Eng spkn; adv bkg acc; ccard acc; golf 5km; tennis; games area; CKE. *"Friendly owner; gd, clean site; basic facs LS; hot water to shwrs only; rocky waterfront adj; gd size pitches; disco every Sat high ssn until v late; Conv Roman ruins & UNESCO site; excel seafood rest 1km; site & area highly rec; conv Bari ferries; gd rest."*
€41.00 **2024**

MONTEFORTINO *2E3* (0.8km W Rural) *42.94495, 13.34017* **Camping Sibilla,** Via Tenna, 63858 Montefortino FM **3387695040; info@campingsibilla.it; www.campingsibilla.it**

A14 exit Civitanova Marche. M'way Macerata take Sarnano exit and on to Amondola. Foll sp for Montefortino. In about 5km, fork R after IP g'ge. Site 200m on L. Med, mkd, hdstg, pt shd, terr, EHU (6A) inc; bbq; twin axles; TV; bus 0.8km; Eng spkn; adv bkg acc; CKE. *"New site opened June 2016; great mountain views; family owned; excel site."*
€25.00, 1 May-10 Nov. **2022**

MONTOPOLI IN VAL D'ARNO *1D3* (1km N Rural) *43.67611, 10.75333* **Kawan Toscana Village,** Via Fornoli 9, 56020 Montópoli (PI) **0571 449032; info@toscanavillage.com; www.toscanavillage.com**

12 (htd)

Bet Pisa & Florence; exit Fi-Pi-Li dual c'way at Montópoli, foll site sps. Turn L bef Montópoli vill - site well sp. 3*, Med, mkd, pt shd, terr, serviced pitches; EHU (10A) €2.50; gas; bbq; red long stay; TV; 15% statics; phone; Eng spkn; adv bkg req; ccard acc; bike hire; golf 7km; CKE. *"Helpful staff; gravel site rds, steep in places; some v sm pitches; spotless facs; gd food in rest; gd pool; well organised; excel for Florence, Pisa & Tuscany; walking dist to Montopoli; beautiful surroundings; reasonably priced rest."*
€43.50 **2024**

MONZA *1C2* (4km N Urban) *45.62305, 9.28027* **Camping Autodromo,** Autodromo Nazionale Monza 20900 **039 339 2665523; info@monzacamping.it or granpremio@monzacamping.it; www.monzacamping.it**

(cont) nr

Fr E exit A4 at Agrate-Brianza; fr W A4 exit Sesto San Giovanni onto S36. Foll sp to Autodromo/Biassono, then to site in Parco Reale complex. NB: Do not go to Monza Centro or exit main rd to Autodromo as no access to site; site clearly sp by g'ge. 3*, Lge, shd, EHU (5A) €6; own san rec; 10% statics; phone; bus to Milan nr; Eng spkn; games area. *"Day ticket for all transport; bus 200m fr gate to Sesto FC (rlwy stn, bus terminal & metro line 1) - fr there take metro to Duomo; pool adj; poor facs; NH/sh stay only for racing."* **€60.00, 31 Aug-9 Sep.** **2024**

NICOTERA *3B4* (3km S Coastal) *38.50755, 15.92666* **Camping Villaggio Mimosa,** Mortelletto, 89844 Nicotera Marina (VV) **0963 81397; info@villaggiomimosa.com; https://www.villaggiomimosa.com/**

12 sand adj

Exit A3/E45 at Rosarno exit. Cross S18 & site sp dir San Ferdinando Porto. Foll sp on SP50 for approx 7km. 3*, Sm, mkd, pt shd, EHU (12A); gas; bbq; twin axles; 40% statics; Eng spkn; games area; tennis; bike hire; boat hire; windsurfing; CKE. *"Some pitches have tight corners for lge o'fits; gd site."* **€42.00** **2024**

ORBETELLO *1D4* (5.5km N Coastal) *42.46341, 11.18597* **Camping Village Obertello,** Strada Gianella 166, 58015 Orbetello **0564 820 201; orbetellocampingvillage@clubdelsole.com; www.orbetellocampingvillage.it**

Fr SS1 Aurelia take exit Albinia. Cont twds Porto Santo Stefano. Campsite on L after 5km. V lge, mkd, hdstg, pt shd, EHU (6A); bbq; cooking facs; TV; Eng spkn; adv bkg acc; games area; bike hire; CCI.
€62.00, 19 Apr-27 Sep. **2024**

ORBETELLO *1D4* (7km N Coastal) *42.49611, 11.19416* **Argentario Camping Village,** Torre Saline, 58010 Albinia (GR) **+39 0564 870068; info@argentariocampingvillage.com; www.argentariocampingvillage.com**

Turn W off Via Aurelia at 150km mark, sp Porto S. Stefano, site on R, clearly sp in 500m. Ignore sps Zona Camping. 1*, Lge, mkd, shd, EHU (6A) inc; 90% statics; phone; adv bkg acc; games area; boat hire; sep car park. *"Better suited for campervans and tent; san facs due for upgrade; excel rest; easy access to beach."* **€42.00, 1 Apr-30 Sep.** **2020**

ORTA SAN GIULIO *1B1* (0.5km N Rural) *45.80125, 8.42093* **Camping Orta,** Via Domodossola 28, Loc Bagnera, 28016 Orta San Giulio (NO) **0322 90267; info@campingorta.it; www.campingorta.it**

Fr Omegna take rd on SS229 for 10km to km 44.5 sp Novara. Site both sides of rd 500m bef rndabt at Orta x-rds. Recep on L if heading S; poor access immed off rd. Med, pt shd, pt sl, terr, EHU (3-6A) €2.50; gas; sw nr; Eng spkn; adv bkg acc. *"Popular site in beautiful location; sm pitches; narr site rds & tight corners; arr early for lakeside pitch (extra charge); slipway to lake; friendly, helpful owner; Orta a gem; waterskiing; noise fr Beach Club at night; €4.50 for lakeside pitches; lakeside walk round peninsular; rec Sacre Monte for St Francis."*
€38.00, 8 Mar-31 Dec. **2024**

ORTA SAN GIULIO *1B1* (2km N Rural) *45.81212, 8.41076* **Camping Verde Lago,** Corso Roma 76, 28028 Pettenasco (NO) **0323 89257; info@campingverdelago.it; www.campingverdelago.it**

Site bet SS229 & lake at km 46, 500m S of Pettenasco on Orta Lake. Gd access. Sm, pt shd, pt sl, EHU (6A) €2.50; bbq; sw nr; TV; 60% statics; Eng spkn; ccard acc; games rm. *"Vg family-run site; friendly, helpful; clean facs but dated; beach; boat mooring; recep 0930-1200 & 1630-1900; excel rest; beautiful setting by lake; if visiting Orta by car take lots of €1 coins for parking; excel."*
€38.00, 25 Mar-16 Oct. **2022**

ORVIETO *2E3* (0.5km S Urban) *42.72379, 12.13162* **Aree di Sosta Parcheggio Funicolare,** Via della Direttissima, 05018 Orvieto (TR) **0763 300161 or 338 6843153 or 328 0644317; renzo.battistelli@hotmail.com; www.orvietoonline.com**

At Orvieto foll sp rlwy stn & funicular parking. Site on L just beyond funicular parking & behind rlwy stn. Foll sp 'Parcheggio Camper'. Sm, hdstg, mkd, unshd, EHU (10A) inc; phone; bus, train 200m; CKE. *"M'vans only but c'vans poss acc LS; conv A1; gd san facs."* **€15.00** **2024**

OSTRA *2E3* (0.2km SW Rural) *43.61032, 13.15351* **Camping 'L Prè,** Viale Matteotti 45, 60010 Ostra (AN) **071 68045; info@lpre.it; www.lpre.it**

Exit A14 at Senigallia onto S360. After approx 10km turn R to Ostra. Sp in vill. 2*, Sm, pt shd, terr, EHU (3A) €2.50; red long stay; games rm. *"Gd san facs; very friendly owners; lovely, quiet, simple site with easy access Ancona, Esini Valley; beautiful views over valley; gd for cyclists; gd place to relax after Venice."*
€24.00, 1 Apr-30 Sep. **2024**

PAESTUM *3A3* (4km N Coastal) *40.42780, 14.98244* **Camping Villaggio Ulisse,** Via Ponte di Ferro, 84063 Paestum (SA) **0828 851095; info@campingulisse.com; www.campingulisse.com**

Foll site sp in cent Paestum, well sp. 3*, Lge, shd, EHU (3A) inc; 80% statics; games area; CKE. *"Direct access to beautiful beach; gd, clean, lovely, friendly site; cash only; gd rest."*
€36.00, 1 Apr-30 Sep. **2023**

PAESTUM *3A3* (5km WNW Coastal) *40.42896, 14.98214* **Campsite Athena,** Via Ponte di Ferro, 84063 Paestum **0828 851105; vathena@tiscali.it; www.campingathena.com**

Site 50km S of Salerno. Foll a'strada to Battipaglia onto main rd to Paestum. Head S on SS18. At rndabt take 1st exit onto SP276, then at next rndabt take 1st exit onto Via della Repubblica. Go thro 1 rndabt, turn L onto SP175, at rndabt take 1st exit onto Via Marittima, L onto Via Poseidonia and 1st L onto Via Ponte di Ferro. Site on R. 3*, Med, pt shd, EHU (5A); twin axles; Eng spkn; CKE. *"Gd site, direct access to beach; takeaway."* **€36.00, 1 Apr-31 Oct.** **2024**

PAESTUM *3A3* (5km NW Coastal) *40.41330, 14.99140* **Camping Villaggio Dei Pini,** Via Torre, 84063 Paestum (SA) **0828 811030; info@campingvillaggiodeipini.com; www.campingvillaggiodeipini.com**

12 sand adj

Site 50km S of Salerno in vill of Torre-de-Paestum. Foll a'strada to Battipaglia onto main rd to Paestum, site sp bef Paestum on rd S18, foll to beach. 3*, Med, mkd, hdg, shd, EHU (6A) inc; bbq; 30% statics; phone; adv bkg acc; ccard acc; games area; CKE. *"Historical ruins nr; narr access rd fr vill due parked cars; lge o'fits may grnd at ent; some sm pitches - c'vans manhandled onto pitches; no dogs Jul/Aug; pleasant site by beach; gd rest; helpful owner; rec."*
€45.00 **2024**

PALMI *3B4* (7km N Coastal) *38.39317, 15.86280* **Sosta Camper Prajola,** Lungomare Costa Viola, 4, 89015 Palmi RC **03662 529692; info@prajola.it**

12 opp

Sp fr camp site San Fantino (Palmi), on beach front, down the hill in 2km. Sm, hdstg, pt shd, EHU (6A); bbq; twin axles. *"Gd basic NH to & fr Sicily; fair."*
€15.00 **2022**

PALMI *3B4* (9.5km N Coastal) *38.40676, 15.86912* **Villaggio Camping La Quiete,** Contrada Scinà, 89015 Palmi (RC) **0966 479400 or 3881080560; info@villaggiolaquiete.it; www.villaggiolaquiete.it**

sand 200m

N fr Lido-di-Palmi on Contrada Pietrenere coast rd dir Gioia Tauro, site sp. 3*, Lge, hdstg, pt shd, EHU (10A) €3; gas; red long stay; 5% statics; phone; Eng spkn; adv bkg acc; ccard acc; CKE. *"Sm pitches; fair sh stay/NH; friendly owner; pitches in ctr of little cottages."* **€30.00, 1 May-31 Oct.** **2023**

PASSIGNANO SUL TRASIMENO *2E3* (0.8km E Rural) *43.18397, 12.15089* **Camping La Spiaggia,** Via Europe 22, 06065 Passignano-sul-Trasimeno (PG) **075 827246; info@campinglaspiaggia.it; www.campinglaspiaggia.it**

€2 (htd) nr

Exit A1 at Bettolle-Valdichiana & foll sp Perugia for 30km. Exit at Passignano Est & foll sp to site. 2*, Sm, mkd, shd, EHU (6A/10A) inc; bbq; red long stay; TV (pitch); phone; bus/train 800m; Eng spkn; adv bkg acc; ccard acc; games area; bike hire. *"Lovely lakeside site; beach for dogs; friendly owner; slipway for boats; nursery; table tennis; lake adj; lge pitches; excel san facs but hot water variable; gd rest; interesting lakeside town; 800m fr the historic cent of Passignano; excel touring base for hill towns."*
€29.00, 27 Mar-13 Oct. **2024**

PASSIGNANO SUL TRASIMENO *2E3* (1km E Rural) *43.18338, 12.15085* **Camping Kursaal,** Viale Europa 24, 06065 Passignano-sul-Trasimeno (PG) **075 828085; info@campingkursaal.it; www.campingkursaal.it**

€1.50

Fr Perugia on S75 to Lake Trasimeno. Exit at Passignano-Est twd lake; site on L past level x-ing adj hotel, well sp. 3*, Med, hdg, mkd, pt shd, pt sl, EHU (6A) €2 (poss rev pol); TV; phone; Eng spkn; adv bkg req; ccard acc; bike hire; CKE. *"Pleasant, lovely site in gd position; vg rest; some pitches have lake view; ltd space & pitches tight; gd clean site; vg san facs; great pool."* **€42.00, 1 Apr-1 Nov.** **2023**

PERTICARA *2E3* (2km N Rural) *43.89608, 12.24302* **Tenuta Perticara,** Via Serra Masini 10/d, 47863 Perticara (PS) **0335 7062260; info@tenutaperticara.com; www.campingperticara.com**

(htd)

Fr A14 at Rimini take S258 to Novafeltria. Foll sp Perticara & site. Steep, hairpins on pt of rte. 3*, Med, hdstg, mkd, hdg, unshd, terr, serviced pitches; EHU (10A) inc; gas; TV; 5% statics; phone; bus; Eng spkn; adv bkg acc; ccard acc; CKE. *"Clean, well-maintained, scenic site; hospitable Dutch owners; many activities arranged; immac san facs; poss diff egress to SW (hairpins with passing places) - staff help with 4x4 if necessary; rough terrain; excel; well run."*
€38.00, 13 May-20 Sep. **2022**

PESCASSEROLI *2F4* (0.5km S Rural) *41.79888, 13.79222* **Camping Sant' Andrea,** Via San Donato, 67032 Pescasseroli (AQ) **0863 912725 or 335 5956029 (mob); info@campingsantandrea.com; www.campingsantandrea.com**

12 (htd) nr

Site sp on R bet Pescasseroli & Opi. If gate clsd ent thro side gate & turn key to open main gate. 3*, Sm, mkd, pt shd, EHU (10A) inc; phone; CKE. *"Beautiful, open pitches in lovely area; clean facs but ltd high ssn; statics (sep area); shop, rest, snacks, bar in town."* **€15.00** **2024**

PESCHIERA DEL GARDA *1D2* (1km N Urban) *45.44780, 10.70195* **Camping del Garda,** Via Marzan 6, 37019 Castelnuovo-del-Garda (VR) **045 7551682; info@delgarda.it; www.delgarda.it**

shgl

Exit A4/E70 dir Peschiera onto SR249 dir Lazise. Turn L in 500m dir Lido Campanello, site in 1km on L on lakeside. 4*, V lge, shd, EHU (4A) inc; gas; sw; 60% statics; phone; adv bkg acc; games area; tennis. *"Busy, well-organised site; helpful staff, discount snr citizens; gd rest; walking & cycling rtes adj; conv Verona."* **€63.20, 25 Mar-4 Nov.** **2023**

ITALY

PESCHIERA DEL GARDA *1D2* (1km N Rural) *45.46722, 10.71638* **Eurocamping Pacengo,** Via del Porto 13, 37010 Pacengo (VR) **045 7590012; info@eurocampingpacengo.it; www.eurocampingpacengo.it**

€2.40

On SS249 fr Peschiera foll sp to Gardaland, Pacengo in 1km. Turn L at traff lts in cent of vill, site on L. 3*, Lge, mkd, pt shd, sl, EHU (4A) inc; sw nr; 25% statics; phone; Eng spkn; adv bkg acc; boat launch; CKE. *"Well-equipped site on shore Lake Garda; helpful staff; some sm pitches; pool adj; espec gd end of ssn; excel rest; conv Verona."* **€36.50, 11 Apr-30 Sep.** **2024**

PESCHIERA DEL GARDA *1D2* (2.5km N Rural) *45.45480, 10.70200* **Camping Gasparina,** Loc Cavalcaselle, 37014 Castelnuovo-del-Garda (VR) **045 7550775; info@gasparina.com; www.gasparina.com**

On SS249 dir Lazise, turn L at site sp. 2*, Lge, mkd, pt shd, sl, EHU (3A) inc; gas; 10% statics; adv bkg acc; ccard acc; games area. *"Popular, busy site; lake adj; variable pitch sizes; lake views some pitches; long lead req."* **€35.00, 1 Apr-30 Sep.** **2024**

PESCHIERA DEL GARDA *1D2* (0.7km W Rural) *45.44555, 10.69472* **Camping Butterfly,** Lungo Lago Garibaldi 11, 37019 Peschiera (VR) **045 6401466; info@campingbutterfly.it; www.campingbutterfly.it**

€5

Fr A4/E70 exit twd Peschiera for 2km. At x-rds with bdge on L, strt over & foll rv to last site after RH bend at bottom. 4*, Lge, shd, EHU inc; gas; sw; 75% statics; adv bkg rec; ccard acc. *"Busy holiday site; conv town & lake steamers; sm pitches; clean san facs."* **€50.00, 9 Mar-10 Nov.** **2024**

PESCHIERA DEL GARDA *1D2* (1km W Urban) *45.44222, 10.67805* **Camping Bella Italia,** Via Bella Italia 2, 37019 Peschiera del Garda (VR) **045 6400688; info@camping-bellaitalia.it;www.camping-bellaitalia.it**

Fr Brescia or Verona on SP11 to Peschiera del Garda, site sp on lakeside. Fr Brescia or Verona on A4/E70 exit at Peschiera on to SP11 in dir of Brescia, site on R in about 2km. 4*, V lge, shd, sl, EHU (16A); gas; bbq; sw nr; bus to Verona; Eng spkn; adv bkg rec; windsurfing; waterslide; games area; bike hire; tennis; archery; CKE. *"Busy, popular site, nr theme park, Aqua World, Verona; suits all ages; v clean; rests gd & gd price; many static tents; gd recep for satellite & wifi."* **€56.50, 16 Mar-26 Oct.** **2024**

PESCHIERA DEL GARDA *1D2* (6km W Coastal) *45.45120, 10.66557* **Camping Wien,** Loc. Fornaci, 37019 Peschiera (VR) **045 7550379; info@campingwien.it; www.campingwien.it**

shgl adj

On Verona-Brescia rd (not a'strada) W of Peschiera, turn R at San Benedetto, turn R 400m after traff lts, site has 2 ents 100m apart. 3*, Med, mkd, hdstg, shd, pt sl, EHU inc (3A); gas; red long stay; 50% statics; phone; bus adj; Eng spkn; adv bkg acc; boating; games area; fishing; ice; CKE. *"Wonderful pool o'looking Lake Garda; walking/cycle path into town; vg site; busy high ssn."* **€52.00, 19 May-30 Sep.** **2023**

PESCHIERA DEL GARDA *1D2* (2km NW Urban) *45.44825, 10.66978* **Camping San Benedetto,** Strada Bergamini 14, 37019 San Benedetto (VR) **045 7550544; info@campingsanbenedetto.it; www.campingsanbenedetto.it**

€1.50-2

Exit A4/E70 dir Peschiera-del-Garda, turn N at traff lts in cent of vill, site on lake at km 274/V111 on rd S11. 4*, Lge, shd, pt sl, EHU (3A) inc; 30% statics; adv bkg acc; games area; bike hire; boat hire; canoeing; windsurfing. *"Pleasant, well-run; sm harbour; site clsd 1300-1500; excel modern rest beside lake; excel new san facs (2017)."* **€54.30, 1 Apr-8 Oct.** **2023**

PIENZA *1D3* (7km E Rural) *43.08089, 11.71159* **Camping Il Casale,** 64 53026 Pienza (SI) **0578 755109 or 333 4250705 (mob); info@podereilcasale.it; www.podereilcasale.com**

12

Fr Pienza dir Montepulciano on S146, turn R in 4km onto sm, gritted track sp Monticchiello. Site in 3km on L sp Podereilcasale. Sm, pt shd, pt sl, EHU (16A) inc; phone; Eng spkn; adv bkg acc; ccard acc. *"8 pitches only for c'vans/mvans; simple farm site; panoramic views; lake adj; rec phone to check availability; v friendly owners, site fees inc breakfast."*
€26.00 **2024**

PIEVE TESINO *1D1* (6km N Rural) *46.11361, 11.61944* **Villaggio Camping Valmalene,** Loc Valmalene, 38050 Pieve-Tesino (TN) **0461 594214; info@valmalene.com; www.valmalene.com**

12 €5 (htd) (htd)

Fr Trento E for 50km on S47. Turn N at Strigno to Pieve-Tesino, site sp. 3*, Med, mkd, pt shd, EHU inc; 10% statics; adv bkg rec; ccard acc; site clsd Nov; sauna; fitness rm; bike hire; games area; tennis. *"Gd base for summer & winter hols; private bthrms avail."*
€32.00 **2022**

PISA *1C3* (0.5km N Urban) **Camper Parking,** Via di Pratale 78, 56100 Pisa, Toscane **+39050555678**

12 nr nr

On Via Aurelia SS1 fork R app Pisa, then turn E approx 1km N of Arno Rv, sp camping. After 1km turn L into Via Pietrasantina. Site on R behind lge Tamoil petrol stn, sp coach parking. Max height under rlwy bdge 3.30m. C'vans acc. Lge, hdstg, unshd, own san req; bus adj. *"Excel NH; parking within walking dist of leaning tower; water & waste inc; plenty of space; san facs open at café opp during day."*
€12.00 **2020**

PISA *1C3* (1km N Urban) *43.72416, 10.3830* **Camp Torre Pendente,** Viale delle Cascine 86, 56122 Pisa **050 561704; info@campingtorrependente.it; www.campingtorrependente.it**

€1.60

Exit A12/E80 Pisa Nord onto Via Aurelia (SS1). After 8km & after x-ing rlwy bdge, turn L after passing Pisa sp at traff lts. Site on L, sp. 1*, Lge, mkd, pt shd, EHU (5A) inc (poss rev pol); gas; bbq; red long stay; TV; phone; Eng spkn; ccard acc; bike hire; CKE. *"Gd base Pisa; leaning tower 15 mins walk; immac, modern, well-maintained san facs; private san facs avail; pitches typically 50sqm; poss tight lge o'fits due narr site rds & corners; many pitches shd by netting; site rds muddy after rain; friendly staff; excel, well-run site; 300m fr Pisa San Rossore rlwy stn, trains to Lucca etc."*
€39.00, 25 Mar-3 Nov. **2024**

"I need an on-site restaurant"

We do our best to make sure site information is correct, but it is always best to check any must-have facilities are still available or will be open during your visit.

PISTOIA *1D3* (10km S Rural) *43.84174, 10.91049* **Camping Barco Reale,** Via Nardini 11, 51030 San Baronto-Lamporecchio (PT) **0573 88332; info@barcoreale.com; www.barcoreale.com**

Leave A11 at Pistoia junc onto P9 & foll sp to Vinci, Empoli & Lamporecchio to San Baronto. In vill turn into rd by Monti Hotel & Rest, site sp. Last 3km steep climb. 4*, Lge, mkd, shd, pt sl, terr, serviced pitches; EHU (3-6A) inc (poss rev pol); gas; red long stay; phone; Eng spkn; adv bkg req; ccard acc; bike hire; games area; CKE. *"Excel site in Tuscan hills; helpful staff; gd touring base; excel mother & fam bthrm; vg rest; poss diff access some pitches but towing help provided on request; unsuitable lge o'fits; well-organised walking & bus trips; excel pool."*
€44.00, 15 Apr-30 Sep. **2023**

POGGIBONSI *1D3* (12km N Rural) *43.58198, 11.13801* **Camping Panorama Del Chianti,** Via Marcialla 349, 50020 Marcialla-Certaldo (FI) **0571 669334; info@campingchianti.it; www.campingchianti.it**

€2 nr nr nr

Fr Florence-Siena a'strada exit sp Tavarnelle. On reaching Tavernelle turn R sp Tutti Direzione/ Certaldo & foll by-pass to far end of town. Turn R sp to Marcialla, in Marcialla turn R to Fiano, site in 1km. NB Some steep hairpins app site fr E. 2*, Med, mkd, hdstg, pt shd, terr, EHU (3A) inc; red long stay; phone; Eng spkn; adv bkg acc; bike hire; CKE. *"Gd tourist info (in Eng); sports facs in area; cultural sites; helpful staff; friendly owner; san facs clean - hot water to shwrs only; 4 excel rests nr; panaromic views; midway bet Siena & Florence; popular site - arr early to get pitch; facs need updating."* **€44.00, 7 Apr-25 Oct.** **2024**

PORLEZZA *1C1* (4km E Rural) *46.04074, 9.16827* **Camping Ranocchio,** Via Al Lago 7,22010 Loc Piano di Porlezza, Carlazzo (CO) **0344 70385 or 62611; campeggioranocchio@gmail.com; www.campingranocchio.com**

€2 (htd)

On main rd bet Menaggio & Porlezza. Ent in vill of Piano on S side. Sp. Steep app in Lugano with hairpin bends; 15% gradient. V narr rd fr Lugano - clsd to c'vans at peak times. 2*, Lge, mkd, unshd, pt sl, terr, EHU inc (6A); gas; sw; TV; Eng spkn; horseriding 2km; fishing; CKE. *"Friendly recep; gd for exploring Como & Lugano; steamer trips on both lakes; lovely, v attractive site; helpful recep; excel corner shop & rest; vg."* **€37.00, 27 Mar-30 Sep.** **2024**

PORTO RECANATI *2F3* (4km N Coastal) *43.47123, 13.64150* **Camping Bellamare,** Lungomare Scarfiotti 13, 62017 Porto-Recanati (MC) **071 976628; info@bellamare.it; www.bellamare.it**

shgl

Exit A14/E55 Loreto/Porto-Recanati; foll sp Numana & Sirolo; camp on R in 4km on coast rd. 3*, Lge, unshd, EHU (6A) €3; gas; 10% statics; phone; Eng spkn; ccard acc; games area; games rm; bike hire; CKE. *"V well-run & laid out site on beach; NH tariff of €17-28 (inc elec) for a pitch at the edge of the site but OK; beach access; gd facs & security."*
€51.20, 20 Apr-30 Sep. **2023**

PORTO RECANATI *2F3* (7.7km NW Urban) *43.44155, 13.61446* **Area Attrezzata Camper Loreto,** Via Maccari, 60025 Loreto **07 19 77 748; info@prolocoloreto.com; www.prolocoloreto.com/area-camper-1.html**

12

Fr A14 S of Ancona, exit at Loreto. Fr town ctr foll sp to campsite. Med, mkd, hdstg, unshd, EHU inc. *"M'van NH; conv for Basilica, beach & Ancona ferries; clean & well run; occasional c'vans allowed if not busy; vg site."* **€12.00** **2024**

ITALY

ITALY

PORTOFERRAIO *1C3* (9km E Rural) *42.80072, 10.36452* **Rosselba Le Palme,** Loc. Ottone 3, 57037 Elba Portoferraio **0565 933 101; info@rosselbalepalme.it; www.rosselbalepalme.it**

sand 0.5km

Fr ferry terminal foll signs 'tutti direzioni'. At 3rd rndabt head twds Porto Azzurro. Take L fork to Bagnaia. Site sp. 3*, Sm, hdg, pt shd, terr, EHU (6A); twin axles; 80% statics; bus adj; Eng spkn; adv bkg acc; CCI. *"Ferry service fr Piombino every 1/2 hr; statics enhance site facs."* **€60.00, 24 Apr-10 Oct. 2024**

POZZA DI FASSA *1D1* (0.5km SW Rural) *46.42638, 11.68527* **Camping Catinaccio Rosengarten,** Via Avisio 15, 38036 Pozza-di-Fassa (TN) **0462 763305; info@catinacciorosengarten.com; www.catinacciorosengarten.com**

€4 nr nr

Fr S SS48 site sp just after San Giovanni. 1*, Lge, hdstg, pt shd, EHU (2A) inc (extra for higher amperage); red long stay; 30% statics; Eng spkn; adv bkg req; ccard acc; site clsd Oct; CKE. *"Superb scenery; helpful staff; luxury san facs; free taxi (2018) to Vigo di Fassa cable car; ski lift 1km; pool 300m; excel site; v convly sited for access to vill & public transport; 20 min walk to Buffaure cable car; ski bus; off clsd 1230-1500."* **€38.80, 1 Jan-9 Apr, 4 Jun-16 Oct, 4 Dec-31 Dec. 2023**

PRATO ALLO STELVIO *1D1* (0.5km E Rural) *46.61777, 10.59555* **Camping Sägemühle,** Dornweg 12, 39026 Prato-allo-Stélvio (BZ) **0473 864410; info@saegemuehle.it; www.saegemuehle.it**

€4 (htd) nr (covrd, htd)

Fr rd S40 turn E at Spondigna onto rd S38 dir Stélvio, site sp in vill. 4*, Med, hdg, mkd, hdstg, pt shd, pt sl, EHU (16A) inc; TV; phone; adv bkg acc; ccard acc; sauna; games area; CKE. *"Excel, well-run site; gd, clean facs; helpful staff; gd walking area in National Park; conv for the reschen pass Austria Italy; ski lift 10km; ski bus; all pitches fully serviced."* **€55.00, 1 Jan-3 Nov & 18 Dec-31 Dec. 2024**

PRATO ALLO STELVIO *1D1* (0.5km NW Rural) *46.62472, 10.59388* **Camping Kiefernhain,** Via Pineta 37, 39026 Prato-allo-Stélvio (BZ) **0473 616422; reception@camping-kiefernhain.it; www.camping-kiefernhain.it**

€4 nr (htd)

Fr rd S40 turn SW at Spondigna onto rd S38 dir Stélvio, site sp in vill. Lge, mkd, pt shd, EHU (6A) €2.50; bbq; red long stay; phone; Eng spkn; adv bkg rec; waterslide; dog shwrs. *"V modern, clean san facs; superb views; sports cent adj; private bthrms avail; facs stretched high ssn; vg value."* **€52.50, 1 May-4 Oct. 2024**

PRECI *2E3* (3km NW Rural) *42.88808, 13.01483* **Camping Il Collaccio,** 06047 Castelvecchio-di-Preci (PG) **0743 665108; info@ilcollaccio.com; www.ilcollaccio.com**

(htd)

S fr Assisi on S75 & S3, turn off E sp Norcia, Cascia. Then foll sp for Visso on S209. In approx 30km turn R for Preci, then L, site sp. Rte is hilly. 4*, Med, mkd, pt shd, terr, EHU (6A) inc (long lead poss req); TV; 20% statics; phone; Eng spkn; adv bkg acc; ccard acc; bike hire; horseriding; tennis; games area; CKE. *"Beautiful views; well-maintained, clean site; pleasant rest; maganificent pool area; sm pitches; gd walking in Monti Sibillini National Park; paragliding; conv Assisi & historic hill towns; excel; well run."* **€40.00, 1 Apr-31 Oct. 2022**

"Satellite navigation makes touring much easier"

Remember most sat navs don't know if you're towing or in a larger vehicle – always use yours alongside maps and site directions.

PREDAZZO *1D1* (2.5km E Rural) *46.31027, 11.63138* **Camping Valle Verde,** Loc Ischia 2, Sotto Sassa, 38037 Predazzo (TN) **0462 502394; info@campingvalleverde.it; www.campingvalleverde.it**

€3.50 (htd)

Exit A22 dir Ora onto rd S48 dir Cavalese/Predazzo. Fr Predazzo take SS50 E, turn R in 1.5km, site on L in 500m. 3*, Med, mkd, pt shd, pt sl, EHU (6A) €2; bbq; sw nr; twin axles; 5% statics; bus 0.5km; Eng spkn; adv bkg acc; ccard acc; games area. *"Excel; bus & cable car rides; walks, cycle tracks & mountain climbs nrby; mini train adj; beautiful site."* **€36.00, 22 Apr-8 Oct. 2023**

PUNTA SABBIONI *2E2* (2km NE Coastal) *45.44560, 12.46100* **Campéole Camping Ca'Savio,** Via di Ca'Savio 77 - 30013 Cavallino Treporti Ca'Savio (VE) **041 966017 or 041 966 570 (mob); info@casavio.it; www.casavio.it or www.campeole.com**

sandy adj

Fr Lido di Jesolo head twd Punta-Sabbioni; at x-rds/rndabt in cent of Ca'Savio turn L twd beach (La Spiaggia) for 800m; turn L into site just bef beach. Or at L turn at rndabt - rd poss clsd at night - cont to Punta-Sabbioni, turn L at sp to beach; L at T-junc, then R at x-rds. 3*, V lge, hdg, mkd, shd, EHU (5A) inc (check pol); gas; TV; 50% statics; phone; bus to Venice ferry; ccard acc; games rm; archery; bike hire; watersports; fishing; kayaking; games area; canoeing; CKE. *"Well laid-out, well-run, busy site - noisy high ssn; helpful staff; conv Venice by ferry fr Punta Sabbioni; excel, clean san facs; facs ltd LS; long, narr pitches; no o'fits over 7m high ssn; access poss diff lge o'fits; gd supmkt; min 3 nights stay high ssn; barriers clsd 1300-1500."* **€40.00, 6 May-24 Sep, Y02. 2022**

PUNTA SABBIONI *2E2* (0.7km S Coastal) *45.44141, 12.42127* **arking Dante Alighieri,** Lungomare Dante Alighieri 26, 30010 Punta-Sabbioni (VE) **+390412909711**

nr nr nr

Take rd Jesolo to Punta-Sabbioni, pass all camps & go to end of peninsula. Turn L at boat piers & foll rd alongside beach; site on L just bef Camping Miramare. Sm, pt shd, EHU (8A) inc; bus 500m; Eng spkn. *"M'vans only; friendly, helpful owner; 10 min walk for boats to Venice; vg."* **€23.00** **2020**

PUNTA SABBIONI *2E2* (1.6km SSW Coastal) *45.44035, 12.4211* **Camping Miramare,** Lungomare Dante Alighieri 29, 30013 Punta-Sabbioni (VE) **041 966150; info@camping-miramare.it; www.miramarevenezia.it**

€4 (htd) nr

Take rd Jesolo to Punta-Sabbioni, pass all camps & go to end of peninsula. Turn L at boat piers & foll rd alongside beach; site 500m on L. 3*, Med, mkd, hdg, pt shd, EHU (6A) inc (rev pol); gas; phone; Eng spkn; adv bkg acc; ccard acc. *"Excel, well-organised, helpful, caring, friendly family-owned site - 10 mins walk for Venice (tickets fr recep) - can leave bikes at terminal; gd security; new pt of site v pleasant wooded area; clean facs; poss mosquito problem; min 3 nights stay high ssn; superior to other sites in area; min stay 2 nights Jul/Aug; sm dogs only; don't miss camping supmkt on way in - an Aladdin's cave; bus to beach; avoid dep on Sat due traff; ferry; Magic of Italy site; highly rec, reasonable mob home rentals; excel staff; close to beach and ferries."* **€41.40, 1 Apr-3 Nov.** **2024**

PUNTA SABBIONI *2E2* (1km SW Rural) *45.44236, 12.42251* **Al Batèo,** via Lungomare Dante Alighieri 19/A, 30013 Cavallino Treporti Venice **040 5301 455 or 041 5301 564; info@albateo.it; www.albateo.it**

12 (htd)

Take rd Jesolo to Punta Sabbioni and go to end of the peninsula. Turn L at boat piers and foll rd along side beach. Site 300 on L. Sm, hdg, shd, bus; Eng spkn; adv bkg acc. *"M'vans only; gd value; Vapporetti to Venice 300m."* **€25.00** **2024**

RAPALLO *1C2* (2km N Urban) *44.35805, 9.2100* **Camping Miraflores,** Via Savagna 10, 16035 Rapallo (GE) **0185 263000; camping.miraflores@gmail.com; www.campingmiraflores.it**

nr

Exit A12/E80 at Rapallo. In 100m fr toll gate sharp L across main rd, sharp L again, site sp 200m on R. Site almost immed beside toll gate but not easily seen. Sp fr town. 2*, Med, hdg, mkd, hdstg, pt shd, terr, EHU (3A) €1.80; gas; red long stay; 10% statics; bus 200m to stn & town cent; ccard acc; sep car park; CKE. *"Excel htd pool adj; gd, modern san facs, refurb (2018); grass pitches for tents, earth only for m'vans & c'vans; v noisy & dusty as under m'way; v friendly staff; ferries to Portofino fr town; conv NH; rec phone ahead if lge o'fit."* **€37.00, 1 Jan-8 Jan, 3 Mar-5 Nov, 5 Dec-31 Dec.** **2023**

RAPALLO *1C2* (2.5km W Urban) *44.35691, 9.1992* **Camping Rapallo,** Via San Lazzaro 4, 16035 Rapallo (GE) **0185 262018; campingrapallo@libero.it; www.campingrapallo.it**

nr nr (htd) shgl 2.5km

Exit A12/E80 dir Rapallo, turn immed R on leaving tolls. Site sp in 500m on L at bend (care), over bdge then R. Narr app rd. Site sp. 2*, Med, hdg, mkd, pt shd, EHU (3A) €2.20; gas; 10% statics; bus (tickets fr recep); Eng spkn; adv bkg acc; ccard acc; bike hire; CKE. *"Clean, family-run site; conv Portofino (boat trip) & train to Cinque Terre; beautiful coastlline; shwrs clsd during day but hot shwrs at pool; v busy public hols - adv bkg rec; awkward exit, not suitable for lge o'fits; NH only."* **€28.50, 15 Mar-15 Nov.** **2024**

RHEMES ST GEORGE *1B1* (3km N Rural) *45.64966, 7.15150* **Camping Val di Rhemes,** Loc Voix 1, 11010 Rhêmes-St George (AO) **0165 907648; info@campingvaldirhemes.com; www.campingvaldirhemes.com**

€2.50 (htd)

Fr S26 or A54/E25 turn S at Introd dir Rhêmes-St George & Rhêmes-Notre-Dame; site on R in 10km past PO; app is diff climb with hairpins. 2*, Med, pt shd, pt sl, EHU (2-6A) €2; 10% statics; Eng spkn; adv bkg acc; ccard acc; CCI. *"Peaceful, family-run site; nr Gran Paradiso National Park; gd walking; excel."* **€26.40, 20 May-10 Sep.** **2024**

RIVA DEL GARDA *1D1* (2.5km E Rural) *45.88111, 10.86194* **Camping Brione,** Via Brione 32, 38066 Riva-del-Garda (TN) **0464 520885; info@campingbrione.com; www.campingbrione.com**

€4 nr (htd)

Exit A22 Garda Nord onto SS240 to Torbole & Riva; on app to Riva thro open-sided tunnel; immed R after enclosed tunnel opp Marina; site ent 700m on R. 4*, Med, mkd, pt shd, terr, EHU (6A) inc; gas; bbq; sw nr; Eng spkn; adv bkg acc; ccard acc; watersports; bike hire; solarium; CKE. *"Olive groves adj; barriers clsd 1300-1500 & 2300-0700; pleasant site with lge pitches; gd, modern san facs."* **€44.00, 9 Apr-25 Oct.** **2022**

ROCCARASO *2F4* (2km NE Rural) *41.84194, 14.10277* **Snow Village Roccaraso (Camping Del Sole),** Piana del Leone, 67030 Roccaraso **0864 62532 or 0379 2037704; info@snowvillageroccaraso.it; www.villaggiodelsole.com**

12 (sm only) nr

Turn E fr S17 at sp Petransieri & site on R in 2km. 3*, Med, pt shd, pt sl, EHU inc (poss no earth - long lead rec); gas; sw nr; 50% statics; bus; ccard acc; CKE. *"Excel & conv National Park; ski school; ltd facs LS; unrel opening, suggest phone to confirm."* **€26.00** **2024**

ROMA *2E4* (8km N Urban) *41.95618, 12.48240* **Camping Village Flaminio,** Via Flaminia Nuova 821, 00189 Roma **06 3332604 or 3331429; info@villageflaminio.com; www.villageflaminio.com**

12 (htd)

Exit GRA ring rd at exit 6 & proceed S along Via Flaminia twd Roma Centrale. In 3km where lanes divide keep to L-hand lane (R-hand land goes into underpass). Cross underpass, then immed back to R-hand lane & slow down. Site on R 150m, sp as Flaminio Bungalow Village. No vehicular access to site fr S or exit to N. Lge, pt shd, pt sl, EHU (3-12A) inc; gas; red long stay; TV; 10% statics; phone; bus (cross v busy rd), train nr; ccard acc; bike hire; site clsd mid-Jan to end Feb. *"Well-run site; excel, clean san facs; poss long walk fr far end of site to ent (site transport avail); poss dusty pitches; take care sap fr lime trees; cycle/walking track to city cent nrby; train 10 mins walk (buy tickets on site); local excursions pick-up fr site (tickets fr recep)."* **€57.00** **2024**

ROMA *2E4* (10km SW Rural) *41.77730, 12.39605* **Camping Fabulous,** Via Cristoforo Colombo, Km 18, 00125 Acilia (RM) **06 5259354; fabulous.huopenair.com**

€1.50 (htd)

Exit junc 27 fr Rome ring rd into Via C Colombo. At 18km marker turn R at traff lts, site 200m on R. V lge, mkd, shd, pt sl, EHU (6-10A) inc; bbq; 80% statics; phone; bus on main rd; Eng spkn; adv bkg acc; ccard acc; tennis; games area; waterslide; CKE. *"Set in pinewoods; gd sh stay, ltd facs in LS; helpful staff."* **€40.00, 1 Apr-2 Nov.** **2023**

ROMA *2E4* (4km W Urban) *41.88741, 12.40468* **Roma Camping,** Via Aurelia 831, Km 8.2, 00165 Roma **06 6623018; roma.huopenair.com**

12 €1.50 nr

Site is on Via Aurelia approx 8km fr Rome cent on spur rd on S side of main dual c'way opp lge Panorama Hypmkt. Fr GRA ring rd exit junc 1 Aurelio & head E sp Roma Cent & Citta del Vaticano. In approx 3km take spur rd on R 50m bef covrd pedestrian footbdge x-ing dual c'way & 250m bef flyover, sp camping; site gates on R (S) in 100m. W fr Rome take spur rd 8km fr cent sp camping just after Holiday Inn & just bef Panorama Hypmkt. At top turn L (S) over flyover & immed R sp camping; site gates on L in 200m. 4*, V lge, hdstg, pt shd, terr, EHU (4-6A) inc; 75% statics; bus to city; Eng spkn; ccard acc; games area; CKE. *"Gd, clean site; excel san facs & pool; friendly staff; popular site - rec arr early; rec not leave site on foot after dark; rest open all year; conv walk to hypmkt."* **€42.20** **2024**

SALBERTRAND *1A2* (1km SW Rural) *45.06200, 6.86821* **Camping Gran Bosco,** SS24, Km 75, Monginevro, 10050 Salbertrand (TO) **0122 854653; info@campinggranbosco.it; www.campinggranbosco.it**

12 (htd) nr

Leave A32/E70 (Torino-Fréjus Tunnel) at Oulx Ouest junc & foll SS24/SS335 sp Salbertrand. Site sp 1.5km twd Salbertrand at km 75. Fr S (Briançon in France) on N94/SS24 to Oulx cent, foll SS24 thro town & foll sp Salbertrand, then as above. 3*, Lge, pt shd, EHU (3-6A) inc; gas; 80% statics; ccard acc; tennis; games area. *"Beautiful setting; excel NH bef/after Fréjus Tunnel or pass to/fr Briançon; gates open 0830-2300; excel, modern, clean san facs; sm pitches; grnd soft in wet - no hdstg; conv for m'way; popular with m'cyclists but quiet at night."* **€28.00** **2022**

SALSOMAGGIORE TERME *1C2* (3km E Rural) *44.80635, 10.00931* **Camping Arizona,** Via Tabiano 42, 43039 Tabiano-Salsomaggiore Terme (PR) **0524 565648; info@camping-arizona.it; www.camping-arizona.it**

€3

Fr fidenza foll sp Salsomaggiore and then at rndabt to Tabiano. Go thro Tabiano and site 500m on L. 4*, Lge, shd, pt sl, EHU (3A) inc (rev pol); 30% statics; phone; bus to Salsomaggiore; waterslide; games area; jacuzzi; sep car park; games rm; tennis; bike hire; golf 7km; fishing. *"Vg site; friendly, helpful staff; interesting, smart spa town; excel touring base; gd for families; san facs vg; best campsite shop; vg rest."* **€37.00, 1 Apr-6 Oct.** **2024**

SAN FELICE DEL BENACO *1D2* (1km E Rural) *45.58500, 10.56583* **Camping Fornella,** Via Fornella 1, 25010 San Felice-del-Benaco (BS) **0365 62294; fornella@fornella.it; www.fornella.it**

€8 (htd) (htd)

N fr Desenzano on S572 twd Salo. Turn R to San Felice-del-Benaco, over x-rds & take 2nd R turn at sp to site. R into app rd, L into site. Rd narr but accessible. Avoid vill cent, site sp (with several others) fr vill by-pass just bef g'ge. 5*, Lge, pt shd, pt sl, terr, EHU (6A) inc; gas; bbq (charcoal); sw; TV; 20% statics; Eng spkn; adv bkg acc; ccard acc; games area; bike hire; games rm; boat hire; windsurfing; tennis; fishing; CKE. *"Family-run site in vg location by Lake Garda; park outside until checked in; recep 0800-1200 & 1400-2000; no o'fits over 7m high ssn; sep car park; excel pool; extra for lge pitches & lakeside pitches; excursions to Venice, Florence & Verona opera; excel rest; gd san facs."*
€50.00, 13 Apr-13 Oct, Y11. **2022**

SAN MARINO 2E3 (7km N Rural) 43.95990, 12.46090 **Centro Vacanze San Marino,** Strada San Michele 50, 47893 Cailungo, Repubblica di San Marino **0549 903964; info@centrovacanzesanmarino.com; www.centrovacanzesanmarino.com**

12 €3 (htd) (htd)

Exit A14 at Rimini Sud, foll rd S72 to San Marino. Pass under 2 curved footbdges, then 800m after 2nd & 13km after leaving a'strada, fork R. Cont uphill for 1.5km then turn R at Brico building, site sp. Steep long-haul climb. 3*, Lge, hdstg, hdg, pt shd, terr, serviced pitches; EHU (6A) inc (poss rev pol); bbq; cooking facs; red long stay; TV (pitch); 10% statics; bus; Eng spkn; adv bkg acc; ccard acc; bike hire; games area; tennis; CKE. *"V busy at w/end - rec arr early; superb hill fort town; excel rest & pool; sm pitches; conv Rimini 24km; solarium; mini zoo; excel, clean site; bus calls at site ent for San Marino."*
€30.00, Y04. **2022**

SAN REMO 1B3 (2.5km W Coastal) 43.802393, 7.745345 **Camping Villaggio Dei Fiori,** Via Tiro a Volo 3, 18038 San Remo (IM) **0184 660635; info@villaggiodeifiori.it; www.villaggiodeifiori.it**

(htd) nr (htd) shgl adj

Fr A10/E80 take Arma-di-Taggia exit & foll sp San Remo Centro. At SS1 coast rd turn R sp Ventimiglia. At 2.5km look for red/yellow Billa supmkt sp on R; 50m past sp take L fork, site on L in 50m. Fr W on A10 take 1st exit dir San Remo - winding rd. Turn R & site on L after Stands supmkt. Fr Ventimiglia on SS1, 150m past San Remo boundary sp turn sharp R (poss diff lge o'fits) to site. 4*, Lge, hdstg, mkd, hdg, pt shd, terr, EHU (3-6A) €4-7; bbq (gas); cooking facs; red long stay; twin axles; 60% statics; phone; train to Monaco & bus San Remo nr; Eng spkn; adv bkg rec; ccard acc; games area; tennis; bike hire; CKE. *"Gd location; well-kept, tidy, paved site; vg, clean facs; beach not suitable for sw; some pitches superb sea views (extra charge), some sm; rd & fairgrnd noise; lge o'fits not acc high ssn as sm pitches; vg rest; conv Monaco; gates locked at night."*
€73.00, 15 Jun-31 Dec. **2022**

SAN VALENTINO ALLA MUTA 1D1 (0.7km N Rural) 46.7700, 10.5325 **Camping Thöni,** Landstrasse 83, 39020 St Valentin-an-der-Haide, Graun **0473 634020; info@camping thoeni.it; www.camping thoeni.it**

12 (htd) nr nr nr

N twd Austrian border site on L on edge of vill on S edge of Lago di Resia. 2*, Sm, unshd, pt sl, EHU 6-16A; site clsd Nov. *"Conv sh stay/NH en rte Austria; cycle rte around lake; scenic area; off open 0900-1000 & 1700-1800; numbered pitches; views; walking rte rnd Haidensee below vill; cable car opens late June."*
€27.00 **2023**

SARNANO 2E3 (3km SSW Rural) 43.01743, 13.28358 **Quattro Stagioni,** Contrada Brilli, 62028 Sarnano **0733 651147; quattrostagioni@camping.it; www.camping4stagioni.it**

12

A14 exit Civitanova Marche. M'way to Macerata as far as Sarnano exit. In Sarnano turn R at sq, foll main rd. Site approx 3km outside Sarnano to the W. 3*, Sm, mkd, pt shd, pt sl, EHU; bbq; twin axles; 60% statics; Eng spkn; adv bkg acc; games area; CKE. *"Fair site."* **€30.00** **2024**

SARTEANO 1D3 (0km W Rural) 42.9875, 11.86444 **Camping Parco Delle Piscine,** Via del Bagno Santo, 53047 Sarteano (SI) **0578 26971; info@parcodellepiscine.it; www.parcodellepiscine.it**

nr

Exit A1/E35 onto S478 at Chiusi & foll sp to Sarteano. Site at W end of vill, sp. 5*, Lge, pt shd, serviced pitches; EHU (6A) inc; 50% statics; Eng spkn; ccard acc; solarium; tennis. *"Clean, well-run; security guard 24 hrs; no vehicles during quiet periods 1400-1600 & 2300-0700; poss long walk to wc/shwrs; Florence 90 mins on m'way, Siena 1 hr; site at 600m, so cool at night; excel."*
€72.00, 1 Apr-1 Oct, Y17. **2023**

SARZANA 1C2 (4km SE Coastal) 44.076651, 9.981182 **Camping Iron Gate Marina 3B,** Viale XXV Aprile 54 19038, Sarzana **0187 676370; info@marina3b.it; www.marina3b.com**

(htd) 1km

Fr A12 exit Sarzana dir S. TR at 4th rndabt (2nd after dble rndabt). 3.1 km or R. Lge, mkd, shd, 65% statics; Eng spkn; ccard acc. *"VG, nice site; gd facs; conv for Cinque Terre towns."* **€20.00, 15 Mar-30 Sep.** **2024**

SARZANA 1C2 (8km S Rural/Coastal) 44.07638, 9.97027 **Camping River,** Loc Armezzone, 19031 Ameglia (SP) **0187 65920; info@campingriver.com; www.campingriver.com**

€3 nr 2km

Exit A12 at Sarzana & foll sp Ameglia & Bocca di Magra on SP432. In 7km turn L into Via Crociata to site (blue sp). Narr app rd with few passing places. 3*, Lge, mkd, pt shd, EHU (3-6A) inc; TV; 50% statics; adv bkg acc; bike hire; games area; tennis 200m; boat hire; golf driving range; rv fishing; horseriding 200m; sauna. *"Gd touring base Cinque Terre; pleasant, helpful staff; vg, well-situated site; gd shop & rest; bus to beach; nice location by rv; dated facs; gd pools."*
€44.00, 12 Apr-30 Sep. **2024**

SAVONA 1B2 (13km SW Coastal) 44.224200, 8.41032 **Camping Leo,** Via Siaggia 4, 17028 Spotorno **019 745184; info@campingleo.it; www.campingleo.it**

nr

Leave A10 sp S8 Spotorno. Immed after rlwy bdge turn R at rndabt into site. Med, hdstg, pt shd, serviced pitches; EHU (3A); bbq (gas, sep area); sw nr; 500m; Eng spkn; adv bkg rec; games area; bike hire. *"Excel."*
€25.00, 1 Feb-4 Nov. **2024**

ITALY

SAVONA *1B2* (2km SW Coastal) *44.29079, 8.45331* **Camping Vittoria,** Via Nizza 111/113, Zinola, 17100 Savona (SV) **019 881439; www.campingvittoria.com**

Exit Savona heading SW, site on L on seashore immed bef Shell petrol stn behind bar Vittoria. 1*, Med, unshd, EHU €2; 90% statics; Eng spkn; adv bkg acc; CKE. *"Excel location with views; busy site; helpful, friendly owner; pitches adj beach; clean, simple facs; ltd sm touring pitches."* **€35.00, 1 Apr-30 Sep. 2024**

> **"There aren't many sites open at this time of year"**
>
> If you're travelling outside peak season remember to call ahead to check site opening dates – even if the entry says 'open all year'.

SENIGALLIA *2E3* (1km S Coastal) *43.70416, 13.23805* **Villaggio Turistico Camping Summerland,** Via Francesco Podesti, 236 Senigallia P.Iva 00207190422 **071 7926816; info@campingsummerland.it; www.campingsummerland.it**

Exit A14/E55 onto SS16 to Senigallia S. Site on R after lge car park at side of rd. 4*, Lge, shd, EHU (5A) €2.50; gas; TV; 10% statics; adv bkg rec; games area; sep car park; tennis. **€42.00, 1 Jun-15 Sep. 2020**

SESTO CALENDE *1B1* (1km N Rural) *45.72988, 8.61989* **Camping La Sfinge,** Via Angera 1, 21018 Sesto-Calende (VA) **0331 924531; info@campeggiolasfinge.it; www.campeggiolasfinge.it**

Take rd fr Sesto-Calende to Angera. Site 1km on L bef junc for Sant' Anna. 2*, Med, mkd, shd, EHU; gas; 90% statics; ccard acc; boating; games area. *"Friendly owners; gd lakeside location; poss mosquitoes; poor facs; lovely pool; excel position for lake Maggiore; within reach of gd shops and rest."* **€39.00, 1 Jan-30 Oct. 2024**

SESTO CALENDE *1B1* (4km N Rural) *45.74892, 8.59698* **Camping Okay Lido,** Via per Angera 115, Loc Lisanza, 21018 Sesto Calende (VA) **0331 974235; campingokay@camping-okay.com; www.camping-okay.com**

Exit A8 at Sesto Calende onto SP69 N dir Angera, site sp. 4*, Med, mkd, pt shd, terr, EHU (6A) €3; sw; TV; 10% statics; Eng spkn; adv bkg acc; watersports; games rm; games area. *"Friendly, welcoming site; private san facs avail; NH pitches by lakeside; gd NH for Amsterdam ferry."* **€42.00, 30 Mar-13 Oct. 2024**

SESTO CALENDE *1B1* (7.5km N Rural) *45.82712, 8.62722* **International Camping Ispra,** Via Carducci, 21027 Ispra (VA) **0332 780458; info@internationalcampingispra.it; www.internationalcampingispra.it**

Site 1km NE of Ispra on E side of lake. 4*, Med, shd, terr, EHU (6A) €3; own san req; bbq; sw; TV; 90% statics; Eng spkn; adv bkg acc; fishing; boating; games area; CKE. *"Gd views of lake; muddy beach; vg rest; nice, peaceful site; friendly, helpful staff; lovely situation on banks of Lake Maggiore; well run; loud music fr bar till midnight."* **€38.90, 5 Mar-16 Oct. 2022**

SESTO/SEXTEN *2E1* (3km SE Rural) *46.66806, 12.39935* **Caravan Park Sexten,** St. Josefstr. 54, 39030 Sexten / Moos **0474 710444; info@caravanparksexten.it; www.caravanparksexten.it**

Fr S49 take S52 SE fr San Candido thro Sexten & Moos. After sh, steep climb site on W of S52 midway bet Moos & Kreuzberg pass. 4*, Lge, mkd, pt shd, pt sl, serviced pitches; EHU (16A) metered; gas; TV; Eng spkn; adv bkg req; tennis; sauna; solarium; CKE. *"Excel, clean facs; Waldbad worth visit; rock climbing wall; lovely scenery; mountain walks; beauty & wellness treatments; v popular & busy site; private bthrms avail; winter sports; v well managed & equipped; rest worth a visit."* **€55.00, Y03. 2022**

SETTIMO VITTONE *1B1* (2.5km N Rural) *45.56474, 7.81668* **Camping Mombarone,** Torre Daniele, 10010 Settimo-Vittone (TO) **0125 757907; info@campingmombarone.it; www.campingmombarone.it**

On E side of Ivrea-Aosta rd (SS26), 100m S of Pont-St Martin. Exit A5 at Quincinetto, turn R onto SP69 across bdge, R at end onto SP26 & site on L in 150m. (App fr S, sp at ent but if overshoot go on 100m to rndabt to turn). Tight ent off busy rd. 2*, Med, pt shd, pt sl, EHU (6A) €2.50; 80% statics; games area; CKE. *"Gd base Aosta valley; superb views; Quincinetto medieval vill walking dist; lovely, grassy, well-kept site; ltd space for tourers; v pleasant, helpful owner who speaks gd Eng, friendly welcome; san facs immac; gd NH; rlwy stn nrby."* **€22.50 2024**

SIBARI *3A4* (4km E Coastal) *39.77944, 16.47889* **Camping Villaggio Pineta di Sibari,** 87070 Sibari (CS) **0981 74135; info@pinetadisibari.it; www.pinetadisibari.it**

Exit A3 at Frascineto onto SS106, then exit at Villapiana-Scalo. Site sp on beach. 3*, Lge, pt shd, EHU (4A) inc; TV; 20% statics; ccard acc; tennis; bike hire. *"Vg beach; site in pine forest; noisy bar/music; gd touring base; watch out for low bdge on app."* **€44.00, 19 Apr-29 Sep. 2024**

SIRMIONE *2G2* (3km E Coastal) *45.45738, 10.64025*
Tiglio, Loc. Punta Grò, 25019 Sirmione **030 990 4009; info@campingtiglio.it; www.campingtiglio.it**

A4 Milan-Verona, exit Sirmione. 1st exit at rndabt onto SP13. 1st exit at next rndabt. Turn L twds Via San Martino. 1st exit at rndabt onto Via Verona. Foll sp to camp. Lge, mkd, shd, EHU inc (4A); bbq; twin axles; 50% statics; bus adj; Eng spkn; adv bkg acc; ccard acc; CKE. *"Gd site; noisy & busy but friendly; on bus rte to Verona."* **€36.00, 18 Apr-30 Sep. 2024**

SIRMIONE *1D2* (3km S Rural) *45.46845, 10.61028*
Camping Sirmione, Via Sirmioncino 9, 25010 Colombare-di-Sirmione (BS) **030 99 04 665; info@camping-sirmione.it; www.camping-sirmione.it**

(cont)

Exit S11 at traff lts sp Sirmione, in 500m R at site sp. 3*, Lge, mkd, hdstg, pt shd, pt sl, EHU (6A) inc; sw; 30% statics; adv bkg acc; ccard acc; games area; watersports. *"Excel lakeside site; facs poss stretched when site busy; excel rest, bar, pool & san facs; lovely walk to Sirmione; highly rec."* **€43.60, 17 Apr-5 Oct. 2024**

"That's changed – Should I let the Club know?"

If you find something on site that's different from the site entry, fill in a report and let us know. See camc.com/europereport.

SORICO *1C1* (0.5km E Rural) *46.17152, 9.39302*
Camping La Riva, Via Poncione 3, 22010 Sorico (CO) **0344 94571; info@campinglariva.com; www.campinglariva.com**

€4 (must be kept on lead) nr

Fr Lecco take SS36 twd Colico & Sondrio. At end of tunnels fork L sp Como & Menaggio. At end of dual c'way turn L onto S340 to Sorico sp Como & Menaggio. Cross bdge & site 500m down lane on L bef cent Sorico, sp Cmp Poncione & La Riva. Easiest app on SS36 on E side of lake (pt dual c'way). Rd on W side narr & congested. 3*, Med, mkd, pt shd, EHU (6A) inc; bbq; sw nr; TV; 50% statics, phone, Eng spkn; waterskiing; bike hire; games rm; boat hire; canoeing; fishing; CKE. *"Excel, family-run site; gd views of lake & mountains; no o'fits over 7.5m high ssn; clean, well-kept & tidy; immac san facs; v warm welcome; less commercialised than some other sites in area; cycle track to vill; poss mosquito problem in Jun; gas 50m; v tidy clean site; friendly helpful owners; rd fr Lugano to Como not adv for c'vans."*
€54.00, 1 Apr-2 Nov, Y12. 2024

SORRENTO *3A3* (3km N Coastal) *40.63541, 14.41758*
Camping I Pini, Corso Italia 242, 80063 Piano-di-Sorrento (NA) **081 8786891; info@campingipini.com; www.campingipini.com**

12 nr 1km

S fr Naples on A3; Exit A3 sp Castellammare di Stabia & take SS145 sp to Sorrento; pass thro vill of Meta; site on R immed over bdge; lge sp on main rd. 1*, Med, hdg, mkd, pt shd, pt sl, EHU (4A) inc; red long stay; 50% statics; bus 50m; Eng spkn; adv bkg acc; ccard acc; CKE. *"Spacious site in mountains bet 2 vills; pool restricted to campers; sh walk to public transport to sites of interest; best site in Sorrento to avoid narr gridlocked rds; old, tired facs (2013); tight narr pitches."* **€47.50 2024**

SORRENTO *3A3* (5km NE Coastal) *40.65953, 14.41835*
Camping Sant Antonio, Via Marina d'Equa 20/21, Seiano, 80069 Vico-Equense (NA) **081 8028570 or 081 8028576; info@campingsantantonio.it; www.campingsantantonio.it**

€3 (not allowed Aug) shgl 100m

Fr A3 exit at Castellamare-di-Stabia. Foll sp for Sorrento; app Vico-Equense take L fork thro tunnel, at end of viaduct R to Seiano-Spaggia. Last site of 3 on L down narr twisting rd after 1km (poss v congested). Access to pitches poss diff due to trees. 3*, Med, shd, pt sl, EHU (5A) inc; gas; 10% statics; phone; bus adj, train 800m; Eng spkn; adv bkg acc; ccard acc; solarium; excursions; boat hire; CKE. *"Ideal base Amalfi coast, Capri, Naples; lovely harbour adj; v helpful, friendly staff; bus & train tickets avail fr site; gd rest."* **€32.50, 15 Mar-31 Oct. 2024**

"I like to fill in the reports as I travel from site to site"

You'll find report forms at the back of this guide, or you can fill them in online at camc.com/europereport.

SORRENTO *3A3* (2km W Coastal) *40.62818, 14.35816*
Camping Villaggio Santa Fortunata, Via Capo 39, 80067 Capo-de-Sorrento (NA) **081 8073574; info@santafortunata.com; www.santafortunata.com**

shgl

Only app fr a'strada, exit Castellamare. Foll sp into Sorrento then sp Massa-Lubrense. Site poorly sp fr Sorrento on R, gd wide ent. 4*, V lge, mkd, hdg, shd, pt sl, terr, EHU (6A) inc; gas; red long stay; TV; 50% statics; phone; bus adj; Eng spkn; sep car park; CKE. *"Gd, clean facs; pitches sm for lge o'fits (7m+) & poss dusty; bus fr gate, ticket fr recep; boat trips to Capri fr site beach; noisy nr gd rest, disco & 18-30 tours; many scruffy statics; facs dated; steep access & tight hairpins to some pitches; friendly, vg site."*
€40.00, 30 Mar-3 Nov. 2022

ITALY

SPERLONGA *2E4* (1km SE Coastal) *41.25514, 13.44625* **Camping Villaggio Nord-Sud,** Via Flacca, Km 15.5, 04029 Sperlonga (LT) **0771 548255; info@campingnordsud.it; www.campingnordsud.it**
sand

Site on seaward side of S213 at km post 15.9. Lge sp visible fr both dirs. Lge, mkd, hdstg, shd, EHU (4A) inc; 10% statics; adv bkg acc; tennis; games area; windsurfing; fitness rm. *"Mostly statics but great location; pleasant site; picturesque beach."*
€48.00, 1 Apr-31 Oct. **2022**

STRESA *1B1* (3.4km NW Urban) *45.91246, 8.50410* **Camping Parisi,** Via Piave 50, 28831 Baveno (VB) **0323 924160; info@campingparisi.it; www.campingparisi.it**
€4 nr nr nr

Exit A26 at Baveno, after x-ing bdge on o'skirts Baveno, turn L off main rd bet Hotel Simplon & Agip g'ge & foll sp. Fr Stresa drive thro Baveno. At end of prom, take R fork at Dino Hotel up a minor 1-way rd (poss congested by parked cars); foll Parisi sp. 2*, Med, pt shd, pt sl, EHU (6A); sw; 10% statics; phone; bus; Eng spkn; adv bkg acc; boat launch; fishing; CKE. *"Well-managed site on Lake Maggiore; fine views; extra for lakeside pitches; frequent lake steamers nr site; gd rests adj; long hose rec for m'van fill up; sm pitches; busy at w/end; sw in lake - supervise children; many repeat visitors; bar adj; clean facs; welcoming recep; conv base for visiting Borromeo Islands."* **€37.70, 1 Apr-30 Sep.** **2023**

STRESA *1B1* (4km NW Rural) *45.91185, 8.48913* **Camping Tranquilla,** Via Cave 2, Oltrefuime, 28831 Baveno (VB) **0323 923452; info@tranquilla.com; www.tranquilla.com**
€2.50 nr

Fr N go into Baveno & turn R 200m past Hotel Splendide; fr S turn L immed after x-ing bdge. Foll brown sp to site up steep hill 1km. 2*, Med, hdg, mkd, hdstg, pt shd, pt sl, terr, serviced pitches; EHU (6A) €2.60; red long stay; 25% statics; train to Milan 2km; Eng spkn; adv bkg acc; watersports; bike hire; car wash; CKE. *"Clean, comfortable, well-managed, pleasant, family-owned site; entmnt (w/end); v helpful staff; sm pitches; conv Lake Maggiore; day trip by train to Milan."* **€41.20, 19 Mar-16 Oct.** **2022**

TERNI *2E3* (7km E Rural) *42.54801, 12.71878* **Camping Marmore,** Loc Campacci, 05100 Cascata-delle-Marmore (TN) **328 677 1534; campingmarmore@gmail.com; www.campingmarmore.it**
€4 (htd)

E fr Terni on S79 dir Marmore & Rieti. Foll site sp. 2*, Med, hdstg, shd, pt sl, EHU inc; sw nr; 90% statics; phone; Eng spkn; games rm; watersports nr. *"Spectacular waterfalls adj & mountain scenery; gd; Casacata Hydro elec, well worth visiting."*
€25.00, 1 Apr-30 Sep. **2024**

TORBOLE *1D1* (0.4km N Urban) *45.8725, 10.87361* **Camping Al Porto,** Via Al Cor, 38069 Tórbole (TN) **0464 505891; info@campingalporto.it; www.campingalporto.it**
€2.50 nr nr

On ent Tórbole fr S take rd twd Riva-del-Garda for approx 600m. Petrol stn & car park on R, turn L into narr lane after shops; site sp. 3*, Med, mkd, pt shd, EHU (5A) inc; bbq; sw nr; red long stay; watersports; CKE. *"Excel san facs; excel site; secure; helpful staff; vill has many rest & sportling locations."*
€39.00, 10 Apr-3 Nov. **2024**

TRENTO *1D1* (12km NW Rural) *46.11111, 11.04805* **Camping Laghi di Lamar,** Via alla Selva Faeda 15, 38070 Terlago (TN) **0461 860423; laghidilamar@gmail.com; www.laghidilamar.com**
€2.50

Head W fr Trento for 10km on SS45b dir Riva-del-Garda/Brescia. Turn R twd Monte-Terlago; site sp on R. Last section via SS45 v steep. 3*, Med, pt shd, terr, EHU (10A) inc; gas; bbq; sw nr; TV; 30% statics; phone; Eng spkn; ccard acc; games rm; bike hire; games area; CKE. *"Excel site; excel new san facs."*
€36.00, 3 Apr-11 Apr, 27 Apr-29 Sep. **2023**

TRIESTE *2F1* (5.5km N Rural) *45.67974, 13.78387* **Camping Obelisco,** Strada Nuova Opicina 37, 34016 Opicina (TS) **040 212744; campeggioobelisco@gmail.com; www.campeggiobelisco.it**
12 €2.50 (cont) nr

Sp fr S58. 2*, Med, hdstg, shd, pt sl, terr, EHU €2.50; own san req; 95% statics; Eng spkn; CKE. *"V steep, narr, twisting ent/exit to site - suitable sm c'vans only & diff in wet; excel views Trieste harbour; interesting tram ride into city fr obelisk; demanding up hill walk to top of site, both Turkish & European wcs."*
€18.00 **2022**

TROPEA *3B4* (7km NE Coastal) *38.70610, 15.97024* **Villaggio Camping Sambalon,** Via del Mare, 89868 Marina-di-Zambrone (VV) **0963 392828; info@sambalon.com; www.sambalon.com**
sand adj

Fr N exit A3 at Pizzo Calabro onto S522 dir Tropea for 20km. Foll sp Marina di Zambrone & site. 4*, Med, mkd, hdstg, pt shd, EHU; TV; 10% statics; adv bkg acc. **€46.50, 20 May-23 Sep.** **2020**

URBISAGLIA *2E3* (5km NE Rural) *43.21136, 13.41544* **Centro Agrituristico La Fontana,** Via Selva 8, Abbadia-di-Fiastra, 62010 La Fontana (MC) **0733 514002**
12

Fr SP77 turn S to Abbadia-di-Fiastra onto SP78. On reaching Abbadia turn L & immed R, then uphill above Monastery for 2km & foll sp to site on R just after sharp RH bend. Sm, pt shd, terr, EHU (6A) inc; bbq; TV (pitch); minigolf; ping pong. *"Fair sh stay/NH; CL-type site on farm; not suitable lge o'fits; attactive countryside; v helpful owners."* **€21.00** **2020**

VENEZIA *2E2* (18km SW Coastal) *45.41916, 12.25666* **Camping Fusina,** Via Moranzani, 93, 30176 Fusina **041 5470055; info@campingfusina.com; www.campingfusina.com**

12 (htd) WD MSP

Exit A4 at sp Ravenna/Chiogga onto SS309 S, & foll sp to site. Take care when turning into rd leading to Fusina as L-hand turning lane used by locals for o'taking. 3*, Lge, pt shd, EHU (6A) inc (poss rev pol); gas; TV; 50% statics; ccard acc; games area; boat hire; CKE. *"Pleasant, busy site; some pitches o'looking lagoon; many backpackers, educational groups & 18-30s; gd san facs; gd public transport/boat dir to Venice; ferry to Greece adj; helpful staff; poss mosquitoes; some ship & aircraft noise + noise fr bar & adj indus complex; some pitches diff due trees & soft when wet; ltd facs LS & poss travellers; new sw."* **€35.00** **2024**

VENEZIA *2E2* (16km W Rural) *45.45222, 12.18305* **Camping Serenissima,** Via Padana 334/A, 30176 Malcontenta **041 5386498 or 041 921850; info@campingserenissima.it; www.campingserenissima.com**

(htd) WD MSP

Exit A4 at Oriago/Mira exit. At 1st rndabt foll sp Ravenna/Venezia; at next rndabt take 1st exit sp Padova/Riviera del Brenta (SR11) twd Oriago. Rv on L, site on R in approx 2km. 3*, Med, mkd, pt shd, EHU (10-16A) inc; gas; 25% statics; phone; Eng spkn; adv bkg acc; ccard acc; boat hire; bike hire; CKE. *"Bus to Venice/ Padua - buy tickets on site; friendly, helpful owners; efficient recep; some sm pitches; excel, v clean san facs; poss mosquitoes; conv Padova; highly rec for Venice; supmkt 3km; vg."* **€37.40, 3 Apr-5 Nov.** **2023**

VERBANIA *1B1* (6km W Rural) *45.93731, 8.48615* **Camping Conca d'Oro,** Via 42 Martiri 26, 28835 Feriolo di Baveno (VB) **0323 28116; info@concadoro.it; www.concadoro.it**

€5 WD MSP sand adj

Foll S33 NW fr Stresa, thro Bavena to Feriolo. At traff lts in Feriolo fork R, sp Verbania & in 800m immed over rv bdge, turn R into site. Clearly sp. 3*, Lge, mkd, shd, pt sl, EHU (6A) inc; 10% statics; Eng spkn; adv bkg acc; ccard acc; games area; windsurfing; bike hire; CKE. *"Helpful staff; excel, clean, modern san facs; discount for local services; dogs not acc Jul/Aug; extra for lakeside pitches; excel, v well run site; beautiful location; busy site."* **€48.00, 1 Apr-10 Sep.** **2024**

VERBANIA *1B1* (9km NW Urban) *45.96111, 8.45694* **Camping Lago delle Fate,** La Quartina, Via Pallanza 22, 28802 Mergozzo (VB) **0323 80326; info@lagodellefate.com; www.campinglagomaggiore.com/en/consorzio-lago-maggiore/campeggio-lago-delle-fate-mergozzo-vb**

€5 WD MSP nr shgl

Fr Verbani on Lake Maggiore drive twrds Mergozzo. Site on LHS just ent Mergozzo. Avoid going thro Mergozzo vill with lgr o'fits. 2*, Sm, hdstg, pt shd, EHU (10A); bbq (elec, gas); sw; twin axles; TV; 10% statics; bus 500m; Eng spkn; adv bkg acc; ccard acc; boat hire; CKE. *"Extra charge for lakeside pitches, slightly bigger with superb views; gd sh stay; town, 5 min walk; gd walking & cycling; vg."* **€55.00, 1 Apr-1 Oct.** **2023**

VERONA *1D2* (1.5km N Rural) *45.44985, 11.00415* **Camping San Pietro,** Via Castel San Pietro 2, 37129 Verona **045 592037; info@campingcastelsanpietro.com; www.campingcastelsanpietro.com**

(cont) WD nr

Exit A4/E70 to San Martino-Buon-Albergo & foll S11 dir Verona cent, site sp adj Castel San Pietro. 1*, Sm, mkd, hdstg, shd, EHU; bbq; 10% statics; bus 1km; adv bkg req. *"Basic site in park, more suited to tents or sm m'vans only; no vehicles/o'fits over 7m; beautiful views over city; easy walk to town cent, but many steps or use funicular 300mtrs; poor & ltd san facs."* **€41.00, 1 Apr-15 Oct.** **2023**

VERONA *1D2* (8km SW Urban) *45.38681, 10.91813* **Agricola Corte Comotto,** Via Comotto, 62, 37062 Alpo di Villafranca **347 5093229; info@cortecomotto.it; www.agricampeggiocortecomotto.it/en/agricamping cortecomotto_verona**

€4 WD MSP nr nr nr

Between Dossobuono and Alpo on LHS of rd. Sm, hdg, pt shd, EHU 8A; bbq (elec, gas); twin axles; train (400m); Eng spkn; adv bkg acc; ccard acc. *"Very good."* **NP 30, Spring-Autumn.** **2023**

VERONA *1D2* (15km W Rural) *45.44557, 10.83447* **Camping El Bacàn,** Via Verona 11, 37010 Palazzolo di Sona (VR) **348 9317204; info@el-bacan.it; www.el-bacan.it**

12 (cont) WD nr nr

Exit A4 onto A22 N & foll sp for Brescia (W) on SR11. Site in 7km on R, sp 150m bef site ent. Sm, hdg, mkd, pt shd, EHU (16A) inc; bbq; TV; bus 1km; Eng spkn; adv bkg acc; ccard acc; CKE. *"Charming, pleasant site on wkg farm; conv Verona, Lake Garda; friendly owner & staff; excel farm shop; highly rec; easy access; vg; gd san facs."* **€30.00** **2023**

ITALY

VERONA *1D2* (7km W Rural) *45.446075, 10.918951*
Agricamping Corte Finiletto, Strada Bresciana 41, 37139 Verona **340 6075017; info@cortefiniletto.it; www.cortefiniletto.it**

Exit A4 onto A22 N & foll sp for Brescia (W) on SR11. Site approx 3km on R. Lge sp with flags flying. Sm, mkd, pt shd, EHU (6A) inc; bbq; bus; Eng spkn; adv bkg acc; ccard acc. *"Kiwi fruit fm; site OAY except for 1st 2 weeks in Nov (harvest time); gd."* **€25.50** **2023**

VIAREGGIO *1C3* (2km S Coastal) *43.85133, 10.25963*
Camping Viareggio, Via Comparini 1, 55049 Viareggio (LU) **0584 391012; info@campingviareggio.it; www.campingviareggio.it**

€4 800m

Fr sea front at Viareggio, take rd on canal sp Livorno; after x-ing canal bdge turn L (but not immed on canal) & 2nd R to site in 2km. 1*, Lge, shd, EHU (4A) (poss rev pol); gas; TV; phone; adv bkg acc; games area; CKE. *"Gd site & facs; no dogs Aug; hot water to shwrs only; cycle rte/footpath to town."* **€32.00, 19 Apr-30 Sep.** **2024**

VIAREGGIO *1C3* (5km S Coastal) *43.82920, 10.2727*
Camping Italia, Viale dei Tigli 52, 55048 Torre-del-Lago Puccini (LU) **0584 359828; info@campingitalia.net; www.campingitalia.net**

sand 1.5km

Fr A12 N exit sp Viareggio, fr S exit Pisa N onto SS1 & turn twd Torre del Lago at S junc, site well sp thro vill. Do not turn L at vill cent but cont for 2km N, then L at rlwy bdge. At rndabt turn L, site on R in 250m. Avoid Viareggio town cent. Med, shd, EHU (6A) €1.30; gas; TV; 10% statics; Eng spkn; adv bkg acc; ccard acc; sep car park; bike hire; tennis. *"Vg for Lucca - Puccini's birthplace; bus tickets fr site for Pisa & Lucca; dogs not acc Jun-Aug; some pitches diff for lge o'fits due trees & low branches; gd clean facs; poss problem with mosquitoes."* **€32.50, 17 Apr-27 Sep.** **2024**

VICENZA *1D2* (9km SE Urban) *45.5175, 11.60222*
Camping Vicenza, Strada Pelosa 239, 36100 Vicenza **0444 582311; info@campingvicenza.it; www.campingvicenza.it**

nr nr

Exit A4 Vicenza Est dir Torri di Quartesole; turn R immed after toll; site on L 300m fr Vicenza exit, hidden behind Viest Quality Inn. Fr city foll sp Padua & a'strada; sp. 4*, Med, pt shd, pt sl, EHU (3A) inc (rev pol); bbq; red long stay; TV; bus; Eng spkn; adv bkg acc; ccard acc; bike hire; tennis; CKE. *"Cycle path to interesting town; functional site; clean san facs; friendly, helpful staff; pleasant site."* **€36.00, 1 Apr-15 Oct.** **2022**

VIESTE *2G4* (2km N Coastal) *41.89901, 16.14964*
Camping Punta Lunga, Loc Defensola, 71019 Vieste (FG) **0884 706031 or 03466 403894; info@puntalung.it; www.puntalunga.it**

(htd) adj

N fr Vieste 1.5km fr end of long beach, turn R at traff lts down narr lane. Site sp. 3*, Lge, mkd, pt shd, terr, EHU (3-5A) inc; gas; TV; 15% statics; phone; bus; Eng spkn; adv bkg acc; ccard acc; canoeing; windsurfing; sep car park; bike hire; CKE. *"Friendly, helpful staff; well-run site on lovely cove; tight pitches - beware pitch marker posts; v clean facs; rec use bottled water; beautiful coastal area; statics sep area; gd rest; lovely cove; excel beaches."* **€49.00, 30 May-15 Sep.** **2024**

VIESTE *2G4* (2km S Coastal) *41.85914, 16.17405*
Camping Adriatico, Lungomare. Enrico Mattei 110, 71019 Vieste (FG) **0884 700954; info@campingadriatico.it; www.campingadriatico.it**

(cont) sand adj

S fr Vieste on coast rd SP53, site on both sides of rd. 2*, Med, mkd, pt shd, EHU (6A) inc; bbq; 10% statics; phone; bus; Eng spkn; adv bkg acc; games area; windsurfing. *"Vg family-run site."* **€34.00, 1 Apr-31 Oct.** **2024**

VOLTERRA *1D3* (1km NW Rural) *43.41271, 10.8509*
Camping Le Balze, Via di Mandringa 15, 56048 Volterra (PI) **0588 87880 or 3791 876712; campinglebalze@gmail.com; www.campinglebalze.com**

nr

Take Pisa rd (S68) fr town; site clearly sp ('Camping' or symbol) after 1km. Watch out for R turn at sharp L corner. 2*, Med, pt shd, pt sl, terr, EHU (6A) inc; gas; bus adj; Eng spkn; ccard acc; CKE. *"Beautifully situated with views of Volterra & hills; gd, adequate san facs; select own pitch; Etruscan walls just outside site; excel site; helpful staff."* **€36.00, 1 Apr-15 Oct.** **2023**

ELBA ISLAND

MARINA DI CAMPO *1C3* (0km E Coastal) *42.75194, 10.24472* **Camping Ville degli Ulivi,** Via della Foce 89, 57034 Marina-di-Campo nell'Elba (LI) **0565 976098; info@villedegliulivi.it; www.villedegliulivi.it**

(€6, dog shwrs) sand adj

Fr Portoferraio take rd sp 'tutti le direzione', then foll sp Procchio, Marina-di-Campo & La Foce, site sp. 3*, Lge, pt shd, EHU (4A) €2.50; gas; 30% statics; adv bkg acc; ccard acc; horseriding 2km; archery; tennis 300m; bike hire; waterslide; golf 15km; watersports. *"Lovely, well-preserved island; gd, v clean, modern site."* **€54.50, 21 Apr-20 Oct.** **2020**

SARDINIA

ALGHERO *3A1* (1.5km N Coastal) *40.57916, 8.31222* **Camping La Mariposa,** Via Lido 22, 07041 Alghero (SS) **079 9950480; info@lamariposa.it; www.lamariposa.it**

sand adj

N fr Alghero on coast rd dir Fertilia. Site on L just beyond pool. 3*, Lge, hdstg, pt shd, pt sl, terr, EHU (6-10A) €3; gas; bbq; TV; 20% statics; bus nr; Eng spkn; ccard acc; bike hire; watersports; games rm; sep car park; CKE. *"Lovely wooded site; gd clean facs; gd security; friendly staff; boat fr Alghero to caves at Cape Caccia or by rd + 625 steps."*
€48.00, 23 Apr-11 Oct. **2022**

CAGLIARI *3B1* (1km SE Urban) *39.21129, 9.12883* **Camper Cagliari Park,** 13 Via Stanislao Caboni, 09125 Cagliari **070 303147; info@campercagliaripark.it; www.campercagliaripark.it**

12

Well sp on main rds into Cagliari. Sm, unshd, EHU (10A) €4; bus 200m; Eng spkn; CKE. *"Gd secure site; v helpful owner; walking dist historical cent, rests etc; c'vans enquire 1st."* **€21.00** **2024**

DORGALI *3A2* (7km W Coastal) *40.28486, 9.63370* **Camping Villaggio Calagonone,** Via Collodi 1, 08022 Cala-Gonone (NU) **0784 93476; info@calagononecamping.com; www.calagononecamping.com**

€5 shgl 400m

Fr S125 turn E twd Cala Gonone, thro tunnel. Site sp on L of main rd. 4*, Med, shd, terr, EHU (6A) €5; bbq; 30% statics; phone; adv bkg acc; ccard acc; games area; tennis. *"Beautiful situation in pine forest on edge of pretty town; nrby coves & grottoes accessible by boat or on foot."* **€44.00, 1 Apr-3 Nov.** **2024**

NARBOLIA *3A1* (6km W Coastal) *40.06956, 8.48375* **Camping Nurapolis,** Loc Is Arenas, 09070 Narbolia (OR) **0783 52283 or 348 8080839(mob); info@nurapolis.it; www.nurapolis.it**

12 sand adj

Fr Oristano take sp to Cuglier on rd SS292i. Site sp fr rd approx 5km fr S. Caterina-di-Pittinura. 3*, Lge, pt shd, EHU (3A) €3; gas; adv bkg acc; ccard acc; tennis; watersports; CKE. *"Site in pine forest; many sports, guided walks Easter to Oct; very pleasant owners."* **€36.50** **2024**

PORTO SAN PAOLO *3A2* (2km S Coastal) *40.85870, 9.64296* **Camping Tavolara,** Loc Porto Taverna, 07020 Loiri-Porta San Paolo (SS) **0789 40166; info@camping-tavolara.it; www.camping-tavolara.it**

€3 sand 500m

On SS125, sp. 3*, Lge, hdg, unshd, EHU (3-6A) €3.50; 25% statics; Eng spkn; adv bkg acc; ccard acc; tennis; bike hire; site clsd Dec & early Jan; CKE. *"Friendly staff; conv ferries & boat trips; pleasant, well managed site; 16km fr Olbia ferries; lovely beach; siesta 1:30-3:30pm; vg."* **€59.00, 22 Apr-14 Oct.** **2024**

PORTO TORRES *3A1* (7km E Coastal) *40.81607, 8.48541* **Camping Golfo dell'Asinara-Cristina,** Loc Platamona, 07037 Sorso (SS) **079 310230 or 335 5409976; info@campingasinara.it; www.campingasinara.it**

sand adj

Foll coast rd SP81 E fr Porto-Torres to site. Sp. 4*, Lge, pt shd, EHU (4A) €4; gas; red long stay; 40% statics; ccard acc; bike hire; tennis; games area; sep car park; CKE. *"Gd position."*
€44.00, 15 May-30 Sep. **2022**

PULA *3B1* (4km S Coastal) *38.96779, 8.97799* **Camping Flumendosa,** Santa Margherita, Km 33.800, 09010 Pula (CA) **070 4615332 or 392 9623094; info@campingflumendosa.com; www.campingflumendosa.com**

€2.50 (htd) sand

Fr Cagliari take SS195 past Pula, sp. Turn L, foll track for 500m to site ent. 3*, Lge, mkd, hdstg, pt shd, EHU (8A); gas; bbq; cooking facs; TV; 30% statics; Eng spkn; adv bkg acc; ccard acc; fishing; guided walks; jeu de boules alley; beach volleyball. *"Beautiful coastline; excel for children; sand flies abound; good, pleasant, friendly site; gd bar/rest; rec Nora for Roman city & beach; conv for lovely coast to W."*
€50.50, 28 Apr-15 Nov. **2024**

PULA *3B1* (4km SSW Coastal) *38.95778, 8.96930* **Camping Cala d'Ostia,** Localita Cala d'Ostia, 09010 Pula **39 070 921470; info@campingcaladostia.com; www.campingcaladostia.com**

Fr Cagliari, take SS195 past Pula. Foll the rd along the seafront about 1km, sp to site. 2*, Lge, pt shd, EHU (13A); bbq; twin axles; bus adj; Eng spkn; games rm; CCI. *"Fair site; busy in high ssn; beautiful coastline; lovely area."* **€35.00, Apr-Sep.** **2024**

SICILY

AGRIGENTO *3C3* (4km SE Coastal) *37.24395, 13.61423* **Camping Internazionale Nettuno,** Via Lacco Ameno 3, San Leone, 92100 Agrigento **0922 416268 or 0922 416983; info@campingagrigento.com or info@campinginternazionalenettuno.com; campingagrigento.com**

12 sand adj

Fr Agrigento to San Leone on SS115, foll rd SE out of San Leone alongside beach until sharp L away fr beach. Turn immed R into lane, site on R. 3*, Med, hdg, hdstg, pt shd, terr, EHU (6A) €2.50 (rev pol); gas; bbq; red long stay; TV; 15% statics; phone; adv bkg acc; ccard acc; CKE. *"Bus to temples at Agrigento; peaceful, unspoilt beach; steep slope to pitches - towed c'vans rec to keep to upper levels if poss; gd rest; take care low branches."* **€27.00** **2024**

ITALY

AGRIGENTO *3C3* (8km S Urban/Coastal) *37.26936, 13.58299* **Camping Valle dei Templi,** Viale Emporium 95, 92100 San Leone **0922 411115 or 350 5348817; info@campingvelledeitempli.com; www.campingvalledeitempli.com**

12 nr 800m

Sp S of Agrigento, foll sp San Leone, site on L bef beach. Lge, hdstg, pt shd, pt sl, terr, EHU (6A) €3; red long stay; 20% statics; bus; Eng spkn; adv bkg acc; ccard acc; tennis; bike hire; site clsd 8 Dec-15 Jan; CKE. *"Gd modern facs; friendly staff; bus to temples fr site ent."* **€34.00** **2023**

"I need an on-site restaurant"

We do our best to make sure site information is correct, but it is always best to check any must-have facilities are still available or will be open during your visit.

AVOLA *3C4* (4km N Coastal) *36.93631, 15.17462* **Camping Sabbiadoro,** Via Chiusa di Carlo 45, 96012 Avola (SR) **0931 822415 or 0338 2003031; info@campeggiosabbiadoro.it; www.campeggiosabbiadoro.it**

12 sand

Fr N exit A18/E45 at Cassibile onto S115 dir Avola, site sp in 4km. Last 500m on narr, winding rd. 3*, Med, mkd, shd, pt sl, terr, EHU (2A) €4; 20% statics; phone; adv bkg acc; ccard acc; horseriding. *"V attractive site with clean, ltd facs; rec visit Noto; well run; dir access to beach; sep car park Jul-Aug; poss muddy pitches after heavy rain."* **€44.00** **2024**

AVOLA *3C4* (5km NE Coastal) *36.93853, 15.17756* **Camping Paradiso del Mare,** Contrada Gallinara Fondolupo, 96012 Avola (SR) **0392 2490440; info@paradisodelmare.com; www.paradisodelmare.com**

nr adj

Best app fr N on S115 fr Siracusa, site on L, well sp. Tight turn if app fr Avola. 2*, Sm, mkd, pt shd, EHU (5A) €3; bus 200m; Eng spkn; CKE. *"Pleasant lovely site by beautiful beach; friendly helpful owners."* **€46.00, 13 Apr-11 Oct.** **2023**

CASTELLAMMARE DEL GOLFO *3C3* (1km E Coastal) *38.02393, 12.89348* **Nausicaa Camping,** C/da Spiaggia-Plaia, Loc Forgia, 91014 Castellammare-del-Golfo (TP) **0924 33030; info@nausicaa-camping.it; www.nausicaa-camping.it**

nr sand adj

Site 1km E fr Castellammare on R of rte 187. Well sp. Awkward ent for lge o'fits as steep ramp. 3*, Sm, mkd, hdstg, pt shd, EHU €3; gas; 10% statics; ccard acc; tennis; CKE. *"Nr Roman temple at Segesta; gd 1st stop fr Palermo if touring historical sites; lovely site on cliff; easy walk to town & access to beach."* **€42.00, 1 Apr-31 Oct.** **2023**

CASTELVETRANO *3C3* (13km SE Coastal) *37.59571, 12.84139* **Camping Athena,** Loc Marinella, Contrada Garraffo, 91022 Castelvetrano (TP) **0924 46132; info@campingathenaselinunte.it; www.campingathenaselinunte.it**

12 nr sand 800m

Exit SS115 (Castelvetrano-Sciacca) at sp to Selinunte, site on L bef Selinunte. 1*, Sm, hdstg, pt shd, EHU (10A) inc; bbq; phone; ccard acc; CKE. *"Can take lger o'fits than Maggiolino site; conv temples at Selinunte; excel facs; gd rest adj."* **€18.00** **2020**

CATANIA *3C4* (6km NE Coastal) *37.53279, 15.12012* **Camping Jonio,** Loc Ognina, Via Villini a Mare 2, 95126 Catania **095 491139; info@campingjonio.com; www.campingjonio.com**

12 nr shgl

SS114 N of Catania, exit Ognina. Fr the Catania ring rd, take exit Catania Centro (San Gregorio) and then Catania E. Foll sp to site. 3*, Med, hdstg, pt shd, terr, EHU (6A) €4; gas; bbq; twin axles; 20% statics; bus to Catania; Eng spkn; adv bkg acc; ccard acc; waterskiing; games area; sep car park; CKE. *"Mt Etna 45 mins drive N; owner v helpful; some pitches sm; subways, scubadiving; gd."* **€39.00** **2022**

CEFALU *3B3* (3km W Coastal) *38.02703, 13.98283* **Camping Costa Ponente,** C de Ogliastrillo, 90015 Cefalù (PA) **0921 420085; info@camping-costaponente.com; http://camping-costaponente.com**

€3.50 sand

Fr Palermo E twd Cefalù, on rd SS113 at km stone 190.3, site sp. Lge, hdstg, shd, terr, EHU rev pol (3A) €5; gas; 10% statics; bus nr; ccard acc; tennis; CKE. *"Sep car park (high ssn); dogs not acc Aug."* **€30.00, 1 Apr-31 Oct.** **2020**

CEFALU *3B3* (5km W Rural) *38.02700, 13.98247* **Camping Sanfilippo,** Ogliastrillo SS113, 90015 Cefalù **0921 420 184; info@campingsanfilippo.com; www.campingsanfilippo.com**

€3.50 150m

Fr Palermo E twds Cafalu on rd SS113. 2*, Med, mkd, hdstg, shd, terr, EHU (4A) inc; bbq; twin axles; 50% statics; bus 300m; Eng spkn; adv bkg acc; games area; games rm; CCI. *"Vg, beautiful site; sea views fr some pitches; newly renovated (2016)."* **€32.00, 1 Apr-31 Oct.** **2023**

FINALE *3B3* (0.5km W Coastal) *38.02305, 14.15388* **Camping Rais Gerbi,** di Triscele Tu.Rist Srl - Finale di Pollina (PA) S.S.113 Km. 172,9 **0921 426570; camping@raisgerbi.it; www.raisgerbi.it**

12 shgl 600m

Direct access fr SS113 immed after bdge W of Finale. 3*, Lge, hdstg, mkd, hdg, pt shd, terr, EHU (6A) €5; bbq; red long stay; TV; 13% statics; phone; bus; Eng spkn; adv bkg req; ccard acc; horseriding 200m; tennis; bike hire; games area; CKE. *"Gd touring base Cefalu & N coast; friendly, helpful staff; excel, clean site & facs."* **€41.00** **2024**

MARINA DI RAGUSA *3C3* (2km E Coastal) *36.78116, 14.56697* **Camping Baia del Sole,** via Maresciallo Scrofani 5, 97100 Marina-di-Ragusa (RG) **0347 8692675; campingbaiadelsolerg@gmail.com; www.campingbaiadelsole.it**

12 adj

Foll sp in Marina di Ragusa for Hotel Baia del Sole. Site in hotel grnds on dual c'way on seafront. 3*, Med, shd, EHU (4A) inc; adv bkg acc; ccard acc; bike hire; tennis. *"Go to recep 1st; no height barrier; sep car park; v quiet."* **€30.00** **2023**

MENFI *3C3* (6km S Coastal) *37.56500, 12.96416* **Camping La Palma,** Contrada Fiore, Via delle Palme 29, 92013 Menfi (AG) **338 8293132 or 2867825; info@campinglapalma.it; www.campinglapalma.com**

12 WD sand adj

Foll sp fr SS115 past Menfi to coast. In abt 3-4km look for campsite sp. Med, hdstg, shd, EHU 16A; gas; bbq; twin axles; TV; 5% statics; Eng spkn; adv bkg acc; games area; CKE. *"Lovely, unspoilt quiet beach (blue flag) with dunes; v helpful owner & staff; family run site; excel."* **€33.00** **2023**

MILAZZO *3B4* (2km N Coastal) *38.26090, 15.24335* **Camping Villaggio Riva Smeralda,** Strada Panoramica 64, 98057 Milazzo (ME) **090 9282980; info@rivasmeralda.it; www.rivasmeralda.it**

12 WD MSP shgl adj

Clearly sp in Milazzo; foll sp Capo-di-Milazzo. Diff app. 1*, Med, hdstg, shd, pt sl, terr, EHU (6A) €3; bbq; twin axles; 5% statics; Eng spkn; adv bkg acc; CKE. *"Gd base for trips to adj isles; site a bit run down; 1 in 5 sl access to pitches, ltd turning space; best for sm m'vans; diving cent on site; excel; v nice site with beautiful views of sea; pitches tight; extremely helpful owners; €3 a night to leave camper to go to Aeolian Islands; vg."* **€35.00** **2023**

OLIVERI *3B4* (1.5km N Coastal) *38.12913, 15.05813* **Camping Villaggio Marinello,** Via del Sole, 17 Contrada Marinello, 98060 Oliveri (ME) **0941 313000 or 0941 526038; marinello@camping.it or villaggiomarinell@gmail.com; www.camping.it/sicilia/marinello or www.villaggiomarinello.it**

12 free (not acc Jul/Aug) WD MSP shgl adj

Exit A20 Falcone dir Oliveri, site well sp. 2*, Lge, hdg, mkd, hdstg, pt shd, EHU (6A) inc; 20% statics; phone; train; Eng spkn; excursions; watersports; tennis; CKE. *"Basic, clean, well-managed site; excel but shelving beach; helpful staff."* **€46.00** **2024**

PALERMO *3B3* (12km NW Coastal) *38.19686, 13.24455* **Camping La Playa,** Viale Marino 55 - 90040 Isola delle Femmine (PA) **091 8677001; campinglaplaya@virgilio.it; www.laplayacamping.it**

WD MSP sand adj

On Palermo-Trapani rd take A29 exit Isola-delle-Femmine & foll sp. 2*, Med, hdstg, pt shd, EHU (6A) inc; gas; bbq; Eng spkn; adv bkg acc; ccard acc; CKE. *"V helpful staff; bus into Palermo hourly; barrier clsd 1400-1600; very clean, well-managed, busy site; manager well versed on local info."* **€47.00, 21 Mar-15 Oct.** **2024**

PALERMO *3B3* (16km NW Urban/Coastal) *38.19805, 13.28083* **Camping Degli Ulivi,** Via Pegaso 25, 90148 Sferracavallo (PA) **091 533021 or 091 530247; mporion@libero.it; www.campingdegliulivi.com**

12 WD MSP nr nr shgl 300m

Fr W on A29 exit sp Tommaso & foll dual c'way twd Mondello. Do U-turn at 1st opportunity to Sferracavallo. Downhill thro vill, site sp, R turn off hg street. 1*, Sm, hdg, pt shd, pt sl, EHU (6-10A) €3; bbq; twin axles; 10% statics; bus to Palermo; Eng spkn; sep car park; CKE. *"Helpful staff; pleasant ambience; beach sand 700m; well-maintained site nr nature park - excel views, popular site."* **€20.50** **2022**

PATTI *B4* (4.8km NNW Coastal) *38.169266, 14.948943* **Camping IL Cicero,** Via Pola 98, 98063 San Giorgio **094 139551 or 347 9989530; info@ilcicero.it; www.ilcicero.it**

(htd) WD MSP nr nr sand; adj

Fr E90 take SS113 to San Giorgio. Site on seafront Med, mkd, shd, EHU (6A) inc; twin axles; 20% statics; 0.5km; games area; games rm. *"V friendly, helpful staff; gd for kids; vg site."* **€37.00, 15 May-30 Sep.** **2023**

PIAZZA ARMERINA *3C3* (4km SE Rural) *37.20239, 14.23155* **Camping Agriturismo Agricasale,** C da Ciavarini, 94015 Piazza-Armerina (EN) **0935 686034; www.agricasale.it**

12 WD MSP nr

In Piazza-Armerina town foll sp twd Mirabella but at rndabt with stone cross bear R (red fox sign) & foll red fox down nar rd to wooded site. Park with care. Sm, pt shd, pt sl, EHU (4A) inc; bbq; TV; Eng spkn; adv bkg acc; CKE. *"Excel site close Palazzo Romana mosaics, pony-trekking, archery & other activities high ssn; all inc rate of €50 avail per day inc excel banquet; site run down."* **€15.00** **2024**

ITALY

PUNTA BRACCETTO 3C3 (0km E Urban/Coastal) 36.81713, 14.46736 **Camping Scarabeo,** Via dei Canaletti 120, Punta-Braccetto, 97017 Santa Croce Camerina (RG) **0932 918096 or 918391; info@scarabeocamping.it; www.scarabeocamping.it**

12 €2.50 nr nr sand adj

W fr Marina di Ragusa on SP80/SC25 coast rd. Site sp. 2*, Sm, hdg, hdstg, pt shd, pt sl, EHU (3-6A); bbq; twin axles; red long stay; 5% statics; phone; Eng spkn; adv bkg acc; ccard acc; CKE. *"Beautiful situation; private bthrm €4; well-maintained, friendly, family-run site; gd, clean, modern facs; vg security; friendly, helpful staff; cars parked sep across rd; excel."* **€40.50** **2023**

PUNTA BRACCETTO 3C3 (0km S Urban/Coastal) 36.81722, 14.46583 **Camping Luminoso,** Viale dei Canalotti, 97017 Punta Braccetto - Santa Croce Camerina (RG) **0932 918401; info@campingluminoso.com; www.campingluminoso.com**

12 sand adj

W fr Marina di Ragusa on SP80/SC25 coast rd. Site sp. 3*, Med, mkd, hdstg, shd, EHU (6A) €5; TV; adv bkg rec; ccard acc; bike hire; CKE. *"Well-run site in gd location; easy access to pitches - suitable lge o'fits/m'vans; excel; modern, immac facs; spacious level hdstg pitches; reliable wifi; helpful English manager; private bthrms avail; direct access to sandy beach; mob shops call daily; ideal long stay in winter."* **€46.00** **2024**

PUNTA BRACCETTO 3C3 (4km SW Coastal) 36.81661, 14.46895 **Camping Baia Dei Coralli,** Punta Braccetto, 97017 Santa Croce Camerina **0932 91 81 92; info@baiadeicoralli.it; www.baiadeicoralli.it**

12 sand

Fr Agrigento take SS115 twds Sircusa to Gela. Turn L onto SP14, cont onto SP13. At rndabt take 3rd exit onto SP20, R onto SP85, L twd Strada Regionale 25. R onto Strada Regionale 24. Campsite on L. 3*, Lge, hdg, hdstg, unshd, EHU (6A); bbq; twin axles; TV; bus; Eng spkn; adv bkg acc; ccard acc; CCI. *"Excel site; v busy in summer."* **€35.00** **2024**

SAN VITO LO CAPO 3B3 (3km S Coastal) 38.15067, 12.73184 **El Bahira Camping Village,** Contrada Salinella, 91010 San Vito-lo-Capo (TP) **0923 972577; info@elbahira.it; www.elbahira.it**

12 shgl adj

W fr Palermo on A29 dir Trapani. Exit at Castellammare del Golfo onto SS187, then turn N onto SP16 sp San Vito-lo-Capo. At Isolidda foll site sp. 4*, Lge, mkd, shd, EHU (6A) inc; bbq; TV; 10% statics; phone; bus nr; Eng spkn; ccard acc; watersports; games rm; sep car park; tennis; excursions; games area; CKE. *"Excel, secure site in vg location; gd facs for families; san facs tired need updating (2014)."* **€26.00** **2024**

SECCAGRANDE 3C3 (2km SE Coastal) 37.43833, 13.2450 **Kamemi Camping Village,** Contrada Camemi Superiore, 92016 Seccagrande-di-Ribera (AG) **0925 69212; info@kamemivillage.com; www.kamemivillage.com**

12 sand 1km

Foll sp fr S115 to Seccagrande & site. 2*, Med, hdstg, pt shd, EHU (6A) €5; 40% statics; Eng spkn; adv bkg rec; tennis; games area. **€37.00** **2024**

SIRACUSA 3C4 (4km SW Rural) 37.03841, 15.25063 **Camping Agritourist Rinaura,** Strada Laganelli, Loc Rinaura, SS115, 96100 Siracusa **0931 721224; sindona.marina@virgilio.it; www.campingrinaura.it**

12 nr sand 2km

S fr Siracusa on S115 twd Avola. Turn R 300m past Hotel Albatros then immed R after rlwy x-ing. Narr lane to site in 300m. 2*, Lge, pt shd, EHU (16A) €3; red long stay; phone; bus 1km; Eng spkn; adv bkg acc; bike hire; CKE. *"CL-type site in lge orchard; basic but adequate san facs; rather neglected LS; helpful owners."* **€27.00** **2024**

TAORMINA 3C4 (10km NE Coastal) 37.93159, 15.35560 **Camping La Focetta Sicula,** Contrada Siena 40, 98030 Sant' Alessio Siculo (ME) **3205 660810; info@lafocetta.it; www.lafocetta.it**

12 sand

A'strada fr Messina to Catania, exit Roccalumera. SS114 thro Sta Teresa-di-Riva to vill of Sant' Alessio-Siculo. Sp at beg of vill. NB Many towns poorly sp. 2*, Med, mkd, pt shd, EHU (6A) €3 gas; red long stay; sep car park; bike hire; games area; CKE. *"Popular winter site; v helpful owner."* **€36.00** **2023**

TAORMINA 3C4 (12km S Coastal) 37.74928, 15.20616 **Camping Mokambo,** Via Spiaggia 211, Fondachello, 95016 Máscali (CT) **095 938731; info@campingmokambo.it; www.campingmokambo.it**

12 nr nr adj

Exit A18/E45 at Fiumefreddo & take S114 sp Catania. In Máscali turn L twd Fondachello. At Fondachello turn R & foll site sp, site 1km on R. 2*, Med, hdstg, pt shd, EHU (3A) €4; bbq; 10% statics; Eng spkn; adv bkg acc; ccard acc; games area; CKE. *"Gd views Etna; conv beach & Taormina; wifi unreliable; no dogs Jul/Aug; poor."* **€31.50** **2023**

TAORMINA 3C4 (7km SW Coastal) 37.8047, 15.2444 **Camping Internazionale Almoetia,** Via San Marco 19, 95011 Calatabiano (CT) **095 641936; campingalmoetia@virgilio.it; www.campingalmoetia.it**

12 shgl 500m

Exit a'strada dir Giardini Naxos. Turn S onto S114 dir Catania, foll sp L onto Via San Marco, site clearly sp. 2*, Med, pt shd, EHU (6A) €2.50; gas; bbq; red long stay; TV; phone; adv bkg acc; bike hire; canoeing; tennis; CKE. *"Conv Etna, Taormina; surrounded by orchards; used by tour groups in motor hotels; site well kept; excel facs; lovely beach nrby."* **€27.00** **2020**

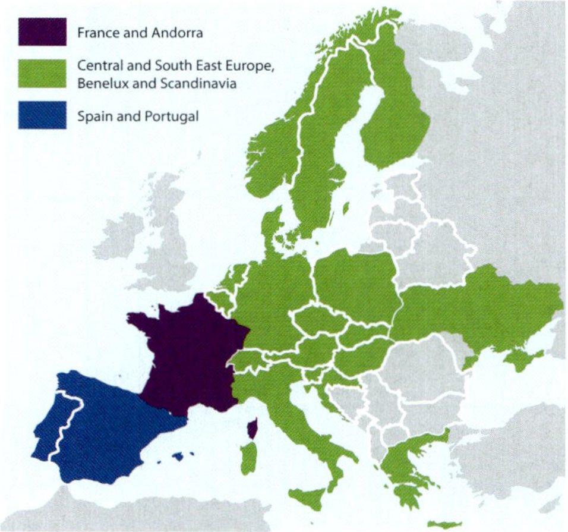

Milano (Milan) to Venezia (Venice) = 274km

	Ancona	Aosta	Bari	Bologna	Bolzano	Brindisi	Como	Cortina d'Ampezzo	Desenzano del Garda	Firenze (Florence)	Foggia	Genova (Genoa)	Grosseto	Imperia	L'Aquila	La Spezia	Livorno	Messina	Milano (Milan)	Napoli (Naples)	Orbetello	Palermo	Parma	Perugia	Pescara	Piacenza	Pisa	Ravenna	Reggio di Calabria	Roma (Rome)	Salerno	Siena	Siracusa (Syracuse)	Taranto	Torino (Turin)	Trento	Trieste	Venezia (Venice)	Verona
Aosta	619																																						
Bari	467	1075																																					
Bologna	220	404	677																																				
Bolzano	498	447	944	278																																			
Brindisi	573	1188	113	786	1062																																		
Como	475	207	929	258	290	1037																																	
Cortina d'Ampezzo	529	543	981	317	102	1090	381																																
Desenzano del Garda	385	296	839	170	188	937	134	243																															
Firenze (Florence)	262	472	724	104	369	836	355	419	261																														
Foggia	343	947	138	552	825	249	803	864	[illegible]	635																													
Genova (Genoa)	508	245	948	299	422	1062	186	497	255	225	842																												
Grosseto	324	556	634	242	512	745	497	561	463	142	552	303																											
Imperia	622	322	1066	403	529	1170	292	602	363	343	946	122	358																										
L'Aquila	203	794	392	411	697	512	675	730	536	372	272	562	305	722																									
La Spezia	428	348	872	212	370	984	274	432	247	146	773	101	232	220	498																								
Livorno	415	419	768	203	446	882	353	506	321	119	678	174	135	295	437	95																							
Messina	910	1445	455	1088	1342	457	525	1367	1469	975	556	1210	893	1317	731	1124	1022																						
Milano (Milan)	426	178	881	212	290	990	50	376	127	301	760	149	438	244	625	223	296	1272																					
Napoli (Naples)	411	962	263	596	858	374	845	1064	746	487	177	718	410	832	247	841	534	731	788																				
Orbetello	308	585	595	275	540	708	525	602	444	170	508	336	41	455	260	260	176	852	471	364																			
Palermo	147	1682	692	1325	1579	694	1565	427	1604	1212	793	1447	1130	1554	968	1361	1265	237	1584	708	1089																		
Parma	314	315	767	98	243	879	170	315	[illegible]	185	644	205	329	310	513	122	194	1398	120	675	358	1127																	
Perugia	141	626	636	264	521	745	511	575	[illegible]	155	550	379	180	501	179	301	272	1127	457	434	169	1127	340																
Pescara	153	766	299	363	643	415	623	676	531	406	191	655	396	762	100	574	526	980	574	388	352	980	458	262															
Piacenza	365	252	815	150	261	933	115	356	[illegible]	242	703	145	379	247	565	162	236	1452	66	725	411	1452	63	399	508														
Pisa	358	401	787	182	446	902	329	487	302	100	700	162	150	270	419	77	19	1279	279	554	179	1279	172	253	499	214													
Ravenna	149	477	605	78	355	716	334	306	245	137	488	374	279	478	353	292	255	1317	285	636	306	1317	173	196	295	229	235												
Reggio di Calabria	910	1441	452	1093	1346	459	1333	1367	1232	975	557	1205	890	1315	728	1128	1018	237	1268	499	576	237	1166	890	741	1219	1035	1086											
Roma (Rome)	286	748	450	379	645	563	632	697	535	276	362	503	192	618	113	427	322	947	571	226	145	942	463	188	206	515	342	382	707										
Salerno	450	1000	240	634	898	355	885	924	787	532	152	763	448	869	286	881	578	684	830	220	405	684	715	442	295	772	599	636	446	260									
Siena	247	535	677	172	435	785	422	486	328	68	590	291	75	411	281	173	121	1165	366	534	105	1165	252	110	379	304	108	205	929	231	480								
Siracusa (Syracuse)	1064	1599	609	1242	1496	611	1482	1521	1386	1129	710	1364	1047	1471	885	1278	1136	154	135	638	1004	259	1315	1044	897	1369	1196	1234	155	859	601	1082							
Taranto	549	1156	98	760	1031	70	1009	1062	922	805	217	1028	722	1149	479	948	850	627	965	305	660	627	852	713	386	906	865	688	392	517	256	755	544						
Torino (Turin)	547	110	1006	333	412	1116	165	503	257	393	883	172	477	208	715	275	345	1607	142	885	502	1607	245	548	699	178	326	405	1375	674	927	463	1524	1089					
Trento	442	394	893	297	60	998	233	135	100	312	773	365	452	475	642	342	413	1525	242	799	485	1525	192	472	582	210	392	296	1286	593	845	381	1442	974	353				
Trieste	506	582	958	295	347	1072	421	236	236	396	839	537	538	643	706	502	492	1607	415	884	567	1607	361	550	652	395	468	288	1374	670	923	465	1524	1045	540	292			
Venezia (Venice)	364	441	816	154	214	931	279	165	147	255	694	399	399	505	566	364	348	1464	274	741	427	1464	218	413	508	255	332	143	1229	533	781	322	1381	899	403	158	159		
Verona	354	331	811	140	155	917	172	236	30	234	689	289	374	388	555	220	295	1439	167	716	403	1439	105	389	503	142	279	215	1206	505	761	295	1356	889	289	103	253	115	
Vicenza	360	376	814	150	183	925	216	167	31	252	693	334	394	439	562	374	347	1464	209	746	424	1464	155	410	505	191	327	166	1223	528	785	322	1381	901	342	144	213	73	52

A
B
C
D
1
2
3
4
BERN
Lausanne
SWITZERLAND
Geneva
Cannobio
Porlezza
Verbania
Stresa
Luino
Como
Courmayeur
Orta San Giulio
Arona
Aosta
Rhemes St George
Sesto Calende
Biella
Settimo Vittone
A9
A4
Milano
NOVARA
Grenoble
A5
see inset on Map
Bardonecchia
A32
TURIN
Salbertrand
211
A7
A21
FRANCE
31
Asti
A21
A22
A13
A33
51
62
12
2
Gap
A6
Alba
Salsomaggiore Terme
PARMA
413
FERRARA
Barolo
30
A26
A7
45
A15
62
A1
MODENA
64
Bologna
21
29
63
28
Genova
Rapallo
12
64
A10
Savona
Deiva Marina
A1
Finale Ligure
Sarzana
A1
Borgo San Lorenzo
San Remo
Diano Marina
Pistoia
Imperia
Viareggio
Lucca
Nice
Monaco
Fiesole
Pisa
Firenze
Figline Valdarno
LIVORNO
A12
Poggibonsi
Volterra
Arezzo
Toulon
Cecina
SIENA
1
2
Castiglion del Lago
Sarteano
1
ELBA
Portoferraio
Marina di Campo
Bastia
Bolsen
Orbetello
1
CORSICA (France)
Aleria
CIVITAVECCHIA
Motorways
Primary roads
Secondary roads
N
W
E
S
All year site(s)
Seasonal site(s)
No sites listed
Bonifacio
0
50
100
150 km
0
20
40
60
80
100 miles

Map 1

E
F
G
H
C
D
1
2
3
4
AUSTRIA
Sesto/ Sexten
Corvara in Badia
Cortina d'Ampezzo
Forni di Sopra
SLOVENIA
UDINE
A23
A27
A28
A4
TREVISO
TRIESTE
Caorle
Bibione
Mestre
Lido di Jesolo
Cavallino
Punta Sabbioni
Chioggia
Pula
RAVENNA
Cervia
Cesenatico
Bellaria
San Marino
Senigallia
Ostra
ANCONA
Porto Recanati
Gubbio
Magione
Urbisaglia
A14
PERUGIA
Assisi
Sarnano
Montefortino
Preci
Castelsantangelo sul Nera
Martinsicuro
Baschi
A1
A24
L'AQUILA
PESCARA
Caprarola
Fiano Romano
Bracciano
A25
Casalbordino
ROMA
Barrea
Vieste
Manfredonia
CAMPOBASSO
FOGGIA
BARLETTA
Sperlonga
Marina di Minturno
BENEVENTO
A16
CASERTA
BARI
ADRIATIC SEA
CROATIA
BOSNIA AND HERZEGOVINA
Sarajevo
Split
Dubrovnic
San Valentino alla Muta
Mals/ Malles Venosta
Prato allo Stelvio
Merano/ Meran
Chiusa/ Klausen
Corvara in Badia
Fie/Vols
Bolzano/ Bozen
Pozza di Fassa
A22
Predazzo
Gravedona
Edolo
Menaggio
Bellagio
Trento
Pieve Tesino
SR50
Lecco
Arco
Riva del Garda
Levico Terme
Torbole
Bergamo
Idro
Malcesine
SP46
SPV
San Felice del Benaco
Bardolino
Vicenza
Manerba del Garda
A35
Milano
Lazise
Desenzano del Garda
A58
Peschiera del Garda
Verona
A21
A31

Map 2

TYRRHENIAN SEA
IONIAN SEA
SARDINIA
SICILY
TUNISIA
ALGERIA
MALTA
Alberobello
Corigliano Calabro
Nicotera
Palmi
Taormina
Catania
Siracusa
Avola
Marina di Ragusa
Punta Braccetto
Piazza Armerina
Agrigento
Seccagrande
Menfi
Castelvetrano
San Vito lo Capo
Palermo
Milazzo
Sorrento
Agerola
Paestum
Narbolia
Cagliari
Porto Torres
Alghero
Porto San Paolo
Dorgali
Pula
Sibari
Tropea
Patti
Cefalu
Castellammare del Golfo
TARANTO
CROTONE
CATANZARO
VIBO VALENTIA
REGGIO DI CALABRIA
MESSINA
POTENZA
SALERNO
NAPLES
RAGUSA
MARSALA
VALLETTA
SASSARI
A14
A2
A3
RA5
A18
A19
A20
A29
Motorways
Primary roads
Secondary roads
All year site(s)
Seasonal site(s)
No sites listed
200 km
120 miles

Map 3

Regions and Provinces of Italy

ABRUZZO
Chieti
L'Aquila
Pescara
Teramo

BASILICATA
Matera
Potenza

CALABRIA
Catanzaro
Cosenza
Crotone
Reggio di Calabria
Vibo Valentia

CAMPANIA
Avellino
Benevento
Caserta
Napoli
Salerno

EMILIA-ROMAGNA
Bologna
Ferrara
Forli
Modena
Parma
Piacenza
Ravenna
Reggio Emilia
Rimini

FRIULI-VENEZIA GIULIA
Gorizia
Pordenone
Trieste
Udine

LAZIO
Frosinone
Latina
Rieti
Roma
Viterbo

LIGURIA
Genova
Imperia
La Spezia
Savona

LOMBARDIA
Bergamo
Brescia
Como
Cremona
Lecco
Lodi
Mantova
Milano
Pavia
Sondrio
Varese

MARCHE
Ancona
Ascoli Piceno
Macerata
Pesaro e Urbino

MOLISE
Campobasso
Isernia

PIEMONTE
Alessandria
Asti
Biella
Cuneo
Novara
Torino
Verbano-Cusio-Ossola
Vercelli

PUGLIA
Bari
Brindisi
Foggia
Lecce
Taranto

SARDEGNA
Cagliari
Nuoro
Oristano
Sassari

SICILIA
Agrigento
Caltanissetta
Catania
Enna
Messina
Palermo
Ragusa
Siracusa
Trapani

TOSCANA
Arezzo
Firenze
Grosseto
Livorno
Lucca
Massa Carrara
Pisa
Pistoia
Prato
Siena

TRENTINO-ALTO ADIGE
Bolzano
Trento

UMBRIA
Perugia
Terni

VALLE D'AOSTA
Aosta/Aoste

VENETO
Belluno
Padova
Rovigo
Treviso
Venezia
Verona
Vicenza

Highlights

Although a tiny country just over 50 miles long, Luxembourg is an economic powerhouse. Luxembourg City is famous for its stunning, medieval old town and for the number of notable museums and galleries that it boasts.

Most of the country is rural, and the beautiful landscapes vary from the micro-gorges of Müllerthal to the vineyards of the Moselle wine region.

Luxembourg cuisine is heavily influenced by its neighbours and in particular has many Germanic influences. Judd mat Gaardebounen, a smoked collar of pork with broad beans, is a particularly popular meal and is widely recognised as one of the country's national dishes.

The Festival of Wiltz is an annual affair that celebrates some of the most talented international musicians. With its open air setting and castle backdrop, it attracts large audiences each year and is considered to be a cultural highlight.

Major towns and cities

- Luxembourg City – this fascinating capital offers UNESCO sites and gastronomy.
- Esch-sur-Alzette – this city has the longest shopping street in the country.
- Diekirck – a city with charming old streets.
- Dudelange – a cultural centre with lots to see including Mount St. Jean.

Attractions

- Mullerthal Trail – explore 112 km of varied landscape, from forests to rock formations.
- Vianden Castle, Vianden – a grand building that originates from the 10th century.
- National Museum of Art and History, Luxembourg City – enjoy a fascinating range of exhibitions from archaeology to fine arts.
- Holy Ghost Citadel, Luxembourg City – a majestic fortress with stunning views.

Find out more

visitluxembourg.lu
info@visitluxembourg.com
+352 (0) 42 82 82 1

Country Information

Capital: Luxembourg City

Bordered by: Belgium, France, Germany

Terrain: Rolling hills to north with broad, shallow valleys; steep slope to Moselle valley in south-east

Climate: Temperate climate without extremes of heat or cold; mild winters; warm, wet summers; July and August are the hottest months; May and June have the most hours of sunshine.

Highest Point: Kneiff 560 m

Languages: French, German, Lëtzebuergesch (Luxembourgish)

Local Time: GMT or BST + 1, i.e. 1 hour ahead of the UK all year

Currency: Euros divided into 100 cents; £1 = €1.20 €1 = £0.84 (Nov 2024)

Emergency numbers: Police 113; Fire brigade 112; Ambulance 112. Operators speak English

Public Holidays 2025: Jan 1; Apr 21; May 1, 9, 29; Jun 9, 23; Aug 15; Nov 1; Dec 25, 26.

There are other dates such as Luxembourg City Feten which are not official holidays but many businesses, banks and shops may close. School summer holidays run from mid-July to mid-September.

Entry Formalities

British and Irish passport holders may stay for up to 90 days in any 180 day period without a visa. You may be asked to show a return or onward ticket at the border to confirm your length of stay, or to prove that you have enough money for your stay.

Your passport will need to have a minimum of 6 months' validity remaining, and be less than 10 years old (even if it has over 6 months left).

Visitors arriving at a campsite or hotel must complete a registration form.

Medical Services

Emergency medical treatment is available on presentation of a European Health Insurance Card (EHIC) or a Global Health Insurance Card (GHIC) but you will be charged both for treatment and prescriptions. Refunds can be obtained from a local sickness insurance fund office, Caisse de Maladie des Ouvriers (CMO).

Emergency hospital treatment is normally free apart from a non-refundable standard daily fee.

Opening Hours

Banks: Mon-Fri 8.30am-12 noon & 1.30pm-4.30pm. Some stay open to 6pm and open Sat 9am-12 noon.

Museums: Tue-Sun 10am-6pm, Thurs late opening 5pm-8pm (check locally); most close Mon.

Post Offices: Mon-Fri 8am-12 noon & 1.30pm-4.30pm/5pm; the central post office in Luxembourg City is open 7am-7pm Mon to Fri & 7am-5pm Sat.

Shops: Mon-Sat 9am/10am-6pm/6.30pm. Some close for lunch and Mon mornings. Large malls may be open to 8pm or 9pm.

Safety and Security

There are few reports of crime but visitors should take the usual common sense precautions against pickpockets. Do not leave valuables in your car.

Luxembourg shares with the rest of Europe an underlying threat from terrorism. Please see gov.uk/foreign-travel-advice/luxembourg before you travel.

British Embassy

Boulevard Joseph II, L-1840
Luxembourg
Tel: (+352) 22 98 64
gov.uk/world/luxembourg

Irish Embassy

Résidence Christina (2nd floor)
28 Route D'arlon, L-1140 Luxembourg
Tel: (+352) 450 6101
embassyofireland.lu

Documents

Money

Major credit cards are widely accepted although there are often minimum amount requirements. Cash machines are widespread. Carry your credit card issuers'/banks' 24-hour UK contact numbers in case of loss or theft of your cards.

Passport

You are advised to carry your passport or photocard licence at all times.

Vehicle(s)

You should carry your vehicle registration document (V5C), insurance details and MOT certificate.

Driving

Alcohol

The maximum permitted level of alcohol is 0.05%. Penalties for driving under the influence of alcohol can be severe. A lower level of 0.02% applies to drivers who have held a driving licence for less than two years i.e virtually nil. Breath tests are compulsory following serious road accidents and road offences.

Breakdown Service

A 24-hour breakdown service 'Service Routier' is operated by the Automobile Club De Grand-Duche de Luxembourg (ACL - acl.lu/en) on all roads, telephone (+352) 26000. Operators speak English. Payment by credit card is accepted.

Child Restraint System

Children under the age of 3 years old must be seated in an approved child restraint system. Children from the ages of 3 to 17 and/or under the height of 1.5 m must be seated in an appropriate restraint system. If they are over 36 kg in weight they can use a seat belt but only if they are in the rear of the vehicle.

Rear-facing child restraint systems are not allowed on seats with front airbags unless the airbag has been deactivated.

Fuel

Petrol stations are generally open from 8am to 8pm with 24-hour service on motorways. Most accept credit cards. It's illegal to carry petrol in a can.

LPG is available at some petrol stations – see (mylpg.eu) and use the drop down menu listed under LPG stations.

Motorways

There are over 150 km of motorways, all of which are toll-free for private vehicles. Motorway service areas are situated at Capellen on the A6 near Mamer, at Pontpierre on the A4, and at Berchem near Bettenbourg on the A3.

Emergency telephones are situated every 1.5 km along main roads and motorways and link motorists to the 'Protection Civile'.

Overtaking

When overtaking at night outside built-up areas it's compulsory to flash headlights.

Parking

Parking is prohibited where there are yellow lines or zigzag white lines. Blue zone parking areas exist in Luxembourg City, Esch-sur-Elzette, Dudelange and Wiltz. Parking discs are available from the ACL, police stations, tourist offices and shops. Parking meters operate in Luxembourg City. Police will clamp or remove illegally parked vehicles.

There are free car parks two to three kilometres outside Luxembourg City and Esch-sur-Elzette from which regular buses leave for the city.

If there's no public lighting when parking on a public road, sidelights must be switched on.

Priority

Where two roads of the same category intersect, traffic from the right has priority. In towns give priority to traffic coming from the right, unless there is a 'priority road' sign (yellow diamond with white border) indicating that the driver using that road has right of way.

Road Signs and Markings

Road signs and markings conform to international standards and are shown in French and German. Traffic lights pass from red immediately to green (no red and amber phase). A flashing amber light allows traffic to turn in the direction indicated, traffic permitting. In Luxembourg City some bus lanes and cycle lanes are marked in red.

Speed Limits

	Open Road (km/h)	Motorway (km/h)
Car Solo	90	130
Car towing caravan/trailer	75	90
Motorhome under 3500kg	90	130
Motorhome 3500-7500kg	90	130

The solo car top speed of 130 km/h (80 mph) is reduced to 110 km/h (68 mph) in wet weather.

The speed limit for drivers who have held a licence for less than a year is 90 km/h (56 mph) on motorways and 75 km/h (47 mph) outside built-up areas. In some residential areas called 'Zones de Rencontre' the maximum permitted speed is 20 km/h (13 mph).

Traffic Jams

Many people travel through Luxembourg in order to take advantage of cheaper fuel and queues at petrol stations often cause jams, in particular along the 'petrol route' past Martelange (N4 in Belgium), at Dudelange on the A3/E25 at the Belgium-Luxembourg border, and near Steinfort on the A6.

Other bottlenecks occur, particularly during weekends in July and August, at the junctions on the A1/E44 near Gasperich to the south of Luxembourg City, and the exit from the A3/E25 at Dudelange. To avoid traffic jams between Luxembourg City and Thionville (France), leave the western ring road around Luxembourg and take the A4 to Esch-sur-Alzette and then the D16. When past Aumetz join the N52 which then connects to the A30 to Metz.

The website (cita.lu) provides webcam views of all motorways and traffic information.

Violation of Traffic Regulations

Police officers may impose on the spot fines for infringement of regulations. These must be settled in cash and a receipt given. Non-residents of Luxembourg can receive penalty points for serious infringements of traffic law.

Winter Driving

Vehicles are required to have M&S (Mud and Snow) marked tyres fitted when driving in wintery conditions (frost, snow, ice etc.). This regulation applies to all drivers, regardless of where the vehicle is registered.

Essential Equipment

Lights

The use of dipped headlights in the daytime is recommended for all vehicles.

Reflective Jacket/Waistcoat

It's compulsory to wear a reflective jacket when getting out of your vehicle on a motorway or main road. Pedestrians walking at night or in bad visibility outside built-up areas must also wear one.

Warning Triangle

A warning triangle must be used if the vehicle is immobilised on the roadway.

Touring

Luxembourg is the only Grand Duchy in the world and measures a maximum of 81 km (51 miles) from north to south and 51 km (32 miles) from east to west. The fortifications and old town of Luxembourg City have been designated as a UNESCO World Heritage site.

Smoking isn't allowed in bars and restaurants. A service charge is usually added to restaurant bills and it's normal practice to leave a little extra if the service is good.

The Luxembourg Card is valid for one, two or three days, and entitles the holder to free public transport, admission to numerous museums and tourist attractions, and discounts on sightseeing trips. It's available from tourist offices, campsites, hotels, information and public transport offices as well as from participating attractions. You can also buy it online at luxembourgcard.lu.

There are many marked walking trails throughout the country, for more information see visitluxembourg.com. A Christmas market is held in the pedestrianised Place d'Armes in Luxembourg City. Others are held in towns and villages throughout the country.

French is the official language, but Luxembourgish is the language most commonly used. English is widely spoken in Luxembourg City, but less so elsewhere.

Camping and Caravanning

There are approximately 120 campsites in Luxembourg; most are open from April to October. Apart from in the industrial south, campsites are found all over the country. The Ardennes, the river banks along the Moselle and the Sûre and the immediate surroundings of Luxembourg City are particularly popular.

Casual/wild camping is only permitted with a tent, not a caravan, but permission must first be sought from the landowner.

Motorhomes

Many campsites have motorhome amenities and some offer Quick Stop overnight facilities at reduced rates.

Electricity and Gas

Most campsites have a supply of between 6 and 16 amps and many have CEE connections. Plugs have two round pins. The full range of Campingaz cylinders is widely available.

Public Transport & Local Travel

Public transport is free for residents and tourists. Travellers no longer need to buy tickets to use local, regional and nationwide trains, trams or buses, however first class travel in trains still has to be paid.

Luxembourg is a compact city and walking around it's easy and pleasant. It's served by an efficient network of buses. Pets are allowed to travel on buses if they can be kept on your lap or on the floor on a leash.

Luxembourg City

Shutterstock/Rudy Balasko

Sites in Luxembourg

BETTENDORF *C2* (1km SE Rural) *49.87262, 6.22137* **Camping Um Wirt,** 12 Rue de la Gare, L-9353 Bettendorf **tel 621 38 38 40; camping@bettendorf.lu; www.camping-bettendorf.lu**

€2.50 WD

Foll the N17/N19 Diekirch/Echternach. Turn R and foll camping signs in Bettendorf. Med, pt shd, EHU (10A); 70% statics; Eng spkn; adv bkg acc; games rm; games area. *"Vg site; gd walking & cycling; open plan, grassy site; rv adj; bowling green; trampoline; tennis court; sports field."* **€25.00, 1 Apr-15 Oct. 2024**

CLERVAUX *B2* (16km SW Rural) *49.97045, 5.93450* **Camping Kaul,** Rue Joseph Simon, 9554 Wiltz **tel 9503591; info@kaul.lu; www.kaul.lu**

€1.50 (htd) WD MSP

Turn N off rd 15 (Bastogne-Ettelbruck) to Wiltz, foll sp N to Ville Basse & Camping. Lge, mkd, unshd, EHU (6-10A) €2.50-2.75; gas; adv bkg rec; tennis; waterslide. *"Gd site; pitches tight for awnings if site full; excel san facs & takeaway; pool adj; local children use playgrnd."* **€30.00, 15 Feb-31 Dec. 2024**

DIEKIRCH *C2* (10km E Rural) *49.86852, 6.26430* **Camping de la Rivière,** 21 Rue de la Sûre, 9390 Reisdorf **tel 836398; campingreisdorf@pt.lu; www.campingreisdorf.com**

€1.50 (htd) WD nr

Fr Diekirch take N19 (sp Echternach) for 10km to where rd crosses Rv Sûre. Site on L after bdge. Med, mkd, pt shd, EHU (6-10A) metered; gas; 20% statics; bus; Eng spkn; CKE. *"Lovely site in beautiful countryside; excel for walking/cycling; helpful, friendly owners; gd touring base."* **€15.00, Feb-Nov. 2024**

> **"There aren't many sites open at this time of year"**
>
> If you're travelling outside peak season remember to call ahead to check site opening dates – even if the entry says 'open all year'.

DIEKIRCH *C2* (0.5km SE Urban) *49.86635, 6.16513* **Camping de la Sûre,** 23, route de la Sûre – L-9390 Reisdorf **tel +352 691 84 96 66; info@campingdelasure.lu; https://campingdelasure.lu**

€2 (htd) WD nr

Fr town cent take N14 twds Larochette, then 1st L after x-ing rv bdge. Well sp. Lge, mkd, pt shd, EHU (10A) €2.50; 50% statics; Eng spkn; adv bkg acc; ccard acc; CKE. *"Nice welcome; excel, clean facs; m'van o'night area outside gates; pleasant rvside site 5 mins walk fr town cent; pool 200m; vg touring base, Battle of Bulge Museum nrby."* **€20.50, 1 Apr-30 Sep. 2020**

DIEKIRCH *C2* (0.9km S Rural) *49.86768, 6.16984* **Camping op der Sauer,** Route de Gilsdorf, L 9234 Diekirch **tel 808590; info@campsauer.lu; www.campsauer.lu**

€2.50 (htd) WD

On rd 14 to Larochette, on S o'skts of Diekirch. 1st L after x-ing rv bdge, site well sp on L past Camping de la Sûre and behind sports facs. Lge, mkd, pt shd, EHU (6A) €3; gas; bus 800m; Eng spkn; adv bkg acc; CKE. *"On banks Rv Sûre; sh walk/cycle to town; spacious site; friendly owners; ltd facs LS; gd, basic site; helpful recep; pool 400m; clean san facs with plenty of hot water; vet is 20 mins walk."* **€25.00, 1 Apr-24 Oct. 2022**

ECHTERNACH *C3* (6km NW Rural) *49.81958, 6.34737* **Camping Belle-Vue 2000,** 29 Rue de Consdorf, 6551 Berdorf **tel 790635 or 808149; campbv2000@gmail.com; campingbellevue.lu**

12 €3 (htd) WD

Nr cent of vill on rd to Consdorf. 2nd of 3 adj sites with facs on L on way out of vill. Lge, hdg, pt shd, terr, EHU (6 or16A) €3.90; gas; bbq; 50% statics; phone; adv bkg acc; games rm; CKE. *"Gd walking; attractive vill with gd rests; open in Jan only if no snow; pitches poss soft after rain; pool 500m; owner's son now running & improving site (2017)."* **€22.00 2023**

ESCH SUR ALZETTE *B3* (2km E Rural) *49.48761, 5.98554* **Camping Gaalgebierg,** 4001 Esch-sur-Alzette **tel 541069; gaalcamp@pt.lu; www.gaalgebierg.lu**

12 (htd)

Sp in cent of town, turn L dir Kayl. Under rlwy bdge sharp R, up steep hill. Lge, hdstg, shd, terr, EHU (16A) €1.50 but elec for heating metered & restricted in bad weather; TV (pitch); 80% statics; bus 1km, train to Luxembourg city; Eng spkn; ccard acc; CKE. *"V clean san facs; gd walks; park & sm zoo adj site; well-kept site; poss boggy when wet."* **€20.70 2024**

ESCH SUR SURE *B2* (1km SE Rural) *49.90693, 5.94220* **Camping Im Aal,** 7 Rue du Moulin, 9650 Esch-sur-Sûre **tel 839514; info@camping-im-aal.lu; www.campingaal.lu**

€2 (htd) WD

Fr N turn R off N15 onto N27 sp Esch-sur-Sûre. Pass thro sh tunnel, site on L in 500m on banks of Rv Sûre. 3*, Lge, hdg, mkd, pt shd, pt sl, EHU (6A) €2; 50% statics; Eng spkn; site clsd 1 Jan-14 Feb; fishing; CKE. *"Well-kept, clean site; gd welcome; gd, modern facs; some rvside pitches; walks along towpath & in woods; cash only; gd for wheelchair users; gd fishing, walking; gd NH & longer; vg."* **€27.00, 12 Feb-11 Dec. 2024**

ETTELBRUCK *B2* (4km E Rural) *49.85043, 6.13461* **Camping Gritt,** 2 Rue Gritt, 9161 Ingeldorf **tel 802018; info@camping-gritt.lu; www.camping-gritt.lu**

€2 (htd) nr

On N15 fr Bastogne turn R at rndabt in Ettelbrück sp Diekirch, go under A7 sp Diekirch. In 3km at end of elevated section foll slip rd sp Diekirch, Ettelbrück, Ingeldorf. At rndabt take 2nd exit sp Ingledorf, site on R over narr rv bdge. Fr Diekirch on N7 fork L twd Ingeldorf. Site on L over rv bdge. Lge, mkd, pt shd, EHU (6A) €2.80; gas; bbq; sw; twin axles; TV; 30% statics; bus/train to Luxembourg City; Eng spkn; adv bkg acc; games rm; tennis nr; fishing nr; CKE. *"Peaceful site; helpful, welcoming Dutch owners; lge pitches with open aspect; gd, modern san facs; recep 0900-1800 high ssn; canoe hire nr; red for groups; pitching still OK after heavy rain; on banks of Rv Sûre (swift-flowing & unfenced); gd walking & sightseeing; rest vg; vg site."* **€31.00, 1 Apr-31 Oct.** 2022

"That's changed – Should I let the Club know?"

If you find something on site that's different from the site entry, fill in a report and let us know. See camc.com/europereport.

ETTELBRUCK *B2* (1.5km W Rural) *49.84600, 6.08193* **Camping Ettelbruck (formerly Kalkesdelt),** 88 Chemin du Camping, 9022 Ettelbrück **tel 00 352 81 21 85; camping@ettelbruck.lu; www.campingettelbruck.com**

€2.50 (htd)

Exit Ettelbrück on Bastogne rd N15. Site visible as app town; approx 200m fr town cent fork L into lane, turn R at sp at foot of hill, steep & narr rd. Site sp fr town. 4*, Lge, mkd, pt shd, terr, EHU (16A) €2.90; TV; 15% statics; phone; Eng spkn; adv bkg acc; CKE. *"Gd, well-maintained, friendly, family-run site in woods; excel san facs; lge pitches; gd walks; train to Luxumbourg city fr town; pool 3km; vg rest."* **€28.50, 1 Apr-30 Sep.** 2022

GREVENMACHER *C3* (0.8km N Urban) *49.68302, 6.44891* **Camping La Route du Vin,** 10 route du Vin, L 6794 Grevenmacher **tel 750234 or 758275; camping@visitmaacher.lu; visitmaacher.lu/camping**

€2 nr nr

Fr E44/A1 exit junc 14 onto N1 to Grevenmacher. After 1km turn R at T-junc opp Esso g'ge. Site sp in town, ent off rndabt. Med, mkd, pt shd, pt sl, EHU (16A) €3; 60% statics; Eng spkn; adv bkg acc; games area; games rm; tennis; CKE. *"Easy walk to town cent; wine festival in Sep; pleasant, well kept site; excel new san facs (2015); boat trips; rvside walks; excel base for touring Moselle & Luxembourg; pool adj; views; helpful staff; excel."* **€22.50, 1 Apr-30 Sep.** 2023

KAUTENBACH *B2* (1km E Rural) *49.95387, 6.02730* **Camping Kautenbach,** An der Weierbaach, 9663 Kautenbach **tel 950303; campkaut@pt.lu; www.campingkautenbach.lu**

12 (htd)

Travelling E fr Bastogne on N84, approx 5km after Luxembourg border take N26 to Wiltz & foll sp to Kautenbach/Kiischpelt. In 10km turn L over bdge into vill, site sp 800m. 3*, Lge, mkd, pt shd, EHU (6A) inc; gas; bbq; TV; 20% statics; phone; Eng spkn; adv bkg acc; ccard acc; site clsd 21 Dec-14 Jan; bike hire. *"Gd for walking & mountain biking; long site along beautiful, secluded rv valley."* **€26.00** 2022

LAROCHETTE *C3* (2km W Rural) *49.78525, 6.21010* **Iris Parc Camping Birkelt,** 1 Um Birkelt, 7633 Larochette **tel 879040; info@camping-birkelt.lu; www.camping-birkelt.lu**

€2.50 (htd) (covrd, htd)

Fr Diekirch take N14 to Larochette; turn R in town on CR118 (N8), foll sp for Mersch. At top of hill foll site sp. Fr Luxembourg take N7 foll sp for Mersch & Ettelbruck (ignore Larochette sp bef Mersch). Turn R bef rv bdge at Mersch onto CR118 & foll rd to o'skts of town. Site on R beyond municipal sports cent - fairly steep, winding app rd. 5*, Lge, mkd, hdg, pt shd, pt sl, serviced pitches; EHU (16A) inc; gas; bbq (charcoal, gas); TV; 50% statics; Eng spkn; ccard acc; golf 5km; tennis; games rm; horseriding; bike hire; sauna; fishing; games area; CKE. *"Excel, well-kept, busy site in pleasant wooded hilltop location; friendly, helpful staff; ideal for families; fitness rm; no o'fits over 9m; canoeing 5km; gd san facs, poss stretched high ssn; access poss diff lge o'fits, care req; late arr report to rest/bar; gd bar & rest, open in LS."* **€40.00, 21 Apr - 9 Sep, H08.** 2022

LAROCHETTE *C3* (7km W Rural) *49.78521, 6.16596* **Camping Nommerlayen,** Rue Nommerlayen, 7465 Nommern **tel 878078; info@nommerlayen-ec.lu; www.nommerlayen-ec.lu**

€3 (htd) (covrd, htd)

N7 Luxembourg to Diekirch. At Mersch N8 E dir Larochette & Nommern. Site is 1km S of Nommern. 5*, Lge, hdg, mkd, pt shd, terr, EHU (10A) inc; gas; TV; 40% statics; Eng spkn; adv bkg acc; sauna; games rm; tennis; bike hire; games area. *"Superb site & facs; private bthrms avail; ideal for families; acc to some pitches diff, site staff will help."* **€40.00, 1 Mar-5 Nov, H20.** 2022

LAROCHETTE *C3* (3km NW Rural) *49.79991, 6.19816* **Camping auf Kengert,** Kengert, 7633 Larochette **tel 837186; info@kengert.lu; www.kengert.lu**

€2.50 (htd) WD MSP (htd)

N8 dir Mersch, CR19 dir Schrondweiler. Site sp fr cent Larochette. 5*, Lge, mkd, shd, sl, EHU (16A) inc; gas; 10% statics; Eng spkn; adv bkg acc; solarium; sauna; CKE. *"Vg facs; Luxembourg Card (red on attractions & public transport) avail at recep; peaceful, friendly site; indoor playgrnd; excel rest; gd local walks/cycle rtes; ltd hdstg for MH's."* **€42.00, 1 Mar-8 Nov. 2023**

LIELER *B2* (0.5km SW Rural) *50.12365, 6.10509* **Camping Trois Frontières,** Hauptstroos 12, 9972 Lieler **tel 998608; info@troisfrontieres.lu; www.troisfrontieres.lu**

12 €2.20 (htd) WD MSP

Fr N7/E421 turn E sp Lieler, site sp. 4*, Med, mkd, pt shd, EHU (6A) €2.75; TV; 10% statics; adv bkg acc; bike hire; games area; games rm. *"V pleasant site; gd touring base; site under new ownership (2014); ACSI registered; discount in LS."* **€32.80 2024**

"I like to fill in the reports as I travel from site to site"

You'll find report forms at the back of this guide, or you can fill them in online at camc.com/europereport.

LUXEMBOURG CITY *C3* (7km S Rural) *49.57220, 6.10857* **Camping Kockelscheuer,** 22 Route de Bettembourg, 1899 Kockelscheuer **tel 471815; caravani@pt.lu; www.ccclv.lu**

(htd) WD MSP

Fr N on A6 then A4 exit junc 1 sp Leudelange/ Kockelscheuer, at top of slip rd turn L N4. After about 1.5km turn R N186 sp Bettemburg/Kockelscheuer & foll camp sp. Foll sp 'Park & Ride', site is 1st R. Fr S exit A3 junc 2 sp Bettembourg & Kockelscheuer. In 700m turn R dir Kockelscheuer & in 3km turn L & foll site sp, rd numberd CR196. 4*, Med, hdg, mkd, pt shd, terr, serviced pitches; EHU (10-16A) metered (check pol); gas; bbq (charcoal, elec, gas); twin axles; TV (pitch); 5% statics; bus to city 400m (tickets fr site recep); Eng spkn; adv bkg acc; ccard acc; games area; CKE. *"Rec arr early afternoon as popular; well-run, clean, pretty site; helpful, pleasant staff; office & gates clsd 1200-1400 & 2230-0700; gd san facs; pitch access on lower level needs care; gd size pitches on terr; poss boggy after rain; sports complex adj; gd dog walks nrby; useful NH for Zeebrugge; pool 4km; excel site; poss to cycle into Luxembourg city; excel."* **€19.50, 24 Mar-31 Oct. 2021**

LUXEMBOURG CITY *C3* (9km S Rural) *49.56907, 6.16010* **Camping Bon Accueil,** 2 Rue du Camping, 5815 Alzingen **tel 367069; www.camping-alzingen.lu**

€3 (htd) WD MSP

Fr Luxembourg city take A3/E25 S, exit junc 1 sp Hespérange. Cont thro town to Alzingen, site sp on R after Mairie, well sp. Med, hdg, mkd, hdstg, pt shd, EHU (16A) inc (poss rev pol); gas; bbq; twin axles; phone; bus to city adj; Eng spkn; adv bkg acc; ccard acc; games area; CCI. *"Pleasant, open, clean, tidy site; gd size pitches; friendly staff; vg, clean, modern san facs; hot water metered; lovely gardens adj; clsd 1200-1400 - ltd waiting space; excel base for city; spotlessly clean; vg site; pool 3km; rec arrive early; bkg rec."* **€21.00, 1 Apr-15 Oct. 2022**

MERSCH *B3* (2km SW Urban) *49.74339, 6.08963* **Camping Um Krounebierg,** Rue du Camping, 7572 Mersch **tel 352329756; contact@camping krounebierg.lu; www.campingkrounebierg.lu**

€2.50 (htd) WD MSP

In Mersch town cent fr main N7 foll site ss. Fr A7, exit Kopstal dir Mersch, then foll site sps. 5*, Lge, hdstg, mkd, hdg, pt shd, pt sl, terr, EHU (6-10A) inc; gas; bbq; twin axles; TV; 20% statics; phone; Eng spkn; adv bkg acc; tennis. *"Gd touring & walking cent; conv for trains to Luxembourg City; htd covrd pool adj; warden v helpful - only on site 2 hrs morning & 2 hrs evening LS; site guarded; excel clean facs; skate park; nice site close to a pleasant town; well laid out; beautiful location; san facs clean."* **€36.00, 25 Mar-31 Oct. 2023**

REISDORF *C2* (0.1km W Urban) *49.86958, 6.26746* **Camping De La Sure,** 23 Route de la Sure, L-9390 Reisdorf **tel 661-151358; reisdorfcamp@gmail.com; www.campingdelasure.lu**

€2.5 WD MSP nr

Reisdorf is bet Diekirch & Echternach. Site sp off the N10 in Reisdorf. NB-2nd site on L after the bdge driving fr Diekirch. Med, pt shd, EHU (10A) inc; bbq (charcoal, gas); TV; 10% statics; bus adj; Eng spkn; adv bkg acc; games area; games rm; CKE. *"V friendly & helpful; gd cycle paths along rv; ACSI; site being upgraded to a hg standard (2015); vg; lovely site by rv; easy walk to town."* **€26.00, 30 Mar-16 Oct. 2023**

REMICH *C3* (4km S Rural) *49.5106, 6.36302* **Camping et Port de Plaisance,** 5447 Schwebsange **tel 23664460; cport-schwebsingen@schengen.lu, www.schengen.lu/port-de-schwebsingen**

nr nr nr

Fr Remich take N10 S on W bank of Moselle. Site 1km E of Schwebsange. Or fr S leave A13 at junc 13 onto N10. Site sp. Sm, EHU (10A) inc; Eng spkn; adv bkg rec. *"rv & port noise; marina & rv activities; red facs LS; pool 4km; gd cycle rtes fr site, main site clsd 2020 but 20 pitches still in harbour inc el pnts, san facs and water."* **€17.55, 1 Apr-31 Oct. 2023**

SEPTFONTAINES *B3* (2.5km NE Rural) *49.69274, 5.98514* **Camping Simmerschmelz,** Rue de Simmerschmelz 1, 8363 Septfontaines **tel 307072; info@simmerschmelz.com; simmerschmelz.com**

€3 (htd)

Head NE fr Arlon sp Mersch. In 4km at Gaichel (Bel/Lux frontier) foll valley of Rv Eisch thro Hobscheid, Septfontaines & in 2km at rd junc turn R. Site on L in 100m. Or fr E25 m'way exit at Windhof. Head N to Koerich & onto Septfontaines, as above. Med, pt shd, pt sl, EHU (6A) €3.75; gas; TV; 40% statics; phone; Eng spkn; adv bkg acc. *"Pleasant site in valley, wet in winter; 1 hdstg pitch; helpful owner."* **€33.75** **2023**

TROISVIERGES *B2* (0.4km S Urban) *50.11908, 6.00251* **Camping Troisvierges (formerly Walensbongert),** Rue de Binsfeld, 9912 Troisvierges **tel 352 - 99 71 41; info@camping-troisvierges.lu; www.camping-troisvierges.lu**

€2 (htd) nr nr

Fr Belgium on E42/A27 exit at junc 15 St Vith on N62 sp Troisvierges. Site sp. 1*, Med, mkd, hdg, pt shd, EHU (16A) €2.50; 10% statics; phone; train 1km; Eng spkn; adv bkg acc; ccard acc; games rm; tennis; CKE. *"Pretty town; pools adj; gd hiking; charming, helpful owners."* **€23.50, 1 Apr-30 Sep.** **2024**

VIANDEN *C2* (1km E Rural) *49.93213, 6.21554* **Camping op dem Deich,** Rue Neugarten, 9420 Vianden **tel +352 83 42 57; https://www.visit-vianden.lu/de/fiche/campingcar/camperpark-vianden**

nr nr nr

Fr Diekirch take N19 E for 3km. Turn L on N17 to Vianden. Site sp 500m fr town cent twd Bitburg. 1*, Sm, hdstg, unshd, EHU (16A) inc. *"Aire de Service for MH's - 16 hdstdg pitches; payment by machine; all pitches line the rv bank; easy walk to sm town with cafes, rest & shops as well as castles; excel scenery."* **€20.00** **2022**

VIANDEN *C2* (2km SE Rural) *49.92673, 6.21990* **Camping du Moulin,** Rue de Bettel, 9415 Vianden **tel 834501; campingdumoulin@vianden-info.lu; https://www.visit-vianden.lu/en/fiche/camping/camping-du-moulin-vianden**

€1.50 (htd)

Fr Diekirch take N17 dir Vianden. In 8km at Fouhren take rd N17B sp Bettel then sp Vianden. Site on R behind yellow Vianden sp. Lge, mkd, pt shd, EHU (10-16A) inc; TV (pitch); phone; Eng spkn; CKE. *"Lovely location; spacious pitches, some on rv bank; gd, modern san facs; superb children's san facs; rv adj; interesting area; rec."* **€17.00, 14 Apr-3 Apr.** **2023**

WASSERBILLIG *C3* (2km SW Rural) *49.70241, 6.47717* **Camping Mertert,** Rue du Parc, 6684 Mertert **tel 621 174 201; syndicat@sit-mertert.lu; www.sit-mertert.lu**

(htd) nr

On E of rte 1 (Wasserbillig-Luxembourg), clearly sp in both dir. Immed R after rlwy x-ing. Site on rv. 3*, Med, mkd, shd, EHU (10A) inc; 70% statics; buses & trains nr; adv bkg acc. *"Grassed tourer area open fr Apr, but owner allows pitching on tarmac rd adj office; excel, clean facs; scruffy statics area; sm boating pond; pool 4km; recep clsd 1300-1500; vg."* **€12.50, 15 Apr-15 Oct.** **2024**

A
B
C
D
1
2
3
4
Motorways
Primary roads
Secondary roads
All year site(s)
Seasonal site(s)
No sites listed
BELGIUM
GERMANY
FRANCE
Liège
Eupen
Spa
Prum
La Roche En Ardenne
Bastogne
Bitburg
Trittenheim
Trier
Florenville
Arlon
Virton
Montmedy
Saarburg
Thionville
Saarbrücken
Metz
Lieler
Troisvierges
CLERVAUX
Kautenbach
Vianden
Esch Sur Sure
Diekirch
Reisdorf
Ettelbruck
Echternacherbruck
Echternach
Larochette
Born Sur Sure
MERSCH
Wasserbillig
GREVENMACHER
Grevenmacher
Septfontaines
LUXEMBOURG
Remich
N7
N15
N11
N1
N10
N6
N5
N4
N2
A7
A1
A6
A3
A13
A4
N
W
E
S
0
10
20
30
40
50 km
0
10
20
30 miles

Netherlands

Shutterstock/Yasonya

Highlights

With a flat landscape that's covered in tulips and windmills, the Netherlands is an enchanting country to explore and is ideal for cyclists. Amsterdam is often the main draw for tourists, and is the home of several museums, including one dedicated to Van Gogh.

The Netherlands is also well known for its beaches, and the coast is a great place to visit for nature lovers and sports enthusiasts alike.

The Netherlands has produced some of the greatest painters in the world, from Rembrandt to Vermeer and Van Gogh to Escher. The Mauritschuis in The Hague houses many famous works of art from the Dutch golden age and is well worth a visit.

Christmas is a time of great celebration for the Dutch, with Sinterklaas a traditional holiday figure based on Saint Nicholas. The giving of gifts on 5 December is a long-held tradition, as is the Sinterklaas parade in mid-November, which is broadcast on national TV.

Major towns and cities

- Amsterdam – this beautiful capital is filled with canals, galleries and pretty buildings.
- Rotterdam – a city famous for its museums and landmark architecture.
- The Hague – a historic city of political and cultural significance.
- Leiden – home of the oldest university in the Netherlands the birthplace of Rembrandt.

Attractions

- Keukenhof, Lisse – one of the world's largest flower gardens and a must-see in the spring.
- Hoge Veluwe, Gelderland – this National Park is a great place for walking or cycling.
- Rijksmuseum, Amsterdam – a national museum dedicated to arts and history.
- Kinderdijk - a beautiful village with the largest collection of old windmills in the Netherlands.

Find out more

holland.com

Country Information

Capital: Amsterdam

Bordered by: Belgium, Germany

Terrain: Mostly coastal lowland and reclaimed land (polders) dissected by rivers and canals; hills in the south-east

Climate: Temperate maritime climate; warm, changeable summers; cold/mild winters; spring is the driest season

Coastline: 451km

Highest Point: Vaalserberg 322m

Language: Dutch

Local Time: GMT or BST + 1, i.e. 1 hour ahead of the UK all year

Currency: Euros divided into 100 cents; £1 = €1.20, €1 = £0.84 (Nov 2024)

Emergency numbers: Police 112; Fire brigade 112; Ambulance 112. Operators speak English

Public Holidays 2025: Jan 1; Apr 18, 20, 21, 27; May 5, 29; Jun 8, 9; Dec 25, 26.

School summer holidays vary by region, but are roughly early/mid July to end August/early September

Entry Formalities

British and Irish passport holders may stay for up to 90 days in any 180 day period without a visa. You may be asked to show a return or onward ticket at the border to confirm your length of stay, or to prove that you have enough money for your stay.

Your passport will need to have a minimum of 6 months' validity remaining, and be less than 10 years old (even if it has over 6 months left).

Visitors arriving at a campsite or hotel must complete a registration form.

Medical Services

Pharmacies (apotheek) dispense prescriptions whereas drugstores (drogisterij) sell only over-the-counter remedies. Pharmacies may require a photocopy of the details on your European Health Insurance Card (EHIC) or Global Health Insurance Card (GHIC). You'll need to show your EHIC or GHIC to obtain treatment by a doctor contracted to the state health care system (AGIS Zorgverzekeringen) and you'll probably have to pay a fee. You'll be charged for emergency dental treatment. Charges for prescriptions vary. Treatment refunds are obtained from AGIS.

Inpatient hospital treatment is free provided it's authorised by AGIS. Local state health insurance fund offices can give advice on obtaining emergency medical services and provide names and addresses of doctors, health centres and hospitals. Tourist Information offices also keep lists of local doctors.

Opening Hours

Banks: Mon-Fri 9am-4pm/5pm (some open Sat).

Museums: Tue-Fri 10am-5pm; Sat & Sun 11am/1pm-5pm.

Post Offices: Mon-Fri 9am-5pm; some Sat 9am-12 noon/1.30pm.

Shops: Mon-Fri 8am/8.30am-6pm/8pm; Sat 8am/8.30am-4pm/5pm; late night shopping in many towns on Thursday or Friday to 9pm. Shops close one day or half day in the week in addition to Sunday.

Safety and Security

Visitors should take care in central Amsterdam (particularly in and around Central Station), in Rotterdam and The Hague, pickpocketing and bag snatching are common. Thieves operate in gangs on the trains and trams.

Ensure you keep your valuables safely with you at all times and don't leave them unattended or hanging on the back of a chair. Bicycle theft is a common occurrence in the major cities.

Fake, plain clothes policemen carrying badges are in action pretending to be investigating counterfeit money and false credit cards. Dutch police don't have badges and plain clothes police will rarely carry out this kind of inspection. Always ask for identity, check it thoroughly and don't allow yourself to be intimidated. Call 0900 8844 to contact the nearest police station if you are concerned or suspicious.

Take particular care when driving, cycling or walking alongside canals.

Avoid confrontation with anyone offering to sell you drugs and stay away from quiet or dark alleys, particularly late at night.

There have been incidences of drinks being spiked in city centre locations. Always be aware of your drink and don't leave it unattended. Young women and lone travellers need to be especially vigilant in these situations.

The Netherlands shares with the rest of Europe an underlying threat from terrorism. Please check gov.uk/foreign-travel-advice/netherlands before you travel.

British Embassy

Lange Voorhout 10, 2514 ED The Hague
Tel: (070) 4270427
gov.uk/world/netherlands

rish Embassy

Scheveningseweg 112, 2584 Ae The Hague
Tel: (070) 3630993
Ireland.ie/thehague

Documents

Passport

Everyone from the age of 14 is required to show a valid identity document to police officers on request and you should, therefore, carry your passport at all times.

Vehicle(s)

When driving carry your driving licence, vehicle registration certificate (V5C), insurance certificate and MOT certificate, if applicable. If driving a vehicle that doesn't belong to you, carry a letter of authority from the owner.

Money

Money may be exchanged at main border crossing posts, major post offices, banks, VVV tourist information offices and some ANWB offices. Other bureaux de change may not give such favourable rates.

The major credit and debit cards are widely accepted but supermarkets will not generally accept credit cards. As a precaution carry enough cash to cover your purchases as you may find that debit cards issued by banks outside the Netherlands aren't accepted. Cash machines are widespread.

Driving

The Dutch drive assertively and aren't renowned for their road courtesy. Pedestrians should be very careful when crossing roads, including on zebra crossings.

Accidents

All accidents which cause injuries or major damage must be reported to the police. Drivers involved in an accident must exchange their identity details and their insurance company contact information.

Alcohol

The maximum permitted level of alcohol is 0.05%. Penalties for driving under the influence of alcohol can be severe. A lower level of 0.02% applies to drivers who have held a driving licence for less than five years.

Breakdown Service

There are emergency telephones every 2 km on all motorways and they are directly linked to the nearest breakdown centre.

The motoring and leisure organisation, the Royal Dutch Touring Club ANWB (anwb.nl), has a road patrol service which operates 24 hours a day on all roads. Drivers requiring assistance may call the 'Wegenwacht' road patrol centre by telephoning 088 2692 888. Alternatively call the ANWB Emergency Centre on (070) 3141414.

Charges apply for breakdown assistance and towing is charged according to distance and time of day. Members of clubs affiliated to the AIT/FIA, such as The Caravan and Motorhome Club, incur lower charges. Payment by credit card is accepted. In some areas the ANWB Wegenwacht has contracts with local garages to provide assistance to its members and affiliates.

Child Restraint System

Children under the age of 18 years, measuring less than 1.35 m must be seated in an approved child restraint adapted to their size (ECE 44/03 or 44/04 safety approved). Children under 3 years old are able to travel in the front if they're seated in a rear facing child seat with the airbag deactivated, and under no circumstances are they allowed to travel in a car with no child restraint system fitted.

Fuel

Unleaded petrol is available from green pumps marked 'Loodvrije Benzine'. LPG (autogas) is widely available along main roads and motorways.

Petrol stations along motorways and main roads and in main towns are open 24 hours, except in parts of the north of the country where they close at 11pm. Credit cards are accepted but some all night petrol stations only have automatic pumps which may operate with bank notes only.

Lights

The use of dipped headlights during the day is recommended.

Low Emission Zones

Low Emission Zones are in operation in 15 cities in the Netherlands. Restrictions apply to freight vehicles over 3500kg and diesel vehicles. Before you travel check urbanaccessregulations.eu.

Motorways

Motorways in the Netherlands are currently toll-free. There are rest areas along the motorways, most of which have a petrol station and a small shop. Tolls are charged on some bridges and tunnels, notably the Westerschelde Toll Tunnel. This road tunnel links Terneuzen (north of Gent) and Ellewoutsdijk (south of Goes) across the Westerschelde. It provides a short, fast route between Channel ports and the road network in the west of the country. The tunnel is 6.6km long (just over 4 miles) and the toll for a car + caravan (maximum height 3m measured from front axle) is €7.45 and for a motorhome €7.45 height under 2.5m) or €18.20 (height over 3m) (all prices for 2024). Credit cards are accepted. Visit (westerscheldetunnel.nl) for more information.

Parking

Parking meters or discs are in use in many towns allowing parking for between 30 minutes and two or three hours; discs can be obtained from local shops. A sign 'parkeerschijf' indicates times when a disc is compulsory. Paid parking is expensive and there are insufficient parking spaces to meet demand.

Clamping and towing away of vehicles are commonplace and fines are high. Check signs for the precise times you are allowed to park, particularly on main roads in Amsterdam.

Priority

Yellow diamond shaped signs with a white border indicate priority roads. In the absence of such signs drivers must give way to all traffic approaching from the right. At the intersection of two roads of the same class where there are no signs, traffic from the right has priority.

At junctions marked with a 'priority road ahead' sign, a stop sign or a line of white painted triangles ('shark's teeth') across the road, drivers must give way to all vehicles on the priority road, including bicycles and mopeds.

Be particularly careful when using roundabouts as on some you have the right of way when on them, but on others you must give way to vehicles entering the roundabout, i.e. on your right.

Trams have priority at the intersection of roads of equal importance, but they must give way to traffic on priority roads. If a tram or bus stops in the middle of the road to allow passengers on and off, you must stop. Buses have right of way over all other vehicles when leaving bus stops in built-up areas.

Roads

Roads are generally well maintained, but are overcrowded and are frequently subject to strong winds. Most cities have a policy of reducing the amount of nonessential traffic within their boundaries. Narrowing roads, obstacles, traffic lights and speed cameras are often in place to achieve this.

Road Signs and Markings

National motorways are distinguished by red signs, and prefixed with the letter A, whereas European motorways have green signs and are prefixed E. Dual carriageways and other main roads have yellow signs with the letter N and secondary roads are prefixed B.

In general road signs and markings conform to international standards. The following are some road signs which may also be seen:

Cycle path

Cycle route

District Numbers

Hard shoulder open as rush-hour lane

Dutch	English Translation
Afrit	Exit
Doorgaand verkeer gestremd	No throughway
Drempels	Humps
Langzaam rijden	Slow down
Omleiding	Detour
Oprit	Entrance
Ousteek u lichten	Switch on lights
Parkeerplaats	Parking
Pas op!	Attention
Stop-verbod	No parking
Wegomlegging	Detour
Werk in uitvoering	Road works
Woonerven	Slow down (in built-up area)

A continuous central white line should not be crossed even to make a left turn.

Speed Limits

	Open Road (km/h)	Motorway (km/h)
Car Solo	80-100	130*
Car towing caravan/trailer	80-90	90
Motorhome under 3500kg	80-100	130*
Motorhome 3500-7500kg	80	80

*Unless otherwise indicated.

Be vigilant and observe the overhead illuminated lane indicators when they are in use, as speed limits on motorways are variable. Speed cameras, speed traps and unmarked police vehicles are widely used. Radar detectors are illegal, with use resulting in a heavy fine.

Motorhomes over 3,500kg are restricted to 50 km/h (31 mph) in built-up areas and to 80 km/h (50 mph) on all other roads. The beginning of a built up area is indicated by a rectangular blue sign with the name of the locality in white. The end of a built up area is indicated by the same sign with a white diagonal lines across it.

Traffic Jams

The greatest traffic congestion occurs on weekdays at rush hours around the major cities of Amsterdam, Den Bosch, Eindhoven, Rotterdam, Utrecht, The Hague and Eindhoven.

Summer holidays in the Netherlands are staggered and, as a result, traffic congestion is not too severe. However during the Christmas, Easter and Whitsun holiday periods, traffic jams are common and bottlenecks regularly occur on the A2 (Maastricht to Amsterdam), the A12 (Utrecht to the German border) and on the A50 (Arnhem to Apeldoorn). Roads to the Zeeland coast, e.g. the A58, N57 and N59, may become congested during periods of fine weather.

Many Germans head for the Netherlands on their own public holidays and the roads are particularly busy during these periods.

Violation of Traffic Regulations

Police are empowered to impose on-the-spot fines (or confiscate vehicles) for violation of traffic regulations and fines for speeding can be severe. If you are fined always ask for a receipt.

Touring

The southern Netherlands is the most densely populated part of the country but, despite the modern sprawl, ancient towns such as Dordrecht, Gouda, Delft and Leiden have retained their individuality and charm. Rotterdam is a modern, commercial centre and a tour of its harbour – the busiest in Europe – makes a fascinating excursion. The scenery in the north of the country is the most typically Dutch – vast, flat landscapes, largely reclaimed from the sea, dotted with windmills.

Some of the most charming towns and villages are Marken, Volendam and Alkmaar (famous for its cheese market). Aalsmeer, situated south of Amsterdam, stages the world's largest daily flower auction.

It's worth spending time to visit the hilly provinces in the east such as Gelderland, known for its castles, country houses and its major city, Arnhem, which has many links with the Second World War. Overijssel is a region of great variety and the old Hanseatic towns of Zwolle and Kampen have splendid quays and historic buildings. Friesland is the Netherland's lake district.

An 'I amsterdam City Card' entitles you to free admission to many of the city's famous museums, including the Rijksmuseum and Van Gogh Museum, and to discounts in many restaurants, shops, attractions and at Park & Ride car parks. It also entitles you to discounts on tours as well as free travel on public transport and a free canal cruise. The card is valid for one to five days and is available from tourist information offices, some Shell petrol stations, Canal Bus kiosks, Park & Ride car parks and some hotels. Alternatively purchase online from iamsterdam.com.

Service charges are included in restaurant bills and tips aren't necessary. Smoking is not permitted in bars or restaurants.

Spring is one of the most popular times to visit the Netherlands, in particular the famous Keukenhof Gardens near Lisse, open from 20 March to 11 May in 2024, see (keukenhof.nl) for more information. Visitors enjoy a display more than seven million flowering bulbs, trees and shrubs.

Camping and Caravanning

There are approximately 2,500 officially classified campsites which offer a wide variety of facilities. Most are well equipped with modern sanitary facilities and they generally have a bar, shop and leisure facilities.

A number of sites require cars to be parked on a separate area away from pitches and this can present a problem for motorhomes. Some sites allow motorhomes to park on pitches without restrictions, but others will only accept them on pitches if they aren't moved during the duration of your stay. Check before booking in.

A tourist tax is levied at campsites of approximately €1.00 per person per night. It's not generally included in the prices quoted in the Site Entry listings which follow this chapter.

The periods over, and immediately after, the Ascension Day holiday and the Whitsun weekend are very busy for Dutch sites and you can expect to find many of them full. Advance booking is highly recommended.

Casual/wild camping is prohibited as is overnight camping by the roadside or in car parks. There are overnight parking places specifically for motorhomes all over the country – see campercontact.nl.

Many campsites also have motorhome amenities and some offer Quick Stop overnight facilities at reduced rates.

Cycling

There are around 33,000 km of well-maintained cycle tracks in both town and country, all marked with red and white road signs and mushroom-shaped posts indicating the quickest and/or most scenic routes. Local tourist information centres (VVV) sell maps of a wide range of cycling tours and cycling fact sheets and maps are available from the Netherlands Board of Tourism in London. Motorists should expect to encounter heavy cycle traffic, particularly during rush hours.

Obligatory separate bicycle lanes for cyclists are indicated by circular blue signs displaying a white bicycle.

Small oblong signs with the word 'fietspad' or 'rijwielpad' indicate optional bicycle lanes. White bicycles and dotted white lines painted on the road surface indicate cycle lanes which may be used by motor vehicles providing they don't obstruct cyclists. Cycle lanes marked by continuous white lines are prohibited for use by motor vehicles.

Cyclists must obey traffic light signals at crossroads and junctions; elsewhere, where no traffic lights are in operation, they must give way to traffic from the right.

Cycle tracks are also used by mobility scooters and mopeds. Pedestrians should be especially cautious when crossing roads, especially on zebra crossings. Look out for both cyclists and riders of mopeds, who often ignore traffic rules as well as red lights. In Amsterdam in particular, many cyclists don't use lights at night.

Bicycles may be carried on the roof of a car providing the total height doesn't exceed 4 metres. They may also be carried at the rear providing the width doesn't extend more than 20 cm beyond the width of the vehicle.

Electricity and Gas

Most campsites have a supply ranging from 4 to 10 amps and almost all have CEE connections. Plugs have two round pins.

The full range of Campingaz cylinders is available.

Public Transport

There's an excellent network of buses and trams, together with metro systems in Amsterdam (called the GVB), Rotterdam and The Hague.

An electronic card 'OV-chipkaart' (OV-chip card) can be bought at vending machines at stations or ticket offices and on board buses and trams and are available for periods from one hour to seven days allowing unlimited travel on trams, buses and the metro.

Children under 12 and people over the age of 65 qualify for reduced fares (show your passport as proof of age). See GVB's website (gvb.nl) for more information.

Tickets must be validated before travel either at the yellow machines on trams and at metro stations or by your bus driver or conductor.

In Amsterdam canal transport includes a regular canal shuttle between Centraal Station and the Rijksmuseum. A 'circle tram' travels from Centraal Station through the centre of Amsterdam past a number of local visitor attractions, such as Anne Frank's house, the Rijksmuseum, Van Gogh Museum and Rembrandthuis.

There are Park & Ride facilities at most railway stations. Secure parking is also offered at 'transferiums', a scheme offering reasonably priced guarded parking in secure areas on the outskirts of major towns with easy access by road and close to public transport hubs.

Transferiums have heated waiting rooms and rest rooms as well as information for travellers, and some even have a shop.

Frequent car ferry services operate on routes to the Frisian (or Wadden) Islands off the north west coast, for example, from Den Helder to Texel Island, Harlingen to Terschelling Island and Holwerd to Ameland Island. Other islands in the group don't allow cars but there are passenger ferry services. In the summer island-hopping round tickets are available to foot passengers and cyclists and are popular for exploring the country.

Sites in Netherlands

ALKMAAR *B2* (7.7km W Rural/Coastal) *52.634290, 4.660384* **De Markiess,** Driehuizerweg 1A, 1934 PR Egmond aan den Hoef **(072) 5062274; info@demarkiess.nl; www.demarkiess.nl**

€2 (htd) nr nr nr 2km; sand

N9 W of Alkmaar. Take Egmond sp. Turn R aft petrol stn. Foll sp to site. Med, unshd, EHU (6A) €3; bbq; TV; bus 2km; Eng spkn; games rm. *"One of best maintained sites; grass like bowling green; no grass cuttings left; spotless facs; recycling; excel."* **€24.50, 30 Mar-30 Sep. 2023**

ALKMAAR *B2* (2.6km NW Urban) *52.64205, 4.72407* **Camping Alkmaar,** Bergerweg 201, 1817 ML Alkmaar **(072) 5116924; info@campingalkmaar.nl; www.campingalkmaar.nl**

€3 (htd) nr

Fr W ring rd (Martin Luther Kingweg) foll Bergen sp, bear R at T-junc & site 150m on L. Site well sp. Med, mkd, hdstg, pt shd, EHU (4-10A) inc; bbq; TV (pitch); 10% statics; bus at gate; Eng spkn; adv bkg acc; ccard acc; golf 2km; CKE. *"Clean, friendly site; decent sized pitches; buses to town; 20 min walk to town cent; cheese mkt on Friday in ssn; pool adj; vg cycling rte into centre; cash/mastercard; gd san facs."* **€29.00, 1 Mar-1 Oct. 2024**

ALMERE *C3* (7km W Rural) *52.35688, 5.22505* **Camping Waterhout,** Archerpad 6, 1324 ZZ Almere **(036) 5470632; info@waterhout.nl; www.waterhout.nl**

€2.50

Exit A6 junc 4, site sp fr slip rd on S edge Weerwater. Med, mkd, shd, EHU (10A) inc; sw nr; TV; 30% statics; phone; bus 200m; Eng spkn; adv bkg acc; CKE. *"Well laid-out site; conv Amsterdam by bus or train - 30 mins; Almere ultra-modern city."* **€27.00, 19 Apr-27 Oct. 2024**

AMERSFOORT *C3* (11km S Rural) *52.07975, 5.38151* **Vakantiepark De Heigraaf,** De Haygraeff 9, 3931 ML Woudenberg **(033) 2865066; info@heigraaf.nl; www.heigraaf.nl**

(htd)

Exit A12 at Maarn junc 21 or junc 22 & foll sp to site on N224, 2km W of Woudenberg. V lge, mkd, pt shd, EHU (4-6A) inc; sw nr; 50% statics; phone; bus 500m; Eng spkn; adv bkg acc. *"Vg, well-managed site; modern san facs; well run site, does not accept Visa."* **€20.00, 26 Mar-30 Sep. 2020**

AMSTERDAM *B3* (12km N Rural) *52.43649, 4.91445* **Camping Het Rietveen,** Noordeinde 130, 1121 AL Landsmeer **(020) 4821468; info@campinghetrietveen.nl; www.campinghetrietveen.nl**

12 nr nr nr

Fr A10 ring rd exit junc 117. At junc off slip rd turn L dir Landsmeer, site sp. Sm, mkd, EHU (10A) inc; sw; bus to Amsterdam 200m; Eng spkn; tennis; adv bkg adv; fishing; bike hire; CKE. *"Vg, pretty lakeside site, like lge CL, in well-kept vill; no recep - site yourself & owner will call; sep field avail for rallies; excel touring base; city 30 mins by bus; san facs inadequate; no wifi;"* **€50.00 2023**

AMSTERDAM *B3* (5km NE Urban) *52.38907, 4.92532* **Camping Vliegenbos,** Meeuwenlaan 138, 1022 AM Amsterdam **(020) 2517800; vliegenbos.sdn@amsterdam.nl; www.amsterdam.nl/vliegenbos**

(htd) nr

Fr A10 Amsterdam ring rd, take exit S116 Amsterdam Noord, at 2nd slip rd turn R sp Noord over rndabt, turn L at next rndabt, then immed sharp R, L onto service rd, site sp. 2*, Lge, hdstg, pt shd, pt sl, EHU (6A) inc; gas; phone; bus to city nr; Eng spkn; ccard acc. *"Sm pitches mainly for tents; ltd EHU; m'vans & c'vans park outside barrier; friendly staff; pool 1.5km; bus tickets to city cent fr recep; cycle path to city cent via free ferry; clean, modern san facs; v well set up."* **€34.00, 1 Apr-31 Dec. 2022**

AMSTERDAM *B3* (6km E Urban) *52.36555, 4.95829* **Camping Zeeburg,** Zuider Ijdijk 20, 1095 KN Amsterdam **(020) 6944430; info@campingzeeburg.nl; www.campingzeeburg.nl**

12 €3

Fr A10 ring rd exit at S114 & foll site sps. Lge, unshd, EHU (6-16A) inc; gas; 10% statics; bus/tram to city nr; adv bkg rec; bike hire. *"Used mainly by tents in summer, but rest of year suitable for c'vans; conv city cent."* **€38.80 2022**

AMSTERDAM *B3* (12km SE Urban) *52.31258, 4.99035* **Gaasper Camping,** Loosdrechtdreef 7, 1108 AZ Amsterdam-Zuidoost **(020) 6967326; info@gaaspercamping.nl; www.gaaspercamping.nl**

€5 (htd)

Fr A2 take A9 E sp Amersfoort. After about 5km take 3rd exit sp Gaasperplas/Weesp S113. Cross S113 into site, sp. 2*, Lge, hdg, mkd, hdstg, pt shd, serviced pitches; EHU (10A) €4.50; gas; 20% statics; Eng spkn; CKE. *"Immac site set in beautiful parkland; well-run with strict rules; night guard at barrier (high ssn); vans must be manhandled onto pitch (help avail); high ssn arr early to ensure pitch - no adv bkg for fewer than 7 nights; metro 5 mins walk (tickets fr site recep); poss cold shwrs & ltd shop LS; gd security; well run site; conv for metro; adv bkg rec high ssn."* **€34.50, 1 Jan-4 Jan, 15 Mar-1 Nov, 28 Dec-31 Dec. 2023**

NETHERLANDS

AMSTERDAM *B3* (15km SW Rural) *52.29366, 4.82316* **Camping Het Amsterdamse Bos,** Kleine Noorddijk 1, 1187 NZ Amstelveen **880 708421; info@camping amsterdam.com; www.campingamsterdamsebos.com**

€3 (htd)

Foll A10 & A4 twd Schiphol Airport. Fr junc on A4 & A9 m'way, take A9 E twd Amstelveen; at next exit (junc 6) exit sp Aalsmeer. Foll Aalsmeer sp for 1km bearing R at traff lts then at next traff lts turn L over canal bdge onto N231. In 1.5km turn L at 2nd traff lts into site. Fr S exit A4 junc 3 onto N201 dir Hilversum (ignore other camp sps). Turn L onto N231 dir Amstelveen, at rd junc Bovenkirk take N231 dir Schiphol, site on R in 200m, sp. 1*, V lge, pt shd, EHU (10A) €4.50; gas; 20% statics; bus to city; Eng spkn; adv bkg acc; ccard acc; CKE. *"Conv Amsterdam by bus - tickets sold on site; poss migrant workers resident on site; san facs stretched high ssn; gd walking & cycling paths; spectacular daily flower auctions at Aalsmeer; waterpark nr; conv bulbfields."* **€28.50, 28 Mar-3 Nov.** **2024**

ANNEN *D2* (3.7km S Rural) *53.03017, 6.73912* **De Baldwin Hoeve,** Annerweg 9, 9463 TB Eext **05 92 27 16 29; info@baldwinhoeve.nl; www.baldwinhoeve.nl**

Fr N34 take Annen exit. Turn R onto Anlooerweg. At rndabt take R dir Eext. Bef underpass take sm service rd on L to campsite. Sm, mkd, unshd, EHU (10A); bbq; twin axles; bus adj; Eng spkn; adv bkg acc; CCI. *"CL type farm site with excel san facs; friendly owners; horses & other livestock; lg group accomodation avail; vg."* **€16.50** **2024**

"There aren't many sites open at this time of year"

If you're travelling outside peak season remember to call ahead to check site opening dates – even if the entry says 'open all year'.

APELDOORN *C3* (10km N Rural) *52.29066, 5.94520* **Camping De Helfterkamp,** Gortelseweg 24, 8171 RA Vaassen **(0578) 571839; info@helfterkamp.nl; www.helfterkamp.nl**

€2.50 (htd)

Leave A50 junc 26; foll sp to Vaassen; site sp on ent to town - 2.5km W of Vaassen. Med, mkd, pt shd, EHU (16A) metered (poss rev pol); gas; sw nr; red long stay; 40% statics; phone; Eng spkn; adv bkg req; ccard acc; bike hire; CKE. *"Excel, immac, well-maintained, busy site in beautiful woodland area; key for shwrs & hot water; v friendly owners; conv for Apeldoorn/ Arnhem areas & De Hooge Veluwe National Park; gd walking/cycling."* **€55.50, 1 Mar-31 Oct.** **2023**

APELDOORN *C3* (10km S Rural) *52.11771, 5.90641* **Camping De Pampel,** Woeste Hoefweg 35, 7351 TN Hoenderloo **(055) 3781760; info@pampel.nl; www.pampel.nl**

€3 (htd)

Exit A1 Amersfoort-Apeldoorn m'way at junc 19 Hoenderloo. Fr Hoenderloo dir Loenen, site sp. Lge, mkd, hdg, pt shd, serviced pitches; EHU (6-16A); adv bkg req; bike hire. *"V pleasant setting 2km fr National Park; go-kart hire; excel facs; free 1-day bus ticket; private bthrms avail; some site rds diff for lge o'fits; vg for children; no dogs high ssn; many mkd walks/cycle paths; friendly staff."* **€46.70** **2023**

APPELSCHA *D2* (4.5km S Rural) *52.92134, 6.34447* **Boscamping Appelscha,** Oude Willem 3, 8426 SM Appelscha **(0516) 431391; info@boscamping appelscha.nl; www.campingalkenhaer.nl**

A28 junc 31 sp Drachten. Turn L onto N381. About 13km turn L onto Oude Willem then take 3rd R, site on L. Lge, mkd, pt shd, EHU (16A); 60% statics; Eng spkn; CKE. *"Neat, friendly, well run site; takeaway; many walking, cycling & riding trails in nrby national park; vg site."* **€24.50, 1 Apr-1 Oct.** **2024**

ARNHEM *C3* (6km W Rural) *51.99365, 5.82203* **Camping Aan Veluwe,** Sportlaan 1, 6861 AG Oosterbeek **(0224) 563109; info@aannoordzee.nl; www.aanveluwe.nl**

€1.80 (htd)

Fr S fr Nijmegen, cross new bdge at Arnhem. Foll Oosterbeek sp for 5km, cont past memorial in Oosterbeek, in 1km turn R at rndabt, 500m L to site. Or fr A50 exit junc 19 onto N225 twd Osterbeek/ Arnhem. In 3km at rndabt turn L, site on L in 500m. Med, pt shd, pt sl, EHU (16A) inc; gas; red long stay; 10% statics; adv bkg acc; sep car park. *"Conv Airborne Museum & Cemetery & Dutch Open Air Museum; sports club bar open to site guests; shwr facs for each pitch; pool 3km; lovely walks."* **€21.00, 29 Mar-28 Oct.** **2024**

ARNHEM *C3* (5km NW Rural) *52.0072, 5.8714* **Camping Warnsborn,** Bakenbergseweg 257, 6816 PB Arnhem **(026) 4423469; info@campingwarnsborn.nl; www.campingwarnsborn.nl**

€3 (htd) nr

Fr Utrecht on E35/A12, exit junc 25 Ede (if coming fr opp dir, beware unnumbered m'way junc 200m prior to junc 25). Take N224 dual c'way twd Arnhem & foll sp Burgers Zoo, site sp. Beware oncoming traff & sleeping policeman nr site ent. Med, pt shd, EHU (6A) inc; gas; bbq; red long stay; 5% statics; phone; bus 100m; Eng spkn; adv bkg acc; ccard acc; CKE. *"Excel, spacious, clean, well-maintained, wooded site; san facs clean; friendly, helpful family owners & staff; airborne museum & cemetery; cycle rtes direct fr site; conv Hooge Veluwe National Park & Kröller-Müller museum (Van Gogh paintings); super site but busy; bus into Arnhem."* **€26.50, 1 Apr-30 Oct.** **2022**

NETHERLANDS

ARNHEM *C3* (9km NW Rural) *52.03192, 5.86652* **Droompark Hooge Veluwe,** Koningsweg 14, Schaarsbergen, 6816 TC Arnhem **(088) 0551596; hoogeveluwe@droomparken.nl; www.hoogeveluwe.nl**

12 €3.50 (htd) (covrd, htd)

Fr Utrecht A12/E35, Oosterbeck exit 25 & foll sp for Hooge Veluwe to site in 4km on R. Lge, pt shd, serviced pitches; EHU (6-16A) inc; gas; 50% statics; Eng spkn; adv bkg acc; ccard acc; sep car park; games area. *"Vg, espec for children; excel site; lots of facs; helpful staff; care needed turning into site area; great value; vg clean san facs; gd rest; conv for Arnhem area, m'way & Ijmuiden ferry port."* **€39.00** **2024**

BERGEN OP ZOOM *B4* (5km SE Rural) *51.46913, 4.32236* **Camping Uit en Thuis,** Heimolen 56, 4625 DD Bergen op Zoom **(0164) 233391; info@campinguitenthuis.nl; www.campinguitenthuis.nl**

€3.5 (htd)

Exit A4/E312 at junc 29 sp Huijbergen & foll site sp. Lge, hdg, pt shd, EHU (4-6A) inc; red long stay; TV; 75% statics; Eng spkn; adv bkg acc; tennis; games area; CKE. *"Spacious site in woodland; gd cycle paths to pleasant town; sep mv places; excel site, v pretty; lge pitches."* **€27.00, 1 Apr-1 Oct.** **2023**

BLADEL *C4* (1.6km S Rural) *51.35388, 5.22254* **Camping De Hooiberg (Formerly Mini-Camping De Hooiberg),** Bredasebaan 20, 5531 NB Bladel **(0497) 369619 or 06 54341822 (mob); info@hooibergcamping.nl; www.hooibergcamping.nl**

(htd)

Exit A67 junc 32 onto N284 to Bladel, turn L at traff lts to Bladel-Zuid, site on L in 2km. Sm, pt shd, EHU (6A) inc; bus adj; Eng spkn; adv bkg acc; sep car park. *"Gd, quiet site; clean san fac; v friendly owner; dogs free; farm shop selling local produce adj; 10 mins fr A67; conv NH & for Eindhoven & Efteling theme park."* **€18.00, 15 Mar-31 Oct.** **2024**

BLADEL *C4* (3km S Rural) *51.34325, 5.22740* **Camping De Achterste Hoef,** Troprijt 10, 5531 NA Bladel **(0497) 381579; info@achterstehoef.nl; www.achterstehoef.nl**

(htd) (covrd, htd)

Fr A67 exit junc 32 onto N284 to Bladel, then Bladel-Zuid, site sp. 5*, V lge, pt shd, EHU (6A) inc; 70% statics; adv bkg acc; ccard acc; waterslide; games area; tennis; games rm; bike hire. *"Private san facs avail."* **€41.70, 5 Apr-29 Sep.** **2024**

BOURTANGE *D2* (1km NW Rural) *53.01014, 7.18494* **NCC Camping 't Plathuis,** Bourtangerkanaal Noord 1, 9545 VJ Bourtange **(0599) 354383; info@plathuis.nl; www.plathuis.nl**

(htd)

Exit A47 junc 47 onto N368 sp Blijham to Vlagtwedde. Turn L onto N365 to Bourtange, site sp on R. Med, hdg, pt shd, EHU 10; bbq; cooking facs; sw; TV; 50% statics; phone; bus; Eng spkn; adv bkg acc; ccard acc; canoe hire; games area; bike hire; fishing; CKE. *"Site adj historic fortress; town 2km fr German border; level pitches, some hdstdng but mainly grass; peaceful atmosphere; gd, clean facs; sm family run site next to marina; cafe at recep; vg; tv recep (Astra)."* **€28.30, 1 Apr-31 Oct.** **2024**

BRIELLE *B3* (1km E Urban) *51.90666, 4.17527* **Camping de Meeuw,** Batterijweg 1, 3231 AA Brielle **(0181) 412777; info@demeeuw.nl; www.demeeuw.nl**

inc (up to 4) sand

On A15/N57 foll sp to Brielle. Turn R after passing thro town gates & foll sp to site. Lge, pt shd, EHU (10A) inc; gas; 70% statics; phone; Eng spkn; bike hire; CKE. *"Historic fortified town; attractive area for tourers; conv Europoort ferry terminal; gd NH/sh stay; phone warden fr recep when arr after 5pm."* **€39.00, 31 Mar-30 Oct.** **2023**

"That's changed – Should I let the Club know?"

If you find something on site that's different from the site entry, fill in a report and let us know. See camc.com/europereport.

BURGH HAAMSTEDE *A3* (3km NW Coastal) *51.71478, 3.72219* **Camping Ginsterveld,** Maireweg 10, 4328 GR Burgh-Haamstede (Zeeland) **(0111) 651590; info@ginsterveld.nl or ginsterveld@ardoer.com; www.ginsterveld.ardoer.com**

sand 2km

SP fr Burgh-Haamstede. Foll R107. Lge, pt shd, EHU (6A) inc; bbq; 50% statics; Eng spkn; adv bkg acc; games area. *"Excel cycling & walking fr site; bicycles; takeaway; vg."* **€46.00, 22 Mar-27 Oct.** **2024**

CADZAND *A4* (2km SE Rural) *51.36099, 3.42503* **Camping De Wielewaal,** Zuidzandseweg 20, 4506 HC Cadzand **(0117) 391216; info@campingwielewaal.nl; www.campingwielewaal.nl**

€2 nr nr nr 3km

Head to Cadzand. Travel 1km SE, site ent on L, 3km NW of Zuidzande. Med, mkd, hdg, pt shd, EHU; bbq; Eng spkn; adv bkg acc; ccard acc; games rm. *"Many cycle tracks; walks fr site; friendly, helpful owners; windmill 1km; highly rec; excel."* **€24.20, 1 Apr-1 Nov.** **2022**

CADZAND *A4* (5km S Rural/Coastal) *51.344562, 3.429860* **Minicamping de Hullu,** Kokersweg 1, 4505 PK Zuidzande **(3111) 7452842**

(htd) 4km

Do not use SatNav. Fr Bruge A11 (new) N253 to Oostburg. N674 thro Zuidzande. Site on L. Sm, shd, EHU (6A) inc; bbq; Eng spkn; adv bkg acc; games area. *"Excel; feels like camping in gdn of stately home; 16 vans when full; views; lawned; no passing traff; spacious."* **NP 20, 20 Apr-15 Sep. 2023**

CALLANTSOOG *B2* (2.5km NE Coastal) *52.84627, 4.71549* **Camping Tempelhof,** Westerweg 2, 1759 JD Callantsoog **(0224) 581522; info@tempelhof.nl; www.tempelhof.nl**

€3.50 (htd) (covrd, htd) sand 1km

Fr A9 Alkmaar-Den Helder exit Callantsoog, site sp to NE of vill. 5*, Lge, mkd, pt shd, serviced pitches; EHU (10A) inc; gas; TV (pitch); 50% statics; phone; adv bkg rec; sauna; gym; bike hire; games area; tennis. *"Superb, well-run site & facs; private bthrms avail; ACSI acc."* **€49.00 2023**

CALLANTSOOG *B2* (3km NE Coastal) *52.84143, 4.71909* **NCC Camping De Ooster Nollen,** Westerweg 8, 1759 JD Callantsoog **(0224) 581281 or 561351; info@denollen.nl; www.denollen.nl**

€3 (htd) sand 1.5km

N fr Alkmaar on A9; turn L sp Callantsoog. Site sp 1km E of Callantsoog. Lge, mkd, pt shd, EHU (10A) inc; gas; red long stay; TV; 40% statics; phone; Eng spkn; adv bkg acc; ccard acc; bike hire; games area; CKE. *"Nature area nr; cheese mkt; clean & superb san facs; pool 400m; supmkt 3km."* **€50.20, 1 Apr-29 Oct. 2023**

DELFT *B3* (4km NE Urban) *52.01769, 4.37945* **Camping Delftse Hout,** Korftlaan 5, 2616 LJ Delft **(015) 2130040; info@delftsehout.nl; www.delftsehout.co.uk**

€3.25 (htd) (htd)

Fr Hook of Holland take N220 twd Rotterdam; after Maasdijk turn R onto A20 m'way. Take A13 twd Den Haag at v lge Kleinpolderplein interchange. Take exit 9 sp Delft (Ikea on R). Turn R twrds Ikea then L at rndabt. Foll sp. Do not use Sat Nav. 4*, Lge, hdstg, mkd, hdg, pt shd, EHU (10A) inc; gas; bbq; red long stay; TV; 50% statics; phone; bus to Delft; Eng spkn; adv bkg rec; ccard acc; bike hire; fishing nr; golf 5km; watersports nr; games rm; CKE. *"Located by pleasant park; gd quality, secure, busy site with excel facs; Holland Tulip Parcs site; helpful, friendly staff; little shd; no o'fits over 7.5m; excursions by bike & on foot; easy access Delft cent; sm m'van o'night area outside site; mkt Thur; excel; site clean & well maintained; gd rest; vg play areas for kids; flea mkt on Sat; gd tram and train svcs to the Hague, Leiden and Gouda fr Delft stn; gd sized pitches; vg MH svr pnt; well stocked shop."* **€33.00, 25 Mar - 1 Nov, H06. 2022**

DELFT *B3* (9.4km SW Rural) *51.95450, 4.28833* **Hoeve Bouwlust,** Oostgaag 31, 3155 CE Maasland **(0105) 912775; info@hoevebouwlust.nl; www.hoevebouwlust.nl**

€2

Fr Hofh on A20 turn N at junc 7. Go thro Maasland on N468. Site on L in 3km. Sm, hdg, pt shd, EHU (10A) €4.50; bbq; twin axles; 10% statics; bus adj; Eng spkn; adv bkg acc; CKE. *"Lots of outdoor activities inc tandem, boating & scotters; v friendly & helpful owners; vg site."* **€20.00, 1 Apr-31 Oct. 2023**

DENEKAMP *D3* (4km NE Rural) *52.39190, 7.04890* **Camping De Papillon,** Kanaalweg 30, 7591 NH Denekamp **(0541) 351670; info@papilloncountry resort.com; www.papilloncountryresort.com**

€4.50 (htd) (covrd, htd)

Fr A1 take exit 32 onto N342 Oldenzaal-Denekamp, dir Nordhorn, site sp on left just bef German border. 4*, Lge, hdg, mkd, pt shd, EHU (6-10A) inc; gas; bbq; sw; red long stay; TV; 5% statics; phone; Eng spkn; tennis; pool paddling; bike hire. *"Super, clean site; friendly site; helpful owners; man-made lake; vg."* **€35.00, 29 Mar-30 Sep, H18. 2022**

DEVENTER *C3* (11km E Rural) *52.25591, 6.29205* **Camping De Flierweide,** Traasterdijk 16, 7437 Bathmen **31 570 541478; info@flierweide.nl; www.flierweide.nl**

Fr A1 junc 25 dir Bathmen. After 1km turn R sp De Flierweide, 800m L onto Laurensweg, thro vill. Cross rlwy, 1st R ontp Traasterdijk. Site on R after 500m at fm buildings. Med, hdg, mkd, hdstg, pt shd, EHU (4-16A) €2.50; bbq; red long stay; 1% statics; Eng spkn; adv bkg acc; bike hire; games area; CKE. *"Walking & cycle rtes; golf nr; boules onsite; excel."* **€24.20, 15 Mar-1 Nov. 2022**

DIEREN *C3* (2.5km NW Rural) *52.06908, 6.07705* **De Jutberg Vakantiedorp,** Jutberg 78, 6957 DP Laag-Soeren **03 13 61 92 20; jutberg@ardoer.com; www.ardoer.com/jutberg**

(htd) (covrd, htd)

Fr A12 take exit 27 onto the A348. Turn L on the N348 into Dieren. Turn L at petrol stn, cont for 2.7km. Foll sp to site. V lge, mkd, shd, pt sl, EHU (6A); bbq; Eng spkn; adv bkg acc; games rm; games area; CCI. *"Hugh pitches, fully serviced; v lively but not noisy; excursions for adults & kids in summer; wet weather diversions; excel san facs; extensive cycle paths thro countryside & forest; excel site."* **€35.20 2024**

DOORNENBURGH *C3* (3km NNW Rural) *51.90416, 5.98529* **Camping de Waay,** Rijndijk 67A, 6686 MC Doornenburg **(048) 1421256; info@de-waay.nl; www.de-waay.nl**

(htd)

A325 S fr Arnhem for 12km turn R onto A15 twrds Tiel, take exit N839 Bemmel. At t-junc foll sp to Gendt. In Gendt take N838. Foll ANWB de Waay sp twrds Angeren. Turn R onto the dyke and site on R. Sm, pt shd, EHU 6A; bbq; TV; 60% statics; Eng spkn; adv bkg acc; waterslide; games rm; bike hire; games area; CKE. *"V helpful staff; takeaway; gd for Arnhem & Nijmegen; ACSI acc; vg."* **€39.00, 1 Apr-30 Sep. 2022**

DORDRECHT *B3* (13km N Rural) *51.89530, 4.72209* **Camping en Feestzall Landhoeve,** Lekdijk 15, 2957 CA Nieuw-Lekkerland **(3184) 684137 or (316) 40487201; info@landhoeve.info; www.landhoeve.com**

(htd)

Fr A15 take exit 23. Take 2nd exit at rndabt and then 3rd exit at next rndabt twrds New Lekkerland. Turn R onto the N480 twrds Streefkerk. Then L onto Zijdeweg & L again at the end of rd. Site in 400mtrs. Sm, unshd, EHU (6A) €2; bbq; Eng spkn; adv bkg acc. *"New htd toilet block (2017); views; 19 windmills at Kinderdijk nrby, Unesco site; like lge CL; vg."* **€23.50, 1 Apr-1 Oct. 2023**

DORDRECHT *B3* (3km SE Rural) *51.80738, 4.71862* **Camping Het Loze Vissertje,** Loswalweg 3, 3315 LB Dordrecht **(078) 6162751; info@campinghetvissertje.nl; www.campinghetvissertje.nl**

€2.50

Fr Rotterdam across Brienenoord Bdge foll sp Gorinchem & Nijmegen A15. Exit junc 23 Papendrecht & turn R onto N3 until exit Werkendam. Turn R & foll sp 'Het Vissertje'. Sm, pt shd, EHU (6A) inc; red long stay; 20% statics; Eng spkn. *"Lovely, delightful site; friendly, helpful manager; modern, clean san facs; gd cycle rtes nr; vg; easy acc to town on local train."* **€27.00, 15 Apr-15 Sep. 2023**

DWINGELOO *D2* (2km SE Rural) *52.82216, 6.39258* **Camping De Olde Bârgen,** Oude Hoogeveensedijk 1, 7991 PD Dwingeloo **(0521) 597261; info@oldebargen.nl; www.oldebargen.nl**

12 €3.5 nr

Exit A28 Zwolle/Assen rd at Spler, turn W sp Dwingeloo, site clearly sp, in wooded area. Sm, mkd, pt shd, EHU (4-6A) inc; 10% statics; Eng spkn; adv bkg acc; CKE. *"Excel, v clean, well-run site on N side Dwingelderveld National Park; gd for walkers & cyclists; v friendly, helpful owners; pool 1.5km; delightful, quiet sitewarden avail 1 hr each morning LS, pitch & pay next day."* **€30.00 2023**

EDAM *B2* (2km NE Coastal) *52.51853, 5.07286* **Camping Strandbad Edam,** Zeevangszeedijk 7A, 1135 PZ Edam **(0299) 371994; info@campingstrandbad.nl; www.campingstrandbad.nl**

(htd) sand adj

Foll N247 Amsterdam-Hoorn; after sp for Edam foll site sp. At traff lts in Edam keep on N247 past bus stn on R, then R at next rndabt. Last 100m to site is single track opp marina. Access thro public car park. 2*, Lge, pt shd, EHU (10A) inc; gas; red long stay; TV; 40% statics; phone; Eng spkn; adv bkg acc; ccard acc; watersports; bike hire. *"Walking dist Edam; landing stage for boats; excel san facs; pool 3km; sm, poss cramped pitches high ssn."* **€34.50, 1 Apr-30 Sep. 2023**

EDAM *B2* (2.5km NE Coastal) *52.52472, 5.06472* **Camping Zeevangshoeve,** Zeevangszeedijk 5-C, 1135 PZ Edam **(061) 7864374; info@zeevangshoeve.nl; www.zeevangshoeve.nl**

€2 opp

Foll coast rd out of Nof old part of Edam past marina along edge of the Markermeer dyke. Site is on L opp the Zeedijk. Sm, pt shd, EHU (6A) Inc; bbq; Eng spkn; adv bkg acc. *"Easy walk/cycle to historic cent of Edam; vg."* **€25.00, 30 Mar-31 Oct. 2023**

EERSEL *C4* (4km SE Rural) *51.33635, 5.35552* **Camping De Paal,** De Paaldreef 14, 5571 TN Bergeijk **(0497) 571977; info@depaal.nl; www.depaal.nl**

€5 (htd) (covrd, htd, indoor)

Fr A67/E34 Antwerp/Eindoven exit junc 32 sp Eersel & bear R onto N284 & stay in R-hand lane. At rndabt take 1st exit onto Eijkereind. In 500m after rndbt turn L at traff lts & foll rd around R & L bend. Take R turn sp Bergeijk after lge church (sm sp on sharp L bend). After approx 5km turn L into site rd. 5*, V lge, pt shd, EHU (6A) inc; gas; bbq (charcoal, gas); TV; 10% statics; phone; games rm; sep car park; bike hire; tennis; watersports 10km; fishing; horseriding 500m; sauna. *"Excel, family-run site set in woodland; espec gd for young children; lge pitches in groups with sep sm play areas; excursions; recep 0900-1800; sm children's zoo; fitness cent; no o'fits over 8m high ssn; conv Efteling theme park, Hilvarenbeek safari park, Oisterwijk bird park; mkt Mon & Tue pm; 1st class facs."* **€47.00, 25 Mar-30 Oct, H04. 2022**

NETHERLANDS

EERSEL *C4* (3.5km SW Rural) *51.33837, 5.29354*
Camping TerSpegelt, Postelseweg 88, 5521 RD Eersel **(0497) 512016; info@terspegelt.nl; www.terspegelt.nl**
(htd) (htd, indoor) sandy beach adj

Exit A67/E34 junc 32 to Eersel. At rndabt turn R, at 2nd traff lts in 1.5km turn L. Site sp 4km on L. 5*, V lge, hdg, mkd, pt shd, serviced pitches; EHU (6-10A); gas; bbq (charcoal, elec, gas); sw; twin axles; TV; 60% statics; phone; bus nrby; Eng spkn; adv bkg rec; ccard acc; tennis; watersports; bike hire; games area; games rm; pump track; mini animal park; CKE. *"Excel site; private san facs avail some pitches; gd pool complex; walking paths adj; sep car parking area; muddy when wet; v busy weekends; excel site for families; vg; highly rec."* **€68.20, 1 Apr-30 Oct. 2023**

EINDHOVEN *C4* (16km S Rural) *51.32887, 5.46160*
Recreatiepark Brugse Heide, Maastrichterweg 183, 5556 VB Valkenswaard **(040) 2018304; info@vakantieparkbrugseheide.nl; www.oostappenvakantieparken.nl/brugse-heide**
(htd) nr (htd)

S fr Eindhoven, exit Waalre; take N69 Valkenswaard; drive thro to rndabt, turn L. At next rndabt strt ahead, at next rndabt turn R, foll sp Achel. Site on L in 1km. 3*, Lge, mkd, shd, serviced pitches; EHU (6A) inc (rev pol); gas; bbq; TV; 40% statics; phone; Eng spkn; adv bkg req; ccard acc; bike hire. *"Excel, friendly site; gd NH en rte Germany; excel san facs."* **€38.00, 1 Apr-31 Oct. 2022**

EMMEN *D2* (6km N Rural) *52.82861, 6.85714*
Vakantiecentrum De Fruithof, Melkweg 2, 7871 PE Klijndijk **(0591) 512427; info@fruithof.nl; www.fruithof.nl**
(htd) (htd)

On N34 N fr Emmen dir Borger, turn R sp Klijndijk, foll site sp. 5*, Lge, mkd, hdg, pt shd, serviced pitches; EHU (6A) inc; gas; bbq; sw nr; red long stay; TV; 50% statics; Eng spkn; adv bkg acc; tennis; games area; bike hire; CKE. *"Excel; v lge busy site; gd san facs."* **€38.80, 5 Apr-23 Sep. 2024**

ENKHUIZEN *C2* (1km N Coastal) *52.70888, 5.28830*
Camping De Vest, Noorderweg 31, 1601 PC Enkhuizen **(0228) 321221; info@campingdevest.nl; www.campingdevest.nl**
€2 sand 800m

When N302 turns R at traff lts, keep strt on to T-junc. Foll site sp to R, site on R in 50m. Sm, pt shd, EHU (4A) inc; 25% statics; Eng spkn; adv bkg acc. *"Gates clsd 2300-0800; easy walk to town cent; lively jazz festival last w/end in May; facs old but clean, well-kept - poss stretched when site full; site inside town walls."* **€27.00, 30 Mar-30 Sep. 2023**

EXLOO *D2* (2km SE Rural) *52.86841, 6.88496*
Camping Exloo, Valtherweg 37, 7875 TA Exloo **05 91 54 91 47 or 05 91 56 40 14; info@campingexloo.nl; www.campingexloo.nl**
12 €1

N34 fr Groningen, exit Exloo. Turn R after vill twd Valthe. Site 2km on L. Sm, pt shd, EHU (6A); bbq; twin axles; TV; Eng spkn; adv bkg acc; CCI. *"Friendly recreation rm; vg site."* **€20.20 2024**

GENDT *C3* (1km E Rural) *51.87599, 5.98900*
Waalstrand Camping, Waaldijk 23, 6691 MB Gendt **(0481) 421604; info@waalstrand.nl; www.waalstrand.nl**
nr

Exit A15 to Bemmel, then Gendt. In Gendt foll sp to site on Rv Waal. Med, mkd, unshd, terr, EHU (6A) inc; gas; TV (pitch); 50% statics; Eng spkn; adv bkg acc; bike hire; tennis. *"Excel, well-kept site; clean, modern san facs; interesting rv traff; v friendly owners; lovely position; gd walks; 6 fully serviced camper van pitches; good views; excel site."* **€35.75, 1 Apr-30 Sep. 2023**

GOES *A3* (12km NW Rural) *51.54200, 3.78000*
De Heerlijkheid van Wolphaartsdijk, Muidenweg 10, 4471 NM Wolphaartsdijk **(0113) 581584 or 06 12612728 (mob); info@heerlijkheidwolphaartsdijk.nl; www.heerlijkheidwolphaartsdijk.nl**
€0.50

Off N256 Zierikzee to Goes rd foll sp Jachthaven Wolphaartsdijk. Shortly after vill turn L twd windmill. Turn R at mini rndabt (ignore camping sp by L turn) sp Arnemuiden, strt on at next rndabt, then L at next rndabt; site on L in 1km on lakeside - ent thro farm gate. Sm, hdg, pt shd, EHU (6-16A) €2.50; sw nr; bus 1km; Eng spkn; sailing; windsurfing; CKE. *"CL-type, farm site; modern san facs; friendly owners; bird reserve opp; excel cycling; rec."* **€19.00, 15 Mar-31 Oct. 2024**

GORINCHEM *B3* (13km E Rural) *51.81845, 5.12563*
Camping De Zwaan, Waaldijk 56, 4171 CG Herwijnen **(0418) 582354; info@rivierenland.biz; http://www.rivierenland.nl**
nr

Exit A15 at junc 29 dir Herwijnen. In Herwijnen turn R at T-junc sp Brakel. Turn L in 500m (Molenstraat). At T-junc turn R (Waaldijk), site on L in 150m on Rv Waal. Sm, pt shd, EHU (4A) inc; 75% statics; Eng spkn; adv bkg rec; CKE. *"Helpful owners; rv adj; ltd but clean facs; 66 m fr Amsterdam ferry."* **€13.00, 15 Apr-15 Oct. 2020**

GOUDA *B3* (10km E Rural) *52.01719, 4.82943* **Camping De Mulderije,** Hekendorpsebuurt 33, 3467 PA Hekendorp **(0348) 563233 or 06 20680521 (mob); info@demulderije.nl; demulderije.nl**

12 €2.5 nr nr nr

Exit A12 junc 14 Woerden onto N204 S. In 5km turn R to Oudewater N228. Cont dir Hekendorp & in approx 2km site sp on R. Narr rd to site. 1*, Sm, hdstg, pt shd, EHU (6A) inc; Eng spkn. *"Vg, clean, friendly site in nature reserve; cycle or boat to Gouda; facs clean attractive position; gd base; narr rd to site not suitable for lge o'fits; no passing places; do not use sat nav."* **€26.00** **2023**

GRONINGEN *D2* (6km SW Urban) *53.20128, 6.53577* **Camping Stadspark,** Campinglaan 6, 9727 KH Groningen **(050) 5251624; info@campingstadspark.nl; www.campingstadspark.nl**

€2.50

Take exit 36-A (dir Drachten) and foll 'Stadspark'. In the park go to the L and foll the sp. Fr Drachten/ Winsum, take exit 36. 2*, Med, shd, EHU (6A) €3.70 (poss rev pol); gas; TV; 20% statics; phone; Eng spkn; adv bkg acc; bike hire; sep car park. *"Municipal site adj parkland with gd sports facs; park & ride into town; plenty of space, tents & vans mixed; extensive cycle paths; car park adj to each set of pitches; gd san facs; well run site; interesting town; pool 3km; friendly helpful staff."* **€32.50, 15 Mar-15 Oct.** **2023**

GULPEN *C4* (1.5km S Rural) *50.80720, 5.89430* **Panorama Camping Gulperberg,** Berghem 1, 6271 NP Gulpen **088 070 8480; info.gulperberg@ europarcs.nl; www.gulperberg.nl**

€4.50 (htd)

Fr Maastricht on N278 twd Aachen. At 1st traff lts in Gulpen turn sharp R & foll site sp for 2km (past sports complex). Narr final app. 4*, Lge, mkd, hdstg, pt shd, terr, EHU (10A) inc; gas; bbq; TV (pitch); 10% statics; phone; Eng spkn; adv bkg acc; games area; bike hire; CKE. *"Nr Maastricht with gd walking/ views; mkd cycle rtes & footpaths; modern, clean facs - poss long walk; beautiful views; v popular site, busy even in LS; excel."* **€37.00, 17 Mar-3 Nov, H12.** **2022**

HARDERWIJK *C3* (13.6km W Rural) *52.340102, 5.505166* **Camping Het Groene Bos,** Green Woudseweg 98, 3896 LS Zeewolde **(036) 5236366; info@hetgroenebos.nl; www.hetgroenebos.nl**

(htd)

Off A305 on minor rd between Kampen & A27. Exit A27 J26 onto 305. Med, mkd, hdg, pt shd, EHU (6-16A) inc; Eng spkn; CKE. *"Vg site; surrounded by woodland."* **€25.00, 1 Apr-11 Oct.** **2023**

HARLINGEN *C2* (2km SW Coastal) *53.16253, 5.41653* **Camping De Zeehoeve,** Westerzeedijk 45, 8862 PK Harlingen **(0517) 413465; info@zeehoeve.nl; www.zeehoeve.nl**

€3.50 (htd) nr adj

Leave N31 N'bound at sp Kimswerd. At rndabt turn L under N31 & foll site sp. Site on R in 1.6km. 3*, Lge, pt shd, EHU (6A) inc; gas; TV; 30% statics; phone; Eng spkn; ccard acc; fishing; bike hire; games area; watersports. *"Roomy, well-maintained, well run, open site; clean modern facs; easy walk to historic town & harbour; interesting area; vg; ACSI acc."* **€40.70, 1 Apr-31 Oct.** **2023**

HELDEN *C4* (2km E Rural) *51.31813, 6.0235* **Camping De Heldense Bossen,** De Heldense Bossen 6, 5988 NH Helden **07 73 07 24 76; heldensebossen@ ardoer.com; www.ardoer.com/heldensebossen**

(covrd, htd)

Fr A67 Eindhoven-Venlo, take exit 38 (Helden). Turn R onto N277 twds Maasbreeseweg. Cont onto N562. Fr Helden dir Kessel. Turn L after 1km. Campsite 1km further on. 5*, V lge, mkd, pt shd, EHU (10A); bbq; twin axles; 65% statics; Eng spkn; adv bkg acc; games area; waterslide; bike hire; CCI. *"Excel site."* **€34.50, 29 Mar-27 Oct.** **2024**

HELLEVOETSLUIS *B3* (2km W Coastal) *51.82918, 4.11606* **Camping 't Weergors,** Zuiddijk 2, 3221 LJ Hellevoetsluis **(0181) 312430; weergors@pn.nl; www.weergors.nl**

€1.60 (htd)

Via m'way A20/A4 or A16/A15 dir Rotterdam-Europoort-Hellevoetsluis; take N15 to N57, exit Hellevoetsluis, site sp. 4*, Lge, hdg, mkd, hdstg, unshd, EHU (16A) €2.80; gas; bbq; TV; 60% statics; Eng spkn; ccard acc; bike hire; tennis; games area; lake fishing. *"Delta works 6km worth visit; bird sanctuary adj; flat site; gd san facs;sep car park; Holland Tulip Parcs site; v friendly, helpful staff; excel rest; gd walking/cycling; excel site; charming owners."* **€19.50, 1 Apr-31 Oct.** **2024**

HENGELO *D3* (7km W Rural) *52.25451, 6.72704* **Park Camping Mooi Delden,** De Mors 6, 7491 DZ Delden **(074) 3761922; info@mooidelden.nl; www.mooidelden.nl**

€3.15 (htd)

Exit A35 junc 28 onto N346 dir Delden. Fr Delden-Oost, site sp. Site ent is R-hand of 2 via barrier (use intercom on arr.) If you have a high vehicle take the turning after Delden-Oost to avoid low rail bdge (3.2m); turn L immed aft lge rv bdge & foll site sp. 3*, Med, mkd, pt shd, EHU (6-10A) €3.40 (poss rev pol); 50% statics; Eng spkn; adv bkg acc; tennis. *"Ideal for touring beautiful pt of Holland; sports complex adj; pleasant, well-kept site; clean facs."* **€30.00, 31 Mar-1 Nov.** **2022**

NETHERLANDS

HEUMEN *C3* (2km NW Rural) *51.76890, 5.82140* **Camping Heumens Bos,** Vosseneindseweg 46, 6582 BR Heumen **(024) 3581481; info@heumensbos.nl; www.heumensbos.nl**

12 €4 (htd) (covrd, htd)

Take A73/E31 Nijmegen-Venlo m'way, leave at exit 3 sp Heumen/Overasselt. Do not re-cross m'way. After 500m turn R at camp sp. Site on R in approx 1.5km, 1km S of Heumen. 5*, V lge, mkd, hdg, shd, EHU (6A) inc; gas; bbq; sw nr; TV; 60% statics; phone; Eng spkn; adv bkg acc; ccard acc; games area; horseriding 100m; games rm; bike hire; tennis; fishing 2km; watersports 6km; jacuzzi; sep car park; CCI. *"Excel, busy, family-run site; modern san facs; lots to do on site & in area - info fr recep; no o'fits over 14m; ideal for Arnhem; WW2 museums nr; activities in ssn; extra €3 for m'vans; noise fr bar high ssn; mkt Sat & Mon in Nijmegen."* **€50.00, H01.** 2022

HOEK *A4* (7km W Rural) *51.31464, 3.72618* **Oostappen Vakantiepark Marina Beach (formerly Braakman),** Middenweg 1, 4542 PN Hoek **(0115) 481730; receptie@vakantieparkmarinabeach.nl; www.oostappenvakantieparken.nl/marina-beach**

€5 (htd)

Sp fr N61. V lge, mkd, pt shd, serviced pitches; EHU (4A) inc; gas; TV (pitch); 50% statics; phone; Eng spkn; adv bkg acc; ccard acc; squash; sailing; tennis. *"Excel for families; lake beach; extensive recreation facs; conv Bruges/Antwerp; extra for lake view pitches."* **€53.00, 1 Apr-31 Oct.** 2022

HOEK VAN HOLLAND *B3* (1.5km N Urban) *51.98953, 4.12767* **Camping Hoek van Holland,** Wierstraat 100, 3151 VP Hoek van Holland **(0174) 382550; info@campinghoekvanholland.nl; www.campinghoekvanholland.nl**

(htd) sand nrby

Fr ferry foll N211/220 Rotterdam. After 2.4km turn L, 50m bef petrol stn on R, sp 'Camping Strand', site 400m on R. 3*, Lge, hdstg, mkd, pt shd, EHU (6A) inc; gas; TV; 60% statics; phone; bus; Eng spkn; sep car park; bike hire; tennis; CKE. *"Open 0800-2300; modern san facs but poss inadequate when site full & long walk fr m'van area; conv ferry; mind speed bumps."* **€37.50, 1 Mar-31 Oct.** 2024

HOEK VAN HOLLAND *B3* (3km N Coastal) *51.99685, 4.13347* **Camping Jagtveld,** Nieuwlandsedijk 41, KV 2691 'S-Gravenzande **(0174) 413479; info@jagtveld.nl; www.jagtveld.nl**

sand 400m

Fr ferry foll N211/220 sp Rotterdam. After 3.2km, turn L at junc with traff lts gantry into cul-de-sac. Site 200m on L. 2*, Med, unshd, EHU (16A) poss rev pol €2; gas; 80% statics; phone; Eng spkn; sep car park. *"Ideal for ferry port; conv Den Haag & Delft; gd, clean, level, family-run site; diff when wet; helpful owners; excel 8km long beach."* **€33.30, 1 Apr-1 Oct.** 2024

HOEK VAN HOLLAND *B3* (3.4km N Rural/Coastal) *52.002950, 4.138390* **Strandpark Vlugtenburg,** 't Louwtje 10, 2691 KR/'s-Gravenzande **(017) 4412420; info@vlugtenburg.nl; vlugtenburg.nl/en/**

12 €3.50 sand; adj

Fr ferry take N211. After passing N220 junc. After tight R-hand bend immed take L between petrol stn & bus shelter. Lge, mkd, unshd, EHU (16A) inc; bbq; 70% statics (sep area); bus adj; Eng spkn; adv bkg acc; ccard acc. *"Vg site; excel for kite & wind surfing; restrictions on dog breeds - check bef travel; conv fr ferry; easy for Delft, The Hague."* **€36.20** 2023

HOORN *B2* (5km SW Rural) *52.63085, 5.00920* **Camping 't Venhop,** De Hulk 6a, 1622GJ, Berkhout **(0229) 551371; info@venhop.nl; www.venhop.nl**

12 €1.50 (htd) nr nr

Fr A7, exit junc 7 dir Avenhorn. Turn L under A7, site sp on R. Med, hdg, mkd, pt shd, serviced pitches; EHU (10A) inc; 60% statics; Eng spkn; ccard acc; sep car park; boat, electric bike & scooter hire; CKE. *"Friendly owner; pleasant, well-run site nr canal; full facs LS; vg, delightful waterside camp; fishing in canal fr some pitches."* **€27.00** 2024

KATWIJK AAN ZEE *B3* (6km E Rural) *52.19990, 4.45625* **Camping Koningshof,** Elsgeesterweg 8, 2331 NW Rijnsburg **(071) 4026051; info@koningshofholland.nl; www.koningshofholland.nl**

€3.25 (htd) (covrd, htd, indoor) sand 5km

Fr A44 (Den Haag/Wassenaar-Amsterdam) exit junc 7 (Rijnsburg-Oegstgeest). In Rijnsburg cont twd Noordwijk. Foll blue & white sps thro Rijnsburg, across a bdge & then R twd Voorhout. Site in 2km. 4*, Lge, hdstg, mkd, hdg, pt shd, EHU (16A) inc; gas; bbq; red long stay; TV (pitch); 35% statics; phone; Eng spkn; adv bkg acc; games rm; bike hire; fishing; tennis; CKE. *"Vg, well-run, busy, friendly site; o'fits over 8m by request; gd for families; excel rest; Holland Tulip Parcs site; excel facs & pool; recep 0900-1230 & 1330-2000 high ssn; sep car park for some pitches; useful tour base for bulb fields; mkt Tues; well maintained; close to beaches and town; rec cash as few cards acc."* **€45.00, 17 Apr-3 Nov, H03.** 2022

KOUDUM *C2* (2km S Rural) *52.90290, 5.46625* **Kawan Village De Kuilart,** De Kuilart 1, 8723 CG Koudum **(0514) 522221; info@kuilart.nl; www.kuilart.nl**

12 €3.35 (htd) (covrd, htd)

Fr A50 exit sp Lemmer/Balk. Foll N359 over Galamadammen bdge, site sp. 5*, Lge, mkd, pt shd, serviced pitches; EHU (6-16A) €1.50-3.60; gas; TV; 50% statics; phone; Eng spkn; adv bkg acc; sailing; watersports; sauna; games area; sep car park; waterslide; CKE. *"Holland Tulip Parcs site; dogs by prior agreement only; private bthrms some pitches; marina."* **€26.00** 2022

LEEK *D2* (1.6km N Rural) *53.171114, 6.382174* **Landgoedcamping Nienoord,** Midwolderweg 19, 9351 PG Leek **(0159) 4580898; info@camping nienoord; www.campingnienoord.nl**

nr

A7 exit 34 Leek. Foll sp immed; Ent to site along slip rd. Med, mkd, hdstg, pt shd, EHU (10A); Eng spkn; ccard acc. *"Site on edge of Nienoord pk; gd fr cycling or walks; vg."* **€22.00, 30 Mar-31 Oct.** **2024**

LEERDAM *B3* (3.4km WNW Urban) *51.905334, 5.061932* **Camping Ter Leede,** Recht van ter Leede 28a, 4143 LP / Leerdam **(0653) 754944; www.camping terleede.nl**

2 max (htd)

Fr Eindhoven take A2 twrds Enspijk. Exit 15 onto N327 to Leerdam. At rndabt take 3rd exit onto Parallelweg. Then 1st exit onto Recht van Ter Leede. Site 2.3km on the right. Hdstg, pt shd, EHU (10A); bbq (elec, gas); Eng spkn; adv bkg rec. *"Site owners v helpful; lovely; pitches well maintained; wc/ shwr clean; v quiet; lovely views; lots of wild birds."* **€23.50, 1 Apr-1 Oct.** **2023**

LEEUWARDEN *C2* (7km W Rural) *53.19484, 5.73785* **Minicamping Van Harinxma,** Marssummerdyk 7, 9033 WD Deinnum **0031 (0) 58 215 04 98; Info@ minicamping-van-Harinxma.nl; www.minicamping-van-harinxma.nl**

Fr S: take N31/N32 twrds Leeuwarden. Turn L on N31 sp Harlingen, turn R to Masum-Harlingen, and imm R sp Ritsumazijl. Foll rd turn L at T- junc, then fork L into no thro rd. Site on L. Sm, hdg, pt shd, EHU (6A); twin axles; TV; Eng spkn; adv bkg rec; CKE. *"Vg; billiards; fishing fr site."* **€12.00, 15 Mar-15 Oct.** **2020**

LEIDEN *B3* (8km N Rural) *52.20984, 4.51370* **Camping De Wasbeek,** Wasbeeklaan 5b, 2361 HG Warmond **71 301 1380; dewasbeek@hetnet.nl**

nr nr nr

Exit A44 junc 4 dir Warmond; in 200m turn L into Wasbeeklaan, then R in 50m. Site sp. Sm, pt shd, bbq; 40% statics; bus 500m; Eng spkn; adv bkg acc; sep car park. *"Attractive, lawned site close to bulb fields; m'vans by arrangement; friendly, helpful staff; some aircraft noise; gd cycling (track to Leiden); dogs free; fishing; boating; birdwatching; lovely sm tidy site; nice area."* **€26.00, 1 Apr-1 Oct.** **2024**

LELYSTAD *C2* (11km SW Rural) *52.48570, 5.41720* **Camping 't Oppertje,** Uilenweg 11, 8245 AB Lelystad **0031 (0)3 20 25 36 93; info@oppertje.nl; www.oppertje.nl**

€2.5 (htd) nr nr nr sandy

Exit A6 junc 10 & take Larserdreef dir Lelystad. In 3km turn L into Buizerdweg & foll sp to site. Med, hdstg, mkd, pt shd, EHU (10A) €3.5; bbq; sw nr; red long stay; twin axles; 20% statics; Eng spkn; sep car park; fishing; CKE. *"Pleasant site in nature reserve; friendly, helpful staff; modern san facs; cycle track adj; excel."* **€23.00, 1 Apr-1 Oct.** **2022**

LISSE *B3* (6km S Rural) *52.22175, 4.55418* **Camping De Hof van Eeden,** Hellegatspolder 2, 2160 AZ Lisse **(0252) 212573; info@dehofvaneeden.nl; www.dehofvaneeden.nl**

Exit A44 junc 3 & turn N onto N208 dir Lisse. Turn R at rest on R bef 1st set traff lts into narr rd, foll rd to end (under A44) to site. 3*, Sm, unshd, EHU (16A) inc; 90% statics; Eng spkn. *"Gd CL-type site, space for 10 tourers (sep area) - rec phone or email bef arr; interesting location by waterway & lifting rlwy bdge; conv Keukenhof; helpful owners; cycling ctr among bulb fields & around lake; excel site; lots of room for MH."* **€45.00, 15 Apr-15 Oct.** **2023**

MAASTRICHT *C4* (11.6km ENE Rural) *50.87276, 5.77056* **Camping 't Geuldal,** Gemeentebroek 13, 6231 RV Meerssen Zuid-Limburg **(043) 6040437; info@camping-geuldal.nl; www.camping-geuldal.com**

Fr Maastrich take A79 exit 2 Meerssen twrds Houthem. Head SW on Eigenweg, turn R onto Geulweg. Cont onto Gemeentebroek. Site on L. Lge, hdg, hdstg, mkd, unshd, EHU (6A); bbq (gas); bus; Eng spkn; adv bkg rec; ccard acc. *"Quiet gd rest; taxi for wheelchair user to city; vg."* **NP 28, 1 Apr-23 Dec.** **2022**

MAASTRICHT *C4* (10km E Rural) *50.84468, 5.77994* **Boerderijcamping Gasthoes,** Gasthuis 1, 6268 NN Bemelen **(043) 4071346 or (06) 54717951; info@ boerderijcamping-gasthoes.nl; www.boerderij camping-gasthoes.nl**

Head for Bemelen, site is sp. Sm, pt shd, EHU (10A); bbq; twin axles; bus; Eng spkn; adv bkg acc; CKE. *"Excel."* **€25.00** **2023**

NETHERLANDS

MAURIK *C3* (2km NE Rural) *51.97605, 5.43020* **Recreatiepark Eiland van Maurik,** Rijnbandijk 20, 4021 GH Maurik **(0344) 691502; receptie@eilandvanmaurik.nl; www.eilandvanmaurik.nl**
€4 (htd)

Exit A15 junc 33 at Tiel onto B835 N & foll sp to Maurik & site on rvside. Or exit A2 junc 13 at Culembourg onto N320 to Maurik. 4*, Lge, pt shd, EHU (10A) inc; gas; TV; 50% statics; Eng spkn; adv bkg acc; tennis; fishing; horseriding; games area; watersports. *"Covrd play area; Holland Tulip Parcs site."* **€42.00, 29 Mar-1 Nov. 2024**

> **"I need an on-site restaurant"**
>
> We do our best to make sure site information is correct, but it is always best to check any must-have facilities are still available or will be open during your visit.

MEERSSEN *C4* (1.6km ESE Rural) *50.87851, 5.77112* **Mooidal Boutique Park (Formerly Camping Meerssen),** Houthemerweg 95, 6231 KT Meerssen **46 202 14 22; info@mooidal.nl; www.mooidal.nl**
nr nr nr

Fr Eindhoven A2, take exit 51, foll Valkenburg sp. Take A79 to Hellen exit 2 Meerssen. L at junc after 400m, site on R. Sm, mkd, pt shd, EHU (6A); gas; bbq; twin axles; 2% statics; Eng spkn. *"Nice, peaceful & relaxing site; v popular with Dutch people; cent for touring the area; excel site."*
€35.00, 1 Apr-30 Sep. 2024

MEPPEL *C2* (15km W Rural) *52.72164, 6.07484* **Passantenhaven Zuiderkluft,** Jonenweg, 8355 LG Giethoorn **(0521) 362312; havensweerribbenwieden.nl/giethoorn**

Turn off N334 sp Dwarsgracht, over lifting bdge, 1st L over bdge, 1st L again, site on R. Sm, unshd, EHU (10A) metered; Eng spkn. *"M'vans only; site run by VVV (tourist board) for m'vans only; ltd EHU; walking dist fr delightful vill on water; all svrs accessed by smartcard purchased from machine on site; CC only."*
€12.00, 1 Apr-1 Nov. 2023

MIDDELBURG *A4* (8km N Rural) *51.55005, 3.64022* **Mini Camping Hoekvliet,** Meiwerfweg 3, 4352 SC Gapinge **(0118) 501615 or (0621) 957185; copgapinge@zeelandnet.nl; www.hoekvliet.nl**
€3 nr nr sand 5km

Fr Middleburg turn R off N57 at traff lts sp Veere & Gapinge, site sp after Gapinge vill. Sm, hdstg, mkd, pt shd, EHU (10A) inc; bbq; TV (pitch); 20% statics; Eng spkn; bike hire; CKE. *"Superb little (25 o'fits) farm site; excel, modern san facs; sep car park; helpful owner; immac san facs; fully serviced pitches; great value."* **€29.00, 1 Apr-31 Oct. 2023**

MIDDELBURG *A4* (7km NE Rural) *51.53863, 3.65394* **Minicamping Trouw Vóór Goud,** Veerseweg 66, 4351 SJ Veere **(0118) 501373; info@trouwvoorgoud.nl; www.trouwvoorgoud.nl**
€1.5

Take Veere rd N out of Middleburg. Site on L in 4km, bef lge g'ge, sp 'Minicamping'. 1.5km SW of Veere. Sm, pt shd, EHU (6A) €2.5; 10% statics; Eng spkn. *"Excel facs; friendly, tidy, spacious, CL-type site; walking dist Veere; no wifi."*
€22.00, 15 Mar-31 Oct. 2023

MIERLO *C4* (1.5km S Rural) *51.43250, 5.61694* **Camping De Sprink,** Kasteelweg 21, 5731 PK Mierlo **(0492) 661503; info@campingdesprink.nl; www.campingdesprink.nl**
€1 nr

Take A67 and exit at Geldrop/Mierlo. Foll sp for Mierlo. Turn R at rndabt onto Santheuvel West fr Geldropseweg. R onto Heer de Heuschweg, R onto Kasteelweg. Site on the L. Med, mkd, hdstg, unshd, EHU (6A) inc; bbq; Eng spkn; adv bkg acc. *"Friendly, helpful staff; all facs immac; excel."*
€26.00, 31 Mar-30 Oct. 2023

NOORDWIJK AAN ZEE *B3* (5km N Rural/Coastal) *52.26817, 4.46981* **Camping De Duinpan,** Duindamseweg 6, 2204 AS Noordwijk aan Zee **(0252) 371726; contact@campingdeduinpan.nl and info@campingdeduinpan.com; www.campingdeduinpan.com**
(htd) nr nr

Exit A44 at junc 3 dir Sassenheim then foll sp Noordwijkerhout. At 5th rndabt (Leeuwenhorst Congress building) turn R then L. Site sp. 2*, Med, mkd, unshd, EHU (10A) inc; gas; 60% statics; phone; ccard acc; sep car park; bike hire; CKE. *"Conv for tulip fields in ssn; pool 2.5km."* **€29.50, 15 Mar-31 Oct. 2024**

NOORDWIJK AAN ZEE *B3* (2km NE Rural) *52.24874, 4.46358* **Camping op Hoop van Zegen,** Westeinde 76, 2211 XR Noordwijkerhout **(0252) 375491; info@campingophoopvanzegen.nl; www.campingophoopvanzegen.nl**
12 €3 (htd) nr sand 2.5km

Exit A44 junc 6 dir Noordwijk aan Zee. Cross N206 & turn R in 1km into Gooweg dir Leeuwenhorst. In 1km turn L into Hoogweg & foll sp to site. Med, hdg, mkd, unshd, EHU (6A) €2.25; phone; Eng spkn; adv bkg rec; ccard acc; games area; bike hire; CKE. *"Gd site; modern san facs; conv bulb fields, beaches."*
€18.00 2024

NOORDWIJK AAN ZEE *B3* (5km NE Urban) *52.26580, 4.47376* **De Wijde Blick,** Schulpweg 60, 2211 XM Noordwijkerhout **(0252) 372246; info@bungalowparkdewijdeblick.nl; www.bungalowparkdewijdeblick.nl**

12 WD MSP 2km

Fr Hague exit L fr N206 at Noordwijkerhout Zuid. Shortly turn R at rndabt 1.3km, turn L at rndabt. Site on Rin 1km (1st bldg after felds). Med, mkd, unshd, EHU (4A) inc; 90% statics; train 10km; Eng spkn; CKE. *"Site with bungalows + statics; very clean facs; friendly, helpful staff; excel wifi; conv for Keukenhof; Flora Holland at Aalsmeer nrby; train to Amsterdam; excel."* **€25.00** **2023**

OIRSCHOT *C3* (1km N Rural) *51.51684, 5.30854* **Camping De Bocht,** Oude Grintweg 69, 5688 MB Oirschot **(0499) 550855; info@campingdebocht.nl; www.campingdebocht.nl**

12 €2.50 (htd) WD

Fr A58/E312 take exit 8 to Oirschot. Site in 4km on Boxtel rd. Site sp. 3*, Med, hdg, shd, EHU (10A) €3; gas; TV; 60% statics; phone; Eng spkn; adv bkg acc; bike hire. *"Gd touring base; gd for families; pleasant town; helpful family run site."* **€30.50** **2024**

OMMEN *D2* (6km W Rural) *52.51911, 6.36461* **Resort de Arendshorst,** Arendshorsterweg 3A, 7731 RC Ommen **(0529) 453248; info@resort-de-arendshorst.nl; www.resort-de-arendshorst.nl**

12 €4 (htd) WD

W fr Ommen on N34/N340 turn L at site sp, then 500m along lane past farm, site on rvside. 5*, Lge, mkd, pt shd, serviced pitches; EHU (10A) inc; gas; sw; red long stay; TV; 50% statics; phone; Eng spkn; adv bkg req; bike hire; games area; CKE. *"Beautiful area; bkg fee; many cycle rtes; pool 3km; gd children's facs."* **€30.00, H02.** **2022**

OMMEN *D2* (4km WNW Rural) *52.532519, 6.385082* **Boerderijcamping Het Varsenerveld,** Emslandweg 14, 7731 RP Ommen **(0529) 453300; boerderijcamping@varsenerveld.nl; www.varsenerveld.nl**

12 (htd) WD MSP

W fr Ommen on N340 turn R after 2km at 1st minor x-rds. Take 2nd L and site on L at flagpole. Sm, pt shd, EHU (10A); bbq (charcoal, gas); twin axles; bus 2km; Eng spkn; adv bkg acc; ccard acc. *"Wkg fm; goats and chickens contained within child petting area; excel."* **€21.00** **2024**

OOSTERHOUT *B3* (6km W Rural) *51.64658, 4.80818* **Koeckers Camping 't Kopske,** Ruiterspoor 75, 4911 BA Den Hout **(0613) 142151; info@campingtkopske.nl; www.campingtkopske.nl**

WD

Leave A59 at junc 32 to Oosterhout W. At rndabt take R for Den Hout. In Den Hout R opp Church. 1st site on L after 1km. Sm, mkd, unshd, Eng spkn. *"Gd cycling area; activity ctr; rest nr; gd."* **€19.00, 1 Apr-2 Oct.** **2022**

OOTMARSUM *D2* (2.5km S Rural) *52.38959, 6.90016* **Camping De Haer,** Rossummerstraat 22, 7636 PL Agelo **0541 291847; info@dehaer.nl; www.dehaer.nl**

€1.50 WD

Site sp 3km S of Ootmarsum. Lge, hdg, mkd, pt shd, EHU (6-10A); bbq; twin axles; TV; 30% statics; bus adj; Eng spkn; adv bkg acc; games rm; bike hire; games area; CKE. *"Many cycle paths fr site; vg."* **€23.20, 1 Apr-1 Nov.** **2022**

OPENDE *D2* (3km SE Rural) *53.16465, 6.22275* **NCC Camping de Watermolen,** Openderweg 26, 9865 XE Opende **(0594) 659144; info@campingdewatermolen.nl; www.campingdewatermolen.nl**

€3 (htd) WD MSP nr

Exit A7 junc 32 dir Kornhorn. In Noordwijk turn L at church & in 2 km turn R into Openderweg. Site in 700m on L. Med, hdstg, mkd, pt shd, EHU (10-16A) inc; bbq; sw; twin axles; TV; 10% statics; phone; Eng spkn; adv bkg acc; ccard acc; CKE. *"Friendly owners; pt of site for NCC members - CMC members welcome but must book ahead; brilliant site with lakes to walk around & woods; hide for bird watching; dogs not acc high ssn; excel; fishing on site; bike hire; €10 dep for key; car free pitches."* **€32.00, 1 Apr-1 Oct.** **2023**

OTTERLO *C3* (2km S Rural) *52.08657, 5.76934* **Europarcs Resort De Wije Werelt,** Arnhemseweg 100-102, 6731 BV Otterlo **(0880) 708090; kcc@europarcs.nl; www.europarcs.nl/vakantiepark/resort-de-wije-werelt**

12 €4 (htd) WD MSP

Exit A50 junc 22 dir Hoenderlo & N304 to Otterlo. Site on R after Camping de Zanding. 4*, Lge, mkd, unshd, EHU (6-10A) inc; 40% statics; phone; Eng spkn; adv bkg acc; ccard acc; games area. *"Excel, well-run site; immac, gd san facs; vg for families; conv Arnhem; gd access to Kroller-Muller Museum; helpful staff."* **€35.00** **2024**

OTTERLO *C3* (2km NW Rural) *52.10878, 5.76040* **Camping 't Kikkergat,** Lange Heideweg 7, 6731 EG Otterlo **(0318) 591794; contact@kikkergat.nl; www.kikkergat.nl**

12 €1 WD MSP

Exit A1/E30 at J17 dir Harskamp. Site on R in 12km, unmade rd. Sm, pt shd, EHU (10A) inc; twin axles; Eng spkn; adv bkg acc; CKE. *"Excel site."* **€22.50** **2023**

PANNINGEN *C4* (4km NW Rural) *51.34894, 5.96111* **Beringerzand Camping,** Heide 5, 5981 NX Panningen **07 73 07 20 95; info@beringerzand.nl; www.beringerzand.nl**

12 €4.85 WD MSP (covrd, htd)

Fr A67 exit at junc 38 twd S, dir Koningslust/Panningen. Site is 3km NW Panningen, down narr lane thro asparagus fields. Med, mkd, pt shd, EHU (10A); bbq; twin axles; Eng spkn; adv bkg rec; games rm; games area; bike hire; waterslide. *"Max 2 dogs per pitch."* **€36.80** **2024**

RENSWOUDE *C3* (2km NE Rural) *52.08435, 5.55069* **Camping de Grebbelinie,** Ubbeschoterweg 12, 3927 CJ Renswoude **(0318) 591073; info@campingdegrebbelinie.nl; www.campingdegrebbelinie.nl**

€1.75 (htd) nr nr nr

Head NW on Dorpsstraat/N224, at rndabt take 1st exit onto Barneveldsestraat, turn R onto Bekerweg, R onto Ubbeschoterweg then turn L. Site on the R. Med, unshd, EHU; Eng spkn; adv bkg acc; games area; CKE. *"Friendly owners; excel cycling with cycle rte adj; conv for Arnhem & Utrecht; peaceful site on former farm; in open countryside; excel value for money."* **€28.30, 1 Apr-8 Oct.** **2022**

RIJSSEN *D3* (7km S Rural) *52.265473, 6.520075* **Camping De Bovenberg,** Bovenbergweg 14, 7475 ST/Markelo **(0547) 361781; info@debovenberg.nl; www.debovenberg.nl**

(htd) sand; adj

Fr A1 J26, foll sp for Markelo. Site name on brown sp. Med, mkd, hdstg, hdg, pt shd, EHU (10A) inc; 5% statics; Eng spkn; CKE. *"Vg; ideal for restful stay; gd NH; away fr rd noise; ideal cycling area; Markelo nrby."* **NP 27, 30 Mar-16 Oct.** **2023**

ROCKANJE *A3* (2km NW Coastal) *51.88000, 4.05422* **Molecaten Park Waterbos,** Duinrand 11, 3235 CC Rockanje **(0181) 401900; info@waterboscamping.nl; www.molecaten.nl/waterbos**

(htd) sand 1km

Site clearly sp fr Rockanje vill. 4*, Lge, hdg, pt shd, EHU (6A) inc; TV (pitch); 80% statics; phone; adv bkg acc; CKE. *"Lovely base for Voorne area; private san facs avail."* **€44.50, 23 Mar-1 Nov.** **2022**

ROERMOND *C4* (15km W Rural) *51.20947, 5.83008* **Camping Geelenhoof,** Grathemerweg 16, 6037 NR Kelpen-Oler (Limburg) **(0495) 651858; info@geelenhoof.nl; www.geelenhoof.nl**

€2.50 (htd)

1km S of Kelpen-Oler; bet Roermond & Weert; exit N280 foll sp; well mkd. Med, hdg, mkd, pt shd, EHU (6A) inc; Eng spkn; adv bkg acc; games area; games rm; CKE. *"Cars not to be parked with c'van; dogs on req; vg site; semi serviced pitches; sep NH; keycard barrier; no twin axles; lake fishing; warm welcome; excel site."* **€29.60, 1 Mar-31 Oct.** **2023**

ROOSENDAAL *B3* (7km S Rural) *51.49430, 4.48536* **Camping Zonneland,** Turfvaartsestraat 6, 4709 PB Nispen **(0165) 365429; info@zonneland.nl; www.zonneland.nl**

(htd)

Take A58 exit 24 onto N262 dir Nispen. Foll site sps. 3*, Lge, hdstg, shd, EHU (4-10A) €2; 80% statics; phone; Eng spkn; adv bkg acc; ccard acc. **€19.00, 16 Mar-28 Oct.** **2020**

ROTTERDAM *B3* (17km SE Rural) *51.83454, 4.54673* **Camping De Oude Maas,** Achterzeedijk 1A, 2991 SB Barendrecht **(078) 6772445; info@recreatieparkdeoudemaas.nl; www.recreatieparkdeoudemaas.nl**

12 (htd)

Leave A29 (Rotterdam-Bergen op Zoom) junc 20 Barendrecht, foll sp for Heerjansdam, site sp. Fr A16 (Breda-Dordrecht) foll Europort sp, then Zierikzee, Barendrecht, site sp. 3*, Lge, pt shd, EHU (10A) inc; TV; 80% statics; phone; ccard acc. *"Excel site on Rv Maas inc sm marina & joins rec park; excel facs; some pitches rough & long way fr facs; ferry fr site in ssn; check recep opening time if planning dep bef midday (espec Sun) for return of deposit & barrier key (€35); entry via new ent past old."* **€25.00** **2022**

ROTTERDAM *B3* (3km W Urban) *51.93100, 4.44200* **Stadscamping Rotterdam,** Kanaalweg 84, 3041 JE Rotterdam **(010) 4153440; info@stadscamping-rotterdam.nl; www.stadscamping-rotterdam.nl**

12 €2

Adj to junc of A13 & A20, take slip rd sp Rotterdam Centrum & Camping Kanaalweg sp to site. Dist fr m'way 2.5km with 3 L turns. 2*, Lge, pt shd, EHU (6A) €3.75; gas; bus; adv bkg acc; ccard acc. *"Gd bus service to city cent; few water taps; pool 500m; friendly staff."* **€25.00** **2022**

SCHIMMERT *C4* (0.6km E Rural) *50.90746, 5.83122* **Camping Mareveld,** Mareweg 23, 6333 BR Schimmert South Limburg **(045) 4041269; info@mareveld.nl; www.campingmareveld.nl**

12 €1.75 (htd)

A76 exit Spaubeek, turn R twd Schimmert. 2nd on the L in Schimmert. Campsite sp. Sm, pt shd, EHU (6A) €2.10; TV; 80% statics; Eng spkn; adv bkg acc; games area. *"Gd cycling/walking fr site; gd site; popular with families; open plan, grassy site."* **€24.00** **2024**

SEVENUM *C4* (5km SW Rural) *51.38310, 5.97590* **Camping De Schatberg,** Midden Peelweg 1, 5975 MZ Sevenum **(077) 4677777; receptie@schatberg.nl and info@schatberg.nl; www.schatberg.nl**

12 (htd) (covrd, htd)

Fr A2/A67 exit junc 38 for Helden; foll sp Sevenum & site by sm lake. 5*, V lge, shd, EHU (6-10A) inc; gas; sw; TV; 60% statics; phone; Eng spkn; adv bkg acc; fishing; bike hire; waterslide; games area; tennis; jacuzzi; sauna; watersports; CKE. *"Excel leisure facs, espec for children; sep pitches for dogs; private san facs some pitches; vg site but impersonal; Holland Tulip Parcs site; tourers pitched amongst statics; Venlo Sat mkt worth visit."* **€41.00** **2024**

'S-HEERENBERG D3 (3km W Rural) 51.87795, 6.21125 **Camping Brockhausen,** Eltenseweg 20, 7039 CV Stokkum **(0314) 661212; campingbrockhausen@gmail.com; www.brockhausen.nl**

€3.45 (htd) nr

Fr A12 exit junc sp 's-Heerenberg, cont past 's-Heerenberg sp & pick up sp to Stokkum & site on L. 2*, Med, mkd, pt shd, EHU (4-6A) inc; TV (pitch); 40% statics; Eng spkn; adv bkg acc. *"V clean, eco-friendly site; facs charged on electronic key; friendly, helpful staff; lovely area walking, cycling; excel."* **€24.00, 1 Apr-31 Oct. 2020**

'S-HERTOGENBOSCH C3 (10km E Rural) 51.6938, 5.4148 **Camping de Hooghe Heide,** Werstkant 17, 5258 TC Berlicum **(073) 5031522; info@hoogheheide.nl; www.hoogheheide.nl**

€4.25

Fr A59/A2 circular rd around 's-Hertogenbosch exit junc 21 dir Berlicum. Foll sp Berlicum & site. Site is NE of Berlicum. 4*, Med, mkd, pt shd, EHU (10A) €3; TV; 70% statics; phone; Eng spkn; adv bkg req; games area; CKE. *"Nice, peaceful wooded site; narr site rds for lge o'fits; tourers on open field; excel."* **€37.80, 27 Mar-4 Oct. 2022**

'S-HERTOGENBOSCH C3 (10km SW Rural) 51.65507, 5.23520 **Topparken Résidence de Leuvert,** Loverensestraat 11, 5266 Cromvoirt **088 5002473; info@deleuvert.nl; www.topparken.nl/residence-de-leuvert**

(htd)

Exit for Cromvoirt fr A59 or A65. Med, mkd, pt shd, EHU (10A) inc; bbq; twin axles; TV; 75% statics; bus 0.5km; Eng spkn; adv bkg acc; games area; games rm; CKE. *"Gd bus access to 's-Hertogenbosch; vg site."* **€28.40, 1 Jan-31 Oct. 2022**

SINT OEDENRODE C3 (3.7km SE Urban) 51.54780, 5.48703 **Landschapsamping De Graspol (Formerly Camping De Graspol),** Bakkerpad 17, 5492 TL Sint Oedenrode **499-338.229; info@degraspol.ni; www.landschapscamping.com**

(htd)

Fr A50 take exit St Oedenrode, dir Nijnsel. Foll sp to site. Med, mkd, pt shd, EHU (16A); gas; bbq; red long stay; TV; Eng spkn; adv bkg rec; bike hire; fishing; games rm. *"Well kept; gd for NH or longer; ACSI; warm welcome; wild flower nature walk."* **€35.50, 1 Mar-1 Oct. 2024**

SLUIS A4 (0.8km N Rural) 51.31395, 3.38863 **Camping De Meidoorn,** Hoogstraat 68, 4524 LA Sluis **(0117) 461662; info@campingdemeidoorn.eu; www.campingdemeidoorn.eu**

€1.75 (htd)

Fr Zeebrugge, ignore 1st turn L to Sluis, cont to rndabt sp Sluis 1km. At windmill keep R (do not go to town cent). After LH bend turn R, foll sps. 3*, Lge, pt shd, EHU (6A) €3; gas; TV; 80% statics; phone; Eng spkn; tennis; CKE. *"Bus to Bruges and Breskens fr rear site ent."* **€33.40, 1 Apr-1 Nov. 2024**

SNEEK C2 (2km E Urban) 53.03557, 5.67630 **Jachthaven Camping De Domp,** De Domp 4, 8605 CP Sneek **(0515) 412559; www.dedomp.nl**

€2 (htd) nr

Fr cent of Sneek on Leeuwarden rd, turn R sp De Domp. 3*, Med, pt shd, serviced pitches; EHU (16A) €4; gas; Eng spkn; adv bkg acc; boating; sep car park. *"Many canals in Sneek; marina on site; easy walk to pleasant town; gd cycling cent; v helpful staff."* **€27.00, 25 Mar-1 Nov. 2023**

STEENBERGEN B3 (5km NW Rural) 51.60887, 4.27303 **Camping De Uitwijk,** Dorpsweg 136, 4655 AH De Heen **(0167) 560000; info@de-uitwijk.nl; www.campingdeuitwijk.nl**

€3.20 (htd) nr

Fr N259 at Steenbergen turn W onto N257 dir Zierikzee. In 2km turn N thro De Heen & turn R at T-junc. Site recep on R, site on L. Do not take c'van to recep, but ent site, park on R & walk back. Med, mkd, pt shd, EHU (4-10A) inc; TV (pitch); 60% statics; bus 750m; Eng spkn; adv bkg acc; games rm; CKE. *"Pleasant, well run, quiet site adj marina; friendly staff; excel; excel cycle rtes; conv for ferry."* **€24.00, 23 Mar-29 Sep. 2024**

TUITJENHORN B2 (4km SE Rural) 52.73495, 4.77612 **Campingpark de Bongerd,** Bongerdlaan 3, 1747 CA Tuitjenhorn **(0226) 391481; info@bongerd.nl; www.bongerd.nl**

€1.90 (htd) (covrd, htd)

N fr Alkmaar on N245, exit at Dirkshorn & foll sp to site. 5*, V lge, mkd, pt shd, EHU (10A) inc; gas; bbq; 60% statics; Eng spkn; adv bkg acc; ccard acc; games area; lake fishing; bike hire; waterslide; tennis. *"Excel, attractive family site; vg facs."* **€56.50, 5 Apr-1 Oct. 2024**

"Satellite navigation makes touring much easier"

Remember most sat navs don't know if you're towing or in a larger vehicle – always use yours alongside maps and site directions.

UDEN C3 (14km E Rural) 51.66309, 5.77641 **Camping Boszicht,** Tipweg 10, 5455 RC Wilbertoord **(0485) 451565 or (06) 12957217; info@boszichtcamping.nl; www.boszichtcamping.nl**

€2 nr

Fr 's-Hertogenbosch on N279 dir Helmond. At Veghel turn L onto N265. Bef Uden turn R onto N264 to Wilbertoord in 11km. Sm, hdg, mkd, unshd, EHU (6A) metered; Eng spkn; games area. *"Family-run farm site in woodland; conv Arnhem, Nijmegen; delightful site."* **€17.00, 30 Mar-1 Oct. 2022**

NETHERLANDS

UTRECHT *B3* (10km NE Rural) *52.13123, 5.22024* **Camping Bospark Bilthoven,** Burg van der Borchlaan 7, 3722 GZ Bilthoven **(030) 2286777; info@bosparkbilthoven.nl; www.bosparkbilthoven.nl**

€3.50 (htd) WD MSP nr (htd)

Exit A28/E30 Utrecht-Amersfoort at exit sp De Bilt & strt to Bilthoven. Approx 3km after leaving m'way (400m S of level x-ing) turn R sp De Bospark Bilthoven. At edge of town foll sps twd lge brown tower & golf course. Site on L. 2*, V lge, pt shd, serviced pitches; EHU (4-6A) inc (poss rev pol); gas; TV; 60% statics; phone; Eng spkn; adv bkg acc. *"Helpful management; quiet but some noise fr air base; 20 mins walk to stn for trains to Utrecht cent; few facs for size of site."* **€35.00, 29 Mar-20 Oct.** **2023**

UTRECHT *B3* (14km E Rural) *52.09272, 5.28287* **Camping de Krakeling,** Woudensbergseweg 17, 3707 HW Zeist **(030) 6915374; allurepark@dekrakeling.nl; www.dekrakeling.nl**

(htd) WD MSP

Fr A12 exit junc 20 Driebergen/Zeist. In Zeist foll dir Woudenberg, site sp. 4*, V lge, mkd, hdg, pt shd, EHU (6-10A) €2.50; sw nr; TV (pitch); 90% statics; phone; bus; adv bkg rec; tennis. *"Gd touring base Amsterdam/Utrecht; pool 3km; friendly; excel, clean facs; adj nature reserve; recep open 0900-1700, clsd for lunch."* **€28.40, 28 Mar-29 Sep.** **2024**

VAALS *C4* (1.5km N Rural) *50.78159, 6.00694* **Camping Hoeve de Gastmolen,** Lemierserberg 23, 6291 NM Vaals **(043) 3065755; info@gastmolen.nl; www.gastmolen.nl**

€2.70 WD nr nr

Fr A76 exit at Knooppunt Bocholtz onto N281 SW to join N278, turn L twd Aachen. Site on L just bef 1st rndabt as ent Vaals. 2*, Med, hdg, mkd, pt shd, pt sl, EHU (6A) €2.70; 10% statics; bus 500m; Eng spkn; adv bkg rec; sep car park; CKE. *"Sm rural site; conv Aachen; vg san facs; diff in wet - tractor avail; mosquitoes; Drielandenpunt 4km, in walking dist (where Netherlands, Germany & Belgium meet); excel."* **€33.00, 15 Mar-31 Oct.** **2022**

VALKENBURG AAN DE GEUL *C4* (13km N Rural) *50.94973, 5.87883* **De Botkoel,** Kerkpad 2, 6155 KJ Puth **(0464) 432374; camping@botkoel.nl; www.botkoel.nl**

€1.50 (htd) WD MSP nr nr nr

Fr W on A2 exit at J4 sp Schinnen. At end of rd turn L, cross x-rds and turn R again on the R until you cross rlwy x-ing, then R on the R. Cont on Stn Street until T-junc, turn L twrds Puth. Uphill to Puth then turn R. At S-turn, turn R into narr rd. Site 200m on L. Sm, unshd, pt sl, terr, EHU; bbq; twin axles; train 1km; Eng spkn; adv bkg acc; games area; CKE. *"Site on fruit fm; views; bike hire; clean facs, rebuilt 2017; excel; conv for Sittard, Maastricht & Aachen; vg; Zoover award site."* **€30.50, 15 Mar-31 Oct.** **2023**

VALKENBURG AAN DE GEUL *C4* (2km N Rural) *50.88013, 5.83466* **Camping de Valkenburg (formerly De Bron),** Stoepertweg 5, 6301 WP Valkenburg **(045) 4059292; info@camping-debron.nl; www.camping-debron.nl**

€5.30 (htd) WD MSP

Fr A79 exit junc 4 dir Hulsberg. Take 3rd exit fr rndabt onto N298, across next rndabt, then L onto N584, site sp. Fr A76 exit junc 3 dir Schimmert, foll sp Valkenburg & site. 4*, Lge, mkd, hdstg, hdg, pt shd, EHU (4-6A) €3-4.50; TV; 30% statics; phone; adv bkg acc; bike hire; games area; CKE. *"Vg, well laid-out site; gd facs; muddy in wet weather; 2 pools with lots of equipment for kids; statics hidden away in the greenery; helpful staff; modern facs; gd for walks; hdstg narr; for privacy book lge grass pitch; little rm for awning plus car."* **€32.00, 1 Apr-20 Dec.** **2024**

> **"There aren't many sites open at this time of year"**
>
> If you're travelling outside peak season remember to call ahead to check site opening dates – even if the entry says 'open all year'.

VALKENBURG AAN DE GEUL *C4* (3km S Urban) *50.85972, 5.83138* **Stadscamping Den Driesch,** Heunsbergerweg 1, 6301 BN Valkenburg **(043) 6012025; info@campingdendriesch.nl; www.campingdendriesch.nl**

€3 (htd) WD MSP nr

Fr A2 dir Maastricht exit sp Valkenburg-Cauberg. Foll sp Valkenburg N590 & take turning sp Sibbe-Margraten. At rndabt foll sp Valkenburg, pass coal mine & turn R in 250m into sm, sl, unmkd ent. Steep turn off main rd into ent. NB L turn into site diff - proceed to rndabt at top of hill & return downhill to site. 2*, Med, mkd, hdstg, pt shd, pt sl, terr, EHU (10A) inc; 10% statics; phone; Eng spkn; adv bkg acc; ccard acc; bike hire; CKE. *"Castle & caves adj; other attractions nr; gd Xmas mkts in caves; easy access Maastricht by bus/train; vg."* **€42.00, 23 Mar-31 Dec, H10.** **2022**

VALKENBURG AAN DE GEUL *C4* (1km SW Rural) *50.85672, 5.81891* **Camping De Cauberg,** Rijksweg 171, 6325 AD Valkenburg **(043) 6012344; info@campingdecauberg.nl; www.campingdecauberg.nl**

€3.10 (htd) WD

Exit A79 sp Valkenburg, foll Sibbe & Margraten sp to town cent. Take R fork in town sp De Cauberg, site on R at top of hill just past end Valkenburg sp. Med, mkd, shd, pt sl, EHU (10A) inc; red long stay; 10% statics; phone; bus; Eng spkn; adv bkg acc; site clsd 1-15 Nov; CKE. *"Excel pool 1km; excel, modern, clean san facs; htd pool 1km; friendly, helpful owner; conv Maastricht; many rests, cafes in Valkenburg."* **€33.00, 22 Mar-27 Oct & 16 Nov-23 Dec.** **2024**

VALKENBURG AAN DE GEUL *C4* (7km W Rural) *50.86057, 5.77237* **Camping Oriëntal,** Rijksweg 6, 6325 PE Berg en Terblijt **(043) 6040075; info@campingoriental.nl; www.campingoriental.nl**

€3.50 (htd) WD MSP nr

(covrd, htd)

Fr A2/E25 exit onto N278 E & in 1km turn L onto N590 sp Berg en Terblijt & Valkenburg. Cont on N590, site on R in 4km at start of vill. 4*, Lge, mkd, pt shd, serviced pitches; EHU (6A) inc (poss rev pol); gas; 10% statics; phone; bus to Maastricht adj; Eng spkn; adv bkg acc; games area; CKE. *"Immac, well-run site; some areas flood in heavy rain; serviced pitch inc TV at extra cost; gd entmnt for young children; conv Maastricht."* **€27.00, Easter-30 Oct.** 2024

VENLO *C4* (22km N Rural) *51.45989, 6.17120* **Camping Landhuis De Maashof,** Veerweg 9, 5973 NS Lottum **07 74 63 19 24; info@demaashof.nl; www.demaashof.nl**

€1.20 WD

Fr A67 Eindhoven - Venlo, take exit 12 onto A73. Then exit 11 twd Horst/Melderslo. Foll sp to Lottum. Foll sp to campsite. Med, pt shd, bbq; twin axles; bus 800m; Eng spkn; adv bkg acc; CCI. *"Cycling, rv bank walks; rose gdn exhibition in vill; lots of rv traff & ferries; working windmill & castle nrby."* **€20.00, 1 Apr-30 Sep.** 2024

WASSENAAR *B3* (1km NW Rural) *52.14638, 4.38750* **Camping Duinrell,** Duinrell 1, 2242 JP Wassenaar **(070) 5155255; touroperator@duinrell.nl; www.duinrell.nl**

12 €6 (htd) WD MSP

(covrd, htd, indoor) sand 3km

Fr Rotterdam in dir Den Haag on A13/E19, then on A4/E19 foll sp for Amsterdam. On A4 keep R onto A12 in dir Voorburg/Den Haag. At end m'way turn R onto N44 sp Wassenaar. In 8km turn L at traff lts immed bef Mercedes g'ge, foll site sp. On arr at site foll sp to campsite not coach park. Not rec to arrive mid-afternoon/early evening due to heavy traff leaving amusement park. 4*, V lge, mkd, hdg, pt shd, serviced pitches; EHU (6A) inc; gas; bbq; TV; 30% statics; phone; Eng spkn; adv bkg acc; ccard acc; waterslide; tennis; sauna; golf 1km; fishing nr; bike hire; games rm; horseriding nr. *"Popular, busy site; no o'fits over 7.75m high ssn; some pitches poss diff access, check bef siting; superb, modern facs; tropical indoor pool; free ent adj amusement park; private san facs avail; sep car park for some pitches; vg security; excel."* **€35.00, H13.** 2022

WEERSELO *D3* (2km N Rural) *52.36530, 6.84285* **Camping De Molenhof,** Kleijsenweg 7, 7667 RS Reutum **(0541) 661165 or 661201; info@demolenhof.nl; www.demolenhof.nl**

€3 (htd) WD MSP

(covrd, htd)

Exit A1 junc 33 dir Oldenzaal then Tubbergen. At Weerselo, foll site sp. 5*, Lge, pt shd, EHU (10A) inc; gas; bbq; TV; TV (pitch); 25% statics; Eng spkn; adv bkg acc; ccard acc; waterslide; golf 10km; bike hire; tennis; fishing. *"Spacious pitches; covrd play area; Holland Tulip Parcs site; spotlessly clean."* **€39.00, 16 Apr-2 Oct.** 2024

WEERT *C4* (9km SE Rural) *51.22480, 5.79916* **Camping Landgoed Lemmenhof,** Kampstraat 10, 6011 RV Ell Limburg **(0495) 551277; info@lemmenhof.nl; www.lemmenhof.nl**

€0.70 (htd) WD nr nr nr

Exit A2 junc 40 dir Kelpen. In 2km at traff lts turn R; in 50m turn R dir Ell. In 2km immed bef vill sp & De Prairie Cafe turn R into Kempstraat, site in 200m. Sm, hdg, mkd, unshd, EHU (10A) inc; Eng spkn; adv bkg acc; CKE. *"Vg; B&B & apartments avail; v friendly helpful owners and friendly local caravaners on site."* **€18.60, 15 Mar-31 Oct.** 2024

WEZUPERBRUG *D2* (0.3km E Rural) *52.84030, 6.72370* **Rekreatiepark 't Kuierpadtien,** Oranjekanaal Noordzijde 10, 7853 TA Wezuperbrug **(0591) 381415; info@kuierpad.nl; www.kuierpad.nl**

12 €5 (htd) WD MSP

(covrd, htd)

Fr A28 m'way exit 31 dir Emmen onto N381. Take exit Zweeloo & turn L immed. Go under viaduct twd Wezuperbrug via Wezup. In Wezuperbrug go over bdge, turn R, site sp. 5*, V lge, pt shd, EHU (6A) inc; gas; sw; TV; 30% statics; phone; boating; games rm; tennis; waterslide; bike hire. *"Excel site; great for kids; vg pool & extensive sports facs; can get busy; sep car park; Holland Tulip Parcs site; some pitches diff to access, narr & steep ent to pitch espec nr the water."* **€53.00** 2024

WEZUPERBRUG *D2* (9km SW Rural) *52.77911, 6.68607* **Camping De Bronzen Emmer,** Mepperstraat 41, 7855 TA Meppen **(0591) 371543; info@de-bronzen-emmer.nl; www.bronzenemmer.nl**

(htd) WD nr

(covrd, htd)

Exit the A37 at Oosterhesselen (N854) twrds Meppen. Foll sp to site. Lge, mkd, pt shd, EHU (10A) €0.40/Kwh; gas; TV; 10% statics; Eng spkn; adv bkg acc; tennis; games area; games rm. *"Cycling off-rd to supmkt; friendly, family site; excel facs; sauna; excel."* **€35.70, 1 Apr-28 Oct.** 2023

NETHERLANDS

WOERDEN *B3* (4km NE Rural) *52.09280, 4.88530* **Camping Batenstein,** Van Helvoortlaan 36, 3443 AP Woerden **(0348) 421320; info@camping-batenstein.nl; www.camping-batenstein.nl**

€1.50 nr (covrd, htd)

Fr A12 exit junc 14 sp Woerden. Twd cent of town, L at rndabt, R at next rndabt, thro rlwy tunnel. L at traff lts, L again at next traff lts, R at camping sp. Ent narr & sm sp. 1*, Med, pt shd, EHU (6-10A) inc; gas; red long stay; 75% statics; phone; bus 750m; Eng spkn; adv bkg acc; ccard acc; sep car park; waterslide; sauna; games area; CKE. *"Gd touring base; el conn by site staff only (locked boxes); san facs cramped but gd quality & clean; conv for ferries."*
€20.80, 29 Mar-27 Oct. **2024**

AMELAND ISLAND

BUREN *C1* (1km N Coastal) *53.45355, 5.80460* **Camping Klein Vaarwater,** Klein Vaarwaterweg 114, 9164 ME Buren **(0519) 542156; info@kleinvaarwater.nl; www.kleinvaarwater.nl**

12 (htd) (covrd, htd) sand 800m

Take ferry fr Holwerd to Nes on Ameland Island. Turn R at rndabt twd Buren & strt on to supmkt. At 3-lane intersection turn L twd beach rd & site. 4*, Med, mkd, pt shd, EHU (16A); gas; bbq; TV; 75% statics; adv bkg acc; tennis; fitness rm; games area; waterslide. *"Nature park adj; site in dunes & forest; ATM; Holland Tulip Parcs site; 10-pin bowling."*
€20.00 **2022**

ZANDVOORT *B3* (5km N Coastal) *52.40415, 4.55180* **Kennemer Duincamping De Lakens,** Zeeweg 60, 2051 EC Bloemendaal aan Zee **(023) 5411570; delakens@kennemerduincampings.nl; www.kennemerduincampings.nl**

(htd) sand 200m

Site sp N of Zaandvoort on coast rd, site in sand dunes. 4*, V lge, unshd, EHU (4-10A) inc; gas; TV; 50% statics; Eng spkn; adv bkg rec; ccard acc; horseriding 300m; games area; windsurfing 2km. *"V busy May/June public holidays; gd facs; excel walking, cycling fr site; welcoming helpful staff; excel spar shop; gd position in National Park; pool 4km; gd for sightseeing in Amsterdam, Haarlem, Aalsmeer flower mkt as well as outdoor pursuits."*
€54.00, 29 Mar-28 Oct. **2024**

ZEVENAAR *C3* (8km S Rural) *51.89666, 6.07041* **Camping De Rijnstrangen,** Beuningsestraat 4, 6913 KH Aerdt **(0316) 371941 or (0612) 559464; info@derijnstrangen.nl; www.derijnstrangen.nl**

12 €2.50 (htd) nr

Exit A12 junc 29 onto N 336 Elten & Lobith. At sp Aerdt turn R onto dyke (narr) & cont approx 1.5km to church. Turn L in 100m, site on R (500m W of Aerdt). Sm, mkd, hdstg, hdg, pt shd, EHU (6A) inc; bbq; cooking facs; twin axles; Eng spkn; adv bkg acc; games rm; bike hire; CKE. *"Friendly, welcoming, helpful owners; gd cycling area with numbered rte; excel htd facs; excel; sep carpark."* **€29.50** **2023**

ZIERIKZEE *A3* (2km N Rural) *51.65683, 3.91242* **Camping 't Uulof,** Zandweg 37, 4301 TA Zierikzee **(0111) 414614; info@tuulof.nl; www.campingtuulof.nl**

€1 nr

SE fr Serooskerke on N59. In 9km just bef traff lts turn L. Site 300m on R; sp fr N59. Sm, pt shd, serviced pitches; EHU (6A) inc; 25% statics; Eng spkn; CKE. *"Lovely site on farm - produce avail; excel san facs, pt unisex; helpful, friendly owner; interesting town, steamer trips; easy cycling to town; peaceful site, friendly & welcoming, lovely home-grown veg."*
€15.50, 1 Apr-1 Oct. **2024**

ZIERIKZEE *A3* (5km N Rural) *51.68048, 3.89847* **Mini-Camping Appelgaerd,** Zandweg 6, 4321 TA Kerkwerve **(0614) 449924; info@appelgaerd.nl; www.appelgaerd.nl**

4km

Fr Zierikzee take N59 dir Serooskerke. Immed turn R onto Zandwek. Cont for 3km, site on L bef vill of Kerkwerve. Sm, hdg, pt shd, EHU (6A) inc; bbq; twin axles; bus 250m; Eng spkn; adv bkg acc. *"Gd cycling, walking & bird watching area; excel site."*
€20.50, 1 Apr-30 Oct. **2024**

ZOETERMEER *B3* (4km W Rural) *52.06716, 4.44862* **Camping De Drie Morgen,** Voorweg 155, 2716 NJ Zoetermeer **(079) 3515107; mail@dedriemorgen.nl; www.dedriemorgen.nl**

Fr Den Haag take A12/E30 sp Zoetermeer. Exit junc 6 sp Zoetermeer cent. In 1.5km turn L onto Amertaweg. In 2km foll sp to Mini-Camping. At rndabt turn R onto Voorweg, site on R. Sm, unshd, EHU (6A) €1.75; Eng spkn; adv bkg acc; sep car park. *"A working farm & farm shop; gd touring base; pleasant staff; peaceful; busy in ssn."*
€14.50, 1 Apr-31 Oct. **2024**

TERSCHELLING ISLAND

OOSTEREND *C1* (0.2km N Rural) *53.40562, 5.37947* **Camping 't Wantij,** Oosterend 41, 8897 HX Oosterend **(0562) 448522 or (06) 20396345 (mob); info@wantij-terschelling.nl; www.wantij-terschelling.nl**
12 €1.75 (htd) nr nr nr sand 2km

Fr Harlingen to Terschelling by ferry. Take rd to Oosterend, site ent on L 250m after vill sp, past bus stop & phone box. Sm, mkd, pt shd, EHU (6A) €3 (poss rev pol); cooking facs; TV; bus adj; Eng spkn; adv bkg acc; CKE. *"Gd area for birdwatching; many cycle/foot paths across dunes; horsedrawn vehicles for conducted tours; Elvis memorabilia 2km at Heartbreak Hotel - rest on stilts; excel site."* **€22.60** **2022**

TEXEL ISLAND

DE KOOG *B2* (0.5km E Rural) *53.09610, 4.76500* **Camping Coogherveld Texel (formerly De Luwe Boshoek),** Kamperfoelieweg 3, 1796 MT De Koog **02 22 31 77 28; www.coogherveld-texel.nl**
(htd) nr sandy 1km

Fr ferry take 501 to De Koog. Sp after ref point 17. R at De Zwaluw Hotel. Site on L after 100m. Med, mkd, unshd, EHU (16A); bbq; 10% statics. *"Excel; gd base to stay; bike hire 0.5 km."* **€32.50, 12 Apr-25 Oct.** **2024**

DEN BURG *B2* (16km N Rural) *53.16987, 4.86072* **Camping de Hoek,** Vuurtorenweg 83, 1795 LK De Cocksdorp **(0222) 316236; saaldehoek@tele2.nl; www.campingdehoek.nl**
€2 (htd) nr nr sandy 1km

Take the main rd fr ferry to top of island, past exit 35, site on L nr end of rd. Sm, pt shd, EHU (16A) inc; bbq; Eng spkn; adv bkg acc. *"Farm site; beatifully kept; lovely fam; by rd but v quiet; cycle path; excel."* **€30.00, 1 Apr-1 Oct.** **2023**

ZUIDWOLDE *D2* (2km S Rural) *52.65822, 6.42726* **NCC Camping De Krententerp,** Ekelenbergweg 2, 7921 RH Zuidwolde DR **(0528) 372847; zuidwolde@ncc.nl; www.ncc.nl**
(htd) nr nr nr

Fr S fr Zwolle exit A28 junc 22 dir Dedemsvaart. Turn L at Balkbrug onto N48, then L at junc Alteveer-Linde to site. Sm, mkd, shd, EHU (4A) €2.75 (long lead poss req); bus 200m; adv bkg acc. *"Peaceful site; friendly, helpful staff; CC members welcome; phone ahead bet 1700 & 1800; htd covrd pool 2km; excel cycling, walking; Zuidwolde beautiful town."* **€12.50, 1 Apr-31 Oct.** **2022**

ZWOLLE *C2* (5km NE Urban) *52.53690, 6.12954* **Camping De Agnietenberg,** Haersterveerweg 27, 8034 PJ Zwolle **(038) 4531530; info@campingagnietenberg.nl; www.campingagnietenberg.nl**
€3.50 (htd)

N fr Zwolle on A28 exit junc 20 Zwolle Oost & turn R at end of slip rd then immed L. In 400m turn L at traff lts into Haersterveerweg & foll site sp. Lge, mkd, pt shd, EHU (10A); bbq; sw nr; TV; 60% statics; Eng spkn; ccard acc; fishing; tennis. *"Excel, family site in pleasant area; gd walking, cycling, water recreation; cars parked in sep areas; single track rd to site."* **€30.00, 29 Mar-31 Oct.** **2024**

ZWOLLE *C2* (6.5km E Urban) *52.524253, 6.167658* **Vecht & Zo,** Hessenweg 14, 8028 PA Zwolle **(06) 24332462; info@vechtenzo.nl; www.vechtenzo.nl**
€2.50 (htd)

Fr J21 on A28 N of Zwolle take N340 in 2km R at sp onto cycleway (row of shops). Sm, mkd, pt shd, EHU (6A) inc (rev pol); bbq; sw; Eng spkn; adv bkg acc; games area; canoes. *"Gd for Gelderland, Kampen, Zwolle; traff noise in day; spotless facs; vg."* **€29.50, 1 Apr-31 Oct.** **2023**

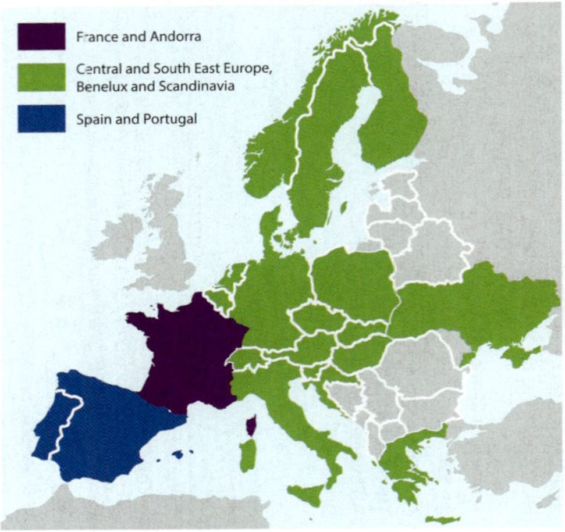

Enschede to Venlo = 200km

	Alkmaar	Amersfoort	Amsterdam	Apeldoorn	Arnhem	Breda	Den Haag (The Hague)	Den Helder	Dordrecht	Eindhoven	Emmen	Enschede	Groningen	Haarlem	Heerlen	Hilversum	Hoek van Holland	Leeuwarden	Leiden	Maastricht	Meppel	Middelburg	Nijmegen	Rotterdam	s-Hertogenbosch	Tilburg	Utrecht	Venlo	Winschoten
Amersfoort	83																												
Amsterdam	40	47																											
Apeldoorn	120	44	87																										
Arnhem	141	51	99	25																									
Breda	145	89	101	141	111																								
Den Haag (The Hague)	85	85	55	133	118	72																							
Den Helder	42	125	82	166	185	189	117																						
Dordrecht	125	76	99	130	102	30	46	168																					
Eindhoven	162	105	120	110	82	57	135	205	92																				
Emmen	179	145	188	120	144	231	227	159	219	225																			
Enschede	194	120	161	76	99	215	224	238	200	180	83																		
Groningen	105	175	203	147	172	263	252	154	248	255	58	147																	
Haarlem	30	67	19	118	114	125	51	72	95	137	211	174	205																
Heerlen	256	195	210	192	158	147	228	301	182	87	310	265	339	229															
Hilversum	69	17	34	72	77	86	82	111	74	101	164	133	193	49	184														
Hoek van Holland	103	105	78	149	137	81	20	138	54	141	250	220	282	63	231	100													
Leeuwarden	111	161	139	130	160	248	189	92	234	242	91	167	66	148	325	147	210												
Leiden	75	75	46	126	110	87	17	116	60	133	219	192	242	42	240	60	37	180											
Maastricht	255	196	214	201	167	148	223	296	181	86	319	264	348	228	24	193	230	335	239										
Meppel	156	91	133	53	88	176	172	177	164	170	50	90	85	156	255	109	210	71	164	264									
Middelburg	201	190	186	233	207	95	134	256	113	155	333	302	362	182	245	198	134	318	147	244	281								
Nijmegen	164	72	120	66	20	100	135	206	99	62	179	134	211	135	142	97	144	194	131	148	124	189							
Rotterdam	102	80	73	129	118	51	21	144	25	113	222	197	257	70	210	77	30	206	35	202	169	104	114						
s-Hertogenbosch	125	71	88	92	66	72	102	171	66	32	204	162	236	103	125	68	109	222	100	124	152	145	45	82					
Tilburg	156	95	114	116	89	25	105	197	60	34	231	186	261	129	125	99	109	246	118	123	176	123	68	81	26				
Utrecht	80	23	37	73	66	73	62	120	60	88	166	140	195	55	180	18	82	182	55	181	111	170	86	57	55	81			
Venlo	225	137	180	125	93	115	193	266	151	56	245	200	274	200	65	163	198	260	195	74	190	212	74	172	95	94	150		
Winschoten	231	191	234	155	189	277	273	189	266	271	54	137	37	257	356	210	298	99	265	365	101	382	225	270	253	277	212	291	
Zwolle	134	70	113	44	66	155	152	157	144	150	77	75	106	136	235	89	177	91	144	244	51	261	104	149	132	156	91	170	121

A
B
C
D
1
2
3
4
Motorways
Primary roads
Secondary roads
All year site(s)
Seasonal site(s)
No sites listed
0 25 50 75 100 km
0 20 40 60 miles
N
S
E
W
NORTH SEA
NEWCASTLE UPON TYNE
HARWICH
HULL
TERSCHELLING
Oosterend
AMELAND
Buren
VLIELAND
Vierhuizen
Emden
N46
GRONINGEN
A7
LEEUWARDEN
Harlingen
N31
Opende
LEEK
De Koog
TEXEL
DEN BURG
A7
Sneek
A7
A28
Annen
ASSEN
Bourtange
Appelscha
N371
N34
Koudum
A32
Exloo
Callantsoog
Wezuperbrug
Dwingeloo
EMMEN
Tuitjenhorn
Enkhuizen
MEPPEL
A37
Zuidwolde
ALKMAAR
HOORN
N50
A28
A9
A7
Edam
Lelystad
Zwolle
OMMEN
A6
Ootmarsum
Zandvoort
AMSTERDAM
HAARLEM
Almere
Harderwijk
Denekamp
Noordwijk Aan Zee
Lisse
A50
Deventer
Rijssen
Katwijk aan Zee
LEIDEN
APELDOORN
A1
Hengelo
Wassenaar
Amersfoort
Otterlo
DEN HAAG
Woerden
Renswoude
A30
Dieren
Delft
UTRECHT
ARNHEM
HOEK VAN HOLLAND
Gouda
Maurik
Zevenaar
ROTTERDAM
A2
Doornenburg
A18
Rockanje
Brielle
Leerdam
S-Heerenberg
Gendt
A15
Gorinchem
A50
DORDRECHT
Heumen
N59
A29
A16
A27
S-Hertogenbosch
Zierikzee
Oosterhout
Uden
Wesel
Steenbergen
Sint Oedenrode
GERMANY
Roosendaal
A73
MIDDELBURG
A58
Bergen op Zoom
OIRSCHOT
Mierlo
Essen
EINDHOVEN
Sevenum
Cadzand
Bladel
A67
VENLO
Hoek
Eersel
Panningen
A2
Helden
Antwerpen
Dusseldorf
Roermond
Ghent
A2
BELGIUM
Koln
Meerssen
Schimmert
Valkenburg aan de Geul
Bruxelles
Maastricht
Gulpen
Aachen
Vaals
Bonn
Liege

Norway

Highlights

Home to soaring fjords, glaciers and polar bears juxtaposed with cosmopolitan cities and vibrant festivals, Norway truly is a remarkable country. The natural landscape must rank as one of the most beautiful in the world, it's easy to see why people become entranced.

With a rich culture spanning centuries from the ancient Vikings to the present day, and plenty of legends, folklore and fairytales in between, Norway is a magical place that invariably delights and inspires its visitors.

The Nobel Peace Prize has, since its inception, been awarded in Oslo by the Norwegian Nobel Committee. Oslo City Hall, where the ceremony is held, is now one of Norway's most famous buildings.

As a country steeped in myths and legends, Norway has a vibrant heritage of story-telling. Trolls are some of the most talked about fairytale creatures, and statues, books and pictures of them can be found all over the country.

Major towns and cities

- Oslo – Norway's capital city hosts numerous festivals throughout the year.
- Bergen – a colourful and peaceful city surrounded by mountains.
- Trondheim – home to the world's most northerly medieval cathedral.
- Drammen – a city with plenty of attractions such as the oldest brewery in Norway.

Attractions

- Heddal Stave Church, Notodden – Norway's largest medieval wooden church.
- Geirangerfjord, Sunnmøre – one of Norway's most breathtaking fjords and a UNESCO site.
- Jostedal Glacier – Europe's largest glacier and an outstanding natural environment.
- The Royal Palace, Oslo - take a tour through some of the most beautiful state rooms.

Find out more

visitnorway.com
hello@visitnorway.com

Country Information

Capital: Oslo

Bordered by: Finland, Russia, Sweden

Terrain: Mostly high plateaux and mountain ranges broken by fertile valleys; deeply indented coastline; arctic tundra in the north

Climate: Moderate climate along coastal areas; more extreme inland with snowy/rainy winters; arctic conditions in the north; summers can be unpredictable and May and June can be cool

Coastline: 25,148km (including islands/fjords)

Highest Point: Galdhøpiggen 2,469m

Language: Norwegian; Sami in some areas

Local Time: GMT or BST + 1, i.e. 1 hour ahead of the UK all year

Currency: Krone (NOK) divided into 100 øre; £1 = NOK 13.92, NOK 10 = £0.72 (Nov 2024)

Emergency numbers: Police 112; Fire brigade 110; Ambulance 113. From a mobile phone dial 112 for any service.

Public Holidays 2025: Jan 1; Apr 17, 18, 20, 21; May 1, 17, 29; Jun 8, 9; Dec 25, 26.

School summer holidays run from mid-June to mid-August.

Border Posts

Borders with Sweden and Finland may be crossed on all main roads. Storskog on the E105, east of Kirkenes, is the only border crossing for tourist traffic from Norway into Russia (visa required).

Duty Free Allowances

Norway isn't a member of the EU and therefore it's possible to import goods duty-free into the country from the EU. Duty-free allowances, which are strictly enforced, are as follows:

- 100 cigarettes or 125g tobacco
- 1 litre spirits and 1½ litres wine
- or 1 litre spirits and 3.5 litres beer
- or 3 litres wine and 2 litres beer
- or 2 litres beer

Goods to the value of NOK 6,000 (including alcohol and tobacco products)

Visitors must be aged 20 years and over to import spirits and 18 years and over for wine, beer and cigarettes.

Entry Formalities

Holders of British and Irish passports may visit Norway for up to three months without a visa.

Food and Medicines

Up to 10kg (combined weight) of meat, meat products and cheese can be imported into Norway from EU countries for personal consumption. The import of potatoes is not permitted but you can take in up to 10kg of fruit, berries and other vegetables. Visitors may only take in medicines for their own personal use with a covering letter from a doctor stating their requirements.

Medical Services

British visitors are entitled to the same basic emergency medical and dental treatment as Norwegian citizens, on production of a UK passport or European Health Insurance Card (EHIC) or Global Health Insurance Card (GHIC), but you will have to pay the standard fees. Ensure you consult a doctor who has a reimbursement arrangement with the NAV (Norwegian Employment and Welfare Organisation). Hotels and tourist offices have lists of local doctors and dentists.

You will have to pay in full for most prescribed medicines which are available from pharmacies (apotek). Emergency in-patient hospital treatment at public hospitals, including necessary medication, is free of charge but you will have to pay for out-patient treatment. NAV Health Service Agencies will reimburse any payments that are refundable.

Mosquitos and midges may be a nuisance at certain times of the year, especially near lakes.

Money

Travellers may import or export currency up to the equivalent of NOK 25,000 in Norwegian and/or foreign notes and coins. Any amount above this must be declared to Customs.

Opening Hours

Banks: Mon-Fri 8am-3.30pm and some open until 5pm on Thurs.

Museums: 9am/10am-4pm/5pm; no regular closing day.

Post Offices: Mon-Fri 8am/8.30am-4pm/5pm; Sat 8am-1pm.

Shops: Mon-Fri 9am-4pm/5pm (Thurs until 6pm/8pm); Sat 9am/10am-1pm/3pm. Some supermarkets and shopping centres are open longer and some open Sun.

Refund of VAT on Export

Some shops have a blue and red sign in their window indicating that visitors may purchase goods free of VAT. For visitors from the UK the purchase price of individual items (exclusive of VAT) must be at least NOK 250. Shop assistants will issue a voucher and on departure from Norway visitors must present goods and vouchers at a tax-free counter situated on ferries, at airports and at main border crossings where a refund of 11-18% will be made.

Regulations for Pets

For details of the regulations regarding the import of pets into Norway, see website: mattilsynet.no (English option) or contact the Norwegian Embassy in London.

Safety and Security

Norway is considered to have lower crime rates than some other European countries, even in the large cities, however you should always take the usual precautions against pickpockets and petty theft, especially in crowded areas. Don't leave valuables in your vehicle.

Following some recent incidents of robbery, the police are warning motorists not to stop in lay-bys overnight. The Norwegian Automobile Association, Norges Automobilforbund (NAF), has also sent out warnings to campsites urging campers to be careful.

If you plan to go off the beaten track or out to sea you should take local advice about weather conditions, have suitable specialist equipment and respect warning signs. Because of Norway's northerly latitude the weather can change rapidly, producing sudden arctic conditions on exposed mountains – even in summer. The winter is long (it can last well into April) and temperatures can drop to minus 25º celcius and below, plus any wind chill factor.

Norway shares with the rest of Europe an underlying threat from terrorism. Please check gov.uk/foreign-travel-advice/norway before you travel.

British Embassy

Thomas Heftyes gate 8, Oslo
Tel: +47 2313 2700
Website: gov.uk/world/norway

Irish Embassy

Haakon Viis Gate 1, N-0244 Oslo
Tel: 22 01 72 00
ireland.ie/en/norway/oslo

Documents

Money

Bank opening hours are shorter than in the UK, especially in summer, but cash machines are widespread. Bureaux de change are found in banks, post offices, airports, stations, hotels and some tourist offices.

The major credit cards are widely accepted (although some supermarkets and petrol stations don't accept credit cards) and may be used at cash machines (minibanks) throughout the country. In remote areas banks and cash machines may be few and far between.

It's advisable to carry your passport or photocard driving licence if paying with a credit card as you may well be asked for photographic proof of your identity. Carry your credit card issuers'/banks' 24-hour UK contact numbers in case of loss or theft of your cards.

Vehicle(s)

Carry your vehicle registration document (V5C), insurance certificate and MOT certificate (if applicable). If driving a borrowed vehicle carry a letter of authority from the owner.

Driving

Alcohol

Norwegian law is very strict: don't drink and drive. Fines and imprisonment await those who exceed the legal limit of 0.02% which equates to virtually zero for at least 12 hours before driving. Random roadside breath tests are frequent.

If you're involved in a road accident which causes damage to property or vehicles or injuries you should not drink any alcohol for six hours following the accident as the police may wish to carry out blood alcohol tests.

If purchasing medicines in Norway you should be aware that some containing alcohol should be avoided if you intend to drive. These are marked with a red triangle.

Breakdown Service

Norges Automobilforbund (NAF) operates a 24-hour breakdown service nationwide. Members of FIA affiliated clubs such as The Caravan and Motorhome Club in need of assistance should call the NAF on 0047 23 21 31 00. Emergency yellow telephones have been installed on difficult stretches of road.

If you're a member of The Caravan and Motorhome Club show your membership card in order to benefit from special NAF rates for breakdown assistance. Some breakdown vehicles have credit card payment terminals; otherwise payment is required in cash.

NAF Veipatrulje (road patrols) operates from mid-June to mid-August on mountain passes and in remote areas but in Oslo, Stavanger and Bergen, they operate all year round.

Child Restraint System

Children of four years and under 135 cm must be seated in a special child restraint system. If in a rear facing system on the front seat, the airbag must be deactivated. A child between 135 and150 cm should use a booster seat with an adult seatbelt. All child restraints must conform to ECE R44-03 or 04 regulations.

Fuel

Prices vary according to region - they are slightly higher in the north and in mountainous areas. Prices can also vary according to whether it's sold in a self-service station or not. There are automatic petrol pumps where payment is made by credit card or cash.

Petrol stations are generally open from 7am to 10pm on weekdays, but in cities you might find some open 24 hours. Petrol stations may be scarce, particularly in the north.

Unleaded petrol is dispensed from pumps marked 'Blyfri'. Not all petrol stations stock diesel. If you fill up with it, ensure that you use the correct pump and don't inadvertently fill with 'Afgift Diesel' (red diesel for agricultural vehicles).

There are very few petrol stations which sell LPG. a list is available at mylpg.eu.

Lights

The use of dipped headlights is compulsory at all times, regardless of weather conditions. Bulbs are more likely to fail with constant use and it's recommended that you carry spares.

Low Emission Zones

There are Low Emission Zones in force in Bergen, Kristiansand and Oslo. See urbanaccessregulations.eu for more information.

Mountain Passes

Always check that any mountain passes you intend to use are open. Some high mountain roads close during the winter, the duration of the closure depending on weather conditions, but many others remain open all year. Other passes may close at short notice, at night or during periods of bad weather. Yellow emergency telephones are installed on mountain passes.

The Norwegian Tourist Board can provide a list of roads which normally close in winter, or contact the Norwegian Public Road Administration (Statens vegvesen) for information about roads, road conditions, mountain passes, tunnels, border crossings, etc.
For enquiries telephone (+47) 22 07 30 00; a list of roads that are closed in winter or which have limited accessibility can be found at (vegvesen.no/en/traffic) and search for Truckers' Guide, or email: truckers.guide@vegvesen.no

Motorways

There are 300 km of four lane motorways signposted by the prefix A, which are situated around the towns of Bergen and Oslo. There are category B motorways with two lanes. Motorways don't have emergency telephones.

There are many toll roads throughout the country and most have an electronic toll system. Vehicles are categorised as follows:

Class 1 – Motorcycles

Class 2 – Car, with or without trailer, with a total weight less than 3,500kg and maximum length of 6m.

Class 3 – Vehicle with or without trailer and a total weight of more than 3,500kg or between 6m and 12.4m in length.

Motorway tolls

The toll system in Norway is fully automated and all foreign and domestic vehichles must pay road tolls in Norway. Toll booths are marked with the sign Automatisk bomstasjon/Automatic toll, and the gate with the camera is marked with the Ikke stopp/Do not stop sign.

Information on tolls for foreign vehicles can be found on autopass.no. To calculate the correct toll rate, you need to register your vehicle on epass24.com.

Tourists are advised to register on EPC before leaving for Norway, although it's not mandatory. If you don't register, you will receive an invoice by post for the sections covered. However, the invoice often takes several months to arrive. Tolls can be paid by bank transfer or online at epcplc.com.

Tolls can be paid in cash or by electronic collection, except for the toll on the Oslo ring road which is automated.

Parking

A white line on the edge of the carriageway indicates a parking restriction. Don't park on main roads if visibility is restricted or where there is a sign 'All Stans Førbudt' (no stopping allowed). If you do so you may have your vehicle towed away. Parking regulations in towns are very strict and offences are invariably subject to fines. Pay and display car parks are in use in the main towns.

Priority

Priority roads (main roads) are indicated by a road sign bearing a yellow diamond on a white background. A black diagonal bar through the sign indicates the end of the priority rule. If you're not travelling on a priority road then vehicles coming from the right have priority. Traffic already on a roundabout has priority and trams always have priority.

Narrow roads have passing places (møteplass) to allow vehicles to pass. The driver on the side of the road where there is a passing place must stop for an oncoming vehicle. However heavy goods vehicles tend to take right of way on narrow roads, especially if travelling uphill, and it may be necessary to reverse to a passing place to allow one to pass.

Roads

The standard of roads is generally good but stretches of major roads may be bumpy and rutted as a result of use by heavy freight traffic. Caravanners in particular should take care to avoid wheels being caught in ruts.

Some roads are narrow, especially in the mountains, and may not have a central yellow line. State roads are shown in red on maps and are asphalted but may not have kerbs and may, therefore, easily become cracked and rutted. Many roads have barriers mounted close to the side of the road.

Secondary roads have a gravel surface that can be tricky when wet and may be in poor condition for some weeks during and after the spring thaw.

Don't assume that roads with an E prefix are major roads - sections of the E39, for example, are single-track with passing places. The E6 road is asphalted all the way to the Swedish border in the south and to Kirkenes in the north.

Some roads in the fjord region have many hairpin bends and can be challenging. Roads may narrow to a single carriageway and single-track bridges often have no advance warning.

Gradients on main highways are generally moderate, not over 10%, but the inside of hairpin bends may be much steeper. There is a gradient of 20% on the E68 from Gudvangen (on the southern tip of the Sognefjord) to Stalheim, but a tunnel under the steepest section of the Stalheim road eliminates this difficult section.

Maps showing roads closed to caravans and those only recommended for use by experienced caravanners, together with rest stops, may be obtained from the Norwegian Tourist Board, Norwegian local road authority offices and from the NAF.

Because of the nature of the country's roads – and the beauty of the scenery – average daily mileage may be less than anticipated. Major repairs to roads and tunnels take place during the summer months and traffic controls may cause delays. Ferries make up an integral part of a number of routes, particularly when travelling north along the coast.

Care should be taken to avoid collisions with elk, deer and reindeer, particularly at dawn and dusk. Accidents involving any kind of animal must be reported to the police.

A number of roads are closed in winter, including the E69 to the North Cape, due to snow conditions; some don't open until late May or early June.

Road Signs and Markings

European highways are prefixed with the letter E and are indicated by signs bearing white letters and figures on a green background, national highways (Riksvei or Stamvei) are indicated by black figures prefixed Rv on a yellow background and local, county roads (Fylkesvei) by black figures on a white background. County road numbers don't generally appear on maps.

Lines in the middle of the carriageway are yellow. Bus, cycle and taxi lanes are marked in white.

Some signs have been introduced, for example a square blue sign showing a car and '2+' in white means that cars carrying more than two people can use bus lanes. Square signs indicate the presence of speed cameras, small rectangular signs indicate the exit numbers on highways and main roads, and a number of triangular signs with a yellow background indicate a temporary danger. Signs advising maximum speeds on bends, obstructions, etc, should be respected.

In addition to international road signs, the following signs may also be seen:

Passing place

Place of interest

Norwegian	English Translation
All stans førbudt	No stopping allowed
Arbeide pa vegen	Roadworks ahead
Enveiskjøring	One-way traffic
Ikke møte	No passing, single line traffic
Kjør sakte	Drive slowly
Løs grus	Loose chippings
Møteplass	Passing place
Omkjøring	Diversion
Rasteplass	Lay-by

Speed Limits

	Open Road (km/h)	Motorway (km/h)
Car Solo	80	90-100
Car towing caravan/ trailer	80	80
Motorhome under 3500kg	80	90-100
Motorhome 3500-7500kg	80	80

Drivers should pay close attention to speed limits, which are in general significantly lower than in the UK. Fines for exceeding speed limits are high and often have to be paid on the spot. Radar detectors are illegal.

In residential areas the speed limit may be as low as 30 km/h (18 mph). Frequent speed controls are in operation. Ramps and speed control bumps are not always signposted.

Vehicles over 3,500kg are restricted to 80 km/h (50 mph) on motorways and highways, regardless of signs showing higher general limits.

Tolls

Toll ring roads are in place around major cities charging drivers to take their vehicles into city centres. There are 3 zones (rings) of toll points in Oslo. In the outer zone you're only charged on entry. In the two inner zones you're charged every time you pass a toll point. Surcharges apply from 6.30-9am and 3-5pm, and for diesel vehicles.
See fjellinjen.no/private/prices for full details.

Because of the mountainous terrain and the numerous fjords and streams, there are many bridges and tunnels where tolls are normally payable.

Tunnels may be narrow and unlit and care is needed when suddenly entering an unlit tunnel from bright daylight. Alternative routes to avoid tolls can be full of obstacles which are not marked on a map, e.g. narrow stretches with sharp turns and/or poor road surface, and are best avoided.

Svinesund Bridge

There is a 700 metre-long bridge linking Norway and Sweden on the E6 at Svinesund (Sweden) – the busiest border crossing between the two countries.

Towing

Drivers of cars and caravans with a combined length of more than 12.4 metres must check from the list of national highways and/or municipal roads may not be allowed on some routes.

You can check this information with The Norwegian Public Road Administration (Statens vegvesen), tel: (0047) 22 07 30 00 from abroad, visit vegvesen.no/en and search for 'Truckers' Guide', or contact the Norwegian Tourist Board or NAF. For a motorhome the maximum length is 12 metres.

Any vehicle towing must have extended towing mirrors fitted.

Some secondary roads have a maximum width of less than 2.55 metres. If your caravan is wider than 2.3 metres and more than 50cm wider than your car, white reflectors must be mounted on the front of your car mirrors.

It's understood that the Rv55 from Sogndal to Lom and the Rv63 north from Geiranger are not suitable for caravans exceeding 5 metres in length, or those without an adequate power/weight ratio.

Traffic Jams

Roads in general are rarely busy but the roads in and around the cities of Oslo, Bergen, Kristiansand and Trondheim suffer traffic jams during rush hours and at the beginning and end of the holiday season. The E6 Oslo-Svinesund road at the border with Sweden and the E18 Oslo-Kristiansand road are generally busy during the June to August holiday period. During the summer you should also expect delays at ferry terminals.

Tunnels

The road network includes approximately 950 tunnels, most of which can be found in the counties of Hordaland and Sogn og Fjordane in western Norway. Most tunnels are illuminated and about half are ventilated. There are emergency telephones at the entrance to tunnels and inside them. Tunnels also have refuges which can be used by motorists in the event of an emergency.

Laerdal Tunnel

The Laerdal Tunnel is situated on road (E16) between Laerdal and Aurland. The toll-free 24.5 km long tunnel is illuminated and ventilated throughout and has a number of caverns at regular intervals which act as turning points and help dispel any feelings of claustrophobia. An alternative route is to take the Rødnes tunnel and then the Rv53, but this involves a steep climb beyond Øvre Ardal.

Lofoten and Vesterålen Islands

The Lofoten Islands can be reached by ferries from Bodø & Skutvik and the Vesteralen Islands can be reached by road (E10) west of Narvik. The individual islands of the Lofoten and Vesterålen groups are connected to each other by bridge or tunnel and the two groups of islands are linked by the E10 Lofast route from Gullesfjordbotn in Vesterålen to Fiskebøl in Lofoten.

Oslo Tunnel

A 3 km long toll-free tunnel runs from east to west Oslo.

Violation of Traffic Regulations

The police are empowered to impose and collect on-the-spot fines for infringement of traffic regulations.

Winter Driving

Vehicles with a total weight of 3,500kg or more must carry chains during the winter season, regardless of road conditions. Checks are often carried out.

Generally, spiked tyres can be used from 1 Nov to the first Sunday after Easter. In an effort to discourage the use of spiked tyres in Bergen, Oslo and Trondheim a fee is payable on vehicles equipped with them.

For vehicles up to 3,500kg the tax is NOK 35 for one day and NOK 450 for a month. For vehicles over 3,500kg the fee is doubled. Daily permits are available through the app Through the app 'Bil i Osl' or from vending machines along major roads into the city marked 'Frisk luft i byen'. Vehicles over 3,500 kg must be equipped with winter tyres on all axles between 15 November and 31 March.

Essential Equipment

Reflective Jacket/Waistcoat

Owners of vehicles registered in Norway are required to carry a reflective jacket to be worn if their vehicle is immobilised on the carriageway following a breakdown or accident. Passengers who leave the vehicle, for example to assist with a repair, should also wear one.

Warning Triangle

An warning triangle must be used if the vehicle has broken down, punctures or is involved in an accident, and could cause danger to other road users.

Touring

International ferry services operate between Norway and Denmark, Germany, Iceland and Sweden. Routes from Harwich to Denmark and Newcastle to the Netherlands are in operation as gateways to Europe and, in addition, a daily overnight ferry service connects Copenhagen and Oslo.

A green 'i' sign indicates a tourist information office which is open all year with extended opening hours in summer, whereas a red sign means that the office is only open during the summer season.

Norwegians take their school and industrial holidays from mid-June to mid-August; travelling outside this season will ensure that facilities are less crowded and more economically priced. Winter brings the inevitable snowfall with some of the most reliable snow conditions in Europe. The winter sports season is from November to April.

Alta, on the coast north of the Arctic Circle, boasts the most extensive prehistoric rock carvings in Europe and has been declared a UNESCO World Heritage Site. Other World Heritage Sites include Geirangerfjord, Nærøyfjord, Bryggen in Bergen and the wooden buildings in Røros.

City cards are available for Oslo and Bergen, giving unlimited free travel on public transport, free public parking and free or discounted admission to museums and tourist attractions. They can be bought from tourist information centres, hotels and campsites in or near the city, from some kiosks or online at visitoslo.com or visitbergen.com.

Wine and spirits are only available from special, state-owned shops (vinmonopolet) usually found in larger towns, and are expensive, as are cigarettes. Beer is available from supermarkets. Smoking in bars, restaurants and public places is prohibited. Tipping is not expected in restaurants.

English is widely spoken, often fluently, by virtually everyone under the age of 60.

Camping and Caravanning

There are more than 1,000 campsites in Norway which are classified 1 to 5 stars and which are generally open between June and mid-August. A camping guide listing a complete overview of Norwegian sites is available from the Norwegian Automobile Association, (NAF), see (nafcamp.no) for more information. Most 3-star sites and all 4 and 5 star sites have sanitary facilities for the disabled and all classified sites have cooking facilities.

Many sites don't open until mid-June and don't fully function until the beginning of July, particularly if the winter has been prolonged. Sites with published opening dates earlier than June may not open on time if the weather has been particularly bad and if, for example, there has been heavy rain and flooding near rivers or lakes where campsites are situated. Campsites which are open all year will usually have very limited facilities for most of the year outside the short holiday season.

Facilities vary; in main tourist centres there are large, well-equipped sites with good sanitary facilities, grocery shops, leisure facilities and attendants permanently on duty. Sites are generally maintained to a high standard of cleanliness. In more remote areas, sites are small and facilities can be basic.

Many small campsites have no chemical

disposal point. Roadside notice boards at the entrance to each local area (kommune) indicate campsites, chemical disposal points (normally sited at petrol stations) and other local amenities. These disposal facilities are usually coin-operated and have instructions in English. In some areas in the north, there may be no adequate arrangements for the disposal of waste water, either on site or in the immediate area, and you're advised to enquire when arriving at a campsite.

The Camping Key Europe may be required at some sites. You can buy the Camping Key Europe on arrival at your first site and will be issued with a temporary card.

There are many sites on the E6 to the North Cape, seldom more than 30km apart. These sites may be subject to road noise. Caravans are allowed to stay at the North Cape but no facilities are available – see Nordkapp later in this chapter and in the Site Entry listing.

In the short summer season, campsites can be crowded and facilities stretched. You're recommended to arrive before 3pm (many sites have a latest arrival time of 4pm) in order to have a better choice of pitches and have the opportunity to erect an awning.

Casual/wild camping is not actively encouraged but the Norwegian 'Right of Access' allows visitors to explore the countryside freely, except for cultivated land, farmland, gardens, nurseries, etc. Off-road driving is not allowed. Visitors must respect nature and take their rubbish away with them when they leave. Open fires (which include Primus stoves) are prohibited in forests or on open land between 15 April and 15 September.

Cycling

Cyclists are fairly well catered for and some areas, such as Vestfold, Rogaland and the Lillehammer area, have a well-developed network of cycle paths. Some old roads have been converted into cycle paths in the mountains and along western fjords. Paths run through magnificent scenery in the Lofoten and Vesterålen Islands in particular, and from Haugastøl in the Hardangervidda National Park to Flåm. A number of tunnels are prohibited to cyclists, but local detours are generally signposted. Information is available at visitnorway.com.

Electricity and Gas

Campsites usually have a minimum 10 amp supply. Plugs are the continental type and have two round pins plus two earth strips. Some sites don't yet have CEE connections. It's recommended that you take an extension cable of at least 50 metres.

There are often problems with both polarity and the earthing of the electrical supply on some sites. Due to its mountainous nature, Norway's electricity supply network is quite different from that found elsewhere in Europe. There is no national grid and electricity systems vary from place to place throughout the country. Any polarity testing system is likely to give false readings. It's understood that progress is being made to improve and standardise the electrical supply throughout the country but you should be cautious and, if in any doubt, ask site staff to demonstrate the integrity of the earthing system before connecting.

Propane gas cylinders are generally widely available from Esso and Statoil petrol stations. You'll need to buy an appropriate adaptor, available from camping shops or Statoil garages. AGA AS dealers will allow you to sell back propane cylinders within six months of purchase prior to leaving Norway at approximately 80% of the purchase price. Statoil garages no longer buy them back, however, some Statoil garages and AGA AS dealers will exchange Swedish Primus propane cylinders for their Norwegian version but won't accept other foreign propane cylinders. There's no refund for the adaptor.

Gas supplies can be conserved by taking advantage of the kitchens and/or cooking facilities available at classified campsites, and using electrical hook-ups at every opportunity.

Motorhomes

Many towns provide parking places for motorhomes close to city centres, known as Bobil Parks, which are open in June, July and August. In general these parking areas provide limited facilities and car and caravan outfits are not permitted. Details, where known, are listed in the Site Entry pages.

Apart from at campsites, motorhome service points are reported to be few and far between and are generally to be found at petrol stations, where water refill may also be available.

The Midnight Sun and Northern Lights

The best time to experience the midnight sun is early or high summer. The sun does not sink below the horizon at the North Cape (Nordkapp) from the second week in May to the last week in July.

Midsummer Night's Eve is celebrated all over the country with thousands of bonfires along the fjords.

You can hope to see the Northern Lights (Aurora Borealis) between November and February depending on weather conditions. You need to go north of the Arctic Circle, which crosses Norway, just south of Bodø on the Nordland coast. Occasionally the Northern Lights may be seen in southern Norway.

North Cape (Nordkapp)

A tunnel links the island of Magerøya, on which the North Cape is situated, to the mainland. North Cape is open from the beginning of May until the end of September, and from the beginning of October to the end of December. Contact the Nordkapp Tourist Office, nordkapp.no, or tel: (0047) 78 47 70 30 for more information.

This is a tourist centre where there are exhibitions, displays, restaurants, shops and a post office, as well as an area of hardstanding for parking. More information is given in the campsite entry for Nordkapp or on the website nordnorge.com. There are no cash machines at North Cape but credit cards are accepted in shops and restaurants, as are euros and sterling.

The true northernmost point of Norway is at Knivskjellodden on a peninsular to the west of North Cape which is marked by a modest monument and a wooden box where you can record your name in a log book. It's possible to walk the 18 km round trip from a car park on the E69 to Knivskjellodden but the walk should not be undertaken lightly.

You can claim a certificate to mark your achievement from the tourist office in Honningsvåg by quoting the reference number of your signed entry in the log book.

The Order of Bluenosed Caravanners

Visitors to the Arctic Circle from anywhere in the world may apply for membership of the Order of Bluenosed Caravanners which will be recognised by the issue of a certificate by the International Caravanning Association (ICA).

Contact bluenosed@icacaravanning.org and attach a photograph of yourselves and your outfit under any Arctic Circle signpost, together with the date and country of crossing and the names of those who made the crossing.

This service is free to members of the ICA (annual membership £20); the fee for non-members is £5. Cheques should be payable to the ICA.

For more information visit icacaravanning.org.

Public Transport

The public transport network is excellent and efficient with bus routes extending to remote villages. For economical travel buy a 24-hour bus pass (campsites often sell them), valid when stamped for the first time. Many train routes run through very scenic countryside and special offers and discounts mean that train travel is reasonably priced. Only Oslo has a metro system. Trams operate in Bergen and Trondheim.

Using domestic public ferry services is often the quickest way of travelling around Norway and from place to place along the coast and within fjords. Most operate from very early in the morning until late at night. Booking isn't normally necessary except in the height of the holiday season when there may be long queues to the more popular destinations. However, internal ferries can be expensive in high season and you might want to plan your route carefully to avoid them.

The ultimate ferry journey is the Norwegian steamer trip (hurtigrute) up the coast from Bergen to Kirkenes. A daily service operates in both directions and the steamer stops at about 30 ports on the way. The round trip lasts eleven days.

The scenic round trip from Bergen or Oslo, 'Norway in a Nutshell', takes you through some of the most beautiful scenery in the country. It combines rail, boat and coach travel on the scenic Bergen railway, the breathtaking Flåm Railway, and takes in the Aurlandsfjord, the narrow Naerøyfjord and the steep Stalheimskleiva. Further details are available from the Norwegian Tourist Board.

You can safely hail a taxi off the street or take one from a taxi stand. Most drivers speak English and all taxis are equipped for taking payment by credit card.

Sites in Norway

ALESUND *1B1* (1km N Coastal) *62.47659, 6.15927* **Ålesund Bobilsenter,** 6002 Ålesund (Møre og Romsdal) **tel 70 16 21 28; www.alesundbobil.no/parkering/hjelsetgarden-bobilparkering**

Foll coast to N of town cent & m'van sps; well sp. Sm, hdstg, unshd, EHU; ccard acc. *"No on-site warden; motor c'vans only; site on water's edge adj sea wall; conv town cent; v nice facs in wonderful location."* **NOK 200, May-Sep.** **2024**

ALESUND *1B1* (3km E Urban/Coastal) *62.46986, 6.19839* **Volsdalen Camping,** Sjømannsveien, 6008 Ålesund (Møre og Romsdal) **tel 70 12 58 90; post@volsdalencamping.no; www.volsdalencamping.no**

(htd)

Foll Rv136 two Centrum, ignore 1st camping sp (Prinsen), take 2nd site sp Volsdalsberga to exit R, up slip rd. At top turn L over E136 then immed R, site on L. 3*, Sm, mkd, hdstg, unshd, terr, EHU (10A) NOK30 (no earth); gas; cooking facs; red long stay; TV; 40% statics; bus 600m; Eng spkn; ccard acc. *"Stunning location; some pitches o'looking fjord; sm pitches; new owners installed cabins; new san facs (2022); clean & tidy; pitch and report to recep if arr before 14:00; town 30 min walk."* **NOK 410, 1 May-1 Sep.** **2022**

ALTA *2G1* (6km S Rural) *69.92904, 23.26136* **Alta River Camping,** Steinfossveien 5, 9518 Øvre Alta (Finnmark) **tel 07 94 03 27 99; post@alta-river-camping.no; www.alta-river-camping.no**

12 (htd)

Fr E6 (by-passing Alta), take E93 S sp Kautokeino. Site clearly sp on L (opp information board). Med, pt shd, EHU (10-16A) NOK30; cooking facs; TV; Eng spkn; adv bkg acc; ccard acc; sauna; CKE. *"Excel facs; o'looks salmon rv; pitches not mkd and close together, some hdstg; elec point poss no earth; facs dated but clean; elec poss no earth."* **NOK 279** **2024**

ALVDAL *1C2* (5km NE Rural) *62.13115, 10.56896* **Gjelten Bru Camping,** 2560 Alvdal (Hedmark) **tel 97 32 35 88; post@gjeltenbrucamping.no; www.gjeltenbrucamping.no**

12

Fr Rv3 join rd 29 at Alvdal. Cross rv opp general store to site on rv bank. 3*, Sm, mkd, pt shd, EHU (10A) NOK40; Eng spkn; fishing; games area. *"V pleasant site; friendly owner."* **NOK 259** **2022**

ANDALSNES *1B1* (11km S Rural) *62.4940, 7.75846* **Trollveggen Camping,** Horgheimseidet, 6300 Åndalsnes (Møre og Romsdal) **tel 07 40 09 20 02; post@trollveggen.com; www.trollveggen.com**

(htd) nr

Sp on W side of E136, dir Dombås. 3*, Sm, mkd, pt shd, terr, EHU (16A) NOK40; bbq; cooking facs; Eng spkn; adv bkg acc; ccard acc; fishing; bike hire; golf 10km. *"Friendly, family-run site; excel touring base; outstanding scenery; at foot of Trollveggen wall - shd fr late afternoon; ideal site for walking in Romsal; on Trollsteig classic rte."* **NOK 294, 10 May-20 Sep.** **2024**

ANDALSNES *1B1* (3km S Rural) *62.55223, 7.70394* **Åndalsnes Camping & Motell,** 6300 Åndalsnes (Møre og Romsdal) **tel 71 22 16 29; epost@andalsnes-camping.no; www.andalsnes-camping.com**

Foll E136 to o'skirts of Åndalsnes. Foll sp Ålesund x-ing rv bdge twd W & L immed. Lge, pt shd, EHU (10-16A) NOK40 (check earth); TV; ccard acc; fishing; boating; CKE. *"Excel facs; rvside, excel mountain scenery; nr Troll Rd & Wall; nice site; grnd can be soft; poss long lead req (poss no earth); gd cent site."* **NOK 284, 1 May-30 Sep.** **2024**

BARDU *2 F2* (2km N Rural) *68.87647, 18.36256* **Bardu Camping & Turistsenter,** Idrettsveien 2, 9360 Bardu (Troms) **tel 77 61 23 00 or 97 41 87 82; haukland@live.no; www.barducamping.no**

12 (htd) nr

Site sp fr E6, N of Setermoen. 3*, Med, pt shd, EHU (10A) NOK50; phone; tennis. *"In valley surrounded by mountains; scruffy but useful NH; only acc Norwegian cc."* **NOK 340** **2023**

BERGEN *1A3* (21km E Rural) *60.37381, 5.45768* **Lone Camping,** Hardangerveien 697, 5268 Haukeland (Horda-Rogaland) **tel 55 39 29 60; booking@lonecamping.no; www.lonecamping.no**

Fr N on E39 until junc with E16. foll sp Voss to rndabt junc with Rv580 sp Nesttun. Foll Rv580 S for approx 5km, site sp on L. Fr S on E39 until Nesttun, foll Rv580 N sp Indre Arna for approx 6km, site sp on R. Recep is sm bureau adj g'ge or, if unmanned, in g'ge. Do NOT go into Bergen city cent. Site is 20km by rd fr Bergen. 3*, Lge, hdstg, pt shd, pt sl, EHU (16A) NOK40; gas; sw; red long stay; TV; 10% statics; phone; bus to Bergen; Eng spkn; ccard acc; site clsd 5 Nov-19 Dec & New Year; fishing; boating; CKE. *"Well-organised; helpful staff; peaceful lakeside setting; superb views; lakeside pitches diff when wet; bus at camp ent for Bergen (35 mins)."* **NOK 326, 5 Jan-19 Apr & 29 Apr-20 Dec.** **2024**

NORWAY

BERGEN *1A3* (17km SE Rural) *60.35220, 5.43520* **Bratland Camping,** Bratlandsveien 6, 5268 Haukeland (Hordaland) **tel 55 10 13 38 & 92 61 52 00 (mob); post@bratlandcamping.no; www.bratland camping.no**

Fr N on E39 until junc with E16, foll sp Voss to rndabt junc with Rv580 sp Nesttun. Foll Rv580 S for approx 4km; site sp on L. Fr Voss on E16, emerge fr tunnel to rndabt, turn L onto Rv580. Then as above. Site 16km by rd fr Bergen. 3*, Sm, hdstg, unshd, EHU (10A) NOK40; cooking facs; TV; 10% statics; bus to Bergen at site ent; Eng spkn; ccard acc; CKE. *"Clean, family-run site; gd, modern san facs; v helpful, friendly owners; conv Bergen, nrby stave church & Grieg's home; great loc."* **NOK 341, 20 Apr-15 Sep.** 2022

BERGEN *1A3* (6km SSE Urban) *60.35405, 5.35962* **Bergenshallen,** Vilhelm Bjerknes Vei 24, 5081 Bergen **tel 55 30 88 50; www.visitnorway.com**

Head SW on E16/E39. Exit onto E39 twrds Stavanger/Rv580, take exit. At rndabt take 3rd exit onto Mindeallé. Turn R to stay on Mindeallé, go thro 1 rndabt, cont onto Rv582. Thro 1 rndabt then at next rndabt take 2nd exit onto Fv252. Turn R onto Hagerups vei, cont onto Vilhelm Bjerknes'vei. Turn L and site is on the R. Sm, hdstg, unshd, EHU (on some pitches); own san rec; train adj. *"28 spaces for MV's only; arrive early; adj to Bergen light Rail - 15 mins to city cent; only fasc are water, emptying toilet & waste disposal; excel location for visiting Bergen; no shwrs or wc."* **NOK 150, 1 May-31 Aug.** 2024

BERLEVAG *2H1* (0.6km E Coastal) *70.85716, 29.09933* **Berlevåg Pensjonat Camping,** Havnagata 8, 9980 Berlevåg (Finnmark) **tel 90 70 45 05; berlevag motell@berlevagmotell.no; www.berlevag-pensjonat.no**

(htd) nr

Leave E6 at Tanabru, foll Rv890 to Berlevåg. Site sp at beg of vill. 3*, Sm, unshd, EHU (16A) NOK40; bbq; cooking facs; TV; phone; Eng spkn; adv bkg acc; ccard acc; CKE. *"Busy fishing port on edge of Barents Sea; museum, glassworks, WW2 resistance history; v helpful staff as site is also TO; site will open outside Jun-Sep on request if contacted ahead; library & lounge; rec arr early; excel site."* **NOK 237, 1 Jun-30 Sep.** 2023

BIRTAVARRE *2G1* (0.7km S Rural) *69.49051, 20.82976* **Camping Birtavarre (TR34),** 9147 Birtavarre (Troms) **tel 47 40 00 34 34; https://arcticexcite.com/bcbpay/**

nr

On E6 Olderdalen to Nordkjosobotn, sp. Or foll sp fr vill. 3*, Med, unshd, EHU NOK45; cooking facs; sw; Eng spkn; ccard acc; CKE. *"Basic site; OK for NH."* **NOK 195, 1 May-15 Oct.** 2024

BODO *2F2* (11km NE Coastal) *67:34136, 14.51261* **Geitvågen Bad & Camping,** Midnattssolveien 653, 8016 Bodø **tel (47) 909 11 777; geitvagen.com**

adj

On ent Bodø on Rv80, turn R onto Rv834 sp Kjerringøy. After 10km turn L at sp, pass car park on R. 1*, Med, hdg, mkd, pt shd, pt sl, terr, EHU 10A (NOK30); cooking facs; sw; twin axles; Eng spkn; adv bkg acc; ccard acc. *"Arr early for pitch with sea view for midnight sun; on rd to Kjerringoy ferry; some pitches hidden among trees with sea views; salwater lagoon; facs adequate but tired; fair."* **NOK 210, 1 Jun-31 Aug.** 2024

BODO *2F2* (28km SE Coastal) *67.23545, 14.62125* **Saltstraumen Camping,** Knapplund, 8056 Saltstraumen (Nordland) **tel 75 58 75 60; saltstraumen@pluscamp.no; www.saltstraumen-camping.no**

12 (htd) nr nr

Fr Bodø take Rv80 for 19km; turn S onto rte 17 at Løding; site sp in Saltstraumen. 3*, Med, hdstg, unshd, EHU (16A) NOK30; gas; bbq; cooking facs; twin axles; TV; 50% statics; phone; bus 300m; Eng spkn; adv bkg acc; ccard acc; fishing; bike hire; boating; CKE. *"5 min walk to Mælstrom, the 'angler's paradise'; v busy high ssn - rec arr early; site a bit tired."* **NOK 400** 2022

BRONNOYSUND *2E3* (14km SW Coastal) *65.39340, 12.09920* **Torghatten Camping,** 8900 Torghatten (Nordland) **tel 75 02 54 95; post@torghatten.net; torghatten.net**

12 adj

Fr Rv17 onto Rv76 to Brønnøysund, foll sp Torghatten. Site at base of Torghatten mountain. Sm, unshd, pt sl, EHU (16A) NOK30; phone; bus; Eng spkn. *"Take care speed humps in/out Brønnøysund; sea water pool adj; vg."* **NOK 280** 2024

"There aren't many sites open at this time of year"

If you're travelling outside peak season remember to call ahead to check site opening dates – even if the entry says 'open all year'.

BYGLANDSFJORD *1B4* (3km N Rural) *58.68895, 7.80322* **Neset Camping,** 4741 Byglandsfjord (Aust-Agder) **tel 37 93 40 50; post@neset.no; www.neset.no**

12 (htd)

N on Rv9 fr Evje, thro Byglandsfjord, site on L. 4*, Lge, unshd, pt sl, EHU (10A) NOK30; gas; bbq; cooking facs; sw nr; TV; 40% statics; Eng spkn; adv bkg acc; ccard acc; windsurfing; bike hire; fishing; sauna; boat hire. *"Wonderful location on lakeside; elk safaris; walks; rafting nr; check elec earth."* **NOK 352** 2024

BYRKJELO *1B2* (0.3km S Rural) *61.73026, 6.50843*
Byrkjelo Camping & Hytter, 6826 Byrkjelo (Sogn og Fjordane) **tel 91 73 65 97; camping@breim.no; www.byrkjelocamping.no**

WD nr nr (htd)

Fr S site ent on L as ent town, clearly sp. 3*, Sm, hdstg, pt shd, EHU (10A) NOK30; cooking facs; 25% statics; phone; Eng spkn; adv bkg acc; ccard acc; solarium; fishing; cycling; CKE. *"Horseriding, mountain & glacier walking; excel, well kept site; great facs."*
NOK 278, 1 May-24 Sep. **2024**

DOMBAS *1C2* (6km S Rural) *62.02991, 9.17586*
Bjørkhol Camping, 2660 Dombås (Oppland) **tel 61 24 13 31; post@bjorkhol.no; www.bjorkhol.no**

(htd) WD MSP

Site on E6. 3*, Sm, pt shd, pt sl, EHU (10A) NOK40 (long lead poss req); cooking facs; 10% statics; phone; Eng spkn; adv bkg acc; CKE. *"A well-kept, friendly, family-owned, basic site; excel mountain walking in area."* **NOK 150, 1 May-1 Sep.** **2024**

DRAMMEN *1C3* (25km SE Coastal) *59.60003, 10.40383*
Homannsberget Camping, Strømmveien 55, 3060 Svelvik (Vestfold) **tel 33 77 25 63 or 91 30 98 52 (mob); post@homannsberget.no; www.homannsberget.no**

MSP adj

Head SW on E18, take exit 25 twr Svelvik/RV319, at rndabt take 3rd exit onto E134. At next rndabt take 1st exit onto Bjørnsons gate/Rv282. Turn L onto Havnegata/Rv319. Cont on Rv319, go thro 1 rndabt. Site on the L. Med, mkd, unshd, EHU; twin axles; adv bkg acc; ccard acc; games area; CKE. *"Vg site; train stn within 20 mins; site is also a strawberry farm & orchard."* **NOK 245, 1 May-1 Sep.** **2024**

EDLAND *1B3* (6km E Rural) *59.72378, 7.69712*
Velemoen Camping, Haukelivegen 6011, 3895 Edland **tel 41 58 87 04; velemoen@frisurf.no; https://visithaukeli.no/overnattingsstad/velemoen-camping**

nr

Fr E site on L off E134 bef Edland; Fr W site is on R, 8km after Haukeligrend on Lake Tveitevatnet. 2*, Sm, hdstg, unshd, pt sl, EHU (16A, no earth); bbq; cooking facs; sw nr; twin axles; red long stay; TV; 10% statics; phone; Eng spkn; adv bkg acc. *"V helpful owner; immac san facs; beautiful lakeside/mountain location; on S side of Hardangervidda National Park; on main E-W rte Oslo-Bergen; excel."* **NOK 250, 15 May-1 Oct.** **2023**

EGERSUND *1A4* (4km N Rural) *58.4788, 5.9909*
Steinsnes NAF Camping, Jærveien 190, Tengs, 4370 Egersund (Horda-Rogaland) **tel 97 40 09 66; post@steinsnescamping.no; www.steinsnescamping.no**

12 WD MSP nr nr

Site located S of Rv44 & on bank of rv; rv bdge at Tengs Bru. 3*, Med, mkd, unshd, EHU (4A) NOK35; bbq; phone; Eng spkn; adv bkg acc; ccard acc; CKE. *"Spectacular rapids 1km (salmon leaping in July); on North Sea cycle rte; horseriding school adj; conv ferry to Denmark or Bergen; vg."* **NOK 230** **2024**

EIDFJORD *1B3* (7km SE Rural) *60.42563, 7.12318*
Sæbø Camping (HO11), 5784 Øvre-Eidfjord (Hordaland) **tel 53 66 59 27 or 55 10 20 48; scampi@online.no; www.saebocamping.com**

(htd) WD MSP nr

Site N of Rv7 bet Eidfjord & Geilo, 2nd on L after tunnel & bdge; clearly sp. 3*, Med, pt shd, EHU (10A) NOK40 (earth fault); cooking facs; boating; CKE. *"Vg; beautiful lakeside setting; adj to excel nature cent with museum/shop/theatre; clean san facs; helpful staff; gd location for walking & cycling."*
NOK 240, 1 May-30 Sep. **2024**

ELVERUM *1D2* (2km S Rural) *60.86701, 11.55623*
Elverum Camping, Halvdan Gransvei 6, 2407 Elverum (Hedmark) **tel 62 41 67 16; booking@elverumcamping.no; www.elverumcamping.no**

12 (htd) WD MSP nr nr nr

Site sp fr Rv20 dir Kongsvinger. Lge, pt shd, EHU (10A); bbq; 20% statics; phone; Eng spkn; adv bkg acc. *"Vg; museum of forestry adj; rlwy museum at Hamar (30km)."* **NOK 300** **2024**

FARSUND *1A4* (6km S Coastal) *58.0663, 6.7957*
Lomsesanden Familiecamping, Loshavneveien 228, 4550 Farsund (Vest-Agder) **tel 04 00 73 30; post@lomsesanden.no; www.lomsesanden.no**

WD sand adj

Exit E39 at Lyngdal onto Rv43 to Farsund & foll camp sps. (NB Rv465 fr Kvinesdal not suitable for c'vans.) 2*, Med, pt shd, EHU (10A) NOK45; TV; 95% statics; Eng spkn; adv bkg rec; ccard acc; fishing. *"Gd site in beautiful location."*
NOK 200, 1 May-15 Sep. **2022**

FAUSKE *2F2* (15km NE Coastal) *67.34618, 15.59533*
Strømhaug Camping, Strømhaugveien 2, 8226 Straumen (Nordland) **tel 75 69 71 06; mail@stromhaug.no; www.stromhaug.no**

12 (htd) WD MSP nr nr nr

N fr Fauske on E6, turn off sp Straumen, site sp. Sm, pt shd, pt sl, EHU (6-10A) inc; cooking facs; red long stay; TV; Eng spkn; boating; fishing. *"Site on rv bank; salmon-fishing in Aug."* **NOK 239** **2024**

FAUSKE *2F2* (5km S Urban) *67.23988, 15.41961* **Fauske Camping & Motel,** Leivset, 8201 Fauske (Nordland) **tel 75 64 84 01; fausm@online.no**

Fr S site on R of E6, approx 6km fr exit of Kvenflåg rd tunnel, & 2km bef Finneid town board. Fr N site on L approx 1km after rv bdge. 3*, Sm, pt shd, sl, EHU (10A) NOK40; cooking facs; sw nr; Eng spkn; adv bkg acc; ccard acc; fishing; cycling. *"Vg; phone ahead LS to check open; v close to E6 rd."* **NOK 312** **2022**

FJAERLAND *1B2* (4km N Rural) *61.42758, 6.76211* **Bøyum Camping,** 5855 Fjærland (Sogn og Fjordane) **tel 57 69 32 52; post@boyumcamping.no; www.boyumcamping.no**

On Rv5 Sogndal to Skei. Shortly after end of toll tunnel on L, well sp. 4*, Sm, hdstg, unshd, EHU NOK75; cooking facs; TV; 30% statics; phone; Eng spkn; adv bkg acc; ccard acc; bike hire; CKE. *"Adj glacier museum, conv for glacier & fjord trips; beautiful location nr fjord (no views); visit Mundal for 2nd hand books; helpful owner; superb, clean site; vg."* **NOK 300** **2023**

FLAM *1B2* (1km WNW Urban) *60.86296, 7.10985* **Flåm Camping,** Nedre Brekkevegen 12, 5743 Flåm (Sogn og Fjordane) **tel 57 63 21 21; camping@flaam-camping.no; www.flaam-camping.no**

Fr Lærdal Tunnel cont on E16 thro 2 more tunnels. At end of 2nd tunnel (Fretheim Tunnel) turn L immed to Sentrum. Turn L at x-rds, site on L. 4*, Med, hdstg, pt shd, pt sl, terr, serviced pitches; EHU (10A) inc; bbq; cooking facs; red long stay; phone; Eng spkn; ccard acc; bike hire; boating; fishing; watersports; CKE. *"Well-kept, friendly, busy, family-run site; no o'fits over 8.5m; excel san facs; conv mountain walks, excel location for Flambana rlwy, Aurlandsvangen 7km - gd shops; gd cycling base; excel."* **NOK 400, 1 Mar-31 Oct.** **2022**

FLEKKEFJORD *1A4* (6km ESE Rural) *58.28868, 6.7173* **Egenes Camping (VA7),** 4400 Flekkefjord (Vest-Agder) **tel 38 32 01 48; post@egenescamping.no; www.2017.egenescamping.no**

Located N of E39 dir Seland. 4*, Med, mkd, pt shd, EHU (5A) NOK40; TV; 75% statics; phone; ccard acc; CKE. *"Ltd facs LS; overflow car park area with facs for tourers 0.5km; lovely situation."* **NOK 250** **2024**

FORDE *1A2* (3km E Rural) *61.44940, 5.89008* **Førde Gjestehus & Camping (SF94),** Kronborgvegen 44, Havstad, 6800 Førde (Romsdal Sogn og Fjordane) **tel 46 80 60 00; post@fordecamping.no; www.fordecamping.no**

Site is on NE o'skirts Forde. At rndabt on E39at Havstad foll sp 'Hospital', site on R in 1km; well sp. Med, mkd, hdstg, pt shd, EHU (16A) inc; cooking facs; sw nr; TV; 10% statics; phone; Eng spkn; adv bkg acc; ccard acc; CKE. *"Pleasant, peaceful site."* **NOK 390, 1 Jan-29 Feb & 15 Apr-1 Oct.** **2022**

FREDRIKSTAD *1C4* (16km SE Coastal) *59.13942, 11.03855* **Bevo Camping,** Bevoveien 31, 1634 Gamle Fredrikstad **tel 94 45 96 73; post@bevocamping.no; www.bevocamping.no**

sand adj

Avoid app fr Fredrikstad. Fr E6 junc 4, take RV110 (Fredrikstad) then L on RV111 & L on RV107 (Torsnesveien). Foll signs to campsite. 3*, Sm, mkd, pt shd, EHU; CCI. *"Isolated site on Oslo Fjord; 15 mins to Gamle Frederikstad by car."* **NOK 280, 28 Apr-8 Sep.** **2024**

GEILO *1B3* (2km NE Urban) *60.54251, 8.23495* **Geilo Hytter & Camping AS (Formerly Breie Hytter & Camping),** Lauvrudvegen 11, 3580 Geilomoen, Geilo **tel 57 99 99 99 (mob); info@campinggeilo.no; www.campinggeilo.no**

Fr Geilo take RV7 twds Gol & Sundre. Site sp, take R into Lauvrudvegen. Sm, unshd, EHU inc; 30% statics; CCI. *"Vg for long or sh stays; pleasant, well kept site in residential area; helpful owner."* **NOK 170** **2024**

GEIRANGER *1B1* (2km NNW Rural) *62.11548, 7.18437* **Grande Hytteutleige og Camping,** 6216 Geiranger (Møre og Romsdal) **tel 70 26 30 68; office@grande-hytteutleige.no; www.grande-hytteutleige.no**

Head N on Rv63, in 2.3km turn L at the foot of zigzags, then 1st R. Site on the L. Sm, pt sl, EHU (16A); cooking facs; Eng spkn; ccard acc. *"Friendly staff; conv for Fjord cruise, steep narr ent; arr early in rainy ssn as some pitches shut if waterlogged, 1st come 1st serve basis as no bkgs; vg site."* **NOK 390, 15 May-15 Sep.** **2022**

GOL *1C2* (3km S Rural) *60.70023, 9.00416* **Gol Campingsenter (BU17),** Heradveien 7, 3550 Gol (Buskerud) **tel 32 07 41 44; booking@golcamp.no; www.golcamp.no**

Ent on R of Rv7 fr Gol twd Nesbyen. 4*, Lge, unshd, pt sl, EHU (16A) inc; gas; cooking facs; sw nr; TV; ccard acc; sauna; games area; CKE. *"Excel; lge extn with full facs across main rd - modern & clean."* **NOK 245** **2022**

GOL *1C2* (2km SW Rural) *60.69161, 8.91909* **Personbråten Camping,** 3550 Gol (Buskerud) **tel 90 78 32 73; leif.personbraten@c2i.net**

12 (htd) WD

Fr Gol to Geilo on Rv7, on L on rvside. 2*, Med, pt shd, EHU (10A); bbq; cooking facs; sw nr; Eng spkn; adv bkg acc; fishing; cycling; CKE. *"On rvside; v pleasant; poss noise fr rd & rv; honesty box if office unmanned; excel NH."* **NOK 298** **2022**

GRIMSBU *1C2* (0km N Rural) *62.15546, 10.17198* **Grimsbu Turistsenter,** 2582 Grimsbu (Oppland) **tel 62 49 35 29; mail@grimsbu.no; www.grimsbu.no**

12 (htd) WD MSP

On Rv29 11km E of Folldal, well sp. 4*, Med, pt shd, pt sl, EHU (16A) NOK30; bbq; cooking facs; sw nr; TV; Eng spkn; adv bkg acc; ccard acc; sauna; boat hire; bike hire; rv fishing. *"Family-run site; fitness rm; private san facs avail; beautiful situation."* **NOK 310** **2024**

GRONG *2E3* (2km S Rural) *64.4604, 12.3137* **Langnes Camping,** 7870 Grong (Nord-Trøndelag) **tel 47 68 83 33; post@langnescamping.no; langnescamping.no**

(htd) WD MSP nr

N on E6 turn off S of bdge over rv on by-pass, site sp. 4*, Med, mkd, hdstg, unshd, EHU (16A) NOK60; bbq; cooking facs; sw nr; TV; 10% statics; Eng spkn; games area; rv fishing; games rm. *"Helpful staff; drying rm for skiers; pleasant, family-run site; Quick Stop pitches; free phone to owner if site clsd; gd facs; access via gravel track."* **NOK 290, 1 Jun-31 Aug.** **2023**

HAMMERFEST *2G1* (1km E Urban) *70.65890, 23.71335* **Storvannet Camping,** Storvannsveien 103, 9615 Hammerfest (Finnmark) **tel 78 41 10 10; storvannet@yahoo.no**

(htd) WD nr nr

Descend into & cont thro town. Turn R immed after x-ing rv bdge. Site at top of Storvannet lake nr mouth of Rv Storelva. Sp. Med, hdstg, unshd, pt sl, EHU NOK40; bbq; cooking facs; sw nr; red long stay; Eng spkn; fishing; CKE. *"Vg; by attractive lake; 2km out of town; poss sightings of reindeer."* **NOK 295, 1 Jun-15 Sep.** **2022**

HAUGE *1A4* (5km NE Rural) *58.36166, 6.30944* **Bakkaåno Camping,** Bakkaveien, Fidje 4380 Hauge i Dalane (Rogaland) **tel 51 47 78 52 or 930 50 219 (mob); visit@bakkaanocamping.no; www.bakkaanocamping.no**

WD MSP

Heading E fr Hauge on Rv44, over rv & immed turn L & foll site sp. Site on L, recep on R over golf course at white house. Rd narr. Med, pt shd, EHU (5A) NOK30; cooking facs; sw nr; 80% statics; Eng spkn; fishing adj. *"Sep area for tourers; friendly, welcoming owners."* **NOK 220, Easter-30 Sep.** **2024**

HELLESYLT *1B1* (0.4km S Coastal) *62.08329, 6.87224* **Hellesylt Camping,** 6218 Hellesylt (Møre og Romsdal) **tel 90 20 68 85; postmottak@hellesyltturistsenter.no; www.hollistay.com/da/Norway/hellesylt/hellesylt-camping**

(htd) WD MSP nr nr shgl

Site on edge of fjord, sp fr cent of vill dir Geiranger. 2*, Sm, unshd, EHU (10A) NOK30; 40% statics; Eng spkn; adv bkg acc; CKE. *"Conv ferry to Geiranger; adj fjord surrounded by mountains - great views; gd rest in local hotel; beautiful church nr."* **NOK 140, 15 Apr-30 Sep.** **2024**

HONNINGSVAG *2H1* (8km NW Coastal) *71.02625, 25.89091* **Nordkapp Camping,** 9751 Honningsvåg (Finnmark) **tel 78 47 33 77; post@nordkappcamping.no; www.nordkappcamping.no**

NOK10 (htd) WD MSP

En rte Nordkapp on E69, site clearly sp. 3*, Sm, unshd, EHU (16A) NOK40; bbq; cooking facs; twin axles; 10% statics; bus 100m; Eng spkn; ccard acc; CKE. *"Vg; reindeer on site."* **NOK 390, 1 May-30 Sep.** **2022**

JORPELAND *1A3* (5km SE Rural) *58.99925, 6.0922* **Preikestolen Camping (RO17),** Preikestolvegan 97, 4100 Jørpeland (Horda-Rogaland) **tel 47 48 19 39 50; info@preikestolencamping.com; www.preikestolencamping.com**

12 WD MSP

Fr S exit Rv13 to Preikestolen to R, site sp. Rd narr in places, care needed. Med, hdstg, unshd, EHU (16A) NOK40; sw nr; red long stay; phone; bus to Preikestolen parking; Eng spkn; adv bkg acc; ccard acc; games area; CKE. *"Marvellous views; poss walk to Pulpit Rock but not easy; conv Stavanger by ferry; excel facs, esp shwrs; midge repellent ess; long lead poss needed; poss no earth."* **NOK 326** **2022**

KARASJOK *2H1* (1km SW Rural) *69.46888, 25.48908* **Camping Karasjok,** Kautokeinoveien, 9730 Karasjok (Finnmark) **tel 97 07 22 25; post@karacamp.no; www.karacamp.no**

12 NOK200 (htd) WD nr

Sp in town; fr x-rds in town & N of rv bdge take Rv92 W dir Kautokeino, site 900m on L. 3*, Sm, pt shd, EHU (10A) inc; Eng spkn; adv bkg acc; ccard acc; CKE. *"Youth hostel & cabins on site; gd, clean site & facs; lge pitches suitable RVs & lge o'fits; sh walk to Sami park & museum."* **NOK 410** **2023**

KAUTOKEINO *2G1* (2.5km S Rural) *68.99760, 23.03662* **Arctic Motell & Kautokeino Camping,** Suomaluodda 16, 9520 Kautokeino (Finnmark) **tel 48 04 09 97; booking@arcticmotel.com; www.arcticmotel.com**

12 (htd)

Well sp fr Rv93. Sm, unshd, pt sl, EHU (10A); 20% statics; Eng spkn. *"No chem disp; Juhls silver gallery worth visit; gd, friendly site."* **NOK 325** **2024**

NORWAY

KILBOGHAMN *2E2* (3km S Coastal) *66.50667, 13.21608* **Polar Camp,** 8754 Kilboghamn (Nordland) **tel 75 09 71 86; post@polarcamp.com or booking@polarcamp.com; https://polarcamp.no/**

12 shgl adj

N on Rv17 sp to L just bef Kilboghamn ferry. Sm, hdstg, unshd, terr, EHU (10A) inc; 10% statics; phone; Eng spkn; fishing. *"Superb location on Arctic Circle; ltd san facs in high ssn; fishing/boat trips arranged; helpful owner; v welcoming."* **NOK 375 2023**

KINSARVIK *1B3* (0.5km SW Rural/Coastal) *60.37426, 6.71866* **Kinsarvik Camping,** RV13, 5780 Kinsarvik (Hordaland) **tel 53 66 32 90; evald@kinsarvikcamping.no; www.kinsarvikcamping.no**

12 nr

Fr SW edge of vill on rv. At Esso g'ge foll sp uphill fr cent of Kinsarvik. 3*, Sm, pt shd, EHU (10A) NOK30 (poss no earth); cooking facs; TV; 80% statics; bus 400m; fishing; CKE. *"Wonderful views over Hardanger Fjord; mv service pnt at Esso g'ge."* **NOK 284 2024**

KIRKENES *2H1* (92km SSW Rural) *69.21283, 29.15560* **Ovre Pasvik Camping,** Vaggetem, 9925 Svanvik **tel 95 91 13 05; atle.randa@pasvikcamping.no; www.pasvikcamping.no**

On the R of Rte 885. Sp fr rd. Sm, hdstg, pt shd, pt sl, EHU; bbq; cooking facs; 50% statics; Eng spkn; sauna; CKE. *"Clean facs, dated & basic; gd for birdwatching; fishing; canoeing; gd."*
NOK 250, Mid Apr-Mid Oct. 2022

KOLVEREID *2E3* (1.7km NW Rural/Coastal) *64.87142, 11.59048* **Kolvereid Familiecamping,** Nedre Kirkasen23, 7970 Kolvereid **tel 976 52727; alfebbe@online.no; www.kolvereidfamiliecamping.no**

12 (htd)

Fr 770 thro Kolvereid past church site to R (twrds Rorvik) sp to Norsjoen. 0.5k on L. Sm, hdstg, unshd, EHU; Eng spkn; ccard acc. *"NH only; near town with shops; cabins avail; simple site; pitch when arr, recep opens at 8pm; near lake; san facs ltd but clean."*
NOK 250 2022

KONGSVINGER *1D3* (10km S Rural) *60.11786, 12.05208* **Sigernessjøen Familiecamping,** Strenelsrud Gård, Arko-Vegen, 2210 Granli (Hedmark) **tel 40 60 11 22; post@sigernescamp.no; www.sigernescamp.no**

(htd)

On N side of Rv2 Kongsvinger to Swedish border, well sp. 3*, Med, pt shd, pt sl, EHU (10A) NOK40; sw nr; 30% statics; Eng spkn; golf adj. *"Gd."*
NOK 390, 1 May-30 Sep. 2023

KOPPANG *1D2* (3km W Rural) *61.57163, 11.01745* **Camping Koppang,** 2480 Koppang (Hedmark) **tel 62 46 02 34; info@koppangcamping.no; www.koppangcamping.no**

nr

Fr Rv3, 25km S of Atna, turn onto Rv30; site on L immed bef rv bdge. 4*, Med, pt shd, pt sl, EHU (16A) inc; gas; cooking facs; TV; 10% statics; Eng spkn; adv bkg acc; ccard acc; fishing.
NOK 350, 1 May-30 Sep. 2023

KRISTIANSAND *1B4* (12km NE Coastal) *58.19011, 8.08283* **Hamresanden Camping,** Hamresandveien 3, 4656 Hamresanden (Vest-Agder) **tel 38 14 42 80; info@hamresanden.com; www.hamresanden.com**

(htd) (htd) sand adj

Fr E18 foll sp Kjevik airport then Hamresanden & site. 3*, Lge, pt shd, EHU (10A) inc; cooking facs; TV; 10% statics; bus; Eng spkn; ccard acc; waterslide; boat hire; games area; tennis; watersports; bike hire.
NOK 295, 1 May-30 Sep. 2024

KRISTIANSAND *1B4* (12km E Rural) *58.12187, 8.06568* **Kristiansand Feriesenter,** Dvergsnesveien 571, 4639 Kristiansand (Vest-Agder) **tel 38 04 19 80; post@kristiansandferiesenter.no; www.krsferiesenter.no**

(htd)

Turn S off E18 jnc 91, 6km E of Kristiansand after Varoddbrua onto Rv401, cont for 5.5km foll sps to site. Rd narr last 3km. 5*, Lge, mkd, shd, sl, EHU (16A) inc; cooking facs; sw; TV; phone; ccard acc; boat hire; fishing; CKE. *"Gd NH; conv for ferry (20 mins); beautiful location; helpful, friendly staff."*
NOK 506, 16 Apr-16 Sep. 2024

KRISTIANSAND *1B4* (2.7km E Coastal) *58.14701, 8.0303* **(Formerly Camping Roligheden),** Framnesveien, 4632 Kristiansand (Vest-Agder) **tel 97 05 97 00 (dial 9 for info in English); post@dyreparken.no; www.dyreparken.no/gjesteinformasjon/roligheden-camping**

nr nr sand adj

Sp fr E18 on N side of town. 4*, Lge, pt shd, pt sl, EHU (25A) NOK40; 5% statics; bus; Eng spkn; ccard acc; CKE. *"Conv for ferry & exploring Kristiansand & district; 40 min walk to town; poss travellers; NH/sh stay only; site v run down; lovely coastal walks."*
NOK 300, 31 May-1 Sep. 2024

KRISTIANSAND *1B4* (23km E Coastal) *58.12551, 8.2310* **Skottevik Feriesenter (AA1),** Hæstadsvingen, 4770 Høvåg (Aust-Agder) **tel 37 26 90 30; post@skottevik.no; www.skottevik.no**

12 nr
nr (htd)

Fr Kristiansand, take E18 E, turn onto Rv401 twd Høvåg; site sp. 4*, Lge, pt shd, EHU (10A) NOK45; gas; Eng spkn; adv bkg acc; ccard acc; golf; CKE. *"Beautiful area; private bthrms avail; 9-hole golf course."* **NOK 205 2024**

KRISTIANSUND *1B1* (3km N Rural) *63.12543, 7.74106* **Atlanten Turistsenter (Formerly Atlanten Motel & Camping),** Dalaveien 22, 6501 Kristiansund (Møre og Romsdal) **tel 71 67 11 04; post@atlanten.no; www.atlanten.no**

12 (htd) WD MSP shgl 2km

Fr Atlantic Rd (Atlanterhavsveien) & Bremsnes-Kristiansund ferry, foll sp on leaving ferry 5km to site. Med, hdstg, pt shd, terr, EHU (6A) NOK40; bbq; cooking facs; phone; Eng spkn; adv bkg acc; ccard acc; CKE. *"Conv Kristiansund & fjords; pool 300m; boat trips to Grip Is with Stave Church; site clsd 20-31 Dec."*
NOK 170 **2024**

KROKSTRANDA *2F2* (0.3km SE Rural) *66.46233, 15.09344* **Krokstrand Camping,** Saltfjellveien 1573, 8630 Krokstranda (Nordland) **tel 75 16 60 02; toverakvaag@msn.com**

(htd) WD MSP

Nr Krokstrand bdge on E6, 18km S of Artic Circle & approx 50km N of Mo i Rana. 2*, Med, pt shd, pt sl, EHU (10A) NOK40; cooking facs; 20% statics; phone; train; Eng spkn; adv bkg acc; ccard acc; fishing; CKE. *"Conv Polar Circle Cent; gd; recep in café opp."*
NOK 420, 1 Jun-20 Sep. **2023**

KVISVIKA *1B1* (8km NE Coastal) *63.10910, 8.07875* **Magnillen Camping,** 6674 Kvisvika (Møre og Romsdal) **tel 71 53 25 59; jarl-mo@online.no; www.magnillen.no**

WD MSP

Fr W turn L off E39 approx 5km after Vettafjellet (N); thro Kvisvika & after another 9km turn L into site; sp. Sm, unshd, serviced pitches; EHU (10A) NOK30; gas; bbq; sw nr; red long stay; 50% statics; Eng spkn; adv bkg acc; ccard acc; boat hire; CKE. *"Site adj sm harbour; gd views."* **NOK 170** **2022**

LAERDALSOYRI *1B2* (26km E Rural) *61.06725, 7.82170* **Borgund Hyttesenter and Camping,** 6888 Borgund in Laerdal **tel 57 66 81 71 or 90 62 08 59 (mob); ovoldum@alb.no; hyttesenter.com**

12 WD MSP

Site on L of E16 just aft Borgunds Tunnel. Well sp in adv aft rd to Borgund Stave Church. Sm, hdstg, unshd, EHU (16A) NOK70; bbq; cooking facs; red long stay; TV; 10% statics; phone; bus 500m; Eng spkn; adv bkg acc; bike hire. *"Gd for Borgund Stave Church, Laerdal tunnel, Glacier ctr & historic rtes; gd."*
NOK 230 **2023**

LAERDALSOYRI *1B2* (0.8km NW Rural/Coastal) *61.10056, 7.47031* **Lærdal Ferie & Fritidspark,** Grandavegen 5, 6886 Lærdal (Sogn og Fjordane) **tel 57 66 66 95; info@laerdalferiepark.com; www.laerdalferiepark.com**

(htd) WD MSP shgl adj

Site on N side of Lærdal off Rv5/E16 adj Sognefjord. 4*, Med, unshd, EHU NOK40 (poss no earth); bbq; cooking facs; red long stay; TV; phone; Eng spkn; ccard acc; games rm; bike hire; golf 12km; boat hire; games area; tennis; CKE. *"Modern, clean, gd value site; excel san & cooking facs; lovely location adj fjord ferry terminal & nr attractive vill; gd touring base; friendly, helpful owners - will open on request outside dates shown; nice site next to Fjord; 10% discount for CAMC members; nr worlds longest tunnel."*
NOK 270, 27 Mar-25 Oct. **2024**

LANGFJORDBOTN *2G1* (1km S Rural) *70.02781, 22.2817* **Altafjord Camping,** 9545 Langfjordbotn (Finnmark) **tel 78 43 80 00; booking@altafjord-camping.no; www.altafjord-camping.no**

(htd) WD nr shgl

On E6, 600m S of exit to Bognelv, site adj to fjord across E6, sp. Dist by rd fr Alta 80km. 3*, Med, hdstg, unshd, terr, serviced pitches; EHU (16A); gas; cooking facs; sw; TV; 50% statics; phone; Eng spkn; ccard acc; fishing; sauna; bike hire. *"Friendly owner; excel views; boat hire; mountaineering."*
NOK 240, 1 Jun-1 Sep. **2022**

LARVIK *1C4* (1km S Urban) *59.04902, 10.03330* **Larvic Bobilparkering,** Tollerudden, Larvik (Vestfold) **www.bobilplassen.no**

12

Fr E18 exit at Rv303 twd Larvik. At rndabt take 1st exit onto Strandpromenaden. Sm, hdstg, unshd, EHU (3A); bbq. *"Gd; parking lot for m'vans; NH only; 8 mkd pitches, honesty box for payment."* **NOK 137** **2022**

LARVIK *1C4* (37km SSW Coastal) *59.00872, 9.70290* **Rognstranda Camping,** Rognsveien 146, 3960 Stathelle (Vestfold) **tel 35 97 39 11 or 92 04 56 61 (mob); post@rognstrandacamping.no; www.rognstrandacamping.no**

12 (htd) MSP sandy adj

Fr Larvik head SW on E18 for 34km. Turn L onto Tangvallveien, R onto Rognsveien. After 1.4km turn L. Then take 2nd L and 1st R. Site on L. Lge, unshd, pt sl, EHU (2 pin); twin axles; Eng spkn; adv bkg acc; CKE. *"Coastal walks; v clean modern facs; 2 areas for sh stay; site popular with MH for NH; vg."* **NOK 320** **2024**

NORWAY

LILLEHAMMER *1C2* (10km S Urban) *61.10275, 10.46278* **Camping Lillehammer,** Dampsagveien 47, 2609 Lillehammer (Oppland) **tel 61 25 33 33; resepsjon@lillehammer-camping.no; www.lillehammer-camping.no**

Exit E6 at Lillehammer Sentrum. Turn 1st R at 1st rndabt, foll rd around Strandtorget shopping cent, cont approx 1.5km along lakeside rd. 4*, Med, mkd, hdstg, unshd, EHU (10A) inc (check earth); gas; TV; phone; Eng spkn; adv bkg acc; ccard acc; CKE. *"Excel san facs, site adj Lake Mjøsa; gd views, conv town & skiing areas; site adj to c'van cent, spare parts etc; facs need updating."* **NOK 360** **2022**

MANDAL *1B4* (3.5km N Rural) *58.04213, 7.49436* **Sandnes Camping,** Holumsveien 133, 4516 Mandal (Vest-Agder) **tel 98 88 73 66; sandnescamping@online.no; www.sandnescamping.no**

On E39 Kristiansand to Stavanger. Turn N onto Rv455, site on R 1.4km. 3*, Med, hdstg, pt shd, EHU (16A) NOK40 (poss rev pol); bbq; cooking facs; sw nr; 5% statics; phone; Eng spkn; adv bkg acc; fishing; boating; CKE. *"Excel, well-kept site; friendly, helpful owners; superb scenery; nature trails thro adj pine forest; Mandal pretty town with longest sandy beach in Norway, conv Kristiansand ferry & Lindesnes, Norway's most S point."* **NOK 284, 1 May-1 Sep.** **2024**

MAURVANGEN *1C2* (0.1km SW Rural) *61.48838, 8.84176* **Maurvangen Hyttegrend Camping,** Besseggen Fjellpark, 2680 Maurvangen VÅGÅ (Oppland) **tel 61 23 89 22; post@maurvangen.no; www.maurvangen.no**

At rv bdge turn off Rv51. Foll sp. Med, hdstg, pt shd, pt sl, EHU (10A) inc; bbq; cooking facs; sw nr; TV; phone; Eng spkn; adv bkg acc; cycling; fishing; CKE. *"White water rafting; gd views; rd 51 poss clsd Nov to mid-May; gd hill walking cent; lovely site."* **NOK 300** **2022**

MELHUS *1C1* (8km NW Coastal) *63.32635, 10.21564* **Øysand Camping (ST38),** Øysandan, 7224 Melhus (Sør-Trøndelag) **tel 72 87 24 15 or 92 08 71 74 (mob); post@oysandcamping.no; www.oysandcamping.no**

Fr Melhus, N on E6; then L (W) onto E39; site sp. 2*, Med, mkd, unshd, EHU (10A) NOK50; bbq; cooking facs; sw nr; red long stay; phone; Eng spkn; ccard acc; games area; fishing adj; boating adj; CKE. *"Fair site with gd views; facs stretched if full; next to Fjord; beach open to day trippers; barrier clsd at night."* **NOK 240, 1 May-1 Sep.** **2024**

MO I RANA *2F2* (17km SW Rural) *66.23307, 13.89178* **Yttervik Camping,** Sørlandsveien 874, 8617 Dalsgrenda (Nordland) **tel 75 16 45 65 or 90 98 73 55 (mob); ranjas@online.no; www.yttervikcamping.no**

Sp S of Mo i Rana, on W side of E6, cross sm bdge over rlwy, diff for long o'fits. Sm, hdstg, mkd, unshd, EHU (16A) NOK 50 (no earth); 50% statics; Eng spkn; adv bkg acc; ccard acc; fishing; CKE. *"Pleasant location on edge fjord; friendly owners; clean, small well-run site; gd new facs (2015); rd works on E6, easier access to site in 2017; kitchen/diner; some road noise."* **NOK 350, 1 Jun-15 Sep.** **2023**

MOLDE *1B1* (4km E Rural) *62.74258, 7.2333* **Camping Kviltorp,** Fannestrandveien 140, 6400 Molde (Møre og Romsdal) **tel 71 21 17 42 or 47 90 14 83 05 (mob); kviltorp.camping@online.no; www.kviltorpcamping.no**

On app fr S, Rv64 (toll) turn L onto E39/Rv62, site on L, sp. Nr airport. 3*, Med, pt shd, pt sl, EHU (16A) NOK35; gas; sw nr; TV; phone; Eng spkn; ccard acc; solarium; boating; fishing; CKE. *"Conv Molde; adj Romsdal Fjord (some pitches avail on fjord-side); wonderful mountain views; excel, clean facs; helpful owners; aircraft & rd noise; gd site; pool 3km; cycle track into Molde; ltd c'van spaces."* **NOK 450** **2022**

MOSJOEN *2E3* (2km E Rural) *65.83453, 13.21971* **Topcamp Mosjøen (Formerly Mosjøen Camping),** Kippermoen, 8657 Mosjøen (Nordland) **tel 75 17 79 00; mosjoen@topcamp.no; topcamp.no/topcamp-mosjoen**

E6 by-passes town, well sp on W side of E6 by rndabt. Fr S only mkd by flag 500m bef rndabt at start Mosjøen bypass. 4*, Med, hdstg, unshd, terr, EHU (16A) inc; twin axles; TV; 40% statics; phone; Eng spkn; adv bkg acc; ccard acc; games rm; CKE. *"Clean, v basic san facs; gd site; gd kitchen facs and san facs, friendly staff; lge spmkt nrby; pizza rest; bowling alley; lively local ctr; gd."* **NOK 479** **2023**

NORDKAPP *2H1* (0.1km S Rural/Coastal) *71.16795, 25.78174* **Nordkapphallen Carpark,** 9764 Nordkapp (Finnmark) **tel 78 47 68 60; reservation.nordkapphallen@scandichotels.com; www.visitnordkapp.net/en/contact**

N on E69. Hdstg, unshd, pt sl, own san req. *"NOK 285 per person for 24hrs (max stay); no other o'night or site charges; 1 Nov-1 Apr private vehicles not permitted - buses in convoy (daily) only; price inc visit to Nordkapp Cent; no facs; very exposed gravel surface; excel for viewing midnight sun."* **NOK 209** **2024**

NOTODDEN *1C3* (1km W Rural) *59.55850, 9.24878* **Notodden Bobilcamp,** Nesøya 11, 3674 Notodden **tel 47 35 01 33 10; notcamp@notoddencamping.com; www.notoddencamping.com**

1km W of Notodden on the E134. Sm, hdstg, pt shd, bus/tram 1km. *"City run stop over; low charge for all facs except electric; no one on site, owner calls in evening."* **NOK 130** **2024**

ODDA *1A3* (2km S Rural) *60.0533, 6.5426* **Odda Camping,** Jordalsveien 29, 5750 Odda (Hordaland) **tel 94 14 12 79; post@oddacamping.no; www.oddacamping.no**

(htd) nr nr

Sp on Rv13; adj sports complex, nr lakeside. 3*, Med, pt shd, EHU (16A) NOK40; bbq; Eng spkn; games area; bike hire; watersports; lake fishing. *"Beautiful area; nr Hardanger Fjord; watersports with canoes for hire; private san facs avail; owner owns a guesthouse where you can use wifi & organise trips."* **NOK 400** **2022**

OLDEN *1B2* (22km S Rural) *61.66513, 6.81600* **Camping Melkevoll Bretun,** Oldedalen, 6792 Briksdalsbre (Sogn og Fjordane) **tel 57 87 38 64; post@melkevoll.no; www.melkevoll.no**

(htd)

Take rte to Briksdal glacier to end of rd. 4*, Med, hdg, unshd, terr, EHU (25A) NOK30; cooking facs; phone; Eng spkn; ccard acc; sauna. *"Walks to glacier; excel views glaciers some pitches; excel."* **NOK 170, 15 Apr-15 Oct.** **2024**

OPPDAL *1C1* (36.4km W Rural) *62.54191, 9.10602* **Gjora Camping,** Fjellgardsvegen 35, 6613 **tel 71 69 41 49 or 91 73 79 75; endre@nisja.no; www.nisja.no**

nr

35km W of Oppdal on Rv70. 1km fr Gjora centre. 3*, Sm, pt shd, EHU (10A) NOK50; cooking facs; twin axles; Eng spkn; adv bkg acc; ccard acc. *"In deep wooded valley on N side of Dovrefjell national pk; gd walking area, especially to Amotan waterfalls; many traditional wooden fmhses nrby; comfortable kitchen/diner; vg."* **NOK 220, 1 May-1 Oct.** **2023**

ORNES *2E2* (7km NW Rural) *66.91327, 13.62995* **Reipa Camping,** N 8140 Reipa **tel 75 75 57 74 or 90 95 60 47; post@reipacamping.com; www.reipacamping.com**

(htd)

Head NE on Havneveien twd Chr. Tidemanns vei/ Rv17, then turn R onto Havneveien/Fv456. Sm, EHU inc (16A); Eng spkn; adv bkg acc; ccard acc; CKE. *"Gd NH on classic Rv17."* **NOK 230** **2024**

OS I OSTERDALEN *1D1* (2km NE Rural) *62.50430, 11.25938* **Røste Hyttetun & Camping,** 2550 Os I Østerdalen (Sør-Trøndelag) **tel 62 49 70 55; post@rostecamping.no; www.rostecamping.no**

Sp on Rv30. 3*, Sm, EHU NOK40; cooking facs; TV; 10% statics; fishing 150m. **NOK 312** **2022**

OSLO *1C3* (5km SE Urban) *59.8984, 10.7734* **Topcamp Ekeberg (Formerly Ekeberg Camping),** Ekebergveien 65, 1181 Oslo **tel 22 19 85 68; ekeberg@topcamp.no; www.topcamp.no**

nr

Fr Göteborg to Oslo on E6 leave 2km bef Oslo; sp Ekeberg, foll sp to site. Fr S on E6 just after passing thro Oslo ent toll take slip rd sp Ekeberg; camp sp about 6km, up 10% hill. 3*, V lge, unshd, sl, EHU ltd (6-10A) inc (long lead poss req & poss rev pol); gas; bus/tram to city - tickets fr site recep; Eng spkn; ccard acc; CKE. *"Insufficient EHU & leads running across rds; area without hook-ups flatter & quieter; use san facs block taps for fresh water; easy access to Oslo cent & places of interest; avoid site during annual children's football tournament end Jul/beg Aug - queues for pitches & facs very stretched; poss ssn workers on site; recep open 0730-2300; helpful staff."* **NOK 355, 1 Jun-1 Sep.** **2024**

OSLO *1C3* (5km W Urban) *59.91802, 10.67554* **Sjølyst Marina Campervan Parking,** Drammensveien 160, Sjølyst Båtopplag, 0273 Oslo **tel 22 50 91 93; bobil@sjolystmarina.no; xn--sjlystmarina-wjb.no/bobil**

Fr E exit E18 at junc after Bygdøy (museums) junc. At rndabt take last exit, go under E18 & into site. Fr W leave E18 at Sjølyst junc, at bottom of slip rd turn R into site. Sm, hdstg, unshd, EHU inc; own san rec; bbq; bus adj; Eng spkn; clsd 2300-0700. *"Gd, basic site, pt of marina; m'vans only - pay at machine; san facs clsd o'night; 30 min walk city cent."* **NOK 300, 1 Jun-15 Sep.** **2022**

OSLO *1C3* (9km NW Urban) *59.9623, 10.6429* **Camping Bogstad,** Ankerveien 117, Røa, 0766 Oslo **tel 22 51 08 00; bogstad@topcamp.no; www.bogstadcamping.no**

(htd) nr

Fr N on E16 cont to E18 & turn E twd Oslo. After approx 7km exit & proceed N twds Røa and Bogstad. Site sp adj Oslo golf club. 4*, V lge, mkd, pt shd, pt sl, EHU (10A) NOK50 (long lead poss req); 25% statics; bus to Oslo 100m; Eng spkn; adv bkg acc; ccard acc; CKE. *"Beautiful area with walking trails; avoid area of site with statics & many ssn workers (behind recep), far end OK with lake views; modern, clean san facs; helpful staff; recep open 24 hrs; conv Oslo cent; bus stop nrby, bus every 10 mins; lake nrby; 30 mins to cent; gd."* **NOK 650** **2020**

NORWAY

PORSGRUNN *1C4* (5km SE Rural) *59.11183, 9.71208* **Camping Olavsberget,** Nystrandveien 64, 3944 Porsgrunn (Vestfold) 35 51 12 05 **tel 91 37 74 70; irene@olavsbergetcamping.no; www.yourvisma website.com/olavsberget-camping-1**

12 (icons) sand adj

Leave E18 at Eidanger onto Rv354 N; foll camp sp for 1km; site on L. Fr Porsgrunn foll Rv36 S; just bef E18 junc turn L; foll sp as above. Med, unshd, pt sl, EHU (16A) NOK30 (no earth); 60% statics; Eng spkn; CKE. *"Well-run site; public access to beach thro site; gd walks in wood; visits to Maritime Brevik & mineral mine, Porsgrunn porcelain factory & shop, Telemark Canal inc boat tour."* **NOK 200** **2024**

RISOR *1C4* (18km SW Coastal) *58.69083, 9.16333* **Sørlandet Feriecenter,** Sandnes, 4950 Risør **tel 37 15 40 80; sorferie@online.no; www.sorlandet-feriesenter.no**

12 (htd) (icons) sand

Fr N take E18 to Sørlandsporten then Rv416 to Risør, then Rv411 to Laget. Foll sp Sørlandet. Fr S exit E18 at Tvedestrand & cont to Laget, then foll site sp. Site is 20km by rd fr Risør. 4*, Med, mkd, pt shd, EHU inc; cooking facs; TV (pitch); 10% statics; Eng spkn; adv bkg acc; bike hire; games rm; boat hire; tennis 1km; watersports. *"Fitness rm; private san facs avail."* **NOK 392** **2024**

RISOR *1C4* (10km W Coastal) *58.72592, 9.07783* **Risør Resort Moen Camping,** 4950 Risor **tel 90 98 19 02; resepsjon@risorresort.no; www.risorresort.no**

12 (htd) (icons) sand

Fr E18 S, L onto 416 twds Risor. Site sp on L. Med, unshd, bbq; cooking facs; TV; 90% statics; Eng spkn; ccard acc; games area; CCI. *"Well cared for, popular site; EHU & water widely spaced; volleyball; boat hire."* **NOK 400** **2024**

RODBERG *1C3* (6.5km SE Rural) *60.23533, 9.0040* **Fjordgløtt Camping,** Vrenne, 3630 Rødberg (Buskerud) **tel 32 74 13 35 or 97 15 96 53 (mob); info@fjordglott.net; www.fjordglott.net**

12 (htd) (icons)

Fr Rødberg on Rv40 dir Kongsberg, take R turn sp Vrenne, cross bdge & foll sp past power stn. 4*, Med, mkd, pt shd, terr, serviced pitches; EHU (16A) NOK30; sw; 40% statics; phone; Eng spkn; ccard acc; fishing; sauna; CKE. *"Lovely views of fjord; excel facs; well kept."* **NOK 268** **2024**

RODBERG *1C3* (10km W Rural) *60.26602, 8.78878* **Uvdal Resort,** N-3632 Uvdal (Buskerud) **tel 32 74 31 08; post@campuvdalcom; campuvdal.com**

(htd) (icons)

Fr Rodberg, take Rv40 W for about 9km. Site on R. Sm, EHU (16A) 30nok; Eng spkn; ccard acc; games area; CKE. *"Family run; level site by rv; fishing & kayaking; vg site."* **NOK 190, 1 May-30 Sep.** **2024**

ROLDAL *1B3* (0.5km E Rural) *59.83103, 6.82888* **Røldal Hyttegrend & Camping,** Kyrkjevegen 49, 5760 Røldal (Hordaland) **tel 07 90 05 44 64; adm@roldal-camping.no; www.roldal-camping.no**

12 (htd) (icons)

Fr E on E134 turn L on ent vill, site sp. 4*, Sm, pt shd, EHU (10A) NOK30; gas; cooking facs; sw nr; TV; 20% statics; phone; Eng spkn; adv bkg acc; ccard acc; CKE. *"Gd walking, angling."* **NOK 206** **2024**

ROLDAL *1B3* (1km SW Rural) *59.83012, 6.81061* **Seim Camping,** 5760 Røldal (Horda-Rogaland) **tel 53 64 73 71 or 97 53 35 17 (mob) or 90 91 90 63 (mob); seim@seimcamp.no; www.seimcamp.no**

12 (htd) (icons) nr nr nr

App fr SW on E134, site sp at ent town. Turn R off main rd & R again. 3*, Med, pt shd, pt sl, EHU (20A) NOK40; Eng spkn; boating; fishing; CKE. *"Gd walks; beautiful views; prehistoric burial mounds & museum on site; poss rd noise."* **NOK 258** **2024**

ROROS *1D1* (0.6km S Urban) *62.57078, 11.38295* **Idrettsparken Hotel & Camping,** Øra 25, 7374 Røros (Sør-Trøndelag) **tel 72 41 10 89; ihotell@online.no; www.idrettsparken.no**

(htd) (icons) nr

Heading twd Trondheim on Rv30 to Røros cent, turn L at rndabt into Peter Møllersvei, over rlwy line, L again & foll sp to site. Sm, unshd, EHU (16A) NOK35. *"Tours of museums & mines; nature reserve & nature park nr; no chem disp - use dump point at fire stn on Rv30; fair NH."* **NOK 300, 1 May-30 Sep.** **2024**

SARPSBORG *1D4* (10km NW Rural) *59.31800, 10.98049* **Utne Camping,** Desideriasvei 43, 1719 Greaker **tel 47 69 14 71 26; post@utnecamping.no; www.utnecamping.no**

12 (htd) (icons)

Leave E6 at junc 9 sp Sollikrysset. Take 118 S (Desiderias vei), 2km to site on R. 3*, Sm, unshd, pt sl, EHU (10A) NOK120; bbq; twin axles; TV; bus adj; Eng spkn; adv bkg acc; ccard acc; games area; CKE. *"Conv acc fr E6; pleasant open site; excel."* **NOK 31** **2023**

SKIBOTN *2G1* (0.4km N Coastal) *69.39397, 20.26797* **NAF Camping Skibotn,** 9143 Skibotn (Troms) **tel 77 71 52 77; www.nafcamp.no/en/camping plasser/3193-Skibotn-Camping**

(icons)

On W of E6 400m N of town. Sm, unshd, pt sl, EHU (10A) NOK25; gas; cooking facs; Eng spkn; fishing. *"NH only, dir access to beach on fjord."* **NOK 200, 1 Jun-31 Aug.** **2024**

SKIBOTN *2G1* (1km SE Rural) *69.38166, 20.29528* **Olderelv Camping (TR30),** 9048 Skibotn (Troms) **tel 77 71 54 44 or 91 13 17 00 (mob); firmapost@olderelv.no; www.olderelv.no**

W of E6 1km N of junc at E8. 4*, Lge, mkd, hdstg, unshd, pt sl, EHU (16A) NOK40; bbq; cooking facs; twin axles; 80% statics; phone; Eng spkn; adv bkg acc; ccard acc; solarium; sauna. *"Well-maintained & clean; dryest area of Troms; vg walking; v busy; vg; car wash."* **NOK 290, 15 May-1 Sep. 2024**

SKJOLDEN *1B2* (3km E Rural) *61.48453, 7.6505* **Vassbakken Camping,** RV 55, 6876 Skjolden (Romsdal SogneFjord) **tel 57 68 61 88 or 57 68 67 00; info@vassbakken.com; www.skjolden.com/vassbakken**

Site on Rv55. Sm, pt shd, EHU (10A) NOK30; sw nr; TV; phone; Eng spkn; ccard acc; fishing adj; sauna. *"Mountain setting; waterfall ad, gd walking & fishing; ltd facs until June."* **NOK 254, 1 May-20 Sep. 2024**

SOGNDALSFJORA *1B2* (15km NE Rural) *61.30738, 7.21500* **Lyngmo Camping (SF16),** Lyngmovegen 12, 6869 Hafslo (Sogn of Fjordane) **tel 57 68 43 66; lyngmo@lyngmoinfo.com; www.lyngmoinfo.com**

Fr Rv55 Sogndal-Gaupne turn L at sp Galden. Immed turn R at camping sp & foll gravel rd down to site on lakeside. 2*, Sm, unshd, pt sl, EHU; cooking facs; sw; 10% statics; phone; Eng spkn; ccard acc; fishing; CKE. *"Beautiful location; steep hill to san facs block."* **19 Jun-24 Aug. 2024**

"I need an on-site restaurant"

We do our best to make sure site information is correct, but it is always best to check any must-have facilities are still available or will be open during your visit.

SOGNDALSFJORA *1B2* (4.5km SE Coastal) *61.2118, 7.12106* **Kjornes Camping & Fjordhytter (Formerly Camping Kjørnes),** 6856 Sogndal (Sogn og Fjordane) **tel 57 67 45 80 or 97 54 41 56 (mob); camping@kjornes.no; www.kjornes.no**

Fr W foll sp in Sogndal for Kaupanger/Lærdal (Rv5) over bdge. Fr E (Rv55) turn L at T-junc with rd 5 over bdge. Site on R; sharp R turn into narr lane (passing places); site ent on R in approx 500m. 4*, Med, hdstg, unshd, pt sl, terr, EHU (10-16A) NOK40 (no earth); cooking facs; twin axles; red long stay; 20% statics; phone; bus 500m; Eng spkn; adv bkg acc; ccard acc; boat launch; fishing; CKE. *"Useful for ferries; stunning location on edge of fjord; superb san facs, the best!; excel site; v highly rec."* **NOK 290 2024**

SOGNDALSFJORA *1B2* (0.1km S Rural) *61.22490, 7.10218* **Stedje Camping,** Kyrkjevegen 2, 6851 Sogndal (Sogn og Fjordane) **tel 57 67 10 12; post@scamping.no; www.scamping.no**

W fr Hella to Sogndal, turn L off Rv55 adj Shell petrol stn, site clearly sp, narr ent. 4*, Med, pt shd, sl, EHU (16A) NOK40 (check earth); sw nr; TV; Eng spkn; watersports; solarium; bike hire; CKE. *"1st gd site after Vangsnes-Hella ferry - in orchard; poss poor facs early ssn; poss v diff in wet for lge m' vans; conv visit to 12th C Urnes stave church."* **NOK 140, 1 Jun-31 Aug. 2024**

SPANGEREID *1A4* (8km S Coastal) *57.99593, 7.09003* **Lindesnes Camping,** Lillehavn, 4521 Spangereid (Vest-Agder) **tel 38 25 88 74 or 91 60 22 76 (mob); gabrielsen@lindesnescamping.no; www.lindesnescamping.no**

Fr E39 at Vigeland turn S onto Rv460 sp Lindesnes lighthouse (Fyr). Approx 8km after vill of Spangereid turn L sp Lillehavn, site sp. Sm, pt shd, pt sl, EHU (16A) NOK40; bbq; cooking facs; phone; Eng spkn; adv bkg acc; ccard acc; CKE. *"Excel, clean, well-run site; pitches not mkd adv early arr."* **NOK 210, 1 Apr-30 Sep. 2024**

STAVANGER *1A3* (3.5km SW Rural) *58.9525, 5.71388* **Mosvangen Camping,** Henrik Ibsens Gate, 4021 Stavanger (Rogaland) **tel 51 53 29 71; post@stavangercamping.no; www.stavangercamping.no**

Fr Stavanger foll sp E39/Rv510; site well sp. Fr Sandnes on E39 exit Ullandhaug; foll camp sp. Med, hdstg, pt shd, sl, EHU (10A) NOK40 (no earth & poss intermittent supply); cooking facs; sw nr; phone; bus; Eng spkn; ccard acc; CKE. *"Excel for wooden city of Stavanger; easy, pleasant walk to town cent; soft grnd in wet weather; facs well used but clean but stretched when site full; helpful manager; excel rustic type of site; bus to cent nr ent."* **NOK 336 2022**

STEINKJER *2E3* (14km N Rural) *64.10977, 11.57816* **Follingstua Camping,** Haugåshalla 6, 7732 Steinkjer (Nord-Trøndelag) **tel 74 14 71 90; post@follingstua.no; www.follingstua.com**

N on E6, site on R, well sp. 3*, Sm, mkd, hdstg, unshd, terr, EHU (16A) NOK50; bbq; twin axles; TV; 60% statics; phone; bus 200m; Eng spkn; adv bkg acc; bike hire; boating; fishing. *"Excel san facs down 10 steps; lake adj; some lakeside pitches; nr Gold Rd tour of local craft & food producers; excel."* **NOK 295 2023**

STEINKJER *2E3* (2km E Urban) *64.02246, 11.50745* **Camping Guldbergaunet,** Elvenget 34, 7716 Steinkjer (Nord-Trøndelag) **tel 74 16 20 45; g-book@online.no; guldbergaunetcamping.no**

(htd) nr nr nr

E fr town cent on E6. Foll Rv762 at 2km L past school. Site at end. 3*, Med, mkd, pt shd, pt sl, EHU 10; bbq; cooking facs; sw nr; twin axles; Eng spkn; adv bkg acc; ccard acc; fishing. *"On peninsula bet two rvs; friendly; gd NH; facs up stairs; 10 mins walk to town along rv; gd."* **NOK 240** **2024**

STOREN *1C1* (1.5km NE Rural) *63.04465, 10.29078* **Vårvolden Camping (ST17),** Volløyan 3A, 7290 Støren (Sør-Trøndelag) **tel 47 75 23 30; varvolden.camping@gauldalen.no; www.facebook.com/people/V%C3%A5rvolden-Camping/100033841465394/**

(htd) nr nr

Leave E6 for Støren & foll site sp. 4*, Sm, unshd, EHU (16A); cooking facs; 20% statics; Eng spkn; CKE. *"Vg."* **NOK 202, 15 May-1 Sep.** **2024**

STORJORD *2F2* (1km SSE Rural) *66.81317, 15.40055* **Saltdal Turistsenter,** 8255 Storjord (Nordland) **tel 75 68 24 50; post@isaltal.no; isaltdal.no**

(htd)

Site is 35km S of Rognan by-pass on E6, 700m N of junc of Rv77, adj filling stn. Med, hdstg, mkd, pt shd, terr, EHU (10A) NOK25; bbq; cooking facs; 99% statics; phone; Eng spkn; adv bkg acc; CKE. *"M'way-style service stn & lorry park; tightly packed cabins & statics; 10 pitches only for tourers; excel rv walks fr site; beautiful area; NH only; secure barrier; clean facs, could be stretched if full."* **NOK 305** **2024**

STRYN *1B2* (10km E Rural) *61.93347, 6.88640* **Mindresunde Camping (SF43),** 6783 Stryn (Sogn og Fjordane) **tel 57 87 75 32 or 41 56 63 16 (mob); post@mindresunde.no; www.mindresunde.no**

(htd) shgl

2nd site on Rv15 on N side of rd. 3*, Sm, mkd, unshd, pt sl, EHU inc (earth prob); TV; Eng spkn; adv bkg acc; car wash; CKE. *"Well-kept, pleasant site; many pitches on lake; friendly staff; site yourself; vg views; excel facs; conv Geiranger, Briksdal glacier & Strynefjellet summer ski cent; gd walking."* **NOK 289, 1 May-31 Oct.** **2024**

STRYN *1B2* (12km E Rural) *61.9314, 6.92121* **Strynsvatn Camping,** Meland, 6783 Stryn (Sogn og Fjordane) **tel 57 87 75 43; camping@strynsvatn.no; www.strynsvatn.no**

On Rv15 Lom to Stryn, on L. 4*, Sm, unshd, terr, EHU (10A) inc (poss earth fault); TV; 20% statics; Eng spkn; adv bkg acc; ccard acc; sauna; CKE. *"Superb site; lake adj; excel facs & v clean, gd views/walking; v friendly owners."* **NOK 336, 1 May-30 Sep.** **2022**

TANA *2H1* (5km SE Rural) *70.1663, 28.2279* **Tana Familiecamping,** Skiippagurra, 9845 Tana (Finnmark) **tel 78 92 86 30; booking@famcamp.no; famcamp.no**

(htd)

On ent Tana fr W, cross bdge on E6, heading E sp Kirkenes; site on L in approx 4km. 3*, Sm, unshd, pt sl, EHU (16A); bbq; Eng spkn; ccard acc; sauna. **NOK 250, 1 May-1 Nov.** **2022**

TENNEVOLL *2F2* (5km SW Rural) *68.67881, 17.91421* **Lapphaugen Turiststasjon,** General Fleischers Vei 365, 9357 Tennevoll **tel 77 17 71 27; postmaster@lapphaugen.no; www.lapphaugen.no**

On the L of E6 approx 60km N of Narvik. Sm, hdstg, unshd, pt sl, terr, EHU (16A) NOK40; bbq; cooking facs; red long stay; 50% statics; Eng spkn; adv bkg acc. *"Gd; sm to med pitches."* **NOK 300, 12 Feb-16 Dec.** **2022**

TINN AUSTBYGD *1B3* (8km S Rural) *59.98903, 8.81665* **Sandviken Camping (TE13),** 3650 Tinn Austbygd (Telemark) **tel 35 09 81 73; post@sandviken-camping.no; www.sandviken-camping.no**

(htd)

Site is off Rv364 on L after passing thro Tinn Austbygd. 4*, Med, pt shd, EHU (10A) NOK35 (check earth); gas; bbq; cooking facs; sw; TV; 10% statics; phone; Eng spkn; games area; boat hire; sauna; games rm; CKE. *"Superb, peaceful location at head of Lake Tinnsjø; sh walk thro woods to shops & bank; conv for museum at Rjukan heavy water plant."* **NOK 450** **2022**

TJOTTA *2E3* (26km N Rural) *65.94692, 12.46255* **Sandnessjøen Camping,** Steiro, 8800 Sandnessjøen, Norge **tel 97 56 20 50 or 75 04 54 40; post@ssj.no; www.ssj.no**

(htd)

Head NW on Rv17 twrds Parkveien. Site is on R. Sm, unshd, pt sl, EHU; bbq; cooking facs; Eng spkn; ccard acc. *"Excel san facs; fjord views; gd hiking & fishing; excel site."* **NOK 250, 1 May-31 Aug.** **2024**

TOSBOTN *2 E3* (550km E Rural) *65.32508, 12.97020* **Tosbotn Camping,** Tosbotn, 8960 Tosbotnet **tel 75 02 61 50; mhermann1955@gmail.com; tosbotn-camping.no**

shingle (1km)

In Tosbotn, sp off Fv76. 25km W of E6, 70km E Bronnoysund. Sm, pt shd, EHU (10A) inc; bbq; sw nr; twin axles; Eng spkn; adv bkg acc; ccard acc. *"V ltd area for campers; boats for hire; facs poor; NH only."* **NOK 300** **2023**

TREUNGEN *1B4* (18km N Rural) *59.15560, 8.50611* **Søftestad Camping,** Nissedal, 3855 Treungen (Aust-Agder) **tel 48 15 95 00; softestadcamping@gmail.com; www.facebook.com/Softestad**

N fr Kristiansand on Rv41 to Treungen, then alongside E edge of Nisser Water to Nissedal, site sp. Sm, shd, EHU (10A) inc; bbq; red long stay; phone; bus adj; Eng spkn; adv bkg acc; CKE. *"Close to Telemarken heavy water plant; beautiful alt rte N fr Kristiansand - rd suitable for towed c'vans; gorgeous views over lake."* **NOK 162, 1 May-1 Sep. 2024**

TROGSTAD *1D3* (6km N Rural) *59.68888, 11.29275* **Olberg Camping,** Olberg, Sandsveien 4, 1860 Trøgstad (Østfold) **tel 07 41 76 56 72; camping@olberg.no; www.olberg.no**

(htd) 3km

Fr Mysen on E18 go N on Rv22 for approx 20km dir Lillestrøm. Site is 2km 2 of Båstad. 3*, Sm, hdg, pt shd, EHU (10-16A) NOK35; bbq; red long stay; TV; phone; Eng spkn; adv bkg acc; ccard acc; tennis 200m; fishing; CKE. *"Site on lge, working farm with elk safaris; local bread & crafts; farm museum; conv Oslo (40km); v helpful staff; ice-skating; gd for NH or longer."* **NOK 274, 1 May-1 Oct. 2024**

TROMSO *2F1* (27km NE Coastal) *69.77765, 19.38273* **Aera (Formerly Skittenelv Camping),** Ullstindveien 736, 9022 Krokelvdalen (Troms) **tel 48251171; hello@aeranord.no; www.aeranord.no**

(htd) (htd)

Fr S end of Tromsø Bdge on E8, foll sps to Kroken & Oldervik. Site on N side of rd Fv53. 4*, Med, hdstg, unshd, EHU (10A) NOK50; bbq; TV; 10% statics; ccard acc; waterslide; fishing; sauna; games rm; CKE. *"Beautiful situation on edge of fjord; arctic sea birds; some facs dated but nice; location o'looking Fjord."* **NOK 320, 15 May-30 Sep. 2024**

TROMSO *2F1* (5km E Rural) *69.64735, 19.01505* **Tromsø Camping,** 9020 Tromsdalen (Troms) **tel 77 63 80 37; post@tromsocamping.no; www.tromsocamping.no**

12 nr

At rndabt on edge of Tromsø take 2nd exit under E8 bdge. Shortly turn R & foll sp. Do not cross narr bdge but turn R then fork L to site. 3*, Sm, unshd, EHU (10-16A) NOK50; Eng spkn; CKE. *"V busy site; surrounded by fast rv after rain; rec visit to Arctic church at midnight; many improvements; gd san facs."* **NOK 475 2022**

TRONDHEIM *1C1* (14km W Rural) *63.45004, 10.20230* **Flakk Camping (ST19),** 7070 Flakk (Sør-Trøndelag) **tel 07 94 05 46 85; contact@flakk-camping.no; www.flakk-camping.no**

nr

Fr N on E6 to Trondheim cent, then foll sp Fosen onto Rv715 W; site sp & adj Flakk ferry terminal; fr S to Trondheim take Rv707 to site & ferry. 3*, Med, unshd, pt sl, EHU (10A) NOK40 (check earth); bus to city; Eng spkn; adv bkg acc; ccard acc; CKE. *"V well-kept site; clean facs; pleasant view over fjord; parts poss muddy after rain; site by ferry terminal (Need to be on R), some ferry noise at night; helpful owner; no earth on elec."* **NOK 440, 1 May-1 Sep. 2022**

ULSVAG *2F2* (3km NE Coastal) *68.13273, 15.89699* **Sorkil Fjordcamping,** Sorkil 8276 **tel 75 77 16 60 or 41 66 08 42 (mob); kontakt@sorkil.no; www.sorkil.no**

(htd) adj

Head NE fr Ulsvag on E6, turn R in abt 2.7km onto site. Sm, mkd, unshd, pt sl, EHU (16A) NOK40; bbq; Eng spkn. *"Lovely site S of ferry; adj Fjord excel for midnight sun and fishing."* **1 May-30 Sep. 2024**

UTVIKA *1C3* (0.5km N Rural) *60.02972, 10.26316* **Utvika Camping (BU14),** Utstranda 263, 3531 Utvika (Buskerud) **tel 32 16 06 70; post@utvika.no; www.utvika.no**

Site on loop rd fr E16 N of Nes twd Hønefoss. Site sp but sp opp site ent v sm. Med, mkd, hdstg, unshd, pt sl, EHU (10A) NOK30; sw nr; twin axles; TV (pitch); 80% statics; Eng spkn; adv bkg acc; CKE. *"Conv Oslo (40km) & better than Oslo city sites; busy, friendly site; san facs inadequate when busy."* **NOK 330, 1 May-1 Oct. 2023**

VADSO *2H1* (18km W Coastal) *70.11935, 29.33155* **Vestre Jakobselv Camping,** Lilledalsveien 6, 9801 Vestre Jakobselv (Finnmark) **tel 78 95 60 64; post@vj-camping.no; www2.vj-camping.no**

12 nr

E fr Tana for approx 50km on E6/E75 dir Vadsø, site sp, 1km N of Vestre Jakobselv. Sm, hdstg, pt shd, EHU (10A) NOK40; cooking facs; 10% statics; bus 1km; Eng spkn; ccard acc; CKE. *"Conv Vadsø & Vardø - interesting towns."* **NOK 278 2022**

VAGAMO *1C2* (1km S Rural) *61.86950, 9.10291* **Smedsmo Camping,** Vågåvegen 80, 2680 Vågåmo (Oppland) **tel 481 21 118; post@smedsmo.no; https://smedsmo.no/**

12

Behind petrol stn on Rv15 twd Lom. 3*, Med, hdstg, unshd, EHU (16A) NOK40; bbq; cooking facs; twin axles; TV; 50% statics; Eng spkn; adv bkg rec; ccard acc; CKE. *"Gd touring base; site now sep fr g'ge; fair."* **NOK 290 2023**

NORWAY

VALLE *1B3* (12km N Rural) *59.2441, 7.4753* **Flateland Camping & Hyttesenter,** 4747 Valle (Aust-Agder) **tel 95 00 55 00; flateland.camping@broadpark.no; www.flatelandcamping.no**

(htd) nr

On W side of Rv9 to Bykle, 1km N of junc with Rv45 Dalen. 2*, Med, pt shd, pt sl, EHU (10A) NOK30; bbq; cooking facs; 20% statics; Eng spkn; ccard acc; boat hire; CKE. *"Pleasant; site yourself; fee collected pm; water trampolin; rvside walks; climbing; excel site."* **NOK 160, 1 Jun-1 Sep.** **2024**

VANG *1B2* (1.7km NW Rural) *61.13032, 8.54352* **Bøflaten Camping,** 2975 Vang I Valdres (Sogn og Fjordane) **tel 90 60 04 89; info@boflaten.com; www.boflaten.com**

(htd) nr

Sp on E16 55km NW of Fagernes. 4*, Sm, pt shd, EHU (10A) NOK40; bbq (charcoal, gas); cooking facs; sw nr; twin axles; 10% statics; phone; Eng spkn; ccard acc; games area; CKE. *"Beautiful area; lakeside; useful NH & gd winter sports site; walks nrby; guided excursions; boat, canoe, bike & TV hire; excel."* **NOK 326** **2022**

VANGSNES *1B2* (3km S Rural) *61.14515, 6.62330* **Tveit Camping (SF32),** 6894 Vangsnes (Sogn og Fjordane) **tel 91 14 18 79; post@tveitcamping.no; www.tveitcamping.no**

(htd) nr nr

On Rv13; sp. 3*, Sm, pt shd, terr, EHU (10A) NOK25; red long stay; TV; 30% statics; phone; boating; bike hire; boat hire; CKE. *"Sw poss off rocky shore; views of Sognefjord."* **NOK 221, 4 May-25 Sep.** **2022**

VASSENDEN *1A2* (2km SW Rural) *61.48785, 6.08366* **PlusCamp Jølstraholmen,** 6847 Vassenden (Sogn og Fjordane) **tel 95 29 78 79; post@jolstraholmen.no; www.jolstraholmen.no**

(htd)

On R of E39, site is 2km SW of Vassenden at Statoil petrol stn. 4*, Med, hdg, pt shd, pt sl, terr, EHU (10-16A) NOK40; bbq; sw; TV (pitch); 70% statics; Eng spkn; ccard acc; fishing; CKE. *"Rv flows thro site; gd facs; ski lift 500m; friendly site; ltd facs for tourers; NH."* **NOK 286** **2022**

VEGA *2E3* (6km S Rural) *65.64353, 11.95110* **Vega Camping,** 8980 Vega **tel 959 73 616; post@vegacamping.no; www.vegacamping.no**

(htd)

Fr Fv90 head NW, take 1st L onto Fv90, turn L twd Fv84, turn R onto Fv84. After 1.6km turn L, then take 2nd L. Site in 450m. Sm, unshd, EHU (16A) inc; cooking facs; sw; Eng spkn. *"Island ideal for cycling/walking; Elder Duck cent; beautiful location; cash only; excel site."* **NOK 250** **2024**

VESTBY *1C3* (3km N Rural) *59.62620, 10.73126* **Vestby Gjestegard & Hyttepark,** Hytteveien 11, 1540 Vestby **tel 47 64 95 98 00; info@vestbyhyttepark.co; www.vestbyhyttepark.no**

Junc 17 on E6. Foll sp. Site behind Esso stn on W of E6. Sm, hdstg, unshd, pt sl, 90% statics; Eng spkn; ccard acc; CKE. *"Limited touring space, mainly chalets; NH only."* **NOK 210** **2022**

VIKOYRI *1B2* (0.2km N Rural) *61.08884, 6.57721* **Vik Camping,** 6891 Vikøyri (Sogn og Fjordane) **tel 57 69 51 25; vikcamping.business.site**

(htd) nr

Sp in cent of Vikøyri dir Ligtvor; 67km N of Voss on Rv13. 2*, Sm, unshd, EHU (10A) (no earth); Eng spkn; CKE. *"Conv for ferry fr Vangsnes, easier access than other sites; gd NH."* **NOK 192, 1 May-30 Sep.** **2022**

VIKSDALEN *1A2* (12km SE Rural) *61.32628, 6.26926* **Hov Camping,** Eldalsdalen, 6978 Viksdalen (Sogn og Fjordane) **tel 57 71 79 37 or 911 88 466 (mob); ottarhov@c2i.net; www.viksdalen.no/hov-hyttegrend**

(htd)

Fr Dragsvik N on Rv13, site is approx 9km S of junc with Rv610, sp. Sm, hdstg, unshd, EHU (8-10A)inc; Eng spkn; ccard acc; bike hire; fishing; CKE. *"Attractive site with boating on lake; wcs by parking area; all other facs 150m; remote area."* **NOK 180, 1 Apr-30 Sep.** **2024**

VOSS *1A2* (0.3km S Rural) *60.62476, 6.42235* **Voss Camping,** Prestegardsmoen 40, 5700 Voss (Hordaland) **tel 56 51 15 97; post@vosscamping.no; www.vosscamping.no**

(htd) nr (htd)

Exit town on E16 & camping sp; by lake nr cent of Voss; app fr W on E16, site visible by lake on R; 2nd turn on R in town to site in 300m. Sm, mkd, hdstg, pt shd, terr, EHU (10A) NOK45; 10% statics; phone; Eng spkn; ccard acc; watersports; bike hire; boat hire; CKE. *"Excel cent for fjords; cable car stn in walking dist; tourist bureau; lake adj; most pitches hdstg gravel but narr/sm."* **NOK 408, 1 May-1 Oct.** **2024**

LOFOTEN ISLANDS

RAMBERG *2E2* (7km W Rural) *68.0975, 13.1619* **Strand & Skærgårdscamping,** 8387 Fredvang **tel 41 60 78 41; mail@fredvangcamping.no; www.fredvangcamp.no**

(htd) sand adj

Foll Fredvang sp fr E10; site sp in vill cent. Sm, unshd, EHU (16A) NOK25; cooking facs; TV (pitch); Eng spkn; boat launch; boat hire; washing machine NOK20; dryer NOK20; CKE. *"View of midnight sun; surrounded by sand beach, sea & mountains; peaceful; gd san facs, tired (unisex), stretched when busy; friendly."* **NOK 300, 20 May-31 Aug.** **2024**

SORVAGEN *2E2* (3km N Coastal) *67.90017, 13.04656* **Moskenes Camping,** 8392 Sørvågen **tel 99 48 94 05; info@moskenescamping.no; www.moskenes camping.no**

(htd) nr

Fr ferry turn L, then immed R opp terminal exit, site up sh unmade rd, sp. Med, hdstg, unshd, terr, EHU (16A) NOK20 (no earth); Eng spkn. *"Excel NH; gd san facs."* **NOK 283, 1 May-15 Sep.** **2023**

"Satellite navigation makes touring much easier"

Remember most sat navs don't know if you're towing or in a larger vehicle – always use yours alongside maps and site directions.

STAMSUND *2F2* (15km N Rural/Coastal) *68.20429, 13.88580* **Brustranda Sjøcamping,** Rolfsfjord, 8356 Leknes **tel 76 08 71 00; post@brustranda.no; www.brustranda.no**

shgl adj

Take E10 W fr Svolvaer ferry for approx 19km. After 3rd bdge turn L onto Rv815. Site on L in 22km. 4*, Sm, pt shd, EHU (10A) NOK70 (poss rev pol); 30% statics; Eng spkn; boat hire; fishing. *"Idyllic setting; mountain views; beach sand 2km; v helpful staff; san facs stretched when site full; highly rec."* **NOK 250, 1 Jun-31 Aug.** **2023**

SVOLVAER *2F2* (15km W Coastal) *68.20573, 14.42576* **Sandvika Fjord & Sjøhuscamping (N09),** Ørsvågveien 45, 8310 Kabelvåg **tel 76 07 45 00; post@lofotferie.no; www.lofotferie.no/sandvika-camping**

Sp on S of E10; app lane thro 1 other site. 4*, Lge, mkd, unshd, terr, EHU (16A) NOK35 (poss rev pol); TV; phone; bus nr; Eng spkn; ccard acc; fishing; sauna; bike hire; boating. *"Ideal for trip thro Lofoten Islands; conv Svolvær main fishing port; vg; beautiful views; helpful staff; currency exchange; san facs stretched in high ssn."* **NOK 330, 15 Apr-30 Sep.** **2024**

SVOLVAER *2F2* (26km NW Coastal) *68.27619, 14.30207* **Rystad Lofoten Camping,** Brennaveien 235, 8313 Kleppstad **tel 47 91658954; kwesteng@gmail.com; www.rystadcamping.com**

Foll E10 W out of Svolvaer. Just bef bdge to Grimsoya Island turn R, sp to Rystad. Site sp fr this junc, about 2km on L. Sm, pt sl, EHU; bbq; sw nr; Eng spkn; CKE. *"Gd for birdwatching; lovely sea views; gd for photographing midnight sun; vg site."* **NOK 259, 1 May-30 Sep.** **2022**

RUNDE ISLAND

RUNDE *1A1* (4km NW Rural/Coastal) *62.40416, 5.62525* **Camping Goksøyr,** 6096 Runde (Møre og Romsdal) **tel 70 08 59 05 or 924 12 298 (mob); camping@goksoyr.no; www.goksoeyr-camping.com**

12

Take causeway/bdge to Runde Island. Turn R off bdge & foll rd round island, thro tunnel. Rd ends 1km after site. 3*, Sm, hdstg, unshd, EHU (16A) NOK30; phone; Eng spkn; adv bkg acc; fishing; bike hire; CKE. *"Excel birdwatching (inc puffins); site on water's edge; boat trips avail; basic facs poss inadequate when site full; owner helps with pitching; vg."* **NOK 222** **2024**

VESTERALEN ISLANDS

ANDENES *2F1* (21km SW Coastal) *69.20410, 15.84674* **Stave Camping & Hot Pools,** Stave 8489 Nordmela **tel 92 60 12 57; info@stavecamping.no; www.stavecamping.no**

(htd) adj

Head S on Storgata/Rv82 twds Stadionveien, cont to foll Rv82, turn R onto Fv976, bear L onto Laksebakkveien, cont onto Fv976; site on L. Sm, unshd, EHU (16A) 40NOK; cooking facs; Eng spkn; ccard acc. *"Excel for midnight sun, hot tubs 250NOK pn."* **NOK 268, 17 May-1 Sep.** **2024**

ANDENES *2F1* (3km SW Coastal) *69.30390, 16.06621* **Whalesafari Andenes Norway (Formerly Andenes Camping),** Bleiksveien 34, 8480 Andenes **tel 41 34 03 88; booking@whalesafari.no and camping@whalesafari.no; www.whalesafari.no/andenes-camping/**

(htd) nr sand adj

Site on L of Rv82, sp. Sm, hdstg, unshd, EHU (16A) inc (check earth); cooking facs; Eng spkn; CKE. *"Nice, sandy beaches; conv whale safari, summer ferry to Gryllefjord & Bleiksøya bird cliff; gd for midnight sun; beautiful location; whale trips."* **NOK 200, 1 Jun-30 Aug.** **2024**

ANDENES *2F1* (9.6km SW Coastal) *69.27552, 15.96372* **Midnattsol Camping,** Gardsveien 8, 8481 Bleik **tel 47 84 32 19; midnattsol.camping@gmail.com; www.midnattsolcamping.com**

15 sand

Take Rte 82 S. Then turn R onto Rte 976 sp Bleik. Site at side of Rte 976 just bef Bleik. Med, mkd, unshd, terr, EHU 16A (NOK50); bbq; cooking facs; TV; Eng spkn; adv bkg acc; recep open 0930-1200; CKE. *"Sea adj; walks; birdwatching; conv for puffin & whale safaris & fishing boat trips; golf & sports grnd adj; lovely site; sea views; friendly owner; lovely setting bet mountain & sea; easy walk to vill shop; excel."* **NOK 235** **2024**

NORWAY

GULLESFJORDBOTN *2F2* (1km NW Coastal) *68.53213, 15.72611* **Gullesfjordbotn Camping,** Våtvoll, 8409 Gullesfjordbotn **tel 47 91 59 75 50; post@gullesfjordcamping.no; www.gullesfjordcamping.no**

(htd) shgl adj

Fr S on E10 then rd 85. At rndabt just bef Gullesfjordbotn take 2nd exit sp Sortland rd 85. Site on R 1km, well sp. 3*, Sm, hdstg, unshd, EHU (16A, poss rev pol) NOK50; cooking facs; phone; Eng spkn; ccard acc; fishing; boat hire; sauna; CKE. *"On edge of fjord; liable to flood after heavy rain; mountain views; gd san facs; friendly owners."*
NOK 256, 15 May-15 Sep. **2023**

RISOYHAMN *2F1* (13km S Coastal) *68.88408, 15.60304* **Andøy Friluftssenter & Camping,** Buksnesfjord, 8484 Risøyhamn **tel 76 14 88 04; booking@andoy-friluftssenter.no; www.andoy-friluftssenter.no**

12 (htd)

Exit E10 onto Rv82 sp Sortland; in 31km at bdge to Sortland do not cross bdge but cont N on Rv82 sp Andenes. Site on R in 38km at Buknesfjord. Sm, hdstg, unshd, pt sl, EHU (10A) NOK50; sw; 50% statics; Eng spkn; adv bkg acc; ccard acc; fishing; CKE. *"Lake fishing; guided mountain walks; easy access for whale-watching; v clean facs; gourmet meals."*
NOK 250 **2022**

SORTLAND *2F2* (2km NW Rural) *68.70286, 15.3919* **Camping Sortland & Motel,** Vesterveien 51, 8400 Sortland **tel 76 11 03 00; hj.bergseng@sortland-camping.no; www.sortland-camping.no**

12

Exit E10 onto Rv82/85 sp Sortland; in 31km turn L over bdge to Sortland, L again at end bdge. Site sp in approx 1km immed past church. Foll rd uphill for 1km, site on R. 4*, Med, hdstg, pt shd, EHU (16A) (no earth) NOK30; gas; cooking facs; TV; phone; Eng spkn; ccard acc; fishing; cycling; gym; solarium; boating; CKE. *"Basic, clean site; v helpful staff; gd base to tour islands; walking; skiing; facs stretched when full; red facs LS."* **NOK 250** **2022**

STO *2F1* (0.7km W Coastal) *69.01922, 15.10894* **Stø Bobilcamp,** 8438 Stø **tel 97 63 36 48; stobobilcamp@gmail.com; www.stobobilcamp.no**

(htd)

Site sp fr cent of Stø. Sm, hdstg, unshd, EHU (16A) NOK30; cooking facs; 10% statics; Eng spkn; fishing; bike hire. *"View of midnight sun; 10min walk to whale boat safari; coastal walks, Queen Sonja's walk fr site, v scenic but poss strenuous; facs stretched high ssn; site open to public for parking."*
NOK 130, 1 May-10 Sep. **2022**

Haugesund to Tromsø = 1932km

	Ålesund	Arendal	Bergen	Bodø	Drammen	Fagernes	Flekkefjord	Førde	Halden	Hamar	Hammerfest	Haugesund	Kirkenes	Kongsvinger	Kristiansand	Kristiansund	Larvik	Lillehammer	Mo i Rana	Molde	Mosjøen	Namsos	Narvik	Notodden	Oslo	Sandnes	Stavanger	Tromsø	Trondheim
Arendal	788																												
Bergen	382	480																											
Bodø	1070	1475	1366																										
Drammen	576	219	447	1366																									
Fagernes	455	421	558	1122	199																								
Flekkefjord	773	189	399	1663	41[illegible]	578																							
Førde	211	584	177	1256	413	283	498																						
Halden	691	262	589	1317	159	310	449	555																					
Hamar	441	395	481	1112	173	146	564	413	234																				
Hammerfest	1916	2321	2212	966	2113	1968	2509	2102	2163	1958																			
Haugesund	518	362	135	1494	387	401	211	313	495	514	2340																		
Kirkenes	2305	2710	2601	1361	2502	2357	2899	2491	3146	2347	501	2729																	
Kongsvinger	544	357	598	1189	137	225	548	518	169	99	2035	538	2424																
Kristiansand	869	69	486	1545	293	487	117	601	320	450	2391	323	2780	425															
Kristiansund	155	867	561	919	589	460	980	347	661	474	1765	655	2154	570	935														
Larvik	673	131	462	1359	95	292	314	496	138	263	2205	392	2594	232	195	737													
Lillehammer	387	406	454	1056	192	114	588	387	307	58	1911	488	2300	161	472	412	281												
Mo i Rana	829	1234	1125	241	1026	881	1422	1548	1076	871	1093	1253	1479	948	1304	678	1118	824											
Molde	80	745	453	946	546	492	939	276	648	413	1792	587	2181	515	822	77	671	348	705										
Mosjøen	736	1141	1032	337	933	788	1329	922	983	788	1175	1160	1571	855	1211	585	1025	731	94	612									
Namsos	538	943	834	572	735	599	1131	724	785	580	1420	962	1801	657	1013	387	827	533	328	637	236								
Narvik	1254	1659	1550	303	1451	1306	1847	1440	1501	1296	659	1678	1047	1373	1729	1103	1543	1249	429	1130	521	751							
Notodden	635	179	403	1337	67	273	329	429	168	237	2797	321	2572	203	252	658	99	250	1096	600	1003	805	1521						
Oslo	576	265	485	1222	41	190	451	465	120	131	2068	445	2457	96	331	601	135	182	981	535	888	690	1406	112					
Sandnes	693	298	215	1569	394	508	108	390	506	566	2415	95	2804	532	226	871	377	571	1328	813	1235	1037	1753	325	435				
Stavanger	581	317	197	1558	409	524	127	377	517	582	2404	77	2793	543	245	860	392	588	1328	801	1224	1026	1742	342	447	15			
Tromsø	1508	1913	1804	562	1705	1560	2101	1694	1755	1550	557	1932	942	1627	1983	1347	1797	1503	682	1384	775	1002	252	1775	1660	2007	1996		
Trondheim	307	754	645	719	546	410	938	532	598	392	1573	775	1955	462	819	199	635	345	478	221	383	190	910	616	503	849	840	1157	
Voss	350	418	101	1267	335	451	423	178	498	358	2113	221	2012	476	423	484	395	332	1026	410	933	735	1451	329	378	295	285	1705	547

A
B
C
D
1
2
3
4
▲ see Map 2
0 25 50 75 100 km
0 20 40 60 miles
N
W
E
S
TRONDHEIM
Melhus
Kvisvika
E39
65
MOLDE
30
ALESUND
Runde
Andalsnes
70
3
Oppdal
Roros
Os I Osterdalen
E6
Hellesylt
Geiranger
E136
30
28
Grimsbu
Alvdal
Stryn
15
VAGAMO
Byrkjelo
55
FORDE
Vassenden
FJAERLAND
Maurvangen
Koppang
5
Ornes
26
Vangsnes
Sogndalsfjora
3
LEIKANGER
Vikoyri
Laerdalsoyri
Vang
LILLEHAMMER
13
Flam
52
VOSS
50
HAMAR
Elverum
BERGEN
7
Gol
GJØVIK
2
Eidfjord
7
13
7
40
Rodberg
7
Odda
4
KONGSVINGER
Tinn Austbygd
Utvika
Roldal
OSLO
Torsby
Edland
2
BÆRUM
9
HAUGESUND
Kongsberg
DRAMMEN
13
Vestby
NOTODDEN
Trogstad
MOSS
Valle
40
STAVANGER
Jorpeland
SKIEN
TØNSBERG
SARPSBORG
Treungen
Porsgrunn
Fredrikstad
SANDNES
450
LARVIK
9
Stromstad
42
Byglandsfjord
Risor
42
42
FLEKKEFJORD
ARENDAL
Vannersborg
Farsund
KRISTIANSAND
Mandal

E
F
G
H
Motorways
Primary roads
Secondary roads
0 50 100 150 km
0 25 50 75 100 miles
N
W
E
S
All year site(s)
Seasonal site(s)
No sites listed
Nordkapp
Honningsvag
Berlevag
Hammerfest
98
Tana
Vadso
E6
Langfjordbotn
Alta
Kirkenes
1
E45
TROMSO
Karasjok
Birtavarre
Andenes
FINNSNES
Skibotn
Kautokeino
Sto
Risoyhamn
VESTERÅLEN
Harstad
Tennevoll
Bardu
Sortland
Storjord
Karesuando
Gullesfjordbotn
LOFOTEN
Svolvaer
NARVIK
Ramberg
Ulsvag
Stamsund
Muonio
Sorvagen
Kiruna
Sodankylä
NORWEGIAN SEA
2
BODO
Fauske
17
Rovaniemi
Kilboghamn
Krokstranda
Mo I Rana
Tjotta
MOSJOEN
SWEDEN
Lulea
Vega
Bronnoysund
Sorsele
Tosbotn
Oulu
RØRVIK
Kolvereid
Skelleftea
NAMSOS
Grong
FINLAND
3
Steinkjer
Stromsund
Umea
see Map 1
Örnsköldsvik
Vaasa
Sundsvall
GULF OF BOTHNIA
Pori
Tampere
4
Gävle
Turku
Helsinki

Poland

Shutterstock/Patryk Kosmider

Highlights

Poland is a country with a deep sense of history, cultural identity and resilience that has been built over thousands of years. The historic and beautiful centre of Kraków is a must see, while the engaging and fascinating museums of Warsaw are also a fantastic experience.

For those looking for relaxation, the Polish countryside is peaceful and unspoilt. There are many hiking trails scattered around the country taking you alongside rivers, through thick forests and around mountains.

Amber, sometimes called the gold of the Baltic, has been crafted in Poland for centuries. Amber products are still produced and sold with the best place to shop being Cloth Hall in the heart of Kraków.

Poland has been producing vodka since the early Middle Ages, and is the birthplace of this spirit. The vodka distilled in Poland is considered some of the finest in the world and vodka tasting events are held around the country.

Major towns and cities

- Warsaw – Poland's capital and the largest city in the country.
- Kraków – a charming and beautiful place that has retained its historic feel.
- Gdansk - a pretty seaside city with a rich history and heritage.
- Wrocław – a city with plenty of landmarks and wonderful buildings.

Attractions

- Main Square, Kraków – a bustling, medieval market square filled with historic buildings and monuments.
- Białowieza Forest – the remains of a primeval forest, home to European bison, ancient oaks and a magical beauty.
- Wieliczka Salt Mine – discover a fascinating mix of history, art and industry in one of Poland's oldest salt mines.

Find out more

W: poland.travel
E: london@pot.gov.pl
T: +44 0208 991 7076

Country Information

Capital: Warsaw

Bordered by: Belarus, Czechia, Germany, Lithuania, Russia, Slovakia, Ukraine

Terrain: Mostly flat plain with many lakes; mountains along southern border

Climate: Changeable continental climate with cold, often severe winters and hot summers; rainfall spread throughout the year; late spring and early autumn are the best times to visit

Coastline: 440 km

Highest Point: Rysy 2,499m

Language: Polish

Local Time: GMT or BST + 1, i.e. 1 hour ahead of the UK all year

Currency: Zloty (PLN) divided into 100 groszy; £1 = PLN 5.11; PLN10 = £1.96 (Nov 2024)

Emergency numbers: Police 997; Fire brigade 998; Ambulance 999. Call 112 for any service.

Public Holidays 2025: Jan 1, 6; Apr 20, 21; May 1, 3; Jun 8, 19; Aug 15; Nov 1, 11 (Independence Day); Dec 25, 26.

School summer holidays run from the last week of June to the end of August.

Border Posts

British and Irish passport holders may stay for up to 90 days in any 180 day period without a visa. You may be asked to show a return or onward ticket at the border to confirm your length of stay, or to prove that you have enough money for your stay.

Your passport will need to have a minimum of 6 months' validity remaining, and be less than 10 years old (even if it has over 6 months left).

Visitors arriving at a campsite or hotel must complete a registration form.

Entry Formalities

British and Irish passport holders may visit Poland for up to three months without a visa. At campsites, reception staff should look after any required registration with local authorities.

Medical Services

For simple complaints and basic advice visit a pharmacy (apteka). In general, medical facilities are comparatively inexpensive and of a good standard. Medical staff are well qualified. English isn't always widely spoken so you may face language difficulties.

You'll need a European Health Insurance Card (EHIC) or a Global Health Insurance Card (GHIC) to obtain emergency treatment from doctors, dentists and hospitals contracted to the state health care system, the NFZ. Reimbursements for any charges that you incur can be claimed from the NFZ office in Warsaw. You'll have to pay a proportion of the cost of prescriptions, which isn't refundable in Poland.

Private health clinics, found in large cities, offer a good standard of medical care.

Opening Hours

Banks: Mon-Fri 9am-4pm; Sat 9am-1pm.

Museums:Tue-Sun 10am-5pm; closed Mon.

Post Offices: Mon-Fri 8am-6pm; Sat 8am-2pm (on rota basis).

Shops: Mon-Fri 11am-8pm; Sat 9am-2pm/4pm; food shops open and close earlier; supermarkets open until 9pm/10pm.

Safety and Security

There is a risk of robbery in tourist areas, particularly near hotels, at main railway stations and on public transport. Passengers are most at risk when boarding and leaving trains or trams. Avoid walking alone at night, particularly in dark or poorly-lit streets or in public parks.

Some tourists have been the target of a scam in which men claiming to be plain clothes police officers ask visitors to show their identity documents and bank cards, and then ask for their PIN(s).

Theft of and from vehicles is common so don't leave vehicle documentation or valuables in your car. Foreign registered cars may be targeted, especially in large, busy supermarket car parks.

Cases have been reported of vehicles with foreign number plates being stopped by gangs posing as police officers, either claiming a routine traffic control or at the scene of fake accidents, particularly in rural and tourist areas. If in doubt, when flagged down keep all doors and windows locked, remain in your vehicle and ask to see identification. The motoring organisation, PZM, advises that any car or document inspection performed outside built-up areas can only be carried out by uniformed police officers and at night these officials must use a police patrol car. Although police officers don't have to be in uniform within built-up areas, they must always present their police identity card.

Don't leave drinks or food unattended or accept drinks from strangers. There has been a small number of reports of drinks being spiked and of visitors having their valuables stolen while drugged.

Poland shares with the rest of Europe an underlying threat from terrorism. Please check gov.uk/foreign-travel-advice/poland before you travel.

British Embassy

ul. Kawalerii 12, 00-468 Warsaw
Tel: (022) 311 00 00
gov.uk/world/poland

Irish Embassy

ul. Mysia 5, 00-496 Warsaw
Tel: (022) 564 22 00
ireland.ie/en/poland/warsaw

Documents

Driving Licence

The standard pink UK paper driving licence is recognised, but if you hold the old style green UK licence or a Northern Irish licence you are advised to update it to a photocard licence in order to avoid any local difficulties.

Passport

You should carry your passport with you at all times.

Vehicle(s)

You must carry your original vehicle registration certificate (V5C), insurance documentation and MOT certificate (if applicable) at all times. You may be asked for these if you are stopped by the police and, in particular, when crossing borders. If you don't own the vehicle(s) you'll need a letter of authority from the owner, together with the vehicle's original documentation.

Money

Cash can easily be obtained from ATMs in banks and shopping centres. ATMs offer an English option.

Major credit cards are widely accepted in hotels, restaurants and shops but you may find that supermarkets don't accept them. Take particular care with credit/debit cards and don't lose sight of them during transactions.

Sterling and euros are readily accepted at exchange bureaux but it isn't possible to exchange Scottish and Northern Irish bank notes in Poland. Carry your credit card issuers'/banks' 24-hour UK contact numbers in case of loss or theft of your cards.

Driving

Poland is a major route for heavy vehicles travelling between eastern and western Europe and driving can be hazardous. There are few dual carriageways and even main roads between large towns can be narrow and poorly surfaced. Slow moving agricultural and horse-drawn vehicles are common in rural areas. Street lighting is weak even in major cities.

Local driving standards are poor and speed limits, traffic lights and road signs are often ignored. Drivers rarely indicate before manoeuvring and you may encounter aggressive tailgating, overtaking on blind bends and overtaking on the inside. Take particular care on national holiday weekends when there is a surge in road accidents.

It isn't advisable to drive a right hand drive vehicle alone for long distances or to drive long distances at night.

At dusk watch out for cyclists riding without lights along the edge of the road or on its shoulder.

Hitchhikers use an up and down motion of the hand to ask for a lift. This may be confused with flagging down.

Accidents

Drivers involved in accidents must call the police, obtain an official record of damages and forward it to the insurance company of the Polish driver involved (if applicable).

Members of AIT/FIA affiliated clubs, such as The Caravan and Motorhome Club, can obtain help from the touring office ('Autotour') of the Polish motoring organisation, Polski Zwiazek Motorowy (PZM), tel: (022) 8496904 or (022) 8499361.

If people are injured, you must call an ambulance or doctor. By law, it's an offence for a driver not to obtain first aid for accident victims or to leave the scene of an accident. In such circumstances the authorities may withdraw a tourist's passport and driving licence, vehicle registration certificate or even the vehicle itself and the penalties can be a prison sentence and a fine.

Alcohol

The permitted level of alcohol is 0.02% which in practice equates to zero. At the request of the police or if an accident has occurred a driver must undergo a blood test which, if positive, may lead to a prison sentence, withdrawal of driving licence and a fine. Penalty points will be notified to the authorities in the motorist's home country.

Breakdown Service

The toll-free telephone number for breakdown assistance throughout the country is 981.

The PZM runs a breakdown service covering the entire country 24 hours a day. Members of AIT and FIA affiliated clubs, such as the Club, should call the PZM Emergency Centre on (022) 5328433. Staff speak English. Roadside assistance must be paid for in cash.

Child Restraint System

Children under the age of 12 years old and under the height of 1.5m must use a suitable restraint system that has been adapted to their size. It is prohibited to place a child in a rear facing seat in the front of the vehicle if the car is equipped with airbags.

Fuel

The usual opening hours for petrol stations are from 8am to 7pm; many on main roads and international routes and in large towns are open 24 hours. Credit cards are widely accepted. LPG (Autogas) is widely available from service stations.

Low Emission Zones

There are Low Emission Zones in force in Krakow and Warsaw. See urbanaccessregulations.eu for more information.

Motorways and Tolls

There are over 4,800 km of motorways and expressways in Poland. Tolls are levied on sections and vary in price, e.g., the A1 Rusocin to Nowe Marzy is PLN 71.00 (2023 prices) for a car towing a caravan weighing under 3500kg.

An electronic toll system (e-TOLL) is in place for vehicles which weigh over 3,500kg, including motorhomes and car and caravan combinations if the total weight is over 3,500kg. Visit etoll.gov.pl for more information.

There are emergency telephones every 2 km along motorways. Recent visitors report that newer stretches of motorway have rest areas with chemical disposal and waste water disposal facilities.

Parking

There are parking meters in many towns and signs display parking restrictions or prohibitions. There are many supervised car parks charging an hourly rate. Illegally parked cars causing an obstruction may be towed away and impounded, in which case the driver will be fined. Wheel clamps are in use.

Sidelights must be used when parking in unlit streets during the hours of darkness.

Priority

Priority should be given to traffic coming from the right at intersections of roads of equal importance, however, vehicles on rails always have priority. At roundabouts traffic already on a roundabout has priority.

Give way to buses pulling out from bus stops. Trams have priority over other vehicles at all times. Where there is no central reservation or island you should stop to allow passengers alighting from trams to cross to the pavement.

In addition to public transport vehicles leaving an official stop, drivers should give way to pedestrians on zebra crossings and to cyclists crossing a cycle lane.

Traffic Lights

All roads are hard surfaced and the majority of them are asphalted. However, actual road surfaces may be poor; even some major roads are constructed of cement or cobbles and heavily rutted. Average journey speed is about 50 km/h (31 mph).

Some roads, notably those running into Warsaw, have a two metre wide strip on the nearside to pull onto in order to allow other vehicles to overtake. Oncoming lorries expect other motorists to pull over when they are overtaking.

Overtake trams on the right unless in a one-way street.

Road Signs and Markings

Road signs and markings conform to international standards. Motorway and national road numbers are indicated in red and white, and local roads by yellow signs with black numbering. Signs on motorways are blue with white lettering and on main roads they are green and white

The following road signs may be seen:

Paid parking between 7am and 6pm

Residential area-predestrians have priority

Toll road

Rutted road

Winding road

Emergency vehicles

You may also encounter the following:

Polish	English Translation
Rondzie	Roundabout
Wstep szbroniony	No Entry
Wyjscie	Exit

Crossroads and road junctions may not be marked with white 'stop' lines, and other road markings in general may be well worn and all but invisible, so always take extra care.

Speed Limits

	Open Road (km/h)	Motorway (km/h)
Car Solo	90	140
Car towing caravan/trailer	70	80
Motorhome under 3500kg	90	140
Motorhome 3500-7500kg	70	80

In built up areas the speed limit is 50 km/h (31 mph) between 5am and 11pm, and 60 km/h (37 mph) between 11pm and 5am.

For vehicles over 3,500kg all speed limits are the same as for a car and caravan outfit. In residential zones indicated by entry/exit signs, the maximum speed is 20 km/h (13 mph). The use of radar detectors is illegal.

Traffic Lights

Look out for a small, non-illuminated green arrow under traffic lights, which permits a right turn against a red traffic light if the junction is clear.

Violation of Traffic Regulations

Motorists must not cross a road's solid central white line or even allow wheels to run on it. Radar speed traps are frequently in place on blind corners where speed restrictions apply. Police are very keen to enforce traffic regulations with verbal warnings and/or on the spot fines. Fines are heavy and drivers of foreign registered vehicles will be required to pay in cash. Always obtain an official receipt.

Touring

Poland's national drinks include varieties of vodka and plum brandy. In restaurants, it's usual to leave a tip of between 10 to 15%.

There are almost 10,000 lakes in Poland, mostly in the north. The regions of Western Pomerania, Kaszubia and Mazuria are a paradise for sailing enthusiasts, anglers and nature lovers. National parks and nature reserves have been created to protect areas of natural beauty,

Two of the most interesting of which are the Tatra National Park covering the whole of the Polish Tatra mountains, and the Slowinksi National Park with its 'shifting' sand dunes.

There are 17 UNESCO World Heritage Sites including the restored historic centres of Warsaw and Kraków, the medieval, walled town of Toruń and Auschwitz Concentration Camp. Other towns worth a visit are Chopin's birthplace at Zelazowa Wola, Wieliczka with its salt mines where statues and a chapel are carved out of salt, and Wrocław.

White and brown signs in cities and near sites of interest indicate architectural and natural landmarks, places of religious worship, etc. Each sign includes not only information on the name of and distance to a particular attraction, but also a pictogram of the attraction, e.g. Jasna Góra monastery. Themed routes, such as the trail of the wooden churches in the Małopolska Region (south of Kraków), are marked in a similar way.

A Warsaw Pass and a Kraków Tourist Card are available, both valid for up to three days and offering free travel on public transport and free entry to many museums, together with discounts at selected restaurants and shops and on sightseeing and local excursions. You can buy the cards from warsawtour.pl and discovercracow.com.

The Polish people are generally friendly, helpful and polite. English is becoming increasingly widely spoken in major cities.

Camping and Caravanning

There are around 250 organised campsites throughout Poland, with the most attractive areas being the Mazurian lake district and along the coast. Campsites are usually open from the beginning of May or June to the middle or end of September, but the season only really starts towards the end of June. Until then facilities may be very limited and grass may not be cut, etc.

You can download details of approximately 160 sites (including GPS co-ordinates) from the website of the Polish Federation of Camping & Caravanning, (pfcc.eu).

Campsites are classified from one to four stars. Category one sites provide larger pitches and better amenities, but it may still be advisable to use your own facilities.

There are also some basic sites which are not supervised and are equipped only with drinking water, toilets and washing facilities. Sites may be in need of modernisation but, on the whole, sanitary facilities are clean although they may provide little privacy. Some new sites are being built to higher standards. A site may close earlier than its published date if the weather is bad.

Many sites are not signposted from main roads and may be difficult to find. It's advisable to obtain a large scale atlas or good maps of the areas to be visited and not rely on one map covering the whole of Poland.

Casual/wild camping isn't recommended and is prohibited in national parks (except on organised sites) and in sand dunes along the coast.

Cycling

There are several long-distance cycle routes using a combination of roads with light motor traffic, forest trails or tracks along waterways. There are some cycle lanes on main roads where cyclists must ride in single file.

Electricity and Gas

The current on most campsites is 10 amps. Plugs have two round pins. There are some CEE connections.

It's understood that both propane and butane supplies are widely available, but cylinders are not exchangeable and it may be necessary to refill. The Club doesn't recommend this practice and you should aim to take enough gas to last during your stay. Some campsites have kitchens which you may use to conserve your gas supplies.

Public Transport & Local Travel

For security reasons recent visitors recommend using guarded car parks such as those in Warsaw on the embankment below the Old Town, in the Palace of Culture and near the Tomb of the Unknown Soldier.

Use only taxis from official ranks whose vehicles have the name and telephone number of the taxi company on the door and on the roof (beside the occupied/unoccupied light). They also display a rate card in the window of the vehicle. Taxis with a crest but no company name are not officially registered.

There are frequent ferries from Gydnia, Swinoujscie and Gdansk to Denmark, Germany and Sweden.

Passenger ferries operate along the Baltic Coast, on the Mazurian lakes and on some rivers, for example, between Warsaw and Gdansk.

There is a metro system in Warsaw. It's possible to buy a daily or weekly tourist pass which is valid for all means of public transport – bus, tram and metro. Buy tickets at newspaper stands and kiosks displaying a sign 'bilety'.

Tickets must be punched before travelling at the yellow machines at the entrance to metro stations or on board buses and trams. You'll incur an on the spot fine if you are caught travelling without a valid ticket.

Niedzica Castle

Sites in Poland

ELK *A3* (3km SW Urban) *53.81545, 22.35215* **Camping Plaża Miejska (No. 62),** ul Parkowa 2, 19-300 Ełk **(087) 6109700; mosir@elk.com.pl; http://mosir.elk.pl/plaza-miejska/camping/**

(htd) nr

Fr town cent on rd 16 take rd 65/669 dir Białystok. After 200m cross rv & immed turn R, site 100m on L. 3*, Sm, mkd, hdstg, pt shd, EHU (10A) inc; cooking facs; sw nr; CKE. *"Gd security; well-maintained, clean site adj town cent & attractive lake; gd touring base lake district."* **PLN 65, 1 Jun-1 Sep. 2022**

FROMBORK *A3* (1km E Rural/Coastal) *54.35877, 19.69572* **Camping Frombork (No. 12),** ul Braniewska, 14-530 Frombork **602 136 245; biuro@campcity.pl; www.campcity.pl**

nr sand 2km

Fr Frombork on rd 504 dir Braniewo, site on L. Med, pt shd, EHU inc; bbq; games area. *"Pleasant, basic site; mv service pnt/chem disp at car wash; san facs tatty but clean (2009); pleasant countryside."* **PLN 60, 1 May-30 Sep. 2024**

GDANSK *A2* (9km E Coastal) *54.37021, 18.72938* **Camping Stogi (No. 218),** ul Wydmy 9, 80-656 Gdańsk **(058) 3073915; jan@camping-gdansk.pl; www.kemping-gdansk.pl**

WD sand adj

E fr Gdańsk on rd 7 (E77) for approx 2km, then L foll sp for Stogi. Then foll tram rte no. 8 to Stogi Plaza/Beach. Site is 100m fr tram terminus, well sp. Med, hdstg, EHU (10-16A) PLN11; bbq; 75% statics; tram 100m; games area; CKE. *"Basic site, more a holiday camp for school groups; ltd facs LS; close to huge, clean beach; gd security; vg site; sep area for m'vans; san facs upgraded (2013)."* **PLN 89, 25 Apr-5 Oct. 2024**

JELENIA GORA *C2* (2km SE Urban) *50.89638, 15.74266* **Auto-Camping Park (No. 130),** ul Sudecka 42, 58-500 Jelenia Góra **(075) 7524525; camping park@interia.pl; www.camping.karkonosz.pl**

12 PLN5 nr nr

In town foll sp to Karpacz on rd 367. Site 100m fr hotel. Well sp. 2*, Med, hdstg, pt shd, terr, EHU (6-10A) PLN10 (poss rev pol); TV; 20% statics; adv bkg acc; ccard acc; tennis 500m; CKE. *"Conv Karkanosze mountains & Czech border; well-run, clean, neat site nr hotel with gd, modern facs; 20 min walk to pleasant town; pool 500m; sports facs 500m; staff friendly, helpful & obliging; conv NH; gd facs."* **PLN 68.31 2022**

KARPACZ *D2* (3km N Rural) *50.80428, 15.76776* **Camping Wiśniowa Polana (No. 142),** Miłków 40A, 58-535 Miłków **504 645 926; wisniowapolana@gmail.com; www.wisniowapolana.pl**

PLN5 WD MSP nr

Fr Jelenia Góra to Kowary on rte 367, turn R at junc with rte 366 at Kowary, site on E of Miłków by rv. Med, hdstg, pt shd, EHU (10A) PLN10; bbq; games area; fishing; CKE. *"Well-kept, guarded site & facs; v friendly staff; 7km fr chairlift onto mountain ridge; gd walking - map fr recep."* **PLN 55, 1 May-30 Sep. 2024**

KARTUZY *A2* (9km W Rural) *54.31983, 18.11736* **Camping Tamowa (No. 181),** Zawory 47A, 83-333 Chmielno **(058) 6842535; camping@tamowa.pl; www.tamowa.pl**

12 WD nr nr

Fr Gdańsk take rd 7 & rd 211 to Kartuzy, cont for approx 4km on 211. Turn L for Chmielno; site sp fr vill on lakesite along narr, bumpy app rd. Med, unshd, terr, EHU (10-16A) inc; bbq; sw nr; bus station 1KM away; Eng spkn; sauna; boat hire; bike hire; CKE. *"Attractive, well-kept site in beautiful location; friendly owner; not suitable lge o'fits; v nice site; shop 0.5m."* **PLN 54 2020**

KATOWICE *D3* (4km SE Rural) *50.24355, 19.04795* **Camping Dolina Trzech Statow (No. 215),** ul Trzech Stawow 23, 40-291 Katowice **(032) 2565939 or (032) 2555388; camping@mosir.katowice.pl; camping.mosir.katowice.pl**

PLN5 (htd) nr nr

Exit A4 at junc Murckowska & foll sp on rd 86 Sosnowiec. In 500m turn R & foll site sp. Med, shd, pt sl, EHU (16A) PLN2.50/kwh; cooking facs; Eng spkn; adv bkg acc; ccard acc; tennis; CKE. *"V clean facs but basic & little privacy; vg."* **PLN 45, 1 May-30 Sep. 2022**

KAZIMIERZ DOLNY *C3* (2km N Rural) *51.33106, 21.95879* **Campsite Pielak,** Pulawska 82, 24-120 Kazimierz Dolny (Lubelskie) **(069) 1047409; www.campingpielaka.pl**

WD MSP 50m

Site sp on the S824 300m N of the town. Sm, pt shd, pt sl, EHU (16A); bbq; cooking facs; twin axles; bus adj; Eng spkn; kayaking; CCI. *"V friendly owners, warm welcome; pool 50m; walking dist to town; close to rv; open grassy site; historic town; excel."* **PLN 94.5, 1 May-30 Oct. 2022**

POLAND

KLODZKO *D2* (13km W Urban) *50.41502, 16.51335* **Camping Polanica-Zdroj (No. 169),** ul Sportowa 7, 57-320 Polanica-Zdrój **(048) 663790204; osir.polanica@neostrada.pl; www.osir.polanica.net/pl**

12 PLN5 (htd)

Foll sp fr rd 8/E67. Site is 1km N of Polanica-Zdrój. Med, pt shd, EHU (6A) PLN9.50; Eng spkn; ccard acc; tennis; CKE. *"Well-run site; clean san facs; helpful warden; many statics adj; easy walk to pleasant spa town - many rests/cafés; wifi free in recep."* **PLN 69.3** **2024**

KOLOBRZEG *A2* (1km NE Coastal) *54.18131, 15.59566* **Camping Baltic (No. 78),** ul 4 Dywizji, 78-100 Kołobrzeg **(094) 3524569 or (0606) 411954 (mob); baltic78@post.pl; www.camping.kolobrzeg.pl**

PLN3 WD MSP nr nr sand 800m

Nr Solny Hotel on NE edge of town over rlwy x-ing; sp fr rndabt in vill. 3*, Med, pt shd, EHU (10-16A) PLN10; red long stay; TV; phone; Eng spkn; adv bkg acc; ccard acc; CKE. *"V helpful staff; easy walk/cycle to town; well kept site with spotless facs; easy walk into town."* **PLN 103, 15 Apr-15 Oct.** **2024**

KRAKOW *D3* (5km N Urban) *50.09454, 19.94127* **Camping Clepardia (No. 103),** ul Pachońskiego 28A, 31-223 Kraków **(012) 4159672; clepardia@gmail.com; www.clepardia.com.pl**

Free WD nr nr

Fr Kraków cent take rd 7/E77 N twds Warsaw for 3km. Turn L onto rd 79 'Opolska' & foll sp 'Domki Kempingowe - Bungalows'. Fr A4/E40 exit onto E462 then S on rd 79 'Pasternik' thro to 'J Conrada & foll sp. Site is nr lge Elea supmkt & Clepardia Basen (sw pools). Med, mkd, pt shd, EHU (6A) PLN20; phone; bus 250m; Eng spkn; CKE. *"Busy site with tightly packed pitches - rec arr bef 1700 high ssn to secure pitch; excel, clean, modern san facs; ltd EHU if site full; muddy in wet weather; dogs free; pool adj; friendly, helpful staff; gd security; well maintained."* **PLN 140, 15 Apr-15 Oct.** **2023**

KRAKOW *D3* (8km S Urban) *50.01546, 19.92525* **Camping Krakowianka (No. 171),** ul Żywiecka Boczna 2, 30-427 Kraków **(012) 2681135; hotel@krakowianka.com.pl or hotel@krakowianka.info; www.krakowianka.com.pl and krakowianka.info**

WD nr nr

Exit A4 at Wezel Opatkowice & head N on E77 twd city cent for approx 3km. After passing Carrefour supmkt on R, turn L at next traff lts & foll site sp. Lge, pt shd, EHU (16A) inc; TV; 10% statics; phone; tram; games area. *"Ltd, basic facs; car wash; conv tram to town; shwrs in hotel v clean & plenty hot water; gd site; pool adj; nice snack/bar."* **PLN 50, 1 May-30 Sep.** **2024**

KRAKOW *D3* (7km SW Rural) *50.04638, 19.88111* **Camping Smok (No. 46),** ul Kamedulska 18, 30-252 Kraków **48 12 429 88 00; info@smok.krakow.pl; www.smok.krakow.pl**

12 PLN10 WD MSP nr

Fr Kraków W ring rd site sp as No 46. Fr S 1st exit immed after x-ing rv onto rd 780 twd Kraków. 3*, Med, shd, pt sl, EHU (5-10A) PLN20; red long stay; Eng spkn; adv bkg rec; windsurfing 6km; CKE. *"On rd to Auschwitz; salt mine at Wieliczka; friendly, well-kept site; spotless san facs; lower field (m'vans) poss muddy after rain - tractor tow avail; poss rallies on site; gd tour base; frequent bus to Krakow connects with trams to cent; cycle rte to cent; gd security; tours with pick-up fr site; excel; v helpful and friendly."* **PLN 150** **2023**

LANCUT *D3* (2km E Urban) *50.070940, 22.254689* **Camping Lancut,** ul. Kazimierza Wielkiego 20, 37-100 Łańcut **(604) 915112 or (602) 252909; biuro@campinglancut.pl; www.camperparklancut.pl/wynajem**

PLN 5 WD MSP nr nr nr

On 94 between Rzeszow and Przeworks. Sm, mkd, hdg, pt shd, serviced pitches; EHU; bbq (charcoal, elec, gas, sep area); cooking facs; twin axles; red long stay; phone; bus; Eng spkn; adv bkg acc. *"Excel; lots to see locally; bike ride off rd; lovely site, 2 years old (2019); modern; helpful American owner; v well kept."* **PLN 51, 1 Apr-30 Oct.** **2024**

LEBA *A2* (2km N Coastal) *54.76150, 17.53833* **Camping Morski (No. 21),** ul Turystyczna 3, 84-360 Łeba **664 258 806; camping.morski@gmail.com; www.camping21.pl**

PLN8 (htd) WD MSP nr sand 150m

N fr Lębork on E214. In Łeba foll sp Camping Raphael & pass rlwy stn on L, over rv bdge twd sea. Site sp. 3*, Lge, mkd, hdg, pt shd, EHU (10A) PLN12; bbq; cooking facs; TV; phone; adv bkg rec; tennis; CKE. *"Nice, well-run site in gd position; modern san facs; pleasant resort; excel; Lacka sand dunes worth a visit."* **PLN 94, 1 May-30 Sep.** **2024**

LEBA *A2* (2km NE Urban) *54.76580, 17.57145* **Camping Przymorze Nr. 48,** ul. Nadmorska 9, 84-360 Leba **059 866 1304; biuro@camping.leba.pl; www.camping-leba.pl/kamery.asp**

(htd) WD MSP sand 0.5km

Take DW214 dir Leba, at rndabt take 1st exit onto aleja swietego Jakuba. Turn R onto Nadmorska & foll sp to camp. Lge, mkd, pt shd, EHU; bbq; TV; 10% statics; phone; bus adj; Eng spkn; ccard acc; CCI. *"Excel site; shops & rest in walking dist; interesting harbour with fresh fish for sale; windsurfing; lovely sandy beach."* **PLN 110, 1 May-30 Sep.** **2024**

LEGNICA *C2* (13km SE Rural) *51.14216, 16.24006*
Camping Legnickie Pole (No. 234), Ul Henryka Brodatego 7, 59-241 Legnickie Pole **(076) 8582397; osir.legnica@wp.pl; www.gokis-legnickiepole.pl**
PLN8 nr

Fr A4/E40 fr Görlitz take exit dir Legnickie Pole/ Jawor, foll sp to vill & site. Sharp L turn after leaving main rd. Site sp on S o'skirts of Legnica on E65 & fr m'way. Sm, pt shd, EHU (10A) inc; CKE. *"Helpful, friendly welcome; clean, basic facs (hot water to shwrs only); poss diff after heavy rain; gd NH on way S; pleasant vill."* **PLN 44, 1 May-30 Sep. 2023**

LEZAJSK *C4* (12km ENE Rural) *50.280257, 22.514233*
Pole Biwakowe Laguna, 37-303 Kuryłówka **(602) 717262; marianszktanny.wp.pl; www.polskicaravaning.pl**
(htd) nr nr sand adj

Thro Kurylowka town. At edge of town foll sp left to Ozanna-Stron. Site on L. 5*, Sm, pt shd, EHU (16A); bbq (charcoal, elec, gas); cooking facs; sw; twin axles; bus; Eng spkn; adv bkg acc; games area. *"Site on lakeside; fishing; grass mowed short; peaceful; Lezajsk monastery 20 mins; cycle path around lake; v friendly; sailing ok; vg."* **PLN 30, 1 May-30 Sep. 2024**

MIELNO *A2* (0.8km E Coastal) *54.26272, 16.07245*
Camping Rodzinny (No. 105), ul Chrobrego 51, 76-032 Mielno **(094) 3189385; recepcja@campingrodzinny.pl; www.campingrodzinny.pl**
PLN5 (htd) WD sand 500m

Fr Koszalin W on rd 11, turn N onto rd 165 to Mielno turn R at rdbt then 1 1/2 km & foll site sp. Site on L thro narr gate bet gardens - easy to miss.
4*, Sm, pt shd, EHU (6A) PLN1.50; bbq; cooking facs; 10% statics; Eng spkn; adv bkg acc; games rm; CKE. *"Easy walk to town; secure, well-kept, family-owned site; gd san facs; Gd site local to beach and shops; friendly owners."* **PLN 88, 15 Apr-15 Nov. 2024**

MIKOLAJKI *A3* (1.5km SW Rural) *53.7954, 21.56471*
Camping Wagabunda (No. 2), ul Leśna 2, 11-730 Mikołajki **(087) 4216018; wagabunda-mikolajki@wagabunda-mikolajki.pl; www.wagabunda-mikolajki.pl**
PLN2.50 shgl 2km

Exit town by rd 16 dir Mrągowo & site sp to L. Med, unshd, pt sl, EHU (16A) PLN13; sw nr; twin axles; TV; 50% statics; phone; Eng spkn; adv bkg acc; games area; CKE. *"Pleasant site nr nice town; san facs adequate but need update (2011); conv Masurian Lakes & historical sites; vg site; 10 min walk into town."* **PLN 82, 1 May-30 Sep. 2024**

MORAG *A3* (11km E Rural) *53.90373, 20.02753*
Camping Kretowiny (No. 247), Kretowiny29, 14-300 Morag **(089) 7582440 or (697) 523402 (mob); info@narie.pl; www.narie.pl**
WD

Fr cent Morąg foll rd 527 S twd Olsztyn but bef exit town, fork L at sp Żabi Róg/Kretowiny. Site sp on Lake Jezioro Narie. 4*, Med, hdg, pt shd, EHU (6A) PLN8; sw; watersports; games area; games rm; tennis; fishing; CKE. *"On shore of lge, lovely lake with sw, boating, fishing; pleasant, attractive site."* **PLN 34, 1 May-30 Sep. 2024**

MRAGOWO *A3* (11km N Rural) *53.94278, 21.32001*
Camping Seeblick, Ruska Wieś 1, 11-700 Mrągowo **(089) 7413155; marian.seeblick@gmail.com; www.campingpension.de**
12 (if on a lead) (htd) WD nr

Fr Mrągowo N on rd 591 dir Ketrzyn, site sp. 3*, Med, pt shd, terr, EHU inc; sw; Eng spkn; boating; games area; tennis. *"Gd but ltd san facs; lots for kids to do; shop nr."* **PLN 50 2020**

"There aren't many sites open at this time of year"

If you're travelling outside peak season remember to call ahead to check site opening dates – even if the entry says 'open all year'.

NIEDZICA *D3* (3.5km SE Urban) *49.40477, 20.33411*
Camping Polana Sosny (No. 38), Osiedle Na Polanie Sosny, 34-441 Niedzica **(018) 3347770; recepcja.polanasosny@gmail.com; www.polanasosny.pl**
12 (htd) WD nr nr

Rte 969 fr Nowy Targ. At Dębno turn R & foll sp to border (lake on L). At 11km pass castle & 1st dam on L twds 2nd Dunajec dam. Site sp. 2*, Sm, mkd, unshd, EHU inc; cooking facs; red long stay; phone; adv bkg acc; watersports; games area; CKE. *"Beautiful, well-maintained site in superb location; friendly, helpful staff; clean, modern san facs; excel walks in mountains; 2km to Slovakian border; quiet but noise fr dam; vg touring base."* **PLN 63.16 2022**

OSWIECIM *D3* (4km S Rural) *50.02262, 19.19891*
Centre for Dialogue & Prayer in Auschwitz, ul Maksymiliana Kolbego 1, 32-600 Oświęcim **(033) 8431000; reception@cdim.pl; cdim.pl/campsite**
12 nr

700m fr Auschwitz 1 museum car park on parallel rd to S, on forecourt of hotel-like building. Sm, hdstg, unshd, EHU inc; bbq; phone; Eng spkn; CKE. *"Conv Auschwitz museum & Auschwitz-Birkenau (3km); clean, modern, lovely site on lawn & among trees; all site powered; gd, clean san facs, similar quality to UK CC sites; friendly, helpful staff; very nice site; excel facs; a gem of a site; highly rec."* **PLN 144 2023**

POLAND

OSWIECIM *D3* (2km W Urban) *50.02895, 19.20054* **Parking Przy Museum Auschwitz,** 32-600 Oświęcim **+48 33 844 8000; www.auschwitz.org/en**

Foll sp to Auschwitz museum fr rd 933. Parking area is on opp side of rd (away fr main car park) by TO. M'vans only. Sm, EHU (6A) PLN7. *"NH only permitted; ltd EHU; allow 4 hrs for museum tour; basically a big car park with a few elec points; wifi at TO or pizza rest."* **PLN 40** **2024**

POZNAN *B2* (5km E Urban) *52.40343, 16.98399* **Camping Malta (No. 155),** ul Krańcowa 98, 61-036 Poznań-Malta **(061) 8766203 or 618766155; camping@malta.poznan.pl; www.norcamp.de/en/poland/camping-155-malta.6236.1.html**

Fr A2/E30 Poznań bypass leave at rte 2/11 dir Poznań. Turn R at traff lts onto rte 5/E261 sp Malta, Zoo & camping, site sp. 4*, Sm, hdg, pt shd, EHU (16A) inc; 80% statics; tram to city; Eng spkn; ccard acc; CKE. *"Clean tidy site on lake with sports but poss unkempt pitches LS; 6 tram stops to Poznań Sq; vg 24-hr security; lake adj; helpful staff; site amongst sports facs by lake."* **PLN 102** **2024**

PRZEWORSK *D4* (1km W Urban) *50.06138, 22.48361* **Camping Pastewnik (No. 221),** ul Łańcucka 2, 37-200 Przeworsk **(016) 6492300; zajazdpastewnik@hot.pl; www.pastewnik.prv.pl**

On N side of N4/E40, sp. 3*, Sm, pt shd, EHU (10A) PLN10; Eng spkn; ccard acc; CKE. *"Conv NH/sh stay with motel & rest; Łańcut Castle & Carriage Museum 25km; elec v dubious, no socket circuit breakers."* **PLN 112, 1 May-30 Sep.** **2024**

SANDOMIERZ *C3* (1km E Urban) *50.68010, 21.75502* **Camping Browarny (No. 201),** ul Żwirki I Wigury 1, 27-600 Sandomierz **(015) 8332703; wmajsak@poczta.fm; www.majsak.pl**

Diff app to site off dual c'way. App on rd 77 fr N only. Avoid town ctr, 2.5 tonne weight limit. 3*, Sm, pt shd, EHU (16A) PLN30; bbq; cooking facs; phone; bus adj; Eng spkn; adv bkg acc; games rm; CKE. *"Attractive sm town in walking dist; vg site; helpful staff; red for 'vans under 5mtrs."* **PLN 110, 1 May-30 Sep.** **2023**

SOPOT *A2* (2km N Urban) *54.46136, 18.5556* **Camping Kamienny Potok (No. 19),** Metropolis Sopot Recreation Center Al. Niepodległości 899 81-861 Sopot **(058) 5500445; metropolis.polmetro@campingsopot.pl; www.kemping19.cba.pl**

Fr Gdańsk rte 27 twds Sopot. Site on R just behind Shell petrol stn. Fr N on rte 6/E28 turn S at Gdynia, onto new section of E28, for 7.5km. Turn L onto rte 220 by 'Euromarket' for 5km. Turn R onto rte 27 (S) twd Gdańsk & site nr Shell g'ge on opp c'way. Lge, mkd, pt shd, EHU (2-20A) PLN10; TV; phone; ccard acc; CKE. *"Pleasant site; friendly & helpful staff; frequent trains for Gdansk 250m; modern, clean san facs; gd security; gd walking/cycling track into town; busy site; upgrades in process (2012)."* **PLN 72, 1 May-30 Sep.** **2020**

SULECIN *B1* (4km S Rural) *52.40911, 15.11761* **Camping Marina (No. 50),** Ostrów 76, 69-200 Sulęcin **505 059 909; biuro@camping-marina.pl; www.camp-marina.pl/index.php**

Cross border fr Frankfurt-an-Oder & take rd 2 to Torzym (35km). In Torzym turn L onto rd 138 dir Sulęcin; thro Tursk & site in 3km. 4*, Med, mkd, pt shd, EHU €2; sw; TV; 10% statics; adv bkg acc; bike hire; fishing; CKE. *"Gd, modern san facs; gd walking/cycling; pleasant, relaxing site; conv Berlin."* **PLN 63, 1 Apr-31 Oct.** **2024**

SUWALKI *A3* (11km SE Rural) *54.0767, 23.0742* **Kajaki Camping Pokoje,** 16-412 Stary Folwark 44, Wigry **(087) 5637789; wigry@wigry.info; www.wigry.info**

Fr Suwalki take 653 dir Sejny. In about 11km turn R in Stary Folwark at PTTK sp. Site on R in approx 100m. Sm, unshd, EHU (10A) inc; bbq; sw nr; Eng spkn. *"Nr lake in National Park; kayaking fr site; vg site."* **PLN 40, 1 May-30 Sep.** **2022**

SWIECIE *B2* (1km S Urban) *53.40321, 18.45574* **Camping Zamek (No. 54),** Zamkowa Street 10, 86-100 Świecie **(052) 3311726 or 604 993 070; recepcja@camping-zamek.pl; www.camping-zamek.pl**

S fr Gdańsk on E75 take rd 1 to Chełmno & Świecie. Cross Rv Wisła & L at x-rds in Świecie cent; site sp at traff lts. 1*, Med, shd, EHU (10A); own san rec; 50% statics; phone; games area; fishing. *"Interesting town & churches; helpful staff; in castle grnds (tower visible fr rd); if gate clsd, ring bell on L; new tolet block (2012)."* **PLN 25, 1 May-15 Sep.** **2020**

SWINOUJSCIE *A1* (2km N Coastal) *53.91709, 14.25693* **Camping Relax (No. 44),** ul Słowackiego 1, 72-600 Świnoujście **(097) 3213912; relax@osir.swinoujscie.pl; www.camping-relax.com.pl**

12 nr 200m

Fr E rd 3/E65 cross rv on free ferry. Fr town cent N for 500m. No vehicle border x-ing fr W. 3*, V lge, shd, EHU (16A) PLN10; cooking facs; phone; adv bkg acc; ccard acc; games rm. *"Nice town; gd beach; gd walking; site popular with families; red snr citizens."* **PLN 65** **2020**

SZCZECIN/STETTIN *B1* (8km SE Rural) *53.39505, 14.63640* **Marina Camping (No. 25),** ul Przestrzenna 23, 70-800 Szczecin-Dabie **(091) 4601165; camping.marina@pro.onet.pl; www.campingmarina.pl**

12 PLN20 (htd) MSP nr

Fr E28/A6 take A10 sp Szczecin. Immed after rlwy bdge turn R sp Dąbie. At traff lts in cent Dąbie turn L, site on R in approx 2km on lake. 3*, Med, pt shd, EHU (6A) inc; sw; bus to Stettin; tennis; boat hire; games area; CKE. *"Pleasant, lakeside site; clean, modern san facs but inadequate if site full; bus tickets fr recep; helpful staff; vg site on lake side."* **PLN 180** **2023**

TARNOW *D3* (2km N Rural) *50.02320, 20.98813* **Camping Pod Jabłoniami (No. 202),** ul Piłsudskiego 28a, 33-100 Tarnów **(014) 6215124; recepcja@camping.tarnow.pl; www.camping.tarnow.pl**

12 WD nr nr nr

E fr Kraków on E40, foll sp to Tarnów 'Centrum'. Turn L by Tesco & foll sp to site. 3*, Sm, pt shd, pt sl, EHU (16A) PLN10; bbq; TV; Eng spkn; CKE. *"Walk to attractive town; pool adj; vg site."* **PLN 85** **2024**

TORUN *B2* (2km S Urban) *53.00062, 18.60847* **Camping Tramp (No. 33),** ul Kujawska 14, 87-100 Torún **(056) 6547187; tramp@mosir.torun.pl; campingtramp.com**

12 PLN20 WD nr nr

Cross bdge S of town & take 1st L at traff lts, site sp in 500m on rvside. 3*, Med, shd, EHU (10A) PLN30; 10% statics; games area; CKE. *"Noisy, busy site but reasonable; walking dist fr interesting old town across bdge; gd security; NH/sh stay only."* **PLN 122** **2023**

UCIECHOW *C2* (1km E Rural) *50.75561, 16.69412* **Camping Forteca,** ul. Wroclawska 12, 58-211 Uciechów (Dolnoslaskie) **(074) 8323008; info@campingforteca.nl; www.campingforteca.nl**

PLN5 WD

Fr cent of Dzierzoniów foll rd 384 twds Lagiewniki and Wroclaw for 4km. In cent of Uciechów go ahead at crossrds. After 400m turn R down gravel track sp to rest and parking. Sm, pt sl, EHU (16A) 15 ZL; bbq; twin axles; 10% statics; Eng spkn; adv bkg acc; CKE. *"Pitches surround lake where sw; fishing and boating permitted; new clean toilet block; helpful, friendly family owners; lake adj; lovely peaceful site LS; open plan, grassy site."* **PLN 88, 1 Apr-1 Oct.** **2024**

USTKA *A2* (1.6km SE Urban) *54.57655, 16.88088* **Camping Morski (No. 101),** ul Armii Krajowej 4, Przewloka, 76-270 Ustka **604 486 413 or 608 402 516; cam_mor@pro.onet.pl; www.morski101.pl**

nr nr 1.3km

Fr Koszalin & Sławno to łlupsk on rd 6/E28 turn L to Ustka. Foll main rd which bears R & foll camping sp to R. After 200m turn R at rndabt & camp on L after 300m. 2*, Sm, pt shd, EHU (6A) inc; bbq; red long stay; tennis; CKE. *"Seaside resort with gd shopping & fishing port; vg for children; gd cycling; gd NH; 30 min walk to town."* **PLN 60, 1 May-30 Sep.** **2024**

WARSZAWA *B3* (13km SE Urban) *52.17798, 21.14727* **Camping Wok (No. 90),** ul Odrębna 16, 04-867 Warszawa **(022) 6127951; wok@campingwok.warszawa.pl; www.campingwok.warszawa.pl**

(htd) WD MSP nr nr

Fr city cent or fr W on E30, take bdge on E30 over Rv Wisła to E side of rv. Then take rte 801 for approx 8km (dual c'way). At rndabt double back for 600m & take 3rd R into Odrębna. Site 200m on R. 4*, Sm, shd, EHU (10-16A) PLN25; gas; bbq; cooking facs; TV; bus/tram adj; Eng spkn; adv bkg acc; ccard acc; games area; CKE. *"Lovely little site; v secure; spotless, modern san facs; helpful staff."* **PLN 180, 1 Apr-31 Oct.** **2023**

WARSZAWA *B3* (4km W Urban) *52.2144, 20.96575* **Majawa Camping (No. 123),** ul Bitwy Warszawskiej 19/20, 02-366 Warszawa-Szczęśliwice **(022) 8229121; biuro@majawa.pl; www.majawa.pl**

WD nr nr

Fr W on E30/rd 2 at junc with E67/rd 8 rd goes S thro tunnel under rlwy then strt on under new over-pass. Site on R in 100m. On E67/rd 8 fr Wrocław app concrete monument 3m high in middle of tramway; turn L at traff lts. Hotel Vera on R, site on L. Fr cent of Warsaw, take rd no. 7/8 700m twds Katowice. Not v well sp fr cent of town. Ent & exit diff due v busy rd. 1*, Sm, pt shd, EHU (6A) PLN15; bbq; 10% statics; phone; bus 500m; Eng spkn; ccard acc; tennis; CKE. *"Easy access to Warsaw & Royal Castle; gd meals at adj bowling alley or Vera hotel; poss lge rallies on site; friendly; poor condition but well positioned to get into city."* **PLN 138, 1 May-30 Sep.** **2024**

WEGORZEWO *A3* (4km SE Rural) *54.18647, 21.77018* **Camping Rusałka (No. 175),** 11-600 Węgorzewo warmińsko-mazurskie Polska **(087) 4272191; camping@cmazur.pl; www.cmazur.pl**

WD nr

Fr rte 63 fr Giżycko to Węgorzewo turn W approx 3km SW of Węgorzewo. Foll sp to site. 2*, Lge, pt shd, EHU PLN8; sw nr; 80% statics; sailing; fishing. *"Lovely pt of Lake District; delightful situation; all facs at top of steep hill."* **PLN 48, 1 May-30 Sep.** **2020**

POLAND

POLAND

WIELICZKA *D3* (1.5km SE Urban) *49.98273, 20.07611* **Hotel na Wierzynka (Formerly Motel Camping Wierzynka),** ul Wierzynka 9, 32-020 Wieliczka **(012) 2783614 / 668 031 352; hotel@nawierzynka.pl; www.hotelnawierzynka.pl**

nr

Site sp fr E40/rte 4 about 2km fr salt mine. Sm, hdstg, pt shd, pt sl, EHU (10A) PLN10 (rev pol); bus to Krakow, train 1km; Eng spkn; ccard acc; bike hire; CKE. *"10 pitches in pleasant setting; helpful staff; facs basic but clean; shwrs erratic; 2km fr salt mines; vg site, local to salt mines; shwr portacabin, but clean."* **PLN 80, 1 May-30 Sep.** **2024**

WROCLAW *C2* (4km NE Urban) *51.11722, 17.09138* **Stadion Olimpijski Camp (No. 117),** ul Padarewskiego 35, 51-620 Wrocław **(071) 3484651**

nr nr

Fr A4 into Wrocław foll N8 sp Warszawa thro city. On N8 dir Warszawa, pass McDonalds, at fork in rd take Sienkiewicza to end, then Rozyckiego to stadium, site on R. If poss foll sp 'stadion' to camp; head for lighting towers of sports stadium if seen thro trees. 2*, Lge, pt shd, EHU (16A) PLN7.50; bbq; 10% statics; phone; tram nr; CKE. *"San facs basic but clean; site run down (2017); gd security; poss noise fr stadium; v conv for city; stop for tram v handy; pool 700m; carpk outside site."* **PLN 110, 1 May-15 Oct.** **2023**

ZAKOPANE *D3* (4km NE Rural) *49.32415, 19.98506* **Camping Harenda (No. 160),** Oś Harenda 51B, 34-500 Zakopane **(018) 2014700; harenda51b@gmail.com; www.harenda.tatrynet.pl**

12 (htd) nr

On main rd to Zakopane fr N, after town sp turn R into petrol stn with McDonalds. Cont to R, pass Cmp Ustep on L then turn L over rv bdge to site in 200m on R. 2*, Med, pt shd, pt sl, EHU (10A) PLN10 (long lead req); bbq; Eng spkn; CKE. *"Gd views Tatra mountains fr site; superb walking; poss rallies on site; poss unkempt LS; laundry done at modest cost; vg rest; rafting (not white water) on Dunajec Rv; Nowy Targ rec; lower site poss muddy in wet weather."* **PLN 52** **2024**

ZAKOPANE *D3* (4km NE Rural) *49.32229, 19.98550* **Camping Ustup (No. 207),** ul Ustup K/5, 34-500 Zakopane-Ustup **(08667) 477791 or 605 950 007 (PL); camping.ustup@gmail.com; www.camping-ustup.pl**

nr nr

Turn R off Kraków-Zakopane rd 47 at petrol stn/ McDonalds just after 1st town sp. Turn R again immed (also sp Cmg Harenda), site on L in 200m. Sm, unshd, pt sl, EHU (10A) inc; bus to town cent; adv bkg acc; CKE. *"Ideal cent for Tatra region; mountain views; excel, family-run site; v welcoming, friendly & helpful owner (ltd Eng); vg, clean san facs; grassy pitches; coach tours arranged fr adj g'ge info desk."* **PLN 81, 1 May-30 Sep.** **2024**

ZAKOPANE *D3* (3km SE Urban) *49.2830, 19.9690* **Camping Pod Krokwia (No. 97),** ul Żeromskiego 26, 34-500 Zakopane **(018) 2012256; camp@podkrokwia.pl; www.podkrokwia.pl**

12 PLN5 nr nr

Sp fr town cent. Fr N 2nd exit at 1st rndbt; strt over at 2nd rndbt; turn R at 3rd rndabt, then R in 250m. Site on L. 3*, Lge, hdstg, shd, pt sl, EHU (10A) inc; bbq; cooking facs; TV; phone; bus to Kraków; Eng spkn; tennis adj; CKE. *"Lge tent area; few mkd pitches; poss scruffy LS; poor san facs; conv town cent; ski slopes & cable cars; rafting on rapids; muddy when set; conv Tatra Mountains; mountain walks; town v touristy; vg loc; ltd facs; free gas stove."* **PLN 65.4** **2020**

ZAMOSC *C4* (1km SW Rural) *50.71919, 23.23908* **Camping Duet (No. 253),** ul Królowej Jadwigi 14, 22-400 Zamość **(084) 6392499; duet@virgo.com.pl; https://pola-namiotowe.info/pl/camping-nr-253-duet,59,podglad.html**

12

Fr Zamość cent W on rd 74, site on R bef Castorama. 1*, Sm, pt shd, EHU PLN12; 10% statics; CKE. *"Walk to attractive town; pool 150m; fair sh stay/NH."* **PLN 59** **2022**

ZGORZELEC *C1* (1km N Urban) *51.15957, 15.00069* **Camping Zgorzelec,** ul Lubańska 1a, 59-900 Zgorzelec **(075) 7752436; it@zgorzelec.eu; https://www.it.zgorzelec.pl**

12

Ent Zgorzelec fr Germany & foll rd sp Zagan. Turn L at traff lts at BP g'ge INTO Lubanska rd sp 351 site on R after 560m, bef downwards hill. Only sp is at camp gate. Sm, unshd, pt sl, EHU inc; CKE. *"Conv NH."* **PLN 60** **2020**

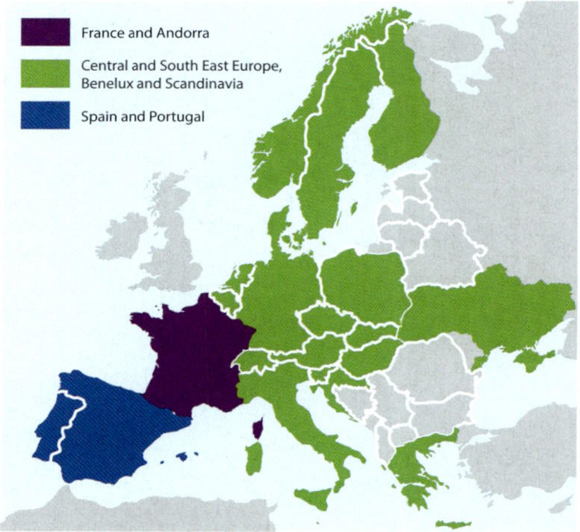

Koszalin to Warszawa (Warsaw) = 436km

	Biala Podlaska	Bialystok	Bielsko-Biala	Bydgoszcz	Czestochowa	Elblag	Gdansk	Gorzów Wielkopolski	Jelenia Góra	Katowice	Kielce	Koszalin	Kraków	Legnica	Lódz	Lublin	Olsztyn	Plock	Poznan	Przemysl	Radom	Rzeszów	Suwalki	Swinoujscie	Szczecin	Torun	Warszawa (Warsaw)	Wroclaw	Zamosc
Bialystok	149																												
Bielsko-Biala	472	543																											
Bydgoszcz	412	392	447																										
Czestochowa	365	410	133	314																									
Elblag	404	320	584	171	451																								
Gdansk	461	379	617	167	473	59																							
Gorzów Wielkopolski	596	603	496	214	415	333	315																						
Jelenia Góra	605	641	348	344	285	515	513	251																					
Katowice	416	485	58	391	75	524	545	456	327																				
Kielce	262	365	207	348	124	461	482	480	415	156																			
Koszalin	596	570	618	198	508	247	188	215	461	560	543																		
Kraków	376	477	86	434	114	567	565	529	403	75	114	621																	
Legnica	567	603	301	288	247	460	455	219	56	291	371	405	341																
Lódz	286	322	252	203	121	325	342	341	313	196	143	395	222	273															
Lublin	127	260	362	421	288	441	500	596	537	323	167	595	269	499	242														
Olsztyn	305	223	537	217	401	99	156	431	536	479	392	344	501	482	279	372													
Plock	267	270	363	150	230	234	276	346	385	305	231	340	327	340	104	271	177												
Poznan	470	488	387	131	289	300	296	131	226	333	354	241	405	170	210	465	323	215											
Przemysl	312	445	319	588	342	622	685	721	618	322	241	778	243	580	384	185	555	444	595										
Radom	184	285	285	322	181	383	444	487	430	232	78	512	192	392	137	107	316	179	358	268									
Rzeszów	297	430	238	513	272	585	642	639	542	243	165	710	165	503	306	170	514	378	517	78	199								
Suwalki	269	117	631	417	497	277	336	613	722	571	449	524	565	675	414	379	200	336	525	562	370	549							
Swinoujscie	730	701	676	312	586	400	341	179	429	636	651	151	701	397	508	728	491	462	297	892	634	816	667						
Szczecin	677	656	603	267	520	374	351	105	356	561	585	160	634	324	446	683	484	415	234	832	585	750	651	110					
Torun	366	347	422	46	290	167	181	260	366	364	307	236	384	312	159	375	172	104	150	542	278	472	370	356	313				
Warszawa (Warsaw)	157	188	355	252	222	280	338	439	452	297	183	436	294	415	136	161	212	112	310	346	103	299	274	601	524	211			
Wroclaw	496	532	230	265	176	436	432	268	109	199	300	420	267	69	204	428	442	276	178	511	321	435	614	442	371	279	344		
Zamosc	180	334	392	514	335	532	589	683	624	367	211	686	320	582	329	90	459	360	554	148	196	155	447	815	770	463	249	508	
Zielona Góra	570	601	387	259	328	430	411	109	142	358	420	322	427	111	301	542	453	351	130	663	433	586	653	290	212	281	413	159	629

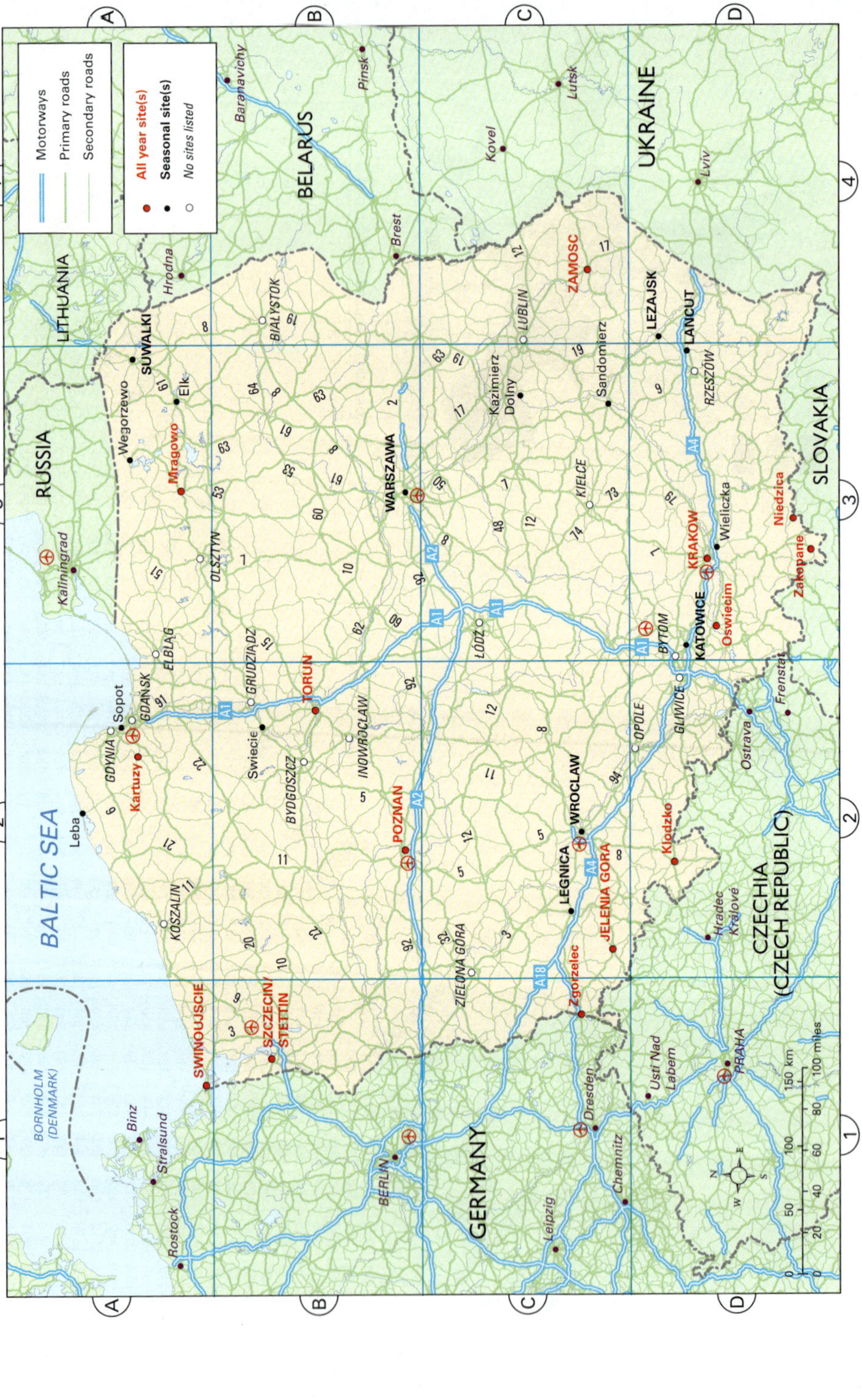
Motorways
Primary roads
Secondary roads
All year site(s)
Seasonal site(s)
No sites listed
BALTIC SEA
RUSSIA
LITHUANIA
BELARUS
UKRAINE
SLOVAKIA
CZECHIA (CZECH REPUBLIC)
GERMANY
BORNHOLM (DENMARK)
SWINOUJSCIE
SZCZECIN/ STETTIN
Karuzy
TORUN
POZNAN
Mragowo
ZAMOSC
KRAKOW
Oswiecim
Zakopane
Niedzica
Klodzko
JELENIA GORA
Zgorzelec
SUWALKI
Wegorzewo
Elk
Leba
Sopot
Swiecie
WARSZAWA
Kazimierz Dolny
Sandomierz
LEZAJSK
LANCUT
KATOWICE
Wieliczka
WROCLAW
LEGNICA
GDYNIA
GDANSK
ELBLAG
OLSZTYN
BIALYSTOK
LUBLIN
KIELCE
LODZ
BYTOM
GLIWICE
OPOLE
INOWROCLAW
BYDGOSZCZ
GRUDZIADZ
KOSZALIN
ZIELONA GORA
RZESZOW
Kaliningrad
Hrodna
Brest
Baranavichy
Pinsk
Kovel
Lutsk
Lviv
Frenstat
Ostrava
Hradec Kralove
PRAHA
Usti Nad Labem
Dresden
Chemnitz
Leipzig
BERLIN
Rostock
Stralsund
Binz
A1
A2
A4
A18
150 km
100 miles

Highlights

With around 3000 hours of sunshine a year, 850 kilometres of spectacular beaches and a wonderfully vibrant and varied landscape, Portugal is a visitor's paradise.

The country has been heavily influenced by its nautical tradition and position on the Atlantic. Many local delicacies are fish-based dishes, such as grilled sardines and salt cod, while some of Portugal's most splendid architecture date from when it was a global maritime empire.

Ceramic tiles, or azelujos, are a common element of Portuguese designs. Often depicting aspects of Portuguese culture and history, these tiles are both beautiful and functional, and are a significant part of Portugal's heritage.

Portugal is the birthplace of port, and the Douro region is one of the oldest protected wine regions in the world. Taking its name from the city of Porto, this smooth, fortified wine is exclusively produced in the Duoro Valley of Northern Portugal.

Major towns and cities

- Lisbon – Portugal's capital is known for its museums and café culture.
- Porto – an extravagant city filled with beautiful and colourful sights.
- Braga – an ancient city with filled with churches and Roman ruins.
- Faro – the prefect base to explore the Algarve.

Attractions

- Jerónimos Monastery – this UNESCO heritage site houses two museums.
- Guimarães Castle – this medieval castle is known as the Cradle of Portugal.
- National Palace of Pena – a striking palace filled with wonderful works of art.
- Lisbon Oceanarium – enjoy stunning living ocean exhibits.

Find out more

visitportugal.com
info@visitportugal.com

PORTUGAL

Country Information

Capital: Lisbon

Bordered by: Spain

Terrain: Rolling plains in south; mountainous and forested north of River Tagus

Climate: Temperate climate with no extremes of temperature; wet winters in the north influenced by the Gulf Stream; elsewhere Mediterranean with hot, dry summers and short, mild winters

Coastline: 1,794 km

Highest Point (mainland Portugal): Monte Torre 1,993m

Language: Portuguese

Local Time: GMT or BST, i.e. the same as the UK all year

Currency: Euros divided into 100 cents; £1 = €1.20 €1 = £0.84 (Nov 2024)

Emergency numbers: Police 112; Fire brigade 112; Ambulance 112

Public Holidays 2025: Jan 1; Apr 18, 20, 25; May 1; Jun 10, 19; Aug 15; Oct 5; Nov 1; Dec 1, 8, 25.

Other holidays and saints' days are celebrated according to region. School summer holidays run from mid-June to mid-September.

Entry Formalities

British and Irish passport holders may stay for up to 90 days in any 180 day period without a visa. You may be asked to show a return or onward ticket at the border to confirm your length of stay, or to prove that you have enough money for your stay.

Your passport will need to have a minimum of 6 months' validity remaining, and be less than 10 years old (even if it has over 6 months left).

Visitors arriving at a campsite or hotel must complete a registration form.

Medical Services

For treatment of minor conditions go to a pharmacy (farmacia). Staff are generally well trained and are qualified to dispense drugs, which may only be available on prescription in Britain. In large towns there is usually at least one English-speaking pharmacy, and all have information posted on the door indicating the nearest pharmacy open at night. All municipalities have a health centre.

State emergency health care and hospital treatment is free on production of a European Health Insurance Card (EHIC) or Global Health Insurance Card (GHIC). You'll have to pay for items such as X-rays, laboratory tests and prescribed medicines as well as dental treatment. Refunds can be claimed from local offices of the Administracão Regional de Saúde (regional health service).

For serious illness you can obtain the name of an English speaking doctor from the local police station or tourist office or from a British or American consulate.

Normal precautions should be taken to avoid mosquito bites, including the use of insect repellents, especially at night.

Opening Hours

Banks: Mon-Fri 8.30am-3pm; some banks in city centres are open until 6pm.

Museums: Tue-Sun 10am-5pm/6pm; closed Mon and may close 12.30pm-2pm.

Post Offices: Mon-Fri 9am-6pm; may close for an hour at lunch.

Shops: Mon-Fri 9am-1pm & 3pm-7pm, Sat 9am-1pm; large supermarkets open Mon-Sun 9am/9.30am-10pm/11pm.

Safety and Security

The crime rate is low but pickpocketing, bag snatching and thefts from cars can occur in major tourist areas. Be vigilant on public transport, at crowded tourist sites and in public parks where it's wise to go in pairs. Keep car windows closed and doors locked while driving in urban areas at night. There has been an increase in reported cases of items stolen from vehicles in car parks. Thieves distract drivers by asking for directions, for example, or other information. Be cautious if you're approached in this way in a car park.

Take care of your belongings at all times. Don't leave your bag on the chair beside you, under the table or hanging on your chair while you eat in a restaurant or café.

Warning flags on Portugeues beaches should be taken very seriously. A red flag indicates danger and you should not enter the water under any circumstance. If a yellow flag is flying you may paddle at the water's edge, but you may not swim. A green flag indicates that it's safe to swim, and a chequered flag means that the lifeguard is temporarily absent. Don't swim from beaches which aren't manned by lifeguards. The police may fine bathers who disobey warning flags.

During long, hot, dry periods forest fires can occur, especially in northern and central parts of the country. Take care when visiting or driving through woodland areas: ensure that cigarettes are extinguished properly, Don't light barbecues, and don't leave empty bottles behind.

Portugal shares with the rest of Europe an underlying threat from terrorism. Please check gov.uk/foreign-travel-advice/portugal before you travel.

British Embassy

Rua de São Bernardo 33,
1249-082 Lisbon
Tel: +351 213 924 000
gov.uk/world/portugal
There is also a British Vice Consulate in Portimão.

Irish Embassy

Avenida Da Liberdade NO 200, 4TH Floor
1250-147 Lisbon
Tel: +351 213 308 200
embassyofireland.pt

Documents

Driving Licence

All valid UK driving licences should be accepted in Portugal but holders of an older all green style licence are advised to update it to a photocard before travelling. Alternatively carry an International Driving Permit, available from the AA, the RAC or selected post offices.

Passport

You must carry proof of identity which includes a photograph and signature, e.g. a passport or photocard licence, at all times.

Vehicle(s)

When driving you must carry your vehicle registration certificate (V5C), proof of insurance and MOT certificate (if applicable) or you may receive an on-the-spot fine.

Money

The major credit cards are widely accepted and there are cash machines (Multibanco) throughout the country. Credit/debit cards may not be accepted for purhcases under 5 euros in taxis, smaller towns, and rural areas. Carry your credit card issuers'/banks' 24 hour UK contact numbers in case of loss or theft.

Driving

Many Portuguese drive erratically and vigilance is advised. By comparison with the UK, the accident rate is high. Particular blackspots are the N125 along the south coast, especially in the busy holiday season, and the coast road between Lisbon and Cascais. In rural areas you may encounter horse drawn carts and flocks of sheep or goats. Otherwise there are no special difficulties in driving except in Lisbon and Porto, which are unlimited 'free-for-alls'.

Accidents

The police must be called in the case of injury or significant material damage.

Alcohol

The maximum permitted level of alcohol in the blood is 0.05% i.e less than in England, Wales and Northern Ireland (0.08%) but the same as Scotland. It reduces to 0.03% for drivers with less than three years' experience. It's advisable to adopt the 'no drink-driving' rule at all times.

Breakdown Service

The Automovel Club de Portugal (ACP) operates a 24 hour breakdown service covering all roads in mainland Portugal. Its vehicles are coloured red and white. Emergency telephones are located at 2 km intervals on main roads and motorways. To contact the ACP breakdown service call +351 219 429 113 from a mobile or +351 707 509 510 from a landline.

The breakdown service comprises on the spot repairs taking up to 45 minutes and, if necessary, the towing of vehicles. The charges for breakdown assistance and towing vary according to distance, time of day and day of the week, plus motorway tolls if applicable. Payment by credit card is accepted.

Alternatively, on motorways breakdown vehicles belonging to the motorway companies (their emergency numbers are displayed on boards along the motorways) and police patrols (GNR/Brigada de Trânsito) can assist motorists.

Child Restraint System

Children under 12 years of age and less than 1.35 m in height aren't allowed to travel in the front passenger seat. They must be seated in a child restraint system adapted to their size and weight in the rear of the vehicle, unless the vehicle only has two seats, or if the vehicle is not fitted with seat belts.

Children under the age of 3 years old can be seated in the front passenger seat as long as they are in a suitable rear facing child restraint system and the airbag has been deactivated.

Fuel

Credit cards are accepted at most filling stations but a small extra charge may be added and a tax of €0.50 is added to credit card transactions. There are some automatic petrol pumps. LPG (gáz liquido) is widely available.

Low Emission Zone

There is a Low Emission Zone in operation in Lisbon. For more information visit urbanaccessregulations.eu.

Motorways

Portugal has approximately 3,000 km of motorways (auto-estradas), with tolls (portagem) payable on most sections. Take care not to use the 'Via Verde' green lanes reserved for motorists who subscribe to the automatic payment system – be sure to go through a ticket booth lane where applicable, or one equipped with the new electronic toll system.

Dual carriageways (auto vias) are toll free and look similar to motoways, but speed limits are lower.

It's permitted to spend the night on a motorway rest or service area with a caravan, although The Caravan and Motorhome Club doesn't recommend this practice for security reasons. Toll tickets are only valid for 12 hours and fines are incurred if this is exceeded.

Vehicle are classified for tolls as follows:

Class 1	Vehicle with or without trailer with height from front axle less than 1.10m.
Class 2	Vehicle with 2 axles, with or without trailer, with height from front axle over 1.10m.
Class 3	Vehicle or vehicle combination with 3 axles, with height from front axle over 1.10m.
Class 4*	Vehicle or vehicle combination with 4 or more axles with height from front axle over 1.10m.

* Drivers of high vehicles of the Range Rover/ Jeep variety, together with some MPVs, and towing a twin axle caravan pay Class 4 tolls.

Mountain Roads and Passes

There are no mountain passes or tunnels in Portugal. Roads through the Serra da Estrela near Guarda and Covilha may be temporarily obstructed for short periods after heavy snow.

Parking

In most cases, vehicles must be parked facing in the same direction as moving traffic. Parking is limited in the centre of main towns and cities and 'blue zone' parking schemes operate. Illegally parked vehicles may be towed away or clamped. Parking in Portuguese is 'estacionamento'.

Priority

In general at intersections and road junctions, road users must give way to vehicles approaching from the right, unless signs indicate otherwise. At roundabouts vehicles already on the roundabout, i.e. on the left, have right of way.

Don't pass stationary trams at a tram stop until you're certain that all passengers have finished entering or leaving the tram.

Roads

Roads are surfaced with asphalt, concrete or stone setts. Main roads generally are well surfaced and may be three lanes wide, the middle lane being used for overtaking in either direction.

Roads in the south of the country are generally in good condition, but some sections in the north are in a poor state.

Roads in many towns and villages are often cobbled and rough.

Drivers entering Portugal from Zamora in Spain will notice an apparently shorter route on the CL527/N221 road via Mogadouro. Although this is actually the signposted route, the road surface is poor in places and this route is not recommended for trailer caravans. The recommended route is via the N122/IP4 to Bragança.

Road Signs and Markings

Road signs conform to international standards. Road markings are white or yellow. Signs on motorways (auto-estrada) are blue and on regional roads they are white with black lettering. Roads are classified as follows:

Code	Road Type
AE	Motorways
IP	Principal routes
IC	Complementary routes
EN	National roads
EM	Municipal roads
CM	Other municipal roads

Signs you might encounter are as follows:

Portuguese	English Translation
Atalho	Detour
Entrada	Entrance
Estacão de gasolina	Petrol station
Estacão de policia	Police station
Estacionamento	Parking
Estrada con portagem	Toll road
Saida	Exit

Speed Limits

	Open Road (km/h)	Motorway (km/h)
Car Solo	90-100	120
Car towing caravan/trailer	70-80	100
Motorhome under 3500kg	90-100	120
Motorhome 3500-7500kg	70-90	100

Drivers must maintain a speed between 40 km/h (25 mph) and 60 km/h (37 mph) on the 25th April Bridge over the River Tagus in Lisbon. Speed limits are electronically controlled.

Visitors who have held a driving licence for less than one year must not exceed 90 km/h (56 mph) on any road subject to higher limits.

In built-up areas there is a speed limit of 50 km/h.

It's prohibited to use a radar detector or to have one installed in a vehicle.

Towing

Motorhomes are permitted to tow a car on a four wheel trailer, i.e. with all four wheels of the car off the ground. Towing a car on an A-frame (two back wheels on the ground) is not permitted.

Traffic Jams

Traffic jams are most likely to be encountered around Lisbon and Porto and on roads to the coast, such as the A1 Lisbon-Porto and the A2 Lisbon-Setúbal, which are very busy on Friday evenings and Saturday mornings. The peak times for holiday traffic are the last weekend in June and the first and last weekends in July and August.

Around Lisbon bottlenecks occur on bridges across the River Tagus, the N6 to Cascais, the A1 to Vila Franca de Xira, the N8 to Loures and on the N10 from Setúbal via Almada.

Around Porto you may find traffic jams on the IC1 on the Arribada Bridge and at Vila Nova de Gaia, the A28/IC1 from Póvoa de Varzim and near Vila de Conde, and on the N13, N14 and the N15.

Major motorways are equipped with suspended signs which indicate the recommended route to take when there is traffic congestion.

Traffic Lights

There's no amber signal after the red. Flashing amber means 'caution' and a flashing or constant red light means 'stop'. In Lisbon there are separate traffic lights in bus lanes.

Violation of Traffic Regulations

Speeding, illegal parking and other infringements of traffic regulations are heavily penalised.

You may incur a fine for crossing a continuous single or double white or yellow line in the centre of the road when overtaking or when executing a left turn into or off a main road, despite the lack of any other 'no left turn' signs. If necessary, drive on to a roundabout or junction to turn, or turn right as directed by arrows.

The police are authorised to impose on-the-spot fines and a receipt must be given. Most police vehicles are now equipped with portable credit card machines to facilitate immediate payment of fines.

Tolls

Portugal uses an electronic toll collecting system. The following motorways have tolls but no toll booths: A27, A28, A24, A41, A42, A25, A29, A23, A13, A8, A19, A33, A22 and parts of the A17 and A4. Tolls for these motorways can be paid by one of the following options:

If you're crossing the border from Spain on the A24, A25 or A22 or the A28 (via the EN13) then you can use the EASYToll welcome points. You can input your credit card details and the machine reads and then matches your credit/debit card to your number-plate, tolls are deducted automatically from your credit card, and the EASYToll machine will issue you a 30-day receipt as proof that you have paid.

If you're entering Portugal on a road that doesn't have an EASYToll machine you can register online or at a CTT post office and purchase either €5, €10, €20 or €40 worth of tolls. For more information visit (visitportugal.com) and see the heading 'All about Portugal' then 'Useful Information'.

Alternatively you can buy or rent a Via Verde transponder device from some motorway service stations, post offices, and on the Via Verde website: visitors.viaverde.pt.

On motorways where this system applies you'll see a sign: 'Lanço Com Portagem' or 'Electronic Toll Only', together with details of the tolls charged. Drivers caught using these roads without a Via Verde transponder device will receive a substantial fine.

The toll roads A1 to A15 and A21 continue to have manned toll booths. Most, but not all, accept credit cards or cash.

Toll Bridges

The 25 April Bridge in Lisbon crosses the River Tagus. Tolls are charged for vehicles travelling in a south-north direction only. Tolls also apply on the Vasco da Gama Bridge, north of Lisbon, but again only to vehicles travelling in a south-north direction. Overhead panels indicate the maximum permitted speed in each lane and, when in use, override other speed limit signs.

In case of breakdown, or if you need assistance, you should try to stop in the emergency hard shoulder areas, wait inside your vehicle and switch on your hazard warning lights until a patrol arrives. Emergency telephones are placed at frequent intervals. It's prohibited to carry out repairs, to push vehicles physically or to walk on the bridges.

Essential Equipment

Reflective Jackets/Waistcoats

If your vehicle is immobilised on the carriageway you should wear a reflective jacket or waistcoat when getting out of your vehicle. This is a legal requirement for residents of Portugal and is recommended for visitors. Passengers who leave a vehicle, for example, to assist with a repair, should also wear one. Keep the jackets within easy reach inside your vehicle, not in the boot.

Warning Triangles

Use a warning triangle if, for any reason, a stationary vehicle is not visible for at least 100 metres. In addition, hazard warning lights must be used if a vehicle is causing an obstruction or danger to other road users.

Touring

Some English is spoken in large cities and tourist areas. Elsewhere a knowledge of French could be useful.

A Lisboa Card valid for 24, 48 or 72 hours entitles the holder to free unrestricted access to public transport, including trains to Cascais and Sintra, free entry to a number of museums and other places of interest in Lisbon and surrounding areas, as well as discounts in shops.These cards are available from tourist information offices, travel agents, some hotels and Carris ticket booths, or by visiting: lisboacard.fr.

When eating out make sure you understand what you're paying for; appetisers put on the table aren't free. Service is included in the bill, but it's customary to tip 5 to 10% of the total if you have received good service. Rules on smoking in restaurants and bars vary according to the size of the premises. The areas where clients are allowed to smoke are indicated by signs and there must be adequate ventilation. Each town in Portugal devotes several days in the year to colourful local celebrations. Carnivals and festivals during the period before Lent, during Holy Week and during the grape harvest can be particularly spectacular.

Camping and Caravanning

There are numerous campsites in Portugal, and many of these are situated along the coast. Sites are rated from 1 to 4 stars.

There are 23 privately owned campsites in the Orbitur chain. Members of the Orbitur Camping Club receive discounts of at least 15% at these sites. You can buy membership at Orbitur sites or via their website: orbitur.pt.

Casual/wild camping is not permitted.

Motorhomes

Some local authorities provide dedicated short stay areas for motorhomes called 'Áreas de Serviçio'. It's rare you'll be the only motorhomers staying there, but take sensible precautions and avoid any that are isolated.

Cycling

In Lisbon there are cycle lanes in Campo Grande gardens, also from Torre de Belém to Cais do Sodré (7km) along the River Tagus, and between Cascais and Guincho. Elsewhere in the country there are few cycle lanes.

Transportation of Bicycles

Only caravans or motorhomes are allowed to carry bicycles/motorbikes at the rear of the vehicle. Bicycles may not extend beyond the width of the vehicle or more than 45cm from the back. Bicycles may be transported on the roof of cars provided that an overall height of 4 metres is not exceeded.

If you're planning to travel from Spain to Portugal please note that slightly different regulations apply and these are set out in the Spain country introduction.

Electricity and Gas

Usually current on campsites varies between 6 and 15 amps. Plugs have two round pins. CEE connections are commonplace.

The full range of Campingaz cylinders is available.

Public Transport

A passenger and vehicle ferry crosses the River Sado estuary from Setúbal to Tróia and there are frequent ferry and catamaran services for cars and passengers across the River Tagus from various points in Lisbon including Belém and Cais do Sodré.

Both Lisbon and Porto have metro systems operating from 6am to 1am. For routes and fares see the websites metrolisboa.pt and metrodoporto.pt. In Lisbon, the extensive bus and tram network is operated by Carris. Buy single journey tickets on board from bus drivers or buy a rechargeable 7 Colinas or Via Viagem card for use on buses and the metro.

If you're planning to move around Porto by bus and metro, you should buy an Andante Tour Card which can be bought and charged at the airport, metro and train stations, some bus stops, kiosks and various other places in the city. For more information, visit: introducingporto.com/andante-card.

Porto also has a passenger lift and a funicular so that you can avoid the steep walk to and from the riverside.

Taxis are usually beige-coloured. In cities they charge a standard, metered fare; outside they may run on the meter or charge a flat rate. Agree a price for your journey before setting off.

Sites in Portugal

ALANDROAL *C3* (13km S Rural) *38.60645, -7.34674* **Parque de Campismo Rural Camping Rosario (Formerly Camping Rosário),** Monte das Mimosas, Rosário, 7250-999 Alandroal **963 679 945; info@campingrosario.com; www.campingrosario.com**

€1 nr

Fr E exit IP7/A6 at Elvas W junc 9; at 3rd rndabt take exit sp Espanha, immed 1st R dir Juromenha & Redondo. Onto N373 until exit Rosário. Fr W exit IP7/A6 junc 8 at Borba onto N255 to Alandroal, then N373 E sp Elvas. After 1.5km turn R to Rosário & foll sp to site. Sm, hdstg, pt shd, pt sl, EHU (6A) €2.35; sw nr; red long stay; TV, Eng spkn; adv bkg acc; boating; fishing; CKE. *"Remote site beside Alqueva Dam; excel touring base; dogs not acc Jul/Aug; ltd to 50 people max; excel site; idyllic; peaceful; clean & well maintained; v helpful owner."* **€22.50, 2 Jan-30 Sep. 2024**

ALBUFEIRA *B4* (3km N Urban) *37.10617, -8.25395* **Camping Albufeira,** Estrada de Ferreiras, 8200-555 Albufeira **289 587629 or 289 587630; geral@campingalbufeira.net or info@campingalbufeira.net; www.campingalbufeira.net**

sand 1.5km

Exit IP1/E1 sp Albufeira onto N125/N395 dir Albufeira; camp on L, sp. 4*, V lge, mkd, pt shd, pt sl, EHU (10-12A) €3; gas; red long stay; TV; 20% statics; phone; bus adj; Eng spkn; ccard acc; games area; games rm; bike hire; tennis; CKE. *"Friendly, secure site; excel pool area/bar; some pitches lge enough for US RVs; car wash; cash machine; security patrols; disco (soundproofed); sports park; pitches on lower pt of site prone to flooding in heavy rain; conv beach & town; poss lge rallies during Jan-Apr; camp bus to town high ssn."* **€27.60 2022**

See advertisement opposite

ALBUFEIRA *B4* (15km W Urban/Coastal) *37.10916, -8.35333* **Camping Armação de Pêra,** 8365-184 Armação de Pêra **282 312260; geral@camping-armacao-pera.com; www.camping-armacao-pera.com**

sand 500m

Fr Lagos take N125 coast rd E. At Alcantarilha turn S onto N269-1 sp Armação de Pêra & Campismo. Site at 3rd rndabt in 2km on L. 3*, V lge, hdg, shd, pt sl, EHU (6-10A) €3-4; gas; TV; 25% statics; phone; bus adj; Eng spkn; car wash; games area; tennis; bike hire; games rm; CKE. *"Friendly, popular & attractive site; gd pool; min stay 3 days Oct-May; easy walk to town; interesting chapel of skulls at Alcantarilha; birdwatching in local lagoon; vg."* **€29.50 2024**

"There aren't many sites open at this time of year"

If you're travelling outside peak season remember to call ahead to check site opening dates – even if the entry says 'open all year'.

ALCACER DO SAL *B3* (1km NW Rural) *38.38027, -8.51583* **Camping Parque de Campismo,** Olival do Outeiro, 7580-125 Alcácer do Sal **265 612303; cmalcacer@mail.telepac.pt**

nr nr nr

Heading S on A2/IP1 turn L twd Alcácer do Sal on N5. Site on R 1km fr Alcácer do Sal. Sp at rndabt. Site behind supmkt. 2*, Sm, hdg, mkd, pt shd, pt sl, EHU (6-12A) €1.50 (rev pol); bbq; phone; bus 50m; Eng spkn; ccard acc; games area; clsd mid-Dec to mid-Jan; CKE. *"In rice growing area - major mosquito prob; historic town; spacious pitches; pool, paddling pool adj; poss full in winter - rec phone ahead; pleasant site behing supmkt; wifi at recep; san facs tired & not clean."* **€15.20, 15 Jan-15 Dec. 2023**

PORTUGAL

ALCOBACA *B2* (3km S Rural) *39.52611, -8.96583* **Camping Silveira,** Capuchos, 2460-479 Alcobaça **262 509573; campingsilveira@gmail.com; www.campingsilveira.com**

S fr Alcobaça on N 8-6 sp Evora de Alcobaça. Site on L in 3km after Capuchos. 1*, Med, hdg, shd, pt sl, EHU (6A) €3; bbq; bus 500m; Eng spkn; adv bkg acc; games rm; badminton; sm library; WiFi access pnt. *"Vg, wooded, CL-type site; friendly owner; gd views; excel facs; pool 3km; excel touring base; site access extremely tight; site overgrown and unkept; Monastry Santa Maria in Alcobaca a must see; fair."*
€13.00, 15 May-15 Sep. **2024**

"That's changed – Should I let the Club know?"

If you find something on site that's different from the site entry, fill in a report and let us know. See camc.com/europereport.

AMARANTE *C1* (3km NE Rural) *41.27805, -8.07027* **Camping Penedo da Rainha,** Rua Pedro Alveollos, Gatão, 4600-099 Amarante **91 549 33 30; ccporto@sapo.pt or geral@amarantecamping.com; www.amarantecamping.com**

Fr IP4 Vila Real to Porto foll sp to Amarante & N15. On N15 cross bdge for Porto & immed take R slip rd. Foll sp thro junc & up rv to site. 2*, Lge, hdstg, shd, pt sl, terr, EHU (10A) inc; TV; phone; bus to Porto fr Amarante; Eng spkn; adv bkg acc; games rm; rv fishing adj; canoeing; cycling; CKE. *"Well-run site in steep woodland/parkland - take advice or survey rte bef driving to pitch; excel facs but some pitches far fr facs; few touring pitches; friendly, helpful recep; plenty of shd; conv Amarante old town & Douro Valley; Sat mkt; not suitable for long o'fits, better for MH's; beautiful cycle route on old rlwy."* **€21.50, 1 Jan-30 Nov.** **2024**

ARCO DE BAULHE *C1* (0.3km NE Rural) *41.48659, -7.95845* **Arco Unipessoal,** Lugar das Cruzes, 4860-067 Arco de Baúlhe (Costa Verde) **968 176246; campismoarco@hotmail.com; www.campismo-arco.com**

Dir A7 exit 12 Mondm/Cabeceiras, 2nd R at rndabt dir Arco de Baulhe. Call and they will lead you in. V narr rd access, no mv's over 7m. Med, pt shd, terr, EHU (6A); bbq; TV; Eng spkn; adv bkg rec; rv. *"New site run by couple with 20 yrs experience; quiet; centrally located for historic towns & nature parks; gd rest; lovely well maintained site with view; excel facs; 100m fr vill cent; beautiful mountain area."*
€23.00, 3 Apr-1 Oct. **2024**

ARGANIL *C2* (3km N Rural) *40.2418, -8.06746* **Camp Municipal de Arganil,** 3300-432 Sarzedo **235 205706; camping@cm-arganil.pt; www.cm-arganil.pt**

Fr Coimbra on N17 twd Guarda; after 50km turn S sp Arganil on N342-4; site on L in 4km in o'skts of Sarzedo bef rv bdge; avoid Góis to Arganil rd fr SW. 2*, Med, pt shd, pt sl, terr, EHU (5-15A) €2.40; gas; bbq; red long stay; TV; phone; Eng spkn; ccard acc; canoeing adj; games area; fishing adj; CKE. *"Vg, well-run site; friendly owner; fine views; gd cent for touring; gd walks; ski in Serra da Estrela 50km Dec/Jan; interesting town; gd mkt (Thu)."*
€12.50, 1 Mar-31 Oct. **2022**

AVEIRO *B2* (14km SW Coastal) *40.59960, -8.74981* **Camping Costa Nova,** Estrada da Vagueira, Quinta dos Patos, 3830-453 Ilhavo **234 393220; info@campingcostanova.com; www.campingcostanova.com**

Site on Barra-Vagueira coast rd 1km on R after Costa Nova. 2*, V lge, mkd, unshd, EHU (2-6A) €2.40; gas; bbq; red long stay; TV; 10% statics; phone; Eng spkn; adv bkg acc; ccard acc; games rm; site clsd Jan; fishing; bike hire; games area; CKE. *"Superb, peaceful site adj nature reserve; helpful staff; gd, hot water to shwrs only; sm pitches; sep car park high ssn; pool 4km; vg; excel cycle track fr site."*
€22.50, 21 Mar-1 Oct. **2024**

AVEIRO *B2* (10km W Coastal) *40.63861, -8.74500* **Barra Camping & Bungalows (Formerly Parque de Campismo Praia da Barra),** Rua Diogo Cão 125, Praia da Barra, 3830-772 Gafanha da Nazaré **(234) 369425 or (929) 056884 (mobile); info@campingbarra.com; www.campingbarra.com**

12 €1.90 WD MSP

sand 200m

Fr Aveiro foll sp to Barra on A25/IP5; foll sp to site. 3*, Lge, mkd, shd, EHU (6-10A) inc; gas; bbq; TV; 90% statics; phone; bus adj; Eng spkn; adv bkg acc; bike hire; games area; games rm; CKE. *"Well-situated site with some pitches in pine trees; recep open 0900-2200; pool 400m; old san facs; m'homes may have to park clse together on hardstanding area in LS; may be rd noise in some areas."* **€22.60** **2024**

"I like to fill in the reports as I travel from site to site"

You'll find report forms at the back of this guide, or you can fill them in online at camc.com/europereport.

BEJA *C4* (2km S Urban) *38.00777, -7.86222* **Parque de Campismo Municipal de Beja,** Avda Vasco da Gama, 7800-397 Beja **284 311911; cmb.dcd@iol.pt; www.cm-beja.pt**

12 WD nr nr nr

Fr S (N122) take 1st exit strt into Beja. In 600m turn R at island then L in 100m into Avda Vasco da Gama & foll sp for site on R in 300m - narr ent. Fr N on N122 take by-pass round town then 1st L after Intermarche supmkt, then as above. 1*, Lge, hdstg, shd, EHU (6A) €1.85; bus 300m, train 1.5km; tennis adj; CKE. *"C'van storage facs; helpful staff; NH only; pool adj; gravel pitches; football stadium adj."* **€10.40** **2024**

BRAGANCA *D1* (12km W Rural) *41.84879, -6.86120* **Cepo Verde Camping,** Gondesende, 5300-561 Bragança **273 999 371; info@montesinho.com; www.montesinho.com/cepoverde-campismo**

€3.50 WD

Fr Spain take IP4 twrds Vinhais/Chaves to skirt Bragança. Site sp fr IP4 ring rd. R off N103, foll lane & turn R at sp. NB Camping sp to rd 103-7 leads to different site (Sabor) N of city. 4*, Med, mkd, hdstg, pt shd, terr, EHU (6A) inc (poss rev pol & long lead poss req); bbq; phone; bus 1km; Eng spkn; adv bkg acc; ccard acc; CKE. *"Remote, friendly, v pleasant, scenic site adj Montesinho National Park; vg value; gd modern san facs; staff v helpful; gd rest with vegetarian options; gd base for Montesinho area; highly rec; v attractive site."* **€28.20, 1 Mar-31 Oct.** **2024**

CAMINHA *B1* (3km SW Coastal) *41.86611, -8.85888* **Camping ORBITUR-Caminha,** Mata do Camarido, N13, Km 90, 4910-180 Caminha **258 921295; infocaminha@orbitur.pt; www.orbitur.pt**

12 €1.50 WD MSP

sand 150m

Foll seafront rd N13/E1 fr Caminha dir Viana/Porto, at sp Foz do Minho turn R, site in approx 1km. Long o'fits take care at ent. 2*, Med, shd, terr, EHU (5-15A) €3-4; gas; red long stay; TV; 5% statics; Eng spkn; adv bkg acc; ccard acc; fishing; bike hire; CKE. *"Pleasant, woodland site; pool 2.5km; care in shwrs - turn cold water on 1st as hot poss scalding; Gerês National Park & Viana do Castelo worth visit; poss to cycle to Caminha; vg site, nr attractive beach and sh walk to pleasant town."* **€33.00** **2023**

CAMPO MAIOR *C3* (2km SE Rural) *39.00833, -7.04833* **Camping Rural Os Anjos,** Estrada da Senhora da Saúde, 7371-909 Campo Maior **268 688138 or 965 236625 (mob); info@campingosanjos.com; www.campingosanjos.com**

12 €1 WD nr

Fr Elvas foll rd N373 to Campo Maior. Foll sm sp thro vill pass green tree and football stadium. Site on L down country lane. Sm, hdstg, pt shd, terr, EHU (6A) €3.20; bbq; TV; phone; Eng spkn; adv bkg rec; games rm; games area; CKE. *"Excel, lovely, peaceful site; v helpful, friendly, caring Dutch owners; gd touring base for unspoiled, diverse area; conv Spanish border, Badajoz & Elvas; 15 Nov-15 Feb open with adv bkg only; max 1 dog per pitch; Campo Maior beautiful, white town; LS call or email bef arr; gd walks & bike rides; v clean shwrs; lake sw 8km; fishing 8km; watersports 8km; modern facs; fantastic views; very relaxing; excel."* **€17.50** **2023**

CASCAIS *A3* (7km NW Urban/Coastal) *38.72166, -9.46666* **Camping ORBITUR-Guincho,** Rua da Areia, 2750-053, Cascais **(214) 870450; infoguincho@orbitur.pt; www.orbitur.pt/camping-orbitur-guincho**

12 €3 WD MSP

sand 800m

Fr Lisbon take A5 W, at end m'way foll sp twd Cascais. At 1st rndabt turn R sp Birre & Campismo. Foll sp for 2.5km. Steep traff calming hump - care needed. 2*, V lge, mkd, hdg, shd, terr, EHU (6A) inc; gas; bbq; sw nr; red long stay; twin axles; TV (pitch); 50% statics; phone; Eng spkn; adv bkg acc; ccard acc; games rm; horseriding 500m; tennis; watersports 1km; car wash; fishing 1km; golf 3km; bike hire; CKE. *"Sandy, wooded site behind dunes; poss stretched & v busy high ssn; poss diff lge o'fits due trees; steep rd to beach; gd san facs, gd value rest; vg LS; buses to Cascais for train to Lisbon; beautiful coastline within 20 min walk; rec lge o'fits prebook to ensure suitable pitch."* **€33.00, E10.** **2022**

CASTELO BRANCO *C2* (6km N Rural) *39.85777, -7.49361* **Camp Municipal Castelo Branco,** Estrada Nacional 18, 6000-113 Castelo Branco **(272) 322577; albigec@sm-castelobranco.pt; www.albigec.pt/pt/equipamentos/parque-de-campismo.aspx**

Fr IP2 take Castelo Branco Norte, exit R on slip rd, L at 1st rndabt, site sp at 2nd rndabt. Turn L at T junc just bef Modelo supmkt, site 2km on L, well sp. 3*, Lge, shd, pt sl, EHU (12A) €2.25; gas; bus 100m; Eng spkn; CKE. *"Useful NH on little used x-ing to Portugal; pool 4km; gd site but rds to it poor."* **€9.00, 2 Jan-15 Nov. 2024**

CASTELO DE VIDE *C3* (7km SW Rural) *39.39805, -7.48722* **Camping Quinta do Pomarinho,** N246, Km 16.5, Castelo de Vide **965 755 341; info@pomarinho.com; www.pomarinho.com**

On N246 at km 16.5 by bus stop, turn into dirt track. Site in 500m. Sm, mkd, hdstg, unshd, EHU (6A) €2.50-3.50; bus adj; Eng spkn; adv bkg acc; bike hire. *"On edge of Serra de São Mamede National Park; gd walking, fishing, birdwatching, cycling; vg; gd views twd Serra de Sao Marmede; recep clsd 1-3pm; not many ehu or flat lge pitches."* **€16.50 2024**

CASTRO VERDE *C4* (1km N Urban) *37.704976, -8.087696* **Parque Campismo Castro Verde,** Rua Timor Lorosae 7780, Castro Verde **286 320150; parque.campismo@cm-castroverde.pt; www.cm-castroverde.pt/pt/553/parque-de-campismo-municipal.aspx**

Sp fr Castro Verde town. Med, hdstg, pt shd, pt sl, EHU; gas; twin axles; TV; Eng spkn; CCI. *"Vg site."* **2024**

CELORICO DE BASTO *C1* (0.7km NW Rural) *41.39026, -8.00581* **Parque de Campismo de Celorico de Basto,** Adaufe-Gemeos, 4890-361 Celorico de Basto **(255) 323340 or 964-064436 (mob); campismo@qualidadedebasto-em.pt; www.portoenorte.pt/pt/onde-ficar/parque-de-campismo-e-caravanismo-de-celorico-de-basto**

E fr Guimarães exit A7/IC5 S sp Vila Nune (bef x-ing rv). Foll sp Fermil & Celorico de Basto, site sp. Rte narr and winding or take the N210 fr Amarente and foll sp to site. 3*, Med, mkd, hdstg, shd, EHU (6-16A) €2-3.20; gas; bbq; sw nr; red long stay; TV; 10% statics; phone; ccard acc; games area; fishing adj; CKE. *"Peaceful, well-run site; gd facs; pool 500m; gd cycling & walking; vg."* **€16.00 2024**

CHAVES *C1* (6km S Rural) *41.70166, -7.50055* **Camp Municipal Quinta do Rebentão,** Vila Nova de Veiga, 5400-764 Chaves **276 322733; parquedecampismo@chaves.pt; www.campismochaves.pt**

Fr o'skts Chaves take N2 S. After about 3km in vill of Vila Nova de Veiga turn E at sp thro new estate, site in about 500m. 3*, Med, hdstg, pt shd, terr, EHU (6A) inc; bbq; sw nr; phone; bus 800m; Eng spkn; adv bkg acc; bike hire; fishing 4km; games rm; CKE. *"Gd site in lovely valley but remote; excel helpful, friendly staff; facs block quite a hike fr some terr pitches, old but clean facs; Chaves interesting, historical Roman town; baker visits every morn; vg rest (clsd Mon in LS) & bar; site clsd Dec; pool adj; easy access; wifi at recep."* **€15.00 2024**

COIMBRA *B2* (6km SE Urban) *40.18888, -8.39944* **Coimbra Camping,** Rua de Escola, Alto do Areeiro, Santo António dos Olivais, 3030-011 Coimbra **239 086902; geral@cacampings.com; www.coimbracamping.com**

Fr S on AP1/IP1 at junc 11 turn twd Lousa & in 1km turn twd Coimbra on IC2. In 9.5km turn R at rndabt onto Ponte Rainha, strt on at 3 rndabts along Avda Mendes Silva. Then turn R along Estrada des Beiras & cross rndabt to Rua de Escola. Or fr N17 dir Beira foll sp sports stadium/campismo. Fr N ent Coimbra on IC2, turn L onto ring rd & foll Campismo sps. 4*, V lge, hdstg, pt shd, pt sl, terr, EHU (6A) inc (rev pol); gas; bbq; sw nr; red long stay; TV; 10% statics; bus 100m; Eng spkn; adv bkg acc; ccard acc; bike hire; games area; tennis; games rm; sauna; CKE. *"Vg site & facs; health club; pool adj; v interesting, lively university town; supmkt & fuel nrby."* **€23.70 2024**

COIMBRAO *B2* (0.5km NW Urban) *39.90027, -8.88805* **Camping Coimbrão,** 185 Travessa do Gomes, 2425-452 Coimbrão **244 606007; campingcoimbrao@web.de**

Site down lane in vill cent. Care needed lge o'fits, but site worth the effort. Sm, unshd, EHU (6-10A) €2.20-3.30; bbq; sw nr; red long stay; TV; bus 200m; Eng spkn; fishing 4km. *"Excel site; helpful & friendly staff; gd touring base; gd loc for exploring; office open 0800-1200 & 1500-2200; canoeing 4km; German owners."* **€18.40 2023**

ELVAS *C3* (2km SW Urban) *38.87305, -7.1800* **Parque de Campismo da Piedade,** 7350-901 Elvas **268 628997 or 268 622877; piedadeconfraria@sapo.pt**

Exit IP7/E90 junc 9 or 12 & foll site sp dir Estremoz. 1*, Med, mkd, hdstg, pt shd, sl, EHU (16A) inc; gas; bbq; phone; bus 500m; CKE. *"Attractive aqueduct & walls; Piedade church & relics adj; traditional shops; pleasant walk to town; v quiet site, even high ssn; adequate san facs; conv NH en rte Algarve; c'vans parked to cls; noisy; facs need updating."* **€20.00, 1 Apr-15 Sep. 2023**

PORTUGAL

ERMIDAS SADO *B4* (11km W Rural) *38.01805, -8.48500* **Camping Monte Naturista O Barão (Naturist),** Foros do Barão, 7566-909 Ermidas-Sado **936710623 (mob); info@montenaturista.com; www.montenaturista.com**

12 €1 WD MSP

Fr A2 turn W onto N121 thro Ermidas-Sado twd Santiago do Cacém. At x-rds nr Areläos turn R at bus stop (km 17.5) dir Barão. Site in 1km along unmade rd. Sm, mkd, pt shd, pt sl, EHU (6A) €3.20; bbq; red long stay; TV; 10% statics; Eng spkn; adv bkg acc; ccard acc; games area; CKE. *"Gd, peaceful 'retreat-type' site in beautiful wooded area; meals Tue, Thurs, Sat & Sun; friendly atmosphere; spacious pitches - sun or shd; rec."* **€27.30** **2022**

EVORA *C3* (3km SW Urban) *38.55722, -7.92583* **Camping Orbitur Evora,** Estrada das Alcaçovas, Herdade Esparragosa, 7005-206 Évora **(266) 705190; infoevora@orbitur.pt; www.orbitur.pt**

12 €4.15 WD MSP

Fr N foll N18 & by-pass, then foll sps for Lisbon rd at each rndabt or traff lts. Fr town cent take N380 SW sp Alcaçovas, foll site sp, site in 2km. NB Narr gate to site. 3*, Med, mkd, hdstg, pt shd, pt sl, EHU (16A) inc (long lead poss req, rev pol); gas; red long stay; TV; phone; bus; Eng spkn; adv bkg acc; ccard acc; games area; car wash; tennis; CKE. *"Conv town cent, Évora World Heritage site with wealth of monuments & prehistoric sites nrby; cycle path to town; free car parks just outside town walls; poss flooding some pitches after heavy rain; beautiful site; gd sized pitches; helpful staff; bread to order; gd cycle track on old rlwy; recently improved EHU and water points (2020); vg, clean san facs; poor water pressure in shwrs."* **€33.80** **2020**

"We must tell the Club about that great site we found"

Get your site reports in by mid-August and we'll do our best to get your updates into the next edition.

EVORAMONTE *C3* (6km NE Rural) *38.79276, -7.68701* **Camping Alentejo,** Novo Horizonte, 7100-300 Evoramonte **268 959283 or 936 799249 (mob); info@campingalentejo.com; www.campingalentejo.com**

12 €1 WD MSP

Fr E exit A6/E90 junc 7 Estremoz onto N18 dir Evora. Site in 8km at km 236. Sm, hdstg, pt shd, terr, EHU (16A) inc; bbq; bus adj; Eng spkn; adv bkg acc; horseriding; CKE. *"Excel site; gd birdwatching, v friendly and helpful owner; conv NH on the way to S; easy parking; excel modern clean facs; gd library in off; bus stop outside gate to Evora; care req ent site; MH stay at lower price if no hookups; improved site; gd; secure."* **€15.00** **2023**

FIGUEIRA DA FOZ *B2* (7km S Urban/Coastal) *40.11861, -8.85666* **Camping ORBITUR-Gala,** N109, Km 4, Gala, 3090-458 Figueira da Foz **233 431492; infogala@orbitur.pt; www.orbitur.pt**

12 €1.50 WD MSP (htd) sand 400m

Fr Figueira da Foz on N109 dir Leiria for 3.5km. After Gala site on R in approx 400m. Ignore sp on R 'Campismo' after long bdge. 3*, Lge, hdstg, shd, terr, EHU (6-10A) €3-4; gas; bbq; red long stay; TV; 80% statics; phone; Eng spkn; adv bkg acc; ccard acc; fishing 1km; car wash; tennis; games rm; CKE. *"Gd, renovated site adj busy rd; luxury san facs (furthest fr recep); excel pool; busy site; in pine woods."* **€43.00** **2022**

GERES *C1* (2km N Rural) *41.73777, -8.15805* **Vidoeiro Camping,** Lugar do Vidoeiro, 4845-081 Gerês **963 414 770; geral@geresvidoeirocamping.pt; www.geresvidoeirocamping.pt**

WD nr nr

NE fr Braga take N103 twds Chaves for 25km. 1km past Cerdeirinhas turn L twds Gerês onto N308. Site on L 2km after Caldos do Gerês. Steep rds with hairpins. Cross bdge & reservoir, foll camp sps. 2*, Lge, hdstg, mkd, pt shd, terr, EHU (10A) inc; bbq; sw nr; phone. *"Attractive, wooded site in National Park; gd, clean facs; thermal spa in Gerês; pool 500m; diff access for lge o'fits, mountain rd; gd walks direct fr site."* **€22.00, 15 May-15 Oct.** **2024**

GERES *C1* (14km NW Rural) *41.76305, -8.19111* **Parque de Campismo de Cerdeira,** Rue de Cerdeira 400, Campo do Gerês, 4840-030 Terras do Bouro **(253) 351005; info@parquecerdeira.com; www.parquecerdeira.com**

12 €4 WD

Fr N103 Braga-Chaves rd, 28km E of Braga turn N onto N304 at sp to Poussada. Cont N for 18km to Campo de Gerês. Site in 1km; well sp. 3*, V lge, shd, EHU (5-10A) €4; gas; sw; TV; 10% statics; bus 500m; Eng spkn; ccard acc; canoeing; bike hire; fishing 2km; CKE. *"Beautiful scenery; unspoilt area; fascinating old vills nrby & gd walking; ltd facs LS; Nat pk campsite; wooded site; san facs modern & clean."* **€30.00** **2022**

GOUVEIA *C2* (7km NE Rural) *40.52083, -7.54149* **Camping Quinta das Cegonhas,** 6290-122 Nabaínhos **238 745886; cegonhas@cegonhas.com; www.cegonhas.com**

12 €1.10 WD MSP nr

Turn S at 114km post on N17 Seia-Celorico da Beira. Site sp thro Melo vill. Sm, pt shd, EHU (6-10A) inc; red long stay; TV; bus 400m; Eng spkn; adv bkg acc; games rm; CKE. *"Vg, well-run, busy site in grnds of vill manor house; friendly Dutch owners; beautiful sm village location conv Torre & Serra da Estrella; guided walks; excel walks; highly rec; beautiful views; great stargazing opps; bread to order; follow dir given as a 1 dir ent."* **€24.50** **2024**

GUIMARAES *B1* (32km E Rural) *41.46150, -8.01120* **Quinta Valbom,** Quintã 4890-505 Ribas **351 253 653 048; info@quintavalbom.nl; www.quintavalbom.nl**

Fr Guimaraes take A7 SE. Exit 11 onto N206 Fafe/ Gandarela. Turn R bef tunnel twds Ribas. Foll blue & red signs of campsite. Med, mkd, pt shd, terr, EHU (10A); bbq; twin axles; Eng spkn; adv bkg acc; CCI. *"Very nice site; friendly, extremely helpful Dutch owners; quiet surroundings; lots of space in beautiful setting; if driving c'van, park at white chapel and call campsite for their 4WD assistance up last bit of steep hill; owner won't acc c'vans over 6mtrs."* **€24.00, 1 Apr-1 Oct.** **2023**

GUIMARAES *B1* (6km SE Rural) *41.42833, -8.26861* **Camping Parque da Penha,** Penha-Costa, 4800-026 Guimarães **253 515912 or 253 515085; geral@turipenha.pt / campismo@turipenha.pt; www.turipenha.pt**

nr

Take N101 SE fr Guimarães sp Felgueiras. Turn R at sp for Nascente/Penha. Site sp. Lge, hdstg, shd, pt sl, terr, EHU (6A) inc; gas; phone; bus; Eng spkn; adv bkg acc; fishing; car wash; CKE. *"Excel v helpful staff; gd but dated san facs; lower terrs not suitable lge o'fits; densely wooded hilltop site; conv Guimarães World Heritage site European City of Culture 2012; cable car down to Guimaraes costs €5 return; excel rest; m'homes must park v close together on higher lvl hard stnding."* **€19.00, 1 May-15 Sep.** **2024**

IDANHA A NOVA *C2* (10km NE Rural) *39.95027, -7.18777* **Camping ORBITUR-Barragem de Idanha-a-Nova,** N354-1, Km 8, Barragem de Idanha-a-Nova, 6060 Idanha-a-Nova **(277) 202793; infoidanha@orbitur.pt; www.orbitur.pt**

12 €1.50 (htd)

Exit IP2 at junc 25 sp Lardosa & foll sp Idanha-a-Nova on N18, then N233, N353. Thro Idanha & cross Rv Ponsul onto N354 to site. Avoid rte fr Castelo Branco via Ladoeiro as rd narr, steep & winding in places. 3*, Lge, hdstg, mkd, shd, terr, EHU (6A) €3-4; gas; bbq; sw; red long stay; TV (pitch); 10% statics; phone; Eng spkn; adv bkg acc; car wash; tennis; fishing; watersports 150m; games rm. *"Uphill to town & supmkt; hot water to shwrs only; pitches poss diff - a mover req; level pitches at top of site; excel."* **€29.40** **2024**

"I need an on-site restaurant"

We do our best to make sure site information is correct, but it is always best to check any must-have facilities are still available or will be open during your visit.

PORTUGAL

LAGOS *B4* (7km W Rural/Coastal) *37.10095, -8.73220* **Camping Turiscampo,** N125 Espiche, 8600-109 Luz-Lagos **282 789265; info@turiscampo.com; www.turiscampo.com**

12 €6 (htd) (covrd, htd) sand 2km

Exit A22/IC4 junc 1 to Lagos then N125 fr Lagos dir Sagres, site 3km on R. 4*, Lge, hdstg, mkd, hdg, shd, pt sl, terr, EHU (6A) inc - extra for 10A; gas; bbq; red long stay; TV; 25% statics; phone; bus to Lagos 100m; Eng spkn; adv bkg acc; ccard acc; games area; tennis 2km; bike hire; games rm; fishing 2.5km; CKE. *"Superb, well-run, busy site; fitness cent; v popular for winter stays & rallies; all facs (inc excel pool) open all yr; gd san facs; helpful staff; lovely vill, beach & views; varied & interesting area, Luz worth visit; vg."* **€50.00, E07.** **2022**

See advertisement on previous page

LAMAS DE MOURO *C1* (2km S Rural) *42.03587, -8.19644* **Camping Lamas de Mouro,** 4960-170 Lamas de Mouro **(251) 466041; geral@camping-lamas.com; www.camping-lamas.com**

12 €2

Fr N202 at Melgaco foll sp Peneda- Gerês National Park, cont R to rd sp Porta de Lamas de Mouro. Cont 1km past park info office, site on L in pine woods. 2*, Med, pt shd, EHU (10A) €3; cooking facs; phone; bus 1km; CKE. *"Ideal for walking in National Park; natural pool."* **€16.00** **2023**

LAMEGO *C1* (0.5km NW Urban) *41.09017, -7.82212* **Camping Lamego,** EN2 Lugar da Raposeira, 5101-909 Lamego **351 969 021 408; campinglamego@gmail.com; campinglamego.wix.com**

12 (htd)

Foll N225. Turn L onto N2. Sm, hdstg, pt shd, EHU (6A) €4; Eng spkn. *"Easy walk to Bom Jesus do Monte; site only suitable for MH's; san facs new & excel (2016); v friendly owners; excel."* **€15.00** **2022**

LISBOA *B3* (17km SW Coastal) *38.653909, -9.238510* **Camping ORBITUR-Costa de Caparica,** Ave Afonso de Albuquerque, Quinta de S. António, 2825-450 Costa de Caparica **212 901366 or 903894; caparica@orbitur.pt; www.orbitur.pt**

12 €3 sand 1km

Take A2/IP7 S fr Lisbon; after Rv Tagus bdge turn W to Costa de Caparica. At end of rd turn N twd Trafaria, & site on L. Well sp fr a'strada. 3*, Lge, mkd, hdg, shd, terr, EHU (6A) €3; gas; bbq; red long stay; TV; 75% statics; phone; bus to Lisbon; Eng spkn; adv bkg acc; ccard acc; car wash; games rm; tennis; fishing; CKE. *"Gd, clean, well run site; heavy traff into city; rec use free parking at Monument to the Discoveries & tram to city cent; ferry to Belém; ltd facs LS; pleasant, helpful staff; pool 800m; aircraft noise early am & late pm."* **€44.00** **2024**

LISBOA *B3* (9km W Urban) *38.72472, -9.20805* **Parque Municipal de Campismo de Monsanto,** Estrada da Circunvalação, 1400-061 Lisboa **(217) 628200; info@lisboacamping.com; www.lisboacamping.com**

12 €2.90 (htd)

Fr W on A5 foll sp Parque Florestal de Monsanto/ Buraca. Fr S on A2, cross toll bdge & foll sp for Sintra; join expressway, foll up hill; site well sp; stay in RH lane. Fr N on A1 pass airport, take Benfica exit & foll sp under m'way to site. Site sp fr all major rds. Avoid rush hrs! 4*, V lge, hdstg, mkd, pt shd, pt sl, terr, serviced pitches; EHU (6-16A) inc; gas; TV; 5% statics; bus to city; Eng spkn; adv bkg acc; ccard acc; tennis; CKE. *"Well laid-out, spacious, guarded site in trees; bank; PO; car wash; ltd mv service pnt; san facs poss stretched when site full but rel and reg cleaned in LS; friendly, helpful staff; in high ssn some o'fits placed on sl forest area (quiet); few pitches take awning; excel excursions booked at TO on site; reg bus service to town; excel rest; bus to Lisbon; san facs dated; expensive for low ssn."* **€40.00** **2024**

LOURICAL *B2* (5km SW Rural) *39.99149, -8.78880* **Campismo O Tamanco,** Rua do Louriçal 11, Casas Brancas, 3105-158 Louriçal **236 952551; tamanco@me.com; www.campismo-o-tamanco.com**

12 (htd) sand 5km

S on N109 fr Figuera da Foz S twds Leiria foll sp at rndabt Matos do Corrico onto N342 to Louriçal. Site 800m on L. 3*, Med, hdstg, mkd, hdg, pt shd, EHU inc (6A) €2.25-3.50, gas; bbq; sw nr; red long stay; twin axles; 5% statics; bus 500m; Eng spkn; adv bkg acc; CKE. *"Excel; friendly Dutch owners; chickens & ducks roaming site; superb mkt on Sun at Louriçal; a bit of real Portugal; gd touring base; mkd walks thro pine woods; v clean; relaxed; sm farm animal area."* **€25.00** **2022**

MEDA *C2* (0.5km N Urban) *40.96972, -7.25916* **Parque de Campismo Municipal,** Av. Professor Adriano Vasco Rodrigues, 6430 Mêda **(351) 925 480 500 or (351) 279 883 270; campismo@cm-meda.pt; www.cm-meda.pt/turismo/Paginas/Parque_Camsimo.aspx**

12

Head N fr cent of town, take 1st R, take 1st L & site on L within the Meda Sports Complex. Sm, hdstg, pt shd, pt sl,. *"Pt of the Municipal Sports Complex with facs avail; conv for town cent & historic ctr; lovely sm site; very friendly; lge pitches; some pull thro; blocks esential; clean modern san facs."* **€16.00** **2022**

MOGADOURO *D1* (1.6km SW Rural) *41.33527, -6.71861* **Parque de Campismo da Quinta da Agueira,** Complexo Desportivo, 5200-244 Mogadouro **279 340 100; geral@mogadouro.pt; www.mogadouro.pt**

€1.50 nr nr

Fr Miranda do Douro on N221 or fr Bragança on IP2 to Macedo then N216 to Mogadouro. Site sp adj sports complex. 2*, Lge, shd, EHU (15A) €2; gas; bbq; TV; phone; bus 300m; Eng spkn; adv bkg acc; tennis; car wash; waterslide. *"Brilliant site in lovely area; value for money; steep hill to town; pool adj; gd touring base."* **€11.50, 1 Apr-30 Sep. 2024**

MONTARGIL *B3* (4km N Rural) *39.10083, -8.14472* **Camping ORBITUR Montargil,** Baragem de Montargil, N2, 7425-017 Montargil **242 901207; infomontargil@orbitur.pt; www.orbitur.pt**

12 €1.50

Fr N251 Coruche to Vimiero rd, turn N on N2, over dam at Barragem de Montargil. Fr Ponte de Sor S on N2 until 3km fr Montargil. Site clearly sp bet rd & lake. 3*, Med, hdstg, mkd, pt shd, terr, EHU (6-10A) €3-4; gas; bbq; red long stay; TV (pitch); 60% statics; phone; Eng spkn; adv bkg acc; ccard acc; fishing; car wash; tennis; games rm; boating; watersports; CKE. *"Friendly site in beautiful area."* **€27.60 2022**

NAZARE *B2* (2km N Rural) *39.62036, -9.05630* **Ohai Nazaré Outdoor Resort (formerly Camping Vale Paraíso),** N242, 2450-138 Nazaré **+351 262 561 800; info.nazare@ohairesorts.com; ohairesorts.com/nazare**

12 €2.10 sand 2km

Site thro pine reserve on N242 fr Nazaré to Leiria. 3*, V lge, hdstg, mkd, shd, terr, EHU (4-10A) €3; gas; red long stay; TV; 20% statics; bus; Eng spkn; adv bkg acc; ccard acc; games area; games rm; bike hire; site clsd 19-26 Dec; fishing; CKE. *"Gd, clean site; well run; gd security; pitches vary in size & price, & divided by concrete walls, poss not suitable lge o'fits, bus outside gates to Nazare, exit down steep hill."* **€42.00 2023**

ODIVELAS *B3* (8km NE Rural) *38.18361, -8.10361* **Camping Markádia,** Barragem de Odivelas, 7920-999 Alvito **(284) 763141; info@markadia.pt; www.markadia.pt/camping**

12 (except Jul-Aug) sand 500m

Fr Ferreira do Alentejo on N2 N twd Torrão. After Odivelas turn R onto N257 twd Alvito & turn R twd Barragem de Odivels. Site in 7km, clearly sp. 3*, Med, hdstg, pt shd, pt sl, EHU (16A) inc; gas; sw nr; phone; adv bkg acc; horseriding; boating; fishing; car wash; tennis; CKE. *"Beautiful, secluded site on banks of reservoir; spacious pitches; pool 50m; gd rest; site lighting low but san facs well lit; excel walking, cycling, birdwatching; wonderful; unmarked sites; long el cable ess."* **€32.00 2024**

OLHAO *C4* (12km NE Rural) *37.09504, -7.77430* **Camping Caravanas Algarve,** Sitio da Cabeça Moncarapacho, 8700-618 Moncarapacho **(289) 791669 / 964 235 050; www.camping.info/en/campsite/caravanas-algarve**

12 nr nr nr sand 4km

Exit IP1/A22 sp Moncarapacho. In 2km turn L sp Fuzeta. At traff lts turn L & immed L opp supmkt in 1km. Turn R at site sp. Site on L. Sm, hdstg, unshd, pt sl, EHU (6A) inc; 10% statics; Eng spkn; adv bkg acc; CKE. *"Situated on a farm in orange groves; pitches ltd in wet conditions; gd, modern san facs; gd security; Spanish border 35km; National Park Ria Formosa 4km; lovely popular site."* **€10.00 2024**

> **"Satellite navigation makes touring much easier"**
>
> Remember most sat navs don't know if you're towing or in a larger vehicle – always use yours alongside maps and site directions.

OLHAO *C4* (2km NE Rural) *37.03527, -7.82250* **Camping Olhão,** Pinheiros do Marim, 8700-912 Olhão **289 700300; parque.campismo@sbsi.pt; www.sbsi.pt**

12 €1.60 1.5km

Turn S twd coast fr N125 1.5km E of Olhão by filling stn. Clearly sp on S side of N125, adj Ria Formosa National Park. 3*, V lge, mkd, hdg, shd, pt sl, EHU (6A) €2.40; gas; red long stay; TV; 75% statics; phone; bus adj, train 1.5km; Eng spkn; adv bkg acc; ccard acc; tennis; games area; horseriding 1km; bike hire; games rm; CKE. *"Pleasant, helpful staff; sep car park for some pitches; car wash; security guard; excel pool; gd san facs; very popular long stay LS; many sm sandy pitches, some diff access for lge o'fits; gd for cycling, birdwatching; ferry to islands."* **€22.30 2024**

OLHAO *C4* (8km NE Rural) *37.07245, -7.79928* **The Lemon Tree Villa (formerly Campismo Casa Rosa),** Apt 209 8700 Moncarapacho **+32 499 83 85 88; info@thelemontreevilla.com; thelemontreevilla.com**

12 (htd)

Fr A22 (IP1) E twd Spain, leave at exit 15 Olhão/ Moncarapacho. At rndabt take 2nd exit dir Moncarapacho. Cont past sp Moncarapacho Centro dir Olhão. In 1km at Lagoão, on L is Café Da Lagoão with its orange awning. Just past café is sp for Casa Rosa. Foll sp. Sm, hdstg, unshd, terr, EHU (6A) inc; TV (pitch); Eng spkn; adv bkg acc; CKE. *"Excel CL-type site adj holiday apartments; adults only; helpful, friendly, Norwegian owners; evening meals avail; ideal for touring E Algarve; conv Spanish border; rec; 30% dep req, no refunds if leaving early; insufficient san facs, but still a gd site; drinkable water taps."* **€13.50 2024**

PORTUGAL

OLIVEIRA DO HOSPITAL *C2* (9km NE Rural) *40.40338, -7.82684* **Camping Toca da Raposa,** 3405-351 Meruge **238 601547 or 926 704218 (mob); campingtocadaraposa@gmail.com; toca-da-raposa.com**

Fr N: N170 Oliveira Do Hospital head SW. Drive thro EM540-2, EM503-1, R. Principal, Estr. Principal and EM504-3 to Coimbra. Foll sp to site. Sm, hdg, pt shd, pt sl, terr, EHU (6A) €2.50; gas; bus; Eng spkn. *"Charming; lovely pool; bar & eve meals; friendly Dutch owner; vg."* **€19.50, 15 Mar-1 Nov. 2023**

ORTIGA *C3* (6km SE Rural) *39.48277, -8.00305* **Parque Campismo de Ortiga,** Estrada da Barragem, 6120-525 Ortiga **241 577200; campismo@cm-macao.pt**

12 nr nr nr

Exit A23/IP6 junc 12 S to Ortiga. Thro Ortiga & foll site sp for 1.5km. Site beside dam. Sm, hdstg, mkd, pt shd, terr, EHU (10A) €1.50; bbq; sw nr; TV; 50% statics; Eng spkn; watersports; CKE. *"Lovely site in gd position; useful NH; dogs free; lge o'fits should avoid acc thro town."* **€21.30 2022**

OURIQUE *B4* (10km S Rural) *37.5675, -8.2644* **Camping Serro da Bica,** Horta da Bica, Aldeia de Palheiros, 7670-202 Ourique **286 516750; info@serrodabica.com; www.serrodabica.com**

12 2 max (htd)

Fr N of IC1 turn R at km post 679.4 & foll sp to site. Fr S go past km post & do U-turn at turn off for Castro da Cola, then as above. 1*, Med, pt shd, pt sl, terr, EHU (10A) €2.50; gas; bbq (elec, gas); red long stay; bus 800m; Eng spkn; adv bkg acc; CKE. *"Pretty, relaxing site; gd walking; v friendly owners; spotless facs; excel."* **€21.30 2024**

"There aren't many sites open at this time of year"

If you're travelling outside peak season remember to call ahead to check site opening dates – even if the entry says 'open all year'.

PENACOVA *B2* (3km N Rural) *40.27916, -8.26805* **Camp Municipal de Penacova (Vila Nova),** Rua dos Barqueiros, Vila Nova, 3360-204 Penacova **919 121967; penaparque2@iol.pt**

nr nr

IP3 fr Coimbra, exit junc 11, cross Rv Mondego N of Penacova & foll to sp to Vila Nova & site. Med, pt shd, EHU (6A) €1; bbq; sw nr; TV; phone; bus 150m; Eng spkn; bike hire; fishing; CKE. *"Open, attractive site."* **€20.00, 31 May-30 Sep. 2023**

PENICHE *B3* (1.5km NW Urban/Coastal) *39.36944, -9.39194* **Camping Peniche Praia,** Estrada Marginal Norte, 2520 Peniche **262 783460; geral@penichepraia.pt; www.penichepraia.pt**

12 €2.10 nr (covrd) sand 1.5km

Travel S on IP6 then take N114 sp Peniche; fr Lisbon N on N247 then N114 sp Peniche. Site on R on N114 1km bef Peniche. 2*, Med, hdstg, mkd, hdg, unshd, EHU (6A) inc; bbq; red long stay; TV; 30% statics; phone; Eng spkn; adv bkg rec; car wash; games rm; bike hire; CKE. *"Vg site in lovely location; some sm pitches; rec, espec LS."* **€18.00 2024**

PONTE DA BARCA *B1* (11km E Rural) *41.82376, -8.31723* **Camping Lima Escape (formerly Entre-Ambos-os-Rios),** Lugar da Igreja, Entre-Ambos-os-Rios, 4980-613 Ponte da Barca **258 588361 or 964 969309; info@lima-escape.pt; www.lima-escape.pt**

€0.60 nr nr

N203 E fr Ponte da Barca, pass ent sp for vill. Site sp N twd Rv Lima, after 1st bdge. 2*, Lge, shd, pt sl, EHU (6A) €1.20; gas; TV; phone; bus 100m; adv bkg acc; fishing; canoeing; CKE. *"Beautiful, clean, well run & maintained site in pine trees; well situated for National Park; vg rest."* **€29.00, 2 Jan-10 Nov, 1 Dec-30 Dec. 2024**

PORTIMAO *B4* (7km W Rural) *37.13500, -8.59027* **Parque Campismo de Alvor (Formaly da Dourada),** R Serpa Pinto 8500-053 Alvor **(282) 459178; info@campingalvor.com; www.campingalvor.com**

12 €2.50 sand 1km

Turn S at W end of N125 Portimão by-pass sp Alvor. Site on L in 4km bef ent town. 2*, V lge, shd, pt sl, terr, EHU (6-16A) €3-5; gas; red long stay; TV; bus adj; fishing; games area; CKE. *"Friendly & helpful, family-run site; office poss unattended in winter, ltd facs & site untidy; excel rest; lovely town & beaches; site much improved, never untidy (2013); v welcoming; popular with wintering Brits."* **€21.50 2024**

PORTO *B1* (17km N Coastal) *41.2675, -8.71972* **Camping Orbitur-Angeiras,** Rua de Angeiras, Matosinhos, 4455-039 Lavra **229 270571; infoangeiras@orbitur.pt; www.orbitur.pt**

12 €4.60 sand 400m

Fr ICI/A28 take turn-off sp Lavra, site sp at end of slip rd. Site in approx 3km - app rd potholed & cobbled. 3*, Lge, shd, pt sl, EHU (6A) €3-4 (check earth); gas; bbq; red long stay; TV (pitch); 70% statics; phone; bus to Porto at site ent; Eng spkn; adv bkg acc; ccard acc; car wash; games area; tennis; games rm; fishing; CKE. *"Friendly & helpful staff; gd rest; gd pitches in trees at end of site but ltd space lge o'fits; ssnl statics all yr; fish & veg mkt in Matosinhos; excel new san facs (2015); vg pool; poss noisy on Sat nights (beach parties)."* **€37.00 2022**

PORTO *B1* (32km SE Rural) *41.03972, -8.42666* **Campidouro Parque de Medas,** Lugar do Gavinho, 4515-397 Medas-Gondomar **224 760162; geral@campidouro.pt; www.campidouro.pt**

Take N12 dir Gondomar off A1. Almost immed take R exit sp Entre-os-Rios. At rndabt pick up N108 & in approx 14km. Sp for Medas on R, thro hamlet & forest for 3km & foll sp for site on R. Long, steep app. New concrete access/site rds. 3*, Lge, hdstg, mkd, pt shd, terr, serviced pitches; EHU (6A) inc (poss rev pol); gas; bbq; sw; TV; 90% statics; phone; bus to Porto; Eng spkn; adv bkg acc; ccard acc; games rm; tennis; boating; fishing; CKE. *"Beautiful site on Rv Douro; helpful owners; gd rest; clean facs; sm level area (poss cr by rv & pool) for tourers - poss noisy at night & waterlogged after heavy rain; bus to Porto (just outside site) rec as parking diff (ltd buses at w/end)."* **€26.00** 2022

PORTO *B1* (9km SW Urban/Coastal) *41.10777, -8.65611* **Camping ORBITUR-Madalena,** Rua do Cerro 608, Praia da Madalena, 4405-736 Vila Nova de Gaia **(227) 122520; infomadalena@orbitur.pt; www.orbitur.pt**

€4.10 sand 250m

Fr Porto ring rd IC1/A44 take A29 exit dir Espinho. In 1km take exit slip rd sp Madalena opp Volvo agent. Watch for either 'Campismo' or 'Orbitur' sp to site along winding, cobbled rd (beware campismo sp may take you to another site nrby). 4*, Lge, pt shd, pt sl, terr, EHU (6A)inc; gas; bbq; red long stay; TV; 40% statics; phone; bus to Porto; Eng spkn; adv bkg acc; ccard acc; car wash; games area; tennis; games rm; CKE. *"Site in forest; slight aircraft noise; some uneven pitches; pitches not mkd out; excel bus to Porto cent fr site ent takes 40 mins - do not take c'van into Porto; facs fine & avail LS."* **€27.50** 2024

SAGRES *B4* (1km N Coastal) *37.02305, -8.94555* **Camping ORBITUR-Sagres,** Cerro das Moitas, 8650-998 Vila de Sagres **282 624371; infosagres@orbitur.pt; www.orbitur.pt**

€1.50 sand 2km

On N268 to Cape St Vincent; well sp. 2*, Lge, hdstg, hdg, mkd, pt shd, EHU (6-10A) €3-4; gas; bbq; red long stay; TV; Eng spkn; adv bkg acc; ccard acc; bike hire; car wash; games rm. *"Vg, clean, tidy site in pine trees; helpful staff; hot water to shwrs only; cliff walks; gd rest; v windy site; new san facs ok; all pitches sl."* **€33.80** 2024

SANTIAGO DO CACEM *B4* (17km NW Coastal) *38.10777, -8.78690* **Camping Lagoa de Santo Andre,** Lagoa de Santo Andre, 7500-024 Vila Nova de Santo Andre **269 708550 / 964 732 193; s.andre@fcmportugal.com; www.fcmportugal.com/parques/santo-andre-2/**

Take N261 sp Melides out of town & foll sps to Lagoa de Santo Andre to site on L of rd. On shore but fenced off fr unsafe banks of lagoon. 1*, Med, pt shd, pt sl, EHU inc (4-6A); sw; boating; fishing. *"Ltd facs LS."* **€19.50, 1 Jan-23 Dec, 26 Dec-31 Dec.** 2024

PORTUGAL

SANTO ANTONIO DAS AREIAS *C3* (5km N Rural) *39.41370, -7.37575* **Quinta Do Maral (Naturist),** PO Box 57, Cubecudos, 7330-205 Santo Antonio das Areias **(963) 462169; info@quintadomaral.com; www.quintadomaral.com**

Take N359 twds Santo Antonio Das Areias/Beira. Pass turn off to Santo Antonio in dir to Beira. At Ranginha turn L to Cubecudos. Turn R past vill sp by a school bldg, keep on this rd for 1.7km. Campsite on L, white hse with blue stripe. Do not use sat nav as they lead to unsuitable rds. Sm, hdg, pt shd, EHU (6-16A); bbq; twin axles; red long stay; TV; 5% statics; Eng spkn; adv bkg rec. *"In S Mamede nature park; vill & castle of Marvao an hr's walk; young, friendly owners; excel."* **€18.50** 2022

SANTO ANTONIO DAS AREIAS *C3* (0km S Rural) *39.40992, -7.34075* **Camping Asseiceira,** Asseiceira, 7330-204 Santo António das Areias **(245) 992940 or (960) 150352 (mob); gary-campingasseiceira@hotmail.com; www.campingasseiceira.com**

nr nr

Fr N246-1 turn off sp Marvão/Santo António das Areias. Turn L to Santo António das Areias then 1st R on ent town then immed R again, up sm hill to rndabt. At rndabt turn R then at next rndabt cont strt on. There is a petrol stn on R, cont down hill for 400m. Site on L. Sm, pt shd, pt sl, EHU (10A) €4; bus 1km; CKE. *"Attractive area; peaceful, well-equipped, remote site among olive trees; clean, tidy; gd for walking, birdwatching; helpful, friendly, British owners; excel san facs, maintained to a high standard; nr Spanish border; excel; ideal cent for walking, cycling, visit hilltop castle Marvao; access & pitches poss tight for lge o'fits."* **€19.00, 1 Jan-31 Oct.** 2024

PORTUGAL

SAO MARCOS DA SERRA *B4* (5km SE Rural) *37.3350, -8.3467* **Campismo Rural Quinta Odelouca,** Vale Grande de Baixo, CxP 644-S, 8375-215 São Marcos da Serra **282 361718 or 915 656685; info@quintaodelouca.com; www.quintaodelouca.com**

€1

Fr N (Ourique) on IC1 pass São Marcos da Serra & in approx 2.5km turn R & cross blue rlwy bdge. At bottom turn L & at cont until turn R for Vale Grande (paved rd changes to unmade). Foll sp to site. Fr S exit A22 junc 9 onto IC1 dir Ourique. Pass São Bartolomeu de Messines & at km 710.5 turn L & cross blue rlwy bdge, then as above. 2*, Sm, pt shd, terr, EHU (6-10A) €3.50; bbq (elec, gas, sep area); sw; twin axles; Eng spkn; adv bkg rec; CKE. *"Helpful, friendly Dutch owners; beautiful views; gd walks; vg; v little shd; access via bad rd; excel; internet free but unreliable and weak signal; fantastic location & facs."* **€23.00, 1 Feb-30 Sep.** 2024

SAO MARTINHO DO PORTO *B2* (1.5km NE Coastal) *39.52280, -9.12310* **Parque de Campismo Colina do Sol,** Serra dos Mangues, 2460-697 São Martinho do Porto **(262) 989764; info@yellohvillage-colinadosol.com; colinadosol.org**

12 €1 sand 2km

Leave A8/IC1 SW at junc 21 onto N242 W to São Martinho, by-pass town on N242 dir Nazaré. Site on L. 3*, Lge, mkd, hdstg, pt shd, terr, EHU (6A) €2.75; gas; bbq; TV; phone; Eng spkn; adv bkg acc; ccard acc; games rm; fishing; site clsd at Xmas; games area; CKE. *"Gd touring base on attractive coastline; mob homes/c'vans for hire; gd walking, cycling; vg san facs; excel site; san facs a bit tired (2013), water v hot."* **€30.50** 2024

SAO PEDRO DE MOEL *B2* (1km E Urban/Coastal) *39.75861, -9.02583* **Camping ORBITUR-São Pedro de Moel,** Rua Volta do Sete, São Pedro de Moel, 2430 Marinha Grande **244 599168; infospedro@orbitur.pt; www.orbitur.pt**

12 €4 (htd) sand 500m

Site at end of rd fr Marinha Grande to beach; turn R at 1st rndabt on ent vill. 3*, V lge, hdstg, mkd, hdg, shd, terr, EHU (6A) inc (poss rev pol); gas; bbq; red long stay; TV (pitch); 10% statics; phone; Eng spkn; adv bkg acc; ccard acc; waterslide; fishing; car wash; tennis; games rm; bike hire; CKE. *"Friendly, well-run, clean site in pine woods; easy walk to shops, rests; heavy surf; gd cycling to beaches; tracks alng coast & inland; São Pedro smart resort; ltd facs LS site in attractive area and well run; bread to order; pitches soft sand & sl."* **€40.00, W18.** 2022

SAO TEOTONIO *B4* (11km W Coastal) *37.49497, -8.78667* **Camping Monte Carvalhal da Rocha,** Praia do Carvalhal, 7630-569 S Teotónio **282 947293; geral@montecarvalhalr-turismo.com; www.montecarvalhaldarocha.com**

12 sand 500m

Turn W off N120 dir Brejão & Carvalhal; site in 4.5km. Site sp. 2*, Med, shd, EHU (16A) inc; gas; bbq; TV; 10% statics; phone; Eng spkn; adv bkg acc; ccard acc; bike hire; car wash; fishing. *"Beautiful area; friendly, helpful staff."* **€37.00** 2024

SAO TEOTONIO *B4* (7km W Coastal) *37.52560, -8.77560* **Parque de Campismo da Zambujeira,** Praia da Zambujeira, 7630-740 Zambujeira do Mar **(283) 958 407; info@campingzambujeira; www.campingzambujeira.com**

€4 sand 1km

S on N120 twd Lagos, turn W when level with São Teotónio on unclassified rd to Zambujeira. Site on L in 7km, bef vill. 2*, V lge, pt shd, pt sl, EHU (6-10A) €3.50; gas; red long stay; TV; phone; bus adj; Eng spkn; tennis. *"Welcoming, friendly owners; in pleasant rural setting; hot water to shwrs only; sh walk to unspoilt vill with some shops & rest; cliff walks; nice site; pool gd; rest food basic; vg facs; v clean site; gd beaches & walks."* **€18.00, 1 Apr-31 Oct.** 2024

SATAO *C2* (12km N Rural) *40.82280, -7.6961* **Camping Quinta Chave Grande,** Rua do Barreiro 462, Casfreires, Ferreira d'Aves, 3560-043 Sátão **232 665552; info@chavegrande.com; www.chavegrande.com**

€2.50 nr nr

Leave IP5 Salamanca-Viseu rd onto N229 to Sátão, site sp in Satão - beyond Lamas. Med, pt shd, terr, EHU (6A) €3.50; gas; red long stay; TV; Eng spkn; tennis; games area; games rm. *"Warm welcome fr friendly Dutch owners; gd facs; well organised BBQ's - friendly atmosphere; dogs leashed; gd touring base; gd walks fr site; excel."* **€20.50, 15 Mar-31 Oct.** 2024

SERPA *C4* (1km SW Urban) *37.94090, -7.60404* **Parque Municipal de Campismo Serpa,** Rua da Eira São Pedro, 7830-303 Serpa **+351 284544290; parquecampismoserpa@cm-serpa.pt; www.cm-serpa.pt**

12 nr nr nr

Fr IP8 take 1st sp for town; site well sp fr most dirs - opp sw pool. Do not ent walled town. Med, pt shd, pt sl, EHU (6A) €1.25; gas; bbq; sw nr; 20% statics; phone; adv bkg acc; CKE. *"Popular gd site; daily mkt 500m; pool adj; simple, high quality facs; interesting, historic town; main site ent may be clsd due to improvement wrks; rec phone ahead bef arr (2019)."* **€10.00** 2024

TAVIRA *C4* (5km E Rural/Coastal) *37.14506, -7.60223* **Camping Ria Formosa,** Quinta da Gomeira, 8800-591 Cabanas-Tavira **281 328 887; info@campingriaformosa.com; www.campingriaformosa.com**

12 €3 (htd) WD MSP sand 1.2km

Fr spain onto A22 take exit junc 17 (bef tolls) Fr N125 turn S at Conceição dir 'Cabanas Tavira' & 'Campismo'. Cross rlwy line & turn L to site, sp. 3*, V lge, hdstg, mkd, pt shd, terr, EHU (16A) €3; gas; bbq; red long stay; TV; bus 100m, train 100m; Eng spkn; adv bkg acc; ccard acc; games area; car wash; bike hire; CKE. *"Excel, comfortable site; friendly, welcoming owner & staff; vg, modern san facs; various pitch sizes; cycle path to Tavira, excel facs."* **€24.00** **2022**

TOMAR *B2* (9km NE Rural) *39.63833, -8.33694* **Camping Pelinos,** Casal das Aboboreiras, 2300-093 Tomar **249 301814; info@campingpelinos.com; www.campingpelinos.com**

WD

N fr Tomar on N110, turn R to Calçadas at traff lts opp g'ge, foll site sp. Steep descent to site. 1*, Sm, pt shd, sl, terr, EHU (6A); bbq (elec, gas); TV; phone; bus 100m; Eng spkn; adv bkg acc; table tennis; CKE. *"Lake sw, watersports & fishing 7km; vg; lovely site; no shops nrby; v helpful Dutch couple; dogs 2 max; walks fr site; ltd wifi on pitch."* **€20.50, 15 Mar-1 Oct.** **2024**

TOMAR *B2* (1km NW Urban) *39.60694, -8.41027* **Campismo Parque Municipal,** 2300-000 Tomar **249 329824 or 249 329800 (town hall); presidencia@cm-tomar.pt; www.cm-tomar.pt**

12 WD MSP nr

Fr S on N110 foll sp to town cent at far end of stadium. Fr N (Coimbra) on N110 turn R immed bef bdge. Site well sp fr all dirs. Med, mkd, pt shd, bbq; TV; Eng spkn; adv bkg acc; ccard acc; CKE. *"Useful base for touring Alcobaca, Batalha & historic monuments in Tomar; conv Fatima; Convento de Cristo worth visit; vg; lovely walk to charming rvside town; easy access for lge vehicle, sh walk thro gdns to Knights Templar castle; pool adj; no longer a camp site: now a free camperstop (2019); all facs avail but no hot water; no security; v rundown site; clean san facs."* **2024**

TORRES NOVAS *B2* (13.5km SE Urban) *39.400100, -8.485829* **Parque De Campismo Municipal Da Golega,** Largo do Parque de Campismo 7, 2150-269 Golega **249 979003; cm-golega.pt**

12 €1.77 WD nr nr

Sp fr main rd. Med, pt shd, EHU (10A); twin axles; Eng spkn. *"Vg; ideal for visiting lovely nature reserve; easy walk to town."* **€10.00** **2024**

VAGOS *B2* (6km W Coastal) *40.55805, -8.74527* **Parque de Campismo da Vagueira,** Rua do Parque de Campismo, 3840-254 Gafanha da Boa-Hora **+351 234 797 526; infovagueira@orbitur.pt; www.orbitur.pt**

12 €1.50 WD MSP sand 1.5km

Fr Aveiro take N109 S twd Figuera da Foz. Turn R in Vagos vill. After 6km along narr poor rd, site on R bef reaching Vagueira vill. 3*, Lge, mkd, shd, EHU (6-16A) €3-4; gas; 90% statics; bus 500m; Eng spkn; adv bkg acc; ccard acc; games area; bike hire; games rm; tennis; fishing 1km; CKE. *"V pleasant & well-run; friendly staff; poss diff access to pitches for lge o'fits; areas soft sand; gd touring base; rest/pool may be closed l/s."* **€21.00** **2022**

VIANA DO CASTELO *B1* (4.6km S Urban/Coastal) *41.67888, -8.82583* **Camping ORBITUR-Viana do Castelo,** Rua Diogo Álvares, Cabedelo, 4935-161 Darque **258 322167; infoviana@orbitur.pt; www.orbitur.pt**

€2.20 WD MSP (htd) sand adj

Exit IC1 junc 11 to W sp Darque, Cabedelo, foll sp to site in park. 3*, Lge, mkd, shd, pt sl, EHU (6A) inc; gas; bbq; red long stay; TV; phone; Eng spkn; adv bkg acc; ccard acc; surfing; fishing; car wash; CKE. *"Site in pine woods; friendly staff; gd facs; plenty of shd; major festival in Viana 3rd w/end in Aug; lge mkt in town Fri; sm passenger ferry over Rv Lima to town high ssn; ferry rec'd over cycling due to busy narr rds; Santa Luzia worth visit."* **€42.00, 1 Feb-3 Nov.** **2024**

VILA DO BISPO *B4* (11km SE Rural/Coastal) *37.07542, -8.83133* **Quinta dos Carriços (Part Naturist),** Praia de Salema, 8650-196 Budens **282 695201; quintacarrico@oninet.pt; www.quintadoscarricos.com**

12 €2.45 (htd) WD MSP sand 1.5km

Take N125 out of Lagos twd Sagres. In approx 14km at sp Salema, turn L & again immed L twd Salema. Site on R 300m. 2*, Lge, pt shd, terr, EHU (6-10A) €3.90 (metered for long stay); gas; red long stay; TV; 8% statics; phone; bus; Eng spkn; adv bkg req; ccard acc; golf 1km; CKE. *"Naturist section in sep valley; apartments avail on site; ltd pitches for lge o'fits; friendly Dutch owners; tractor avail to tow to terr; noise fr adj quarry; area of wild flowers in spring; beach 30 mins walk; buses pass ent for Lagos, beach & Sagres; excel."* **€28.00** **2024**

PORTUGAL

VILA NOVA DE CERVEIRA *B1* (5km E Rural) *41.94362, -8.69365* **Glamping de Cerveira (formerly Parque de Campismo Convívio),** Rua de Badão, 1 Bacelo, 4920-020 Candemil **+351 251 08 06 13; info@glampingdecerveira.com; www.glampingdecerveira.com**

€1.10

Fr Vila Nova de Cerveira dir Candemil on N13/N302, turn L at Bacelo, site sp. Sm, pt shd, terr, EHU (6A); bbq; red long stay; Eng spkn; adv bkg acc; games rm; CKE. *"V helpful Dutch owners; gd area to visit; vg."* **€13.50, 1 Mar-15 Oct.** **2023**

VILA NOVA DE MILFONTES *B4* (1km N Coastal) *37.73194, -8.78277* **Camping Milfontes,** Apartado 81, 7645-300 Vila Nova de Milfontes **(283) 996140; reservas@campingmilfontes.com; www.campingmilfontes.com**

12 €1 sand 800m

S fr Sines on N120/IC4 for 22km; turn R at Cercal on N390 SW for Milfontes on banks of Rio Mira; clear sp. 3*, V lge, mkd, hdg, pt shd, EHU (6A) inc (long lead poss req); gas; TV; 80% statics; phone; bus 600m; ccard acc; CKE. *"Pitching poss diff for lge o'fits due trees & statics; supmkt & mkt 5 mins walk; nr fishing vill at mouth Rv Mira with beaches & sailing on rv; pleasant site; helpful staff; gd cycle ride to Porto Corvo; attractive town; gd coastal walks; chge for pool; site on edge of lovely vill."* **€25.60** **2024**

VILA REAL *C1* (1km NE Urban) *41.30361, -7.73694* **Camping Vila Real,** Rua Dr Manuel Cardona, 5000-558 Vila Real **259 324724; camping.vilareal@gmail.com; https://www.campingvilareal.com/**

nr

On IP4/E82 take Vila Real N exit & head S into town. Foll 'Centro' sp to Galp g'ge; at Galp g'ge rndabt, turn L & in 30m turn L again. Site at end of rd in 400m. Site sp fr all dirs. 2*, Med, pt shd, pt sl, terr, EHU (6A); gas; bbq; 10% statics; phone; bus 150m; tennis; CKE. *"Conv upper Douro; pool complex adj; gd facs ltd when site full; gd mkt in town (15 min walk); Lamego well worth a visit; excel rest adj."* **€15.80, 1 Feb-31 Dec.** **2023**

VILA REAL DE SANTO ANTONIO *C4* (14km W Rural) *37.18649, -7.55003* **Camping Caliço Park,** Sitio do Caliço, 8900-907 Vila Nova de Cacela **281 951195; geral@calico-park.com; www.calico-park.com**

12 €1.60 sand 4km

On N side of N125 Vila Real to Faro rd. Sp on main rd & in Vila Nova de Cacela vill, visible fr rd. 1*, Lge, hdstg, shd, pt sl, terr, EHU (6A) €2.80; gas; red long stay; 80% statics; phone; Eng spkn; adv bkg acc; ccard acc; bike hire; CKE. *"Friendly staff; noisy in ssn & rd noise; not suitable for m'vans or tourers in wet conditions - ltd touring pitches & poss diff access; gd NH."* **€17.00** **2022**

VILA REAL DE SANTO ANTONIO *C4* (3km W Coastal) *37.17972, -7.44361* **Parque Municipal de Campismo,** 8900 Monte Gordo **281 510 000; geral@cm-vrsa.pt; www.cm-vrsa.pt/pt/menu/459/parque-de-campismo.aspx**

12 €3 sand 100m

Fr Faro on N125 turn R sp Monte Gordo. Site on sea front in 500m. Or fr Spain over bdge at border, exit junc 9 to Vila Real over rlwy line. Strt over rndabt & turn R at T-junc, site sp just bef ent town. 1*, shd, Pt sl, EHU (10A) €1.90 (long cable poss req); gas; bbq; red long stay; TV; 10% statics; phone; bus, train to Faro 3km; Eng spkn; ccard acc; canoeing; CKE. *"Former campsite now MH stop; sp through town; san facs avail but shwrs cold water; MH svr pnt."* **€13.50** **2024**

VILAMOURA *B4* (4.8km N Rural) *37.112371, -8.106409* **Vilamoura Rustic Motorhome Aire,** N125 436A, 8100 Consiguinte, Loule **289 149315 or 918 721948 or 917 428356 (mob); vilamoura.rustic@gmail.com; www.vilamourarustic.scatterlings-of-africa.com**

12 €1 5km

Fr A22 (tollrd) take exit for Quarteria and drive for 3km for exit Quarteira/Portimao. Turn R at exit to join N125 and drive for approx 6km W direct to site. Sm, hdstg, pt shd, EHU (6A) €0.50 per KW; bbq; twin axles; TV; bus 200m; Eng spkn; adv bkg acc; games area; bike hire. *"Boutique, adults only (18+), MH & c'van Aire; outdoor cinema; Sky Sports; events throughout the year; vg; run by past CAMC memb."* **€10.00** **2024**

Miranda do Douro to Vila Real de Santo António = 688km

	Aveiro	Beja	Braga	Bragança	Castelo Branco	Chaves	Coimbra	Elvas	Évora	Faro	Fundão	Guarda	Leiria	Lisboa (Lisbon)	Miranda do Douro	Mourão	Portalegre	Portimão	Porto	Sagres	Santarém	Setúbal	Sines	Valença	Viana do Castelo	Vila Formoso	Vila Real	Vila Real de Santo António	Vila Verde de Ficalho
Beja	408																												
Braga	129	500																											
Bragança	285	558	214																										
Castelo Branco	225	274	318	288																									
Chaves	235	630	140	106	341																								
Coimbra	77	339	186	298	156	260																							
Elvas	379	162	478	445	155	496	253																						
Évora	325	77	432	485	198	513	258	84																					
Faro	535	164	639	732	442	723	468	328	245																				
Fundão	227	317	263	253	43	175	150	198	239	483																			
Guarda	163	361	263	200	92	240	156	247	290	538	57																		
Leiria	143	276	248	368	174	327	77	252	201	417	199	230																	
Lisboa (Lisbon)	273	179	383	503	247	480	206	206	131	295	300	362	146																
Miranda do Douro	320	572	280	76	287	180	313	442	487	732	252	195	387	607															
Mourão	365	110	490	533	260	575	322	101	66	276	303	356	265	193	552														
Portalegre	258	180	365	382	94	440	191	64	105	351	136	185	167	216	382	173													
Portimão	508	105	607	680	379	725	443	267	185	61	465	476	381	295	682	215	288												
Porto	74	445	65	219	261	170	121	364	372	578	208	209	191	317	254	407	303	552											
Sagres	556	153	655	728	407	773	491	315	233	109	513	524	429	343	730	263	336	48	600										
Santarém	205	198	310	426	177	388	140	174	120	338	220	292	78	80	445	186	148	336	251	384									
Setúbal	309	144	418	525	261	500	240	171	96	260	347	391	182	47	576	161	195	260	355	308	113								
Sines	390	99	497	609	305	570	323	193	109	201	348	397	262	162	592	209	214	140	433	147	184	119							
Valença	180	560	66	280	373	208	241	529	487	696	365	316	297	436	352	544	418	658	116	706	364	466	548						
Viana do Castelo	147	520	50	264	342	192	196	437	446	651	314	283	263	395	340	509	379	625	77	673	322	423	507	51					
Vila Formoso	193	400	290	226	135	269	190	290	271	575	111	44	259	428	175	336	228	507	240	555	333	439	380	358	342				
Vila Real	163	560	95	119	268	643	190	425	448	641	222	166	262	412	188	510	363	660	100	708	321	432	506	165	150	200			
Vila Real de Santo António	594	120	693	688	396	815	529	284	200	66	560	492	463	350	688	234	308	126	639	174	400	312	264	761	728	535	742		
Vila Verde de Ficalho	465	60	560	626	334	680	399	222	140	230	377	430	338	241	627	68	246	182	511	230	261	204	160	622	583	460	614	183	
Viseu	84	445	191	220	171	173	89	326	341	547	77	77	161	330	234	401	259	650	132	698	219	321	404	255	237	107	99	562	501

ATLANTIC OCEAN
SPAIN
Vigo
Ourense
Vila Nova de Cerveira
Lamas de Mouro
Caminha
A3,IP1
Ponte da Barca
Viana do Castelo
Geres
Braganca
EN103
Chaves
A28,IC1
BRAGA
A24,IP3
ER206
Arco de Baulhe
A11
A7,IC5
A4,IP4
EN217
Guimaraes
Celorico de Basto
EN221
Amarante
Vila Real
EN214
Porto
Penafiel
Lamego
A1,IP1
A24,IP3
EN226
Meda
Salamanca
EN327
EN228
EN102
Aveiro
A25,IP5
VISEU
A25,IP5
Vagos
GUARDA
Ciudad Rodrigo
Oliveira do Hospital
Gouveia
A17,IC1
EN1;IC2
Figueira da Foz
Penacova
EN 230
COVILHÃ
Arganil
Coimbra
EN112
ER233
Lourical
IC2;EN1
IC8
A23,IP2
EN239
Coimbrao
EN238
ER112
Sao Pedro de Moel
A13,IC3
IC8
LEIRIA
CASTELO BRANCO
Nazare
Tomar
Alcobaca
A23,IP6
Ortiga
Caceres
IC1
Torres Novas
Santo Antonio das Areias
A15-IP6
A1,IP1
Castelo de Vide
EN243
EN2
EN119
PORTALEGRE
A8,IC1
EN245
EN246
Montargil
A10
A13,IC3
EN 251
Campo Maior
EN10
EN119
EN251
EN114
Elvas
Mérida
Odivelas
A13,IC11
Badajoz
Evoramonte
A6,IP7
Cascais
LISBOA
A6,IP2,IP7
Alandroal
A2
A6,IP7
SETÚBAL
Evora
ER2
A2,IP1
EN380
EN256
Alcacer do Sal
ER2
ER384
Santiago do Cacem
BEJA
Ermidas Sado
Serpa
N
W
E
S
Vila Nova de Milfontes
EN263
EN122
Castro Verde
Ourique
A2,IP1
EN2
EN122
Sao Teotonio
ER266
Sao Marcos da Serra
Seville
Vila Real de Santo Antonio
Huelva
A22
A22
Lagos
Vilamoura
Tavira
Sagres
Albufeira
Olhao
FARO
0 25 50 75 100 125 km
0 20 40 60 80 miles
Motorways
Primary roads
Secondary roads
All year site(s)
Seasonal site(s)
No sites listed

Slovakia

Highlights

Well known for the sheer volume of castles to be found, Slovakia is a country rich in culture. It retains much of its sense of tradition, both in its beautiful medieval towns such as Levoča or Bardejov and in the small villages dotted around the countryside.

A relatively small country with an untamed and diverse wilderness, Slovakia is a great place for those wanting to experience new and different landscapes on a daily basis.

Slovakia has a rich tradition of folklore, and festivals celebrating local folk customs are found throughout the country. The oldest of these is held in Východná, and showcases parades, music, costumes and local crafts.

There are several speciality foods found in Slovakia, one of which is bryndza, a creamy sheep's cheese known for its strong smell. It's the main ingredient of Bryndzové Halušky, a dish made of potato dumplings, bryndza and bacon and considered the national speciality.

Major towns and cities

- Bratislava – a unique capital with a hilltop castle overlooking the city.
- Košice – the well-preserved historical centre is full of heritage sites.
- Prešov – a tourist favourite with many attractions.
- Žilina – packed with museums and historic buildings.

Attractions

- Tatras National Park – with a rich variety of flora and fauna there's plenty to discover in this gorgeous landscape.
- Spiš Castle – the sprawling remains of a 12th century castle that now houses a fascinating museum.
- Nedbalka Gallery, Bratislava – admire the works of Slovakian artists from the 19th century to the present day.

Find out more

slovakia.travel
info@slovakia.travel

Country Information

Capital: Bratislava

Bordered by: Austria, Czechia, Hungary, Poland, Ukraine

Terrain: Rugged mountains in the centre and north; lowlands in the south

Climate: Continental climate; warm, showery summers; cold, cloudy, snowy winters; best months to visit are May, June and September

Highest Point: Gerlachovský štít 2,655m

Languages: Slovak, Hungarian, German

Local Time: GMT or BST + 1, i.e. 1 hour ahead of the UK all year

Currency: Euros divided into 100 cents; £1 = €1.20, €1 = £0.84 (Nov 2024)

Emergency numbers: Police 112; Fire brigade 112; Ambulance 112

Public Holidays 2025: Jan 1, 2, 7; Feb, 15, 16, 17; Apr 18, 21; May 1, 2; Nov 11.

School summer holidays are from the beginning of July to the end of August

Entry Formalities

British and Irish passport holders may stay for up to 90 days in any 180 day period without a visa. You may be asked to show a return or onward ticket at the border to confirm your length of stay, or to prove that you have enough money for your stay.

Your passport will need to have a minimum of 6 months' validity remaining, and be less than 10 years old (even if it has over 6 months left).

Visitors arriving at a campsite or hotel must complete a registration form. All foreign visitors are required to show proof of medical insurance cover on entry.

Medical Services

Medical facilities are variable. Whereas the standard of care from doctors is good, many hospitals suffer from a lack of maintenance. The biggest problem you'll probably encounter is language, as nurses and ancillary workers may not speak English.

There's a reciprocal health care agreement with the UK for urgent medical treatment and you should present a European Health Insurance Card (EHIC) or a Global Health Insurance Card (GHIC). Emergency treatment is from doctors and dentists contracted to the Slovak health insurance system, but you'll be asked for payment and follow on costs could be considerable. Hospital patients are required to make a financial contribution towards costs. Charges incurred are not refundable in Slovakia.

A 24 hour first aid service exists in provincial and district towns, as well as in some small communities. For minor ailments, the first call should be to a pharmacy (lekáren) where staff are qualified to give advice and may be able to prescribe drugs normally available only on prescription in the UK.

Hepatitis A immunisation is advised for long stay travellers to rural areas, and those who plan to travel outside tourist areas.

Opening Hours

Banks: Mon-Fri 8am-3pm/5pm.

Museums: Tue-Sun 10am-5pm; closed Mon.

Post Offices: Mon-Fri 8am-6pm; Sat 8am-1pm.

Shops: Mon-Fri 7am-6pm; Sat 7am-12 noon. Hypermarkets usually open Sun.

Food Shops: Mon-Fri 7am-6pm; Sat 7am-12pm.
Department Stores - Mon-Sat 9am-9pm

Safety and Security

Most visits to Slovakia are trouble free. However, there's a risk of petty theft, particularly in Bratislava, and pickpocketing is common at tourist attractions and in some bars. When placing your jacket on the back of a chair in a restaurant make sure you don't leave valuables in the pockets. Don't put handbags on the floor or under chairs, where they may be vulnerable to theft. There have been occurrences in Bratislava of visitors being offered 'spiked' drinks and subsequently being robbed.

Visitors entering Slovakia via the border crossings on the D2 and D4 motorways should be extremely vigilant. While you leave your vehicle to buy petrol or a motorway vignette, a tyre may be deliberately damaged. Once you're back on the road and have driven a few kilometres other motorists will flag you down under the pretext of offering assistance. In these circumstances you should stay in your vehicle with the doors locked and call the police (dial 112) or the emergency service of the Autoklub Slovakia Assistance (ASA) on 18112.

Robberies from parked cars are on the increase. Cameras, mobile phones and tablets are as attractive as cash and credit cards; don't leave them or other valuables unattended.

If you intend to ski or hike in the Slovak mountains you're recommended to have sufficient insurance to cover rescue costs should the Slovak Mountain Rescue (HZS) be called out. Take heed of any instructions issued by HZS; if you ignore their advice you may be liable to a heavy fine.

Taking photos of anything that could be perceived as a military establishment or of security interest may result in problems with the authorities.

Slovakia shares with the rest of Europe an underlying threat from terrorism. Please check gov.uk/foreign-travel-advice/slovakia before you travel.

British Embassy

Panska 16, 81101 Bratislava
Tel: (02) 5998 2000
gov.uk/world/slovakia

Irish Embassy

Mostova 2, 81102 Bratislava
Tel: (02) 3233 8700
Ireland.ie/bratislava

Documents

Passport

Carry your passport at all times as it's an offence to be without it and you may be fined and held in custody for up to 24 hours. Keep a photocopy of the details page separately. Ensure your passport is in a presentable state as the authorities can refuse you entry if it's worn or damaged or looks as if it may have been tampered with.

Vehicle(s)

You should carry your vehicle registration certificate (V5C), at all times together with your driving licence, insurance certificate and your vehicle's MOT certificate (if applicable).

Fines may be imposed by police patrols if you cannot produce these documents on request.

Money

Exchange kiosks often offer poor exchange rates and there's a risk of being robbed by thieves nearby. Scottish and Northern Irish bank notes will not be exchanged.

Cash machines which accept UK debit or credit cards are common but do not rely on finding one in remote areas. Shops, particularly in the main tourist areas, increasingly accept credit cards but are sometimes reluctant to accept cards issued by foreign banks. If you intend to pay for something by card do check first that the shop will accept it and that it can be read. You should also check your statements carefully for transactions you did not make.

Driving

The standard of driving isn't high and sometimes aggressive with drivers going too fast, especially in bad weather, tailgating and overtaking dangerously. Drive defensively and allow yourself more 'thinking time'. Beware of oncoming cars overtaking on your side of the road, especially on bends and hills.

Accidents

If your vehicle is damaged when you enter Slovakia the border authorities must issue a certificate confirming the visible damage. While in the country if an accident causes bodily injury or material damage exceeding a value of approximately €4,000 it must be reported to the police immediately. If a vehicle is only slightly damaged both drivers should complete a European Accident Report. In the case of foreign motorists driving vehicles registered abroad, it's advisable to report the accident to the police who will issue a certificate which will facilitate the exportation of the vehicle.

Alcohol

Slovakia has a policy of zero tolerance for drinking or consuming drugs before driving. Police carry out random breath tests and you'll be heavily penalised if there's any trace of alcohol in your system.

Breakdown Service

The motoring organisation, Autoklub Slovakia Assistance (ASA), operates an emergency centre which can be contacted 24 hours a day by dialling 18112 or +421 2 49 20 59 49. Operators speak English.

Child Restraint System

Children under the age of 12 years and anyone under 1.5 m in height must not travel in the front seat of a vehicle. Child restraint seats must be used for any children weighing less than 36 kg.

Fuel

Diesel is sold in service stations with the sign 'TT Diesel' or 'Nafta'. LPG is widely available and is sold under the name ECO Auto-gas or ECO Car-Gas – see mylpg.eu/stations/slovakia for a list of outlets. If driving a vehicle converted to use LPG you must be in possession of a safety certificate covering the combustion equipment in your vehicle.

Some service stations on international roads and in main towns are open 24 hours but in other areas they may close by 6pm. Credit cards are generally accepted. Service stations may be hard to find in rural areas.

Lights

All vehicles must use dipped headlights at all times.

Motorways

There are approximately 500 km of motorways. Bratislava has direct motorway connections with Prague and Vienna. Emergency phones are placed along motorways and callers are connected directly to the police.

Vehicles using motorways and selected highways must display an e-vignette which can be purchased at online at eznamka.sk, at border crossings, petrol stations or post offices. Charges for vehicles up to 3,500kg with or without a caravan or trailer are as follows (2024 prices): €12 for a period of 10 days and €17 for one month. The road from the Austrian border crossing at Berg to Bratislava is free of charge.

Motorhomes over 3,500kg are considered private vehicles and can buy the above vignettes as long as you're able to show the Vehicle Registration Certificate (V5) and it shows that the vehicle has fewer than 9 seats. Without the V5, drivers of vehicles over 3,500kg must pay motorway tolls by means of an electronic toll collection unit fitted to their vehicle. Tolls vary according to distance driven, vehicle weight and emissions classification. For information see emyto.sk or telephone +421 235 111 111.

Parking

Visitors are warned to park only in officially controlled parking areas since cars belonging to tourists may be targeted for robbery. There are many restrictions on parking in Bratislava and fines are imposed. Wheel clamps are used in main towns and vehicles may be towed.

Continuous white/yellow lines indicate that parking is prohibited and broken white/yellow lines indicate parking restrictions.

Priority

At uncontrolled crossroads or intersections not marked by a priority sign, priority must be given to vehicles coming from the right. Drivers must not enter an intersection unless the exit beyond the crossing is clear.

Drivers must slow down and, if necessary, stop to allow buses and trams to move off from stops and to allow buses to merge with general traffic at the end of a bus lane. A tram turning right and crossing the line of travel of a vehicle moving on its right has priority once the driver has signalled his intention to turn. Trams must be overtaken on the right but do not overtake near a tram refuge.

Roads

Roads are relatively quiet and are generally well maintained. They often follow routes through towns and villages, resulting in sharp bends and reduced speed limits.

Many main roads, although reasonably good, have only a single carriageway in each direction making overtaking difficult.

In winter, north-south routes through Slovakia can be challenging as they pass through mountain ranges. The passes of Donovaly (Ružomberok to Banská Bystrica), Veľký Šturec (Martin to Banská Bystrica), and Čertovica (Liptovský Mikuláš to Brezno) are the most frequented. Slow moving vehicles travelling uphill should pull over at suitable stopping places to allow vehicles to pass.

Road Signs and Markings

Road signs and markings conform to international standards. The following signs may also be seen:

Slovak	English Translation
Dialkova premavka	By-pass
Nemocnica	Hospital
Jednosmerny premavka	One-way traffic
Obchadzka	Diversion
Průjezd zakázaný	Closed to all vehicles
Zákaz parkovania	No parking
Zákaz vjazdu	No entry

Signs indicating motorways are red and white and signs on motorways or semi-motorways have a green or blue background; on other roads signs have a blue background.

Sat Nav/GPS Device

A GPS device must not be placed in the middle of the windscreen where it will impede the driver's view.

Speed Limits

	Open Road (km/h)	Motorway (km/h)
Car Solo	90	130
Car towing caravan/trailer	90	90
Motorhome under 3500kg	90	130
Motorhome 3500-7500kg	90	90

Motorhomes over 3,500kg are restricted to 80/90 km/h (56 mph) on motorways and to 80 km/h (50 mph) on other main roads and dual carriageways. Do not exceed 30 km/h (18 mph) when approaching and going over level crossings.

Speed limits are strictly enforced. Carrying and/or use of radar detectors is prohibited.

Traffic Lights

A green arrow together with a red or amber light indicates that drivers may turn in the direction indicated by the arrow provided they give way to other traffic and to pedestrians. A green arrow accompanied by an amber light in the form of a walking figure means that pedestrians have right of way.

Violation of Traffic Regulations

Police are empowered to collect on the spot fines for contravention of driving regulations. An official receipt should be obtained.

Winter Driving

In winter equip your vehicle(s) for severe driving conditions and fit winter tyres, which are compulsory when roads are covered in snow or ice. Carry snow chains and use them when there's enough snow to protect the road surface.

Essential Equipment

First aid kit

A first aid kit is compulsory in all vehicles.

Reflective Jacket/Waistcoat

If your vehicle is immobilised on all roads outside a built up area, or if visibility is poor, you must wear an EU approved reflective jacket or waistcoat when getting out of your vehicle. Passengers who leave the vehicle, for example, to assist with a repair, should also wear one.

Warning Triangles

Carry a warning triangle which, in an emergency or in case of breakdown, must be placed at least 100 metres behind your vehicle on motorways and highways, and 50 metres behind on other roads.
The triangle may be placed closer to the vehicle in built-up areas. Drivers may use hazard-warning lights until the triangle is in position.

In case of breakdown, vehicles left on the edge of the carriageway will be towed away after three hours by the organisation in charge of the motorway or road at the owner's expense.

SLOVAKIA

Touring

Smoking isn't allowed on the premises where food is served and a partial smoking ban is in force in some bars and cafés which have a dedicated area for smokers. A tip of between 5 to 10% is usual in restaurants. It's normal to give taxi drivers a small tip by rounding up fares to the nearest 50 cents.

Mains water is heavily chlorinated and may cause stomach upsets. Bottled water is available.

The highest peaks of the Tatras mountains are covered with snow for approximately four months of the year.

There are a number of UNESCO World Heritage sites in Slovakia including the town of Bardejov, the mining centre of Banská Štiavnica, the 'gingerbread houses' of Vlkolínec village, Spiš Castle, wooden churches in the Carpathian mountains and the caves of Aggtelek Karst and Slovak Karst.

Slovakia has over a thousand curative mineral and thermal springs, together with extensive deposits of high quality healing peat and mud reputed to cure a variety of diseases and ailments. Visitors from all over the world attend these spas every year.

The Bratislava Card valid for one, two or three days, offers discounts and benefits at various museums, attractions, restaurants and cafés. In addition, it offers free access to public transport and a free one hour walking tour of the Old Town. The card can be obtained at tourist information centres, at the central railway station and at hotels.

German is the most common second language, English isn't widely understood or spoken.

Camping and Caravanning

There are approximately 175 campsites (Kemping or Autocamp) which are classified into four categories. Sites generally open from mid-June until mid-September, although some are open all year. The season is slow to get going and sites which claim to open in May may not do so or offer only minimal facilities.

Campsites' standards vary and facilities may be basic. Many consist mainly of cabins and chalets in various states of repair, while others form part of the facilities offered by hotels, guest houses or leisure/thermal spa complexes. Campsite prices and the cost of living are still relatively low.

Casual/wild camping isn't permitted; sleeping in a caravan or motorhome outside a campsite isn't allowed.

Cycling

There are a number of long distance cycle tracks throughout the country including alongside the River Danube between Bratislava and the Gabčikovo Dam. See slovakia.travel for more information.

Cyclists must ride in single file on the right hand side of the road or may use the verge outside built up areas. Children under 10 years of age may not ride on the road unless accompanied by a person over 15 years of age.

Electricity and Gas

Usually the current on campsites varies between 10 and 16 amps. Plugs have two round pins. Some campsites, but not all, have CEE connections.

It isn't possible to purchase Campingaz International or any other of the gas cylinders normally available in the UK. Sufficient supplies for your stay should be taken with you. Many sites have communal kitchen facilities which enable visitors to make great savings on their own gas supply.

Public Transport

From April to September hydrofoil services operate from Bratislava to Vienna and Budapest.

In Bratislava bus, trolley bus and tram tickets are valid up to 60 minutes up to 90 minutes at night and weekends. Buy them from kiosks and yellow ticket machines. You can buy tickets valid for one or several city zones for 24, 48 or 72 hours or for seven days. Ensure that you validate your ticket on boarding the bus or tram.

Passengers aged 70 and over travel free; carry your passport as proof of age. You must buy a ticket for dogs travelling on public transport and they must be muzzled.

You must also purchase a ticket for large items of luggage. See (imhd.sk) for more information.

Sites in Slovakia

BANSKA BYSTRICA *B2* (11km W Rural) *48.7540, 19.0552* **Autocamping Tajov,** 97634 Tajov **(048) 4197320; ks.rovdyklev@rovdyklev; www.velkydvor.sk/en**

12 (htd) nr

Fr Tajov dir Kordíky. Site well sp 2km NW of Tajov. Sm, unshd, pt sl, EHU (6-10A) inc; TV; bus; CKE. *"Lovely setting in wooded valley; friendly welcome."* **€16.00** **2022**

BANSKÁ ŠTIAVNICA *C2* (6.7km E Rural) *48.447462, 18.983303* **Camping Studenec,** 969 01 Banský Studenec **907 418 033 or 907 746 303; info@campingstudenec.eu; www.campingstudenec.eu**

€1.5

Fr Banska Stiavnica take 2536 (sp Bansky Studenec) for 5km. At end of vill turn L sp Studenec. At next junc go strt on gravel track for 50m. Sm, unshd, pt sl, EHU (16A) inc; bbq; cooking facs; sw nr; bus 500m; Eng spkn. *"Well run site; excel facs; extensive views; rural walks & biking; conv Bansky Stiavnica; poss open off ssn esp w/ends; excel."* **€22.00, 1 Jul-31 Aug.** **2023**

BRATISLAVA *C1* (9km NE Urban) *48.18801, 17.18488* **Autocamping Zlaté Piesky,** Senecká Cesta 12, 82104 Bratislava **(02) 44257373 or 44450592; kempi@netax.sk; www.intercamp.sk**

€2

Exit D1/E75 junc sp Zlaté Piesky. Site on S side of rd 61 (E75) at NE edge of Bratislava. Look for pedestrian bdge over rd to tram terminus, ent thro adj traff lts. If x-ing Bratislava foll sp for Žilina. In summer a 2nd, quieter, drier site is opened. For 1st site turn L when ent leisure complex; for 2nd site carry strt on then turn R. Med, shd, EHU (10A) €3 (long lead poss req); sw; phone; tram to city; Eng spkn; golf 10km; tennis; fishing; CKE. *"Basic site on lge leisure complex; no privacy in shwrs; ltd hot water; muddy in wet; security guard at night & secure rm for bikes etc but reg, major security problems as site grnds open to public; pedalos on lake; helpful, friendly staff; interesting city."* **€13.00, 1 May-15 Oct.** **2022**

BREZNO *B3* (6km SE Rural) *48.79501, 19.72867* **Camping Sedliacky Dvor,** Hliník 7, 97701 Brezno **(048) 911 078 303; info@sedliackydvor.com; www.sedliackydvor.com**

€1

Fr cent of Brezno at traff lts nr Hotel Dumbier take rd 530/72 SE sp Tisovec. In approx 5km cross rlwy line & ent vill of Rohozná. At end of vill turn L after Camping sp. Site in 500m. Sm, pt shd, EHU (10A) €3.25; cooking facs; Eng spkn; adv bkg acc; games area. *"Excel site in lovely orchard setting; welcoming Dutch owners; camp fires in evening; excel facs."* **€22.50, 15 Apr-31 Oct.** **2024**

CEROVO *C2* (8km E Rural) *48.25228, 19.21783* **Farm & Camping Lazy (Formerly Camping Lazy),** Cerovo 163, 96252 Cerovo **(0)908590837 or (0)915155309; info@minicamping.eu; www.minicamping.eu**

S fr Zvolen on rd 66 dir Krupina. S of Krupina turn L onto rd 526 to Bzovik. After church in Bzovik turn R sp Kozí Vrbovok, Trpin & Litava. Cont thro Litava (agricultural co-operative, Družstvo, on R) & cont for approx 5km to T-junc with bus shelter & turn R. Do not foll sp Cerovo on R but cont to forest & look out for sm lane & site sp to R. Sm, pt shd, pt sl, EHU (4-6A) €2.50. *"Site on working farm; ideal for nature lovers, hikers, dog owners; some statics (equipped tents); pleasant, helpful owners; dogs free; v clean, modern facs."* **€16.00, 1 May-30 Sep.** **2024**

LEVOCA *B3* (5km N Rural) *49.04982, 20.58727* **Autocamping Levočská Dolina,** 05401 Levoča **(053) 4512705 or 4512701; rzlevoca@pobox.sk**

12 €1.50 nr

Site on E side of minor rd 533 running N fr E50 at Dolina to Levočská Dolina. Steep ent; ltd access lge o'fits. Med, pt shd, sl, EHU (16A) €3; TV; Eng spkn; CKE. *"Diff in wet weather due v sl grnd; friendly staff; interesting old town; ski lift 2.5km; Spišský Hrad castle worth visit; walks in forests around site."* **€18.00** **2022**

LIPTOVSKY MIKULAS *B3* (11km NW Rural) *49.13608, 19.5125* **Resort Villa Betula (formerly Penzión),** 03223 Liptovský Sielnica **(907) 812327; villabetula@villabetula.sk; www.villabetula.sk**

12 €7

Fr rd 18/E50 exit onto R584 to Liptovský Mikuláš, site on N of lake 6km past Autocamp. 3*, Med, unshd, EHU (10A) inc; sw nr; phone; Eng spkn; ccard acc; bike hire; jacuzzi; sauna; CKE. *"Family-friendly, gem of a site in wonderful area of lakes, mountains & forest; welcoming, helpful owners; v clean & well-kept; vg rest; site at rear of hotel; excel for long or sh stay."* **€34.00** **2022**

NITRIANSKE RUDNO *B2* (1km N Rural) *48.80457, 18.47601* **Autocamping Nitrianske Rudno,** 97226 Nitrianske Rudno **(090) 5204739; info@camping-nrudno.sk; www.camping-nrudno.sk**

€1

E fr Bánovce & Dolné Vestenice on rd 50, turn N onto rd 574. Site on shore of Lake Nitrianske Rudno, sp in vill. 2*, Med, pt shd, EHU €2.50; cooking facs; sw; 10% statics; adv bkg acc; watersports; games area; CKE. *"Welcoming, helpful owner; pleasant location."* **€13.00, 1 Jun-30 Sep.** **2022**

SLOVAKIA

PIESTANY *B1* (2.6km S Urban) *48.576469, 17.833889* **Camping Pullman,** Cesta Janka Alexyho 2, 92101 Pieštany **(033) 7623563; info@campingpiestany.sk; www.campingpiestany.sk**
€2

On rd 507 500m Sof junc with 499 (immed E of rv bdge). Sm, unshd, EHU (6A) €5; bbq; cooking facs; TV; 20% statics; train 2km; Eng spkn; adv bkg acc; games rm; bike hire; CCI. *"Canoing on rv adj; rvside walk to town; reg trains to Bratislava 50mins (taxi to stn €8 or free parking nr stn); pleasant parks in town ctr; bar/rest in town; vg."* **€26.00, 15 Apr-15 Oct.** 2023

PREŠOV *B4* (13km W Rural) *49.00386, 21.08145* **Autokemping A Motorest Kemp,** Chminianske Nová Ves, District Prešov 082 33 **0517 795190 or 0905 191056 (mob); kemppo@kemppo.sk; www.kemppo.sk**
€2

Fr W on Rte 18/D1/E50, take exit twd Vit'az/ Hrabkov, site on R. Sm, pt shd, EHU €4; gas; bbq; cooking facs; twin axles; Eng spkn; ccard acc; games area; CKE. *"Site behind motorest Kemp on Rte 18; campers kitchen; recep in rest; 5 chalets for rent on site; fair site."* **€15.00, Feb-Dec.** 2024

ROZNAVA *B3* (6km E Rural) *48.64920, 20.59796* **Autocamping Krásnohorské,** Hradná 475, 04941 Krásnohorské Podhradie **(058) 7325457**

E fr Rožňava on rd 50/E571 foll sp Krásnohorské Podhradie. Site under shadow of castle. Sm, pt shd, 80% statics. *"Lovely setting in pine woods; primitive facs but plenty of hot water; conv for cave visits."* **€10.00** 2020

TATRANSKA LOMINICA *B3* (2.6km S Rural) *49.14974, 20.27968* **Camping Rijo (formerly Jupela),** Dolny Smokovec, 3705981 Vysoke Tatry **(421) 911 616530; rijocamping@rijocamping.eu; www.rijocamping.eu**

Fr Tatranska Lominca travel W on 537 take L turn twrds Nova Lesna. Foll sp to site. Sm, pt shd, EHU 16A €3.50; bbq; adv bkg rec. *"Beautiful location nr to mountain torrent; conv for walking in Takranska; basic clean san facs; lovely spot; walks and scenice drives."* **€13.00, 7 May-16 Sep.** 2024

TERCHOVA *B2* (3km SW Rural) *49.24779, 18.98866* **Autocamp Belá,** Nižné Kamence, 01305 Belá **(041) 5695135 or (905) 742514; camp@bela.sk; www.campingbela.eu**
12 €1

Fr Zilina foll rd 583 twd Terchová. Site on L 3km after vill of Belá. 2*, Med, pt shd, EHU (10A) €3; bbq; cooking facs; 10% statics; tennis. *"Delightful rvside site; gd welcome; clean, modern san facs; conv walking in Malá Fatra mountains."* **€20.50** 2022

TRENCIN *B2* (2km N Urban) *48.90011, 18.04076* **Autocamping Na Ostrove,** Ostrov, 91101 Trenčín **(032) 7434013 or (905) 633905; campingtn@gmail.com; visit.trencin.sk/autocamping-na-ostrove**
€1.50 nr

Fr SW on rd 61/E75 cross rv at Hotel Tatra, 1st L dir Sihot, go under rlwy bdge. 1st L, then immed 1st L again, then R at stadium, cross canal to island, site on L. Sm, unshd, serviced pitches; EHU (10A) €3; cooking facs; 90% statics; Eng spkn; CKE. *"Popular NH en rte Poland, rec arr early high ssn; on rvside in run down pt of town adj sports stadium; adj delightful town with fairy-tale castle; pool 500m; poss waterlogged in wet; facs old but clean - some lack privacy."* **€18.00, 1 May-15 Sep.** 2024

Martin to Wien (Austria) = 298km

	Banská Bystrica	Bratislava	Budapest (Hungary)	Komárno	Košice	Liptovský Mikuláš	Lučenec	Malacky	Martin	Nitra	Prešov	Poprad	Považská Bystrica	Rimavská Sobota	Svidník	Trencín	Trnava	Wien (Austria)	Zvolen
Bratislava	214																		
Budapest (Hungary)	183	201																	
Komárno	167	106	94																
Košice	218	404	282	330															
Liptovský Mikuláš	75	291	260	246	166														
Lučenec	77	243	160	168	161	151													
Malacky	223	42	242	144	417	290	258												
Martin	64	233	246	197	225	63	140	232											
Nitra	114	98	165	72	310	194	152	111	142										
Prešov	201	413	316	361	35	140	194	429	199	321									
Poprad	120	335	286	288	110	57	123	343	116	233	84								
Považská Bystrica	120	174	306	210	283	118	197	171	61	144	260	176							
Rimavská Sobota	103	274	187	194	132	132	25	287	164	177	165	97	223						
Svidník	259	471	371	415	90	195	251	484	256	373	55	135	313	221					
Trencín	145	125	281	161	332	166	183	129	103	99	302	222	47	212	360				
Trnava	169	60	209	117	361	238	204	63	182	54	372	287	120	231	422	74			
Wien (Austria)	281	68	244	175	473	358	314	109	298	125	483	400	240	340	537	194	126		
Zvolen	22	201	162	147	213	99	56	210	85	101	225	142	145	82	280	132	154	267	
Žilina	89	205	273	215	254	87	167	202	26	142	226	145	32	190	282	76	153	271	112

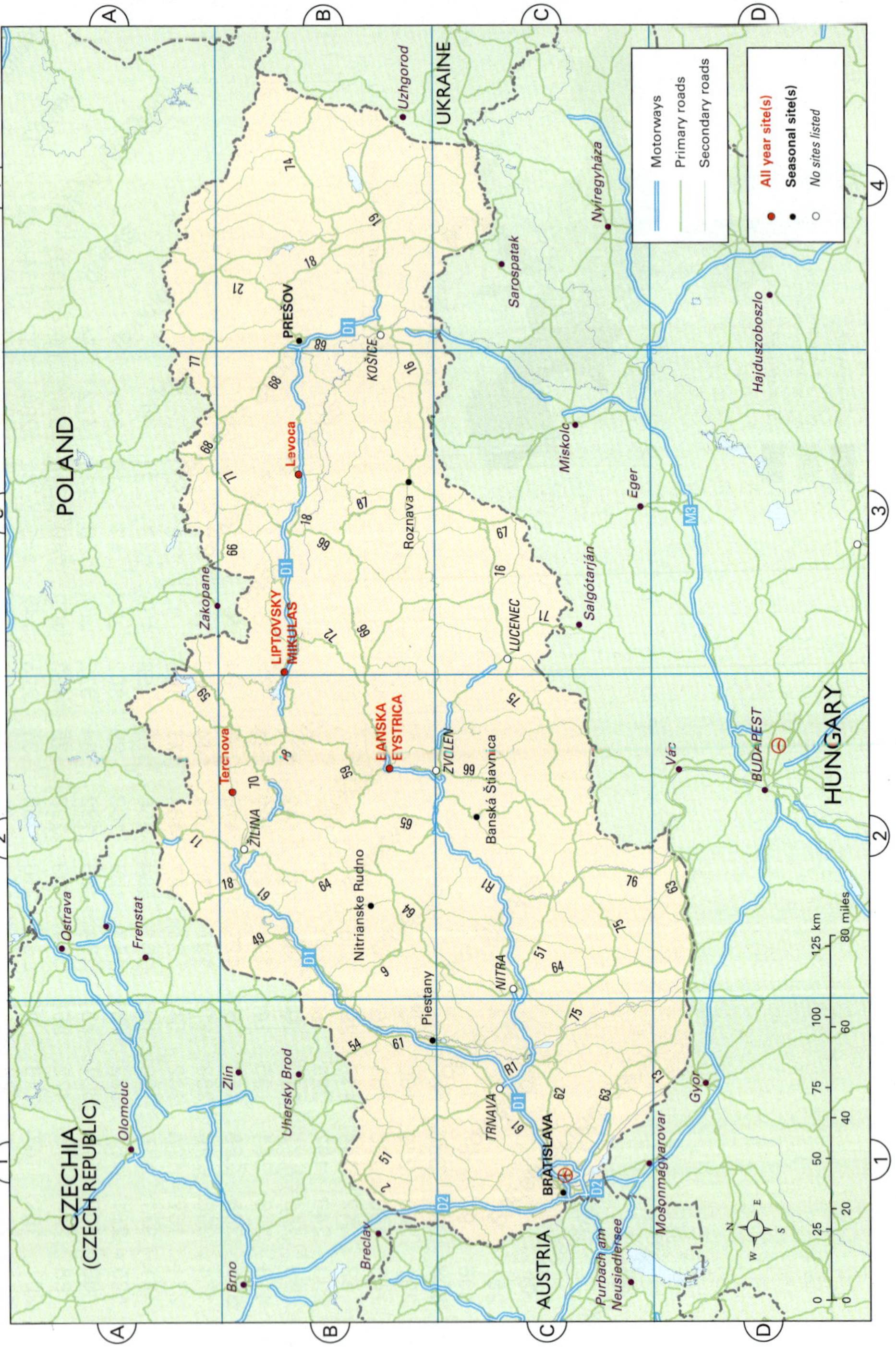
POLAND
UKRAINE
CZECHIA
(CZECH REPUBLIC)
AUSTRIA
HUNGARY
Motorways
Primary roads
Secondary roads
All year site(s)
Seasonal site(s)
No sites listed
Terchova
LIPTOVSKY MIKULAS
Levoca
BANSKA BYSTRICA
PREŠOV
KOŠICE
ŽILINA
ZVOLEN
LUCENEC
NITRA
TRNAVA
BRATISLAVA
Roznava
Banská Štiavnica
Nitrianske Rudno
Piestany
Zakopane
Uzhgorod
Sarospatak
Nyiregyháza
Miskolc
Eger
Salgótarján
Vác
BUDAPEST
Hajduszoboszlo
Gyor
Mosonmagyarovar
Purbach am Neusiedlersee
Breclav
Brno
Uhersky Brod
Zlín
Olomouc
Ostrava
Frenstat
D1
D2
R1
M3
A
B
C
D
1
2
3
4
0
25
50
75
100
125 km
0
20
40
60
80 miles

Slovenia

Highlights

Equipped with an extraordinarily pretty landscape, Slovenia is deeply in tune with its natural surroundings and is one of the greenest countries in Europe. Outdoor pursuits are wholeheartedly embraced here and are top of the list when it comes to attractions.

There's also plenty to see and do for history fans to see and do - this small country boasts around 500 castles and manor houses. Not to be missed are the hilltop castles of Bled, Ljubljana and Predjama.

Slovenia is one of the world's most biologically diverse countries, and despite its small size is home to an estimated total of 45,000 – 120,000 species.

Slovenia is also a key centre for winter sports, with major competitions and events held in the country on a regular basis. Kanin, the highest ski centre in Slovenia, offers the opportunity to ski to neighbouring Italy.

Major towns and cities

- Ljubljana – a charming capital with an old-world feel.
- Maribor – this vibrant city holds many events throughout the year.
- Celje – an ancient settlement with Celtic and Roman origins.
- Kranj – a lively city with a castle and 14th century church.

Attractions

- Bled Castle – a medieval castle overlooking the popular Lake Bled, and one of the most visited attractions in the country.
- Tivoli Park, Ljubljana - home to botanical gardens and a museum.
- Škocjan Caves – an extraordinary series of caves renowned as a natural treasure.
- Predjama Castle, Postojna – a gothic castle built 700 years ago into the mouth of a cave.

Find out more

slovenia.info
info@slovenia.info

Country Information

Capital: Ljubljana

Bordered by: Austria, Croatia, Hungary, Italy

Coastline: 46.6km

Terrain: Coastal strip on the Adriatic; alpine mountains in west and north; many rivers and forests

Climate: Mediterranean climate on the coast; hot summers and cold winters in the plateaux and valleys in the east; spring and early autumn are the best times to visit

Highest Point: Triglav 2,864m

Languages: Slovenian; Serbo-Croat

Local Time: GMT or BST + 1, i.e. 1 hour ahead of the UK all year

Currency: Euros divided into 100 cents; £1 = €1.20, €1 = £0.84 (Nov 2024)

Emergency numbers: Police 113; Fire brigade 112; Ambulance 112. Operators speak English

Public Holidays 2025: Jan 1, 2; Feb 8; Apr 20, 21, 27; May 1, 2; Jun 8, 25; Aug 15; Oct 31; Nov 1; Dec 25, 26.

School summer holidays are from the last week in June to the end of August

Entry Formalities

British and Irish passport holders may stay for up to 90 days in any 180 day period without a visa. Following Brexit you may be asked to show a return or onward ticket at the border to confirm your length of stay, or to prove that you have enough money for your stay.

Your passport will need to have a minimum of 6 months' validity remaining, and be less than 10 years old (even if it has over 6 months left).

All foreign nationals must register with the police within three days of arrival in Slovenia. Campsites carry out registration formalities, but if you're staying with friends or family you or your host will need to visit the nearest police station to register your presence in the country.

Medical Services

British visitors may obtain emergency medical, hospital and dental treatment from practitioners registered with the public health service, Health Institute of Slovenia (HIIS) on presentation of a European Health Insurance Card (EHIC) or a Global Health Insurance Card (GHIC). You'll have to make a contribution towards costs which will not be refunded in Slovenia. Full fees are payable for private medical and dental treatment.

Health resorts and spas are popular and the medical profession uses them extensively for treatment of a wide variety of complaints.

Opening Hours

Banks: Mon-Fri 9am-12 noon & 2pm-5pm; closed Sat/Sun

Museums: Tues-Sun 9/10am-5/6pm. Most closed Mon.

Post Offices: Mon-Fri 8am-6pm; Sat 8am-12noon.

Shops: Mon-Fri 8am-7pm/9pm; Sat 8am-1pm.

Safety and Security

Slovenia is relatively safe for visitors but the usual sensible precautions should be taken against pickpockets in large towns and cities. Do not leave valuables in your car.

Western Slovenia is on an earthquake fault line and is subject to occasional tremors.

If you're planning a skiing or mountaineering holiday, contact the Slovenian Tourist Board for advice on weather and safety conditions before travelling. You should follow all safety instructions meticulously, given the danger of avalanches in some areas. Off-piste skiing is highly dangerous.

Slovenia shares with the rest of Europe an underlying threat from terrorism. Please check gov.uk/foreign-travel-advice/slovenia before you travel.

British Embassy

Trg Republike 3, 1000 Ljubljana
Tel: +386 1 200 3910
gov.uk/world/slovenia

Irish Embassy

Palaca Kapitelj 1st Floor
Poljanski nasip 6
1000 Ljubljana
Tel: +386 1 300 8970
ireland.ie/ljubljana

Documents

Driving Licence

All European countries recognise the EU format paper UK driving licence introduced in 1990. However, it's a legal requirement to show your driving license with a form of photographic identification, such as your passport, if your driving licence doesn't include a photograph.

Passport

Carry a copy of your passport at all times as a form of identification.

Vehicle(s)

You should carry your vehicle documentation, i.e. vehicle registration certificate (V5C), insurance certificate, MOT certificate (if applicable) and driver's licence.

If you're driving a hired or borrowed vehicle, you must be in possession of a letter of authorisation from the owner or a hire agreement.

Money

Cash machines are widespread and the major credit cards are widely accepted. Carry your credit card issuers'/banks' 24-hour UK contact numbers in case of loss or theft of your cards.

Driving

Accidents

Any visible damage to a vehicle entering Slovenia must be certified by authorities at the border. All drivers involved in an accident while in the country should inform the police and obtain a written report (Potrdilo). Drivers of vehicles which have been damaged will need to present this police report to Customs on departure.

Alcohol

The maximum permitted level of alcohol in the blood is 0.05% i.e less than in England, Wales and Northern Ireland (0.08%), but the same as Scotland. If a driver is under the age of 21 or has held a driving licence for less than two years the permitted level of alcohol is zero. The police carry out tests at random.

Breakdown Service

The motoring organisation, Avto-Moto Zveza Slovenije (AMZS), operates a 24 hour breakdown service which can be contacted by telephoning 1987. On motorways, using a mobile phone, call the AMZS Alarm Centre in Ljubljana on +386 1 5305 353 or use the emergency telephones on motorways and ask for AMZS assistance.

Charges apply for repairs or towing, plus supplements at night, weekends and on public holidays. Credit cards are accepted.

Child Restraint System

Children under 12 years of age and under the height of 1.5 metres must use a suitable child restraint system for their size and age.

Fuel

Petrol stations are generally open from 6am or 7am to 8pm or 9pm Monday to Saturday. Many near border crossings, on motorways and near large towns are open 24 hours. Credit cards are accepted.

Visit (mylpg.eu/stations/slovenia) for a list and interactive map of LPG stations in Slovenia,

Lights

Dipped headlights are compulsory at all times, regardless of weather conditions. Bulbs are more likely to fail with constant use and you are required to carry spares. Hazard warning lights must be used when reversing.

Motorways

There are around 625 km of motorways (autoceste) and expressways (hitre ceste) with more under construction. For more information about motorways see the website dars.si.

There are service areas and petrol stations along the motorways and emergency telephones are situated every 2 km.

Emergency corridors are compulsory on motorways and dual carriageways. Drivers are required to create a precautionary emergency corridor to provide access for emergency vehicles whenever congestion occurs. Drivers in the left-hand lane must move as far over to the left as possible, and drivers in the central and right-hand lanes must move as far over to the right as possible.

Motorway Tolls

Drivers of vehicles weighing up to 3,500kg must purchase an electronic vignette for use on motorways and expressways. The e-vignette is available from petrol stations in Slovenia, neighbouring countries, some shops at the border, from the club AMZS, and online at evinjeta.dars.si/en. The cost of a 7-day e-vignette is €16, 1 month is €32 and an annual is €117.50 (2024 charges).

Tolls for vehicles over 3,500kg are collected electronically by means of a small box (called a DarsGo) installed in your vehicle. For more details, see the DARS website: dars.si.

Karawanken Tunnel

The 8 km Karawanken Tunnel links the E61/A11 in Austria and E61/A2 in Slovenia. The toll is €8.20 for a car and caravan or motorhome up to 3,500kg (2024 charges). For motorhomes over 3,500kg, the toll is paid with the DARS electronic payment system. Visit (dars.si/Karavanke_tunnel) for more information.

Parking

Parking meters are used in towns. In city centres white lines indicate that parking is permitted for a maximum of two hours between 7am and 7pm, a parking ticket must be purchased from a machine. Blue lines indicate places where parking is allowed free of charge for up to 30 minutes. Vehicles parked illegally may be towed away or clamped.

Priority

At intersections drivers must give way to traffic from the right, unless a priority road is indicated. The same rule applies to roundabouts, i.e. traffic entering a roundabout has priority.

Roads

International and main roads are in good condition. Secondary roads may still be poorly maintained and generally unlit. Minor roads are often gravelled and are known locally as 'white roads'. Road numbers aren't often mentioned on road signs and it's advisable to navigate using place names in the direction you're travelling.

Roadside verges are uncommon, or may be lined with bollards which make pulling over difficult. Where there's a hard shoulder it's usual for slow vehicles to pull over to allow faster traffic to overtake.

The capital, Ljubljana, can be reached from Munich, Milan, Vienna and Budapest in less than five hours. There are numerous border crossings for entry into Slovenia.

Care should be taken, especially on narrow secondary roads, where tailgating and overtaking on blind bends are not unknown. Drive defensively and take extra care when driving at night. Be prepared for severe weather in winter.

Information on roads may be obtained by telephoning the AMZS Information Centre on (01) 5305300.

Road Signs and Markings

Road signs conform to international standards. Motorway signs have a green background and national road signs a blue background. On your travels you may see the following signs:

Mountain pass

School area

Toll: Vignette/ card or cash

Speed Limits

	Open Road (km/h)	Motorway (km/h)
Car Solo	90-110	130
Car towing caravan/trailer	90	100
Motorhome under 3500kg	90-110	130
Vehicle over 3500-7500kg	80	80

Motorhomes over 3,500kg are restricted to 80 km/h (50 mph) on open roads, including motorways. Other speed limits are the same as for solo cars. Areas where speed is restricted to 30 km/h (18 mph) are indicated by the sign 'Zone 30'.

When visibility is reduced to 50 metres the maximum speed limit is 50 km/h (31 mph).

Traffic Jams

Slovenia is a major international through-route and bottlenecks do occur on the roads to and from Ljubljana, such as the E61/A2 from Jesinice and the E57 from Maribor. Traffic queues can be expected from May to August on the roads around Lake Bled and to the Adriatic and on the E70/A1 motorway near the Razdrto toll station and near Kozina and Koper.

Tailbacks also occur at border posts near the Karawanken Tunnel, Ljubelj and Šentilj/Spielfeld particularly at weekends.The motoring organisation, AMZS, provides traffic information in English – telephone (01) 5305300 or see their website: amzs.si.

Violation of Traffic Regulations

The police have powers to stop drivers and levy heavy on-the-spot fines, including penalties for speeding, driving under the influence of alcohol and for using mobile phones without properly installed wireless headsets (bluetooth). Jaywalking is an offence and you could be fined if caught. Fines must be paid in local currency and you should obtain an official receipt.

Winter Driving

From 15 November to 15 March, and beyond those dates during winter weather conditions (snowfalls, black ice, etc), private cars and vehicles up to 3,500kg must have winter tyres on all four wheels or, alternatively, carry snow chains. Minimum tread depth of tyres is 3mm.

Essential Equipment

First aid kit

Although a first aid kit is not compulsory in all vehicles, it's recommended

Reflective Jacket/Waistcoat

In the event of vehicle breakdown on a motorway, anyone who leaves the vehicle must wear a reflective jacket.

Warning Triangles

Vehicles towing a trailer must carry two warning triangles (single vehicles require one). In the event of a breakdown to vehicle and trailer combinations, one triangle must be placed at the rear of the towed vehicle and another at the front of the towing vehicle at a distance which ensures maximum safety and visibility.

At night, drivers must use hazard warning lights or a torch in addition to the warning triangles.

Touring

A 10% tip is usual in restaurants and for taxi drivers.

The capital, Ljubljana, is a gem of a city with many Baroque and Art Nouveau influences. The works of the world renowned architect Jože Plecnik are among the finest urban monuments in the city. A Ljubljana Card is available for one, two or three days and offers free travel on city buses, tourist boat trips, the funicular, guided tours and the tourist train to Ljubljana Castle, plus free admission to museums and discounts at a wide range of shops, restaurants and bars. You can buy the card at the main bus and railway stations, hotels and tourist information centres or from visitljubljana.si.

Visit the largest cave in Europe is situated at Postojna, south west of Ljubljana. Also worth visiting are the mountains, rivers and woods of Triglav National Park, which covers the major part of the Julian Alps, together with the oldest town in Slovenia, Ptuj, and the city of Maribor. In Lipica take a guided tour around the stud, home to the world famous Lipizzaner horses.

There's a hydrofoil service between Portorož and Venice from April to November.

Slovenian is the official language although most Slovenians speak at least one other major European language and many, especially the young, speak English.

Camping and Caravanning

There are over 60 organised campsites in Slovenia rated one to five stars. They're usually open from May to October, but some are open all year. Standards of sites and their sanitary facilities are generally good. Campsites on the coast are mostly statics and can be overcrowded during the peak season.

Casual/wild camping is not permitted.

Cycling

There are some cycle lanes which are also used by mopeds. Cyclists under the age of 15 must wear a safety helmet.

If using a vehicle bike carrier which overhangs by over one metre at the rear of a vehicle, you need to affix a 30 cm square red flag or panel. At night the overhanging load must be indicated by a red light and a reflector. Loads may only project rearwards; they must not overhang the sides of vehicles.

Electricity and Gas

Usually the current on campsites varies between 6 and 16 amps. Plugs have two round pins. Hook-up points on most campsites conform to CEE standards.

Campingaz cylinders cannot be purchased or exchanged.

Recent visitors report that it's possible to have gas cylinders refilled at Butan-Plin on Verovškova Ulica 70, Ljubljana. The Caravan and Motorhome Club doesn't recommend this practice and you should aim to take enough gas to last during your stay.

Public Transport

There's an extensive bus network in Ljubljana. Buy a yellow 'top-up' Urbana card for a one-off payment of €2 from news-stands, tobacconists, tourist information offices or the central bus station.€50 of credit can be added at the same locations or at the green Urbanomati machines around the city. Touch the card to one of the card readers at the front of the bus and €1.30 will be deducted allowing 90 minutes of unlimited travel. Taxis are generally safe, clean and reliable. Fares are metered. For longer distances ordering a taxi by phone will attract lower rates.

Lake Bled

Shutterstock/Zdenek Matyas Photography

Sites in Slovenia

BLED *B2* (12.5km SE Rural) *46.326170, 14.234771* **Turistična kmetija Hribar,** Brezje 14, 4243 Brezje **40 260 414; breda.policar@gmail.com; www.turisticna-kmetija-hribar.si**

12 nr nr nr

Exit m'way sp Brezje and turn L to Brezje. Turn R at rndabt sp Brezje. On reaching Brezje bear R and cont past firestn. At T-junc turn R. Cont for 300m (ignoring Sat Nav) until you see sm residential carpk on R. Now turn sharp L and go straight thro metal gates to site. Sm, pt shd, EHU (16A) €3.50; bbq (charcoal, elec, gas); cooking facs; red long stay; 5% statics; bus 1km; Eng spkn; adv bkg acc; ccard acc. **€24.40** **2024**

BLED *B2* (4km SE Rural) *46.35527, 14.14833* **Camping Šobec,** Šobčeva Cesta 25, 4248 Lesce **(04) 5353700; sobec@siol.net; www.sobec.si**

€9

Exit rte 1 at Lesce, site sp. 5*, Lge, pt shd, pt sl, EHU (16A) inc; red long stay; TV; Eng spkn; ccard acc; bike hire; CKE. *"Excel, tranquil rvside site in wooded area surrounded by rv; friendly, helpful staff; lge pitches; clean san facs; gd rest; gd walking/cycling; many sports & activities; real camping atmosphere, plenty of space; def rec; rv pool; beautiful area; conv NH en-rte to Croatia."* **€58.40, 15 Apr-1 Oct.** **2023**

BLED *B2* (6km SE Urban) *46.34772, 14.17284* **Camping Radovljica,** Kopališka 9, 4240 Radovljica **(04) 5315770; info@camping-radovljica.com; www.camping-radovljica.com**

nr nr

Exit A1/E61 junc Bled/Bohinj, site in cent of Radovljica bet bus & train stn sp Camping & Sw. Med, pt shd, pt sl, EHU (16A) inc; red long stay; 10% statics; bike hire. *"Vg; security gate; vg, clean san facs; fitness rm; gd NH; pool adj; friendly staff."* **€38.00, 1 Jun-15 Sep.** **2024**

BLED *B2* (4km SW Rural) *46.36155, 14.08066* **Camping Bled,** Kidričeva 10c, SI 4260 Bled **04 5752000; info@camping-bled.com; www.camping-bled.com**

€3 nr nr (htd, indoor) shgl

Fr Ljubljana take E16/A2 & exit dir Bled/Lesce. At rndabt take 2nd exit for Bled & cont along rd 209. In Bled take rd around lake on L (lake on R), site sp - winding rd. 5*, Lge, mkd, pt shd, pt sl, EHU (16A) inc (long lead req some pitches - fr recep); gas; bbq; sw nr; twin axles; red long stay; TV; bus to Ljubljana adj; Eng spkn; ccard acc; games rm; fishing; white water rafting; games area; horseriding; bike hire; dog shwrs; CKE. *"Beautifully situated nr lake; m'van & car wash; busy, popular, well-run site; well-drained in bad weather altho lower pitches poss muddy; v gd, modern, clean san facs, stretched in ssn; helpful, efficient, friendly staff; spa cent nrby; paragliding; conv Vintgar Gorge, Bled Castle, Lake Bohinj, Dragna Valley; excel walking/cycling around lake; excel rest; arr acc anytime; free WiFi throughout site."* **€25.00, 1 Jun-30 Sept, X03.** **2024**

See advertisement

BOHINJSKA BISTRICA *B1* (0.8km NW Rural) *46.27438, 13.94798* **Camping Danica Bohinj,** Triglavska 60, 4264 Bohinjska Bistrica **(04) 5721702; info@camp-danica.si; www.camp-danica.si**

12 €6 nr

Site on o'skts of vill clearly sp. 3*, Med, pt shd, EHU (6A) inc (long lead poss req); gas; red long stay; 10% statics; Eng spkn; ccard acc; tennis; canoe hire; kayak hire; fishing; CCI. *"Excel site, spacious, open, attractive site in beautiful valley; fly-fishing; gd walking & climbing; gd, clean san facs but poss stretched high ssn; conv bus to Ljubljana & Lake Bohinji."* **€58.60** **2023**

BOVEC *B1* (1km E Rural) *46.33659, 13.55803* **Autocamp Polovnik,** Ledina 8, 5230 Bovec **(05) 3896007; kamp.polovnik@siol.net; www.kamp-polovnik.com**

Sp on rd 206 down fr Predil Pass (1,156m - 14% gradient) fr Italy - do not turn into vill. Site 200m after turn to Bovec. 3*, Sm, pt shd, EHU (16A) €2.50 (poss rev pol); bbq; ccard acc; tennis; fishing; CKE. *"Helpful staff; clean facs; muddy when wet; friendly staff."* **€30.00, 1 Apr-15 Oct. 2024**

BOVEC *B1* (9km E Rural) *46.33527, 13.64416* **Camping Soča,** Soča 8, 5232 Soča **(05) 3889318; kamp.soca@siol.net / booking@kamp-soca.si / info@kamp-soca.si; https://kamp-soca.si/**

€1 (htd) nr nr

Sp on S side of rd 206 in national park, nr turning for Lepena approx 3km bef Soča vill. 3*, Lge, pt shd, terr, EHU (6A) inc; bbq; red long stay; TV; 50% statics; Eng spkn. *"Beautiful situation in rv valley; gd, modern san facs; gd walking, rafting; gd touring base Triglav National Park; rv adj; excel; braziers and wood avail; walking and cycling tracks fr site."* **€35.00, 1 Apr-31 Oct. 2024**

BREZICE *C3* (5km S Rural) *45.89138, 15.62611* **Camping Terme Čatež,** Topliška Cesta 35, 8251 Čatež ob Savi **(07) 4936700; info@terme-catez.si; www.terme-catez.si**

€4 (htd)

Exit E70 at Brežice, foll brown sp to Terme Čatež, then site sp. 5*, Lge, mkd, pt shd, EHU (10A) inc; gas; bbq; TV; 50% statics; Eng spkn; adv bkg acc; ccard acc; games rm; canoeing; fishing; bike hire; sauna; golf 7km; games area; boating; tennis; CKE. *"Site in lge thermal spa & health resort; many sports, leisure & health facs; shop nr; thermal water complex, inc 10 outdoor & 3 indoor pools, waterfalls & whirlpools, etc; select own pitch - best at edge of site; gd family site; conv Zagreb; fitness studio; san facs dated (2013); not value for money."* **€67.00, X05. 2024**

KAMNIK *B2* (1km NE Urban) *46.22724, 14.61902* **Kamp Resnik,** Nevlje 1a, 1240 Kamnik **51 346 543; info@kampresnik.com; www.kampresnik.com**

nr nr

Fr Ljubljana foll rd sp Celje then turn N for Kamnik. Fr Kemnik by-pass (E side of rv) bear R thro 2 sets traff lts, site 200m on L just after sports cent - site ent not obvious, turn bef zebra x-ing opp pub. Fr E on rd 414, site sp. 2*, Med, pt shd, EHU (10A) €3; gas; 5% statics; bus; Eng spkn; adv bkg acc; ccard acc; golf nr; CKE. *"Conv Ljubljana & Kamnik Alps; friendly staff; pleasant, well-kept; thermal spa nrby; pool adj; new excel extra shwrs (2018); views of Kamniska Alps; short stroll into town; rly stn 1km."* **€17.00, 1 May-30 Sep. 2024**

KOBARID *B1* (1km NE Rural) *46.25070, 13.58664* **Kamp Koren,** Drežniške Ravne 33, 5222 Kobarid **(05) 3891311; info@kamp-koren.si; www.kamp-koren.si**

€2 (htd) nr

Turn E fr main rd in town, site well sp dir Drežnica. 4*, Med, pt shd, EHU (16A) €5; red long stay; TV; Eng spkn; ccard acc; bike hire; canoeing; CKE. *"Vg, clean facs but stretched; friendly, helpful staff; pitches cramped; pleasant location in beautiful rv valley; excel walk to waterfall (3hrs); WW1 museum in town; lge elec lead poss req."* **€36.00 2023**

KOPER *D1* (7km N Coastal) *45.57818, 13.73573* **Camping Adria,** Jadranska Zesta 25, 6280 Ankaran **(05) 6637350; camp@adria-ankaran.si; www.adria-ankaran.si**

€4 adj

Fr A1/E70/E61 onto rd 10 then rd 406 to Ankaran. Or cross Italian border at Lazzaretto & foll sp to site in 3km. Site sp in vill. 4*, Lge, mkd, shd, EHU (10A) €3; bbq; 60% statics; bus 500m; ccard acc; tennis; bike hire; waterslide; sauna. *"Old town of Koper worth a visit; 1 Olympic-size pool; Vinakoper winery rec N of site on dual c'way; poss noisy groups high ssn; insect repellent req; private san facs avail; clean san facs but red LS; gd rest; has beach but not picturesque; vg."* **€55.00, 8 Apr-15 Oct. 2023**

KRANJSKA GORA *B1* (14km E Rural) *46.46446, 13.95773* **Camping Kamne,** Dovje 9, 4281 Mojstrana **(04) 5891105; info@campingkamne.com; www.campingkamne.com**

€2 (htd) nr nr

Sp fr rd 201 bet Jesenice & Kranjska Gora, 2km E of Mojstrana. Do not go thro vill of Dovje. 3*, Sm, hdstg, pt shd, terr, EHU (6A) €2.50-3.50; red long stay; TV; 10% statics; bus to Kranjska Gora fr site; Eng spkn; bike hire; tennis; fishing; CKE. *"Conv Triglav National Park & border; views Mount Triglav; warm welcome; ltd san facs stretched high ssn; hiking; friendly helpful staff; gd cycling along old rlwy track; steep site; some pitches sm, some with good views; tap for filling aquarolls at bottom of site."* **€31.00 2024**

KRANJSKA GORA *B1* (4km E Rural) *46.484438, 13.837885* **Camping Spik,** Jezerci 21, 4282 Godz Martuljek **51 634 466; info@camp-spik.si; www.camp-spik.com**

(htd) (htd)

Fr Ratece foll rd past Kranjska Gora to Gozd. Thro vill, bear L over rv bdge, site ent immed on L adj hotel. 3*, Lge, mkd, shd, EHU (10A); bbq (charcoal, elec, gas); red long stay; twin axles; 40% statics; phone; adv bkg acc; ccard acc; bike hire; fitness rm; tennis adj; sauna; climbing wall. *"Conv Kranska Gora National Park; max 2 dogs; vg rests in KG; gd walking & cycling; LS check in at hotel; gd facs; next to Spa Hotel."* **€33.70 2024**

LENDAVA *B4* (2km S Rural) *46.55195, 16.45875* **Camping Terme Lendava (Part Naturist),** Tomšičeva 2a, 9220 Lendava **(02) 5774400; info@terme-lendava.si; www.terme-lendava.si**

12 €3 (htd) nr (covrd, htd)

Site well sp, adj hotel complex. 3*, Med, pt shd, EHU (16A) €4; TV; 10% statics; adv bkg acc; ccard acc; waterslide; sauna; bike hire; tennis; games area. *"Conv Hungarian & Croatian borders; private bthrms avail; fitness rm; use of spa inc; naturist pool; unisex san facs."* **€45.00** **2024**

LJUBLJANA *C2* (5km N Urban) *46.09752, 14.51870* **Ljubljana Resort,** Dunajska Cesta 270, 1000 Ljubljana **(01) 5890130; ljubljana.resort@gpl.si; www.ljubljanaresort.si**

12 €6 (htd)

Fr Maribor take A1 twd Ljubljana, at junc Zadobrova take Ljubljana ring rd twd Kranj & exit junc 3 sp Lj - Ježica, Bežigrad. At x-rds turn R twd Črnuče along Dunajska Cesta, turn R 100m bef rlwy x-ing. Fr N (Jesenica/Karawanken tunnel) exit A2/E66 at junc 13 sp Ljubljana Črnuče & foll rd for 3.5km; at rndabt junc with Dunajska Cesta rd turn R (1st exit); site on L in 200m. 4*, Lge, mkd, hdg, pt shd, EHU (10A) inc; bbq (elec, gas, sep area); 10% statics; phone; bus to city at site ent (tickets at recep); Eng spkn; ccard acc; horseriding 500m; rv fishing; tennis; bike hire; games rm; CKE. *"Busy site by rv; gd rest; naturist sunbathing adj pool; dishwash area; red facs LS; archery; fitness club; pitches nr hotel poss noisy due late-night functions; whirlpools; htd pool complex adj; some pitches muddy when wet; conv for city; cycle & walking path along Rv Sava; friendly, helpful staff."* **€57.50, X04.** **2023**

MARIBOR *B3* (5km SW Urban) *46.5355, 15.60508* **Camping Centre Kekec,** Pohorska ulica 35c, 2000 Maribor **040 665 732; info@cck.si or bernard@cck.si; www.cck.si**

12 €5 (htd) nr nr

Fr S on A1 exit Maribor Jug; foll rd until you see Bauhaus shopping cent on the R, turn L at this x-rd; turn R after approx 400m; turn L after approx 100m; site on L after approx 3km opp the Terano Hotel. Sm, mkd, hdstg, unshd, pt sl, terr, EHU (25A) €5; bbq; Eng spkn; adv bkg acc; ccard acc; CKE. *"Rec for larger o'fits as lge pitches avail but care with narr ent rd; v nice site."* **€31.20** **2023**

NAZARJE *B2* (7km W Rural) *46.31166, 14.90916* **Camping Menina,** Varpolje 105, 3332 Rečica ob Savinji **51219393; info@campingmenina.com; campingmenina.com/en**

12 €3

Fr rte E57 bet Ljubljana & Celje, turn N twd Nazarje, then dir Ljubno for 3km. Site sp. 4*, Med, mkd, hdstg, shd, EHU (6-16A) €3; sw nr; 10% statics; Eng spkn; adv bkg acc; bike hire; CKE. *"Helpful owners; delightful site in woodland; very ltd facs in winter."* **€26.00** **2022**

NOVA GORICA *C1* (7km SE Rural) *45.94182, 13.71761* **Camping Lijak - Mladovan Farm,** Ozeljan 6A, 5261 Šempas **(0) 5 30 88 557 or (0)31 894 694; camp.lijak@volja.net; www.camplijak.com**

€1 (htd) nr

Fr Nova Gorica take rd 444 twd Ljubljana/Ajdovščina. Site on L bef turn-off to Ozeljan. Sm, pt shd, EHU (10A) €3 (poss long lead req); bbq; 10% statics; phone; bus; Eng spkn. *"Farm site in wine-growing area; weekly wine tasting; hang-gliding area, enthusiasts use site; friendly owner; gd san facs."* **€35.50, 15 Mar-31 Oct.** **2024**

"There aren't many sites open at this time of year"

If you're travelling outside peak season remember to call ahead to check site opening dates – even if the entry says 'open all year'.

NOVO MESTO *C3* (11km SW Rural) *45.76735, 15.05150* **Campsite Polje,** Meniška vas 47, 8350 Dolenjske Toplice **40 466 589; info@kamp-polje.si; kamp-polje.si**

(htd) nr

W fr Novo Mesto on 419 to Dolenjske Toplice. Foll sp. Hdstg, mkd, pt shd, EHU (16A); bbq (charcoal, elec, gas); sw nr; twin axles; Eng spkn; adv bkg rec; ccard acc; bike, canoe and scooter hire; fishing. *"Ideal NH or longer; forest on one side, fields other; ACSI discount."* **€18.00, 1 Apr-5 Nov.** **2024**

PIVKA *D2* (3km S Rural) *45.708997, 14.192552* **Camp Plana,** Selce 66, 6257 Pivka **(07) 0668668; camp.plana@gmail.com; camping-plana.com**

€2

Fr the border with Croatia at the end of E61/A7 foll rte 6 to Pivka. Site sp on R off rte 6. Sm, hdstg, pt shd, EHU (10A) €7; cooking facs; sw nr; twin axles; TV; Eng spkn; adv bkg acc; games area. *"Excel."* **€34.00, 1 Apr-31 Oct.** **2023**

PORTOROZ *D1* (3km S Coastal) *45.50138, 13.59388* **Camping Lucija,** Obala 77, 6320 Portorož **(05) 6906000; camp.lucija@sava.si; www.camp-lucija.si**

€5 adj

Fr Koper (N) on rd 111, turn R at traff lts in Lucıja. Take next L, then 2nd L into site. Nr Metropol Hotel, site sp. 3*, Lge, pt shd, serviced pitches; EHU (6-10A) €4.50; 60% statics; Eng spkn; ccard acc; bike hire; CKE. *"Conv Piran old town by bike or bus; sea views; sep area for tourers, extra for beach pitch; sm pitches; vg facs; busy site; gd public beach; noise fr disco opp till 4am."* **€37.00, 11 Mar-2 Nov.** **2022**

See advertisement on page 731

POSTOJNA *C2* (5km NW Rural) *45.80551, 14.20470* **Camping Pivka Jama,** Veliki Otok 50, 6230 Postojna **(05) 7203993; avtokamp.pivka.jama@siol.net; www.camping-postojna.com**

(htd)

Fr N or S Exit A1/E61 strt over traff lts, R at rdbt then bear L at next, foll sp to caves grotto (Postojnska Jama). Pass caves on R & then foll signs for Predjama Castle. 3km after caves site sp. Narr, winding app rd. 3*, Lge, hdstg, shd, pt sl, terr, EHU (6A) €3.70 (rev pol); cooking facs; 50% statics; Eng spkn; adv bkg acc; ccard acc; tennis; CKE. *"Gd forest site; gd rest with live Tirolean music; gd san facs, needs updating (2017); used as transit to Croatia, open 24 hrs; caves 4km a must visit (take warm clothing!)."* **€32.00, 15 Apr-31 Oct, X09. 2022**

PREBOLD *B3* (0.2km N Rural) *46.24027, 15.08790* **Camping Dolina,** Dolenja Vas 147, 3312 Prebold **(03) 1692488; camp@dolina.si; www.dolina.si**

12 €2 nr nr (htd)

On A1/E57 turn R 16km fr Celje sp Prebold & foll sp, site on N edge of vill. 3*, Sm, unshd, EHU (6-10A) €3.30; gas; red long stay; bike hire; CKE. *"Gd clean facs but no changing area in shwrs; helpful, friendly owner; conv Savinja valley; gd walking."* **€20.00 2022**

"That's changed – Should I let the Club know?"

If you find something on site that's different from the site entry, fill in a report and let us know. See camc.com/europereport.

PREBOLD *B3* (0.4km N Rural) *46.23832, 15.09266* **Camping Park,** Latkova Vas 227, 3312 Prebold **38641472496; info@campingpark.si; www.campingpark.si**

(on lead) (htd) nr

Fr A1/E57 or rd 5 exit at Prebold. Foll site sp for 400m, cross Rv Savinja & site on L. 2*, Sm, shd, EHU (6A) inc; bbq; Eng spkn; adv bkg acc; games area; CKE. *"V pleasant, well-kept site but ltd facs; pleasant walks by rv; helpful owners own adj hotel; gd walking & cycling."* **€20.00, 1 Apr-31 Oct. 2020**

PREBOLD *B3* (15km W Rural) *46.24458, 14.943502* **Camping Podgrad Vransko,** Praprece 30, 3305 Vransko **651 22 91 55; www.camp-vransko.com**

12 (htd)

Foll sp off A1 at Vransko. Site 0.5km NW of town. Well sp. Sm, hdstg, mkd, pt shd, EHU (16A); bbq (charcoal, elec, gas); Eng spkn; ccard acc; games rm; games rm. *" New site (2018); v friendly, helpful owners; MH disposal; panaramic views."* **€23.00 2024**

PTUJ *B4* (3km NW Rural) *46.42236, 15.85478* **Autokamp Terme Ptuj,** Pot V Toplice 9, 2250 Ptuj **(02) 7494100; info@terme-ptuj.si; www.terme-ptuj.si**

12 €4 (htd) nr (covrd, htd)

S fr Maribor on A4 or rd 1/E59; turn L onto rd 2 sp Ptuj (exit junc 2 fr A4); on app Ptuj foll sp Golf/ Terme Camping to L off rd 2; site after leisure complex on Rv Drava. Diff to find when app fr SW on rd 432. 4*, Med, pt shd, EHU (10A) €4; gas; bbq; red long stay; phone; Eng spkn; tennis; waterslide; golf 1km; bike hire; games area; CKE. *"Helpful staff; clean san facs, poss stretched high ssn; pitches muddy in wet; superb water park free to campers; lovely area; sauna; steam rm; castle & monastery in Ptuj old town worth a visit; fitness rm; weekly bus to Vienna; new san facs (2013)."* **€58.00 2024**

ROGASKA SLATINA *B3* (12km S Rural) *46.16499, 15.60495* **Camping Natura Terme Olimia,** Zdraviliška Cesta 24, 3254 Podčetrtek **(03) 8297836; info@terme-olimia.com; www.terme-olimia.com**

(htd) nr (covrd, htd)

Fr Celje take rte E dir Rogaška Slatina. Turn S sp Podčetrtek just bef Rogaška. Site on L (waterchutes) alongside Rv Solta on Croatian border in approx 10km. 5*, Sm, unshd, EHU (10-16A) €3.20; TV; phone; adv bkg acc; ccard acc; bike hire; waterslide; golf 4km; tennis; horseriding 2km; sauna; fitness rm; CKE. *"Aqualuna Thermal Pk adj; vg walking country with wooded hillsides."* **€36.20, 15 Apr-15 Oct. 2022**

SKOFJA LOKA *B2* (12km E Rural) *46.17455, 14.41720* **Camping Smlednik (Part Naturist),** Dragočajna 14a, 1216 Smlednik **1 36 27 002 or 40 840 050; smlednik.camp@gmail.com; www.dm-campsmlednik.si**

€1

Fr Ljubljana N on E61 take turning W onto rd 413 sp Zapoge & Zbilje. After Valburg & bef x-ing rv turn R to Dragočajna & site. Lge, pt shd, terr, EHU (6-10A) €3-4; bbq; 80% statics; Eng spkn; tennis; canoeing; CKE. *"Pleasant rvside location; steep site; sep sm naturist site; shwrs poss only warm as solar powered; ltd facs LS; poss muddy when wet."* **€24.00, 1 May-15 Oct. 2024**

VIPAVA *C1* (2km S Rural) *45.832168, 13.971053* **Kamp Tura,** Gradišče pri Vipavi 14a, 5271 Vipava **659-93 00 67; info@kamp-tura.si; www.kamp-tura.si**

12

Foll sp fr Vipava. Steep, narr approach, not suitable for units over 5m. TV; Eng spkn; Ccard acc. *"Gd facs; helpful owner; gd walks/climbing."* **€32.00 2024**

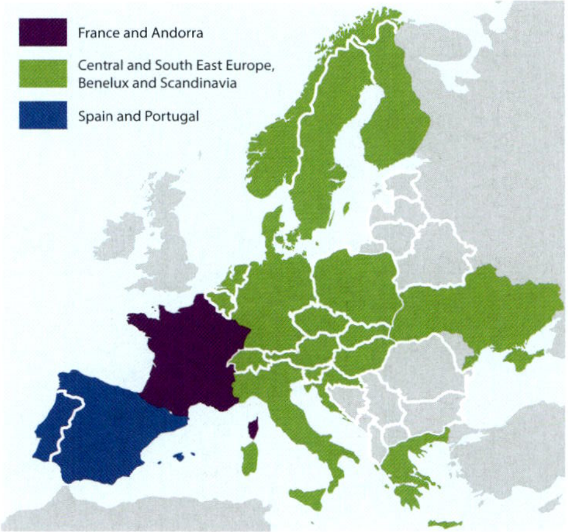

Kocevje to Rogaška Slatina = 176km

	Bled	Bohinj Bistrica	Brezice	Celje	Dravograd	Ilirska Bistrica	Jesenice	Kobarid	Kocevje	Kranj	Ljubljana	Maribor	Murska Sobota	Nova Gorica	Novo Mesto	Postojna	Ptuj	Rogaška Slatina	Tolmin
Bohinj Bistrica	20																		
Brezice	165	180																	
Celje	129	143	76																
Dravograd	176	191	135	61															
Ilirska Bistrica	137	154	181	159	203														
Jesenice	11	37	168	134	181	139													
Kobarid	106	126	219	197	244	140	95												
Kocevje	124	139	91	144	191	102	127	156											
Kranj	31	46	135	99	149	110	34	109	95										
Ljubljana	57	74	104	76	123	79	62	119	61	30									
Maribor	180	198	126	51	59	210	185	248	195	151	127								
Murska Sobota	237	252	186	108	119	265	240	305	252	210	184	56							
Nova Gorica	165	91	209	188	232	91	171	53	129	138	109	236	295						
Novo Mesto	131	148	42	95	154	144	134	185	48	104	74	147	201	175					
Postojna	107	124	149	127	174	33	110	104	74	80	51	181	238	61	114				
Ptuj	184	199	130	55	109	212	189	252	200	154	132	27	66	242	149	182			
Rogaška Slatina	163	180	58	35	97	191	168	232	176	136	110	48	106	219	98	163	53		
Tolmin	101	58	204	181	232	128	106	14	142	96	104	232	293	41	169	89	239	218	
Velenje	138	157	98	24	39	166	143	206	151	111	83	73	128	195	120	140	77	59	191

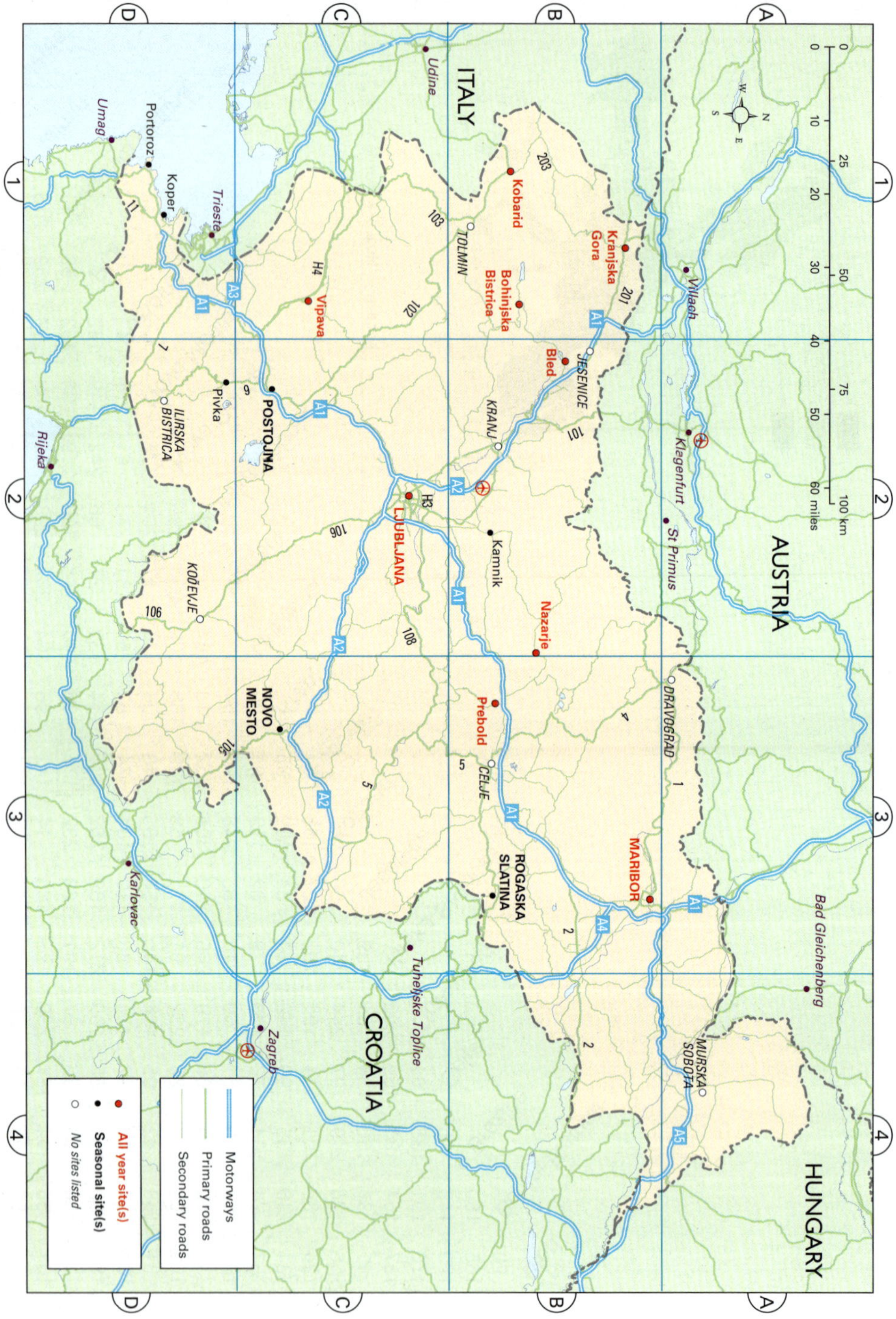
AUSTRIA
ITALY
CROATIA
HUNGARY
Villach
Klagenfurt
St Primus
Bad Gleichenberg
Udine
Trieste
Portoroz
Koper
Umag
Rijeka
Karlovac
Zagreb
Tuheljske Toplice
Kranjska Gora
Kobarid
Bohinjska Bistrica
Bled
JESENICE
TOLMIN
KRANJ
Vipava
POSTOJNA
Pivka
ILIRSKA BISTRICA
LJUBLJANA
Kamnik
Nazarje
KOČEVJE
NOVO MESTO
Prebold
CELJE
DRAVOGRAD
MARIBOR
ROGASKA SLATINA
MURSKA SOBOTA
Motorways
Primary roads
Secondary roads
All year site(s)
Seasonal site(s)
No sites listed
0 10 20 30 40 50 60 miles
0 25 50 75 100 km

Spain

Plaza Espana, Seville

Shutterstock/May_Lana

Highlights

Boasting lively cities, beautiful beaches and an energetic and diverse culture, it's easy to see why Spain is one of the most popular destinations in the world.

From Gaudi's Sagrada Familia in the bustling centre of Barcelona to the ancient monuments of Andalusia, Spain has a rich history to explore. After a long day of sightseeing, what better way to relax that on one of Spain's many beaches, with a glass of sangria in hand.

Music and dance are deeply ingrained in Spanish culture, and the flamenco is one of the best loved examples of the Spanish arts. Known for its distinctive flair and passion, this dance is now popular worldwide, but there's nowhere better to soak in a performance than in its homeland.

Tapas and sangria are some of Spain's most popular fare, but there's plenty of choice for those looking to try something different. Orxata is a refreshing drink made of tigernuts, water and sugar, and is served ice cold.

Major towns and cities

- Madrid – this vibrant capital is filled with culture.
- Barcelona – a city on the coast, filled with breathtaking architecture.
- Seville – known for stunning architecture, tapas and Flamenco dancing.
- Valencia – set on the Mediterranean sea, this city has numerous attractions on offer.
- Malaga - this coastal gem has plenty of history and culture to absorb.

Attractions

- Prado Museum, Madrid - housing over 8000 paintings and sculptures including works by Francisco de Goya.
- Sagrada Familia – Antoni Gaudí's basilica is one of Barcelona's most famous sights.
- Alhambra – a stunning 13th Century palace fortress near Granada.

Find out more

spain.info

Country Information

Capital: Madrid

Bordered by: Andorra, France, Portugal

Terrain: High, rugged central plateau, mountains to north and south

Climate: Temperate climate; hot summers, cold winters in the interior; more moderate summers and cool winters along the northern and eastern coasts; very hot summers and mild/warm winters along the southern coast

Coastline: 4,964km

Highest Point (mainland Spain): Mulhacén (Granada) 3,478m

Languages: Castilian Spanish, Catalan, Galician, Basque

Local Time: GMT or BST + 1, i.e. 1 hour ahead of the UK all year

Currency: Euros divided into 100 cents; £1 = €1.20, €1 = £0.84 (Nov 2024)

Emergency numbers: Police 092; Fire brigade 080; Ambulance (SAMUR) 061. Operators speak English. Civil Guard 062. All services can be reached on 112.

Public Holidays 2025: Jan 1, 6; Apr 17, 18; May 1; Aug 15; Oct 12; Nov 1; Dec 6 (Constitution Day), 8, 25, 26.

Several other dates are celebrated for fiestas according to region. School summer holidays stretch from mid-June to mid-September.

Entry Formalities

British and Irish passport holders may stay for up to 90 days in any 180 day period without a visa. You may be asked to show a return or onward ticket at the border to confirm your length of stay, or to prove that you have enough money for your stay.

Your passport will need to have a minimum of 6 months' validity remaining, and be less than 10 years old (even if it has over 6 months left).

Visitors arriving at a campsite or hotel must complete a registration form.

Medical Services

Basic emergency health care is available free from practitioners in the Spanish National Health Service on production of a European Health Insurance Card (EHIC) or a Global Health Insurance Card (GHIC). Some health centres offer both private and state provided health care and you should ensure that staff are aware which service you require. In some parts of the country you may have to travel some distance to attend a surgery or health clinic operating within the state health service. It's probably quicker and more convenient to use a private clinic, but the Spanish health service will not refund any private health care charges.

In an emergency go to the casualty department (urgencias) of any major public hospital. Urgent treatment is free in a public ward on production of an EHIC or GHIC; for other treatment you will have to pay a proportion of the cost.

Medicines prescribed by health service practitioners can be obtained from a pharmacy (farmacia) and there will be a charge unless you're an EU pensioner. In all major towns there's a 24 hour pharmacy.

Dental treatment is not generally provided under the state system and you will have to pay for treatment.

The Department of Health has two offices in Spain to deal with health care enquiries from British nationals visiting or residing in Spain. These are at the British Consultate offices in Alicante and Madrid, Tel: +34 96 521 6022 or +34 91 714 6300.

Opening Hours

Banks : Mon-Fri 8.30am/9am-2pm/2.30pm, Sat 9am-1pm (many banks are close Sat during summer).

Museums: Tue-Sat 9am/10am-1pm/2pm & 3pm/4pm-6pm/8pm. Sun 9am/10am-2pm; most close Mon.

Post Offices: Mon-Fri 8.30am-2.30pm & 5pm-8pm/8.30pm, Sat 9am/9.30am-1pm/1.30pm.

Shops: Mon-Sat 9am/10am-1.30pm/2pm & 4pm/4.30pm-8pm/8.30pm; department stores and shopping centres don't close for lunch.

Regulations for pets

Dogs must be kept on a lead in public places When travelling by motor vehicle, the use of an approriate restraint, like a seat belt harness, a cage or pet carrier is recommended.

Safety and Security

Street crime exists in many Spanish towns and holiday resorts. Keep all valuable personal items such as cameras or jewellery out of sight. The authorities have stepped up the police presence in tourist areas but nevertheless, you should remain alert at all times (including at airports, train and bus stations, and even in supermarkets and their car parks).

In Madrid particular care should be taken in the Puerto de Sol and surrounding streets, including the Plaza Mayor, Retiro Park and Lavapies, and on the metro. In Barcelona this advice also applies to the Ramblas, Monjuic, Plaza Catalunya, Port Vell and Olympic Port areas. Be wary of approaches by strangers either asking directions or offering help, especially around cash machines or at tills, as they may be trying to distract attention.

A few incidents have been reported of visitors being approached by a bogus police officer asking to inspect wallets for fake euro notes, or to check their identity by keying their credit card PIN into an official-looking piece of equipment carried by the officer. If in doubt ask to see a police officer's official identification, refuse to comply with the request and offer instead to go to the nearest police station.

The dedicated English-speaking police helpline +34 90 210 2112 is no longer operational. If you need to report a crime while on holiday you must file a report at the nearest police station.

Motorists travelling on motorways – particularly those north and south of Barcelona, in the Alicante region, on the M30, M40 and M50 Madrid ring roads and on the A4 and A5 – should be wary of approaches by bogus policemen in plain clothes travelling in unmarked cars. In all traffic related matters police officers will be in uniform. Unmarked vehicles will have a flashing electronic sign in the rear window reading 'Policía' or 'Guardia Civil' and will normally have blue flashing lights incorporated into their headlights, which are activated when the police stop you.

In non-traffic related matters police officers may be in plain clothes but you have the right to ask to see identification. Genuine officers may ask you to show them your documents but wouldn't request that you hand over your bag or wallet. If in any doubt, converse through the car window and telephone the police on 112 or the Guardia Civil on 062 and ask them for confirmation that the registration number of the vehicle corresponds to an official police vehicle.

On the A7 motorway between the La Junquera and Tarragona toll stations be alert for 'highway pirates' who flag down foreign registered and hire cars (the latter have a distinctive number plate), especially those towing caravans. Motorists are sometimes targeted in service areas, followed and subsequently tricked into stopping on the hard shoulder of the motorway. The usual ploy is for the driver or passenger in a passing vehicle, which may be 'official-looking', to suggest by gesture that there's something seriously wrong with a rear wheel or exhaust pipe. If flagged down by other motorists or a motorcyclist in this way, be extremely wary. Within the Barcelona urban area thieves may also employ the 'punctured tyre' tactic at traffic lights.

In instances such as this, the Spanish Tourist Office advises you not to pull over but to wait until you reach a service area or toll station. If you do get out of your car when flagged down take care it's locked while you check outside, even if someone is left inside. Car keys should never be left in the ignition.

Spain shares with the rest of Europe an underlying threat from terrorism. Please check gov.uk/foreign-travel-advice/spain before you travel.

Coast guards operate a beach flag system to indicate the general safety of beaches for swimming: red – danger / don't enter the water; yellow – take precautions; green – all clear. Coast guards operate on most of the popular beaches, so if in doubt, always ask. During the summer months stinging jellyfish frequent Mediterranean coastal waters.

There's a risk of forest fires during the hottest months and you should avoid camping in areas with limited escape routes. Take care to avoid actions that could cause a fire, e.g. disposal of cigarette ends.

Respect Spanish laws and customs. Parents should be aware that Spanish law defines anyone under the age of 18 as a minor, subject to parental control or adult supervision. Any unaccompanied minor coming to the attention of the local authorities for whatever reason is deemed to be vulnerable under the law and faces being taken into a minors centre for protection until a parent or suitable guardian can be found.

British Embassy & Consulate-General

Torre Emperador Castellana
Paseo De La Castellana 259d
28046 Madrid
Tel: +34 91 714 6300
gov.uk/world/spain

British Consulate-General

Avda Diagonal 477-13
08036 Barcelona
Tel: +34 93 366 6200

There are also British Consulates in Alicante and Málaga.

Irish Embassy

Paseo De La Castellana 46-4
28046 Madrid
Tel: +34 91 436 4093
ireland.ie/madrid

There are also Irish Honorary Consulates in Alicante, Barcelona, Bilbao, Málaga and Seville.

Customs Regulations

Under Spanish law the number of cigarettes which may be exported is set at 800. Anything above this amount is regarded as a trade transaction which must be accompanied by the required documentation. Travellers caught with more than 800 cigarettes face seizure of the cigarettes and a large fine.

Documents

Driving Licence

The British EU format pink driving licence is recognised in Spain. Holders of the old style all green driving licence are advised to replace it with a photocard version. Alternatively, the old style licence may be accompanied by an International Driving Permit available from the AA, the RAC or selected post offices.

Passport

Visitors must be able to show some form of identity document if requested to do so by the police and you should carry your passport or photocard licence at all times.

Vehicle(s)

When driving in Spain it's compulsory at all times to carry your driving licence, vehicle registration certificate (V5C), insurance certificate and MOT certificate (if applicable). Vehicles imported by a person other than the owner must have a letter of authority from the owner.

Money

All bank branches offer foreign currency exchange, as do many hotels and travel agents.

The major credit cards are widely accepted as a means of payment in shops, restaurants and petrol stations. Smaller retail outlets in non commercial areas may not accept payments by credit card – check before buying. When shopping carry your passport or photocard driving licence if paying with a credit card as you will almost certainly be asked for photographic proof of identity.

Keep a supply of loose change as you could be asked for it frequently in shops and at kiosks.

Driving

Drivers should take particular care as driving standards can be erratic, e.g. excessive speed and dangerous overtaking, and the accident rate is higher than in the UK. Pedestrians should take particular care when crossing roads (even at zebra crossings) or walking along unlit roads at night.

Accidents

The Central Traffic Department runs an assistance service for victims of traffic accidents linked to an emergency telephone network along motorways and some roads. Motorists in need of help should ask for 'auxilio en carretera' (road assistance). The special ambulances used are connected by radio to hospitals participating in the scheme.

It's not necessary to call the emergency services in case of light injuries.

A European Accident Statement should be completed and signed by both parties and, if conditions allow, photos of the vehicles and the location should be taken. If one of the drivers involved does not want to give his/her details, the other should call the police or Guardia Civil.

Alcohol

The maximum permitted level of alcohol in the blood is 0.05%. It reduces to 0.03% for drivers with less than two years experience, drivers of vehicles with more than 8 passenger seats and for drivers of vehicles over 3,500kg. After a traffic accident all road users involved have to undergo a breath test. Penalties for refusing a test or exceeding the legal limit are severe and may include immobilisation of vehicles, a large fine and suspension of your driving licence. This limit applies to cyclists as well as drivers of private vehicles.

Breakdown Service

The motoring organisation, Real Automóvil Club de España (RACE), operates a breakdown service and assistance may be obtained 24 hours a day by telephoning +34 91 594 9347.

RACE's breakdown vehicles are blue and yellow and display the words 'RACE Asistencia' on the sides. This service provides on the spot minor repairs and towing to the nearest garage. Charges vary according to type of vehicle and time of day, but payment for road assistance must be made in cash.

Child Restraint System

Children under the age of 12 years old and under the height of 1.35m must use a suitable child restraint system adapted for their size and weight (this does not apply in taxis in urban areas). Children measuring more than 1.35m in height may use an adult seatbelt.

Fuel

Credit cards are accepted at most petrol stations, but you should be prepared to pay cash if necessary in remote areas.

LPG (Autogas) can be purchased from over 100 outlets. Details of sales outlets throughout mainland Spain can be found on mylpg.eu.

Lights

The use of dipped headlights is compulsory for all vehicles on all roads at night and in tunnels. Bulbs are more likely to fail with constant use, always carry spares.

Dipped headlights must be used at all times on 'special' roads, e.g. temporary routes created at the time of road works such as the hard shoulder, or in a contra-flow lane.

Headlight flashing is only allowed to warn other road users about an accident or a road hazard, or to let the vehicle in front know that you intend to overtake.

Low Emission Zones

There are Low Emission Zones in many towns and cities in Spain.
Please see urbanaccessregulations.eu for the most up-to-date information.

Motorways

There are approximately 17,000 km of motorways and dual carriageways in Spain. The main sections are along the Mediterranean coast, across the north of the country linking the Basque region to the Mediterranean and around Madrid.

Roads marked AP (autopista) are generally toll roads and roads marked A (autovía) or N (nacional) are dual carriageways with motorway characteristics – but not necessarily with a central reservation – and are toll-free. Tolls are charged on most autopistas but many sections are toll-free, as are autovias. Exits on autopistas are numbered consecutively from Madrid. Exits on autovias are numbered according to the kilometre point from Madrid.

Many different companies operate within the motorway network, each setting their own tolls which may vary according to the time of day and classification of vehicles.

Avoid signposted 'Via-T' lanes showing a circular sign with a white capital T on a blue background where toll collection is by electronic device only. Square 'Via-T' signs are displayed above mixed lanes where other forms of payment are also accepted.

Rest areas with parking facilities, petrol stations and restaurants or cafés are strategically placed and are well signposted.

Emergency telephones are located at 2 km intervals.

Motorway signs near Barcelona are confusing. To avoid the city traffic when heading south, follow signs for Barcelona, but once signs for Tarragona appear follow these and ignore Barcelona signs.

Mountain Passes and Tunnels

Some passes are occasionally blocked in winter following heavy falls of snow. Check locally for information on road conditions.

Parking

Parking regulations vary depending on the area of a city or town, the time of day, the day of the week, and whether the date is odd or even. In many towns parking is permitted on one side of the street for the first half of the month and on the other side for the second half of the month. Signs marked '1-15' or '16-31' indicate these restrictions.

Yellow road markings indicate parking restrictions. Parking should be in the same direction as the traffic flow in one way streets or on the right hand side on two way streets. Illegally parked vehicles may be towed or clamped but, despite this, you will frequently encounter double and triple parking.

In large cities parking meters have been largely replaced by ticket machines and these are often located in areas known as 'zona azul', i.e. blue zones. The maximum period of parking is usually two hours between 8am and 9pm. In the centre of some towns there's a 'zona O.R.A.' where parking is permitted for up to 90 minutes against tickets bought in tobacconists and other retail outlets.

In many small towns and villages it's advisable to park on the edge of town and walk to the centre, as many towns can be difficult to navigate due to narrow, congested streets.

Madrid

In Madrid, there's a regulated parking zone where parking spaces are shown by blue or green lines (called SER). Parking is limited to one or two hours in these areas for visitors and can be paid by means of ticket machines of by mobile phone.

Pedestrians

Jaywalking isn't permitted. Pedestrians may not cross a road unless a traffic light is at red against the traffic, or a policeman gives permission. Offenders may be fined.

Priority and Overtaking

As a general rule traffic coming from the right has priority at intersections. When entering a main road from a secondary road drivers must give way to traffic from both directions. Traffic already on a roundabout (i.e. from the left) has priority over traffic joining it. Trams and emergency vehicles have priority at all times over other road users and you must not pass trams that are stationary while letting passengers on or off.

Motorists must give way to cyclists on a cycle lane, cycle crossing or other specially designated cycle track. They must also give way to cyclists when turning left or right.

You must use your indicators when overtaking. If a vehicle comes up behind you signalling that it wants to overtake and if the road ahead is clear, you must use your right indicator to acknowledge the situation.

Roads

In recent years some major national roads have been upgraded to Autovías and have two identifying codes or have changed codes, e.g. the N-I from Madrid to Irún near the French border is known as the A1 or Autovía del Norte. Autovías are often as fast as autopistas and can be more scenic.

Roads managed by regional or local authorities are prefixed with the various identification letters such as C, CV, GR, L or T.

All national roads and roads of interest to tourists are generally in good condition, are well signposted, and driving is normally straightforward. Hills often tend to be longer and steeper than in parts of the UK and some of the coastal roads are very winding, so traffic flows at the speed of the slowest lorry.

As far as accidents are concerned the N340 coast road, especially between Málaga and Fuengirola, is notorious, as are the Madrid ring roads, and special vigilance is necessary.

Road humps may be high, putting low stabilisers at risk.

Andorra

The best free road to Barcelona from Andorra is the C14/C1412/N141b via Ponts and Calaf. It has a good surface and avoids any high passes.

The N260 along the south side of Andorra via Puigcerda and La Seo de Urgel also has a good surface.

Road Signs and Markings

Road signs conform to international standards. Lines and markings are white. Place names may appear both in standard (Castilian) Spanish and in a local form, e.g. Gerona/Girona, San Sebastián/Donostia, Jávea/Xàbio, and road atlases and maps usually show both.

You may encounter the following signs:

Spanish	English Translation
Carretera de peaje	Toll road
Ceda el paso	Give way
Cuidado	Caution
Curva peligrosa	Dangerous bend
Despacio	Slow
Desviación	Detour
Dirección única	One-way street
Embotellamiento	Traffic jam
Estacionamiento prohibido	No parking
Estrechamiento	Narrow lane
Gravillas	Loose chippings/gravel
Inicio	Start
Obras	Roadworks
Paso prohibido	No entry
Peligro	Danger
Prioridad	Right of way
Salida	Exit
Todas direcciones	All directions

Many non motorway roads have a continuous white line on the near (verge) side of the carriageway. Any narrow lane between this line and the side of the carriageway is intended primarily for pedestrians and cyclists and not for use as a hard shoulder.

A continuous line also indicates 'no stopping' even if it's possible to park entirely off the road and it should be treated as a double white line and not crossed except in a serious emergency. If your vehicle breaks down on a road where there's a continuous white line along the verge, it should not be left unattended as this is illegal and an on the spot fine may be levied.

Many road junctions have a continuous white centre line along the main road. This line must not be crossed to execute a left turn, despite the lack of any other 'no left turn' signs. If necessary, drive on to a 'cambio de sentido' (change of direction) sign to turn.

Traffic police are keen to enforce both the above regulations.

Watch out for traffic lights which may be mounted high above the road and hard to spot. The international three colour traffic light system is used in Spain. Green, amber and red arrows are used on traffic lights at some intersections.

Speed Limits

	Open Road (km/h)	Motorway (km/h)
Car Solo	90-100	120
Car towing caravan/trailer	70-80	80
Motorhome under 3500kg	80-90	100
Motorhome 3500-7500kg	80	90

In built-up areas speed is limited to 50km/h (31mph) except where signs indicate a lower limit. Reduce your speed to 20km/h (13mph) in residential areas. On motorways and dual carriageways in built-up areas, speed is limited to 80km/h (50mph) except where indicated by signs.

Outside built-up areas motorhomes under 3500kg are limited to 100km/h (62mph). Those over 3500kg are limited to 90km/h (56 mph) on motorways and dual carriageways. On other main roads motorhomes under 3500kg are limited to 80-90km/h (50-56mph) hose over 3500kg are limited to 80km/h (50mph).

It's illegal to use or transport radar detectors.

Foreign Registered Vehicles

When a radar camera detects a foreign registered vehicle exceeding the speed limit, a picture of the vehicle and its number plate will be sent not only to the relevant traffic department, but also to the nearest Guardia Civil mobile patrol. The patrol will then stop the speeding vehicle and impose an on the spot fine which non-residents must pay immediately, otherwise the vehicle will be confiscated until the fine is paid.

This is to prevent offenders flouting the law and avoiding paying their fines, as pursuing them is proving costly and complicated for the Spanish authorities.

Towing

Motorhomes are prohibited from towing a car unless the car is on a special towing trailer with all four wheels of the car off the ground.

Any towing combination in excess of 10 metres in length must keep at least 50 metres from the vehicle in front except in built-up areas, on roads where overtaking is prohibited, or where there are several lanes in the same direction.

Traffic Jams

Roads around the large cities such as Madrid, Barcelona, Zaragoza, Valencia and Seville are extremely busy on Friday afternoons when residents leave for the mountains or coast, and again on Sunday evenings when they return. The coastal roads along the Costa Brava and the Costa Dorada may also be congested. The coast road south of Torrevieja is frequently heavily congested as a result of extensive holiday home construction.

Summer holidays extend from mid June to mid-September and the busiest periods are the last weekend in July, the first weekend in August and the period around the Assumption holiday in mid-August.

Traffic jams occur on the busy AP7 from the French border to Barcelona during the peak summer holiday period. An alternative route now exists from Malgrat de Mar along the coast to Barcelona using the C32 where tolls are lower than on the AP7.

The Autovía de la Cataluña Central (C25) provides an east-west link between Gerona and Lleida via Vic, Manresa and Tàrrega.

There's fast access from Madrid to La Coruña in the far north-west via the A6/AP6.

Information on road conditions and traffic delays, can be found on: infocar.dgt.es/etraffic.

Violation of Traffic Regulations

The police are empowered to impose on the spot fines. Visiting motorists must pay immediately otherwise a vehicle will be confiscated until the fine is paid. An official receipt should be obtained.

An appeal may be made within 15 days and there are instructions on the back of the receipt in English. RACE can provide legal advice, visit the website (race.es) or tel: 900 100 992.

Essential Equipment

Reflective Jacket/Waistcoat

If you're required to leave your vehicle when stopped on a carriageway or on the side of the road outside of a built-up area, you must wear an EU approved reflective jacket or you could be fined.

This also applies to passengers who may leave the vehicle.

Reflectors/Marker Boards for Caravans

Any vehicle or vehicle combination, i.e. car plus caravan over 12 metres in length, must display reflector marker boards at the rear of the towed vehicle. These aluminium boards must have a yellow centre with a red outline, be reflective and comply with ECE70 standards.

They must be positioned between 50cm and 150cm off the ground and must be 500mm x 250mm or 565mm x 200mm in size. Alternatively a single horizontal reflector may be used measuring 1300mm x 250mm or 1130mm x 200mm.

To buy these aluminium marker boards visit hgvdirect.co.uk, or tel: 01335 470 009. Contact your local dealer or caravan manufacturer for advice on fitting them to your caravan.

Warning Triangles

Use of the V16 emergency beacon is gradually being phased in as a replacement to the warning triangle.

From 1 July 2023 to 1 January 2026 drivers are free to use V16 luminous device or the emergency triangles on motorways, although the traditional warning triangles will still be mandatory on conventional roads for the time being.

Motor vehicles must carry two warning triangles that should be placed at least 50 metres behind and in front of broken down vehicles, The use of warning triangles will be prohibited on 1 January 2026.

Touring

A fixed price menu or 'menú del dia' offers good value. Service is generally included in restaurant bills but a tip of approximately €1 per person up to 10% of the bill is appropriate if you have received good service. Smoking isn't allowed in indoor public places, including bars, restaurants and cafés.

Spain is one of the world's top wine producers, enjoying a great variety of high quality wines of which cava, rioja and sherry are probably the best known. Local beer is generally drunk as an aperitif to accompany tapas.

Spaniards tend to get up later and stay out later at night than their European neighbours. Out of the main tourist season and in non-tourist areas it may be difficult to find a restaurant open in the evening before 9pm.

Taking a siesta is still common practice, although it's now usual for businesses to stay open during the traditional siesta hours.

Spain's many different cultural and regional influences are responsible for the variety and originality of fiestas held each year. Over 200 have been classified as 'of interest to tourists' while others have gained international fame, such as La Tomatina mass tomato throwing battle held each year in August in Buñol near Valencia. Find a full list of fiestas via the website (spain.info) or from tourist offices. Each town will also celebrate its local Saint's Day which is always a very happy and colourful occasion.

The Madrid Card, valid for one, two, three or five days, gives free use of public transport, free entry to various attractions and museums, as well as free tours and discounts at restaurants and shows. You can buy the card from (introducingmadrid.com) or by visiting the City Tourist Office in Plaza Mayor, or on Madrid Visión tour buses.

Similar generous discounts can be obtained with the Barcelona Card, valid from two to five days, which can be purchased from tourist offices or online at (barcelonacard.org). Other tourist cards are available in Burgos, Córdoba, Seville and Zaragoza.

The region of Valencia and the Balearic Islands are prone to severe storms and torrential rainfall between September and November and are best avoided at that time. Monitor national and regional weather on the WMO website: wmo.int.

Gibraltar

For information on Gibraltar contact:

Gibraltar Government Tourist Office
150 Strand, London WC2R 1JA
020 7836 0777
visitgibraltar.gi

There are no campsites on the Rock, the nearest being at San Roque and La Línea de la Concepción in Spain. The only direct access to Gibraltar from Spain is via the border at La Línea which is open 24 hours a day. You may cross on foot and it's also possible to take cars or motorhomes to Gibraltar.

A valid British passport is required for all British nationals visiting Gibraltar. Nationals of other countries should check entry requirements with the Gibraltar Government Tourist Office.

There's currently no charge for visitors to enter Gibraltar but Spanish border checks can cause delays and you should be prepared for long queues. As roads in the town are extremely narrow and bridges low, it's advisable to park on the outskirts. Visitors advise against leaving vehicles on the Spanish side of the border owing to the high risk of break-ins.

An attraction to taking the car into Gibraltar includes English style supermarkets and a wide variety of competitively priced goods free of VAT. The currency is sterling and British notes and coins circulate alongside Gibraltar pounds and pence, but note that Gibraltar notes and coins are not accepted in the UK. Scottish and Northern Irish notes are not generally accepted in Gibraltar.

Euros are accepted but the exchange rate may not be favourable.

Disabled visitors to Gibraltar may obtain a temporary parking permit from the police station on production of evidence confirming their disability. This permit allows parking for up to two hours (between 8am and 10pm) in parking places reserved for disabled people.

Violence or street crime is rare but there have been reports of people walking from La Línea to Gibraltar at night being attacked and robbed.

If you need emergency medical attention while on a visit to Gibraltar, treatment at primary healthcare centres is free to UK passport holders under the local medical scheme. Non UK nationals need a European Health Insurance Card (EHIC). You're not eligible for free treatment if you go to Gibraltar specifically to be treated for a condition which arose elsewhere, e.g in Spain.

Camping and Caravanning

There are more than 1,200 campsites in Spain with something to suit all tastes – from some of the best and biggest holiday parks in Europe, to a wealth of attractive small sites offering a personal, friendly welcome. Most campsites are located near the Mediterranean, especially on the Costa Brava and Costa del Sol, as well as in the Pyrenees and other areas of tourist interest. Campsites are indicated by blue road signs. In general pitch sizes are small at about 80 square metres.

Many popular coastal sites favoured for long winter stays may contain tightly packed pitches with long-term residents putting up large awnings, umbrellas and other structures. Many sites allow pitches to be reserved from year to year, which can result in a tight knit community of visitors who return every year.

If you're planning to stay on sites in the popular coastal areas between late spring and October, or in January and February, it's advisable to arrive early in the afternoon or to book in advance.

if you're planning a visit to a site out of season, always check it's opening dates first. It's common for many 'all year' sites to open only at weekends during the winter.

Facilities may be very limited.

Motorhomes

A number of local authorities now provide dedicated or short stay areas for motorhomes called 'Áreas de Servicio'.

For details see the website (lapaca.org) for a list of regions and towns in Spain and Andorra which have at least one of these areas.

It's rare that yours will be the only motorhome staying on such areas, but take sensible precautions and avoid any that are isolated.

Some motorhome service points are situated in motorway service areas. Use these only as a last resort and don't be tempted to park overnight. The risk of a break-in is high.

Recent visitors to tourist areas on Spain's Mediterranean coast report that the parking of motorhomes on public roads and, in some instances, in public parking areas, may be prohibited in an effort to discourage wild camping. Specific areas where visitors have encountered this problem include Alicante, Dénia, Palamós and the Murcian coast. Police are frequently in evidence moving parked motorhomes on and it's understood that a number of owners of motorhomes have been fined for parking on sections of the beach belonging to the local authority.

Cycling

There are more than 3,300 km of dedicated cycle paths in Spain, many of which follow disused railway tracks. Known as 'Vias Verdes' (Green Ways), they can be found mainly in northern Spain, in Andalucia, around Madrid and inland from the Costa Blanca. For more information see the website (viasverdes.com) or contact the Spanish Tourist Office.

There are cycle lanes in major cities and towns such as Barcelona, Bilbao, Córdoba, Madrid, Seville and Valencia. Madrid alone has over 100 km of cycle lanes.

It's compulsory for all cyclists, regardless of age, to wear a safety helmet on all roads outside built-up areas. At night, in tunnels or in bad weather, bicycles must have front and rear lights and reflectors. Cyclists must also wear a reflective waistcoat or jacket while riding at night on roads outside built-up areas (to be visible from a distance of 150 metres) or when visibility is bad.

Cyclists have right of way when motor vehicles wish to cross their path to turn left or right, but great care should always be taken. Don't proceed unless you're sure that a motorist is giving way.

Spanish regulations stipulate that motor cycles or bicycles may be carried on the rear of a vehicle providing the rack to which the motorcycle or bicycle is fastened has been designed for the purpose.

Lights, indicators, number plate and any signals made by the driver must not be obscured and the rack should not compromise the carrying vehicle's stability.

An overhanging load, such as bicycles, should not extend beyond the width of the vehicle but may exceed the length of the vehicle by up to 10% (up to 15% in the case of indivisible items). The load must be indicated by a 50cm x 50cm square panel with reflective red and white diagonal stripes. These panels may be purchased in the UK from motorhome or caravan dealers/accessory shops. There's currently no requirement for bicycle racks to be certified or pass a technical inspection.

If you're planning to travel from Spain to Portugal please note that slightly different official regulations apply. These are set out in the Portugal Country Introduction.

Electricity and Gas

The current on campsites should be a minimum of 4 amps but is usually more. Plugs have two round pins. Some campsites don't yet have CEE connections.

Campingaz is widely available in 901 and 907 cylinders. The Cepsa Company sells butane gas cylinders and regulators, which are available in large stores and petrol stations, and the Repsol Company sells butane cylinders at their petrol stations throughout the country.

French and Spanish butane and propane gas cylinders are understood to be widely available in Andorra.

Public Transport

Madrid boasts an extensive and efficient public transport network including a metro system, suburban railways and bus routes. You can purchase a pack of ten tickets which offer better value than single tickets.

Tourist travel passes for use on all public transport are available from metro stations, tourist offices and travel agencies and are valid for one to seven days – you will need to present your passport when buying them. Single tickets must be validated before travel. For more information visit crtm.es.

Metro systems also operate in Barcelona, Bilbao, Seville and Valencia and a few cities operate tram services including La Coruña, Valencia, Barcelona and Bilbao.
The Valencia service links Alicante, Benidorm and Dénia.

Various operators run year round ferry services from Spain to North Africa, the Balearic Islands and the Canary Islands. All enquiries should be made through their UK agent:

Southern Ferries
22 Sussex Street
London
SW1V 4RW
southernferries.co.uk

Sites in Spain

AGUILAR DE CAMPOO *1B4* (3km W Rural) *42.78694, -4.30222* **Monte Royal Camping,** Carretera Virgen del Llano 34800 Aguilar de Campóo (Palencia) **979-18 10 07; info@campingmonteroyal.com; www.campingmonteroyal.com**

12 nr

App site fr S on N611 fr Palencia. At Aguilar de Campóo turn W at S end of rv bdge at S end of town. Site on L in 3km; sp at edge of reservoir. Fr N take 3rd exit fr rndabt on N611. Do not tow thro town. 2*, Med, mkd, shd, pt sl, EHU (6A) inc; sw; twin axles; 50% statics; ccard acc; horseriding; watersports; fishing; lake 400yds; CKE. *"Useful, peaceful NH 2 hrs fr Santander; ltd/basic facs LS & poss stretched high ssn; barking dogs poss problem; friendly staff; gd walking, cycling & birdwatching in National Park; unrel opening dates LS; facs and site run down (2019); poor."* **€22.00** **2024**

"There aren't many sites open at this time of year"

If you're travelling outside peak season remember to call ahead to check site opening dates – even if the entry says 'open all year'.

AGUILAS *4G1* (2km SW Coastal) *37.3925, -1.61111* **Camping Bellavista,** Ctra de Vera, Km 3, 30880 Águilas (Murcia) **968-44 91 51; info@campingbellavista.com; www.campingbellavista.com**

12 €2.50 nr sand 300m

Site on N332 Águilas to Vera rd on R at top of sh, steep hill, 100m after R turn to El Cocon. Well mkd by flags. Fr S by N332 on L 400m after fuel stn, after v sharp corner. Sm, hdg, hdstg, pt shd, pt sl, EHU (10A) €5.20 or metered; gas; bbq; red long stay; 10% statics; Eng spkn; adv bkg acc; ccard acc; bike hire; CKE. *"Gd autumn/winter stay; clean, tidy site with excel facs; ltd pitches for lge o'fits; helpful owner; fine views; rd noise at 1 end; excel town & vg beaches; v secure site."* **€34.20** **2024**

AGUILAS *4G1* (11km NW Rural) *37.45387, -1.64488* **Camping La Quinta Bella,** Finca El Charcon 31, 30889 Aguilas **968 43 85 35; campingquintabella@gmail.com; www.quintabella.com**

12 (htd) nr

Fr AP7 exit at junc 878 onto RM11. Foll sp to Los Arejos. In 2km turn R foll sp to site. Med, mkd, hdstg, EHU; gas; bbq; twin axles; 30% statics; Eng spkn; adv bkg acc; ccard acc; CKE. *"V lge pitches; ideal for carnival & Easter parades; v friendly English owners; boules; m'homes should have other transport; excel."* **€20.00** **2022**

AINSA *3B2* (2.5km N Rural) *42.43593, 0.13606* **Camping Peña Montañesa,** Ctra Ainsa-Bielsa, Km 2.3, 22360 Labuerda (Huesca) **974-50 00 32; info@penamontanesa.com; www.penamontanesa.com**

12 €4.50 (htd) (covrd, htd, indoor)

E fr Huesca on N240 for approx 50km, turn N onto N123 just after Barbastro twd Ainsa. In 8km turn onto A138 N for Ainsa & Bielsa. Or fr Bielsa Tunnel to A138 S to Ainsa & Bielsa, site sp. NB: Bielsa Tunnel sometimes clsd bet Oct & Easter due to weather. 4*, Lge, mkd, shd, EHU (6A) inc; gas; bbq (elec, gas); sw nr; TV; 30% statics; phone; adv bkg acc; ccard acc; tennis; games rm; bike hire; sauna; fishing; canoeing; games area; horseriding; CKE. *"Situated by fast-flowing rv; v friendly staff; Eng spkn; gd, clean san facs; pitching poss diff due trees; no o'fits over 10m; nr beautiful medieval town of Ainsa & Ordesa National Park; excel."* **€26.95, E12.** **2022**

AINSA *3B2* (1km E Rural) *42.41944, 0.15111* **Camping Ainsa,** Ctra Ainsa-Campo, 22330 Ainsa (Huesca) **974-50 02 60 or 603-83 60 63; info@campingainsa.com; www.campingainsa.com**

€2.20 nr

Fr Ainsa take N260 E dir Pueyo de Araguás, cross rv bdge, site sp L in 200m. Foll lane to site. Sm, pt shd, terr, EHU €4.75; gas; TV; 50% statics; phone; ccard acc; games rm; CKE. *"Pleasant, welcoming, well-maintained site; fine view of old city & some pitches mountain views; vg san facs; not suitable lge o'fits; gd pool."* **€24.00, Holy Week-30 Oct.** **2024**

AINSA *3B2* (6km NW Rural) *42.43004, 0.07881* **wecamp Pirineos (formerly Camping Boltaña),** Ctra N260, Km 442, Ctra Margudgued, 22340 Boltaña (Huesca) **900-05 60 03; hola@pirineos.wecamp.net; wecamp.net/en**

€6-7 (htd) (htd)

Follow N260 NW for 5km. After petrol stn turn L sp Barcabo. Cross bdge and keep L. Site ent on R in 1km. 1*, Lge, hdstg, mkd, hdg, shd, pt sl, terr, EHU (4-10A) €6.50; gas; twin axles; red long stay; 30% statics; phone; Eng spkn; adv bkg acc; ccard acc; horseriding 500m; fishing 600m; clsd 15 Dec-15 Jan; bike hire; games area; tennis 1km; games rm. *"Conv Ordesa National Park; adventure sports; san facs stretched high ssn; friendly, helpful staff; Ainsa old town worth visit; excel."* **€25.00, Apr-Oct.** **2024**

ALBARRACIN *3D1* (2km E Rural) *40.41228, -1.42788* **Camp Municipal Ciudad de Albarracín,** Camino de Gea s/n, 44100 Albarracín (Teruel) **978-71 01 97 or 657-49 84 33 (mob); campingalbarracin5@hotmail.com; www.campingalbarracin.com**

Fr Teruel take A1512 to Albarracín. Go thro vill, foll camping sps. 2*, Lge, pt shd, pt sl, EHU (16A) €3.85; gas; bbq; 10% statics; phone; adv bkg acc; ccard acc; CKE. *"Gd site; immac san facs; pool adj in ssn; sports cent adj; gd touring base & gd walking fr site; rec; friendly staff; gd rest & shop; views striking, gd Sierras; site extended to nearly dbl; Albaraccin beautiful ancient town."* **€20.00, 4 Mar-27 Nov.** **2024**

ALBERCA, LA *1D3* (6km N Rural) *40.52181, -6.13762* **Camping Sierra de Francia,** Ctra Salamanca-La Alberca, Km 73, 37623 El Caserito (Salamanca) **923-45 40 81; info@campingsierradefrancia.com; www.campingsierradefrancia.com**

Fr Cuidad Rodrigo take C515. Turn R at El Cabaco, site on L in approx 2km. Med, mkd, hdg, shd, EHU (3-6A) €3.75; gas; bbq; 10% statics; ccard acc; horseriding; bike hire. *"Conv 'living history' vill of La Alberca & Monasterio San Juan de la Peña; dogs free; excel views."* **€23.50, 1 Apr-15 Sep.** **2023**

ALCALA DE LOS GAZULES *2H3* (4km E Rural) *36.46403, -5.66482* **Camping Los Gazules,** Ctra de Patrite, Km 4, 11180 Alcalá de los Gazules (Cádiz) **956-42 04 86; info@campinglosgazules.com; www.campinglosgazules.com**

12 €2

Fr N exit A381 at 1st junc to Alcalá, proceed thro town to 1st rndabt & turn L onto A375/A2304 dir Ubriqu, site sp strt ahead in 1km onto CA2115 dir Patrite on v sharp L. Fr S exit A381 at 1st sp for Acalá. At rndabt turn R onto A375/A2304 dir Ubrique. Then as above. Med, mkd, pt shd, pt sl, EHU (10A) €5.25 (poss rev pol); red long stay; TV; 90% statics; phone; adv bkg acc; bike hire; CKE. *"Well-maintained, upgraded site; take care canopy frames; sm pitches & tight turns & kerbs on site; friendly, helpful staff; ltd facs LS; ltd touring pitches; attractive town with v narr rds, leave car in park at bottom & walk; gd walking, birdwatching."* **€35.00** **2024**

ALCANAR *3D2* (4km NE Coastal) *40.53986, 0.52071* **Camping Estanyet,** Paseo del Marjal s/n 43870, Les Cases d'Alcanar (Catalonia) **977-73 72 68; reservas@estanyet.com; www.estanyet.com**

12 €3.50 (htd) shgl adj

Leave Alcanar to N340 at lLes Cases D'Alcanar foll camping signs. Fr AP7 Junc 41 fr N or Junc 43 fr S. Med, hdg, hdstg, pt shd, EHU (10A) €6.50; bbq (charcoal); 10% statics; phone; adv bkg acc; ccard acc; CKE. *"Gd; friendly owners; but ltd facs esp LS."* **€41.00** **2024**

ALCARAZ *4F1* (6km E Rural) *38.67301, -2.40462* **Camping Sierra de Peñascosa,** Ctra Peñascosa-Bogarra, Km 1, 02313 Peñascosa (Albacete) **639 37 17 89; informacion@campingpenascosa.com; www.campingpenascosa.com**

12 €2

Fr N322 turn E bet km posts 279 & 280 sp Peñascosa. In vill foll site sp for 1km beyond vill. Gravel access track & narr ent. 2*, Sm, mkd, hdstg, shd, terr, EHU (6A) €4; gas; ccard acc; bike hire; CKE. *"Not suitable lge o'fits or faint-hearted; pitches sm, uneven & amongst trees - care needed when manoeuvring; open w/end in winter; historical sites nr."* **€21.00** **2022**

ALCOSSEBRE *3D2* (2.5km NE Rural/Coastal) *40.27016, 0.30646* **Camping Ribamar,** Partida Ribamar s/n, 12579 Alcossebre (Castellón) **683 46 93 69; info@campingribamar.com; www.campingribamar.com**

12 €1.90 sand 100m

Exit AP7 at junc 44 into N340 & foll sp to Alcossebre, then dir Sierra de Irta & Las Fuentes. Turn in dir of sea & foll sp to site in 2km - pt rough rd. Med, hdstg, mkd, hdg, pt shd, pt sl, terr, EHU (6/10A) €4.50-6.50 (metered for long stay); gas; red long stay; TV; 25% statics; Eng spkn; adv bkg acc; tennis; games area; games rm; CKE. *"Excel, refurbished tidy site in 'natural park'; warm welcome; realistic pitch sizes; variable prices; excel san facs."* **€35.00, W04.** **2022**

ALCOSSEBRE *3D2* (2.5km S Coastal) *40.22138, 0.26888* **Camping Playa Tropicana,** Camino de l'atall s/n, 12579 Alcossebre (Castellón) **964-41 24 63; info@playatropicana.com; www.campingplayatropicana.com/**

12 (htd) sand adj

Fr AP7 exit junc 44 onto N340 dir Barcelona. After 3km at km 1018 turn on CV142 twd Alcossebre. Just bef ent town turn R sp 'Platjes Capicorb', turn R at beach in 2.5km, site on R. Lge, mkd, pt shd, terr, serviced pitches; EHU (10A) €4.50; gas; red long stay; TV; 10% statics; Eng spkn; adv bkg rec; ccard acc; bike hire; car wash; watersports; games area; kayak hire. *"Excel facs & security; beauty salon; superb well-run site; vg LS; ACSI acc; poss rallies Jan-Apr; management v helpful; poss flooding after heavy rain; pitch access poss diff lge o'fits due narr access rds & high kerbs; cinema rm; take fly swat!"* **€56.00** **2024**

ALGAMITAS *2G3* (3km SW Rural) *37.01934, -5.17440* **Camping El Peñon,** Ctra Algámitas-Pruna, Km 3, 41661 Algámitas (Sevilla) **955-85 53 00; info@algamitasaventura.es; www.algamitasaventura.es**

12 nr

Fr A92 turn S at junc 41 (Arahal) to Morón de la Frontera on A8125. Fr Morón take A406 & A363 dir Pruna. At 1st rndabt at ent Pruna turn L onto SE9225 to Algámitas. Site on L in approx 10km - steep app rd. Sm, hdg, mkd, hdstg, pt shd, EHU (16A) €3.32; gas; bbq; 50% statics; adv bkg acc; ccard acc; site clsd 13-24 Nov; games area; CKE. *"Conv Seville, Ronda & white vills; walking, hiking & horseriding fr site; excel rest; excel, clean san facs; vg site - worth effort to find."* **€15.00** **2022**

ALHAURIN DE LA TORRE *2H4* (4km W Rural) *36.65174, -4.61064* **Camping Malaga Monte Parc,** 29130 Alhaurín de la Torre (Málaga) **951-29 60 28; info@malagamonteparc.com; www.malagamonteparc.com**

12 €1.70 (htd) nr

W fr Málaga on AP7 or N340 take exit for Churriana/Alhaurín de la Torre. Thro Alhuarín de la Torre take A404 W sp Alhaurín el Grande, site on R, sp. Sm, hdstg, hdg, mkd, shd, pt sl, EHU (6A) inc; bbq; TV; 10% statics; bus 200m; Eng spkn; adv bkg acc; ccard acc; golf nr; CKE. *"Vg site; well-appointed, clean san facs; friendly Welsh owner; all facs open all year; sm pitches; gd position to tour Costa Del Sol."* **€25.00** **2024**

ALICANTE *4F2* (12.5km NE Coastal) *38.41333, -0.40556* **Camping Bon Sol,** Camino Real de Villajoyosa 35, Playa Muchavista, 03560 El Campello (Alicante) **626 219 880; info@campingbonsol.es; www.campingbonsol.es**

12 sand

Exit AP7 N of Alicante at junc 67 onto N332 sp Playa San Juan; on reaching coast rd turn N twds El Campello; site sp. 2*, Sm, mkd, hdstg, pt shd, serviced pitches; EHU (10A); red long stay; adv bkg acc; ccard acc; CKE. *"Diff ent for long o'fits; helpful friendly staff; poss cold shwrs; vg."* **€20.00** **2022**

ALLARIZ *1B2* (1.5km W Rural) *42.18443, -7.81811* **Camping Os Invernadeiros,** Ctra Allariz-Celanova, Km 3, 32660 Allariz (Ourense) **988-44 20 06; reatur@allariz.gal; www.allariz.gal/reatur/camping**

12 €2

Well sp off N525 Orense-Xinzo rd & fr A52. Steep descent to site off rd OU300. Height limit 2.85m adj recep - use gate to R. 3*, Sm, pt shd, EHU (6A) €4.50; gas; red long stay; 10% statics; Eng spkn; adv bkg req; ccard acc; horseriding; bike hire; CKE. *"Vg; steep slope into site, level exit is avail; pool 1.5km; site combined with horseriding stable; rv walk adj; facs v clean; hot water; short rv side walk to interesting town; site sp in town as Camping Hippe."* **€28.00** **2024**

ALMERIA *4G1* (23km SE Rural/Coastal) *36.87266, -2.006404* **wecamp Cabo de Gata,** Cala del Cuervo, s/n, 04116 Las Negras, Almería **900-05 60 03; hola@cabodegata.wecamp.net; www.wecamp.net**

12 €6-7 sand

Exit m'way N340/344/E15 junc 460 or 467 sp Cabo de Gata, foll sp to site. Lge, mkd, hdg, shd, EHU (6-16A) €4.60; gas; bbq; red long stay; TV; 10% statics; bus 1km; Eng spkn; adv bkg acc; ccard acc; tennis; bike hire; games area; excursions; games rm; CKE. *"M'vans with solar panels/TV aerials take care sun shades; gd cycling, birdwatching esp flamingoes; diving cent; popular at w/end; isolated, dry area of Spain with many interesting features; warm winters; excel site."* **€22.00** **2024**

See advertisement

ALMERIA *4G1* (18km W Coastal) *36.79738, -2.59128* **Camping Roquetas,** Ctra Los Parrales s/n, 04740 Roquetas de Mar (Almería) **950-34 90 85 or 950-34 38 09; info@campingroquetas.com; www.campingroquetas.com**

12 €2.90 WD MSP shgl 400m

Fr A7 take exit 429; ahead at rndabt A391 sp Roquetas. Turn L at rndabt sp camping & foll sp to site. 3*, V lge, pt shd, EHU (10-16A) €6.35-7.45; gas; red long stay; TV; 10% statics; phone; bus 1km; Eng spkn; adv bkg rec; ccard acc; tennis; CKE. *"Double-size pitches in winter; helpful staff; gd clean facs; tidy site but poss dusty; artificial shd; many long term visitors in winter; gd dedicated cycle path along sea front."* **€26.00, E30.** **2022**

ALMERIA *4G1* (4km W Coastal) *36.82560, -2.51685* **Camping La Garrofa,** Ctra N340a, Km 435.4, 04002 Almería **950-23 57 70; info@lagarrofa.com; www.lagarrofa.com**

12 €2.40 WD MSP shgl adj

Site sp on coast rd bet Almería & Aguadulce. Med, mkd, shd, pt sl, EHU (6-10A) €4.30-4.90; gas; red long stay; 10% statics; phone; bus adj; sep car park; games area; CKE. *"V pleasant site adj eucalyptus grove; helpful staff; modern, clean facs; sm pitches, not rec lge o'fits; vg."* **€20.50** **2024**

ALQUEZAR *3B2* (1.5km SW Rural) *42.16454, 0.01527* **Camping Alquézar,** Ctra. Barbastro s/n. 22145 Alquézar, Huesca **34 974 318 300; camping@alquezar.com; campingalquezar.com**

12 WD MSP

A22 Huesca - Barbastro. Take N240 W of Barbastro, dir Barbastro. Then A1232 & A1233 to Alquezar, foll camping sp. Med, mkd, hdstg, pt shd, terr, EHU (10A) inc; bbq; twin axles; Eng spkn; adv bkg acc; ccard acc. *"Tricky access; hard 2km walk up hill to old town; interesting town & selection of walking rtes; gd."* **€30.00** **2023**

ALTEA *4F2* (4km S Coastal) *38.57751, -0.06440* **Camping Cap-Blanch,** Playa de Albir, 03530 Altea (Alicante) **965-84 59 46; info@camping-capblanch.com; www.camping-capblanch.com**

12 WD MSP nr shgl adj

Exit AP7/E15 junc 64 Altea-Collosa onto N332, site bet Altea & Benidorm, dir Albir. 'No entry' sps on prom rd do not apply to access to site. 1*, Lge, hdstg, pt shd, EHU (5-10A) €3.50; gas; red long stay; TV; 10% statics; Eng spkn; ccard acc; car wash; golf 5km; watersports; tennis. *"V cr in winter with long stay campers; lge pitches; Altea mkt Tues; buses to Benidorm & Altea; handy for lovely beach; most pitches hdstg on pebbles; excel loc; excel walking/cycling."* **€38.00** **2024**

AMETLLA DE MAR, L' *3C2* (3km S Coastal) *40.86493, 0.77860* **Camping Ametlla,** Paratge de Santes Creus s/n, 43860 L'Ametlla de Mar (Tarragona) **977-26 77 84; info@campingametlla.com; www.campingametlla.com**

12 (htd) WD MSP shgl 400m

Exit AP7 junc 39, fork R as soon as cross m'way. Foll site sp for 3km - 1 v sharp, steep bend. Lge, hdstg, mkd, hdg, pt shd, terr, EHU (5-10A) inc; gas; bbq; red long stay; TV; 10% statics; phone; Eng spkn; adv bkg acc; ccard acc; games rm; bike hire; fitness rm; games area; CKE. *"Conv Port Aventura & Ebro Delta National Park; excel site & facs; can cycle into vill with mkt; dogs free; diving cent; delightful site."* **€41.50** **2022**

AMPOLLA, L' *3C2* (2km SW Coastal) *40.79940, 0.69974* **Camping L'Ampolla Playa,** Playa Arenal s/n, 43895 L'Ampolla **977-46 05 35; reservas@campingampolla.es; www.campingampolla.es**

WD MSP 50m

Exit AP7 at junc 39A twds S on N340 to km 1098. Turn L onto TV3401 sp L'Ampolla. At rndabt after1 km go L twds L'Ampolla and at next rndabt take 1st exit alongside campsite to ent. Med, hdstg, hdg, mkd, shd, EHU (5-10A); bbq; twin axles; train/bus 1km; Eng spkn; adv bkg acc; games area; CCI. *"Kite surfing; natural park of Ebro Delta; cycling; historic ctrs; vg."* **€34.00, 4 Mar-1 Nov.** **2022**

ARANDA DE DUERO *1C4* (3km N Rural) *41.70138, -3.68666* **Camping Costajan,** Ctra A1/E5, Km 164-165, 09400 Aranda de Duero (Burgos) **947-50 20 70; campingcostajan@camping-costajan.com; www.guiacampingfecc.com/campings/costajan**

Sp on A1/E5 Madrid-Burgos rd, N'bound exit km 164 Aranda Norte, S'bound exit km 165 & foll sp to Aranda & site 500m on R. 3*, Med, shd, pt sl, EHU (10A) €5 (poss rev pol &/or no earth); gas; bbq; 10% statics; phone; Eng spkn; adv bkg acc; tennis; games area; CKE. *"Lovely site under pine trees; poultry farm adj; diff pitch access due trees & sandy soil; friendly, helpful owner; site poss clsd LS - phone ahead to check; many facs clsd LS & gate clsd o'night until 0800; recep poss open evening only LS; poss cold/tepid shwrs LS; gd winter NH; vg site for dogs."* **€20.00 2024**

ARANJUEZ *1D4* (2.5km NE Rural) *40.04222, 3.59944* **Camping International Aranjuez,** Calle Soto del Rebollo s/n, 28300 Aranjuez (Madrid) **918-91 13 95; info@campingaranjuez.com; www.camping aranjuez.com**

Fr N (Madrid) turn off A4 exit 37 onto M305. After ent town turn L bef rv, after petrol stn on R. Take L lane & watch for site sp on L, also mkd M305 Madrid. Site in 500m on R. (If missed cont around cobbled rndabt & back twd Madrid.) Fr S turn off A4 for Aranjuez & foll Palacio Real sp. Join M305 & foll sp for Madrid & camping site. Site on Rv Tajo. Warning: rd surface rolls, take it slowly on app to site & ent gate tight. 3*, Lge, mkd, hdg, unshd, pt sl, serviced pitches; EHU (16A) €4 (poss no earth, rev pol); gas; red long stay; 10% statics; phone; ccard acc; rv fishing; bike hire; games area; canoe hire; CKE. *"Well-maintained site; gd san facs; rest vg value; some lge pitches - access poss diff due trees; hypmkt 3km; some uneven pitches - care req when pitching; pleasant town - World Heritage site; conv Madrid by train; excel site; free train to Royal Palace each morning; shop & rest clsd Tuesdays."* **€35.00** 2022

ARBIZU *3B1* (2km S Rural) *42.89860, -2.03444* **Camping Arbizu eko,** NA 7100 km 5, 31839 Arbizu **848-47 09 22; info@campingarbizu.com; www.campingarbizu.com**

Fr A10 Irurtzun to Altsasu exit 17 onto NA-7100. Site on R in 1km. Med, EHU (16A) inc; bbq; twin axles; TV; Eng spkn; adv bkg acc; ccard acc; fishing; games rm. *"Stunning views of mountains fr site; excel, clean shwr block; v helpful, friendly staff; lots to do in area; gd size pitches; best site; lge open camping area; popular sw."* **€28.00, 7 Jan-23 Dec.** 2024

ARENAS, LAS *1A4* (1km E Rural) *43.29973, -4.80321* **Camping Naranjo de Bulnes,** Ctra Cangas de Onís-Panes, Km 32.5, 33554 Arenas de Cabrales (Asturias) **985-84 65 78; info@campingnaranjodebulnes.com; www.campingnaranjodebulnes.com**

Fr Unquera on N634, take N621 S to Panes, AS114 23km to Las Arenas. Site E of vill of Las Arenas de Cabrales, both sides of rd. 2*, V lge, mkd, pt shd, pt sl, terr, EHU (10A) €3.50 (poss rev pol); gas; TV; bus 100m; ccard acc. *"Beautifully-situated site by rv; delightful vill; attractive, rustic-style, clean san facs; wcs up steps; poss poor security; conv Picos de Europa; mountain-climbing school; excursions; walking; excel cheese festival last Sun in Aug; excel rest, bars in vill; lovely."* **€34.00, 2 Apr-9 Oct.** 2023

ARIJA *1A4* (1km N Rural) *43.00064, -3.94492* **Camping Playa de Arija,** Avda Gran Via, 09570 Arija (Burgos) **942-77 33 00; info@campingplayadearija.com; www.campingplayadearija.com**

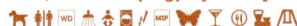

Fr W on A67 at Reinosa along S side of Embalse del Ebro. Go thro Arija & take 1st L after x-ing bdge. Go under rlwy bdge, site well sp on peninsula N of vill on lakeside. Or fr E on N623 turn W onto BU642 to Arija & turn R to peninsula & site. NB Rd fr W under repair 2009 & in poor condition. Lge, shd, EHU (5A) €3; bbq; sw; 10% statics; phone; bus 1km; watersports; games area; CKE. *"Gd new site; gd birdwatching; LS phone ahead for site opening times."* **€14.00, Easter-15 Sep.** 2024

AROSTEGI *3B1* (0.9km W Rural) *42.9375, -1.6927* **Camping Izarpe,** Ctra Gulina-Aroztegi, km 12,8 31867 Aroztegi, Valle de Atez **848 68 14 00; info@campingizarpe.com; www.campingizarpe.com**

N bound on A15 14km fr exit 97. S bound on N121A 14km fr Arraitz-Orkin. Daylight rec. Sm, mkd, unshd, pt sl, terr, EHU (10A); 60% statics; ccard acc; games area. *"Gd NH in LS; sm shop open till 8pm; off open mornings; rest clsd Mondays LS; gd."* **€30.50** 2021

AURITZ *3A1* (3km SW Rural) *42.97302, -1.35248* **Camping Urrobi,** Ctra Pamplona-Valcarlos, Km 42, 31694 Espinal-Aurizberri (Navarra) **948-76 02 00; info@campingurrobi.com; www.campingurrobi.com**

NE fr Pamplona on N135 twd Valcarlos thro Erro; 1.5km after Auritzberri (Espinal) turn R on N172. Site on N172 at junc with N135 opp picnic area. Med, pt shd, EHU (5A) €4.90; gas; bbq; 20% statics; phone; Eng spkn; ccard acc; horseriding; tennis; bike hire; CKE. *"Excel, busy site & facs; solar htd water - hot water to shwrs only; walks in surrounding hills; ltd facs LS; poss youth groups; overprices; poor wifi; clean; gd local walks."* **€31.30, 1 Apr-1 Nov.** 2023

AYERBE *3B2* (1km NE Rural) *42.28211, -0.67536* **Camping La Banera,** Ctra Loarre Km.1, 22800 Ayerbe (Huesca) **974-38 02 42 or 659-16 15 90 (mob); labanera@gmail.com; www.campingayerbe.com/camping_Ayerbe/index.html**

€2 nr

Take A132 NW fr Huesca dir Pamplona. Turn R at 1st x-rds at ent to Ayerbe sp Loarre & Camping. Site 1km on R on A1206. 2*, Med, mkd, pt shd, terr, EHU (6A) €2.60; gas; cooking facs; red long stay; TV; Eng spkn; adv bkg acc; ccard acc; CKE. *"Friendly, pleasant, well-maintained, peaceful, family-run site; facs clean; pitches poss muddy after rain; helpful owners; wonderful views; close to Loarre Castle; care req by high o'fits as many low trees; area famous for Griffon Vultures which inhabit tall cliffs nr Loarre."* **€17.50, 1 April-3 Nov.** **2024**

BAIONA *1B2* (5km NE Urban/Coastal) *42.13861, -8.80916* **Camping Playa América,** Ctra Vigo-Baiona, Km 9.250,Aptdo. Correos 3105 - 36350 Nigrán (Pontevedra) **986-36 54 03 or 986-36 71 61; oficina@campingplayaamerica.com; www.campingplayaamerica.com**

sand 300m

Sp on rd PO552 fr all dirs (Vigo/Baiona) nr beach. Med, mkd, pt shd, EHU (6A) €5; gas; bbq; 60% statics; bus 500m; Eng spkn; adv bkg acc; bike hire; CKE. *"Friendly staff; pleasant, wooded site; gd."* **€25.50, 16 Mar-15 Oct.** **2024**

BAIONA *1B2* (1km E Coastal) *42.11446, -8.82588* **Camping Bayona Playa,** Ctra Vigo-Baiona, Km 19, Sabarís, 36393 Baiona (Pontevedra) **986-35 00 35; campingbayona@campingbayona.com; www.campingbayona.com**

12 €3.50 sand adj

Fr Vigo on PO552 sp Baiona. Or fr A57 exit Baiona & foll sp Vigo & site sp. Lge, mkd, pt shd, EHU (10A) €5.90; gas; red long stay; 50% statics; phone; adv bkg req; waterslide; CKE. *"Area of outstanding natural beauty with sea on 3 sides; well-organised site; excel, clean san facs; avoid access w/end as v busy; ltd facs LS; tight access to sm pitches high ssn; gd cycle track to town; replica of ship 'La Pinta' in harbour."* **€29.40, E49.** **2022**

BAIONA *1B2* (8km SW Coastal) *42.08642, -8.89129* **Camping Mougás (Naturist),** As Mariñas 20B, Ctra Baiona-A Guarda, Km 156, 36309 Mougás (Pontevedra) **986-38 50 11; info@campingmougas.es**

Fr Baiona take coastal rd PO552 S; site sp. Med, mkd, pt shd, EHU €4.65; bbq; 80% statics; phone; Eng spkn; ccard acc; fishing; games area; tennis; CKE. *"Excel staff; lovely site on rocky coast; gd for watching sunsets; gd NH; o'looks beach; vg."* **€29.00, 18 Mar-27 Mar & 15 May-15 Sep.** **2022**

BALAGUER *3C2* (8km N Rural) *41.86030, 0.83250* **Camping La Noguera,** Partida de la Solana s/n, 25615 Sant Llorenç de Montgai (Lleida) **973-42 03 34; info@campinglanoguera.com; www.campinglanoguera.com**

12 €3.50

Fr Lleida, take N11 ring rd & exit at km 467 onto C13 NE dir Andorra & Balaguer. Head for Balaguer town cent, cross rv & turn R onto LV9047 dir Gerb. Site on L in 8km thro Gerb. App fr Camarasa not rec. Lge, hdstg, mkd, pt shd, terr, EHU (6A) €5.15; gas; bbq; red long stay; TV; 80% statics; phone; Eng spkn; adv bkg acc; ccard acc; games area; CKE. *"Next to lake & nature reserve; gd cycling; poss diff lge o'fits; friendly warden; gd facs."* **€37.70** **2023**

BALERMA *2H4* (1km S Coastal) *36.72202, -2.87838* **Camping Mar Azul,** Ctra de Guardias Viejas, S/N 04712 Balerma **950-93 76 37; info@campingbalerma.com; www.campingbalerma.com**

12 €2.60 100m

Exit junc 403 off A7/E15 for Balerma. Site in 6 km. Lge, hdg, mkd, hdstg, shd, EHU (16A) €0.35 per kw; bbq; twin axles; red long stay; TV; 4% statics; bus 1km; Eng spkn; adv bkg acc; games area. *"Lge car park; excel."* **€28.60** **2022**

BANYOLES *3B3* (2km W Rural) *42.12071, 2.74690* **Camping Caravaning El Llac,** Ctra Circumvallació de l'Estany s/n, 17834 Porqueres (Gerona) **972-57 03 05; info@campingllac.com; www.campingllac.com**

12 €2.30 (htd)

Exit AP7 junc 6 to Banyoles. Go strt thro town (do not use by-pass) & exit town at end of lake in 1.6km. Use R-hand layby to turn L sp Porqueres. Site on R in 2.5km. Lge, mkd, pt shd, EHU €4.60; sw; red long stay; 80% statics; bus 1km; site clsd mid-Dec to mid-Jan. *"Immac, ltd facs LS & stretched high ssn; sm pitches bet trees; pleasant walk around lake to town; site muddy when wet."* **€30.00** **2022**

BEAS DE GRANADA *2G4* (0.8km N Rural) *37.22416, -3.48805* **Camping Alto de Viñuelas,** Ctra de Beas de Granada s/n, 18184 Beas de Granada (Granada) **958-54 60 23; info@campingaltodevinuelas.com; www.campingaltodevinuelas.com**

12 (htd)

E fr Granada on A92, exit junc 256 & foll sp to Beas de Granada. Site well sp on L in 1.5km. Sm, mkd, pt shd, terr, EHU (5A) €3.50; bbq; red long stay; 10% statics; bus to Granada at gate; Eng spkn; CKE. *"In beautiful area; views fr all pitches; 4X4 trip to adj natural park; gd; conv for night halt."* **€26.00** **2024**

SPAIN

SPAIN

BEJAR *1D3* (15km SW Rural) *40.28560, -5.88182* **Camping Las Cañadas,** Ctra N630, Km 432, 10750 Baños de Montemayor (Cáceres) **927-48 11 26; info@lascanadas.es; www.lascanadas.es**

12 (htd)

Fr S turn off A630 m'way at 437km stone to Heruns then take old N630 twd Béjar. Site at 432km stone, behind 'Hervas Peil' (leather goods shop). Fr N exit A66 junc 427 thro Baños for 3km to site at km432 on R. 3*, Lge, mkd, shd, pt sl, EHU (5A) €4; gas; red long stay; TV; 60% statics; Eng spkn; ccard acc; fishing; bike hire; games area; tennis; CKE. *"Gd san facs but poss cold shwrs; high vehicles take care o'hanging trees; gd walking country; NH/sh stay."* **€25.00** **2022**

BENABARRE *3B2* (0.5km N Urban) *42.1103, 0.4811* **Camping Benabarre,** 22580 Benabarre (Huesca) **974-54 35 72; aytobenabarre@aragon.es**

nr

Fr N230 S, turn L after 2nd camping sp over bdge & into vill. Ignore brown camping sp (pt of riding cent). Med, hdstg, pt shd, EHU (10A) inc; phone; bus 600m; tennis. *"Excel, friendly, simple site; gd facs; gd value for money; v quiet LS; warden calls 1700; mkt on Fri; lovely vill with excel chocolate shop; conv Graus & mountains - a real find."* **€26.00, 9 Apr-11 Dec.** **2024**

BENAJARAFE *2H4* (3km E Coastal) *36.71962, -4.16467* **Camping Valle Niza Playa,** Ctra N340, km 264,1 ES-29792 Benajarafe **952 51 31 81; info@campingvalleniza.es; www.campingvalleniza.es**

12 (htd) 50 mtrs

On N340 (old coast rd), bet Torre Del Mar and Benajarafe. Lge, hdstg, hdg, mkd, pt shd, EHU (10-16A); bbq; twin axles; red long stay; TV; 20% statics; phone; bus 100m; Eng spkn; adv bkg acc; bike hire; games rm. *"Gd site; gymnasium; free yoga twice a week."* **€33.00** **2023**

BENICARLO *3D2* (2.6km NE Urban/Coastal) *40.42611, 0.43777* **Camping La Alegría del Mar,** Ctra N340, Km 1046, Calle Playa Norte, 12580 Benicarló (Castellón) **964-47 08 71; info@campingalegria.com; www.campingalegria.com**

12 (htd) adj

Sp off main N340 app Benicarló. Take slip rd mkd Service, go under underpass, turn R on exit & cont twd town, then turn at camp sp by Peugeot dealers. Sm, hdstg, mkd, hdg, pt shd, EHU (16A) €4.90; gas; bbq; red long stay; twin axles; 40% statics; phone; bus 800m; Eng spkn; ccard acc; games rm; CKE. *"Friendly British owners; access to pitches variable, poss diff in ssn; vg, clean san facs; Xmas & New Year packages; phone ahead to reserve pitch; excel; well run site."* **€30.00** **2022**

BENICASSIM *3D2* (0.9km E Coastal) *40.05709, 0.07429* **Camping Bonterra Park,** Avda de Barcelona 47, 12560 Benicàssim (Castellón) **964 30 00 07; info@bonterraresort.com; www.bonterraresort.com**

12 €3 (htd) (covrd, htd) sand 300m

Fr N exit AP7 junc 45 onto N340 dir Benicàssim. In approx 7km turn R to Benicàssim/Centro Urba; strt ahead to traff lts, then turn L, site on L 500m after going under rlwy bdge. 4*, Lge, hdstg, mkd, shd, pt sl, serviced pitches; EHU (6-10) inc; gas; bbq; sw nr; red long stay; TV; 15% statics; phone; train; Eng spkn; adv bkg acc; ccard acc; gym; games rm; tennis; bike hire; games area; CKE. *"Fabulous, excel site in gd location; excel cycle tracks & public trans; lovely beach; reasonable sized pitches; no o'fits over 10m; no dogs Jul/Aug; well kept & well-run; clean modern san facs; access to some pitches poss diff due to trees; sun shades some pitches; winter festival 3rd wk Jan; Harley Davidson rallies Jan & Sep, check in adv; highly rec; flat rd to town; excel facs; sep car park; ACSI card acc; site organises trips out; gd rest; excel."* **€60.00, E19.** **2022**

BENICASSIM *3D2* (4.5km NW Coastal) *40.05908, 0.08515* **Camping Azahar,** Ptda Villaroig s/n, 12560 Benicàssim (Castellón) **964-30 35 51 or 964-30 31 96; campingazahar.benicasim@gmail.com; www.campingazahar.es**

12 €4.07 (htd) sand 300m

Fr AP7 junc 45 take N340 twd València; in 5km L at top of hill (do not turn R to go-karting); foll sp. Turn R under rlwy bdge opp Hotel Voramar. Lge, mkd, unshd, pt sl, terr, EHU (4-6A) €2.90 (long leads poss req); gas; red long stay; 25% statics; phone; bus adj; Eng spkn; adv bkg acc; ccard acc; bike hire; CKE. *"Popular site, esp in winter; access poss diff for m'vans & lge o'fits; poss uneven pitches; organised events; tennis at hotel; gd walking & cycling; gd touring base."* **€48.00** **2023**

BENIDORM *4F2* (5.6km N Coastal) *38.56926, -0.09328* **Camping Almafrá,** Partida de Cabut 25, 03503 Benidorm (Alicante) **965-88 90 75; info@campingalmafra.es; www.campingalmafra.es**

12 (htd) (covrd, htd)

Exit AP7/E15 junc 65 onto N332 N. Foll sp Alfaz del Pi, site sp. 5*, V lge, hdstg, mkd, hdg, pt shd, EHU (16A); bbq; red long stay; twin axles; TV (pitch); 20% statics; bus; Eng spkn; adv bkg acc; games rm; jacuzzi; sauna; gym; games area; tennis; CKE. *"Tennis, Alfaz del Pi a sh walk away; private san facs avail; wellness/fitness cent; reg bus into Benidorm; excel."* **€15.00** **2022**

BENIDORM *4F2* (1.5km NE Urban) *38.54833, -0.09851* **Camping El Raco,** Avda Dr Severo Ochoa, 19 Racó de Loix, 03503 Benidorm (Alicante) **965-86 85 52; info@campingraco.com; www.campingraco.com**

12 €1.15 (covrd, htd) 1.5km

Turn off A7 m'way at junc 65 then L onto A332; take turning sp Benidorm Levante Beach; ignore others; L at 1st traff lghts; strt on at next traff lts, El Raco 1km on R. Lge, hdstg, mkd, hdg, pt shd, pt sl, serviced pitches; EHU (10A) metered; gas; bbq; TV; 30% statics; bus; Eng spkn; games area; CKE. *"Excel site; popular winter long stay but strictly applied rules about leaving c'van unoccupied; EHU metered for long stay; friendly helpful staff; two pin adaptor needed for elec conn."* **€34.00** 2024

BENIDORM *4F2* (3.6km NE Urban) *38.55564, -0.09754* **Camping Villamar,** Ctra del Albir, Km 0.300, 03503 Benidorm (Alicante) **966-81 12 55; camping@campingvillamar.com; www.campingvillamar.com**

12 (covrd, htd) sand 2km

Exit AP7 junc 65. Down hill twd town, turn L at traff lts into Ctra Valenciana, turn R where 2 petrol stns either side of rd, site on L. V lge, mkd, pt shd, terr, serviced pitches; EHU (16A) €3.50; gas; red long stay; TV (pitch); 60% statics; phone; adv bkg acc; games rm. *"Excel site, esp winter; gd security; v welcoming; gd walking area; excel food; spotless san facs; great value; excel food; bus to town."* **€28.00** 2024

BENIDORM *4F2* (1km E Coastal) *38.5449, -0.10696* **Camping Villasol,** Avda Bernat de Sarriá 13, 03500 Benidorm (Alicante) **965-85 04 22; info@camping-villasol.com; www.camping-villasol.com**

12 (htd) (covrd, htd, indoor) sand 300m

Leave AP7 at junc 65 onto N332 dir Alicante; take exit into Benidorm sp Levante. Turn L at traff lts just past Camping Titus, then in 200m R at lts into Avda Albir. Site on R in 1km. Care - dip at ent, poss grounding. 3*, V lge, hdstg, mkd, shd, EHU (5A) €4.28; red long stay; TV (pitch); 5% statics; phone; Eng spkn; adv bkg acc; ccard acc; games area; laundromat; basketball court; petanque pitches. *"Excel, well-kept site espec in winter; medical service; currency exchange; some sm pitches; friendly staff."* **€35.00** 2022

BENQUERENCIA *2E3* (2km SW Rural) *39.29626, -06.10109* **Camping Las Grullas (Naturist),** Camino Valdefuentes 4, 10185 Benquerencia **34 634 264 504; info@lasgrullas.es; www.campinglasgrullas.es**

(htd)

Take EX-206 to Miajadas. After 30km take 2nd turning to Benquerencia (close to Valdefuentes vill). Site on R after 2.5 km. 1*, Sm, mkd, hdg, pt shd, EHU (4-6A) inc; twin axles; Eng spkn; adv bkg acc. *"Over 16's only; close historic town; no childrens facs; v helpful owners; gd walks fr site; vg."* **€25.00, 1 Apr-16 Oct.** 2022

BIELSA *3B2* (8km W Rural) *42.65176, 0.14076* **Camping Pineta,** Ctra del Parador, Km 7, 22350 Bielsa (Huesca) **974-50 10 89; info@campingpineta.com; www.campingpineta.com**

€2.50

Fr A138 in Beilsa turn W & foll sp for Parador Monte Perdido & Valle de Pineta. Site on L after 8km (ignore previous campsite off rd). 2*, Lge, pt shd, pt sl, terr, EHU (6A) €5 (poss rev pol); gas; bbq; 10% statics; phone; ccard acc; bike hire; games area; CKE. *"Well-maintained site; clean facs; glorious location in National Park."* **€27.00, 25 Mar-2 Oct.** 2022

BILBAO *1A4* (18km N Coastal) *43.38916, -2.98444* **Camping Sopelana,** Ctra Bilbao-Plentzia, Km 18, Playa Atxabiribil 30, 48600 Sopelana (Vizcaya) **946-76 19 81 or 649-11 57 51; reservas@campingsopelana.com; www.campingsopelana.com**

12 sand 200m

In Bilbao cross rv by m'way bdge sp to airport, foll 637/634 N twd & Plentzia. Cont thro Sopelana & foll sp on L. 1*, Med, hdg, sl, EHU (10A) €4.50; own san req; gas; red long stay; 70% statics; Eng spkn; adv bkg req; CKE. *"Poss strong sea winds; ltd space for tourers; pitches sm, poss flooded after heavy rain & poss diff due narr, steep site rds; ltd facs LS; helpful manager; site used by local workers; poss clsd LS - phone ahead to check; gd NH/sh stay only."* **€36.00** 2022

BILBAO *1A4* (2.5km W Urban) *43.25960, -2.96351* **Bilbao Hostel (formerly Motorhome Parking Bilbao),** Monte Kobeta 31, 48001 Bilbao **688 809 399 or 944 655 789; kobetamendi@suspertu.net; bilbaohostel.net**

A8 m'way, Balmaseda exit, dir Altamira - Alto de Kastrexana. Med, unshd, terr, EHU inc; bus adj; ccard acc. *"MH's only; on hill o'looking Bilbao; ehu & water to each pitch; v conv for visiting city by bus (every 1/2 hr); max stay 2 days; clsd 1st week of Jul; vg; full security."* **€17.00, 17 Mar-9 Jan.** 2023

BLANES *3C3* (1km S Coastal) *41.65933, 2.77000* **Camping Blanes,** Avda Vila de Madrid 33, 17300 Blanes (Gerona) **972-33 15 91; info@camping blanes.com; www.campingblanes.com**

12 WD MSP sand

Fr N on AP7/E15 exit junc 9 onto NII dir Barcelona & foll sp Blanes. Fr S to end of C32, then NII dir Blanes. On app Blanes, foll camping sps & Playa S'Abanell - all campsites are sp at rndabts; all sites along same rd. Site adj Hotel Blau-Mar. Lge, mkd, shd, EHU (5A) inc; gas; phone; bus; Eng spkn; ccard acc; solarium; bike hire; watersports; games rm. *"Excel site, espec LS; helpful owner; narr site rds; easy walk to town cent; dir access to beach; trains to Barcelona & Gerona."* **€49.00** **2023**

BLANES *3C3* (1.5km SW Coastal) *41.66206, 2.78046* **Camping Solmar,** Calle Cristòfor Colom 48, 17300 Blanes (Gerona) **972-34 80 34; campingsolmar@ campingsolmar.com; www.campingsolmar.com**

WD MSP sand 150m

Fr N on AP7/E15 exit junc 9 onto NII dir Barcelona & foll sp Blanes. Fr S to end of C32, then NII dir Blanes. On app Blanes, foll camping sps. Lge, mkd, hdg, shd, EHU (6A) inc; bbq; red long stay; 10% statics; bus 100m; adv bkg acc; ccard acc; games area; games rm; tennis; CKE. *"Excel site & facs; dogs free."* **€39.40, 2 Apr-12 Oct.** **2023**

See advertisement

BOCAIRENT *4F2* (9km E Rural) *38.75332, -0.54957* **Camping Mariola,** Ctra Bocairent-Alcoy, Km 9, 46880 Bocairent (València) **962-13 51 60; info@ campingmariola.com; www.campingmariola.com**

12 (htd) WD MSP

Fr N330 turn E at Villena onto CV81. N of Banyeres & bef Bocairent turn E sp Alcoi up narr, steep hill with some diff turns & sheer drops; site sp. Lge, hdstg, pt shd, EHU (6A) inc; bbq; cooking facs; twin axles; TV; 50% statics; phone; Eng spkn; adv bkg acc; ccard acc; games area; games rm; CKE. *"In Mariola mountains; gd walking; bicycles; superb tranquil location in Sierra Mariola National Park, excel walking & cycling, great for dogs, friendly family atmosphere."* **€22.00** **2024**

BOSSOST *3B2* (3km SE Rural) *42.74921, 0.70071* **Camping Prado Verde,** Ctra de Lleida a Francia, N230, Km 173, 25551 Era Bordeta/La Bordeta de Vilamòs (Lleida) **973-64 71 72; info@campingpradoverde.es; www.campingpradoverde.es**

12 (htd) MSP

On N230 at km 173 on banks of Rv Garona. Med, shd, EHU (6A) €5.50; TV; 10% statics; bus; ccard acc; bike hire; fishing; CKE. *"V pleasant NH."* **€22.00** **2022**

SPAIN

BROTO *3B2* (1.2km W Rural) *42.59779, -0.13072*
Camping Oto, Afueras s/n, 22370 Oto-Valle De Broto (Huesca) **974-48 60 75; info@campingoto.com; www.campingoto.com**

On N260 foll camp sp on N o'skts of Broto. Diff app thro vill but poss. Lge, pt shd, pt sl, EHU (10A) €3.80 (poss no earth); gas; bbq; adv bkg acc; ccard acc. *"Excel, clean san facs; excel bar & café; friendly owner; pitches below pool rec; some noise fr adj youth site; conv Ordesa National Park; gd site, pleasant."*
€30.00, 5 Mar-15 Oct. **2024**

BROTO *3B2* (7km W Rural) *42.61576, -0.15432*
Camping Viu, Ctra N260, Biescas-Ordesa, Km 484.2, 22378 Viu de Linás (Huesca) **974-48 63 01; info@campingviu.com; www.campingviu.com**

12 (htd)

Lies on N260, 4km W of Broto. Fr Broto, N for 2km on rd 135; turn W twd Biesca at junc with Torla rd; site approx 4km on R. Med, pt shd, sl, EHU (5-8A) €4.20; gas; bbq; phone; adv bkg acc; ccard acc; games rm; bike hire; horseriding; CKE. *"Friendly owners; gd home cooking; walking adj; skiing adj; car wash; fine views; highly rec; climbing adj; clean, modern san facs; poss not suitable for lge o'fits."* **€17.40** **2022**

BURGOS *1B4* (4km E Rural) *42.34111, -3.65777*
Camp Fuentes Blancas, Ctra Cartuja Miraflores, Km 3.5, 09193 Burgos **947-48 60 16; info@campingburgos.com; www.campingburgos.com**

12 €2.47 (htd)

E or W on A1 exit junc 238 & cont twd Burgos. Strt over 1st rndabt, turn R sp Cortes & then L. Look for yellow sps to site. Fr N (N627 or N623) on entering Burgos keep in R hand lane. Foll signs Cartuja miraflores & yellow camp signs. 3*, Lge, mkd, shd, EHU (6A) inc; gas; TV; 10% statics; phone; bus at gate; Eng spkn; ccard acc; games area. *"Neat, roomy, adj woodland; some sm pitches; ltd facs LS; poss v muddy in wet; easy access town car parks or cycle/rv walk; Burgos lovely town; gd NH to Portugal or France; San Rafael dated; gd bus to town; excel, well maintained busy site; gd shd; gd facs; helpful staff; gd mv service pt; gd rest."* **€30.00** **2024**

CABRERA, LA *1D4* (1km SW Rural) *40.85797, -3.61580* **Camping Pico de la Miel,** Ctra A-1 Salida 57, 28751 La Cabrera (Madrid) **918-68 80 82 or 918-68 95 07; info@picodelamiel.com; www.picodelamiel.com**

12 (htd)

Fr Madrid on A1/E5, exit junc 57 sp La Cabrera. Turn L at rndabt, site sp. Lge, mkd, pt shd, pt sl, EHU (10A) €4.45; gas; red long stay; 75% statics; phone; Eng spkn; adv bkg acc; ccard acc; tennis; games area; sailing; windsurfing; squash; fishing; CKE. *"Attractive walking country; conv Madrid; mountain-climbing; car wash; ltd touring area not v attractive; some pitches have low sun shades; excel san facs; ltd facs LS."*
€28.00 **2023**

CACERES *2E3* (6km NW Urban) *39.48861, -6.41277*
Camp Municipal Ciudad de Cáceres, Ctra N630, Km 549.5, 10005 Cáceres **927-23 31 00; reservas@campingcaceres.com; www.campingcaceres.com**

12

Fr Cáceres ring rd take N630 dir Salamanca. At 1st rndbt turn R sp Via de Servicio with camping symbol. Foll sp 500m to site. Or fr N exit A66 junc 545 onto N630 twd Cáceres. At 2nd rndabt turn L sp Via de Servicio, site on L adj football stadium. Med, mkd, hdstg, unshd, terr, EHU (10A) €4.50; gas; bbq; TV; 15% statics; bus 500m over footbdge; Eng spkn; adv bkg acc; ccard acc; games area; CKE. *"Vg, well-run site; excel facs; ACSI acc; v helpful staff; vg value rest; gd bus service to and fr interesting old town with many historical bldgs; excel site with ensuite facs at each pitch; individual san facs each pitch; location not pretty adj to football stadium & indus est; town too far to walk; v lush, free use of spa; Lydl 1.6km."* **€26.00**
2022

CADAQUES *3B3* (1km N Coastal) *42.29172, 3.28260*
Camping Cadaqués, Ctra Port Lligat 17, 17488 Cadaqués (Girona) **93 626 8900; hola@cadaques.wecamp.net; www.wecamp.net/destinos/cadaques**

shgl 600m

At ent to town, turn L at rdbt (3rd exit) sp thro narr rds, site in about 1.5km on L. NB App to Cadaqués on busy, narr mountain rds, not suitable lge o'fits. If raining, rds only towable with 4x4. 3*, Lge, hdstg, mkd, pt shd, sl, EHU (5A) €5.95; gas; Eng spkn; ccard acc; sep car park. *"Cadaqués home of Salvador Dali; sm pitches; medical facs high ssn; san facs poss poor LS; fair, red facs in LS next to m'way so poss noisy but gd for en-route stop."* **€35.00, Easter-17 Sep.** **2024**

CALATAYUD *3C1* (15km N Rural) *41.44666, -1.55805*
Camping Saviñan Parc, Ctra El Frasno-Mores, Km 7, 50299 Saviñan (Zaragoza) **976-82 54 23; info@campingsavinan.com; www.campingsavinan.com**

12 €2.70

Exit A2/E90 (Zaragoza-Madrid) at km 255 to T-junc. Turn R to Saviñan for 6km, foll sps to site 1km S. 2*, Lge, hdstg, pt shd, terr, EHU (6-10A) €4.60; gas; 15% statics; phone; ccard acc; site clsd Jan; tennis; horseriding; CKE. *"Beautiful scenery & views; some sm narr pitches; rec identify pitch location to avoid stop/start on hill; terr pitches have steep, unfenced edges; many pitches with sunscreen frames & diff to manoeuvre long o'fits; modern facs block but cold in winter & poss stretched high ssn; hot water to some shwrs only; gates poss clsd LS - use intercom; site poss clsd Feb."* **€24.00** **2023**

SPAIN

CALELLA *3C3* (2km NE Coastal) *41.61774, 2.67680* **Camping Caballo de Mar,** Passeig Maritim s/n, 08397 Pineda de Mar (Barcelona) **937-67 17 06; info@caballodemar.com; www.caballodemar.com**

€2.20 sand adj

Fr N exit AP7 junc 9 & immed turn R onto NII dir Barcelona. Foll sp Pineda de Mar & turn L twd Paseo Maritimo. Fr S on C32 exit 122 dir Pineda de Mar & foll dir Paseo Maritimo. Lge, mkd, shd, EHU (3-6A) €3.40-4.40; gas; bbq; red long stay; 10% statics; Eng spkn; adv bkg acc; ccard acc; games area; games rm; CKE. *"Excursions arranged; gd touring base & conv Barcelona; gd, modern facs; rlwy stn 2km (Barcelona 30 mins); excel; pitches sm for twin axles; noise fr locals on site."* **€69.00, 23 Mar-29 Sep.** **2024**

"I need an on-site restaurant"

We do our best to make sure site information is correct, but it is always best to check any must-have facilities are still available or will be open during your visit.

CALIG *3D2* (1km NW Rural) *40.45183, 0.35211* **Camping L'Orangeraie,** Camino Peniscola-Calig, 12589 Càlig **34 964 765 059; info@campingorangeraie.com; www.campingorangeraie.com**

€8 10km

On AP7 exit 43 Benicarlo-Peniscola. 1st R at rndabt to Calig then foll sp to campsite. Fr N340 exit N232 to Morella, then after 1.5km turn L to Calig CV135, foll sp to campsite. 5*, Med, mkd, hdg, pt shd, terr, EHU (6A) or (10A); bbq; twin axles; red long stay; 15% statics; bus 1km; Eng spkn; adv bkg acc; waterslide; games area. *"Excel site."* **€33.00, 1 Apr-31 Dec, E43.** **2022**

CALPE *4F2* (0.3km NE Urban/Coastal) *38.64488, 0.05604* **Camping Calpe Mar,** Calle Eslovenia 3, 03710 Calpe (Alicante) **965-87 55 76; info@campingcalpemar.com; www.campingcalpemar.com**

12 (htd) nr sand 300m

Exit AP7/E15 junc 63 onto N332 & foll sp, take slip rd sp Calpe Norte & foll dual c'way CV746 round Calpe twd Peñón d'Ifach. At rndabt nr police stn with metal statues turn L, then L at next rndabt, over next rndabt, site 200m on R. Med, hdstg, mkd, hdg, unshd, serviced pitches; EHU (10A) inc (metered for long stay); bbq; red long stay; TV; 3% statics; phone; bus adj; Eng spkn; adv bkg acc; ccard acc; ice; games area; games rm; dog wash; CKE. *"High standard site; well-kept & laid out; Spanish lessons; gd security; excel; extra lge pitches avail at additional charge; car wash; gd for long stay, friendly staff; sep car park; close to beach and Lidl."* **€35.00** **2023**

CAMBRILS *3C2* (1.5km N Urban/Coastal) *41.06500, 1.08361* **Camping Playa Cambrils Don Camilo,** Carrer Oleastrum 2, Ctra Cambrils-Salou, Km 1.5, 43850 Cambrils (Tarragona) **977-36 14 90; camping@playacambrils.com; www.playacambrils.com**

€4.35 (htd) sand adj

Exit A7 junc 37 dir Cambrils & N340. Turn L onto N340 then R dir port then L onto coast rd. Site sp on L at rndabt after rv bdge 100m bef watch tower on R, approx 2km fr port. V lge, mkd, hdg, shd, EHU (6A) inc; gas; red long stay; TV; 25% statics; bus 200m; Eng spkn; adv bkg req; ccard acc; tennis; watersports; games rm; bike hire; boat hire; CKE. *"Helpful, friendly staff; children's club; cash machine; doctor; cinema; sports activities avail; Port Aventura 5km; 24-hr security; vg site."* **€48.00, 15 Mar-16 Oct.** **2023**

"Satellite navigation makes touring much easier"

Remember most sat navs don't know if you're towing or in a larger vehicle – always use yours alongside maps and site directions.

CAMBRILS *3C2* (11km SW Coastal) *41.02512, 0.95906* **Camping Miramar,** Ctra N340, km 1134 43892 Mont-roig del Camp **977-81 12 03; recepcio@camping-miramar.com; www.camping-miramar.es**

Fr the AP7 take exit 37 to the N340. Turn L at KM134 to campsite. Sm, pt shd, EHU (6A) €5.20; bbq; twin axles; red long stay; 75% statics; bus; Eng spkn; adv bkg acc. *"Site on beach, walking, sw, snorkelling; vg."* **€39.00, 1 Jan-30 Nov.** **2023**

CAMBRILS *3C2* (8km SW Coastal) *41.03333, 0.96777* **Playa Montroig Camping Resort,** N340, Km1.136, 43300 Montroig (Tarragona) **977 810 637; info@playamontroig.com; www.playamontroig.com**

(htd) (htd) sand adj

Exit AP7 junc 37, W onto N340. Site has own dir access onto N340 bet Cambrils & L'Hospitalet de L'Infant, well sp fr Cambrils. 5*, V lge, mkd, shd, pt sl, serviced pitches; EHU (10A) inc; gas; 30% statics; phone; Eng spkn; adv bkg acc; ccard acc; games rm; games area; golf 3km; tennis; bike hire; CKE. *"Magnificent, clean, secure site; private, swept beach; skateboard track; some sm pitches & low branches; cash machine; doctor; 4 grades pitch/price; highly rec."* **€53.00, 1 Apr-30 Oct.** **2022**

See advertisement opposite

CAMBRILS *3C2* (8km SW Coastal) *41.03333, 0.96777* **Playa Montroig Camping Resort,** N340, Km1.136, 43300 Montroig (Tarragona) **977 810 637; info@playamontroig.com; www.playamontroig.com**

(htd) (htd) sand adj

Exit AP7 junc 37, W onto N340. Site has own dir access onto N340 bet Cambrils & L'Hospitalet de L'Infant, well sp fr Cambrils. 5*, V lge, mkd, shd, pt sl, serviced pitches; EHU (10A) inc; gas; 30% statics; phone; Eng spkn; adv bkg acc; ccard acc; games rm; games area; golf 3km; tennis; bike hire; CKE. *"Magnificent, clean, secure site; private, swept beach; skateboard track; some sm pitches & low branches; cash machine; doctor; 4 grades pitch/price; highly rec."*
€53.00, 1 Apr-30 Oct. **2022**

CAMBRILS *3C2* (1.8km W Urban/Coastal) *41.06550, 1.04460* **Camping La Llosa,** Ctra N340 Barcelona a Valencia, Km 1143, 43850 Cambrils (Tarragona) **977-36 26 15; info@camping-lallosa.com; www.camping-lallosa.com**

12 €3.50 sand

Exit A7/E15 at junc 37 & join N340 S. Head S into Cambrils (ignore L turn to cent) & at island turn R. Site sp on L within 100m. Fr N exit junc 35 onto N340. Strt over at x-rds, then L over rlwy bdge at end of rd, strt to site. V lge, hdstg, shd, EHU (5A) €5; gas; red long stay; 50% statics; phone; bus 500m; Eng spkn; ccard acc; car wash. *"Interesting fishing port; gd facs; excel pool; gd supmkt nrby; poss diff siting for m'vans due low trees; excel winter NH."* **€51.00** **2024**

CAMBRILS *3C2* (8km W Coastal) *41.03717, 0.97622* **Camping La Torre del Sol,** Ctra N340, Km 1.136, Miami-Playa, 43300 Montroig Del Camp (Tarragona) **977 810 486; info@latorredelsol.com; www.latorredelsol.com**

(htd) sand

Leave A7 València/Barcelona m'way at junc 37 & foll sp Cambrils. After 1.5km join N340 coast rd S for 6km. Watch for site sp 4km bef Miami Playa. Fr S exit AP7 junc 38, foll sp Cambrils on N340. Site on R 4km after Miami Playa. Site ent narr, alt ent avail for lge o'fits. 4*, V lge, hdg, mkd, shd, EHU (6A) inc (10A avail); gas; bbq; TV; 40% statics; Eng spkn; adv bkg acc; ccard acc; squash; games rm; gym; tennis; sauna; bike hire; golf 4km. *"Attractive well-guarded site for all ages; sandy pitches; gd, clean san facs; steps to facs for disabled; whirlpool; jacuzzi; access to pitches poss diff lge o'fits due trees & narr site rds; skateboard zone; radios/TVs to be used inside vans only; conv Port Aventura, Aquaparc, Aquopolis; cinema; disco; highly rec, can't praise site enough; excel."*
€67.52, 15 Mar-30 Oct, E14. **2022**

SPAIN

CANET DE MAR *3C3* (1.5km E Coastal) *41.59086, 2.59195* **Camping Globo Barcelona,** Ctra N11, Km 660.9, 08360 Canet de Mar (Barcelona) **937-94 11 43; camping@globo-rojo.com; www.globo-rojo.com**

€5.50 shgl adj

On N11 500m N of Canet de Mar. Site clearly sp on L. Gd access. 4*, Med, hdstg, mkd, hdg, shd, EHU (10A) €6; gas; bbq; red long stay; TV; 10% statics; phone; Eng spkn; adv bkg acc; ccard acc; horseriding 2km; sep car park; games area; watersports adj; bike hire; tennis; CKE. *"Excel facs; friendly, family-run site; busy w/end; slightly run down area; conv Barcelona by train (40km)."* **€42.00, 1 Apr-30 Sep.** 2023

CANGAS DE ONIS *1A3* (16km E Rural) *43.33527, -4.94777* **Camping Picos de Europa,** Avin-Onís, 33556 Avín, **985-84 40 70; info@picos-europa.com; www.picos-europa.com**

12

E80, exit 307. Dir Posada A5-115. Loc on the rd Onis-Carrena, 15 km fr Cangas de Onis and 10 km fr Carrena, foll sps. 2*, Med, hdg, mkd, pt shd, terr, EHU (6A) €3.80; gas; 10% statics; phone; Eng spkn; adv bkg acc; horseriding; CKE. *"Owners v helpful; beautiful, busy, well-run site; vg value rest; modern san facs; poss diff access due narr site rds & cr; some sm pitches, lge o'fits may need 2; canoeing on local rvs; conv local caves, mountains, National Park, beaches; highly rec."* **€27.00** 2024

CANGAS DE ONIS *1A3* (3km SE Rural) *43.34715, -5.08362* **Camping Covadonga,** 33589 Soto de Cangas (Asturias) **985-94 00 97; campingcovadonga@hotmail.es; www.camping-covadonga.com**

N625 fr Arriondas to Cangas de Onis, then AS114 twds Covadonga & Panes, cont thro town sp Covadonga. At rndabt take 2nd exit sp Cabrales, site on R in 100m. Access tight. 1*, Med, mkd, pt shd, EHU (10A) €3.50 (no earth); red long stay; bus adj; adv bkg acc; CKE. *"Sm pitches; take care with access; site rds narr; 17 uneven steps to san facs; conv for Picos de Europa."* **€22.00, Holy Week & 15 Jun-30 Sep.** 2023

CARBALLO *1A2* (15km N Coastal) *43.29556, -8.65528* **Camping Baldayo,** San Salvador de Rebordelos, 15105 Carballo **981-73 95 29; campingbaldayo@yahoo.es; www.campingbaldayo.com**

12 sand 200m

Access via DP-1916 fr Carballo. Turn L in vill and foll sp. App rds are unmade. On site access rds are narr with sharp corners, diff for long o'fits. 2*, Med, hdg, mkd, hdstg, pt shd, pt sl, terr, EHU (3A) €1.50; bbq; twin axles; 75% statics; phone; adv bkg acc. *"Sm pitches & narr camp rds poss diff lge o'fits; poss unkempt LS; nrby lagoon with boardwalk and bird hides; beach popular for surfing & watersports."* **€16.50** 2023

CARIDAD, LA (EL FRANCO) *1A3* (3.6km W Rural) *43.55635, -6.86218* **Camping A Grandella,** 33746 Valdepares (Asturias) **985-866 338; info@campingagrandella.com; campingagrandella.com**

12 €1

Sp fr N634/E70. 1*, Med, pt shd, EHU €3.50; 10% statics; bus 200m; site clsd mid-Dec to mid-Jan. *"Attractive little site; well-situated."* **€18.00** 2024

CARRION DE LOS CONDES *1B4* (0.4km W Rural) *42.33506, -04.60447* **Camping El Edén,** Ctra Vigo-Logroño, Km 200, 34120 Carrión de los Condes (Palencia) **979-88 07 14**

Fr N231 take junc 85, go S then L at 3rd rndabt to ctr. Site sp on L. 2*, Med, mkd, pt shd, EHU (6A) €3.50; gas; bus 500m; Eng spkn. *"Pleasant walk to town; basic rvside site; recep in bar/rest; site open w/ends only LS; fair NH; quite lively in high ssn; nice site in interesting town on pilgrim rte; no lts in san block."* **€30.00, 1 Apr-30 Oct.** 2023

CASPE *3C2* (12km NE Rural) *41.28883, 0.05733* **Taiga Resorts (Formerly Lake Caspe Camping),** Ctra N211, Km 286.7, 50700 Caspe (Zaragoza) **951 20 45 31; hola.caspe@taigaresorts.com; www.taigaresorts.com/en/taiga-lake-caspe.html**

€3.75

Fr E leave AP2 or N11 at Fraga & foll N211 dir Caspe to site. Fr W take N232 fr Zaragoza then A1404 & A221 E thro Caspe to site in 16km on L at km 286.7, sp. 2*, Med, hdstg, hdg, mkd, pt shd, EHU (5-10A) €5.60; gas; 10% statics; phone; Eng spkn; adv bkg acc; fishing; sailing; CKE. *"Gd, well-run, scenic site but isolated (come prepared); avoid on public hols; site rds gravelled but muddy after rain; sm pitches nr lake; gd watersports; mosquitoes; beware low branches."* **€37.00, 1Mar-10 Nov.** 2024

CASTELLO D'EMPURIES *3B3* (4km NE Rural) *42.26460, 3.10160* **Camping Mas Nou,** Ctra Mas Nou 7, Km 38, 17486 Castelló d'Empúries (Gerona) **972-45 41 75; info@campingmasnou.com; www.campingmasnou.com**

€2.35 (htd) nr 2.5km

On m'way A7 exit 3 if coming fr France & exit 4 fr Barcelona dir Roses (E) C260. Site on L at ent to Empuriabrava - use rndabt to turn. 3*, Lge, mkd, shd, EHU (10A) €4.90; bbq; red long stay; TV; 5% statics; phone; Eng spkn; ccard acc; tennis; games area; CKE. *"Aqua Park 4km, Dali Museum 10km; gd touring base; helpful staff; well-run site; excel, clean san facs; sports activities & children's club; gd cycling; excel; vg rest."* **€52.50, 8 Apr-24 Sep.** 2023

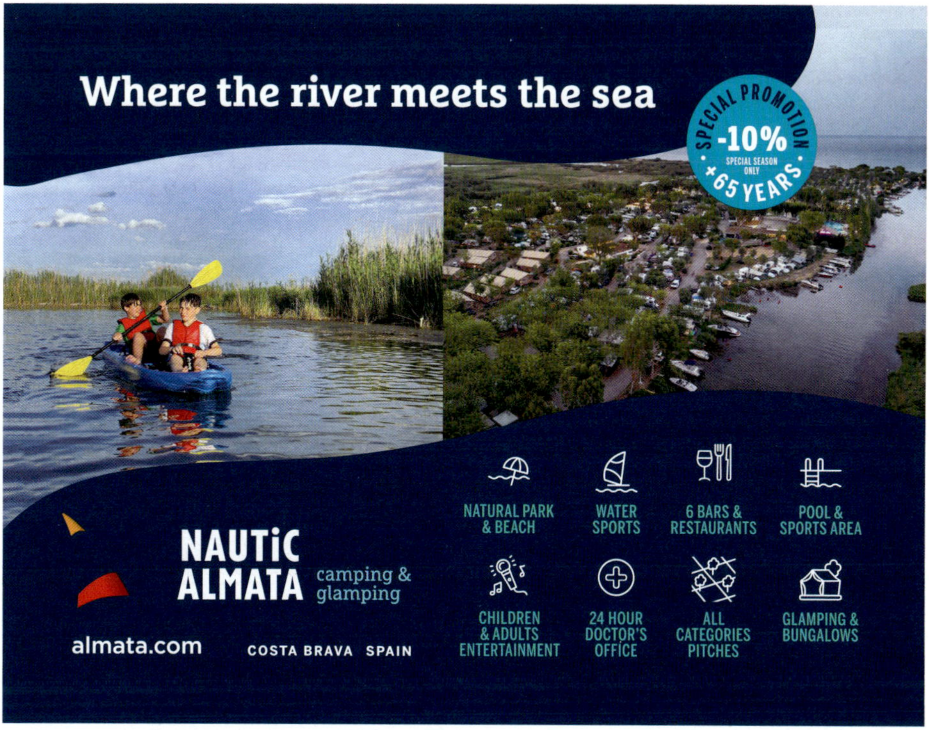

CASTELLO D'EMPURIES *3B3* (4km SE Coastal) *42.20725, 3.10026* **Camping Nautic Almatá,** Aiguamolls de l'Empordà, 17486 Castelló d'Empúries (Gerona) **972-45 44 77; info@almata.com; www.almata.com**

€6.40 sand adj

Fr A7 m'way exit 3; foll sp to Roses. After 12km turn S for Sant Pere Pescador & site on L in 5km. Site clearly sp on rd Castelló d'Empúries-Sant Pere Pescador. Lge, pt shd, EHU (10A) inc; gas; TV; adv bkg acc; sailing school; tennis; bike hire; horseriding; games area. *"Excel, clean facs; ample pitches; sports facs inc in price; disco bar on beach; helpful staff; direct access to nature reserve; waterside pitches rec."* **€59.00, 16 May-20 Sep. 2022**

See advertisement

"There aren't many sites open at this time of year"

If you're travelling outside peak season remember to call ahead to check site opening dates – even if the entry says 'open all year'.

CASTELLO D'EMPURIES *3B3* (1km S Coastal) *42.25563, 3.13791* **Camping Castell Mar,** Ctra Roses-Figueres, Km 40.5, Playa de la Rubina, 17486 Castelló d'Empúries (Gerona) **972-45 08 22; info@camping-castellmar.com; www.camping-castellmar.com**

sand 100m

Exit A7 at junc 3 sp Figueres; turn L onto C260 sp Roses, after traff lts cont twd Roses, turn R down side of rest La Llar for 1.5km, foll sp Playa de la Rubina. 4*, Lge, mkd, hdg, pt shd, serviced pitches; EHU (6-10A) inc; gas; bbq; TV (pitch); 30% statics; phone; Eng spkn; adv bkg acc; games rm; CKE. *"Pitches poss unsuitable lge o'fits; gd location; excel for families."* **€52.00, 22 May-19 Sep. 2024**

CASTRO URDIALES *1A4* (1km N Coastal) *43.39000, -3.24194* **Camping de Castro,** Barrio Campijo, 39700 Castro Urdiales (Cantabria) **676 40 57 45; info@campingdecastro.com; www.campingdecastro.es**

sand 1km

Fr Bilbao turn off A8 at 2nd Castro Urdiales sp, km 151. Camp sp on R by bullring. V narr, steep lanes to site - no passing places, great care req. 2*, Lge, unshd, pt sl, terr, EHU (6A) €3; 90% statics; phone; bus; Eng spkn; adv bkg acc; CKE. *"Gd, clean facs; conv NH for ferries; ltd touring pitches; narr, long, steep single track ent; great views over Bilbao bay."* **€27.00, 13 Feb-10 Dec. 2024**

SPAIN

CERVERA DE PISUERGA *1B4* (0.5km W Rural) *42.87135, -4.50332* **Camping Fuentes Carrionas,** La Bárcena s/n, 34840 Cervera de Pisuerga (Palencia) **979-87 04 24; campingfuentescarrionas@hotmail.com; campingfuentescarrionas.com**

nr nr

Fr Aguilar de Campóo on CL626 pass thro Cervera foll sp CL627 Potes. Site sp on L bef rv bdge. Med, mkd, pt shd, EHU €3.50; 80% statics; bus 100m; games area; tennis; CKE. *"Gd walking in nature reserve; conv Casa del Osos bear info cent; rest/bar area busy at wkend; new gd clean san facs; site busy with wkenders in statics or cabins; owners v helpful and pleasant; well maintained."* **€21.00, Holy Week-30 Sep.** **2023**

CIUDAD RODRIGO *1D3* (1.5km S Rural) *40.59206, -6.53445* **Camping La Pesquera,** Ctra Cáceres-Arrabal, Km 424, Huerta La Toma, 37500 Ciudad Rodrigo (Salamanca) **923-48 13 48; campinglapesquera@hotmail.com; www.campinglapesquera.es**

12

Fr Salamanca on A62/E80 exit junc 332. Look for tent sp on R & turn R, then 1st L & foll round until site on rvside. 2*, Med, mkd, pt shd, EHU (6A) inc; sw nr; TV; phone; ccard acc; fishing adj; CKE. *"Medieval walled city worth visit - easy walk over Roman bdge; gd san facs; vg, improved site; friendly nice sm site next to rv, gd for NH; lovely town; v helpful staff."* **€13.50** **2023**

COLOMBRES *1A4* (3km SW Rural) *43.37074, -4.56799* **Camping Colombres,** Ctra El Peral A Noriega Kml - 33590 Colombres (Ribadedeva) **985 412 244; campingcolombres@hotmail.com; www.campingcolombres.com**

12 (htd) sand 3km

Turn off A8/E70 at J277. 3rd exit then 2nd exit fr rndabts. East on N634 then R opp petrol stn. Site to L 1km. Med, mkd, pt shd, terr, EHU (6A) €4.20; bbq (sep area); twin axles; 10% statics; Eng spkn; ccard acc; games area; CKE. *"Quiet, peaceful site in rural setting with fine mountain views; v helpful owners; nice pool; excel san facs; well kept & clean; immac, modern san facs; dogs free; gd walking."* **€43.60** **2023**

COMILLAS *1A4* (1km E Coastal) *43.38583, -4.28444* **Camping de Comillas,** 39520 Comillas (Cantabria) **942-72 00 74; info@campingcomillas.com; campingcomillas.com**

nr sand 800m

Site on coast rd CA131 at E end of Comillas by-pass. App fr Santillana or San Vicente avoids town cent & narr rds. Lge, hdg, mkd, pt shd, pt sl, EHU (5A) €3.85; TV; phone; adv bkg acc; CKE. *"Clean, ltd facs LS (hot water to shwrs only); vg site in gd position on coast with views; easy walk to interesting town; gd but rocky beach across rd; helpful owner; pitches inbetween 2 rds."* **€33.00, Holy Week & 1 Jun-30 Sep.** **2023**

COMILLAS *1A4* (5km E Rural) *43.38328, -4.24689* **Camping El Helguero,** 39527 Ruiloba (Cantabria) **942-72 21 24; reservas@campingelhelguero.com; www.campingelhelguero.com**

(htd) sand 3km

Exit A8 junc 249 dir Comillas onto CA135 to km 7. Turn dir Ruiloba onto CA359 & thro Ruiloba & La Iglesia, fork R uphill. Site sp. Lge, mkd, pt shd, pt sl, EHU (6A) €4.35; 80% statics; Eng spkn; ccard acc; tennis 300m; bike hire; CKE. *"Attractive site, gd touring cent; clean facs but some in need of refurb; helpful staff; night security; sm pitches poss muddy in wet; v gd."* **€30.00, 1 Apr-30 Sep.** **2022**

COMILLAS *1A4* (3km W Rural/Coastal) *43.3858, -4.3361* **Camping Rodero,** Ctra Comillas-St Vicente, Km 5, 39528 Oyambre (Cantabria) **942-72 20 40; campingrodero@gmail.com; www.campingrodero.com**

sand 200m

Exit A8 dir San Vicente de la Barquera, cross bdge over estuary & take R fork nr km27.5. Site just off C131 bet San Vicente & Comillas, sp. Lge, mkd, pt shd, pt sl, terr, EHU (6A) €3; gas; 10% statics; phone; bus 200m; adv bkg acc; ccard acc; games area; CKE. *"Lovely views; on top of hill; friendly owners; site noisy but happy - owner puts Dutch/British in quieter pt; sm pitches; poss run down LS."* **€29.00, 15 Mar-30 Sep.** **2024**

CONIL DE LA FRONTERA *2H3* (3km NE Rural) *36.31061, -6.11276* **Camping Roche,** Carril de Pilahito s/n, N340 Km 19.2, 11149 Conil de la Frontera (Cádiz) **+34 956 442 216; info@campingroche.com; www.campingroche.com**

12 €3.75 sand 2.5km

Exit A48 junc 15 Conil Norte. Site sp on N340 dir Algeciras. Lge, hdstg, mkd, pt shd, EHU (10A) €5; red long stay; TV; 20% statics; Eng spkn; adv bkg acc; ccard acc; games area; games rm; tennis. *"V pleasant, peaceful site in pine woods; all-weather pitches; friendly, helpful staff; special monthly rates; clean san facs; superb beaches nr; excel facs; lack of adequate management."* **€30.00, W02.** **2022**

CONIL DE LA FRONTERA *2H3* (1.3km NW Rural/Coastal) *36.29340, -6.09626* **Camping La Rosaleda,** Ctra del Pradillo, Km 1.3, 11140 Conil de la Frontera (Cádiz) **956-44 33 27; info@campinglarosaleda.com; www.campinglarosaleda.com**

12 (except 15 Jun-15 Sep, otherwise in sep area €5) sand 1.3km

Exit A48 junc 26 dir Conil. In 2km at rndabt foll sp Puerto Pesquero along CA3208. Site sp on R. 4*, Lge, hdstg, mkd, pt shd, pt sl, terr, EHU (5-10A) inc; gas; sw; red long stay; 10% statics; phone; Eng spkn; adv bkg acc; car wash; CKE. *"Well-run site; friendly, helpful staff; gd social atmosphere; sm pitches not suitable lge o'fits but double-length pitches avail; poss travellers; pitches soft/muddy when wet; lge rally on site in winter; gd walking & cycling; sea views; historical, interesting area; conv Seville, Cádiz, Jerez, day trips Morocco; If low occupancy, facs maybe clsd and excursions cancelled."* **€38.00** 2022

CORDOBA *2F3* (8km N Rural) *37.96138, -4.81361* **Camping Los Villares,** Ctra Los Villares, Km 7.5, 14071 Córdoba (Córdoba) **857 89 09 02 or 621 24 54 82; reservas@campinglosvillares.es; www.campinglosvillares.es**

12

Best app fr N on N432: turn W onto CP45 1km N of Cerro Muriano at km 254. Site on R after approx 7km shortly after golf club. Last 5-6km of app rd v narr & steep, but well-engineered. Badly sp, easy to miss. Or fr city cent foll sp for Parador until past municipal site on R. Shortly after, turn L onto CP45 & foll sp Parque Forestal Los Villares, then as above. Sm, hdstg, shd, sl, EHU (15A) €4.30 (poss rev pol); gas; red long stay; 10% statics; bus 1km; CKE. *"In nature reserve; peaceful; cooler than Córdoba city with beautiful walks, views & wildlife; sm, close pitches; basic facs (v ltd & poss unclean LS); mainly sl site in trees; strictly run; suitable as NH; take care electrics; poss no drinking water/hot water."* **€17.70** 2024

CORTEGANA *2 F2* (1.2km NW Rural) *37.91348, -6.82820* **Camping Ribera Del Chanza,** Avenida de las Norias, 21230 Cortegana **959-50 79 65 or 601 22 24 34 (mob); info@campingdecortegana.es; http://www.corteganacamping.com/**

12 €1.50 nr nr

Fr N435 dir Portugal at top of hill 2nd L sp Camping. After 200m cross rndabt into Av de las Norias. Site at end of road in 500m. Sm, mkd, pt shd, pt sl, EHU €5; bbq (sep area); TV; 500m; Eng spkn; adv bkg acc; ccard acc. *"Site in easy walking distance to Cortegana; town has gd supermkts and shops; restored medieval castle; walking/mountain biking trails in surrounding hills; site closed Christmas week; excel."* **€15.50** 2024

CORUNA, LA *1A2* (11km E Rural) *43.348194, -8.335745* **Camping Los Manzanos,** Olieros, 15179 Santa Cruz (La Coruña) **981-61 48 25; informacion@campinglosmanzanos.com; campinglosmanzanos.com**

App La Coruña fr E on NVI, bef bdge take AC173 sp Santa Cruz. Turn R at 2nd traff lts in Santa Cruz cent (by petrol stn), foll sp, site on L. Fr AP9/E1 exit junc 3, turn R onto NVI dir Lugo. Take L fork dir Santa Cruz/La Coruña, then foll sp Meiras. Site sp. 3*, Lge, pt shd, EHU (6A) €4.80; gas; TV; 10% statics; phone; Eng spkn; adv bkg req; ccard acc; CKE. *"Lovely site; steep slope into site, level exit is avail; helpful owners; hilly 1km walk to Santa Cruz for bus to La Coruña; gd rest; conv for Santiago de Compostela; excel."*
€27.50, 22 Mar-30 Sep. 2023

COTORIOS *4F1* (2km E Rural) *38.05255, -2.83996* **Camping Llanos de Arance,** Ctra Sierra de Cazorla/Beas de Segura, Km 22, 23478 Cotoríos (Jaén) **953-71 31 39; arancell@inicia.es; www.llanosdearance.com**

12 nr

Fr Jaén-Albecete rd N322 turn E onto A1305 N of Villanueva del Arzobispo sp El Tranco. In 26km to El Tranco lake, turn R & cross over embankment. Cotoríos at km stone 53, approx 25km on shore of lake & Río Guadalaquivir. App fr Cazorla or Beas definitely not rec if towing. Lge, shd, EHU (5A) €3.21; gas; bbq; 2% statics; phone; ccard acc; CKE. *"Lovely site; excel walks & bird life, boar & wild life in Cazorla National Park."* **€18.50** 2024

COVARRUBIAS *1B4* (0.5km E Rural) *42.05944, -3.51527* **Camping Covarrubias,** Ctra Hortigüela, 09346 Covarrubias (Burgos) **616-93 05 00; proatur@proatur.com; www.proatur.com**

12 nr

Take N1/E5 or N234 S fr Burgos, turn onto BU905 after approx 35km. Site sp on BU905. 3*, Lge, mkd, pt shd, pt sl, EHU (12A) €3.90; gas; 90% statics; phone. *"Ltd facs LS; pitches poss muddy after rain; charming vill; poss vultures; phone to confirm if open."*
€18.50 2024

CREIXELL *3C3* (3km SW Coastal) *41.14851, 1.41821* **Camping La Noria,** Passeig Miramar 278, 43830 Torredembarra **977-64 04 53; info@camping-lanoria.com; www.camping-lanoria.com**

adj

Just outside Torredembara, going N on the old coastal N340 rd. Lge, hdstg, hdg, mkd, pt shd, EHU (6A) €5; bbq; twin axles; red long stay; TV; 60% statics; bus adj; Eng spkn; adv bkg rec; games area; games rm. *"Adj to Els Muntanyans Nature reserve, with walks & birdwatching; rail 1.6km; beach has naturist area; some noise fr train line bet beach & site; vg; conv for town; sep beach area for naturist."* **€43.50, 1 Apr-1 Oct.**
2023

SPAIN

CREVILLENT *4F2* (8km S Rural) *38.17770, -0.80876* **Alannia Costa Blanca (formerly Marjal Costa Blanca),** AP-7 Salida 730, 03330 Crevillent (Comunidad Valenciana) **965-48 49 45; www.alanniaresorts.com/**

12 €2.20 (htd)

Fr A7/E15 merge onto AP7 (sp Murcia), take exit 730; site sp fr exit. 4*, V lge, hdstg, mkd, hdg, pt shd, serviced pitches; EHU (16A) inc; gas; bbq; sw; twin axles; TV; 30% statics; phone; Eng spkn; adv bkg acc; ccard acc; tennis; bike hire; games area; games rm; CCI. *"Superb site; car wash; hairdresser; doctor's surgery; gd security; excel facs; wellness cent with fitness studio, htd pools, saunas, physiotherapy & spa; tour ops; new site, trees and hedges need time to grow; lge pitches extra charge; excel, immac san facs; nr to Elfondo birdwatching; v helpful staff."* **€47.50, W05.** **2022**

See advertisement opposite

CUBILLAS DE SANTA MARTA *1C4* (4km S Rural) *41.80511, -4.58776* **Camping Cubillas,** Ctra N620, Km 102, 47290 Cubillas de Santa Marta (Valladolid) **983-58 50 02 or 983-58 51 74; info@campingcubillas.com; www.campingcubillas.com**

12 €2 nr

A-62 Exit 102 Cubillas de Santa Marta. Fr N foll slip rd and cross rd to Cubillas de Santa Marta the site is on the R in 200m. Fr S take exit 102 take 5th exit off rndabt, cross over m'way and then 1st L. Site on R in 200m. Lge, hdg, mkd, unshd, pt sl, EHU (6-10A) inc; gas; bbq; red long stay; 50% statics; phone; ccard acc; site clsd 18 Dec-10 Jan; CKE. *"Ltd space for tourers; conv visit Palencia & Valladolid; rd & m'way, rlwy & disco noise at w/end until v late; v ltd facs LS; NH only; 2.5h fr Santander; adequate o'night stop."* **€26.00** **2024**

CUDILLERO *1A3* (2.7km SE Rural) *43.55416, -6.12944* **wecamp Cudillero,** Ctra Playa de Aguilar, Aronces, 33150 El Pito (Asturias) **900-05 60 03; hola@cudillero.wecamp.net; www.wecamp.net**

€6-7 (htd) sand 1.2km

Exit N632 (E70) sp El Pito. Turn L at rndabt sp Cudillero & in 300m at end of wall turn R at site sp, cont for 1km, site on L. Do not app thro Cudillero; rds v narr & steep; much traff. Med, mkd, hdg, pt shd, EHU (6A) €4.50; gas; TV; phone; bus 1km; adv bkg acc; games area; CKE. *"Excel, well-maintained, well laid-out site; some generous pitches; gd san facs; steep walk to beach & vill; v helpful staff; excel facs; vill worth a visit, parking on quay but narr rds; diff to get to vill, very steep; sm crowded pitches."* **€23.00, Apr-Sep.** **2024**

"I like to fill in the reports as I travel from site to site"

You'll find report forms at the back of this guide, or you can fill them in online at camc.com/europereport.

CUDILLERO *1A3* (2km S Rural) *43.55555, -6.13777* **Camping L'Amuravela,** El Pito, 33150 Cudillero (Asturias) **985-59 09 95; camping@lamuravela.com; www.lamuravela.com**

€1 sand 2km

Exit N632 (E70) sp El Pito. Turn L at rndabt sp Cudillero & in approx 1km turn R at site sp. Do not app thro Cudillero; rds v narr & steep; much traff. Med, mkd, unshd, pt sl, EHU €4.10; gas; 50% statics; ccard acc. *"Pleasant, well-maintained site; gd clean facs; hillside walks into Cudillero, attractive fishing vill with gd fish rests; red facs LS & poss only open w/ends, surroundings excel."* **€26.00, Holy Week & 1 Jun-30 Sep.** **2023**

CUENCA *3D1* (8km N Rural) *40.12694, -2.14194* **Camping Cuenca,** Ctra Tragacete, Km8, 16147 Cuenca **674 29 88 68; info@campingcuenca.com; www.campingcuenca.com**

€1

Fr Madrid take N400/A40 dir Cuenca & exit sp 'Ciudad Encantada' & Valdecabras on CM2110. In 7.5km turn R onto CM2105, site on R in 1.5km. Foll sp 'Nalimiento des Rio Jucar'. 3*, Lge, pt shd, pt sl, terr, EHU (6-10A) €4; gas; 15% statics; phone; Eng spkn; adv bkg acc; games area; tennis; jacuzzi; CKE. *"Pleasant, well-kept, green site; gd touring cent; friendly, helpful staff; excel san facs but ltd LS; interesting rock formations at Ciudad Encantada."*
€21.00, 19 Mar-11 Oct. **2024**

DEBA *3A1* (6km E Coastal) *43.29436, -2.32853* **Camping Itxaspe,** N634, Km 38, 20829 Itziar (Guipúzkoa) **943-19 93 77; itxaspe@hotmail.es; www.campingitxaspe.com**

nr nr shgl 4km

Exit A8 junc 13 dir Deba; at main rd turn L up hill, in 400m at x-rds turn L, site in 2km - narr, winding rd. NB Do not go into Itziar vill. Sm, mkd, pt shd, pt sl, EHU (5A) €4; gas; bbq; 10% statics; adv bkg acc; solarium; CKE. *"Excel site; helpful owner; w/ends busy; sea views; Coastal geology is UNESCO site, walking fr site superb."* **€58.00, 22 Mar-22 Sep.** **2024**

DEBA *3A1* (5.7km W Coastal) *43.30577, -2.37789* **Camping Aitzeta,** Ctra Deba-Guernica, Km. 3.5, C6212, 20930 Mutriku (Guipúzkoa) **943-60 33 56; aitzeta@hotmail.com; www.campingseuskadi.com/aitzeta**

nr sand 1km

On N634 San Sebastián-Bilbao rd thro Deba & on o'skts turn R over rv sp Mutriku. Site on L after 3km on narr & winding rd up sh steep climb. Med, mkd, pt shd, terr, EHU (4A) €3; gas; phone; bus 500m; CKE. *"Easy reach of Bilbao ferry; sea views; gd, well-run, clean site; not suitable lge o'fits; ltd pitches for tourers; helpful staff; walk to town; basic facs but gd NH."*
€20.00, 1 May-31 Oct. **2022**

DELTEBRE *3D2* (8km E Coastal) *40.72041, 0.84849* **Camping L'Aube,** Afores s/n, 43580 Deltebre (Tarragona) **977-26 70 66; campinglaube@hotmail.com; www.campinglaube.com**

sand adj

Exit AP7 junc 40 or 41 onto N340 dir Deltebre. Fr Deltebre foll T340 sp Riumar for 8km. At info kiosk branch R, site sp 1km on R. 2*, Lge, mkd, hdstg, pt shd, EHU (3-10A) €2.80-5; red long stay; 40% statics; phone; CKE. *"At edge of Ebro Delta National Park; excel birdwatching; ltd facs in winter; sm pitches; pricey; interesting local rest."*
€50.20, 1 Mar-31 Oct. **2023**

SPAIN

DENIA *4E2* (3.5km SE Coastal) *38.82968, 0.14767* **Camping Los Pinos,** Ctra Dénia-Les Rotes, Km 3, Les Rotes, 03700 Dénia (Alicante) **965-78 26 98; lospinosdenia@gmail.com; www.lospinosdenia.com**

12 €3 nr shgl adj

Fr N332 foll sp to Dénia in dir of coast. Turn R sp Les Rotes/Jávea, then L twrds Les Rotes. Foll site sp turn L into narr access rd poss diff lge o'fits. 2*, Med, mkd, pt shd, EHU (6-10A) €3.20; gas; bbq; cooking facs; red long stay; TV; 25% statics; phone; bus 100m; Eng spkn; adv bkg acc; ccard acc; CKE. *"Friendly, well-run, clean, tidy site but san facs tired (Mar 09); excel value; access some pitches poss diff due trees - not suitable lge o'fits or m'vans; many long-stay winter residents; cycle path into Dénia; social rm with log fire; naturist beach 1km, private but rocky shore."* **€26.40** **2024**

DOS HERMANAS *2G3* (3km SW Urban) *37.27731, -5.93722* **Camping Villsom,** Ctra Sevilla/Cádiz A4, Km 554.8, 41700 Dos Hermanas (Sevilla) **954-72 08 28; campingvillsom@hotmail.com; campingvillsom.com**

On main Seville-Cádiz NIV rd travelling fr Seville take exit at km. 555 sp Dos Hermanos-Isla Menor. At the rndabt turn R (SE-3205 Isla Menor) to site 80 m. on R. 3*, Lge, hdg, mkd, hdstg, pt shd, pt sl, EHU (8A) inc (poss no earth); gas; bus to Seville 300m (over bdge & rndabt); Eng spkn; adv bkg acc; ccard acc; CKE. *"Adv bkg rec Holy Week; helpful staff; clean, tidy, well-run site; vg, san facs, ltd LS; height barrier at Carrefour hypmkt - ent via deliveries; no twin axles; wifi only in office & bar area; pitches long but narr, no rm for awnings; dusty, rough, tight turns; c'vans parked too cls."* **€24.00, 10 Jan-23 Dec.** **2023**

EL BARRACO *1D4* (6.6km SW Rural) *40.428630, -4.616408* **Camping Pantano del Burguillo,** AV-902 Km 16 400, El Barraco **678-48 20 69; info@pantanodelburguillo.com; www.pantanodelburguillo.com**

€2

31km S of Avila on N403, take AV902 W for 5km. Site on L beside reservoir. Sm, mkd, hdstg, pt shd, EHU inc; bbq (sep area); ccard acc. *"Mainly residential c'vans, but staff very welcoming; a bit scruffy; open hg ssn & w'ends only; fair."* **€30.00, 22 Jun-10 Sep.** **2023**

ELCHE *4F2* (10km SW Urban) *38.24055, -0.81194* **Camping Las Palmeras,** Partida Deula 75, 03330 Crevillent (Alicante) **660 06 19 82 or 965 40 01 88 or 966 68 06 30; laspalmeras@laspalmeras-sl.com; www.laspalmerasresort.com**

12 nr

Exit A7 junc 726/77 onto N340 to Crevillent. Immed bef traff lts take slip rd into rest parking/service area. Site on R, access rd down side of rest. Med, hdstg, mkd, pt shd, EHU (6A) inc; 10% statics; ccard acc; CKE. *"Useful NH; report to recep in hotel; helpful staff; gd cent for touring Murcia; dogs free; gd rest in hotel; gd, modern san facs; excel."* **€28.00** **2024**

ESCALA, L' *3B3* (0.5km S Urban/Coastal) *42.1211, 3.1346* **Camping L'Escala,** Camí Ample 21, 17130 L'Escala (Gerona) **972-77 00 84; info@campinglescala.com; www.campinglescala.com**

nr 300m

Exit AP7 junc 5 onto GI623 dir L'Escala; at o'skts of L'Escala, at 1st rndabt (with yellow sp GI623 on top of rd dir sp) turn L dir L'Escala & Ruïnes Empúries; at 2nd rndabt go str on dir L'Escala-Riells, then foll site sp. Do not app thro town. Med, mkd, hdg, pt shd, serviced pitches; EHU (6A) inc; gas; bbq; TV; 20% statics; phone; Eng spkn; adv bkg acc; car wash; CKE. *"Access to sm pitches poss diff lge o'fits; helpful, friendly staff; vg, modern san facs; Empúrias ruins 5km; vg."* **€44.50, 12 Apr-21 Sep.** **2024**

ESCALA, L' *3B3* (2km S Coastal) *42.11027, 3.16555* **Camping Illa Mateua,** Avda Montgó 260, 17130 L'Escala (Gerona) **972-77 02 00 or 972-77 17 95; info@campingillamateua.com; www.campingillamateua.com**

€3.60 sand adj

On N11 thro Figueras, approx 3km on L sp C31 L'Escala; in town foll sp for Montgó & Paradis. Lge, pt shd, terr, EHU (5A) inc; gas; red long stay; 5% statics; Eng spkn; adv bkg req; watersports; games area; tennis; CKE. *"V well-run site; spacious pitches; excel san facs; gd beach; no depth marking in pool; excel rest."* **€58.40, 11 Mar-20 Oct.** **2024**

ESCALA, L' *3B3* (3km S Coastal) *42.10512, 3.15843* **wecamp Cala Montgó,** 17130 L'Escala (Gerona) **900-05 60 03; hola@calamontgo.wecamp.net; www.wecamp.net**

€6-7 sand 850m

Exit AP7 junc 5 twd L'Escala then turn R twd Cala Montgó & foll sp. Med, mkd, shd, pt sl, terr, EHU (6A) €4; gas; red long stay; TV; 15% statics; phone; bus 500m; Eng spkn; adv bkg acc; ccard acc; fishing; tennis; car wash; CKE. *"Pleasant, clean site in pine forest; gd san facs; lge pitches; vg; rest and pool clsd Sept."* **€28.00, 10 Apr-13 Oct.** **2024**

ESCORIAL, EL *1D4* (6km NE Rural) *40.62630, -4.09970* **Camping-Caravaning El Escorial,** Ctra Guadarrama a El Escorial, Km 3.5, 28280 El Escorial (Madrid) **918 90 24 12 or 02 01 49 00; info@camping elescorial.com; www.campingelescorial.com**

12 (htd)

Exit AP6 NW of Madrid junc 47 El Escorial/ Guadarrama, onto M505 & foll sp to El Escorial, site on L at km stone 3,500 - long o'fits rec cont to rndabt (1km) to turn & app site on R. V lge, mkd, hdstg, pt shd, EHU (5A) inc (long cable rec); gas; bbq; TV; 80% statics; Eng spkn; adv bkg acc; ccard acc; tennis; games rm; horseriding 7km. *"Excel, busy site; mountain views; o'fits over 8m must reserve lge pitch with elec, water & drainage; helpful staff; clean facs; gd security; sm pitches poss diff due trees; o'head canopies poss diff for tall o'fits; facs ltd LS; trains & buses to Madrid nr; Valle de Los Caídos & Palace at El Escorial well worth visit; cash machine; easy parking in town for m'vans if go in early; mkt Wed; stunning scenery, nesting storks; well stocked shop; v well run; 20min walk to bus stop for El Escorial or Madrid; rec; gd for families; gd pool."* **€37.50** **2023**

ESTARTIT, L' *3B3* (1km S Coastal) *42.04972, 3.18416* **Camping El Molino,** Camino del Ter, 17258 L'Estartit (Gerona) **972-75 06 29**

sand 1km

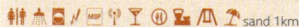

Fr N11 junc 5, take rd to L'Escala. Foll sp to Torroella de Montgri, then L'Estartit. Ent town & foll sp, site on rd GI 641. V lge, hdg, pt shd, pt sl, EHU (6A) €3.60; gas; bus 1km; adv bkg rec; games rm. *"Site in 2 parts - 1 in shd, 1 at beach unshd; gd facs; quiet location outside busy town."* **€28.00, 1 Apr-30 Sep.** **2022**

See advertisement

ESTARTIT, L' *3B3* (2km S Coastal) *42.04250, 3.18333* **Camping Les Medes,** Paratge Camp de l'Arbre s/n, 17258 L'Estartit (Gerona) **972-75 18 05; info@camping lesmedes.com; www.campinglesmedes.com**

12 €2.60 (htd) (htd, indoor) sand 800m

Fr Torroella foll sp to L'Estartit. In vill turn R at town name sp (sp Urb Estartit Oeste), foll rd for 1.5km, turn R, site well sp. Lge, mkd, shd, serviced pitches; EHU (6A) €4.60; gas; red long stay; TV; 7% statics; phone; Eng spkn; adv bkg acc; sauna; games area; tennis; horseriding 400m; car wash; games rm; watersports; solarium; bike hire; CKE. *"Excel, popular, family-run & well organised site; helpful, friendly staff; gd clean facs & constant hot water; gd for children; no dogs high ssn; no twin axle vans high ssn - by arrangement LS; conv National Park; well mkd foot & cycle paths; ACSI acc."* **€45.60** **2023**

ESTEPAR *1B4* (2km NE Rural) *42.29233, -3.85097* **Quinta de cavia,** A62, km 17, 09196 Cavia, Burgos **947-41 20 78; reservas@quintadecavia.es**

12

Site 15km SW of Burgos on N side of A62/E80, adj Hotel Rio Cabia. Ent via Campsa petrol stn, W'bound exit 17, E'bound exit 16, cross over & re-join m'way. Ignore camp sp at exit 18 (1-way). Site at 17km stone. 2*, Med, pt shd, EHU (6A) inc; 10% statics; ccard acc; CKE. *"Friendly, helpful owner; gd rest; conv for m'way for Portugal but poorly sp fr W; poss v muddy in winter; NH only; food in rest vg and cheap; can get to Bilbao ferry in morn if ferry is mid aft; elec security gate; lit at night; gd NH; new san facs (2018); site 2723 feet abv sea level, cold at night; gem of a site; site being improved (2019)."* **€20.00** **2024**

ESTEPONA *2H3* (7km E Coastal) *36.45436, -5.08105* **Camping Parque Tropical,** Ctra N340, Km 162, 29680 Estepona (Málaga) **952-79 36 18; parquetropicalcamping@hotmail.com; www.campingparquetropical.com**

€2 (covrd, htd) shgl 1km

On N side of N340 at km 162, 200m off main rd. 2*, Med, mkd, hdg, pt shd, terr, serviced pitches; EHU (10A) €4; gas; red long stay; 10% statics; phone; bus 400m; Eng spkn; adv bkg acc; golf nr; horseriding nr; CKE. *"Tropical plants thro out; clean facs; tropical paradise swimming pool; wildlife park 1km; helpful owners."* **€34.80** **2023**

ETXARRI ARANATZ *3B1* (2km N Rural) *42.91255, 2.07919* **Camping Etxarri,** Parase Dambolintxulo, 31820 Etxarri-Aranatz (Navarra) **948-46 05 37; info@campingetxarri.com; www.campingetxarri.com**

€2.15

Fr N exit A15 at junc 112 to join A10 W dir Vitoria/Gasteiz. Exit at junc 19 onto NA120; go thro Etxarri vill, turn L & cross bdge, then take rd over rlwy. Turn L, site sp. Med, hdg, pt shd, EHU (6A); gas; bbq; 95% statics; phone; Eng spkn; ccard acc; games area; archery; cycling; horseriding; CKE. *"Gd, wooded site; gd walks; interesting area; helpful owner; conv NH to/fr Pyrenees; youth hostel & resident workers on site; san facs gd; various pitch sizes & shapes, suitable for sm-med MH; NH only."* **€41.80, 1 Mar-1 Nov.** **2022**

FIGUERES *3B3* (12km N Rural) *42.37305, 2.91305* **Camping Les Pedres,** Calle Vendador s/n, 17750 Capmany (Gerona) **972-54 91 92 or 686-01 12 23 (mob); info@campinglespedres.net; www.campingalbera.com/nl/index.htm**

(htd) nr

S fr French border on N11, turn L sp Capmany, L again in 2km at site sp & foll site sp. Med, mkd, pt shd, pt sl, EHU (6-10A) €4.50; 20% statics; phone; Eng spkn; adv bkg acc; ccard acc; CKE. *"Helpful Dutch owner; lovely views; gd touring & walking cent; gd winter NH."* **€39.40** **2024**

FIGUERES *3B3* (8km NE Rural) *42.33902, 3.06758* **Camping Vell Empordà,** Ctra Roses-La Jonquera s/n, 17780 Garriguella (Gerona) **972-53 02 00 or 972-57 06 31 (LS); vellemporda@vellemporda.com; www.vellemporda.com**

€4.50 (htd)

On A7/E11 exit junc 3 onto N260 NE dir Llançà. Nr km 26 marker, turn R sp Garriguella, then L at T-junc N twd Garriguella. Site on R shortly bef vill. Lge, hdstg, mkd, hdg, shd, terr, EHU (6-10A) inc; gas; bbq; red long stay; TV; 20% statics; phone; Eng spkn; adv bkg acc; ccard acc; games rm; games area; CKE. *"Conv N Costa Brava away fr cr beaches & sites; 20 mins to sea at Llançà; o'hanging trees poss diff high vehicles; excel."* **€48.00, 1 Feb-15 Dec.** **2023**

FOZ *1A2* (11km E Coastal) *43.56236, -7.20761* **A Gaivota Camping (formerly Poblado Gaivota),** Playa de Barreiros, 27790 Barreiros Lugo **982-12 44 51; www.agaivotacamping.com**

opp

Junc 516 on A8, on to N634 to Barreiros. Foll sp to the R in Barreiros. Rd winds down to coast for 2km. Site on L, parallel with sea. Sm, hdg, shd, EHU (6A); bbq; Eng spkn. *"Excel."* **€30.00, 21 Mar-15 Oct.** **2022**

FRANCA, LA *1A4* (1km NW Coastal) *43.39250, -4.57722* **Camping Las Hortensias,** Ctra N634, Km 286, 33590 Colombres/Ribadedeva (Asturias) **985-41 24 42; lashortensias@campinglashortensias.com; www.campinglashortensias.com**

€5 nr nr sand adj

Fr N634 on leaving vill of La Franca, at km286 foll sp 'Playa de la Franca' & cont past 1st site & thro car park to end of rd. Med, mkd, pt shd, pt sl, terr, EHU (6-10A) €5; gas; phone; bus 800m; Eng spkn; adv bkg acc; ccard acc; bike hire; tennis; CKE. *"Beautiful location nr scenic beach; sea views fr top terr pitches; vg."* **€28.50, 5 Jun-30 Sep.** **2023**

FRESNEDA, LA *3C2* (2.5km SW Rural) *40.90705, 0.06166* **Camping La Fresneda,** Partida Vall del Pi, 44596 La Fresneda (Teruel) **978-85 40 85; info@campinglafresneda.com; www.campinglafresneda.com**

Fr Alcañiz S on N232 dir Morella; in 15km turn L onto A231 thro Valjunquera to La Fresneda; cont thro vill; in 2.5km turn R onto site rd. Site sp fr vill. 2*, Sm, hdg, mkd, pt shd, terr, EHU (6A) inc; gas; red long stay; phone; Eng spkn; ccard acc; CKE. *"Narr site rds, poss diff lge o'fits; various pitch sizes; gd; adv bkg adv; v helpful owners."* **€34.00, 24 Mar-1 Oct.** **2024**

FUENTE DE PIEDRA *2G4* (0.7km S Rural) *37.12905, -4.73315* **Camping Fuente de Pedra,** Calle Campillos 88-90, 29520 Fuente de Piedra (Málaga) **952-73 52 94; info@campingfuentedepiedra.com; www.camping-rural.com**

€3

Turn off A92 at km 132 sp Fuente de Piedra. Sp fr vill cent. Or to avoid town turn N fr A384 just W of turn for Bobadilla Estación, sp Sierra de Yeguas. In 2km turn R into nature reserve, cont for approx 3km, site on L at end of town. 2*, Sm, mkd, hdstg, pt shd, pt sl, terr, EHU (10A) €5; gas; bbq; red long stay; 25% statics; phone; Eng spkn; ccard acc; CKE. *"Mostly sm, narr pitches, but some avail for o'fits up to 7m; gd rest; san facs dated & poss stretched; poss noise fr adj public pool; adj lge lake with flamingoes (visible but access is 4.8km away); gd."* **€16.00** **2023**

SPAIN

FUENTEHERIDOS 2F3 (0.6km SW Rural) 37.9050, -6.6742 **Camping El Madroñal,** Ctra Fuenteheridos-Castaño del Robledo, Km 0.6, 21292 Fuenteheridos (Huelva) **669 43 46 37; info@campingelmadronal.com; www.campingelmadronal.com**

12

Fr Zafra S on N435n turn L onto N433 sp Aracena, ignore first R to Fuenteheridos vill, camp sp R at next x-rd 500m on R. At rndabt take 2nd exit. Avoid Fuenteheridos vill - narr rds. 2*, Med, mkd, pt shd, pt sl, EHU €3.20; gas; bbq; 80% statics; phone; bus 1km; horseriding; car wash; bike hire; CKE. *"Tranquil site in National Park of Sierra de Aracena; pitches among chestnut trees - poss diff lge o'fits or m'vans & poss sl & uneven; o'hanging trees on site rds; scruffy, pitches not clearly mkd; beautiful vill 1km away, worth a visit."*
€13.00 **2024**

GALLARDOS, LOS 4G1 (4km N Rural) 37.18448, -1.92408 **Camping Los Gallardos,** 04280 Los Gallardos (Almería) **950-52 83 24; reception@campinglosgallardos.com; www.campinglosgallardos.com**

12 €2.25

Fr N leave A7/E15 at junc 525; foll sp to Los Gallardos; take 1st R after approx 800m pass under a'route; turn L into site ent. Med, mkd, hdstg, pt shd, serviced pitches; EHU (10A) €3; gas; red long stay; 40% statics; adv bkg acc; ccard acc; tennis adj; golf; CKE. *"British owned; 90% British clientele LS; gd social atmosphere; sep drinking water supply nr recep; prone to flooding wet weather; 2 grass bowling greens; facs tired; poss cr in winter; friendly staff."* **€21.00** **2023**

GANDIA 4E2 (4km NE Coastal) 38.98613, -0.16352 **Camping L'Alqueria,** Avda del Grau s/n; 46730 Grao de Gandía (València) **962-84 04 70; lalqueria@lalqueria.com; www.lalqueria.com**

12 €1.90 (htd) nr (covrd, htd) sand 1km

Fr N on A7/AP7 exit 60 onto N332 dir Grao de Gandía. Site sp on rd bet Gandía & seafront. Fr S exit junc 61 & foll sp to beaches. 3*, Lge, hdstg, mkd, pt shd, EHU (10A) €5.94; gas; red long stay; 30% statics; phone; bus; adv bkg acc; ccard acc; games area; jacuzzi; bike hire; CKE. *"Pleasant site; helpful, friendly family owners; lovely pool; easy walk to town & stn; excel beach nrby; bus & train to Valencia; shop & snacks not avail in Jul; gd biking; no dogs over 10kg; m'van friendly; site scruffy but san facs gd; gd location; rec; gd location bet old town & beach; gd cycling & walking."*
€42.00 **2024**

GARGANTILLA DEL LOZOYA 1C4 (2km SW Rural) 40.9503, -3.7294 **Camping Monte Holiday,** Ctra C604, Km 8.8, 28739 Gargantilla del Lozoya (Madrid) **918-69 52 78; monteholiday@monteholiday.com; www.monteholiday.com**

12 €2.80 - €3.20

Fr N on A1/E5 Burgos-Madrid rd turn R on M604 at km stone 69 sp Rascafría; in 8km turn R immed after rlwy bdge & then L up track in 300m, foll site sp. Do not ent vill. Lge, pt shd, pt sl, terr, EHU (7A) €4.30 (poss rev pol); 80% statics; phone; bus 500m; Eng spkn; adv bkg acc; ccard acc; CKE. *"Interesting, friendly site; vg san facs; gd views; easy to find; some facs clsd LS; lovely area but site isolated in winter & poss heavy snow; conv NH fr m'way & for Madrid & Segovia; excel wooded site; v rural but well worth the sh drive fr the N1 E5; clean; lovely surroundings."* **€35.40, E04.** **2022**

GAVA 3C3 (5km S Coastal) 41.27245, 2.04250 **Camping Tres Estrellas,** C31, Km 186.2, 08850 Gavà (Barcelona) **936-33 06 37; info@camping3estrellas.com; www.camping3estrellas.com**

€4.90 (htd) (htd) sand adj

Fr S take C31 (Castelldefels to Barcelona), exit 13. Site at km 186.2 300m past rd bdge. Fr N foll Barcelona airport sp, then C31 junc 13 Gavà-Mar slip rd immed under rd bdge. Cross m'way, turn R then R again to join m'way heading N for 400m. 3*, Lge, mkd, pt shd, pt sl, EHU (5A) €6.56 (poss rev pol &/or no earth); gas; bbq; TV; 20% statics; phone; bus 400m; Eng spkn; adv bkg acc; ccard acc; tennis; CKE. *"20 min by bus to Barcelona cent; poss smells fr stagnant stream in corner of site; poss mosquitoes."*
€52.50, 15 Mar-15 Oct. **2024**

GERONA 3B3 (8km S Rural) 41.9224, 2.82864 **Camping Can Toni Manescal,** Ctra de la Barceloneta, 17458 Fornells de la Selva (Gerona) **972-47 61 17; campinggirona@campinggirona.com; www.campinggirona.com**

nr nr

Fr N leave AP7 at junc 7 onto N11 dir Barcelona. In 2km turn L to Fornells de la Selva; in vill turn L at church (sp); over rv; in 1km bear R & site on L in 400m. NB Narr rd in Fornells vill not poss lge o'fits. 1*, Sm, mkd, pt shd, pt sl, EHU (5A) inc (poss long lead req); gas; train nr; Eng spkn; adv bkg acc; ccard acc; CKE. *"Pleasant, open site on farm; gd base for lovely medieval city Gerona - foll bus stn sp for gd, secure m'van parking; welcoming & helpful owners; lge pitches; ltd san facs; excel cycle path into Gerona, along old rlwy line; Gerona mid-May flower festival rec; gd touring base away fr cr coastal sites."*
€23.00, 1 Jun-30 Sep. **2024**

SPAIN

GIJON *1A3* (9.5km NW Coastal) *43.58343, -5.75713*
Camping Perlora, Ctra Candás, Km 12, Perán,
33491 Candás (Asturias) **985-87 00 48; recepcion@
campingperlora.com; www.campingperlora.com**

🐕 👫 🚿 wc ♿ ⚓ ☕ 💧 ⊘ ♨ ▽ 🍴 ⊕ 🛒 🏪 ⛲ 🏖 sand 1km

Exit A8 dir Candás; in 9km at rndabt turn R sp
Perlora (AS118). At sea turn L sp Candás, site on
R. Avoid Sat mkt day. 2*, Med, mkd, unshd, pt sl,
terr, serviced pitches; EHU (10A) €3.50; gas; red
long stay; 80% statics; phone; bus adj; Eng spkn;
ccard acc; watersports; fishing; tennis. *"Excel; helpful
staff; attractive, well-kept site on dramatic headland
o'looking Candas Bay; ltd space for tourers; easy
walk to Candás; gem of a site; train (5 mins); excel
fish rests; no mob signal; facs gd & clean, ltd LS; rec."*
€27.50, 18 Jan-10 Dec. 2024

GORLIZ *1A4* (1km N Coastal) *43.41782, -2.93626*
Camping Arrien, Uresarantze Bidea, 48630 Gorliz
(Bizkaia) **946-77 19 11; reception@campinggorliz.
com; www.campinggorliz.com**

🐕 €1 👫 wc ⚓ 💧 ⊘ ▽ 🍴 ⊕ 🛒 🏪 ⛲ 🏖 sand 700m

Fr Bilbao foll m'way to Getxo, then 637/634 thro
Sopelana & Plentzia to Gorliz. In Gorliz turn L at
1st rndabt, foll sps for site, pass TO on R, then R at
next rndabt, strt over next, site on L adj sports cent/
running track. Not sp locally. Lge, pt shd, pt sl, EHU
(6A) inc; gas; bbq; red long stay; 60% statics; phone;
bus 150m; Eng spkn; ccard acc; CKE. *"Useful base for
Bilbao & ferry (approx 1hr); bus to Plentzia every 20
mins, fr there can get metro to Bilbao; friendly, helpful
staff; poss shortage of hot water; very cramped; no
mkd pitches."* **€36.00, 1 Mar-31 Oct.** 2022

GRANADA *2G4* (4km N Urban) *37.19832, -3.61166*
Camping Motel Sierra Nevada, Avda de Madrid 107,
18014 Granada **958-15 00 62; campingmotel@
terra.es; www.campingsierranevada.com**

12 🐕 👫 wc ⚓ 💧 ♿ ⊘ ♨ MSP ▽ 🍴 ⊕ 🛒 🏪 ⛲ ✏ 🏊 (htd)

App Granada S-bound on A44 & exit at junc 123,
foll dir Granada. Site on R in 1.5km just beyond bus
stn & opp El Campo supmkt, well sp. 3*, Med, mkd,
hdg, pt shd, pt sl, serviced pitches; EHU (8A); cooking
facs; red long stay; bus to city cent 500m; Eng spkn;
adv bkg acc; ccard acc; sports facs; games rm; CKE. *"V
helpful staff; excel san facs, but poss ltd LS; 2 pools adj;
motel rms avail; can book Alhambra tickets at recep
(24 hrs notice); conv city; excel site."* **€40.00** 2024

GRANADA *2G4* (15.3km NE Rural) *37.22657, -3.49151*
Alto de Vinuelas, Ctra Beas de Granada s/n, Beas de
Granada 18184, Granada. **958-54 60 23 or
647-30 78 12; info@campingaltodevinuelas.com;
www.campingaltodevinuelas.com**

12 🐕 👫 ♿ ⊘ 💧 ▽ 🍴 ⊕ 🛒 🏊

Fr A92 take exit 256 twds Beas de Granada and
then foll signs to campsite 1.5km fr junc. 1*, Mkd,
EHU (10A) inc; gas; twin axles; TV; bus; ccard acc;
horseriding. *"Wonderful views of Sierra Nevada
fr campsite; biking; adventure sports; gd site for a
long peaceful stay or v conv for a NH; ACSI red."*
€28.00 2024

GRANADA *2G4* (13km E Rural) *37.16085, -3.45388*
Camping Las Lomas, 11 Ctra de Güejar-Sierra, Km 6,
18160 Güejar-Sierra (Granada) **0034 958 484 742;
info@campinglaslomas.com; www.campinglas
lomas.com**

12 🐕 €4 👫 (htd) wc ⚓ 💧 ♿ ⊘ ♨ MSP ▽ 🍴 ⊕ 🛒 🏪 ⛲
🏊 🏊

Fr A44 exit onto by-pass 'Ronda Sur', then exit onto
A395 sp Sierra Nevada. In approx 4km exit sp Cenes,
turn under A395 to T-junc & turn R sp Güejar-Sierra,
Embalse de Canales. After approx 3km turn L at
sp Güejar-Sierra & site. Site on R 6.5km up winding
mountain rd. 3*, Med, mkd, hdg, pt shd, terr, serviced
pitches; EHU (10A) €5 (poss no earth/rev pol); gas; red
long stay; bus adj; Eng spkn; adv bkg req; ccard acc;
sports area; kids entertainment; minigolf; playground;
hiking and cycling areas; CKE. *"Helpful, friendly
owners; well-run site; conv Granada (bus at gate);
waterskiing nr; access poss diff for lge o'fits; excel san
facs; gd shop & rest; beautiful mountain scenery; excel
site."* **€30.00** 2022

> # "I need an on-site restaurant"
>
> We do our best to make sure site information
> is correct, but it is always best to check any
> must-have facilities are still available or will
> be open during your visit.

GRANADA *2G4* (10km SE Urban) *37.12444, -3.58611*
Camping Reina Isabel, Calle de Laurel de la Reina,
18140 La Zubia (Granada) **958-59 00 41; info@
campingreinaisabel.com; www.campingreinaisabel.es**

12 🐕 👫 (htd) wc ⚓ 💧 ♿ ⊘ ♨ ▽ 🍴 ⊕ 🛒 🏪 🏊

Exit A44 nr Granada at junc sp Ronda Sur, dir Sierra
Nevada, Alhambra, then exit 2 sp La Zubia. Foll site
sp approx 1.2km on R; narr ent set back fr rd. 2*,
Med, hdg, hdstg, pt shd, EHU (6A) poss rev pol €4.20;
gas; red long stay; TV; phone; bus; Eng spkn; adv bkg
rec; ccard acc; CKE. *"Well-run, busy site; poss shwrs v
hot/cold - warn children; ltd touring pitches & sm; poss
student groups; conv Alhambra (order tickets at site);
shwr block not htd; tight site; elec unrel."* **€25.85**
2023

GUADALUPE *2E3* (1.5km S Rural) *39.44232, -5.31708*
Camping Las Villuercas, Ctra Villanueva-Huerta del
Río, Km 2, 10140 Guadalupe (Cáceres) **927-36 71 39
or 927-36 75 61; www.campinglasvilluercas
guadalupe.es**

👫 ⚓ 💧 ⊘ ▽ 🍴 ⊕ 🛒 ⛲ 🏊

Exit A5/E90 at junc 178 onto EX118 to Guadalupe.
Do not ent town. Site sp on R at rndabt at foot of
hill. 1*, Med, shd, EHU €2.50 (poss no earth/rev pol);
ccard acc; tennis. *"Vg; helpful owners; ltd facs LS; some
pitches sm & poss not avail in wet weather; nr famous
monastery."*
€14.50, 1 Mar-15 Dec. 2024

GUARDAMAR DEL SEGURA *4F2* (4km N Rural/Coastal) *38.10916, -0.65472* **Alannia Guardamar (formerly Camping Marjal),** Ctra N332, Km 73.4, 03140 Guardamar del Segura (Alicante) **965-48 49 45; reservas@alannia.com; alanniaresorts.com/es/resorts/alannia-guardamar**

12 €2.20 (covrd, htd) sand 1km

Fr N exit A7 junc 72 sp Aeropuerto/Santa Pola; in 5km turn R onto N332 sp Santa Pola/Cartagena, U-turn at km 73.4, site sp on R at km 73.5. Fr S exit AP7 at junc 740 onto CV91 twd Guardamar. In 9km join N332 twd Alicante, site on R at next rndabt. 5*, Lge, hdstg, mkd, hdg, pt shd, serviced pitches; EHU (16A) €3 or metered; gas; bbq; red long stay; TV; 50% statics; phone; Eng spkn; adv bkg rec; ccard acc; bike hire; tennis; sauna; CKE. *"Fantastic facs; friendly, helpful staff; excel family entmnt & activities; recep 0800-2300; sports cent; tropical waterpark; excel; well sign-posted; lge shwr cubicles; highly rec."* **€67.00** **2023**

GUARDIOLA DE BERGUEDA *3B3* (3.5km SW Rural) *42.21602, 1.83705* **Camping El Berguedà,** Ctra B400, Km 3.5, 08694 Guardiola de Berguedà (Barcelona) **938-22 74 32; info@campingbergueda.com; www.campingbergueda.com**

On C16 S take B400 W dir Saldes. Site is approx 10km S of Cadí Tunnel. Med, mkd, hdstg, pt shd, terr, EHU (6A) €3.90 (poss rev pol); gas; bbq; TV; 10% statics; phone; Eng spkn; games area; games rm; CKE. *"Helpful staff; vg clean san facs; beautiful, remote situation; gd walking; poss open w/ends in winter; highly rec; spectacular mountains/scenery; gd touring area; rec Gaudi's Garden in La Pobla."* **€39.00, 1 Apr-1 Nov.** **2024**

HARO *1B4* (0.6km N Urban) *42.57824, -2.85421* **Camping de Haro,** Avenida de Miranda 1, Haro, La Rioja, 26200 **941-31 27 37; campingdeharo@fer.es; www.campingdeharo.com**

€3.50 (htd) (htd)

Fr N or S on N124 take exit sp A68 Vitoria/Logrono & Haro. In 500m at rndabt take 1st exit, under rlwy bdge, cont to site on R immed bef rv bdge. Fr AP68 exit junc 9 to town; at 2nd rndabt turn L onto LR111 (sp Logroño). Immed after rv bdge turn sharp L & foll site sp. Avoid cont into town cent. 2*, Med, mkd, hdg, pt shd, EHU (6A) inc; gas; bbq; 70% statics; phone; bus 800m; Eng spkn; adv bkg acc; ccard acc; site clsd 9 Dec-13 Jan; car wash; CKE. *"Clean, tidy, well run, lovely site - peaceful LS; friendly owner; some sm pitches & diff turns; excel facs; statics busy at w/ends; conv Rioja 'bodegas' & Bilbao & Santander ferries; recep clsd 1300-1500 no entry then due to security barrier; excel & conv NH for Santander/Bilbao; lge o'night area with electric; big, busy, vg site; easy walk to lovely town; san facs constantly cleaned!"* **€32.40, 28 Jan-11 Dec, E02.** **2022**

HARO *1B4* (10km SW Rural) *42.53017, -2.92173* **Camping De La Rioja,** Ctra de Haro/Santo Domingo de la Calzada, Km 8.5, 26240 Castañares de la Rioja (La Rioja) **941-30 01 74; info@campingdelarioja.com**

(htd)

Exit AP68 junc 9, take rd twd Santo Domingo de la Calzada. Foll by-pass round Casalarreina, site on R nr rvside just past vill on rd LR111. 3*, Lge, hdg, pt shd, EHU (4A) €3.90 (poss rev pol); gas; 90% statics; bus adj; adv bkg acc; ccard acc; bike hire; tennis; clsd 10 Dec-8 Jan; site clsd 9 Dec-11 Jan. *"Fair site but fairly isolated; basic san facs but clean; ltd facs in winter; sm pitches; conv for Rioja wine cents; Bilbao ferry."* **€36.00, 10 Jan-10 Dec.** **2022**

"Satellite navigation makes touring much easier"

Remember most sat navs don't know if you're towing or in a larger vehicle – always use yours alongside maps and site directions.

HECHO *3B1* (1km S Rural) *42.73222, -0.75305* **Camping Valle de Hecho,** Ctra Puente La Reina-Hecho s/n, 22720 Hecho (Huesca) **974-37 53 61; campinghecho@campinghecho.com; www.campinghecho.com**

12 (htd)

Leave Jaca W on N240. After 25km turn N on A176 at Puente La Reina de Jaca. Site on W of rd, o'skts of Hecho/Echo. 1*, Med, mkd, pt shd, pt sl, EHU (5-15A) €4.20; gas; 40% statics; phone; bus 200m; ccard acc; games area; CKE. *"Pleasant site in foothills of Pyrenees; excel, clean facs but poss inadequate hot water; gd birdwatching area; Hecho fascinating vill; shop & bar poss clsd LS except w/end; v ltd facs LS; not suitable lge o'fits; gd rest in vill."* **€27.00** **2022**

HORCAJO DE LOS MONTES *2E4* (0.2km E Rural) *39.32360, -4.65003* **Camping Mirador de Cabañeros,** Calle Cañada Real Segoviana s/n, 13110 Horcajo de los Montes (Ciudad Real) **926 77 54 39; info@campingcabaneros.com; www.campingcabaneros.com**

€2 (htd) nr (indoor)

At km 53 off CM4103 Horcajo-Alcoba rd, 200m fr vill. CM4106 to Horcajo fr NW poor in parts. Med, hdstg, mkd, pt shd, terr, serviced pitches; EHU (6A); gas; bbq; red long stay; TV; 10% statics; phone; adv bkg rec; ccard acc; tennis 500m; games area; bike hire; games rm; laundry facilities; lounge; playground; free Wi-Fi zone; bio park area; CKE. *"Beside Cabañeros National Park; beautiful views; rd fr S much better; lovely site; clean san facs; covered pool; terraced gravel pitches; friendly staff; remote; walking; cycling; petrol stn no longer in Horcajos."* **€28.00, 14 Feb-9 Dec, E38.** **2023**

SPAIN

HORNOS *4F1* (9km SW Rural) *38.18666, -2.77277* **Camping Montillana Rural,** Ctra Tranco-Hornos A319, km 78.5, 23292 Hornos de Segura (Jaén) **680 15 87 78; jrescalvor@hotmail.com; www.clubrural.com/cabana/jaen/hornos/camping-montillana_134745**

Fr N on N322 take A310 then A317 S then A319 dir Tranco & Cazorla. Site nr km 78.5, ent by 1st turning. Fr S on N322 take A6202 N of Villaneuva del Arzobispo. In 26km at Tranco turn L onto A319 & nr km 78.5 ent by 1st turning up slight hill. Sm, hdstg, mkd, pt shd, terr, EHU (10A) €3.20; 5% statics; phone; Eng spkn; adv bkg acc; CKE. *"Beautiful area; conv Segura de la Sierra, Cazorla National Park; much wildlife; lake adj; friendly, helpful staff; gd site."*
€16.00, 19 Mar-30 Sep. **2024**

HOSPITAL DE ORBIGO *1B3* (1.3km N Urban) *42.4664, -5.8836* **Camp Municipal Don Suero,** 24286 Hospital de Órbigo (León) **987-36 10 18; camping@hospitaldeorbigo.com; www.hospitaldeorbigo.com**

nr

N120 rd fr León to Astorga, km 30. Site well sp fr N120. Narr rds in Hospital. Med, hdg, pt shd, EHU (6A) €1.90; bbq; 50% statics; phone; bus to León 1km; Eng spkn; ccard acc; poss open w/end only mid Apr-May; CKE. *"Statics v busy w/ends, facs stretched; pool adj; phone ahead to check site open if travelling close to opening/closing dates."*
€15.00, Easter-1 Oct. **2022**

> **"There aren't many sites open at this time of year"**
>
> If you're travelling outside peak season remember to call ahead to check site opening dates – even if the entry says 'open all year'.

HOSPITALET DE L'INFANT, L' *3C2* (2km S Coastal) *40.97722, 0.90083* **Camping El Templo del Sol (Naturist),** Polígon 14-15, Playa del Torn, 43890 L'Hospitalet de l'Infant (Tarragona) **977-82 34 34; info@eltemplodelsol.com; www.eltemplodelsol.com**

Leave A7 at exit 38 or N340 twds town cent. Turn R (S) along coast rd for 2km. Ignore 1st camp sp on L, site 200m further on L. Lge, hdg, mkd, pt shd, pt sl, serviced pitches; EHU (6A) inc; gas; red long stay; TV; 5% statics; Eng spkn; adv bkg req; ccard acc; INF card. *"Excel naturist site; no dogs, radios or TV on pitches; cinema/theatre; solar-energy park; jacuzzi; official naturist sand/shgl beach adj; lge private wash/shwr rms; pitches v tight - take care o'hanging branches; conv Port Aventura; mosquito problem; poss strong winds - take care with awnings."*
€43.00, 1 Apr-22 Oct. **2022**

HOYOS DEL ESPINO *1D3* (1.5km S Rural) *40.34055, -5.17527* **Camping Gredos,** Ctra Plataforma, Km.1.8, 05634 Hoyos del Espino (Ávila) **920-20 75 85; campingredos@campingredos.com; www.campingredos.com**

nr

Fr N110 turn E at El Barco onto AV941 for approx 41km; at Hoyos del Espino turn S twd Plataforma de Gredos. Site on R in 1.8km. Or fr N502 turn W onto AV941 dir Parador de Gredos to Hoyos del Espino, then as above. 2*, Sm, pt shd, pt sl, EHU €2.90; gas; sw nr; adv bkg acc; horseriding; bike hire; CKE. *"Lovely mountain scenery; beautiful loc in forest nr rv, san facs basic, mountain walks."* **€17.20, 1 Mar-30 Nov.** **2024**

HUMILLADERO *2G4* (0.5km S Rural) *37.10750, -4.69611* **Camping La Sierrecilla,** Avda de Clara Campoamor s/n, 29531 Humilladero (Málaga) **951-19 90 90; info@lasierrecilla.com; www.campinglasierrecilla.com**

12 €1.50 (htd) nr (htd)

Exit A92 junc 138 onto A7280 twd Humilladero. At vill ent turn L at 1st rndabt, site visible. Med, hdstg, mkd, pt shd, pt sl, terr, serviced pitches; EHU (10A) €3.50; bbq; 10% statics; Eng spkn; adv bkg acc; CKE. *"Excel new site; gd modern, san facs; vg touring base; gd walking; horseriding, caving, archery high ssn; Fuentepiedra lagoon nrby; lots of facs clsd until Jun/Jul."* **€24.00** **2024**

IRUN *3A1* (2km N Rural) *43.36638, -1.80436* **Camping Jaizkibel,** Ctra Guadalupe Km 22, 20280 Hondarribia (Guipúzkoa) **943-64 16 79; recepcion@campingjaizkibel.com; www.campingjaizkibel.com**

sand 1.5km

Fr Hondarribia/Fuenterrabia inner ring rd foll sp to site below old town wall. Do not ent town. Med, hdg, hdstg, pt shd, terr, EHU (6A) €4.35 (check earth); bbq; 90% statics; phone; bus 1km; Eng spkn; adv bkg acc; ccard acc; tennis; CKE. *"Easy 20 mins walk to historic town; scenic area; gd walking; gd touring base but ltd turning space for tourers; clean facs; gd rest & bar; helpful staff; gd lndry facs."*
€39.50, 28 Mar-15 Nov. **2023**

IRUN *3A1* (6km W Coastal) *43.37629, -1.79939* **Camping Faro de Higuer,** Ctra. Del Faro, 58, 20280 Hondarribia **943 64 10 08; faro@campingseuskadi.com; www.campingfarodehiguer.es**

12 €1.20 adj

Fr AP8 exit at junc 2 Irun. Foll signs for airport. At rndabt after airport take 2nd exit, cross two more rndabts. 2nd exit at next 2 rndabts. Cont uphill to lighthouse & foll signs for Faro. Med, mkd, hdg, unshd, pt sl, terr, EHU (10A) €5.20; bbq; cooking facs; TV; 50% statics; phone; Eng spkn; adv bkg acc; bike hire; games rm; waterslide; games area. *"Vg site on top of winding rd, is v busy outside; sep ent & exit; exit has low stone arch, be careful when leaving."*
€23.00 **2024**

ISABA *3B1* (13km E Rural) *42.86618, -0.81247*
Camping Zuriza, Ctra Anso-Zuriza, Km 14, 22728 Ansó (Huesca) **974-37 01 96; contacto@camping zuriza.es; www.campingzuriza.es**

On NA1370 N fr Isaba, turn R in 4km onto NA2000 to Zuriza. Foll sp to site. Fr Ansó, take HUV2024 N to Zuriza. Foll sp to site; narr, rough rd not rec for underpowered o'fits. 1*, Lge, pt shd, pt sl, serviced pitches; EHU €6; 50% statics; phone; ccard acc; CKE. *"Beautiful, remote valley; no vill at Zuriza, nearest vills Isaba & Ansó; no direct rte to France; superb location for walking; best to call prior to journey to check opening dates."* **€18.00, 1 Jul-31 Oct.** **2023**

ISLA *1A4* (1km NW Coastal) *43.50261, -3.54351*
Camping Playa de Isla, Calle Ardanal 1, 39195 Isla **942-67 93 61; consultas@playadeisla.com; www.playadeisla.com**
sand adj

Turn off A8/E70 at km 185 Beranga sp Noja & Isla. Foll sp Isla. In town to beach, site sp to L. Then in 100m keep R along narr seafront lane (main rd bends L) for 1km (rd looks like dead end). Med, mkd, pt shd, pt sl, terr, EHU (3A) €4.50; gas; 90% statics; phone; bus 1km; ccard acc; CKE. *"Beautiful situation; ltd touring pitches; busy at w/end."* **€26.40, Easter-30 Sep.** **2024**

ISLA CRISTINA *2G2* (4km E Coastal) *37.20555, -7.26722* **Camping Playa Taray,** Ctra La Antilla-Isla Cristina, Km 9, 21430 La Redondela (Huelva) **959-34 11 02; info@campingplayataray.es; www.camping taray.com**
12 sand adj

Fr W exit A49 sp Isla Cristina & go thro town heading E. Fr E exit A49 at km 117 sp Lepe. In Lepe turn S on H4116 to La Antilla, then R on coast rd to Isla Cristina & site. 2*, Lge, pt shd, EHU (10) €4.28; gas; red long stay; 10% statics; phone; bus; ccard acc; CKE. *"Gd birdwatching, cycling; less cr than other sites in area in winter; poss untidy LS & ltd facs; poss diff for lge o'fits; friendly, helpful owner; san facs basic, poor; not rec."* **€30.00** **2024**

ISLARES *1A4* (1km W Coastal) *43.40361, -3.31027*
Camping Playa Arenillas, Ctra Santander-Bilbao, Km 64, 39798 Islares (Cantabria) **942-86 31 52; cueva@ mundivia.es; www.campingplayaarenillas.com**
nr sand 100m

Exit A8 at km 156 Islares. Turn W on N634. Site on R at W end of Islares. Steep ent & sharp turn into site, exit less steep. 1*, Lge, mkd, pt shd, EHU (5A) €4.63 (poss no earth); gas; bbq; TV; 40% statics; phone; bus 500m; adv bkg rec; ccard acc; bike hire; horseriding; games area; CKE. *"Facs ltd LS & stretched in ssn; facs constantly cleaned; hot water to shwrs and washing up; rec arr early for choice of own pitch, and avoid Sat & Sun due to parked traff; conv Guggenheim Museum; excel NH for Bilbao ferry; beautiful setting."* **€30.60, 24 Mar-30 Sep.** **2022**

JACA *3B2* (10km N Rural) *42.624191, -0.543496*
Solopuent Camping, Ctra Bescos de la Garcipollera s/n 22710, Castiello de Jaca **621 40 20 95; recepcionsolopuent@gmail.com and booking@ apartamentos3000.com; www.solopuent.com**
(htd) nr nr (htd) shgl

Fr N240 take N330A/N330 to Castiello de Jaca. Turn R and cross bdge over rv and take rd to site 450m on R. Sm, mkd, pt shd, EHU (10A) inc; gas; bbq (charcoal, elec, gas, sep area); cooking facs; twin axles; TV; 50% statics; phone; bus/train; Eng spkn; adv bkg acc; ccard acc; games area & rm. *"Excel loc beside rv & vill; clean facs; flat pitches; min 10A supply for aldi heating, c'van shwr & cooking; wonderful mountain views, rv walks, wildlife; gd cycle rtes; excel."* **€35.00, 1 Jan-5 Nov, 4 Dec-31 Dec.** **2024**

JACA *3B2* (2km W Urban) *42.56416, -0.57027*
Camping Victoria, Avda de la Victoria 34, 22700 Jaca (Huesca) **974-35 70 08; campingvictoria@ eresmas.com; www.campingvictoria.es**
12 (htd)

Fr Jaca cent take N240 dir Pamplona, site on R. Med, mkd, pt shd, EHU (10A) €5; bbq; 80% statics; bus adj. *"Basic facs, but clean & well-maintained; friendly staff; conv NH/sh stay Somport Pass."* **€24.00** **2023**

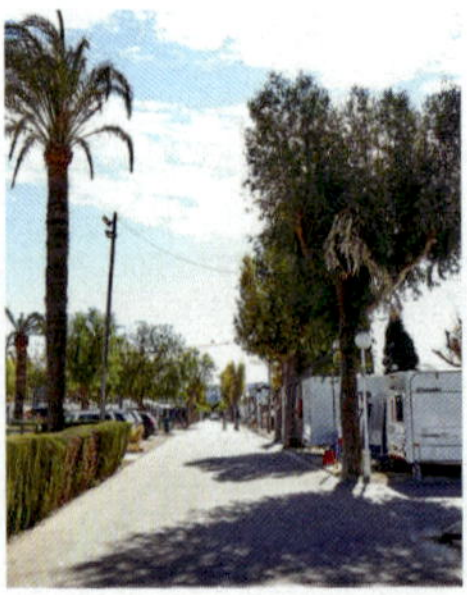

SPAIN

JAVEA/XABIA *4E2* (1km S Rural) *38.78333, 0.17294* **Camping Jávea,** Camí de la Fontana 10, 03730 Jávea (Alicante) **965-79 10 70; info@campingjavea.es; www.campingjavea.es**

12 €2 nr sand 1.5km

Exit N332 for Jávea on A132, cont in dir Port on CV734. At rndabt & Lidl supmkt, take slip rd to R immed after rv bdge sp Arenal Platjas & Cap de la Nau. Strt on at next rndabt to site sp & slip rd 100m sp Autocine. If you miss slip rd go back fr next rndabt. Lge, mkd, pt shd, EHU (8A) €4.56 (long lead rec); gas; bbq; red long stay; 15% statics; adv bkg acc; ccard acc; games area; tennis; CKE. *"Excel site & rest; variable pitch sizes/prices; some lge pitches - lge o'fits rec phone ahead; gd, clean san facs; mountain views; helpful staff; m'vans beware low trees; gd cycling; site a bit tired but gd."* **€35.00** **2022**

See advertisement

JAVEA/XABIA *4E2* (3km S Coastal) *38.77058, 0.18207* **Camping El Naranjal,** Cami dels Morers 15, 03730 Jávea (Alicante) **965-79 29 89; info@campingel naranjal.com; www.campingelnaranjal.com**

12 (htd) sand 500m

Exit A7 junc 62 or 63 onto N332 València/Alicante rd. Exit at Gata de Gorgos to Jávea. Foll sp Camping Jávea/Camping El Naranjal. Access rd by tennis club, foll sp. Med, hdstg, mkd, pt shd, EHU (10A) inc (poss rev pol); gas; bbq; red long stay; TV; 35% statics; phone; bus 500m; Eng spkn; adv bkg acc; ccard acc; bike hire; tennis 300m; games rm; golf 3km; CKE. *"Gd scenery & beach; pitches poss tight lge o'fits; dogs free; excel rest; immac facs; tourist info - tickets sold; rec; ACSI rate."* **€33.50** **2023**

LAREDO *1A4* (0.5km W Urban/Coastal) *43.40888, -3.43277* **Camping Carlos V,** Avnda Los Derechos Humanos 15, Ctra Residencial Playa, 39770 Laredo (Cantabria) **942-60 55 93; info@campingcarlosv.com; www.campingcarlosv.com**

€2.14 sand 200m

Leave A8 at junc 172 to Laredo, foll yellow camping sp, site on W side of town. Med, mkd, pt shd, EHU €2.60; gas; bus 100m; CKE. *"Well sheltered & lively resort; sm area for tourers; gd, clean, modern facs."* **€25.00, 6 May-30 Sep.** **2024**

"We must tell the Club about that great site we found"

Get your site reports in by mid-August and we'll do our best to get your updates into the next edition.

LAREDO *1A4* (3km W Coastal) *43.41176, -3.45329* **Camping Playa del Regatón,** El Sable 8, 39770 Laredo (Cantabria) **942-60 69 95; info@camping playaregaton.com; www.campingplayaregaton.com**

sand adj

Fr W leave A8 junc 172, under m'way to rndabt & take exit sp Calle Rep Colombia. In 800m turn L at traff lts, in further 800m turn L onto tarmac rd to end, passing other sites. Fr E leave at junc 172, at 1st rndabt take 2nd exit sp Centro Comercial N634 Colindres. At next rndabt take exit Calle Rep Colombia, then as above. 2*, Lge, mkd, pt shd, EHU (6-10A) €4.30; gas; red long stay; 75% statics; bus 600m; Eng spkn; adv bkg acc; ccard acc; horseriding nr; CKE. *"Clean site; sep area for tourers; wash up facs (cold water) every pitch; gd, modern facs; gd NH/sh stay (check opening times of office for EHU release); gd bird watching; lovely loc in nature reserve; easy cycle to town; free solar powered phone charging; hot water in main washing up area."* **€32.40, 22 Mar-11 Oct.** **2024**

LEKEITIO *3A1* (3km S Coastal) *43.35071, -2.49260* **Camping Leagi,** Calle Barrio Leagi s/n, 48289 Mendexa (Vizcaya) **946-84 23 52; leagi@camping leagi.com; www.campingleagi.com**

sand 1km

Fr San Sebastian leave A8/N634 at Deba twd Ondarroa. At Ondarroa do not turn into town, but cont on BI633 beyond Berriatua, then turn R onto BI3405 to Lekeitio. Fr Bilbao leave A8/N634 at Durango & foll B1633 twd Ondarroa. Turn L after Markina onto BI3405 to Lekeitio - do not go via Ondarroa, foll sp to Mendexa & site. Steep climb to site & v steep tarmac ent to site. Only suitable for o'fits with v high power/weight ratio. Med, mkd, unshd, pt sl, serviced pitches; EHU (5A) €3.90 (rev pol); 80% statics; ccard acc; CKE. *"Ltd facs LS; tractor tow avail up to site ent; beautiful scenery; excel local beach; lovely town; gd views; gd walking; san facs under pressure due to many tents; bus to Bilbao & Gurnika."* **€39.00, 1 Mar-1 Nov. 2024**

LEON *1B3* (7km SE Urban) *42.5900, -5.5331* **Camping Ciudad de León,** Ctra N601, 24195 Golpejar de la Sobarriba **987-26 90 86 or 666-03 98 85; reservas campingleon@gmail.com; sites.google.com/site/campingleon/**

€1.50

SE fr León on N601 twds Valladolid, L at top of hill at rndabt & Opel g'ge & foll site sp Golpejar de la Sobarriba; 500m after radio masts turn R at site sp. Narr track to site ent. Sm, shd, pt sl, EHU inc (6A) €3.60; gas; bus 200m; Eng spkn; adv bkg acc; bike hire; tennis; CKE. *"Clean, pleasant site; helpful, welcoming staff; access some sm pitches poss diff; easy access to León; shwrs need refurb (2015); ltd public trans to and fr town."* **€19.00, 1 Jun-20 Sep. 2024**

"I need an on-site restaurant"

We do our best to make sure site information is correct, but it is always best to check any must-have facilities are still available or will be open during your visit.

LEON *1B3* (12km SW Urban) *42.51250, -5.77472* **Camping Camino de Santiago,** Ctra N120, Km 324.4, 24392 Villadangos del Páramo (León) **987-68 02 53; info@campingcaminodesantiago.com; www.campingcaminodesantiago.com**

Access fr N120 to W of vill, site sp on R (take care fast, o'taking traff). Fr E turn L in town & foll sp to site. Lge, mkd, pt shd, EHU €3.90; gas; red long stay; 50% statics; phone; bus 300m; adv bkg acc; ccard acc; CKE. *"Poss no hot water LS; facs tired; pleasant, helpful staff; mosquitoes; vill church worth visit; gd NH."* **€18.60, 23 Mar-30 Sep. 2024**

LINEA DE LA CONCEPCION, LA *2H3* (3.6km N Urban/Coastal) *36.19167, -5.3350* **Camping Sureuropa,** Camino de Sobrevela s/n, 11300 La Línea de la Concepción (Cádiz) **956-64 35 87; camping@asansull.org; www.asansull.org**

12 sand 500m

Fr AP7, ext junc 124. Use junc124 fr both dirs. Just bef Gibraltar turn R up lane, in 200m turn L into site. Fr N on AP7, exit junc 124 onto A383 dir La Línea; foll sp Santa Margarita thro to beach. Foll rd to R along sea front, site in approx 1km - no advance sp. App rd to site off coast rd poss floods after heavy rain. Med, mkd, hdstg, hdg, pt shd, EHU €4.30; phone; Eng spkn; adv bkg acc; site clsd 20 Dec-7 Jan; CKE. *"Clean, flat, pretty site; vg, modern san facs; sm pitches & tight site rds poss diff twin axles & l'ge o'fits; sports club adj; quiet but noise fr adj sports club; ideal for Gibraltar 4km; stay ltd to 4 days; wifi in recep only; sh stay only."* **€20.00 2022**

"Satellite navigation makes touring much easier"

Remember most sat navs don't know if you're towing or in a larger vehicle – always use yours alongside maps and site directions.

LLANES *1A4* (8km E Coastal) *43.39948, -4.65350* **Camping La Paz,** Ctra N634, Km 292, 33597 Playa de Vidiago (Asturias) **985-41 12 35; delfin@campinglapaz.com; www.campinglapaz.eu**

€2.50 sand adj

Take Fr A8/N634/E70 turn R at sp to site bet km stone 292 & 293 bef Vidiago.Site access via narr 1km lane. Stop bef bdge & park on R, staff will tow to pitch. Narr site ent & steep access to pitches. Lge, mkd, shd, terr, EHU (9A) €4.82 (poss rev pol); gas; bbq; TV; phone; Eng spkn; adv bkg acc; ccard acc; fishing; golf 4km; watersports; games rm; horseriding; CKE. *"Exceptionally helpful owner & staff; sm pitches; gd, modern san facs; mountain sports; excel views; cliff top rest; superb beaches in area."* **€37.25, Easter-30 Sep. 2023**

LLANES *1A4* (3km W Coastal) *43.42500, -4.78944* **Camping Las Conchas de Póo,** Ctra General, 33509 Póo de Llanes (Asturias) **985-40 22 90 or 674-16 58 79 (mob); campinglasconchas@gmail.com; www.campinglasconchas.com**

sand adj

Exit A8/E70 at Llanes West junc 307 & foll sp. Site on rd AS263. 2*, Med, pt shd, sl, terr, EHU (6A) €3.20; 50% statics; phone; bus adj. *"Pleasant site; footpath to lovely beach; lovely coastal walk to Celorio; stn in Póo vill; gd pitches for tourers; gd clean san facs; gd WiFi at recep."* **€20.00, 1 Jun-15 Sep. 2024**

SPAIN

LLANES *1A4* (5km W Coastal) *43.43471, -4.81810* **Camping Playa de Troenzo,** Ctra de Celerio-Barro, 33595 Celorio (Asturias) **985-40 16 72; info@campingtroenzo.com; www.campingtroenzo.com**

sand 400m

Fr E take E70/A8 exit at junc 300 to Celorio. At T-junc with AS263 turn L dir Celorio & Llanes. Turn L on N9 (Celorio) thro vill & foll sp to Barro. Site on R after 500m (after Maria Elena site). 2*, Lge, pt shd, terr, EHU (6A) €2.51; gas; 90% statics; phone; Eng spkn; adv bkg acc; CKE. *"Lovely, old town; most pitches sm; for pitches with sea views go thro statics to end of site; gd, modern facs; gd rests in town; nr harbour."* **€21.00, 16 Feb-19 Dec.** **2024**

LLORET DE MAR *3B3* (1km SW Coastal) *41.6984, 2.8265* **Camping Santa Elena-Ciutat,** Ctra Blanes/ Lloret, 17310 Lloret de Mar (Gerona) **972-36 40 09; santaelena@gsala.cat; www.campingsantaelena.com**

12 shgl 600m

Exit A7 junc 9 dir Lloret. In Lloret take Blanes rd, site sp at km 10.5 on rd GI 682. V lge, pt sl, EHU (5A) €3.90; gas; phone; Eng spkn; games area; CKE. *"Ideal for teenagers; cash machine."* **€34.60** **2022**

LOGRONO *3B1* (2km N Urban) *42.47122, -2.45493* **Camping La Playa,** Avda de la Playa 6, 26006 Logroño (La Rioja) **941-25 22 53; info@campinglaplaya.com; www.campinglaplaya.com**

12 €2

Leave Logroño by bdge 'Puente de Piedra' on N111, then turn L at rndabt into Camino de las Norias. Site well sp in town & fr N111, adj sports cent Las Norias, on N side of Rv Ebro. 1*, Med, hdg, shd, EHU (5A) €4.80; gas; sw nr; 80% statics; tennis; CKE. *"Sh walk to town cent; ltd facs LS & site poss clsd; vg; nr rest."* **€25.00** **2022**

LORCA *4G1* (8km W Rural) *37.62861, -1.74888* **Camping La Torrecilla,** Ctra Granada-LaTorrecilla, 30817 Lorca (Murcia) **968-44 21 36; campinglatorrecilla@hotmail.es; www.allyouneedinmurcia.com/en/accomodation-and-transport/camping-la-torrecilla-7884/**

12 (htd) nr

Leave A7/E15 at junc 585. In 1km turn L, site well sp. Med, hdstg, mkd, pt shd, pt sl, EHU (6A) €3.88; gas; bbq; red long stay; TV; 95% statics; phone; bus 1km; Eng spkn; ccard acc; games area; tennis. *"Ltd touring pitches & EHU; friendly, helpful staff; excel pool; vg san facs."* **€20.00** **2024**

LUARCA *1A3* (2km W Coastal) *43.55116, -6.55310* **Camping Playa de Taurán,** 33700 Luarca (Asturias) **985-64 12 72 or 619-88 43 06 (mob); tauran@campingtauran.com; www.campingtauran.com**

€1 shgl 200m

Exit A8/N634 junc 471 sp Luarca, El Chano. Cont 3.5km on long, narr, rough access rd. Rd thro Luarca unsuitable for c'vans. Med, hdg, pt shd, pt sl, EHU (10A) €3.50; gas; bbq; red long stay; phone; bike hire. *"Sea & mountain views; off beaten track; conv fishing & hill vills; peaceful, restful, attractive, well-kept site; beach sand 2km; steep access to beach; excel."* **€18.50, 1 Apr-30 Sep.** **2024**

LUMBIER *3B1* (1.3km S Rural) *42.65111, -1.30222* **Camping Iturbero,** Ctra N240 Pamplona-Huesca, 31440 Lumbier (Navarra) **948-88 04 05; iturbero@campingiturbero.com; www.campingiturbero.com**

nr

SE fr Pamplona on N240 twds Yesa Reservoir. In 30km L on NA150 twds Lumbier. In 3.5km immed bef Lumbier turn R at rndabt then over bdge, 1st L to site, adj sw pool. Well sp fr N240. 2*, Med, mkd, hdstg, hdg, pt shd, EHU (5A) €4.95; gas; bbq; 25% statics; bus 1km; tennis; CKE. *"Beautiful, well-kept site; clean, basic facs; pool 100m; excel touring base; open w/end only Dec-Easter (poss fr Sep) but clsd 19 Dec-19 Feb; eagles & vultures in gorge & seen fr site; hang-gliding; gd for NH or long breaks; helpful staff; Lumbier lovely sm town."* **€27.40, 15 Mar-15 Dec.** **2022**

"There aren't many sites open at this time of year"

If you're travelling outside peak season remember to call ahead to check site opening dates – even if the entry says 'open all year'.

MACANET DE CABRENYS *3B3* (1km S Rural) *42.37314, 2.75419* **Camping Maçanet de Cabrenys,** Mas Roquet s/n, 17720 Maçanet de Cabrenys (Gerona) **667-77 66 48 (mob); info@campingmassanet.com; www.campingmassanet.com**

€5.50 (htd)

Fr N, exit AP7 junc 2 at La Jonquera onto N-II dir Figueres; at km 767 turn R onto GI-502/GI-503 dir Maçanet de Cabrenys; turn L 500m bef vill; site sp. Or fr S, exit AP7 junc 4 at Figueres onto N-II dir France; at km 766 turn L onto GI-502 dir Maçanet de Cabrenys; then as above. Sm, hdstg, mkd, pt shd, sl, terr, EHU (10A) €6.50; gas; bbq; TV; 10% statics; Eng spkn; adv bkg acc; ccard acc; games rm; bike hire; CKE. *"Cycle rtes fr site."* **€30.00, 1 Mar-31 Dec.** **2024**

MADRID *1D4* (13km S Urban) *40.31805, -3.68888* **Camping Alpha,** Ctra de Andalucía N-IV, Km 12.4, 28906 Getafe (Madrid) **916-95 80 69; info@campingalpha.com; www.campingalpha.com**

12

Fr S on A4/E5 twd Madrid, leave at km 12B to W dir Ocaña & foll sp. Fr N on A4/E5 at km 13B to change dir back onto A4; then exit 12B sp 'Polígono Industrial Los Olivos' to site. 2*, Lge, hdg, hdstg, pt shd, EHU (15A) €5.90 (poss no earth); 20% statics; phone; Eng spkn; adv bkg acc; ccard acc; games area; tennis; CKE. *"Lorry depot adj; poss vehicle movements 24 hrs but minimal noise; bus & metro to Madrid 30-40 mins; sm pitches poss tight for space; vg, clean facs; helpful staff; NH or sh stay."* **€28.00** **2022**

MADRIGAL DE LA VERA *1D3* (0.5km E Rural) *40.14864, -5.35769* **Camping Alardos,** Ctra Madrigal-Candeleda, 10480 Madrigal de la Vera (Cáceres) **927-56 50 66; info@campingalardos.com; www.campingalardos.com**

12

Fr Jarandilla take EX203 E to Madrigal. Site sp in vill nr rv bdge. Med, mkd, pt shd, EHU (6-10A) €4; bbq; sw nr; TV; 95% statics; phone; Eng spkn; adv bkg acc. *"Friendly owners; ltd facs LS; beautiful scenery; excel touring area; ancient Celtic settlement at El Raso 5km."* **€24.60** **2024**

MANGA DEL MAR MENOR, LA *4G2* (3.5km W Urban) *37.6244, -0.7447* **Caravaning La Manga,** Autovia Cartagena - La Manga, exit 11, E-30370 La Manga del Mar Menor **968-56 30 19; lamanga@caravaning.es; www.caravaning.es**

12 €2

Take Autovia CT-32 fr Cartagena to La Manga; take exit 800B twds El Algar/Murcia; keep L, merge onto Autovia MU312; cont to foll MU-312; cont onto Ctra a La Manga & cont onto Av Gran Via; site clearly sp. Lge, hdstg, hdg, pt shd, serviced pitches; EHU (10A) inc; bbq; sw nr; 10% statics; bus to Murcia and Cartagena; Eng spkn; adv bkg acc; ccard acc; watersports; tennis; games rm. *"Immac, busy, popular site; Mar Menor shallow & warm lagoon; open air cinema & children's programme high ssn; lovely location & gd for golfers; horseridng nrby; recep open 24 hrs; Mar Menor well worth visiting; vg rest; gd for families; outdoor fitness; some narr site rds & trees - rec park in car park on arr & walk to find pitch; gd walking; gym; sauna; jacuzzi; mountain biking; bird sanctuary; poss lge rallies on site Dec-Mar; excel; friendly, helpful staff; immac facs."* **€38.00** **2022**

MARBELLA *2H3* (14km E Coastal) *36.48910, -4.74146* **Kawan Village Cabopino,** Ctra N340/A7, Km 194.7, 29604 Marbella (Málaga) **952-83 43 73; info@campingcabopino.com; www.campingcabopino.com**

12 first dog free (covrd) sand 200m

Fr E site is on N side of N340/A7; turn R at km 195 'Salida Cabopino' past petrol stn, site on R at rndabt. Fr W on A7 turn R at 'Salida Cabopino' km 194.7, go over bdge to rndabt, site strt over. NB Do not take sm exit fr A7 immed at 1st Cabopino sp. Lge, mkd, pt shd, pt sl, EHU (6-10A) inc (poss long lead req); bbq (elec, gas); TV; 50% statics; bus 100m; Eng spkn; ccard acc; golf driving range; archery; games area; games rm; watersports; CKE. *"V pleasant site set in pine woodland; rd noise & lge groups w/enders; marina 300m; busy, particularly w/end; varied pitch size, poss diff access lge o'fits, no o'fits over 11m high ssn; blocks req some pitches; gd, clean san facs; feral cats on site (2009)."* **€42.00, E21.** **2022**

MARBELLA *2H3* (7km E Coastal) *36.50259, -4.80413* **Camping La Buganvilla,** Ctra N340, Km 188.8, 29600 Marbella (Málaga) **952-83 56 21 or 952-83 19 73; info@campingbuganvilla.com; www.campingbuganvilla.com**

12 €4 sand 350m

E fr Marbella for 6km on N340/E15 twds Málaga. Pass site & cross over m'way at Elviria & foll site sp. Fr Málaga exit R off autovia immed after 189km marker. Lge, shd, pt sl, terr, EHU (16A) inc; gas; bbq; red long stay; TV; 40% statics; phone; Eng spkn; adv bkg acc; ccard acc; fishing; tennis; games rm; CKE. *"Relaxed, conv site; helpful staff; excel beach; no dogs Jul/Aug; bus stop to Marbella at ent; 20min walk to nice beach; bigger & more shaded pitches at top of site."* **€25.00** **2022**

"That's changed – Should I let the Club know?"

If you find something on site that's different from the site entry, fill in a report and let us know. See camc.com/europereport.

MARIA *4G1* (8km W Rural) *37.70823, -2.23609* **Camping Sierra de María,** Ctra María a Orce, Km 7, Paraje La Piza, 04838 María (Málaga) **620-23 22 23; www.campingsierrademaria.es**

12

Exit A92 at junc 408 to Vélez Rubio, Vélez Blanco & María. Foll A317 to María & cont dir Huéscar & Orce. Site on R. Med, mkd, pt shd, pt sl, EHU (16A) €3.75; 10% statics; adv bkg acc; ccard acc; bike hire; horseriding; CKE. *"Lovely, peaceful, ecological site in mountains; much wildlife; variable pitch sizes; facs poss stretched high ssn; v cold in winter; v helpful mgrs, gd food in rest."* **€23.00** **2022**

MARINA, LA *4F2* (1.5km S Coastal) *38.12972, -0.65000* **Camping Internacional La Marina,** Ctra N332a, Km 76, 03194 La Marina (Alicante) **965-41 92 00; info@campinglamarina.com; www.lamarinaresort.com**

12 €2.14 (htd) (covrd, htd) sand 500m

Fr N332 S of La Marina turn E twd sea at rndabt onto Camino del Cementerio. At next rndabt turn S onto N332a & foll site sp along Avda de l'Alegría. 5*, V lge, hdstg, mkd, hdg, shd, terr, serviced pitches; EHU (10A) €3.21; gas; red long stay; TV; 10% statics; phone; bus 50m; Eng spkn; adv bkg acc; ccard acc; watersports; games rm; solarium; fishing; sauna; tennis; games area; waterslide; CKE. *"Popular winter site - almost full late Feb; v busy w/end; disco; clean, high quality facs; various pitch sizes/prices; fitness cent; bus fr gate; gd security; car wash; security; excel rest; gd site; v helpful; hire cars avail; fantastic site."* **€65.00** **2022**

See advertisement

MATARO *3C3* (3km E Coastal) *41.55060, 2.48330* **Camping Barcelona,** Ctra NII, Km 650, 08304 Mataró (Barcelona) **937-90 47 20; info@campingbarcelona.com; www.campingbarcelona.com**

€4 sand 1.5km

Exit AP7 onto C60 sp Mataró. Turn N onto NII dir Gerona, site sp on L after rndabt. Lge, hdstg, mkd, shd, EHU (6A) €5.50; gas; red long stay; TV; 5% statics; Eng spkn; adv bkg acc; ccard acc; games area; games rm; CKE. *"Conv Barcelona 28km; pleasant site; shuttle bus to beach; animal farm; friendly, welcoming staff."* **€45.70, 4 Mar-1 Nov.** **2024**

MAZAGON *2G2* (10km E Coastal) *37.09855, -6.72650* **Camping Doñana Playa,** Ctra San Juan del Puerto-Matalascañas, Km 34.6, 21130 Mazagón (Huelva) **959-53 62 81; info@campingdonana.com; www.campingdonana.com**

12 €4.10 sand 300m

Fr A49 exit junc 48 at Bullullos del Condado onto A483 sp El Rocio, Matalascañas. At coast turn R sp Mazagón, site on L in 16km. V lge, hdstg, mkd, pt shd, EHU (6A) €5.20; 10% statics; bus 500m; adv bkg acc; games area; site clsd 14 Dec-14 Jan; watersports; bike hire; tennis; CKE. *"Pleasant site amongst pine trees but lack of site care LS; ltd LS; lge pitches but poss soft sand; quiet but v noisy Fri/Sat nights; new (2014) lge shwr block on lower pt of site."* **€35.00** **2024**

SPAIN

MENDIGORRIA *3B1* (0.5km SW Rural) *42.62416, -1.84277* **Camping El Molino,** Ctra Larraga, 31150 Mendigorría (Navarra) **948-34 06 04; info@campingelmolino.com; www.campingelmolino.com**

Fr Pamplona on N111 turn L at 25km in Puente la Reina onto NA601 sp Mendigorría. Site sp thro vill dir Larraga. 1*, Med, mkd, pt shd, serviced pitches; EHU (6A) inc; gas; bbq; TV; phone; adv bkg acc; ccard acc; games area; canoe hire; waterslide; tennis; clsd 23 Dec-14 Jan & poss Mon-Thurs fr Nov to Feb, phone ahead to check; CKE. *"Gd clean san facs; solar water heating - water poss only warm; vg leisure facs; v ltd facs LS; for early am dep LS, pay night bef & obtain barrier key; friendly, helpful staff; statics (sep area); lovely medieval vill."* **€29.60, 1 Feb-15 Dec.** **2022**

MERIDA *2E3* (4km NE Urban) *38.93558, -6.30426* **Camping Mérida,** Avda de la Reina Sofia s/n, 06800 Mérida (Badajoz) **924-30 34 53; info@campingmerida.com**

12 €1.65

Fr E on A5/E90 exit junc 333/334 to Mérida, site on L in 2km. Fr W on A5/E90 exit junc 346, site sp. Fr N exit A66/E803 at junc 617 onto A5 E. Leave at junc 334, site on L in 1km twd Mérida. Fr S on A66-E803 app Mérida, foll Cáceres sp onto bypass to E; at lge rndabt turn R sp Madrid; site on R after 2km. 2*, Med, mkd, pt shd, pt sl, EHU (6A) €3.30 (long lead poss req & poss rev pol); gas; TV; 10% statics; phone; CKE. *"Roman remains & National Museum of Roman Art worth visit; poss diff lge o'fits manoeuvring onto pitch due trees & soft grnd after rain; ltd facs & run down in LS; conv NH; taxi to town costs 5-9 euros; grass pitches; bread can be ordered fr rest; poss nightclub noise at w/end."* **€21.00** **2024**

MIAJADAS *2E3* (14km SW Rural) *39.09599, -6.01333* **Camping-Restaurant El 301,** Ctra Madrid-Lisbon, Km 301, 10100 Miajadas (Cáceres) **927-34 79 14; camping301@hotmail.com; www.camping301.com**

12

Leave A5/E90 just bef km stone 301 & foll sp 'Via de Servicio' with rest & camping symbols; site in 500m. Med, pt shd, EHU (8A) €5.50 (poss no earth); gas; TV; phone; ccard acc; CKE. *"Well-maintained, clean site; grass pitches; OK wheelchair users but steps to pool; gd NH; gd bird life."* **€24.00** **2022**

MOJACAR *4G1* (9km S Rural) *37.06536, -1.86864* **Camping Sopalmo,** Sopalmo, 04638 Mojácar (Almería) **950-47 84 13 or 660-73 53 68; campingsopalmo@gmail.com; campingsopalmo.com**

12 €1 shgl 1.7km

Exit A7/E15 at junc 520 onto AL6111 sp Mojácar. Fr Mojácar turn S onto A1203/AL5105 dir Carboneras, site sp on W of rd about 1km S of El Agua del Medio. Sm, hdstg, mkd, pt shd, terr, EHU (6A); gas; bbq; twin axles; 10% statics; Eng spkn; adv bkg acc; CKE. *"Clean, pleasant, popular site; remote & peaceful; friendly owner; gd walking in National Park; lovely san facs; gd."* **€31.00** **2024**

MOJACAR *4G1* (0.5km W Rural) *37.14083, -1.85916* **Camping El Quinto,** Ctra Mojácar-Turre, 04638 Mojácar (Almería) **950-47 87 04; campingelquinto@hotmail.com**

12 €1 nr

sand 3km

Fr A7/E15 exit 520 sp Turre & Mojácar. Site on R in approx 13km at bottom of Mojácar vill. Sm, hdstg, hdg, mkd, pt shd, EHU (6-10A) €3.21; gas; bbq; red long stay; phone; Eng spkn; adv bkg acc; CKE. *"Neat, tidy site; mkt Wed; close National Park; excel beaches; metered 6A elect for long winter stay; popular in winter, poss cr & facs stretched; security barrier; poss mosquitoes; drinking water ltd to 5L a time."* **€32.50** **2024**

MONCOFA *3D2* (2km E Urban/Coastal) *39.80861, -0.12805* **Camping Mon Mar,** Camino Serratelles s/n, 12593 Platja de Moncófa (Castellón) **964-58 85 92; info@campingmonmar.com; www.campingmonmar.com**

12 (htd)

shgl 200m

Exit 49 fr A7 or N340, foll sp Moncófa Platja passing thro Moncófa & foll sp beach & tourist info thro 1-way system. Site sp, adj Aqua Park. 2*, Lge, hdstg, hdg, pt shd, serviced pitches; EHU (6A) inc; gas; bbq; red long stay; 80% statics; phone; bus 300m; Eng spkn; adv bkg acc; ccard acc; CKE. *"Helpful owner & staff; rallies on site Dec-Apr; mini-bus to stn & excursions; sunshades over pitches poss diff high o'fits; excel clean, tidy site."* **€32.00** **2024**

MONESTERIO *2F3* (3km S Rural) *38.06276, -6.24689* **Camping Tentudia,** CN 630 Km 727, 06260 Monesterio (Badajoz) **924-51 63 16; ctentudia@turiex.com; www.camping-extremadura.com**

On E803/A66 N Mérida-Sevilla take exit 722 and foll dir to Monesterio then Santa Olallio - don't take rd into Nature Park. Med, mkd, hdstg, shd, terr, serviced pitches; EHU (15A); red long stay; Eng spkn; adv bkg acc; ccard acc; horseriding nr; bike hire; CKE. *"Gd stopping place in quiet area; Sep '99 future of site uncertain, contact in advance; site a little run down; poss rd noise fr A66."* **€20.00, Easter-15 Sep.** **2024**

MONTBLANC *3C2* (1.5km NE Rural) *41.37743, 1.18511* **Camping Montblanc Park,** Ctra Prenafeta, Km 1.8, 43400 Montblanc **977-86 25 44 or 492-28 38 48; montblancpark@capfun.com; www.capfun.com/camping-espagne-catalogne-mont_blanc_park-FR.html**

12 €4.50 (htd)

Exit AP2 junc 9 sp Montblanc; foll sp Montblanc/Prenafeta/TV2421; site on L on TV2421. 4*, Med, hdg, pt shd, pt sl, terr, EHU (10A) inc; bbq; red long stay; 50% statics; phone; Eng spkn; adv bkg acc; ccard acc; CKE. *"Excel site; excel facs; lovely area; many static pitches only suitable for o'fits up to 7m; Cistercian monestaries nrby; conv NH Andorra."* **€39.50** **2024**

SPAIN

MONTERROSO *1B2* (1km S Rural) *42.78720, -7.84414* **Camp Municipal de Monterroso,** A Peneda, 27560 Monterroso (Lugo) **982-37 75 01; campingmonterroso@aged-sl.com; www.campingmonterroso.com**

WD nr nr

Fr N540 turn W onto N640 to Monterroso. Fr town cent turn S on LU212. In 100m turn sharp R then downhill for 1km; 2 sharp bends to site. Sm, hdg, mkd, pt shd, pt sl, EHU (10A) €3.50; Eng spkn; games area; CKE. *"Helpful staff; v quiet & ltd facs LS; pool adj; vg."* **€21.00, 30 Mar-24 Sep.** **2023**

MONZON *3B2* (5.7km NE Rural) *41.93673, 0.24146* **Camping Almunia,** Calle del Nao 10, 22420 Almunia de san Juan **696-77 18 51; camping-almunia@hotmail.com; www.camping-almunia.es**

12 WD MSP

Foll the A-22 to Monzón. Turn R onto the A-1237 to campsite. Sm, hdstg, pt shd, terr, EHU (6A) €4; bbq; twin axles; adv bkg acc. *"Friendly German couple; Monzon splendid medieval castle to visit; conv NH."* **€13.00** **2024**

MORELLA *3D2* (2km NE Rural) *40.62401, -0.09141* **Motor Caravan Parking,** 12300 Morella (Castellón)

12 WD MSP

Exit N232 at sp (m'van emptying). Sm, hdstg, pt shd,. *"Free of charge; stay up to 72 hrs; clean; superb location; lge m'vans acc; excel Aire with fine views of hilltop town of Morella (floodlit at night), clean, well maintained."* **2024**

MOTILLA DEL PALANCAR *4E1* (10km NW Rural) *39.61241, -2.10185* **Camping Pantapino,** Paraje de Hontanar, s/n, 16115 Olmedilla de Alarcón (Cuenca) **969-33 92 33 or 689 24 17 50; pantapina@hotmail.com; www.campingpantapino.eu**

12 €1.50 WD MSP

Fr cent of Motilla foll NIII; turn NW onto rd CM2100 at sp for Valverde de Júcar; site on L just bef 12km marker. 2*, Med, mkd, pt shd, pt sl, serviced pitches; EHU (6A) €4; gas; bbq; 40% statics; adv bkg acc; ccard acc; tennis; bike hire; horseriding; games area; CKE. *"Clean, attractive site but tatty statics; poor facs; gd size pitches; resident owners hospitable; poss clsd in winter - phone ahead to check; vg; san facs old but clean; ltd facs LS; gd NH; poss problem with earth on elec."* **€18.00** **2024**

MOTRIL *2H4* (3km SW Urban/Coastal) *36.71833, -3.54616* **Camping Playa de Poniente de Motril,** 18600 Motril (Granada) **958-82 03 03; info@campingplayadeponiente.com; www.campingplayadeponiente.com**

12 €1.50 (htd) WD MSP adj

Turn off coast rd N340 to port bef flyover; at rndabt take rd for Motril. Turn R in town, site sp. Lge, hdstg, mkd, pt shd, EHU (6-10) €3.35; gas; bbq (elec, gas); red long stay; 40% statics; bus; Eng spkn; adv bkg acc; ccard acc; bike hire; games rm; horseriding; tennis; golf; games area. *"Well-appointed site but surrounded by blocks of flats; gd, clean facs; helpful recep; gd shop; access diff for lge o'fits; poss lge flying beetles; excel long stay winter; lovely promenade with dedicated cycle track."* **€35.00** **2023**

MUNDAKA *3A1* (1km S Coastal) *43.39915, -2.69620* **Camping Portuondo,** Ctra Amorebieta-Bermeo, Km 43, 48360 Mundaka (Bilbao) **946-87 77 01; recepcion@campingportuondo.com; www.campingportuondo.com**

12 500m

Fr Bermeo pass Mundaka staying on main rd, do not enter Mundaka. Stay on Bl-2235 sp Gernika. After approx 1km site on L down steep slip rd. Med, pt shd, terr, EHU (6A) €4.20; 30% statics; train 800m; adv bkg rec; ccard acc; site clsd end Jan-mid Feb. *"Excel clean, modern facs; pitches tight not suitable for lge o'fits; popular with surfers; conv Bilbao by train; site suitable sm m'vans only; v ltd touring space; ent is very steep single track."* **€35.00** **2022**

MUROS *1B1* (7km W Coastal) *42.76100, 9.11100* **Camping Ancoradoiro,** Ctra Corcubión-Muros, Km.7.2, 15250 Louro (La Coruña) **981-87 88 97; wolfgangh@hotmail.es or campingancora@outlook.es; www.campingancoradoiro.com**

WD nr nr sand 500m

Foll AC550 W fr Muros. Site on L (S), well sp. Immed inside ent arch, to thro gate on L. 1*, Med, hdg, mkd, pt shd, terr, EHU (6-15A) €3.50; phone; bus 500m; adv bkg acc; watersports; CKE. *"Excel, lovely, well-run, well-kept site; superb friendly site on headland bet 2 sandy beaches; welcoming owner; excel rest; excel san facs; poss diff for lge o'fits; beautiful beaches; scenic area."* **€24.00, 25 Apr-16 Sep.** **2024**

MUXIA *1A1* (10km E Coastal) *43.1164, -9.1583* **Camping Playa Barreira Leis,** Playa Berreira, Leis, 15124 Camariñas-Muxia (La Coruña) **981-73 03 04; playaleis@yahoo.es; www.campingplayadeleis.es**

12 €1 WD sand 100m

Fr Ponte do Porto turn L sp Muxia; foll camp sp. Site is 1st after Leis vill on R. 1*, Med, mkd, pt shd, terr, EHU €3.50; bbq; TV; ccard acc; CKE. *"Beautiful situation on wooded hillside; dir acces to gd beach; ltd, poorly maintained facs LS; mkt in Muxia Thurs; scruffy & rundown; basic san facs."* **€16.00** **2024**

NAVAJAS *3D2* (1km W Rural) *39.87489, -0.51034*
Camping Altomira, Carretera, CV-213 Navajas Km. 1, E-12470 Navajas (Castellón) **964-71 32 11; reserva@campingaltomira.com; www.campingaltomira.com**
12 (htd) (htd)

Exit A23/N234 at junc 33 to rndabt & take CV214 dir Navajas. In approx 2km turn L onto CV213, site on L just past R turn into vill, sp. 4*, Med, hdstg, pt shd, terr, serviced pitches; EHU (6A) inc; gas; bbq; sw nr; red long stay; TV; 70% statics; phone; bus 500m; Eng spkn; adv bkg acc; ccard acc; games rm; tennis; bike hire; fishing; CKE. *"Friendly welcome; panoramic views fr upper level (steep app) but not rec for lge o'fits due tight bends & ramped access/kerb to some pitches; gd birdwatching, walking, cycling; vg, useful NH & longer; excel; stunnng waterfall with sw nrby; site renovated; excel pitches, fully serviced, new excel san facs (2019); gd loc."* **€36.00, E18.** **2022**

NOIA *1B2* (5km SW Coastal) *42.77198, -8.93761*
Camping Punta Batuda, Playa Hornanda, 15970 Porto do Son (La Coruña) **981-76 65 42; camping@puntabatuda.com; www.puntabatuda.com**
12 (htd) nr sand adj

Fr Santiago take C543 twd Noia, then AC550 5km SW to Porto do Son. Site on R approx 1km after Boa. 3*, Lge, mkd, pt shd, terr, EHU (3A) €3.74 (poss rev pol); gas; red long stay; 50% statics; Eng spkn; adv bkg acc; tennis; CKE. *"Wonderful views; htd pool w/end only; exposed to elements & poss windy; ltd facs LS; hot water to shwrs only; some pitches very steep &/or sm; gd facs; naturist beach 5km S."* **€23.60** **2024**

NOJA *1A4* (20km W Coastal) *43.46306, -3.72379*
Camping Derby Loredo, Calle Bajada a lay Playa, 19 39160 Loredo **942 504106; info@camping loredo.com; campingloredo.com**
12 €2 nr sand adj

Fr Santander on S10 twrd Bilbao. L at J12, foll CA141 to Pedrena/Somo. After Somo L onto CA440 Loredo. On ent Loredo L sp @400m Playa Deloredo.' Med, mkd, pt shd, EHU; gas; twin axles; 70% statics; Eng spkn; ccard acc. *"Gd loc by beach; watersports; not suitable for lge o'fits; surf board hire; busy; friendly site with fams and surfers; gd."* **€25.20** **2023**

NOJA *1A4* (1km NW Coastal) *43.49012, -3.53765*
Camping Playa Joyel, Playa del Ris, 39180 Noja (Cantabria) **942-63 00 81; info@playajoyel.com; www.playajoyel.com**
sand adj

Fr Santander or Bilbao foll sp A8/E70 (toll-free). Approx 15km E of Solares exit m'way junc 184 at Beranga onto CA147 N twd Noja & coast. On o'skirts of Noja turn L sp Playa del Ris, (sm brown sp) foll rd approx 1.5km to rndabt, site sp to L, 500m fr rndabt. Fr Santander take S10 for approx 8km, then join A8/E70. 4*, V lge, mkd, pt shd, pt sl, EHU (6A) €6.30; gas; bbq; TV; 40% statics; phone; Eng spkn; adv bkg acc; ccard acc; sailing; windsurfing; jacuzzi; tennis; games rm; CKE. *"Well-organised site on sheltered bay; cash dispenser; very busy high ssn; pleasant staff; hairdresser; car wash; no o'fits over 8m high ssn; gd, clean facs; superb pool & beach; recep 0800-2200; some narr site rds with kerbs; midnight silence enforced; highly rec."* **€48.30, 3 Apr-27 Sep, E05.** **2022**

NUEVALOS *3C1* (1km N Rural) *41.21829, -1.79292*
Camping Lago Park, Ctra De Alhama de Aragón a Cillas, Km 39, 50210 Nuévalos (Zaragoza) **976-84 90 38; lagoresort@gmail.com; www.lagoresort.com**
12 nr nr

Fr E on A2/E90 exit junc 231 to Nuévalos, turn R sp Madrid. Site 1.5km on L when ent Nuévalos. Fr W exit junc 204, site well sp. Steep ent fr rd. 4*, V lge, hdg, mkd, pt shd, terr, EHU (10A) €5.40; gas; bbq; red long stay; 10% statics; bus 500m; adv bkg acc; fishing; games area; boating; CKE. *"Nr Monasterio de Piedra & Tranquera Lake; excel facs on top terr, but stretched high ssn & poss long, steepish walk; lake nrby; ltd facs LS; gd birdwatching; bar 500m; only site in area; gd; very friendly owner; an oasis en rte to Madrid in picturesque setting; vg rest; gd welcome; pool not open yet (2016); rec."* **€29.50** **2022**

OCHAGAVIA *3A1* (0.5km S Rural) *42.90777, -1.08750*
Camping Osate, Ctra Salazar s/n, 31680 Ochagavia (Navarra) **948-89 01 84; info@campingosate.net; www.campingosate.net**
12 €2

On N135 SE fr Auritz, turn L onto NA140 & cont for 24km bef turning L twd Ochagavia on NA140. Site sp in 2km on R, 500m bef vill. Med, mkd, pt shd, serviced pitches; EHU (4A) €5.50; gas; bbq; 50% statics; Eng spkn. *"Attractive, remote vill; gd, well-maintained site; touring pitches under trees, sep fr statics; facs ltd & poss stretched high ssn; site clsd 3 Nov-15 Dec & rec phone ahead LS; facs require maintenance (2018); TO v helpful; gd walks fr site."* **€22.00** **2023**

SPAIN

OLIVA *4E2* (2km E Coastal) *38.93278, -0.09778*
Camping Kiko Park, Calle Assagador de Carro 2, 46780 Playa de Oliva (València) **962-85 09 05; info@kikopark.com; www.kikopark.com**

12 €2.95 (htd) WD MSP (covrd) sand adj

Exit AP7/E15 junc 61; fr toll turn R at T-junc onto N332.At rndabt turn L foll sp Platjas; next rdbt take 1st exit sp Platja; next rndabt foll sp Kiko Park. Do not drive thro Oliva. Access poss diff on app rds due humps. Lge, hdstg, mkd, hdg, shd, serviced pitches; EHU (16A) inc; gas; bbq; sw nr; red long stay; phone; Eng spkn; adv bkg acc; ccard acc; horseriding nr; watersports; games rm; bike hire; fishing; games area; tennis; windsurfing school; golf nr; CKE. *"Gd, family-run site; whirlpool; spa; very helpful staff; vg, clean san facs; excel rest in Michelin Guide; pitch price variable (lge pitches avail); cash machine; beauty cent; access tight to some pitches."* **€65.50, E20.** **2024**

See advertisement

OLIVA *4E2* (3km SE Coastal) *38.90555, -0.06666*
Eurocamping, Ctra València-Oliva, Partida Rabdells s/n, 46780 Playa de Oliva (València) **962-85 40 98; info@eurocamping-es.com; www.eurocamping-es.com**

12 €2.16 (htd) WD MSP sand adj

Fr N exit AP7/E15 junc 61 onto N332 dir Alicante. Drive S thro Oliva & exit N332 km 209.9 sp 'urbanización'. At v lge hotel Oliva Nova Golf take 3rd exit at rndabt sp Oliva & foll camping sp to site. Fr S exit AP7 junc 62 onto N332 dir València, exit at km 209 sp 'urbanización', then as above. Lge, hdstg, mkd, hdg, pt shd, EHU (6-10A) €4.64-6.70; gas; bbq; red long stay; TV; phone; ccard acc; bike hire; CKE. *"Gd facs; busy, well-maintained, clean site adj housing development; helpful British owners; beautiful clean beach; gd rest; gd beach walks; cycle rte thro orange groves to town; pitch far fr recep if poss, night noise fr generators 1700-2400; recep clsd 1400-1600; highly rec; rest stretched; busy site."* **€45.00** **2024**

OLIVA *4E2* (3km S Coastal) *38.89444, -0.05361*
Camping Olé, Partida Algua Morta s/n, 46780 Playa de Oliva (València) **962-85 75 17; campingole@hotmail.com; www.camping-ole.com**

12 €3.15 (htd) WD sand adj

Exit AP7/E15 junc 61 onto N332 dir Valencia/Oliva. At km 209 (bef bdge) turn R sp 'Urbanización. At 1st rndabt, take 2nd exit past golf club ent, then 1st exit at next rndabt, turn L sp ' Camping Olé' & others. Site down narr rd on L. Lge, hdstg, mkd, hdg, pt shd, EHU (6-10A) €5.74; gas; bbq; red long stay; 15% statics; phone; Eng spkn; adv bkg acc; ccard acc; bike hire; tennis 600m; fishing; golf adj; games rm; horseriding 2km; CKE. *"Many sports & activities; direct access to beach; excel site; rest across rd very nice; gd value; pool only opens 1st July."* **€50.00** **2024**

OLVERA *2H3* (4.2km E Rural) *36.93905, -5.21719*
Camping Pueblo Blanco, Ctra N384, Km 69, 11690 Olvera (Cadiz) **619 45 35 34; info@campingpueblo blanco.com; www.campingpuebloblanco.com**

12 €1.50 WD MSP

Bet Antequera and Jerez de la Frontera, on the A384, at 69km marker. About 3km bef Olvera on the R. Wide driveway 600m to the top. Lge, unshd, pt sl, terr, EHU (16A) €4; bbq; red long stay; TV; Eng spkn; adv bkg acc; games rm. *"Site has 360 degree mountain views; ideal for walking; 12 bungalows; pool games area; bird watching and Pueblo Blanco; vg site, but not quite finished."* **€27.50** **2024**

OROPESA *3D2* (4.2km N Coastal) *40.12125, 0.15848*
Camping Didota, Avenida de la Didota s/n, 12594 Oropesa del Mar (Castellón) **964 31 95 51 or 635 65 28 10; info@campingdidota.es; www.campingdidota.es**

12 WD sand

N on rd E-15 fr València to Barcelona, bear L at exit 45 sp Oropesa del Mar. Turn L onto N-340. Turn R at next exit, then cont strt at rndabt onto on Avenida La Ratlla. Foll camping sp. Med, pt shd, EHU (6-10A) €4.30; gas; 10% statics; adv bkg acc; ccard acc. *"Gd site, helpful friendly staff; excel pool."* **€45.00** **2024**

OROPESA *3D2* (3km NE Coastal) *40.12786, 0.16088* **Camping Torre La Sal,** Camí L'Atall s/n, 12595 Ribera de Cabanes (Castellón) **964-31 95 96 or 627-79 34 14; info@campingtorrelasal.com; www.campingtorrelasal.com**

12 (except Jul/Aug) (htd) nr (covrd, htd) shgl adj

Leave AP7 at exit 44 or 45 & take N340 twd Tarragona. Foll camp sp fr km 1000.1 stone. Do not confuse with Torre La Sal 2 or Torre Maria. 1*, Lge, hdstg, mkd, hdg, pt shd, EHU (10A) €4.20; gas; bbq; red long stay; TV; 10% statics; bus 200m; Eng spkn; adv bkg acc; ccard acc; tennis; games area; CKE. *"Clean, well-maintained, peaceful site; elec metered for long stays; night security guard."* **€28.90** **2024**

OROPESA *3D2* (3.5km NE Coastal) *40.1275, 0.15972* **Bravo Playa Camping Resort,** Cami L'Atall s/n, 12595 Ribera de Cabanes (Castellón) **964-31 95 67; camping@bravoplaya.com; www.bravoplaya.com**

12 (htd) (covrd, htd) shgl adj

Leave AP7 at exit 45 & take N340 twd Tarragona. Foll camp sp fr km 1000 stone. Site adj Torre La Sal 1. 1*, Lge, hdstg, mkd, hdg, pt shd, serviced pitches; EHU (10A) inc; gas; red long stay; TV; 10% statics; Eng spkn; adv bkg acc; games area; tennis; sauna; CKE. *"Vg, clean, peaceful, well-run site; lger pitches nr pool; library; more mature c'vanners very welcome; many dogs; poss diff for lge o'fits & m'vans; excel rest; excel beach with dunes; excel site, spotless facs, highly rec."* **€60.00** **2024**

PALAFRUGELL *3B3* (5km E Coastal) *41.9005, 3.1893* **Kim's Camping,** Calle Font d'en Xeco s/n, 17211 Llafranc (Gerona) **972-30 11 56; info@campingkims.com; www.campingkims.com**

sand 500m

Exit AP7 at junc 6 Gerona Nord if coming fr France, or junc 9 fr S dir Palamós. Foll sp for Palafrugell, Playa Llafranc. Site is 500m N of Llafranc. 3*, Lge, hdstg, mkd, hdg, shd, sl, terr, EHU (5A) inc; gas; bbq (gas); red long stay; TV; 10% statics; phone; Eng spkn; adv bkg acc; ccard acc; watersports; golf 10km; games area; excursions; tennis 500m; games rm; CKE. *"Excel, well-organised, friendly, fam run site; steep site rds, new 2nd ent fr dual c'way fr Palafrugell to llafranc for lge o'fits & steps to rd to beach; bike hire 500m; guarded; discount in high ssn for stays over 1 wk; excel, modern san facs; beautiful coastal area; mostly gd size pitches."* **€57.00, 14 Apr-24 Sep.** **2023**

PALAFRUGELL *3B3* (5km S Coastal) *41.88879, 3.17928* **Camping Moby Dick,** Carrer de la Costa Verda 16-28, 17210 Calella de Palafrugell (Gerona) **972-61 43 07; info@campingmobydick.com; www.campingmobydick.com**

€3.30 nr shgl 100m

Fr Palafrugell foll sps to Calella. At rndabt just bef Calella turn R, then 4th L, site clearly sp on R. Med, hdstg, pt shd, sl, terr, EHU (10A); TV; 15% statics; phone; bus 100m; Eng spkn; adv bkg acc; ccard acc; CKE. *"Nice views fr upper terraces; gd rest; very friendly; very pretty sm resort; lovely coastal walks; gd value; excel; lovely sea views; great site."* **€35.00, 25 Mar-30 Sep.** **2022**

PALAMOS *3B3* (1km N Coastal) *41.85044, 3.13873* **Camping Palamós,** Ctra La Fosca 12, 17230 Palamós (Gerona) **972-31 42 96; campingpal@grn.es; www.campingpalamos.com**

€2 nr (htd) shgl adj

App Palamós on C66/C31 fr Gerona & Palafrugell turn L 16m after overhead sp Sant Feliu-Palamós at sm sp La Fosca & campsites. Lge, pt shd, pt sl, terr, EHU (4A) €2.70; gas; 30% statics; phone; ccard acc; golf; tennis. **€40.00, 27 Mar-30 Sep.** **2024**

PALAMOS *3B3* (2km NE Coastal) *41.87277, 3.15055* **Camping Benelux,** Paratge Torre Mirona s/n, 17230 Palamós (Gerona) **972-31 55 75; www.cbenelux.com**

sand 1km

Turn E off Palamós-La Bisbal rd (C66/C31) at junc 328. Site in 800m on minor metalled rd, twd sea at Playa del Castell. Lge, hdstg, mkd, pt shd, terr, EHU (10A) €6.90; gas; bbq; red long stay; TV; 30% statics; phone; Eng spkn; adv bkg acc; ccard acc; CKE. *"In pine woods; many long stay British/Dutch; friendly owner; safe dep; clean facs poss ltd LS; car wash; currency exchange; poss flooding in heavy rain; rough grnd; marvellous walking/cycling area; many little coves."* **€36.70, 24 Mar-25 Sep.** **2022**

PALAMOS *3B3* (3km W Coastal) *41.84700, 3.09861* **Eurocamping,** Avda de Catalunya 15, 17252 Sant Antoni de Calonge (Gerona) **972-65 08 79; info@euro-camping.com; www.euro-camping.com**

€4 sand 300m

Exit A7 junc 6 dir Palamós on C66 & Sant Feliu C31. Take exit Sant Antoni; on ent Sant Antoni turn R at 1st rndabt. Visible fr main rd at cent of Sant Antoni. 1*, V lge, mkd, hdg, shd, serviced pitches; EHU (6A) inc; bbq; red long stay; TV; 15% statics; phone; Eng spkn; adv bkg acc; ccard acc; games area; games rm; tennis; golf 7km; waterpark. *"Excel facs for families; fitness rm; doctor Jul & Aug; car wash; lots to do in area; excel; lots of ssnal pitches; immac san facs; generous flat pitches; waterpark 5km; helpful, friendly staff."* **€54.00, 28 Apr-17 Sep.** **2023**

PALS *3B3* (6km NE Coastal) *41.98132, 3.20125* **Camping Inter Pals,** Avda Mediterránea s/n, Km 45, 17256 Playa de Pals (Gerona) **972-63 61 79; interpals@interpals.com; www.interpals.com**

€3.50 (htd) nr sand 600m

Exit A7 junc 6 dir Palamós onto C66. Turn N sp Pals & foll sp Playa/Platja de Pals, pass Camping Neptune sp on L then Golf Aparthotel on R. At rndbt take 2nd exit, site clearly sp on L approx 500m. Lge, shd, pt sl, terr, EHU (5-10A) inc; TV; 20% statics; phone; adv bkg acc; golf 1km; tennis; bike hire; watersports; games area; CKE. *"Lovely, well-maintained site in pine forest; poss diff lge o'fits - lge pitches at lower end of site; naturist beach 1km; modern, well-maintained facs."* **€55.60, 1 Apr-25 Sep. 2024**

PALS *3B3* (6km NE Coastal) *42.0012, 3.19382* **Camping Playa Brava,** Playa Pals, 17256 Pals (Gerona) **972-63 68 94; info@playabrava.com; www.playabrava.com**

nr sand adj

App Pals on rd 650 fr N or S. Avoid Pals cent. Fr by-pass take rd E sp Playa de Pals at rndabt. In 4km turn L opp shops, in 400m turn L past golf course, site on L bef beach. Avoid Begur & coast rd. 3*, Lge, shd, EHU inc; gas; bbq (charcoal, elec, gas); sw nr; adv bkg acc; tennis; car wash; bike hire. *"Guarded; gd facs for children & families."* **€69.00, 15 May-12 Sep, E35. 2022**

PALS *3B3* (1km E Rural) *41.95541, 3.15780* **Camping Resort Mas Patoxas,** Ctra Torroella-Palafrugell, Km 339, 17256 Pals (Gerona) **972-63 69 28; info@campingmaspatoxas.com; www.camping maspatoxas.com**

12 €6.20 (htd) sand 4km

AP7 exit 6 onto C66 Palamós/La Bisbal, turn L via Torrent to Pals. Turn R & site on R almost opp old town of Pals on rd to Torroella de Montgri. Or fr Palafrugell on C31 turn at km 339. 3*, Lge, mkd, shd, terr, serviced pitches; EHU (5A) inc; gas; red long stay; TV; phone; Eng spkn; adv bkg req; ccard acc; bike hire; games area; tennis; site clsd 14 Dec-16 Jan; golf 4km; CKE. *"Excel; recep clsd Monday LS; gd security."* **€69.00, E45. 2022**

PALS *3B3* (4km E Rural) *41.98555, 3.18194* **Camping Cypsela,** Rodors 7, 17256 Playa de Pals (Gerona) **972-66 76 96; info@cypsela.com; www.cypsela.com**

sand 1.5km

Exit AP7 junc 6, rd C66 dir Palamós. 7km fr La Bisbal take dir Pals & foll sp Playa/Platja de Pals, site sp. 5*, V lge, hdstg, mkd, hdg, shd, serviced pitches; EHU (6-10A) inc; gas; bbq; sw nr; red long stay; TV; 60% statics; Eng spkn; adv bkg acc; ccard acc; tennis; golf 1km; games rm; bike hire; CKE. *"Noise levels controlled after midnight; excel san facs; mini golf & other sports; free bus to beach; private bthrms avail; 4 grades of pitch/price (highest price shown); vg site."* **€48.00, 4 May-10 Sep, E36. 2022**

PAMPLONA *3B1* (7km N Rural) *42.85776, -1.62250* **Camping Ezcaba,** Ctra a Francia, km 2,5, 31194 Eusa-Oricain (Navarre) **948-33 03 15; info@campingezcaba.com; www.campingezcaba.com**

12 €2.95

Fr N leave AP15 onto NA30 (N ring rd) to N121A sp Francia/Iruña. Pass Arre & Oricáin, turn L foll site sp 500m on R dir Berriosuso. Site on R in 500m - fairly steep ent. Or fr S leave AP15 onto NA32 (E by-pass) to N121A sp Francia/Iruña, then as above. Med, mkd, pt shd, pt sl, EHU (10A) €5.50; gas; phone; bus 1km; adv bkg acc; horseriding; tennis. *"Helpful, friendly staff; sm pitches unsuitable lge o'fits & poss diff due trees, esp when site full; attractive setting; gd pool, bar & rest; ltd facs LS & poss long walk to san facs; in winter use as NH only; phone to check open LS; excel cycle track to Pamplona; quiet rural site; gd facs not htd."* **€23.60 2023**

PARADA DE SIL *1B2* (3km NW Rural) *42.38941, -7.58885* **Camping Cañón do Sil,** Lugar de Castro s/n, 32740 Parada de Sil **988 408 762; info@canondosilcamping.com; www.canondosilcamping.com**

12 nr

OU-0604 to Ctra De Castro, turn R on OU-0605. Turn L to Ctra da Castro, site on L. Med, pt shd, terr, EHU €4. *"Amazing location on the edge of Rv Sil Gorge; gd walks fr site; vg."* **€23.00 2022**

PENAFIEL *1C4* (1km SW Rural) *41.59538, -4.12811* **Camping Riberduero,** Avda Polideportivo 51, 47300 Peñafiel **983-88 16 37; info@campingriberduero.com; www.campingriberduero.com**

€1.50 (htd)

Fr Valladolid 56km or Aranda de Duero 38km on N122. In Peñafiel take VA223 dir Cuéllar, foll sp to sports cent/camping. Med, mkd, hdstg, shd, EHU (5A) €5; gas; red long stay; TV; 20% statics; phone; bus 1km; Eng spkn; adv bkg acc; ccard acc; site open w/end only LS; bike hire. *"Excel, well-kept site; interesting, historical area; ideal for wheelchair users; sm pitches and access diff due to trees."* **€30.00, 22 Mar-6 Oct. 2024**

PENISCOLA *3D2* (2km N Coastal) *40.37916, 0.38833* **Camping Los Pinos,** Calle Abellars s/n, 12598 Peñíscola (Castellón) **964-48 03 79; info@campinglospinos.com; www.campinglospinos.com**

12 1.5km

Exit A7 junc 43 or N340 sp Peñíscola. Site sp on L. 1*, Med, mkd, hdg, pt shd, EHU (10A) €5.95; gas; bbq; TV; 10% statics; phone; bus fr site; Eng spkn; adv bkg acc; games rm. *"Narr site rds, lots of trees; poss diff access some pitches; vg."* **€30.00 2022**

300
sunny
days
a year
120 kilometers of beaches of all kinds and more than 300 days of sunshine a year.

PENISCOLA *3D2* (2km NW Rural) *40.40158, 0.38116* **Camping Spa Natura Resort,** Partida Villarroyos s/n, Playa Montana, 12598 Peñíscola-Benicarló (Castellón) **964-47 54 80; info@spanaturaresort.com; www.spanaturaresort.net**

12 €3 (free LS) (htd) (htd) sand 2.5km

Exit AP7 junc 43, within 50m of toll booths turn R immed then immed L & foll site sp twd Benicarló (NB R turn is on slip rd). Fr N340 take CV141 to Peñíscola. Cross m'way bdge & immed turn L; site sp. 3*, Med, hdstg, mkd, shd, serviced pitches; EHU (6A) inc; gas; bbq; red long stay; twin axles; TV; 50% statics; phone; bus 600m; Eng spkn; adv bkg acc; ccard acc; games rm; tennis; waterslide; car wash; sauna; games area; gym; bike hire; CKE. *"Vg site; helpful, enthusiastic staff; c'van storage; spa; wellness cent; jacuzzi; gd clean san facs; wide range of facs; gd cycling."* **€40.00, E23.** **2024**

PILAR DE LA HORADADA *4F2* (4km NE Coastal) *37.87916, -0.76555* **Lo Monte Camping & Caravaning,** Avenida Comunidada Valenciana No 157 CP 03190 **00 34 966 766 782; info@camplinglomonte-alicante.es; www.campinglomonte.com/en/**

12 €1 (htd) (covrd, htd) 1km

Exit 770 of AP7 dir Pilar de la Horadada; take the 1st L. 4*, Med, mkd, hdg, serviced pitches; EHU (16A) €0.40; bbq; Eng spkn; adv bkg acc; ccard acc; bike hire; games rm; CKE. *"New site; superb facs, exceptionally clean; great location, lots of golf & gd for walks & cycling; rec; excel; gym/wellness cent; beautifully laid out; neat; gd pool; v gd rest; isolated, nothing around site."* **€49.00** **2023**

PINEDA DE MAR *3C3* (1km SW Coastal) *41.61827, 2.67891* **Camping Bellsol,** Passeig Maritim 46, 08397 Pineda de Mar **937-67 17 78; info@campingbellsol.com; www.campingbellsol.com**

Fr N, take exit AP7 Junc 9 & immed turn R onto N11 dir Barcelona. Foll sp Pineda de Mar and turn L twd Paseo Maritim at exit at rv x-ing. Fr S on C32, exit 122 dir Pineda de Mar & foll dir Paseo Maritim & Campings fr same rndabt. Beware narr rds at other turnings. Lge, hdstg, shd, EHU (4A); twin axles; red long stay; 15% statics; bus nrby, train 800m; Eng spkn; adv bkg acc; CKE. *"V friendly & helpful staff; walking; bike & moped hire; sea fishing trips; vg."* **€34.60, 19 Mar-31 Dec.** **2022**

PLASENCIA *1D3* (4km NE Urban) *40.04348, -6.05751* **Camping La Chopera,** Ctra N110, Km 401.3, Valle del Jerte, 10600 Plasencia (Caceras) **927-41 66 60; lachopera@campinglachopera.com; www.campinglachopera.com**

12

In Plasencia on N630 turn E on N110 sp Ávila & foll sp indus est & sp to site. 3*, Med, mkd, pt shd, EHU (5A); red long stay; twin axles; Eng spkn; adv bkg acc; ccard acc; tennis; bike hire; games area; CKE. *"Peaceful & spacious; much birdsong; conv Manfragüe National Park (breeding of black/Egyptian vultures, black storks, imperial eagles); excel pool & modern facs; helpful owners; shop (Jul & Aug); Carrefour in town; 35 min walk to town; vg."* **€26.60** **2024**

PLASENCIA *1D3* (14km S Rural) *39.94361, -6.08444* **Camping Parque Natural Monfragüe,** Ctra Plasencia-Trujillo, Km 10, 10680 Malpartida de Plasencia (Cáceres) **927-45 92 33 or 605-94 08 78 (mob); contacto@campingmonfrague.com; www.campingmonfrague.com**

12 (htd)

Fr N on A66/N630 by-pass town, 5km S of town at flyover junc take EXA1 (EX108) sp Navalmoral de la Mata. In 6km turn R onto EX208 dir Trujillo, site on L in 5km. 3*, Med, hdg, pt shd, pt sl, terr, EHU (10A) €4; gas; bbq; TV; 10% statics; phone; Eng spkn; ccard acc; tennis; archery; bike hire; horseriding; games area. *"Friendly, helpful staff; red ACSI; vg, gd rest; clean, tidy, busy site but poss dusty, hoses avail; 10km to National Park (birdwatching trips); rambling; 4x4 off-rd; many birds on site; excel year round base; new excel san facs; discounted fees must be paid in cash; pitches muddy after heavy rain; peaceful; interesting over Halloween."* **€20.40** **2024**

PLAYA DE ARO *3B3* (2km N Coastal) *41.83116, 3.08366* **Camping Cala Gogo,** Avda Andorra 13, 17251 Calonge (Gerona) **972-65 15 64; calagogo@calagogo.es; www.calagogo.es**

€2 (htd) sand adj

Exit AP7 junc 6 dir Palamós/Sant Feliu. Fr Palamós take C253 coast rd S twd Sant Antoni, site on R 2km fr Playa de Aro, sp. 3*, Lge, pt shd, pt sl, terr, serviced pitches; EHU (10A) inc; gas; bbq; red long stay; TV; Eng spkn; adv bkg acc; boat hire; tennis; games area; golf 4km; bike hire; games rm. *"Clean & recently upgraded san facs; rest/bar with terr; no dogs Jul/Aug; diving school; site terraced into pinewood on steep hillside; excel family site."* **€52.00, 16 Apr-18 Sep.** **2022**

PLAYA DE ARO *3B3* (2km N Coastal) *41.83666, 3.08722* **Camping Treumal,** Ctra Playa de Aro/ Palamós, C253, Km 47.5, 17250 Playa de Arro (Gerona) **972-65 10 95; info@campingtreumal.com; www.campingtreumal.com**

sand adj

Exit m'way at junc 6, 7 or 9 dir Sant Feliu de Guixols to Playa de Aro; site is sp at km 47.5 fr C253 coast rd SW of Palamós. 1*, Lge, mkd, shd, terr, EHU (10A) inc; gas; 25% statics; phone; Eng spkn; adv bkg acc; ccard acc; car wash; sports facs; games rm; tennis 1km; bike hire; golf 5km; fishing; CKE. *"Peaceful site in pine trees; excel san facs; manhandling poss req onto terr pitches; gd beach."* **€49.00, 31 Mar-30 Sep. 2022**

POLA DE SOMIEDO *1A3* (0.3km E Rural) *43.09222, -6.25222* **Camping La Pomerada de Somiedo,** 33840 Pola de Somiedo (Asturias) **985-76 34 04; csomiedo@infonegocio.com**

nr nr

W fr Oviedo on A63, turn S onto AS15/AS227 to Augasmestas & Pola de Somiedo. Site adj Hotel Alba, sp fr vill. Route on steep, winding, mountain rd - suitable sm, powerful o'fits only. Sm, mkd, pt shd, EHU €4.20. *"Mountain views; nr national park."* **€19.00, 1 Apr-31 Dec. 2022**

PONFERRADA *1B3* (16km W Rural) *42.56160, -6.74590* **Camping El Bierzo,** 24550 Villamartín de la Abadia (León) **987-56 25 15; info@campingbierzo.com; www.campingbierzo.com**

12 nr

Exit A6 junc 399 dir Carracedelo; after rndabt turn onto NV1 & foll sp Villamartín. Bef ent Villamartín turn L & foll site sp. 2*, Med, pt shd, EHU (3-5A) €5; phone; bus 1km; adv bkg acc; CKE. *"Attractive, rvside site in pleasant, lge, level grassed area with mature trees; gd, clean facs; friendly, helpful owner takes pride in his site; Roman & medieval attractions nr; sm rv beach adj; no bus svrs into Ponferrada."* **€22.00 2024**

PONT DE SUERT *3B2* (16km NE Rural) *42.51900, 8.84600* **Camping Taüll,** Ctra Taüll s/n, 25528 Taüll (Lleida) **973 69 61 74; campingtaull@gmail.com; www.campingtaull.com**

12 €3 (htd) nr nr nr

Fr Pont de Suert 3km N on N230 then NE on L500 dir Caldes de Boí. In 13km turn R into Taüll. Site sp on R. 1*, Sm, pt shd, pt sl, terr, EHU €6; 30% statics; clsd 15 Oct-15 Nov; CKE. *"Excel facs; taxis into National Park avail; ltd touring pitches; suitable sm m'vans only; many bars & rest in pretty vill."* **€28.50 2024**

PONT DE SUERT *3B2* (5km NW Rural) *42.43944, 0.69860* **Camping Baliera,** Ctra N260, Km 355.5, Castejón de Sos, 22523 Bonansa (Huesca) **974-55 40 16; info@baliera.com; www.baliera.com**

12 €3.80 (htd)

N fr Pont de Suert on N230 turn L opp petrol stn onto N260 sp Castejón de Sos. In 1km turn L onto A1605 sp Bonansa, site on L immed over rv bdge. Site sp fr N230. Lge, mkd, shd, pt sl, terr, EHU (5-10A) €5; gas; bbq; TV (pitch); 50% statics; phone; Eng spkn; ccard acc; rv fishing; horseriding 4km; site clsd Nov & Xmas; bike hire; golf 4km; CKE. *"Excel, well-run, peaceful site in parkland setting; walking in summer, skiing in winter; excel cent for touring; conv Vielha tunnel; weights rm; all facs up steps; pt of site v sl; helpful owner proud of his site; clean facs, some rvside pitches."* **€32.40 2024**

"I need an on-site restaurant"

We do our best to make sure site information is correct, but it is always best to check any must-have facilities are still available or will be open during your visit.

PORT DE LA SELVA, EL *3B3* (3km W Coastal) *42.34222, 3.18333* **Camping Port de la Vall,** Ctra Port de Llançà, 17489 El Port de la Selva (Gerona) **972-38 71 86; portdelavall@terra.es**

€2.95 shgl adj

On coast rd fr French border at Llançà take GI612 twd El Port de la Selva. Site on L, easily seen. Lge, pt shd, EHU (3-5A) €6; gas; 10% statics; phone; adv bkg acc; ccard acc. *"Easy 1/2 hr walk to harbour; gd site; sm pitches & low branches poss diff - check bef siting; san facs v clean."* **€29.00, 1 Mar-15 Oct. 2022**

POTES *1A4* (1km W Rural) *43.15527, -4.63694* **Camping La Viorna,** Ctra Santo Toribio, Km 1, Mieses, 39570 Potes (Cantabria) **942-73 20 21; info@campinglaviorna.com; www.campinglaviorna.com**

(htd)

Exit N634 at junc 272 onto N621 dir Panes & Potes - narr, winding rd (passable for c'vans). Fr Potes take rd to Fuente Dé sp Espinama; in 1km turn L sp Toribio. Site on R in 1km, sp fr Potes. Do not use Sat Nav. Med, mkd, pt shd, terr, EHU (6A) €3.40 (poss rev pol); bbq; bus 1km; Eng spkn; adv bkg acc; ccard acc; bike hire; CKE. *"Lovely views; gd walks; friendly, family-run, clean, tidy site; gd pool; ideal Picos de Europa; conv cable car, 4x4 tours, trekking; mkt on Mon; festival mid-Sep v noisy; some pitches diff in wet & diff lge o'fits; excel san facs; voted 8th best camp in Spain; excel."* **€30.10, 1 Apr-1 Nov. 2023**

SPAIN

POTES *1A4* (3km W Rural) *43.15742, -4.65617* **Camping La Isla-Picos de Europa,** Ctra Potes-Fuente Dé, 39586 Turieno (Cantabria) **942-73 08 96; campinglaislapicosdeeuropa@gmail.com; www.campinglaislapicosdeeuropa.com**

Take N521 W fr Potes twd Espinama, site on R in 3km thro vill of Turieno (app Potes fr N). 2*, Med, mkd, shd, pt sl, EHU (6A) €4 (poss rev pol); gas; bbq; red long stay; 10% statics; phone; Eng spkn; adv bkg acc; ccard acc; horseriding; cycling; CKE. *"Delightful, family-run site; friendly, helpful owners; gd san facs; conv cable car & mountain walks (map fr recep); many trees & low branches; 4x4 touring; walking; mountain treks in area; hang-gliding; rec early am dep to avoid coaches on gorge rd; highly rec; lovely loc, gd facs."* **€23.00, 1 Apr-15 Oct. 2023**

PUERTO DE MAZARRON *4G1* (5km NE Coastal) *37.5800, -1.1950* **Camping Los Madriles,** Ctra a la Azohía 60, Km 4.5, 30868 Isla Plana (Murcia) **968-15 21 51; info@campinglosmadriles.com or reservas@campinglosmadriles.es; www.campinglosmadriles.com**

12 (htd)

shgl 500m

Fr Cartegena on N332 dir Puerto de Mazarrón. Turn L at rd junc sp La Azohía (32km). Site in 4km sp. Fr Murcia on E15/N340 dir Lorca exit junc 627 onto MU603 to Mazarrón, then foll sp. (Do not use rd fr Cartegena unless powerful tow vehicle/gd weight differential - use rte fr m'way thro Mazarrón). Lge, hdg, mkd, hdstg, pt shd, pt sl, serviced pitches; EHU (10A) €5; gas; red long stay; bus; Eng spkn; adv bkg req; ccard acc; games area; jacuzzi; CKE. *"Clean, well-run, v popular winter site; adv bkg req; some sm pitches, some with sea views; sl bet terrs; 3 days min stay high ssn; v helpful staff; excel."* **€38.40 2024**

PUERTO DE SANTA MARIA, EL *2H3* (2km SW Coastal) *36.58768, -6.24092* **Camping Playa Las Dunas de San Antón,** Paseo Maritimo La Puntilla s/n, 11500 El Puerto de Santa María (Cádiz) **956-87 22 10; info@lasdunascamping.com; www.lasdunascamping.com**

12 sand 50m

Fr N or S exit A4 at El Puerto de Sta María. Foll site sp carefully to avoid narr rds of town cent. Site 2-3km S of marina & leisure complex of Puerto Sherry. Alt, fr A4 take Rota rd & look for sp to site & Hotel Playa Las Dunas. Site better sp fr this dir & avoids town. 3*, Lge, pt shd, pt sl, EHU (10A) inc; gas; 30% statics; phone; Eng spkn; adv bkg rec; ccard acc; sports facs; CKE. *"Friendly staff; conv Cádiz & Jerez sherry region, birdwatching areas & beaches; conv ferry or catamaran to Cádiz; facs poss stretched high ssn; pitches quiet away fr rd; take care caterpillars in spring, poss dangerous to dogs; dusty site but staff water rds; gd; excel facs; busy; guarded; excel new shwr block (2016); pool adj; old elec conns."* **€26.00 2024**

RIAZA *1C4* (1.5km W Rural) *41.26995, -3.49750* **Camping Riaza,** Ctra de la Estación s/n, 40500 Riaza (Segovia) **921-55 05 80; info@camping-riaza.com; www.camping-riaza.com**

12 (htd)

Fr N exit A1/E5 junc 104, fr S exit 103 onto N110 N. In 12km turn R at rndabt on ent to town, site on L. Lge, hdg, unshd, EHU (10A) €4.70 (rev pol); bbq; 30% statics; phone; bus 900m; Eng spkn; adv bkg acc; games rm; games area. *"Vg site; various pitch sizes - some lge; excel san facs; easy access to/fr Santander or Bilbao; dogs free; beautiful little town."* **€25.00 2023**

RIBADEO *1A2* (12km N Rural/Coastal) *43.554004, -7.111085* **Rinlo Costa Camping,** Rua Campo Maria Mendez, s/n 27715 Rinlo **679-25 52 81; info@rinlocosta.es; www.rinlocosta.es**

12

Fr N634 take LU141 twrds Rinlo. Over rly bdge (0.5km) take 1st L and foll rd round for another 0.5km. Turn L and site ahead on R. Sm, EHU (6A) €4.50; bbq; cooking facs; bike hire. **€24.00 2023**

RIBADEO *1A2* (4km E Coastal) *43.55097, -6.99699* **Camping Playa Peñarronda,** Playa de Peñarronda-Barres, 33794 Castropol (Asturias) **985-62 30 22 / 616-602 496; campingpenarrondacb@gmail.com; www.campingplayapenarronda.com**

sand adj

Exit A8 at km 498 onto N640 dir Lugo/Barres; turn R approx 500m and then foll site sp for 2km. 2*, Med, mkd, pt shd, EHU (6A) €4 (poss rev pol); gas; bbq; red long stay; 10% statics; phone; Eng spkn; games area; bike hire; CKE. *"Beautifully-kept, delightful, clean, friendly, family-run site on 'Blue Flag' beach; rec arr early to get pitch; facs clean; gd cycling along coastal paths & to Ribadeo; ltd facs LS, sm pitches; gd sized pitches, little shd."* **€23.60, Holy Week-25 Sep. 2024**

RIBADESELLA *1A3* (3km W Rural) *43.46258, -5.08725* **Camping Ribadesella,** Sebreño s/n, 33560 Ribadesella (Asturias) **985 858293 or 699-79 02 31; info@camping-ribadesella.com; www.camping-ribadesella.com**

€2.50 (covrd, htd)

sand 4km

W fr Ribadesella take N632. After 2km fork L up hill. Site on L after 2km. Poss diff for lge o'fits & alt rte fr Ribadesella vill to site to avoid steep uphill turn can be used. Lge, mkd, pt shd, pt sl, terr, EHU (10A) €5; gas; bbq; red long stay; Eng spkn; adv bkg acc; ccard acc; tennis; games area; games rm; CKE. *"Clean san facs; some sm pitches; attractive fishing vill; prehistoric cave paintings nrby; excel; not much shd; steps or slopes to walk to top rate facs; 35min easy downhill walk to town, shorter walk down steep lane to beach; rec; terr site; rest has cvrd terrace and lovely views."* **€36.00, 12 Apr-22 Sep. 2024**

RIBADESELLA *1A3* (8km W Rural/Coastal) *43.47472, -5.13416* **Camping Playa de Vega,** Vega, 33345 Ribadesella (Asturias) **985-86 04 06; info@campingplayadevega.com; www.campingplayadevega.com**

sand 400m

Fr A8 exit junc 336 sp Ribadesella W, thro Bones. At rndabt cont W dir Caravia, turn R opp quarry sp Playa de Vega. Fr cent of Ribadesella (poss congestion) W on N632. Cont for 5km past turning to autovia. Turn R at sp Vega & site. 3*, Med, hdg, pt shd, terr, serviced pitches; EHU €4.15; bbq; TV; phone; bus 700m; ccard acc; CKE. *"Sh walk to vg beach thro orchards; beach rest; sm pitches not suitable lge o'fits; poss overgrown LS; immac san facs; a gem of a site; beware very narr bdge on ent rd."* **€27.00, 15 Jun-15 Sep.** **2023**

RIBES DE FRESER *3B3* (0.5km NE Rural) *42.31260, 2.17570* **Camping Vall de Ribes,** Ctra de Pardines, Km 0.5, 17534 Ribes de Freser (Girona) **972-72 88 20 or 620-78 39 20; info@campingvallderibes.com; www.campingvallderibes.com**

12 €4.60 (htd) WD nr

N fr Ripoll on N152; turn E at Ribes de Freser; site beyond town dir Pardines. Site nr town but 1km by rd. App rd narr. Med, mkd, pt shd, terr, EHU (6A) €4.30; 50% statics; train 500m; CKE. *"Gd, basic site; steep footpath fr site to town; 10-20 min walk to stn; cog rlwy train to Núria a 'must' - spectacular gorge, gd walking & interesting exhibitions; sm/med o'fits only; poss unkempt statics LS; spectacular walk down fr the Vall de Nuria to Queralbs."* **€23.00** **2024**

ROCIO, EL *2G3* (2km N Rural) *37.14143, -6.49059* **Camping La Aldea,** Ctra del Rocío, Km 25, 21750 El Rocío,Almonte (Huelva) **959-44 26 77; info@campinglaaldea.com; www.campinglaaldea.com**

12 €4.25 (htd) WD MSP (htd)

Fr A49 turn S at junc 48 onto A483 by-passing Almonte, site sp just bef El Rocío rndabt. Fr W (Portugal) turn off at junc 60 to A484 to Almonte, then A483. 3*, Lge, hdstg, mkd, hdg, pt shd, EHU (10A) €6.50; gas; bbq; red long stay; 30% statics; phone; bus 500m; Eng spkn; adv bkg acc; ccard acc; horseriding nr; CKE. *"Well-appointed & maintained site; winter rallies; excel san facs; friendly, helpful staff; tight turns on site; most pitches have kerb or gully, van washing facs; pitches soft after rain; rd noise; easy walk to interesting town; avoid festival (in May-7 weeks after Easter) when town cr & site charges higher; poss windy; excel birdwatching nrby (lagoon 1km); beautiufl site; gd pool & rest."* **€19.00, E24.** **2022**

RONDA *2H3* (1km S Rural) *36.72111, -5.17166* **Camping El Sur,** Ctra Ronda-Algeciras Km 1.5, 29400 Ronda (Málaga) **952-87 59 39; info@campingelsur.com; www.campingelsur.com**

12 €1.70 (htd) WD MSP nr

Site on W side of A369 dir Algeciras. Do not tow thro Ronda. Med, mkd, hdstg, pt shd, sl, terr, EHU (5-10A) €4.30-5.35 (poss rev pol &/or no earth); red long stay; phone; Eng spkn; adv bkg acc; CKE. *"Gd rd fr coast with spectacular views; long haul for lge o'fits; busy family-run site in lovely setting; conv National Parks & Pileta Caves; poss diff access some pitches due trees & high kerbs; hard, rocky grnd; san facs poss stretched high ssn; easy walk to town; friendly staff; vg rest; excel."* **€27.00** **2024**

ROSES *3B3* (2.5km W Coastal) *42.26638, 3.15611* **Camping Salatà,** Port Reig s/n, 17480 Roses (Gerona) **972-25 60 86; info@campingsalata.com; www.campingsalata.com**

€2.80 (htd) WD (htd) sand 200m

App Roses on rd C260. On ent Roses take 1st R after Roses sp & Caprabo supmkt. Lge, mkd, hdstg, pt shd, EHU (6-10A) inc; gas; red long stay; 10% statics; phone; Eng spkn; adv bkg acc; ccard acc; CKE. *"Vg area for sub-aqua sports; vg clean facs, but not enough; dogs not acc Jul/Aug; red facs LS; pleasant walk/cycle to town; overpriced."* **€50.70, 12 Mar-31 Oct.** **2022**

SABINANIGO *3B2* (6km N Rural) *42.55694, -0.33722* **Camping Valle de Tena,** Ctra N260, Km 512.6, 22600 Senegüe (Huesca). **974-48 09 77 or 974-48 03 02; correo@campingvalledetena.es; www.campingbungalowsvalledetena.es/**

12 €2.70 (htd) WD MSP

Fr Jaca take N330, in 12km turn L onto N260 dir Biescas. In 5km ignore site sp Sorripas, cont for 500m to site on L - new ent at far end. Lge, mkd, unshd, terr, serviced pitches; EHU (6A) €6; TV; 60% statics; phone; Eng spkn; adv bkg acc; sports facs. *"Helpful staff; steep, narr site rd; sm pitches; hiking nrby; excel, busy NH to/fr France; rv rafting nr; rd noise during day but quiet at night; beautiful area; in reach of ski runs; v busy."* **€21.00** **2024**

SALAMANCA *1C3* (17km NE Rural) *41.05805, -5.54611* **Camping Olimpia,** Ctra de Gomecello, Km 3.150, 37427 Pedrosillo el Ralo (Salamanca) **923-08 08 54 or 620-46 12 07; info@campingolimpia.com; www.campingolimpia.com**

12 €1 (htd) WD

Exit A62 junc 225 dir Pedrosillo el Ralo & La Vellés, strt over rndabt, site sp. Sm, hdg, pt shd, EHU €3; phone; bus 300m; Eng spkn; adv bkg acc; site clsd 8-16 Sep; CKE. *"Helpful, friendly & pleasant owner; really gd 2 course meal for €10 (2014); handy fr rd with little noise & easy to park; poss open w/ends only LS; excel; grass pitches; clean facs; perfect; some pitches tight."* **€16.00** **2023**

SPAIN

SALAMANCA *1C3* (5km E Rural) *40.97611, -5.60472* **Camping Don Quijote,** Ctra Aldealengua, Km 1930, 37193 Cabrerizos (Salamanca) **923-20 90 52; reservas@campingdonquijote.com; www.camping donquijote.com**

sand 200m

Fr Madrid or fr S cross Rv Tormes by most easterly bdge to join inner ring rd. Foll Paseo de Canalejas for 800m to Plaza España. Turn R onto SA804 Avda de los Comuneros & strt on for 5km. Site ent 2km after town boundary sp. Fr other dirs, head into city & foll inner ring rd to Plaza España. Site well sp fr rv & ring rd. 3*, Med, hdstg, mkd, hdg, pt shd, EHU (10A) inc; bbq; twin axles; 10% statics; phone; bus; Eng spkn; adv bkg acc; ccard acc; rv fishing; CKE. *"Gd rv walks; conv city cent; 45 mins easy cycle ride 6km to town along rv; rv Tormes flows alongside site with pleasant walks; friendly owner; highly rec; new excel san facs (2016); v friendly; 12 min walk to bus stop; may not be suited for lge units; some late-night functions on w/ends."* **€23.60, 1 Mar-3 Nov. 2024**

SALAMANCA *1C3* (7km E Urban) *40.94798, -5.61456* **Camping Regio,** Ctra Ávila-Madrid, Km 4, 37900 Santa Marta de Tormes (Salamanca) **923-13 88 88; recepcion@campingregio.com; www.campingregio.com**

Fr E on SA20/N501 outer ring rd, pass hotel/camping sp visible on L & exit Sta Marta de Tormes, site directly behind Hotel Regio. Foll sp to hotel. 3*, Lge, mkd, pt shd, pt sl, EHU (10A) €3.95 (no earth); gas; TV; 5% statics; phone; bus to Salamanca; Eng spkn; ccard acc; car wash; bike hire; CKE. *"In LS stop at 24hr hotel recep; poss no hdstg in wet conditions; conv en rte Portugal; refurbished facs to excel standard; site poss untidy, & ltd security in LS; hotel pool high ssn; hypmkt 3km; spacious pitches but some poss tight for lge o'fits; take care lge brick markers when reversing; hourly bus in and out of city; excel pool; bar and restaurant on site; vg; facs up to gd standard & htd; highly rec."* **€23.00, E26. 2022**

SALAMANCA *1C3* (3km NW Rural) *40.99945, -5.67916* **Camping Ruta de la Plata,** Ctra de Villamayor, 37184 Villares de la Reina (Salamanca) **923-28 95 74; recepcion@campingrutadelaplata.com; www.campingrutadelaplata.com**

€1.50 (htd)

Fr N on A62/E80 Salamanca by-pass, exit junc 238 & foll sp Villamayor. Site on R about 800m after rndabt at stadium 'Helmántico'. Avoid SA300 - speed bumps. Fr S exit junc 240. Med, hdg, mkd, pt shd, pt sl, terr, EHU (6A) €2.90; gas; TV; bus to city at gate; golf 3km; CKE. *"Family-owned site; some gd, san facs tired (poss unhtd in winter); ltd facs LS; less site care LS & probs with EHU; conv NH; helpful owners; bus stop at camp gate, every hr."* **€27.00 2024**

SALOU *3C2* (1km S Urban/Coastal) *41.0752, 1.1176* **Camping Sanguli,** Paseo Miramar-Plaza Venus, 43840 Salou (Tarragona) **977-38 16 41; info@sangulisalou.com or booking@sangulisalou.co; www.sanguli.es**

(htd)

sand 50m

Exit AP7/E15 junc 35. At 1st rndbt take dir to Salou (Plaça Europa), at 2nd rndabt foll site sp. 5*, V lge, hdstg, mkd, shd, pt sl, serviced pitches; EHU (10A) inc; gas; bbq; red long stay; TV; 35% statics; phone; bus; Eng spkn; adv bkg rec; ccard acc; games area; waterslide; games rm; jacuzzi; car wash; tennis; CKE. *"Quiet end of Salou nr Cambrils & 3km Port Aventura; site facs recently updated/upgraded; fitness rm; excursions; cinema; youth club; mini club; amphitheatre; excel, well-maintained site."* **€75.00, 5 Apr-3 Nov. 2024**

SAN FULGENCIO *4F2* (7km ENE Coastal) *38.12094, -0.65982* **Camper Park San Fulgencio,** Calle Mar Cantábrico 7 Centro Comercial las Dunas (Alicante) **491 791 18 07 70 or 346 53 08 19 96; sanfulpark@gmail.com; www.camperparksanfulgencio.com**

Fr N on AP7, take exit 740 twd Guardamar; At rndabt exit onto CV-91. 2nd exit at next rndabt then 3rd exit at another rndabt and stay on CV91. Take 1st exit at rndabt onto N-332, merge onto N332 and go thro 1 rndabt. At next rndabt take 3rd exit onto Calle Mar Cantabrico, go thro next rndabt and site is on the L. Sm, hdstg, unshd, EHU (5A) inc; bus to Alicante 150m; Eng spkn. *"Sm m'van only site; gd facs; 1.75km to wooden area nr beach & sea; friendly helpful owner; gd atmosphere; Sat mkt; vg."* **€14.00 2024**

"Satellite navigation makes touring much easier"

Remember most sat navs don't know if you're towing or in a larger vehicle – always use yours alongside maps and site directions.

SAN ROQUE *2H3* (7km NE Rural) *36.25031, -5.33808* **Camping La Casita,** Ctra N340, Km 126.2, 11360 San Roque (Cádiz) **956-78 00 31**

€2.67 sand 3km

Site sp 'Via de Servicio' parallel to AP7/E15. Access at km 119 fr S, km 127 fr N. Site visible fr rd. Lge, pt shd, pt sl, terr, EHU (10A) €4.54; red long stay; 90% statics; phone; bus 100m; Eng spkn; adv bkg req; ccard acc; horseriding; CKE. *"Shwrs solar htd - water temp depends on weather (poss cold); san facs poss unclean; friendly staff; conv Gibraltar & Morocco; daily buses to La Línea & Algeciras; ferries to N Africa (secure parking at port); golf course next to site; great rest; poor site."* **€39.50 2022**

SAN SEBASTIAN/DONOSTIA *3A1* (7km W Rural) *43.30458, -2.04588* **wecamp San Sebastián (formerly Camping Igueldo),** Paseo Padre Orkolaga 69, 20008 San Sebastián (Guipúzkoa) **900-05 60 03; hola@sansebastian.wecamp.net; www.wecamp.net**

12 €6-7 sand 5km

Fr W on A8, leave m'way at junc 9 twd city cent, take 1st R & R at rndabt onto Avda de Tolosa sp Ondarreta. At sea front turn hard L at rndabt sp to site (Avda Satrústegui) & foll sp up steep hill 4km to site. Fr E exit junc 8 then as above. Site sp as Garoa Camping Bungalows. Steep app poss diff for lge o'fits. Lge, mkd, hdg, pt shd, terr, serviced pitches; EHU (10A) inc; gas; red long stay; TV; phone; bus to city adj; Eng spkn; CKE. *"Vg, clean facs; sm pitches poss diff; spectacular views; pitches muddy when wet; excel rest 1km (open in winter); pool 5km; frequent bus to beautiful, interesting town; new pool (2017)."* **€22.00** **2024**

See advertisement

"There aren't many sites open at this time of year"

If you're travelling outside peak season remember to call ahead to check site opening dates – even if the entry says 'open all year'.

SAN TIRSO DE ABRES *1A2* (0.5km N Rural) *43.41352, -7.14141* **Amaido,** El Llano, 33774 San Tirso de Abres **623-38 31 00; amaido@amaido.com; www.amaido.com**

Head N on A6 twds Lugo & exit 497 for N-640 twds Oviedo/Lugo Centro cidade. At rndabt take 4th exit onto N-640, turn R at LU-P-6104, turn R onto Vegas, then take 2nd L. Site at end of rd. Med, hdg, pt shd, terr, EHU (6A); bbq; twin axles; TV; adv bkg acc; bike hire; games area. *"Lovely wooded site set in a circle around facs; farm animals; vg site."*
€20.00, 10 Apr-15 Sep. **2024**

SAN VICENTE DE LA BARQUERA *1A4* (1km E Coastal) *43.38901, -4.3853* **Camping El Rosal,** Ctra de la Playa s/n, 39540 San Vicente de la Barquera (Cantabria) **942-71 01 65; info@campingelrosal.com; www.campingelrosal.com**

sand adj

Fr A8 km 264, foll sp San Vicente. Turn R over bdge then 1st L (site sp) immed at end of bdge; keep L & foll sp to site. Barier height 3.1m. Med, mkd, pt shd, pt sl, terr, EHU (6A) €4.80; gas; phone; Eng spkn; adv bkg acc; ccard acc; CKE. *"Lovely site in pine wood o'looking bay; surfing beach; some modern, clean facs; helpful staff; vg rest; easy walk or cycle ride to interesting town; Sat mkt; no hot water at sinks."*
€27.00, 1 Apr-30 Sep. **2024**

"That's changed – Should I let the Club know?"

If you find something on site that's different from the site entry, fill in a report and let us know. See camc.com/europereport.

SAN VICENTE DE LA BARQUERA *1A4* (6km E Coastal) *43.38529, -4.33831* **Camping Playa de Oyambre,** Finca Peña Gerra, 39540 San Vicente de la Barquera (Cantabria) **942-71 14 61; camping@oyambre.com; www.oyambre.com**

(covrd, indoor) 800m

E70/A8 Santander-Oviedo, exit sp 264 S. Vicente de la Barquera, then N634 for 3 km to Comillas exit on the Ctra La Revilla-Comillas (CA 131) bet km posts 27 and 28. 4*, Lge, hdg, mkd, pt shd, terr, EHU (10A) €6; gas; 40% statics; bus 300m; Eng spkn; adv bkg acc; ccard acc; gym, two pools, playground, laundry service, horseback riding, biking, hiking, golf; CKE. *"V well-kept site; clean, helpful owner; quiet week days LS; gd base for N coast & Picos de Europa; 4x4 avail to tow to pitch if wet; some sm pitches & rd noise some pitches; conv Santander ferry; immac san facs; excel site; staff speak gd english; rest rec; gd base to tour N coast & Picos de Europa."* **€32.00, 4 Mar-30 Oct.** **2022**

SANT PERE PESCADOR *3B3* (1km SE Coastal) *42.18180, 3.10403* **Camping L'Àmfora,** Avda Josep Tarradellas 2, 17470 Sant Pere Pescador (Gerona) **972-52 05 40; info@campingamfora.com; www.campingamfora.com**

€4.95 (htd) sand adj

Fr N exit junc 3 fr AP7 onto N11 fro Figueres/ Roses. At junc with C260 foll sp Castelló d'Empúries & Roses. At Castelló turn R at rndabt sp Sant Pere Pescador then foll sp to L'Amfora. Fr S exit junc 5 fr AP7 onto GI 623/GI 624 to Sant Pere Pescador. 4*, V lge, mkd, hdg, pt shd, serviced pitches; EHU (10A) inc; gas; bbq (charcoal, elec); red long stay; TV; 15% statics; phone; Eng spkn; adv bkg acc; fishing; horseriding 5km; bike hire; games rm; windsurfing school; tennis; waterslide; ice; CKE. *"Excel, well-run, clean site; no o'fits over 10m Apr-Sep; helpful staff; immac san facs; gd rest; private san facs avail; poss flooding on some pitches when wet; Parque Acuatico 18km."*
€60.40, 14 Apr-27 Sep, E22. **2024**

See advertisement above

"I like to fill in the reports as I travel from site to site"

You'll find report forms at the back of this guide, or you can fill them in online at camc.com/europereport.

SANT PERE PESCADOR *3B3* (2km SE Coastal) *42.16194, 3.10888* **Camping Las Dunas,** 17470 Sant Pere Pescador (Gerona) (Postal Address: Aptdo Correos 23, 17130 L'Escala) **972-52 17 17 or 01205 366856 (UK); info@campinglasdunas.com; www.campinglasdunas.com**

€4.50 sand adj

Exit AP7 junc 5 dir Viladamat & L'Escala; 2km bef L'Escala turn L for Sant Martí d'Empúries, turn L bef ent vill for 2km, camp sp. V lge, mkd, pt shd, pt sl, serviced pitches; EHU (6A) inc; gas; bbq; TV; 5% statics; phone; Eng spkn; adv bkg req; games area; games rm; tennis; watersports; CKE. *"Greco-Roman ruins in Empúries; gd sized pitches - extra for serviced; busy, popular site; souvenir shop; money exchange; cash machine; doctor; excel, clean facs; vg site."* **€72.50, 15 May-15 Sep.** **2024**

See advertisement opposite

SANT PERE PESCADOR *3B3* (3km SE Coastal) *42.17701, 3.10833* **Camping Aquarius,** Camí Sant Martí d'Empúries, 17470 Sant Pere Pescador (Gerona) **972-52 00 03; info@campingaquarius.com; www.campingaquarius.com**

€4.10 sand adj

Fr AP7 m'way exit 3 on N11, foll sp to Figueres. Join C260, after 7km at rndabt at Castello d'Empúries turn R to Sant Pere Pescador. Cross rv bdge in vill, L at 1st rndabt & foll camp sp. Turn R at next rndabt, then 2nd L to site. Lge, pt shd, serviced pitches; EHU (6-15A) €4-8; gas; red long stay; 10% statics; phone; Eng spkn; adv bkg rec; games rm; car wash; games area; CKE. *"Immac, well-run site; helpful staff; nursery in ssn; cash point; vg rest; windsurfing; vast beach; recycling facs; excel site, highly rec, gd value ACSI site; wind gets v high."* **€56.70, 15 Mar-2 Nov.** **2024**

SPAIN

SANT PERE PESCADOR *3B3* (1.3km S Coastal) *42.18816, 3.10265* **Camping Las Palmeras Costa Brava,** Ctra de la Platja 9, 17470 Sant Pere Pescador (Gerona) **972-52 05 06; info@campinglaspalmeras.com; www.campinglaspalmeras.com**

€4.50 (htd) sand 200m

Exit AP7 junc 3 or 4 at Figueras onto C260 dir Roses/Cadaqués rd. After 8km at Castelló d'Empúries turn S for Sant Pere Pescador & cont twd beach. Site on R of rd. 1*, Lge, mkd, shd, serviced pitches; EHU (5-16A) €3.90; gas; TV; phone; Eng spkn; adv bkg acc; games area; bike hire; games rm; tennis; CKE. *"Pleasant site; helpful, friendly staff; superb, clean san facs; cash point; gd cycle tracks; nature reserve nrby; excel."* **€47.70, 15 Apr-5 Nov.** **2022**

See advertisement

SANTA ELENA *2F4* (0.4km E Rural) *38.34378, -3.53612* **Camping Despeñaperros,** Calle Infanta Elena s/n, Junto a Autovia de Andulucia, Km 257, 23213 Santa Elena (Jaén) **953-66 41 92; info@campingdespenaperros.com; www.campingdespenaperros.com**

Leave A4/E5 at junc 257 or 259, site well sp to N side of vill nr municipal leisure complex. 3*, Med, mkd, hdstg, pt shd, serviced pitches; EHU (10A) €4.25 (poss rev pol); gas; red long stay; TV (pitch); 80% statics; phone; bus 500m; adv bkg acc; ccard acc; CKE. *"Gd winter NH in wooded location; gd size pitches but muddy if wet; gd walking area, perfect for dogs; friendly, helpful staff; clean san facs; disabled facs wc only; conv national park & m'way; gd rest; sh walk to vill & shops; site v rural; beautiful area."* **€24.00** **2022**

SANTA MARINA DE VALDEON *1A3* (0.6km N Rural) *43.13638, -4.89472* **Camping El Cares,** El Cardo, 24915 Santa Marina de Valdeón (León) **987-74 26 76; campingelcares@hotmail.com**

€2.10

Fr S take N621 to Portilla de la Reina. Turn L onto LE243 to Santa Marina. Avoid vill (narr rd), go to Northern end of vill bypass. Site is sp on L. 2*, Med, pt shd, terr, EHU (5A) €3.20; 10% statics; phone; bus 1km; ccard acc; CKE. *"Lovely, scenic site high in mountains; gd base for Cares Gorge; friendly, helpful staff; gd views; tight access - not rec if towing or lge m'van."* **€26.50, 1 Jun-15 Oct.** **2022**

SANTA POLA *4F2* (1km NW Urban/Coastal) *38.20105, -0.56983* **Camping Bahía de Santa Pola,** Ctra de Elche s/n, Km. 11, 03130 Santa Pola (Alicante) **965-41 10 12; info@campingbahiasantapola.com; www.campingbahiasantapola.com**

(htd) sand 1km

Exit A7 junc 72 dir airport, cont to N332 & turn R dir Cartagena. At rndabt take exit sp Elx/Elche onto CV865, site 100m on R. Lge, hdstg, mkd, pt shd, EHU (10A) €3; gas; red long stay; TV (pitch); 50% statics; phone; bus adj; Eng spkn; adv bkg acc; ccard acc; CKE. *"Helpful, friendly manager; well-organised site; sm pitches; recep in red building facing ent; excel san facs; site rds steep; attractive coastal cycle path."* **€25.00** **2024**

SANTAELLA *2G3* (5km N Rural) *37.62263, -4.85950* **Camping La Campiña,** La Guijarrosa-Santaella, 14547 Santaella (Córdoba) **957-31 53 03; info@campinglacampina.com; www.campinglacampina.com**

€2

Fr A4/E5 leave at km 441 onto A386 rd dir La Rambla to Santaella for 11km, turn L onto A379 for 5km & foll sp. 2*, Sm, mkd, hdstg, pt shd, pt sl, EHU (10A) €5.50; gas; bbq; red long stay; TV; bus at gate to Córdoba; Eng spkn; adv bkg acc; ccard acc; CKE. *"Fine views; friendly, warm welcome; popular, family-run site; many pitches sm for lge o'fits; guided walks; poss clsd winter - phone to check; helpful & knowledgable owner; great site."* **€30.00, E25.** **2022**

SANTANDER *1A4* (5km NE Coastal) *43.48916, -3.79361* **Camping Cabo Mayor,** Avda. del Faro s/n, 39012 Santander (Cantabria) **942-39 15 42; info@cabomayor.com; www.cabomayor.com**

adj

Sp thro town but not v clearly. On waterfront (turn R if arr by ferry). At lge junc do not foll quayside, take uphill rd (resort type prom) & foll sp for Faro de Cabo Mayor. Site 200m bef lighthouse on L. Lge, mkd, unshd, terr, EHU (10A) inc; gas; TV; 10% statics; phone; bus to Santander nrby; Eng spkn; CKE. *"Med to lge pitches; site popular with lge youth groups hg ssn; shwrs clsd 2230-0800; conv ferry; pitches priced by size, pleasant coastal walk to Sardinero beachs; gd NH; well organised & clean; gd facs but dated; no hot water for washing up; excel; gd welcome."* **€40.40, 27 Mar-12 Oct.** **2023**

SANTANDER *1A4* (12km E Rural) *43.44777, -3.72861* **Camping Somo Parque,** Ctra Somo-Suesa s/n, 39150 Suesa-Ribamontán al Mar (Cantabria) **942-51 03 09; somoparque@somoparque.com; www.somoparque.com**

1.5km

Fr car ferry foll sp Bilbao. After approx 8km turn L over bdge sp Pontejos & Somo. After Pedreña climb hill at Somo Playa & take 1st R sp Suesa. Foll site sp. Med, pt shd, EHU (6A) €3 (poss rev pol); gas; 99% statics; Eng spkn; site clsd 16 Dec-31 Jan; CKE. *"Friendly owners; peaceful rural setting; sm ferry bet Somo & Santander; poss unkempt LS & poss clsd; NH only."* **€32.00, 1 Mar-15 Nov.** **2024**

SANTANDER *1A4* (8km W Coastal) *43.47678, -3.87303* **Camping Virgen del Mar,** Ctra Santander-Liencres, San Román-Corbán s/n, 39000 Santander (Cantabria) **942-34 24 25; cvirdmar@ceoecant.es; www.campingvirgendelmar.com**

12 sand 300m

Fr ferry turn R, then L up to football stadium, L again leads strt into San Román. If app fr W, take A67 (El Sardinero) then S20, leave at junc 2 dir Liencres, strt on. Site well sp. 2*, Lge, mkd, pt shd, EHU (4-10A) €4; red long stay; bus 500m; adv bkg acc; CKE. *"Basic facs, poss ltd hot water; some sm pitches not suitable lge o'fits; site adj cemetary; phone in LS to check site open; expensive LS; gd for ferry; recep not v friendly."* **€27.00** **2024**

SANTANDER *1A4* (2km NW Coastal) *43.46762, -3.89925* **Camping Costa San Juan,** Avda San Juan de la Canal s/n, 39110 Soto de la Marina (Cantabria) **942-57 95 80 or 629-30 36 86; info@hotelcostasanjuan.com; www.hotelcostasanjuan.com**

12 sand 400m

Fr A67 take S20 twds Bilbao, exit junc 2 & foll sp Liencres. In 2km at Irish pub turn 1st R to Playa San Juan de la Canal, site behind hotel on L. Sm, pt shd, EHU (3-6A) €3.20 (poss rev pol); TV; 90% statics; bus 600m. *"NH for ferry; muddy in wet; poss diff lge o'fits; gd coastal walks; 2 pin adaptor needed for elec conn."* **€28.70** **2024**

SANTIAGO DE COMPOSTELA *1A2* (3.5km NE Urban) *42.88972, -8.52444* **Camping As Cancelas,** Rua do Xullo 25, 35, 15704 Santiago de Compostela (La Coruña) **981-58 02 66 or 981-58 04 76; info@campingascancelas.com; www.campingascancelas.com**

12

Exit AP9 junc 67 & foll sp Santiago. At rndabt with lge service stn turn L sp 'camping' & foll sp to site turning L at McDonalds. Site adj Guardia Civil barracks. NB-Do not use sat nav if app fr Lugo on N547. 2*, Lge, mkd, shd, pt sl, terr, EHU (5A) inc; gas; bbq; TV; phone; bus 100m; Eng spkn; CKE. *"Busy site-conv for pilgrims; rec arr early high ssn; some sm pitches poss diff c'vans & steep ascent; gd clean san facs, stretched when busy; gd rest; bus to city 100m fr gate avoids steep 15 min walk back fr town (LS adequate car parks in town); poss interference with car/c'van electrics fr local transmitter, if problems report to site recep; LS recep in bar; arr in sq by Cathedral at 1100 for Thanksgiving service at 1200; helpful owner; vg rest onsite; excel site; facs v clean; wifi vg."* **€39.90** **2024**

SANTILLANA DEL MAR *1A4* (2.5km E Rural) *43.38222, -4.08305* **Camping Altamira,** Barrio Las Quintas s/n, 39330 Queveda (Cantabria) **942-84 01 81; nfo@campingaltamira.es; www.campingaltamira.es**

Clear sp to Santillana fr A67; site on R 3km bef vill. 2*, Med, mkd, pt shd, pt sl, terr, EHU (16A); gas; TV; 30% statics; bus 100m; Eng spkn; adv bkg req; ccard acc; horseriding; CKE. *"Pleasant site; ltd facs LS; nr Altimira cave paintings; easy access Santander ferry on m'way; gd coastal walks; open w/end only Nov-Mar - rec phone ahead; excel; san facs v clean & modern; local rests nrby."* **€28.00, 10 Mar-7 Dec.** **2022**

SANTILLANA DEL MAR *1A4* (1km NW Rural) *43.39333, -4.11222* **Camping Santillana del Mar,** Ctra de Comillas s/n, 39330 Santillana del Mar (Cantabria) **942-81 82 50; www.campingsantillana.com**

12 5km

Fr W exit A8 junc 230 Santillana-Comillas, then foll sp Santillana & site on rd CA131. Fr E exit A67 junc 187 & foll sp Santillana. Turn R onto CA131, site on R up hill after vill. 3*, Lge, pt shd, sl, terr, EHU (6A) inc (poss rev pol); gas; 20% statics; phone; bus 300m; Eng spkn; horseriding; bike hire; tennis; golf 15km; CKE. *"Useful site in beautiful historic vill; hot water only in shwrs; diff access to fresh water & to mv disposal point; narr, winding access rds, projecting trees & kerbs to some pitches - not rec lge o'fits or twin axles; car wash; cash machine; poss muddy LS & pitches rutted; poss travellers; gd views; lovely walk to town; poor facs (2014); NH."* **€25.00** **2023**

SPAIN

SANTO DOMINGO DE LA CALZADA *1B4* (3.6km E Rural) *42.44083, -2.91506* **Camping Banares,** Ctra N120, Km 42.2, 26250 Santo Domingo de la Calzada **941-34 01 31; info@campingbanares.es; www.campingbanares.es**

12

Fr N120 Burgos-Logroño rd, turn N at Santo Domingo, foll sp Banares & site. 4*, Sm, unshd, pt sl, EHU (5-10A) €5.50; gas; 90% statics; Eng spkn; adv bkg acc; ccard acc; games area; tennis; CKE. *"Interesting, historic town; shops, bars, rests 3km; NH only."* **€32.60** **2022**

SANXENXO *1B2* (4.5km SW Coastal) *42.39254, -8.84517* **Camping Playa Paxariñas,** Ctra C550, Km 2.3 Lanzada-Portonovo, 36960 Sanxenxo (Pontevedra) **986-72 30 55; info@campingpaxarinas.com; www.campingpaxarinas.com**

sand adj

Fr Pontevedra W on P0308 coast rd; 3km after Sanxenxo. Site thro hotel on L at bend. Site poorly sp. Fr AP9 fr N exit junc 119 onto VRG41 & exit for Sanxenxo. Turn R at 3rd rndabt for Portonovo to site in dir O Grove. Do not turn L to port area on ent Portonovo. Lge, mkd, shd, pt sl, terr, EHU (5A) €4.75; gas; bbq; red long stay; TV; 75% statics; phone; bus adj; Eng spkn; adv bkg acc; ccard acc; CKE. *"Site in gd position; secluded beaches; views over estuary; take care high kerbs on pitches; excel san facs - ltd facs LS & poss clsd; lovely unspoilt site; plenty of shd."* **€32.00, 17 Mar-15 Oct.** **2022**

SANXENXO *1B2* (3km NW Coastal) *42.41777, -8.87555* **Camping Monte Cabo,** Soutullo 174, 36990 Noalla (Pontevedra) **986-74 41 41; info@montecabo.com; www.montecabo.com**

12 sand 250m

Fr AP9 exit junc 119 onto upgraded VRG4.1 dir Sanxenxo. Ignore sp for Sanxenxo until rndabt sp A Toxa/La Toja, where turn L onto P308. Cont to Fontenla supmkt on R - minor rd to site just bef supmkt. Rd P308 fr AP9 junc 129 best avoided. Sm, mkd, pt shd, terr, EHU €4.25; red long stay; TV; 10% statics; phone; bus 600m; Eng spkn; adv bkg acc; ccard acc; CKE. *"Peaceful, friendly site set above sm beach (access via steep path) with views; sm pitches; beautiful coastline & interesting historical sites; vg."* **€28.25** **2023**

SAX *4F2* (6km NW Rural) *38.56875, -0.84913* **Camping Gwen & Michael,** Colonia de Santa Eulalia 1, 03630 Sax (Alicante) **965-47 44 19 or 7718 18 58 05(UK)**

nr nr

Exit A31 at junc km 191 & foll sp for Santa Eulalia, site on R just bef vill sq. Rec phone prior to arr. Sm, hdg, hdstg, unshd, EHU (3A) €1. *"Vg CL-type site; friendly British owners; beautiful area; gd NH & touring base; c'van storage avail; 3 rest nrby."* **€15.00, 15 Mar-30 Nov.** **2022**

SEGOVIA *1C4* (2km SE Urban) *40.93138, -4.09250* **Camping El Acueducto,** Ctra de la Granja, 40004 Segovia **921-42 50 00 / 681-38 219 0; informacion@campingacueducto.com; www.campingacueducto.com**

nr

Turn off Segovia by-pass N110/SG20 at La Granja exit, but head twd Segovia on DL601. Site in approx 500m off dual c'way just bef Restaurante Lago. Lge, mkd, pt shd, pt sl, EHU (6-10A) €5; gas; bbq; 10% statics; phone; bus 150m; bike hire; CKE. *"Excel; helpful staff; lovely views; clean facs; gates locked 0000-0800; gd bus service; some pitches sm & diff for lge o'fits; city a 'must' to visit; bus stop and gd spmkt 10min walk; site muddy after rain; unfriendly new owner (2018); cycle path to city; gd hot shwrs."* **€34.00, 15 Mar-15 Oct.** **2024**

SENA DE LUNA *1A3* (1km S Rural) *42.92181, -5.96153* **Camping Río Luna,** Ctra de Abelgas s/n, 24145 Sena de Luna (León) **987-59 77 14 or 685-89 15 21; info@campingrioluna.com; www.campingrioluna.com**

(htd)

S fr Oviedo on AP66, at junc 93 turn W onto CL626 to Sena de Luna in approx 5km. Site on L, sp. 1*, Med, pt shd, EHU (5A) €3.80; bbq; sw nr; TV; phone; adv bkg acc; ccard acc. *"Vg, scenic site; walking, climbing; cent for wild boar & wolves; rural, rustic site; hot shwrs."* **€18.00, Easter & 1 May-30 Sep.** **2024**

SEO DE URGEL *3B3* (8.5km NW Rural) *42.37388, 1.35777* **Camping Castellbò- Buchaca,** Ctra Lerida-Puigcerdà 127, 25712 Castellbò (Lleida) **973-35 21 55; info@campingsdelleida.com; www.campingsdelleida.com**

€3.60

Leave Seo de Urgel on N260/1313 twd Lerida. In approx 3km turn N sp Castellbò. Thro vill & site on L, well sp. Steep, narr, winding rd, partly unfenced - not suitable car+c'van o'fits or lge m'vans. Sm, mkd, pt shd, pt sl, EHU (5A) €5.85; phone; adv bkg acc. *"CL-type site in beautiful surroundings; friendly recep; basic fac's."* **€30.00, 1 May-30 Sep.** **2024**

SITGES *3C3* (2km SW Urban/Coastal) *41.23351, 1.78111* **Camping Bungalow Park El Garrofer,** Ctra C246A, Km 39, 08870 Sitges (Barcelona) **938 94 17 80; camping@grupolasinia.com; www.campingelgarrofer.com**

€2.65 (htd) shgl 900m

Exit 26 on the C-32 dir St. Pere de Ribes, at 1st rndabt take 1st exit, at 2nd rndabt take 2nd exit, foll rd C-31 to campsite. V lge, mkd, hdstg, hdg, pt shd, serviced pitches; EHU (5-10A) €4.10 (poss rev pol); gas; TV; 80% statics; phone; bus adj; Eng spkn; adv bkg acc; ccard acc; games rm; tennis 800m; car wash; site clsd 19 Dec-27 Jan to tourers; windsurfing; games area; horseriding; bike hire; CKE. *"Great location, conv Barcelona, bus adj; sep area for m'vans; pleasant staff; recep open 0800-2100; gd level site; quiet; gd old & new facs."* **€40.00, 22 Feb-15 Dec.** **2024**

SORIA *3C1* (2km SW Rural) *41.74588, -2.48456* **Camping Fuente de la Teja,** Ctra Madrid-Soria, Km 223, 42005 Soria **975-22 29 67 or 625-93 14 27; camping@fuentedelateja.es; www.fuentedelateja.es**

nr

Fr new ring road SO-20 follow Madrid to S edge of town. Take exit 8 sp Redonda then R at rndabt. 2*, Med, mkd, pt shd, pt sl, EHU (6A) €3 (poss no earth); gas; bbq; TV; 10% statics; phone; Eng spkn; adv bkg acc; ccard acc; CKE. *"Vg site; excel, gd for NH; vg san facs; interesting town; phone ahead to check site poss open bet Oct & Easter; hypmkt 3km; easy access to site; pitches around 100sqm, suits o'fits upto 10m; friendly staff, access fr 9am."* **€23.30, 1 Mar-31 Oct.** **2024**

SUECA *4E2* (5km NE Coastal) *39.30354, -0.29270* **Camping Les Barraquetes,** Playa de Sueca, Mareny Barraquetes, 46410 Sueca (València) **961-76 07 23; info@barraquetes.com; www.barraquetes.com**

sand 350m

Exit AP7 junc 58 dir Sueca onto N332. In Sueca take CV500 to Mareny Barraquetes. Or S fr València on CV500 coast rd. Foll sp for Cullera & Sueca. Site on L. Med, mkd, pt shd, EHU (10A) €5.88; gas; bbq; red long stay; twin axles; TV; 70% statics; phone; bus 500m; Eng spkn; ccard acc; games area; waterslide; tennis; windsurfing school; CKE. *"Quiet, family atmosphere; conv touring base & València; quiet beach 8 min walk; helpful staff; gd."* **€45.50, 16 Jan-14 Dec.** **2023**

TAPIA DE CASARIEGO *1A3* (2km W Rural) *43.54870, -6.97436* **Camping El Carbayin,** La Penela, 33740 **985-62 37 09 or 711-72 07 53; info@campingelcarbayin.com; www.campingelcarbayin.com**

12 sand 1km

Take N634/E70 (old coast rd parallel to A8-E70) to Serantes, foll sp to site bet N634 and sea. 2*, Sm, mkd, pt shd, pt sl, EHU (3A) €3; 10% statics; phone; bus 400m; adv bkg acc; ccard acc; fishing; watersports; CKE. *"Gd for coastal walks & trips to mountains; gd; new san facs."* **€22.50** **2024**

TARAZONA *3B1* (8km SE Rural) *41.81890, -1.69230* **Camping Veruela Moncayo,** Ctra Vera-Veruela, 50580 Vera de Moncayo (Zaragoza) **976 64 90 34; antoniogp@able.es**

12 nr

Fr Zaragoza, take AP68 or N232 twd Tudela/ Logroño; after approx. 50km, turn L to join N122 (km stone 75) twd Tarazona; cont 30km & turn L twd Vera de Moncayo; go thro town cent; site on R; well sp. Med, hdg, mkd, pt shd, pt sl, EHU; gas; adv bkg acc; bike hire; CKE. *"Quiet site adj monastery; friendly owner; gd."* **€26.00** **2023**

TARIFA *2H3* (10km NW Coastal) *36.06908, 5.68036* **Camping Valdevaqueros,** Ctra N340 km 75,5 11380 Tarifa **34 956 684 174; info@campingvaldevaqueros.com; www.campingvaldevaqueros.com**

12 €4 sandy 1km

Campsite is sp 9km fr Tarifa on the N340 twds Cadiz. Lge, pt shd, pt sl, EHU (6A); sw; TV; 50% statics; phone; Eng spkn; adv bkg rec; games area; bike hire. *"Excel site; watersports nrby."* **€35.00** **2022**

"I need an on-site restaurant"

We do our best to make sure site information is correct, but it is always best to check any must-have facilities are still available or will be open during your visit.

TARIFA *2H3* (3km NW Coastal) *36.04277, -5.62972* **Camping Rió Jara,** Ctra N340, km 81, 11380 Tarifa (Andalucia) **956-68 05 70; campingriojara@terra.com; www.campingriojara.com**

12 €3.50 sand 200m

Site on S of N340 Cádiz-Algeciras rd at km post 81.2; 3km after Tarifa; clearly visible & sp. 2*, Med, mkd, pt shd, EHU (10A) €4; gas; adv bkg acc; ccard acc; fishing; CKE. *"Gd, clean, well-kept site; friendly recep; long, narr pitches diff for awnings; daily trips to N Africa; gd windsurfing nr; poss strong winds; mosquitoes in summer."* **€45.00** **2024**

TARRAGONA *3C3* (0.6km NE Urban/Coastal) *40.88707, 0.80630* **Camping Nautic,** Calle Libertat s/n, 43860 L'Ametlla de Mar Tarragona **977-456 110; info@campingnautic.com; www.campingnautic.com**

Fr N340 exit at km 1113 sp L'Amettla de Mar (or A7 exit 39). Over rlwy bdge, foll rd to L. Turn R after park and TO on R, foll signs to campsite. Lge, hdstg, pt shd, terr, EHU; TV; 25% statics; phone; bus 500m, train 700m; Eng spkn; adv bkg acc; games area; CCI. *"Vg site; tennis court; 5 mins to attractive town with rest & sm supmkt; lge Mercadona outsite town; site on different levels."* **€40.00, 6 Apr-3 Nov.** **2024**

SPAIN

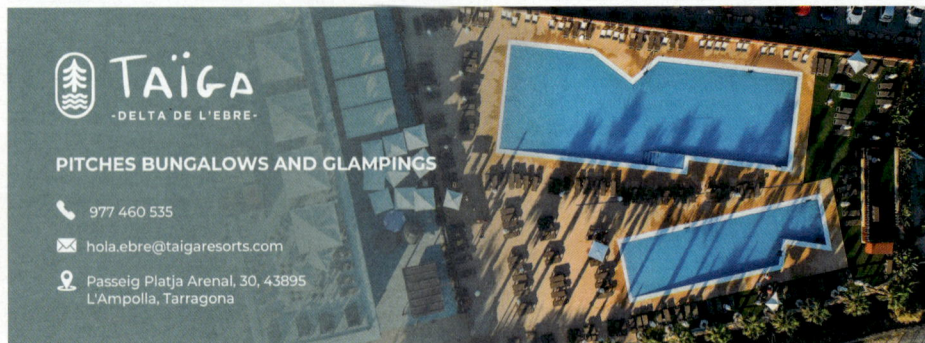

TARRAGONA *3C3* (5km NE Coastal) *41.13019, 1.31170* **Camping Las Palmeras,** Ctra. N 340, P.Km 1168, 43007 Tarragona **977 20 80 81; laspalmeras@laspalmeras.com; www.laspalmeras.com**

€5 sand adj

Exit AP7 at junc 32 (sp Altafulla). After about 5km on N340 twd Tarragona take sp L turn at crest of hill. Site sp. 1*, V lge, mkd, pt shd, EHU (6A) inc; gas; red long stay; 10% statics; phone; ccard acc; games rm; tennis; games area; CKE. *"Gd beach; ideal for families; poss mosquito prob; many sporting facs; gd, clean san facs; friendly, helpful staff; naturist beach 1km; supmkt 5km; excel site."*
€45.00, 2 Apr-12 Oct. **2024**

"Satellite navigation makes touring much easier"

Remember most sat navs don't know if you're towing or in a larger vehicle – always use yours alongside maps and site directions.

TARRAGONA *3C3* (7km NE Coastal) *41.12887, 1.34415* **Camping Torre de la Mora,** Ctra N340, Km 1171, 43008 Tarragona-Tamarit **977-65 02 77; info@torredelamora.com; www.torredelamora.com**

€3.65 sand adj

Fr AP7 exit junc 32 (sp Altafulla), at rndabt take La Mora rd. Then foll site sp. After approx 1km turn R, L at T-junc, site on R. Lge, hdstg, pt shd, terr, EHU (6A) €5.20; gas; red long stay; 50% statics; bus 200m; Eng spkn; adv bkg acc; ccard acc; tennis; golf 2km; CKE. *"Improved, clean site set in attractive bay with fine beach; excel pool; sports club adj; conv Tarragona & Port Aventura; various pitch sizes, some v sm."*
€61.40, 22 Mar-12 Oct. **2024**

TARRAGONA *3C3* (12km E Coastal) *41.1324, 1.3604* **Camping-Caravaning Tamarit Park,** Playa Tamarit, Ctra N340, Km 1172, 43008 Playa Tamarit (Tarragona) **977-65 01 28; resort@tamarit.com; www.tamarit.com**

€4 (htd) (htd) shgl adj

Fr A7/E15 exit junc 32 sp Altafulla/Torredembarra, at rndabt join N340 by-pass sp Tarragona. At rndabt foll sp Altafulla, turn sharp R to cross rlwy bdge to site in 1.2km, sp. V lge, hdstg, hdg, shd, pt sl, serviced pitches; EHU (10A) inc; gas; bbq; red long stay; TV; 30% statics; phone; Eng spkn; adv bkg rec; ccard acc; games area; watersports; tennis; CKE. *"Well-maintained, secure site with family atmosphere; excel beach; superb pool; private bthrms avail; best site in area but poss noisy at night & w/end; variable pitch prices; beachside pitches avail; cash machine; car wash; take care overhanging trees; Altafulla sh walk along beach worth visit; excel."*
€65.00, 14 Mar-16 Oct. **2022**

TOLEDO *1D4* (3.5km W Rural) *39.86530, -4.04714* **Camping El Greco,** Ctra Pueblo Montalban, Km.0.7, 45004 Toledo **925-22 00 90; info@campingelgreco.es; www.campingelgreco.es**

12 (htd)

Site on CM4000 between CM40 ring road & Puenta de la Cava bridge. Fr E foll yellow sp. Fr W look for 5 flagpoles on L next to Cirgarral Del Santoangel Custodio. 3*, Med, hdstg, hdg, mkd, pt shd, pt sl, EHU (6-10A) inc (poss rev pol); gas; bbq; phone; bus to town, train to Madrid fr town; Eng spkn; ccard acc; games area; CKE. *"Clean, tidy, well-maintained; all pitches on gravel; easy parking on o'skts - adj Puerta de San Martín rec - or bus; some pitches poss tight; san facs clean; lovely, scenic situation; excel rest (expensive); friendly, helpful owners; vg; dusty; gd rest; site poss neglected during LS; gd pool, closes fr 15 Sept; cheap bar; nice, neat site; mv service pnt basic; sh walk to city."* **€32.30** **2024**

TORDESILLAS *1C3* (1km SSW Urban) *41.49584, -5.00494* **Kawan Village El Astral,** Camino de Pollos 8, 47100 Tordesillas (Valladolid) **983-77 09 53; info@campingelastral.es; www.campingelastral.com**

12 €2.35 (htd) WD MSP

Fr NE on A62/E80 thro town turn L at rndabt over rv & immed after bdge turn R dir Salamanca & almost immed R again into narr gravel track (bef Parador) & foll rd to site; foll camping sp & Parador. Poorly sp. Fr A6 exit sp Tordesillas & take A62. Cross bdge out of town & foll site sp. Med, hdstg, hdg, mkd, pt shd, EHU (5A-10A) €3.60-5 (rev pol); gas; TV; 10% statics; phone; Eng spkn; ccard acc; tennis; bike hire; rv fishing; site open w/end Mar & Oct; CKE. *"V helpful owners & staff; easy walk to interesting town; pleasant site by rv; vg, modern, clean san facs & excel facs; popular NH; excel site in every way, facs superb; various size pitches; worth a visit; conv o'night on rte to S of Spain/Portugal; pull thro pitches avail; excel."* **€46.92, E03. 2022**

TORLA *3B2* (1.5km N Rural) *42.63948, -0.10948* **Camping Ordesa,** Ctra de Ordesa s/n, 22376 Torla (Huesca) **974-11 77 21; camping@campingordesa.es; www.campingordesa.es**

€3 WD nr

Fr Ainsa on N260 twd Torla. Pass Torla turn R onto A135 (Valle de Ordesa twd Ordesa National Park). Site 2km N of Torla, adj Hotel Ordesa. Med, pt shd, serviced pitches; EHU (6A) €5.50; 10% statics; phone; bus 1km; Eng spkn; adv bkg rec; ccard acc; tennis; CKE. *"V scenic; recep in adj Hotel Ordesa; excel rest, helpful staff; facs poss stretched w/end; long, narr pitches & lge trees on access rd poss diff lge o'fits; ltd facs LS; no access to National Park by car Jul/Aug, shuttlebus fr Torla."* **€22.60, 28 Mar-30 Sep. 2022**

TORRE DEL MAR *2H4* (1.6km S Coastal) *36.7342, -4.1003* **Camping Torre del Mar,** Paseo Maritimo s/n, 29740 Torre del Mar (Málaga) **952-54 02 24; info@campingtorredelmar.com; www.campingtorredelmar.com**

12 WD MSP nr nr shgl 50m

Fr N340 coast rd, at rndabt at W end of town with 'correos' on corner turn twds sea sp Faro, Torre del Mar. At rndabt with lighthouse adj turn R, then 2nd R, site adj big hotel, ent bet lge stone pillars (no name sp). 2*, Lge, hdg, mkd, hdstg, shd, serviced pitches; EHU (16A) €4.40 (long lead req); gas; red long stay; TV (pitch); 39% statics; phone; tennis; CKE. *"Tidy, clean, friendly, well-run site; some sm pitches; site rds tight; gd, clean san facs; popular LS; constant hot water; poorly laid out; poss flooding in parts of site; conv for town."* **€39.00 2022**

TORRE DEL MAR *2H4* (1km W Coastal) *36.72976, -4.10285* **Camping Laguna Playa,** Prolongación Paseo Maritimo s/n, 29740 Torre del Mar (Málaga) **952-54 06 31; info@lagunaplaya.com; www.lagunaplaya.com**

12 WD MSP sand 1km

Fr N340 coast rd, at rndabt at W end of town with 'correos' on corner turn twds sea sp Faro, Torre del Mar. At rndabt with lighthouse adj turn R, then 2nd R, site sp in 400m. Med, pt shd, EHU (10A) inc; gas; bbq; 80% statics; Eng spkn; adv bkg acc; fishing; games rm. *"Popular LS; sm pitches; excel, clean san facs; gd location, easy walk to town; NH only; well shaded; pleasant little seaside town."* **€33.00 2024**

TORRE DEL MAR *2H4* (3km W Coastal) *36.72526, -4.13532* **Camping Almayate Costa,** Ctra N340, Km 267, 29749 Almayate Bajo (Málaga) **952-55 62 89; info@campingalmayatecosta.com; www.campings.net/almayatecosta**

WD MSP sand 50m

E fr Málaga on N340/E15 coast rd. Exit junc 258 dir Almería, site on R 3km bef Torre del Mar. Easy access. 4*, Lge, mkd, hdstg, shd, EHU (10A) €5.10; gas; bbq; red long stay; phone; Eng spkn; adv bkg acc; ccard acc; golf 7km; car wash; games rm; CKE. *"Helpful manager; pitches nr beach tight for lge o'fits & access rds poss diff; vg resort; excel."* **€40.00, 1 Jan-31 Dec. 2022**

"There aren't many sites open at this time of year"

If you're travelling outside peak season remember to call ahead to check site opening dates – even if the entry says 'open all year'.

TORRE DEL MAR *2H4* (7km W Coastal) *36.71967, -4.16471* **Camping Valle Niza Playa,** Ctra N340, km 264, 1 29792 Valle Niza/Malaga **952-51 31 81; info@campingvalleniza.es; www.campingvalleniza.es**

12 WD shgl

A7 Malaga-Motril exit 265 Cajiz Costa; at T-junc L onto N340 Coast rd twd Torre Del Mar. Site in 1km. 1*, Med, mkd, pt shd, EHU (6-10A); bbq; twin axles; TV; 50% statics; bus 0.3km; adv bkg acc; ccard acc; games area. *"Gdn ctr adj; poor beach across rd; gd."* **€33.00 2023**

TORREVIEJA *4F2* (7km SW Rural) *37.97500, -0.75111* **Camping Florantilles,** Ctra San Miguel de Salinas-Torrevieja, 03193 San Miguel de Salinas (Alicante) **965-72 04 56; camping@campingflorantilles.com; www.campingflorantilles.com**

12 WD MSP sand 5km

Exit AP7 junc 758 onto CV95, sp Orihuela, Torrevieja Sud. Turn R at rndabt & after 300m turn R again, site immed on L. Or if travelling on N332 S past Alicante airport twd Torrevieja. Leave Torrevieja by-pass sp Torrevieja, San Miguel. Turn R onto CV95 & foll for 3km thro urbanisation 'Los Balcones', then cont for 500m, under by-pass, round rndabt & up hill, site sp on R. Lge, hdg, mkd, hdstg, pt shd, terr, EHU (10A) inc; gas; bbq; TV; 20% statics; adv bkg acc; ccard acc; golf nr; horseriding 10km; games rm; CKE. *"Popular, British owned site; fitness studio/keep fit classes; workshops: calligraphy, card making, drawing/painting, reiki, sound therapy etc; basic Spanish classes; 3 golf courses nrby; no o'fits over 10m; recep clsd 1330-1630; walking club; friendly staff; many long-stay visitors & all year c'vans; suitable mature couples; own transport ess; gd cyling, both flat & hilly; conv hot spa baths at Fortuna & salt lakes."* **€30.00, E11. 2022**

TORROELLA DE MONTGRI *3B3* (6km SE Coastal) *42.01111, 3.18833* **Camping El Delfin Verde,** Ctra Torroella de Montgrí-Palafrugell, Km 4, 17257 Torroella de Montgrí (Gerona) **972-75 84 54; info@eldelfinverde.com; www.eldelfinverde.com**

€4 WD MSP sand adj

Fr N leave A7 at junc 5 dir L'Escala. At Viladamat turn R onto C31 sp La Bisbal. After a few km turn L twd Torroella de Montgrí. At rndabt foll sp for Pals (also sp El Delfin Verde). At the flags turn L sp Els Mas Pinell. Foll site sp for 5km. 4*, V lge, mkd, pt shd, pt sl, EHU (6A) inc; bbq; TV; 40% statics; ccard acc; games rm; horseriding 4km; windsurfing; fishing; tennis; bike hire; CKE. *"Superb, gd value site; winter storage; excel pool; wide range of facs; sportsgrnd; hairdresser; disco; no o'fits over 8m high ssn; dogs not acc high ssn; money exchange; clean, modern san facs; all water de-salinated fr fresh water production plant; bottled water rec for drinking & cooking; mkt Mon."* **€68.78, 17 May-20 Sep. 2023**

TORROX COSTA *2H4* (2km NNW Urban) *36.73944, -3.94972* **Camping El Pino,** Urbanización Torrox Park s/n, 29793 Torrox Costa (Málaga) **952-53 00 06; info@campingelpino.com; www.campingelpino.com**

12 €2.50 WD nr sand 800m

Exit A7 at km 285, turn S at 1st rndabt, turn L at 2nd rndabt & foll sp Torrox Costa N340; in 1.5km at rndabt turn R to Torrox Costa, then L onto rndabt sp Nerja, site well sp in 4km. App rd steep with S bends. Fr N340 fr Torrox Costa foll sp Torrox Park, site sp. Lge, mkd, shd, terr, EHU €3.80 (long lead req); gas; bbq; red long stay; 35% statics; phone; Eng spkn; games area; golf 8km; car wash; CKE. *"Gd size pitches but high kerbs; narr ent/exit; gd hill walks; conv Malaga; Nerja caves, Ronda; gd touring base; noise fr rd and bar; san facs adequate."* **€18.00 2024**

TOSSA DE MAR *3B3* (3km SW Coastal) *41.71509, 2.90672* **Camping Cala Llevado,** Ctra Tossa-Lloret, Km 3, 17320 Tossa de Mar (Gerona) **972-34 03 14; reservation@seagreen.fr; www.calallevado.com**

WD MSP shgl adj

Exit AP7 junc 9 dir Lloret. In Lloret take GI 682 dir Tossa de Mar. Site well sp. 4*, V lge, mkd, shd, terr, EHU (5-10A) €3.50; gas; TV; 10% statics; phone; Eng spkn; adv bkg acc; waterskiing; tennis; windsurfing; games area; boat trips; sports facs; fishing; CKE. **€64.00, Holy Week & 1 May-30 Sep. 2022**

VALENCIA *4E2* (23km N Coastal) *39.601, -0.2709* **Camping Valencia,** Carrer Rio Turia, 1 46530 Playa de Pucol **961 46 58 06; info@campingvalencia.com; www.campingvalencia.com**

2 max WD MSP sandy 200m

Fr S: Take V21, exit at Pucol, foll sp Playas. Fr N: Take A7, exit at Pucol, foll sp Playa de Puzol. 3*, Lge, mkd, hdstg, unshd, serviced pitches; EHU (10A); bbq (elec, gas, sep area); sw nr; twin axles; red long stay; 20% statics; phone; Eng spkn; adv bkg acc; ccard acc; games area; games rm. *"Excel."* **€58.00, 3 Feb-5 Nov. 2023**

VALENCIA *4E2* (16km S Rural) *39.32302, -0.30940* **Camping Devesa Gardens,** Ctra El Saler, Km 13, 46012 València **961-61 11 36; contacto@devesagardens.com; www.devesagardens.com**

12 (htd) WD MSP 700m

S fr València on CV500, site well sp on R 4km S of El Saler. Med, hdstg, mkd, pt shd, EHU (7-15A) €5; gas; bbq; 70% statics; phone; bus to València; adv bkg acc; ccard acc; horseriding; tennis. *"Friendly, helpful staff; site has own zoo (clsd LS); lake canoeing; excel; san facs being refurb (2017); lovely pool area; easy access to tourist areas."* **€68.00 2023**

VALENCIA *4E2* (9km S Coastal) *39.39638, -0.33250* **Camping Coll Vert,** Ctra Nazaret-Oliva, Km 7.5, 46012 Playa de Pinedo (València) **961-83 00 36; info@collvertcamping.com; www.collvertcamping.com**

€4.28 sand 500m

Fr S on V31 turn R onto V30 sp Pinedo. After approx 1km turn R onto V15/CV500 sp El Salar to exit El Salar Platjes. Turn L at rndabt, site on L in 1km. Fr N bypass València on A7/E15 & after junc 524 turn N twd València onto V31, then as above. Turn L at rndabt, site in 1km on L. 2*, Med, hdg, mkd, shd, EHU €4.81 6A; gas; bbq; red long stay; 20% statics; phone; bus to city & marine park; Eng spkn; adv bkg acc; ccard acc; car wash; games area. *"Hourly bus service fr outside site to cent of València & marine park; helpful, friendly staff; san facs need update sm pitches; conv for F1."* **€22.00, 16 Feb-14 Dec. 2024**

VALENCIA *4E2* (9.5km S Urban/Coastal) *39.38880, -0.33196* **Camping Park El Saler,** Ctra del Riu 548, 46012 El Saler (València) **961-83 02 44; info@campingparkelsaler.com; www.campingparkelsaler.com**

sand 300m

Fr València foll coast rd or V15 to El Saler. Site adj rndabt just N of El Saler. Med, hdstg, hdg, mkd, pt shd, EHU (6A) inc; 50% statics; phone; bus at gate; Eng spkn; CKE. *"Very conv València - hourly bus; tow pin adaptor needed for conn cable; narr pitches & ent."*
€25.00 **2024**

VALLE DE CABUERNIGA *1A4* (1km E Rural) *43.22728, -4.28970* **Camping El Molino de Cabuérniga,** Sopeña, 39510 Cabuérniga (Cantabria) **942-706 259; info@campingcabuerniga.com; www.campingcabuerniga.com**

Sopeña is 55 km. SW of Santander. Fr A8 (Santander - Oviedo) take 249 exit and join N634 to Cabezón de la Sal. Turn SW on CA180 twds Reinosa for 11 km. to Sopeña (site sp to L). Turn into vill (car req - low bldgs), cont bearing R foll sp to site. Med, shd, EHU (6A) €6.00; gas; bbq (charcoal, elec, gas, sep area); phone; bus 500m; adv bkg acc; ccard acc; tennis; fishing; CKE. *"Excel site & facs on edge of vill; no shops in vicinity, but gd location, rds to site narr in places; lovely; open, level site with trees & well mkd pitches; lovely stone bldgs; mkd walks to nrby vill."* **€29.00, E29.** **2022**

VECILLA, LA *1B3* (1km N Rural) *42.85806, -5.41155* **Camping La Cota,** Ctra Valdeluguercs, LE321, Km 19, 24840 La Vecilla (León) **987-74 10 91; lacota@campinglacota.com; www.facebook.com/campinglacota/**

Fr N630 turn E onto CL626 at La Robla, 17km to La Vecilla. Site sp in vill. Med, mkd, shd, EHU €3.50; 50% statics; train nr; ccard acc; games area. *"Pleasant site under poplar trees - poss diff to manoeuvre lge o'fits; open w/ends out of ssn; gd walking, climbing nr; interesting mountain area; NH only."*
€21.00, 23 Mar-30 Sep. **2024**

VEJER DE LA FRONTERA *2H3* (10km S Coastal) *36.20084, -6.03506* **Camping Pinar San José,** Carretera Vejer, Caños de Meca, Km 10.2, Zahora 17, 11159 Barbate, Cadiz **951-12 90 02; info@campingpinarsanjose.com; www.campingpinarsanjose.com**

€2 sand 700m

Fr A48/N340 exit junc 36 onto A314 to Barbate, then foll dir Los Caños de Meca. Turn R at seashore rd dir Zahora. Site on L, 2km beyond town. Med, mkd, shd, EHU inc; TV (pitch); 10% statics; adv bkg acc; games area; tennis. *"Excel, modern facs."*
€64.00 **2024**

VELEZ MALAGA *2G4* (16km NNW Rural) *36.87383, -4.18527* **Camping Rural Presa la Vinuela,** Carretera A-356, 29712 La Viñuela Málaga **691-473 472; info@campinglavinuela.es; www.campinglavinuela.es**

€1.10

Site is on A356 N of Velez Malaga adjoining the W shore of la Vinuela lake. Fr junc with A402, foll sp to Colmenar/Los Romanes. Stay on A356(don't turn off into Los Romanes). Site is on R approx 2.5km after turn for Los Romanes, next to rest El Pantano. Sm, hdstg, mkd, hdg, pt shd, terr, EHU (5A); TV; 20% statics; Eng spkn; adv bkg acc; games area; games rm. *"Excel site."* **€26.00** **2024**

VIELHA *3B2* (7km N Rural) *42.73649, 0.74640* **Camping Verneda Mountain Resort,** Ctra Francia N230, Km 171, 25537 Pont d'Arròs (Lleida) **973-64 10 24 or 606-75 63 93; info@campingverneda.com; www.campingverneda.com**

€2.50

Fr Lerida N on N230 twd Spain/France border, site on R adj N230, 2km W of Pont d'Arròs on rvside, 1km after Camping Artigane. Lge, mkd, hdg, pt shd, EHU (16A); twin axles; TV; 10% statics; Eng spkn; adv bkg acc; ccard acc; horseriding; bike hire; games rm; CKE. *"Gd area for walking; site closed Nov then open weekends only Dec-Mar; well-run site; gd facs; lovely clean site in beautiful Val d'Aran; GR-211 long distance footpath runs along with pleasant shady walks to Es Bordes vill (2km) or Viella (6km); vg."* **€39.00** **2022**

"That's changed – Should I let the Club know?"

If you find something on site that's different from the site entry, fill in a report and let us know. See camc.com/europereport.

VIELHA *3B2* (6km SE Rural) *42.70005, 0.87060* **Camping Era Yerla D'Arties,** Ctra C142, Vielha-Baquiera s/n, 25599 Arties (Lleida) **973-64 16 02; yerla@coac.net; www.aranweb.com/yerla**

(htd) nr nr

Fr Vielha take C28 dir Baquiera, site sp. Turn R at rndabt into Arties, site in 30m on R. Med, shd, EHU (4 10A) €4.25-5.15; gas; 10% statics; phone; bus 200m; ccard acc; CKE. *"Pleasant site & vill; skiing nr; ideal for ski resort; san facs gd; gd walking; OK for sh stay."* **€33.10, 1 Dec-14 Sep.** **2024**

SPAIN

VILANOVA I LA GELTRU *3C3* (3km NW Urban) *41.231846, 1.690732* **Camping Vilanova Park,** Ctra Arboç, Km 2.5, 08800 Vilanova i la Geltru (Barcelona) **938-93 34 02; info@vilanovapark.com or reservas@vilanovapark.com; www.vilanovapark.com**

12 €8.65 (htd) (covrd, htd) sand 3km

Fr N on AP7 exit junc 29 onto C15 dir Vilanova; then take C31 dir Cubelles. Leave at 153km exit dir Vilanova Oeste/L'Arboç to site. Fr W on C32/A16 take Vilanova-Sant Pere de Ribes exit. Take C31 & at 153km exit take BV2115 dir L'Arboc to site. Fr AP7 W leave at exit 31 onto the C32 (A16); take exit 16 (Vilanova-L'Arboc exit) onto BV2115 to site. Parked cars may block loop & obscure site sp. V lge, hdstg, mkd, hdg, pt shd, terr, serviced pitches; EHU (10A) inc (poss rev pol); gas; bbq (elec, gas); sw nr; red long stay; TV; 50% statics; phone; bus directly fr campsite to Barcelona; Eng spkn; adv bkg req; ccard acc; horseriding 500m; games rm; bike hire; sauna; fishing; tennis; golf 1km; CKE. *"Gd for children; excel san facs; gd rest & bar; supermarket well stocked; gd winter facs; jacuzzi; spa; fitness cent; helpful staff; gd security; some sm pitches with diff access due trees or ramps; conv bus/train Barcelona, Tarragona, Port Aventura & coast; away from town on top of hill; mkt Sat; excel site; superb."* **€39.77, E08.** **2022**

See advertisement

"I like to fill in the reports as I travel from site to site"

You'll find report forms at the back of this guide, or you can fill them in online at camc.com/europereport.

VILANOVA I LA GELTRU *3C3* (3km NW Urban) *41.231846, 1.690732* **Camping Vilanova Park,** Ctra Arboç, Km 2.5, 08800 Vilanova i la Geltru (Barcelona) **938-93 34 02; info@vilanovapark.com or reservas@vilanovapark.com; www.vilanovapark.com**

12 €8.65 (htd) (covrd, htd) sand 3km

Fr N on AP7 exit junc 29 onto C15 dir Vilanova; then take C31 dir Cubelles. Leave at 153km exit dir Vilanova Oeste/L'Arboç to site. Fr W on C32/A16 take Vilanova-Sant Pere de Ribes exit. Take C31 & at 153km exit take BV2115 dir L'Arboc to site. Fr AP7 W leave at exit 31 onto the C32 (A16); take exit 16 (Vilanova-L'Arboc exit) onto BV2115 to site. Parked cars may block loop & obscure site sp. V lge, hdstg, mkd, hdg, pt shd, terr, serviced pitches; EHU (10A) inc (poss rev pol); gas; bbq (elec, gas); sw nr; red long stay; TV; 50% statics; phone; bus directly fr campsite to Barcelona; Eng spkn; adv bkg req; ccard acc; horseriding 500m; games rm; bike hire; sauna; fishing; tennis; golf 1km; CKE. *"Gd for children; excel san facs; gd rest & bar; supermarket well stocked; gd winter facs; jacuzzi; spa; fitness cent; helpful staff; gd security; some sm pitches with diff access due trees or ramps; conv bus/train Barcelona, Tarragona, Port Aventura & coast; away from town on top of hill; mkt Sat; excel site; superb."* **€39.77, E08.** **2022**

VILLAFRANCA *3B1* (1.5km S Rural) *42.26333, -1.73861* **Camping Bardenas,** Ctra NA-660 PK 13.4, 31330 Villafranca **948-84 61 91; info@campingbardenas.com; www.campingbardenas.com**

12 (htd)

Fr N leave AP15 at Junc 29 onto NA660 sp Villafranca. Site on R 1.5km S of town. Med, hdstg, unshd, bbq; 30% statics; ccard acc; games rm; CCI. *"Gd site for winter stopover en rte to S Spain; facs ltd in severe weather; excel rest."* **€27.00** **2024**

VILLAFRANCA DE CORDOBA *2F4* (1km W Rural) *37.95333, -4.54710* **Camping La Albolafia,** Camino de la Vega s/n, 14420 Villafranca de Córdoba (Córdoba) **957-19 08 35; informacion@camping albolafia.com; www.campingalbolafia.com**

€2.80

Exit A4/E5 junc 377, cross rv & at rndabt turn L & foll sp to site in 2km. Beware humps in app rd. Med, hdstg, hdg, mkd, pt shd, EHU (10A) inc (long lead poss req); bbq; twin axles; TV; 10% statics; phone; bus to Córdoba 500m; Eng spkn; CKE. *"V pleasant, well-run, friendly, clean site; watersports park nrby; bar and rest clsd end May; ok for stopover."* **€21.70, 15 Feb-9 Dec.** 2023

VILLANANE *1B4* (0.8km N Rural) *42.84221, -3.06867* **Camping Angosto,** Ctra Villanañe-Angosto 2, 01425 Villanañe (Gipuzkoa) **945-35 32 71; info@camping-angosto.com; www.camping-angosto.com**

(htd) (covrd, htd)

S fr Bilbao on AP68 exit at vill of Pobes & take rd to W sp Espejo. Turn L 2.4km N of Espejo dir Villanañe, lane to site 400m on R. Med, mkd, pt shd, EHU €4.15 (long cable poss req - supplied by site); bbq; TV; 50% statics; phone; Eng spkn. *"Beautiful area; friendly, helpful staff; open site - mkd pitches rec if poss; gd rest; conv NH fr Bilbao; wonderful site; in LS site seems close but call nbr on gate; site long way fr main rd; poss narr vill app rds."* **€27.00, 15 Feb-30 Nov.** 2024

VINAROS *3D2* (5km N Coastal) *40.49363, 0.48504* **Camping Vinarós,** Ctra N340, Km 1054, 12500 Vinarós (Castellón) **964-40 24 24; info@camping vinaros.com; www.campingvinaros.com**

12 €3 (htd) nr nr shgl 1km

Fr N exit AP7 junc 42 onto N238 dir Vinarós. Straight on at first 2 rndabt, at 3rd rndabt turn L (3rd exit) dir Tarragona. Site on R at Km1054. Lge, hdstg, mkd, hdg, pt shd, serviced pitches; EHU (6A) inc; gas; red long stay; 15% statics; phone; bus adj; Eng spkn; adv bkg rec; ccard acc; CKE. *"Excel gd value, busy, well-run site; many long-stay winter residents; spacious pitches; vg clean, modern san facs; elec volts poss v low in evening; gd rest; friendly, helpful staff; rec use bottled water; currency exchange; Peñíscola Castle & Morello worth a visit; easy cycle to town; ok stopover."* **€13.00** 2023

VINUELA *2G4* (7.5km NW Rural) *36.87383, -4.18527* **Camping Presa La Viñuela,** Ctra A356, km 30 29712 Viñuela **691-47 34 72; info@campingla vinuela.es; www.campinglavinuela.es**

12 €1.10

Site on A356 N of Velez Malaga adjoining the W shore of la Vinuela lake. Fr junc with A402, foll sp to Colmenar & Los Romanes. Stay on A356 (don't turn off into Los Romanes). Site is on R approx 2.5km after the turn for Los Romanes, next to El Pantano rest. 2*, Sm, hdstg, mkd, shd, terr, EHU (5A); TV; 20% statics; Eng spkn; adv bkg acc; games rm; games area. *"Excel site; fab views."* **€33.00** 2024

VINUESA *3B1* (2km N Rural) *41.92647, -2.76285* **Camping Cobijo,** Ctra Laguna Negra, Km 2, 42150 Vinuesa (Soria) **975-37 83 31; recepcion@ campingcobijo.com; www.campingcobijo.com**

Travelling W fr Soria to Burgos, at Abejar R on SO840. by-pass Abejar cont to Vinuesa. Well sp fr there. Lge, pt shd, pt sl, EHU (3-6A) €4-5.70 (long lead poss req); gas; bbq; 10% statics; phone; Eng spkn; ccard acc; bike hire; CKE. *"Friendly staff; clean, attractive site; some pitches in wooded area poss diff lge o'fits; special elec connector supplied (deposit); ltd bar & rest LS, excel rests in town; gd walks."* **€26.30, 1 Apr-1 Nov.** 2023

VITORIA/GASTEIZ *3B1* (5.5km SW Rural) *42.83114, -2.72248* **Camping Ibaya,** Nacional 102, Zuazo de Vitoria 01195 Vitoria/Gasteiz (Alava) **945-14 76 20 or 627-07 43 99; info@campingibaia.com; www.campingibaia.com**

12 €2.20

Fr A1 take exit 343 sp N102/A3302. At rndabt foll sp N102 Vitoria/Gasteiz. At next rndabt take 3rd exit & immed turn L twd filling stn. Site ent on R in 100m, sp. Sm, mkd, hdstg, pt shd, pt sl, EHU (6A) inc; gas; bbq; phone; Eng spkn; CKE. *"NH only; gd, modern san facs; phone ahead to check open LS; fair site; sometimes noisy; close grouped sites."* **€29.50** 2024

VIVER *3D2* (3.5km W Rural) *39.90944, -0.61833* **Camping Villa de Viver,** Camino Benaval s/n, 12460 Viver (Castellón) **676 64 00 32; info@ campingvilladeviver.es; www.campingvilladeviver.es**

€3.10 (htd) nr

Fr Sagunto on A23 dir Terual, approx 10km fr Segorbe turn L sp Jérica, Viver. Thro vill dir Teresa, site sp W of Viver at end of single track lane in approx 2.8km (yellow sp) - poss diff for car+c'van, OK m'vans. Med, hdg, pt shd, terr, serviced pitches; EHU (6A) €3.80; red long stay; TV; 10% statics; phone; Eng spkn; adv bkg acc; ccard acc; CKE. *"Improved site; lovely situation - worth the effort."* **€19.00, 1 Mar-1 Nov.** 2024

SPAIN

ZARAGOZA *3C1* (6km W Urban) *41.63766, -0.94227*
Camping Ciudad de Zaragoza, Calle San Juan Bautista de la Salle s/n, 50012 Zaragoza **876-24 14 95; info@zaragozacamping.com; www.zaragoza camping.com**
12 €3.75 (htd) WD MSP

Fr western ring rd Z40 go E on N11A Av Manuel Rodriguez Ayuso. Pass one rndabt then R onto C San Juan Batista de la Salle to 2nd rndabt, u-turn to find site ent on R in 150m. Lge, hdstg, mkd, pt shd, pt sl, EHU (10A) €5.75; bbq; twin axles; TV; 50% statics; Eng spkn; adv bkg acc; games area; tennis. *"Modern san facs; conv site in suburbs; gd sh stay; poss noisy (campers & daytime aircraft); gd food at bar; helpful staff; gd NH from Bilbao ferry; plenty of trees for shade; busy site."* **€36.00** **2024**

ZARAUTZ *3A1* (3km NE Coastal) *43.28958, -2.14603*
Gran Camping Zarautz, Monte Talaimendi s/n, 20800 Zarautz (Guipúzkoa) **943-83 12 38; info@grancampingzarautz.com; www.grancamping zarautz.com**
12 (htd) WD MSP 1km

Exit A8 junc 11 Zarautz, strt on at 1st & 2nd rndabt after toll & foll site sp. On N634 fr San Sebastián to Zarautz, R at rndabt. On N634 fr Bilbao to Zarautz L at rndabt. Lge, hdstg, mkd, hdg, pt shd, pt sl, terr, EHU (6-10A) inc; gas; bbq; TV; 50% statics; phone; train/bus to Bilbao & San Sebastian; Eng spkn; adv bkg acc; ccard acc; golf 1km; games rm; CKE. *"Site on cliff o'looking bay; excel beach, gd base for coast & mountains; helpful, friendly staff; some pitches sm with steep access & o'looked fr terr above; sans facs upgraded but poor standard and insufficient when cr; excel rest; pitches poss muddy; NH for Bilbao ferry; rec arr early to secure pitch; v steep walk to beach (part naturist); gd for NH; excel train service to San Sebastian; gd shop on site; ACSI discount."* **€32.30** **2023**

ZARAUTZ *3A1* (8km E Coastal) *43.27777, -2.12305*
Camping Orio Kanpina, 20810 Orio (Guipúzkoa) **943-83 48 01; info@oriokanpina.com; www.oriokanpina.com**
WD MSP nr sand adj

Fr E on A8 exit junc 33 & at rndabt foll sp Orio, Kanpin & Playa. Site on R. Or to avoid town cent (rec) cross bdge & foll N634 for 1km, turn L at sp Orio & camping, turn R at rndabt to site. Lge, mkd, pt shd, pt sl, EHU (5A) inc; gas; 50% statics; phone; Eng spkn; adv bkg acc; ccard acc; car wash; tennis; CKE. *"Busy, well maintained site; flats now built bet site & beach & new marina adj - now no sea views; walks; gd facs; friendly staff; useful NH bef leaving Spain; interesting sm town."* **€36.00, 1 Mar-12 Nov.** **2022**

León to Valladolid = 134km

	Albacete	Alicante	Almeria	Andorra-la-Vella	Badajoz	Barcelona	Bilbao	Burgos	Cáceres	Cádiz	Ciudad Real	Córdoba	La Coruña	Gibraltar	Gerona	Granada	Guadalajara	Huesca	León	Lérida (Lleida)	Madrid	Málaga	Murcia	Ourense (Orense)	Oviedo	Pamplona (Iruña)	Salamanca	San Sebastián (Donostia)	Santander	Santiago de Compostela	Segovia	Sevilla	Soria	Tarragona	Teruel	Toledo	Valencia	Valladolid	Vitoria (Gasteiz)
Alicante	172																																						
Almeria	370	296																																					
Andorra-la-Vella	711	686	998																																				
Badajoz	523	694	605	1062																																			
Barcelona	539	516	810	182	1025																																		
Bilbao	645	818	959	533	694	620																																	
Burgos	489	657	799	578	537	584	157																																
Cáceres	503	675	652	958	90	919	605	446																															
Cádiz	619	688	848	1312	342	1285	1049	900	389																														
Ciudad Real	208	379	408	851	318	812	586	424	325	462																													
Córdoba	355	524	333	1061	273	892	796	636	318	263	199																												
La Coruña	863	1029	1170	1168	774	1120	645	536	683	1070	799	997																											
Gibraltar	603	612	349	1335	490	1127	1069	911	537	148	518	317	1220																										
Gerona	642	615	908	206	1125	100	721	683	1020	1379	912	1009	1214	1227																									
Granada	362	354	167	1057	438	868	830	673	487	335	278	166	1043	259	968																								
Guadalajara	308	483	619	603	460	563	395	240	352	719	248	458	668	732	663	492																							
Huesca	494	570	828	259	799	275	323	358	694	1055	588	797	905	1071	374	830	338																						
León	583	756	898	824	495	785	360	202	409	796	511	733	334	1007	884	762	389	560																					
Lérida (Lleida)	514	491	801	196	867	157	464	428	761	1122	655	865	974	1139	256	861	408	117	630																				
Madrid	251	423	563	661	402	621	396	237	297	663	190	402	610	674	721	433	58	398	334	465																			
Málaga	475	481	218	1205	437	998	940	782	505	264	387	187	1153	130	1097	129	602	940	877	1010	544																		
Murcia	151	76	220	779	677	591	795	639	656	613	357	445	1010	537	690	280	460	611	734	583	334	408																	
Ourense (Orense)	773	944	1085	1062	645	1028	606	447	557	945	699	922	175	1195	1127	955	578	803	271	871	520	1066	920																
Oviedo	700	873	1015	885	614	903	305	322	525	914	641	851	340	982	1004	885	508	626	118	703	452	997	850	338															
Pamplona (Iruña)	601	675	971	384	754	438	160	204	653	1068	597	807	738	1081	537	841	349	162	403	280	409	952	712	650	462														
Salamanca	462	633	762	813	298	777	395	236	208	601	354	529	472	747	878	629	270	554	199	622	213	756	613	346	314	441													
San Sebastián (Donostia)	692	767	1031	463	770	530	120	233	679	1132	659	869	764	1143	629	903	441	255	433	372	470	1014	807	679	423	93	469												
Santander	642	816	957	628	663	693	110	156	574	1056	583	793	546	1067	793	827	394	430	293	537	394	936	793	544	207	266	364	226											
Santiago de Compostela	871	1045	1184	1177	759	1131	658	550	670	1058	808	1012	62	1296	1232	1055	780	918	348	988	623	1165	1019	113	352	751	460	777	561										
Segovia	339	511	651	685	384	652	355	197	298	749	277	497	560	761	750	519	144	426	245	494	87	630	487	466	363	370	164	429	360	575									
Sevilla	490	609	423	1199	217	1044	934	775	263	125	339	140	947	273	1151	256	596	935	672	1003	538	220	532	821	789	945	474	1012	837	922	561								
Soria	472	549	795	488	580	453	258	142	491	894	421	631	676	905	553	665	172	229	342	299	231	775	589	573	465	176	324	268	297	671	195	771							
Tarragona	442	417	710	280	934	99	556	519	832	1060	649	796	1061	1029	198	769	476	209	720	90	534	899	490	962	835	372	713	464	629	1071	585	953	390						
Teruel	243	317	578	512	702	410	488	372	600	873	397	596	908	845	509	605	244	255	573	320	302	716	358	805	690	355	514	450	527	920	390	749	231	309					
Toledo	241	411	526	727	369	694	465	309	264	583	120	321	675	637	792	398	130	467	393	536	71	508	390	580	511	477	235	541	464	689	159	457	303	605	339				
Valencia	192	167	461	520	717	350	634	517	636	808	398	545	961	778	449	520	411	398	685	324	350	650	241	783	803	502	563	594	673	974	441	699	376	251	145	371			
Valladolid	445	614	757	698	415	664	281	123	325	713	377	578	455	867	761	630	251	440	134	508	195	737	593	355	252	327	115	354	249	468	112	589	211	598	441	257	544		
Vitoria (Gasteiz)	603	741	916	477	652	529	66	115	562	1016	540	751	649	1025	630	785	352	256	314	374	352	895	752	560	381	95	351	119	174	662	311	825	191	489	421	422	575	235	
Zaragoza	424	500	758	292	726	297	321	287	620	989	515	725	834	999	396	758	267	73	488	141	325	867	541	731	604	174	480	269	399	847	354	864	157	229	180	397	328	369	261

Portsmouth
Plymouth, Portsmouth
Gorliz
Bilbao
Castello d'Empuries
Islares
Laredo
Noja
Santander
Santillana del Mar
Comillas
San Vicente dela Barquera
Valle de Cabuerniga
Colombres
Potes
La Franca
Llanes
Santa Marina de Valdeon
Ribadesella
Cangas de Onis
Gijon
Oviedo
Cudillero
Pola de Somiedo
Sena de Luna
Ribadeo
San Tirso de Abres
Foz
La Coruna
Carballo
Santiago de Compostela
Muros
Monterroso
Parada de Sil
Allariz
Ourense
Sanxenxo
Vigo
Baiona
Ponferrada
Hospital de Orbigo
León
Villamanan
Carrion de los Condes
Cervera de Pisuerga
Aguilar de Campoo
Castrojeriz
Estepar
Burgos
Santo Domingo de la Calzada
Haro
Aranda de Duero
Cubillas de Santa Marta
Valladolid
Tordesillas
Riaza
Gargantilla del Lozoya
La Cabrera
Segovia
El Escorial
Guadalajara
Madrid
Aranjuez
Toledo
El Barraco
Oropesa
Salamanca
Bejar
Plasencia
La Alberca
Ciudad Rodrigo
Bragança
Vila Real
Braga
Porto
Guarda
Castelo Branco
Aveiro
Coimbra
Leiria

Map I

PORTUGAL
Leiria
Santarém
Portalegre
Elvas
LISBOA
Evora
Beja
Portimão
Faro
Oropesa
Toledo
Caceres
Benquerencia
Horcajo de los Montes
Miajadas
CIUDAD REAL
BADAJOZ
Merida
Santa Elena
LINARES
Villafranca de Cordoba
Cortegana
Fuenteheridos
Cordoba
JAÉN
SEVILLE
Santaella
Dos Hermanas
HUELVA
Isla Cristina
Mazagon
El Rocio
Fuente de Piedra
Humilladero
Beas de Granada
Granada
Algamitas
Vinuela
Velez Malaga
Motril
Balerma
Ronda
MÁLAGA
Puerto de Mazarron
CÁDIZ
Alhaurin de la Torre
Torrox Costa
Torre del Mar
Benajarafe
Estepona
Marbella
Conil de la Frontera
Vejer de la Frontera
San Roque
La Linea de la Concepcion
GIBRALTAR (U.K.)
Tarifa
EXA1
A5
A4
A36
AP36
CM42
A43
A41
A58
A66
A32
A44
A45
A49
A92
AP4
AP46
A7
AP7
A381
A48
N400
N420
N401
N502
N521
N430
N432
N435
N433
N322
N316
N340
Motorways
Primary roads
Secondary roads
All year site(s)
Seasonal site(s)
No sites listed
N
E
S
W
0
50
100
150 km
0
20
40
60
80 miles
E
F
G
H
1
2
3
4

Motorways
Primary roads
Secondary roads
All year site(s)
Seasonal site(s)
No sites listed
see inset on Map 4
FRANCE
MEDITERRANEAN SEA
MINORCA
MAJORCA
Marseille
Montpellier
Beziers
Narbonne
Toulouse
Montrejeau
Tarbes
Pau
Biarritz
Mundaka
Lekeitio
Deba
Zarautz
San Sebastian/Donostia
Irun
Etxarri
Aranatz
Arbizu
Aurtiz
Arostegi
Ochagavia
Isaba
Hecho
Lumbier
Pamplona
Mendigorria
Vitoria/Gasteiz
Logroño
Villafranca
Tarazona
Vinuesa
Soria
Calatayud
Nuevalos
Zaragoza
Jaca
Torla
Broto
Bielsa
Ainsa
Alquezar
Bossost
Vielha
Balaguer
LERIDA/LLEIDA
Montblanc
Salou
Cambrils
L'Hospitalet de l'infant
L'Ametlla de Mar
L'Ampolla
Deltebre
Arnes
Vinaros
Benicarlo
Peniscola
Calig
Alcossebre
Benicassim
CASTELLO
Moncofa
Navajas
Albarracin
A8
A1
A15
AP1
AP15
AP68
N121
N232
N122
N234
NIII
N330
A23
A22
AP2
A2
N240
N230
N211
N420
N11
AP7
N320
A40
PM27
C712
A
B
C
D
1
2
3
4

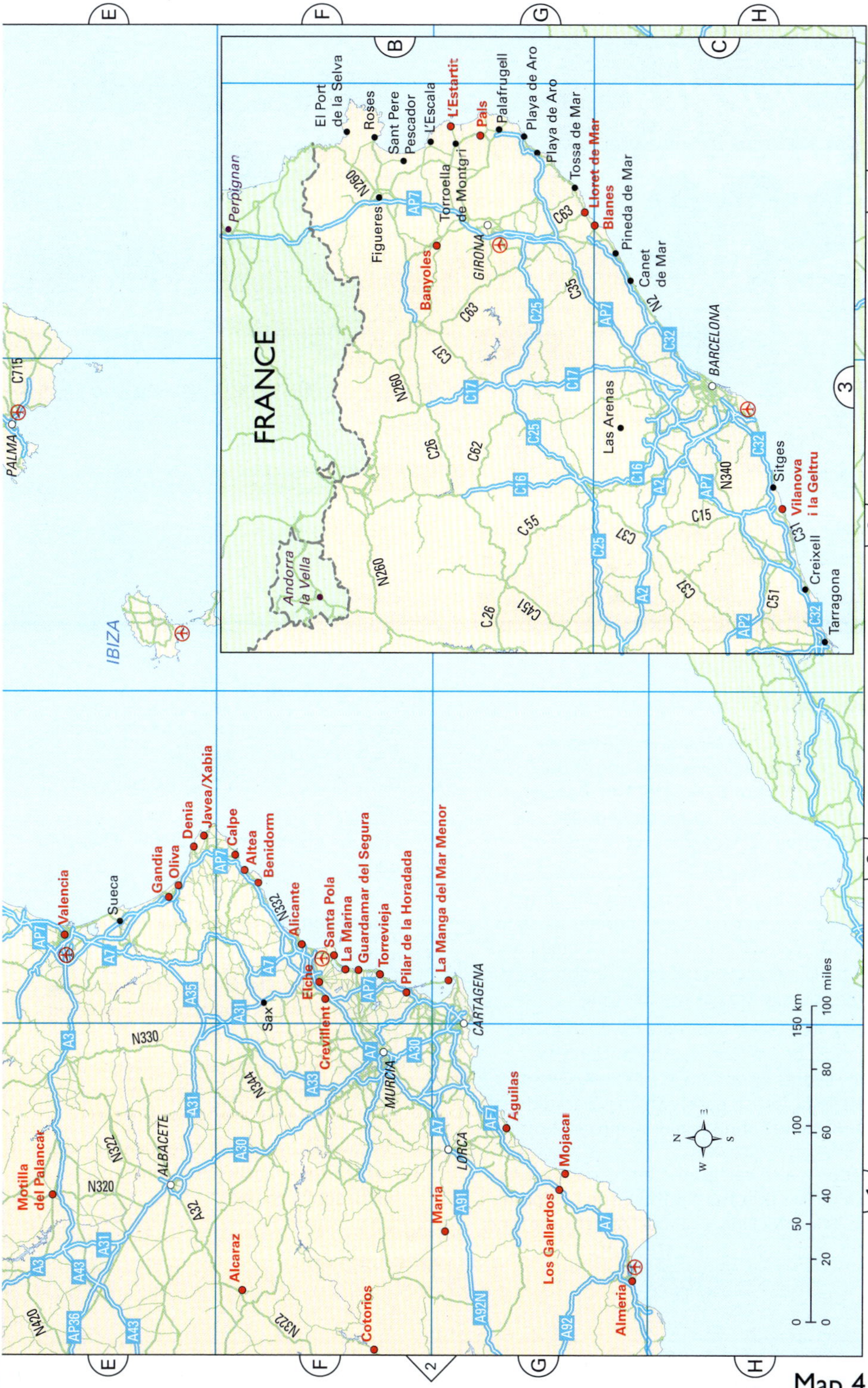
FRANCE
Perpignan
Andorra la Vella
El Port de la Selva
Roses
Sant Pere Pescador
L'Escala
L'Estartit
Pals
Palafrugell
Playa de Aro
Playa de Aro
Torroella de Montgrí
Figueres
Banyoles
GIRONA
Tossa de Mar
Lloret de Mar
Blanes
Pineda de Mar
Canet de Mar
BARCELONA
Las Arenas
Sitges
Vilanova i la Geltru
Creixell
Tarragona
N260
AP7
C63
C35
N2
C25
C37
C17
C26
C62
C16
C32
N340
A2
C15
C55
C31
C451
C51
AP2
PALMA
C715
IBIZA
Valencia
Sueca
Gandia
Oliva
Denia
Javea/Xabia
Calpe
Altea
Benidorm
Alicante
Santa Pola
La Marina
Guardamar del Segura
Torrevieja
Pilar de la Horadada
La Manga del Mar Menor
CARTAGENA
Elche
Crevillent
Sax
MURCIA
Aguilas
Mojacar
LORCA
Maria
Los Gallardos
Almeria
Motilla del Palancar
ALBACETE
Alcaraz
Cotorios
N330
N332
N344
N322
N320
N420
A3
A7
A35
A31
A33
A30
A32
A43
AP36
A91
A92N
A92
E
F
G
H
B
C
1
2
3
4
N
E
S
W
150 km
100 miles
0
20
40
50
60
80
100

Sweden

Shutterstock/Leonid Andronov

Highlights

Renowned for combining simple beauty with functionality, Sweden is one of the design capitals of the world. This is shown in everything from Gothic cathedrals and Baroque palaces to its more modern creations.

As one of Europe's largest, least populated countries Sweden has a lot of green space to enjoy. An extensive network of national parks and trails mean even the most remote parts of the country are easily accessible.

Due to its shorter summers, Sweden makes the most of the long days by packing as many events into them as possible. One of these is a crayfish party, which is a traditional summertime eating and drinking celebration.

Sweden is also celebrated for its rich variety of children's literature, with Astrid Lindgren's Pippi Longstocking, or Pippi Långstrump, one of the most well-known creations.

Major towns and cities

- Stockholm – a dynamic capital city which is the home of the Nobel Prize.
- Gothenburg – this port city has plenty of history on show.
- Malmö – a green city with plenty of beautiful parks.
- Uppsala – this city has ancient roots and boast a dominating cathedral and castle.

Attractions

- Vasa Museum, Stockholm – This fascinating museum features a fantastically preserved shipwreck from the 17th century.
- Sigtuna – the oldest town in Sweden, boasting a picturesque medieval centre filled with restaurants, shops and cafés.
- Drottningholm Palace – A residence of the Swedish royal family, this stunning palace has beautiful gardens.

Find out more

visitsweden.com

Country Information

Capital: Stockholm

Bordered by: Finland, Norway

Terrain: Mostly flat or gently rolling lowlands; mountains in the west

Climate: Cold, cloudy winters, sub-arctic in the north; cool/warm summers. The best time to visit is between May and September; August can be hot and wet. Be prepared for occasional sub-zero temperatures and snowfalls, even in summer months

Coastline: 3,218km

Highest Point: Kebnekaise 2,104m

Language: Swedish

Local Time: GMT or BST + 1, i.e. 1 hour ahead of the UK all year

Currency: Krona (SEK) divided into 100 öre; £1 = SEK 13.92, SEK 100 = £7.18 (Nov 2024)

Emergency Numbers: Police 112 (or 11414 for non-emergency calls); Fire Brigade 112; Ambulance 112. Operators speak English

Public Holidays 2025: Jan 1, 6; Apr 18, 20, 21; May 1, 29; Jun 6, 8, 21; Nov 1; Dec 25, 26.

School summer holidays are from early June to the second or third week of August

Border Posts

There are approximately 40 customs posts along the Swedish/Norwegian border. They are situated on all main roads and are normally open Mon to Fri from 8.30am - 4pm/5pm.

Travellers with dutiable goods must cross the land borders during hours when the customs posts are open. However, travellers without dutiable goods may cross the border outside customs post opening hours. The main border posts with Finland are at Haparanda, Övertornea, Pajala and Karesuando.

Customs Regulations

Visitors arriving from an EU country via a non-EU country (e.g. Norway) may bring quantities of tobacco and alcohol obtained in EUcountries, plus the amounts allowed duty-free from non-EU countries. However, you must be able to produce proof of purchase for goods from EU countries and goods must be for your personal use.

Entry Formalities

British and Irish passport holders may stay for up to 90 days in any 180 day period without a visa. You may be asked to show a return or onward ticket at the border to confirm your length of stay, or to prove that you have enough money for your stay.

Your passport will need to have a minimum of 6 months' validity remaining, and be less than 10 years old (even if it has over 6 months left).

Medical Services

Health care facilities are generally very good and most medical staff speak English. Thre is no GP system; instead visit the nearest hospital clinic (Akutmottagning or Värdcentral) and present your passport and a European Health Insurance Card (EHIC) or a Global Health Insurance Card (GHIC). You'll be charged a fee for the clinic visit (free for anyone under 20) plus a daily standard charge if it's necessary to stay in hospital.

Prescriptions are dispensed at pharmacies (apotek) which are open during normal shopping hours. Emergency prescriptions can be obtained at hospitals. Dentists (tandläkare or folktandvård) offer emergency out-of-hours services in major cities but you may have to pay the full cost of treatment.

The use of mosquito repellent is recommended, particularly from mid-June to September when mosquitos are most common. Mosquitos are generally more often encountered in the north of Sweden rather than the south.

Visitors to remote areas should consider the relative inaccessibility of the emergency services. In northern Sweden mobile phone coverage does not generally extend beyond main roads and the coast.

Opening Hours

Banks: Mon-Fri 9.30am-3pm or 5pm and until 5.30pm one day a week in larger towns. Many banks do not handle cash after 3pm and some banks will not handle cash at all.

Museums: Check locally, opening hours vary.

Post Offices: Post offices no longer exist. Mail is dealt with at local shops, kiosks and petrol stations; opening hours vary.

Shops: Mon- Fri 9.30am-6pm or 7pm and longer in larger towns. Sat 9.30-2 or 4pm. Shops generally close early the day before a public holiday.

Regulations for Pets

In order to protect the countryside and wildlife, dogs are not allowed to run off the lead from 1 March to 20 August and at other times in certain areas.

Dogs travelling directly from the UK and Ireland must be microchipped and have an EU pet passport. For more information please visit the website (jordbruksverket.se) and go to the 'Animal' section.

Safety and Security

Pickpocketing is common in major cities where tourists may be targeted for their passports and cash.

In recent years there have been incidents of 'highway robbery' from motorhomes parked on the roadside, especially on the west coast between Malmö and Gothenburg.

Sweden shares with the rest of Europe an underlying threat from terrorism. Please check gov.uk/foreign-travel-advice/spain before you travel.

British Embassy

Skarpögatan 6-8
115 93 Stockholm
Tel: 08 671 3000
Website: gov.uk/world/sweden

Irish Embassy

HOVSLAGARGATAN 5
111 48 Stockholm
Tel: 08 5450 4040
Website: dfa.ie/sweden

Documents

Driving Licence

A UK driving licence is only valid when it bears a photograph of the holder, i.e. a photocard licence, or when it's carried together with photographic proof of identity, such as a passport.

Money

A growing number of shops, cafes and restaurants do not accept cash. Having a credit or debit card is essential for many transactions. Major credit cards are widely used both for major and minor transactions and cash machines (Bankomat or Minuten) are widespread. It's advisable to carry your passport or photocard driving licence if paying with a credit card as you may be asked for photographic proof of identity.

Driving

Accidents

In the case of an accident it's not necessary to call the police unless there are injuries to drivers or passengers and/or vehicles are badly damaged, but drivers are required to give their details to the other persons involved before leaving the accident scene. A driver leaving the scene of an accident without following this procedure may be fined.

If you are involved in an accident with a possible third party claim, you are strongly recommended to report the accident to the national Swedish insurance bureau which will act as claims agent. Contact Trafikförsäkringsforeningen in Stockholm, tel: 08 522 78200, email: info@tff.se, website: tff.se.

Accidents involving wild animals (e.g. elk, reindeer, bear, wolf, etc) must be reported to the police immediately by calling 112 or 11414 and the spot where the accident took place must be marked by putting up reflective tape or anything clearly noticeable so that the police can find it easily.

Collisions must be reported even if the animal involved is not injured. After reporting the accident and marking out the place, a driver may leave. Accidents involving smaller animals (badgers, foxes, etc) need not be reported.

Alcohol

The maximum permitted level of alcohol in the blood is 0.02%. Penalties for driving under the influence of alcohol are extremely severe. The police carry out random breath tests. If the level of alcohol exceeds 0.02% a fine will be imposed and driving licence withdrawn.

This level is considerably lower than that permitted in England, Wales and Northern Ireland (0.08%) and equates to virtually zero. A level exceeding 0.1% is considered to be severe drink driving for which a jail sentence of up to two years may be imposed and licence withdrawn.

Breakdown Service

The motoring organisation, Riksförbundet M Sverige (known as the 'M'), does not operate a breakdown service. It does, however, have an agreement with 'AssistanceKåren' (a nationwide road service company) which operates a 24-hour, all-year service and can be contacted free on (020) 912 912 or 08 627 5757 from a foreign-registered mobile phone. Phone boxes are becoming quite scarce and it's advisable to carry a mobile phone. There are normally no emergency telephones along motorways or dual carriageways. Charges for assistance and towing vary according to day and time and payment by credit card is accepted.

Child Restraint System

Children under the height of 135cm must be seated in a child restraint or child seat. A child aged 15 or over, or 135cm in height or taller, can use normal seat belts in the car. Children under the height of 140cm are only allowed in the front seat if the passenger seat airbag has been deactivated.

Fuel

Petrol stations are usually open from 7am to 9pm. Near motorways and main roads and in most cities they may remain open until 10pm or even for 24 hours. Outside large towns garages seldom stay open all night but most have self-service pumps (possibly not for diesel) which accept credit cards. In the far north filling stations may be few and far between so keep your tank topped up. Credit cards are accepted.

LPG (known as gasol) is sold at a very limited number of petrol stations mainly located in central and southern Sweden.

Lights

Dipped headlights should be used at all times, regardless of weather conditions. Bulbs can fail with constant use and you're recommended to carry spares.

You can use fog lights when visibility is poor but they must not be used together with dipped headlights.

Vehicles parked or stopped on a poorly lit road at night, including dawn, dusk and bad weather, must have their parking lights switched on.

Low Emission Zones

There are Low Emission Zones (Miljözen) in Gothenburg, Helsingborg, Lund, Malm, Mölndal, Stockholm, Umea and Uppsala. Stockholm also has a Zero Emissions one. Please see urbanaccessregulations.eu for the most up-to-date information.

Motorways

There are over 1,900 km of motorway and 560 km of semi-motorway or dual carriageway, all confined to the south of the country and relatively free of heavy traffic by UK standards. There are no service areas or petrol stations on motorways; these are situated near the exits and are indicated on motorway exit signs. Please note that there are no petrol stations close to the 110 km Uppsala to Gälve motorway.

Overtaking

Take care when overtaking long vehicles. A typical long-distance Swedish truck is a six-wheeled unit towing a huge articulated trailer, i.e. a very long load.

Many roads in Sweden have wide shoulders or a climbing lane to the right of the regular lane and these permit drivers of slow moving vehicles or wide vehicles to pull over to allow other traffic to pass. These climbing lanes and shoulders should not be used as another traffic lane.

Parking

Parking meters and other parking restrictions are in use in several large towns. Vehicles must be parked facing the direction of the flow of traffic. Wheel clamps are not in use but illegally parked vehicles may be towed away and, in addition to a parking fine, a release fee will be charged.

In an area signposted 'P' parking is permitted for a maximum of 24 hours, unless otherwise stated.

Priority

Vehicles driving on roads designated and signposted (with a yellow diamond on a black background) as primary roads always have priority. On all other roads, as a general rule, vehicles coming from the right have priority, unless signs indicate otherwise. This rule is sometimes ignored however, especially by vehicles on roads regarded as major roads but not signposted as such.

At most roundabouts signs indicate that traffic already on the roundabout has priority, i.e. from the left.

Give trams priority at all times. Where there is no refuge at a tram stop, you must stop to allow passengers to board and alight from the tram.

Roads

The condition of national and country roads is good although some minor roads may be covered with oil-gravel only. Road surfaces may be damaged following the spring thaw, and some may be closed or have weight restrictions imposed during that period. Gradients are generally slight and there are no roads unsuitable for towing. Road repairs tend to be intensive during the short summer season. See the website (trafikverket.se) for information on major roadworks and road conditions.

There's a good road link with Norway in the far north of Sweden. The Kiruna-Narvik road is open all year from Kiruna to the border. It's a wide road with no steep gradients.

There's generally little or no heavy goods traffic on roads during the Christmas, Easter and midsummer holidays or on the days preceding these holidays so good progress can be made.

Road Signs and Markings

Road signs and markings conform to international standards. Warning lines (usually on narrow roads) are broken lines with short intervals which indicate that visibility is limited in one or both directions; they may be crossed when overtaking. Unbroken lines should not be crossed at any time.

National roads (riksvägar) have two-digit numbers and country roads (länsvägar) have three-digit numbers.

Roads which have been incorporated into the European road network – E roads – generally have no other national number.

Direction and information signs for motorways and roads which form part of the European road network are green. Signs for national roads and the more important country roads are blue. Signs for local roads are white with black numerals.

The following are some other signs that you may see:

Passing place

Additional stop sign

Accident

Swedish	English Tanslation
Enkelriktat	One way
Farlig kurva	Dangerous bend
Grusad väg	Loose chippings
Höger	Right
Ingen infart	No entrance
Parkering förbjuden	No parking
Vänster	Left

Speed Limits

	Open Road (km/h)	Motorway (km/h)
Car Solo	60-100	90-120
Car towing caravan/trailer	80	80
Motorhome under 3500kg	60-100	90-120
Motorhome 3500-7500kg	70-100	90-120

Speed limits are no longer based on the category of road but on the quality and safety level of the roads themselves. As a result limits may vary from one town to another and along stretches of the same road. It's advisable, therefore, to pay close attention to road signs as speed limits are strictly enforced. If in doubt, or if no speed limit is indicated, you're advised to keep to 70 km/h (44 mph) until you see a speed limit sign.

Outside built-up areas, including expressways, speeds up to 100 km/h (62 mph) may be permitted according to road signs, providing a lower maximum speed is not applicable for certain vehicle categories. Vehicles with trailers must never exceed 80 km/h (49mph). On motorways the maximum permitted speed is 110 or 120 km/h (68 or 74 mph). During the winter a speed limit of 90 km/h (56 mph) is in force on some motorways and dual carriageways. This limit is signposted.

In most residential areas and during certain periods in areas near schools, speed is limited to 30 km/h (18 mph) according to road signs. Periods indicated in black mean Monday to Friday, those in black in brackets mean Saturday and the eves of public holidays, and those indicated in red mean Sunday and public holidays.

Speed limits for motorhomes under 3,500kg and privately registered motorhomes over 3,500kg are the same as for solo cars. Speed cameras are in use on many roads. The use of radar detectors is not permitted.

Tolls

Tolls for private vehicles have now been introduced. The Motala by-pass (on road 50m in central Sweden) the toll will be 5 SEK and for the Sundsvall by-pass (on E4 in northern Sweden) the toll will be 9 SEK. Göteborg(E6) 9-22 SEK.

Toll Bridges

The Øresund Bridge links Malmö in Sweden with Copenhagen in Denmark and means that it's possible to drive all the way from mainland Europe by motorway. The crossing is via a 7.8 km bridge to the artificial island of Peberholm and a 4 km tunnel. Tolls (payable in cash, including EUR, SEK or DKK or by credit card) are levied on the Swedish side and are as follows for single journeys (2024 prices subject to change)

Vehicle(s)	Price
Solo car or motorhome up to 6 metres	455 DKK
Car + caravan/trailer or motorhome over 6 metres	910 DKK

Vehicle length is measured electronically and even a slight overhang over six metres will result in payment of the higher tariff.

Speed limits apply in the tunnel and on the bridge, and during periods of high wind the bridge is closed to caravans. Bicycles are not allowed. Information on the Øresund Bridge can be found on www.oeresundsbron.com.

Svinesund Bridge

There's a 700 metre bridge linking Sweden and Norway on the E6 at Svinesund.

Traffic Lights

A green arrow indicates that traffic may proceed with caution in the direction of the arrow but pedestrians must be given priority. A flashing amber light indicates that a crossing/turning must be made with caution.

Violation of Traffic Regulations

Police are authorised to impose and collect fines for violation of minor traffic offences which must be paid at a bank, normally within two to three weeks. Offences, which may qualify for a fine include driving without lights in daylight, speeding, lack of a warning triangle, not having a nationality plate or sticker (UK or IRL), or a dirty or missing number plate.

If a fine is not paid and the driver is a resident of another EU country, notice of the fine will be forwarded to the authorities in the driver's country of residence.

Winter Driving

The winter months are periods of severe cold and you should be prepared for harsh conditions. The fitting of winter tyres is compulsory for vehicles from 1st December to 31st March in the event of severe winter road conditions, i.e. the road is covered with ice or snow, or if the road is wet and the temperature is around freezing point. Trailers towed by these vehicles must also be equipped with winter tyres. Snow chains must be used where indicated by road signs.

Essential Equipment

Warning Triangle

It's compulsory for foreign registered vehicles to carry a warning triangle.

Touring

Ferry services connect Sweden with Denmark, Estonia, Finland, Germany, Latvia, Lithuania, Norway and Poland; some services only operate in the summer. Full details are available from visitsweden.com. Scheduled car ferry services also operate between the mainland and the island of Gotland during the summer season.

In the south and centre the touring season lasts from May to September. In the north it's a little shorter, the countryside being particularly beautiful at each end of the season. Campsites are most crowded over the midsummer holiday period and during the Swedish industrial holidays in the last two weeks of July and first week of August. Tourist attractions may close before the end of August or operate on reduced opening hours.

Sweden has 15 UNESCO World Heritage sites and 30 national parks which, together with nature reserves, cover eight percent of the country. Information on national parks and nature reserves is available on naturvardsverket.se.

Inland, particularly near lakes, visitors should be armed with spray-on, rub-on and electric plug-in insect repellent devices as mosquitoes and midges are a problem.

Discount cards are available in Stockholm and Gothenburg offering free public transport and free admission to many museums and other attractions, plus free boat and canal sightseeing trips. Buy the cards at tourist information offices, hotels, kiosks, some campsites and online. For more information please see gocity.com/en/stockholm or goteborg.com.

Local tourist offices are excellent sources of information and advice; look for the blue and yellow 'i' signs. Information points at lay-bys at the entrance to many towns are good sources of street maps.

A good-value 'dagens rätt' (dish of the day) is available in most restaurants at lunchtime. A service charge is usually included in restaurant bills but an additional small tip is normal if you have received good service.

The most popular alcoholic drink is lager, available in five strengths. Wines, spirits and strong beer are sold only through the state-owned 'Systembolaget' shops, open from Monday to Friday and on Saturday morning, with branches all over the country. Light beer can be bought from grocery shops and supermarkets. The minimum age for buying alcoholic drinks is 20 years at Systembolaget and 18 years in pubs, bars and licensed restaurants.

It's not permitted to smoke in restaurants, pubs or bars or in any place where food and drinks are served.

Camping and Caravanning

Camping and caravanning are very popular, but because summer is short the season is brief - from May to early September, although winter caravanning is increasing in popularity. High season on most sites ends around the middle of August when prices and site office opening hours are reduced or sites close altogether. There are more than 1,000 campsites, about 350 of which remain open during the winter particularly in mountainous regions near to ski resorts. Those that are open all year may offer fewer or no facilities from mid-September to April and advance booking may be required.

In late June and July advance booking is recommended, especially at campsites along the west coast (north and south of Göteborg), on the islands of Öland and Gotland and near other popular tourist areas.

Approximately 500 campsites are members of the SCR (Svenska Campingvärdars Riksfärbund – Swedish Campsite Owners' Association), which are classified from 1 to 5 stars. Visitors wishing to use these sites must have a Camping Key Europe card. You can buy the Camping Key Europe at campsites and you'll be given a temporary card, or you can order it in advance from camping.se/en for 199 SEK (2024 prices). If ordering in advance you should allow at least three weeks for delivery.

Also aim to arrive by mid afternoon to get a better pitch, since many Swedes arrive late.

It's reported that hand basins on sites often do not have plugs so it's advisable to carry a flat universal plug when touring.

Many sites have a 'Quick Stop' amenity which provides safe, secure overnight facilities on, or adjacent to, a site. This normally includes the use of sanitary facilities. 'Quick Stop' rates are about two thirds of the regular camping rate if you arrive after 9pm and leave before 9am.

Casual/wild camping is normally permitted (except in National Parks and recreational areas), however for security reasons it's not recommended to spend the night in a vehicle on the roadside or in a public car park. Instead use the 'Quick Stop' amenity at campsites. In any event local parking rules and signposting should always be observed.

Alternatively there are around 150 organised 'ställplatser' mainly intended for motorhomes but generally car and caravan outfits may also use them for an overnight stay at the discretion of the site's manager.

Most designated rest areas along highways are owned and managed by the Vågverket (Swedish Roads Administration) which, although not officially ranked as 'ställplatser', offer adequate parking space and various facilities for motorhomes staying overnight. A map showing these rest areas is available at local tourist offices.

Cycling

The network of cycle lanes in Sweden is growing rapidly and many cycle routes are named and signposted. In some cases cycle lanes are combined with foot paths - see: svenska-cykelsallskapet.se.

The 'Sverigeleden' cycle trail covers the whole country and connects all major ports and cities. The 190 km cycle route along the Göta Canal from Sjötorp on Lake Vänern to Mem on the Baltic coast is relatively flat and hence a very popular route.

The wearing of a safety helmet is compulsory for children up to the age of 15 and is recommended for everyone.

Electricity and Gas

On campsites the current is usually 10 amps or more and round two-pin plugs are used. CEE connections are becoming standard.

Propane (gasol) is the gas most widely obtainable at more than 2,000 Primus dealers; you'll need to buy an appropriate adaptor. It's understood that it's possible to sell back your propane cylinder at the end of your holiday and outlets will also exchange the corresponding Norwegian Progas cylinders. Recent visitors report that major distributors will refill cylinders but they must be of a recognised make/type and in perfect condition.

Butane gas is available from a number of outlets including some petrol stations. It's understood that Campingaz 904 and 907 cylinders are available but recent visitors report that they may be difficult to find, and virtually impossible in the north of the country. For more information on butane suppliers contact the Swedish Campsite Owners' Association (SCR) by email: info@scr.se

Ensure that you are well-equipped with gas if venturing north of central Sweden as it may be difficult to find an exchange point. Many sites have communal kitchen facilities which enable visitors to make great savings on their own gas supply.

The Midnight Sun and Northern Lights

The Midnight Sun is visible north of the Arctic Circle from about the end of May until the middle of July.

The Northern Lights (Aurora Borealis) are often visible during the winter from early evening until midnight. They are seen more frequently the further north you travel. The best viewing areas in Sweden are north of the Arctic Circle between September and March.

The Order of Bluenosed Caravanners

Visitors to the Arctic Circle from anywhere in the world may apply for membership of the Order of Bluenosed Caravanners which will be recognised by the issue of a certificate by the International Caravanning Association (ICA).

Contact bluenosed@icacaravanning.org and attach a photograph of yourselves and your outfit under any Arctic Circle signpost, together with the date and country of crossing and the names of those who made the crossing.This service is free to members of the ICA(annual membership £20 plus a £5 joining fee).

Cheques should be payable to the ICA. Please see (icacaravanning.org) for more information.

Public Transport & Local Travel

Stockholm has an extensive network of underground trains (T-bana), commuter trains, buses and trams. Underground station entrances are marked with a blue 'T' on a white background. You can buy single tickets for one of three zones at the time of your journey, or save money by buying tickets in advance. A discount applies if you are aged 65 or over. Single tickets and prepaid tickets are valid for one hour after beginning your journey. Travel cards offer reduced price public transport in Stockholm for periods of 1, 3, 7 or 30 days – see (sl.se/en/in-english) for details of routes, fares and tickets.

For information on public transport systems in Göteborg and Malmö, see vasttrafik.se and skanetrafiken.se.

Stockholm is built on an archipelago of islands and island hopping ferries operate all year. You can buy single tickets or an island hopping pass for use on the Waxholmsbolaget and Cinderella fleet of ferries.

Confirm your taxi fare before setting off in the vehicle. Some companies have fixed fares which vary according to the day of the week and time of day. A full price list must be on display. Payment by credit card is generally accepted. It's usual to round up the fare shown on the meter by way of a tip.

Sweden is a country of lakes, rivers and archipelagos and, as a result, there are over 12,000 bridges. Road ferries, which form part of the national road network, make up the majority of other crossings. Most ferries are free of charge and services are frequent and crossings very short.

A congestion charge apples in Stockholm and Göteborg from Mon to Fri from 6.30am to 6.30pm For more information go to transportstyrelsen.se. In some other towns traffic restrictions may apply during certain periods and these are signposted.

When giving directions Swedes will often refer to distances in 'miles'. A Swedish 'mile' is, in fact, approximately ten kilometres. All road signs are in kilometres so if a Swede tells you it's 3 miles to a town, expect the journey to be around 30 km.

Hamburgsund

Shutterstock/TTphoto

Sites in Sweden

AHUS *2F4* (1km NE Urban/Coastal) *55.94118, 14.31286* **First Camp Ahus,** Kolonivägen 59, 29633 Åhus **(044) 248969; ahus@firstcamp.se; firstcamp.se**

12 (htd) WD MSP nr nr sand 150m

Take rd 118 fr Kristianstad SE twd Åhus. Site well sp fr ent to town. 3*, Lge, mkd, hdstg, pt shd, EHU (10A) SEK29; bbq; 10% statics; Eng spkn; ccard acc; sauna; site clsd 3 Nov-16 Dec; CKE. *"Gd base for walking, cycling, watersports; htd pool 300m; excel fishing; famous area for artists."* **SEK 260** **2022**

"There aren't many sites open at this time of year"

If you're travelling outside peak season remember to call ahead to check site opening dates – even if the entry says 'open all year'.

ALMHULT *2F3* (2km N Rural) *56.56818, 14.13217* **Sjöstugans Camping (G5),** Campingvägen, Bökhult, 34394 Älmhult **(0476) 71600; info@sjostugan.com; www.sjostugan.com**

(htd) WD MSP nr sand adj

Fr Växjö SW on rd 23, at rndabt turn W to Älmhult. Fr town cent turn N on Ljungbyvägen, site in 1.5km on lakeside, well sp. 3*, Med, pt shd, pt sl, EHU (16A) SEK45; bbq; cooking facs; twin axles; 25% statics; bus 500m; Eng spkn; adv bkg acc; ccard acc; canoe hire; sauna; games area; CKE. *"Some lakeside pitches; well-kept site; lake adj; 1st Ikea store opened here in 1958; v helpful staff; excel."* **SEK 350, 1 May-30 Sep.** **2023**

AMAL *2E2* (1km SE Urban) *59.0465, 12.7236* **Örnäs Camping (P2),** Gamla Örnäsgatan, 66222 Åmål **(0532) 17097; Info@destinationamal.nu; https://destinationamal.se**

12 (htd) WD MSP nr nr

Leave rd 45 to Åmål, site sp. 4*, Sm, hdstg, pt shd, pt sl, terr, EHU (10A) inc; red long stay; 10% statics; Eng spkn; ccard acc; boat hire; fishing; bike hire; tennis; CCS; sauna. *"Gd views Lake Vänern; lake adj."* **SEK 370** **2023**

ARBOGA *2G1* (13km S Rural) *59.28134, 15.90509* **Herrfallets Camping (U14),** 73293 Arboga **(0589) 40110; reception@herrfallet.se; www.herrfallet.se**

12 (htd) WD MSP

Foll sp fr E20/E18, turn off at Sätra junc twd Arboga, cross rv. Foll sp to Herrfallet/Västermo. 4*, Med, mkd, pt shd, serviced pitches; EHU (10A) SEK40; bbq; sw; phone; ccard acc; boating; bike hire; sauna; CKE. *"Lovely spot on edge Lake Hjälmaren."* **SEK 270** **2022**

ARJANG *2E1* (26km SE Rural) *59.30399, 12.44662* **Camping Grinsby,** Grindsbyn 100, Sillerud, 67295 Årjäng **(0573) 42022; info@campgrinsby.eu; https://campgrinsby.eu**

SEK15 (htd) WD MSP

On E18 SE fr Årjäng & Sillerud, turn L at site sp. Site in 2km on Stora Bör lake. Med, hdstg, pt shd, terr, EHU (10A) inc; bbq; cooking facs; sw nr; 10% statics; phone; Eng spkn; adv bkg acc; ccard acc; games rm; bike hire; boat hire; CKE. *"A 'wilderness' site in beautiful setting; many walking paths; friendly, helpful staff; vg san facs."* **SEK 430, 1 May-3 Sep.** **2023**

ARJEPLOG *1C2* (1.5km W Rural) *66.05007, 17.86298* **Kraja Camping (BD1),** Krajaudden, 93090 Arjeplog **(0961) 31500; kraja@silverresort.se; www.kraja.se**

12 (htd) WD MSP (htd) sand

NW fr Arvidsjaur thro Arjeplog vill to site on R. 3*, Lge, unshd, EHU (16A) SEK40; bbq; cooking facs; sw nr; twin axles; TV; 90% statics; phone; bus 500m; Eng spkn; adv bkg acc; sauna; boating; fishing; CKE. *"Gd cent for local Lapp area; hotel on site with full facs; 20 touring pitches; v pleasant & helpful staff; keypad security at night; excel Sami silver museum in town."* **SEK 275** **2023**

ASARNA *1B3* (9km S Rural) *62.56340, 14.38786* **Kvarnsjö Camp,** Kvarnsjö 696, 84031 Åsarna **(0682) 22016; info@kvarnsjocamp.com; www.kvarnsjocamp.com**

12 WD MSP

Fr N on E45 3km after Åsarna turn R onto rd 316 dir Klövsjo. In 8km turn L sp Cmp Kvarnsjö. In 8km cross rlwy, thro vill, site on L in 1km. Fr S 9km after Rätan turn L dir Klövsjo. In 1.5km bear R at Y-junc site in 4km. 3*, Sm, hdstg, unshd, terr, EHU (10A) SEK50; Eng spkn; adv bkg acc; sauna; CKE. *"CL-type family-run site o'looking woods & mountains; excel walking, fishing; boating, fresh bread/breakfast in high ssn."* **SEK 300** **2023**

BERGKVARA *2G4* (1km E Coastal) *56.39043, 16.09061* **Dalskärs Camping,** Dalskärvägen11, 385 40 Bergkvara **(0709) 415567; info@dalskarscamping.se; www.dalskarscamping.se**

WD MSP (htd) sand adj

Exit E22 in Bergkvara twd Dalskärsbadet, site sp. 3*, Med, mkd, pt shd, EHU SEK40; 10% statics; phone; Eng spkn; ccard acc; games area; sauna; bike hire; boat hire. *"Gd family site; san facs adequate; excel rest; scenic location."* **SEK 355, 24 Apr-11 Sep.** **2024**

BOCKSJO *2F2* (5km NW Rural) *58.68058, 14.59911* **Stenkällegårdens Camping Tiveden,** 54695 Stenkällegården **(0505) 60015; kontakt@stenkallegarden.se; www.stenkallegarden.se**

N on rd 49 fr Karlsborg, turn L at Bocksjö, site sp on L in 2km. Pt of rte single track with passing places. 4*, Med, mkd, pt shd, pt sl, terr, EHU (10A) SEK40; bbq; cooking facs; sw; TV; 30% statics; Eng spkn; ccard acc; fishing; boat hire; sauna; site clsd last 2 weeks Apr & 1st 2 weeks Oct; CKE. *"Gd cycling; mkd walking trails; spacious, sheltered site; clean san facs; skiing on site in winter; Tividen National Park 5km."* **SEK 250** **2022**

BORAS *2E3* (2.5km N Urban) *57.73885, 12.93608* **Caming Borås Salteman (P11),** Campinggatan 25, 50602 Borås **(033) 353280; info@borascamping.com; www.borascamping.com**

Exit N40 fr Göteborg for Borås Centrum; foll sps to Djur Park R42 to Trollhätten thro town; well sp. 4*, Med, mkd, pt shd, pt sl, EHU (10-16A) inc; cooking facs; twin axles; TV; 10% statics; bus 350m; Eng spkn; adv bkg acc; boating; CKE. *"Gd pitches adj rv with paths; quickstop o'night facs; gd zoo 500m; pool 500m; gd, clean facs; nr sports stadium/tennis courts."* **SEK 370** **2023**

BORENSBERG *2G2* (1.5km S Rural) *58.55663, 15.27911* **Strandbadets Camping,** 59030 Borensberg **(0141) 40385; info@strandbadetscamping.se; www.strandbadetscamping.se**

Foll sp for Camping Gota Canal fr Rd 34 thro town & across canal. Site 2nd site on R. 3*, Med, pt shd, EHU (10A) SEK60; cooking facs; sw; 10% statics; fishing. *"Gd base for Östergötland & Lake Vättern area; cycle rte along Göta Canal."* **SEK 280, 22 Apr-11 Sep.** **2023**

DOROTEA *1C3* (0.5km SW Rural) *64.25850, 16.38833* **Doro Camping,** Storgatan 1A, 91731 Dorotea **(0942) 10238; info@doro.camp; www.dorocamping.com**

Site on E side of E45. 3*, Med, pt shd, pt sl, EHU (10A) SEK50; cooking facs; sw; 10% statics; Eng spkn; sauna; site clsd Nov; golf; fishing. *"Site being extensively redeveloped (2019); most impressive rest."* **SEK 350** **2024**

ED *2E2* (2km E Rural) *58.89931, 11.93486* **Gröne Backe Camping (P8),** Södra Moränvägen 64, 66832 Ed **(0534) 10144; info@gbcamp.nu; www.gbcamp.nu**

App Ed on rd 164/166, site sp on Lake Lilla Le. 3*, Med, shd, pt sl, EHU (10A) SEK40; sw; ccard acc; sauna; bike hire; CKE. *"Excel for boating."* **SEK 291** **2022**

EKSJO *2F3* (1km E Rural) *57.66766, 14.98923* **Eksjö Camping (F13),** Prästängsvägen 5, 57536 Eksjö **(0381) 39500; info@eksjocamping.se; www.eksjocamping.se**

Site sp fr town cent on rd 33 twd Västervik, on lakeside. 3*, Med, shd, EHU (10A) inc; sw nr; 10% statics; phone; ccard acc; boating; fishing; bike hire; CKE. *"Gd cent glass region; attractive countryside & old town."* **SEK 340** **2023**

FALKOPING *2F2* (2km W Rural) *58.17595, 13.52726* **Mössebergs Camping & Stugby (R7),** Scheelegatan, 52130 Falkoping **(0515) 17349 or 07072 56493; mossebergscamping@telia.com; www.mossebergscamping.se**

Exit rd 184 at Falköping; foll Int'l Camping sps or sps to Mösseberg; site also sp fr rds 46 & 47 & in town. Site on plateau overlkg town. 3*, Med, mkd, pt shd, EHU inc; cooking facs; sw nr; 10% statics; phone; ccard acc; sauna; CKE. *"Pool 400m; site has barrier."* **SEK 375** **2023**

FILIPSTAD *2F1* (1km N Rural) *59.72035, 14.15899* **Munkeberg Camping (S5),** Skillervägen, 68233 Filipstad **(0590) 50100; alterschwede@telia.com; www.munkeberg.com**

Fr Karlstad take rd 63 to Filipstad. In town foll sp for rd 246 twd Hagfors, site sp in town. 3*, Med, pt shd, pt sl, EHU (10A) SEK30; sw; 10% statics; adv bkg acc; fishing; boating; CKE. *"Beautiful lakeside site; gd for touring old mining district."* **SEK 208** **2022**

GADDEDE *1B2* (0.4km NE Rural) *64.50400, 14.14900* **Gäddede Camping & Stugby,** Sagavägen 9, 83090 Gäddede **(0672) 10035; info@gaddedecamping.com; www.gaddedecamping.se**

On ent Gäddede cent on rd 342, turn R & site in 500m on R, sp. 3*, Med, mkd, pt shd, EHU (10A) SEK50; TV; 40% statics; Eng spkn; adv bkg acc; ccard acc; games area; canoe hire; games rm; sauna; fishing; CKE. *"Gd touring base 'Wilderness Way'."* **SEK 198** **2022**

GALLIVARE *1C2* (1km S Urban) *67.1290, 20.6776* **Gällivare Campingplats (BD5),** Kvarnbacksvägen 2, 98231 Gällivare **(0970) 10010; info@gellivarecamping.com; www.gellivarecamping.com**

On E45 app fr SW on R immed after bdge. 3*, Sm, mkd, hdstg, unshd, EHU (10A) SEK50; bbq; cooking facs; sw nr; twin axles; TV; 50% statics; phone; Eng spkn; ccard acc; bike hire; sauna; games area; CKE. *"Helpful, friendly owners; pleasant pitches on rvside; gd facs; daytime cafe opp; rest & shops 1km; sep car pk."* **SEK 240, 13 May-27 Sep.** **2023**

GAMLEBY *2G2* (1km SE Coastal) *57.88475, 16.41373* **KustCamp Gamleby (formerly Hammarsbadets),** Hammarsvägen 10, 59432 Gamleby **(0493) 10221; info@campa.se; www.campa.se**

sand adj

On E22 Kalmar-Norrköping, foll sp to site 2km off main rd. 4*, Med, mkd, pt shd, terr, EHU (10A) SEK45; sw; 10% statics; phone; ccard acc; boat hire; tennis; Quickstop o'night facs; sauna; bike hire; CKE. *"Clean, well-kept, relaxing site."* **SEK 312, 1 May-15 Sep. 2022**

GESUNDA *1B4* (2km N Rural) *60.90100, 14.58500* **Sollerö Camping,** Levsnäs, 79290 Sollerön **(0250) 22230; info@sollerocamping.se; www.sollero camping.se**

12

Fr Gesunda take bdge to Sollerön Island in Lake Siljan. Site immed on R on reaching island; clearly visible fr bdge. 3*, Lge, pt shd, pt sl, EHU (16A); sw nr; adv bkg acc; ccard acc; tennis; boat hire; sauna; canoe hire; CKE. *"Beautiful outlook to S across lake; gd base for Dalarna folklore area; gd site & facs; every 7th day is free."* **SEK 350 2024**

GOTEBORG *2E3* (4km E Rural) *57.7053, 12.0286* **Lisebergsbyn Camping Kärralund (O39),** Olbersgatan 1, 41655 Göteborg **(031) 840200; lisebergsbyn@liseberg.se; www.liseberg.se**

12

Exit E6/E20 junc 71 onto rd 40 E & foll sp Lisebergsbyn, site well sp. Lge, unshd, pt sl, terr, EHU (16A) inc; gas; bbq; cooking facs; twin axles; TV; 25% statics; phone; tram 400m; Eng spkn; adv bkg rec; ccard acc; games area; CKE. *"Boat trips arranged; vg, well-run site; LS arr early to obtain barrier key; poss travellers on site; cycle path to Liseberg amusement park & town cent; impressive, organised & professional staff; red LS & Sun-Fri; lovely site; san facs outstanding."* **SEK 450 2023**

GOTEBORG *2E3* (7km W Urban) *57.70413, 12.02989* **Lisebergs Ställplats,** Olbersgatan 9, 416 55 Göteborg **031 840 200; lisebergsbyn@liseberg.se; www.liseberg.se**

12

Take Backebogatan to Litteraturgatan. Then E6 and Delsjövägen to Olbersgatan. At rndabt take 1st exit to Olbersgatan, Turn R & R again, site on L. Sm, hdstg, mkd, pt shd, EHU (10A) inc; own san rec; bbq; Eng spkn; adv bkg acc; ccard acc. *"Tram at bottom of hill past main site ent, main site off will help with travel info etc; excel."* **SEK 240 2022**

GRANNA *2F2* (0.5km NW Rural) *58.02783, 14.45821* **First Camp Gränna,** Hamnen, 56300 Gränna **(0390) 10706; granna@firstcamp.se; www.grannacamping.se**

nr

In cent of Gränna down rd twd Lake Vättern, sp Visingsö Island. 3*, Lge, unshd, EHU (10A) metered + conn fee; sw; TV (pitch); CKE. *"Ballooning cent of Sweden; Visingsö Island, Brahehus ruined castle, glass-blowing 3km; vg site; gd location; some cottages; excel, clean san facs, excel camp kitchen."* **SEK 300, 30 Apr-3 Oct. 2022**

GREBBESTAD *2E2* (1km S Coastal) *58.6832, 11.2625* **Grebbestads Familjecamping,** Rörvik, 45795 Grebbestad, Sverige **(0525) 61211; info@ grebbestadfjorden.com; www.grebbestad fjorden.com**

12 sand 150m

Exit E6 at Tanumshede sp Grebbestad; foll rd thro vill, past harbour; site on R approx 500m after harbour. 4*, Lge, mkd, unshd, pt sl, EHU (10A) SEK50; cooking facs; 80% statics; phone; Eng spkn; adv bkg acc; ccard acc; games area; sauna; CKE. *"Well-maintained site 500m fr busy fishing/yachting harbour; meadowland; htd pool 1km; excel mv services; helpful staff; vg facs, lge cr noisy site."* **SEK 350 2024**

"That's changed – Should I let the Club know?"

If you find something on site that's different from the site entry, fill in a report and let us know. See camc.com/europereport.

HALMSTAD *2E3* (10km S Coastal) *56.59033, 12.94430* **Gullbrannagården Camping (N27),** 31031 Eldsberga **(035) 42180; info@gullbranna garden.se; www.gullbrannagarden.se**

12 sand 500m

Fr S site sp on E6. Lge, pt shd, pt sl, EHU SEK45; cooking facs; 60% statics; Eng spkn; adv bkg acc; games rm. *"Christian-run site; church & bible classes; alcohol discouraged; OK for those of like mind."* **SEK 290 2022**

HAMBURGSUND *2E2* (1km S Coastal) *58.54075, 11.28240* **Rorviks Camping,** Rorviksangen 15 45747 Hamburgsund **05 25 33 573; info@rorviks camping.se; www.rorvikscamping.se**

Take exit 103 on the E6 (bet Tatum V-Munkedal). Foll 163 W to Kville. Turn L to Hamburgsund, cont S 1km. Campsite on R. Lge, mkd, hdstg, pt shd, EHU (10A) inc; bbq; cooking facs; twin axles; 10% statics; bus 1km; Eng spkn; adv bkg acc; games area; CCI. *"Quiet, low key site in a great area; vg."* **SEK 430, 1 May-31 Aug. 2024**

SWEDEN

SWEDEN

HAMMERDAL *1 B3* (2km S Rural) *63.57513, 15.34286* **Camp Route 45,** Fyran 210, 83341 Hammerdal **(070) 6076892; info@camproute45.com; camproute45.com**

12 nr

0.5km off E45 outside Hammerdal, 65km N Ostersund. 3*, Sm, hdstg, unshd, EHU (10A) SEK60; cooking facs; sw nr; twin axles; Eng spkn; adv bkg acc; ccard acc; sauna. *"Canoes for hire; English run; comfortable kitchen/diner; elk hunting in season; cafe with burgers; english breakfast; poss mosquitoes; pleasant, well kept site; excel."* **SEK 240** **2023**

HAPARANDA *1D2* (15km N Rural) *65.9620, 24.0378* **Kukkolaforsen Camping (BD27),** Kukkolaforsen 184, 95391 Haparanda **(0922) 31000; info@kukkolaforsen.se; www.kukkolaforsen.se**

12 (htd)

On rd 99 on banks of Rv Tornionjoki. 3*, Med, pt shd, EHU (10A) inc; TV; phone; adv bkg acc; ccard acc; sauna; bike hire; fishing; CKE. *"Friendly staff; rv rapids."* **SEK 390** **2023**

HARNOSAND *1C3* (2.5km NE Coastal) *62.64451, 17.97123* **Sälstens Camping (Y21),** Sälsten 22, 87133 Härnösand **(0611) 18150; salsten.camping@telia.com**

(htd)

On Gulf of Bothnia, E of town & on S side of inlet; exit off E4; foll sp for Härnösand town cent, then intn'l camping sp; then site. 3*, Sm, mkd, pt shd, terr, EHU (10A); TV; Eng spkn; CKE. *"Folk museum in town; excel site."* **SEK 250, 15 May-31 Aug.** **2022**

HEDESUNDA *2G1* (5km SE Rural) *60.35000, 17.02100* **Hedesunda Camping,** Övägen 68, 81895 Hedesunda **(070) 5443713; info@hedesundacamping.se; www.hedesundacamping.se**

(htd) nr

Exit rd 67 L at sp Hedesunda. Foll camp sp thro Hedesunda; past church, cont about 4km to Hedesunda Island. 3*, Sm, pt shd, EHU (6A) SEK30; gas; cooking facs; sw nr; red long stay; TV; Eng spkn; fishing; boat hire; CKE. *"Peaceful, lakeside site; organised activities in ssn; helpful staff."* **SEK 260, 1 May-31 Oct.** **2022**

HELSINGBORG *2E4* (5km S Coastal) *56.0034, 12.7300* **First Camp Råå Vallar,** Kustgatan, 25270 Råå **(042) 182600; raavallar@firstcamp.se; www.firstcamp.se**

12 (htd) sand

Exit E6 into Helsingborg onto rd 111 to Råå, foll sp to camp. 3*, Lge, pt shd, EHU (10A) SEK50; gas; 10% statics; phone; ccard acc; Quickstop o'night facs; golf 5km; fishing; sauna; CKE. *"Excel, secure site with gd facs; sports cent 2km; friendly, helpful staff; excursions to Copenhagen via Helsingør or Landskrona; town bus excursions to King's Summer Palace daily; boat trips to glass works at Hyllinge."* **SEK 410** **2022**

HOGANAS *2E4* (8km N Rural) *56.27061, 12.52981* **First Camp Mölle (M1),** Kullabergsvagen, 26042 Mölle **(042) 347384; molle@firstcamp.se; www.firstcamp.se**

(htd) 1.5km

Site is S of Mölle at junc of rds 11 & 111, at foot of Kullaberg. 5*, Lge, unshd, pt sl, EHU (10A) inc; cooking facs; 10% statics; Eng spkn; ccard acc; games area; golf; Quickstop o'night facs; sauna; fishing. *"Steep slope to san facs; walking; Krapperups Castle & park sh walk fr site; excel outdoor activities."* **SEK 417, 1 Apr-30 Sep.** **2022**

HOVA *2F2* (8.7km NE Coastal) *58.90998, 14.28995* **Otterbergets Bad & Camping,** 54891 Hova **050633 127 or 0738064 935; info@otterbergetscamping.com; www.otterbergetscamping.com**

adj

Fr Laxa take E20 rd; site sp approx 4km fr Hova; drive 2 km thro woods to site. Med, mkd, pt shd, EHU (16A) SEK50; bbq; cooking facs; 10% statics; Eng spkn; adv bkg rec; sauna; CCI. *"Attractive site with private access to lake; events held such as fishing competition & trade fairs (when site may be busy); v helpful Dutch owners; recep 0800-2200; san facs vg; excel."* **SEK 300, 15 Apr-1 Nov.** **2023**

JOKKMOKK *1C2* (3km SE Rural) *66.59453, 19.89145* **Arctic Camp Jokkmokk,** Notudden, 96222 Jokkmokk **(0971) 12370; arcticcamp@jokkmokk.com; arcticcampjokkmokk.se/**

12 (htd) (htd)

Sp fr rd 45. In Jokkmokk take rd 97 E, site in 3km on N side of rd situated bet rv & rd. 4*, Lge, mkd, pt shd, EHU (10A) SEK40 (poss rev pol); sw nr; 10% statics; Eng spkn; adv bkg acc; ccard acc; bike hire; waterslide; fishing; sauna; CKE. *"Friendly, clean, well-maintained site 5km inside Arctic Circle; gd area for Sami culture; excel playgrnd; lakeside setting, gd pool; late arrival area."* **SEK 260** **2023**

JOKKMOKK *1C2* (3km W Rural) *66.60500, 19.76200* **Skabram Stugby & Camping,** Skabram 206, 96299 Jokkmokk **(0971) 10752; info@skabram.se; www.skabram.se**

12 (htd)

Site sp fr E45 along rd 97, Storgatan. Sm, hdstg, pt shd, EHU (16A) SEK70; bbq; cooking facs; sw nr; twin axles; 10% statics; Eng spkn; adv bkg acc; sauna; fishing; boating. *"Vg; canoe & dog sleigh trips; relaxing site; lovely sm fm type site; v quiet location; gd san facs."* **SEK 230** **2023**

JONKOPING *2F3* (2.5km E Urban) *57.7876, 14.2195* **Villa Björkhagen,** Friggagatan 31, 55454 Jönköping **(036) 122863; info@villabjorkhagen.se; www.villabjorkhagen.se**

12 (htd) WD MSP

Fr N exit E4 junc 99 or fr S exit E4 junc 98a & foll sp Rosenlund/Elmia & site sp nr exhibition cent. Site on Lake Vättern. 4*, Lge, mkd, pt shd, pt sl, EHU (10A) SEK35; sw nr; TV (pitch); 50% statics; phone; ccard acc; fishing; bike hire; Quickstop o'night facs; sauna; CKE. *"Gd rest; prone to flooding after heavy rain; some facs run down & site untidy (2010); htd covrd pool complex, waterslide 300m; site charges increase considerably during exhibitions & site v full; pitches well mkd; easy walk into town along sea front."* **SEK 265** **2024**

KALMAR *2G3* (2km S Coastal) *56.64975, 16.32705* **First Camp Stensö,** Stensövägen, 39247 Kalmar **(0480) 88803; stenso@firstcamp.se; www.stensocamping.se**

WD MSP sand adj

Fr E22 foll sp Sjukhus (hosp) then camping sp - this avoids town cent. Fr town cent, site sp. 4*, Lge, mkd, shd, pt sl, EHU (10A) SEK40 (check pol); cooking facs; 10% statics; phone; Eng spkn; ccard acc; boating; fishing; Quickstop o'night facs; cycling; CKE. *"Conv Öland Island (over bdge); glass factories in vicinity; walking dist to town; helpful, friendly staff; new clean san facs (2014); excel."* **SEK 276, 27 Mar-30 Sep.** **2022**

KARESUANDO *1D1* (2km SE Rural) *68.43396, 22.51577* **Karesuando Camping,** Laestadiusvägen 185, 98016 Karesuando **(0981) 20139; karesuando.camping@hotmail.com; karesuandocamping.blogspot.com**

WD MSP

Travelling N on E45, in town cont past bdge to Finland onto rd 99 for approx 2km; site on L. App fr Finland, turn L after x-ing bdge; cont on 99 for 2km. Sm, unshd, EHU (10A) 50; bbq; twin axles; 50% statics; Eng spkn; adv bkg acc; sauna; games area; CKE. *"Model Sami vill on site; cash point in PO; poss mosquito prob; canoe hire avail; gd view of midnight sun on rv; unmkd pitches, fills up quickly."* **SEK 300, 18 May-18 Sep.** **2023**

KARLSHAMN *2F4* (3km SE Coastal) *56.15953, 14.89085* **Kolleviks Camping (K7),** Rådhusgatan 10, 374 81 Karlshamn **(0454) 810 00; info@karlshamn.se; www.karlshamn.se**

(htd) WD MSP sand adj

Fr E22 dir Karlshamn & Hamnar (harbour), then site well sp. 3*, Med, mkd, pt shd, pt sl, EHU (10A) SEK45; red long stay; 25% statics; Eng spkn; adv bkg acc; ccard acc; canoeing; Quickstop o'night facs; CKE. *"Helpful owner; attractive location inc harbour; gd base for area; ltd facs LS; well-kept site; facs tired, poss stretched when busy."* **SEK 155, 26 Apr-14 Sep.** **2020**

KARLSKRONA *2G4* (2km NE Coastal) *56.1729, 15.5675* **Dragsö Camping,** Dragsövägen 14, 37137 Karlskrona **(0455) 15354; info@dragso.se; www.dragsocamping.se**

(htd) MSP nr nr adj

Foll app to town cent, taking m'way. At end of m'way foll sp to Dragsö. Site sp - on its own island. Lge, mkd, pt shd, EHU (10A) inc; TV; 10% statics; Quickstop o'night facs; fishing; bike hire; sauna; boating; CKE. *"Sea bathing; rocky cliffs; scenic beauty; gd."* **SEK 323, 1Apr-10 Oct.** **2024**

KARLSTAD *2F1* (9km W Rural) *59.36233, 13.35891* **BomstadBaden,** Bomstadsvägen 640, 65346 Karlstad **(054) 535068; info@bomstad-baden.se; www.bomstadbaden.se**

12 WD MSP sand

2km S of E18 on Lake Vänern. Foll sp thro woods. 4*, Lge, shd, pt sl, EHU (10A) SEK50; bbq; sw; phone; adv bkg acc; bike hire; fishing; canoeing; CKE. *"Excel base; beautiful site in trees; gd walks on mkd trails."* **SEK 290** **2024**

KATRINEHOLM *2G2* (2km S Rural) *58.9696, 16.21035* **Djulö Camping (D6),** Djulögatan 51, 64192 Katrineholm **(0150) 57242; info@djulocamping.se; www.djulocamping.se**

12 MSP nr nr

At Norrköping on E4 cont twd Stockholm for about 3km, turn L onto rd 55 N twd Katrineholm. Camping site sp in 2km. 3*, Lge, hdstg, pt sl, EHU (10A) SEK35; gas; sw; adv bkg acc; ccard acc; games area; bike hire; fishing; boating; CKE. *"On lakeside in lge park; well-run, friendly site."* **SEK 291** **2022**

KIL *2F1* (7km N Rural) *59.54603, 13.34145* **Frykenbadens Camping (S17),** Stubberud, 66591 Kil **(0554) 40940; info@frykenbaden.se; www.frykenbaden.se**

12 WD MSP

Fr Karlstad take rd 61 to Kil, site clearly sp on lakeside. 4*, Lge, pt shd, pt sl, EHU (10A) inc; sw; TV; phone; adv bkg acc; fishing; Quickstop o'night facs; boat launch; bike hire; CKE. *"Very clean, spacious waterfront site; sauna SEK5; barrier key."* **SEK 395** **2023**

KIRUNA *1C1* (1.6km NE Urban) *67.8604, 20.2405* **Ripan Hotel & Camping,** Campingvägen 5, 98135 Kiruna **(0980) 63000; info@ripan.se; www.ripan.se**

12 (htd) WD nr (htd)

Site sp fr town cent. 3*, Med, hdstg, mkd, unshd, EHU (10A) inc; TV (pitch); Eng spkn; ccard acc; sauna. *"No privacy in shwrs; easy walk to town; public footpath thro site (top end) - poss v noisy & disruptive; trips to Kirunavaara Deep Mine fr tourist info office; no security fence."* **SEK 323** **2022**

SWEDEN

SWEDEN

KIVIK *2F4* (1.6km N Rural/Coastal) *55.69135, 14.21373* **Kiviks Familjecamping (L35),** Väg 9, 27732 Kivik **(0414) 70930; info@kivikscamping.se; www.kivikscamping.se**

shgl 1km

On rd 9 o'looking sea, sp. 3*, Med, mkd, unshd, EHU SEK35; bbq; cooking facs; TV; 20% statics; phone; Eng spkn; ccard acc; CKE. *"Steam rlwy w/end in summer at Brösarp; cider/apple area; easy walk to town; rev pol certain pitches."* **SEK 230, 16 Apr-9 Oct.** **2022**

KOLMARDEN *2G2* (2km SE Coastal) *58.6597, 16.4006* **First Camp Kolmården,** 61834 Kolmården **(011) 398250; kolmarden@firstcamp.se; www.firstcamp.se**

(htd) adj

Fr E4 NE fr Norrköping take 1st Kolmården exit sp Kolmården Djur & Naturpark. Site on sea 2km bef Naturpark. 4*, Lge, pt shd, terr, EHU (10A); cooking facs; TV; 10% statics; phone; ccard acc; waterslide; sauna; bike hire; boat hire; CKE. *"Gd site; nr to Kilmarden zoo & aquarium; well mkd pitches."* **SEK 428** **2024**

KUNGALV *2E2* (1km SE Rural) *57.86211, 11.99613* **Kungälvs Vandrarhem & Camping (O37),** Färjevägen 2, 44231 Kungälv **(0303) 18900; info@kungalvsvandrarhem.se; www.kungalvsvandrarhem.se**

(htd)

Exit E6 junc 85 or 86 & foll sp Kungälv cent, then sp 'Bohus Fästning'. Site sp. 3*, Sm, mkd, hdstg, shd, EHU (12A) SEK40; bbq (gas); red long stay; 10% statics; bus adj; Eng spkn; ccard acc; CCI. *"Site adj Bonus Fästning (fort) & Kungälv Church (17th C) on rv bank; find pitch & check in at recep 0800-1000 & 1700-1900; door code fr recep for san facs; gd NH."* **SEK 250, 15 Apr-30 Sep.** **2024**

KUNGSHAMN *2E2* (2km NE Coastal) *58.36569, 11.28077* **Swecamp Johannesvik,** Wagga Nordgard 1, 45634 Kungshamn **(0523) 32387; info@johannesvik.nu; https://johannesvik.nu/**

(htd) shgl adj

Fr E6 rte 171 to Askum, dir Kungshamn, thro Hovenaset, over bdge. Ent to site on R (sp). 4*, Lge, mkd, unshd, terr, EHU inc; gas; bbq; cooking facs; red long stay; TV; Eng spkn; adv bkg acc; CKE. *"Barrier card SEK150 dep; dep req; shwr card SEK6 (3mins); gd."* **SEK 400** **2023**

LANDSKRONA *2E4* (4km N Rural) *55.90098, 12.8042* **Borstahusens Camping (M5),** Campingvägen, 26161 Landskrona **(0418) 108 37; bokning@motesplatsborstahusen.se; www.motesplatsborstahusen.se**

(htd) adj

Exit E6/E20 at 'Landskrona N' & foll sp for Borstahusen 4.5km fr E6/D20. 3*, Lge, unshd, EHU (10A) SEK40; TV; 50% statics; phone; Eng spkn; ccard acc; tennis; golf; bike hire; CKE. *"Gd, pleasant, well run site on edge of Kattegat; htd pool 2km; sm pitches; game reserve; boat to Ven Island fr town; adj sea but no views; chalets & holiday packages."* **SEK 320, 21 Apr-11 Sep.** **2024**

LEKSAND *2G1* (4km SW Rural) *60.73061, 14.95221* **Västanviksbadets Camping (W12),** Siljansnäsvägen 130, 79392 Leksand **(076) 81 28 510; info@vbcl.se; www.vbcl.se**

(htd)

L off Borlänge to Leksand rd at Leksand S, dir Siljansnäs. Site ent clearly visible on R in 3km at W end Lake Siljan at Västanvik. Med, mkd, unshd, pt sl, terr, EHU (10A) SEK45; bbq (sep area); cooking facs; sw; TV; 10% statics; Eng spkn; adv bkg acc; ccard acc; Quickstop o'night facs; boating; bike hire; fishing. *"Attractive site on lakeside; friendly welcome; ltd facs LS; lakeside pitches avail; keycard for all facs; Dalarna/Lake Siljan traditional heart of Sweden; excel."* **SEK 292, 30 Apr-6 Sep.** **2024**

LIDKOPING *2 F2* (24.4km N Rural) *58.67381, 13.21283* **Lacko Slott Camping,** Läcko Slott Kållandsö, 53199 Otterstad **(5104) 84668; info@lackoslott.se; www.lackoslott.se**

nr nr lake 50m

On Lake Vanern, 25km N of Lidkoping, sp fr Lacko. Sm, hdg, mkd, shd, EHU (10A) inc; cooking facs; sw nr; bus; Eng spkn; adv bkg acc; ccard acc. *"Medieval Lacko Castle 100m; Naturum nature and visitor ctr with rest 150m; mostly individual pitches hidden in woods (no lake views) on promontory opp castle; barrier key; bkg rec; lovely site; excel."* **SEK 350, 1 May-30 Sep.** **2023**

LIDKOPING *2F2* (32km NE Rural) *58.624003, 13.383631* **Kinnekulle Camping & Stugby,** Strandvägen, 53394 Hällekis **(0510) 544102; info@kinnekullecamping.se; www.kinnekullecamping.se**

(htd) adj, sand

Turn off E20 at Gotene for Hallekis. Outskirts of Hallekis foll sp (ignore MH NH sp) rd passes factory & heads into woods. Site in 3km. 4*, Lge, mkd, pt shd, pt sl, terr, EHU (10A) SEK 25; 30% statics; Eng spkn; ccard acc; CKE. *"Vg; local walks in woods & hillside; barrier key card."* **SEK 390, 13 Apr-9 Sep.** **2023**

LJUNGBY *2F3* (1km N Urban) *56.84228, 13.95251* **Ljungby Camping Park,** Campingvägen 1, 34122 Ljungby **(0372) 10350; reservation@ljungby-semesterby.se; www.ljungby-semesterby.se**

(htd)

Exit E4 at Ljungby N, site sp. 3*, Med, shd, EHU (10A) SEK35; ccard acc; cycling; CKE. *"Adv bkg ess high ssn; htd pool adj."* **SEK 256, 1 May-31 Aug.** **2022**

LJUSDAL *1B3* (3km W Rural) *61.83894, 16.04059* **Ljusdals Camping (X21),** Ramsjövägen 56, 82730 Ljusdal **(0651) 129 58; info@ljusdalscamping.se; www.ljusdalscamping.se**

(htd)

Leave Ljusdal on Rv83 dir Ånge, site on R in 3km. 3*, Med, pt shd, EHU (10A) SEK40; cooking facs; sw nr; 10% statics; Eng spkn; adv bkg acc; ccard acc; bike hire; games area; sauna; CKE. **SEK 295** **2024**

LULEA *1D2* (8km W Coastal) *65.59565, 22.07221* **First Camp Luleå (BD18),** Arcusvägen 110, 97594 Luleå **(0920) 60300; lulea@firstcamp.se; www.firstcamp.se/lulea**

12 (htd) WD MSP sand adj

Exit E4 on R 500m N of Luleälv Rv bdge. Foll sp 'Arcus' (recreation complex). 3*, V lge, mkd, pt shd, EHU (10A) inc; cooking facs; TV; phone; Eng spkn; adv bkg acc; ccard acc; tennis 300m; car wash; sauna; bike hire; CKE. *"Excel family site; many sports facs; san facs poss stretched high ssn; htd pool complex 700m; suitable RVs & twin axles; adj rlwy museum."* **SEK 365** **2024**

MALMO *2E4* (11km N Coastal) *55.68873, 13.05756* **Habo-Ljung Camping (M23),** Södra Västkustvägen 12, 23434 Lomma **(040) 6411000; info@lomma.se**

(htd) WD MSP sand adj

Turn off E6 dir Lomma, head N for Bjärred, site on L. 3*, Lge, pt shd, EHU (10A) SEK40; bbq; cooking facs; 5% statics; phone; Eng spkn; ccard acc; CKE. *"Conv NH; vg; location for wind & kite surfing; 20 min walk along beach to town."* **SEK 396, 15 Apr-15 Sep.** **2024**

MALMO *2E4* (7km SW Urban) *55.5722, 12.90686* **Firstcamp Sibbarp – Malmö (formerly Malmö Camping),** Strandgatan 101, Sibbarp, 21611 Limhamn **(040) 155165; malmo@firstcamp.se; www.firstcamp.se**

12 (htd) WD MSP sand 250m

Fr Öresund Bdge take 1st exit & foll sp Limhamn & Sibbarp, then int'l campsite sp. Fr N on E6 round Malmö until last exit bef bdge (sp), then as above. Fr Dragør-Limnhamn ferry turn R on exit dock. Site in 1km on R, nr sea, in park-like setting. 4*, V lge, mkd, hdg, pt shd, pt sl, EHU (16A) inc (poss rev pol); gas; bbq; cooking facs; twin axles; TV; 20% statics; phone; bus to Malmo; Eng spkn; ccard acc; games rm; windsurfing; games area; bike hire; CKE. *"Easy cycle to town cent; facs poss stretched high ssn; v busy city site; well-laid out; pool 400m; conv Öresund Bdge; lovely site; v friendly, helpful staff; gd clean new (2016) san facs blocks."* **SEK 420** **2023**

MALUNG *2F1* (1km W Rural) *60.68296, 13.70243* **Malungs Camping (W22),** Bullsjövägen, 78235 Malung **(0280) 18650; info@malungscamping.se; www.malungscamping.se**

12 (htd) WD

Fr Stöllet take rd 45 to Malung, site sp. 3*, Lge, pt shd, EHU (10A) SEK40; TV; ccard acc; car wash; fishing; Quickstop o'night facs; bike hire; boating; CKE. **SEK 260** **2022**

MARIESTAD *2F2* (2km NW Rural) *58.7154, 13.79516* **Ekuddens Camping (R2),** Ekuddenvägen 50, 542 45 Mariestad **(501)106 37 or (0771) 101 200; ekudden@firstcamp.se; www.firstcamp.se/destinationer/ekudden-mariestad**

12 MSP (htd)

Fr E20 take turn off twd Mariestad. At 1st rndabt foll ring rd clockwise until site sp on Lake Vänern. 4*, Lge, shd, EHU (10A) SEK40; gas; phone; ccard acc; bike hire; golf 2km; sauna; Quickstop o'night facs; CKE. *"Gd views fr lakeside pitches; friendly, helpful staff; gd san facs."* **SEK 294** **2024**

MARKARYD *2F3* (0.5km N Urban) *56.46475, 13.60066* **Camping Park Sjötorpet (G4),** Strandvägen 4, 28531 Markaryd **(0433) 10316; info@markarydscamping.se; www.markarydscamping.se**

(htd) WD MSP

E4 fr Helsingborg (ferry) site is bet E4 N turn to Markaryd & rd 117, sp. Narr app. 3*, Sm, pt shd, pt sl, EHU (10A) inc; cooking facs; sw; 10% statics; phone; Eng spkn; ccard acc; boating; fishing; bike hire; CKE. *"Excel san & cooking facs; well-run site; new owners (2017), helpful; barrier may clse 7pm."* **SEK 400, 12 Apr-29 Sept.** **2023**

MARSTRAND *2E2* (1.4km NE Coastal) *57.89380, 11.60510* **Marstrands Camping (036),** Långedalsvägen 16, 44030 Marstrand **(0303) 60584; info@marstrandcamping.se; www.marstrandscamping.se**

(htd) WD MSP shgl

Exit A6 dir Kungsälv/Marstrand & foll rd 168 to Marstrand. Site sp on Koön Island. App rd to site v narr. 4*, Med, pt shd, pt sl, EHU (10A) inc; cooking facs; TV; 50% statics; adv bkg acc; ccard acc; CKE. *"Ferry to Marstrand Island; recep not staffed in LS."* **SEK 425, 12 Apr-2 Oct.** **2023**

MELLBYSTRAND *2E3* (1km N Urban/Coastal) *56.51961, 12.94628* **Mellbystrands Camping (formerly Marias),** Norra Strandvägen 1, 312 60 Mellbystrand **(0430) 28585; info@mellbystrands.se; www.mellbystrands.se**

(htd) WD MSP sand adj

20km N of Båstad, exit junc 41 fr E6 W onto rd 24, site sp off coast rd N. 4*, Lge, mkd, hdg, pt shd, EHU inc; cooking facs; TV; bus 500m; Eng spkn; adv bkg acc; games rm; CKE. *"Vg site beside dunes; beautiful beach."* **SEK 320, 21 Apr-26 Aug.** **2024**

MELLERUD *2E2* (15km N Rural) *58.81968, 12.41519* **Haverud Camping,** Kanalvagen 4, 464 72 Haverud **(0530) 30770; hafrestromsif@telia.com; https://www.hafrestromsif.se/haveruds-camping**

nr

Signposted in Haverund. Sm, mkd, hdstg, unshd, terr, EHU SEK40; sw nr; Eng spkn; CKE. *"Self pitch on arr, fees collected am or pay at visitors ctr at canal; gd."* **SEK 210, 25 Apr-14 Sep.** **2023**

SWEDEN

MELLERUD *2E2* (4km SE Coastal) *58.68933, 12.51711* **Vita Sandars Camping,** 46421 Mellerud **(0530) 12260; mail@vitasandarscamping.se; www.vitasandarscamping.se**
(htd) (htd)

Fr S on rd 45 take Dalslandsgatan Rd on R & foll sp. Fr N turn L twd Sunnanåhamn, Vita Sandar. 4*, Med, pt shd, EHU (10A) SEK50; cooking facs; sw; TV; 20% statics; ccard acc; waterslide; games area; tennis; bike hire; Quickstop o'night facs; sauna; fishing; boat hire; CKE. *"Pleasant family site in pine trees; excel sw."* **SEK 420** **2024**

MELLERUD *2E2* (2km W Rural) *58.71288, 12.43231* **Kerstins Camping (P21),** Hålsungebyn 1, 46494 Mellerud **(0530) 12715; epost@kerstinscamping.se; www.kerstinscamping.se**
(htd)

Fr Mellerud on rd 166 dir Bäckefors & Ed, site sp. 3*, Sm, mkd, hdg, pt shd, EHU (10A) SEK50; bbq (sep area); cooking facs; TV; 15% statics; phone; Eng spkn; adv bkg acc; games rm; CKE. *"Pleasant area; excel; sm site with open outlook to fmland on 1 side; vg site."* **SEK 275, 14 May-9 Sep.** **2023**

"I like to fill in the reports as I travel from site to site"

You'll find report forms at the back of this guide, or you can fill them in online at camc.com/europereport.

MORA *1B4* (0.5km N Urban) *61.00853, 14.53178* **Firstcamp Moraparken Camping,** Parkvägen 1, 79237 Mora **(0250) 27600; moraparken@firstcamp.se; https://firstcamp.se/destinationer/moraparken-dalarna**
(htd) nr nr (covrd, htd)

Fr SW site sp on rd 45. Or foll sp in town cent; site in 400m. Recep in adj hotel. 4*, Lge, mkd, pt shd, pt sl, EHU (10A) inc; TV; 10% statics; Eng spkn; ccard acc; sports facs; Quickstop o'night facs; fishing; waterslide; games rm; CKE. *"Excel site; ltd facs LS & poss unclean; suitable RVs & twin axles; conv for bear sanctuary at Orsa."* **SEK 370** **2023**

NOSSEBRO *2E2* (0.5km N Urban) *58.19195, 12.72161* **Nossebro Camping,** Marknadsgatan 4, 46530 Nossebro **(0512) 57043; nossebrobadochcamping@essunga.se; www.essunga.se**
nr (covrd)

N fr Alingsås on E20; exit N to Nossebro, site in 16km. Clearly sp. 3*, Sm, unshd, pt sl, EHU inc; 10% statics; fishing; boat hire; sauna; bike hire. *"Vg NH; sports grnd adj; stream thro site."* **SEK 200, 25 Apr-31 Aug.** **2024**

NYNASHAMN *2H2* (1km NW Coastal) *58.90717, 17.93805* **First Camp Nickstabadet,** Nickstabadsvägen 17, 14943 Nynäshamn **(08) 52012780; nickstabadet@firstcamp.se; www.firstcamp.se**
(htd) nr adj

Fr Stockholm on Rv 73 to Nynäshamn. Foll site sp, turning R at ICA supmkt, then immed L (sp poss cov'rd by hedge.) 4*, Med, pt shd, pt sl, EHU (10A) SEK50; cooking facs; 10% statics; train 600m; Eng spkn; games area; site clsd mid-Dec to mid-Jan; Quickstop o'night facs; waterslide; bike hire; CKE. *"Gd site; ferries to Gotland & Poland."* **SEK 343** **2022**

OREBRO *2G2* (3km S Rural) *59.2554, 15.18955* **Gustavsviks Camping (T2),** Sommarrovägen, 70229 Örebro **(019) 196900; camping@gustavsvik.com; www.gustavsvik.se**
(htd) (covrd, htd)

Foll sp fr E18/E20 & rd 51 to site. 5*, V lge, mkd, pt shd, pt sl, serviced pitches; EHU (10A) SEK80 (poss rev pol); gas; bbq; cooking facs; sw nr; TV (pitch); 10% statics; phone; bus; Eng spkn; ccard acc; waterslide; solarium; gym; golf nr; CKE. *"Excel family site; excel facs; gentle stroll to town; very highly rec; beautiful site."* **SEK 240, 15 Apr-6 Nov.** **2022**

ORSA *1B4* (1km W Rural) *61.12090, 14.59890* **First Camp Orsa,** Timmervägen 1, 79431 Orsa **(0250) 46200; orsa@firstcamp.se; www.orsacamping.se**
(htd) nr (htd)

Sp fr town cent & fr rd 45. 4*, V lge, pt shd, EHU (10A) SEK50; cooking facs; sw; TV (pitch); 5% statics; phone; tennis; canoe hire; fishing; waterslide; bike hire; sauna; CKE. *"Excel countryside; bear reserve 15km; gd general facs but ltd LS."* **SEK 375** **2022**

OSKARSHAMN *2G3* (3km SE Coastal) *57.2517, 16.49206* **Gunnarsö Camping (H7),** Östersjövägen 103, 57263 Oskarshamn **(0491) 77220; gunnarso@firstcamp.se; www.firstcamp.se**
(htd)

Fr E22 dir Oskarshamn, site sp on Kalmar Sound. 4*, Med, pt shd, EHU (10A) SEK35; TV; 40% statics; phone; adv bkg acc; ccard acc; watersports; sauna; CKE. *"Beautiful location; many pitches with gd views; gd walking/cycling."* **SEK 332, 1 May-15 Sep.** **2022**

OSTERSUND *1B3* (3km SE Rural) *63.15955, 14.6731* **Östersunds Camping (Z11),** Krondikesvägen 95, 83146 Östersund **(063)14 46 15; ostersundscamping@ostersund.se; www.ostersundscamping.se**
(htd) nr

At Odensala on lakeside, well sp fr E14. 4*, Lge, mkd, hdstg, pt shd, pt sl, EHU (10A) SEK60 (poss rev pol); cooking facs; TV (pitch); 80% statics; phone; bus; ccard acc; sauna; tennis; CKE. *"Gd NH; very helpful staff."* **SEK 200** **2024**

PAJALA *1D1* (1.5km SE Rural) *67.20381, 23.4084* **Pajala Camping (BD8),** Tannavägen 65, 98431 Pajala **(073) 364 52 78; pajalacamping@gmail.com; https://www.pajalacampingroute99.se/**

12 (htd) WD MSP

Site sp fr rd 99. 2*, Med, mkd, hdstg, pt shd, FHU (10A) SEK30; cooking facs; red long stay; TV; Eng spkn; adv bkg acc; ccard acc; sauna; tennis; bike hire; CKE. *"Clean, well-presented site; delightful owner; salmon-fishing in rv in ssn (mid-Jun approx)."* **SEK 190** **2022**

RAMVIK *1C3* (1km S Rural) *62.79911, 17.86931* **Snibbens Camping,** Snibben 109, 87016 Ramvik **(0)73 696 1325; info@snibbenscamping.com; www.snibbenscamping.com**

(htd) WD MSP nr

Fr S on E4, 23km N of Härnösand; after high bdge sighted take slip rd dir Kramfors; site sp in 2.5km on L just bef Ramvik. 4*, Med, mkd, pt shd, pt sl, EHU (16A) SEK20; cooking facs; sw nr; TV; 10% statics; bus; Eng spkn; ccard acc; boat hire; fishing; CKE. *"Helpful owners; delightful site with lakeside setting; v peaceful even when busy; spotless facs & lovely camp kitchen with seating areas inside & out; conv Höga Kusten suspension bdge; delightful site in beautiful surroundings."* **SEK 415, 6 May-11 Sep.** **2024**

RATTVIK *1B4* (1km W Rural) *60.88891, 15.10881* **Firstcamp Enåbadet – Rättvik (formerly Siljansbadet Camping),** Enåbadsvägen 8, 795 32 Rättvik **(0248) 56118; enabadet@firstcamp.se; https://firstcamp.se/destinationer/enabadet-rattvik**

WD MSP nr nr

Fr S on rd 70 thro Rättvik. Immed outside town turn L at rndabt, site sp on Lake Siljan. Height restriction 3.5m. 4*, V lge, mkd, pt shd, EHU (16A) inc; bbq; cooking facs; sw; twin axles; TV; 15% statics; bus/train; Eng spkn; ccard acc; games area; boat hire. *"Lovely scenic lakeside location; conv town cent; excel san facs; excel site."* **SEK 300, 26 Apr-6 Oct.** **2023**

SAFFLE *2F2* (6km S Rural) *59.08326, 12.88616* **Duse Udde Camping (S11),** 66180 Säffle **(0533) 10800; duseudde@firstcamp.se; www.duseudde.se**

12 MSP

Site sp fr rd 45. 4*, Med, shd, pt sl, EHU (10A) SEK50; sw; red long stay; 20% statics; phone; bus; ccard acc; watersports; sauna; bike hire; Quickstop o'night facs; CKE. *"Place to relax; pool 6km; useful base for Varmland area with nature walks."* **SEK 180** **2022**

SARNA *1B3* (1km S Rural) *61.69281, 13.14696* **Särna Camping (W32),** Särnavägen 6, 79090 Särna **(070) 3330518; info@sarnacamping.se; www.sarnacamping.se**

WD MSP nr nr shgl

Turn R off rd 70 opp fire stn. 3*, Med, pt shd, terr, EHU (10A) SEK35; adv bkg acc; sauna; bike hire. *"Beautiful setting o'looking lake; pleasant town."* **SEK 245, 19 May-30 Sep.** **2022**

SIMRISHAMN *2F4* (2km N Coastal) *55.57021, 14.33611* **Tobisviks Camping (L14),** Tobisvägen, 27294 Simrishamn **(0414) 412778; info@tobisvikscamping.se; www.tobisvikscamping.se**

12 WD MSP nr nr (htd)

By sea at N app to town. 4*, Lge, pt shd, EHU (10A) SEK50; TV; phone; ccard acc; watersports; CKE. **SEK 210** **2022**

SKANOR *2E4* (2km SE Coastal) *55.39750, 12.86555* **Calsterbo Camping & Resort,** Strandbadsvägen, 23942 Falsterbo **(040) 6024020 or (414) 401180; info@falsterboresort.se; falsterboresort.se**

(htd) WD MSP sand 200m

Fr E6/E22 exit to W sp Höllviken onto rd 100. Foll sp Skanör/Falsterbo. Site sp on L at rndabt at ent to town, dir Falsterbo. 4*, Lge, mkd, hdstg, pt shd, EHU (10A) SEK50; bbq; cooking facs; TV; 50% statics; bus; Eng spkn; ccard acc; CKE. *"Conv Viking Vill museum; nature reserve adj; gd birdwatching, cycling; vg; aircraft noise (under flight path Copenhagen airport); new management, new recep & ongoing work on facs (2017)."* **SEK 325, 29 Apr-28 Sep.** **2023**

SKELLEFTEA *1C2* (1.5km N Rural) *64.76156, 20.97513* **Skellefteå Camping (AC18),** Mossgaten, 93170 Skellefteå **(0910) 735500; skelleftea camping@skelleftea.se; www.skelleftea.se/skellefteacamping**

12 (htd) WD MSP nr nr (htd) sand 5km

Turn W off E4; well sp behind g'ge. Also sp as Camping Stugby. 4*, Lge, mkd, unshd, pt sl, EHU (16A) inc; bbq; cooking facs; TV; 10% statics; phone; Eng spkn; ccard acc; waterslide; tennis 150m; sauna; fishing; bike hire; games area; CKE. *"Friendly, clean site in pine trees on sheltered inlet; lge pitches suitable RVs & twin axles; Nordanå Cultural Cent & Bonnstan Church Vill in walking dist; if site clsd book in at Statoil stn 500m S on E4 at rndabt; excel san facs, lgr camp kitchen, helpful staff, lge supmkt nrby."* **SEK 400** **2023**

SKELLEFTEA *1C2* (7km NE Coastal) *64.77681, 21.11993* **Bovikens Havsbad,** 931 99 Skellefteå **070 670 10 28; info@bovikenshavsbad.se; www.bovikenshavsbad.se**

WD sand adj

Site sp off E4, site in 5km. 3*, Med, mkd, pt shd, EHU; TV; 10% statics; Eng spkn; adv bkg acc; ccard acc; tennis nr; CKE. *"Gd family site by secluded beach; friendly owner; excel birdwatching; avoid shwr cubicles with elec heaters nr floor level; v nice!"* **SEK 360, 16 May-14 Sep.** **2024**

SODERHAMN *1C4* (10km SE Coastal) *61.24843, 17.19506* **Stenö Havsbad Camping (X9),** Stenövägen, 82022 Sandarne **(0270) 75150; stenocamping@soderhamn.se; www.stenohavsbad.se/**

Exit E4 at sp Bollnäs-Sandarne (S of Söderhamn turn), foll sp Sandarne at Östansjö, turn L at camping sp. 4*, Lge, shd, EHU (10A) SEK50; cooking facs; TV; 10% statics; phone; bus; adv bkg acc; ccard acc; games area; CKE. *"Adj nature reserve."* **SEK 307** **2022**

SODERKOPING *2G2* (1km N Rural) *58.49163, 16.30618* **Skeppsdockans Camping (E34),** Dockan 1, 61421 Söderköping **(0121) 21621; info@soderkopingscamping.se; www.soderkopingscamping.se**

On E22 immed N of canal bdge. 2*, Sm, mkd, unshd, EHU SEK40; cooking facs; sw; TV; Eng spkn; ccard acc; bike hire; CKE. *"On side of Gota Canal; peaceful."* **SEK 220, 30 Apr-2 Oct.** **2022**

SORSELE *1C2* (0.4km W Rural) *65.53428, 17.52663* **Sorsele Camping (AC21),** Fritidsvägen 10, 92432 Sorsele **(070)18 27 886; info@sorselecamping.se; www.sorselecamping.se**

N on rd 45/363 fr Storuman to Arvidsjaur. In Sorsele vill turn W for 500m; site sp. Med, unshd, EHU (16A) SEK35; TV; 10% statics; phone; ccard acc; bike hire; canoeing; fishing; CKE. *"Nature reserve; hiking; interesting ancient Lapp vill; friendly, welcoming; attractive site."* **SEK 249** **2024**

STOCKHOLM *2H2* (15km N Rural) *59.43821, 17.99223* **Rösjöbadens Camping (B1),** Lomvägen 100, 19256 Sollentuna **(08) 962184; info@rosjobaden.se; www.rosjobaden.se**

Take E18 m'way N fr Stockholm, sp Norrtälje. Pass Morby Centrum on L after 7km. Take Sollentuna exit, turn L & foll Sollentuna rd 265/262 for approx 5km. At 2nd set of traff lts with pylons adj, turn R on sm rd, clear sp to site. 3*, Lge, pt shd, pt sl, EHU (16A) SEK50; bbq; cooking facs; twin axles; TV (pitch); 90% statics; bus 150m; Eng spkn; adv bkg acc; Quickstop o'night facs; boating; fishing; CKE. *"Conv Morby Centrum, lge shopping cent, petrol, metro to city; pleasant walks in woods & lakeside; lake sw fr pontoons; san facs adequate; staff uninterested; site run as a residential site; fair."* **SEK 360** **2023**

STOCKHOLM *2H2* (12km SW Urban) *59.29558, 17.92300* **Bredäng Camping (A4),** Stora Sällskapetväg, 12731 Skärholmen **(08) 977071; bredangcamping@gmail.com; www.bredangcamping.se**

Exit E4/E20 to Bredäng junc 152 & foll sp to site. 3*, Lge, mkd, hdstg, pt shd, serviced pitches; EHU (16A) SEK40; cooking facs; TV; 30% statics; Eng spkn; adv bkg acc; ccard acc; Quickstop o'night facs; bike hire; sauna. *"Facs ltd LS & poss stretched in ssn; v helpful staff; overspill 3km at Sätra Camping; battery-charging; conv for Stockholm; shopping cent & metro with free car park about 700m; lake adj; access to Stockholm also poss by lake steamer fr pier (high ssn) - 10 min walk; well-run site; metro 700m; vg forest walks."* **SEK 358, 18 Apr-9 Oct.** **2022**

STOCKHOLM *2H2* (10km W Rural) *59.33731, 17.90105* **Ängby Campingplats (A3),** Blackebergsvägen 25, 16850 Bromma **(08) 370420; reservation@angbycamping.se; www.angbycamping.se**

On E4 fr Stockholm take rd 275 W twd Vällingby. At rndabt turn L for rd 261 dir Ekerö, then R sp Sodra Ängby, site sp. 3*, Med, mkd, pt shd, pt sl, EHU SEK35; sw nr; TV (pitch); 10% statics; phone; train; Eng spkn; ccard acc; waterslide; tennis; sauna; CKE. *"Sh walk to metro stn, 20 mins to city; gd situation; walk/cycle to Drottningsholm Palace; some sm pitches; poss diff pitching for lge o'fits; lack of privacy in shwrs; san facs stretched high ssn & need update; ltd facs LS; workers living on site; site poss muddy after rain; helpful staff."* **SEK 333** **2022**

STROMSTAD *2E2* (3km S Coastal) *58.91350, 11.20531* **Lagunen Camping & Stugor,** Skärsbygdsvägen 40, 45297 Strömstad **(0526) 755000; info@lagunen.se; www.lagunen.se**

On Uddevalla rd 176 out of Strömstad. Site on L. 4*, Lge, pt shd, pt sl, EHU inc; cooking facs; TV; 10% statics; adv bkg acc; ccard acc; bike hire; boat hire. *"By lakeside (long stay); barrier card preloaded with shwr money."* **SEK 385** **2023**

STROMSUND *1B3* (1km SW Rural) *63.84651, 15.53378* **Strömsunds Camping (Z3),** Näsviken, 83324 Strömsund **(0670) 16410; turism@stromsund.se or stromsunds.turistbyra@stromsund.se; www.stromsund.se/stromsundscamping**

W of rd 45, over bdge S of main town on lakeside. 4*, Lge, pt shd, pt sl, EHU (10A) SEK40; cooking facs; 10% statics; phone; ccard acc; bike hire; fishing; boat hire; CKE. *"In 2 parts: W side has main facs but E quieter; go to g'ge adj when site office clsd."* **SEK 260** **2023**

SUNDSVALL *1C3* (4km SE Urban/Coastal) *62.3585, 17.37016* **First Camp Fläsian - Sundsvall,** Norrstigen 15, 85468 Sundsvall **(060) 554475; sundsvall@firstcamp.se; https://firstcamp.se/destinationer/flasian-sundsvall**

12 (htd) WD MSP sand adj

Clear sps on E4 in both dirs; site on E coast side of rd. 3*, Med, mkd, pt shd, terr, EHU (10A) inc; cooking facs; Eng spkn; adv bkg acc; ccard acc; fishing; CKE. *"Sea view all pitches; gd access even in wet; suitable RVs & twin axles; if recep clsd, site yourself & pay later; helpful staff; some traff noise; sw pools in Sundsvall; clean san facs."* **SEK 300** **2023**

SVEG *1B3* (0.6km S Rural) *62.03241, 14.36496* **Svegs Camping (Z32),** Kyrkogränd 1, 84232 Sveg **(0680) 13025; info@svegscamping.se; www.svegscamping.se**

12 (htd) WD nr nr

Just S of traff lts at junc rds 45 & 84. Opp Statoil at rear of rest, well sp. 2*, Med, mkd, pt shd, EHU (16A) SEK65; bbq; cooking facs; twin axles; TV; 15% statics; phone; bus 300m; Eng spkn; adv bkg acc; ccard acc; games area; bike hire; CKE. *"Gd for sh stay/NH; htd pool 500m; many cabins used as long stay family units; san facs excel; well organised & run."* **SEK 330** **2023**

TIMMERNABBEN *2G3* (1.5km S Rural/Coastal) *56.94405, 16.46708* **Camping Timmernabben,** Varvsvägen 29, 38052 Timmernabben **(0499) 23861; timmernabben-camp@telia.com**

12 (htd) WD shgl adj

Turn off E22, site sp. Med, mkd, shd, pt sl, EHU (10A) inc; bbq; Eng spkn; games area; tennis; CKE. *"Tranquil site; delightful views; gd walking & windsurfing; paths on site not wheelchair-friendly."* **SEK 271** **2022**

TORSBY *2F1* (16km N Rural) *60.275763, 13.029961* **Camping 45,** Overbyn 53, 68594 Torsby **(560) 31169; kontakt01@camping45.com; www.camping45.com**

12 WD (htd)

18km N fr Torsby on L of E45 immed after g'ge. Sm, pt shd, EHU (10-16A) SEK60; bbq; cooking facs; sw nr; twin axles; TV; 30% statics; bus 100m; Eng spkn; adv bkg acc; sauna; games rm; bike hire. *"Vg site; green key eco award site; guided walks; canoe hire; friendly, helpful staff."* **SEK 260** **2023**

TORSBY *2F1* (5km S Rural) *60.09168, 13.03045* **Torsby Camping Svenneby,** Bredviken, 685 33 Torsby **(0)560 71095; info@torsbycamping.se; www.torsbycamping.se**

WD MSP

On shore of Lake Fryken, sp fr rd 45. 4*, Med, EHU (10A) inc; sw; red long stay; TV; 80% statics; ccard acc; watersports; sauna; CKE.
SEK 260, 1 May-15 Sep. **2024**

TRANAS *2F2* (3km E Rural) *58.03548, 15.0309* **Hättebadens Camping (F1),** Hätte, 57393 Tranås **(0140) 17482; info@hattecamping.se; www.hattecamping.se**

12 MSP nr nr

On W edge Lake Sommen on rd 131, sp. 4*, Med, mkd, pt shd, EHU (10A) SEK40; sw; 20% statics; phone; Eng spkn; ccard acc; boating; fishing; Quickstop o'night facs; bike hire; CKE. *"Generous pitches; spacious site; gd, clean facs."* **SEK 220** **2022**

"I need an on-site restaurant"

We do our best to make sure site information is correct, but it is always best to check any must-have facilities are still available or will be open during your visit.

TRELLEBORG *2E4* (4km E Coastal) *55.3638, 13.20933* **Trelleborg Strand (Formerly Camping Dalabadet),** Dalköpingestrandväg 2, 23132 Trelleborg **(0410) 301770; info@trelleborgstrand.se; www.trelleborgstrand.se**

(htd) WD MSP nr nr

Bet sea shore & rd 9 (Trelleborg-Ystad), E of town. Foll sp fr town. 4*, Med, pt shd, EHU (16A) inc; cooking facs; TV (pitch); 20% statics; phone; ccard acc; tennis; sauna. *"Conv for ferries; gd; helpful recep; ltd fac LS."* **SEK 350, 27 Apr-30 Sep.** **2023**

TROLLHATTAN *2E2* (1km N Urban) *58.29206, 12.29848* **Trollhättans Camping Hjulkvarnelund (P7),** Kungsportsvägen 7, 46139 Trollhättan **79 077 95 16; city@stenrosetscamping.se; https://camping.se/en/camping/2898/Trollhattans-Camping-City**

WD MSP nr

Foll rd 45, site sp adj rv/canal. 3*, Med, pt shd, pt sl, EHU (10A) inc; Eng spkn; tennis; CKE. *"Access to Trollhätte Canal; beautiful, spacious wooded site; cycles; easy walk to town & impressive gorge/waterfall; htd pool 300m; modern, clean san facs poss stretched high ssn."* **SEK 295, 1 May-6 Sep.** **2023**

UDDEVALLA *2E2* (9.5km W Rural) *58.3306, 11.8222* **Unda Camping (O30),** Unda 149, 45194 Uddevalla **(0522) 86347; info@undacamping.se; www.undacamping.se**

12 (htd) WD MSP

Exit E6 junc 96 Uddevalla N onto rte 44 twd Uddevalla Centrum. Site sp in 1km on R. 4*, Lge, pt shd, pt sl, EHU (10A) SEK50; cooking facs; TV; 80% statics; phone; Eng spkn; adv bkg acc; ccard acc; boat hire; fishing; sauna; bike hire; CKE. *"Lovely situation in nature reserve; o'flow area when full; Quickstop o'night facs; recep hrs erratic LS; cr in high ssn; WiFi nr recep."* **SEK 380** **2020**

SWEDEN

ULRICEHAMN *2F3* (3km S Rural) *57.77055, 13.40173* **Camping Skotteksgården (P34),** Gamla Marbäcksvägen, 52390 Ulricehamn **(0321) 13184 or (0705) 613184; skotteksgarden@telia.com; www.skottek.cc**

(htd) MSP

On rd 40 take dir Centrum. Foll sp Skotteksgården to Tranemo. 4*, Sm, mkd, hdstg, unshd, serviced pitches; EHU SEK70; cooking facs; sw nr; 10% statics; phone; ccard acc; boat hire; sauna; fishing; bike hire; CKE. *"Friendly, helpful owner; cycle path adj; OAY, winter on req."* **SEK 302, 1 May-30 Sep.** **2023**

UMEA *1C3* (6km NE Coastal) *63.84210, 20.33815* **First Camp Nydala – Umeå,** Nydalasjön 2, 90654 Umeå **(090) 702600; umea@firstcamp.se; www.firstcamp.se**

12 WD MSP (htd)

Sp fr E4 to N of town on lakeside. 5*, Lge, mkd, pt shd, serviced pitches; EHU (10A) inc; sw nr; 10% statics; bus; ccard acc; tennis; games rm; waterslide; games area; CKE. *"Attractive site; lge pitches suitable RVs & twin axles; excel service block; conv E4; pitches muddy in wet weather; shop, rest & pool clsd in LS."* **SEK 299** **2022**

UNDERSAKER *1B3* (22km SW Rural) *63.1660, 13.0590* **Camping Vålågården,** Östra Vålådalen 120, 83012 Vålådalen **070-63 70 725 (Marie); marie@valagarden.se; www.valagarden.se**

12 (htd) WD

E14 to Undersåker, turn S at hotel sp Vålådalen. Site on L. Sm, pt shd, EHU (10A); cooking facs; TV; 20% statics; Eng spkn; ccard acc; sauna; CKE. *"Hiking in surrounding nature reserve; magnificent mountain scenery; friendly owners."* **SEK 210** **2022**

UPPSALA *2H1* (2km N Urban) *59.87133, 17.61923* **Fyrishov Camping (C12),** Idrottsgatan 2, 75333 Uppsala **(018) 7274950; reception.fyrishov@uppsala.se; www.fyrishov.se**

12 WD MSP nr nr

Exit E4 Uppsala N; in 300m at rndabt foll sp Strangnas, Sala. In 2.25km exit via slip rd sp Bjorklinge, Fyrishov. At rndabt foll sp Fyrishov, in 1.6km at traff lts turn R & immed R. Site in Fyrishov Park adj sw & sports complex. 3*, Med, unshd, EHU (10A) SEK45; bus; ccard acc; CKE. *"Within easy access of city cent; pool adj (sports complex behind pool); fair NH."* **SEK 225** **2022**

URSHULT *2F3* (1km N Rural) *56.54476, 14.80703* **Urshults Camping (G7),** Sirkövägen 19, 36013 Urshult **(0477) 20243; info@urshult-camping.com; www.urshult-camping.com**

(htd) WD MSP

Rd 30 S fr Växjö, turn W onto rd 120 at Tingsryd. In 10km at Urshult turn R, site sp on lakeside. 3*, Med, pt shd, EHU (10A) inc; cooking facs; sw nr; 10% statics; Eng spkn; CKE. *"Well-run site; lovely lakeside location with boat/canoe hire on site; nr Kurrebo gardens & museum; vg."* **SEK 310, 27 Apr-15 Oct.** **2023**

URSHULT *2F3* (10km NW Rural) *56.58466, 14.69491* **Getnö Gård Naturcamping (G24),** Lake Åsnen Resort, 36010 Ryd **(0477) 24011; info@getnogard.se; www.getnogard.se**

(htd) WD MSP

W fr Urshult on rte 120 to junc with rte 126; turn NW onto rte 126, site in 7km via Ålshult to Getnö Gård. Site on shore Lake Åsnen. 4*, Med, mkd, pt shd, pt sl, EHU (10A) Inc; cooking facs; red long stay; 10% statics; phone; Eng spkn; adv bkg acc; fishing; canoe hire; CKE. *"Beautiful location in private nature reserve; lake adj; needs care & attention; facs dated."* **SEK 320, 1 May-10 Oct.** **2023**

VARBERG *2E3* (8km N Coastal) *57.1826, 12.22076* **Kärradal Camping,** Nisebäcksvägen 1, 43295 Varberg **(0340) 622377; karradal@firstcamp.se**

WD MSP sand 500m

Fr S exit E6 junc 55 Varberg N & foll sp Tångeberg & Kärradal. Fr N exit junc 56 & foll sp Värö & Åskloster, then Kärradal & site. 3*, Lge, mkd, pt shd, EHU SEK40; cooking facs; TV; 80% statics; phone; Eng spkn; ccard acc; bike hire; games area; CKE. *"Rec arrive early afternoon high ssn; o'flow field has minimal san facs, but clean."* **SEK 340, 23 Apr-5 Sep.** **2024**

VASTERVIK *2G3* (3km SE Coastal) *57.73823, 16.66846* **Vastervik Resort,** Lysingsvägen, 593 53 Västervik **(0490) 258000; vastervikresort@vastervik.se; www.vastervikresort.se/**

12 (htd) WD MSP (htd) sand adj

On coast 3km SE of town. Fr E22 foll sp around S ring rd; on app to Västervik. Site well sp fr E22. 5*, V lge, pt shd, serviced pitches; EHU (10A) inc; cooking facs; 10% statics; ccard acc; tennis; bike hire; sauna; boat hire; waterslide; golf. *"Lovely, family site in landscaped, coastal woodland; easy access to islands by wooden footbdge fr site; o'night m'vans area; adj to bay; in HS EHU's taken by late afternoon."* **SEK 450** **2022**

VILHELMINA *1C2* (1.5km SE Rural) *64.62131, 16.67846* **Saiva Camping (AC4),** Baksjön 1, 91231 Vilhelmina **(0940) 10760; info@saiva.se; www.saiva.se**

(htd) WD

Sp on E site of rd 45. 3*, Med, pt shd, EHU (10A) SEK30; TV; 10% statics; phone; ccard acc; tennis; bike hire; CKE. *"Gd; excel san facs in log style cabins, v helpful staff, lovely lakeside setting; lake beach."* **SEK 180, 20 May-1 Oct.** **2022**

VILHELMINA *1C2* (5km NW Rural) *64.64998, 16.59240* **Kolgärdens Camping,** Lövliden 16, 91292 Vilhelmina **(0940) 10304; kolgarden@vilhelmina.ac; www.kolgarden.se**

12 (htd) nr

Site sp fr E45 N of Vilhelmina. Sm, pt shd, EHU (10A) SEK30; cooking facs; TV; 50% statics; Eng spkn; sauna; fishing. *"Wonderful lakeside location; clean san facs; helpful, pleasant owner; highly rec."* **SEK 320** **2023**

VINSLOV *2F4* (0.5km N Rural) *56.10988, 13.91245* **Vinslövs Camping (L2),** Troed Nelsongatan 18, 28833 Vinslöv **(070) 2077679; info@vinslovscamping.se; vinslovscamping.se**

12 nr nr nr

Site sp of rte 21. 2*, Sm, mkd, pt shd, EHU (6A) SEK40; cooking facs; 20% statics; bus 500m; CKE. *"Htd pool adj."* **SEK 120** **2022**

YSTAD *2F4* (3km E Coastal) *55.43286, 13.8650* **Ystad Camping (Formerly Camping Sandskogens),** Österleden, 27160 Ystad **(0411) 19270; info@ystadcamping.se; www.ystadcamping.se**

12 nr sand 100m

On N side of rd 9. 4*, Lge, mkd, shd, EHU (10A) SEK55; TV; 10% statics; phone; ccard acc; CKE. *"On Baltic coast; cycle path to beautiful town; mkd walks nrby; gd site, well-managed site; extremely helpful Eng spkn staff; high ssn expect queues checking in; CKE card req; metered shwrs; Wallander TV series studios site nr site, tours avail; cramped pithces; san facs stretched when busy."* **SEK 400** **2023**

OLAND ISLAND

BYXELKROK *2G3* (1km N Coastal) *57.33013, 17.01211* **Neptuni Camping (H41),** Småskogsvägen 2, 38075 Byxelkrok **(0485) 28495 or 070 5428495 (mob); info@neptunicamping.se; www.neptunicamping.se**

adj

Fr S on rd 136 thro Böda, at Byxelkrok turn R past harbour for 200m. Site on R. 4*, Med, pt shd, EHU (16A) SEK80; phone; Eng spkn; ccard acc; games area; CKE. *"Conv touring base N Öland, sh walk to harbour, rest & supmkt."* **SEK 330, 29 Apr-2 Oct.** **2023**

DEGERHAMN *2G4* (12km S Rural) *56.23778, 16.4530* **Ottenby Vandrarhem & Camping (H57),** Ottenby 106, 38065 Degerhamn **(0485) 662062; info@ottenbyvandrarhem.se; www.ottenbyvandrarhem.se**

12 (htd) nr (htd)

Rd 36 S to Ottenby, bear R for 4km, site on R at youth hostel. Sm, unshd, EHU (10A) SEK50; cooking facs; 10% statics; phone; ccard acc; bike hire. *"On edge Ottenby nature reserve; excel walks & birdwatching - ssn geared to bird migration; poss noise fr late arr & early risers as no barrier; dogs free; World Heritage Site on S pt of island."* **SEK 260** **2023**

"Satellite navigation makes touring much easier"

Remember most sat navs don't know if you're towing or in a larger vehicle – always use yours alongside maps and site directions.

LOTTORP *2G3* (3km N Coastal) *57.17876, 17.03746* **Sonjas Camping (H39),** John Emils Gata 43, 38074 Löttorp **(0485) 23212; info@sonjascamping.se; www.sonjascamping.se**

(htd) (htd) sand adj

Fr Kalmar over bdge to Öland Island, take rd 136 N thro Borgholm. Cont to Löttorp, site sp. 5*, Lge, mkd, pt shd, EHU (10A) SEK45; cooking facs; 10% statics; adv bkg acc; bike hire; sauna; tennis; fishing; CKE. *"Vg beach; excel family site; vg touring base."* **SEK 364, 1 May-4 Oct.** **2022**

Motorways
Primary roads
Secondary roads
All year site(s)
Seasonal site(s)
No sites listed
0 50 100 150 200 km
0 40 80 120 miles
N
W
E
S
A
B
C
D
1
2
3
4
NORWEGIAN SEA
NORWAY
FINLAND
GULF OF BOTHNIA
Tromso
Skibotn
Karasjok
Karesuando
Muonio
Kiruna
Pajala
Gallivare
Rovaniemi
Jokkmokk
Mo I Rana
Arjeplog
Haparanda
Kemi
Lulea
Sorsele
Oulu
Skelleftea
Vilhelmina
Gaddede
Dorotea
Steinkjer
Stromsund
Umea
Trondheim
Hammerdal
Undersaker
ÖRNSKÖLDSVIK
Vaasa
Ostersund
Oppdal
Asarna
Harnosand
Sundsvall
Sveg
Ljusdal
Sarna
Tamper
BOLLNÄS
Soderhamn
Lillehammer
Orsa
Mora
Rattvik
Gesunda
see Map 2
Turku/Abo
99
95
97
94
92
90
87
86
84
83
70

E
F
G
H
1
2
3
4
▲ see Map 1
Malung
Leksand
FALUN
GÄVLE
BORLÄNGE
Hedesunda
Kongsvinger
Torsby
Oslo
Bærum
Uppsala
Filipstad
VÄSTERÅS
Kil
Arjang
KARLSTAD
Arboga
STOCKHOLM
Orebro
Saffle
Stromstad
Amal
Ed
Katrineholm
Nynashamn
Mellerud
Mariestad
NYKÖPING
Hamburgsund
Bocksjo
NORRKÖPING
Kolmarden
Borensberg
Kungshamn
Soderkoping
Uddevalla
VANNERSBORG
LINKÖPING
Trollhattan
Falkoping
Tranas
Granna
Marstrand
Kungalv
Gamleby
Goteborg
Ulricehamn
JÖNKÖPING
Vastervik
Hova
Boras
VISBY
Eksjo
Kungsbacka
Byxelkrok
Oskarshamn
Lottorp
Timmernabben
VÄXJÖ
Ljungby
Halmstad
Kalmar
Almhult
Markaryd
Urshult
Degerhamn
Hoganas
Karlshamn
Vinslov
Helsingborg
KRISTIANSTAD
KARLSKRONA
Ahus
Landskrona
Kobenhavn
Kivik
Rockildo
Malmo
Simrishamn
Skanor
ENMARK
Ystad
Trelleborg
E4
E18
E20
E6
E6/E20
27/40
40
73
N
W
E
S
0
50
100
150 km
0
20
40
60
80 miles

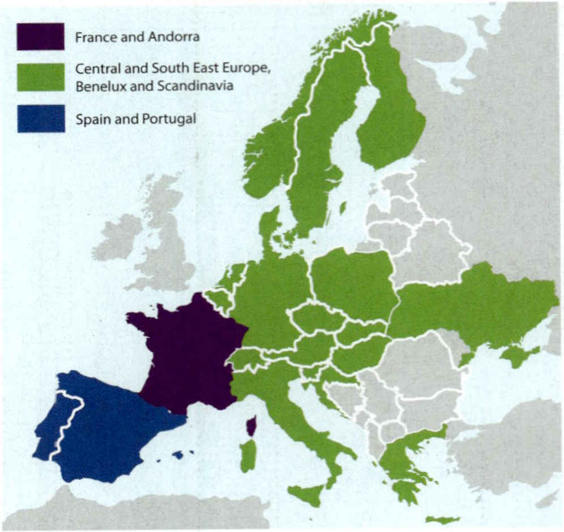

Karlstad to Varberg = 322km

	Borlänge	Dorotea	Falun	Gävle	Göteborg (Gothenburg)	Halmstad	Helsingborg	Härnösand	Jokkmokk	Jönköping	Kalmar	Karlskrona	Karlstad	Kiruna	Malmö	Norrköping	Norrtälje	Örebro	Östersund	Skellefteå	Skövde	Stockholm	Sundsvall	Söderhamn	Tarnaby	Umeå	Uppsala	Varberg	Västerås
Dorotea	563																												
Falun	20	544																											
Gävle	113	571	93																										
Göteborg (Gothenburg)	445	978	470	521																									
Halmstad	524	1062	542	587	144																								
Helsingborg	603	1140	616	673	225	79																							
Härnösand	371	258	352	264	774	848	933																						
Jokkmokk	1022	429	1003	887	1431	1503	1581	490																					
Jönköping	366	923	384	436	152	165	236	693	1347																				
Kalmar	501	1099	514	533	337	242	295	789	1445	218																			
Karlskrona	586	1185	599	624	335	212	210	876	1531	227	92																		
Karlstad	216	739	233	319	251	387	459	583	1232	241	468	463																	
Kiruna	1171	642	1165	1068	1592	1651	1742	825	213	1503	1605	1679	1378																
Malmö	653	1196	678	727	279	138	66	986	1636	289	288	206	521	1802															
Norrköping	254	826	272	292	322	335	406	551	1201	172	245	332	228	1359	458														
Norrtälje	232	731	247	167	549	558	635	424	1077	401	478	566	354	1228	689	236													
Örebro	167	730	184	235	285	361	435	494	1144	198	359	396	111	1306	489	118	243												
Östersund	389	176	365	397	806	882	966	241	605	749	920	1014	564	812	1029	682	552	557											
Skellefteå	724	293	705	615	1127	1206	1277	358	300	1049	1142	1226	929	466	1342	908	781	846	463										
Skövde	308	838	331	381	159	225	302	639	1289	85	299	312	162	1446	360	215	392	146	662	993									
Stockholm	212	739	226	175	475	491	564	430	1084	332	406	494	310	1242	622	166	71	195	562	786	343								
Sundsvall	317	227	297	212	728	796	882	57	546	642	741	825	533	866	929	495	375	443	185	412	534	382							
Söderhamn	185	494	166	81	592	662	738	189	839	508	604	690	393	997	802	359	237	303	321	542	455	245	133						
Tarnaby	807	244	788	815	1223	1306	1384	572	435	1167	1343	1429	983	648	1440	1099	975	974	420	463	1032	983	597	738					
Umeå	591	175	568	483	996	1072	1152	224	424	911	1012	1091	796	605	1206	767	642	704	366	135	830	652	275	406	352				
Uppsala	162	670	172	106	459	559	627	365	1016	398	471	562	285	1175	681	228	74	177	499	714	322	71	316	175	914	582			
Varberg	517	1049	541	592	77	70	151	846	1500	173	308	283	322	1653	205	343	568	358	870	1208	224	500	794	660	1293	1066	529		
Västerås	133	710	140	146	388	462	548	402	1056	298	396	474	215	1215	608	152	151	104	536	759	249	108	352	219	954	622	75	452	
Växjö	485	1042	497	556	232	133	188	815	1464	123	110	108	368	1614	195	289	519	321	871	1171	207	447	762	628	1286	1031	512	197	429

Switzerland

Highlights

A country of mountains, lakes and natural beauty, Switzerland's high alpine peaks make it one of the world's top destinations for winter sports.

Inside the cities, you'll find a world that compliments the outstanding landscape while providing a modern and vibrant outlook on life.

There is an endless supply of places to visit and experience, with mouth-watering chocolates and cuckoo clocks just the tip of the cultural iceberg.

Switzerland is renowned for being a hub for winter sports enthusiasts, but there are also a variety of traditional competitions such as Schwingen, a type of Swiss wrestling and Hornussen, a strange mixture of golf and baseball, which are still practiced today.

Switzerland also produces a delicious variety of food, with cheese being one of its specialities. Types such as Emmental and Gruyère are used to make fondue, which is often associated with the skiing culture of the Alps.

Major towns and cities

- Zürich – there are tons of museums and cultural sites in this metropolitan capital.
- Geneva – this breathtaking city is one of the world's most diverse.
- Basel – a world-leading city of culture and arts.
- Lausanne – this city has a stunning view of Lake Geneva and the Alps.

Attractions

- Jungfraujoch – admire unrivalled views from the highest railway station in Europe.
- Château de Chillon, Veytaux – an island castle on Lake Geneva.
- Kapellbrücke, Lucerne – Europe's oldest wooden covered footbridge.
- Rhine Falls, Shaffhausen – discover Europe's largest waterfall.

Find out more

myswitzerland.com

info@myswitzerland.com

Country Information

Capital: Bern

Bordered by: Austria, France, Germany, Italy, Liechtenstein

Terrain: Mostly mountainous; Alps in the south, Jura in the north-west; central plateau of rolling hills, plains and large lakes

Climate: Temperate climate varying with altitude; cold, cloudy, rainy or snowy winters; cool to warm summers with occasional showers

Highest Point: Dufourspitze 4,634m

Languages: French, German, Italian, Romansch

Local Time: GMT or BST + 1, i.e. 1 hour ahead of the UK all year

Currency: Swiss Franc (CHF) divided into 100 centimes; £1 = CHF 1.12, CHF 10 = £8.95 (Nov 2024)

Emergency numbers: Police 117; Fire brigade 118; Ambulance 144 or 112 for any service

Public Holidays 2025: Jan 1; Apr 18, 21; May 29; Jun 9, 19; Aug 1 (National Day); Nov 1; Dec 25, 26.

School summer holidays vary by canton but are approximately from early July to mid/end August.

Entry Formalities

Holders of valid British or Irish passports may enter without a visa for up to 3 months.

Medical Services

There are reciprocal emergency health care arrangements with Switzerland for EU citizens.
A European Health Insurance Card (EHIC) or a Global Health Insurance Card (GHIC) will enable you to get reduced cost for emergency treatment in a public hospital but you'll be required to pay the full cost of treatment and apply afterwards for a refund from the Department for Work & Pensions on your return to the UK. Ensure that any doctor you visit is registered with the national Swiss Health Insurance Scheme. Dental treatment is not covered.

You'll have to pay 50% of the costs of any medically-required ambulance transport within Switzerland and/or Liechtenstein, including air ambulance.

If you're planning sports activities, such as skiing and mountaineering, your holiday insurance should be extended to cover these activities and should also include cover for mountain rescue and helicopter rescue costs.

Opening Hours

Banks: Mon-Fri 8.30am-4.30pm (some close for lunch; late opening once a week to 5.30pm/6pm in some towns).

Museums: Check locally as times vary.

Post Offices: Mon-Fri 7.30am-6pm (smaller branches may close for lunch); Sat 7.30am-11am.

Shops: Mon-Fri 8am/8.30am-6.30pm/7pm (closed lunch time) & Sat 8am-4pm/7pm; shops close early on the eve of a public holiday.

Safety and Security

Most visits to Switzerland and Liechtenstein are trouble-free and the crime rate is low. However, petty theft is on the increase and you should be alert to pickpockets and thieves in city centres, railway stations, airports and public places.

You should be aware of the risks involved in the more hazardous sports activities and take note of weather forecasts and conditions, which can change rapidly in the mountains. You should be well-equipped; do not undertake the activity alone, study the itinerary and inform someone of your plans. Off-piste skiers should follow the advice given by local authorities and guides; to ignore such advice could put yourselves and other mountain users in danger.

Switzerland and Liechtenstein share with the rest of Europe an underlying threat from terrorism. Please check gov.uk/foreign-travel-advice/switzerland before you travel.

British Embassy

Thunstrasse 50
3005 Berne
Tel: +41 (0)31 359 7700
gov.uk/world/switzerland

Irish Embassy

Kirchenfeldstrasse 68
CH-3000 Bern 6
Tel: +41 (0)31 350 0380
ireland.ie/berne

Customs

Alcohol and Tobacco

Switzerland is not a member of the EU and visitors aged 17 years and over may import the following items duty-free:

200 cigarettes or 50 cigars or 250 g tobacco

5 litres of alcoholic drink up to 15% proof

1 litre of alcoholic drink over 15% proof

All goods are duty free up to a total combined value of 300 CHF, including alcohol and tobacco products.

Caravans and Motorhomes

Caravans registered outside Switzerland may be imported without formality up to a height of 4 metres, width of 2.55 metres and length of 12 metres (including towbar). The total length of car + caravan/trailer must not exceed 18.75 metres.

Food

From EU countries you may import duty free per person 1 kg of meat and/or meat products (excluding game).
Importing foodstuffs of animal origin from outside the EU is prohibited.

Refund of VAT on Export

A foreign visitor who buys goods in Switzerland in a 'Tax-Back SA' or 'Global Refund Schweiz AG' shop may obtain a VAT refund (7.7%) on condition that the value of the goods is at least 300 CHF including VAT. Visitors should complete a form in the shop and produce it, together with the goods purchased, at customs on leaving Switzerland. See globalblue.com for more information.

Documents

Vehicle(s)

Carry your original vehicle registration certificate (V5C), MOT certificate (if applicable) and insurance documentation at all times. Drivers may be asked to produce proof of vehicle ownership at the border and failure to do so may mean that entry into Switzerland is refused. If you're driving a vehicle which doesn't belong to you, you should be in possession of a letter of authorisation from the owner.

Money

Prices in shops are often displayed in both Swiss francs and euros. Major credit cards are widely accepted, although you may find small supermarkets and restaurants do not accept them. Recent visitors report that some retail outlets may accept only one kind of credit card (MasterCard or VISA), not both, and it may be advisable to carry one of each. You may occasionally find that a surcharge is imposed for the use of credit cards.

Carry your credit card issuers'/banks' 24-hour UK contact numbers in case of loss or theft of your cards.

Driving

Accidents

In the case of accidents involving property damage only, when drivers decide not to call the police, a European Accident Statement must be completed.

In the case of injury or of damage to the road, road signs, lights etc, the police must be called.

Alcohol

The maximum permitted level of alcohol in the bloodstream is 0.05%. A lower limit of 0.01% applies to new drivers of up to three years. A blood test may be required after an accident, and if found positive, the penalty is either a fine or a prison sentence, plus withdrawal of permission to drive in Switzerland for at least two months. Police carry out random breath tests.

Breakdown Service

The motoring and leisure organisation Touring Club Suisse (TCS) operates a 24-hour breakdown service, 'Patrouille TCS'. To call for help throughout Switzerland and Liechtenstein, dial 140. On motorways use emergency phones and ask for TCS.

Members of clubs affiliated to the AIT, such as the Club, who can show a current membership card will be charged reduced rates for breakdown assistance and towing, according to the time of day and/or the distance towed. Payment by credit card is accepted.

Child Restraint System

Vehicles registered outside of Switzerland that are temporarily imported into the country, have to comply with the country of registration with regards to safety belt equipment and child restraint regulations.

All children up to 12 years of age must be placed in an approved UN ECE R44.03 regulation child restraint, unless they measure more than 150cm and are over seven years old.

Fuel

Prices of petrol vary according to the brand and region, being slightly cheaper in self-service stations. Credit cards are generally accepted.

On motorways, where prices are slightly higher, some service stations are open 24 hours and others are open from 6am to 10pm or 11pm only, but petrol is available outside these hours from automatic pumps where payment can be made by means of bank notes or credit cards.

See mylpg.eu/stations/switzerland/ for a list of outlets and a map showing their location.

Lights

Dipped headlights are compulsory at all times, even during the day. Bulbs are more likely to fail with constant use and you're recommended to carry spares.

Motorways

There are over 1,500 km of motorways and dual carriageways. To use these roads motor vehicles and trailers up to a total weight of 3,500kg must display a vignette. Motorists using roads to avoid motorways and dual carriageways may find it necessary to detour through small villages, often with poor signposting. In addition, due to a diversion, you may be re-routed onto roads where the motorway vignette is required.

If you have visited Switzerland before, make sure you remove your old sticker from your windscreen.

There are emergency telephones along the motorways.

Mountain Roads and Tunnels

One of the most attractive features of Switzerland for motorists is the network of finely engineered mountain passes, ranging from easy main road routes to high passes that may be open only from June to October. In the Alps most roads over passes have been modernised. Please note the Umbrail Pass is not recommended for caravans. Passes have a good roadside telephone service for calling aid quickly in the event of trouble.

A blue square sign depicting a yellow horn indicates a mountain postal road and the same sign with a red diagonal stripe indicates thfe end of the postal road. On such roads, vehicles belonging to the postal services have priority.

During certain hours, one-way traffic only is permitted on certain mountain roads. The hours during which traffic may proceed in either or both directions are posted at each end of the road.

Speed must always be moderate on mountain passes, very steep roads and roads with numerous bends. Drivers must not travel at a speed which would prevent them from stopping within the distance they can see ahead.

When it's difficult to pass oncoming vehicles, the heavier vehicle has priority. Slow-moving vehicles are required by law to use the lay-bys provided on alpine roads to allow the free flow of faster traffic. This is the case where a car towing a caravan causes a queue of vehicles capable of a higher speed.

Parking

Parking in cities is difficult and it's worth using the numerous Park & Ride schemes which operate around major towns and cities. Illegal parking of any kind is much less tolerated in Switzerland than in any of its neighbours and fines are common for even minor violations.

Pay and display car parks and parking meters are used throughout the country and permitted parking time varies from 15 minutes to 2 hours. Feeding meters is not allowed. Wheel clamps are not used, but vehicles causing an obstruction may be removed to a car pound.

You may park in a 'blue zone' for limited periods free of charge providing you display a parking disc in your vehicle. These are available from petrol stations, kiosks, restaurants and police stations.

Parking in a red zone is free for up to 15 hours with a red parking disc available from police stations, tourist offices, etc.

Parking on pavements is not allowed. Do not park where there is a sign 'Stationierungsverbot' or 'Interdiction de Stationner'. Continuous or broken yellow lines and crosses at the side of the road and any other yellow markings also indicate that parking is prohibited.

Priority

In general, traffic (including bicycles) coming from the right has priority at intersections but drivers approaching a roundabout must give way to all traffic already on the roundabout, i.e. from the left, unless otherwise indicated by signs. However, vehicles on main roads – indicated by a yellow diamond with a white border or a white triangle with a red border and an arrow pointing upwards – have priority over traffic entering from secondary roads.

Please be aware sometimes pedestrians have right of way and will expect vehicles to stop for them.

Roads

Switzerland has over 84,000 kilometres of well-surfaced roads, from motorways to local municipal roads, all well-signposted. Four-wheel drive vehicles must not be driven off road local authority permission.

During daylight hours outside built-up areas you must sound your horn before sharp bends where visibility is limited. After dark this warning must be given by flashing your headlights.

Dial the following numbers for information:

162: Weather information

163: Road conditions, mountain passes, access to tunnels and traffic news

187: In winter, avalanche bulletins; in summer, wind forecasts for Swiss lakes

It's also possible to obtain updated information on road conditions via teletext in larger motorway service areas.

Motorway Tax

To be able to use national roads (motorways and semi-motorways) in Switzerland, motor vehicles and trailers up to a total weight of 3,500kg must have a vehicle sticker (vignette). The sticker is valid for 14 months from December 1 every year and costs 40 CHF (2024 price). An additional fee is charged for caravans and trailers. The sticker allows multiple re-entry into Switzerland during the period of validity.

If you enter a motorway or semi-motorway without a sticker you'll be fined 200 CHF and also the cost of the sticker. The stickers can be bought from custom offices, petrol stations or TCS offices in Switzerland or alternatively they can be purchased from the UK before travelling by calling the Swiss Travel Centre on 0207 420 4900.

Heavy Vehicle Tax

Vehicles (including motorhomes) over 3,500kg must pay a lump-sum heavy vehicle tax (PSVA) on entry into Switzerland which is applicable for all roads. This charge applies for every day you're in Switzerland and your vehicle is on the road. For a 10-day pass (valid for a year) you self-select the days that your vehicle is on the road and, therefore, you're not penalised if your motorhome is parked at a campsite and not driven on a public road. This heavy vehicle tax applies to any Swiss road and replaces the need for a motorway vignette.

This particular tax is only payable at the border on entry into Switzerland and if there is any doubt about the exact weight of your vehicle it will be weighed. An inspection may be carried out at any time and is likely at the exit border. Failure to pay the tax can result in an immediate fine.

Road Signs and Markings

Road signs and markings conform to international standards.

White lettering on a green background indicates motorways, whereas state and provincial main roads outside built-up areas have white lettering on a blue background. This is the reverse of the colouring used in France and Germany and may cause confusion when driving from one country to the other.

Road signs on secondary roads are white with black lettering.

The following are some road signs which you may encounter:

Postal vehicles have priority

Parking disc compulsory

Slow lane

One-way street with a two-way cycle lane

Speed Limits

	Open Road (km/h)	Motorway (km/h)
Car Solo	80-100	120
Car towing caravan/trailer	80-100	100
Motorhome under 3500kg	80-100	120
Motorhome 3500-7500kg	80-100	100

The fundamental rule, which applies to all motor vehicles and bicycles, is that you must always have the speed of your vehicle under control and must adapt your speed to the conditions of the road, traffic and visibility. On minor secondary roads without speed limit signs speed should be reduced to 50 km/h (31 mph) where the road enters a built-up area. The speed limit in residential areas is 30 km/h (18 mph). Speeding fines are severe.

When travelling solo the speed limit on dual carriageways is 100 km/h (62 mph) and on motorways, 120 km/h (74 mph) unless otherwise indicated by signs. On motorways with at least three lanes in the same direction, the left outside lane may only be used by vehicles which can exceed 80 km/h (50 mph).

Motorhomes with a laden weight of under 3,500 kg are not subject to any special regulations. Those over 3,500 kg may not exceed 80 km/h (50 mph) on motorways.

In dual carriageway road tunnels, speed is limited to 100 km/h (62 mph); in the St Gotthard tunnel and San Bernardino tunnels the limit is 80 km/h (50 mph).

It's illegal to transport or use radar detection devices. If your GPS navigation system has a function to identify the location of fixed speed cameras, this must be deactivated.

Traffic Jams

Traffic congestion occurs near tunnels in particular, during the busy summer months, at the St Gotthard tunnel on Friday afternoons and Saturday mornings. When congestion is severe and in order to prevent motorists coming to a standstill in the tunnel, traffic police stop vehicles before the tunnel entrance and direct them through in groups.

Other bottlenecks occur on the roads around Luzern (A2) and Bern (A1, A6 and A12), the border crossing at Chiasso (A2), the A9 around Lausanne and between Vevey and Chexbres, and the A13 BellinzonaSargans, mainly before the San Bernardino tunnel.

Traffic Lights

Outside peak rush hours traffic lights flashing amber mean proceed with caution.

Violation of Traffic Regulations

The police may impose and collect on-the-spot fines for minor infringements. In the case of more serious violations, they may require a deposit equal to the estimated amount of the fine. Fines for serious offences are set according to the income of the offender. Drivers of foreign-registered vehicles may be asked for a cash deposit against the value of the fine.

Winter Driving

Alpine winters often make driving more difficult. You should equip your vehicle(s) with winter tyres and snow chains and check road conditions prior to departure. A sign depicting a wheel and chains indicates where snow chains are required for the mountain road ahead. Snow chains are compulsory in areas where indicated by the appropriate road sign. They must be fitted on at least two drive wheels.

Essential Equipment

Warning Triangles

All vehicles must be equipped with a warning triangle which has to be within easy reach and not in the boot.

Touring

The peak season for winter sports is from December to the end of April in all major resorts. February and March are the months with the most hours of winter sunshine and good snow for skiing. Summer skiing is also possible in a few resorts. Information on snow conditions, including avalanche bulletins, is available in English on the website: slf.ch/en.

Besides being famous for watches, chocolate and cheese, the Swiss have a fine reputation as restaurateurs, but eating out can be expensive. Local beers are light but pleasant and some very drinkable wines are produced.

There are a number of UNESCO World Heritage sites in Switzerland including the three castles of Bellinzona, Bern Old Town, the Monastery of St John at Müstair, the Jungfrau, the Aletsch Glacier and the Bietschhoorn region.

Liechtenstein is a principality of 160 sq km sharing borders with Switzerland and Austria. The capital, Vaduz, has a population of approximately 5,500 and German is the official language. The official currency is the Swiss franc. There are no passport or Customs controls on the border between Switzerland and Liechtenstein.

Camping and Caravanning

There are approximately 340 campsites available to touring caravanners, with around 100 sites remaining open in winter. Some sites may be nearly full with statics, with only a small area for tourers.

There are 24 Touring Club Suisse (TCS) sites and affiliated sites classified into five categories according to amenities available. All TCS campsites have a service station with facilities for emptying sanitary tanks. For further information and current rates see tc.ch/de/camping-reisen.

The Swiss Camp Sites Association (VSC/ACS) produces a camping and road map covering approximately 180 sites, including charges and classification. For more information see swisscamps.ch.

The Swiss are environmentally conscious with only limited scope for removing waste. Recycling is vigorously promoted and it's normal to have to put rubbish in special plastic bags obtainable from campsites. A 'rubbish charge' or 'entsorgungstaxe' of approximately CHF 3 per person per day is commonly charged.

A visitors' tax, varying according to the area, is levied in addition to the site charges.

The rules on casual/wild camping differ from canton to canton. It may be tolerated in some areas with the permission of the landowner or local police, or in motorway service areas, but local laws – particularly on hygiene – must not be contravened. For reasons of security the Club recommends that overnight stops should always be at recognised campsites.

Cycling

Switzerland has approx 9,000 km of cycle trails, including nine national cycle routes, which have been planned to suit all categories of cyclist from families to sports cyclists. Maps of cycle routes are available from schweizmobil.ch. Routes are marked by red and white signs. The problem of strenuous uphill gradients can be overcome by using trails routed near railway lines. Most trains will transport bicycles and often bicycles are available for hire at stations. Switzerland Tourism can provide more information.

Children under the age of 7 may only cycle on the road if accompanied by a person over 16 years of age.

Bikes may be carried on the roof of a car providing they are attached to an adequate roof rack and providing the total height doesn't exceed 4 metres. Bicycles carried on special carriers at the rear of a vehicle can exceed the width of the vehicle by 20 cm on each side, but the total width must not exceed 2 metres. The rear lights and number plate must remain visible and the driver's view must not be obstructed.

Electricity and Gas

Usually current on campsites varies between 4 and 16 amps. Plugs have two or, more usually, three round pins. Some campsites have CEE connections. Some may lend or hire out adaptors – but do not rely on it – and it may be advisable to purchase an appropriate adaptor cable with a Swiss 3-pin plug. Adaptors are readily available in local supermarkets.

The full range of Campingaz cylinders is available from large supermarkets.

Public Transport & Local Travel

Some towns are inaccessible by road, e.g. Zermatt and Wengen, and can only be reached by train or tram.

The Swiss integrated transport system is well known for its efficiency, convenience and punctuality. Co-ordinated timetables ensure fast, trouble-free interchange from one means of transport to another. Yellow post buses take travellers off the beaten track to the remotest regions.

In addition to efficient inter-city travel, there is an extensive network of mountain railways, including aerial cableways, funiculars and ski-lifts.

Half-fare tickets are available for attractions such as cable cars, railways and lake steamers. Switzerland Tourism offers a public transport map and a number of other useful publications. For more information see swisstravelsystem.com.

All visitors to campsites and hotels in Interlaken are issued with a pass allowing free bus and train travel in the area.

A ferry operates on Lake Constance (Bodensee) between Romanshorn and Friedrichshafen (Germany) saving a 70 km drive. The crossing takes 40 minutes. For more information telephone 071 466 78 88 or visit bodensee-schiffe.ch.

A frequent ferry service also operates between Konstanz and Meersburg on the main route between Zürich, Ulm, Augsburg and Munich (Germany). The crossing takes 20 minutes. For more information visit stadtwerke-konstanz.de.

Principal internal ferry services are on Lake Lucerne between Beckenried and Gersau, see autofaehre.ch and on Lake Zürich between Horgen and Meilen, see faehre.ch. All these services transport cars and caravans.

Château de Chillon

Shutterstock/saiko3p

Sites in Switzerland

AIGLE *C2* (1km N Rural) *46.32385, 6.96206* **Camping de la Piscine,** Ave des Glariers 1, 1860 Aigle **024 466 26 60; contact@campingdelapiscine.ch; www.campingdelapiscine.ch**

CHF4

Turn W off N9 (Aigle-Lausanne) at N edge of Aigle, site sp. Foll rd for 400m, site past pool on L. 3*, Med, pt shd, EHU (4A) CHF3.50 (adaptor avail); gas; 10% statics; Eng spkn; adv bkg acc; ccard acc; fishing; bike hire; tennis; CKE. *"V helpful owner; vg, well-maintained site; pleasant town & gd touring base; outlook on to vineyards; easy flat walk into town, about 10 mins."* **CHF 35, 6 Apr-30 Sep. 2024**

ALTDORF *B3* (2km N Rural) *46.89256, 8.62800* **Remo-Camp Moosbad,** Flüelerstrsse 122, 6460 Altdorf **041 8708541**

12

Exit A2 at Altdorf junc 36. Foll sp Altdorf to rndabt & turn R. Site 200m on L adj cable car & sports cent. 2*, Sm, pt shd, EHU (10A) CHF3 (adaptor loan); bbq; 80% statics; phone; Eng spkn; CKE. *"Ideal windsurfing; useful NH en rte Italy; friendly welcome; excel san facs; excel rest; superb views; gd base for train trip over St Gotthard pass; plenty to see & do in Altdorf; public pool & waterslide adj; bus & cable car combos avail."* **CHF 27.7 2022**

ANDELFINGEN *A3* (1km NE Rural) *47.59698, 8.68376* **TCS Camping Rässenwies,** Alte Steinerstrasse 1, 8451 Kleinandelfingen **079 238 35 35; raessenwies@tcs-ccz.ch; www.tcs-ccz.ch**

CHF3.50 nr

On N4 Schaffhausen-Winterthur rd, site well sp in Kleinandelfingen, on Rv Thur. 2*, Sm, unshd, EHU CHF3.50; gas; fishing. *"Beautiful area; v friendly."* **CHF 43, 20 Mar-4 Oct. 2024**

BASEL *A2* (10km S Urban) *47.49963, 7.60283* **Camping Waldhort,** Heideweg 16, 4153 Basel-Reinach **061 7116429; info@camping-waldhort.ch; www.camping-waldhort.ch**

CHF3 nr

Fr Basel foll m'way sp to Delémont & exit m'way at Reinach-Nord exit; at top of slip rd, turn R & L at 1st traff lts (about 300m). Site on L in approx 1km at curve in rd with tramway on R, sp. Basel best app off German m'way rather than French. Lge, mkd, pt shd, EHU (6A) inc; gas; 50% statics; tram 500m (tickets fr recep); Eng spkn; adv bkg acc; ccard acc; CKE. *"Rec arr early in high ssn; helpful staff; gd sized pitches; m'van pitches sm; excel san facs; gates clsd 2200-0700; site muddy when wet; excel art museums in Basel."* **CHF 37, 1 Mar-29 Oct. 2024**

BASEL *A2* (18km S Rural) *47.45806, 7.63545* **TCS Camping Uf der Hollen,** Auf der Hollen, 4146 Hochwald **061 7120240; platzkommission@tcscampingbasel.ch; www.tcscampingbasel.ch**

12 (htd)

Exit A18 at Reinach-Sud dir Dornach, S thro Dornach dir Hochwald, uphill thro forest to site. 2*, Med, mkd, pt shd, EHU CHF3; 90% statics; adv bkg acc; games area; CKE. *"Gd views; peaceful, pleasant site; buy day pass on bus."* **CHF 35 2022**

BELLINZONA *C3* (2.6km N Urban) *46.21186, 9.03831* **Camping Bellinzona (formerly Bosco di Molinazzo),** Via San Gottardo 131, 6500 Bellinzona **091 829 11 18; info@campingbellinzona.ch; www.campingbellinzona.ch**

CHF4

Fr A13 exit Bellinzona Nord, foll rd over rv & rlwy bdgs. In approx 200m on R, immed after rd to Gorduno, site sp in 200m down ramp to R just bef Shell g'ge. 3*, Med, pt shd, sl, EHU (6A) CHF4; gas; bbq; TV; 20% statics; adv bkg acc; ccard acc; bike hire; tennis; golf; CKE. *"Pleasant & attractive city; gd NH en rte Italy; rv adj; san facs stretched high ssn & site overcr; early arr site yourselves & report later - instructions on barrier."* **CHF 52, 1 Apr-9 Oct. 2024**

BERN *B2* (4km S Rural) *46.93285, 7.45569* **Camping Eichholz,** Strandweg 49, 3084 Wabern **031 9612602; info@campingeichholz.ch; www.campingeichholz.ch**

Exit A1/A12 & take 2nd turn-off sp Bern/Bümplitz dir Belp & airport. Turn L under A12 & foll sp Wabern & site. 4*, Lge, hdstg, shd, EHU (rev pol) CHF3.50; gas; bbq; tram; Eng spkn; adv bkg acc; ccard acc; fishing; bike hire; tennis. *"Walk to Bern by rv (steep climb); clean, modern san facs; helpful staff."* **CHF 43, 20 Apr-30 Sep. 2024**

BERN *B2* (8km NW Rural) *46.96375, 7.38420* **TCS Camping Bern-Eymatt,** Wohlenstrasse 62C, 3032 Hinterkappelen **031 9011007; camping.bern@tcs.ch; www.campingtcs.ch**

CHF6 (htd) (htd)

Fr E on A1 exit junc 33 sp Bern Bethlehem; foll sp for Wohlen & site. In 200m turn R at bottom of hill into site on shores Wohlensee. Fr W take Brunnen-Bern exit, then sp to Wohlen. Access for lge o'fits poss diff. 4*, Lge, hdstg, pt shd, EHU (6A) inc; gas; bbq (charcoal, gas); TV; 80% statics; bus to Bern nrby; ccard acc; sep car park; games area; games rm; bike hire; fishing; CKE. *"Recep 0830-1100 & 1700-2000 high ssn, but site yourself; various pitch sizes; clean facs; no o'fits over 8m high ssn; helpful staff; daily mkt in Bern; 2 supmkt nrby; excel."* **CHF 56, 1 Mar-10 Nov. 2023**

SWITZERLAND

BIEL/BIENNE *B2* (20km SW Rural) *47.08556, 7.11726* **Camping Prêles,** Route de la Neuveville 61, 2515 Prêles **032 3151716; info@camping-jura.ch; www.campingpreles.ch**

CHF2 (htd)

App Biel fr N on rd 6 approx 2km bef town; immed after emerging fr 2nd long tunnel turn R then L sp Orvin. Cont thro Orvin to Lamboing, in Lamboing turn L dir La Neuveville to Prêles. Drive strt thro vill & look out for tent sp beyond vill when descending hill. App fr S on rd 5 poss via Neuveville or Twann but steep climb, tight bends & narr vill rds. Lge, shd, pt sl, EHU (10A) CHF3.50; gas; bbq; red long stay; 10% statics; adv bkg acc; ccard acc; games rm; bike hire; watersports 5km; horseriding; tennis; CKE. *"Nice scenery & gd views; peaceful site surrounded by woods & meadows; sep car park high ssn; recep clsd 1130-1400 & after 1800."* **CHF 38.5, 1 Apr-15 Oct. 2024**

BOURG ST PIERRE *D2* (0.5km N Rural) *45.95265, 7.20740* **Camping du Grand St Bernard,** 1946 Bourg-St Pierre **0 79 370 98 22; reservation@camping grand-st-bernard.ch; www.campinggrand-st-bernard.ch**

nr nr nr

Fr Martigny S to Grand St Bernard Tunnel. Site well sp in cent of vill. 1*, Med, unshd, EHU (4A) CHF3.50; gas; Eng spkn; ccard acc; CKE. *"Conv St Bernard Tunnel; htd pool adj; gd views."* **CHF 32, 1 Jun-30 Sep. 2022**

BRIENZ *B2* (2km SE Rural) *46.75069, 8.04838* **Camping Seegartli,** 3855 Brienz **033 951 1351; www.camping-seegaertli.ch**

Fr Interlaken take N8 sp Luzern/Brienz. Take Brienz exit, ignore sp to site to R & take L in 1km bef Esso stn, sp Axalp. Site in 500m on R immed after passing under rlwy. Site on E shore of lake, next to sawmill. 2*, Sm, pt shd, pt sl, EHU (10A) CHF3; sw; Eng spkn; fishing; watersports; tennis; CKE. *"Beautiful lakeside situation; well-kept site; friendly owner; lakeside pitches boggy in wet weather; long hose req for m'van fill-up; arr bef noon in ssn; no dogs."* **CHF 33, 1 Apr-31 Oct. 2022**

BRIENZ *B2* (3km SE Urban) *46.74811, 8.04769* **Camping Aaregg,** Seestrasse 22, 3855 Brienz **033 9511843; mail@aaregg.ch; www.aaregg.ch**

CHF5 (htd)

Fr Interlaken take N8 sp Luzern/Brienz. Take Brienz exit, ignore sp to site to R & take L in 1km bef Esso stn, sp Axalp. Site in 500m on R after passing under rlwy. Site on E shore of lake, next to sawmill. 5*, Med, mkd, hdstg, pt shd, serviced pitches; EHU (10A) CHF7; sw nr; red long stay; train nr; Eng spkn; adv bkg rec; ccard acc; CKE. *"Excel, busy site on lakeside; lakeside pitches sm; pool 500m; ideal touring base; excel, modern san facs; many attractions nrby."* **CHF 51, 1 Apr-31 Oct, S02. 2023**

BRIG *C2* (3km E Rural) *46.31500, 8.01369* **Camping Tropic,** Camping TROPIC Vandyck-Gasser family 3911 Ried-Brig **027 9232537**

On Brig-Domodossola rd on Swiss side of Simplon Pass. Fr Brig, exit Simplon rd at sp Ried-Brig Termen. Site on L in 500m. Fr Simplon foll sp to Ried-Brig, site in vill. 1*, Med, pt shd, sl, EHU CHF3; gas; TV; Eng spkn. *"Useful CL-type NH to/fr Italy; welcoming & helpful owners; superb scenery; san facs adequate."* **CHF 24, 1 Jun-15 Sep. 2020**

BRIG *C2* (1km S Rural) *46.30838, 7.99338* **Camping Geschina,** Geschinastrasse 41, 3900 Brig **027 923 0688; www.geschina.ch**

CHF2

Foll sps twd Simplon Pass, site on R at 700m, behind pool at rv bdge. Best app fr Glis. 4*, Med, pt shd, pt sl, EHU (10A) CHF2.50; gas; red long stay; Eng spkn; adv bkg acc; fishing; CKE. *"Friendly, well-kept, family-run site; vg san facs; superb mountain & glacier views; ideal for Rhône Valley & Simplon Pass; pool adj; sh walk to town."* **CHF 29, 1 Apr-15 Oct. 2022**

BRIG *C2* (6km SW Rural) *46.30177, 7.93010* **Camping Thermal Brigerbad,** Thermalbad 1, 3900 Brigerbad **027 9484837; camping@brigerbad.ch; www.thermalbad-wallis.ch**

(covrd, htd)

To ent Brigerbad, access the "Kantonsstrasse", which is the main rd bet Visp and Brig. Once on this rd look out for blue bdge which leads directly to the Brigerbad. Lge, pt shd, EHU €3.60; bbq; twin axles; Eng spkn; adv bkg rec; waterslide; games area; bike hire. *"Sauna landscape; fitness rm; vg; dogs allowed in sep area."* **CHF 45, 1 May-31 Oct. 2023**

BRUNNEN *B3* (5km E Rural) *46.99030, 8.63394* **Camping Ferienhof Rüti,** Rüti 4, 6443 Morschach **41 8205309; info@ferienhof-rueti.com; www.ferienhof-rueti.ch**

12 (htd)

N4/E41 S thro Brunnen tunnel, take next L sp Morschach, thro vill & site on R bef cable car. Sm, mkd, pt shd, pt sl, EHU (6a) inc; bbq (charcoal, gas); sw nr; TV; bus adj; Eng spkn; ccard acc; games rm; games area; CKE. *"Panoramic views; on hobby farm with donkeys, mini-pigs, hens etc; excel site, quiet."* **CHF 29 2024**

BRUNNEN *B3* (1km NW Rural) *47.00076, 8.59149* **Camping Urmiberg,** Gersauerstrasse 75, 6440 Brunnen **041 8203327; fragen@campingurmiberg.ch; www.campingurmiberg.ch**

CHF3 (htd) nr nr nr

Exit A4 Brunnen Nord dir Weggis. Site sp opp Urmiberg cable car stn. Sm, pt shd, EHU (16A); bbq (elec, gas); sw nr; 60% statics; bus or boat; Eng spkn; adv bkg acc. *"Peaceful, clean, family-run site; wonderful views; excel."* **CHF 40, 1 Apr-15 Oct. 2024**

SWITZERLAND

BUCHS *B4* (0.5km W Rural) *47.16663, 9.46524* **Camping Werdenberg,** Camping Werdenberg Marktplatz 9470 Buchs **081 7561507; info@verkehrsverein-buchs.ch; https://www.verkehrsverein-buchs.ch/camping**

CHF2 nr

Fr bdge over Rv Rhine at Buchs on rd 16 dir Werdenberg & Grabs. Turn L at parking/camping sp, thro car park to site. 3*, Sm, unshd, EHU (16A) CHF4; gas; sw nr; adv bkg acc. *"Vg, attractive setting by lake with views of old town & castle; friendly owners; gd base for Liechtenstein, Appenzell & Vorarlberg; walking; plenty of activities mini golf etc; htd pool 2km; extra charge for vans over 5m; gd for families."* **CHF 34, 1 Apr-31 Oct.** **2020**

BUOCHS *B3* (1km N Rural) *46.97950, 8.41860* **TCS Camping Buochs Vierwaldstattersee,** Seefeldstrasse, 6374 Buochs-Ennetbürgen **041 6203474; camping.buochs@tcs.ch; www.campingtcs.ch**

CHF4 nr

Fr W on N2 m'way, exit junc 33 Stans-Süd & bear L. Foll sp Buochs. At 1st x-rds in Buochs, turn L to Ennetbürgen, in approx 1km R twd lake, sp. Fr E exit junc 34 for Buochs, turn L onto Beckenriederstrasse; at x-rds in cent of town turn R dir Ennetbürgen & foll sp as above. 3*, Med, mkd, pt shd, EHU (10A) CHF3.50 (adaptor avail); gas; sw nr; TV; 50% statics; Eng spkn; ccard acc; tennis; games rm; bike hire; fishing; CKE. *"Gd NH twd Italy; helpful staff; well-maintained facs; fine views; boat trip tickets sold on site; ferry close by; if recep clsd find own pitch & sign in later; pitches not draining well after heavy rains; v friendly staff; picturesque site; pool adj; site being redeveloped winter 2016-17."* **CHF 50, 4 Apr-4 Oct.** **2022**

BURGDORF *B2* (1.4km SE Rural) *47.05241, 7.63350* **TCS Camping Waldegg,** Waldeggweg, 3400 Burgdorf **344 222460**

nr nr

Exit Bern-Basel N1 m'way at sp Kirchberg. Site in Burgdorf clearly sp. App over narr (2.7m) humpback bdge. 3*, Med, pt shd, EHU (10A) CHF4; adv bkg acc; golf; tennis; fishing. *"Conv Bern; old town of Burgdorf v interesting; pool 200m; friendly staff; clean san facs; gd NH."* **CHF 35, 1 Apr-30 Oct.** **2022**

CHUR *B4* (2.6km W Rural) *46.85605, 9.50435* **Camping Au Chur,** Felsenaustrasse 61, Obere Au, 7000 Chur **081 2842283; info@camping-chur.ch; www.camping-chur.ch**

12 CHF3 (htd) nr

Site sp fr Chur Süd a'bahn exit, foll sp with tent pictogram (easily missed). 3*, Lge, pt shd, EHU (10A) CHF3.50; gas; TV; 65% statics; bus nr; Eng spkn; ccard acc; tennis; games area; CKE. *"Well-ordered, clean site; sm area for tourers; htd pool 200m; sm pitches; gd, modern facs; v soft when wet; helpful, friendly owners; interesting, old town."* **CHF 16** **2022**

DISENTIS MUSTER *C3* (1.6km S Rural) *46.69620, 8.85270* **TCS Camping Disentis,** Via Fontanivas 9, 7180 Disentis-Mustèr **081 9474422; camping.disentis@tcs.ch; www.campingtcs.ch**

CHF6 (htd)

Fr Disentis S twd Lukmanier Pass for 2.5km. Site on L. 3*, Lge, pt shd, EHU (6-10A) CHF4; gas; bbq; cooking facs; sw; TV; 25% statics; Eng spkn; adv bkg acc; ccard acc; tennis; bike hire; CKE. *"Excel san facs; pool 2.5km; historic old town; gd walks."* **CHF 56, 26 Apr-29 Sep.** **2022**

EVOLENE *C2* (0.8km S Rural) *46.11080, 7.49656* **Camping Evolène,** Route de Lannaz 1983 Evolène / Valais **027 2831144; info@camping-evolene.ch; www.camping-evolene.ch**

CHF3 (htd) nr

Fr Sion take rd to Val d'Hérens. As app Evolène take L fork to avoid vill cent. Proceed to Co-op on L, turn sharp R & 1st L to site. Site sp. 3*, Sm, unshd, EHU (10A) CHF4; gas; 5% statics; Eng spkn; adv bkg acc; ccard acc; bike hire; CKE. *"Mountain scenery; ACSI; well-kept site; snowboard hire; vg san facs; attentive owners; x-country ski hire; sh walk to vill cent, poss cr."* **CHF 43, 15 May-15 Oct.** **2020**

FAIDO *C3* (2.4km SE Rural) *46.47134, 8.81771* **Camping Gottardo,** 6764 Chiggiogna **091 8661562; schroeder.camp@vtxmail.ch; www.campinggottardo.ch**

CHF2 (htd)

Exit A2/E35 at Faido, site on R in 500m, sp immed bef Faido. 3*, Med, pt shd, terr, EHU (6A) CHF4; gas; red long stay; 10% statics; phone; bus 400m; Eng spkn. *"On main rd fr Italian lakes to St Gotthard Pass; interesting vill; poss diff for lge o'fits, espec upper terrs (rec pitch bef white building); excel facs; gd bar & rest - home cooking inc bread, pastries; friendly, helpful staff; access to pitches v ltd in snowy conditions; excel NH."* **CHF 36, 1 Mar-1 Nov.** **2024**

FILISUR *C4* (2.6km W Rural) *46.67176, 9.67408* **Camping Islas,** 7477 Filisur **081 4041647; info@campingislas.ch; www.campingislas.ch**

(htd)

Fr Tiefencastel take dir Albula. At Filisur foll camping sp. Long, single track rd to site. 3*, Med, hdstg, unshd, EHU (10A) CHF2; gas; bbq; TV; 70% statics; phone; Eng spkn; adv bkg acc; ccard acc; fishing. *"Gd touring base; informal management; euros acc; train to Davos free with guest card supplied; excel san facs."* **CHF 52, 1 Apr-31 Oct.** **2024**

SWITZERLAND

FLEURIER *B1* (1.4km NW Rural) *46.90643, 6.57508* **Camping Val de Travers,** Belle Roche 15, 2114 Fleurier **032 8614262; romane.camping2114@outlook.com; www.j3l.ch/en/P45336**

CHF3 (htd)

On Pontarlier (France) to Neuchâtel rd, site sp in Fleurier to L at start of vill. 2*, Med, pt shd, EHU (4A) CHF3; gas; 15% statics; Eng spkn; adv bkg acc; ccard acc; rv fishing; tennis; games area; bike hire. *"Helpful owners; htd pool 2km; wild chamois on rocks behind site visible early morning; vg."* **CHF 22, 17 Apr-26 Sep.** 2022

FRIBOURG *B2* (13km N Rural) *46.87827, 7.19121* **Camping Schiffenensee,** Schiffenen 15, 3186 Düdingen **026 4933486; info@camping-schiffenen.ch; www.camping-schiffenen.ch**

CHF3

Exit A12 Bern-Fribourg at Düdingen & foll rd for Murten (sp). Ent poss tight lge o'fits. 4*, Lge, mkd, pt shd, EHU (10A) CHF3; 80% statics; bus; Eng spkn; adv bkg acc; tennis; CKE. **CHF 27, 1 Apr-31 Oct.** 2022

GENEVE *C1* (8km NE Urban) *46.24465, 6.19433* **TCS Camping Geneva Vésenaz (Formerly Pointe à la Bise),** Chemin de la Bise, 1222 Vésenaz **022 7521296; camping.geneve@tcs.ch; www.campingtcs.ch**

CHF6

Fr Geneva take S lakeside rd N5 sp Evian to Vésanez 4km. Turn L on Rte d'Hermance (D25) at traff lts & foll sp to site in 1km. 4*, Med, pt shd, EHU (4-10A) inc (adaptor on loan, rev pol); gas; sw; TV; 60% statics; bus to Geneva; Eng spkn; ccard acc; bike hire; fishing; CKE. *"Pleasant, lovely site; excel lake & mountain excursions; helpful staff; muddy when wet; bus & boat pass fr recep; some early morning aircraft noise."* **CHF 64, 28 Mar-6 Oct.** 2023

> **"There aren't many sites open at this time of year"**
>
> If you're travelling outside peak season remember to call ahead to check site opening dates – even if the entry says 'open all year'.

GENEVE *C1* (9km W Rural) *46.20111, 6.06621* **Geneva City Camping (previously Camping du Bois de Bay),** Geneva City Camping Bois de Bay Route de Bois - de - Bay 19 CH-1247 SATIGNY **022 3410505; contact@geneva-camping.ch; www.geneva-camping.ch**

CHF3.50 (htd)

Fr A1 exit sp Bernex, then foll sp to Vernier, site sp. 4*, Lge, hdg, pt shd, EHU (6A) CHF4.50; gas; bbq; 40% statics; Eng spkn; ccard acc; tennis 2km; CKE. *"V friendly; modern san facs; park & ride bus to city; don't be put off by indus site outside site."* **CHF 43, 1 Mar-31 Dec.** 2020

GRUYERES *C2* (2km N Rural) *46.59515, 7.08069* **Camping Les Sapins,** 1664 Epagny-Gruyères **026 9129575; info@gruyeres-camping.ch; www.gruyeres-camping.ch**

CHF3 (htd) nr

Foll rd S fr Bulle sp Châteaux d'Oex. Site on L of rd sp Gruyères-Moléson. 3*, Med, pt shd, EHU (4A) CHF3; gas; 60% statics; phone; adv bkg acc; tennis. *"Neat, tidy site; Gruyères lovely medieval town; visits to cheese factory; lovely countryside; easy reach E end Lake Geneva; supmkt & fuel 2km."* **CHF 33.2, 1 Apr-30 Sep.** 2023

GRUYERES *C2* (6km S Rural) *46.56080, 7.08740* **Camping Haute Gruyère,** Chemin du Camping 18, 1667 Enney **026 9212260; camping.enney@bluewin.ch; www.camping-gruyere.ch**

12 CHF5 (htd) nr

Well sp fr N (Gruyères) but not by name - foll TCS sp, not well sp fr S. Site E of rd fr Bulle to Château d'Oex, 1km S of Enney vill. Beware trains on x-ing at turn in. Diff final app, single track around blind bend. 3*, Med, hdstg, unshd, EHU (10A) CHF4.50; gas; red long stay; TV; 95% statics; adv bkg acc; ccard acc; fishing; bike hire. *"Vg, modern san facs; minimal area for tourers; bread to order; mainly level cycle rte to Gruyeres; new management (2016); not rec, NH only."* **CHF 38** 2023

GSTAAD *C2* (2km NW Rural) *46.48119, 7.27269* **Camping Bellerive,** Bellerivestrasse 38, 3780 Gstaad **033 7446330; bellerive.camping@bluewin.ch; www.bellerivecamping.ch**

12 CHF2.70 (htd)

App fr Saanen turn R bef Gstaad, sp. 3*, Sm, mkd, hdstg, pt shd, EHU (12A) CHF2.70; gas; TV; 60% statics; Eng spkn; adv bkg acc; tennis; fishing. *"Gd touring, walking, winter sports; rvside site; sm pitches; pool 700m; skiing; buy Gstaad Card for rd, rail & mountain transport."* **CHF 29** 2022

GUDO *C3* (2km W Rural) *46.17080, 8.93170* **Camping Isola,** Via al Gaggioletto 3, 6515 Gudo **091 859 32 44; info@campingisola.ch; www.campingisola.ch**

CHF4 (htd)

(htd)

Exit A2 at Bellinzona Sud dir Bellinzona (47), turn L at major traff lts sp Locarno. Cross rv & m'way, cont thro Gudo, site on L in 500m, sharp L into site v narr rd, poorly sp. 4*, Lge, mkd, hdg, pt shd, EHU (10A) CHF40; 95% statics; site clsd mid-Dec to mid-Jan. *"Delightful, well-kept site; NH pitches poor with inadequate elec supply; easy access fr main rd; mainly statics creating cr; v sm pitches not suitable for lge o'fits."* **CHF 41, 15 Jan-15 Dec.** 2024

HAUDERES, LES *D2* (2km N Rural) *46.09303, 7.50560* **Camping Molignon,** Route de Molignon 183, 1984 Les Haudères **027 2831240; info@molignon.ch; www.molignon.ch**

12 CHF3.20 (htd)

Fr Sion take rd to Val d'Hérens, turn R 2.5km after Evolène. Site sp. Rd fr Sion steep, twisting & narr in places. 4*, Med, mkd, pt shd, terr, EHU (10A) CHF3.80; gas; TV; 15% statics; phone; Eng spkn; adv bkg acc; ccard acc; CKE. *"V friendly owner; ski lift 3km; ideal for mountain climbing & walking; beautiful location."*
CHF 36 **2024**

INNERTKIRCHEN *C3* (1.5km NW Rural) *46.70938, 8.21519* **Camping Aareschlucht,** Hauptstrasse 34, 3862 Innertkirchen **033 9712714; campaareschlucht@bluewin.ch; www.camping-aareschlucht.ch**

CHF2 (htd) nr nr

On Meiringen rd out of town on R. 3*, Sm, pt shd, EHU (6-10A) CHF3; gas; bbq; 30% statics; Eng spkn; adv bkg acc; ccard acc; games rm; sep car park; CKE. *"Excel site; clean facs; gd walking; gd touring base Interlaken, Jungfrau region; pool 5km; conv Grimsel & Susten passes; rv walk to town."*
CHF 24, 1 May-31 Oct. **2022**

INTERLAKEN *C2* (5km NE Rural) *46.70761, 7.91330* **Camp au Lac,** 3852 Ringgenberg **033 8222616; camping@au-lac.ch**

12 CHF2

Fr Ringgenberg to Brienz, site sp on R when exit Ringgenberg. Cont under rlwy viaduct to site. 3*, Med, pt shd, pt sl, EHU (6A) CHF3 (long cable poss req); 25% statics; bus; Eng spkn; adv bkg acc; ccard acc; CKE. *"Excel site; private access to lake; magnificent setting."* **CHF 36** **2022**

INTERLAKEN (NO. 01) *C2* (8km W Rural) *46.68004, 7.81669* **Camping Manor Farm,** Seestrasse 201, 3800 Interlaken-Thunersee **033 8222264; info@manorfarm.ch; www.manorfarm.ch**

12 CHF4 nr

Fr W on A8 exit junc 24 Interlaken West & foll sp Thun & Gunten. At rndabt take 2nd exit twd Thun, sp Gunten; pass Camping Alpenblick on R, then site on L after bdge. 5*, V lge, mkd, pt shd, serviced pitches; EHU (6A) CHF4 (adaptor avail); gas; bbq (charcoal, gas); sw nr; TV; 25% statics; Eng spkn; adv bkg req; ccard acc; watersports; boat hire; golf 300m; fishing; games rm; horseriding 3km; bike hire; CKE. *"Site on banks of Lake Thun; excel views; gd sized pitches; helpful staff; immac san facs; o'fits over 8m by request; money exchange; variable pitch price; excel facs for children; steamer boat trips; excursions; bkg fee; cable car & chairlift nrby; local bus pass provided free; gd walking; if staying on Super pitch, water hose with pressurised valve fitting req; site v easy to find; v pleasant and well looked after; if taking an awning a storm strap req."* **CHF 37.5** **2024**

See advertisement

INTERLAKEN (NO. 02) *C2* (5km W Rural) *46.67969, 7.81764* **Camping Alpenblick,** Seestrasse 130, 3800 Unterseen-Interlaken **033 8227757 or 8231470; info@camping-alpenblick.ch; www.camping-alpenblick.ch**

12 CHF3 (htd)

Fr W on A8 exit junc 24 Interlaken West & foll sp Thun & Gunten. At rndabt take 2nd exit twd Thun, sp Gunten. Site adj Motel Neuhaus & Rest Strandbad on Gunten-Thun rd. 4*, Lge, mkd, pt shd, EHU (10A) CHF4.50 (rev pol); gas; bbq; sw nr; 30% statics; phone; bus fr site ent; Eng spkn; ccard acc; watersports; fishing; golf adj; CKE. *"In beautiful situation; mountain views; excel, modern facs; bread baked on site; lake steamers fr hotel opp; gd walks nr; free bus pass to town; cycle rte to Interlaken; CHF1 to fill m'van water tank; max 2 dogs; adv bkg attracts surchage; pool 3km; site next to shooting club, poss noisy."* **CHF 55** **2023**

SWITZERLAND

INTERLAKEN (NO. 04) *C2* (4.2km W Rural) *46.68555, 7.83083* **Camping Lazy Rancho,** Lehnweg 6, 3800 Unterseen-Interlaken **033 8228716; info@lazyrancho.ch; www.lazyrancho.ch**

CHF3 (htd)

Fr W on app to Interlaken, exit A8/A6 junc 24 sp Interlaken West. Turn L at slip rd rndabt then at rndabt take a sharp R turn (foll camping sp Nos. 3-5); at Migrol petrol stn foll sp for Lazy Rancho 4 (narr rd on L just bef Landhotel Golf); it is 2nd site. Cent of Interlaken best avoided with c'vans or lge m'vans. Rec arr bef 1900 hrs. 4*, Med, hdg, mkd, hdstg, pt shd, serviced pitches; EHU (10A) inc (adaptors provided); gas; bbq; cooking facs; TV (pitch); 30% statics; phone; Eng spkn; ccard acc; bike hire; horseriding 500m; fishing nr; tennis 2.5km; games rm; watersports nr; CKE. *"Superb views Eiger, Monch & Jungfrau; no o'fits over 7.5m high ssn; ideal for touring Interlaken, Bernese Oberland; fitness cent/spa; friendly, caring, helpful owners; sm pitches; recep 0900-1200 & 1330-2100 high ssn; 5 mins to bus stop nr Cmp Jungfrau; ask about Swiss red fare rlwy services - excel value; immac, outstanding, well-maintained site & facs; brilliant site."* **CHF 53, 14 Apr-2 Oct, S01.** **2022**

INTERLAKEN (NO. 05) *C2* (2km W Rural) *46.68688, 7.83411* **Jungfrau Camp,** Steindlerstrasse 60, 3800 Unterseen-Interlaken **+41 76 295 0511; info@jungfraucamp.ch; www.campinginterlaken.ch or www.jungfraucamp.ch**

CHF4 (htd)

Leave N8 at exit Unterseen. In approx 600m turn R at rndabt & foll sp to site. 4*, Med, pt shd, EHU (10A) CHF4; gas; sw nr; 40% statics; bus adj; Eng spkn; adv bkg acc; tennis. *"Visits to all Bernese Oberland vills; views of Jungfrau, Mönch & Eiger; some noise fr shooting range at w/end; town in walking dist; excel, relaxing, well-run site; high standard san facs; poss ssn workers in summer."* **CHF 50, 15 Jun-20 Sep.** **2022**

INTERLAKEN (NO. 08) *C2* (3km S Rural) *46.66111, 7.86453* **Camping Oberei,** Obereigasse 9, 3812 Wilderswil-Interlaken **033 8221335; info@campingwilderswil.ch; www.campinginterlaken.ch or www.campingwilderswil.ch**

CHF2 (htd) nr

Fr Interlaken by-pass take rd sp Grindelwald & Lauterbrunnen to Wilderswil. Site sp 800m past stn on R in vill. Narr ent. 3*, Med, mkd, pt shd, pt sl, EHU (6A) CHF3; gas; TV; bus adj, bus/train nr; Eng spkn; adv bkg acc; CKE. *"Well-managed, relaxing, family-run site in superb scenic location; helpful owners; grnd sheets supplied if wet/muddy; blocks provided; gd, clean facs; gd touring cent; easy walk to rlwy stn; guest card gives free local train & bus travel; pool 3km; excel rec high ssn."* **CHF 43.3, 1 May-30 Sep.** **2024**

INTERLAKEN (NO. 10) *C2* (0.7km N Rural) *46.69125, 7.89353* **TCS Camping Boenigen Brienzersee (formerly Seeblick),** Campingstrasse 14, 3806 Bönigen **033 8221143; camping.boenigen@tcs.ch; www.campingtcs.ch**

CHF5 (htd) nr

Fr A8 exit junc 26 Interlaken-Ost dir Bönigen; on ent vill turn L, site sp on Lake Brienz. 4*, Med, hdstg, shd, EHU (6A) CHF4; gas; sw; TV; 10% statics; phone; Eng spkn; ccard acc; boating; fishing; golf 4km; CKE. *"Ideal for fishing or boating; v helpful, friendly owner; clean facs; htd pool & paddling 200m; excel site; excel position walking & cycling into Interlaken."* **CHF 44, 28 Mar-6 Oct.** **2024**

KANDERSTEG *C2* (15km N Rural) *46.58188, 7.64150* **Camping Grassi,** 3714 Frutigen **033 6711149; campinggrassi@bluewin.ch; www.camping-grassi.ch**

12 CHF1.50 (htd) nr

Exit rd to Kandersteg at Frutigen-Dorf & in 400m L to site in 500m. 4*, Med, pt shd, EHU (10A) CHF3; gas; red long stay; TV; 50% statics; phone; Eng spkn; adv bkg acc; tennis; bike hire; fishing. *"Walking rte dir fr site to spectacular pedestrian suspension bdge; htd covrd pool 1km; 10 min walk to town."* **CHF 29** **2024**

KANDERSTEG *C2* (1.3km NE Rural) *46.49800, 7.68519* **Camping Rendez-Vous,** 3718 Kandersteg **033 6751534; rendez-vous.camping@bluewin.ch; www.camping-kandersteg.ch**

12 CHF3 (htd)

In middle of Kandersteg turn E dir Sesselbahn Öschinensee; site sp. 3*, Med, hdstg, pt shd, pt sl, terr, EHU (10A) (adaptors avail); gas; bbq; Eng spkn; adv bkg acc; ccard acc; games rm; bike hire; CKE. *"Excel, well-supervised site; htd pool 800m; chair-lift adj; excel walking."* **CHF 39** **2024**

KREUZLINGEN *A3* (0km E Rural) *47.64676, 9.19810* **Camping Fischerhaus,** Promenadenstrasse 52, 8280 Kreuzlingen **071 6884903; info@camping-fischerhaus.ch; www.camping-fischerhaus.ch**

(htd)

Fr Konstanz take rd 13 dir Romanshorn. Turn L at sp 'Hafen/Indus Est' off main lakeside rd, Kreuzlingen-Arbon. Camping sps fr 5km SE at Customs in Konstanz. 4*, Med, unshd, EHU (10A) inc; gas; bbq; twin axles; 60% statics; phone; bus 100m; train 1km; Eng spkn; adv bkg acc; fishing; tennis; games area. *"Facs for statics excel, but for tourers v basic; gates clsd 1200-1400 & 2200-0700; gd cycle paths."* **CHF 60, 28 Mar-21 Oct.** **2023**

LANDERON, LE *B2* (0.3km S Rural) *47.05216, 7.06975* **Camping des Pêches,** Route du Port, 2525 Le Landeron **032 7512900; info@camping-lelanderon.ch; www.camping-lelanderon.ch**

A5 fr Neuchâtel, exit Le Landeron or La Neuveville; foll site sp. 4*, Med, mkd, pt shd, serviced pitches; EHU (15A) CHF3.50; gas; TV; 60% statics; Eng spkn; adv bkg acc; ccard acc; sep car park; bike hire; tennis; fishing; CKE. *"Sep touring section on busy site; htd pool 100m; walks by lake & rv; interesting old town."* **CHF 32, 1 Apr-15 Oct. 2022**

LAUSANNE *C1* (9km E Rural) *46.48973, 6.73786* **Camping de Moratel,** Route de Moratel 2, 1096 Cully **021 7991914; camping.moratel@bluewin.ch; https://spbmc.ch/camping**

Fr Lausanne-Vevey lakeside rd (not m/way), turn R to Cully; sp thro town; site on R on lake shore. Ent not sp. 3*, Sm, hdg, hdstg, mkd, pt shd, EHU (3-5A) CHF3; gas; sw; 80% statics; bus, train, ferry; adv bkg acc; boating; fishing. *"Vg value; attractive, clean site with beautiful views; rec adv bkg for lakeside pitch; friendly staff; siting poss diff for lge o'fits; pool 3km; gd location for best pt Lake Geneva; vg value."* **CHF 40, 20 Mar-20 Oct. 2023**

LAUSANNE *C1* (3km W Rural) *46.51769, 6.59766* **Camping de Vidy,** Chemin du Camping 3, 1007 Lausanne (Genferseegebiet) **021 6225000; info@clv.ch; www.clv.ch**

12 CHF2 (htd) adj

Leave A1 at Lausanne Süd/Ouchy exit; take 4th exit at rndabt (Rte de Chavannes); in 100m filter L at traff lts & foll site sp to L. Site adj to HQ of Int'l Olympic Organisation, well sp all over Lausanne. 4*, Lge, mkd, pt shd, EHU (10A) CHF4; gas; bbq; TV; 80% statics; bus to Lausanne 400m; Eng spkn; adv bkg acc; ccard acc; watersports; bike hire; games rm; tennis 1km; CKE. *"Excel lakeside site in attractive park; friendly staff; sm pitches; gd train service to Geneva; sports & recreation area adj; conv m'way; recep 0800-2100 high ssn; no o'fits over 8m high ssn; free bus passes for unltd bus & Metro tavel in Lausanne; gd san facs (updated 2018); gd cycling."* **CHF 38 2023**

LAUTERBRUNNEN *C2* (1km S Rural) *46.58788, 7.91030* **Camping Jungfrau,** Weid 406, 3822 Lauterbrunnen **033 8562010; info@camping-jungfrau.ch; www.camping-jungfrau.ch**

12 CHF3 (htd)

S o'skirts of Lauterbrunnen sp at R fork, site in 500m. 5*, Lge, hdstg, pt shd, terr, serviced pitches; EHU (16A) CHF2.5 (metered in winter, poss rev pol); gas; red long stay; TV; 30% statics; phone; Eng spkn; adv bkg rec; ccard acc; tennis; bike hire; CKE. *"Friendly, helpful welcome; fine scenery, superb situation in vertical walled valley; rlwy tickets sold; sep car park when site full; ski bus; ATM; close to town & rlwy stn to high alpine resorts; ski & boot rm; superb facs; clean; shop gd; pool 600m; excel site."* **CHF 50, S15. 2023**

LAUTERBRUNNEN *C2* (3.6km S Rural) *46.56838, 7.90869* **Camping Breithorn,** Sandbach, 3824 Stechelberg **033 8551225; info@campingbreithorn.ch; www.campingbreithorn.ch**

12 CHF1 nr

Up valley thro Lauterbrunnen, 300m past Trümmelbach Falls to ent on R. 3*, Med, unshd, EHU (10A); gas; bbq; 60% statics; phone; Eng spkn; adv bkg acc; tennis; fishing; CKE. *"Quiet site in lovely area; arr early high ssn; fine scenery & gd touring base; friendly helpful owners; frequent trains, funiculars & cable cars fr Lauterbrunnen stn (4km); Schilthorn cable car 1.5km; excel cent for mountain walking & cycling; pool 3km; excel, clean facs; cash only."* **CHF 31 2023**

LEUK *C2* (15km N Rural) *46.38119, 7.62361* **Camping Sportarena,** 3954 Leukerbad **027 4701037; info@leukerbad.ch; https://www.sportarenaleukerbad.ch**

CHF2 (htd) nr

Exit A9 at Susten & foll sp N to Leukerbad, site sp. 3*, Med, hdstg, pt shd, pt sl, terr, EHU (10A) CHF5; bbq; TV; 20% statics; Eng spkn; adv bkg acc; games area. *"Beautiful situation; sports cent adj; pleasant, helpful staff; htd covrd pool 200m; attractive little town; cable cars; thermal pools nr; walks; vg."* **CHF 30, 1 May-31 Oct. 2020**

LEUK *C2* (4km SE Rural) *46.29780, 7.65936* **Camping Gemmi,** Briannenstrasse 4, 3952 Susten **027 4731154 or 4734295; info@campgemmi.ch; www.campgemmi.ch**

CHF3

Foll A9/E27 SE; then nr Martigny take A9/E62 to Sierre; then take E62 thro Susten. After 2km, by Hotel Relais Bayard, take R lane (Agarn, Feithieren), ignoring sp Camping Torrent, & foll Alte Kantonstrasse sp Agarn. Turn R at site sp into Briannenstrasse; site in 200m. 4*, Med, mkd, pt shd, pt sl, serviced pitches; EHU (16A) inc; gas; bbq (elec, gas); sw nr; TV (pitch); 5% statics; Eng spkn; adv bkg acc; ccard acc; tennis; golf; bike hire; horseriding nr; CKE. *"Outstanding site; friendly, helpful, hardworking owners; indiv san facs some pitches; no o'fits over 9m high ssn; private bthrms avail; gd stop on way Simplon Pass; various pitch prices; barrier clsd 2200-0800; pool 600m; excel walking; conv A9."* **CHF 40, 1 Apr-2 Oct, S12. 2022**

LEUK *C2* (3.7km SW Rural) *46.30702, 7.61101* **Camping Monument,** Alter Kehr 33, 3952 Susten **027 473 18 27; camping.monument@hotmail.com; www.campingmonument.ch**

Fr Visp twds Sion, foll E62 (blue sp); site sp on R approx 3km after passing thro Susten. Lge, hdg, mkd, pt shd, pt sl, EHU (10A); bbq; twin axles; 10% statics; CKE. *"Lovely, well maintained sw pool; site partly in pine forest & in lge grassy fields; spacious open pitches; mountain views; walking tracks fr site; gd site."* **CHF 37, 1 May-21 Sep. 2024**

SWITZERLAND

LOCARNO *C3* (14km E Rural) *46.16978, 8.91396* **Park-Camping Riarena,** Via Campeggio, 6516 Cugnasco **091 8591688; info@campingriarena.ch; www.campingriarena.ch**

CHF4

Exit A2/E35 Bellinzona-Süd & foll sp dir airport. Bear R at rndabt & foll site sp to Gudo, site on R in 2km. 4*, Med, mkd, shd, EHU (10A) CHF5 (adaptor avail); gas; twin axles; red long stay; bus 0.5km; Eng spkn; adv bkg acc; ccard acc; bike hire; games area. *"Friendly, family-run site; excursions arranged; gd cycle rtes; gate shut 1300-1500; clean san facs; dusty site; beware acorn drop September; vg."*
€62.70, 21 Mar-17 Oct. 2024

LOCARNO *C3* (2km S Urban) *46.15587, 8.80258* **Camping Delta,** Via Respini 7, 6600 Locarno **091 7516081; info@campingdelta.com; www.campingdelta.com**

Fr cent of Locarno make for prom & foll sp to Lido. Site in 400m past Lido on L. Fr Simplon Pass SS337 fr Domodossola to Locarno clsd to trailer c'vans; narr rd with many bends. Site well sp fr m'way. 5*, Lge, mkd, hdg, pt shd, EHU (10A) CHF5; gas; sw nr; Eng spkn; adv bkg req; bike hire; kayak hire. *"No access for vehicles 2200-0700; superb location walking dist Locarno; no radios or musical instruments allowed; fitness rm; excel facs but long walk fr S end of site; premium for lakeside pitches."*
CHF 82, 1 Mar-31 Oct. 2024

"That's changed – Should I let the Club know?"

If you find something on site that's different from the site entry, fill in a report and let us know. See camc.com/europereport.

LOCARNO *C3* (9km NW Rural) *46.22436, 8.74395* **TCS Camping Bella Riva,** 6672 Gordévio **091 7531444; camping.gordevio@tcs.ch; https://www.campinglariva.com/**

CHF5

Fr W end of A13 tunnel under Locarno foll sp Centovalle & Valle Maggia. In 3km turn R to Valle Maggia. Stay on rd which bypasses Gordévio (approx 5km), site on L. 4*, Lge, pt shd, EHU inc (10A) CHF4.50; gas; sw; TV; 30% statics; Eng spkn; adv bkg acc; ccard acc; tennis; fishing; sep car park; bike hire; CKE. *"Attractive region; well-run site; lge tent area adj; bus to vill nr site."* **CHF 48, 1 Apr-2 Nov.** 2022

LUGANO *D3* (7km W Rural) *45.99534, 8.90845* **Lugano,** Via alla Force 14, 6933 Muzzano-Lugano **091 9947788 or 091 9858070 LS; camping.muzzano@tcs.ch; https://www.tcs.ch/de/camping-reisen/camping-insider/campingplaetze/tcs-campingplaetze/campingplatz-lugano-muzzano.php**

12 CHF6 (htd)

Leave A2 at Lugano Nord & foll sp Ponte Tresa & airport. In Agno turn L at traff island; foll camping sp. In 800m, just after La Piodella town sp, look for sm sp at rd junc with tent symbol & TCS sticker. NB This may appear to direct you to your R but you must make a 180° turn & take slip rd along R-hand side of rd you have just come along - app rd to site. 4*, Lge, mkd, pt shd, serviced pitches; EHU (10A) inc (long lead poss req, avail fr recep); gas; bbq; TV; 10% statics; Eng spkn; adv bkg acc; ccard acc; watersports; games area; horseriding 6km; tennis; games rm; fishing; CKE. *"Idyllic location; pitches nr lake higher price; o'fits over 7.5m HS; sep car park; modern san facs; no cats; access to pitches poss diff lge o'fits; boating 6km; train to Lugano 1km, or easy drive; ideal for Ticino Lakes; day/eve aircraft noise; barrier clsd 1200-1400."* **CHF 37, S10.** 2022

LUZERN *B3* (3km E Rural) *47.0500, 8.33833* **Camping International Lido,** Lidostrasse 19, 6006 Luzern **041 3702146; luzern@camping-international.ch; www.camping-international.ch**

12 CHF5 (htd) nr

Fr bdge on lake edge in city cent foll sp Küssnacht & Verkehrshaus. Turn R off Küssnacht rd at traff lts by transport museum (sp Lido), site 50m on L beyond lido parking. Fr A2/E35 exit Luzern Centrum. 4*, Lge, mkd, hdstg, pt shd, EHU (16A) CHF4.50; gas; bbq; sw nr; 10% statics; phone; bus, 200mtrs; Eng spkn; adv bkg rec; ccard acc; boat trips; boat launch; CKE. *"Ltd touring pitches cr in peak ssn, early arr rec; pool adj (May-Sep); recep open 0830-1200 & 1400-1800 high ssn; money exchange; recep in bar LS; clean, well-maintained facs stretched high ssn; lake ferry 200m; helpful staff; pleasant lakeside walk to Luzern; conv location; excel rest in Wurzenbach; transport museum worth a visit; well-run site; free local bus tickets avail."* **CHF 50.6** 2023

MARTIGNY *D2* (1km S Urban) *46.09788, 7.07953* **TCS Camping Martigny (formerly Camping Les Neuvilles),** Route du Levant 68, 1920 Martigny **027 7224544; camping.martigny@tcs.ch; www.campingtcs.ch**

CHF5 (htd)

Exit A9/E62 dir Grand St Bernard to Martigny. Camping poorly sp fr town; foll Expo sp, ent past cemetary. (sat nav poss inacurate). 4*, Lge, mkd, hdstg, unshd, EHU (6-10A) CHF4.50; gas; TV; 65% statics; Eng spkn; adv bkg acc; ccard acc; fishing; bike hire; tennis; CKE. *"Excel san facs; conv Valais & Mont Blanc area; Martigny pleasant town; gd cycling."*
CHF 45, 1 Apr-31 Oct. 2024

MEIRINGEN *C3* (1.5km NW Rural) *46.73431, 8.17139* **Alpencamping,** Brünigstrasse 47, 3860 Meiringen **033 9713676; info@alpencamping.ch; www.alpencamping.ch**

CHF3 (htd) nr

Leave A8, then take rd11/6 twd Brünig Pass. On entering Meiringen, at 1st rndabt foll camp sp L to site. 4*, Med, unshd, EHU (10A) CHF7; gas; bbq; cooking facs; 70% statics; bus 200m, train 1.3km; Eng spkn; adv bkg acc; site clsd Nov; CKE. *"Meeting point of alpine passes; friendly, family-run site; excel, modern san facs; vg walking/cycling; beautiful site with gd views; fair."* **CHF 46, 1 Jan-31 Oct & 1 Dec-31 Dec. 2023**

"I like to fill in the reports as I travel from site to site"

You'll find report forms at the back of this guide, or you can fill them in online at camc.com/europereport.

MEIRINGEN *C3* (14km NNW Rural) *46.78499, 8.15157* **Camping Obsee,** Campingstrasse 1, 6078 Lungern **041 6781463; camping@obsee.ch; www.obsee.ch**

12 CHF3 (htd) nr

S fr Luzern on N8 to Sachseln. Exit m'way for rte 4 to Brienz; thro Lungern; R at end of vill & site on R on lakeside. Best app fr Luzern - turn fr Interlaken diff for lge o'fits. Lge, pt shd, pt sl, EHU CHF3; gas; sw; TV; 95% statics; Eng spkn; fishing; tennis; games rm. *"Well-kept site in beautiful situation - ski cent; cable rlwy adj; 10 mins walk to vill; sm area for tourers; vg rest; easy access by rd or train to attractions; Swiss adaptor & poss long lead for elec."* **€51.20 2024**

MENDRISIO *D3* (8km NW Rural) *45.88921, 8.94841* **Camping Monte San Giorgio,** Via Ala Caraa 2, 6866 Meride **091 6464330; info@montesangiorgiocamping.ch; www.montesangiorgiocamping.ch**

CHF5 nr (htd)

Fr A2/E35 exit Mendrisio, then foll sp Rancate & Serpiano. Steep climb. Site on L to S of vill. 4*, Med, hdstg, pt shd, pt sl, EHU (4A) CHF4.50; gas; TV; 20% statics; Eng spkn; adv bkg acc; ccard acc; lake fishing; sep car park. *"Attractive, peaceful setting away fr traff; Unesco World Heritage vill; pitches uneven in parts & v sm, some surrounded by other pitches - make sure you can get off with o'fit; site clsd to arr 1100-1700; conv Milan by train."* **CHF 49, 1 May-26 Sep. 2022**

MORGES *C1* (2km S Rural) *46.50360, 6.48760* **TCS Camping Morges,** Promenade du Petit-Bois 15, 1110 Morges **021 8011270 or 091 9858070 LS; camping.morges@tcs.ch; www.tcs.ch/de/camping-reisen/camping-insider/campingplaetze/tcs-campingplaetze/campingplatz-morges.php**

CHF5

Exit A1/E25 at Morges Ouest, then foll sp to lake. Site well sp on Lake Léman N shore adj pool. 3*, Lge, mkd, unshd, EHU (6A) inc (adaptor/long lead avail); gas; bbq; sw nr; TV; 15% statics; Eng spkn; adv bkg acc; games rm; bike hire; watersports; tennis 500m; boating; CCI. *"Pleasant site but sm pitches; htd pool in complex 200m (high ssn) inc; helpful staff; clean san facs; conv Lausanne, Geneva & some Alpine passes; o'fits over 8m on req; town car pk adj for late arr, not part of site; easy walk to town & stn; cycle path around lake; Swiss adapter/lg lead avail to rent, expensive; vg."* **CHF 60, 1 Apr-4 Oct. 2023**

MURG *B3* (0.5km N Rural) *47.11543, 9.21445* **Camping Murg am Walensee,** 8877 Murg **081 7381530; info@camping-murg.ch; www.murg-camping.ch**

CHF4.50 nr

Exit A3 junc 47 dir Murg, site sp on lake. Med, pt shd, EHU (10A) CHF3.70; sw nr; 30% statics; phone; adv bkg req. *"Spectacular outlook at water's edge; sm pitches; beautiful setting; boat trips adj; cable car 4km; vg."* **CHF 49, 1 Apr-15 Oct. 2024**

MUSTAIR *B4* (0.5km E Rural) *46.62405, 10.44933* **Camping Muglin,** Via Muglin 223, 7537 Mustair **081 8585990; info@campingmuglin.ch; www.campingmuglin.ch**

CHF4.20

On rd 28 to Mustair. Foll sp. Med, mkd, unshd, EHU (13A) CHF3.80; bbq; TV; adv bkg acc; games rm. *"Beautiful views; serviced pithces; walking rte fr site; lge sauna."* **CHF 42.7, 22 Apr-29 Oct. 2023**

NEUCHATEL *B1* (13km NE Rural) *47.00198, 7.04145* **TCS Camping Gampelen,** Seestrasse 50, 3236 Gampelen **032 3132333; camping.gampelen@tcs.ch; www.campingtcs.ch**

CHF6 (htd)

Foll TCS camping sp fr turning off N5 in Gampelen - approx 4km fr vill, on lakeside. 3*, V lge, mkd, pt shd, serviced pitches; EHU (4-6A) inc (adaptor on loan, rev pol); gas; bbq; sw; red long stay; 80% statics; Eng spkn; adv bkg acc; ccard acc; tennis; archery; golf; fishing; watersports; CKE. *"In nature reserve; office/barrier clsd 1200-1400; office & shop hrs vary with ssn; gd, modern facs; helpful staff; Euros also acc; vg cycling around lakes."* **CHF 62, 10 Apr-13 Oct. 2023**

SWITZERLAND

SWITZERLAND

ROMANSHORN *A4* (5km SE Rural) *47.53620, 9.39885* **Camping Seehorn,** Wiedehorn, 9322 Egnach **071 4771006; info@seehorn.ch; www.seehorn.ch**

CHF5 (htd)

Site is 2km E of Egnach, dir Arbon. 4*, Med, mkd, pt shd, pt sl, serviced pitches; EHU (15A) inc; gas; TV; 60% statics; phone; adv bkg acc; fishing. *"Direct access Lake Constance; sep car park high ssn; statics sep; excel facs; great loc; cycle paths around lake; friendly recep."* **CHF 53.3, 1 Mar-31 Oct.** **2024**

SAANEN *C2* (0.3km S Urban) *46.48738, 7.26406* **Camping Saanen (formerly Beim Kappeli),** Campingstrasse, 3792 Saanen **033 7446191; info@camping-saanen.ch; www.camping-saanen.ch**

CHF3 (htd) nr

On edge of vill bet rv & light rlwy. Site sp fr town cent. 3*, Med, pt shd, EHU (6-13A) CHF4; 50% statics; Eng spkn; ccard acc; tennis; site clsd Nov; fishing. *"Beautiful walks; neat site; excel, clean facs; pool adj; buy Gstaad card vg value."* **CHF 30** **2024**

SAAS FEE *D2* (4.6km NE Rural) *46.11588, 7.93819* **Camping am Kapellenweg,** 3910 Saas-Grund **027 9574997; camping@kapellenweg.ch; www.kapellenweg.ch**

CHF2.50

Fr Visp, take Saas Fee rd to Saas Grund, cont twd Saas Almagell, site on R after 1km. 3*, Sm, pt shd, pt sl, EHU CHF3; gas; Eng spkn; fishing; golf. *"Ideal for walking; family-run site; clean san facs; beautiful scenery; if recep clsd, site yourself; bus or walk (50 mins) into town; excel site."* **CHF 34, 10 May-13 Oct.** **2024**

SAAS FEE *D2* (5km NE Rural) *46.11368, 7.94136* **Camping Mischabel,** Unter den Bodmen, 3910 Saas-Grund **027 9571608; mischabel@hotmail.com**

CHF2.50

Fr Visp take Saas Fee rd to Saas Grund & cont twd Saas Almagell for 1.2km. 3*, Med, pt shd, EHU (10A) CHF3; TV; Eng spkn; adv bkg acc; fishing; boating; CKE. *"Lovely scenery; gd walking; helpful, friendly staff."* **CHF 63, 1 Jun-30 Sep.** **2024**

SAAS FEE *D2* (5km E Rural) *46.11150, 7.94238* **Camping Schönblick,** 3910 Saas-Grund **027 9572267; schoenblick@campingschweiz.ch; www.camping schweiz.ch**

(htd) nr

Fr Visp take Saas Fee rd to Saas Grund & cont twd Saas Almagell for 1.5km. Site on R over rv. 2*, Sm, hdstg, unshd, EHU (10A) CHF3; gas; TV; 25% statics; adv bkg rec; ccard acc; fishing; tennis; horseriding. *"Site ideal for walking & mountain scenery; winter & summer skiing; navette 50m; open Oct-May with adv bkg only; facs ltd LS."* **CHF 29** **2024**

ST GALLEN *A4* (9km N Rural) *47.46191, 9.36371* **Camping St Gallen-Wittenbach,** Leebrücke, 9304 Bernhardzell **071 2984969; campingplatz.stgallen@ccc-stgallen.ch; www.ccc-stgallen.ch**

CHF3

Exit A1/E60 St Fiden. L in Wittenbach cent at site sp. Cross Rv Sitter on sharp R bend, turn sharp R at sp. 3*, Med, hdstg, pt shd, EHU (6A) CHF4 (adaptor loan); gas; bbq; TV; 30% statics; bus; Eng spkn; adv bkg acc; ccard acc; canoeing; golf 10km; bike hire; CKE. *"Gd base for S shore of Bodensee; pleasant rvside setting; friendly staff."* **CHF 32, 12 Apr-4 Oct.** **2022**

ST MARGRETHEN *A4* (3km E Rural) *47.45114, 9.65650* **Strandbad Camping Bruggerhorn,** 9430 St Margrethen **071 7442201**

nr

Exit N1/E60 dir St Margrethen, site well sp. 3*, Med, pt shd, EHU (10A) CHF2.50 (adaptor avail); gas; sw; Eng spkn; adv bkg acc; tennis; CKE. *"Picturesque, clean site; vg shwrs; sports cent adj; helpful staff."* **CHF 36, 1 Apr-31 Oct.** **2022**

"We must tell the Club about that great site we found"

Get your site reports in by mid-August and we'll do our best to get your updates into the next edition.

ST MORITZ *C4* (1km S Rural) *46.47843, 9.82511* **Camping St. Moritz,** 7500 St Moritz **081 8334090; info@camping-stmoritz.ch; www.camping-stmoritz.ch**

CHF4 (htd) nr

Turn S off rd N27 immed after park & ride car park. Site 1km fr vill of Champfer. 3*, Med, mkd, pt sl, EHU (6A) CHF4 (adaptor on loan); gas; sw nr; Eng spkn; ccard acc; bike hire; tennis; CKE. *"Gd walking area, nr St Moritz & Maloja & Julier passes; site v high & cold (poss snow in Aug); san facs stretched when site full; sh walk town cent."* **CHF 52, 20 May-28 Sep.** **2022**

SCHAFFHAUSEN *A3* (18km ESE Rural) *47.66216, 8.84034* **Camping Wagenhausen,** Hauptstrasse 82, 8260 Wagenhausen **052 7414271; info@campingwagenhausen.ch; www.campingwagenhausen.ch**

CHF4 (htd)

Turn R off Stein-am-Rhein/Schaffhausen rd, site sp. 4*, Med, mkd, pt shd, pt sl, serviced pitches; EHU (10A) CHF3; bbq (gas, sep area); sw; twin axles; TV; 80% statics; bus nrby; Eng spkn; adv bkg acc; ccard acc; fishing; CCI. *"Vg; direct access to Rv Rhine; rvside footpath; lovely site; excel san facs; easy walk into town; beautiful old town; cafe's & rest aplenty."* **CHF 47.5, 1 Apr-30 Oct.** **2024**

SCHAFFHAUSEN *A3* (3km SE Rural) *47.68763, 8.65461* **Camping Schaffhausen (formerly TCS Camping Rheinwiesen),** Hauptstrasse, 8246 Langwiesen **052 6593300; info@camping-schaffhausen.ch; www.camping-schaffhausen.ch**

Fr N, S & W on A4/E41 exit Schaffhausen & foll sp 'Kreuzlingen' on rd 13. Fr E on rd 13 pass under rlwy bdge to Langwiesen about 3km bef Schaffhausen; site sp at Feuerthalen (tent sp only - no site name) down narr rd on L on Rv Rhine. 3*, Med, mkd, pt shd, EHU (4A) inc (adaptor avail); gas; bbq (charcoal, gas); sw; TV; 30% statics; phone; Eng spkn; adv bkg acc; ccard acc; games rm; horseriding 3km; fishing; CKE. *"Excel site in beautiful location; covrd pool 4km; conv Rhine Falls & Lake Constance; pitches on rvside (rv v fast-moving & unfenced); no o'fits over 7m high ssn; clean, adequate san facs; grass pitches poss muddy after rain; poss tight access to pitches; gd facs sm children; gd cycling."* **€52.00, 24 Apr-7 Oct. 2024**

SEMPACH *B3* (1.5km S Rural) *47.12447, 8.18924* **TCS Camping Sempach,** Seelandstrasse, 6204 Sempach Stadt **041 4601466 or 091 9858070; camping.sempach@tcs.ch; https://www.tcs.ch/de/camping-reisen/camping-insider/campingplaetze/tcs-campingplaetze/campingplatz-sempach.php**

CHF6 (htd)

Fr Luzern on A2 take exit sp Emmen N, Basel, Bern. Join E35 & cont on this rd to exit at Sempach sp. Site well sp. 4*, Lge, mkd, unshd, EHU (13A) inc (adaptor avail); gas; bbq (charcoal, gas); sw nr; TV; 60% statics; Eng spkn; adv bkg acc; ccard acc; bike hire; watersports; fishing; golf 5km; tennis; games rm; CKE. *"Excel location on Sempacher See, 10 mins drive fr m'way & attractive town; no o'fits over 9m high ssn; sep car parks high ssn; sm pitches; helpful staff; rest & beach open to public; water & bins far fr many pitches; poss tight parking; ltd facs LS; private san facs avail; lakeside walk to Sempach."* **CHF 35, 4 Apr-7 Oct, S08. 2022**

"I need an on-site restaurant"

We do our best to make sure site information is correct, but it is always best to check any must-have facilities are still available or will be open during your visit.

SIERRE *C2* (3km NE Rural) *46.30215, 7.56420* **Camping Swiss Plage,** Campingweg 3, 3970 Salgesch **027 4556608; info@swissplage.ch; www.swissplage.ch**

CHF3.50

Fr A9/E62 exit at Sierre, turn L & go over bdge, Foll sp Salgesch & Site. Fr town site well sp. 4*, Lge, shd, EHU (10A) CHF3.60; gas; sw; Eng spkn; adv bkg req; ccard acc; tennis. *"Pleasant site in lovely location."* **CHF 39, Easter-15 Oct. 2022**

SILVAPLANA *C4* (0.6km SW Rural) *46.45671, 9.79316* **Camping Silvaplana,** 7513 Silvaplana **081 8288492; reception@campingsilvaplana.ch; www.campingsilvaplana.ch**

CHF3

Exit by-pass rd at S junc for Silvaplana (opp camp site). In 100m after g'ge turn R & site sp via underpass, on lakeside. When app fr Julier Pass foll sp for Maloja Pass as above. Lge, pt shd, pt sl, EHU (16A) CHF3.50; gas; sw; 80% statics; Eng spkn; ccard acc; fishing; tennis; watersports. *"V beautiful location; gd walking; hiking; climbing; vg watersports & windsurfing; pool 3km; excel facs for m'vans; 2.5% surcharge on ccard."* **CHF 45, 13 May-20 Oct. 2024**

SOLOTHURN *B2* (2km SW Rural) *47.19883, 7.52288* **TCS Camping Lido Solothurn,** Glutzenhofstrasse 5, 4500 Solothurn **032 6218935 or 091 9858070 LS; camping.solothurn@tcs.ch; www.campingtcs.ch/solothurn**

CHF6 (htd)

Exit A5 dir Solothurn W, cross rv bdge. At traff lts turn L & foll sp to site (new rd 2009). 4*, Lge, mkd, pt shd, serviced pitches; EHU (16A) inc; gas; bbq; cooking facs; sw nr; TV; 20% statics; bus 200m; Eng spkn; adv bkg acc; ccard acc; games rm; bike hire; tennis 200m; fishing; boat hire; golf 100m; games area; CKE. *"Gd touring base by Rv Aare; no o'fits over 12m high ssn; lge pitches; htd pool adj; excel facs; helpful staff; 20 mins walk to picturesque town; excel cycling paths."* **CHF 37, 28 Feb-29 Nov, S13. 2022**

SPIEZ *C2* (6km SE Rural) *46.65880, 7.71688* **Camping Stuhlegg,** Stueleggstrasse 7, 3704 Krattigen **033 6542723; campstuhlegg@bluewin.ch; www.camping-stuhlegg.ch**

12 CHF3 (htd) nr (htd)

13km fr Interlaken on hillside on S side of Lake Thun. Advise app fr Spiez. Fr Spiez rlwy stn heading SE turn R over rlwy bdge; foll sp Leissigen & Krattigen for 5km. In Krattigen after modern church turn R (low gear), site 500m on R. To avoid going thro Spiez town, leave Bern-Interlaken m'way at junc 19. Foll dir to Aeschi. At rndabt in Aeschi turn L to Krattigen. Turn L after 1m opp wood yard into Stuhleggstrasse. Site in 300 yds. 4*, Lge, pt shd, pt sl, terr, EHU (10A) CHF4 (some rev pol); gas; 60% statics; phone; adv bkg acc; ccard acc; site clsd last week Oct to end Nov; CKE. *"Excel well-kept, well run site; immac facs; helpful friendly staff; recep clsd 1300-1500; mountain views; gd dog-walking in area; scenic rtes fr site; ski bus; free bus service with Guest Card; gd rest; bread can be ordered."* **CHF 40 2024**

SUR EN *B4* (0.4km NE Rural) *46.81859, 10.36594*
Camping Sur En, 7554 Sur En (Graubünden)
079 0111147; wb@sur-en.ch; www.sur-en.ch
CHF3 (htd)

Visible in valley fr rd 27. Steep access. Sm, unshd, EHU (6-10A) CHF3 (long lead poss req, warden has adaptors); bbq; 30% statics; Eng spkn; ccard acc; CKE. *"Superb facs in out-of-the-way spot; great atmosphere for nature lovers/walkers/cyclists; ski lift 7km; gd for dog walking but tick treatment ess; free ski bus; no ccard."* **CHF 38** **2024**

SURCUOLM *B3* (0.7km N Rural) *46.76053, 9.14324*
Panorama Camping Surcuolm, Via Principala, 7138 Surcuolm, Switzerland **081 9333223; info@camping-surcuolm.ch; www.camping-surcuolm.ch**
CHF3 (htd) nr

Fr N19 to Ilanz & in Ilanz foll sp Valata & Obersaxen. In Valata turn L to Surcuolm, site on L. This is only rec rte - steep climbs. 4*, Med, unshd, pt sl, EHU (16A) metered; 10% statics; bus 500m; adv bkg acc. *"Mountain views; ski lift nr; popular winter site; quiet in summer; excel facs."* **CHF 41** **2020**

SURSEE *B2* (3km W Rural) *47.17505, 8.08685*
Camping Sursee Waldheim, Baslerstrasse, 6210 Sursee
041 9211161; info@camping-sursee.ch; www.camping-sursee.ch
CHF3 nr

Exit A2 at junc 20 & take L lane onto rd 24 dir Basel/Luzern. Turn R at traff lts, foll rd 2 turn R at 2nd rndabt dir Basel to site. 3*, Sm, hdstg, pt shd, pt sl, EHU (10A) inc; gas; bbq; sw nr; TV; 70% statics; Eng spkn; adv bkg acc; games rm; bike hire; CKE. *"Pretty site; excel san facs; gd train service to Luzern; sh walk to town cent; popular NH; gd touring base; v helpful owner; acc Euros; recep clsd 12:00-15:00."* **CHF 36, 1 Apr-29 Oct.** **2023**

TENERO *C3* (1.5km E Rural) *46.16890, 8.85561*
Camping Campofelice, Via alle Brere, 6598 Tenero
091 7451417; camping@campofelice.ch; www.campofelice.ch
nr

Fr A2 take Bellinzona S exit & foll sp Locarno on A13. In about 12km take Tenero exit, at end slip rd foll sp to site. V lge, mkd, pt shd, serviced pitches; EHU (10A) inc; gas; red long stay; 10% statics; Eng spkn; ccard acc; tennis; CKE. *"Expensive but superb, attractive & well-equipped, v clean facs; boat moorings; pool 8km; min stay 3+ nights high ssn."* **CHF 55, 14 Mar-27 Oct.** **2023**

TENERO *C3* (1km SW Urban) *46.17292, 8.84808*
Camping Miralago, Via Roncaccio 20, 6598 Tenero
091 7451255; info@camping-miralago.ch; www.camping-miralago.ch
CHF3 (htd) (htd)

Turn L off A13 Bellinzona/Locarno rd at Tenero & foll camping sps. 5*, Med, mkd, unshd, EHU (10A) inc; bbq; sw nr; bus adj; Eng spkn; adv bkg acc; ccard acc; games area; CKE. *"Beautiful area; ltd facs LS; lake steamer pier lakefront camping; sm pitches with no privacy hdgs; fairly new san facs; beautiful location, no rd noise."* **CHF 55** **2024**

ULRICHEN *C3* (1km SE Rural) *46.50369, 8.30969*
Camping Nufenen, 3988 Ulrichen **027 9731437; info@camping-nufenen.ch; www.camping-nufenen.ch**
CHF2 nr

On NE end of Ulrichen turn R on Nufenen pass rd. After rlwy & rv x-ing (1km), site on R. 3*, Med, pt shd, EHU (8A) CHF3.50; red long stay; 50% statics; phone; adv bkg acc; tennis 2km; CKE. *"Pleasantly situated, mountainous site with gd local facs; gd walking; san facs basic but clean; pool 6km; recep open 0800-2100, clsd 1230-1400; gd NH."* **CHF 37, 1 Jun-30 Sep.** **2023**

ULRICHEN *C3* (8km SW Rural) *46.46480, 8.24469*
Camping Augenstern, 3988 Reckingen **027 9731395; info@campingaugenstern.ch; www.camping augenstern.ch**
CHF2

On Brig-Gletsch rd turn R in Reckingen over rlwy & rv, site sp. 3*, Med, unshd, EHU (10A) CHF4.50; 20% statics; golf; fishing; CKE. *"Nr Rv Rhône & mountains; htd pool adj."* **CHF 37, 1 Jan-15 Mar, 11 May-16 Oct & 14 Dec-31 Dec.** **2022**

VADUZ (LIECHTENSTEIN) *B4* (7km S Rural) *47.0866, 9.52666* **Camping Mittagspitze,** Saga 29, 9495 Triesen **392 2688; info@campingtriesen.li; www.campingtriesen.li**
CHF4

On rd 28 bet Vaduz & Balzers, sp. Poss diff for lge o'fits. 4*, Med, hdstg, pt shd, terr, EHU (6A) CHF5; gas; bbq; 80% statics; Eng spkn; ccard acc; fishing. *"Pretty site in lovely location; excel touring base; site yourself, recep open 0800-0830 & 1900-1930 only; fitness trail; steep, diff access to pitches & slippery when wet; beer garden; gd rest."* **CHF 42, 1 Mar-31 Dec.** **2022**

VALLORBE *B1* (0.7km SW Urban) *46.71055, 6.37472*
Camping Pré Sous Ville, 10 Rue des Fontaines, 1337 Vallorbe **021 843 22 52; yvan.favre@vallorbe.com**
nr

Foll camping sp in town. 3*, Med, mkd, pt shd, EHU (10A) CHF5; gas; 20% statics; Eng spkn; fishing; games area; tennis; CKE. *"Gd, clean facs; gd size pitches; site yourself if warden absent; htd pool adj; conv for Vallée de Joux, Lake Geneva & Jura; views down valley."* **CHF 37, 15 Apr-15 Oct.** **2022**

VILLENEUVE *C1* (12km W Rural) *46.38666, 6.86055*
Camping Rive-Bleue, Case postale 68, 1897 Le Bouveret
024 4812161; info@camping-rive-bleue.ch; www.camping-rive-bleue.ch
CHF3.30 nr

Fr Montreux foll sp to Evian to S side of Lake Geneva. Turn R after sp 'Bienvenue Bouveret'. Foll camp sp to Aqua Park. Site on R approx 1km fr main rd. 4*, Lge, mkd, pt shd, EHU (10A) CHF6 (adaptor avail - check earth); gas; sw; 20% statics; Eng spkn; adv bkg acc; watersports; tennis; waterslide; sep car park; CKE. *"Well-maintained, well-ordered, completely flat site in lovely setting on lake; friendly staff; water/waste pnts scarce; vg facs but red LS; 15 mins walk to vill with supmkt; conv ferries around Lake Geneva; cars must be parked in sep public car park; gd cyling area; free bicycles for 4 hrs fr vill; pool adj; 1st class san block."* **CHF 43.7, 1 Apr-12 Oct. 2023**

VILLENEUVE *C1* (5km W Rural) *46.39333, 6.89527*
Camping Les Grangettes, Rue des Grangettes, 1845 Noville **021 9601503; noville@treyvaud.com; www.les-grangettes.ch**
12 CHF3 (htd)

Fr N9 Montreux-Aigle rd, take Villeneuve exit, at end slip rd turn N twds Villeneuve. At 1st traff lts turn L to Noville, turn R by PO, site sp. Narr app rd. 4*, Med, mkd, unshd, EHU (10A) CHF4; sw; 80% statics; phone; Eng spkn; sep car park; fishing; boating. *"Beautifully situated on SE corner Lake Geneva o'looking Montreux; sep tourer area; pool 3km; poss noisy in high ssn."* **CHF 42.8 2024**

VITZNAU *B3* (0.5km SE Rural) *47.00683, 8.48621* **Camping Vitznau,** Altdorfstrasse, 6354 Vitznau **041 3971280; info@camping-vitznau.ch; www.camping-vitznau.ch**
CHF5 (htd)

On E edge of Vitznau, sp. Fr Küssnacht twd Brunnen turn L at RC church with tall clock tower. 4*, Lge, hdstg, pt shd, terr, EHU (16A) CHF5 (adaptors on loan); gas; sw nr; red long stay; 40% statics; Eng spkn; adv bkg rec; ccard acc; tennis; CKE. *"Excel, v clean, family-run site; friendly owner will help with pitching; max c'van length 7m high ssn; sm pitches; some site rds tight & steep; recep closes 1830 hrs; fine views lakes & mountains; Quickstop o'night facs CHF20; many activities inc walking; gd dog-walking; conv ferry terminal, cable cars & mountain rlwy (tickets avail on site); gd saving by using 'tell-pass'; lake steamer to Luzern 500m; gd pool, sm shop."* **CHF 42.66, 1 Apr-2 Oct, S05. 2024**

WINTERTHUR *A3* (3km N Rural) *47.51965, 8.71655*
Camping am Schützenweiher, Eichliwaldstrasse 4, 8400 Winterthur **052 2125260; campingplatz@win.ch; www.camping-winterthur.info**
12 CHF3 (htd) nr

Fr A1/E60 exit Winterthur-Ohringen dir Winterthur, turn R & foll site sp, site adj police stn in about 200m. 2*, Sm, shd, EHU CHF4; gas; 8% statics; phone; bus 250m, train; Eng spkn; CKE. *"Helpful owner; office open 0900-1100 & 1830-1930 to register & pay; find own pitch outside these hrs; sm pitches; pool 3km; gd NH; fairly gd site."* **CHF 38 2023**

ZERMATT *D2* (6km N Rural) *46.06450, 7.77500*
Camping Alphubel, 3929 Täsch (Wallis)
027 9673635; welcome@campingtaesch.ch; www.campingtaesch.ch
CHF2 (htd) nr nr

Turn down R-hand slip rd over level x-ing & bdge after rlwy stn in Täsch, & foll sp to site. S bend bdge poss diff for lge o'fits at app. 2*, Med, unshd, EHU (10A) CHF5 (long lead poss req); Eng spkn; tennis; fishing. *"Conv for frequent train to Zermatt fr vill; recep clsd 1200-1400; superb scenery & walking; htd pool 1km; helpful owner; vg, modern san facs; excel."* **CHF 36, 8 May-14 Oct. 2024**

ZUG *B3* (2km E Rural) *47.17806, 8.49438* **TCS Camping Zug,** Chamer Fussweg 36, 6300 Zug **041 7418422; camping.zug@tcs.ch; www.campingtcs.ch**
CHF6 (htd)

Fr A4/E41 take A4a Zug-West, site sp on R in 3km on lakeside. Fr Zug take Luzern rd for 2km. Site on L under rlwy. 3*, Med, mkd, pt shd, EHU (6A) inc; gas; sw; 40% statics; phone; Eng spkn; ccard acc; tennis; fishing; games area; bike hire; CKE. *"Easy walk to town; pool 3km; new (2018) young owners; v clean & tidy; lovely location."* **CHF 48, 29 Mar-14 Oct. 2023**

ZUG *B3* (11km SE Rural) *47.127781, 8.591945*
Campsite Unterägeri, Wilbrunnenstraße 81, 6314 Unterägeri **041 7503928; info@campingunteraegeri.ch; www.campingunteraegeri.ch**
12 (htd) pebble lake adj

Fr Zug take rd to Unterageri. Site sp fr vill. 4*, Lge, hdstg, mkd, pt shd, EHU (10A) inc (rev pol); gas; sw; 40% statics; Eng spkn; adv bkg acc; ccard acc. *"Excellent sw in lake; cycling/walking; recep clsd 1200-1400; vg."* **CHF 56 2023**

ZURICH *A3* (4km S Rural) *47.33633, 8.54167*
Camping Zurich Fischers Fritz, Seestrasse 559, 8038 Zürich-Wollishofen **044 4821612; camping@fischers-fritz.ch; www.fischers-fritz.ch**
CHF3

Fr city foll rd 3 (twd Chur) on S side of lake; foll camping sp. 1*, Lge, hdstg, pt shd, EHU (6A) CHF6; gas; bbq; sw; 80% statics; bus; Eng spkn; ccard acc; tennis; fishing; watersports. *"Parking in Zürich v diff, use bus; sm area for tourers; pool 3km; conv NH, v sm pitches; cycling into Zurich poss; only 52 plots; tent spaces."* **CHF 51.5, 1 May-30 Sep. 2023**

ZWEISIMMEN *C2* (1km N Rural) *46.56338, 7.37691* **Camping Fankhauser,** Ey Gässli 2, 3770 Zweisimmen **033 7221356; info@camping-fankhauser.ch; www.camping-fankhauser.ch**
12 (htd) nr nr nr

N6 exit Spiez, then foll sp Zweisimmen. On o'skts of town turn L at camping sp immed bef Agip petrol stn, site on L immed after rlwy x-ing. 4*, Med, pt sl, EHU (10A) CHF3.50 or metered; bbq; 90% statics; phone; Eng spkn; adv bkg acc; fishing; golf; CKE. *"Gd NH; pool 800m."* **CHF 28 2022**

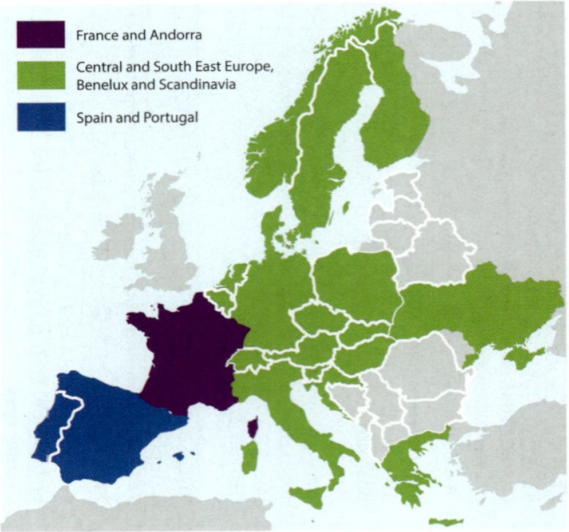

Lausanne to Zermatt = 170km

	Altdorf	Basel	Bellinzona	Bern	Brig	Chur	Delémont	Disentis	Fribourg	Genève (Geneva)	Gstaad	Innertkirchen	Interlaken	La Chaux-de-Fonds	Lausanne	Lugano	Luzern	Martigny	Neuchâtel	Olten	St. Gallen	St. Moritz	Schaffhausen	Scuol/Schuls	Sion	Vaduz (Liechtenstein)	Winterthur	Zermatt	Zug
Basel	144																												
Bellinzona	110	244																											
Bern	155	98	255																										
Brig	118	192	161	166																									
Chur	181	230	115	243	175																								
Delémont	151	44	292	93	182	239																							
Disentis	62	204	80	177	108	66	268																						
Fribourg	188	132	286	35	178	275	124	211																					
Genève (Geneva)	319	268	420	172	216	410	261	324	141																				
Gstaad	159	204	223	81	91	272	172	183	66	145																			
Innertkirchen	68	187	126	91	77	153	178	88	126	263	97																		
Interlaken	99	155	195	59	75	210	144	120	93	230	63	34																	
La Chaux-de-Fonds	189	103	291	68	164	274	61	245	66	145	149	160	126																
Lausanne	257	205	358	107	152	348	201	262	73	62	83	201	166	96															
Lugano	132	264	29	281	189	142	275	108	312	449	284	154	220	315	382														
Luzern	42	102	142	116	151	141	109	103	149	280	134	46	74	145	219	166													
Martigny	281	231	240	136	82	371	225	188	101	136	74	156	192	159	73	267	250												
Neuchâtel	196	142	295	47	142	285	81	223	44	122	149	138	104	23	74	320	155	146											
Olten	96	53	197	69	159	181	64	160	99	235	156	103	122	102	172	220	57	201	111										
St. Gallen	179	191	218	205	289	105	201	156	236	371	318	210	256	237	310	244	139	336	245	145									
St. Moritz	201	313	152	327	242	86	323	145	360	459	406	199	298	362	432	177	218	332	369	268	188								
Schaffhausen	147	159	246	173	262	182	169	209	206	340	291	215	229	208	279	275	110	305	216	115	82	269							
Scuol/Schuls	253	305	186	319	279	105	315	169	348	485	375	256	284	352	425	214	215	337	362	260	181	62	252						
Sion	170	253	215	162	53	401	250	161	129	161	120	115	88	190	99	241	273	27	166	225	356	296	326	317					
Vaduz (Liechtenstein)	110	206	147	203	206	32	213	98	237	371	304	186	241	271	310	184	115	262	249	160	58	117	136	99	221				
Winterthur	119	133	219	145	232	158	141	180	177	311	216	125	188	179	249	243	81	279	188	89	59	245	29	233	299	84			
Zermatt	245	212	185	202	28	199	206	136	204	239	194	114	161	188	170	224	174	99	164	186	325	278	296	313	72	243	267		
Zug	67	125	166	137	181	115	135	130	169	305	164	75	103	172	241	193	28	265	182	79	112	197	82	189	293	86	51	219	
Zürich	65	112	196	123	211	117	122	127	158	292	191	105	128	156	228	223	59	258	165	66	83	201	51	194	280	93	22	245	30

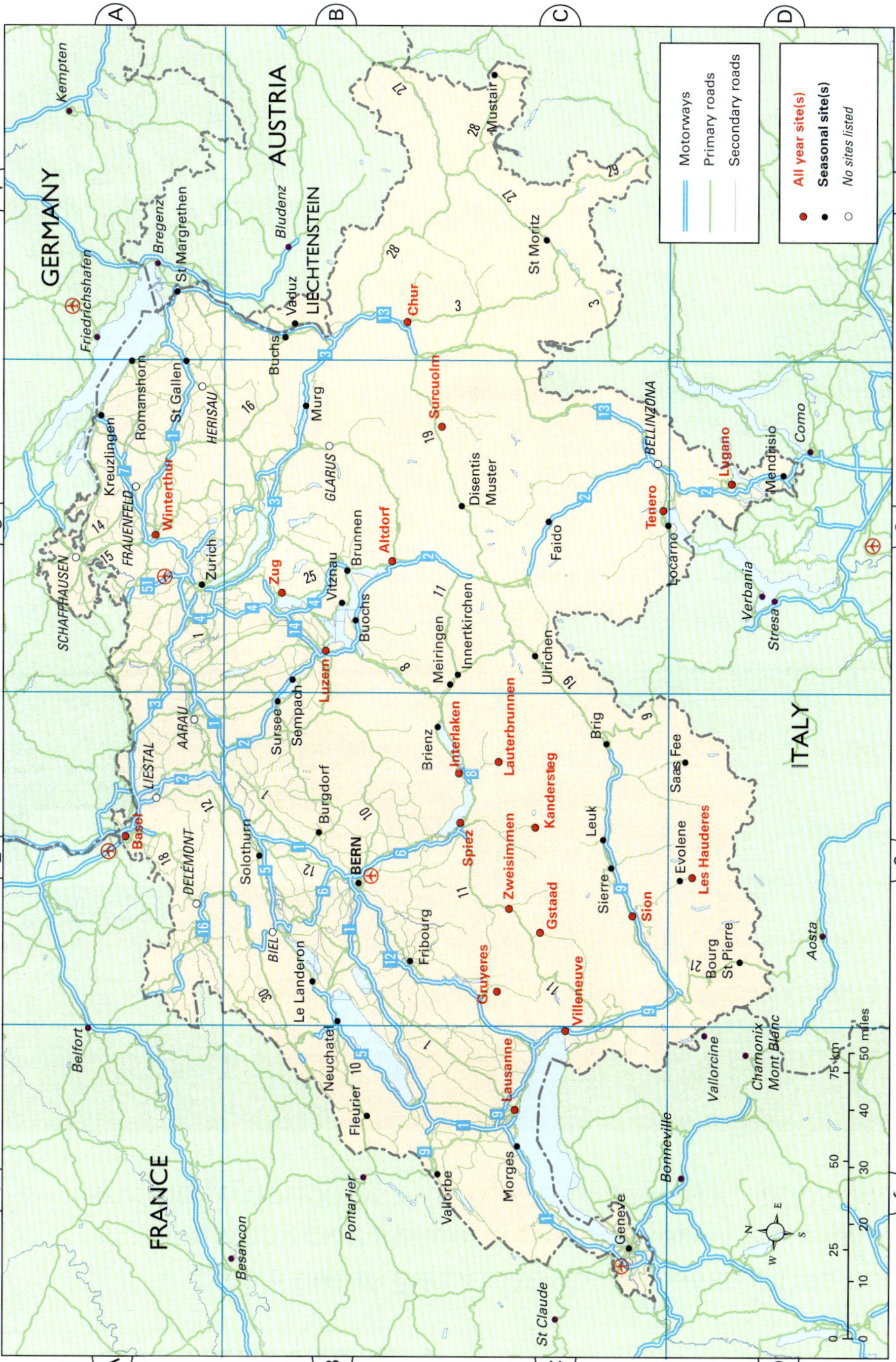
Motorways
Primary roads
Secondary roads
All year site(s)
Seasonal site(s)
No sites listed
GERMANY
AUSTRIA
LIECHTENSTEIN
FRANCE
ITALY
Kempten
Friedrichshafen
Bregenz
Bludenz
St Margrethen
Vaduz
Buchs
Romanshorn
St Gallen
HERISAU
Kreuzlingen
FRAUENFELD
Winterthur
SCHAFFHAUSEN
Zurich
Murg
GLARUS
Chur
Surcuolm
Mustair
St Moritz
Disentis Muster
Brunnen
Altdorf
Zug
Vitznau
Buchs
Luzern
Meiringen
Innertkirchen
Sursee
Sempach
AARAU
LIESTAL
Basel
DELEMONT
Solothurn
Burgdorf
BERN
Brienz
Interlaken
Lauterbrunnen
Spiez
Kandersteg
Zweisimmen
Gstaad
BIEL
Le Landeron
Fribourg
Gruyeres
Neuchatel
Fleurier
Vallorbe
Lausanne
Morges
Villeneuve
Geneve
Sion
Sierre
Leuk
Brig
Saas Fee
Evolene
Les Hauderes
Bourg St Pierre
Ulrichen
Faido
BELLINZONA
Tenero
Locarno
Lugano
Mendrisio
Como
Verbania
Stresa
Aosta
Chamonix Mont Blanc
Vallorcine
Bonneville
St Claude
Pontarlier
Besancon
Belfort
0 10 25 20 30 50 40 75 km 50 miles

Site Report Form

If campsite is already listed, complete only those sections of the form where changes apply or alternatively use the Abbreviated Site Report form on the following pages.

Sites not reported on for 5 years may be deleted from the guide

Year of guide used	20..........	Is site listed?	Listed on page no...........	Unlisted	Date of visit	......../........./.........

A – CAMPSITE NAME AND LOCATION

Country		Name of town/village site listed under *(see Sites Location Maps)*			
Distance & direction from centre of town site is listed under *(in a straight line)*	...................km	eg N, NE, S, SW	Urban	Rural	Coastal
Site open all year?	Y / N	Period site is open *(if not all year)*	................./................. to ..../.................		
Site name				Naturist site	Y / N
Site address					
Telephone		Fax			
E-mail		Website			

B – CAMPSITE CHARGES

Charge for outfit + 2 adults in local currency	PRICE		

C – DIRECTIONS

Brief, specific directions to site (in km) *To convert miles to kilometres multiply by 8 and divide by 5 or use Conversion Table in guide*	
GPS	Latitude...*(eg 12.34567)* Longitude...*(eg 1.23456 or -1.23456)*

D – SITE INFORMATION

Dogs allowed	DOGS	Y / N	Price per night .... *(if allowed)*
Facilities for disabled			
Public Transport within 5km	BUS / TRAM / TRAIN	Adj	Nearby
Reduction long stay	RED LONG STAY	Credit Card accepted	CCARD ACC
Advance bookings accepted/recommended/required		ADV BKG ACC / REC / REQ	
Camping Key Europe or Camping Card International accepted in lieu of passport			CKE/CCI

E – SITE DESCRIPTION

SITE size ie number of pitches	Small Max 50	SM	Medium 51-150	MED	Large 151-500	LGE	Very large 500+	V LGE	Unchanged
Pitch features if **NOT** open-plan/grassy		HDG PITCH	Hedged	HDG PITCH	Marked or numbered	MKD PITCH	Hardstanding or gravel	HDSTG	Unchanged
If site is **NOT** level, is it		PT SL	Part sloping	PT SL	Sloping	SL	Terraced	TERR	Unchanged
Is site shaded?		SHD	Shaded	SHD	Part shaded	PT SHD	Unshaded	UNSHD	Unchanged
ELECTRIC HOOK UP *if not included in price above*	EL PNTS				Price...			Amps......................	
% Static caravans / mobile homes / chalets / cottages / fixed tents on site								................% STATICS	
Serviced Pitched	Y / N				Twin axles caravans allowed?			TWIN AXLES Y / N	

You can also complete forms online: camc.com/europereport

CUT ALONG DOTTED LINE

E – SITE DESCRIPTION CONTINUED...

Phone on site	PHONE		Wifi Internet	WIFI
Television	TV RM	TV CAB / SAT	Playground	PLAYGRND
Entertainment in high season	ENTMNT		English spoken	ENG SPKN
Motorhome Service Point	Y / N			

F – CATERING

Bar	BAR	On site	or	Within 2km	
Restaurant	REST	On site	or	Within 2km	
Shop(s)	SHOP(S)	On site	or	Within 2km	
Snack bar / take-away	SNACKS	On site	Y / N		
Cooking facilities	COOKING FACS	On site	Y / N		
Supplies of bottled gas on site	GAS	Y / N			
Barbecue allowed	BBQ	Charcoal	Gas	Elec	Sep area

G – SANITARY FACILITIES

WC	Heated	HTD WC	Continental	CONT	Own San recommended	OWN SAN REC
Chemical disposal point		CHEM DISP				
Hot shower(s)	SHWR(S)	Inc in site fee?		Y / N		
Child / baby facilities *(bathroom)*		FAM BTHRM		Launderette / Washing Machine		LNDRY

H – OTHER INFORMATION

Swimming pool	POOL	HEATED	COVERED	INDOOR	PADDLING POOL
Beach	BEACH	Adj	or ....km	Sand	Shingle
Alternative swimming *(lake)*	SW	Adj	or ....km	Sand	Shingle
Games /sports area / Games room	GAMES AREA		GAMES ROOM		

I – ADDITIONAL REMARKS AND/OR ITEMS OF INTEREST

Tourist attractions, unusual features or other facilities, eg waterslide, tennis, cycle hire, watersports, horseriding, separate car park, walking distance to shops etc	YOUR OPINION OF THE SITE:	
	EXCEL	
	VERY GOOD	
	GOOD	
	FAIR	POOR
	NIGHT HALT ONLY	
Your comments & opinions may be used in future editions of the guide, if you do not wish them to be used please tick		

J – MEMBER DETAILS

ARE YOU A:	Caravanner		Motorhomer		Trailer-tenter?	
NAME:			MEMBERSHIP NO:			
			POST CODE:			
DO YOU NEED MORE BLANK SITE REPORT FORMS?			YES		NO	

Please use a separate form for each campsite and do not send receipts. Owing to the large number of site reports received, it is not possible to enter into correspondence. Please return completed form to:

The Editor, Overseas Touring Guides, East Grinstead House
East Grinstead, West Sussex RH19 1UA

Please note that due to changes in the rules regarding freepost we are no longer able to provide a freepost address for the return of Site Report Forms. You can still supply your site reports free online by visiting camc.com/europereport. We apologise for any inconvenience this may cause.

Abbreviated Site Report Form

Use this abbreviated Site Report Form if you have visited a number of sites and there are no changes (or only small changes) to their entries in the guide. If reporting on a new site, or reporting several changes, please use the full version of the report form. **If advising prices,** these should be for an outfit, and 2 adults for one night's stay. **Please indicate high or low season prices and whether electricity is included.**

Remember, if you don't tell us about sites you have visited, they may eventually be deleted from the guide.

Year of guide used	20..........	Page No.	....	Name of town/village site listed under	
Site Name				Date of visit	......./......./........
GPS	Latitude...(eg 12.34567) Longitude...(eg 1.23456 or -1.23456)				

Site is in: Andorra / Austria / Belgium / Croatia / Czech Republic / Denmark / Finland / France / Germany / Greece / Hungary / Italy / Luxembourg / Netherlands / Norway / Poland / Portugal / Slovakia / Slovenia / Spain / Sweden / Switzerland

Comments:

Charge for outfit + 2 adults in local currency	High Season	Low Season	Elec inc in price?	Y / N	.............amps
			Price of elec (if not inc)		.............amps

Year of guide used	20..........	Page No.	....	Name of town/village site listed under	
Site Name				Date of visit	......./......./........
GPS	Latitude...(eg 12.34567) Longitude...(eg 1.23456 or -1.23456)				

Site is in: Andorra / Austria / Belgium / Croatia / Czech Republic / Denmark / Finland / France / Germany / Greece / Hungary / Italy / Luxembourg / Netherlands / Norway / Poland / Portugal / Slovakia / Slovenia / Spain / Sweden / Switzerland

Comments:

Charge for outfit + 2 adults in local currency	High Season	Low Season	Elec inc in price?	Y / N	.............amps
			Price of elec (if not inc)		.............amps

Year of guide used	20..........	Page No.	....	Name of town/village site listed under	
Site Name				Date of visit	......./......./........
GPS	Latitude...(eg 12.34567) Longitude...(eg 1.23456 or -1.23456)				

Site is in: Andorra / Austria / Belgium / Croatia / Czech Republic / Denmark / Finland / France / Germany / Greece / Hungary / Italy / Luxembourg / Netherlands / Norway / Poland / Portugal / Slovakia / Slovenia / Spain / Sweden / Switzerland

Comments:

Charge for car, caravan & 2 adults in local currency	High Season	Low Season	Elec inc in price?	Y / N	.............amps
			Price of elec (if not inc)		.............amps

Please fill in your details and send to the address on the reverse of this form.

You can also complete forms online: camc.com/europereport

CUT ALONG DOTTED LINE

Year of guide used	20..........	Page No.	....	Name of town/village site listed under		
Site Name				Date of visit	......./......./........	
GPS	Latitude..(eg 12.34567) Longitude..(eg 1.23456 or -1.23456)					
Site is in: Andorra / Austria / Belgium / Croatia / Czech Republic / Denmark / Finland / France / Germany / Greece / Hungary / Italy / Luxembourg / Netherlands / Norway / Poland / Portugal / Slovakia / Slovenia / Spain / Sweden / Switzerland						
Comments:						
Charge for outfit + 2 adults in local currency	High Season	Low Season	Elec inc in price?	Y / N	............amps	
			Price of elec (if not inc)		............amps	

Year of guide used	20..........	Page No.	....	Name of town/village site listed under		
Site Name				Date of visit	......./......./........	
GPS	Latitude..(eg 12.34567) Longitude..(eg 1.23456 or -1.23456)					
Site is in: Andorra / Austria / Belgium / Croatia / Czech Republic / Denmark / Finland / France / Germany / Greece / Hungary / Italy / Luxembourg / Netherlands / Norway / Poland / Portugal / Slovakia / Slovenia / Spain / Sweden / Switzerland						
Comments:						
Charge for outfit + 2 adults in local currency	High Season	Low Season	Elec inc in price?	Y / N	............amps	
			Price of elec (if not inc)		............amps	

Year of guide used	20..........	Page No.	....	Name of town/village site listed under		
Site Name				Date of visit	......./......./........	
GPS	Latitude..(eg 12.34567) Longitude..(eg 1.23456 or -1.23456)					
Site is in: Andorra / Austria / Belgium / Croatia / Czech Republic / Denmark / Finland / France / Germany / Greece / Hungary / Italy / Luxembourg / Netherlands / Norway / Poland / Portugal / Slovakia / Slovenia / Spain / Sweden / Switzerland						
Comments:						
Charge for outfit + 2 adults in local currency	High Season	Low Season	Elec inc in price?	Y / N	............amps	
			Price of elec (if not inc)		............amps	

Your comments & opinions may be used in future editions of the guide, if you do not wish them to be used please tick ....

Name ....

Membership No. ....

Post Code ....

Are you a Caravanner / Motorhomer / Trailer-Tenter?

Do you need more blank Site Report forms? YES / NO

Please return completed forms to:

The Editor – Overseas Touring Guides
East Grinstead House
East Grinstead
West Sussex
RH19 1FH

Please note that due to changes in the rules regarding freepost we are no longer able to provide a freepost address for the return of Site Report Forms. You can still supply your site reports free online by visiting camc.com/europereport.
We apologise for any inconvenience this may cause.

You can also complete forms online: camc.com/europereport

Index

A

Abbreviated Site Report Forms .... Back of guide
Abbreviations 11
Abbreviations (mountain passes & tunnels) 42
Accessing the Internet 77
Accidents and Emergencies .... 59 & country intros
Acknowledgements 8
Alcohol (legal limits) .... Country Intros
Alps (passes & tunnels) 43
AUSTRIA 78

B

Beaches (Safety) 66
BELGIUM 101
Breakdown Service .... Country Intros
Booking a Campsite 72
Booking your Ferry 27
British Consular Services Abroad 71
British & Irish Embassy Contacts .... Country Intros

C

Camping & Caravanning .... Country Intros
Camping Key Europe 14
Campsite Entries (explanation) 9
Campsite Fees .... 6 & 74
Campsite Groups 76
Campsite Safety 66
Caravan Spares 37
Caravan Storage Abroad 73
Car Spare Kits 37
Channel Tunnel 28
Club Sites Near Ports 29
Club Together 77
Complaints 76
Contact Details - Sites .... Individual Site Entries
Converting Gradients 42
Counrty Highlights .... Country Intros
Country Information .... Country Intros
Credit and Debit Cards 26
CRIS document 17
CROATIA 118
Currency .... Country Intros
Customs Allowances 20
Customs Regulations 20
Cycling .... Country Intros
CZECHIA 134

D

DENMARK 149
Documents .... 14 & Country Intros
Driving in Europe 32
Driving Licence 14
Dynamic Currency Conversion 26

E

E10 Petrol 32
Electrical Connections 62
Electricity .... 62 & Country Intros
Emergency Cash 26
Emergency Services .... Country Intros

E cont...

Essential Equipment .... 35, 39 & Country Intros
European Accident Statement 23
European Health Insurance Card (EHIC) 59
Explanation of a Campsite Entry 9

F

Facilities and Site Description 73
Ferry routes and Operators 30
Final Checks (motoring) 31
Finding a Campsite 73
FINLAND 168
First Aid 60
Food (Customs) 21
Foreign Currency Bank Accounts 25
FRANCE 180
Fuel .... 32 & Country Intros

G

Gas .... 64 & Country Intros
Gas on Ferries and Eurotunnel 28
General Advice (campsites) 76
GERMANY 476
GREECE 540

H

Hazard Warning Lights 36
Headlight flashing 36
Hired or Borrowed Vehicles 18
HMRC Advice Service 21
Hooking up to the Mains 63
HUNGARY 552

I

Insurance: 22
- Caravan Cover 22
- Vehicle Insurance 22
- Holiday .... 24 & 60
- Home 24

Internet access 77
ITALY 564

L

Lakes (Safety) 66
Legal Costs Abroad 23
Lights 35
Liquified Petroleum Gas (LPG) 32
Local Currency 25
Low Emission Zones .... 33 & Country Intros
LUXEMBOURG 612
Lyme disease 61

M

Major Alpine Mountain Passes 43
Major Alpine Rail Tunnels 52
Major Alpine Road Tunnels 53
Major Pyrenees Mountain Passes 55
Major Pyrenees Road Tunnels 58
Major Towns & Cities .... Country Intros

Index

M cont...

Medical Services .... 59 & Country Intros
Medicines (Customs) 21
Mobile Internet 77
Mobile Phones 77
Money .... 25 & Country Intros
Money Security 70
MOT Certificate 18
Motorhomes Towing Cars 33
Motoring .... Country Intros
Motorway Tolls .... Country Intros
Motorways .... Country Intros
Mountain Passes & Tunnels .... 43 & 55
Mountain Pass Information 41
Municipal Campsites 74

N

Nationality Plate 36
Naturist Campsites 74
NETHERLANDS 622
NORWAY 648

O

On the Ferry 24
On the Road Safety 68
Opening Hours .... 74 & Country Intros
Overnight Stops 74
Overseas Site Night Vouchers 72
Overseas Travel Service 72
Overtaking .... Country Intros

P

Parking .... Country Intros
Passport 15
Pedestrian Crossings 34
Personal Possessions (Customs) 20
Personal Security 69
Pets on Campsites 75
Pets on Ferries and Eurotunnel 28
Pet Travel Documentation 16
Plants (Customs) 21
POLAND 678
PORTUGAL 693
Preparing for your Journey 31
Prices 74
Priority .... 33 & Country Intros
Public Holidays .... Country Intros
Public Transport .... 33 & Country Intros
Punctures 38

R

Radar Detectors .... Country Intros
Radio and Television 77
Reflective Jackets/Waistcoats 36
Registering on Arrival 76
Returning Home (Medical Advice) 61
Reversed Polarity 64
Rivers (Safety) 66
Roads .... Country Intros
Road Signs and Markings .... Country Intros
Route Planning 36

S

Safety and Security .... 66 & Country Intros
Sanitary Facilities 73
Satellite Navigation/GPS .... 7 & 36
Satellite Television 77
Schengen agreement 15
Seat Belts 37
Shaver Sockets 64
Site Hooking up Adaptor 64
Site Location Maps .... End of Site Entries
Site Opening Dates .... Individual Site Entries
Site Prices .... Individual Site Entries
Site Report Forms .... 7 & 859
SLOVAKIA 715
SLOVENIA 725
SPAIN 737
Spare Wheel 37
Spares 37
Speed Limits .... Country Intros
Sun Protection 60
SWEDEN 810
SWITZERLAND 835

T

Television 77
Tick-Borne Encephalitis 61
Touring .... Country Intros
Tourist Information .... Country Intros
Towbar 37
Traffic Jams .... Country Intros
Traffic Lights .... 34 & Country Intros
Travelling with Children 17
Travel Money Cards 25
Tyre Pressure 38
Tyres 37

V

Vehicle Tax 18
Vehicle Registration Certificate (V5C) 18
Vehicles left behind abroad 23
Violation of Traffic Regulations .... Country Intros
Visas 19

W

Warning Triangles 39
Water 61
Weight Limits 31
Winter Driving 38
Winter Sports 71

PEFC Certified
This product is from sustainably managed forests and controlled sources
PEFC
PEFC/16-33-254
www.pefc.org